CONDUCTORS ANTHOLOGY

Volume 2

Conducting and Musicianship

A compendium of articles from *The Instrumentalist*
from 1946 to 1992 on score study, conducting techniques,
rehearsals, and musicianship.

Second Edition, 1993

Interpretive Analyses of Band Repertoire

⌒⌒⌒⌒⌒

Percy Aldridge Grainger's

Lincolnshire Posy

An Interpretive Analysis
by Frederick Fennell

There had been some precedent in American musical life for the arrival on our shores of Percy Aldridge Grainger. We had already welcomed the likes of Louis Antoine Jullien, that early swooner among public entertainers, as conductor of his "evenings" in 1853; and Jenny Lind, the Swedish nightingale who would win all hearts, as well as any number of widely heralded tenors, violinists, and pianists.

Grainger had been nothing less than a smashing success ever since the start of his European pianistic career in 1901, and tours to Australia, New Zealand, South Africa, Norway, and Denmark, together with his steady emergence as a composer, had made him an outstanding young musical personality. The difference was the fact that Grainger, in his conscientious objection to the war then raging in Europe, had come to stay. Before leaving England in 1914, Percy Grainger had established most of the patterns of thought and action that he would follow for the rest of his extraordinary life. His emergence as the leading folk song collector of his day had earned him an enviable position in that vital preoccupation then beginning to surface in England among the leading composers, including Holst and Vaughan Williams.

Grainger did most of his folk song collecting in rural England during the summer months, dead concert periods prior to the emergence of our now-feverish summer festival activity. He made this available time count in his usual efficient way, helping to rescue the English folk song from extinction. And he pursued the subject with a kind of fanaticism that one grows to know as standard with him on all subjects, once joined.

These folk song collecting journeys began in the summer of 1905 with Grainger seeking out his sources by walking on foot from town to town, music pad in hand. He would hastily write down in his own kind of musical shorthand what he had heard, spending his evenings at the local inn transcribing the day's discoveries. Skillful though he became at this, it bothered him that he could not immediately chart the subtleties of inflection that fascinated him so much in the highly personal interpretation of each singer. He was struck by their individuality, excited at their unfettered flights of creative fancy, and admired their freedom from those shackles sometimes forged in conservatories and opera houses like those he had come to know from his studies in Frankfurt. His "Program Note" in the *Posy* score contains sensitive character sketches of the folk singers whose tunes he used in the six-movement work. On returning to London each folk song, minutely documented, was pasted in huge accountant's ledgers, now in the Grainger Museum in Australia.[3]

On his next visit to North Lincolnshire in 1906, he fulfilled his desire to be 100% faithful to those he called "Kings and Queens of Song" by taking along one of Thomas Edison's new cylinder-disc phonographs. Now he had it all — the words, the dialect, the tune, the pitches, the inflections, the tone, the rhythms — a completely faithful, endlessly-and-exactly-repeatable account of what those fast-disappearing folk singers had inherited and how, in turn, they had added their own particular contributions to the interpretation.[4]

Grainger in Milwaukee for the *Lincolnshire Posy* premiere performance, 1937

The Score

As soon as the front cover of this unique and unprecedented score has been turned back, it's reader is quickly introduced to the exciting intellect and the impassioned musical beliefs of a totally extraordinary man. Issues are joined immediately in his note "To Bandleaders," a collection of thoroughly-considered, absolutely unguarded observations and statements; more follow in his "Program Note."

Everything about the score, beginning with the words and culminating in the music, is a whole new invitation to music itself — a ringing manifesto around which those who truly believe in the potential of wind band music can regroup, re-evaluate, and rejoice. I have not ceased to do since first reading this marvellous score.[5]

Readers should number every bar in each movement, separately, prior to transfering any suggestions from these pages to those of the score and of each individual part.

To Percy Grainger, detail was a discipline, documentation a passion. Desiring and obviously getting complete control of every aspect of the publication of his music he probably controlled his off-beat "compressed score", the color of its covers (the *Posy* lettered in his own hand was originally issued in a bright Lincoln green), the layout of the pages, and the inclusion of his personal observations, historical references, and performance philosophies. With this clear obsession for minutiae and the obvious need to right the wrongs as he saw and heard them, it is difficult to understand the presence in this material of errors and inconsistencies on a scale rarely found in any publication. There is little doubt that they contribute greatly to abandonment of performance. These are corrected in the 1987 full score edition.

Grainger must bear the burden of responsibility for the mistakes. Perhaps his insistence on a completely free hand backfired, editors and proofreaders at Schott, London removing themselves from the project altogether, leaving the monumental job of proofing (without a full score) in Percy's hands, too. Once he had approved the proofs the responsibilities were his alone. However, the continued re-printing of *Lincolnshire Posy* in the same condition that its composer (presumably in haste) submitted it to the publisher 40 years ago, is a disgrace. Artistic and editorial irresponsibility of this magnitude are difficult to imagine, but unfortunately this publication remains as a vivid and bitter example of both.[6]

1. "Lisbon" (72 bars). § Brisk, ♩ = 116, with plenty of lilt. The mode is mixolydian on A♭ with that key as the harmonic center and the D♭ signature as a writing convenience. Grainger "noted down" this tune in 1905, during the first of his three summers in Lincolnshire and began to use it as composition material a year later.

The "Lisbon" tune [1-17], first set forth and harmonized in the seven parallel major triads of the mode is intended to present the material in a diffused profile, listener and player alike knowing

Percy Aldridge Grainger (1892-1961): "Lincolnshire Posy. British Folk-Music Settings No. 34, [based on] English Folksongs gathered in Lincolnshire (England)...and set for Wind Band (Military Band)" (1905 to 1937), copyright 1940 by Percy Aldridge Grainger, published by Schott & Co., Ltd., London, plate no. 5009; G. Schirmer, Inc., sole agents for U.S.A.; 1 to 9 line "compressed full score" 41 pages.

Scored for piccolo, 2 flutes; 2 oboes, english horn; 2 bassoons, contra bassoon; clarinets: E♭, B♭, 1-2-3, alto, bass; saxophones: soprano, alto 1&2, tenor, baritone, bass; 4 horns in E♭ [now F]; 3 cornets or trumpets, flugel horn; 2 tenor, 1 bass trombone; treble clef baritone, bass clef euphonium, tubas; string contrabass; kettledrums (3), snare drum, bass drum, cymbals, glockenspiel, xylophone, chimes, Swiss hand bells.

1. "Lisbon" (Sailor's Song), 2. "Horkstow Grange" (the Miser and his Man — a local Tragedy), 3. "Rufford Park Poachers" (Poaching Song), 4. "The Brisk Young Sailor" (who returned to wed his True Love), 5. "Lord Melbourne" (War Song), 6. "The Lost Lady Found" (Dance Song).

Performance time is approximately 15 minutes.

The first performance of three unidentified movements[1] was March 7, 1937 in Milwaukee, Wisconsin at the 8th Annual Convention of the American Bandmasters Association, when the composer conducted The Milwaukee Symphonic Band, sponsored by Local 8, A.F.M. The date of the first complete performance is probably unknown, but I suspect it took place on Saturday May 29, 1937 at Town Hall, New York City when Grainger guest conducted the band of the Ernest Williams School of Music at that institution's "4th Annual Composition Contest and Band Festival"[2].

from the outset that this is a different kind of band music. Vital to this diffusion is the necessity for perfect balance between the three lines, so that none emerges as the lead. In scoring it for the pair of muted trumpets on the top two lines to be matched in intensity and projection by a muted horn doubled by bassoon, Grainger has presented the player and conductor with challenge no. 1 in bar no. 1. Oblivious of the fact that the horn and bassoon don't always grow with ease in many a band director's country garden, the composer scores only from his keen sense of color in mixing these tonal "pigments," topping off the timbres in a typical Grainger touch at the tune's conclusion with a dash of the different — his rudely-interrupting saxophones [14].

Grainger's initial measure has five silent pulses; all parts not playing in this first phrase should count this as part of their total bars of rest. The conductor must tell the players to count from the first of the silent pulses, which he should beat with clarity for everyone.

His tempo is unmistakably clear, both as to metronome-speed and verbiage. These, together with the "detached" short-long style, might be achieved, if any further clarification is necessary, by saying the iambic articulation: tee T A H tee T A H tee T A H T A H. These parts should carry Grainger's full request "...with plenty of lilt."

The 16-bar melody (A-A-B-A) is fully stated four consecutive times, each exposition being set in its own harmonic and instrumental surroundings. It is variation around the tune, not on it, and for this its composer wastes no time in revealing his weakness for the sounds of massed reeds. These punctuated by the kettledrums (no damping, please) dominate the second setting of "Lisbon"; his essentially detached articulation is contrasted here at the tune's B section [25-29] by the legato characteristics of the instruments playing in the two bottom staves. It is necessary to remind everybody with the tune in the top staff, marked "detached", that they must play it "clingingly", Grainger's preferred term (rather than legato or sostenuto) in his own language — "blue-eyed English".[7] As the tune's second statement is concluded [31-33] the rising figure in the oboes must be played as *forte* as possible.

Grainger's call to the reeds to play it "gently" at the beginning of the tune's third statement [34] is exactly the right request, for it is a very beautiful setting. The *dolce* on the parts loses something in the translation. He might also have asked for a "clinging" character to every eighth following a quarter, beginning with the G^b major triad that starts it off on its diatonic/chromatic wanderings. Solo players suit the intimacy of the scoring [34 to 60]. Every note here must be played as sustained as possible, including all the passing-tones. At its *piano* dynamic, the whole really charms, even when the horns burst in with their heroic intrusion, blowing a counter-tune based on the first phase of "The Duke of Marlborough".[8]

After the conductor with neat and appropriate pulsing has the quiet reed beginning in hand he must vigorously address the horns (backed by assorted reeds and brasses), making sure that his gestures and manner suit what they play while still keeping a penetrating ear on the wandering reeds as their sounds follow the outlines of musical interest established by the horns. As setting III concludes, the string bass and bass clarinet should be urged to build up the sound of their low E^bs in bar 48, the lowest tones in the variation. The music fairly glides along with Grainger at ease in a rhythmic-harmonic style totally his. The little reminder in bars 45 and 46 of the sax's earlier intrusion should not go unnoticed as setting III leads to IV, where simple two-part counterpoint between the reeds with distant echoes of "the Duke of Marlborough" in the horns provide pleasant playing and listening.

Then, again, Grainger bursts in with an intruding sound, [60] this one from among those that probably began to hatch in his head when he was a boy in Australia responding to the skirling of the bagpipes while imagining what a whole band of them might sound like tuned to different drones. I can hardly contain myself when this chord is sounded. Its expectancy is totally delightful. Grainger asks that it be played "nasal, reedy" — and he really means it. I'm rarely satisfied with the sounds players provide until, in desperation, I ask them to "really honk it!" Perhaps some of this grows from my feeling that Grainger has under-marked the dynamic; to get what he told me he liked, it can't be played less than *forte*. But I would not want my request for a solid "honk" to be misconstrued as license to make bad sounds which are never welcome. "Nasal" and "reedy" they must be; when blown full and vibrant they can be memorable.

The conductor should study this sonority with the players, constructing the chord, interval on-top-of-interval, all sustaining until every instrumental line is sounding, vibrant and full. The composer's texture consists of a widely-spaced D^7 chord beneath an A^b inverted pedal-point with G^b, A^b, and E^b passing-thru; but it is all those low-reed registers that color-up the music, the scoring (emphasizing the tritone's top two intervals) that guarantees at least a portion of its composer's textural requests. The conductor who hesitates slightly before unleashing this marvellous moment [60] will find that this framing of the sound provides a clarity not otherwise available.

As the high tide of "Lisbon" recedes and its composer winds it down in rhythmic extension and augmentation, a satisfying musical statement is withdrawn and completed in the same condition of charm with which it began. The vital harmony line [69-72] assigned to english horn, clarinet III, and tenor sax should be dominated by the english horn, for its timbre is able to penetrate the surrounding heavy scoring in favor of A^b and E^b. A brief but convincing fermata added to the final bar seems appropriate to a satisfying conclusion.

2. "Horkstow Grange" (The Miser and his Man — a local Tragedy). 37 bars. $\frac{4}{4}$ and various quarter-note metric signatures, slowly flowing, $\quarternote$ = about 76, D^b. Grainger first "noted down" this tune in that 1905 visit to Lincolnshire and then put it on the phonograph for the first time a year later; he never set the tune for any other instrumental or vocal ensemble, except for the version for two pianos.[9]

"Horkstow Grange," a pleasantly situated eighteenth-century farm house, stands beside the B 1204 road to South Ferriby and about 8 miles north of Brigg.[10] The song's narration of "local history" tells a tale of brutal violence suddenly erupting against an oppressive overseer by "his man" who obviously just couldn't take it any more; one market day he rose up and with a club released his long-pent emotions — "A local tragedy", indeed. Reading the full lyric[11] and recoiling at its horrors it is difficult, perhaps, to lay those words on top of Grainger's completely un-violent and sonorous setting of the tune. Obviously, he chose to set it as a kind of requiem to both men and their "falling out" rather than to react creatively to the violence in the words.

Here is one of the truly great pieces of band music — just 37 bars long, but so over-spilling with pathos, so emotionally packed as to belie their less than three minutes of running time. That its composer could pack this much profound and fervent beauty into less time than it takes to play many a quick-step march is one more measure of his genuine creative talent.

This beautiful music probably lay within him for a long time. Certainly he could hardly have been inspired to this lofty *"requiescat in pace"* from the very perfunctory rendition of it that was re-phonographed as sung by George Gouldthorpe in 1908. But Grainger obviously heard and felt within the tune that great underlying sadness which is sometimes the ultimate distillation of violence.

"Horkstow Grange" begins with the most legato anacrusis that players and conductor can produce; in addition to "slowly flowing" Grainger might have added "feelingly." It is an up-beat expressing all that follows, not a mere antiseptic interval of a perfect fourth through which an A♭ and D♭ are connected. The scoring of this interval for saxes, baritone, and all horns fixes the horns as the dominant color with their noble, haunting sound so wonderfully suitable to Grainger's requiem in the major mode. All players can enhance the expressive character of this beginning by pushing a special amount of air into the instruments just before they move from the A♭ to the D♭. All conductors can contribute to it through a slow and intense upward motion that stretches these intervals as expressively as possible.

The complete song encased within the full A♭ octave scale is stated four times with scant melodic alterations other than those convenient to rhythmic purpose, and all but the third statement (in the solo trumpet) are cast in D♭ Major. Harmonic underpinnings, however, are never the same, growing ever-richer as each use of the tune unfolds. The simple gift of subtle harmonic variation present in all of these expositions grants Grainger a very special place in music for the band.

The accent in bar 6 for the supporting F minor chord should be, like the seven other accents in the piece, highly expressive, *molto tenuto*, and in no way percussive. Each of the four times Grainger approaches the final cadence [8, 17, 27, 36] on the dominant A♭, the rhythmic juxtaposition between the tune and its accompaniment may be clarified for all by writing the following visual aids in the parts above the line:

Example 2

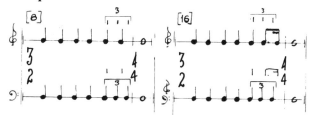

That all may know critical performance details it is recommended that this much ✗ of the grace-note minus pitch be written as a cue in all parts above the staff and just preceding the first note played by those instruments that accompany the "high reeds" as the second statement begins in bar 10. The "high reeds" are to be instructed to play this ornamentation before the beat.

Everybody's musical line should then stride forward, "singingly," with every player contributing ultimate breath support to a vibrant sonority of the most resonant balance. The conductor could contribute to the horizontal intensity with every technical resource of hands and arms, face and body. These total intensities which subsequently spill over into bar 14 cannot be so great at bar 10 that this further generation of them lacks the

Example 1 [1-9]

dynamic and emotional contrast — *forte* to *fortissimo*. When Grainger asks that all should "soften" in bar 15, this cannot apply to the horns, especially the first, for this line must continue to soar from its beginning on the G♭ in bar 14 reaching its zenith on the D♭ in bar 16.

When all have arrived at bar 17 there begins a diminuendo of nuance, orchestration, and color as part of the composer's F♭7 harmonic fabric, delicately touched-up by that rarely-used military band dimension, the pianissimo snare drum.[12] Its roll must be close and fast. To project the desired texture the player should practice and play this roll in the center of the head; it is easier at the edge, but the sound is simply not the same.

As the solo trumpet spins-out the superimposed A♭ *Horkstow* tune above this pedal, the critical entrances of the three clarinets and alto sax are vital to the color texture; conductors should bring each instrument in with precision on their part if with no punctuation by the players. The harmonic change a half-step up to the F7 at bar 25 fairly invites one to "linger" as the composer directs. The sound also invites the stress of a heavy weight being lowered on to it. In the interest of the two closing phrases in the trumpet [25 & 26, 27, 28, 29] it is desirable to terminate the first of these on the last note (E♭) of bar 26, and to begin a new phrase on the next G♮ with the advantage of fresh breath support; the G is much more important in Grainger's approach to the coming E♭ cadence than his printed phrasing allows it to be.

Grainger has so skillfully varied his harmonizations in the first three settings of the tune, never moving it off of its D♭ center, that when he moves into its fourth statement by way of the A♭7 chord to the D♭7 at bar 30, it all sounds very fresh and different — yet the *Horkstow* tune has never been changed.

Suspended cymbal (and that formerly-mysterious snare drum) must be careful not to override their sound into bar 30, joining the crescendo rather than leading it, following similar cares into bar 34 where the kettledrums must also pace the crescendo by listening to all that is happening in the group; cymbal and kettledrums must let the sound ring free at bar 34.

The majesty and grandeur of this final setting of *Horkstow Grange* [30-37] calls for playing of the highest order based upon endlessly superb breath support and opulent tone production. The lofty concept in these pages grants Grainger a very large niche in music written for the military band, one now uniquely his own. At its conclusion, conductor and players should remain motionless for about five seconds prior to release of the music's tension.

It always seems that this music possesses the magical power to draw from players that final thrust of good sound, that exhilarating climactic resource they aren't even sure they can produce — but it comes! The eighths especially challenge the low reeds and brass, and the trumpet must be able to generate the last full ounce of an intense crescendo leading to the grace note [36] that caps

Grainger's great climax with an expressive utterance that throbs with genuine musical passion. The final ornament also must be lyrically expressed and the closing fermata one of very long duration.

3. "Rufford Park Poachers" (Poaching Song). Flowingly ♪ = about 132, although I have now adopted ♪ = 160 as the tempo.[14] 103 bars, with multiple metric meters in alternation 4/8, 5/8, 3/4, 2/4, 3/8, 4/4 . Noted down and phonographed August 4, 1906 at Brigg, Lincolnshire. The tune and its expressive performances by Joseph Taylor so bewitched Grainger that he told me he was simply unable to choose between the different versions, which Taylor always seemed able to deliver with such conviction. And so, in his usual uncompromising way he set half of his full realization of it in two different versions, leaving the choice to the performers. The two principal differences between versions A and B are keys (F minor or C minor) and instrumentation, together with 7 bars where the composer seemingly could not choose between rhythmic options offered by the folksinger [7, 11, 12, 20, 47, 48, 49]. There is, of course, the matter of his beloved soprano saxophone which may also be used with Version A. The conductor must select one version or the other and then — as Grainger warns (in score and parts) ". . .be careful to let the band know which version is to be played." Version A, especially for the elegant sonority of its F minor tonality and a greater richness in its scoring has always been my preference. Performance suggestions for Version A apply to Version B, with allowance for those obvious differences in rhythm and tonality.

The story in "Rufford Park" (Percy corrected my pronunciation from "roughered" to "rooofered ") is told in five substantial stanzas each 18 measures in length (except for the third, with 15) unfolding the events surrounding the surreptitious nocturnal taking of game from somebody's private hunting preserve, punishment for which was sometimes extreme. Risking that, the daring raiders here described became the subject for one of the most poignant of all the folksongs Grainger found, and Joseph Taylor's singing of it is the most outstanding of all the Grainger cylinders I have heard. The composer's obvious fascination with the tune was certainly born in Taylor's superb singing of it. The song does not appear elsewhere in the gatherings from Lincolnshire. With total disregard for any fixed meter, Taylor let the words take him rhythmically wherever he chose to go melodically (Grainger's earliest notation of the tune appears in *Journal of the Folk-Song Society No. 12*, part 3, volume III).

Having once heard Taylor's memorable performances with their unfettered rhythmic flow, the multi-metered musical realization that we have was Grainger's only way to go. Selecting once more his favorite form, he is into theme and variation without delay. The tune, essentially Dorian, lent itself to immediate imitation, so here also begins the contrapuntal "complication" that unfortunately has caused so many conductors to bypass this marvelous music.

I am convinced that Grainger also unknowingly defeated himself visually. All that ink, all that busy printing, all that contradictory information emanating from the two versions (unfortunately printed on the same page) simply bewilders even the most conscientious players.[15] By the time the eye has leaped across music it is not supposed to read, fighting off instinct and training to respond to what is on the page, vital rhythmic and harmonic changes have transpired. Once out of these patterns, the player — rarely ever able to get back in — frustrates himself, his colleagues, and the conductor. *Lincolnshire Posy* then either winds up back in the file or is performed minus this magnificent movement.

Even without the visual problem, there is still the strict canonic imitation (2 eighth notes later) complicated by the uneasy presence of all those "mixed-up" meters. Performance problems persist, even though many young players have told me that they find Grainger's wide spacings of the tune at three octaves apart over a five-octave range to be an exotic playing and listening experience. Certainly there was nothing else like it at the time of its writing.

To play this movement we must remind those players who cannot absorb a simultaneously-sounding rhythmic/melodic signal contrary to their own that they must not listen to what is going on around them at that particular time. This is one of those contradictory experiences in which music abounds, to be sure — we have spent so much time telling our young players that they must always listen.

The same study/rehearsal procedures suggested for those difficult and slow contrapuntal excursions in Holst's *Hammersmith*[16] are recommended for the beginning and ending of "Rufford Park Poachers." Study must begin with individual mastery of each single line. Particular care for the strict observance of every nuance, exactly when given, will fulfill Grainger's intentions, for the nuances must be as strict, contrapuntally, as are the rhythms and intervals.

Study of the beginning and ending of "R.P.P." might begin with the conductor making copies[17] of pages 11, 12, 13, 14 and 23 of his corrected compressed score for distribution to the 6 players involved: piccolo, E♭ clarinet, B♭ clarinet, bass clarinet, oboe, and trumpet. With these excerpts from the score in front of them, the players and conductor should listen together to an accurately-recorded performance of these two passages, endeavoring to capture their character in timbre, nuance, rhythm, and that all-important element of perfect imitation in strict canon. Each player could alternate concentration between his own and another's line, absorbing as much of the whole as this sort of visual/aural contrapuntal osmosis might provide.

Among the options available is the following obvious set of patterns:

Example 3 [1-18]

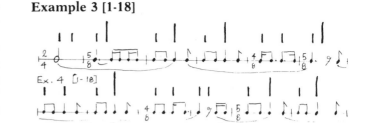

Grainger has prescribed "flowingly" as the essential character of this music. With this pervasive primary charge, conductors — first being certain of their own convictions and totally prepared for their teaching — should coach each player separately; performance in front of the whole band should be delayed until the playing of bars 1-18 and 85-103 is absolutely secure. Nothing so unnerves, frustrates, or bores a large group as does sitting there while four players and a conductor do their homework.

When this individual practice of the beginning and ending is achieved, I have found it helpful to start the players off by asking them to sing it in unisons/octaves at their most convenient vocal register. The tune spans but one E♭ octave and its intervals are no challenge. The conductor should then ask that all four begin on their first dotted-quarter note and sing together from bars 2 through 18. A hasty look at bars 2 and 3 shows that the melody is the same for all four instruments, with the lower two following along two eighth notes behind the upper two. For bars 85-103 the two upper line singers begin on their first quarter-note [85] at the same time that the bottom two line singers start on their half-note.

Once the music is achieved vocally, those hazards contributed to this music by the contraptions for which it is scored may be somewhat lessened and the whole problem might be conquered with lasting musical benefits that should long transcend the performance of this fascinating piece. The study might be completed by writing out a full score for each player with proper transpositions for the E♭ and B♭ instruments so everyone may then experience the playing of these two excerpts from the score.

It should be apparent immediately that the eighth note is the unit common to all measures for all players; Grainger's metronome mark at ♪ = 132 (revised to 160) sets the pace and establishes the conductor's patterns as pulses in those quarters or their nearest values equalling 3 eighths. Inasmuch as challenges in this piece are visual and aural the composer might have helped us all by always writing those bars of four pulses as $\frac{4}{8}$, rather than the $\frac{2}{4}$ which he used in random fashion up to bar 50. What transpires from that bar forward to bar 82 demands the $\frac{2}{4}$; whereas up to that point it is merely a confusion to the player who must think and see only eighth notes as the governing pulse. Bars 1-18 and 85-103 are free of this inconsistency.

Players, cautioned by conductors who we will assume have studied and solved the problem, must be certain to grant full value in these bars to all notes of longer value that precede notes of shorter duration.

Those continuing phrases that begin after the eighth note rest are critical to the rhythmic imitation, and they, too, must be begun exactly on time (without accent) and played at absolutely full value. Their up-beat characteristics contribute to what seems to be a natural tendency to rush them.

And it must be remembered by all that the flowing performance and high musicality desired through these two previous examples transpires in a contrapuntal situation where one player's zigging occurs while another player zags. The marvelous recorded example of Joseph Taylor's warmly expressive singing of this melody is a great performance guide.[18] Barring its availability, keep everything expressive with soft-textured rhythms and ornaments.

The most difficult part of the conductor's contribution to the successful playing of this music when grouping the eighths together is the need for absolute physical control of upward motion — our least developed technical motion, which has been sacrificed, I presume, to our over-concern for the beginning of the bar rather than its continuation or conclusion.[19]

Grainger's pattern of 5 is consistently 2+3 for all but 4 of the 18 measures [2, 6, 14, 98], and in these bars, those with 3+2 (piccolo and solo clarinet, then E♭ clarinet) should defer to those with 2+3, and these measures should be marked to convey this information.

Next comes *Stanza II* and its challenge of the composer's inner rhythm and harmony assigned to clarinets in two triads spaced at the octave. Surrounded above and below by quiet pedal points in reeds and string contrabass, these undulating sounds and pulsations always seem difficult to achieve, free from error. Grainger's error-filled parts are a real detriment to his music here. Like the beginning and ending of this movement, those who play (including the solo trumpet II) must be thoroughly trained in the proper performance of bars 18-45 prior to rehearsal of the whole band.

Again, these players and conductor together, but working apart from the band should listen to an error-free and musically acceptable recording while reading their music to implant its sounds in their musical and mental storage bank. Next all might say the rhythms, sustaining the notes their full value. After this when the instrument adds its dimension to the rest of the complexities, it all might seem to be a little less difficult.

If all of these study assists do not work, the conductor may then conduct each eighth note pulse [1 to 45 and 85 to 103] with the clear understanding that this must not reduce a beautifully flowing musical idea down to a choppy recitation of unexpressive eighth notes. Should the single eighth be adopted, the conductor should confine his motions to their clear minimum.

Colored by the presence of the tritone (D♮ to A♭), these two parallel triads with their diminished 5th establish immediately a warm, lush, homophonic texture, that — together with

Example 4. [24-35]

their encapsulating F♮ pedal points — afford an effective contrast to the starkly-spaced polyphonic fabric of *Stanza I*. These sounds from the clarinets always benefit from the most vibrant character that players can contribute; this "accompaniment" might well borrow its tonal commitment from most of the composer's charge to the companion solo soprano brass player: ". . .very feelingly, very vibrato." This constantly shifting harmonic substance draws upon 11 different three-note chords moving up and/or down and mostly in parallel motion by major or minor 2nds. Clarinet III along with the alto clarinet an octave below and always the bottom of the three voices make the first non-parallel sound in their move to the D♭ concert in bar 19; both instruments must push an extra amount of air into that D♭ to make its accent glow with vibrant intensity. The alto clarinet line is so vital to harmonic fullness here that, should the conductor have two bass clarinets and but one hesitant player of the alto instrument, one of the bass clarinets should double the alto clarinet line while the second bass player stays with the pedal point; Grainger provided this convenient cue in the part all the way to bar 46.[20]

These 28 bars [18-48] never come with ease, and I suspect that it is the aforementioned visual complexity, together with the constantly changing irregular rhythms and harmonic wanderings that combine to confuse the players in this ostinato-like passage. In what I know as his desire to erase the bar line (his folksingers had none) Grainger resorted to use of the tie across the bar line 14 times in *Stanza II*. Thus he generated inner rhythms and unknowingly contributed to the performance problem for those with the ostinato shown in example 4. The conductor should teach the players that these ties across the bar line *are* part of the problem. Like the exposition of the tune in *Stanza I*, every crescendo and diminuendo, properly played, is also part of the solution.

If it would assist I would not hesitate to convert the $\frac{2}{4}$ s to $\frac{4}{8}$ s; the parts should also be marked — every part — with the pulse patterns that the conductor intends to use. And the conductor must then be consistent and clear in their execution.

Problems begin for all when any note value here is not played or conducted to the full — even beyond the full. The eighths always seem to suffer, mostly I suspect because they precede the "sacred" bar line and because they are at the end of the $\frac{5}{8}$, an "irregular" rhythmic unit. The conductor can help out by making every motion be flowing, "cool," and almost vertical in direction. Upward flow, extended beyond the usual dimension to incorporate the fifth eighth or the three sixteenths in those patterns, contributes greatly to the smooth, fully-flowing character of the music. The pattern and its proportions might match what is shown in example 5.

For the expressive conductor it is not merely the space to be covered or its direction that are of primary concern. Of equal importance is the intensity with which these are pursued, and for this,

one must be at least on the fringe of command in all physical facets of conductor technique.[21]

Stanza II affords the opportunity to introduce readers to what I have come to call the "up-beat down beat," and this occurs at each of the seven $\frac{5}{8}$ s between bars 22 and 38. These brief units serve the composer's musical grammar, much as a comma clarifies structural content in prose or poetry. Each $\frac{5}{8}$ occurs after notes of longer duration and serves to extend and to stress those points where the folksinger took his time before proceeding to the next line of thought. Thus, it seems to me, these units are more up-beat in character than down, and this is why I suggest that the conductor be rid of one more down pulse (amidst this profusion of them) by spinning another up-pulse off the last quarter note pulse in the bar that precedes it. The pattern is shown in example 6.

Motion upward, slow and intense, covering more territory than a $\frac{5}{8}$ bar is usually programmed to get, provides that stretch so desirable to the music and affords, as well, a special identification for these seven critical pivotal points in the music's performance. Moving this music safely through its first 45 bars is a genuine test of a conductor's ability to lead.

Example 5   **Example 6**

The solo flugelhorn (or trumpet, or cornet) has just begun to sing *Stanza II* above the ostinato in the clarinet family when, at the end of its first phrase, Grainger adds a sinister comment on that voice through his extension of it in muted Trumpet II. This is the first of four such complementary fragments, each treated a bit differently. The chromatically descending triplet, always played in crescendo/dimuendo then becomes the basis for composing the two important five bar dividers [46-50 & 63-67] that Grainger used to separate Stanzas II, III, and IV. Both dividers seem fervent outpourings of his own deep feeling for English "Yeoman-artists," for their "grandeur and sturdiness." These brief creations are among the high points in the *Posy*, with their composer reaching moments of ultimate excitement as the second one tops the first.

Trombones lead off this development with their sonorous downward chromaticism [46] which is under-marked in dynamic, increasing *mf* to *f* being minimal for proper projection in crescendo. Their answer in clarinets and horns, followed by the same material spaced rhythmically in soprano and mid-range brass, is then overpowered by the triplet figure bringing the first divider to its resonant conclusion in C minor. All players here [50] should cap their climaxing crescendo with a great pushing-off of the sound on the second pulse of the $\frac{2}{4}$ bar; aided in this by the sounds from the kettle-drum and suspended cymbal (the dynamics scrupulously observed) the whole gets a great boost from that single bass drum note [50].

The conductor here fulfills his pulse-keeping duties, beckons the important entrances to begin, keeps a penetrating ear out for balances, and lets it all happen until the C minor cadence [50] when the great sound must be ceased and then resumed with gestures of both force and clarity. All players with the five-octave G's at the end of bar 50 must separate that note from the previously suggested push-off, make it long and intense, then be on their way with the exciting Dorian setting of *Stanza III*.

The composer's indication that the tempo here should be "somewhat faster" is out of step with his metronome mark ♩ = 80, which is 35 points slower than his initial, and last suggested pulse. "Somewhat" is exactly what he really meant, so he told me when I brought him the tape in preparation for a recording. This was my choice because of the coming change of mood at bar 68, with which he also agreed.

Grainger's brilliant[22] (possibly even unprecedented) musical idea in the rapidly reiterrating trumpet notes ("triple-tongue as fast as possible — no set number of notes to the beat") moves their parallel triads in startling chromatic descent the distance of a tenth over the next 12 bars. The bass trombone, for instance, plays a completely chromatic scale passage descending for an octave and diminished fifth over the 11 bars between 51 and 62. The harmonic backbone to the great five octave spacing of the tune in the low reeds and brass, together with the sustained fabric scored in the 2nd and 3rd staves of bars 19 and 20 provides a joyous and robust setting of what had first been stated as a quiet little tune, appropriate for easy imitation. Here, as in that initial statement, the nuances (the swells and fades) are not cosmetic to the music but integral to it.

The second divider begins with yet another compelling instrumental touch — the piccolo, at the piano dynamic, amidst all this regenerating sound; but that marvelous little instrument has a way of getting through the screen of sonority around it. Then Grainger lets loose with all the trombones and baritone for another go at his divider material, piling-on the sonorities that culminate in his great "slow-off" on the Gb7 with the F♮ and Gb each striving to be dominant, as they should. Again he turns to that magnificent, much abused instrument, the bass drum, to cap it all when the brass and others have given everything they can.

I know few more satisfying moments in band literature than those which follow as Grainger

---

Mixed Meters and Mixed Blessings

Music pulsing in 5s or 7s continues to plague performance by many young American musicians, who seem to be fatally locked into only the duple or triple pulse. For some, I suspect it may even be a nightmare from which there is no awakening. In our country we continue to suffer a general lack of any serious pursuit of the basic elements of music separate from the simultaneous challenge of producing sounds on an instrument of one kind or another. Because of our failure to grasp the unending values of fundamental music studies free of an instrument's complications, frequently we have had to rely on the intelligence, the talent, and the gift of rhythm granted to the smallest segment of our students — always in the hope that they who do not have problems of the pulse might pull their less gifted peers (and some of us equally ineffective conductors) through the music of Charles Ives, Aaron Copland, Igor Stravinsky, or Percy Grainger.

The Crusaders might have eased these pains had they brought back from their excursions to the Middle East (1096-1271) the songs and dances in 5, 7, 11, and 13 that went with the percussion instruments that they did so successfully transplant to the popular culture of Europe. Perhaps we should be grateful for the magnificent triangles, tambourines, cymbals, and kettledrums they carried home, and conclude that their physical strength probably surpassed their aural dictation skills.   *FF*

---

leads the listener away from the tension so carefully constructed and into the relaxed warmth of his richly chromatic harmony for *Stanza IV*. Led by one of his favorite instrumental blends (horns and saxes), the tune winds its way above the wandering chromaticism, which idea was spawned in that first muted trumpet figure in bars 24-26, and appears here again, sounding somewhat less sinister in these expansive Db Major surroundings. Grainger's harmonies fairly glide from bar to bar and he invites the conductor to join that freedom of motion in his suggestion of a "waywardly" tempo. With all of this the conductor must lead the players in the constant heave and swell of sound that occurs in almost every measure.

As *Stanza IV* winds down, the composer directs that the music should "slow off lots," and I have found it necessary for good ensemble to have the conductor dictate each of the four notes in bar 82. With the resumption of the music's "1st speed" and the statement of *Stanza V*, the conductor and players again assume the rhythmic posture discussed for the beginning of the piece. For everybody's rhythmic security in the final "slow off" it is suggested that the conductor should beat every eighth-note pulse in the last four bars, beginning this by beating the last two eighths in bar 99.

It may be helpful to seat the six solo players together in a cluster at the center front of the band where they can hear each other to the best advantage, and where the visual challenge may also be overcome.

Percy Grainger's great pioneer belief in the

musical resource of the military band so eloquently set forth in this music remains an open challenge to us all. And how strange all of this must have seemed to the musicians who played it under Percy's unorthodox conducting for the first time — wherever that was. Lacking probable contact with the evolution of composition and its performance practices pursued as an accepted part of the profession by orchestral and chamber music players, bandsmen at this time were probably confused or dismayed by this new style, and disenchanted with the composer of *Country Gardens* "— a good man gone mad!" I imagine there was many a laugh in Milwaukee at Percy's expense that 7th of March 1937 — laughs from the musicians, the audience, and most of the bandmasters, and much unkind muttering behind the mouthpieces about the ". . .eccentric piano player who thought he was a composer." But if there was laughter of derision then, nobody's laughing at Percy Grainger anymore.

4. "The Brisk Young Sailor" (who returned to wed his True Love). 48 bars. B♭ throughout, ¾ Sprightly, ♩ =about 92. Percy Grainger's contact with this folksong began in the summer of his 1906 journey to Lincolnshire and ended with this version of it for the *Posy* 30 years later. He finished this setting after he and his wife Ella had returned to White Plains following their trip to Milwaukee for whatever of it was played for the first time at that ABA convention.

I do not remember seeing the designation "clarinet choir" in any previous work, the scoring for which reveals much of the richness inherent in this collective sonority. Once again, Grainger was far ahead of everybody, and unfortunately, too many of us "everybodies" were the nation's band directors.

As always with Grainger, the whole tune is apparent as well as present, with the five variations developed around it rather than on it.

I have found it secure to write in every part that all should count from the first beat of the first bar, and then to indicate these two initial pulses with small but positive delivery — a special emphasis going to the second. This is particularly necessary for conductors whose habit is to conduct "extra" preparatory beats.[23] Grainger's pulse (♩=about 92) does not seem "Sprightly" enough to me. Perhaps he chose it out of consideration for the rapid finger activity that goes with the sextolet embellishment in the high reeds that is his very attractive comment on the tune's third statement. But the players always rise to the occasion, and a brilliant performance in rehearsal (after a little work) usually elicits the approbation of shuffling feet or even applause from their colleagues. Try a speed of ♩=108 with editings shown in example 7.

As the first statement of the tune concludes [9] it is imperative for proper balance that all possible low reeds (bassoon II, contrabassoon, bass saxophone/contrabass clarinet) build up the sound of the low B♭, for the chord tends to be over-scored in favor of F♮, its fifth. The connecting link between statements three and four provided by the quartet of horns [17] needs a quick flair crescendo to start it off. It is sometimes difficult to discern in Grainger's music whether the difference between identical figures disimilarly scored are intentional

Example 7 [18-25]

Editing of music examples, shown in gray, is by Frederick Fennell.

PICC. FLUTES, CLAR.

Piccolo octave higher

mf

louder

Louder all you can

variants or simple inconsistencies. One among these questions is raised between bars 11-12 and 35-36. Surely, the second of these must sound as short and detached as the first, but Percy's eighths in the trumpets, horns, and baritones [35-36] won't necessarily be as short as the same figures so effectively written for the reeds in bars 11-12; the visual comparison is in favor of the reeds' sixteenths, but each conductor must make this decision.

A different and yet more costly inconsistency is that between the word of the score and what appears in the parts at bar 41. Here [40] where resonant and pleasantly scored reeds and horns are to be answered [41] by snarling brass — marked *angrily* in the score — the parts merely carry the comparatively bland direction that it be played sonorously! And the contradictory alteration in meaning is his own doing, for the publisher merely printed what he wrote for each individual part.[24] The snarling must be of gathering intensity straight through the five triads of harmonic change (C♭, A♭, D, G, D♭) into the sixth, a cluster of a diminished fifth, augmented and perfect fourths, topped by a major 3rd.

All conductors know how difficult it is to achieve the next passage or one like it in any piece of music such as bar 42, with its simultaneous demands ("slow off" and $>$) coupled to the ensemble challenge offered by Grainger's two-piano-like writing between the top and bottom staves. Here the pulses of eighths must lead those above who play a sixteenth later; and those who play the sixteenths should neither play them short nor muddy the sound with length. A plain and vibrant sixteenth will work if it is properly placed. Everybody has to work at achieving this demanding single measure. Players frequently tend to start off at less than Grainger's *forte* dynamic and are then reluctant to diminish their sound proportionally. The six eighths are units of measurement set out for all and they should provide an accurate dynamic-gauging guide for the conductor, who will remind the players.

The conductor's contribution to all of this might be reduced to the simplest of motions — offering six pulses all delivered in the same place with identical bottom points and gradually smaller, slower spacings, keeping everybody's vision concentrated on the exact "when." Resumption of the tempo where the little coda/extension [43-48] needs projection of the motive from bar 2 leads to the delicate and difficult passage for clarinets I & II. It is in the best interests of everybody to make these two lines a solo passage for two players. Soft staccato articulation with a bit of diminuendo in the last four sixteenths leads to Grainger's highly individual closing chords which, with their major-sixth inverted pedal-point come out being two combinations of major triads [47] B♭ over F♭ and [48] B♭ over D♭. Their scoring in the reeds with the alto saxophone lead has always struck me as a quaint and charming Grainger farewell to American popular music of the twenties. A little of that special ballroom vibrato colors the cadence here

in fine style.

After all those heavy demands everybody endured in the preparation and performance of "Rufford Park Poachers," "The Brisk Young Sailor" comes as a relief from tensions, especially for the conductor who can sort of stand back for some of it and thoroughly enjoy listening as the music goes past, dipping the hand in when needed. After getting things started and bringing the first statement to conclusion with a clear release of the dotted quarter [9], the conductor's next concern must be for precise ensemble in bars 11-12. Then, after the horn flair and the entrance of the solo baritone [17], there is little a conductor can contribute to the rapid reeds except perhaps to join — with appropriately sculptured gestures — the high rise and fall [21-22] to the exciting conclusion [24-25]. The brief three-part contrapuntal excursion [25-33] only needs a firm hand at its conclusion [33], leading to the fifth statement/variation which needs steady control all the way to the end of the movement where the previously-discussed conductor's participation is needed for the last seven bars.

5. "Lord Melbourne" (War Song). This is a variant of "The Duke of Marlborough" folksong; "Sung by Mr. Wray and phonographed — 'Thrice & noted' by P.A.G. at Brigg, — Lincolnshire 28 July 1906; this version for military band (worked out and scored, Feb. 1937)." No key signature, free time, various tempi and metrics ($\frac{1}{8}$, $2\frac{1}{2}\frac{1}{4}$, $1\frac{1}{4}$, $\frac{2}{4}$, $\frac{3}{8}$, $\frac{4}{4}$, $\frac{5}{4}$, $\frac{4}{8}$, $\frac{3}{4}$); 59 bars.

Here, in the opening statement of Grainger's "Lord Melbourne" we meet anew the military band's original free-thinking spirit. But any unsuspecting bandmaster who might have ventured an innocent look at this first page (29) in 1940 might have thought that Grainger was the military band's original nit-wit! — music without a time signature, 7 random note values stretched over a span of 35 impacts before a bar line. Grainger called it "free time," and for it he endeavored, once again, to instruct his interpreters in the performance of an unconventional music by simple verbal explanation of his purpose.

His notabene (N.B.) printed in the score at the beginning of the fifth movement, offers two interpretive guides: the opening phrase written in traditional note values, minus the arrows used in the score, but explaining their purpose. His call for music that sounds "Heavy, fierce" (it is a "War Song") with each note in the brass to be played forte and "fairly clingingly" tells us the essentials in our approach to stylistic performance. Unfortunately, however, the words of the folksong are missing; and to me they are the real key to these great moments in the band's music.

During a visit with him in early January 1958, prior to the Eastman Wind Ensemble's Mercury session of *Posy*, I caught Percy in a mood of great candor and creative reminiscence. We were discussing my part in making "Lord Melbourne" work, and he said the answer was in the words. Once again we were off to the fireproof basement to get the copy I still have of *The Journal of the Folk Song Society*, first singing through all of this lengthy saga, as he had set it and published it in 1925. We were headed back up to his music room when he paused at the foot of the stair and said: "The first time I went to Brigg I was urged by locals to go to a pub where one of its regulars was considered to be the best singer of 'the Lord,' as he called it. As you know, my dear Frederick, I have always been free of the habits [he was vegetarian, never smoked, offered me a light red wine at dinner] and I just could hardly make my way into that smelly, evil place — but I did — and I'm glad. This day all the poor man could bring himself to remember was the first phrase which he fairly bellowed-out in hesitant, if gleefully inebriated joy:"

Example 8

It is this mangy doggerel version and the breezy spirit in Percy's superb imitation of a happy inebriate that have stuck with me ever since. I have "sung" it for an uncountable number of groups in rehearsal, and each time, these words and my bellowed imitation of Percy's imitation never fail to make "the Lord" come alive!

This is where the stretches on the first quarter of each phrase come from. It was, Grainger said, as though the man was trying to remember the next word before plunging into his performance. Matching the words to the notes as illustrated, the reader sees, for instance, that ♪♩=BATTLE, while the elongated Is and other stretched vowels are my attempt to communicate to others what Grainger so vividly imparted to me. It may be used or ignored but the conductor is urged to find some departure from the simple note values in keeping with the composer's directions at the head of the score. My own architecture for "Lord Melbourne" divides it into *13 lines:* Line 1 [1], 2 [1 — from A], 3 [2-8], 4 [9-13], 5 [13-18], 6 [18-23], 7 [23-27], 8 [27-35], 9 [35-43], 10 [44-48], 11 [49], 12 [50-54], 13 [54-59].

Excellent results may be had when the conductor jabs both hands down and out from the body, covering identical territory in the repetitious delivery of the down-pulses so clearly indicated by the arrows. But I urge conductors to join the in-

testinally fortitudinous character of this music no matter how it is conducted; the "cadencial" half notes are easily wiped away with a wave of the left hand. The release of the final half note in bar 1 (the whole of page 29 is bar 1!), climaxed by the crescendo roll of the kettledrum should find the conductor's hands/arms stopped at a point of positive attention from which the preparation for bar 2 may be executed as clearly as possible. And here the conductor might think of Grainger's ⅝ bar as a ⅝ in which the first pulse is silent but present as the preparation for the entrance of the trumpet, horns, baritone, and saxes. To execute in "strict time" the conductor simply raises both hands 3 inches and stops; the players enter and the conductor proceeds down for the 2½/₄. It is another example of what might be called the "up-beat down-beat" and it serves with clarity to invite the solo trumpet to begin the lyrical statement that follows.

It is desirable to secure the performance of Grainger's vacillating harmony (E7 — Dm7) [2-7] before joining it to the solo trumpet; and I have found it functional to indicate a square, brittle three-pulse pattern in the ⅜ [7] to set up a clear dictation of the rhythm in bar 8. The punctuations in the quarter-note brass that accompany the tune should be as resonantly short in bars 10-11 as they are sustained and separated in bar 12.

The bass drum termination of that great Dm7 chord [13] is clearly written as an eighth note. I was never satisfied with that sound and early-on in my rehearsals of this piece I decided to dampen the kettledrum after impact and to let the bass drum's wonderful resonance die a natural death. As the sound is about to decay completely, moves to resume the music are executed. If the group is secure, give the 4th pulse only; if there is any insecurity, giving three and four will assist the players to precisely establish the "lively, playful" tempo with which all must deal for the next 19 bars, offered in four short segments (lines 5, 6, 7, 8).

Grainger has chosen his words very carefully to describe style and pulse. These, along with strict attention to articulation and nuance, provide as clear a performance plan as anybody could want. However, two aspects need the conductor's special care: (1) space which must separate all eighths, and (2) precise evaluation of tempo and note value in the ⅜ bars [15-20-29]. Players tend to hurry the 2nd eighths when offered in pairs, and to rush ahead with the ⅜s as a kind of triplet played on its hasty way to the following downpulse.

The fascinating variety offered in the scoring of these four settings (percussion punctuations define them clearly) testify to Grainger's vivid aural imagination, courageous conviction, and positive commitment to the wind band medium. He said it all in the second paragraph of his "Program-note on 'Lincolnshire Posy'," and these 36 remarkable pages of music that follow are its manifestation. Performance of the 3rd setting (line 7) is given over to the baritone solo [23-27] and marked to be played "easy going." The player must be urged to project this music far beyond his position in the group's physical setup (the F tends to be sharp). The clarinets at the cadence [27] should make their "gurgley" comment with special emphasis from Clarinet III, playing in major 2nds with its neighbor.

Line 8 [27-35] is extremely compact and, as was sometimes typical of its composer, flits quickly from idea to idea. In the midst of this rhythmically vital material the sudden presence of the huge B♭ chord that errupts in the reeds at bar 32 is always an anticipated joy. The crescendo should be tremendous with an appropriately vibrant push-off at its release.

As line 8 concludes [33-35] with Grainger's "slow-off," the 16ths and 8ths might be played properly long if the conductor elects to pulse bar 33 in 4. The arresting sound that is left by bassoon, sax, and horns as the great D major chord of bar 34 is released for the beginning of bar 35 never fails to be a striking aural experience — a Dm9 played piano to the third power emerging from such an open D major triad — *forte* to the third power. It is another Grainger first for band music. The conductor should let this quietly diffused sonority hang well in fermata before proceeding to line 9. Balance in this fermata is extremely critical, the players being careful to keep the listener off balance in never offering prominence to either the E or the F natural.

All my life I have been a whistler (frequently I am sure to the aggravation of others) and in this way have decided many personal musical matters in great privacy minus the presence of any instrument. Some pieces fit that format as though designed for it, and a great deal of Lincolnshire Posy is one of them. Line 9 [35-43] of "Lord Melbourne," made for the piccolo, whistles with natural ease. Although Percy heads it off "in time," I have always felt it to be a free-sounding tune that fairly invites a reflective kind of improvisitory character; and so did he with his directions to the oboe and piccolo that they play the 16ths "fast." Unfortunately, he neglected to so inform the rest of the players in these measures [37 and 41]; so unless the conductor writes the same word in these bars for the saxes and horns, one more incommunicative condition exists for the conductor and the players.

At each of the 10 critical changes of harmony that occur along the contour of the melody [36 to 43] the players need every ensemble security that the conductor can provide. The patterns and stretches shown in example 9 usually work for me.

The poignancy with which Grainger addresses himself to line 10 [44-48] is all there in the harmony, the voice leading, and the "lingeringly." If this is insufficient, the conductor should apply to all instruments what Grainger expressed for his favorite instrument, the soprano sax, when he wrote out its part: "Solo, vibrato, appassionato." This descending inner passage must be projected as all players begin to "louden" all they can toward line 11 [40-49], to the "free time" [49] when, once more, the brass and kettledrums restate the opening material. This time it is varied, of course, both harmonically and rhythmically forward from the 3rd chord of "slightly faster." On their way to this point, the clarinets should play every note in measures 44 to 48 to their maximum duration — molto tenuto or, as Grainger might have expressed it "very clingingly" with each accent played as expressively as possible. This line is topped off by the ultimately expressive and tenuto entrance of trumpet I [48] as it bridges the music into line 11 [49]. The tenor sax, horn II, and euphonium carrying the tonality from the D minor triad to the diminished seventh by way of the A♭ in bar [46] must indeed follow Grainger's encouragment to "louden all you can."

Notice that Grainger adds fermatas at both of the cadence chords in this next "free time," and that the richness in his harmony grows with each chord (Bm, Em, Am9, B♭maj7 E9, F♯7) to the G Major over the D minor, where only the three horns must make this colossal crescendo that so gloriously completes bar 49. Although the horns don't like to do it, raising the bells is a legitimate practice and is never more effective than in this place where it really brings the sound "to the fore." The conductor must address some very clear and appropriate gesture to the horns for their crescendo; but whatever may be applied here physically, it will be the conductor's straight-on look at the horn section that will bring the crescendo and secure its release as well.

Example 9 [35-43]

Line 12 [50-54] consists of five of the greatest measures in the piece, headed by the impetuous statement of the tune in Grainger's powerful four octave scoring for the high reeds, backed by those marvellously sonorous punctuations in the brass, low reeds, and precussion. Balances are critical in these chords and to be certain that all the players in the group hear what these harmonic changes contribute to the excitement in the music I suggest that the conductor ask that these chords be studied first as fermatas — just for the listening. When later played short, as written, they may then have a greater meaning for all. The three vital notes: G♯ [50] to A♮ then to G♮ [51] do not project through the density of Grainger's rich scoring without reminding the players of their importance. Although the score allows the percussion a *fff*, it is better reduced to *f* in the interest of balance, although cymbals and bass drum should not dampen their eighths [50-51-52].

Then comes this forceful rhythmic presentation in that same scoring for low reeds, brass and percussion. If all will back off one dynamic level, waiting until bar 52 for Grainger's *fff*, the effect of it all will be heightened (see Ex. 10).

Example 10 [52]   **Example 11 [59]**

It is, of course, a harmonization of notes 6 thru 8 "...English man..." of line 1, and it is almost impossible to overplay this passage, so do request the players to project it. In the 6 sets of triplets that follow [53-54], the phrasing emphasis should be toward the 6th set, approached through the "slow off" with its long eighths. This last triplet can then be an anacrusis to the final "free time" [D-55].

Again, the horns should put the bells up for their "very brassy" heroic contribution [53-54]. The snare drum and suspended cymbal will contribute the most if they delay the peaking of their crescendo until the 3rd pulse of bar 54, spilling their sound over into the "free time," which for the only time in "Lord Melbourne" is scored for the full band. It is line 13, and Grainger faithfully uses every note of the opening line while composing

below it as effective and as positive a conclusion as one can imagine. And how exciting it is to relive each time, the surprise one always experiences the first time that this great pylon of brass blows the first of the three final chords below the tune's last three notes.

After a great many exciting, mostly error-free performances of this work, marred only by a faulty release of the final chord — one of the high brasses failing to time the physical factors and holding past the cut-off — I have removed the fermata and added the visual release on an additional next down pulse in all of the parts (see example 11). This way I can judge the length of that final bar by what I think the brass can sustain after all of the demanding blowing that preceeds it, and still be certain of a clean release that grows out of the five pulses. It is always easy for us conductors to stand there, shaking both hands and pleading with every facial expression for the brass to give, *give*, GIVE! But sometimes they have already given, and this spectacular ending washes out simply because we have not properly estimated how much water there was in the well. The players, too, can judge their reserve of sound and time its release when they can see how long the "fermata" will be.

6. "The Lost Lady Found" (Dance Song) English folksong noted down by Lucy E. Broadwood from the singing of her Lincolnshire nurse Mrs. Hill (1893) and set for Military Band by P.A.G. in 1937 from an earlier one "tone-wrought for mixed voices and 9 or more instruments in 1910." No key signature (Dorian mode on D) ¾ , no meter changes, 146 bars. Full instrumentation, plus "tuneful" percussion.

Grainger was as moved by the words of the folksongs that he set as he was possessed by the tunes. The simplicity of the "Lost Lady" melody contrasts the complexity of the nine verses in which her story is told.[26] Stolen by gypsies, her uncle is falsely suspected of having done away with her in order to acquire her estate. Her sweetheart, searching everywhere, eventually came across her in Dublin. Returning home, the united pair arrived in time to prevent her uncle's hanging for the alleged crime. The final verse completes the tale:
"Then straight from the gallows they led him away,
    The bells they did ring, and the music did play;
  Every house in the valley with mirth did resound,
    As soon as they heard the lost lady was found."
It is easy to see Grainger being carried away by this, turning his fancy for variations around a theme rather than on it to these nine different dimensions in harmony and orchestration.

Verse 1 [1-17] is safely begun when the conductor writes in every part: "count from l," so that players entering at measure 18 know that no "free beat" is given. The conducting style (one pulse to a bar) should reflect the short, driving character of the music with clear emphasis on the first beat accents and the third beat *sforzandi*, indicating as well the important length of the dotted quarter that ends each four-bar phrase. Grainger's "short" describes the other articulation very clearly.

Verse 2 [17-33] adds harmonic punctuations beneath the same tune. Be sure to stress the rich content of bars 26 and 27, with special emphasis on the B♮ in bar 27. Carry the ensemble precision achieved in the unison statement of Verse 1 into the rhythmic developments of Verse 3 [33-49].

Verse 4 [49-65] is a tonal, rhythmic, and textural variation beneath a beautiful solo for the piccolo. With its utter contrast in legato it demands that the conductor join the change of style by adopting appropriately smooth and "pulseful" gestures. These might consist of a pattern executed at the conductor's discretion that only delivered *one* and *three* of the bar. But whatever is adopted, the conductor will probably have to remind the players that the third pulse of each bar must be full and vibrant, and that each of the three bars [52, 56, and 64] will have to be especially legato. The unfortunate and unnecessary hazards usually surrounding performance on the alto clarinet bid me to suggest that the conductor use the cue for that line provided in the bass clarinet part [50 to 66].

Verse 5 [65-81] extends the spirit of the preceding variation and is so utterly rich in its thick doublings and lush in its harmonies that I was not surprised to find out that this is the verse when the lost lady flies into her sweetheart's arms. (I discovered a copy of the folksong after I knew the music). It is always difficult to keep the band at its minimum dynamic here where everything sounds so warm and inviting, but the conductor must be sure that *pianissimo* prevails; small, smooth, "pulseful," and inviting gestures fit the music.

Verse 6 [81-97] begins with an ensemble hazard between the short notes of the reeds and the longer values of the saxes, horns, and tenor brass. This can only be solved by listening, but it will help if visual aids are written in the parts of all players involved (Example 12).

Verses 7 and 8 [97-113, 113-129] herald the joyous closing of the piece and for its principal rhythmic projection Grainger borrows the figure he introduced in Verse 3, starting with the horns:

Typical of the good composer, Grainger keeps building on this good and driving rhythm, even bringing it into the high woodwinds, tastily, two bars "too soon" [112]. This is a touch that never fails to tickle me as Grainger then continues to pour on the instruments and the decibels in Verse 8 until everything happening at the middle phrase [122-129] so completely swamps the tune — intentionally, I'm sure — that the orchestration tail wags the folksong dog.

But it all comes back together as Percy begins Verse 9 [130] with its happy ringing of the bells in fulfillment of the text with the tune now unmistakably present. His term, "tuneful percussion" so aptly described the vibracussion family in 1937. And it was Grainger who was first to hear that the most undeveloped sonority in the military band was that of its percussion section, with particular concern for the mallet instruments.[27] Had he lived to enjoy the percussion virtuosity that he helped to stimulate, he'd have been the most energetic member of the percussion clan, for he was there before anybody!

But his bells do ring, and his music does play as at last the lost lady is found and his *Lincolnshire Posy* comes to its brilliant conclusion. As the wayward trumpets lead the whole band in its paean of joy, the bass drum has the final say.

A compelling momentum has built up in this set of variations, and it is not necessarily easy for the conductor to slow it down (or "off," as Grainger says) without some plan. Mine is to join the group in changing from the one pulse to three in bar 141, affording us all the visual and aural control so necessary to this imposing conclusion.

Final Thoughts

I knew before I began that it would be impossible to write a worthy comprehension of a masterpiece, a work I am only now beginning to really know after long study, frequent rehearsal, and repeated performance. My time with its composer was all too short, but what there was has shaped

Example 13 [97-99]

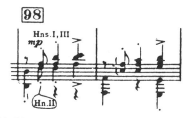

Example 12 [81-89]

15

me greatly. His marvellous spirit and his magnificent devotion to the whole art of music live for me in all of those pieces of his we discussed together, sitting in those "B♭" rocking chairs on the porch at 7 Cromwell Place in White Plains, New York. He could look a hole straight through me with those honest, and now sad blue eyes; behind them — and through the tone of resignation in the voice — I grew to know that his life didn't quite add up to the lofty aims of his youth. The failure of most of us to give his band music much of a view until a spurt toward the end, together with the complete "cold-shouldering" of *Lincolnshire Posy* weighed heavily on his vanishing spirit. Abdominal cancer, of course, was steadily destroying what had been a magnificent body.

Percy once called his music "...a pilgrimage to sorrows."[28] And he meant these sorrows to be tears of discouragement at the public's rejection of his serious music, of his failure as a composer. But we must know that our tears must be shed in grateful joy and in thanks to him for *Lincolnshire Posy*, great music, uniquely and extraordinarily his. ∎

Notes

1. Review, *The Milwaukee Sentinel*, March 8, 1937 by Hans F. Emmerling who observed that as a "special guest" Mr. Grainger offered "three parts of the yet unfinished 'Lincolnshire Posy.'" I am convinced that he undertook this composition in acknowledgement of his recent election to honorary membership in the A.B.A., and because he sincerely believed in the band and its future as reflected in the prestige of this association. A news story in the same paper on the same date offered a figure of 7,000 in attendance, that 15 bandmasters rehearsed the group between 9 a.m. and 4 p.m. with rehearsal time pro-rated to each conductor at 3 times what it took to play his music, the whole overseen by a timekeeper with a stopwatch. Grainger must have found this to be anything but fun, for in addition to whatever he played of the *Posy* (most likely I-II-VI; movement IV was not yet scored) he also had to prepare his long, very difficult, and extremely strenuous *Lads of Wamphray March* for this same concert.

2. Seeking to interest Carl Fischer, Inc. in the publication of his "...most recent composition for military band..." he invited the editor to attend this concert and sent him a broadside announcement of it (letter and broadside in the author's collection). The American trumpet virtuoso, Don Jacoby, who played first trumpet as a student in the Williams Band at this performance, confirms the premiere.

3. Grainger often took me with great pride to his incredibly well-organized two-room fireproof shelter dug beneath the backyard and connected to the basement of his very large frame house at 7 Cromwell Place, White Plains, New York. Who but Grainger would have thought of such a simple but effective way to protect his most precious possessions? Every imaginable article used by him from his old army boots, walking sticks, and back packs, to most of his repertory piano music, some manuscripts, publication proofs, and these 10" X 20" ledger books, was already neatly tagged and stored in sturdy dry-goods boxes. When he died, all the shippers had to do (in fulfillment of his will) was to come pick it up and send it to the museum he had founded (and even helped lay brick to build) on the grounds of the University of Melbourne, Parkville, Victoria, Australia. He had already collected and sent there a variety of ethnomusicological artifacts; first editions of his music are also displayed.

4. Representative samplings of these cylinder recordings may be heard on a long-play disc called ENGLISH FOLK SONGS, *Unto Brigg Fair;* Leader 4050; 2 sides, texts of the songs, copious notes, and illustrations are included.

5. Conductors should really prepare a time, possibly apart from rehearsal, when all of the introductory notes Grainger wrote for this piece can be read to the entire group. Any "wayward" reactions from students (or players of any age) may be overridden by his unmistakable passion for these subjects and his positive manner of their expression. We are all so far behind in the aesthetics or the expressiveness of our art that we should cherish and share these marvelous words with each other, preoccupied as we have become with the musical symbols and their always elusive pursuit.

Additional reading for conductors should include Grainger's forward to *The Band's Music*, by Richard Franko Goldman. There are also two biographies currently available, *Percy Grainger — the Inveterate Innovator*, by Thomas C. Slattery, The Instrumentalist Co., 1974; *Percy Grainger* by John Bird; Paul Elek, London, England, 1976. All Grainger students will want to secure *A Complete Catalogue of the Works of Percy Grainger*, edited, catalogued, and with a foreword, afterword, and explanatory notes by Teresa Balough, The University of Western Australia, Department of Music, 258 pages, 1975; available in the U.S.A. from Theodore Front, 131 N. Robertson Blvd., Beverly Hills, California 90211, as is the Paul Elek publication of John Bird's book.

6. G. Schirmer, Inc., the U.S. agent for the publisher Schott & Co., Ltd., 48 Great Marlborough Street, London W.1., U.K.; the copyright was Grainger's.

7. For further explanation, see author's box in the performance essay on Grainger's *Irish Tune* and *Shepherd's Hey*, and the Slattery and Bird books mentioned in note 5.

8. Grainger's brief but superb brass ensemble composition, "The Duke of Marlborough Fanfare," British Folk-Music setting No. 36 published by Schott & Co. 1949, was written in Coral Gables, Florida March 5-6, 1939 while he was there as soloist with the University of Miami Symphony. It is a searing and haunting cry-out against war, and a work every bandmaster should know and own.

9. Recorded on EMI Records HQS 1402 by Leslie Howard and David Stanhope, duo pianists, with 10 other Grainger pieces under Percy's own

title: "Room-Music Tid-Bits and other Tone Stuffs."

10. Bob Thomson's words from the booklet accompanying ENGLISH FOLK SONGS (note 4).

11. The lyrics for Horkstow Grange are provided by Bob Thomson in his notes for the *Leader* recording (note 4):

In Horkstow Grange there lived an old miser,
You all do know him as I've heard say.
It's him and his man that was named John Bowlin'
They fell out one market day.
    Pity them who see him suffer,
    Pity poor old Steeleye Span;
    John Bowlin's deeds they will be remembered;
    Bowlin's deeds at Horkstow Grange.
With a blackthorn stick John Bowlin' struck him,
Oftens had threatened him before;
John Bowlin' turned round all in a passion,
He knocked old Steeleye onto t'floor.
    Pity them who see him suffer, [etc.]
John Bowlin' struck him quite sharply;
It happened to be on a market day.
Old Steeleye swore with all his vengeance,
He would swear his life away.
    Pity them who see him suffer, [etc.]

12. P.A.G. called it the "side drum," a traditional usage. I suspect that it is so-called in the English language because in its ancient origin as an outdoor military instrument there was no other simple way to carry the drum except hung from the shoulder by a sling which throws the drum off to the side on the march. During its symphonic metamorphosis composers should have re-labeled the instrument a soprano snare drum. The bass drum, properly pegged in its register, and likewise of ancient origin was not called a "front drum," although it should have been and for the same physical reason that it must be slung from the shoulders and rest on the body's front when carried. When it was moved indoors it was cradled and played in this same position and remained so (against the law of gravity) until the percussion ensemble, the wind ensemble, and the many composers who were creating both groups placed it in the horizontal position at the beginning of the second half of the 20th century.

13. Grainger was a pioneer explorer of the wide range of percussion sonorities as applied to music for the band, including what he called, appropriately, "tuneful percussion." His ethnomusicological interest led him to spend much time investigating and playing the extensive collection of percussion instruments in the Rijksmuseum at Amsterdam, Holland in the earliest years of his tours as a piano virtuoso.

14. The final autograph of the compressed military band score reveals the most unfortunate of the many errors in the printed score of "Rufford Park," for the unit of speed is clearly given there as an eighth (rather than the quarter note shown in the published score), both at the beginning and at bar 83. The autograph of the version for two pianos is the same as that for military band. Grainger, however, never corrected my tempo (using the misprinted quarter note) when I took him a pre-recording session rehearsal tape. Both of us followed my score, noting the many corrections I had made, but nothing was said about this considerable and critical difference in speed. However, I find the piece to lose its charm at the composer's indicated tempo ($\flat$=132). It relates in no way to Joseph Taylor's singing of it, he being closer to the quarter note unit (see note 4); but at a pulse of $\flat$ =132 boredom sets in, and when Grainger published this folk song for the first time in the 1908 Journal, he indicated the singer's pulse at $\flat$ =160!

15. P.A.G. knew it would be so, for he wrote as follows in a letter "To the editor" at Hawkes & Son, London dated July 1, 1938, at which time he was obviously in serious negotiations with that very important band firm on the publication of *Posy*. In his detailed directions concerning the format of the printed parts, he wrote as follows: "The 2 versions of Rufford Park Poaches [sic] makes a regrettable complication, but seems to me unavoidable."

16. See pages 30-37 in the author's study/performance essay on *Hammersmith* in Basic Band Repertory, the British Band Classics.

17. *The United States Copyright Law, A Guide for Music Educators* is issued jointly by several national organizations and available from the Music Educators National Conference. The reader-conductor-teacher is advised to procure and read this document for proper copyright use in the classroom.

18. See note 4.

19. Consult author's article, "The Calisthenics of Conducting," *The Instrumentalist*, November 1978, pages 16-20.

20. The score should indicate this vital cue.

21. See note 19.

22. See "Program note on Lincolnshire Posy" on page 76 of the full score edition, Ludwig Music, Inc., 1987. It is destructive to rehearse, but at performance, the players must spend it all.

23. The certain snobbishness about not giving preparatory pulses argues against the fact that among our principal responsibilities as conductors is to give information — not withhold it.

24. A careful comparison of each master brass part written in his own hand, and in obvious haste, contains the bland, *sonore*. In the matter of haste and as some explanation of the plethora of errors and their proliferation in the material, it must be remembered that Grainger received his letter of commission from the A.B.A "...to write two pieces for band for their annual Grand Concert and Convention at Milwaukee in March 1937..." in December 1936. His biographer, John Bird (see footnote 5) writes that he "...composed three of the movements in the remarkably short time of four days." All the parts were written out in ink in his own hand from the compressed score, the absence of a full score making a positive check of what he seems to have composed as he extracted, literally impossible.

25. See footnote 4; the full and "proper" text of "Lord Melbourne" is published in Bob Thomson's superb notes to the recording listed here.

26. The lyrics, too extensive to print here, are available only in the 1907 Boosey & Co. edition

Grainger credits in the upper left box at the head of this movement.

27. He used them melodically, enjoying the articulate penetration of the xylophone and the ringing quality of all of the metals. When he scored "Spoon River" for orchestra (published in 1929) he specified a part for "steel marimba," looking ahead to the coming of the vibraphone! It would remain for mid-twentieth century composers such as Warren Benson and Karel Husa to further apply

Grainger's "tuneful percussion" to the wind group. Most band composers were simply slow to see and hear their long-available vibracussion resource. Anyone who has read this study/performance essay this far, should read Grainger's "Preface to *Spoon River*," included as Appendix C, pp's 285-291 of John Bird's biography (see footnote 5).

28. Quoted by John Bird, p. 164, from "Grainger's Anecdotes."

The following corrections to the Schott & Co., Ltd. 1940 printing of Lincolnshire Posy *accompanied Frederick Fennell's essay/performance analysis, which appeared in* The Instrumentalist *in 1980. Since then Fennell has prepared a corrected full score edition, published by Ludwig Music, which he discusses at the end of this article.*

Errors

"Lisbon"

All Parts: Change title to "Lisbon."

[10] Part: Clarinets II, III, alto and bass — critical cue line is falsely labeled as clarinet 2, instead of trumpet II.

[3-7-15] Part: Trumpet I — remove the tie between the F's.

[30] Parts: Tenor sax — change *f* to *mf*.

[31] Part: Kettledrums — change dynamic from *p* to *mf*.

[42] Part: Trumpet III — relocate measure one bar later than printed.

[43] Part: Horn I — add *ff*.

[50] Part: String contrabass — correct the number of measures rest from 8 to 10.

[50] Part: Alto Sax II — add *<* .

[60] Score: Bottom staff — change dynamic to *f*.

[63] Part: alto and bass clarinet — remove *f*.

[72] Part: Flute — change *pp* to *p*.

[72] Score: add fermata.

"Horkstow Grange"

The title should be corrected on score and parts, to *Horkstow*, in addition to the following corrections and/or additions:

[2] Part: Horns I and II — add *<* .

[5] Score: Bottom staff — add *mp* to the dotted half.

[7,8] Part: Clarinet II — change dynamic to match score.

[7] Part: Alto clarinet — remove crescendo.

[9,10] Part: Bassoon and Baritone Sax — make slur as in score.

[10] Part: Alto clarinet — remove slur.

[10] Part: Alto clarinet — add *mf*.

[13] Part: String contrabass — correct impossible page turn, by cutting the page between the first and second staves of page 2.

[14] Part: E♭ clarinet — add accent to the 4th note.

[14] Score: Bottom staff — add *mp* at dotted quarter.

[15] Part: Flute — add soften.

[18] Part: Bassoon — make dynamic *ppp*.

[19] Parts: English horn and trumpet III — correct 19 to 17 .

[21] Part: Baritone sax — remove *<* and add it at bar 23.

[25] Part: Alto clarinet — correct ♩ to ♪ .

[25] Part: Alto clarinet, alto sax, bassoon — change dynamic to *p*.

[25] Part: Horns I, II — change *mf* to *f*.

[25] Part: Horn I — correct D♮ to D♭ concert on the dotted quarter.

[26] Score: add diminuendo throughout this bar as in trumpet I part.

[29] Score: 2nd staff — add *pp* cresc.
3rd staff — add *p* cresc., as in parts.

[29] parts: Soprano sax — change *mf* to *f*.

[30] Score: 2nd and 3rd staves — add *>* to quarter note.

[30] Parts: Flute — add slur from bar 29.
Score: Add Flute slur from bar 29.

[30-37] Score: 1st staff — transfer the many overlapping phrasings from all of the parts.

[33] Part: Clarinet III, bassoon — correct the half note to a whole note to match the score.

[33] Score and Part: Cymbal — clarify "soft drum stick"[13] as being kettledrum stick.

[33 & 34] Score and Parts: Add *≥* to the last eighth note of bar 33 (♩ ♪) and following the first half note of 34 (♩).

[37] Part: Flute — add fermata.
Baritone — add *p > pp*.

"Rufford Park Poachers"

The following extensive list of critical errors for *Version A* must be corrected in the score and parts: Corrections for *Version B* are a challenge I leave to the reader who, if patience is matched to curiosity, will surely find both to provide a great satisfaction. I acknowledge in admiration and with thanks the assistance of the players of the 1957-58 Eastman Wind Ensemble whose brilliant playing of *Lincolnshire Posy* at their Mercury Record session on March 2, 1958 at the Eastman School of Music in Rochester, New York won for them the unique recognition of that performance as being one of "the 50 best recordings" of the *Centenary of the Phonograph* (100 years of recorded sound, 1877-1977) by David Hall, of *Stereo Review*. Together we began the endless task of correcting the errors in the printed music. Additional acknowledgement for this search is extended to numerous colleagues, among them Donald S. George, Jack W. White, Robert Pinto, Joseph

Kreines, William D. Nicholls, and H. Robert Reynolds.

[1] Score: Change unit from ♩ to ♪ = 132.

[2] Score: E♭ Clarinet is cued in Oboe I (not Flute I — the piccolo part is cued in Flute I).

[5] Part: Bass Clarinet — 16th not printed clearly.

[6] Part: Flute I — correct last note from F to C in piccolo cue.

[6] Part: Piccolo — add *p*.

[6] Part: Clarinet I — correct to written a.

[7] Part: E♭ clarinet and bass clarinet — correct 1st eighth to G concert.

[16] Score: 2nd and 3rd staves — extend beam to connect last four notes = ♪♪♪♪

[16] Part: Piccolo — remove *poco rit.*

[17] Score: Upper stave – time signature missing.

[17] Part: Bass clarinet — remove *ritard*

[18] Part: Bass clarinet — remove *a tempo*.

[18] Part: English horn — relocate [18] from [19].

[18] Part: Horn I-II — this bar is missing in the cue from Trumpet I.

[19] Part: English horn — reverse the last two notes = ♪♩ ♪♩

[20] Score: Solo soprano brass line — the dot is missing on the quarter note.

[20] Part: Clarinet II — remove eighth note flag on 3rd note = ♪♩♩

[23] Part: Tuba — measure is missing.

[24] Part: Trumpet I — correct the second 16th note to a written F♮.

[30] Part: Alto clarinet — change ⅜ to ⅜ .

[32] Part: 1st alto sax — should have half note.

[46] Part: Trumpet III — tie to next bar missing.

[47] Part: Treble clef baritone — delete everything in ♭ th bars and substitute rests.

[47] Part: Horn IV in F - second note should be E♭.

[48] Part: Clarinet II — remove the dot on the dotted half note; revise rhythm to ♪♩.

[48] Part: Clarinet II & III — reverse the values on the last two notes and remove slur (make ♩♪).

[49] Part: Clarinet — dot missing on dotted half.

[49] Part: Horns — slur missing.

[49] Part: Euphonium — remove E♮ whole note, and substitute part identical with the baritone.

[52] Part: Trombones — remove ⅜ .

[53] Part: Clarinet I & II — correct written G♯ to:

[54] Part: Horns III and IV in E♮ — change whole note rest to quarter rest.

[57] Part: Flute — make slur as in score.

[60] Part: Alto clarinet — articulate as in score.

[62] Part: Clarinet II — move accent from 2nd note to last.

[62] Part: Horns I-II and III-IV — the vital figures indicated in the score are missing in the parts.

[63] Score: Top staff — whole note needs a stem and a dot.

[64] Part: Baritone sax — remove *subito*.

[64] Score: 2nd staff (trombones, baritone) — remove dot from dotted half.

[65] Part: Clarinet I & II — reverse the rhythm of the last two notes and remove the tie in Clarinet II.

[65] Part: Horns I & II — reverse the rhythm of the last two notes.

[65] Part: Trumpet I & II — correct the 3rd note

to written B♮.

[66] Score: Top staff — add ¼ .

[67] Part: Piccolo — add *slow off*.

[68] Part: Bass clarinet — change first note to written C♭ .

[72] Score: 2nd staff — add *pp* at end of >.

[72] Part: Trumpet II — one too many bars; eliminate the cue bar, last in line 4 in the part.

[75] Part: Euphonium — change > to this bar only.

[75] Score: Bottom staff — 3 is missing over the sixteenths.

[75] Part: Bassoon I — 3 is missing over the sixteenths.

[78] Part: Flute and E♭ Clarinet — remove tie to 2nd pulse.

[81] Part: Trumpet III — no fresh slur.

[82] Score: 3rd staff — Add >.

[83] Score: Change unit from ♩ to ♪ = 132.

[83-86] Part: Tuba — change ¼ to ⅔ , put stems on the whole notes.

[90] Part: Oboe I and Bassoon I — dot missing on quarter.

[95] Part: E clarinet — correct first note to written B♮ .

[95] Part: Flute I — missing first note, in the piccolo cue.

[98] Part: Oboe I — correct rhythm in part as in score.

[99] Part: Bassoon I — last note correct from ♪ to ♩.

[100] Part: Bassoon I — correct the part to match the score.

"The Brisk Young Sailor"

These errors must be corrected in the score and parts:

[1] Part: Clarinet I — slur missing over the first two notes.

[8] Part: Basson — remove slur.

[11, 12] Part: Flute; Oboe; Bassoon; Clarinets I, II, III; Alto and Bass clarinets — remove all lines from the eighths to sixteenths as in the score.

[17] Part: All horns — correct dynamic to *mp*.

[17] Score: Delete reference to horn III cue in tenor sax.

[25] Part: Oboe — add slur to sixteenths.

[28] Part: Oboe — change last ♫ to ♫

[38] Part: Baritone — change > to *sf*.

[39] Part: Euphonium — change last ♪ from F♮ to G♮.

[41] Part: All brass — change sonorous to *angrily*.

[42] Part: Soprano sax — remove crescendo.

[43] Part: Soprano sax — remove *ff*, make *mf*.

[46] Part: Bassoons, tenor and baritone sax — 1st note should be a quarter.

"Lord Melbourne"

The following errors and/or omissions must be corrected in the score and parts:

[1] Part: Trumpet I — 14th note, add stem and flag to make it an eighth.

[1] Score: 2nd staff 14th note — remove eighth-note flag.

[1] Part: Horns III & IV in F — 4th, 5th, 6th notes of letter A correct the notes ot E F♯ G / C D E.

[1] Part: All horns in E♭/F — 9th note of letter A correct eighths to sixteenth.

[1] Part: Horn IV — 11th note of letter A correct to F♯ concert.

[1] Part: Trumpet II — four notes before measure 2 tie the two eighths, remove accent.

[1] Part: Trumpet I — 9th note of letter A correct eighth to sixteenth.

[9] Part: Horns I & II — dynamic should be *ff*.

[9] Part: Trombones I & II — dynamic should be *ff*.

[9] Part: Trombones I & II — remove accent on 6th note.

[9] Part: Euphonium — remove accent on 6th note.

[10] Part: Horns, trumpets, baritone, euphonium, tuba, percussion, kettledrum, and string bass — "Strict time" is missing.

[12] Score: Upper staff — add dots to half notes.

[12] Part: Trombone III — remove crescendo.

[13] Part: Horn IV in F — correct note to A concert.

[15] Part: Bassoon — correct ₂ to ₈ .

[16] Part: Clarinet I — add *piano*, last eighth.

[16] Part: Alto sax — line missing on first note.

[19] Part: Trumpet I — 4th pulse, correct ♩ to ♪♪ .

[20] Part: English horn — dot missing on first eighth.

[20] Part: Alto sax I — correct first note to written G♮ .

[21] Score: Top staff — second note is Clarinet II, not I.

[22] Part: Trombone I — correct 3rd note from B♮ to A♮ .

[23] Part: Trumpet II — dot missing below eighth.

[24] Part: Baritone — "easy going" missing.

[27] Part: Trumpet I — correct time from ₂ to ₄ .

[29-30] Part: Bass Clarinet — part written major 2nd too low; transpose up.

[30] Part: Trumpet II — correct first note to a half.

[32] Part: Baritone — correct ₈ to ₂ .

[33] Part: Trumpets I & II — 5th note, correct F♮ concert to F♯ .

[33] Part: Trumpet II — correct *pp* to *f*.

[34] Part: Flute I — ₈ missing.

[34] Part: Alto Sax I — ₈ missing.

[34] Part: Bassoon — relocate 34 here.

[39] Part: Horn I — note must be F♯ concert.

[43] Part: Horns I & IV in E♭ — dot missing on half.

[47] Part: E♭ Clarinet — this bar with its proper rest and ₈ signature is missing.

[48] Part: Clarinet II — remove dot from half note; add one to the first eighth.

[48] Part: Alto Sax I — add dot to half note, remove dot from quarter note, and remove superfluous dotted eighth.

[48] Part: Alto Sax II — make repairs as above and remove eighth flag.

[49] Part: Horns — bracket missing on quarter triplet.

[49] Part: Horns I — 4th note from end of bar correct D♯ to D♮ in E♭ parts (to C♮ in F parts).

[49] Part: All horns — add "to the fore" on last fermata.

[49] Part: Trombone I — final fermata correct note to B♮ .

[49] Part: Baritone & Euphonium — delete the crescendo on final fermata.

[49] Part: Horns I & II — remove false bar line after half note fermata.

[50] Score: Third staff down — remove the ♯; it relates to nothing.

[53] Part: Oboe, Clarinet III, Alto Sax I, Tenor Sax — the dot is missing from the half note.

[53] Part: Horns III & IV — add "very brassy."

[53] Part: Trumpet II *ff*, not *fff*.

[54] Part: Clarinet I — correct time to ₂ .

[55] Part: Clarinet II — accent missing on 4th note.

[55] Part: Trombone III — accent missing on 4th note.

[55] Part: Trombone III — 8th note in the measure should be A♭ .

[56] Part: All parts — "Strict time" is missing.

[58] Part: Tenor sax — first 8th should be staccato.

[58] Part: Trombone I — first note is F♮ .

"The Lost Lady Found"

The upper righthand information box on page 35 of the score lists 1927 as the date of this version; it should be 1937. These errors must be corrected in the score and parts:

[25] Score: Correct last quarter to two eighths.

[34-48] Part: Flutes, Oboes, E♭ Clarinet, Clarinets I & II — add accents to the first note in each bar.

[49-65] Part: Piccolo — identify these small cue notes as the solo for piccolo.

[57] Part: Alto Clarinet — correct last two eighths to a quarter.

[61] Part: Piccolo — correct last quarter to two eighths.

[86] Part: Trombone II — dot missing, half note.

[91] Part: Horns I & II — remove diminuendo.

[108] Part: Alto Sax I — correct the rhythm as in score.

[113] Part: Baritone — make last quarter into two eighths.

[121] Part: Alto Sax I — make last quarter into two eighths.

[121] Score: Bottom line — remove final quarter note; add quarter rest.

[127] Part: Flutes — add staccato on last two eighths.

[145] Part: Piccolo — dot missing on half note.

[145] Part: Bassoons — add fermata.

Frederick Fennell and Percy Aldridge Grainger

Full Score Edition

Repeated study and performance of *Lincolnshire Posy* since its appearance in various 1980 issues of *The Instrumentalist* continued to reveal a galloping amount of errors, omissions, and inconsistencies numbering well over half a thousand in the parts alone for the 1940 edition. This data, voluminous and cumbersome to codify, simply reached beyond a practical list of errors as had sufficed for the earlier study/performance essays. My solution for these problems was to assemble a thoroughly correct full score from Grainger's original manuscript parts; Grainger, it must be noted, never made a full score. In 1987, when it was discovered that the composer's 1940 copyright had not been renewed and that the *Posy* was in the public domain, a new set of parts matching the new score also were assembled. The copyright was applied for and granted. For the correction of errors, etc., in the 1940 edition discussed here, the reader is referred to the full score edition, *Lincolnshire Posy*, composed by Percy Aldridge Grainger, published by Ludwig Music, Inc., Cleveland, Ohio in 1987.

Correction of the *Posy*'s errors really began with the players of the Eastman Wind Ensemble in their preparation for the 1958 Eastman/Mercury Recording. Colleagues Donald S. George, Jack W. White, Robert Pinto, Joseph Kreines, William P. Nicholls, H. Robert Reynolds, and Donald Hunsberger had lent their valuable support. Two new strong allies were found in Ward Hammond, who would engrave the new full score edition, and in Tim Topolevsky who also joined me in the painstaking examination of Grainger's manuscripts, compressed score and parts, and every scrap of paper about *Lincolnshire Posy*. This material had generously been loaned on microfilm by the Grainger Museum Board, University of Melbourne, Parkville, Victoria, Australia. This resource offered what, after 40 years of study I believe to be the best available information about Percy Aldrige Grainger's masterpiece.

Frederick Fennell
June 1988

September, 1978

Percy Aldridge Grainger's Irish Tune from County Derry and Shepherd's Hey

An Interpretive Analysis
by Frederick Fennell

Percy Grainger was an avid and highly successful collector of English folk songs, a summertime pursuit that began at the same time he emerged as a concert pianist and composer at the turn of the 20th century. These song-gathering expeditions would eventually provide the source for many of his compositions, the foremost being *Lincolnshire Posy*. On the way to that masterpiece, which slumbered within him for over 30 years, he spent his considerable energies composing, among numerous other scores, a series of what he called *British Folk Music Settings*. The series, which eventually totalled 43, was conceived to be sung, played at one or more pianos, or performed by strings, orchestras, or military bands.

Grainger's rich, piquant harmonies were cast within a framework of great rhythmic vitality which provided attractive program material for easy listening. Such pieces quickly swept him to a lofty position among the composers of the post World War I period.

Country Gardens was his most popular composition, but he lived to rue the day he had ever written it, feeling that it had robbed him, in his maturity, of a listening audience for his other equally serious but more personal creations. No matter how he beheld them, these superb instrumental settings are the harmonizations and the orchestrations so many of us have come to know as representative folksongs of rural England. They are undeniably his.

Percy Grainger served in the U.S. Army from 9 June 1917 to 6 February 1919. His life as a musician at Fort Hamilton, New York must have been one continuous band clinic. Already hailed as one of the world's great pianists, he was not one to pass up any opportunity to learn. He chose, among other interests, to practice the saxophone, more to learn about that whole family of instruments than to endeavor to become a "90-day wonder" on the B$\flat$ soprano. He never ceased to praise its beauty of tone and splendid lyric quality, or to register his strong if questionable belief that the whole family of saxophones was superior to that of the clarinet.

When transferred to Governor's Island he began to conduct what he was composing, including these band settings of *Irish Tune* and *Shepherd's Hey*. His continual interest thereafter in writing music for this type of ensemble makes Grainger's volunteer war-time service a positive gift to us all.

Irish Tune from County Derry is credited by Grainger as having been collected by "Miss J. Ross, of New Town, Limavady Co. Derry, Ireland, and published in the Petrie Collection of Ancient Music of Ireland, Dublin 1855." His setting of it for piano solo was among his first compositions. It is No. 6 in the *British Folk Music Settings* series and was preceded by an *a capella* version for mixed voices, which Grieg greatly admired. That was followed by the famous arrangement for strings and horns.

The military band version is Grainger's final treatment of *Irish Tune* and its harmonic content (up a half step from E major) is a literal transcription of the setting for strings. But his scoring for the military band reveals a concept of instrumental voicing that for the band was daring, rich and varied, in the vein of originality in band music that we admire so much in the two Suites by Gustav Holst (both of which Percy told me he did not know when he wrote this piece in 1918).

Grainger obviously heard everything. His consummate knowledge of instrumental voicings as they appear in *Irish Tune* reveals an acute, almost innate awareness of how to bring out the best in all the instruments. From bar one Grainger's score looks different: he has the tune in the bass clef, and that is the top clef of the three, with the ones for treble harmony and counter *cantilena* (flowing melody) tucked in the middle. I know of no band music set in this voicing before this piece. Immediately and vividly apparent are the long legato lines, all six of them moving in stately procession along the staves. The tune in these 32 bars is eloquently assembled and exquisitely balanced.

That this beautiful music came to Grainger from a pure and expressive crucible of Celtic folk art shows his affinity toward almost all of those cultures surrounded by the eastern North Atlantic Ocean and most of the North Sea; his antipathy to things Germanic, save for the music of J.S. Bach, was complete and unchanging.

Irish Tune from County Derry

The formal construction of *Irish Tune* may be analyzed in a variety of ways, for example: A - B - A - C (16 bars) D - D - E - A (16 bars), with the essential structure and rhythmic flow clearly relating each phrase and section to the other.

The melody ranges over an octave and a fifth (I suspect that the low C♯ is Grainger's), and is certainly a textbook chapter on "melodies and how they are made." The listener and performer are carefully led through easily-heard intervals to appropriate points of repose, then led again by thematic restatement to a mid-point that might itself have been a satisfying conclusion. The whole first half of the melody is neatly encased within the scope of a single octave (D to D). But then [17] the second section moves immediately through an upper F major tetrachord into the tessitura of the baritone voice. These same intervals are restated with insistence, gathering dynamic intensities of their own, until everything spills over into the high A that prepares the final phrases.

The individual lines and their assignment to instru-

mental timbres proceed with balanced logic from phrase to phrase with the same clarity that emerges in the opening bar. Even though mixing dark timbres can be dangerous business in these registers of the key of F, Grainger takes no chance that his tune will be buried. The inclusion of trombones assures that the light of the melody will shine through all that surrounding darkness; and all textures which support harmonically are designed to blend.

Grainger's masterful counter *cantilena,* spun out above the beautiful tune, is among his most notable achievements. It fits its parent melody as though conceived simultaneously. To me, this together with the whole harmonization is the quintessence of the Grainger gift to us all.

With the fulfillment of the first climax of intensities and at the height of the melody [26], he skillfully withdraws from this pileup of heavy sonorities into a quiet release that brings the first section to a perfect conclusion, having led us through one complete musical experience.

The second statement [33] commences in a contrasting way: the tune, cast in pianissimo plus, is now passed to the soprano line and the whole scheme is elevated; the lucid harmony which supports that voice in the flute is distributed among four other lines assigned to complementary reeds. Grainger's classical sense of part writing and the essentially vocal ambiance that one finds within it continually lead the music on, to one appealing instrumental entry after another [36-47].

These instrumental entrances are judiciously selected to increase the harmonic and linear tension that is carefully built and then released in the sonorous F major chord [48], which brings this first section of the second statement to its intense middle cadence. Then come the great singing sonorities of the final phrases and the first employment of all the instruments. Their apex of sound [58], led by screaming French horns (forte to the 4th power), is one of the great moments in band music, and Grainger's sensitive release from this magnificent climax is a withdrawal as carefully planned and as beautifully balanced as was the instrumental buildup that preceded it. The recession from these great sounds to the quiet cadence contains that gift of genius which so frequently elevates his settings of other people's tunes into a sphere that makes their music become his.

Conducting Challenges

A tempo that works is always the initial responsibility of the conductor. In this case the composer has done everything to provide guides to a proper tempo, beginning with that typical Graingerism: "Flowingly," and continues with two equally characteristic descriptions: "Very feelingly" and "gently but feelingly," and there is of course his metronome marking of ♩=80.

It should be obvious from all of this that Grainger hoped he might avoid having his interpreters choose a pulse that would find the music wallowing around in a pool of sentimental slush, the players gasping for breath, and those beautifully-proportioned lines sagging at every seam. "Dyingly but gaspingly" might better describe what is frequently heard rather than what is prescribed. Conductorial maturity regardless of age may be said to have arrived to some degree when one no longer conducts slow music too slowly or fast music beyond its pace.

A tempo that works is always an initial responsibility of the conductor, and everything plays beautifully at Grainger's 80 pulses. The casting of these as quarters in $\frac{4}{4}$ for the military band as opposed to his setting in eighths at $\frac{4}{4}$ for the string orchestra version always causes me to pause and think before I conduct one or the other. In either case the initial silent pulse must be definite and inviting. Obviously he is depending on the simple visual flow of quarters to provide the bandsman with a pulse projection that encases his rhythmic needs within a single bar. Average band players and bandmasters in 1918 may not have been secure with 8 slow pulses to a measure, and if Bandsman 2nd Class Percy A. Grainger's experiences at Ft. Hamilton and Governor's Island had taught him so, this is probably why this version moves by the quarter-note.

Balances demand careful listening with all lines subjugated to the melody, which must be projected with greatest breath support in full keeping with Grainger's exhortation to ultimate expression. The five different instrumental sonorities that he has selected [1-16] require careful balance within themselves, that they may blend into a homogeneous sonority.

I have usually been happiest with this sound when I add more horns and urge the trombones to carry the leading quality, using as many baritones as available, but asking them to let their numbers, in a solidly supported *piano*, blend with the trombones, rather than dominate them. All should play vibrantly, especially the trombones. Note that way back in 1918, Grainger was asking that the baritone and tenor sax play with vibrato. All must play with the greatest possible sostenuto, clinging to every note for its full value and beyond, seeking the ultimate ensemble as the lines move in their marvelous way.

The line above the tune, the one I call the *cantilena* (cornet 1, horn 1, soprano sax), has a special presence. Grainger sought to color it through his inclusion of the soprano sax amongst the sonorities of the brass. The present publication does not include a soprano sax part, although it is mentioned in the score and the publisher has promised to restore it. A soprano saxophone player can use the 1st cornet part for the first 16 measures.

The *cantilena* must not be so unobtrusive as to lack presence as sounds begin to build in the second section (D) [17]; intensities generate of themselves, peaking at the climax [25 & 26] in an unmistakable musical fulfillment. But it is the closing, the releasing phrase [28-32] that demands the greatest discipline, the ultimate in breath support, the complete conductorial control of nuance and sonority.

As the first complete statement approaches its conclusion [29], all should release the G7 chord deftly and cover that release with sufficient resonance to allow a skillful breath with which to finish the phrase [29-32].

The beginning of the second statement [33] seems to demand five solo players, to be joined by a sixth where a choice between tenor sax and bassoon may be made

for that important lowest line [37]. This suggested contrast, achieved by thinning the texture, follows the thick richness which is the hallmark of the first statement. Vibrant solo playing here is certain to bring sonic and artistic rewards, allowing critical control of the delicate nuances and minimum dynamics, all of this under the aura of expressiveness that has been so lovingly instilled by the composer.

All instruments may be utilized as more and more instrumental voices gather around the action [41] and the midway point is reached [48]. In the interest of effective ensemble and the momentary emotional release to be found here, the conductor should extract the ultimate in tonal support from the players toward that release leading to the great *tutti* at [49]. All parts with a whole note at measure 48 should be edited as in this example for the 1st cornet:

And now everybody should be at it, playing vibrantly with a great singing sound. Whenever the excitement of playing such beautiful music grows as it does here all players must remember the constant need for the ultimate in breath support to drive the airstream on through the instruments. When vibrancy is added to all of this the music seems to soar off into a sonic realm that transcends the mere instruments producing it.

Every line is important, and it is up to the conductor to be sure that lines do not become buried within instrumental textures just about as thick as one is likely to find. As the music begins to *louden* [56] all must remember that any accents are to be played *espressivo* and *tenuto*. In the gathering excitement, the conductor and the players must hold sound in reserve for each pulse. Grainger's request for sound must be served by those horns, cornets, clarinets, oboes, and saxes who must literally thrust their rising F major triad up through the rest of the band. It is vital to remember that the pulse of the music must continually press the great sounds forward, keeping the melodic line aloft and driving the rich harmonies to their climax [58].

The suspended cymbal [56-60] should be used to heighten the excitement of the climax, not to dominate it. The "soft drumstick" indicated should be a pair of felt kettledrum sticks or yarn-wound marimba mallets.

The Final Cadence

"Slow off lots" and "soften gradually" tell us what we need to know; if everything is kept as expressive as possible, the steady approach to the final cadence shimmers in beautiful sounds, capped by the closing harmonies of the horns and trombones.

The final F major chord is a typical Grainger voicing and its balance is not easy to achieve. The close intervals in the two bottom octaves (with their "forbidden" doubled 5th, a C natural) are more a pianoforte voicing than anything else. Scored for the bassoon, baritone sax, and the baritone, this 5th of the chord is certain to be present.

It has long been my feeling that *Irish Tune* from measure [49] to the end is among the most demanding scores for the conductor in the basic band repertory, and the first of these demands is that of keeping the music moving while all revel in the great bath of sounds that Grainger has provided. I resort to a basic large pulse of two beats to the bar after establishing tempo in bar [49], returning to four pulses at "Slightly Slower" where the conductor should indicate with steadily rising motion the stretch of the fourth quarter-note in measure [57]. The 4-pulse continues to the end. When the conductor keeps the two fermatas of bar 63 moving upward, all is in position for the final fermata and its appropriate descending physical motion. Players and conductor should remain motionless for about five seconds after the sound has ceased, to continue the spirit of the music in the silence that grows from its termination.

Shepherd's Hey

In addition to Grainger's explanations in the score, a "Hey" may have taken its name as a dance from *haie*, the French word for hedge. The dancers were probably arranged in two hedge-like rows. This may be why the composer begins his setting of it with two parallel lines of music instead of stating the tune simply by itself before variating it. The sixteen bars in each of the six variations are constructed with two identical eight-bar phrases and within these there is an inner repetition of four bars. Thus:

$$a4 + a4 = A8$$
$$b4 + b4 = \underline{B8}$$
Total: 16 bars

Grainger pits one set of timbres against another, exposing the alto saxophone in a solo statement, (and demanding the soprano from the start). When the score says alto sax, it is the 2nd alto sax part that contains the solo. It is possible that Grainger's sax section consisted of soprano, alto, tenor, and baritone saxes. Following the 1st alto sax part throughout, it appears to be a transposition of what may have originally been a soprano part. Every instrument must play this opening statement with a real staccato, but the 2nd alto sax and bassoon answer [6-9] should be played with a contrasting, almost legato articulation. This sets up the bouncing staccato of the first presentation of part B.

Variations

In the first variation, Grainger has established his basic plan: embellishment by instrumentation and composition, using articulation, nuance, and dynamic, while always maintaining the faithful presence of the full tune. Each variation begins in a different dressing, projects a different character, sets and achieves a complete expression within its 16-bar capsule. And of course Grainger mixes sounds with the palate of a gourmet cook.

Variation 2 [18-33] contains another instrumental Graingerism in that fast burst of sound in the reeds [21-22]. He revelled in such flights of virtuosity in his own compositions and in playing the music of others; he liked it here so much that he couldn't resist it the next time it came along [37-38].

Variation 3 [34-49] finds the top line of the score devoted to the xylophone, in 1918 a fresh new sound for band music. I note especially its *glissando* which joins the reeds in that second burst of sound at measure [37]. The *pesante* does not necessarily mean "slow-down" [42-48]. In measures 42-48 the basses must not bog down the sound when they have part B of the tune. The last bar of this variation with its resonantly-scored B♭7 at *subito fortissimo* must have no diminuendo and must be sharply attacked; Grainger's thick bass/pianoforte scoring should prevail as well. As the "A" part concludes, the composer could not resist a quote from *Country Gardens,* given to the cornets [40-41].

Variation 4 deals in delicate textures, with the alto sax lead surrounded with more "tuneful percussion" walking above the melody. For the first time, to my knowledge, the pianoforte makes its appearance in a piece for band. Its presence with the reeds, playing in solid keyboard octaves [50-57] contributes a facile sound, giving the music a fresh lift as well as a striking character. Nobody was scoring music quite like this for military band in 1918. But even Grainger, "the inveterate innovator," had to list the piano as *ad libitum*. Band concerts were mostly outdoor affairs in 1918; mobility and the risk of rain meant everything had to be doubled within the standard band instruments. Today, however, this hobble must be removed; every school has a piano and plenty of students who play.

Another of this composer's typical rhythmic figures is found in the mid-cadence approach of measures [56-57]. Players consistently have difficulty with the fluency expected in this passage. It seems to become mired in its own ornamentation; clarinets III and IV, 2nd alto and tenor sax must conquer this by careful practice. Grainger has asked that this music sound playful *(giocoso)*, but I have never known it to come through by itself. It could be that the *tenuto* lines on the quarter and half note interfere with clarity. I suggest that the *tenuto* lines be removed, that the first two quarter notes be played short and vibrantly and that a great energy be thrust into the ornamentation.

The conductor must exhort the players to react immediately to Grainger's call for contrast in the change of texture and tone in measure [57] where suddenly everybody must play as expressively legato as possible. The composer's dynamics for tenor sax, bass clarinet and tubas assigned to the descending chromatic crescendo in bar [61] are insufficient for this important line; the conductor must increase the dynamic levels by half of the printed indications (*mezzo forte* becomes *forte*). As Variation 4 concludes, the cornets must be sure that the tune projects.

As Variation 5 begins it is necessary to clarify the tutti articulation as being *marcatissimo*. The xylophone provides point to the sound, as does the glockenspiel [66-73], but its pointed attacks (especially with brass mallets) are followed by the resonant ring that is its basic acoustical property and which colors Grainger's block chords (also given to the piano). What follows [70-74] is as typical a Grainger rhythmic and harmonic combination as one can find in these folk music settings. Some might call these passages influenced by the cake walk or early jazz, and that may be true, too; but I think it is what Percy was always calling the "fierceness" in his music. These phrases must be played with that "marcatissimo" he requested at the beginning of this variation; in subsequent scores he would have labelled such passages to be played "hammeringly," as he did in his *Lincolnshire Posy*.

Conductors will have to urge their low reeds and brass to inject forward motion into the last four eighth notes of bar [73] to connect the first half of the variation to the next half without cloddiness. This forward thrust should be maintained as these instruments carry the tune to its conclusion. At measures [80-81] all the high reeds and high brass are indulged with the previous "Graingerism," leading to the $\frac{3}{2}$ turn-around. Here, for the first time since it began, *Shepherd's Hey* comes to a pause; here, also for the first and only time in these two scores, it is time to correct printing errors.

Remove the superfluous dot on the score's third quarter notes (two upper staves) in bars [74], [75], and [79]; and correct the bass drum part to conform to the score at the fifth quarter-note of the $\frac{3}{2}$ bar. The part erroneously assigns this vital note to the cymbals, whereas the low frequency impact of the bass drum when struck with a hard and heavy beater provides the ideal cap to the tutti crescendo of this important structural junction in the music.

Now comes the final variation, an ever-accelerating romp that the conductor can lead with small but constantly pressing gestures. Those playing the on-and-off quarters and eighths here must play them with brevity, precision, and drive. The presence of the piano in all of this, hammering out its great din-producing octaves in both hands is much too desirable to remain *ad lib*. Grainger's music generates so much exciting sound as it gathers speed that at its height, it is desirable to momentarily back off on the volume for all instruments, including the percussion in the score's two bottom staves [95, 96, 97].

The *Prestissimo* [98] has a chance to be more than a jumble of uncalculated noise when the conductor and players take it apart slowly, marking the notes gathered under the eighth-note beam with those numbers that the composer did not provide (6's, 7's, 9's). When Grainger tells the xylophone player to "roll the hammers about on any notes" [98-99] he expects the choices to be random, and the effect is glorious. When this very effective ending has been carefully rehearsed, *Shepherd's Hey* concludes with a kind of shout from the brass and percussion, plus that enormously effective and necessary glissando of the entire white keyboard, top to bottom on Percy's own instrument. It was a resource for sound that he could hardly resist. ∎

Grainger's Language

It is perhaps painfully difficult for some people at this distance in time from Grainger's formative years in Frankfurt and London (1895-1914) to view his nationalism and his rugged individualism with much appreciation of his methods in projecting those "tone thots" to others through the five-line staff and those unusual accompanying adjectives.

Readers must consult both the Slattery[1] and Bird[2] biographies for a proper discourse on his philosophy called "blue-eyed English," but even if one knew nothing of the reasons behind it, the Grainger adjective is unmistakably clear to all who read the English language.

It is a sad observation that the publisher, for whatever the reason, could not accept Grainger's personal expressions (i.e., slacken, louden, slow off lots, etc.), humoring him it seems by allowing them to appear as one of his "eccentricities" in the score, but denying him completely their inclusion in the published parts. The conductor always benefits from careful study of each separate part as it has been extracted from the score in any published work for band. When this is done with Grainger's music it is revealed that the publisher chose to translate Grainger's extraordinary English into Signor Fischer's ordinary Italian. In his campaign to cast musical expression in the language of the composer who wrote it and the player who would perform it, Grainger was merely extending to his music what Robert Schumann and Claude Debussy had previously adopted in theirs as the full and proper use of a native language to convey those expressions and directions which are a vital part of composition. In Grainger's case, the use of unique expressions in English removes the mystery while still maintaining the magic.

The conductor should correct the parts to conform to the language in the score.

1. *Percy Grainger, the Inveterate Innovator* by Thomas C. Slattery, The Instrumentalist Co., Evanston, Illinois, 1974.

2. *Percy Grainger* by John Bird, Paul Elek, London, England, 1976.

Percy Aldridge Grainger's

Country Gardens

An Interpretive Analysis
by Frederick Fennell

Country Gardens was Percy Grainger's most popular composition and, though he lived to rue the day he had put his name to it[2] — feeling that it had undermined his more personal creations — he did not always hold it in artistic contempt. When I wrote him in 1959 requesting a line or two about eleven of his orchestral pieces to be included in the liner notes I was writing for an orchestral album I had just recorded, he cheerfully responded:

"The Morris Dance tunes 'Country Gardens' and 'Shepherd's Hey'[3] are instrumental versions of songs long popular in the English countryside under the titles 'The Vicar of Bray' and 'Keel Row.' When Cecil J. Sharp discovered the Morris Dance versions around 1908, he sent them to me with the remark: 'I think you will find them effective to arrange.' But I did not arrange 'Country Gardens' until I was a Bandsman in the U.S. Army. Our band would take part in Liberty Loan drives and I would be asked to improvise at the piano —

without much response from the audience. But I thought of 'Country Gardens' as a likeable and lively little tune that might please. So I tried it and, sure enough, it was popular at once. So I wrote it down in the barracks."[4]

Grainger might have added the adjectives "catchy" and "simple" to describe the tune's appeal to his 1918 war bond listeners, and we, too, may do so for audiences anywhere to this day. Minus any introduction, it attracts immediate attention as the first music descends its bouncing way, uninterrupted for six notes of the E♭ major scale, then glides through the last two (see music example). All of this is then reconfirmed as a literal re-statement in the next four bars; more and different bouncing rhythm intrigues the listener who, after the briefest such excursion, is then led comfortably through a third playing of the original idea. It's the same a-a-b-a sequence that has provided the standard form for so many American popular songs. At bar 17 the tune moves to the sub-dominant for another gently-gliding two bar sequence that ends securely for listeners with that final turn they have heard three times before.

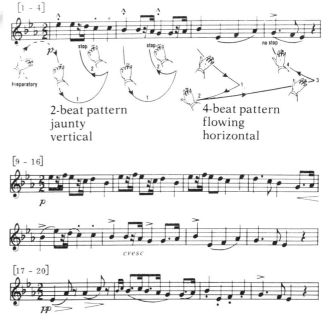

The key phrase in the popular appeal of this music is "listener security" which probably (and innocently) evolved over a number of years through repeated folk use of the tunes for Morris dancing. Its balance in construction is simple and superb (see chart).

Percy Aldridge Grainger (1882-1961) *Country Gardens*. British Folk-Music Settings No. 22. Copyright 1931 by G. Schirmer, Inc. New York, Special Edition No. 60 (plate No. 35227), 8-line synoptic score, in the instrumentation by Tom Clark;[1] edition is octavo: piccolo, flute 1-2; oboe 1-2, bassoon 1-2; clarinet: E♭, solo-1-2-3, alto, bass; saxophone: soprano, alto, tenor, baritone, bass; 4 horns; cornet 1-2, trumpet 1-2, flugelhorn; trombone 1-2-3; treble clef baritone, bass clef euphonium, tuba; percussion: xylophone, glockenspiel, snare drum, bass drum, cymbals; 82 bars, E♭ major, 2/2, *Allegro moderato* ♩ = *circa* 96 *con leggero movimento*; duration: 3:30.

5-Part Rondo, ABABA

Large Form	Measures	Internal Form	Harmony	Dynamics
		Rounded Binary:		
A	[1-4]	a	I	*p*
	[5-8]	a		*mf*
	[9-12]	b		*p*
	[13-16]	a		
		Rounded Binary:		
B	[17-20]	a'	IV	*pp*
	[21-24]	a'		
	[25-28]	b	I	*mf*
	[29-32]	a		
A	[33-48]			*ff*
B	[49-64]			*mf* *p-mf* *cresc.*
A	[65-82]			*ff*

The obvious original purpose of the tune was to lead dancers, not to confuse them. It is not difficult to imagine why it enjoyed such immediate popularity as a keyboard piece, especially with Grainger projecting the music through his considerable gifts for tonal and rhythmic expressivity at the piano.

We who play it with instrumental ensembles should approach the music in equal concern for its simple, expressive nature, and with a light touch, even in the fortes; 47 of the 82 bars have dynamic shading less than forte and those contrasts within the 47 bars are the conductor's principal concern in the preparation and performance of this piece. In his band instrumentation of it, Tom Clark has been sensitive to textural variance in maintaining the bright character of the piano original.

Conductors interested in developing a technique in arms, hands, and baton that looks like this music sounds will find the first complete statement [1-16] of *Country Gardens* to be attractive basic study material. Separated, then connected, the music of the first four bars presents some possible and simple reactions to what is seen (see conducting diagram in the music example). The size of the area covered is dictated by the dynamic level: piano. For the literal repeat of bars 5-8, the size of the gestures increases by the dynamic level, now revised to mezzo forte. Those insistent and jagged impulses at the beginning of B [17] urge the conductor to deliver small but very precise gestures that are neatly (and only) up and down, fitting the concise and, again, miniature character of the music.

The first two phrases at ② are set off by contrasts — rhythmic, harmonic, textural, and dynamic that are genuinely charming, anticipated with a personal pleasure to me that is always fulfilled. As in all of these wonderful settings, the tunes are from the British folk, but the harmonies by which we know all of Grainger's enormous output of them are Grainger's. Here, of course, is where his extraordinary keyboard facility, and the inquisitive aural imagination that propelled it, combine to offer us such wholly satisfying musical experiences.[5]

Simplicity of presence best describes the conductor's suggested role during the playing of the B sections [17-32 and 49-64]. We might think of appropriate physical reactions that come out as "feeling" *tenuto, sostenuto, pianissimo,* endeavoring to join the graceful contour in the rise and fall of its first four measures, making certain that the players do not clip the eighth-notes; invite them to concentrate on the sounds here, not on the silences.

A final performance suggestion: keep the overall sound of the *fortissimo* tutti at ④ from dispelling the simple charm created in the previous music; something less than the letter-of-the-dynamics law is appropriate as is a light touch throughout, regardless of how great the sound. ∎

Footnotes:
1. The composer elected not to do the orchestral version which was arranged by another of the Schirmer house writers, Adolf Schmid (Galaxy No. 269); a box in the band score (certainly placed there by P.A.G.) informs the bandmaster that "string-bass and harp (or any other parts) from Adolf Schmid's arrangement...may be used with this band arrangement."
2. John Bird quotes him as once having written: "The typical English country garden is not often used to grow flowers in; it is more likely to be a vegetable plot. So you can think of turnips as I play it." John Bird, *Percy Grainger,* Paul Elek, London 1976, p. 161.
3. "Morris is a term that is used by the folk in a generic sense to cover several forms of dance....It is danced normally by six men: three on a side. They carry a white handkerchief in each hand, or else a stick in one or both hands, and these are employed rhythmically during the dance. Pads of small bells are strapped on to the dancers' shins and the ringing of the bells emphasizes the rhythm of the step. The costume...is always decorated with gaily coloured ribbons and usually with hats ornamented with flowers and ribbons;" excerpted by the author from *Groves Dictionary of Music and Musicians,* fifth edition, New York 1970, Volume III, pp. 232-3.
4. Letter to the author quoted in the liner notes, *Country Gardens* and other favorites by *Percy Aldridge Grainger,* Frederick Fennell conducting the Eastman-Rochester Pops Orchestra, Mercury Records, Golden Imports (reissue) SRI 75102.
5. Johannes Brahms' 21 *Hungarian Dances* for piano four-hands, and Antonin Dvorak's 16 *Slavonic Dances* for orchestra also endlessly enrich one's musical education and pleasure in much the same way.

Percy Aldridge Grainger's
Molly on the Shore

An Interpretive Analysis
by Frederick Fennell

The composer chose two Irish Cork Reel tunes,[2] "Temple Hill" and "Molly on the Shore," and set them as a single composition. All of the materials used in the piece are identified in the list of music examples which serve as the basis for writing this study/performance essay: *Molly on the Shore* (Molly), *Temple Hill* (Temple), Grainger counter tunes (Percy), and ostinatos (Ostinato).

Grainger's deft and free interplay of these tunes, plus the presence of his own appropriate support material as mucilage for the whole, provides music cast with freedom in a basic rondo form.[3] The simple walking *basso ostinato* in 5ths and 7ths (Ostinato I) with which the work begins proved to be such an attractive musical device that the composer used it in one fashion or another for almost half of the piece. In its original application for the "string four-some" and then for orchestra, Grainger had at his disposal the easily repeatable and invariably resonant resource of *pizzicato* strings. In this transfer to the band (up a half-tone from G) he used the clarinets and bassoons. It would be useful if the sound of *pizzicato* strings were in everybody's ear, beginning with conductors themselves.

The *pizzicato* characteristic, as sound, may be described: perfectly articulate, desirably resonant. If obvious technical wind approaches do not produce the proper sound, the conductor should not hesitate to invite string players to bring their instruments to band rehearsal for what could be a vivid demonstration that might long transcend the moment or the piece. In any case the conductor should avoid sound that is brittle and dry, but still

secure proper spacing of the notes from all who contribute to the five *ostinatos* so vital to this music. In the original string version the opening Ostinato I for instance, employed four highly resonant open strings G-D/D-A from the violin and cello, a resource not to be duplicated by wind instruments, to be sure, but a tonal character wind performers should strive to approximate.

These conveniently functional "one-size-fits-all" accompanimental figures[4] were highly suited to Mr. Grainger's purposes, running unchanged for 15 of the 17 measures needed to expose Molly I/II.

The observant conductor sees at once that the compass of Molly I is a minor seventh E♭-D♭ while Molly II covers an octave and minor third of the A♭ key-scale. They vary in that the first tends to noodle while the second skips. Productive study of this music benefits from its having possessed one with that sometimes maddening presence in which the tune keeps popping out of the mouth, involuntarily and at unpredictable moments; friends have admonished: ". . . you're whistling it again!" That is a very good condition for the conductor to be in if not such a happy one for those around him. However, the tunes must own you, you and the players.

As one is being "taken-over" by Molly I it would be well to think of the seven recurrences of the eighth-note triplet as performed lazily and very *legato*, distinctly different from the eighth/sixteenths figure as in bar 6:

MUSIC EXAMPLES

EIGHT-BAR SEQUENCES, 1 through 18,

BEGIN AT 27

The sixteenths demand compact energy. The performance challenge presented to player and conductor at measure 19 when the composer chose to score Molly III/1 in the nether regions of the reeds is in no way eased by his having cued it for the low brass. If the reeds need assistance here it would be best not to muddle the sound by using all notes in the brass bass cue; use only those that might contribute to clarity, such as:

All accented notes here must be energetic, brief, and resonant, and the rhythmic contribution of the clarinets the same, with special rhythmic attention on the part of everybody to the cadence at measure 26. The conductor's contribution to Molly III/1 might be a highly concentrated, repetitious, slanted gesture that departs from the traditional one-two pattern until that motion fits the music in bar 22:

This action might support the "passage-is-all-accent" concept in its performance and serve, as well, to bring Molly III/1 to the cadence which also introduces the next developments at measure 27 where Grainger joins Molly I/2 and Ostinato I/2. Since the music began, dynamic levels have been subdued at *piano/pianissimo* and as the sound begins to swell in bar 28 the conductor's charge is to build it to bar 35. Measure 27 also marks the beginning of a set of 18 sequences, eight bars long which take *Molly on the Shore* to its coda and conclusion.

The third of these sequences in measure 43 introduces the second Cork Reel,[5] *Temple Hill*. When Grainger found the two tunes they were printed in reverse order from the way he used them. Presumably he heard *Temple Hill* as dominant in feeling and, therefore, the perfect foil for the alternating tonic/dominant properties so prevalent in *Molly's* beginning and further underlined by his first *ostinato*. His sequence weds the two, permanently, and here he begins to contribute his own "countertunes" (identified as Percy) that match so appropriately the two reels.

Temple Hill is not as busy a tune as *Molly*, which seems to relate to the fife or some other flute-like folk instrument, whereas *Temple Hill's* elements add up to folk fiddle playing. Temple I/1 plus Percy I, then Temple II/1 close-off the long A part of Grainger's *rondo*.

From the height of the initial *crescendo* at measure 35 the observant conductor will have seen that the principal task is to maintain close control over those eight-bar sequences that continually unfold in constant contrast. The conductor's study of the score prior to rehearsal offers, among many values, an overview of the composer's plan for his music, an assessment of his means to compositional ends, a graph-like table of tonal, rhythmic,

Percy Aldridge Grainger, *Molly on the Shore*, Irish Reel set for Military Band, No. 23 of British Folk Music Settings, published in a variety of scorings by Schott & Co., London; this edition copyright 1962 by Ella Strom Grainger, published by Carl Fischer, Inc., New York; scored for military band 1920 as a birthday gift to his mother, Rose;[1] *Presto*, ♩=112/126, A major, *alla breve*, 195 bars, time: *circa* 4:15; journal No. J270, plate No. N3905; five-line condensed score: piccolo, flute 1-2, oboe 1-2, bassoon 1-2; clarinet: E♭, B♭ 1-2-3-4, alto, bass, EE♭ contrabass; saxophone: alto 1-2, tenor, baritone; 4 horns, 4 cornets, 3 trombones, treble clef baritone, bass clef euphonium, tuba, string contrabass; kettledrums, bells, vibraphone, snare drum, bass drum, cymbals.

and dynamic intensities. There is, as well, a scale of unfolding musical importance by which one is able to control the large and diverse elements of the ensemble that must bring them all to musical life.

With the introduction of *Temple Hill* at measure 43 and its swells and fades, these characterisically expressive elements demand faithful execution by all, with the players responding immediately to both of these; the conductor's patterns might reflect the music and its nuances in this way:

The score is at its first dynamic peak at measure 51 (Temple II/1) in the fourth of the 18 sequences; the first three strong impacts and those that follow in support of the tune should be played sticky — resonantly, and separated. We might borrow these characteristics from the physical action in the three down bows required of the "string foursome" in Grainger's original version of the Reels, and perhaps he borrowed those heavy impacts from footwork appropriate to such an Irish dance. The conductor's motions might join this idea, too, for accentuation is mandatory.

That busy and difficult fragment in triplet eighths [52, 56, 57, 58] given to clarinets 3 and 4 must be heard and will be if rescored to add the power of a pair of alto saxophones. These measures will also benefit from a re-balance of all quarter notes reduced to *forte*; the termination of sequence 4 is a very sudden *diminuendo* on the third pulse of bar 58.

If the conductor has joined the action of these previous *forte* measures, a sudden reduction in the size of any motion on the third pulse of bar 58 to small, neat, minimum pulsing will be appropriate to the subdued manner of Grainger's statement of Molly I/3. These small gestures are more effective when brought in front of the body. A *tenuto* line placed on all eighths on the third pulse in the accompaniment in bar 62 adds to the secure production of the vital harmony. In his constant variance of the material which supports the reel tunes, Grainger reveals, once again, his remarkable musical imagination.[7] From that seemingly inexhaustible resource he offers the hop/skip grace note treatment (play them crisply, please) that ends Molly I/3. The same *tenuto* line suggested for measure 62 is also needed for a resonant harmonic resolution on the last eighth of bar 66.

After an effective and active contrapuntal imitation of Molly II/3 as his 6th sequence, Grainger allows everybody the first moments of relaxation in a piece that seems never to stop; but this breathless, exhausting pace is how it is with Irish Reels. Everything is momentarily *legato* and very expressive as Molly III/2 is varied rhythmically to achieve the brief change of pace at measure 75. This is the only time that any bit of either *Temple Hill* or *Molly on the Shore* is changed in any way over the course of 193 bars, save from major to minor mode. Conductor motion, of horizontal design, enhances the music, but it must be the character of it that relaxes, not its tempo.

This brief respite from action ends, however, in sequence 8 at measure 83 when Molly I/4 is joined by Percy II, the composer's bold contribution to contrast, carefully matched by rhythmic differences in the accompaniment for every four-bar section.

The conductor's responsibilities to these rapid-ly-changing musical scenes continue to mount, but it is aural comprehension and dynamic balance that dominate them more than technical concern or involved cuing. Within each sequence lie contrasts within contrasts through ever-changing scorings and their rhythmic underpinnings.

Textures begin to thicken and decibels rise in sequence 9, where, in addition to Molly III/3, Grainger adds his third composed countertune (Percy III) and begins the second of his *ostinatos* (Ostinato II/1). The *fortissimo* countertune is a passionate expression in its rapid swells and fades and its ever-gathering range, topped-off by an arresting chromatic outburst in the cornet and alto sax as the transitional cadence figure in bars 97-98; he would use this same sort of dramatic device again in "Rufford Park Poachers" 17 years later.[8] His second *ostinato* given to bells and vibraphone (motor off, no pedaling) creates the repetitious jangle needed to go with static but vital inner harmonies. Grainger had marked them to be played "richly" and the countertune to sound "feelingly" in the original version for strings.

The sudden dynamic drop to *piano/pianissimo* for sequence 10, (Temple I/2) rests upon the dramatic drone of pedal fifths Ab-Eb with the other lines weaving about as they contribute to Ab minor. The vibraphone now carries the *ostinato* alone, implying Bb minor for the next 24 bars; bells provided the cutting edge for the *fortissimo* of sequence 9, but that would be inappropriate here.

All of the conductor's subtle *legato* energy is attracted by Grainger's equally subtle but sinister coloring of the harmony at the beginning of sequence 11. Drawing clarinets 3 and 4 down to their lowest note, from the half step above, the color of the music is darkened in a way that he seems to have understood with uncommon insight. It has been my experience that players frequently shy away from this unique sonority which only the clarinet produces, but if the low Eb concert is played as a very sticky note, stuck as well to the coming D and blown to it with just the right amount of air for a very quick *crescendo* and a tasty diaphragm accent, the musical result will fulfill much of Grainger's hope for these three passes at a very fascinating sound. He did not put a top on the *crescendo;* the conductor's good taste will have to decide that.

The listening conductor will also be aware of the importance of the descending scale fragment that glues sequence 11 to 12 at measure 115. In the materials log (see music examples) this is Temple I/3 plus Percy I/2. That critical observation about the scale fragment also happens to lead the performers to the most subdued sounds yet encountered and in another variant of key — Bb minor — which holds tonal attention for the next 16 bars, along with a generous amount of Eb minor in both relationship and implication. The *ostinato* veers toward Bb minor because the ear accepts it from the Db in the drone pedal point.

Thus, with this triad of minor keys (Eb-Gb-Bb), Grainger has made a considerable departure from his initial harmonic comfort in Ab which has held for more than half of *Molly on the Shore*. Having arrived at this state, he requests minimum dynamic balances in threes, as well — *piano, pianissimo, pianississimo*.

All players must observe principles of group dynamics (see box) as sequence 12 builds over the eight bars from its three minimum levels to the *fortissimo* at sequence 13 in measure 123, for Temple II/3 and the brightness of G♭ major. While the conductor is observing the composer's dynamics at measure 139 for sequence 15 (Molly II/5) care must be taken to assure the dominance of the *Molly* tune over the heavily-scored sound for every other line. Compromise is the plan here where all but the tune must be reduced by half, to *forte*.

Grainger's fourth countertune [147] combined with Molly I/6 is almost on par with Molly I at sequence 16 and this sets up the complex mixture of three principal resources that combine at measure 155 to produce sequence 17 (Molly III/4, Percy III/2, and Ostinato IV). Again, conductors who expect a convincing performance of this very typical Grainger grab-bag of interesting musical ideas will have to sort them out according to player strength and value of material as each line seeks to be heard. There is a lot of sound here and very busy action demanding critical listening on the podium where the concerned conductor with ear and eye carefully focused on these exciting developments must plan ahead for the rapid evaporation of all that sound in a single bar [162].

Eyes and ears concentrated on the suspended cymbal in measures 157-158 should encourage the player to join the music making, not obliterate it, and to use a bright, thin plate (15") with yarn vibe mallets. The conductor and the group must quickly surrender their previously busy, high-dynamic involvement to the composer's now quiet and poignant final setting, in F minor, of the *Temple Hill* reel (Temple I/4, Ostinato V). The compositional Grainger is seated again at his reed organ, drawing both *ostinato* and drone from the two fourths (C-F/G-C) that are fundamental intervals of that Reel tune. Conductors, in study and reflection, grow to know something of a composer's writing habits; with Grainger they cannot help but be impressed by his use of the simple, yet highly effective devices — drone and *ostinato* (pedal-point), the one to slow things down and the other to keep them moving. Here he combines the two with a third element, hushed dynamics, in this abrupt withdrawal from that wide-open music making. The quiet drone cools the harmonic heat of sequence 18 while the vibraphone's gradually fading *ostinato* helps the conductor and first clarinet (best reduced to solo) maintain the drive inherent in the dance.[10]

Here is yet another opportunity for the conductor to work in minimum motion for the good of all with a precise, confidential kind of pulsing that, though small, is utterly clear and contributive to what is happening as the piece begins to wind down. Both the *ostinato* and drone pedal-point thin out and disappear together leaving the critical harmonic turn-around [178] to the home key of A♭ with the principal clarinetist. As this recession of activity unfolds, the conductor can enjoy the rewarding communication with the players that subtle cuing brings to music making, once the material is securely rehearsed; the eyes have it when it comes to ultimate musical communication.

Group Dynamics

The conductor's overview study of the 18 sequences, already mentioned, should have revealed a high priority for carefully-controlled levels of sound. To secure these is, in my experience, the greatest of all performance challenges, and the reasons why are as elusive, perhaps, as the proper balances themselves.

Energy dominates the physical elements that generate sound produced on any instrument or with any voice. Energy sources for strings — the bow and left hand — are clearly measurable visually; but the energy source of instruments played with the breath is almost completely hidden.

Among the primary reasons for dynamic imbalance in a large group is the absence of a concept of group dynamics — squarely the responsibility of the conductor/teacher once basic tonal security is achieved. The problem begins when players are first gathered in the most elementary of teaching units. A section's concept for *mezzo-forte*, for instance, is too frequently accepted by the conductor as the aggregate of ten or more players' production of their individual *mezzo-forte*, from which it is certain that nothing resembling a true ensemble *mezzo-forte* is ever to ensue.

It is a performance discipline in ensemble musicianship that can and must be taught, re-taught, and insisted upon by the conductor until it is an accepted, immediate, and positive ensemble reaction. Stated plainly and simply, we do not do our job, and neither do the players. We err when we don't know the score and/or when the technique to impart what we do know is lacking; they play/sing only the notes when we let them get away with that. It is almost as though, in our teaching/rehearsing we subscribe to some curious belief that a composer conceives the sounds first and then arbitrarily decorates them, spreading-on the dynamics, the nuances, much in the same way that icing is added to the top of a cake. Wrong. All is conceived simultaneously as integral to the whole.

Group dynamics — whatever they may be — are gauged by the size of the section and are observed regardless of the style of the music, the name of the composer, or the period of the composition. Stylistic subtleties within these bounds are easily settled, but never until fundamental allegiance to the ensemble's non-negotiable dynamic levels is met. Meeting them is what we conductors do the least faithfully, regardless of what group we lead or when these infractions occur in its life or ours. We blithely allow a host of excuses to block our hearing or to short-circuit what should be our absolutely positive physical reaction to the negative signal coming from false readings of the *group* decibel meter. Those false readings by performers must be corrected at once, pleasantly but firmly, and insisted upon constantly. A guide that serves the extremes in dynamics reminds the individual: *In* pianissimo *hear only your stand partner; in* fortissimo *hear only yourself.*[9]

The effectively simple musical hinge that is Grainger's bar 178 needs lots of air from everybody, especially flutes in that part of their low register as they come on while the clarinet recedes with its return to Molly I/7 and Percy IV/2. Percy asks the first violin in his original version to play this transition "smoothly," but he neglected to request the same of the clarinet(s); I add it to my parts.

Everything from measure 179 to the end gives me the feeling of coda — Molly, pianissimo, Percy IV dropped an octave, resonant punctuations in the clarinets as at the beginning; a close look at the bottom stave [183-186] reveals the composer's "merrie" memory of his opening ostinato. Then, it all comes to its charming conclusion with the most delicately possible exposition of Molly II, deliciously scored for the minimum reed sonorities.

The role of the conductor in almost all optional music-making is that conscience-searching dilemma known in sports as the judgement call. Conductors happily have the quiet of study and reflection in these matters denied to the judge or referee in competitive sports. However, while musical decisions may not add up to who wins or loses, there is that even-greater, though gossamer bottom-line for the artist/teacher — the musical conscience. Mine tells me to reduce all playing to one-on-a-part (save for flutes until measure 187) from measure 178 through the down-pulse of the final bar. These last nine measures, in spirit, are akin to Mendelssohn's "Scherzo" from *A Midsummer Night's Dream* and Berlioz' "Queen Mab" from the *Romeo and Juliet Symphony*. All of the band then joins in the final flourish, which benefits from an open character in the ornamentation and a reduction to *forte* from Grainger's outlandish *forte* to the fourth power (!) for the *tutti* conclusion.[11]

In summary, the conductor has, in this seemingly innocent "British Folk Music Setting" a superb opportunity to assess many skills/controls, both visual and aural: dynamics from no place to everywhere, myriad articulation, shifting instrumental colors, and galoping musical ideas wide enough to arrest any genuinely serious musical director about to try to bring them to life. The sequences offer any conductor 18 eight-measure technical etudes that are certain to test basic skills in a musically rewarding environment. *Molly on the Shore* is one of Percy Grainger's most successful pieces and no responsible conductor of the band's basic repertory can afford not to know it. ■

Errors:

score [55]	2nd stave, remove "wild" *mf*
part [64]	clarinet III and IV, exchange the printed bottom line of the page (measure 64 is the first bar) with the next-to-bottom line; measure sequence will then be proper.
part [73]	Horn III change 1st note from A♭ to B♭.
part [91-97]	Baritone sax, notes are a major 2nd too low, correct to D-D/D-A/D-D/D-B/D-D/D-A/D-D.
score [94]	3 missing from triplet.
part [98]	E♭ clarinet, 2nd note change from A♮ to G♮.
score [119]	bottom stave, 1st note, flat missing.

Footnotes
1. The original setting for "string four-some" (1907), British Folk Music Setting No. 1, was dedicated to the memory of Edvard Grieg; the initial Fischer edition for Band was a "double-number" printed with *Colonial Song*.
2. Numbers 901 and 902 of "The Complete Petrie Collection of Ancient Irish Music," ed. Charles V. Stanford, Boosey and Co., London.
3. I/A: A1 1-10, B1 11-18, C1 19-26, A2 27-34, B2 35-42, D1 43-50; II/B A3 59-66, B3 67-74, C2 75-82, F1 and A4 83-90, C3 91-98, D2 (over A♭ pedal-drone) 99-106, E2 (ditto) 107-114, D3 (over G♭ pedal-drone) 115-122, E3 123-130; III/A: A5 131-138, B4 134-146, A6 147-154 (countertune used at coda), B5 155-162, D4 163-170 (over drone F-C/G-C), E4 171-178; *Coda*: A7 179-186 (countertune from 147), B6 187 to end; for definition of *Rondo* see Apel, Willi: *Harvard Dictionary of Music*, Harvard University Press, 1944, 19th printing 1968, pps. 87-88, 651-652.
Grainger wrote me about his own contributions to the score: "In setting *Molly on the Shore* I strove to imbue the accompanying parts that made up the harmonic texture with a melodic character not too unlike that of the underlying reel tune." — letter dated 6 August 1959.
4. Morton Gould's deep admiration for Percy Grainger and his music may be reflected in his use of this same *ostinato* for the beginning of his charming and highly original *Pavane*, 2nd movement of the *American Symphonette No. 2*.
5. The reference is to County Cork, Ireland.
6. Read the ultimate treatise on the subject by a man who really knows: Erich Leinsdorf, *The Composer's Advocate*, New Haven, Yale University Press, 1981.
7. Grainger's ultimate excursion into variance and a revelation of his seemingly inexhaustible imagination in scoring is his orchestral work, *Greenbushes*, an 8:30 recitation of instrumental and manipulatory wonders. Conductors will recognize the tune as the same one at the *Poco Allegro* middle section of Vaughan Williams' *Love Song*, "My Bonnie Boy" from the *Folk Song Suite* (*The Instrumentalist*, June 1976, reprinted in the *Basic Band Repertory, British Band Classics*).
8. See *Lincolnshire Posy*, movement III, "Rufford Park Poachers."
9. A quote from #21 of my "31 Points for Performance" published in thousands of industry music folders seen throughout the country since 1969.
10. The entire harmonic/instrumental resource here benefits from the reduction to one-on-a-part. For the Mercury Recording I made with the Eastman-Rochester "Pops" Orchestra Percy sent me his personally edited set of parts; the chime (A♭ in the band version) heard in that record on the 3rd quarter of bars 174 and 176 was one of his most effective "after-thots."
11. Grainger is well-known to those informed about his life and work to be a man of exuberant excesses, the ultimate of which must obviously have been his total addiction to *work*. He did everything to excess — he was even Percy Grainger to excess to some people, I'm sure, but they were the losers. Conductors/performers, however, must face his dynamics excesses with a not-always easy modification, but they all know in dimensions: *pppp/ffff*, that the one is rarely heard with substance and the other is never produced without distortion.

Percy Aldridge Grainger's
The Immovable Do

An Interpretive Analysis
by Frederick Fennell

Percy Grainger's large foot-pumped reed organ dominated a fair portion of the downstairs front music room of his sizeable frame house in White Plains, New York where he lived while in the United States and not off on his transcontinental journeys. I'm sure that he did much compositional improvising at that organ while musical ideas simmered within. It was one of his joys, and he played on it for me every time I visited. He loved its gentle tone, its constant production of sounds. He said they didn't fade like "that *helpless* piano over there," pointing to the instrument that had brought him such fame so quickly when he was only in his mid-twenties. Once at my request he played (and unforgettably so) the three final chords of "Lord Melbourne" pumping furiously with his feet, knee on the swell bar, all stops out, reveling in the sounds that were anything but helpless. He said the organ was such a desirable instrument for him as a composer because on it he could freeze any sound he could finger, hold it in its own space, listen to it with greatest penetration at any dynamic, decide whether he really liked it or not — not just for itself but for its relationship to what surrounded it.

With this fascination for the reed organ (minus any pedals, of course) it is no surprise that he eventually came upon the idea of writing a piece that would harness the instrument's most fearsome operational hazard — the reed that gets stuck. When that happens, this note (technical term: cipher) will sound as long as there is any air in the wind chest; and no matter what the performer may attempt to play, the constant presence of this wild note will be heard. One of Grainger's biographers, John Bird, writes of Percy's typical reaction to this kind of technical misfortune:

> One morning in 1933 Grainger had sat down at his harmonium and discovered that the mechanics of the high C had broken and it was ciphering through whenever he played. Turning the fault to good use he decided to improvise around the note and very soon had created one of his most unusual and engaging compositions, which he eventually called *The Immovable Do*.[2]

The result of this incident is a charming piece that provides several desirable bonuses beyond its listening and playing enjoyment as music. Void of any technical difficulties and playable by almost any band out of its musical diapers, the music offers players the charm of innocent dissonances and the exoticism of parallel harmony. It is a superb and uncomplex vehicle for developing the listening habit — the constant presence of the common tone provides an intriguing opportunity to study pitch relationships.

A long-time avoider of formality of any kind and as a seeker of his own way to go in musical architecture, as well, Grainger liked to indulge himself in musical profiles which he called "Rambles" and *Immovable Do* is one of them, for it certainly rambles along like a rose unpruned in a basic two-part form within four principal shoots. The first music heard once the cipher is established is an eight-bar idea that, though it dominates with the big two of its three exposures, is never heard again after the last of them [40-47]. Shoot no. 2 in its two hearings [14-17] and [48-55] always complements idea no. 1, and like it, is not heard again. What remains of the structure is a pair of developmental ideas [20-23], [36-39], [62-65] and [32-35], [58-60], [84-86]. There is generous use of extension and lots of free rambling, but perhaps it is basically a two-part form: [1-39] ABCADC; [40-120] ABDC(ext),D, Coda.

There is no question, however, about the presence or form of the music's inspiration, "The Cyphering C." As Grainger employs it this is both a drone and an inverted pedal point, probably the longest one in music. Here in bar one is the conductor's first challenge, the octave C. After the pitch and blend of the four reeds that the composer has selected to imitate his harmonium have joined in common purpose, the conductor might consider this option for the music's beginning: show all four pulses in the fermata bar, but place the fermata on the second pulse, then use pulses three and four to establish the tempo ($\quarternote = 112$). All cipher players should use the extra time given

Percy Aldridge Grainger (1882-1961), "The Immovable Do"[1] (or "The Cyphering C") for Wind Band (Military Band) or Wind Groups. Composition begun 1933, completed and scored 1939, copyright 1941 by Percy Aldridge Grainger, published by G. Schirmer Inc., New York, (plate no. 39219). The 7- to 10-line concert key score shows the distribution of parts for performance by four different instrumental combinations: wind band, woodwind choir, clarinet choir, and saxophone choir.

Wind-band scoring: piccolo 1-2, flute 1-2-3-4, oboe 1-2; bassoon 1-2, contra; clarinet E♭, B♭ 1-2-3-4-5 (6-7 substitute E♭ and alto), alto, bass; saxophone: soprano, alto 1-2, tenor 1-2, baritone, bass; 4 horns (F or E♭); cornet 1-2-3, trumpet 1-2, trombone 1-2-3; baritone treble, euphonium, tuba; string contrabass; kettledrums, side-drum, triangle, cymbals, bass drum.

There are 120 bars, F major, $\frac{4}{4}$, stridingly, ♩=about 112; playing time 4:00. The conductor must thoroughly absorb the composer's notes and performance advice on the fly-leaf of the score.

them by the fermata on the second pulse to quickly adjust any variance in pitch. Grainger's 112 is the proper tempo and should be observed without compromise.

There never seems to be sufficient presence in the opening bass line unless bassoon II and bass clarinet increase their dynamics to some acceptable degree above the printed *mezzo-piano*. In his customarily ideal concept of the forces that would play his music, Percy Grainger (like all composers) assumed the inclusion of an experienced player of the string contrabass performing on a first-class instrument. That, unfortunately for this and other of his scorings, is rarely fulfilled for the variety of reasons mentioned elsewhere in these essays.[3] The beginning of *Immovable Do* is not the same without the pizzicato bass which provides (as does no other instrument) a pointed character to the blended sound, and effectively generates the forward striding drive requested by the composer.

The music's origin and composition at the harmonium is unmistakably and consistently evident in the first of two dozen *crescendos/diminuendos* yet to come and more properly designated in the organists terminology as swells. One also knows this terminology in nuances from any time spent making music in company with British musicians. These specific swells < > in which the dynamic of the music rises and falls, are produced on the pedal-pumped harmonium (or reed organ) by moving the knee to the right against the swell bar that is located at knee level when seated; the bellows must be pumped simultaneously. The whole set of reeds reacts to the opening and closing of the swell box by the swell bar, providing a perfectly balanced *crescendo* and *diminuendo*. Grainger's application of this control of nuance in each of the sets of measures where the swells occur is immediately apparent in any view of all but 8 of the 20 pages in the score. And those pages on which a rise and fall does not occur, invariably show *tutti crescendi* or *diminuendi* in progress.

The critical observance here is the *tutti* condition in the nuances.

All players must contribute to the swell, evenly up and down in imitation of the mechanical performance guaranteed on the harmonium by that instrument's swell bar/swell box device.

Crescendo and *diminuendo* ought to be observed as precisely as this in all concerted music making, and here in an innocent piece by Percy Grainger is a pleasant opportunity for conductor and player to practice this rewarding process.

The conductor's score at measure 24 provides a broadside view of music that is solidly and stridingly under way, and with all of the thick-textured sound thus generated the conductor must make sure that the tone of the dominant (C♮) at the conclusion of measure 27 is not buried by its accompanying passing tones.

Grainger's brief extensions [30-31] and [56-57] calling for color contrasts in the solo instruments that then lead to important developmental extensions demand thorough control of their variety in texture, and the conductor must listen to everything that is happening. In the first of these two developments [36-39] the composer has offered a pedal point (in low reeds and brasses) as well as the inverted pedal point in the ever-present cipher (in the high reeds). If the conductor will concentrate on listening to these outer extremes and on all the fill in the middle, the total may not add up to a muddle. Another teaching opportunity is offered here to isolate and identify the sounds being made, skills that are vital to the development of aural comprehension.

The obvious thickness in most of the voicing in *Immovable Do* does have its contrasts, such as the second statement of B [48-55]. It is desirable to reduce the players to 15 soloists in these eight bars regardless of the size of the group. The four voices, plus cipher, treat the sensitive sonorities in miniature, the *tutti* being restored at measure 58.

The conductor's part in all of this is invariably *legato* participation in movement that is mostly horizontal, keeping the pulse in its stride while tending to balances created by Grainger's extensive use of the swell bar, as in this extension phrase:

[58-61]

The players should not be expected to provide control of these nuances without some help from the conductor. The degree of the swells may be governed by the size of the conductor's gesture; and the degree of appropriateness is governed by the conductor's taste.

The development of short phrases begun at measure 56 and used as extensions calls for clarity in balance that the conductor must discover in the score, such as: who has the lead at measure 62? The soprano instruments grouped in the top line of the brass staves have it, then pass it to the top reeds for the first formidable *crescendo* in the work. It is a wise caution to reduce the *crescendo* in the snare drum [62-65] until after the brass have begun theirs in measure 64, and to reduce the terminal dynamic for the drum's final eighth to *forte*. If the bass drum's single note [65] is played on a resonant instrument and not dampened too quickly it will be that instrument's surviving frequencies that will be the last sound heard from the *crescendo* rather than the snare drum's overpowering presence, as is too often the case.

In the decay of the *fortissimo tutti* that concludes measure 65 the music then proceeds most effectively when assigned to solo players with the *tutti* restored at measure 70, where one of Grainger's typically fetching variants of previous material provides conductor and player with excellent opportunities to study balance. The scoring is about as thick as it can get, thick and resonant. The *sforzandi* laid on top of the *pianissimo* (also within the *pianissimo* dynamic) provide yet another balance challenge with that articulation. In these four measures the conductor can achieve both character and precision by concentrating on the *sforzandi*, rather than following the customary pattern of four.

Meanwhile, the cipher sounds-on incessantly, colored by a variety of instruments that blend with the flute family and with each other, covering a range from one to four octaves, sometimes swelling with the rest or keeping its impersonal character as the drone it is. For some players it may be necessary to take a breath when none is indicated, and when this is necessary the exit and re-entry must be in a feathered sound with no obvious attack. The cipher is a most unusual aural opportunity for those who contribute to it, and pitch adjustment (or criticism of others) is not its only challenge. *Immovable Do* is a ramble in form and harmonic process. Those who play this common tone can hear clearly what is rambling around them and the conductor should take time to remind all players that this is happening, that it all works in every bar, and that the harmonic procession passing beneath their ciphering C could pause at any one of its vertical moments and the resulting sonority would work. Why not try pausing in rehearsal, any place, just to check it out?

The conductor's lot with the rest of the band will be a happier one if the *crescendo* of the suspended cymbal at measure 74 is delayed until measure 77, then allowed to ring free; neighboring players will also appreciate a slight reduction in the amount of sound.

Immovable Do next develops that character which its composer described elsewhere as fierceness [78-91], with full-throttled execution of the piece's climactic use of parallel triads in contrary motion and with subito *pianissimo* followed by roaring *crescendos*. It is one of the places in his unorthodox conducting of his own music that I remember most vividly; he simply stood before the band, head down but with both arms flailing wildly up and down from the elbow; with him it was very effective for it drove the band through these passages [78-80 and 84-86] and served to offset his questionable directive in the score: "as heavy as possible." The customary interpretation that these words elicit can bog a group down in a mire not intended; perhaps this is why P.A.G., the conductor, felt it necessary to resort to his flailing technique.

The harmonic and rhythmic material of bar 86 is more important than the *decrescendo;* remove it and ask kettledrums and bass drum to let their last eighth ring until the next bar; suspended cymbal should reduce dynamic to *forte* at bar 89.

If conductors lead the group to stretch its *crescendo* at measure 89 by their stretch of the fourth quarter, this will prove to be an effective thrust toward the high point in that three-octave line in the low instruments that then descends its way through hemiola in *diminuendo* to measure 93. Once there, the listening conductor will quickly accept the composer's advice to keep the "Top voice to the fore." The "cipher" is once again extended to the bass line in pedal point and this, together with close register scorings above it, do bury the lead voice. The conductor will also have to listen to the snare drum and gauge the level of its *crescendo*. The triangle's 15 markings of the pulse [101-104] are a bright and welcome touch as Grainger continues his long extension of fragments from the basic material which peaks at measure 110.

The conductor may find it an acceptable interpretation to slacken the tempo slightly at 110, for this is what Grainger did at that rehearsal where he flailed so effectively. The conductor may also find it an acceptable performance aid to suggest that players of the rising bass line should think $\frac{12}{8}$ and make the three notes full and broad in their *crescendo*. Those with the swells above the bass should wait for the first quarter, play with minimum attack, then swell gloriously; the snare drum should reduce the *fortissimo* dynamic by half, and the kettledrum should know that its swell while the band lingers on the cadence [113] is a very tailored touch to four of the piece's most charming bars.

Finally then, in one great swell, Grainger fulfills with happy dispatch what probably began as an annoyance. ∎

Footnotes
1. There exists the term and function in sight-singing known as "movable do" in which "do" is the name given to the keynote of every scale; another widely-practiced system, however, has "do" immovably fixed as C natural, regardless of the key of the musical material. Mr. Grainger's "do" is immovable.
2. John Bird, *Percy Grainger*, Paul Elek, London 1976, pp. 216, 217.
3. See footnote 8, author's study/performance essay, Grainger's *Children's March*

Corrections: all in the parts
Flute [75]: 4th quarter, correct D to C
Alto sax [75]: move *sfz* from 1st to 2nd quarter
Euphonium [82]: change quarter on 3rd beat to two eighths
Tuba [82]: see above for euphonium
Kettledrums [83]: *piano* missing
Bassoons, trombone III, euphonium, tuba, string contrabass [118]: change first half to E♭

Percy Aldridge Grainger's
Colonial Song

An Interpretive Analysis
by Frederick Fennell

Grainger, composing in the 1920s, White Plains, New York

Courtesy, Robert Simon, Jewel Dimensions

Percy Grainger (born in Australia) responded to my request for a note about this music as follows: "Much of my music was composed as a tribute to the scenery and people of my favorite countries. Thus *Colonial Song* was an attempt to write a melody as typical of the Australian countryside as Stephen Foster's exquisite songs are typical of rural America."[1]

Colonial Song is another result of his productive

time as a World War I U.S. (recently naturalized) Army bandsman in the New York City area, spent mostly in the sympathetic company of Rocco Resta, a bandmaster who was interested in what Grainger had to offer as a composer, as well as a famous pianist, fledgling oboist, and a full-time devotee of the saxophone. The music contains none of the folk song elements so closely associated with him. It is one of his considerable challenges to conductor and players, for together they must be at peace about the tonal balance and interpretive demands of the work; all begin to present themselves in bar one.

After first numbering every measure in the score and parts, the next favor conductors can do for the composer, the players, the performance, and themselves, is to purchase a bottle of liquid paper and take the time to remove by white-out every staccato dot from the score and parts — every one of them. This is very "wet" music and anything that contributes to "dryness" in the customary visual interpretation of a note simply has to go. Even after this visual purging is accomplished, the conductor's principal performance problem still will be: variety in fullness of sound from every note, regardless of its metric value.[2]

As a conductor I invite readers to address themselves, as conductors, to these five principal challenges to be found in *Colonial Song*:

First, it is a superb study in ensemble playing, because of the concentration so essential to the listening process which must be developed simultaneously with the performance techniques.

Second, there is the raw challenge of developing a singing, vibrant, ultimately sustained tonal production in great variety.

The third might be tonal balance, textural clarity growing out of the above together with the colorful spectrum of sound so present in Grainger's thickly-scored music; this requires everybody's full use of their ears, and of their complete breath resource.

Fourth, the piece is a very good lesson in basic accompanying, rare in this literature.

Fifth, it is an excellent study in rubato — those many nuances, rhythmic and tonal, that are the essence of romantic Italian opera where a single, innocent-looking "little sixteenth note" changes everything.

I am sure that other and longer lists of interest might be assembled but these five areas would surely be their progenitors. Readers of the score are well into them by the time Mr. Grainger has exposed the first stanza of his *Song* for its only time [1-11], and the first three can be found in bar one.

I believe the first two silent pulses have been placed there intentionally, that we conductors should use them to assist in making secure the technical production of the ensemble's initial sound; it can be a wonderfully evocative blend from the six different instruments. After everything is in tune and blended, those open pulsations can be an invitation to a mysterious kind of music making conjured up in Grainger's sonic alchemy. To this end the conductor could instruct the players to begin the unison G with the most solidly breath-supported *piano* of which they are capable, allowing absolutely minimum articulation and no vibrato; none until the fourth pulse is about to surge. Then both vibrato and crescendo lift us all through that fourth pulse into the glorious E♭ major from which we will not depart for the whole of the piece. If the conductor seeks to find it, the first note can glow with a warm ethereal incandes-

Percy Aldridge Grainger (1882-1961): *Colonial Song* arranged for military band by the composer, fall 1918 after several previous settings including the principal one for symphony orchestra (1912). This edition copyright 1962 by Ella Strom Grainger, published by Carl Fischer, Inc., New York, J582 (plate No. N 3904), 3 line condensed score; piccolo, flute 1-2; oboe 1-2; bassoon 1-2; clarinets: E♭, B♭ 1-2-3-4, alto, bass, contrabass; saxophones: alto 1-2, tenor, baritone; 4 horns in F, 4 cornets in B♭; 3 trombones, treble-bass clef baritones, tuba, string contrabass; harp, piano (*ad libitum*); percussion: kettledrums, tam-tam, suspended cymbal, snare drum. All versions of the music were composed as a "yule gift" to his mother, Rose; 72 bars, E♭ major, 4/4, "Fairly slow (m.m. ♩ = about 58) Richly, broadly, and with ample swells." Duration: 6:00.

cence that can establish the character of the rest of the performance; it must happen within the prescribed dynamic range. The instruments need a special push of air just before bar 2 begins.

After many rehearsals, performances, and one recording session, I have concluded that Grainger's initial metronome mark is fourteen points too fast to allow his music to sound "Richly, broadly, and with ample swells." This considerable departure (♩ = 44) from the composer's direction is not a random choice; it results from a carefully-considered overview of the composer's nine additional adjustments in tempo with which the conductor also must be concerned.[3]

For the leader and the players it is helpful to view this music as horizontal; arch-like though the four melodies may be, the strands of harmony that accompany them are linear. To the physical manifestation of these musical ends the conductor could contribute confined but intense motions that are much more left and right than up and down, saving upward motion for the final pulse in those bars where the elasticity that the composer has built into the phrases invites musical stretching. The conductor can supply this according to taste, using carefully spun-out upward motions for its achievement [3-5-8] in the first of the Grainger tunes. The third of these phrases in bar 8 invites an extension of the sound, ultimate *diminuendo*, followed by deft connection between that fading sonority and the subtle resumption of the music in the following measure. The accompaniment then must begin at a genuine *piano* "to the third power" (see measures 1 to 11).

The second melody invites forward motion to go with its more simple beginning and restrained character. The conductor should elicit from the alto saxophone player (only one perferred) a warm and well-projected sound, backing the solo with subdued, carefully-balanced and yet warm-sounding lines of accompaniment. A refreshing clarity in performance by any large group is offered by reducing the scoring to eleven solo players [12-20]. At the third phrase the conductor might add the inner pedal-point in the horns that served Grainger's orchestral setting so effectively and which I

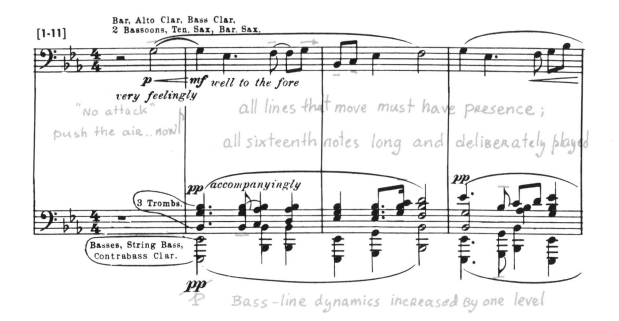

find strangely absent in the band version; it knits the harmonies (E♭, B♭, A♭):

[16-17]

The conductor should also consider using the kettledrum in substitution for the three critical pizzicato punctuations scored for string contrabass [15, 17, 20], and in the first one [15] the note in the score must be corrected from E♭ to G; this note would be bass clef bottom line and the other two 3rd space E♭ unless a 30" or larger kettle is available for the lower E♭. In the bands I hear and guest conduct, the presence of the kettledrums unfortunately stands 20 to 1 over the string contrabass. These notes are not cued for any instrument, but they may not be left out. The kettledrum, tastefully played and allowed to resonate beyond the note value, is the only acceptable substitute, if such there be for the plucked sound of the open G string of the string contrabass.[4]

Next, the entrance of the oboe and horn [18] attract the conductor's eye and ear where the bright color of a vibrant oboe joins the equally vibrant saxophone in an impassioned close to this second melody; the horn's role, however obvious, is one for which the conductor should share visual and manual concentration with the oboe and saxophone.

Percy Grainger's third melody given to the trumpet with the two countermelodies for baritone and saxophone [21-28] does not present any particular challenge to the conductor, but the accompaniment scored in the bottom stave does. Here is where that bottle of white correction fluid already should have done its work in the score and parts. It is suggested that all single eighths from bar 21 to the end of the piece be played as vibrant, full-valued eighths, not only non-staccato, but its diametric opposite: *tenuto*.

Our challenge here in these arpeggiations and single punctuations is to bring to the sound of the reeds that natural overhanging resonance which is a fundamental tonal property of string and keyboard instruments. This music was originally conceived for them and is not easily produced by wind instruments with anything approximating a similar sonority. The conductor should demonstrate this resonance factor at the piano for all the band to hear. Ask the players of keyboard percussion instruments to demonstrate it; and don't forget to ask any of the "acoustic guitars" to do the same — clarinetists, it seems, resist the composer's suggestion that they play these notes "quasi pizz."[5]

In addition to whatever sonic examples you use, ask the reed and brass players to employ the standard orchestral string practice of dividing on the stand the music written to be played by both players. The outside chair plays what is written (in this case with staccato dots removed) and the inside chair plays the same notes but plays them slurred and at half the dynamic level used by the player who produces the separated notes. This applies to all of the measures between bars 21 and 35, 37 and 38, 44 and 53, 56 and 65 — 37 bars of the piece. This also applies to every rising or falling sequence of 2, 3, 4, or 5 eighth notes, whether found within the bar or over the bar line. Here is how it would look/sound at the second statement of the composer's third melody:

[28-30]

[28-30]

Single eighths for all instruments are to be played very resonantly and vibrantly; detached notes in groups of two and more must be separated and played with this same vibrant and resonant character. The result of all of this should be a pleasantly-heard and acceptable approximation of the pizzicato strings, the piano, and the harp that are all so vital to this music. I know that it works.

If the conductor may have decided to move the tempo slightly (♩=58) for the third tune at measure 21, it is wise not to begin the *ritard* at the front of bar 27 but rather to reserve that as lead-in for the brief pull-back in bar 28 that then sends the music moving forward at the *piu mosso*. The "short" fermata in bar 32 is better removed and replaced with *tenuto* on that single note; it is more hesitation than an interruption of the melodic flow.

The conductor, probably thoroughly involved in the rising tide of great sounds as the composer rhapsodizes on his dramatic melody [37-46] is urged to approach it with less of a fermata but with great broadening of the pulse through which, it is hoped, the director will allow the contrary-running ascending and descending scales by the reed players to be filled with ample air.

Most of *Colonial Song* has proceeded with few problems for the conductor, but now they begin to appear with Grainger's slightly more complex extensions to his musical ideas. All has flowed with the least departure from the basic four-pulse, except for the two cadence *ritenutos* [28], [35-36]. As the previously horizontal, transparent, linear character of the music gives way to dense, vertically-constructed blocks of sound, the conductor's concern for what all players need to feel, hear, and see in pulses by the eighth note invites patterns that communicate those pulses to everybody. In these divisions of 3, 6, and 8 the conductor is cautioned against any heaviness in motion that may creep into execution, particularly when an inordinate amount of space is covered with the arms. Control is what is required here, and concentrated action is its strong ally.

Those final three eighths in bar 43 need the ♩=44 directly above the *meno mosso*, not two inches behind it; if the down-pulse eighth — the G♭ major triad — is a long, sticky *tenuto* followed by a substantial physical and musical breath (at the eighth rest) for those playing the top-line triad, that will set-up the greater sound inherent in the quarter note that follows [44]. That sound will be enhanced if the conductor reduces the composer's dynamic for the suspended cymbal and tam-tam at the peak of their crescendo from triple to single *forte*: these sounds should ring to silence after being struck; two marimba mallets make the tam-tam sound more appropriate.

If things are proceeding by the eighth note, the conductor has a fair chance of assisting the ensemble with its horizontal and vertical functions in measures 44, 45, and 46. These bars also may need some stretching of the final pulse into a *divided eighth note*.

The music returns to the quarter-note pulse (♩= 56) immediately in bar 47 and continues with appropriate stretches by the conductor, in rubato

[49, 50] until the middle of bar 51 when what amounts to a tasty *ritenuto* by the eighth note concludes these freely-felt embellishments: as in romantic Italian opera, a sixteenth note does make a dramatic difference. These lead to four additional measures of extension, all in E♭ and B♭; the tempo resumes in four at bar 52. Grainger's *molto ritenuto* begun at bar 53 and intended to fill a listening span of 24 eighth notes, slows down the repetitious action too soon. I believe his purposes in this extension are better served when the *ritard* begins on the 3rd quarter-pulse of bar 54. Glockenspiel, harp, and piano (and all the band) should be told that the final three notes of the *ritard* of bar 55 will be cue pulses, visually and manually dictated.[6]

If the conductor uses the release of the fermata [55] as a repetition of the eighth pulse of that bar and resumes by the quarter note (♩=54) in tempo after a musical breath, the continuity of the music is carried forward; once again the conductor has an opportunity to withdraw in minimum presence [56] while the cornet leads the band with its second solo.[7]

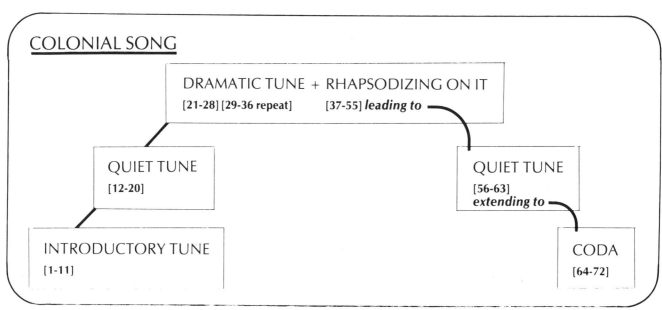

COLONIAL SONG

DRAMATIC TUNE + RHAPSODIZING ON IT
[21-28] [29-36 repeat] [37-55] *leading to*

QUIET TUNE
[12-20]

QUIET TUNE
[56-63]
extending to

INTRODUCTORY TUNE
[1-11]

CODA
[64-72]

A single thirty-second note can always change everything too, as is evident at the conclusion of bar 59 where the low reed F converts the G minor chord to a flat seventh, setting up Grainger's spaciously sonorous harmonic variation at bar 60. The tubas should be added to this sound (as cued) and the conductor should ask the 1st bassoon to play this F and the succeeding notes in unison with the 2nd bassoon, returning to the 1st part at the 2nd quarter note in bar 62. With all of the low Fs available for the concluding of bar 59 the conductor will then have to remind the players that their thirty-second note must be long, stickily *tenuto*, played *mezzo-forte* and then separated from the following down-pulse. These same directions should also be applied to the last note in bar 61. Band members should be cautioned to listen carefully, and to play the down-pulses in bars 60 and 62 only after they have heard the two thirty-second notes that precede them. For most of the band, it is a critical matter of listening; for those who play the thirty-second notes it is a vital matter of execution.

Clarification of the speed of the *meno mosso* [62] at ♩=48 suggests, as well, that the same tempo should replace *molto ritard poco a poco* heading the music in the next two bars [63, 64], placing the *molto ritard* at the beginning measure [65]. A steady *diminuendo* must be the conductor's companion to this *ritard*, reducing the sound to its minimum.

Percy Grainger's coda for *Colonial Song* is one of his most personal expressions, a badge of sounds and who plays them, by which he would be recognized in a company of wind band musicians anywhere. *A tempo* allows an effective *molto ritard* in the following measure where the composer's directions as to what should be happening are crystal clear — in the score, that is. He simply neglected to write the two fermatas in a single one of the parts, and Grainger always extracted his own parts from the score and supplied them to his publisher!

All of his bass-line reeds share the role of importance with the top-line tune at the coda's beginning. The conductor must blend the tam-tam and suspended cymbal with the other instruments in what they contribute to this eerie evaporation of pleasant sounds; again marimba mallets on the tam-tam are better than any standard beater. Directions are clearly printed indicating when instruments are added to the orchestration and when they stop playing. A note in the part for piano and harp admonishes the players not to ". . . end their runs together;" the vibraphone could be added to this measure, pedal down, playing its full-range chromatic scale, motor off, vibrating beyond the last note to be struck. If all that remains before the final silence is a pair of flutes, *pianissimo*, the conductor and the players effectively will have served the composer.

When Grainger's strikingly original conclusion to this piece brings the music to its close, a personal expression, indeed, has been shared between a composer and his players. ∎

Footnotes:
1. Letter to the author dated August 6, 1959.
2. For many players the "look" of a sixteenth note, for instance, does not change, sometimes well into the years of tonal development and the acquiring of complex performance techniques. That little black symbol — standing alone or beamed to different note values — remains a beacon for speed, a lighthouse flashing its warning: "look out — play it fast, play it short." Of course, it is mathematics going in, but it must come out as music; that, among other factors, is where the habits of listening to others and remembering what one learns about stylistic nuances separate musicians from technicians.
3. Specifically: [12] ♩=52, [21] ♩=58, [28] ♩=63, [36] ♩=54, [43] ♩=44, [56] ♩=54, [62] ♩=48, [66] ♩=52, [68] ♩=56.
4. Grainger owed the presence and acceptance of the string contrabass in his military band to his British cousins who put it there; we have it in our concert band and wind ensemble because a part for it frequently was included in British publications that were staple items in the repertory of the school band from the time of its emergence as an organized student and contest activity in the early 1920s. (See footnote 8 to my study/performance essay for Grainger's *Children's March*.

5. The composer simply transferred to the reeds notes given in his earlier orchestral scorings for the harp, piano, and/or pizzicato strings. These are the places in the band setting where it is suggested that the staccato articulation be removed. Grainger's resonant orchestral sonorities are clearly audible in the recording of the work which I made with the Eastman-Rochester Pops Orchestra, and this was recorded in the frontal 3 microphone pick-up established by the distinguished recording engineer, C. Robert Fine, with no microphone placed by the harp or piano. That these sounds under discussion do not transfer without loss of resonance to staccato-articulated flutes, clarinets, and other band instruments is a miscalculation of the composer. Robert Schumann (1810-1856) was similarly less successful in much of his symphonic scoring deeply rooted as it was in his extraordinary keyboard facility and experience; study of any Haydn symphony from No. 88 onward could have helped this. Grainger depended on the piano and harp in this piece to the extent that the single part serving both carries a box with this information: "If you have several harps and (or) pianos handy, use them all."
6. In the British Band Journal tradition, this vital part is printed boldly in the kettledrum part; it appears as a cue in the drum part and this frequently results in its not being played at all.
7. I have enjoyed the darker sound of the flugelhorn in place of cornet, its solo ending at bar 62 when the cornet must resume with the lead.

Percy Aldridge Grainger

Ye Banks and Braes O' Bonnie Doon

An Interpretive Analysis
by Frederick Fennell

Rural Scotland

Photo courtesy of World Design Tours Inc.

In this simple and sensitive setting of a simple, sensitive Scottish tune, Percy Grainger has provided all bands with a charming piece in his inimitable — unmistakably personal style. The full tune is set twice with no introduction or extended close and there is not one non-legato note to be found from its beginning to its end. Basic melodic material is the simple pentatonic scale that fits the key of F major with the 4th and 7th intervals always absent in the tune but present when appropriate in the two harmonizations:

Example 1

Grainger's appropriate harmonic support for the five-note melody creates the mood — a feeling of peaceful undulation as though it was his intention here to suggest the presence of the river itself. And the melody, probably an old pipe-tune, may be assessed as A-A-B-A in form.[3] The composer chose to give this tune to the principal alto saxophone from his favorite family of all musical instruments, and then backed its sonority with a unison doubling of "second" instruments (oboe, clarinet, cornet); together they play the complete melody both times and they are the tune's only keepers.

And so in the study of the score prior to rehearsal the conductor is advised to use *only the full* score.[4] With it one sees at a glance that — of the 21 lines of music present in the first statement, 4 are for the tune and 17 are not, and to know which is which is the conductor's principal concern in establishing proper balances. Without the full score, one sees none of this. These ratios of sound prescribed by the composer do look fine on paper but they will fail to produce that blend of tune and harmony he expected unless all harmony players subject themselves to the melody. Here is one more opportunity for the players to learn the truth of that ancient performance adage: "...if you can't hear the tune you are playing too loudly." And this, of course, only holds when the melody is being played at its proper level of sound and with that intensity in projection that was assumed for it by the composer.

For all of us who conduct groups where the sound comes mainly from wind instruments this means that we must convince ourselves and our players that it is *air*, solidly and endlessly supported — air thrust vibrantly all the way through the instrument that makes this projection possible. It is air that elevates the music, air that *makes* the music.

Of "Ye Banks and Braes..."[5] it may be said that — like so many pieces of music, its character can be established within the first few notes. A performer's concept of its interpretation may even be settled here. A listener's reception of that interpretation also may be grasped with more than the mere comprehension of these initial sound signals. We are careless, too frequently, with this vital projection to the listener of all that we feel and know of a creative idea in the first moments of its unfolding.

Grainger's opening intervals (C to F), following his "slowly flowing" guide-line invite playing that is as sustained as possible with the C up-beat as extended in length and played with as little "attack" as possible. If the conductor can encourage the players of the tune to push a little, special amount of air into the sound just as they are about to move from the C to the F, this subtle crescendo colors the beginning of it all in a pleasant and expressive delivery.

The conductor who gives the players of this opening C the confidence of a firm but expressive set of the 4th and 5th pulses prior to it has a fair chance of hearing the kind of beginning I have attempted to describe. It has a chance of happening when all, including the conductor breathe rhythmically and together. Filled to overflowing with a special kind of innocent intensity the tune begins to unfold in its simple way. It is four bars old when the "Scotch" rhythmic element separates it from other cultural or geographical roots:

Example 2

Percy Aldridge Grainger (1882-1961): "Ye Banks and Braes O' Bonnie Doon. British folk-music settings no. 32. Scottish folk-song set for wind band (military band) with or without organ (or harmonium) or for wind choirs with or without organ (or harmonium). Copyright 1936 by Schott and Co., Ltd., London; copyright 1949 by Percy Aldridge Grainger, International Copyright secured; printed in the U.S.A." Available from G. Schirmer, Inc., New York, plate no. 42115; three-line condensed and full scores available.

F major, $\frac{6}{8}$, slowly flowing; 33 bars; duration *ca.* 2:00; minimum of 34 players required. Scored for piccolo; 2 flutes; 2 oboes (English horn *ad. lib.*); 2 bassoons; clarinets: E♭, B♭ 1, 2, 3, 4, alto, bass; saxophones: 2 alto, tenor, baritone; 4 horns; 3 cornets; 2 trumpets; 3 trombones; euphonium (treble clef baritone part provided); tuba; string contrabass; among the several *ad. lib.* parts which the composer and publisher provide are those for additional 2nd and 3rd reed and brass instruments which, along with a part for organ or harmonium, thicken the texture of rich sounds to be heard in the basic 34 player instrumentation listed above.[1]

The score in its original version was first performed on May 23, 1903 by a chorus of single voices, whistlers, and harmonium at a concert organized at her home in London by Grainger's then composer patroness, Mrs. Frank Lowrey (as we know, he then became his own patron with some assistance from Gardiner and Quilter); the whistlers were his closest friends and fellow composers;[2] Grainger played the harmonium. The wind band version dates from 1932.

Its stylistic performance may be achieved as follows:

Example 3

Give the F its full value, plus, then skillfully release it as a tenuto while having planned a momentary hesitation before playing the "Scotch" figure, lowering a special and carefully weighted amount of sound on the second F; it is a matter of wait and weight in the expressive touch that sets this figure off from other elements around it. Each conductor must decide whether or not such an interpretation is either necessary or desirable and, if either, just when to employ it according to individual taste.

After an expressive repetition of the first 4 bars as the second A phrase and a careful approach to the cadence bar [9], the conductor might secure the appropriate release of the F major chord by indicating a gentle withdrawal from the 5th pulse as the common terminal for all sound. And, of course, this release sets up the continuation of the tone with the anacrusis to that ever-gathering B phrase. Each of the four C naturals [10, 11, 12] assumes a continually greater emotional and structural significance as they seem to invite,

Percy Grainger, pianist and composer

penetrating perception to the balances within the movement of each of the lines which weave this fabric of sound, and in so doing, to encourage and to assist the players to listen to their performance so that all may strive together to achieve the composer's intention. Listening demands are not complex in this music, and since they are as rewarding as they are simple, the conductor should seize this opportunity to make the players aware of their place within the harmonic content and of the composer's skillful if uncomplicated manipulation of the lines by which the aggregate music is created.

Indications for a tempo that is "slowly flowing" at a pace of 104 to the eighth are clear declarations that the conductor's pulse in six should keep all those eighths flowing and organized. It would be helpful to all if the conductor took advantage of the available space in upward vertical motion when executing the opening anacrusis and similar stretch-points in the melody.[7] Helpful, as well, would be the conductor's awareness of horizontal flow within other elements in the music using this in contrast to those vertical phrase-endings.

Viewing the first page of the full score through the gauze of slitted eyelids that are almost closed one sees a pattern of wiggly lines and stable supports — things that move and things that do not — all of them contribute to a texture that undulates:

Example 4

If this "view" is acceptable to the conductor as a kind of guide, the markedly horizontal motions made to join that sort of action are suggested by the music's intervalic and rhythmic designs, and the pattern of conducting it might look more like this:

Example 5

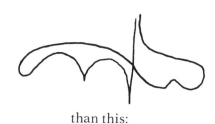

than this:

Example 6

through their re-emphasis, a constant stretching until they spill-over into the D above that releases the insistently built-up tension.

Grainger's harmony for this phrase is carefully generated to grant a special emotional tonal identity to the entire content of bar 13, his compositional goal reached by way of the three bars that precede it. In study of the score the conductor readily can find the composer's purpose stated in these harmonic progressions. They are developed with no notes of the F major scale altered until the 3rd chord of the bar of release [13] when the richness of the tritone (F to B) then allows him to slip conveniently into the dominant 7th and on to the closing repetiton of the A phrase — again without resort to any altered notes; there is, in fact only one altered note in the whole first statement of the 16-bar tune — the raised 4th (B♭ to B) that afforded the harmonic and emotional turn-around in bar 13 described above.[6]

The conductor's purpose in the rehearsal of this deceivingly simple-seeming music is to *listen* with

As always for the conductor, the great challenge is to make the page come alive, to reach beyond the mere translating of symbols into sounds — remarkable though that process may be when executed simultaneously by a large body of players at any stage in their development.

Many lines of sound for "Ye Banks and Braes" in the wind band setting are drawn from Grainger's original concept of the piece as one for harmonium. That instrument's (or the organ's) capability to produce endless sound as long as the performer pumps the bellows and depresses the keys is clearly evident in viewing the first page of the full score. Pedal-points in bassoon II, baritone sax, and trombone III, together with those extended inner harmonic lines running in clarinet III, cornet III, horns I and II, and trombone I demand solid breath support and mature control. Playing the piece is one way to develop both.

The conductor who may be obliged to accommodate players whose development is in-process should adjust the breathing between those players so that it is staggered, closing those open holes in the music that the composer has skillfully endeavored to avoid. Study the overlaps in the second phrase (B-A) [10-17]; there are five different phrasings in bars 10-11 alone. When these and the continuing rhythmic intensities are combined with those harmonic and melodic properties already discussed — together with faithful observance of dynamic balances, the result is that satisfaction in a musical phrase which one seeks to enjoy again and again.

As the first statement of the tune comes to its quiet close, Grainger's request that we "slow off" is more than a quaint substitute for the customary Italian, French, or German terms usually affixed to closing cadences. It is stylistic character — not merely a slower pulsation with which this close should be infused and Grainger's words say it all. His suggestion that the fermata be "short" allows for a satisfying momentary pause in the music's flow while providing an overlap in the sound for those who release, breathe, and continue with the tune's second statement.

The conductor is cautioned not to stop the beat on this fermata, for it is — after all, a pause and not a terminal. One might avoid a stop by moving the fermata in technical execution from the 4th to the 5th pulse and then to resume "in time" on the 6th eighth of bar 17. It is, again, the technical influence of the organ/harmonium overlap, and as the flow resumes, balance in dynamics becomes critical. The prevalence of flutes in many bands where they frequently outnumber clarinets bids caution that they do not bury the tune which is still limited to those few instruments which have played it from its beginning. As the flutes climb ever-higher to their G, balance problems mount with them. The conductor will suggest, of course, that those players unable to reach the upper octave will play where convenient.

The composer's suggestion that the cantilena above the tune be played "sweetly" invites performance that begins with a stretched character and is then energized by a subtle crescendo as it carries its motion over the bar-line to the first note of bar 18. Keeping the melody aloft and applying such adjustments as breath demands the conductor may lead this first portion of the second statement through its fascinating unfolding with the same ease that worked for the first. When the lines begin to cross each other again [26] and the texture thickens, the harmonic and rhythmic energy rises to its height at bar 30. Strict observance by conductor and players of each of Percy Grainger's precise verbal directives will surely lead all to his clearly specified performance intentions.

Those players, especially the low brass, who have accented sixteenths and continuing eighths [29, 30, 31] should remember that these punctuations are under the slur and they are intended to be played deliberately and expressively. Those rising scale fragments in the high reeds [26, 27, 28] that then extend to the full F major scale [28, 29] contribute a growing intensity that tops all other elements, mounting to the climax of the setting at bar 30.

A final suggestion to the conductor bids that an uncommon amount of air be thrust through those instruments, at the moment of execution, that are assigned to the *glissando* [33]. Contemporary terminology calls it a "fall" (Grainger would have used it had he known), but no matter what its identity it requires an extraordinary amount of air to make it happen, and speed is not necessarily desirable in its execution. It may be better, on the other hand, to think this as a relaxed and happy sigh of satisfaction.■

Notes
1. There was no need for percussion, Grainger's "personal discovery;" of all *ad lib* instruments the most desired color here is provided by the English horn. The score does not so indicate, but the conductor should know that the tubas have the full bass-line as a cue [2-17]. The consistent weakness of the bass voice in the average band suggests that this cue be played in the quiet dynamic indicated for other similar instruments.
2. Among them were Roger Quilter and Cyril Scott; for this source and an amusing peek into an early incident in P.A.G.'s early manhood see: *Percy Grainger;* John Bird, Paul Elek, London 1976, pp's 74-75.
3. A [1-5] A [6-9] B [10-13] A [14-17]
4. Rare though they be in the Grainger repertory, more will probably not be published unless this simplest of them all is not made a part of every band library.
5. A brae is a hillside along a river.
6. Regardless of the terminology applied to them, the 1st and 3rd chords in bar 13 are constructed of two minor triads topped by a major triad.
7. See bars 1, 5, 9, 17, 18, 20, 25, 29, 33.

Children's March
by Percy Aldridge Grainger

An Interpretive Analysis
by Frederick Fennell

Percy Grainger once held very high rank among pianists appearing before the public, and that position launched the international career that led to his acceptance as a composer. His ability to sell tickets as a recitalist supported his composition habit for most of his peripatetic life, and though he grew to loathe the piano, public concerts, and all they represented, it was his keyboard facility and reputation that allowed the development of the unusual musical personality which was so closely wed to all the rest of him.[2]

When he was attached to U.S. Army Bands in the New York area during an enlistment in World War I he used available time to great advantage, eventually turning his interests as a composer to re-scoring for military band the music he had already written for orchestra, such as *Colonial Song, Irish Tune*, and *Shepherd's Hey*. The original composition from this period is *Children's March*. It is an original work, to be sure, but it is so closely cast in the style of his famous folk song settings that it is frequently and casually accepted as being one of

them. This character is apparent from the opening phrase, as folk-song-like a tune as one could imagine. Grainger the composer was an obvious product of his environment. He had lived with English folk song for so long that much of its tonal, melodic, and rhythmic character seems by this time to have become a subconscious presence.

He considered *Children's March* to be the first composition for band utilizing the piano[3] and I have seen no score which refutes the statement. From musical experiences while attached to the military he was aware of the band's mostly *al fresco* function, ceremonial and otherwise, where a piano in any state of acceptable operation would be rare indeed. What he wrote for the piano is offered as an option and cue-scored to cover the notes. Inevitably of course, there is no acceptable substitute for the instrument; however, it is difficult to accept in Grainger's cued substitutions his strange avoidance of those keyboard percussion instruments which he so firmly championed in other scorings of this period, principally *Shepherd's Hey*. If he had dared once, why not twice?[4]

These considerations are stated as a basic principle that permeates the scoring. In one's study of the full score,[5] which Frank Erickson and the publisher provide with the revised version, the sonority of the piano as an integral element in the composer's concept of the piece becomes critical to the conductor's eventual fulfillment of responsibility to the composer.[6]

The Structure

Children's March has many characteristics of a march, but not its usual form. It is actually a five-part rondo (ABABA — similar to the return of A in early European marches), with an introduction and coda; and is devoted mostly to the keys of F, B♭, and A♭ major with some excursions to relative tonality plus inevitable Grainger chromaticism (see chart).

Instrumental color makes its bid for the conductor's attention from the very beginning. The composer's unison mixture of English horn and bassoon, alto and tenor saxophone — pairs of double and single reeds — join to create a very attractive sonority as they play what at first may seem to be a straight-off statement of the march offered in the title; but that simple pentatonic tune (F major without B♭ and E♮) on second look turns out to be the introduction. Performers and listeners won't meet these fetching ideas again for 351 bars.

The conductor's first responsibility, as always, is the right tempo, which the composer has given here with simple clarity: *Fairly Fast* (♩. = about 126). The wisdom of his choice and its effectiveness is immediately evident when the conductor sets the metronome at 126 then reads the score straight through. Observing the relentless drive of the music in the first hours of study establishes this tempo priority; and right with it comes the conductor's responsibility to dynamic balances which are of primary concern in the performance of this piece.

Opening instrumental colors in the solo and accompanying reeds also establish that this is to be a piece dominated by them; there are but 14 of the 413 measures which are given exclusively to the brass and percussion, and — unusual for a march of any kind — there are only 110 bars (roughly ¼) that are scored *tutti*.

Grainger's life-long fancy for the reeds was fed its full ration during his Army days. Richness of sound in the scoring for anything such as this introduction was something he could hear anytime he presented Bandmaster Rocco Resta with score and parts. My request to Grainger for a word about the music brought the reply: "*Children's March* was specially written to use all the forces of the Coast Artillery Band in which I was serving in 1918."[7]

The conductor should be sure to establish the legato character of the opening tune making certain that players use the composer's *espressivo* to the full, avoiding any accentuation at the beginning of each two-bar segment, securing full value from each note. This trochee meter (long-short) all too

Five-Part Rondo Form: Introduction, ABABA, Coda

(number each measure of the score for immediate reference)

Large Form	Measures	Internal Form	Key
Introduction	[1-16]	a(8) + b(8)	leads to
	[17-20]	vamp-like transition	F
A	[21-36]	⌐a(8) repeat	
	[37-52]	⌊b(8) repeat	(iii-vi-ii-V-I)
	[53-68]	⌐a(8) a-var.(8)	
	[69-84]	⌊b(8) repeat	(iii)
	[85-100]	⌐a-var.(8) repeat	
	[101-116]	⌊b(8) repeat	(iii)
B	[117-132]	⌐a(8) repeat	B♭: I
	[133-160]	⌊b(8) repeat w/extensions & variations	(iii pedal)
	[161-164]	vamp-like trans. (4)	
	[165-180]	⌐a(8) repeat	
	[181-196]	⌊c(8) repeat	
A	[197-212]	⌐a-var.(8) repeat	B♭
	[213-228]	⌊b(8) repeat	E♭: iii
	[229-236]	⌐a-var.(8)	E♭: I
	[237-251]	⌊b(8) repeat	(iii)
	[252-266]	trans. (15)	
B	[267-282]	⌐a(8) repeat	A♭
	[283-302]	⌊b(8) repeat w/extensions & variations	(iii pedal)
	[303-306]	vamp-like trans. (4)	
	[307-322]	⌐a(8) repeat	
	[323-338]	⌊c(8) repeat	
A	[339-354]	⌐a-var.(8) repeat	A♭
	[355-370]	⌊b(8) repeat	(iii)
Coda	[371-386]	16 meas. from introduction (w/variations)	B♭
	[387-402]	16 meas. from section Ab	
	[403-413]	11 measure extension	

Percy Aldridge Grainger (1882-1961) *Children's March* "Over the Hills and Far Away" for Military Band (piano ad libitum). Based on the piano solo of the same name (copyright 1918 by Percy Grainger and published by G. Schirmer). That 48-measure composition (marked ♩.=116) is the main theme (measures 21-68) of the band version.

Composed fall 1916-February 1918 and scored summer and fall 1918-February 1919.[1] Copyright 1919, by Percy Grainger and originally published by G. Schirmer, Inc., New York, as Schirmer's Compendium, No. 29; (plate no. 28980); revised version by Frank Erickson, copyright 1971 by G. Schirmer, Inc.

The original edition has a score of 2-5 lines. The revised edition has both a full and a condensed score, including parts for piccolo; flute 1-2; oboe 1-2; English horn; bassoon 1-2; clarinets: E♭, B♭ 1-2-3-4, E♭ alto, B♭ bass, E♭ and BB♭ contrabass; saxophones: alto 1-2, tenor, baritone; 4 horns in F; 4 cornets in B♭; 3 trombones; treble clef baritone, bass clef euphonium; tuba; string contrabass; percussion: kettledrums, glockenspiel, chimes, xylophone, cymbals, tam-tam, wood block, castanets, tambourine, snare drum, bass drum; piano.

The revised edition eliminates the original scoring and parts for D♭ piccolo and flute, bass oboe, contrabassoon, soprano and bass saxophones, horns in E♭, treble clef tenor horns and trombones, and contra sarrusophone in E♭.

There is a ⅜ meter signature throughout; 413 measures; performance time *ca.* 7:00.

Dedication: "For my playmate beyond the hills" [Karen Holten, a Scandinavian beauty].

First performance: New York by the Goldman Band, June 6, 1919, the composer conducting, Ralph Leopold, piano.

frequently invites an indifferent response which must be avoided:

Example 1

The conductor who is able to coax "wet" (as opposed to "dry") sounds from the clarinet choir players providing harmonic and rhythmic support [measures 2, 4, 6, 10, 12] will find these bouncy impacts to be as appropriate to performance as the vibrant harmonies of the closing cadence. "Wet" as a sonority adjective invites a vibrant and solidly-supported resonant tone that contains maximum richness regardless of brevity and separation. Both qualities must be present here where richness of tone and balance in sound supersede articulation.

To suggest these properties, the conductor should demonstrate them at the piano, where the critical element of resonance, regardless of articulation, is almost impossible to avoid:

Example 2

[1-2]

The necessity for "wetness" is further revealed when the piano joins the low brass in the extension [17-21], where the scoring offers greater space between sounds. When the piano is absent, the conductor must remind the tubas and contrabass clarinet that their lines carry the lead, and be sure the trombones always keep a piano-like resonance in what they play.

The band's bass deficiency presents itself as the principal tune is exposed at measure 21. Grainger's (or any composer's) line for the string bass looks very convincing — *looks,* but almost never *sounds* that way. Raising the dynamic level is not necessarily the answer, even though a forced sound from a single player is probably better than none at all.[8]

Grainger's granting the first statement of the tune to the 2nd bassoon is very much in keeping with his liberal views of the art. I recommend that the kettledrum be added to the cadential F on the second pulse of bar 36. Its presence will fortify the piano's octave, or supply that note if the piano is absent. I recommended the same doubling for the cadences in bars 51-52 and 59-60. In the absence of the piano, the conductor must strive to secure from the mid to low-range brass as fully compensating a sound as is possible toward the end of the first full statement of the recurring rondo theme [52].

The composer's inevitable change of texture from detached to legato [61-68] also brings the music up to its highest elevation thus far, a point toward which the conductor should lead the players with positive, appropriate, inviting gestures suggested by the music itself. Here also is where, in the 62nd bar of his music, the composer uses the seventh scale step, E♮, in the melody for the first time — a moment I always enjoy in preparation and fulfillment. All eight bars of this section might have been directed to be played "feelingly;" its concluding figures [65-66] come off better musically when the dot on the 4th eighth is played "wet" rather than short and "dry."

The phrase "somewhat clingingly," directed to the brass in their only soli statement in the piece [85-92], might be interpreted: "play all the notes and their articulations at face value." As Grainger's scoring thickens [93] the conductor should opt for the piccolo cue and also be happy that once there was money in the budget for that good E♭ clarinet. The music needs these two powerful instruments on the top of the sound. It will be desirable ensemble discipline for cornets, the trombone, and the conductor to rise from their *forte* crescendo and sink back with the subito *mezzo piano* at measure 93.

Another conductor judgment in editing occurs in measures 97-116 where everything that resonates and penetrates like the sound of the composer's piano is nowhere to be found in the cue scorings. Judicious application of all the "tuneful percussion" was never more appropriate than here. As the A section is concluded, the conductor is cautioned against that invitation to distortion presented by Mr. Grainger's *tutti fortissimo*

[115-116] in which the brass and percussion will surely bury everybody else unless their mark is reduced by two-thirds to *forte*.

The B section [117-196] unfolds major developments in the composition, shifting the harmonic center up a 4th to B♭ where at the outset the conductor's two principal concerns are tonal character and dynamic balance. It is critical for all of us who study and conduct Grainger's wind band pieces to remember his assumption that the music would be played by those who, like himself, were thoroughly professional performers. Contemporary facts of professional life have shifted the balance of performance toward the average American school musicians, in whose hands Grainger's nuances are not always as easily observed as he conceived them.

It is totally unrealistic (in spite of our outstanding groups) that the average choir of clarinets, plus the oboe and saxophone, will produce the balances Grainger heard in his head when he scored this musical idea. Alto and bass clarinet dynamics here must be raised from piano/pianissimo to mezzo forte/forte (as most of these players conceive sound level) and played with appropriate air support.[9] As this part offers its refreshing new material, the textural mixture requires the conductor to blend the solo sounds of the oboe, clarinet, and saxophone and to secure from these players stylistic unanimity in note-value and nuance.[10] These materials offered first in simplicity, later will appear twice [267 and 307] at full-throttle settings that swing along in solid block scorings; they contrast and complement to these extents:

Example 3a

Example 3b

The conductor's further consideration in tonal presentation as this B section unfolds is for a sustained and expressive character from all players, not just those with the tune. Unless the low clarinets are unusually strong, the cue in the bassoons is a must, as is the addition to score and parts of that very expressive Grainger directive — "feelingly."

The six notes in the horn [119] will not be lost on the inquisitive conductor, for they beg the repetition they receive as ostinato in 95 of the remaining 293 bars of the piece. These repetitious, agitated rhythmic pedal points do not always transcribe successfully from their piano origin to the saxophone or cornet;[11] when the horns are exposed to the task, those players must prepare with care. The ultimate use of this arresting ostinato figure is reserved for the *fortissimo* octaves in the cornets, where it serves as compositional glue for the bridge [252-266] that leads to the B part's second appearance, beginning at measure 267.

Fierceness

Grainger seems to have been pleased when performers perceived the element of "fierceness" in his music; "Lord Melbourne" comes quickly to mind. We have also seen him deal in quick jabs of sound that he intended as "fierce" without so indicating. Two possible excursions into unlabeled "fierceness" are found in cadences ahead:

Example 4 [131-132]

Example 5 [187-188]

The conductor's challenge in both examples is to dig out the bass lines, which do not sound on their own. Where the baritone sax will invariably be the savior of Example 4, its curious absence from the "fierceness" of Example 5 is a condition the conductor can correct by giving it the line Erickson gave to the E♭ contrabass clarinet; grumbling "fierceness" is appropriate. Between these two examples there occurs this flaring outburst —

Example 6

[143]

— a sound born into the saxophone and curiously absent here; do not hesitate to reassign this intentionally arresting eruption to include the alto saxophone (see measure 293). Fourth in these observations on working toward "fierceness" is the six-bar A♭ major scale excursion employed to set-up the restatement of the B section — a "fierce," solid *tutti* (see Example 7).

Here the conductor/teacher challenges the players to infuse these contrary-running scales with the greatest energy; but as this swirling ferocity is completed, all should save some of that invigoration for a crescendo in the final bar. It also is possible that the *least* physical motion by the conductor could be the *most* effective — standing back in performance letting it all happen from the players, joining the motion as the tune resumes at measure 267. A final observation on "fierceness:" the composer's charge to all the horns at measure 213 that they play "as violently and roughly as possible" — *fortissimo* — is a dangerous request in the world of today's terrific hornists who are ready and eager to comply!

In absence of the E♭ clarinet, the ostinato at measure 173 doesn't have quite enough bite in the sound; double with the piccolo sounding with the flutes. Another Grainger outburst in the saxophones [175] (same as "Dublin" — *Lincolnshire Posy* Part I) should be played "fiercely"; but when, at last, the inevitable contrasting and strikingly fresh new material comes in the up-beat to measure 181, every line in the score should carry the greetings: "tonefully," "feelingly to the fore"! This is a musical utterance to treasure. Its composer has waited patiently to give it to us, setting it up so we could hardly fail to respond. Next comes the inevitable Grainger descending chromaticism beneath the two-bar three-times-repeated new material, the chromatics later to be carried all the way in the piano and the reeds while the brass peal out the tune [323].

For its bold statement starting at measure 189 it is unfortunate to lose the piano's contribution to variety in orchestration. In the piano's absence, the glockenspiel can contribute brightness if the conductor gives just the top notes to that instrument. You will also find it rewarding to add a crescendo to all the reeds sustaining the composer's extended length through the dotted half at measure 193.

A Recapitulation?

Diminuendo of dynamic and orchestration returns the music to square one, where it seems, momentarily, that a traditional recapitulation has begun [197]; but this feeling is dispelled in that shatteringly "violent" horn entrance [212] that begins 24 bars of wide-open offerings which, at their height, are replaced by the dramatic *subito pianissimo* at measure 237. The momentum of the music then continues to re-gather, storm-like, with its insistent oncoming eighths.

The conductor, observing everything — especially balances — gauges the levels of sound so that this series of climaxes is not one in which one climax outdoes the other. On the contrary, each must proceed with a sense of order toward the apex of choice.[12] The conductor also may wish to compensate for a missing piano's fortissimo hammerings [269, 273, 277, 281, 282] by giving these notes to all available keyboard percussion, and to keep an ear open for the projection of that quadruplet in the cornets, horns, trombones, and baritone at measure 274 which makes what its composer probably thought was "...a grand effect!" It's the only duple moment in the piece; the low brass and conductor should be laying for it — "fiercely!"

Another conductor care in this portion of the composition is the balance of all players contributing to the harmonic change of F minor — G minor 7 — C minor [281-282] carried mostly by horns and trombones. Percussion should not bury their colleagues here, but in the interest of harmony and with general availability of pedal kettle-drums, the conductor should alter the printed notes for them (which distort) to conform to those for the tubas (which do not).

The effective use of the wood block [282] requires a good wrist to play the part with one hand;

Example 7

[261-266]

when two hard xylophone sticks are used, there need not be any accentuation. Reference to the earlier reed flair [143] finds Grainger's scoring in measure 293 to be truly "fierce."

If the conductor has absorbed that metronomic drive mentioned at the outset of this study/performance essay, the momentum of *Children's March* should be a thorough presence by the time the band is negotiating Grainger's rhythmic and harmonic extensions that prepare the final assaults on his B section tunes [307-339].

It is prudent at this point in our overview of the music to clarify that Grainger did not consider the composition to be variations on his themes, varied though his manipulations of the material may be. For the most thorough statement by him on the subject of variation I urge you to consult *The Percy Grainger Companion*.[13]

This is demanding music, almost constantly articulated. Fatigue becomes a performance factor, particularly when nuance is a vital part of repetition as in the four bars preceding measure 304.

Grainger has used his B section's principal theme twelve times before altering a single note of it, and thus we have become familiar with this line:

Example 8

[117-120]

Being a good and always interesting composer, he saved a little something to top what had gone before; here is how he did it for *Children's March:*

Example 9

[315-318]

This happy little touch, the high F — an elevation of a perfect fourth rather than giving us the minor second for the 13th time — unfortunately is inundated by the ostinato and all the sound around it, as only the full score shows for bar 317. The F scored for 2nd cornet is obliterated by the D♭ of the 1st cornet hard at the ostinato figure. One way to let this bright moment be heard is to double the F concert in the 1st cornet in bar 317, passing the ostinato in that bar to the 3rd cornet; there is already plenty of D♭ in other soprano brass.

Those three arch-like brass octaves for the statement starting at measure 323 should be insistently offered, no two being alike in intensity, but growing all the way into that rugged terminal in the saxes and brasses [328-330]. And as this is happening in the brass, the D♭ major scale rising 2½ octaves in the reeds fairly vaults them into their final statement of the tune [331]; add crescendo to all of the rising reeds, and be sure they support the tone with maximum air.

As the *March* begins to wind down, that A♭ statement of the main tune (beginning at measure 339) falls into an ungrateful register. The conductor must ask the saxophones and horns to compensate. The final statement of that theme is somewhat ironically given to the E♭ clarinet at the bottom of its register, doubled by the alto saxophone. The conductor withdraws to minimum gestures as the sounds of the *March* recede to its introduction/restatement [371-386] now pitched a 5th lower in B♭ and cast in the reflective character of a lazy legato. The nervous agitations — $\frac{6}{8}$ ♪ ♪ ♪ — with which the piece began are gone. The composer now indulges himself in familiar harmonies and retrospective voicings for his favorite reeds for the last time in *Children's March*.

The last part of the coda [387], dark and empty, with its fragmentation, augmentation, and more than a slight touch of "beyond-the-hillness" is left to the pungent solo bassoon. Everyone in the band should sit motionless until the conductor's arms are lowered to signal the end of the music: atmosphere!

The Grainger touch — originality — in his use of the marimba stick to strike into sound the lowest B♭ on the grand piano string calls for a healthy stroke, as can be heard in his performance at the piano in the recording he made with *The Goldman Band*.[14] It is no mere "effect" but a simple and (to him) obvious sonority resource.[15] Others have found that similar uses for the piano make it fair game in the world of sounds; but, again, Grainger had already been there. His sensitivity to space is wonderfully applied to the quietly dramatic closing of *Children's March*. The silences say so much — as though he were walking away glancing back over his shoulder as his playmate gradually disappears "beyond the hills...and far away." ■

Errors

[3] part: tenor sax, reverse rhythm ♩ ♪
[11] score: English horn, complete the note as C
[16] score and parts: 2nd horn, correct written B to C (F concert)
[68] score: trombone I, remove "sax" from cue indication
[72] score: E♭ clarinet, remove the A
[76] part: tuba, note does not print, lower octave
[99] part: flute II, 4th eighth is D, change to F
[111] part: baritone, 1st note change from A to G
[163] part: baritone, change F to C, play as note, not cue
[188] part: E♭ clarinet, change 4th sixteenth from G to F♯
[227] part: E♭ clarinet, last eighth change from E to D
[228] part: 1st alto sax, dotted quarter rest missing
[228] part: baritone, 2nd quarter change from A♭ to G
[237] part: xylophone, this and all succeeding tied dotted quarters and quarters are to be rolled
[262] part: horn II, 5 not clear in bars rest

[273] score: piano, treble clef for bottom stave
[274] part: 1st and 2nd cornets, remove slur over the quadruplet
[275] part: baritone, add A♭ downbeat to finish the line
[281] score: add ♮ to 2nd note of the triplet
[281] part: cornet II, remove ♯ before the B in triplet, make B♮
[281] score: 1st cornet, eighth rest missing after triplet
[318] score: clarinet I, correct last two eighths as G, F
[338] part: oboe I, change quarter to E
[394] score: bassoon, fill in the note heads F, G

Footnotes

1. Also published for two pianos (Music Room Tit-Bits No. 4) and in Adolph Schmid's considerably truncated setting for theater orchestra.
2. Two biographies are currently available: *Percy Grainger — The Inveterate Innovator*, by Thomas C. Slattery, The Instrumentalist Co., 1974; and *Percy Grainger*, by John Bird, Paul Elek, London, England, 1976.
3. Letter to the author dated January 6, 1959.
4. Frank Erickson's revised edition avoided their use either as substitute for or adjunct to Grainger's cue-scorings which seems odd in the era of keyboard percussion so well under way by the time of his revision of the score; his cautious avoidance of any "tampering" with the score is an honest if unproductive observance of what the composer offered. I feel no reluctance to apply the whole range of basic keyboard percussion, including the new electronic bass marimba and the now always-available electronic piano to performance of this music. I saw *three* solovoxes attached to various keyboards in Grainger's home at White Plains; I think he would have gone all the way.
5. Erickson generously supplied me with this quotation concerning the score: "At the time of this revision I was doing some work as an editor for G. Schirmer. I was familiar with the piece but had never seen the score; no one has written better band music or worse scores. This was a typical Grainger condensed score and completely inadequate. My method of working was to construct a full score in reverse: that is, each part was taken individually and written into the full score. The parts were all re-engraved with changes in small details, but the original was adhered to as closely as possible."
6. It is both the potential force and clarity of articulation, together with the ringing long beyond their sounding that makes application of all keyboard percussion, plus kettledrums, so appropriate to this score. The conductor who is not familiar with these instruments — their range and characteristics or the wide variety of sounds produced by every kind of mallet — is urged to study the subject thoroughly, seeking professional advice. In the parlance of today's bumper communication, the sticker for *Children's March* should read: THINK KEYBOARD.
7. Letter to the author dated August 6, 1959.
8. This unrealistic presence of the string bass reaches its most ridiculous proportions at an all-state band when one sees a single instrument stuck way back in a group numbering over 100 players. Amplification of it usually results in feedback or distortion; the power of an electric bass guitar rarely brings musical satisfaction to all parties. That single acoustic bass player who did come to the festival may take home a worthwhile personal music experience; but there, as in Mr. Grainger's *pianissimo* backing of this theme, what transpires is strictly music for the eyes.

Rocco Resta and Percy Grainger in 1916

9. Bassoons should play the cues at 117.
10. The original publication contained wordless music [117-137 and 165-172] for "vocal male quartet;" in their absence the music ". . . can be sung by the members of the band not playing their instruments at this particular moment," according to the composer, once again ahead of the pack.
11. Again, the keyboard percussion can substitute; or, in their absence, a small and large triangle could put up a little appropriate jangle [132-144]. Considering the composer's fascination with clanging metals, it seems strange that he would avoid the triangle here.
12. I opt for measures 307-322 and 323-331.
13. *The Percy Grainger Companion*, edited by Lewis Foreman; London 1981, Thames Publishing; p. 141. Sole Distributor is T.R.N. Music Publisher, Box 1076, Ruidoso, New Mexico.
14. *Band Masterpieces*, The Goldman Band, Richard Franko Goldman, conductor; Decca Records, Inc.; DL 8633.
15. There is no worthy substitute for what is scored, but the tam-tam comes closest. Its effectiveness will be enhanced if the conductor experiments for the desired sound. Two instruments will make acceptable sounds if they are contrasting in size and pitch, and played with the same marimba mallet that Grainger prescribed for the piano (do not use the standard tam-tam beater). All percussion should treat this concluding section subtly. A tambourine with ".000" sandpaper glued to the head near the rim guarantees a sometimes risky performance with the thumb. Ornaments come before the beat. Mounted castanets assure three impacts, or the player may hold the traditional instrument at a raised horizontal angle, grasping the upper clapper with one hand while producing the three impacts with two fingers on the suspended lower clapper.

Percy Aldridge Grainger

Hill-Song No. 2

An Interpretive Analysis
by Frederick Fennell

A Necessary Preamble

Percy Grainger sent me a note about the music:

I have always been in love with the wildness, the freshness, and the heroic qualities of hill countries, hill peoples, and hill musics. This love of the hills was brought to a head in 1900 by a three-day's walk I took in Argyleshire, in the Western Highlands of Scotland. I was entranced by the sound of the bagpipes (which is my favorite of all musical sonorities) and by the sound of some oriental double-reeds that I heard at about the same time. I felt a great urge to weave these fierce nasal sounds into a polyphonic weft. The result was my *Hill-Song No. 2* [he meant No. 1] composed in 1901-1902 which consisted of both fast and slow elements, scored mainly for double-reed instruments (6 oboes, 6 English horns, 6 bassoons, etc.).

Wishing also to write a bagpipe-like *Hill-Song* that consisted only of fast and energetic elements I wrote my second *Hill-Song* in the period 1902-1907 [of] material culled from *Hill-Song No. 1* and partly of new energetic material I composed in 1907. This time the scoring, for 24 instruments, was mainly for a mixture of double-reeds and single-reeds.

This is probably the first time in known music that such a large body of solo winds was brought together in chamber music. . . . In writing my *Hill-Songs* I was not concerned with man's impressions of nature, but strove, as it were, to let the hills themselves express themselves in music.[4]

Whether his final statement is achieved or not, it is more than the hills that were to speak for themselves through this music. Percy Aldridge Grainger speaks for *himself* here, not through his familiar agents — deft and arresting manipulation of folk-song material, however charming or bold. This is not another of what have been described as those ". . . delightful but secondary pleasantries . . . ."[5] This is the music *he* wanted to write; the score and each part emphatically state: "composed by Percy Aldridge Grainger."

The conductor's comprehension of many elements in *Hill-Song No. 2* might be considerably enhanced through an acquaintance with bagpipe basics.[6] Their simple and constant tone source is air

Grainger's Argyleshire Piper Tune

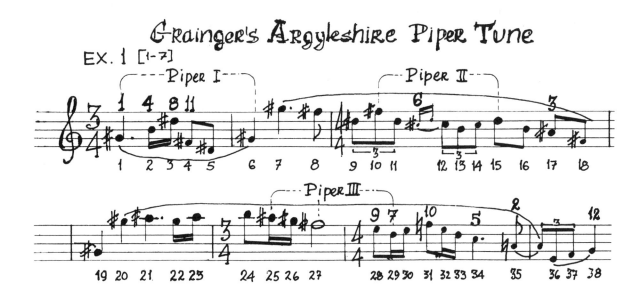

EX. 1 [1-7]

A Complex and Extraordinary Score

received from the player by a blow-pipe with which air is stored in a bag clutched under the left arm, pumped to pressure that activates four covered double-reeds. Three reeds are fixed drones (two tenor and one bass), and one serves as a conically-shaped instrument, the chanter, containing seven finger holes and one thumb hole. The piper produces tunes above the independent and always-present drones (see the low reeds in the score at measures 1-3 and 85-96) by manipulating finger combinations on the holes. The right thumb supports the chanter while the left thumb controls the "speaker function" of the thumb hole. The range is nine notes up from G♮ with both C and F being close to C♯ and F♯.

With its handy air storage bank the instrument is capable of spinning out such long lines as those with which Grainger establishes the basic character of this music. Articluation is by accurate and forceful throwing of flat fingers onto the holes and by a spring-like lift away. Complex ornaments — beats, ripples, or throws — add rhythmic color to bagpipe music and it is their spirit as well as their sound that is helpful to our understanding of Grainger's view of it all as reflected in his music.[7]

Hill-Song No. 2 begins with this freely-wandering musical statement which I have chosen to call *Grainger's Argyleshire Piper Tune*.

Three fragments from it, identified as *Piper I, II,* and *III* are principal material from which most of the music evolves. Numbers above the staff identify the twelve notes of the chromatic scale on G♯ in order of appearance; those below the staff allow quick reference to notes not included in the *Pipers*. The conductor who is preparing for the rehearsal of this score might copy the above *Argyleshire* example and keep it handy for reference while working through the score; *Argyleshire* in full never returns again.

Grainger certainly achieves in this opening phrase his desire to write bagpipe-like music demanding a "fierce and keen" approach. The conductor's first challenge in a journey that is full of them, is to get the oboes, bassoons, and low clarinets to play "skirlingly" (with a shrill, piercing, unrelenting sound; also, the sound of the bagpipe — reedy, nasal) without resort to burlesque, bad taste, poor intonation, or any comic quality whatsoever. Complete absence of vibrato matches bagpipe tone for the melody and drone; lots of edge on all sounds is appropriate in these first seven measures, but the pipes end at the third

A Formal Rebellion

That Grainger's initial musical statement [measures 1-7] never returns again[8] is fully in keeping with his personal rebellion as a composer against traditionally formal structure. Memories of an idea — even one as bold as this opener — may float in and out, but they do not do so at pre-determined junctions dictated by those forms with which he was so thoroughly familiar; as a young pianist playing the music of others these were fine, but increasingly anathema to him as a composer. This particular antipathy makes critical scrutiny of these results of his personal and constructional abhorences a dilemma that is in no way easily reconciled.

Readers may already be aware that I have often resorted to highly personal modes in analytical

technique just to approach Grainger's exposition of a very long train of ideas — logical, fetching, and rewarding but somewhat out of phase with those familiar guidelines in text book analysis that serve other music with common ease. As sympathetic investigators of Percy Grainger's music we have to dig deeper, one more time, for the music (like the man) simply does not fit with convenience into everybody's comfortable B♭ cubby-hole; hence the absence of any structural formal analysis. analysis.

Our greatest ally in these considerations is the composer-approved published full score, the one *he* made, and it is the first of but two that exist from among his many large works for winds.[9] Errors in score and parts are minimal and the publisher accepted his personal terminology.

pulse of bar 7. Grainger uses the clarinet family to affect withdrawal from his "fierce" piping and the solo oboe's entrance, "feelingly," changes the character of the music at once. Subsequent directions provide all conductors with sufficient description of the composer's wishes, sonically and emotionally. Grainger uses *all* of these words: "toneful, tonefully, feelingly, fiercely, brassy, screamingly, explosive, snarlingly, shatteringly, skittishly, supportingly, clingingly, hugely, playfully, boldly, skirlingly, singingly, passionately, reedy, nasal, [and] throbbingly."

Complete concentration on *Argyleshire* is essential to learning this score. Memorizing it so that it can be sung, whistled, played, or recalled in silence makes this wide-ranging idea a part of life. Its 38 notes (12 plus 26 repeats) cover an octave and a fifth. Additional resources found in five consecutive bars at the halfway mark in the score, together with an existing idea from bar 28 complete the *Hill-Song* resource.

Characteristic "Scottish" ornamentation, the common mordent, is present 26 times. Economy of gesture in the conductor's manner should reflect great and concentrated horizontal intensity minus tension, all resources pointing toward the first high point at the A# in bar 4. Once a conductor develops the habit of looking at every bit of music expecting to detect minute particles as well as the bold chunks of a composer's material, he is on the way to total score comprehension; *Hill-Song No. 2* presents constant opportunity for the practice of this critical skill. In addition to those easily-identifiable large portions of *Argyleshire* the observant conductor sees Grainger's application of a procedure basic to composition in the major/minor mode — an uninterrupted scale, this one descending an octave and a minor third in the second bassoon and baritone sax [4-5-6] as solid base for the wayward tune and its wandering chromatic harmony.

The conductor's first of many adjustments in balance comes in bar 7 during the bridge between the first and second extended phrases: maintain the *forte* at measure 7 in the low reeds, but adjust the *piano* in measure 9 to *mezzo-forte*. There's never enough bottom sound to this phrase [7-14].

A bird's-eye view is frequently the conductor's most helpful guide to a score's thematic and in-

Percy Aldridge Grainger (1882-1961), *Hill-Song No. 2*, composed in 1907 and scored to be played by "a solo wind ensemble (23 or 24 wind instruments and cymbal) or band or symphony orchestra (omitting trombones, tuba, and violins)." Copyright 1950 by Leeds Music Corporation (now Belwin-Mills); presently available from T.R.N. Publishing Co., P.O. Box 1076, Ruidoso, New Mexico, in licensed reprint. Also published in 1922 for two pianos by G. Schirmer, Inc., New York. Neither the full score nor the parts have plate numbers and the work is not otherwise identified by a publisher catalog number. It is dedicated to Grainger's close friend H. Balfour Gardiner,[1] although the published score carries no inscription. The dedication and the customary Grainger note about the music are found on the inside cover of the dust jacket for the parts, as is his time and place table for its composition.[2]

Scored for piccolo, flute 1-2, oboe 1-2-3, English horn, bassoon 1-2, double bassoon; clarinet: E♭, B♭ 1-2-3, alto, bass; saxophone: soprano, alto, tenor, baritone; cornet 1-2, horn 1-2, trombone 1-2-3, baritone, euphonium, tuba; cymbal.[3] Score nomenclature guides the conductor through a maze of performance couplings, left here to personal preferences.

Time: *ca.* 5:00; "fierce and keen, at fast walking speed," ♩=120, multiple meters, no key signature, 141 bars.

strumental "topography;" standing up and back with *Hill-Song* open on the desk to pages two and three, for example, it becomes apparent that Grainger constantly passes the action from one instrumental solo or set to another. Refocussing down to close-range, the conductor finds the first use of notes 10-15 of *Piper II* [measures 7-9] as another link, this to the second major phrase (oboe), seen to be *Piper III*, a descending four-note whole-tone fragment of notes 25-28 that is then ascended — a figure seen in many a guise in measures ahead. The first ten notes in the oboe all come in sequence from bars 5 and 6, notes 24 to 34. When the passage ends in bar 14 important intervalic and rhythmic material not found in *Argyleshire* has also been exposed.

The conductor will have noticed a lean but strong musical character as the lines move left to right sparsely distributed amongst the solo players and their few collaborators, the music flowing with natural ease through the nine meter changes that lead it to its second bridge [21-23].

There are 88 meter changes to be negotiated by the conductor and players in this piece. They structure the steady unfolding of the composer's ideas, granting him as much freedom to roam here, musically, as his free spirit beckoned him to wander at will amidst Scottish highlands. In addition to being able to read and execute these changes of order, the conductor is urged to let the *content* of a measure or a sequence of change absorb the eye, then the brain, and not merely react to the numerals which indicate change. Musical content is what eventually will fix the metric value in the brain anyhow, so why not try writing out the melodic line of those sequences that at first seem bothersome? Use the pitches and rhythms, but leave out any numerical guide:

In this fashion the conductor conducts music, not changes in time signature. Concentration on content brings its ultimate reward — logic; once content controls comprehension there simply isn't any other way that the composer could have written the music; and there isn't any other way to conduct it, either. The conductor then is in control of the music being played.

A thickening of the sound is immediately apparent at measure 16, the sound building and peaking as familiar Grainger parallel triads descend in whole-tones (*Piper III*); the first musical and instrumental climax is reached in bar 20. The conductor's part in this, first of all is to have the score with both the bird's-eye and microscopic views, the latter showing a G major seventh chord at the beginning of bar 19 in which the tenor sax alone has the vital fifth, D♮; the ear should also tell that the second bassoon part here needs to have its A corrected down to G. Players seem reluctant to push all the air into the instruments required to project this sound to the printed *fortissimo*. The conductor's motion terminating the action leading to bar 19 might be *down* and *out* from the body, well energized and planned as the thrust from which, after indicating a long eighth, there is physical recoil appropriate to the descending music in bars 19 and 20; the motion might resemble this pattern:

Next comes that wonderfully screetching bit of descending parallelism led by piccolo and E♭ and B♭ clarinet offering nine consecutive whole tones [20-21-22] that the conductor must assure be played with accents under the slur and strong breath action. Because the passage seems to have a built-in slow-down, you may wish to ask players to add arrows pointing forward on their parts in these measures as a reminder to keep the music moving.

A conductor seeking to be free from the tyranny of beating patterns might elect to do here what this same composer told us to do at the beginning of "Lord Melbourne" in *Lincolnshire Posy*[10] — at

least for seven of the nine high energy sounds:

The conductor's return to the beat pattern clues those who need to know that Grainger's next bridge — a grumblingly fascinating low reed flourish fashioned from the first five notes of *Argyleshire* — is about to set up a harmonically rich development, exclusively in the mid-to-low reeds and clearly manufactured from bars 7 and 8. Just to guarantee length for the quarter *and* length plus deliberation for the eighths, motion might include patterns similar to these:

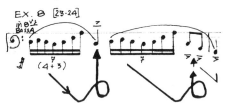

Following the composer's directive it is suggested that players be instructed to organize the seven notes as four-plus-three, throwing a special "toneful" force into the final three and extending the first with *tenuto* added to that note in each group. The next music [24-27] is highly horizontal, suggesting that a conductor who is aware will find ways to transmit this to the players — obviously something opposite to that suggested in example 7. Economy of gesture may not seem to correlate with dynamic and directive; but each, at greatest intensity will eventually prove to be what both the players and the music need, rather than large flailing gestures.

Half-way through the horizontal passage just discussed, the music has passed a third of its longest consecutive meter line, six bars of ¾; in them we also have been introduced to the composer's adaptation of the technical pipe terminology, the "throw." Given to the oboes and clarinets with Grainger's most personal instruction that they play it "fiercely," this arresting musical idea heralds developments of a like intensity down through the group that will also reach upper tessitura ranges in the high reeds. Grainger uses the single bar, 32, as a rhythmic cadence, and the conductor has a special duty to control it with firm hands, preventing the players from hurling their sound into bar 33 until the phrasing of silence — however slight — allows the first idea to be achieved and the coming one to be properly separated from it. A short vertical line inserted in all parts helps:

A close look at bar 33 finds those consecutively-numbered notes for *Argyleshire*; and all of its twelve tones will be found between the final eighth of bar 36, and the climax at bar 42 — a measure that is derived from measures 19 and 20. The conductor's control of the sustained bagpipe-like character of this music greatly depends upon control of dynamics and insistence upon the function of nuances as printed. When Grainger indicates a spread in sound from *fortissimo* in the clarinet family to *pianissimo* for the suspended cymbal, that is exactly what he expects to get. The same, unfortunately, may be said for customarily strident sound and ferociously poor intonation when these many reeds are carried up to *tessitura ultimo* in measures 41 and 42, the composer expecting *forte* to the third power! The conductor must control the quality and guard against the tendency to play sharp as instrumentalists scale their way up to G6. The suspended cymbal is a favorite Grainger high intensity magnifier, and here — as in *Lincolnshire Posy* — the conductor must not allow that player to bury every sound in the vicinity; the vibrating plate should join the activity, not obliterate it.

Grainger's complete control of his resources is very impressive; the completion of one use of *Argyleshire* that began in measure 36 and ended in measure 42 is overlapped in that bar by yet another serving as withdrawal material from the work's second climax. This attractive music in the second flute will be used later. The observant conductor sees and hears that the bottom falls out of the sound at the end of measure 43; keep the low reed level at *mezzo-forte* with *crescendo* to *forte* at measure 46.

Grainger's notes (see footnote 2) inform us that he had written so much of this music in the summer of 1902 in bits and pieces. The next of these pieces [29-34] is a charming bit of polyphony between clarinet and oboe, also drawn from *Argyleshire*. To support this activity the low reeds must increase their dynamic to *mezzo-forte*.

Observing the generous use of whole-tone fragments and scales here, we are reminded that Claude Debussy's whole-tone and musical masterpiece, *The Afternoon of a Faun* had its premiere in 1892 and Grainger must have known and admired it. However, Grainger used whole-tones in quite his own way.

In his concept of the scoring the composer specified that clarinet III was intended to be the instrument in A, desiring to have the low Ds needed in the final eleven bars played by the clarinet family. The substitute part in B♭ serves until measure 131 when the bassoon, in cue, must assume the range and in doing so raise its dynamic level to *mezzo-forte* for vital harmonic presence. On the assumption that the B♭ clarinet is used most commonly in performances of *Hill-Song No. 2* the conductor will have the opportunity to become more familiar with the A clarinet transposition (down a minor third from written) as what is seen in the score is converted to what must be heard. Clarinet

III demands a solo player equal to the other soloists.

Highlands scenery shifts quickly in *Hill-Song* — something like showing slides of photos taken on a summer holiday, jumping from one place to the next with fast commentary in between. The peaceful vista of Argyleshire high country which Grainger has offered, for instance, in the seven quiet measures for solo reeds and horn [49-55] suddenly is shattered by the *forte* D♭ major outburst in the brass at measure 56, followed by the *fortissimo* skirling of all instruments used in performance of our extremely agitated, compressed expression drawn from the material he used first in withdrawal from *Argyleshire's* initial statement [7-8-9]. Of the eleven notes in this passage, seven come directly and in order ending with the saxophones' quoting of *Piper III* while cornet I rudely intrudes on the saxophone cadence with a direct quote from bars 7 and 8.

As we move to the next scene [56] we are faced, once again, as in *Lincolnshire Posy*, with Grainger's personal metric quirk, $1\frac{1}{2}{4}$, a peculiarity that has probably used up more rehearsal time and generated more unnecessary player frustration than any of his rugged musical individualities. That he simply sees it as a quarter note and half a quarter note certainly adds up to three eighth notes ($\frac{3}{8}$), which is what the conductor, seeking performance security should enter in the parts after the $1\frac{1}{2}{4}$ has been removed with whiteout. Why he created the problem, adding to the stress in agitated places, (see also "Lord Melbourne" in *Lincolnshire Posy*) and elected to use $\frac{3}{8}$ in a lyrical context [98 and 120] has never been clear to me. Perhaps Grainger was thinking of the connotation of these meters — $\frac{1\frac{1}{2}}{4}$ for agitation and $\frac{3}{8}$ for lyricism.

I suggest that the entire passage [56 through 60] be conducted by the eighth note, at least until the conductor and players feel secure with large pulsing (and perhaps even then). Use precise and economical gestures and remind the cornet player to allow an uncommon amount of space between the E that ends bar 60 and the B which begins bar 61 and *Hill-Song's* next developments; it is a matter of rhythmic phrasing which is of extreme importance.

As the previous view of Grainger's hills turns to the next vista the conductor returns to keeping the larger pulse, and with his musical microscope is aware at once that the new-sounding material [61-62] is right out of *Argyleshire* (notes 21-22-23-24). It is not transitional or fragmentary in its presence for it becomes the prime rhythmic force in important future developments [75 through 83]. Then, just as the conductor is adjusting the players to one change and helping them to generate quick *crescendos* followed by subito *pianos*, a really new musical idea [99] descends in clarinet III, five minor thirds bordered by two major thirds, material so important that the conductor should strike the composer's *decrescendo* and keep the full sound down to the low B♭; the descent in pitch is *decrescendo* enough.

At this point Grainger is busy weaving that "polyphonic weft" he mentioned in his letter, reaching back to his second major oboe solo [9-14] to pluck its last eight notes [13-14] for a pair of lines in the alto and tenor sax, supported by the cornet that, like the *Argyleshire* quote two bars previously, will have extensive use up ahead. And if this was not sufficient evidence of manipulative skill, he adds yet another idea buried deeply in the bass clarinet that is soon to be dug up and displayed "hugely to the fore" in the horns. But for now the conductor must raise the dynamic level to *forte* if the bass clarinet is ever to be heard (see example 3).

Our next glimpse of the highlands as they "speak for themselves," of course, is a series of richly-scored mostly parallel harmonies[11] unique to Grainger's love of the sounds of the reeds and his skill in writing for them. The full score shows it all, and as Grainger prepares his coming new material, the conductor might consider the importance of the utmost extension of the final sound in bar 66 allowing the last passing tones C♭ and D♭ to color the D♭ chord as all release a full sound and wait for a rhythmic phrasing before proceeding with the next music at bar 67:

EX. 10 [66-67]

Nobody writing music for the wind band anywhere in the world was in any way on Grainger's

wave length in these early years of composition and neither, it seems, were any of its bandmasters and orchestral conductors; he found a few of the former after he came to the United States. *Hill-Song No. 2* was not and is not what the world of music knows as "band music." He simply put on paper to the best of his remarkable ability the music that was in his heart, the wonderful sounds he heard in his head and of which he knew the instruments to be capable regardless of the name or philosophy of the group that might play them or the "traditions" which he felt were stifling their musical growth. The rest would have to wait until conductors emerged to see and hear what he had conceived; the long wait would discourage him greatly.[12]

The music which began to heat up at measure 56 now gathers the momentum which the composer had so carefully generated. For the first time in the score [71] he turns squarely to the few brasses he elected to use and gives them the charge of carrying the pace to the reeds, some down to the bottom of the range for their "fiercely"-conceived set of descending pylons of great sounds; five consecutive major fifths, a new version of his hint in clarinet III [63] now going full blast into yet another fulfillment of an earlier idea.

Rhythmic energy developed from the figure: ♪ ♪♪ ♪ ♪♪ drawn from bars 13 and 14 extends through the next ten bars and can be seen and heard in five exact sequences [79 to 84]. Solo soprano and alto sax now emerge with a figure (whole-tone in the soprano) that was exposed in bar 11; the conductor must increase the dynamic for both instruments to *forte*. That figure which Grainger had buried in the bass clarinet a few measures ago now erupts in the horns [80] in an unmistakably "gutsy" fashion, the rhythmic sequence gathers sound, and the two cornets splitting the whole-tone idea from measures 20-21-22, along with the presence of the rest of the brass, lead all to *Hill-Song's* great climaxes.

As the single reeds and flutes rise up through the only scale in the entire piece (Lydian on F♭) the conductor should broaden the pace beginning with the first triplet and allow the players a full breath before they begin it. Keeping the cymbal at a level no more than *mezzo-forte* will allow the scale its great moment, and the reeds their ultimate *crescendo*.

Almost A Recap

Arriving at bar 85 we have come to what is the closest spot in *Hill-Song No. 2* that we might label "recapitulation." It surely is a reminder of the beginning, but with everything now at full throttle. The whole of the eleven climactic bars is underpinned with a massive pedal point/drone in all the bassoons, euphonium, and tuba; other low reeds contribute to it when not needed for thematic duties. Altogether the drone/pedal lasts for 34 quarter notes. The first two-and-a-half bars of *Argyleshire* are here in all the skirling reeds; they hurl their sounds into the throws [87,91,93,96] doing a kind of battle with the brass, and winning for a change! It is all very "fierce" — Grainger's favorite quality and one so thoroughly woven into the texture of the sonorities and their registers that it was not necessary for him to again assign the word.[13]

These many exciting excursions into dramatic sound are a challenge to any conductor. Cool control judged by the heave and swell of musical emotions growing out of score knowledge and stylistic comprehension guide the group to their awareness of the music's meaning. After *Argyleshire* there are no "tunes" in *Hill-Song No. 2*. Putting together a solid grasp of Grainger's remarkably fragmented music is the conductor's challenge. What is offered here is but one conductor's view in a long search for that grasp. And that frequently includes a lot of agony in what one thinks, feels, hears, and concludes that he must do to serve the composer beyond a literal reading of his notes.

Ask the players for that last ounce of support for the B♭7 chord that concludes the long pedal/drone; the music needs that last extra effort so that the harmonic confirmation which it represents brings a major segment of the piece to that point in its architecture where something else is certain to take place. Here it is after the downpulse of bar 96; add *tenuto* lines to every eighth there, then pick up the still skirling solo reeds and flutes with their final "throw" in the piece.

The observant conductor, perhaps will have noticed in other score study that Grainger's sense of musical architecture includes the gift of appropriate withdrawal from high energy writing to a conclusion that is more than just the end of a piece of music. As the long winding-down begins, the brass have been withdrawn for the rest of the work; poignant descending harmonies hint at previous material until the clarinet states what had been connecting material complementing the flute and bass clarinet quoting [61-62-63] two octaves apart, both in low registers. Again the conductor must raise the dynamic level for the B♭ and bass clarinets and for the solo oboe which returns the music back to Grainger's first material to follow the initial statement of *Argyleshire* [7-8]. The conductor will also want to be mindful of the needs of each of the solo instruments and their accompaniment as they carry the line down, as though Grainger's walk in the high country was over and he, too, had begun his descent. It is an emotional wind-down, too; for the solo players it is low register as well — flute to low D♭, oboe to low B♮, soprano sax to E♭ and, finally English horn to low D♯ — ironically the G♯ concert with which the piece began; the undermarked soprano sax quoting *Piper II* must hold the stage, however briefly.

I think this final portion is more than good composition; I do think Grainger may have been recounting his own inevitable descent from the high hills; his walk was finished and this was his way of expressing that. And it definitely is a bright feeling that he brings to these closing statements of what the hills probably meant to him. In the long passage for the solo flute, joined by piccolo, the feeling is major, not the dark G♯ minor with which the piece began, and instead of continuing a feeling of descent, he allows himself one more "climb" up to

the heights by way of this soaring statement by the flute.

Whatever may be read into this music it is fact, not fancy, that the flute line starts with positive borrowings from the beginning of *Argyleshire* and that from the last note of bar 116 (B♮) through the first C♮ of bar 121, Mr. Grainger — once again — has exhausted all twelve notes, this time of the chromatic scale on B♮ and in the span of nineteen notes.

When the flute has come to rest on its A♭ in bar 124 so, too, has the music in *Hill-Song No. 2* for the first time since the piece began. This is the first tonal pause with no motion and it sets up clarinet III with final borrowings from bar 63, again undermarked in dynamic. From bar 126 to the end all material is taken from those critical measures [7 and 8] beginning with the beautifully poignant (and treacherous) solo for E♭ clarinet. The conductor must decide with the player whether to pulse the $\frac{2}{2}$ bar in two or four; that probably will be settled by the player's concern for the security of the high C♮. Whatever is adopted, the conductor should stress the lyric quality throughout, allowing the player to breathe before the quarter note triplets (getting out of the way) and granting the player full freedom of expression. The A♭ pedal point, of the same 31 pulse duration as that which supported the great climax, is a genuine breath challenge to any player; where to breathe, if at all, must be settled with each player. The conductor is reminded that he must adjust the balance upward for the bassoon's cue for clarinet III (in A) in measures 131 to the end. Full license for lyricism goes to the oboe as the conductor plans the steady slowing of the pulse to the final *fermata*. Grainger just didn't want it to end, ever. Editing the parts might show the breathing as follows:

Ex. 11

This study/performance essay concludes the Grainger series, a total of ten studies devoted to much of the man's unique legacy to the band. Readers, I trust, may want to write their own study plan for other pieces of his. If this final essay may at times have seemed to be in-depth thematic, theoretical detective work, that is because *Hill-Song No. 2* is just that kind of piece. I could have used a guide when I began to study the work 33 years ago. It is among Grainger's least played scores and is possibly his greatest composition; it requires a tremendous amount of study time on the part of conductor and players. Not much of its charm lies conveniently on the surface and it most likely doesn't get played by many bandmasters for that primary reason.

All of us owe Percy Aldridge Grainger more than we can ever repay, but a carefully studied and sincere performance of *Hill-Song No. 2* would be an honest initial premium. ∎

Five sides of Percy Aldridge Grainger, 1933

Footnotes

1. Gardiner paid for the musicians' costs and rental of Percy Hall in Tottenham court, 1907, so that Grainger could actually hear his *Hill-Song No. 2*; John Bird, *Percy Grainger*, p. 131; Paul Elek, London 1976.

2. "The musical material of *Hill-Song No. 2* was composed as follows: bars 1-11, 126-134, 139-141, date from March 16, 1901, and thereabouts in Frankfurt-am-Main. Bars 13-23, 35-47, 49-52, 66-80 date from the latter half of the summer of 1902, at Waddeson. All other bars date from April 3-6, 1907, and thereabouts, in South Kensington, London."

3. This unusually limited use of percussion is highly appropriate to the music.

4. A letter from the composer dated January 16, 1960 from Rochester, Minnesota where he had gone to the Mayo Clinic for treatment of the cancer that would consume him in less than a year. The letter was in response to my need for a personal word for my liner notes to accompany the Eastman Wind Ensemble's Mercury Recording that was to be released in the spring. Grainger's letter also said that he was "...unspeakably happy about *Hill-Song No. 2*."

5. Grainger quoted in a newspaper article.

6. See, Francis Collinson, *The Bagpipe*; Routeledge & Kegan Paul; London, Henley, and Boston, 1975; or that entry in any standard musical reference work.

7. Readers may find it helpful in study of this score to listen to the author's recording of *Hill-Song No. 2* with the Eastman Wind Ensemble in the Eastman/Mercury Series recorded in May, 1959 and first released in the album *Diverse Winds* MG 50221/SR 90221, and subsequently recoupled with all materials of British Band Classics, Volume 1. SRI 75011.

8. Neither does the first eleven-bar statement of another Grainger original, *Colonial Song*; see that study/performance essay

9. Mills Music, Inc., published *The Power of Rome and the Christian Heart* in 1953.

10. See the study/performance essay, *Lincolnshire Posy*.

11. It was both entertaining and informative to hear Percy Grainger improvise at his reed organ, his love of such parallel harmony inevitably taking over from other devices; pianistic ability at his level is constantly a compositional resource when great handfuls of sound await the fingers that produce them.

12. One of his most painful statements about this is one he wrote to accompany a display of his published scores in The Grainger Museum, University of Melbourne. "I do not mind being 'found wanting,' as long as I am weighed in the balance, first. But I (in common with most composers) do not like to be condemned unheard. And the non-performance of my serious compositions is the more insulting in view of the fact that several of my pieces are said to be 'known wherever music is made.' . . . . This long display of the first editions of my published compositions may seem, to the thoughtless, a proof of my 'success' as a composer; in reality it marks the measure of my artistic defeat. The bulk of these works are not 'alive' — for music that is not heard is not alive, and the bulk of my music is never heard. . . . Where musical progress and compositional experiments are discussed my name is never mentioned. Can a more complete aesthetic failure be imagined? Not by me." Quoted from Bird Ibid. p. 206.

13. With his passion to inform, the pages of music sometimes carry too much information, such as the first oboe part to *Hill-Song*, which in addition to carrying 100 of the 141 bars also contains cues for others.

Corrections

[12] part: trombone III, $\frac{4}{4}$ missing
[33] part: trombone II, correct rhythm to:
[G4] part: bass clarinet, top beam missing, all notes on 2nd pulse
[G9] part: cornet I has last two quarters written as eighths
[70] part: cornet II, last quarter rest is missing
[87] part: oboe I-II and English horn, remove bracket from downbeat; make triplet only over 16ths
[132] part: oboe 1, correct part from $\frac{2}{2}$ to $\frac{2}{4}$

October, 1985
February, 1988

Alfred Reed's Armenian Dances, Parts I and II

A Rehearsal Analysis

by Harry Begian

Author's Note: The type of analysis I have written should be more meaningful to band conductors than the usual, cut-and-dried formal/harmonic analysis. Band conductors should be able to do that type of analysis for themselves, while close observation of conductors in rehearsal too often reveals that they can't identify the trouble-spots in a work or know what to do even if they do recognize them. Most of the problems of the score discussed here relate to the factors of performance such as style, tempo, rhythm, accentuation, and balance. I have tried to identify where the problems may occur and offer practical means of curing those problems.

Part I is the first movement of a suite, with Part II constituting the three remaining movements of the work in its entirety. Part I is based on five authentic Armenian folksongs from the collected works of Gomidas Vartabed (1869-1935), Armenian clergyman and ethnomusicologist. The five songs that Alfred Reed has treated freely and developed into an extended symphonic rhapsody, are — in their phonetic spelling — as follows:

1. "Tzirani Tzar" — The Apricot Tree
2. "Gakavi Yerk" — The Partridge's Song
3. "Hoy, Nazan Eem" — Hoy, My Nazan
4. "Alagyaz" — A Mountain in Armenia
5. "Gna, Gna" — Go, Go

While the opening song ("Tzirani Tzar") is a sentimental song with a declamatory beginning, the song that follows it is a simple, childlike tune by contrast ("Gakavi Yerk") both in rhythm and tempo. "Hoy, Nazan Eem" is a highly rhythmic dance-song, followed by a sharply contrasting song of stately and lyrical mood ("Alagyaz"), and ending with the delightful and humorous laughing-song, "Gna, Gna." Part I of *Armenian Dances* takes about 10½ minutes to perform.

"Tzirani Tzar" (The Apricot Tree; 1-29)

The opening tempo of the work should most likely be played in a slightly faster tempo than suggested in the score, at about ♩=60. This will provide a little movement to the song without making it sound hurried or taking anything away from its musical effect; therefore, the opening motive in trumpets should be played more like 16th notes rather than 32nds. The scalar accompanying figures in soprano woodwinds in the opening should not stand out so prominently as to obscure the

tune in any way. Measures 1 and 2 of the timpani part should be played with some prominence, finishing in measures 4 to 5 with rhythmic deliberation and with a slight accent on the final F. Percussionists will invariably "thump" or play too loudly on such a figure, and the conductor should correct this inclination.

The brass melodic line, from measure 1 through 8 should be heard above everything else. From measure 5 through 7 the 32nd-note turns in clarinets should be played with a breath accent on the first note of each group of notes.

A clean and rhythmically exact pick-up indication from the conductor is necessary leading into measure 9 for those continuing the melodic line in the woodwinds. Care must be exercised in playing the florid countermelodic line at measure 9 in baritones (euphonium), tenor saxophone, and so on because this material is second in importance only to the melody. The triplet 32nds should be played quickly and lightly, in the manner of triplet-grace notes, followed by broadly played 8th notes with fuller sound than the triplets. Because baritones (euphoniums) always seem to be too timid and often don't sound through in the ¾ measure (12), the conductor should at least give them a cue with his eyes.

The descending bass line in octaves leading to the English horn entry with the tune (14) is an extremely important line that should serve as a lead-in to the solo. This bass line sounds best when played with a crescendo, tapering off at the end so that the English horn entry can be clearly heard. The excellent coloristic change that occurs with the English horn entry should stand out (as to volume). The conductor will find that the English hornist will, more often than not, have to be urged to play out and project the solo line. Should it be necessary to use the alto saxophone on the solo, the player should not be permitted to play it with as fast a vibrato as we would ordinarily expect on that instrument. The point to be made here is that excessive vibrato use would be contrary to this style of folk tune.

Returning to the opening section of "Tzirani Tzar," measure 19 should be treated with deliberation, preceded in measures 17 and 18 with a cumulative crescendo which is most dependent on the countermelodic material noted previously from measure 9 and onward, and now treated as the melodic line. The subtle changes in the return to the original of the opening must be clearly delineated from measure 19 onward: the trombone's answer to the trumpet motive (♪ ♫♩) in measure

19, the beat delay in the timpani entrance in the same measure, the new horn use for continuation of the trombone line, and the ascending bass clarinet line (written as a descending passage earlier) are some of the changes in treatment that should be clearly heard. The bass line in measures 19-21 should be played legato-like and sound just short of slurring and with very little tongue.

Measures 23-26 find the composer extemporizing along the lines of the original tune but with his own melodic material which leads to a transition into the new material of "Gakavi Yerk" in measure 30. It should be mentioned at this point that although the composer has entitled this work *Armenian Dances*, the first two materials he presents are actually songs and not dances. Understanding this fact should help the conductor to arrive at a more convincing musical treatment of these two materials as to style and expression. "Tzirani Tzar" is a sentimental, reflective type of song, slow in nature and somewhat sad, whereas the "Gakavi Yerk" is a simple, lighthearted, childlike song which should move along at a lively pace.

"Gakavi Yerk" (Partridge's Song; 30-68)

The oboe ending of the first song (30) elides with the accompanimental, harmonic rhythm and tempo set-up of the new song in measure 30 requiring that both materials be heard distinctly. Because of the lighthearted, childlike simplicity of the new material between measures 30-68, I would suggest a tempo of ♩ = 104. To play this song at the suggested tempo in the score tends to change the character of the tune (which I first heard sung so many years ago) and gives it a weightiness and cumbersome quality with which I disagree.

Application of a crescendo-diminuendo in the accompanimental figure in basses and horns in measures 30 and 31 can provide a little more interest for listeners than playing these measures at the same dynamic as I have heard in so many performances. Treatment of the tune from measure 32 onward should be simple and lighthearted and with tenuto applications on the first of the two slurred 8th notes on beats 1 and 3, as follows: | ♫♩ ♫♩ | .

The tenutos on beats 2 and 4, as indicated by the composer, should also be carefully observed be-

Armenian Dances (Part I) was completed in the summer of 1972 and premiered by the University of Illinois Symphonic Band at the C.B.D.N.A. Convention in Urbana, Illinois on January 10, 1973. The work was commissioned by Harry Begian, Director-Emeritus of Bands at the University of Illinois, who also conducted its first public performance. The Sam Fox Publishing Company of New York published Part I in 1974, and since then the work has become a staple of the band repertory, being played by concert bands and wind ensembles throughout the world. Its composer, Alfred Reed, considers the *Armenian Dances* one of his most successful and musically satisfying works, and the longest work that he has written for the band medium. The premiere performance of the *Dances* was received with great enthusiasm, and the work has emerged as probably the finest band composition to come out of the 1970s.

cause this will give an authentic lilt to the song. The cornet solo in measures 44 and 45 can be played by the 1st trumpet and should again be played with tenuto over each pair of slurred 8th-note groupings. The accompanying 8th-note figures against the cornet solo will sound better musically if played with slight accents on the offbeats as follows: | ♪ ♫♫ ♫ | .

Whenever the oboe carries the melodic lead in this section of the work the conductor will invariably have to ask that the player project his tone; most oboists take the dynamic indications too literally and get covered up in consequence. The countermelody in woodwinds is so well-conceived and tuneful from measure 59 on that there is always the urge to overplay it dynamically, resulting in covering of the harmonized melody in flutes and trumpets. The melodic passage for horns in measures 65 and 66 is hard to play as suggested in the score and parts; it comes through much cleaner and musically, I think, when each pair of 8th notes is slurred, thus; ♫♫♫ , as they are

in the tune of "Gakavi Yerk." If this suggested procedure (of slurring pairs of 8th notes) is employed, the players should also apply a slight tenuto on the first 8th of each pair of 8ths, using a very light tongue on each beat. The trumpets in measures 67 and 68, more often than not, will not be heard; the problem seems to be that most trumpet players don't understand that they must play muted parts at a louder dynamic than when playing *senza sordino*. The flute and piccolo answer to the muted trumpets should be clearly heard and the final note treated as a short hold in preparing for the mixed meter section and tempo of "Hoy Nazan Eem" which starts with the downbeat at measure 69. A clear and highly rhythmic preparatory beat should be indicated when coming out of the hold I have suggested on the end of measure 68. The preparatory beat should be in the time value of a quarter note in the new tempo of "Hoy Nazan Eem" (69).

"Hoy Nazan Eem" (Hoy, My Nazan; 69-185)

The material for the third section of *Armenian Dances* is a danced-song. The lyrics have to do with a young man who is singing about his girl friend and is usually sung and danced to a ⅝ meter. Reed's ingenious treatment of the tune in a ⅝ setting with shifting twos and threes gives the tune a delightful twist yet confounds so many band conductors and their players. I, myself, had to relearn "Hoy Nazan Eem" in Reed's ⅝ treatment before taking the work into rehearsal.

I would suggest a little faster tempo in the ⅝ section that would be more in keeping with the tempo at which the original dance-song is played (♪=192). It should be noted that there is a certain legitimacy to Reed's treatment of this tune in ⅝ since so many Armenian, Greek, and near-Eastern dances are done to 5, 7, and 9 (2+2+2+3, or variations of the same). The amazing thing about the dancing of these asymmetric rhythms is that the dancers never seem to miss a beat in the most complex settings, and are always aware of where in the bar the three-factor occurs!

The uneasiness conductors and players, alike, seem to display in handling asymmetric meters has been evident too often in many of the performances I have heard of *Armenian Dances* and other works involving asymmetric rhythms. Often the uneasiness has been even more evident through the clumsiness with which many conductors convey these rhythms with their batons. One frequent error is to lengthen the time-duration of the two-factor in the measure so that it comes out actually to the listener as a three, thus causing a 2+3 to sound as 3+3. A sure cure for conductors with this tendency is to sing the tune at a slower tempo while tapping 8th notes with the left hand and conducting with the right hand. After mastery at a slower tempo, the tempo can be increased until the required tempo is reached.

Another frequent error in conducting asymmetric meters is where the conductor glosses over the three-factor in the measure, making it come out as a triplet (three in the time of two 8ths in a ⅝, for example). This type of error is invariably attended by a rather blasé and loose stick technique while the conductor seems oblivious to the fact that he is actually shortening the measure in time value by one 8th quantity. In these cases, the ⅝ comes out 𝅘𝅥𝅮𝅘𝅥𝅮𝅘𝅥𝅮 or 𝅘𝅥𝅮𝅘𝅥𝅮𝅘𝅥𝅮 , the ⅞ becomes ‒ ‒ ‒ or ‒ ‒ ‒ , and the uneven 9 becomes 𝅘𝅥𝅮𝅘𝅥𝅮𝅘𝅥𝅮𝅘𝅥𝅮 . Conductors who fall into this rhythmic trap seem never to become aware of their error. I know of a case where a most highly consid-

ered contender for a university band conducting position was immediately dropped from contention when his performance tape of an asymmetric piece sounded as ⁶⁄₈ rather than the ⅝ notation.

In preparation of *Armenian Dances* prior to rehearsal, it would be wise for the conductor to sing through the melodic line from measure 69 through 185 while tapping the 8th notes, lightly but *evenly* with the left hand and conducting with the right hand. When this has been done accurately and without hitches several times in a row, then he can feel sure about rehearsing and teaching the ⅝ section properly. A conductor's insecurity in handling asymmetric meters will never go by unnoticed in a high school or college band (or orchestra). Rehearsals should never become the place for the conductor to practice or learn how to execute an asymmetric meter correctly!

In teaching a fast ⅝ , where the conductor must indicate one beat for two 8th notes and another (longer) beat for three 8th notes, it would help to give a quick wrist movement, in strict time, on the final 8th of a three 8th-note grouping before proceeding to the next grouping of 8th notes, whether they are two or three. The following diagram shows what I mean:

The important thing to remember is that the third 8th note of a three group must be executed in strict tempo and as a very small movement. Practicing this technique in front of a mirror while counting aloud would be most helpful to the conductor who feels insecure in conducting fives, sevens, and uneven nine pulses. In counting aloud, it would also be helpful to slightly accent the first 8th of each grouping of either two or three 8ths, as follows:

This same drill might even be used in rehearsal with the entire band counting aloud, while indicating accents on the first note of each two or three 8th-note groups. Such a recitation drill is the easiest way to teach a young group of players how to play a five, seven, or uneven nine pulse measure. When the accents are played on the first 8th note of each grouping, and the recurring 8th rhythm held in strict time, everything falls into place, and the tune and rhythm take on an authentic sound. One other caution in the ⅝ section of *Armenian Dances*: players should observe the composer's slurs and staccato indications most carefully; and finally, the conductor should reassure all solo entries by cueing them in clearly (72 - alto saxophone; 76 - oboe; 86 - clarinet section, and so on.)

There will always be some hesitation in the correct rendition of the occasional $\frac{6}{8}$ measures that occur (as in measures 174 and 176); the general tendency is to contract them and play them as measures of five. The conductor can quickly correct this error by explaining the occasional $\frac{6}{8}$ measures as melodic cadential measures with a feel

of ♩ ♪♩ . Singing a common rhythmic pattern with its accentual inflections is very often the most efficient way to correct an incorrectly inflected rhythmic pattern. It should also be noted that a sung example is the method most frequently relied upon by conductors of major symphony orchestras. It has always puzzled me why band conductors seem to avoid using such an efficient method of rote-teaching to correct or explain a simple rhythmic inflection to their players.

Finally, there is the invariable problem in getting players to enter on time in the concluding $\frac{3}{8}$ measures (82-85) of this section of the work. Players will invariably hesitate before their entries in these measures; most likely because they have been playing in $\frac{5}{8}$ and $\frac{6}{8}$ for some considerable time and don't catch the metric change quickly. The composer's use of the $\frac{3}{8}$ meter is both rhythmically and accentually the correct one for this ending, but the conductor may wish to conduct these last four measures as a group (which they are) indicating a four-pulse stick pattern such as he would use in a $\frac{12}{8}$ bar of music. This device usually clears up any hesitancy of entry in horns (183), trombones (184), and tubas plus timpani (185). If the conductor chooses to use this technique, he should be sure to explain it to his players.

"Alagyaz" (Name of an Armenian mountain; 186-223)

It is extremely important for the conductor to treat the rests between this and the previous section (185) in the tempo that is to *follow* in measure 186. In performances of this work that I have heard, the conductors too often treated the rests in the time of the previous $\frac{3}{8}$ measures because they have obviously misread the composer's indication of ♩ = ♪ in the score at measure 185. The music seems to demand a break of substantial duration between the two adjacent sections of the work at this point and one might even consider a "pause" of two or three beat values in the oncoming tempo. At any rate, to go *subito* from "Hoy, Nazan Eem" into "Alagyaz" seems so abrupt and unmusical that a very definite separation between the two sections is imperative.

The "Alagyaz" section comes as almost a relief for most players and conductors after playing through the $\frac{5}{8}$ section. The general tendency in the new section is (unconsciously) to play it at a tempo that is too fast, at a louder dynamic level than necessary, and with little thought given to expression. An additional error in playing this section is to overplay the excellent countermelodic lines. Not only are the countermelodies good, but they are technically easy to play. As a result, the euphoniums (194-201) and the clarinets (202-205) often tend to cover the melodic lines.

The rich textural treatment, plus the simple harmonic setting of the tune, can result in poor balance throughout this section. The conductor, therefore, has to listen attentively to make sure that the melodic line is always clearly heard and that all other parts are in proper balance to it. The final measures of this section of the work (221, 222, and 223) form the concluding chord of "Alagyaz" and a short, but deceptively quiet and gradually slower tempo change acts as a transition into the *Allegro vivo con fuoco* at measure 224.

"Gna, Gna" (Go, Go!; 224-end)

The title of the final tune in *Armenian Dances* in translation, "Go, Go!", provides some indication to the spirited nature of this dance tune. Reed's choice of a tempo of ♩ = 138 is a wise one since the tune can be circle-danced and sung at that tempo. To play it at a faster tempo and present it as a sheer technical display is to destroy its simple charm. The sheer vitality and forward mobility of the tune does not call for an excessive tempo but rather a staccato and accented style in playing it. The finale section can, however, be played at a much brighter tempo (381 to the end), for it becomes obvious that the composer is now using the dance tune for a rousing coda to the work.

My experience with introducing this section of the work to any group is that the cornet and oboe duets from measure 381 on are most often underplayed dynamically and that the players must be asked to make themselves heard to balance the duet parts. All accompanimental parts must be held down dynamically at the piano level indicated by the composer.

The opening ♪-note *sffz* should be played both hard and short in both brasses and percussion, with the piccolo being clearly heard ♪♪♪ . This (224) should come as a musically contrived surprise and contrast in dynamic and tempo to the short transition which precedes it.

Measure 226 will invariably present a problem because too many players tend to play the figure

♪ ♫♪ with the two 16th notes *on the beat*, rather than after, as notated. This is a strange tendency because, as mentioned earlier, the same kind of rhythmic pattern (♫. as in the opening) is so often played incorrectly, with the 16ths being played *before the beat*. The cornet sustained E (226-228) should only enforce the clarinet crescendo on the same note without covering the clarinet tone.

The sustained D pedal in trombones and euphonium should also be held under the clarinets as to volume.

In measures 234, 272, 276, and so on, we return again to the rhythmic figure already mentioned ( ); and, again, in each instance the old tendency of playing the two short notes before the beat will come forth. Simply asking the players to play the first 16th on the beat and *with an accent* will often cure the problem.

Close attention should be given the euphonium counterline in half notes (272-281) so that they are played in an accented manner and with detachment. The crescendos indicated along with the upward movement of the half notes (272-281) can add so much more musical excitement when adhered to with the same kind of treatment given to measures 288-300, a parallel segment on a different tonal level.

The technical difficulties of the 1st clarinets in measures 308-315 can only be remedied through individual slow practice and sectional rehearsals, while making sure that all the Cs in this passage are C♯s, and not C♮s. The unisonal horn passage (312-324) will require sectional work in order to make it sound as intended — with abandonment.

The oboe and tenor saxophone parts from measures 329-333 are rarely projected clearly. When this is the case, it would be wise to ask the alto saxophone and the cornets to play the cues in their parts. My preference in this passage is to use the duet in muted cornets rather than saxophones. In the parallel passage (338-345), no doubling is necessary because the duet stands out clearly.

The crescendo which starts at measure 343 must be well contrived so as to peak with the playing of the figure of the percussion in measures 347-348.

The height of the dance comes at the section marked *furioso* and should be played loudly and with abandon. Incidentally, the section from 357-377 deviates from Armenianate musical procedures and infuses a bit of central-European dance music; but no matter, because the *furioso* section does evoke the excitement of the climactic part of the circle-dance. As suggested earlier, the ending section of the work, beginning at measure 381, can be played faster than ♩ =138 indicated at the beginning of the movement. A faster tempo from 381 onward (♩ =148) adds a certain flair, drive, and brilliance to the ending of this work.

The 8th-note passage in brasses (414-417) should be played with detachment (staccato) and should not be rendered as overly loud or blatant. The beginning of the trilled A in horns and the D roll in timpani should be well-accented and the 8th notes in the final three measures played both short

and hard with great emphasis placed on the glissandi parts in the final cadence so that they are played with a resounding crescendo, bringing the work to a brilliant and exciting close.

Part II of Alfred Reed's *Armenian Dances* was completed in 1977 and received its premiere by the University of Illinois Symphonic Band in the Great Hall of the Krannert Center for the Performing Arts on March 12, 1978. Part II was commissioned after the highly successful premiere of Part I in 1973, as the result of the composer's continuing interest in the folk music collection of Gomidas Vartabed, the Armenian clergyman and ethnomusicologist. [Harry Begian's analysis of Part I appears in the October 1985 issue of *The Instrumentalist*.] Reed realized that this body of folk music had been virtually untapped as bases for extended composition for the band medium.

The commission was underwritten by the Armenian General Benevolent Union's Alex Manoogian Cultural Fund, and the work was dedicated "To Dr. Harry Begian." The premiere performance was enthusiastically received with the composer in attendance at the concert. Part II was published shortly after its premiere by

Harry Begian

Internationally-known conductor Harry Begian, former director of bands at the University of Illinois (1970 to 1984), Michigan State University, and Wayne State University, has resumed an active role in conducting as the director of the 1985-86 Purdue Symphony Band. Begian, who organized and conducted his first band and orchestra while in his teens, has appeared as guest conductor, adjudicator, clinician, and lecturer throughout the United States, Canada, and Australia. His more than 60 LP records with the University of Illinois Symphonic Bands comprise one of the largest and finest collections of recorded performances in existence. A charter member of the American School Band Directors Association, Begian is also a member of the American Bandmasters Association, the College Band Directors National Association, and an honorary member of the National Band Association. He holds degrees from Wayne State University and a doctorate from the University of Michigan.

Birch Island Music Press (C.L. Barnhouse, Oskaloosa, Iowa).

Alfred Reed's *Armenian Dances* Parts I and II constitutes one of the finest band works to emerge from the 1970s. It is performed by symphonic bands and wind ensembles all over the world and has gone through several printings. Reed claims the work to be his finest and his most extended piece for symphonic band. In completing Part II Reed has actually given the band repertoire a full-length symphony based on Armenian folk music. The symphonic form emerges on hearing the entire work, Parts I and II: a long first movement that is rhapsodic in nature; a second movement in song form; a third movement that is a dance in §; and a long final movement in quasi-rondo form.

Above all, Reed's exceptional abilities as composer and arranger have again shown him to be a master of his craft. In the *Armenian Dances* he has captured the styles, the tempos, and the subtleties of these simple folk songs and dances. As I have often told him, "My only regret is that my father didn't live to hear your setting of the *Armenian Dances*; he would have loved them, just as I do."

"Hov Arek" (The Peasant's Plea)

It often helps the conductor to know the nature of a particular song so he can determine the music's style, tempo, and mood. "Hov Arek," as described in the historical and descriptive notes of the score, is basically a lyrical song requiring much expression. At the same time, it is rather melancholy because the singer is pleading for the mountains to send a breeze to relieve the oppressive heat. Alfred Reed's setting for concert band provides conductor and players every opportunity to interpret the music with as much expression and feeling as they are capable.

The tempo indication on the score is ♩=42, which is a mite slow; the song seems to drag and sound rather dull. A tempo of around ♩=50 makes quite a difference in the movement and will yield a more convincing interpretation. The original setting of "Hov Arek" for solo voice and piano in *Hai Knar: A Collection of Peasant Songs* by the Armenian musicologist and clergyman Gomidas Vartabed (Paris, 1938), contains a tempo indication of ♩=60.

For the opening of "Hov Arek" the conductor should attempt to create a pensive mood through the shimmering sound called for prior to the melodic entry of the English horn just before measure 9. The sextolets of the introduction should be played as 2+2+2, not 3+3. The vibraphone and bell parts, featuring two against three, need to be clearly heard against the woodwind sextolets along with the gentle harp glissandos. The tremolando-legato in the clarinets, saxophones, and flutes helps to establish the pensive mood. Musicians should take care in performing the sextolet groups so that they sound at the same dynamic level in the flutes, clarinets, oboes, then flutes again. The sextolets in the oboe duo, measure 5, rarely come off to my satisfaction; the passage is scored at the bottom of the oboe register, where it is most difficult to produce the delicate and soft dynamic of flutes and clarinets. The cuing indicated for a pair of alto saxophones is much preferable to the oboes. The function of the brasses in the introduction is to provide a soft yet subtle A minor tonality and sonority as background for the florid woodwind parts. In measures 7 and 8 the syncopated figures sound best when played in a slightly detached staccato-legato manner so that the syncopations are heard.

The composer's choice of the English horn to play the song beginning at the end of measure 8 reaffirms the original pastoral and melancholy qualities of the music. The English horn solo is cued for oboe and alto saxophone for bands lacking either an English horn or a proficient player. When an alternate for the English horn is necessary, the saxophone is the preferred instrument. The following example shows a suggested stylistic interpretation of the tune:

The oboe and clarinet entrances preceding measure 17 should be played 3+3,  with a crescendo to forte, presenting the tune in octaves with answering countermelodies in the low woodwinds, measures 18-24. The diminuendo in measure 24 needs to be observed with the eighth-note countermelody linking the next section of the tune in the clarinets and saxophone, measure 25. The concert D on the first beat of measure 25 should be lightly articulated, as it is in measure 26, and not tied over from the previous measure. This is consistent with Gomidas's setting. In fact, both measures 25 and 26 would sound better if played as follows:

Measures 29 to 32 form a dynamic build-up to measure 33, with the full band playing the tune and imitative answers in horns and tenor saxophone. The climax of the tune subsides in measures 39 and 40, returning to a lighter texture and softer dynamic in measures 41 to 49. From

49 on the music returns to the original woodwind texture of the tune and accompaniment heard earlier at measure 9. The melodic answer in the cornets, measures 53 and 54, and accompanying brasses provides a fresh coloristic change and might be played with one on a part, permitting the first cornet to play this answering phrase with good vibrato, molto espressivo.

The English horn once again takes the tune at the end of measure 56 in the same manner as in measure 8. Here the accompaniment contains the addition of a highly ornamented and florid triplet line that functions as a duet with the melody. Conductors need to be sure that this part maintains its secondary place of importance and does not cover the melody. Because of the technical requirements of the florid triplet lines, players often tend to attach more significance to that part than needed by overplaying.

A problem of balance often begins at measure 65; instruments playing the florid triplet figures tend to cover up the clarinet melody and the answering baritone lines. The fragmented tune with its successive imitative answers needs to be clearly projected with the more technical triplet lines kept in a secondary role.

The closing section of the movement begins at measure 69, continuing with melodic fragments in measures 70 and 71. The flutes and oboe complete a return through measure 72 to the final section of the closing material, measures 73-77. The composer here uses the same musical material in the closing as he does in the opening of the movement. He has, however, shortened it and reversed the instruments playing the sextolets (clarinets, then flutes). The vibraphone part, along with muted cornets and low brass, is again heard reaffirming the opening A minor mode. The conductor should subdivide measure 75 and distinctly conduct the ascending eighth notes in the vibraharp, bells, and harp. The cup-muted trombone parts should be played in the Lombardic style (an accent on the short note) and exactly right on beat one in measure 76. The final A, sounded in both timpani and string bass, must be softly played but distinctly heard, and allowed to resonate.

"Khoomar" (Wedding Dance)

The second movement of Part II is a delightful setting of a wedding dance tune from the Gomidas collection. Here the composer has turned a simple six-bar melody into a musical gem. Through the application of his craft, both as arranger and composer, Reed has captured the spirit and style of this ethnic tune.

The tempo indication of ♩=54-60 is much in keeping with this kind of dance tune in ⅝ meter. It is also the same tempo Gomidas indicated in the vocal setting for soprano soloist and chorus.

The use of a small high-pitched drum or tom-tom for rhythmic accompaniment adds another touch of stylistic authenticity, while the harp and bells add a touch of refinement and grace to a light-hearted, light-footed wedding dance. The following musical examples show the original tune as Gomidas notated it and how Alfred Reed slightly altered it for the band setting:

The reader will note that the original tune is eight measures long and without any cadential points at the ends of the phrases. Reed's additions of the cadential resting points and the small melodic and rhythmic alterations make the tune sound much more refined and graceful than the original; the changes are stylistically compatible as well as musically convincing. The cadential additions contrast Reed's treatment of the first five measures with the four-measure original without a cadential rest point. His extension of the second phrase from the second ending to the end again lengthens the repeat of the first phrase through elision with the original's second strain and added cadential measure.

The movement begins with oboes and clarinets playing the tune in duet in G major. In measure 3 the first horn should play the rhythmic figure with the following inflections:

This horn figure needs to be heard clearly against the tune and with long dotted eighths, short sixteenths, and accents on beats 3 and 6. Give the quarter notes of the melody in measures 3 and 8 their full value with quick releases on beats 3 and 6 so that the horn accents on those beats are also clearly heard. The flute figure in measures 5 and 6 will complement the melody if played with a diminuendo; otherwise, it seems to stand out with little relationship to the tune. When played as suggested the passage provides a graceful link to the second phrase of the melody.

The musical materials from measure 14 to 35 are the composer's own creation. They are so convincing in their stylistic agreement with the original tune that one would never suspect an interpolation, added to round out the original brief folk tune.

A glance at the first trumpet melodic lead-in preceding measure 22 can cause a conductor to think that it is incorrectly spelled, because the sonority at 22 is basically a minor sound. Further investigation will show the sonority to be bimodal (A minor in trumpets and D minor in trombones) or an 11th chord built on D. In spite of such analysis, the major inflection, as notated, is what the composer really wants because all such lead-ins that follow are built on the major tetrachord. The dotted rhythmic figure, ♩. ♫ ♩., used extensively throughout the wedding dance, is common to most Armenian dances in ⅜ meter and should be played with full value given to the dotted note, a short 16th note, followed by a short eighth note, just as the composer indicates.

Looking ahead in the score, however, one notes indications of a quite different inflection of the dotted-rhythmic figure in measures 62-65. The composer clearly indicates tenuto on beats 3 and 6 in this particular passage, only to revert to the earlier shortened style on beats 3 and 6 at measures 134 to 137. The lengthened third and sixth beats are indicated as such in agreement with the underlying legato lines with full eighth notes on those same beats.

The melodic fragments in the horns from measures 26 to 30, with the supporting legato treatment of the woodwinds, should be carefully balanced and made to project in the playing of this section. The F pedal, measures 26 through 34, signals the forthcoming key change and the full band sounding of the original tune in B♭ major at measure 35. The crescendo from measure 31 to 35 needs to develop with ever-increasing intensity, with a flourish and sweep of woodwinds and harp into measure 35. After the first few measures of full band tutti, measures 35 to 39, Reed reduces the instrumentation and the earlier woodwind texture reappears, now accompanied by all horns playing the important rhythmic figure in measures 40 and 42.

The section of music from 48 on is a return to material heard at 14, with variation. This time a duet appears in the cornets and trombones with scalar flourishes in the woodwinds. The dynamic contrasts from ff to mp in measures 54 to 55 add a delicacy to the cadence, only to be led by the cornets into a brief developmental section, measures 56 to 61, with a bridge from 62 to 69. The G minor section starting at measure 66 functions in two ways: it serves as an ending to the development section that precedes it, and it prepares for the new material presented at measure 72. The saxophone and flute duets that follow should be played in a veiled manner, molto espressivo. The excellent countermelody underlying this section in the clarinet and tenor saxo-

phone should be heard against the duets and along with rhythmic figures of the tom-tom and timpani, measures 72-87.

The delicate obbligato in the oboe, beginning in measure 80 and ending in the bassoon in measures 86 and 87, always seems to be buried by the other parts. Oboists, even the most experienced ones, tend to play the part timidly and, more often than not, with the wrong rhythmic and stylistic inflections. These problems can be solved if the player is asked to project the oboe sound so that it can be heard and to play the obbligato as follows:

At measure 88 the clarinetist should slightly accent the eighth-note entrance in order to be clearly heard and give the dotted eighths that follow full value, performing them with fuller sounds than the preceding notes. The solo horn countermelody, measures 88 to 91, must be heard along with the clarinet melody, as well as the answering fragments in 92 through 94. The D pedal in measures 95 to 97 heralds the return to G minor at 98, with a complete return to G major, the original key and melodic material from the beginning of the movement. The return of the tune at 102 recalls music of an earlier section (measures 40-55) in B♭ major with slight variations. The double appoggiaturas in the melody sound best if accented and played quickly, measures 111 and 113.

The coda, or closing section, begins at measure 125 in a rather subtle manner, only to burst forth in full tutti, forte, and varied in measures 129 to 133. The second section of the coda contains rhythmic play on the dotted note and functions in the dual role of linking and returning the music to the final section of the coda, measure 135. A gradual diminuendo from measure 125 to the end of the movement, along with the descending slurred line in the tenor saxophone and the pulsating rhythmic figure of the timpani, are effective touches. The final measures of "Khoomar" can be stylistically delicate when played as follows:

144
1st and 2nd Clarinets

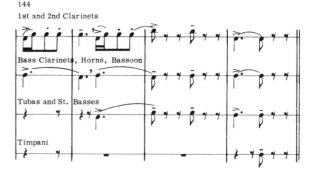

"Lorva Horovel" (Songs from Lori)

The final movement of this work is rhapsodic in nature and presents several tunes of national character. An analysis of the movement reveals at least five distinctly contrasting musical materials (tunes), treated in a quasi-rondo manner:

Quasi-Rondo Form:
    Introduction 1-22
    First Material 23-38
    Second Material 39-169
    Third Material 170-179
    Fourth Material 180-201
    Third Material 202-215
    Second Material 216-317
    Fifth Material 318-326
    Second Material 326-368
    Closing Section 369-391

The introduction to the movement begins dramatically with trumpets and cornets loudly sounding the marcato eighth notes in octaves, which lead to the opening motive, measures 3 through 7. In addition to using hard, marcato attacks, the eighth notes should be slightly detached throughout the introduction. The woodwind motivic figures in measures 3 to 6 need to begin with sharp attacks to give distinctly separated statements of the motives:

Conductors should exaggerate the crescendos indicated in measures 7 and 18 that lead into the *sffz* accents and rumbling diminuendos at 8 and 20. A clear entry cue for the woodwinds in measure 12 is necessary, because players will tend to want to begin this entry on beat 5, just as the first entry in measure 2 was performed. The flourish of the timpani and gong solo have to be clearly heard and the gong needs to sound into measure 23. The timpani and cymbal parts, measures 13 to 20, should be played prominently with hard accents.

In measure 22 the conductor should pause long enough to allow the gong sound to nearly die away before proceeding into measure 23. Here the musical material will sound best when all players perform with a full tone, using a light tongue ("dah, dah, dah"). The return of the opening motive of the movement in the muted trumpets and trombones, measures 28 and 29, should be played in the same manner as in the opening measures. The sixteenth-note entries at the end of measure 30 in the low clarinets, bassoons, and trombones, measures 28 and 29, should be played as follows:

Shortening the first eighth note in measure 32 delineates the phrasing clearly. The sixteenth notes in all parts in measures 34 and 36 should again be accented as they were earlier.

Through repeated performances of this work, I have learned that the molto ritardando of measure 38 is much more effective if started earlier, in measure 37; a sudden change of tempo seems unmusical. By beginning the ritardando in measure 37 the conductor can slow down the tempo enough to subdivide the beats for the long hold of the D♭ of the clarinets and a clear statement of the timpani flourish, which needs to be prominent. The softer the clarinets can play this note, the more exciting it will be in anticipating what is to follow.

The new material after measure 39 is a fast dance common to Eastern Armenians. Though the score indicates a tempo of ♩=176-184, a tempo of ♩=148 would be musically more effective and in keeping with the tempo at which such tunes are actually danced. Most players tend to play this dance tune,

with little or no attention to the composer's indications of the shortened second eighth note in each duplet. The conductor will have to ask his musicians to play the tune as follows in order to achieve an authentic style:

The rest of this particular dance is quite obvious and needs little comment, except to say that the ⌢ figure in measures 104 and 108 should be played with sharp accents on the short 32nd notes, exactly as shown in the measures that follow and in the introduction to this movement. When played in this manner, the ensemble achieves a stylistic consistency along with a clear definition of the important rhythmic figure it accompanies.

Measures 162 through 169 function as a bridge to the molto sostenuto section. This transition can become a problem for the conductor in getting from a rapid tempo with the quarter-note unit into a much slower tempo with the eighth-note unit within the space of two measures. One choice the conductor has is to start slowing the tempo in measure 168 while subdividing measure 169 at a tempo of ♪=120. The other choice is to start a poco a poco ritardando in measure 166 (timpani solo), arriving at measure 169 at ♪=120 with subdivided beats. In either case, the subdivision and treatment of the eighth note as the unit of time is extremely important in forming the transition into the 5/8 at measure 170. The subdivision at measure 169, at the 120 tempo, sets up the tune that follows and allows the conductor to give a clear cue to the flutes before measure 170.

The new tune occurring at measure 170 is also from the Gomidas collection of Armenian folk music. Here again Reed has slightly reworked the melody, refining the simple tune while preserving its style. The composer uses this tune both as prelude and postlude to the main material of this section, measures 180 to 201. The tempo at 170 is the same as that indicated in the folk song collection of Gomidas but should be slowed down to about ♪=108 at measure 180. The song presented at 180 is distinctly different from what precedes it.

Familiar to most Armenians, "Giligia" (Cilicia), is sung at the slower tempo indicated. Because the words of the song relate to longing for country and lost homeland, the slower tempo of ♪=108 is preferable to ♪=120. The clarinet and baritone tune at measure 180 should project the dynamic rise and fall of the melody with as much expression as possible to relate the sentimental qualities of the melody and text. A slight change of articulation in the flute entrance at measure 183 would be helpful, if played as follows: ♩♩♩♩ | ♩♩♩ . The eighth notes in measures 187 and 191 are often played too detached, giving the impression of sounding as sixteenths with sixteenth rests. To be consistent with the style, these measures should be played staccato-legato, with slight detachment and using a light ("dah") tongue articulation: ♩♩♩♩ . The volume and tempo can be increased slightly at measure 192, with slight ritenutos applied in both measures 195 and 199. Measures 200 and 201 should be handled with extreme care, because they serve the dual function of providing melodic continuity while returning to the earlier material of the 5/8 section at measure 170. When the "Giligia" tune is played at the suggested tempo of ♪=108, it would be good to play measures 200 and 201 with an even broader ritardando and crescendo before resuming the 120 tempo.

In the flute and horn duet lines in measures 207 through 215, a slight separation between beats 2 and 3 would heighten the lines, while slight accents on beat 3 of measures 171, 176, 203, and 208 can add an expressive element. The long hold in measure 215 should be played pianissimo, with the harp and triangle clearly heard. The grace notes in measures 216 and 217 should be treated as acciaccaturas (short, on the beat, and with the half notes accented), with each successive entrance clearly heard in measures 216 through 237. The arpeggiated crescendo in the piccolo, E♭ clarinet, and first trumpet needs to stand out clearly above anything else in the band at measures 238 and 239 and reach a climax at measure 240 in the trumpets, cymbals, and triangle. The low brass and horn parts that follow from 240 to 244 should lead into the loudly accented detached quarter notes of the brasses, heralding a return to the harmonic/rhythmic accompanimental material, measures 253-256, with a full return to the presto tune at 257.

The presto tune must be played in the same manner as in the beginning of the movement, with emphasis on the melodic lines in the bassoons, saxophones, and baritones, measures 285 to 289, with the cornets and xylophone clearly heard in measures 289 to 293. The crescendo and dynamic rise of the horn line (up to a high B♭) in measures 295 and 296 is a thrilling high point and a demanding part. If the horn section is not up to the demands of the part, the conductor should use saxophones and cornets, which have the horn parts cued.

At measure 318 saxophones, horns, and baritones introduce a distinctly new melodic fragment. This new melodic material needs to be heard above the noodling of the woodwind parts.

The closing section (coda) of the work begins at measure 354 with the often repeated figure, ♪♩♪ | ♪♩♪♩ . It is answered by descending scales in the woodwinds, capped off by a loud percussion exclamation, ♩♩ | ♪ sff , in measure 364. The harmonic buildup on the diminished seventh chord in the trombones from measure 369 leads to the trumpet, trombone, baritone, and low woodwind eighth-note rhythm/melodic figures, which are an inversion of the original presto tune. These same figures, with sharp brass accents, measures 376 and 378, reach a climax at measure 381 with the horns and cornets hammering at the rising half-step duplets in measures 381-384. The diminished sonority with added seventh and half-step tremolos in the saxophones sustain the half-step interval important to the woodwinds in bringing the work to a brilliant close and a scalar flourish ending in E♭. □

Emperata Overture

The Composer's Thoughts on Interpretation

Claude T. Smith

Claude T. Smith drawing by Al Kennedy

One of a set of four (W. Francis McBeth, Clare Grundman, Frank Erickson) reproductions 14 x 17 on 65-pound acid-free library stock paper being sold by Wingert-Jones Music, Inc., Kansas City, Missouri.

What makes for great musical interpretation is often elusive. I always like to work for the correct and most musical interpretation. At times I feel I'm very good at it, and at other times I know I have missed completely.

When I was teaching in high school, I entered a brass choir in the state music festival/contest. We had prepared a work in great detail and were confident of our performance. The day came for us to be judged, so we gave it our best. We felt sure that we had our I, the "Superior" rating. About an hour later, one of the members of the ensemble came flying down the hall with an incredulous look on his face. He said he had seen our rating, a II. I couldn't believe it, so I went to the festival headquarters to review the rating sheet. For sure, our rating was a II. In reading down the adjudication sheet, I saw that all areas of the performance were graded I, except interpretation. A comment at the bottom of the sheet read: "Fine brass choir and good choice of music, but I didn't care for your interpretation." The fact that the judge didn't like my interpretation was a real shock, for the selection performed was one of my compositions.

As a composer, I certainly am thrilled to hear one of my works performed, especially when all avenues of musical expression have been exhausted. I admire conductors who are masters in the art of interpretation, for interpretation is the final and most important ingredient towards the successful rendition of any musical composition.

There will be those times, and they are rare, when the music speaks the exact concept of the composer. At such moments the precise volume is reached; the technique is flawless; and the fermata is held — neither too long, nor too short — but just right. It's that time when both the harmony coupled with a beautiful melody cause the hair on the back of one's neck to stand up, and the rhythm is so pulsating that it stirs one's body to get up and dance. Truly, music should move us to respond emotionally, intellectually, and physically. These three responses ensue when matters concerning interpretation are given maximum consideration.

Claude T. Smith is a native of Missouri who received his education at Central Methodist College (Fayette, Missouri) and at the University of Kansas (Lawrence). He has over 70 published works and is active as a clinician and guest conductor throughout the United States and Canada. Mr. Smith has taught instrumental music in the public schools of Nebraska and Missouri, served on the faculty at Southwest Missouri State University, and is currently a staff composer for Jenson Publications, and composer and educational consultant for Wingert-Jones Music.

Regardless of the apparent quality of any piece of music on paper, each performance determines its ultimate fate; and our judgment of the work is usually based completely on the interpretation it receives. Each individual musician, the conductor, and the composer all share in its destiny. The composer through certain signs, symbols, and words gives those involved with the creation of sound a clear set of instructions concerning tempo, volume, articulation, style, etc. To what degree these instructions are met is out of the composer's hands once the work is shaped by the musicians and conductor even though they are obligated to honor the creator's intent.

Whereas the solo performer has complete control over the interpretation, in ensemble performance the players and conductor share in sensing the composer's ideas. Because the conductor is the leader, final judgment regarding interpretation rests there. The conductor will feel free to deal with interpretation when the ensemble has complete control of the music's technical demands. I have never heard a composition performed musically when the group has had trouble with range, technique, key, or rhythm. These considerations, plus tone and physical maturity, have a great effect on the emotional impact of the music. When these considerations are within the players' grasp, a musical experience is possible. We must also have a meeting of the hearts and minds between the ensemble and the conductor to insure that the ultimate aesthetic experience is achieved. When sound compels us to smile, to cry, to tap our feet, while it simultaneously stimulates the intellect, then our objective has been met. If at least one of these responses is not apparent, then the presentation will have been as inspiring as the bland and sterile sound of Muzak.

The Overture

These remarks on my work, *Emperata Overture* include my views not only as its composer, but also as a teacher and a conductor. Please enter measure numbers on your score.

The opening tempo is marked Allegro. I have not specified an exact tempo, as I feel there is reasonable latitude regarding choice of tempo. A speed of $\quarternote = 132$ allows the melody to sing and the rhythm to have an energetic pulsation.

In measure 9 we find the first of several asymmetric measures. The indication $\eighthnote = \eighthnote$ is the key to performing these measures successfully. Proper execution is accomplished in measures 8, 9, and 10 with a constant eighth-note feel. When confronted by asymmetric time signatures, indicate the beat pattern to the performers. In the case of this $\frac{7}{8}$ measure, the pattern is $3+2+2$. My more recent compositions indicate all asymmetric measures with the beat pattern on both the score and parts. When this work was composed, asymmetric patterns were uncommon in band music; and I was often called upon to interpret such rhythms by letter, person-to-person contact, and by telephone. I know my wife had to wonder about my sanity upon hearing me sing and articulate these patterns by phone from coast-to-coast.

Measure 10 begins the first full statement of one of the two principal themes upon which the work is based. Let the melody "sing." That may seem like an obvious statement, but much of the band music I hear lacks melodic expression. Perform the melody as an eight measure phrase. Be sure the quarter note triplet is played evenly. As you know, this rhythm is sometimes given a tango treatment by being played as $\eighthnote\ \quarternote\quarterdot\ \eighthnote$. At slower tempos the figure is usually rushed.

An unusual asymmetric pattern is found in measure 17. Certainly the common pattern for $\frac{9}{8}$ time is $3+3+3$, but here it is $2+3+2+2$.

The first tutti playing is heard in measure 18. At this point the countermelody in the horns needs to be brought out because it is new material. Use the saxophone cue and other cues throughout the piece, if necessary, to establish proper balance. Also, at this point, observe that the percussion are only accompanying and should not overbalance the rest of the ensemble. The percussionists playing tom-toms, bass drum, and timpani should choose mallets that will complement the ensemble. Avoid mallets that are too soft because these parts need to have a clean, well-defined sound.

The section beginning at measure 26 presents one of two secondary themes. Be careful to balance the timbre of the clarinet and oboe. A slight crescendo in measure 26 and a diminuendo in measure 27 works nicely. Do the same when the figure repeats. Rhythmic instability often occurs in measure 28 because the players listen to each other rather than subdivide the beat and that causes a time delay between entrances. Precision is sometimes a problem in measures 34-37 as the upper woodwinds tend to rush.

At measure 45 the third trombone needs to be very strong to bring out the pedal sound. Also let the timpani be forceful coming out of the phrase at measure 45. A crescendo by the horns in measure 48 will allow the chord in the next measure to have strength and resonance. The same is true in measures 52 and 53. Bring out the dissonance between clarinet I and II in measure 55. Following the fermata in the next measure, the chords in the lower voices need to be well spaced as indicated by the breath mark. The conductor must be very distinct with subdivision through the ritard because the timpani player often plays either too few or too many notes going into the fermata. Also, firmly conduct the second clarinet in measure 56, as these notes finalize the harmonic direction of the first part of the overture.

The Andante introduces the second principal theme. At measure 63, I prefer that the tune be played by the solo flute. A flowing, expressive style is achieved through dynamic change and a sensitive vibrato. Furthermore, I always take a slight ritard in measure 66. In measure 70, a tenuto, or even a brief fermata, is acceptable on beat four. The oboe countermelody should highly complement the melody in measures 67-70. Here is how I would edit this phrase:

The second subordinate theme is introduced in measure 71. This section is best performed in a rubato style. Measure 72 has a good feel with a tenuto on beat four, and I like a slight ritard on beat three in measure 74. Dictate the eighth notes in measure 76, and don't allow the crescendo to peak too early. A tenuto in measure 80 on beat four gives the horn player the opportunity to execute a firm pickup into the solo. The conductor should allow the horn soloist to have complete freedom during the ritard in measure 86, and it may be necessary for the second horn player to assist the soloist on the final note of the solo.

Measures 87 and 88 are among the most difficult in the entire work. A subtle clarinet attack is not easy due to the tessitura of the section. I believe the triplet is best executed when the conductor indictates each note. The next measure demands firm chords and a strong dissonance. The relief should be felt when the dissonance resolves to consonance.

The most emotional moments of the piece occur in measures 93-104. There are several dramatic dissonances as well as dynamic changes that must be played with the proper tension and release that characterize such romantic devices. In measure 94 the ritard must be greater than the earlier statement of this material; it really is *molto* ritard. The impact of the bass drum and crash cymbals in measure 95 must be realized. A vital measure, one that is rarely played well, is measure 97. Here the trombone crescendo must be forceful, and the F♯ against the G must "cry" for resolution. Relief is further provided in the next measure as the tuba states the melody in its inverted contour, and the muted brass provide a subtle accompaniment. The clarinet draws this section to a close with a free variation of the theme that should be played with a relaxed rubato feel.

The dynamic power igniting the allegro section that follows must be evident. The timpani player must not be timid with the rhythmic motif. At this point the conductor needs to guide the players through several development devices that climax in the final measures. The modulation that takes place during the sequence of chords in measures 115-119 is often played poorly. Check the accidentals closely. The beat pattern is again 3+2+2 in the ⅞ measure.

The fugato, measures 123-154, is edited so the subject is always the strongest voice. In measures 134 and 142, the indication for the trill to continue for two measures is an error. The trill should cease after the first measure. Don't let the low voices pull the tempo down during the phrase that begins in measure 147.

At measure 155 the two secondary themes are sounded together. There is usually a tendency for the cornets to lag behind the band. I find in other selections, as well as my own, that those playing legato usually fall behind those players with staccato material when they play simultaneously. The instruments playing *fp* will want to crescendo through measures 163 and 164, so hold them back. They may also crescendo too quickly in measure 165 and 166.

Balance is the primary concern from measures 167 through 180. The horns often get covered up; thus the cue again may be useful. The trombones are a vital part of the scoring, because they provide the rhythmic drive that allows the work to finish with energy and vitality. Be certain that measures 167-173 are at a true forte level of volume. The volume change to fortissimo together with the key change, the playing of the two principal themes together, and the rhythmic accompaniment all should combine to create an exciting finale.

The interpretation given *Emperata Overture* or any other composition is the lifeline connecting the written page with the true concept of the music. At no time can we be satisfied with a nondescript, lackluster playing of notes and rhythm. My greatest musical thrills have been when every detail of musical expression has been uncovered. What a great opportunity we have as musicians, for we surely can affect the pulse of the human body, the thought processes, and the soul. This surely is an opportunity to savor. ■

What's In a Name

For many composers, the task of naming a composition may be as difficult as composing the music. Titles are often a problem for me and selecting one for this work was no exception. Originally it was *Overture for Winds and Percussion*, but that had already been used. After many considerations, *Emperata Overture* seemed to be the best choice. The word emperata has no specific meaning but it is an intriguing word.

Emperata Overture was published in 1964 by Wingert-Jones Music, Inc. (2026 Broadway, Box 1878, Kansas City, Missouri). A free conductor's score is available from the publisher. A definitive recording by the University of Kansas Concert Band on an album entitled *Accent On Claude T. Smith* may be obtained from the publisher or local dealers.

Emperata Overture:

A Second Opinion

BY ARNALD D. GABRIEL

There is no greater area of disagreement in music than interpretation. Balance, intonation, blend, precision, tone quality, and dynamics can all be defined or demonstrated in fairly precise terms; but interpretation is subjective and often ambiguous. In *The Composer's Advocate, A Radical Orthodoxy for Musicians*, Erich Leinsdorf takes issue with traditional ideas of interpretation. He argues that if the composer has not indicated a particular nuance, it should not be added by the performer. Leinsdorf's critics charge that his interpretations are sterile, but I applaud his dogmatism, even when I disagree with him on matters of interpretation. In many cases too much has been done by arrangers, editors, and publishers to obscure the composer's intentions. How then do conductors know how much liberty to take? The answer lies somewhere between being a slave to the printed page and injecting the music with personal ideas that may be foreign to the composer's intentions.

The subtitle of this article, "A Second Opinion," stems from the fact that Claude Smith offered an interpretive essay on his work in the November 1982 issue of *The Instrumentalist*. Though it may seem presumptuous to comment on a work already discussed by its composer, my goal is to offer another interpretation based on my own study, performance, listening, and responses.

If possible, you should read the following analysis with a numbered score in hand. My plea to composers is to indicate measures with numbers instead of letters. Some composers give numbers in multiples of five, which is better than letters; but I suggest that measure numbers placed at structural points would be more helpful still. Insert numbers at the beginning of the exposition, the development, and each section of a rondo; also use them at repeats, at fermatas, and anywhere else that would be a logical place to begin rehearsing.

The allegro indicated at the beginning of *Emperata* allows some liberty, but I recommend a tempo of ♩=128-144. It always bothers me to see the conductor beat out an entire measure before the first entrance of the tom-tom and timpani. If the conductor and the percussionists are looking at each other, a single, precise preparatory beat should be sufficient to ensure a confident entrance. The brass section has a tendency to enter late in the first measure and then rush to get the three eighth notes in on time. Start earlier and then don't rush.

In measure seven the syncopated pedal F is often lost due to incorrect interpretation of the accent. I frequently ask groups for the explanation of an accent, with only mixed results. For every rule there is an exception; but in general, players should attack an accented note one dynamic above the prevailing one, drop to a lower level immediate-

ly, and space continuing accents to effect a good marcato. This allows the musician to prepare the tongue and the breath for the next accent. If the dynamic level is dropped properly in bar seven, the pedal F has a better chance of being heard.

There are two problems in measure nine: the eighth notes are often played unequally, and there is so much concern over the asymmetrical meter that the decrescendo is seldom observed. I suggest an approach to teaching irregular compound meters to players who have difficulty with the ⅞ measure: musicians are taught to play in ⅞ from their first lessons in the form of the B♭-major scale. Have the group play up and down the scale in eighth notes (♩=136) while you conduct 3+2+2. The band will feel the grouping of the eighth notes as they observe your pattern. When all are comfortable with the concept apply it to measure nine. This approach can be used to teach ⅞ in all its forms (3+2+2, 2+3+2, and 2+2+3).

At measure 10 rehearse each element separately. Remember that the first fortissimo occurs at bar 174, which is a long way off. To achieve contrast, underplay the mezzo forte in the clarinets, changing it to mezzo piano and the accompaniment to pianissimo.

Although interpretation is indeed based on feeling, I am disturbed when teachers ask that the three quarter notes in measures 12 and 26 be "felt." A triplet is a mathematical absolute that should be analyzed and taught rhythmically:

Once this is understood, the middle two notes are simply tied:

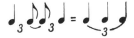

The eight-measure phrase in measures 10-17 can be approached in at least two different ways: either as a single eight-measure crescendo-diminuendo, or as two phrases of four measures each. The second interpretation makes more sense because the crescendo and diminuendo follow the rise and fall of the line.

In the trombone part I recommend a slight accent on the second half of the second beat in measures 11, 13, and 15. It not only feels right, but a similar accent occurs on the same figure in the percussion parts at B and at D. The interpretation of the figure will then be consistent throughout.

If measure nine has been thoroughly learned, measure 17 should present no problem, because the concept extends to all irregular compound meters. The pattern is 2+3+2+2.

Defining balance in measures 18-36 is difficult because every band has different instrumentation. A mezzo forte for three flutes of the United States Air Force Band is quite different from a mezzo forte for 14 flutes of a 48-piece high school band. Because it is difficult for a composer to score specific dynamics applicable to every band, he often will mark a uniform dynamic up and down the score. It is the conductor's responsibility to adjust the dynamics of a polyphonic section like B. I nearly always hear too much upper woodwind here and rarely enough horn, which presents the new material.

There are two major considerations for the B section. First, the horn line should be rehearsed along with the upper woodwind line at D to assure a consistent interpretation. This reveals that the horns have dots over the fourth beat in measures 19, 21, and 23, while the woodwinds have none in measures 39, 41, and 43, a discrepancy that strikes me as a misprint. Second, rehearsing the percussion at B simultaneously with the trombones reinforces the importance of adding accents to the trombone part in measures 19, 21, and 23.

At the end of this phrase, measure 25, I disagree with the dynamic markings. I prefer that the entire band make a crescendo to the third beat along with the upper winds for a consistent, confident phrase ending.

The upper woodwind music at letter C is often rushed. This secondary theme should contrast with the song-like statement at A. Several words come to mind: giocoso, scherzo, playful, sprightly, dance-like. In addition to consciously maintaining a steady tempo, add an accent to the first eighth note and a dot under the second (which is slurred to the first) to evoke the proper spirit. Separate the syncopated notes in measures 21, 27, and 35 for a light, airy effect. In measures 28 and 32 the same articulation of the eighth notes should be applied not only to the clarinet and oboe, but also to the horn, trombone, and flute (♪♪♪).

At D work for a balance of the principal elements. Add accents in the horn and trombone parts to match the percussion in measure 39.

At measure 45 judicious use of felt pads on the timpani heads is desirable to eliminate unwanted ring, which tends to obliterate rhythmic definition. Use hard mallets for clarity of articulation.

The four-measure phrase at bars 47-50 (repeated, 51-54) should crescendo two measures and dimenuendo two measures, peaking on the A♭ chord above the B♭ pedal in bar 49. Measures 50 and 54 should follow the previously established articulation. In bar 56 the first and third clarinets should start their dimin-uendo at the beginning of the measure, while the second clarinet maintains intensity until the resolution on the third beat; the second should then dimenuendo to blend with the first and third clarinets. It is advisable for the timpanist to memorize measures 55-57 to ensure the ritardando, cutting off with the conductor in measure 57. Eye contact is critical here. The conductor should insist that all low brass and woodwind that play the G-major chord in bars 57 and 58 watch the stick, again to ensure a satisfying resolution to the first moment of repose in the composition.

The andante section commencing at measure 59 is often taken too slowly. Remember that andante is literally a walking tempo. In the flute solo at measure 63, the oboe countermelody at 67, and the ensuing phrases, a line under the first 16th note of each group (♪♪♪♪) will help to discourage rushing. In addition to a slight crescendo of two measures and a dimenuendo of two measures, I recommend a rubato that can only be described as an imperceptible two-bar accelerando followed by an undiscernible ritardando. There has rarely been a better example of subtle phrasing than the combination of oboist Marcel Tabuteau and flutist William Kincaid, both formerly of the Philadelphia Orchestra. One allegedly said to the other, "Let's think a ritardando at this point, but don't play it."

The ritardando in measure 70 is usually incorrectly followed by a space. Although it is a phrase ending, there is no written rest. It is very effective to begin the G section hard against the concluding C major of measure 70.

At the piu mosso it is likely that the cornets will overplay the indicated dynamic of piano. They may insist upon invoking that ubiquitous "faster is louder" rule, in which case the conductor should invoke a more valid truism: If you want it louder merely request it; but if you want it softer, insist on it.

While there is no articulation marking for the eighth notes in measures 75 and 76, I suggest a tenuto on the first of the two slurred notes. An accent could exaggerate the desired effect. Leaning slightly on the first of the two eighth notes and easing off the second creates a passionate yet sensitive effect. Be sure that bar 77 is not overplayed or anticipated. There is still a long way to go to the fortissimo in measure 174.

With the plethora of upper woodwinds in most bands, it may be difficult to hear the countermelody of the cornet at measure 77. Insist on the necessary transparency.

From measure 81 to 86 I recommend one clarinet to a part to ensure better intonation and to be certain that the accompaniment does not intrude upon the horn solo. It is also a good idea to have the clarinets play the three-measure phrases in one breath (measures 81-83 and 84-86).

Give the horn some liberty in measure 86, allowing the resolution at 87 to settle for an instant while all the clarinets prepare for the attack on the D-major arpeggio. The written C in the alto sax part is a misprint; it is actually a cue for the horn. The first of the clarinet 16th notes in measure 87 should have a line over it to ensure security and confidence, and to counter the tendency to hurry the figure. In measure 88 the first and second clarinets should begin their diminuendo immediately on the third beat, pointing up the suspension in the third clarinet, which should then diminuendo on the E. Encourage the clarinets to hold the C-major chord, melting into the warmth of the A♭ sonority in measure 89.

Measures 89 through 93 should be treated just as measures 71 through 75. The fortissimo at bar 95 should not be as strong as the one to come at bar 174. It should, however, arrive with a broadening of the tempo in bar 94, clinging to the last eighth note of the measure, resulting in a satisfying delay of the sub-climax. Prolong the harmonic dissonance created by the D-major sonority in the trombones against the C major of the rest of the band in measure 96. The first and second trombones should begin their diminuendo on the first beat of bar 98; but delay the third trombone's diminuendo until the third beat of bar 98.

For transparency of texture there should be only one player to a part in the cornets and horns from 99 to 104. The tuba can then express its mournful inversion comfortably. Give the solo clarinet complete freedom in bars 102-104. It is one of those times during which it is best for the conductor to step aside, assuming that the clarinetist has been properly coached on how to play the rubato.

The horn and clarinet entrances at measure 107 are generally overplayed. Though they should be soft for greater contrast with things yet to come, be sure that the figure does not lose its intensity. A hushed excitement can be expressed by a diaphragmatic accent on each note. In measures 115 to 118 use the interpretation mentioned earlier for similar passages (♩ ♩). At bar 120 the accents need not be overdone; it is preferable to play the unaccented notes softer. Save it for the climax.

The principal theme returning in bar 123 has already been discussed. In the interest of consistency I recommend that you rehearse the figure found in the woodwinds at O, the cornets at P, and the horns at Q simultaneously in all three parts. It will sound rather Coplandesque with the open fourths and fifths, but it will give those sections of the band an opportunity to play the figure together, eliminating any personal interpretations. The natural tendency for the cornets to drag and the clarinets to rush at bar 155 can result in disaster if left unchecked.

Though the flute part at measure 167 is indicated 8va, it should be approached cautiously. Have you ever heard 14 high school flutists play high C in tune? Could 14 Jean-Pierre Rampals play high C in tune? While the composer's intention is clearly to add more and more brilliance as the finale approaches, editing the flute part may be in order here.

The quarter-note triplet in measure 173 should launch the climactic T section with gusto and bravura. For cleaner ensemble I suggest that the players with the half and quarter-note triplet (♩ ♩) play a quarter note followed by a quarter rest and another quarter note (♩ 𝄽 ♩).

The final C-major sonority in measure 183 is preceded by two measures of dissonances in the second alto sax, third cornet, and second horn. This delicious effect is rarely heard, especially if the high C of the flutes is not adjusted. I further recommend that the dissonances be doubled by additional players to achieve the desired balance. To avoid stalling the forward momentum of the brilliant codetta, the quarter note on the third beat of measure 183 should be played as an eighth note followed by an eighth rest.

Yes, there is a fortissimo in the final measure. Save some energy for it and approach it as an exclamation point at the end of this magnificent musical essay.

Emperata Overture is a jewel. Examine its many facets to reveal its multi-colored brilliance and subtle hues. My interpretation is not definitive; try other approaches until a composite becomes a reflection of your own feelings. ∎

Arnald D. Gabriel is chairman of the performing arts department at George Mason University in Fairfax, Virginia, where he directs the university symphony orchestra. Recently retired from the United States Air Force after a 36-year military career, Gabriel served as conductor of the U.S. Air Force Band, Orchestra, and Singing Sergeants from 1964 to 1985. He is a Contributing Editor of The Instrumentalist.

February, 1981

From the Composer-Conductor

Analysis of *Sketches On a Tudor Psalm*

Fisher Tull

I believe that musicians are the products of their environments; and I know the principle applies to my evolution as a composer. While in high school I began experimenting with simple arrangements for our student dance band and (on at least one occasion) for the marching band. While an undergraduate student at North Texas State University, I wrote dozens of jazz arrangements for the Lab Band plus many commercial arrangements for several of the "big bands" in the Dallas area where I regularly played on weekends. I even made a short arrangement of a Gershwin tune which was used as an encore on a university orchestra concert. When I joined the faculty at Sam Houston State University in 1957 as director of the Jazz Ensemble and the Brass Choir, it seemed natural to compose and arrange music for these groups.

Fisher Tull, professor and chairman of the Department of Music at Sam Houston State University (Huntsville, Texas), is a graduate of North Texas State University. In addition to teaching and administrative activities, Tull is the composer of over 50 works, the majority of which are for band, orchestra, and instrumental chamber ensembles. His earliest works for band are recorded on the Golden Crest "Authenticated Composers Series," and volume two, comprising band works published between 1977 and 1981 is scheduled for release in early 1981. Tull frequently appears as guest composer, conductor, and lecturer on campuses throughout the country.

My first "serious" compositions were *Liturgical Symphony* and *Variations on an Advent Hymn*, both for large brass-percussion ensemble and both based on sacred music. These two works represent a link between my arranging and the emergence of actual composition techniques. *Liturgical Symphony* uses six borrowed tunes with little development (almost a medley in fact) whereas *Variations on an Advent Hymn* consists of a theme with four extensive variation sections.

Encouraged by the acceptance of *Toccata* (the 1970 A.B.A. Ostwald winner) I was motivated to try my hand at another band work in theme-and-variation form similar to *Variations on an Advent Hymn*. I considered using a number of tunes found in the *Episcopal Hymnal* but always seemed to gravitate to Thomas Tallis' setting of the second psalm. My reluctance to finalize this choice was caused by the awareness that Ralph Vaughan Williams had used the same material for his *Fantasia* for Double String Orchestra (1910), a work with which I was quite familiar. Nonetheless, against the advice of some of my colleagues, I decided to take the plunge.

After locking away my Vaughan Williams score and record, my first step was to consult Tallis' original setting which is found in *Musica Disciplina*, Vol. II, pp. 198-199. In this version the

> *Numbering each measure of the score will facilitate quick reference to passages discussed in this article.*

79

Example 1. Theme

Original setting

Hymnal setting

melody is in the tenor voice, but otherwise the harmony is essentially the same as the setting in the *Episcopal Hymnal* (No. 424, second tune). Example 1 shows the first phrase of each version.

The second phase of the process was to seek out elements in the music that would lend themselves to variation techniques. The most obvious rhythmic characteristic was the uneven measuring of the phrases which prompted the use of multimeter in the variations. Harmonically, Tallis' music was quite consonant and typical of 16th-century modal style. Of interest, however, was the juxtaposition of major and minor triads over the same root resulting from the application of *musica ficta* principles at cadential points. This feature gave rise to the harmonic motif used in the introductory measures and in several linking passages throughout *Sketches:*

Example 2. Harmonic Motif

Fmin. Fmaj.7

Brief Thematic and Structural Analysis

Introduction (1-10)

1-5	Harmonic motif (brass) followed by motif 2
6-10	Harmonic motif (woodwinds) followed by motif 2

Theme (11-87)

12-33	Theme (sax, horns, oboes)
34-40	Harmonic motif followed by motif 2
41-67	Restatement of theme
67-87	Harmonic motif, development of motif 5

Development by Continuous Variations (88-266)

88-100	Ostinato (percussion, trombone)
101-104	Motif 1 (horns, cornets)
111-150	Melody derived from retrograde of theme (see example 4)
151-176	Development of motifs 1, 1a, 2
177-199	Development of motif 6
200-212	Development of motifs 4, 2
213-242	Combination of motifs 5 and 1
243-261	Conclusion of development with harmonic motif and motifs 2, 6

Recapitulation and Coda (262-335)

262-268	Harmonic motif (woodwinds), motif 6 (chimes)
269-298	Theme in augmentation followed by motif 2
299-310	Last half of theme (tutti)
311-335	Coda based on motifs 3, 1

The most abundant and promising thematic germs were the melodic fragments that lent themselves so readily to motivic and sequential development. They are identified by numbers in example 3. The parenthetical notes represent modification of given pitches which were occasionally used.

Choosing appropriate tempi for the two sections is perhaps the fundamental and most perplexing problem to be solved. The allegro tempo initiated at measure 88 is best determined by a comfortable, but not rapid, double-tongue rate for the trumpets at measure 110. I find this to fall within the bounds of 132 and 144, so my indication on the score (♩ = 132) is slightly on the slow side.

Conversely, my indication for the opening section (♩ =ca. 88) should be considered on the faster side of a very flexible pace calling for considerable rubato and stretching of the beats as dictated by the conductor's sensitivity. My own preferences are mentioned in several instances that follow.

In conducting the opening $\frac{5}{4}$ measures, one must be cognizant of the division into 3+2 or 2+3 and the use of appropriate beat patterns. For example, the first two measures demand 3+2 whereas, in the third measure the stress requires 2+3. The pattern can usually be discerned by observing the notation and the harmonic rhythm.

The introduction calls for a degree of exaggeration of the dynamic swells. In both statements of the harmonic motif, a clear climax should be reached at the third measure of the passage. Note that the woodwinds receive support by the addition of saxophones plus the muted trumpets which should be brought to the fore in measure 8.

At measure 11, the woodwinds tender a transparent background which should diminish to the softest possible level at measure 12. The alto clarinet is essential to the composite texture; therefore, if it is not available, the notes must be assigned to a second bass clarinet player. The tessitura of the opening theme for solo saxophone is admittedly not in the most gratifying register; however, it allows for a certain pungent tone quality when played softly but with full support. The subsequent passing of the melody from saxophone to horns, then to oboes and finally to clarinets must be accomplished with smoothness and perception by the entering players. I usually make a slight rallentando into the cadence at measure 34.

Whereas the first thematic statement by solo saxophone is taken in fairly strict time, the restatement beginning in measure 41 allows for considerable rubato since it is without an underlying rhythmic accompaniment. I stretch the three quarter notes leading into measure 43, then press ahead with the woodwinds in measures 43-44, slowing the pace in measure 45 via a tenuto on the third beat, and continue in similar fashion to measure 56 where a pronounced allargando is appropriate. At measure 58, the breath should be taken rather quickly. I ask the brass to fade well into the fourth beat of measure 60 to insure a smooth connection with the woodwinds.

For me the soaring horn obligato at measure 62 is one of the highlights of this section; but care is required to see that the horn does not overpower the melody in 1st flute, 2nd oboe, 1st clarinet, and tenor saxophone. Again the woodwinds should fade well into the last beat of measure 64 to achieve an uninterrupted transition. In measures 65-66, I ask the 2nd horn to articulate clearly the syncopated pedal point.

The contrapuntal section for solo woodwinds [72-78] offers a playful contrast to the preceding

Example 3. Thematic Motifs

material and presages the allegro development section to follow. A strict pulse at ♩ = 88 is appropriate here. Observe that the solo E♭ clarinet is assigned the melody in measures 80-83. Cues appear in the 1st oboe part but, if the E♭ clarinet is lacking, the notes are best taken by the second chair 1st clarinet player. The subtle reference to motif no. 2 by 2nd and 3rd clarinets in measures 84-85 should emerge clearly.

In the establishment of the allegro tempo beginning at measure 88, the timpani should be played molto staccato in order to match the effect stated by the tenor drum and timbales. At measure 95 the trombones must be encouraged to imitate the articulation of the percussion with equal weight and attack on both sixteenth notes. I ask for a "tat-tat" (♫) as opposed to the jazzier "tah-dat" (♬) which one often hears. Also, the bass trombone G♭ in measures 98, 99 and 100 demands a pronounced marcato style so that the composite trombone figuration results in ♫ . In measures 101 and 103 (and later in 164 and 166) the timpanist should strive to imitate the articulation of the horns from the preceding beat. By judicious dampening, the timpanist can approximate the ♪♪♪♪ effect. The tambourine, beginning at measure 111, should be placed head up on a flat surface and struck with a hard mallet.

Example 4. Theme Modification

Beginning at measure 111 the long line derived from the retrograde notes of the theme (see example 4) requires careful control as it ascends in pitch and volume to a peak at measure 136. The clarinets should initiate the line very softly and should increase only slightly to measure 199. The addition of the saxophone timbre at measure 199 should be suppressed by asking them to begin as softly as possible. Specific points of crescendo are measures 121, 125, and 128-129. Flutes, oboes, and E♭ clarinet should enter at measure 130 at a volume soft enough to allow a pronounced crescendo at measures 134-135. Woodwinds should stress heavily the quarter notes in measure 136. All of the above must be supported by the punctuations of the brasses which should build to a savage quality by measures 134-138.

At measures 160-161, strongly defined articulations are required from the woodwinds. In order to achieve this, I ask the players to mark their parts: ♪ ♪♫ | ♫♫♫ |♩. | A similar style is mandatory for measures 172-175.

The imitative brass pyramid on motif no. 4 at measures 202-205 necessitates a degree of stress on each beat in order to delineate the asymmetric meter. The concerted climax to this section at measure 206 calls for sustained legato-tonguing from the brasses. At measure 210 the whip demands a large slapstick constructed from hinged slats. The whip stroke at measure 211 should be reduced to mezzoforte.

Due to the rapid tempo, the grace notes in measure 219 must be played as quickly as possible *before* the beats. At measure 222 the conductor should use every means at his disposal to bring forth the figure in horns and saxophones. At measure 225 a diminuendo culminating in a piano at measure 226 should be inserted for all brasses. The sustaining pedal is required for the chimes at measures 235-236. Here, the horns must pierce through the mass of sound as must the 1st trombones at measure 238 in order to capture the full dramatic impact prior to the return to the allegro tempo at measure 239.

I have been asked why I did not notate measure 242 in § meter with upper woodwinds playing the characteristic rhythm: ♩♫♩♫ as opposed to the more complex notation in the score. The answer is seen in the 3rd clarinet and bassoon line which maintains the triple-simple meter; nonetheless, the upper woodwinds should adhere to the agogic stress on the fourth eighth note of the measure. At measures 243-246 the woodblock should be felt only as a support to the accents of the muted horns. On the other hand the snare drum and whip at measure 251 serve as a springboard for the horns and saxophones which should enter with the utmost authority at measure 252.

Sketches On a Tudor Psalm was composed in 1971 and published by Boosey and Hawkes in 1973 (Q.M.B. 386) with a 59-page full score and standard symphonic band instrumentation. A miniature score (free) and a cassette recording ($1 postage/handling) can be secured from the publisher.

The 11-minute composition was first performed by the Sam Houston State University Symphonic Band on February 10, 1972 at the Texas Music Educators Association Convention in Fort Worth. The work is dedicated to this group and to its conductor since 1964, Ralph L. Mills, in appreciation of the many fine performances, recordings, and premieres of my works.

F.T.

Example 5. Part Modification

The inclusion of the percussion section in a bit of antiphonal interplay at measures 256-260 acknowledges this group as the third "choir" of the wind band. Now, almost a decade later I would substitute roto-toms for the snare drum and tom-toms for the tenor drum to produce a more literal imitation of the melodic motif initiated in measure 256. The conductor may feel free to modify the parts as shown in example 5.

The timpanist should once more strive for a staccato effect by dampening each tone as quickly as possible at measure 260. At measure 267 care should be given toward achieving equal balance among the solo woodwinds with special attention to the triplet figuration for 2nd flute. The expansion of motif no. 2 in trumpets and trombones at measures 173-237 (and later in 187-290) presents rhythmic problems which are best solved by rehearsing first without the ties.

If one is aware that measures 298-299 represent the ultimate climax of the work, then the material

from measure 267 forward is recognized as a gradual ascent to this peak of intensity. The surge in measures 294-296 consisting of octave A's and quickening Phrygian scales serves to create a feeling of anxiety prior to the brass entrance at 297. In order to enhance this the duration of measure 297 may be greatly lengthened as long as the tension continues to grow. Notice that the trumpets and trombones are held in reserve until measure 299 where they serve to prolong and augment the climactic effect. I must confess to a preference for a more dramatic pace ($\downarrow$= *ca.* 69) at measure 298 followed by a slight pressing ahead at measure 302 with an establishment of the indicated tempo ($\downarrow$=88) by measure 306.

In this section the upper woodwinds should not breathe with the brass lest the continuity of this significant passage be broken. Apart from "sneak breaths" while sustaining the high A's, piccolo, flutes, oboes, 1st and 2nd clarinets should break only after the dotted half-note in measure 301. It is especially important to maintain the integrity of the line throughout measure 302 when the brass break for a breath. Bass instruments assigned a whole note followed by a quarter rest should sustain their pitches into the fifth beat of measure 302. The two choirs should again cling to their phrase endings during the antiphonal exchanges in measures 306-309. A slight rallentando in measure 310 preceding the cadence is appropriate but the strict tempo of $\downarrow$=88 should be respected at measure 311.

I have had several conductors tell me they felt the ending of this work was too abrupt. Curiously enough, my original draft of the ending located the final chord one measure sooner, but I decided later to delay it by inserting the timpani solo. It should be observed that the final Phrygian cadence of the recapitulation occurs at measure 311, the remaining material serving as cadential prolongation in the form of a coda. Nevertheless, I understand this concern and have no argument with those who slow the tempo dramatically at measure 333 (as I do) or even with some who play this measure twice prior to the final chord.

In conclusion I reassert my respect for all conductors who approach the score with the proper balance of scholarly intellect and musical instinct. In my opinion there is no such thing as a single definitive interpretation of any work; there is rather an ongoing collaboration between composer and conductor, both seeking a common goal. It is my hope that these comments will encourage this objective. ■

Christian Steiner

Peter Mennin's *Canzona*

An Interpretive Analysis

BY BARRY E. KOPETZ

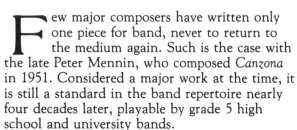

Few major composers have written only one piece for band, never to return to the medium again. Such is the case with the late Peter Mennin, who composed *Canzona* in 1951. Considered a major work at the time, it is still a standard in the band repertoire nearly four decades later, playable by grade 5 high school and university bands.

Peter Mennin was born on May 17, 1923 in Erie, Pennsylvania, and developed an interest in composition at an early age, completing his Symphony No. 1 at 18. This interest led him to composition studies at Oberlin in 1940 and later at the Eastman School of Music.

Early on Mennin was recognized as an outstanding American composer. His free-spirited approach fell into no particular school of compositional style; he allowed the basic materials of his craft to dictate direction, rather than forcing ideas into a predetermined form. This approach did not keep him from creating solid musical structures in his works. Mennin expressed his ideas fluently, regardless of form.

Mennin once told a writer for *Music Clubs Magazine,* "I like to work at long stretches, from early morning to night. I compose without a piano or any other musical instrument. I think that a work is completely scored before I put a note on paper." Apparently he was able to decide on form and orchestration in his head and then simply transfer the mental score to paper. This procedure seems to have worked well for Mennin, because his output is an enviable one by any standards. His works include nine symphonies, a piano concerto, a cello concerto,

works for chamber orchestra, string orchestra, chamber ensembles, and solo piano, and one composition for band.

After concluding his compositional studies, Mennin received a Guggenheim fellowship in 1948 and another in 1956. He taught at the Juilliard School of Music prior to being named director of the Peabody Conservatory at the age of 35. He served in this capacity from 1958 to 1962, when he was named president of the Juilliard School. He spent the remainder of his career there, guiding the school's move to the Lincoln Center for the Performing Arts in 1969 and serving until his death in 1983 as an administrator and composer.

Mennin had progressive views on the training of musicians and conductors. It was his contention, as reported in the May 1958 issue of *Musical America,* that most conservatory training for conductors was mere stick-waving. While at Peabody he began a program to assist gifted young conductors in developing the skills necessary for professional success. A committee that included Charles Munch, Eugene Ormandy, Fritz Reiner, Max Rudolf, and George Szell oversaw this three-month program. Mennin believed

Barry E. Kopetz is currently on the faculty of the University of Minnesota, where he conducts the symphonic band, teaches band arranging, and directors the marching band. A published composer and arranger, he will be teaching a new course, conducting wind literature, this spring. Kopetz is active as an adjudicator and guest conductor.

that students seeking careers in music needed to make music at the highest levels, and he was willing to go to great lengths to provide such programs.

As a practicing composer, Peter Mennin held strong opinions about the compositional process. Because he believed that composition was an individual matter, he disliked the idea of compositional schools; it was unthinkable for him to write in a style interchangeable with that of another composer. Mennin firmly believed that a composition should state something personal and that it must come from within. In the November 1980 issue of *Musical America*, Charles B. Sutton quoted him as saying, "A composer can't rely on outside stimuli. He must have inner stimuli. I would continue to be a composer whether I were here or in Timbuktu." Fortunately, Mennin followed his own advice in his approach to composition.

Walter Hendl's article, "The Music of Peter Mennin" in the *Juilliard Review*, Spring 1954, provides some information about Mennin for the interested conductor. Hendl suggests that "all of Mennin's craft is directed toward achieving the dramatic whole." The composer is adept in his use of motives and their exposition, and does not try to fit his ideas into anything resembling sonata form.

Mennin's melodies are generally diatonic; he uses half-step progressions to quickly change tonal centers. The composer shows a predilection for the intervals of the diminished fifth and augmented second, using the latter to create major/minor ambiguity. His melodies are exceedingly long, with no particular antecedent-consequent phrase structure and no strong dependence on the bar line.

Mennin is perhaps most interesting in his approach to harmony. In "The Music of Peter Mennin," Hendl states that "some triads have been restored to important levels of power and given contemporary significance by such means as added notes, bitonality, and a kind of inflection unknown in the 19th century."

Mennin uses instrumental choirs to create contrast in *Canzona*. He treats the woodwind and brass choirs as distinct units, retaining their individual identities even when the full ensemble is playing. Percussion instruments are sparsely scored, in the manner of orchestral percussion writing.

Commissioned in 1950 by Edwin Franko Goldman through the League of Composers, *Canzona* was published by Carl Fischer, Inc. Goldman had already enjoyed a long career as the conductor of a professional band, which gave him the opportunity to play much of the music that had been written or transcribed for concert band. Along with many other bandmasters Goldman longed for a high-caliber concert band repertoire. He believed the future health of the concert band depended on the development of such a repertoire by current composers. At the time *Canzona* was commissioned, most composers felt they could not advance their careers by writing for concert band, and few were doing so. Commissioning composers was one of the only ways Goldman and others could encourage first-rank composers to produce works for concert band.

In choosing the title "Canzona," Peter Mennin intentionally evoked an earlier compositional style, giving it a 20th-century definition. His use of the term does not imply a strict adherence to any of the 16th- and 17th century instrumental forms of that name, one of which eventually evolved into sonata form, but he seems to have adopted the sectional nature of the early canzonas as a structural principle for this work. More generally, the composer himself acknowledged the influence of Renaissance polyphony

Formal Structure

A	B	a1	b1	a2	b2	B	
Chorale	First Theme	Triadic Motive	3-Bar Motive	Triadic Motive	3-Bar Motive	First Theme	
1-6, 7-12	12-26	26-30	31-33, 34-36	37-41	42-44	45-55	

A	C	c1	C	c2			
Chorale	Second Theme	Rhythmic Bridge	Second Theme	Rhythmic Bridge			
56-63	64-71	72-75	76-88	89-96			

B	b3	a3	b4	B	C	B	A
First Theme	3-Bar Motive	Triadic Motive	3-Bar Motive	First Theme	Second Theme	First Theme	Chorale
97-112	108-112	113-117	118-120	121-126	127-135	136-146	147-156

on his compositional style. Some of his harmony could be described as polyphonic, in that it results from the carefully blended interaction of melodic lines. The alternation between the homophonic style of the chorale section and the canonic imitation of the thematic sections is another organizing principle. On the largest scale, the chorale serves an important unifying function, delineating the work's major sections.

Mennin treats thematic material less by development than by repetition with subtle rhythmic and melodic variations. He uses this concise approach in *Canzona*, varying the basic material throughout the work by augmentation, transposition, canonic imitation, and timbral alteration. Virtually all the melodic material in the piece is derived from the dramatic opening, a bold chorale in polychords.

Chorale

This music requires a forceful, accented style and should be played at Mennin's indicated tempo ($\downarrow = 126$). Balance is essential to this passage and should not be sacrificed for the sake of dynamic effect. It is possible to analyze this beautiful chorale using traditional harmonic analysis, but the non-tendential movement of the chords defies such an analysis. The sounds seem to have been conceived sheerly for the qualities they represent, and their effect on the listener is magnificent. These marvelous chords depend heavily on precise balance, which is important to stress in early rehearsals of the piece. The written C♯ by the first cornet and trumpets in measure five should be attacked firmly to maintain intensity and tempo.

The second statement of this brilliant chorale occurs at letter A, with the upper woodwinds added to the scoring. Here the percussion parts should receive emphasis by using decisive accents, which enhance the natural forward momentum of the material. Mennin already begins to achieve variety by rhythmically modifying the chords in the second statement. Though the harmonies achieved through contrary triadic motion are similar to those in the first six measures, the slight changes in orchestration — use of upper woodwinds and sparse percussion — show the ability of the master craftsman to create additional tension and momentum. It is this beautifully conceived

chorale that offers a firm means of establishing form within the work.

The first theme appears at letter B. In a program note published by Carl Fischer, the composer calls it a "broad melodic line supported by powerful rhythmic figurations."

First Theme

Here the conductor has to propel the melodic line forward in a cantabile style, interpreting it expressively by using tension and motion in the forearm and baton. At the same time the staccato accompaniment should be clean, precise, and subordinate to the thematic material in the upper woodwinds and the first cornet. Mennin quickly reveals his penchant for long melodic lines, this one stretching for a full 14 measures plus an additional eighth note. Balanced phrases are non-existent, and there is little sense of influence from the barline on the theme. This ingeniously conceived first theme is full of syncopations and melodic repetitions, all smoothly blended into an arresting melody.

One of the compositional devices Mennin uses extensively in *Canzona* is canonic imitation, carefully crafted to create both melodic and harmonic interest. The first such occurrence is in measure 21, 10 bars after B, in the low brasses and reeds. The conductor should provide a precise downbeat to assure accurate rhythmic placement of this syncopated thematic material. The entrance is in two octaves with a tonal center of D minor. At letter C the imitation ends abruptly with a pleasing though unexpected rhythmic diversion.

One factor contributing to the unity of *Canzona* is Mennin's reuse of material with such craft that the listener is barely aware of the close relationship between what is new and what was previously heard. An example of this occurs at letter C, where the composer introduces a series of parallel triads in first inversion in the B♭ clarinets and an octave lower in alto and tenor saxophones; it is essentially accompanimental material, which the composer is now bringing to the fore as melody.

Triadic Motive

Here the conductor should dispense with the espressivo beat pattern so critical at letter B and instead conduct in a crisp, staccato style. The incessant eighth notes in the low reeds and low brass require light, delicate attacks, achieved with a small beat pattern whereby the tip of the baton stops concisely on each count. This eighth-note material in the bass is intervalically related to the first theme and is another example of Mennin's thematic economy.

Although the three-bar melodic motive at letter D sounds like a new theme, it closely resembles the first theme in its syncopations, stepwise melodic motion, and cantabile style. It is, however, more rhythmically vigorous than the first theme.

Three-Bar Motive

Mennin follows its introduction by repeating the idea at measure 34 before returning to punctuated, rhythmic triads at letter E. A third statement of the three-bar motive reappears within an increasingly thickening texture at measure 42 as the composer drives toward the magnificent canon at letter F based on the all-important first theme. It is easy for the conductor to lose sight of the importance of the melodic material within the texture at letter D, unless he makes some interpretive decisions prior to the rehearsal. As before, an espressivo beat pattern combined with a careful balancing of the accompanimental figures yields excellent results.

The composer brings his creative abilities to bear at letter F, developing material he has thus far presented. He offers the first theme in a four-octave span in the key of F minor, followed one bar later by a low brass and reed entrance a perfect fifth lower on B♭. Here the conductor should simply stand aside and enjoy the glorious counterpoint, intervening only to maintain proper balance between the melodic lines.

Mennin modifies the first theme at measure 52 as he approaches the dramatic return of the opening chorale. He rescores this restatement for the entire ensemble at a *fff* dynamic; the rhythmic variation of the chords further demonstrates the supreme subtlety with which Mennin treats material and creates interest. Conductors should enhance this exciting return of the chorale with large, accented motions of the baton, allowing

for the increased dynamic level indicated on the score. For the listener this second appearance of the chorale provides a second pillar in the overall construction of the piece.

The second theme, the beautiful, cantabile melody at letter H, is based on chord tones from the first theme but is in a contrasting, lyrical style.

Second Theme

Again parallel triads, this time in second inversion, are used as harmonic accompaniment; and syncopations provide tension and release. The light, separated bass figure recalls earlier material.

During score study the conductor should sing the melody many times to develop his own interpretation of it; he should not allow the sustained half notes in the clarinets and French horns to overpower the beautiful melodic statement by the flutes and oboes. The thinly scored texture at letter H provides a welcome contrast to the preceding chorale, revealing Mennin's masterful ability to keep the proportions of the structure clearly in mind throughout the composition. There is no spot where the listener feels that the composer is rambling or searching; every note has an important role to fill.

Another short rhythmic transition appears at letter I, this one sufficiently new and different to generate tension leading up to a second presentation of the second theme, the cantabile melody at letter J. As he did with the first theme, Mennin presents this melody in canonic imitation at measure 81 followed six bars later by a second entrance a minor third lower. Conductors need to balance the melodic lines so they do not lose expressiveness; one helpful approach is to experiment with the number of players on each part.

After another rhythmic interlude at letter K, the first theme returns in augmentation.

This time the theme is laced with new melodic material in the upper woodwinds.

Baton motions full of energy and intensity are required to draw Mennin's thick, dark melodic line from the ensemble. He has indicated the desired balance at letter L: the bass line should clearly predominate.

Six bars after letter L, in measure 102, the composer emphasizes the augmentation of the theme by presenting three bars of it in canon. The entrances are layered so that although they are melodic in nature, their interaction provides a harmonic foundation for the return of the three-bar motive in measure 108.

The woodwind choir at letter M serves as a bridge that leads to a new contrapuntal section at N, setting up the most fascinating counterpoint yet provided. Numerous melodic elements emerge in stretto at letter N: the three-bar motive, followed immediately by the first theme in canon. It is easy to overconduct this intense passage of music. Alerting performers to the im-

portance of not playing each note *ff* will lend clarity to the texture of this thickly scored section.

A stroke of genius follows at letter O as the composer begins the second theme in augmentation, then reverts to its original rhythmic values after two bars.

This is followed by a brief triadic entrance in the cornets, whose contrary motion against the bass line recalls the opening chorale, another subtle

Errors in the Score and Parts

4	Score: Cornet 3 - add slur between D and C#.
7	Part: Horn 4 - add the accent on beat 4.
9	Score and Part: Clarinet 1 - add slur beginning with the D on "and" of beat 2, extending to the C on "and" of beat 3.
9	Part: Baritone T.C. - eliminate sharp sign before the B.
10	Score and Part: Clarinet 2 - sharp sign missing before F on beat 3; carries to the F on "and" of 4.
12-13	Part: Flute - the first full measure plus the first two eighths of the next measure should be marked 8va.
12	Part: Oboes - part is written in only one octave; Oboe 1 should be 8va until the end of beat 2 in measure 17.
13	Score: Alto and tenor sax - add eighth rest to beat 3.
13	Score: Oboe - add staccato mark to the fourth eighth note (A).
14	Parts: Horn 1, 2, 3, 4 - missing ⎯⎯
15	Part: Basses - add flat to the first quarter-note B.
17	Part: Bass clarinet - eliminate stray flag connecting the first eighth note and the quarter note.
19	Part: Cornet 1 - slur should extend to the end of beat 3.
19	Parts: Horn 1, 2, 3, 4 - missing ⎯⎯
19-20	Part: Tenor sax - missing ⎯⎯
20	Part: Alto sax - missing ⎯
20	Parts: Horn 1, 2, 3, 4 - missing ⎯
21	Score and Part: Baritone sax - add tenuto mark to final quarter note.
21	Parts: Baritone T.C., B.C. - add tenuto mark to final quarter note.
22-23	Part: Cornet 1 - add slur connecting beat 3 to the first beat of the next measure.
29	Score: Trombone 1 - add staccato to E♭.
30	Part: Clarinet 1, 2, 3, - slur should connect on-

	ly the first two sixteenth notes.
31	Score and Part: Tenor sax - add natural sign before E on beat 4.
33	Part: Clarinet 1 - staccato mark over the sixteenth-note F# should be eliminated.
34	Part: Trombone 3 - add staccato marks to the first two eighth notes.
34	Score: Baritone - add slur beginning on beat 2 and extending to the end of beat 3.
41	Parts: Piccolo and flute - slur should connect the first two notes only.
47	Part: Alto clarinet - remove staccato mark from below the first note.
51	Score: Bassoon 1 - add sharp before the note F.
51	Score and Part: Baritone B.C. - add flat sign before the D.
51	Part: Baritone T.C. - add flat sign to the E.
52	Score and Part: Tenor sax - add flat sign before E.
53	Score: Trumpets - add staccato marks to two eighth notes on beat 3, and to the final eighth note.
53	Part: Baritone B.C. - add flat sign before the E.
53	Part: Baritone T.C. - change beat 3 from a D to an F (concert E♭).
54	Score: Trumpets - add staccato marks to all notes except the two sixteenths.
55	Part: Alto sax - add accent to B♭ on beat 3.
55	Score and Part: Baritone B.C. - add flat sign before the D.
55	Part: Baritone T.C. - add flat sign to the E.
58	Part: Bassoons - staccato missing from eighth note on beat 3.
72	Part: String bass - add flat sign to the quarter-note E.
76	Score: Bassoon - eighth-note G should be indicated for both parts.
84	Score and Part: Bass clarinet - add flat sign to half-note B on beat 2.

unifying device.

The first theme makes its final appearance at letter P in canon with the entrances a fifth apart as before. Mennin cleverly drops the dynamic level here, allowing the conductor to rebuild the intensity as he approaches letter Q; conductors should carefully rehearse this passage to assure a gradual crescendo from letters P to Q. The climactic appearance of the chorale at the end of the piece, with a thematic fragment superimposed in the upper woodwinds, is simply breathtaking and constitutes a final structural pillar for the work. Allowing a small amount of space between the chords in the brass, saxophone, and lower reed chords at letter Q will produce a cleaner, more vibrant interpretation of this exciting ending. Winds and percussion should listen carefully to balance each other, and the ringing of the cymbal crashes should not be dampened in any fashion. This extended chorale leads to the punctuated fanfare on a D major seventh chord at measure 154 by trumpets, horns, and upper woodwinds that concludes *Canzona*.

Will *Canzona* be regarded as a masterwork for band in years to come? The piece does not sound as contemporary today as it did when first published in 1954; more recent band compositions give the percussion section an importance equal to that of the woodwinds and brass. The technical requirements for players are not as great as those of many contemporary works. It would be a mistake, however, to overlook this marvelous piece amid today's new works. *Canzona* is challenging music for the band medium, written by a major composer; as such it merits the attention of every serious band conductor. Careful study of the score will continue to yield many rewards for performers, conductors, and listeners alike. □

85	Score: Oboe - 3rd note is an E, 4th note is C (score unclear).
91	Part: Clarinet 1, 2, 3 - staccato mark missing form the final eighth note.
100	Score: Oboes are missing staccato marks on beat 3.
101	Part: Clarinet 1 - slur should extend to the third note (D).
106	Part: Bassoons - missing ⟨decrescendo/crescendo⟩
108	Score and Part: Bass clarinet - add tenuto marks to both half notes.
112	Score: Bassoon 1 - slur missing between F and E.
113	Part: Percussion - missing decrescendo in bass drum part.
115	Part: Flute - slur between G♭ and F sixteenth notes is missing.
116	Part: Clarinet 3 - staccato mark missing from eighth-note A on beat 2.
117	Part: Flute - slur missing between first two sixteenths on beat 4.
120	Score: Oboe - add staccato mark to D eighth note on "and" of two.
121	Part: Clarinet 3 - remove staccato mark from below the first note.
122	Score: Alto sax - slur missing between final 2 notes in 2nd part.
123	Score: Alto sax - slur missing between first 2 notes in 2nd part.
123-4	Part: Cornet 3 - add slur between beat 3 and the eighth note in measure 124.
124-5	Part: Bassoons, baritone sax - slur missing between beat 3 and the first beat of the next measure.
125-6	Part: Cornet 3 - add slur to the final two eighths extending to the dotted quarter G in the next measure.
126	Score: Cornets 1, 2, 3 - slur needs to carry over from previous page.
126	Part: Horn 2 - missing staccato marks on beat 2 plus "and" of 3.
126	Score: Horns 1, 2, 3, 4 - add staccato marks to 2 eighth notes on beat 2, and the eighth-note on "and" of beat 3.
127	Part: String bass - add staccato mark to the eighth-note.
132	Score and Part: Oboes - add sharp to the fourth eighth-note (C).
132	Score and Parts: Trombone 2, 3 - add staccato mark to the eighth-note.
136	Score: Horn 3, 4 - add staccato mark on the "and" of beat 2.
138-9	Part: Bass clarinet - slur missing between beat 3 and the first eighth of bar 139.
140-1	Part: Bass clarinet - slur missing between eighth-notes beginning on beat 4 and the dotted quarter in the next measure.
141	Score and Part: Alto sax - add sharp in front of the F.
141	Score: Baritone sax - add accent to quarter note on beat 3.
142	Part: Baritone B.C. - add flat sign before the B.
142	Part: Baritone T.C. - eliminate the sharp sign before the C.
148	Score and Part: Trumpet 2 - add sharp before the first eighth-note (C).
152	Part: Alto clarinet - slur missing between the quarter-note on beat 2 and the D♯ eighth-note on beat 3; staccato mark missing from same D♯.
153	Part: Oboes - slur beginning on beat 3 should continue over to the note A on beat 4.
153	Score: E♭ clarinet - add flat sign to final quarter-note G.
153	Parts: Clarinets 1, 2, 3 - slur should extend from the four sixteenths to quarter-note on beat 4.
156	Parts: Alto clarinet, bass clarinet, bassoons, alto sax, tenor sax, baritone sax - final accent should be ∧.
156	Part: Trombone 1 - add accent ∧ to final pitch.
156	Score: Cornet 1, 2, 3 - questionable staccato mark on final pitch.
pages 12-15	Trombone, baritone, bass, and string bass staves are labeled incorrectly. The parts appear in the proper order.

Ingolf Dahl's *Sinfonietta for Concert Band*

An Interpretive Analysis

BY BYRON ADAMS

I ngolf Dahl is an example of a European-born composer who entered so completely into the musical life of his adoptive country, and made such an influential contribution to its music that he is considered an important American composer. Born in Hamburg, Germany in 1912 to a family of mixed German-Swedish background, Dahl and his siblings received music lessons and encouragement in their musical interests. In 1931 Dahl entered the Hochschule für Musik in Cologne, where he studied composition with Philipp Jarnach, an associate of Busoni. He left the Hochschule in 1933 and went to the Zurich Conservatory where he studied with Volkmar Andreae, conductor of the Tonhalle Orchestra of Zurich. Dahl was interested in other disciplines besides music, however, and spent the years between 1933 and 1938 studying art history at the University of Zurich.

A composer, conductor, and author, Byron Adams is Visiting Assistant Professor at the University of California, Riverside. The author gratefully acknowledges the following who were of assistance in the preparation of this article: Frederick Lesemann and the staff of the U.S.C. Music Library, Thomas C. Duffy, William Schaefer, and the late Robert Wojciak.

Dahl emigrated to America in 1939 and settled in Southern California. He quickly became an important figure in the musical life of the area as a pianist and conductor, especially in the performance of contemporary music. He became acquainted with Stravinsky in 1942 and audited a series of master classes given in Los Angeles by Nadia Boulanger two years later.

In 1945 Dahl was appointed to a position on the music faculty of the University of Southern California, a post he held for the rest of his life. During his tenure at U.S.C. he taught orchestration, theory, composition, conducting, music history, and literature as well as conducting the collegium musicum and, from time to time, the university orchestra. Dahl was an inspired and effective teacher whose students include Michael Tilson Thomas, Robert Linn, and Donal Michalsky. Dahl began to receive wider attention in the early 1950s. He was awarded a Guggenheim Fellowship in 1952, taught at Tanglewood in 1951, and acted as Music Director of the Ojai (California) Festival in 1964 and 1965. He maintained a busy schedule until his health deteriorated in the late 1960s and died in Switzerland on August 7, 1970.

Dahl was a vigorous, curious, forthright, and witty man with a deep love of nature. He was an accomplished mountaineer, with over a hundred peaks to his credit in Southern California alone. His sense of humor is vividly suggested by the enjoyment he derived from accompanying the British music hall singer and comedienne Gracie Fields. Dahl's personal and artistic independence allowed him to gain the respect of both Stravinsky and Schoenberg at a time when acquaintance with those rival masters was widely considered mutually exclusive. (Dahl assisted in translating both Stravinsky's *Poetics of Music* and the text of Schoenberg's *Pierrot Lunaire*, and made piano reductions for Stravinsky's ballets *Danses Concertantes* and *Scènes de Ballet*.)

Dahl was particularly interested in the expressive possibilities inherent in wind instruments. In 1942 he wrote the *Allegro and Arioso* for woodwind quintet and two years later composed the well-known work *Music for Brass Instruments*. The bright, clean, and colorful timbres of wind and brass instruments were well suited to Dahl's clear, concise style.

William Schaefer, then conductor of the U.S.C. Trojan Symphonic Band, recalls urging Dahl to write a piece for concert band, and also the composer's initial response: "I *hate* bands!" Due in part to Schaefer's persistence, Dahl eventually overcame his reluctance and began to sketch a work for band in 1959, originally entitled *Serenade*. This project gained added impetus the following year when the Northwestern and Western Divisions of the College Band Directors' National Association commissioned Dahl to compose a work for concert band.

Dahl was a meticulous and self-critical composer. The holograph sketches for the *Sinfonietta* are evidence of a long creative process. Dahl was acutely aware of the problems faced by wind players; he was in the habit of carrying around scraps of manuscript paper containing short passages of his work-in-progress and consulting players on technical details and articulation. Dahl's procedure was to search incessantly for the inevitable note choices. The formal plan of the piece was sketched as a sequence of events, sometimes including timings and estimates of the number of measures, that suggest some sort of musical blueprint. The sketches and partial short score are covered with successive revisions made in a wide variety of colored inks and pencils. The process of revision often continued past the premiere; Dahl made revisions in the *Sinfonietta* until its publication in 1969.

Aside from Dahl's painstaking manner of working, the composition of the *Sinfonietta* was slowed by the composer's heavy schedule of performing and teaching, and by illness. Although

the premiere was scheduled for the spring of 1961, the official first performance of the *Sinfonietta* was given by William Schaefer conducting the Trojan Symphonic Band of the University of Southern California on January 12, 1962. Early interpreters of the score, aside from Schaefer, included Donald McGinnis, John Paynter, and Donald Hunsberger. Dahl himself conducted it at the 1964 C.B.D.N.A. Convention in Tempe, Arizona. The following analysis uses the score of the *Sinfonietta* published in 1969 by Alexander Broude, Inc.

Dahl said he wanted to write a piece that had "a serenade tone with symphonic proportions." Furthermore he designed the work to reflect both the acoustical properties and idiomatic qualities of the instruments. Because of the nature of the overtones generated by wind instruments, Dahl decided to use a tonal idiom (the tonal center of the *Sinfonietta* is A♭), and said he chose to emphasize "open, i.e. consonant intervals."

These choices did not preclude the use of the serial procedures that fascinated Dahl; rather it led him to employ what he describes in the introductory notes to the score as a six-tone set made up of consonant intervals that allow for a wide assortment of triadic structures:

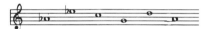

Combining the prime form of this hexachord with its inversion at the interval of the major sixth (I^9) results in what Dahl refers to as a twelve-tone row, although he did not strictly maintain the order of the notes in this row:

Dahl uses the prime form of the six-tone set to generate thematic material, such as the main theme, which opens the third movement:

Harmonic structures are also derived from the set. These are frequently triadic because of the intervallic construction of the set; other harmonic structures, such as quartal harmony, are present as well. Here are two quartal chords found one bar before rehearsal letter P in the first movement:

Photo courtesy of Brent Pierce

The set is further used to provide tonal motion and points of tonal polarity throughout the score. This is especially evident in the tonal plan of the variations in the third movement, which is a series of tonal poles based on a cycle of fifths.

Two subsidiary motives in the *Sinfonietta* assist in generating thematic material. The first, referred to here as motive X, is a small thematic cell that lends itself to a variety of permutations, including octave displacement, one of Dahl's favorite developmental devices:

Motive X

This thematic cell consists of an upper or lower neighbor figure, usually, but not invariably, followed by an interval of a third. This motive, as well as the six-tone set, outlines the first theme of the rondo section of the first movement, initially stated at rehearsal letter B:

The second of these motives, called here motive

Y, is a scalar pattern that Dahl calls a tetrachord:

Motive Y

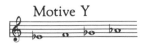

This motive is especially prominent in the second movement, although it appears in the first three bars of the *Sinfonietta* stated in retrograde in the bass clarinet and horn.

Dahl's treatment of serial techniques gives unity to the thematic, harmonic, and tonal elements of the *Sinfonietta*. He is not dogmatic or rigid in his handling of these procedures, using the order of the notes in the set with freedom. He does not hesitate, for example, to repeat notes. Dahl, like the 20th-century Swiss composer Frank Martin, realized that he could adapt serial techniques to enrich an already developed compositional style; he felt no desire to encumber his art with the aesthetics of 20th-century German Expressionism.

The overall form of the *Sinfonietta* is that of a concise symphony in three movements — "Introduction and Rondo," "Pastorale Nocturne," and "Dance Variations."

In his introductory notes to the score, Dahl wrote that this three-movement design is "akin to an arch or to the span of a large bridge: the sections of the first movement correspond, in reverse order and even in some details, to the sections of the last." While the first and third movements share material, albeit in a sophisticated manner often not readily apparent to the listener, the second movement, cast in ternary form, completes the arch. The gavotte of the B section of the second movement is the center of the entire *Sinfonietta*; Dahl describes it as "a center stone which does not weigh heavily." Dahl further emphasizes the archlike structure of the score by bringing back the introduction from the first movement as the final music in the last movement. It is unfortunate that, like Prokofiev in his Seventh Symphony, Dahl acquiesced to pressures from various sources and provided an alternate loud, fast ending for the *Sinfonietta*. Not only does Dahl's alternate ending mar the delicate and carefully planned formal balance of the entire work, it is distinctly inferior to the poetic, hushed conclusion that was his original conception.

The first seven bars of the "Introduction and Rondo" are a wonderful musical joke that recalls those of Haydn: the music begins amorphously and atonally, gradually groping towards a cadence on A, only to suddenly and deceptively resolve to A♭. The rest of the introduction consists of an off-stage fanfare for three trumpets (or cornets) that states the basic musical material of the entire work in embryo. In a lecture given at the C.B.D.N.A. convention, Dahl likened this fanfare to the ceremonial processional music played by 18th-century musicians as they entered a room for a performance.

The rondo proper begins at rehearsal letter B (example 6), with a marchlike theme, which is immediately stated in a varied form. A transitional passage at E leads to the second section at F, which proves to be a miniature ternary form. The first part of this second section is found between F and G and contains a theme played by the trumpets and trombones five bars after F that is related to the marchlike theme. The second part of this section begins at G with a figure played by the saxophones and double reed instruments and concludes five bars after H; the first part returns at I. An oboe solo seven bars after J leads to a truncated restatement of the marchlike theme.

The next section, from K to O, contains a series of developments of material from the second section. The passage six bars before L is clearly derived from the music first stated at F, for example, and the flute trills at M turn out to be a varied retrograde of the trombone melody

at five bars after F. A forceful canonic passage at O prepares for what Dahl calls a "cadenza-like modulatory episode for the clarinet section" at P; Dahl said this extraordinary section was "inspired, I do not hesitate to admit, by a wonderful performance William Schaefer gave of Weber's Concertino played by the full clarinet section." This episode moves rapidly through tonal areas that touch upon each note of the prime form of the six-tone set (A♭ E♭ C G D and A). When the cadenza reaches the tonal area of A, the rondo section returns in A♭ at R, thus repeating the deceptive harmonic gesture of the introduction. A varied return at V of the brass fanfare of the introduction leads to the high-spirited conclusion, which contains material that will form the opening of the third movement along with the drum and piccolo formula that traditionally opens a march. The overall form of the first movement is therefore an arch enclosed within an arch:

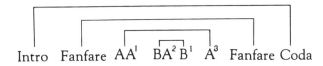

Intro Fanfare AA¹ BA²B¹ A³ Fanfare Coda

The second movement, "Pastorale Nocturne," is a simple ternary form. The first section is a free fugue whose subject, based on motive Y, is always evolving. A waltz is superimposed upon the fugue in a manner reminiscent of the collages of Charles Ives, whose music Dahl performed and admired. The central section is an airy, elegant, and uncomplicated gavotte, after which the material from the first section returns, ending with a poignant solo for the alto clarinet that echoes the clarinet section solo that opened the movement.

The final movement, "Dance Variations," begins with the main theme, which is the most overt statement of the six-tone set in the entire *Sinfonietta* (example 3). This theme will be present in all of the variations, serving as a continuously evolving *basso ostinato* in a way similar to Vaughan Williams's treatment of the passacaglia theme in the last movement of his Fifth Symphony. The first section of this movement falls into three parts. A restatement and expansion of the theme at A constitutes the first part, while the second part at C is marked "con tutta forza." The third and final part of this section, between E and H, contains two distinct elements, the first played by the horns and trombones at E and the second found in the baritone and tuba at one after G.

The second section, which is tripartite, begins at I with mysterious and pointillistic music; across this eerie musical landscape flits a scrap of theme marked "giocoso" at J. A brief transition prepares for the appearance of a shapely and expressive melody, derived from the set, played by the flutes and oboes at M, which is repeated at N by a solo horn. This section concludes with a brief reminiscence at O of the pointillistic texture at I.

The third section of this movement recapitulates material from the first section in different order: Tempo I to P recalls the music from A to C, while the passage from Q to R is a variant of the one between E and G. A transitional crescendo at R prepares for the climax at S, which is analogous to the "con tutta forza" music at C. Then the main theme is stated in its original form, leading through a transitional passage that returns the "giocoso" theme at J to an audibly recognizable variant of the introduction to the first movement. The return of this fanfare suggests that the musicians have completed their work and are ready to depart. The *Sinfonietta* draws to a serene conclusion as the instruments leave one by one, playing fragments of the six-tone set as they go.

The form of the "Dance Variations," like that of the "Introduction and Rondo," is one of an arch enclosed within an arch. The first movement proceeds away from the music of the introduction, while the last movement moves toward the fanfare in reverse order towards a restatement of the introduction. The form of the *Sinfonietta* as a whole can thus be compared to a large, subtly organized musical palindrome, or the play of arches in a Gothic cathedral.

Intro I II III Coda

Like a cathedral architect, Dahl is never obvious or crudely symmetrical in designing his proportions. His lively rhythms, irregular phrase lengths, and constant variations banish any hint of rigidity from the *Sinfonietta*.

The technical demands made by the *Sinfonietta* on a conductor's technique and musicianship are formidable. One basic requirement is that the conductor's baton technique be precise without becoming pedantic, fluid without losing impetus, and buoyant without sacrificing control. The clarity of the conductor's beat patterns determines the rhythmic vitality of the performance. If the conductor allows the first and last movements to rush, the wealth of rhythmic and thematic detail will become obscure, while the second movement has to maintain an inexorable forward momentum if it is to retain the listener's interest. The conductor should strictly follow Dahl's metronome markings.

One aspect of the conductor's technique especially tested by the *Sinfonietta* is clear, alert, and consistent cueing. Many of the cues in the *Sinfonietta*, such as the alto saxophone entrance five bars after E in the first movement, occur on off beats. A particularly complex passage for cues is the pointillistic music at I in the "Dance Variations," which the conductor needs to carefully work out in advance and diligently rehearse. Due to the nature of Dahl's orchestrations, instrumentalists may have long periods of rest, entering only to play a few isolated yet important notes; take, for example, the brief bassoon figure three bars before the end of the second movement.

The amount of detail in the *Sinfonietta* makes considerations of balance particularly important; the thematic line can be obscured at times by the vivacious and complicated accompanimental material. Such a passage occurs four bars after T in the "Introduction and Rondo," where the trombones, marked piano, are easily covered by the elaborate clarinet figuration (also marked piano) that occurs one bar later. Solos should be clearly delineated, such as the bassoon solo two bars after C in the second movement or the horn solo one bar before N in the last movement.

Dahl's articulation and dynamic markings, if scrupulously observed, will greatly aid in distinguishing the foreground from the background elements. Dahl was deeply concerned with articulations and dynamics, putting markings into his early sketches for the *Sinfonietta*. That he wanted them to be vivid is illustrated by this note on one of the holograph sketch pages: "Note in this score 'staccatissimo' always means: as short as possible — a peck."

The final aspect a conductor must bring to the *Sinfonietta* is interpretive insight. This work does not play itself; an accurate but uncommitted performance of just the notes on the page would be deadly. Dahl was an excellent conductor whose performances were noted for their clarity, maturity, and, above all, sense of line. If this sense of logical linear direction is missing from a performance of the *Sinfonietta*, the carefully planned formal balances will fall to pieces. In addition to communicating the formal balance, the music needs to be animated by a lively and informed expressivity. The conductor who lacks a taste for musical wit should not attempt this work. The *Sinfonietta* is more than a testimony to its composer's intelligence and skill, because it also reflects something of Ingolf Dahl's sense of humor, clarity of thought, and utter maturity. To be completely successful the interpreter must bring similar qualities to the performance of this delightful score. □

An Interpretive Analysis

Karel Husa's *Music for Prague 1968*

BY BYRON ADAMS

Karel Husa was galvanized by the invasion of his native Czechoslovakia by Soviet troops in August of 1968, particularly the entry of the invading army into Prague, the city of his birth, where several members of his immediate family still lived. After a sleepless night monitoring radio broadcasts for news of the situation, Husa began sketches for a composition. A recent commission from the Ithaca College Concert Band gave the impetus for these initial ideas. In the short space of seven weeks, working at a high pitch of excitement and inspiration, Husa composed *Music for Prague 1968* with the score completed in October.

Music for Prague 1968 was first heard in a semi-private performance at Ithaca College by the Ithaca College Concert Band conducted by Kenneth Snapp on December 13, 1968. The same conductor and ensemble gave the official public premiere on January 31, 1969 at an M.E.N.C. convention in Washington, D.C. Husa subsequently prepared a version of *Music for Prague 1968* for standard orchestra, which was first performed on January 31, 1970 with the composer conducting the Munich Philharmonic Orchestra. Since its premiere the work has received over 7,000 performances around the world. Among the distinguished interpreters of the score are Frederick Fennell, Erich Leinsdorf, William D. Revelli, Stanislaw Skrowaczewski, and John P. Paynter. While reviewing this analysis, readers should follow the concert band score of *Music for Prague 1968*, using the 1986 edition published by Associated Music Publishers.

Husa had long planned to write a piece to celebrate the beauty of his native city, but after the events of 1968, the emphasis necessarily became Prague's tragic history. The central musical idea of *Music for Prague 1968* is the first four bars of the 15th-century Hussite war song "Kdož jste boží bojovníci" ("Ye Warriors of God and His Law"). This melody has been repeatedly used by Czech composers when writing about their homeland: it was used by Dvořák in two concert overtures, *Domov můj*, Op. 62 (*My Home*, 1882) and the *Husitská dramatická ouvertura*, Op. 67

(*Hussite Overture*, 1883); by Josef Suk in his symphonic poem *Praga* (*Prague*, 1904); and most notably by Bedřich Smetana in *Tábor* (*The Camp*, 1878) and *Blaník* (1879), the final two symphonic poems of his cycle of six entitled *Má vlast* (*My Country*, 1874-1879). By using this war song Husa places *Music for Prague 1968* directly in the tradition of compositions that deal with the history of the Czech nation. The use of the Hussite war song in the timpani in *Music for Prague 1968* deliberately recalls Smetana's similar scoring of this melody in *Tábor* from *Má vlast*. Any Czech concert audience would understand the allusion instantly, given the opportunity.

Husa had previously used traditional Czech melodies as the basis for such scores as the *Evocations of Slovakia* (1951) for clarinet, viola, and cello, and the *Eight Czech Duets* (1955) for piano. *Music for Prague 1968*, however, is the first of Husa's scores to combine an existing traditional melody with the personal and experimental serial procedures found in such works as the *Poem* (1959) for viola and chamber orchestra and *Mosaiques* (1961) for orchestra. Every thematic element in *Music for Prague 1968* can be traced to the first four bars of "Ye Warriors of God."

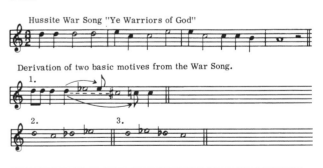

Hussite War Song "Ye Warriors of God"

Derivation of two basic motives from the War Song.

Byron Adams is Visiting Assistant Professor at the University of California, Riverside. He holds degrees from Jacksonville University, the University of Southern California, and Cornell University, where he received his doctoral degree studying composition with Karel Husa. One of Adams's own compositions was performed at the 26th Warsaw Autumn International Festival of Contemporary Music.

From the implications of these four bars, Husa has derived two 12-note sets that contain between them all of the score's basic motives:

Set II also contains the origin of the most important recurring harmonic ideas in *Music for Prague 1968*: three chords that Husa refers to as the chorale chords.

Husa never employs these 12-note sets in a rigid manner; rather, he uses serial procedures to promote the greatest possible thematic unity through motivic interrelation. He does not allow serial procedures to become merely systematic. Husa frequently alters the order of notes within a set to suit his expressive purposes.

The overall form of *Music for Prague 1968* is that of a symphony in four movements – "Introduction and Fanfare," "Aria," "Interlude," and "Toccata and Chorale." Within this large structure Husa uses cyclic return of ideas; music from the first movement returns in both the "Aria" and the "Toccata and Chorale." This use of cyclic procedure includes the use of musical symbolism; the resolve of the Hussite war song, the sounds evoking the bells of Prague, and the opening piccolo solo representing a bird call. In the composer's words the bird call is a "symbol of the liberty which the City of Prague has seen only for moments during its thousand years of existence" [foreword to the score of *Music for Prague 1968*, Associated Music Publishers, Inc.]. Other musical symbols recur throughout the score.

The first four bars of the "Introduction and Fanfare" contain the basic musical ideas of the entire piece in embryo: the motive stated in the piccolo; the three chorale chords in the flutes, clarinets, and horns; and the Hussite war song outlined by muted timpani. These ideas are developed and extended throughout as the introduction proceeds, growing increasingly more intense until the savage brass fanfare erupts at rehearsal letter C. In the remainder of the movement Husa opposes the ideas of the introduction with those of the fanfare, each section growing more restless and complex. A massive climax is achieved from G to H, only to dissipate quickly to a reminiscence of the piccolo and quiet timpani with which the movement began.

The second movement, "Aria," is both the most systematically serialized and formally subtle of the four movements. Husa superimposes a modified song form (ABB'A') on an underlying expressive structure organized like the arch of a huge span of continually developing melody. The A section of the song form is a melody derived from set II, played by saxophones and low clarinets accompanied by an ostinato in the percussion that is constructed by the rotation of the same set. Beginning with nervous rhythmic figures in the upper woodwinds four bars after J, the first part of the B section contains a prominent return at K of the chorale chords from the first movement.

The second part of the B section commences at the entrance of the bassoons, low clarinets, and saxophones seven bars after K; this is imperceptibly transformed into the middle of the main melody of A six bars after L. The rising progress of the underlying expressive structure can be followed from the beginning of the "Aria" by tracing the pedal points, starting low in the tubas and ascending through the ensemble, to the climax at K. Husa derives these pedal points from the pitches of set II in free augmentation.

The "Interlude" is scored exclusively for the percussion: the snare drum and vibraphone are the soloists accompanied by three percussionists playing a variety of instruments selected to evoke bell-like sonorities. Like the Danish composer Carl Nielsen, Husa sometimes assigns personality traits to given instruments. In this movement the snare drum has an elemental, menacing, and militaristic quality, while the vibraphone symbolizes a human voice growing increasingly agitated. The accompanying percussion parts suggest the bells of Prague ringing a warning against the approach of the invaders; these parts are rhythmically serialized and organized in a palindromic structure that progresses from the beginning to O and then reverses itself in inversion.

The concluding movement, "Toccata and Chorale," is a sectional form reminiscent of the "Introduction and Fanfare." The 19-bar introduction has two parts, the first being seven bars that contain a rhythmic motive of repeated notes in groups of five. (Rhythmic figures of five units have appeared previously in each of the preceding movements.) The second part of the introduction contains fragmentary motives that coalesce into the 17-bar first theme played by the clarinet at A:

From B to C this theme is subjected to a brief development leading to a second theme played by the trumpet section at C. This theme is a 17-bar period organized as two asymmetrical antecedent/consequent phrases separated by rests and accompanied by high woodwinds and percussion:

At D a restatement of the first theme begins an elaborate development that continues until F, when the second theme undergoes an extended development. The procedure used to build this first large formal unit of the "Toccata and Chorale" recalls the French Baroque *doublé*, a formal procedure in which a concise unit is immediately followed by a longer, more elaborate treatment of the same material. We might note that Husa has long been interested in music of this period, having produced performing editions of Lully and Delalande.

Beginning at I both of these themes are combined in development, and during this section material from the preceding movements begins to reappear. At I, for example, the last three pitches of set II appear in the flutes, oboes, and E♭ clarinet. Material from E in the "Introduction and Fanfare" is recalled in the alto saxophone eight bars after K, while five bars after L the trumpets play a rhythmically transformed version of the fanfare material from the first movement and pitched percussion play the Hussite war song. One bar later the trombones, baritones, tubas, and string bass begin a version of the chorale chords heard in the first and second movements. The Hussite war song makes a dramatic appearance nine bars after M, leading to a return at N of the rhythmic motive of five repeated notes with which the movement opened.

The next section, from O to 12 bars after Q, corresponds to the section in the "Introduction and Fanfare" from C to E, with slight differences in rhythmic adjustment, register, and musical detail. The rest of Q is a brief transition from this material to the grand, augmented statement at R of the chorale chords by the brass, saxophones, and low woodwinds. Eleven bars after R the opening rhythmic motive of five repeated notes returns.

After a brief pause the coda begins at S; this is the "chorale" section to which the movement's title refers. The Hussite war song, which dominates this coda, is heard *fortissimo* in the timpani one bar after S, followed by an instrumental statement of the song's first of the two phrases. This is interrupted by a five-note rhythmic figure in the woodwinds and percussion. After the second phrase of the war song is stated, the menacing snare drum of the "Interlude" returns at V (there is no letter U), sounding its rigid and militaristic rhythmic pattern over a 12- to 16-second passage of controlled aleatoric playing by the winds and percussion. This aleatoric section is constructed of many of the main motivic fragments of *Music for Prague 1968* in their most ele-

mental form. The terror and dismay of this section suggests the wildness of a fearful crowd. A metered bar of snare drum solo is followed by a tutti statement of the first phrase of the Hussite war song, which overpowers the snare drum. The second measure of this two-bar phrase is repeated, and then the last two notes of this second bar (C and E) are repeated as a gesture mingling defiance, resolve, and hope. The Hussite war song remains unfinished; so too the search for freedom is never finished.

The conductor who undertakes a performance of *Music for Prague 1968* faces five basic challenges. The first of these involves his baton technique, which must be absolutely precise and controlled if the music is to have continuity. The rhythmic vitality of *Music for Prague 1968* depends on the clarity of the conductor's beat patterns, especially in the fast sections of the "Introduction and Fanfare" and the "Toccata and Chorale." The conductor needs to resist the temptation to be carried away by the music and begin to rush, which can mar the precision of the rhythmic values (such as can happen with 16th notes in the brass fanfare at C in the first movement). Allowing the beat pattern to become too large can retard the forward impetus of the music and cause the carefully planned formal proportions to fall apart. Cues need to be absolutely confident and consistent from rehearsal to performance, especially at such spots as the cue to the suspended cymbals at C in the first movement or the off-beat cue to the muted trombones 12 bars after A in the last movement. The players must feel absolute confidence in the conductor if they are to be able to interpret their often taxing parts with conviction.

The second challenge combines these technical considerations with an element of the conductor's basic musicality: the ability to remember and control tempo relationships. It is vitally important that the forward motion be consistently maintained throughout *Music for Prague 1968*. The musical argument and the formal design are predicated upon the continuity of tempo, which is as important in the slower passages in the "Introduction and Fanfare" and in the "Aria" as it is in the faster sections. The "Toccata and Chorale" in particular should have a cumulative effect, and the music from K to the coda must move inexorably ahead toward the approaching tragedy. Wherever Husa has indicated a single unmodified metronome marking, such as the ♩ =52 at the beginning, it must be precisely followed; when a possible range of metronome markings is given, such as the opening of the last movement, ♩ = *ca.* 120-126, the faster tempo is preferable.

The third challenge for the conductor presented by *Music for Prague 1968* is the balancing of instrumental forces so that the basic thematic

III. Interlude

continuity emerges with optimum clarity. The main thematic line always needs to be balanced against an often complex and elaborate background. Without careful differentiation between the various elements, the composition can degenerate into a series of loud gestures without melodic content, and the success of *Music for Prague 1968* is predicated largely upon the primacy of its melodic line. Even a cursory study of the score will reveal the care with which Husa has indicated the relative importance of the different elements through his orchestration and expressive markings.

Solutions to problems of balance in the first movement include doubling the flute flutter tonguing the low C♯ if only one flute cannot be heard, making sure that the baritone saxophone solo from B to C stands out strongly from the accompanying texture, and reducing the dynamic marking of the trumpets from *fortissimo* to *forte* for the first three bars of E so that the winds can be heard, as Husa himself does whenever he conducts the work. In the second movement the saxophones should gradually *diminuendo* five bars after L and become quiet only at M. Husa omits the *poco dim.* marking in the percussion one bar before M.

In the "Interlude," the vibraphone solo needs to be distinctly differentiated from the accompanying bell-like percussion. The additional snare drums, which enter for the terrific roll that concludes this movement, should have staggered entrances and each should begin *piano*.

Problems of balance in the "Toccata and Chorale" are found nine bars before F, where the piccolos have to strongly reinforce the trumpets to help them in this difficult passage. Husa recommends the use of any extra trumpets to double the low Gs and F♯s here. From J to K the *glissandi* should predominate. especially the trombone *glissandi*, which should give the impression of a wailing siren. At five bars after L, the pitched percussion have to play the Hussite war song loudly enough so that it sounds both brilliant and resolute.

Attention to details of dynamics is the conductor's next challenge in *Music for Prague 1968*. Although the score is conceived on grand terms, it makes its most complete impression only if the details are carefully and lovingly prepared, rather like the way the details of a great fresco by Delacroix contribute to the viewer's impression of the whole. Such details are found in the first movement in the trumpet section six bars after E, where each trumpeter should have his bell in the air, *campana in aria*, so that the colors of the different types of mutes are heard; at eight bars after K, where each of the trumpets needs to clearly articulate the different rhythmic patterns while playing at high volume, in order to give the impression of the cruel brilliance of a giant searchlight; and at H, where the varied grace notes have to be accurately differentiated by each trumpet in turn. In the "Aria" the upper woodwinds must crescendo continually after their *forte-piano* attacks at M. Another important dynamic consideration in this movement is that the figure in the marimba and vibraphone one bar after K should be particularly brilliant. The principal detail in the "Interlude" is attention to the accents marked throughout the parts, but especially in the opening snare drum solo. A crucial detail in the "Toccata and Chorale" comes in the handling of the snare drum solo in the coda: at V the snare drum takes its tempo from the preceding adagio (♩ = *ca.* 44), and there is no breath mark in the snare drum part, which continues without a break from the aleatoric section into the next metered bar.

The final challenge for the conductor of *Music for Prague 1968* is to realize fully the work's message and dramatic content. For example, the fanfare at C in the "Introduction and Fanfare" has to be both machinelike and aggressive. The thematic line of the "Aria" needs to rise in an unrelenting curve of anguish and despair. The

"Interlude" must unite the mysterious beauty of the bell sonorities with a sense of increasing dread. The "Toccata and Chorale" should hurtle to its noble and tragic conclusion. When Husa conducts *Music for Prague 1968*, he emphasizes the resolve of the ending by holding the last note, which is marked both with a *fermata* and the direction *lunga,* for eight or nine seconds, beginning moderately loud and growing to a massive final sustained sonority. Many a performance of *Music for Prague 1968* has been robbed of its impact by a conductor content merely to cue in the ensemble and count seconds at V in the last movement rather than indicate to the players through some gesture the terrifying expressive implications of this passage. Every bar of *Music for Prague 1968* is infused with the burning sincerity and compassion of its composer; the interpreter of this masterpiece of the contemporary wind ensemble repertoire must come prepared with an equal commitment to the task of bringing the music to life.   □

Errata

Errors in the Score
for Editions Published before 1986
Movement I
   Page 10, bar one, flutes 1 & 2: the word *tutti* is missing in the score and parts.
   Page 10, bar four, baritone: the word "mute" is missing; the baritone is unmuted at C.

Movement II
   Page 31, early editions of the score had ♪ = ca. 60-66 rather than the correct ♩ = *ca.* 60-66.
   Page 41, bar one, vibraphone: there should be a dyad with the D5 and the F3 played together.

Movement III
   Page 48, two bars before P, vibraphone: the direction "not necessarily in tempo" should finish on the third beat.

Movement IV
   Page 55, bar four, baritone: "mute" is omitted in score and parts; the baritone should remain muted until four bars before K.
   Page 65, bar two, xylophone: the last note of this bar should be an E♭.
   Page 88, bar six, contrabassoon and string should have this:

   Page 91, bar one, trumpet 4: the D should be tied over from the preceding bar.
   Page 98, bars one and two, flute 1: the flute should play an F6, not an A6.

Errors in Parts
Movement I
   Page 9, bar four, clarinet 1, division 3: there should be a dotted half note on beat two.

Movement II
   Page 39, bar one, trumpet 3: the notes should read the same as the score.

Movement IV
   Page 52, rehearsal letters A-B, bassoon 2: the number of bars should read 8-8-1.
   Page 56, bar three: bass clarinet should have a quarter note on beat five rather than beat four.
   Page 98, bar four, horn 2; the tempo marking of *adagio* is omitted.

Discography for
Music for Prague 1968

Concert Band
University of Michigan Symphony Band,
   Karel Husa, conductor, Golden Crest: CRS-4134 (White Horse Pike and Ehrke Road, Ancora, New Jersey), presently unavailable.
University of Texas Symphonic Band, William
   J. Moody, conductor, Belwin-Mills: BP-136

Orchestra
Louisville Orchestra, Jorge Mester, conductor,
   Louisville Orchestra: LS-722

Karel Husa—

Apotheosis of This Earth

There are times when an artist feels the need to express in his work an idea concerning the present state of world affairs. I must say that I was never concerned with such ideas in my music until the summer of 1968 when I wrote the *Music for Prague, 1968*. Although I have previously composed pieces with titles expressing their character or mood, most of my works have no programmatic elements. While this is evident with respect to my Quartets, Concertos, Symphony and Sonata, it also applies to my *Apotheosis of this Earth*. This work has no detailed "program" of any kind, but it does attempt to express musically the present alarming and tragic situation of mankind on this planet. Here is the complete text as it appears in the "Note" of the score.

The composition of *Apotheosis of this Earth* was motivated by the present desperate state of mankind and its immense problems — war, hunger, and ecological disaster. Man's brutal possession and misuse of nature's beauty — if continued at today's reckless speed — can only lead to catastrophe. The composer hopes that the destruction of this

We are proud to announce that Karel Husa has recently joined the Board of Advisors of The Instrumentalist. *A former student of Arthur Honegger and Nadia Boulanger, Husa has been Professor of Composition and Director of the Cornell University Symphony and Chamber Orchestras since 1954. During 1972-73 he visited campuses of some 20 universities and schools of music where he lectured, directed seminars, and guest conducted festivals and concerts of his own music. Last spring, a new version of his* Apotheosis of this Earth *(for orchestra and chorus) was premiered by the Cornell Orchestra and Chorus in Carnegie Hall, the John F. Kennedy Center, and on the Cornell Campus.*

beautiful earth can be stopped, so that the tragedy of destruction (musically projected here in the second movement) and the desolation of its aftermath (the "Postscript" of the third movement) can exist only as fantasy, never to become reality.

In the first movement, "Apotheosis," the earth first appears as a point of light in the universe (the soft A played at the beginning by the glockenspiel). As our memory and imagination approach it, the earth grows larger and larger, and we can even remember some of its tragic moments (as struck by the xylophone near the end of the movement). This picture of the earth coming gradually back to us was the reason for my construction of a *crescendo* taking 9 minutes — from the beginning to the climax of this movement (when the xylophone starts the anguished solo).

The second movement, "Tragedy of Destruction," deals with the actual brutalities of man against nature which lead to the destruction of our planet. The earth dies as a savagely and mortally wounded creature.

The last movement is a "Postscript," full of the realization that so little is left to be said. The earth has been pulverized into the universe, the voices scattered into space. Toward the end, these voices — at first computer-like and mechanical — unite into the words "this beautiful earth," simply said, warm and filled with regret . . . and one of so many questions comes to our minds, "Why did we let it happen?"

It is always more or less a step into the unknown when one writes a piece, using devices which have not been explored previously. I did not know, for instance, how many of the young players in bands would know how to finger some of the quarter-tones, but I was amazed by the quality of young performers in colleges, universities and even high schools. Their technical skills, quick understanding, and ability to realize musical ideas have resulted in some excellent performances of this composition. I did not expect when I wrote this work that so many ensembles would be able to perform it so well. The only problem — and one I did not expect — is the narration of the syllables and broken words leading to the phrase "this beautiful earth" in the last movement. I realize now that a player who is uninhibited with his instrument, is able to express warmth, gentleness, tragedy, and despair through his tone production, is shy to say a word or two on stage. In all the performances I have conducted or heard, the spoken word is never loud enough until the whole sentence is said in m. 57 (and this is sometimes too loud!). For the last spoken section (mm. 63-64) it may even be preferable to have one person in the front of the ensemble to say the phrase simply, but with sincere emotion.

The following comments — more specific in nature — may be helpful in the rehearsal and performance of this piece.

First Movement

MM. 23-24: The melody line in these three measures is split up between the alto clarinet (g), the bassoon (f#), and the bass clarinet (1/4 tone higher than d). These notes should be smooth and heard clearly as a melodic line. Similar broken up melodic lines appear in mm. 53 (horns and tenor sax) and 68 (trumpets, horns, and trombones).

M. 80: The flutter tonguing of the muted trombones together with the marimba tremolo must be audible and become stronger and stronger (until m. 108), leading into the muted, flutter tongued trumpets.

MM. 1-134: The tension should increase progressively without "falling down" until m. 134. Here the xylophone will beat the 32nd notes as strongly and loudly as possible but not faster than indicated. (Sometimes I hear them played so fast that they resemble tremolos.)

There should be a 15-20 second pause between the first two movements.

Second Movement

General: The low pedal notes of all instruments must always be loud and powerful. One string bass cannot provide a strong enough bass line, so I suggest using 2, 3, or even 4 string basses.

MM. 75-82: The trumpet entrances should be accented and strong.

M. 82: Starting here, the fugato has to come out phrase by phrase from all entering instruments.

MM. 120-121: This aleatory passage is notated approximately in seconds — but the exact timing will depend on the strength, power or speed of the movement. It is up to the conductor to sense the moment in which the crescendo has reached its maximum, and consequently he must know whether prolonging these measures will weaken the effect. The same is true for all free passages in this work.

MM. 129-131: The glockenspiel, vibraphone, xylophone, and bel lyra must sound as "alarming" as possible and the indicated crescendi and decrescendi should be respected.

MM. 135-140: The big bass drum and the low, long sound of the large gong (struck with gong mallets) should cause an "explosion" of sounds which culminate in m. 140 with crash cymbals and suspended cymbal.

End: At the end of this movement the percussion will slow down progressively and freely, and all instruments will get softer in the last two measures.

There should be only a very short pause between the second and third movements.

Third Movement

Opening: The entrances of the clarinets should be heard, only gently, as a "pulse" or "wave" somewhere in space. This same effect should be evident in mm. 14-16 (clarinets) and 16-19 (horns).

M. 24: The entrance of the medium tom-tom (struck with medium sticks) should come out as a continuation of the spoken sounds. The rhythm of the spoken sounds as well as of the tom-toms must be precise sextuplets (as written). These sounds are to remind us of some computer-like beeps scattered in the universe.

M. 55: The sound of the xylophone is important. It should be a gentle sound (no hard sticks), precise, and in the octave as written — not one octave higher as it is sometimes played.

End: The "signal" sounds in the last 5 measures (xylophone) should be played softer and softer until they virtually disappear — but no ritardando should be made. The conductor must decide how many repetitions of the last measure are to be taken. I have conducted from 3-7 repetitions depending on the impact of the performance and the quietness of the audience.

A Warning

I have used the word, "Apotheosis," in the title because of its reference to the glorification of a once great being which has passed away. I certainly hope that our beautiful earth will not have to be glorified in this way, but I cannot hope to remedy or even affect this situation in any way except through music. So I have composed this work as a kind of warning which, perhaps, will play at least a small part in preventing such a tragedy. ∎

Basic Band Repertory
Suite of Old American Dances

Frederick Fennell

Robert Russeli Bennett's long-standing presence as a composer on the American music scene was expanded in 1947 to include the band. The score was *Suite of Old American Dances.* Long an indispensable third of the typical production troika for Broadway shows (the other two, of course, are the lyricist and composer) it has always been his special gift as a peerless arranger of other men's music to transform a composer's precise — or sometimes very sketchy — musical outlines into a working theater format. The stars and their rehearsal accompanists, the chorus and dance coaches, and finally the orchestra in the pit must have their own scores from which to learn and play the performance. No small task, and one in which Russell Bennett's gifts and skills as a composer and orchestrator make him the ultimate catalyst for the creation of the final show.

And this becomes the version by which millions of theater goers, record and radio listeners will come to know the music of *Oklahoma, South Pacific,* or *The Sound of Music,*[1] listing but three of his many masterful achievements. At age 85 he is spiritually as involved as ever with this uniquely American contribution to music theater.

But there is that individually creative side to this man who has done so much for other men's music, and this *Suite* is one of its brightest examples. The *Suite of Old American Dances* owes its existence to a concert which the League of Composers presented on January 3, 1948 at Carnegie Hall, New York, in honor of Edwin Franko Goldman's 70th birthday; the Goldman band performed a memorable program of original works guest conducted by Walter Hendl and Percy Granger. Russell and his wife Louise attended. He has told me that on that evening he was overwhelmed by the wonderful sounds that the band can make, especially, he said, indoors where acoustics like those at Carnegie are on the side of the composer and performer and where all the extraneous outdoor intrusions of aircraft and

Frederick Fennell is currently the adjunct professor in conducting at the Catholic University of America School of Music. In addition to teaching conducting he is the conductor of the Concert Orchestra.

automobiles do not defeat the common cause of music making.

And he knew the wonderful sounds early-on, for his father was a bandmaster in Kansas City, and he too, had been an Army bandmaster in the First World War. But it had been a long time since he'd been to a band concert, and thus stimulated he began work on the *Suite* immediately. Other work interfered and two years were to elapse before it was finished and played for the first time by the band which had inspired it. No full score was ever written by Bennett and none is presently available from the publisher. He wrote out the parts, one at a time from the short score, over a period of two years.[2] Months would elapse between the writing of the second and then the third clarinet part, for instance. He would return to New York after a period away scoring a new show, dash off another part and leave again for other work. The cohesive nature of the writing, of course, shows none of these peripatetic pursuits.

The scoring, however, shows his long service to the theater, revealing a superior knowledge of voice leading and projecting — perhaps technique of the sort one can't really learn but merely perfect.

I know no music for band quite like this, except his other attractive *Symphonic Songs*. It makes me feel that the music had long cooked within, was all worked-out, and simply awaited time for transfer from the brain to the page. It was the first original score of its kind for band; the composer has also scored it for orchestra.

Pursuit of the style is the ultimate reward in this very pleasant music. Style is its essence, listening and playing-enjoyment its *raison d'etre*.

I. Cake Walk (228 Bars) $\frac{2}{4}$

A tempo that works is what makes the music go, and here one finds considerable margin in opinion. The composer's simple indication is *"Allegretto in two"* with no metronome mark. I've heard it played at the speed of a *galop*, not necessarily effectively; I feel happy with the metronome pulsing at c. 108 for the quarter note.

The cakewalk as a dance has its origin among American Negroes in the post Civil War plantation days when, according to authority,[3] one of the principal after-work diversions was dancing to com-

pelling rhythms and tunes played on the banjo, America's unique folk instrument. When the body simply could not stand still as the music was played, hand clapping, foot stomping, and fancy stepping was the inevitable result. What later became known as two-beat strutting led to contests among dancers in which a pastry or cake was awarded to the one who had performed the most outstanding, the most intricate kinds of steps or walks. Its legacy, two-beat jazz in various delineations including the fox-trot, was to dominate popular music for the time to come.

But I do not think that this "Cake Walk" should be confused with the Charleston, another two-beat dance of the later 1920s. The Charleston is usually pictured as a more frenzied dance with much emphasis on kicking-out with hands thrust high, whereas the more smooth action of the body erect and in that easy rocking motion associated with the strut as a dance seems to argue in favor of a more relaxed pulse. All of the dances which emerged from the post Civil War's most successful entertainment enterprise, the minstrel show, were influenced by two-beat syncopation growing out of the minstrel show walk-around. This was well under way before the war; it flowered later in the music of Scott Joplin (1868-1917) born after the peace and destined for success as a writer of great piano rags. The recent rediscovery of Joplin has led us in a return to more easy ways with cakewalks and has brought on renewed interest in this score by Russell Bennett.

Robert Russell Bennett, (born 1894) *Suite of Old American Dances* for Concert Band; *Cake Walk, Schottische, Western One-Step, Wallflower Waltz, Rag*; copyright 1950 by Chappell & Co., Inc., New York; 3 line condensed score in concert pitch, 32 pages; time for performance ca. 16:30; scoring: piccolo, 2 flutes, 2 oboes, English horn; clarinets: E♭, solo, 1st, 2nd, 3rd, alto, bass; 2 bassoons, 2 alto, tenor, baritone saxes; solo & 1st, 2nd, 3rd cornets, 2 trumpets, 4 horns, 3 trombones, treble and bass clef baritones, tubas, string contrabass; kettledrums, snare drum, cymbals, triangle, two blocks, sandpaper, bass drum, bells, vibraphone, and xylophone; no key signatures used, score or parts.

Before applying what follows in this study, the reader should first number each measure of the movements separately in the score; and performance preparation will be aided greatly by numbering each bar of every part. The rehearsal numbers are too far apart for the efficient detailed work the music demands, especially in the absence of a full score. Success in one's performance of "Cake Walk" is pretty much decided by how things go in the first 15 bars. All notes in the first two bars, when played with the longest articulation that time and separation will allow, are certain to set the style for what follows. Two different articulations produce two obviously different results.

Ex. 1a

Ex. 1b

I have come to prefer 1a. for a variety of reasons but principally because it helps the piece to play in the loose, easy manner that both avoids a brittle texture and aids in the prevention of that tense character which is the almost certain result with the average group when adopting 1b. All must meet the composer's challenge and maintain a positive pulse in the long, tied F natural [2-4]. A small, neat, rhythmic beat suffices here while the composer suspends the motion of the music as soon as he begins it, then resumes his syncopated way with the rhythmic development of this opening music [1-15]. Here, at bar 5, is where everybody needs the conductor and that clear down-beat we all know is the first condition in this art. And we had all better be there with it and with that clear preparation for it that allows all to happen. And what precedes this down-beat is always as important as its execution. The players, with their many physical and mechanical challenges can't receive what they need to see (and feel) at the point of execution, alone; then it is too late.

Planning is the conductor's business; executing is for the players and the conductor to achieve together as a result of that planning. The up-pulse

(two) at bar 4 sets up the conductor's physical rhythmic explosion in bar 5 where the down pulse is all that is really important; the second pulse in this measure and the down pulse in the next [6] hardly need be given, so the conductor is out of the way once things have gotten started; after all, what can any conductor do after executing its beginning?

But the conductor must be there with a carefully-prepared second pulse in bars 6, 8, 11; and the first one in bar 10 as Russell Bennett pushes his syncopated developments at half and double speed [5 to 11] with a rhythmic escalation culminating in the big sounds [11]. It is a real harmonic climax too, this A-over-E♭ triad combination. There the score and parts do not show the obviously *forte* dynamic that the composer has baked into his music; it should be added to both, as should a vertical line before the last eighth in bar 11 that indicates to all the separation of that sound from what precedes it.

If the conductor gives a vigorous and precise second pulse, that may help to bring off the big sound in question. I have always found it necessary to build up the sound of the B♭ in this chord. Once he gets there the composer again suspends the pulse — this time over the bar-line. The strong confirmation of his idea, now stated in 3 octaves, leads to the simplicity of the traditional 4-bar vamp that sets up the tune's first full statement at [1].

These first 21 introductory bars are as neat a commercial package as one is likely to find. Their architecture is charming, wonderfully proportioned, their harmonic and rhythmic content satisfying, intriguing, and faithful to purpose; the scoring is superb.

The music at [1] seems to work best in rehearsal when the conductor establishes security in the accompaniment prior to combining that with the tune, establishing crisp and resonant on-and-off beat patterns in the score's bottom line to be mixed with their extremely legato counterparts in the reeds scored in the top line. I have grown to favor a doo-doo — da-doo-doo articulation for the tune in the brass with special emphasis on the soft-textured eighth in the middle of the syncope.

Once again, an easy rocking motion, side-to-side, is suggested to impart the spirit of the music. If the conductor is not inhibited but subtle in his motions, the group rarely fails to respond to this

---

The Score

The condensed score is a genuine frustration. The conductor, who must have all information, is denied it. Its continued publication as the only score available is an open invitation to dishonesty, an insult to intelligence that must dominate study and control performance. The information it withholds, the knowledge it denies, the music it buries within its ignorant outlines is a denial of the search for truth and the pursuit of knowledge that lie at the root of all education.

ff

immediate imparting of the style, and should the conductor prefer to stand erect and motionless, the group should still be urged by him to adopt a loose rather than a tense posture in what they play. The two eighths following each syncope must always be placed and separated with utmost care. The sustained low B♭ which ends the two cake walk statements, never to return this way again, benefits from being blown in a fat sonority by cornets, baritones, and trombones. The conductor's role in this section should be unobtrusive tending of the rising legato triads in the reeds, shaping the sounds with appropriate, small horizontal motions. When the character of the music changes at ②　the bright modulation to E♭, doo-doo becomes tee-tee; and rhythmic ensemble problems begin to appear. The sixteen bars after ② present several challenges (see example 2):

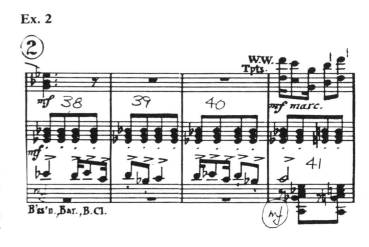

Ex. 2

1. Cakewalks and ragtime have as part of their fascination the sometime avoidance in the melody of synchronous juxtaposition of their rhythm with that of its persistent one-two accompaniment [50 to 54]. The syncopes generate forward-feeling motion here and elsewhere, obliging players and director to avoid any rushing by careful observance of all note values and by extremely careful placement and separation of the two eighths (see example 1) however they appear.

2. Reeds and trumpets (and conductors) might avoid the tendency to jump into bar 42 by adding the vertical line before that eighth, and then to refrain from rushing ahead in the ragtime rhythm at bar 45.

3. As that line continues, the answering sixteenths in the cornets [46 & 47] must be of full value and without hurry; when these same instruments go on to comment on the cakewalk figures with their tied eighths and quarters, it is desirable to soften the texture of these octaves; accents like these (∧) appear for the first time in the piece and generate harsh properties of intonation and quality, unless they are softened. It may be desirable to remove them altogether.

4. The galoping syncopation so solidly scored [50 to 54] invites solid playing, with every accent emphasizing the sticky character of each attack, culminating in the added crescendo over the four sixteenths with which this development is concluded.

Form of "Cakewalk"	
Bar	Section
[1-21]	Introduction
[22-37]	A
[38-57]	B
[58-68]	A
[69-91]	C
[91-97]	bridge (from A)
[98-129]	D
[130-139]	bridge #1 (from A)
[140-147]	bridge #2 (from D)
[148-166]	bridge #3 (from D)
[167-186]	A
[187-208]	B, plus extensions
[209-228]	D plus extensions = coda

The composer withdraws [54-57] from this high point by way of an extension of his first vamp [18-21]. This connection passes through what should be a four-bar diminuendo from the *forte* that is almost hidden in bar 46. The conductor's two-pulse pattern should reflect the shape of this diminuendo. If this is conducted as it is expected to be played, a proper and satisfying bridge will be made between musical ideas. This leads to Bennett's compressions of the cakewalk idea [61-66]. He taunts listeners and challenges interpreters with his back-and-forth play between B♭ and E♭ [61-66]; we have to help everybody out by building up the dynamic of the baritones in these measures to at least *forte*. This line furnishes the inner core to an intriguing passage that finally becomes his third musical idea, but only after he has arrested all motion with the big D pedal in horns and baritones; don't rush into this attack too soon, either, and do spread the diminuendo over both bars.

Here is another moment when the conductor can refrain from the usual big one-two/up-down motion of hand or arm: the pulse must be kept with clarity as the conductor's descending arms and hands join the diminuendos, but the physical action should be as sparse as is the composer's music.

Dynamics need clarification at ③ triads in the upper-line reeds should be *piano* (the tune in the middle is *mezzo-forte*) and the bottom rhythmic accompaniment should also be adjusted to *piano*. *Forte* should be a surprise at bar 61 as should the new material at bar 69.

The conductor has the chance to launch the new idea by providing a particularly expressive down pulse at bar 69, inviting the players by this action to produce equally expressive music, vibrant and legato, throughout the eight notes. Add a line above this first eighth and avoid any percussive quality in the attack. The floating legato feeling (try *dolce*) suggested for these first eight notes (here and at bars 77-79) may be contrasted through a positive change in the character of the five notes that follow. Remember that Bennett's accents are within the *piano* dynamic while giving the five note phrase a little kick.

The next four bars at ④ and their succeeding development [81-84] should be clarified in score and parts as being *pianissimo* and with that same floating and expressive character previously suggested, except for the baritones who must play with a strong *mezzo-forte* as they remind us that this is a cakewalk; their figure must come through.

If we are lulled into the dreamy state, we are awakened [85] with the big tutti version of bars 69-71. The conductor, joining the action with a precise first beat followed by the appropriate legato must be aware of the ensemble's need for a firm hand in these six bars and at their equally vital terminal [91]. I have always found it helpful to write accents (shown as > in example 3) in all instruments carrying the two upper lines and to emphasize the length of the quarter note at bar 90.

Full value in that quarter note aids ensemble at bar 91, avoiding any hurry coming into the cakewalk rhythm that follows. This is another point at which that rhythm becomes hard to handle when the players rush ahead; once again, the "cool" approach helps to avoid that. The diminuendo approaching ⑤ is difficult to achieve, possibly because of the energy that is generated between the reeds and trumpets as they alternate the cakewalk rhythm at the *forte* level.

The following bars introduce new musical material (his 4th idea) in the spirit of the initial cakewalk as the composer spins out an augmentation of that resource in rich, sonorous harmonies, above which dart continuous cakewalk fragments. Once the conductor has established the tutti *piano* dynamic through the diminuendo to ⑤, all that is necessary from the podium is careful maintenance of pulse and balance between all the forces providing these very pleasant sounds; large and heavy conducting is not appropriate here. The accents in bars 105 & 107 are expressive rather than percussive, and the important D to C/D to C♭ [110-113] scored for brasses in octaves should be projected beyond the printed dynamic. The rise in

Ex. 3

106

sound to bar 116 should fall again in bar 117 so that the greater crescendo and decrescendo prior to 6 makes its full effect; all bass instruments should raise their dynamic level here to match their solid accents.

The quality of tone in the sustaining reed G♮ at this point is enhanced when the accent is removed, but the matter of its customarily sharp intonation needing the careful attention of all players must allow for the diminuendo which should be added to all of these parts two bars before 6; then all should observe the dynamic of *piano*.

The two statements at 5 & 6 where the initial cakewalk rhythm is superimposed upon its augmentation provide convincing evidence that the articulation suggested in example 1a is desirable for the ensemble. When the two rhythms are combined, players on the top line are obliged to match those on the bottom. The tendency of the top line to rush ahead when playing the articulation in example 1b becomes apparent immediately. Thus, it seems it might even be desirable to begin the rehearsal of the main idea of "Cake Walk" at 5, rather than at the first bar of the piece.

This is frequently my practice with music which has rhythmic difficulty common to most of the group or when a stylistic characteristic is exposed at the music's beginning in a single instrument or in a section, later to be played by all. I do it to give confidence to the players. The security which is to be experienced when all share a common problem can sometimes hasten its solution. I even begin pieces at the end rather than at the beginning just so that all may know the goal toward which we must work.

Measures 128-147 are developmental extensions of earlier ideas presenting no problems save to keep the sixteenths moving [132, 133 & 136, 137, 138] by adding arrows pointing forward in these bars. It is also idiomatic to add the accents in bars 138 & 139.

Ex. 4

Ex. 5

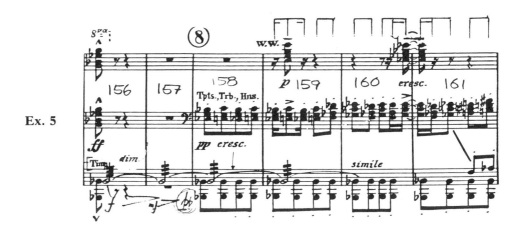

All the brass playing the *fortissimo* E♭ major statement of Bennett's 4th idea [149-154] should do so in great sostenuto up to bar 155 and then drive their short eighths to bar 156 as the kettledrum's dramatic roll sets up the next developmental extensions. The diminuendo in the roll should be made specific in both the score and part (see example 5). The extension at 8 presents a rhythmic ensemble challenge to all of the reeds, piccolo down through alto clarinet. The problem is when to play and how long to make the sound. I believe it should be long and the visual aid suggested above the top line in example 5 has proven to be useful in this syncopated melee. It helps the player to know what the other rhythms are, providing security rather than chancy stabs in the musical dark.

As "Cake Walk" is working toward its goal at [11], it seems desirable for the conductor to make certain minor adjustments in the dynamic structure to heighten the arrival of that climax: [10] begins *forte* as printed; subito *piano* at bar 199 with crescendo to *mezzo-forte* [200-203] when the crescendo begins in earnest over the next 6 bars, with ultimate crescendo in bars 207 & 208. The very slightest, quickest musical breath before the climactic A♭ chord at [11], plus the ultimate accent, serves to heighten this exciting moment. If the conductor paces the approach to it with appropriate physical manifestation of the sound, he usually finds the group ready to provide it. The rising chromatic scales [221-224] played in crescendo above the driving bass line lead to the final cakewalk flourish. The composer has led the listener so carefully that audiences invariably applaud on impulse at its conclusion.

Concern for listener reaction, and thus for the most successful presentation of the music offers this possible re-ordering of the five movements: III-IV-V-II-I; when a shortened version of the suite is desired, try III-II-I. After conducting this music for a quarter century I'm convinced that "Rag," the listener, and the *Suite* benefit from re-order.

One of the critical shortcomings of this condensed score is the absence, save for two indications in "Cake Walk," for instance, of any percussion information, including the vital kettledrum solo [225-226] at its conclusion. But what is happening in percussion textures in this whole suite is so vital that the conductor is obliged to write its music in the white spaces of the score, however scarce and irregular they may be.

Reference in movements 1, 3, and 4 to "muffled" (snare drum) means to release the snare strainer and to play with a wood drumstick. Time does not allow the engaging of the snares in "Cake Walk" at bar 148; use a tom-tom. The bass drum's low frequency reinforcement of the last eighth in bar 11 demands low frequency tuned heads. Bennett's brush on the snare drum (or cymbal) is barely audible at [4] in the large groups that play this piece, and so it might be desirable to substitute the stick played lightly on top of the cymbal, *piano*, about four inches from the edge.

At the time the score was published the notation (now passé) always indicated a cymbal sound, crashed or suspended, and so it appears frequently in the percussion parts for this piece, first at bar 85, and frequently throughout. In Bennett's calligraphy I think it always means suspended and choked. A popular technique among set players in the 1920s was to place a stick in the left hand and hold it under the cymbal, pressed tightly up against it with the thumb. They would release the tension with the left hand when they struck the cymbal with a stick held in the right hand, and then would squeeze the left thumb-held-stick against the plate. This created that additional zap from the stick which made a distinct "zizzly" kind of sound. It is most appropriate here and elsewhere throughout the suite when these cymbal notes marked ♪ appear. The important kettledrum roll and diminuendo [156 & 157] needs to

Percussion

The drum set has become a standard part of the ever-expanding percussion profile in today's concert band, wind ensemble, pep band, and at orchestral pops concerts. Today's set player has unlimited facility (which strangely is not always applied to stand-up percussion), peerless technique, and that all-important total control producing a variety of percussion sounds in the hands and feet of a single player. This person also usually provides his own superior equipment, including a variety of well-tuned non-snare skins and a host of plates, all in appropriate sizes and timbres.

Section playing as a substitute for what Robert Russell Bennett has written in this piece is usually a cloddy corruption of those sounds when produced by a facile pit drummer — the player I think he had in mind. A compromise between the set and the section works well. The conductor can work up any variation of the following:

• All suspended cymbal and snare drum parts to the set player, with the use of his bass drum and hi-hat to add to the rhythm — but only as two-beat, on-off playing.
• Concert bass drum for the solo places, especially, and throughout as desired, but with the drum free of damping devices.
• Crash cymbals reserved for the great climaxes, coordinated with the set player.
• Small things like sandpaper, triangle, and two blocks shared by two section players.
• Vibraphone, glockenspiel, xylophone by a single section player.
• Kettledrums by that player.

In my set I provide these seven players with seven carefully annotated and identified published parts.

ff

be clarified at the bottom end of that diminuendo as being *piano*, and the roll is more effective when it does not fade too soon. Amidst the happy din of bars 167 to 170 the snare drum must be cautioned against burying everything else, and the bright triangle roll which follows [171-174] should be tied. When the suspended cymbal heightens the chromatic scales [221 & 223] a big 22" ride cymbal is what the textures demand; obviously, the score must be annotated to identify the kettledrum solo in bars 225 & 226, and the final eighth in bar 228 must be dampened quickly by all percussion. Two corrections must be made in the score. At bar 105 the G♭ is misplaced; remove it and then add the flat before the E. At the first eighth note in bar 115 add the flat to the first G, bottom line.

II. Schottische: (89 bars) $\frac{4}{4}$ Moderato (in two or fast four)

I have preference for the latter pulse (four, c. ♩=132) which holds the performance precisely together. The composer needs no introduction for this tune with which the piece begins and ends. The attractive music and its superb scoring that occupies the middle of this basically three-part form provides a period piece in the style made popular by radio dance bands such as that led by Larry Clinton.[4]   Any quick analysis of both the harmony and its instrumentation shows Bennett's skillful use of the octave in doubling the voices that produce these pleasant sounds.

```
Form of "Schottische"
   Bar      Section
[ 1-30]      A
[31-42]      B
            (31-38 B¹; 39-42 B²
[43-48]      C
[49-64]      B material
            (49-52 fragment, 53-64 B plus development
             and B²
[65-79]      A
[80-89]      Coda
```

If the clarinets can produce a sonority at the beginning and at [5] that resembles sub-tone[5] an effect once used extensively in commercial popular music, it will be appropriate, if not necessary, to the style. Low brass and sandpaper are the simple accompaniment. The two sand blocks are played with quick, short, opposite motions of the hands, covering no more than 1-1/2" to 2" (up & down) with the two blocks never being separated — the string player's martele stroke of the bow. Bennett does not say so, but to me the presence of the sandpaper and the charm of the music has always added up to a great soft shoe dance. Players have the tendency to reach the downbeat of the 4th bar too soon, and should the conductor wish to avoid this here and in bars 11, 22, 68 & 74, a short vertical line placed just before that bar line frequently helps. Avoiding yet another visual inconsistency, a line placed above the final quarter note (upper staff instruments) in bars 13, 15, 77 & 79 assures its length.

The xylophone's effective color [27-28] must come from the hardest mallets, and all reeds and brass that play the three-note flare at bar 29 should surely place it before the beat. The bass drum's bump on the 4th pulse of bar 30 should be damped.

Now comes the Larry Clinton sound from [2] all the way to the end. When things are played loose in all that follows, it seems to come off much more successfully than when they are played tight — especially all sixteenths, the eighth-note triplets, and the quarter notes which should be played "wet" rather than "dry"; the half notes need to be articulated. Experience urges caution against a common visual/aural error in bars 31, 32, 33, 35, 37, 53, 54, 55, 57, & 59 where the eighth note should not be caught up in the sixteenth note patterns that precede it; put a line above those eighths to achieve distinction and length.

All remains basically sonorous and "wet" until bar 61 when shorter articulation becomes the way

of the triplets as all make the greatest crescendo to the subito *mp* at [5] when the blocks[7] and sandpaper return. As the "Schottische" ends, the brass and reeds in [88] should be asked to provide a vibrant, resonant eighth before the reeds gurgle their way to its conclusion.

This is the sort of music a conductor can really enjoy if that is the inclination. Mostly what we might do is to keep that pulse clear and small, to lay back and then join the action when that seems to be the call; this is fun music! For it there are these corrections: 1st clarinet, bars 15 & 79 — correct the written G to G♯, last quarter note; E♭ clarinet — the *pianissimo* is missing in the four sixteenths at bar 26; all percussion — add *forte* to the down pulse at bar 29; clarinet III at bar 77 — correct the written F♮ to F♯ on the sixteenth notes; flutes I & II, score and parts, bars 39 & 49 — correct the last triplet to read G♭ - F♮ - E♮.

III. Western One-Step (242 Bars) $\frac{2}{4}$

The composer informed me that this is also a dance known as the "Texas Tommy," an obviously bright-eyed tune with an equally bright-eyed tempo (ca. ♩ = 132), *Allegro ma non troppo*. That zizzly stick-under-the-cymbal type sound (quickly choked) launches this music in exactly the proper 1920s spirit. Here the conductor must give a very precise initial beat and continue to emphasize the first pulse in bars 3, 5, 6, 7, 8 & 10. After six rhythmic and harmonic feints at the three eighth-note figure (basic musical mucilage in this piece) R.R.B. tops the introduction with the seventh of these figures, laying down three ever more rich harmonies to do it: A♭₇, G₇, and G♭₉ plus the E♭ that was there from bar 1. The harmonic changes on the way must be stressed, but it is vital that the players should hear each chord in bar 9 slowly and separately, leading to the terminal c minor at [1] Syncopation is dominant in the tune of this dance as it was in "Cake Walk," but the rhythmic underpinnings come from the jazz pianist's left hand and the reach to go with it.

```
Form of "Western One-Step"
   Bar       Section
[  1-9  ]     Introduction
[ 10-35 ]     A
[ 36-67 ]     B
[ 68-97 ]     C
[ 98-118]     B
[119-148]     D
[149-188]     E
[189-204]     B
[205-220]     Coda (A fragment plus B fragment
               in major)
```

After joining the action already described, the conductor can reduce participation at [1] to small pulse keeping with great attention to dynamics, textures, and the steady, driving movement of the rhythm. But, as always, what the conductor cannot reduce is constant listening — listening to and for everything. And this music is so pleasant to listen to as the conductor's part in the music making follows its rise and emphasis, its fall and shade. When the third of the "One-Step's" five separate and very charming ideas unfolds at 4 the conducting is most effective if it can be in the smallest motion. One must possess unusually cool conducting skills to be able to catch those last eighths that tantalize in bars 77 & 79, 93 & 95 without causing more trouble to the ensemble than such a move may be worth. For the big sounds at 5 it is frequently more desirable to join the A-C-Eb-G chord (look out for a sharp C here) sustained in the upper reeds then punctuated by all [101, etc.] than it is to work at the bottom-staff music for baritones and trombone.

One way for the conductor to try to achieve subito *piano* at bar 114 is to hang with the up-position of the second pulse in the previous bar, making almost no following motion until the big five-octave C that begs *fortissimo* participation as "Western One Step's" large third idea gives way to the fresh chamber-music-like fourth idea. Again, the conductor who withdraws to simple but precise housekeeping duties will find that the built-in propulsion of the music, along with first class listening, does most of the conducting all the way to 7 where one might then join effectively in producing the flare in the reeds (get them to open it up) and the solid block ensemble sounds that follow.

Just following the sights and sounds on these pages, matching their vertical and horizontal contours, provides us with ample guides to conducting. "Less can be more" is frequently the music director's best conscience; and the theory is eminently applicable to the long build-up of the piece's initial idea, now returning at 10 as the beginning of the coda. And when all these repetitions and accumulations have led us to the kettledrum's dramatic contribution [221-222], we conductors might still simply join the action that follows rather than to superimpose ourselves upon it. We are very much needed to control the great diminuendo [235 to the end] that does not necessarily happen without us, but which is so vital a part of this effective ending to a very exciting piece of music.

These few corrections match the parts to the score: horn IV, bar 10 — correct the rhythm as in the score; piccolo, flutes, oboe I, Eb clarinet, bar 149 — make it *forte* as well as *sforzando*; score, bar 176 — on the bottom staff *piano* is missing as is *forte piano* in bar 179 and at innumerable other places on the bottom staff throughout the suite where the copiest neglected to include any dynamic or nuance; horn I, bar 196 — a flat is missing on the quarter note B; trombone II, bar 237 — correct notes to C-B-A♮-A♯; alto sax II, bar 238 — correct the 3rd eighth note to a written B♮.

And here are a few additional suggestions for the conductor: edit the quarter notes throughout so they are long; the brush on the cymbal is inaudible with any but the smallest group, so try a drum stick played lightly on top at bars 70, 71, etc.; re-

mind the xylophone player that R.R.B. means hard mallets regardless of dynamics at bar 67, etc.; the passage at bars 132-135 can be played by the piccolo and flute if there are ensemble problems with the trumpet; at bars 205 through 208 start the diminuendo from a *mezzo-forte*; urge the kettledrummer to play bars 221-222 with one hand, not to dampen the eighths [223, 225, 227, 229], and to alter his C to Ab at bars 234-235, playing the ornament before the beat.

IV. Wallflower Waltz (122 bars) $\frac{3}{4}$ Tempo di Missouri Waltz[8] (in three).

The music and the spirit of its title add up to me as a tempo of circa 96-104 to the quarter note. A goodly amount of air support is demanded of the flute player and this plus excellent rhythm must come from the English horn (or oboe) as Russell Bennett does a superb job of melodic wandering, seemingly in search of a tune (or its key center) in this simple and sometimes dangerous introduction. This material (which also serves as the coda) is not used elsewhere. The squareness that is inherent in the dotted-eighth/sixteenth figure which dominates here seems to call for a slight ritard and diminuendo that the composer assumed, perhaps, a sensitive conductor might wish to contribute before he embarks on the waltz itself. At the resumption of the tempo at 1 these matters are of concern to the discerning band director:

1. Establish the balance and blend between the muted brass and the clarinets; as to blend, the conductor has the option to play with or without vibrato, and here it seems most appropriate to opt for the cool, non-vibrato sounds of what used to be called close harmony; all sounds in the top two staves must be played to their maximum notational value with no diminuendo from anybody and with tasteful modification of the accent ($\wedge$) into a soft-tongued articulation. The sixteenths [25-32] should be *leggiero* in character and played close to the coming note.

2. For balance one must look closely at the parts and condensed score to discover where the tune is in this voicing. It is complete only in the top line of the solo & 1st cornet part, which should blow as the lead voice, the one to which all others should listen. Portions of it are in the 2nd and the 3rd clarinet, but their sounds are secondary to the lead cup-muted cornet which plays the tune in example 6.

3. Bennett's scoring for the waltz's traditional one-two-three is left simply to the first three horns, the tubas, and the string contrabass; no additional instruments are appropriate here. He avoids the obvious resource of any percussion instrument and assigns the rhythmic role very effectively to tubas and horns with the added fillip of the string contrabass which, I submit, is more effective as a resonance here and necessary as a rhythm when played *pizzicato* and the dynamic raised to *mezzo-forte*. Let all notes vibrate; *arco* is obviously appropriate from bars 32 to 44 with *pizzicato* again in the cadence [46 & 47] and return to *arco* the 3rd beat of bar 47, the rest as printed. Be

Ex. 6

certain that the horns play a resonant staccato at [1] that upholds the space Bennett has placed between each eighth note. As the fourth of the six ideas in "Wallflower Waltz" concludes, it is appropriate to delay the diminuendo until its final bar [46].

	Form of "Wallflower Waltz"
Bar	*Section*
[1- 16]	Introduction = A
[17- 24]	B
[25- 32]	C
[33- 46]	D
[47- 62]	E
[63- 98]	F
[99-122]	Coda

The conductor knows whether or not the tempo chosen for the first idea at [1] is the right one when the performance arrives at bar 55 with its following sparse material and a waltz with no oom to go with 43 bars of pah-pah while the composer enjoys himself with eight literal restatements of the same 4-bar tune. The piece ends with the vibraphone's five notes that might be marked in the part as "on cue" so that the conductor may dictate them at will.

V. Rag: (200 bars) alla-breve, Gaily, in easy two (= c. 100).

Easy is the word here, but not as an adjective describing the grade of the music, for, as all who have ever played it know, this is anything but an easy piece. What Robert Russell Bennett has in mind, I think, is an easy, loose character in the overall sound of the whole piece; avoid speed. This might mean precision without a feeling of regimen, togetherness that is a feeling as well as an intellectually-ordered response — knowing where you are in the music without worrying

about what is keeping you off those four basic guideposts in every bar, and having the faith in this feeler instinct that it will not only keep you out of trouble but will reward you gloriously for having tried to join it.

Cakewalks and ragtime are so tied in to the evolution of jazz that all of us who conduct can hardly remain uninformed of that history.[9] And it is, for many people, still basically an aural history, with stylistic evolution and performance characteristics being difficult to document with mere words or musical symbols.

Our inadequacies as players, teachers, and conductors begin showing up at bar 10 where any tension that may be present is certain to bring on more. The conductor who chooses an articulation that sounds something like "dah" with a soft d, rather than one that sounds like "tee" may find that the first step has been taken to loosen up the players and establish the style. And then if any rushing ahead can be avoided in the gathering storm of eighth notes leading to [1], the major challenges of the introduction can be met.

The rag (or ragtime) rhythm at [1] is an educational encounter of the first kind. Among several approaches to this problem/opportunity are these three: (1) plow right in with what is printed at [1] and let the eighths fall where they may; (2) begin with sectionals or one-on-one instruction; (3) teach everybody to sing the entire rag in unison/octaves in their own voice and at the most convenient register.

I prefer number 3. "If you can't sing it, you can't play it" was never more true than here. Those who have difficulty with this rhythm seem to benefit from a patient process of orientation to the figure itself prior to its superimposition on the basic two-pulse of each bar; try reorganizing it into two bars of $\frac{12}{8}$ (see example 7).

Ex. 7.

Ex. 8.

Ex. 9

At the outset of any process of orientation to this ragtime rhythm it is critical to avoid an accent on the first of the three eighths, no matter how they are organized.

For those who relate to numbers, the study shown in example 8 can be added to your ragtime pedagogy.

To bring the entire band into the problem, copy example 9 and distribute it to each player; don't put it on the chalkboard, for they must learn to associate the study with what they see on their music stand.

Remind everybody to "keep cool" as you first of all teach those who need to know how, to make the phonetic sound ("phono") of the three slurred eighths. After the whole study is thoroughly under control, the two-pulse should be established. Hand claps or finger snaps do this effectively. It is important that the instrument be laid aside so there will be neither technical nor tonal distractions.

After much giggling and a few hilarious breakdowns, the conductor can usually move into the serious achievements of the study. At first, everyone should conquer the top line. As it progresses, the study might be executed; with the ragtime being carried only by those whose band parts have the ragtime; the rest of the band would sing what is on their band parts. The following is a suggested order of happenings when the phonetic approach is adopted: (1) begin by saying the "da-dl-a" in monotone, being careful then and thereafter to have all observe the dynamics and to avoid accenting anything; (2) add pitches if the players can do so; (3) sing what is written for everybody at 11 ; (4) play at 11 ; (5) listen to my recording[10]; (6)pray.

The second portion of "Rag's" first complete statement [25-42] does not necessarily play by itself, but compared to those difficult seven bars at 1 it seems to. All should retain the loose character within the precision of these next bars with particular care to observe the difference between two similar-looking passages (see example 10).

"Rag's" second major section in this three-part form begins with a basic two-bar jazz ostinato that is repeated sixteen times, above which two very attractive ideas are set forth. The infectious low brass ostinato is all the encouragement that conductor and players should need. The ear will tell you what to do in bars 51-58 and in bars 69-74. Grace notes sprinkled into the third extension of section B are to be played in a highly expressive, non-percussive fashion.

As for the conductor's function in this music, the composer has helped us all by making it rather conductor-proof, as is the nature of the popular idiom. But we are needed in the four-bar crescendo approach [85-88] to the return of the rag at 6 , just to keep everybody from rushing into its difficulties, which are formidable enough without hurrying.

Extending the rag figure, prior to presenting his third idea, Russell Bennett demands the most solid, full-value, heavily accented control from all the low brass [105-112]. Here the conductor can easily become a liability rather than an asset if any movements are too large or if more than a simple, clear two-pulse is what is offered to all the players.

Comes now Bennett's third musical idea, the necessary contrast to all the great rhythmic driving we have enjoyed in the first two sections of his rag. If the conductor is again withdrawn, tending to balance, texture, nuance, and offering minimum but effective pulses, the music tends to

Ex. 10.

take care of itself until the short bridge in the clarinets that connects the two parts of section C. In addition to using appropriately small, disconnecting gestures, the score and parts should be edited to assure separation of the figures, as follows:

Ex. 11

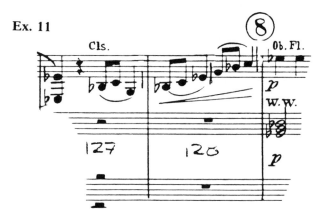

I've seldom heard enough sound in the bass clarinet line at bars 134 through 142. Taste rules the passage, but the dynamic must be raised. Using the solo baritone to lead into the bell-like triads, Bennett moves his flute and oboe solo of bars 129-143 two and one-half octaves down to the low, low brass, continues to the bells, and inevitably brings back the rag to be faithful to his form, and thus brings to fulfillment a very charming and happy piece of the band's basic literature.

Corrections and Suggestions: On the score, identify the octave on the top line, as solo & 1st clarinet, 2nd & 3rd clarinet; and show the entrance of eighths [10] as clarinets 1 & 3, top line

Form of "Rag"	
Bar	*Section*
[1-16]	Introduction
[17-36]	A¹
[37-42]	bridge
[43-58]	B¹
[59-68]	B²
[69-88]	B³, plus extension
[89-100]	A²
[101-112]	A³
[113-128]	C¹
[129-142]	C²
[143-160]	C¹
[161-176]	bridge
[177-200]	A² and A³

[12] clarinets solo & 2nd; the vital descending quarters at bar 28 should be labeled 1st alto and 2nd cornet; at bar 52 check the pitch for flutes, oboes, and clarinets (F♯-E♮-E♭); and at bar 189 add the rehearsal letter 12 .

E♭ clarinet part, bar 17 — a slur is missing on the last 3 eighths; 2nd oboe part bar 22 — correct the third eighth to B♭; 1st trombone part bar 107 — remove this extra measure; 1st flute part, bar 111 — correct the 1st note from A♭ to B♭; 1st bassoon part bar 180 — correct the rhythm by converting G to G♭ quarters into eighths; snare drum part bar 197 — the roll is missing from the last eighth and the following quarter.

Use a very articulate kettledrum stick at bar 3, and don't dampen the suspended cymbal or kettledrum too quickly at [1] and succeeding places.

1. Richard Rodgers' music for "Victory at Sea," the great World War II documentary was another of Bennett's remarkable enhancements of minimum materials supplied by a colleague.
2. Karl L. King (1890-1971) wrote marches the same way, working only from the solo cornet part which he wrote first; propped up in front of him at his writing desk, he then filled in the rest of the band out of his head. One summer in the early 1950s I watched on two successive mornings at his office in Fort Dodge, Iowa as he wrote most of the parts to *Tiger Triumph*, carried on business in the music store and regaled me with stories of his life in the circus — all at the same time.
3. Gilbert Chase, *America's Music from the Pilgrims to the Present*, McGraw-Hill, 1955, pp's 439-440.
4. Leo Walker, *The Great Dance Bands*, Howell-North Books, 1964, p. 78.
5. A clarinet sound on the very threshold of audibility (usually played into a microphone) — very breathy and mostly limited to the chalumeau register. Multiple players can provide this sound very effectively if it is requested.
6. Garnet paper #80 (9" x 11") is recommended. The coarse grit is necessary for projection. A very workable and speakable

pair of sand blocks can be made at minimum cost by cutting the paper in half at the 5-1/2" middle, and mounting it with upholstery tacks on two pieces of p;ine 7-1/2" x 9-1/2" x 7/8".
7. Two temple blocks played with soft rubber mallets or a piccolo block and a regular wood block played with hard xylophone mallets may be used here.
8. Harry S. Truman of Independence, Missouri, 33rd President of the United State, was in office when Bennett (also from Missouri) wrote this music; Truman liked to play the piano for fun and his favorite piece was *The Missouri Waltz*, well known then because of him.
9. Among many highly informative texts on this subject is the following paperback edition: Marshall Stearns, *The Story of Jazz*, Oxford University Press, 1977.
10. The recording which The Eastman Wind Ensemble and I made on May 14, 1953 is still available in its most recent reissue on Mercury Records Golden Import series #SRI 75068. This debut recording holds a record for professional symphonic recordings that has not been equalled or surpassed: 43 minutes of marketable music for 80 minutes of recording time — less than two takes for each of the six titles.

October, 1979

Russian Christmas Music

Alfred Reed

I have always believed that a composer speaks best, if he must speak at all, in (or through) his music rather than about it; certainly he should be wary of attempting to explain it in words. Inasmuch as Russian Christmas Music *is successful as music, very little expository comment is required, except perhaps some historical and biographical material to include in the inevitable program notes. However, the suggestion that perhaps an article dealing with this work from the composer-conductor's point of view might be of some practical assistance to others engaged in studying and preparing it for performance, seems to me to have a good deal of merit. The following observations, therefore, dealing with my own experiences with this music as a conductor, are offered in the hope that they may be of some help to others.*

First and foremost, as always, must come the matter of tempi, which in my view lies at the heart of all successful interpretations of every kind of music ever written and performed, be it a 32-bar pop tune, a 5-hour music-drama, or anything in between.

The troublesome fact is that there really cannot be one, absolutely cast-iron, unchangeable tempo for every work under every possible set of performance conditions, even with professional groups. Such matters as the size of the group, the ability level of its members, and the acoustical conditions under which the performance will take place, all play a part in determining the tempo to be taken at any point in the music. I'm assuming that the overriding desire of the conductor and players is not just to play the work, but to perform it so the audience can always hear with maximum clarity and ease what the composer wishes them to hear. This objective can be surprisingly troublesome. Arturo Toscanini once said (and not in jest, either) that every piece has three different tempi: the tempo the conductor decides on when he is sitting quietly in his studio studying the score; the tempo he takes at rehearsal; and, finally, the tempo he actually takes at the performance.

I have repeatedly found that when a large band plays in a resonant hall, the faster sections must be taken just a shade slower than if the hall were "drier" (less resonant). The change has been necessary not because the players were unable to play the passage clearly and cleanly, but because the audience could not hear it clearly. Conversely, the slow passages played in a very "dry" hall might need to be taken a bit faster in order to maintain smooth sostenuto because the hall will not provide the reverberation that helps to produce a feel-

Alfred Reed is professor of music at the University of Miami, where he holds a joint appointment in the theory-composition and music education departments, and supervises the music merchandising degree program. He has over 200 published works and his role as a guest conductor and clinician has taken him to 46 states, Europe, Canada, Mexico, and South America.

ing of sustained, unbroken tone. Under such varying acoustical conditions, any conductor who would insist on playing such passages at the exact metronome marking given in the score, thinking that he would be doing the composer a service by remaining absolutely true to his stated intentions, would actually be doing him a disservice instead.

Metronomical, exact tempi may be useful in the practice studio for development of technique and rhythmic concentration; but except for dancing and marching, or interpretively, to give the idea of soulless machinery in action or feeling, they should not have, and cannot have, any place in living, breathing, human-feeling music. This is the whole philosophical point: soulless as against soulful, mechanical as against human.

A Vocal Concept

The *Russian Christmas Music* is based throughout on actual liturgical themes or carols and original material conceived in the spirit of that musical language. The Eastern Orthodox Church (of which the Russian church forms a part) admits no instrumental music in its services, believing that one should worship only with the human voice. Therefore it is obvious that literally every note, every rhythm, every melodic, harmonic, or rhythmic inflection in this score should produce an impression of singing, regardless of texture or tempo. After all, is not the human voice, basically, a wind instrument also?

This vocal concept becomes the key factor in the proper approach to interpretation of this music (I am tempted to say, of all successful music as well, from any period), and every passage in this score should be conceived as being sung by either a soloist or massed choirs.

The composition is in four connected sections, opening with a re-harmonized setting of an old Russian Christmas carol, the "Carol of the Little Russian Children." The feeling here should be one of gently, somewhat restrained movement. I have attempted to indicate this feeling by suggesting a divided three-beat, with the eighth-note at approximately 72 on the metronome; however, I would not fault any conductor who takes this section (up to measure 13 at least) somewhat freely: for example, holding on to the final quarter note in measures 4 and 5 and again in measures 9 and 10 just a shade beyond strict tempo in order to build up the small crescendi and the change of chord each time, rather than playing them mechanically, exactly in the basic beat. I have also found it expedient to beat the first three measures in a slow three, because nothing actually moves here except the chime notes. As a conductor, I indicate each of these with an entrance cue to help the chime player establish his pedal note figure as quickly

and painlessly as possible. Then, with a divided up beat on the last beat of measure 3, the rhythmic pattern beginning with the theme in measure 4 can be readily established for those instruments entering at that point.

Of course all eighth notes in this entire section, from measure 4 through 31, must be long eighths, whether tongued (legato) or slurred, and never cut short at any time.

At measure 13 the tempo should be picked up slightly and no rubato indulged in until the ritard in measure 21. Although the passage could be taken in a broad three-beat, I would still subdivide the first beat only in each measure except the last, so the eighths and sixteenths do not sound rushed, despite the slightly faster tempo.

At measure 22 we return to the original tempo, and maintain a divided beat, as formerly, even in the broad cadence passage in the brass beginning at 26 and extending for the last two measures of ¾ tempo. The effect intended here is of a great, organ-like swell of tone underneath and around the stationary pedal point in the 1st trumpets, which is then answered by the woodwind choir, as an echo effect, in the last four measures before measure 32. It is important to note that the main melodic line in this brass passage lies in the 2nd trumpet, 1st cornet and 1st trombone; because this line is not in the uppermost sounding part, the conductor must take pains to make certain listeners can hear it clearly, and without effort.

---

35 Years of Progress

Needless to say, I was pleased to see that the *Russian Christmas Music* has been included in the high school band category of "The Instrumentalist's Basic Library" (July 1979, page 19), all the more, perhaps, because the work will be celebrating its 35th anniversary this year. It was first performed in December 1944, and has been active in the repertoire continually since 1948, despite the fact that it remained in manuscript until 1969, when it was finally published [Sam Fox, 170 NE 33rd St., Fort Lauderdale, Florida.] No better indication of the success of the music program in our schools and colleges need be given than the simple fact that when this work was offered to one of our leading publishers in 1948 after it had been selected as one of the three prize-winning scores in the 1947 Columbia University sponsored contest for new, serious music for the symphonic band, it was politely rejected with a note to the effect that very few, if any, high school bands in the country could undertake a piece of such length (about 14 minutes) and such difficulty (in the key of D major concert). Now, today, we find this music chosen for high school bands to consider as part of their basic library. Surely this situation must be gratifying to all of us, not just the composer, and something for all to take a justifiable amount of pride in having seen develop in this country.

A.R.

116

I have found that beating the last four measures before measure 32 in a simple three and then four-beat pattern will help hold the final long cadence together just a bit better; there seems to be no need to subdivide any of the beats here.

The big crescendi of the timpani and suspended cymbal should not begin until the first beat of the final ($\frac{4}{4}$) bar before measure 32; after the cut-off of the woodwinds, horns, and baritone on the second beat of this measure, the conductor may make a ritardando, if he wishes, to prolong the percussion crescendo a bit, and permit the timpanist and suspended cymbal player to develop it to a greater extent than might otherwise be possible, and thus make the entry of the next section even more exciting. However, the crescendo should not be overdone to the point where the trombone entry at measure 32 even though a solid forte, will sound weak by comparison with the timpani cymbal roll; the rolls are designed to lead into the trombone statement of the theme, not to take away from it.

At measure 32 the marking for the trombones is *marcato ma sostenuto*, and my experience with this passage leads me to stress the fazct that marcato does not necessarily mean cutting short note values; it refers only to the quality of the attack. Thus, the problem with this trombone passage at measure 32 and again at measure 43 is to combine a marcato attack with a full sostenuto on each note (particularly the quarter notes). Here again, the question of tempo will rest with the ability of the trombone section to not only combine the marcato attack and sostenuto of the notes, but to do so with a consistent forte that retains its sonority throughout five full measures (in one breath!) and does not begin to die away until measure 37 . . . and then not all at once, but gradually, over the next two full measures. When this phrase returns at measure 43 the forte sostenuto must be maintained for an ever greater length of time, because although the number of measures remains the same, two of those measures have been enlarged to $\frac{3}{2}$ time.

In contrast to the trombone line, the answering woodwind, saxophone and horn line (joined by cornets the second time), although equally sustained in nature, demands a legato tongue attack ($\flat$ $\flat$ $\flat$). The problem here is for the listener to be aware of six attacks on the same tone (the second time, eight) with no spaces between them. In my experience this effect has not always been too easily achieved by various performers, despite the apparent simplicity of the texture.

The slight ritard two measures before measure 55 is more easily achieved if the conductor begins to beat four on the third measure before measure 55 (but without making any ritard at all in this measure, merely changing from two to four so the basic quarter and half notes will sound the same in length), and then begin the ritard in the second bar before measure 55. Taking one thing at a time will enable the players to bring off the effect with a little less effort. If desired, the conductor can also hold the final chord before measure 55 a

shade longer, to enable the diminuendo in the brass to come down even more, depending on his taste, before beginning the next section.

Throughout this next section, from measure 55 through measure 85, the half note is the established basic beat, and should be taken only as fast as the shortest-note patterns — the sixteenth note groups in the woodwind and saxophones beginning at measure 67, and the trumpet-trombone interjections beginning at measure 77 — can be played clearly and cleanly. Even though these patterns may be considered as of secondary (even tertiary) importance in the general texture, they must sound clear or else no matter how fast the tempo may be taken, the music will actually sound slower to the listener. The phenomenon is caused by the ear trying to slow down an unclear performance in an attempt to hear it better. The effect is purely psychological, of course, but the net result to the listener is the same: uncertainty. What the conductor and performers are attempting to achieve is a brilliant effect of velocity that the ear can grasp without effort.

A Difficult Feat

I consider the eight short measures from measure 55 until measure 63 to be one of the most difficult passages in the whole work to bring off with the full effect intended, particularly at the indicated tempo (or faster). The problem here is how to progress from a quiet beginning through five canonic imitations (the last four coming just one measure apart) and at the same time build up volume to just the point where the outburst of the trumpet-trombone choir comes at exactly the right dynamic level, as a climax to the whole section. Accomplishing this feat will require the most careful adjustment of entrances and crescendi by each of the instruments or sections making each of the thematic entrances, and a final "last gasp" crescendo by the flutes, oboes, English horn, 2nd B♭ clarinets, alto saxophones, horns, and 1st and 3rd cornets on the last three counts of the measure before measure 63.

Also, in each of the various entrances throughout this section, the first quarter note has a line under it, to indicate that it is to be atttacked gently, sustained for full value, and never cut short in any way. When the theme bursts forth in the brass beginning at measure 63 the same articulation is needed, but even more so. The quarter notes are held full value even though they are now strongly attacked (*sempre marc.*) each time; only the eighth notes are slightly cut in order to allow a little air space between them, and thus give a feeling of lift and movement despite the heavy sound of the full brass. From measure 63 through the first half of measure 71, the main melodic line is in the middle-low register of the 2nd and 3rd trumpets; it must not be allowed to disappear, especially because the 2nd and 3rd trombones are playing the theme with them not in parallel harmony (as the 4th trumpet does), but in contrary motion a good portion of the time. The 1st trombone, playing the main melodic line an octave lower than the 2nd and 3rd trumpets, is designed to strengthen that line, but experience has shown, particularly in younger bands, that it too has a tendency to disappear. (Players must be taught to move more air through their instruments as they play in the lower ranges if they expect to remain at the same dynamic level, let alone make a crescendo.)

When the theme returns at measure 76 with full woodwinds, saxophones and horns, the quarter notes must once again be held for full value and the eighth notes cut slightly. The bells and xylophone should be played with hard mallets to make their etching of the melody as distinct as possible. Of course, the cornets should hold their chords at no more than a forte level so the theme can be heard without effort. The trumpet-trombone interjections on the other hand, coming as they do in between the phrases of the theme itself, can be strongly accented at a true fortissimo. When played on the proper instruments and mouthpieces in the proper style, the difference in weight and color between the trumpets and cornets can be heard distinctly.

At the climax of this passage two measures before measure 86, the trumpet-cornet chord must be attacked *sffz* and then dropped immediately to forte (not lower) so that the *fff* trill in the woodwinds and saxophones may have time (a full measure) in which to establish itself in the listener's ear in all its brilliance, before it is overcome by the molto crescendo of the trumpets and cornets in the last measure before measure 86. The long timpani roll in G beginning at measure 63, despite the fortissimo marking, must never be allowed to swamp any of the lines above it. There is even an indication of a little less forte at measure 76 to be sure the themes in the relatively weaker woodwinds, saxophones and horns come through. The exact dynamic level of this continued roll, to provide a background of excitement and motion against the remainder of the texture, must be left to the conductor's discretion; then the final crescendo, three measures before measure 86, can be as big as the timpanist's ability will permit. Most important of all, though, is that the roll give the impression of fast motion; there should be as many strokes of the sticks as possible, regardless of dynamic level.

From measure 86 until measure 118 we have a transition passage linking the second and third sections of the work, which introduces a new theme played by the solo English horn. The passage can be beaten throughout or the conductor can permit the player some leeway in the interpretation of the two solo passages, especially after the low woodwinds drop out on the first beat of measure 93. Both approaches can work; the one used will depend on the rapport between soloist and conductor, as established in rehearsal. In my own performances, I usually indicate only the first beats of each bar from measure 93 through measure 97, while the soloist is permitted to develop the line a bit freely, like a cantor would in singing a passage to his congregation. If this approach is followed, I suggest beginning to beat strict tempo once again at measure 98 so the entrance of the

flutes, piccolos, oboes, E♭ clarinet and triangle at measure 99 will be firm and convincing. The same procedure should be followed for the repetition of the phrase, beginning with the second entrance of the English horn solo at measure 105. Here again, after the accompanying lines drop out, the solo line may proceed freely until measure 113, at which point the conductor will once again beat clearly, beginning with the downbeat of that measure, so the entrances on the third beat of the measure will once again be firm.

The Third Section

The third section, beginning at measure 118 ($\frac{6}{4}$), is one long song, written mostly in two-measure phrases, to be delivered as smoothly and flowingly as possible, with never a bumpy entrance, shortened notes, or a break in the legato sound of the various lines. The six-beat melody must flow at all times, and the actual tempo taken will depend in large measure on the ability of the string bass players, to execute the long walking bass line with continual smoothness, precision, and clarity of sound. The several crescendi and decrescendi written in the string bass part are there to emphasize certain important changes of direction of the line, as well as to indicate the harmonic relationships between the line and the chordal texture above it. They should be observed carefully so the line will never sound monotonous or (as in the passacaglia) like a ground bass that continually repeats itself and hence is of relatively little importance after the first one or two hearings, except as a basis for the tonal structures erected above it. This section could even be considered as two-part counterpoint with a third added line: the melody in the top voice, the walking bass, and the bass of the chordal texture itself.

In measures 128-129 and again in measures 132-133, the function of the walking bass line is taken over by the bells; the change of color and register of this line serves to throw the passage into high relief momentarily, before the first part of the song is repeated with instrumental variations at measure 134 and the walking bass resumes its original position and color in the string bass(es). Here again, the overall tempo must, in part, be decided by the ability of the percussionist playing the bells to be able to enunciate the line clearly and without loss of fluidity.

The decrescendo in the last three beats of measure 141 should be sufficient to allow the solo oboe, coming in with the pick-up phrase to the next measure, to be heard clearly, without having to force the tone.

The third section really comes to a close in the G-major cadence chord in measure 150. The next 15 measures, a transition passage to the final sections of the music, are based on the melody played by the solo English horn. Again, the passage may either be conducted throughout or played freely by the soloist, with the conductor merely indicating the first beats of each bar during the solo until the final two measures before measure 166. A continuous beat must be established beginning with the downbeat of measure 166 so the entrance of the horns on the third beat, and their subsequent change of notes may be firm. A small point, but one of some importance here, is that the conductor should be careful not to hold the fermata on the final measure before measure 166 too long, or else the English horn player may literally run out of wind and end his phrase before the all-important downbeat of the next measure.

The fourth, and final, section of the work begins at measure 166 with a 22-measure crescendo that is achieved both by introducing more and more instruments into the musical texture and by increasing the individual dynamic level. The percussion section dynamics require the most careful control in order to maintain a feeling of mounting excitement and tension as the masses of tone of the different choirs are added, but still to avoid peaking too soon and thus creating a feeling of anticlimax when measure 188 is finally reached. Once again, the proper tempo is of the utmost importance in enabling all of these things to be done with full control and no undue strain. The rhythm of the chimes and bells must be absolutely firm and steady, and the roll on the deep timpani must again contain many individual strokes, despite the pianissimo required here. The crescendi on the phrases in the trombones alone, and then the trombones and horns together, must be very large, beginning as soon as the tone is struck and continuing steadily up to the fortissimo.

Although the timpani crescendo is indicated as beginning in measure 177, where the roll merges into a steady triplet rhythm, it must be carefully controlled in its growth so the forte at measure 185 is neither reached too soon nor becomes so loud that the interchanges of choirs and lines above it are swamped in its sound.

At measure 185 the tempo is picked up slightly, and the fanfare-like figures in the trumpets, trombones, and cornets must each cut through the moving harmonic masses, each one making a larger crescendo until the downbeat of measure 188 is reached.

The conductor must make certain that the basic beat here at measure 188 ($\frac{4}{4}$) remains exactly the same as in the preceding three measures ($\frac{6}{4}$) even though the measure grouping changes. I have found it a bit of a problem at times, especially for the timpani, to maintain the same basic beat while playing the duplets at measure 188 immediately following 11 measures of triplets. The effect here is of a broadening of feeling even though the basic tempo remains the same. The broadening is already written into the music so the conductor should beware of attempting to broaden the feeling still further by slowing down the beat itself. I do not believe it will work even half so well that way, and, besides, the slower tempo will almost surely cause unnecessary strain on the brass who are asked to play forte sostenuto in the chordal hymn commencing at that point.

The ritard leading into the subdued middle section chorale at measure 200 must not begin until the downbeat of measure 199, after the downward rushing sixteenth-note figures of measure 198 have been completed, a procedure that will help

the execution of each of those figures and insure a smooth connection from one group of instruments to another where this is required by the ranges involved. Once into measure 199, however, the ritard may be as broad (or as little) as the conductor in his judgment may wish.

A Powerful Piano

The chorale beginning at measure 200 should be taken only as slowly as the various instruments and choirs involved in these relatively long phrases can manage them without loss of beauty of sound in the piano and pianissimo required. There is no excitement at this point in the score due to rhythmic motion or fast-moving lines, the harmony returns to a simple modal combination of intervals, the colors are subdued and the tempo is slow, but the sound, the tone, must still be alive, vibrant and sonorous, even though soft in volume. Brahms in his rehearsals used to ask the orchestra for "a right powerful piano, gentlemen," and this phrase stayed in the minds of quite a few of the players who heard it. The same applies here. Again, this is an effect not always easily obtained even with a professional group.

At measure 211 the music is at its softest, even softer than at the beginning of this section, and then gradually gathers strength during the next eight measures to begin the final section. Here again the goal is a carefully controlled, dynamic crescendo that peaks at just the right point: the entrance of the full brass chorale at measure 219.

In the last two measures before measure 219 we have an example of the doubling of the horns by the cornets, in an attempt to strengthen the former as they climb into the sky, and yet to permit their essential tone color to prevail throughout. I am convinced that this doubling of horns with cornets played with deep cup mouthpieces, will give the horns all the support they need without robbing them of that tremendously exciting and penetrating sound that they, of all the instruments, can produce in such climatic passages, and which so excites us when we hear it.

Although an accelerando is indicated in the score at this point, I have found that some conductors (including myself) have at times elected not to make the accelerando, and then attack the new tempo on the downbeat of measure 219, believing, no doubt, that the excitement of the horn line in the preceding two measures is enhanced by this holding back. Once more, I can only say that I have heard this done convincingly in the past; this option, like others discussed in this article, rests with the taste of the conductor.

From measure 219 to the end the general effect is that of two massed choirs singing antiphonally and then joining together for the final coda at measure 236. The tempo should be broad and never rushed, but with a feeling of movement nonetheless. The walking bass lines of the third section are briefly brought back here as an enhancement of the brass chorale and the woodwind/saxophone/horn descant; and the two measures just before measure 236 unite all three in a massive final cadence leading to the long pedal tone in pure, rhythmic, and ornamental forms simultaneously, while the trumpet-trombone choir reprises the opening of the fourth section as a kind of "Amen" with horn/cornet/saxophone interjections.

The tempo taken in this coda will once again be influenced by the degree of sostenuto attainable by the brass, and the maintenance of the highest possible intensity of tone throughout. In the final crescendo (next-to-last measure) the conductor may (if he wishes and his brass section is capable) make a slight ritard until the full growth of the crescendo is reached before the cut-off on the downbeat of the last bar.

With a large concert band I have found a second set of timpani, bells and chimes to be most useful in these last two sections of the score, particularly if they are set up on the opposite side of the group from the first, or main set. This second set of instruments can enter at measure 188 and play until measure 200, rest until measure 219, when they should be ready to enter again at measure 221 and then play, together with the first set, until the end.

The effect of the bells and chimes coming from both the left and right sides of the group, and the extra definition (assuming precise pitch and perfect coordination) of the second set of timpani strengthening the first, produces a most powerful impression, and certainly heightens the intensity achieved in these final portions of the music.

I am indebted to Don Marcouiller, for a most novel treatment of this music in its last section. The *Russian Christmas Music* has become an annual tradition, closing each season's Christmas concert at Drake University. Don has added a fine organ to assist in the long pedal notes from measure 166 through measure 196, and again from measure 236 to the end, and two additional sets of trumpets and trombones, as left and right antiphonal choirs in the organ loft, joining the trumpets and trombones in the band from measure 219 to the end, with the organ also adding its weight to the final cadence chords at measure 236. Truly a festive, brilliant, and jubilant sound. ∎

The Three Versions

Many of those who have read the program note printed in the score of the published edition have asked me just what differences there are between the three versions of the music: the original manuscript of 1944; the first revision of 1946, which was played in manuscript for the next 20 years; and the second revision, which became the published version of 1969, representing, presumably, my final word on the subject. Many of the inquiries have hinged on the question of whether there are many (or any) changes in the basic musical texture itself (its themes, harmonic and contrapuntal treatments) or whether the changes were largely those of instrumentation, or both. I am grateful for the interest such questtions have shown, but to answer them in detail would require another article as long as this one. Suffice it to say that there were just five minor changes in the basic musical texture itself, involving the addition of only two new measures in all, between the first revision of 1946 and the final revision 22 years later. All of the other changes were matters of notation and instrumentation, based on my developing concepts of what were the most efficient methods of getting the music to sound in performance.

The *Russian Christmas Music* was the work of a young man taking his first steps in writing large-scale forms for large-scale performing groups, and represented his first major work for concert or symphonic band. His experience, plus the pressure of having to produce a score of such dimensions in a little less than two week's time, may explain his later desire to improve the notation, instrumentation, and even a little of the basic music. All of this was possible when the rush of immediate events had passed and he could review the work with a bit more coolness and

objectivity in the light of his own later experience with it in rehearsal and performance. All composers at some time in their careers experience the same feelings when they look back on their earlier work, thinking they could now improve the piece. But both Brahms and Stravinsky, who attempted to do this with earlier pieces of theirs, pointed out afterwards how dangerous it is for the older master to tinker with the work of the younger apprentice where truly creative efforts were involved. For some 20 years I resisted the attempt to revise the first revision of this work; but when the opportunity to have it published came along, I felt I had to make some purely technical adjustments of notation and instrumentation to make matters easier for the conductor and players; but changing the basic music itself was something else again, and very few changes were made. If it becomes a question of changing the basic texture in order to improve it, as both Brahms and Stravinsky soon realized, where does one stop? To completely recompose the younger man's work might very easily (in fact, probably would) create a substantially new and different work; and in the process some of the very essence of the piece, including that which originally gave it its charm and claim to attention, might be lost.

So the *Russian Christmas Music* remains almost exactly the same work it was when commissioned less than three weeks before its first performances. It is the work of an ardent, music-drunk, young composer whom I have some difficulty in recognizing these many years later, but who continues to be grateful for the numerous expressions of gratitude and enthusiasm from thousands of performers and hundreds of conductors since, to say nothing of their audiences.

A.R.

Some Remarks on Berlioz' Symphony for Band

BY C.B. WILSON

The *Symphonie Funèbre et Triomphale* of Hector Berlioz has been the subject of numerous comments in these pages in recent years. Today, there should be little doubt about either the merit of the work or the significance of Berlioz' contribution to the nineteenth-century repertoire for winds and percussion. Questions have been raised, however, about the historical roots of this symphony. The purpose of this article is to show that the *Symphony Funèbre* is representative of Berlioz' style as well as illustrative of the French tradition in the 19th century.

Berlioz' Symphonic Output

Although Berlioz was practical, conservative, and very much "in the mainstream" in a number of respects, there are numerous contexts in which he could be considered an innovator or experimenter. His innovative qualities can be readily observed when one attempts to categorize his output generically. The works of most of the significant classic or romantic composers can usually be catalogued without difficulty: so many symphonies, so many sonatas, so many quartets, etc., with a relatively small number of pieces left over to be designated "miscellaneous." It is much more difficult to do this with the Berlioz works. The editors of the *New Berlioz Edition*[1] have tried to meet this challenge by using somewhat broader classifications for most of his output (secular works, sacred works, orchestral and instrumental works, miscellaneous vocal works), with only two specifically generic categories: operas and symphonies.

Even the category of symphonies, however, encompasses a variety that one does not typically encounter in the works of other major composers. Although they all bear kinship to the term, each of the four works that Berlioz called "symphony" has a distinctive premise: (1) *Symphonie Fantastique*, a program symphony for orchestra; (2) *Harold in Italy*, a program symphony for solo viola and orchestra; (3) *Romeo and Juliet*, a "dramatic" symphony for solo voices, chorus, and orchestra; and (4) *Symphony Funèbre et Triomphale*, a ceremonial symphony for military band, later revised to include string orchestra and chorus.

Some critics have been reluctant to admit that the *Symphonie Funèbre* can be legitimately termed "symphony." Obviously, its three-movement scheme does not adhere to a strict "text-book" definition. However, the fact that this symphony, like the other Berlioz symphonies, is a unique, one-of-a-kind composition, simply confirms the imaginative creativity of an artist who let his purposes shape a work, rather than the conventions of his time.

C.B. Wilson is Executive Assistant to the Dean at the Cleveland Institute of Music. He holds a Ph.D. in musicology from Case Western Reserve University and has taught in all fields of music.

Some Historical Matters

Details concerning the composition of the *Symphonie Funèbre* can be found in numerous sources, including the forward to the score provided in the *New Berlioz Edition* and William Workinger's article in the December 1969 issue of *The Instrumentalist*. For purposes of the present article, it is important to note that the content and scope of the work were influenced by certain external conditions. First, the work was commissioned by the French government for a particular ceremonial occasion, with each of the three movements playing a specific role in the ceremony. Second, the nature of the ceremony dictated the musical forces available, namely a military band. In short, and regardless of possible earlier sources of inspiration, the work as it stood in 1840 was not conceived as an artistic abstraction for an idealized performance medium in the concert hall; it was composed to implement a patriotic event, for execution out-of-doors by a large ensemble of military musicians performing on wind and percussion instruments.

The Symphony's conception as a work for military band is clear upon examination of the manuscript (but not entirely autograph) score. Types of instruments and their order in the layout of the score are typical for military compositions of the time: D♭ piccolos, E♭ flutes, E♭ clarinets, B♭ clarinets, oboes, natural horns (various keys), natural trumpets (various keys), valved cornets (various keys), trombones, ophicleides, bass clarinets, bassoons, and percussion (including *Pavillon Chinois*). Of particular interest in this type of score layout is the placement of oboes after clarinets, and the grouping of bass instruments, which places bass clarinets and bassoons after ophicleides.

Various aspects of the Symphony's scoring were no doubt affected by Berlioz' use of this standard military layout. One probable instance occurs in the finale at m. 97, the point at which the texture consists of three lines. In the original score, each line was assigned to instruments written on adjacent staves: line one, staves 1, 2, 3, and 4 (piccolo, flute, E♭ clarinets, B♭ clarinets I); line two, staves 5, 6, 7, 8, and 9 (B♭ clarinets II, oboes, horns); and line three, staves 17, 18, 19, and 20 (ophicleides, bass clarinets, bassoons).[2] This common Berlioz procedure, known as "layered scoring," would certainly be affected by the type of score layout used. Additional examples of this procedure are found throughout the work, and include the scoring of the opening melody of the first movement.

---

1. *New Edition of the Complete Works of Berlioz* (Kassel: Bärenreiter, 1967).
2. In the modern edition, the stave grouping is 1, 2, 4, 5; 3, 6, 10, 11, 12; and 7, 8, 19.

Performances of the Work Conducted by Berlioz

Berlioz, in addition to his many accomplishments as composer, critic, author, and impressario, was of course also one of the first significant nineteenth-century conductors. He conducted the Symphony in whole or in part on 20 separate occasions between 1840 and 1855. In the Official First Performance, which took place on July 28, 1840, the first and third movements (both marches) were played several times as the procession moved to the *Place de la Bastille*. The middle movement was performed during the ceremonial blessing; and the final rendition of the last movement was obscured by the now-famous commotion by the troops of the National Guard. Approximately 200 musicians took part.

Of the nineteen performances after the première, only three featured the entire work with band alone. Twelve of the nineteen utilized orchestra and chorus in addition to band, and the last twelve apparently did not include the first movement. To interpret these facts within the context of the time, Berlioz probably found the Symphony (generally without the first movement) to be more satisfactorily executed by a combination of winds, percussion, strings, and voices than by band alone. Of course, it is quite possible that this was due to the fact that his concerts were usually *orchestral* concerts, which, when the situation demanded, could be augmented by additional winds, solo voices, or chorus. Had he been a conductor primarily at *band* concerts, other circumstances would have prevailed, and the statistics would permit different observations.

Berlioz did not conduct the Symphony during the final twenty years of his life, although he continued to perform his earlier symphonies until the end of his conducting career. The final tour to Russia in 1867-68, for example, included performances of the first three symphonies, but not the *Symphonie Funèbre*. Whatever the reason for this (perhaps to be able to pay more attention to later works such as *Damnation of Faust,* perhaps because in certain situations the work would have been inappropriate), a comparison of the number of performances of the Symphony to those of other major works suggests that the band composition was not really slighted. For example, the popular overture *Roman Carnival,* written four years after the *Symphonie Funèbre,* received approximately the same number of performances under Berlioz' baton.

Some Sources of Berlioz' Style

Berlioz championed Beethoven in a number of ways, as critic, author, and conductor among others. As a composer, he was greatly inspired by Beethoven from the time of the performances of the master's symphonies at the *Conservatoire,* beginning in 1828.

No fewer than eighteen examples of Beethoven's music appear in Berlioz' *Treatise on Instrumentation* (by comparison, none appear in Rimsky-Korsakov's treatise). Further, the *Symphonie Fantastique* can be linked to the five-movement scheme and the programmatic aspects of the "Pastoral" Symphony, *Harold in Italy* can be associated with the Seventh and Ninth Symphonies, and *Romeo and Juliet* (with soloists and chorus) clearly drew inspiration from the Ninth as well.

The evidence of Beethoven's impact upon Berlioz is quite clear, but it would be misleading to suggest that Berlioz, by virtue of his admiration for Beethoven, had rebelled from or rejected the French tradition. This is particularly true in the case of the *Symphonie Funèbre* and other "architectural" works, and is a view strongly supported by Brian Primmer in a recent publication dealing with Berlioz' style.

> How much Berlioz' music was a part of his native tradition, how deeply national rather than nationalistic it was at all times, can be seen by even a cursory glance at the scores of some of his predecessors and contemporaries. The massing of large forces in contrasting and complementary bodies, vocal and instrumental, was one of the commonest textures of the Revolutionary Period...Patriotic compositions for two, three or four choirs and orchestra were a commonplace of the time. There is nothing original in conception about the layout of Berlioz' *Te Deum, Grande Messe de Morts* or *Symphonie Funèbre et Triomphale.* Indeed, the opposite is the case. Since they were all destined for great national occasions, what else could a truly French composer do?[3]

Numerous composers participated in the establishment of this tradition, including such notables of their day as Gossec, Grétry, Méhul, LeSueur, and Reicha. *François Joseph Gossec* (1734-1829), for a time conductor of the National Guard Band and one of the most important composers of his time, has been identified as a "revolutionary" and a "republican" composer. One of several works he composed to commemorate the revolution, *Le Triomphe de la Republique,* was a band piece scored for piccolo, flutes, clarinets (in C, Bb and A), oboes, bassoons, horns, trumpets, trombones, drums, and cannon. Like Berlioz, his output included a *Requiem,* a *Te Deum* (which required 300 winds and 1200 voices), and a Christmas oratorio, *La Nativité* (which utilized an "invisible" chorus of angels backstage).
André Ernest Modeste Grétry (1741-1813), a Belgian living in Paris, was known mainly as a dramatic composer. His interests, however, extended to the impact of physical space upon musical effect, as well as the use of music for public and ceremonial purposes.

3. Brian Primmer, *The Berlioz Style* (London: Oxford University Press, 1973), pp. 4-5.

Étienne Nicolas Méhul (1763-1817), who was admired by Beethoven (and who therefore perhaps caused the Germanic tradition to be distilled by that of the French), composed several pieces for band. Among his contributions are those associated with instrumental color and effect; one example of this is the opera *Uthal* (1806), in which violins are omitted entirely. Like Berlioz, he was influenced considerably by Gluck.

Jean François LeSueur (1760-1837) and *Anton Reicha* (1770-1836) were both teachers of Berlioz at the *Conservatoire*. Of the two LeSueur was more closely associated with music for the republic, and, like his contemporaries, was interested in the effects of physical space and large forces. Both men experimented with instrumental color: among other examples, one can cite the twelve harps in LeSueur's opera *Les Bardes* and the eight timpani in Reicha's work for double chorus and orchestra, *Die Harmonie der Sphären*.

All of these composers are relegated to a few lines (at most) in the currently standard music history texts. Their impact upon French music was considerable, however, going far beyond the brief remarks made here. As contributors to the French tradition, they significantly influenced Berlioz' style in general and the *Symphonie Funèbre* in particular.

Berlioz' Style as Illustrated in the Symphonie Funèbre

The stylistic aspects of the *Symphonie Funèbre* can be ascertained by examining the way in which various elements have been employed in the work by Berlioz, and its Berliozian qualities can be determined by the relative consistency with which he utilized these elements in his other works. Although a number of musical elements could be isolated for analysis, these remarks will focus primarily on some aspects of melody, harmony, rhythm, and orchestration.

Melody

Among the melodies used by Primmer to illustrate that which is "characteristic" of Berlioz are the two principal themes of the first movement of the *Symphonie Funèbre*.[4] Like the *idée fixe* from *Symphonie Fantastique*, these two melodies have several interesting features, including their unusual length, their lack of strict symmetry, and their organic growth. The first theme (m. 4) is nineteen measures in length and analyzed by Primmer as being in phrases of 2, 2, 2, 4, and 9 measures respectively. The second theme (m. 95) contains thirty measures in eleven units of 4, 2, 2, 5, 1, 4, 3, 2, 2, 2, and 3 measures. The unusual length and asymmetrical construction of these melodies are closly linked to the matter of organic growth. In other words, the use of a variety of techniques to extend the basic figures or patterns of the melodies results in the need to stretch the boundaries of the common, square, eight- or sixteen-measure units one might expect in the works of less original composers. After brief reference to the fact that the first melody is later expanded to a twenty-four measure unit, let us turn to the equally interesting melodies of the second movement (Examples 1, 2).

The melody of Example 1 links the recitative portion of the movement with the main material shown in Example 2. The seventeen measures of the first example (in four phrases of 4, 4, 4, and 5 measures) bear similarities to the first theme of the first movement: there is comparative "squareness" in the opening portion with expansion in the second half; a significant portion of the second half consists of a gradually rising line leading to a climax; and of course there are the more obvious relationships of the dotted rhythmic patterns and the melodic skip of a fourth.

The second melody (Ex. 2) is by far the longest of those examined here: 44 measures. Like its counterpart in the first movement, this is the more complex of the two melodies in this movement with twelve phrases in a pattern of 4, 4, 4, 4, 3, 4, 3, 4, 4, 2, 2, 6. Similarly, its length offers opportunities for more than one climax. However, the orchestration of the second half of this melody presents an interesting difference; the shifting of colors between soloist and ensemble rather than the more static quality of a single timbre on the melody throughout produces a kind of kaleidoscopic effect.

The melodies found in the final movement are much less irregular, probably due to the more martial, "apotheosis-like" character. The main tune (Example 3) is most notable for its early pitch climax, two wide and expressive leaps (of a seventh and a sixth respectively), and the similarity of its opening line (a diatonically descending fourth) to portions of the second movement.

Each of the melodies described has Berliozian characteristics, and yet they are each very different. To indulge in one other passage by Primmer,

> Berlioz' melodies are extended and asymmetrical because these characteristics are part of their very nature. The expressive character of his art demands it so. He is not out to astonish...but to express, in wholly musical terms, the plentitude of contrasts which taken together make up Life as the Romantic felt it.[5]

---

4. *Ibid.*, p. 18 *ff.*
5. *Ibid.*, p. 43.

Harmony

Like all musical elements, the term "harmony" has a number of implications. Here, three facets of harmony will be touched upon: (1) the "vertical" structure of individual chords; (2) the "horizontal" matter of chord progression (or chord succession) and its relationship to melody; and (3) the broader aspect of key relationships. In each facet one can sense a "characteristic" approach by Berlioz.

The vertical structure of Berlioz' chords is amazingly conventional. In the *Symphonie Funèbre,* as in his other works, he employs mostly simple triads, dominant sevenths, and diminished chords. (Today, Berlioz is sometimes accused of over-using diminished sonorities, but no doubt the effect was more dramatically successful in his own era.) Chord resolutions were at times more unconventional, but this falls into the realm of the second facet, chord progression.

Chord progressions are among the most interesting

of Berlioz' procedures, and although almost always logical (often, however, with a nod to the logic of *linear* writing), they sometimes defy standard, "functional" analysis. In this regard, some critics have insisted that he did not understand or know how to write conventional progressions. On the other hand, one can say that he started with the same basic chords and used them in a more expressive way; in other words, he broadened the system.

Berlioz often altered the harmonies of a specific melody or fragment upon its repetition, a procedure one might call harmonic development. The recapitulatory statement of the second theme of the first movement is illustrative of a more traditional procedure: it is harmonized exactly as the earlier expository statement (although the key, of course, has been changed). In fact, most of the thematic recurrences in the Symphony, including those of the march tune in the finale, bear unchanged harmonizations. In this sense, the work is more conservative, more in the Eu-

Example 1. Symphonie Funèbre, Second Movement, mm. 40-56.

Example 2. Symphonie Funèbre, Second Movement, mm. 58-101.

Example 3. Symphonie Funèbre, Third Movement, Main Theme.

124

ropean "mainstream," than some of Berlioz' other compositions.

The key relationships of the Symphony mix traditional procedures (in a general context) with more "characteristic" Berlioz techniques. In the first movement (F minor), the expository statement of the theme in the relative major is traditional, while the recapitulatory statement of this theme and the coda in the tonic major are more Berliozian. A move to the subdominant (B♭) for the opening of the second movement is traditional, in contrast to the less-conventional shifts within the movement (to E minor, E♭, and G). The change from G to B♭ for the finale is typical for Berlioz and a common procedure (modulation by third) for the entire Romantic Period. The sudden shift near the end of the movement to A major before closing in the home key of B♭ is dramatic and highly characteristic of Berlioz.

Rhythm

The significance of rhythm in Berlioz' works has been discussed by a number of writers.[6] However, it is difficult to point out any consistency in Berlioz' rhythmic usage beyond the appropriateness and skillful manipulation of the rhythmic aspects of a particular piece.

In the *Symphonie Funèbre* the rhythmic configuration of ♩ ♫♩ ♩ (and its variants) in the first movement has been frequently cited. Beyond the obvious musical unity obtained thereby, one can also comment upon the sheer practicality of using this ostinato-like figure to set and sustain the cadence of the march. Other, more subtle, rhythmic procedures can also be discerned. In the rather short "development" section, the "tune" given in the bass instruments is rhythmically telescoped from three measures to two and finally to one (mm. 125ff., 138 ff.), a device which heightens the effect of subsequent statements of principal thematic material (mm. 135, 148). The pace of the coda is subtly ritarded by the utilization, in the upper woodwinds, of sixteenth notes slowed to triplets, then to eighths (mm. 269-72).

The significance of rhythmic factors in the last two movements is less obvious than in the first. One interesting relationship is the persistence of a pattern of long-short-short or long-short values in the melodies of both the "Oraison Funèbre" and the "Apothéose."

Orchestration

The effect of the instrumentation and score arrangement of the Symphony upon some aspects of the orchestration was mentioned earlier in the context of layered scoring. Another contributing factor to this procedure in the Symphony was Berlioz' use of specific instrumental groups as units, which might fulfill a variety of functions. In most of his works, a delineation between strings, woodwinds, and brasses can often be observed. These units might be assigned to the functions of counterpoint, sustained harmony, and melody (respectively), although other combinations and function-assignments are also possible. In the Symphony the basic tripartite delineation

(in the absence of strings) was often high woodwinds, natural brass (horns and trumpets), and chromatic brass (often doubled by low woodwinds for bass strength). One such example in the first movement (m. 58) includes (a) flutes, oboes, high clarinets and bassoons, (b) horns and trumpets, and (c) cornets, trombones, ophicleides, bass clarinets and contrabassoon, as the three groups.

The gradual addition of instruments during a long crescendo to implement the dynamic change is common for Berlioz, and its inclusion in the Symphony is hardly surprising. A good example of this procedure is illustrated by the passage in the first movement at m. 14, which moves from soft to loud by m. 21 as nine different parts are added.

Another practice that occurs rather often in Berlioz' compositions, especially in the brass parts, is one in which an individual instrumental part is temporarily diverted from a unison or octave line to sound in harmony with the parts remaining on the line. The contexts in which the procedure occurs suggest a direct relationship to the physical and/or aesthetic limitations of the instruments involved. I have referred to this procedure as "compensatory harmony."[7] The employment of the procedure can be observed in several of the brass parts in the Symphony, and will be discussed more fully in a subsequent article dealing with performance problems in this work.

Although this "architectural" work by Berlioz is one which contributed to the allegation that he was always bombastic and required only large forces to achieve his ends, the Symphony is characteristic in yet another way. In spite of the large forces used, Berlioz required a full *tutti* only a relatively small part of the time. Even when the optional parts are excluded (contrabassoon, bass trombone, timpani, strings, and chorus), the full force of all instruments assigned to a given movement was employed in less than twelve percent of the total number of measures. For a work originally intended for outdoor performance, this is rather remarkable.

Some Conclusions

The information presented here clearly does not represent all of the stylistic aspects of the Symphony or of Berlioz' total output. There is enough evidence, however, to support the notion that the *Symphonie Funèbre* is a significant and characteristic example of Berlioz' style, showing both German and French influences. If the work has been overlooked, this is most likely due to (1) its existence outside of the *orchestral* tradition; (2) its nature as a ceremonial piece for a specific occasion; and (3) the absence, during most of its existence, of regularly organized ensembles of a size appropriate for its performance. Today, of course, most major college and university music departments could mount a performance of the work without any difficulty — for its historical interest as well as its intrinsic musical value. ■

6. One recent example is Edward T. Cone, "Inside the Saint's Head," *Musical Newsletter*, Vol. I, No. 3 (July 1971), pp. 3-12.
7. The procedure and its implications are treated in more detail in the author's "Berlioz' Use of Brass Instruments" (Unpublished Ph.D. dissertation, Case Western Reserve University, 1971).

A Rehearsal Analysis of
Praise Jerusalem!

BY HARRY BEGIAN

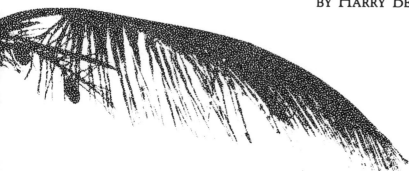

The work opens with a flourish on a rhythmic motive of three short notes followed by a long one. This important figure is recalled throughout the piece. After the conductor indicates subdivided preparatory eighth notes on counts three and four, the opening figure needs to be played with deliberation. The first note of the triplet should be clearly attacked with an accent. Cornets in duo rhythmically echo the opening figure of the first measure, followed by a flurry of woodwind triplets along with scalar runs in the bells and chimes. The bitonal sonority of the opening measures creates an ambiguous tonal center, which resolves to D minor in measure 4 as the horns and cornets play the opening phrase of *Kovia Yeroosaghem!* When the phrase ends in measure 8, fanfarelike interjections sound from the brasses through the crescendo and *sffz* release in measure 11.

After a long pause soli flutes play the hymn with a lightly textured clarinet accompaniment. Two oboes distantly echo the fanfare trumpet figures heard earlier. In measures 16 to 17 the oboes should imitate the trumpet's style while playing at a softer dynamic. In measures 17 to 18 the horn inversion of the trombone figures

Internationally known conductor Harry Begian is Director Emeritus of the University of Illinois Bands. He was a member of the music faculty of the University of Illinois from 1970-1984, and after a one-year retirement served as conductor of the Purdue Symphony Band in West Lafayette, Indiana for two years. He holds degrees from Wayne State University and a doctorate from the University of Michigan. Begian, who organized and conducted his first band and orchestra while in his teens, has appeared as a conductor, adjudicator, and lecturer throughout the United States, Canada, and Australia, and currently maintains a busy schedule with these activities. Last November he appeared as guest conductor of the Detroit Symphony Orchestra.

from measure 8, along with the D pedals in the vibraphone, timpani, and bass clarinets in octaves, should be heard through measure 20. The ornamented and delicate downward play of the oboe duet, measures 18 to 20, should be light and graceful but audible above the pedal. At the woodwind entry preceding measure 21, the composer departs from the hymn tune and uses original material to bring the introduction to a close in measure 30. The brief timpani solo, measures 28 to 29, ends with the now well-established figure of three short notes followed by a long one; it is answered by the chimes in augmentation, and then answered by a short eighth note, like a period at the end of a sentence, in the timpani and string bass on the third beat of measure 30.

With the introduction now complete, we hear the theme *Kovia Yeroosaghem!* in its entirety. The composer's setting of this ancient Easter communion hymn is in A minor. The mood and intent of the hymn are of joy and praise — "Praise the Lord, O Jerusalem; Christ is Risen from the Dead, Alleluia!" The music might better be played at a tempo of about ♩=72. A slower tempo, as indicated in the score, gives the hymn a melancholy air.

I should mention that the composer has exercised some license in presenting the *Kovia* melody. By excluding five measures of the original tune, he has achieved a compactness that enhances the original. The extended phrase endings with trumpet fanfares that Reed uses give the melody a length of 27 measures, instead of the 29 measures in *Chants of the Divine Liturgy of the Armenian Apostolic Orthodox Church.* Reed presents the hymn in homophonic style, ending it on a Picardy third, which is the same as sung in the Armenian Easter service. Underlying the final chord, the timpani provides the rhythmic movement into the first variation. Serving as a link, the timpani is important and should be heard as a solo.

The tempo indication at 58 of ♩=72 seems slow for Variation I, though ideal for the theme section that preceded it. To show contrast with the tempo of the theme and in keeping with the light, detached style of Variation I, consider a tempo of about ♩=92. The conductor should test for tempo choice by playing the first flute part, measures 59 to 67, and the alto saxophone solo from 67 to 74. This slightly faster tempo generates the necessary rhythmic propulsion, while being more compatible with the "lightly and detached" style requested in the score. After the diminuendo ending of the theme in measure 57, the hard, short accent from the brasses and percussion at measure 58 should come as a sudden surprise. Establish the new tempo immediately, locking in and maintaining it without deviation throughout this variation.

The solo saxophone entry at 67, in diminution, should start with an accented eighth-note anacrusis. The solo needs to be played with the same detached style established by the flutes at the beginning of this variation. The English horn and tenor saxophone will need to focus on projecting the thematic material so that they are heard in measures 71 to 76. The persistent sounding of sixteenth notes up to measure 78 gives the movement drive and vitality; these have to be clearly heard and played with rhythmic precision whenever present in the music.

New material based on a theme fragment appears at measure 78. This section sounds best when all the eighth notes are played for their full value followed by the lighter sixteenths. The phrasing of the flute line in measures 83 to 88 takes on more character if played as follows:

The ascending solo line of the alto saxophone should stand out against the descending flute line, measures 85 to 88, with tongued accents on the written C♯s in measure 88 as well as measure 89. Following the slurred sixteenths, do not allow the flutes and saxophones to slur into the half notes, or their arrival at measure 88 may be imprecise. This arrival may contribute to an equally imprecise entry of the sixteenth notes in measures 88 and 89. Muted trumpets and trombones should accent their entries on the sustained dominant pedal with a crescendo on concert E and resolution to A minor at measure 93.

At this point the clarinets play the flute line in A minor from the beginning of this variation. All the horns enter at measure 103 playing the opening phrase of *Kovia.* Cornets, oboes, and E♭ clarinet enter in canonic imitation before the horns complete their thematic statement. The material from measure 115 to 124 is basically the same as that in measures 78 to 88, with horns sounding forth the theme with an inverted ending, measures 124 to 127. The first horn, timpani, and vibraphone set up the closing section at measure 127 with driving sixteenth notes, while the tuba and bass clarinets sustain a pedal A. The trio of trombones are answered by trios of trumpets, clarinets, and flutes. As they move upward with staccato eighth notes and diminuendo, they should end pianissimo in measure 132 with the sounding of the triangle solo (a small triangle, please). The anacrusis of each group of four eighth notes, from trombones through flutes, should be accented in measures 127 to 132.

Variation II is a beautiful piece of writing. While appearing deceptively simple in its technical requirements, the setting offers a musical challenge to conductor and players alike. It demands slow, sustained playing of great musical sensitivity and expression. The tempo indication is ideally suited to the pensive, almost melancholy mood of the variation. It requires intense score study to ferret out the thematic fragments the composer has so artfully concealed. The rhythmic and modal changes bring out an entirely different aspect of the *Kovia* tune. Shown here are only four such transformations of the thematic material:

Without further discussion of Variation II, I leave it to conductors to decide how they will teach and direct this section. Espressivity is a subjective matter; no two conductors should be expected to feel or express a piece of music, especially a slow work, with the same tempos, nuances, dynamic inflections, or phrasings. These matters should be left for conductors to decide for themselves. Variation II comes to a cadential close on a Picardy third (as the Introduction did) and the clear pealing of the chime at measure 171.

After a brief pause the conductor should go directly into Variation III, which begins with a sharply punctuated, loud A in octaves in the brasses, as well as the saxophones and percussion. The dotted rhythm, the propulsive element throughout this variation,

should be sounded with an accented first note followed by short sixteenth and eighth notes, played ♩. ♪♪ , not ♩. ♪♪ . The crescendo in the 9/8 measure, with its scalar flourishes in the woodwinds, leads up to the fortissimo statement of

the cornet and woodwind figure, ♪♪♪ ♪. . The horn, trombone, and timpani, which follow in quick answers, should stand out boldly in measures 176 and 177 along with the bells and chime in octaves. The hymn tune in the trumpets and cornets should ring out boldly in marcato style with full value placed on the dotted-quarter notes. The counterlines and scalar flourishes, measures 178-185, should not take predominance over the thematic material in octaves in the trumpets and cornets.

The material from measures 185 to 194 functions as a transitional section leading to a variant of the *Kovia* theme in the English horn. For those bands without an English horn the use of either saxophone or cornet is optional. The dotted rhythm in the horns provides the rhythmic momentum beneath the English horn melody and has to project up to measure 201 along with the vibraphone in measures 194 to 201. The oboe's continuation of the English horn melody should sound as an extension of the theme, though with a definite coloristic change. The tuba takes up the dotted rhythm at measure 202 with the clarinets carrying the tune; important answers sound from the oboe and first horn, measures 202 to 205. The bassoon, tenor saxophone, and baritone counterlines in this same section should not be given prominence. The delicate melody in the flute, measures 205 to 211, is enhanced when played as follows (the horn quartet answering as noted in the score):

Apply these same approaches to accents and style in the clarinets, alto saxophones, bassoons, trumpets, flutes, and English horn between measures 222 to 231. Measures 232 to 235 serve as a transition; the music modulates, returning to the A minor tonality and dotted rhythmic figure heard in the beginning of this variation. The crescendo starting at measure 236 climaxes in the full band at measure 240, followed by full and clearly articulated answers in the soprano woodwinds in measure 240.

Measures 244 to 252 herald the approaching end of the movement, the closing section, measures 251 to 258. The section from 253 to the end of the variation should be played with abandon in bells and chime; the first trumpets play the *Kovia* motif as cadential material. From the strong material in A minor that ends the variation, the music abruptly changes tonal levels to E♭. A descending figure in low woodwinds, baritone, and tuba, as well as the cornets moving in contrary motion in measures 259 to 260, helps establish a musical mood for the variation to follow. The sustained sonority in measures 260 and 261 on the notes B♭, C♭, D, and E♭ provides the notation for the chime solo.

The score does not show a tempo indication after the poco rallentando in measures 260 to 262. I found a tempo of about ♩=40 appropriate for Variation IV. Obviously the solo instruments are scored to suggest the melismatic chants of a priest or cantor. The sounding of chimes and the sustained choirlike chords in the accompaniment set up a church atmosphere. The solo lines of Variation IV should be played rather freely, in the style of a cadenza, against the softly sustained chords of the clarinets. The conductor should indicate the chime entries with small motions of the left hand, as well as show the chord releases in measures 264 and 265 in the same manner. Follow the releases with an upward stroke of the right hand on the "and" of beat four.

The rhythmic figure in the solo clarinet at measure 266 should be played as follows:

The solo clarinetist needs to observe the composer's dynamics, especially the diminuendo after the sustained D, the high point of the phrase. The solo flute should enter with full sound and vibrato, then continue in the same style as the clarinet. The horn section entry at measure 267 recalls the trombone motif at the beginning of the work and needs to be played with short sixteenth notes and accented quarters.

The horns will need to project the *Kovia* motif so as to be heard against the solo flute. At the return of the solo clarinet at measure 272, the first two notes should be played deliberately. The phrase, played ritenuto, should elide imperceptibly with the ending flute F♯. The upward run in thirty-second notes needs to be performed at a tempo where every note is heard. The solo clarinet has to sound above all the other moving clarinet parts in measures 273 to 274, because this material is a fragment from the second phrase of the *Kovia* hymn. Variation IV ends with a hold on C♯ in measure 276, which seeks resolution to the D that begins the final variation. The conductor may wish to make a short

break to heighten the dramatic impact of the opening of the final variation.

Variation V begins with a commanding rhythmic figure that later becomes the second subject of a double fugue. What follows is the most exciting and technically well crafted of all the variations and is as fine a piece of contrapuntal writing as exists in the band repertoire. In testing for tempo, I found that ♩=96 provides both subjects with the easy, comfortable drive that musicians ordinarily associate with fugal procedures. The opening trumpet figure at measure 277 sounds more musical if the eighth note is shortened and accented, thus:

The tendency to give the longer notes in a musical passage their full values would render this figure with less spirit.

The timpani solo in measures 277 to 278 should be played with a dynamic equal to the trumpets as should the echoing trombone parts in measures 279 and 280. Horns and cornets sound the first fugue subject accompanied by strong eighth-note chords in the brasses and percussion, measures 282 to 285. The first subject is derived from the opening phrase of *Kovia* played in diminution. The anacrusis of the horn entry should be well accented in order to be heard. Apply the same accents to the successive entries as the fugue progresses. It is the conductor's responsibility to cue each subject entry and to maintain a steady, driving tempo throughout this variation. At measure 307 the second subject is presented and should be answered with the rhythmic motif sounding clearly in the timpani and in the cascading effect of the clarinets and saxophones in measure 311.

A buildup of dynamic intensity beginning at measure 314 arrives at a climactic level at 318 when the full band returns to the second subject. The episodic material from measures 330 to 341 is similar to the first fugue subject in stretto. The music continues diatonically upward, becoming increasingly louder from measures 343-346, arriving at a strettolike section in measures 347-350. The principal fugue subject returns at 353 in shortened form in the clarinets, trumpets, and cornets and finally arrives at the full dominant sonority in measure 359. At this point the horns and cornets come to the fore with the melodic material and a return to the fanfare material in the trumpets at 363. Measures 363 to 371 complete a full return to the *Kovia Yeroosaghem!* melody as the finale of the work. We now have the ancient hymn in all its grandeur, with brass choir, bells, and chimes triumphantly proclaiming, "Praise the Lord, O Jerusalem; Christ is Risen from the Dead, Alleluia!" □

A Composer-Conductor's View

Kaddish

W. Francis McBeth

How do you as a conductor address your task of re-creating a musical work? How does anyone re-create anything? It's very simple if you have a set of instructions, and the musical score is basically just that. Unfortunately, it is also a very antiquated and inexact set of instructions attempting to explain one of the most complicated reconstruction ventures that man has ever devised: the re-creation of a designated period of time containing sound and all of its related elements raised to the level of art. What a task. It can't be done by amateurs.

To re-create music we must go beyond mere instruction into the realm of understanding. No one can truly re-create a musical score without understanding the principles upon which it was created, but the conductor must understand intent as well because the principles of construction and intent dictate style.

The editor's intent in this series is for the composer to give help to the conductors in the performance of a particular work. I will do the same, but I hope in the process I can give you insights that should be used with any work. We have chosen *Kaddish*, as the vehicle for this discussion. It was commissioned by Howard Dunn and the Richardson (Texas) High School Band. Mr. Dunn, who also directed the Lake Highlands High Band is a highly respected musician who is presently conductor of the Wind Ensemble and the University Symphonic Band at Southern Methodist University. When he called me about a commission, I told him that I was very despondent over the illness of James Clifton Williams (one of my college

teachers) and that our telephone communication that week (I had been calling every few weeks during that last hospital stay) was such that I knew it was to be our last. I asked Mr. Dunn if he would allow me to write a work in Jim's memory to which he answered in the affirmative. I hope you realize that it is most unusual for a man to agree to a commission written to the memory of someone else; Mr. Dunn was not only agreeable but encouraged me to do so. At that time I felt I could never write another note until this specific work was done. I give you this particular background because it is desperately important to you in understanding the attitude of the work. Now to the performance.

When approaching a work, the fundamental, the basic first simple step is to find its scale. The scale is the basic building material of any musical work, and will tell you much about the basic style that is desired. Hindemith said in regard to scale, "The carpenter would not think of disregarding the natural properties of his wood and putting it together any old way, without regard to its grain."

To find the scale that *Kaddish* is built on, go to the first non-percussion note of the work (measure 3, example 1). It starts on C in the top voice and progresses upward C, D♭, E♭ and F. The bottom voice starts on the same C and progresses C, B♭, A♭, G♭ and F. The outer voices both start on C and end on F, but look what they form. The upper voice forms the first four notes of the Phrygian scale (ascending) on C, and the lower voice forms the first five notes of the Phrygian scale (descending) on F (see example 1).

Example 1

W. Francis McBeth is professor of music and resident composer at Ouachita University, Arkadelphia, Arkansas, and has written extensively for band, orchestra, and chamber ensembles. He received his degrees from Hardin-Simmons University, the University of Texas, and the Eastman School of Music.

These two contrary Phrygian scales in example 1 cadence on a major triad. The widest harmonic interval of a major triad (the perfect fifth) constitutes the second ingredient of the motive. The first is the bottom tetrachord of the Phrygian scale, the second the interval of the perfect fifth. The entire work is built on these two ingredients.

At this point we must deviate from the music to learn one of the most important facts for any conductor, young or old.

Isn't it fascinating or tragic how many musicians don't understand music. Music can be enjoyed without being understood, but it can't be conducted without understanding.

Music has been called the universal language — I don't think so. Music is the least understood of all the arts.

Let me try to explain the one most basic step, the one most important understanding, the one single historical fact that will initiate the beginning of the understanding of how music is built. Have you ever wondered why all the arts reached an artistic level hundreds of years before music? Have you ever wondered why the Greeks left masterpieces in all the arts except music?

This is the reason: all arts except music were an extension of man and nature and took their departure and development from a reflection of man and nature; music could not. For hundreds of years music was a non-artistic collection of melodies and rhythm relegated to song and accompaniment, dance and accompaniment, completely detached from artistic development. Music did not become art until the invention of the motive. It was the motive and the development of it that allowed music to join the ranks of artistic achievement. Before the motive, music was a song or dance. After the invention of the motive, music became an art in the skilled manipulation of an idea that required ingenious craft and fertile imagination that carried the listener on a journey of logical and skilled development of ideas produced through sound. If you stop and reflect on this, it was a breakthrough that is easily on the level of putting a man on the moon. It was the only artistic breakthrough in the history of man that was not connected with nature, but dealt with the emotional, mental, and spiritual side of man.

But all things come to those who wait. It was this late discovery that placed music far above all the other arts because of its separation from nature and caused it to hold a stature in art that evoked the famous quote, "all art aspires to the level of music."

Young conductors, please don't leave me now. I can hear your brain thinking, "He's getting into philosophy and I need help on the podium." You must trust me that what I have just said is the beginning "key" to the understanding of a composition and without this understanding one cannot conduct, one can direct but not conduct.

If music became art when the motive was invented, then your understanding of a work begins with the understanding of its motive and the development thereof. Now write this down and

Now hold everything. Don't leave me. I can hear all those young bandmasters out there saying to themselves, "I don't need to know that," but that's the price of being young. You really do need to know that, and I will explain why.

We all know that when a scale ascends, it makes a slight crescendo, and when a scale descends, it does the reverse — a principle that we have all been taught. When speaking of pre-20th century scales, this is 99% correct, with one exception. The Phrygian scale also crescendos while descending to the tonic in the lower tetrachord.

Without the knowledge of this fact the motivic development in the entire work will be misinterpreted. I will point out many specific examples as we proceed.

memorize it: the initial statement of the motive will dictate the style of the work.

Back to *Kaddish*. The conductor who has no idea that the first statement of the motive in measures 3, 4, 5 and 6 (example 1) is the ascending Phrygian tetrachord in the first clarinets and horns and that simultaneously with it is the descending Phrygian tetrachord in the third clarinets and horns and ramifications manifested in the tetrachord discussed earlier, will completely miss the style of the work.

If the motive and repetitive development of it raised music to the level of art, it would naturally follow that the conductor's stylistic treatment of the motive would be the basic step to correct interpretation. I have stated the two components of the motive. Now let's trace it through the work.

You will notice that in the first two measures of the work (example 1) the chimes state the minor second (C – D♭) which is the characteristic Phrygian interval of the motive. Students tend to play one of the two notes louder than the other. This is usually caused by the right hand being stronger than the left (or vice versa for left-handed students). Work for equal volumes. Many times switching hands will correct it.

In measure three we start with the original statement. It is stated three times, simultaneously ascending and descending plus harmonization.

These three statements set the tone for the entire work. They cannot be played using a metronome tempo. The most subtle of rubato must be used in the second measure of each statement with a little more in the third. These are tempo variances that cannot be written in the music because if they were written in they would be overdone. A conductor either feels the correct rubato here or he doesn't. There is no in between. The crescendo is never done enough in the third measure of each statement. Nuance must be exaggerated in all music, but it is imperative in romantic music.

Bands enter so loudly at the *p* that I wish I had written a *pp* there. In other words, the entry is softer and the end of the crescendo reaches a higher volume than most conductors achieve here.

The sixth measure of example 1 where the timpani and bass drum enter is the touchiest part of the piece from the beginning to letter B, and is extremely difficult to get correct. The first note in the timpani and bass drum is usually too soft in most bands, with the last note usually being too loud. This must be repeatedly worked with the bass drum and timpanist because incorrect volumes here will destroy this section. The crescendo which starts immediately each time, is usually incorrectly started in the second measure in which they play, and that is too late.

Beginning at letter B the double motive becomes accompaniment in the upper woodwinds with the motive becoming the chant in the lower brass and woodwinds. From this point on, the simultaneous use of the motive ascending and descending plus harmonization will be referred to as the double motive (example 2).

The repetition of the double motive as accompaniment continues to repeat until letter C.

The double motive as accompaniment in the flutes and clarinets naturally will not use the dramatic quality that is needed in the lower brass and woodwinds.

This accompaniment figure seems to give bands a problem. It is devised so that the effect produced will be that of four 16th notes per beat, although no separate lines show this. If you will rehearse the flutes and clarinets without the slurs, they will learn their rhythms faster. Rehearse the flutes alone with the glockenspiel, then the same with the clarinets and chimes. The clarinets and flutes have difficulty making the three measure crescendo starting three before letter C. They will wait and make it on beat four before letter C. You must work this crescendo because the woodwinds won't do it on their own. The repeated notes in the

Example 2

Example 3

chant (G's in third measure, example 2) should crescendo, going back to the original volume on the first note that follows the repetition. This should be done in every similar measure in the work.

At letter C (example 3) the upper woodwinds will never play a true *ff*.

They will have to be forced to do so. The *ff* volume should cover four full counts before the decrescendo starts. The woodwinds will erroneously start the decrescendo two counts early. Upper woodwinds in the band are not as used to major volume changes as the brass are. It will take special work to insure that the clarinets and flutes will decrescendo to a *pp* and in one measure get

back to a *ff*. The chordal ostinato in the sixth measure of letter C must not be separated. The trumpet entrance and the following brass entrances are *pp* (marking is *p*) with no vibrato.

At letter D (example 4) the upper woodwinds will never come in loud enough.

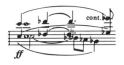

They should enter like a cry in the night and sustain the *ff* for four full beats. In measure two (example 4) there should be a slight accelerando to beat three with measure three having a ritard to atempo at measure four of letter D. Why didn't I write it in? The answer is that if I had, it would be overdone. Just feel it. Again, there should be no separation when the tubas start the chordal ostinato.

Example 4

At letter E (example 5) overdo the crescendo in the horns in the first measure, but do not overdo it in the saxes. Keep the horn sound as the predominate texture. Again in the second measure of letter E overdo the crescendo with the clarinets.

At letter F a major problem arises (example 6). There are three distinct motivic developments going on simultaneously. They are:

1. All players who begin with a white note are playing a chorale over a pedal. The chorale is a harmonization of the descending motive.

2. The horns, saxes, and bassoons are playing a dramatic setting of the motive ascending.

3. The upper woodwinds are playing the descending motive preceded by the fifth with the Phrygian tonic removed.

Now let me explain the interpretation of this section using our previous breakdown.

1. This chorale should be sustained at *ff*. They will not do this without your help. The whole notes in the second and third trombones will always tend to decrescendo in each measure unless you bring it to their attention.

2. The horn must use a brassy attack on each accent. There is no real separation, but if the attacks are strong enough, the natural decay will give a correct allusion of separation.

3. The upper woodwinds have a moving ostinato using a variation of the motive. Following the leap of each fifth, the descending Phrygian interpretation should be used; but you notice it is always 4, 3, 2, with what looks like 1 but is not 1 (or tonic). It is the first note of the new fifth. In other words, in the first measure of letter F a slight crescendo should occur with notes D, C, B♭, but A♮ would be the note of resolution (measure 2, beat 2). A♭ occurs instead, which is the start of the next fifth leap. A return to the original volume occurs on each of the bottom notes of the interval of the fifth. Think of it this way: leap the fifth and crescendo for three notes (D, C, B♭), return to original volume on the next note (A♭), and repeat for each sequence.

134

Example 5

Example 6

Example 7

At letter G we get a bold statement of all the components of the motive in the trumpets and horns (example 7).

In the first two measures of letter G (trumpets and horns) we have the ascending motive, the leap of the perfect fifth followed by the descending motive at *fff*. The mistake usually made here is that the trumpets and horns will invariably decrescendo the descending motive (second measure, notes 2, 3, 4). The reverse is correct, so at least stay the same.

Measure three after letter G has a decrescendo on the fourth beat. I'm sorry I put this in. They always drop too much here. A decrescendo from *fff* to *ff* is very little.

The entrance of the trombones is written at the volume of *p* followed by the crescendo solely to disguise the entrance. you may get to the *ff* earlier than it is marked.

Many conductors have been taught that the (∧) articulation marking separates notes. Not so. It affects only the attack or beginning of the note. Don't use any separation. The natural decay from that hard attack gives the illusion of separation without the loss of sound.

The flams in the timpani and bass drum must be open and the volume *ff* without being overdone.

From letter H to I all of the lines that start with the leap of the upward fifth should be done in a singing manner, very cantabile, especially the horn line (example 8).

Starting in the second measure of letter I all the advice I gave for letter F applies in exactly the same manner.

At the second measure of letter J (example 9) we have a massive harmonization of the ascending and descending motive (simultaneously). The problem here is keeping the trombones at a continuous *ff* with no separation. It is so strong here that they unconsciously do a series of decrescendos just from fatigue. Notice that it takes at least five trombones.

The major mistake in this section is the failure to get to *p* after

Example 8

Example 9

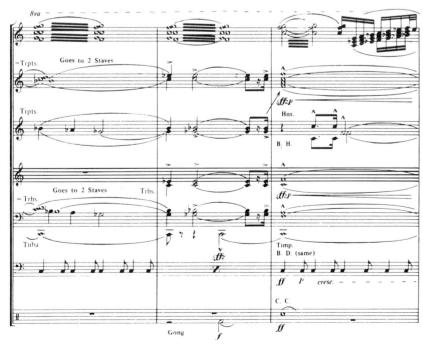

the *sffzp* (fifth measure of letter J and like occurrences). If it isn't done, the horns cannot be heard performing our old friend, the perfect fifth in its most dramatic setting. The other problem here is getting a true *sffz* in the tubas, baritone sax, and bass clarinets. These all occur three times before the end.

Again five measures from the end (example10) there is an *sffzp* with the horns coming in *ff*. When the horns enter, the rest of the band should only have reached about an *mf* from their crescendo. This is very seldom done correctly.

The heartbeat in the timpani and bass drum throughout are usually done too loudly or too softly. Use your good taste as to the correct level.

You must approach this work with your best understanding of romanticism, and it should be readily seen by your physical attitude on the podium. Let the band know the intent of the work before any rehearsing is started.

Remember that the volume

Example 10

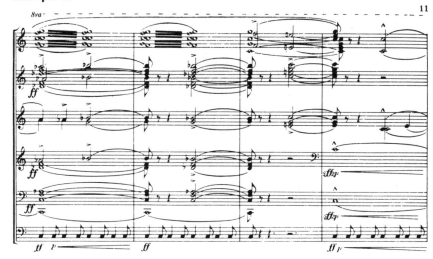

variances are desperately important to achieve the dramatic effect that is necessary. This work is a combination of all the emotions that surround the death of a friend — cries, shouts, resignation and sorrow — but the work should end as an alleluia, an affirmation of life.

In the beginning of this article I talked to you about what finally lifted music to the level of art. I believe that a conductor can

take a work written on the level of art and by complete disregard of its re-creation can bring it down to non-art. In music, and only music, a work of art can be less than art depending upon the re-creator (the conductor).

It is my hope that these comments will help you re-create my intentions. Ours is the highest of the arts, the understanding of it will afford you the highest of joy and fulfillment. ∎

October, 1970

Performance Problems in Mozart's Serenade in Bb, K. 361

David Whitwell

Discussion of this masterwork might properly begin with the title. Mozart called the work *Gran Partitta,* and a partita, or perhaps divertimento, is exactly what the piece is. These terms appear frequently in the large body of serious, original wind music from this period, which is only now being uncovered. The more familiar term, "serenade," like its cousin, "tafelmusik," is used by European musicologists with definite prejudice toward wind music. So if we reject Mozart's title, we must accept the lighter, outdoor connotations of the serenade. For those who may examine this manuscript, while the title is in Mozart's hand, the signature and date are not; they are in a later hand.

Two Separate Compositions?

One interesting question which awaits further study is the original order of the seven movements. A num-

bering system, which seems to be in Mozart's hand, at the top of each movement leads one to believe that this material may have originally been two separate compositions, organized as follows:

Largo-Allegro	*Adagio-allegretto*
Menuett (first)	*Menuett (second)*
Adagio	*Theme and Variations*
Allegro (Finale)	

A four movement work with the minuet preceding the slow movement is common in music of this period. It reflects not a symphony-form, with reversed movements, but the older divertimento form of fast-minuet-slow-minuet-fast, with the second minuet omitted. It would appear that we have here two works of this nature, with the second lacking the final fast movement.

Serenade No. 10 in B♭ for 13 Wind Instruments, K. 361

Instrumentation: 2 oboes, 2 clarinets, 2 basset horns, 4 horns, 2 bassoons, and string bass.

Available on Angel, London, Vanguard, and Decca recordings; published by Broude Bros., Eulenberg, and Musica Rara.

The remaining point regarding the score itself is the bass part, which Mozart called, "Contra Basso." The Köchel *Catalog* makes the following, very definite statement:

In the autograph Mozart asks for neither kontra-bass nor kontrafagott, but merely "Contra Basso."[1]

This is not true. Even a cursory glance through the score reveals such words as "pizzicato" and "arco," which prove Mozart *did* ask for a specific instrument. We could forgive the editors of the Köchel *Catalog* for this oversight, were it not for the fact that it is another example (among hundreds) of the careless scholarship which permeates this catalog. Another conspicuous error in the catalog is the dating of this composition. This aspect has been discussed in some detail earlier in these pages.[2]

Problems in Articulation

A number of articulation problems arise from the fact that there are inconsistencies in the manuscript. These occurred because Mozart assumed certain markings would be clear to the musician of his day; it did not occur to him that they might *not* be clear 200 years later. For example, Mozart used the *slur* to establish basic legato character, but he often did not carefully place the actual slur mark nor did he foresee the current strict views on this matter. This may be seen in the following passage from the "Finale," where Mozart only wrote out these three parts (the rest being indicated by shorthand).

Other inconsistencies in the manuscript occur from Mozart's manner of composition. He composed the melodic line, or lines, for rather long sections before he returned to fill in all voices. Sometimes this results in a refinement found in some middle voice, as for example, in bar 22 of the first movement. Here the B♭ horns alone have the articulation ⌢ as opposed to *staccato*, a softening most appropriate considering what follows.

Mozart left to the player a few of the more obvious articulations, such as the following missing tie in the fifth movement:

Sometimes Mozart used articulation marks in a *negative* sense, as in bar 6 of the opening "Largo." Here Mozart did not intend for the basset horn to play staccato, but rather *non*-legato in contrast with the oboe.

It is worthy of note that only Mozart would have introduced a B♮ here immediately after the B♭ cadence.

The earliest editors and publishers of Mozart's music created additional articulation problems, many related to a confusion at the time between baroque and classic phrasing. One such editorial change, which still appears in publications, is bar 31, first movement:

Published:

Manuscript:

Examples such as this one in which editors have changed the phrasing to fit the meter (rather than the melody) are numerous in current publications of this work. In most cases, Mozart clearly wrote what he wanted in the manuscript.

In many cases editorial changes have occurred which defy explanation. The second ending of the first minuet's first trio certainly takes on a different character as it leads to the *da capo:*

Published: *Manuscript:*

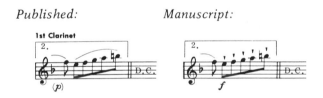

A few comments should be made regarding performance practices. First, there is one articulation problem which is a special one in the music of Mozart. The composer, in a desire to indicate a pause or breath, frequently was careless in the exact duration of rests. Often, if performed literally, such examples are heard as being weak at moments of strong harmonic interest.

In the following, if the basset horns play what is *written*, their sound will have stopped before the resolution in the oboe. Nothing could be further from Mozart's intent.

The reader will also notice that the articulation and dynamic markings in the above example (bar 12, first movement) do not conform with the normal published versions. Again, the autograph is the most logical in the first place. An additional point here is that in all voices except the oboe Mozart wrote a quarter tied to an eighth-note, rather than the easier dotted-quarter note, for the *forte* chord. His point was that the second beat must be *felt*, as a springboard for the oboe solo.

Finally, articulation markings are often a clue to tempi in 18th century music. In the "Adagio" of the fifth movement, the following original articulation is an obvious guide to tempo, for at a definite speed it no longer sounds lyrical.

In the second minuet's second trio, Mozart in his articulation proves that he intended the trio to be conducted in one beat per bar, rather than three.

Published:

Manuscript:

Mozart was also very careful in this manuscript in notation of *crescendi*. For example, there are several instances where he spelled the word in syllables spread under three or four measures. Modern editions usually condense this to "cresc." under the first bar of such phrases.

There is one use of *crescendo* so rare that I have seen no other example of it in 18th century manuscripts. It reflects the problem that the word itself does not

indicate how loud the player is to play at its conclusion. In bar 22 of the fifth movement, Mozart does exactly this, seen here as it appears for the bassoon.

It is generally understood today that in music of this period *fp* and *sfz* meant only *accent* at the established dynamic level. Our accent mark (>) was not known. In this composition Mozart even uses the two at the same time, implying he held no distinction. An example of the proof that *fp* meant only an accent is found in bars 35-36 of the first movement, where the forte level is already established. Obviously, Mozart did not intend some sudden drop to piano (which would be the reverse of today's use of *fp*). The forte which appears in bar 37 undoubtedly means *piu forte*, a practice which continues through Beethoven.

On the other hand, there are two examples in publications of this work in which editors have taken *separate* forte and piano markings of Mozart and combined them into an unintended *fp*. These are bars 131-133 of the sixth movement and bars 25-26 of the "Finale." The *correct* dynamics as found in the manuscript are, respectively:

A few of the dynamic errors are of such a scale as to alter the fundamental interpretation. First, in bars 59-61 and 184-186 of the first movement, modern editions create a most awkward syncopation, while in the

Problems in Dynamic Markings

Of the many Mozart manuscripts this writer has been able to examine, none has been so carefully marked with regard to dynamics; yet many interpretative problems have been created by modern editions. The opening measures offer a perfect example:

David Whitwell is conductor of the San Fernando Valley State College Wind Ensemble and Chamber Orchestra and is conductor of the Los Angeles Orchestra Club. He has conducted major professional orchestras in Europe, the United States, and South America.

Present day interpreters have been puzzled by these dynamic markings which, if taken literally, result in comedy in their sudden and extreme change on each third beat. Some have suggested that perhaps Mozart really intended a *diminuendo* and that he merely marked the extremities. The fact is that *none* of these dynamic markings are in the manuscript! The first markings are *piano* for the sustained voices in bar three and for all other voices in bar four. The source of the error is the word "dolce" which appears under the solo part in the manuscript, but not, ironically, in published editions. The word *dolce* was often used exactly as we use the word *solo* today, meaning "project" rather than "sweetly." To add to the confusion, early editors translated this word to read *piano*. Therefore, we can suppose that some early editor assumed that the work must begin *forte*, then forced all accompanying voices to read *piano* in order that the "piano" solo might be heard. It is my feeling that Mozart intended the entire passage to be *forte*, until he marked it otherwise, which he soon did in every voice.

138

manuscript Mozart clearly placed the *fp* at its more natural and logical location.

Published: *Manuscript:*

Modern editions of the slow movement have distressingly difficult placements of the *fp,* such as in bar 9 where it appears in three different locations within the bar. In the manuscript it appears only under the fourth beat, in all voices.

Finally, there are entire sections which are published incorrectly. In the manuscript there is no indication that the over-all dynamic level of the first minuet's first trio be *piano,* although this does seem to be a reasonable assumption. More questionable is one of the subordinate sections of the "Finale," bars 57-63. This has always been published as *piano,* while in the manuscript it is clearly *forte!*

Problems in Ornamentation

Ornamentation in Mozart is usually not so great a problem, because he tended to follow his father's advice that composers should write out in full any ornament which might not be clear to the performer.

There is one ornament in this composition (bar 16, first movement) which has caused a dilemma for many conductors.

Common practice would realize this as ♪♪ ;

it has been published in at least one edition as ♪♪. However, I believe that neither was intended by Mozart. First of all, Mozart *did* write out several ornaments in this movement. Bar 72-73 is clearly such a case as is the beginning of the development section, bar 92 (which is the source for one publisher's decision regarding bar 16, even though they are completely unrelated musically). All that we know for sure about bar 16 is that by *not* writing out the ornament, Mozart felt it would be obvious. This eliminates the ♪♪. solution. In this particular context it would be more natural to play the appoggiatura before the beat, rather than the conventional ♪♪ , which disturbs the meter. As a matter of fact, in the manuscript when this appoggiatura first appears, the principal note seems to have been written first, with the ornament wedged in before it as an after-thought. *Before* would

have to be, in spite of the appearance on paper, before the bar line. The same problem exists in bar 2 of this movement, where any resolution on the beat forms a dissonance rare in the style.

A very fascinating example of a written-out ornament appears in bar 17 and 41 of the "Adagio."

Bar 17 :

This looks, at first sight, like another instance of an omitted tie (which, in fact, one publisher adds). However, a tie is impossible when one understands that this is a written-out ornament, which another composer might have written thus:

Mozart apparently foresaw that a musician seeing the principal note as "C" and the potential dissonance, might be afraid to play four sixteenth-notes, so he wrote it out. We can clearly deduce Mozart's thought process from the manuscript when this ornament appears in the recapitulation, bar 41. It should be remembered that Mozart wrote with such facility that he usually composed recapitulations without bothering to look back at the exposition, hence the delightful changes found in Mozart recapitulations. Mozart came to this spot and began to write the more conventional appoggiatura form. He then remembered his thought process regarding the performer, crossed out the appoggiatura and wrote it out as four sixteenth-notes! In the manuscript, bar 41 looks something like this:

These few comments only touch the surface of the interesting study which is possible whenever original sources are available, a study equally necessary in the orchestral repertoire. In the case of this manuscript we are fortunate indeed, for it resides permanently in Washington, D.C.[3] To connoisseurs of wind music, it is one of our greatest national treasures. ∎

[1] Köchel **Catalog** (6th ed.), pg. 379.
[2] David Whitwell, "A Case for the Authenticity of Mozart's Arrangement of 'Die Entführung aus dem Serail' for Wind Instruments," **The Instrumentalitst** (November, 1969).
[3] Xerox copies may be ordered for approximately **$11.00**. Requests should be addressed to Chief, Photoduplication, Library of Congress, Washington, D.C.

The Holst Suite in E♭

Frederick Fennell

These interpretive convictions and editorial observations continue to evolve as they do for all artists, but what is set forth here is exactly the way I behold this remarkable music at this writing.

Frederick Fennell is Conductor-in-Residence at the University of Miami School of Music, where he is Music Director of the Symphony Orchestra and Symphonic Wind Ensemble. He is also Resident Conductor of the Miami Philharmonic Orchestra. Well known as Founder/Director of the Eastman Wind Ensemble, he was a member of the faculty at Eastman for many years.

Gustav Holst. *First Suite in E♭ for Military Band*, Opus 28a (1909). 3 movements: "Chaconne" (Allegro moderato), "Intermezzo" (Vivace), "March" (Tempo di marcia). Initial copyright by Boosey & Company for the U.S.A., 1921 (renewed for all countries 1948); issued in the U.S.A. by Boosey & Hawkes as Quarto Military Band Journal No. 120. It was first published in the original scoring: flute, piccolo, 2 E♭ clarinets, 2 oboes, B♭ clarinets (solo-1st, 2nd, 3rd), alto saxophone, tenor saxophone, 2 bassoons, 4 horns in E♭, B♭ cornets (solo-1st, 2nd), 2 trumpets in B♭, 3 trombones, euphonium, basses, timpani, snare drum, bass drum, cymbals, tambourine, and triangle, with condensed score only (as in the composer's original scoring). A group slightly larger than the official 28-piece British army band was thus required to play it. Subsequently, additional parts were added for alto clarinet, bass clarinet, and fluegel horn, probably at the suggestion of Albert Austin Harding (*ca.* 1932), to have the score conform to instrumentation standards in American school band contests. The parts for baritone and bass saxophone/contrabass clarinet were the idea of the publisher, who issued a full score in 1948 which had been made from the parts of the original publication and which also incorporated all of the above-mentioned additions, their errors and omissions.

It is essential that readers have a copy of the score. First, number each bar of the score, beginning with the up-beat quarter note as [1] and continue consecutively through the entire *Suite*. There are 132 bars in the "Chaconne," 142 in the "Intermezzo" [133-274], and 179 in the "March" — 453 in all.

Holst and Vaughan Williams

The photograph is copyrighted by G. & I. Holst Ltd; reproduced, with permission, from *Holst*, by Imogene Holst (Great Composers Series). Faber & Faber, Ltd, London.

Gustav Holst (1874-1934) produced this cornerstone of modern wind band literature when he was 35 years old. Though Holst's scoring reveals a classical knowledge of part writing and acute awareness of orchestral traditions, it is truly conceived in terms of the military band medium. Unlike so many of his colleagues, he achieved this new concept of band scoring without being hampered by his consummate knowledge of orchestral principles; he was, in fact, guided by them. He was both a violinist and trombonist. Although no facts prove him experienced with military bands, it seems difficult to otherwise comprehend his knowledge of the medium or the skillful simplicity with which he managed it.

According to all available information, the *Eb Suite* was not solicited; it certainly was not commissioned. It did, however, fit neatly into the fabric of sound that was (and is) characteristic of the British military band, our English brethren having long ago settled the hash of instrumentation to their obvious satisfaction.

The composition did not really become a part of the repertory of bands, either in England or in America, for many years to come, but it is an unquestioned masterpiece viewed from any point of consideration. Holst wrote nothing about it and provided no detailed notes to the bandmaster, save to inform him cryptically, as follows, on the first page of the two-line condensed score (the only one published with the original 1921 edition):

> As each movement is founded on the same phrase, it is requested that the *Suite* shall be played right through without a break. It is suggested that in the absence of a string bass, the *ad lib* part for that instrument in the "Intermezzo" shall not be played on any brass instrument, but omitted, excepting where the notes are cued in other parts. Also in the absence of timpani, the *ad lib* part for the latter is to be omitted entirely.

And this, indeed, is enough — provided one then pursues the minutely detailed study of Holst's score that is expected of any responsible conductor. A good portion of my lifetime has gone to just such an examination of this piece, both score *and* individual parts.

What we seek here is knowledge of the style, the real key to the art of the conductor.

Feeling that I must share these long-distilled thoughts with others, I have undertaken this personal view which may serve as a study-performance guide to colleagues. When used in conjunction with the recording which I made of it over twenty years ago with the Eastman Wind Ensemble (recently reissued for the third time by Mercury Records, SR1 75011), one may evaluate and/or equate print to sound and choose whatever course of interpretation he so desires.

Chaconne

A chaconne is a type of continuous variations which take place over a repeating harmonic pattern or ground bass. The first movement of Holst's *Suite* is built on an 8-bar ground bass.

The bass melody is presented in 16 different statements: 12 are strict; 2 are strict inversions in the relative key of C minor; 1 is an inversion in the dominant; and the final statement hovers between the *Suite's* key of Eb and the flat seventh key of Db. Thus, the work is a set of 15 variations above the basic tune (or ground bass), which is *always* present.

Taking a closer look at the actual scoring at the opening of the movement, one sees that the Db piccolo is a superfluous line. In addition, the line assigned to the contrabass clarinet (one of the added parts — not written by Holst) intrudes on the brass texture, so it is preferable to preserve the original brass bass line octaves of the euphonium and basses and leave out the reeds entirely. The first "variation" [9] continues with cornets and trombones, confirming the emphasis of low brass in the opening statement, and then is followed by a contrasting second "variation" in the reeds [17]. Although the list of instrumentation in the left hand margin does not say so, the part for 1st Bb cornet is divided, and the bottom line is not duplicated in any other soprano brass. (The out-dated designation, solo *and* 1st cornet, was probably Holst's original intention.) In this and all other parts where the bottom line indicates 2nd instruments, it is wise to clearly label the part as such in order to guarantee that it will be played.

The choice of tempo for Holst's *Allegro moderato* can only be made after careful consideration of all of the "Chaconne" ground bass statements leading to the *Maestoso* at F, the first indicated departure from the initial pulse. As a result of these considerations of pattern and style, I place the pulse of the quarter note in the neighborhood of 88.

Because the full score was constructed at a later date from the parts written and presumably proofed by Holst, as well as from parts that were added later (and were never seen by Holst), a host of omissions and errors have crept into the score which make accurate study and performance almost impossible. The first of these omissions is the serious absence (in the full score) of his note to the conductor previously quoted;* the second is the absence of a *legato* indication for the low brass that was clearly printed in the condensed score; and at [9] trombones should play *piano*, and I would add the further adjective, *sostenuto*.

With the entrance of the reeds [17], the irrepressive expressivity of the music begins to unfold and with it comes the need to reduce the doubling of oboe and clarinet to solo players. The next serious omission is the absence of a *staccato* articulation for the figure in the reeds in [24] ; it is clearly present in the condensed score but missing in the full score until [A]. The importance of establishing the *staccato* articulation becomes apparent when one sees that the figure it generates continues unchanged for 18 more bars.

The *mf* [25] reached after the *crescendo* in [24] should be transferred to all reeds and their articulation set as . After a similar *crescendo*, indicated in [32], the low reeds underpinning "variation 4," and all eighths should continue to be short and precise. Trumpets [32] should modify balance downward, so that their stationery octaves do not bury the moving woodwind lines. The fluegel horns doubling trumpets here do so throughout the *Suite* (for all but 9 bars); they are not essential to performance and, when used, balance must be adjusted so the preferred trumpets always predominate.

At the beginning of "variation 5" [41], delete the *tenuto* placed between the bass and percussion lines in the score — the latter are incapable of playing it, the former must play its opposite, and Holst did not use it in his original condensed score. If any *tenuto* is to be indicated at all in this crowning "variation" of the first portion, it should be incorporated into the *legato* excursions of the reeds. Using "stretched" sixteenths in these slurred scale passages will help emphasize the basic pulses which all the brass and percussion are now punctuating with their short and resonant chordal presentation of the chaconne tune

(the tune itself is played by trombones in octaves). The *fortissimo*, which is ambiguously tucked between the saxes and cornets in the full score, should be added for all brass [41].

The marvelous writing for the reeds in this 5th "variation" [B] demands expressive playing by all, with rising *crescendi* following the heave and swell of the scale-wise passages. The players will need to produce their maximum sonority with ultimate support and the best possible quality of tone. One always has to remind the woodwind players that the final bar of this passage is the one that crowns it; thus, they must be careful not to squander their breath early in the variation and be buried by the brass! Holst requests that the whole be played *Brilliante*; to this end I have always felt it my duty as an interpreter to re-group the four note phrases in 44 as follows,

so that the pulses follow the chaconne-tune punctuations and provide a stronger upbeat for the following scale passages.

Many interpretations of *peasante* are possible [50]. In this instance my preference is for long and heavy detached eighth's which do not slow up the pulse but which add the element of breadth demanded. I add a Brahms-like articulation: . The mid-range and high brass, which present the chaconne tune (in the highest voice, the 1st cornet) along with a chordal harmonization, must pour out their sound in the most sustained, sonorous fashion and with particular care for impeccable balance. Near the end of this "variation" (6), in the octave passages which appear in the basses [55-58], the upper octave is preferable; and the bassoon line [56-57] should be corrected to match the other bass instruments. At this point Holst neglected to put a bottom on his *diminuendo* approaching the next variation [C], so we must elect to terminate these bass lines in *piano* [58].

The *piano* dynamic is retained throughout "variation 7" [57-65] and, with the instrumentation reduced to clarinets and horns, the composer achieves the intimacy of chamber music. In the next "variation" (8), the composer's choice of the E♭ clarinet [67-71] must be preferred to the cued part in the 1st clarinet, at least it should not be left out, as is too often the case.

Holst reaches the midway point in this piece after 9 literal statements in E♭ (*i.e.*, after "variation 8"), then turns his "Chaconne" on its harmonic axis [73-97], inverting its intervals at this poignant moment so that the key moves into the relative C minor. These turn-about intervals

---

*The note does appear in the condensed score which is included in the complete sets currently published by Boosey & Hawkes.

(which appear again at the beginning of the 3rd movement) all come from a perfect inversion of the chaconne tune in the cornets and euphonium. By the way, the baritone sax is an intruder at this point and should be removed until F.

The simple ostinato-like figure in bassoons and basses D ("variations 10-11"), punctuated by duple strokes on the bass drum and enhanced by the distant presence of the suspended cymbal, must be at the *pianissimo* level with the bassoon quality slightly prevalent [82-97]. The suspended cymbal should be a large, thin, high-pitched plate (about 18"), and the bass drum should be played with a soft articulating beater "stroking" a resonant, undamped head.

Next, along with the return of the chaconne tune in its original version at E ("variations 12-13"), comes the vital counter-tune [100] in 2nd clarinet, alto clarinet, and alto saxophone; and of these, the most urgent sonority is that of the saxophone. In spite of the importance of the counter-tune line, these instruments, even when bolstered by 3rd clarinet, bass clarinet and tenor saxophone [106], add up to the lines least likely to be heard amidst the on-coming power of the brass — *unless* the conductor insists on their clear projection all the way to F. Here ("variation 14"), for the first time since the "Chaconne" began, Holst alters the pace of his music, indicating a steady slowing of the pulse to the conclusion of the movement, 18 measures later.

Concerning the previous percussion build-up [107], it seems prudent for the sake of balance to restrain any percussion *crescendo* until [115], the approach to F, at which point all percussion that can should ring to natural decay. All rising lines [121-122] must *crescendo ultimately* to [123], the last presentation of the chaconne tune.

Trombones [128-129] must provide the utmost expression in their performance of the quarter- and half-notes that lead to the final bars. If the bass drum is damped in any way (rags, paper, head tape, feathers, etc.), it will be robbed of one of its great moments in band literature [128-132]. When the player uses a hefty beater providing weight as well as directness-to-head texture, the bass drum strokes will lead inevitably to that ultimate sound in the low brass and reeds on the down pulse of [131] — to which a *sforzando* must be added. Conductors must be certain that all low reeds, low brass, and percussion cease their sound after the beginning of the final measure.

These final bars in the "Chaconne" — marvelously overwhelming — build to their great climax through the harmonic richness and rhythmic thrust of the trombones in the last 6 measures. At the height of the climax, cornets and horns join the trombones. The half note, one bar prior to the fermata, must not suffer a lack of intensity because of faltering breath sup-

port. This "suspension," with its always surprising upward resolution, benefits greatly from a relentless *crescendo* which one must add [131] to all the parts. A quick gasp for the final fermata guarantees a fresh attack and allows the Eb pedal-point to sound.

We must all be certain to check dynamic and harmonic balances in this final chord, with the awareness that Holst scored the G♮ (third of the chord) very thinly. It appears in the 2nd clarinet and as the bottom note of a divided 2nd cornet part. Ego being what it frequently is, 2nd cornet players are not likely to want to be *second* 2nd cornets — and they may not play the lower note at all — resulting in the loss of the G beneath an avalanche of high Bb's and Eb's. The fluegel horn parts doubling the trumpets could help, but it is essential to preserve the divisi balance in the 1st and 2nd cornets, with emphasis on the bottom line. Snare drum rolls should be tied [123-130], but this should end in bar [130] to allow the great attack at [131].

Specific conducting challenges in the "Chaconne"

The challenges begin, as they do in all scores, with one's comprehension of the overall concept of the piece. Conducting techniques can then be applied to the score in the simplest of ways — by making the physical involvement a linear duplication of the very piece itself, the size or intensity of gesture matching the music as seen and heard, always complementing the articulation required of the players and following, with absolute fidelity, the dynamic unfolding of each of the "Chaconne's" 16 statements.

For myself, I have never been able to start by beating just the third pulse with which it all begins. I feel it necessary to provide 1 & 2, since these pulses always seem to help launch this wonderful piece with utmost security to all. As with all scores, the answers to the conductorial questions are to be found *only* in the music itself. If we emphasize the *legato* aspects of [1-23] in our conducting, the players will surely comply, just as they will respond to appropriate invitations to *staccato* [24-40] — or to the demanding combination of both textures [42-47]. Maintaining the initial pulse (♩=ca. 88) through all the chaconne "variations" until the *Maestoso* at F (♩=ca. 72) is standard interpretive procedure, as is the license to restrain it ever-so-slightly at the poignant midway juncture where Holst turns it around [73-74].

Intermezzo: Vivace

The tempo taken here should be on the bright side and one everybody can live with — at both the *vivace staccato* opening and at the *l'istesso tempo* C, with its more *legato* mood. I recorded it at 152 to the pulse, though it does not need to be that bright to be effective.

The "Intermezzo" has two essential ideas — first a light and bright, almost brittle vertical texture at the opening and then the dark, sonorous horizontal-linear development so beautifully set forth at C. Each, clearly fashioned from the chaconne tune, has its say in a full exposition, after which Holst ingeniously combines the two with remarkable effectiveness in the deceivingly simple-sounding counterpoint that is as charming as it is masterful. Band music like this simply did not exist before Holst.

The Eb clarinet is a must for this music — as it is for all British band literature, but nowhere is that fact more blazing than in the opening of this intermezzo, where two are required. If only one Eb clarinet is available, the 2nd Eb part can be played on Bb clarinet (cued in the 1st clarinet part — but without articulation, nuances, or dynamics; you must provide them if you choose to use this inadequate substitute). Lacking any Eb instrument at all, you might use the 1st part cue in the flute and write the 2nd Eb part for 2nd flutes a third below it. In any case, a matched sonority is desired here.

The alto clarinet note in the first bar is not Holst, nor is it necessary. And since the C concert appears in both the 1st trumpet and 1st cornet parts, it can (and should) be taken out of the 1st cornet, so that player may be securely muted and ready for his solo — ready, that is, if you have him play it at all. This brings us to a vital decision: is the muted cornet solo [134] an intentional double or is it a back-up in absence of the oboe? I am convinced of the latter: Holst was probably observing an ancient British army band security measure — scoring an important part for a reliable instrument in case of rain, when delicate instruments such as the oboe would have to be packed away in their cases. Remembering that British bands, then and now, are principally outdoor groups and that they rarely appear with more players than in Holst's original instrumentation, one can and should make appropriate judgments within artistic conscience toward our customarily larger indoor groups. *The sound*, then, is that provided by the doubled oboes and clarinet, upon which it seems that the solo cornet, however well played, is an intruder [134-157, 175-190, 248-255, 259-272]. Holst's composition is so securely crafted that any cross-cueing destroys the lines, bloats the textures. Here is a great lesson in clarity of concept, cleanliness of sonority.

The timpani ostinato at A benefits from sticks that produce a crisp texture, such as those of wood covered with one layer of chamois, sticks of hard felt, or yarn vibe mallets. Anything that helps contribute head texture in place of the customary muddle made by the booming sound of standard sticks is desirable here and at F.

All brass and percussion should delay their *crescendo* until 3 bars before B, and all reeds with sixteenth-note runs should begin their passages *forte*, then *crescendo* [171-174]; percussion should vibrate freely at B.

The *legato* tune at C provides superb opportunities for solo playing on all parts, should the conductor elect to perform this section as a chamber music work (with one-to-a-part); it also works well for multiple players, though the former is always preferable. The alto clarinet line [225-228] should be re-written to match the solo cornet. (Note also that a quarter rest is missing in the individual flute part at [227].)

When the tune from the first section returns [231], there occurs the classic editorial error. The tune should be played by the euphonium/baritone, but some editor or other assigned it to, of all instruments, the alto clarinet! Be sure to write the tune into your score in the correct place (for euphonium), and remind the players that the tune is written into the euphonium parts in both clefs as a cue; it must be played by the best solo performer. In addition, that tune should have the same articulation (*♩. ♪ ♪*) in bars [234, 235, and 238], as printed in the alto clarinet part and the euphonium treble clef cue (in the individual parts). The correct articulation is missing in [238] on the alto clarinet line in the full score and in all 3 measures in the cue on the euphonium bass clef part.

A number of other corrections will also be necessary in this movement. There are printing errors in the rhythms of bars [136-137] (oboe), [152-153] (piccolo), [169] (timpani), [195] (1st cornet), and [251] (1st clarinet). The 2nd horn part in F [231] should be corrected from printed F♮ down to Eb. The bass clarinet, in both score and parts, has an E♮ instead of the correct pitch, Eb [246]. The euphonium articulation in [257-258] should match that for tenor saxophone. All reeds in bar [207] should play long quarters. The tambourine figures (*♫♫♪ ♫♫♪*) beginning in [254] play easily and sound properly when the player is seated with the instrument head down on the knees, the wrists resting on the near rim, and the finger tips playing the rhythm on the opposite rim. One final and vital correction to make in both score and parts: bass clarinet and tenor saxophone rhythm [269] must conform to that of the euphonium.

Specific conducting challenges in the "Intermezzo"

After the pulse has been established, the conductor can be of the greatest assistance to his players by letting *them* play while he gets as far out of the way as his pulse-tending and balance-preserving responsibilities allow. A precise beginning always helps, and in such instances as this, the visual physical manifestation of taking a breath frequently guarantees a good beginning. Harmonic balance in the short opening chord can be established in rehearsal by first having the chord sustained to establish proper distribution and to allow the players to hear where they fit into the overall sonority of this brief but highly resonant C minor triad. Stylistic interpretation of the rhythmic germ in the second measure of this movement (♩ 𝅘𝅥𝅮 | 𝅘𝅥𝅮 ♩ 𝅘𝅥𝅮 | 𝅘𝅥𝅯𝅘𝅥𝅯𝅘𝅥𝅯 | 𝅘𝅥𝅯𝅘𝅥𝅯𝅘𝅥𝅯 | 𝅗𝅥) obliges the players to offer a steady syncopation and to avoid any rush to the following dotted eighth, a dictum which should be followed throughout the entire piece. The conductor's physical movements in the first section of the "Intermezzo" should be as precise in their economy and vertical in their action as they must be horizontal and flowing for the second section beginning at C — gesture reflecting the sound of the music, action joining the music making.

The long *crescendo* of dynamics and instrumentation from A to B is one the conductor should join only according to the needs of ensemble, urging the players to listen intensely to each other as well as taking what they need from him.

Before leaving the "Intermezzo," attention must be called to an early imperfection in the printing plate for solo clarinet in bars [204-206]; some parts I have seen are badly smeared, garbling the notes and rhythms. Conductors whose parts appear this way are urged to copy those measures boldly and correctly and to paste those parts over this unfortunate production error.

March: Tempo di marcia

Many a tempo is possible here, so long as the marvelous driving spirit in what starts out to be a great British brass band quick-march is unmistakably present. My recorded tempo is on the bright side, with a pulse of about 138, but any reading between 128-132 would also be appropriate. I can never resist the desire to add *molto crescendo* to the trill in the reeds in the 2nd bar [276], so that it spills full-tilt into the next bar. The quarter notes in the first three bars (the intervals here are derived from the chaconne tune, see bars [73-74]) must be played both short *and* detached (short alone is not enough). The great booming sound of the bass drum that follows must be free

of damping devices, the head struck with a heavily-weighted beater that produces a good tone without thudiness or distortion.

The 4th bar [278] contains a curious and unnatural dynamic indication, *subito mezzo forte*. The fact that this is engraved in the solo cornet part *only* (not in other brass) and did not appear in the original condensed score is one more painful reminder that the full score was made from error-plagued parts. Thus, the dynamic in the full score must be corrected to a *fortissimo* for all brass. A *sforzando* may be added and, if desired, a *diminuendo* resulting in an effective dynamic of something less than *fortissimo*. These remarks also apply to bar [302] (the passage beginning in [278] is repeated in [302-310]).

After the initial *staccato* indications [275-277], nothing appears in any score or part as to how the music should be played. I can't imagine that it would be played in any *sostenuto* fashion, but your players ought to see your preference written clearly on the music. The dotted quarters [287, 288, etc.] should be long and vibrantly attacked; all repeated quarters [289-294] might be reduced in volume, allowing the moving parts to be heard with ease. The vital descending scale-lines beginning in horns [299], then in trombones [300] are essential to the effectiveness of the section's next to last cadence, which occurs just before the repetition of the passage that first appeared in [278-286]. There should be a tasteful balance between the brass and percussion throughout this opening section [to 310], without domination by the percussion.

Since B suddenly appears in bar [345], the double-bar key change to Ab (concert) [311] was obviously intended to be letter A, but this vital rehearsal letter is missing in both scores and all parts. The cymbal used in the opening measures of this second section might be a large suspended plate (20″) that affords a different tone from that used in the "brass band" statement of the first section. This sound should decay to its own infinity (blending with the *diminuendo* in the brass).

Now comes the "Land of Hope and Glory" version of Holst's great chaconne tune [314]. It should be played with the broadest support, the most open of sounds — in the great *sostenusto* tradition of the singing chorus; the sculptured lines of the tune fairly beg the conductor to follow their continuing contours. And when the *staccato* soprano brass and trombones enter to punctuate all of this [354-361], their presence must be felt and heard. Since the entry of the oboe at B is of greater importance than its dynamic allows, it should be built up to *forte* before receding to the printed dynamic (*mf*).

Thus far in the movement we have had the "brass band," then the "Land of Hope and Glory" version of the chaconne tune, and now comes the "village wind band" [362-371] for its brief but memorable rustic contribution, ending at C. To set this off, it is best to change the first half note in bar [362] to a quarter, insert a quarter rest, then accent the (second) half note and be off on this wonderful *staccatissimo* venture. The condensed score calls for a *diminuendo* for all reeds two bars before C, but in the full score this indication appears only in the flute part; all other reeds (in the full score and parts) should conform to the condensed score.

At C there begins a series of unfortunate (if necessary) page turns in the 1st and 2nd clarinets, then in the solo and 3rd. They are unfortunate because they invariably cause sloppy entrances and create harmonic imbalances when the page is slow in coming over. Since there is no better place to turn, even if one writes these crucial bars on the third page, the best solution seems to be a quick turn (V.S. — *volti subito*) by the inside player.

The transition from Ab [362] through C Major [371] and G Major [383] to what the British call "the home key" — Eb [397] — is one of the magical places in all music to me. With genius shining through every bar, Holst uses the inversion fragment he set up in the "Chaconne" [89-90] in the euphonium [374-380] (players never seem to respond enough to this) and then the trombones [380-382] who ought to overpower the whole band with an ultimate *crescendo* into the G Major chord at the double bar [383].

Again — a plea for an undamped bass drum with a heavy, hard beater to make the moments in [386, 390] memorable, and a call for the greatest sound that low brass can provide at [392] when Holst demands a final thrust for the repetition of his opening "March" statement. Reeds [393-396] must pour out their sound to take all into the final contrapuntal statements (D to [427]) where both tunes of the "March" ("brass band" tune and chaconne tune) play marvelously together.

A major correction must be entered in the parts for flute, piccolo, Eb clarinet, solo-1st and 3rd Bb clarinets in bar [398], since all should conform to the lines of the 1st cornet; the final quarter note should be an Ab concert, not Bb as is printed in score and parts. At [422] it is the 1st cornet that must correct his note to Bb concert rather than the Ab printed for him. Holst uses this different figure from the one just corrected [398] because of the figure in bar [424] (which does not correspond to the figure in [400]). Another omission occurs in [407-419]; the slur that should cover the triplet figure in the reeds is missing in the full score, condensed score, and all parts; it should be added but *not* to the 1st cornet which

should remain detached. Flute and piccolo must be corrected in score and parts in bar [417] where the triplet is printed a major 2nd too high.

Lines from [427] to [436] cannot be too *legato*, and a *crescendo* seems demanded from all — especially the moving brass at [435-436] leading to the *meno mosso* at [437] (which should be *subito*). Percussion should begin their rolls here *piano* then quickly *crescendo*. A final bit of broadening and *crescendo* on the half note in [442] added to all the brass and a roll and *crescendo* in the timpani will set up the *piu mosso* at [443].

A final correction (to go with obvious printing errors in [375, 420, 431, 432]) concerns the pitches in the tenor saxophone in [451-452]; the part should read as follows:

This rising scale must be played with a *crescendo* in all the reeds.

All trills in [445] should be launched with accents. How many times have you seen *forte to the 4th power* in any music? With all the high brass driving to the end and with trombones at their final thrusts of thematic material, Holst's masterpiece comes to its exciting conclusion.

Specific conducting challenges in the "March"

With the matter of pulse settled at a pace that the brass can enjoy, the conductor should once again stand back and enjoy the music, joining the phrasing at cadence points and following the rhythmic exposition with minimal physical expenditure. When the texture and line change at A, so should the conductor, using appropriate horizontal gestures of his choice as companions to the music making, with concentration on the phrasing.

The perfunctory "beater of time" is vastly out of place here; certainly, this is one of the most appropriate places for a conductor to make the vital observation that the music can go on without him and his incessant chopping of the air. Contrary to the apprehension that this might be a discouraging experience to the ego, becoming a "listener" can be a vivid and exciting experience for the conductor. One thing I have learned in a conducting career of forty years is that for all of us, players and conductors, the answers to making music are to be found in listening, not in looking; and this genuine masterpiece of music literature can help you to become a listener in the most rewarding of ways.

If you really wish to become a true conductor of the band's repertory, I beg you to learn this score completely, to study it from every conceivable approach. Live with it, learn it any way you can, but know it, and when you come close to knowing *it* you will know a great deal about a lot of other music as well. You can, in fact, become self-educated in theory, counterpoint, form, scoring, composition, *and conducting* — if you really know this score . . . but that will probably take a lifetime to achieve.

As basic band repertory, *The E♭ Suite* should be studied often by all groups and performed with the frequency that material of this dimension deserves. I can't imagine life without it. ■

Postscript

Shortly after this initial piece in our Basic Band Repertory series was published, the manuscript of the *Suite in E♭ for Military Band* surfaced for the first time. The full score always existed and it could have answered all the questions which were raised in my initial study and in the minds of other conductors whose pursuit of definite answers in this score has been an equal frustration.

As a result of all scholarship on behalf of this music, a new and correct edition in full score has been prepared by Colin Matthews under the supervision of Imogen Holst, incorporating observations found in my April 1975 study and combining appropriate information to be found only in the holograph score with those practical aspects that must be considered for contemporary U.S. concert band performance. This score is expected to be released by the publishers in the near future.

Among the salient observations of the original score are these points of interest:

• Holst made his own condensed score written at the bottom of the full manuscript score.

• A vital part (curiously labelled *ad lib*) written by Holst for the treble clef baritone was eliminated by the editors of the 1921 set of parts, but they did cannibalize it into many different instrumental lines: alto clarinet, bassoon, alto, tenor, baritone saxes, horns, cornets, trumpets, flugelhorn, and trombone (when there was no instrument available, the notes were simply left out). This is curious policy, when in both British and American bands the baritone and euphonium have long been partners, and both are essential to the full achievement of Holst's original musical ideas. The absence of this part is how we lost that vital passage in the *Intermezzo* [223-240].

• The manuscript had a part for string contrabass.

• Additional pages equal in length to the following study might be published in a microscopic view of Holst's very fascinating manuscript.

• Conductors who wish to perform the Suite in its holograph edition will find an excellent guide to that rewarding pursuit available from Frank Battisti, New England Conservatory, Boston, Massachusetts.

• Holst wrote this direction in the original score (published only in the condensed): "As each movement is founded on the same phrase it is requested that the Suite shall be played right through without a break." This has led to performance in which *Chaconne* is segued to *Intermezzo* and *Intermezzo* to *March* with no more than an quarter-note's separation; literal interpretive license, to be sure — but I find it difficult to move immediately from the enormous emotional conclusion of the *Chaconne*, for instance, without at least a breather or two in which to savor all that magnificent accumulation of the forces that create it. Beautiful jewels need a proper setting.

September, 1975

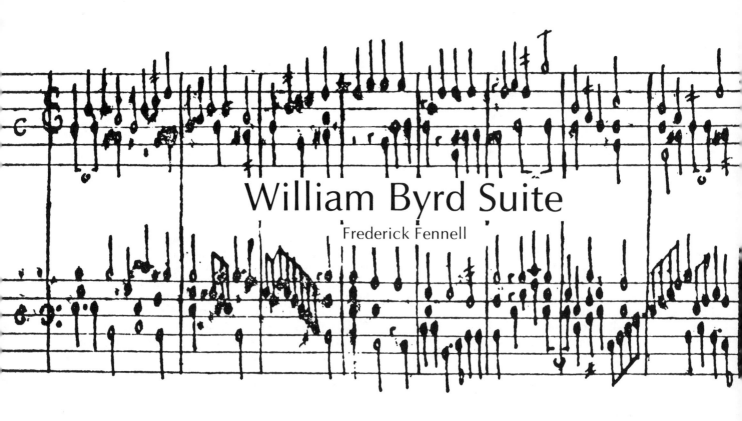

William Byrd Suite
Frederick Fennell

So much precious rehearsal/teaching time is squandered because we do not take the interest and the time to write into our scores and parts those minimal articulations, nuances, dynamics, and all other interpretive guides that can save so much time — and in terms of the wind player's embouchure — so much "skin."

Conductors of the great and endless orchestral literature work from scores and parts that show these editorial and performance notes on every page, inherited in many an instance from the lifetime experiences of legendary maestros and players who, together, established modern orchestral playing techniques. How can today's conductor of bands expect to really make it with clean pages, especially in an ensemble whose performance traditions have so recently begun?

William Byrd *Suite*, selected from the Fitzwilliam Virginal Book and freely transcribed for military band by Gordon Jacob in 1923. Published in 1924 by Boosey & Co. as No. 3 in the 149th series of their Military Journal in what they called the Kneller Hall Series (after the Royal School of Music at Twickenham). The original plate numbers H11072 were preserved by the current publishers, Boosey & Hawkes, as part of the

1960 U.S. edition. The original (this is what is available today) is scored for piccolo, 2 flutes, 2 oboes, 2 bassoons, E♭ clarinet solo, 1st, 2nd, 3rd, 3rd B♭ clarinets, alto and bass clarinet, alto and tenor saxophone (no baritone), a quartet of horns in F, 1st and 2nd B♭ cornet, 1st and 2nd B♭ trumpet, 3 trombones, baritone (no treble clef part published), basses, timpani, triangle, chimes, snare drum, bass drum, cymbals.

Conductors should avoid the automatic doubling of the B♭ bass clarinet with the B♭ contrabass clarinet throughout this *Suite*; those who choose to employ the contra should edit the bass clarinet part to be played only as a bass line doubling, avoiding all other doublings. The absence of any baritone sax part prevents the automatic employment of that line in erroneous double for the E♭ contra-alto.

The original 3-line condensed score from which I worked (as well as from a study of every individual part) was what was available when I recorded this work with The Eastman Wind Ensemble for Mercury Records in 1958 (recently re-released as Golden Import Stereo SR 1 75028). Performance time is 18 minutes. The full score and new edition published in 1960 was made from the parts and, like the Holst *Suite in E♭*, it unfortunately incorporates their errors.

148

THE MAYDENHEAD

of the first musicke that

euer was printed for the VIRGINALLS.

COMPOSED

By three famous Masters: William Byrd, Dr. John Bull, & Orlando Gibbons.

Gentlemen of his Maiesties most Illustrious Chappell.

Dedicated to all the Louers and Lovers of Musick.

Ingrauen

by William Hole.

for

DOROTHIE EVANS.

Cum

Privilegio.

Printed at LONDON by G. Lowe and ... are to be solde at his howse in Loathberry.

William Byrd (1542/3-1625), a pupil of Thomas Tallis, was a famous organist (Lincoln Cathedral), master of the Queen's Royal Chapel, and a prodigious and prolific composer for voices and for the keyboard instruments of his day, principally the virginal. The limited sonority of the virginal led to the development of a florid style to sustain the tones that emanated from the very small lap-size oblong box in which the instrument was housed. Byrd was a master of this magnificent medium, and many of his pieces for it can be found in a collection of music known today as the *Fitzwilliam Virginal Book*. The original collection is now in the Fitzwilliam Museum at Cambridge. An American reprint of these two volumes, edited by J.A. Fuller Maitland and Barclay Squire, is available from Broude Bros., New York. Jacob's work is based on six of the pieces in the collection: "The Earle of Oxford's Marche" (Vol. 1, p. 259); "Pavana" (Vol. 11, p. 174); "Jhon come kisse me now" (Vol. 1, p. 10); "The Mayden's Song" (Vol. 11, p. 126); "Wolsey's Wilde" (Vol. 11, p. 157); and "The Bells" (Vol. 1, p. 69). These pieces may also be found in Volumes XVIII, XIX, and XX of the collected works of Byrd, edited by Edmund Fellowes and published in 1950 by Stainer & Bell Ltd., London.

The United Kingdom celebrated the tercentenary of Byrd's death in 1923 and Jacob probably undertook these unprecedented, unusual, and extremely sensitive settings for military band as part of that observance. Their publication in 1924 coincided with Vaughan Williams' *Toccata Marziale, Folk Song Suite,* and Holst's *Second Suite in F,* making available four of the band's great scores in a single bountiful year.

I first came upon a set of parts somewhat accidentally in 1934 as part of a gigantic give-away sale of band inventory by the Toronto firm of Whaley &

Royce. I had just begun the Eastman Symphony Band and desperately needed a library. I took the mimeographed announcement of the sale to Dr. Howard Hanson who gave me the funds to purchase a whole $50 worth! And for that amount I acquired the Holst *E Flat* and "Mars" from *The Planets*, Rossini/Respighi/Godfrey *La Boutique Fantasque*, the MacDowell *Woodland Sketches* and the Smetana *Moldau* (the last two in the great Winterbottom arrangements)...plus this *William Byrd Suite* (I remembered the name Byrd from my high school harmony class where we had sung some of his madrigals).

My first performance of Jacob's work was in 1941 with the Eastman Symphony Band. The careful preparations which preceded the 1958 recording session resulted in what have to be my best observations of this music; when one compares his score, annotated (and with all measures numbered) as suggested here, with that performance and chooses his own way, he will have these points of departure as a guide to a genuine masterpiece in this medium.

This music by Byrd, written originally on a 6-line staff, sounds somewhat modal, quite different from the more "familiar" harmonic language developed in the 18th century. And it is this remarkable modal technique and its highly developed art of imitation, frequently bordering on canon, that gives this music its thoroughly unique harmonic substance so remarkably refreshing today.

The Marche

"The Earle of Oxford's Marche," or the Marche Before The Battell (from that Suite of 15 movements also freely adapted by Jacob) is characterized by extremely florid writing. Jacob's version is a very satisfying if considerably truncated transcription of the original. It conjures up in a vivid picture the noble procession of a man of great dignity and regal bearing.

A choice of pulse something slower than the ♩=80 in the score seems to afford the music a desired pace, and to his *Un poco piu pomposo* Jacob might well have added *sostenuto molto*. The great demand for a very sustained character to *every note* that is not clearly detached becomes a major stylistic consideration in the performance of this superb music. This is a particular demand in all scale and scale-fragment passages with which the developments of each variant abound and which grow in rhythmic intensity and frequency to the end.

Jacob's careful concern that the basic long-short articulation be preserved throughout the piece is set forth in his consistent insistence on Byrd's basic melodic figure (Ex. 1). The players must not ever be allowed to relinquish this vital grasp on the music's underpinnings, and the conductor must contribute meaningful physical participation to that end while still maintaining the *legato/sostenuto*. These are tough orders, and they make the piece as good a test of one's fundamental conducting techniques as can be found. But, unless the conductor provides more than just pulse points [1-3] [17-20] [25-28] to the development of the figure shown in Ex. 1, the *sostenuto* yet striding character in the music is certain to wane.

Ex. 1

The conductor might well borrow here from that great bank of appropriate conductorial techniques derived from string bowing, employing his baton or hand in the vertically slanted up-and-down motions made when bowing this passage (Ex. 2). Remembering that the bow draws no tone unless it moves, the conductor is thus more certain to contribute "tone" in his conducting of these sustained sounds, while indicating the lifted separation that the two up-bow motions suggest.

Ex. 2

Jacob also provided a complete dynamic and nuance profile for Byrd's music. Here is wedding of shading to substance that seems impossible to imagine was not there until he established it, so perfectly does it fit Byrd's music. Such sensitivity in adaptation for another's music is rarely granted, Jacob joining Rimsky-Korsakov and Ottorino Respighi among the elite in this field. His treatment of intensities, leading from the quiet beginning to [6], building once more to the heights of a carefully engineered summit of sound at the conclusion, is, like his similar sensitivities throughout the rest of the *Suite*, nothing less than a remarkable achievement.

The entire harmonic fabric of the "Marche" is developed from but five triads (F, C, G, and Bb major, c minor) — by no means a limited resource to William Byrd. It is this resource, together with fascinating rhythmic variety, that will challenge the conductor. In pursuit of a proper style one is immediately aware of the critical balances which Jacob has built into his scoring, as well as the importance of establishing and maintaining a desirable pulse.

The judicious use of percussion throughout the *Suite* stimulates the imagination to enhance the percussion still further in terms of color and texture. It is important to use loosely tuned, undamped bass drum heads, with a cylinder free of rags, paper, or other stuffing, and stroked by articulate beaters of firm texture and weight. Those who listen to our recording will note that the snare drum is doubled by a loosely tuned field drum and tenor drum, the latter played with wood. Snare and field drums, only, highlight the solo passage [15-16] which ends the first phrase; they dominate the sound at bar [40]. (When you listen to the recording, be sure to listen for the clarity in the deliberate spacing at bar [40].)

The proper rudimental terminology for the figure in Ex. 3 is *drag*, a term which may even have been

Ex. 3

derived from a technique of "dragging" the stick across the head to make its sound. Its counterpart in

pitched notation is a single mordent, and proper notation requires the slur as I have used it in Ex. 3. Thus, I have added the slur to the 118 bars in my score where the publisher has neglected to provide it. Missing slurs (or ties) should also be added in the following bars for the snare drum: [35-38, 44-48, 50, 54-55, 76-80, 82-86, 93-94, 97-108, 110-112].

The conductor must maintain strict dynamics [4] to [5], granting the flute, piccolo, and Eb clarinet a special vibrant resonance to their grace notes [45-46] and demanding a true *forte* at [47] when the solo clarinet joins them, the band meanwhile having made no *crescendo* until the end of bar [48]. Now, at [5] things are beginning to open up, and to complete the phrase at [48] the flute, piccolo and Eb clarinet flourish [49] should precede the beat. Cornet, trumpets, trombones should back off to *mezzo piano* at [50 and 52] to allow build-up without dominating. Jacob put no top on the clarinet *crescendo* at [50] which I make *fortissimo*. Horns should cap this whole development with a *fortissimo* outburst at [54] joined by another reaching *crescendo* in the high reeds.

Byrd's next variation, [6] to [7], demands the utmost in *legato* playing from the solo reeds with all digging deeply to bring out the bottom contours. Brass at [6], when *legato*, must be extremely so as is required throughout the "Marche."

Jacob scored a demanding and frequently undoubled part for Eb clarinet, voicing it on equal terms with a single solo flute and clarinet. For this reason and because its characteristic timbre provides that bright sound which only the Eb clarinet possesses, this instrument is essential to the overall balance. In the absence of the Eb it may be necessary to transcribe that part for no less than a pair of piccolos.

Sonorities really begin to build as [8] is approached, and I have frequently found it a challenge to prevent groups from rushing ahead at this point. The Byrd/Jacob line in [77-78] needs special care and should be played as in Ex. 4 (the vertical slash indicates a

Ex. 4

phrase-wait for the next dotted quarter). The vitality of the line assigned to 1st and alto clarinet, alto and tenor sax, bassoons and baritone between [9] and [10] never seems "fulfilled" in its present scoring. If you share this feeling with me, you might wish to relieve the four horns of their *continuo* assignment and rescore the passage for them; it is both appropriate and effective.

The eighth notes scored for cymbals and bass drum at [10] should be played as undamped half-notes [89-91], as they are notated at [93-94], and nothing should be dampened to the end. The last eighth of the figure in all reeds and soprano brass at [89] and in succeeding measures should be extended with ultimate vibrancy and support (Ex. 5). The

Ex. 5

rhythmic phrasing evident in the recording between [92-93] is stylistically appropriate. Trombones always need to be begged for more sound here [96-100], so you might remind them by adjusting the dynamic to *fortissimo*.

The "Marche," which proceeded from the beginning with no change of pulse, demands careful preparation for the final *molto ritardando al fine*. The safe approach is to indicate the 4-pulse in [110] to avoid ensemble problems that can arise if one waits until [111] to slow down a going group. Jacob took his wonderful percussion touch in [113] from a line in the Byrd original and used it as effective imitation of the whole band. I prefer not to dampen the cymbals before [114]. The final high reed flourish should come just before the last downbeat; and I have always liked to support that with a low F on my biggest kettledrum.

Pavana

In Jacob's version this wonderfully beautiful slow music has 29 bars which were selected from the 56 in Byrd's original (it was in a minor). At the outset each line fairly begs for a single player all the way, save for bars [22-24], but that is a matter of individual preference. Throughout the piece, and particularly for the twenty pairs of sixteenths (and all sixteenths in general), there must prevail the most sustained character possible in the playing.

Though this is extremely slow music, I would caution against conducting the eight pulses. Use a slow, flowing four; eight pulses tend to rob the music of its marvelous direction, its genuine grandeur and dignity. In this, as in all such matters, the conductor must think of the music, of the composer, and of the player, not of his own problems as the leader. I know of no better teacher of a true *legato* in conducting than this "Pavana," and there are not many works in original band literature that afford these same productive teaching resources to the players at the same time.

The first phrase ends with one of those marvelous strung-out cadences that account for every sixteenth pulse. To achieve the ultimate tonal support that is needed here, the final measures of the phrase should be played as in Ex. 6.

Ex. 6

That wonderfully rich E♭ major sound at [2] that builds to the D major at [20] does not seem to me to need the cymbal crash intended to cap it; feeling this an intrusion, I suggest its modification or elimination, but I do feel that the bass drum contributes to the low frequencies as a vital part of the texture.

The "Pavana's" glorious climax at [3] and beyond demands the utmost *sostenuto* launched from sticky accentuations (Ex. 7) with each of the reeds or brass

Ex. 7

answering each other in perfect imitation, even endeavoring to outdo each other in the musical intensity of their *sostenuto*. All of this leads to Jacob's perfectly planned *diminuendo*, setting up the final phrase and terminal cadence. The difficulties of resolving the upper reed trill and turn [24], as well as those musical ideas that follow, might be approached as in Ex. 8 [24-29] — a method which I feel has never failed to bring clarity to this most beautiful music.

Ex. 8

The final widely-spread chord in the trombones and tubas is still as delightful a "surprise" to me now as it was the first time I heard it. I so cherish this sound that I do not wish to hear even my own favorite instruments, the kettledrums. But at [3] I do want to hear them, so I make them follow the tonal bass line by rewriting Jacob's roll on D and G [22-23] to B♭ and C — certainly no uncommon demand with the prevalence of today's multiple machine drums. It is preferable to use the now customary set of four 23″-26″-29″-32″, and in this case to assign the B♭, C, and D to the three lowest drums, having already altered the non-bass G [19] to upper E♭, so that this doubles the tubas. If one is going to play my suggested tonal editings on two pedal timpani, it will be necessary for the player to dampen between the B♭ and C — assuming the D is set up on the high drum. I'll never know how the cymbal came to be left out of our recording [22-24], but it *is* glaringly absent.

Jhon come kisse me now

One of Byrd's most fanciful pieces, it was originally written in G major as a series of 16 phrase variations over 96 bars, all phrases of which were to be repeated. Jacob chose eight of the phrase variations for this work and scored them with great skill and keen sympathy, casting Byrd's characters, so-to-speak, with remarkable insight in their most appropriate roles.

Imitation is established at the beginning and pursued throughout. Gathering rhythmic and tonal complexity marks the development of the first six variations. The piece then settles down in two final contrasting variations, the 7th being as *sostenuto* as the 8th is *staccato*. But *en route* there is so much interesting musical countryside, beginning with this view of a simple, but volatile idea (Ex. 9). It is wise to establish at the outset the length and character of

Ex. 9

the third note (Byrd's quarter with Jacob's dot on it). I hold this dot to be an expressive articulation, one indicating a vibrantly, resonantly-supported ringing sound, released before the 4th quarter to be sure — but not until it has been vibrantly held for the "right" length of time. And if you really try to achieve that "right" length and sound, you'll know when you've found it. Entreat the players to listen for it; believe me, you'll both know when it happens!

The length of the first dotted quarter note, established (again by tonal *support*) as a *tenuto*, is so vital to the study, rehearsal, and performance of this music. This opening figure appears in 40 of the 67 bars and its guises are as varied amidst surrounding textures as they are numerous; so you will be wise to establish what you want at the very beginning here both in your ear *and* on the page (which to the players must be a calligraphic extension of *exactly* how you want the passage to be played — how you have *decided* it should sound).

The descending figure of "variation 2" ① and succeeding reed figures must continue the sustained *legato* of the opening. In [21] the placid character of the music suddenly changes. Resonance marks should be added to the eighths as in Ex. 11, for all similar figures in [21-39]. The impetuosity of this figure (Ex. 10) and attendant lateness of reaction in the

Ex. 10

players may both be served by writing "Don't be late" on every part [21-27]. Jacob's "very smoothly" [35] in the trombone applies to all similar lines between ④ and ⑤ . "Variation 6," a rugged essay for brass and percussion, needs appropriate drive from all.

Percussion throughout "Jhon" might make appropriate adjustments to the light textures of the first six "variations" — using a bright-sounding triangle with a light beater and a piccolo snare drum tightly tuned and played with light sticks (in contrast to the deeper textures suggested for the "Marche"). The exposed *piano* figures in the snare drum [8, 18, 20, 24] can be played with more clarity if the player uses one stick in his best hand. Neither the triangle nor the bass drum should be damped during this movement. Drum rolls [41-48, 53, 56] should be tied and so, too, should all the 47 drags.

Like so many band sets prior to 1950, this one simply lumps all of the percussion on one page under the innocuous label: "Drums." In the small British regimental band for which it was published, three players for everything was sometimes a luxury, but our multiple player sections need multiple parts. I suggest that conductors carefully label this single part, as furnished in duplicate by the publisher, for the separate instruments. My set has five parts isolated as follows: (1) snare, field, and tenor drums; (2) bass drum; (3) cymbals and triangle; (4) chimes; (5) kettledrums (for which I have written my own appropriate part). These meticulously edited parts contain *everything* pertaining to size, beaters, sticks, textures, duration, and musical cues. My score lists these groupings and so does the library's list of parts. Leave nothing to chance.

The Mayden's Song

Like its predecessors in this *Suite*, "The Mayden's Song" starts innocently enough with the brass unison/ octaves in a sonorous statement of the whole 16-bar tune which is then literally restated five more times. But before these variations end, powerful things will have been heard, and Jacob's remarkable gifts as an orchestrator will have once more illuminated Byrd's impressive music. Again the character of the playing must be sustained, deliberate — smoothly ordered, and with ultimate breath support. The care and vitality with which fingers activate keys, valves and slides will contribute those rhythmic impulses which grant the music its distinguished character — and without which that important condition is glaringly absent.

With but three exceptions [31, 95, 96] *every* phrase or fragment, melodic or contrapuntal, and *every* supporting harmonic texture begin on the anacrusis. Hence, it is imperative that the conductor establish these upbeats at the outset, and they should be so sustained as to have a stretched character beyond that customarily granted. This is especially appropriate to the 8th bar of every 10-bar phrase and obviously apparent where Jacob's *crescendo* confirms it [8-82-92]. Each third pulse, every four bars, needs some special care in its intensification; adding a line above each entering 8th ② to ③ and each 16th ③ to ④ reminds the players of this. Flutes, E♭, solo, and 1st clarinets must provide both reach and stretch [40-41] when register adds its challenge.

These same players then commence that delicate embroidery in the 16ths which decorates the fourth version of the tune ③ to ④ . The music will take on a special sheen when solid breath support, smoothly deliberate fingers and rhythmic pulsations combine, especially at the tie. Also in the interest of sonority and style, I suggest the replacement of all dots with dashes over the 8ths which end the 16th note fragments [50 to 60].

Removal of the slur and substitution of *marcato* [60-61-62] for alto and bass clarinet, alto and tenor sax, bassoons, and baritone will enhance these important lines, while all reeds down through 3rd clarinet should play bar [62] as in Ex. 11. The innocence

Ex. 11

with which "The Mayden's Song" began passes with the rugged *marcato* of "variation 4." The brass should be exhorted to the production of fat, healthy sounds and to listen for their vital place in the brief but fascinating contrapuntal bout at ⑤ . Byrd's florid keyboard style is exemplified by the brilliant lines for the reeds from bar [79] to the end. And the whole complicated development concludes in sonorous brilliance capped by the simplicity of the single *fortissimo* F major triad in the brass which should fade in *fermata* to a solid *piano*.

Percussion points include undamped triangle [48-60], as well as undamped bass drum and cymbals [65]. Snare drum should delay its *crescendo* until the end of [64] to allow a difficult tuba part to sound. All percussion should be sure to separate the sounds in [68-69]. Snare drum slurs are missing in [73, 74,

76, 77, 94], as are slurs for every *drag*. Help the percussionists to listen by writing the word "wait" just before [89]. In the interest of clarity, you might consider changing the "distorting" snare drum roll on the half note [97] to eight 16ths matching the brass and reed rhythm. In that same bar the use of bass drum and cymbals will damp and choke the eighth.

Wolsey's Wilde

Byrd's original was in C with a meter of 12/4; Jacob has preserved his two-part structure while adjusting the metric flow to 6/8. If you feel that the piece can be played by your group at Jacob's tempo (♩=88), I'm sure it would be a brilliant and convincing experience. However, I have always preferred a slower pace (regardless of the ability of the performing group). My recorded tempo was 66.

Once again we are confronted by a fascinating score fashioned from the simple harmonic resource of but three basic chords (Bb, F, Eb — with a one-chord assist from f minor [36]). The remarkable melodic variation and rhythmic gifts of Byrd seem without end. So, too, do his and Jacob's sense of proportion. Stylistic considerations begin with the stickiest up-beat everybody can play followed by a short, resonant and explosive down pulse [1-3-5-6], and continue throughout with every sensitivity to this inventive essay in Bb. Scrupulous fidelity to all contrasting dynamics is basic to the style.

An inconvenient page turn in the tuba part [23, 24, 25] can be solved by copying those bars on page 3 of that part and turning in the next bar rest [26]. All reeds, horns, and baritone should take a phrasing breath before the final Bb chord.

The Bells

Byrd's original for "The Bells" was 102 bars of C major. In Jacob's transposition to Bb it is an impressive ground bass, an essay of 98 bars based entirely on a harmonic fabric of two chords, Bb and a quasi-F major, which always has the same voicing and

Ex. 12

pattern (Ex. 12). From the outset, imitative counterpoint sets the form of the piece, and the most vital harmonic aspect of the contrapuntal texture is the gathering sonority of ringing, undamped bells — pealing bells running gloriously into each other's tones, all the tones of a Bb major scale in one octave.

Beginning with tubas and kettledrums, 56 bars [1-56] are developed above this bell-like bass line (Ex. 13). This is followed by a 9/8 version of the bass

Ex. 13

[57-68] with various permutations of the basic tones (Bb-C-D-Eb-F). With appropriate restraint Jacob waits until bar [69] to score the chimes using only the upward Bb tetrachord to cap the sounds of Byrd's bells by the greatest brass bell-ringer of them all, the horns, who top it at [9] .

The score should indicate a compatible unit pulse (♩=♩.) at [5] and the reverse at [8] , but it does not. Conductors should be aware of the flat pitch character of all these G naturals (submediant to the Bb tonality) and generally exhort the players to keep the pitch aloft in these initial 12 bars [57-68]. The first scale fragment passages [13-19], [23-26] benefit from an intensification of the dotted eighth (Ex. 14), as do the 9/8 figures (Ex. 15) at [5].

Ex. 14

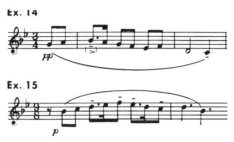

Ex. 15

A note to the kettledrummer that "Wolsey's Wilde" is all in Bb should help the player tune for the beginning of "The Bells." Jacob's very limited kettledrum part (61 bars — only 7 lines of music for the entire *Suite*) seems hardly adequate for a work of these dimensions. Since the part ends in "Bells" at [6] , I suspect that this player would be free to play the chimes which join the texture at this point. British arrangers frequently group vibracussion with the kettledrums. Those who choose, as did I, to add the kettledrums to the end will have no difficulty fashioning appropriate music from the obvious bass line. Chimes must have their own part and for further rhythmic and tonal interest you might consider the option of both removal of the tie in that part [96-97] and the addition of the bass drum, cymbals, and kettledrum, making the percussion read as in Ex. 16.

Ex. 16

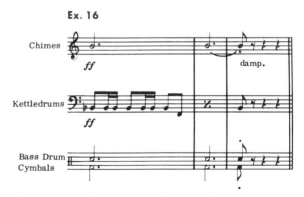

Thus concludes one of the band's most unusual scores, one of its great pieces, and one I cannot imagine would not be a primary part of every conductor's repertory, a piece he would play with calculated frequency both as a study work and a performance vehicle. It is also one of those works from which he may perform as many or as few movements as fit his study and performance plans. I frequently excerpt from it for festival groups for it is, and long has been, a vital part of my repertory.

Points of Correction

"The Marche"

[26] Baritone — part and full score. The sixth 16th-note should be B♭ (the three-line condensed score is correct).

[55-56] Alto clarinet, alto saxophone — parts. A slur is missing (full score is correct).

[57] Basses — parts. Add *piano* on the first beat.

[59] Alto clarinet, alto saxophone — full score. Last 16th should be corrected from B to G (parts are correct).

[64] E♭ clarinet correct 2nd 16th to B

[69] Oboe — part. Change the two eighths to a dotted eighth and sixteenth (full score is correct).

[91-92] 1st clarinet — part. Add a slur covering both bars (full score is correct).

[98] Baritone — parts and full score. Add an accent to the first note and slur the first two eighths to agree with the 1st and 2nd trombone.

[103-104] Snare drum — full score. Add slurs to show continuing roll.

[104] Snare drum — part. Add flags to half note.

[105] Basses — parts and full score. Change all three notes to C (condensed score is correct).

[114-115] Flutes & piccolo, E♭ clarinet — parts and scores. The flourish should come before the beat.

"Pavana"

[6] Flute — part. The 16th flag is missing on the first pair of notes (full score is correct).

[12] 2nd cornet — full score. Correct to read as in Ex. 17 (the part is correct).

[15] 1st cornet — part. Add a third flag to the 16th note figure, making it a 32nd note figure (full score is correct).

[21] Alto clarinet, alto saxophone — full score and parts. Change the trill on D♯ to one on F♯.

[23] 1st cornet — full score. A 16th flag is missing (part is correct).

Ex. 17

"Jhon come kisse me now"

[6] E♭ clarinet — score. The last note should be E (part is correct)

[8] Baritone — score and part. Articulations should conform to basses, bassoons, clarinets.

[9-10] Alto clarinet, alto saxophone — parts. A slur is missing (score is correct)

[36] All parts, 2nd clarinet and down — full score. Key signatures are missing.

[39] 1st clarinet, 2nd cornet — score and parts. The fifth 8th-note must be E♭ concert, but all E's after that must be natural.

Ex. 18

[48] Bass drum and cymbals — score and parts. Add ties as shown in Ex. 18.

[59] 2nd clarinet — part. Change the first note to C (score is correct).

"The Mayden's Song"

[16] 2nd clarinet — part. The part should have two quarter-note rests.

[19] 1st cornet — part. Add a 16th flag following the dotted 8th (score is correct).

[43] Flutes & piccolo — part. The second beat should be two 8ths (score is correct).

[63] 1st cornet — part. Remove the 16th flag from the last note in the measure (score is correct).

3rd trombone — part. Remove the diminuendo and insert a crescendo (score is correct).

[65] 2nd cornet — score and part. Add an accent.

[81] E♭ clarinet — score and part. Add an accent on the first note.

[82] solo clarinet dot missing 1st 8th.

[86-87] E♭ clarinet — part. Add a slur on the third beat (score is correct).

[97-98] 2nd cornet — part. The fortissimo and diminuendo should be moved from [97] to [98].

"Wolsey's Wilde"

[1] Alto clarinet, alto saxophone — parts. Add a *piano* on the fourth beat (score is correct).

[2] Solo clarinet — part. Add a slur (score is correct).

[6] Piccolo — part. Add a slur (score is correct).

[8] Snare drum — score. The first 3 notes should be 8ths (part is correct).

[1, 2, 4, 6, 15, 16, 19, 20, 21, 22, 25, 37, 39] Snare drum — score and parts. Add slurs.

[20] 2nd cornet slur missing.

[30] Solo clarinet — part. The last note should be a quarter (score is correct).

[31] Alto clarinet, alto saxophone — parts. The first two notes should be 8ths (score is correct).

"The Bells"

[50-56] Timpani — score and parts. Add slurs to rolls.

[56] Timpani — score. Remove superfluous 8th rest (part is correct).

[57] Solo clarinet — part. Correct rhythm to read as in Ex. 19.

Trumpets — part. Add 9/8 meter signature.

[59] 1st cornet — part. Add a slur to the first two beats (score is correct).

[61] Flute — part. Add 16th flags (score is correct).

[69, 70, 81] 1st cornet — part. Add 16th flags (score is correct).

[74] Tuba — score and parts. Remove the 3 that appears above the 16ths; this should not be a triplet.

[75-79] Trumpets — parts. Dots are missing from all half and quarter notes (score is correct).

[85] 1st and 2nd trombones — parts. The accents and articulations in the parts should conform to those in the score. ∎

BASIC BAND REPERTORY

Vaughan Williams'

Folk Song Suite

Frederick Fennell

This is another in a series of articles by Frederick Fennell on basic band repertory. Earlier articles covered Holst's *Suite in E♭* (April 1975, pp. 27-33) and Gordon Jacob's *William Byrd Suite* (September 1975, pp. 35-41). Dr. Fennell looks back over his 40 years as a conductor and discusses those compositions which he considers to be the basis of the band literature, focusing primarily on those things of interest to fellow conductors.

It is essential that readers have a copy of the score while reading this article. First, number each bar of the score, beginning each movement [1]. There are 132 bars in the "March" ("Seventeen come Sunday"), 97 in the "Intermezzo," and 113 in the "March" ("Folk Songs from Somerset").

Ralph Vaughan Williams (1872-1958). *Folk Song Suite* for Military Band. Initial copyright 1924 by Boosey & Co., London (Plate No. H 11065); presently available in the U.S.A. through Boosey & Hawkes, New York. Three movements: (1) "March" ("Seventeen come Sunday"), (2) "Intermezzo" ("My Bonny Boy"), (3) "March" ("Folk Songs from Somerset"). Full score and condensed score; scored for flute (*divisi* in only 4 measures) and piccolo, 2 oboes, E♭ clarinet (a 2nd E♭ is scored in the 3rd movement), B♭ clarinet (1st, 2nd, 3rd), alto clarinet, bass clarinet, 2 bassoons, saxophones (alto, tenor, baritone, bass/contrabass clarinet), B♭ cornets (solo and 1st — *divisi* in only 9 measures — 2nd), 2 B♭ trumpets, 4 horns in E♭ (F parts come with the set), trombones (2 tenor, 1 bass), bass clef euphonium (treble part comes with the set), basses, string contrabass, kettledrums (only in the middle movement; their absence in the outer movements is obviously intentional), triangle, snare drum, cymbals, bass drum.

Folk Song Suite reveals Vaughan Williams* interest in and association with the folk song movement which swept through England toward the close of the nineteenth century. His wife, Ursula, wrote: "Folk music weaves in and out of his work all through his life, sometimes adapted for some particular occasion, sometimes growing into the fabric of orchestral writing."[1] The suite, *English Folk Songs*, was written for the Royal Military School of Music at Kneller Hall. After the first performance on July 4, 1923, *The Musical Times* reviewer commented, "The good composer has the ordinary monger of light stuff so hopelessly beaten."[2] Vaughan Williams had been particularly happy to undertake the *Suite*, according to his wife, as he enjoyed working in a medium new to him.

*This composer's name is one of the most frequently mispelled among all composers: "Vaughn" is incorrect.

Frederick Fennell is conductor-in-residence at the University of Miami School of Music in Florida, where he is music director of the Symphony Orchestra and Symphonic Wind Ensemble. Well known as the founder/director of the Eastman Wind Ensemble, he was a member of the faculty at Eastman for many years. His classic recording of the "Folk Song Suite" with the Eastman Wind Ensemble is still available (Mercury SRI 75011).

"A military band was a change from an orchestra, and in his not-so-far off army days he had heard enough of the 'ordinary monger's light stuff' to feel that a chance to play real tunes would be an agreeable and salutary experience for Bandsmen."[3]

At the head of his condensed score (the only one available until the mid-1950's) the composer gave the following credits, not printed in the full score: "The tune, 'My Bonny Boy', is taken from 'English County Songs' by kind permission of Miss L.E. Broadwood, J.A. Fuller-Maitland Esq., and the Leadenhall Press. The tunes of 'Folk Songs from Somerset' are introduced by kind permission of Cecil Sharp, Esq."

1. March — "Seventeen come Sunday"

Folk song materials used in the first "March" are "Seventeen come Sunday" [4-17] and "Pretty Caroline" [32-63]. The other dominating tune [64-96] is a Vaughan Williams original. Characteristically in robust contrast to the other two tunes (in the key of f minor), it is wonderfully folk-like, an irresistible jig-tune.

"Seventeen come Sunday" is in the Dorian mode and the musical rhythm follows that in the extended text, taking stress from the words (Ex. 1). Vaughan Williams probably found this tune from among the many notations by Sharp, Broadwood, and others.[4]

Ex. 1.

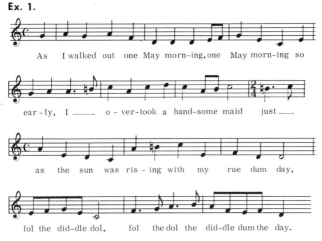

As I walked out one May morn-ing, one May morn-ing so

ear-ly, I ___ o - ver-took a hand-some maid just ___

as the sun was ris - ing with my rue dum day,

fol the did-dle dol, fol the dol the did-dle dum the day.

"Pretty Caroline" [32-63] is a straight-forward tune in Ab that perfectly sets up the composer's own melody [64]. In spite of its demands on the stamina of all players, the section [64-96] must be repeated to fulfill the form. Vaughan Williams seemed fascinated with the compelling rhythm of his tune, but he shows that he is "the good composer" by departing from its pattern twice at the proper moments [82-86]. "Pretty Caroline" returns [96] before the *da capo* return to "Seventeen come Sunday," extending the form to that of a small arch. The listener, the player, and the conductor are guided through the "March" by a simple and effective harmonic scheme which leads comfortably through related keys: f minor, Ab major, back to f minor. A bold declaration then concludes the movement — the Picardy third in F major.

Conducting Challenges

One tempo must suffice for all three tunes in this movement, and if played in the area of ♩=120 the

music moves brightly without being pushed. Strict dynamic control must be established in the first four bars for the *pianissimo* which follows in the "Seventeen come Sunday" tune with its constant shift of phrase emphasis. Here we could all convey the vital elements of irregular stress that are so much a part of the rhythmic freedom in British folk tunes,[5] by conducting the stresses where they fall, not merely beating continually a perfunctory pulse of two. The music simply demands something else (Ex. 2, measures [8-11]). At the mid-cadential figure [39-40] and similar places, an *espressivo* added to the *cantabile* already indicated greatly enhances the music. In these bars all parts should carry the nuance ＜＞

Ex. 2.

(stress)   (stress)

In "Pretty Caroline" once again we face the question of doubling in *piano* solo passages (clarinet and cornet) when the work is performed indoors. This problem occurs in all but 4 of the 33 bars of the complete exposition of "Pretty Caroline." I now resolve the question by eliminating the solo cornet from the doublings [32-55], allowing the clarinet plus the flute [40] plus the oboe [48] to carry the tunes in contrasting and reinforcing timbres all the way to [60], where the solo clarinet is eliminated and the solo cornet plays the tag-line phrase as a refreshing change of color. Thus, the clarinet also has a brief rest prior to the taxing 6/8 passage ahead. When "Pretty Caroline" returns again [97, second ending], the clarinet is silent and the cornet plays the tune to [105], then gives it back to the flute and clarinet until [125] when the cornet completes it alone to the *da capo*.

To add further expansions of color and register, remove *loco* from the piccolo part [56-60] and add the piccolo in the same register [121-125].

Vaughan Williams was not explicitly clear about the length of the dotted eighth-note figure which dominates his jig [64-96]. We see it clearly only in the initial figure, in the piccolo, flute, and Eb clarinet parts only. This might then be taken as the preferred articulation and transferred to all other parts. I have

Ex. 3.

always preferred the long, *tenuto* eighth followed by very *staccato* eighths (Ex. 3).

2. Intermezzo — "My Bonny Boy"

The middle movement, a 3/4 *Andantino* in f minor and F major, uses the folk songs "My Bonny Boy" and "Green Bushes." These 97 bars, among the best in any band music, probably began to take shape in Vaughan Williams' brain as early as 1905 when, as his wife observed, he noted the "Bonny Boy" tune at King's Lynn.[6] The beautifully scored f minor chord with which the movement begins seems to demand an initial dynamic marking greater than the *pianissimo* indicated. If the players begin *mezzo-piano*, they can make an effective *diminuendo* so the chord at the movement's beginning will be less static.

Then at [2] the conductor must choose his solo player between the oboe and cornet. Perhaps one player's security, virtuosity, beauty of tone, or musicality may make the decision obvious. But if not, I always prefer the plaintive, expressive quality of the oboe in this solo and ask the cornet to be at rest in this whole opening statement (except for [16] and the first note of [17]. The oboe timbre here should fit the darker aspects of the key and help emphasize the emotional content of the tune's expressive words, indicating a departed love.

> "Now once I was courted by a bonny, bonny boy,
>   I loved him I vow and protest;
> I loved him so well, so very, very well,
>   That I built him a bower in my breast,
>   That I built him a bower in my breast."

Various notations of this principal song contain basic, similar elements, including the elongation of the pulse at the emotional junction of the words and melody. This is one such version provided by Karpeles,[7] here transposed to Vaughan Williams' key:

that I built him a bower in my breast

Vaughan Williams never varies the meter from 3/4, but his *crescendo-diminuendo* [14] gives some indication of the stress a folk singer might give to the word, and conveys, as well, his expressive intent in this phrase. (Before I knew of this version documented by Karpeles I had been instinctively stretching this bar the last time it comes [91].)

The composer's familiarity with English folk song at it roots clearly shows in the "Intermezzo" movement. After the "exposition and development" of the first tune, "My Bonny Boy," the second tune, "Green Bushes" is introduced and forms the middle section. The songs he heard in the counties and shires were traditionally sung unaccompanied except, perhaps, by a drone, which instrument he imitated here in the sparse underpinnings of the clarinets and horns ("Poco Allegro — Scherzando"); all the melodic elements move neatly above this static f minor/Major harmonic foundation. Here again, we notice how important the *tune* is over any harmonic accompaniment, as it was to the singers of these folk songs. Vaughan Williams' remarkable musical comprehension (recall his classic orchestral setting of "Greensleeves") has served to acquaint us with beautiful tunes through his highly effective settings — simple, sensitive, and charming.

When "My Bonny Boy" returns [77 to end], a favorite Vaughan Williams harmonic technique (parallel triads above the tune in the bass) brings back the dolorous character of the movement's beginning. Here we are treated to the work of a master, the imprint of whose craft is unmistakable; these simple measures could only have been penned by R.V.W.

The confusing designation, *solo*, is still to be found in some publications. One reason might be that from the band's beginning, the clarinets and cornets were the keepers of the melody. But somewhat later the trombone, euphonium, saxophone and xylophone were also featured solo instruments, though there was not such a designation on the parts or in the score.

This custom is probably held over from a past time when the exalted position of "up-front soloist" also brought with it military rank, financial advantage, and a certain social distinction. Then, too, so much of band tradition was borrowed from orchestral custom. The titular and spiritual leader of the orchestra has always been the concertmaster, who is the principal of the many violins and spokesman for all the strings. The concertmaster/mistress at the conductor's left is the ready recipient of the conductor's handshake greeting extended to the entire group. For the band this is something of a dilemma. To many of us, the principal clarinetist still gets the conductor's greeting, even though a band's flutes may equal or outnumber the clarinets; and that long walk back through the players to the principal cornet is one rarely taken by conductors of today's wind groups.

Regardless of the historical reasons, however, the time has come for publishers to dispense with the designations "solo clarinet" and "solo cornet" in today's band music.

Conducting Challenges

The choice of tempo should be an *andantino* close to ♩=72 to move the line without pressing the soloist. In spite of the sad character of the words, the music should not sink to a maudlin drawl that dies in a sagging melodic line. The soloist, by the way, should be reminded (if necessary) to extend the final note of the fourth phrase [15] to the very end of the bar. This G♮ is too frequently cut short and creates an awkward gap in the line, simply because of the upward leap of a 7th into the next bar. (A quick glance at the score will show that the coming passage is well-covered elsewhere.)

If an E♭ clarinet is missing (an unfortunate absence), the line [20-40] must be given to the piccolo to play in unison with the flute. The texture demands that little bit of higher melodic penetration to enhance the beautiful winding lines of the oboe and B♭ clarinet. The cadence and connecting link in the clarinet [40-42] must be played by a single performer. The conductor should then allow the clarinet soloist some freedom, but he might suggest a slight *ritenuto* leading into "Poco Allegro (Scherzando)." Here it may feel comfortable to establish the new pulse (*ca.* ♩.=54, or ♩=160) by launching it in a neat, small, precise pulse of three, moving into the more desirable one beat per bar at the first convenient place [46], continuing thus until it is necessary [73] to prepare the *ritenuto* and the return in *diminuendo* to the opening tune.

The expressive character of "Green Bushes" in Vaughan Williams' setting [43-77] calls for more of a "half-*staccato*" (line over the dot above the note) rather than the short *staccato* articulation frequently heard. Cymbals [58-74] should be a small thin pair, struck together without damping.

Preservation of the dynamic balances and subtle nuances in this middle section [43-77] is vital to the sensitive setting of the tune, as is the need for extremely solid breath support for everything going on here (including the triangle and cymbals!). The overlapping figures in the reeds (played with long eighths at the end of the slurs) should fairly shimmer in a vibrant *pianissimo* exchange above the solo alto reeds, cornet, and euphonium. These solo players should be encouraged to sing out at the top level of their printed *mezzo-forte* dynamic.

The return of "My Bonny Boy" at *Tempo primo* [77] is a tricky spot for achieving good tonal balance, and if the baritone and bass saxophone players have any difficulty in providing the written *pianissimo* here, I would not hesitate to replace them with the more frequently secure low brass blend. (Note that the composer has already omitted the bassoons and bass clarinet at this point.) Approaching the F major final cadence, it seems important and necessary to enhance the balance in the bass lines with the following expressive dynamics:

The *crescendo* in the final chord, preceded by the composer's built-in *ritenuto* through augmentation, should not exceed a level of *mezzo-forte*.

3. March — "Folk Songs from Somerset"

The final movement, in Bb major, is in a 2/4 *Allegro*. A tempo about ♩=128 is recommended. Folk song materials used are "Blow away the morning dew," "High Germany," "The tree so high," and "John Barleycorn." A second Eb clarinet appears in this movement [23-24, 63-64], and its notes are sufficiently important in that register to warrant transferring them to 2nd flute and 2nd oboe, since these instruments are doubling the 1st parts here.

Vaughan Williams is very specific about articulations in this piece, but I would urge the conductor to keep the *marcato* dotted eighths long enough [28-29, 41-42], and to scrupulously avoid any harsh or strident brass sounds in the sixteenths following the dotted eighths.

The score does not point out that the pulse should remain the same at the 2/4 and 6/8 change at [69] but the conductor should assure it. In this "Trio" it seems desirable to stress the *sostenuto* character of the tune to contrast with the more driving first portion of this "March" movement. I always have to coax the charming counterline out of the unison trumpets [81-84] and from the solo cornet at [85-88], and it helps to raise their dynamic marking from the writ-

ten *piano* and *pianissimo* to a singing *mezzo-forte*. Good tone quality must be the first consideration for all of the brass when the 2/4 section returns [89].

To lead into the 1st ending before the *da capo* [108], I have always felt that making a well-paced *ritenuto* in these final four bars is a valid interpretive license. I was privileged to attend most of the series of lectures Vaughan Williams gave at Cornell University in November, 1954, and on one occasion I took along this score to discuss with him. When I asked what he thought of this interpretive change, he said: "I like it — use it." The *Folk Song Suite* is indeed an altogether "agreeable and salutary experience for bandsmen" — and for conductors, too! ■

Corrections

The full score to *Folk Song Suite* was made from the parts, but it is less error-filled than the Holst (*Suite in Eb*) and Jacob (*William Byrd Suite*) scores discussed earlier in this series. In the absence of any rehearsal numbers in the music, it is urgent that the score be numbered at every bar and the parts at the head of each line, to facilitate rehearsal.

March — "Seventeen come Sunday"

[5, 16] Solo and 1st cornet — part. Correct *senza solo* to read *senza 1st*.

[67] 2nd cornet — part. Some parts may have a printing error which makes the first eighth note look like a dotted eighth.

[72] Eb clarinet — part. Correct rhythm in first half of the bar to read ♩. ♪ (full score is correct).

March — "Folk Songs from Somerset"

Solo and 1st cornet — part and score. Throughout this movement the *divisi* presents a visual problem. Clarify and assign each part when *divisi* occurs.

[1] Solo clarinet — part. The 16th flag is missing on the first pair of notes.

[15, 55] Triangle — score and part. Slur missing.

[34, 36, 40, 43] Snare drum — score and part. Slur missing. All drags and flams throughout the score and parts need slurs.

[56] Solo cornet — score and part. Because of the previous *tutti*, part should indicate *solo* on last eighth note.

[70,88] All reeds playing trill — score and parts. Trill should be slurred into [71] and [89].

[112] All reeds (Bb clarinets and up) — score and parts. 32nd-note flourish should be slurred into the downbeat at the repeat [71].

1. Ursula Vaughan Williams, *R.V.W.: A Biography of Ralph Vaughan Williams* (London: Oxford University Press, 1964), pp. 150-153.

2. *Ibid.*

3. *Ibid.*

4. Maud Karpeles, *An Introduction to English Folk Song* (London: Oxford University Press, 1973).

5. See Percy Aldridge Grainger's Forward to *Lincolnshire Posy* (London: Schott & Co., Ltd., 1939).

6. Vaughan Williams, op. cit.

7. Karpeles, op. cit.

This is the fourth in a series of articles by Frederick Fennell on basic band repertory. Earlier articles covered Holst's *Suite in E♭* (April 1975), Gordon Jacob's *William Byrd Suite* (September 1975), and Vaughan Williams' *Folk Song Suite* (June 1976). Dr. Fennell looks back over his 40 years as a conductor and discusses those compositions which he considers to be the basis of the band literature, focusing primarily on those things of interest to fellow conductors. His discussion of the Vaughan Williams works stems from his personal conversations with the composer, as he describes below.

"Vaughan Williams visited the United States for the last time in November, 1954, when he delivered a series of lectures at Cornell University. He granted me a brief interview while at Cornell, and with scores in hand, I visited him to discuss *Folk Song Suite* and *Toccata Marziale*.

"When I spoke of my long admiration for *Toccata,* he was surprised and seemed pleased that anybody in the U.S. knew of it, since it had been pretty well ignored in England. This remarkable score dates from 1924. And that is all anybody seems to know about it at this writing. I do not know the location of the manuscript, nor why or for whom it was written. I spent what precious little time I had talking with him about the music, not about its origin. I realized very soon that this was an error, for he died before I found out the story behind *Toccata.*

"The recording which I made one year later (1955) with the Eastman Wind Ensemble has recently been re-released by Mercury Records. The performance embodies my feelings for the piece and projects the spirit of my conversation with Vaughan Williams."

Vaughan Williams' Toccata Marziale

Frederick Fennell

Ralph Vaughan Williams (1872-1958). *Toccata Marziale*. Copyright 1924 by Hawkes & Son, London; presently available through Boosey & Hawkes, New York (Quarto Military Band Edition No. 234, Plate No. H.&S. 6239). B♭ major, 3/4 *Allegro maestoso;* 157 bars; duration *ca.* 5:00; minimum of 36 players required. Full score (made from the parts in the mid-1950s) and condensed score; 2 flutes and piccolo, 2 oboes, 2 bassoons, clarinets (E♭, solo, 1st, 2nd, 3rd, alto, bass, and contrabass), saxophones (soprano, alto, tenor, baritone, and bass), 4 horns in F, cornets (solo and 1st, 2nd), B♭ trumpet*, trombones (2 tenor, 1 bass), bass clef euphonium (treble part comes with the set), basses, string contrabass, kettledrums, triangle, snare drum, cymbals, and bass drum.

The band of the Royal Military School of Music (Kneller Hall) played the premiere in 1924 at Wembley Stadium in London under the direction of Lt. H.E. Adkins, as part of the British Empire Exposition. Hawkes & Son issued it in a Souvenir Edition (No. 473) of music for military band in commemoration of the Exposition.[1]

*T*occata Marziale was Vaughan Williams' second work for band, and it is one of the most significant pieces of music ever contributed to band literature. Like Holst's *Suite in E♭,* also conceived for the band medium, it is a supreme example of what a master composer can contribute to the musical literature of this unfortunately neglected ensemble. It is an original work, first-rate by any standard of measurement. *Toccata* is a contrapuntal masterpiece in which textures are juxtaposed in massed effects with large sections of reeds and brasses, making it difficult to imagine this work being performing by any ensemble but a large wind band.

Harmonically, it is typical of Vaughan Williams' style in 1924 (*cf.* Overture to *The Wasps* and *Symphony No. 2,* "London"), with its diatonic movement of parallel major and minor triads and free manipulation of major, minor, and whole-tone scales. Michael Kennedy, Vaughan Williams' biographer, believes that some elements of the *Symphony No. 6* were ". . .anticipated in *Toccata Marziale* twenty years before,"[2] and that the *Toccata* ". . .contains a 'tryout' of the marvellous hieratic writing for brass [in *Job*] that dominates [Vaughan Williams'] work from 1926 onwards."[3] A great rhythmic vigor, as the title suggests, permeates the whole score, propelling the strong contrapuntal lines throughout the vividly clear harmonic textures.

Toccata Marziale is a supreme example of what a master composer can contribute to the literature of this unfortunately neglected ensemble.

Toccata's superb scoring brilliantly reveals the fundamental properties of the band's sonority and its instrumental virtuosity and color, with strong emphasis on the fine gradations between long and short, *forte* and *piano.* It is regrettable that this piece, such a faithful conception of the wind band as a medium of musical expression, has not been performed with more frequency commensurate with its musical value.

The word "toccata" comes from the Italian, *toccare,* "to touch." Hence its association with the early Baroque virtuoso keyboard pieces written by Frescobaldi and others. Describing Frescobaldi's toccatas, Willi Apel writes in the *Harvard Dictionary of Music* (1964, p. 750):

> They are written in a succession of quickly changing "scenes," an interesting exhibition of overflowing imagination without any restraining and binding principle of form.

Professor Apel could just as well have been writing the perfect program note for *Toccata Marziale.*

A choice of tempo must be based upon a combination of the indicated tempo *Allegro maestoso,* the sound of the music itself, the consideration of clarity, and finally the title — "martial toccata." Somewhere in all of this lies a pulse that works; try ♩=104-112. I find that this allows it all to move while harnessing the music's undeniable thrust, affording that majesty suggested in the tempo description "maestoso."

The Main Motive

Vaughan Williams' overflowing imagination and his unrestrained approach to form make *Toccata* a small masterpiece of musical construction. He builds the entire piece from a single motive (Ex. 1), out of which he creates a busy network of countermelodies, echo fragments, and accompanimental patterns.

Ex. 1 [1]

The piece is barely four bars old when the entire instrumental machinery is at work on this main germ idea: the low reeds and brasses play it as a rock-ribbed bass line [1-4], to be immediately capped by a martial fanfare in the horns and trombones in the same measures (idea I, derived from the major motive beneath it). This contrapuntal community, heavily populated with parallel thirds, is joined by another motivic answer (II) in [5]. These ideas are hammered away with more parallelism to the transitional bar [8], leading on to another derivative idea (III) in [9], which is accompanied by a bass pattern built on fourths (see summary on next page).

The spirit in which the first two notes of *Toccata* are launched has important consequence for the

remainder of the piece. These notes

Ex. 2

benefit greatly from the traditional separation which is articulated almost automatically by first rate bands and orchestras. It is separation with just the slightest hesitation, and without it something stylistically rewarding is missing.

To conduct the opening bars, give the silent second and third beats prior to the up-beat eighth-note to assure a solid, secure beginning; everybody has a chance to feel the pulse. Then immediately, the driving sixteenths begin propelling the basic ideas throughout *Toccata*. The *staccato* of the sixteenths is as vital to them as the *tenuto* length and separation of the eighths which follow [4]. These eighths must be restrained to control what might otherwise run away. The sometimes desirable ensemble practice of reducing the volume of sustained sounds to heighten important moving voices is not desirable in this piece, where all the lines are drawn to be played without dynamic reduction. (The opening eight measures illustrate two such equivalent lines, both assigned a *forte* dynamic.)

The first contrasting melodic idea (III) appears next [9]. It is built on a fragment of the main motive and explores a reduced dynamic level *(mezzo-forte)*, with *legato* textures in both the parallel triad sixteenths and in the important bass figure which accompanies them. This bass line is present in about

one-third of the 157 bars and assumes varied appropriate forms in support of the particular musical ideas. The super *legato* of the slurred sixteenths here, and the lengthy quarter note followed by the two brief, separated eighth-notes are contrasts which must be observed. The conductor has to work with the ensemble to achieve these contrasts; my experience convinces me that a full and vibrant *legato* is more difficult to achieve than the *staccato* in these passages.

Bar [10] contains the rhythmic figure ♫♩ , which is one that will grow in importance throughout the work. The challenge which this presents comes not only from the precision necessary in the sixteenths and eighths, but also in the care with which any following impulse is placed — avoid the tendency to play it too soon. It will help the players to be reminded that the sixteenths are the essential backbone throughout the entire piece.

Vaughan Williams makes many sophisticated ensemble demands on those who perform his *Toccata Marziale*, including strict control of nuance and absolute observance of printed dynamic levels. The latter is present in the brief connecting link [15], where he expects a reduction from *forte* to *piano* in only two eighth-notes. This is highly important in performance:

Ex. 3 [15]

Summary of Motives & Derivative Ideas

161

Within this new *piano,* another outgrowth of the germ motive makes its appearance, scored for reeds and crisply etched by the snare drum (idea IV). (Throughout, the snare drum should be thin, tightly tuned, and played with sparkle; please allow the cymbals, bass drum, and triangle to ring.) The figure at [18] should stress the important rising interval of the fourth since it is borrowed from the first bars of the piece. It serves the performance well if all parts have accents written in over these notes, including all rising intervals of a fifth which are obviously related [17-22].

A Newly-Derived Idea

Toccata is 22 bars old when a major melodic idea (V) is introduced. It is cleverly related to the opening motive:

Ex. 4

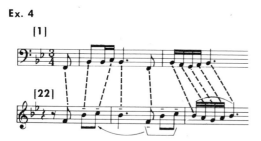

This melody will appear in approximately one-third of the total piece, dominating the high intensity portions. Here at [22], as it often happens in British band literature, the conductor must choose between two solo instruments, oboe and cornet. Others may not agree, feeling that the doubling is intentional. But as I have previously stated in other discussions in this repertory series, when the thicker-textured scoring and higher dynamic levels diminish to sparser instrumentation, all instrument parts should be taken by solo players. In this particular decision, I prefer the oboe for its plaintive, expressive quality.

All players must strive to achieve the lyricism in this infectious little tune [V], emphasizing the *legato* sixteenths [24]. The idea so obviously delighted Vaughan Williams that he couldn't resist the invitation to treat it in *stretto* among the alto reeds, bass reeds, and euphonium. Counter to this there also runs an independent *cantabile* line in the bassoon and horn which foreshadows an upcoming new melody [53]. Thus at [22] we are treated to a fascinating contrapuntal melange: the tune V leads the way, its accompanimental figure running in counterpoint with itself, while the hint of the melody-to-be runs through the middle!

Just when we have settled down to these quiet delights, tastily garnished with delicate percussion, the melody idea V is again hurled at us [26], quickly transformed to a fierce *fortissimo* utterance in the trombones and euphoniums. This is hastily countered [27] by an answering fanfare fragment in horns and cornets.

Clarinets and others pick up a countermelodic line in [26], and the conductor and players must make sure that this line comes through in spite of all the heavy competition from the brasses. The following editing usually helps, adding accents and a *crescendo* [26-28]:

Ex. 5 [26-28]

Alternating heavy and light textures becomes the pattern as the composer pursues the rhythmic development of his material, adding accents to shift the metric feeling:

Ex. 6 [32-34]

and moving the bar line around at will:

Ex. 7

The subtle articulation in all these voices [30-34] demands detailed study by conductors and absolute observance by players. Heavy *tenuto* is indicated by the lines over the notes, emphatic impact by the accents, and an unyielding flow of sound from the *legato* slurs.

Some of the most marvelous reed writing I know comes next [35-40] where, along with the second *fortissimo* statement of melody idea V in the brass, these remarkable lines are laid down (see Ex. 8).

Ex. 8 [35-40]

On examination of the full score, the intriguing cross-rhythms in the "swinging" clarinets and saxophones should be immediately apparent, and I re-affirm my fervent admiration for this music when I say "it swings." I have enjoyed performances in which, responding to my request, players have played these sixteenths with the "jazz feel." Those stark contrasts in *marcato* [34-36] and *legato* [37-40], vital elements in *Toccata*, are vividly set forth in the brasses in these same measures — and the contrasts must be *stark!* The *stretto*-like statement of the first four eighths in [41-43] demands a good *marcato* quality, and a super separation between the eighths will assure that detached articulation.

Bars [44-47] then reveal the development of melody idea V, the results of which re-appear in an extended quotation before the close of the piece (compare [44-45] with [140-142], and [47] with [144-146]). The *legato* syncopes (syncopated notes) which occur throughout the piece (see [9-10, 38-40, 45, 100, 132-133], and [139-141]) are of stylistic importance to the performance, and a short release of the eighth before the quarter note must be scrupulously avoided.

Folk Song Interlude

The main motive of the opening and its counter-melody I, briefly quoted in subtle disguise in the c minor statement at [51], lead deftly to the introduction at [53] of Vaughan Williams' lovely folk-song melody, offered in contrast and earlier hinted at [23] and [29-30]. This folk-like modal tune is totally unlike any other idea in the score. It must be played in ultimate singing *legato* with the most expressive *cantabile*. Because it is assigned [53-57] to 3rd clarinet, alto reeds, horns, and euphonium (previous carriers of the secondary counterpoint [23-26]), the theme gives the impression of a major new voice.

One familiar with the music of Vaughan Williams grows to expect a line of similar lyricism in anything he wrote. Although the essential character of *Toccata* changes here, where the composer decorates his wonderfully arching melody with cascading lines in the two clarinets and flute [53-58], the accompanying bass idea reminds us, even in *pianissimo*, that old contrapuntal obligations are present, and we see that new ones are versatile [61-64], where the main opening motive and the new folk melody

are happily joined while the latter counterpoints within itself.

The pentatonic character of the bridge [65-68], over a descending version of the bass idea, leads *Toccata* to fascinating harmonic developments as the music momentarily becomes less contrapuntal. A fragment idea of the folk melody originates in [47] (see also [144-146]). A whole-tone scale feeling pervades much of these developments [69-90], generated by both the scale fragments in the reeds [75-78] and the parallel descending major triads in the brasses [70-71] and [73-74] .

Vaughan Williams' rhythmic diminution (two 3/8's within a 3/4 bar at [70]) must *not* result in a 1920s jazz interpretation — avoid any false accents:

Ex. 9 [70]

The bass drum (no rags inside or tape on the heads, please) should simply enhance the *crescendo* here [70], not dominate it; write in a maximum of *mezzo-piano* over it to insure balance. The parallel triad idea, which first appeared in [11] as a connecting device, now becomes augmented over four bars [75-78], to provide slowly-paced rising triads through the running reed passages.

The excitement of this *crescendo*, which is built into the harmonic scheme, requires an adjustment of the printed clarinet dynamics — this fabulous passage must be heard! Start from *mezzo-forte* in [75], reach *forte* in [77], and end with *fortissimo* in [78]. (The strong independence written into the four Bb clarinet parts begs for equal distribution of the players among the four lines; there is a minimum of doubling in any of them. It is desirable to assign the strongest players as the four principals and spread clarinet strength throughout the sections.)

The harmonic tension here [75-78] is built around the E pedal point in flute, piccolo, soprano sax, 1st and 2nd horns, and 2nd cornet, and it is so important to the total substance of the music that conductor and players must not allow the pitch to be buried beneath the rising excitement (see Ex. 10).

In the long seven-bar *diminuendo* which follows [78-84], the trills in clarinets, saxophones, and cor-

Ex. 10 [75-78]

net benefit from a punching kind of accent. The absence of the brass and string bass from the F pedal point [85] in favor of the quality of horns, saxes, and bassoons is the touch of skill; it also sets up the entrance of all the low brass for the "recapitulation" (*pianissimo*, in the key of Gb beginning with the pickup to [91]). The suspended cymbal, scored to color the low reed and kettledrum [85-87] should be a thin, bright plate played with soft-textured sticks. All reeds playing eighth-notes [89-90] should ignore the *diminuendo* until the last three notes before [91], and maintain a highly vibrant quality throughout these two bars of thematic extension.

Contrapuntal Ingenuity

At [91-94], with the literal transposition to Gb of the first four bars of *Toccata*, Vaughan Williams embarks on yet another exciting contrapuntal excursion during which he treats us to a viruoso display of his compositional gifts. Above the opening germ motive, most of the contrasting folk melody appears in a *cantabile* statement [93-95]; horns and middle reeds engage in a *stretto* of the germ motive with basses [95-97], while upper reeds contribute an "oriental" version of idea II [96-98], with an upper brass statement of the folk melody at the same time [97-99]. Next [100-105], there follows a restatement of melody idea III (from [9-14]), this time with the high brass adding the folk melody [101-102], which then passes to the low brass [103-104] as the high reeds quote the bass idea; the low trombones join with low reeds in a canon with the folk melody, above and below which the high reeds and low valve-brass engage in a canon with another earlier rhythmic idea. Ideas jam up as we are led on with material fashioned from the bass idea plus new rhythmic fragments from III:

Ex. 11 [109-111]

This figure possesses great drive, and Vaughan Williams harnesses it to full extent as he approaches the exciting return of the home key of Bb in a majestic *allargando* [116], the only change of tempo in

Ex. 12 [116]

the piece. At the *allargando*, stress the subtle variation (rhythmic and in voicing) between horns and high trombones and among cornets, trumpet and the rest of the low brass.

Now comes the full statement of melodic idea V, with its counterline, and from [120-139] we have a restatement of bars [26-45]. At [134-137] (and also [40-43]) emphasize the importance of the *fortissimo* pedal point in the middle reeds and horns, and add *sforzando* when it changes to Eb. In the canonic statement at [134-137] between reeds and cornets, there must be no slackening of the necessary tonal intensity. In fact, at the final bar of this section [143], *molto crescendo* should be added to every rising part:

Ex. 13 [143]

At [144] the composer continues to borrow from the quarter note triads of [47], extending them to nine pulses which move harmonically through parallel triads from Bb to Gb. Be sure to scrupulously avoid the usual natural tendency toward *diminuendo* in this harmonic descent, and instead press forward to the third beat of [146], which should be *fortissimo* in all instruments with a *mezzo-forte* for the percussion. The gradual *crescendo* from *piano* to *fortississimo* [147-end] must be strictly observed, but the higher dynamic level must be attained early enough to project the important scale passages in the reeds [146-151]. Throughout this final section [147-153], all the hard-hitting fragments of the major germ motive must be brittle and detached. The horns, cornets, and trumpets here contribute something "new-sounding" — a rhythmic motto theme which comes from the germ rhythm:

Ex. 14 [147-149]

The rugged, relentless *basso ostinato* on Gb, which begins in [146] and grows dynamically by gradual addition of the low brass instruments, could be augmented by having kettledrums play Ab instead of the Db. This Gb-Ab *ostinato* is the foundation of everything here, including the implied whole-tone scales in the reeds. It amounts to one of the great moments in band music, culminating at [153] in an apotheosis of swirling whole-tone scales on Bb and F above a pitchless percussion pedal point (modify it to *mezzo forte*). It all ends in the great and final parallelism of Gb-Bb-C-Bb. Cymbal might be added to the final release.

Thus concludes a great British band classic. There was no piece like it before in band literature, and I know of none written in the following half-century that compares to it. Here is a work of principal significance by a man in complete control of all phases of a superior technique, written in 1924 for a medium that was perhaps not yet ready to receive it. In 1923, a music reviewer wrote of the premiere of R.V.W.'s other original work for band, *Folk Song Suite:* "The good composer has the ordinary monger of light stuff so hopelessly beaten."[4] Half a century later, the works of "the ordinary mongers of light stuff" are still high on the lists of what bands study and perform in the schools of America, while performances of *Toccata Marziale* are strangely infrequent.

We conductors who shy away from demanding contrapuntal works of this dimension are probably to blame for such infrequent performances. But today the contrapuntal experience is sought out by so many young players who are eager to come to grips with this sort of intellectual and musical complexity. We are denying them a vital experience by avoiding such music, just because it may not play with ease . . . at first. The *Toccata* is difficult rhythmically, not because of complex or diverse meters, but in the sophisticated placement of simple fundamental rhythmic impulses and in the constant demand for vitality of tonal production in their precise execution.

The part writing is superb, but the demands are there: all instruments must play in all registers, and there must be utmost control of articulations from super detached to the greatest *sostenuto*. All this drapes Vaughan Williams' remarkable contrapuntal fabric over a rhythmic framework to make it, like all great pieces, a lesson in orchestration. *Toccata* most definitely was not written for players or conductors faint of heart, but since we are now producing an ever-abundant number of first-class conductors to lead the excellent players we've always had, *Toccata Marziale* seems certain to be studied and performed more frequently in the years ahead — with obvious rewards to all. ∎

Corrections

[1] 1st and 2nd trombone — parts. Bar line missing.

[8] 2nd clarinet — part. Flat missing on first eighth note.

[11] Tenor sax — part. Change second eighth note to written F.

[13] 1st and 3rd horns — parts. Correct second eighth note from E to written D.

[14] 2nd cornet — part. Correct last quarter note to C from D.

[10] E♭ clarinet — part. Extend slur over the sixteenths to the eighth note.

[17] 3rd clarinet — part. Fourth eighth note should be B♭.

[17] 1st bassoon and euphonium (treble clef) — parts. Third eighth note should be G♭.

[18] 2nd clarinet — part. Clarify second of two sixteenths — should be an A♮.

[20] 2nd clarinet — part. Four eighth notes should be sixteenths.

[24] Oboe — part and score. Last eighth note should be an F♮.

[31] 2nd and 3rd clarinets — parts. Remove dot on first eighth note in second pair of eighths.

[32] Oboe — part. Change fourth sixteenth note to E♭.

[35] Bass clarinet — part. Slur missing over first four sixteenths.

[42] 2nd trombone — part. Second eighth should be E♭.

[43] 1st and 3rd clarinets — parts. Add staccato dots.

[47] Bass trombone — part. Remove dot from first eighth note.

[48, 49] Euphonium, treble clef — part. Last eighth should be C concert.

[49] Trumpet — part. Remove *diminuendo* under last six sixteenths and move to [50].

[60] 3rd clarinet — score. Correct first two eighth notes to written A and G.

[60] 3rd and 4th horns — parts. Correct note to written E♮.

[70] 1st horn — score. Correct fifth eighth note to B♮.

[70] Solo cornet — part and score. Correct first note to written G♯.

[70] 1st trombone — part. Tie the two C's.

[83, 84] 2nd clarinet — part. Print the flats and sharps on the trills.

[90] Oboe — part. Correct first eighth note to C♮.

[92] Euphonium, treble clef — part. Add flat on first sixteenth note.

[96] Oboe — part. Second rest should be an eighth, not a quarter rest.

[100] E♭ clarinet — part and score. Remove the dot from the first eighth note.

[100] 1st and 3rd horns — parts and score. Correct third eighth note to B♮.

[103] Soprano sax — score. Correct first note to written G.

[106] E♭ clarinet — part. Last four sixteenths should be eighth notes.

[136] 1st clarinet — part. The printed sixteenths should be eighth notes.

[144] Snare drum — part and score. Dynamic should be *forte*.

[145] Snare drum — part and score. Remove *diminuendo*.

[146] Alto clarinet and sax — parts. Correct first eighth note to E♭ concert.

[148] Solo and 1st clarinet — score. Slur the first four sixteenth notes.

[151] 1st trombone — part. Second eighth note should be flatted.

[156] 2nd cornet — part. Correct fifth eighth note to E.

[157] 2nd trombone — part. Remove the *piano* dynamic.

1. Michael Kennedy, *The Works of Ralph Vaughan Williams* (London: Oxford University Press, 1964), p. 495.
2. *Ibid.*, p. 224.
3. *Ibid.*
4. Quoted by Ursula Vaughan Williams in *R.V.W.: A Biography of Ralph Vaughan Williams* (London: Oxford University Press, 1964), pp. 151-152.

Gustav Holst's Hammersmith

Frederick Fennell

This is another in a series of articles by Frederick Fennell on basic band repertory, beginning with the British classics. Earlier articles covered Holst's *Suite in Eb* (April 1975), Gordon Jacob's *William Byrd Suite* (September 1975), Vaughan Williams' *Folk Song Suite* (June 1976), and Vaughan Williams' *Toccata Marziale* (August 1976). Fennell looks back over his 40 years as a conductor and discusses those compositions which he considers to be the basis of the band literature, focusing primarily on those things of interest to fellow conductors.

A copy of the score is essential to readers. Number the bars 1-436.

When Holst was offered the BBC commission that became *Hammersmith*, 19 important years had passed since last he addressed himself to the military band. His daughter Imogen describes the Holst *Hammersmith* creative posture: "Nineteen-thirty was one of the best years for composing that Holst had known . . . for the first time in his life. . . filled with a sense of well-being, he. . .enjoyed bringing all his energy to the works he had been commissioned to write." Robert Cantrick further establishes the *Hammersmith* profile: "This was his first task of writing wind-instrument music for professionals, the two early suites for military band in Eb and F, and the mature 'Moorside Suite' for brass band, having been written for amateurs. He conceived the new piece with great seriousness of purpose." [1]

The composition was named after a section of London called Hammersmith, a west metropolitan borough on the Thames River. It was more than home and workshop to Holst for most of his life while he also served as musical director at the St. Paul's Girls' School. He signed the title page of the score: "St. Paul's Girls' School/Brook Green/London W.6." The school no longer stands, but about the place, the man, and his music, Imogen Holst writes:

> The mood out of which the music had grown was a mood that had haunted him for nearly forty years: during his solitary walks in Hammersmith he had always been aware of the aloofness of the quiet river, unhurried and unconcerned, while just around the corner there was all the noise and hustle and exuberant vulgarity of the Cockney crowd...[4]

In spite of which she firmly believes that

> *Hammersmith* was not programme music. It was the outcome of long years of familiarity with the changing crowds and the changing river....In *Hammersmith* the river is the background to the crowd: it is a river that 'goes on its way unnoticed and unconcerned.'[5]

This score's dedication, "To the Author of 'The Water Gypsies'," acknowledges Alan P. Herbert's 1930 novel of that name in which a working-class girl from Hammersmith lives in two opposite worlds at once, sharing her life with a painter and a Thames River character whom Cantrick describes as an "illiterate bargee." The girl's irreconcilable personal dilemma obviously appealed to Holst.

Form

The *Hammersmith* form may be identified as a double arch of the two inner *Scherzos* resting on a center podium (Lento) and supported at the outer extremities by the two abutments of Poco adagio:

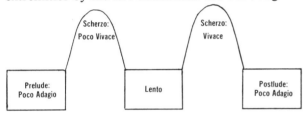

Prelude

Performance challenges begin with the choice of a tempo that suits the dark mood of the *Prelude*:

Ex. 1 [1-12]

Noting that Holst reserved Molto adagio for the final statement of the Prelude [422], and desiring the establishment of a legato movement, a pulse somewhere in the vicinity of ♩ = 60 allows it all to breathe and to play. From the outset one sees that this is indeed a serious piece for serious players who are in complete control of every aspect of performance. The ostinato with which the writing for low brass begins, set in ¾ time, employs the "white notation" (half-note) concept of lines which are slow-moving and of sustained character. Its visual intention is obvious, but its asset to material explored in adagio bars [1-42] carries liabilities when rhythmic complexities join, as in the piccolo [43] and trumpets [47], and for all

instruments [249-283] and [397-436]. The average 20th-century player somehow continues to reject this seemingly wise notational practice. Holst's obvious desire to harness the slowest pulse to the slowest-looking notation for the *Prelude* and to gain visual drive by casting the *Scherzo* in the familiar eighths and sixteenths ought to work automatically — but it does not unless the conductor and the players really work at it.

In his adoption of the half note as the "white" unit of time (¾) in the *Prelude*, Holst was obliged to use the *breve* ‖o‖ in bar [6] and subsequent measures where musical material called for two whole notes in a bar. This old note-value sign was part of mensural notation which served composers for about three and a half centuries up until around 1600, when present notational values came into use. *Alla breve* ¢ derives, of course, from that same mensural legacy.

Another visual liability which probably confuses some young players in this uncompromising and sophisticated score is the general absence of key signatures and the frequent use of accidentals. Key signatures are used only for convenience in the opening polytonal *Prelude* and twice in the *Scherzo*. Holst even abandoned at the final Poco adagio [397] those signatures he felt obliged to provide for the first one. Young players trained to keep eyes on the left margin may feel lost at first in this sea of unorthodox band sound, devoid of these familiar aids to musical navigation.

The first harmonic challenge is the juxtaposition of the horns' extended E major line [4] with the F minor ground bass of the low valve-brass. With this attractive polytonal joining of dark sonorities Holst demands the most intense and unwavering sostenuto to evoke the sight of slowly passing water running thick, deep, and inexorably out to sea. Breath factors and skillful, deliberate valving in support of this effect contribute to a performing difficulty that is further compounded by the triple challenges of intonation, the darkest sound, and the most restrained dynamics. It would be wise for the conductor and all players involved in the

> The first performance of the original military band score was played by the Kiltie Band of the Carnegie Institute of Technology in Pittsburgh, on April 14, 1954 with Robert Cantrick conducting. This puzzlingly long-delayed premiere of what to any eyes should have been an obvious masterpiece was the direct result of Cantrick's curiosity and indefatigable pursuit of the score. His fascinating tale is told in the journal *Music and Letters*.[2] This account, together with two remarkable writings[3] about the score by Holst's devoted and articulate daughter, Imogen, must be considered basic to any thorough study of the score, containing as they do a host of vital facts and penetrating analyses. A copy of the original manuscript from which Cantrick extracted the parts and subsequently conducted the premiere can be found in the special documents section of the library of the College at Buffalo, SUNY, Buffalo.
>
> The instrumental resources Holst chose for this score should be faithfully preserved in its performance. *Hammersmith* was a serious commission from a thoroughly professional source, perhaps for a specified instrumentation, and this scoring is very close to the minimum British military band. There is no place here for alto, bass, and contrabass clarinets (or the baritone sax), and the five optional instruments may easily be left out. It is superbly weighted just as Holst scored it, including the necessary equal distribution of the four clarinet parts.

opening 42 bars to thoroughly study and rehearse this section prior to assembling the whole group.

When in [22-42] Holst exchanges flutes and bassoon for the horns on the upper line and the horns join the ostinato, a subtle color change occurs as the tune is extended to octaves. A vital color also has been added in the character of the E♭ clarinet [28-42] — a color in this register not found on the B♭ instrument. Throughout these opening bars [1-42] the option in favor of solo players is desirable.

When the quiet of the running Thames is pierced by the piccolo at [43] with its first statement of what Cantrick calls the "challenge theme," the seemingly ordered world of the *Prelude* reveals musical emotions not necessarily apparent on the surface. The three trombones [44] quietly pick up the previously stated horn harmonic materials, moving in ghostly half-step triads E major to F major above the incessant ostinato, topping their eerie presence with a full and quiet upward glissando of the two triads [46]. This is a great moment in band music, when the customarily "commercial" (sometimes vulgar) glissando — a simple mechanical fact of life to the unique brass sonority-resonance of the trombone — becomes a moving and subtle creative stroke. In these wonderful moments [44-46] the haziness at the beginning of the *Prelude* seems about to lift — when abruptly the *fff* trumpets [47] transform the piccolo's quiet "challenge theme" into a searing, almost frightening arrest of any tranquillity. (In the orchestral score Holst indicated over the trumpet entrance here: "Solo, coarse tone.") In this line, which the piccolo introduced at [43], freedom of interpretation should transcend a metronomic statement of this extended fanfare idea:

Ex. 2 (Fennell's markings are shown in gray)

Gustav Holst (1874-1934). *Hammersmith — Prelude and Scherzo*, Opus 52. Boosey & Hawkes Quarto Military Band Edition No. 225, copyright 1956 by Hawkes & Son Ltd. (London), Plate No. 18086, printed in U.S.A. Performance time *ca.* 14:00, 436 bars. Only the full score is published; scored for piccolo, 2 flutes (2nd interchangeable as 2nd piccolo), 2 E♭ clarinets (2nd optional), 2 oboes (2nd optional), solo, 1st, 2nd and 3rd B♭ clarinets, alto and tenor saxophones, 2 bassoons (2nd optional), 4 horns in F (3rd and 4th optional), solo, 1st and 2nd B♭ cornets, 2 B♭ trumpets, 3 trombones, baritone bass clef (treble part included with the set), basses, kettledrums, xylophone, glockenspiel, snare drum, triangle, cymbals, bass drum, and gong.

Hammersmith was commissioned by the British Broadcasting Company in 1930 ostensibly for performance by its military band. No performance ensued, and after completing the commission Holst then transcribed the military band score for orchestra. The publishers issued the orchestral version (also Opus 52) in a miniature score printed in England as Plate No. 18862, copyright 1963.

Numerous performances as the conductor of different groups have exposed this problem to me, and I find that both announcements of this theme suffer when absolute fidelity to the background rhythm is breached, especially in the tied quarter/half-note and the dotted eighths. Do not hurry the quarter-note triplet.

At [48-61] the new material (parallel fifths in triple meter) introduced by the cornet and trombone, then passed in octaves to the four clarinets, bridges *Prelude* to *Scherzo*:

Ex. 3 [52-61]

These connecting devices serve also to wind down the incessance of the opening ostinato, now reduced to its first four notes, which gathers "visual" momentum in its $\frac{3}{2}$ setting and finally dissolves through accelerando into repeated 5ths and 4ths, as though groping its way up from the depths toward the fresh and brighter color of the *pp* alto saxophone motive. The essence of the *Scherzo* is now upon us.

Performance Suggestions

Throughout this profound and enigmatical *Prelude*, all players not contributing to the sounds of the piece should be advised that their motionless silence also contributes to the total atmosphere. (I believe it appropriate to suggest to those not playing that they should concentrate on the music being made, to seek by transference of thought to be tuned-in to what is transpiring.) Horns, baritones, basses — however anxious they may be to expel water from their instruments — must refrain from any motion until after the flute and clarinet are well into their exposition of the *Scherzo* material. Solo saxophone, accompanying clarinets, tenor saxophone and bassoons also should be as motionless as possible in the fermata which precedes the *Scherzo*.

So, too, should the conductor. Throughout the *Prelude*, considerable demands on his technical equipment include the absolute necessity for intense horizontal pulsing that is sostenuto molto; the minimum gesture is what the music demands. Here again, everyone benefits from strong visual communication as a vital part of total control.

To attain these ultimate intensities in the low brass and horn phrasings [4-21], the conductor must be in complete communication with the players, indicating the breathing along with them in the most obvious fashion while he conducts, overseeing one of the most treacherous stretches of quiet legato music-making in all of the band's literature. And as if all of this walking on musical eggs was not enough, Holst compounds the act by finishing off his *Prelude* in a steady acceleration of pulse over continual evaporation of sound. Keep everything small and under cool control.

Scherzo

Hammersmith's first three tempo indications are all *poco* (also a favorite condition of Brahms) — Poco adagio, Poco animato, and now for his *Scherzo*: Poco vivace. Indications of hesitancy? Perhaps, but rather than that I feel comfortable seeing them; *poco* controls

my concept of these principal tempo characters. From here on [62-227] the bar pulses are always equal, not eighth-note units.

The melodic material of the *Scherzo* grows out of the opening three-part invention:

Ex. 4 [62-72]

The second *Scherzo* motive, a $\frac{6}{8}$ counterline in the flutes, occurs at [73], joining the invention subject:

Ex. 5 [73-86]

The third motive appears in the piccolo and E♭ clarinets at [87], which leads into additional contrapuntal material and an energetic woodwind line at [92]:

Ex. 6 [87-95]

Further material in the section includes this *Scherzo* version of the "challenge theme":

Ex. 7 [171-174]

With these ideas must also be added the rising scale-wise material first exposed in the horns, baritones, and basses in [108-110], and later in [343-346]:

Ex. 8 [108-110]

an idea which subsequently [138-141] in this harmonic version becomes vital to the *Scherzo*:

Ex. 9 [138-141]

Holst mixes all these ideas at will, sometimes combining, frequently fragmenting the first six notes of Ex. 4, and usually binding the first and third notes of the "invention subject" with the convenient mucilage of steadily falling chromatic sixteenths that are the closing idea of the principal *Scherzo* subject. In this contrapuntal *Scherzo* the free interplay of ideas is not

169

bound by a fixed formal structure. Holst goes where he likes, when and how he likes — but all is yet fiercely disciplined. So too, must be the players and their conductor.

Performance Suggestions

It is necessary to achieve ultimate *separation* as well as *brevity* in the staccato character of the *Scherzo's* opening intervals, dominated by 4ths and 5ths. Once again the composer seeks to aid the cause of his music by a particular notation, grouping or separating the eighths for the eye the way he wants them to fall upon the ear:

Ex. 10 [62-64]

Holst cautions against overdoing the accents, but they are a vital part of the texture. I have found it necessary to remind players to provide full note value to the quarter note in [90] and the half in [91] the many times these figures occur:

Ex. 11 [89-92]

These obvious editings help to avoid the kind of diminuendo that happens in passages like this when the players become too concerned with what lies ahead, frequently at the expense of the desired sustained sound. It is hoped that with these signs of caution, and with the mark for breath in [91], all the reeds will not rush ahead into the rhythms of the following bar [92]. Also, baritones and basses must be urged to increase their tone at [F] [114], for their *p* is not sufficient to underpin the beginning of the stretto of Ex. 4 material that begins there. This stretto demands the same detachment previously discussed for Ex. 4 — short notes are simply not enough, as one's initial experiences with this difficult figure are certain to reveal.

With his characteristic rhythmic subtlety, Holst first suspends forward motion by repeating chromatic material borrowed from earlier bars (at [E]):

Ex. 12 [136-139] Concert Score

Caution is needed in the interpretation of the *pesante* in the lower brass [139-141] to avoid a heaviness that stalls. My preference in *pesante* eighths is for long and heavy detached notes which add the element of breadth demanded while not slowing up the pulse. (I add a Brahms-like articulation: ♪♪♪ .)

Then, through augmentation, Holst withdraws all forward propulsion:

Ex. 13 [142-145] Concert Score

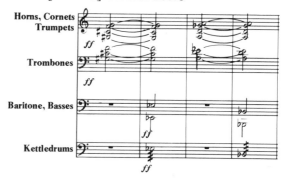

The prominent interval of a 4th which is introduced in all brass instruments in [143] and [145] will, with its inversion, dominate the music through bar [227].

The entrance of the kettledrums at [143] is the first percussion scoring in *Hammersmith*, and its 14 bars are its total use in the entire piece. One wonders why — and so it seems did Holst himself when he sat down to rescore the work for orchestra, for he then extended the kettledrum writing.

All reeds (including the extreme-range piccolo) benefit from playing their exciting *ff* passage [146-159] as legato as possible, using particularly long quarters. This statement of the second *Scherzo* motive, the ⁶⁄₈ melody, screams its way above the brass, who play their now-truncated reiteration of Ex. 13. The massive chord idea of Ex. 13 returns again [160-165] before Holst breaks everything off with the dramatic silence [166] that precedes this searing sonority of perfect 4ths, augmented 4ths, and minor 2nds:

Ex. 14 [166-167] Concert Score

Holst relentlessly drives home the dissonances — minor 2nds and 9ths — setting the tension, first with that silence, then suspending it all while thrusting the basses upward and framing the sound to set up the *Prelude's* "challenge theme" in the cornets at [171]. The six-note figure of its third measure [173] then becomes development material in the reeds [177] above leaping augmentations in the low brass [187-188] of the *Scherzo's* invention subject, to be joined then by all three contrapuntal ideas. A new and arresting octave fanfare idea is then introduced in the brass [209-215], and it appropriately confuses the diverse rhythmic elements (two against three) fighting to be heard:

Ex. 15 [209-215]

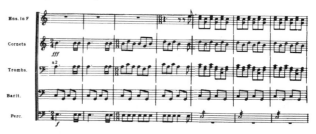

Holst then winds down the enormous momentum he has generated by use of the static sonorities [221-227] that are suspended above his still-present basic rhythmic materials in 2nds, 4ths, and 5ths, and next by the thinly-scored support for a dolefully expressive alto saxophone solo [228-241] that spins out its augmentation of the $\frac{6}{8}$ *Scherzo* melody in $\frac{3}{4}$. Once-blaring brasses, now muted in *ppp* [241], interrupt the action briefly in a fermata on one of *Hammersmith's* principal harmonic resources, the augmented minor 7th chord. Below this at the *Tempo primo*, the solo tuba returns sarcastically to the original *Scherzo* subject [242] two and a half octaves below its initial flute statement. Baritone and trombones finally fragment it [246-248], leaving it unresolved.

Specific Notes on Performance

Within this first exposition of the *Scherzo* lie these further observations:

Percussion:

Holst's use of the instruments is integral to the music, not merely cosmetic to it.

• Examination of the kettledrum part, which plays in [143], reveals no cues — they should be added at [125], writing in the prominent alto sax part [127] and the piccolo/E♭ clarinet line [128-132].

• The glockenspiel's contribution to reed texture [H] to [I] is enhanced when played with brass mallets.

• Cymbals used at [166] should be a large bright pair, at least 20".

• Holst patiently withheld the bass drum until he needed it for ultimate low frequency impacts at [168, 170].

• He was similarly patient about the xylophone with its great ability to penetrate all sound around it, hoarding its use until [K] to top the reed ostinati [187-197].

• The snare drum is reserved for pairing with its traditional partners, the trumpet/cornet, in [209-221, 319-324], and it has only another single flam [331]. The player should be instructed to release the snares when finished with his first passage [222], to avoid picking up sympathetic vibrations from the coming solo saxophone.

• Tenuto is not possible on the glockenspiel in the way one produces it on non-percussion instruments, so all one can do to observe Holst's tenuto line on the quarter notes [304-305] is to play it with the smallest stress of sound greater than the other notes. This *pp* glockenspiel line is a master-stroke in scoring for resonance with the muted cornet, and it is well served by white plastic mallets on the bells.

• Holst has need for but one *p* triangle stroke in the entire score, at [311].

• If but two percussion players are to be used, the flam on the snare drum in [331] may be played with xylophone mallets, in order to be ready for the xylophone part at [336].

• The dynamic in the suspended cymbal [384-395] should be reduced to *mf*, and white plastic xylophone mallets should be used on top of the plate in order to expose the running lines in the reeds above.

• The gong at Poco adagio [397] is difficult to play — one cannot prime it because of the silence that precedes it. A low-pitched, very sensitive gong played with a proper mallet will guarantee that the gong will speak, but *pp* is what one hopes for.

Bass Instruments:

• Because of the gathering excitement in the middle of the first *Scherzo* exposition I caution against the tendency to slow down in the upward leaps of minor 9ths in all bass instruments [170-186]. Writing arrows pointing forward usually accomplishes this:

Reeds:

• As natural as a crescendo in the rising scales of the reeds [201-202] seems, it is unwritten (but necessary) and should be added to the parts.

• The articulation possibly indicating staccato quarters in the solo alto sax line [228-241] should be modified to avoid playing any short notes.

Lento

Holst has carefully bound together the pulses of the five major segments of *Hammersmith* from the *Scherzo* onward: quarter equals quarter, half equals half. At the conclusion of his bridge [228-248] from the first *Scherzo* to the *Lento* at [249], he clearly requests a measured silence before the entrance of the solo clarinet. The parts for the six solo reed lines in [249-275] must be edited for every possible security to the players. Once again we are confronted with the hazards of "white notation," now further compounded by rhythmic subdivision creating long-line visual problems within a single bar. Marking in the six pulses of the $\frac{3}{2}$ bars, the repeated accidentals, and other aids to performance might help, as shown in this example:

Ex. 16 [268-269]

Once the six solo players have these markings to help, they must first carefully study the music with a metronome and then see the conductor for individual coaching. After each player has been thus briefed, the six can gather alone to improve the chance that the passage will be played with reasonable accuracy. It is vital that the players observe the dynamics as each line unfolds, for Holst has called for a healthy sound, not a *pp*. The long breaths for clarinet [256-260] and flute [262-265] obviously need a second player to assist. Throughout the *Lento*, the eighth-note triplets should be played *tranquillo*, not staccato, adding the slur articulations as shown above in Ex. 16.

Holst's merciless request that the solo tenor sax descend *pp* to the bottom of the range in [271] creates a marvellous sound that I can't imagine scored any other way. Plainly, no other instrument has this sound, and its injection (instead of the bassoon) into the "traditional" chamber music mixture of flute, oboe, and clarinet is another indication that *Hammersmith* is indeed a serious piece for serious players.

Performance Suggestions

As a contrapuntal study, apart from its beauty as music, the *Lento* portion of *Hammersmith* provides a musical experience not previously available in band literature. And when his counterpoints have run their course, Holst simply turns to a haunting harmonization of the contrapuntal subject by an octet of brass [275], with some of the counterpoint remaining as the basses imitate the cornets three octaves below. All players should fully extend the sound through bar [279], then breathe together for the following phrase. (Mark all the brass parts and score for a breath before [280].) The 1st cornet must know how vital is the sound of his lower octave to the scoring here.

These are among Holst's great moments, the whole *Lento* being a remarkable example of composition as the subject constantly shifts center, rising steadily in range and complexity until reaching the surprising entrance of the brass in [275]. I recommend that the flute and oboe [256-275] play their lines with intense vibrato, but that the clarinet and tenor sax bring ultimate support, non-vibrato, to the color of what they play. At [275-283] all the brass should also play with greatest support, non-vibrato but not non-espressivo!

Conducting Challenges

I consider the *Lento* and the related final *Poco adagio* [397] to be among the most difficult musical and technical challenges in all band literature. The first demand is for what we frequently lack the most — a controlled, intense legato beat that is compact, definite, horizontal, and tranquil all at once. As a guide to the players I have found that it is secure and productive to conduct the three long pulses as far as M [261], when beating the shorter six pulses becomes mandatory until the fifth pulse of bar [262]. The entering oboe solo here needs no subdivision, nor does anything until bar [261], but from there on all six pulses should be given through the termination of the solo reeds [275]. The entrance of the brass octet here obviously is again in three pulses.

One only discovers many of the performance problems when carefully examining the pages from which the players read, for the conductor's score, contrary to belief, does not necessarily tell all. Spending some time with the parts reveals, for instance, that there are no cues for the 1st and 2nd trombones over the 25 very slow and complex measures of *Lento* preceding their important entrance at [275] — an absence which does not contribute to player security. Add a prominent cue.

Scherzo

Three times previously — [59-61], [226-227], and [242-244] — Holst has bridged major developments with the rising figure of 4ths and 5ths. Here at [282-283] the figure appears again to lead the *Lento* section into the last *Scherzo* (Vivace $\frac{2}{4}$) and to contribute the common tempo through equal pulses ($\d = \d$). As he made heavy range demands on the tenor sax in the *Lento* [271], Holst here expects the piccolo and E♭ clarinet to play rapidly and repeatedly, staccato *pp*, in not necessarily convenient registers.

The "Poco" is dropped from Vivace this time, as

previously extended ideas are telescoped to quickly recapitulate all of the *Scherzo* motives, bringing the listener rapidly again, at [324], to what was the initial high point of the composition — [219] — from which Holst had made his skillful withdrawal to the alto sax bridge. Now suddenly, the third *Scherzo* motive is dramatically hurled at us in massive octaves, in augmentation and Allargando beginning at [325]. The Holst sense of pace here is remarkable indeed; so, too, is his harmonic sensitivity in leading the listener, who may now be confused with the complexities of Holst's compressed musical materials. Clarity comes with the huge octave passage [325] that once more orients the listener to the third *Scherzo* motive. But Holst cannot be content with one idea at a time, so beneath this third motive the principal *Scherzo* invention idea rises and falls in counterpoint to it.

I have always been unable to suppress my instinct to linger just a bit on the first B♭ with which the Allargando begins, mainly to let it sink in deeply as the ultimate *ff* result of the crescendo which began at [315] as *Scherzo* motives were piled on top of each other. The *a tempo* at T [330] must begin unhesitatingly in the first eighth-note on the second beat — everything must go forward with utmost energy. All of the editing suggestions previously discussed for brevity and detachment in every eighth-note must be repeated here, and the individual parts should emphasize this energy with written accents at the beginning of each ♪♪♪ figure throughout this section [330-342].

The half-note augmentations [367-370] prior to X continue in the beat pattern of two-in-a-bar to secure things before changing the beat to one-in-a-bar at X. This is because it is the bar pulses of the $\frac{3}{4}$ at X which are equal to the previous $\frac{2}{4}$ pulse, not the quarter note unit. All the reed and horn parts must be marked *molto legato* to Y [384]. The energy and precision demanded here suggest that the conductor return to a vigorous two-beat to assist the brass with their rising figures two bars before Y.

Conducting again in $\frac{2}{4}$ prepares the conductor to contribute to the ensemble's need for a strong central pulse as Holst's animated version of the first static *Scherzo* dissonance drives forward in a growing, swirling confusion of conglomerate ideas [383-396]. All players will be looking for whatever is the conductor's appropriate gesture to assure the sudden, dramatic cessation of all this sound at [396]. All should freeze, the only allowable motion being that through which the conductor (after a brief pause) sets in motion the basses' closing ostinato.

Poco Adagio

With the appearance of the final *Poco adagio* at [397] the tutti playing is finished, but though they may cease to contribute, all players other than the handful that do play must continue to concentrate along with the soloists. Again, no moving about, and certainly no clean-up chores, are appropriate here. The gong in [397] should ring to natural decay, and the first statement by the solo oboe of the "challenge theme" must be languidly played (Mahler would have cautioned with *nicht eilen*, not hurried). The soloist's part should carry a written reminder to this effect, as well as a line over the first G♯ in bar [398] to insure that vital length.

The piccolo's staccato in [399] is not merely a matter of texture — it is essential to the rhythmic structure of this music. The player must be reminded here of the judicious use of silence, as indicated by the four eighth-note rests in [399]. I have sometimes found it more difficult to secure a proper eighth rest than the notes which follow. There is simply no substitute for the metronome in the practice of such passages. In bars [400-402] it is a further aid to the player to add a line to the sixteenth-note that is tied to the previous note, to avoid the tendency to hurry. It is misleading to see only one articulation guide in this Poco adagio — the staccato shown at [399]. All lines eventually move to very legato, and the parts must be edited accordingly:

Ex. 17 [400]

The xylophone player [402-405] must concentrate on the three long half-note lines in the basses which lead to his entrance — a cue showing the piccolo and flute parts in [402] would help. The player should be instructed to "think staccato" and to use white plastic mallets; his part might be edited this way, correcting the visual groupings of eighths:

Ex. 18 [402-405]

As was suggested in Ex. 16, each solo part here must be edited to contain every visual security to the players, and the soloists should rehearse separately. Throughout the difficult bass lines with which *Hammersmith* begins and ends, the breathing seems to fall logically. It is hoped that after taking maximum breath before the quarters in [412] (horns), no breath would be necessary until after the half-note at [415].

The single *pp* note assigned to the bass drum at Molto adagio [422] is one that can be heard only when the drum is as free of all foreign matter as it was when it left the factory. Up to the very conclusion Holst deftly mixes the colors of the low brass, leading the listener off into the infinity of the composer's unfettered spirit and imagination. Things remain as they have been since the beginning — unresolved, probing. At its conclusion I still do not feel a terminal cadence.

Not much comes easily in this remarkable score, except that it all seems to have come freely from within its creator who probably carried it around inside his head for a long time before committing it to paper. Holst obviously treasured *Hammersmith*, for it is one of the few scores that he set twice for an instrumental group. Why the BBC never performed it or why there is no word whatsoever about it from anybody except his friend and musical confidante, Vaughan Williams, is a mystery.

Holst and Vaughan Williams met occasionally to try out each other's new works on the piano. After what must have been a big evening on December 12,

1930 in the music room at the St. Paul's Girls' School, Vaughan Williams sent Holst a letter recapping that meeting and speaking at length about Holst's *Choral Fantasia*, an opera (*The Wandering Scholar*), and *Hammersmith*. "The one thing I can't yet quite get hold of is 'Hammersmith' — but you are (like your daughter) a realist and you are almost unique in that your stuff sounds better when it is played on the instrument it was originally written for."[6]

And so it does. I have always felt *Hammersmith* as a mystic experience, and thus did Holst write in a philosophical essay (1920): "I suggest that all mystical experiences (like all artistic ones) are either illusions or *direct and intimate realizations*...I do not know if they are illusions or whether they alone are real and the illusion the world we live in."[7] This is the essence of *Hammersmith*. ∎

(For additional information see Fennell's postscript, p. 49.)

Corrections

The following corrections in the published score and parts of *Hammersmith* are needed. Some corrections have been made in later printings of this work.

[28-29] Score. Remove the "s" from oboes (solo at this point). point).

[74-75] 1st flute — part. Impossible page turn; having 2nd flute turn the page is not satisfactory. Secure a second copy of page 1 and hinge the right edge to the left of page 2.

[101-102, 104-105] Trumpet — part. Accent missing (as shown in cornets).

[109-110] Horn I & II — part and score. The A♭ in [109] and the D♭ in [110] should be A♮ and D♮.

[125] Alto sax — part. Change the eighth-note from G to F.

[139] Tuba — part. The second eighth-note in the lower octave should be G, not A.

[177] 1st clarinet — part. The first eighth-note should be E♭, not E♮.

[225] Tuba — part. Quarter note rest missing.

[273] Oboe — part. The first note of the last triplet should be corrected to D.

[274] Solo clarinet — part. Remove "à 2" (solo player only).

[330] 1st & 2nd trombones — part. First eighth-note rest looks unclear.

[346] Tuba — part. Add missing ♯ to the first note.

[350] Basses — part. The accent is missing on the dotted quarter.

[386] Bassoon — part. Note should be G♯, not B♯.

[406] Basses — part. Correct second half-note to G.

[407] Oboe — part. The last note of the last triplet should read E, not F♯.

1. Robert Cantrick, "'Hammersmith' and the two worlds of Gustav Holst" (London: *Music and Letters*, Oxford University Press, pp. 211-220, Vol. 37, No. 3, July 1956).

2. Cantrick, *Ibid.*

3. Imogen Holst, *Gustav Holst* (London: Oxford University Press, 1938), p. 144; also, Imogen Holst, *The Music of Gustav Holst* (London: Oxford University Press, 1968), pp. 125-128. A digest from this book of her description of the Hammersmith neighborhood is printed on the inside of the back cover of the *Hammersmith* band parts.

4. Imogen Holst in *The Music of Gustav Holst*.

5. Imogen Holst in *The Music of Gustav Holst*, p. 125.

6. Ralph Vaughan Williams and Gustav Holst, *Heirs and Rebels*, letters written to each other and occasional writings on music, edited by Ursula Vaughan Williams and Imogen Holst (London: Oxford University Press, 1959), p. 75.

7. Imogen Holst in *Gustav Holst*, pp. 195-196.

Gustav Holst's Second Suite in F for Military Band

Frederick Fennell

My long love affair with representative pieces of British military band music has always been dominated by the works of its two greatest masters, Holst and Vaughan Williams. Their combined contributions to this mostly underprivileged musical literature amounts to five! Between them could have been viewed a-way-to-go in composition for military band; sadly, however, only their countryman and then-youthful colleague, Gordon Jacob, took up their lead. Nobody on the continent responded to their unmistakable thrust, and here at home that "inveterate innovator," the *real* Percy Aldridge Grainger, remained mostly undiscovered. A quarter of a century would pass before Morton Gould, Vincent Persichetti, Russell Bennett, or Clifton Williams would take up his own highly individual role in the evolution of what Holst and Vaughan Williams had so promisingly held forth.

Here at the beginning of that lonely road is one of those five little masterpieces, music unquestionably and enthusiastically basic to the repertory.

Gustav Holst's original manuscripts for the two military band *Suites* are now deposited in the British Museum, and a copy of the *Suite* discussed here was available for comparison.[1] Inasmuch as these articles are addressed to the available published edition, I will not dwell on the extensive variances between the printed score and the manuscript, save to correct or

adjust where the original clarifies long-observed questions.

I. March
Performance challenges begin in the first two bars, where Holst scored only for euphonium and basses. I do not find the editor's addition of low reeds to be of any help. It has always seemed best to leave the first two bars to low brass and high reeds, securing from them both as much cleanliness as constantly repeated playings in search of the lightest texture can produce. The dynamic must be an honest *forte*, the rising character of the scale fragment must be brilliant — played in crescendo. I have also found it productive to rehearse the first five notes extremely slowly and with greatest emphasis on their detachment, gradually speeding the pulse until the proper articulation is achieved, as is the ultimate separation.

On first-hearing one might be tempted to conclude that the little brass band from the *March* in the *First Suite* is back again, Holst so scoring the beginning of his *Morris Dance*.[2] But two short phrases later the whole band is at this happy-sounding business. The moving line in 2nd cornet/1st trumpet [6-10-18-30] must be projected; in these same bars a long, vibrant release in all brass is desirable. As the answering phrase is exposed, all horns, low reeds, and low brass must always dig out the descending scale fragment [16] and [40].

Ex. 1 [16] and [40]

The quiet, contrasting, and answering phrase in upper reeds [19-26] should not be too clipped; try this editing:

Frederick Fennell is conductor-in-residence at the University of Miami School of Music in Florida, where he is music director of the Symphony Orchestra and Symphonic Wind Ensemble. Well known as the founder/director of the Eastman Wind Ensemble, he was a member of the faculty at Eastman for many years. His recording of the Holst Second Suite with the Eastman Wind Ensemble is available (Mercury Golden Import 75011).

Gustav Holst (1874-1934) *Second Suite in F for Military Band*. Opus 28b. Copyright 1922 by Boosey & Co., London; (Plate No. H10472); Quarto Military Band (Q.M.B.) Edition No. 201; presently available in the U.S.A. through Boosey & Hawkes, New York. Four movements: (1) March, (2) Song Without Words "I'll love my love", (3) Song of the Blacksmith, (4) Fantasia on the "Dargason." Full score and condensed score. Scored for C flute and piccolo (no divisi), oboe, E♭ clarinet, B♭ clarinets (solo, 1st, 2nd, 3rd), E♭ alto clarinet, B♭ bass clarinet, 2 bassoons, saxophones (soprano, alto, tenor, baritone, bass/contrabass clarinet), B♭ cornets (solo and 1st, 2nd), 2 B♭ trumpets, 4 horns in F, trombones (2 tenor, 1 bass), euphonium, basses, snare drum, bass drum, cymbals, tambourine, triangle, anvil. Performance time: ca. 10:30.

The score, dating from 1911 is dedicated to James Causley Windram, but when it was first performed and by whom is not known.

Ex. 2 [19-20]

Holst's autograph shows "Fl Picc" in the instrumentation, but he never clarifies the use of the piccolo in *March* or *Song without words*, and specifies but the final ten bars of *Fantasia* as being piccolo. Perhaps he meant the piccolo to be coupled constantly to the flute, but that doubtful matter must be settled by each individual conductor; the flutes and/or piccolo are never *divisi* in the whole score. Constant pairing certainly puts a top on this music when it is played throughout by large festival bands. I prefer to "score"[3] the piccolo as reinforcement, with the ratio of 1 piccolo to 2 flutes. Generally I save it for the second statement [23-26] of the answering phrase rather than using it constantly. The effective tonal resource of the low to mid-register of the piccolo is too frequently by-passed in wind band scoring in favor of its obvious function in the upper octaves and to the loss of its remarkable colors when played in unison with the flute, particularly in subdued dynamics.

Interpretive judgement suggests that the cymbals, crashed on the 2nd half at [42] be allowed to ring and decay as do the sustained sounds in the upper reeds [43-46]. A single damped half note from the cymbal opposes all other textures or rhythmic functions in this very effective descending bridge from "Morris Dance" to "Swansea Town." This diminuendo has no terminal dynamic; I suggest *piano* be added to score and parts. Holst also left open the level of sound in the euphonium at [46] expecting, perhaps, that all would instantly recognize its music to be the tune — a condition much too risky to assume. The part and score should be edited to read *solo* and *mezzo-forte* (*soli* in large festival bands) for the euphonium.

Holst's wonderful setting here of "Swansea Town" (located in Wales) has become a classic statement of some of the tonal resources of the euphonium over this range of an octave and a minor third (E3 to G4). Its 32 bars make it the longest uninterrupted euphonium solo known to me in band literature. My interpretive markings are shown in Ex. 3.

Editor's note: Most music examples have been photographed (with permission) from the condensed score published by Boosey & Hawkes, copyright 1922. Frederick Fennell's markings are shown in gray.

This is the sixth in a series of articles by Frederick Fennell on basic band repertory, beginning with the British classics. Earlier articles covered Holst's *First Suite in E♭* (April 1975), Gordon Jacob's *William Byrd Suite* (September 1975), Vaughan Williams' *Folk Song Suite* (June 1976), Vaughan Williams' *Toccata Marziale* (August 1976), and Gustav Holst's *Hammersmith* (May 1977). Fennell looks back over his 40 years as a conductor and discusses those compositions which he considers to be the basis of the band literature, focusing primarily on those things of interest to fellow conductors.

A copy of the score is essential to the readers' understanding. Number the bars I (1-159), II (1-37), III (1-33), IV (1-211).

The scale fragment [77-78] played by the trombones, which leads to the large *tutti* statement of "Swansea Town", is too important not to be identified by a dynamic; start it off at least *mf* and build the crescendo to *ff* very quickly. The crescendo for the snare drum roll in these same measures should be delayed until G when its rapid increase to [81] joins the textures rather than fights them. The roll at bar [81] is not only inappropriate, the composer never wrote it in the original score; delete the roll and add flams to the following half notes. Bass drum and cymbals together should make here a "...most joyful noise," putting out their maximum good sounds for the *ff* [81], allowing the sound to decay without damping to a re-adjusted dynamic in bar [83] that is no more than *mf*. Players should be cautioned not to lose the pulse in bar [82] and to avoid being late in the following bar. Everyone (but especially the low brass) must be cautioned here against any slowing of the pulse; believe me, it seems built into the music.

The entire group should play this whole exposition [78-110] with a full, vibrant, and exuberant sound, listening attentively for their balances within Holst's rich and sturdy harmonic setting, being careful to always let the tune dominate. As the melody approaches its final phrase, trombones, euphoniums, and basses [102-106] may use an especially clear articulation that they should also *avoid* as the octaves and unisons [107-108] bring this melodic statement to its positive conclusion. And that conclusion is, I think, intentionally indefinite; the conductor must decide for himself how long he thinks Holst wants the half to sound, for it surely must end resoundingly.

Next there occurs one of those seemingly unavoidable visual complexities in notation made all the more involved by the amount of black ink required to com-

Ex. 3 [46-78]
Euphonium

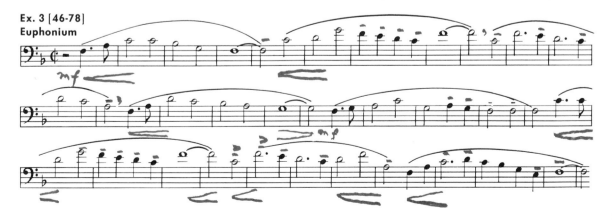

municate what is happening at this important juncture in Holst's formal structure. First, there is the need to indicate the eventual *fine* ending to the piece, followed by the traditional double bar, followed then by the change of key from F Major to B♭ minor (lots of ink for the C players), and the change of rhythmic pulse from *alla breve* to ⁶⁄₈ — the whole visual mélange including the presence of the rehearsal letter H. It is small wonder that the following crucial *ff* B♭ minor downbeat frequently loses out to all that precedes it, even when the players have seen it more than the first time; the conductor must overcome the obvious visual hazard shown in Ex. 4.

It may be that Holst was sensitive to the problem of clutter and did not also add *L'istesso tempo* to the already tangled jungle of information, but the conductor must be sure that the previous half now equals the dotted quarter. And I think it is necessary to add *ff* to all of the parts to assure the proper dynamic level at H.

The folk tune "Claudy Banks" is another of those sturdy melodies fairly brimming with vitality, and it should be played at a healthy *mf* and with the full, vibrant sound of unison clarinets in the chalumeau register. This must be backed by the *piano* rhythmic/harmonic ostinato in the mid-to-low brass and low saxes that emphasizes the harmonic changes occurring on the eighths, all of which should be edited with the *tenuto* line (see Ex. 5).

Clarinet players need to be cautioned against two common hazards in "Claudy Banks": (1) the low-pitch tendency of their written E♭ [113] and (2) non-support of the tied dotted quarter and quarter [115]. This figure occurs 14 times between [111-159]; some initial indication for the need of its absolute length may assure its continual fulfillment.

Holst's second setting of "Claudy Banks" in the same key begins at J as a *p/pp* tutti for reeds and brass, demanding all instruments *except* bass drum and cymbals. The *pp* brass pin-pricks of sound contrast with Holst's three octave distribution of the tune over that wide gamut in the reeds: all should be cautioned against any hint of the coming crescendo until it actually begins a patient 11½ bars later [147]. Mean-

while, let the tune in the reeds move in animated legato and make the eighths in the brass sparkle in vibrant staccato. Holst's delicate application of the snare drum as the only percussion presence here completes a textural spectrum that simply did not exist for the military band prior to him and I have not seen any evidence that Holst's remarkable grasp of the medium was picked up by anybody until Vaughan Williams and Gordon Jacob scored their masterful contributions to music for the British military band.

The absence of the snare drum in the bars before the quick crescendo to K does begin, sets up that crescendo — which the whole band will have to be reminded must progress from *p* to *ff* in but 4½ bars. This crescendo, in my experience, does not come easily, and the re-entry of the snare drum to assist, should drive the band toward the great sound at K. Now the drum is remarkably silent (a Holst talent, too) while the previously *tacet* bass drum and cymbals emphasize the joy of this brilliant final statement of "Swansea Town"; let the percussion ring here, then dampen just before the *da capo* at [159], allowing the brass and percussion to give point to the lengthy tones in the reeds.

The simple optics of a long *da capo*, such as occurs in "March" frequently robs the reading (and sometimes the performance) of ensemble security. It is a very good idea to practice this visual feat (moving the eyes from lower right to upper left). For those who leave nothing to chance, a special written reminder on the parts would be appropriate. Holst's use of the *dal segno* sign (𝄋) at the conclusion of his exposition of *March*, [159] and its presence at the first bar of the piece are superfluous; *da capo*, D.C., Italian for "from the head" ("from the beginning") being all that is necessary here.

Conducting Challenges

The beginning of the *Suite* needs the conductor's ultimate concentration of physical and mental energy; after a speed of pulse has been established in rehearsal: ♩=128-132, what the players need the most is a clear, small, forceful and focussed initial beat. One's habits in matters of preparatory movement must serve this

Ex. 4 [107-111]

Ex. 5 [112-116]

176

concentration on the part of the group. Depending upon the degree of sophistication in playing, preparatory pulses established by small lip movements frequently assist those who most need this visually-available-but-subtle rhythmic security.

A crisp beat should lead the group into the desired playing style, with the conductor's gestures reflecting the music's phrases and joining the levels of sound laid down by Holst's orchestration; a happy music such as this must not be conducted in a bland, perfunctory manner. The conductor who "makes like the music" will surely wind up with his hands, baton, and arms at some sort of up/in position when arriving at the third quarter of bar [18] where Holst's first quiet, contrasting phrase is about to begin. Again, fluent movements — minute, like the music's sounds, are dictated by those sounds.

The four bar diminuendo [43-46] to "Swansea Town" might be made through a series of rhythmically falling gestures — leaf-like and begun on the second half of [42] when the conductor's arm might be extended up and away from the body at an angle about 45° to the floor. The pattern might look like this:

Ex. 6

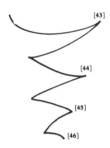

Once the dynamic level and style are established for the euphonium solo, the conductor will contribute the most by contributing the least at "Swansea Town," a minute, neat bit of musical house keeping sufficing for the whole 32 bars. Some small but meaningful acknowledgement of the subtle rhythmic comments in trombones, basses, and snare drum at the turn-around in the tune's middle [60, 61, 62] is appropriate for the conductor.

As these 32 bars end, the conductor should be concentrating his energy toward the trombones and their scale fragment [77-78] which heralds the big tutti [78]. Previous reference to the built-in slow-down tendency in this music [G] to [H] demands that the conductor plan to prevent it as follows: reaffirm the two-pulse for the whole group at [G] by conducting a vigorous two-beat for the first four bars, then deftly move into motions which almost indicate a single rather than a duple pulse. This may help to keep the low reeds moving forward and to do this without un-called-for accentuation or separation.

Music for the snare drum should be edited in bar [77] to delay the bulk of the crescendo until [G] where it should really begin *mf* and build quickly to *ff* at [81]. The whole group should play the first four half notes at [G] in crescendo, and when they have spent their resources the conductor should direct his interest to the bass drum and cymbals.

The conductor who carefully anticipates the final sounds in bar [110], saving a telling and vigorous

gesture for bar [110] that may be topped by a yet more vigorous *and* explosive downbeat at [H], will surely help to overcome the visual challenge here which has already been discussed.

Developments at [H] with "Claudy Banks" bid the conductor's attention to the full-throated *mf* that clarinets and saxes should provide. His contribution to that should be some supple application of a flexible left hand and a tenuto baton that covers more horizontal motion than it provides vertical emphasis. These movements will assist the previously discussed musical challenges of this music. As the dynamic level is raised at [I], so too, should the conductor's contribution join that elevation of interest — and it might be done with forward and outward elongated pulses of *one* for the first two bars, as motion then recedes to that which is appropriate to the tutti *p/pp* of the second statement at [J].

Here I have always felt the necessity to provide the most compact staccato pulse I can generate, taking my lead not from the tune in the reeds but from the punctuating eighths in the brass and snare drum. I feel the tune can take care of itself, but the rest of the score needs my careful and concentrated attention.

The balance, the clarity, the texture, the beginning of the coming excitement all must be expressed in the hands, the stick, the face. This absolute control of elements must continue with no hint of crescendo until [147] when gesture, inviting and sure, must lead all to the final *ff* that concludes the full statement of this first movement. Conviction within these terminal gestures must serve, as well, to prepare all for the *da capo*; the conductor whose final motion in bar [159] has brought him into a position where both hands are *up* and *in* (at shoulder height), is then ready to deliver that precise initial pulse that is the need of basses and euphoniums at the *da capo*. When *March* concludes, the conductor's final gesture should reflect Holst's intentionally indefinite ending, and this might be done by executing a rapid and small full circle of contrary motion in both hands on that final down-pulse.

II. Song without Words: "I'll love my love"

The folk song basis for this hauntingly beautiful tune in Holst's tastefully simple setting is a Cornish contribution to the literature. Cornwall is located at the very southern and western tip of England at Land's End. This maritime locale is the source for the words and they the reason why a song of love is cast in the Dorian mode and set in the dark key of F minor. Sad words are sung in six verses by a young maiden driven into Bedlam[4] in grief over her lover's having been sent to sea by his parents to prevent their marriage. Holst has captured the pathos and heartbreak of that unhappy situation in one of the band's rare pieces on the quiet and tender side.

In the original manuscript Holst scored the piece for but 18 instrumental lines,[5] and any bandmaster who so elects to play it this way will be rewarded in a manner that is difficult to describe; in its customary performance with multiple doublings it can also be a moving musical experience. Balance and color with sostenuto and intensity become the principal objectives in the conductor's pursuit of mood, regardless of what forces are used. Once the missing dynamics are added,

177

the conductor has to deal with customarily absent or weak sounds in the alto clarinet,[6] and, in its absence, to balance saxes, bassoons, horns, and clarinets; but if, as so often happens, he fails to re-score the Eb clarinet's concert C (written A) and the alto clarinet's sounding Ab (written F), there is none of that vital 3rd in Holst's sensitively-scored F minor sonority. Other harmonies also demand their presence.

In the playing of each bar in this melody every entrance must be tenuto, every note must be sostenuto, and every exit must be reluctant. The additional markings shown in Ex. 7 fulfill those needs. The falling/rising lines which accompany and vary the tune's second setting need similar care in phrasing and intensity (see Ex. 8).

The solo cornet's fermata [32] must be left with a skilful, minimum break in the sound, but any break in the breath support will surely invite disaster. The conductor should avoid any complicated cut-off gestures here; simply resume the pulse with the soloist on the fourth quarter. Holst's manuscript contained a slur over the two final 8ths, which would aid the player to continue a singing quality in the phrase. The waiting euphonium, 2nd cornet, tenor sax, and 2nd clarinet would welcome a cue of those two last cornet 8ths following the fermata, and the final five bars might be edited as shown in Ex. 9.

The alto sax must be reminded that the pitch of the D concert [35] tends to be sharp and must be supported with the greatest intensity; the final F concert in that bar and the Ab which follows must not be hurried. I realize that my addition of a fermata at the final sound — the second pulse of the last bar — is an arbitrary decision. But, without it, I feel that the conclusion comes too suddenly, too abruptly — especially when the trombones withdraw before the basses have secured their not-so-easy low F. The F minor triad in cornets and trombones, underpinned by the basses (and the added euphonium) provide a satisfying conclusion to a beautiful piece.

Ex. 7 [2-18]

Oboe solo with clarinet

Ex. 8 [18-22]

Ex. 9 [31-37]

Ex. 10

I love my love be - cause I know my love loves me.

Conducting Challenges

"I'll love my love" is a challenge to any conductor's control of subdued timbres and a test of his technical mastery of those physical pursuits that produce an intense sostenuto. Throughout these 37 bars there is no printed dynamic greater than *piano*, and much of it is less than that. Intensity, concentrated in hands and face, with sostenuto arms to support the transmission of a kind of visual vibrancy works very well in this music. And in addition to the value of things horizontal in the generation of this sostenuto, there is the necessity of providing that carefully-controlled upward motion by which — *and only by which* — the conductor can stretch the initial anacrusis and all other 4-pulses throughout this music. The well-trained group that turns this sort of phrase at the conductor's subtle behest plays with a maturity in phrasing that is a delight to hear.

Ad libitum does not always imply ritenuto, so one might resort to other appropriate freedoms the two times Holst employs this device [15 & 16], [31 & 32]. The words from which the phrase is derived are the key to its interpretation (see Ex. 10). In its second offering the conductor must deal with one of his most delicate responsibilities in the release of the quiet fermata; here, as is so frequently the case, the simplest way to release the sound and then to resume it is to *repeat the pulse* on which the fermata was established in the first place, thus to provide a timed, or rhythmic release that is within the pulse of the music at its inception. As the music concludes, the minimum motion is what is appropriate, as is a tasteful phrasing of the final five notes, each of which should be dictated by minute down-pulses in the left hand; the final release of the imposed fermata might also be given by the left hand.

III. Song of the Blacksmith

Gustav Holst has fashioned the words and music of this unique Hampshire folk song into 33 of the most original and exciting bars in band music. Never, in my experience, have players of any age or degree of sophistication failed to respond to this wonderful piece. Its title has always conjured up for me the vivid picture of a brawny man, drenched in perspiration, clad in heavy dark clothes fronted by a leather apron to deflect the sparks. I spent enough time as a child pumping the bellows for the forge in our shop at home to carry the unmistakable and pleasant aroma of the fire and its red-hot metal with me all my life. Remembered, as well, is the sound of the anvil and the hammer — and especially the *weight* of any blacksmith's tool. Holst has captured it all — rhythmically, harmonically, dynamically!

His guide to its proper tempo is encased within the traditional Italian terms: *Moderato e maestoso*. It is further indicated in the weight of a heavy hammer and the time required for its efficient wielding against the glowing iron. Also, the words (which I never knew until the final research for this paper was undertaken) are rather descriptive of the sound.

Kang kang kang ki-ki kang kang kang ki-ki kang kang

With all of this assistance it seems impossible that anybody could play the piece as fast as 132 beats to the quarter note, but I have so heard it. A pulse of 96 to 100 allows the scene to be re-created in style.

Rehearsal for *Song of the Blacksmith* should begin by asking the saxes and contra clarinet to be tacet until bar [7]; Holst did not score them, and this magnificent brass texture does not need them. Asking the percussion to be silent (only during the following rehearsal), the conductor should then ask the brass to play each chord in the first two bars *on his cue*, and to sustain each sound long enough to let the players hear it in isolation, to adjust the balance, and to enjoy the richness of Holst's harmony. The staccato articulation does not seem to describe "Kang" (the word-sound to be matched by instruments). Hammer blows, steel-on-steel that produce a ringing resonance are what one should strive to achieve, with all the players granting their impacts the space that characterizes the repeated blow of the hammer.

I have even found it productive in achieving the proper attack and ring for these notes, to have the anvil played — *for rehearsal purposes only* — on every eighth note rest [1-4] to help establish the sound in their ears *before* the brass play it. If they earnestly attempt to match the anvil's attack and ring, the style of the music should be just that much more quickly achieved.

The standard anvil offered by leading percussion manufacturers certainly provides what Holst requires; in its absence the best substitute I have found is a 2 foot length of standard galvanized water pipe, with a 3½-inch inside diameter. This can be held in one hand by a length of rope passed through it and knotted. When struck with an ordinary claw hammer, the proper sound will surely result.

As one is conducting those slow, separated rehearsal playings of these chords, their key names should be identified for all to hear, for everybody plays a changing sound on every note. When this sequence is then undertaken in performance tempo, the result should be gratifying to all.

The first six bars, constructed of 3 two-bar phrases are identical harmonically and serve as the ideal preamble to the folk song itself. As Holst thins the scoring [5-6] the diminuendo must proceed to *piano* then be wiped away by the *forte* entrance of the unison statement of the tune. With this great effect going on in the twelve lines of reeds and horns it is usually difficult to get all the others to suppress their enthusiasm to join in with the tune, but they must observe their *piano* hammering.

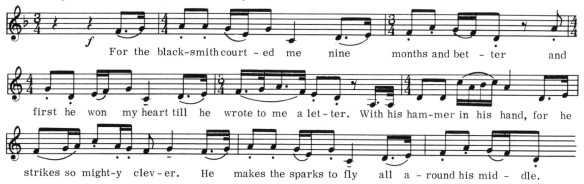

For the black-smith court - ed me nine months and bet - ter and

first he won my heart till he wrote to me a let - ter. With his ham-mer in his hand, for he

strikes so might-y clev - er. He makes the sparks to fly all a - round his mid - dle.

Ex. 12 [22-24]

The vitality of this music overwhelms me. Holst's anapest hammering figure ♩♫ appears 21 times. With its 20 counter-figures ♪♩♫ and all that "rhythmic silence", the title is fulfilled. In his setting for men's voices, the hammer figures employ very appropriate words (see Ex. 11).

As the second setting of the tune begins, there invariably occurs at the quarter rest just prior to B the most frequently played error in my experience with band music. It happens when players are so caught up in Holst's hammering ostinato that they go on with the 8ths as they fail to observe the quarter rest which is there *simply* so that the composer could pass the tune, unaccompanied, to the solo cornet. I have added the warning WAIT at this point to all of my parts for low brass, reeds and 2nd cornet.

The solo cornet player should be encouraged to sing this entrance with great vibrancy and a bright sound. This pivotal and contrasting passage [15-18] suggests that the character of the eighths in the accompanying brass be softened and that the tenuto lines on the quarters be observed to the full, so that the coming crisp tune-imitating answers in the cornet and clarinets will find their proper setting.

Holst's restraint in withholding the anvil [19] is now the listener's reward. The player should strike the anvil firmly, in the real spirit of the blacksmith, no dynamic being assigned. When Holst is about to bring it all together at C a *slight* broadening of the syncope in the previous bar played in crescendo, *f* to *fff*, really sets up the final, powerful tutti statement (see Ex. 12).

As the third part of this suite approaches its close, the composer prepares the listener by six repetitions of the same chord (it is also the first chord of this part) and these are split in the middle by the vital silence of the quarter rest in bar [32]. The conductor should surely provide positive visual control in this bar; strip movement of everything superfluous as you

prepare the brilliant final D major chord. This is another of those moments when the conductor's ultimate invitation to music-making could be heightened by movement up, out, and away from the body. The final chord is scored in favor of the F♯, but if the first trombone supplies full intensity to the high A, the chord will be just that much more brilliant. Remember that a fermata held too long is not always effective. If the player of the suspended cymbal in bar [33] is not skilful in grasping the plate (it should be thin, high pitched, and played with red rubber xylophone mallets), a second player could accomplish this quick cessation of sound.

IV. Fantasia on the "Dargason"

The composer has prescribed his tempo, not at the customary place at the head of this music, but 57 bars into it, at C : "One beat in a bar but keep the same pace as before."[7] The traditional Italian tempo indication (*Allegro moderato*) offers scant guidance to the conductor; I have always preferred ♩.=160.

The "Dargason"[8] tune is stated perfectly in 25 consecutive repetitions over 200 bars, each "variation" being different in orchestration and harmonization. The joining of the "Dargason" with the 64 bars of "Green Sleeves" (yes, that is the original folksong spelling) passes that melody through eight "Dargasons"; the final 11-bar section is a coda.

The first hazard is the beginning in the solo saxophones[9]. These players must be thoroughly instructed in the ways of this music and play with absolute control of themselves and their instruments. In this iambic figure ♪♩ ♪♪ ♪♩ ♩ all players *throughout the piece* must be made aware of the incessant, driving character of the "Dargason" music, and should go for the quarter note and toss-off the eighth, making the quarter vibrant, tenuto, and long. This figure always benefits from constant stretching, a condition not always easily achieved when panic consumes the player and tense "freezing" on the eighths robs the passage

180

of the light character one associates with whistling a little ditty such as this. I recommend that you try to whistle the "Dargason", for that experience may tell you more about how you want it played than all the words or musical examples I could muster.

The conductor's role in getting this music going consists mainly of avoiding any contribution to tension, and in providing the rhythmic clarity with which he hopes to infuse the music itself. The critical anacrusis allows the conductor to employ what I have come to describe as the "up-beat down-beat." One can, of course, simply give two small beats — down and up, and — if all has been well rehearsed the piece should begin as intended.

In the "up-beat down-beat" the conductor first gives a very small down blip (a characteristic of the great conductor Fritz Reiner), then raises both arms and hands about four inches, stopping firmly at the top which becomes the down pulse of the standard one-two beginning. The difference is that this motion places the anacrusis (upbeat) motion *on the up*. If solo sax players are on the conductor's wave length, the aesthetic benefits to this always-tricky beginning are worth the chance. The conductor then continues in the pulse of one, rather than two. After all, what can the conductor do about the saxophone performance here, anyhow? Why not (in addition to praying) simply help them to get started, then get out of the way.

And when this problem of the saxophone beginning has been solved, along comes the equally-demanding clarinet entrance. The conductor must concentrate on the sax, providing a compact and precise down pulse every two bars [9-15] to be sure that the sax will not be late with that figure.

As Holst begins his harmonic developments at [A] it is desirable to assist those resonances with length and vibrancy in the eighths and with skillful, soft tonguing at the tied dotted quarters and dotted halves (see Ex. 13).

The long crescendo [25-40] is easy for the players to ignore and that may be avoided by either writing the full word in bars [29] and [37] or by using a stretched-out version of the symbol. The fifth "variation" at [B] has the whole band at work on "Dargason" and some editing will add vitality (see Ex. 14).

The tambourine at [B] plays better if held in the best hand, the head struck for the quarters with the first-joint fingers of the opposite hand and the rolls articulated with those open fingers; the touch of bright color in the triangle rolls illumines the transition as Holst prepares the listener for the Green Sleeves counter-tune. As far as I have been able to discover, this use of the wonderful Elizabethan tune by Holst is the first by any composer.[10] It fits the "Dargason" as though the two were meant for each other. The nobility of its character unfolds as the clarinets, then the solo cornet join at 8-bar junctions — the oboe, flute, and piccolo peeking in-and-out with reminders that the "Dargason" is still present.

All solo entrances must be labelled *cantabile*. As this middle section of the basic three-part form concludes and Green Sleeves gives way to "Dargason", the dynamic in the euphonium must be adjusted in the score and part to at least *mf*, and the tubas should raise their level of sound to at least *mp*.

Holst reminds us at [D] that the two-pulse must be resumed — but only for the eight bar phrase to [E] where, once again, the conductor should return to a pulse of one. A vigorous two-pulse should be resumed at [113] to establish the security of the duple pulses [117-119] and to control the great sounds with which this 14th "variation" on the "Dargason" is so abruptly concluded.

The trills in the high reeds [113-116], brilliantly highlighted by the tambourine and triangle rolls, should be played with all possible speed, and the dotted quarters in cornets/trumpet should be reduced in volume in favor of the tune in the mid-to-low brass and reeds. All could play that last bar [120] before [F] in crescendo, giving length to the first quarter. It might even be desirable as a contribution to the shock value of the subito *p* at [F] for the players to be reduced one

Ex. 13 [17-21]

Ex. 14 [41-44]

to a part for that next full "Dargason"; urge the bassoons, bass clarinet, and euphonium to increase the dynamic level of their rising chromatic line to *mp*; and return to the one-pulse. Then, as the full band begins its crescendo to [137], employ the two-pulse and gradually increase the size of the gesture to match (or to lead) the rising sound.

As Holst approaches his ultimate wedding of the two tunes at $\boxed{G}$, the cornets (unless they play a real *ff*) are hard-pressed to provide sufficient "Dargason" amidst the excitement created by all the rest of the band. Those big sounds in the dotted halves should be left, with long lines added to every part to indicate resonance in the resolving sounds on the following eighths. (The harmonic transition concludes on the deceptive cadence with the D minor chord at $\boxed{G}$.)

The composer has been hoarding the bass drum since the end of the first movement, but here it is again, teamed with its ancient partner the paired cymbals — each instrument contributing its bright and dark sound in alternation as the ultimate contribution to the approach of this first real climax in the piece. The bass drum must resonate freely with no damping devices employed. However both the bass drum and cymbals must *join*, not *obliterate* the textures around them.

At $\boxed{G}$ a dramatic elision occurs and after 17 entirely different presentations surrounding the "Dargason" the composer arrives at the fruition of his ideas. And it is here that all of the conductor's feelings and skills must also come together. The composer has provided a tremendous sonic and metric achievement out of his apparent genius; what the conductor can contribute out of his knowledge, his feeling, and his experience is that ultimate musical catalyst — the proper pulse with which to bind all of this together.

To these ends, the reeds with their statement of "Dargason" must stretch every quarter and eighth, *molto sostenuto*, and every part must be edited to so indicate. This, of course, is in opposition to the throwaway suggestion about the eighth offered to the saxes in the tune's initial statement, but here the figure should allow the conductor to provide the intensity stretch that must go with the up-beat to the *fff* statement of the Green Sleeves tune [146]. This is not liable to happen unless all players with the "Dargason" stretch every note in the two bars where it begins [145-146]. All parts should be edited, adding *molto sostenuto* at $\boxed{G}$.

The bass drum roll (use a pair of articulate beaters) contributes less distortion [147-148] if its dynamic is reduced to *f*. Those who follow with keen observance the scoring for horns in most British military band music find a pair of instruments to be the customary need — and so it is with *Second Suite*, where the second pair (horns III and IV) are separated from the first pair for but 24 bars in the whole score [146-170], when Holst uses them in unison with other instruments to bolster the Green Sleeves tune while horns I and II play sustained harmony. In the original score this was sketched in on the very bottom line.

It is essential to the full contour of the melody that all players on Green Sleeves reach down for the phrase-ending D concert in bar [154]. (That vital note is frequently underplayed;) And when these same players

sustain their A♮ concert for two bars [161-162] they should do so in crescendo, the better to restate the phrase that follows.

Holst's *coda* begins at $\boxed{H}$, having started his withdrawal from Green Sleaves prior to it but keeping its spirit in the elongated melody which he fashioned for the solo cornet [177-184]. He then expands on its last two bars by creating from them a harmonic bridge in the clarinets [185-192] above the "Dargason" in the solo euphonium emphasizing the low reed and brass pedal point with a *pp* bass drum roll. Again, the resolving harmony in the eighths must have the benefit of a tenuto line. When the trombones and euphonium pick this up and extend it, they must tongue the resolving eighth [195 & 199].

In many ways, these concluding moments are the most difficult in the whole score, and unless they are thoroughly rehearsed, thoroughly understood by all of the band (especially those who play only the last chord), this very effective ending can be a disaster! These measures are masterful composition. After all of the foregoing busy-ness they wind down Holst's previous complexities with remarkable simplicity.

The low reeds added by the editor [192 to the end] are a positive intrusion to me; certainly, the last eleven bars — up to the final chord — belong to the five solo players of the original score. These five players should be rehearsed before any play-thru by the whole group is attempted. After each player has thoroughly mastered his separate part, rehearsal follows at the same physical distances apart that they will eventually play with the group. If the three muted cornets are evenly balanced in their harmony, the rest of the problems lie with the solo piccolo and tuba, who — though they be the largest and smallest of their kind and are played four octaves apart — must play precisely together in this bizarre little duet. Both should be aware that what is happening (before Holst's free composition in the final five bars) is the obvious fragmentation of the first half of "Dargason" [201-205]. Both must know that silence is the challenge as well as sound. Silences, which serve the composer so well are frequently more of a challenge to players than sounds, however complex, and silence in these final eleven bars must be firmly under the control of the pulse of the music.

The piccolo's first hazard is the *ppp* dynamic; adjust that to *p* and insist on solid breath support as you remind the player of the lyricism in these first two fragments; edit score and part with long tenuto lines. The final F major scale should rise in expressive soft staccato to the trill; begin the low E♮ at least *mp*; add the slur into the final bar where the player must make the F♮ eighth extremely secure in rhythmic placement and tonal support (see Ex. 15).

The solo tuba, with its sudden establishment of a duple pulse has the initial responsibility for rhythmic stability; these first three eighths and those that follow must be played separated and resonantly short; the crucial bar for the tuba is [206] which must not be hurried as seems the natural tendency. It would add great security to the feelings of both solo players if their parts were edited to include all of the music played by the opposite instrument. If the cue were written in a contrasting color I'm sure that its presence would replace anquish with charm and anxiety with security.

Frederick Fennell with Imogen Holst at her home in Aldeburgh, England (December 1973). The music rack was used by Gustav Holst.

Ex. 15 [201-211]

The closing bars should be rehearsed repeatedly to make them secure, with all the band knowing exactly what is to happen. To this end the whole band might have a cue of the piccolo and tuba music written in the parts [207-211]. With this, the final *ff* might always be neither a disaster nor a different sort of surprise than Gustav Holst intended it to be.

I have heard convincing performances with the last chord played long, but I prefer a short and very solid sound. Regardless of the length, it must be a sound that brings this classic of British military band music to a positive and satisfying conclusion.

Corrections

The following corrections in the currently-available published score and parts of *Second Suite in F for Military Band* are needed.

I. March

Opus number on the full score should read: Opus 28b.

The single page allotted by the publisher for all the percussion parts (labeled "Drums") is too cluttered; purchase additional parts and identify each instrument separately.

[3] Full Score should read: (Morris Dance)

[3] Score and part: *f* missing in snare drum.

[22] Score: triangle roll missing.

[36] Score and parts: all brass articulations should match solo cornet.

[51] Score: one ledger line missing in euphonium; must be 3 above bass clef (G4).

[61-62] Score: snare drum rhythm exactly as tuba has been left out; urge player to execute in his single best hand.

[81] Score and part: remove the snare drum roll, play half note.

[95-98] Score and part: remove all snare drum rolls; they are not in the autograph (flams preferred).

[110] Score and part: remove snare drum roll; not in autograph.

[110] Parts: 1st and 2nd trombone have impossible page turns; adjust.

[128] Score: alto sax, tie missing on first two notes.

[132] Score: basses, *mf* missing.

[135] Score: tenor sax tie missing on first two notes; euphonium flag missing from the second note, should be an eighth.

[136] Part: 2nd bassoon last eighth should be F♮.

[140] Score: flute and piccolo, add flag to second note, should be an eighth.

II. Song without words "I'll love my love"

[1] Score: tuba *pp* dynamic missing.

[2] Score: oboe *p* dynamic missing.

[17] Part: Alto sax rehearsal letter A misplaced, should be moved to bar 18.

[18] Score: Solo cornet dynamic should be *mp* and marked "solo".

[26] Part: Solo cornet half note should be dotted half.

[32] Score/part: the composer's manuscript shows slurs on the last two eighths of the solo cornet line.

[35] Score: Alto sax should be marked "solo".

III. Song of the Blacksmith

[3] Score: Remove *f* in Euphonium

[5] Score and parts: all should begin diminuendo at 3rd eighth (composer's manuscript).

[15] Score: Contra clarinet, 2nd cornet, basses — *mf* is missing.

[19] Part: 1st clarinet rhythm on 2nd beat is garbled; correct as in score (four 16ths).

[21] Score: Suspended cymbal crescendo missing.

[28] Part: Tuba 4/4 time signature missing.

[28] Part: cymbal *fff* missing.

[32] Score/parts: All brass articulation should conform to printed solo cornet (staccato).

[33] Part: flute and piccolo. Change Gb to F#.

IV. Fantasia on the "Dargason"

[33-40] [51-52] [55-56] Score and parts: triangle roll missing.

[58] Score/part: Euphonium; composer's manuscript reads "solo" (Green Sleeves), *mp, cantabile.*

[66] Score/part: solo cornet remove the single G (should be full measure rest).

[75] Score/part: Solo cornet add *cantabile.*

[88] Part: tenor sax impossible page turn; write D on the next page.

[120] Score/part: Tambourine and triangle change roll to a struck dotted quarter, add rest (composer's manuscript).

[140] Score: flute and piccolo delete accent.

[183] Score: triangle roll missing (composer's manuscript).

[203 & 207] Score: Tuba eighth rest missing after initial eighth note.

[210] Score: *senza sord* is misplaced at the bass sax line; it belongs to all the cornets.

Notes

1. Like the *First Suite in Eb* (which manuscript unfortunately was not available to me during the writing of that initial essay in this series), there are innumerable variances between what Holst wrote and what his editor prepared for publication. For a full and proper comparison one should put the two side-by-side — a comparison I intend to make at another time. One example of the difference is the basic instrumentation. Holst's manuscript for the *Second Suite in F*, was scored for flute/piccolo in Db, Eb clarinet, oboe, clarinets (I, II, III), Eb sax, bassoons, Bb cornet (I, II), horns (I-IV) in Eb and F, Bb sax, trombones (I-II-III), euphonium, bass, the same percussion as the published version, plus his reduction of the score for the piano. The additional six reed parts and those for two trumpets were not Holst's idea.

Also, the autograph tells us that Holst originally started the first movement with an entirely different tune, mostly in F minor (rather than the present one in F Major) which he identified as "Young Reilly", and scored fully for 30½ bars; a modulation to F Major then led to the present edition's bar [46] at "Swansea Town." Holst then drew full page crosses through these 30½ bars, abandoned them and started all over again. He did not throw away this original version, but I do not know if he ever used "Young Reilly" again. The initial idea is interesting enough, but the judgement which led Holst to what he published shows his recognition of better material once he had written it.

The manuscript reveals, as well, a different pen for the now-published first 46 bars, as though he wrote them later when Boosey & Co. published the *Suite* nine years after it was written. From his use of short-cuts in writing techniques for duplicate scoring and in the careless way he left customarily precise articulations and dynamic unresolved, it is apparent that Holst was in a hurry with this piece.

One further observation from Holst's manuscript is his decision there (not fulfilled by his editor) to abandon, on page 4 of his score, the solo/1st clarinet split. He finished the whole score with lines for but three clarinets; the solo/1st part (and that for ripieno clarinet which came with the original set) are the idea of the publisher, perhaps to meet some specification laid down for British Army purchase.

2. The reader should enjoy Percy Grainger's description of the morris dance included in the score of *Shepherd's Hey* (No. 21 of British Folk Song Settings; New York 1918, Carl Fischer, Inc.). The man wearing his May hat pictured on the cover of the initial issues of the Eastman Wind Ensemble Mercury record containing Grainger's *Lincolnshire Posy* was a morris man, not the conductor, as is sometimes humorously assumed.

3. (1) *March*: [2-18] 8*va* bassa; [19-22] tacet; [23-26] as written; [35-46] 8*va* bassa; [78] thru first half [82] as written; [98] to [159] 8*va* bassa. (2) *Song Without Words:* [1] thru 1st quarter [12] tacet; [12-24] 8*va* bassa; [15-19] tacet; [20] 8*va* bassa, play 2 eighths and half only; [21-24] tacet until 4th quarter [24]; play 8*va* bassa thru dotted half [26] [26] last quarter thru 3rd quarter [28] tacet; 4th quarter [28] thru dotted half [30] 8*va* bassa; [32] whole bar 8*va*; tacet the rest. (3) *Song of the Blacksmith*: play all as indicated for second flute in score. (4) *Fantasia*: [40-56] play as written; [57-71] tacet; [72-120] 8*va* bassa; [128] to end as written.

4. The English noun for a hospital for the mentally ill, after the corruption in pronunciation for such a hospital in London, St. Mary of Bethlehem. Holst's setting of the full six verses for men's voices (TTBB) was published in 1925 by J. Curwen and Sons, Ltd., with the melody identical to the band version. The choral arrangement tells the tale from the male point of view: "Abroad as I was walking, One evening in the Spring, I heard a maid in Bedlam so sweetly for to sing; Her chains she rattled with her hands and thus replied she: "I love my love because I know my love loves me!" (2) O cruel were his parents who sent my love to sea, And cruel was the ship that bore my love from me! Yet I love his parents since they're his, although they've ruined me. I love my love because I know my love loves me! (3) With straw I'll weave a garland, I'll weave it very fine; with roses, lillies, daisies, I'll mix the eglantine; And I'll present it to my love when he returns from sea. For I love my love, because I know my love loves me. (4) Just as she sat there weeping, her love he came on land, then hearing she was in Bedlam, he ran straight out of hand; He flew into her snow-white arms, and then replied he: "I love my love because I know my love loves me." (5) O yes, my dearest Nancy, I am your love, also I am returned to make amends for all your injury; I love my love because I know my love loves me." (6) so now these two are married, and happy may they be Like turtle doves together, in love and unity. All pretty maids with patience wait that have got loves at sea; I love my love because I know my love loves me."

5. Flute, oboe, Eb & 3 Bb clarinets, alto sax, 2 bassoons, 2 cornets, 2 horns, 3 trombones, euphonium, and tuba.

6. It *does not* have to be this way; *no* instrument will sound when played by one who does not play very well, as is the frequent fate of the alto clarinet at the hands and breath of so many immature players.

7. Holst might have indicated the same conditions for his first movement, too — inasmuch as the same tempo must prevail throughout the *March*. In both parts the first tempo is clearly dictated by the music that comes second. The technical dangers inherent at the beginnings of these two outer movements sometimes dictate too firmly what the tempo will be — the tuba's articulation controlling the one and the saxophone's tone and technique affecting the other. Both of these limitations obviously must be overcome if these pieces are to move along at the pace built into them.

8. The Oxford Companion to Music, p. 297, describes it thus: "Dargason: An English folk tune, used from the 16th century onwards for a country dance." Holst used the same tune in his *St. Paul's Suite* for string orchestra which he composed in 1913 for the Girl's School where he taught for most of his life; this was two years after he wrote the *Suite in F*.

9. The autograph score shows a very different pen for the Bb sax" (as Holst identified the tenor instrument) as though this doubling was added at publication time for security, as was the cue in the 1st Bb clarinet that is also in the autograph: the alto clarinet line here is a publisher addition.

10. Vaughan Williams's use of Green Sleeves in his famous setting for the opera, "Sir John in Love," where it is sung by Mistress Page in Scene 1, Act III, dates from 1929, 18 years after this one by Holst. ∎

(left margin, vertical) THE STARS AND STRIPES FOREVER ★ EL CAPITAN MARCH ★ NATIONAL EMBLEM MARCH ★ THE THUNDERER MARCH

(right margin, vertical) ★ THE THUNDERER MARCH ★ NATIONAL EMBLEM MARCH ★ EL CAPITAN MARCH ★ THE STARS AND STRIPES FOREVER

Behold the Lowly March

BY HARRY BEGIAN

For too many years I believed that there was a traditional or authentic way to perform most marches. When I questioned various Sousa Band members about how Sousa directed his own marches, however, I learned that he didn't always perform the same march in exactly the same way. Hearing William Revelli's album, *Hail Sousa*, with the University of Michigan Band was proof to me that the conductor's musical convictions, imagination, and sense of style can transform a march into a spirited piece of music. Marches that I had discarded as bad pieces came out as musical gems on the *Hail Sousa* album and in the live performances Revelli presented.

I was so excited by what I learned from Revelli's treatment of marches that I wrote one of only two fan letters I have ever written to a band conductor. Since then I have listened closely to directors known for their march interpretations to learn how they achieve such conviction of style, tempo, and expression. Rather than copy someone else's authentic performance, my musical objective is to study each march and interpret it to the best of my musical ability and understanding for the enjoyment of my audiences, my players, and myself.

Too many American band directors imitate the interpretations of other conductors; they have to be told how to play or conduct a piece of music. This is particularly true regarding the "authentic" performance of a march — any march. The recent influx of edited versions of standard marches is proof that directors have an insatiable need to be told how to play a march. In the field of orchestral conducting the opposite is true; no two orchestral conductors would want to approach the same piece with the same tempos, expressions, or styles. Just listen to three or four prominent orchestral conductors perform any movement of a standard symphony to hear how each approaches the same composition in entirely different ways regarding tempos, expressive phrases, and style.

This being so, why do band conductors try to copy each other's interpretations of a particular march? Why do directors hesitate to study the march form and come up with their own musical convictions about the music's best style, tempo, and expression? Those who shun the march and openly boast about how long it has been since they last performed one are either musical snobs or simply haven't taken the time or exerted the effort to learn the musical possibilities of even the lowliest march.

Historically, the march was often the optional movement in the classical suites of Haydn and Mozart, and even Beethoven wrote military marches. The great Viennese symphonists used the march form in their compositions, as well as Mahler, Hindemith, and Stravinsky. If our great orchestra and band conductors show musical regard for style and care in their interpretations of marches, why do band directors ignore this indigenous musical form? The answer to this question is three-fold: a lack of interest in and study of the march form; a general discomfort regarding style, tempo, and musical spirit of marches; a failure of band directors to apply their own musical imaginations to the march.

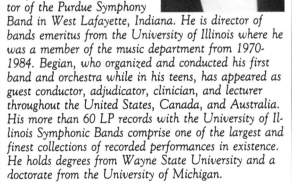

After a one year retirement, internationally-known conductor Harry Begian returned to the podium in 1985 as conductor of the Purdue Symphony Band in West Lafayette, Indiana. He is director of bands emeritus from the University of Illinois where he was a member of the music department from 1970-1984. Begian, who organized and conducted his first band and orchestra while in his teens, has appeared as guest conductor, adjudicator, clinician, and lecturer throughout the United States, Canada, and Australia. His more than 60 LP records with the University of Illinois Symphonic Bands comprise one of the largest and finest collections of recorded performances in existence. He holds degrees from Wayne State University and a doctorate from the University of Michigan.

Over the years through study and listening I have developed the following approaches to interpreting marches. These are only some possibilities for the performance of a march and are not to be regarded as telling band directors "this is how to play a march."

Style. A march is not a sacred piece of music that has to be played at a certain tempo, in a certain style, or with a certain kind of interpretation. In performance the march should reflect the conductor's musical convictions — how he perceives the piece — after he thoroughly studies it. Because a copy of someone else's interpretation can never be as good as the original, each conductor should operate within his own sense of musicality and develop convictions about the musical possibilities he sees in the score.

Score preparation. Study a march in the same way that you would any other piece of music, examining style, tempo, expression, and contrast and unity. Learn the melodic line well so that you arrive at solid convictions about phrasing, articulation, dynamic contrasts, and accents. Look for special obbligato passages and musical figures as well as important bass lines that may be hidden. Because the general style of a march is detached and spirited, look for any possibilities for a legato treatment to offer contrast. Consider the repeats of strains to vary dynamics and heighten obbligatos or countermelodies (during the baroque era a repeated strain of music was often varied in some way).

Trio sections of most marches offer the possibility for the clarinets to play the melody in the *chalumeau* register. Look for this possibility and use it when appropriate to provide textural variety and contrast. Also, consider dynamic contrast in final strains of a march that has a good obbligato scored against the melody (*p* the first time; *ff* the last time).

Observe the general form (repeats and *D.C.* indications), especially in European marches because most of them are written in the minuet and trio form of the classical orchestra suites and the dance movements of the classical symphonies. American marches are composed in an abbreviated form (the minuet and trio form is a rarity) to be played without *da capo*. For a march with a *D.C.*, play only second endings in the *da capo* section.

When marches have an exceedingly long strain with a repeat that does not allow for good contrast the second time through, consider taking the second ending. Symphony orchestras follow this practice when performing the exposition sections of standard symphonies. Why fuss about whether or not to repeat a long march strain, particularly if there is no way to vary the repeated strain?

Tempo. Test the tempo of each march you perform, and never play all marches at the same tempo. Most American military marches and almost all ⁶₈ marches sound best at about ♩ =120. However, circus marches and most of Henry Fillmore's marches sound best at ♩ =148-152, with the circus galops sounding best at ♩ =180-192.

Know that European march tempos vary from country to country; American band conductors often play them too fast. The *Grove's Dictionary of Music and Musicians* relates that the British quick-step march can vary from ♩=108-120. Spanish *paso dobles* (two-steps) are played at ♩=112, and most German marches sound best at ♩=112-116. While tempos in Italian marches can vary anywhere from ♩=116-160, French marches are generally the fastest of the European genre and sound best at ♩=144. To arrive at a convincing tempo for a march, play or sing the march tune to yourself, finding a suitable tempo within the guidelines just listed.

Dynamics. Check the dynamic ranges and changes throughout the march by playing or singing through the music. Look for and mark the score with melodic and dynamic highpoints. Such climaxes are often found in the second and final strains of a march and are usually indicated by the composer. Too often, however, march composers are not specific in using accents and articulation marks or writing percussion parts with care. These composers probably have assumed that conductors and bandsmen understand the musical principles and performance practices regarding marches. Such an assumption is nothing new because even the master composers prior to the classical period gave little or no indication regarding tempo, dynamics, or style for their works.

In march performance it is the responsibility of the conductor to determine the music's particular tempo, style, and phrasing. Such decisions are a test of the conductor's musicality, aural perceptions, and intuitive thinking; a copied interpretation of another performance can never come off in a spirited or convincing manner. Musical mimicry has become a way of life for too many band conductors, particularly in playing marches. Why not take a tip from the professional conductors of some of our top bands? Studying, listening, learning, and evolving valid musical approaches will ultimately reflect musicality, spirit, and personal conviction to all the music we perform — and most particularly to the performance of the lowly march. ■

The first requirement in the proper interpretation of a march should be knowing the tune so well that you can play or sing it from beginning to end. As a test, try to write the complete march tune in manuscript. Only then can you make decisions regarding tempo, style, and each of the other factors that influence the interpretation of a march.

Because most marches are written in a detached style, listen and look for stretches of legato sections, which most often occur in the trio tune. Legato passages can provide a pleasing departure and contrast to a detached style throughout a single march. The following trio to Sousa's march, *The Directorate*, affords contrast in both legato and staccato articulation within the same tune.

In the next example from *Pasadena Day*, Vessela indicates that the trio melody should be performed legato all the way, and even indicates the particular phrasing he wants to hear from the clarinets and baritones that is so typical of Italian symphonic march trios.

Karl King's trio tune in *March Ponderoso* is legato throughout and based on four-measure phrases.

In *His Honor*, Henry Fillmore handles the first-time trio tune in eight-measure phrases with a contrasting accent each time on the highest note of the melodic line in the fifth measure. Fillmore's use of the eight-measure phrase, rather than the common four-measure phrase, is due to the fact that most of his marches in alla breve are to be played from 148-152 beats per minute.

It is a proven fact that on various occasions Sousa and other march composers would play the same march differently than its printed form. So, why not do the same and try your own musical ideas and approaches to the playing of a trio tune? Don't look to edited editions and mimic the way that a famous band conductor does it. Never hesitate to use your own artistic judgment and imagination; exercise your personal musical style and sense of expression when interpreting a march.

All marches have their own tempos. As jazz musicians put it, "The music must swing." Richard Wagner said it even better: "The right comprehension of the melos (melody) is the sole guide to the right tempo; these two things are inseparable. The one implies and qualifies the other."

To arrive at the right tempo for a march, sing or play the music at different tempos until you reach the one that is most convincing. Although it is an accepted fact that most American military marches were originally written for marching or parade use, it is musically ridiculous to play them around 120 beats per minute, which is the accepted military cadence. These marches, however, can be changed to a faster tempo for concert performance. For instance, can you imagine how dull the following extract from Fillmore's *Orange Bowl* would sound at 120?

When it comes to European marches, we American band conductors do commit some real musical sins regarding tempos. In typical fashion, we don't take the time to listen to recorded performances of the various outstanding European bands playing the marches of their national composers.

Because we sometimes fail to research professional journals for interpretations of European marches, we often play them in wrong tempos. A perfect example is the improper tempo used for Jaime Texidor's *Amparito Roca*, a well-known, frequently played Spanish march. Though this work is in the Spanish *paso doble* style, for years I have heard it played at breakneck speeds instead of the tempos used by Spanish bands. Try playing or singing the following extracts from *Amparito Roca*, first at 160 and once again at 112. Then imagine how these passages would sound with a good band.

When played at 160 by most bands the fluid qualities of the first passage would come forth in a blurred, fake-sounding fashion; and the precision of the flute obbligato in the second passage would be lost. Note that the articulation of the second example is the way Spanish bands play the trio obbligato. Shouldn't we try to play Spanish *paso dobles* at their proper tempos and in the Spanish style?

What about British military marches? How often do we hear Kenneth Alford's *Colonel Bogey* at a tempo that destroys the character and lilt inherent in that great march? Try a tempo of 112 on *Colonel Bogey* and see if it isn't a convincing tempo, especially on the second strain bass tune. Then, play or sing the following example from *Flag of Victory* by Franz von Blon at around 108 (this tempo is more compatible with the pre-World War I German "goose-step" style of marching).

Italian marches are indicated in a variety of tempos. Generally lyrical in nature, they feature wide dynamic ranges and make greater use of refined, songlike sections. Italian and Spanish marches are similar in their lyrical approach, yet the melodic differences between the two cannot be mistaken. The next example is from *March Electric* by Guiseppe Creatore; the music is unusual because it is to be played around 152 – 160, more scherzo than march.

Most French marches I have played or conducted are the fastest in the European march group and sound best around 144. Although few American bands play French military marches, the following excerpt from Planquette-Rauski's *Sambre et Meuse* is typical in style and tempo:

The French march generally lacks the lyrical lines and soaring countermelodies of the Spanish, Italian, and German marches. It is texturally leaner and the melodies tend to be less lyrical but more rhythmically rigid. The trio tunes in many French marches are accompanied by the following characteristic two-measure drum beat:

In addition to the differences in march tempos, I also want to discuss rhythm. All of the military or parade marches have one thing in common — they must be played in precise rhythm; a steady pulse has to be maintained throughout. Although a conductor can choose to make a slight change in the overall interpretation of a concert or operatic march (faster or slower), there should be no deviation in tempo or rhythm from the beginning to the end in a military (parade) march.

When playing marches, most bands tend to vary the rhythmic pulse; the more experienced and technically proficient players will occasionally hurry toward cadences and endings, while less technically proficient players tend to drag tempos. A band that plays a march in detached style often shortens longer note values which starts to pull the tempo and destroys the rhythmic pulse. Younger, inexperienced players who don't understand the basic detached style of the march, often do not separate notes properly, and by hanging on to longer notes, give an imprecise pulse. One of my teachers said that a rhythmic pulse could be maintained if every note of one beat or more in duration were given its full value. Over the years, I have applied that advice and taken it one step further to include giving full value to dotted notes.

Hurried attacks after a rest often contribute to rushing; the longer the rest, the greater the tendency to anticipate the next attack. In the following example from the break strain of *His Honor* by Fillmore, I've used an "X" to show where hurried, imprecise attacks often occur.

Having discussed the variety of tempos and the rhythmic feel of marches in ¢ and ²⁄₄ meter, something should also be said about marches in ⁶⁄₈. A close examination shows that most ⁶⁄₈ marches sound best at around 120. There are exceptions, such as *In Storm and Sunshine* by J.C. Heed, which sounds best at an up tempo, yet the generalization still holds. Just recall such familiar ⁶⁄₈ marches as *Washington Post, Black Jack, Salutation, King Cotton,* or *Liberty Bell* and this generalization becomes more valid. *The Free Lance March* is the only ⁶⁄₈ march of Sousa's I can recall that sounds convincing at a tempo faster than ♩.=120. (I like it at 132.)

Young bandsmen, particularly those at the junior and senior high levels, seem to have particular difficulties in performing a ⁶⁄₈ march well. The rhythms usually lack precision and the result is a rhythmically clumsy performance that fails to have the unique lilt of the $\frac{6}{8}$ march. The rhythmic figures that seem to lack precision most include the following:

$\frac{6}{8}$ [musical notation] is too often played [musical notation] or as

[musical notation]

$\frac{6}{8}$ [musical notation] is often played to sound like $\frac{2}{4}$ [musical notation]

$\frac{6}{8}$ [musical notation] is almost played in $\frac{2}{4}$ and sounds

$\frac{2}{4}$ [musical notation]

$\frac{6}{8}$ [musical notation] comes forth sounding like

$\frac{2}{4}$ [musical notation]

Before playing the figures up to tempo, slowly practice and drill these and other rhythms in $\frac{6}{8}$ to help clear incorrect performances. Teach players the rhythmic feel of a $\frac{6}{8}$ march by having them recite rhythmic drills by rote in unison, using the syllables, "ONE-a-da, TWO-a-da." These syllables have the added advantage of being short enough to recite rapidly (up to ♩=152). To see how easily the articulation is and how rapidly syllables can be said, try reciting them in the following common rhythm patterns:

$\frac{6}{8}$ [musical notation] 1 ⅞ da 2 ⅞ da — Recite using a staccato articulation, making sure there is silence on the rests.

$\frac{6}{8}$ [musical notation] 1 – da 2 – da — Sustain the "ONE" and "TWO" for the length of a note in $\frac{6}{8}$ and say or sing the eighth notes softer than the quarter notes.

$\frac{6}{8}$ [musical notation] 1 du du 2 —— — Use a voice that is loud on the quarter note, light and quick on the two 16th notes, loudest and with a full beat on the dotted-quarter note.

$\frac{6}{8}$ [musical notation] rest dudu 2 – dudu 1 — Whisper "REST," then recite the remainder of the figure in tempo.

Using syllables in drilling rhythms becomes a bit more difficult when a series of 16ths is involved. They can be executed as follows:

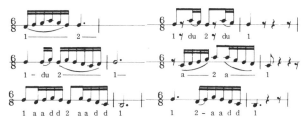

Interpretation in music is generally understood to mean the personal and creative elements that a player or conductor reflects in the performance of a composition. A

performance should show the musician's familiarity with the work and convey his musical concept of it. When playing any piece, he needs to be faithful to the composer, while at the same time perform the music as he perceives it. By copying another musician's interpretation, the imitator only robs himself of the sheer joy of re-creating that work.

If we believe that conductors should enjoy the privilege of interpreting music to suit their ideas and tastes, then no two conductors should interpret a march in exactly the same way. They might agree on style and choose a similar tempo; but their thinking may be completely different about phrasings, dynamics, or accents. Though conductors should understand their responsibilities to the composer, they should also realize their positions as middlemen between players and the listening audience.

I have evolved the following musical concepts through performing, studying, and listening to march interpretations by many conductors who play them well. The examples I have chosen demonstrate basic principles that I use in march interpretation. They are not presented as models of how you should play a particular march. If these principles make musical sense to you, then apply them; if they do not make sense, simply reject them.

• *Phrasing* in most marches refers to short phrases that are highly regular and either in four- or eight-measure lengths. The four-measure length is the common phrase in march tunes; it would be difficult to find more than a handful of marches that use eight-measure phrases. There just aren't many long-line tunes in marches. The following examples are typical of four- and eight-measure phrases:

• *Style* in marches can be shown in many ways — tempos, opposing dynamics, staccato and legato contrasts, accents, highlighting countermelodies, variations, and obbligatos. In the following examples, the first one demonstrates dynamic contrast in a tune that moves upward; the second shows two contrasting phrases.

189

B.B. and C.F.   J. Ord Hume

Though Sousa's march, *The University of Illinois*, is not printed as a legato tune, the next example shows my own concept of how I want to hear the trio melody played. This is one of the lesser-known Sousa marches; I regard it as one of his very best.

The next two excerpts show some possibilities for accenting and highlighting these well-known trombone/baritone countermelodies in two of Sousa's greatest marches, *Semper Fidelis* and *The Stars and Stripes Forever*. The markings and symbols explain how I would want to hear them played. In the first countermelody, treating the tied eighth-note (following the dotted-halves) as a 16th accomplishes two things musically: it clears up the articulation of the downward run and makes it possible to play the notes in time and with rhythmic precision. When held full value, the tenuto marks over the quarter note in measures four and six give this three-note figure (♪♩♪) the lilt and swing that Sousa used so often in his ⅜ march melodies. The separations marked before each of these figures lend clarity to the melody and help avoid the rhythmic blurring that often occurs when this obbligato is played in quasi-legato fashion. The character of the countermelody is obviously marcato and detached; attempting to play it as a long-line, eight-measure legato melody would certainly destroy the flavor of the tune.

The character of the second countermelody in the next example is lost if there is no break in measure two between the dotted-half note and the quarter note, and if the quarter notes are played full value and not detached. A slight detachment between dotted-quarter and eighth

notes in the third measure is consistent with the style of the countermelody while accenting the eighth note ensures rhythmic precision. Though the markings in these examples may look exaggerated or overdone to some, they represent, as nearly as possible, how these countermelodies sound best.

An exceptional, well-conceived piccolo-flute obbligato appears in the trio of Sousa's original march, *The Free Lance: On to Victory*; but it is seldom heard in performances of the work. Most band conductors seem unaware of its existence and often perform one of two edited versions of the march that use a watered-down rendition of the obbligato as well as the entire march. Hopefully, the eight-measure excerpt from the beginning of this brilliantly written obbligato will encourage more conductors to try the original march.

The final example is a charming, yet well-hidden and rarely heard horn line from Fillmore's *Golden Friendships*, a march written in ⅜ . It appears in the second strain of the march, which also includes a rather unique treatment of the bass line. A conductor has to study all the parts to this march to discover these hidden or obscure lines because a full score to the work is not available. Such musical items will never be heard in performance if conductors confine their knowledge of a march to the bare basics — melody, harmony, and rhythm.

Band conductors who study and look beyond the essentials may discover that even the lowliest march can be valuable music that deserves to be interpreted according to personal musical ideas and tastes. That, dear reader, is the musical challenge a march can offer. ■

April, 1986

Sousa

PERFORMANCE NOTES: THE STARS AND STRIPES FOREVER

BY KEITH BRION

Sousa in his study, 1928

These performance notes are reprinted with the permission of Hal Leonard Publishing. They correspond directly to the complete concert band arrangement of The Stars and Stripes Forever March *edited by Keith Brion, available through Hal Leonard Publishing, P.O. Box 13819, Milwaukee, Wisconsin; $45.*

Written in 1896, *The Stars and Stripes Forever* is the most celebrated American march. The following notes provide a representation of the music as it was performed by John Philip Sousa and his band in concert. It differs from both the heavily orchestrated marching band versions published by Sousa and from those editions published after his death.

Sousa's Band was exclusively a concert band that performed mainly in concert halls, theaters, and opera houses. During the first season of a newly composed march Sousa would verbally indicate various changes to his players that included deletions in doublings, octave switches, and accents. Sousa tried these alterations in concert, during the daily give-and-take between himself and his virtuoso

musicians. Shortly, they would settle into a standard concert procedure for each march. In addition to Sousa's verbal suggestions, the nuances created by his musicians during hundreds of performances allowed each composition to reach its full musical potential. This process created the "Sousa sound" and thus made Sousa's performances of his own music unique.

When a march had proven to be a hit, it was added to the Sousa encore books — a bound volume of the 100 most popular encore selections. From these 100, 8 to 10 were chosen for performance at each concert. Sousa's altered performance versions of his marches remained fairly constant through the years, even though the players continued to read the music from the original published march-size

parts, which were heavily orchestrated and largely unmarked. The Sousa style was merely passed on to new members by word of mouth from their older "side-partners." While these changes are sometimes difficult to pinpoint, they must be considered authentic clues to accurately interpreting Sousa's music.

Today, 50 years after Sousa's death, these ideas are corroborated by a small number of surviving pencil markings in the Sousa Band encore books. They also live in the contemporary performance practice of the marvelous Allentown Band, which began to play the marches in this way during Sousa's lifetime and continues to do so today. This band, which was conducted from 1925-75 by Albertus Myers, a former Sousa cornetist, has maintained the tradition. In the same aural and oral manner

A band director for 25 years, Keith Brion now portrays the March King in Sousa revival concerts throughout the country.

191

used by the Sousa Band, section by section, older members pass the information to younger ones, and all play from unedited parts.

These Sousa performance practices create musical rewards and provide a freshness of texture, shading, and dynamics. The alterations heighten the music's form and add to the full effect of the composition. The trimming of instrumentation allows many sections to become more delicate and dance-like. By contrast, this lightness of texture illuminates the power of the battle scenes and grandioso finales that conclude the march.

These comments and performance suggestions will help your band recreate the sound of a concert performance of *The Stars and Stripes Forever* as played by the Sousa Band with Sousa conducting.

Sources for these comments include the original full-score manuscript; the first two printings; recordings; and primary and secondary sources from former Sousa band members.

Sousa's musical changes were often deletions of instrumentation. In the case of *The Stars and Stripes Forever* these included elimination of the trumpets and trombones at the first statement of the second strain; elimination of the percussion at the first trio; and elimination of the trumpets and the trombones at the first and second trio. In addition, the clarinets stayed in their lower octave the first time through the second strain and during the first two trios.

Study of the Sousa Band encore books has revealed some interesting information. The flute section played from published D♭ piccolo parts, while the bass clarinet played a tenor saxophone part. Parts that are more idiomatic for these instruments are now provided. A harp part was added by Sousa in 1910 and was used regularly after that time. The trumpet I and II parts and timpani part were added after Sousa's death. Upbeat snare drum accents were also used in the final grandioso, which Sou-

sa's drummers began to use during the ragtime era.

Performance Suggestions

m. 5 a) Sousa added both length and weight to the first note of this bar. The length helps to correct the natural tendency to arrive at the second beat too soon.

b) Keep the short notes light and dance-like (leggiero).

c) Tubas should phrase in this manner:

Play the 32nds as pickups to the next beat: In the actual bass parts, however, the music is notated in the following way, reminding the players to legato tongue the first note of each group of 32nds as well as the dotted eighth.

Written:

m. 12 The volume and length of notes should be held until the moment the downbeat of m. 13 begins.

m. 13 These phrases should be light as well as piano. This delicate dance-like quality is found in the first strain of many Sousa marches.

m. 22 The woodwinds play marcato style and with solid volume; the phrasing should sound quite similar to the way it is played by

On tour, 1926: Jay Sims, trombonist; Winifred Bambrick, harpist; John Dolan, cornet soloist; Sousa; Marjorie Moody, soprano; Gus Helmecke, bass drummer

the brass instruments when the strain repeats.

m. 38 The snare drum part has strong accents on beat two, suggesting the feeling of a misplaced downbeat. When the second strain is repeated these accents become even more prominent.

m. 53 The trio melody may be treated as an aria. Trio pickups should be fully supported with a singing, well-blended tone. In Sousa's version for orchestra, the violins play this passage "sul G" (on the G string). This smooth, rich, cantabile string sound is a good model for band performance. The accents (bar 55) are achieved by the use of breath accents to enlarge the tone. Color should not

192

change; the desired effect is a sudden deepening of the texture. Rhythm is supplied by the attacks of tubas, trombones, and horns.

m. 54 This part was played by a harp in the Sousa Band. A marimba may be used as a substitution.

m. 87 Quarter note staccatos are played as medium length staccatos; the releases are lightly clipped.

m. 90 Trombones: to facilitate the slur from B♭ to A♭, switch to 5th position on the repeated B♭.

m. 94 In the Sousa Band this solo was played by the bass drum/attached cymbal player using his bass drum beater. A suspended cymbal played with the butt end of a snare stick may be used; or it may be performed effectively with a pair of crash cymbals.

m. 110 On the second statement of the trio, allow the saxophone and euphonium a bit more prominence than in the first statement of the trio. The melody must be kept expressive and alive without overbalancing the piccolo solo.

When *The Stars and Stripes Forever* was written in 1896, the D♭ piccolo was widely used in the bands and Sousa composed a solo that lies very naturally for it. Today, because the C piccolo is by far the more prevalent instrument, the *Stars and Stripes* solo is somewhat trickier. The following suggestions will facilitate C piccolo performance:

a) the first note:

is played:

fingered:

lift LH 2, 3, 4 fingers as a group

This trill fingering provides the best pitch and tone color and most closely approximates the sound of the corresponding D to E trill on the D♭ piccolo.

b) the second note:

is fingered:

For most C piccolos, this fingering is necessary for both pitch and accuracy of range. Using rapid air support, hyper-ventilate this note using the articulation syllable, "tee(t)," lightly clipping the ending.

c) the third note:

Keeping the same support, change to an "ah" syllable so that the note is not obscured by the high brilliance of the preceding pitches, and make it project as much as possible.

m. 110-113 Use the air to connect the musical motives in four-bar phrases.

m. 111 Piccolo: It is necessary to play these notes extremely short. Use the syllables "duckie duck-a," and double tongue on a legato breath line. Accent the final quarter note so it will project with an intensity that equals the high register notes.

m. 113 Piccolo: Sustain all trills full length.

m. 162 Sousa vigorously objected to the practice of slowing the tempo on these descending chromatics.

m. 166 Trumpets and trombones: The act of standing will increase volume many times without extra push. A *piu forte* volume is suggested. Do not force.

m. 166 Note the accents in the snare drum part; this accent should come squarely on the upbeat. The style is that of an accented five-stroke roll with a light flam attack. The snare drum part is written:

and is played:

The sticking never changes. The flam is played softly; it is used to start the head vibrating for the heavy upbeat accent. To adapt the length of the roll to the tempo re-

Sousa and his mother, 1907

193

quirements of the conductor, the roll may be extended in length through the use of multiple rebounds.

General Comments

Short notes are always short, but played delicately and lightly clipped. While short notes are slightly softer than longer ones, pitch and tone are always heard in the shortest notes.

the tuning pitch low.

Bass Drum - 34-36" in diameter. Use a calf batter head or both calf heads. Use standard beaters.

Cymbals - 16"-18" heavy. They should be able to produce a hard, clear attack for time as well as a satisfying, deep tone for large crashes. If two performers are available, use smaller, heavy cymbals for rhythm, and larger cymbals for accents and crashes. A

the entrance of their solo, and omitting the second preserves tonal balance when the trumpets and trombones are not playing.

Choreography

The piccolos (Sousa's entire flute section doubled piccolo for the solo), and the trumpet and trombone sections all marched to the front of the stage apron to perform their featured passages. The picco-

Premier performance of Royal Welch Fusiliers March, *1930: British ambassador, President Hoover, and Sousa*

Long notes and tied long notes are always held to the extremes of their values in both melodic or countermelodic passages. Long notes or slurs are never shortened before a short note. Long notes found in supporting harmonies are sometimes shortened or played with a tapered ending.

Percussion

The following percussion equipment will help make the tone qualities of Sousa's sound possible:

Snare Drum - 6½" x 14" or deeper, up to 12" x 15". Do not double snare drum parts except in solo drum passages. Use gut snares only and calf batter heads. Keep

cymbal attached to the bass drum will provide the most characteristic sound.

Performance Options for the Conductor

1. Sousa sometimes eliminated the repeats of the first and second strains.

2. Marimba may be substituted for the harp solo.

3. Trumpets and trombones may lay out for the second dogfight – this facilitates marching to the front of the stage and magnifies their effect in the finale.

4. The piccolos may eliminate both dogfights. Eliminating the first keeps the high octave fresh for

los stood directly in front of Sousa's podium, remaining there until the end of the march. During the second dogfight, the cornets marched to positions at Sousa's left; the trombones were to his right. As each section left their chairs to come forward, they began by stepping off on the left foot. Instruments were raised together on the first beat of the bar preceding their musical entrance. After the final stinger of the march, all sections pivoted on the next (silent) beat and immediately marched in step to their seats. In Sousa's performances an American flag was lowered at the rear of the stage at the grandioso. ■

Norman Dello Joio's
Variants on a Mediaeval Tune

by Barry E. Kopetz

Norman Dello Joio is an important American composer who has taken composition for the wind band seriously. His music shows the influences of jazz and dance and the teachers with whom he studied. Dello Joio's first teacher was his father, a church organist in New York; he later studied composition at The Juilliard School and at Yale University with Paul Hindemith. Each affected the young composer.

Dello Joio's major contributions to the repertoire of the wind band include *Variants on a Mediaeval Tune* (1963), *Scenes from the Louvre* (1966), and *Fantasies on a Theme by Haydn* (1968). More recently Dello Joio wrote *Concertante for Wind Instruments* (1973), *Satiric Dances* (1975), and *Colonial Ballads* (1979). The *Variants on a Mediaeval Tune* was his first work for band and has achieved lasting success.

Source of *In dulci jubilo*

The melody entitled *In dulci jubilo* has been borrowed by a number of fine composers, not the least of whom is J.S. Bach. The melody is used in the Christmas carol *Good Christian Men, Rejoice*, but has origins older than music historians are able to trace. Some of its earliest uses date back to the early 16th century and Martin Luther, whose 95 theses posted on the church door at Wittenberg altered the liturgy and also changed the accompanying music. According to musicologist Gustav Reese, the earliest music of the Lutheran church came from

Barry E. Kopetz is currently an associate professor of music at the University of Minnesota, where he conducts the symphonic and marching bands. He also teaches a graduate course in conducting wind literature and a course in band arranging. He is a published composer and arranger and in demand as a guest conductor and adjudicator. His background includes teaching instrumental music in grades five through twelve in Ohio and South Carolina as well as directing bands at the university level.

two distinctively varied origins: the chants of the Catholic and the pre-Reformation churches (predominantly German, religious songs), and a large second category encompassing several classes of music. One of these categories included non-liturgical pieces, some of which were already centuries old.

As a part of its reforms, the early Lutheran church sang in the vernacular rather than in the traditional Latin, hence the mixed Latin-German hymn known as *In dulci jubilo* became "nun singet und seid froh." Martin Luther and others frequently borrowed music from other sources, sometimes writing new verses and at other times modifying the music. Thus, the origins of *In dulci jubilo* remain clouded, but the melody has rich musical potential and serves as the basis for a number of musical compositions.

Variants on a Mediaeval Tune was commissioned by the Mary Duke Biddle Foundation for the Duke University Band and received its premiere on April 10, 1963. While the form of the piece is a straightforward theme and variations, the five exquisite variations are creative in content and orchestration.

Introduction

The opening cornet fanfare proclaims the beginning of the piece in bold fashion. The conductor should give an exact preparatory beat to clarify the tempo of the rapidly articulated passage that follows. Too often these first notes are performed either out of tempo or clumsily by an over-anxious section of first cornets. One way to resolve this problem is to write the subdivision over the first measure in each of the first cornet parts so that the performers can visualize the placement of these important notes.

Another exercise that will further illuminate this passage is to have the cornets practice playing a full 32nd-note group on the first third of beat one.

Dello Joio uses the introduction to set the tone of the entire work. He scores the first chord sounded by the brasses in measure 1 using pitches from the first two measures of the melody:

The conductor should encourage the brasses to play full chords in measures 1-3, then establish a legato beat pattern to help draw the melody from the clarinets in expressive fashion. In measure 5, we find the first occurrence of

hemiola, a technique Dello Joio uses abundantly. Here, the conductor should make clear the primary beats of each measure and devise a way to achieve clarity in the remaining portion of the measure. This occurs again in measure 8, though the hemiola is now divided between the soprano register woodwind instruments and the low reeds and brasses.

Theme

The conductor should give the ensemble a clear release on the downbeat in measure 12 and another to the sustaining clarinets at the end of the measure. The first statement of the theme now begins quietly, shared by the piccolo and bass clarinet. The term *semplice* is all the instruction that is required for the ensemble and conductor to interpret this passage. Before the first rehearsal, the conductor should make sure that a good clarinetist has prepared the important E♭ alto clarinet solo beginning in measure 17. If the instrument is unavailable, copy the part out for a second bass clarinet. The conductor should encourage the performers to play *cantabile* throughout this introduction of thematic material by using an *espressivo* beat pattern.

The second statement of the theme begins equally plainly in the bassoon at the end of measure 21. It may be that the composer wants to present the origin of the melody as clearly as possible before diverging into the five wonderfully imaginative variations. After the melody passes to the first clarinet in measure 23, the harmonic activity of the bassoon counterpoint builds intensity that is finally released on the downbeat of measure 26. Here, the piccolo, flutes, and second clarinets sing the glorious conclusion of the melody. Dello Joio concludes the presentation of the theme as it began, reminding the listener of the cornet introduction, now supported by new harmonic underpinnings that give no hint of the music that will follow. The conductor should give a definite downbeat in measure 33 to give the first cornet the impetus to play this important part. Again, a reminder written on the part will help.

Within the first 34 bars, the composer sets a precedent for ample use of unusual harmonies in the five variations to follow. Similarities in orchestration between key sections also help to unify the work. The composer often uses the interval of a major second at the root of his voicings (see trombone 1 and 2 in the first measure), a technique that provides wonderful opportunities for creative harmonic structure. Here, Dello Joio has incorporated a harmonically ambiguous version of the theme:

The use of the minor third (G to B♭) in measure 17 versus the major second (G to A) in measure 15 highlights the contrast that Dello Joio exploits fully during the variations. His harmonic language is fresh and unique as he moves freely through various tonal centers.

Variation I

As the ensemble diminuendos in measure 34, the conductor should give a clear cue to the percussionist about to begin the snare drum solo. It is critical to establish a definite tempo at this juncture or the ensemble will start unevenly. The important entrance of the eighth-note ostinato in measure 36 should be perfectly metronomic for the variation to properly continue its forward motion. This passage is an excellent example in the wind repertoire of how much the string bass pizzicato can add to the texture. Without it, the passage is not quite the same.

There are five measures of soft intensity before the entrance of a rapid, terse, three-octave melodic fragment in the piccolo, flute, and oboe. This material is presented with such speed that it is scarcely apparent that it is based on notes two through five of the melody. The passage also draws attention to the contrast betwen the major and minor third, a contrast that Dello Joio takes great joy in highlighting.

The conductor need only provide steady, precise pulses and encourage rapid, light articulations in order to achieve proper execution of these measures. The contrasting sixteenths in the E♭ clarinet part are not doubled elsewhere in the texture, so make sure the player brings them out.

The trumpet melody in measure 42 bears a marked resemblance to the opening notes of the piece. The final two notes in the first trumpet in measure 42 (G to A) and measure 43 (G to B♭) demonstrate early in the variation how cleverly the composer can weave the original melody into the composition. It is an interesting study for the dedicated conductor to examine the work carefully and identify all such occurrences. It is in the course of such study that the high level of Dello Joio's craftsmanship is revealed.

Cue the punctuated entrances of the brass and percussion in measures 42 and 43, and provide a sharp downbeat to the clarinets in measure 44.

Because the brasses are still *fortissimo*, the second pulse of this measure should indicate a softer dynamic for the clarinets in the same tempo. Any fluctuation at this point weakens the forward motion of the variation. It is better to take the variation at a slightly slower tempo than the indicated *Allegro deciso* (♩ = 120) than to mar its momentum with a careless slowdown in tempo.

The entrance of the second phrase of the melody in syncopation occurs in measure 46 over the eighth-note ostinato. The conductor should establish full quarter notes while maintaining the incessant sixteenths and eighths in the accompaniment. In measure 48, the dynamics at the expressive entrance of the second alto and tenor saxophone, along with alto clarinet, are not mismarked. Rarely do performers adequately project this important ascending line so that it cuts through the texture. Have your players focus on bringing this important line to the fore.

The first pulse of measure 50 should be accented, setting up a major contrast to the previous measure. Have the player elevate the crash cymbals after the attack, allowing them to ring brilliantly. This measure marks another way in which Dello Joio subtly varies and reuses previous material. The rhythmic drive of the sixteenth notes is the same as at the beginning of the variation but now one full step higher in pitch, shifting the tonal center of the variation. The composer uses this opportunity to wander harmonically from the tonal center of G established at the beginning of the variation.

The conductor's task remains modest until the first note of measure 57, where he should give an emphatic downbeat to electrify the measure. The outline of the augmented seventh chord in the upper register should be clearly audible, and each quarter note should be conducted with equal weight. Measure 58 is harmonically identical; a crisp beat will help to achieve clarity in the sixteenth notes. It will help to encourage an exaggerated staccato from the ensemble here.

A return to the tonal center of G occurs at measure 59, accompanied by the familiar eighth-note ostinato established at the beginning of the variation. Dello Joio immediately begins to obscure the harmonic direction by layering perfect fourths on top of one another:

To enhance the crescendo leading to measure 63, play softly in the preceding measures and avoid making the crescendo too quickly. The upper woodwinds in measure 63 play, in strict time, the melody first introduced by the trumpets in measure 42. Variation I concludes as it began: abruptly, and with exciting rhythmic drive.

Variation II

What the conductor does during rests is sometimes more important that what he does while the music is in motion. At the end of the first variation, for example, the conductor might conduct beats three and four in the tempo of the next variation, or he might remain motionless for an instant and simply start the next variation in the new tempo with a preparatory beat. Either way, the conductor should prepare the ensemble for the *pesante* style of the next variation.

Use small, heavy motions with the baton at the beginning of Variation II, and appropriately larger motions to indicate the crescendo at the end of measure 69. The dramatic melodic fragment introduced by the cornets in measure 70 stresses the importance of the minor third in Dello Joio's compositional plan. The composer achieves some semblance of melodic unity in measure 73 by restating the material from measure 1, now presented by the trumpets, baritone, and first trombone. Dello Joio continues to obscure the tonal direction here with a contrasting ascending line in the bass instruments.

Each conductor makes interpretive decisions throughout a work, and the second variation of *Variants on a Mediaeval Tune* is certainly no exception. One question to consider is how to differentiate between melodic and accompanying material. Dello Joio successfully blurs the distinctions in this wonderful set of variations, but studying the score with this question in mind will help in developing an interpretation. A related question is whether differentiation exists between the melodic and accompanying material throughout the work. Confronting such questions when studying the score provides the key to uncovering important issues relating to balance and interpretation. It also assists the conductor in better understanding the work holistically.

In measure 76, the melodic material in the woodwinds and low brass is derived from the theme, and the three-octave distance between the voices is a beautiful effect. Use the baton with long, stretched motions to bring out the *cantabile* quality called for by the composer. The sparse texture over measures 80 to 84 calls for delicate control, yet the conductor should preserve a singing style. Minimal arm motion with a fluid, graceful pulse from the wrist should provide what is needed. There is ample opportunity for musical flexibility as long as the ensemble carefully follows the conductor.

At measure 85 the sense of motion accelerates, due in part to repeated triplets and syncopation on the note G. Once established, these rhythmic patterns allow the conductor to turn to shaping the melodic material in the upper woodwinds. This continues through the crescendo leading to measure 89, where the ensemble should articulate the chord on beat one without taking a breath. The impact of measure 89 is lessened considerably when the ensemble breathes before the attack. Be sure that the musicians carefully mark their parts to insure proper execution. Providing a firm pulse to the low brass on beat two will discourage players from rushing the 32nd-note figure in measures 89 and 90. Finally, the conductor must have a clear vision of the musical results he wants to achieve in the final bars of the variation. Simply keeping time will not be sufficient. Conducting with an expressive beat pattern and implying the appropriate amount of tension with the baton and forearm will bring the desired response from the ensemble.

Variation III

The delicate beginning of the third variation requires excellent communication between the conductor and the five solo musicians. The percussionist playing the snare drum part should not accent any of the sixteenth notes; these four notes are often uneven or rushed. Having the performer indicate a silent quarter note on the next count will help eliminate this problem. The conductor has to establish strict tempo, avoiding any fluctuation, as the ensemble approaches measure 103. If the tempo is unsteady, the result may be disastrous. Having the ensemble articulate sixteenth notes on the syllable "tah" or "tee" during the first two measures in rehearsal will help stress the importance of even tempo and accurate subdivision.

The conductor can assist the ensemble immeasurably in this variation by executing short, precise motions with the tip of the baton. Once the sixteenth notes begin, they continue throughout the variation, disappearing only in the 3/4 measure 120 and the first two counts of measure 138. Make the ensemble aware of the importance of maintaining light, even articulation when playing passages of repeated sixteenth notes.

After passing an F♯ triad from the upper woodwinds to the low brass in measure 103 (a four-octave drop in the space of four counts), Dello Joio presents *In dulci jubilo* hidden within the rapidly articulated sixteenths of the E♭ and first B♭ clarinet parts:

Xylophone, bells, and upper woodwinds contribute their contrasting colors while highlighting important melodic and harmonic notes. At once, listeners can sense that the ideas from previous variations have been subtly modified.

Articulation poses a problem in this variation. Writing the word "lightly" on every part will remind players of how best to approach it. Once they master the rapid, light articulation the variation will float along on its own. Indeed, the music should sound effortless, even though the musicians may be working very hard. Be sure to give an adequate number of cues for entrances that require complete sections to continue the sixteenth notes. Also cue important entrances by the percussion section. Remind the percussionists not to rush the sixteenths leading into measure 139; they need to help the ensemble avoid a faulty attack on the final staccato sixteenth note of the variation.

Variation IV

The beginning of Variation IV contrasts with what has just transpired. The rich, dark quality of the bassoon and bass and alto clarinets is a welcome change from the electrifying intensity of the conclusion of Variation III. The conductor should indicate exactly what he expects stylistically on the opening triplet, lest the low reeds play the passage monotonously. The performers have to execute the duple and triple subdivisions of each count with the utmost precision if this opening melody is to be musical. In short, the players need to carefully prepare the rhythmic details so they can give full attention to the conductor. Attention to phrasing is also critical to the successful performance of this delicate passage. The conductor should keep the tip of the baton moving slowly and gracefully throughout in order to give the music a sense of motion. Assigning fewer players to a part in the opening measures may allow for greater flexibility and better balance. The snare drum roll in measure 147 should be nearly inaudible, though even in quality.

As the ensemble grows in both volume and intensity in measures 148 to 150, the musicians should not overplay the dynamic level in measure 151. Inserting the word *subito* before the *mf* in each part will help resolve this problem. Approach the next four measures in moderate rubato style, adding a slight acceleration at measure 155. Bring out the horn and second and third clarinet parts at measure 160, being careful to keep the ensemble in balance at the same time. Allowing a slight *ritardando* on the last two counts of measure 161 will reveal a musical approach to the return of the melodic material in the following measure.

Measures 167 to 180, the remaining measures of the variation, are among the most beautiful in the repertoire. They should be conducted as expressively as possible, *molto legato*. Care must be taken to prepare the dotted eighth-sixteenth figure in measures 167 and 169. Alert the low reeds to the fact that the rhythm is not the same as the double-dotted-eighth/ thirty-second-note rhythm at the beginning of the variation. Provide clear pulses on beats two and three.

Variation V

The final variation is a fitting, spirited conclusion to the work. You may choose to dispense with keeping time in measure 180 if you give a clear preparatory beat in the new tempo prior to measure 181. Once the proper tempo is established, the music fairly drives itself along. You may do more damage than good by overconducting in these measures, so step back and enjoy the music as it joyously evolves.

I have seen this variation conducted in a variety of patterns. Some conductors group the measures in fours, some in twos. A few conduct almost entirely up/down, one pulse to the measure. Personal comfort and confidence is important here, though I admit a preference for conducting the passage in four, each beat equalling one full measure. Experimenting in front of a mirror will help you find what seems appropriate to achieve the proper style. After all, it is the sound of the music that is important; and if the conductor is able to achieve what is intended through conducting the entire passage in one, then the question of pattern is moot.

Portions of Variation V require a fluid pattern in order to achieve the liquid expression that is called for. The conductor may choose to switch to a more punctuated ictus when encountering the accented sections of hemiola, such as the one found in measures 189 to 191. Do not allow the tempo to change during these four measures. After alternating legato melodic phrases with sections of hemiola, Dello Joio breaks the pattern by bringing the timpani in *fortissimo* in measure 221. This entrance should be strong, then diminuendo quickly in the second measure in order to prepare for the lovely return of the melody in the first clarinet and first and third horns. Again, an expressive pattern is appropriate in order to achieve a lyrical quality.

The entrance of the piccolo, flute, and glockenspiel at measure 243 provides a charming, joyful change in the texture. The composer designates this lively passage as the most prominent, because it is clearly based on the melody. Even separation is required from the upper woodwinds both here and at measure 251; hence, a crisp staccato from the baton is in order with an appropriate, quick rebound. In measure 252 be sure to insist upon adequate balance from the bassoon and bass clarinet; too often this important passage is lost.

To reintroduce the section of hemiola in the cornet parts, let the crash cymbals resonate loudly and freely. Rhythmic intensity continues to grow until the music reaches an important climax at measure 275. Here begins the magnificent three-part canon so carefully anticipated by Dello Joio. The conductor needs to do very little other than provide the pulse necessary to allow the music to soar to its fullest heights. Do not obscure the trumpet entrance at measure 279; the cue should be one of ample volume.

Dello Joio indicates no dynamic level softer than fortissimo from the beginning of the canon until the final notes are played. Conductors should alert performers to the danger of peaking too early if the dynamic levels are taken literally.

Dynamic control is necessary in order to expose the dramatic trumpet part in measure 305 as well as the cornet/horn combination two measures later. This is where the conductor must be conscious of the dynamic direction of the music. It is easy to become so captivated with the exciting rhythmic and melodic fervor that the last five measures lose intensity. Improper pacing of the music from measure 275 to the end may cause the ensemble to peak early, resulting in an anticlimatic ending. Occasionally practicing the final five measures at the beginning of rehearsals will help remind players of what needs to occur if the piece is to end with the excitement it deserves. The final note should be in good balance and have adequate length and resonance for the piece to end satisfactorily. □

Hindemith's Symphony for Band

An Interpretive Analysis

by Barry E. Kopetz

Paul Hindemith was a rare musician known not only for his talent as a composer but also for his work as a professional violist, conductor, and teacher. Born in 1895, he received his education at the Hoch Conservatory in Frankfurt. He taught composition in Berlin in 1927, but under Nazi pressure eventually moved to the United States and taught at Yale University. In his later years Hindemith taught and conducted in the United States and Europe. He died in Frankfurt in 1963.

Hindemith's works fall into several periods. His early works bear similarity to the style of the late 19th-century composers. During the early 1920s the young composer went through an experimental period. Works of this time show jazz influences, atonality, impressionism, and

expressionism, though none were to become mainstays in his musical language. His mature style became somewhat neo-Classical, borrowing from baroque textures and forms. In his mature period Hindemith wrote the Symphony in B♭ for Concert Band (1951). Published by Schott, the work is available in the United States through the European American Music Distributors in Valley Forge, Pennsylvania.

Before composing the Symphony for Band Hindemith wrote a large amount of music for winds, including instrumental sonatas that continue to be performed regularly as well as chamber pieces for various wind combinations. Hindemith wrote the Symphony for the United States Army Band; he conducted its premiere on April 5, 1951. It is his lone contribution to the literature for full concert band, although other works have been transcribed.

Movement I - Moderately fast, with vigor (♩ = 88-92)

The maturity and craftmanship of Hindemith's contrapuntal technique shows immediately in this dramatic movement. Set in sonata-allegro form, the movement opens boldly with a unison

Barry E. Kopetz is on the faculty of the University of Minnesota, where he conducts the chamber winds and the symphonic band, teaches band arranging, and directs the marching band. A published composer and arranger, Kopetz is active as an adjudicator and guest conductor.

statement of the first theme by the cornets and trumpets.

Hindemith wastes no time in establishing a clear tonal focus around the pitch B♭, though he varies the tonal center within the melodic material. Extensive use of the interval of the fourth is one of his distinguishing characteristics both within his melodic and harmonic scheme, and progressions of seconds often form the substance of his melodies.

The first movement requires a concise preparatory beat in the precise tempo to get things started. The woodwind performers also require an exact tempo in order to execute their rapid figurations confidently.

Note carefully the pitches in the first measure of the bassoon and bass parts.

Hindemith often makes subtle connections such as this; these five notes are the same as those that begin the second theme later in the movement. Make them prominent, placing them in the ear of the listener from the beginning.

At first glance it may seem impossible to cue all of the entrances. Only adequate rehearsal time will dictate which you choose to cue, but consider cueing the first horn entrance in measure 4 and the trombone entrance in measure 5, being careful not to let these color additions affect the natural progress of the melody. Hindemith's writing for winds stands out among other compositions of the era for its soloistic qualities. His masterful color combinations demand that the listener hear thematic material as a unit even though new tone colors enter briefly. The final portion of the first theme (shown in measures 7-10 of the first example) consists of a descending, reiterated four-note motive in the cornets and trumpets. A legato beat pattern with appropriate indications for dynamic contrast will help to attain a smooth conclusion to this important thematic material.

In the second statement of the first theme, given by the upper woodwinds, the first note of the melody is shortened by a full count. Hindemith delegates the accompaniment to the cornets and trumpets, which is a complete reversal of roles. Players should continue to perform the melody "vigorously," as marked, and the conductor should continue to direct attention to maintaining good balance. Note that the snare drum roll is at the *pp* level. Because the snare is used so sparingly, be sure that its presence adds rather than detracts; it should be soft.

The composer concludes the second presentation of the second theme with the same four-note motive as before. Hindemith begins shifting the tonal direction by stating the motive with seven successive entrances, the first four beginning on different pitches (study measures 17-23). Remember to shape each motive while encouraging the woodwinds to maintain the vitality necessary to propel the music forward. Study the entire section thoroughly until you are fully aware of the musical problems present.

Two measures (24-25) of melodic material in the trumpets and trombones bring the exposition of the first theme to close. Use progressively larger pulses to bring this section to a satisfactory conclusion on the downbeat of measure 26 in a balanced *ff* F triad. The third appears only in the first clarinet part and one in the flute tremolos.

After a brief two-measure introduction the first oboe introduces the second theme.

The relationship between this and previously presented material quickly becomes apparent. For example, the first four notes appeared in the opening measure of the piece, the dotted quarter-eighth note rhythm is reused, and the wide skips in the angular melody are all present in the previous thematic material. At the bassoon entrance in measure 28 a four-note idea is presented in counterpoint with the second theme, repeating itself when the melody comes to moments of repose.

The tenor saxophone begins what appears to be a second repetition of this material in measure 33, but ends abruptly as the clarinet enters in measure 36 on melodic material used to tonally diverge. Use a firm pulse here to indicate the immediate dynamic change. In measure 38 Hindemith incorporates material from the first theme, teasing the listener by blurring the tonal center. Be sure to note the beginning pitch on each entrance, starting with the solo and first clarinet in measure 36 to see how quickly Hindemith accomplishes these shifts.

The second complete repetition of the second theme begins in measure 41 in the B♭ clarinets. The quarter-note counterpoint provided earlier by the bassoon is replaced by light staccato notes in the horn and soft, delicate, melodically based ornamentation in the flute and piccolo, all based upon the first five notes of the first theme. Continue to insist upon an expressive interpretation of the thematic material; at the same time, keep the accompaniment light. Heavy pulses have no place in this texture.

The glockenspiel, while marked *piano*, outlines important notes of the second theme, so make sure it is precisely aligned with the clarinets. Prevent the ensemble from rushing the intensifying passages in measures 46 through 50, otherwise the final notes in measure 50 will make a poor preparation for the music to follow.

One of the great challenges of conducting the first movement of Hindemith's Symphony for Band is bringing this past section to a precise conclusion and providing the proper size pulse to begin the third theme in measure 51.

Third Theme

Be careful not to slow down in your attempt to achieve the contrasting soft dynamic level. Consider a legato beat pattern, stretching each pulse fully to assist in achieving the lyrical quality of this gorgeous three-octave unison passage. Don't over-emphasize the written crescendos in the score; they should be no louder than *mp* or *mf* at the conclusion of the crescendo.

Horns

Treat the $\frac{5}{4}$ meter in measure 72 carefully, deciding before the first rehearsal whether to conduct short-long or long-short. The latter seems more natural because of the way the baritone saxophone, cornets 2 and 3, baritone, and bass drum parts are notated. It also helps the players accurately place the eighth note at the end of the bar. Five measures later, the $\frac{3}{8}$ bar also requires attention. If you believe a *ritardando* is in order, then conduct three beats to the measure and make an abrupt release.

After pausing, provide an exact downbeat for the alto clarinet and alto saxophones to begin the development section. Take care to establish *l'istesso tempo*. While the conductor appears to have an easy job keeping time at this point, the delicate balances require a keen ear. Parts enter and exit rapidly, but don't get so caught up in cueing entrances that you neglect to provide a sense of direction. Making a slight separation between the persistent dotted eighth-sixteenth rhythm will help to maintain the tempo, rhythmic drive, and clarity.

Creative orchestration abounds during the coming measures, so the conductor must be prepared to balance the multitude of entrances. Adhering to the indicated dynamic levels will help clarify the musical line. Be sure to keep the snare drum at *pp* at measure 99, and bring the brasses and clarinet to a full *ff* before the dynamic change at 104. Note the unexpected prominence of the flute and baritone part and the *mf* trill in clarinet 3. The music continues to flow easily until measure 129 with the entrance of the solo cornet part again based upon previous material.

Solo Cornet

As the fugal subject passes from cornets on to other instruments, be careful to see that the theme maintains its forward motion and buoyancy; do not allow the thickening texture to slow the tempo. Lead up to the magnificent *ff* of the thematic material in augmentation at measure 147 with a long, even crescendo. Conduct the $\frac{3}{4}$ at 149 either in one or in a rapid three, depending upon the effect you want to make with the second dotted quarter note in those parts having two dotted quarters. Conducting the measure in three provides better clarity to the ensemble but tends to place additional stress on the second dotted quarter.

The recapitulation of the first movement begins in measure 155 with the clarinets playing figurations similar to those found in the first bar Hindemith reintroduces the first theme scored in parallel fifths at measure 157 followed one bar later by the second theme in bass clarinet, first bassoon, and baritone saxophone. The basses can help maintain a steady tempo by playing their quarter notes precisely.

At letter L the solo clarinet takes the first theme, while the second theme is scored above the clarinet in the first flutes. Subdue the supporting trills in clarinets 2 and 3, as well as horn 1 and 2. Watch the tempo in the next several bars; use a progressively smaller beat pattern as the music cadences obscurely in measure 183. A small *ritardando* is in order here.

When the third theme returns, consider having the players stagger the breathing until the downbeat of measure 191 so as to achieve an unbroken line. All must play as one.

Give trombones and horns a firm cue at measure 191 to emphasize the importance of this entrance. Here it is scored for more instruments than in the exposition, and the increased weight demands a larger pulse. At the third presentation of the third theme at measure 197 Hindemith adds weight by including more cornets on the part as well as adding the euphonium and timpani. Though the music feels as if it could build no further, the music rises to new heights with the fourth repetition of the third theme at measure 203. Beware of letting the music get out of hand at this point with all musicians playing *ff*. Maintain good balance, especially making sure that all of the moving eighth notes can be clearly heard.

Scoring of the final four measures emphasizes the unison woodwind line. Rehearse the woodwinds to ensure good balance among parts. Then rehearse the punctuated brass chords that accompany the woodwind line, making sure players put the proper amount of separation between quarter notes. Players often rush these quarter notes, so provide a clear, concise pulse.

Movement II – Andantino grazioso (♩ =56)

The second movement could be outlined roughly as A-B-AB(combined)-Coda. Except for a brief *ff* outburst at measure 84, the entire movement is thinly scored to emphasize the woodwinds.

Striking the proper balance between the two primary lines is important in the opening measures of the second movement. In the duet between the solo cornet and the first E♭ alto saxophone the instruments play an equally important role in the exposition of the first theme.

Both players need to adhere to the dynamics.

The shifting meters and grace note/quarter note accompaniment blur the barlines, so don't slavishly emphasize the beginning of measures simply because the barline happens to be present. Before the ensemble rehearses this opening material, rehearse only the two solo lines apart from the ensemble so the musicians understand the interplay of their parts. When rehearsing uneven measures, such as those in $\frac{5}{4}$, keep the musical line and excellent precision in the accompaniment foremost in your thoughts.

At measure 12, when the first theme repeats, Hindemith reverses the original roles played by the two solo lines. Note that he alters the melodic material in measure 16 in a way that resembles the reiterated trumpet motive from the first movement. (See the last four measures of the first example.) A series of parallel 11th chords in the trumpets supporting the tenor saxophone melody (measures 21-26) prepares the listener for the first unison presentation of the first theme.

First Theme

Exert firm, but not rigid, control over the ensemble in order to encourage a musical performance here. Give special attention to the accompaniment interacting between the upper woodwinds and the horns. It should add a fresh, new appearance to the melody, without covering it.

Measure 38 begins a partial presentation of the first theme in the solo cornet part, which is interrupted by a melodic fragment in trombones 2 and 3.

Trombones

The musical fragments that follow simply die away during the next seven measures. Give clear pulses to help the flutes play together during the *ritardando* in measures 47 and 48.

Hindemith remains true to his tendency to write in sectional form, finishing the previous theme quietly and beginning a contrasting, fresh idea. The second theme, marked "fast and gay," bursts forth in solo and first clarinets.

Second Theme

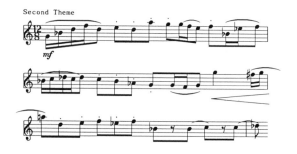

Marking the important lines both in the score and the individual parts will help you emphasize the imitation between parts. The tambourine part lends itself beautifully to the spirit of this theme; the player should strike it lightly, minimizing residual sounds.

Do everything possible to set and maintain a light, buoyant style. Small, light pulses will allow for the gentle dynamic shadings that add so very much to this section. You will need to make a larger downbeat at measure 62 to achieve the *f* indicated, but try to maintain the lightness. At measure 66 the glockenspiel should play softly, preferably with brass mallets.

Measure 71 requires a great effort to achieve the startling change of character. A pronounced, dry beat will help maintain precision and bring out the accent at the end of each beat. It will also help the ensemble avoid the urge to rush. Hindemith no sooner establishes new material than he wanders off into a brief but lovely imitative interplay between the piccolo and the two flute parts. Overcoming the conducting challenge presented here requires a combination of deliberate score study with accompanying practice in front of a mirror.

The meter from the end of measure 72 through measure 75 remains compound triple, while the scoring clearly remains duple. You may either stay in the meter designated on the score or switch to a two-pulse pattern beginning with the downbeat of measure 73. As long as the parts are clearly marked and the players understand the reason for the change, such a modification presents no problem. If this helps the performance, by all means make the change.

The second theme returns at measure 77 scored exactly as it had been at measure 49, but Hindemith quickly diverges from it. The entrance of the rhythmic cornet parts and the trombone arpeggios informs us that new and exciting material is about to be heard.

Trombone

Give adequate attention to the crescendo as you approach the exciting music at measure 84.

Trombone 1

Trombones 2–3

Horns 1–4

204

This is powerful music, and it is the only time in the movement that Hindemith unleashes all of his forces. Emphasize the important melodic material in the horns and trombones during this glorious three-measure outburst.

Following the repeated 16ths that predominate in the woodwinds from measures 87 through 90, Hindemith combines both themes beginning in measure 91. Because the entire ensemble is marked *piano* (except for the *pianissimo* tambourine and the *mf* horn and baritone saxophone), listen for textural clarity. Cue the important entrances.

A second repetition of the combined themes begins at measure 102, new instruments adding to the increasing volume. The composer begins diverging in measure 106, with the saxophones presenting material played by the solo cornet in measure 16. Glockenspiel, flute, oboe, and clarinets are also combined masterfully here using material from measures 66-71. Consider marking the primary beats on each of the flute parts as well as the piccolo in measures 112 through 115. While the location of the pulse is obvious, the diversity of rhythms in these parts requires careful execution because of the underlying parallel chords now present in the cornets and trumpets.

The final return of the combined first and second themes begins at measure 117, with the two presented simultaneously. The woodwinds practically float through their final four measures as the trombones wander melodically. Using a small, smooth pulse will help to achieve the musical precision needed here.

The sectional nature of the second movement demonstrates Hindemith's ability to use and reuse materials freely in counterpoint, creating a sense of tension and release through contrapuntal means. While the general tonal focus is centered around the pitch G, Hindemith moves about freely. The use of the stable G triad to conclude the movement, while typical of the composer, provides a satisfying conclusion to this fascinating movement.

Movement III – Fugue, Rather broad ($\downarrow$ = 100)

The third movement abounds with energy and unusual orchestration. Hindemith begins by teasing the listener with an eight-measure introduction that seems to have little chance of going forward. After the fermata in measure 8, maintain the original tempo in the next measure before establishing the new tempo at letter A. Trumpets and cornets 2 and 3 are the carriers of the first theme, which is used as the basis of a fugue.

First Theme

As the composer has marked the score "fast, energetic," a crisp, two-beat pattern seems in order. Be sure that the players are sensitive to achieving proper balance as the horns and baritone enter on the fugue subject in measure 17.

Hindemith uses canon beginning in measure 26 and again in measure 45, where the accompanimental figures must remain *p* as the ensemble approaches the section of stretto that begins at D in measure 54. Typical use of the stretto technique with a fugue subject has the melodic material enter in rapid succession, and the stretto is used to bring the fugue to conclusion.

The composer's indication of *scherzando* at E implies a somewhat lighter beat from the conductor in order to draw the appropriate qualities from the repetitive woodwind figures. First alto saxophone plays the entire first theme, which leads to new thematic material. Ask a percussionist to strike a small triangle with a thin beater to delicately color this transition.

The first appearance of the second theme occurs in unison, performed by the combined bass clarinet and bassoons beginning in measure 77.

Second Theme

One of the qualities that was fresh about Hindemith's scoring techniques was his willingness to place primary thematic material in the hands of less common instruments, and this is only one such example. Cohesiveness is achieved in a variety of ways, in this case through melodic unity. The similarity between this and previously stated material is readily identifiable. The second theme occurs three times between measures 77-88, overlapping in the second and third entrances. At measure 77 the *espressivo* requires a fluid, liquid pattern to produce the desired results.

Letter G introduces a harmonized setting of the second theme, with sporadic accompaniment based upon the first four notes of the fugue subject. Here we find an example of the composer's inventive scoring procedures: oboes on the outside voices of a triad; E♭ soprano clarinet on the third (see measure 89). The theme is scored in three voices over the course of the next 10 bars before the texture thins at measure 99. From here until measure 110, an imitative section requires careful cueing.

This harmonized theme continues in the clarinets at measure 110, slightly varied. This presentation is more rhythmically vital than the statement in unison, and the accompanimental figures are reminiscent of the fugue subject. When this harmonized material returns seven measures later in measure 116, it requires attention to balance, because the harmonized melody is now at a two-octave spread (flutes 1, 2 and oboe versus first alto, tenor, and baritone saxophones). Maintain a lyrical quality throughout this expressive passage. The section concludes with another section of stretto (measures 122-135) based on the first three notes of the second theme.

With the reappearance of the *scherzando* at J, the listener expects to hear a recapitulation of previous material, but instead the music appears to gradually lose momentum and lead to an unstable cadence. At the *tempo primo* at L, both themes are presented simultaneously in counterpoint, and the conductor should perform this passage energetically, giving the musicians pronounced pulses. Charles Gallagher discusses the fugal treatment of the themes in an excellent article in the Spring, 1966 issue of *The Journal of Band Research*.

One of the potential dangers in conducting the third movement of the Symphony is that the music may reach a musical peak at the wrong place, such as at M. The dramatic return of the first theme from movement one in augmentation is thrilling, given simultaneously with the two themes from the final movement.

First Theme

Still, we need to restrain ourselves and our musicians, because more exciting music is about to begin.

The music reaches a new level of intensity at measure 197 as the brasses boldly proclaim a melodic fragment in harmony taken from the first example. Brass phrasing during this dramatic buildup determines the results of this section. Cue the musicians playing imitatively at O. The snare drum needs a special cue for his roll.

The Symphony culminates in a 13-measure coda that begins at measure 213. All of the band's forces are now present, playing *ff*, so listen to be sure that the descending melodic material in cornets 1-3, trombone 1, and glockenspiel come through, along with the important answer in the bass clarinet, bassoon, trombones 2-3, and tuba. Cornets, trumpets, bass clarinet, bassoons, and divisi tubas announce the ending with a fanfare beginning in measure 218. A small *crescendo* added to the dotted quarter-note chords in measures 220-221 will elevate the ensemble for an exciting conclusion.

The Symphony in B♭ for Concert Band illustrates that the wind band is a viable, artistic performance medium. Hindemith pushed the limits of various instruments of the band, confidently giving important exposed lines to instruments rarely receiving such attention. Fewer doublings than usual result in purity of color.

It is easy to speculate why Hindemith gave but one major work to the band medium. During his career, getting orchestral performances of his works was considered far more prestigious than writing and conducting pieces for bands. Today, although his orchestral works such as *Mathis der Maler* and his numerous solos are performed extensively, his chamber works for winds are relatively obscure. (When was the last time you heard a live performance of his Septet for Wind Instruments?) The argument of the last four decades holds: if the wind profession is to have the standard body of repertoire we so crave then we, the conductors, must give composers reason to put their best efforts into pieces for wind and percussion combinations. Without a forum for their works, first-rank composers will write for other mediums. By giving excellent performances of the great original works for band we can help convince new composers of the value of writing for wind band. □

Frescobaldi's Toccata

An Interpretive Analysis by Barry E. Kopetz

Some years after the publication of Earl Slocum's band adaptation of *Toccata*, it was discovered that the original was not composed by Frescobaldi but by Gaspar Cassadó, who wrote the piece, copyrighted in 1925, for cello and piano in the style of Frescobaldi. During Girolamo Frescobaldi's life (1583-1643) the Baroque texture of chordal harmony gradually replaced the Renaissance's contrapuntal writing for multiple parts. Three principles guided the style of early Baroque music: sectional form, variation in melodic procedures, and a distinct polarity between the bass line and the upper voices. Composers created several types of instrumental works from these ideas, including pieces of a rhapsodic character that were similar to this one. Although this information changes program credits, *Toccata* is still a superb piece, and it gives bands a rare opportunity to play in the early Baroque style.

Dramatic contrasts dominate this music in Frescobaldi's style, including dissonance and the piece's multi-sectional form of alternating tempi between slow *grave* sections and faster lively passages. These contrasts and the piece's Baroque style affect how a conductor approaches *Toccata*.

The preparatory beat indicates the style of articulation and dynamic for the opening C minor triad. Strive for breadth of tone and good balance without accents. Brass players of the Baroque period utilized variety in articulation, and a softer approach is called for here. Indicating four pulses in the opening measure may help the ensemble gauge breath requirements for the second measure; the four beats should gradually decrease in size and not imply an accent at the beginning of measure 2. By not taking a breath before the second measure the melodic entrance is smoother, but if the ensemble breathes there, give a clear release before the downbeat of the second measure. I prefer using only timpani in the percussion section.

The challenge of the *Grave* is to maintain the musical tension at the tempo indicated. Use

---

Barry E. Kopetz is director of bands at the University of Utah in Salt Lake City where he conducts the Wind Symphony. Kopetz is active as a composer, guest conductor, and adjudicator.

elongated beat patterns that stretch the dramatic chord changes, and the brass chords should not overpower the woodwinds. With a tempo that is not rigid the section should be played *mp* so the first inversion C major triad in measure six is heard with the *legato* eighth notes of the upper woodwinds. It is difficult to achieve balance in measure 7 because the second flutes and second and third clarinets are the only instruments playing the descending sixteenth notes while the remainder of the ensemble increases in volume. Mark the parts to indicate less *crescendo* and insist that the alto saxophones and horns can hear the woodwinds.

The ornaments in measure 10 are difficult for students, starting with the grace notes, succeeding trill, and the resolution to the sixteenth note followed by a half note in measure 11. It is musically correct to place the grace notes on the beat, borrowing time from the following note. The upward grace notes to the G that prepares the trill are not as difficult as its conclusion. Subdivide the fourth beat and add a bit of *ritardando* to this material. *On Playing the Flute* by Johann Joachim Quantz offers a good description of the performance of Baroque ornaments.

The cadence to the E♭ major triad in measure 11 can be marred by a poor release; extend the triad slightly for musical satisfaction, but then emphasize the ensuing dissonance on the third beat. The C minor triad, supported by an octave D in the bassoons and alto and bass clarinets, is a delightful dissonance that resolves quickly,

making a return to the original tempo appropriate.

If the entrance of the melodic line by the unison flutes and first B♭ clarinet in measure 12 is a little loud at *mf*, adjust the dynamics accordingly. Pause slightly at the saxophone, first cornet, and timpani entrance on the down-beat of measure 14. Slocum scores the first inversion C major triad widely, discounting the root in the timpani, with the first cornet and second clarinet providing the fifth. The dissonant D♭ entrance against this C major triad creates wonderful tension that most conductors enjoy thoroughly.

This music also has many diminished fourths, tritones, and augmented triads, most often in the first inversion. The chord structures between measures 12 and 19 effectively build and release tension. The composer gradually intensifies the music into measure 16 through a series of upward half-steps in the bass line. At measure 16, conduct the music freely to sweep through the scalar passage of the upper woodwinds supported by the first inversion D♭ triad. Count three provides a glorious example of tension resolving a beat later to a B♮, producing the infamous tritone. Linger here to emphasize the musical tension created by these tones.

Add a *ritardando* to measure 17 as the tutti ascending line highlights the second inversion G

major triad. Stretch the octave C on count 3 in the upper woodwinds to bring out this climactic moment of the *Grave*.

Make a diminuendo immediately in measure 18, earlier than marked, with precise releases by second and third cornets and in measure 19 by the first cornet and piccolo. This cadence often is ruined by poor releases, which can be remedied by conducting the cadence precisely so the lower neighboring tones of count two change together and players know where to breathe and have enough air to play the low octave on count three. Maintain some baton motion in the fermata to keep the decaying G major triad alive; a sideways motion works well. As you release this triad, pause briefly before the *allegro giusto* section in E♭ major, giving a clear upbeat to set the new tempo for the horns, who should memorize measure 22 to play precisely together.

In measures 22 and 26 the flutes, clarinets, bassoons, and trombones should mark their parts *tenuto* so the eighth note resonates. Cornetists today usually articulate tah-tah-tah-tah or use the syllable tee for a sharper attack; Baroque trumpet players might have played tah-dah-tah-dah. Experiment with tonguings for a more interesting interpretation but maintain the tempo in measure 23 to keep the low brass and low woodwinds together on their descending sixteenth notes.

The second and fourth horns may sound weak at the end of this measure, but adding the first and third horns will augment them to balance the sound going into measure 24. Measures 26 and 27 are similar to 22-23, but the final concert E♭ should be stretched.

Emphasize the echo effect in measures 28-29 with woodwinds playing *mp* at the end of 28 for a richer contrast. For good balance in the syncopation, the trombones should play softly while the oboes play out.

Horns should be aware that their broken chords fit with the alto saxophone's arpeggio in measure 30. To keep the horns together, it may help for all horns to play the entire arpeggio.

The melodic fragments in the next three measures use the tone colors of different instruments; have players maintain the same *mf* dynamic. At the end of measure 33 emphasize a more legato style on the *anacrusis*. The horns, baritone, and cornets share the melodic line and should be balanced dynamically.

The woodwinds echo the legato brass motive in measures 34-35, emphasizing dominant to tonic harmony. Add intensity for the second statement in measures 36 and 37 from D to G minor.

The five measures at letter C are one musical thought growing to the fortissimo fermata in measure 42 incrementally. Drop the dynamic level at the end of each bar but keep the overall motion forward toward the octave G, letting the players take a full breath to play the final unison G with certainty. Players can manage this by staggering their breathing just before the G cadence, which resolves to C minor only in the next measure (at letter D).

The upbeat to this resolution can be difficult for the horns and trombone to play together. Conductors can use the release of the octave G as the preparatory beat for their entrance or they can release, pause briefly, and give a separate upbeat to re-establish the tempo. After the third trombone, string bass, and tuba start their pedal point *fp*, they should make a crescendo to the unison sixteenth notes in measure 46. Upper woodwinds, horns, and baritone tend to drag in this tutti passage.

Conductors should have an exact tempo and intention in mind to begin the Tranquillo section at letter E; control the slowing with clear, gentle beats to lead into it gracefully. The dynamics are difficult to balance in the tranquillo. The woodwinds should play their scales evenly, without the brass covering them; mark the low brass and woodwind parts *mf* or *mp*, using only small *crescendi* and *diminuendi* to support the scales. Rehearsing the brass and low woodwinds separately gives them more opportunity to learn the purpose of the reduced dynamics.

The low brass and reed players tend to drag the octave skips at the end of measures 51-52, but a slightly slower tempo and softer dynamics can accommodate them, as well as the first cornetist, whose part is not doubled. Playing the final sixteenth notes staccato in measure 54 seems out of character, as is too much *ritardando*.

Slow the *Pesante* at letter F to a more dignified tempo, not overdoing the accents in the cornets, trumpets, and baritone. Bring out the horn line in measures 56-59 with a slower tempo, allowing adequate time for the melodic eighth notes to sound. Give the last eighth note enough length to conclude the phrase before the abrupt tempo change by placing a *tenuto* mark over it.

A clear separation before the new tempo makes bridging the two sections relatively easy. Subdivide the fourth beat so that the first clarinets do not flounder on their first *anacrusis* to the *Allegro giusto*. Conductors should plan this bridge before the first rehearsal.

The *Allegro giusto* at letter G contains some of the most delightful music within the *Toccata*. A comfortable start and good balance between the first clarinet and its accompaniment are essential, so adjust dynamics and doublings judiciously. One player is enough on the alto saxophone part and helps intonation. The first clarinets lead here and should have a light, consistent articulation, though their sixteenths should not be too short; at their entrances the flute and E♭ clarinet should play their sixteenths evenly. The oboe balances the first clarinet in measure 61 as do clarinets two and three in measure 63.

Conductors should clarify the upper woodwind balance in measures 64-67. In measure 67 subdividing the last two beats makes the *molto rit.* transition to the *Grave* more graceful.

Conduct the *Grave* in four, stretching out each pulse. Make sure all players have the *con fantasia* clearly marked; adding an *accelerando* here and interpreting freely can bring freshness to the performance.

Start the *diminuendo* in measure 71 before it is indicated, but have clarinets play out their moving parts. Rushing at letter I can ruin the passage's quiet delicacy. Subdivide at the end of measure 72 to help the clarinet begin its thirty-second notes gracefully, using a small smooth beat and avoiding gestures that invite emphasis. If the oboist listens carefully to the first clarinets in measures 73 and 76, the thirty-second notes harmonize the conclusion of the ascending line. Having the alto saxophones play softly balances with the clarinets in measures 73-76; using one on a part helps intonation and balance in such places as the flute's high B♭ in measure 76. Rehearse second and third clarinets and oboe at measure 77 in their descending harmonic changes; this miniscule accompaniment to the flute line is wonderful music that should be heard clearly.

The last thirty-second notes of measure 78 are especially difficult to play together musically. The first clarinet and horn entrance at the *ritardando* before letter J can spoil this beautiful music, so subdivide the last beat into four units while slowing the tempo and give clear beats at

letter J. Continue conducting the ensuing measures in four; marking the subdivision in all of the parts before the rehearsal saves time.

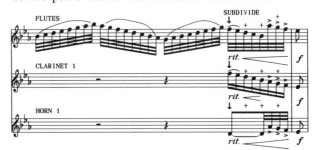

Once the tempo is established at J the music plays itself until measure 82, but bring out the woodwind arpeggios in measures 79 and 80, making sure the brasses and low woodwinds do not dominate. Subdivide in the *molto rit.* to make the return of the *Allegro giusto* dramatic. The fanfare concert E♭ in the first cornet and trumpet at measure 85 adds a bit of bravura to this restatement and should be heard both here and again at measure 89 where it joyously heralds the piece's conclusion.

Conductors have flexibility in the tempo of the last two measures; they may wish to subdivide all eighth notes, adding a *molto rit.* to this glorious ending. If a breath is needed, it can be taken between counts three and four so long as the phrasing remains clear. The final release should resonate, allowing the audience to savor the conclusion of Slocum's beautiful arrangement for wind band. □

Errata

Score: 7-8, slur should continue on the next page of the score in trumpets and horns; 10, E♭ clarinet add *dim.*; 14, clarinet 1 add *"divisi"*; 15, oboe, E♭ clarinet, horns 3-4 add *crescendo*; 17, flute 2, oboe 2 add *tenuto* to C on count 4; 17, clarinet 3, alto sax. add *cresc.* to counts 1 and 2; 24, horns 3-4 remove *staccato* from count 3; 29, oboe add an accent on count 1; 30, cornet 2-3, trumpet 2 add *mf* dynamic; 32, oboe add an accent on count 1; 32, tenor sax. second note should be B♭, not B♮; 33, horns, baritone add *mf* dynamic; 38-39, oboe 2 correct score to match the part; 39, cornet 3, trumpets add a slur to the two sixteenth notes on the second half of count 2; 46, alto clarinet add the tie from the previous page to the first quarter note; 51, bassoon add *a2* designation; 51, horn 4 add slur to the two sixteenth notes; 52, horns add *dim.* for 2 counts; 54, clarinet 1 add *"divisi"*; 55, trumpets indicate "first part only" beginning with the two sixteenth notes; 57, cornet 2, trombone 1 break the beam from the eighth note on count 3 to the eighth note on count 4; 59, trumpets add an accent to the first eighth note; 60, string bass indicate the entrance of the string bass on the first count; 64, oboe add *dim.* and *cresc.*; 73-75, oboe continue slur to include both thirty-second notes; 75, flutes extend slur to F on count 3, add slur to first two sixteenth notes on "and of three"; 80, horns 1-2 add *mf* on count 3; 85, trumpets add *a2* designation; 86, bassoon 2, baritone sax, bass, string bass, timpani add the tie from the previous page to the first quarter note on the last page of score; 86, timpani change dotted quarter note to a quarter note tied to an eighth note (see the part).

Piccolo: 39, modify the last two eighth notes to be sixteenth notes; 69, add an accent to the first sixteenth note on count 3; 80, add **∧** to the note C on count 3; 82, add *molto rit.*, add *cresc.*

Flute 1: 15, extend the *crescendo* to the end of the measure; 17, move *ff* dynamic to the note C on count 3; 35, clarify the eighth note beam; 43, add *a tempo*; 54, clarify the last sixteenth note as F; 59, remove the accent on count 4; 79-80, the thirty-second note slur should not include the note E♭ on count 2.

Flute 2: 17, extend the *crescendo* to the

end of the measure; 54, remove the slur from count 4; 59, remove the accent from count 4; 79-80, the thirty-second note slur should not include the note E♭ on count 2.

Oboe 1: 15, extend the *crescendo* to the end of the measure; 17, add *crescendo*; 29, add an accent to the dotted quarter note B♭; 54, add an accent to count 3; 59, remove the accent from count 4; 69, add *ff* dynamic, add *con fantasia.*

Oboe 2: 11, remove "soli"; 17, add *crescendo*, add *ff* dynamic on count 3; 32, add an accent to the first eighth note; 39, add *f* dynamic to the sixteenth notes at the end of the measure; 41, extend the *crescendo*; 54, add an accent on count 3; 59, remove the accent from count 4; 69, add *con fantasia.*

E♭ Clarinet: 9, clarify the last note as written F; 11, remove "soli"; 67, slur only the first two notes on count 3.

1st B♭ Clarinet: 10-11, add a *diminuendo* beginning on count 3; 54, add an accent to the first sixteenth note B♭ on count 3; 60, remove the *staccato* from the final sixteenth note A on count 3; 62, remove the *staccato* from the final sixteenth note E on count 3; 72, add *dim.* to count 4; 82, remove *staccato* from the final sixteenth note A on count 2.

2nd B♭ Clarinet: 54, add an accent to the first sixteenth note B♭ on count 3; 62, remove the *staccato* from the final sixteenth note E on count 3; 72, move the *rit.* to begin on count 3; 75, tie the half note C to the first eighth note; 82, remove *staccato* from the final sixteenth note A on count 2.

3rd B♭ Clarinet: 3, begin *crescendo* on count 1; 54, add an accent to the first sixteenth note B♭ on count 3; 67, add an accent to the G♯ on "and of three"; 69, add an accent to the first sixteenth note on count 3; 72, move the *rit.* to begin on count 3; 82, remove *staccato* from the final sixteenth note A on count 2.

E♭ Alto Clarinet: 3, begin *crescendo* on count 1; 41, remove the accent from the note A on count 1.

B♭ Bass Clarinet: 10, delay the *dim.* until count 3; 69, add *con fantasia.*

Bassoon 1: 10, delay the *dim.* until count 3; 45, clarify the accent on count 1; 52, slur the first two sixteenth notes on count 4; 69, add *con fantasia*; 82, place the *crescendo* beneath this measure rather than earlier.

Bassoon 2: 10, delay the *dim.* until count 3; 82, extend the *crescendo* to the end of the measure.

1st E♭ Alto Saxophone: 23, the horn cue notes are missing from the part; 27, add *f* dynamic to the horn cue; 69, add *con fantasia*; 81, remove the extraneous *crescendo.*

2nd E♭ Alto Saxophone: 7, add *crescendo* to the entire measure; 23, add *f* dynamic to the cue; 51, *p* dynamic is not present on the score; 64, add *p* dynamic at the conclusion of the *dim.*; 69, add *con fantasia*; 81-82, move the *crescendo* from m. 81 to m. 82; 83, last two sixteenth notes should be changed to read written "C to B."

B♭ Tenor Saxophone: 5, the *diminuendo* begins on count 1; 18-19, *dim.* continues to count 3 of m. 19; 54, connect the second eighth note stem to the beam; 69, add *con fantasia.*

E♭ Baritone Saxophone: 15, lengthen the stem on the F half note; 69, add *con fantasia*; 89, the first note should be a dotted half note.

1st B♭ Cornet: 5, add a slur to the quarter notes B to C♯; 19, add a *fermata* on count 3; 28-29, the order of these two measures is reversed; the oboe cue should be the measure before B; 46, add *mf* dynamic to the two sixteenth notes; 55, add accents to the final two sixteenth notes; 69, add accent to the first sixteenth note on count 3.

2nd B♭ Cornet: 7, remove the *tenuto* mark; 40, move *poco rall.* to begin on count 3; 69, add *con fantasia*; 81, add accents to the two sixteenth note Cs on "and of two."

3rd B♭ Cornet: 40, move *poco rall.* to begin on count 3; 69, add *con fantasia*; 83, remove extraneous *staccato* mark from the first note; 87, clarify the first note as written C.

1st B♭ Trumpet: 5, begin *dim.* at the beginning of the measure; 7-8, add a slur from the eighth note F to the B♭ in m. 8; 51, add *f* dynamic; 66, add *cresc.* designation on count 3; 69, add *con fantasia.*

2nd B♭ Trumpet: 5, begin *dim.* at the beginning of the measure; 17, remove *dim.* marking at the conclusion of the measure; 39, add *cresc.* at the beginning of the measure concluding on count 3; 67, add a slur to the quarter notes C to B, change *molto cresc.* to *molto rit.*; 69, add *con fantasia.*

1st F Horn: 7-8, continue the slur to the half note E♭; 18-19, begin the *dim.* on count 3 concluding at the *p* dynamic of m. 19; 69, add *con fantasia.*

2nd F Horn: 27, add *f* dynamic to the two sixteenth notes; 59, add a *tenuto* mark to the final eighth note A; 69, add *con fantasia*; 72, add *rit.* on count 3.

3rd F Horn: 16-17, delay the *crescendo* until count 1 of m. 17; 20, clarify the slur between the final two sixteenth notes; 55, add *mf* dynamic to the final two sixteenth notes; 69, add *con fantasia*; change the final eighth note from written G to F.

4th F Horn: 59, add a *tenuto* mark to the final eighth note A; 69, add *con fantasia*; 85, remove the extraneous ink marking.

1st Trombone: 10, begin *dim.* on count 3; 11, add *p* dynamic to the bassoon cue; 69, add *con fantasia*; 72, move the *rit.* to count 3.

2nd Trombone: 10, begin *dim.* on count 3; 56, add an accent on the first eighth note, A♭; 69, add *con fantasia*; 82, add *cresc.*

3rd Trombone: 16-17, move the *cresc.* to begin on count 1 of m. 17; 48, add *cresc.*; 69, add *con fantasia*; 81-82, move the *cresc.* from m. 81 to m. 82.

Baritone (bass clef): 43, remove the accent; 47, remove the accent; 69, add *con fantasia*; 89, change the final quarter note to F.

Baritone (treble clef): 41, begin the *cresc.* on count 3; 43, remove the accent; 47, remove the accent; 69, add *con fantasia*; 81-82, move the *cresc.* to m. 82; 83, remove the extraneous ink mark; 87-88, add a tie between the two whole notes; 89, change the final quarter note to written F.

Basses: 1, clarify the first note; 10-11, add *dim.* beginning on count 3; 17-18, move the *cresc.* to m. 18 beginning on count 1; 26, clarify the first note as a dotted half note; 40, *poco rall.* begins on count 3; 42, the part is missing the *fermata*; 45, add *cresc.*; 69, add *con fantasia*; 81-82, move the *cresc.* to m. 82; 88-89, add a tie to the dotted half note E♭.

String Bass: 40, *poco rall.* begins on count 3; 41, *cresc.* begins on count 3; 45, add *cresc.*; 51-52, extend the *cresc.* to the end of the measure; 69, add *con fantasia.*

Percussion: 1, clarify how to conclude the snare and bass drum rolls, decide on whether or not the timpani part continues its roll into m. 2; 41, add *cresc.* to timpani roll; 58, add *f* dynamic to the timpani part; 69, add *con fantasia*; 71, remove *dim.* from timpani part (unless you prefer to start the *dim.* at this point); 90, add accents to the quarter notes in the bass drum part.

January, 1992

Clifton Williams'
Dedicatory Overture

by Barry Kopetz

Clifton Williams wrote *Dedicatory Overture* for the opening of a new music building on the campus of Evansville College and created a piece that abounds with musical substance. It opens with a dignified fanfare that should be played with authority, firmly, and without undue accent until the B♭ triad on the third count of measure three. Too often the opening lacks authority because of mushy attacks from the trombones, baritones, and trumpets scored in octaves; write an accent in parentheses above the first note in each part. Ensembles should follow the clearly indicated phrasing for each fanfare. Brass players should stop the sound with breath rather than tongues

and listen to achieve a uniform release of dotted quarter notes followed by a breath mark. Encourage players to intensify the half note tied to the quarter note, and be sure the music does not lose its forward direction.

It helps to explain how this wonderful passage is built upon D minor followed by a D minor seventh chord and that accurate intonation is especially important. Emphasize the B♭ triad on count 3 of measure 3 with a slight *accelerando* to *più mosso*. The percussion are in command here, and a deeper snare or a field drum is preferable for this ceremonial music. In measure 5 the wind and percussion release should not be too abrupt. Rehearse this several times while percussionists listen and then attempt to match the releases of the wind players. Allow the natural resonance of the triad to decay before beginning the second fanfare in measure 6.

This fanfare is similar to the first, returning to *tempo primo*. The D minor seventh on count three of measure 8 is invariably unbalanced with the C played by the first horn and second alto saxophone and the upper octave C carried by the third clarinet and English horn. Too much alto saxophone spoils the balance. If there is no English horn, third clarinets should play out more. Students will learn the importance of balancing chord tones from working on this in rehearsals. At letter A the fanfare returns for the third time, but with increased harmonic tension that is released on the downbeat of measure 17. Listeners accustomed to the D minor seventh found in measure 13 may be puzzled by the B♭ major seventh of measure 15. The fifth of the chord is conspicuously absent, except in the first bassoon part; the composer probably wanted the first bassoon to play D a minor third lower than the written F because all other instruments are scored on B♭, D, or A.

The three octave A, prominent throughout measures 13 through 16, becomes the source of immense tension. Note its use in measures 13 and 14, first as the fifth of the D minor seventh, then as the seventh of the B♭ major seventh. In measure 15 it is pitted against the E♭ triad scored in the saxophones, low reeds, and brasses. The tension is increased by the *crescendo* leading the ensemble to the first inversion A major triad at measure 17, and the conductor should prepare the ensemble for this resolution from the first measure of music. This is the first musical peak, a moment of musical glory, emphasized by the first entrance of the crash cymbals but spoiled by the slightest *diminuendo*. Add an arrow to each part to remind students that even long tones should have forward motion. The downbeat of measure 19 provides the abrupt release, which the composer intensified by adding a *staccato* marking. Consider providing this pulse, and stopping at the bottom without rebound; the next three counts are silent, creating tension, and no further motion from the conductor is necessary until the next measure. A controlled, precise upbeat on count 4 of measure 19 is all the ensemble requires to play the first note of measure 20 with authority.

At letter B the tonal center suddenly changes, and the fanfare material of the opening measures returns, now centering on a G minor triad. Although there are no additional markings that indicate a more accented style of articulation, emphasizing the measures beginning at 20

produces satisfying results. The increased activity of supporting parallel triads in measure 20 adds to the tension. Phrase the melodic material at letter B the same as before; the first syncopated entrance should be clean. Note the well-balanced series of triads, A♭, B♭, and C minor scored in the saxophones, trumpets 2 and 3, horns, and trombones. Work for balance among the chord tones; rushing the sixteenth note G-D-G entrance in the bass part of measure 21 destroys the otherwise dramatic formation of the G tonal center. Playing the two sixteenths *staccato* assists ensemble clarity.

Beginning at letter B the music is extended and transposed to the new pitch level; the accompanying parts give intensity and vibrance; increase the size of the beat pattern and use crisper baton motions to indicate more pronounced attacks. The score shows no dynamic contrasts between letter B and measure 28 but slightly modifying the dynamic levels enhances the performance. Mark the low reed and low brass eighth notes *mf* in measure 24 and add a *diminuendo* to the dotted half note in the alto and tenor saxophones, trumpets 2 and 3, horns, and trombones. Maintain the *mf* dynamic, intensity, and clarity through measures 25 and 26. Cue the suspended cymbal, and begin a *crescendo* at measure 27 to bring out the bold, fanfare-like triplets. The music should culminate in the emphatic *fortissimo* on the first count of measure 28. During this dynamic increase, conduct in *marcato* style, with each note separated rather than short. Avoid the infamous brass tongue-cut-off in executing these resonant eighth and sixteenth notes in measures 25-27.

The snare drum at measure 28 should match, not overpower, the winds. This passage is a wonderful augmentation of the fanfare passages that dominate the music to this point; make the most of this modification in measures 28 through 30. In 28 and 30 approach the descending A, F♯, A minor third in the melody in a more lyrical fashion while those playing the descending bass line continue in an accented style for contrast.

There is a natural *diminuendo* at measure 31 on the whole note; let the sound decay in all parts with the moving line remaining *f*. This adds musical presence to the low reeds and brass. Point out that melodic material in measure 28 through 31 is based upon a D major seventh chord while the descending line increases tension and harmonic instability. Demonstrate the musical construction by rehearsing only the D major triad in measure 31, then add the moving line below. Decrease the size of the pulse in measure 31 if you choose to decrease the volume.

Barry Kopetz is director of bands at the University of Utah. A published composer and arranger, Kopetz is active as an adjudicator and guest conductor.

Give a strong downbeat at letter C to the low reeds and brass; it is important that the trumpets, trombones, and baritones enter at the proper dynamic on count 2. The addition of the D major triad over the B♭ pedal creates an augmented harmony full of musical tension. Clipping the last two eighth notes in measures 32 and 34 seems out of character for this passage; playing these notes at full value eases this introductory section to a more sensitive conclusion.

Listen for pitch problems stemming from improper breath support in measures 35 through the fermata in measure 39. Emphasize note length and fullness of tone as the long *diminuendo* over these bars comes to a graceful conclusion. The composer toys with the listener, vacillating between D major triads and B♭ augmented triads before coming to rest upon a C major triad, while the bass line returns to the pedal B♭. The final F♯ to B♭ in measure 34 leaves the listener wondering where the music is going.

The second section of music begins at letter D in the key of F major, and the third inversion C7 of measure 39 does not resolve according to standard rules of voice leading but moves to a fully scored F major triad. Williams allows the conductor to decide how to bridge the cadence in 39 to the new music about to begin. Allow the final chord in measure 39 to decay to *pianissimo* before releasing it; then pause briefly before providing a simple downbeat in the new tempo, *Andante, quasi hymn*. Tempos between ♩=69-76 work well here.

Few times in wind music does the composer allow the conductor so much flexibility in interpretation. The "alma mater" begins at letter D, and conductors should provide the necessary *tempo rubato* to bring this music to its full expressiveness. Pitch improves dramatically if students sing the lines one at a time.

The ensemble should think of the music from letter D to the end of measure 51 as a complete idea played in one breath, achieving this by staggering the breathing and elongating pulses three and four at the conclusion of each three-measure phrase. This will bridge such measures as 45 to 46, in which the moving quarter note bass line should lead to the downbeat of the following phrase. Add a *crescendo* and *diminuendo* to parts with the unresolved *appoggiatura* on count 1 (see measures 42, 48, and 51) to emphasize the resolutions highlighted by the timpani roll.

The first entrance of the bells in measure 52 adds a delightful quality to the full texture of the chorale. Because the score is marked *poco animando*, the mallet player should watch the conductor as the tempo increases rather than imagining the part in the previous tempo. Brass mallets played at *mp* are best for this part. Measures 52 through 57 may be grouped as one idea with staggered breathing, and try adding a *diminuendo* in measure 54 and a *crescendo* in measure 56 to obtain a fresh interpretation.

Hold the A minor triad on the downbeat of measure 57 before providing a gentle pulse resolving it to the second inversion C7 chord. Provide the ensemble with a breath by releasing the chord, pausing briefly, and providing a downbeat at measure 58, indicating a warm entrance at the pianissimo level. The F major triad on the first count of measure 58 should be played no louder than *pp*, but not at the expense of good tone. Rehearse your ensemble on this entrance by varying the dynamic level until you achieve this. The softer the ensemble plays this passage, the more dramatic the *crescendo* becomes at measure 60, which leads to the musical climax in measure 61. Cue the percussion section in measure 60 and mark parts appropriately in measure 62 to bring out the moving eighth-note line.

If the piece ended here, there would be some sense of musical satisfaction, but Williams extends his mood through four measures of fully scored woodwind choir, minus the piccolo, contrabass clarinet, and baritone saxophone. These measures should have dynamic contrast so the music does not stagnate. Often students lack enthusiasm for the dynamic change to *mf* in measure 66. Encourage the second oboe, second clarinets, and first alto saxophone to bring out their accented concert C on count 2 because it is the only chord tone changing and is often not clearly audible.

The addition of trumpets and horns in measure 68 should balance carefully with the woodwinds. The low brass and reeds D♭ major triad on count three should provide a marked change. Indicate the accent with a decisive pulse, and cue the bass drummer, who should let vibrations resonate freely. The melodic passage of measures 68 through 71 should not be entirely at the same dynamic level; add a *crescendo* beginning in measure 68, concluding on count 1 of the next measure with a small *diminuendo* on the two quarter notes at the end of measure 69. Control the *diminuendo* in measure 71 through a series of pulses gradually decreasing in size and intensity.

Measures 72 to 75 are simply enchanting. Based on the opening and fanfare, the music is decidedly simple: a melodic line played by first flute, first B♭ clarinet, and baritone all in three different octaves. First oboe and E♭ clarinet play a secondary line in one octave, and second B♭ clarinet and first horn an octave lower. The balances between these two lines are delicate. All other players sustain a D minor triad as the melodic lines weave towards a restful conclusion. The addition of the single bell tone in measure 72 adds color to these measures, and a small amount of *ritardando* in measure 75 concludes this transition with grace; conduct these measures *legato* connecting each note to the succeeding one.

The drum cadence at letter F provides an abrupt change. The rhythm of this material and the rhythm of the melody entering eight bars later in measure 84 is the same. Add rehearsal numbers to all parts at measures 84, 100, and 118 to save rehearsal time. Measure 84 begins with melodic material from the original fanfare scored in two octaves. Play this music with precision and in *marcato* style. One performer straining for notes and missing destroys this passage; it may help to reduce the number on each part. Mark the word precisely on all parts at measure 84, and make sure the percussionists are persistent in their entrances on the second half of count 2. This seemingly new melodic material has its roots in the opening fanfare: the composer reiterates the melodic line in canon up a fifth from its original pitch level. The descending whole note line in measure 92 should balance with the melodic line, and continue in the *marcato* style; if the secondary line lacks intensity and enthusiasm so will the primary melody above.

For consistent articulation play the second quarter note in measure 100 *staccato* throughout all parts. Although these eight measures are marked *f*, the nature of the melodic line demands a lighter style. Use a smaller beat pattern, stopping the motion of the baton sharply for accurate subdivision in the percussion. Drop the ensemble dynamic level to *mf* at measure 106, adding a *crescendo* to the six eighth notes in measure 107, which will lift the ensemble intensity at measure 108. The following measures are often uneven in piccolo, flutes, clarinets, alto saxophone, and, for two measures, timpani and snare drum. Consider adding a

tenuto mark above each quarter note to give the line breadth and a *diminuendo* to the accompanying quarter-eighth notes in measure 109. Descending to a dynamic of *mf* improves clarity among the three competing ideas. Note how the composer increased the complexity of the music by simply adding an additional part.

The music rises to new intensity in measure 118, seeming at first to be a literal repetition of the eight measures from 100 through 107. Aside from the snare drum becoming an integral part of the texture, and the bass line's pedal A, these measures seem the same as 100-107 until the subtle but effective change in measure 121. By altering the ascending eighth notes preceding measure 122, the composer raises the pitch a whole step, adding variety and additional intensity. Ask for a fraction more volume but don't sacrifice balance and clarity. Use a *crescendo* to lead the ascending melodic line in measure 125 to the musical peak at letter I. The passage at letter I is difficult to perform musically. For balance and momentum, try rehearsing second and third clarinets, alto and tenor saxophones, and baritones as a unit, balancing them so the second B♭ clarinet is as loud as the first alto saxophone. Then balance the second clarinet and the first alto saxophone against the same melodic material an octave lower in the tenor saxophone and the baritone horn. The elongated bass line should not delay the syncopation in measure 128 and cause a loss of tempo; even the slightest change of pace harms the musical continuity. Note the augmentations of the fanfare material in measures 126 through 143 throughout the upper woodwinds that guides the intensity of the music over the next 18 bars. Balance this against the countering bass line and unison horns. The music grows in intensity as it approaches the two-note *anacrusis* to measure 144. If the ensemble drags here, the conductor is to blame. These measures should float, not plod.

Conduct the *anacrusis* to letter J with a firm upbeat. In measures 144, 150, and 154 Williams restates the same material, each time up a full step from the previous presentation. Bring out

the bass drum part in measure 144 and in similar passages, and the cymbal crash on count 1 of measure 146 should ring freely. Measure 150 is a truncated version of the material at 144, and the volume and intensity level of the music should jump one notch. Note the change in articulation on the two eighth notes in measure 155. Gradually conduct in a *legato* style at measure 157, and consider adding *tenuto* marks to the quarter notes in measure 159. Remove the incorrect ties in the score in measures 160 and 161 in the oboes, English horn, clarinets 2 and 3, alto saxophones, and horn 2 to match the individual parts. Add a touch of *ritardando* two measures earlier than the indicated *molto rall.* in 160 to provide a more gradual transition into the *Adagio* at measure 162, which is nothing more than the opening fanfare played lyrically by the solo horn. Cut the number of flutes playing the octave C's down to one or two for good balance and pitch with the E♭ clarinet. Hold the notes in the higher octave for full value and balance with the melodic line of the first horn. Controlling the decreasing volume of the next four measures and the implied *ritardando* are the keys to interpreting this brief transition. In the absence of the E♭ clarinet, the A triad on count 3 of measure 165 is incomplete in the upper register. If you don't have an E♭ clarinet, write out the final two notes of that part for one first clarinet to play. The addition of the bells playing the C of this triad should not be too pronounced and its decaying resonance may serve as a guide for the release.

The *Allegretto* presents the melody of the chorale theme stated at letter D in a rapid series of eighth notes answered by a second series of

Fennell on J. Clifton Williams

Clifton Williams was a proud and true product of the American schools band movement. From early boyhood in the town of Traskwood, Arkansas where he was born in 1923 he played in the band. By high school he qualified for membership in the Little Rock High School band as an accomplished horn player. When L. Bruce Jones, the Little Rock director moved on to Louisiana State University, Williams followed. By that time the creative urge was upon him and composition had moved into his music world; at L.S.U. he became a pupil of Helen Gunderson.

From Louisiana he went to the Eastman School of Music for a master's degree and studied with Bernard Rogers and Howard Hanson. Then his academic appointment to the theory/composition faculty of the University of Texas at Austin School of Music became the scene of further development. While he was at Rochester's Eastman School he participated in the school's unique Annual Symposium of New Orchestrated Music. Seeing the example and feeling the need for a similar exposure and gathering of kindred souls, he organized the Southwestern Composers Symposium at Austin. He was its tireless driving force for many years as he and his colleagues sought to make their area aware of their music for orchestra. As a teacher at Austin he numbered among his outstanding students W. Francis McBeth and James Barnes Chance.

In his work as a teacher, composer, and organizer for creativity — in these customary pursuits for recognition as a composer Clifton Williams toiled for years in the vineyards of the orchestra with scant harvest, but when he put *Fanfare and Allegro* together for band in the early 1950s he was off and running, fast and far.

His new piece for band set a style that he would follow with total reward beginning with it having won the first ABA/Ostwald Prize in 1956 and publication that same year. *Symphonic Suite* (it won ABA/Ostwald No. 2), *Pastorale, Festival, Variation Overture,* and *Symphonic Dances* Nos. 2 and 3 list a few of the important scores he produced.

Williams joined the faculty of the School of Music at the University of Miami in 1966 as composer in residence, a position he held until his death in 1976. As that true product of the American school band movement, his music, the bountiful harvest, continues to serve.

— notes by Frederick Fennell

eighths outlining familiar harmonies. There are two complementary lines played over a C pedal point in the low reeds, tuba, string bass, and timpani. Each measure of 7/4 equates to three measures of the chorale theme and all lines should be played *legato*. The addition of new parts at measure 170 adds too much volume at once if it is not controlled, and the ensemble should continue the flowing lines of the last four measures. Do not simply beat time in a 7/4 pattern or in a 4 followed by a 3 pattern; this music is *molto legato* and should be shaped freely.

Give a small cue to the suspended cymbal and snare drum on the fifth count of measure 171, and imply the rapid *crescendo* by increasing the size of the beat pattern. The section from measure 166 up to the *crescendo* leading to measure 172 is in the original key of the chorale, F major. This *crescendo* moves the ensemble into A♭ major, while the C pedal point continues. The first four phrases of the chorale occur in the new key as the texture thickens with the addition of trombones and horns. The bass drum adds to the intensity towards the resolution at the *Maestoso*, and the conductor should keep the ensemble from overplaying before the proper musical moment.

The effect created on the downbeat of the *Maestoso* is sometimes ruined by those instruments carrying the pedal point. Players get bored with their parts from measure 166 through 175 and their sound and attention to proper breathing suffer unless those holding the pedal mentally sing the melody to give their parts a different sense of direction. Players should take in enough air to avoid breathing before playing the D♭ on the downbeat of the *Maestoso*. If those holding the pedal gasp for air just before this note sounds, it lacks impact. This entrance should provide the same sense as the opening fanfare.

In the *Maestoso* bring out the augmented opening fanfare material and draw attention to the shortened version the composer has used in wind and percussion parts. Avoid a *diminuendo*, either *subito* or gradual in measures 179 and 180 by sustaining the D♭ triad and adding a slight increase in volume approaching measure 181. It should be noted that throughout the *Maestoso* there are numerous inconsistent articulation markings in the score. Beginning in measure 176 the baritone has a number of *tenuto* markings not found in the first trombone and trumpet parts. This becomes consistent in measure 186.

Treat each fanfare the same way as the one marked at letter N, with each note receiving full value and not being overly accented.

The final measures of *Dedicatory Overture* contain a myriad of entrances. Work on these measures at the beginning of rehearsal before other portions. In measure 191 Williams scores an incessant concert F in the upper woodwinds emphasized through the use of a trill, and in the texture beneath, the remaining instruments are equally insistent upon their first inversion C♭ triad. Highlight this harmonic tension by adding a *crescendo* into the first inversion D♭ triad of measure 193. The release on count three must be exact, and it would help the percussion to have parts marked *subito mf* on the third count of measure 193. Do not conduct the final count of the *fermata*, but indicate the increase in volume by widening the space between baton and left hand. Giving an accented downbeat on the first count of measure 194 provides a release to the percussion while giving the proper tempo to the winds entering on the second count. In measure 194, keep the musicians from overblowing at the juncture of the first inversion D♭ triad to the second inversion C♭ major seventh because these chords sound odd when certain tones receive more weight than others. Rehearse them without the percussion so the musicians are sensitive to balance and blend.

Mark the percussion parts *subito mf* in measure 195 and consider dropping the dynamic further to prepare the percussion section's final *crescendo*. The space between the release and the C♭ major seventh and the entrance of the F triad, a tritone, give this entrance a sense of finality. This is partially because of the tension of the previous five measures, which stretch out in a manner that leaves the audience anxious for a conclusion. This final chord should be worth the wait and a sideways baton stroke seems out of place. Simply lift the baton, give a sharp downbeat, and the percussion are sure to follow.

Dedicatory Overture is a popular piece with young wind and percussion students lucky enough to experience the piece. The lovely chorale provides many opportunities for lyrical phrasing and interpretation. If the chorale section is used as a warm-up, students soon achieve accurate tuning and proper breathing. Continued score study and performances of this marvelous work will provide conductor, students, and audiences with great musical pleasure. □

Charles Ives's
Variations on America

by Barry E. Kopetz

A business man who made a fortune selling insurance, Charles Ives (1874-1954) composed music at night, when all the day's work was finished. He was an innovator who foreshadowed many compositional techniques others later used. His self-imposed isolation from the mainstream of composition allowed him the luxury of not having to please an audience. In short, Ives wrote for himself.

Ives composed the *Variations on America* when he lived in Danbury, Connecticut, and it has become the most well known of his works of this period. Originally written for organ in 1891-1892, the variations are humorous in character and full of surprises. Two of the interludes are polytonal, and the composer later made the following observation, which appears in John Kirkpatrick's book *Charles E. Ives Memos.*

> In the manuscript at the bottom of p. 8, there are two rhythms made by off-accents:

> In some of these passages, the lower pedal rhythm keeping the regular ¾ is omitted — this is often done in jazz today. Also [there are] short interludes between variations (right hand starting Hymn in F, left hand Hymn in G♭, as a kind of canon together). These lasted only five or six measures, and Father would not let me play them in the Brewster concert, as they made the boys laugh out loud.

In his teenage years Ives was concerned about differences in his music, feeling that he was expected to conform in musical style. The following passage is from the book, *Charles Ives and His America* by Frank R. Rossiter:

> The young composer feared that his deep interest in serious music might alienate him from the common people of Danbury and, in particular, from his male peers. His ingenious response to the threat was *Variations on America*, in which he not only used musical unorthodoxy to assert his independence from the genteel musical life of the ladies of Danbury, but also, by the very act of doing so, asserted his oneness with the democratic and masculine vernacular life of the town. In his experimentation, he was just "cutting up," just "being one of the boys." At the same time he was being seriously patriotic.

Barry E. Kopetz is an associate professor of music at the University of Minnesota and conducts the Chamber Winds, the Symphonic Band, and the Marching Band. He also teaches wind literature, conducting, and band arranging.

The wind version, transcribed from William Schuman's orchestral version by William E. Rhoads and published by Theodore Presser remains true to the original in most respects. This is the music of young Charles Ives at his best: rebellious, witty, and willing to throw in a few musical jokes just to see who is listening.

Allegro maestoso

Begin with a firm downbeat in the first measure and a resonant eighth note. The dotted-quarter note may be separated from the eighth note at the end of the measure or given full value; either interpretation is satisfactory, but the ensemble should be consistent in approach. I prefer a slight separation between the dotted-quarter and the eighth note.

After the dotted-eighth sixteenth rhythm in measure 2, which should be exact, there is another interpretive decision on count two as to how long the tied quarter note should resonate. The organ score has a quarter note (no tie), but an organ performance of the work gives an entirely different impression. Allow the note to resonate, releasing it on count three. Consider modifying the bar, adding an eighth note on count three so the release occurs slightly later than indicated. Above all, listen to a performance of the work or purchase a recording of the original version for organ; your opinion will never be the same. Treat measures 3 and 4 in similar fashion to measures 1 and 2.

After releasing on count three in measure 4, immediately change to *legato* style in measure 5. Ensembles often slow down at this point, which destroys the dynamic build-up between measures 5 to 8. It is possible to vary these measures using the organ score as a guide. The music reveals no bass pulse on count one in measures 5, 6, and 7 (see the alto clarinet, baritone saxophone, and string bass parts). Experiment by removing the notes on count one, leaving only the eighth note

Measures 5 to 8

on count three in these parts. This gives the upper woodwinds different weight with only arpeggios beneath their melodic statement, which closely matches the organ version. The melodic voices should not be covered by the ascending arpeggios. Slowly increase beat size so

that the crescendo leading to measure 8 is gradual and effective.

Add a light accent on count two in measure 8 so the entrance of horns 2-4 and trombones 1-2 is heard. (This is also present in the organ version.) These instruments form a second inversion C7 chord voiced exactly as in the original version, and its presence briefly adds a change of color to the full ensemble.

Measure 9 should be a literal restatement of the first two measures. The descending eighth notes in the upper woodwinds are a series of wonderful triads and seventh chords and should sound like balanced chords. If desired alter measures 10 and 11 to match the organ version. The dynamic of *fff* can easily be overemphasized in the band version; the organ part has only *mf*, a considerable difference. If you decide on the softer approach, mark the parts clearly; one mismarked part can ruin an otherwise good performance.

One of the most delightful moments in the opening statement occurs in measure 13. The horns play a descending figure with bells up on concert A♮ and clash dramatically with the G♯ in trombone 1. Encourage the first trombone to play out because student musicians fear that the G♯ is a wrong note: the louder the better here. This is a classic example of the type of humor Ives created with dissonance; he wanted his peers to snicker.

For contrast conduct the *poco ritard* of measures 15-16 more slowly than indicated; the vivid change of orchestration to the clarinet choir and the soft *piano* dynamic also provide contrast. If an alto clarinet is not available, use a tenor saxophone on the cues because the final note is not doubled.

At letter C return to the original tempo with a brilliant tone quality. Conduct to add length to the quarter notes in measure 17, and consider removing the staccato marks in the low brass so players know to imitate organ pedals. The moving eighth-note bass line should be prominent and precise. At the conclusion of this line allow the quarter note on count two in measure 22 to resonate; release the quarter note in this measure and prepare the ensemble for the somber D minor cadence in measures 23 and 24 with a slow, smooth preparatory pulse on count three. In measure 23 the first clarinet part should be loud enough for the sixteenth notes on count two to balance with the oboes, flutes, and bassoons.

The familiar opening statement reappears; again use a precise upbeat to prepare for the first note and conduct the passage in the same robust manner as before. The first entrance of the xylophone at letter E should set the style for the next three measures with crisp separation and a steady *crescendo*. In measures 29 - 32 the timpani and string bass should perform the single G on count two to add articulation to the bass clarinet color, something that cannot be imitated by a wind instrument. This note is played in the pedals of the organ version; sustain it because it is the only note on count two that is not marked staccato.

Ives marks measure 31 "slower" in the original version rather than *poco ritard*; the conductor has more freedom than the concert band arrangement suggests. In releasing the quarter note at the conclusion of count one, use the opposite hand to build the *crescendo* indicated in the score. Be sure not to release the half note too soon. A close look at the C7 chord shows that the fifth of the chord is present on count one, but after the release the third inversion of the chord remains, minus the fifth. Pointing this out helps the release and balance of these chords. In measure 29 the xylophone part is written for two players; as in measure 32, try using one performer rolling the top note and a second performer on the bottom note to produce a smoother roll than is possible with one player. Both players should use the same mallets for this option.

The presentation of *America* at letter F, again in F major, is the purest version of the theme in the work and the greatest diversion from the original score. In the organ score Ives wrote the four-part chorale with *forte* dynamics without ornamentation; it is a traditional, patriotic statement. Rehearse the chorale tune first, adding woodwinds when they are aware of subtle tempo variations. The woodwind parts emphasize the rhythm of the melody; align them accurately with the chorale.

In this section use the baton to conduct the short, precise woodwind parts and the opposite hand for the chorale. Rehearsing the parts separately helps, especially if you change the dynamics in each phrase. Because the *pizzicato* string bass is not cued in any other part, it helps to copy the part (in the proper octave) for solo tuba. While tuba is not the best substitute, the bass line may not be heard if the string bass is absent. Note that the second trombone is slurred one octave higher than the string bass.

The flams in the snare drum part at 33 should be soft and precise. The bell part in measure 38 contrasts with a *forte*; the notation of the bell part in measure 46 suggests a roll on the first count, building to a single attack on count two. As with the earlier xylophone part, I prefer having one bell player for each note, for a more sustained roll. This is a delicate spot, even at the *mf* level; play with confidence because this is the first presentation of the tune on which Ives bases the entire piece.

Variation I

Instead of the indicated tempo of ♩ = ca. 60 conductors may wish to mark parts Moderato, the original tempo. If this variation is performed too slowly the sixteenth notes do not come alive. Often the passage seems too soft, although it is appropriately marked *forte*. It should be played out rather than as an accompaniment; Ives wanted this part to be prominent. To maintain the proper dynamic ask wind players to stagger their breathing so the line does not lose momentum. Conduct with full, long beats throughout the section.

Those playing the constant sixteenths at measure 52 are often short of air after the preceding passage; the *crescendo* on count two adds to the problem. Encourage musicians to plan their last breath before measure 52 to complete the passage at the correct dynamic.

Measures 52 and 53

Rehearse this measure alone, removing the tie from the trill on count two to the first thirty-second note on count three. Practicing the passage as an ensemble and articulating the first thirty-second note makes it clear that the trill and the thirty-second notes are not played the same way. Once this is established, return the tie to the music. The other danger is rushing count three rather than starting on the upbeat. Rehearsing this bar at a slower tempo is helpful.

The next section is frantic with thirty-second notes in the piccolos, flutes, and E♭ clarinet. Keep a steady tempo, perhaps limiting the number of flutists for the sake of clarity. The skip between the first note and the second at the beginning of each beat will be out of tempo unless rehearsed sufficiently. The slurred thirty-second notes in measure 52 should be precise so those entering in the next measure play lightly and in tempo. For this reason I avoid the natural tendency to ritard to the end of measure 52. Indicate a light accent at the beginning of each thirty-second note unit in measure 53 to maintain tempo.

Measures 53 and 54

Cue the oboes, clarinets, bassoons, and xylophone in measure 54; maintain tempo and a *forte* dynamic at this entrance and the one two measures later. I added the word "subito" to woodwind parts at measure 57 to emphasize dynamic contrasts, which are not part of the original but are effective additions to the band version.

In measure 58 of the organ version, Ives writes a *ritard* at the beginning of the measure and adds a *fermata* to the quarter note on count three. This provides a welcome change from the incessant sound of the upper woodwind line. In the full score the eighth note in measure 58 of the woodwind parts is not aligned properly with the sixteenths in the cornets and the xylophone.

In the original version Ives repeats the section between measures 53 and 60; measure 60 is modified using a first ending. It is not practical to make such an addition to the wind version without the conductor scoring a first ending and adding it to each part. However, the wind version has a noticeable change in measure 60. At the end of the descending chromatic scale there is a staccato eighth note and a rim shot in the snare drum part. The organ version has a quarter note on the final count of measure 60, and it is logical to allow a full count before going on. This is another instance in which several interpretations are possible, although the rim shot seems out of place if you select a long final note.

Variation II

Variation II contrasts starkly with the first variation. The tempo marking is approximate and may be played in a slower, more somber way. Phrasing in *tempo rubato* is acceptable here; study the chromatic movement carefully to produce the balance you want. The first oboe and first horn parts are solos that should dominate, while balanced, internal voices play *pianissimo*.

The arranger's choice of *espressivo legato* is perfect for the music at this point, but I prefer a slower tempo to highlight Ives's interesting chromatic wanderings in the clarinets and bassoons. The muted trumpets on descending diminished triads in measure 66 provide a color change and adding *diminuendo* and *ritardando* here is appropriate. Trumpet 1 with the melody should never be covered completely. Balance with tension and release produce subtle dynamic contrasts. Consider changing the dynamic level of the unison bassoons at measure 70 from *mf* to *f* to continue the dynamic of the preceding trombone line.

The final two measures of this variation should be *molto ritardando*. The descending first trombone line adds musical interest, particularly the final sixteenth and eighth notes. The humor of the cadence becomes more obvious by gently emphasizing the descending third trombone on the downbeat of measure 74. Ask for a little more from the oboist on count two and from the first trombone playing the B♮ on the second quarter of count two. I subdivide this entire measure to indicate these changes.

Measures 73 and 74

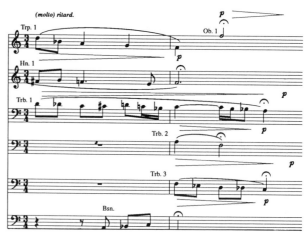

Interlude

At measure 75 the chorale is in the upper woodwinds in F major over pedals alternating between D♭ and C, while the second entrance of the chorale one measure later is in the key of D♭ major; the resulting clashes are wonderful. Conduct these measures ponderously, with long, full sounds. While the upper woodwinds are slurred, emphasize the second entrance in the horns and low brass, which is marked "Sw. pp" in the organ score. There are several ways to balance this passage; keeping the three competing forces in check is best. The organ score indicates ad lib from measures 75 to 83, so vary the tempo to suit your ideas. In this brief passage a slow tempo gives extra tension, making the next variation that much more enjoyable. One way to play the final chord of this interlude is with a *fermata* on it, keeping hands in motion for a sostenuto effect. Conduct the final release to indicate the tempo that follows.

Variation III

Delightful in every respect, the third variation is reminiscent of an amusement park. Conduct the melodic line in the oboes with long quarter notes. Because the first trombones are playing eighth notes with the oboes' quarters, be sure that the difference in note values is maintained. Adding *tenuto* marks to the oboe parts helps this inherent problem. The organ score has longer notes in the melodic parts than in the accompaniment; I group the staccato trombone parts with the bassoon line in measures 84 through 94. The second sixteenth note on count two of the bassoon part does not have a staccato marking, and both notes should have full value. I have the suspended cymbal struck with a plastic tipped drum stick for clarity and not dampened. The percussion section should play lightly.

A common problem in beginning this variation is erratic tempos; rehearse a controlled release in measure 83 so the ensemble begins the third variation together.

Count two of measure 94 brings many parts together on an A diminished chord, resolving to a B♭ minor triad. Because this clever bit of harmony goes by quickly, it sometimes lacks the precision of the music preceding it. Rehearse this passage to highlight the *poco rit.* that follows. Carefully place the final eighth note in measure 94, and subdivide the three eighth notes of measure 95 to control the chord progression.

Measures 94 and 95   *poco rit.*

Increase the size of your beat on these eighth notes, concluding with a brilliant *forte* on count two on the first inversion D♭ triad. Indicate with the baton rebound the tempo for the solo flutist's sixteenth notes at the end of the measure. This measure can be disastrous if musicians do not understand the conductor's intentions. Cue clarinet and percussion sections as you release the D♭ triad in measure 95; low reeds, euphonium, and string bass are often timid about playing measure 97 at the proper volume.

At the end of measure 97 the anacrusis is rarely as prominent as it should be. Encourage clarinetists to play out and project the exercise-like figures over the next 12 bars. Except for proper note lengths, the melodic parts require little attention here. It is almost impossible to maintain tempo in this passage if the gyrating first clarinet and the divided alto saxophones do not master their parts and perform the passage smoothly and gracefully.

Approach the anacrusis at the end of measure 103 as before, requesting *ff* from those instruments about to play this passage. Seek precision in measures 104 through 107; the sixteenth notes should be played as if by one hand on a keyboard. The addition of the bells at 104 stands out if the percussionist uses brass mallets. Add a *tenuto* mark to the score and parts to be sure the dotted eighth note on count two of measure 107 receives full length before the ensemble members breathe. If you conclude measures 108-109 *molto ritardando* to emphasize the end of this busy passage, add a *crescendo* at the beginning of measure 109. A brief delay after holding the *fermata* gives the interpretation more interest and prepares for the last three bars of

this variation. After the release remain motionless for a split-second, then conduct the rebound in the proper tempo to cue the first cornet. Basses and horns should play notes accurately and with full length; these eighth notes are not marked staccato. Be sure to conduct the dramatic change of dynamics occurring in the horns at measure 111. Copying the piccolo line in the trumpet and horn parts in measures 112 and 113 overcomes precision problems; conduct these measures with progressively smaller pulses from the wrist to indicate proper articulation of this delicate ending.

Variation IV

In the organ score Ives adds "Polonaise" to Variation IV, referring to a Polish dance with a repeated rhythmic pattern in a stately tempo. The band score tempo marking of ♩ = 126-132 seems fast compared to the original marking; a slower, deliberate approach to the variation is more appropriate.

During the brief pause beginning this variation, give a deliberate preparatory beat in the new tempo. The low brass and reed entrance should be exact because the third cornet, horns, and trombones depend on it to play the repeated rhythm of the polonaise. The castanets and tambourine should be prominent without being loud. Students always laugh at the first rehearsal of this variation, but this is Ives, the humorist, at his best.

The bass player is often so excited to play a solo in bar 116 that he does not balance with the same line two octaves above in the first cornet part; encourage boldness with balance. Start the variation in measure 114 using short, crisp baton motions for the staccato accompaniment. Change to a *legato* beat pattern when the cornet and bass enter, but the accompaniment should continue with precise articulation.

In the measures following 119 the castanets should play *crescendos* during each entrance; the starting dynamic for each tambourine roll is *mf*. At measure 126 the slurred accompaniment parts often slow the tempo slightly; conduct in *legato* style at the exact tempo and ask all to listen to the descending melodic line in the first cornet and bass. A cue to the snare drum in measure 127 assures that the following sixteenths will be played with the brass. In measure 129 the third cornet, horns, and first trombone slur the first two eighth notes together; I place a staccato mark over the second eighth note to separate it slightly from the dotted eighth note on count two. The rest of the measure should also be played staccato. Stop the baton on count two to show the desired space, then increase the pulse size on count three to conduct the *crescendo*.

At letter M the woodwinds join the texture;

the grace note/eighth note addition should be heard. Rehearse the piccolo, flutes, Eb clarinet, and the second cornet as a group so that each hears these pitches in the ensemble. In measures 136-137, the third trombone, euphonium, and bass parts are a continuation of the idea started on count two. Bass clarinet, bassoons, and baritone saxophone in measure 137 continue the idea.

The conclusion of this variation depends on the beginning tempo. If taken at ♩=ca. 126-132, a small ritard is satisfactory; if a slower, Polonaise tempo was chosen, *molto ritardando* is effective with a longer final eighth note. In the organ version Ives indicated a full quarter note followed by two quarter rests.

Interlude

The four-bar interlude after Variation IV is the phrase, "from every mountainside, let freedom ring." Conduct *legato* , and players should not breathe after the second bar of the phrase. The *crescendo* should not be too strong and a peak of *mp* is more graceful than the *mf* indicated.

The arranger's dynamic level of *p* at measure 142 is subject to interpretation because in the organ score Ives indicates the Swell at *ppp* and the Great and Pedal at *ff*. The second cornet part in measure 143 should be changed from written Ab to Bb to produce the harmony the composer intended.

Measures 142 and 145

Variation V

Select a tempo for this variation based on Ives' instructions for the organist: "Allegro - as fast as the pedals can go." Imagine the young composer's feet romping over the organ pedals and the audience laughing during the performance. Many wind performances of this variation are too fast; if the solo first cornet part at 146 is too brisk, measures 152 to 159 can sound out of control.

To prepare the ensemble for this variation conduct an upbeat on count three in the new tempo, making the downbeat the release for the previous chord in 145; or conduct the release and pause briefly before beginning the variation. The flute trio is a welcome contrast to the somber mood of the Interlude; give each quarter note full length because flutists may separate the notes because the cornet line is staccato.

Conduct long beats to obtain the desired note length, but encourage the cornetist to play lightly and delicately. The cornet part drives the music forward, so the flutes should not slow the tempo even slightly. Conduct with short, crisp motions to bring the passage back in tempo should this occur. Find two cornetists with similar tone quality for the overlapping beginning at 150.

At letter P parts should be marked Allegretto; Ives clearly intended this passage to be slower than "as fast as the pedals can go," but too often it sounds like a continuation of the previous music in the same tempo. Slowing even a fraction allows the sixteenth-note chirps in the upper woodwinds to come through. Give a strong cue to the saxophones and the Bb clarinets at the end of measure 159 so the anacrusis to letter P at the *forte* level provides the correct dramatic change. A small *ritardando* in this measure gives more control to the next bar if you take the section Allegretto.

Indicate strong accents to the woodwinds in measures 160-164. I prefer a space between the dotted eighth-sixteenth note in measure 165 accompanied by a staccato sixteenth note before broadening the pulse on counts 2 and 3.

Letter Q is scored for full ensemble at *fortissimo*. The danger here is overbalance in the low brass/low reed parts because they are heavily doubled. This is the way Ives wrote the original pedal part, so it may be just what he wanted. The cornet and horn parts have a breath mark at the end of measures 167, 171, and 173, but not at the end of measure 169. If you choose this phrasing, add the breath marks to the score. Measures that have several successive two-note groups of sixteenths should be planned in advance, because the second note of each group is often clipped. Perhaps add a staccato marking to these notes; if a longer note is played, establish its length early in rehearsals and play it consistently. Consider bringing the baton to a complete stop on count three of measure 177 to emphasize the abrupt conclusion of this punctuated passage. Pause briefly here before giving the downbeat in the new tempo to start measure 178 exactly and to allow musicians to catch their breath before returning to the introductory material.

Letter R begins with the idea of the opening measures, although it is not a literal restatement. The third and fourth horns and the trombones should play their repeated sixteenths boldly. Their incessant, repeated pitches, coupled with the snare drum part, should be exact because they set the tempo. Brasses should double-tongue the passage for clarity. Gradually increase beat size in measures 179 and 181, again stopping the baton on count three to add emphasis. Give special attention to the bass drummer on count three in measure 181; his is a lonely addition that makes an important difference.

Ives now writes some of his most daring music. The low brass/reed performers will have no problem playing their simple melody, but the woodwinds who play sixteenths grouped in threes have a challenge. The accents seem logical because in the organ version Ives also beams the sixteenths in groups of three. The ensemble should relax and swing with the rhythm. In measures 183 and 185, emphasize the two sixteenths that occur on the and of two to prepare for the final two sixteenths. The 1st notes in measures 183 and 185 often smear together if the tempo is unstable. Rehearse this sixteenth note passage until it is clean and precise. Measures 182 to 185 are marked "ad lib." in the original, so take some liberties with the tempo. "Ad lib" is certainly easier for one musician at the keyboard, but a free approach here produces fresh results.

Measures 186 to 189 must have been Ive's favorites. The thrilling bass line brings the piece to an exciting conclusion. If the low brass cannot maintain the tempo, try a slower tempo of ♩=89-92 for better control of the bass line. Upper woodwind players will misplace grace notes if the bass line changes tempo. The eighth notes sound marvelous when stretched to their full length, but they should be no longer than

unadorned eighth notes scored in the cornets, saxes, and horns.

Consider adding a *crescendo* in measure 190 as the brasses and lower woodwinds engage in a powerful exchange. I use two players on suspended cymbal here, one using a drum stick on the off-beats and the second using yarn mallets to play the suspended cymbal roll in the next measure. The decay during the *tremolo* in measure 191 should be quick, almost *fp*, and then swell rapidly to *ff* in measure 192. During rehearsal, stop and hold the G minor triad on the first count of measure 192. This chord is brilliant and resonant, and it helps for the ensemble to stop and listen to it and the next two chords. Once they hear each chord tone, they will play the three chords vibrantly. This is a magnificent moment; do not rush through it.

For precision, subdivide the triplet in measure 193, giving equal weight to each note. The two chords with *fermatas* do not have accompanying accents; conduct them in a broad style that describes weight of sound rather than point of attack. Space between the *fermatas* is a matter of preference; I indicate space only before the final chord in measure 194. The ensemble should drop to a true *piano* before beginning the *crescendo* that concludes the work.

Charles Ives wrote this marvelous lighthearted organ work for himself. It is full of humor, pokes fun at a number of musical stereotypes, exasperates those who dislike discordant sounds, and yet, in Ives' own way, is intensely patriotic.

Errata

Score

11 String Bass: add "arco" to the score.

15 Bassoon: add *p* dynamic to Bass Clarinet cue.

15 Tenor Sax: add *p* dynamic to the Alto Clarinet cue.

17 Baritone Sax: add *ff* dynamic.

17 String Bass: add "pizz." to the score.

18 Trombones, Euphonium: add a breath mark at the end of the measure.

29 Alto Sax 1: add crescendo to Alto Clarinet cue.

37 Tenor Sax: add a natural sign to the final eighth note A on count 3.

40 Clarinet 2: add a natural sign to the G on count 3.

43 Flute: add a natural sign to eighth note F on second half of count 3.

44 Bass Clarinet: the grace note on count 3 should be A♯ and the eighth note should be B♮.

45 Clarinet 3: add a natural sign to eighth note D on count 2; add natural sign to eighth note C on count 3.

47 English Horn: add natural sign to D sixteenth on count 3.

47 String Bass: add "arco" to the score.

54 Bass Clarinet: add *f* dynamic to the bassoon cue.

55 Piccolo, Flute: add a natural sign to the A on the seventh thirty-second note on the third count; E♭ clarinet add a sharp to the F on the seventh thirty-second note on the third count.

74 Bass Clarinet: add a diminuendo concluding with a piano dynamic level.

84-94 Euphonium: add articulation marks to bassoon cue; also add *mf* to measure 84.

91 Baritone Sax: change the final eighth rest to an eighth note F.

95 Baritone Sax: add a crescendo concluding with a dynamic of forte.

96 Bass Drum: add *p* dynamic.

99 English Horn, E♭ Clarinet, Clarinets 2-3, Cornet 1: add breath mark after quarter note on count 2.

102 Euphonium, String Bass: add accents to the two thirty-second note figures.

106 Oboe 2: the first quarter should be changed from D to E♭.

108 Alto Sax 2: add a slur to the first two sixteenths on count two.

110 Cornet 1: add *dim.* to the entire measure.

110 Horns: add "open" designation.

111 Cornet 1: add *mp* dynamic.

114 String Bass: add "pizz." to the score.

114 Timpani: change dynamic to *f*.

117-121 Tambourine: modify dynamic at the beginning of each crescendo to be *mf*.

120 Castanets: start *f* and crescendo to *ff*.

121-127 Castanets: add *f* plus a crescendo to each measure.

126 Cornets, Horns, Trombone 1 and 2: add staccato to the first two sixteenths.

127 Cornets, Horns, Trombone 1 and 2: add staccato to the first two sixteenths and to the final eighth note.

128 Cornets, Horns, Trombone 1 and 2: add staccato to all notes.

129 Cornets, Horns, Trombone 1 and 2: add staccato to the first sixteenth note and to all successive notes.

130 Castanets: add *f* dynamic.

133 Add a breath mark to all melodic parts after the final quarter note.

139-140 Snare Drum, Castanets: add *dim.* concluding with a *p* dynamic.

139 Tambourine: add *mf* dynamic on count 3 and a *dim.*

140 Tambourine: place *mp* on count 1; add *dim.* beginning on count 3.

141 Tambourine: add *p* dynamic.

142 Basses: add *espr. legato*.

143 Cornet 2: first dotted quarter note should be written B♭ (see organ score).

146 Flute 1: designate that the part divides into flute 1 and flute 3.

155 Oboe 1, Clarinet 1: add breath mark after count 3.

164 Clarinets 2-3: add *a2* designation.

165 Flute: add the designation "loco."

166 String Bass: add "arco" to the score.

167, 171, 173 Cornets 1-3, Horns 1-4: add a breath mark at the end of each measure.

172 Alto Sax 1: add slur to the first two sixteenth notes.

175 Basses: remove low octave G on count 1.

185 Clarinet 2: add *a2* designation on final sixteenth.

185 Alto Clarinet: add sharp sign to two sixteenth note Gs on second half of count 2.

189 Trombone 2: remove upper octave from the score; these notes are not present on the part.

192 Flute 2: change sixteenth note D to C natural.

Parts

Piccolo - 191 Extend cresendo to the end of the measure.

Flute 1 - 11-12 Extend *dim.* to the *mf* in measure 12; 23 add "2 players" designation to the part; 43 add natural sign to the G eighth note on count 3; 45 add natural sign to the G eighth note on count 3; 98 add "Fl. 1 play top"; 109 add fermata to the quarter notes on count 2; 186, 193 add "Fl. 1 play top."

Flute 2 - 11-12 Extend *dim.* to the *mf* in measure 12; 39 add grace note B♮ to the final note; 43 add natural sign to G eighth note on count 3; 45 add natural sign to G eighth note on count 3; 190-195 add the 8va designation to the part.

Oboe 1 - 23-24 Move molto rit. designation to measure 23; 29 add staccato marks to first two eighth notes; 29-32 continue crescendo mark to measure 32; 61 add "espr. legato" and "in one breath" to the part; 74 change *mp* dynamic to *p*; 94 remove tenuto marks from the dotted quarter note F; move poco rit. designation to the next measure; 152 add "1 player" designation; 177 add crescendo beginning on count 1 and extending to count 3.

Oboe 2 - 23 correct the spelling of the word molto; 24 move molto rit. to the beginning of the measure; 54 add *f* dynamic; 94 move poco rit. to the next measure; 130 add *f* dynamic; 133 add breath mark after count 3; 177 add crescendo to the measure.

English Horn - 43 Remove the sharp sign from the grace note B on count 3; 45 add a natural sign to the D on count 3; 47 add *f* dynamic.

E♭ Clarinet - 47 Add *f* dynamic; 53 add a sharp sign to the fifth thirty-second note F on count 3; 55 add a sharp sign to the seventh thirty-second note F on count 3.

Clarinet 1 - 5 Add legato designation; 29 add staccato to the second eighth note; 43 add staccato to the last four eighth notes in the flute cue; 65-66 remove the diminuendo; 85 remove the breath mark at the end of the measure; 94 move poco rit. to the next measure; 142 cancel 2 flats, add F♯ to the key signature; 156 change the bottom pitch from E to D; 186 add ♩ = ca. 100 to the part.

Clarinet 2 - 33 Change "2nd A. Sax" cue to "1st A. Sax"; 65-66 remove the diminuendo; 85 remove the breath mark at the end of the measure; 141 add a double bar at the end of the measure; 159 remove "tutti"

223

designation; 165 add crescendo beginning on count 2; 176 add tenuto to the quarter note.

Clarinet 3 - 16 Remove poco rit.; 142 cancel 2 flats, add F♯ to the key signature; 173 add an accent to the final eighth note; 174 add an accent to the first eighth note; 177 add a crescendo to the entire measure; 183 add a natural sign to the final sixteenth note A on count 2.

Alto Clarinet - 5-7 Remove the staccato marks; 25 add *ff* dynamic; 65 continue the slur to include the third eighth note; 109 move the poco rit. to the beginning of the measure; 131 remove the breath mark at the end of the measure.

Bass Clarinet - 17 Add *ff* dynamic; 23 add *p* dynamic to the bassoon cue; 54 add staccato to the first sixteenth note of the bassoon cue; 70 add *mf* dynamic to the bassoon cue; 74 add dim. concluding with a piano dynamic level; add a fermata to the cue; 102 change the first eighth note from E♭ to C; 142 eliminate the two flats; add an F♯ to the key signature; 174 add staccato to the first eighth note.

Bassoon 1 - 15 Add *p* dynamic to bass clarinet cue; 47 add legato tongue designation to the part; 54 add *f* dynamic; 57 add *p* dynamic; 61 add *pp* dynamic; 72 add a flat sign to the first eighth note E; 85 add a staccato mark to the second eighth note; 109 remove the crescendo; 141 add *p* at the conclusion of the dim.; change the signature to one flat; 164 add staccato marks to the first four eighth notes; 177 move the crescendo to begin on count 2; 182 add the rehearsal letter "S"; remove it from its position at measure 184; 184-185 add a crescendo mark; place *fff* under the final sixteenth in measure 185.

Bassoon 2 - 15 Add *p* dynamic to bass clarinet cue; 53 add the slur from the previous measure; 74 add a fermata to the dotted-half note; 84 add staccato to the first eighth note; 90 add staccato to the second eighth note; 109 remove the crescendo; 141 the key change should be modified to one flat; 164 add staccato marks to the first four eighth notes; 177 move the

crescendo to begin on count 2; 184-185 add a crescendo mark; place *fff* under the final sixteenth in measure 185.

Alto Saxophone 1 - 103 Add *ff* dynamic to the last two sixteenth notes; 165 add a crescendo beginning on count 2; 183 change *fff* to *ff*; 186 add *f* dynamic; 189 place an accent on the quarter note G.

Alto Saxophone 2 - 43 Add staccato marks to the last four eighth notes; 45 add a natural sign to the final eighth note E in the English horn cue; 133 add a breath mark at the end of the measure; 182 change the dynamic to *mf*; 183 change the dynamic to *ff*; 184 change the dynamic to *mp*.

Tenor Saxophone - 15 Add *p* dynamic to the alto clarinet cue; 75 add *ff* dynamic; 94 add *p* dynamic; 97 add staccato to the first eighth note; 101 add an accent on count 2; 185 change dynamic to *fff*; 192 add *ff* dynamic.

Baritone Saxophone - 84 Add *f* dynamic to the bass clarinet cue; 95 add *f* dynamic; 97 add staccato to the first eighth note; 139-140 add diminuendo; 160 add staccato to the final two eighth notes; 165 add crescendo beginning on count 2; 170 add staccato mark on E eighth note on count 2; 185 change dynamic to *fff* at the end of the measure.

Cornet 1 - 110 Add staccato to G♭ eighth note; add dim. to the entire measure; 116 add "1 player" designation to the part; 185 change the dynamic at the end of the measure to *fff*.

Cornet 2 - 25 Add *f* dynamic; 114-115 add staccato marks to each note in these two measures; 127 add staccato mark to the final eighth note; 129 move the crescendo to begin on count 2; add staccato to the final four notes in the measure.

Horn 1 - 29-31 Add *p* dynamic to measure 29; add crescendo marking; 61 add "solo" designation; add espr. designation; 73 begin dim. on count 1; 81 add a breath mark after the quarter note; 110 add dim.; 118 remove the *f* dynamic; 129 add crescendo beginning on count 2; 142 add

" ♩ = ca. 56" to the part; 177 add crescendo beginning on count 2; 178 add *f* dynamic.

Horn 2 - 142 Add " ♩ = ca. 56" to the part; 177 add crescendo beginning on count 2; 178 add *f* dynamic.

Horn 3 - 129 Add staccato to the sixteenth note after the dotted eighth note; 142 add " ♩ = ca. 56" to the part; 176 add staccato to the first eighth note; 178 add staccato to all of the sixteenth notes; 179 add staccato to the eighth note; 180 add staccato to all of the sixteenth notes.

Horn 4 - 128 Add staccato to all of the notes; 133 add staccato to the final eighth note; 142 add " ♩ = ca. 56" to the part; 176 add staccato to the first eighth note on count 2; 178 add staccato to all of the sixteenth notes; 179 add staccato to the eighth note; 180 add staccato to all of the sixteenth notes.

Trombone 1 - 74 Add a natural sign to the sixteenth note C on the second half of count 3; 118 add staccato to the final eighth note; 177 modify the crescendo to begin on count 2.

Trombone 2 - 95 Remove the staccato from the E♭ eighth note; 177 modify the crescendo to begin on count 2.

Trombone 3 - 88 Add staccato to the first two eighth notes; 130 add *f* dynamic.

Euphonium B.C. - 84 Add *mf* to the bassoon cue; 97 add the word subito after the *ff*; add *staccato* to the E♭ eighth note; 160 add *mf* dynamic.

Baritone T.C. - 84 Add *mf* to the bassoon cue; 97 add the word subito after the *ff*; add *staccato* to the F eighth note; remove staccato from the last two eighth notes; 176 add staccato to the first eighth note B; 185 change the dynamic to *fff*.

String Bass - 12 Move *mf* to the first quarter note; 49 place slur from the D to the B♭; 97 add the word subito after the *ff*; add staccato to the E♭ eighth note; remove staccato from the last two eighth notes; 106 add an accent to the G♮ on count 2; 111 change the dynamic to *mp*; 169 add staccato to the first eighth note C; 170

remove staccato from the first eight note; start slur on count 1 extending to the eighth note G on count 2; place staccato on the G eighth note on count 2; 172 add staccato to eighth note B♭ on count 2; 174 add staccato to eighth note B♭ on count 2; 176 add staccato to eighth note C on count 2; 183 add slur from A to B♭ on count 2; 190 remove double bar; 193 add *ff* dynamic.

Basses - 61 Add *pp* to string bass cue; 73-74 move dim. to begin on the dotted half note in the string bass cue; 95 add crescendo on count 1; add *f* dynamic under count 2; 108 extend the first slur to encompass the third eighth note A♭; 111 change the dynamic to *mp*; 125 remove the breath mark; 170 remove the staccato from the first eighth note; begin the slur on count 1 extending to the G eighth note on count 2; add staccato to the G on count 2; 172 add staccato to the B♭ eighth note on count 2; 173 add staccato to the final eighth note F♯; 174 add staccato to the B♭ eighth note on count 2; 176 add staccato to the C eighth note on count 2; 183 slur A eight note to B♭ sixteenth note.

Timpani - Add tunings throughout the part; 114 change the dynamic to *f*; 130 add *f* dynamic; 139-140 begin dim. in measure 139; move the designation rit. poco a poco to measure 139; 193 add "rolls" to counts 2 and 3.

Percussion 1 - 54 Change the 7 count rest to 6; create a measure and add two quarter rests and a quarter note rim shot in measure 60 at the *f* dynamic (the rim shot is missing from the part); 96 add *p* dynamic; 139-140 add dim. to snare drum part.

Percussion 2 - 120-127 Castanets: start *f* and add crescendo at the beginning of each group of notes (see indications on the part); 130 change dynamic to *f*; 133 tie eighth note roll to the eighth note in the next measure.

Percussion 3 - 38 Change dynamic to *f*; 56 count 3 should be modified to be two sixteenth notes followed by an eighth note; 174 xylophone should add D eighth note on "and of 3" in harmony with present G; 184 change dynamic to *mp*. □

July, 1991

Composer Comments on *Elegy*

by Mark Camphouse

Although I am a product of some of the midwest's finest school band programs, my earliest, most inspirational musical experiences were steeped in vocal and orchestral traditions. My father sang to me as a child, and my wife, Elizabeth, is a gifted soprano. As a Chicago-trained brass player, I apply vocal style, so this engrained lyricism and my fascination for the warmth and variety of the orchestral palette were crucial to the evolution of *Elegy* for band.

My earliest works were for orchestras, not bands, and my first large ensemble conducting experience was with a summer festival orchestra, and except for chamber music, I play trumpet only with symphony orchestras. My boyhood heroes, along with Mickey Mantle, Roger Maris, and Whitey Ford, were Aaron

Copland, Leonard Bernstein, and Adolph Herseth. Those baseball greats played for the same team, as did those musicians, each of whom played with the orchestra. My early experiences were primarily orchestral, but the passage of time and the influence of my college band director, John P. Paynter, stimulated me to write for band. Paynter was a musical father figure, whose persuasive powers on and off the podium still amaze me. Most important, however, was my realization that the essence of human creativity is that the medium isn't the message; the message is the message. When judging a work, musicians should remember what American composer Bernard Rogers emphasized while teaching at the Eastman School of Music: "there is only honest or dishonest music." If the message is honest, the music will likely stand the test of time with performers and audiences.

Conductors debate the challenges of leading a band rather than an orchestra, but I do not know any serious composer who has not found composing for band to be the greater challenge, especially during the orchestration process. It requires great care and more time to achieve transparency of texture, contrast, and balance in band scoring. For example I spent four weeks composing *Elegy*, but orchestrating the work took over fourteen weeks. Although there are many fine orchestration teachers and texts, the best teachers of orchestration are not professors or textbooks, but masterpieces written by great composers throughout history. Indeed, music libraries make it possible for any of us to study orchestration with the world's greatest composers. Band conductors and composers are responsible for the future of band composition, conducting, and performance, and I hope *Elegy* has some of the aesthetic qualities our medium deserves and needs.

In addition to being a tribute to my late father, the work's lyricism and rich harmonies are a musical memorial to the sacrifices made by the U.S. Armed Forces in defense of freedom.

Elegy's inspiration came from a four-minute (1981) work I wrote for an *a capella*, eight-part chorus entitled "Morning," based on a poem of the same title by Scottish writer and poet John Henry Mackay (1864-1933):

And tomorrow the sun will shine again,
and on the path that I shall follow
it will reunite us, the blessed ones,
amidst this sun-breathing world.

And to the shore, broad and blue with the waves
we shall go down quietly and slowly.
Mute we shall look into each other's eyes,
and upon us will descend the great silence of love.

The following excerpts are phrases from my choral work, "Morning," that were the source for *Elegy*'s themes and unified its scoring.

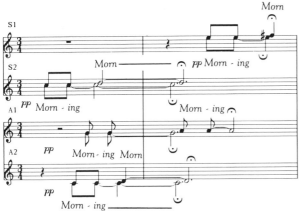

Introduction to "Morning"; see the oboe and English horn parts in measures 31-34 and the brass parts in measures 104-108.

Excerpt of "Morning"; see trumpets and trombones measures 125-131

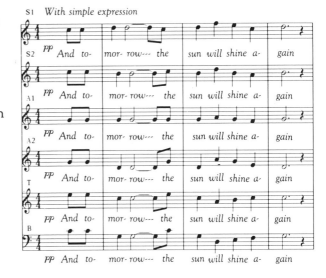

Excerpt of "Morning"; see horns "Nobilmente" measures 170-177.

Fragments of other themes come from sketches made in 1983 of an unperformed orchestral work based on the hymn "The Church In The Wildwood," by William S. Pitts. My earliest memories are of my father singing me to sleep with this simple tune:

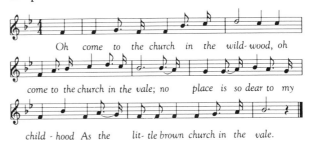

Solo horn foreshadows the hymn tune in measures 39-43. Tubular bells and harp provide a complete but well-camouflaged statement of the melody in measures 125-131 amidst a polytonal layered texture, which features a brass chorale (see the second musical example), saxophone quartet, modal upper woodwinds, and a G♭ pedal point in low reeds, low brass, and timpani. Solo horn refers again to the hymn tune in measures 180-182 as do flute and glockenspiel from measure 187 to the end. A more thorough investigation of harmonic movement and musical form is best left to those not intimately involved in the creative process.

While I share many composers' aversions to assigning difficulty levels to works, conductors will find *The Instrumentalist* gave *Elegy* a grade six and the 1990 National Band Association's list gave it a five. Most difficult are the exposed solo passages, trumpet and horn tessitura, and maintaining intensity of tone and expression during extended phrases at contrasting dynamic levels. Although the work's tempos are slow (♩ =56-80) throughout, there are many important metronomic changes and subtle fluctuations in tempo that are crucial to the pacing of the work.

Tasteful and accurate releases are also important throughout *Elegy*. Too often releases are secondary to attacks, while I believe they are of equal importance. I also gave considerable attention to economy of orchestration, with one and two players per part designated throughout the work. Adhering to these indications will enhance textural transparency and clarity of musical line. Strive for delicacy and transparent texture during the 20-measure introduction featuring solo flute. I also recommend subdividing the first four beats of measure 97 (⅗) for rhythmic precision in trumpet and trombone parts.

Most conductors and players, and therefore audiences, assume the work reaches its climax at measure 170, the "Nobilmente," which is, for better or worse, achieved with Wagnerian aplomb. Do invite all players to reach and maintain a rich, round, dark, orchestral *fortissimo* here. However, the most powerful moment and true climax in the chromatic progression of measure 180 should be marked by a warm, quiet intensity, a controlled power at *pianissimo*. Make the *meno mosso*, *trattenuto*, and *tenuto* indications

leading to this moment happen. Listen for harp, solo horn, and tubular bells here. Strive to achieve serenity during the final eight measures of the work, which does not reach it's peaceful, if unresolved, conclusion until all tubular bell sounds die away to nothing. (*estinguendosi al niente*).

Vocal and orchestral performance experiences give band composers a valuable perspective, which they should apply with integrity to this art. I hope that *Elegy* contains some of the qualities the band repertoire deserves and needs.

Commissioned by and for The United States Marine Band, *Elegy* was composed between June and October 1987, and premiered at a concert celebrating the 190th anniversary of The Marine Band on July 11, 1988 at the Kennedy Center in Washington, D.C. *Elegy* was runner-up for the 1989 Ostwald Award for band composition sponsored by the American Bandmasters Association. Published by TRN Music, *Elegy* appears on the compact disc "Marine Band Showcase - Volume II," which also includes original works for band by Beethoven, Warren Benson, Percy Grainger, Walter Piston, and Saint-Saëns. ☐

Mark Camphouse is associate professor of music and director of bands at Radford University in Virginia. He holds undergraduate and graduate degrees from Northwestern University. His most recent work, based on Jack London's To Build a Fire, *received a Kennedy Center premiere by the United States Army Band.*

September, 1991

Gossec's Military Symphony in F

An Analysis by Barry Kopetz

In addition to his works for winds, Francois-Joseph Gossec (1734-1829) wrote operas, oratorios, symphonies, vocal pieces, and considerable chamber music. During the French Revolution Gossec was director of the Musical Corps of the National Guard, for which he wrote marches and selections for combinations of wind instruments. Most were intended to inspire patriotism at ceremonial functions.

Gossec wrote the piece for pairs of piccolos (doubling on C flutes in the second movement), oboes, clarinets, bassoons, horns and trumpets

in F, plus serpent (or string bass), timpani, and bass drum. As this ensemble of 13 wind instruments plus percussion was a much smaller ensemble than the modern wind band, conductors might cut some players when performing this work and should omit some of

Barry Kopetz is director of bands at the University of Utah. A published composer and arranger, Kopetz is active as an adjudicator and guest conductor.

the heavy doublings of parts. Keeping the original scoring in mind, the conductor has flexibility to determine balance.

Numerous editorial inconsistencies mar the published version and are listed in the errata at the end of this article.

First Movement: *Allegro Maestoso*

This simple, straightforward movement is a binary form in F major, with each section repeated in its entirety; conductors should not skip the repeats. Begin conducting with a preparatory beat for the opening series of F major triads. At a tempo of ♩=96-100, the dotted eighth-sixteenth figure on counts three and four of the first measure will not sound rushed. This is dignified music, and achieving a proper mood is difficult at too rapid a tempo. The accented opening notes should receive sufficient stress, and a slight separation between the dotted quarter and eighth notes in the second measure and between eighth notes in measures 2 through 4 fits the style of the music.

The first of the major discrepancies in the published arrangement is at letter A. The accent on the downbeats of measures 5 and 7 is marked Λ in some parts and > in others; the former may sound forced. Whichever accent you choose, modify the parts consistently.

At measure 5 give a strong downbeat with little or no rebound for the *subito piano* on the second eighth note. Each successive beat should be short and clipped and the repeated B♭ triads balanced and resonant. Mark the crash cymbals entrance on the first count of measure 5, bringing out the short sixteenth-note figure in the solo and first clarinets in measure 6. Pay attention to the clarinets and baritone/tenor saxophone, which tend to rush this passage, particularly if the tempo is too fast from the beginning. The size of the baton beats should reflect the dynamic contrasts of measures 5 and 7.

The eighth-note F triad on the last half of count four in measure 8 is an anacrusis to the emphatic chords of the following measure and is occasionally underplayed. Give it proper accent and separation; players should think of the triad as an integral part of the next two measures.

The legato in measure 11 is an effective contrast after the punctuation of the first 10 measures. Adjust the balance of the C major triad so the ascending C major scale in the low brass and reeds clearly projects. Only the first horn plays the harmonic line in the second stave of measures 11-12; bring it out to compliment the step-wise motion of the scale below. Decide what length to give the first eighth note of count two in measure 12; many players group this eighth with the ensuing series of staccato eighth notes, thus clipping it shorter than necessary.

The original parts contain no articulation marks or slurs here, leaving phrasing to the discretion of the conductor. I leave the slur as printed, giving the concluding eighth note its full value, and completing the measure with light, resonant, slightly separated eighth notes. A similar approach is appropriate for the melodic line in measure 13, played by alto, bass, E♭ contrabass clarinet, bassoon, and euphonium. These instruments are not indicated in the score, and a reminder helps.

Play the four sixteenth notes at the end of measure 14 evenly without a hint of acceleration. In measure 15 it is difficult to resolve the G7 half-note chord to a staccato eighth note as indicated in many of the parts; consider deleting the staccato marking and resolving to a full-length eighth-note C major triad. Use a similar approach in measures 16-18.

The key to the dynamic contrasts in measures 19 and 20 is not to allow the ensemble either to *diminuendo* or shorten the quarter note on count two. Avoid rushing the *forte* repeated notes on the first two counts or losing tone control; this wonderful dynamic contrast is easily ruined by one or two musicians playing too loudly and spoiling the balance.

After conducting a light series of staccato eighth notes on the F triads in measure 21, maintain the same even beat in the following measure so the ascending sixteenths in thirds remain in tempo. If the final staccato quarter note on count three of measure 22 is clipped with a "tut" sound, it will be too short to make the chord quality apparent. Your gesture on count three should indicate appropriate note length.

Consider dropping the dynamic from *piano* to *pianissimo* at measure 23 before beginning the *crescendo* culminating in measure 26. In measures 23-24 hold the final eighth note in each of the three-note slurs for its full value (not staccato). Write the entrance of the snare drum roll in the score at measure 25.

The snare drum and crash cymbal parts are controversial; some conductors omit them entirely. They are not indicated in the original parts but many have been used in performances. The published arrangement includes snare drum, bass drum, and crash cymbals, with few indications of percussion accents, which should be added to suit your interpretation.

Beginning in measure 23, Gossec uses the secondary dominant G triad (V of the key of C major) to start an extended cadence culminating in the repeated C major triads of measures 26 and 27. Emphasize this brief departure from the key of F major with a *crescendo*, and conduct the concluding chords in measure 27 and the downbeat of the repeat to measure 1 with authority. I practice the repeat at each rehearsal rather than saving time by skipping it, or at least play the first few measures of the repeat before proceeding.

At letter C the second section begins with C major triads and a cymbal crash, which I prefer to omit; there are differing versions in parts and score. Give the first three measures and the first count of measure 31 a strong conducting pattern and sustain the first two dotted half notes right up to count four. The first note of measure 31 is *forte*, with woodwinds entering on the second half of the first count at *piano*; conduct the downbeat with a small rebound and continue the measure with a smaller beat. This movement builds tension from the F triad of measure 32 to the fully diminished C♯ seventh chord in measure 33, which may be emphasized by adding a small *crescendo* in measure 34. It helps to write the timpani entrance in measure 35 on the score. The contrasting lyricism of measures 34 and 35 prepares listeners for the incessant octave Cs in the next two measures as the descending cadential triads increase the tension.

F Triad   C♯ dim   *mf*   +Timp.   etc.

The words *poco rit.* do not appear in the original parts in measures 38-39; a slight *ritardando* is acceptable, but precision on the descending eighth notes in measure 39 is more important. Often ensembles are unprepared for the *crescendo* into measure 40, and thus the first chord at D lacks authority. Staggered breathing approaching D should help achieve an even crescendo.

The first four measures of letter D reprise measures 1-4 and should be interpreted similarly. Measures 44 and 46 have confusing articulations, including *sfz* plus either a hard or regular accent, all of which should be deleted and replaced by your choice of accent. I prefer the *sforzando*, which implies an immediate drop in dynamics to *piano*, followed by a *crescendo*. If you use the

cymbal crashes here, add them to your score as a reminder.

After the B♭ clarinet's sixteenth-note parallel thirds in measures 45 and 47, the euphonium and tuba should respond boldly and in tempo. Indicate in your score that flutes enter *fortissimo* on count four of measure 47. Emphasize the trombone entrance on the accented eighth notes in measure 47.

The trumpet and horn fanfare at letter E is important but should not overpower the descending line in the baritone saxophone and euphonium at measure 51. Measures 52-53 are identical to 21-22, though at different pitch levels. In the published score the ascending line of the later two measures is slurred, culminating with a staccato quarter, while in the earlier measures the ascending notes are marked staccato. The original parts indicate no articulation in either case, so it seems appropriate to phrase the two passages identically. I delete the slur in measure 53 and add staccato markings to each note.

Play measures 54-56 similarly to measures 23-24, but making a stronger *crescendo*. Emphasize the extended cadence by accenting the syncopations and restraining the upper woodwinds from rushing the *mi-re-do* sixteenth-note figure in measures 57-58. Consider adding an accent to the A in each of these groups and encouraging musicians to stretch the length of each figure's concluding F eighth note. The low brass may separate the eighth notes in the final descending arpeggio, and the quarter-note F triads of the concluding measure should also be slightly separated; indicate this separation with crisp baton motions.

Second Movement: *Larghetto (Pastorale)*

The score fails to identify each voice as it plays, and the first four measures contain chord tones that are not present in any of the parts. Conductors should study the individual parts to determine which instruments play at various times.

A common complaint is that bands have few instruments to play the uppermost voices, and the mid-range instruments sound overly strong because of numerical advantage. The opening of the second movement is a prime example of this problem. The condensed score indicates a heavily doubled F major triad on the first count of measure 1; if the chord is played in balance, the top should be prominent as the melodic line. The part assignments, however, make balance difficult to achieve.

On the top line flute 1 and solo B♭ clarinet carry the melody, and the piccolo sounds the first two notes of the melody an octave higher, then drops out for the next nine counts. Interestingly, this melodic line is played an

octave lower only by the first horn, with the first two notes played in the same octave by the first alto saxophone, first cornet, and first trumpet. Theoretically the higher octave should be heard more clearly because of its *tessitura*, but in performance the mid-range instruments may predominate. The balance should be modified by changing the dynamics of the lower-octave instruments or by cutting instruments from the texture completely.

Conductors should approach rescoring with caution, but in this case Gossec's original scoring had only the first flute in the top octave and first clarinet and first oboe in the second octave carrying the melody. In making this work available for modern bands, the arrangers voiced the parts so balance is difficult to achieve.

The E♭ clarinet part in the opening is essential to the harmony; if an E♭ clarinet is not available, transpose the part for B♭ clarinet and have one first clarinet play it throughout the movement.

Many performances of this pastorale are marred by imprecise rather than fluid chord changes. Begin with a *legato* beat pattern to elicit the necessary volume and encourage players to listen to the delicate balances. On count four of the first measure the size of the conductor's beat should reflect the abrupt dynamic change. The quarter note in counts four and five of measure 2 should have full value, though a hint of

diminuendo is musically appropriate. This chord should be released cleanly; adequate breath support will help intonation here and at similar releases.

A tempo too slow or too rapid will adversely affect the melodic line. I encourage conductors to sing the lines freely to find the tempo that feels right, perhaps ♩=72-80. Because the movement should be conducted in six with eighth notes receiving the beat, the music can stagnate.

After repeating the first four measures, the second-inversion B♭ triad in measure 5 calls for a broad approach to begin the second section. Consider omitting the accent completely and striving for breadth rather than emphasis of attack. The articulation marks for baritone in the score do not match the part; delete the *tenuto* and staccato marks and add a slur from count four of measure 5 to the final eighth note in measure 6.

Like the first four measures, measures 5-8 constitute a question-answer phrase structure. The score's notation of measure 6 is deceptive: the eighth rest on count six in the top stave makes it appear no woodwinds play on the final count, but the clarinet parts have an F triad, doubled in baritone and tenor and baritone saxophones, which should be added to the score as a reminder.

Repeated dominant sevenths in measures 9 through 11 resolve to tonic F triads; then accented secondary dominant (G7) chords in measure 12 resolve to the dominant C triad on count four of the same measure. In measure 11 add the trumpet and horn fanfare part to the score so you will conduct it with emphasis.

Modify the notation of the bass part in measures 9-11 using the bassoon part as your guide. In the published version all of measure 12 is *forte*. A worthy alternative is playing *forte* on the first count and *piano* on the fourth as marked in the original parts.

Following the fermata in measure 12 the movement's final four bars call for the same approach as the opening four measures, perhaps holding the final chord slightly longer and adding a slight *diminuendo*.

Third Movement: *Allegro*

After the delicate second movement the robust *Allegro* is a welcome change. Separation between triads is in order throughout the first four measures. Because the published version assigns so many players to a bass line originally intended for bassoon and string bass, this part often lags behind and overshadows the rest, but a tempo of approximately ♩ = 104 aids clarity.

Add an E♭ clarinet and solo B♭ clarinet cue to the sixteenths that appear at the end of measure 4 in the score. The original parts called for piccolo and first oboe to carry this line as well, and both could be added here. Players tend to execute these three pitches in a variety of tempos, so careful beat subdivision and diligent rehearsal are necessary.

Conducting measures 5-10 in graceful fashion provides a refreshing contrast to the punctuation of the first four measures. In an attempt to fill out the harmony, the arrangers added a part for oboes and second clarinet that is not in the original.

Give this lyrical secondary part a sense of melodic direction rather than merely treating it as added harmony. The bass line may be played broadly with little accent to support the smooth melodic line through these measures. The melody is played by the flutes, E♭ clarinet, and solo clarinet, and each trill should be concluded precisely. Adding appropriate subdivision markings above the measures in question establishes each note's exact rhythm.

Conduct measures 9-10 with a light, playful beat to contrast with the powerful descending arpeggio of measure 11. In measure 9 indicate in the score that the bass part is also played by clarinets two and three, alto clarinet, and bass clarinet. The string bass has an important *pizzicato* quarter note on the first count of both of these measures.

After a bold reading of the C major arpeggio and repeated G octaves in measures 11 and 12, conduct the half notes of the next measure *legato* with a slight *crescendo* on the second half note along with a decay to the quarter note on the first count of measure 14; play these measures a dynamic level softer than indicated. Modify the slur in the top stave of measures 15-16 to match the articulation of measures 13-14.

The *tutti* of measures 17 through 20 should be played with a marked style befitting the end of the section. If you use the crash cymbals part, add a whole note entry on the first count of measure 17 with an accent. As with

repeats in the first two movements of the work, the *Allegro*'s first section should be repeated in its entirety.

The octave G in measure 21 initiates a smooth excursion away from the tonic key of C major. If the first three measures of this section are performed without hint of accent, the *forte* scale passage of measure 24 will come as a delightful surprise. Players often are unsure of the tempo in measure 24 and articulate too forcefully and hurry to the end of the bar. Guard against this by marking "Do Not Rush" in the parts.

The alternating quarter-note chords of measures 27-30 should receive equal weight and length; in measures 28 and 30 add the horn chords to the third stave of the score. Measures 31-38 should make musical sense instead of being a series of two-measure ideas; measures 31-34 and 35-37 invite some rise and fall, but only so the music flows naturally into the aggressive scale passage in measure 38.

The section from letter M to the end should be played in a stately, accented style. Change the slur in measure 40 to include only the two sixteenths but not the quarter notes, and add the cymbal crash to the score on the first count of measure 39.

The final four bars (measures 41-44) feature two counterlines: one on stave two for alto and tenor saxophones, alto clarinet, and horns, and another on stave three for bass clarinet, trombones, and euphonium.

Conductors tend to balance these lines with the harmonized melody in the top stave; I have even heard performances in which these two lines overshadowed the primary material. An examination of the original parts, however, reveals that these two counterlines are entirely the work of later arrangers. Rehearse the passage without these parts so players are aware of the original material before adding the other parts to enhance rather than dominate. Overemphasizing these parts gives the concluding phrase a contrapuntal character that seems inconsistent with the overall style of the work.

Although band repertoire has expanded rapidly in recent decades, little music written specifically for large

bands is available from earlier periods. *Military Symphony in F* may never rank among the masterpieces for band, but as conductors endure criticism for performing only contemporary music, Gossec's piece offers an attractive alternative. Appropriate for relatively young musicians, this grade three work gives ensembles an opportunity to perform period music written expressly for winds and allows conductors to introduce students to the wide variety of music available for bands. □

Errata

Editor's note: Measure numbers are identified by Arabic numerals.

Score, Movement I: 2 - add accents on remaining notes in top and bottom staves; 5 - change to cl. 2-3; 6 - add *staccato* on eighth notes in staves 2, 3; 7 - add *staccato* marks to the eighth notes in stave 3; 8 - add *staccato* on eighth note on count three in top stave; 11 - change to hn. 1; 13 - change to hns. 2-4; 14 - accent on first sixteenth on count 4, move *f* from 15 to last quarter on 14, accents on counts 2 and 4 in bottom stave; 15 - remove fl. from top stave; 15, 17 - trill B♮ in top stave; 24 - remove *staccato* from fourth eighth note, top stave; 25 - change accents to *staccato* on second stave; 26 - accents on first two sixteenths in each stave; 33 - change *tenuto* to *staccato* on first C♯ in second stave; 35 - add whole note G timpani roll; 40 - accents on counts 3-4 in bottom stave; 41 - accent all remaining notes in each stave; 44, 46 - cymbal crashes on count 1; 45, 47 - remove *staccato* from count three, top stave; 47 - accent on first sixteenth note on count 4, *ff* on this note; 48 - trill on half note, remove accent from eighth note on count three, top stave; 49 - change dotted quarter G in top stave to a half note; 50 - add trill in top stave; 55 - add snare drum roll; 56 - accents on eighth notes in each stave; 57 - redraw accents in top stave to emphasize syncopation in second stave; 58 - remove accents from count two in top stave, accents on offbeats of counts two, three; Movement II: 1 - add bells on count 1; 5-6, 7-8: remove articulation in second stave and add a slur beginning on F quarter note on count 4; 7 - accent on first quarter note, top stave; 9 - indicate entrance of timpani; 9-11: in second stave tie quarter note C to eighth note C in next measure, accent quarter note; 11 - accent on final quarter note in bottom stave; Movement III: 1 - letter I on first measure; 4 - *mf* on sixteenths in top stave; 5-6, 7-8: slur from first half note to quarter note E in top stave; 9 - add cl. 2-3 on bottom stave; 10 - slur half note and two quarter notes in top stave; 13 - change to *mp*; 13, 15 - accent on half notes and quarter notes in second stave; 15-16: articulation same as 13-14; 18-20: add accents to trombone/baritone part in the third stave; 21 - *tenuto* on half notes in top stave; 23 - *mf* on first eighth note in top stave, remove *staccato* on count 1 in staves 2-3; 28, 30 - remove slurs from two eighth notes and replace with accents; 32 - remove *staccato* from quarter note on count 1, third stave; 32, 35 - accent on final quarter note in third stave; 33 - change to hn. 1-2; 37 - accent on horn entrance in second stave; 40 - only slur two sixteenth notes.

Piccolo, Movement I: 1 - change to *f*; 14, 16 - change accent to ＞; 17 - remove *staccato* from eighth note; 24 - *staccato* on first eighth note and final four eighth notes in flute cue; 31 - *staccato* on last five eighth notes in flute cue; 34-36: slur includes first quarter note in 36; 47 - accent on first sixteenth note B♭; 48, 50 - remove dot from half note, *staccato* on eighth note C tied to half note, add eighth rest after eighth note; 57 - accent on first eighth note and on each eighth note A on the off-beats; 58 - accents on two A sixteenth notes; Movement III: 14 - remove slur from two eighth notes and add *staccato*, slur final two quarter notes, place accent on quarter note B; 16 - accent on quarter note B on count 2.

1st Flute, Movement I: 7 - change accent to ＞; 17 - trill on last half note, change last count to *p*; 23 - change to *p*; 25 - remove accents and add *staccato*; 31 - change to *p*; 34-35 - tie two A quarter notes; 47, 49 - change accent to ＞; 48 - remove *staccato* on count 3; 53 - change to *mp*; 56 - *crescendo*; Movement II: conform to score dynamics; 11 - third note is B♭; Movement III: 1 - change to *f*; 13 - change to *mp*; 24 - change to *f*.

2nd Flute, Movement I: 14 - accent on first sixteenth note; 17 - change to *p* on count 4; 19 - change to *mp*; 20 - add *p*; 23 - change to *p*; 25 - change accents to *staccato*; 31 - change to *p*; 47, 49 - change accents to ＞; 53 - change to *mp* 56 - *crescendo*; Movement II: conform to score dynamics; III: 24 - change to *f*.

1st Oboe, Movement I: 7 - change accent to ＞; 37 - change first eighth note to a G; 48, 50 - change quarter note F on count 3 to an eighth note, add eighth rest after eighth note; 51 - slur to count 3; 55 - *crescendo* entire measure; 56 - final four eighth notes are C-B♭-A-G, *crescendo* entire measure; 57-58 - accent on first sixteenth note of each group, accent on first note of 57; Movement II: 6 - change D on count 3 to E♭; 11 - *crescendo*; Movement III: 1 - change to *f*; 9 - change to *mp*; 13 - change to *mp*; 32 - slur form grace note to final quarter note A.

2nd Oboe, Movement I: 5, 7 - change accent to ＞; 48, 50 - change quarter note E on count 3 to an eighth note, add eighth rest after eighth note; 56 - final four eighth notes are A-G-F-E, *crescendo* entire measure; 57-58: accent on first sixteenth note of each group, accent on first note of 57; Movement II: 2 - slur to last quarter note, 9 - *crescendo*; Movement III: 1 - change to *f*; 9 - change to *mp*; 13, 15 - change to *mp*; 27, 29 - quarter notes on counts 1 and 3 and quarter rests on counts 2 and 4.

E♭ Clarinet, Movement I: 9-10 - accents on each note; 14 - dot half note, remove quarter note on count 3, accent on first sixteenth note; 15, 17 - remove *crescendo*, remove *staccato* from eighth note; 16 - accent on first sixteenth note D; 23, 24 -*crescendo* to end of measure; 48, 50 - remove *staccato* from eighth note D; 56 - second and third eighth notes are D and F; 57-58: accent on first sixteenth note of each group, accent on first note of 57; Movement III: 5-8: trill on dotted eighth notes; 9 - *staccato* on two quarter notes in oboe cue; 10 - slur entire measure; 21 - *tenuto* on cued half notes; 31, 33, 35, 37 - change accents to ＞.

Solo Clarinet, Movement I: 5, 7 - change accent to ＞; 14-15: slur includes half note and first eighth note in 15, remove accent from half note in 15, remove *ff* in 15; 23 - begin *crescendo* on count 3; 44, 46 - change accent to *sfz*; 47 - *mf* dynamic at end of *crescendo*; 52 - remove accent from first eighth note, change to *mp*; 54, 55: *crescendo* to end of measure; 57-58: accent on first sixteenth note of each group, accent on first note of 57; Movement II: 9 - begin *crescendo* on count 4; Movement III: 4 - change to *mf*; 9 - *staccato* on two quarter notes in cue; 10 - slur entire measure; 14 - accent on C quarter note on count 2; 21 - *tenuto* on cued half notes; 24 - change to *f*.

1st Clarinet, Movement I: 5, 7 - change accent to ＞; 14 - change to *f* at end of measure; 23 - change to *p*; 39 - move *poco rit.* to count 3 of previous measure; 47 - *mf* at end of *crescendo*; 49 - accent on first sixteenth note; 52 - change to *mp* on second eighth note; 53 - *staccato* on quarter note on count 3; 57-58: accent on first sixteenth note of each group, accent on first note of 57; Movement II: 9 - begin *crescendo* on count 4; Movement III: 4 - change to *mf*; 9 - *staccato* on two quarter notes in cue; 10 - slur entire measure; 13 - change to *mp*; 21 - *tenuto* on cued half notes; 23 - quarter note cue on count 1, notes are G and E.

2nd Clarinet, Movement I: 15 - remove *staccato* from D on count 3; 39 - move *poco rit.* to count 3 of previous measure; 44, 46 - change accent to *sfz*; 47 - *mf* at end of *crescendo*; 52 - remove accent from first eighth note, move *mp* to second eighth note; 54, 55 - *crescendo* to end of measure; 57-58: accent on first sixteenth note of each group, accent on first note of 57; Movement II: 9 - *mf*, begin *crescendo* on count 4; Movement III: 15 - remove *p*; 24 - change to *f*; 39 - accent on quarter note B.

3rd Clarinet, Movement I: 12 - remove *staccato* from eighth note A on count 2; 14, 16 - change accent to ＞ on first sixteenth note; 23-25: *crescendo* to end of each measure; 24 - sixth eighth note is E on and of 3; 34 - change to *mf*; 39 - *crescendo* to end of measure; 44, 46 - change accent to *sfz*; 47 - accent on first sixteenth on count 4, change to *mf*; 49 - accent on first sixteenth note; 52 - move *mp* to second

eighth note; 54, 55 - *crescendo* each measure; 56 - accents on final four eighth notes; 57-58: accent on first sixteenth note of each group, accent on first note of 57; Movement II: 5 - move *p* from count 3 to count 4; 9 - begin *crescendo* on count 4; 10 - *staccato* on last three eighth notes; 11 - accents on counts 1 and 4; Movement III: 15 - remove *p*.

Alto Clarinet, Movement I: 2 - accent on each note; 7 - accent on quarter note A; 11 - add *mf*; 17 - accent on half note E; 24 - add *p*, *staccato* on last four eighth notes, *crescendo* beginning on count 3; 25 - *staccato* on eighth notes; 26 - add *ff*, accent all notes; 33 - remove slur from first note and replace it with *staccato*; 41 - accents on eighth note E and quarter note F♯; 42, 43 - accent each note; 53 - *staccato* on eighth note B; 54 - *crescendo*; 55 - add *mf*, *crescendo*; 56 - accent on each note, *crescendo* entire measure; Movement II: 9 - *staccato* on last three eighth notes, begin *crescendo* on count 4; 10 - *staccato* on last three eighth notes; Movement III: 24 -change to *f*; 41 - change eighth note on second half of count 3 from C♯ to B.

Bass Clarinet, Movement I: 14 - accent on quarter note C♯ on count 2; 20 - add *p* to eighth note D on and of 3, remove *p* from next measure; 39 - move *poco rit.* to count 3 of measure 38; 54 - add *p*; 56 - accents on eighth notes, change to *ff*; Movement II: 1, 3, 13, 16 - remove *staccato* from eighth note; 5, 7: remove *staccato* from count 3; Movement III: 14 - *staccato* on eighth note A.

E♭ Contrabass Clarinet, Movement I: 2 -accents on unmarked eighth notes; 14 - accents on counts 2 and 4, *f* on count 4; 26 - accents on two sixteenth notes; 41 - accents on unmarked notes; 56 - accents on eighth notes; Movement III: 13 - change to *mp*; 23, 32, 34, 36, 38 - remove *staccato* from first quarter note.

1st Alto Saxophone, Movement I: 5, 7 - change accent to ＞; 26 - accent on first note in measure; 33 - *staccato* on first eighth note, final two eighth notes are G♯ and F♯; 44, 46 - remove accent; 47 - accent on final eighth note; 53 - *staccato* on count 1; 56 - change accents to *staccato*; Movement II: 1-2 - slur horn cue; 9 - change accent to ＞, begin *crescendo* on count 4; Movement III: 5 - change alto clarinet cue to *mf*; 9 - add *mp* to cue; 11 - change to *ff*.

2nd Alto Saxophone, Movement I: 5, 7 - change accent to ＞; 15, 17 - remove *crescendo*; 32 - change to *p*; 33 - *staccato* on first eighth note, final two eighth notes are G♯ and F♯; 38, 39 - cue is hn. 2, move *poco rit.* to count 3 of 38; 44, 46 - remove accent; 45 - *staccato* on last eighth note; 47 - slur from sixteenths to eighth note D, change *staccato* on final eighth note to an accent; 51 - accent on quarter note F♯ on count 4; 53 - *staccato* on eighth note D; 56 - change *staccato* to accents; 59 - change three final quarter notes from written E to F♯; Movement II: 2, 14 - final two notes in horn cue are an eighth note A and a quarter note C♯; 9 - change accent to ＞, start

231

crescendo on count 4; Movement III: 5 - change to *mf*; 9 - add *mp*; 11 - change to *ff*; 39 - accent on whole note A.

Tenor Saxophone, Movement I: 5 - change accent to >; 6 - *staccato* on first sixteenth note, begin slur on second sixteenth; 8 - change final eighth note *staccato* to an accent; 13-14: tie G whole note to half note in next measure; 21-22: add *staccato* to cue; 24 - change to *p*, *crescendo*; 25 - remove slur, add *staccato* on first three eighth notes; 46 - remove accent; 47 - change *staccato* on last note to an accent; 48 - change final eighth note from written E to D; 54 - remove accent; Movement II: 2, 14 - final two notes in horn cue are an eighth note G and a quarter note C; 5, 7 - add *p* to count 4; 9 - *crescendo* on count 4; 11 - accent on counts 1 and 4; Movement III: 5 - change to *mf*; 9, 10 - change accent on first eighth note to a *staccato*; 9 - add *mp* to first note of slur; 17 - add *ff*; 27 - first quarter note is written C; 32 - remove accent from G quarter note on count 4; 39 - change accent to >.

E♭ Baritone Saxophone, I: 11 - add *mf*; 12 - remove *staccato* from quarter note A; 13 - change written A to D; 14 - change half note B to E; 21-22 - add *staccato* to cue; 23-24 - remove *staccato*; 45, 47 - *staccato* on eighth note on count 1; 47 - change *staccato* on last note to an accent; 52 - remove accent from first eighth note; 55 - *crescendo*; 56 - change *staccato* to accents, *crescendo*; Movement II: 1 - designate hn. 4 cue; 9 - *crescendo* on count 4; Movement III: 5 - change to *mf*; 6 - accent on second quarter note; 14, 16 - *staccato* on eighth note E; 23 - remove accent from quarter note G♯; 24 - change first eighth note to written A.

1st and 2nd Bassoon, Movement I: 2 - accents on unmarked notes; 5-7: add *staccato*, *staccato* on first five eighth notes, move *f* to final eighth note D; 19 - add *p* to count 3; 23 - change to *p*; 26 - accents on two sixteenth notes; 34-36: bsn. 2 slur B♭ dotted half note to G dotted half note, slur from quarter note G on count 4 to eighth note C on count 1 of 36; 36, 37 - accent on C on and of 1; 38 - move *poco rit.* to count 3; 41 - accent on unmarked notes; 47 - accent on final eighth note A; 48 - bsn. 2 note is F; 52 - *mp* on second eighth note; 54, 55 - *crescendo*; 56 - add accents; Movement

II: 9 - add ties to bsn. 2; 16 - slur to final note; Movement III: 5 - remove a2, accent on count 1; 9, 10 - *staccato* on first eighth note, begin slur on second eighth note, *mp*; 14, 16 - *staccato* on eighth note G; 24 - change to *f*; 30 - begin slur on eighth note C; 31-32 - slur to first quarter note of 32; 33-34 - slur to first quarter note of 34; 41 - accent on first quarter note.

1st B♭ Cornet, Movement I: 2, 3 - accents on unmarked notes; 15, 17 - remove *staccato* on count 3; 26 - accents on two sixteenth notes; 44, 46 - remove accent; 52 - change accent to *staccato*; 54 - change to *p*; 55 - *mf*; Movement II: 5, 7 - change count 4 to *p*; Movement III: 22 - *tenuto* on half notes; 40 - only slur two sixteenth notes, accent on first quarter note.

2nd B♭ Cornet, I: 5-6, 7-8: change cue to hn. 3, *staccato* on cued notes; 15 - remove *crescendo*; 44, 46 - remove accents; 52 - change accent to *staccato*; 54, 55 - *crescendo*; Movement II: 7 - *tutti* on count 1; Movement III: 26, 30 - remove slur from two eighth notes, change to accents.

1st and 2nd Trumpets in B♭, I: 5, 7 - change accents to >, add *staccato* to horn cue, add *p* to cue; 8, 9 - add *staccato*; 15, 17 - remove *staccato* from eighth notes; 38-39 - *poco rit.*; 40 - *a tempo*; 44, 46 - remove accent; 48, 50 - change accents beginning on and of 3 to *staccato*; 49, 51, 52 - change accents to *staccato*; Movement II: 9 - *mf*; 11 - remove *staccato* from eighth notes; Movement III: 24 - change to *f*; 28 - 2nd trumpet note is written E, remove slur, add accents on two eighth notes; 30 - remove slur, add accents; 40 - only slur two sixteenth notes, accent on first quarter note B.

1st Horn, Movement I: 5, 7 - change the accent to >, *staccato* on remaining eighth notes; 8 - remove accent on count 1, final eighth note *f* and accented; 16-19: remove *staccato* from eighth notes; 21-22: *staccato* on all notes; 33 - *staccato* on first eighth and final five eighth notes; 44, 46 - remove accent; Movement II: 9 - *crescendo* beginning on count 3; Movement III: 14, 16 - *staccato* on eighth note; 21 - change accents to *tenuto*; 21-23: slur count 1 of 23, *mf*; 22 - remove accent from count 1; 24 - *f* on second eighth note; 33 - change accent to >.

2nd Horn, Movement I: 5, 7 - change accent to >, *staccato* on remaining eighth notes; 8 - remove accent on count 1, final

eighth note *f* and accented; 15-18: remove *staccato* from eighth notes; 21-22: *staccato* on all notes; 27 - *D.C.*; 33 - *staccato* on first eighth and final five eighth notes; 44, 46 - remove accent; Movement II: 9 - *crescendo* beginning on count 3; Movement III: 14, 16 - *staccato* on eighth note; 21 - change accents to *tenuto*; 21-23: slur count 1 of 21 to count 1 of 23, *mf*; 22 - remove accent from count 1; 23 - remove accent from final quarter note F♯; 24 - *f* on second eighth note; 33 - change accent to >.

3rd and 4th Horns, Movement I: 5, 7 - change accent to >, *staccato* on remaining eighth notes; 6 - remove accent on count 1, all notes *staccato*; 8 - write out repeated measure and add an accent to and of 4; 33 - remove written D from fourth horn part, double third horn; 39 - move *poco rit.* to count 3 in 38; 44, 46 - remove accent; 48, 50 - remove *ff*; Movement II: 9 - *crescendo* beginning on count three; Movement III: 14, 16 - *staccato* on eighth note; 23 - remove accent from final quarter note A/D.

1st Trombone, Movement I: 5, 7 - change the accent to >; 38 - change accents to *staccato*; 44 - remove accent; 47 - *staccato* on first eighth note; 52-53 - add *staccato* to bsn. cue; Movement II: 9 - *crescendo* on count 4; Movement III: 11 - change to *ff*; 23 - remove accent from final quarter note; 31, 35 - change accent to >.

2nd Trombone, Movement I: 1, 5, 7 -change accent to >; 38 - change accents to *staccato*, change to *mf*; 45, 47 - *staccato* on first eighth note; 50 - remove accent from A quarter note on count 3; Movement II: 9 - *crescendo* on count 4; Movement III: 11 - change to *ff*; 24 - change to *f*; 32, 36 - accent on final quarter note A; 35 - accent on whole note G; 39 - change accent to >.

3rd Trombone, Movement I: 15, 17 -remove *staccato* from eighth note; 19 - *f*; 38 - change accents to *staccato*; 39 - change accent to >; 47 - *staccato* on first eighth note; 50 - remove accent from count 3, slur half note B♭ to quarter note A; 52 - change *staccato* to accents; 56 - *crescendo*; 57 - *ff* at conclusion of *crescendo*; Movement III: 11 - change to *ff*.

Euphonium, Movement I: 5 - change accent to >; 23-25: remove *staccato*; 27 -*D.C.*; 35 - remove accent from quarter note G; 36 - remove *crescendo*; 38, 39 -

move *poco rit.* from next measure to count 3 of 38; 44, 46 - remove accent; 47 - *staccato* on first eighth note, change final *staccato* to accent; 56 - *crescendo*; Movement II: 11, 12 - remove slur from final quarter note C to eighth note B♭; Movement III: 11 - change to *ff*; 23 - remove accent from final quarter note G.

B♭ Baritone T.C., Movement I: 5 -change accent to >; 23-25: remove *staccato*: 27 - *D.C.*; 36 - remove *crescendo*; 36, 37 - add accents on eighth notes; 38 -move *poco rit.* from next measure to count 3 of 38; 44, 46 - remove hard accent; 45 - *staccato* on final eighth note C; 47 - *staccato* on first eighth note, change final *staccato* to accent; Movement II: 11, 12 - remove slur from final quarter note D to eighth note C♯; Movement III: 11 -change to *ff*; 23 - remove accent from final quarter note A.

Bass, Movement I: 5, 7 - change accent to >; 15 - remove *staccato* from eighth note; 23-24: remove *staccato*, *p* plus *crescendo*; 38 - change accents to *staccato*; 44 - remove accent; 56-57: change to *f*, *crescendo* to *ff* in 57; Movement II: 9 - begin *crescendo* on count 4; Movement III: 11 - change to *ff*; 23 - remove accent from final quarter note G.

String Bass, Movement I: 2 - accents on unmarked notes; 38, 39 - move *poco rit.* from next measure to count 3 of 38; 40 - accents on counts 3 and 4; 41 - accents on unmarked notes; 56 - accents on eighth notes; Movement III: 23 - remove accent from final quarter note G; 39 - accent on whole note F.

Percussion: Decide whether or not to use part. If using printed page, add accents and dynamics that fit your interpretation. The following are suggestions: Movement I: 30-31 - decide upon use of crash cymbals, score and part do not match; 45 - *f*; 46 - *sfz* and *crescendo* to *f*; 56 - *crescendo*; Movement III: add appropriate points of accentuation.

Timpani, Movement I: 5, 7 - change accent to >; 15, 17 - remove *crescendo*; 38 - remove accent; 38, 39 - *crescendo*, move *poco rit.* to count 3 of 38; decide whether to observe this cymbal part or one on score; 57 - *ff*; Movement II: 13 - dotted quarter note F octaves in bell part, separate performer plays bells; 18-19: change timpani pitch to D. □

October, 1992

An Analysis of Chance's
Incantation and Dance

by Barry E. Kopetz

John Barnes Chance had a short but successful career as a composer for band, chorus, orchestra, and chamber ensembles. Born in Beaumont, Texas in 1932, he studied with Kent Kennan, Paul Pick, and Clifton Williams at the University of Texas and was recognized early in his career and rewarded with a composer-in-residence award from the Ford Foundation Young Composers Project that brought composers into schools to teach and compose. His residence for the Young Composers Project was at Greensboro Senior High School in North Carolina and he composed his first work for band, *Incantation and Dance*, for this ensemble and its director, Herbert Hazelman. Chance initially called the piece *Nocturne and Dance* and it was a fresh and original composition that is still performed

frequently at band festivals throughout the country.

Chance wrote only a few works for band in his short life. Some of the most performed include *Elegy*, *Variations on a Korean Folk Song*, *Introduction and Capriccio*, and *Blue Lake Overture*. In 1972 at age 40 he was electrocuted in his backyard by a fence carrying a strong electric current.

An incantation is a chanting of magical words or a formula for casting a spell or performing magic. From the composition's opening *misterioso* flute note, this musical incantation is unlike other selections in the standard repertoire. A thirteen-measure first theme is the basis for virtually all of the melodic material in the piece and should be clear and precise. The ascending minor third is important to the structure of the work, and using fewer flutists may improve intonation. Conduct this section *molto legato*, clearly indicating phrase endings in a quiet, controlled manner.

Chance lets us hang precariously on every note before the first Bb clarinet, bass clarinet, and BBb contrabass clarinet entrance in measure 4. This is followed by one of the harmonic devices that becomes a pillar of the composition, the harmonically ambiguous sustained pedal appearing first in the BBb contrabass clarinet and cued in the string bass. Do not omit this note in the absence of these instruments, but write it into one tuba part. With the exception of a brief transition to Db in measure 9, the first theme is in phrygian mode and cadences on D in measure 13 before the *Poco piu mosso* moves to new melodic material.

m. 15 to 19

In measure 15 this motive appears in modified form and loosely based around D. All entrances after the first begin with the first four notes of the phrygian scale and end with a descending minor third. The entrances are one count apart in rapid succession and at the interval of a fifth. This harmony accompanies the modified first theme in measures 19-26. If there is no alto clarinet, write out measures 17-26 for a second bass clarinet; the part is an octave below the second clarinet and not doubled anywhere else.

Give clear cues and releases for low reeds and clarinets in the delicate opening measures; there is so little harmonic clutter here that poor releases are obvious. The subtle shadings of *crescendi* and *diminuendi* are important to bring this music to life.

When the first theme begins again in measure 19, the texture becomes heavier as Chance drops two octaves from the original unaccompanied flute to bassoon, contrabass clarinet, and tuba. Keep the accompaniment moving in this section and dynamics *mp* to *mf*; any more will lessen the later contrast.

The flute trill beginning in measure 19 is the first extended pedal; the slightest bump will draw attention away from the melodic passage below. Alternating entrances on the trill contribute to the mood of the incantation.

While measures 26-32 are clearly part of the incantation, the melody is only a rhythmically modified and augmented version of the first theme with parallel major thirds as the unifying element. The melody appears in the top voice, and the parallelism in lower harmony as the tonal center shifts to what appears to be E major with a Db pedal point and the first percussion entrance, a *pianissimo* bass drum roll.

Measures 26-32

With only the horns absent, measure 26 is the first full ensemble passage; rigorously adhere to a piano dynamic in all parts. These measures sound insecure if players do not count carefully and change chords at the wrong moment; indicate the rhythm of the melodic line to minimize this error. In addition, balance the triads so they are not mainly upper voice. In the absence of two baritones have the student play the bottom notes beginning in measure 26; the upper note is doubled in the tenor saxophone while the lower is doubled only in the bass clarinet.

Use progressively larger pulses for the crescendo in the Db pedal at measure 29 and have those playing triadic parts breathe after the half note in measure 30 to support the transition to *presto*. Chance closes the largo section with triads which ascend a minor third, going to great lengths to have unity during the first thirty-two measures. A small amount of *ritardando* in measure 32 prepares the exciting, rhythmic motives at the beginning of the *presto*.

At the *presto* give an accurate release of the eighth note on the first count of measure 33. With maracas, the mood changes, and the percussion motives are the foundation for the remainder of the composition. Label each motive beginning at measure 35 through the end of the piece. The claves play rhythmic motive *a*, perhaps the most powerful of the five motives, in

Barry E. Kopetz is director of bands at the University of Utah in Salt Lake City where he conducts the Wind Symphony. Kopetz is active as a composer, guest conductor, and adjudicator.

measures 35-52, and each motive serves as an *ostinato* two measures in length repeated over and over. Sectional balance is important because the parts are layered; each motive is equal in texture but may be hampered by inadequate equipment, such as using soft mallets that produce insufficient volume.

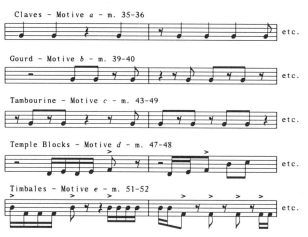

An accurate tempo at the *presto* will establish the percussion motives and missed or incorrect entrances can be avoided with cues. Keep the pedal subdued and use staggered breathing.

Students playing the A pedal often believe they have a boring, unimportant part and lose concentration, causing the note to lack intensity. By marking the percussion entrances on their parts, they will learn to change to the D pedal in measure 53 at the right moment; one player coming in *ff* and heavily accented at the wrong moment will ruin the *subito* dynamic shift by the clarinets, saxophones, and horns at measure 54. Similarly, mark the crescendo in measures 52-53 to preclude anyone playing it early. Cue the first timpani entrance at measure 53 because two measures later it inherits the rhythmic motive *a*.

The series of ascending major triads beginning on F in measure 54-55 are a premonition of what follows. Give a clear beat on count one of measure 54 for a precise entrance of the parallel major triads in clarinets, saxophones, and horns; each section has a complete triad with the fifth doubled at the octave in the outside voices, C-F-A-C. If the alto clarinet is missing, write out the part for a second bass clarinet and in the absence of other parts, make good decisions regarding balance, making sure all four voices are covered.

Chant-Like Motive (m. 57 - 59)

Perhaps nowhere in the piece does the word incantation have a more precise application than

in measures 57-69 with accented repeated triplets sounding like a chanted spell. This passage should not be underplayed and is marked both *feroce* and *fff*.

The ascending minor thirds at the conclusion of each incantation are often played without confidence and precision as the result of poor articulation, producing a muddy, hesitant conclusion to what should be powerful and dramatic. Rehearse the passage slowly and gradually build speed, adding a small crescendo over the final three notes. It is better to take the *presto* at a slower tempo than to stumble through the notes. Cue the woodwinds on count four of measure 59 and in other similar passages as they enter at the same tempo the brass set in the previous measures.

Ensemble balance is important in measure 63-64 for the music to maintain forward motion; it is not enough for the winds to articulate cleanly. The harmonized minor thirds should be at the indicated *ff* for woodwinds and *f* for brass. Rehearse these measures slowly so players can hear the woodwind and brass balance. In this section, the whip is heard for the first time, and Chance remarks in the score it "must be extremely loud and sound like a real whip, or else should be omitted." Make one from two two-by-fours and a hinge; commercially available whips are often too soft and lack crispness.

Rehearse measure 69 slowly and pay close attention to the saxophones' conclusion of the A♭ triad with the familiar three note pattern. Saxophonists often articulate these notes late; a small space before the first sixteenth note helps correct this. In measure 70, there are two unaccompanied whip cracks played *ff* to herald the end of the incantation and beginning of the dance. Cue the whip and do not miss the change of meter to $\frac{3}{4}$. By treating the notes after the whip-cracks in the upper woodwinds and trumpets as an anacrusis to the dance, there is less temptation to rush them. Hold the ensemble back and maintain *l'istesso* tempo.

As the dance begins in measure 71, the meaning of the motives becomes clear. The second theme is based on the first theme and played by the first and second trumpets in measures 71-75. It is a two-measure melodic idea repeated and followed by an uneven subdivision in measure 75. The two measures of melody form the basis of the dance section, which is structured in loose A-B-A-B-A form. The first five measures are defined not so much by melodic content as by the accompanying rhythmic motives, first *a* in the claves, then *c* in the tambourine. The two-measure melody has roots in several of the rhythmic motives, namely interaction between motives *a*, *b*, *c*, and *d*, and is a carefully planned compositional technique that gives the piece unity. The piccolo and flutes play only a portion of motive *d* to support the melodic line of the trumpets in measures 71-75 and the horns have a series of parallel major triads in measures 71-72 corresponding to rhythmic motive *c*. Conduct these measures with sharp, concise motions befitting the dance-like qualities.

Dance Theme (m. 71 -75)

The first seven measures of the next section are also defined by the accompanying rhythmic motives. The tonal center has shifted from G to D and the melody at measure 76 is now in the B♭ clarinets and alto clarinet, but with a twist. The bass clarinet and bassoon have rhythmic motive *f* that adds a wonderfully awkward momentum when coupled with the BB♭ contrabass clarinet's off-beat part, motive *g*.

The second theme repeats the two-measure melody three times, but with a variation the third time as the starting note shifts to concert E♭. Motives *f* and *g* continue, and the horns add a fragment of melody in the rhythm of motive *a*; this statement ends in measure 82 with a return of the anacrusis that started the dance.

Measures 83-87 correspond exactly with measures 71-75 in terms of proportion, key, and rhythmic motives, but Chance reversed the brass and woodwind sections. The horns maintain supporting parallel triads, but the primary color should be the woodwind section. In spite of the

rhythmic drive, there is no percussion beginning in measure 71.

Just as the clarinets and bassoons had the theme in measures 76-82, trombones and low brass inherited it in measure 88-94. Motive *f*, previously in the bass clarinet and bassoon, is divided between baritone, bass trombone, and tuba but essentially remains unchanged. The trumpet and trombone entrance at measure 92 is the third time the two measure melodic idea is heard in major sixths. The fifth and final time the second theme is heard begins with the anacrusis in measure 94 and the full ensemble playing the dance, highlighted with motive *a* in the timpani, crash cymbals, and whip. It is easy to get caught up in the excitement of the music at this point, but all parts should balance.

After a cadance on E♭ in measure 100 there is rapid movement to A in the clarinets. This transition lasts only six counts but prepares the first new melodic material since the beginning of the piece. Conduct these two measures forcefully, indicating *fff* accents before the diminuendo in measure 101.

Chance now presents the third theme, an octave-based melody that occurs between measures 101-104 over a pedal point reflecting the melodic material in measures 15 and 16. Listen to the counterline in the bass and contrabass clarinets to be sure it is played correctly and at the right time. Some conductors use an uneven beat in measures 102-103 to emphasize the melodic line, and others change the meter through measure 114. This creates a slightly varied rhythmic sense in the third theme and if used, mark all parts carefully in advance of the first rehearsal. The advantage to staying in four throughout is musicians seem to play with more confidence, particularly those on the pedal point. The accents in parentheses (>) show which tones to stress.

Third Theme: m. 101 - 106

A gradual increase in volume builds tension in the third theme at measure 110 along with intervallic skips and accents, and the horn entrance in measure 113. The fanfare-like melody beginning on count four of measure 114 releases the tension as trumpets and trombones return with the first theme pitched in D♭.

First Theme - Fanfare Style: m. 114 - 123

The ascending sixteenth notes in the woodwinds from measure 115-121 appear chromatic, but examination reveals this is not so. In measure 115 the oboe part is a D♭ mixolydian scale for the first eight notes repeating the first four notes one octave higher on count four. This is not unusual and the entire line uses a series of parallel major triads. If

students just stab at the notes, the passage will lack the swell Chance intended. Rehearse these measures slowly so finger patterns become natural and students hear the inner parts. There is an exception to the series of major triads in measure 119 when the second clarinet creates a G minor triad with a concert B♭. It is possible Chance meant to write concert B♮ here and some conductors change this.

Cue the brass triads in measure 121 and note that as before, the scoring doubles the fifth of each triad in the outer voices. This melodic sequence prepares the modified first theme now in the low brass and low reeds in measures 122-129. Give a clear release for the entire ensemble on count three of measure 126 before beginning an aggressive pattern on count four and cuing the bass drummer. An implied *sfz* is important on the first count of measure 127, but should be followed by ever smaller beats to achieve the *molto diminuendo*.

Measures 130-147 mark the return of the incantation, specifically the percussion motives that introduced the dance; but are in the same sequence as before, but now occur every two measures instead of four. The A pedal point is still present supporting a B major triad with an F♯ to G tremolo.

Flutes often miss the sixteenth note passage in measure 140 unless cued. Give releases for low reeds and horns in measure 142 and cue the first clarinets on the melodic fragment that recalls the very first notes. Encourage clarinets to play evenly, not overdoing the accent on the final note of each grouping; this melodic fragment aligns with motive *d* in the percussion. Cue the flutes again on the scale passage in measure 147.

Chance now offers a soft version of the *a* motive in measure 151-165 as an ostinato introduction to the horns who play a harmonized version of the first theme in G minor. The first clarinets begin a counterline under the horns in measure 152 that is strikingly similar to the clarinet part of measure 142; this part, marked *pp*, rarely has enough presence and should be brought out for balance. The flute entrance at measure 155 should balance with the horns and clarinets.

Chance abruptly modulates to B♭ major using only the F to B♭ eighth notes in measures 165-166. Trumpets solidify this with parallel triads played fortissimo and the woodwind entrance on the *d* motive. The cymbal crash in measure 170 should be cued, played at the proper dynamic, and allowed to vibrate. The excursion into B♭ major ends on count four of measure 171 as the anacrusis leads back to G minor. Conductors should consider stopping the baton abruptly on count 4 to avoid indicating that the ensemble should play loudly in measure 172; the bass and contrabass clarinets have *subito piano* on the and of four in measure 171 to begin this contrast. Use short, crisp baton motions in measures 172-175 and mark the clarinets *pp* so the flute entrance has more impact without excessive volume.

Recall now the A-B-A-B-A form of the dance in measures 71-99 because the material beginning in measure 176 is similar. Variety comes from the orchestration, but the phrase groupings are identical. Precision between the flutes and clarinets can be a problem at measure 176, and between the bass and contrabass clarinets in measure 181. Bring out the solo second clarinet at measure 185 as it harmonizes the melody a sixth below; the player is usually surprised how important the second part is.

The whip crack at measure 188 signals the descending octave scale passages that have not appeared before and swirl up and down. All other material, both melodic and motivic, is the same, though percussion accents in the crash cymbals and whip fall earlier in the dance than previously. An interesting variation occurs in measures 188-191. The first measure of motive *a* is excluded in the contrabass clarinet, baritone, and tuba; only the second measure off-beats are found.

The excitement of the music in measures 193-199 is the result of combined rhythmic elements in all voices. There is so much going on that no one voice carries the melody. The horns, second and third clarinets, and alto clarinet have harmony in measures 193-196 that should be heard within the busy texture. Percussionists should think of their notes as part of one of the motives to achieve a line. At measure 197 the harmonized line exists between trumpets and trombones. The fifth and final recap of the second theme occurs in measures 200-205.

Chance intersperses two-measure percussion motives with material heard only once. Measures 207-210 are an augmented version of the combined octave skips in measure 101 (the third theme) and the chant-like triplets in measures 57-70. Conduct these measures aggressively with large accentuated beats but no *diminuendo* between the half notes in measure 207. The accented quarter note triplets should be heavily accented without sacrificing good tone quality in measures 209 and 214.

Augmentation of Third Theme: m. 207 - 210

With all but the flutes and trumpets playing the anacrusis to the modified second theme in measure 216, it seems, for an instant, the full ensemble will play with little direction. A subtle change of eighth notes instead of sixteenths in measures 217 and 223, and the 3+3+2 subdivision in measure 221 are hints of differences in approach. These changes culminate at measure 226, the coda, where motives *a* and *d* are modified and combined in preparation for the final trumpet and trombone fanfare fragment based on the first theme. The woodwind sixteenths conclude on a tremolo in measure 230, and the brass statement of measure 232 heralds the final three measures. At the climax the trumpets, oboes, and clarinets have a G major triad while all other voices conclude on a concert G covering six octaves.

Incantation and Dance never fails to delight both ensembles and audiences. With a relatively small amount of melodic material, Chance created a remarkable piece that is brimming with rhythmic vitality. A pioneer in using percussion, he was one of the first to use temple blocks in such a bold manner. *Incantation and Dance* is a valuable addition to the band repertoire, and musicians cannot help but wonder what John Barnes Chance might have written in later years.

From Nocturne and Dance to Incantation and Dance

The Genesis in Greensboro

A biographical sketch of John Barnes Chance for his publicity recounts that the Beaumont, Texas lad was nicknamed Barney to get around his mother's objections to people calling him Jack. Chance described his piano teacher, Miss Jewell Harned, in glowing terms but remarked that under her tutelage he "made rapid progress as a pianist, reaching a level of proficiency by the age of twelve that he never surpassed but, indeed regressed from until today he plays the piano in a loud and ugly manner typical of most composers." At Beaumont High School Chance played in the school orchestra: "It was this opportunity to hear and take part (as a percussionist) in the performance of Beethoven, Schubert, and Shostakovich that lured him into the dubious career he thereafter pursued." He began composing in high school first for orchestra, completing what was "destined to be the only movement of that symphony he finished because soon after he went away to college and discovered what he had feared - that it was not only 'not modern' but was, worse yet, sort-of-Rachmaninov."

After studying at the University of Texas, he married and two years later became a member of the Fourth U.S. Army Band in San Antonio. He arranged music for and conducted the band, but continued to compose chamber and orchestral music; in 1958 he became a member of the Eighth U.S. Army Band in Korea. Returning to Austin, Texas after his discharge from the army, he was manager of a component high fidelity store until the Ford Foundation selected him to be part of a composer-in-residence project.

For the project Chance spent the 1960-61 school year at the Greensboro, N.C. public schools and wrote seven pieces for school ensembles, including his first band composition, *Nocturne and Dance*, which became *Incantation and Dance* in later revisions. Chance worked with Herbert Hazelman, the high school band director and later the custodian of many of Chance's scores

and memorabilia. (While obtaining photographs for this article we first learned that while Hazelman was growing up in Asheville, N.C. his music director was Traugott Rohner, during his second and third year of teaching.) In a report to the Ford Foundation Hazelman includes comments about how audiences and students reacted to Chance's compositions, providing an interesting historical perspective. Of the *Incantation and Dance*, first performed in November 1960, Hazelman wrote: "The *Incantation and Dance* is a brilliant piece for band which has been very well received by students, townspeople, critics, musicians, and

educators alike. At the Asheville concert, the piece received an ovation." Of Chance's *Blessed Are They That Mourn* Hazelman wrote that the composition for voices, strings, horns, and bass drum received a "splendid" audience response, and "students liked the work but were not overly enthusiastic." Students and audiences liked his *Wgoom*, a quickstep march written as a tongue-in-cheek parody, and *Satiric Suite for String Orchestra*.

According to Hazelman, his most popular work was *Capriccio*, a piece for piano and 24 winds that received an ovation at each performance and was "a brilliant work which students adore." His *Ballad and March* for band

238

accompanying chorus also was popular among students and received an ovation in Asheville. Chance's last work for Greensboro was *The Noiseless, Patient Spider* for girls' voices and flutes, and it had not been performed when the foundation report was written.

Copies of original materials for *Nocturne and Dance* still exist at Greensboro Senior High School, though Hazelman speculates that Chance destroyed the original score when he revised it as *Incantation and Dance*. The original included a performance note that Chance wanted Boosey and Hawkes to publish with their edition of the work. In this note, that was omitted, he asks directors to caution students not to play unintended accents in the syncopated measures, so that an effect of mixed meters comes through.

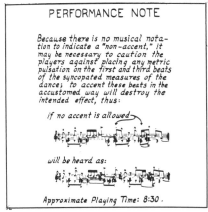

A more interesting discovery was that the original *Nocturne and Dance* contained 31 measures not found in the revised edition. Beginning at measure 205, Chance takes the third theme through a 15 measure ostinato build-up starting in the first clarinet and expanding, part-by-part, until it includes the entire woodwind section.

This ostinato also includes a dynamic pyramid, becoming louder with each entrance, until its conclusion at measure 220. The brass anacrusis to measure 220 signals a fanfare-style statement of the first theme over ascending sixteenths in the woodwinds, reminiscent of measures 203-204 in the Boosey and Hawkes score.

Both versions merge at measure 238 in the original, or 207 in the revised edition, on the third theme now played by the full band. With the exception of the baritone part, the orchestration is identical, but in a different key.

Why Chance deleted these measures from *Incantation and Dance* is a matter of speculation, but the tightened revised version has become a band classic and more than lives up to its original good reception.

Errata

Score: 8, Bassoon: add the tie from the previous measure; 19, Clarinet 3: add p dynamic; 55, Clarinet 2, 3: add an accent to the eighth note; 59, Timbales: add an accent to the eighth note on count 2; 64, Trumpet 1-2: add 'open' to the score; 69, Baritone: add a ∧ to the final note; 71, Alto & Tenor Sax: add f dynamic to the cue; 74, Trumpet 1-2: add a ∧ to the eighth note E; 75, Alto Sax: change the first staccato mark to an accent; 75, Alto Sax: remove the staccato mark from the final eighth note in the horn cue; 75, Horn 1-2: add a staccato mark to the second eighth note; 76, Tenor Sax: add continuation of the slur from the previous measure; 80, Bassoon: add f dynamic; 81, Clarinet 2: the third eighth note should be written Ab not Bb; 81, Alto Clarinet: add a slur to the final three eighth notes; 86, Alto & Tenor Sax: add the slur from the previous measure; 88, Bassoon: add an accent to the D; 74, Trumpet 1-2: add a ∧ to the eighth note E; 93, Trombone 1-2: add a staccato mark to the eighth note C; 93, Tuba: add a staccato to the final note; 99, Alto Clarinet: change the accent on the A to ∧ ; 100, Bassoon: clarify the end to the slur on the final 16th note; 100, Horn 3-4: add an ∧ accent; 108, Alto Clarinet: add a staccato mark to the first note; 111, Alto Clarinet: add an accent to the E eighth note on count 4; 113-114, Oboe: add crescendo culminating in ff dynamic; 117, Bassoon: add a natural sign to the second 16th note on count 4(A); 118, Alto Sax: add a flat sign to the first 16th note (E); 127, Trumpet 3-4: add a2 designation; 129, Tambourine: add the trill designation to the second half note; 141-142, Alto Sax: add a slur from the dotted quarter note across the measure line; 148-166, Bassoon cue: copy the articulation marks and slurs from the bass clarinet part; 155, Bass Clarinet, Contrabass Cl.: remove the staccato from the final eighth note; 156, Flute: remove the whole rest; add half note Eb plus half rest, add tie and slur from previous measure; 156, Trombone 1-2, Bass Trombone: add a tenuto mark to the quarter note; 157, 159, 163, Note that the Eb (concert Ab) in the horns appears here, but not at measure 151. When compared to the

Nocturne and Dance

Incantation and Dance

trombone cue (A natural), it is clear that the conductor must decide upon the intent of the composer and make the score and parts consistent. My preference —change the Eb's on the score to E natural; 165, Trombone 1-2, Bass Trombone: add 'open' designation to the score; 166, Baritone: add a ∧ to the F eighth note; 171, Bassoon cue: copy the articulation marks from the bass clarinet part; 172, Alto & Tenor Sax: add an ∧ to the second note; 172, Alto & Tenor Sax: add p dynamic to the cue; 181, Bassoon: add the slur from the A to the F♯; 181, 183, Clarinet 1: add ∧ to the B eighth note on count 2; 183, Clarinet 1: add an accent to the C♯ on count 4; 188, 190, Woodwinds: decide if it is necessary to add the natural signs to count 3, the second 16th and to count 4, the second 16th; 189-190, Timpani: remove the slur; 191, Horn 1-2, 3-4: add an accent to and of three; 191, Trombone 1-2: add a staccato mark on the first note; 192, Clarinet 1: remove the sharp sign from the final F; 193, Bassoon: add an ac-

cent on the second eighth note; 193, Baritone Sax: add an accent to the final note; 198, Trumpet 3-4: add a staccato mark to the first note; 199, Trumpet 3-4: add a2 designation on and of 2; 200, Piccolo, Flutes, Clar. 1-3, Alto Cl., Bsn., A. Sax, T. Sax: modify the slur to begin on the first 16th note. Currently, it appears to be a continuation of a previous slur; 200, 202, Alto & Tenor Sax: add a natural sign to count 3, the second 16th note; and to count 4, the second 16th note; 202, Clarinet 2-3: change the first note on count 2 to written E; 203, Alto Sax: remove 8va designation; 204, Horn 1-2: change the ∧ on the first note to an accent; 204, Trumpet 1-2: add a ∧ on and of three; 205-211, Gourd: the part is not notated on the score, but present on the part; 205, Timbales: add an accent to the first 16th note; 206, Tambourine: add an accent on the eighth on and of three; 207, Tambourine, Claves: add an accent to the eighth note; 209, Flute: the bottom note of the second quarter should be B, not A (part is correct); 210, Tim-

bales: add accents on the first note of count 1 and the fourth note of count 2; 211, Timbales: add an accent on and of 1; and of 2; and of 3; and of 4; 211, Tambourine: add an accent on the eighth on the and of three; 212, Alto Sax: on count 3, change the natural sign on the second 16th to a flat sign; 212, Timbales: add an accent; 212, Tambourine, Claves: add an accent to the eighth note; 213, Oboe: add a sharp sign to 16th note A on count 4; 216, Horn 1-2, 3-4: add a flat sign to the second 16th note; 217, Horn 3-4: remove the dot from the quarter note A; 218, 223, Piccolo: add staccato to the first eighth note Eb; 219, Trombone 1-2; add a staccato mark on the first note; 220, Trumpet 1-2: add ∧ on eighth note; 222-223, Baritone Sax: slur the quarter note C to the eighth note D; add staccato to the D; 222-224, Whip: add ∧ accent; 223, Oboe: final eighth note C should be Cb.

Piccolo: 95, add an eighth rest on and of one; 194, add an ∧ to the G♯ 16th note; 203-204, add the slur; 218, 223, add staccato on the first eighth note Eb.

Flutes: 73, add an accent on the eight note Eb; 74, slur C-D-Eb together; add an accent to the Eb; 95, add a ∧ to the eighth note G; begin the slur on the first 16th note; 187, add a slur to the two 16th notes; 208, 213, add a sharp sign to the A 16th note, third 16th note on count 4.

Oboes: 86, add staccato to the first eighth note C on count 4; 234, the final 16th note should be C, not Eb.

Bb Clarinet 1: 70, add a ∧ accent to the first note; 106, add a slur to A-G, the second and third eighth notes; 119, add a flat sign to B on count 4, the second 16th note; 160, add a slur to the first note, only the tie is present; 184, add an accent to the C♯; 216, remove the ∧ accent from the 16th note F; add a beam to the first two notes to create two 16th notes; 217, remove the staccato from the first note and change it to a ∧ accent; 221, add an accent to the first note F.

Bb Clarinet 2: 85, the accent on count 2 should be changed to a ∧; 88, add an accent to the eighth note E; 95, add a ∧ to the eighth note A; 112, add an accent to the final eighth note; 174, add ∧ to the eighth note D; 194, 196, add a ∧ to the eighth note Ab; 210, change the accent to ∧; 217, change the staccato mark on the first note to a ∧; remove the staccato from the dotted quarter note G.

Bb Clarinet 3: 83, add a ∧ to the eighth note A; 85, change the ∧ to an accent; 86, add a slur to the 16th notes D-E; 88, add an accent to the eighth note E; 94, add a slur to the 16th notes E-F; 174, add a staccato to the first note C; 192-193, carry the slur over to the eighth note E; 217, add ∧ accent on the first note; 222, add ∧ accent to the G eighth note on and of 2.

Alto Clarinet 53-54, add a tie to the

eighth note G; 59, the two sixteenths-eighth should be written F♯-G♯-A; 88, add an accent to the eighth note B; 95-98, remove the flat sign from the B sixteenth note; 112, add an accent on the final eighth note; 112, change the fourth 16th note to written G; 209, remove the flat sign from the third quarter note F; 217, add an accent to the quarter note C; 221, add an accent on the first note, C.

Bass Clarinet: 88, add an accent to the eighth note E; 193, add sf to the second eighth note and to the last eighth note; 194-198, add sf on the second eighth note in each of these measures; 221, change the ∧ on the F♯ to an accent.

BB♭ Contrabass Clarinet: 104, add the tie from the previous measures; 165, add ff to the final eighth note; 187, decide if the note should be marked sf or p; 193, add a staccato to the second eighth note.

Bassoons: 84, add staccato to the eighth note D; 88, add an accent to D; 100, add a slur to the four 16ths on count four; 102, add a ∧ accent on the A♭; 117, add a natural sign to the second 16th note on count 4 (A); 193, add an accent on the second eighth note; 204, add an accent on the eighth note G; 213, add a ∧ accent.

Alto Saxophone 1: 27, add a slur beginning on the eighth note B; 75, change the first staccato mark to an accent mark; 98-99, slur the F♯ to the G; 109, add a slur to C-E-C; 110, add a slur on the last two eighth notes; 14, add an accent to the fourth eighth note; 172, articulation on the first note in the cue should be staccato, not ∧ ; 202, add a natural sign to count 3, the second 16th note (E).

Alto Saxophone 2: 71, add f dynamic to the cue; 75, change the first staccato to an accent; 80, add mp dynamic to the cue; 110, add a slur to E-E-D beginning on count 2; 172, add p dynamic to the cue; 200, 202, add a natural sign to the second 16th note E on count 3; 203, remove the 8va designation; 216, remove the ∧ from the 16th note C.

Tenor Saxophone: 75, change the first staccato to an accent; 122, remove the flat sign from the third 16th note A; 126, add an eighth rest after the D eighth note; 141, clarify the slur to begin on the dotted quarter note E♭ in the cue; 196, add a slur to the A♯-B 16th notes; 200, 202, add a natural sign to the second 16th A on count 3 and the second 16th E note on count 4; 207-215, note that the Tenor Sax

is divisi in the part like the Baritone though not on the score. Decide how to divide if one on a part. Ex. Bar. take top note; T. Sax take the bottom note; 216, add a ∧ to the first 16th note E.

Baritone Saxophone: 69, add a crescendo; 118, add the continuation of the slur from the previous measure; 171, clarify the accent on and of 2; 181, add f dynamic to the cue; 197, add an accent on the F♯; 198, change the staccato on the first note to ∧ ; 200, 202, add a natural sign to the second 16th on count 3 and to the second 16th note on count 4; 218, add a staccato to the first note.

Horns 1&2: 55, add diminuendo; 63, add sf on count 4; 74, add an accent on and of 3; 75, add an accent on the first eighth note; 125, add crescendo; 188, add 'open' designation; 225, part does not match the score, but the part is probably correct (see m.220).

Horns 3&4: 63, add sf on count 4; 72, add an accent to the final eighth note; 75, add an accent on the first eighth note; 100, add an ∧ accent; 172, add 'muted' designation; add staccato to the first note; 188, add 'open' designation;198, add a ∧ to both notes; 203, add ∧ to the final eighth note; 205, add a ∧ accent; 208, the last notes should be changed to A♭/F; 218, add a slur to the two 16ths; 234, remove the extra accent from the first note; add a ∧ accent to the final note.

B♭ Trumpets 1&2: 70, remove the ∧ accent from the second note; 72, add staccato to the first eighth note; 201, add a slur from the final eighth note to the next measure.

B♭ Trumpets 3&4: 94, add a crescendo; 116, add an accent to the eighth note A♭; 119, add a ∧ to the dotted half note; 209, 214, the fifth note in Trumpet 4 is missing the ledger line for C♭;235, add a ∧ .

Trombones 1&2: 98, add staccato on the first note; 210, add a ∧ accent.

Bass Trombone: 68-69, add the tie; 92, change the staccato on the F♯ to an ∧ ; 98, add staccato on the first note; 165-166, note that the glissando is not present on the score; decide whether to utilize or not; 201, 203, add a ∧ on B♭ eighth note; 218, the final eighth note is F♯, not F natural; 234, remove the staccato from the first note.

Baritone BC: 29-30, add a slur beginning on the eighth note; 140, add a ∧ to the

A♭, 191, add a ∧ to the F eighth note; 210, add a ∧ to the D♯; 215, add a ∧ to the D natural.

Baritone TC: 28-29, add a slur beginning on the dotted quarter note in m. 28 to the dotted quarter in 29; add a dot to the bottom note (D) in measure 28; 79, the final eighth note should be written E, not G; 122, change the C♯ to C natural; 168, the C natural is missing the ledger line; 191, add a ∧ to the G eighth note; 202, add an accent on the eighth note A; 210, add a ∧ to the E♯; 215, add a ∧ to the E; 216, remove the ∧ accent from the F 16th note; 218, add a slur on the two 16ths D-E; 219, add staccato on the first note; 223, add a ∧ on the eighth note E; add a slur to the two 16ths D-E.

Tubas: 96, add a ∧ to the final eighth note F.

Timpani: 69, add staccato to the final note; 95, add a ∧ to the E♭; 149, add staccato to the final note, F; 158, add staccato to the final note, E♭; 192, change the staccato mark to an ∧ ; 199, add sf to the D eighth note; 225, add staccato to the E♭.

String Bass (Not on the score): 82, remove the sf from the final note; 83, remove the sf from the first note; 101, change the dynamic to mp; 104, add a tie from the previous measure; 165, add ff to the final eighth note; 193, add sf to the second eighth note; 208, add 8va designation to E♭ (out of range on some string basses).

Percussion: 57, Tambourine: part is missing; remove the whole rest and copy the part from the score; 68, Timbales: add an accent to the 16th note on and of four; 69, Tambourine: change quarter rest to an eighth rest followed by an eighth note; 96, add ∧ to the Whip part; 135, Tambourine: add an accent to the final eight note; 199, Bass Drum: change f dynamic to sfz; 210, Timbales: add accents on the first note and on count two; 211, Timbales: remove the accent from the first note; add an accent on and of one; place an accent on and of four; Tambourine: add an accent to the eight note on and of three; 215, Timbales, add an accent on the first 16th note; remove the accent from the fourth 16th note; 223, Timbales, add an accent on and of two; 228, Tambourine: add a ∧ to the dotted half note roll; 233-234, Whip: add a ∧ to the quarter note; 234, Tambourine: change the quarter rest on count four to an eight rest followed by an accented eighth note; 235, copy the accents from the score to the parts.

June, 1990

Gordon Jacob's *An Original Suite*

An Interpretive Analysis by Barry E. Kopetz

Gordon Jacob composed such works for winds and percussion as the *William Byrd Suite, Music For a Festival, Giles Farnaby Suite, Flag of Stars, Tribute to Canterbury, Fantasia* (for euphonium and band), and *Old Wine in New Bottles* (for chamber winds).

Though Jacob's interest in wind music is well known, few people are aware of his other contributions as author, editor, and film scorer. He wrote a number of books, including *How to Read a Score, The Elements of Orchestration,* and *The Composer and His Art.*

Jacob was born in London on July 5, 1895 and received his education from both Dulwich College and the Royal College of Music, earning a Doctor of Music degree in 1935. He became a member of the faculty of the Royal College of Music in 1926. A long line of his composition students, including Malcolm Arnold, Antony Hopkins, and Bernard Stevens, went on to successful careers.

An Original Suite is a work in three compressed movements. Unlike the suites of folk songs by Holst and Vaughan Williams, *An Original Suite* comprises newly composed material, hence the title. The instrumentation is that of the British military band: 1 flute and piccolo, 1 oboe, solo B♭ clarinet, 1st, 2nd, and 3rd B♭ clarinets, alto and bass clarinet, 1 alto saxophone, tenor saxophone, baritone saxophone, bass saxophone (or B♭ contra bass clarinet), 1st and 2nd cornet, 1st and 2nd trumpet, 4 horns, 3 trombones, baritone, tuba, string bass, snare drum, bass drum, crash cymbals, and triangle.

Movement I. March

Jacob begins this march in the simplest of all ways: unaccompanied snare drum. Establish a precise tempo here to begin the piece with the appropriate dignity. In measure 3 the winds introduce the first theme, an eight-measure melody centered on G natural minor.

The first note should resonate with quality, so the tempo in the preceding measure must be exact. Use a small beat pattern here and carefully balance the supporting harmonic parts. Measure 11 brings a *forte* repetition of this thematic material, with upper woodwinds joining the texture. Note the first appearance of the crash cymbals. Pay attention to consistent phrasing and articulation, and indicate an unhurried, even quality for the sixteenth-note passages in measures 17-18. Be sure to remove the trill and grace notes from the score in measure 16; they are not present on any of the parts. Two bars of descending transitional material in measures 19-20 close this brief section.

The second theme begins at B and is in the same tempo, but ensembles tend to rush these delightful *staccato* notes. The conductor should maintain the tempo using light, concise pulses, but should not allow the notes to be so short that the ensemble produces a "tut" sound. Each note should have a resonant quality with all the elements of good tone that are produced on longer pitches. The second theme is structured in two 4-bar phrases, only the eighth bar differs from the fourth.

Barry E. Kopetz, an associate professor of music at the University of Minnesota, conducts the Chamber Winds, the Symphonic Band, and the Marching Band. He also teaches wind literature conducting and band arranging.

During the final measure (28) of the theme, ensembles tend to rush as the crescendo heralds the return of the first theme fragment. The conductor should maintain firm control while gradually increasing the size of the pulse in order to prevent a surge in tempo. It helps the percussion section if you add the important entrance of the triangle part to the score in measure 25.

The music returns to a portion of the first theme in measure 29, now supported by a series of descending major thirds in the brasses and woodwinds that give the effect of chromatic harmony. Encourage the performers to stretch each note to the fullest by appropriately drawing pulses with the baton. In measure 33, two augmented VII-I cadences lead the music into two measures of unison transitional material.

Letter C begins *fortissimo* in the brass with a one-measure descending bass line, which repeats six times before moving to a new pitch level in measure 42. It serves as the harmonic support for the third theme, beginning with a five-note anacrusis in measure 37.

The accented *marcato* style of the music calls for a sharp, aggressive beat pattern by the conductor. Ensembles invariably play beats three and four of measure 40 inaccurately because of the quintuplet followed by four sixteenths. Consider having the ensemble articulate the passage several times so the change becomes natural.

The third theme is essentially a two-bar idea, repeated. In measure 42 Jacob moves the material to a different series of pitches, but the idea remains the same. The four measures that follow, 42-45, lead to a return of a modified second theme in measure 46, now adorned with an agile upper countermelody in the flute and E♭ clarinet. The snare drum can help achieve an increase in tension in measures 44 and 45 by playing a sustained even roll to lead into the large bass drum and cymbal crash on the down

beat of measure 46. While the section is marked *ff sempre*, the conductor should ensure clarity of line throughout these measures, perhaps by changing the dynamics in some of the parts to achieve this.

At D the composer uses the rhythm of the first measure of the second theme as the basis of his transitional material. The conductor has an opportunity to build tension during the following four measures; a long *crescendo* gives the most musical effect. Conduct these measures with a precise, accented style on the pertinent counts, being careful to provide a progressively larger pattern as you approach the *sff* in measure 54. Jacob teases the listener by beginning what appears to be another repetition of the first theme; instead he provides a graceful transition that leads to the lyrical pentatonic melody beginning in measure 58.

For a fourth theme the composer created a beautiful melody requiring few notes, and measures 58-64 show his purpose. The thematic material, seven measures long, contains two 3½ measure phrases based on the first six counts of the theme. Through simple extension Jacob created a longer, unified whole.

The contrasting brass writing that begins in the middle of the measure 61 provides a delightful change for the listener, and the gentle triangle attacks on the first three counts offer a beautiful

accompanying resonance to the brasses. The conductor should approach the entire expressive passage with a fluid, *legato* beat pattern, and it helps to mark the melodic parts with the term *espressivo*.

The composer moves the melodic material up a step to C minor at measure 65, modifying the melody slightly in the process but maintaining the 3½ measure unit. A slight increase in the dynamic level heightens this change of key. The return of the melody to its original pitch at measure 72 is accompanied by a parallel line in the third clarinet, bass clarinet, bassoons, tenor saxophone, and baritone saxophone. This additional line harmonizes the original melody at the interval of a third until joined by another line in measure 74. The addition of this third line creates parallel triads in the first inversion

243

(measure 74), eventually leading to the return of the first theme at measure 76. Do not allow the snare drum part to overpower the texture in the measure before F; keep the sixteenth notes even and in the proper tempo.

A distinct, dotted eighth-sixteenth passage accompanies the return of the first theme. This brassy punctuated line is reminiscent of bold, British majesty, an exciting melodic transformation.

The conductor should insist through gesture that the band play the passage in the indicated *marcato* style. The melodic material diverges in its eighth measure at 83 and glides gracefully into the second theme. Steady tempo is critical at this juncture because a rapid scale passage accompanies the second theme. As before, small light pulses help the ensemble maintain tempo. Often this woodwind passage sounds like a frantic race to play all the notes in the given time. For the sake of clarity and good balance, the conductor should use only one flute along with the piccolo and the E♭ and solo clarinets and should encourage balance and matching dynamic variations within the line.

Use strong, fully stretched pulses in measures 92-95. Immediately decrease the size of the pulse for the *piano* dynamic on beat two of measure 96. Maintain strict tempo so the solo and first clarinet cadence just after beat two will be accurate; these instruments enter off the beat and add the root to the augmented triad each time in measures 96-97. Keep the pulses small and precise throughout these measures so the ensemble entrance in measure 98 is accurate and *piano*. Gradually increase the size of the beat throughout the next two measures, conducting the eighth-note triads with quick, sharp motions to get precise attacks on each of these chords.

The movement ends as it began, with a bold unaccompanied snare drum. The bass drum note on the second count of measure 101 should be precise and have sufficient length and volume. The G major triad in the brasses and low reeds on beat three should be breathtaking for the ensemble and the listener alike; keep the initial attack soft enough so all performers, not just the

top ones, can *crescendo*. End this movement with conviction, giving an aggressive, exact release.

Movement 1 — March

Introduction Snare Drum m. 1-2	1st Theme A m.3-10	1st Theme (2x) A1 m. 11-18	Transition (1st th. based) m. 19-20
2nd Theme B m. 21-28	1st Theme A2 m. 29-33	Transition (1st th. based) m. 34-35	Introduction 2 (1 m. repeated) m. 36-37
3rd Theme C m. 38-45	2nd Theme B1 m. 46-49	Transition (2nd th. based) m. 50-53	1st Theme Incomplete m. 54-57
4th Theme Pentatonic mel. D m. 58-64	4th Theme (up a step) D1 m. 65-71	4th Theme Pentatonic mel. D2 m. 72-75	1st Theme (+ marc. brass) A3 m. 76-83
2nd Theme (+ ww C. mel) B2 m. 84-91	1st Theme (from m. 29-32) A4 m. 92-95	Coda (based on m.33 + sn. dr. intro) m. 96-102	

Movement II. Intermezzo

The *Harvard Dictionary of Music*, defines an intermezzo as a "character piece, suggestive of the somewhat casual origin of a piece, as if it were composed between works of greater importance." In *An Original Suite* the music is anything but incidental. This gentle, lovely movement is full of emotion. While it begins in C major, its primary focus is A natural minor. Its one theme is 17 measures in length and is the basis for the entire movement, which has a phrase structure of 4+4+4+5.

Begin the movement with a relaxed, clear preparatory pulse, directed to the solo alto saxophone. Prepare the performers for the *rubato* nature of the music, which should flow freely but with subtle, changing pulses: strict tempo has no place here. Conduct with a *rubato* style and place a slight *ritardando* at the end of the phrases (measures 4, 8, 12, 17).

The indicated tempo (♩ = 80) seems a little

too fast for this gorgeous, lyrical movement. Sing through the theme many times before the first rehearsal to develop an interpretation and tempo that feels correct. The challenge is to communicate this interpretation to the ensemble through the craft of conducting.

The theme in phrases one, two, and four begins in exactly the same fashion and ends the same way; only the middle of each phrase is different. The conductor who realizes this can make important decisions regarding tension and release within each phrase. The third phrase, by nature of its difference from the others, requires an approach that heightens its musical interest. Consider accelerating slightly during measures 9 through 12, playing the third and fourth phrases at an increased dynamic level before cadencing softly. Slow, *legato* pulses will assist the conductor in drawing the expressive phrases from the ensemble. The size of the beat and gesture should inform the musicians of the musical peak in the middle of the final phrase. The entrance of the soft snare drum roll in measure 14 with its accompanying *crescendo* and *diminuendo* helps in achieving a musical interpretation. Retreat from this musical pinnacle rapidly so that the music ends quietly in measure 17. The delayed arrival of the third in the solo clarinet and first horn in measure 17 should be apparent within the texture of the music. Request a little more from these two musicians and indicate a musical breath before beginning the melody a second time on beat three of measure 17.

The second presentation of the melody in measures 18-34 is exactly as the first, only the accompaniment changes. Jacob has woven beautiful, moving lines underneath his melody that serve both as accompaniment and secondary melodic material. A little extra preparation, singing each part and adding notations to the condensed score, will help the conductor understand the importance of these linear parts and shape the lines more musically.

The repetition of this melody presents the challenge of phrasing the primary theme adequately while continuing the gentle, flowing character of these other important lines. Rehearse these secondary lines without the melodic material, as these parts should provide an unbroken, balanced accompaniment to the melody. The musical peak occurs in the same place in the melody as before (measure 31); make sure that the low brass *crescendo* does not cover the melody.

It is easy to end this theme and rush into the quasi-developmental section that begins in

measure 35. Consider placing a *tenuto* mark over the eighth note on beat two that concludes the second presentation of the melody (measure 34) to allow the ensemble to cadence gracefully before continuing. After another musical breath, begin the next section in an unhurried and relaxed style, but be mentally prepared for the musical excitement that follows.

As with most music there are many ways to interpret given sections, and the next 13 measures provide conductors ample creative opportunity. One interpretation is to think of this section as a long *crescendo* culminating in the *fortissimo* in measure 44, gradually retreating to *pianissimo* on the down beat of measure 48. Whatever your plan, let the ensemble in on the secret. Otherwise the music in these measures may stagnate. The composer cleverly takes fragments of his previous melodies and uses them to create musical motion during these precious measures. I prefer to linger on the second quarter note in measures 36, 38, and 40 for musical effect. This brief sequence reaches higher in each appearance and the dynamics should follow along appropriately. The next three bars, measures 41-44, are based on the figure of an eighth followed by two sixteenths that first appears in measure 14, and provide increasing tension. Approach these measures with vigorous pulses that gradually increase in size and tension. Use a slight *accelerando* during these measures, then slow down gradually between measures 44 and 48. Rehearse these measures carefully; fine performances of this movement have ended abruptly, with the ensemble and conductor simply rushing through these measures in one tempo.

Perhaps nowhere in the movement is the condensed score less help to the conductor than at letter C. Examine the parts carefully for the clues necessary to derive meaning from the music. The triplets flowing beneath the texture are played by B♭ clarinets one, two, and three. The indicated "Hns. sust." in measure 48 does not provide a remote idea as to what they are sustaining; however, the part reveals a concert F♯ in octaves, which changes to F, E♭, and D over the next few bars, still in octaves. The conductor should add these notes to the score as a reminder, as well as the solitary triangle entrance on the down beat at letter C.

The melodic line in measure 48 is based on material first presented in measure 9 and requires *molto legato* technique. Take care that the accompaniment doesn't cover the melodic line during this delicate passage. Decrease the dynamic level slightly in measure 53 when the flute and cornet answer the melody of the

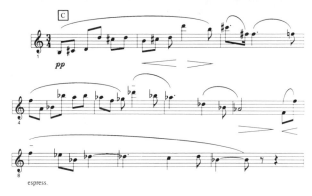

clarinets. Then slightly lessen the pace during measure 56 to glide effortlessly into the deceptive cadence at letter D at a slightly slower tempo, approximately ♩ = 72. A slower tempo here heightens the contrast of the surge that follows in the next measures.

Letter D brings the music to a relaxed passage centered around B♭ natural minor. Jacob appears to wander aimlessly, almost as if he is not sure where to go next with his ideas, but nothing could be further from the truth. The character changes quickly, and the conductor and the ensemble should be ready for the three sixteenths that begin the increase in motion at the end of measure 61. Indicate a building intensity, volume, and tempo during measures 62 and 63. The *fortissimo* E♭ eleventh chord on the down beat of measure 65 should sound with a resolution as should the two brass repetitions (minus horns) at the end of the measure. To accurately place this important sixteenth note in the brass, indicate a clear release of the previous chord precisely on beat two to help the ensemble subdivide the sixteenth note. Ensembles often end up performing it as a thirty-second note, not together, and definitely not balanced. These two brass chords are another peak, and their balance and accurate placement are important to bringing this section to a musical close. Maintain a steady tempo on the accented eighths in measure 65 and the first beat of 66, beginning a slight *ritardando* from this point until letter E.

The music moves so gracefully into letter E that the listener scarcely notices that it ever left the original melody during the previous section. A wonderful transition takes place during measures 66 and 67; exert gentle control over the slightly declining tempo in order not to rush the tempo at letter E. Jacob craftily returns to the original melody, but not at the point of its beginning. Rather he enters on the third phrase (measure 9) as if nothing had been different during the previous section. Ensembles often play too loudly and too fast here. Proceed with

the next nine measures as if there were no more music to be played and the ensemble were approaching a final cadence on the down beat of measure 76. Here the composer begins his simple *coda* based upon a melodic fragment from the last two eighth notes in measure 6 and all of measure 7. He states this material in some modified form five times as the music flows to a restful conclusion.

On the quarter note on beat three of measure 85, it seems as if the music may travel no more. The fifth entrance of the melodic material now mournfully sounds in the low brass and low reeds, just prior to the A minor triad played by the brass in measure 87. Give the ensemble a light, precise pulse to begin (not attack) this note in a *legato* style; listen to the slow bass drum roll that enters with the brass as your model. Bring the woodwinds in lightly, and in good balance; a missed or late entrance at this point spoils this beautiful ending. Release the brasses gently, keeping the baton moving slowly to encourage the woodwinds to execute their *diminuendo* evenly and musically. Pause briefly after the final release before turning to the third movement.

Movement 2 — Intermezzo

Theme (alto sax solo) (4+4+4+5) A m. 1-17	Theme (upper ww's) (4+4+4+5) A1 m. 18-34	Quasi-devel. (based on mel. fragments) m. 35-47	Devel. contd. (based on m. 9 +other fragments) m. 48-67
Theme (based on m. 9-17 A2 m. 68-76	Coda (based on cad. material m. 76-90		

Movement III. Finale

Jacob opens his Finale in somewhat the same fashion as he began the first movement: simply. The clarinets and saxophones immediately begin to play B♭ scale passages in § as opposed to the ¾ meter of the other parts. The conductor should provide a preparatory beat that clearly indicates §, switching to a precise pulse on the first beat of the second measure that clearly implies the proper subdivision. Make an appropriate rebound of the baton during the first bar, stopping cleanly on beat one of the second measure to prepare the brass for their I-V-vi progression at the end of measure 2. Beginning in measure 3, the entering melody requires more attention than the continuing clarinet/ saxophone line. Maintain a precise beat with little rebound. Jacob is quick to confuse the listener concerning key: the opening two bars give the impression of B♭, but the melodic material beginning in measure three indicates G minor.

This movement is sectional in nature, and the first melody lasts a full 23 measures. This long idea falls into an A-B-A structure; the A sections are seven measures each and the B section is eight.

The conductor's beat should reflect the punctuated, exciting style of the music. Insist on textural clarity at measure 10, perhaps cutting the volume back even though the dynamic indication is *forte*. The A theme returns in measure 18, subtly altered as a series of parallel first-inversion major triads in the clarinets and cornets. Do not allow the tempo to falter during these two soft, *legato* bars. Consider adding a *crescendo* in measures 18 and 19 leading to the *fortissimo* in measure 20, and be careful that the ensemble does not rush.

The second section is essentially two 4-measure melodic ideas, repeated at a new pitch level. It begins on a soft note leaving the listener wondering what has become of the melodic material. ⃞B

The rapid series of sixteenth notes in the woodwinds need to be played easily and evenly. The conductor should indicate a rapid *crescendo*, then decrease the size of the pulse immediately in measure 27 when the music drops to *piano*. The entering flute, piccolo, and first clarinet (not

marked on the score) on the descending arpeggio on beat two of measures 26, 28, 34, and 36 should maintain the momentum. These players should be aware that they are part of a melodic line already in progress and should blend dynamically during their brief appearance, marking their parts appropriately.

The four bars from measures 29-32 seem to depart stylistically from what has just transpired. Pay special attention to accents and their correct placement, especially the *sforzando* on beat two of measure 32.

Measure 40 concludes the second repetition of this theme; next, the composer begins a series of arpeggios accompanied by forceful eighth notes on "and-one." Rehearse the two items separately so that the ensemble is aware of the content and the need for precision. The arpeggios should be exact and have adequate volume. The eighth notes need to start softly, then crescendo rapidly and dramatically to the *sforzando* on the down beat of each measure. Maintain balance in each note of these chords and insist that the brass not overblow. Think of each of these bridge measures as slightly louder than the previous one so that the *fortissimo* at letter D builds from a gradual *crescendo* in the previous four measures.

The music returns to the first theme at measure 45, scored with a punctuated off-the-beat accompaniment but remaining 23 measures in length. Because the accompaniment in measures 45-51 plays exclusively off the beat after the first note, the conductor should give the ensemble a dry beat with no rebound. You need rhythmic precision here; eliminate any motions that will draw the ensemble to play early.

At measure 52 the B section of the melody takes on a new appearance through the use of the 6/8 accompaniment used earlier to support the first phrase. Cornets outline the melodic idea in a series of rapidly articulated sixteenths; this passage needs to align perfectly with the upper woodwind melody. Not apparent in the score, the cornet parts alternate groups of sixteenths, rather than one part having the entire passage. Cutting back the cornets to one on a part may help achieve the desired clarity and balance. Add the important triangle entrance in measure 56 to the score; it should be cued by the conductor. The third phrase begins in measure 60, but the dynamic leap that occurs earlier in measure 20 finds no place in this presentation. Maintain a small pulse to make sure the flutes and upper woodwinds do not miss this important difference. The last three clarinet eighth notes in measure 66 are important and lead the

Suite

ensemble back to a repetition of the entire section; neglecting them will lead to a ragged transition.

The exact repetition of measures 25-66 gives the Finale the shape that Jacob desired: A-B-A-B-A (coda). The coda begins at measure 67 through the use of a single four-measure

measures 74-75

phrase from the beginning of the B section. Measure 71 is a stroke of scoring genius from the master: a C♭7 with the seventh serving as the bottom note (third inversion). Jacob has the bass instruments attack the seventh followed by a partial arpeggio outlining only the root and fifth in the upper woodwinds. He now borrows the fanfare-like idea from movement two, measure 64, and states it with authority, completing the seventh chord. This he repeats in measure 72, using an F7, again with the seventh in the root. Studying measures 74 and 75 reveals a cleverly disguised progression of inverted C♭7 to F triads and inverted F7 chords leading to C♭ triads. The composer still manages to cadence in B♭ on the first count of measure 75 before concluding the movement with an implied V-I cadence. The conductor needs full command of all forces in measures 71 and 72, using strong, accented pulses. Have the

ensemble drop down to f or mf at measure 73 to prepare for a *crescendo* that continues through the unison B in the final measure; this helps to obtain proper balance as the upper woodwinds aggressively navigate their arpeggios in measures 74 and 75. You may slightly delay the final accented B♭ in octaves for musical reasons; the amount of accent left to each conductor's discretion. Allow the bass drum and cymbals to resonate freely until the final release.

Movement 3 — Finale

Introduction WW scales (7+8+7) m. 1-2	A 1st Theme A-B-A1 (8+8) m. 3-24	B 2nd Theme C-C1 m. 25-40	Bridge WW arpeggios accented cad. m. 41-44
A 1st Theme A—B—A1 (7+8+7) m. 45-66	B 2nd Th. (2x) C-C1 (8+8) m. 25-40	Bridge (2x) WW arpeggios accented cad. m. 41-44	A 1st Th. (2x) A-B-A1 (7+8+7) m. 45-66
Coda (2nd Theme, Bridge + scales m. 67-78			

Errata

Movement 1: March

4   Bass Cl.: remove tenuto mark from quarter note B on count 4; Bsn. 2: add tenuto mark to E♭ qtr. note

6   Cornet 1 (same as solo cornet part): add slur from dotted qtr. note A to 8th note B

7   Oboe: add staccato marks to final 2 8th notes; Solo Cl.: add staccato to final 8th note

10   Score: add slur to qtr. notes in 2nd stave; Solo Cl.: slur ends on final 16th note G; Cornet: 1: add accent to count 2

11   Flute: add note to play piccolo 8va basso for 2 bars; Cornet. 1: add forte dynamic; Score, Trom. 1, Bari. Sax., Str. Bass: add staccato to 1st 8th note

12   Score, Bari. Sax., B♭ Contra Bass Cl., String Bass: add tenuto marks to qtr. note on count 2

13   Score, Trom. 2: add staccato to 1st 8th note; Cornet 1: add staccato to 8th note on count 1

14   Cornet 2: remove tie to the 1st 8th note

15   Score: add staccato 8th note G on beat 4; Bsn. 2: remove staccato from G 8th note

16   Score: remove trill from beat 3; remove grace notes; add tenuto marks on final qtr. and 2 8th notes; Bsn. 2: remove staccato from G 8th note; Trom. 3, Bass: remove staccato from 8th note on count 1

17   Cl. 3: slur should connect entire measure; Trom. 3: add crescendo to forte and a diminuendo

18   Score: add staccato marks to D and C 8th notes in 3rd stave; Score, Tpt. 1: start slur on dotted qtr. G and finish on final 16th note F; Trom. 1, 3: remove staccato mark on count 1

19   Score: slur 1st 2 8th notes in 2nd stave; add staccato to 2nd 8th note

21   Bass Cl.: add piano dynamic to measure; B♭ Contra Bass Cl., String Bass: add staccato on count 1

22   B♭ Contra Bass Cl.: add staccato on count 1

23   B♭ Contra Bass Cl.: add staccato on count 1

26   Trom. 2: add staccato marks to 3 A 8th notes

28   Trom. 2: add staccato to final 4 8th notes

29   B♭ Contra Bass Cl.: add staccato on count 1; Cornet 1: change final 8th note to D

31-32   Score: change all tenuto marks to accents

31   Trom. 1: change final 8th note to C

33   Cornet 1, Str. Bass: add staccato to 8th note on count 1; E♭ Cl.: add staccato on beat 3

34   Bari. Sax.: remove slur from count 2; replace with staccato marks

35   Bass Cl.: count 3, 2nd 16th should be changed to an A; Bsn. 1-2: connect slurs on counts 3 and 4

38   Score: add staccato to G 8th note on count 4, top stave; Cl. 3: slur extends to the 8th note A on count 4; Bsn. 1-2, Tenor Sax., Bass: add marcato beneath the measure

38-43   Score: add accents to all 8th notes in 2nd stave; add accents to all half and qtr. notes in 3rd stave; Oboe: change 2 16ths to 2 32nd notes

39   Flute: add tenuto marks to counts 3, 4

41   Flute: add tenuto marks to counts 3, 4

42-43   Cl. 3, (Alto Cl.), Alto Sax.: change staccato marks on final 2 8ths to accents

42   Bsn. 1-2: add ff *sempre* beneath the

measure; Cornet 1: add staccato marks to 1st 4 8th notes; add accent to count 3; add staccato to 8th note E on count 4; Trom. 2: extend slur to include 8th note D on count 4

44   Flute: add tenuto marks to counts 3, 4

45   Score: add staccato marks to 1st 4 8th notes; add tenuto mark to count 3; Flute: add tenuto to count 3

45   Bass Cl.: remove staccato mark from F♯ qtr. note; B♭ Contra Bass Cl.: remove tenuto mark on count 1

46-49   Solo Cl., Cl. 1, 2, 3, Alto Cl., Alto Sax., Hn. 1-4, Cornet 1-2, Trpts.: add 2 tenuto marks, 4 staccato marks to each measure (added for score and part consistency)

50   Cornet 1: add accents to 1st 2 qtr. notes

51   Cornet 1: add accents to 1st 2 qtr. notes

52   Bass Cl.: add accent to qtr. note F; B♭ Contra Bass Cl.: add accent to count 1; Cornet 1: change slurs over 16th notes to "slur-2-tongue-2"; add accents to 8th notes on 1st and 3rd counts

54   Score: add slur from qtr. note D to 8th note F in top stave

58   Bari. Sax.: add piano dynamic

60   Bsn. 1: extend slur past end of measure

60-61   Bsn. 2: continue slur to the 2 qtrs. in measure 61

64   Trom. 1: add staccato to D and F 8th notes

67-68   Bari. Sax.: continue slur from measure 67 to the 2 qtrs. in measure 68

68-69   Cornet 1: start slur on D-E qtr. notes and connect to next measure

75-76   Trom. 2: extend slur to 8th note B♭

76   Solo Cl.: slur from qtr. note E to final 8th G; Trom. 3: add marcato beneath measure

77-78   Bari. Sax.: slur qtr. note A to 8th note E

77 Str. Bass: change accent on E to ∧

78 Score: add slur from qtr. note D to 8th note F in top stave; Solo Cl.: slur from qtr. note E to final 8th G; Trom. 1: add accent to final qtr. note B♭

80 Flute, Oboe, E♭ Cl.: add 2 staccato marks on beat 3; also add staccato mark on beat 4 in flute, oboe, and E♭ clarinet

81 Score: end 8va designation on count 4; E♭ Cl., Oboe, Cl. 2-3, Alto Cl., Alto and Tenor Sax., Euph.: add tenuto mark on qtr. on count 3

82 Trom. 1: change all E♭'s on counts 2, 3, and 4 to D

83 Oboe, Solo Cl., Cl. 1-3, Alto Cl., Alto Sax.: add slur from trill on count 3 to last note in measure; Cornet 2, Trom. 1-2: add two staccato marks to the 8th notes on count 2

87 Score: add staccato marks to 8th notes in staves 2 and 3

91 Score: add piano dynamic before crescendo; Score: add staccato marks to all 8th notes in staves 2 and 3

92 Score, Flute, Cl. 2, Bass Cl., Bari. Sax., B♭ Contra Bass Cl., Str. Bass: add staccato on 1st 8th note; Cornet 1: add forte dynamic

93 Bass Cl.: add tenuto marks to all 4 qtr. notes

94 Bsn. 1: remove staccato mark from 8th note D; Oboe: move ff dynamic to count 2

94-95 Score: change tenuto marks to accents in staves 2 and 3

96 Bari. Sax.: add slur from A♯ to B; B♭ Contra Bass Cl., Str. Bass: add staccato on 1st 8th note; Trom. 2: add staccato underneath the accent on count 1; Euph.: add accent over staccato mark on count 1

97 Bari. Sax.: add staccato on G 8th note

100 Score: add staccato on 1st 8th note

101 Score: add staccato to G 8th note in 3rd stave; B♭ Contra Bass Cl.: add staccato to count 3 8th note; Bass Cl.: add ∧ accent to half note E

Movement 2: Intermezzo

1 Alto Cl.: part is identical to alto sax. part. Consider deleting solo line at beginning; Score: tie qtr. note C in 2nd stave across the bar line (see cl. 2); Bsn. 2: dynamic for cue is *pp*

2 Alto Sax., Alto Cl.: end slur on dotted qtr. note, start new slur on next 8th

4 Bass Cl.: change written A 8th note to F

5 Score: add crescendo to measure

5-7 Bari. Sax.: slur from 2 8th notes to half note C♯ in measure 7

6 Score: add diminuendo to measure; Bass Cl.: last 8th in bar should be changed from F♯ to E

6-8 Bass Cl., Bsn. 1: continue slur to half note in measure 8

7 Cl. 1: continue slur to measure 9 with no break

7-8 Bsn. 2: slur in cued part should continue to the half note in measure 8

9 Cornet 1: add cresc. and dim.

10 Oboe: begin slur on final 8th and connect to slur in measure 11

11 Bsn. 2: add crescendo to part

11-12 Cornet 1: slur entire 2 measures together; Trom. 2, 3: add slur beginning on 1st qtr. note, ending on 3rd qtr. in measure 12

13-14 Score: end slur on last 8th note of measure; begin new slur in next measure;

Bari. Sax., Str. Bass: add crescendo beginning under last 2 8th notes; begin diminuendo in the middle of the next measure

14 E♭ Cl.: slur extends over entire measure plus next 3 8th notes

15 Score, Euph.: continue slur over 3rd stave into next bar, ending on dotted qtr. in measure 17; Bsn. 2: add piano dynamic; Bari. Sax.: add piano dynamic; slur carries over to next measure

16-17 Hn. 1, 2: tie final 8th note A to 1st 8th in next measure

17-26 Score: take copy of cl. 2 and add slurs to 2nd stave of score

23 Oboe: add slur to final 2 8th notes and connect to next measure

25 Score, Oboe: slur last 2 8th notes together

26 Score: slur ends on final 8th note; Bsn. 2: place slur from qtr. note G♯ to A in next measure; Str. Bass: add crescendo marking

27 Score: slur ends on dotted qtr., 8th note G begins next slur

28 Tenor Sax.: add slur to 3 qtr. notes

29 Tenor Sax.: slur 1st 3 qtr. notes together

30 Score: add 2 tenuto marks to last 2 8ths beneath bottom stave; Bari. Sax., Contra Bass Cl.: add 2 tenuto marks on 8th notes on count 3; Str. Bass: remove slur on count 3, add 2 tenuto marks

32 Flute: add dot to qtr. note C, remove 8th rest

31 E♭ Cl.: add tenuto to 8th on count 2; extend slur over entire measure; Bass Cl.: remove tenuto mark on count 1, add tenuto mark to 2nd qtr. note; Cornet 1, Bari. Sax., Contra Bass Cl.: add tenuto to 8th note on count 2

36 Score: add piano to beginning of crescendo

39-40 Score: indicate flute 8va in top stave; Score: add tenuto mark under dotted half note in the bottom stave; Bari. Sax.: add tenuto mark under dotted half note

41 Score: add slur to the 8th and 2 16ths at the end of the 2nd stave

41-43 Score: add tenuto marks to each qtr. note in the bottom stave

42-43 Bari. Sax.: add tenuto marks to all qtr. notes

43 Bass Cl.: add tenuto marks to all 3 qtr. notes; Contra Bass Cl.: add tenuto mark to qtr. note on count 1; Cornet 1: Continue slur to qtr. note G

44 Bass Cl., Bsn. 2: add staccato to 8th note on count 1; Score: add staccato mark under B♭ 8th note in bottom stave

46 E♭ Cl.: add natural sign in front of 8th note G

48-49 Score: slur extends across the bar line in 1st stave

49 Score: triplet part slur ends on last note of measure, begins anew in next measure

54 Score: triplet part ends at conclusion of the last note of count 2, begins anew on the next count

55 Score: espressivo designation is missing

57 Oboe: connect 1st 8th note to the slur

57-58 Score: connect all 3 8ths at the end of the 3rd stave to the slur in measure 58

59 Score: add piano under final 8th in top stave

59-60 Score: tie dotted half note F in 3rd stave to next measure

61 Bsn. 1: remove crescendo

63 Contra Bass Cl. add tenuto marks to last 2 qtr. notes, add flat sign to lower octave D

64 Contra Bass Cl.: add tenuto to count 1

65 Bass Cl.: add accent to 1st 8th note B natural

67 Flute: add diminuendo underneath the measure

68-69 Score: connect slur to next measure in top stave

69 Str. Bass: change final pitch to E on count 3

71 Bass Cl.: change slur to encompass only the 3rd count; Bari. Sax.: change slur over counts 3-4 so that the 1st 8ths are slurred, and the last 2 receive tenuto marks

72 Solo Cl.: remove tenuto from count 1, extend slur over entire measure

73 Bass Cl., Bsn. 1-2, Contra Bass Cl., Str. Bass: add tenuto mark to the 1st qtr. note

73-74 Bari. Sax.: add tenuto marks to last 4 8th notes plus 1st qtr. in next measure; Contra Bass Cl.: add tenuto mark on count 1

74 Score: add tenuto to qtr. note in 2nd and 3rd staves; Bass Cl.: remove accent from count 1, add tenuto mark on count 1; slur the last 4 8th notes together; Str. Bass: add tenuto to qtr. note on count 1

74-75 Score: begin slur on final 8th note E in top stave and continue into next measure; Hn. 1, 2: break slur in 1st part at conclusion of measure 74

75 Str. Bass: add diminuendo for the entire measure

77 Bass Cl.: change crescendo to diminuendo

78 Bsn. 1: add *pp* dynamic to end of diminuendo; remove *pp* from measure 79

78-80 Hn. 1, 2, 3, 4: slur extends to 1st qtr. of measure 80; Hn. 1, 3: new slur begins on 2nd qtr.

79 Bsn. 1: place *pianissimo* at the beginning of measure 78

79-80 Score: extend slur to include qtr. and 8th note A in next measure

82 Bsn. 1, Contra Bass Cl.: add diminuendo beneath measure

83-86 E♭ Cl.: break slur at conclusion of the 2nd 8th in measure 84; connect slur between measures 84 and 85

84 Score: end slur on 2nd 8th note G, begin new slur on next 8th note A

84-85 Cl. 1: continue slur between measures

86 Score: end slur on final 8th note in the measure on staves 2 and 3; Str. Bass: change dynamic to *ppp*

Movement 3: Finale

3 Score: add *sf* to 8th note in 3rd stave

7 Flute: add staccato to 8th note G

8 Score: add accent to 1st and 3rd 8th notes in top stave; Flute: remove staccato on 1st 8th note; replace it with an accent

9 Score: remove accent on count 2 in 2nd stave; Bass Cl.: add crescendo under last 2 8th notes; Str. Bass: remove staccato marks over final 2 8th notes

10 Score, Oboe: change accents on 1st 2 8th notes to tenuto marks; Cl. 3: add tenuto mark to qtr. note A

12 Score: add staccato to 8th note G on count 2; Cornet 1: add staccato marks to 2 16ths plus 8th note

13 E♭ Cl.: add staccato on 1st 8th note B

14 Score: add 2 staccato marks to count 2, top stave

Grainger's Lost Letters on *Lincolnshire Posy*

by Mark Grauer

"When an audience of 7,000 or more sits through a concert nearly two and one-half hours in length, it would appear that the attraction is fairly genuine. And when the tremendous program is gleefully welcomed from beginning to end, the sage reporter will hazard the guess that the listeners thought it great." (Milwaukee Journal review, Monday, March 8, 1937)

With these opening comments, Richard Davis, music critic for the *Milwaukee Journal*, began his review of the Grand Concert of the American Bandmasters Association's 1937 convention in Milwaukee, Wisconsin. This concert was filled with much of the best music of the day under the batons of the greatest directors of the era, including Percy Grainger conducting the first performance of *Lincolnshire Posy.*

Joseph Bergeim was a Milwaukee director and composer who organized the 1937 A.B.A. convention. He died in 1968 and left an attic filled with stacks of Boosey & Hawkes band method books, notebooks of harmony notes from a correspondence course in the early 1930s with F.H. Losey, a multitude of band and theory textbooks, and even a few old band uniforms. At the bottom of one box I found an old concert folder filled with photographs; including some autographed photos

Percy Grainger (signature)

Percy Grainger on *Lincolnshire Posy:* I would like as many alto and bass clarinets as possible, and the more flutes and piccolos the better.

from Charles O'Neill, A.R. McAllister, Harry Stares, and Karl King, as well as pictures of bands that Bergeim had conducted. In the back of this yellowed band folder was a brown envelope that contained a variety of correspondence regarding the 1937 A.B.A. National Convention, letters of congratulation from Erik Leidzen, Edwin Franko Goldman, Frank Holton, Frank Simon, and Herbert L. Clarke and a telegram that slid out of the pile.

> 1937 Feb 3 PM 6:02
> Joseph Bergeim, 3010 North 9 St Milw
>
> Grainger coming to Milwaukee to conduct his compositions stop Letter follows.
>
> Edwin Franko Goldman

The American Bandmasters Association commissioned Grainger in December 1936 to write two band works to premiere at the upcoming convention. Goldman persuaded Grainger to conduct the world premiere of these works. Attached to Goldman's telegram were three letters, including one dated August 1936 from Frank Simon, president of A.B.A., declaring "...nothing would please me more than to have our next convention in your wonderful city...I think that a great concert with an array of Bandmasters, such as we have, could fill the great auditorium of yours."

The other two letters in this group were written in January and February 1937 by Edwin Franko Goldman, the honorary life president of A.B.A. Goldman wrote of trying to get N.B.C. to broadcast the grand concert at the end of the annual convention. He proposed that the band remain after the concert "and repeat the three or four most important numbers" a second time for a radio broadcast from 11:35 pm to midnight. He felt that the publicity the national broadcast would bring the band movement outweighed the concern of getting money for the broadcast, but it is not clear whether the broadcast was made.

I also found in this envelope five letters from Percy Aldridge Grainger to Joseph Bergeim in February and March, 1937. They were amazingly well preserved, the paper still crisp and unyellowed with the passage of the years, and provide a rare insight into the preparations for the premiere of two Grainger works for band, the *Lads of Wamphray March* and *Lincolnshire Posy*.

The correspondence between Joseph Bergeim and Percy Grainger began as Bergeim organized the convention. The first of the letters was dated February 22, 1937 with Grainger inquiring when he should arrive in Milwaukee for the rehearsals, adding, "Mr. Goldman suggests that I send you the band parts of my numbers as soon as possible. This I shall do after returning to White Plains on Feb. 24, as soon as possible. 3 numbers of the Suite I can send you around Feb. 25, the March a day or so later, & the 2 other numbers of the Suite later still." Four days later Grainger wrote: "Today I am sending you the band parts (almost complete; there may be soprano saxophone & string bass parts to follow) of 3 numbers of my *Lincolnshire Posy*. (The other 2 numbers of Linc. Posy I will bring with me to Milwaukee). Tomorrow I expect to send you the band parts of *Lads of Wamphray March* (almost complete)."

The letter suggests he arrived in Milwaukee Friday morning March 5 at "about 8:00 or 9:00 o'clock" so he would "be ready for a band rehearsal at about 9:00 (or 10:00) o'clock in the morning". On February 27 Grainger had completed *Lads of Wamphray March* and sent the parts to Bergeim in Milwaukee with the following letter: "I am sending you today the band parts of the *Lads of Wamphray March* all except the following parts: all saxophones, alto clarinet, bassoons I & II. These I

Mark Grauer is the band and orchestra director at John Marshall High School in Milwaukee, Wisconsin and assistant conductor of the Cudworth-Milwaukee American Legion Band, formerly called the Blatz Band or the Milwaukee Symphonic Band. He notes the assistance of Thomas Slattery, Burnett Cross, Stewart Manville, and several of the musicians who performed at the Lincolnshire Posy *premiere in 1937, with special thanks to Frederick Fennell for encouragement on this article.*

must send or bring later." Then came a surprising passage as Grainger continued his instructions regarding the band for the performance:

> Mr. Goldman says you are going to have plenty of alto & bass clars (6 of each?). I would like awfully if as many as possible alto & bass clars took part in my pieces. Also the more flutes & piccolos double any flute & picc. parts the better.

This is intriguing because many conductors believe that *Lincolnshire Posy* is best performed as a wind ensemble piece with only one or two players on each part. This request was repeated before the convention, in Grainger's final letter dated March 1, 1937:

> Mr. Goldman says you are going to have 4 alto clars & 4 bass clars...I shall bring 2 parts for alto cl. & 2 parts for bass clar of the numbers not already sent. Will you (if possible) have an extra alto cl. & extra bass clar. part made of the numbers already sent -if convenient?
>
> I appreciate yr wanting the parts promptly & will do my best - I sat up last night writing parts & have worked thru 4 complete nights already.

Grainger worked diligently to complete the scoring in time for the performance in Milwaukee. He wrote to Bergeim of his travel plans to insure he had enough time to take care of all the perform-ance details. In the letter of March 1 he writes: "As I cannot rehearse with the band until Sunday morning, my wife & I will not arrive in Milwaukee before Saturday evening...We shall go straight to Hotel Schroeder & I will be available there that evening to correct any mistakes in my band parts your people may have discovered."

He was scheduled to conduct five movements on the concert. Two were unfinished, but he worked feverishly and rehearsed all five movements with the band at the Ernest Williams Band School in Brooklyn, New York before sending them to Milwaukee. The letter continues: "Two more numbers of the 'Linc. Posy' I am rehearsing tomorrow afternoon (Wed) in Brooklyn. After the rehearsal I am planning to hand them to Mr. Goldman (who leaves tomorrow afternoon for Milwaukee) so he can give them to you on Thursday evening. If Mr. Goldman can do that it will be safer and quicker than any other way."

The convention began on Friday, March 5, and the members were treated to a number of concerts on Friday and Saturday. On Friday the band-masters enjoyed a concert performed by the University of Wisconsin Band with Ray Dvorak and a host of guest conductors. Captain Harry Stares, resplendent in his red and white socks with a bright blue full dress kilt, was the highlight of the first concert. Saturday afternoon's concert featured the Milwaukee All-City High School

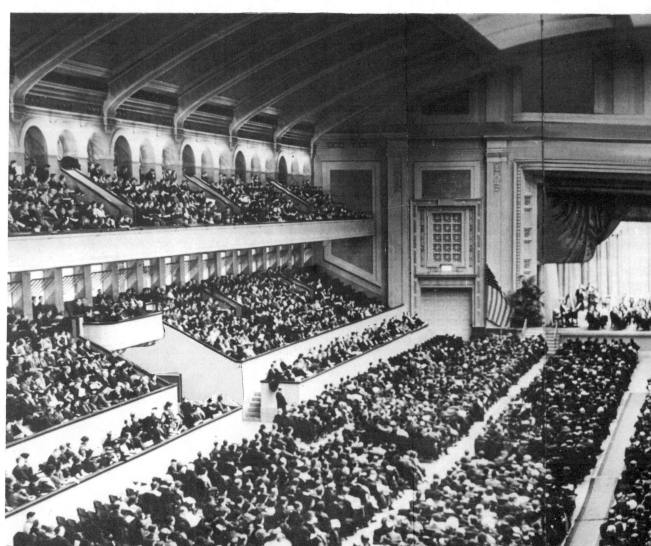

Band with another slate of famous guests upon the podium. The concert was followed by the annual banquet of the A.B.A. membership at the Hotel Schroeder. Meanwhile, in a room in the same hotel, Percy Grainger had arrived and went over his new pieces.

Sunday was a busy convention day, and the band for the Grand Concert had assembled in the Milwaukee Auditorium to rehearse with the numerous conductors. The rehearsal began promptly at 9:00 a.m. and lasted until 4:00 p.m., and reportedly each of the fifteen conductors was allotted three times the length of the piece they conducted for rehearsal. The newspaper reported that there was even a timekeeper with a stop watch to ensure that no director took more than his share. After his allotted time, Grainger gave an interview to a Milwaukee Sentinel reporter. When asked about composition, he asserted that a composer's "work is all done in his head....I do all my work while walking around in my comfortable if somewhat expansive army boots. This writing business is merely thought transference for the instrumentalists' benefit." The newspaper account describes how, after smoothing his attire and hair, he "hustled off to the Auditorium to usher into the musical world his *Lincolnshire Posy* and *Lads of Wamphray*".

What the reporter did not know was that the rehearsal had been difficult for Grainger. The band, sponsored by the Local #8 of the Musicians Union, was made up primarily of members of the band from the Blatz Brewery American Legion Post and for the occasion was called the Milwaukee Symphonic Band. These players were unaccustomed to the complex harmonies and rhythms that *Rufford Park Poachers* and *Lord Melbourne* presented. Grainger maintained his calm throughout the rehearsal but was frustrated by the difficulties the band had with his music. He later wrote that the band was "keener on their beer than on the music". Finally the decision was made to drop the two difficult movements from the performance. Musicians who played in the band for that performance still remember how informal Grainger was during the rehearsal. One man described him as "very persuasive" and "very loose jointed" on the podium, in contast to the more dictatorial style of many conductors of that era.

The band for the Grand Concert had 86 members: 6 flutes/piccolos, 2 oboes, 1 English Horn, 24 B♭ clarinets, 4 alto clarinets, 2 bass clarinets, 1 contrabass clarinet, 2 bassoons, 1 contrabassoon, 2 alto saxophones, 1 tenor saxophone, 1 baritone saxophone, 1 bass saxophone, 4 cornets, 4 trumpets, 7 horns, 5 trombones, 1 baritone, 2 euphoniums, 6 tubas, 2 string basses, 5 percussion, 1 harpist, and 1 organist. The concert began at 8:15 p.m. in the Milwaukee Auditorium on Sunday, March 7, 1937. The literature selected for

A.A. Harding, Glenn Cliff Bainum, Harold Bachman, Harry Stares, Ray Dvorak, and Joseph Bergeim

the program was challenging for any band, and the conductors were demanding. Eight of the seventeen selections were premiere performances.

Program

"The American Bandmaster" (First Performance) by J. Gigante, conducted by Joseph Bergeim, North Division H.S., Milwaukee, Wisconsin

Malaguena (First Performance) by E. Lecuona, arr. by Paul Yoder, conducted by Harold Bachman, University of Chicago

"Builders of Youth Overture" (First Performance) by Charles O'Neill, conducted by Captain Charles O'Neill, 22nd Regiment Band, Quebec

Selections from "The Bartered Bride" by B. Smetana, conducted by Raymond Dvorak, University of Wisconsin

Overture to "Salvador Rosa" by Antonio Gomes conducted by Captain Taylor Branson, U.S. Marine Band

"The Music Goes Round and Round" arranged and conducted by Captain Charles Benter, U.S. Marine Band

"His Honor" by Henry Fillmore, conducted by Henry Fillmore, Cincinnati

"Fraternity Overture" by Herbert L. Clarke, conducted by Herbert L. Clarke, Long Beach Municipal Band, California

Festival March (First Performance) by Henry Hadley, conducted by A.R. McAllister, Joliet H.S., Illinois

"Buffo" (The Buffoon) (First Performance) by Ernst Toch, arranged and conducted by Glenn Cliff Bainum, Northwestern University

Overture to "Prince Igor" by Borodin, conducted by A.A. Harding, University of Illinois

"Barnum and Bailey's Favorite" by K.L. King, conducted by Karl L. King, Fort Dodge Municipal Band, Iowa

"Lincolnshire Posy" (First Performance) by Percy Grainger, "Lads of Wamphray March" (First Performance) conducted by Percy Aldridge Grainger, White Plains, New York

"Holiday Overture" (First Performance) by Erik Leidzen, conducted by Edwin Franko Goldman, The Goldman Band, New York City

"Mardi Gras" from Mississippi Suite by Ferde Grofé, conducted by Frank Simon, ARMCO Band, Cincinnati Conservatory of Music

"The Stars and Stripes Forever" by John Philip Sousa, conducted by Frank Simon

Approximately 7,000 people attended the program, largest ever to that time for an A.B.A. Grand Concert. Both Milwaukee newspapers carried extensive coverage of the convention and also reviewed the concert. Emmerling wrote of the band's performance: "The Milwaukee Symphonic Band acquitted itself nobly of its exacting task. Performing effectively so varied a program as that

Joseph Bergeim (1895-1968) became the band director at North Division High School in Milwaukee in 1925 and remained there until his retirement in 1953. By 1930 his group was the Wisconsin State Champion Band and soon thereafter he was elected to membership in American Bandmasters Association. He collaborated with Joseph Skornicka in writing the Boosey & Hawkes' *Band Method* and *Band School* technique books, and on several Rubank method books. His forte was that of composer and arranger of band music, and he wrote 60 marches, including *The Skywriter*, *Chimes of Victory*, and *Music in the Park*. His marches were delightful and tasty and the trios always had terrific melodic lines.

Bergeim was an exacting conductor, and many of his students still work as professional musicians. During his tenure at North Division High School, it was not unusual for Edwin Franko Goldman, Percy Grainger, Frank Holton, and others to drop in to work with his band. Bergeim conducted and played baritone horn in various ensembles including the Blatz Brewery American Legion Post Band and the Mukwonago, Wisconsin Fireman's Band, taking a trolley car more than 30 miles each way to reach Mukwonago.

offered last night, and under the leadership of 13 directors of decided individuality is asking pretty much of anybody's band." After describing the various pieces on the program, he continued with these comments about Grainger's works: "Karl L. King preceeded the appearance on the podium of one of the bandmasters' special guests, Percy Grainger, whose first offering was three parts of the yet unfinished "Lincolnshire Posy." Mr. Grainger's second offering, also brand new, was a lengthy concert march, "Lads of Wamphray" which he composed on a train about a week ago. The train ride was probably a tedious one."

The reviewer from the *Milwaukee Journal*, Richard Davis, also noted the success of the concert and commented upon the musicianship of the band: "The concert did demonstrate that Milwaukee has band musicians who can meet the demands of men who presumably are most exacting. The program, moreover, was a thorough test. All the refinements and experiments of modern band music were introduced at one time or another and there could have been no complaint with the way the bandsmen met the difficulties. And the night program was played after a day of rehearsing under the different conductors. It would be hard to imagine an ordeal more severe."

However, Davis was not as generous with Grainger's compositions in his review: "And there is much to be said for the virility and honest directness of the old school band music. When composers attempt too much, as Percy Grainger

unmistakably did in the pieces he presented Sunday night, there is no gain, but rather a loss."

Several days later on March 10 while journeying home from Milwaukee, Grainger wrote another letter to Bergeim. "We cannot thank you enough for all your many kindnesses! It was such a joyous occasion & you made everything so comfortable & practical for us.
Would it be too much to ask you to let me have one of each of the evening papers about the concert - if convenient?
What a lot of beautiful copying of the parts of my pieces you had done! May I pay for these? I am so glad to have these extra parts."

Any disappointment Grainger may have felt about the first performance of *Lincolnshire Posy* and *Lads of Wamphray* did not dissuade him from seeing these compositions published and performed. All five movements of *Lincolnshire Posy* were performed three months later by the Goldman Band in New York City. The Milwaukee Symphonic Band is still in existence today, known as the Cudworth-Milwaukee American Legion Band and is the oldest American Legion Band in the United States.

My explorations into the works of Joseph Bergeim led to a fascinating look at the premiere of one of the masterworks for band. Particularly through Grainger's comments about his preferred instrumentation, his composition and intentions have come alive. In spite of Grainger's frantic efforts to complete the work on time, he produced a milestone in band literature. □

Remembering How Grainger Conducted *Lincolnshire Posy*

by Harry Begian

When Harry Begian was a student at Wayne State University, the band performed Lincolnshire Posy *under the direction of Percy Grainger on two of his visits to the campus. The following are recollections of Grainger's musical interpretation and comments.*

Grainger was such a remarkable personality that we hung on everything he said or did. He had a tremendous knowledge of music of all periods but came across as a non-conformist and an eccentric. On several occasions some of us asked Grainger a wide variety of questions about his music and about music in general. Quite often his answers were laced with references to Renaissance or English Tudor music or facts about English history that influenced music. Percy Grainger was the most knowledgeable musician

these undergraduates had ever met. At one concert we heard Grainger as piano soloist when the band accompanied him in a performance of the Grieg Piano Concerto. What we heard and saw of Grainger on this occasion was a musical artist who had wonderful control of his instrument. As a conductor Grainger was not the most graceful person on the podium; his physical movements were rather rigid, jerky, and he jabbed a lot, especially in *marcato* and accented passages. He used his left hand sparingly in conducting and kept it in his trouser pocket most of the time. He didn't cue with his hands, giving cues by gazing in the appropriate direction. When he used his left hand, it was often rather spasmodic.

In rehearsal Grainger's keen ears detected the slightest imperfections of rhythm, style, or

> On two occasions Grainger conducted the "Rufford Park" section at half the tempo indicated. The tempo printed on the score is wrong.

balance, although he seemed less likely to correct slight pitch deficiencies saying, "Strict in-tuneness is a pedant's goal, not a practical musician's."

Grainger spoke softly with a decidedly British accent and had a high-pitched voice. His speech was sprinkled with invented words: undowithoutable, intuneness, art-skills, personality-impresses, upbuild, race-redeeming, mankind-rescuing, blind-to-gain, and saviour-heros. Grainger stood out in a crowd as the individualist and eccentric that he was.

Although he dressed informally, favoring short-sleeved cotton shirts open at the collar, white-duck trousers, army boots, and a Harris-tweed jacket, he was neat and clean. I first saw Grainger five minutes before the first rehearsal he conducted at Wayne State University as he walked down the street to the band building in frigid weather with a knapsack on his back but without a hat or coat. He came into the building, went directly to the band director's office, shed his jacket, got out his scores, and was on the podium at the appointed time.

Grainger was certainly not conservative or traditional in his music, dress, speech, conducting, or philosophy. He was different in so many ways that he seemed to be from another place, even another planet; yet what he said was so incisive that there was never any doubt about what he said. It came as a shock to see him at concert time, elegantly dressed in tails, presenting a striking picture.

In rehearsals Grainger was strictly business: no diversions, story-telling, or joking; his mind concentrated on only the music. When he stopped, he told why and explained how to correct the problem. Because we played *Lincolnshire Posy* from his manuscript parts, there were mistakes; when he heard a mistake, he jumped from the podium with a pencil in hand, raced over to the player, and corrected the part on the spot. He raced back and jumped up on the podium calling out a rehearsal number. Grainger always moved quickly in rehearsals but never seemed to be in a rush with players. Although his conducting and baton technique were not refined, he spoke succinctly and positively about what he wanted to hear.

The rehearsals and concerts Grainger led at Wayne State University are unforgettable memories. I can recall them as clearly as though they took place a year ago; each tempo, style, and inflection that Grainger asked for in his music is still vivid. I particularly liked the folk-tunes Grainger used in *Lincolnshire Posy* and was impressed by his rich harmonies, the wind sonorities and the mixed meters, polytonality, and polyrhythms.

I asked him about the mixed meters in the folk songs in *Lincolnshire Posy*; he replied that they were notated rhythmically and metrically as they had been sung for him.

I believe conductors should study and perform music as they hear and feel the tempo, style, and balance; but in the case of *Lincolnshire Posy* I make an exception. When I played this work under the composer's direction, the tempos, styles, and balances were matters of conviction with him; and I always try to reproduce them as nearly as he did. Having said this, I will add that it is hard for me to accept some of the performances by some fine conductors and bands over the years.

For those directors who are interested in how Grainger approached this enduring masterpiece, here are some of the nuances of Grainger's performances at Wayne State University.

"Lisbon" (Sailor's Song) is a strophic song, and each appearance of the theme is treated as a variation. The timpani arpeggio on A♭ should be heard beginning in measure 19, but should not blot out the tune. The "Duke of Marlborough" countermelody in the horns at measure 36 should be heard, but again not cover the melody in the clarinets. Often horns play this countermelody so loudly that balance is destroyed and the tune is not heard. The sonority that Grainger terms nasal and reedy in the low reeds is rarely heard at measures 60-63, and the final cadential resolution in measures 71-72, B♭ concert resolving to C concert, is often underplayed by tenor saxophone and English horn.

"Horkstow Grange" (The Miser and his Man, a local Tragedy). Once again Grainger treats a folk-song strophically with variations. Grainger never played this movement as slowly as I so often hear it played; in fact, he played it somewhat faster than the ♩.= about 76 indicated in the score. The slurs in this movement should be treated as phrase indicators so the dotted-eighth and sixteenth figures are clearly defined and heard. Most players tie the 16ths to the dotted 8ths, and the result is a quarter note and not ♫. Play the melodic grace-note in the woodwinds in measure 10 cleanly and rhythmically by treating it as a sixteenth note pickup and stressing beat one ♪|♩♩♩|. Grainger asked the soloist in measure 19 to play meditatively while applying his own dynamics with a bit of ritenuto (linger) at measure 25. His use of a sixteenth note pickup to the tune in measure 30 confirms this treatment of the grace note at measure 10 and the grace note in the final measure as well.

"**Rufford Park Poachers**" (Poaching Song). Many conductors and players have difficulty understanding the metrics, expressive qualities, and proper interpretation in the canonic section of the opening and closing sections of this movement. Even Grainger seemed to have difficulty memorizing the metric changes in this movement and invented what he referred to as a "seeing eye score". He used a special score, which was color coded (water colors) painted on ordinary 20 lb. grocery bags. He painted the notation in various colors on the unstaffed grocery bag sheets in a large notation about six inches high to show the correct metrical schemes. The metrical changes could not be missed on that large score, but the only difficulty was that it conveyed only note values and metric changes without indicating what the notes were.

Even today most conductors have difficulty teaching and conducting this movement; imagine how unusual it seemed to the university band conductors in the early 1940s. I think that the "Rufford Park Poachers" and "Lord Melbourne" movements should be audition requirements for any band conductor applying for a university position. These two movements reveal a conductor's baton technique, metrical and rhythmic understanding, musical flow, expressiveness and pacing.

Over the years I have been astonished to hear this movement performed at break neck speed. The indicated tempo of ♩ =132 is an error! On each of the two years Grainger conducted *Lincolnshire Posy* with our university band, he used a tempo only half this fast, one close to ♪ =132. Some otherwise excellent performances of this piece are ruined by playing it at ♩ =132 and producing something that sounds like the accompaniment to a Mickey Mouse movie.

Though ♪ =132 is an appropriate tempo, Grainger conducted this movement using a quarter note beat at ♩ =66, and the tune sounded as it would with a folksinger.

Another misunderstanding about "Rufford Park Poachers" is that Grainger preferred Version B over Version A. We did read through Version B once in rehearsal because many of the players were eager to hear the difference. Although our soprano saxophonist played the solo in Version B beautifully, Grainger performed Version A at both concerts. This is a contradiction because he stated his preference that the solo be played on a soprano saxophone, an instrument he played in an army band during World War I.

"**The Brisk Young Sailor**" (who returned to wed his true love) is again an eight-bar song treated strophically with variations. Grainger conducted this at about ♪ =92 as the score indicates and made the tune sound sprightly, by styling it as

The tune is deceptively simple but is technically complicated and demanding in measures 11-12 and the woodwind obbligato that moves like a whirlwind in measures 18-25. Grainger took some time to balance the fugato section between oboe, soprano saxophone, and bassoons in measures 25-34, which is a section conductors should carefully work out. The balance of the obbligato to the baritone solo from measures 18-25 is a rare instance of questionable scoring; the part calls for

Percy Grainger

robust baritone playing to cut through the accompanying woodwind obbligato. Grainger did not slow the tempo leading to the hold at the end of measure 39 or in 40-41, but this never convinced me musically. I perform this by slowing down progressively from meausres 39 through 42, resuming the original tempo at measure 43.

The stretto-like coda in measures 43-45 was clearly pronounced in clarinets, trumpet, and trombone but Grainger carefully balanced the clarinets in measure 46 and the second alto saxophone resolution of A♭ to F in measures 47-48. Grainger maintained the same tempo from measure 43 to the end; he did not slow down in measures 46-48 as is often heard in present day performances.

"Lord Melbourne" (War Song), along with "Rufford Park Poachers," has problems for both players and conductors in the opening and sections at letters B and C. Grainger conducted both sections at ♩=100 and insisted that all eighth and sixteenth notes receive their full lengths.

This treatment contradicts notations in the score page under N. B. in which he explains two ways to play the opening phrase and adds that, "The bandleader should give free rein to his rhythmic fancy just as folk singers do," and that "each note with an arrow above it may be beaten with a down beat." Grainger did not follow these instructions when he conducted this movement but always kept strict time, conducting a regular three-pulse on the triplets and long fermatas on all half notes at phrase endings.

Grainger picked off the eighth note anacrusis at measure 2 without much preparation and asked the horns for sharp accents and a big crescendo in the measure before B. The tempo at measure 14 was considerably faster than the ♩= about 92 as indicated in the score and slowed down with the baritone entry at measure 24, resuming the faster tempo with the brass entry in measure 28.

The rhythmic interpretation of the clarinet melody at measure 45 is almost always played incorrectly; instead of playing the triplet in one beat as notated, it is invariably played.

The fermatas in measures 50-51 can be conducted either by indicating a release of the held note on beat two and giving a sharp beat three, or by making beat three the release of the fermata. Grainger gave the release after beat two and a sharp beat three. In the final two measures, the descending melodic line should not be covered up by the ascending, descant-like part in the soprano brass.

"The Lost Lady Found" (Dance Song) is the easiest of the six movements to conduct and play, but there are some important sylistic and interpretive ideas that Grainger made clear. In rehearsing this movement the style of the tune is generally

staccato throughout, with the heaviest accents on the first beat. Accents marked *sf* on the third beats correspond to short, violent kicks that Grainger mentions in his prefatory notes. The full brass chords in measure 18 are to be sharp and short but should not overwhelm the melody.

Grainger asked the horns and baritones to play the accompaniment figures with the eighth notes more like sixteenths This interpretation seemed to give a lift to the tune. At measure 50 the piccolo and alto clarinet tune three octaves apart should be legato, and the quarters tongued with a "dah" syllable. Beginning in measure 50, players often mistake the phrase lines of the melody for slurs, and play the repeated quarters as half notes.

The countermelody in saxes, horns, and tenor brass from measure 82-93 is often overplayed; Grainger stressed that the melody was not to be covered at any time. He asked for a solid crescendo from measure 122 to 130, where the tuneful percussion, as he called it, came in for a rousing ending. As loud as this ending was played, audiences often did not seem to realize that this was the end of the piece. At the completion of *Lincolnshire Posy* there always seemed to be a long silence before the applause began.

The popularity of the Grainger composition seems to grow with the passage of time, and the applause for this work may never stop. □

Harry Begian has appeared as a conductor, adjudicator, and lecturer in the United States, Canada, and Australia and is Director Emeritus of the University of Illinois Bands

Vincent Persichetti's *Psalm for Band*

by Barry E. Kopetz

Vincent Persichetti was a rarity among composers of his time, writing many works for band while others wrote one or two. Conductors are indebted to him for his efforts during the struggle for professional recognition of the band.

Persichetti was born in Philadelphia in 1915 and studied theory, piano, and organ. By the age of 16 he was already a church organist in Philadelphia. He received his undergraduate training at Combs College and advanced degrees at the Philadelphia Conservatory, studying composition with Paul Nordoff and Roy Harris and conducting with Fritz Reiner. His commissions included works for the Philadelphia Orchestra and the Koussevitsky Foundation.

In an article by Rudy Shackelford for the 1982 spring issue of *Perspectives of New Music* Persichetti was asked how he began writing for band and replied,

> I haven't as yet become involved in writing for the band! My earliest works were stimulated by the sound of winds. In 1926 my grade-school chamber group — oboe, horn, and bassoon (the Angelucci brothers), plus soprano sax, violin, and piano — performed arrangements of hotel and symphony music. Then, in 1929, came my Op. 1, *Serenade for Ten Winds* and in 1934 the *Pastoral for Woodwind Quintet*. I'd been composing in a log cabin schoolhouse in El Dorado, Kansas, during the summer of 1949, working with some lovely woodwind figures, accentuated by choirs of aggressive brasses and percussion beating. I soon realized the strings weren't going to enter, and my *Divertimento* began to take shape.

Persichetti's attitude toward the band, a word he did not avoid using, solidified in his early years. In a 1964 article on his *Symphony No. 6 for Band* that appeared in the *Journal of Band Research* he said, "One should no longer apologize for the word (band). Band music is virtually the only kind of music in America today (outside the pop field), which can be introduced, accepted, put to immediate use, and become a staple of the literature in a short time."

Moderato

In the beginning of *Psalm for Band* (Elkan-Vogel) Persichetti designates the three B♭ clarinets as solo instruments. To convey the delicate scoring, make sure that the solo clarinets balance with the bass clarinet, giving equal weight to each part. The tempo at the opening, ♩=104 seems a bit fast for this gorgeous music. A slightly slower tempo at about ♩=96 gives the musicians and the audience the chance to enjoy every rich tone of this hymnlike presentation. Give a definite preparatory beat, and take care that the four musicians crescendo and diminuendo while maintaining proper balance. One player producing more or less than the others detracts from this music.

Conduct a large crescendo in measure 8 to prepare for the fortissimo horn, euphonium, and tuba entrance in the following measure. Broaden your beat patterns, striving for the fullest note length possible. The widely spaced major and minor triads of these bars allow each instrument's color to be clear, and the contrast of these chords to the homogeneous sound of the clarinets is wonderful, but the bass drum roll should not overpower the brasses in measure 11.

In the opening of *Psalm* Persichetti treats the

Barry E. Kopetz, an associate professor of music at the University of Minnesota, conducts the Chamber Winds, the Symphonic Band, and the Marching Band. He also teaches wind literature, conducting, and band arranging.

band as a chamber ensemble, a basic characteristic of his scoring. Full band sound is not part of his general palette, and he expands the musical color through combinations of instruments without disturbing the continuity. Asymmetric phrase units are present but emerge so naturally they are hardly noticeable. For example, in measures 8 and 9 the composer overlaps phrases to achieve musical continuity, a frequently used technique in the piece; listen to be sure the sections hold phrases to full length.

Measure 12 reveals another of Persichetti's essential characteristics, tonal ambiguity. As the brasses release a Bb triad on count one, the tutti clarinets enter on a perfect fifth, Bb and F. The listener is left to wonder if he is hearing major or minor. Persichetti's purpose is not clear until a measure later on count two when the important second clarinet line resolves on concert Db. When conducting the passage be sure that each passing tone gives life to the forward motion of the phrase, and encourage the musicians to bring out the moving lines in such passages. The suspense for the listener is delightful.

In measure 17 the somber, dark quality of the trombone section provides a color contrast to the dominant clarinet sound of the preceding phrase, again highlighting the chamber aspect of Persichetti's scoring technique. The composer often uses only the colors essential to reveal his plan, which requires confident players to perform soloistic lines. Continue to give smooth, legato pulses to ensure the flow of the music intended by the composer.

Bring to the fore the cornet solo in measure 24 to magnify its melodic importance. Balance the upper woodwind E major triad carefully at measure 27, and allow the quarter notes to be prominent. This is the most rhythmically active bar up to this point. Be certain to examine the two-octave chord change on count one of measures 27 through 29 because the progression (E major-D maj7-E major) occurs extensively throughout the *Psalm for Band*. It is a harmonic structural unit that serves to unify the entire piece.

The three-part writing that begins at measure 27 continues at measure 34, now in one octave, heavily doubled. Be sure to study these measures carefully, noting which parts carry similar lines. The composer already begins to achieve a sense of unity by reusing material from measures 12-17, though in slightly abbreviated form.

Conduct the cornet and trumpet entrance in measure 38 with a firm pulse to emphasize the unifying effect of the Ab-Gbmaj7-Ab progression. Take care to switch to an espressivo beat pattern on the down beat of measure 42. Too often conductors indicate this pulse in a way

that sends the wrong interpretive message to the ensemble. Practicing in front of a mirror may help overcome this problem.

One charming aspect of the opening of the *Psalm for Band* is the ease with which Persichetti moves from triad to triad. In his book, *Twentieth-Century Harmony*, Persichetti wrote,

> Any tone can succeed any other tone, any tone can sound simultaneously with any other tone or tones, and any group of tones can be followed by any other group of tones, just as any degree of tension or nuance can occur in any medium under any kind of stress or duration. Successful projection will depend upon the contextual and formal conditions that prevail, and upon the skill and the soul of the composer.

In essence, the composer should be able to place sound after sound in musical fashion, and Persichetti's mastery of this is fascinating to observe.

In measure 45 the composer again blurs the major/minor distinction on count one. The Bb clarinets release a second inversion B minor triad just as the horns and euphonium enter on B major. This tonal ambiguity is emphasized at measure 48 where the woodwinds sustain an A major triad while the flutes, Eb clarinet, and first cornet outline a melodic idea centered on A minor. Balance the woodwind chord so the expressive nature of the melody comes through the texture.

Measures 52 and 53 exemplify how Persichetti achieves unity in part by using a specific sequence of chords transposed to various pitch levels; here the progression appears again in the woodwinds. It is easy for the music to become somewhat stagnant between the first measure and the first tempo change at measure 82, so emphasize an expressive approach to musical phrasing and remember the key unifying elements to keep these passages flowing.

Measure 58 contains the timbral interchange that Persichetti uses so effectively. Brass section writing is followed by woodwind section writing with the composer taking advantage of color differences and chord relationships. Conduct these measures with authority because they are intended as dramatic statements, and maintain good balance between the brass and woodwind chords. Do not allow the woodwinds to play their entrances with less boldness than the brasses or you will not achieve the desired effect. Be sure that the ensemble knows exactly what to expect musically as a result of each gesture.

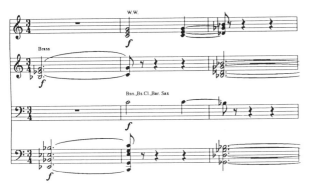

The first count of measure 66 is an important climactic moment in the *Psalm* because the full ensemble plays simultaneously for the first time. While it is not indicated on the score, the conductor may want to emphasize the Gb major triad through an agogic accent. Persichetti rarely uses the full force of the ensemble in this manner, so it seems only fitting to savor this moment in the music.

At measure 73 Persichetti returns to the unadorned clarinet texture of the opening measures, minus the bass clarinet. Conduct in a legato pattern listening for precise changes in the quarter notes. The solo bass in measure 78 provides the root of the A major triad and should be in proper balance with the Bb clarinets. Encourage the tubist to treat the music as if he were part of the clarinet section. Also note the importance of the eighth notes in the bass drum part, which should be full and well rounded (no accents and no muffling of the drum).

Now comes one of the more delicate portions of this opening section. The entrance of the oboes, bassoons, and saxophones in measure 82 is often strained in quality. Consider using one oboe and balance the oboe and bassoons carefully against the full saxophone section. Too loud an entrance destroys the transition to the approaching piu mosso; starting the notes weakly is even less desirable. Be sure that all musicians breathe deeply and have adequate air to achieve the pianissimo. If you do not use the Eb alto clarinet in your ensemble, consider giving the concert Bb to the first chair second clarinet. This important note is doubled in the second alto saxophone, but the clarinet color adds a warm quality to the sound. A small amount of ritardando during measure 82 will assist in providing a most musical contrast to the piu mosso.

It is interesting to note that the texture at the beginning of the piu mosso is the same used to begin the piece: three solo clarinets plus bass clarinet. To leave no question in the minds of the performers about the new tempo, provide a clear, smooth change of pulse to achieve the character being established. The beat pattern should remain legato, and use appropriate decay at the various cadential points.

A careful study of the measures beginning at 83 reveals interesting information for the conductor. The composer begins his music with a three-measure phrase on a Gb triad, following with a two-measure phrase. Neither phrase concludes with a sense of finality in a traditional sense; the listener expects more. Persichetti simply reuses the same material in measure 88, up a step in Ab minor, overlapping this second three-measure phrase with another two-measure phrase. Note how often Persichetti uses the quarter note on count four followed by the half note and quarter to complete phrases. For example, an extension based upon this rhythmic

Photo by Louis Ouzer

figure begins with the anacrusis to measure 93. He uses this particular idea many times throughout the music, and being aware of its importance will assist in decisions regarding dynamic shading. Careful study of each phrase as a small unit and within the entire work will allow the conductor to develop a sense of the music's high points and points of rest.

Persichetti again presents his melodic material in measures 97 through 99, one half step higher in G major. The music seems to move with increasing intensity due to the new pitch level, and the addition of the euphonium to the bass clarinet part provides a subtle contrast in orchestration. Consider adding intensity to this restatement and a bit more volume. Provide the ensemble with necessary momentum leading to the crescendo in measure 103, and encourage the percussionist on suspended cymbal to play out in measures 102 through 105 to assist in building intensity. Note the repeated rhythmic unit at the end of many phrases, which the composer uses to lend additional unity to his ideas.

The woodwind choir, minus the bass clarinet and the baritone saxophone, provides a dynamic climax on the final count of measure 108 and the next measure, containing wonderful chords that should be full of emotion. Conduct them with appropriate emphasis to obtain the rich fortissimo Persichetti requests.

One way to interpret the measures from 110 to 116 is to think of them as one musical idea constructed from small units. The three chords that begin in measure 110 foreshadow the Allegro Vivace that occurs later in measure 127; conduct them with vitality and authority. The timbral interchanges that occur the composer again scores in chamber fashion to emphasize the color differences of the various brasses. Not readily apparent are the voicing similarities between these measures and previous measures, which lend unity to the music. Conduct these measures with the knowledge that they are leading to the full brass choir on the final count of measure 115, and maintain this dramatic feeling until the resolution upon the Eb triad in measure 117.

One of the most precious passages in the *Psalm* is the series of chords in measures 117 through 119 in the flutes, oboes, Eb clarinet (doubled in the first oboe), and solo Bb clarinet. The flute line is reminiscent of the melodic materials first introduced by the solo Bb clarinet at measure 83 and should be clearly heard. In addition this line serves an important harmonic function by providing an independent voice in the chord progression and, hence, should balance carefully with the other parts. To achieve this balance consider decreasing the number of flutes to two. Provide a cue to the first cornet and horns in measure 119, and help the first cornetist resist the tendency to rush to the concert A♮ on count four. This passing tone changes the chord from a C♯ minor to first inversion A major triad, before finally resolving on a B major triad; listeners should enjoy the passing tone before cadencing in the following measure. Give equal care to similar upward moving resolutions, which occur throughout the piece. Do not allow the ensemble to play them as just notes; they are important linear ideas that bring order to Persichetti's design.

Between measures 122 and 126, a ritardando brings this beautiful first section of the work to a restful conclusion, which should be a musically satisfying statement. Consider reducing the number of clarinets to one on a part from measures 123 to 126 to achieve a balance and effect similar to the beginning of the composition.

Allegro Vivace

At letter E the second major section of the *Psalm* begins, offering a complete change of character. Persichetti replaces the quiet, restful nature of the earlier music with aggressive chords played marcato and rapid, swirling scalar passages in the woodwinds. The section begins with bold chords from the trumpet and cornets doubled an octave lower in the euphonium and trombones. Bass drum and tenor drum add resonance to the third chord and should be played with a solid attack. The chord sequence is the same one introduced earlier (A-G maj7-A), but in the new, fiery tempo of the Allegro Vivace, the sequence sounds fresh and new. Note the tenuto marks over the brass quarter notes and be sure that the ensemble gives these notes adequate length.

An accurate tempo is all-important at this juncture. If the conductor sets the tempo too fast for the ensemble, the music sounds frantic and out of control. If it is too slow, the music loses its vitality and natural musical momentum. Persichetti's designation of ♩=152 provides for maximum excitement in this music, but ensemble clarity and control is crucial. Rehearse this section carefully, slowly at first; and perform it only as rapidly as the ensemble is capable. I have heard excellent performances of this music at a slightly slower pace. The only danger is that the conductor will choose an overly ambitious tempo and place the ensemble at risk. It is better to carefully select and maintain the tempo throughout than to start too fast and have to slow down as the music propels itself forward. In short, be sure the preparatory pulse is exact.

Conduct with the necessary energy to bring this music to life. The pulses should be crisp, quick, and imply the length note desired from the brasses. The addition of the bass drum

playing on the rim at measure 133 provides an important contrast, which should be as rhythmically precise as the upper woodwinds it is supporting. The oboes, E♭ clarinet, and the B♭ clarinets present new material placed in polytonal fashion above supporting chords in the trombones and horns. Such clear polytonal relationships are present throughout Persichetti's music and are characteristic of his style within the *Psalm*.

At measure 135 woodwinds and brass appear to be engaged in a rival relationship. The brasses offer the familiar three-chord sequence, while the woodwinds reiterate the little rhythmic motive first introduced at measure 133, now in three octaves. Precise, short motions of the baton will assist the woodwinds in performing these driving staccatos. Following a brief section based on the interval of a descending minor third (measures 138 to 141), the first cornet begins a melodic line based on the same interval, but having its upper notes ascending in whole tone fashion. Be sure this line receives emphasis, and provide an appropriate accented gesture on count three of measure 142 for the instruments providing accents beneath the melodic idea.

A gesture of syncopation on count four of measure 143 will encourage the woodwinds and horns to be precise as they enter. Studying the next few measures again reveals how cleverly Persichetti is able to repeat material with subtle modification. His mastery of using the smallest melodic/rhythmic fragment and uncovering its potential is remarkable. To fully appreciate this facet of the *Psalm*, the conductor should spend hours studying this score and deciding the relative importance of all the parts. Often, the material that seems to be accompanimental is far more important than it appears at first glance. An examination of all brass, saxophone, bassoon, and bass clarinet parts from measures 144 to 147 illustrates this point.

The second appearance of the full ensemble playing simultaneously appears on beat two of measure 149. This sequence of chords should have maximum impact because the composer uses the combined forces infrequently at the fortissimo level. Stretch each motion of the baton to draw these rich, triadic sounds from the ensemble, being careful to maintain the tempo.

The brass section needs to play with confidence during the measures beginning at 152. These melodic fragments all hold equal importance and should balance dynamically. I prefer to drop the dynamic level slightly at measure 152 and provide a long crescendo from this point up to measure 160. Bring out the descending low brass line at 158 by conducting in a precise, accented style.

The material at measure 160 demonstrates the composer's ability to present a unison melodic line that is brimming with life and propulsion. Conduct aggressively, being careful that the ensemble does not shorten the second eighth note in measure 161; add a tenuto mark over this note. At measure 161 the tenor drum is an equal partner in the exchange, so the performer should play in a forthright manner using the stick or mallet preferred by the conductor. This tenor drum part bridges the woodwind line to the alto/tenor saxophone and horn parts, and the accented staccato from the brasses and saxophone on count one of measure 162 must be precise and secco. The music is sheer fun at measure 164 with the woodwinds almost scolding the brass section. Be sure the brass responses are properly punctuated and not rushed. I think of the measures from 164 to the end of 169 as one cohesive unit made up of three shorter phrases in a 2-2-3 structure, which gives order to the music.

Persichetti adorns the repeat of the melodic material at measure 171 with a countermelody in the piccolo, flutes, Eb clarinet, second Bb clarinet, and first alto saxophone. This counter-line has a fuller, broader quality than the melody and should be treated as such. The ensuing hocket in the horn and low brass in measure 174 is a delightful change of pace and should literally jump from the texture. Note that the chords outlined by this appearance are the same three the composer has used so profusely to lend unity to the piece. The bass drum part (again on the rim) at measure 175 is a rhythmically contrasting part, providing momentum; it should be cued. The tenor drum serves a similar function in measure 179, providing a sense of steady eighth notes to the music. Without this part, accurately played at the proper dynamic, the natural momentum of the music is lost.

Precision is the key in measures 181 and 182 in the horns and low brass. Provide an accented, secure pulse on count two in measure 182 to insure accurate placement of the two sixteenths in the tenor saxophone, horns, and euphonium. Do not lose sight of the important upper woodwind entrance in the same measure, and insist that musicians play the sixteenths in measure 183 with precise authority; add a tenuto to their final eighth note to ensure its proper value.

A firm cue to the trumpets at measure 184 will secure their important duet. The texture and style of this passage bear strong similarity to a segment in movement six of Persichetti's *Divertimento for Band* (measures 51-58). It pits the two trumpets against an incessant upper woodwind line that is highlighted by a crescendo leading to a brilliant rhythmic passage. In the *Psalm* allow the saxophones and horns to frolic happily in the exuberant passage at measure 188. Do not underplay the accented entrance of the upper woodwinds and the cornets in measure 189; rather conduct them with accented, crisp motions from the baton.

I prefer to approach measure 192 in a style more relaxed than the music that precedes it, almost legato. The music returns to its aggressive character soon enough, so the conductor and ensemble should take advantage of this brief respite. Note the polytonality beginning at measure 198 between the cornet/trumpet versus the horn and trombones. The upper woodwinds enter on a melodic motive that appears to be wedded to neither of the existing tonalities, creating the sense that a third tonality may be present. This is terse, emotional music, which the conductor should emphasize through expressive gestures.

The composer reintroduces material at letter J that was first introduced at letter G, but he now adds accompaniment to the texture for the sake of variety; it is clearly the same material. Persichetti begins combining various melodic and rhythmic elements in a texture that approaches layering, massing one idea on top of another. Here we find many of the composer's ideas: the hocket figure and the addition of the unifying three chord idea presented in augmentation at measure 207. The music should build in intensity through the conductor's progressively larger, intense pulses throughout the exciting section. At measure 209 the upper woodwinds will take care of themselves if they have been maintaining the tempo up to this point. Give your attention to the bold chords from the various brasses, because these triads provide an effective contrast to the woodwinds and should receive emphasis.

A wonderful unifying effect occurs at letter K with the reintroduction of the music from letter C, now fully scored for woodwind choir and euphonium. True to his desire for color contrast, Persichetti scores the second phrase in the cornets and trumpets. Here, be absolutely certain that the tempo does not falter. Conduct this brief passage dolce as indicated in the score, being wary of the natural tendency to slow down.

The composer continues to achieve unity through such techniques as matching the same relative key relationship at the second entrance of the melody (measure 223) to that used earlier in the first presentation (measure 97). Again, Persichetti varies the orchestration but keeps the same elements and the same tonal relationships. I believe that the expressivo attached to the horn entrance at measure 225 applies to everyone; it is a wonderful place to engage in the entire ensemble playing expressively.

The chords at measure 230 should receive dramatic accents to prepare for the ritardando in the next two measures. This slowing of pace prepares us for the brisk Coda that will bring the *Psalm* to its exciting resolution. Allow the resonant quality of the bass drum to be heard as the crescendo proclaims the approaching change of tempo.

The conductor should provide the ensemble with a clear, accurate change of tempo at letter L. Though I prefer to linger on count three of the previous measure, then provide an upbeat on count four in the precise tempo indicated at the Più Mosso, any number of solutions are possible. Be sure that what you choose is consistent from rehearsal to rehearsal. The upper woodwinds are depending for their very lives upon the conductor at this point. Any indecision on their part regarding tempo will lead to a disastrous passage for the next few measures. Consider starting the brasses a little softer than marked in measure 234, allowing for a small crescendo on each quarter note sequence of chords.

The primary difficulty in the Coda is in maintaining tempo and balance from letter L until the final chord has sounded. Rehearse the various components as follows: upper woodwinds; horns alone; and all other parts. By simply developing an awareness of texture among the musicians, you will help reduce the number of precision problems in the ensemble as the piece races to its conclusion.

Cue the horns in measure 242 with authority, being certain that good pitch and tone quality are the first priority both on the unison notes and the two-part harmony in the following measure. Conduct measure 244 with sharp motions of the baton, each pulse increasing in size and intensity. The final count of measure 244 is often rushed, which leads to an inaccurate attack on the B♭ triad in the final measure. Alert the ensemble to this pending danger, perhaps adding the designation "do not rush" to each part. Students do get caught up in the emotion of the music and rush as a matter of course. Carefully rehearse the ensemble in this final segment, so everyone has full knowledge of the desired conclusion.

Work for a balanced B♭ triad on the final eighth note. Even notes that are marked accented and staccato should have resonance, and so rehearse them diligently to provide a fitting climax to the music.

During his career Vincent Persichetti provided a substantial body of literature for the American wind band. His *Divertimento for Band* and the *Symphony No. 6 for Band* are among the standard repertoire and ensembles perform them often. The serious conductor of music for winds will find a wealth of enjoyment in studying the *Psalm for Band*. It is an excellent work by this serious composer of band music, and performances of it will be enriching for the ensemble and conductor alike. □

Errata

Score

9	Horn: add *forte* dynamic to horn parts
47	Horn III: add tenuto mark to half note E
71	Tenor Sax: add accent to dotted half note
73	Percussion: add quarter note on count one of bass drum part marked *piano*
105	Percussion: add quarter rest to count four of suspended cymbal part
135	Baritone Sax: remove whole rest, add eighth note B on count one; add slur from pre-previous bar; add necessary rests to complete the measure
151	Tenor Sax: add slur to final two eighth notes
165	B♭ Clarinet 3: add slur between F eighth note and D dotted quarter
166	Alto Sax: add slur to eighths on count three, add slur to eighths on count four
167	Alto Sax: add slur from F♯ eighth to E quarter note; begin slur on final eighth note E
170	Alto Clarinet, Tenor Sax: add accent to eighth note on count three
171	Tenor Sax: add slur to final two eighth notes
174	Percussion: add quarter rest to count four of tenor drum part
179	Basses: add *mf* to final eighth note
180	Alto Sax: add "a2" designation
180	Percussion: add eighth rest on count four to bass drum part
182	Baritone Sax: add slur to first two eighth notes
182	Percussion: remove eighth note flag from note on count three
183	Cornet 1: add staccato to final eighth note A
183	Trombone 2, 3: add beginning of slur to quarter note G
183	Euphonium: add staccato to accented quarter note
184	Tenor Sax: continue slur from previous measure
188	Baritone Sax: add accent to final eighth note
188	Basses: add accents to two D♭ eighth notes
200-201	Piccolo: extend slur to first eighth in next measure
203	Baritone Sax: add accent to quarter note C♯
208	Horns: add accents to all eighth notes
211	Trombone 1: remove tie at beginning of measure
224	Percussion: add *pp* to quarter note
227	Tenor Sax: clarify half note as written G
239	Horn: add accents to eighth note in horn parts
240	Piccolo: add staccato to F eighth note on count four
242	Cornet 1: add slur from previous page to first note

Parts

Piccolo - 138 Add staccato to accent; 245 add staccato to accent.

C Flute I and II - 150 Change first eighth note to C; change second eighth to B♭; 231 *Rit.* missing from part.

Oboe I and II - 168 Add accent to eighth note C; 187 add slur to sixteenths on and of three and eighth note on four; 211 add accent to eighth note B on count one; 241 add staccato eighth note G on count four.

E♭ Clarinet - 138 Add staccato to accent; 150 remove tie from two eighth notes; 241 add staccato to eighth note E on count four.

B♭ Clarinet I - 34 Change quarter note on count three to written F; 160 add letter G designation to the part; 241 add staccato eighth note A on count four.

B♭ Clarinet III - 81 Add dot to the half note; 94 clarify first note as a half note; 102 add *cresc.* designation to the half note; 104 clarify second half note as G♯; 138 add staccato to the accent; 167 add slur between B eighth and A quarter note; 185 remove slur from beginning of count three; start slur on sixteenth note A; 240 add accent to first note; 241 add staccato to eighth note A on count four; 242 add staccato to the accent.

E♭ Alto Clarinet - 69 Clarify first pitch as written E♭; 122-123 add slur over these two measures.

B♭ Bass Clarinet - 1 Add "Solo" designation to part; 20 add "Tutti" designation to part; 95 add dot to half note A♭; 122-123 add slur under these two measures; 180-181 add *crescendo*; 182 add slur to first two eighth notes.

Bassoon I and II - 134 Clarify pitch as whole note C; 145-147 add staccato to each accent; 245 clarify final articulation underneath second bassoon part.

E♭ Alto Sax I and II - 53 Remove dot from half note; 133 add staccato to eighth note on count three.

B♭ Tenor Sax - 167 Remove # sign from F eighth notes.

E♭ Baritone Sax - 76 Add *piano* dynamic.

B♭ Cornet 1 - 160 Add staccato to accent; 244-245 remove slur; add accents to last two eighth notes in 244.

B♭ Cornet 2 - 142 Add staccato to eighth note F♯ on count three; 244-245 remove slur; add accents to last two eighth notes in 244.

B♭ Cornet 3 - 244-245 Remove slur.

B♭ Trumpet I and II - 244-245 Remove slur; add accents to last two eighth notes in 244 in top part.

F Horn I and II - 70-71 Remove *crescendo*; 115 add staccato to accent.

F Horn III and IV - 159 Add staccato to first eighth note; 208 add accents to all three eighth notes; 230 add staccato to accent; 234 add staccato to accent.

Trombone 1 - 244-245 Remove slur; add accents to last two eighth notes in measure 244.

Trombone 2 - 182 Add staccato to accent; 221 clarify first note as a half note C♯; 244-245 remove slur; add accents to last two eighth notes in measure 244.

Trombone 3 - 140-141 Begin slur on final eighth note B♭ and continue to dotted half note C; 213 remove accent from D♭ eighth note.

Euphonium - 164 Add staccato to accent; 183 add staccato to accented quarter note; 188 remove staccato marks.

Basses - 71 Remove extraneous ink mark; 115 add flat sign to half note C; also add dot after half note; 160 add staccato to accent; 188 add accents to D♭ eighth notes.

Percussion - 71 Move *mp* marking to underneath the second quarter note in Bass Drum part; 105 change final dynamic to *forte*; 123 add diminuendo between the half note and quarter note; 159 remove staccato from final eighth note; 202 add *mf* dynamic to tenor drum part.

Conducting and Rehearsal Skills

～～～～

Interpretation

Unlocking the Drama in Music

by W. Francis McBeth

To discuss the interpretation of music is the most difficult of all pedagogical efforts because it does not fall into the category of technique, and we bandmasters are known for our mastery of the technical. Interpretation resides in a special world and can only be called forth by understanding a composition's reason for being through the intent of its creator. The composer's intent can never be understood technically, but only through an understanding of why it was created—what the work is trying to accomplish and where it is going. Real art is never created just to add to the sum total of anything; it is created for a reason. The reason, or what the music is trying to do, is the key.

Music was present many thousands of years before it was elevated to the level of art, much later than its companions of literature, sculpture, drama, and painting. Its status as an art is actually quite recent if several hundred years is considered recent in comparison to thousands of years for literature. The pre-art existence of music relegated it to song and dance, and it is no surprise that early concert music and words were almost inseparable. In music with words the interpretation is usually self-evident. It was with the coming of purely instrumental concert music that a conductor, and later an interpreter, was necessary.

Scarlatti wrote 51 operas, and a hundred years later Beethoven wrote one, but nine symphonies. While Scarlatti's music was supported by the church or the patron system, Beethoven had to fill a theater with purely instrumental music, without words to guide them. It is evident the attraction of drama, painting, and literature to the populist, but what is the appeal of purely instrumental music? I believe that without good and logical interpretation this appeal is completely lost, especially for music composed in the last two hundred years. Not only is the appeal lost but a level of boredom can be created that is unattainable in the other arts. I have never seen a painting as boring as a boring piece of music. This is partly caused by individual choices on the length of time spent with a painting, while with music you are trapped by time determined by someone else.

Although there are many boring compositions, any work can be lowered to that level by poor interpretation, especially in the 20th century literature. Boredom in the classroom is the greatest crime a teacher can commit. In music it is death.

Berlioz wrote in his treatise on conducting:

"Among creative artists the composer is almost the only one depending upon a host of intermediaries between him and the public—intermediaries who may be intelligent or stupid, friendly or hostile, diligent or negligent. It is in their power either to carry his work on to brilliant success or to disfigure, debase and even destroy it.

Singers are often considered the most dangerous of these intermediaries; I believe that this is not true. In my opinion, the conductor is the one whom the composer has most to fear. A bad singer can spoil only his part, but the incapable or malevolent conductor can ruin everything."

When a close friend of mine is judging and hears a terrible band attempt one of my pieces, they love to send a copy of the tape to me. When I see them they always ask how I felt when I heard it. They are surprised when I reply that it didn't bother me. It doesn't bother me at all, because everyone who heard that band knew something on stage was horribly wrong. What does bother me, I should say tears my heart out, is when a great band with superb pitch, excellent balance, and all the techniques plays a piece of mine and completely misses the interpretation. This is so upsetting because the audience does not know anything is wrong with the band and assumes something is wrong with the composition. When the interpretation is missed with a 19th century work, it just seems dull; but if it is missed with a 20th century piece, it sounds silly and awkward.

A potentially great film can be destroyed by the cutters. If it is cut well there is a logical and dramatic sense of the occurrence or progression of events. If it is cut poorly the logic of occurrence is confused (e.g. *Heaven's Gate*). In a well-cut film the form cannot be changed by the viewer or projectionist because the time element is unchangeable. In music this is the case only with electronic music on tape. When a musical work is "cut" well the

---

W. Francis McBeth is professor of music, chairman of the theory/composition department, and resident composer at Ouachita University in Arkadelphia, Arkansas. His education was received from Harding Simmons University, The University of Texas, and the Eastman School of Music.

form will be good, but the time element is at the discretion of each conductor.

In discussing the elements of interpretation, tempo would seem to be the simplest to correct or perform right, but it is the one element that if incorrect will destroy a good work immediately. In 19th century music tempo is usually indicated by terms. In the 20th century it is more specifically denoted with actual metronome markings. How, then, can there be any mistake in tempo in a work marked by a metronome indication. Easily.

First, composers very often put the wrong tempo on their music. This would seem impossible, but the tempo that seems best at the writing desk is very seldom the best on the podium. Most composers are not conductors, and the true tempo for a work can only be felt in a physical performance. Tempo is like water, it seeks its own level and this seeking only occurs in actual performance.

To avoid this problem I never publish a metronome marking until I have conducted the work at least five times in public performances. I say public performance because this is not always the same feel as at rehearsals.

Shostakovich marked the opening of his Symphony No. 5 as ♪ = 76—a very specific marking. Dimitri Mitropoulos, who I consider the best interpreter of Shostakovich, took it at ♪ = 94 and then sped up six to eight counts at rehearsal number [2]. This is a major discrepancy of about 20 counts between composer and conductor. Why did Mitropoulos do this? Because he felt it is the best tempo, and I agree it is the most logical and musical.

Much band music and some orchestral tempi are chosen by the conductor solely from the gymnastics approach. At a concert last year two conductors seemed intent on showing how fast the outstanding band could play. The performance was a musical disaster by a great band solely because of tempo. I judged a tape this year in which the percussion variation in James Barnes' "Paganini Variations" was impeccably performed at almost twice the tempo it should have been played. It caused this wonderful variation to sound silly.

Why are so many band conductors, and soloists, concerned with speed over music? I include soloists because as the conductor of the Arkansas Symphony, I directed many concerts with guest soloists. I can't remember a soloist wishing to take a tempo too slow, but often too fast. I once was forced to conduct the finale of the last movement of the Tchaikovsky Violin Concerto (last Tempo Primo to the end) in a fast one at the soloist's insistence. Why did the performer insist on a tempo that was musically disastrous? He wanted the audience to applaud what Furtwängler referred to as a "gymnasium performance." Furtwängler also said, "When a person recites a poem or gives a lecture, he endeavors in the first instance to enunciate the words in such a manner that their sense is intelligible." Wagner, in his book on conducting, states, "His choice of tempi will show whether he understands the piece or not."

How does one determine the correct tempo? A great first step is to sing it! I repeat for emphasis, *sing it*. Wagner said that it is almost impossible to choose the wrong tempi if you sing it. You have heard the first four notes of the Beethoven Fifth many different ways, some with the first three notes fast, short and clipped, others with the first three notes too long and exaggerated rubato with a huge space before the fourth note. Sing those four notes out loud while conducting, and it is difficult to do them wrong.

Wagner said, "Our conductors so frequently fail to find the true tempo because they are ignorant of singing. These people look upon music as a singularly abstract sort of thing, an amalgam of grammar, arithmetic, and digital gymnastics."

Involved in tempo is the choice of rubato. William F. Santleman once told me after I had complimented his rubato in "Andrea Chenier," "You can't teach rubato. A conductor can either do it or he can't." I think I agree that it probably cannot be taught, but musicianship and musicality may be, and it is the guiding factor in rubato.

Although tempo is the Achilles heel in interpretation, volume variants is the Moriarty, the ever present hidden nemesis. When I speak of volume variants, many think that I am talking only of playing loudly or softly. Volume variants include so many aspects of playing—articulation, the accent is a volume variant; phrasing, the phrase ending is a volume variant; the complete curve of a phrase is a volume variant, the crescendo, the decrescendo, the timpani volume, and just plain louds and softs.

The composer primarily speaks through volume variants and dissonance with melody and rhythm a distant second. I have sat many times with composers as they listen to their own works. They always mumble throughout the entire performance. The mumbling invariably goes like this:

"Too fast—louder trombones, louder—too loud trumpets—come on timpani, we can't hear that—no, no *sffzp*, band, *sffzp*—can't hear the tubas." When it's one of my works, my wife has to listen to all the mumbling.

I never hear composers mumble, "Oops, the flutes are sharp—poor subdivision in the clarinets—brass balance is poor," they always speak of tempi and volumes. This tells me that composers and most band directors are primarily concerned about two different aspects of the performance: the director with technique and the composer with interpretation. The performance should have both; but no matter how good the band is, poor interpretation destroys the music, poor technique only hurts it.

Why are volumes so difficult to sense? One seldom hears the Brahms Second performed with different volume concepts, but you surely will with "Fanfare and Allegro." I have never heard a composer conduct one of his pieces without pleading for more volume from the timpanist. Most high school timpanists just can't play at a fortissimo, and it's so easy. The same is true for French horns.

After I have rehearsed an all-state band for two hours, I invariably hear from a player or band director, "Oh, you want the horns and timpani to play real loud," to which I reply, "No, not at all. I want the same volume at an *ff* from them that Hanson wants in his music or Ansermet uses in Stravinsky. I want the same timpani volume at *ff* that the timpanist in the Chicago Symphony uses." It's not a matter of skill or technique, experience, or age.

Correct interpretation is the re-creation of the composer's intent. As I said before, in music with text the intent is more obvious. In purely instrumental music the conductor must understand what the composer is trying to accomplish, what problem he is trying to solve. Stravinsky said, "I cannot compose until I have decided what problem I must solve." I would state it differently: I cannot compose until I have decided what effect I wish to achieve.

The effects that I am trying to achieve are not mysteries known only by the chosen. Ninety percent are written on the page. When I use the term "composer's intent," I am not speaking of some hidden meaning or an idea that is difficult to comprehend: I mean primarily what is written on the paper. Many times I have said to high school honor bands, always on the first day, that they should consider a career as band clinicians. It is good travel, you meet wonderful people, and you don't have to know anything. You just show up and tell the musicians what is printed on their parts. This is an over-simplification, but not by much.

In my work "Masque" (pronounced *Mask* by the way not *Mosque*) there are two measures that I have seldom heard done correctly. There are two adjacent measures in which the band has an *sffzp* $<$ *ff* over three beats at a tempo of 156. Most bands will not get down to the *p* or up to the *ff* because it happens so fast. When I point this out in clinics, I play a tape of it being done perfectly by a high school band from Kaho, Japan. The extreme quick change of volume is so exciting, and invariably someone will say, "How do we know that is the effect you want?" I reply, "How else can that marking be done? I know of no other way." It's printed on the paper; a *sfmf* $<$ *f* is wrong. A director would never change a note or chord, but they frequently change the volumes. The volumes are more important than the notes. The problem is that most conductors think they are performing

them correctly. There are seldom inconsistencies with orchestral directors, yet I wonder why there are the extreme differences among band directors. Could it be that so many young bands are not mature enough to handle the literature they attempt to play?

The effect to be achieved is not difficult to understand. The difficulty is in the degree of drama that various conductors choose to achieve it. Musical nuance must be exaggerated. From the composer's pen to the conductor, through the ensemble to the audience, so much can be lost in the translation. Art is not an experience of reality; it is one of exaggeration.

If nuance is underplayed, music withers into just acoustical pitches that don't offend. Exaggerated nuance affects the listener in a myriad of responses, none of which is boredom.

I do not wish to leave the impression that a given work is supposed to be the same no matter who conducts it. There can be a wide range of personal variations of interpretation by different conductors. This is one of the great enjoyable advantages that orchestrated music, performed by humans, has over electronically produced tape music. There are sections in certain works that I have chosen to perform differently than anyone else. This is my artistic prerogative, but it seldom has to do with tempo and never with volumes or specifically designated markings.

It is in tempo and specific markings that the interpretation of band music suffers so. Don't forget why you became a musician. It was because of a love affair with sound. It was not from a love affair with organization, techniques, or competition, no matter how commendable these efforts may be. A musical experience has no substitute; and when it is experienced by the band, the conductor, and the audience, it is desired above all else. ☐

The Conductor's Responsibilities

by Harry Begian

As a college student many years ago, I read that a conductor has three responsibilities: to composers, to players, and to his audiences. This declaration of a conductor's responsibilities made such good sense that I have tried to adhere to it throughout my career as a conductor and teacher. At the many excellent concerts I have attended over the years, I have learned that most conductors of bands, orchestras, and opera accept these responsibilities, reflecting them in the music they choose to perform.

Audience attendance at symphony orchestra, opera, and university band performances reached an all-time high into the 1960s. Most conductors seemed committed to presenting performances of the best music available for the listening pleasure of their audiences. From the 60s until the present, symphony and opera attendance have held their own while attendance at university band concerts has dropped.

Decline in the size of band audiences is a major concern for many band conductors and has been the topic of panel discussions and seminars throughout the country. While many reasons are advanced for the causes, one never hears or reads that perhaps the main reason for the decline is poor programming. Far too many band conductors have forgotten, or consciously dismissed, a proper balance of musical responsibilities to both audiences and players.

In the book *Music After Modernism* Samuel Lipman states, "The audience, which can give its immediate and warm-hearted approval to performers who play known and beloved music, can in no direct way influence composers; yet the long-run approval of the composer by the audience is vital for the composer's self regard...not only can the composer not be told what to do...but the audience cannot long be expected to support what it neither likes nor understands."

Our many fine college and university bands had for years preserved band traditions and served as models for the band movement in this country. They charted the directions in which bands developed instrumentation and the music

Harry Begian holds degrees from Wayne State University and the University of Michigan. Director Emeritus of the University of Illinois Bands, Begian has appeared as a conductor, adjudicator, and lecturer in the United States, Canada, and Australia.

photo by: Steve J. Sherman

they played. In the late 1960s and into the 70s, one began to hear from a small group of university band conductors that they did not care to program traditional music from the band's limited band repertoire; they would devote their musical energies to the performance and propagation of new music, original band works in the contemporary idiom.

This approach to band programming had a direct influence on the younger generation of band conductors being trained by our universities. When this younger generation entered the conducting profession they adopted the programming philosophies of their mentors. Many of them became so intent on personal expression that they showed little or no responsibility for exposing players and concert audiences to a variety of styles and periods of music.

It is my opinion, shared by a great number of band conductors, that programming of a preponderance of one kind of music is short-sighted and cheats our players. Through lopsided programming that stresses only new, original, or contemporary band works, an aura of musical monotony is created, seriously affecting the performers' enthusiasm and curtailing audience attendance at concerts. Such messianic programming should be reconsidered if conductors are to accept their musical responsibilities to student players and audiences seriously. This does not in any way imply that conductors should lower their musical standards or pander to only that which audiences and players enjoy. Nor does it mean that we should revert to playing the inane and poorly transcribed music of the past.

University band conductors definitely have a responsibility to present new, original band works on their concerts; but they should exercise greater care in selecting music that is artistically sound, displays solid composer craftsmanship, and has intrinsic musical worth. Examples of works that meet these criteria are the following: *...and the mountains rising nowhere...* by Joseph Schwantner, *Divertimento for Band — "On Winged Flight"* by Gunther Schuller, *Symphony No. 2* by David Maslanka, and *Symphony No. 3* by Alfred Reed. Earlier original contemporary works for band that meet the highest musical standards are the *Symphony in Bb* by Paul Hindemith, *Theme and Variations Op. 43a* by Arnold Schoenberg, *Sinfonietta* by Ingolf Dahl, Symphony for Band by Vincent Persichetti, *Dionysiaques* by Florent Schmitt, *Lincolnshire Posy* by Percy Grainger, *La Fiesta Mexicana* by H. Owen Reed, *Music for Prague 1968* by Karel Husa, *Hammersmith* by Gustav Holst, *Armenian Dances Parts I and II* by Alfred Reed, and *Fiesta del Pacifico* by Roger Nixon. The myopic view

that foists only one type of music on audiences and players is wrong, both educationally and ethically.

It is amazing that after numerous discussions about the pros and cons of transcriptions over the past 50 years that band conductors haven't come to realize there are basically only two types: good ones and bad ones. Transcriptions by Harding and Hindsley of the Richard Strauss tone poems are well crafted and suited to performance by the finest bands, as is Guy Duker's scoring of Respighi's *Pines of Rome*. In selecting transcribed works for performance one learns that the transcriber is an important indicator of the work's musical quality and the craftsmanship displayed in its setting for band. A conductor can rest assured that the transcriptions done by reliable transcribers such as Leiden, Calliet, Reed, Paynter, Grundman, or Curnow, to name only a few, will be suitable and sound well when played by a wind band. To me the reasons for this are obvious: these arrangers are familiar with a wide range of music, are sympathetic to the wind band medium, and understand its timbral and coloristic potentials.

To conductors who regard all transcriptions as anathemas, I say that transcriptions have been considered a legitimate practice throughout the history of Western music. Bach, Mozart, and Liszt are but a few of the great composers who transcribed music of their own as well as that of other composers. Unfortunately, there are far too many bad transcriptions for band: transcriptions unsuited to band performance or executed so poorly they discredit the original composition. Unacceptable transcriptions are those in which the transcriber has freely changed harmonies, textures, and rhythmic figures or made deletions.

However, having listed these objectionable transcription practices I would also venture to say that many bands today perform in concert as many bad original works as bad transcriptions. In consideration of this, I believe conductors need to review the band transcription literature and sort out those that are worthy of performance. This we must do. The disinterested players and apathetic audiences are saying it is not justifiable to play music only because it is new, original, or contemporary music for band.

American society has always had a fascination with all that is new, whether in trends, clothing, automobiles, or music. With the desire to see the band's repertoire grow, band conductors clutch at any new music written for the medium. This is understandable; what is not acceptable is that too often we equate the word "new" with the word "good". Too few conductors take the time to study a score for themselves instead of relying on the assessment of others. Because these conductors don't trust their musical perceptions or intuition, they seek outside help to select music and decide how to play it. Conductors who ask others what to play and how to play turn out carbon copy performances that can never convey commitment or strong convictions about the music.

When teaching graduate music students, it is distressing to observe how little they know about music literature and music history. This leads me to believe that very few band students ever play or hear music of the masters in their high school or college bands. It may also indicate that many of them do not attend symphony orchestra concerts and operas. In pondering this matter I have come to the conclusion that their playing experiences are confined to the new educational music published for bands and a type of "non-music music" (it looks like music, reads like music, but sounds terrible).

I believe strongly that band players who never experience the expressive qualities of good music in performance and who are continually forced to perform music of inferior or questionable quality will leave our bands or give up their instruments altogether. The drop in enrollment in some university bands and music departments bears this out, and I am certain this trend is due in part to the quality of music played in high school. The monotony of playing and hearing the same kinds of musical sounds, textures, and rhythmical devices can only discourage and disappoint our players and audiences.

Having isolated programming as the main reason band conductors fail to fulfill their responsibilities to composers, players, and audiences, it is time to suggest what can be done to correct the matter. In doing so I speak from 50 years of experience. Over that period of time I have conducted many excellent bands, symphony orchestras, and a few operatic productions. I have been fortunate through most of my career to play for fairly large audiences. I have never experienced a dropout problem with any of the groups I have conducted. I believe that this has been largely because of the music we played and the manner in which we presented it in concert.

Much of what I learned about performance, conducting, and programming came from intensive listening and observation of professional musicians. Through listening to players and observing concert-goers I learned much more about music, programming, and a conductor's musical responsibilities than I ever did in a college classroom. Early in my conducting career I concluded that concert audiences attend concerts to hear performances of a variety of music played well, with serious

conviction. I also developed sensitivity and regard for the musical likes and dislikes of players. I came to the realization that sincere commitment to what we perform is immeasurably effective in the final outcome of how well a musical work is performed.

In conclusion, I offer what I believe to be truths and guidelines for conductors. First and foremost, band conductors should concern themselves with fulfilling their responsibilities to composers, players, and audiences. To do this they must perform the very best music available, prepare it well, and present it to a public audience with strong commitment and musical conviction. A good work presented in a shoddy performance will not credit the composer and will not bring pleasure to players or audiences.

Play a variety of types of music and structure programs with the principles of unity, variety, and contrast in mind. Include some high-quality trancriptions in your concerts, making sure that they are faithful to the original work and that they are musically convincing.

By all means, include good contemporary works in your programs. If you study them thoroughly and prepare them with care, you will reflect credit on the composer. Select, organize, and present balanced programs. Avoid programming only one kind of music for public presentation; repetitive sounds and techniques are boring. Resist the notion that the words new and original are synonymous with good. Feature fine soloists on your concerts, both vocal and instrumental. Finally, do include a lowly march or two, even if you play them as encores. Audiences love them and want to hear them played well by a good band. □

The Score

Mechanics of Preparation

by W. Francis McBeth

How does a person learn a score? Volumes have been written on this subject, but how does one actually learn a score or a poem or a role in a play?

Seventeen years ago I became the conductor of the Arkansas Symphony in Little Rock and was faced with the challenge of learning scores of up to an hour in length. A conductor's first employment with a professional orchestra is an overpowering experience in score study. This is a far different experience from university conducting, which covers only about a tenth of the literature a professional orchestra performs. An hour-long symphony is about a hundred times harder to learn than ten 10-minute works; it might seem that it should only be ten times harder, but this is not so for many reasons. It is a shock how quickly the repertoire learned in university years and in prior performing experiences is consumed.

After about 1½ seasons, a full-time orchestra will go through a young conductor's repertoire, and he will begin to leave duplicate scores in other rooms and spend all available time studying. I mention all this to explain why I had to start learning scores faster than ever before and what I learned from it.

The first step in score study is to memorize the score, and the second is to decipher the composer's intent. The third step is to determine the conductor's concept of what he expects to hear. The fourth step involves the technical approaches that we have all been taught, such as form and harmonic usage.

In using the word memory I do not mean you should know the alto clarinet or viola note on beat 3 in measure 126 or the rehearsal letters by recall. Rather I mean knowing by memory the

W. Francis McBeth is professor of music, resident composer, and chairman of the theory-composition department at Ouachita University, Arkadelphia, Arkansas, and has written extensively for band, orchestra, and chamber ensembles. He is a former conductor of the Arkansas Symphony at Little Rock and has conducted extensively in the United States and abroad. McBeth's formal education is from Hardin-Simmons University, the University of Texas, and the Eastman School of Music.

sequence of events of the work and being able to sing it from beginning to end.

When I make this statement in clinics, there is often one person who gets a bit upset. This is a natural reaction to something he thinks he cannot or does not need to do. I disagree that he cannot do it; but I agree that it is not always necessary. In fact there are some scores that are not worth learning, not because of the quality of the scores but how they are used. If it is a training piece for a beginning band to learn various aspects of mechanical technique, and if you conduct four periods of this level a day, it's not worth memorizing. However, I don't know how one could keep a score out of memory by sheer osmosis.

Some conductors define score memory as knowing every note that each instrument has in any given measure, while others define memory as knowing the melody all the way through. I define score memory, or more accurately the memory that I use, as a memory knowledge of the order of occurrence in the composition.

If the word memory disturbs you, please note that the superb book by Elizabeth Green, *The Modern Conductor*, one of the few books on conducting that discusses score study in depth, does not use the heading of score study or score preparation. The chapter devoted to this subject is titled "Memorizing the Score." It does not say learning, preparing, or studying the score. It speaks only of memorizing the score and gives the best information about how memory works, and I recommend Chapter 17 to all of you.

Once you memorize the score you know the order; once you know the composer's intent, then you know the plot. Once you know the order of events and the plot, you are almost there.

Most articles on score study start with the analysis of form. Trust me, you do not need to know the form first. What difference does it make if it is *rondo concertant, sonata allegro,* or *stollen-stollen-abgesang?* Form becomes obvious once you have memorized the work, and another major heresy on my part is that the form of a work has never aided me in learning it. It must help someone because almost everyone lists it as the first step in score study, but I cannot comprehend how it helps initial learning. The only way it could is for each separate form to be exactly alike in time (minutes passed) and occurrence. I do not mean that form is not important, because I know the form of every piece I conduct. I do mean that it is not a useful first tool for memory. In memorizing a poem, did you ever have to know the form first? Form is not a roadmap, and every *sonata allegro* is different. When a score is memorized, the form is obvious.

Perhaps those who recommend learning the form first are using the wrong term. To most musicians and all music academia, the word form pertains to a prescribed structure that results from the composer's manner of presenting and developing the ideas in a work. Many use the term form when they actually mean the unfolding of a work (what I call the sequence of occurrence). These are two completely different aspects. Orchestration has much more effect upon memory of occurrence than knowledge of the form.

The architectural study of form in college has never helped a composer learn form. Form is more complicated and important than superficial structure. The name form should be changed to glue. Form is what holds a piece together. One can have perfect architectural form and the piece can fall apart formally, but then that's another discussion.

To return to my first step — memory. I don't mean that you must conduct without a score, which can be used as an occasional reference during a concert, but you should have memorized the score to the point that if it falls off the stand you will be no worse off. At times I use a score for a concert when I have not used one in rehearsal, and always when a group is a bit shaky and may need extra help with a problem. Sometimes I put a paper clip in a score and open it only to a specific page I have trouble remembering.

Conducting from memory always produces the most musical performance for many reasons. Herbert von Karajan said about driving fast cars, a hobby we had in common, that conducting from memory is like driving a fast car to your ultimate potential on a road course that you know from memory: you will brake and accelerate at exactly the correct instant. When driving a course that you don't know, you brake early and accelerate late. It's the same for conducting: without having to watch for road signs, a smoother and more musical product results.

Composers have a particular problem that most conductors do not, and I usually use a score when conducting my own music. I have heard so many comments over the years, such as, "I don't understand; you didn't use a score on any piece except the one you wrote." The reason for this is that when you have composed music for 35 years, your brain can easily shift into another piece you have written. I don't conduct from the score, but use it to remind myself now and then as to which piece I'm conducting.

Baroque music is the most difficult music to memorize because of its constant similarity. It's like driving through a tunnel: the scenery does not change. Twentieth-century music is the easiest — the scenery is in neon.

If the first step in score study is memory, then how does one memorize a score? In the 1950s public education tried to get away from memorization and replace it with logic. Twenty years later it dawned on educators that if you can't remember it, you don't know it. Knowledge is memory, wisdom is not.

Although I cannot explain memory, I know the process for achieving it is repetition, an ugly word in modern education: the repetition of singing through the score and playing through the score on a keyboard or a recording. A recording can be detrimental if you tend to take only the recording's interpretation. Listening to Reiner with Strauss, Mitropoulos with Shostakovich, or Ansermet with Stravinsky can be a plus, but usually bandmasters will listen to a recording by the local Presbyterian junior college band, and this can be disastrous.

Singing while conducting or playing through a piece is far superior because you memorize faster when you participate instead of just listen. Listening is the slowest way to memorize and has interpretational pitfalls.

Try conducting through a score while singing it, silently, to yourself. You can silently sing melody, harmony, and percussion at the same time — try it. Not only is it possible, but there are never wrong notes or pitch problems in silent score singing. I have found that conducting while silently singing the score is the fastest method of score memory. While singing, you can stop and check the score at each mistake or error. This activity follows knowing the harmonies; it cannot precede it.

Learning the composer's intent (plot) comes from understanding music and how composers speak through sound. I don't know how it can be done without an understanding of composition, which should be the one required course for all music majors; yet only 2% study it.

I don't know how one can fully understand anything that another does without ever having tried to do it. It does not mean one should be good at it or successful at it, only that they have tried it. No one can appreciate a great bull fighter, a great aviator, a great sailor, or a great trumpet player if he has never tried it. Trying to understand music without having tried to create it makes it a longer road.

The composer's intent is the most overlooked element among wind conductors and is the most important aspect in music. Without the recreation of the composer's intent, the exercise of performance is futile. Wilhelm Furtwangler said, "Everything purely mechanistic is a matter of training. But that understanding from which the word art derives has nothing whatever to do

with training." This is a debatable statement, but the older I become the more I understand his point. I have asked a hundred conductors if *rubato* can be taught, and they all said yes, immediately. I wish I knew how to teach it. It is either right or wrong, and I can't explain it to another. I can tell a student that it is too fast or too slow, neither of which would happen in the first place if he could feel it. How is feel taught?

To understand the composer's intent, begin with the simplest and most often violated aspect, executing what is on the written page. Hundreds of times, I have stopped conducting a high school honor band and said, "When you get back to your schools, you should talk to your counselor about being a clinician. It's great fun and wonderful travel and you don't need to know anything. You only have to make the band members play what is printed on their parts." This is almost true. The first day of an all-state is primarily forcing the students to do what is printed on their parts. How many times have you been a participant in the following scene:

Conductor: "Timpanist, what does your part say?"

Timpani: "What? Where?"

Conductor: "The note you just played, what is the volume marking?"

Timpani: (Long pause) "Double *f*" (the reply is never *fortissimo*).

Conductor: "Why did you play *mezzo-piano?*"

Timpani: (No response).

I know this sounds simplistic, but 80% of the time I conduct where the music has already been prepared, the volumes are not correct (99% with the timpani).

A composer speaks through many techniques, but the one most used is volume variance, with dissonance running a close second. Volume variance covers much more than louds and softs and includes most articulation markings, and goes through style and down to phrase endings. However, let's not get complicated and stay with louds and softs and the graduation between them. Incorrect volumes will kill the composer's intent faster than anything other than an absurd tempo. Even slight tempo changes can harm it. I have a tape on my desk on which the slow tempos are ten counts too fast and the fast tempos are ten counts too slow; it destroys the entire effect. Why is slow music usually conducted too fast?

A few years ago I was in the audience when an excellent honor band performed a work of mine. The tempo was excellent and all the technical aspects were good, but the pianissimos were mezzo-piano and the fortissimos were mezzo-forte. I don't know when I was ever more embarrassed to take a bow. The work is a dramatic work that I am fond of, and it sounded silly and made no sense. This isn't a rare occurrence; it happens more often than not.

We could go into other aspects of understanding the intent of the composer, but the execution of what is printed is a major first step.

Step three is the conductor's concept. In score study the conductor decides what he wants to hear and with what attitude and balance. Most young conductors are not sure what they want and accept what comes out as long as it is in tune — a disastrous approach. Young conductors worry about pitch and tempo; neither has

anything to do with score study. Good pitch is assumed, and the tempo is written on the score.

Before the downbeat I know exactly what I want to hear; if it is not what I expect I stop and force it into what I want. The first element that affects my ear and brain is always attitude; the second is balance. Young conductors stop for wrong notes; I never do unless it happens twice. Notes mean nothing; attitude is everything. Don't confuse attitude with composer's intent. Attitude is the conductor's intent, which he hopes is part of the composer's intent, but he has no way of knowing for sure.

Step four of score study is learning technical aspects. Hundreds of classes and articles cover analysis of form, harmonic understanding, and rhythmic complexity. To understand controlled dissonance is to understand balance; to understand harmony (18th to 20th century) is to understand volume. These are most important. I do not make light of the technical aspects, which are essential but are easily accomplished.

I realize that I am in the minority on a final aspect of score study, that of marking the score. When I was young I marked much of the score because I was taught to do so. I found that my usual markings in an hour's work caused me to spend more time reading markings than listening because the eye and ear do not work together. Once the eye goes to the page, the ears shut down about 40%. It was a great revelation to me that if I had to mark the score, I didn't know the score. I recently read an article on how to mark a score, but I feel that if you need to mark the score, you do not know the composition. We are not learning a score; we are learning a musical work.

Except for enlarging the numerals in multiple meter changes, one must know all the things that are usually marked. I realize that this may be heresy, but I believe that a marked score is an unlearned score. To a lesser degree this is also true with the players' individual parts.

After a recent concert I erased the markings from the parts and found three players that had circled, usually three or four times, the *ff* at the opening measure. If players need additional reminding that the work starts *ff*, then they either have no concept of the piece or their brains have been somewhere else during all of the learning process (rehearsal). I may be the only conductor who asks the ensemble not to mark their parts unless the marking is to correct an error, to change the printed material, or as logistics for the percussion. I want players to know how the piece goes; it is too late to read at the concert. I am not talking about bow markings, but I am tired of all those pencils clicking when I want everyone to remember and understand what I am saying.

I hope these thoughts are helpful to young conductors. Expanding your score study will build confidence and enhance the pleasure that comes from being in complete control. I leave you with this one important thought: you are not learning a score; you are learning a musical composition. ☐

Suggestions for Marking the Score

by Frank Battisti and Robert J. Garofalo

There are three types of score markings and annotations a conductor can use during score study and the pre-rehearsal phase: markings for analysis; markings for interpretation, including editorial corrections and adjustments; and markings of the score and parts for podium conducting. Analytical and interpretive markings are an integral part of the score study process. Marking the score and parts for podium conducting belongs to the pre-rehearsal phase of a conductor's preparation and follows the score study process; therefore, do not mark the score for podium conducting until you have thoroughly studied the music and have developed a clear interpretive image of the work in your mind.

Make score markings and annotations with a dark, erasable lead pencil, such as a number two bonded lead pencil, to facilitate changes. The score used for study should not be the one used for podium conducting, because in the process of analyzing the music, score pages become cluttered with markings and annotations. It is usually best to prepare a fresh score with selective markings for podium conducting.

Marking the Score for Analysis

The ideas, procedures, and symbols suggested below are offered to guide the inexperienced conductor. As a rule write in the score any important fact, question, or insight discovered during analysis, if you do not want to lose track of it. Write score entries in the margins or within the music itself. Keep a note pad and manuscript paper handy to write additional notes.

Begin the analysis by identifying phrase units. As you read through the score, mark off phrases and periods with a single vertical line or slash beneath the bottom staff of each score brace or page. Use double vertical lines to indicate large sections or subsections of the music and tally the measures as shown in the example. Identify subphrases and mark them at the top of the score brace using brackets.

Phrase structure tallies at the beginning of each section and at the top of the score brace

(4+6=10)

make it easier to see the phrasing of the music. In addition to the brackets shown in the first example, you may wish to use different symbols to mark off phrase units of varying lengths. For example:

3 measure unit:

4 measure unit:

5 measure unit:

The next step is to identify the important melodic ideas beneath the bottom staff of each score brace where they begin in the music. Using traditional labels, identify melodies as Theme 1, 2, 3; Theme A1, A2, B1, B2, or by their musical or stylistic characteristics, such as Maestoso Theme, Scherzo Idea, Cantabile Melody, Martial Tune, Countermelody 1, and so on. Use any descriptive label as long as it represents the music appropriately and is meaningful to you. After indicating phrasing and thematic ideas on the score, go back to the first page of the music and label each section according to its overall form. If the composition is in sonata allegro form, you would mark the sections introduction, exposition, development, recapitulation, and coda.

Identify and mark important compositional techniques used by the composer to transform melodic ideas where they appear on the score page. If you encounter familiar musical material that appeared earlier in the piece, be sure to compare the related passages, measure by measure, and mark any changes observed in the repeated passage. Composers often find subtle and interesting ways to vary musical ideas when they reappear in a composition. Such changes provide important clues to the interpretation of the music. If a composer does not vary the reused materials, note that in the score; for example, *Exact repeat of letter A, for 15 measures,* which will remind you to skip analysis of the repeated passage and move ahead to the next section of the composition.

When analyzing chords, cadences, and harmonic progressions using the full score, examine each structure vertically from the bottom up. First study the bass clef instruments — timpani, string bass, tuba, euphonium, trombones — because these instruments often provide information that will help you grasp the chord structure quickly. If a complex chord is difficult to understand in a full score, construct a condensed piano score version of the structure somewhere on the score page where there are rest measures in the music, or in the margins of the score page, or on an insert sheet. The tonal idiom of the music usually dictates the symbols used for the harmonic analysis of a specific composition: for compositions written in a traditional harmonic style, use Roman numerals or letter name chord symbols; for contemporary compo-

sitions that employ nontraditional harmonic idioms, devise your own symbols and abbreviations to identify chord structures. For example, indicate bichordal sonority as fmi/C, or cluster as Cl: C, C#, D, D#, E. For guidance in analyzing contemporary harmonic idioms, read the supplemental materials listed at the end of the article.

As you analyze the orchestration of a composition, it helps to mark such specific scoring techniques as unisons, octaves, 3rds, and 6ths in the music:

Un.   (8va   (3rds   (

For complex melodic doublings draw a schematic diagram of the orchestration at the top of the page.

Orchestration scheme of the beginning of Charles Gounod's *Petite Symphony for Winds.*

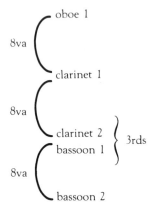

Identify vertical doublings of chord tones in traditional music by outlining the notes with geometric shapes.

* diamond = 7th	◇	* circle = 3rd	O
* triangle = 5th	△	* square = root	□

Marking the Score for Interpretation

Marking the score for interpretation is not as clear a process as marking it for analysis because musical expression is difficult to annotate, but a young conductor should make interpretive markings in the score to remember the musical concepts. An experienced conductor may need a few interpretive markings, but many accomplished conductors insert their interpretive markings in their scores. Interpretive markings are personal; here are some guidelines for marking scores.

Tempo/Meter/Rhythm
Clarify tempi with metronome markings where none are given.
Clarify tempo relationships when necessary (a quarter note in ⅔ meter = an eighth note in

Frank Battisti is conductor of the Wind Ensemble at the New England Conservatory in Boston, Massachusetts. A recognized authority on wind literature, he has conducted wind ensembles and bands for over 30 years.

Robert J. Garofalo is professor of music and head of graduate programs in instrumental conducting at the Benjamin T. Rome School of Music of The Catholic University of America in Washington, D.C. He has authored five books and more than two dozen articles and music publications.

This article is adapted from an appendix "Marking the Score" in a newly published book, Guide to Score Study for the Wind Band Conductor, *by Frank Battisti and Robert Garofalo. Used with permission, Meredith Music Publications, 170 N.E. 33rd Street, Fort Lauderdale, Florida.*

§ meter.

Indicate interpretive tempo adjustments with an arrow pointing to the right for accelerando and to the left for ritardando.

Indicate brief interpretive hesitations or pauses such as before the final chord with the symbol "v."

Clarify subgroupings of asymmetrical meters as in ⅞ = 4+3.

Clarify passages requiring superimposed meters (two measures of ¾ meter to be interpreted as one measure of 3/2 meter with a subdivided beat).

Melodic Phrasing

Clarify the interpretation of ornaments and embellishments according to period performance practices.

Indicate the expressive high point in a phrase with a vertical arrow.

Expressive high point (most intensity) in a phrase.

Indicate a phrase separation with brackets and a comma.

Break in phrase.

Indicate *no breath* or *no break* in the phrases with brackets and a dotted line arrow.

No break in phrase

Indicate a suspension or appoggiatura for expressive emphasis with a slash through the note head and a tenuto mark in parentheses.

Slightly emphasize a note by lengthening it.

Orchestration and Texture

Clarify how specific instrumental lines should be interpreted (NV = no vibrato, ST = straight tone, VIB = vibrato).

Indicate desired textural sound by writing in such descriptions as transparent, opaque, resonant, vibrant, and so on.

Dynamics

Clarify crescendos and decrescendos when the beginning and ending dynamic levels are not marked.

Clarify balances by adding or adjusting dynamic markings; cross out printed dynamics and insert new markings in parentheses.

Clarify balances between primary and subordinate parts at the top of the score. For example, f/mf = melody at forte and accompaniment at *mezzo-forte*.

Mark the climax and subclimax phrases by writing the words at the top of the score.

Stylistic Articulations and Expressive Terms

Indicate separation and articulation of notes by using vertical lines between them.

Separate and articulate each note.

Add or adjust stylistic articulations of melodic lines (legato, staccato, marcato, tenuto, polyarticulations).

At appropriate places in the score, write in your own musical or descriptive words; for example, leggiero, con fuoco, molto expressivo, dramatic, flowing, calm and relaxed; and so on.

Editorial Corrections and Adjustments

Score study includes two categories of editorial changes: corrections and adjustments. Make editorial corrections to a score that contains obvious errors, misprints, and omissions, ranging from such things as wrong notes, pitches, or rhythms, to missing accidentals, dynamics, or articulations, to incorrect key signatures, or even misplaced or missing rehearsal numbers and letters. The list is almost endless. Correct these errors as soon as you discover them and keep a separate list of score and past errors for future reference.

Editorial adjustments, commonly called retouching, are frequently made to orchestral works written before 1825 because many wind instruments were incapable of playing the entire chromatic scale. Early orchestral scores are sometimes adjusted to accommodate modern instruments. Score adjustments of this type rarely occur in band music because most original wind band literature dates from the 20th century.

A good example of score retouching a wind band orchestration is Paul Hindemith's *Konzertmusik fur Blasorchester*, Opus 41. The baritone and the bass tuba move in octaves or in unison except for the low E♭ in the baritone part at letter G. Hindemith wrote this piece for three-valve baritones, but the baritone passage should be rewritten for the modern 4-valve instrument, which can play all of the notes.

Other practical reasons for adjusting a score are the need to accommodate different skill levels of individual players, the limitations of the ensemble, or acoustic characteristics of the auditoriums. Even slight score adjustments should be made with consideration of the composer's intent: adjustments should bring clarity to the interpretation without changing the underlying spirit of the composition.

Suggested Reading

Techniques of Twentieth-Century Composition. Leon Dallin (Wm. C. Brown)
Introduction to Schenkerian Analysis. Allen Forte and Steven E. Gilbert (W.W. Norton & Company, Inc.)
Analytic Approaches to Twentieth-Century Music. Joel Lester (W.W. Norton & Company, Inc.)
Composition with Pitch-Classes: A Theory of Compositional Design. Robert Morris (Yale University Press)
Serial Composition and Atonality, 2nd edition, revised. George Perle (University of California Press)
Twentieth-Century Harmony. Vincent Persichetti (W.W. Norton & Company, Inc.)
Basic Atonal Theory. John Rahn (Longman, Inc.)
Music of the Twentieth Century: Style & Structure. Bryan R. Simms (Schirmer Books)   □

August, 1980

Score Study and Preparation

Donald Hunsberger

The task of delving into a new score and assimilating each interpretive and technical component appears formidable, even forbidding, to many conductors. The fear is frequently compounded when the score includes new compositional techniques, expanded orchestrational devices, strange harmonic resources, and complex rhythmic concepts.

Actually, musicians who have successfully completed four or more years of university-level training possess sufficient musical knowledge for any such task. What they may lack and must develop is the ability to internalize, retain, and transfer information from all musical experiences — past, present, and future.

Most band and orchestra conductors proceed to the podium through a series of performance opportunities as players of wind, percussion, or string instruments. Thus, their personal contact with music has come from playing a single line of music. Pianists encounter the complexity of many notes on two clefs, and organists add the third element of the feet. However, the conductor must

---

Donald Hunsberger is the conductor of the Eastman Wind Ensemble and professor of conducting and ensembles at the Eastman School of Music.

deal with every facet of a multi-staved full score; and for most people this responsibility requires considerable expansion of thinking and additional musical development.

All too frequently a conductor feels overwhelmed by the enormity of the score study process, and forgets or even subconsciously blocks out important musical information. The feeling can be alleviated by establishing correct study procedures that are designed to stimulate thought processes and promote the transfer of ideas and experiences, using an individualized approach that is most compatible with each conductor's ability and learning patterns.

The Checklist

I find a valid analogy between the pre-flight procedures employed by pilots and the conductor's approach to score study. Just as the pilot systematically reviews every system in the plane before undertaking actual movement and flight, so must the conductor assess and review every musical system involved in the preparation of the score. The examination process includes a methodical look at compositional techniques, formal design, harmonic scheme, melodic development, rhythmic motives, orchestrational devices, physical conducting requirements, and most important, interpretative nuances.

The "Score Study Checklist" and accompanying glossary have been prepared as a means of stimulation for the conductor, a quick-reference process which lists techniques that may be included in the score under consideration. Not every element will be found in each work studied, and possibly new techniques or combinations of old ones will be encountered; but using the checklist will help the conductor place all his accumulated knowledge in perspective and provide starting points for the various areas of analysis and study. The final goal should be a total command of, and ease with, every note and marking on the page, providing a state of mind in which the music and the composer are paramount, and allowing the rehearsal to be an area where the music and the performers meet at the highest level of potential achievement. This procedure eliminates the practice of a conductor coming to rehearsal with only a cursory knowledge of the score and proceeding to learn more as he hears sounds from the ensemble and connects them with marks on the page, a situation devastating to the conductor (who is constantly on the defensive) and the ensemble (which never reaches its musical potential).

Correct and systematic score study can lead to rehearsals in which the only surprises are pleasant ones — those of the discovery of yet another level of beauty or excitement — achieved while making the composer's written intentions come to life.

Score Study Checklist

Melodic
___ 1. tertian harmony scale
___ 2. modal scales
___ 3. pentatonic scales
___ 4. whole tone scale
___ 5. synthetic scale
___ 6. dodecaphonic
___ 7. free tonality
___ 8. serial
___ 9. other: _____

Form
___ 1. single movement
___ 2. multiple movement
___ 3. binary (AB)
___ 4. ternary (ABA)
___ 5. arch (ABCBA; ABCDCBA)
___ 6. rondo (ABACABA)
___ 7. variation of #3 through #6
___ 8. sonata
___ 9. fugue
___ 10. passacaglia; chaconne
___ 11. variation
___ 12. other: _____

Harmonic
___ 1. tertian (triadic)
___ 2. polytriadic
___ 3. quartal
___ 4. quintal
___ 5. modal
___ 6. polychordal
___ 7. parallelism
___ 8. tonal center
___ 9. serial
___ 10. ostinato
___ 11. cluster
___ 12. other: _____

Rhythm - Meter
___ 1. traditional (duple, triple)
___ 2. asymmetric meters
___ 3. changing signatures
___ 4. unusual meters
___ 5. displaced (shifting) accents
___ 6. change of meter
___ 7. metrical modulation
___ 8. alea-proportional
___ 9. other: _____

Orchestration
___ 1. strings
___ 2. winds - brasses
___ 3. percussion - keyboards
___ 4. wind ensemble
___ 5. symphonic band
___ 6. exotic timbral
___ 7. other: _____

Interpretation
___ 1. stylistic indicators:
    a. tempo indication
    b. dynamic scheme
    c. phrasing markings
    d. tension and release
    e. accent scheme
    f. character indications
    g. linear flow
    h. other: _____
___ 2. major expressive qualities
___ 3. foreign language terms/translations
___ 4. historical performance or stylistic considerations

Score Study Checklist Glossary

Melodic

1. *tertian harmony scale* — use of twelve chromatic tones based upon major, minor, diminished, augmented triadic (in thirds) movement.

2. *modal scales* — seven-tone scales each containing 5 whole steps and two half-steps (8th tone being the octave).

3. *pentatonic scale* — a five-note scale (6th note being the octave); diatonic and chromatic intervals.

4. *whole tone scale* — a six-note scale with each interval a whole tone (2 semi-tones).

5. *synthetic scales* — scale patterns created through the combination of modal patterns, key signatures, or other existing scale patterns.

6. *dodecaphonic (duodecuple)* — The use of the twelve tones within the octave in an ordered sequence; each must be sounded before any one tone or its permutation is repeated. The twelve tones are called a tone row, and are for melodic purposes only. Each is treated equally with no implication of tonality.

7. *free tonality* — tonal center present with free and equal use of remaining eleven tones.

All musical examples (other than La Bohème *by Puccini) are by Donald Hunsberger.*

8. *serial* — sets of tones in a pre-determined order; no tone is repeated until entire set is sounded; tones may be repeated or used in any octave freely as long as the order of the row is left undisturbed. Tones may be made into harmonic structures.

Harmonic

1. *tertian* (triadic) — chords built on succession of major and minor thirds; extensions (diatonic and chromatic) are used plus added tones. Basic triads are labelled major, minor, augmented, and diminished.

2. *polytriadic* — use of two or more superimposed triads (any type).

3. *quartal* — chords built on a succession of fourths (perfect, augmented).

4. *quintal* — chords built on a succession of fifths (perfect, diminished, augmented).

5. *modal* — chords and progressions constructed from modal scale patterns; use of two or more modes simultaneously.

6. *polychordal* — chords contructed by superimposing tertian, quartal, quintal, or modal structures.

7. *parallelism* — pattern of a fixed structure (ex.: triads, M, m, d, a) on any scale degrees.

8. *tonal center* — the use of a predominant tone to which all other tones relate; similar to a tonic though not necessarily tertian harmony; may also serve as a "pedal."

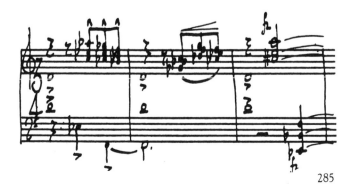

9. *serial* — chords constructed through use of the tones in the row; may be in order (strict) or freely adapted.

10. *ostinato* — repeated melodic or harmonic figure usually in the same voice and at the same pitch [example: a)melodic b)harmonic/rhythmic].

11. *cluster* — chords of consecutive seconds; may be mixed whole step and half step.

Form

1., 2. *single, multiple movements* — substantial, isolated sections, musically strong to stand by themselves; examine for common or related factors in melodic, harmonic, rhymthic, stylistic, orchestration development, key relationships, etc.

3., 4., 5., 6., 7. *binary, ternary, arch, rondo* — most commonly used process to identify sections within individual movements; many variations and ordering of sections are possible. Example: a Sousa march might be listed as:

Intro-AA-BB-C-D-C[-D-C]. Following the introduction, the first strain (A) is repeated, followed by the second strain (B), also repeated. The trio (C) and the breakstrain (D) may be presented with varying repeats.

8. *sonata* — classical form consists of: exposition-development-recapitulation-coda. Vari-

ations include introductions (frequently in contrasting tempi), double or triple theme expositions, contrasts between themes in key choice, style, and mood; use of cadenzas, double developments, binary sonata — or sonatina-form, rondo-sonata (ABA C AB'A) with alternate exposition of themes and return of the principal theme.

9. *fugue.* Baroque fugue (Bach) begins with theme (subject) in one voice followed by statements of the subject in remaining voices; as succeeding voice begins the subject, preceding voice begins the counterpoint. If counterpoint is systematically presented with each statement of the subject, it is termed a *countersubject.* The second statement of the subject is in a dominant relationship to the first statement and is called the *answer;* if the intervallic presentation is identical, it is termed *real,* if altered it is termed *tonal.* Compositional devices employed in fugal development include augmentation, diminution, stretto, inversion, double fugue, among others.

10. *passacaglia, chaconne.* Traditionally, the passacaglia employed a theme in the bass voice, in $\frac{3}{4}$ meter (i.e. *Passacaglia and Fugue in C minor* -J.S. Bach) while the chaconne presented a chordal progression as the basis for the variations. The terms have become interchanged and one must assess the variations today under a joint title. (Mov. 1, *Suite in E-flat,* G. Holst, begins the theme statement in the bass voice, major key tonality, $\frac{3}{4}$, passes it to the treble voices and presents it in chordal fashion — all under the title *Chaconne!*).

11. *variation.* The variation concept is usually applied to a melodic line, a harmonic progression or a rhythmic motive; it may incorporate the entire original idea in some form of variant or a portion. In the *free variation* the original material may be presented in a variant, then used as a springboard for free composition based on the style of the original thought.

Rhythm - Meter

1. *traditional* (duple, triple) — the use of 2-4-6-8, 3-6, 1 primary beats to a measure; the use of primary and secondary weight pulses. Use of *hemiola,* the superimposition of two beats over three and vice versa.

2. *asymmetric meters* — the use of unequal durations (2+3, 3+4, etc.) consistently within the traditional measure concept. The common asymmetric meters and beat divisions are:

$\frac{5}{4}, \frac{5}{8}$ = 2+3 or 3+2

$\frac{7}{4}, \frac{7}{8}$ = 4+3 or 3+4 or 2+2+3 or 2+3+2 or 3+2+2

$\frac{9}{4}, \frac{9}{8}$ = 4+5 or 5+4 or 3+2+4 (or variations thereof)

$\frac{11}{4}, \frac{11}{8}$ = 4+4+3 or 4+3+4 or 3+4+4 (or variations thereof)

3. *changing signatures* — dividing a line or progression through the use of bar lines on important points of stress (the use of accented points independent of traditional meter).

4. *unusual meters* —though frequently asymmetric in nature, these signatures present the pulse sub-division over the common metric pulse:

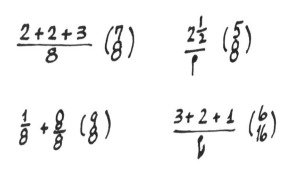

5. *displaced (shifting) accents* — the use of traditional meter with accented points highlighted through articulation or dynamic means.

6. *change of meter* — the change of meter signature over a bar line with a common metric unit between each provides a common (♪) basic pulse with the feeling of changing signatures and somewhat that of shifting accents.

7. *metrical modulation* — a change in meters or tempo through common metric units or pulses that remain constant; usually accompanied by a change in metronomic pulse. The ♩ assumes a longer value than if (♪) was used; the ♪. is much faster due to its equivalency to the previous.

8. *alea, proportional* — the composer provides pitches, time frames, dynamic markings, and stylistic suggestions for the performer who interprets the indications in a free or fixed manner. The performer is an active participant in the composition/performance process, adding emotional and technical vitality to the composer's desires. Each score should contain an explanation, or key, illustrating how the composer wishes each event to be performed.

Play the five pitches in order at a pianissimo level, as fast as possible, for a period of ten seconds.

During the twenty-five second time frame, play the indicated sounds (↓ = lowest possible note; ↑ = highest possible note; ■ = cluster with inclusive pitches) dividing the frame into approximately equal divisions. These events are sometimes dictated by a leader or performer independently.

Orchestration

1. *strings.* The timbral quality of the orchestra is set first by the size of the string section; the massed sound of a large section more adequately balances a full wind/brass complement [3-3-3-3 (fl, ob, cl, bsn) 4-3-3-1 (trpt, horn, trb, tuba)]. Dynamic levels and the balancing of lines must be determined by the size of each string section, the style of the composition and the composer's stated priorities. The conductor must be aware of timbral possibilities of each period, orchestra instrumentation, and balancing requirements.

2. *winds-brasses.* During the Classical Era, winds in orchestra were 0-2-0-2/2-(2); expanding with addition of flutes, clarinets, trombones, and tuba plus auxiliary instruments — piccolo, English horn, E♭ clarinet, bass clarinet, contrabas-

soon — to the present-day orchestra wind section of 3(P)-3(EH)-3(E♭,bcl)-3(Cbn) 4-3-3-1 for which an emerging repertoire is constantly developing.

3. *percussion-keyboards.* Formerly limited to timpani, snare drum, bass drum, cymbals, bells, chimes, xylophone, and "traps", the well-equipped percussion section encompasses all the keyboard percussion, many sizes and timbres of drums, cymbals, gongs, and various metal bells (concert band compositions frequently require 5 percussionists plus the timpanist). The piano and celeste are commonplace instruments in the contemporary ensemble.

4. *wind ensemble.* The contemporary symphonic wind ensemble program encompasses repertoire from chamber size up to the massed or doubled symphonic band. The concept calls for single players to each part (an orchestra concept versus the massed or doubled parts of the symphonic band), thus presenting concert programs with varying sizes of ensembles, each constructed according to the composer's wishes. (This is in contrast to the symphonic band where a fixed ensemble is formed which then performs each composition with exactly the same instrumentation and personnel.) In the performance of English military band compositions — usually originally written for ensembles of fewer than 30 players — the wind ensemble conductor employs two or three performers to each clarinet part to establish the predominance of that timbre and melodic carrier.

5. *symphonic band.* The symphonic band concept employs multiple performers to each voice part which in turn, have been standardized into "preferred" instrumentations by organizations such as the American Bandmasters Association, the American School Band Directors Association, the College Band Directors National Association and the Music Publishers Association, among

others. The timbral difference between the multiple performers to each part and the single performer to each part remains one of the prime differences separating the two concepts; otherwise each is absorbing the best features of the opposite program into its format.

6. *exotic timbral qualities.* The control over weights and balances plus unlimited timbral qualities have led to an adaptation of exotic orchestration and harmonic resources for orchestral wind ensembles and bands. The use of the expanded percussion section with water gongs, bowed steel bars and cymbals, multiple keyboards, amplified instruments, animal bells, plus singing, speaking, whistling, in addition to the various muted possibilities have placed composers such as Messiaen, Husa, Schwantner among others in a class of their own.

Interpretation

1. *stylistic indicators.* The overall "feel" of a composition becomes apparent upon reading through the score for each movement in a cursory manner, observing each of the listed indicators, their consistent use, and the way in which they affect the melodic, harmonic, and rhythmic development. As each assumes a scheme or organized process of employment, the conductor applies a subjective approach to the music in addition to the more technical objective approach. It is this last step that separates the technical reproducers from the feeling, flexible interpretors; even the most stark or harshly-etched contemporary compositions still contain emotional development areas; the conductor uses the indicators as a continual guide.

2. *major expressive qualities* — perceived differently by each conductor, they include each of the aforementioned qualities under the five preceding major headings. Each conductor must

---

How Long Does It Take?

How long the conductor spends, on the average, studying a new score or re-acquainting himself with one of the staple items in the basic repertoire depends on his mental agility and ability to recognize and retain the various components of the score. Every person has certain capabilities which serve as minimum standard measures and every person possesses the potential for growth and improvement; what must be brought into play is a process that combines all this talent, experience, and previous knowledge.

As an example, I believe that a conductor with a few years working experience approaching a work like the *Folk Song Suite* of Ralph Vaughan Williams should expect to spend a minimum of five hours per movement over a period of a few weeks.

Consider that the formal design is straight forward and easily charted, the melodic lines are clear for comparative study, harmonically it is purely triadic, the rhythms are uncomplicated, and the toughest nut — the interpretative elements — should come alive through the study and repeated singing of individual lines. The orchestration, English military band style, is easily analyzed and charted. However, merely tracing each line from beginning to end, identifying the purpose of each note in itself takes much time. One should not hurry the learning process, but rather proceed in a slow and orderly fashion, adding information and experience with every study session.

For a complex contemporary composition, a period of several months of living with the score still may not provide the security we seek.

train himself to respond to each area, analyze the indicator, interpret through the techniques of the ensemble, and bring the music to a living entity.

3. *foreign language terms/translations.* The conductor must be aware of every indication on the score page that provides some form of interpretative assistance; far too often conductors will pass through the study period and move into actual rehearsal of a work without full knowledge of non-English language terminology. Not only does this hamper complete develoment of analytical and interpretative abilities, but also leads the individual performer in the ensemble to follow the conductor's lead and pass through rehearsals and performance without complete knowledge.

4. *historical performance or stylistic considerations.* When performing works of any period (the contemporary composition has its own performance practices just as does the Baroque or Renaissance composition), read as much as possible concerning the period, its instruments, the interpretation of improvised or ornamented figures, the original timbres of the instruments and ensembles. Numerous sources from each period plus musicological research leads one to an authoritative performance that may be presented today with modern instruments.

Marking the Score

Each conductor should develop a system of entering meaningful indications in the score that contributes to his understanding of the music. Score entries may be useful during three distinct portions of the process: (1) score learning, (2) editorial, and (3) performance (including rehearsal).

The score learning process must be a multi-layer venture during which the conductor makes notes on additional information, correlation between different facets of composition and performance practices, and the results of specific projects such as harmonic realizations of vertical structures, identification of melodic material or contrapuntal devices, analysis of rhythmic motives and subsequent development, examination of scoring practices or systems, translation of foreign language instructions, and outline of the macro-form and sub-divisions.

These notes are informational stepping stones, reminders for later score study sessions and possibly for rehearsal procedures. The markings should be entered onto the margins surrounding the actual stave areas, keeping the printed music area as clean as possible. (I frequently construct a separate notebook or insert manuscript paper or blank pages into the score of a complex contemporary composition; the extra space provides a place for notes or analyses that would otherwise obliterate the printed page.)

The learning process should progressively pursue yet another facet of the score in each study session. One should set a goal for each session rather than somewhat aimlessly wandering through the pages looking here and there for previously identifiable material or possibly new correlations to be discovered. Isolate one of the six major areas and study it specifically in order to fulfill everything available in the sub-listings. Obviously your mind will spot other areas simultaneously, thus adding to the wealth of information you are gaining.

Remember, your ultimate pre-rehearsal/performance goal is to feel secure and accountable for every note and marking on the score page. This is not quite as formidable a task as imagined, for just the knowledge of scoring systems and the subsequent reduction of many individual voice parts to their original triadic or post-triadic state offers a vastly-reduced musical landscape with which we must work. Another comforting thought lies in the knowledge that, in most instances, you have already seen or heard many of the individual or grouped lines previously in other works.

One must develop and maintain an aural memory — a retention of every sound you have performed or heard coupled with the visual comfort of a score page bearing those particular voicings. The examples available are far too numerous to list — merely think about a particular ensemble — the Classical orchestra of 1770-1800, for example. The melodic process is a gracious long spinning of notes conceived as consonant or dissonant in the simplest triadic harmonic sense. The harmonic motion was not quick or chromatic as in later decades, but rather a statement of major-minor, dominants, secondary dominants for modulation, plus occasional pedals for development purposes. The orchestra in its early days consisted of Violin 1 as the main melodic carrier, Violin 2 as a melodic/harmonic voice, constantly supporting and reinforcing Violin 1 in unison, octaves, thirds, and sixths. Until the viola, cello and bass divided into three identifiable voice parts, all three performed the bass voice part in two enclosed octaves. The wind counterparts to this practice presented Oboe 1 doubled with or replacing Violin 1, Oboe 2 serving the same function with Violin 2, and the bassoon with the bass voice. The two horns played harmonic series tones serving as harmonic pedals and fillers; the oboes also served harmonic support duties. Once the timbral quality of Violin 1 is learned, then coupled with Oboe 1, likewise for the remainder of the voices, the learning of a second or third symphony cast in the same mold should not be nearly so difficult, based on the assumption that a sound seen and heard is remembered.

The editorial process is used to clarify ambiguities in the score. No composer, editor, transcriber, or arranger enjoys hearing that a conductor spent time correcting errors, adding articulation marks, adjusting dynamics, lining up vertical sonorities, or multiple entrances, but all this frequently must be done. If a conductor is to be in complete command of all his faculties, both personal and musical, while on the podium, then he must be in command of every note and mark on the page. This means frequently double-checking all doubled or coupled lines to compare articulations, making certain that the envelope of each crescendo-decrescendo dynamic requirement has established levels (traditionally left open for maximum interpretative freedom) at each of its three critical points: rise, steady state, decay ($p < f > p$). Contemporary music, in particular, requires a much tighter control over such matters.

In this line of thinking one must condemn the use of reduced or condensed scores for any ensemble music beyond the most elementary level where doublings and line assignments remain constant once assigned. The military band journal with its myriad cues and safety doublings normally carries a condensed score, leaving the diligent, industrious conductor with the task of spreading the individual parts out over a large surface and comparing the parts for inner voice doublings and weights and marking important considerations into the score.

Performance process markings are the type which will illuminate areas for instant recognition during rehearsal or performance. This includes the enlargement of meter signatures, reminders of what follows after a page turn, quick multiple entrances, asymmetrical meters in rapid order, orchestration couplings, etc.

Frequently, conductors enter performance markings into their scores too early in the learning process. If done in bold sweeps or slashes, or in vivid colors, these markings may have the effect of reassuring the conductor that a certain element occurs or enters, and the conductor learns the marking rather than the actual notes and timbral result. This can happen with massive color-coding in which the dynamics are one color, section entrances another, etc. All this art in many layers of color may separate the conductor from the final, most important levels of score learning — the identification of, and with, each mark on the page.

290

Part II

A conductor should begin his search into the score with the belief that while he may not understand certain aspects of the music at sight, there are actually few scores that are impenetrable after several study sessions. And remember, none of us is alone in our frustrations when trying to overcome unfamiliar or difficult territory. The method is based on an organized, systematic approach, working from areas of familiarity to those of doubt and indecision, building cornerstones of knowledge and experience in an orderly and controlled manner. The checklist provides a basic group of compositional techniques, formal considerations, orchestration, and interpretative guidelines which are to serve as musical stimuli for analysis. Many more may be added by each conductor in the development of a personalized procedure.

While some conductors are fortunate in experiencing new techniques on a regular basis, others must begin from an elementary position each time a new compositional style is encountered. Regardless, each person must pass through every trying stage of assimilating all musical requirements of each work, always working to build speed in understanding. One satisfaction in this process lies in the conductor's eventual complete command of all the musical forces, in comparison to the individual performer who masters one part and becomes only conversant with the others.

During the past decade and a half I have encountered many new scores and techniques through reading student works and presenting first or second performances of many compositions still in manuscript. One work which presented a continuing interpretative question was Aaron Copland's *Emblems*, commissioned by the College Band Director's National Association. Since first hearing the work in the early 1960s, I studied and performed *Emblems* several times, each reading with a feeling that there was something elusive in the middle section (rehearsal number 17 through 40; marked *Quite Fast* ♩ =126). Convinced that *Emblems* is indeed a serious work in the wind repertoire, I recorded the work on Mercury Records with the Eastman Wind Ensemble, all the while pondering the question of that elusive area. It seemed to be only a series of unrelated individual isolated sections interspersed between rests. Finally, after applying a score checklist approach to the work, I became convinced that the problem was mine, not Copland's and that the ordering of notes was ingenious, the open pointalistic score was unique, and my problem lay in understanding the formal layout.

Following a friend's suggestion, I began looking at the section with an overview rather than trying to discover the position and meaning of each note and rest. I did this by singing through that section at a faster tempo while conducting only one beat per measure. Soon I had a feeling of sounds and silences in a well-established order. Slowing the tempo down to m.m. =126 the whole area now made sense musically and flowed along. In rehearsals I tried the "greater overview" approach with the players, but found that the technique was more applicable for the conductor, who has the advantage of the full score and can see the relationships between sections. Single line performers feel more secure with individual beat patterns.

For a thorough understanding of the following section, the reader should secure a copy of the score for Canzona by Peter Mennin (Carl Fischer, Inc.)

Making Notes

Many conductors make notes during score study that serve as a visual record of the many things they know must eventually become a part of their aural memory. The notes printed here, made during first, second, and later levels of appraisal, contain *Score Checklist* items plus off-hand observations. As you prepare such a list, leave ample room on each page for additions to be gleaned from subsequent study sessions. The listing of such items on separate pages and not on the score is more attractive to me than over-marking the score, which can become a hindrance during performance.

In addition to standard abbreviations for individual instruments (fl= flute, ww= woodwind, br= brass, etc.) I use the following: ml= melodic line; bg= background; rhy/har= rhythm/harmony.

First Level Appraisal

copyright 1954
Allegro Deciso ♩ =126
duration ca. 5:00
full concert band (no Cb clar, no percussion listed on score pg. 1)

- Title suggests a multi-section work. Is this a reflection of the form or a programmatic/descriptive title?
- Rehearsal numbers separate major sections developed through change of thematic material, variations, orchestration, etc.
- Score written with no key signatures; accidentals before each note, good for whole measure.
- Polytriadic writing: beginning, A minor over D minor, G major over E minor, C major over B minor, etc.; are more than two triads used in composition?
- Much fugal writing; augmentation of ml; subject in bass voices frequently.
- Rhy/har bg often doubled in traditional hns/saxs scoring (provides thickness and loss of individual section timbre).
- Cornets and trumpets used interchangeably, no real separation of timbre.
- Articulation markings, particularly slurs, appear more string-oriented than wind; short, choppy lines under *cantabile* marking.
- Br bass voice overused with tutti ww choir rather than pure indigenous ww bass quality.

291

- String bass heavily doubled with tuba; perhaps more pizz for projection; use with ww bass alone?
- Short phrases with new material or variation of previous material; melodic lines primarily step-wise outlining triadic shape; often difficult to tell new lines from variation on previous line.
- Short open spaces of silence; important to preserve these "windows" for contrast of thick scoring, and concentration of sound in middle register.
- Percussion writing restricted to orchestral type timpani plus snare, bass drum, cym in explosive inserts, crescendi; no outlining or highlighting of melodic material.
- Variations on earlier material: how done? rhythmic? original orchestration plus added texture? any harmonic variations? melodic variations?
- Bass voices divided in pointillistic style; require rehearsal for tight ensemble, balance, clarity of lines.
- Ending requires support of tone plus constant building right up to last 3-4 measures; no reduction of intensity permitted.
- Fugal stretto at short distance — one measure, sometimes in similar timbres; requires projection of each line.
- Compositional style produces feeling of flow; development of material is natural, not forced or contrived; short phrases
- have solid relationship and blend one into another; only constant element is crescendo ending phrase and leading into next (occurs 11 times).

The first level comments are the result of a general perusal through the score and should be re-examined later. You will change your mind about the analysis each time you go through the score; what this first level appraisal has provided is a number of written thoughts which you may later amend or even replace completely. Far too much analysis is done "off the top of the head" and valuable time is wasted by repeating the same mental exercise if you do not notate your thoughts as you progress.

Second Level Appraisal

A second sweep through the score, obviously a more in-depth approach, may well produce additional information. Always remember that each individual will find what is most vital to him at the time, so you should expect great variation from person to person. The second level appraisal list printed here is what I found during my analysis plus what surfaced as I re-read the information. My list includes melodic material, formal design, harmonic and rhythmic considerations, and, again, commentary for future consideration. This "talking to yourself" while studying is an easy way to discuss questions and a logical step in amassing information, all built upon your experiences,

knowledge, and imaginative thinking. As in long examinations, do first what you can accomplish easily and then use the remaining time to return to the tough problems.

Themes

Rehearsal Letter/ Measure No. (Theme No.)	Comments (See music examples for themes and bass lines)
1-6 (1,1a)	brass/sax, timp; no tuba, s.b., timp. *Theme 1a* begins m2, beats 3,4.
A/7-11 (1b)	rhythmic variation, tutti orchestration.
B/12-25 (2)	bg: rhy/har in hns/sax; *bass line #1.*
21-25 (2)	fugal entrance in low ww/br
C/26-30 (3)	cl/sax triadic scoring (omit brass bass if sufficient ww bass); s.b. to pizz; *bass line #2a.*
D/31-36 (4)	*4a:* 3 meas *4b:* 3 meas; pointillistic divisi bass voices; *bass line 2b.*
E/37-41 (3)	tutti var. of mm26-30.
42-44 (4)	tutti var.; *Question:* are themes 3 and 4 actually one complete ml or two separate yet similar lines?

Bass Lines

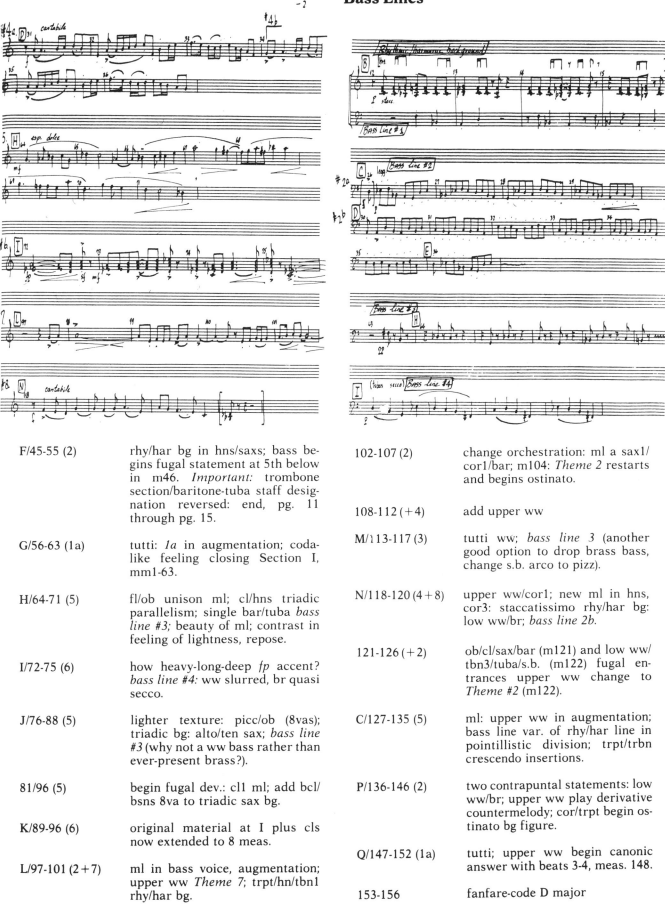

F/45-55 (2)	rhy/har bg in hns/saxs; bass begins fugal statement at 5th below in m46. *Important:* trombone section/baritone-tuba staff designation reversed: end, pg. 11 through pg. 15.
G/56-63 (1a)	tutti: *1a* in augmentation; coda-like feeling closing Section I, mm1-63.
H/64-71 (5)	fl/ob unison ml; cl/hns triadic parallelism; single bar/tuba *bass line #3;* beauty of ml; contrast in feeling of lightness, repose.
I/72-75 (6)	how heavy-long-deep *fp* accent? *bass line #4:* ww slurred, br quasi secco.
J/76-88 (5)	lighter texture: picc/ob (8vas); triadic bg: alto/ten sax; *bass line #3* (why not a ww bass rather than ever-present brass?).
81/96 (5)	begin fugal dev.: cl1 ml; add bcl/bsns 8va to triadic sax bg.
K/89-96 (6)	original material at I plus cls now extended to 8 meas.
L/97-101 (2+7)	ml in bass voice, augmentation; upper ww *Theme 7;* trpt/hn/tbn1 rhy/har bg.
102-107 (2)	change orchestration: ml a sax1/cor1/bar; m104: *Theme 2* restarts and begins ostinato.
108-112 (+4)	add upper ww
M/113-117 (3)	tutti ww; *bass line 3* (another good option to drop brass bass, change s.b. arco to pizz).
N/118-120 (4+8)	upper ww/cor1; new ml in hns, cor3: staccatissimo rhy/har bg: low ww/br; *bass line 2b.*
121-126 (+2)	ob/cl/sax/bar (m121) and low ww/tbn3/tuba/s.b. (m122) fugal entrances upper ww change to *Theme #2* (m122).
C/127-135 (5)	ml: upper ww in augmentation; bass line var. of rhy/har line in pointillistic division; trpt/trbn crescendo insertions.
P/136-146 (2)	two contrapuntal statements: low ww/br; upper ww play derivative countermelody; cor/trpt begin ostinato bg figure.
Q/147-152 (1a)	tutti; upper ww begin canonic answer with beats 3-4, meas. 148.
153-156	fanfare-code D major

Still More Analysis

Again, this second analysis should not be considered complete, but another step along the path to complete understanding of the score. *Canzona* is relatively accessible to most conductors due to the extremely sectional nature of the composition and the fact that the rehearsal numbers reflect major changes of technique. Nevertheless, the act of charting the work measure-by-measure leads to an in-depth realization of the musical potential of the composition, solidifies one's musical thoughts, and suggests proper rehearsal procedures. At this point, it may be fruitful to raise more questions for contemplation:

• How to keep this work from sounding too sectional? How to "glue together" the short phrases and variations while maintaining a clarity in the fugal passages?

• The scoring is traditional English military band journal scoring with substantial doublings both for timbre and for safety in unknown ensembles. How to establish good balances, clear timbres, and individual section sounds?

• The percussion writing is limited and somewhat restricted to explosive qualities and crescendi; this must be contained within the context of the dynamic and interpretative scope of the work.

• The middle register of the band, (F3 to C5) is heavily scored and doubled. To what extent should these textures be thinned for the wind band of the 80s?

• Where to program this work on a concert? (Full and powerful in sound, contrasting cantabiles, 5 minutes in length.) Beginning of first half? Second half? Close of either half? Between two extensive low-dynamic works?

The next excursion into the score will probably produce some answers for the questions raised during the first two study sessions, and will concentrate on the remainder of the major areas in the *Score Checklist* that are still left uncovered. Again, I must stress the fact that the exact sequence of events must be at the discretion of each individual conductor who is establishing his own mode of study. At this point in the study of *Canzona* I would certainly investigate the articulation markings; the printed style of writing suggests string bowings rather than wind markings.

Score study and score marking involves more than a dispassionate analysis of printed facts; it requires personal participation — singing through each line or playing individual parts on a keyboard instrument. This act approximates the sensation experienced by the individual performer and provides the realization of a given melodic line, the weight and length of stressed notes, the articulations necessary for one note to pass to another musically, etc. These thoughts may be entered into the score proper as they may well be helpful during the rehearsal process.

The music example shows my re-marking of *Theme #2* at rehearsal letter B that I used for further study, based on personal criteria:

• Singing through the line exactly as printed produces a sectionalized, almost choppy feeling, alleviated only by the composer-originated marking of *cantabile*. While this marking may well be sufficient for solo performers or chamber music performers, the use of this term combined with the few printed slurs, staccato marks, and (most important) lack of marks over some notes, will certainly lead to confusion in a massed wind organization, particularly a younger ensemble.

• I am constantly searching for methods to introduce a breadth of sound into wind performance as I feel that many conductors and performers have not yet escaped the inherent wind band approach to performance that is more vertical in nature than linear. The mere fact that the majority of wind organizations spend a disproportionate amount of time performing music where the attack of each tone is of more importance than the duration or release of the tone (i.e. in marches and most outdoor compositions) leads one to create (or recreate) articulation schemes to introduce this important element into the concert wind ensemble.

• Syncopation figures and notes tied over a bar line require special attention to ascertain sufficient length for the interpretive qualities desired. In these instances I mark a tenuto dash to indicate breadth of tone, and to eliminate chopping the smaller note values.

• Notes with staccato marks must be examined carefully for length consideration and separation from the preceding note as well as the following note. I personally prefer a staccato-tenuto approach which establishes a "lifting" effect rather than a quick release of the tone. This is in line with the thought that every tone has a life of its own, however short, and must have ample time to be sounded and heard.

• The most important consideration in *Canzona* markings is the lack of substantive indications to support the printed *cantabile*. Here I apply a dotted slur to indicate the length of the musical thought which includes open "windows" of rest space as well as sounded pitches.

• Accents must be evaluated for several factors, including quality of initial attack, length and breadth of the stress, weight of the tone in timbre, and relationship of the accented note to those surrounding it. I frequently prefer a deeper leaning into the note rather than merely a strong stroke of the tongue on the impetus of the attack as this provides more breadth to the sound.

All the above discussion leads to the realization that the conductor, as the representative of the composer, must frequently contribute his wealth of knowledge and experience in addition to the written desires of the composer for the welfare of the performance. I have worked closely with composers who possess an extremely fine-honed knowledge of their own craft and the rehearsal techniques necessary to bring their compositions to musical fruition. Unfortunately, I have also worked with composers whose creations were a part of a mental-emotional experience devoid of instrumental technique practicality and whose compositions required a re-working of practically every measure to insure an adequate performance.

If each conductor can develop an appreciation of each aspect of the score through a process such as the *Score Study Checklist,* he will be equipped to approach the podium confident that he has investigated every known resource of musical activity. This knowledge will offer security — both musical and personal — and will lead him to consider the composer and his contribution the most important element of the conductor's craft. In turn this wonderful realization will offer the conductor full access to the glorious experience of creating an audible performance from a silent score. ■

Selected Bibliography

The texts listed below may be of benefit during score study periods for reference and explanation of the various compositional techniques listed in the *Score Study Checklist.* An additional source is the bibliography included in the books listed, especially the first entry by Fink and Ricci. This list is by no means complete and should be considered as a basic guide to a further insight into the various areas of analysis under consideration.

The Language of Twentieth Century Music, Robert Fink and Robert Ricci, Schirmer Books, 1975.

Form and Orchestration, Schirmer Books, Gardner Read, 1980.

Techniques of Twentieth Century Composition, third edition, Leon Dallin, W.C. Brown, 1974.

Twentieth Century Idioms, G. Welton Marquis, Prentice-Hall, 1964.

Twentieth Century Harmony, Vincent Persichetti, W.W. Norton, 1961.

Form in Tonal Music, Douglass Green, Holt, Rinehart and Winston, 1966.

The Technique of Orchestration, second edition, Kent Kennan, Prentice-Hall, 1970.

New Directions in Music, David Cope, W.C. Brown, 1971.

The Art of Wind Playing, Arthur Weisberg, Schirmer Books, 1975.

New Music Vocabulary: A Guide to Notational Signs for Contemporary Music, Howard Risatti, University of Illinois Press, 1975.

Editor's Note: The two compositions discussed in this article have been recorded by the Eastman Wind Ensemble on Mercury Records. The Peter Mennin *Canzona* was recorded by Frederick Fennell and the Eastman Wind Ensemble in 1954 on *Mercury MG50084.* The Aaron Copland *Emblems* was recorded by Donald Hunsberger and the Eastman Wind Ensemble on November 7, 1978 and recently released on *Mercury Golden Imports SRI 75132.*

Score Reading — The Silent Skill

BY FRANK BATTISTI

*My approach is to look at the score until
I know it and can read it like a book.*
— Frederick Fennell

Score reading is a complex process that
involves the conductor's musical imagination, intuition, inner hearing ability,
memory, feelings, and emotions. By reading
through a score many times, the conductor
becomes personally involved with the composer's music in a nonanalytical way. His
goal should be twofold: to acquire a
skeletal image of the music, an overview of it that he can hear with unbroken continuity in his mind
without referring to the
score; and to develop an
intuitive musical feeling
for the expressive content
and form of the image.
The following guide-
lines will help con-
ductors read and
study scores
more effec-
tively.

Editor's Note: A work in progress, Music is the
Score! *is a guide to score study for the wind band
conductor co-authored by conductor Frank Battisti
and Robert Garofalo, Professor of Music at the
Catholic University of America in Washington,*
*D.C. The book dissects score study into a four-step
process: score orientation, score reading, score analysis, and score interpretation. This article extracts
Frank Battisti's comments regarding the second step,
score reading.*

The novice conductor who has a new or unfamiliar score in front of him should first determine an appropriate slow reading pulse for the music based on the knowledge of all of the tempo indications in the piece. If two or more tempo markings appear in the work, he has to be aware of them before setting a first reading pulse. The tempo he chooses should allow him to read the score and hear the music (imagine the sound) without stopping.

Score reading, like reading a book, involves continuous eye movement through musical notation. Once the conductor begins, he should not stop. The moment he stops, he begins studying the score, which is a different process. Until one has developed enough skills and had enough experience, the beginning reading tempo will probably be slower than the indicated tempo found in the score.

On the first read-through the conductor should approach the task with an open mind so that he is able to grasp whatever comes through naturally. He shouldn't have any preconceived list of items to look for when he starts reading the score. He should not force the process of looking for anything specific; rather, he should just read and discover the piece naturally and spontaneously. The music's inherent content and expressive meaning gradually should become apparent with subsequent readings of the score.

The inexperienced conductor should try to read the entire page of music, measure by measure from left to right, up and down. Success at score reading will vary from individual to individual; an inexperienced conductor at first may be able to read only the melody, while the young conductor whose major instrument is percussion may focus on the percussion parts in the score. That's fine. With more experience at score reading, each conductor gradually will improve his ability to imagine sound from music notation.

To read even a relatively simple wind band score with some degree of fluency, a conductor needs to possess at least average inner hearing ability. He also needs to be familiar with traditional harmony, standard musical terms, and the transpositions of instruments, as well as be able to instantaneously transpose nonconcert pitch instrument lines. The conductor who tries to read a score that is beyond his musical skills and knowledge won't be able to do it. He will have

to stop frequently to figure out the music, and won't be able to read it without stopping.

Let me explain it this way. If a person opens a medical book and begins to see unfamiliar terms, charts, graphs, diagrams, and so on, he instinctively knows that he won't be able to read and understand what is there. He almost immediately says to himself, "This is a book that I cannot read." The same is true for score reading.

The best way to develop score reading skill is to silently read and reread a lot of scores. The conductor should begin with short, easy pieces, then gradually increase the difficulty of the scores. Conscientiously applying this step will greatly improve his ability to read a score.

Of course, the conductor first has to decide whether or not he is able to read the score in front of him. He has to determine if his skills and knowledge are on a par with the task of reading the music at hand. If they are not, he will be wasting his time.

The conductor who wants to learn or perform a score that is too difficult to read should omit the score reading part of the study process, going ahead to analyze the music. He does not have to slow read the score many times in order to learn the music; he can get by without applying the second step. However, an inability to read the score with some degree of fluency is a clear signal that he will have to work hard at correcting apparent deficiencies in his training.

It is not always possible to identify which specific musical elements will stand out to the conductor as he reads the score. Experience has shown that the melody is one of the first elements to emerge during score reading. However, conductors notice other elements as well. Tempo markings, time signatures, or key changes; a climactic phrase or an orchestrated crescendo; an instrument or section entrance; an embellishment or stylistic articulation; an ostinato rhythmic pattern; a cadence or chord progression; even such things as repeat signs or rehearsal numbers may strike the reader.

The inexperienced reader may be able to see, hear, and absorb only one or two musical elements in a composition with each reading of the score. On the other hand, an experienced score reader may be able to deal with several of them at the same time. Once he identifies and remembers an element, he will recognize it every time he sees it. The process of score reading has a lot to do with one's musical memory; however, remembering what is in the music should occur naturally from many readings of the score. A conductor should not force himself to memorize the music. Gradually he will begin to achieve a sense of the complete score.

Score reading is similar to a scavenger hunt where you discover one clue after another until eventually the clues lead you to the object. It is

Frank Battisti is conductor of the Wind Ensemble at the New England Conservatory in Boston, Massachusetts. A recognized authority on wind literature, he has conducted wind ensembles and bands for over 30 years. He is Past-President of the College Band Directors National Association, founder of the National Wind Ensemble Conference, and a member of the Standard Music Award Panel for A.S.C.A.P. He is a contributor to many journals and magazines, and in 1986 was a Visiting Fellow at Clare Hall College, Cambridge University, England.

a matter of discovering, identifying, and relating. When you are on a scavenger hunt you pick up a clue and go to a spot. At that spot you pick up the next clue, which helps you to continue. In reading scores you identify musical clues — motives, themes, shapes, events, and so on. The more clues you can identify, remember, and connect, the clearer the object becomes. Eventually, with enough musical clues, you achieve the goal.

What is the goal, you ask? The conductor should be able to put away the score, then carry some sort of skeletal sound image of the music in his head so that his mind is always working on it. He needs to get to this stage as quickly as possible. The best way to do it is to read the score as frequently as possible.

Score reading is like walking down a path through the woods with an alert, concentrated mind and an observant and perceptive attitude. Each time you do it, you discover something new in the environment. If you do it three, four, or five times every day, eventually you will get to know the path and its environment so well that you will be able to walk through it with your eyes closed, yet being able to see, hear, and smell the surroundings.

While score reading the conductor should allow his feelings and ideas about the expressive content of the music to develop. To do that he should give free rein to his musical imagination, letting his emotional response unfold naturally and spontaneously. Most important, he should not deny any intuitive musical responses that occur as he reads the score. Later he may change his ideas about the music, but not in this step of the process.

If certain parts of the music are still unclear after several readings, the conductor should go back to the music and focus on the specific passages he can't remember. At this time he should actually study the score, taking a concentrated look at it. This does not mean he should analyze the score. He needs to figure out what is going on at those points in the music so he can remember them in the context of the score. His goal is not to deal with details, but to have an outline of the sound of the entire work with unbroken continuity.

To check his memory of the score, the conductor has to provide time during score reading to replay the music in his mind without looking at the score. If there are gaps or breaks in the image after several readings, he needs to study those passages in the context of the entire piece.

I believe it's difficult to put a time limit on the practice of score reading, going from step two (score reading) to step three (score analysis) in the process of score study. It depends on the length and complexity of the composition and the conductor's skill at score reading. He should be prepared to spend whatever time is necessary

— two, three, or four weeks or months. Sometimes it takes years to be able to read a score in a natural way.

It is important for the conductor to avoid analyzing the music in this step of the process simply because score study does not start with analysis; one should not get there too soon. The conductor needs to explore the terrain — roam around the landscape, if you will — before beginning to dig the well. Once familiar with the terrain, he will be ready to organize an expedition to explore the details. If the conductor stops his exploration of the musical landscape by studying detail, he could get so far involved with the detail that he might begin to build a premise from a limited perspective. This can be dangerous because during the early stages of score study it is difficult to know whether or not the detail being examined is important or not.

By reading the score many times every day, the conductor should be able to formulate conclusions based on his knowledge, imagination, and intuition. For example, if he thinks that the piece is in sonata-allegro form, then he will be looking for the recapitulation. He can't do that as quickly if he begins to analyze details of the music. By the time one conductor completes an analysis of the harmony of the first page of the score, another conductor could finish several readings of the entire piece and have a better overall idea of the composition. Because the

A Tasty Analogy

If I were a chef and had to prepare a meat dish, I would have to decide how to cook the meat. I could put it in the oven and let it simmer slowly in its own juices, or I could put it in the pressure cooker or microwave oven to cook it very fast. Each cooking method would give the meat a different kind of taste, flavor, and aroma — a different result.

Now, if someone gave me a new score, requesting that I conduct the piece in 24 hours, I could prepare that score in the given time limit. But I will tell you one thing: it wouldn't be a pleasant experience. It would be very hard work, and the main objective would be to learn it in a manner that enabled me to conduct a rehearsal of the piece in 24 hours. When I have to prepare a score that way, the result is likely to be superficial. Unfortunately, far too many conductors do it just that way, and they do it with the aid of a record or cassette tape.

composer presented an entire musical conception in the score, the conductor should start by reading the whole piece, not by analyzing the details. To me it is a wholistic approach.

For a long, multi-movement work — a suite, concerto, or symphony — the conductor should read and reread one movement at a time, making sure he has some grasp of the music's content before moving on to the next movement. This is a practical matter because the novice conductor may not be able to read through an entire multi-movement score.

The conductor should avoid using the piano or other keyboard instrument to help acquire a mental image of the music. Though it's true that the piano is a powerful tool to develop external hearing skills, using the piano to hear the score diminishes the challenge of developing inner hearing ability. The conductor should go to the piano only as a last resort.

Some experienced professional conductors play through their scores at the piano, but I am not talking about professionals; I am addressing the young, inexperienced conductor who needs to develop score-reading skill. Score reading has nothing to do with one's ability to play the piano; it has everything to do with one's inner hearing ability. A professional conductor doesn't use the piano as a crutch to hear what is in a score; he uses it as an instrument to play the music. A young conductor will never learn how to read a score with fluency by pounding out the music on the piano. He has to learn how to play it in his mind, using his musical imagination and inner hearing ability.

Another temptation to avoid is listening to a recording or cassette tape performance of a work when studying the score. Listening to a recording of a work during the reading step does not help to develop an inner hearing ability. While listening the conductor doesn't read the music, he follows it. Following along in the score and actually reading the music are two entirely different processes. The distinction is very important. A recording gives you too much, too soon; it gives you everything. The danger is that the conductor may be tempted to imitate what he is hearing. Imitation is not the ultimate goal of score study; a unique, personal interpretation is.

It is clear that the conductor cannot always take the time to study a score this slowly if he is under pressure to prepare a work for rehearsal and performance in a short amount of time. For example, when I gave the premiere of Michael Colgrass's *Winds of Nagual*, I was under tremendous pressure to learn the score quickly; the ink was still drying on the last pages of the score when it was time to begin rehearsing the piece. As soon as I had received the manuscript score I began studying and analyzing the music so that I could conduct the music. Although we were able to perform the work satisfactorily, it was not an enjoyable experience.

By contrast, here is an example of how the score reading process should function. Recently I gave a performance of Persichetti's *Masquerade*. I had been reading and studying this piece since it was published in 1966. During that time I had often taken this score out of the file to read.

One day, as I was reading the score, it suddenly came to me: "I've got to perform this work; it's a wonderful piece of music!" By this time I knew the piece quite well. I had been accumulating knowledge, musical ideas, and a feeling for the piece for many years, free from the pressure of getting it ready for a performance. This experience is very different from cramming.

The conductor who studies a score and simultaneously tries to prepare it for performance restricts his creative imagination because his mind is diverted to dealing with practical rehearsal items. The best time to study a score is when there is no pressure to perform the work; without performance pressure the conductor's imagination has more time to explore the possibilities, to blossom and unfold. □

Guidelines for Score Reading

1. Establish a comfortable reading tempo. Before you begin to read the score, choose a tempo that allows you to read and hear the music as a flowing, continuous sound in your mind.
2. Don't stop. Use a metronome to assure a continuous forward reading movement. (Do not use a metronome if there are asymmetrical meters or tempo changes in the music, especially ritardandos and accelerandos, etc.)
3. Use your intuition and musical imagination. Let your subjective, nonanalytical feelings and emotions about the music surface naturally. Give yourself the freedom to respond spontaneously to the music as you read the score.
4. Don't analyze the music. Avoid being concerned with details of the score, and don't linger over uncertainties. Allow the elements of the music to emerge naturally in any way, shape, or form.
5. Don't try to memorize the music. Don't force the process by trying to absorb more than what comes naturally to you. With subsequent readings of the score, an outline of the music will gradually emerge in your mind. Don't make memorization the priority; let it be the result of the exploration.
6. Use any music reading method you are comfortable with to silently read the score. Sing to yourself using neutral syllables, movable do, fixed do, letter names, or numbers. If you can't read transposed instrument lines at concert pitch, then read the transposed lines in your mind as they appear in the score.
7. Do not use the piano.
8. Do not listen to recordings of the work.
9. Allow sufficient time for score reading. Read through the score slowly several times every day.
10. Periodically evaluate your ability to hear music in your mind.

EMULATE THE PROFESSIONAL

Harry Begian

Development of an effective rehearsal procedure, with its accompanying techniques, is probably the most important problem that faces a conductor. A career as conductor on either the professional or amateur level is often measured in terms of improvement in rehearsal techniques and improving effectiveness in the use of rehearsal time. As the conductor becomes increasingly proficient in attaining more musical results in a given amount of rehearsal time, he can feel that he has improved the application of conducting and rehearsal techniques. If he should continue in the same old ways, year after year, without learning the importance of time, and how to use it well in rehearsal, there has obviously been no improvement.

One of the greatest fallacies among school music conductors and conductors of essentially amateur groups is the concept that the rehearsal techniques of their groups should be different from those employed with professional ensembles. As a result, most conductors of such groups develop a "school-marmish" approach which is a far cry from professional rehearsal procedures. Such a difference in approach would be tolerable if it achieved the intended aims, but invariably it seems to miss the essential purposes underlying rehearsals. Since the problem is a common one confronting amateur music-making situations, it is surprising that it is rarely hinted at or discussed. Obviously, all concerned can benefit from a discussion of this problem. It must first be presumed, however, that such discussion relates to conductors of groups which have achieved a level of technical and musical maturity that will benefit from a professional-type approach to rehearsals and performance. The following remarks are therefore directed to conductors of high school, college, and civic musical organizations who have as their aim the better utilization of whatever alloted rehearsal time they now enjoy.

In most fields of endeavor the amateur very often looks to the professional as a person to emulate. The professional musician has usually trained long and hard in his chosen specialization and, through experience, has learned to apply his talents in such a way as to derive maximum results with minimum wasted time and effort. A professional approach to one's work is often a way of life which implies involvement and commitment that are at one and the same time practical, artistically demanding, and effective in their results. Such beliefs, when applied to conducting amateur groups, can improve any rehearsal situation. Briefly stated, there should be no difference in the approach to rehearsals of

Harry Begian is director of bands at Michigan State University. He holds the bachelor's and master's degrees from Wayne State University and a doctorate from the University of Michigan. Prior to his appointment at MSU he was director of the band at Cass Technical High School in Detroit for 17 years and director of the Wayne band for three years. He has served as a guest conductor, adjudicator, and clinician throughout the Midwest, and is a new member of The Instrumentalist's Board of Advisors.

professional or amateur groups. The only difference we can allow is for the technical and musical abilities (or inabilities) of the particular organization involved.

Obviously, those who do not have professional musicians to work with are not able to make the same exacting demands as those who do. Their general aims, terminology, and techniques can and should be the same, however. So many amateur groups suffer at the hands of conductors who are unaware of what can reasonably be expected of them. Such conductors constitute a majority, far outnumbering those whose demands border on the impossible. Too few conductors challenge the performers enough or help them realize their potentials fully. It is too easy to subscribe to an attitude that good, solid music-making is beyond the grasp of most young players and to conduct rehearsals accordingly. Such an approach is often disguised as "fun through music" and comes out as sheer bad music-making. It is too often accompanied by dull, labored, and fruitless rehearsing which completely misses the exhilaration and accomplishment characterising those rehearsals that achieve a *musical* objective through time-tested and professional means.

What, then, are the necessary ingredients of a solid, professionally-oriented rehearsal procedure, and how can they be applied to improve the quality of rehearsals and performances of amateur groups? It would seem that we must first of all try to adapt the techniques, demands, and reasonable expectations of the professional conductor.

Basic to any rehearsal procedure must be a plan of action. It must be thought out clearly beforehand and embrace what is to be rehearsed with a clear idea of how much time to devote to each phase of the rehearsal. Robert Shaw, one of the great choral conductors of our time, has been heard to remark that he knows how many minutes of rehearsal time he will allow for a certain difficult passage. Any professional conductor has to plan his rehearsals carefully to be certain that he will cover a specified amount of music in a given amount of rehearsal time. It would seem that a conductor of an amateur ensemble could do the same. In fact, how can he afford to do less?

It would seem unthinkable for a competent conductor to start rehearsal on a work which he has not studied. Can conductors of amateur groups approach a new work any differently when the technical and musical understanding of their group is far less than that of the professional? Obviously, the school music conductor should have as much information about a work as possible before going into the rehearsal room. Otherwise the rehearsal will be wasted and reduce itself to a search (on the part of conductor *and* ensemble) to learn what the music is and what it is trying to say.

Once in rehearsal the conductor must impose a no-

nonsense atmosphere of rehearsal discipline. Undisciplined and aimless rehearsals can only lead to poor performance, poor attitudes, and the false concept that music-making is a game rather than a serious business. Again, we can learn from the professional rehearsal atmosphere, which is disciplined, practical, and efficient in its procedures. The conductor must set the "tone" of his rehearsals by constantly demanding more of himself than of the performers. By such example he can rightfully expect something from the players in return. The "personality conductor," the "talking conductor," or the "story-telling conductor" only wastes valuable rehearsal time and avoids the true purposes of the rehearsals. An efficient conductor knows what he is after, tries to explain it with minimum verbiage, and develops his technique to the point where he does not have to stop for every little correction. But, when his technique cannot accurately convey what he is seeking musically, he must stop and explain.

Too often a business-like, tight, no-nonsense type rehearsal may seem to connote a harsh, unbending approach. This need never be if the conductor seizes opportunities in rehearsal to release built-up tensions. No rehearsal atmosphere should exclude humor as an important ingredient. A conductor who fails to share the humor of certain occurrences in amateur rehearsals is less than mindful of the players' emotional needs. The ability to "change gears" when the occasion permits or demands it should be regarded as both welcome and healthy, and can only make for better feeling and understanding between a conductor and the musicians.

The conductor with a good set of ears and a knowledge of musical styles is never at a loss as to what to say or do in rehearsal. At any given moment there are sounds to be heard, evaluated, and possibly corrected. So as not to demoralize the ensemble through infinite picking away at details, the conductor must have established in his mind which mistakes need immediate attention and correction and those mistakes which tend to correct themselves. Musical mistakes of a basic nature such as wrong notes, wrong rhythms, or wrong styles should be immediately identified and corrected. To permit such mistakes to pass without challenge can only have a cumulative effect and cause greater problems later. Some sort of priority scale must be operative at rehearsals so that the conductor does not concern, or prematurely bog down, a group with subtle refinements and problems while there are still problems of a basic nature to be worked out. It is of prime importance that the conductor have an established, over-all concept of a work as he re-creates it, and this concept *must* be in accordance with the demands of the score. In order to achieve something approaching his idealized concept, a conductor must constantly stress proper balances, dynamics, intonation, and nuances. These elements, along with the basic ones mentioned earlier, constitute the purposes behind all rehearsals, and must be dealt with constantly. The proficient conductor is much like a doctor in that his chief concerns are to diagnose what is wrong and to recommend its cure. Most conductors of amateur groups tend to be competent diagnosticians who are at a complete loss when it comes to effecting cures of musical ailments. Unfortunately, when a cure is not offered the musician, the problem persists or becomes intensified.

Advocacy of a "tight" rehearsal too often conjures a rather nasty picture of shackling the musical expression of performers. Once again, we refer to general professional procedures and recognition by the conductor of those passages which allow for individual expressiveness. More often than not, the player is permitted to perform a passage of soloistic nature as he hears and conceives it. Obviously, something must be left to the performer's judgment, *if* he is sufficiently mature musically. The conductor need impose his will only when the player is stylistically at odds with correct performance practices or what he, the conductor, knows to be correct. In such instances, desirable changes can be induced through subtle suggestion rather than direct means. Or if player-ego may suffer, the problem can be discussed outside the rehearsal room, in private.

One of the greatest rehearsal aids is the ability of a conductor to convey his musical concepts through singing. The professional conductor will invariably demonstrate in this manner, and yet too few school conductors have adapted this valuable technique. What better way to explain something musically than through singing? The most eloquent verbalization could not begin to convey how we want a thing to sound, nor present a clear representation of the idea in terms of musical sounds. One need not have a fine singing voice to demonstrate what he wants in terms of rhythms, dynamics, phrasing, or stylistic intent. The conductor who depends more on involved and lengthy explanation rather than singing examples wastes more rehearsal time than is necessary. Can it be that school conductors have rebelled so completely against the rote approach that they are ignoring its usefulness in rehearsal situations?

The conductor's ego too often impedes, rather than helps, a rehearsal. The conductor who is overly-concerned with how he "looks" in rehearsal is sure to lose the respect of the ensemble. There is nothing more aggravating to competent players than to be lectured and drilled on passages which do not present musical problems. Too often, these are passages where the conductor had anticipated problems. If such trouble spots do not develop as expected, the conductor should be grateful for one less reason for stopping the rehearsal momentum. Yet we so often see players subjected to lengthy, seemingly "rehearsed" explanations of problems that have not presented themselves. It is almost as though the conductor, having reasoned how to treat the anticipated problem, feels that he must release this information even if things go right.

The most unforgivable exercise of conductor ego is the practice of diversionary tactics, used by some to cover up their own obvious errors. How often have we witnessed rehearsals in which some unsuspecting player is blamed for the conductor's mistake? This has to be the most fatal mistake in the conductor-player relationship. If indulged in frequently enough, it can ultimately erode any respect that players feel for a conductor. And yet, unwillingness to admit to an honest mistake seems beyond many conductors. Such an attitude implies that players are unaware of the conductor's fallibility; this is an insult to their intelligence. A conductor might far better admit to his mistakes and, by so doing, let his organization recognize that he is human and capable of error. The conductor of a fine junior high school group would find it hard to cover up a conducting mistake convincingly; yet conductors often employ deception with mature, adult musicians.

Conductors of amateur and school groups too often display a self-consciousness in rehearsal that is never evident in the professional rehearsal. The seeming lack of concentration displayed by such conductors is in basic contradiction with the production of fine results. A person who is self-conscious while conducting a rehearsal risks developing a similar response from the players. His goal should be complete self-involvement and commitment to the music being studied. When he achieves this he will no longer feel restricted.

Finally, something should be said briefly about the conductor-player relationship. Implicit to a successful interaction of the two parties is mutual rspect. Each side needs the other's respect; the conductor without a group of players to conduct has no function, while the group without a conductor can only reflect a wide range of disjointed ideas and approaches to rehearsing and performing. It is the conductor's task (mission) to unite divergent individual attitudes and concepts and to di-

rect their abilities toward a common musical ideal. This can only be achieved through musically demanding rehearsals during which the time is wisely spent in an atmosphere of mutual respect. Though the essential purpose of rehearsals is the detection and elimination of errors and wrong concepts, all opportunities to compliment exceptional performance should be enthusiastically and genuinely recognized. The most demanding conductor will find that players will try to meet his most exacting requests if he will but keep them in the realm of the attainable and show a genuine regard for the players, their musical abilities, and their personalities. In return he must be much more than a "nice guy." He must be most demanding of himself in doing all that can be done to prepare and conduct his organization in a professional atmosphere. Sincerity and musical honesty must motivate his actions and comments in rehearsal at all times, and he must radiate nothing less than complete commitment to and involvement with the music. This is the way of the professional conductor—should it not also be the way of conductors of amateur groups? ■

May, 1991

Learning From A Legend

by John Knight

For the better part of this century conductors have modeled their techniques after Arturo Toscanini, whose style comprised preparation, precision, and objective interpretation. Beat preparation, however, was Toscanini's most effective tool; it was preparation, not the beat's sharpness or accuracy, that influenced his orchestral sound.

Max Rudolf agreed with the primary importance of gesture: "The more the conductor can express in these gestures, the more response he will get from the players in the way of shading, articulation, and expression."[1] Conductor Wilhelm Furtwangler also found essential the exactness of that "brief, often tiny movement of the downbeat, before the point of unified sound is reached in the orchestra."[2]

N.B.C. Symphony members believed Toscanini's art of preparation was one of his great conducting secrets. When Toscanini conducted the Vienna Philharmonic in 1936, bassoonist Hugo Burghauser observed:

> Toscanini was able to project whatever was in the score and in his mind. The conception of great interpretation, of what it should be, can quite often be found in fine artistic minds; but to project such ideas into the orchestra unmistakably, by technical means that are absolutely convincing — which Toscanini did — this is a sort of miracle which I can explain in part only as a result of a real capability of telepathic communication; and in fact he rarely used words to communicate what he wanted. About half a

bar before the occurrence of a detail in the music you saw already on his face and in his gesture what he was coming to and would want. This was extraordinary: the parallel conducting of what was going on now and what was coming the next moment. It was an entirely unheard-of ability, almost like the clairvoyance of a seer.[3]

A Toscanini interpretation is marked secondly by precision or line clarity, and many of his contemporaries were critical of this. According to Schonberg, Guido Ricordi attacked Toscanini in the *Gazzetta Musicale*, claiming his execution was rigid, that he lacked poetry. "Ricordi said that Toscanini's conducting of *Falstaff* resembled that of a 'mastadonic mechanical piano.' Later on, Ricordi changed his mind, as did virtually everybody else."[4] Toscanini's technique was precise, winning from an ensemble unanimous, split-second, accurate responses.

The paradox is that Toscanini's baton technique was far from technically exceptional. According to David Walter of the N.B.C. Symphony:

> Toscanini's conducting movements didn't beat time in accordance with the traditional skeletal configurations.... They delineated the musical flow,...breaking the prison of these config-

John W Knight is professor of music education and conductor of the Symphonic Band at Oberlin College, Ohio. He holds a doctorate from Louisiana State University.

urations. And so while they were the most expressive movements and gestures of any conductor, they didn't always answer the orchestral players' well-known question: 'Where's the beat?' "[5]

Violinist Joseph Gingold related that "It wasn't the beat of a specialist in virtuoso conducting; it was the beat of a musician who had a stick and could show whatever he wished with it."[6]

Samuel Antek wrote:

> We usually think of virtuoso baton technique in a more spectacular sense, such as beating complicated rhythms, giving very sure, positive entrances, and managing sudden changes of tempo. These are, in a sense, the more obvious conductorial appurtenances. What Toscanini sought was something much rarer, something beyond the rules and textbook formulas. Toscanini never sought, nor did he ever seem aware of, the easy, practical, safe approach to conducting and music making. The secret of Toscanini's conducting is that he never concerned himself with the mere mechanics of stick waving. He was primarily interested in the musical problem and its solution. He was not too concerned with helping the orchestra mechanically, and I always felt that he himself did not know quite what he was doing with the baton. He often spoke contemptuously of those who studied or taught conducting per se. I felt he would rather die than conduct mechanically for ensemble reasons, in order to obtain what he felt should be achieved by the men.[7]

In light of this how could Toscanini achieve such precision and clarity? Leopold Stokowski offered an answer:

> His beat breaks every academic rule — yet it is always clear and eloquent. But it is between the beats that something magical happens: one can always tell when he has reached the half-beat or the three-quarter beat, even when he does not divide his beats; and it is this certainty and clarity of beats which creates such a perfect ensemble when he conducts.[8]

Toscanini discarded standard beat patterns, substituting one that outlined the musical line's rise and fall. He realized standard baton technique produces an orchestral sound equal to it, where concentration is on rhythm, not musical line. Toscanini conducted subtle nuances between the beats.

Toscanini's arrival marked the end of the subjective conducting exemplified by Hans Von Bulow and Gustav Mahler. "Toscanini was the pivotal conductor of his period: the strongest influence, the one who marks the transition from the Wagner style to 20th-century objectivity. He ended up the greatest single force on today's conducting."[9]

According to George Szell, "Whatever you think about his [Toscanini's] interpretation of a specific work, [the idea] that he changed the whole concept of conducting and...rectified many, many arbitrary procedures of a generation...before him is now authentic history." Szell claimed Toscanini served as a "not too useful model" for generations of conductors, so fascinated they were unable to see him critically or follow with discrimination. "However, he did wipe out the meretricious tricks and the thick encrustation of the interpretive nuances that had been piling up for decades."[10] Spike Hughes substantiated this: "To clear the romantic grime off the classics was one of Toscanini's greatest achievements." To clean up "a romantic work like the Tchaikovsky *Pathetique*, and to know when to stop the operation before the music is stripped of its character and genuine emotional quality is little short of a miracle."[11]

Toscanini sought the composer's intentions. He had read about many stylistic, interpretive dilemmas, and came to the conclusion there was no conclusion. He believed it was futile for a conductor to attempt an authentic performance style. Instruments, pitch, and concepts had changed, and Beethoven would not recognize a 20th-century performance of his music. To Toscanini, truth was in the notes, and to interpret a composer's intentions a conductor must rely on musicianship, taste, and instinct.

Rehearsing Beethoven's *Eroica Symphony* Toscanini said, "The tradition is to be found only in one place — in the music! Some say this is Napoleon, some Hitler, some Mussolini. For me it is simply *allegro con brio*."[12]

Alan Schulman, cellist with the N.B.C. Symphony, said,

> What struck all of us, and what we talked about, was Toscanini's total honesty, his total dedication, his subordination of himself to the composer's demands. This honesty and sincerity continued through the years. He tried to get as close as one could to the truth in a piece of music.[13]

Whether Toscanini discovered composers' intentions is irrelevant; in his quest he enhanced music with a purpose and integrity that remain standards of conducting excellence today. ☐

Footnotes:
1. Max Rudolf, *The Grammar of Conducting*, p. 251.
2. Harold C. Schonberg, *The Great Conductors*, p. 257.
3. B.H. Haggin, *The Toscanini Musicians Knew*, pp. 156-157.
4. Harold C. Schonberg, *The Great Conductors*, p. 255.
5. B.H. Haggin, *The Toscanini Musicians Knew*, p. 20.
6. *Ibid.*, p. 136.
7. Samuel Antek, *This Was Toscanini*, p. 146.
8. David Ewen, *The Man With The Baton*, pp. 175-176.
9. Harold C. Schonberg, *The Great Conductors*, p. 252.
10. *Ibid.*
11. Spike Hughes, *The Toscanini Legacy*, p. 383.
12. *Ibid.*, p. 39.
13. B.H. Haggin, *The Toscanini Musicians Knew*, p. 25.

Remembering Toscanini

As a 16-year-old in the North Little Rock, Arkansas high school band, I was introduced to the magnetism of Arturo Toscanini when my director suggested band members study a recording of Beethoven's *Egmont Overture* to help us play a transcription of the work. I purchased a recording of the overture by the N.B.C. Symphony conducted by Maestro Toscanini. That night, while listening to the fantastic performance, I heard the highest standards of uncompromising musicianship and realized for the first time what music was about. The magic of that moment has been with me ever since. I began a life-long study of Toscanini and his interpretations and have received a wonderful musical education along the way. During two visits to Toscanini's birthplace in Parma, Italy I was able to retrace the legacy of his home and the Conservatory where he studied.

Arturo Alessandro Toscanini was born March 25, 1867 to Claudio and Paolina Toscanini in a poor district of Parma called Oltretorrente, "the other side of the stream." It is easy to walk from the main street of Parma, one section of which is named Viale Toscanini, cross the bridge, and locate his birthplace at Borgo Rudolfo Tanzi, no. 13.

The Toscanini home has undergone restoration and is now a museum filled with memorabilia from a career in music spanning three-quarters of a century. I could imagine Toscanini drawing inspiration from the personal items I viewed throughout the home.

In the first room I saw an original score of *Parsifal*, impeccably neat and easy to read, though the barlines were erased, I assumed by Toscanini. Nearby was a picture of Cosima, Wagner's wife and daughter of Franz Liszt. Recalling Toscanini's passionate love of Wagner's music, I remembered that he gave the first Italian performances of *Gotterdammerung, Tristan,* and *Siegfried* and was the first Italian conductor invited to conduct at the Bayreuth festival by Siegfried Wagner, the composer's son, in 1930 and 1931.

A bust of Toscanini's idol, Giuseppe Verdi, sat in a corner and autographed pictures of Verdi hung on the wall. Toscanini played cello under Verdi's direction and later conducted many of Verdi's operas with Verdi's documented approval.

Many portraits and pictures of the Toscanini family were displayed, including one of his wife, Carla, in her wedding dress when they married in 1897. They had three children: Walter who married Cia Fornaroli; Wanda who married pianist Vladimir Horowitz; and Wally, the former Countess Castelbarco. Among these pictures is one of the great young conductor and close friend of Toscanini, Guido Cantelli, dated March 25, 1956, only a few months before his untimely death in a plane crash on November 23. Because Toscanini himself was in bad health at this time he never heard of Cantelli's death.

On a table is a collection of Shakespeare's complete works, which Toscanini often quoted from memory, and next to it a death mask of Puccini, a close friend of Toscanini for many years. Toscanini led the premières of *La Boheme, The Girl of the Golden West,* and *Turandot.* Puccini said of Toscanini, "He conducts a work not just as the written score directs, but as the composer imagined it in his head, even though he failed to write it down on paper."

During the trip I visited the Conservatory of Music where Toscanini studied as a scholarship student at the age of nine. He graduated in 1885 at the age of 18 with high honors in cello, piano, and composition. The dean of the Conservatory allowed me to see several compositions written by Toscanini while he was a student.

A Toscanini room at the Conservatory was filled with momentos of his career, including a Steinway piano covered with autographed pictures of Verdi, Puccini, Debussy, Mascagni, along with many photographs of Wagner given to Toscanini by the Wagner family. The score of Verdi's *Falstaff* with interpretation notes written by Toscanini in the margins is in the room as well. The dean's secretary told me that as a young student, Toscanini would sneak out of the Conservatory at night by going out the window and climbing down a tree to swim in the nearby stream. Such a story made him seem all the more human, amid all these intimate treasures. Being alone in that room for over an hour I experienced a range of emotions — humilty, nostalgia, thankfulness for the gift of Arturo Toscanini — and the same thrill that charged through me 30 years ago when I heard the *Egmont Overture.*

Before leaving Italy I visited the cemetery where Toscanini is buried in Milan. Standing by his tomb I could visualize the crowd of 40,000 mourners who stood in the rain Febraury 18, 1957 for his funeral. I thought of the hymn from Verdi's opera, *Nabucco,* which Toscanini conducted at Verdi's funeral in 1901 and then was played for Toscanini — "Fly my thoughts on golden wings." □

The Toscanini home in Parma, Italy

Creative Conducting Techniques

by John W. Knight

"I should like to put on record here that in my experience every innate talent — in music as in many other fields — usually goes through three phases of development: in the first, one can do everything; in the second, one becomes unsure of oneself, loses one's ability, searches, doubts, experiments, learns, matures; the third begins when the assurance of the first gradually returns, now enhanced and made conscious by the experience one has gained. Scarcely any artist is wholly spared these growing pains." — Bruno Walter, *Of Music and Music Making.*

As conductors we strive for musical excellence within ourselves and our ensembles, and our growth as a conductor is a lifetime goal. A necessary step in this process is to become aware of technical problems with the baton. "Technical control is indispensable to artistic mastery. Technique is style's liberator," Charles Ives said.

Unfortunately many conductors become enamored of stick technique and tend to overconduct, confusing their ensemble with large beat patterns. A clear stick technique is important, but mere mechanical clarity is not enough. According to Bruno Walter, "By concentrating on precision, one arrives at technique; but by concentrating on technique one does not arrive at precision." In the second stage of growth and development the conductor becomes aware of the difference between timebeating and creative conducting.

The most effective conducting is simple and economical. Indeed, as the Hungarian conductor Arthur Nikisch said, "Technique is the ability to make use of one's means with the least effort and the greatest effect." This master level of ar-

tistic simplicity requires creativity in selecting the appropriate gesture for each musical nuance. For the technique of the stick to express depth of musical feeling, there should be considerable variation in the size of basic beat patterns.

Conductors usually learn the basic beat patterns for the traditional and asymmetrical meters by imitating the two-dimensional diagrams found in conducting textbooks. The normal field of beating the frames is between the waist and shoulders, with the baton in front of the body. There are times, however, when it is justified to leave this area for a more emotional interpretation. When we go beyond the standardized baton technique, some wonderful and creative communication happens.

Think of dynamics as having weight, height, and depth. For example, to contrast the boldness of the first subject of Mozart's *Jupiter* Symphony against the lightness of the second subject, think of the first theme as having weight and depth and keep the baton at a lower plane, more out in front of the body. Conversely, for the second subject, let the baton float at approximately eye level with a minimum of movement, but bring it closer to the body.

John W. Knight is an associate professor of music education and conductor of the Symphonic Band at Oberlin College. He also maintains an active schedule as adjudicator, clinician, lecturer, and guest conductor throughout the United States and Europe. He received a Ph.D. from Louisiana State University.

For a dramatic forte, as in *The Great Gate of Kiev*, think of channeling the energy from your body through small intense beats instead of forcing the sound from your ensemble with large beats. Also use a sudden drop of the baton for the accents in measures 2-6 and 8.

Preparatory Beats

Conductors should telegraph what is going to happen in the music before it happens. Our best tool for this is the preparatory beat with the appropriate facial gestures. According to Max Rudolf, "the more the conductor can express in these gestures, the more response he will get from the players in the way of shading, articulation and expression." Conductor Wilhelm Furtwängler explained, "Great conducting lies entirely in the preparation of the beat, not in the beat itself — in the brief, often tiny movement of the downbeat, before the point of unified sound is reached in the orchestra. The manner in which these preparations are shaped determines the quality of the sound with the most absolute exactness."

Each nuance of the music, not just those at the beginning of the composition, should be prepared. The beat of preparation indicates the tempo, mood, dynamics, shading, articulation, precision of attack, and the concept of sound that you have in mind; it is what happens between the beats that communicates the artistry of the music.

To insure an interpretation of depth and breadth, be sure to use the appropriate facial gestures with your prep beat. A preparatory beat without appropriate facial gesture is a wasted effort. Practice exaggerated facial gestures to convey the emotion of the music, gradually refining your expressions. Study the facial gestures of such actors as Laurence Olivier and George C. Scott to see how they convey depth of emotion with the minimum of effort.

Many consider Arturo Toscanini a master at using appropriate facial gesture to guide musicians. Bassoonist Hugo Burghauser describes Toscanini guest-conducting the Vienna Philharmonic: "About half a bar before the occurrence of a detail in the music you saw already on his face and in his gesture what he was coming to and would want. This was extraordinary: the parallel conducting of what was going on now and what was coming at the next moment. It was an entirely unheard-of ability, almost like the clairvoyance of a seer."

Anticipatory Beat

Another conducting gesture closely related to the preparatory beat is the anticipatory beat. The major difference is that the preparatory beat is usually in strict tempo, while the anticipatory beat comes slightly before the beat and the ensemble plays a fraction behind the ictus. The anticipatory beat was an innovation of Arthur Nikisch (1855-1922), who conducted the Leipzig, Berlin, Boston, and London orchestras. It was later adopted by Furtwängler; and until his recent death, the greatest exponent of this method was Herbert von Karajan, conductor of the Berlin Philharmonic. While this technique is frequently used in Europe, especially in Germany, most American ensembles find it confusing and prefer playing with the beat. The technique is difficult to master, but is useful in setting the mood of compositions starting quietly or for cueing instruments that respond slowly in the bottom register, such as double reeds and low brass.

The bassoon solo at the beginning of Tchaikovsky's Sixth Symphony can be tricky if the reed doesn't respond at a soft dynamic level, but an anticipatory beat allows the bassoon and bass players to synchronize their entrances. Once the bassoon sounds the low E, the conductor can conduct in tempo.

Releases

A musical tone has four parts: preparation, start, sustaining the sound, and release. This cycle repeats itself throughout a composition.

When working on baton technique, conductors often neglect releases. Problems with releases, especially after fermatas, can arise when conductors use more beats than are necessary to elicit a clear release. Remember Toscanini's admonishment, "there are no cadenzas for the baton."

Release gestures should put the baton in position for the next beat. Many conductors use the script "e" ↪ release motion, but it puts the baton out of position for the next beat and can elicit an unpleasant accent and "tut" tongue stop if it is done in an abrupt manner. However, the script "e" release can be effective if you reverse the direction ↩. The following two examples demonstrate its exactness.

$$\left|\begin{matrix}4\\4\end{matrix}\ \overset{\frown}{}\ \ . \quad \quad - \ \right|$$
ff   pp

Stop the baton on beat one but keep the left hand moving to sustain the sound. Stop the sound using a reverse script ℒ with the left hand and at the same time let the baton float upward to eye level to be in position for the staccato quarter notes.

For this release repeat beat three with the baton but use a piano staccato gesture to prepare the fourth beat. The *morendo* (dying away of sound) release with strings can be done effectively by slowly relaxing the facial gestures and bringing both hands down to the side. At the last instant gently bow your head; no definite cut-off is needed.

Sustain the fermata with the left hand and baton. At the exact moment of release use a reverse script ℒ staccato gesture with the baton to prepare for the second measure. This can be especially effective if you lower the baton for the *ff* sound.

Winds require a definite cut-off, so after bowing your head bring it back to the original position, in rhythm, for the cut-off.

A good place to use the *morendo* cut-off with winds is in the final few measures of the first movement of Tchaikovsky's Sixth Symphony. Sustain the brass with the baton but let it float down slowly. Use the left hand to gently lift the timpani's eighth notes. The final eighth notes in the timpani will serve for the release of the brass. Wait at least three to five seconds before you move to maintain the fermata.

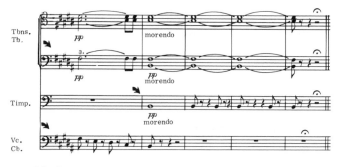

Clicking

A useful technique in clarifying the beat is clicking. This is a short, quick, and precise beat usually made with only the fingers or wrists. It is a silent motion, but if a sound were audible it would resemble the click of a metronome. Click-

ing was a favorite technique of Fritz Reiner. As a student of Nikisch, Reiner became one of the world's greatest baton technicians and got fantastic results with minimal effort. A master of the tiny beat, Reiner used the technique of clicking whenever his ensemble began to drag. As he made his beat smaller, his players would watch him more closely, much like an actor who whispers his lines so his audience listens intently.

Clicking can bring out notes with intensity, delineate a change of tempo, or encourage precise rhythmic entrances.

A precise click on beat four will help the entering brass shift to the new tempo.

Lincolnshire Posy has many pitfalls for the conductor. Clicking provides one solution in measure 13 of "Lord Melbourne," which has a difficult entrance for saxophone and horn.

Make a staccato click inward (not upward, because that will put you out of position) on beat four to prepare for the new tempo at measure 13.

Clicking is helpful in measure 50 of the same movement.

Using the left hand for the cut-off tends to confuse players because of the superfluous movement. Omit the left hand and use only the baton for clarity. Stop on beat two and let the baton float to the right and then give a precise *inward* click on three to release the fermata and prepare the eighth on the "and" of three.

In the first movement of Beethoven's Ninth Symphony an intense click on the following notes clarifies the rhythm.

The introduction to Tchaikovsky's Fourth Symphony can also be better prepared if you incorporate the click.

A conductor can create a beautiful effect in measure five of the finale to Beethoven's First Symphony by using clicking and the anticipatory beat. The introduction is conducted in 4/8, and the classical fermata is usually held for nearly twice its value.

Use the left hand to sustain the intensity. Release the *ff* fermata by repeating beat one with a high rebound to prepare the *p* entrance of the violins; wait a second after the fermata for the silence to change moods. Prepare the *p* pick-up on beat four by using a small but rhythmic click on beat three. Without the click the music usually sounds like  .

Give full value to the eighth notes in measures two, three, and four by pulling the sound with the baton. Don't move on the rests; let the baton be neutral. Remember in this music the preparation is more important than the beat itself. Let the size of the gesture of preparation look like the music before it happens. The first beat of the fifth measure is traditionally delayed a second; give the anticipatory beat and wait for the violins. In the same measure give a gentle click on three and lead the violin to the fermata and let the sound decay naturally. Release the fermata with the left hand and give a precise click inward on beat two to prepare the *allegro molto*.

Legato

Leopold Stokowski once said that "music is a painting on a canvas of silence," and it is a good definition to remember when conducting legato. Indeed conducting is the art of painting in sound because we transform the written notes into artistic motion.

For the legato beat use the flexible wrist of a painter. Try switching from the traditional palm-downward grip on the baton to the palm sideways grip, opening the palm more to draw the sound from the ensemble. With a legato beat the conductor should concentrate on the rebound. The curves and pulling of the sound on the rebound of the beat will shape what occurs between beats. Georg Solti has said that the talent of a conductor can be measured by his ability to pull sound from the orchestra.

A good way to pull sound from an ensemble is to point the tip of the baton down and slowly let it float upward, feeling the resistance of 16th-note subdivision in the baton. For example, the second movement of *Lincolnshire*, "Horkstow Grange," starts with the most beautiful and noble pick-up in all band literature. To prevent the horns from rushing the quarter note keep the tip

of the baton down and feel the 16th-note subdivision before resolving to the D♭.

At measure 25 in the same movement Grainger invites the trumpet to linger on the first note. Again think of the 16th-note subdivision and use a gentle click to pull the sound.

In pulling the sound feel the resistance in the baton and follow the melodic contour with a similar baton movement.

Few conductors feel in control when conducting a slow legato. The third movement of Beethoven's Ninth Symphony challenges the conductor to demonstrate a perfect legato; the instruments should sing without letting the musical line sag. In an example like this, weaken the second and fourth beats in the first measure but still feel the internal subdivision. Follow the melodic contour and feel the resistance in the baton. Think of the baton moving as a bow on a string instrument.

Backbeat "Hot Stove" Technique

Many conductors avoid the backbeat technique with the accelerated rebound (♪.) because frequent use will cause the piece to drag as the ensemble comes in on the reboud instead of the ictus. The backbeat technique is effective in measure 45 of "The Lost Lady Found" from *Lincolnshire Posy*, which has a tricky entrance for the trombones.

The music has a pulse of one beat to the measure and the trombones invariably enter late unless you use an accelerated rebound.

To get the necessary lift and break on the first and fourth beats of Arnold's *Four Scottish Dances* the backbeat would be appropriate.

This technique may be used when you want a slight interruption between measures. The Germans call this the *Luftpause* (air break) and designate it with a comma at a moment of musical tension. The *luftpause* technique is vital in the music of Mahler and Bruckner, which has many changes of tempos and moods.

Use the backbeat technique on four but do not go up for the rebound. Instead let the rebound on four  go at a right angle

and stop. The speed of the rebound will serve for a clean release. After the release go up for the preparation of the *ff* whole note.

Circles in Conducting

The master of the circular beat was Arturo Toscanini. A videotape of Toscanini conducting the Overture to *La Forza del Destino* shows how he used this technique to build the intensity in a crescendo and the reverse the circle for a decrescendo. Because of the lack of an ictus, the circle may be used for an accelerando and ritard. To give the music a sense of forward motion, try using the half circle to give a gentle lift to the following articulation:

The wonderful curving contour of the melody from the first movement of the Tchaikovsky Symphony *Pathetique* is ideal for the circle method.

Do a gentle click on beat three to prepare the eighth-note pickup. On the "and" of three use a reverse circle for the pickup to put you in position for the first measure. Use the same technique for the second measure.

Hemiola Beat

A classic example of the hemiola beat is the finale of the Schumann Piano Concerto. Many a conductor has met disaster with this difficult three-against-two syncopation. Conducting these measures in the traditional one-beat-to-the-bar approach creates a stiff interpretation unless the conductor has perfect rhythmic control. One solution would be to think of the measures in 3/2 instead of 3/4 and use a three-beat pattern.

Countless examples of the use of hemiola beat can also be found in the wind music of Robert Jager's *Third Suite* (Waltz) and the trio section of Dvorak's *Serenade for Winds*.

One of my favorite examples of the hemiola beat can be found in Tchaikovsky's *Serenade for Strings*. This technique will give you perfect control of the stringendo and ritard.

The conducting patterns we use today have been in existence only since the days of Berlioz, and conducting is still a relatively young art. Creative conductors transform two-dimensional patterns into creative gestures. Before we ask the ensemble to perform with expression and clear articulation, we should impose the same standards on our conducting. □

Recommended Reading

The Grammar of Conducting, *Max Rudolf, Schirmer Books, 1980.*

The Great Conductors, *Harold C. Schonberg, Simon and Schuster, 1967.*

The Toscanini Legacy, *Spike Hughes, Dover Publications, 1969.*

The Toscanini Musicians Knew, *B. H. Haggin, Horizon Press, 1967.*

Of Music and Music-Making, *Bruno Walter, translated by Paul Hamburger, W. W. Norton, 1961.*

Conducting Irregular Meters

by John Knight

During my formative years as a conductor I was fascinated by irregular meters and the beat patterns used in conducting. This interest started when I watched Sir John Barbirolli and the Houston Symphony perform Tchaikovsky's *Symphonie Pathétique*. As I sat in the balcony that night armed with the Belwin-Bonanza edition of the score, I anxiously waited to see how Maestro Barbirolli would conduct the famous ⅝ meter in the second movement. During the week before the concert I practiced the ⅝ beat pattern shown in my conducting textbook in front of a mirror, and I felt ready to mount the podium if Sir John should falter.

To my surprise Barbirolli did not use the beat pattern I had practiced but a smaller, graceful, and asymmetrical beat pattern.

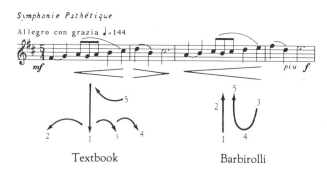

He started the movement with a definite beat, but soon seemed to disappear deep into the music, becoming an artistic monitor of sound rather than a beater of rhythm.

It was an eye-opener to realize his beat pattern came from the music itself and not from a conducting textbook. Until then I had thought that textbook patterns were used by the great conductors. I now view advice in textbooks as painting by numbers. Watching Barbirolli that night it became clear that the music as the conductor internalized it shaped the pattern, not a rigid academic design. After the concert I wrote down three rules that have helped me to grow as a conductor. Good conductors make the beat pattern look the way the music should sound; conducting patterns are usually appropriate variations of the basic beat patterns from one to four; keep them simple, clean, and stay out of the way of the ensemble.

Arturo Toscanini also believed in simple beat patterns that did not always conform to the textbook patterns. Recordings of Toscanini conducting are available on R.C.A. video tapes and are great teaching tools. To see him conduct Respighi's *Pines of Rome* is a revelation in precision, pacing, and clarity; Toscanini kept his beat patterns located almost all at the same place in front of his body. He based his ⁶₄ pattern on a ¼ frame with 1, 2, 3 as repeated downbeats and 4, 5, 6, conforming to the 2, 3, and 4 of a ¼ beat pattern.

John Knight is a professor of music education and conductor of the Symphonic Band at Oberlin College. He also maintains an active schedule as adjudicator, clinician, lecturer, and guest conductor throughout the United States and Europe. He received a Ph.D. from Louisiana State University.

In the chant section marked *ancora piu mosso* Toscanini conducts the $\frac{5}{4}$ meter with four repeated downbeats, hitting at the same spot, and coming in and up with his wrist for the fifth beat.

The repeated downbeats give the chant a clarity and strength not heard in other interpretations.

Many conductors use another pattern in this $\frac{5}{4}$ section of *Pines of Rome*, a $\frac{4}{4}$ frame with a repeated 4th beat.

The repeated 4th beat is also effective for the $\frac{5}{4}$ measure found in the finale of Shostakovich's Symphony No. 5.

An example of when not to beat time is the opening promenade from the Mussorgsky-Ravel, *Pictures At An Exhibition*. Set style and tempo with the trumpet player in advance and get out of the way until bar three. The $\frac{5}{4}$ bar is usually conducted as 2 + 3 and the $\frac{6}{4}$ measure as 3 + 3.

Arturo Toscanini

Try Toscanini's technique in the $\frac{5}{4}$ and $\frac{6}{4}$ measures, placing the beats close together in front of your body within a $\frac{4}{4}$ frame.

Other meters become simple when broken down into basic beat patterns. In Hindemith's Concerto for Orchestra think of the $\frac{7}{4}$ meter in a $\frac{3}{4}$ frame with repeated beats on one, two, and three.

The $\frac{7}{4}$ meter found in the Walton Viola Concerto flows better using a four-beat frame, erasing the score's dotted bar lines, giving a definite downbeat and repeating beats 2, 3, 4.

Walton, Viola Concerto

Polymeters occur when two or more different metric schemes appear simultaneously in a composition, usually related by a common beat, unit, or subdivision.

An early example of polymeters is the ballroom scene in Mozart's *Don Giovanni* where three orchestras play in three different meters while Masetto and Don Giovanni sing in ⅜ and 2/4.

Many conductors show this with one downbeat per measure while others ignore the bar line and use a weak three, allowing the ⅜ and 2/4 to fit in as best they can.

Don Giovanni

Many band compositions include polymeters, an example being the second movement of Symphony in B♭ by Hindemith. Starting in measure 97 there are three different metric schemes, a 3/2 meter concurrent with a 12/8 and 6/8, but through careful analysis it is possible to find one single meter that works smoothly. In the Hindemith that is a 3/2 beat pattern. Ignore the 12/8 bar line and use a subdivided 3, not a 6/4 pattern as that would shift the metric emphasis to 1 and 4 instead of 1, 3, and 5.

In the 1960s and 1970s composers used notation that many performers did not know how to interpret or count. Conductors had to find new gestures to communicate the scores to players. As W. Francis McBeth wrote, "The compositional devices of Penderecki, Husa, and Nelhybel must be completely understood by the conductor before they can become effective.... The days when a band director can just beat frames are long gone" *(Effective Performance of Band Music).* Despite the music's apparent difficulty, conductors should continue to keep patterns simple and clean, making them reflect the music's sound.

John Barnes Chance's *Blue Lake* uses irregular note groups carried over bar lines. Unless band members feel subdivisions, the ensemble suffers rhythmically. Directors can conduct measures 69, 70, and 71 in several ways; one is a basic four-beat pattern.

A better solution is to ignore the bar line and interpret the three measures in 6/8 and 9/8, using a two-beat pattern (6/8) in measure 69, and a three-beat pattern (9/8) when the sixteenth-notes begin in measures 70 and 71 with a rest on the third beat of 71. This solution produces control in the *allargando* and emphasizes the correct subdivision.

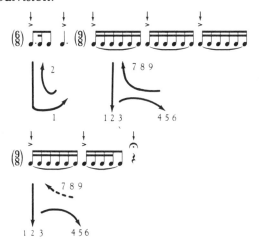

Conducting the measures as a partial $\frac{12}{8}$, full $\frac{12}{8}$, and $\frac{6}{8}$ is a third possibility. The first measure becomes a fourth beat pick-up followed by a four-beat pattern in the second measure and a two-beat pattern for the third. By using either a standard or an asymmetrical beat pattern, the conductor simplifies complicated scoring.

In trying to eliminate a sense of meter and tempo, composers often create ambiguous notations that confuse performers. Gardner Read comments, "Too frequently the obscurities of avant-garde musical thinking are surpassed by the obscurities of its notation—a closed book to all but a small inner circle of initiated professional musicians" (*Music Notation: A Manual of Modern Practice*).

Conductors encounter nonmetrical organization not only in music of the 1960s and 1970s,

but in classics like Percy Grainger's *Lincolnshire Posy*. Among the mixed meters of the fifth movement, "Lord Melbourne," Grainger indicated free time at measure 9. Conduct this measure with ten symmetrical downbeats as indicated by the arrows.

Another alternative is to give three symmetrical downbeats for the first three quarter notes and an elongated downbeat for the fourth beat with a quick rebound on the eighth and quarter combination. The fifth beat would revert back to a symmetrical downbeat; conduct the quarter-note triplet in a three-beat pattern; and the half note in a two-beat pattern.

Grainger gave an explanation of the zero tempo passage, indicated by the symbol ⊙, in his score notes: "In the passages marked Free Time the bandleader should slightly vary his beat lengths with that rhythmic elasticity so characteristic of many English folk singers and especially characteristic of George Wray, the singer of the song. The opening phrase may be taken

or

or in any other suitable arrangement of slightly varying beat-lengths. The bandleader should give free reign to his rhythmic fancy, just as folk singers do. Give each note with an arrow above it a downbeat. Regular beat-lengths and conventional beat-gestures are taken up wherever there are bar lines and time signatures."

Grainger, Lincolnshire Posey, Mvt. 5, Lord Melbourne

There are several alternatives available to directors conducting nonmetrical compositions. Dictated single-beat patterns occur most frequently and may take the form of a single beat per note as in "Lord Melbourne." A durational beat is an indication of the chronological passing of time as exemplified in Krzysztof Penderecki's *Pittsburgh Overture*. A suggestion is to use an elastic downbeat to indicate the duration of the measure. In measure 31 of *Pittsburgh Overture* give two downbeats per measure with time estimates so that the performers can anticipate the length of each free episode.

Thomas Tyra discussed the conductor's responsibility in his analysis of the performance problems in the *Pittsburgh Overture*. "He must, through some visual means, indicate to the performer the durational progress of the measure.... One possible solution is to let one hand, or arm, act as the hand of a clock which describes a circle whose circumference, from six o'clock to six o'clock, would indicate the duration of the measure. By watching this motion the performer would be able to see how quickly the measure was moving and begin and end his material at the approximate point in the measure shown in his part" ("The Analyses of Three Twentieth Century Compositions for Wind Ensemble").

Pittsburgh Overture

Ferruccio Busoni eloquently said, "Music was born free, and to win freedom is its destiny." As composers break away from tradition by negation of the bar line and disintegration of metrical regularity, conductors should give up absolute control of the ensemble and act as a monitor to allow the performers more interpretive freedom. This freedom is more in keeping with the wishes and philosophy of contemporary composers. □

November, 1990

The Challenge of Asymmetric Meters

by John W. Knight

Composition techniques in contemporary wind literature have extended musical horizons, but they have simultaneously created interpretive problems for the conductor. According to Gunther Schuller, the complexities of the new approaches to composition require fundamental reevaluation of conducting techniques. In *The Conductor's Art* Schuller says, "The demands made by the music have multiplied; and the conductor's art, if it is to continue to serve the music, must reflect these increased demands." If a conductor does not acquire the techniques necessary to control contemporary meters, he may shy away from rhythmically challenging works with asymmetric meters, additive meters, combined meters, fractional meters, polymeters, and others.

Of the irregular meters the simplest to understand are the asymmetric meters, those that are a combination of simple meter and compound meter. I suggest that when directors conduct asymmetric meters at fast tempos they follow these guidelines for interpretation:

• a basic premise of contemporary music is that the value of eighth notes should remain equal.

John W. Knight is an associate professor of music education and conductor of the Symphonic Band at Oberlin College. He also maintains an active schedule as adjudicator, clinician, lecturer, and guest conductor throughout the United States and Europe. He received a Ph.D. from Louisiana State University.

- to conduct a combination of simple and compound meters, extend one or more of the beats to keep the eighth notes constant.

- the internal grouping of the eighth notes dictates an extended beat. For example, $\frac{7}{8}$ | ♫ ♫♫ ♫ | requires an asymmetric three-beat pattern with an extended second beat.

- appropriate conducting patterns are asymmetrical variants of the basic beat patterns.

- there is a direct relationship between an asymmetrical beat pattern and a basic beat pattern. In other words, $\frac{5}{8}$ is related to $\frac{2}{4}$ with an extended beat; $\frac{7}{8}$ and $\frac{8}{8}$ are related to $\frac{3}{4}$; and $\frac{9}{8}$, $\frac{10}{8}$, and $\frac{11}{8}$ are related to $\frac{4}{4}$.

- there should be a lilt on the asymmetric part of the beat, achieved by pulling the wrist and decelerating the baton's velocity to include the extra notes.

Apply these guidelines to the following etude using small, precise, rhythmic beats and giving equal weight and baton velocity to the simple meters and more lilt and deceleration to the extended beats, but do not drag when going from the asymmetric to the simple meter. Draw a vertical line in the score above the extended beat as a visual aid, especially for works at fast tempos.

Asymmetric meters were late in coming to the school band movement. At the turn of the century Charles Ives was at the vanguard of rhythmic innovations in orchestral music. Later, Stravinsky scored rhythmically difficult passages that seem tame compared to today's challenges. His *Symphony of Wind Instruments* (1920) and *Concerto for Piano and Wind Instruments* (1924) are notable compositions for wind band that use asymmetric meters.

The monumental work, *Lincolnshire Posy*, by Percy Grainger (1940) is replete with metrical innovations, and Frederick Fennell's 1952 recording with the Eastman Wind Ensemble made many school directors aware of this magnificent composition. A notable example of a $\frac{5}{8}$ asymmetric meter occurs in the third movement of Grainger's *Lincolnshire Posy*, "Rufford Park Poachers," measures 6-10. Although the time signature changes frequently from $\frac{5}{8}$ to $\frac{4}{8}$, Grainger says, "The only players that are likely to balk at these rhythms are seasoned professional bandsmen, who think more of their beer than of their music."

Meter

Asymmetrical 2
Extended beat 2

Try conducting the excerpt from *Lincolnshire Posy* in $\frac{5}{8}$ in an asymmetric two-beat pattern with an extended second beat for a smoother sound, allowing the point of the baton on the extended second beat to drop lower than the ictus of the first beat. Think of the extended second beat in compound time and let it float more. The $\frac{4}{8}$ measures are conducted in a regular two-beat pattern.

After *Lincolnshire Posy* many composers decided that irregular rhythms were viable for school ensembles, and that the band could perform contemporary music. Some of us first encountered asymmetric meters in Gordon Jacob's difficult work, *Flag of Stars*, published in 1956, which has a tricky meter starting at letter C: $\frac{5}{8}$ ($\frac{2}{8} + \frac{3}{8}$)

Then along came a high school band director in Chillicothe, Missouri by the name of Claude T. Smith who wrote *Emperata Overture* (1964); its $\frac{7}{8}$ and $\frac{9}{8}$ measures were some of the most misplayed measures of the mid 1960s, as conductors frequently treated the asymmetric measures as triplets instead of three constant eighths. Eventually, musicians understood the mysteries of $\frac{7}{8}$ and $\frac{9}{8}$ and looked forward to compositions that contained these new meters. Conduct the $\frac{7}{8}$ measure with an asymmetric three-beat pattern, extending beat one. Again allow the point of the extended first beat to drop lower than the second and third beats for a smoother pattern. Conduct the $\frac{9}{8}$ measure in an asymmetric four-beat pattern with an extended beat two.

Widespread acceptance of Smith's scoring of asymmetric meters opened the door for other composers, and today band literature abounds with them. Asymmetric meters appear in the exciting composition *Aegean Festival Overture* (1967) by Andreas Markis. Originally scored as an orchestral overture, Major Bader later arranged it as a concert overture for band. It is conducted in an asymmetric three-beat pattern with an extended beat one.

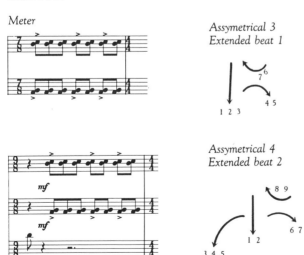

The fourth movement of Alvin Etler's *Concerto for Clarinet* (1964) dispenses with traditional time signatures and uses only numerators to indicate the eighth-note division of units within each beat. Measure 7 should be read as being in ⅝, measure 8 in ⅞, measure 9 in 9/8, and measure 10 in ¾.

To gain control of asymmetric meters at a slow tempo, subdivide the beat. Louisiana State University's L. Bruce Jones developed this exercise to teach control of basic subdivision: begin with ⅝ and accelerate until you reach ¼, then accelerate to ¾, then to ⅝, accelerating further until the tempo is in 1.

Repeat the exercise backwards decelerating, and be sure the tempo is the same when shifting from one meter to the next.

The following etude is a tricky combination of regular and subdivided asymmetric meters and develops baton control to correctly prepare articulations and dynamics before they happen. Use only the forearm on the downbeat and a flexible wrist on the subdivisions. Later refine the subdivision by moving the baton with only the fingers. Never let the subdivision be obtrusive. Check your tempos with a metronome and come out of the fermatas with a clean release. For an additional challenge repeat the etude backwards.

An example of subdivided asymmetric meter is in Alfred Reed's *El Camino Real* (1984). To achieve the *molto tenuto* and expressiveness of this melody, use the following diagrams.

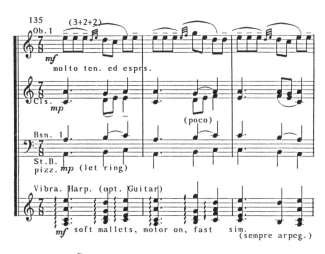

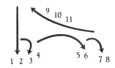

Conducting pattern for a basic frame of five

Conducting pattern for a basic frame of three

Conduct measure 212 of the same movement in an asymmetric four-beat pattern with an extended second beat and subdivided third and fourth beats.

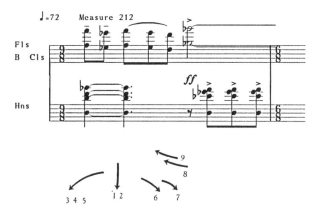

When conducting asymmetric meters remember that the appropriate conducting patterns are asymmetrical variants of the basic beat patterns from one to six. To achieve the necessary lilt of the combination of simple and compound meters, extend or subdivide one or more of the beats depending on the tempo, making the subdivision as unobtrusive as possible. The most important guideline to always remember, however, is the value of the eighth notes must remain constant. □

Conduct the ⅞ measures in a (♪=92) subdivided three-beat pattern with an extended one. The ⅞ is also a basic subdivided three-beat pattern with extended first and third beats.

There are times to give the fractional values beneath the melody a subdivided beat for control and intensity. The Andante section from the *Aegean Festival Overture*, measure 200, calls for a gentle but rhythmic subdivision of the meter.

Recommended Reading

Gunther Schuller, "Conducting Revisited," in *The Conductor's Art*, ed., Carl Bamberger (McGraw Hill).

W. Francis McBeth, *Effective Performance of Band Music* (Southern Music Company).

Nicolae Malko, *The Conductor and His Baton: Fundamentals of the Technique of Conducting* (Welhelm Hanson).

John Knight "Graphic Analysis of Conducting Techniques for Irregular Meters and Nonmetrical Organizations Found in Selected Twentieth-Century Band Literature (Ph.D. dissertation, Louisiana State University, 1979. University Microfilms: 80-13, 126, Ann Arbor, Michigan).

The Calisthenics of Conducting

Frederick Fennell

In its final form — in performance — conducting is a silent art. At least, it ought to be, for, when the begging, pleading, cajoling, the castigation and the singing, screaming, yelling, and pounding, and stamping of rehearsal have been spent, the performance must proceed with none of these. Better to be rid of all that in the first place. But rid or not, some physical manifestation of the music will have to take its place, sooner or later. We can all learn immensely from a mime; try Marcel Marceau as a model.

The communication of musical ideas is basic to conducting, and although there is no single way to achieve that communication, we must have a technique to translate musical thoughts and silences. For me, there is no doubt that the body — and I mean the whole body — can and must be a vital part of this translation process.

When we exchange our instrument or voice for the conductor's podium, the body frequently becomes lost in the transfer. Actually the body is the conductor's instrument, not the people making the music in front of us.

Frederick Fennell is conductor-in-residence at the University of Miami School of Music in Florida, where he is music director of the Symphony Orchestra and Symphonic Wind Ensemble. Well known as the founder and director of the Eastman Wind Ensemble, he was a member of the faculty at Eastman for many years.

For conductors nothing comes before knowledge of the music, how the music goes, why it goes, and how it should sound. Knowledge of the score and the technique to transmit that knowledge remain our two inseparable reasons to exist. But the body must be prepared in order for this to happen, its physical operation developed by proper exercise. If the body is so controlled that our actions become almost second nature, we are free to unplug our usually stuffed-up ears and learn how to listen. Listening is the most difficult thing that all of us have to do as musicians. It is not a casual, simple task to free the body of its tensions so we can hear the music, but this is absolutely basic to all music making, and especially to conducting.

All athletes carefully prepare the body to perform. The lengthy heating-up process that precedes what the pitcher hopes will be nine winning innings of baseball is part of the great ritual of the game. None of us would think of launching into a set of tennis or a round of golf without at least a few practice swings, but I'm afraid we too often head to the conductor's pitching mound for those nine grueling innings of musical baseball with almost no warm-up whatsoever.

There are many conductors who insist on elaborate warm-up routines for the players in their bands and orchestras, but do nothing to prepare themselves. Here are some physical passports to your own conductorial good health by way of a few old-fashioned calisthenics.

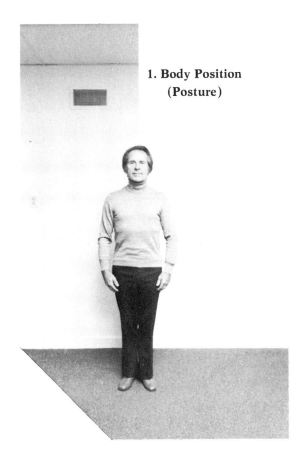

1. Body Position (Posture)

Bring heels together and balance the body weight on the ball of the foot, distributing it to your convenience, then think of your body as rising from this base as does a beautifully proportioned wine goblet. Check your knees and thighs and make sure that these areas are free of tension. At the waist-line area, we may come to our first physical problem. This is because of lack of control at the table and because we forget that distended abdominal areas act to slow down other physical responses.

At upper chest and shoulders, we arrive at those parts of the body that are so important in what we do as conductors. Here at the top of the chest is where we imagine that we are suspended by two imaginary hooks which are drawn up by wires hung from the heaven of music to elevate the whole body above its earthly roots. Only when so elevated is the dancer ready to dance, the conductor ready to conduct.

Elevate the head along with the chest and keep the shoulders relaxed; with arms hanging at our sides we present a body that is organized, balanced, and poised for action.

Beginning by putting yourself together like this is a basic calisthenic, both of mind and body; it may be compared to removing an instrument from its case and assembling it for playing. One just doesn't slap a bassoon together with a few fast moves and start blowing. Remember: the body must be prepared to conduct and as carefully assembled as any instrument.

2. Up on Toes, Breathing

While in the position of Exercise One we must now practice inhaling and exhaling breath into the body using only the abdominal muscle areas and the diaphragm, no chest or shoulder action. Deep, full controlled breathing is a vital part of all of the calisthenics and no activity of this kind should ever be undertaken without this parallel construction on breathing life's oxygen into the body.

Now that we are organized and breathing, movement can begin. Using those remarkable hinges we call toes, raise your body upward *slowly*. Pause briefly on tip toes and then return. Breathe in as you rise, out as you return.

3. Arms Up From Side

Building on this, let's add the raising of the arms out in front and angled away from the body, rising on the toes, elevating the body on those wires from heaven, and then breathing as we go.

Now relax the body, put the feet apart and carefully but firmly rub out the muscles of the shoulders and arms.

4. The Trunk — Twist and Turn

Let us return to body position No. 1 and place the hands on the hips, fingers forward, thumbs back. Inhale, then slowly bend the torso forward from the hips, lowering the head with the body and exhaling to a point of pause; then begin to inhale and to return the upper torso to the initial body position.

Now, carefully begin to rock the upper torso from side to side. Don't do any of these body movements too quickly or violently; let your muscles and sockets have some warning about what's coming. Return to Position No. 1. Begin to turn the trunk 90° to the left and right of the body center.

Let the outer shoulder (upper arm) do the leading, and as you get into the swing of this movement, raise the parallel heel away from the floor and involve the knee, the ankle, and the toes in this operation as well. All of our downbeats directly involve the spinal area, so all of the body system that supports that stem of the skeleton must be alive and working. Also do this movement with the feet apart.

Next, proceed slowly and cautiously to a nearly full turn of the upper torso. Waking up dormant joints and muscles can be a tricky operation. For the full twist and turn you'll probably have to keep both feet on the floor and use your hands on the hips to push you around. You can also do this with the arms extended outward.

5. Arms Up and Around: Shoulder Wheels

Our arms are connected to the shoulders in a swivel capable of full wheeling movements in nearly all directions. The big conducting gestures begin with this exercise, and it is here, too, where the calisthenics are most directly tied to the use of the lower arm, also basic to all conducting technique.

Before starting the shoulder wheels, prepare the arm and its shoulder socket by straight-up motions of the full arm, borrowed from our third calisthenic when we raised the arms to shoulder height as we come up on the toes. Now let's raise the arms all the way up — slowly — first in front, then at an angle, then at the sides. (Look out for this one, it may catch you in the upper arm.) Remember to breathe deeply as you exercise. Now rub out the arm muscles, breathe deeply, rest briefly.

Wheeling the arm from the shoulder one can feel something of the centrifugal action which seems to force the blood out to the tingling fingertips. Begin with the right arm; body in position, head up, oxygen flowing. Cock the right arm out to the side, fingers extended slightly upward, palm flat, the hand slightly above the shoulder.

Slowly and with control, lower the arm toward the left, moving clockwise. Bring it over, across, and in front of the body; then up and around past the left shoulder, and above the head. Repeat. Make four revolutions and stop where you began. Breathe as you work. Rub out the muscles again. Repeat the entire procedure using the left arm.

Next, raise both arms to the previous initial position. (Watch your body position and posture continually). Then bring both arms together in counter-clockwise action for four revolutions. Wheel the arms rapidly in all directions following these basic procedures; also move the arms in parallel, rather than in contrary motion.

6. Knee Spring

I am aware that many books on conducting either ignore or discourage the bent knee. I use it as the music urges me to. I really feel the need to cushion those sometimes massive down pulses that one finds in music of every kind. If you desire to use your whole body in what you do as a conductor, this kind of poise and motion will surely keep you in balance while granting a vibrant and resilient involvement with that music. I also find that one foot placed slightly farther forward (for me it's the right foot) assists in this motion. Use a repeated light springing action at the knees. Breathe deeply as you work.

7. Forward Bend — Hand to Opposite Knee

Yet another waker-upper for the spine and the legs (as well as the back, the hand, and the arms) is this combination of motions: With feet apart and arms raised, bend carefully forward, place the right fingertips on the left knee cap; raise up, pause, then execute this motion to the opposite knee. Inhale as you raise the arms and exhale as you bend to touch the knee.

8. Arm Thrusts

Calisthenic No. 5 with its wheeling motions of the full arms was a good preparation for this exercise. Begin with Body Position and with the hands drawn up into a firm fist with the arms cocked upward from the elbow. Thrust the arms outward at the shoulders through a 180° arc in front of the body. Use considerable push, opening the closed fist at the end of each stroke; then return the arm and hand to the initial cocked position for each thrust, breathing as you go.

Practice using this exercise to throw a cue to an imaginary player. It is a conducting move I could never do without, after I saw Sir Thomas Beecham deliver it.

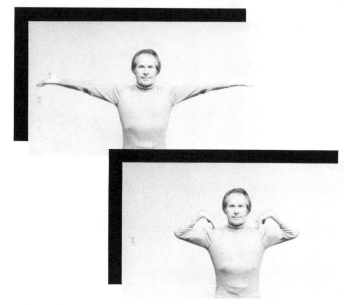

9. Rhythmic Slap of the Legs

To begin this calisthenic we again assume Body Position with the arms raised to the sides. We will rhythmically slap the sides of the legs in an even and intense movement. Begin with the arms elevated, then drop them sharply for two counts; raise them again for two counts, pause, and repeat. Rhythmically count out loud the four points of cadence to help you judge the movement of the arms through the space between the beginning position and the slapping action on the legs. Going down is easier than finding the place to stop when raising the arms again. One of this calisthenic's most beneficial by-products is that it makes us conscious of the muscles in the arms, shoulders, and back by which the arms are elevated.

10. Shake Out the Hands, Flick the Fingers

This is an appropriate place to shake out the hands. Extend the arms away from the body once again and let the fingers fly around as you turn the wrist in alternate motions. After random shaking, flick the fingers rhythmically, stopping the hand between each flick.

11. Extended Arms, with Circles

You've probably noticed how much emphasis is placed on calisthenics that develop the muscular system of the shoulders and arms. Since much conducting is done with the arms raised in front of the body, the muscular systems which support those arms must be developed and maintained.

In this exercise we extend the arms outward and move them in circles both clockwise and counterclockwise. When this gesture is adapted on the smaller scale used in conducting, we have these very useable little circles that afford us a gently turn of a phrase or a tender release of a quiet fermata.

12. The Hinges

The body contains a remarkable series of over 30 hinges on both sides that hold us together. These begin at the outer extremity of the foot where the first of our hinges is the one in the middle of the big toe; and the next one hinges the toe to the foot. Without these two hinges we would lose our sense of balance. (We musicians need this toe for more than tapping.) We overwork the jaw hinge and underwork those ultimate hinges in the eyes. Our final calisthenics involve the hinge of the arm and the hand.

Stand and assume the Body Position, again with your arms outstretched to the sides. With the palms up bring the tips of the fingers to the top of the shoulder — alternately at first, then together. Next, turn the arm to the front and continue. Touch the shoulder and breathe rhythmically as you go.

With the arms raised at shoulder height and extended away from the shoulder hinge at a 45° angle (palms facing inward), bend the hands back as far as they will go; when the hands are bent back to this physical stopping point, begin to bring the wrists together slowly, keeping the arms at shoulder height and the hands bent back.

When the wrists are joined, invert the hinge position of the wrist and join the finger tips; now begin to draw the hands apart to their previous outer position, keeping the hands parallel to the front of the body.

When the arms are returned to the initial position of this exercise, bend the hand back again to its stopping point and carefully connect that action to the inward movement of the arms for the continuation and repetition of the motion.

This smooth hinge action is extremely useable in legato, and when the palms are flattened parallel to the floor we have a technical application of the calisthenics of the arms and hands that is undeniably musical.

There are several movements of the karate-chop variety that warm up the wrist, hand, and lower arm. They, too, have their own application to conducting. (In fact, I know a one-time great oboe-player-turned-pop-conductor who made a fortune with it as he asked the audience to "sing along.")

Before we leave the hinges, let's return to that motion with the arms out and the palms down: to make this study a telling success, please take a coin and place it on the fingers. The purpose of this, of course, is to get you to keep your palms down as you move the hand into any desired position and (on all levels) as you employ all of the hinges of the hand, arm, and shoulder — all *without dropping* the coin.

Most of these calisthenics should also be done in the swimming pool, where, up to the neck in water, all are able to become keenly aware of the resistance which the water offers; this must then be transferred to the execution of all arm and hand movements when the water no longer offers that unmistakable field against which muscular development must be undertaken. The air around us must present that same resistance mentally that the water provides and which can only be achieved "on dry land" by the greatest and most intense muscular awareness — and the ultimate in muscular control.

Why should you expect to conduct without physically conditioning your body? The physical resources of your body are yours alone, so use them well. The simple and basic calisthenics we have been exploring are but a few of the many you can apply to overcome what we thought were the limitations of our body. Use your imagination to devise your own additional calisthenics. When our body is in complete control, when its motions are habitual and free flowing, we are able to concentrate on listening while we shape the music produced by the groups we conduct. ∎

The Composer Conducts

Vaclav Nelhybel

The composer and conductor are two independent agents functioning on two very remote levels.

The composer operates as an individual. He is ego-centered and the impulse for his action comes from within. His tools are a collection of disciplines geared to enable him to translate individual sounds and complex simultaneities of sounds, rhythms, and tone colors into visual symbols. He must choose his materials carefully in order to achieve a constant relation of all elements resulting in his own musical style. Finally, he has to mold all the chosen shapes into the tight framework of a structural form. He does not *hear*, but *imagines* sounds, combining them vertically and organizing them horizontally. All of this happens only in his mind. The piano is of very limited help. He can rely only on previous experiences with performances of his own works or on the analysis and study of recordings.

The conductor, on the other hand, operates with live sounds produced by a collective body of individual players. The composer's score is the point of departure for his activity, and the performing group is the material that he is working with. His tools are a collection of virtually the same disciplines as those of the composer, but they are geared to enable him to understand the composer's score and to imagine its actual sound. From the printed page, the conductor must find the thematic elements and their interaction; he must recognize the structural make-up of the composition and have the know-how to materialize all this into live sound. The conductor is the mediator between the composer and the performing musicians. First he has to "de-compose" the work in his own mind and then he has to re-create it in live sound. In this phase of his activities he communicates the printed score to the musicians and leads them in the final communication of the composer's ideas to the listeners through the medium of performance.

Vaclav Nelhybel, born in Czechoslovakia in 1919, is now an American citizen and a composer of considerable influence. Since coming to the U.S. in 1957, he has devoted most of his time to composition but has still been able to give lectures, clinics and guest conduct throughout the country.

The Guest Composer/Conductor

Let us take an actual situation — I am in a high school band room with a group I have neither seen nor heard and with whom I am supposed to perform some of my own compositions.

During the ten years that I have been a guest-conductor I have developed a certain system, an unwritten checklist for this type of situation. First, I look at the band and check the size and instrumentation. I might find a preponderance of brass instruments, a great number of B♭ soprano clarinets and only one bass or contrabass clarinet (perhaps none), a disproportionate number of saxophones, and so on. Although I have not yet heard a single note played by the band, I already have some information on possible balance problems that will have to be taken into consideration.

The warm-up starts, and I begin to check my visual findings with the actual sound. I might find out that this band does have overpowering, brilliant trumpets and trombones, yet the tuba sound is not focused enough and the horns should be doubled in number to match the rest of the brass; the woodwinds might be top-heavy and the double reeds might be below the general technical level of the band. The *percussion* might be only a glorified *drum* section, with inadequate efficiency and subtlety in the mallet instruments. (Fortunately, this is less and less true.)

While standing in front of a performing group as the conductor of my own music, I too have to make up my mind on how to transfer the printed page of a score into sound.

Of course, I do have the considerable advantage of knowing the score thoroughly. . . but I am still functioning only as the re-creator of a score.

During the warm-up, I have learned about the balance, sound quality, and dynamic sensitivity of the band, and I have gauged the players' reactions to the conductor's baton. Following the warm-up, I usually ask the local director to take the band through a part of the composition that I am supposed to conduct, so that I can measure the overall technical efficiency of the band as well as make an evaluation of the individual sections. After the band has played for about five minutes, I am quite aware of its good and bad qualities, and it is time for me to go into action.

Let us assume the band has many weaknesses and is not well-enough prepared. Now I will have to decide what I might be able to change in the short rehearsal time available and to what degree I will have to compromise — or in general, what kind of adjustment I will have to make in order to achieve the maximum result that I think I can reach with this band, without damaging the composition. (It is in this area that the composer/conductor has a unique insight.)

Very often a rather minor slowing-down of a fast tempo can result in a more relaxed and convincing performance. Whenever I feel that the players are struggling with fast passages, I find the tempo at which they can play all the notes comfortably without neglecting dynamic and other markings. If that tempo turns out to be somewhat slower than necessary to achieve the required drive of the music, I will still maintain the adjusted (slower) tempo and try to compensate for the lowering of the speed by other means, according to the specific character of the composition. In many situations of this kind, a strong emphasis on detailed dynamics and somewhat exaggerated expressive phrasing will result in a convincing rendition of the composition. It is important to remember that, even though the technical difficulties that necessitated the adjusted tempo occurred only in *one* segment of the composition, the whole movement (or perhaps the entire composition) will have to be adjusted. A movement with the tempo indication *allegro con brio* might become an *allegro poco marcato*. It will still be an allegro, a little heavier, maybe, and more dramatic, but because the whole movement was stretched out and intensified expressively, no real damage was done.

The same thing — in reverse — can be done with very slow movements. Breathing and intonation problems caused by long sustained phrasing can at times seriously impair the projection of the musical content. Speeding up a heavy, very slow dramatic

movement will result in a somewhat lyrical, lighter performance, but strict consistency in the adjustment will justify the change of tempo. (In this respect it would be interesting to compare the great and yet quite different performances of the same compositions by the Italian Toscanini and the German Furtwängler.)

Perhaps because of the finger technique of young players, the question that band directors ask me most frequently is: "How fast do you want such and such a composition to be played?" Whenever I don't know the band (and the conductor), my answer is never a dogmatic metronomic indication. The more mature (musically) and the more efficient (technically) the band is, the faster you can play the fast movements and the slower the slow ones.

The right choice of tempo for the band is, I feel, the first and most important decision to be made. A major misjudgment of tempo can result in a total misrepresentation of the score, even if the musicians are able to play all the notes with all the markings. Music lives in time, and therefore the right tempo is the first concern for me.

After I have found what I feel is the right tempo, I concentrate on dynamics, a vital and structurally important dimension of music. The lack of dynamic differentiation is a rather frequent problem in band performances, so I spend considerable time in the rehearsal to make the players aware of the expressive power of dynamics. Dynamic differentiation of culmination points and long stretched build-ups, the variety of shapes of expressive dynamic curves in phrases, sudden dynamic contrasts — these are some of the dynamic guidelines that I try to establish in great detail and on whose execution I insist relentlessly.

Tempo and dynamics are the first two elements that a conductor must deal with in his approach to any composition. This, then, is the very general answer that I would give when asked how my music should be performed: choose the tempo in which the players are able to execute all the notes with all expressive markings; if the chosen tempo is either slower or faster than indicated in the score, compensate with dynamics by over-emphasizing all expressive markings in fast movements, and de-emphasizing slightly in slow movements. Whatever the situation, a logical relation between tempo and dynamics must be maintained. Without it, a convincing performance cannot be achieved. ∎

December, 1968

VACLAV NELHYBEL'S CONCEPT OF CONDUCTING

Joel Blahnik

The subject of this article is an examination of the function of the conductor, as presented by Vaclav Nelhybel during his conducting class at Bemidji State College in August, 1967. It is not a literal transcript of the lectures, but rather a recollection from my notes taken during the classes. What follows may be thought of as being the words and/or thoughts of Mr. Nelhybel, coming from him directly rather than through me.

Basically, there are three phases in the work of a conductor:
1. The *study of the score* before the first rehearsal;
2. The communication of the score to the musicians during the *rehearsals;*
3. The *performance,* during which the conductor communicates the composition, through his ensemble, to the audience.

Study of the Score

Conducting is musicianship in the broadest sense of the word. An essential prerequisite in musicianship for a conductor must be his ability to analyze *in detail* the score to be performed. The conductor must "decompose" the score in order to become aware of its content. The first step in the study of a score is to look for the *shape* of the musical composition. This inlcudes the basic division of the composition into sections, changes of tempo, and other general facts obvious at a first reading of the score. To define the shape means to collect the obvious facts and thus get oriented—in a general way—about the composition. The actual qualitative study begins with the examination of the form. In contrast to shape, which states the general outline of the composition, form is the result of complex structural interrelations between all components of the work.

There are two basic structural relation patterns in music: (1) repetition (exact or modified) and (2) contrast. Let us take, for example, a simple and quite common formal layout, the A-B-A song form. A composition with the shape A-B-A is structurally based on the

Vaclav Nelhybel

principle of repetition (A . . . A) and contrast (the B between the two A's). The repetition of a section in a composition is almost never identical, except in a Da Capo restatement, as, for instance, in marches. If nothing else, the orchestration is changed in order to achieve the finality of the restatement of the initial section, thereby defining it as the concluding one. If the repetition of the first section were identical, the composer would set the listener back to the beginning of the composition. This is virtually impossible: time cannot be turned back. The first section (A) was followed by a contrasting section (B), and this established in the mind of the listener two elements, close to each other (because they are part of one piece of music), but at the same time antagonistic (because of their contrasting character). The restatement of the first section (A) is never perceived by the

Joel Blahnik is head director of the two wind ensembles which comprise the symphonic band at Nathan Hale High School in West Allis, Wisconsin. He is a graduate of the Lawrence Conservatory in Appleton, Wisconsin and studied there with Fred Schroder. The wind ensembles, under his direction, will present a lecture-demonstration on Vaclav Nelhybel at the Wisconsin State Music Convention in Madison in January. The Symphonic Band has also performed at halftime for the Green Bay Packers football games.

327

listener in the same way as when it was played the first time. The first section entered the "uncommitted" mind of the listener; the restatement, however, reaches the listener's mind when it is saturated with the contrasting section, which just preceded, and therefore the restatement of the first section has to regain the attention of the listener. Very often the restatement of section A will be varied not only instrumentally but also structurally. The restatement may be shorter, less narrative, and more dramatic (or vice versa) than the initial statement, and it may even retain some elements of the preceding contrasting section. There might be a new countermelody in the accompaniment, derived from the thematic material of the contrasting section, or certain orchestration patterns, typical of the contrasting B section, might be integrated into the orchestration of the restated A section. The restatement might be extended by a repetition of the A section, with the theme of the B section as a strong antagonistic countermelody. In a coda, thematic elements of both the A and B sections might be welded into one organism—and so on.

When we described the potential changes in the structure of the A section, which was repeated after a contrasting B section, we touched briefly on a *third structural relation*, a relation that is more than just an exact or modified repetition or a sequence of two contrasting elements: the *antagonistic involvement* of contrasting thematic material. The strongest application of this principle is in the development section of the sonata-allegro form, but we can find this element of development even in compositions of limited size and modest sophistication.

The few preceding thoughts are only suggestions on how to proceed when defining the form of a composition: first, study the shape and then the interrelation of all the elements involved, i.e., the inner form.

Now, let us examine the individual layers of the overall structure. Of vital importance in defining the structural whole of a composition is the *tempo;* not only the choice of the basic tempo, expressed in most cases by metronomic markings, but also in the deviations from it: meno mosso, piu mosso, agitato, accelerando, ritardando, etc. All deviations from the basic tempo of a composition represent changes in its kinetic pulsation and therefore are some of the most powerful tools in molding the amorphous shape of a composition into a communicative, organic musical form.

The overall *dynamic outline* of a composition is equally important. Speeding up or slowing down the basic tempo, and increasing or decreasing the loudness of sound, if done with the utmost awareness and control, contribute substantially to the excitement of a performance. Crescendo and accelerando, diminuendo and ritardando, are expressions of kinetic energy in action, and music, as art moving in time, depends on kinetic energy. Tempo and dynamics are the most important ingredients in building climaxes, which are the points of reference for the listener; they are two ever present elements, a kind of common denominator for the composition as a whole, and therefore their control and handling is of primary importance.

Then follows the detailed analysis of the *thematic make-up* of the composition: What is the main theme, what is the secondary theme? Is there any interrelation between them? Based on what? Are the themes, in the course of the composition, going through a changing evolution, or do they remain intact throughout? Are any segments from a theme developed into a figure accompanying the contrasting theme? Is the flow of the composition achieved by alternating restatements of the themes, or are the themes going through dramatic developments in which the entity of a theme is split into fragments, each functioning as a theme? Do the two (or more) themes clash in an antagonistic confrontation? These are just a few examples of the type of questions the conductor has to ask himself when studying the thematic make-up of a composition.

The next layer to be studied is the *vertical organization.* Some sections will be purely homophonic-harmonic, other sections harmonic with a countermelodic strand of various degrees of thematic importance, and other sections will be polyphonic in the academic sense —fugue, canon, or freely imitative. Each of these situations requires a different balancing of the overall sound.

The *rhythmic make-up* of the composition as a whole deserves to be studied separately. Rhythm is spaced time, and time is the primary ingredient in music. Section after section should be examined for its rhythmic characteristics and compared with other sections so that one becomes aware of the rhythmic interrelations within the composition.

Meter should be treated in the same way. The whole composition should be examined in order to find out if the indicated meter signature is the *actual* meter, or if in certain instances the music "walks" the given time signature. Sometimes the melody "runs away" from the regular meter, which is clearly maintained in the accompaniment, or vice versa.

After having studied the individual structural elements of a composition separately, the conductor should look for the relationships between them. He may find, for example, that in a composition which is basically homophonic, every repetition of the theme, stated almost without melodic modification, is accompanied by a distinct countermelody. This constant factor must be kept in mind by the conductor who should, therefore, always treat the countermelody in the same way: as an expressive but only secondary melodic strand, or as an outline of important harmonic notes resulting in a continuous melodic line, or, if derived from a contrasting theme, as a challenging antagonist of the main theme. These are just a few potential situations.

What is important is the consistency in the rendition of consistent structural patterns in a composition. The consistency of the interrelations of *all* elements in a composition is musical *style*, which constitutes the "personality" of an artistic work.

The expressive means and the *expressive intensity* of a composition should be the subject of a separate study: How does the composer build a melodic line? Is it one long, singing line, or is it a sequence of short melodic fragments, separated by short rests, yet belonging together? Do the crescendos and diminuendos coincide with the mounting and falling of the melodic curve? Where is the culmination point in each theme, and how is the melodic climax achieved? What harmonic means are used to stress the expressive content of the melodic line? What rhythmic and metric patterns are used to generate the mounting and falling of the melody? This kind of analysis must be continued until the expressive means of the composition are thoroughly understood.

Rehearsal

Before starting to rehearse, the conductor has to have a concept of the composition and must possess the technical means to transform the preconceived image of the composition into musical sound. During his study of the score he must spend considerable time imagining what will happen in the rehearsal. He must be able to recognize those sections in the composition where his ensemble may run into difficulties. Is the problem purely technical? Is it a problem of dynamic balance, or does the difficulty lie in the antiphonal interplay between two or more instrumental groups? Or—let us not underestimate this—is the cause of the problem just a lack of instant involvement of the player after a long rest? A great time-saver in rehearsing is the readiness of the conductor to handle a situation in which not only one but several problems emerge simultaneously.

When rehearsing, the conductor should apply all the knowledge gained from the study of the score. First of all, he should explain briefly the overall form of the composition. Then he should have the main theme played and point out its characteristics and personality, demonstrate all of the additional thematic material, and describe the structural make-up of the work, section after section. The description should always be in *concrete* terms. For example: "The clarinets play the harmonized main theme and the baritones join them with a countermelody which is derived from the contrasting theme . . ." The players should be made aware of the character of the music at every instant of the composition. For example: "Here there is a quiet statement of the main theme in the double reeds; in the next ten measures, the final portion of the main theme is repeated; the harmonic changes in the repetition and the addition of low saxophones and clarinets result in an expressive restlessness, strongly contrasting with the quietness of the first statement of the theme." And so on, through the entire piece. The conductor must always be scrupulously specific; by giving the exact measures that he is talking about and naming the instruments involved, he will sustain the attention of the players while he is talking. Above all, the conductor must convey to the players the outline of expressive intensity of the composition as a whole. Control of dynamics is one of the means which will indicate the vitally important direction in which the music is moving and will point up the organic relation of the actually sounding tones to those preceding and those following. For example: you can play a scale twice, each time with completely different musical meaning; the first time, the inital seven ascending notes are striving to reach for the upper octave which will, in this case, sound like the climax of the phrase; or, vice versa, the first note of the same scale can be played so emphatically that it will become the most important tone of this eight note phrase, and the remaining seven ascending notes will sound as if they were "running away" from the emphatic first note. The player must always remember that musical sound is "going somewhere," but it is up to the conductor to point out the actual direction of a phrase or section—and of

the whole movement, too. It is not surprising that players who are aware of the direction of a phrase will play with much better intonation, even though not one word has been said about pitch. A feeling on the part of the player that he is playing unrelated notes is very often the main cause for inferior intonation. The conductor should make the players sing phrases in order to allow them to feel the whole design of the phrase before they start playing it. This technique should be employed frequently.

The conductor must be a teacher of his ensemble. He must systematically work at blending the independent playing of his musicians into coherent, organic ensemble music-making. To achieve this, the conductor sees to it that the individual players are continuously aware of their function within the ensemble. For example, the musician, before entering after a rest, has to listen to the playing of the ensemble and has to know the purpose and function of his entrance. Is it an unexpected introduction of some thematic material, a dynamic surprise? Or is he taking over the melodic line from another instrument—and should therefore match its dynamics and tone color in order to make his entrance as unobtrusive as possible? Or is his function to add new tone color to the existing sound, without raising the dynamic level? There are many possibilities. The conductor must get each of his players to develop enough musical thinking and creative hearing so that each, by himself, will be able to subordinate his line to the overall sound of the ensemble. Being aware of the specific purpose and function of his individual line within the overall sound of the ensemble makes the musician feel important. He is therefore willing, and even eager, to participate, to the utmost of his abilities, in the intricate game of pushing and pulling forces within the musical structure of a composition.

To generate a specific expressive mood in the music requires the active, creative participation of all players involved. Each of the players is like one of many painters who simultaneously adds strokes of color to one vast canvas. This poetic awareness must be coupled with physical involvement in the dynamic and rhythmic shaping of the phrases. Music is always motion: a steady walk or a painfully exhausting run uphill, a rush down with constantly increasing energy, a tense reaching for the top or a pulling on a heavily charged chord, a sudden break-down or a sudden outburst. In music, like in any human physical activity, everything is energy.

In order to achieve the correct curve of a difficult musical phrase, it is of great help to have the musicians act out some of the movements of the sounds and, at the same time, have them sing the rhythm of the notes on any pitch, while concentrating solely on the direction of the curve of energy in the phrase. A sforzato-piano, a strong crescendo or decrescendo of short duration, the final fermata of a composition in fortissimo, with a short crescendo before the final release—these are some of the situations where "dancing out" the music helps to obtain a convincing interpretation from the ensemble.

Teaching is the most important function of a conductor. By unveiling the energetic forces behind the notes, the conductor guides the players to the essence of music. The individual player begins to become involved and to identify himself physically and mentally with the sounds that he is producing; even a single note begins to have a meaning and a function related to the whole structure. Once the conductor has made his players think and hear structurally, once they begin to participate creatively in the music-making, he has achieved the communication that is essential between himself and his ensemble. The players become a flexible instrument, capable of communicating with the listening audience. This leads us to the third and final function of the conductor, the conducting of a performance.

Performance

In the rehearsal the conductor is free to use any means to communicate with his players: the verbal approach, in conveying the analysis of the score, by using metaphoric stimulation to set a poetic mood in the mind of the players; and the non-verbal approach, through expressive and meaningful baton techniques. During the performance, however, the conductor has only the non-verbal means at his disposal. (In this résumé of a lecture which lasted a whole week I have purposely omitted the problems of baton techniques and will concentrate only on the musical dimension of conducting.)

During the performance, the conductor has at his disposal, in addition to his two hands (and a baton, usually), an extremely efficient instrument of communication with his players: his eyes. In order to start the first note of a composition, all the players must be completely focused, mentally, on the expressive intensity of the music to be performed. The conductor does not need to be a mime, but his face should to some degree mirror the mood of the music. He should insist, as much as possible, on *eye contact* with all his players, not only at the very beginning of the music, but also during the whole composition. Eye contact is a must before an important entrance of a group of instruments, or of one solo player, after a long rest. The conductor has to look at the group of players, which is about to enter, a few measures before their actual entrance. If the entrance is difficult to count, the conductor should show the number of measures to go before the entrance with the fingers of his left hand. This gives the players a feeling of security and confidence. This same eye contact and counting of measures is a great help to the unfortunate snare drummer who had to play the same rhythmic pattern for 24 measures and has to be prominently present with a new rhythmic pattern in the 25th measure. A soloist must look at the conductor before his difficult entrance, and the conductor should cue him by breathing with him. If eye contact is established, very often a little motion of the conductor's head is sufficient as a cue. This eye-cuing somewhat relieves the left hand and thus permits it to fulfill its most important function, that of controlling the expression and dynamics of the ensemble. Of course, this requires *memorization* of the score—not necessarily of the complete score so that the director is able to conduct without it—but of sections in which the players need close eye contact with the conductor. Such *sectional memorization* is an absolute must. *In critical moments there is no substitute for eye contact between the conductor and his players.* Not only is the conductor sure that the players are "awake" and ready to go, but he also will get from the players their utmost because of this face-to-face confrontation before an entrance. The eye contact bridges over the physical distance between the conductor and the players and this psychological closeness between the players and the leader is the secret of the conductor's control during the performance. This ability to control his ensemble is, after all, the very essence of the function of a conductor. ∎

August, 1989

Rehearsal Techniques

by Paul Kirby

Conducting a rehearsal of a professional ensemble usually involves only teaching one's concept of music to the players because they can solve technical problems for themselves. With student ensembles the task also involves teaching the performers the technical skills to achieve the musical concept.

The biggest difference between professionals and amateurs is a difference in consciousness about playing. Once players understand the concept of a piece they can correct themselves if one person strays from the rhythm or enters at the wrong time. Rehearsing younger players involves raising their consciousness so that they have a sense of the music as a whole.

Conducting a rehearsal is like studying a score, in that you alternate between analyzing material and assimilating it. Both procedures are important, and if you keep them in balance you will achieve an overview both of the details and the overall flow of the music.

As you rehearse your ensemble, consider whether you are covering both the nuances and

Paul Kirby directs the Iowa State University Symphonic Orchestra and the Central Iowa Symphony. He was music director and conductor of the Houston Youth Symphony and Ballet for eight years. He holds degrees from the University of Michigan, Michigan State University, and Rice University.

the big picture. To do this, you need to be aware of the difference between conducting and teaching. If you are drilling a section, don't conduct; this way, students will not get into the bad habit of ignoring you when you conduct.

Young students struggling with posture, position, fingering, and other technical problems have trouble watching and responding to a conductor, so I merely establish the tempo by counting out loud and have them practice together without me at first. If they need to hear a beat to keep together, use an amplified metronome, the piano, tapping, or clapping to create an audible beat.

Students are more likely to remember the details of the rehearsal if they write down your comments. Probably the best way to encourage this is to place a large pencil box near the door for those who forget theirs. If you find yourself having to make the same comment twice, stop the group and say, "Write it down," then allow the students enough time to do so. Writing instructions on the music is an especially good reminder for ensembles that do not rehearse daily.

Clear instructions from you can go a long way toward smooth rehearsals. When you ask the ensemble to begin playing at a certain point in the score, do not say, "Start two after letter B." Such a request is confusing; students may not know the difference between one after B and two after B. Identifying the place as the second measure of letter B is clearer.

When asking the group to count a substantial number of measures to find a starting point or to identify a problem, ask them to count together. For example, you might say, "Start counting at letter C; now count forward with me, one, two, three, etc." Develop a consistent style of stating such requests.

In general, if a piece is particularly difficult for the group it is better to begin with sectional rehearsals and teach the piece part by part; this way you can give instructions and anticipate problems. If you begin by reading the piece, the ensemble members are more likely to fake it and begin developing bad habits.

When a particular mistake consistently resists correction, I have the group play the passage both the correct and the wrong way, one after the other, to help the students hear the differences.

In rehearsing a passage that has only a few technical problems, try to incorporate musical expression as soon as possible. In early rehearsals ignore minor technical imperfections and ask for a better sense of tone quality and phrasing. Make sure the weight of the phrase is where it belongs and that the music moves in the proper direction. Insist upon accurate dynamics and

nuances right from the start, and give much attention to consistency of style. Often when students concentrate on such nuances technical problems work themselves out without any special attention.

If a work presents a significant number of difficulties, try starting near the end, working out that section, moving back a little, working out that section, playing to the end, and so on until you have covered the entire trouble spot. This gives the group the psychological advantage of understanding where the music is going and knowing it can get there, which can be especially useful for pieces with many tempo or meter changes. Rather than stumbling through, having to stop and start over at each change, the ensemble is usually able to manage the transitions effectively.

Of course you will occasionally have to rehearse some passages slowly to achieve clarity. It can also be useful, though, to play a passage faster than the specified tempo. This gives the group a better sense of forward motion and the overall layout of the work, as well as helping to cement technical improvements.

Besides changing rehearsal tempos, a couple of other techniques can solve specific problems of rhythmic precision. Try having the ensemble play the notes staccato, even pizzicato for strings. As the players listen to themselves, they will hear minor rhythmic imprecisions much more readily; this increased awareness will help them correct themselves without more extensive drilling.

Another useful technique for problems of rhythmic precision is to stop conducting altogether. Sometimes using a metronome or tapping on a music stand helps straighten out rhythm problems, but try asking the group to play as if it were a chamber ensemble: no conductor is present and no beat is audible. For certain passages this can work wonders, because the group has to listen carefully to avoid crashing.

For technically difficult passages of even notes (all 16th, 8ths, or equal triplets, for example) practice the notes in dotted rhythms.

Written

Practiced like this

like this

like this

or like this

When trying to achieve better intonation in a moderately paced or fast section I like to conduct the passage in question at a comfortable tempo, working with players to identify the notes that need the most adjustment. We then play the music again at the same tempo, attempting to anticipate and make the needed adjustments. This tends to work better than stopping the flow of the passage and tuning specific notes.

Intonation is only as good as the players' listening skills. Focusing the students' attention on all details of the music helps, because only by listening carefully can they achieve good balance, rhythmic precision, proper phrasing, and articulation. Careful listening should also help them to hear intonation deficiencies. Teach your students the correct ways of adjusting pitch on their instruments and then encourage them to apply these techniques while rehearsing passages that need improved intonation. Young players often lack confidence in choosing the right direction to adjust a pitch. I urge them to be willing to experiment. I also try to build their confidence with praise for recognizing an out-of-tune note, even if they adjust it incorrectly. Occasionally you will still need to use an electronic tuning machine or stop to tune specific notes.

Of course a well-organized room set up in advance with proper lighting and spacing is important; remember to place chairs and stands so that players can see the baton with their peripheral vision. Although it may seem corny, I post signs and pictures around the room to boost morale and encourage good playing habits. Ensemble members cannot help but see them, read them (especially if they are in large block letters), and be affected by them. Think of the effect on the performer if every time he looks up he sees a huge sign that says "Solid Breath Support" or "Cougar Band Pride."

Organize a rehearsal the way you would an individual practice session: warm-up, working out of problems, sight-reading, and playing through pieces. The order can vary somewhat. Devising a routine for tuning will help save time in the warm-up; you may also want to include a routine of exercises to develop technical skills. Drilling difficult passages, taking sections of pieces apart, and working on ensemble problems will take most of your rehearsal time.

Pacing rehearsals so that the group moves just a little faster than is easily comfortable encourages better concentration and harder work. Try to keep in mind the amount of talking versus playing and the amount of synthesis versus analysis that goes on. How much time do you spend working with sections or individuals? If such work fails to yield results fairly quickly, you may want to move on to something else and handle the difficulty at another time.

Making announcements in the middle of a rehearsal works well because it provides a short break and change of pace for players. In longer rehearsals, such as those with community or youth orchestras, I make announcements just before the break. In this way I take advantage of the students' natural desire to start playing at the beginning of the rehearsal. In general, variety helps keep players' attention.

Consider rehearsals as a series of events leading up to a performance. This can be difficult for an inexperienced conductor. Although you don't want the ensemble to peak too soon, you should strive to have the music in fairly good shape before the last few rehearsals; this will leave you time to solidify and polish the playing. It is a good idea to schedule an extra rehearsal or two at the outset in case you need to pick up slack later. If weather, illness, a fire drill, or any other problem forces you to curtail or cancel a rehearsal, you will have some extra time built into the sequence. If it turns out that the ensemble doesn't need this extra time, you can always cancel a rehearsal at the end or use the time to listen to recordings or sight-read. It is more difficult to schedule an extra last-minute rehearsal to make up for unforeseen problems than it is to cancel or replan one.

Players tend to feel better about a rehearsal that runs for an hour and a half if it were originally was scheduled to run two hours rather than one hour. However, never let an elementary or junior high ensemble special rehearsal out early. The parents will not be there to pick up their children, and it is not productive to have young students waiting for more than five minutes or so with nothing specific to do.

In the rehearsal itself, consider the players' motivation in determining how you will behave. If your ensemble has good enrollment and has had strong support from its audiences, you can afford to be relatively serious and businesslike a good deal of the time. If your group does not have such a positive attitude about itself, or if it is a group of volunteers whose commitment is not solid, it may be more important to make sure the rehearsals are more fun. You can lighten up occasionally without compromising your musical standards as long as you continue to set goals.

There's an old adage that says "If the final rehearsal goes well, the performance will be poor." Sometimes directors consciously attempt to prevent this. I once heard of a conductor who purposely would sabotage his own final rehearsal if he thought it was going too well. I believe this approach compromises one's integrity. It's true that if an ensemble peaks in the final rehearsal and gives an especially exciting reading, the actual concert will then seem disappointing even if it goes rather well. It is also possible that a good final rehearsal can lead to an overconfident attitude and perhaps a disappointing performance. If a group has just completed an excellent final rehearsal, you may want to warn the players of these possibilities.

To build a group's confidence, keep the carrot fairly close to your players: set reasonably attainable goals. Be sure to praise the group for each achievement before moving on to more advanced goals. Everyone loves praise.

Inexperienced conductors often point out all of the errors they hear without realizing that it is equally important to compliment the good aspects of the playing. Some of us (I plead guilty), however, tend toward a routine of praise followed by correction: "That was very good, but..." If your responses are too predictable, you lose effectiveness.

Shake up the routine occasionally by rotating the seating of an ensemble. Your concert seating arrangement is not necessary for every rehearsal. Putting the weaker musicians in the front allows the director to give them more help and allows them to hear the rest of the ensemble more clearly. Meanwhile, seating stronger players toward the back challenges them to maintain their usual good contact with the conductor and the music from greater distance. Flexibility and creativity in changing the seating play from time to time can provide an additional element of variety to the routine.

Should the director give instructions while the ensemble is playing? This is controversial; some fine conductors I know eschew the practice on principle. I do it quite a bit, especially when I believe I can accomplish a minor adjustment, quicken the rehearsal pacing, adjust a stylistic problem, or get a lost performer back on track. To be effective, however, you should use only brief, authoritative commands, such as "Letter C!" or "Short! Separate more!" Whatever commands you give, be sure to look directly at the student as you speak. Try to give all of the members, particularly those in back, the impression that you are keeping an eye on them.

Musicians at all levels enjoy increasing their understanding of the music they play. The exciting performances that result will reward everyone involved. □

February, 1970

WITH OR WITHOUT BATON?

Lewis Harlow

This is a personal experience report on conducting, sometimes (for what I considered very good reasons) with a baton and sometimes (for other seemingly good reasons) without a baton. There will be no moral at the end and no attempt to sway any conductor who may have developed fixed habits in the practice of his profession.

The idea of conducting with two bare hands came to me during an April week in the late 1930's.. I was still an impressionable young band leader then and I had accepted the baton unquestioningly as the badge of my profession. On this particular week, Stokowsky and the

Philadelphia Orchestra were on tour, and they had chosen Monday night for a concert at Boston's Symphony Hall, a place convenient for me to attend live performances. On Wednesday of the same week, Toscanini and the New York Philharmonic, also on tour, scheduled their Boston concert at the same Symphony Hall. And to make matters even more enjoyable, Koussevitsky and the Boston

Lewis Harlow was educated at Harvard University where he studied under Walter Spaulding, Archie Davison, and Ed Hill. He received the Payne award and continued his studies in Paris.

Symphony were at home and playing their regular Friday-Saturday subscription series.

Here was the opportunity of a lifetime for a young band leader to observe and benefit from the conducting techniques of three of the greatest men in the trade, and I attended the programs of all three. It would be presumptive and tasteless for me to say that one was "better" than another, but the results attained were quite different and you can take your choice as to which you prefer.

Stokowsky offered a quality of tone that seemed completely detached from the mechanical processes of music making. I lost Stokowsky and I lost his musicians as living people. I could only hear — and think about — the composition as a message from the composer.

Toscanini was crystalline in a material sort of way. I was always aware of the man Toscanini and his human musicians. When Brahms doubled a pair of clarinets with a pair of bassoons, I could not hear a composite tone but rather the four instruments exactly as Brahms had scored them.

Koussevitsky, when the spirit moved, could cajole or drive more musicianship, more precision, more technique, and more virtuosity out of his players than merely human minds and fingers are capable of delivering. On this occasion, the spirit moved happily.

Stokowsky conducted without a baton. I had heard through the grapevine that this had been his regular practice for some years previous, and in a 1969 televised Stokowsky performance which I "attended" in my living room, I can report that he is still conducting without a baton.

Toscanini conducted without a baton. This was a shocker to me and others. In opera, I had seen him throw or "lose" his baton up into the flies in a paroxysm of rage or other emotion, but always it was retrieved for him or replaced as quickly and unobtrusively as possible. At Symphony Hall, he started the concert batonless and persisted throughout. Perhaps he had heard about the Stokowsky technique and was curious or competitive. We will never know. For the record, I later saw him on a few occasions and he was again using a baton.

Koussevitsky conducted with a baton. His results were usually superbly precise, but I have never witnessed as seemingly inept and uncertain baton technique as was his regular habit. In fact, I could not bear to watch it. If I wanted to enjoy the music, I would watch the tympanist or the harpist — or even pretend to read my program notes.

This Koussevitsky phenomenon mystified me for all of 20 years, but then I happened onto what may be the answer. Leonard Bernstein had been a pupil of Koussevitsky's, and in the late 1950's Bernstein came to Boston to guest conduct the Boston Symphony Orchestra. I attended his open rehearsal and the program started with a very straightforward Mozart symphony, a piece that this orchestra and this conductor could have presented sympathetically and accurately with no rehearsal at all. Bernstein, an excellent technician and communicator in any category of orchestral music, stopped the players again and again to plead that they "relax" and "play together" on their own.

Perhaps this was the disclosure of the Koussevitsky secret. Infinite rehearsal and then a self-containing performance with a minimum of molestation from the podium.

After this threefold orgy of objective concert going, it was natural that I would make some practical use of what I had seen and heard. As I drove to my band rehearsal the following week, I had already decided to try conducting without a baton. I liked what I had heard from Stokowsky, and if Toscanini could make the transition abruptly with no apparent loss of his communicative powers, why couldn't I do the same?

My band of the moment was a pretty good one, and we played a repertory considerably more demanding of leader communication than the fundamental display of two, three or four beats to the measure. The band was small, mostly adult, and professional to the extent that the modest gross receipts from all public appearances were distributed to the band members as a semi-annual dividend. The leader did not share in this melon cutting; he was on an annual retainer from the largish manufacturer who dominated the smallish town in which he was located — and sponsored many of the town's social activities. Locally, the band played a summer series of ten concerts in the little circular bandstand on the common, and in the winter there was an occasional concert, minstrel show, or other event involving public assembly. Out of town, there were concerts, parades on all holidays, firemen's musters, and the like.

But back to the rehearsal that was to be my first experiment at batonless conducting. I began it with a note by note story of my experiences of the previous week. I had seen and heard two of the best conductors of the era working without baton. Obviously, their objective was better performance from their musicians that would result from better communication between conductor and players. If this was the new thing, why shouldn't we try it? At our own more modest level of leader ability to ask and player ability to respond, perhaps we could improve our own net result. My band seemed interested and willing to try the experiment, so I distributed the parts for the "Prelude" to *Die Meistersinger* and we went to work, first at sightreading and then at as much refining as the two-hour rehearsal would allow.

For my part, I was too busy communicating to give any thought to the fact that I was doing it with two bare hands. The transition from baton was natural and effortless. I did not feel awkward, embarrassed, or handicapped in any way. It was as though the baton had never been a part of my earlier life.

My band never played better. They knew it and enjoyed the experience to the utmost. They gave me a level of musicianship and alert attention that we had never before shared. I responded in turn, asked for the impossible, and got it.

I am sure that my batonless conducting deserved only a small part of the credit for the result attained. Much more important was the discussion that had started the rehearsal. Never before had I used the word "communication" in talking to this band or any other. The idea of sharing as a confidence the mechanical aspects of the relationship between conductor and players was as new to me as it was to them. With all of us thinking about this hitherto secret facet of ensemble playing, we all responded at a level higher than our fondest dreams.

At the end of the rehearsal, no one packed up to go home. We sat around and talked. At future rehearsals, of course, I would conduct without baton, but what about the visual tradition that the baton is the badge of the leader? It was agreed that I would not use a baton in our public performances before our local audience; these people knew us well, liked the music we played, and the way we played it, and would not be needing the extra pretense of professionalism. It was agreed that I would conduct with baton on out-of-town jobs; here we were being hired by relative or absolute strangers, and the money they were investing in the presence of a small professional band should bring them a traditional band leader with baton.

Time passed with the new rules in effect, and I began to notice a secondary benefit. With this new general consciousness of the visual aspects of "being a band," I began to see better polished instruments and better pressed uniforms and a more businesslike and punctual approach to the bandstand at concert starts and after intermissions. The symptom first showed itself on the out-of-town jobs, but eventually it became standard practice even at home.

On those occasions when, by our set of rules, I conducted with baton, the band seemed to feel that I was working under a handicap and that it was up to them to be especially attentive and responsive to my fumbling communication.

Not infrequently, there would be calls for me to serve as guest conductor of amateur bands. The situation usually provided minimum time (or no time at all) for rehearsal, and I have usually found the establishment of rapport with amateur musicians to be a slow process. Here there was need for instant dignity and at least the look of competence. I used a baton — as assurance to my musicians that I was really a band leader. My audience of strangers too, would react more favorably to the music if the unknown substitute conductor looked traditional on the podium.

On other occasions, I conducted in a theater pit for one-time events and promotions that ran the full range from amateur musical shows and local beauty contests to celebrity welcomings and political rallies. Here my responsibility was to show up with an appropriate library and an assortment of 20 men or so whom I had recruited from Local Nine of the American Federation of Musicians. These men I conducted with bare hands. Top-flight professional instrumentalists are very worldly and they have their own criteria with which to judge the competence of their conductor. A baton would not have kidded them at all and it was up to me to prove my musicianship in other ways that they knew well. Also, I wanted to get the best possible music out of them in return for the union scale that I was paying. In this kind of work, the audience was not to be considered at all. They would be watching what was happening on the stage above.

I have never conducted a band at a televised halftime ceremony at a football game. If this situation should arise, I would use a baton. However well the band might know me and be ready to respond to my most delicate expression of demand, I would use a baton for the sake of the television audience. The television picture at halftime is painted with a broad brush and all possible visual symbolism is helpful to the whole.

Choral conducting

I have observed that batonless conducting is quite common in choral music. Probably the less likely of two reasons is that the conductor has come directly out of the ranks of the chorus being conducted; the use of a baton

might seem austentatious to this conductor.

I prefer to believe the following reason, though. I assume that every choral conductor *is* schooled, probably schooled in conducting and surely in other aspects of music which include time beating and note values. Given this benefit of the doubt, the choral conductor has good reason to lead his chorus with bare hands. This chorus is almost surely amateur, and it may even learn its songs by rote — with less than a nodding acquaintance with measure bars and the like. In front of such a chorus, it is expedient that the conductor stick to the rhythm of the melodic line and possibly even forget the fundamental idea of beats to the measure. Certainly neither of his hands should be encumbered by a baton, and there are many occasions where he may wish that he had a third hand.

When I was guest conducting a chorus I did as the Romans do. If the regular conductor who preceeded me used a baton, I used a baton. If not, I didn't. This was just to save confusion and misunderstanding. If the chorus seemed to have learned its music by rote, I conducted by rote, waving jerkily on the dotted rhythms and freezing on the sustained syllables. To an instrumentally oriented conductor, this was not easy, but my effort was sincere. Whatever the handicaps, my objective has always been the best possible performance from the conditions at hand.

Any rule is said to be proved by one exception. The occasion for my exception was an emergency. The regular conductor of this chorus was ill, and I was called in to finish the preparation of Brahms' *Song of Destiny,* the work to be included in an otherwise instrumental program and the whole to be conducted by the orchestra conductor. I knew that the choral conductor ahead of me did not use a baton, but that the orchestra conductor to follow me did use a baton, and would use it in the Brahms. I did not know the chorus — except that it was somewhat dependent on rote conducting. I was to have two rehearsals to get the chorus ready for the big event and I began with a complete explanation of the situation. The conductor of the public performance would be using a baton, and as they, the chorus, would probably be baton shy, I had decided to use a baton in these rehearsals. I would use it in the professional manner. Except for cuing their entrances, I would simply beat time, and this would be the very least assistance that they could expect from the orchestra conductor to come.

The rehearsals were accompanied by piano, with the pianist handling the unusual assignment alertly and sympathetically. The chorus also rose to the challenge and in the course of the two rehearsals learned to follow me precisely — and to find a new kind of meaning on the printed pages of their octavo parts.

We all knew that they had done well and that they had gained the confidence they might have needed. I congratulated them, and also told them that I would be at their concert. I attended, and was very proud of "my" chorus.

Through all of the above experiences, I have failed to mention one item. What is my innermost personal attitude toward conducting without a baton? I approve of the technique wholeheartedly. I am sure that I conduct better without than with. Without a baton, I feel that I am communicating more eloquently to my musicians. The proof of this is that they seem to understand me and give me the extra musicianship for which I ask. ∎

The Compleat
Conductor Stuart J. Ling

Perhaps the most important aspect of personality is the ability to communicate clearly with the performers. The conductor must quickly be able to determine and point out what is wrong, and he has to indicate practically in the same instant how the error might be corrected. The outstanding conductor also needs an almost poetic command of the language. One maestro said to his string players, "Play with more sound. That white, worn, washed-out sound of last week's laundry isn't good enough."

I believe that a sense of humor is a valuable tool for a conductor. His humor reflects a positive outlook that embraces a tension-releasing wit. A conductor whose group had just sight-read a piece commented, "It's not bad reading; it just doesn't sound much like the piece." As his group began another composition the same conductor said, "You can tell how fast the music goes if you look at the baton."

Musicianship

We assume too often that a conductor is a musician. Any music teacher knows that musicianship is measurable in amounts and varies from person to person, from the conductor who plays a full orchestral score at the piano to the person who barely hears what is happening as he conducts. Most of us find our place somewhere between these extremes. The best conductor, though, needs to know what is supposed to be happening and the extent to which it is actually occurring. Thus, the conductor's musicianship involves awareness of pitch, tonal quality, rhythm, dynamics, style, phrase, balance, clarity, and an ability to deal with these elements in many combinations. Here is where the conductor's ear-training, music theory know-how, applied music instruction, music literature studies, and other formal musical learning pay off. Natural talent, though, which has a way of shining through, cannot be ignored. For instance, a failure to hear what is happening because of an inability to discriminate among the sounds cannot be corrected by formal training.

Because conducting skills are so important to successful teaching, I observed a dozen or so excellent conductors in rehearsal during this past year in order to discover the factors that contribute to their effectiveness. Six major considerations emerged from my observation.

Personality

Personality is what the student feels about the conductor as a person. Impressions say a great deal about the chemistry operating between people, and if a conductor doesn't measure up, he is faced with a nearly-insurmountable obstacle.

The conductors I observed ran the gamut of physical characteristics, so I am not associating personality with physical appearance. However, I must admit that each conductor was in his own way "distinguished" in appearance; each communicated a self-confident presence to the performers. This is an attitude that says, "I know more about this music than anyone in this room, and I can help you perform it in a satisfying manner if you will permit me."

Stuart J. Ling is professor of music and director of bands at The College of Wooster.

Preparation of the Score

Even though most conductors study scores, they do not agree on how to do it. For some it means marking every entrance in colored pen. For others it means repeated listening to a record until that particular version becomes a part of the conductor's being. Some sing each part from the score, and still others reduce the score so that it is manageable at the piano. I know some conductors who examine each part to uncover problem areas such as fingering, bowing, and articulation. Many conductors memorize scores, a practice I find fascinating but one which is probably not required to conduct effectively.

Surely all of these techniques are helpful, but it is also possible that some of the learning done by the conductor will happen during rehearsal. This is not all bad; conductors need to be flexible enough to change approaches and expectations during a rehearsal. The basic ideas, though, must be in mind before the first rehearsal to make the most efficient use of rehearsal time and to instill confidence in the performers.

Technique

In spite of the concentration on specific technique in elementary conducting classes, it's difficult to prove that technique is the most important factor of a conductor's success. It seems far more important that the performers understand the conductor's directions. Over a period of time, students and professionals can become used to almost any conductor's style, but conductors must know these things:

• What beat preparation to give. Most shaky entrances are the conductor's fault.

• How to cue. This is needed especially when players have to count long rests. The conductor needs to make eye contact in sufficient time to permit an unhurried, confident response.

• Direct tempo changes. It helps the players greatly if the conductor makes tempo changes the same way each time. The conductor who slights transitions in rehearsals is asking for trouble in performances.

• Left hand techniques. Nearly all good conductors avoid "mirror" conducting. The left hand should indicate dynamic changes, accents, cues, and phrasing, for instance. If it is used sparingly, the left hand can signal the performers that something special or different is about to occur. The left hand functions best as an alert.

• Indicating mood. Beating time is the conductor's least important function; communicating mood is far more important. This may be done with the hands, body, face, eyes, mouth, or eyebrows.

• Communicate style with the right hand. The good conductor makes his beat communicate the proper sound character — staccato, marcato, heavy, bouncy, legato, for example. A deaf person watching the conductor should be able to interpret his style.

• Beating precisely. Performers must know where the beat is, and they must be able to distinguish each measure's "one" from the other beats. There must be a point which designates where the beat occurs. Some conductors believe all beats should originate at the same point.

Procedure

The good conductors I observed established and maintained a rehearsal procedure. This includes a tuning exercise, warmups, and indicating what music will be played. If this does not change from rehearsal to rehearsal, a minimum of time is wasted and the players settle into a productive routine.

Correcting errors is an important consideration, too. Options range from stopping for every mistake to not stopping at all in the hope that repetition will automatically eliminate most errors. The consistency of the method is more important than the specific procedure because an established routine lets the performers meet the conductor's musical expectations quickly.

Even though some procedural details may seem minor, these matters affect the group significantly. For instance, the good conductors I visited started and ended their rehearsals on time. These groups knew exactly how long the rehearsal would last and worked hard during the entire rehearsal. To clarify expectations further the conductor should distribute a complete schedule of rehearsals and performances at the beginning of a year or season. Schedule conflicts are more likely to surface early, and satisfactory solutions are easier to reach this way.

If challenges are permitted, the procedure must be established clearly, and rules for absences and tardiness must also be clear to all. Problems are less likely to develop when each student knows exactly what the conductor expects.

Leadership

Leadership encompasses everything discussed earlier, and it is impossible to over-emphasize its importance. A musical group is not a democratic organization in any sense of the word, and there must be no mistake about who is in charge. One of the conductors I visited said, "Play this piece at my tempo. My salary is 20% more than yours." At any given moment the conductor should feel more qualified to be on the podium than anyone in the organization. Everything the conductor says or does should demonstrate this belief. Nothing is more devastating to the morale of a musical organization than a disorganized leader.

Furthermore, leadership includes paying attention to the smallest detail, but they must be taken care of subtley. Librarians should handle music; a secretary should take the attendance; section leaders should manage their sections; stage managers should handle equipment. All of these people need to function efficiently so the director is free to devote his attention to any extraordinary problems that occur and to conduct the rehearsal.

Leadership also includes managing other details, like gathering information to make announcements and seeing that officers and committees are functioning properly. But no outside business should be permitted to interfere with rehearsal time. I recall an incident involving several key players who were caught between baseball practice and a band recording session. The director wasted no time calling the baseball coach who very obligingly made baseball practice an hour later. Not every conflict can be resolved this way, but I am convinced that this director would have left no stone unturned to free his students from an uncomfortable dilemma.

A good leader will project an image that inspires his students, too. A lazy director will not encourage student diligence, and a slovenly director will not motivate student neatness. A director who requires little will get what he requires, but an enthusiastic director has a better chance to evoke his students' active participation. Each good director I visited was hard-working, well-groomed, demanding, and possessed unflagging enthusiasm for his art.

In addition, good leaders delegate every possible duty to a responsible person or group. One does not have time to be in charge of every activity or phase of an operation. So the successful director needs the help of the parents' group, school administration, alumni office, assistant directors, officers, local merchants, and others. Without such help the director has too little time for the music.

Good musical leaders communicate the importance of what they are doing to the performers and stress that the best possible performance of the music now on the music stand before them is the most important thing they can do with their lives at that moment. His devotion to music must be clear and overriding so that these signals are clearly received by the students.

One may fall short in one or more of these areas and still be successful. But one final aspect I've seen is that even the best, most knowledgeable conductors are also humble. One well-known conductor I observed said, "The person who nails heels on shoes learns all there is to know about it in three weeks. You can conduct all your life and never learn all you need to know." ∎

337

The Band Conductor as Musician and Interpreter

Walter Beeler

Donald Hunsberger

Leonard B. Smith

Harry Begian

Walter Beeler

Walter Beeler, Assistant Dean of the School of Music at Ithaca (N.Y.) College, has been confined by illness to his home for many months. He has written and arranged various compositions for band and is the author of numerous articles on band directing.

The professional literature already abounds with excellent and comprehensive counsel on band techniques necessary to develop the "perfect" organization; but very little has been written concerning the aesthetic requisites of the band conductor.

It is my belief that evaluations of band directors are not based on the same criteria as those directed toward orchestra conductors. Bandsmen tend to be judged by the completeness, quality and finesse of their organizations, whereas orchestra conductors are appraised largely by their interpretive ability. Until band conductors are afforded the privilege of critical evaluation as musicians, band music will never be taken seriously by the concert-going public.

With these thoughts in mind, several well-known and respected band conductors were asked for their general philosophy of conducting, the devices through which they reach an audience, and the manner in which they create music out of notes. They were also requested to discuss problems inherent in the band as a vehicle for producing music. Finally, it was suggested that they offer bandsmen advice or assistance in producing musical performances.

Donald Hunsberger

Donald Hunsberger is Associate Professor of Music at the Eastman School of Music and the conductor of the Eastman Wind Ensemble. He holds the B.M., M.M., and D.M.A. degrees from the Eastman School of Music.

The young conductor entering the music profession today faces a totally different world than did his predecessors of the past few decades. Previously unimaginable scientific discoveries, the shifting of attitudes in social mores concerning the role of the authority figure in society, plus economic developments which threaten the solidity and, in fact, the very existence of arts and performing organizations — all these affect the young musician seeking a leadership role and seriously challenge the traditional patterns of training associated with his chosen profession.

The preparation of the young conductor has traditionally been rooted in a few areas: musical analysis, baton technique and body movement, repertoire (usually of a particular performing medium such as orchestra, chorus or band), instrumental techniques, etc. What is also necessary in this preparation are some guidelines . . . a credo that will provide feasible artistic and professional goals.

To assist the search for such principles, I have turned to an article by Dr. Howard Hanson in which he listed the attributes that he felt contributed greatly to the phenomenal success enjoyed by the late Emory Remington during his forty-nine year career of teaching trombone at the Eastman School of Music. These included: (1) professional knowledge without pedantry, (2) enthusiasm mixed with dedication, (3) perfectionism without sadism, and (4) a belief in the supreme importance of the individual and the development of his ability. Since all forms of music training, be it in the classroom, the private studio, or the rehearsal room, are dependent upon the type of dedicated teaching exemplified by Mr. Remington, these tenets can be examined with the needs of the young conductor in mind.

Professional Knowledge without Pedantry

The conductor's craft is basically one of communication. His understanding of the composer's desires may be considered *interpretation* and his ability to successfully communicate this interpretation to his performers is a major portion of his leadership role. It is his responsibility to stimulate the individual artistic efforts of each performer while coordinating these individuals into a cohesive, disciplined ensemble.

In order to develop his communicative skills, a conductor will have to be proficient in a number of background areas. Some of these include: *historical perspective*, encompassing socio-economic structures, performance styles and traditions, and an understanding of the position of the arts in man's thinking throughout each century; *compositional practices*, a knowledge which aids the conductor in his search for the composer's true intents and wishes including his individual concept of orchestration; *theoretical practices* (easily the most pedantic unless considered a part of compositional practices) which assist the conductor in the analysis of vertical structures and contrapuntal devices; *instrumental techniques,* the knowledge of each instrument (including the human voice) as it functions individually and in combination with other instruments; *conducting skills,* the so called "baton technique" — the actual communication tools; *psychological relationships,* the role of the leader and his involvement with other persons working together toward a common goal — an artistic performance.

Each of these plays an integral part in the preparation of the young conductor and remains a vital part of his daily existence; he must rely on each for the value it offers but must not permit any one to supersede any other.

Enthusiasm Mixed with Dedication

The history of the school music program in the United States is filled with chronicles of the deeds of many dedicated men and women who have made music performance universally accepted as an essential portion of our daily lives. Everyone now has an equal opportunity to share the joys and rewards of playing an instrument or singing in an ensemble of quality standards. This is directly attributable to these great individuals — persons with foresight, ambition, enthusiasm, and above all, a dedication to the ideal that there will always be something finer than that which exists today.

Perfectionism without Sadism

Perhaps the most difficult of all the decisions a young conductor must face is that of his relationship with his performers during rehearsal times and performances. It is all too frequent that one observes a conductor attempting to gain the attention (and respect) of his players through dictatorial tactics based primarily on fear techniques. I find it most difficult to believe a person can artistically express himself while under a barrage of indignate, disrespectful commands. Every conductor must seek to develop a sense of respect for each of his players and offer every element of human dignity. In return, he may expect to earn the respect, admiration and loyalty of his performers only through a total command of his professional knowledge coupled with an obvious display of his love for music performance. Fear does not engender respect, it only serves to stultify the conductor in his leadership role. This is all involved in that most important developmental consideration that the conductor must have . . . *a belief in the supreme importance of the individual and the development of his ability.*

To quote once more from Dr. Hanson's description of Emory Remington . . . "he didn't teach trombone; he taught people." Isn't this what conducting is really all about — the introduction of people to music, the development of techniques to perform this music and the transmission of the composer's thoughts to the audience? The conductor is a "middle man" in the composer-ensemble-audience relationship, a most important link in the creative processes who must have the tools to utilize, and the proper spirit to develop, the best possible from his performers.

What a wonderful description to have applied to a successful conductor . . . "he didn't just conduct; he taught people." ∎

Leonard B. Smith

Leonard B. Smith has performed as first trumpet player for a vast array of orchestral conductors and has long been referred to as "America's Premier Cornet Soloist." Presently, he is also conducting the Detroit Concert Band.

Everything that goes on in a band or an orchestra should pass through the conductor's brain first. Not only must the conductor understand the uses and limitations of every instrument, he must be trained and skilled in many areas — in theory, counterpoint, sight-singing, dictation, and ear training, as well as baton techniques. There is nothing which will evoke accuracy and attention to detail, on the part of the performers, as much as a capable and discriminating conductor who *hears* what goes on in an ensemble. The ability to immediately correct a note by indicating what wrong note was played and what the right note should be *commands* respect. And this can be done on the spot, without resorting to a minute study of the score. But it takes practice if these skills are to be developed and maintained.

Some areas of conducting can be taught quite readily — how to indicate 3/4, 6/8, 5/4, etc. But other aspects of conducting, such as the ability to communicate one's interpretation of a work through a clear visual definition of every tone, shading, accent, dynamic, etc., do not rely entirely on mechanical movements and so cannot be learned very easily. Perhaps the only way to understand these "other" aspects of conducting is through careful observation of those "great" conductors whose ability to communicate on the interpretative level allows them to produce that vitality and energy which is felt by everyone — performer, conductor, and listener alike.

Of the vast array of orchestral conductors for whom I have played, there are relatively few whom I would choose to designate "great" conductors. However, Bruno Walter, Fritz Reiner, Eugene Ormandy and Victor Kolar are four who readily come to mind as fitting that category. Though each was completely different from the other in his style of conducting, they all had that vitality-energy, or "charisma," and it could be felt by musicians and audience alike.

Not infrequently, Bruno Walter conveyed his wishes to players by giving them the feeling that he had an orb or sphere in front of him which he could mould. He was able to "draw" the music to him, out of the players. He would look, for instance, at the first violins, shake his head slowly back and forth and half close his eyes. His outstretched hands would impress one that he was attempting to bring their vitality to his (which was, in fact, what he was doing). It always seemed to me that he came to the podium with the greatest of respect for the composer's wishes. I believe he regarded the possession of his talent a great privilege to be used to the best of his ability.

Fritz Reiner was a superb technician with the baton. On occasion, he would point it straight up in the air and then, with a snap of his wrist, he would dip the baton

---

Bruno Walter. . . could mould
Fritz Reiner. . . superb technician
Eugene Ormandy. . . makes music
Victor Kolar. . . neat as a pin

---

and his whole body would sway in consonance with the music, his left hand outstretched and almost making a fist. Then he would look down to the floor and suddenly up again, taking in the entire orchestra with a single sweeping glance. He was always aware of what went on. When a solo passage was performed exactly the way he wanted it, he would communicate his appreciation to the player by turning up the palm of his left hand — anyone who ever played for Reiner can demonstrate that little mannerism. And how welcomed the little gesture was — sometimes even more rewarding than the paycheck! He was a "gratifying" conductor to play for, and such a far cry from some conductors who, lacking any real depth of perception into the science and art of conducting, are not only seldom aware when a passage has been performed as desired, but who usually are "busy" conducting the second violins or violas at that moment!

Eugene Ormandy is, indeed, one of the greatest! I have seen him come on stage for a concert or broadcast rehearsal, see a "cold" score (i.e., one which has just been prepared in manuscript) for full orchestra with chorus and solo vocal line, and then proceed to read and conduct it flawlessly. Some lesser "lights" placed in that same circumstance have promptly turned the stick over to the concertmaster and made a bee-line into the control booth to "hear the balance" (when in fact, they were hoping to get a chance to brief themselves on the unfam-

iliar score).

Ormandy made, and still makes music — and he can do it with any fine team of players. Many years ago, I helped him recruit a band for the U.S. Navy in Philadelphia. I still have recordings of the network broadcasts we did with this band. Ormandy's conducting comes through like a shining light. You cannot see it on the record but you can hear it!

Victor Kolar, in my estimation, was also one of the greats. He was brought to this country by Walter Damrosch, along with Georges Barrere, Pierre Henrotte, Carl Heinrich, et al. Kolar later became concertmaster with Victor Herbert and, in addition, was a fine pianist and excellent composer.

Kolar was as neat as a pin in both his personal demeanor and his attention to musical details. I don't think I ever played the 4th or 5th Tchaikovsky symphonies with anyone who so correctly and consistently achieved the "right" tempo. He understood the stretto and, in Tchaikovsky, this reveals the whole structure and subsequent interpretation. I well recall one instance in which the eminent pianist Sergei Rachmaninoff (who incidentally, was not overly demonstrative) turned to the orchestra to compliment Kolar, stating that he had finally received the finest accompaniment for his concerto.

Reiner, Ormandy and Kolar were frequent guest conductors on the famous network broadcasts, the Ford Sunday Evening Hour. Some of us in the orchestra would delight in querying these conductors about their opinions of the previous week's program. We would say: "How did you like the Strauss waltz we did last week?" Invariably, they would respond with, "Oh, all right, I suppose, but wait 'til this week. This will be *real* Strauss."

I can state this for myself, and I rather imagine that any of my colleagues reading this will readily confirm it, that the Strauss waltz interpretations in the hands of either Ormandy, Kolar or Reiner would satisfy any discriminating listener — musician or layman. And each interpretation was completely different from the other, yet containing all the inherent charm and elegance in the music.

Whether he conducts a band or an orchestra, a fine conductor can lift his musicians to new levels of artistic accomplishment through his keen understanding of all the "dialects" of music. The most reliable way I have found to evaluate a conductor is not by his "press," his body gyrations, or his use of the baton, but by feeling what his musical interpretation does *to* and *for* me. If he breathes life into the music and I can sense that energy-vitality at work, then I know he is a fine conductor.

■

Harry Begian

Harry Begian is Director of Bands at the University of Illinois. Before coming to Champaign-Urbana, he held similar positions at Michigan State University and Wayne State University.

Conductors of all musical organizations, on whatever level or in whatever situation they work, should

take occasional inventory of themselves. They should evaluate those musical concepts and procedures they have learned and are constantly applying; assess their strengths, weaknesses, and musical shortcomings; honestly evaluate those areas that should be developed and improved technically and conceptually; then actively work and study toward the desired ends. Such an inventory is essential if one wishes to improve his musical and general effectiveness as a conductor.

Every conductor reflects the great variety of musical experiences, influences, learning, listening, and observation to which he has been exposed during his lifetime. The player experience is most basic and it is to be hoped that all conductors have been so exposed. To have played good music in fine musical organizations under musically demanding conductors can only be regarded as a positive experience. On the other hand, negative playing activities under poor conductors, of poor or worthless music, can only serve to create false musical concepts and goals. It then becomes obvious that the conductor who has not been exposed to positive performance experiences has some lost ground to recover. This he can try to do through study, concert attendance, score study, observance of professional rehearsals, and listening to recorded performances of great soloists, conductors, and ensembles. The importance of one's role as performer cannot be overestimated, for it can teach us much about literature, general programming principles, the values of proper organization, and procedures of concert preparation and presentation.

Studio experience in the study of an instrument with a master teacher is an absolute necessity to the development of a competent conductor. It was through the studio experience that I learned what an artist-teacher demands of a student in terms of musical exactitudes, interpretation, and regard for the printed musical page. There is no doubt that the musical demands made of me in the studio have become a part of my rehearsal and performance procedures and expectations as a conductor. Exposure to more than one excellent artist-teacher can only tend to broaden a conductor's views and soon reveals the fact that there can be more than one valid solution for a musical problem.

The listening experience, which we must seek throughout our careers, is also extremely valuable. It is only through hearing a variety of live and recorded performances that we learn to evaluate on the basis of style, tempo, contrast, unity and variety. It is also through these aural exercises that we learn to listen critically and to develop our own tastes. And such analytical listening will allow us to determine what styles,

sonorities, textures, or balances we will strive to achieve in our own rehearsals and performances.

Observation of other conductors in rehearsal can be of great value to all of us even though we may have our own established ways of rehearsing. If we feel, as we should, that we do not have all the answers, we can learn from observing other conductors. By emulating the greatest strengths of the professional conductor, we assimilate new or better techniques than we presently have. Even a negative evaluation of another conductor's techniques can work to our own positive gain. In such instances we are forced to discard techniques, procedures, or mannerisms which would seem foreign to our physical or aesthetic make-up or beliefs.

The educative process of the conductor never ends. He must keep on studying scores, reading, listening, evaluating, for as long as he continues in this work. For him there can be no complacency, nor can he afford the luxury of feeling that he has all the answers. He must remain a "student" of music throughout his career, always seeking to improve his musical knowledge and refining his musical approach in both rehearsal and performance. As time passes he will often be forced to evaluate what he does and how he proceeds musically so as to keep with the times. He will have to keep abreast of the new music and bring what critical ability he has developed to bear on what new material is musically worthy of preparation and performance by his organizations.

Finally, the conductor must be ever open to self-evaluation and self-criticism if he is going to improve. He must be able to turn his critical abilities on himself just as he does with the members of the ensembles he conducts. After a performance he must be able to admit to those things which he could have done better and be pliable enough to try to improve on the next performance. He will find it most helpful to have a trusted, interested, and highly competent musician friend who can act as critic and tell him truthfully what was both bad and good about his performances. When such a critic is of high musical calibre and the conductor can accept reliable criticism without suffering ego-damage, he has indeed found a true friend and guide. ∎

November, 1967

The Problems of the Conductor:
I. Leading People in
a Musical Experience William Cramer

It was my good fortune to have been a student at the Domain School for Conductors during the regular summer seasons of 1951 through 1957. Here in the little

William F. Cramer is associate professor of music at Florida State University, teaching lower brass, brass choir, and conducting, as well as graduate courses in symphonic literature. He has B.S. and M.A. degrees from Ohio State University and earned the Ed.D. from Florida State University. Dr. Cramer studied under Pierre Monteaux from 1951 to 1957.

town of Hancock, Maine, amidst pastoral surroundings, some 50 students from the professional, semi-professional, and academic world gathered around the world-renowned Pierre Monteux to study the standard orchestra repertoire through actual performance.

It was Mr. Monteux's avowed purpose to pass on to a new generation of conductors the tradition which he had inherited from the great conductors of his younger years—men like Richter, Nikisch, Weingartner, and Strauss. Tacitly, the students realized two other benefits —the benefit of Mr. Monteux's personal acquaintance with many composers (including St. Saëns, Debussy, Ravel, and Stravinsky) and the benefit of his personal study of other works.

Customarily, the repertoire for any given summer might be announced a full year in advance, thus affording the students ample opportunity to study the works. Then for three and one half hours each morning, the students would assemble as an orchestra to perform for each other as each took his turn as conductor. Mr. Monteux generally sat in the midst of the orchestra, remarking with a twinkle in his eye, "Don't pay any attention to me—I play third bassoon."

During my first week at the school, we noted a single person who observed the sessions from one of the vacant seats in the hall. We learned that he was a well-known critic who had reviewed many of Mr. Monteux's concerts. After a few days he was overheard to comment to the administrative director. "I feel that very few of the student conductors are really leading the orchestra—they are following the concertmaster." As I continued to play for each student and observe, I had to agree with the critic. It appeared that less than 10% of the class had the gift of real leadership.

What then were the qualities in these few that set them apart from the rest of the class? Were there characteristics in the competent conductors that could be identified and passed on as teachable techniques?

Four characteristics seemed to fit into this category.

1. The competent conductor is *prepared*. He has a plan of action.

a. He knows the score in every way that it is possible to know it—melodically, harmonically, rhythmically, structurally, historically, etc. He has a concept of the composer's intent—the poetic image—and has resolved his own differences with the composer's wishes. He has predetermined the obvious troublesome spots in the score and is ready to cope with them—even to preventing their occurring. He knows the phrasing patterns and cadences so that he might begin at the obvious musical point rather than at an arbitrary measure.

b. Equally important, he knows *the musicians and their potential*. He knows what he can require of them as humans while trying to reach the musical ideal—the poetic image. He knows when a mistake by a musician is an obvious slip which is instantly "corrected" by an exchange of eyes; but he also recognizes the mistakes in concept that must be corrected by explanation. He knows when to encourage and when to ignore.

c. The competent conductor also understands the particular *situation* and adjusts or adapts as is needed. He knows that rehearsal and concert are not the same thing. He knows that different halls will produce different resonances and will require different tempi. He knows that the musicians will play differently under different circumstances.

The fact that he knows, and knows that he knows, affects his demeanor to such a degree that professional musicians can fairly well determine as he takes his position on the podium that they will play the music *with* him rather than *for* him.

2. The competent conductor immediately establishes and maintains *visual communication* with the musicians.

There is no point in giving the signal to begin unless the musicians are looking at the conductor, and the conductor cannot know that they are looking at him unless he looks at them, so in effect they must "swap eyeballs." Since music is a continuous unfolding of the musical experience the conductor and musicians must be in continual contact with each other.

There are those musicians who will insist they can see the conductor "out of the corner of their eye." That may be so, but there is no way for the conductor to know that. When the conductor sees that a musician is ready to receive a cue, and when the musician sees that the conductor knows the music so well and is personally interested in giving a cue to a particular musician, each builds up confidence in the other and the whole ensemble plays with greater conviction.

A sweeping gesture to the cymbal player for a fortissimo crash has no meaning if the cymbal player is not looking, while a simple exchange of glances will suffice if he is looking.

3. The competent conductor uses *universal hand signals* to convey his wishes as the musical experience unfolds. Universal in this sense means common to all, understood in every situation. To that end, a down beat must be only a down beat. To finish off a down beat with an up gesture is only to give a second down beat which then causes all metrical patterns to look alike. The gestures used by the conductor must indicate (1) the exact moment when the beat begins, (2) the exact part of the metrical pattern being executed, (3) the rate of speed at that moment, and (4) to some limited extent, the style of the music at that given moment.

The conductor's real task at this point is to *help* the musicians, not to confuse them. Music is an aural art, not a visual art. Therefore all extraneous choreographic gestures are meaningless. While they may delight the ladies in the audience, they perhaps betray the conductor's emotional ardor, or even portray an egotistical nature. In any event, they will certainly confuse the beginner and will annoy skilled musicians even to the point that they do not look at the conductor *at all*, since in their eyes, his "performance" is for the audience only.

4. The competent conductor *listens* and continuously evaluates what the musicians are producing. It is not enough to blow the whistle for the dog and pony show to begin, to fit one's own choreography to the act as it unfolds, and then to receive applause when it is finished. Also, it is not enough to give the down beat and then follow the score with one's left forefinger, grimacing from time to time at the wrong notes or insecure entrances. The conductor must be *in charge*. Each performance is a new experience which must be shaped for that moment and for that duration. No military commander would write a battle plan, assign tasks, and then walk away from it. He would keep in constant touch with his troups to be absolutely certain they were giving their best under those circumstances.

Under normal conditions musicians want to do their best. If the conductor will just believe this he will find it very much easier to relax and enjoy the musical experience rather than "keep score" with great anxiety.

The conductor must also beware of merely beating time to a mental recording which he is playing back in his own head. Rather he must be tuned into the performance at hand. The act of listening, of responding to "feedback," is one of the most elementary examples of cybernetics in this modern age.

In light of the above observations a working definition evolves: *Conducting is the art of leading people for the purpose of recreating a musical experience.* Specifically,

a. Conducting is an *art* insofar as there are no exact procedures or ingredients, but there are well defined principles. Further, the principles are consistent and should have their own integrity.

b. The conductor *leads* rather than drives, pushes, follows, or threatens.

c. The conductor does not lead sopranos and altos, nor violins and violas, but rather *people* who desire to sing or people who desire to play. If one wishes to play the piano he gets a piano, if the trombone—a trombone, if the violin—a violin; but when one wishes to conduct, he does not simply get a baton—he must gather *people* around him. These people will really want to play, to be lead, encouraged, molded, guided—even loved.

d. Insofar as the conductor's primary responsibility is to be faithful to the composer's wishes, he can only *recreate* the musical experience as originally conceived by the composer. While it is true that no two performances are alike and therefore each performance is a new experience, the conductor should always be striving for the *composer's* intent.

e. The ultimate goal is the realization of the *musical experience*. If the applause or spoken congratulations are given merely for an outstanding technical performance, then the composer may have been denied a fair hearing. A concert is not a circus act and the conductor is not a ringmaster.

The summer sessions passed on, as did the great Monteux; yet music and aspiring conductors live on. If we are to do justice to this music and avoid the pronouncements of the critic we must develop *leadership*. The musical experience must transcend those who recreate it. ■

II. Interpreting Dynamics

William Schaefer

There are many factors in music which affect dynamics other than the familiar markings. Whereas some composers have tried in part to indicate relative dynamics, i.e., marking melodies louder and accompaniments softer, raising dynamic levels when few play and decreasing the indication when many play, this is the exception and not the rule. More generally, the same dynamic marking is given to all parts, and the consideration of countless other factors is left to the player and his conductor. Brahms once responded to a question regarding instructions for performance of his music with the comment that if he were writing for a musician, additional comments were unnecessary, and if he was not, they wouldn't help.

Young players tend to feel that each dynamic marking should have a specific meaning: so many decibels. But as Toscanini once told one of his instrumentalists—there are a thousand fortes; use the one that fits. In the most flagrant disregard of musical factors which affect dynamics, some groups demonstrate their idea that pp—ff means inaudible to unbearable. They permit melodies to be unheard, percussion out of balance, the highest or loudest instrument to dominate the music constantly.

What factors, other than markings in the music, affect the individual player's dynamic within an ensemble? Let us first establish the fact that it is everyone's responsibility to make the balance work. When two voices do

William Schaefer is director of bands at the University of Southern California at Los Angeles and prior to joining the faculty at USC he held a similar position at the Carnegie Institute of Technology. He also heads the wind instrument department at the university and is a frequent adjudicator and guest conductor.

not balance, both are incorrect and they should adjust to each other. Whereas it is the responsibility of a person playing a melody to play out, it is also the responsibility of the person with the accompaniment to hold back.

The following terms, while not defined as dynamic terms, have a significant affect on dynamics:

Solo—alone, but important, above the accompaniment, hence louder.

Soli—all parts so marked are important, hence somewhat louder.

Tutti—all are playing, hence less from each individual.

Expressivo—expressively, importantly. Be sure you are heard, hence louder.

Dolce—sweetly, also used to identify a passage that must sing over the music, hence louder. Often misleadingly defined as sweetly and *soft*.

All parts should be heard at all times and each instrument should always be audible in the total sound. This necessitates a considerable adjustment on the part of players of instruments that can dominate the sound too easily, especially the louder and higher instruments. There is a tendency for the first clarinetist and cornetist of the band to play as if they *always* have the melody—and for others in the same choirs to play as if they never do. Percussionists are often inclined to overplay louder indications, without reference to their relationship to the actual sound of the moment. To solve these problems, the following considerations should be given attention:

When instruments are sharing the same part, the level

should be suggested by the weakest instrument, not the strongest. (Heed well, trumpets!)

All voices playing in the same rhythm should balance equally. This requires that the higher parts be held back and the inner voices brought forward, that stronger instruments yield to weaker ones.

Melody should prevail against accompaniment in contrasting rhythm.

The fewer players involved at any given time, the more each individual player must contribute; the more players involved, the less each individual needs to contribute. The hall must be filled with music and a feeling of strength given to the music even when the fewest are playing at the softest indicated level. On the other hand, the most extreme ffff played by the entire ensemble should never result in more sound than the hall or the audience can absorb. Furthermore, this heavy sound should not result in the weaker instruments being covered by the stronger, but an equal sharing of the sound among all choirs and voices. Thus solos and chamber music episodes have to be pushed forward, and tutti passages played with restraint. Unfortunately, this does not seem to coincide with the instincts of young people.

A hypothetical formula helps to put this problem into perspective: take the dynamic marking, increase by one level if the melody and decrease by one if the accompaniment, multiply it by the size of the hall, and divide by the number playing to determine how the individual should play. Although this will not result in a specific dynamic level, it does lead to a realization of the effect on the individual of varying instrumentation within the ensemble.

An instrumentalist must learn to match his surroundings. For example, a horn player playing in a woodwind quintet should look around and say "with me are a flute, an oboe, a clarinet, and a bassoon. I play the strongest instrument here and must lower all dynamic indications accordingly to balance." The same horn player in a brass sextet should identify himself as the weakest voice of that group, and therefore raise all dynamic markings to match the sound of the ensemble.

Similarly, within a large group, the instrumentation is constantly changing, and this requires a constant reevaluation of balance and its effect on the individual player. Here are a few specific examples: Baritones and tubas with woodwinds in band, frequently found in older scores, must play delicately, bassoon-like.

Horns and saxophones must constantly adjust to their varying assignment to the woodwind and brass choirs.

Percussion must constantly be sensitive to the sound which they hear about them. A ff does not necessarily call for the ultimate sound. Basically, except in solo passages, they should decorate, not dominate, the music. Percussion players should stay inside the sound; they should not lead crescendos but support them, making sure they never cover the melodic and harmonic texture of the music.

Clarinets and flutes must compensate for the tendency of their instruments to be overly brilliant in the higher registers. The music should determine the dynamics, not the instrument.

Trumpets (cornets) must be aware of whether they are doubling a woodwind instrument, for when they do they must not sound like soloists but partners.

Melodies must always be heard. This is easy in the highest or loudest instruments, but difficult in inner or weaker voices. The problem is increased by the reaction of players, since the melody so often does appear in the highest voice they may not react properly when it is elsewhere. Thus in a fugue, when the voices enter from the lowest voice and proceed gradually to the highest voice, it works easily, for the melody is always in the highest part. But when the order of voices is changed each new voice must be projected, and continuing voices must yield to it.

This problem is sometimes compounded by assigning all strong players to the top part and weaker players to other voices. The inclination in this direction seems especially strong in some bands. Though there may be a certain logic for this in the marching band, reasonable equality of weight between voices is essential in the concert band.

Horizontal balance in music is equally important to vertical balance. Horizontal balance involves the consideration of what comes before and after the episode being played. Figures being played by various sections of the organization must be played in a consistent manner. There must not be a sagging or an explosion of the music due to a change of color. It pays to rehearse a piece with its accompaniment only—to be sure there is a matching of dynamics and style, and likewise, with melodies alone to achieve a matching of melodic material.

All dynamic shadings should be relative to the music. Swells, fp, sfz, accents, etc. should be considered in the light of the passages in which they occur, since none has a specific meaning. *Avoid excesses.* A 20th century style explosive sfz would sound ridiculous in a 17th century work. Furthermore, a sfz in a melody as used by some composers, may be merely identifying the climax of a phrase.

The items mentioned are by no means a complete listing. There are many other influences on dynamics: the crescendo of a rising line and the diminuendo of a falling line, the tendency of a phrase to swell, the inclination to accent changes of pitch in a line which is essentially static, the emphasis of the fastest moving notes in some passages, and the reverse of this in others, etc.

In summing up the problem of dynamics, one must finally say that it *does* take a musician to bring a musical performance into perspective with regard to dynamics. In the training of young performers and conductors it is well to include as many specific matters which affect dynamics as possible. In the final analysis, though it is still the intuition of the musician, undergirded by fine training, which resolves this, along with all the other matters which culminate in artistic performance. ■

III. Maintaining Discipline in Bands and Orchestras

Edwin Kruth

One of the most critical aspects of the teaching profession is discipline and all its ramifications. Surprisingly, the subject of discipline is seldom discussed in education journals and teaching textbooks. Possibly the reason for the lack of available literature is that most experienced educators realize that many discipline procedures emerge from the individual teacher's personality. Each individual has his own "discipline" based upon his entire orientation to the classroom. His role, as it is eventually determined through interaction with students and the general classroom environment, is his discipline. The major question consistently appears to be: is this orientation *enough* for the teacher, especially the inexperienced one. Another possible reason for the lack of literature is the fact that discipline by formula is difficult because ready-made rules do not always fit the many variables experienced in ensemble performance.

In today's society teachers are faced with increasingly complex problems when dealing with large musical organizations. Current literature on general curriculum emphasizes permissiveness. Teaching for responsibility, duty, and obligation is often neglected in the general classroom and emotional distortion is frequently miscast under the terms "individualism" and "creativity." Personal grooming, "fad" clothing styles, and, most unfortunately, a reluctance of some schools to take a firm stand in discipline matters, present major problems. Some parents, as well as students, become irate at the very suggestion of moderation and conformity in grooming. The projection of a musical image, visual, as well as aural, is rapidly becoming a crucial problem with an increasingly large number of music teachers. For effective performance, unanimity of concept *in appearance* is as essential as unanimity of sound. Unless music teachers present a united front on the propriety of dress, grooming, and general behavior, we can expect serious consequences in the future.

A highly structured conformity to a group discipline is by no means designed to restrict a student's creativity, imagination, and freedom of expression. Freedom of expression and individualism in performance should be encouraged to grow and flourish in developmental situations parallel to the disciplined experiences of a large group. One cannot exist without the other. These abilities are encouraged to grow and mature in individual study, small ensemble experience, and even, in some schools, through composition. The disciplined environment described in this article is concerned with providing opportunities for the young student to develop control of creative talent and to learn to mold this music talent within a carefully structured environment. One of the reasons so many creative individuals are not successful is that they never learn to *control* their abilities within a disciplined environment.

A student recently was told that he could not become a member of a band unless he cut his hair. His reply was "What does that have to do with music?" The answer of course, is that a conductor of a music group must be concerned with the visual as well as the audible. The cultivation of ideals and attitudes in the minds of individual pupils and the development of the person as a responsible individual to the group goals as well as to his own are essential. If this is not recognized, participation in a music group is eliminated. This attitude is not to minimize the importance of the music itself, it simply recognizes the entire musical experience as an educational function. In public education we are helping students to be responsible members of society as well as helping them to become competent musicians. As instruction is concerned with intellectual stimulus and direction, discipline is concerned with emotional stimulus and direction. All influences that enter into the determination of school conduct and performance should be recognized as coming within the province of discipline.

The general concept of discipline has changed a great deal in the past few decades. Formerly discipline was thought of as obedience to authority. Pupils were expected to do the tasks set for them and to ask no questions. In case they failed to obey, prescribed punishments were given for definite offenses. Recent literature in the field of mental hygiene has done much to bring about a change in the concept of discipline, which is increasingly being thought of as a means of developing the best personality possible for every pupil. This should not be interpreted to mean freedom of the individual without responsibility. Instead of using punishment or retribution as the means of securing control, emphasis is being placed more and more on guidance. In the past, teachers have dealt primarily with symptoms rather than cause. Today teachers endeavor to understand the forces acting on their pupils. According to current mental hygiene, discipline needs to be thought of more in terms of self-control and self-direction. The conductor cannot argue with this fact in principle.

Every element in school control has both positive and negative aspects. The positive or constructive aspect is the really significant one. We have learned that

Edwin Kruth is coordinator of instrumental music and director of bands at San Francisco State College. He received the B.M. and M.M. degrees at the University of Michigan and the Ed.D. degree at Stanford University. He is a clarinetist and a recognized authority on woodwind instruments.

there is little value in curbing bad conduct without stimulating a desire for better conduct in its place. Unacceptable behavior is not eliminated until the behavior can be appropriately redirected; unless punishing the wrong somehow causes confirmation of the right, we may always be suspicious of its efficiency. The acceptable way must be clearly indicated. Educators and administrators too often forget that education and learning should involve changes in behavior, supposedly in a desirable direction. This "desirable direction" must be made clear to every student.

An understanding of the above general concepts is important. However, the uniqueness of bands and orchestras demands a certain type of discipline somewhat removed from the general classroom approach. The moment a student becomes a member of a group, either in concert or rehearsal, he must understand that many elements of a democratic situation cease to operate. If self-oriented needs are allowed full expression both productivity and satisfaction suffer because group goals cannot be attained. The role of the conductor must be clearly defined and the importance of the group paramount. On the other hand, the conductor must be constantly aware of individual needs and response. Often an inexperienced teacher is insensitive to "feedback" and thus becomes completely ineffective in rehearsal. A conductor should constantly imagine that he has a line of communication running to and from each student. A dynamic exchange of covert, overt, and concomitant ideas pass from the conductor to the player and from the player to the conductor. The communication is *not* one way. A conductor is communicating with the entire group only when he is aware of this almost magnetic exchange. In rehearsal or in concert, individual needs must be subservient to the group, as determined by the conductor. Of course, recognition of the importance of the individual by the conductor must always be in evidence in his individual personal relationships with students. We, as teachers, owe it to each pupil to help him develop good citizenship. The work of the rehearsal demands that the pupil be orderly, systematic, and cooperative so that maximum communication and learning can take place. Students like good management and appreciate a well disciplined music environment. In turn, the public is quick to judge the teacher, the school, the administration, and the student by the type and effectiveness of order that is maintained at all music functions.

As mentioned previously, the constructive type of discipline is most effective—not discipline that simple matches infractions with penalities, but the kind that aims to help the student grow in the ability to discipline himself. The type of discipline that is desired is neither tough nor sentimental and recognizes that when constructive measures have failed with an offender, the welfare of the group and school will be protected by demanding conformity. Discipline should cause students to desire not to trespass on the rights of the group. Discipline procedures should help students to realize that there is no freedom without responsiblity. Constructive discipline cannot be treated as a problem, or even a series of problems to be solved. It is a continuous process of adopting ways and means to the accomplishment of predetermined purposes. It is primarily a process of prevention rather than a cure of misbehavior. The fol-

lowing constructive techniques in discipline may be helpful to inexperienced teachers and useful for review by all teachers as guidelines in establishing an environment in which maximum communication can take place. Within this environment, the conductor can best combat forces which tend to destroy the image and effectiveness of bands and orchestras.

1. In rehearsal, *pace* is paramount. Keep things moving. Never waste time.
2. Keep your objectives clear and attainable for the group.
3. Be organized and efficient in your administration.
4. Utilize the students' aid in management and in establishing policy on dress, grooming, and promptness.
5. Never start a rehearsal late.
6. Always concentrate on the development of tradition and spirit within the group.
7. Study the community and home life of pupils for guidance in handling cases of discipline.
8. Always reflect an impression of firmness and certainty. (Lack of specificity and definiteness in role expectation leads to conflict.)
9. Have rehearsals carefully planned and scores well prepared.
10. Good order may vary according to accepted standards within a system or building.
11. Routine specific activities.
12. Maintain at all times: clarity of speech, good personal appearance, optimism, reserve, enthusiasm, fairness, sincerity, sympathy, vitality, and scholarship.
13. An attempt should be made to develop and maintain a condition of rapport (i.e., cooperation and sympathetic understanding between conductor and students).
14. Freedom must not be permitted to degenerate into license. Too much freedom is neither good for the individual nor the group.
15. It is better to be too strict in the beginning than to be too lenient. It is easier to "let down" than it is to "tighten up" on matters of conduct.
16. Indulgence of pupils tends to build disrespect. If every shortcoming is excused, new problems soon appear.
17. It is usually effective to point out to older students their responsibility in influencing the younger students and to secure their cooperation.
18. Stop the little things that could cause future discipline problems.
19. Use special occasions to illustrate to the students that you are interested in them as individuals.
20. Learn the names of students quickly.
21. Call upon students who do not appear to be attentive.
22. Always be available and interested in a student's personal problems.
23. Never use sarcasm or ridicule.
24. Always refrain from punishing the group because of the mistake of an individual.
25. Do not expect threats to produce desirable results.
26. The deprivation of certain privileges is often effective. Privileges belong to those who merit them, not to those whose conduct is in conflict with the best interests of the individual and the group.
27. It is often wise to let the offender "meditate" for an hour or so before talking to him.
28. Do not hurry in decisions regarding punshment.

29. When the case is settled, drop it. Never carry a grudge.

30. At *no* time in *any* punishment, verbal or otherwise, refer to the parents or the home training of the student.

There are three basic rules for punishment. *First,* the certainty of punishment is a much better deterrent than severity. Under effective discipline, severe punishment should be rare, but minor penalties should be used systematically to hold up the standard of work and to check incipient tendencies to violate the group code which should be determined jointly by the conductor and the group. *Second,* there must be justice tempered by kindness. Nothing undermines confidence in a teacher quicker than an unjust punishment. *Third,* the punishment should be adapted to the offense both in degree and kind. There can be no such thing as a punishment that is not painful, but over-severity is sure to cause a bad reaction. Appoint a disciplinary committee of students to hear cases and recommend punishment. Remember we, as educators, are interested in *self*-direction and *self*-discipline, not in the discipline of humiliation.

Although the above statements apply to classroom situations as well as to the rehearsals, they are not general platitudes to be ignored. All too often rehearsals are completely wasted because a lack of communication exists between the conductor and the musicians, primarily because of discipline problems. The effective teacher communicates and relates to his students in a complete and penetrating manner at all times. He is conscious at all times of the importance of effective discipline procedures as they relate to his own personality within the teaching environment. He never rationalizes.

We, as conductors, should never allow a student's personal idiosyncrasies to detract from the image of the performing group. No student is "needed" that badly. As stated before, in many instances parental and general school permissiveness often contribute to serious discipline problems in our school bands and orchestras. Discipline functioning within the confines of group objectives is mandatory with respect to the worth and dignity of the individual and the necessity for effective communication both visual and aural. The individual serves the group; in turn, the group serves the individual. Without group and individual discipline, and unanimity of attitude and method on the part of the music educators, music can never maintain its stature within the academic structure of the school curriculum. ∎

May, 1970

THE INTERPRETATION OF DYNAMIC MARKINGS

Henri Temianka

In the primitive language of musical annotation nothing is more bewildering than the composer's dynamic markings. *Forte* marks the composer, usually abbreviated to a simple *f;* or *piano,* abbreviated to a puny *p.* Yes, but how loud is loud, how soft is soft? To make matters worse, most printed editions do not confine themselves to conveying the composer's authentic intentions. Almost invariably, an editor has found it necessary to enlighten us as to the true intentions of the composer. More often than not these editors are not eminent concert artists with a lifetime of experience in interpreting the great literature. They are, all too frequently, armchair strategists who have never tested their sometimes bizarre theories on a live audience. In some editions separate editors have been retained for the separate instruments, one giving his own interpretation of the violin part of a sonata, the other concentrating on the piano part of the same composition. Similar monstrosities exist in string quartet editions. I have the distinct impression that in several instances these editors were retained only after the publisher had made sure that they were not on speaking terms with each other. Not only are they not on speaking terms with each other, they also hold diametrically opposed views. Thus, any resemblance between the bowings and phrasing marks of the one editor and the other are purely coincidental. Furthermore, some of these editors appear to look upon the composer as a simpleton who had some unaccountable facility for throwing notes together. By the time it came to adding the dynamics, the composer's meager mental resources had given out. That, at least, is the inescapable conclusion when one views the music. Line after line is pockmarked with hysterical exhortations such as *ffff, pppp,* etc. Sometimes these dynamic indications are so numerous that it would require one full-time specialist to attend to the dynamics while somebody else played the notes. Nothing can obscure the true meaning of a piece of music as effectively as excessive dynamic indications. Brahms, who sometimes indulged in this failing when first writing a piece of music, would later remove most of his dynamic markings, saying: "Bad musicians can't use them, and good musicians don't need them.'

It is interesting to observe the usage and development of dynamic markings by composers. As we go back to such 17th century composers as Corelli, and 18th century composers as Bach and Handel, dynamic indications are exceedingly rare. In orchestral compositions, the composers relied primarily on juxtaposition of orchestra and soloist for dynamic contrast. If the whole orchestra played, the *concerto grosso,* one automatically had something resembling a *forte.* When the orchestra stopped momentarily, while the concertmaster continued, usually with the aid of one other violin and a cello, and possibly the harpsichord or organ, a dynamic contrast resembling a *piano* was achieved, on the principle that three players sound softer than 30. With the disappearance of the *concerto grosso* and the evolution of the virtuoso solo concerto, beginning with Haydn and Mozart, dynamic markings became the object of the composer's more precise attention. The Mannheim composers, of which Johann Stamitz was the most famous representative, developed an extraordinary new device, a graduated crescendo. Mozart was enormously impressed with this remarkable discovery when he visited Mannheim and incorporated it in the symphonies he wrote immediately thereafter. The device was developed to a shameless degree of melodramatic effectiveness by Rossini, who delighted in long, drawn-out orchestral crescendi that started with an almost inaudible whisper and built up gradually to a deafening explosion. (It seems a shame that Rossini did not live to witness the eardrum-shattering era of hi-fi.)

It was Beethoven, the innovator in so many areas, who revolutionized the art of dynamics by introducing the unexpected. Until then, dynamics had been staid, stylized, and stagnant. If an eight bar phrase started out *forte*, it was pretty well predictable that it would stay *forte* for eight bars, more often than not followed by a *piano* repetition, in accordance with established custom that required an echo effect. Beethoven changed all that. For the first time in the history of music, jagged *sforzandi* appear where they are least expected, as well as off-beat sudden *pianissimos*, or equally unexpected *fortissimos*. In doing so, Beethoven created extraordinary dramatic suspense and made dynamics an integral part of the composition. No longer did the interpreter have the latitude of saying, as he might in Bach or Haydn: "Let's play the next eight bars *piano* and then go back to a *forte*." Beethoven's off-balance accents and dynamics must be observed meticulously if the performer hopes to do justice to the master's intentions. If he does not, he is bound to fail. However, even if he does observe the markings, that is no guarantee of success. The crude language of musical annotation even as used by Beethoven leaves much unclear. As an example, almost no composer, including Beethoven, ever indicates how far a crescendo is supposed to go. Should it go to *forte*? *Fortissimo*? A mere *mezzo forte*? Take the following passage in Beethoven's Opus 30, No. 2 (C minor Sonata for Violin and Piano) 1st Mvt. bar 86-87.

There are many other baffling aspects to the dynamic markings of composers. Brahms opened up a whole new "can of worms" when he favored the designation *pf* by which he meant *poco forte*. Many performers are so conditioned to play loudly at the sight of the letter *f* that they begin to slaver like Pavlovian dogs at the sight of one, regardless of the fact that this one is preceded by a *p*. What Brahms means here is not "loud," but a "little loud." Now, you may argue that being "a little loud" is somewhat like being "a little pregnant." But let us be patient with Brahms' peculiar terminology. It is quite evident that Brahms wants us to be louder than *piano*, but softer than *forte*. So, why didn't he indicate *mezzo forte*? I think Brahms' reasoning may have been that many players take a *mezzo forte* as a license to play *forte*, and, as I understand it, Brahms wanted to be sure that the player went no more than one little notch beyond an ordinary *piano*. Here is a typical example of a *poco forte* in Brahms' G Major Sonata for Violin and Piano:

1st mvt. rehearsal No. 14 in the Peters Edition (Flesch-Schnabel)

Until Mahler, toward the end of the 19th century, it was rare for a composer to indicate varying dynamics between one instrument and another in chamber music or orchestral music. If a certain phrase is marked *piano*, every instrument in the orchestra has the same *piano* indication, regardless of the fact that 50 string players may easily drown out one solo flute. In a *forte* passage, the danger of secondary voices drowning out the leading ones are even more obvious. In the following passage of Beethoven's *Fifth Symphony* one frequently hears nothing except a shattering blast from the trumpets.

Violins

The 30 times reiterated *C* of the trumpets, doubled by French horns and timpani, easily drowns out everything else.

It was Mahler who systematically began to differentiate between the volume of sound required from each player or group of players in order to achieve an ideal orchestral balance. One instrument may have a *mezzo forte* marking, while simultaneously another has *pianissimo*, and a third, *forte*. One group of instruments may have a crescendo, while another remains static. One may of course argue that the role of properly balancing the instruments belongs to the conductor, and that, if he is a good enough musician, the composer should not have to trouble himself with this aspect of the performance. Mahler was a great conductor himself, hence this very special preoccupation with balance. Furthermore, orchestras had become so large, and orchestrations so complex and subtle, that it became necessary to give the interpreter some additional indications as to what was expected of him.

In the classical repertoire, where such diversified markings are missing, I am a strong believer in training the orchestra players to the highest possible level of musical understanding and sensitivity. I rarely confine myself to telling an accompanying body of string players to play softer. Rather, I ask them to write the name of the leading instrument above that passage. The players, most of whom do not familiarize themselves with the score of an orchestral composition, are then more likely to listen for the instruments that have the leading voice, and it is my experience that this approach leads to a greater individual concern for balance and musical understanding.

The insensitivity of many orchestral players and their failure to listen carefully to what goes on elsewhere in the orchestra, is beautifully illustrated by the famous story of the bass player in the Paris Opera Orchestra who had held the job for a lifetime. One morning at rehearsal he said to the bass player standing next to him: "Hey, Gaston, I had an extraordinary experience last night! It was my day off, so I decided to go and sit in the audience for once and listen to a performance of *Carmen*. I had the surprise of my life when the orchestra came to that spot where we play:

You'll never guess what goes on up front in the violin section while we do that! They're playing:

The story is really not too far-fetched. Frequently, when I see the strings sawing away furiously in a difficult, rapid passage, and I call their attention to the fact that the oboe is playing an enchanting melody which they are drowning out, a look of absolute wonder comes on their faces when the melody is finally revealed. The problem that we are dealing with in an orchestra is in reality the problem of human relationships on every level. For it is the sign of a healthy ego to tackle one's own problems first. That's what the fiddles are doing when they are so furiously preoccupied with a difficult accompanying passage. But it is a sign of greater maturity to want to hear and understand also what others have to say, to communicate with them on their level. In an orchestra this means playing softly enough so that everyone can be heard. To achieve this blend of expressing oneself, while also enabling the other fellow to express himself, is what it is all about. That's what makes the correct interpretation of dynamics such a subtle art.

The proper treatment of a printed crescendo is almost worthy of an article by itself. Crescendos come in many sizes. If it is a short crescendo, say one bar long, one can see the light at the end of the tunnel even before one starts. It is quite another matter when dealing with a protracted crescendo, such as Beethoven's extraordinary crescendo in the first movement of the *Pastoral Symphony*, which takes 38 bars to achieve its climax.

There isn't a performer in the whole world who can hope to make an actual note-by-note crescendo over so long a period of time. After six or seven bars at most, he will be spent, incapable of any further increase in volume for the next 32 bars. To achieve the effect that Beethoven demands here, we are forced to resort to what I call a "terraced crescendo." This means that, instead of making a continuous crescendo, one moves to the next dynamic level only every few bars, staying on that particular terrace until it is time to move to the next. This has to be figured out very carefully and precisely notated in the music. In the case of the particular Beethoven example one would start with an almost inaudible *ppp*, and at intervals of four bars move to *pp*, *p*, *mp*, *mf*, *f*, etc. Nonetheless, the change from one level to the other is not affected abruptly, but with a subtle crescendo just before the next phrase is due.

Many players do not realize that making an effective crescendo is often not exclusively a matter of playing louder and louder. There is also the matter of intensify-

ing the quality of the sound itself, as the crescendo, racing towards its climax, demands an intensification of the dramatic impact. Here is where it becomes important for the string player to move the bow closer to the bridge, while simultaneously quickening his vibrato. In a string quartet it is vital that there be a clearly spelled out agreement among the players as to the manner in which a crescendo will be graded. If matters are left unsaid, one player may produce one type of crescendo, while the second produces another type of crescendo, and the third one still another. It should be self-evident that such a crescendo, lacking in unanimous purpose and execution, will miss its mark. During the many years that I functioned as first violinist of the Paganini Quartet, we frequently engaged in crescendo and decrescendo exercises in order to achieve this unanimity. We would also take turns playing the same crescendo for each other, in order to make sure that everyone knew what the others were doing. It is, of course, equally important to arrive at a unanimous verdict as to the *character* of a crescendo and its maximum volume. All crescendos are not necessarily dramatic. For instance, we find in Beethoven crescendos of one bar starting from a *pianissimo*. The next bar is marked *piano*. One can become involved in endless, hairsplitting arguments as to whether Beethoven wanted a crescendo only leading to the *piano* in the next bar or a much bigger crescendo followed by a *piano subito*. One could wish that Beethoven had given the interpreter more precise instructions at this point.

Another major factor in determining one's dynamics is the combination of instruments. In a string quartet with its four homogeneous instruments, the most ethereal *pianissimo* will carry and be heard. But the moment the giant grand piano is added to the group, as in the Brahms *Piano Quintet*, the picture changes. Here, if the four string players are to tell their story effectively, if they are to hold their own and match Brahms' massive piano writing, all of the dynamics have to be raised by one degree.

I do not believe in adjusting one's dynamic scale according to the varying acoustical properties of auditoriums around the world. Certainly the temptation is strong to force when a hall is particularly dead, but it doesn't work. To change one's scale of dynamics on the spur of the moment while standing on a concert stage is tantamount to destroying months of painstaking work. The subtleties of carefully wrought quartet dynamics in particular cannot be altered lightly or suddenly. It is one of the frustrations the seasoned concert artist learns to take in stride. I once heard of a famous French concert pianist, a beautiful and temperamental young woman, who became so infuriated at the bad acoustics of the hall she played in and the sound of the unfamiliar grand piano, that she snarled and gave it a vicious kick. It's the only time I have ever felt that pianists have an advantage over string players! ■

Henri Temianka is String Clinic Editor of The Instrumentalist. *He is conductor, concert violinist and professor of music at California State College in Long Beach, and also conducts the California Chamber Symphony, a virtuoso group of 40 players which offers an annual concert series in Los Angeles. The founder of an orchestra series,* Concerts for Youth, *he has also been a conductor and commentator for the Symphonies for Youth presented by the Los Angeles Philharmonic.*

Crosscurrents After 170 Years

by John W. Kinght

Prior to 1800 orchestras relied on a musician at the harpsichord, usually the composer, for the beat, while other groups employed someone to strike the floor with a stick or stamp his foot to set the tempo. As music grew more complex it became increasingly difficult for ensembles to play without direction or for the composer to conduct from the keyboard. Thus, a figure eventually stepped to the front of the orchestra and waved a rolled-up paper or violin bow to keep the tempo, and on April 10, 1820 Ludwig Spohr initiated an historic change by using a baton with the London Philharmonic. Spohr later recreated the event, which is documented in *The Romantic Period of Music*.

> I then took my position with the score at a separate music desk in front of the orchestra, drew from my pocket my directing baton, and gave the signal to begin. Quite alarmed at such a novel procedure, some of the directors [other conductors of the day] would have protested against it; but when I pleaded with them to grant me at least one trial, they became pacified....Surprised and inspired by the result, the orchestra immediately after the first movement of the symphony expressed aloud its unanimous assent to the new mode of conducting. The triumph of the baton as a time giver was decisive.[1]

Despite Spohr's breakthrough, performers still shared conducting duties, and occasionally confusion resulted when three or more musicians directed at the same time. The unfortunate players had to choose between the gestures of the pianist at the keyboard, the bow waving of the first violinist, and even the composer giving signals.

From his first experience with the baton, Mendelssohn realized the importance of a single conductor. Nonetheless, divided authority persisted and at a London performance in 1847 as Mendelssohn conducted his *Elijah*, the concertmaster frequently beat time with his bow and blocked Mendelssohn's view of the orchestra.

Through Mendelssohn's tenacious efforts, he made the public aware of new conducting methods and approaches; today we recognize him as one of conducting's first practitioners and the originator of the classical style that continues to the present. While Mendelssohn based his style on precision

Franz Liszt

clarified through the baton, Franz Liszt brought a creative impulse and subjective interpretation to conducting. In the mid-19th century conductors no longer looked upon themselves as mere timekeepers, but saw themselves as intepreters.

Mendelssohn believed that conductors should provide an objective interpretation of the score and emphasize rhythmic control. Liszt had no interest in a literal or strict interpretation and promoted freedom of beat patterns, flexibility of rhythm, and exaggeration of nuance for dramatic effect.

Based on the observations made by contemporaries of the two men, we can now detect the

John W. Knight is an associate professor of music education and conductor of the Symphonic Band at Oberlin College. He also maintains an active schedule as adjudicator, clinician, lecturer, and guest conductor throughout the United States and Europe. He received a Ph.D. from Louisiana State University.

formation of two schools of conducting. In 1829 Edward Devrient, the German baritone, outlined his opinion of the duties of a conductor as follows:

> The continued beating throughout a movement, which must necessarily become mechanical, vexed me and does so still. It always appeared to me that the conductor ought to beat time only when the difficulty of certain passages, or unsteadiness of the performers, rendered it necessary. Surely the aim of every conductor should be to influence without obtruding himself. [2]

Mendelssohn, a friend of Devrient, met those qualifications, and Devrient obviously was pleased. "Many whole sections were often beaten through, but Felix, as soon as large sections were running smoothly, dropped his baton and listened with seraphic transport, occasionally beckoning with eye or hand."[3]

Such serenity was absent from Liszt's conducting, as Ferdinand Hiller described a Liszt performance in 1853. "He does nothing but keep changing the baton from one hand to the other — sometimes, indeed, laying it down altogether — giving signals in the air with this or that hand, or on occasion with both, having previously told the orchestra not to keep too strictly to the beat."[4]

Liszt did not maintain strict tempos and said that mere time beating was "enough to beat down the life-nerve of a beautiful symphonic performance."[5] He played the piano in phrases, and he conducted the same way, because he felt regular accents with a heavy beat at each bar line were obtrusive to the music. Liszt emphasized thematic elements of each piece and discarded standard beat patterns, outlining instead the rise and fall of the musical line. Liszt felt standard baton techniques produced a mechanical orchestral sound that emphasized rhythm instead of the complete musical line. George Smart, an English conductor who introduced the works of Beethoven and Schumann to London audiences, commented that the expressive beat of Liszt caused "plenty of twisting of the person."[6]

Such movement contrasted with Mendelssohn's style, which was refined and never theatrical. His austerity on the podium reflected his classical training. Schumann noted his approval of Mendelssohn's style: "It was a joy to watch, and note how with his eye he anticipated and communicated every meaningful turn and nuance, from the most delicate to the most robust, an inspired leader plunging ahead, in contrast to those conductors who threaten with their scepters to thrash the score, the orchestra, and even the audience."[7]

Violin virtuoso Joseph Joachim described Mendelssohn as conducting "almost without motion, but [using] extremely lively gestures through which it was possible to transmit the spirit of his personality to chorus and orchestra, to correct little errors with a flick of his finger."[8]

Mendelssohn relied on precise baton technique, which gave him the appearance of calmness and clarity. His refinement extended to his baton, a whalebone stick covered with white leather to match his white gloves. Mendelssohn was the first conductor to fully use a baton to emphasize rhythm and control.

Liszt's podium style reflected his temperament; he felt the baton should be used with "care, suppleness, and knowledge of effects of coloring, rhythm, and expression." Unfortunately his actions on the podium were often misunderstood. Joseph Joachim observed:

> At the conductor's desk Liszt makes a parade of moods of despair and the stirrings of contrition...and mingles them with the most sickly sentimentality and such a martyrlike air that one can hear the lies in every note and see them in every movement...I have suddenly realized that he is a cunning contriver of effects who had miscalculated.[9]

Liszt's advanced techniques were not appreciated by those who favored the classical conducting style. He believed that the conductor should be the servant of the public, while Mendelssohn maintained that conductors should be the servant of the score, using technique that was free of subjective emotions. Such strictness of performance stemmed from rigorous rehearsals with the conductor firmly in control. In 1841 Mendelssohn described his experience as guest conductor of the Berlin orchestra, which was noted for being unruly when its regular leader was away.

Felix Mendelssohn

Georg Solti

At the first rehearsal the orchestra was disposed to behave badly. Disorder and arrogance prevailed, and I could not believe my eyes and ears. At the second rehearsal, however, I turned the tables. It was my turn to be rude. I punished half a dozen of them, and now they regard me as another Spontini. Since then there has been no sulking. As soon as they see me, they are attentive and they do their best. Instead of being haughty they are now obsequious; they bow and scrape.[10]

With his own orchestra at the Gewandhaus in Leipzig, Mendelssohn raised the performance level by playing only the finest music and approaching each score with classic integrity. Composer Julius Benedict recounted an occasion when Mendelssohn requested this respect for the score.

Once, while conducting a rehearsal of Beethoven's Eighth Symphony, the admirable allegretto in B♭ not going at first to his liking, he remarked smilingly that "he knew every one of the gentelmen engaged was capable of performing, and even composing, a scherzo of his own but that just now he wanted to hear Beethoven's, which he thought had some merits."[11]

This literal recreation of the composer's intent included a fastidious interpretation of every musical notation. No longer were players allowed a mediocre reading of their parts; and the conductor demanded meticulous attention to tempo, balance, and nuances of expression. Through such rehearsals the Gewandhaus became an orchestra unequaled in Germany.

Liszt also had rigorous rehearsals, but they followed a different pattern. He used preliminary sectional rehearsals to work on tone color, rhythm, and expression. Liszt gives an interesting picture of his ideas on rehearsal techniques in his directions of the score of his *Symphonic Poems.*

At the moment I would like to remark that the usual mechanical, cut and dried performance customary in many cities be avoided and in its place the new period style which stresses proper accentuation, the rounding off of melodic and rhythmical nuances be substituted. The life-nerve of a symphonic production rests in the conductor's spiritual and intellectual conception of the composition, it being assumed of course, that the orchestra possesses the necessary power to realize this conception. Should the latter condition be absent, I recommend that my works be left unperformed.[12]

Liszt believed that the concept of a musical work was more important than what was printed on paper and that the composer cannot "put down in black and white everything that gives a performance character and beauty."[13] His interpretation and intuition resulted in a performance of Wagner's *Tannhauser* that was a union of two minds. Wagner described the experience:

Though mainly concerned with the musical rather than the dramatic side, [the performance] filled me for the first time with the flattering warmth of emotion roused by the consciousness of being understood by another mind in full sympathy with my own. I saw Liszt conduct a rehearsal of *Tannhauser* and was astonished at finding my second self in his achievement. What I had felt in composing music, he felt in performing it; what I wanted to express in writing it down, he produced in making it sound.[14]

Mendelssohn and Liszt initiated two divergent approaches to interpretation, the elegant and the passionate. Mendelssohn was like a mirror, reflecting the composer's image; Liszt, a prism, producing a personal synthesis of the musical parts. The art of conducting had developed into the classical and romantic schools, respectively.

Nowhere were the ideas of these two men more

David Zinman

opposed than in their concepts of tempo, with Mendelssohn emphasizing strict rhythms and metronomic exactness, and the antithetical Liszt stressing subtle nuance, flexible rubato, and the expressive qualities of romanticism.

Liszt could not be chained to the formality of classicism in conducting. Long before he ever picked up a baton, his virtuosity at the keyboard instilled abandonment in him. At the piano he had played in phrases, ignoring the bar line, modifying tempos to the benefit of expression and drama. Once applied to the art, these characteristics became the pioneering step that turned conducting away from classicism and into romantic expression. Always seeking an expressive interpretation, Liszt could not hold to a basic tempo and was critical of the shortcomings he saw in the printed work:

> Although I have tried through exact markings of the dynamics, the accelerations and slowing up of the tempo, to clearly indicate my wishes, I must confess that much, even that which is of the greatest importance, cannot be expressed on paper. Only a complete artistic equipment on the part of the conductor and players, as well as a sympathetic and spiritually enlivened performance can bring my works to their proper effort.[15]

According to Stoessel, Liszt used a concept that was more than simple rubato. "It was a rise and fall, slowing and speeding, variation of tempo, with the use of ritards to link contrasting passages."[16] Liszt tried to define the indefinable and to draw universal rules from what basically were his own intuitions.

Wagner, who built on the ideas of Liszt and became a giant in the history of conducting, recognized the importance of tempo. He believed the proper tempo depended upon a correct understanding of the *melos*, the spiritual melody of the piece: "It is unnecessary to give the exact tempo since a gifted conductor will find the right one and the untalented will never grasp it regardless of what the score says."[17]

True tempo to Liszt varied according to the rise and fall of the expressive content, but Mendelssohn was completely against rubato tempo because it was sentimental and distracting. Mendelssohn preferred to emphasize rhythm and control, and demanded a sense of rhythm from his players. With such clarity and precision, he naturally enjoyed fast tempos.

After watching Mendelssohn direct a rehearsal of Beethoven's Eighth Symphony, Wagner made this comment about tempo:

> As to conducting, he personally informed me once or twice that too slow a tempo was the devil, and he would rather choose to take things too fast, that a really good performance was a rarity at any time, but that it was possible to delude the audience so that a bad one would not be too much noticed, and that this was best done by not lingering too long on the piece, but passing rapidly over it.[18]

However, it is not possible to make a true estimation of Mendelssohn's tempo from the previous statement, because Wagner's voice "is the only major dissenting viewpoint about Mendelssohn's ability as a conductor, and that alone makes it suspect."[19]

The creative forces of Mendelssohn and Liszt ignited a revolution in the art of conducting, and through their efforts the status of conductors rose from that of crude time beaters to polished interpreters. The conflicting styles are the foundations of conducting techniques today, and the classical and romantic characteristics are the elements from which conductors now choose. Some modern conductors faithfully represent the composer's intention, while others reflect themselves in the works they conduct. Mendelssohn dominated the period of conducting from 1830 to 1850, but as the passion and freedom of Liszt's performances came to tion, while others reflect themselves in the works they conduct.

Mendelssohn dominated the period of conducting from 1830 to 1850, but as the passion and freedom of Liszt's performances came to public attention, the younger generation abandoned convention.

Liszt succeeded in freeing the spirit of the composition from the limitations of bar line rhythm by a new style of conducting gestures. He used both hands for cues, conducting in phrases instead of in strict beats, showing new shadings of expression. By giving the art these techniques, musicians recognize Liszt as the founder of modern conducting, but the spirit of Mendelssohn's classical style was never completely extinguished. The most recent philosophy in conducting does not follow any one school of thought; contemporary conductors balance classical and romantic attitudes. This eclecticism, though, is only the temporary top of the pyramid that continues to rest on the foundation started by Mendelssohn and Liszt a century ago. ☐

Footnotes
1. Kenneth B. Klaus, *The Romantic Period in Music*, p. 263.
2. Harold C. Schonberg, *The Great Conductors*, p. 89.
3. *Ibid.*, p. 118.   4. *Ibid.*, p. 162.
5. Eleanor Perenyi, *Liszt, The Artist as Romantic Hero*, p. 291.
6. Schonberg, *The Great Conductors*, p. 161.   7. *Ibid.*, p. 120.
8. Herbert Kupferberg, *The Mendelssohn's: Three Generations of Genius*, p. 138.
9. Schonberg, *The Great Conductors*, p. 161.   10. *Ibid.*, p. 121.
11. Kupferberg, *The Mendelssohns*, p. 138.
12. Albert Stoessel, *The Technic of the Baton*, p. 5.
13. Schonberg, *The Great Conductors*, p. 160.
14. Sacheverell Sitwell, *Liszt*, p. 214.
15. Perenyi, *Liszt, The Artist as Romantic Hero*, p. 5.
16. Stoessel, *The Technic of the Baton*, p. 5.
17. Schonberg, *The Great Conductors*, p. 136.
18. Heinrich Eduard Jacob, *Felix Mendelssohn and His Times*, p. 312.
19. Schonberg, *The Great Conductors*, p. 124.

Rehearsal Techniques

Distraction — An Overlooked Technique

by Victor Bordo

The effective director goes into rehearsal with an efficient strategy based on what is already known:

- Rehearsal time is too limited.
- Ensemble members have short attention spans.
- The actions of the conductor produce reactions in the students which can be anticipated. As educators, we are responsible to see that students graduate having gained the knowledge and appreciation of great music literature. Using distraction, an often overlooked technique, is one way to help.

The Strategy

Distraction can be used as a valuable tool in many interesting ways to keep the ensemble involved in the music. Some effective techniques include:

- Relating a humorous incident to relieve tension.
- Telling interesting anecdotes about composers and famous instrumentalists.
- Discussing important facets of the music to make it interesting.
- Enjoying a moment of great passion when the music swells and reaches an inspirational level in a demanding piece of literature.

Having a plan is essential, and knowing when to alter the plan to keep the ensemble interested is paramount. Begin the rehearsal with some basic fundamentals, but only for a brief period. The fundamentals could include reviewing scales in all keys (four minutes or less) and playing a chorale for tuning purposes (three minutes or less).

When you are ready to work, spend 15 to 25 minutes on the most difficult selection of the day. Students should anticipate this time as the most intense period of the rehearsal. Develop a detailed plan of attack for the most challenging selection; and offer students plenty of drill, but change, as needed, from one knotty section to another. Pay attention to your students. If they tire, switch to something else. Divert their attention, but always with quality literature. Players can handle a reasonable period of intensive rehearsal if they know some relief will follow it.

After 20 years of working with high school bands and nine years with an adult community band, I find that both types of ensembles tire about half way into the period. Depending on how well the intensive period of rehearsing is going, I may insert a livelier selection about half way through the period. It can be a spirited march (I generally don't rehearse them) or some show tune that provides a contrast to the more serious piece I've been rehearsing. Using this type of distraction seldom fails to pick up the pace of the rehearsal and restore the energy packed response that is needed. At this point, well into the second half of the rehearsal, I can drill some passage that requires physical dexterity, but not a lot of mental strain, for at least 10 minutes.

For about the last eight minutes of the rehearsal, I again use music that is light and entertaining. I am always amazed that the players, no matter what the age level, leave the room humming the last piece we played. They seem to forget about the intensive drilling that went on.

I use less and less of the distraction technique as the group becomes more involved with a major work. Sound bizarre? The approach has worked for me with such works as the *Symphony in Bb* by Hindemith, *Russian Christmas Music* by Alfred Reed, *Festive Overture* by Shostakovitch, and *Diamond Variations* by Robert Jager. The technique also works with younger students. You just have to shorten the intense part of the rehearsal, slightly lengthen the drill section, and keep a good supply of those lighter, livelier peices on hand.

As a conductor, I have found that using distraction has kept me from getting bored during the rehearsals. The trick is to pick quality literature, regardless of whether it is a standard or something from the popular field. There are some other helpful off-shoots of this techniques:

- Students become accustomed to a fast-paced rehearsal and are so attentive that they don't miss anything.
- The ensemble covers more literature.
- The literature in the folder is not there just to be readied for performance.
- Sightreading skills improve.
- Rehearsals become a highlight of the school day.

If you are a new director, try the technique of distraction for your rehearsals; you'll like it and so will your students. ■

Victor Bordo is coordinator of music for the Ann Arbor Public Schools and founder/director of the Symphony Band of Ann Arbor.

Rehearsal Techniques

Harmony — Developing Listening Skill in Rehearsal

by Manuel Alvarez

Of the three primary elements of music — rhythm, melody, and harmony — band directors spend countless hours of rehearsal time correcting rhythmic patterns, coordinating rhythmic passages, discussing melodic shapes, and determining phrase lengths. Harmony, on the other hand, is seldom mentioned. As a result, students fail to learn the relationship of harmony to the other elements of music; have trouble in determining the shape of a melody or the length of a phrase; and do not know how to listen for, or respond to, the subtle dynamic changes that occur within harmonic progressions. These players continue to spin out linear phrases on their instruments, unaware of the vertical sonorities being created by the ensemble.

Perhaps one reason conductors do not teach harmony is because they believe that students first need a working knowledge of theory — defining terms, labeling harmonic functions, spelling out chord types. It is no wonder that some conductors have been reluctant to include lessons in harmony during rehearsals. After all, how much material can be taught during a 40-minute session? However, as Leonard B. Meyer states in his book, *Explaining Music*, "you don't have to know why a bicycle is rideable in order to know how to ride a bicycle." Here is an approach to teaching harmony that does not involve theory.

Dynamic Tension

In the book, *Sound and Symbol*, Victor Zuckerkandl presents the idea that all tones contain some degree of dynamic tension. Scale tones 1, 3, 5, and 8 are inactive (they have no dynamic tension); 4 and 6 are mildly active; and 2 and 7 are strongly active. Carrying this idea one step further, harmonic functions also contain varying degrees of dynamic tension. A tonic chord contains little dynamic tension because all of the tones of the chord are inactive; a subdominant chord contains some dynamic tension because two tones of the chord are mildly active; a dominant chord contains a great deal of dynamic tension because two tones of the chord are strongly active. Following this idea, it's possible to classify harmonic functions according to the amount of dynamic tension they contain.

Less Tension-----More Tension
I   vi   iii   IV   ii   V   vii

It is interesting to see the similarities between this system and the traditional harmonic classification system. Other than the position of the mediant chord, the two classification systems are virtually alike.

Rehearsal Techniques

Music scholars, such as Jerome Bruner, author of *The Process of Education* and Edwin Gordon, *Learning Sequences in Music*, advocate that students learn how to discriminate between differences in sound before learning how to read or write music or understand theory. By using the following teaching techniques along with the music example from *Tipps, No. 29* by Hovey, you can help students learn to hear harmonically.

Tipps, no. 29, Nilo W. Hovey

• Begin with chord progressions of tonic and dominant harmonies. After a few rehearsals, introduce subdominant chords.

• Sing or play the root of the tonic chord on a neutral syllable for the duration of a chord progression (line A).

• Listen for tension points. If tension occurs while singing or playing the tonic tone (tonal syllable *do* or *la*), resolve the note downward to the leading tone (*ti* or *si*), which is the most active tone of the dominant chord (line B, measure four).

• Continue to listen for tension points. If tension occurs while singing or playing the leading tone, resolve the note upward to the tonic tone, which is the least active tone of the tonic chord (line B, measure five).

• To discriminate between tonic and subdominant functions, sing or play an upward arpeggio pattern on tonic chords, *do-mi-sol-mi-do*, and then downward on subdominant chords, *do-la-fa-la-do*. Note that both arpeggio patterns begin on the tonic tone (line C). Eventually students will be able to scan the chords and hear the tones in their heads rather than to have to sing the arpeggio patterns (line D).

• Sing or play with the fullest intensity on dominant chords; less intensity on subdominant chords; and the least intensity on tonic chords (line E).

Advantages

There are several advantages to learning this technique. First, it is simple because it consists of only two tones (scale degrees one and seven). Second, it can be used for both major and minor tonalities. Third, it can be used for both root position and inverted chords. Fourth, it emphasizes the development of the ear rather than the eye. Finally, the technique can be learned without a knowledge of theory.

After students are able to discriminate between the primary harmonic functions in warm-up books, continue with this newly acquired skill in concert selections. The following passages from standard wind repertoire include dynamic markings to indicate whether the harmonic direction is away-from or toward the tonic chord. In performance, demonstrate these changes of intensity in as subtle a manner as possible. Later try extracting similar passages from other literature you have selected for performance.

Trauersinfonie, Richard Wagner

Serenade for 13 Winds, op. 7, Richard Strauss

Serenade no. 10, Movement One, Wolfgang Amadeus Mozart

Fairest of the Fair, John Philip Sousa

Overture for Winds, op. 24, Felix Mendelssohn

"La Paix" from *Royal Fireworks Music*, George Frideric Handel

When introducing this technique do not use larger or smaller conducting gestures to anticipate the changes of dynamic tension. Remember, the purpose of the approach is to develop listening skills, not visual ones. When students learn to respond to the harmonies being played, you can strengthen the changes of dynamic tension with appropriate gestures. As a result students will not only respond to conducting gestures, but more importantly, to the changes of dynamic tension they have heard and felt. This simple technique allows students to gain valuable insight into an element of music that has been largely neglected. ∎

Manuel Alvarez is conductor of the Symphonic Wind Ensemble at the Hartt School of Music of the University of Hartford in Connecticut.

References

Brocklehurst, Brian, *Response to Music*, Routledge & Kegan Paul.

Bruner, Jerome, *The Process of Education*, Harvard University Press.

Clifton, Thomas, lectures.

Gagne, Robert, *The Conditions of Learning*, Holt, Rinehart and Winston.

Gordon, Edwin, *Learning Sequences in Music*, G.I.A. Publications.

Meyer, Leonard B, *Explaining Music*, University of California Press.

Pike, Alfred, "A Phenomenological Approach to Tonal Imagery," *Journal of Existentialism*. Vol. 8, (Fall 1967), 67-73.

Zuckerkandl, Victor, *Sound and Symbol*, Princeton University Press.

January, 1985

Rehearsal Techniques

Rehearsal Reminders

by John Koshak

Previously I have discussed how to study and mark a score, how to improve your baton technique, and how to communicate better with your ensemble. In rehearsal, all these skills must come together. The first step toward a well-organized rehearsal is to draw up a rehearsal plan.

As you first study a score, you should note where performance problems will be, keeping these observations in mind as guidelines for your rehearsal. Next, whether you are rehearsing a three-minute work or a complete symphony movement, you will need to divide the material into sections. (Sometimes the form of the work will suggest natural divisions.) To play your rehearsal, you should know how long each section takes to play. For example, the exposition may be four minutes long. To gauge the amount of time you will need to work out the problems in the section, your written plan should include specific notes as to what areas you will rehearse. For example, you might write: Flutes I & II, letter A — tune octaves and work out syncopated rhythms.

A general rehearsal format might be:
  9:00 A.M. - Tune
  9:05 A.M. - Recapitulation (You don't have to start a rehearsal at the beginning of a composition.)
  9:25 A.M. - Announcements and assignments
  9:30 A.M. - Exposition
  9:50 A.M. - Rehearsal ends (Extend this plan for longer rehearsals.)

Assuming that you know the score and have a rehearsal plan, let's go now to the actual rehearsal.

Sitting

All too often, conductors insist that players sit up straight and hold their instruments in the proper positions. However, sitting up is not enough; we must go back a step. What a musician sees when he walks into a rehearsal affects his attitude and the results. A confused, disorderly room makes it impossible to achieve high rehearsal goals. If necessary, take five minutes from the rehearsal and arrange the room in a way that reflects the high standards you want to set. To encourage positive attitudes, make sure your rehearsal room is neat, well-organized, and properly set up.

Next, consider the position of the player. He must sit so that he can always see the conductor as well as the music. The player must also be able to see over and around the players in front of him. For orchestras, it is important to have the outside players (traditionally, the first violins and cellos) turned straight ahead, or possibly a little toward the audience. The inside firsts and cellos must be turned on an angle toward the conductor and audience. In the correct sitting position, the players can see the conductor and the instruments face the audience, increasing the potential volume of sound directed toward the listeners.

Warm-up and Tuning

For accurate tuning, players must be warmed up. Professional musicians will arrive in time and assume the responsibility to warm up. Younger musicians, though, need to be taught. If done properly, individual warm-ups can be more beneficial and less time-consuming than group warm-ups. If you are working with a young ensemble and feel that the group warm-up is a better learning experience, make sure it is related to the music you will be rehearsing, not an isolated exercise or the same scale repeated daily.

Tuning is a process that you must teach starting at the very beginning stages of music study. When working with inexperienced musicians, use the words high and low rather than sharp or flat. This choice of vocabulary will make the concepts understandable. Remember that players can make mistakes while tuning. Be patient; you will probably be surprised at how much musicians can do on their own when they have been given the necessary guidance, knowledge, and encouragement.

Follow individual tuning by tuning sections -- woodwind, brass, strings -- and then the full group. It is imperative that players not tuning remain quiet so that their colleagues in the other sections can tune properly. Tuning is an ongoing process; no group in the world is in tune after the first tuning at the beginning of a rehearsal or concert. You must guide your musicians throughout the rehearsal, teaching them to constantly listen to themselves and the ensemble and to adjust their instruments for intonation when necessary.

Bowing

Many things affect the sound of an orchestra, but your approach to bowing will have the greatest impact. A particular bowing will produce a specific sound, and you must use your eyes and ears to determine whether bowings are consistent. Each string player must bow in the same direction, in the same part of the bow, with the same amount of pressure and in the same style. Never let up on the demand that all string players do everything the same, except of course when variations are called for.

Bowing Techniques

Here again, the conductor assumes the role of the teacher. The more experienced the string players, the less the conductor must actually teach, and the better string players in the orchestra should be used as resources to help the conductor decide what technique should be used. Still, the conductor must be aware of the bowings that the ensemble will need. As you study a score, visualize what bowing techniques will be required to

Watching the Conductor

No matter how experienced or inexperienced the players, many musicians simply ignore the person on the podium. Why? The fault must lie with the conductor. Insistence on a standard is

one of the most difficult expectations to maintain. Many times, conductors just give up, beating time and ignoring the musicians, while the musicians, in turn, ignore them. In order to lead an ensemble you must have eye contact with the players. Insist on this and continually expect it. Most important, be certain that you look at the players, not the score, and then you will be one step ahead in expecting the musicians to watch you.

achieve the sound you hear in your mind. For a review of basic techniques and as a guide for teaching bowing techniques for young players, I recommend the fine book by Elizabeth Green, *Orchestral Bowings and Routines* (Ann Arbor, Michigan: Campus Publishers).

If you are not a string player, the best way for you to understand bowing techniques is to study them with teachers. When you do this, remember that your primary goal is to become a better conductor. Don't just learn to play the instrument; study also how it works and what role bowing techniques play in developing orchestral sound. If you are a string player, think beyond performing and use your knowledge to imagine the total orchestral sound. Whatever your performance background is, remember that you are now the conductor.

Winds and Percussion

As with string instruments and bowing techniques, the key to understanding wind and percussion instruments is continuous study. No one learns enough in the conservatory or at college to conduct an ensemble. A bit of self-analysis is in order to make sure that you are striving to grow as a person, musician, teacher, and conductor. This growth includes understanding the techniques that are used in all sections of the group so that you can in turn teach your players. Wind and percussion players, for example, should know the meaning of the words *pizzicato* and *spiccato* so that when they are playing in an orchestra they can listen for these styles and effects in the strings and respond accordingly. If a *pizzicato* passage is played first in the strings and later in the woodwinds, the woodwinds should play the notes with the length set by the strings. Uniformity is, once again, the goal, and teaching various sections of the group to perform notes and phrases in the same style will bring the ensemble closer to a "one-instrument" sound.

Sightreading

Among professional orchestras, British groups are thought by many to be the best sightreaders. A major reason for this is that the orchestras are expected to play two or three different programs each week in addition to making recordings. Although this kind of demanding schedule may not produce the most memorable and perfect performances, repeated sightreading experience does increase a performer's ability to sightread quickly and perform orchestral works with minimal rehearsal.

Sightreading need not be separated from normal rehearsals. The first time you conduct a work that is being prepared for a concert, treat it as sightreading. Take the piece in tempo, expecting the performers to play as many notes as possible and as expressively as possible. It's okay to stop and start again, but really work on training the ensemble to look ahead and respond quickly. If you include other works just for sightreading, be certain to maintain your performance goals. Don't sightread at a slower tempo or forget about dynamics. Strive to make sightreading a truly meaningful experience.

Form and Style

Too often, musicians perform with insufficient musical knowledge. Your musicians should know how the music they are playing is put together. Take time to discuss the form of the composition, including simple structural analysis, important themes, and the development of the work. Also, explain the history behind the performance practices of various compositional periods. More experienced performers will be accustomed to these traditions, but younger players need you to explain the historical precedents for bowing practices, note lengths, trills, and textures.

Even professional players sometimes go about playing every day without digging into what lies beyond the notes. Many string players bow a certain way just because they have always done it that way, never exploring new and possibly better methods. I remember a wonderful lady in one of my orchestras who, when I asked her why she was bowing a certain way, would reply, "It feels good." Instead of choosing a bowing because it feels comfortable, encourage your string players to think first about the bowing practices and styles of the period of the composition.

Listening

Music, the "Listener's Art" — this is often said, but do conductors and musicians actually practice it? Too often, valves are pushed, strings are touched, and keys are pressed, but the ears sleep. Musicians don't listen enough to what they play. As the conductor, you're lucky; all of the parts are in front of you in your score. The poor clarinetist has only his part, one line. Worse off yet is the timpanist, with a few notes and 124 measures of rests. Your job is to guide the musicians through the listening process, helping them relate their parts to the compositional whole.

Encourage members of the ensemble to listen as if they were part of a string quartet or brass quintet, being aware of pitch, style, rhythm, chords,

form, orchestration and the often-neglected modern melodies, harmonies, and rhythms. (I isolate the last three because unfortunately, today's musician is still often a product of only past traditions and theories.) Ensemble members can achieve these goals by aiming for three things: one musical concept, a one-instrument precision of sound, and uniformity of style. If the musicians can play with the pitches, style, and rhythms all perfectly matched, the ensemble will realize the joyous occasion of a very special musical experience.

Being a conductor is a special role in life. You must earn this privilege of being a leader among musicians. Make the most of it and then you, your musicians, and your audience will reap the rewards and joys of music. ■

John Koshak is director of orchestras and professor of music at Chapman College in California and music director of the International Youth Symphony Orchestra. He received a bachelor's degree from Pennsylvania State University, a master's degree from Columbia University, and a conducting diploma from the Mozarteum in Salzburg, Austria.

Score Reading:
Transpositions and Clefs

by Robert J. Garofalo

S core reading is a complex process that requires specialized skills. Reading a score for instruments in several different keys, especially a band score with the parts spread around the page, can often frustrate a director.

The conductor can transpose the parts in a full score through two approaches: the interval of transposition method or the clef substitution method. Using the interval of transposition method, one thinks up or down a certain interval. For example, to read an F French horn part, you transpose the notes down a perfect fifth to see and hear the correct concert pitches.

With the clef substitution method the conductor replaces the original clef with a different clef and key signature, then reads the part at concert pitch without transposing the music. With this method the conductor has to adjust the octave for any instruments not in the key of C in order to get the correct register or tessitura. Experience has shown that the clef substitution method, if learned thoroughly, is an accurate and fluent way to read all the parts in a full score. Every aspiring conductor should learn how to use it.

A t first glance it may appear to the un-informed musician that having parts in several keys unnecessarily complicates the process of reading a full score. As the composer Arthur Honegger points out in his book *I*

Am a Composer, the score should be a clear sound image of the music, and not a picture puzzle. There are, however, practical as well as historical reasons why instruments are built in different keys.

There are several important factors to keep in mind when using the interval of transposition method to read a score. In scores from the 19th and 20th century horn and trumpet parts sometimes appear without key signatures; composers would write in accidentals in the music as needed. This procedure follows the old practice of notating these parts.

Composers and arrangers sometimes write bass clarinet parts on the bass staff to avoid writing ledger lines below the treble staff. When this occurs, the octave transposition is omitted. Thus, the B♭ bass clarinet sounds a major second lower than written on the bass staff, and the A bass clarinet a minor third lower.

Finally, all horns sound lower than written

Robert Garofalo is a professor of music and head of the graduate program in instrumental conducting at the Benjamin T. Rome School of Music of The Catholic University of America in Washington, D.C. He is cofounder and artistic director of the Eternal Winds of Washington, a professional wind symphony, and from 1978 to 1988 was conductor of Heritage Americana, a mid-19th century cornet/saxhorn brass band. Garofalo holds music degrees from Mansfield University and The Catholic University of America.

when the part appears on the treble staff. The easiest way to remember the intervals of transposition for horns is to imagine a note on the third space of the treble staff (C), letting it represent the written note for any transposing horn part. Following the C are the notes produced by horns pitched in different keys. The interval difference between the written C and the pitch key of any given horn gives the interval of transposition for that instrument.

Remember that the B♭ (alto) horn refers to the high-pitched French horn, not the upright alto horn sometimes used in marching bands. Also, the B♭ basso horn refers to the low-pitched French horn, not the tuba.

When horn parts are written on the bass staff, be sure to carefully examine the music to determine which system of notation is used — old or new. With the old notational practice, most horn parts written in bass clef will sound higher than written:

B♭ (alto) horn sounds up minor 7th
A horn sounds up major 6th
G horn sounds up perfect 5th
F horn sounds up perfect 4th
E horn sounds up major 3rd
E♭ horn sounds up minor 3rd
D horn sounds up major 2nd
C horn sounds as is
B♭ basso horn sounds down major 2nd

For all of these horns, except the C and B♭ basso horns, simply reverse the direction and invert the interval of transposition when the part appears in the bass staff and the old notational practice is used. With the new notational practice that some early 20th-century composers initiated to avoid confusion, horn parts that appear in the bass staff sound lower than written just as they do in the treble staff.

The Clef Substitution Method

The three clef symbols that are used in music today are corrupted versions of the letters they represent:

    𝄞 = G clef

    𝄡 = C clef

    𝄢 = F clef

Editor's Note: A work in progress, Music is the Score: A Guide to Score Study for the Wind Band Conductor, *is co-authored by Robert Garofalo and Frank Battisti. The book dissects score study into a four-step process: score orientation, score reading, score analysis, and score interpretation. This article extracts Robert Garofalo's comments regarding score reading.*

In music written before the middle of the 18th century each of these clefs regularly appeared in different positions on the five-line staff. The reason was simply to avoid writing ledger lines. For example, each part for the human voice had its own movable C clef — soprano clef, mezzo-soprano clef, alto clef, tenor clef, and baritone clef — whichever corresponded best to its range or tessitura.

Most musicians today are familiar with only two of the five movable C clefs — alto and tenor. The alto clef, of course, is used regularly by the viola; and the tenor clef is sometimes used by the trombone, bassoon, and cello.

To fluently employ the clef substitution method, one needs not only to be thoroughly familiar with all of the movable C clefs, but also to be highly skilled at reading them. The following overview shows the different clefs used in the method.

	Clef	Pitch of Transposing Instrument
	1. G Treble clef	
Movable C Clefs	2. C Soprano clef	A
	3. C Mezzo-soprano clef	F
	4. C Alto clef	D or D♭
	5. C Tenor clef	B♭
	6. C Baritone clef	G
	7. F Bass clef	E♭ or E

On a staff, the clefs are used as follows:

Instruments in E♭

One of the easiest and most frequently used substitution clefs is the bass clef, which may be used in place of any E♭ or E instrument part that is written in the treble clef. To read any E♭ instrument part at concert pitch, substitute the bass clef and the concert pitch key signature for the clef and key signature given in the part, then adjust the octave, if necessary, to get the correct tessitura.

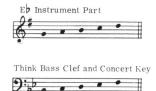

Think Bass Clef and Concert Key

Adjust octaves as follows:

- 2 octaves up ↑ for E♭ soprano clarinet and E♭ trumpet/cornet
- 1 octave up ↑ for E♭ alto clarinet and alto saxophone, and E♭ horn
- No adjustment necessary for E♭ contra-alto clarinet and E♭ baritone saxophone

Instruments in E

To read any E instrument part at concert pitch, substitute the bass clef and the concert pitch key signature for the clef and key signature given in the part, then adjust the octave to get the correct register.

E Instrument Part

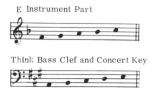

Think Bass Clef and Concert Key

Adjust octaves as follows:

- 1 octave up ↑ for E horn
- 2 octaves up ↑ for E trumpet/cornet

Not all accidentals appearing in a transposed part remain the same when a clef substitution is made. To achieve accuracy with the method, you need to know exactly which notes and accidentals are altered and which pattern of adjustment applies. There are two basic patterns of accidental adjustments.

Pattern A is for instruments pitched in flat keys – E♭, B♭, F, and D♭ :

    natural becomes a flat   ♮ = ♭

    sharp becomes a natural   ♯ = ♮

    flat becomes a double flat   ♭ = ♭♭

Pattern B is for instruments pitched in sharp keys – E, A, D, G:

    natural becomes a sharp   ♮ = ♯

    sharp becomes a double sharp   ♯ = ×

    flat becomes a natural   ♭ = ♮

Remember that these adjustment patterns only apply to the accidental pitch notes of the home key of the instrument; all other accidentals remain the same after the substitution clef is applied. For E♭ instruments accidental changes only occur on the notes B, E, and A and always follow Pattern A.

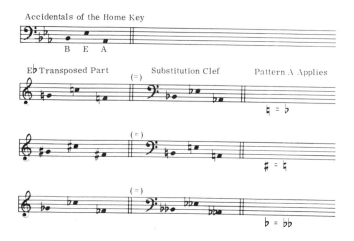

Accidentals of the Home Key

B E A

E♭ Transposed Part   Substitution Clef   Pattern A Applies

♮ = ♭

♯ = ♮

♭ = ♭♭

For E instruments accidental changes will only occur on the notes F, C, G, and D, and will always follow Pattern B.

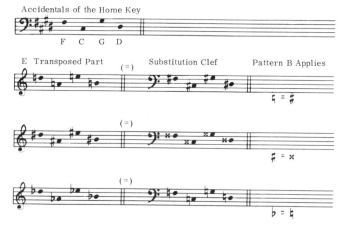

Accidentals of the Home Key

F C G D

E Transposed Part   Substitution Clef   Pattern B Applies

♮ = ♯

♯ = ×

♭ = ♮

One of the best ways to gain an understanding of the bass clef as a substitution clef is to look at musical examples that clearly show its application. The next example illustrates the substitution of the bass clef for different E♭ and E instrument parts.

Written Part

Substitution Clef, Concert Key, and Pitches

E♭ Soprano Clarinet (E♭ Trumpet)

mf
(Think 2 octaves up)

mf

f

f

Table of Wind Band Instruments and Transpositions

Flutes
Db Piccolo - Up 1 octave + minor 2nd
C Piccolo - Up 1 octave
C Flute - As written
G Alto Flute - Down perfect 4th
C Bass Flute - Down 1 octave

Oboes
Oboe - As written
Oboe d'Amore - Down minor 3rd
English Horn - Down perfect 5th
Hecklephone (bass oboe in C) - Down 1 octave

Clarinets
Eb (Soprano) - Up minor 3rd
D (Soprano) - Up major 2nd
C (Soprano) - As written
Bb (Soprano) - Down major 2nd
A (Soprano) - Down minor 3rd
F Basset Horn - Down perfect 5th
Eb Alto - Down major 6th
Bb Bass - Down major 9th
A Bass - Down 1 octave + minor 3rd
Eb Contra-alto - Down 1 octave + major 6th
Bb Contra-bass - Down 2 octaves + major 2nd

Bassoon - As written
Contrabassoon - Down 1 octave

Saxophones
Bb Soprano - Down major 2nd
Eb Alto - Down major 6th
Bb Tenor - Down major 9th
Eb Baritone - Down 1 octave + major 6th
Bb Bass - Down 2 octaves + major 2nd

French Horns
Bb (Alto) - Down major 2nd

A - Down minor 3rd
G - Down perfect 4th
F - Down perfect 5th
E - Down minor 6th
Eb - Down major 6th
D - Down minor 7th
C - Down 1 octave
Bb (Basso) - Down major 9th

Trumpets
F - Up perfect 4th
E - Up major 3rd
Eb - Up minor 3rd
D - Up major 2nd
C - As written
Bb - Down major 2nd
A - Down minor 3rd

Low Brass
Bb Trombone (tenor or bass) - As written
Bb Euphonium/Baritone Horn (treble clef) - Down
   major 9th
Bb Euphonium/Baritone Horn (bass clef) - As written
Tuba/Sousaphone (Bb, C, Eb, F) - As written

String Instruments
Double bass - Down 1 octave

Percussion
Timpani - As written
Marimba - As written
Vibraphone - As written
Xylophone - Up 1 octave
Chimes - Up 1 octave or as written
Chimes - Up 1 octave
Celesta - Up 1 octave
Orchestral Bells - Up 2 octaves
Crotales - Up 2 octaves

The movable C clef may be substituted for five different treble clef transposing parts as follows:

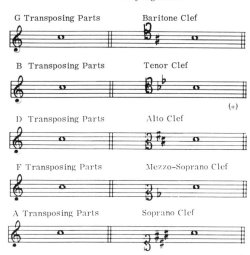

Substitute this Clef and the Concert Pitch Key Signature

(+) The alto clef may be substituted for D♭ instruments such as the D♭ piccolo. For this instrument, Pattern A applies to accidentals falling on the notes B, E, A, D, and G of the home key. Also, adjust the notes two octaves higher.

Instruments in A
1. Substitute the soprano clef and concert pitch key signature.
2. Change only the accidentals falling on the Notes F, C, and G using Pattern B.
3. No octave adjustment is necessary for A clarinet, A trumpet, A horn, or oboe d'amore.

Instruments in F
1. Substitute the mezzo-soprano clef and concert pitch key signature.
2. Change only the accidentals falling on the note B using Pattern A.
3. No octave adjustment is necessary for F horn, English horn, or basset horn.

Instruments in D
1. Substitute the alto clef and concert pitch key signature.
2. Change only the accidentals falling on the notes F and C using Pattern B.
3. Adjust the octave as follows:
   • For D trumpet and D clarinet think one octave higher.
   • For D horn no adjustment is necessary.

Instruments in B♭
1. Substitute the tenor clef and concert pitch key signature.
2. Adjust only the accidentals falling on the notes B and E using Pattern A.
3. Adjust the octaves as follows:
   • For B♭ soprano clarinet, B♭ soprano saxophone, B♭ trumpet/cornet/fluegelhorn and B♭ French horn (alto), think one octave higher.

• For B♭ bass clarinet, tenor saxophone, baritone horn/euphonium (treble clef), and B♭ basso French horn no adjustment is necessary.
• For B♭ contrabass clarinet and bass saxophone, think one octave lower.

Instruments in G
1. Substitute the baritone clef and concert pitch key signature.
2. Adjust only the accidentals falling on the note F using Pattern B.
3. Adjust the octave as follows:
   • For G alto flute and G horn think one octave higher.

The following example illustrates the application of the movable C clef to various transposed parts.

Here's a final word of caution. The clef substitution method won't work if a transposing part is written enharmonically, or if it employs the bass clef (e.g., bass clarinet, French horn).

The ability to read different clefs with skill and fluency is the key to unlocking transposed parts in a full score. To improve your clef reading skills, I suggest the following sequence of study.

1. Sing melodies that contain the following movable C clefs: soprano, mezzo-soprano, alto, tenor, baritone.
2. At the keyboard, play one, two, and then three-part exercises that use the movable C clefs.
3. Play Bach chorales (or other four-part

exercises) that contain the original clefs printed on separate lines.
4. Read (sing or play at the keyboard) transposed instrument parts using the clef substitution method.

Once you have developed some facility at reading clefs and applying the substitution method, begin to read (and play at the keyboard, if possible) simple transposed scores. Score reading is a complex, translative skill that needs to be developed sequentially. You should read scores regularly and frequently, starting with simple music at first, then gradually moving to more difficult scores. With disciplined daily practice you should begin to develop fluency at applying the clef substitution method. □

March, 1978

A Survey of Ambiguous Wind Articulations

Gary Stith

A large number of articulation markings found in wind music have long seemed nebulous directions as to how the music should be performed. In his excellent book, *Effective Performance of Band Music* (Southern, 1972), W. Francis McBeth devotes one complete chapter to the responses from American composers and conductors to a survey regarding five articulation markings ( ). The responses were so interesting and enlightening that I decided to continue this research. The new survey was very similar to McBeth's. It asked for general

definitions of four different, but equally ambiguous, articulations.

Twenty distinguished American composers and conductors received a copy of the survey and were asked to respond to the following questions:

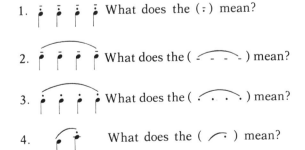

Gary Stith directs the high school wind ensemble and teaches instrumental music at Holland Central School in Holland, New York.

Additional comments were also welcomed.

Some of those surveyed wrote back saying that they found it impossible to respond. One reason given was that it was not possible to interpret the markings without seeing the specific musical example because the interpretation is dependent on the style of the period and the tradition of the composer.

Here are the interpretations offered by the seven musicians who were able to respond.

1. How do you interpret ♪ ♪ ♪ ♪ ?

Keith Brion, conductor-in-residence at Yale University: Three-fourths of the normal value, unended release (no mark on release).

Arnald D. Gabriel, conductor of the U.S. Air Force Band and Orchestra: The tenuto implies holding the note its full or slightly longer than its full value. This will depend on how rhythmic the accompaniment is. The dot indicates a slight space between the notes. I firmly believe that we in wind performance should borrow the down bow marking (⊓) to make clear from an audible and visual standpoint this articulation. Each note is attacked with the down bow held as long as possible without diminuendo and the bow quickly retaken for the next and similarly played note. This example is especially effective for young players.

Karel Husa, professor of composition at Cornell University: I think of these attacks as long quarter notes (expressed by the tenuto mark) with little staccato accents. They will, however, be detached from each other; otherwise said, the player will attack the note as if it were a staccato marking only, but will hold the note nearly as long as a quarter note with the shortest possible breaks between them. A possible variation of the notation could be:

♪ ♪ ♪ ♪

Ronald LoPresti, professor of composition at Arizona State University: I've never used this. The two marks of tenuto and staccato seem to cancel each other.

Weston Noble, chairman of the music department at Luther College, Decorah, Iowa: It is very difficult to explain these markings verbally. One almost has to hear them and then adjust the player's style accordingly. This first one is unusually difficult, and to be honest with you I do not take it very seriously. I interpret it as a half-staccato, half-marcato. So, a slight detachment. Or a broad staccato. One must first determine the general overall style of the selection and adjust from there.

Vincent Persichetti, professor of composition at Juilliard School of Music: Some pressure (slightly accented) and slightly separated.

H. Robert Reynolds, conductor of the University of Michigan Wind Ensemble: Slight separation but basically long notes.

2. How do you interpret ♪ ♪ ♪ ♪ ?

Keith Brion: This is a *du* articulation begun with *a too*. The note values sound almost too long for the rhythm. The feeling is like that of full string bows. ⌒ indicates a strong phrasing connection.

Arnald D. Gabriel: I would assume that this articulation is to be used on different pitches because a repeated pitch with this marking would result in a sustained whole note. If there is no rhythmic pulse the slurred notes can be held longer than usual. Even though more difficult, the notes can be held longer, even with a rhythmic pulse, but great flexibility and sensitivity would then be required in the accompaniment. This articulation is used often in operatic repertoire for a dramatic effect.

Karel Husa: I assume that this articulation is used mainly in slow or moderate tempos. The dash and slur marking, it seems to me, came into wind phrasing from string bowing called "louré," meaning a stroke which slightly separates the notes on one bow (thus the slur). Perhaps it could mean the same for winds: to separate the notes very slightly and in a very sensitive espressivo way on one uninterrupted breath. It has been used by composers in very delicate accompaniments and sometimes even in very expressive melodies. By the slur, the composer also meant to express that the notes are not independent, but that they relate to each other.

Ronald LoPresti: Hold each tone for its full value, touching each with the tongue lightly.

Weston Noble: A legato, but yet a slight feeling of detachment between notes. The notes are played long, but not with a full legato, and yet with more weight than a normal legato.

Vincent Persichetti: Some pressure (slightly accented) and smoothly phrased (sustained).

H. Robert Reynolds: Connection with pulsation on each note mostly with the breath.

3. How do you interpret ♪ ♪ ♪ ♪ ?

Keith Brion: Slightly shorter than the no. 1 *du* articulation. Half the normal note value, but with a phrasing connection across each note, regardless of separation. Unended release.

Arnald D. Gabriel: This is one of the most effective articulations available in the wind repertoire of articulations, and in my view it is not used often enough. Once again I would like to borrow from string bowings, not because winds should try to sound like strings, but what happens with the bow on the string is obvious whereas what happens in the diaphragm, lungs, and mouth of the wind player is not so obvious. In string playing, this articulation is referred to as louré bowing and was developed during the Romantic period to produce a very pulsating, almost passionate kind of playing. The tempo is usually fairly slow. The violinist plays all four quarter notes in one bow on one pitch. To identify the quarter notes a slight pressure is applied as the bow is being drawn so that there is no break in the sound. Of course, I have heard violinists argue over this articulation, but it certainly results in a smooth, long-line, connected kind of playing. Wind players should merely attack the note. To identify succeeding pitches they should create a pulsation by using the diaphragm but absolutely no tongue.

Karel Husa: The slur here also expresses a relationship between the slurred notes, but the notes are to be played shorter than in articulation no. 2. Normally, we say that a note with a point is shortened approximately to its half value (♩ = ♪ in this case), but this again varies with the tempo; when faster, the note will be even longer than half of its value. I would recommend not breathing within the slurs.

Ronald LoPresti: Half staccato. Articulate each tone lightly with space between each quarter. Usually played 𝄞

Weston Noble: A staccato, but yet a slight feeling of legato on each note. The same as in articulation no. 2, but in reverse — notes played short, but not as short as a full staccato and with less weight than a normal legato.

Vincent Persichetti: Slight separation between tones, not accented, but liquid.

H. Robert Reynolds: Separation, generally with lightness. Sometimes the slur marking is used as a phrase marking.

4. How do you interpret ♩ ♩ ?

Keith Brion: Last note half value, unmarked release. Usually a feminine ending with less pressure on the second note, less weight of tone.

Arnald D. Gabriel: Because the second note has a leger line through it and seems to be higher in pitch, the player slurs from the first to the second, making the second note shorter than the first. How short depends on the style. For an upward interval of this kind it is almost always artistically correct to make a diminuendo to the second note.

Karel Husa: I explain this example perhaps in another notation: ♩ ♪ As in articulation no. 3 the point on the second note would shorten it to approximately half its value, but again depending on the speed of the music. There has been no clarity as to this staccato second note: should it be slightly accented as staccato notes usually are, or should it be without an accent, with the first note heavier and the second a light resolution? This depends on many factors such as the beat (in Classical music) on which it is written. If it is on a first and second beat in a moderately fast $\frac{3}{4}$ meter, the effect will be stronger-lighter, but if it falls on the third and first beat in the same meter, it will sound lighter-heavier. Some modern composers have indicated an accent (>) together with the point, when they actually wanted that short note to be strong; on the other hand, when no accent was written, the note is to be played lighter than the first one. I think that composers often did not take the time to write out an eighth note and a rest and simply put a dot on a quarter note.

Ronald LoPresti: The second tone is touched lightly with the tongue, but is of a shorter duration than notated in order to prepare the tongue for the next attack. "T" "T"

full value

Weston Noble: An easy release of the note, shorter than a normal quarter, but yet not a short staccato release. A modified staccato release.

Vincent Persichetti: A smooth phrase leading to a shortened and slightly tongued tone.

H. Robert Reynolds: The second note is released, but not articulated.

Additional Comments
Keith Brion: There are three staccato articulations:

TooT = ended staccato
Too = unended staccato
Toot = lightly clipped

♪ = at least full value

♪ = 3/4 value

♪ = 1/2 value

♪ = 1/4 value

♪ = as short as possible
staccatissimo

Arnold D. Gabriel: Notation and articulation markings are at best arbitrary, nebulous, and inadequate. They mean different things to different composers, conductors, and players. Additionally, to take a group of notes out of context compounds the problem because the style, tempo, etc. of the piece is not known and can and does affect the interpretation. Finally, there is no definitive interpretation of any phase of the musical art, because music is an art, not a science, and is therefore subject to very personal considerations. With these thoughts in mind the preceding is my humble and personal approach to the problems you present.

Karel Husa: Many markings, including the above ones, depend on numerous factors, among them the speed of the music (the same notation will sound differently in a lyrical, emotional passage than it would in a scherzo-like or satirical phrase). The modern composers were aware of some of the inadequacies of the notation and tried to be as precise as possible. May I cite Stravinsky, Bartok, Webern, Berg, and Prokofiev; their scores, together with many others, are notated nearly as close as possible to avoid any doubt. As far as the old music is concerned, a knowledge of the common practice during Baroque, Classical and Romantic music is necessary to solve these interpretative problems in different circumstances.

Ronald LoPresti: Articulations 1, 2, 3, and maybe 4 originated from concepts of bowing stringed instruments:

All upbows with a slight break between each tone.

Group staccato : All upbows with a definite separation between each tone.

Vincent Persichetti: These articulations always seem slightly ambiguous. I hope your article can help all of us.

H. Robert Reynolds: Articulations 1, 2, and 3 are often used by composers who are writing string music. These are generally string bowing and articulation markings, thus:

Articulation 1 is a detaché bowing or separate bows on the string with slight separation.

Articulation 2 is generally played with a louré bowing with all four notes on the same bow with a slight pulsation on each note.

Articulation 3 is generally off-the-string bowing or the same bow stroke.

It would also be absolutely essential to know the context in which these were used and to know the dynamic and speed of the selection or passage. All articulation markings are subject to interpretation based upon the music and other instruments playing. It is also imperative to know the composer and his history of using these markings. Even a commonly used marking such as an accent (>) sounds different in Haydn, Beethoven, Brahms, Stravinsky, and others. To isolate these markings for a definitive statement to me is impossible. ■

September, 1980

How to Improve Rehearsals

Manny Brand

For many instrumental directors rehearsal preparation too frequently consists of simply grabbing the director's folder along with a splintered baton, and racing to the podium. The rehearsal that follows is likely to be unproductive and disorganized. Students easily detect an unprepared director and quickly tire of rehearsals in which musical progress is not made quickly.

Good rehearsal preparation means that prior to stepping on the podium the director has a clear concept of what he expects to achieve.

The amount of rehearsal time devoted to warming up, tuning, and rehearsing is based on such factors as the frequency of rehearsals, the maturity and attention span of the students, and the performance schedule. Many directors correlate their rehearsal schedule with specific goals within set time limitations, as shown by the 60-minute junior high school band rehearsal schedule printed here.

Using this kind of rehearsal schedule lets the director formulate clear goals for each rehearsal. When pre-planning takes place, the director and the students realize the importance of accomplishing certain goals during the rehearsal. Thus, these rehearsals tend to be musically productive and gratifying, and each day the director and students can leave the rehearsal hall with a feeling of accomplishment.

Effective Rehearsal Procedures

Too often conductors say, "Try it again at letter B," hoping the students will improve through mere repetition. They seldom do. Every time a director stops the group, a clear and specific suggestion or direction needs to be given prior to the second playing; and the more specific the suggestion, the greater the likelihood it will be implemented. For example, the director who says, "Trumpets, let's

Manny Brand is assistant professor of music education at the University of Houston.

hear measure 40 again, and this time use your third valve slide for the D," is more likely to improve trumpet intonation than the one who says, "Trumpets, be careful of your notes; try it again." Remember, every correction should name the band section, the specific error committed, and

60-Minute Junior High Concert Band Rehearsal	
2:07	Warm-up and tuning Goals: Use concert F and C scales to work on clearer articulation, and use concert D scale to work on ♩ rhythm.
2:17	Administrative announcements: Pictures to be taken on Tuesday; student assistant checks roll.
2:19	Review familiar piece; "Overture in B♭" Goal: Check balance, especially in brass section, and be sure second and third parts can be heard.
2:25	Introduce new work: "Fantasia in B Major" Goals: Read through the piece and work on flute and oboe parts.
2:40	Detailed work on "Burnished Brass" Goals: Work on lower brass from letter C and trumpets from letter E.
2:55	Sight read "Parade Precision"
3:03	Review familiar piece: "Star Wars Theme"
3:07	Dismissal

suggest a musical prescription needed for improvement.

Sometimes it is necessary to work with just one section during a full band rehearsal; but it is often possible to turn a sectional problem into a learning experience for the entire band. For example, if the saxophones are having difficulty with a quarter-note triplet figure, write the rhythmic problem on the board for a class drill. As the saxophones' rhythmic error is corrected, others are also learning, and because everyone is playing, discipline problems are less likely to occur.

Using advance verbal cues such as "don't breathe here," or "clarinets, piano," means the director will stop and start the group less often, so musical progress is achieved more quickly.

Pace

The director who always pauses to gather his thoughts after stopping the group to make a comment, and then punctuates every few words with "ah" or "um," or whose long-winded and vague comments are unnecessarily repetitive, or who fumbles through the folder to find the next piece, is the director who slows the rehearsal pace to the point of boredom.

Conversely, many of us have observed conductors whose rehearsals seem purposeful and fast-moving as they generate a sense of continual progress.

Being able to give musical corrections and suggestions in a concise manner is the first characteristic of good rehearsal pacing; students listen when the director speaks because his comments are pertinent, musically helpful, and stated briefly.

Directors who are prepared for each rehearsal, set specific goals within allotted time limitations, and use an efficient and fast-paced approach, find their rehearsals to be enjoyable, as well as effective in the creation of better performing organizations. ∎

February, 1976

Productive Rehearsals

C.B. Kreichbaum, Jr. and Jacquelyn Dillon

The primary objectives in planning a good rehearsal should be (1) to use every minute in the most efficient manner, and (2) to plan so that every person will be playing during as much of the period as possible. Here are some ideas to help you achieve your goals.

Preparation for the Rehearsal

1. Set up the rehearsal room ahead of time. Cases should be out of the way so that the teacher is free to move about without disturbing students.

2. Know the places in the music that you plan to rehearse. Identify each by rehearsal number or letter.

3. Put the titles of the compositions on the board in the order that they will be rehearsed so the students can have the music ready.

C.B. Kreichbaum is Supervisor of Music and Band/Orchestra Director for the North Olmsted (Ohio) City Schools. He is also guest conductor for all-state orchestras and festival bands, adjudicator, and clinician for Scherl and Roth, Inc.

Jacquelyn Dillon is a professional cellist and clinician for Scherl and Roth, Inc. As a recruiter, coordinator, and teacher she helped establish many successful string programs.

4. Place any new music in the folders or on the stands. On the board list music to be turned in at end of the rehearsal.

5. See that the measures in your score and the students' parts are numbered correctly.

6. Have suggested fingerings and uniform bowings marked in critical areas on the students' music.

7. Choose performance music, especially for young training groups, that helps teach technical difficulties. Music is needed that allows for work in such areas as intonation, rhythm, vibrato, bow control, tone, shifting, balance, etc. It is also important that music be planned for the whole year just as it is planned for each daily rehearsal. A long-range, flexible plan should include specific areas and goals that are necessary to move the group ahead.

The Actual Rehearsal

1. Stop as little as possible and only for a good reason. Briefly tell the group why you stopped and say enough to enable students to correct mistakes.

2. Make sure that your students understand that they can apply the solution of one particular prob-

lem to other compositions. Never say "Do this" without telling them why. Impress upon them that "Whenever you have this situation, this is what you do."

3. Make certain that the students understand the purpose behind the drills that you require them to play. Drills should be related to problems in the music and/or extracted from the music itself.

4. Work on music of various levels of difficulty so that students of all abilities find something challenging and rewarding in each rehearsal.

5. Don't use the time of an entire group to work on individual or small group problems. Schedule sectionals or small-group rehearsals to work on such areas as fingerings, bowings, seating, tone production, etc. Large group rehearsals should be reserved for problems involving the whole ensemble and devoted to areas such as balance, phrasing, intonation, rhythm, style, dynamics, tutti passages, etc.

6. Going through a piece of music over and over again will not correct all the problems. It may be a good idea to first give the group a feeling for the "full sweep" of a piece, but then tear the music apart and work on specific problems.

7. Work on one problem at a time until it is corrected before attacking another one.

8. Stop only if you think the students are not aware of their mistakes or do not know what to do about them. Many mistakes will correct themselves — some will not. The teacher must be able to distinguish between them. Generally problems such as tone, intonation, balance, and phrasing won't correct themselves and should be discussed.

9. Establish an order of importance for rehearsing problems, such as rhythm, tone, notes (including intonation), expressiveness, and style. This can apply to all rehearsals at all levels. Before a concert you may have to change this order to improve the overall effect.

10. Establish the concept that it is not how many notes you play, but rather, how you play them that is most important. Students must realize that correct notes, rhythm, and good intonation are where music making *begins*, not where it ends. They must also be made to understand that the accompanying passages are essential to every piece and provide excellent opportunities for the player to concentrate on the style, dynamics, and phrasing.

11. Tempos are relative and should be selected with the capabilities of the group in mind.

12. When preparing for a performance, be sure to rehearse all the music all the way through.

The Psychological Angle

1. Tell your students that they are working for perfection and that they cannot stop until this goal is reached; however, to avoid frustration, they must know that if they don't achieve this particular goal, they are not total failures.

2. Give constant encouragement, but never let students think they have achieved absolute perfection, or many will stop trying. Set goals that are a bit out of reach of the group — but never make them so far removed as to seem unobtainable. Say such things as,

"That was better, now we need to do this."

3. Teach students to have pride in their playing and always play to the best of their ability. The teacher should insist on high standards, give the group the tools to achieve the goals set for them, and convince the students that the goals are worth achieving.

4. Students should realize that you have nothing personal against them when you criticize their playing. Remember — positive reinforcement while the music is being learned and praise when the goal has been achieved can do wonders for morale.

5. You must realize that anything that the students need to know you must teach. If the students are lacking in some area, teach it to them, without complaining. After all, that's why you were hired. If they already knew everything, you'd be out of a job.

6. Teach intelligent playing — make sure students think about what they are doing and why, so that they can eventually function without you and make musical decisions on their own.

7. When preparing for concerts and contests "overlearn" the music so that the students will be able to perform well under pressure.

8. If much of the rehearsal has been spent in intense work on a small portion of the composition, it would be a good idea, at the end of the period, to put the problem spot back into the context of the music and let the students see the progress that has been made.

9. Try to end all rehearsals on a positive note. Let the group feel successful by playing something that shows improvement, or some piece that they especially like.

10. Let each student know that it is his responsibility to play with the utmost musical integrity and as though it were a solo performance. If the performer is unable to do this and is faking the music, the director has either chosen music that is too difficult or has not rehearsed it properly.

Continuing Objectives

In order to improve the quality of your group and raise their level of understanding of the music, keep the following items in mind for your rehearsals:

1. Note posture and holding positions, embouchures, left and right hand positions, and make any necessary corrections.

2. Teach basic rhythms so that the level of sight-reading can improve.

3. Work on tone production, control, and intonation.

4. Improve technical facility so the group can progress to more difficult music and/or concentrate on musical problems.

5. Teach musical concepts in the works you are studying.

6. Briefly discuss the style, historical background and the composers of the music you are playing.

7. Develop an awareness for the overall form of the compositions and their basic harmonic structure.

Some of the techniques that we've suggested may already be part of your routine. By integrating the other ideas into your rehearsals, you can get the most out of the time you have with your musical organizations. ∎

A Symphony Player Looks at Conductors

Kurt Loebel

The following comments and observations are based on over twenty years of playing in the first violin section of the Cleveland Orchestra, for the most part under George Szell but also under the leadership of a great many other conductors. In some instances my experiences with a conductor involved periods of several weeks or perhaps just several days. The personal and cultural background of each conductor varied, but the conditions such as rehearsal time, rules of conduct, acoustic conditions and orchestra personnel remained basically the same.

The list of conductors begins with Felix Weingartner, under whom I played while still a student in Vienna. Later, as a professional in the U.S. (with the Dallas Symphony 1945-47 and the Cleveland Orchestra 1947-present), I played under Ancerl, Ansermet, Beecham, Bernstein, Dorati, Goldovsky, Golschman, Karajan, Kletzki, Krips, Kubelik, Leinsdorf, Markevitch, Monteux, Munch, Ormandy, Paray, Rudolf, Schmidt-Isserstedt, Shaw, Steinberg, Stokowski, Susskind, Van Beinum, and Walter. Among the younger generation, there were Abbado, Barenboim, Ceccato, Craft, Fruhbeck de Burgos, Haitink, Kertesz, Lane, Levine, Maazel, Ozawa, Pretre, Previn, and Schippers. Composer-conductors have included Boulez, Chavez, Copland, Enesco, Foss, Hanson, Kodaly, Maderna, Schuller, Stravinsky and Villa-Lobos, and violinist-conductors were Goldberg, Menuhin and Oistrakh. Franz Allers, Leroy Anderson, Victor Borge, Duke Ellington, Arthur Fiedler, Andre Kostelanetz and Henry Mancini, known in the world of lighter music, have also led the Cleveland Orchestra. In addition to these famous names there were countless other wielders of the baton, all of whom contributed to my understanding of this hard-to-define profession called conducting.

The requirements of mastering the art of conducting are such that few can hope to attain a high level. A rare combination of musicianship, discipline, charisma, psychological insight, ruthlessness, business sense and acting ability, as well as unusual physical and mental strength are essential. To be able to command orchestra and audience alike, additional non-musical considerations enter into the picture, such as good looks and knowledge of many related fields, including art, literature, politics, history, and a world outlook acquired by travel and social relationships.

A conductor cannot live in an ivory tower, and a complete knowledge of the score, obtained by continuing and relentless study, is only the beginning. A monastic and lonely existence, at least in part, must be taken for granted.

In working relationships with other musicians, one must find a middle ground between comradeship and distance, friendliness and firmness, humor and seriousness, inspiration and calculation, emotion and intellect. The conductor must display authority without suppression or capricious, dictatorial manners. He must be able to hide his weaknesses, yet be humble enough to admit a mistake. The words chosen in such an instance should never be apologetic, but phrased in a simple, human, perhaps humorous fashion. There can be no faking in front of trained musicians; an orchestra will instinctively make a fairly accurate appraisal of a conductor's ability in a comparatively short time.

The remarks made in this article are based on experience in a professional orchestra and may need some modification in the case of student and amateur groups. But the basics remain the same for all situations involving the relationship — artistic and personal — between conductor and players. The player must be convinced that the conductor is involving himself in a common, artistic endeavor and not using the musicians for purposes of self-glorification or choreographic exhibitionism for the sake of audience approval. If the conductor demands of himself as much or more than he does of the players, there will hopefully be no more than a small degree of opposition to his demands. It is necessary that he know more, however, than those he attempts to direct, guide, teach, cajole, inspire or collaborate with. If he cannot measure up to this requirement, his effectiveness will be minimal, discipline will be non-existent, and music making will become impossible. His convictions must be strong enough to be transmittable to musicians and audience alike, and his courage must outweigh the critical comments by insiders and outsiders, as well as professional advice offered by overly ambitious players. In other words, he must remain his own man, avoid favoritism, and not falter from his position of polite but flexible authority.

For the purpose of learning how to conduct, a poor orchestra will be of greater benefit to the conductor than a fine, highly professional one, because a poor orchestra will offer far greater opportunities for self-analysis, experimentation and correction. The highly-polished orchestra will only prevent the conductor

Kurt Loebel was a violinist with the Dallas Symphony before joining the first violin section of the Cleveland Orchestra in 1948. He holds degrees from the Cleveland Institute of Music and became a faculty member there in 1950.

from becoming aware of his shortcomings and do for the conductor what he should learn to do for himself. Although the old cliche "There are no bad orchestras, only bad conductors" is an over-simplification, there is some truth in it. The better the orchestra, the more apparent the personality of the conductor. However, it is often obvious that a fine orchestra will play well in spite of the conductor. An uncommitted orchestra can drag the standard toward mediocrity in a matter of hours, while a dynamic, knowledgeable and strong conductor can elevate the same body of players to great heights in the same amount of time. It takes a long time to build an orchestra but only hours to destroy it — unless the idealism of the players is so uncommonly high that their pride and self-esteem prevent such disintegration.

There are no steadfast rules which assure success to a conductor. One can, however, offer a variety of Do's and Don'ts based on observation and experience. These must be molded to the conductor's individual personality so that they reinforce his basic nature and character, instead of appearing as inflexible, calculated tricks.

It has been said repeatedly that conductors are born and not made. This may be so, but if you want to be a conductor, remember that you too are mortal and perhaps born with a slight birth defect. Surely this kind of humility, however well disguised, may be the wisest attitude to take if you hope to be taken seriously as a leader of men.

Don'ts

Don't Talk Too Much

Your job is to make music with your hands. There is no point in stopping to tell the orchestra about making a crescendo which they can already see in print. If you conduct it, chances are they will do it. If it isn't printed (and you still want it), you should still conduct it. Talking about it will make the musicians doubt your ability to conduct; they will be annoyed by unnecessary stopping, and become angry about your underestimating their intelligence. Be economical, don't live from hand to mouth.

Don't Whisper

Since you want to be efficient and in a position of authority, your announcements should be clear, audible and to the point. If you whisper, the players in the back will think that you are indulging in a private flirtation with the players in front. This will contribute to their already deflated egos and minimize their contribution to the orchestra's performance.

Don't Sit Down

It impairs the player's view of your beat, detracts from your physical image as a leader, and invites mental laxity. Besides, it looks lazy and some players feel that you are being overpaid anyway.

Don't Repeat Ad Nauseam

If you stop to repeat measures, sections or movements, be sure to explain your purpose. Meaningful repetition or even sheer mechanical drilling will not

be resented if it is justified. Should you ask for repetition for your own practice, say so. The orchestra knows instinctively that "practice is for them who needs it!"

Don't Neglect the Downbeat

Remember that there is only *one* downbeat in each bar. Should your downbeat move up or sideways by mistake, you will cause much unnecessary confusion. When a player has several bars of rest to count, your downbeat remains his only guide; without a clear downbeat he is sunk, unless he can absolutely count on your cue. But since you are busy conducting, you cannot possibly indicate all the cues. This should encourage you to think, however, that you will not get a precise and convincing entrance, especially of an entire section, by relying on the counting of individual players.

Once you have conducted for awhile, you will be in danger of believing that you do not have to conduct clear beats any longer, that you are only "making music" and interpreting. You may believe that the orchestra knows the music and doesn't need your beat any longer. Unfortunately, you cannot hear their complaints in the dressing room and they will hesitate to tell you that your beat is unintelligible; nonetheless, it still pays to conduct (diagram: downbeat pattern 1→2→3) instead of (diagram: pattern 1,2,3).

Don't Be Surprised If . . .

When the rehearsal has gone on for awhile, the musicians look at their watches instead of your beat.

Don't Hide the Beat

Your beat is the most vital thing you have to offer. It must be visible to everyone, no matter where they sit in the orchestra. Its purpose is to express clarity and precision for the guidance of the musicians who are trying to express your ideas via their instruments. The fact that your podium choreography might excite the audience and mislead the rational thinking process of the critics is only an unfortunate concomitant.

Don't Knit

It is true that Toscanini used circular motions. Unless you are convinced that you are another Toscanini, try clear, straight patterns. Incidentally, contrary to your emotional inclination, if you want the orchestra to play faster, use smaller instead of larger motions.

Don't Conduct the Melody

All the musicians know the melody. So does the audience. Where the orchestra needs you is either for rhythmic control, proper balance, logic in contrapuntal textures, exact attacks and releases, and control of dynamic gradations.

Don't Make Faces

You will not impress the orchestra by staring at the players or by inspirational facial expressions directed at the ceiling as if you were in direct communication with God. Nor should your head be buried in the score, even if the score isn't buried in your head.

It is equally pointless to memorize for the sake of impressing everyone that the cello passage begins three measures before letter K. Let your face honestly express the emotions the music arouses in you.

Don't Scream, Threaten or Throw Fits

It serves no purpose. You will be ridiculed and become the victim of artistic hostility which might lead to sabotage and resentment. If the orchestra is not making the effort it is capable of, do not threaten to cancel the concert or walk out, because they will say to themselves "go ahead, walk out!" An unruly, frustrated and lethargic orchestra can be changed suddenly to an attentive, cooperative and motivated group by a calm remark such as: "Sometimes I wonder whether you care about your work!" The old traditional, temperamental, autocratic, prima-donna type of conductor is on the way out. The Union and/or Orchestra Committee will give you a hard time and it is questionable whether you can really carry out your threats. If you are attempting to achieve your goals by instilling fear or guilt, you may see some temporary results. In the long run, the disadvantages for you and the orchestra will outweigh any temporary triumphs.

Don't Believe That Musicians Aren't People

There is no evidence that musicians are in any way different from other people. Contrary to popular belief based on romantic fiction, there is no mode of human behavior by which musicians can be categorized.

Don't Belittle Players

To embarrass, belittle or criticize musicians in front of the entire orchestra is a poor investment. So is the habit of calling a few key players by their first names or "my dear," while you address the others as "you there in back." If you want the orchestra to work for you or with you, this is a sure way to get them to work against you.

Don't Encourage Advice from the Faculty

The best place to learn is from well-intended musicians...but in the privacy of your studio. Allowing verbal advice in front of the orchestra, be it from key players you respect or self-appointed experts, will reduce your effectiveness. In addition, it causes confusion, waste of time, jealousy and orchestral malaise.

Don't Show Off Your Knowledge

It is worthwhile to understand that the musicians basically resent having to conform to your "authentic" interpretation. They each have their own and think they know better, so don't rub it in. They are likely to be cynical about any display of theoretical knowledge on your part. They know that it is easier to talk about it than to do it on the instrument. This should not convert you, however, to docile humility, breast-beating and apologetic self-accusation.

Don't Say: "You're Out Of Tune!"

Good players are constantly trying to play in tune. Good intonation is not an absolute thing, but a matter of compromise. There have been many instances of top musicians disagreeing on the exact pitch of a given note. It is not enough for the conductor to tell the players to fix it. The conductor is the "fixer," and is responsible for tuning of such things as woodwind chords or brass chorales by asking the players to conform to his concept of acceptable intonation.

Don't Be Misled by Ovations

It is possible to be deceived by premature success. Critics and audiences are fickle. A performer can be a hero one day and a bum the next as far as the public is concerned.

Don't Take Solo Bows

If your achievements are legitimate and honest, you will not lack approval, especially with the conductor's image in today's concert world. However, with rare exceptions, the stick makes no sound, the musicians make the sound. To share with them the recognition for your labors will assure their good will and enthusiasm. The solo bow will do the opposite; besides, the orchestra may even be impressed enough to stay seated and give you a hand all on their own.

Don't Use Clip-On Ties

If you are a good conductor, you'll get excited by the music and you may move a lot. Clip-on ties fall off. There is nothing more comical, pathetic and helpless than an un-tied conductor.

Don't Conduct Music You Don't Believe In

For political reasons and other strategic considerations, you will not escape the fate of having to perform certain pieces against your will. However, by and large, you won't be able to make someone believe in something unless you do.

The Fifth Commandment

In addition to honoring your father and mother, honor the composer. Orchestra members lose respect when you say, "Don't play too loud, you're spoiling *my* diminuendo!" But it isn't *your* diminuendo, it's the composer's.

Don't Think Conducting Is Easy

...nor playing easier than conducting.

Do's

Do Get to Know the Orchestra

This poses a serious problem, since at the present time few conductors are able to spend more than a few days with an orchestra. They will frequently step off a jet, have a few rehearsals and concerts and embark for their next engagement in some other part of the world. It is questionable whether music making of significance can ever be achieved by such a method, which corresponds to a parent bringing up a child by monthly visits.

Do Know How to Rehearse

To avoid tedium and routine, some of which is unavoidable, treat every composition as if it were new, in rehearsal as well as in concert. Each rehearsal is a new performance, just as each concert is a rehearsal for the next performance. This means constant re-study of even the most familiar score. New compositions should be sight-read and checked for mistakes well enough in advance. This will also give the player an idea of which passages need individual practice.

Rehearsing seems to divide itself into two opposing methods, rather than a combination of both. It's either (1) play through the work with no attention to detail except for an occasional outcry of delight or disgust or (2) the drudgery of minute assembling of each part. In such a case, you ask the piccolo, double bass and 4th horn to play the few measures they have in common, and after that the violins and harp several other such measures. While all this goes on, the orchestra gets bored and restless, talks too much and waits for the rehearsal to end. The concert then provides the first opportunity to put the whole thing together. It's like repairing a watch and returning it to the customer before winding it to check whether or not it is actually running. Only by experience is it possible for the conductor who has never played in an orchestra, or possibly never played an instrument at all, to learn what needs rehearsing and what doesn't. Therefore, there is no better training for the conductor than to play some instrument in the orchestra. Many fine conductors begin as instrumentalists.

Traditionally, and mostly for good reasons, there are sections in string parts which are meant to be "faked," usually for some coloristic purpose. It is important to know where these are. It wastes time and causes unnecessary antagonism to demand that these be played letter perfect. Serious players will try to play them anyway because they feel unclean having to fake. On the other hand, it demoralizes a player when no attempt is made to rehearse a difficult but playable technical passage. I know of one conscientious musician who, after 2½ hours of sloppy rehearsal, said: "I'm going home to play a Bach chorale and take a shower!"

Do Say "We" Instead of "I"

It is important for the musicians to be made to feel that they are part of a common endeavor. Since it is inevitable that a good conductor will impose his musical ideas on the orchestra and thereby reduce their individuality as performers (if not completely erase it), the only choice left to the conductor is to convince the musicians that he shares with them the aim of putting their combined efforts at the service of the composition. If the conductor can earn this degree of respect for his integrity, he might hope to successfully dominate 100 egos confronting and constantly challenging him.

Do Demand Perfection

Demand perfection, because you won't get it. First of all, because it doesn't exist. Secondly, because the benefit of personal recognition to the player, with the

exception of a few solo players, is not worth the sacrifice and effort which perfection demands. However without the specific insistence that at least an attempt at perfection be made, mediocrity will be the end result. Don't demand unreasonably or capriciously, and be sure to set a fitting example by demanding equally much of yourself. Should the quest for perfection be strictly technical, guard against defeating your efforts by creating undue nervous tension or emotionless, mechanical, chrome-plated replicas of notes. To perfect perfection, make it unnoticeable.

Do Know Your Transpositions

If the orchestra ever finds out that you don't (and some conductors go for years without being found out), you've had it.

Do Know How to Mark Parts

One of the most laborious but necessary preparations for a good performance is a well-marked and legible part. Be sure all the parts have the same letters or numbers, because much valuable time is lost in confusion if they don't. More often than not, markings on Xerox copies of handwritten manuscripts are not legible. This refers especially to bowings, since no person other than a string player could possibly understand how many problems, frustrations, fights and misunderstandings can result from the primitive choice of either going upbow or downbow. Should you not be a string player, let your concertmaster initiate you into the fraternity of bowing specialists. You won't go wrong by asking your string players to make their bowings fit the music, instead of the other way around.

Do Know How to "Do Something"

Many times the score says nothing — no crescendo, no diminuendo, no forte, no piano. Just little naked black notes. However, just because it says nothing, doesn't mean you do nothing. The magic seems to lie in not doing too little or too much. If you do nothing except be a human metronome, the musicians will also turn into metronomes (so will the audience). If you turn into a choreographer, you don't provide the technical guidance needed by the players. Finding a meaningful balance between inspiration and perspiration, between being a traffic cop and a poet, a scholar and an exhibitionist, a preacher and a disciple, produces a good conductor.

Do Know How to Play the Piano

The most obvious and practical reason for this is the need for preparatory piano rehearsals with soloists. You will probably want to coach them — and come to an agreement with them *before* rehearsing with the full orchestra. The experience of playing piano or celeste in the orchestra is indispensable; there you can observe other conductors and get the feel for being a player. You will learn about how other instruments are played, what the problems are and how to solve them. You will learn that players who have long rests sometimes read magazines or even listen to a transistor radio if their favorite ball club is playing a World Series game. You will also learn that most inside chair string players are tempted to play to the last note on each page, instead of turning in time for the outside player to see the top of the next page.

As a pianist you can also play chamber music and accompany others, all of which teaches you how to follow and adjust. Strangely enough, if you are going to be the authoritative leader, one of the best things to know is when to do nothing and follow the orchestra. There are moments when doing nothing is more profitable. And above all, as a pianist you can play the entire literature and acquire a well-rounded musical outlook.

Do Know How to Ignore the Recording

Only the strongest can resist the temptation to listen to conductor X's recording to either confirm, imitate or reject. Orchestra members suspect that some conductors are walking around the living room learning next week's program "by proxy" and on some occasions, conductors have been caught in their studios in the middle of an illegitimate relationship with the record player. Records, in a sense, are a falsehood. They have been spliced together from little crumbs of "good takes" while the "bad takes" end up in the garbage can. One movement might have been recorded Friday and one on Saturday. A couple of out-of-tune notes might have been mysteriously replaced by correct ones, weeks later by recording editors. Even the "authentic" recording with the composer himself conducting, may have to be taken with a grain of salt, because he may have been sick, aging, or performing under less than optimum conditions over which he had no control. Your live performance will have no such protection and will have to be given without the aid of electronic flattery. So back to the printed score!

Do Know Languages

There are instructions to be read in foreign languages and if you can't understand them, you're licked. What is worse is not being able to pronounce them properly. The musicians are lying in wait to prove that you really aren't superior to them and they won't miss an opportunity to catch your slightest weakness. Don't say Tschaikowsky (as in "cow") or try to fake a Russian accent, which might prove that you are as phony as the orchestra thinks you are.

Do Beware of the Strauss Waltz

The unrehearsed Strauss Waltz has been the cause for many a catastrophe. The repeats and da capos are confusing, and the parts are traditionally a mess, because each conductor uses different repeats. Just because you gave a triumphant performance of the Beethoven 9th does not guarantee that in a Strauss Waltz one part of the orchestra won't still be playing after-beats, while the other half is on the introduction to the next waltz — unless you rehearse it as seriously as the Beethoven 9th.

Do Know That an Orchestra Is Not a Chorus

Choral conductors, either by accident or design, are a different breed. The problem could be solved by their awareness of this fact. They have been trained to conduct words and phrases, all of which is most natural, musical and artistic. However, orchestral music is written only in measures with bar lines that impose symmetrical conducting patterns, often in the manner of a Prussian Army formation. The musicians want to know what bar they are in (not knowing drives them to drink) and only a clear beat keeps a player in the musical bar and out of the neighborhood bar. If you are a choral conductor working with an orchestra and you can take time off from singing the words with the chorus, remember the down beat has also an upbeat.

Do Know How to Treat Musicians

Within each orchestral musician is buried a conductor, frustrated soloist or both. The antagonism they feel for the conductor is traditional, implacable and part of the routine. To a few musicians, the check will be more important than the music, but that doesn't mean they would quit music for more money. It only means their enthusiasm for music needs to be rekindled by an inspiring conductor, a demanding one, or preferably by a combination of both. The conductor can learn from the players and, if he is tactful and shrewd, it can be done in such a way that the newly-acquired information can be presented by the conductor as if it were his own. How to make the player feel important without flattery is an art in itself, and this particular artform is still in its infancy. ∎

Rehearsing for a Musical Life

by Frank Battisti

Rehearsals are where teachers do a lot of teaching and students a lot of learning about music. It is the heart of the instrumental curriculum in many public school programs and the place students learn to create, share, and develop music appreciation. Teacher preparation for rehearsals is important, and the first step is formulating long-range musical objectives:

Musical skills and knowledge. Encourage each student to develop the self-discipline of daily practice, which should include work on private-lesson material and the school ensemble music. The goals should be improved tone, technical skills, and dynamic/expressive range. Provide students with recommended lists of recorded artists and ensembles and a calendar of live music performances. Listening to music and attending live performances are very important components in a student's music education. In this way the student's individual and ensemble performance standards will be expanded and their knowledge of literature increased.

Collaborative skills. The teacher should guide students in selecting ensemble activities and encourage participation in large and chamber ensembles as well as solo performances. Chamber music offers the most effective and efficient way to develop important ensemble skills that will also improve the student's performance in large ensembles. Chamber music also exposes students to repertoire they can pursue throughout their lives.

Musical values and musical appreciation. It is important for teachers to monitor what music students listen to. An individual reveals his values through the things he buys and the

Frank Battisti is conductor of the Wind Ensemble at the New England Conservatory in Boston, Massachusetts. A recognized authority on wind literature, he has conducted wind ensembles and bands for over 30 years.

activities he chooses on his own. If teachers hope to influence and expand these values it is important to understand students' current musical tastes. Through lessons and rehearsals directors can influence these; it is also important for students to attend performances by good instrumentalists and ensembles. Local concerts may provide opportunities for this, otherwise directors should arrange bus transportation to out-of-town events. By hearing great music performed by experts, students will develop good musical values.

Discuss with students the music rehearsed or listened to; explain your musical values and challenge students to consider theirs.

Creative potential. Create opportunities for students to express themselves as soloists with large ensembles as well as in chamber groups or in solo performances. Help them understand that music offers them an opportunity to express and share creativeness with

others. Encourage students to develop the ability to improvise and compose music.

Response to sound and gestures. In music we communicate with sound and gestures; teach students to listen, look, and respond. They should always listen to the sounds created around them and respond to these. Explain that conductors communicate through gestures and how important it is that they watch for these special communications and respond in the complex interactions involved in music making.

Preparation of music and public performances. Directors can share their music values and performance standards and imbue students with a desire for excellence through responsible preparation for performances. By showing interest and respect for each composer and composition, conductors will become models for students. Try to make every composition come alive musically and discuss with stu-

dents the character of a work. Motivate them to strive for tonal beauty, technical clarity, and proper style in playing solos and ensemble music. By projecting dedication as a musician and person, a director can become a living example of musical values and habits.

In selecting music to use with the ensemble directors should seek repertoire that is interesting and imaginative in developing the musical elements of melody, harmony, texture, rhythm, and form. The music should provide opportunities for teaching musical concepts about form and construction and help students to grow technically. Each part should be as interesting as possible, and students like pieces in which everyone is part of the action with tubas playing melodies as well as bass lines, and horns playing more than off-beats.

Select music that fits the instrumentation of the ensemble, but if a wonderful piece calls for several instruments that are missing, directors might still be able to perform the piece with reasonable substitutions. Make sure this is done in a way that preserves the musical integrity of the piece. I can remember performing parts of the Mozart *Serenade No. 10 K. 361* with my high school students using 3 horns and 1 euphonium instead of the 4 horns called for in the score. I told the euphonium player to sound like a 4th horn, and it sounded great.

The technical and musical challenges of the music should be compatible with the skills of the ensemble. Music entailing months of drill should be passed over in favor of literature that allows students to approach the expressive character and nature of the music. Literature with excessive technical levels denies students the opportunity to reach this expressive level of music making.

Select music with a variety of styles, from contemporary, avant garde, Renaissance, Baroque, Classical, Romantic, popular, and jazz. This makes it possible to teach history, various musical styles, and performance practices. Include music with textures ranging from delicately scored passages for soloists and small groups to fully scored compositions for the entire ensemble.

Another important consideration in selecting music is whether it is appropriate for the occasion. For example, the Wagner *Trauersinfonie* might not be appropriate for a Fourth of July concert but it could be suitable for a concert of remembrance on Veteran's Day.

Before any rehearsals the conductor should thoroughly study the score and arrive at interpretations. In studying a score the conductor should be able to hear all parts at least individually, perhaps collectively. A complete knowledge of all musical elements in the score and a clear concept of the form and shape of the work are necessary for an effective and efficient rehearsal.

It is important to establish a procedure before giving the first beat so students will know what they are expected to do prior to the sounding of the first note in rehearsal. This should include specific information on how they should warm up, and the importance of long tones and slow scales while concentrating on good tone production and intonation. With an electronic tuner each student can complete preliminary tuning before sitting down for the rehearsal.

Post the sequence of works for the next several rehearsals for students to see as they enter the rehearsal room, together with any notices and announcements. These will help rehearsals operate smoothly and save time.

Chairs and stands should be arranged before students arrive, and percussion and other large equipment, reeds, mutes, and pencils should be in place.

Assemble a complete set of parts in folders with individual names on them so each student has a set of parts to mark and practice.

The rehearsal room should be interesting; post pictures of students and the ensemble in action, and enlist a student not in the ensemble to take photographs during rehearsals and concerts. Students love to see pictures of themselves.

The director has the dual responsibilities of teaching (sometimes) and conducting (sometimes). Some things one might do as a teacher (counting out loud or tapping beats on a music stand) should be avoided by conductors. Students in a large ensemble should be lead by a conductor, not a teacher. Conductors should communicate and provoke musical response by means of gestures, not speech. To keep the two roles separate in the students' eyes, operate as a teacher from a position off the podium. Move to the podium when conducting.

Formulate specific goals before beginning rehearsal. A clear idea of what is to be accomplished keeps the rehearsal focused. Set realistic goals and don't attempt to accomplish more than can be done well in the amount of time available. The rehearsal plan should have a good balance between tension and relaxation by using music of contrasting styles: lyrical vs. high energy, soft vs. loud, slow vs. fast music. Introduce new works that build on what has been studied, rehearsed, and performed, but introduce works that expand students' musical knowledge and skills.

Be yourself and develop a personal rehearsal style. Create a friendly, comfortable environment in which students feel encouraged to participate and express themselves as individuals. Be a positive, sensitive, and committed leader.

Give clear, focused instructions during rehearsals and always look at students when conducting or giving instructions. Insist that students bring a pencil to rehearsals to mark parts when something is changed, added, or emphasized.

Encourage students to practice their parts at home by emphasizing that if everyone comes prepared each day, the rehearsal room will not become a drill shed. Establish that the rehearsal room is a place where individuals share the excitement of creating music. Try to provoke students into commitment by making demands that are significant enough to warrant commitment.

Display joy when exciting things happen and congratulate students when they do something well, either individually or collectively. Encourage students to support each other and acknowledge good playing.

Rehearsals should begin with a warm-up procedure, perhaps using scales and chorales to get students listening. I ask students to sing and play during the warm-up session and begin by solfeging scales, then having students sing them, and finally play the material on their instruments. During the course of the year, I expand their knowledge and ability to solfege music with larger intervals. The second part of the warm-up is spent singing and playing chorales, with students striving for good tone quality, intonation, and balance.

The warm-up segment is a wonderful opportunity to teach basic musicianship skills and music theory, stressing ear training and listening. Give no downbeat until every eye is on the conductor, and demand this concentration throughout. Vary the material used in the warm-ups so students remain alert.

Establish general rules for listening. Teach students to listen from back to front, from tubas in the back to the piccolo in the front, and from bottom to top, tuning notes in a vertical structure from the lowest root in the chord.

Remind the students to achieve balance by listening to others. Good balance is impossible without listening to others in the ensemble. Explain how dynamics are determined by the smallest voice in the texture, not the loudest. A tuba playing with a flute should get down to the flute dynamic level. Brass should play with woodwinds at the woodwind's dynamic level.

A conductor sets the tempo but it is up to the students to maintain it. This is possible only if everyone feels a strong inner pulse. Allow the ensemble to play without a conductor so it is necessary for every student to feel the pulse and increase the level of listening. Marches are good for developing an inner feeling of pulse and subdivision. These skills are essential for developing good rhythm and movement.

Instead of always using rehearsal numbers or letters, refer to a specific section within the form of the piece, as by starting at "the beginning of the Trio" instead of "number 15" or "the recapitulation of the first theme played by the clarinets" instead of "number 65." This takes more time but the long-term rewards are great as students will gradually expand their understanding of musical forms.

Make sure that students understand all terms and symbols found in the music they rehearse by using correct musical vocabulary. Encourage proper musical speech in the rehearsal room in the same way a chemistry teacher encourages scientific terms in a chemistry class.

During rehearsals invite individuals to play passages in a manner that expresses how they feel about the music. Take time to allow students to discover that arriving at ensemble expression is a give and take process of sharing and caring.

When students know something about the composer and the piece be-ing rehearsed, the experience is richer and more meaningful. Either the teacher can provide this background or students can research and report back about the composer and music, citing other works by the composer. Facilities might be set up in the school or department library for the purposes of expanding students' musical horizons.

If reading new music is a regular part of your rehearsal plan, try reading music chronologically to teach music history. I have created an art gallery in the music department for prints of paintings that correspond stylistically with the music rehearsed. When we read Norman Dello Joio's *Scenes from the Louvre*, I displayed prints of paintings from the Louvre.

Don't waste rehearsal time on sections that involve only a few people, but instead assign one student to schedule and lead a rehearsal for those involved. This gives students a sense of contributing to the improvement and success of the group. If there are strong section leaders, allow them to conduct sectional rehearsals. This allows still more students to contribute to the ensemble's progress and development.

Conductors who thoroughly understand a score can efficiently prepare for a concert. With efficient rehearsals, there should be time for other important activities during the rehearsal period, such as student recitals of solo and chamber music literature. This is a wonderful complement to the large ensemble experience.

Recording rehearsals on audio and video tape is a valuable aid to both conductors and students in observing and evaluating their techniques, including teaching procedures, conducting techniques, and verbal instructions. Verify that you do not talk or look at the score too much — eyes should be on the students. Your rehearsal procedure should include everyone in the rehearsal activity; don't neglect any individual or section. Good pacing of the rehearsal is important to maintain student interest and concentration. The tape allows a conductor to evaluate listening skills during the rehearsal. Was every problem identified or did some bad intonation or incorrectly played rhythm escape detection? Finally, determine if all rehearsal goals were achieved.

If rehearsal tapes are available to students they can also evaluate what happened, especially if you assist them in learning what to listen and look for in a rehearsal. The tapes should make students more aware of what they are doing and clarify what is needed to improve their performance level. Try to evaluate rehearsal tapes immediately so changes can be initiated to improve the next rehearsal.

Another consideration is striking a balance between rehearsal time and the number of public performances for the ensemble. With too many concerts there is inadequate time to explore other excellent compositions and do a thorough job of teaching. Try to arrive at a concert calendar that allows sufficient time to explore the music and prepare for excellent performances.

Composing music can be an exciting experience for students. Inaugurate a project in creativity that encourages them to compose a work for their instrument, perhaps beginning with something in the style of one piece they have studied. Allow time in rehearsals to play and evaluate these compositions and to help students improve their skills. Through this experience some students will develop a drive to study harmony and orchestration.

This creative activity can be complemented by commissioning a composer to write a piece for the ensemble. It is probably best to commission someone familiar to you or the school or to ask for recommendations from respected musicians. Having a composer write a piece for a group of students is an exciting event for which students will work enthusiastically to prepare for the premiere. Be sure to bring the composer to your school for the week before the premiere to participate in the final preparations and the concerts.

Rehearsals that stimulate students through studying and performing great literature develops their potential to appreciate and create good music. The good musical values that are derived from this kind of music education will enhance the quality of life for every student. ☐

Band Conducting as a Profession

H. Robert Reynolds

What distinguishes the activity of the conductor from that of all other musicians? That he does not play himself, but guides and influences the playing of others. It is not before he enters on the professional phase of his vocation that he can really come to know the handling of his instrument, the orchestra[1].

This instinctive faculty for immediately transmitting one's own musical impulses to the orchestra is the sign of true talent for conducting.[2] — *Bruno Walter*

We prepare ourselves to be conductors through formal training at colleges, universities, and conservatories in the areas of music history, music theory, counterpoint, composition, and orchestration. We learn our craft by studying a number of instruments in order to more fully understand the complete scope of our profession. We also acquire skills in non-verbal communication and score reading through courses in the art of conducting. Prior to this comprehensive study of music, each potential band conductor should have achieved some degree of competence on at least one wind or percussion instrument. The importance of this competence as a performer cannot be underestimated; a conductor must develop his own musical sensitivity as a participant before he can hope to inspire and guide others in making music. This is not to say that all musically sensitive performers are capable of being fine conductors — it is only to suggest that few musically sensitive conductors have become so without first having experienced the role of the musically sensitive performer. Furthermore, it is my personal conviction that a conductor should make every effort to continue performing on his instrument — not only to set an example for his students, but to better understand the performers in his ensembles.

Appreciation of music of all mediums is an important characteristic of the *musical* band conductor. Such a conductor studies not only the great wind masterpieces, but also constantly reacquaints himself with the great symphonies and string quartets, as well as the numerous masterpieces in all other areas of music. The recent compositions of Elliott Carter, Gunther Schuller, or Pierre Boulez are of just as much interest to him as the latest work from the pen of Karel Husa. He will seek out opportunities to hear chamber music, new music ensembles, and the finest symphony orchestras. Such a conductor, for example, may decide to take time out from the many activities of the Mid-West Band and Orchestra Clinic in Chicago each December to walk a few blocks to hear the Chicago Symphony perform, and he will recognize that this experience might well be more valuable to his growth as a band conductor than any of the scheduled activities of the clinic.

Growth is perhaps the most important element in the musicianship of a successful band conductor. The music world is changing at such a rapid rate that constant study, exploration, and open-mindedness are necessary if one is not to fall hopelessly behind. The ability to grow and to expand our range of knowledge is particularly important to those of us associated with the wind band for we have a unique place in the music of the future. We must be alert and able to respond to the new opportunities presented to us, or we will find that once again the world of music has by-passed our medium.

Concept of the Score

The question is often asked, "How do you study a score?" There is no system which applies to all scores and all conductors. One approaches a new score as one approaches a crossword puzzle — by trying to discover several key ideas that will lead to a complete understanding of the work. Each composition is a new experience and presents a challenge to the conductor. And it is here that the conductor calls upon his study of theory, counterpoint, form, history and other aspects of his formal and informal training. Naturally, knowledge of the composer's complete works, styles, and biography is of vital importance as are specific facts regarding the piece under study and its relation to the other works by the composer.

Implicit in "knowledge of the score" is the conductor's personal concept of all details such as balance, weight, emphasis, and phrasing which make one conductor's interpretation different from that of another. Most composers expect the conductor to use his own musical judgement to interpret the idea of the composition. As an example, several years ago I was rehearsing *Emblems* by Aaron Copland while the composer himself was present. When I looked through the score in my study, I felt that the tempo marked in one section was too fast. During the rehearsal of this section, I turned to Mr. Copland to ask if the section was too slow for his liking. He commented that he would have conducted it faster, but that it was musical and should not be changed to the faster tempo indicated. I offered to change the tempo to suit him, but he insisted that it be an interpretation which I felt best for his piece. Composers, with the exception of Stravinsky and a few others, expect the conductor to bring his own interpretation to the work, as long as it is consistent with stylistic traditions of the per-

H. Robert Reynolds is the Director of the Band Department at the University of Wisconsin. He also remains active as a French horn player and is in constant demand as a clinician.

iod and other guidelines already mentioned.

If the conductor has studied the composition in a detailed manner, he will be more efficient in rehearsal. In order to discover problems quickly and solve them rapidly, he must be familiar with a work in all of its details. If he is not so prepared, the conductor will be forced to establish balance and interpretation on the basis of spontaneous, casual adjustments (and this is the mark of a conductor who learns the composition as he rehearses it). Eugen Jochum, a well-known European conductor, states this idea very well.

> His [the conductor's] own inner analysis of the composition, the identification with the will of the composer, precedes his work with the orchestra. It would be too late to come to his conception of the piece when working with the orchestra, although certain aspects can still be perfected by actually hearing the work.[3]

There is no fixed formula for successful score study. Each conductor must find his own technique. When I asked Frederick Fennell how he studies a score his answer was, "I just live with it." One never reaches the end in the study of a score. It is a constant process involving the combination of one's total knowledge of music with an understanding of the myriad of details which make up a specific work — and all of this before the first rehearsal takes place!

Baton Technique

Motion is the language of conducting; through motion the conductor displays his inner-most sensitivity toward the music as a physically sounding medium. The conductor is constantly either sensitizing the musicians to his visual signs — because they are effective means of communication — or desensitizing the musicians to these signs because they tend to be monotonous or awkward and convey only the most elementary musical aspects of pulse, volume, and general style.

A common problem to many band conductors is the "visual screen." A conductor sets up a barrier to communication by using large and repetitious motions. In order for the conductor to get the attention of the performers, he must somehow break through this "visual screen" of non-communicative motions. Unfortunately, some conductors attempt to do this by using even larger motions than before, creating an even greater barrier — and the cycle continues.

We have all observed a large number of band conductors whose conducting technique could best be described as "unrefined." These conductors seem to feel that they must constantly supply energy (through frantic, non-stop arm-waving) to the music-making machine. The fact is, however, that even a moderately good ensemble is capable of a good deal of independence. That is, once a certain tempo, volume or style is established, a group will usually maintain it. Once the ensemble has established a *forte* volume, it is unnecessary for the conductor to constantly conduct *forte* — although an occasional reminder is helpful. The same is true of general style and pulse. After the speed of a piece with a strong steady pulse is set, the conductor is free to help in other more subtle areas of interpretation.

It is important to understand when and what *not* to conduct. It is a well-known fact that most inexperienced conductors tend to over-conduct, thus limiting their effectiveness by setting up the visual screen mentioned earlier. To overcome this habit, the conductor must consciously eliminate the sameness of beat and energy of motion. Appropriate and varied conducting gestures will command the attention and response of the players; unnecessary or monotonous ones will cease to have any effect at all.

Once the conductor has eliminated the visual screen and learned to communicate visually, he must, of course, have something to say. Performers look for and receive from a conductor's motions not only when, how loud and how fast to play, but an infinite variety of subtle messages on all aspects of the music. In order to communicate these subtleties the conductor must feel the music as physical texture and describe it visually to the players. To a sensitive conductor, music is not only an aural art but a physical art as well. For example, accents in the music of Haydn, Bee-thoven, Brahms, Wagner, and Stravinsky not only *sound* different but *feel* different. The ability to respond physically to music is essential if a conductor is to convey, through outward motions, his understanding and interpretation. He must *feel* the power of the final movement of *Symphony in B♭* by Hindemith or the fragile texture of the second movement of the *Sinfonietta* by Ingolf Dahl. His sensitivity must be refined beyond whole movements or compositions to include individual phrases, fragments and even isolated sounds. It is this ability to understand and communicate the physical element of music that too often is missing from an otherwise technically superb conductor.

Personal Characteristics

Perhaps the most elusive aspect of conducting is the psychological impact of the personality. This aspect was described by Elizabeth Green in her excellent book, *The Modern Conductor*, as "impulse of will."[4] It is that intangible quality which is so essential to the successful conductor. William Steinberg, well-known music director of the Pittsburgh Symphony says, "The only factor that counts is the power of his [the conductor's] personality."[5] The conductor must certainly have confidence, poise, enthusiasm, and eye contact. It is also imperative for him to understand group psychology, motivation techniques, and to display musical sensitivity. "He who cannot deal with people or exert his influence on them is not fully qualified for this profession."[6]

Bruno Walter was not only one of the great conductors, but he was also very articulate when writing about his profession. His personal philosophy is one which has guided me for some time. He expresses this philosophy so well in these words:

> I realized that I was certainly not cut out to be a ruler or despot, but rather to be an educator who, as we know, methodically uses his empathy with others for gaining influence over them. My task was now to enforce the powerful, nay, irresistible demands of my musical personality by means of that empathy; to uphold my own ideals uncompromisingly without violation of other people's.... In general it can be

said that a violent manner of deal-ing with people will either be de-feated by their resistance or result in their intimidation. On the other hand, the milder methods of psy-chological empathy, persuasion, and moral intermediation will have an encouraging and productive effect.[7]

When a well educated conductor who has prepared the score, has the ability to communicate visu-ally, and has personal qualities en-abling him to lead others stands before his ensemble — whether or-chestra or band — he has an awe-some responsibility. He has the re-sponsibility to make music. Serge Koussevitzky, conductor of the Bos-ton Symphony orchestra from 1924 to 1949, comments on precisely this point:

Nowadays we can often hear "au-thorities" exclaim, in reviewing a performance: "Let the music speak for itself!" The danger of this maxim lies in its paving the way for medi-ocrities who simply play a piece off accurately and then maintain that he "let the music speak for itself." Such a statement is not right, in any event, because a talented artist ren-ders a work as he conceives it, ac-cording to his own temperament and insight, no matter how painstakingly he follows the score markings. And the deeper the interpreter's in-sight, the greater and more vital the performance.[8]

This responsibility which Kousse-vitzky understood so well may seem obvious, but it is often the greatest weakness of band conductors. How often it is in our band world that the conductor uses his abilities only to put the elements of music in or-der. Tone quality, intonation, pre-cision, correct notes, balance, dy-namic and articulation markings are all important and must receive sufficient attention if they are not to detract from the music making process, but we must never lose sight of the larger purpose of our role as conductors — that of inter-preters. And as interpreters we must constantly call upon our knowledge, training, and unique artistic sensitivity to enable us to fulfill this most challenging role. Viewed in this light, the profession of band conducting assumes a depth and potential of exciting proportions. ∎

1. Bruno Walter, *Of Music and Music Mak-ing* (New York: Norton, 1961), p. 83.
2. *Ibid.*, p. 112.
3. Carl Bamberger (ed.), *The Conductor's Art* (New York: McGraw-Hill, 1965), pp. 258-259.
4. Elizabeth A.H. Green, *The Modern Con-ductor* (Englewood Cliffs, NJ: Prentice Hall, 1961), p. 60.
5. Bamberger, p. 306.
6. Bruno Walter, p. 111.
7. *Ibid.*, p. 120.
8. Bamberger, p. 144.

September, 1979

Conductor As Marksman

Donn Laurence Mills

Some conductors will tell you that only the composer's marks should appear on scores and parts, and that anything else is graffiti. Others mark scores and parts me-ticulously, covering pages with cryp-tic diagrams and poetic descriptions. Obviously professional musicians know from experience how to play characteristic styles and patterns and may even resent being told what to do. Students, however, need more guidance; and well-marked parts are welcome. Of course the conductor's own study habits bene-fit from marking student parts. By going over what the players see, a conductor can anticipate difficulties and plan more efficient rehearsals.

In the case of pit work markings are crucial as cuts, repeats, cues, fermatas, transpositions, sudden tempo changes, and special effects are normal occurrences. But notes in the score concerning balance and interpretation ("go," "move," "bring out") are important to the conduc-tor's concept of the music and do more harm than good if written into the parts. There they destroy the spontaneity and the effects of good stick technique.

Of course there's always the possi-bility that a conductor may change his mind about interpretation, or the performance situation may dic-tate something different from the conductor's original intent. Flexi-bility is important, but players may get the idea that the conductor has exercised poor judgment and now must waste valuable rehearsal time correcting his own mistakes. Respect fades. A conductor must be sure of his decisions before passing out the music. Trial and error methods have no place in the conductor's craft. For the player a rehearsal is a reve-lation; for the conductor it's a con-firmation.

A few years ago at a conductor's seminar sponsored by the American Symphony Orchestra League and the Cincinnati Symphony, an am-bitious participant came armed with a set of parts that were loaded with detailed instructions. Using colored pencils and magic markers, he had interpreted just about every note and rest in the score, leaving nothing to chance. As he stood before the orchestra, he was like Zeus looking down from Mt. Olympus. The or-chestra need only follow his written commands and the result would be dazzling perfection.

This conductor was a pianist whose knowledge of orchestral in-struments came from basic college instrumental courses and fingering

Don Laurence Mills is the NSOA con-tributing editor. He holds music de-grees from Northwestern University and Eastman School of Music. A conductor and music educator, he is also the American educational director for the Yamaha Music Foundation of Tokyo.

charts. His bowings were theoretically possible but unstylistic, his dynamics based on stereo recordings made in a studio with eight microphones and a mixer. His phrasing was strangely mannered, and there were stern admonitions to "Look up," "Be careful here," and "Give it all you've got" (which the brass did with obvious relish). He instructed the violins to play *spiccato* at the frog and the woodwinds to triple-tongue a figure which could easily have been single-tongued.

As you might guess, the orchestra revolted, compelling him, out of self-defense, to demand that his markings be obeyed. The result was a musical and personal disaster. Max Rudolf (Cincinnati's conductor at the time), wonderful mentor that he is, counseled the young conductor afterwards, impressing him with the need for both wisdom and humility. Actually he was a talented musician and a reasonably skillful conductor. Had he relied on his stick technique and essential markings, the players would have gladly given him what he wanted.

This man persisted in learning how to conduct and is today leading a major orchestra in the southwest. His interpretations are artistic and he knows what he wants. I've been told by members of his orchestra that he now has section leaders mark the parts. They listen to what he wants, make practical suggestions, and then translate the ideas into messages the players can understand. This conductor would probably fail as a high school director because he doesn't know instrumental techniques, but with the pros he succeeds because they know the techniques and he has learned to respect that. He still doesn't know flute fingerings or horn embouchure problems in the low register or string-crossing requirements (although he's learned a thing or two over the years), but he knows music, and his players do the rest.

I recently wrote to the principal players of 25 major orchestras to discover what professional musicians think about playing from conductor's markings. Different instrumental points of view emerged, but there was remarkable agreement. To the question, do you like to work from a part that's been previously marked in detail by a conductor, 18 said "yes," 2 "no," and 5 said

that it depended on their respect for the conductor as a musician. They said detailed markings insulted their musicianship and intelligence.

When I asked if they found conductor's marks misleading or uncharacteristic the emphatic answer was yes; musical taste and instrumental understanding were the chief issues. Comments were added that it was particularly irksome when conductors ignored their own markings.

Only one person from the brass section said yes to wanting to do all the markings as the section leader. Articulation and dynamics was the unanimous answer given for what markings were appreciated the most. And, when I asked what markings they found annoying, players mentioned duplications (sfz combined with an accent, for example), arbitrary fingerings, words of encouragement, "anything in ink," circling or underlining, unstylistic bowings. Professionals seem to want clarification from the conductor's pencil, not lessons.

Parts have personal significance to a musician. He knows every smudge, wrinkle, and dot; and he relates the sounds he hears with every cue, rest, or sustained note on the page. He likes to make his own marks, marks meaningful to him. If we over-mark we rob him of his contribution and invite passivity.

In the case of school orchestras, markings are mostly reminders and reinforcements of instructions that will be made from the podium. Everything must be explained and demonstrated to students while they're learning the tricks of the trade, and it's agonizing to repeat instructions over and over because players are careless or don't remember. Part of our job as teachers is to train students in the fine art of using a pencil. Microscopic editing of parts by the conductor can deprive students of an opportunity to actively participate in the rehearsal process. We should mark essential things, of course, but leave some things for the player to add.

What a pleasure to go through a clean, new set of parts. Most of us use rental or library parts, however, and it's not unusual to find that the previous users have neglected to erase their markings. I'm sure you've seen, as I have, violin parts with up-

bows, down-bows, dots, slurs, accents, instructions in various colors in both pencil and ink crossed-out, written-in, changed, and changed back again (with some droll comments from the part's previous users) all layered on top of one another until the original notation is unreadable. The confusion of contradictory markings can reduce rehearsals to frustrating, boring question and answer periods as musicians and conductor struggle to unscramble the mess. Every player deserves a part he can read, and every conductor deserves to be free of unnecessary aggravations. The job of marking and erasing can be given to librarians, special people

---

Information that should be written in the player's part

- Added dynamics
- Articulation (staccato/legato)
- Accents
- Phrasing, breathing (uniformity)
- Cues, cuts, repeats, ritards, cessura, etc.
- Type of equipment (sticks, mutes)
- Tempo changes or unusual beat patterns
- Added lines for impossible page turns
- Re-orchestrations
- 𝄐 if something is tricky or dangerous
- Special effects (such as peculiar tone qualities)
- Unusual fingerings or position shifts (student or amateur orchestras only)
- Anything that clarifies or simplifies complicated or confusing notation

---

Information that should not be written in the player's part

- Obvious things which are there already (like "*divisi*" or accidentals)
- Cute comments or poetic imagery ("Like a puff of smoke")
- Uncharacteristic brainstorms the conductor may live to regret ("ffff," 𝄐, or odd phrasing, for example)
- Words of encouragement ("Don't give up," "Do your best," "Congratulations")
- Happy faces, cartoons or jokes (They won't be humorous the 2nd, 3rd, or 4th time around)
- Obscure directions ("Fat sound," "Easy," "With drive")

assigned to the job, an assistant conductor, or section leaders who transcribe such things as bowings and special notes from the conductor's score. Marking is a valuable experience for those advanced players who are bored or impatient with routine rehearsing, too, as it provides them with an opportunity to learn something about instrumentation, composition, and interpretation.

As we all know, eye communication between player and conductor is important. Even more important is the visual contact between a player and his music. If we give him the information he needs through both verbal and written instructions, he'll be able to give us his best effort. ∎

September, 1978

So You Want to Conduct

Frank B. Wickes

There is a tendency today among some of our college graduates in instrumental music education to want to pass from the ranks of experienced student performer directly to conductor without acknowledging the important intermediate step known as "teacher." Often their immediate goal is to conduct a group similar to the college band in which they participated. This pipedream is frequently nurtured by the presence of some outstanding high school programs nearby.

The college music graduate comes by this desire to conduct quite naturally. Many have apprenticed for the band world since the fifth grade or earlier; they have spent up to 12 years participating in bands, orchestras, and/or small ensembles at all levels. Often they have played before solo and ensemble judges for years and have performed for college applied music juries. While in college they get high grades in conducting courses and learn all of the band instruments well enough to meet the requirements for the degree. Frequently we hear them say, "I can't wait to get out and conduct."

Editor's Note: With this article, we welcome Frank B. Wickes to these pages as the contributing editor for the National Band Association column. Since 1973 he has been director of bands at the University of Florida in Gainesville. From 1967 to 1973 he directed the Fort Hunt High School Band in Fairfax County, Virginia. During this period the group performed at the Mid-West Band and Orchestra Clinic and won first place at the Virginia Beach Music Festival.

So they get their first job and in the early weeks they suddenly learn their greatest lesson. Whammo — their band breaks down trying to sightread. What's more, the tone of the band in immature, the pitch is poor, and the rhythm is wrong. Technique, precision, balance, blend, and proper articulation are completely lacking. Style is a word their students seem not to understand, not to mention expression or musicality.

To add to the musical chaos there are interruptions for P.A. announcements, discipline problems, equipment failures, improperly passed out music and absence from class. If they are high school directors they are "blessed" with the marching band responsibility. Suddenly reality sets in. They have to build their own kind of program from scratch. They must spend most of their rehearsal time teaching. Baton usage diminishes because they have to stop too often. These aspiring conductors begin to fall into a rut and join the vast throng in our profession known as "time beaters."

A closer analysis of the background of many young teachers will show that very little actual conducting is done by most teachers before their student internships. College conducting classes provide only a few opportunities. Prior to college, very few are tapped as student conductors or drum majors. Later, opportunities to conduct the college band are almost nonexistent. In short, the teachers' conducting experiences have not been nearly as significant as their performance experiences.

Is it possible to realize these early goals of wanting to be a conductor? My experience has been that it is possible if the young teacher will persevere, practice, and observe a few evaluative measures. Listed below are a few suggestions which can help young teachers realize some of their conducting aspirations:

• Review the five basic beat patterns which will suffice for much of the band repertoire: non-espressivo, legato-espressivo, full staccato, light staccato, and marcato. (These patterns are diagrammed very clearly in *The Grammar of Conducting*, by Max Rudolf, published by G. Schirmer). Unfortunately we see band directors who use a legato-espressivo/non-espressivo combination to the exclusion of all the others.

• Avoid constant two-arm conducting. In order to eliminate this habit, practice with the left hand resting on your belt buckle.

• Conduct all major dynamic contrasts with a distinct change in the size of the beat pattern. However, if you are a large or tall person, avoid excessively large gestures.

• If you use a baton, occasionally practice true espressivo passages without the baton. This helps the wrists to become more flexible.

• When standing on the podium, learn to stand still. Too many directors shift weight nervously, "pace" back and forth across the podium, lean forward too much, or bend the knees excessively. Also, keep your coat buttoned and make sure the podium is the proper size and height for your stature.

• As much as possible, keep your head out of the score while conducting. Get in the habit of memorizing marches as a first step to eliminating the need for a score. This will take some study as your concert selections become more complex, but it will allow you to focus your attention on the melodic line and will force you into eye contact with members of your ensemble.

• In rehearsals, periodically check yourself for correct tempos with a metronome. It is common tendency to speed up selections as the group becomes more proficient and especially when the adrenalin is flowing at concert time. Practice various conducting patterns using arbitrarily selected tempo markings. Teachers often know where 120 beats per minute (or 60) is, but they have difficulty with tempos like 48, 80, 96, or 152.

• Have access to a musical dictionary and study Italian, German, and French musical terms. Our solo literature is filled with them. Do this with articulation markings, tempo markings, and style indications. We tend to forget some of these over a period of time.

• Use the next to the last rehearsal before a concert to videotape your podium technique. This way small faults can be observed, corrected, and practiced with the group before the concert. Don't attempt this on the final rehearsal because a change of conducting technique at the concert itself may confuse immature performers.

Teaching is one of the most rewarding of professions. Band directors are always proud when admirers refer to them as good teachers. They are especially proud, however, when someone approaches them after a performance and says, "What a fine job of conducting." Work at it. It's well worth the effort. ■

The College Conductor

Henri Temianka

There exists a quaint notion among many people, including music students, that the art of conducting is primarily, and perhaps exclusively, a matter of "baton technique." If you have that mysterious technique, you are a conductor. If you don't, forget it! Of all the simplistic statements, this one takes the cake. The baton can only serve as a vehicle for what must first exist inside the mind and heart of the conductor, waiting to be expressed. Rhythm, tempo, style, dynamics, instrumental balance, the mood of a particular piece, intonation—these are only a few of the basic qualifications a conductor must satisfy before he can hope to use the baton effectively.

Given all these attributes, he must now learn to use his hands (regardless of whether he elects to use a baton or not), developing his own particular style of "body English." This body language is admittedly one of the great and fascinating mysteries of the art of conducting. One may be a great musician and never acquire that particular art at all. In the case of Wilhelm Furtwängler, the great German conductor, the language of his movements was so mysterious that only his intimates, those who had played under him for a considerable time, knew how to respond. Before the opening chord of a symphony, he would suddenly break out in convulsive motions that to the untrained eye suggested the possibility of a nervous disorder. These seemingly uncoordinated motions were followed by a fraction of a second of total silence and then, miraculously, without any apparent signal from the conductor, the 100-man orchestra sounded a chord of incredible unity and beauty. When Furtwängler guest-conducted elsewhere the magic didn't work; his style was too intensely personal.

As a college conductor, Furtwängler would have been a failure; also Toscanini. Sir Thomas Beecham, on the other hand, would have been a sensational success on the campus. Let me explain why. It stands to reason that working with college students requires some special qualifications. In the first place, most college students have limited ensemble experience, sometimes none. Whatever they play, they are playing for the first time, not the 500th time, as is the case with so many professional players. Extreme clarity in conveying one's intentions, therefore, becomes exceedingly important. In most instances the professional player can be relied upon to make his entrance without a cue from the conductor. Students are infinitely more dependent on cues. There is a considerable danger in this for the conductor, who can easily deteriorate into a cueing machine. A man can keep awfully busy just giving cues, and doing it, be lulled into a false sense of achievement. A conductor who gives all the cues may have little time left to make music.

There are many other duties and dangers inherent in the job of the college conductor. A professional player who is habitually late or absent from rehearsals, or who doesn't practice his part knows he

Henri Temianka is String Clinic Editor of The Instrumentalist. *He is conductor, concert violinist and professor of music at California State College at Long Beach, and also conducts the California Chamber Symphony, a virtuoso group of 40 players which offers an annual concert series in Los Angeles.*

will be fired. His livelihood is at stake. College students have a much better deal. Certainly, the grading system can be used to punish them, but it is a weapon that should be used only as a last resort. First, the conductor has to be sure not to punish a student unfairly—and college students have a positive genius for thinking up excuses that sound legitimate! One of the trumpeters has a sore on the inside of his cheek, way back where it can't be seen. He is careful to make it clear, that although he is in mortal agony, he will play if I insist, thereby putting the onus on me. Students have dental troubles and treatments, appointments with the draft board, sick relatives, and flat tires and broken engines 10 times the national average. Only a monster would give them bad grades when they are already enduring such terrible suffering and anguish.

A little sympathy and a sense of humor go a long way in dealing effectively with such problems, two good reasons why Toscanini and Furtwängler would not have made good college conductors. I am not among those who believe that students today are less serious about their work than the previous generation. When I was a student at the National Conservatory in Berlin, I discovered a providential little knot on the side of one of the fingers of my left hand. I carefully painted the knot with iodine whenever it suited my purpose, occasionally submitting it to the school doctor for inspection. He always shook his head sympathetically and recommended a rest.

I have learned that the best way to deal with all these threats to the health of the young generation is the preventative medicine of enthusiasm and joy in making music. Every rehearsal should be an exhilarating, creative experience. To achieve this is not always easy, and occasionally impossible, but it is nonetheless the one major goal to be kept in mind constantly.

Another matter of vital importance is to have a concrete, exciting project for the group at all times. You may say: "There should be enough excitement in learning to play a Beethoven or Brahms Symphony." Perhaps there should be, but there isn't, or at least it does not last long enough. There is a world of difference between learning a piece just for the sake of learning, and learning it against the challenge of an immovable performance date that draws closer with the passing of every hour. Students need this kind of challenge. The greater the challenge, the tougher the obstacles, the more they will dedicate themselves to the task of succeeding.

There are plenty of exciting concert projects for students, provided one has a little ingenuity and luck. Last semester my orchestra at the California State College at Long Beach presented a concert at the headquarters of Synanon, which is popularly thought of as the phenomenally successful rehabilitation center for drug addicts. (In point of fact, it is very likely the most drug-free place in California.) The concert at Synanon was a beautiful affair. After the concert, a buffet-style supper was served, very simply, and students and residents got along with each other so famously that the orchestra was asked to come back at least once or twice a year.

Another splendid opportunity materialized in Palm Springs. In return for a free concert, community leaders offered the students full hospitality and a sightseeing program. There must be many unexplored opportunities for such friendly exchanges, and if the conductor of a college ensemble has a bit of Sol Hurok in him, he will explore them.

I believe in giving gifted students every opportunity to try out and conduct their own compositions in rehearsals, and to appear as soloists and conductors in rehearsals and public performances. I also believe in bringing celebrated musicians to the campus, because the students are enormously stimulated by working with them. Aaron Copland and Darius Milhaud each came to the California State College at Long Beach campus for a visit of several days, rehearsing and conducting concerts of their own music. After paying their fee and all promotional expenses, we still had a substantial amount of money left for the music scholarship fund.

I think it is important to end every rehearsal on a happy, constructive, optimistic note. No matter how wearing the work may have been and no matter how badly some of it may have gone, it is advisable to end the rehearsal with something that is full of vim and vigor, something that the players know well enough to end the rehearsal cheerfully.

Whenever possible, the positions of the players in a student ensemble should remain flexible. Even if the second clarinetist is manifestly inferior to the first one, there is frequently one movement in a symphony or suite in which the first clarinet part is simple enough to permit a switching of the players without devastating results. These are considerations that the conductor of a professional ensemble need not be concerned with, but the conductor of a student group will ignore them at his peril. Every conductor must be a morale-builder if he hopes to be successful. The differences between one performing group and the other lie not in the principle but in the method.

I am a great believer in sectional rehearsals. When a large ensemble is going full-blast, many technical inadequacies are swept under the rug. When space permits, I like to have several rehearsal rooms in operation simultaneously during the first part of my college orchestra rehearsals. The first violin section rehearses separately under its concertmaster; the second violins, under their leader, do their woodshedding in another room; similarly, the violas, celli, and basses. The woodwinds take up a sixth room, the brass section a seventh, and the percussion players still another room. I make the rounds, supervising the activities. It is astonishing how much can be achieved in this manner in a short period of time, and when the whole orchestra is assembled after intermission, the results are often nothing less than spectacular.

I am against studying the same composition for too long a time. Six weeks to two months should be the absolute maximum. After that, little is to be gained from further study. The players become stale, lose their enthusiasm and concentration, and frequently end up playing worse rather than better. Anyone who has ever squeezed the juice out of a lemon knows that extracting the last drop requires an effort out of all proportion to the earlier bountiful harvest. A conductor with a command of good rehearsal techniques will relinquish his grip before extracting the last tortured drop.

Imaginative, broadly based programming is another matter of vital importance. It behooves the conductor of a student group to remember that the young people of today are not happy with a diet consisting exclusively of classics and romantics, or even the so-called contemporaries. What a middle-aged conductor may regard as far-out and *avant-garde,* is a natural language for the young generation. Music that includes electronic devices has a place in the repertoire of today. College conductors who live in the past will soon lose contact with their students. Jazz too, plays a legitimate role in today's repertoire. The largely spurious distinction made for so long between "serious" music and other kinds has all but disappeared from the scene. It is a truism that there are only two kinds of music: good and bad. In a recent concert at the University of California at Los Angeles, I devoted the first part of the program to Mendelssohn and Respighi, the latter part to the premiere of a work called *Dialogs for Jazz Quintet and Orchestra,* by the immensely gifted Lalo Schifrin. The public acceptance was total at least in the sense that the audience appeared to give the work the same undivided, unprejudiced attention as to the classical, "serious" composers. What is true for mature audiences is of course truer still for college students.

No one is more familiar than I with the frustrations the college conductor has to endure. They range from the technical variables between one player and another (they are one and all entitled to an education), to the mysterious mid-term slump that sets in, to absenteeism, to the strange disappearance of parts, (especially those that are hard to replace), and every other form of irresponsibility. But whatever these frustrations are, they are outweighed by the genuine sense of achievement and exhilaration that comes from reaching out to the new generation. The "generation gap" need not be any greater than it has ever been. At any rate, we are lucky in our profession. For those students who are inclined toward music and join a college ensemble soon discover that great music brings people of all ages together, enabling them to share the same emotions and experiences. ∎

November, 1965

The Basic Gesture

RALPH G. LAYCOCK

♫ "ONE, TWO, THREE, FOUR." And with their director's traditional two taps of the baton on the music stand, followed by a verbal count-down, (count-up?) the Nowhere High School Orchestra had gotten under way. They did quite well, too, until the double-bar where the tempo changed to a three-four allegro, but there the ensemble suffered so badly that their mentor was forced to stop them, rap twice, and count to three so that they could *allegretto* their way on through to the second double-bar, at which point they successfully recaptured Tempo I and brought the piece to a conclusion.

But the festival was a different and sadder story. The clicks were there, but some of the members did not realize that their conductor was mouthing the numbers silently so the first attack was very ragged. The three-four was a scramble for several measures, but they did remember the recapitulation and were able to finish nicely. In total, though, they just did not seem to be a group that could respond to anything quite on time.

Was it really their fault? Perhaps not. True, their director had become habituated to the baton-rapping and the count-down because they did not start unitedly and in tempo without it, and he had only slackened the pace of the allegro because the basses dragged so badly when he tried to take what he knew to be a more appropriate tempo. But after all, is it not his obligation to *teach* his players to respond instantly and authoritatively, not only to the written music, but also to his interpretation of it? How often is an adjudicator tempted to go down on stage and give one good clean down-beat just to see what might happen!

I understand that Frederick Fennell tells conducting students that in case of trouble they are to look for it about twelve inches in front of their nose. This strikes me as such excellent advice that I propose to examine what goes on there for the remainder of the article. (In the following discussion, I take for granted the use of a baton, fourteen inch fibre-glass preferred, firmly believing that training with one is indispensable even if, and perhaps especially if, the student later chooses to do without it. I am also an advocate of a free and supple wrist, the use of which is strongly recommended in any experimenting done in accord with the suggestions below.)

The Basic "One-Beat" Gesture

Though there are countless sources

wherein one may find patterns customarily used in conducting complete measures of various meters and tempos, there seem to be few which really go into detail about the elements of the basic gesture itself and the function served by each. This seems to me to leave the conductor in a position relatively like that of the young musician who is shown four quarter notes per measure, but told nothing of their musical meaning and so is content to play them mechanically without any inflection or style. The conductor who merely goes through a standard pattern thirty times in thirty measures is doing little to help his group perform either precisely or musically by his motions, forfeiting thereby his most important means of communication with his organization.

On the premise that a *beat* is not a *point* in time but rather an expanse of time, may I present what seem to me to be the four elements of the conducting gesture which serve to give meaning to this important musical unit. Though they may at times be run together so as not to be distinctly identifiable as individual actions, none-the-less all are embodied in a successful and meaningful gesture. In order, they are 1) *preparation*, 2) *ictus*, 3) *rebound*, and 4) for the want of a better name, *connection*.

1) *Preparation*—Usually the musical meaning of a beat must be indicated *before* it actually begins. For this reason, the gesture must commence during the previous beat if the performers are to have time to see it, recall its meaning, recall what they should do about it, and then initiate the physical activity necessary to execute it properly. It is usually identifiable as a speeding up of the baton's motion just before the *ictus*.

2) *Ictus*—That infinitely short moment where the beat begins, (the "click" of the beat) usually indicated by some change of direction and/or speed of the baton.

3) *Rebound*—The "change of direction or speed" above-mentioned, commencing at the "click" and continuing until the *connection*.

4) *Connection*—That portion of the beat between the end of the *rebound* and the beginning of the next *preparation*. If the music is fast or staccato it may take the

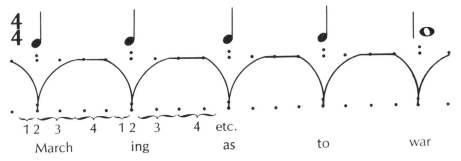

1 2 3 4 1 2 3 4 etc.

March ing as to war

form of an almost dead stop in the baton's motion. In slow or flowing music it may be nothing more than a slight slowing of the baton's travel as it glides into the next *preparation*.

These may most easily be demonstrated in a "one-beat" gesture, a down-up motion that can be done in a vertical straight line. But lacking the live example, let us imagine that the tip of the baton is tracing its action on moving graph paper in the fashion of a seismograph stylus.

Accented Gesture

Assuming a piece of the nature of the universally known "Onward Christian Soldiers," performed with a little accentuation and "military" feeling at a tempo of approximately a quarter note = 90, the "picture" might well turn out something like this: (Starting at the third measure avoids, for now, the problem of the "cue" beat.)

It is important to note that:

1) In the *preparation*, even though it takes only about one-eighth of a beat, a definite increase in the speed of the baton tip is shown. (This acceleration is a troublesome problem for most beginning conductors, a decrease of speed sometimes becoming habitual among the less confident who do not insist that their group keep right up with them. They slow down the beat to avoid getting ahead of the players but actually make it im-

possible for the group to catch up because of the deceptive gesture which reaches its *ictus* later than it should have.)

2) The *ictus* is a sharp click. The baton, traveling at its greatest downward speed, is suddenly reversed in direction of travel, and moves upward at its greatest upward rate of speed. This gives both a firm visual indication of the tempo and a command that the notes be given some individual accent, as required by the military feeling.

3) The *rebound* begins its upward travel at high speed, slowing down (coasting), as it reaches the top. It lasts noticeably longer than does the *preparation*, much of this time being spent in slowing down.

4) The *connection* in this fairly quick, accented pattern takes the form of a dead stop (or very nearly so) for an appreciable amount of time (more than a quarter of a beat), separating the *rebound* and *preparation* very distinctly and giving further indication of the non-legato interpretation.

The motion of the baton might well be compared to that of the hand in throwing a ball against the ground and then catching it at the top of its rebound. The actual throwing motion is equivalent to the *preparation;* the quick change of direction resembles the *ictus;* the upward reach becomes the *rebound;* and the catching and momentary holding of the ball cor-

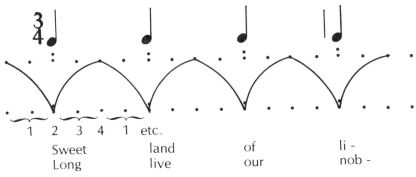

1 2 3 4 1 etc.

Sweet land of li -
Long live our nob -

responds to the *connection*.

Failure to achieve these changes of pace (best handled by the free and supple wrist), is responsible for a good deal of uninspiring and lethargic conducting, which in turn produces performances that suffer from the same faults. But we must remember that it is in the mind and heart that the original inspiration must be born—the conductor who does not sense that the piece should be performed with energy will not conduct in such a fashion as to inspire anyone. We must also be aware that inexperienced performers must be educated to understand the baton's message and taught to handle their instruments so as to produce the desired result before the gesture alone will be effective.

Legato Gesture

As an example of a contrasting gesture let us use measure three of "My Country, 'Tis of thee," ("God Save the Queen"). Still demonstrating a "one-beat" pattern, the graph might appear somewhat like this:

In contrast to the earlier more accented example, our graph points up the following:
1) The *preparation* takes proportionately a much larger portion of the beat, approximately one-half. The increase in speed is not nearly as great but still is evident in the last fraction of its duration. (Good definition of the "click" is almost impossible without some such acceleration.)
2) The *ictus* is not so sharply "clicked." This is in character with the more legato approach. (Remember, this is a horizontal graph of a vertical action. The apparently wider angle indicates only less speed, not the actual pattern traced by the baton.)
3) The *rebound* is proportionately (as well as actually) longer, taking approximately the first half of the beat. There is also less

change of speed because it starts slower than did the earlier one.
4) The *connection* is much smoother. With the *rebound* and *preparation* each taking a greater proportion of the beat, the *connection* becomes merely the change of direction from up to down, avoiding a dead stop which would tend to break up the legato mood.

In this example it is well to think of the baton as being continually in motion, accelerating slightly into the *ictus* and slowing down slightly into the *connection*, not unlike the swing of a pendulum, if one does not regard the change of direction in either case as an actual "stop."

Application to Other Standard Patterns

The "one-beat" pattern was chosen deliberately because the desired points could be made with the simplest possible explanations. And many subtleties of rhythm and emotion can be indicated clearly by variations in the speed and/or proportion of the beat allotted to each of these basic elements.

However, there is relatively little call for the "one-beat" pattern, so our previous comments must now be stretched out along the paths taken by the tip of the baton in the more usual and more complicated standard patterns. Two comments may suffice:
1) Along these paths, the changes of speed pointed out above should be carefully planned for and executed. For example, in an uncomplicated four-beat pattern at any tempo, there should be *appropriate* changes of speed at all appropriate places—an increase during the *preparation* for each beat and a decrease as the *rebound* coasts in to the *connection*, no matter what direction the baton may be traveling at the moment.
2) Where a change of direction occurs, its angularity is affected by the character of the piece:

a) The more staccato or forceful the music, the more angular are the changes of direction, e.g.

Allegro con fuoco

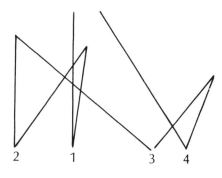

b) The more legato or expressive the music, the more curved are the changes of direction, e.g.

Andante espressivo

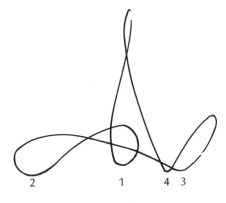

Perhaps I should make it clear that the above suggestions carry full force only in measures that are primarily in one mood, whatever that may be, and not rhythmically complicated. The problems brought on by changing rhythms, dynamics, scoring, emotional stresses, tempos, etc. may well demand that each measure be conducted somewhat differently, and this will be discussed in future articles. But the acquisition of a clear, precise and expressive basic gesture is certainly the most important first step along the road to mastery of the baton. ∎

The Anatomy of a Rehearsal

Kenneth G. Bloomquist

Rehearsal Room Atmosphere

One objective of each rehearsal is that the ensemble should be able to do something at the end of the session that it couldn't do at the beginning. This simple statement has implications that are surprisingly complex. By examining each phase of a rehearsal it is possible to come close to establishing the best way to get the most done in the shortest amount of time.

Studies have shown that the environment has an effect on the way people work. Distractions, poor lighting, improper materials, even decor are some concerns.

Keep a Clean and Carefully Arranged Rehearsal Room. This means that extra chairs and stands are stacked or removed, and musical instruments not in use should be properly stored. In other words the rehearsal set-up should be as orderly as the set-up on the concert stage. Ideally, this would demand that the rehearsal room not be in use during the period prior to the rehearsal, but because this may not be possible, you may want to start the rehearsal a few minutes late while a few students set the stage for the efficient rehearsal.

Maintain Proper Lighting. This is extremely important in an ensemble rehearsal. The musicians should not have to compromise posture and instrument position by leaning forward or squinting in order to see the music.

Eliminate Outside Distractions. Personally, I like a room without windows. With windows uncovered, rehearsal effi-

Kenneth Bloomquist is director of bands and professor of music at Michigan State University.

ciency can be affected by good or bad weather, visual activity outside, and noise. Drapes or Venetian blinds are a simple solution to the problem, and in some cases they improve the acoustical properties of the room as well. Placing the ensemble with their backs to the windows is also possible.

Eliminate a Visable Clock. Ideally, time should fly in a rehearsal. Realistically this won't happen for all performers all of the time, but clock watching in rehearsals does not help the music unless the clock is used as a metronome. You should keep track of the time or have the concertmaster keep you informed.

Designate Areas for Storage of Books, Coats, and Instrument Cases During Rehearsals. This can be a problem in many rooms depending on the availability of space. Do not permit material other than that necessary for the rehearsal to be taken to the chair in the rehearsal room. It is messy, distracting, and provides the means for some to concentrate on other matters. Solving this problem in some rehearsal rooms may be perplexing, but it is important enough to insist on a solution.

Have Students Maintain a Decorum As They Enter the Rehearsal Room. Students must realize that they are special people doing a special job requiring a special room. Dignity and seriousness of purpose should prevail in a rehearsal. The degree to which this can be accomplished is probably directly proportionate to the pride of the students and the influence of the conductor. It can set the tone for the work about to be done.

Rehearsal atmosphere can be

ignored and good rehearsal results may still be possible. But if better results can be achieved with attention to rehearsal room atmosphere, then that atmosphere must be examined and properly adjusted. Just as a church uses soft music and lighting to aid a quiet, prayerful entry into the worship service, just as a factory uses background music to provoke efficiency, just as a football team uses the crowd, marching band, and cheerleaders to motivate the team, so the conductor must use the atmosphere of the rehearsal room to benefit an efficient rehearsal.

Warm-Up and Tuning

The warm-up and tuning phase of the rehearsal usually reveals the philosophy, maturity, training techniques, and attitudes of a conductor. It is at this time when the self-discipline and practice habits of the ensemble and the influence of the conductor are most evident.

Various research projects, papers, and books have validated the fact that pitch will vary on instruments relative to the rehearsal room temperature and as a result of warming up. Therefore, warming up first is necessary to be able to tune reliably.

The warm-up should be done either individually or within the ensemble with prescribed direction and pace. The warm-up should make it possible for each player to execute every facet of necessary performing ability — range, facility, tone, dynamics, attack, etc.

Individual warm-up is probably the preferred method for the simple reason that each player can proceed at his own pace and in his own way;

however it is not feasible because there is not enough time in a typical school rehearsal schedule and unfortunately, many students do not have the ability or self-discipline to warm-up properly. The following steps can be used for ensemble warm-up.

• Step 1 (30-60 seconds). Sound concert B♭ using a tuning device, clarinet, oboe, or trumpet and then have the students match the pitch. This is not the time for tuning but the moment when the ensemble finds a pitch center from which to proceed.

• Step 2 (2-3 minutes). Perform a chorale, march, alma mater, or any short selection with the following characteristics: no extreme registers, full ensemble scoring, and dynamic levels that permit individuals to hear themselves.

• Step 3 (2-3 minutes). Play something in a contrasting style. If the warm-up music was a chorale with concentration on tone and legato style playing, conclude with either a short selection that focuses on articulation or play unison pitches, chords, or scales with specified attack patterns. If the warm-up number was a march, perform long tones or sustained chords, scales, or chorales that emphasize tone quality and legato playing. This warm-up schedule takes only five to seven minutes. Ideally, this is not enough time, but it is realistic for most rehearsal schedules and it should permit reasonably reliable tuning.

Tuning

Ensemble tuning can take from a few minutes to a few hours, and many musicians have probably observed a rehearsal where every moment was used for tuning. While this is easy to understand and might be justifiable in some cases, it may not be the wisest use of an entire rehearsal. There are some basic ideas that are primary to understanding the problem of tuning.

• The student must know when he is out of tune in order to be able to play in tune.

• Almost everyone can learn to play in tune and recognize pitch variance.

• A student must learn the tuning peculiarities of his particular instrument. For example, flutes tend to be sharp in the upper register, trumpets are flat on D4, etc. When learning how to tune and in practic-

ing tuning, students should know which pitches tend to be sharp or flat on their particular instrument, and the conductor must know all of the many tuning peculiarities for every instrument.

• Students should not be afraid or concerned if occasionally they are unable to decide whether a pitch is sharp or flat. Tone quality, for instance, can make tuning more difficult at times. The problem can be alleviated by making larger tuning adjustments, i.e., going very sharp or very flat before returning to the pitch center. For example, valve brasses can pull out their tuning slides and then slide up to arrive at the pitch center, much like a trombone.

• Be aware of the effect of rehearsal room temperature on tuning. In a room below 70° F it is difficult to stay in tune because the instruments will cool off quickly when they are not played constantly.

• The longer brass and woodwind instruments are played, the sharper the pitch tends to be, up to a point. This degree of sharpness will vary for each family of instruments.

Here is a tuning procedure you can follow:

• Step 1. Sound concert B♭. If you are not using an electronic or fixed pitch device, have the solo clarinet, oboe, or trumpet sound the pitch while watching a stroboscope. It is unreasonable to expect the 1st chair player at any level, public school or university, to always give a perfect tuning pitch.

• Step 2. Have the woodwinds and the horns match this pitch. Each member must play loud enough to hear himself but soft enough to permit others to hear themselves.

• Step 3. Sound concert B♭ again and have the brasses, minus the horns match the pitch. Again, the students should be asked to be dynamically astute.

• Step 4. Sound concert A for the string bass and for further tuning of the woodwinds and horns.

• Step 5. Play an unmeasured scale slowly to further establish the pitch center on more than one or two notes.

• Step 6. If time permits and the ability of the ensemble warrants it, play a chorale or series of chords to further establish good intonation on something other than unison or octave exercises. (Of course this

technique should also be used in the context of the music being rehearsed.)

I also often tune a particular troublesome note or chord in the first selection to be rehearsed, or take time to point out tuning problems in a particular register of a specific instrument. In other words the tuning process can be continued. In fact I think it should go on, but within the context of the rest of the rehearsal.

Ensembles bored with the routine of predictable warm-ups and tuning are, unfortunately, all too common. Challenging and interesting warm-up material executed by the conductor with purpose and enthusiasm is essential. Tuning that isolates problems and identifies individuals who are in error is mandatory if tuning is to be meaningful. This is the conductor's first moment of truth in the rehearsal. He must evaluate pitch, be able to state the direction of pitch change, and reverse a decision if he's called it wrong.

The director's constant analysis of tuning and his willingness to realize that there is always something to learn about the subject is essential for the growth and effectiveness of both the conductor and his ensemble.

Problem Solving

The main portion of most rehearsals (after the warm-up and tuning) is usually spent in problem solving with the intended result being the making of music. There are many ways to solve problems. The method outlined here represents one approach with the ideas being adaptable to any routine.

There is one truth that must be accepted before this portion of the rehearsal can be considered a success: At the end of the rehearsal, the ensemble must be able to perform something better than they could at the beginning of the rehearsal. This accomplishment might consist only of a technically difficult four measures, a complex rhythmic figure, or the tuning of intervals in a passage involving extreme registers. Whatever it is, it must be improvement that is obvious to all participants. In other words, the rehearsal must be worth having and worth attending.

Before the downbeat is given, the following considerations should be checked.

• *Music Stand Height.* Is it high enough for the player to look at the music and see the conductor, at least with peripheral vision? (Marches printed on quick-step size paper may be paper clipped to the top of the folder in order to facilitate eye contact.)

• *Players Per Music Stand.* Are there more than two people per stand? There should not be if correct body position and instrument position is desirable. The instrument, eyes, and body should be facing the conductor.

• *Posture.* Is the body in a position forward on the chair, sitting erect, with the knees down and the legs relaxed with both feet on the floor) that permits maximum attention to the requirements of the rehearsal?

To illustrate the correct placement of a music stand, ask the musicians to put their instruments in playing position and to look at the last note of the first selection to be rehearsed. Then raise your baton within the conducting field, and ask the musicians if they can see the baton without looking at it (peripheral vision). If they cannot see the baton ask them to adjust their music stands or body position so they can.

Begin the rehearsal (after the warm-up and tuning) by playing a selection, or part of a selection, as close as possible to the designated tempo. After playing a passage the analytical phase of the rehearsal begins. The key word is isolate. Identify the elements of the music by isolating them and pointing out the problems to the students. Assume the band has played through a traditional march and is going to rehearse by practicing only the first few measures. Isolate the component parts of those measures.

1. *First Attack.* Did everyone start together? Did the musicians take a rhythmic breath with the preparatory beat? It is important to know that the air stream on wind instruments should not be stopped or frozen before release. The air never stops moving.

2. *Balance.* Is every chord heard in such a way that no single pitch can be heard more than another? (Of course melodic and occasional harmonic considerations may alter this equality.) I usually balance chords by starting with the lower pitches and building to the soprano instruments. You will most likely find yourself asking for more volume from the middle or alto line or second and third part instruments and less from the first or top soprano line instruments. A good rehearsal device is to play an alla breve march in slow $\frac{4}{4}$ time or the quick $\frac{6}{8}$ march in a slow six beats per measure. When doing this, listen only for the balance of parts.

3. *Blend.* Direct your attention to the instrumental blend by listening for tone qualities that do not fit the ensemble sonority. Bad blend or tone quality can often be mistaken for bad balance — and certainly the two can be interrelated. It is in this phase that the conductor must identify individuals and initiate remedial work. If a student's tone quality cannot be changed, it may be necessary to ask the individual to play softer than is indicated in the music. This need not be a demeaning experience for the student, it is simply a corrective action, the same as correcting wrong notes, rhythmic mistakes, and intonation problems. The sonority of the entire ensemble is largely dependent on this isolated area.

4. *Tuning.* It is important for musicians to know what the chords sound like when they are played in tune. Whatever tuning reference is used make sure it is in tune before starting to tune intervals and chords. I often use the tuba as the starting point. It is common for that instrument to go sharp after a "heated" rehearsal, but it is advisable to check the pitch on an electrical tuning device before beginning the process. When musicians do hear a chord in tune it is usually easier for them to repeat it by doing what they did again (lipping up or down) and listening for that gorgeous in-tune sound.

5. *Style.* This area is too often ignored as an ensemble technique, particularly if there are strong lead players executing their parts correctly. It is mandatory to know which style is required — detached, legato, cantabile, classical, romantic, baroque, etc. — and find an example to imitate. Sloppy or inconsistent execution of style separates the good band from the great band. Conductors usually take special note to find out the style of a selection, to understand it, and to be prepared to make value judgments as to its execution during the course of rehearsal and performance.

6. *Phrasing.* The shaping of a phrase is too often confined to starting and stopping the band together. Though this is important it should not be the only end result of good phrasing. The conductor needs to teach all aspects of phrasing, (including breathing, dynamics, accent, emphasis, tension, release, and precision), being sure that those who are playing non-melodic lines also know where the phrases are. These players then must feel the melodic progression and shape their lines the same as the melodic phrase.

7. *Playing Facility.* Conductors must be concerned with getting correct notes at the correct time. The danger is being satisfied with correct execution as the end result. Actually it is the beginning of making music.

After isolating these components the band should be able to execute a musical phrase perfectly. If the music isn't performed as well as the finest ensemble, further remedial action and work is required. It may be impractical or unnecessary to emphasize each isolated component in each measure of each selection. Transfer of learning and musical expertise may negate the need for continuous isolation. It is important to be prepared to diagnose trouble, isolate the problem, solve it, and get on with the rehearsal.

Content and Planning

Some of the many factors influencing the content of a rehearsal include the age of the members, the length of the rehearsal, the difficulty and the style of the repertoire, the proximity of the rehearsal to the concert, and the performance ability of the musicians. Consider the following plan, based on 60 minutes of rehearsal.

Section I. Warm-up and Tuning (10 minutes)

This topic was discussed completely in Part II (*The Instrumentalist*, March 1981). It should be mentioned that the students' schedules prior to the rehearsal will determine the content of this section. If individual warm-up and tuning time is available, this section can be short. If warm-up and tuning can be done only in rehearsal, this section will need to be longer.

Section II. Problem Solving (30 minutes)

This subject was covered in Part III of this series (*The Instrumentalist*, April 1981). If all execution problems have been solved, more rehearsal time could be spent on other sections. If problem solving is needed, here are some points to consider.

1. Don't work too long on a seemingly impossible passage. Repetitive, shorter drills accomplished during many rehearsals may be a better way.

2. Don't spend too much time with only a part of your ensemble. You could bore and lose the others quickly.

3. If all players are involved and progress is evident, extensive time can be spent on isolated passages.

4. Don't let individuals hide. Ask your students to play alone, in pairs, or small groups. They must realize they are all equally important.

5. Don't stop unless there is a problem; and each time you do stop, express a specific, clear, and concise reason.

6. Don't be too talkative; let your baton say it.

7. Recognize accomplishments and establish new goals.

Section III. Reviewing and Solidifying Material (15 minutes)

This section of the rehearsal is usually the most enjoyable because everyone feels the results of their musical efforts.

1. Playing through the portion of the music that has just been drilled will solidify the problem solving that has just taken place. It provides proof of accomplishment.

2. Continue to play the repertoire that has been learned in the past days and weeks. If reviewing is not done on a regular basis, problems which were once solved will soon need to be solved again.

3. As the run-through takes place, continue to point out melody lines, supporting lines, harmonic structure, countermelody, form, style, etc., working toward student understanding of the repertoire.

4. This process is sometimes called "routining" because it permits the musician to develop reliable performance habits based on a familiar routine that leads to self-confidence. If the performer can execute the repertoire with a degree of relaxation, then thought can be directed to the real task of musical expression.

Section IV. Sightreading (5 minutes)

This aspect of music making is of great importance for the performer, particularly when auditioning for ensembles at the high school, college, or professional level. Most auditioners, conductors, and teachers equate the person who is a good sightreader with the one who will require a miniumum of rehearsal to achieve a high level of performance. Although this is not necessarily true for every performer, there is evidence to support the practice of evaluating a musician's capabilities through sightreading. It should be included in a daily rehearsal routine. The ability to sightread effectively can be learned by most musicians. Here are some considerations that must be brought to the sightreader's attention.

1. Rhythm — The single, most important aspect of effective sightreading is comprehending the rhythm. To practice, set your instrument aside, and concentrate on the notes alone. Set a tempo and use a single pitch to sing the rhythm.

2. Facility — Limited technique hampers sightreading ability. If the player comprehends the rhythm, it is then important to keep the tempo going and "fake" through the notes until adequate facility is gained.

3. Reading Ahead — The musician's eye movement must be steady, always looking a few notes to a measure or more ahead of the notes being played. If a mistake is made, the player should not look back to see what went wrong, or his problems will increase.

4. Posture and Position — It is essential that the musician use every aid at his disposal. Refer to this section in Part III which gives detailed information as to music stand, body, and instrument position relative to the conductor.

5. A Check List — Scan the following before sightreading: key signature, time signature, tempo, repeat signs (*Coda*, *Dal Segno*, and *Da Capo*), style indicators (*Maestoso*, *Grazioso*, *Grave*, etc.), dynamics, and problem areas (rhythm patterns, unusual intervals, awkward fingerings, accidentals, phrasing, and range).

With some practice this scanning can be done in a matter of minutes. It is important to practice the technique of preparing to sightread before the actual challenge of playing the music at first reading.

The time frames for each of these four sections of a rehearsal can be shortened or lengthened to suit the conductor, based on the performance needs at the moment. It is my belief that all the sections should be used at each meeting. Close attention to content and planning will provide the excitement, challenge, accomplishment, tension and relaxation which should be a part of every rehearsal.

Conductor Concerns

Special attention is given to the rehearsal conductor in this final part of the "Anatomy of a Rehearsal." The conductor's intelligence, talent, organizational skill, knowledge of the profession, and courage to honestly self-evaluate are measured in the degree of success or failure of the ensemble rehearsal. These obvious concerns are identified to complete this anatomy.

• *Knowledge of the Literature.* It should go without saying that the conductor should know the score. Faking with little more than a beat pattern is not enough. The score should be researched, studied, and marked to assure a meaningful rehearsal. Research should include knowledge of the composer, period, and style, as well as performance requirements peculiar to the selection.

• *Organizing the Rehearsal.* The conductor should plot each phase of the rehearsal, identifying goals and planning their accomplishment. The informed conductor should be able to anticipate the problems that will be encountered in a rehearsal and be aware of the time needed to be spent on each. Understanding the score and knowing the ensemble's weaknesses will help the director to plan an efficient rehearsal.

• *Pace.* Keeping the rehearsal moving is important. Good pacing is directly related to the conductor's leadership skills and effectiveness in dealing with people. The conductor's unique personality as well as complete preparation and planning for rehearsals is important. Look around at the faces in your rehearsal room and have the courage to assess your effectiveness. Pace could be a factor.

• *Percussion Section.* It is awkward to isolate a section as needing attention. However, anyone with public school experience knows the percussion section is of common concern. The playground atmosphere of the fascinating equipment is a natural environment for non-musical activity. Organization is essential and prescribing the exact arrangement of instruments is just as important for the percussion as it is for the winds. Choosing a percussion section leader and assigning jobs to individual section members is a director's responsibility that requires careful consideration. Provide extra chairs for percussionists not involved in a particular selection

• *Self-Evaluation.* Much evaluation is left up to the annual contest rating, but regular self-evaluation can serve as one facet of an ongoing analysis of personal effectiveness. Conductors, you should have the courage to

• listen to recordings and compare what you hear with the sounds coming from your band,

• go to conventions and concerts and listen honestly,

• go to contests and take what is coming to you,

• invite proven conductors to work with your ensembles,

• change rehearsal techniques and/or examine your philosophy of education if things are not working,

• invite student evaluation.

There are many ways to improve. These are some. Good luck.

Over-Conductors: Heed!

Maurice Faulkner

School music organizations usually succeed or fail because of the abilities of their leaders. By the same token, the magnificent symphonic orchestras and bands reach pinnacles of perfection based upon the skills of their conductors.

When a conductor over-conducts, extraneous movements detract from the efforts of the musicians. What constitutes over-conducting? First of all, when a conductor waves both arms unnecessarily, the right arm may provide the beat, but the left arm continues to wave with the rhythm of his right as if he couldn't keep time properly unless the two arms were synchronized! If both arms are moving smoothly with a real affection for the phrase line and the subtleties of the musical expressiveness, then perhaps the two arms are essential. Usually, though, a muscle-bound, two-armed time-beater does not control his ensemble sensitively.

The over-conductor usually will show off his skills by cueing every instrumental entrance, often failing to produce a careful phrase line of the ensemble because his attention to cues has interfered with his interpretative skills. Some professionals, such as Lorin Maazel of the Pittsburgh Symphony, are so well acquainted with scores that they can conduct from memory; not everyone possesses this skill. The superb professional musicians he directs probably could play most of the works without a conductor, though; much of his conducting is superfluous. In fact, his cueing for operatic performances sometimes creates a busier effect than the actions on the stage.

Some young conductors may beat too hard, causing the group to attack each measure with a hard tone quality. Some professional baton artists, too, have made this a trademark of their musical efforts. The Boston Symphony's Seiji Ozawa often forces the orchestral tone with a powerful beat, and, from this writer's point of view, an unnecessarily strident quality results. This is not the fault of the Boston musicians, for Ozawa also produces this effect with the Vienna Philharmonic and the Berlin when he serves as a guest with those organizations.

The young conductor should select a first-rate example of a conducting specialist whose work satisfies him and try to copy his style. For my taste, Herbert von Karajan, with his easy, soft beat and infrequent cues, expresses the essence of the scores with little excess motion. His program of Wagner masterpieces at a Salzburg Festival, all conducted without a score, reached the peak of sensitive interpretation. A less graceful baton wielder, Carlo Maria Giulini, creates the same feeling of serenity while developing the power essential to the

393

fortissimos.

At the Salzburg Festival some years ago, von Karajan was responsible for conducting the Cleveland Symphony one evening. After the performance of one of the works on the program, a Clevelander told me, "We certainly had a difficult time following his beat, but he sure let us play with our hearts!"

Depend upon your musicians and realize that they are talented, even when they are only beginners. The finer the musician, the less help he needs from the conductor. A well-trained orchestra or band should be able to play effectively without a conductor. Try it sometime on a concert and you will soon discover whether you have taught them properly.

September, 1980

Conducting From Memory

Donn Laurence Mills

Standing before a group of musicians without benefit of a score is like walking the high wire without a net. Such a feat of daring impresses audiences, and even members of an orchestra, but it's risky. Also any evidence of the conductor's insecurity may be interpreted by others as confirmation he is really just a faker or show-off of less than genius caliber.

Conductors began conducting from memory in the 19th century, when artists were advertised as virtuosos and wizards. As the conductor's power and prestige increased, his need to appear super-human grew accordingly. Fascinated audiences, entranced by the notion that the conductor was creating the music out of his own mind, loved the idea.

Undeniably, some egotistical conductors glossed over their mistakes or took foolish chances, but others did develop truly remarkable score memories by limiting their repertoire to a handful of standard works, which they repeated over and over. These maestros became high priests of the podium.

Today opinions differ concerning the wisdom of conducting from memory. Most big league conductors carry a few standard, oft-repeated works in their heads; but the frequency of

Donn Laurence Mills is the NSOA contributing editor. He holds music degrees from Northwestern University and Eastman School of Music. A conductor and music educator, he is also the American educational director for the Yamaha Music Foundation of Tokyo.

concerts and variety of repertoire allow little time for complete memorization. Today's conductor is also less of an idol than before; his eminence is shared more equally and fairly with the other musicians on stage. Display of virtuosity has been largely replaced by integrity and scholarship; but it would be a mistake simply to dismiss memorization as passe or fraudulent. Consider some of the disadvantages of conducting with a score.

• The presence of a score, no matter how little it is needed, places a small barrier between conductor and orchestra. When the eyes or the left hand are occupied with it, communication is interrupted and the conductor is momentarily out of touch with the players.

• A printed score necessarily organizes music into pages and segments rather than phrases and sections. Each page allows only a small glimpse of the whole picture, forcing the conductor to concern himself with trees rather than the forest.

• Because we depend most heavily on our visual sense, a phenomenon attributed to our relating knowledge to reading, we tend to hear what we see, trusting our eyes and ignoring our ears. Visual impressions are so strong, we continue to see notation even after we look away from the music.

The Value of Memorization

Separating music from notation allows the conductor to operate in a purely artistic medium. Form, orchestration, dynamics, and line are dealt with

in abstract dimension. The conductor's eyes have the freedom to roam about the orchestra and communicate with the players.

It isn't necessary to memorize an entire program or even a long piece. Something short or part of a piece will do at first to get used to the experience. You needn't let anyone know you're doing it, either; just don't open the score. If you memorize just one piece per program, you'll soon have a sizable repertoire. Memorizing unusual or insignificant music is probably not worth the effort, and complicated music is not worth the risk.

How to Memorize a Score

Absolute familiarity with the music is the pre-requisite to memorization. In fact, it's probably never wise to perform a piece from memory before you've had a chance to conduct it in performance using the score. The memorizing process is identical to regular score study except that you need to give yourself little tests as you labor along. Close your eyes and conduct your imaginary philharmonic through passages you've studied thoroughly.

Resist the temptation to think only melody. Sing the inside lines, too. As you go through the piece, think ahead to the next phrase, entrance, and pitch. Write out tricky passages on manuscript paper first by copying, then from memory. Try sections at rehearsals to see how you get along. Most conductors listen to recordings to check their memories. Of course, don't mimic the interpretation or be lulled by a false sense of security just because the recorded performance doesn't fall apart when you lose your way. Confident conducting from memory comes from successful experiences and much practice.

When you can sing any part of the piece, and when you know the inside parts, entrances, releases, the number of bars in critical passages, every nuance and stylistic marking, the form; and when you can begin conducting from memory at any point, then you're ready to conduct completely from memory. At first, you'll see notes and pages in your head. You'll picture the score, knowing the position on the page of every line and rehearsal number; but after a few repetitions you'll be operating intuitively without visual references. That's an exhilarating experience.

Conductors of professional orchestras aren't the only ones to conduct from memory. I've known school and community conductors who do it regularly with great success. They are respected for it by colleagues and students alike. Conduct something from memory at your next concert and experience a new level of artistic satisfaction. ∎

January, 1977

How to Rehearse —
A Lesson from Stokowski

Legh W. Burns

We were all there. The University of Miami Symphony Orchestra, rehearsed, capable, and hot. The concert was to take place the following weekend, and our guest conductor for the occasion had just arrived. Leopold Stokowski. He stood quietly on the podium, dignified, powerful, and with the awe of us all surrounding him. He was being introduced by John Bitter, our regular (not to say ordinary) conductor and former pupil of Maestro Stokowski. The day was especially hot and the introduction, because of the circumstance and association, extra long. Accolades like "superior musician" and "pioneer" began to make their way back to the trumpet section where I sat. "Inspirational," they continued, "influential." The maestro looked down at the music (among other pieces, this concert was to feature the Tchaikovsky *Symphony No. 4).* His face was expressionless, the thin strands of white hair in careful disarray.

Finally the introduction came to an end. Mr. Stokowski was presented to us, and the applause burst forth from the orchestra with a spontaneity and obvious sincerity that

Legh W. Burns is currently conductor of the University of Oklahoma Symphony Orchestra, a post he assumed in 1973. His conducting experience also includes the University of Denver Symphonic Band, the Washington D.C. Chamber Ensemble, and the Festival Chamber Orchestra of Denver. He has studied conducting with Renee Longy, Modest Alloo, Pierre Monteux and Richard Lert.

impressed me very much. We waited for the acknowledgement from the maestro. A "thank you" for certain, followed by the usual "nice to be here" and perhaps a story or two of the Stokowski-Bitter association that would start the rehearsal off on a cordial and familiar footing. We waited. Still, the gaunt, lined face looked at the stand. Silence. Then, the head finally lifted and he spoke: "Tchaikovsky please, 1st movement." After that, things happened so fast our heads spun. No one had his music ready, and the resulting shuffle of parts was clearly annoying to Maestro Stokowski. "Letter A," was followed all but simultaneously by a downbeat. Letter A? Half of us hadn't found our music yet. The trumpet section, never noted for being on top of things, grumbled the loudest.

Well, it went on like that for the entire week. We were angry at first, half at Mr. Stokowski for moving at an intolerable speed and half at ourselves for letting *his* half make us angry. The second rehearsal found us determined to stay with him, and towards the end of it we were all speed readers. You would have thought Evelyn Woods was on the podium. Well, it got better and better. Rehearsals became a challenge, and the intensity with which Mr. Stokowski approached *each note* began to be infused in us as well. Everything improved. Everything! As this transformation was taking place, I began to develop a warm affection for him. He had a technique

of rehearsal I had never seen before. It moved very fast but always with a purpose. We soon learned to stop when he did, for the direction (which soon supplanted correction) was only given once.

By concert time, we were all inspired as we had never been before, and speaking for myself, as I have not been since. The concert was outstanding. I have played many concerts since, but will remember that one above all others.

That was almost twenty years ago, and I think the principle still holds. Maestro Stokowski had shown us not only outstanding musicianship, not only total dedication to his art, not only inspirational leadership, but a rehearsal technique as well. It was a technique that was comfortable to him, and one he made comfortable for us. When I decided to move from performance in the trumpet section to conducting, it soon became apparent to me that knowledge of the music and ideas on its interpretation were not enough. The *how* of music making is also crucial. In short, a personal rehearsal technique is a part of one's conducting musicianship that must be practiced, developed, and natural.

A reporter once asked Spencer Tracy if he had any advice to give young, aspiring actors; some wisdom he had gleaned from all his experience; some pearl that would inspire the neophyte to stick in there, no matter what. Tracy's answer? "Learn your lines." The same is obviously true for us. Nothing, no rehearsal technique, no pyrotechnical baton technique, no amount of dramatic words and gestures will save a rehearsal for which we are not prepared. Leopold Stokowski's dramatic entrance into our first rehearsal years ago would be recalled as so much charlantanism if he had not immediately shown himself to be the consummate musisian he is. So let's leave that as understood. Learn your music; know it thoroughly. Only after that can you start thinking about your rehearsal techniques.

The technique of rehearsing an ensemble is often either taken for granted or overlooked altogether. How many times have we tossed off an unproductive rehearsal as "just one of those days," or found fault with the members, or blamed it all on the low pressure area that was settling over the community. I have heard them all and, like you, have used those excuses and probably others. The fact is, however, bad rehearsals are almost invariably the fault of the person on the podium.

How to avoid it? The first step would seem to be an admission that all rehearsals will not be jewels. You will not receive that warming shuffle of feet each time you finish. There will still be times when your members will be looking at the clock after only fifteen minutes of the rehearsal have passed. Next, have a plan, a style if you will, and follow it. Schedules and personalities are different, of course, and one plan will not work for all. However, some plan will work, some variant, if practiced prior to the rehearsal.

I think it best if I tell you what I do during the rehearsal rather than suggest something for you to try. First of all, I keep the hour immediately prior to the rehearsal free, allowing nothing save an emergency situation to interrupt. During this time I map out specifically those things I want to accomplish during the rehearsal. I mean pieces, movements, rehearsal numbers, and specific notes of specific instruments in those specific places. If letter A is a problem, we start there. What's the matter? Intonation? (Always.) Balance? (Often.) Trumpets have the wrong music up? (All too frequent.) An immediate attack on a problem starts the rehearsal off on a footing that says at least two

things to the ensemble: (1) we're under way, and I (the orchestra member) had better be ready, (2) the old boy has rehearsed his score and is ready for this rehearsal. Am I? Nothing will inspire your members to the careful preparation of their parts faster than your demonstration of the careful preparation of your score, which they will realize, contains all their parts. When you encourage them to practice their parts by themselves, you are in addition strongly implying, "because I've practiced mine."

Once a score has been thoroughly worked on with respect to the ensuing rehearsal and the purposes of the rehearsal established, I write it down. I've found that it's a big help to write the order of the rehearsal on a separate sheet of paper which I place on a stand to the side of the podium. By "order," I mean the priority of things to be done. In my preparation for the rehearsal, I list rehearsal spots in the order they occur, going back later to number them according to their importance for that particular rehearsal. But having carefully organized my rehearsal into areas of priority, I studiously avoid trying to cover everything on that sheet. It's for reference, and I feel that allocating specific amounts of time to each area is too frustrating for me. Sometimes I get well into the list, other times only to the second or third item.

This ties in with something else that is really the crux of my rehearsal procedure: A rehearsal must be kept moving at all times. Anytime you find yourself in a situation where you can't say anything constructive (which of course includes praise for a job well done) and find yourself either at a loss for something to say or reduced to the giveaway phrase "let's do it again from the beginning," your rehearsal is lost for the day, and everything, most of all the music, will be better served if you close it up and go home. Keep it moving! For example, I make it a practice to begin talking immediately after indicating that we are stopping. It serves several purposes. One, that the comment or correction is important enough to stop for. Two, that, by speaking to it immediately, I have attached a certain amount of urgency to it, and by not letting anything else enter their minds

between playing and correcting, I have probably avoided a slump, however slight, in the energy of the rehearsal. Also, I rarely stop for obvious errors. The error of a missed note, or entrance is apparent to all, and time is lost by stopping to underline it. Repeated offenses of the same nature require attention, of course. And, errors of intonation, however obvious, are corrected immediately; not grimaced or laughed at; and certainly not passed off with a generalized correction of "you're out of tune." This latter evasion is simply an admission that you don't hear it any more critically than that. Rather, a short, decisive indication of whether the person is flat or sharp is given immediately.

Also, when a problem area has been isolated and the section(s) identified, we all have those performers try their parts alone *right then*. On the first hearing, you must make the decision on whether or not the problem can be solved today and, if not, just how much progress toward that end can be accomplished. It's crucial, I believe, for that decision to be made on the *initial* hearing and the problem left, without regrets, when you've done all you can. How many times have you witnessed or been part of a rehearsal in which the conductor rehearses a section over and over, when everyone in the room (with the possible exception of the conductor) knows it simply will not improve any more today. Hear . . . diagnose . . . give specific direction for the solution . . . rehearse until the problem is either solved or until everyone understands what he must do individually to effect a solution — *and move on!*

There will be times, of course, when just a little extra time will eliminate the problem that day. It's almost always worth the extra time, providing you don't overdo it. One way I've found to make this extra effort and time a little less trying on those sections not directly involved is to include one or more of them after the problem has been isolated and rehearsed several times. For example, if the initial area of concern involves the violas, you may have as many as fifty or sixty other members sitting through your rehearsal of the viola part. Their interest in the violas' difficulty is short-lived at best, and you will lose them — irretrievably — if you aren't aware of them, as well as the errant violas. It's a case of the cure being worse than the disease. The viola part may or may not improve, but, the longer you exclude the rest of the ensemble from the rehearsal, the more surely are you diminishing their energy and interest. All right, you've made the decision that you want to spend an extra five or six minutes on this section because you can get it all cleared up today. Fine. But on the next time through include, say, the bassoons or flutes or whomever, just to keep them involved in the rehearsal. It matters little that these extra parts do not in any way resemble the problem the violas had to begin with; what's important is that others are involved, and the orchestra has moved along a little faster and more smoothly. And, if you vary the "extra" sections, you'll find that everyone is more alert and, more importantly, listening better. Incidentally, I have found this to be especially effective in keeping the wind section involved. By the very nature of the string parts, the winds are often the ones left sitting most of the time.

The final ingredients to successful rehearsals are, I think, introspective, very personal, and difficult to write about objectively. They involve attitudes and the realization of what kind of person we really are when in the role of conductor. It has often been said that conducting is an extension of one's personality. That's true, of course, and the key word is, "extension." We must really *know* ourselves before we can *be* ourselves. Some isolated reflection into what kind of person we really are, is necessary before the personality can be extended sufficiently. The attitudes we take to each rehearsal also play a large part in the predetermination of the success or failure of that day's effort. Whatever your attitude, it must reflect your feelings honestly. They will vary, of course. There will be days when pressures, related or not, will affect the way you present yourself to the ensemble and to the music. Take stock of yourself; be honest and thorough in your self-evaluation of attitude, preparedness, and yes, degree of inspiration. It really helps.

Finally, a short word about our feelings concerning rehearsals. How do we view them? What are the main reasons for today's get-together? Aside from the obvious learning process, there is a larger reason which pervades every one I conduct. Music, unlike any other art form, is an instantaneous phenomenon. Each note, alone or in combination, is special, and will sound different each time it is performed. There can be no exact duplication of live music, no dwelling on a particular sound the same way each time. This is true whether you are on the second or seventeenth repetition. Each time is unique. If you can convey to your ensemble with your own preparation, dedication, appreciation, and attitude, just how extraordinary each sound is, each time it is performed, and how fortunate we are to engage in its beauty, the real gift of music will make rehearsals the most rewarding times of your life. ∎

January, 1971

Pianissimo !

Donn Laurence Mills

Pianissimo! Even the sound of the word creates a feeling of hushed excitement doesn't it? It can be more powerful than the mightiest *fortissimo* . . . and far more difficult to achieve. As every experienced instrumentalist knows, playing *pianissimo* is one of the most challenging accomplishments in the entire vocabulary of the musician. How many school organizations have you heard that could really play softly? I mean produce a *real* pianissimo. Not many, I'm sure. Inexperienced musicians find playing loud-louDER-LOUDER no problem at all, and many can, with effort, scale the volume down to a strained *mf*, but there is a giant step between what generally passes for pianissimo and the real thing.

After striving futilely to get a group or a soloist to play pianissimo, too many conductors and teachers settle for a compromise. The temptation, of course, is to scale one's own dynamic levels higher so that *pp* only *sounds* pianissimo in comparison to the overpowering red-faced, distorted and indistinguishable fortissimo at the other end of the scale. Adrenal-motivated students usually equate loudness with excitement and quiet with dullness as we know from the wattages unharnessed by today's amplifiers! Probably even our terms "loud" and "soft" are poor expressions because of their ambiguity. "Soft" has a more common tactile meaning: "gentle, giving way easily under pressure," and certainly not all quiet music is meant to be gentle or smooth! Some *pp* has enormous electricity and tension in it. In this regard I'm especially fond of an Eskimo word "Qarrtsiluni," an expression usually translated as "silence about to burst." The well-executed pianissimo has just this quality about it.

Let's concentrate our efforts on the more difficult quiet dynamics. What can we do to pull the volume

Donn Laurence Mills is Director of Orchestral Activities at the University of Oklahoma where he conducts the University Symphony and Opera performances. Prior to assuming his present position, he was Musical Director of the Royal Winnipeg Ballet of Canada. Mr. Mills has studied conducting with Max Rudolf, Pierre Monteux, and Sixten Ehrling. He is the author of a soon to be released book on conducting. His degrees (in composition) are from Northwestern University and from the Eastman School of Music.

down to a near-silence without losing tonal substance or pitch? Here are some ways I've found successful in working with university, all-state and amateur instrumentalists — and even with some professional groups.

1. Maintain a silent rehearsal room. General noise level (even from conversation) has a great negative effect on the feeling for pianissimo. Music should grow out of silence, not be extracted from noise. A hushed atmosphere is electric, tense. This is the environment best suited to the mood of pianissimo.

2. Speak softly to the group or even whisper when rehearsing quiet passages. Shouting PIANISSIMO ! ! does not bring about the desired reaction. A musician responds to verbal stimuli involuntarily, so try putting a tone of awe and expectancy in your voice and see if the players' response doesn't reflect it.

3. Keep the beat patterns small using as little motion as possible. This allows the music to float along airily. A heavy beat will contradict any sense of lightness or flow and result in choppy, impulsive playing. It is almost impossible to play softly while watching a vigorous baton. Try it.

4. When rehearsing, scale dynamic levels down degree by degree. Establish a scale of 1 to 10 with the group. Using a chord or single note, ask everyone to play a "comfortable" middle-range dynamic. Label it "5." Then increase and decrease the volume and establish numerical values accordingly all the way from 10 (loudest) to 1 (softest). Let the individual players experience for themselves the varying degrees of dynamics with a numerical scale concept. You may wish to refer to dynamics by numbers entirely. In many ways it is more easily comprehended than arbitrary Italian terms.

5. Rehearsal warm-ups may well include crescendo - diminuendo drills to help the individual player establish dynamic control. This can be done by sections, tutti, or individuals. Practice it by having the sections play "dynamic counterpoint" whereby one section makes a crescendo, another a decrescendo, a third holds a steady "piano" and so on. The possibilities are infinite.

6. Never be satisfied with a pianissimo! Don't give up too soon. If you insist on it stubbornly enough, you just might get it! Give up after a few polite requests and you never will.

7. It's disheartening to have a group achieve a beautiful pianissimo at a rehearsal and then, because of excitement, over-play at a performance. It's happened to all of us. Caution your group ahead of time to be on guard against this happening and suggest that they write a reminder to themselves in their music. A large SHHH! or QUIET!! or DOWN TO NOTHING! pencilled over a particular passage catches the player's eye far more effectively than a tiny *pp* shyly peering out from beneath a crowded staff.

8. Practice the *fp* effect with your group. The sharp forte attack followed by an immediate drop in dynamics is a particularly effective way to call attention to one's *emotional* reaction to pianissimo. Making a musician *aware* of the desired effect solves a large part of the problem of achieving it. Conductors often make the mistake of assuming that musicians understand exactly what is required, when in reality they neither understand nor hear with the perspective of the conductor.

9. We all know it is easier to play softly in the lower part of an instrument's range than in the middle or upper ranges (with a few exceptions). Therefore try having players reverse this natural tendency by playing a low note *ff* and answering it with a higher note *pp* (continually increasing the interval). This requires a lot of control and concentration, but eventually the habit of playing "pitch dynamics" (higher-louder: lower-softer) is overcome. It is also easier to practice playing softly if tonguing is temporarily eliminated or the upper 1/3 of the bow is used or vibrato is discontinued and other similar technical impediments are removed. Scales, by the way, are doubly valuable if practiced pianissimo.

Of course any instrumentalist needs to acquire *basic* techniques of pianissimo playing. For the wind player it means developing good breath control, a light, free tonguing ability, and a carefully executed vibrato which helps to secure the pitch and regulate the flow of air. For the percussionist it means developing a flexible wrist action and an awareness of the varied timbres available to him on different parts of a drum head or battery instrument. The string player must understand the functions of his bow and how he can achieve pianissimo effects by taking more notes per bow, playing near the fingerboard, using the upper part of the bow only and varying the speed of the bow stroke.

Discover Fundamental Concepts

The imaginative teacher will probably allow the student to discover such things for himself through experimentation. Set up a problem: "Here are two measures to be played pianissimo; how can we do it?" By allowing the student to find an answer through trial and error or by having him select the best solution from several demonstrated by the teacher (noting the cause and effect), fundamental concepts will evolve which can be applied to many situations where pianissimo is called for.

10. Make a great issue of dynamics at every rehearsal. Use a tape recorder to prove to the group how little dynamic range they are using (they always *think* they're doing it until they hear the playback). Even when sight-reading, make sure the players pay attention to all dynamic levels without depending upon your podium gyrations to get a reaction. The necessity to over-conduct is a reflection upon the rehearsal technique of the conductor, not an indictment of the group.

Impress upon your group that dynamics are essential to the music, not something added later for decoration. After experiencing the thrill of a real pianissimo sound they will discover a new world of musicianship and will be on their way to artistic maturity. ∎

Candid Thoughts
on Rehearsal Techniques

Milton Goldberg
as told to G. Jean Smith

All articles written about rehearsal techniques stress the importance of the conductor's complete mastery and understanding of the score. But there is an even more important consideration for the school orchestra conductor — that of preparing the players. Unless each individual player has mastered his own part, the orchestra will not perform as successfully as possible. Sectional string rehearsals can help considerably in working out any rough spots by acquainting students with difficult fingerings and bowings. And carefully marked parts can certainly save precious rehearsal time.

The orchestra's seating plan and physical setup is also an important factor in the success of a performance. Percussion students should place drum equipment and music stands so that they can face the director at all times. Seated players, especially the string players, should be encouraged to raise their music stands high enough to be able to also see the conductor's beat in their line of vision. In general, the taller the conductor, the higher the music stand.

Tuning is a prime consideration for the effective rehearsal and concert. Don't hesitate to stop and tune when it is needed. Hot stage lights may raise the pitch of the wind instruments, so a conductor should be prepared to check the tuning after the first 20 minutes. To facilitate string tuning, insist on tuning adjusters for every

G. Jean Smith has taught in Virginia Public Schools, at Madison College (Harrisonburg, VA) and at the Indiana State University Lab School. She holds degrees from the Eastman School of Music (B.M., cello), the University of South Dakota (M.M., Mus. Ed.), and Catholic University (Ph.D., Musicology) — and is currently editor of the NSOA Bulletin.

steel string.

Unexpected problems may contribute to intonation difficulties. Here are a few practical suggestions for dealing with these problems. Besides using graphite (or soft pencil) for sticking pegs, rub some on the nut and bridge at the point of contact with the string to prevent unnecessary wear and tear on the string winding. Bridges on new string instruments may slip sideways, thus changing the pitch seconds after tuning. A little chalk or rosin applied to the exact places where the legs of the bridge touch the belly will keep things in control and save much precious rehearsal time. For all tuning purposes, a battery operated oscillator-tuner will be very helpful before and during the rehearsal and concert. In fact, it is necessary on-stage equipment for every concert.

Time savers in tuning for rehearsal are essential. Learn to skim through string tunings by lining up youngsters for a quick check. Pre-tuning all large string instruments just before the rehearsal period saves headaches and time. Tune all winds after strings are set.

Many college students who have completed practice teaching requirements at the high school or junior high level may discover, upon accepting an elementary school position, that rehearsal techniques differ considerably from their secondary school experience. With 4th, 5th, and 6th graders, a great deal of drill and repetition will be required. Rehearsing in a spirit of good humor with an underlying seriousness will be effective in keeping student interest and giving them that sense of pride needed to raise their standards for fine performances.

Certain rehearsal techniques can cut down disasters in performance. For example, call out key rehearsal numbers so that percussion and wind players with long rests can learn to keep their place by recognizing the music in those sections. At a concert, the director can "mouth" the rehearsal numbers. Should there be a false start, a miscounted entrance, or any other serious mistake which interferes with the total orchestra sound, a conductor would be well advised to stop immediately and begin again or indicate a nearby rehearsal letter and continue with the performance. With older students, one can take a more professional approach.

How quickly does your orchestra respond to your *first* down beat? We have a signal that is a real attention getter. When our rehearsal is ready to start, lights out means quiet and we're ready to begin. The agenda is on the board with any important announcements. Talking is minimal so that we can get to the music. When preparing to play in an unfamiliar hall, we go through at least one piece before the program, even if we have to play in front of the arriving audience. It is always a good idea to play a few opening chords at the beginning to avoid starting cold. If the orchestra cannot get into a new hall for rehearsal before the performance, the conductor should check it out for resonance and dead spots. If last minute substitutions on solo parts are necessary, then explain it to the audience. They will certainly be sympathetic when they know what the problems are. On one occasion the first trumpet player was unexpectedly absent from our final concert featuring an important solo part. At the last minute, it was impossible to get a substitute for the part and the other players just weren't quite up to it. With a sympathetic audience, our orchestra had the confidence to proceed successfully. At times a broken string or, even worse, a broken tailgut will leave the concertmaster without a playable instrument. If students know ahead of time that they should pass the instrument down to the last player, a disaster can be averted.

There are a number of minor precautions that can be taken to avoid problems at concerts. Advise the clarinet and oboe players to save good reeds for the concert, and to have a spare on hand. An emergency cello endpin holder can be made by laying a folded chair flat on the floor, inserting the leg of the chair behind the cellist's chair leg and sticking the endpin into the wooden or metal part of the back of the folded chair. Cloth cases can be useful for emergencies

only — they're subject to damage if used often. When on tour we use folding stands. We crimp the top section of the tube (which fits into the desk part) to make it hold as one unit and carry them in a circular waste basket to keep them all together. This way we don't lose parts and can carry as many as 30 at one time. It is a good idea to see to it that every child has his own piece of music. Usually, we purchase the largest orchestra set possible to ensure enough for everyone. And even if parts are lost, there is always one more left for that emergency. Having extra parts on hand is a lifesaver. To preserve music, we bind separate parts to used file folders and cut them to fit so that each sheet has a backing and cover. This is especially important for old music that is used frequently for special occasions such as graduation exercises and assemblies. It is absolutely essential to

check all audio-visual equipment in advance. If you know that your program is to be taped, try to time it so that you know when half the time is up. You don't want the reel to be changed in the middle of a piece.

A recent national educational television documentary entitled, "Rehearsal with Stokowski" was most effective in demonstrating how to use rehearsal time successfully. The rehearsal began with two polite requests for "quiet please" and one angry, violent, resounding "QUIET!" which cleared the air for the balance of the session. The speed with which Maestro Stokowski stopped, counted bars, made corrections, and began again with the complete cooperation of his orchestra was an excellent demonstration to all viewers of how professionals work. This may well be the lesson that we are looking for. ∎

January, 1992

Rehearsal Preparation

by Max Dalby

Having heard much about the importance of preparing for rehearsals, you may still not be clear about what is involved in a detailed score analysis that produces efficient rehearsals.

After selecting music which seems appropriate for your group, analyze its harmonic texture and tonal nature. Notice instrumentation, key signatures, tempo and dynamic markings, modulations and other obvious clues, and mark places in which difficulties might occur with a colored pencil. It helps to know the historical setting in which the music was written. Each general historical period, Renaissance, Baroque, Classical, Romantic, and 20th Century, has identifiable structural elements such as repeat of sections, polyphonic and monophonic texture, rhythmic and harmonic repetition, melodic lines and accompaniment figures, *Da Capo* and *Dal Segno* locations. Understanding where these common elements occur will improve rehearsal effectiveness.

In looking at the score, you may be

overwhelmed by all of those notes plus transpositions on the full score; remember that in music with traditional harmony most parts can be reduced to chords of three or four notes. Study the condensed piano score that is usually furnished and analyze the harmonic progressions, using such shorthand chord symbols as CM, Cm, C7, and indicate these on the score. Play them on a piano and memorize the changes, or use a recording to compensate for inadequate keyboard skills. You may be more comfortable identifying chords as they appear in theory exercises. Indicate passing tones, suspensions, non-harmonic notes, embellishments, and other movements as they occur. Instrument parts written in bass clef are non-transposing, as are the flute, oboe, and mallet parts in the treble clef; it helps to review B♭, E♭, and F transpositions to make all parts fit the piano score. Most traditional music can be analyzed harmonically in this fashion, and doing so will give you confidence as you approach the anal-

Max Dalby in 1973

During 28 years on the faculty of Utah State University, Max Dalby served as director of bands, chairman of the music department, coordinator of music education programs, conductor, and teacher. Prior to this, he established the instrumental music program of San Diego Diocese elementary school system in 1946.

ysis of contemporary music, with chord clusters, polytonality, and unusual interval relationships.

Examine the score or the individual parts if a full score is not furnished to determine if players have the range, endurance, and dynamics for the music. Notes above the staff for cornets/trumpets and third octave notes for flutes may take skills the students have not acquired.

Brass players attempting music beyond their abilities develop poor tone production habits and may damage embouchures trying to play loudly and high and sabotage learning correct playing techniques, which develop only over a period of many months by long-tone and flexibility exercises, daily technical studies, and gradual extension of range.

Anticipating Intonation Problems

Often intonation problems are inherent in the nature of the music or in the instruments of the band. Many composers, even some writing for young bands, work in keys that expose the intonation deficiencies of wind instruments. Keys nearest those in which band instruments are built are usually easier to play in tune and may account for many band directors who choose to stay in familiar territory.

Close score examination may reveal such problems as chords in which cornets play major thirds or, worse, minor sevenths, using one and three, or three-valve combinations; you will be forgiven for writing another note of the chord for cornets and giving the major third or minor seventh to trombones to play in tune with a simple slide movement and without losing tone quality.

Trombonists have problems if they learned basic scale positions from pitches dealt them by baritone players using three-valve instruments that do not humor B and C second line and space in bass clef down to proper pitch. Remind trombonists that positions should be shortened as the slide moves upward, lengthened as it moves downward.

Many young players are conditioned to accept acute degrees of sharpness in ensemble playing, especially flute at the *forte* or *fortissimo* level in the third octave, the cornets/trumpets and the trombones and euphoniums on high F and G Concert, and most alto saxophones playing written Ds, Gs, As, and high

Cs in the second octave. Oboes, bassoons, and clarinets have critically sharp notes as well. Horns are sharp when the slides are not pulled correctly or when hands are not placed properly in the bells. These conditions add up to considerable sharpness; it is a wise band director who copes with it early in each school year.

A director can anticipate and solve many problems by identifying out-of-tune notes on all wind instruments, knowing how to bend them to required pitch, and locating these on a score in advance of rehearsals, and by reviewing common causes of intonation problems.

• Careless warm-up procedures, and the B♭ tuning syndrome, by which band members and some directors assume that tuning one note in octaves will achieve good intonation.

• Correct and alternate fingerings and positions, and tuning at extreme dynamic levels.

• Brass instruments with stuck tuning slides and dented or dirty tubing.

• Clarinet tuning barrels should be 2 5/8 inches; short barrels should be pulled and tuning rings inserted. If the second space A key opens too far, stack small squares of plastic tape beneath the key until the pitch is lowered to an accurate whole step with G.

• Bassoons with wrong or unclean bocals and oboes and bassoons with reeds too long or too short, too hard or too soft.

• Flute cleaning rod marks not in the center of embouchure holes.

• Bass clarinets and saxophones held incorrectly. Use of jazz modified sax mouthpieces. Octave keys and right hand bank of keys open too far.

• Timpani not tuned accurately.

• Improper use of right hand in bell by horn players.

Technical and Rhythmic Aspects

Next investigate the technical and rhythmic aspects of the music: fingering, positioning, striking and rhythmic patterns related to tempo. Difficult music usually involves complicated rhythmic patterns and rapid notes that some players may sight-read without error while others take several weeks of practice to learn the parts. It helps to work with some students individually or in small groups before scheduling full rehearsals of certain compositions. Woodwind parts are usually more difficult technically than brass or percussion parts, especially in transcriptions.

Although technically difficult music is often impressive in performance, many directors spend inordinate amounts of time learning it. Certainly it is easier to motivate technical development than to refine tonal concepts or to open a Pandora's box of intonation problems. Most students who practice consistently can develop a remarkable amount of dexterity with little help from teachers and do so even with wrong fingerings and positions, poor tonal quality, and terrible intonation. Many bands never get beyond this point yet play with vitality and obvious enjoyment; critical listeners are less enthusiastic.

Technical facility and accurate reading ability are important, of course, for a great quantity of band music is technically and often rhythmically very difficult. As players develop impressive manipulative and rhythmic skills to meet the challenges of this kind of music, encourage them to also concentrate on tone control.

Interpretation: Style and Expression

Style is basically the treatment of notes through slight alteration of note values and volume (accent or stress). It is what is done to notes that is not indicated but is implied by the character of the music, involving tempo, articulation, dynamic elements, and the effect of traditional performance practices on the interpretation of certain pieces.

Much of the music you will conduct has been recorded by competent professional or other groups. If you are not intimately acquainted with music you plan to perform through your playing or listening experience, the recordings will help you analyze the stylistic elements.

Proper style is learned through imitation; by singing or playing you can demonstrate how a rhythm should sound, including the accent or stress given to certain notes. Style is most effectively taught by analysis of how individual notes are treated.

March Tempo

Don't ask for short or shorter notes unless you have specified with chalk board notations the normal note values.

Staccato notes should be preceded by silence, which means the note

401

before a staccato note should be shortened. Analyze the treatment of groups of notes (phrases) through inflection of all four elements of musical sound: duration, intensity or volume, timbre, and, occasionally, pitch. Expressive phrasing is best taught by imitation, and success here depends upon your competence in demonstrating how fragmentary cues reflect a composer's intent, and how the four elements are melded into emotional and intellectual reactions that enable players to identify with the spirit, mood, and purpose of the music.

The key to expressive playing is how students' attitude toward the music influences the performance. This attitude depends upon your imagination and ability to stimulate the students to share your commitment and react to your emotion in revealing the unseen meaning of notes on the score.

Many musical terms give important clues as to the style and emotional content of music: *cantabile, spiritoso, tranquillo, scherzando, eleganza, funebre, dolce, legato, marcato, portato.* Look up the meanings of unfamiliar words; they convey important interpretive messages.

Do not expect a definitive performance of anything, but your approaches should closely resemble those of respected conductors. If there are no recordings or historical references delineating the style of the music, study the recording of a similar piece of music from the same period.

Vocal music, in which meaning is more easily presented than in instrumental music, is frequently a kind of program music, having meaning in relationship to something basically non-musical, often begetting its own expressive qualities. Such music is usually more susceptible to interpretive analysis than instrumental music. The expressive qualities inherent in band music are, as a rule, less easily discovered.

Superior vocal performance has much to offer wind instrument players. To learn expressive playing, students should experience the physical involvement singers feel, that instrumental notes are to melody as words are to sentences. When students sing an accent value, stretch a note, condense a note, or create a rise and fall of dynamic interest, they are learning vocal musical communication. The next step is transferring these sensations to the single vowel and limited consonant sounds of instruments as students gain insight into expressive playing.

Encourage students to improve their ability to listen critically by studying performances on all instruments and groupings, especially string quartets. Students may not become individually creative, but each should experience at one time or another the thrill of performing when all musical elements come together at the right time and place.

Conducting Skills

In preparing for rehearsals, many school directors lose sight of the importance of communicating effectively and eloquently with the baton, the symbol of musical authority. Diligent practice before a mirror of all movements is necessary to elicit unified responses from your band in matters of tempo, dynamics, precision, and style. You will save valuable rehearsal time with clear and self-assured baton movements, teaching young musicians to respond to traditional conducting gestures.

Limitations in baton technique have little effect on tone quality or intonation, but they influence dynamic levels, rhythmic accuracy, ensemble precision, style, and the overall expressiveness of your group.

Train your students to memorize certain passages that are critical to expressive unity: phrase beginnings and endings, climaxes, dynamic shading, and effects resulting from accents, tempo, and style changes. Unless students memorize such parts, they cannot see the expressive guidance of the conductor.

Proper baton cues eliminate the need for such verbal superfluities regarding tempo or legato style.

When you assume the mantle of conductor you become in a sense an actor with a part to play; lose yourself in the role. By conducting with recordings and videotaping your movements you will overcome self-consciousness and gain confidence. Although graceful and authoritative conducting may not improve the sound or pitch, it will certainly give students faith in your knowledge of the score. They will also learn to depend upon consistency of cueing, tempos, style, and dynamic levels. Poor conducting habits detract from the music and engender feelings of uncertainty and sometimes embarrassment in the band, while good posture, a confident attitude, and elegant conducting movements create an impression of professional competence and impart an air of dignity to a con-

cert performance.

When preparing for rehearsals consider these suggestions to improve your conducting image:

• In giving tempo indications before a piece begins, do so with one hand in front of your body where it will not be seen by the audience. Most tempos can be given by a preparatory baton movement if the group, including percussionists, learns to take a breath with the movement.

• Do not develop the habit of counting off. This lazy technique teaches band members to listen for words and ignore the baton. When standing behind the band or a section giving instructions, however, a verbal signal eliminates trips to the podium.

• Do not tap on the stand for attention; this is amateurish.

• After raising the baton, survey the group, check posture and eye-contact. Do not give the baton cue until you have the undivided attention of every member of the group, but there should be no talking or whispering once you have ascended the podium.

• After an interruption in the playing, give the band clear direction about where to resume playing. Whenever possible begin on a phrase line, but students should number all measures, lightly and in pencil, in music that will have intensive drill.

• Use composers' names to identify alphabetical rehearsal letters which sound alike to avoid confusion, such as Arensky for letter A, Bach or Beethoven for B, Chopin for C, Debussy for D, which helps students become familiar with proper pronunciation.

• Use facial and mouth expressions with baton movement to indicate how notes begin and end. Try "ooo" for a pianissimo sound that should have no consonant beginning, "poo" for one with a gentle onset, "too" or "tah" for one louder with more definition, and "pah" for a strong entrance. Students will appreciate these facial cues.

Directors sometimes forget that a public or music festival performance is an opportunity to display what the group can do, not what it cannot do. With thoughtful music choices, meticulous score preparation, and well-organized rehearsals, the group can reach the high performance levels for which we all strive. ☐

Instrumentation

Is the Composer's Prerogative

Keith Wilson

THE PHENOMENAL GROWTH IN THE number and quality of bands in the United States and the significant place they have assumed in music education in most schools and colleges make it difficult to understand why many musicians, including a considerable number of band conductors and especially composers, still ask: "What is a band?" Since the very beginning of the school band movement, with its accompanying contests and festivals, instrumentation has been a primary concern of conductors, composers, publishers, and instrument manufacturers—in short, of everyone connected in any way with bands. Band directors' associations have devoted countless hours in committees and general sessions to the study and discussion of this controversial subject.

Many feel that, in spite of all these efforts, little, if any, progress has been made. They point out that there is not even agreement on a name for this group of wind instruments and that a contest in semantics has developed, creating even more labels to add to the already existing ones of concert band, symphonic band, symphony band, wind ensemble, symphonic wind ensemble and wind symphony. The critics can rightly complain, furthermore, that it is still possible to buy a "full" set of published parts having not only fewer multiple parts, but lacking even in some of the individual parts available in the "symphonic" set. This implies that either the full set

Keith Wilson is Professor of Music at Yale University and director of the music division of the University's Summer School of Music and Art. Under his direction, the Yale University Band toured Europe in 1959 and 1962. In addition to serving as president of the College Band Directors National Association, Mr. Wilson retains membership in the American Bandmasters Association, the Musical Educators National Conference, and other professional organizations.

is incomplete, or the added parts in the symphonic set are unessential, thereby entirely negating the importance of several instruments considered by many conductors to be indispensable in a "complete" instrumentation.

Difficult to Set a Standard

Many reasons for this situation are obvious. In the first place, there are so very few professional bands to set a standard for the educational field. (It is interesting to note in this respect that the few in existence, such as the service organizations in Washington, D.C., and Mr. Goldman's, are all simply called bands without the status-seeking prefixes considered so essential by most of us in schools and colleges.) In the second place, since the vast majority of bands are in educational institutions—where consequently, all levels of technical and musical development exist and where inevitable personnel changes occur every year—it is virtually impossible for all bands to have an identical "standard" instrumentation. A third important reason is the simple fact that very few of the conductors of even our finest professional and college bands agree in complete detail on just what the ideal instrumentation of a band should be.

Some Progress

However, I think that we are much closer to a definition of band than the foregoing would indicate. For several years, the CBDNA's Committee on Band Instrumentation has worked untiringly to arrive at such a definition. The 1960 and 1962 national conferences provided many revealing and encouraging results. Prior to the 1960 conference, several composers and publishers had been invited to meet with CBDNA representatives and to speak

at the conference. The recommendations of the committee concerning instrumentation, the speeches by composers, publishers, and conductors, and the vote on the recommendations by the membership present have been published in the proceedings of the conference and elsewhere, so will not be repeated in this article. Summarily, the most impressive aspect of the conference was the virtually unanimous agreement on many points of discussion. The points of serious controversy usually involved single instruments, such as the alto oboe (English horn), the contrabassoon, the soprano and bass saxophones, the E♭ cornet, and whether it was advisable to divide the clarinet and cornet sections into two or three parts. Most significant of all was the fact that the composers present, all of whom had written extensively for band, were in disagreement to the same extent as the conductors.

The Composer's Freedom

This brings us to the main premise of this article. Composers do not want to write for precisely the same instruments in every band piece—nor should they. When the composer writes for orchestra, he is not *required* to provide a part for piccolo, alto oboe, contrabassoon, cymbal, or any other instrument. He scores only as he sees fit. He often tries new ideas, such as subdividing the two main sections of violins.

I maintain, then, that the instrumentation of the band should not be absolutely defined but must be as flexible as that for orchestra or any other ensemble. Certainly, there now is a recognized basic instrumentation including sections of flutes, double reeds, clarinets (alto, bass, and contrabass), saxophones, cornets and trumpets, horns, trombones, baritones, tubas, and percussion. We

403

conductors must realize that the time has come for the composer, and not us, to determine just how the basic and auxiliary instruments in each of these sections are to be employed. Let the composer divide the clarinets and cornets as he sees fit, and let him write for piccolo, alto flute, alto oboe, contrabassoon, soprano saxophone, Eb cornet, or any other instruments, whenever they are required to convey his musical thoughts. It is our responsibility to acquire these auxiliary instruments and to develop a few "doublers" to play them when the occasion arises but not to consider each a permanent addition to the instrumentation with music written for it in every composition.

Financial Problem of the Band Composer

We have achieved much in our efforts to bring the band to a high level of musical potential; but, if bands are to gain the artistic stature and the literature conductors are constantly striving for, we must make it possible for composers to express their creative talents as they see fit, and not as we prescribe. Equally important, they must receive just financial remuneration.

The speeches by the composers and publishers mentioned above contained numerous reminders that the lack of a standard instrumentation for bands was not as major an obstacle in enticing composers to write for this medium as was the lack of a satisfactory monetary return on their investment of time and talent. It was pointed out that orchestra commissions usually range from $1,000 to $5,000 with ensuing royalties, performance and recording fees. But, as stated before, most bands are in educational institutions which pay no performance fees (few band pieces are recorded commercially), so the band composer can normally expect to realize only his 10 per cent on the purchase price of an undetermined number of sets of parts each of which may be performed any number of times with no further remuneration for him. This financial problem is one that can be resolved only thru deliberations among composers, licensing agencies, and school administrators. However, conductors should be cognizant of the seriousness of the situation and be prepared to lend their support to any arrangement which will provide greater inducement to our major composers to utilize the band medium for their creative talents.

When the composer can feel free to write for band as he would like—without being restricted and inhibited by all the confusing, precautionary advise usually offered him by conductors and publishers—and when he can be assured of a financial return equal to that provided by other media, then, and only then, can the problems of band instrumentation and worthwhile literature be resolved.

Band Instrumentation

A Symposium

I
The Concert Band

HERBERT WINTERS HARP

DURING THE PAST FIFTY years a great deal has been done toward developing the band into a satisfactory medium of musical expression. Both wind and percussion instruments have been improved mechanically and acoustically. Instrumentation has been varied to give greater sonority and better blend of tone.

Arrangers are not only transcribing more compositions from the repertoire of the orchestra, but modern composers are writing band compositions. Public schools are making a very important contribution in developing better players and creating a demand for better band music. These developments and others constitute an unending effort to place the band on a higher musical level.

Whether much more progress can be made with the band without modifying its instrumentation is questionable. Perhaps the traditional band is an inferior vehicle of musical expression.

This inferiority, if it exists, might stem directly from the use of the clarinet as the main section of the band. Even though the clarinet is a very lyrical instrument when played well and even though it has great flexibility, it does possess certain inherent weaknesses. In the first place, rapid articulation is limited on the clarinet because of the inability of most clarinet players to use double and triple tongue. In the second place, the clarinet tone, while highly refined as a solo instrument, does not seem to fulfill its promise of greater richness as the number of clarinets is increased. With each added clarinet the collective tone becomes more strident, and its tone no longer blends in the same manner that only two or three clarinets blend with other woodwind instruments.

What is the answer? Should bandsmen continue to follow the same fifty-year-old pattern? Should they endeavor to improve the clarinet section and encourage great composers to compose for band on the assumption that music originally intended for band will approach the desired level of tonal perfection?

Research Program

The State Teachers College at Fredonia, a division of the State University of New York, has established a program of research in music and music education, and each year a symposium will be presented in conformity with this policy. This year the topic, "Can Flutes Revolutionize the Modern Band?" was chosen because the wind teachers of this school were agreed that the flute offers a great number of possibilities as a substitute for the inadequate clarinet.

The intonation problem, it was thought, would be no worse than with clarinets; the potential from the standpoint of articulation seemed much greater; and the opportunity for the use of vibrato appeared as a distinct advantage over the clarinet. As for tone quality, no one could predict what thirty flutes as the main section of a band would sound like, but acoustically it offered good possibilities.

The experiment involved the use of two 65-piece bands. One had a main section of flutes, and the other, a control band, had standard instrumentation. The procedure of the experiment was to have a selection performed in sequence by the experimental and then by the control group.

Instrumentation for the experimental band was as follows:

2 Piccolos (C)

3 1st Flutes
4 2nd Flutes
6 3rd Flutes
7 4th Flutes
3 Alto Flutes (G)
1 Bass Flute (C)[1]

4 Soprano Clarinets
2 Alto Clarinets
3 Bass Clarinets

2 Oboes
2 Bassoons

2 Alto Saxophones
2 Tenor Saxophones
1 Baritone Saxophone

1 1st Cornet
1 2nd Cornet
1 3rd Cornet
2 Trumpets
4 Horns

1 Euphonium

2 Tenor Trombones

1 Bass Trombone

2 Tubas (B Bb)

2 Bass Viols
Snare Drum
Cymbals
Bass Drum
Tympani

This instrumentation was selected with the hope of obtaining enough volume from the flute section so as not to disturb the basic setup of the brass section. No brass parts were eliminated, but the players were restricted to one on a part.

The instrumentation of the regular Symphonic Band being used in the investigation differed from the experimental group by having only one piccolo, three flutes, no alto or bass flutes, and eighteen soprano clarinets.

The following program was selected by the symposium committee:

Two Moods (Overture) __ _Grundman_
Experimental arr. Theodore Petersen
Prelude in Bb Minor_____
_____ _Bach-Moehlmann_
Experimental arr. A. Cutler Silliman
The Gods Go A-Begging (Ballet Suite) _____ _Handel-Beecham_
Introduction, Allegro, Bouree
Experimental arr. Robert Marvel
Symphony No. 1, "Nordic"_____
_____ _Hanson-Maddy_
Second Movement
Experimental arr. Theodore Petersen
Pictures at an Exhibition_____
_____ _Moussorgsky-Leidzen_
Promenade, the Hut of the Baba-Yaga, The Great Gate of Kiev
Experimental arr. A. Cutler Silliman

In the case of the orchestral compositions the transcriptions were made from the original scores by members of the college faculty.

Factors controlling the selection of the compositions were as follows:

a. Requirement that they be representative of the repertoire of high school bands

b. The necessity of using compositions of moderate difficulty because high school flutists were included in the experimental band

c. Desirability of selecting music that would display flute tone and articulation and at the same time answer the question of whether the volume produced by thirty flutes would be adequate to balance the brasses

A serious attempt was made to obtain an accurate evaluation of this experiment from the one hundred high school band directors in the audience and from faculty members who worked with the unit in one capacity or another. The evaluation was ascertained by means of a comparative evaluation sheet which was filled out by the audience of directors while the numbers were being played.

Each arranger explained, preceding the performance, how he had handled the voicing of instruments. The experimental band played his arrangement, and then the regular Symphonic Band arrangement was presented.

A careful tabulation of the answers was made with the following results:

Is the massed tone quality of the flutes better than the massed tone of the clarinets? _Yes, 73%; no, 27%_[2]

Is the massed articulation of the flutes better than the massed articulation of clarinets? _Yes, 50%; no, 50%_[3]

Is the low register of the flute section acceptable in this medium? _Yes, 60%; no 40%_

Does the massed vibrato of flutes produce a warmer tone color than the clarinets which employ no vibrato? _Yes, 95%; no 5%_

Does the flute section make for a better blend than that achieved by the clarinet section? _Yes, 75%; no, 25%_

Does the flute section make for a greater variety of tone color than that found in the clarinet section? _Yes, 23%; no, 77%_

Do you feel that the experimental band is potentially capable of performing:

(a) more transcriptions (orchestral) than our present band? _Yes. 70%; no, 30%_

(b) more flexibly than our present band? _Yes, 50%; no, 50%_

(c) as expressively as the conventional concert band? _Yes, 55%; no, 45%_

Do you think the band scoring for this flute band was satisfactory? _Yes, 100%_

---

[1]We were able to obtain one bass flute in C, but it arrived too late to use in the band. Judging from what that bass flute sounded like, it is extremely doubtful whether it ever would be a worth-while addition to the band. It is a difficult instrument to play, and the tone is quite weak in the medium low and low register.

[2]A magnificent tone color was produced by the flute section in all registers. This color was greatly enhanced by the use of the three alto flutes. However, with a section having twenty-eight flutes the use of at least six or eight alto flutes would have been more satisfactory.

[3]It may be said here that even though the flutes offered a greater potentiality with their better flexibility of tonguing, this advantage was offset by their inability to "cut through" the band. Even though the flutes could tongue faster, the rapid passages lacked clarity and definition.

405

Do you feel that the scoring would be improved by employing:

(a) Flutes and clarinets evenly divided? *Yes, 70%; no, 30%*

(b) Clarinets on the lower parts and flutes on the higher? *Yes, 69%; no, 31%*

(c) More alto flutes in the lower voicing? *Yes, 82%; no, 18%*

(d) Piccolo doubled with first flute? *Yes, 40%; no, 60%*

(e) Piccolo doubled with first and second flutes? *Yes, 16%; no, 84%*

Is the volume of the flute section adequate in balancing the remainder of the band? *Yes, 100%* (Inadequate in middle and low register except when few brasses were used)

Under the heading of "additional comments," the chief criticism was lack of variety in tone color of the flute section; it became a bit monotonous.

Conclusions

Looking at the above evaluation as a whole, the conclusion might be reached that the substitution of a flute section for the clarinet section is the answer to the band problem. However, such is not the case. Certain answers must be qualified, and, upon closer examination, the discovery is made that certain of the negative answers outweigh several of the affirmative ones.

In summarizing this experiment it may be said in general that the flute tone with its vibrato produced a warmth of tone that just cannot be achieved by clarinets. The blend was also excellent. Yet with these advantages in tone, three distinct faults were apparent: (1) the inadequacy of the volume in the middle and low register; (2) the lack of variety in tone color; and (3) the lack of clarity in regard to articulation.

Within the limits of this experiment we have drawn the following conclusions:

(1) In a band of this size at least ten or fifteen clarinets and a good number of alto, bass, and contra bass

Herbert Winters Harp has been trumpet instructor and director of band, State University of New York, Teachers College, Fredonia, N.Y., since 1946. Before that he had been director of bands at Syracuse U., and had had nine years experience teaching instrumental music in public schools. He has played trumpet in the Utica and Syracuse symphonies and in the Erie Philharmonic. He earned his B.M. and his M.M. at the Eastman School of Music.

clarinets should be retained.

(2) There is a definite place in band for a complete section of ten to fifteen flutes, including approximately four alto flutes.

(3) The flute should function as a complete section and take over from the clarinets the work in the high register.

The capabilities and limitations of the flute, as a section, are now known to us, and we have gained an insight into what might be expected of the flute in the future symphonic band.

II
The Concert Band

MARK H. HINDSLEY
University of Illinois

THE concert band began to move indoors many years ago, but it probably has retained too many of the characteristics of the outdoor band.

Our standards of performance have risen considerably during this period, and the instrumentation has changed to quite a degree to reach those standards, but I believe there is further need for refinement. I believe that we need to reconsider and re-evaluate the instrumentation of the concert band and our method of scoring for it.

It is probable, too, that bands as a whole have grown too large and that there has been considerable carelessness in maintaining numerical balance of the instruments. As a result, the band tone has become too thick, heavy, and elephantine, thus breeding carelessness in execution and other lack of finesse.

It is possible to have a good concert band of 90 to 120 players though a completely instrumented and balanced group can be had within the range of 50 to 70 players. In fact, it is desirable to keep the band within the lower range unless the proficiency of the membership is unusual, for good players are required if a large group is to play as a cohesive unit.

I should like to see flutes given more prominence in the concert band. They should replace the clarinets in much of the high register work. Ordinarily, flute parts should be written in two parts with provision for fur-

ther divisi work. One piccolo is usually sufficient within the flute section, but occasionally more piccolos will be needed for unison or divisi work. I should like to see at least six flutes in a smaller band, and I would like to try up to eighteen or so in the largest band.

I believe that one oboe on a part is adequate for any size band. The difficulties of intonation and blend make doubling on this instrument a hazard. A complete section should include two oboes and one English horn, the latter to be used as the occasion demands. With an English horn available, much melodic and ensemble work could profitably be assigned to it.

In general, the same comments may be made with regard to the saxophone section. A quartet of saxophones, with two altos, one tenor, and one baritone, is quite adequate for any size band. There is not quite so much hazard in doubling the alto and tenor saxophones as in doubling the oboes; yet I feel that four are sufficient. The bass saxophone is a good instrument if played well; yet it is less valuable than other bass woodwinds and would serve only to duplicate them. I would consider the bass saxophone an optional instrument, and, furthermore, I can see no reason for having a higher saxophone tone than the alto.

More Bassoons

In contrast to oboes and saxophones, it is my belief that it is profitable to double the bassoons. While they have unusual intonation problems, they are more flexible in intonation and will blend with each other and with other instruments better than the other two instruments named. They are extremely versatile in technique and range, and in a large band the reinforcement of their tone by doubling is often very desirable. Two bassoons are adequate in a small band, but I would use a half dozen in a large group. The contrabassoon may be used as a doubling instrument by one of the regular bassoon players.

The clarinets, of course, are the basic woodwind family. With the abundance of flutes indicated earlier as being desirable, I see no reason for using the E♭ soprano clarinet except for special occasions.

The number of B♭ soprano clarinets may vary from twelve in the small group to twenty-five or thirty in the extremely large organization. The bottom of the clarinet tone may be taken care of by two to six bass clarinets and one to three contra-bass clarinets.

Alto Clarinet

There is no real objection to the alto clarinet between the soprano and the bass clarinets, but this is one instrument that I believe we can eliminate without serious handicap. The register is well taken care of otherwise, and, although the alto clarinet tone is distinctive, it does not seem to be essential. It is perhaps because of these factors that arrangers in general have not assigned independent parts to the alto clarinet. For the present, at least, I believe that it is better economy to use players regularly on the soprano and bass instruments.

A valuable supplement to the bass woodwinds is the string bass. String basses and contrabass clarinets work very well together. From one to four string basses may be used, depending on the number of contrabass clarinets and brass basses.

The brass section is, perhaps, more standardized than the woodwinds. I should use from four to nine cornets, two to four trumpets, five to nine French horns, three to eight trombones, two to four baritones, and three to six tubas. The flugelhorn I would use only as a doubling instrument when that texture of tone is desired for a solo or ensemble passage.

A percussion section of from four to six players would complete the normal band instrumentation, exclusive of such instruments as harp, celeste, marimba, etc., for which other players might have to be called when these instruments are essential to the score.

It is obvious that if we are to make fullest use of an instrumentation such as that outlined above, the scoring must be in keeping with the character of the instrumentation. Much of the recent scoring is basically good for this combination, but the standard arrangements of several years ago will need rearranging or re-editing to fit the new conception of the concert band.

Re-Edit Music

For example, as mentioned earlier, extremely high clarinets should be avoided except when power is necessary, with the flutes and piccolos taking over in the top register. Much doubling on other parts, such as those for horns and bassoons, should be avoided. There should be liberal markings of one player to a stand or one player to a part to achieve correct balance and color. With sufficient bass reeds and string basses, the tubas may be used more sparingly in delicate work. Percussion parts should be edited to make sure that they are essential and not written just to make sure that the players are kept busy.

Artistic Medium

It is my belief that we have at our disposal a marvelous group of instruments with which to work, instruments that can contribute to an aesthetic concert band ensemble. Many of them are still quite imperfect, particularly from the standpoint of intonation, but I believe many corrections can be made as we demand finer performance.

We also have at our disposal a great body of fine music although it still is our own responsibility to arrange and edit this music for its most effective performance. The concert band is becoming more and more recognized as a high artistic medium of expression, and we can well hope for further significant contributions to the original music for higher study and performance.

Mark H. Hindsley, director of bands at the University of Illinois, has been on the faculty there since 1934. During World War II he was in the Air Corps, serving three years as music officer and six months on the faculty of Biarritz American University in France. He has held numerous offices in professional organizations, is author of *School Band and Orchestra Administration,* **and has several published compositions to his credit. He has rendered notable service at contests, festivals, and clinics in more than twenty states. Graduate (A.B. and A.M.) Indiana University.**

III
The Small Band

TRAUGOTT ROHNER
Northwestern University

ALTHOUGH THERE ARE more small high school bands than there are large ones, instrumentation of bands is usually patterned after the latter.

As a result, band arrangements for Class C and D bands vary considerably in their attention to basic details, and reveal a monotonous insistence on following the patterns suitable only for full concert bands.

The director of the small band is continually trying to reach for an instrumentation which he rarely achieves. It is a most discouraging situation for the serious bandsman.

The small band deserves a special instrumentation which is designed to fit. A professional band sounds fine with a small number of players, even though there may be only one player to a part or one player to an instrument. With student bands this is not practical. The number of parts and different instruments must often be limited.

Three well-known arranger-composers (Buchtel, Fred, Yoder) were asked to list a minimum basic instrumentation. All agreed on the following parts:

3 Clarinet
3 Cornet-trumpet
1 Baritone
2 Trombone
1 Tuba
1 Percussion

They differed somewhat in other respects, but they agreed upon the above. This, then, we might call "Basic Instrumentation No. 1."

It is amazing how well this limited instrumentation can sound when the parts are arranged skilfully and when they are played well. Add a piccolo and a bell lyra part, and the band becomes an excellent group for marching purposes.

What instruments should be added next? To No. 1 let's add the following and call it "Basic Instrumentation No. 2":

2 Flute-piccolo
2 Horns in F
2 Sax (Eb alto, Eb baritone)

As can be seen, Basic Instrumentation No. 2 uses six additional parts and three different additional instruments. Not only do these provide considerably more variety in tone color, but at the same time they increase the problems of developing a superior band.

Neither of the foregoing two suggested instrumentations will be published without the usual number of parts for the instruments not listed in this basic instrumentation; however, the music is to be written to sound well with only the basic. The director will then know that additional parts are optional.

Let us be practical in our goals. It is high time that the small band is given more attention. Those directors who have heard the Chicago Salvation Army Staff Band, an all-brass group, can attest to the high quality of the sounds that can come forth from a band with limited instrumentation. Then, too, the clarinet trio, the trumpet trio, and the various brass ensembles are all considered as legitimate groups. Certainly a band can sound well which consists of multiples of these groups.

This statement is in no way a reflection on the double reeds and the other instruments not listed; they should be added just as soon as the director has the time to develop good players on them. Too many bands suffer because the director spreads his time too thinly over too many different instruments and parts. A band of limited instrumentation playing well will always sound better than one with more different instruments playing poorly.

Use Basic First

Arranging music for limited instrumentation does not mean that small bands should not perform music for full concert instrumentation if they have the instruments and the players. But to rob an already weak clarinet section just to get some oboe and bassoon players is not a practical procedure. The same statement will hold true in respect to any of the other instruments not listed in either of the two Basic Instrumentations.

Preparing for Band Festivals

by Lacey Powell

Preparing concert bands for district or state festivals takes commitment and organization from directors and students. Although contests are part of state music education programs, band directors and administrators often disagree about the value of participating in competitive music events. Some endorse competition; others find fault. Festivals can be a valuable experience for a band, but the director's attitude toward ensemble ratings is important because it affects how well students perform and how much they enjoy the event.

Many schools use contest results to justify music programs; some schools' curriculum is structured around contests, which need not be a detriment to music programs if the contests motivate the students to reach musical goals.

Often students fear competition out of fear that they will fail. Students who think they will succeed work towards the goal. For this reason many directors postpone entering state festivals and compete at the district level. Festivals offer the opportunity to motivate students to achieve a specific goal and offer an evaluation of the educational program for the director.

Selecting music is an important part of preparation; compositions should complement the instrumentation and proficiency of the players. Choose music that enhances the band's strong sections and challenges the group musically. Performing music that is too difficult puts excessive demands on the weaker players and only strengthens bad habits. Choose a variety of styles of music that the players can perform expressively; music of good quality generally has contrasts in style, moods, and periods. Do not select music to impress colleagues, but pick music that is best for the band. By balancing musical and technical demands, the program can interest players, adjudicators, and audiences.

Reading through a large amount of music gives students a voice in the selection. Look beyond free promotional recordings of last year's programs and find compositions and alternates that contain significant musical concepts. The music selected bears directly on motivation and is an important part of guiding students to goals beyond the next concert.

The next step is to number the measures in the conductor's score; students should use it as a guide for numbering parts to save rehearsal time. All players should keep pencils in their folders and mark comments from the director during rehearsals.

Motivate students by using an adjudication form, listing criteria, to familiarize them with the rating system and the musical standard. Discuss the adjudicator's comments from last year in order to avoid similar mistakes. Ratings and comments are sometimes put to good use by directors, but more frequently, they are ignored and some of the same problems occur year after year.

As rehearsals progress, pace the sessions so the band peaks at the proper time. Use experienced players as models; students are eager to serve in leadership roles such as maintaining a contest bulletin board.

A typical problem facing directors is a large gap in proficiency between the players because the more mature musicians learn their parts early and become bored as rehearsals continue. Negotiate a pact with the band; each player pledges to practice the festival music an agreed amount of time daily,

Lacey Powell is associate professor of music at the University of South Alabama and has degrees from Troy State University, VanderCook College of Music, and the University of Alabama.

and directors promise to study the scores and practice conducting. During this period give better players other performance opportunities to keep them challenged and interested: solo and ensemble performances, recitals, playing for community service groups, school assemblies, and churches. Establish specific goals so players learn how to practice regularly and carefully.

Learn both the full and condensed scores early in order to know how the piece sounds, improve analytical techniques, and allow for creative editing; recordings are valuable aids for interpretation. For example, improve the sonority or tone color of the band by reducing the doublings or simplifying a part so that inexperienced players can contribute.

Carefully plan each rehearsal, stating goals before starting. Remind students that there are a specific number of rehearsals before the festival to prevent them from thinking in terms of days or weeks.

Begin each rehearsal with a warmup period, conditioning players to become mentally and physically prepared for concentration. Establish a mature concept of sound and tone production through the use of some memorized material. Each player should execute every phase of performing ability, so watch for individual problems with register, articulation, and technique. If sound and tone quality are lost later in the rehearsal, return to warmup material.

To avoid burnout and loss of interest, rehearse more than the festival selections; include sight-reading in the routine, rehearsing the music after sight-reading to avoid developing sloppy habits. Teach students to transfer learned concepts by recording the sight-reading sessions, analyzing errors, and correcting them.

Schedule section rehearsals early to detect errors and prevent students from practicing mistakes, and so that the last week is not overcrowded. The technique of spot rehearsing makes rehearsal more interesting by identifying problems and suggesting how to practice difficult sections.

Assign strong players to inner parts to improve balance. Recording an occasional rehearsal gives students an opportunity to hear the overall sounds; a videocassette recorder has the added advantage of letting players see themselves.

To realize the true sound and color potential of the band experiment with different seating arrangements, such as having the ensemble face a new direction to alter acoustics; leave the podium occasionally to listen from the rear of the room; invite a guest conductor to give an objective evaluation; become familiar with the performance hall and adjust the style, tempo, or dynamics to compensate for the reverberation or the lack of it. Be alert and listen to the band objectively, and try to hear each player individually prior to the festival. Seek musical excellence in the rehearsal hall because students will become less proficient under stress. Prepare the music so that players feel confident performing it.

Make detailed plans for the day of the festival and develop student leaders with responsibilities for music, judges' scores, bus list, the sign on the bus, repair kit with extra reeds and oil, first-aid kit, set-up crew for the concert stage, loading crew, and bus captains to introduce chaperones and drivers.

Plan the festival day to the minute, allowing sufficient time for travel, meals, and warmup. Good planning improves a director's confidence, and this will ease students' nervousness.

Students should arrive at school dressed in travel attire. Begin the day by warming up with breathing exercises, chorales, and scales to condition the embouchure for playing later in the day. Check every music folder, and hold a brief meeting for band members, parents, and administrators discussing expectations for the day, standards of behavior, guidelines for etiquette and conduct, and a careful diet naming foods to avoid.

Upon arrival at the festival site, students should change into concert dress and meet in the warmup room with instruments. Hold deep breathing exercises and warm up for a minimum of five minutes, reminding students to keep instruments at body temperature during tuning. Use a strobe to check several pitches on each instrument and then check unisons in each section by ear. Make an acoustic check of the hall prior to warmup by listening to a well-balanced band perform.

Have a set-up crew ready to prepare the stage if this service is not provided by the host. Enter the stage with a rehearsed standard to ensure a positive first impression. Bands that are confident, neat in appearance, sit down quietly, allow sufficient space for individual players, adjust music stands to a proper height, and sit erectly with good posture so that each player can see the director impress adjudicators.

Players can adjust to the hall and relieve nervous tension by playing a note, chord, or scale for an acoustic check. Do not rehearse a section of the music or play a chorale because it may display problems to the judges. Remind students that physical exercises reduce nervousness: breathe deeply 10 times to exchange the oxygen in the system or gently bite the tongue to secrete saliva.

After the concert program, students should go to the assigned sight-reading room. Before the festival, rehearse sight-reading procedures, using contest regulations so the students know how to study the music with concentration. Tell players what to do about cues: not to play any or play only for missing instruments. In most festivals, bands read a march and an overture or a chorale and overture; study the overture first to allow sufficient time for it and to leave the march or chorale fresh in the players' minds.

Listening to other bands perform is an exceptional educational opportunity; assign a specific number of bands for each student to hear and have the students complete an evaluation sheet with comments about each band. Study the judges' comments and suggestions and use this constructive criticism as a basis for future plans.

The preparation and experience of performing in a festival provides motivation for individuals and groups and can improve a band's skill and performance. Festivals represent an important part of the year's schedule, but should not control the curriculum. □

Score Preparation

BY SONJA REHBEIN

*Y*ou have just come back from the new music clinic with the piece that is going to be the hit of the concert. Or is it? Will you put as much effort into preparing the music as you did into choosing it?

There are as many ways to prepare a piece for performance as there are conductors, and each conductor may rehearse a composition differently, depending upon the individual requirements of the work and the abilities of his group. Certain criteria, though, bear consideration, regardless of the rehearsal method you choose.

Score Study

Just as you expect each performer to prepare his part, it is up to you to study yours. Begin by examining the instrumentation. Is it standard or does it call for some unusual instruments? If there is a bassoon solo, do you have a player who can handle it, or can some other instrument substitute? Sometimes it is possible to simplify a solo without losing the effect; in other cases, it is better to wait to perform the work with a fully competent player.

Effects such as muting, unusual percussion sounds, imitation of natural, mechanical, or electronic sounds may call for some imagination and planning ahead on your part. A piece entitled *Morning Commuter* (Richard Spinney, Belwin Mills), for example, has a section portraying a fender-bender between two cars, an effect that the percussion section can create by dumping one garbage can full of metal and glass into another empty garbage can.

In some cases you can show students alternative ways to play special effects. Young trumpet players usually have difficulty reaching the bell with the left hand to play a "wah-wah" effect such as the one in *Clarinet Rag* by James Ployhar (Belwin Mills). Have the players use a plastic coffee cup instead of the hand; it may change the intended tone slightly, but that is better than not including the effect at all. By checking the score ahead of time, you can anticipate such problems and have solutions ready.

Another aspect to consider early on is the ranges of the instruments that the piece requires. While young first trumpeters may occasionally be able to force out high Gs, sustained or repeated Gs throughout the work may rule out programming the composition. Even if the players can manage the high notes, playing out of range can affect the pitch and tone quality of the performance. Young clarinetists playing above G in the clarino register can make an otherwise well-played piece unbearable for listeners.

Look over the score for challenging rhythms and tempos, remembering that one affects the other. Even if the rhythms in a work do not go beyond quarter notes, the tempo required may not be within the capabilities of the performers. Rhythm can also affect the speed of a piece: a march in 𝄴 is usually played at a slower tempo than one in 𝄵, 𝄴 , or 𝄵 .

Watch for rhythms that should

be interpreted differently from what the notation indicates. Many times, a swing-style work will be written as a dotted eighth note followed by a sixteenth note but should be played as a triplet pattern, a quarter note followed by an eighth note:

John Edmondson's *Dixieland Dazzle* (Discovery Series, Hal Leonard) uses eighth notes throughout the music but indicates that the triplet pattern may be substituted, as in

Keep an eye out for difficult fingerings, especially in the woodwinds; they can complicate the execution of otherwise simple rhythms. A rhythm may seem straightforward until a clarinetist tries to play C to E♭ in the clarino register and finds that he doesn't know the necessary alternate fingering. Young students may also find it difficult to cross back and forth over the break at a quick pace.

Analysis of phrases will reveal much about the overall structure of a composition. Locating the measure groupings and themes, finding melodic devices such as imitation and repetition, and pointing out dynamic variations will help you draw your students' attention to subleties in the music and elements of the composer's style. It also helps the students and the conductor to observe how one section of a piece relates to another. A challenging work becomes much less intimidating when you point out to students that the first 16 measures are repeated twice later in the music. With 48 measures suddenly learned, the students may feel a greater sense of accomplishment.

Scan the work for modulations that lead to new key signatures. New or seldom used keys require extra attention before register changes can be negotiated smoothly. Look for problems that may arise due to accidentals, and be ready to rehearse chords as well as melodies. Often the marches that sound the best are those that have been rehearsed with careful attention to the chords that embellish the melodies, though the audience may only be aware of the appealing beat and melody.

Finally, ask yourself whether the parts will sustain your students' interest. If the trombones repeat the same phrase throughout the entire work while the rest of the instruments have more complex parts, the composition may be just the remedy for lack of confidence in weaker players. For players of ability that is average or better, this much repetition may stunt interest. A work with a familiar melody but with many triplets in the rhythm may be a good choice if your students need work in that area. Ultimately, the decision depends on your group's strengths and weaknesses.

Rehearsal Techniques

Every director should be videotaped during rehearsal as an aid in studying personal conducting habits. A videotape will pick up nuances that might otherwise be missed. It does not take much bounce in a pattern, for example, to make the beats difficult to discern. Unconscious habits such as directing more to one side than the other, adjusting glasses, or not looking at the performers can detract from the quality of a performance.

Be aware of posture, deportment, and facial expressions; extraneous movements affect the audience as well as the performers. Practice so that your left and

right hands can operate independently of each other. While the right hand, properly trained, is mainly for giving the tempo, beat pattern, and character, the left should assist the right with expression. Providing cues that do not fit into the beat pattern and underscoring the gestures of the right hand are the primary functions of the left hand.

In Bartók's *Three Folk Songs* arranged by Anne McGinty (Hal Leonard), for example, the saxophones and horns have a fermata that ends one section but should be sustained while the next section is begun. One hand must cue the held note while the other cues the entrance to the next passage. This requires practice, perhaps in front of a mirror, so that the effect is not one of calisthenics.

Although it is true that musicians who have been counting rests in the music should not require an entrance cue, young students often just need the reassurance of the conductor's attention. A cue can also remind players of the character of the entrance (*marcato, fortissimo, cantabile*, etc.) and help them come in more precisely.

The rehearsal of a piece may begin with a review of any familiar keys or with practice of any new or infrequently performed keys. Using a band method that features a section in the key(s) to be performed can provide an effective tool in aiding a group to becoming comfortable in a new key.

A method book may also be used to work out any potential difficulties posed by new time signatures and specific rhythms. Introducing ⅜ meter for the first time by playing progressive exercises in a method can make the concept easier to understand. These same exercises can be used in succeeding rehearsals as warmups leading to practicing particular pieces in ⅜. To master short patterns, have students first count, clap, and tap, then practice on a single tone, and finally use the music.

Sight-reading of the piece may

be attempted either before or after the key and rhythm work. Generally, if a group can read through the piece without falling apart, it is within their capabilities. If you expect a work to be especially difficult for your group, play a recording before attempting to sight read it. Your group may become inspired to play an arrangement with more accuracy and expression after listening to a recording of the original composition.

The form of the work will become more apparent to students if you rehearse, for example, all "A" sections of a composition in rondo form, then the "B" sections, and so on. A theme with variations may become easier as the students become aware of how a theme has been changed with each variation.

There are a number of arrangements of familiar works in which changes of style are easy for students to grasp. *A New Wrinkle on Twinkle* (James Ployhar, Belwin Mills), *Variations on a Theme by Mozart* (Anne McGinty, Hal Leonard), and *Around the World with This Old Man* (Gerald Sebesky, C.L. Barnhouse) are just a few examples. In a case like Vaclav Nelhybel's *Ballad* (J. Christopher Music Co.), in which the variations on the theme are more sophisticated, it is worthwhile to spend some time showing how the themes are transformed.

Whatever the form, it is necessary to practice going from section to section so that the change — whether a thematic variation, time change, or key modulation — will be smooth and natural. The faster a change occurs, the more practice it may need to be performed correctly. One method is to start slowly on either side of the change and work through it repeatedly until it is accurate. Then the tempo

Sonja Rehbein is a band instructor at St. Francis Middle School in St. Francis, Minnesota. She is currently doing graduate work at St. Cloud State University in St. Cloud, Minnesota.

can be increased until the change can be performed musically.

The relationship of the various parts must strike a balance. One approach is to work on each section separately and then gradually bring them together. First, rehearse all of the melody voices. After rehearsing the bass line alone, add it to the melody. Gradually add the first harmonic part, the second, and finally the percussion.

Besides achieving clarity, this procedure helps give the various sections a sense of identity and importance. Some of the underlying nuances that might be lost without individual attention to inner lines may surface, using this technique. In a work like *Fisherman's Evening Song* (Lloyd Conley, Studio PR), a nautical Breton air, the distant hornpipe melody in the trombones is a special effect that can easily

become lost. Working through the parts section by section can bring out that voice and maintain the integrity of the score.

Paying attention to musical details will help you bring out the best that your group has to offer. All the great conductors have stressed the importance of score study. It is no less important for the director of a school band than for the conductor of the New York Philharmonic. ■

October, 1950

For best results and best appearance you had better

Stick To Your Stick

NEWELL H. LONG

BEFORE we break up our batons for kindling and join the Stokowski-Mitropoulos-and-others school of batonless conducting, let's examine the advantages and disadvantages of that little piece of wood which we wave in front of a group of instrumental musicians.

Correctly employed, the baton is an extension of the right hand, the right hand and forearm, or the entire right arm, depending upon whichever magnitude of motion is demanded by the musical situation. The baton serves to magnify the movements of the hand or arm and makes them more easily seen by the performers. Since the baton adds to the visibility of the conductor's beat, it is possible to reduce the amplitude of the arm's movement and still keep the beats clearly discernible. This permits the conductor to utilize smaller and less tiring motions for the basic meter indica-

tions.

The conscientious director will find plenty of physical exertion in his work without waving around an arm weighing several pounds instead of a stick weighing a few ounces. Furthermore, the conductor has a greater total range of time beating amplitude and will have more reserve left for the music's climaxes.

While it is true that the baton is less personal than the hand, the baton does impart a certain authority to the person who wields it. As a uniform gives authority to the man directing traffic on a busy corner, so the baton gives authority to the right hand in its time-beating function. Because some conductors with limited technic or musicianship do little more than beat time, they are frequently referred to as "mere time beaters." Nevertheless, the function of providing the necessary metrical signals to

NBC Photo
LEOPOLD STOKOWSKI

RCA Victor Record Photos
DIMITRI MITROPOULOS

VLADIMIR GOLSCHMANN

PIERRE MONTEUX

keep all the performers in the same part of the measure at the same time has always been, and remains, the first duty of any conductor.

There are Few Advantages

Against these advantages of greater visibility of beats, less fatigue, greater range of amplitude, and sense of authority, what are the advantages of using no baton? Although many conductors, whom we have observed using batons, are truly eloquent with them in slow, legato motions, there is the possibility of more pliable and plastic beats with the hand free of the stick when the tempo is slow and the style sustained.

The possibility of the hand providing a more personal communication to the band or orchestra than the baton has been mentioned earlier. However, the eyes and facial expressions are capable of forming much stronger avenues of personal connection between conductor and players than either hand or baton.

One technical problem wherein the presence or absence of a baton seems pertinent is the rebound after the point of the beat. Conductors who place the point at the lowest position

reached in each beat, indicating the continuation of the sound through the beat by an upward rebound, are apt to fall into either or both of two difficulties. First, since all the rebounds are upward, all the beats are likely to look like down beats, particularly to players seated to the extreme right or left. Second, a sluggishness of player-response may develop, as the band or orchestra members may easily fall into the habit of waiting for the rebound before starting the sound due on that beat.

While this very questionable habit of conducting with the up-beat (the rebounds) has been seen to develop in both stick-wavers and non-stick-wavers, the writer feels that the tendency to do so is greater among directors who have discarded the baton. It behooves every director to check his right hand patterns from time to time in order to guard against those all-too-easily acquired flourishing rebounds, which can destroy the clarity and precision of the beat.

Without a baton to extend the arm movements, some conductors allow their bodies to bend and sway excessively. Unless the person is naturally poised and graceful, these energetic

movements of the torso may appear awkward and comical to an audience.

There are recognized, competent professional conductors who use batons, and equally recognized and competent ones who do not; but before deciding which group to emulate, before throwing away that slender bit of wood that is your conductor's insignia, you should be sure you have so thoroughly mastered the mechanics of conducting that your beats will be lucid, not ludicrous, precise, not precipitous, and graceful, not grotesque. Be certain that when you conduct without the baton you don't appear to be cranking an old "Model T," strewing daisies over the musicians, or throwing peanut shells over your right shoulder!

Newell Long is assistant dean and professor of music education in Indiana University, and president of North Central Division, MENC. Taught formerly at Central State Teachers College, Michigan, and Calumet City, Ill. Holds master's degrees from Northwestern and Indiana. Composer and arranger of materials for school bands, orchestras, and ensembles. Past president, Indiana Music Educators Assn. Founder and former editor, *Indiana Musicator*.

October, 1966

HOW TO MEMORIZE

HENRI TEMIANKA

There is no such thing as a really bad memory. People who think they have a bad memory simply have not learned how to use it. All the things in life which we do well we have trained ourselves to do, usually over a long period of time: speaking, reading, writing—all the things we now take for granted.

Similarly, a good musical memory is acquired through careful training.

Undeniably, some are more naturally gifted than others. The kind of memory with which musicians like Dimitri Mitropoulos and George Szell are blessed is entirely exceptional. Mitropoulos' memory was photographic. His knowledge of the score did not only include all the notes and dynamic mark-

ings; it extended to the letters and bar numbers. I remember my amazement when, rehearsing Lalo's *Symphonie Espagnole* with him, he stopped the orchestra and, with no score in sight, called out: "Gentlemen, let us start again eight bars before letter *M*, please."

Szell's memory is equally prodigious. Once we spent a summer vacation together in Tremezzo on Lake Como in Italy. Szell had brought little music with him, and I had nothing except the Beethoven and Schubert sonatas which we were preparing for our duo-concerts the following season. There was little to do on those quiet summer evenings—an occasional bridge game with Artur Schnabel who lived next door or a stroll

along the lake terminating with a glass of grappa on the terrace of a cafe. Soon we were spending our evenings, and many of our days, making music in the hotel lounge for our own amusement and that of any guest who happened by. It was a typical businessman's holiday.

In the course of the first week, we went through practically every violin concerto and sonata I had ever learned, Szell playing the piano part without music and helping me out whenever my memory failed me. He never skipped one bar of a tutti, even when it was as extended as the introduction to the Beethoven or Brahms *Concertos*. We had a boundless appetite for music, playing as many as six and

413

seven major works at one session. At this rate the violin repertoire could not last forever. Soon we were down to the dregs, shamelessly playing Ernst's "Othello" Fantasy and Paganini's "God Save the Queen" variations.

I thought this was the end; I was mistaken. For Szell it had only been the beginning, a pleasant appetizer. The next evening he sat down at the piano and started out playing the overture to Mozart's "Don Giovanni." But he did not stop after the overture. He stopped three hours later, having played the entire opera from memory and sung the text to it. It is only fair to state that, as a singer, Szell was a poor second to Caruso, particularly when he took on vocal duets and quartets single-handedly. His desperate efforts to sing bass and colorature parts simultaneously sometimes caused the music-loving Italian waiters acute anguish.

After recovering from his efforts over "Don Giovanni," Szell played Richard Strauss's "Till Eulenspiegel" as an encore.

Some days later, when a goodly part of the opera repertoire had been disposed of, someone referred to the fact that a gifted man by the name of Beethoven had written some quartets. This was the trigger mechanism that set off a colossal new orgy of music, this time chamber music.

Everything from Beethoven's Opus 131 to Schubert's glorious two cello quintet emerged from Szell's infallible mental filing system.

Szell once told me that he occasionally had to make an effort not to memorize a new piece accidentally, as it became burdensome, particularly when he anticipated dropping the piece from his repertoire after one or two performances.

"Of course," you will say, "all this is very nice for Szell and Mitropoulos, but how are we ordinary mortals to memorize our music?"

There are a number of ways. The most widely used and most wasteful way is to play a piece over and over again until it "sinks in." This is mental saturation bombing. Indiscriminately, the player repeats the entire piece from A to Z ad nauseam, unmindful of the fact that 90% of it has automatically registered in his mind after the first few playings. If he ultimately does memorize the piece, chances are he will be sick to death of it.

There are far more effective techniques of memorizing, and they are available to everyone. You must learn to look at your music as if it were an architect's blueprint. A good composer is something of an architect and mathematician. He writes according to a definite floor plan. When you understand the plan, the composition as a whole is much more easily memorized. I cannot help thinking that if Bach had been trained as an architect, he would have built cathedrals to rival those of Strasbourg and Chartres. And Mozart, as a mathematician, might have followed in the footsteps of Newton and Pascal. Look at the phenomenal games of mathematical gymnastics that Mozart occasionally indulged in for pure amusement. I have one composition of his for two violins, but there is only one part from which to play. It is laid flat on the table, and while one violinist plays from top to bottom, his partner stands at the opposite end of the table and starts playing the last note of the piece, playing backwards to the beginning. You see, every note is actually two different notes. The middle G played by the one violinist reads D to his partner who is looking at it upside down from the other end of the table. The composition is of course mathematically constructed and has a plan that anyone can grasp.

This affinity between music and mathematics does not necessarily work equally well in reverse. There is the story of Artur Schnabel playing sonatas with Einstein who was a passionate amateur violinist. The great physicist and the famous pianist had a good deal of trouble agreeing on tempo and rhythm. Finally, according to the legend, Schnabel stopped in exasperation and exclaimed: "For goodness sake, Albert, can't you count to four!"

Mozart's penchant for mathematics is also revealed in the astonishing musical dice game he composed. This unique composition consists of one hundred and seventy-six separate slips of paper, each containing one bar of music. These slips can be combined in hundreds of different ways, each representing a complete and logical composition. The various combinations are obtained by throwing a pair of dice, one throw for each bar. After each throw you consult the key list provided by Mozart and pick a corresponding bar of music. What you end up with in this game is a waltz of thirty-two bars, completely harmonized and playable. If you just keep shaking those dice, you may combine enough waltzes to last a lifetime.

The first rule then, for someone who desires to gain an insight into the technique of memorizing, is to study a score with the mind alone. Play it once or twice if you wish, or listen to it once or twice. But after that, away with the violin or piano; the time is not nearly at hand. That first theme, of how many bars is it constituted? To what key does it modulate? Where does the development section begin? Where is the recapitulation? In what form is the piece written? Sonata form? Variation form? Rondo?

All this is just the ground plan. Now you begin to sing the piece to yourself. Here is where you can make your waste time productive. You should do your singing quietly, inwardly. The memorizing process can be successfully applied while waiting for a bus or riding in it. You can apply it in the bathtub and in bed. If you are at a boring party, you can apply it with immense success while someone else is holding forth. This, of course, you only do when you are in the advanced stages of memorizing a piece and can work on it without having the score with you. I have done some of my best work while mechanically nodding to a dinner partner who was haranguing me. How often have I observed a musician like Monteux thoughtfully tapping the table with his fingers, absently humming between two morsels of lobster Newburg, while someone else was telling a story. What was he humming? Obviously, next week's symphony program. On one occasion I had no knowledge of the program chosen. I carefully watched Monteux at the dinner table, and suddenly I knew, beyond the shadow of a doubt what he was rehearsing underneath his lobster-soaked mustache. It was so obvious: The March to the

Gallows, from the *Symphonie Fantastique* by Berlioz. How did I know? I caught him making a characteristic sucking sound, which I knew was not directed at the lobster. For those who knew Monteux's mannerisms, it was clear that here was an imperative summons to the trombones.

Among the true masters of music there are many who will not even begin to practice a composition on their instrument until they have mentally and musically almost completely mastered it. Unfortunately, a great many students do exactly the opposite. They practice and practice a given piece on their instruments until they are mentally, emotionally, and physically stale, and their musical vitality has gone down the drain.

Those same students will pack up their instruments after a practice period and promptly forget about the whole composition. To the contrary, with the instrument out of the way, you can really rise above the mechanical impediments of execution. Now your mind can work unfettered. Instead of exhausting yourself at the double task of simultaneously conquering technical obstacles and memorizing as well, do your memorizing separately.

I once witnessed Yehudi Menuhin apply this strategy in a masterful and, I would say, rather daring way. He had programmed two new contemporary pieces, a slow number by the South American Guarnieri and a rapid one by the Englishman Arthur Benjamin. All kind of unexpected things had happened to interfere with his practice schedule and the day of the concert came without Yehudi being ready.

I was staying with him at the time and drove with him to the concert. We rested for awhile at the hotel during the afternoon and then Yehudi got up to begin the usual pre-concert routine. He was about to start shaving when he remembered the two new pieces, threw the scores on my bed and asked me to follow them while he whistled the music. With that he disappeared into the bathroom and began to shave and whistle. Soon he reappeared with his face full of soap, the music emerging from behind a mass of white blobs.

I had to stop him after four bars because he had skipped a couple of notes. I made the correction and he continued. A little later I had to stop him again. Thus we continued, Yehudi whistling, I playing Beckmesser. When we got to the end, he started over again. He did not repeat the old mistakes but he made a smaller batch of new ones. At the fourth try the piece was note-perfect. Then we rehearsed the other piece.

That evening Yehudi played both compositions perfectly, by memory.

One need have neither the facility nor the daring of Menuhin to apply the same technique successfully, in a more leisurely way.

Far be it from me to suggest that the task of memorizing should be entirely one of mental and intellectual slavery. As I have said at the beginning, much of it comes, thank heavens, entirely naturally and subconsciously. Listening to recordings while following the score is extremely helpful.

A certain amount of mechanical drudgery is unfortunately inevitable, for fast passages can only be secured by the development of an automatic mechanism, a kind of finger memory so rapid that it runs ahead of the conscious mind and functions independently of it.

Finally, a great many home performances are required before you are really ready. You should perform the piece with a pianist to become thoroughly familiar with the whole score, not just the solo part.

One more thing: the ability to memorize must be developed through regular training and habit. No matter how difficult you find it, impose upon yourself or your pupil the task of memorizing at least one piece every month. You will discover for yourself what astonishing developments can occur in the course of a few brief months, a year at most.

After dwelling so extensively on the part that conscious and intellectual efforts play in our work, I do wish to emphasize the enormous part played by our subconscious mind. These subconscious functions, of which we know so little, must be allowed to function as freely as possible.

I remember one occasion when I had a particularly bad time trying to memorize a piece; when it mended in one place, it broke in another. Finally, I gave up in despair and tossed it aside. One month later, on a sudden impulse, I started playing it, just to see how much of it still remained. To my amazement, it went faultlessly, with not one break from beginning to end. It was an extraordinary manifestation of the subconscious work that had gone on in my mind after I had discarded the piece.

I hope I have made clear my belief that too much intellectual probing can be as harmful as too little. You know the sad story of the centipede? One day he was sauntering along happily when another animal came along and said: "Hello, Mr. Centipede. Tell me, what method do you use in walking? Do you say to yourself: 'Now foot 77; now foot 34; now foot 13?'"

The centipede replied: "I have never thought about it, I just walk. Give me a minute to figure it out." He stood there for a little while, thinking hard. Then, suddenly, he cried out: "I can't walk anymore; I'm paralyzed!" ∎

Rehearsals Should Be Fun

Joseph E. Maddy

The co-founders of the National Music Camp at Interlochen, Michigan—the late Thaddeus P. Giddings with the writer of this article.

MEMBERS OF SCHOOL music organizations are always eager to do their very best when rehearsing worth-while music under capable and enthusiastic conductors. All they need is encouragement and guidance to develop their learning powers as well as to learn the music at hand. Opportunities to hear professional recordings of the numbers in rehearsal will often do more good than hours of drilling and lecturing.

There is a vast difference, or there should be, between rehearsing a professional musical group and a school group. Professional musicians are supposed to know the music and they need only to check up on a few difficult passages and to learn what the conductor intends to do in the way of changing tempos and personal items of interpretation. The school musician, on the other hand, needs first to learn what the music is all about, how difficult it is, and what the music is supposed to interpret.

The Conductor

The school music director who apes the professional conductor makes more work for himself and his students and ends up with a bad temper and meager results arrived at by the long, dreary, unpleasant way. Sarcasm has no place in teaching, any subject, anywhere.

There are two major types of conductors, *playing* conductors and *talking* conductors. The more a conductor talks, the longer it takes him to teach his players the music.

There is no truer maxim than the familiar *We learn to do by doing.* We all know that a student will learn more about playing any musical instrument by trying it himself for half an hour than he could possibly learn by listening to many hours of lecturing without making a noise on the instrument.

Playing music is fun. The better you play the more fun it is. The more music you play, the better you *can* play; and there is plenty of good music to be played. Playing a great amount of good music, with brief periods of suggestions by the conductor, is the best way to develop enthusiasm as well as musicianship in your musical organizations.

What are the principal things a conductor must teach his players? First, he must teach them to keep going, to find their places if they lose them, to feel rhythm and to read rhythm. Second, he must teach them to follow his directions. There is only one way to do this; keep changing tempos until the players can't be lost. The school conductor should never play a piece in the same tempo twice in succession, or his players will take that tempo and force him to follow them. Third, he must teach the players what he means by every gesture and baton movement he makes. The major gestures and baton movements should be those which have become standardized through the years. In this way the players will be able to perform under other conductors when occasion demands.

Be Prepared

The conductor should have high ideals, musically and morally, and should set a good example for his students. He should know the music he is to teach before he attempts to teach it. A floundering conductor cannot maintain the respect of his pupils any more than could an English teacher who couldn't read or speak English.

Many conductors forget all about the passage of time when they are conducting. Every rehearsal should be carefully planned in advance with each item planned. This plan should be followed strictly until a habit is formed.

Every rehearsal should begin with a familiar piece. Follow this by the principal work or works to be learned. Next, go over partially learned material and some sight-reading pieces. End with a familiar piece. The rehearsal program should be put on the board where the students can see and follow it. Here is a sample rehearsal program:

MONDAY
11:00 Intonation c h o r d s and scales.
11:05 Review: *El Capitan*
11:10 New: *Oberon*
       Dream Pantomime
11:45 Sight Reading: *Bolero*
11:55 Review: *Mardi Gras*

Getting Results

Every time a piece is played in rehearsal there should be some noticeable improvement over the last playing, so that the players will realize that the repetition was for a purpose as well as for fun. Two or three brief stops when reviewing a number may bring quick responses and immediate improvement, once the players realize that each stop is for a more satisfactory performance.

At the close of each rehearsal the conductor should go through his scores and make notes for the next rehearsal, while the day's efforts are still fresh in his mind. With carefully made rehearsal notes on what to stress at the next rehearsal, he will get results in a fraction of the time otherwise needed.

Every school music organization is a co-operative project requiring the highest type of teamwork. The director is the captain of the team. He must play *with* the team as well as command it. If he does his part well and uses only worth-while music, the organization will develop that "team spirit" which spells success in any enterprise.

Developing Musicianship

The Elements of Artistry

by Gunther Schuller

The source of all our motivation and inspiration as musicians are compositions, the creations of great composers. Our interpretation of the music should be based on those sources, those scores, and a full knowledge of the style and musical language peculiar to each great composer. I strongly oppose the over-individualized, even at times arrogantly arbitrary, approach to horn playing or any instrumental playing that to some degree ignores or rejects the composer's notations, and bases the interpretation on largely extra-musical considerations.

For a Beethoven Symphony all we have is the score, which I consider a sacred document. We can also look at the original autograph and compare it with various editions (most musicians do not bother to do that), but in the end those are the only sources we have. The entire information available to us is that score. The details of making a smooth slur or using the correct breathing technique are subservient to rendering, as authoritatively as we can, the message left by the composer.

There is more factual information available in the scores than we generally assume. By factual information I mean the unequivocal evidence contained in the notation as to how we should proceed.

It is unfortunate that we are often at the whim of conductors who tend to ignore information in the scores and instead interpret willfully or freely. As horn players, we have to collaborate with them in their willful interpretation. This is one of the difficult aspects of being a professional orchestral horn player; musicians sitting in the orchestra are often finer artists than their conductors and are nonetheless subservient to a wrong interpretation. To survive professionally we do what the conductor wants; there is no way around that. If eighty musicians interpreted a work in eighty different ways, there would be utter chaos. Music comes together in one person's interpretation, but in general we are not conscientious enough about the concrete factual information contained in the score, which in most cases is the only reliable document left by the great composers.

After two seasons as principal horn with the Cincinnati Symphony, Gunther Schuller played with the Metropolitan Opera Orchestra for fifteen years, nine as principal. He is acknowledged as a composer, author, musicologist, publisher, and conductor.

I have the concept of musicians, whether horn players or any other instrumentalist, as being like a spider sitting in the middle of a web maintaining all the different strands or as being at the center of a wheel with fourteen spokes radiating out and representing the mental and physical activities to be accomplished more or less simultaneously.

A musician should think of himself as being two persons, two musicians in one: one produces a series of actions in playing, while the other sits outside and listens critically to the sounds produced. One produces the required musical result, while the other listens and appraises that result. Musicians do a certain amount of this automatically in listening to rhythm, intonation, clean attacks, and other technical considerations. That is only the minimum, and only by going much beyond that can the highest levels of artistic playing be reached.

Through my experience as a composer and performer I created this wheel to show in a simple, graphic way what musicians should do. It represents what musicians are obligated to recreate in acoustical terms as they perform a piece of music.

The first spoke of the wheel is following the conductor; this needs little further explanation and is self-evident. The second is more complicated: read and register in our minds *all* the information contained on the part or the score. Unfortunately many musicians pass over much of that basic information: dynamics, for example, or phrasings for

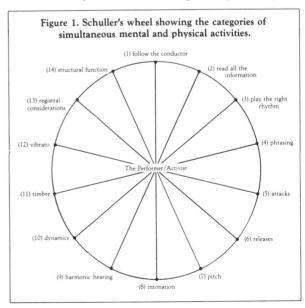

Figure 1. Schuller's wheel showing the categories of simultaneous mental and physical activities.

(1) follow the conductor
(2) read all the information
(3) play the right rhythm
(4) phrasing
(5) attacks
(6) releases
(7) pitch
(8) intonation
(9) harmonic hearing
(10) dynamics
(11) timbre
(12) vibrato
(13) registral considerations
(14) structural function

The Performer/Activist

articulations. Often there is a primary drive to just get the note at the expense of other things, but we are obliged to read whatever information there is, whether above or below the note, at the beginning of a phrase or during it. While the information in such early composers as Bach or Handel may be scant, the notations of 19th century and contemporary composers are much more meticulous and precise and give us written and verbal indications of all kinds, including very detailed dynamics. The common practice of reading the notes first and later reading the dynamic is, to my mind, all wrong. This is essentially a limited and crude way to play music. Our minds, when well trained, are quite capable of reading all the information on a particular line or part. This is an ability or discipline one has to develop; but, it is our obligation as good and intelligent musicians to read everything at first glance, to avoid performing only a part of the composer's message.

The next and obvious obligations are playing the right rhythm and phrasing (#3 and #4). These include all aspects of phrasing: slurring, tonguing of various kinds or degrees, shaping the phrase, and identifying the structural and ensemble functions of rhythms and phrases.

When thinking of attacks and releases (#5 and #6) it is important to realize that there is not just one attack available on an instrument but an almost infinite variety of gradations of attacks. Although we are generally taught rather well how to attack a note, we are rarely taught how and when to release a note. There are many stylistic and technical considerations in releasing a note. In most Romantic music it is quite proper to taper a note into silence by degrees, depending on the tempo of the music. In contemporary music complex and precise rhythms are common; we have to be much more conscientious and precise about releases. This may include even an abrupt, audible release that would be inappropriate in a Brahms symphony, but just what is called for in a piece by Webern, Boulez, or Carter (or even Schuller).

In the case of *Klangfarbenmelodie* (a tone-color melody) with the melody or theme divided into several instrumental timbral segments and played by five different instruments, the first player hands the last note over to the next player, who hands the last note to the next player in the melodic line, as in a relay race. The timing and nature of the release of the last note is critical to making the tone-color melody a complete entity rather than five separate segments. I believe that musicians should concentrate more on the release of notes than is generally the case.

Pitch, intonation, and harmonic hearing (#7, #8, and #9) are all related, but alas often quite neglected. There are many aspects to this. A horn player who sees an A in an F-horn part may think of an A, but of course it is really a D. I submit that it is essential to know this is a D and not an A. That A is a fictional, not notational, abstraction; we should not play a note with some kind of ab-stract or absolute pitch. Every note we will ever play should be slightly differently tuned in relation to the specific harmonic context and depending upon a host of other factors that include a particular horn's intonation. It may be necessary to adjust the natural intonation of a note that is slightly flat on your horn, but if the relative harmonic tuning of that note needs to be slighty sharp at this moment then you adjust accordingly. You cannot allow the note to be flat. This in turn depends on knowing what pitch you are actually playing, not some transposed or fictional note, and the harmonic context in which it exists.

A knowledge of theory, harmonic voice-leading, and harmonic functions is necessary. Granted, you may not be able to adjust the tuning while sight-reading a piece unknown to you, but the second time you should make intonational and harmonic adjustments. You cannot adjust correctly while reading, thinking, and hearing only F-horn notes.

A Mozart piece will not say, "Watch out, the music is now moving to G minor." All your part will show is a written C (in Bb horn). You should know that you are not playing a C but a Bb and that this Bb is the minor third in the key of G minor, which should be tuned differently than when it is the major third in Gb major

Near the beginning of Debussy's *Afternoon of a Faun* from a single soft C♯ minor chord in the clarinets and oboes the horn emerges on an E concert, the minor third. Suddenly the music moves to a Bb seventh chord, making the end of that E a leading tone. To do full intonational and harmonic justice to those two chromatically remotely related chords, you have to start on the low side of the E and as it moves toward the F (in the Bb chord) you raise it slightly to its leading-tone feeling. If you read and think of B and C (in F-horn), neither of these notes being in those two stated chords, you obviously will not play with the correct intonation.

These three elements - pitch, intonation, and harmonic hearing (or intervallic hearing) - should be part of your critical awareness as you play. Know what you have to do through hearing, thinking, and listening, and develop that other person - that other outside ear - which says, "Did I do what I was meant to do? Was that note in tune or was it still a little flat because the third valve on my horn is a little flat?"

Three related areas are important: dynamics, timbre, and vibrato (#10, #11, and #12). Dynamics, like intonation, may be absolute or relative, and composers have different ways of notating them. In the Beethoven Eighth at one climactic point in the first movement there is a chord written triple forte for every part (flute, oboe, clarinet, horns, and violins) and it is what we might call an absolute dynamic. In Beethoven's day it was a notational convention to write all dynamics at any given point the same for every instrument. It wasn't until the end of the century that vertically differentiated dynamics in scores emerged, as in Strauss or Mahler. In the Beethoven example horns should play at a relative dynamic: relative to the other instruments because a horn *fff* is about five times as loud in that register as, for instance, the loudest note the flutes or violins can produce. If the horns and trumpets play a true triple forte, they will wipe out the rest of the orchestra. To achieve the effect the composer intended brass players should consider the dynamic limitations of other instruments.

In a Mahler symphony there might be five different dynamics at one place in the score. Mahler often marked trumpet and percussion parts down to balance them against acoustically weaker instruments: that is why relative dynamics are relative to the prevailing, over-all dynamic so as to fit the context of that passage.

The same applies to timbre, tone color, and sonority. Each horn player has an absolute or basic sonority, the sound that player and horn produce. It is each player's obligation to color that timbre and adjust that sonority to what is called for in the music. No one can just decide to impose a sound on a piece, no matter who the composer or what the instrumental textures. The absolute aspects of timbre, just like absolute dynamics, are of little use in orchestral playing. In a typical concert you will play with a sound that sometimes blends with the brass section and at other times with the woodwinds or strings. Sometimes this means blending with the brighter sound of trumpets and trombones, or with the darker sounds of a tuba or bassoon, or the softer, dulcet sounds of a clarinet, in each case with an infinite variety of tone colors.

The basic techniques available to change tone colors are related. One is the rate of air speed and the volume of air being used. Balance this against the resistance from the instrument, another variable that affects the flow of the air stream. There are other physical variables as well, such as opening or closing the teeth, the mouth cavity, and the throat. Those three physical attributes can be used flexibly; with them one can do much to control and vary timbre and tone color. Horn players have a fourth device that nobody else has: the hand in the bell. It acts like a rudder to steer the sound in a variety of ways.

Vibrato is another aspect hornists use to brighten or darken the sound. I do not refer to the specific techniques of throat, head, or hand vibrato, but rather to the speed, the degree of pitch variation, and intensity of vibrato. Horn players in France used to take even the simplest stationary harmonic notes, as in a Haydn symphony, and turn on the vibrato, thereby often covering up the true melody and diffusing harmonic clarity. (Horn players in France do not play that way anymore, I'm happy to say.)

On all instruments, but particularly the horn, there are problems of register and registral projec-

tion (#13): the horn projects differently in different registers. For example, the concert C5 projects easily through almost any orchestral balance; it is often difficult to play softly enough (in Mozart, for example). Conversely, moving down two octaves to concert C3 we have about one-tenth the projection of a concert C5. Because of the way notes project or do not project, horn players should ask themselves whether the register they are to play in is weak or strong, adjusting the ensemble context. Here again that other half of you should be listening to the playing half. When players do not compensate for the varied acoustical projection, section balance will suffer. This is why so often in a horn section the first horn is clearly heard, the third and second somewhat less, and perhaps the fourth not at all.

Finally, there is the question of structural and thematic functions (#14) - whether playing a solo or some other primary material, or secondary material such as a countermelody, or even a tertiary line or single harmony note. It is important to know what you are playing and to play in an intelligent, understanding way, realizing the function of your note or notes in the overall structure and continuity.

These fourteen functions - control points, as it were - are the full circle of what musicians should do, not only successively but mostly simultaneously. You cannot, of course, accomplish all this at first because there are thousands of variables to control in building a solid technique. This level of artistry is a goal musicians should strive to achieve and maintain throughout their professional careers. When all fourteen components work together, playing becomes a pleasure as you approach a nearly perfect realization of the composer's intentions. □

J.J. Johnson —
Expanding the Envelope

by Lida Belt Baker

Establishing himself as the definitive bop-era trombonist while still in his 20s, J.J. Johnson has inspired and influenced generations of jazzmen. He performed with, among others, Count Basie, Illinois Jacquet, and Miles Davis, and formed the much recorded trombone duo with rhythm, Jay and Kai. Later he pursued a career writing music for films and television.

Many aspiring jazz players don't understand the role of practice. They think that a jazz artist appears on stage and simply emotes. How do you feel about this?

I've found that out just with my limited experience with clinics. I've tried to drive the point home to young players that they have got to practice. You always have to practice. There won't come a time when you won't have to practice anymore. As long as you are going to perform, you've got to practice.

One of the most dramatic examples of the importance of practice is once many years ago when Miles Davis played at one of the clubs in the Village with his quintet: Miles, Coltrane, Red Garland, Philly Joe, and Paul Chambers. They played their normal set, which was exciting to say the least, then they'd take a 35 or 45-minute intermission, at which point John Coltrane would always go down to the basement and practice until it was time to go back on the bandstand again. This meant that he played all night long without letup. I don't know of any more dramatic example of the fact that you've got to practice. We all know what that did for Coltrane; he became the ultimate improvisor.

That's inspiring for young students or older players who need to get back on track again. I can't imagine that ever happening to you.

I think getting off the track happens to most jazz musicians. You go through cycles of frustration and cycles of exploration. You need to take stock of what you are doing. Maybe

that's good. I like to think that these periods are indicative of growth. You don't reach a certain status where there's nothing else to do, nothing else to gain. There's always more to learn; you never really master an instrument. Sometimes I think that I'm a slave to the trombone; in a sense I am. Ted Nash, a studio man in L.A., finally gave up playing because he said that the hassle of keeping his chops up and keeping his playing mechanism in tip-top form got to the point where there was no joy in it. He said that when it got to be a drag he knew that it was time to get out.

I can relate to what he said about the hassle of having to keep up. It takes dedication and discipline, especially when there is no gig in

sight. That's difficult; I know that for a fact. We all know how intensely we practice when the gig is approaching, but when there is no work in sight, you just have to practice as hard, and you always look for a little edge, a little something extra: another dimension, another tone color, or something.

That's always been something that I liked about your playing. In the 1940s you had already established a style that set the standard for every trombone player that's come after you, but you didn't stop there.

One of the things that I try to pass along to younger players is the fact that jazz by its very nature is a restless music. It won't stay still; it won't behave. You can't just put it over here and say, "Now be quiet and don't say anything." It won't allow that. It must evolve; it must reach out and explore. When Dizzy and Bird came on the scene there was a hue and cry, "What is this crazy music with flatted fifths called bebop?" Obviously, it prevailed. I think it will always be that way. When something new comes along there will be resistance to it at first. When Miles recorded *Bitches Brew* there was a great hue and cry, from the critics, the media, everybody but especially his adoring fans. They raised a big ruckus about it. "He can't desert us like this and go off into another world like that," they said; but that's what he did.

It's difficult for kids coming up now because they don't have the opportunities to play with older musicians as you did with the Basie Band. Who are some of the players who influenced you?

One of my favorite stories that I pass along to young students is about my time with Basie, sitting next to Dickie Wells who was the lead trombonist and the featured trombonist of the band at that time. He was a tall, rangy, handsome man who could have been a movie star. Somehow, when he stood up to play his solos, he seemed to tower over the orchestra. Of course, this is magnified by the fact that I was in awe of him. I was a kid from Indianapolis sitting next to this monster trombone player who did not play a lot of notes, did not play pyrotechnics or play into the stratosphere. He just played a few well-chosen notes with great feeling and great depth of emotion. He played very few notes but it was the inflection that he put on those notes that made his playing so

---

Lida Belt Baker is a music researcher and lecturer at Indiana University and a free-lance musician and writer whose areas of specialization include jazz history and performance, ethnomusicology, oral history, and the creative process in music. She is the co-author of The Black Composer Speaks *and has written a number of articles on contemporary composers and musicians.*

outstanding. Kids nowadays are obsessed with a thousand notes and playing faster and higher, so to find out that I was in awe of someone who didn't play a lot of notes gives them something to think about.

Another favorite story is about the first trombonist I heard play in a manner other than the way trombonists played up to that point. His name was Fred Beckett. He never was well known and never reached a high profile status in the classic sense. He was with a territory band called Harlan Leonard's Rockets. I happened to hear a recording where he played a 16-bar solo, and I was just amazed. He was the first trombonist I heard play in a linear style. He would play lines that were beautiful. Unfortunately, he passed away in his 30s; he was with Lionel Hampton at the time. He would have been a force to be reckoned with had he continued in jazz.

I've often noticed that when you're on the stand you have the sets planned out as to which tunes you will call and who will play on what. It seems that often everybody plays on every tune, and after a while that gets old to the audience.

I've seen the edge you need to be a good performer fall off because things were not well thought out and were falling apart at the seams. I've seen the reverse where people had their act together and planned in advance. Seeing both sides of the coin, I hope something good has rubbed off on me.

People often talk about a certain level of spontaneity in this music that is necessary for a good performance.

No question about it. Normally Miles is a featured act on a show that has three or four acts. Usually, the featured act plays last, that's common practice, but not Miles. Miles plays first. You know why? Ever have the experience where you wait and wait, and by the time you play, you've lost that edge? That will never happen to Miles. Miles plays when he's fresh and spontaneous; he gets out and is gone by the time the last act plays. You'll never hear Miles who waited through three acts and has lost his sharp, very fine, well-honed edge. Nobody in the audience wants to know that he's been waiting around and has lost his edge. If they paid $20 or $30 a ticket, they want blood. You can't blame them. They deserve the best performance you are capable of.

When you were learning to improvise as a young player, what kinds of stages did you go through?

I'm sure that all of us first begin by emulating the people who we idolize. I guess personalizing my playing began during practicing. At first you practice the customary scales and long tones and arpeggios. Somewhere along the line you begin to incorporate some of yourself in this routine.

One of the reasons I ask is that you are the person who brought the instrument into the modern era. You did things that no one had thought of before, and you looked at the trombone in a way that people had never looked at it before. It fascinates me that you could do this when there really wasn't a precedent to follow. How did you do it?

Two or three words come to mind: naive, reckless, and a little crazy. The other words that come to mind are practice, practice, practice. I had encouragement from people like Dizzy when I was struggling with lines of bebop tunes. I recall Dizzy planting seeds, saying, "J.J., try it this way." I was amazed when it worked out because Dizzy is not a trombone player and nobody realized that he knew anything about trombone technique, but he did. He'd show me little tricks with the slide and sure enough, it would be easier. It wasn't only Dizzy, though. People planted little seeds here and there that paid off dividends later in a big way. One who really helped me was Illinois Jacquet. I played in his band for a while. We called it the Little Big Band: two trumpets, trombone, tenor sax, baritone sax, and a rhythm section. Jacquet was a great source of encouragement, although most people don't associate him with bebop. Jacquet was a wonderful bebopper, but he would do it offstage, over in the corner somewhere when he practiced. He played marvelous bebop, but then he went onstage and played the show he was famous for, honking and screaming. "C'mon, J.J., let's play this line in unison," he'd say, and then he'd tell me that I could do it. He was always a source of encouragement, and after a while I began to believe him. I was lucky to be exposed to such people.

The thing that is the most exciting about your playing is that you take chances.

Test pilots have a term called the "envelope" for when a pilot goes to a certain speed, after which he no longer has control. Up to that point, the plane is under his control. That fine line between being in control and out of control is the edge of the envelope. Once you cross that line, anything can happen. In playing we have our envelope. When I take chances, I'm trying to expand my envelope. The challenge of life is like that; we try to expand our envelopes by expanding our capabilities. Many times we go past the envelope with disastrous results.

Do you think that playing every night makes a big difference?

I have an old saying, "You have to play to play." Playing frequently and playing hard makes you play better. Unfortunately, there is no substitute.

Many people think that you quit playing for an extended period of time because you became so active as a writer.

I never stopped playing entirely. I did some studio work and infrequently played jazz festivals. I practiced a little almost every day.

Are you getting to work as much as you want to? The thing I'm concerned about is if there are enough venues left to play in.

It's tough. As I test the waters and do some research, I've found that players today have to supplement their income by taking on activities such as clinics. You have to be versatile; it's not like the old days.

What are your thoughts on clinics?

For a long time I shied away from that area. It felt awkward to stand before a bunch of intelligent, aspiring musicians and paint a rosy picture of the music business when we all know how rosy it is not. As I addressed the students at a clinic at the University of North Texas, I couldn't help but think of what would happen to all these wonderful musicians once they left school; schools like Indiana University and Eastman. Once they leave schools that have high-powered jazz programs, what will these gifted, talented musicians do with their lives? They can't all be Stan Getz, Miles Davis, or John Coltrane. Some of them will be sidemen somewhere and some will wind up in education, but overall, what are we going to do with all these musicians? It's a little disturbing to think about.

What do you like to listen to and do you have particular favorites?

When I just listen for fun my selections fall into all kinds of crazy categories: classical, jazz, non-jazz, but my favorite is Stravinsky. I must have five versions of *Le Sacre*, three or four different versions of *The Firebird Suite*, several versions of *Petrouchka*, and a gem of a piece called *Fireworks*. Of course, I have several recordings of *L'Histoire*, which is classic Stravinsky. I love Hindemith's orchestral works, but one of my favorite pieces is his *Kleine Kammermusik*. It's wonderful, and I never tire of hearing it. It's loaded with goodies. I also like to listen to the Bartok Concerto for Orchestra as well as his piano concertos. One of my favorite Bartok pieces is *The Miraculous Mandarin*. I tend toward the classical modernists. I'm big on Ravel, especially *Le Tombeau de Couperin*.

When I get into a real orchestration frame of mind, I go big into Richard Strauss: *Ein Heldenleben*, *Til Eulenspiegel*, *Salome*, those are my favorites. I'm big on Tomita; he's a Japanese synthesizer composer. He's recorded *Le Sacre* on synthesizer; it's incredible programming. He made a big splash a few years ago with a record called *Snowflakes Are Dancing*. It's a marvelous work. That's the kind of listening I do. Of the film composers I enjoy listening to Jerry Goldsmith is at the top of the list. He has a grip on the art, technique and craft of film composition. Film composition doesn't get a lot of attention; it's frowned upon in some circles. It is subservient to the film but by its nature it has to be. The film is first and the music is part of the film, but there is a certain know-how that only some guys have and Jerry Goldsmith is one of them. John Williams is another. James Horner is one of the newer guys, and he's really coming along; he's quite talented.

Writing for films is another ball game.
It's another world.

I read somewhere that Quincy Jones was responsible for getting you started in film writing.

He had heard some stuff I had done that led him to believe I should take a stab at film composition. He told me to come out to California to have a go at it.

Had you though about doing something like that before?

Not seriously. The thought had crossed my mind but I never paid any attention to it; finally I did.

Did you go through an apprenticeship out there? I understand that you worked a good deal with Earle Hagen.

Well, you're not going to be ready for this but the apprenticeship began in New York two or three years prior to moving to California. M.B.A. Music offered me a position as staff composer and arranger to produce music for television and radio commercials. I worked there for three years and learned the mathematics of film composition. It all begins with the premise that 35mm film (the industry standard) runs through a projector at the rate of a foot and a half of film per second. Earle Hagen put out a book called *Three Equals Two* (three feet of film equals two seconds). That is the basis for all film mathematics. It gets quite complicated after that, but it begins with that simple premise. Fifty percent of your work in film composition has to do with the mathematics.

Sometimes you wonder if you'll ever get to putting notes down on a page because you are so preoccupied with numbers, footage, film counts, and synchronization points; but that's where writing for films has to begin because the picture is first and the music is second. People look down on film composition for that reason. Years ago an enterprising film producer said to Igor Stravinsky, "We would love for you to write the music for our film." Igor agreed and the producer told him how it would work. "We'll shoot the picture. We'll edit the picture. We'll re-edit the picture, and after all that's done we'll show you the picture. Then we'll discuss what we would like to have in the way of music for the picture, and then you write it." Stravinsky said, "Oh no, it can't be that way. The way it will have to be if I write it is first I will write the music, then you will produce the picture according to the music I have written." I love that story.

I'm sure that when you first view a movie, you often have a different idea about what music should be written for it than the movie's producer.

A number of film composers have had their scores thrown out and have been paid very high fees in full, the most famous being *2001: A Space Odyssey*. The original score was written by Alex North, who is one of the granddaddies of film composition. Everybody who has his right mind knows that he wrote a marvelous score for that movie; he's incapable of writing a bad picture score. Nonetheless, it was thrown out because it was not what Kubrick had in mind. He was paid in full and they threw it out. This happens frequently and it has become a status symbol. Anyone who hasn't had a film score thrown out on him ought not to be in the business.

Was writing for television similar to writing for films?

Yes, it's the same math although they don't have to use only 35mm anymore. The basic premise of film production remains.

What are some of your current projects?

I've got a couple of things on the back burner that could get off the ground floor someday. When I first got interested in clinics, one consideration was a clinic book or clinic library. I began to entertain all kinds of crazy, grandiose ideas of what the instrumentation ought to be. I was naive enough to think I could write a book for six or seven woodwinds, five or six trumpets, three or four French horns, tuba, and harp. I began to talk to people who were active in the clinic scene and they quickly brought me down to planet Earth. What would happen is that I'd write all this music but it would never get played anywhere. Nobody has that kind of setup. I got a grip on reality: four trumpets, four trombones, five saxes.

At one clinic I related this grandiose, naive dream of mine to some of the directors present. They got a big laugh out of it as I had hoped they would. There was one high school band director who said, "J.J., I for one hope that you never give up those ideas. Someday go after that dream, write for three French horns and harp. Some of us will see to it that it gets played because we want to hear it." I loved that guy for saying that. The others applauded him. That's my arranger/orchestrator mentality asserting itself. I like the colors and textures. There is nothing like French horns. There is nothing like harp, and I'm not talking about the cliche harp glissandos, I'm talking about harp writing. Listen to Benjamin Britten's *Four Sea Interludes.*

Another thing I'd like to try is to interface my trombone with synthesizers. I have had some experience with this. When I worked for M.B.A. in New York, they bought one of the first Moog synthesizers. They dispatched me to Trumansburg, New York where the Moog factory was at that time, to take a cram course in Moog synthesizer programming and patching. That's where I got hooked on synthesizers, and I've been hooked ever since. I went through a phase during my film composing career in California where I owned quite an elaborate array of analog synthesizers. I had two Arp 2600s, which are big, modular synthesizers, and I had a lot of sequencers and phase shifters. I used all this stuff in my film writing. Unlike the synthesizer scores that are going around now, I wrote for acoustic instruments as well. I've always felt that the best synthesizer colorations were synthesizers used in conjunction with acoustic instruments. I learned a lot from Earle Hagen about incorporating the synthesizer into the orchestration or giving it another color. If you put a synthesizer on a flute line or a unison trumpet line it gives it another texture, another timbre; it can be very effective. Of course, we're all concerned with the threat of

synthesizers putting musicians out of work. The threat is real and we can't shove it aside or ignore it because it won't go away. I am concerned with the fact that there are synthesizer scores where the entire score is performed without acoustic instruments; this is putting musicians out of work. This is a real threat that we will have to deal with, and I don't know the answer. Nonetheless, there are interesting things going on in synthesizer technology.

One of the things I learned was to interface and trigger the synthesizer with the sound of the trombone. I found a small company in California that made a pitch-to-voltage converter, and I had one of my mouthpieces wired so that when I played the trombone it would trigger the synthesizer. I tried this in a recording session and it worked well. If you listen to the cut called "Mr. Clean" on the Fantasy album, *Tentacles,* you will hear the trombone with three other voices parallel with it. What's happening is that the trombone triggers an Oberheim synthesizer expander module in parallel so that you hear three lines instead of one. The next time you listen to it you'll notice that it's a trombone with two synthesizer voices stacked in fourths. There is nothing new about this but I would like to further explore that area. □

September, 1992

Teaching Musicianship with Games

by Max Dalby

Band students will not become musicians simply by sitting through band rehearsals day after day. Only with carefully organized instruction to guide them through the fundamentals of musicianship will they acquire the skills and concepts to play outstanding music. Many texts offer suggestions concerning this subject, but an important source of information is Philip Farkas' "The Art of Musicianship," a book that should be included in every band director's library.

One of the most effective methods for developing musicianship is using games that offer variety and excitement. One game each day is adequate and should take about seven minutes of rehearsal time, except when explaining a new concept or describing a homework assignment. By using warm-up exercises throughout the year, you will teach specific skills and improve overall musicianship.

I have found Leonard Smith's *Treasury of Scales*

is effective basic material for many of the games that develop musical concepts. The *Treasury* consists of 96 harmonized scales all beginning and ending on the tonic chord in root position; each of the twelve major and minor scales is written for every instrument and played over four-note harmony. When used by imaginative band directors it provides an endless variety of material.

When students develop proper fingerings, positions, and embouchure placement, they can learn tonal control and dynamic variation, intonation, rhythmic structure, style, articulation, and expressive playing. The exercises in *Treasury* are appropriate for bands of any size or instrumentation with students who can tune unisons and octaves, know the chromatic scale, and are comfortable in the keys found in intermediate band music; harmonic treatments are traditional, so students quickly understand how sounds relate to others, developing a sense of tonality and pitch. The first few days of using *Treasury* should include one or more of the scale harmonizations followed by one of the games.

Intonation Games

For intonation games to be successful, students should know that temperature affects pitch and how to adjust for good intonation. They should develop a characteristic tone with steady pitch, but realize that intonation problems exist whenever there are two or more players. They should also be accustomed to hearing well-tuned intervals through the band tuning process.

With this understanding directors can present the harmonic series, describing how it influences scales and intervalic relationships and determines alternate, harmonic fingerings. To illustrate the harmonic series, divide a string on a cello or bass to demonstrate not only the string vibrating in its mathematical parts to the eighth partial, but also the individual notes of the harmonic series by fingering the bowed string at one-half, one-third, one-fourth, one-fifth, one-sixth, one-seventh, and one-eighth the total length. A wind example could be a tuba playing a harmonic series on Bb1 or a flutist on C4 to show that every fundamental produces the sames series of overtones. If any of the partials are not in tune with the pitches generated by the fundamental, beats will occur. Adding a trombone or baritone to the octave BBb demonstrates this as beats will occur if an octave is not perfectly in tune. When the BBb is in tune, add another trombone on a fifth above the first octave, one two octaves above the fundamental, and two others playing D and F. Tune the triad and add a trumpet on Ab concert, and a horn to demonstrate upper partials by playing the open notes of the series, C, E, G, Bb, C, D, and E. This exercise helps band members understand how they are bound by the harmonic series when trying to eliminate beating in traditional harmonic situations.

The Tempered Scale Game

Through many years of listening to music via radio and T.V. young musicians are conditioned to the tempered scale. Nearly every child can accurately sing the song "Do, Re, Mi," and most fifth and sixth graders can detect notes that do not agree with temperament.

Many intonation problems result from imperfections existing in the incompatibility of the tempered scale with the same pitches in the harmonic series. In *Acoustics of Music*, Wilmer Bartholomew states, "The expansion of the octave ratio is incommensurable with the expansions of the ratios of all other intervals. This means that we can never hope to arrive at a true octave on a tone by stepping off any true interval except the octave interval itself. In other words, a twelve-tone division of the octave is necessarily imperfect because of the

nature of the number series itself."

J.S. Bach was the first to widely use the tempered scale, with octaves divided into equal half steps, sharp major thirds, and very sharp minor sevenths, making it possible to play in tune in every key. An effective introduction to the tempered scale is to play middle C on the piano and have students sing a major third above. Invariably they will sing a pure third, the one produced by the harmonic series. Then play E on the piano demonstrating the piano pitch is higher.

The chart below shows how to alter pitch from tempered tuning to pure harmonic tuning, with all changes to the upper tone in a chord:

major third, lower 1/7 of a semitone
minor third, raise 1/6 of a semitone
perfect fourth, lower 1/50 of a semitone
perfect fifth, raise 1/50 of a semitone
augmented fifth, lower 1/4 of a semitone
major sixth, lower 1/6 of a semitone
minor sixth, raise 1/7 of a semitone
minor seventh, lower 1/3 of a semitone

In the tempered scale game students sing the first phrase of "Do, Re, Mi," listen as a cornet or baritone player repeats the song with no attempt to humor the notes, and judge which notes do not agree in pitch. It is interesting to discover how quickly students will identify notes played out of tune. An electronic device, well-tuned piano, or keyboard percussion instrument will verify student evaluations, which should continue in different keys with other instruments.

The Bad Note Game

With the exception of trombones, intonation problems are inherent in the construction of wind instruments. Acoustically, they cannot be built to play true intervals in more than one octave without compromises unless players use dynamics, embouchure, and mechanical adaptation to bend notes to the correct pitch. Although these imperfections occasionally produce acceptable or perfect harmonic pitches by accident, compromises built into wind instruments can create problems even in unison and octave tuning. Directors should identify the notes on each instrument that are not in tune and understand how to correct the problem.

Intonation problems are apparent on trumpet when playing a scale from C#4 to A4 and further demonstrated by three trumpet players, two sustaining a perfect fifth of G4 and D5 and the third on B4, but using all three valves. The sharp third caused by using that fingering on B4 is obvious. For an even more dramatic effect, set up a Db con-

During 28 years on the faculty of Utah State University, Max Dalby served as director of bands, chairman of the music department, coordinator of music education programs, conductor, and teacher. Prior to this, he established the instrumental music program of San Diego Diocese elementary school system in 1946.

cert triad, lowering the third and adding the seventh on trumpet using the three-valve combination. The sharpness resulting from this is almost impossible to humor down to pitch because the tempered minor 7th alone is one-third of a half-step sharp and the three-valve combination is almost one-half step sharp in the tempered scale. It would probably be easier to bend a C up to the proper pitch.

To play the bad note game students use an electronic tuner to identify notes that are more than five to seven cents or one one-hundredth of a half step sharp or flat and complete a chromatic scale chart showing which notes to humor. This game is best played in pairs with one student playing while the other controls the tuner and registers the results.

The Beating Game

Beats are caused by mismatched frequencies and, with the exception of minor seconds, are the signal to make pitch adjustments. Playing A440 against A444 results in four strong pulsations heard each second as the vibrations match and amplify each other. Slow beating is often acceptable, but as it increases in speed, auditory discomfort results. Other more serious problems can be caused by beating; pilots of multi-engine piston airplanes were required to match propeller pitches to avoid excessive beats caused by mismatched frequencies that would dislodge engines from mountings.

Begin by deliberately mistuning a unison between two students, or mistune one player with an electronic tuner. Continue playing out of tune until there are eight or ten beats per second and students call for mercy. A minor second will also cause rapid beating that cannot be eliminated. Learning to recognize this sound as distinguished from excessive pitch aberration is another challenge to be met. When it is obvious all students hear the beats proceed to show how to humor or bend notes to the correct pitch.

Pitch-bending aids in good intonation and can be accomplished in many ways.

Volume: Increasing volume on flutes, oboes, and bassoons generally raises pitch while decreasing volume lowers pitch. Single reed instruments are the reverse; pitch goes down with increases in volume and up with decrescendos. In the higher register, brass players first tend to play flat at full volume but they become sharp as lip pressure increases; regardless of the volume most young players are flat on low notes, with some exceptions.

Clarinets and saxophones: Except for brass players on 1st and 3rd and three-valve combinations, clarinets have the greatest problems in humoring notes as they play at or near the top of their pitch to begin while other instruments are typically played in the center. Pitch is affected by altering pressure on the reed; raising the clarinet bell or lowering the jaw flattens it while lowering the bell raises pitch slightly. Humor notes on alto and bass clarinets in the same manner.

Control saxophone pitch with the same jaw motion used for vibrato, down to lower it and forward to make it higher. Alternate fingerings, opening or closing vent holes near the note, and changing the oral cavity can all affect pitch. On alto saxophones, lower A5 by depressing the F♯ key and C♯6 by pressing down the right hand bank of keys; raise C♯5 by using long fingering or opening the second side key. Tenor and baritone saxophones have their own peculiarities and these alto options are not always useful.

Air Stream: Flute players can flatten pitch by lowering the jaw or head and shaping the air stream, directing it down, and raise pitch by lifting the head or moving the jaw forward. Oboists and bassoonists raise the pitch when more reed is taken into the mouth and lower it by taking in less reed.

Trumpet, trombone, euphonium, and tuba players can raise pitch by directing the air stream upward to the top of the mouthpiece and can lower pitch by directing the air stream downward toward the bottom. Students should use first valve triggers and third valve slides on cornets and trumpets properly and understand the fourth valve on euphoniums and tubas. When compared to the tempered scale brass instrument fifth partials are slightly flat and sixth partials very sharp.

Horns and trombones: Horn players tune with the right hand in the bell: farther in to lower the pitch, out to raise. Trombonists have the easiest task of all; they just move the slide. Professionals often tune first position slightly sharp so there is some leeway in both directions.

The Humoring Game

The humoring game is played by having one member of a section demonstrate pitch bending for the others and followed by the entire band practicing this section by section. Except for trombonists, changing dynamic levels is a desirable method for tuning unisons because it changes pitch without affecting tone quality. Other tuning methods can be used if changing dynamic levels does not have the desired effect.

Tuning the Unison Game

With two players on like instruments, have one sound any note which the other matches, humoring it up or down until any beats disappear. When the notes match, the first player nods approval but if the second player cannot find the pitch, start over with a new pitch. The game continues with the first player sounding a note one half-step or a whole step above the original. After several successes the students reverse positions, and the game should continue each day until everyone understands how it works. Then the director should assign pairs of like instruments to practice tuning unisons as a homework assignment, over time adding a third and fourth player until entire sections can eliminate beats while playing unisons.

The Unisons Game, Part 2

Another game alerts students to problems with unisons in single reed instruments with opposite pitch tendencies. When a clarinet and flute play F concert at the *mf* level, the pitch should be fairly close. As each player diminishes to *pp*, the clarinet will go sharp, the flute flat, and beats occur. When dynamic levels are reversed the pitches will pass each other with the flute pitch going above the clarinet and the clarinet below the flute. To correct this the flutist can change the pitch with jaw or head movement, and the clarinetist can add all right hand fingers and, if necessary, the third and fourth fingers of the left hand to open G.

Tuning the Octave Game

This game is the same as unison tuning. Beats occur if the second octave does not match the pitch of the second partial; partials in the harmonic series are numbered from the fundamental up, the first overtone being the second partial. Note that it is more difficult to tune clarinets in octaves than to tune them with other instruments because acoustically they lack even-numbered overtones.

Tuning the Major Triad Game

Treasury of Scales works well in tuning major triads, especially number 19 in Eb concert, with the scale in the bass. After playing the last chord, Eb in root position, students should sing the chord tones, up and down, to determine which note of the triad is written in their part. With this goal accomplished, conductors play the broken chord on the piano and have students sing the notes in every key from the changing fundamental bass note. It is important for students to be able to identify where in the triad a note falls as well as to recognize that all major triads sound alike, no matter what the key. Accurate tuning cannot be achieved until students understand relationships of notes in a chord structure. Return to number 19 in *Treasury* and ask students to play their corresponding note in each triad; including all octaves, and backing up if errors develop. Through singing and playing, most students can find the chord root, third, and fifth.

Tune the root unisons and octaves first, then begin thirds and fifths by asking a tuba or trombone player to sound Eb in octaves. Have students listen for and sing Bb, the third partial, generated by the in-tune octave to create a perfect fifth. Finally, have the band play the complete chord again and tune. Delete all players on three or five,

but ask those on five to sing the fifth with the original tuba and trombone octave.

Continue working until one and five are accurate, involving all players even though the notes are not in their parts. When one and five are in tune, the third of the triad, the fifth partial, will be audible.

If problems still exist at this point, simplify the game by using a bass clarinet unison fifth over a tuba root, third partial over fundamental, then add a trombone or baritone to amplify the second partial or octave. If the partials are in tune, the fifth partial, or third of the triad, is clearly heard; adding a soprano voice on the third will aid in identification. By writing these notes on the chalkboard band members can see what this chord looks like, furthering their understanding.

Play through number 19 again to evaluate the band's progress. Once students have heard major triads in pure harmony, with every partial in tune and in balance, strong fundamental and octaves, slightly weaker fifth, and less tonal weight on the third, they will be inclined to duplicate them in other harmonic situations.

Tuning the Minor Triad Game

Begin with an in-tune perfect fifth, deleting the root, and tune the minor third as a major third below the fifth. When satisfactory, add the root remembering that minor thirds cannot be tuned without beats because the root generates a major third partial that beats against it.

Tuning the Minor Seventh Game

Use the same tuning approach as for major triads, then add the minor seventh.

The Inversions Game

Inversions of chords are more difficult to tune as the bass produces a series of overtones in conflict with primary overtones. The solution is to find the root, tune the notes above, then add the voices below. Bass line players can occasionally find their pitch through difference tones, the lower members of the harmonic series produced by two in-tune upper partials; however, teaching bass line players to be in tune with tempered intervals is the most practical method.

There are intonation problems between instruments of the same family as a result of differences in diameter, bore, and placement of valves and tone holes. Ensemble intonation can be improved by using similar mouthpieces, reed strengths, and correct embouchures.

These games isolate tuning problems but improving simpler harmonies also affects intonation in complex harmonies. Tuning unisons, octaves and fifths accurately allows band members to match the tempered scale that pianists and keyboard percussionists use. If a band adds a few pure thirds and minor sevenths to some harmonies, they can sound exceptionally good. Learning tuning fundamentals in traditional harmony also helps adjusting to tempered tuning in 20th century music where complex rhythmic structures, wide intervals, dynamics, and style overshadow harmony. In romantic and contemporary music, pure harmony and perfect intonation are lesser goals than the model of well tempered intonation with occasional glimpses of pure harmony.

Students are usually surprised when they see a demonstration of the differences and compromises between pitches in pure harmony and those in temperament. They will seek pure harmony when they recognize the advantages of bending pitch to achieve intonation. What directors should keep in mind, during this often frustrating procedure, is that working toward improved intonation means a better band. ☐

December, 1975

Gerard Schwarz Talks About Phrasing

Barbara Jepson

"**Y**ou must make the phrasing in this movement absolutely free — otherwise, it can start to sound repetitious."

At the podium is Gerard Schwarz, the 27-year old co-principal trumpet with the New York Philharmonic. Twice a week Schwarz conducts classes in orchestral repertoire for winds, brass and percussion at the Juilliard School of Music.

Today the students are playing through Bruckner's *Symphony No. 7* in E Major. Schwarz conducts with broad, expressive gestures, stopping the students frequently until he is satisfied that they understand the style of the piece — *and* the phrasing. Schwarz has a reputation for smooth, careful phrasing in his own playing, along with some definite ideas on how wind players can transcend "just getting the notes."

The following interview took place in one of the many dressing rooms reserved for musicians at Avery Fisher Hall. It ended just in time for Schwarz to warm up for the 8:30 concert.

Tell us about your class at Juilliard. What is its purpose?

The class is designed to prepare students for future orchestral positions by exposing them to the standard orchestral repertoire and by giving them a sense of the style of works from different periods. But I aim for something more — I try to help my students develop a style of their own.

How do you do that in a two-hour class that plays through one major orchestral work per week?

By getting them to think for themselves, especially when it comes to phrasing. I'm not going to try to impose my ideas on them — I'd like them to impose their ideas on me, to inspire me. I ask them to study and experiment with a particular phrase or group of phrases. If they resist, I threaten to tell them how to play it — note by note. *That* usually works! Then, when they've come up with something, I toss out my own ideas. I'll sing or play a phrase to help get it across. Over a period of time, they begin to develop their own concepts. They learn when to listen to the second horn, when to imitate someone else, when to put a little of themselves into their parts, and when to play it straight. Ultimately they develop a style of their own and learn how to teach themselves a new piece, which is a very important beginning.

What about accuracy, rhythm, intonation and overall technique?

Each of these things is an important part of music. I spend a lot of time correcting rhythm and intonation. But all of my students are taking private lessons, and about two-thirds of their lesson time is spent on technique. So I try to concentrate on musicality in the class.

430

Unfortunately, many wind players are taught to get the notes correct, and *then* to work on phrasing and dynamics. At the very least, this method is inefficient — it means students may have to re-learn a piece. At worst, they may never learn to go beyond just getting the notes and a good sound. My view is that the initial concept, and the initial effort, must be a musical one. I try to get my students to work towards musical perfection the first time around.

With that goal in mind, what do you recommend for the student who wants to develop more than technical proficiency?

The talented student must look to great conductors and performers for inspiration. This is one area of instruction that many otherwise excellent wind instrument teachers neglect. They don't open their students' eyes to outstanding musicians who play other instruments. If you want to learn more about Beethoven, how to play Beethoven musically, you don't listen to his wind music. You listen to Serkin! I would like to see teachers spend more time on musicality, not just technique.

Which do you think conductors value more in a player, accuracy or musicality?

If you ask the top conductors what they look for in a player, most of them will tell you accuracy. Stokowski summed it up beautifully once, when I was playing in the American Symphony Orchestra: "The French horn is so hard to play that I prefer a horn player who is not too inspired musically. If he gets the notes, then *I'll* make the music." From the wind player's standpoint, however, that's not enough. For example, many orchestral trumpet parts are relatively simple, and just playing the right notes can get boring...if that is as far as you go. Working out the phrasing helps make your job more meaningful.

What do you aim for in your own orchestral playing?

I try to understand what is going on around me rather than just my own part. I study the score before a performance, and try to see how my part fits into the whole. This helps me to know when I can put a little of my own personality into my playing, and when I must be an accompanist only. You can't go overboard. You can't express too much of yourself. There are many times when it's best to play it absolutely straight. It varies according to the nature of the piece, who is conducting, and what he is asking for. But even when I accompany, I try to have a sense of how my accompanying fits into the whole.

For example, the other night the orchestra performed Beethoven's *Concerto No. 3* for piano in c minor. In the first movement, I play a very simple series of notes with the woodwinds (see example).

With *crescendos* and *decrescendos* added, here is how most musicians would phrase the line:

And I think trumpet players should complement this material by phrasing along with the oboe.

This kind of approach enables me to be involved even when playing a simple part. I guess it's all part of my particular philosophy — technical proficiency will always be important, but perfection of technique must go hand-in-hand with perfection of musical concept.

Barbara Jepson is a free lance writer and amateur pianist from Brooklyn Heights, New York. She has studied at The Mannes College of Music.

Expression and Style
in
Band and Orchestra Playing

MERLE J. ISAAC

ONE who listens to many school bands and orchestras in public performances cannot fail to observe certain common strengths and weaknesses. In general, when bands and orchestras participate in contests and festivals, all of the members play the right notes, but all too often they do not play the notes right.

Playing the right notes involves mainly the mechanical process of putting down the right fingers in the right place at the right time. This is not always an easy job. In very fast or difficult music this process often taxes the ability of the player so that we must be content if he does play the right notes at the right time.

But music, if it is to be real music, demands more than this of the player. In addition to the right note at the right time, listeners of serious music demand that the tone quality be good. Whether the tones be long or short, loud or soft, they must be acceptable to the ear as musical tones. Listeners demand, even more, that the tones be fairly well in tune. Most listeners are reasonable about this and do not expect tones to be scientifically in tune. We do insist, however, that the tones be well enough in tune to satisfy the ear. Even persons who know very little about music can usually tell whether or not it is in tune and they just don't like sour notes. It can be said with certainty that music, to be acceptable, must consist of tones whose tone quality and intonation are satisfactory.

One of the things that make the difference between mediocrity and superiority in music is expression. Children in the primary grades al-ways talk with expression, yet they do not always read aloud with expression. Like the young readers who pronounce all of the words correctly, but without expression, many of our school band and orchestra members play all of the notes correctly, but without expression. They play the right notes, but they do not play the notes right.

Musical expression is generally regarded as something quite mysterious and spiritual. The ability to play with expression is popularly believed to be a gift and either you have it or you don't have it. This may be true so far as artist musicians are concerned, but any ordinary musician can learn to do certain things that will make his playing more expressive and more enjoyable.

Dynamic Contrast

Let us consider one of the simpler kinds of music, a march. If a march is played from start to finish with all of the tones produced correctly as to pitch and duration, but with each and every note played equally loud, we are not satisfied with the result. Generally, we expect the trio strain to be played softly the first time through. This device of playing a middle section softer than the rest of the composition is an elementary form of musical expression. Certainly there is nothing mysterious or spiritual about it. It is done mechanically: the players just don't blow so hard or they don't pull so much on the bow. How does this device apply to more difficult music? Nearly every musical composition sounds more effective if at least one strain is played with reduced volume.

Another device that is commonly used with simple music is that of playing the melody louder than the accompaniment. This device is just as applicable to more difficult music. With band music, especially, the heavy tubas and the penetrating horns often provide an accompaniment that quite overbalances the melody played by the clarinets. While all parts are equally important, not all parts should be equally loud.

Getting back to our simple march, the first count in each measure is usually played louder than the others. Also, there is a heavy bass tone and a bass drum beat on this first count. This gives us accent and rhythm, and helps folks to keep step when marching. Much concert music also requires this accent, though not always to the same degree nor with the same regularity. The character of the music determines the amount of rhythmic stress required.

Phrasing Gives Meaning

In language, one of the important things to consider in making speech expressive is phrasing. We do this naturally in everyday conversation. A phrase is a group of related words expressing an incomplete thought. In music, a phrase is a group of related tones expressing an incomplete musical idea. When talking, we emphasize certain words and syllables and minimize others. We can actually omit certain words and syllables without being misunderstood. In making music expressive we must stress certain phrases and play others softer and lighter. Within a musical phrase certain tones must be emphasized, sometimes by making them louder and sometimes by playing the other tones softer. The final note of a phrase is often played very softly and lightly. (We "kiss the phrase good-bye, rather than kick it good-bye.") The difference between a loud tone and a soft tone need not be great, but unless there is some difference there is likely to be little or no musical expression.

One way to decide what to do with a phrase is to sing it. Singers usually have words to help them, and vowel and consonant sounds give color, variety, and emphasis. Singing an instrumental phrase, without words, making some tones loud and some soft, will usually give a clue as to how the phrase may be played with expression. As the word is used here, expression is largely a matter of loud and soft. Playing loudly or softly involves mechanical processes that are neither poetic nor esthetic. Musical expression is produced by mechanical means. Knowing what to do involves intelligence and taste, but doing it is a matter of mechanics.

What is Style?

Another quality of music that is too much neglected by our school bands and orchestras may be termed style. In its simplest form this means tones separated or tones connected. Our youngest players join all of their tones the same way, about midway between connected and separated. Generally, however, players on stringed instruments tend to play everything connected, while brass players tend to separate the tones.

Different melodies require different styles and combinations of styles. A slow andante song-melody requires that most of the tones be played very smoothly and many tones should be slurred for maximum smoothness. Many rhythmic, marcato, march melodies, on the other hand, require that the tones be separated rather widely for effective performance. Playing tones connected or separated is purely a mechanical process, yet it does much to make music interesting, enjoyable, and expressive. Let a violin section play Schubert's MARCHE MILITAIRE, the first theme after the introduction, first connecting the tones and

then separating them, and anyone can see the great difference. Played one way, the melody sounds like a spirited march. The other way, alas, is too often the way we hear it.

Most melodies, as found in instrumental music, are to be played neither with all of the tones connected nor with all of the tones separated. Here is where taste and intelligence are needed. Musicians must decide which tones are to be connected and which are to be separated. Also, when tones are to be separated, how much they are to be separated. The best answer to this whole question will be given by an artist musician, one born with great talent. But any good player can work out some kind of an answer, and often it will be more than satisfactory.

Everything in the preceding paragraphs concerning expression and style is based upon the concept that expression is largely a matter of loud tones and soft tones and that style is a matter of tones connected and tones separated. (In both cases there are many degrees and shadings.) This is, of course, an oversimplification, but it is a good starting point. It is of sufficient validity to warrant serious study by every school band and orchestra teacher who feels that his pupils might play with more expression or with better style. This concept is put into practice by purely mechanical means and every school musician has the ability to do what is necessary, although some will be more skillful than others.

Use Recordings

The director's responsibility lies in teaching the players which notes to play loud or soft, which notes to play connected or separated, and in both cases to what degree. The director must decide upon an interpretation and then teach it to the players by various methods. One thing that can help directors in deciding upon an interpretation is a recorded professional performance. A record may be played many times, in whole or in part, while one is listening to the various devices employed to make the music more expressive, interesting, and enjoyable. Certain tones are accented and separated, certain chords are sustained very softly, some phrases are played with boldness while others are soft and tender. An idea that is good

for a fine symphony orchestra may also be an idea that is good for a school orchestra. Most of our ideas are borrowed or adapted. Why not borrow the best? Professional musicians play Mozart and Beethoven according to tradition. What is traditional interpretation but imitating excellent performances that have been heard and studied? School directors can help their students greatly by studying recordings, analyzing them, and teaching their players to produce similar results within their abilities.

What about much of the music used by school bands and orchestras that is not recorded? Of course, if the music has been carefully edited and is published with marks of expression, tempo indications, and suggestions to the conductor, be sure to try them. However, if the music has few printed suggestions, the director must use his intelligence, imagination, judgment, and good taste. Assuming that he has mastered one instrument and that he has performed and listened to much great music, the director has a background to draw upon for ideas, devices, and methods. We should put as much care into the interpretation of a melody in an easy overture as we would put into the interpretation of a theme in a symphony. Our pupils who play or hear the easier melody for weeks or months deserve to hear it played with the best interpretation that we can give it. These pupils may never play the symphony. Their closest contact with music may be through the easy overture. It is the teacher's responsibility to provide his pupils with experiences which are genuinely musical and meaningful.

It might be well, at this point, to digress for a moment and urge teachers to use great care in the selection of material to be played by their musical organizations. Some music is such that the players cannot help but play it expressively. Other music is such that even an artist cannot make it sound well. School musicians will play with more expression if they play music which appeals to their emotions.

Other Methods
After the teacher has selected a composition and has decided upon

the interpretation (tempo, style, and expression) he can and should employ several methods to teach his players. It is usually advisable to place in the music certain marks such as bowings and articulations. Well schooled professional musicians know how to bow certain types of passages, but we should help our younger musicians by marking the bowings for them. Accent signs, dots, breath marks, and marks which indicate crescendo and decrescendo also may be helpful.

There are many things in music, however, which cannot be put on paper. Some of these can be taught by singing (or even talking) to the players. Some things the director may be able to demonstrate on an instrument. (This is one of the most effective methods.) Sometimes it is well to let the players listen to a recording, listening many times to the same passage, with certain salient features pointed out, analyzed, and made clear.

In addition to all of these methods it is necessary for the director to call the players' attention to the desired interpretation not once but at every rehearsal until it becomes part of the melody itself and the players cannot think of it in any other way. This does not mean that there is one right interpretation, and one only. On the contrary, there are often several ways of playing a passage effectively. But with school musicians it is well for the director to decide upon one interpretation and then not change it unless there is a good reason.

Most school bands and orchestras, when playing in public, play the right notes, but too often they do not play the notes right. Their music is played without expression or style. Much of that which is lacking may be supplied, in a simple way, merely by playing some tones and passages loudly while playing others softly, and by making some tones connected and others separated, with many intermediate degrees and shadings.

Musical expression, then, is not spiritual or mysterious, but is based upon the use of good taste and common sense (judgment and intelligence) based upon experience, and is put into practice by purely mechanical means, blowing or bowing harder or easier or not at all. Music educators, directing our youth, have a great responsibility which they should face unafraid. School musicians have always been taught how to play the right notes. Now, more of them must be taught how to play the notes right!

July, 1990

The Strobe
A Forgotten Friend

by Frank Wickes

A band director I knew refused to accept a job offer until the band's parent organization agreed to purchase a 12-window strobe. They did, and he took the job; but not everyone shares his opinion about this often misunderstood piece of equipment. Several years ago when a prominent guest conductor came to my school, he walked into the bandroom, pointed to the strobe, and said in a loud voice, "What's that doing in here? Get rid of it. You shouldn't be using that machine!" I was surprised at his comments until I realized that he ordinarily worked with professionals, not students.

Many high school band directors use a strobe to help tune their bands. A few years back while adjudicating a high school-level contest, I was amused when a band director rolled a strobe onto the stage in front of the band, audience, and judges. Tuning each player to a B♭ concert pitch, he delayed the festival 15 minutes beyond the allotted time. He managed to get the band fairly well in tune on B♭, but ironically the group's piece was Bach's *Fantasia in G major*; from the opening chords the band was out of tune.

A 12-window strobe is expensive but worth the investment if used properly. The finest students I have taught, those who now play professionally or teach at the university level, spent hours practicing in front of a strobe. Doing so sharpens a player's pitch discrimination and helps him understand the intonation idiosyncrasies of his instrument.

To use a strobe effectively, a player needs a quality instrument, including mouthpieces and reeds, as well as good tone production, because good intonation and good tone are inseparable. Playing with a proper embouchure, the student needs to be able to

sustain a tone at a *forte* level with a supported air stream for several counts.

Before attempting to tune to a strobe, players should warm up; the length of time depends on the instrument. Frequently students using a strobe check only one pitch, usually concert B♭; this limits the strobe's effectiveness and does little to solve other intonation problems. Conductors can assist students by teaching basic tuning concepts before introducing the strobe. In rehearsals I use it only occasionally to check an individual or section. Use the following notes for basic tuning: flutes, A4; oboes, A4; clarinets, F4 (concert E♭4), then lower octave G3 (concert F3); bassoons, F3 followed by A3; alto and baritone saxes, C5 (concert E♭4) followed by F♯4 (concert A4); tenor saxes, C5 (concert B) followed by C6 (concert B♭5); trumpets, G4, C5 (concert F4 and B♭4); French horns, C4, B4, B♭4, and A4 (concert F4, E4, E♭4, and D4); trombones and baritones, F3, B♭3, tubas, F2, B♭2; string bass, G-D-A-E, tuned by using harmonics.

Frank B. Wickes, president of the National Band Association, is director of bands at Louisiana State University in Baton Rouge.

Procedures for Individual Practice

Once you calibrate the strobe according to instructions in the owner's manual, learn how the strobe windows correspond to the notes on the instrument. Experiment by lipping notes up or down to make them more flat or sharp, which will help place pitches better with increased practice and improved pitch discrimination.

Practice the chromatic scale in front of the strobe while looking at the windows. Play long tones, letting each note sound until the strobe wheel displays a continuous pattern. If the pattern is moving, lip the notes up or down until the pattern slows or stops. Players who do not lip notes easily should practice the technique until they master it. Always try for the most beautiful tone possible. Pure tones register on the strobe as a clear pattern.

After slowing or stopping the strobe display pattern on each note, again practice the chromatic scale in long tones, this time starting the note without looking at the windows. Once you think the note is in tune, look at the corresponding window and adjust the pitch accordingly.

In the early stages of strobe practice looking at the windows will help you make proper adjustments with the lipping muscles. After much repetition, you will not only begin to memorize the placement of each pitch, your ear will also begin to hear it. After all, hearing consistently is the ultimate goal. Unless they are unusually precocious, most students do not hear

deviations of eight cents (hundredths of a semitone) or less. With continued strobe practice, young musicians will refine their sense of pitch discrimination.

Tips for Effective Strobe Practice
• Practice the complete practical range of the instrument, and especially emphasize the extreme high and low registers.
• Play long tones at different dynamic levels: *pianissimo*, *mezzo piano*, *forte*, and *fortissimo*.
• Practice using all types of mutes, because each can alter the pitch.
• Check the pitch each time you change a reed or mouthpiece.

The Strobe Test
Pair students as practice partners and develop a strobe test in which they work together every few months. Give one student a sheet of manuscript paper showing the notes of the complete practical range of the instrument, and have him record the strobe results by marking the deviation in cents for example, +6, 0, -7 below each note on the staff while his partner plays. The player should not look at the strobe windows during the test. I recommend three of these strobe tests per marking period.

Individual strobe practice and strobe testing make long-tone study more interesting and help students locate and correct inherently out-of-tune notes. Good intonation in ensemble playing is not an exact science, and practice with a strobe will improve pitch flexibility. Many

students believe that the strobe is absolute, but when playing in an ensemble strobe-perfect notes are not necessarily in tune. With flexible intonation players will adjust to each other and group intonation will improve.

Some years ago a member of the Philadelphia Orchestra was asked how the group played so perfectly in tune. He responded that they didn't; it only sounded that way because they all played out of tune together. This is flexible intonation.

Nothing separates strong concert bands from weak ones more quickly than poor intonation; good intonation starts with the director. Teaching students to hear both horizontal and vertical pitch relationships takes time and patience. Using the strobe, you can help students refine pitch in both ensemble and individual performance. □

Listening for Improved Intonation

by Lacey Powell

Perhaps no problem in instrumental music is more complex and discouraging to directors and students than faulty intonation. Even though the subject is addressed in volumes of journal articles and is discussed in clinics, lectures, and workshops, intonation problems continue.

Often the responsibility for intonation is left to the strobe tuner or to the director's ears. As a result, stu-

dents learn not aurally but visually, or by the commands, "pull it out" or "push it in." They wait for the tuner or director to tell them whether they are in tune, and if not, whether they are flat or sharp. They then assume they will remain in tune for the rest of the rehearsal and do not understand why they are admonished just a few minutes later for playing out of tune. To break this cycle, it helps to not only tune the instrument, but to make the student an active participant in

the process.

Begin working on intonation with the first lesson. Unless students be gin with correct posture, embouchure, and breath support, it will

Lacey Powell is an associate professor of music at the University of South Alabama. He has served as president of Alabama Bandmasters Association and Alabama Music Educators Association.

be impossible for them to play in tune. Before initiating any training in tuning, confirm that students can correctly produce a tone; an aural concept of good tone is necessary as a foundation. Diagnose the quality of the sound the student produces, and be ready to provide a demonstration of the quality you want him to produce. Recordings, advanced students, or you can be excellent models.

After establishing fundamentals, assign a carefully ordered repertory to develop technical skills and aural sensitivity. Students learn to listen carefully when provided with materials that permit discrimination, such as slow melodic selections in homophonic texture. Chord progressions or Bach chorales work well for this. Avoid extreme ranges and dynamics; the point to stress is nuance, not bombast.

An accurate sense of pitch perception and discrimination is best developed through the human voice. Start this training with a class of beginners; older students will feel inhibited. Beginning students respond positively when the technique is introduced naturally as a play-sing-play approach, using a neutral syllable *oo, loo, ah,* or *lah.* Charles Elliott's 1972 study in the *Journal of Band Research* investigating singing in the beginning band class concluded that students who vocalize have a superior ability to discriminate between pitches, to relate sounds to notation, and mentally convert notation into sound. Students also become more sensitive to pitch if they are required to correctly finger the notes while singing the pitches. The goal is to help students form in their musical ear a clear mental picture of the notes. A word of caution here: check to make sure that students sing with good tone supported by adequate breath, not in loud playground voices.

Francis McBeth in his book *Effective Performance of Band Music* states, "Pitch is a direct result of balance," and continues, "If the conductor cannot describe to his band his concept of balance and how to achieve it, then he is leaving to pure chance the sound of the ensemble." When taught and practiced regularly, this concept will help students become better listeners. Using the term oneness and asking them to match each other gives the students something specific to listen for. It is useless to ask a player simply to listen. Listen for what? Instead, ask, "Who do you hear playing the melody?" This will help students relate to the concepts of balance in the section and across the ensemble.

Parts that move together in octaves are rarely balanced. Usually the fault lies in the predominance of the upper voices. The mathematical ratio of two notes an octave apart is 1:2. The higher pitch, having double the cycles per second, requires more control of the dynamics for proper balance and pitch. Explaining this to students may help them realize the nature of the problem.

Players soon become aware of the characteristically out-of-tune notes on the instruments. Fifth and sixth partials and 1-2-3 or 1-3 valve combinations frequently cause problems for young brass players, while throat tones on the clarinet or open tones on other reeds pose their own challenges to woodwind players. As the players increase their ranges, they add bad notes along with good.

The late James Neilson wrote a helpful booklet called *The Overtone Principle* (available from the G. Leblanc Company) that explains the acoustics of wind instruments. A fingering system and alternate finger system are provided. With such knowledge of pitch tendencies, advanced players can learn to compensate when making a crescendo or decrescendo, which causes pitches to go sharp or flat. They become aware that flutes and brass instruments go sharp when playing a crescendo and flat while playing a decrescendo, while the reeds must compensate for reverse pitch changes. It's little wonder that bands experience serious intonation problems when dynamics change.

Using a strobe in the practice room allows students to find the proper tuning position and to discover characteristically bad notes. Because most instruments need to tune to several pitches to be accurate, it may be helpful for you to use a sequence of four or five tones when tuning the ensemble. When players attempt to tune from matching only one pitch, they may set the embouchure differently than when using a pattern of several notes. Mark Hindsley in his article "Intonation for the Band Director" (*The Instrumentalist,* January 1972) recommends a sequence of pitches appropriate to each instrument rather than the same concert pitch for all the instruments. It is also easier and more accurate for students, especially younger players, to hear intonation problems when playing several tones centered around a tuning note than it is to match a single pitch against a constant tone.

Have students practice with the strobe in pairs, with one student serving as monitor for the other player, who plays into the strobe without looking at it. Begin this training with like instruments, then when students master the lessons, have dissimilar instruments pair up. Initial exercises consist of long tones, chromatic and diatonic scales, and intervals.

Students should continue this procedure until they can play a scale in tune. At that point they can add to the routine crescendos, decrescendos, and extended ranges. When pairs of students continue to practice matching pitches without using the strobe, they develop skills of concentrated listening and immediate adjustment.

At this point students begin to recognize beats and are aware when they disappear. One technique to sensitize them further to beat listening is to have two students play a unison simultaneously without adjusting, allowing the unison to sound out of tune. Gradually, one should adjust to eliminate the beats while the other remains constant. In this way students learn to concentrate and to listen for a oneness of pitch. As players attempt to correct tuning deficiencies, they learn to make subtle embouchure adjustments rather than constantly changing the length of the instrument. Notes can be humored as follows: flute — direction of air; reeds — firmness of embouchure; brass — lip tension, aperture; horn — hand position; all — amount of velocity of air and alternate fingerings. Lip buzzing on brass instruments will promote accuracy; students learn to feel the pitch and become aware of their ability to adjust while playing a centered pitch.

As the performers learn to recognize when they are in tune, they can compare and match their own pitches with the ensemble. Ask the ensemble to play pitches 1 2 3 4 in a named key. On the fourth step of the scale, point to a section or to an individual to continue playing as the ensemble releases the pitch. Then direct steps 5 6 7 8 in the same way to introduce the half step in each tetrachord. Finally, direct the playing of pitches 1 2 3 4 5 and tune the fifth degree of the scale.

Participating in small ensembles is the best way for students to learn to tune accurately. The independence required in such ensembles helps them develop sensitivity beyond that which they would learn in a large group. Once learned, this skill will stand students well in any size ensemble. ☐

The Director's Intonation Checklist

Preparation for Good Intonation

• Develop a course of study that includes intonation proficiency

• Provide students with a good visual and aural model to imitate

• Teach woodwind players to balance a throat-register note against a long-tube note when they tune.

• Require students to mark the correct location of the tuning mechanism rather than starting from scratch at each rehearsal.

• Mark music "↑" or "↓" to remind players of needed adjustment.

• Remind players that vibrato should be used to enhance tone quality, not to mask intonation problems.

• Teach students to use alternate fingerings.

• When possible, match instruments by brand and model. This will improve intonation from the outset.

• Adjust music stands high enough to maintain correct posture and playing position of instruments.

• Seat the flutists in an arrangement that does not require them to stretch their neck muscles to look up at the conductor. Allow sufficient space for the players to hold their instruments correctly. Cramped flutists droop at the elbow, which worsens intonation.

• Schedule solo and ensemble activities as a year-round activity. Assign student leaders to manage scheduling groups for rehearsals.

• Encourage students to occasionally practice in the dark; it promotes concentrated listening.

• Provide opportunities for students to play by ear.

• Remember the effect temperature has on intonation. Is your rehearsal hall too hot or too cold?

• Record rehearsals often. Check the pitch level on the strobe.

While Tuning

• Recognize and compliment good intonation.

• Tune at mezzo forte.

• Adhere to the pitch standard of A-440.

• Tune lower voices in the ensemble first.

• Have students listen to the quality of sound to judge whether it is flat or sharp. A strident, pinched sound is usually sharp; a flabby, dull, unsupported tone is usually flat. Encourage students to strive for a centered tone.

• Play, sing, and play while tuning. Listen both for vertical and horizontal intonation.

• Sing with enthusiasm, concentration, and confidence when demonstrating.

• Have students warm instruments to body temperature before attempting to tune.

Teaching Intonation to Beginners

by Paula Crider

Technically, the band is proficient, but too many intonation problems marred a good performance." From my experiences with adjudicating bands across the country, I hear enough evidence to support the fact that music educators are generally competent at teaching technique, but lack an organized approach to teaching how to play in tune. By incorporating intonation as a fundamental part of technique, students develop the habit of listening while playing.

Sing the music. Faulty intonation results when students don't know how to listen. Singing requires listening, so have beginners sing every line before playing it. By progressing from scalewise patterns to intervals, a format used in most beginning method books, young musicians learn to sightsing without realizing that it might be difficult. Try using singing as a regular part of rehearsals with junior high and high school groups as well. If students have never sung before, experiment by having each section hum its note when a chord is out of tune. Next ask students to play the chord, then change to humming when you give the cutoff. If your students are listening, the chord should be in tune. You can transpose to a comfortable octave if necessary. Students are often inhibited the first time you ask them to sing. With a little practice, however, they can become more confident singers and will enjoy performing compositions that involve singing as well as playing. Including such a number on a concert not only improves singing and listening skills, but also provides variety for the audience.

Develop an intonation chart. Using a tuner, work with each student to create an intonation chart that will make him aware of the general pitch tendencies of his instrument as well as his own inherent intonation problems. For example, flutes are generally flat in the low register and sharp in the third register, whereas clarinets are generally sharp in the throat tones and flat in the third register. After the student warms up, have him turn away from the tuner, then play a chromatic scale from the lowest practical note to the highest. Using the intonation chart, write down the pitch tendency of each note shown on the tuner's display. Use a plus sign to show the number of cents sharp, +3, and a minus sign to indicate the cents flat, -2. A zero means the note is in tune. Have the student keep his chart in his music folder for reference. After he memorizes all tones over five cents sharp or flat, ask him to make a second chart with the goal of improving the readings from the first chart. When you evaluate the intonation chart, offer suggestions for alternate fingerings and slide compensations to improve intonation.

Listen to beats. A musician who listens can tell whether a pitch is sharp, flat, or in tune; students can learn this response by eliminating the acoustical phenomenon of beats, which result when notes are not in tune. Have two trumpet players sound an open tone with the tuning slide on one instru-

Intonation Chart

Name _____

Instrument _____

	1st 8va	2nd 8va	3rd 8va	4th 8va	Notes/comments
B♭					
B					
C					
C♯					
D					
D♯					
E					
F					
F♯					
G					
G♯					
A					

1. Warm up carefully and tune properly.

2. Play a chromatic scale, beginning on the lowest practical note on your instrument. Continue to the highest practical note.

3. Do not look at the strobe while making this chart. Your partner should mark the number of cents sharp or flat for each note.

ment pulled out as far as possible. Ask the class members to close their eyes and use their hands to represent the frequency of beats, moving them rapidly at first, then slowing them as the trumpeter pushes the tuning slide back in. When no beats are heard, all hands should be still. With this exercise you can observe each student's aural perception.

I teach my high school students intonation by assigning unison scales; the goal is to play eight notes perfectly in tune. Scale ranges correspond to ability; a beginning trumpeter plays from C4 to C5; a more advanced student from G4 to G5, and the most advanced player from C5 to C6. Set the

metronome at ♩=60, and ask the student to hold each scale tone for four counts, then let him identify which notes are out of tune. This assignment teaches students to concentrate on tuning as well as how to listen and adjust. It builds confidence in listening abilities, encourages the use of alternate fingerings and slide positions, and emphasizes good tone production. Consequently, I spend less time addressing intonation problems in rehearsal.

Using a tuner daily and telling students if they are sharp or flat doesn't train them to listen. Instead, ask the ensemble members to tune to a sounding pitch and let them adjust them-

selves, offering help only if someone cannot make the correct adjustment. It is also a good idea to inspect each student's instrument for needed repairs, such as warped pads on woodwinds and dents in critical segments of brass tubing, to alleviate potential intonation problems.

Exemplary intonation is no accident. If you approach intonation with the same resolve you apply to sight-reading and building technique, your students will learn to play in tune. □

Paula Crider is an associate professor and assistant director of the Longhorn Bands at the University of Texas. She is the former director of the Crockett High School Bands in Austin, Texas.

Misleading Music Notation

by Bruce Berr

That children are impressionable makes a teacher's job easier, but misconceptions in the first years of music study snowball and impede progress at the intermediate level. Concentrated work can solve these problems later, but it is far better to avoid mistaken impressions in the first place. Music notation is an area that often creates long-term problems.

It is remarkable that our traditional music notation system conveys the artistic conceptions of so many composers. Perhaps one reason it has functioned well for so long and for so many is that it looks the way it sounds, most of the time. Our notation system easily handles elements such as up and down, intervals, and meter, but other aspects of standard music notation can be visually deceiving, especially to beginners. Certain symbols communicate technical details, but their appearance creates an impression contrary to musical reality.

Consider eighth notes. In a piece where the quarter note is the unit of beat, passages of consecutive eighth notes tend to have forward momentum toward the next non-eighth of longer note value. Pairing eighth notes communicates the music's basic pulse and indicates that those notes

subdivide the beat into two equal parts, but it fails to show the eighth notes' forward momentum.

Sometimes eighth notes are beamed in larger groups to help communicate this feeling:

Even this notation is deceptive to young eyes because it does not go far

enough. The longer beam stops one note short, creating the illusion that the eighths are unconnected to the half note. The longer the beam of eighth notes, the more resolutely they appear separate from their destination, whereas the opposite is true. An unconventional but more accurate visual representation might be the following:

To avoid this problem, make sure a student's first exposure to eighth

439

notes is not through notation or terminology but through experience. Play familiar pieces that use eighth notes and ask students to count along as you play. Through such eurythmic activities as clapping and tapping, pupils feel the forward motion of eighth notes. Teaching by rote gives students aural and physical experiences with eighth notes before they encounter the pitfalls of notation and terminology: "Eighth notes? Are there eight to a beat?"

In teaching eighth notes, use short basic patterns beamed in pairs to communicate how eighth notes subdivide the beat, clapping or tapping these rhythms while counting. All these short segments should end on a strong note or beat.

In choosing a pattern, try to avoid examples that create a suspended feeling by ending on a half beat.

After mastering short patterns, students can read and play short pieces using them; then you should emphasize their musical aspects. A useful technique is having students circle each set of eighth notes and the concluding long note.

Then ask students to play the circled segment, making the eighth notes sound as if they point to the note at the end of the circle. Here is a slightly more advanced example.

Use these techniques at more advanced levels to teach sixteenth notes and other subdivisions of the beat. At all levels students should learn the basic musical concept that short notes frequently create motion toward longer notes.

Bar lines can be even more deceiving to beginning students, who see separate notes inside closed boxes as communicating that notes in a measure are segregated from and unrelated to notes in other measures. Mu-

sic publishers often leave a fraction of an inch of blank space at the beginnings and ends of measures for visual clarity, compounding the problem. Bar lines and measures are accurate notations of the music's basic pulse, but visually they misrepresent the forward flow of the music. A student's earliest perceptions of these symbols frequently lead to faulty practice and unmusical playing.

There are several easy and effective teaching techniques to circumvent this problem. Have students clap and count consecutive measures of quarter notes with vocal inflections to indicate musical direction, creating mid-measure momentum to propel the music over the bar line and decreasing in intensity until the next cycle. The second half of a measure moves toward the next downbeat, and the first half relaxes after the downbeat. It helps to explain that some beats in a measure look forward and others look backward. Another effective image is that some notes lean in one direction and some lean in another, as when this example is counted in ¼.

Count ¾ this way:

Count ¼ by raising the voice pitch and intensity when approaching beat one and lowering it afterwards. This *sprechstimme* technique is useful and fun in group lessons; children love the strange mixture of spoken and sung numbers, yet the exercise teaches them an important musical concept, which can be applied to a longer phrase.

Not all music in these meters behaves this way all the time, but these exercises overcome the visual tyranny of the bar line. The traditional appearance of measures and bar lines in printed music suggests that the last note in a measure is the end of something, whereas frequently it is a helping note, pointing the way to a more important subsequent note. Put the

musical meaning of beat one in perspective: what gives the downbeat its significance is not an accent but rather the notes before and after it. Use this process as a point of departure for music in which the metric phrasing is not clear-cut.

Publishers frequently lay out music so a piece fits onto complete pages, stretching some measures and squeezing others. To children a series of widely spaced quarter notes implies that they are unrelated, while small measures with notes jammed together may inspire a student to rush. Page turns blur a student's comprehension of the larger sections of a piece of music; teachers exacerbate this with practice assignments determined by page rather than by musical form. Even a clef change sometimes creates the illusion that a long and beautifully arched phrase has an ugly zigzag in the middle of it. A double bar at a change of key signature within a piece may seem to indicate a point of repose, whereas the musical content moves through the key change with great momentum.

The most important step in dealing with notational pitfalls is to take a fresh look at familiar symbols, to see the notation through a child's eyes. This requires seeing familiar groups of symbols with a fresh, almost naive outlook. It is your responsibility to show students how to deal with discrepancies between the musical sound and the way it is notated, so they understand that our notation system is sometimes inadequate to communicate even the simplest elements of music. Those students who learn how to interpret written symbols in a musical way right from the start may become good musicians, not just good readers. □

Bruce Berr, an assistant professor and coordinator of piano pedagogy at the Chicago Musical College of Roosevelt University in Chicago, is completing a doctoral degree at Northwestern University. He co-authored a collection of supplementary piano teaching pieces, Musical Pictures, Volume 1a, *recently published by CPP/Belwin.*

Teaching Rhythm with Games

by David W. Roe

Games can be a valuable tool for teaching a variety of musical concepts. I have developed three group activities that can help teach rhythm and orchestration to my high school instrumental classes; the complexity of these games varies if longer or shorter note values are used. The first two are effective as warm-up exercises in the first five minutes of class to focus students' attention on a common activity.

The Elimination Game

Ask a student to create a one- or two-measure rhythmic pattern in a specific meter, for example a one-measure pattern in 4/4 using only quarter, eighth, and sixteenth notes.

The pattern should be interesting and playable by the whole class. Write the pattern on the board, explaining any special note groupings; for example, write ♪♪♪ as ♫. Then ask the class to play the pattern in unison or octaves using a specific pitch, such as concert F. Once the class can play the pattern correctly, the elimination game begins: ask a student to eliminate one note in the pattern and replace it with its equivalent rest value. As the process continues, replace consecutive rests with a longer rest where appropriate; for instance, ⁊⁊ becomes ⁊ unless the second eighth rest falls on the beat. The class then plays the new rhythmic pattern, and the process continues until only one note remains in the pattern.

You can also divide the class into two teams and award points for playing each version of the pattern correctly.

Rhythmic Composition Game

This activity teaches rhythmic execution and encourages creativity.

Begin as in the elimination game by asking a student to create an interesting two-measure rhythmic pattern in a specific meter, using specific notes and rest values. Write the pattern on the board and ask the class to play it on a specific pitch, then ask a second student to create a second pattern using the same assigned values and meter but rhythmically different from the first pattern. For example, where the first pattern has longer note values, the second might use shorter values. After the class plays the second pattern, continue with a third pattern in the same fashion. Once the class plays all three patterns correctly, divide it into three groups to play all three patterns simultaneously. You can divide by instrumental sections, or divide each section into three parts to perform the pattern as a trio using any instrumental combination. You can also add the element of pitch, assigning a different pitch to each of the three patterns (for example, concert F, concert A, and concert C).

In notating the patterns on the board, be sure that all beats in the measure line up properly.

David W. Roe is a composer, trombonist, and music educator in Scarborough, Ontario, Canada, where he teaches instrumental and vocal music at Wexford Collegiate Institute. He holds a Music Baccalaureate in music education from the University of Toronto and M.M. and D.M.A. degrees in composition from the University of Miami, Florida.

Orchestration Game

I use this activity with my second-year high school students. Each class produces a composition, and the classes exchange pieces and perform them.

Ask your class to write a four-bar composition titled "Bells," following these specifications: limit pitches to the notes of the E♭ major triad (concert pitch); use ⁴/₄ or ³/₄ meter; stay within a comfortable range for each instrument; make the parts rhythmically independent; write the piece in proper score order and form; and include appropriate dynamics. Explain the notes of the E♭ major triad; correct notation of various note and rest combinations in ⁴/₄ or ³/₄ meter; the range and transposition of each instrument in the class; proper score order and form; possible dynamic levels; the key signature for E major and how to notate it in treble, bass, and alto clefs; and key signatures for transposing instruments. The class should also consider whether dynamic levels should be the same for each instrument, how the instruments sound in various registers, and whether to assign shorter or longer rhythmic values to higher- or lower-pitched instruments.

April, 1991

Bells No. 1

Flute
Bells

Clarinet

Alto Sax

Trumpet

F Horn

Bells No. 2

Tuba
Flute
Bells

Clarinet
Trumpet
Tenor Sax

F Horn

Trombone

Cymbals

Ideas for Teaching Rhythm

by James Warrick

Evaluating student comprehension of rhythmic values is difficult. Teaching rhythm usually evolves into a math lecture on fractions followed by a class performance of rhythms, but the problem with this method is knowing which students understand the lesson when only the loudest players are discernible. By approaching rhythm through subdivision and duration, I have developed a method that works with individuals or groups and objectively measures student progress while teaching notation.

Prepare a handout containing rhythms in ⁴/₄ time and instruct students to decide the appropriate subdivisions and write them in. This will often lead to a discussion about what subdivision is, how rhythmic stability comes from subdividing a measure into smaller units, and why a player should mentally count divisions of beats while playing long notes.

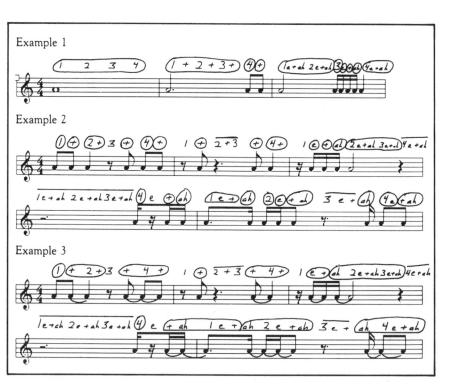

Example 1

Example 2

Example 3

442

When analyzing whole, half, or quarter notes, have students consider the quarter note as the largest subdivision in any measure. A whole note would be subdivided as

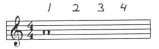

When a measure contains an eighth note, it should be subdivided as

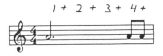

When a measure contains a sixteenth note, they would write:

Instruct students to circle the durations of the subdivided notes. In the previous three examples, the students should write and circle as in example 1 on this page.

At this point I can see if students understand note values, and they can see that the articulation of each note begins with the first circled subdivision. They will also see that notes with longer values have larger circles; and shorter, faster notes have smaller circles.

To teach students how to notate rests, have them leave rest subdivisions uncircled, but draw a line over combined subdivisions to show the duration of a rest: the longer the line, the longer the rest, as in example 2.

In example 3, because ties connect the values of notes, a circle encompasses the combined durations. At this point, students often ask if rests can be tied. Of course they are not, but the question leads to a thought-provoking discussion.

Demonstrate the difference between correct and efficient notation. While this rhythm is correct,

this is more efficient notation for seeing the beats.

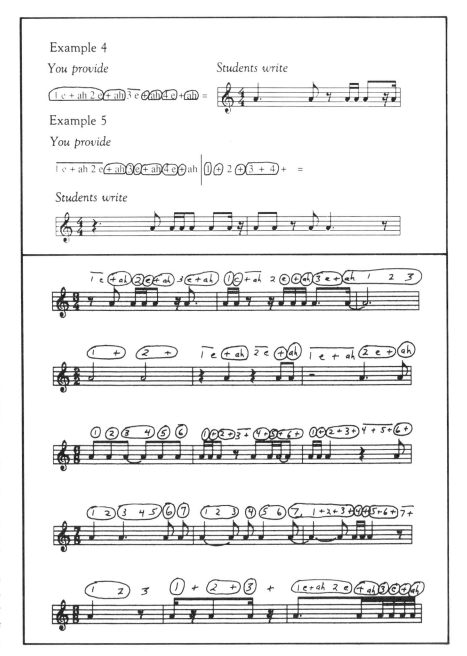

Example 4

Example 5

I explain that while inefficient notation will be noted on the first two quizzes, points will not be deducted until the third quiz.

Have students clap the rhythms while saying the subdivisions, and sometimes it helps for half the students to count the subdivision while the other half claps. A drum machine or an amplified metronome can be effective in demonstrating rhythms.

Students now have all the tools to notate music and construct rhythms from the circled subdivisions and durations in worksheets or quizzes, as in examples 4 and 5. It will also give them an opportunity to write musical notation.

The final part of a quiz is performing on their instruments the rhythms analyzed on the written portion of the

test. A few days after returning corrected quizzes, I have students record a cassette tape at home of the rhythms on the quiz. Above is an example of a homework sheet of rhythms in various time signatures analyzed by ninth grade students.

Until I used this system to teach and test rhythmic understanding, younger students had difficulty performing and understanding such complicated rhythms as the ones on this quiz, but after a few classes using this method, students are capable of figuring out rhythms on their own. You will even begin to see band music marked with subdivisions and durations. □

James Warrick directs bands at New Trier High School in Winnetka, Illinois, and has taught at all grade levels.

Teaching Rhythm Reading

by Daniel Kazez

Rhythm notation is a complex and imperfect system; most time signatures don't mean what they appear to say, most notes don't end when it seems they should, and a rhythm can change identity depending on the context. A widespread misconception of rhythm pedagogy is that subdivision is the answer to all rhythm woes; the opposite is closer to the truth. Teach students to read rhythms in much the same way they learn to read English: syllable by syllable, or word by word, not letter by letter. They become familiar with such recurring groups of letters as at: bat, cat, fat, hat, mat. The letters "at" are an indivisible unit students learn to recognize, and these word units are plentiful: it, bit, fit; aught, caught, naught; ate, bate, fate; and so on.

Students should read rhythms as a group of notes called a rhythm cell; but unlike syllables in English, there are only a few cells. Nearly all rhythm patterns in simple meters of $\frac{2}{4}$, $\frac{3}{4}$, and $\frac{4}{4}$ contain the following fundamental cells:

You can create most rhythm patterns, such as dotted notes, double dotted notes, syncopation, two-against-three, four-against-three, by combining the fundamental cells.

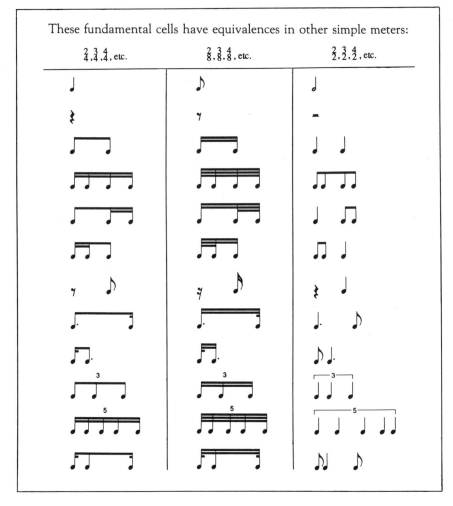

These fundamental cells have equivalences in other simple meters:

Each of these derivative patterns can be transformed for meters with different beat units.

In such compound meters as $\frac{6}{8}$, $\frac{9}{8}$, and $\frac{12}{8}$ cells can generate most compound meter rhythm patterns:

Daniel Kazez, an assistant professor of music at Wittenberg University, has published articles on intonation, relaxation in string performance, and cello technique, in such journals as The American String Teacher, Music Educators Journal, Triad, The Instrumentalist, and the College Music Society's Symposium. He is author of the college textbook Rhythm Reading: Elementary Through Advanced Training.

Students who learn these fundamentally difficult passages in solos, etudes, and ensembles. By working on each cell as an indivisible unit, students will come to recognize and perform them correctly. It helps them if you use speech cues to introduce a fundamental cell and have them say or sing the rhythm with a word attached.

After a time they should drop the word, but they will naturally associate the rhythm with the word and perform it correctly. The speech cue is a well-known technique, and the following words fit well with simple meters:

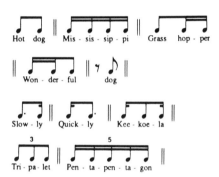

Select words to introduce a new rhythm that match the notes in accents as well as syllables, and modify the words to fit the ages of the students. A five-year-old will enjoy saying "lol-li-pop, lol-li-pop" when learning a rhythm cell, but may have trouble saying or understanding "won-der-ful, won-der-ful":

The words you choose should match only the rhythm, not a combination of the rhythm and the underlying beat. For example, many instructors teach two-against-three and three-against-two using the words "not dif-fi-cult":

This may work for pianists who control both the rhythm and the beat; but it won't work for students who have to impose the rhythm over an existing beat. Instead, this rhythm should be taught as a combination of fundamental cells.

Speech cues are a tool, not a crutch, and once students master the cell, they should drop the word and perform the rhythm alone.

A music teacher who is a capable performer provides a service to students by demonstrating elements of good technique and musicianship. However, teachers should avoid spoon-feeding music to their students. Teaching by demonstrating good technique can help or hinder students' learning depending upon the circumstances. Many well-known music educators, such as Carl Orff and Zoltán Kodály suggest that students should read music only after they can sing or play an instrument proficiently, just as they learn to read after they can speak. In *The Kodály Context* (Prentice Hall) Lois Chosky says, "The teaching order is always sound to sight, concrete to abstract." You can incorporate this concept by demonstrating difficult rhythms and having students mimic you as you clap, tap, or sing a rhythm, then have them perform it in the music.

On the other hand, when more advanced students encounter rhythmically challenging material, mimicry is rarely a beneficial technique; encourage students to figure out the passage on their own by discerning an apparently new rhythm pattern as a combination or permutation of fundamental cells they have mastered. Compared to mimicry, this approach demands more time and energy of both teacher and student, but in the long run develops rhythmically self-sufficient students, and the ensemble will have more time making music rather than learning how to play the notes.

After explaining a rhythm concept, ask students questions to test their understanding of the mathematical foundations of notes and rests in the time signature.

1. How many eighth notes are in a quarter note?
2. ♩ ♩ = what single note?
3. ♩. = what two notes tied together?
4. 𝅝 = ♩♩♩ : True or False?
5. Which of the following are equivalent?
   a: ♩. b: ♩♩ c: ♩♩
6. Draw a quarter note.
7. Identify this note: ♪
8. In 𝄴 , what does "2" mean?
9. In 𝄴 , what does "8" mean?
10. What would the time signature be for the following measure?

    | ♩ ♩. ♪ |

11. Write and perform eight measures in 𝄴 using ♪ , ♩. , and ♩ .
12. Mark the location of each beat in the following: (*include one or two lines of rhythm*)
13. Which of the following measures has the wrong number of beats? (*include one or two lines of rhythm*)

Eventually, students will decipher and perform most rhythms.

Rhythm notation has evolved over the last 2,000 years from a system that vaguely indicated relative durations to one that specifies meter, tempo, and duration of sound and silence. It is the precision and detail of our rhythm notation that seems confusing and contradictory to students. A serious shortcoming of rhythm notation is its inability to indicate the difference between simple and compound meter.

Whether meters like 𝄴 and 𝄴 can function as compound is debatable. Although many music theorists claim that such meters are never compound regardless of the tempo of the passage, other theorists, such as S. Kostka and D. Payne state that a "fast waltz or scherzo is almost always notated as simple triple, usually 𝄴 . The aural effect is of one beat per measure, for which we might use the term compound single" (*Tonal Harmony: With an Introduction to Twentieth Century Music*). Most professional performers count one beat per measure when playing fast passages in $\frac{3}{4}$, $\frac{3}{8}$, and $\frac{3}{16}$.

Students almost always end notes too soon, short-changing long notes. They assume, for example, that a two-beat note should end on beat two. In fact, if a half note starts on beat one of the measure, then it must end at the beginning of beat three. Tell students to imagine that they have a two-hour class: if it starts at 1:00, then it ends at 3:00.

Because the music that follows the symbols **C** and **¢** looks the same, many students think that these two terms are synonymous; so in **¢** help students be aware of the half-note beat. Although **C** is often known as common time, it is not an abbreviation for this term. In the Middle Ages the geometrically perfect circle stood for triple meter (three representing the perfection of the Holy Trinity). An imperfect circle, somewhat like a **C** , stood for duple or quadruple meter. From this music theorists use **C** to indicate $\frac{4}{4}$ and **¢** (**C** cut in half) to indicate $\frac{2}{2}$.

Several common tempo markings originally had meanings subtly different from those musicians use today, and understanding these meanings sheds light on possibilities for inter-

	Simple meters	Compound meters
Meaning of the upper number	Number of beats in each measure	Number of largest possible subdivisions of the beat in each measure
Meaning of the lower number	Value of one beat	Value of one subdivision of the beat
Examples:	$\frac{2}{4}, \frac{3}{4}, \frac{4}{4}$ and $\frac{2}{8}, \frac{3}{8}, \frac{4}{8}$ and $\frac{2}{2}, \frac{3}{2}, \frac{4}{2}$	$\frac{6}{8}, \frac{9}{8}, \frac{12}{8}$ and $\frac{6}{4}, \frac{9}{4}, \frac{12}{4}$
Value of one beat:	Never a dotted note	Always a dotted note

pretation. For example, in the greater part of the 17th and 18th centuries, *adagio* meant at ease, not simply slow; *allegro* meant cheerful or joyful; *presto* meant fast, not very fast.

This rest ▬ has two possible meanings: a whole note rest, or a whole measure rest. If the rest stands alone in a measure, it indicates a whole measure rest, regardless of the meter. In meters longer than $\frac{4}{4}$, such as $\frac{3}{2}$ or $\frac{4}{2}$, if ▬ appears in a measure with other notes or rests, it represents a whole note rest.

Double dotting is a subject yielding to much controversy. Many scholars suggest that dotted notes in music in the style of a French overture should be performed double dotted.

In teaching college sight-singing classes, I find that nearly all freshmen music majors, regardless of their performance ability, suffer from rhythm misconceptions. They rarely understand the difference between simple and compound meters (they count $\frac{6}{8}$ in six rather than two) and overuse subdivision when learning music; they shortchange long notes. Students should learn these by the end of the first year of music study, whether in choir, band, orchestra, or private lessons. Despite all the imperfections of its notation, rhythm should be neither difficult to teach nor to learn. The difference comes with using the proper teaching strategies. □

May, 1989

Sight-Reading: Is It A Lost Art?

by Paula A. Crider

"**D**irectors who teach by rote should be imprisoned for child abuse!" This scathing epithet was delivered by Warren Benson during his visit to the University of Texas campus last fall, and it serves as an apt edict for those who teach by rote. It is easy for any instructor to fall into the habit of singing rhythms to students rather than helping them understand how to perform rhythms at sight. This writer found an easy way to break the rote teaching habit: she told her band members that any time she was guilty of singing a rhythm, the first student to raise his hand would earn five dollars. Thirty-five dollars later, this director was cured.

Sight-reading can and should become an enjoyable part of every rehearsal, even during marching season. Learning to sight-read competently will help students reduce the time it takes to prepare each piece.

Preparation

Before school begins, take the time to go through your library and organize several large stacks of music. Each stack should begin with easy-level pieces and progress to more challenging ones. Include all forms and styles from jazz to aleatory. Old overtures make excellent sight-reading material, and the classic standard marches are great technique builders.

A director must be able to quickly scan a score for cogent points. You can hone your score-reading skills by keeping unread scores handy, then when a free moment is available, scan a score for one minute, jotting down all salient points. At the end of the minute, slowly and carefully read through the music to discover any important areas you might have missed. With practice, you will overlook little. Observing sight-reading contests can also be educational: watch an old pro at work for a most enlightening experience.

Teach the Basics

Rhythm. Five minutes a day of well-planned, progressive rhythmic studies will yield remarkable improvements in students' understanding of rhythms. Never assume anything when teaching rhythm; it is wise to begin at square one rather than risk learning gaps. First, establish a workable counting system; Ralph Hale's *Rhythm Slides* and counting system are an example of outstanding pedagogical aids for the teaching of rhythm. Other resources that might prove useful are Hovey's *Advanced Technique for Bands*, Yaus's *101 Rhythmic Rest Patterns*, Smith's *Symphonic Rhythms and Scales*, Colin's *Develop Sight-Reading*, Haines and McEntyre's *Division of the Beat*, and Berryman's *Rhythm Patterns*.

Worksheets prepared in advance provide a quick method of checking students' progress. To create interest, place a challenging rhythm on the board each day and invite students to perform it correctly. Ask students for their ideas, and provide some incentives. For example, each week offer a pizza party to the section with the most successful rhythmic readers. Teaching rhythm can be enjoyable if you approach it creatively, rather than as a dreaded activity.

Key. While some students may dazzle you with scale pyrotechnics, few young musicians have the knowledge to write out scales. That's because much of their learning has been by rote. This problem is easily solved by teaching basic concepts of music theory such as the order of sharps and flats and the logic behind key signatures.

Ask students to spell scales while fingering them. Give written tests. Hold a spelling bee in which you give students a key and ask them to spell the corresponding scale, or give the number of sharps or flats and ask them to name the corresponding key. I always include spelling bees early in the year for my ninth grade musicians. The students learn about keys through enjoyable, spirited competition. Frank Erickson's arrangement of *Prelude Through All Major Scales*, based on Beethoven's Op. 39, is an excellent source for teaching awareness of key signature. After one reading of this piece, challenge students to play through the entire work without missing a key change (those who do drop out). This kind of exercise can be a real eye-opener.

Style. The proper execution of musical style, taught in an organized, systematic way, is another often-ignored aspect of sight-reading. To alleviate this problem, incorporate the various articulations into a daily warm-up routine, then assign a style exercise on a scale pattern. Several minutes of individual instruction will yield amazing improvements in articulation throughout the ensemble. Hear students individually during sectionals, or during rehearsals. Ask an assistant or private teacher to help you by working with students individually as the rehearsal proceeds. Read, rehearse, and program a wide variety of contrasting styles to achieve desired results in this most important area. Carol Butts' "The High School Band Clinic" is an excellent source for style and for articulation exercises.

Musicianship. I shall never forget the first time my high school band not only showed technical mastery of a sight-reading piece, but also played musically. The enthusiasm for this accomplishment brought about a loud, spontaneous cheer and an unforgettable gleam of satisfaction and understanding in my students' eyes. Students need to be able to perform a variety of dynamics so that they can create nuances in phrasing. Choose literature and warm-ups that require a wide range of dynamics, and encourage students to perform expressively. Make all aware of the long note rule: "When holding a note of two counts or more, chances are that someone else may have a more important part; so listen, determine the musical function of your note, and balance accordingly."

Sight-reading procedures. Establish a rehearsal environment that is conducive to good sight-reading. Allow for a brief period of silence for the students to scan the sight-reading piece. At the end of this study period, have students turn their stands around to face the conductor, then ask questions concerning tempo,

style, meter and meter changes, accidentals, difficult rhythms, dynamics, and other details of performance. The first time you ask students to do this, they may not give many correct answers; however, once they learn to quickly scan and retain important details about the music, they will make far fewer errors.

When preparing for a sight-reading competition, it is important to rehearse exactly as you will handle yourself in the sight-reading room. Directors should practice pacing instructions so that they fit comfortably into the time allowed, regardless of score length. Following a first reading, it is often helpful to replay a few problem spots. A few words of encouragement and a more successful rendition of a section can help build confidence.

Conducting techniques. Good eye contact is essential for successful musical communication. Conductors should conduct the ensemble, not the score. Insist on good eye contact at all times. Stop if you find yourself conducting the tops of heads. Varying style, tempo, and dynamics on warm-ups is an excellent way to encourage good eye contact. A good indication that students are not watching the conductor is if the band continues to play after the conductor has given the cut-off. Insist on clean and immediate cut-offs. Expressive, non-verbal communication between musicians and conductor can be a musically rewarding experience.

Teaching young musicians to become successful sight-readers is a challenge that requires instructors to present fundamental musical concepts in an organized format for each rehearsal. The results will make the art of making music much more enjoyable. □

Paula Crider is an associate professor and assistant director of the Longhorn Bands at the University of Texas. Prior to this appointment she directed the Crockett High School Bands in Austin, Texas for many years.

Basic Phrasing

David Sweetkind

Private teachers and organization conductors perpetually implore students to "phrase," "sing," or "play expressively." More often than not, bewildered inexperienced players have either no idea how to satisfy the conductors' demands or a completely erroneous conception of the directors are after. Expressive playing mistranslated becomes anything from excessive use of vibrato to an increased amount of instrument and body wiggling. How many instrumentalists, however, have actually been taught to "play musically?" This article attempts to set forth, on a most basic level, six concrete suggestions for phrasing which, if followed, should guide a student toward a basic feeling for a musical phrase and should help to eliminate the all-too-frequently-heard dull performance. The idea that playing all notes and markings on the printed page constitutes a musically perfect performance appears to be all too prevalent among students—and in a small voice I will add, *even among many teachers.*

I have purposely omitted any mention of differences in historical style; a basic sense of phrase must first be developed before more subtle differentiations are attempted. No clean cut division between these six rules is possible, as suggestions in each category must interact upon one another. It must be assumed that the player has enough control of his instrument to play fairly evenly—tonally, technically, and dynamically.

Rise and Fall

The normal phrase, like the spoken

David Sweetkind is associate professor of music at the Univeristy of Georgia in charge of teaching woodwinds and woodwind ensembles. Awarded the Bachelor and Master of Music degrees at the Yale School of Music, his doctorate is currently in progress at Boston University. Mr. Sweetkind has served as clarinetist with the New Haven Symphony, the Connecticut Symphony, and the 7th Army Symphony. For three years he was assistant conductor of the Yale University Band.

sentence will rise in both pitch and volume toward the middle and fall off at the end. The instrumentalist must follow this same curve, even if the composer's markings indicate no dynamic change. The melodic line simply marked *piano* is too often played in a monotonous mumble. A composer will usually note a marked dynamic difference, but will leave to the discretion of the performer the normal shaping of a line. What if the general shape of a line is a fall rather than a rise? The answer is the same—crescendo as the line moves downward. A falling phrase played at constant volume will appear to be gradually weakening; an increase in volume in a falling line is needed to counteract this tendency. Try to find the musical high point of a phrase and aim toward this. Once the climax is reached the point of relaxation at the end of the phrase can be aimed for.

A drama critic once deftly slashed an actor by writing, "His performance ran the gamut of emotions from A to B." How often this occurs in music! Many students attempting to give a feeling of rise and fall to a line underdo the dynamic variation and never manage to communicate a tension and relaxation of any sort to the listener. The following five rules should help to answer, "How can I be sure I am making enough variation?" and "How much can I make?"

Play Each Note Differently

The rule applies not only to repeated notes, but also to any group of notes in succession. It must first be established that a single note communicates no meaning; only in context and through a relationship of qualities can a note make sense. The Italian Renaissance painter Titian is purported to have said concerning the ever present difficulty of obtaining a true flesh tone, "Give me the color of mud and I can turn it into the most beautiful flesh

by virtue of the colors with which I surround it." Each note is but part of a musical thought or idea, and a player must find the function of the note within the context.

To form a shapely phrase the notes must always be aiming toward or returning from a high point. Ask yourself, "Is this note to be played louder or softer than the previous one? Why?" Granted this is often a sticky problem when one is concerned not only with a line, but also with a combination of melody, harmony, and rhythm. However, at the basic level, a sense of phrase direction can be considered the most important first step. When aiming toward a climax each successive note must be louder and conversely should be softer coming to rest toward the end of a phrase. Subtleties can be added after the general framework of the phrase is clear in the player's mind.

The player must vary rhythm as well as volume. (Is there a sudden change which must be brought out? Is the rhythm incisive or languid? Is the rhythmic character changing?) Articulation constitutes another significant aspect. (Should one note be attacked more strongly than another for emphasis? Will more or less separation aid to put across the composer's idea?). A droning performance can be compared to the monotone of a dull story teller, the average performance to the amenities of every day chit-chat, while the dynamic and polished words of a fine professional actor, poetry reader, or orator. To play each note differently establishes a starting point, possibly too calculated, but a beginning in bringing some life or spirit to a musical line.

Bring Out The Moving Notes

In playing a phrase expressively, too many performers attempt to accentuate the long notes and skim over those tones which move more quickly. This leads to backward phrasing. Over emphasis of a long note sounds labored or ludicrous, ranging from extreme distortion and interrupting of the phrase to the siren effect *a la* Jerry Colona. If the most expressive notes were the long ones, the piano would long ago have been discarded as a useless music making instrument, for here a note can only diminish in sound after being struck. The moving notes are direction and can be used in sequence—one against or in conjunction with another to bring out a musical line effectively. A long note usually functions as a resting point and in this instance must be a relaxation from tension. When a long note is the height of a phrase, the note must be properly led up to as there can be no climax without a buildup. A climax can be said to be no more than the sum total of the tension leading to it. Do not save expression for the climax; it will be too late.

Rapid notes are often played as though the composer put them in the music merely to fill up space for lack of a better idea. Unfortunately this sometimes seems true, but more often faster moving notes will automatically heighten excitement and must be brought to the fore rather than sloughed off or underplayed.

Exaggerate

Rarely must a student be admonished for over-phrasing. Even those students aware of the necessity of convincing phrasing usually fall far short of even the minimum amount of dynamic, rhythmic, or articulation variety imperative to an exciting musical performance.

The problem of projecting to an audience is not peculiar to the music field. An actor on a stage points with not one, but two fingers. To an audience this looks normal; a one fingered gesture would hardly be emphatic enough. Likewise the musician must learn to play what he would at first consider to be a bit larger than life-size to put across his and the composer's intentions. When most students feel they are exaggerating to the point of grotesqueness, the phrase is usually just beginning to take shape to the listener. A session with a tape recorder usually illustrates this quickly and vividly to the student.

The weakest instrumentalists, in respect to projecting well, seem to be those who have always been section players where most contrast was obtained by differences made by orchestration to show contrast between sections of the band or orchestra, rather than by articulation and dynamic variation within one's own line. A simple looking string of eighth notes on a page can be made to sound lively, curt, choppy, smooth, expressive, driving, legato, etc. depending on articulation used, stress on notes, and rhythmic thrust employed. Each eighth note does not serve the same purpose, and these notes must not all be treated alike. Likewise, a group of dotted eighths and sixteenths should range from smooth and expressive to clipped and martial depending on the length of each note, length of the rest between the first and second notes, degree of accent, and the attack on each of the notes in the group. Which does the composer want? What style will best put across his intention?

Examine Phrase Relationships

One phrase is like one note—only a part of a larger unit. As a play is divided into acts, scenes, and lines, so is a piece of music divided into movements, phrases, and notes. All must relate to one another by means of similarities and differences. Students should be made conscious early in their training of this type of relationship. Call it form if you will, but it must be understood that a two measure phrase might relate to the next two measures, possibly followed by a four bar phrase and that all three phrases actually constitute but one still larger phrase. For example, once a student learns the relationship between the following three phrases, he must attempt to construct a cohesive and interesting line like this. Works must be examined for major and minor climaxes, contrasting sections, and larger groupings than just the small phrase. First-grade-reader phrasing (John is a boy. He has a ball. It is a new ball. He got it for his birthday.) must advance to greater understanding of more complex relationships and continuity of ideas. (John, the boy, has a new ball which he got for his birthday).

Point of View

The performer must attempt to discern the intent of the composer in each work. No composer consciously attempts to write bland music, though many performances are played as if blandness were the composer's primary preoccupation. First, the general character of the piece must be ascertained. Is it a strong virtuoso work? Is it lyrical? Is it whimsical? Within this larger framework there will always be contrast and these contrasts must be brought out. If the first theme is strong and the second lyrical, a player must be sure to bring out this difference. Too often a common denominator is found between opposite poles of expression.

All music strives for an optimum balance between likeness and difference. A cohesive lyrical passage must hold together, but must be played in absolute contrast to a rhythmically dynamic section in the same piece or movement. A performer should constantly ask himself questions such as, "Is this phrase more or less intense than the previous one?" "Is the rhythm becoming more or less exciting?" "Does the harmony increase or decrease in tension here?" "Is the general melodic excitement heightening or lessening?" In general, if the music is slow and lyric, emphasize long melodic phrases, dynamics, and minimize sharp articulation. If a work is supposed to be fast and light, articulate cleanly, lightly, and with deftly placed accents. *Do not play noncommittally* any more than you would consider delivering a speech in a monotone. The performer's job is to convince.

When an instrumentalist is made conscious of the need for phrasing, when he listens to fine players phrasing well, and seriously attempts to cross over from the world of notes to the realm of music, he realizes better the supreme importance of control in playing—far more control than he has ever needed or used, and usually more than he is capable of producing. This alone can be a great stimulus in a "back to the woodshed" movement—not only for the player to work on actual phrasing problems, but to work toward technical improvement to attain better command of his instrument so that he may cope more easily with the musical problems.

449

Flexibility of Tempo

Ralph G. Laycock

"Uh-one, uh-two, uh-one, two, three, four!" With the tempo thus firmly established, the stage band was off and running — running at a fixed tempo that was *not* to be altered for the duration of that particular composition. And rightly so, for much dance-oriented music demands an unchanging pulse; and the ability to manage all of the appropriate expressive effects without sacrificing the security of that pulse is imperative for a successful performance.

Just as unyielding must be the tempo of a parade band charged with the responsibility of keeping countless feet in step for marches of a half-hour or more in length. Unfortunate is the company, and in serious trouble is the band (especially the bass drummer) who does not possess this inner metronome.

The Sacred Beat

For that matter, *any* music organization that cannot, when it is called for, maintain a steady tempo through thick and thin (scoring), through loud and soft (volume), through fast and slow (rhythmic patterns), sacrifices much of its potential effectiveness. The audience, even if only subconsciously, is aware of this unrhythmic character and is let down, rather than buoyed up by such a performance.

But many of us, having grown up in an atmosphere where "the beat" is practically sacred, tend to apply this same rigid yardstick to the performance of all types of music. "If it is not metronomically exact, it cannot be correct," we say. In my own case, I remember how (as a fledgling performer and conductor) only a printed *ritard, accelerando*, or other specific instruction could induce me to vary the tempo in the slightest. To do

so otherwise seemed somehow rather sinful! It took a long time to overcome the slightly "guilty" feeling that came over me when (even though armed with the "authority" granted by some famous conductor's recording) I took liberties with the composer's tempo.

Stilted performances of this kind are all too common. Conductors "slow-march" their groups, heads erect, eyes forward and looking neither to right nor left, through delicate flower gardens, oblivious to either the beauty or the perfume. The result is that such music seems to have been played only because, like the garden, it was in the direct line of march, and had to be traversed in order to get to the next "exciting" portion. Whatever the reason for such insensitivity (and there are many reasons that for the time and place may seem temporarily valid), the music has been robbed of much of its interest, meaning and very reason for being. Everyone within hearing is the loser.

In the belief that recognizing the problem is itself the first step in the correction thereof, may I suggest what may be some of the reasons for insensitive performance in the hope that they will serve as a springboard for the readers' imaginative thinking. *But whatever the extenuating circumstances, the entire responsibility for success lies squarely on the shoulders of the conductor-teacher. No immature group is able to perform more sensitively than they are taught or conducted. The conductor must not only be able to feel such subtleties, but must be able to communicate his feelings to the students with sufficient conviction that they accept them, and, in turn, communicate them effectively to the audience.*

Here Are the Excuses

For now, let us examine the "excuses." (Next month we will make suggestions for the elimination of the need for them.)

1. Much of this type of music is actually more difficult to perform effectively than many pieces that are faster and mechanically more challenging: (a) Tone, intonation, precise but gentle attacks and releases, blend and *all* of the other fundamentals are more exposed, particularly in solo and other prominent voices. (b) The music is more subtle and demands more maturity to appreciate and to perform it authentically. (c) Minute changes of tempo are difficult for inexperienced players to recall exactly and bring off unitedly.

2. Immature students may find such music less interesting: (a) They may well think that it is "easy" or even "dull" and, as such, not worth their full attention and concentration. (b) Some players may have few notes or even no notes at all, becoming a discipline problem through sheer boredom. (c) Their lack of an exact sense of tempo and their careless counting (after all, *who* should have to count quarter notes!), shows up most obviously in such music.

3. Rehearsal problems: (a) The students' lack of interest and their consequent inattention may lead to inefficient rehearsal, or even to resistance to *any* rehearsal on such a piece. (b) The eternal problem of insufficient rehearsal time may lead to neglect of the "easy" music so that faster and/or more technically difficult parts can be mastered. (c) The conductor may fear that such delicate nuances will be forgotten by some of the players in the nervousness and tension of the eventual performance and, in consequence, may feel that time spent

on them would only be time wasted. (d) The conductor's gestures may not be sufficiently clear and accurate to secure (and insure) perfect ensemble in such matters, in which case it would be frustrating to all concerned even to rehearse such effects. (e) If the conductor does not understand the subtleties of such a piece, he may, unfortunately, contribute to the seriousness of any or all of the above-mentioned problems.

Although the above list makes no claim to being complete, it perhaps points arrows in several directions from which difficulty may come — the exact nature of which is only clearly apparent when it reveals itself. The solution may differ somewhat in each case.

The story is told that Toscanini, in going over the score of one of Verdi's operas with the composer prior to its first performance, pointed out a place where he felt that a slight ritard, although not indicated would be effective. Verdi enthusiastically agreed, commenting that it was just what he wanted, whereupon the conductor asked why it had not been written into the score. Verdi's reply was to the effect that, "If I had marked it, most conductors would have overdone the ritard."

Whether it be true or not, it is entirely within the realm of possibility, and, as such, points out three important considerations: (1) changes of tempo are not always marked; (2) when marked, they are often exaggerated; and (3) some composers would rather have none at all than to have them overdone. Mature composers often leave interpretive details in the hands of others whom they hope will be mature performers alert to the subtleties that cannot always be put down on paper.

Composers in earlier times were not as careful to indicate their desires as they are now. They may not have realized that they were writing for posterity—next Sunday's service was all too close at hand, and they had to get the notes copied in time for tomorrow's rehearsal. Since they were going to conduct personally and their musicians were accustomed to their manner of interpretation, minor details could safely be left for explanation during the rehearsals.

Even careful composers often leave us very much on our own in many matters, not the least of which concerns tempo and its variation.

How can we know exactly what is desired?

We cannot know for sure what the composer intended but we can develop and exercise our own best judgment with the knowledge that after all of the possibilities have been examined, it is still the conductor's obligation and privilege to do what that judgment tells him is best for his group at this time. (And it is also his obligation to realize that if his group cannot hope to give a fairly authentic performance at *this* time, he should postpone or cancel any public performance of any piece!)

Leaving aside the vast area of *indicated* tempo changes, many of which are too often disregarded or overdone, let us consider a number of situations wherein tempo changes of varying degree may be appropriate even though they are not indicated.

Changes of Basic Tempo

1. Changes of texture—thinning, thickening or altering the texture through addition, subtraction or substitution of a number of instruments may indicate a new mood which may benefit from a slightly faster or slower tempo.

2. Changes of rhythmic vitality —when a "busy" rhythmic feeling gives way to a relaxed, less energetic one, a slightly slower tempo may be helpful in setting the new emotional climate. But be aware that the very relaxation of the rhythmic tension may in itself be sufficient and that a slower tempo could overdo the effect, producing lethargy rather than only relaxation.

3. Style of music—music from the renaissance and romantic periods may, on the whole, be performed more flexibly than classic or late baroque. Fast music usually must be more "metronomic" than slow, but slow music with many small notes and/or repeated rhythmic patterns needs a steady pulse. Dance music which by design becomes more and more animated may call for accelerando, either section by section or a continual

speeding up.

4. Repetition of a complete segment of a rhythmic piece may gain by being performed faster and more excitingly or slower and more majestically. Particularly is this true on the final portion of a sectional work such as a march.

5. Endings—the ending of a slow piece may slow down still further in order to finish calmly; the ending of a fast piece may be accelerated in order to finish with a rousing climactic feeling; a long coda may do both in turn depending on the mood desired at any particular moment.

6. Harmony—the amount and speed of harmonic movement may influence the tempo. For instance, a theme which has several changes of harmony per measure may have to be performed more slowly than one which has only one change per measure (or even fewer) so that the harmony can produce its full effect. . . especially when the theme is a repetition which is much more richly harmonized than an earlier version.

7. Melody—a minor statement of a theme originally in major may possibly gain from a slower tempo if it is intended to produce a somber effect. A jagged melody with many skips may perhaps be more effective if performed a little slower than a similar one that is more step-wise.

Whereas the above considerations refer most directly to over-all changes of tempo that continue at this new pace for a number of measures or even for entire sections, there are many occasions where a more transitory dislocation of the pulse may be effective.

Momentary Changes of Tempo

1. Slower pieces, especially those of a folk or hymn-like nature without many "extra" notes can usually be performed flexibly. Among the more normal places for slight rubato are climaxes, where a prolonging of the most important note(s) is effective, and at phrase endings, where a slight ritard can provide a relaxation similar to that which a period produces at the end of a sentence—a moment wherein the audience can take a mental breath and prepare for the next phrase.

2. Fermatas—are often preceded by a slight ritard for the same rea-

son that one slows down before bringing an automobile to a stop—there is no "shock" when the momentum entirely ceases. But, on the contrary, there are times in dramatic pieces where the abrupt stop is precisely what is called for.

3. Climactic notes or phrases may profit from being prolonged. In the case of high notes it may be explained as being similar to having climbed to the top of a high mountain—one would certainly wish to stand there a few moments to enjoy the view and the exhilaration before going on down the other side. Among individual notes this may take the form of an agogic accent—the prolonging of even a single important 16th note then hurrying on—thereby giving it a desirable prominence without having to play it louder or accent it unduly.

4. Silences—are sometimes intended to actually heighten the tension in a manner similar to a rhetorical question, or to let any tension evaporate. Proper handling of them, which may include extending them longer than may have otherwise seemed proper, may enhance their effect. But remember that the entire organization must still be "feeling" the musical effect and act accordingly. For instance, in a tense silent pause the conductor must maintain (and insist that everyone in the group maintain) a posture of tense "suspended animation," otherwise the effect is utterly destroyed!

5. *Scherzando*—this joking style may well call for slight rubato effects in order to maintain the light-hearted mood.

6. Accompaniment—melodies with minimal accompaniment such as long-held notes, or with no accompaniment at all, including but not limited to cadenza-like construction, often can be performed flexibly, even if their basic tempo is quite fast.

7. Dynamic changes—(a) *pp subito* after a loud passage may warrant waiting a moment for the sound to die away so that the first quiet notes can be heard. (b) gradual changes of dynamics may call for gradual changes of tempo, e.g., a long crescendo may be accompanied by a gradual *accelerando*, the resulting *stringendo* driving on

to a climax; a long *diminuendo* may be enhanced by a gradual ritardation as an aid in relaxing the mood. (c) *crescendo-decrescendo* at the climax of a phrase may call for a broadening of the tempo in order to allow its full effect of power or heaviness.

8. Momentary harmonic effects—a strong dissonance, an unexpected harmonic shift, etc., may often be highlighted by a slight prolongation.

All of the above situations have had one thing in common—the tempo has been changed because the musical effect called for it, and to have failed to make such a change would have lessened the expressiveness of the composition. But there are other situations where the tempo change is necessary for purely mechanical reasons, and only if subtly handled will it avoid interference with the continuity or the expression. Indeed, it should, if possible, be so adroitly managed that it *seems* to actually enhance the expression. Some of these situations are:

Mechanical Problems

1. Taking a breath—many musical phrases cannot be performed in one breath, particularly those played by a solo instrument. Here, if the musical pulse will allow it, a slight ritard just before the breath is taken will make the necessary hesitation seem less obviously a delay. At times a competent performer might even be able to make such a "natural" ritard that he would convince the audience that the ritard was called for in the original and therefore, having time to spare anyway, he merely took a breath in the slight break that was already available to him. (Usually the previous note would have to be released somewhat abruptly, the breath taken very quickly and the next note started before the "momentum" had entirely died.)

2. Extreme changes of position and/or register—may take more than the "printed" time if they are to be made accurately and confidently. If so, a slight ritard just before the shift will prepare the listener for the hesitation, serving a purpose similar to that in No. 1 above.

3. Difficult technical passages—

wherein, if the tempo need not be absolutely rigid, it is sometimes possible to "ease" into such a spot, gain speed as the difficulty is passed, and make the passage even more exciting than it would have been had it been played "straight."

4. Bow direction—a passage containing a number of dramatic successive down-bows, in order for each note to reach its full sound and projection, may have to be taken somewhat slower than the prevailing tempo, but this change may itself help reinforce the intense emotional effect desired.

Any dislocation of rhythm or tempo must be negotiated impeccably if it is to add to the musicality of the passage. But this is particularly difficult for immature groups to do unitedly, and their attempts could easily result in seemingly nothing but poor ensemble.

"In order to use a metronome, one should first get a pail of water. Then one should place the metronome in the pail of water. Thereafter, one should sip, each morning, two tablespoonfulls of the water."

In words to this effect did Charles Foidart, late violist of the Paganini String Quartet, express his opinion that rigid "metronomic" playing leaves much to be desired. It is an over-statement, to be sure, for there are valid uses of this accurate, insensitive disciplinarian, but, nonetheless, his words are not without merit so far as public performance is concerned.

So if we can agree that flexibility of tempo in places where none is indicated can at times be possible, permissible and even obligatory, a few generalizations (to which the usual exceptions are appended without saying), regarding its employment may be appropriate:

(1) Fast music tends to be "tight" and unyielding tempo-wise, for while the momentum itself is providing a good deal of musical exhilaration, it is simultaneously legislating against sudden tempo changes which would be as disconcerting to an audience as is a sudden, unexpected sharp turn in a speeding auto. So, unless a deliberate "shock" effect is called for, judicious *bending* of the tempo is usually more in order.

(2) Slow music, on the other

hand, usually has much less forward thrust, so variation of the pace is not only less disturbing, but is actually capable of adding a new expressive dimension while avoiding the tendency to "plod" that might otherwise make itself apparent.

(3) Immature performers find both extremes of tempo difficult to manage. Even though the rhythmic drive of a fast tempo may carry them along with it, their technique and rhythmic sense are not sufficiently developed to insure an immaculate rendition. The consequent lack of precision robs the performance of its rhythmic vitality. In slow music where this natural driving force is blunted, their rhythmic immaturity makes it difficult for them to maintain a perfectly steady tempo even though they can solve the mechanical problems. In either case, then, the added problem of speeding up or slowing down only compounds their difficulties.

(4) In the many circumstances wherein unmarked flexibility *may* be proper (see Part II of this series —November 1970), it is necessary to use good judgment as to where, when, and how much to employ. This wisdom must extend far beyond the individual occurrence, for such effects should complement each other throughout an entire piece or even a multi-movement work.

(5) The effective use of flexibility can have a definite bearing on the choice of a basic tempo, for with it a piece can be kept constantly interesting at a slower pace than would otherwise be satisfying. In fact, an unnecessarily fast tempo makes it impossible (see #1 above) to give sufficient "breathing space" for such effects to be utilized. (I will never forget the young man who, in his audition for a scholarship, spoke so proudly of his high school band, which had played a certain piece at the spring festival at a tempo of "at least a hundred and sixty when it was only marked a hundred and twenty!"

(6) It is *not always* necessary to "catch up," (as is often inferred in definitions of *rubato*) when one leaves a little extra space between phrases, spreads a climax a bit,

or otherwise deliberately holds back the tempo momentarily. The two effects are not necessarily identical.

(7) The rate of change of speed in an *accelerando* or a *ritardando* is often increased toward the culminating point of the effect. For instance, in a long *accelerando* one would usually increase the speed only slightly during the first portion and then increase it more and more obviously during the latter portion, making the greatest change just before the end of the *accelerando*.

Analysis of Performance

(1) As an introduction to careful study of analysis, listen to a number of performances of the same expressive piece as done by different organizations, among which might well be that of your own group. It would be helpful to record a tape containing a specific excerpt as done by each of the performers so that you could immediately compare the smallest details of interpretation. With score at hand, listen actively by setting up a "solid beat" either mentally or by means of a finger snap and/or arm movement, (a metronome is too difficult to get synchronized). This should make it possible for you to hear the tiniest alteration from steady tempo.

(2) Mark the score lightly in pencil with some simple sign indicating the type and degree of change. Many conductors use a **wavy** line ∿∿∿∿∿ to show *ritardando,* the degree of change being shown by the height of the "wave," as on a bumpy road—the going is the slowest where the road is the roughest. For *accelerando,* one or more arrows pointing to the right, ⟶ ⟶ indicate when to move ahead. Thus, a *ritardando* followed by an *a tempo* might appear as ∿∿∿⟶ Placed in a prominent position on the score page, such an indication is not only easier to see than the fine print often employed for such important interpretive details but it also shows more precisely just where and how the effect is to be handled.

(3) As you listen to the various versions, try to decide what effect is created by each. One ritardation may seem to relax quite comfortably; another may hesitate questioningly and then relax; still another may seem like an interruption of a mood that will not allow itself to be discarded. Acceleration may portray increased joy, renewed vigor, or even greater anger of terror. In any case, you should endeavor not only to explain to yourself what *does* seem to happen, but also to find a good reason why and how the performer made it happen that way, whether or not you at that moment agree with his interpretation. All of this activity is aimed toward helping you gain judgment and taste as to what is appropriate and what is not, so that you will be better able to decide for yourself what *you* would do in a similar situation.

(4) It follows naturally that you should expand your intensive listening far beyond this single excerpt, using your growing awareness of the uses of flexibility to first recognize and then to judge the success of the performance in this respect. Do not confine your listening to only band or orchestra, but seek out all types of performance (piano or vocal solo, duo sonata, opera, etc.) through all periods of music, thereby gradually learning what is proper in any given instance.

(5) It has sometimes seemed to me, when listening to tapes of my rehearsals and concerts, that what had seemed to be a very satisfying tempo alteration in the live situation seems overdone when heard through a loudspeaker. I am not sure why this is so; if it has also happened to you, you might want to employ a slightly greater degree of flexibility in a live performance than was displayed on a recording. (I invite readers' comments on this —or any other item)

Personal Conviction

But what should you do? Follow the recording of *maestro x,* as is occasionally noted on the scores sent up to the adjudicators at the spring festival? Possibly so, for a while at least, *if both you and your group are capable of doing so.* But the more you think on it and work at it, the more you are apt to find that you have minor, then perhaps even major disagreements with some part of almost any recording. Indeed, in listening to any one conductor's treatment of the same piece at different stages of his career, you may well find that he has made very significant changes in his interpretation.

You will probably come to have firm convictions about such matters (and *should* do so) only after much thought, experimentation and further listening. Listening should include playbacks of your own work so that, no longer concerned primarily with "putting out," you can devote your entire attention to a reflective analysis of what is "coming back." You should guard against letting "rehearsal" tempos and ensemble problems put you unwittingly into a strait-jacket, unable to move freely enough to express yourself convincingly.

So, before rehearsals, during rehearsals, and after rehearsals, become intimately acquainted with all of the musical ideas in the score. Sing them, listen to them, play them on the piano or on any other instrument on which you are able to perform artistically. You can save much precious rehearsal time by experimenting with different degrees of flexibility and coming to at least tentative decisions as to your desires. It may be that you will discover conflicting interpretations, each of which seems to have a certain degree of validity, and that you will be able to make your final choice only after hearing them all well-performed "in full and living color."

On the basis of your best judgment, (see preceding articles) decide *Where* you wish to employ tempo flexibility, *How Much* will be appropriate, and *What Purpose* will be served by it. (Although you may well revise your thinking as the result of actual rehearsal, you cannot be convincing in your conducting if you yourself are not convinced as to exactly what you wish to do.) To other considerations, add the following:

1. Fermatas may, in some instances, actually become rhythmic extensions of the pulse rather than complete stoppage of that pulse, i.e., they may feel best when held a *precise* number of beats or measures rather than for some indefinite length of time. (Counting on through fermatas in recorded performances may prove to be instructive in this regard.)

2. In long *poco a poco accelerando* or *rallentando* passages it may be helpful to insert appropriate metronome markings at the beginnings of important major ideas as a guide to the over-all tempo curve. (The entire first major portion of the Finale of the Shostakovich *Fifth Symphony* could well be so interpreted, and the metronome marks are already there.)

Physical Preparation

1. Work out what seems to be a satisfactory manner of conducting each passage and master it thoroughly before appearing in front of your group. In fact, exploring one or more alternate ways might sometimes be worth doing.

2. Mark the score clearly. Use underlining, encircling, large overwriting in colored pencil, tenuto mark or abbreviation, wavy line (for slower), arrow (for faster), fermata, comma, cut-off mark, or any of the above combined with numbers indicating where in the measure they take effect. Indeed, any symbol you may desire can be used as long as it will be unerringly meaningful to *you* when needed.

3. Insist that each player habitually makes it his own responsibility to be able to see you clearly and easily *at all times*. You should not even have to check on this once it is established.

From the myriads of possible situations and conditions, we will select only a few elementary ones:

1. *When slowing down.* Delay the beginning of the rebound, then, with wrist bent downward, pull the baton up so that the tip appears to be dragged upward. Lift the wrist and tip just before beginning the next downward stroke. This type of action will give the players almost a full beat's warning that the next beat will be later than steady tempo would demand. If necessary, and particularly in longer passages, gradually introduce subdivision of the beat, first as a casual rebound timed to fit the subdivision, and then as a more independent and important action which will take control of the group.

2. *When speeding up.* Flip the wrist upward sooner and more sharply so that the tip of the baton precedes the wrist and arm in the upward motion. The quicker rebound will thus alert the players to the quicker tempo desired. If necessary, and again particularly in longer passages, gradually suppress the weaker beats and give the pulse with fewer but stronger gestures. (Even though a piece be marked in 4/4, it is often easier for a group to achieve and/or maintain a really fast tempo when guided by two moderately fast but firm gestures per measure, rather than by four very fast but meaningless ones.)

3. *Tenuto on one note.* If long, stop the baton at the very beginning of the beat pattern; then, after an appropriate amount of time, use the remainder of the beat's gesture to indicate when the *next* beat will come. If short, merely slow down the baton at the beginning of the beat; then use the last portion of the beat to move back into tempo.

4. *"Phrasing"* (as in giving time for a breath in a chorale-like piece). Treat it similarly to the tenuto, using the remainder of the beat to indicate the cut-off and to serve as the cue for the next beat. By means of a proper selection of speed of the baton during the silence, the timing of the next entrance can be suitably gauged.

5. *Fermata.* If no cut-off is needed, treat similarly to the tenuto. If a prolonged silence follows the cut-off, make the cut-off by repeating the gesture for the beat, stopping at the beginning of the repeated beat gesture (similar to the long tenuto). Then use the remainder of that beat as a cue for the next entrance after an appropriate silence. If the pause lasts more than one beat, make the pause gesture on the next-to-last beat if possible, saving the last beat to serve as a combined cut-off and cue to the next entrance.

6. *In a complicated passage.* The left hand may be used for individual cut-offs and/or cues, but use it identically *every* time.

7. *As a warning.* Before coming into a touchy change of pace, the conductor may use a deliberately smaller-than-normal pattern. On arriving at the passage in question, his larger gestures will then automatically command attention. The left first finger may be held aloft to serve a similar purpose.

You should use as *few* gestures as possible, teaching the players to subdivide mentally, and to check their ensemble through careful listening. Too often, conductors merely clutter the air with gestures that are either too quick and too late to be useful, or too cumbersome to allow the music to flow naturally.

Rehearsal Suggestions

1. Using a chorale-like piece in which all players have identical rhythmic values, conduct all types of rhythmic dislocations, including *ritard, accelerando, piu mosso* and *meno mosso, tenuto, fermata* with and without cut-off, silent pauses, etc. Explain your actions verbally when and as necessary, but then expect the students to read them visually thereafter. This will help you to gain stick control and confidence, and will give them valuable experience in reading and following such nonverbal communication. Indeed, by this means you may, perhaps for the first time, convince them that they must *always* watch you. Then, even in music which is rhythmically steady, you will have the constant contact necessary for making changes in balance, style, etc.

2. When first rehearsing flexible passages, you may find it advisable to over-do subtle effects so that *everyone* realizes exactly where each effect is to take place. Then, in later rehearsals, you will be able to minimize the changes without fear that someone will forget or totally disregard them. ("You and I may very well be the only people in the auditorium who are really aware that we are doing this at this point.")

3. To check their understanding of your conducting gestures, have the students count aloud in the smallest subdivision needed in the passage in question, (e.g., in constant eighth or sixteenth syllables) as you conduct. Then have them say *tah* at the start of their own notes. Drill and explain until you are certain that they all understand.

4. Try alternate ways of conducting complicated passages and then, when the students understand them, ask them which way gets the message across most clearly. Your main aim is to communicate unequivocally, so even if their consensus surprises you, use the one

that "makes it" unless you feel that it results in an unmusical interpretation. However, the temporary use of an unmusical solution may clarify the problem, and make the final choice more effective.

5. If you fear that your conducting gestures alone have been insufficient to show the *reason* for the change in tempo, explain it in words. Does it add tension? Relax tension? Hesitate in order to gather strength before driving on? Add momentum in order to drive on immediately? Add a triumphant feeling? A funereal one? Affection? Whimsy? The students will perform more convincingly if they all have a common purpose.

6. Complicated ensemble problems may possibly best be solved by first rehearsing the passage slowly in a steady tempo so that each performer comes to understand how his part fits with all others. (He may even find it helpful to write, on his own part, important notes that fall between those that he is to play.) When all are able to play their parts knowledgeably and well, they will then be able to add the flexibility . . . efficiently and confidently.

7. As a test of their security, have the group (after careful rehearsal) play the passage without you, perhaps at first in steady tempo, but then with what they consider to be the appropriate amount of tempo change. When they are successful in this endeavor they will be able to follow you easily and confidently if your gestures are adequate.

8. Have one person play the main melodic or rhythmic figure as a solo, varying the degree or type of flexibility from one time to another, and have everyone else "accompany" him, fitting their parts to his.

9. When playing well-known songs, have the students think the words to avoid "chopping off" the final notes (syllables) of phrases. If breaths are needed before continuing, a slight, but probably permissible delay may be necessary before the next attack.

10. Have the students mark their parts, in soft black pencil, similarly to your marked score (see above).

Paradoxically, in order to make the marks meaningful to themselves, they may have to erase marks placed there by previous performers and then mark the parts in their own hand.

11. When you have experimented enough that you are quite sure of the degree of flexibility you wish to use, be quite consistent from then on. Thereby the students will learn to judge the amount of breath, the number and/or speed of travel of their bows, the timing of *crescendos* or *decrescendos* so as to end them effectively and together. If a fermata does become a rhythmic extension (see above), tell the students how many beats or measures you expect to hold it so that they can be with you in spirit as well as in body at its conclusion.

12. *Occasionally* in tight rehearsal of a touchy place, hold back unexpectedly. Those who fall into the trap (and probably everyone else!) will not need to be told to watch carefully at that spot in the future. Although I have heard of conductors who do such things in order to "keep the players on their toes" during a concert, I feel that it creates unnecessary anxiety in the players' minds, not to mention the violence it does to a truly sensitive musical interpretation.

Even if at first it seems to take too much time, to sound too laborious or to seem hardly worth all of the effort, know that as the students learn to handle and to appreciate the expressive possibilities of flexibility of tempo, their attitude will change. They will accomplish such effects much more easily and readily, and everyone will find the music to be more rewarding. I recall the disparaging remarks passed by a couple of directors who were part of a group watching the efforts of a guest conductor who was attempting to instill some of this delicacy into a large and unwieldy clinic band. I also recall (with more relish) the audible sighs of enjoyment that involuntarily escaped these same directors the first time a particularly sensitive *rubato* effect "came off."

How thrilling it is to hear good music performed musically! ∎

Teaching Artistry

by Donn Laurence Mills

When Isaac Stern plays a passage on violin —

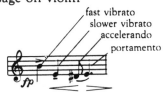

audiences melt. James Galway's fingers dance across his flute to produce a rapid passage like the spray from a mountain stream. Delightful. Both musicians can infuse a few notes with emotional impact not found anywhere on the printed page. In fact, it is artistic revelations such as these that drew most of us into musical careers. As a result many of us have become educators to pass along our discovery to others. It's not so easy, however.

Kids aren't artists. Most young students cannot channel their sense of creative freedom and imagination into their music. When they play a simple passage, the result is raw and uninteresting. Can an instructor get an average 14-year-old to play like an artist? Why must a school group always sound like a bull in a china shop?

The Starting Point

Notes themselves are just the starting point, even if they are played correctly and in tune. Musical notation is only the tip of a fathomless mysterious iceberg. As with anything else, instructors need to lay out some kind of plan or curriculum for teaching artistic subtleties — dynamics, articulation, tone color, phrasing, vibrato, and countless other nuances that transform notes in music.

Emotional Growth

Emotions grow with the rest of the body. Adults who have achieved emotional stability tend to forget what a youngster's feelings are like. Educators can't expect children to feel the way an adult does. We think a child can control his moods, show compassion, or respond to slow, sad music as we do. Unfortunately, he can't. His beat is up, his emotional range limited and superficial. Loud, fast, exciting, rhythmic, sometimes maudlin — these are the responses the young musician lives with. A child grows from a self-centered pleasure-seeker to an empathetic perceptive adult in gradual stages; he learns those more mature responses slowly through life experiences and by observing others. The seeds of emotional response are there, but they will not flower without influence and guidance. We all know adults who have missed out on this development and have never been able to appreciate the power of the fine arts. Unfortunately, there are many former high school orchestra and band students who never got that far, either.

For most children under the age of 12, music is merely amusing. Expecting elementary school students to comprehend or even like Rachmaninoff or Mahler would be like describing the Florida Everglades to an Eskimo. We have to work with students at their level of understanding. That doesn't mean music has to be obvious or trashy. Just as young children paint in primary colors — reds, blues, and yellows — at this early stage we need to focus on the raw materials of rhythm and melody. The subtleties we can teach at that age are dynamics and articulation.

Junior High Students

When youngsters reach junior high school, they are ready to stretch their emotional vocabularies a bit more. Unfortunately, their physical growth complicates things. With emotions on a roller coaster, students are disoriented, confused, and shy. We can introduce musical styles and bring them along technically, but we shouldn't expect outpourings of tender emotion. Students are too self-conscious for that even if they are naturally sensitive people. The junior high level is a good time to bring in clinicians to demonstrate musical techniques. Let your students hear fine performances in concerts and recordings; tape your students and let them try out different ways of performing a passage. Vary your conducting style to draw players away from their music stands. They may not respond quickly, but they are learning. Students at this age are just too inhibited to let go.

High School Musicians

On the other hand, the high school student is eager to explore the mysteries of music and the emotions that are welling up from within him. He knows he feels something spiritual, but he doesn't know how to make it happen musically. Most high school musicians are unable to execute interpretative ideas, but they can recognize them when played by others. The high school student may over-respond to one piece and be completely bored by another. He tries to understand his emotions and is apt to make superficial value judgments. The director needs to guide the student through the problems of peer pressure and distractions.

The college and community level band or orchestra is the spawning ground for artistry. Here players have reached an advanced level of technique and want to participate in the highest forms of music making. Working with professional repertoire, the conductor himself must have artistic qualities. At the podium he explores every shading and emotional nuance in the music.

Artistic Freedom

If you think your students are ready for artistic freedom and musical sensitivity, I offer these training suggestions:

Exposure. It is difficult to describe a musical nuance in words. Music teaches music; good music must be heard. By listening to fine artists playing their interpretative ideas, students learn to feel the emotional excitement of a musical passage. It is a powerful lesson. Make sure your students attend good concerts; play short examples of fine music on recordings. Whenever possible, bring in professionals to demonstrate their skills. People imitate what they like. The more artistry students hear, the more artistically they will perform.

Musical Rehearsals. Often artistry is set aside in rehearsals. Some directors feel that nuances can be added only after players nail down the notes. Too often the time never comes. Provide your groups with little chunks of expression. Don't wait to add interpretation until after a piece has been rehearsed to death. Allow time here and there for lessons in musicality. It's better to play one less piece on a program and spend the time on careful interpretative work than to play more music less artistically.

Use of Tapes. Students can be their own best teachers. By recording a passage, playing it back, and then repeating it again, the young musician hears the differences that subtleties make. Apply this technique to individuals or the entire band or orchestra. Recording sessions, going over sections of pieces

with several takes, brings about dramatic progress.

Solo and Ensemble Experiences. Because private teachers work on details and usually demonstrate playing techniques, they are able to develop artistic concepts in their students more quickly than players in larger groups. In a large section or full band, an artistic player is easily buried by a heap of clumsy colleagues. Educators can overcome this problem by working with small ensembles. Here students develop sharper listening habits and have more personal responsibility for their parts than in the full, and often louder, band or orchestra. If possible have only a few students from a section experiment with several interpretations while others listen or vote for the best choice.

Easier Repertoire. Artistry is often best obtained through simpler music. When the technical challenges are overwhelming, students usually forget about interpretation. Give your groups some music that is below their grade level and polish it carefully. See if you can get the clarinet players to sing out on a melodic passage of half notes; insist that the brass make a smooth *diminuendo* on the last chord.

Musical Development. Students learn by doing. You know the way you would like a passage played, but if you impose only your ideas, students won't discover the process for themselves. Let several people interpret one line of music and ask the other ensemble members which is more effective and why. Every time someone does play something beautifully, it should be noticed and praised. One brief passage may serve as an example for an entire piece.

Artistic Vocabulary. Put lists of musical terms and concepts on a

wall chart. Make sure your ensemble understands them.

Time and Space in Music

Students are often unaware of the importance of time or space in music. They either rush the music or maintain such a rigid beat that any chance of rising and falling with the musical line is lost. Pressing forward at the end of every bar robs the music of its most human characteristic; adhering to a strict beat makes it become like a machine. Music must breathe to survive. I suspect that during many students' first music lessons teachers stress tempo and counting so heavily that young players are forever conditioned to put the beat ahead of everything else. Achieving ebb and flow, or musical flexibility, is one of the areas teachers need to work toward from the earliest days of instruction. The beat is important, but only as it serves the musical elements of melody and harmony.

As a mature musician, you understand the balance of these elements. You want your ensemble to be flexible, responsive, and intuitive. When you change tempo or have a spontaneous interpretative idea, you expect your players to follow. There are school groups like that, and they developed these qualities because their conductors taught artistry at every rehearsal. Such conductors are as insistent about style as they are about sharps and flats. These educators are passing along the secrets of musical sensitivity to their students. Hopefully those students will mature into real musicians and, more important, music lovers. ∎

Donn Laurence Mills, conductor, composer, and music educator, is Director of Research and Development for the Yamaha Music Education Division. He holds music degrees from Northwestern University and the Eastman School of Music.

Making Musicians

by Gordon Peters

Author's Note: I am on a campaign to make musicians out of people who study how to play instruments! It seems the theory professors in our universities are teaching performers comprehensive musicianship from both the composer's and theoretician's point of view. For the most part, the instrumental instructor has become a teacher of the techniques of the instrument and little more. It has been my experience that most instrumentalists today do not know what to do with an eight-bar phrase. They know very little about either the qualities that determine an interpretation or the meaning of style; they have become horizontal-linear players of a series of notes, the faster played (and in the case of brass, the louder), the better.

What we need is a Department of Interpretation and Style, related to the music that players prepare for auditions and use in the field, rather than esoteric exercises from texts. The answers to music-making are found in the score of the composer — the complete score — and from the insight, talent, and imagination of the player. Combining these facts with the ability to observe all the details of the composer, will make many more listeners and players happier with their musical experiences.

— G.P.

Instrumental Mastery or Musical Illiteracy?

Conceiving music aurally, rhythmically, and interpretively before playing or conducting it has become all but a lost art. Instrumentalists first play through a work or listen to a recording of it to hear what the music sounds like.

A recent survey of 43 young musicians attending a Civic Orchestra seminar found only three who were able to hear a simple tonic-dominant-tonic exercise by looking at it. One person admitted that he always plays through a work first to see what it sounds like; most players do. Their inner ears are not sufficiently trained to study music away from instruments and teachers. What has happened to the art of solfège, which requires the musician to hear before singing? Is it not the responsibility of teachers to fill the void between musicians' goals and inadequacies, using and teaching the skill of aural conception as a primary tool?

Much to Think About

Many years ago on educational television, Pablo Casals was asked, "Maestro, how do you study a piece of music that is new to you?" He replied, "Well, I sit in a chair and study it until I learn it. After I learn it, I put it down and go to my cello and play it." Certainly there is much to think about here: a trained, aural-perceptive ability; strict attention to the composer's instructions; and considerations for such technical aspects as bowings and fingerings as well as such interpretive dimensions as phrase contours and climax points. Maestro Casals not only learned the music, but memorized it before using his instrument!

Studio teachers have increasingly ignored this art of the inner ear because they have to cover so much technique and literature that there isn't time for solfège; and theory instructors are so busy teaching intellectual analysis and theoretical systems that they do not have the necessary hours to prepare musicians to be complete and competitive performers.

Few players leaving music schools today can intelligently discuss phrasing. Most cannot coherently and concisely define the terms "interpretation" or "style." Theory teachers confronted with this issue often respond by telling of their fine sight-singing class or text. We all know, however, that in large classes students cheat (they sing behind the beat and follow one or two of the diligent or gifted leaders, or sing "in the cracks" to disguise the fact that they can't hear pitch relations). No real discipline or sight-singing is developed in large classes; this is a subject that must be taught individually or in small groups. The class is an uncomfortably expensive option for music department administrators who must watch their budgets. However, instructing small classes is the only effective way to teach an absolutely vital skill.

Instructors' Excuses

I recall that during my days as a theory fellow at the Eastman School of Music, Allen McHose, chairman of the department, held weekly department meetings. Each week, he would ask how much time instructors had spent working with classes on sight-singing. Almost with exception I heard the same types of excuses:

• "Oh, we only had time for 20 minutes last week."

• "Oh, we got behind; there was an exam to prepare for."

• "We were correcting papers."

Are instructors teaching theory for theory's sake, or are they relating it to the needs of the performing musicians? Why, for that matter, is the teaching of beginning theory in most music schools relegated to junior faculty or even to graduate-level teaching assistants, the least efficient and least experienced instructors? Surely the subject merits more careful attention from senior faculty members who would do the job to far higher standards.

At a recent seminar, Samuel Hope, the executive director of the National Office for Arts Accreditation in Higher Education, observed:

> Behind the interpretation of a work of music there has to be a tremendous amount of basic musical skill. When we talk about musical training, I think we might well focus on those basic skills that are necessary to enable the creativity...of the composer to come forward (through the interpretive skills of the performing musician).

Considering the state of the art and the inability of students to play beautiful and musically logical phrases on their instruments, educators should raise questions about the current systems of producing musicians — the issues of defining interpretation and style, of learning efficient practice techniques, of effectively using the metronome and tape recorder, and of knowing the skills looked for at job interviews and auditions. All of these need careful examination to determine whether we are producing instrumentalists or musicians, technicians or artists. ■

Gordon Peters is the administrator and conductor of the Civic Orchestra of Chicago, which is the training orchestra of the Chicago Symphony Orchestra. He is also principal percussionist in the Chicago Symphony and was formerly Percussion Clinic editor for The Instrumentalist.

May, 1985

The Education of the Performer

by Robert Weirich

Faculties everywhere spend a lot of time in committee meetings discussing "the program." We endlessly revise and modify requirements in the hope of devising a curriculum that will turn every one of our students into first-class musicians. How many juries should they play? How many recitals? How many years in a major ensemble? Should we require this class or strongly recommend that one? We have these meetings year after year because no one program will work for every student. By now most faculty members know this, but we keep on looking. If we just keep trying, perhaps we'll get it right.

A performance study program is an especially tough nut to crack. We can assign technical exercises to improve the fingers. We can teach courses in music history and theory. We can put the students through performance requirements in which they show how much the technical exercises and the courses in history and theory have helped. Unfortunately, none of this guarantees that first-rate performers will emerge from the system. Even the students with talent can go through such a program and not know what it is to be responsible, expressive, and artistic performers.

We need to examine the nature of the performer and the kind of training that is needed to create one. We have the capacity in the American university system to inspire our performance students a great deal more if we are willing to challenge established notions a bit.

Every performer needs the following assets:

• Sensitivity to sound (a good ear)
• Complete physical control (a great technique)
• Keen intellectual command (head)
• Sensitive emotional response (heart)
• Communicative projection (personality)

The musician is only able to communicate his thoughts and feelings through the sound he is able to create. He needs extraordinary sensitivity to the evocative powers of sound — the ability to conjure up tangible images through intangible auditory impulses. He should have a personal indentification with the sound he produces so that performer and sound are one. When you think of the truly great artists, the first thing that comes to mind is their sound. Artists like Stoltzman, Rampal, Perlman, and Horowitz each have a sound about their playing that immediately identifies them. During the days that Heifetz, Piatigorsky, and Rubinstein played together as a trio, it was said that people felt great pleasure just hearing them tune. How can we promote this?

Technical control is in large part physical. A pianist should exercise complete control over fingers, hands, arms, shoulders, torso, posterior, and feet. Even that is a partial list. Practicing scales is the tip of the iceberg. What we are really talking about is the physical ability to produce that intangible sound with each and every note. Are we teaching this?

Intellectually, performers should coherently organize an entire composition, relating each note in the piece to every other note, as well as

459

*Performers are responsible for touching
in others that which music touches in them.
Can this be taught in a program?*

understanding the place of the composition in the historical panorama of larger thoughts and actions. Performers should be able to memorize — an intellectual *and* physical feat. They should be of analytical persuasions if their performances are to have lasting value. Many child prodigies fall by the wayside because they are not able to analyze the music or what they are doing; they are simply good imitators. The most difficult task for performers is to rationally understand the first two abilities or needs: to be able to recognize that almost mystical sound, and the physical necessities of achieving it. The flimsy, dull, irrational mind cannot meet these demands.

Performers should be capable of great emotional response. They respond to the music only when it touches something they can hold onto, cherish, remember in dark times — in short, something they can love. Response also suggests responsibility. Performers are responsible for touching in others that which music touches in them. A great performance is one in which the listener comes away feeling exalted by the beauty of the music and renewed by the emotional truths that the music holds. Performers are responsible as the medium through which this exaltation and renewal can take place. Can this be taught in a program?

Performers should have the desire and ability to project all of the above to an audience, living with the rapid pulses, rushing adrenalin, and the fear of repudiation that goes with the act of performance. There is a great deal at stake and the pressure is sometimes overwhelming. Yet it is in performance that all of one's strivings come together; the sound, the body, the mind, the heart are all united in the attempt to touch. How is this taught?

If music-making is to be imaginative, music education itself must be at least as inventive and designed for the whole being.

What Are the Possibilities?

Teaching a student musician to listen to sound involves training the ear to concentrate with an intensity bordering on the maniacal. The ear should become a magnet for every aspect of the sound produced: the attack, the sustaining quality, the decay, the joining of one pitch to the next, the blending of the voices of a chord, and the movement of one harmony to the next. Learning this sensitivity to sound should involve more than a couple of ear training classes taught by a graduate assistant. What

about a class that cleans out the ears of the students? Immerse them in electronic music, African music, John Cage's music of chance. What about a class that trains them to ascertain pitch and duration to a more exact degree than we presently require? The putting together of notes and harmonies is an extraordinary lesson in the nature and power of sound. Why not require at least a term of composition? No less an authority than Schnabel advised his students to spend some time every day putting notes down on paper.

With all of these possibilites, ensemble instruction in many schools consists of four years of membership in a band, orchestra, or chorus. All too often, however, this requirement is an excuse for putting bodies on stage. Ensemble instruction should be, among other things, a workshop in sound. Four years of burial in the back of the clarinet section does not help the weaker student improve.

What about the way we teach technique? Can we improve that? The study of instrumental technique takes place in the studio, but there is more to playing a scale than moving one finger followed by another. Is an anatomy class designed for musicians out of the question? Actors take movement classes; is there a musical equivalent? The dreaded physical education classes of high school days failed because they concentrated on brawn rather than brain. If students understood how yoga, swimming, or gymnastics enhanced inner balance, the smooth interaction of muscle groups, and the sequence of preparation, execution, and recovery, might it not affect the physical aspects of their playing, too? All of these things are as much a part of instrumental technique as they are a description of the ideal tennis stroke. Yet we do not encourage this kind of thinking.

We are probably most successful in our present system of education in the realm of training the intellect. We have theory courses that teach form and analysis. We have history courses to fill out students' understanding of the events surrounding a composer and his work. What we do not have is a way of integrating these courses into the fundamental experience of performing. Is it time for the applied teacher to teach an occasional class in analysis, showing that it is indeed important to know where the recapitulation begins? Is it time for the classroom teacher to visit an occasional lesson to see that the esteemed artist-teacher does not fill up fifty minutes talking about the color of the sunset in the coda? At long last, might we have learned that it takes more than music courses to train the mind? For too many years we have given short shrift to the role of foreign languages, mathematics, logic, art history, literary criticism, and philosophy in the music curriculum. The present ratio of one liberal arts course per term to three or four in music is not necessarily the best. What about intellectual recreation? How many students at your school know how to play chess?

You may have supplied answers to these rhetorical questions. The most important question remains: What can we do about any of this? Whose responsibility is it?

The applied teacher and the conductor have the most power to effect change. They are the people who see the students regularly on a one-to-one basis. They have the most influence, for better or worse. Students are not likely to be open to the fullness of the musical experience unless these two crucial figures encourage and lead the way. If the advisor does not suggest foreign language study, the applied teacher should. If the conductor cannot demonstrate what is meant by listening with magnetic ears, how can students be expected to pick it up in any other class? No matter how much thought is given to a program, integrated or otherwise, the private teacher and the conductor have the lion's share of responsibility for the musical education of students — an awesome and frightening fact.

The performance qualities most difficult to teach are the capacity to respond emotionally to music, and the ability to communicate that response to an audience. Our usual procedure is to avoid dealing with these matters altogether, falling back on the old explanation of "they either have it or they don't." Talent surely helps, but that is not enough.

The fact that few musicians agree on the role of emotion in music is one hindrance. There has been a continuous swing of the pendulum through musical history, ranging from the Apollonian elegance of the Classics to the Dionysian excitement of the Romantics. In our own century we have had both: composers as diametrically opposed as Stravinsky and Rachmaninoff were alive and working as contemporaries. The fact remains, however, that most teachers active today were trained in the period that favored Neo-Classicism and ultra-rational serialism. Composers of this music wanted nothing to do with emotions, and said so. Conductors such as Toscanini made a religion out of fidelity to the score and we have learned that lesson well, but it does not help us go beyond the printed notes to an awareness of that which the music touches.

Sometimes I ask my piano students what the composer is trying to say emotionally in a given passage in, say, a Chopin ballade. The usual response is embarrassment, and then a half-hearted stab at, perhaps, "sadness." It isn't too long before we begin to discuss the meaning of the word emotion. Quite a number of students are even more uncomfortable with this. They feel that emotion cannot be defined; that it is a private matter, hidden in the subconscious. For the most part, they are happy to leave it there.

I ask them if Chopin had emotions. Of course. How do you know? It's in the music. How do you know? Well, listen to this, you over-intellectual professor! Hear that falling minor second? Listen to that resigned cadence. Suddenly they play with conviction and true feeling.

I wish it were that easy. In that scenario the student felt several emotions: embarrassment, indignation, fear, possibly defensiveness, and finally the resignation and melancholy of the music. He also felt the desire to communicate this last feeling, to touch another person with his own insights into human emotion. Students cannot be taught to feel those emotions. They can, however, be taught to be aware of them. This awareness allows them the objectivity to consider the emotion in the light of day, as it were, turning it this way and that to refine and focus its communicative potential.

Again we can take a lesson from our friends in the theater. Actors study the Stanislavsky Method, which suggests that the performer study a character, be aware of the emotions of that character, and then feel those emotions by recalling an event from the actor's own past in which the same emotions were present. It is a practice that not only acknowledges the primacy of the emotional message of art, but also integrates the personal experiences of the performer with the work at hand.

The emotional content of music and the ability to communicate it are closely related. Both depend in large part on how much fledgling performers love their work. Again, the love itself cannot be taught, but the teacher can encourage it and help the students become aware of this love. More often than not, our work as educators can be thought of as a process of unlocking or tapping potential, not of building one block at a time. Of course, it is necessary to put certain pieces in place. Performers' needs can be built up methodically; the sensitivity to sound, the physical technique, and the perceptual as well as the conceptual capacities of the mind can all be taught. Getting to that reservoir of artistry in every student is another matter. Finding it and helping the students to accept their capacity to feel and touch is perhaps the greatest and most rewarding task of the teacher.

We teach performance, but performance is not a product. It is not something you can put on a shelf and admire. What we really teach is a way of living, a pursuit of life in which all sides of our being are put to use: sensory, physical, intellectual, spiritual.

Socrates implored his students, "Know thyself." Thomas Carlyle suggested, "Know thy work and do it." Performing is a remarkable synthesis: it is certainly work, and the study of performing is in a sense the growing awareness of self and its abilities. The daily focusing of physical, mental, and spiritual energies in one direction causes students to probe ever deeper into self to find greater stamina, more intellec-tual discipline, and a truer response to their own humanity. Even if students do not make a living in music, the study of music will have helped them know themselves; they will do whatever they do better because of that study.

Robert Weirich is associate professor and chairman of piano at Northwestern University in Evanston, Illinois. He received his formal training at Oberlin Conservatory and the Yale University School of Music.

December, 1981

Teaching Basic Musicianship

Ed Solomon

There are certain fundamental techniques of basic musicianship which are an essential element of early band experience. Their presentation at the appropriate time can enhance interpretive skills and lead young musicians into the area of expression, control, and performance skill.

Phrasing and Musical Arithmetic

I teach basic phrasing as an introduction to musical form by fragmenting the four-bar phrase. Two measures make a fragment, two fragments make a phrase, two phrases make a musical sentence, two sentences make a paragraph.

From this format students explore simple song form and examine each of the folk song examples in the method book. Often one section of the band plays the music while the rest of the group sings. They examine the song's sentence structure for punctuation. When does the comma appear? Is it an exclamatory sentence? Does it ask a question? Is there a stress point or a catch phrase? Is it necessary to subdivide a word rhythmically? How does the word structure affect the rhythmic content?

This is not a complicated process and it helps students understand what must be done when playing four-bar phrases. It also makes rehearsal procedure smoother, because they understand what it means to begin at the "third phrase" or the "last phrase," and it establishes a basis from which to examine other musical forms.

Articulation

To teach *staccato* and *legato* we examine chorales and hymns and contrast them with marches.

For drill purposes I incorporate scales and articulations in the warm-up to explore *legato* ("touching notes that make wall to wall sound"), and *staccato*, ("notes that bounce").

Staccato separation is the most difficult to teach. If students get the idea that *staccato* means short, it is difficult to change their minds. They will try to play long notes faster or "spit" them out like an automatic weapon.

I use the idea of bouncing a ball. Basketballs, tennis balls, and ping-pong balls bounce at various speeds, because of their different sizes. Their size compares favorably with the value of a note, and helps youngsters understand the "dribbling a ball" approach to *staccato*.

Some easy rules include:
• The second note of a slur is played shorter and softer than the first.

• A note followed by a rest is short. (♪ 𝄾 ♩ 𝄾)
• Unless marked, the last note of a phrase is never chopped off.

Using a down-up stick pattern, I ask students to play when the stick comes down and stop when it comes up. This controlled, play-stop style allows for as much or as little space between the notes as is needed for good playing. In the warm-up, students follow the stick on major scales. Playing

Ed Solomon is a staff member of the New Braunfels (Texas) Public Schools. He earned his degrees from Central State University in Oklahoma and North Texas State University (Denton), and is associate conductor of the Greater San Antonio Youth Orchestras.

four notes on each pitch (or three or two or one), I dictate long or short notes and try to trick those who may not be watching. A mobile hangs from the ceiling of the band hall. It is a large, styrofoam eye-ball, pierced by a long baton. An attached sign reads: "Keep Your Eye On The Stick." It moves in the slightest breeze, continually looking around the room as a constant reminder. Needless to say the eye receives many comments from the students and, while somewhat crude, it gets the point across.

Dynamics and Line Development

Continuity within a melodic line is the result of phrasing; the line's direction is like a connect-the-dot picture. If we were to connect musical notes with a pencil line, a graph-like picture of peaks and valleys would show the ups and downs of the melody. Here are expressions I use often:

• "If the line goes up, make a *crescendo*; if the line goes down, make a *decrescendo*."
• "Look for the high point of the phrase or sentence."
• "If you must break the phrase to breathe, do it after the longest note."
• "Lower voices *crescendo* as the line goes down, and *decrescendo* as the line goes up. Contrary motion requires contrary dynamics."
• "It's better to leave out a note to take a breath than to chop one in half."
• "Stagger the breathing and sneak back in. Don't jump back in and let everyone know you were gone."

Dynamics

Considerations for dynamics include several admonitions: "Don't play any louder than lovely." "Don't take a breath during a *crescendo* or a *decrescendo*." "Listen. Does the musical line call for more or less volume?" "Whole notes don't sit there, they grow or swell." "Support the long notes and go the full value — go to the beat or the bar line."

Tone Color

We all talk about tone color, but often find it difficult to describe to students. I find they learn through experiments with sound values. For instance, we listen to the alto saxophone and flute in octaves and compare that sound to when they play in unison. We also contrast the sounds of the brass and woodwind choirs. The saxophone quartet and the brass quartet are similar, and yet have a particular color.

A simple eight-bar, four-part exercise can provide a tremendous learning experience in exploring different sound colors. Discuss what instrumental groupings will present a dark color. Try combining horns, low clarinets, low brass, and low woodwinds. Re-voice the exercise creating a different tone quality. Work for bright red, or yellow, or orange, or chocolate fudge sounds. Cool ice blue, for instance, is a straight flute sound with no vibrato, a little oboe, and bells. (Remember the tingling tartness of Sprite?) Putting sound into a context students can understand will enhance their appreciation of the delicate balance problems which will present themselves with each new musical experience.

Style and Interpretation

The approach I use to teach style is based on the students' awareness of the background music in their favorite T.V. shows or movies. I explain that the music they hear matches the mood and/or action of what they see happening. I also point out how inappropriate some music would be to certain situations. My examples are far fetched but effective: a mountain road chase does not lend itself to a frilly waltz, nor does a prize fight scene from *Rocky* warrant the *Rustle of Spring*.

A group of recorded theme excerpts from T.V. will bring an instant response from students. Whether the name of the show is immediately recalled or not, students instantly recognize the context of the excerpt and make an association with certain emotions.

We all remember drop-the-needle tests from our music literature courses, but do we use that technique, particularly for our young students? Why not? *The Bad News Bears* uses light classical and familiar opera themes as its background music. I try to establish an action or create a mood to begin a discussion on the style and character of the music. With a touch of drama and a little imagination, it is relatively simple to make up a story that fits a musical selection. An inventive mind can easily expand this imagery. Often the students' imaginations are freer than the instructor's, and they take great delight in creating make-believe situations and narrating musical action.

A simple three note exercise from a warm-up drill can be the motif for an experiment in style. Have the band play concert F, go down to concert Bb, and then to the upper octave concert Bb. Explore this theme as a march, as an opening to a hymn, have it articulated as a slur, or ask them to play it as a bugle call.

"Imagine a rocky coast line shrouded in fog. A cold breeze is coming off the crashing waves along the beach. Silently out of the fog comes the dragon head of a Viking long boat. Standing in the bow is a warrior blowing a ram's horn." Have the horns play the exercise and notice how imagining a story has increased their awareness and musical effort.

"In the distance the mournful call is answered." Ask the cornets or trumpets to play the same exercise at a *pianissimo* level. If this doesn't raise goose bumps, there is something wrong with you, or your group is not as sensitive as it should be.

The creativity that this approach generates is worth every effort. You'll notice the excitement of your young musicians as their musical awareness increases. It is one of the greatest rewards we teachers have. ■ **Ed Solomon**

Style—
The Most
Abused
Musical Element

John W. Grashel

In contest and other performance situations, most bands manage to play correct notes, rhythms, and articulations. However, style is the element that separates excellent ensembles from their mediocre counterparts. It permeates the overall musical effect of any instrumental group. While many stylistic factors are regularly misinterpreted, several elements seem to fall into "most abused" category:

1. Failure to hold notes full value, often resulting in chopped phrases
2. Misinterpretation of accents
3. Failure to space notes properly
4. Confusion concerning expressive indicators

A currently popular composition among secondary school bands is Jim Swearingen's *Exaltation* (C.L. Barnhouse Company, 1978). Its inclusion on state contest lists and widespread appearance on concert programs indicates the acceptance of this fine work. Not surprisingly, the composition contains numerous opportunities for abusing stylistic components that would affect its overall performance.

Chopped Phrases

Like the speaker who allows sentences to tail off into miscomprehension, the band that does not observe proper phrase lengths is jeopardizing the listener's musical understanding. The problem of holding notes full value is critical at any point in a phrase; however, it is especially crucial at phrase endings.

Measures 20-29 of *Exaltation* (example 1) provide several illustrations of the potential problem. The upper woodwind line (which crescendos with the entire ensemble throughout the phrase) should not be broken as suggested by the slur marks, but

needs to be carried through to the syncopated rhythmic unison in measures 27-29. The eighth-note run into measure 27 must lead directly into the syncopated passage. Concurrently, the lower brass and woodwind unison contains similar phrasing problems, and staggered breathing might be appropriate, particularly for less experienced groups. The unison cornet, alto saxophone, and horn line is a third area of potential phrasing inaccuracy. It is all too easy to cheat on the whole notes, playing them as dotted half-notes.

This excerpt exemplifies some of the nontraditional phrase lengths, common among modern compositions. Make sure the ensemble is aware of the entire musical content of the phrase, and does not play a collection of isolated motives. What's good material to train members to play to the end of phrases? Chorales are excellent sources for developing this skill because they demand that the band hold notes full value, enhance intonation awareness, and aid in achieving balance. Fortunately, many beginning method series introduce chorale-style material early in the learning sequence. Such "chestnuts" as James Ployhar's arrangement of *Navy Hymn* (Byron-Douglas Publications, 1964) and Frank Erickson's *Balladair* (Bourne Comany, 1958) and *Air for Band* (Bourne Company, 1956) are excellent pedagogical compositions for young ensembles.

John Grashel is assistant professor of music education at the University of Kansas (Lawrence) where he teaches undergraduate and graduate courses and coordinates the student teaching program. He previously taught instrumental music at both the middle school and high school in Grove City, Ohio.

Misinterpretation of Accents

It is important for band members to differentiate between accents that imply full value, the ones that indicate separation, and those that combine both categories. *Exaltation* offers splendid examples of these types. Measures 28 and 29 (example 1) include three stylistically different accents in the span of five beats. The first beat staccato note (♪) should be a short, but not heavy accent. The following syncopated, accented quarter-notes (♩) should be slightly louder with just a touch of separation. The marcato accent on the first beat of measure 29 (♩) indicates a short, heavy

articulation. Because these accents are scored in unison for the entire group, it becomes necessary for each musician to understand as well as observe the different markings. The warm-up period is an ideal time to teach these accents. Incorporate them into scale drills, either in unison or combined with long notes or contrasting patterns.

In his book *Instrumental Music Pedagogy* (Prentice-Hall, Inc., 1973) Daniel Kohut identifies several types of accents. This brief discussion (pages 173-176) should be reviewed by every ensemble conductor.

Example 1. *Exaltation*, measures 20-29

All musical examples of *Exaltation*
© 1978 by C.L. Barnhouse, Oskaloosa, Iowa
Used by permission of the publisher.

465

Example 4. Measures 44-51

Confusion Concerning Expressive Indicators

Many bands sound computerized — note-wise correct and exact — yet, they are musically lifeless and sterile. Lack of dynamic contrast and insensitivity to the musical line regarding tempo are obvious manifestations of this problem. The conductor should let the melody (and the technique and musicianship of the group) influence the tempo. Though the music should not be "milked" for its own sake, implied rubatos and accelerandi should not be ignored. Except for certain forms, such as marches and some dance movements, tempo must be pliable.

The *Slowly espressivo* section beginning at measure 44 is a case in point (example 4). Although no dynamic variation is indicated in the accompaniment voices, the horn line implies crescendo and decrescendo in relation to the ascending eighth-notes. Similarly, the tempo should also reflect the movement of the eighth-notes and their resolution on the whole notes. This rubato feeling will add immeasurably to the musicality of the performance. At measure 48 the alto saxophone soloist must soar above the background material, but like the horn accompaniment figure, be always sensitive to implied crescendi and decrescendi as dictated by the melodic line.

Exaltation certainly does not illustrate every potential stylistic problem that will confront music educators. There are no dotted eighth-sixteenth note rhythms — arguably the single most abused stylistic factor. This composition does serve as a valuable source for teaching the elements of music as well as providing excellent program material.

Style is the most pronounced indicator of musical maturity in school instrumental ensembles. As music educators, we must teach this vital element of musical performance during rehearsals and select music that enhances the development of a stylistically correct performance. ∎

Space Notes Properly

A common problem related to accents concerns the spacing of notes. While some accents imply space, the shortening of note values can result in a typical problem called rushing. In *Exaltation* this tendency may be encountered in the lower brass and woodwind figures from measures 72-79 (example 2). Performers must be conditioned to fill up the note values with silent space and not rush the next staccato eighth-note. Drills with a metronome will help students in performing these rhythms correctly.

The syncopated rhythm in measures 33-34 offers another illustration of the importance of spacing (example 3). This unison syncopation must be accurately played by each band member to facilitate clean and precise articulation. The snare and bass drum parts, correctly performed, can assist the ensemble in achieving the required crisp and separated concept.

Example 3. Measures 33-34

Example 2. Measures 72-81

467

Time in Your Hands

Vaclav Nelhybel

"Time" has always been a vital part of music. Several centuries ago music was, in fact, defined as "consumption of time" — *ars musica: temporis consumptio.*

In purely monodic music (Gregorian chant) the organization of time was concerned only with the driving force that propels the melodic line. In the two-part organum of the 10th century, both melodic lines were synchronized by means of numerical relations between them. During the Renaissance, counterpoint served to structure the consumption of time numerically among several simultaneous melodic lines.

The consonance and dissonance that appeared in the 16th-century modal counterpoint and the tonic-subdominant-dominant sequence in baroque and post-baroque harmonic cadences were also devices for propelling music through time. The interaction of consonance and dissonance created a driving force that made the musical structure move forward. All these techniques maintained and regulated the flow of music.

A new and revolutionary element was introduced by Claudio Monteverdi in his operas and madrigals: the expression through music of human emotions (from calm tenderness to turbulent rage). In addition to requiring all the melodic lines to move in a coordinated manner, his music necessitated changes in speed as it progressed through different emotions: it required variation in *tempo.*

Conducting Implications

Tempos and tempo changes present challenges to the director. He should be able through his conducting to maintain a steady tempo as well as to proceed through tempo changes smoothly. Sometimes (certainly when no tempo indication is provided) he must know how to choose appropriate tempos. Specific guidelines for dealing with some of the most frequent and typical tempo/conducting problems are provided in the discussion of several band compositions that follows.

Canzona *by Peter Mennin*
Published by Carl Fischer, 1954

Canzona is a rather exceptional example, as it is a concert piece with one single tempo (Allegro Deciso ♩= 126) and one time signature throughout its entirety.

Vaclav Nelhybel, composer of such widely-played pieces for band as Trittico Sine Nomine *and* Symphonic Movement, *is also well-known as a guest conductor.*

There are no tempo changes whatsoever — not even a ritardando or allargando at the end. In this case, it is best to try to "memorize" the tempos. Keep your pocket-size metronome with you, take the reading of a tempo, and from time to time check with the metronome to see if you still remember the exact pulsation. In performance, find an unobtrusive way to take the metronome reading just before you start conducting and then check the recording of your performance to see how well you maintained the tempo throughout the whole composition. The *Canzona* — or any march — would be a perfect choice for checking the consistency of your tempo.

When you study a composition that you will conduct for the first time, make a chart of all the tempos, (provided there are tempo changes in the composition - see Ex. 1). The more complex the composition, the more advisable it is to make such a chart, for to see the numerical relations of the tempos aids in the overall study of the composition.

Ex. 1 Tempo Charts

Creston: Prelude and Dance
  Maestoso (♩=58)
    Fermata on last beat of measure 7
    Fermata on last 3 beats of measure 42
  Allegro (♩=120)
    Steady tempo throughout, except for a poco ritardando before the last chord

Hanson: Chorale and Alleluia

  ♩ =50, doubles at [7]
  ♩ =112 at 8
  ♩ =120 at 14

  ¾ to ¼ at [21] (♩=40)

Bernstein: Overture to Candide

  Allegro molto con brio (♩=152)
  Piu mosso (o=96) in measure 231

Nelhybel: Festivo
  Allegro marcato [meas. 1-29]
  Allegro con fuoco [30-86]
  Meno mosso [87-132]
  Allegro [133-171]
  Grave [172-end]

There are no simple solutions...

...each composition has its own tempo problems

Prelude and Dance *by Paul Creston*
Published by G. Ricordi, 1960

This work contains a Maestoso (♩=58) and an Allegro (♩=120). The numerical relation of the two tempos is 58:120. By changing the 58 to 60, we obtain a simple ratio of 60:120 or, scaled down, 1:2, which means that the Allegro is twice as fast as the Maestoso. Therefore the quarter note of the Allegro equals the eighth note of the preceding Maestoso.

The following suggestion may prove helpful in handling the fermata in [meas. 7] (see Ex. 2). Decide

Ex. 2 Creston: Prelude and Dance (measures 7 and 8)

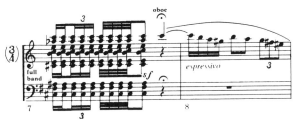

on the number of beats you wish the fermata to be held. Then, when you reach the third beat in [meas. 7], conduct the fermata with your hands as usual (indicating no beats). Meanwhile, continue to count silently the number of beats — perhaps five, for example. On your "silent" fifth count, your hands should make the pick-up gesture that will mark the end of the fermata and at the same time lead the performers into the next segment of the composition (which has the same tempo).

This technique of counting out a fermata should also be used in [meas. 42] (see Ex. 3). The hands hold the fermata on the dotted half note for five beats (or any other number you decide upon). While the hands are holding the fermata, count the beats silently, "One, two, three," and then subdivide the quarter-note beats into two eighth notes each, "Four and five and." On the "and" after "five" the hands make an eighth-note pickup gesture, marking the end of the fermata and at the same time establishing the new, faster tempo, in which a quarter note equals the preceding slower

tempo's eighth note. This method of changing the tempo applies only if the ratio of the two tempos is 1:2, which means the second tempo is twice as fast (sometimes indicated as "Doppio Movimento").

Chorale and Alleluia *by Howard Hanson*
Published by Carl Fischer, 1960

The initial tempo is ♩=50. At [7] the tempo doubles: Doppio Movimento, ♩=100. Here the change of tempo is not preceded by a fermata (see Ex. 4). In the

Ex. 4 Hanson: Chorale and Alleluia (rehearsal no. 7)

measure before [7] the hands will beat one, two, three. Meanwhile, count silently the subdivided eighth notes, "one and two and three and four and." On the fourth beat the hands start beating the subdivided eighth notes, thus establishing the new tempo, in which a quarter note equals an eighth note from the preceding tempo.

At [8] the tempo is increased from 100 to 112 and at [14] it is increased further (from 112 to 120). Practice these three tempos with a metronome: 100, 112, and 120. Memorize them. Check the recording of your rehearsals. You must feel these tempos; there is no numerical crutch to help you.

At [20] the meter is ¾ and the tempo is ♩=120 (see Ex. 5). At [21] the meter changes to ½ (Largamente Molto) with the indication that one beat (one half note) equals an entire preceding measure (of ¾ meter). The last measure of [20] consists of three quarter notes, each played ♩=120. Therefore, the duration of the whole measure is ♩.=40. In this case we actually

Ex. 3 Creston: Prelude and Dance (measures 41-43) Allegro (♩ = 120)

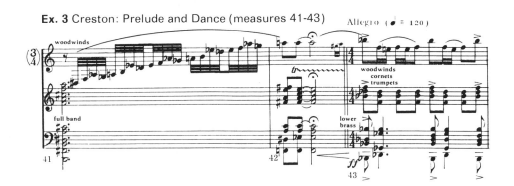

469

have a 1:1 relationship. The whole last measure of [20] is ♩=40 and the half note (one beat) in the new tempo is also at MM40. Whenever there is a relatively low number relation between the rhythmic values of two different tempos, you can devise a method that allows you to anticipate the pulsation of the time unit from the tempo that follows. At [20] the hands beat distinctly the three quarter-note beats per measure. Because the counting unit of the succeeding tempo is equal to the duration of a whole measure in the present tempo, you count mentally the whole measures, "One, two, three, four." On four, the hands can join your silent counting and direct the last measure before the tempo change with *one* large beat for the whole measure, as an upbeat to the ¾ in the next tempo. The size and duration of the one beat in the last measure of [20] will be identical with the size and duration of each of the beats in the ¾ measure at [21]

Overture to Candide *by Leonard Bernstein*
(arranged for band by Walter Beeler)
Published by G. Schirmer, 1960

We cannot reduce the two numerical tempo indications, ♩ = 152 in the Allegro molto con brio and o=96 in the Piu mosso, to give us a method of conducting as we were able to do in the *Chorale and Alleluia*. Basically, Bernstein's *Candide* is a composition with one tempo, Allegro molto con brio, ♩=152. In its 230 measures the music flows and dances in an exciting, irregular meter, but the pulsation remains always the basic half note at MM152. What follows (from [meas. 230] to the very end) is a brilliant, whirlwind-like coda. The music flows *una battuta* — conducted one beat per measure. The conductor has to be able to switch to the faster tempo in [231] with complete assurance and ease (see Ex. 6).

The duration of a half note in the Piu mosso is actually ♩=192. The ratio of the half notes in the two tempos is thus 152:192. The only way that you can learn to switch from one tempo to the other is to practice, to check yourself with the metronome, and

to memorize the abrupt change. Record your rehearsals and check to determine whether you maintained the Allegro molto and whether the jump into the Piú mosso tempo was correct.

Festivo *by Vaclav Nelhybel*
Published by Franco Colombo, 1968

This composition contains only verbal tempo indications; there are no metronome markings at all. I did not indicate numerically how fast the individual sections should be played because I did not consider the *actual number* of beats per second vitally important. What is, however, vitally important is the *relationship* between the various tempos:

Allegro marcato — a comfortably fast, well marked tempo.

Allegro con fuoco — another Allegro, this time *con fuoco*, "with fire," therefore somewhat faster (How many students know what *con fuoco* means?)

Meno mosso — slower. How much slower? This section is conceived as a strongly contrasting middle section. The slowing down of the tempo emphasizes the contrasting character of the music. It is left up to the individual conductor to choose the degree of contrast between the two tempos.

Allegro — About the same tempo as the Allegro con fuoco. This section has the same function as the varied restatement of section A in an A-B-A form.

Grave — A total breakdown of the hectic pulsation of the Allegro.

To make a tempo chart of *Festivo* is quite simple, and it is up to the conductor to create the right balance between the individual sections. I have heard many different approaches to the coordination of the tempos in *Festivo*, reflecting the artistic taste of each conductor and the ability of his band.

There are no simple solutions in dealing with tempos. Each composition has its own tempo problems. Using the metronome frequently, making charts of the tempos and thus visualizing their numerical relationships and interactions will help the conductor in his score preparation. ∎

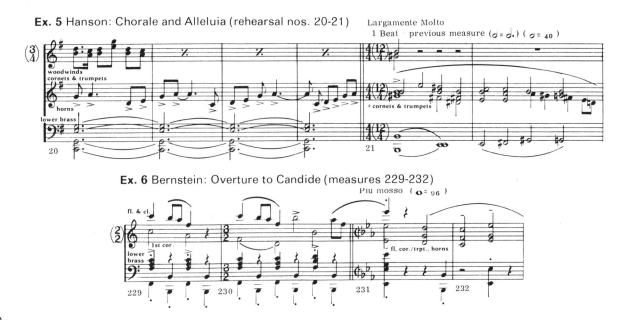

Ex. 5 Hanson: Chorale and Alleluia (rehearsal nos. 20-21)

Ex. 6 Bernstein: Overture to Candide (measures 229-232)

Develop Creative Musicians

by Frank Bencriscutto

Music offers a phenomenon capable of expressing the highest feelings to which humanity aspires. The ultimate goal of music education is to teach us to love this great force not as an amusement or merely an ornament, but for its ennobling energy, for its power of making us better by awakening within each individual a perception of what is good and beautiful.

This is indeed an exciting thought; but, in reality, I find it necessary to ask if music education has become an obsolete label — whether or not we have the right to identify with such a calling.

The Creative Core of Music

Fulfilling such a goal requires the stimulation and cultivation of creative thought, response, and action. Is music functioning as a creative discipline or are students parroting the dictates of a conductor without understanding any meaning? Certainly more of the latter than the former predominates.

Educational leaders agree that among the failings in the educational process, stifling the individual's creative capacity stands out as a salient thorn in the flesh of human fulfillment. All of which leaves a most crucial gap for music and the fine arts to fill. The challenge then — to cultivate the creative core of music — must be uppermost in our minds.

To an alarming extent, music instruction, as now realized in the schools, is similar to teaching a student to recite a poem or sing a song in a foreign tongue without teaching him the meaning of the words. Teachers accomplish these lessons by dictating pitch inflection, pauses, emphasis, breathing, intensity, and style, just as all the musical elements are now dictated to students in many school performing groups.

The motivation for such achievements is also similar: a degree of fun, and some emotional releases, to name a few. Is it not frightening to consider such a restricted comparison; but, can it be denied that this is all too often the truth of the matter?

Motivation for Musical Progress

Consider the means by which educators motivate students for musical progress: orchestra and band public appearances and competitions, competition for chair placement, grades, contest ratings, and so on. Each of these is not bad in itself. Rather, it is the fact that these considerations for participating in music are primary, and too often the only ones in the student's mind. In the final analysis, the values attained through this perspective are as artificial as the motivation.

Is it any wonder that administrators are harboring thoughts of excluding music programs in public schools? You should remember that many of the present administrators played an instrument in band or orchestra. In most cases, adults who participated in music during their school days look back and say, "it was fun," or "we had a great group." Rare is the individual who will state: "Through music I developed a sense of beauty, of goodness, and love;" or "The idealism inherent in music and the fine arts provide the key to the improvement of humanity." Even though these values are being gained in varying degrees in all our music programs, whether the students are aware of them or not, it is imperative that educators more actively emphasize, cultivate, and seek them out.

Certainly idealism may not be completely realistic, but, realistically, the striving toward idealism is our only chance for music programs to survive. Only to the degree music is taught as a creative discipline will it survive and function in its essential capacity as a guide for man's rational intellect.

Creative Thinking

Psychologists conclude that such goals as a fully functioning, mentally healthy, well-educated, vocationally successful individual are undeniably related to the individual's creative fulfillment. There are several abilities involved in creative thinking:

- Sensitivity to problems
- Fluency (ability to produce a large number of ideas)
- Flexibility (ability to produce a variety of ideas or manners of approach)
- Originality
- Elaboration
- Redefinition

How well music can meet these requirements!

Studies have shown that about 70 percent of those who will score in the upper 20 percent on a test of creativity would not score in the upper 20 percent on an intelligence test (Paul Torrance, *Creativity*, National Education Association). If creative development is soon to become a primary concern of education, music and the fine arts should lead the way. Proper creative development, however, requires that the full music discipline be taught: theory, literature, performance, aesthetics, and philosophy.

Because most schools provide students with little or no opportunity for more than performance, it is necessary for performance directors to assume the responsibility of exposing the students to these other phases of music study. In the end, the students will become excited about them, the organizations will improve, and music will gradually bear the fruit of human development.

Food for Thought

It is for this reason I co-authored the method book, *Total Musicianship*, for which I now have developed a four-year set of lesson plans to be used in rehearsal warm-up. At a summer camp where I put the book's ideas into practice, students wrote short musical compositions as well as brief essays about music. The following excerpts provide food for thought, as

well as excellent material to add to programs for parents and the general public to read.

Frank Bencriscutto is director of concert bands and jazz ensembles at the University of Minnesota. He has studied at the University of Wisconsin, Northwestern University, and the Eastman School of Music and holds a doctor of musical arts degree.

When I hear great music, it makes me think about the problems and joys of life, and makes me want to do something to help solve those problems and keep the joys alive...If more people in the world could have just one musical experience, I think our world would be a lot better place to live in. —Jane (15 years old)

To really listen to a composition in the true sense one must let his imagination fly unhindered to its beckoning power. One flies to a world where everyday troubles and cares are forgotten and soothed by the magical world of music. After a trip such as this we return refreshed and uplifted far more than we shall ever realize. How wonderful it is to have such a world at our beck and call — the world of music. — Kathy (15 years old)

Music can say in a few measures what philosophers say in a thousand words. This is the power of music and so many people never experience it. — Gary (16 years old)

I think the main cause of the dishonesty and falsehood in the world today is the stress put on material things and money...Music is the one unifying element in the world. It is important to have communication in the world, and what is a truer, more honest means of communication than music?... To create something gives one a deeper meaning of life. If everyone were properly educated to understanding, how could there be anything but truth and peace in the world? — Heidi (15 years old)

January, 1987

Stressing Fundamentals

BY DONALD DEROCHE

Several years of listening to college entrance auditions have convinced me that few high school students receive adequate training in the fundamentals of playing their instruments. College freshmen frequently have difficulties reading basic rhythms, playing major scales, and tuning to a pitch given at the beginning of a rehearsal. Teachers too often feel pressure to prepare pieces for performance and neglect the basic training of students. They forget that they are teachers who sometimes conduct, not conductors who sometimes teach. It is important to teach fundamentals to students while they are in grammar school, or at the latest by

the time they reach ninth grade. The high school group these students later participate in will be able to play more interesting music with greater competence, consuming less rehearsal time.

Rhythmic Training. To sightread well, it is important for students to develop motor functions rather than just an intellectual understanding of pulse and subdivision. A good way to do this is to create a sequential set of rhythms that move from simple quarter-note and quarter-rest patterns through increasingly complex patterns of sixteenth notes and triplets. These rhythmic materials should add new patterns slowly, allowing plenty of practice on each pattern, because repetition

is fundamental to motor development. Two excellent books that provide rhythmic sets for instrumental teaching are *Teaching Rhythm* by Joel Rothman (JR Publications) and *Winning Rhythms* by Ed Ayola (Neil Kjos).

Spend 10 minutes each day having students clap rhythms and count with rhythmic syllables. If they have trouble translating this skill to playing rhythms on their instruments, have them clap or count and then play the rhythms on their instruments using a single pitch. (One director has all ninth-grade students buy drumsticks; he then sets up long boards across chairs and has the whole class play the rhythms in unison.) Test your

472

students about every 10 days with a metronome running to keep track of their progress.

Teaching basic learning skills as well as musical skills often requires patience on the part of both student and teacher. Students who have not been required to go through a regimen before may become impatient at first, but with a little encouragement from a sensitive teacher, they soon learn that the rewards justify the investment, and subsequent drills meet with less resistance. Moreover, by presenting challenges and rewards, you not only help your students to improve their playing, but you teach them techniques they can apply to other situations.

Technical Training. High school students are capable of developing not only fast fingers but accurate note placement. Accuracy is essential to good technique: speed alone means little. A good way to develop accuracy is to have students play a passage or study with the metronome, beginning at a tempo slow enough that they can play it without errors. After they can play the passage 10 times without a mistake, increase the speed by one metronome mark and have them play it three times without mistakes. Gradually accelerate in this way until performance tempo is attained. To solidify the gains have students go through the regimen several days in succession. The goal is to be able to play the passage accurately every time; getting through it once is only the beginning of developing technique.

Practicing. If we could place a hidden camera to watch our students practice we would find them playing non-stop through passages, spending little time on correcting errors and a good deal of time on various distractions. Students need guidance to establish practice habits. Explain that they should have a place where they will be undisturbed and a specific practice time set aside each day.

In the first week of class spend time supervising individual students as they practice. Show them how to use the metronome and point out errors that they may not perceive as mistakes. These class practice sessions are often best done with training groups or with new students in sectional rehearsals. (In college ensembles, they can be led by graduate students.) Particularly unorganized students may benefit from an after-school session every day for a week or two. Though you may never persuade every student to practice efficiently every day, you can improve their approach to learning and elevate the group's performance level.

Tone. Whenever college freshmen tell me that they have never heard a fine professional play their instrument, either live or on a recording, it comes as a surprise. Conception of a characteristic tone quality is entirely mental; one should be able to close his eyes and imagine a perfect tone. Before this image becomes personal, though, the student needs some idea of what a good tone is. This can be achieved by listening to good players, even on recordings. Private teachers, local professionals, and visiting professional groups offer additional opportunity to hear good tones. It is important that students listen to good playing and understand that they should emulate both tone and style. Students should listen critically to their own tones — their good and bad characteristics — and learn to improve them.

Intonation. Often high school seniors come to a college entrance audition not knowing how to tune with the piano. When I guest conduct I often find students who don't know what to listen for when tuning. They don't know if they should push in or pull out and have no notion of what it means to play in tune with themselves. Wind instrumentalists need to know the typical intonation problems of their kind of instrument as well as specific problems on their own horn. They can then be taught how to compensate for these problems and, most impor-

tant, to listen. Time can be spent in rehearsal having individuals tune intervals and triads with the class involved in listening for problems and suggesting solutions. The concept of tuning to A440 and staying down to the pitch level of mallet percussion and keyboards is important.

Band and orchestra directors should agree to tune to the same pitch level. When orchestral conductors complain that brass play with strained tones, less accuracy, and poorer pitch than when they play in band, I always check the tuning of the strings. It is invariably too high for good wind playing. I like to use electronic tuners because I haven't found a high school clarinet, oboe, or trumpet consistent enough to allow me to teach good tuning habits.

Equipment. Problems of intonation, tone, range, and technique are all affected by the quality and condition of the performer's equipment. Take time before classes begin in the fall to ascertain that all school instruments are in working order. Spend rehearsal time at the beginning of the year and again at mid-year actually inspecting individual instruments. Instruct the students on how to maintain and repair their instruments. Emphasize that the mouthpiece or reed has a dramatic effect on tone.

Because students need a solid foundation on which to build playing skills, it is essential that teachers have a plan for their instruction that includes setting high standards and testing to be sure they are upheld. The result will be less time spent learning those three contest pieces we depend on to help maintain the illusion of a superior program, and more time with interesting music and interested students. ∎

Donald DeRoche is a member of the faculty of the DePaul University School of Music in Chicago, where his duties include conducting the Wind Ensemble and Symphonic Band. He is also Chairman of the Department of Music Education. He holds graduate and undergraduate degrees from the University of Illinois and is currently pursuing a Ph.D. at Northwestern University.

Concentrate on Sound

by Dale Clevenger

Tone production is the result of what I do, my personality, and how I hear the horn. Why I hear horn tone a particular way reflects the conditioning by people who took an interest in me, showed me the ropes, and inspired me to listen to records and broadcasts. I was allowed to hear, and made to hear, the different tones produced by fine players; from them I assimilated my concept of horn tone.

I gravitated toward a certain sound because I admired the performances of several fine musicians. One outstanding horn player in this country was Bruno Jaenicke, who made a famous recording in 1927 that I bought for $1.98 in 1953. The sound of that man's instrument caught my ear as no one else's has. Freiburg was one of the Viennese horn players I heard in person in Pittsburgh playing the Schubert Octet. I felt the Viennese sound was closest to the ideal of how a horn ought to sound. One of his successors, Roland Berger, is in Vienna now and played solo horn for 25 years, then moved down to third horn of his own choice. There were some earlier, great horn players who never were recorded.

I believe each of us has a personality that develops as we grow up and would be apparent regardless of what career we choose. I was fond of music very early and wanted to play horn in an orchestra by the time I was 14, but until I graduated from college and started auditioning I didn't know where I would end up. I had listened to most of the first horn players in orchestras who recorded and knew of the very best playing by Jimmy Stagliano, Mason Jones, Myron Bloom, Phil Farkas, Joe Singer, Dick Moore, Jimmy Chambers, John Barrows, and Gunther Schuller. I still remember how they sounded.

I have a record of Rudy Puletz playing first horn in the second and fourth movements of the Mahler 4th Symphony with the New York Philharmonic under Bruno Walter. It is a gorgeous, creamy, beautiful, reposeful sound.

Sound is the essence of expressiveness; it is the reason I play the horn and everybody else plays the instrument of his choice. I was captivated by the horn's sound. The cello didn't get me at the time, nor did the oboe, bassoon, or trumpet; the sound of the horn is what got me. Once you learn how important the sound of an instrument is, you start listening and imitating. Imitation is one of the most important keys to playing music; everybody in the arts imitates somebody. When you become good enough, you break off, let your own personality take over, and hope your imagination will go beyond whatever you have imitated.

This happened to me two years after I joined the Chicago Symphony, when William Steinberg came to conduct Strauss' *Ein Heldenleben*. I knew Steinberg from playing as an extra with the Pittsburgh Symphony years before, and after the concert in Chicago I went in to chat with him about the old days with the Pittsburgh Symphony and its 1964 tour. I commmented about the just completed concert and how I had tried to make the beautiful horn solo at the end sound like Bruno Jaenicke. Steinberg was a fast retorter and snorted out the command, "Sound like Clevenger!"

This started me thinking that I had the job and should let my personality take over and play with my own sound. I stopped thinking about playing like someone else and more about, "This is my sound; this is what I have to offer, and I hope you like it."

Some horn players have a beautiful sound but are limited technically. There are a certain number of notes on the instrument that are must-do's, necessities. On the horn the notes span about four octaves, but beyond the matter of range is the technical consideration of starting those notes. I can name a minimum of five ways to start and end a note and a maximum of infinity. A note is a note, but the register and the sound can be different. The more an artist can do with these, the better he is equipped.

Then there is the area of dynamics, loudness and softness, the steps between *fff* and *ppp*. These go all the way to infinity, but logically nobody can play that many. So there are notes, beginnings and endings of notes, phrases, and dynamics as well as sound, color, timbre, and tone quality. These are the basics. Some people don't think about them and just play whatever comes out. It is a simplification to say you should be able to play three ways: darker, lighter, and the base tone.

In discussing color, dynamics, and style, the horns more than any other instrument are pivotal. Horns play in big orchestras, brass quintets, woodwind quintets, solos, with each other, and with strings. We have to adapt the sound to each of these situations. In the Schubert 8th Symphony when the bassoons have the lead and the horns have chords, we need to support them with a bassoon sound. At other times the horn has the lead.

Accents add emphasis to notes and are part of sound, style, phrasing, nuance, and blending. What I try to teach students is to stop looking at the parade through the knothole in the fence and look over the top of the fence, where they can hear and see much more. Expand your horizons. There are physical things that can affect sound, such as octave placements, the bore of the horn, the size of the bell, the kind and thickness of the metal, whether it is spun from one piece or put together from two or three pieces, whether it is hand-hammered, how thick it is if hand-hammered; all these things affect timbre. Nothing affects tone more than the human ear. Students should listen, study and work at it, imitate, and try to discover new sounds.

I would not talk about the shape of the mouth in terms of there being only one successful way to play, but I certainly believe it is important to experiment and to discover through trial and error how raising the jaw makes the oral cavity smaller, raises the pitch, and makes the sound thinner, drier, and less interesting. By letting the jaw down consciously, saying eeeoooowuuu, you change the mouth cavity and the tone color.

It is equally important to know what to do with your lips inside the mouthpiece. I demonstrate for students where I place the mouthpiece on my lips when playing a low middle register tone, doing something that looks rather grotesque. Once I get the tone going, I let what is outside the mouthpiece cave in or the cheeks puff out, but I can keep the tone exactly the same. Then I gradually perform what John Barrows called facial isometrics: strengthen, tighten, and change from a loose face to a tight face, keeping the tone the same. By isolating the flesh inside the mouthpiece that keeps the air moving steadily, I maintain a sound virtually the same with major facial muscle changes. I can change inside the mouthpiece in one second and absolutely destroy the tone.

On the subject of pressure, I am not a non-pressure player because I don't believe non-pressure gets the sound. I have never had a student who did it successfully. They are basket cases if they try to play this way because they cannot produce a fine sound.

By playing one note from *ppp* to *fff*, the embouchure and the facial muscles will change noticeably, and the mouth cavity probably changes. What goes on physically with the body, however, with the oral cavity, the face, the hand position, is only interesting information, not the criteria for how we sound. Our ears and minds control everything; I learned that from Arnold Jacobs, and it amazes me. I just had my eyes examined by a doctor whose specialty is the relationship between what the eyes perceive and how the brain handles the information. Some of her comments were quite interesting because a regular opthalmologist doesn't talk about what the brain does but only about visual perception. For instance, the brain uses only part of its capacity to control involuntary actions within our bodies, such as breathing, which takes two percent of the brain's capacity. If a person has emphysema, it takes in excess of ten percent of the brain's capacity; that's a large percentage for lung activity. If ten percent of the brain's capacity deals with involuntary functions, we have ninety percent left to think about things such as playing an instrument. If we use twenty percent primarily thinking about technique, how tight our face is, or where our tongue touches, we have taken away from the brain's potential to function.

To the extent we overdo thinking about the physical part of playing, we minimize attention to the mental part: how we want to sound, where we want to phrase, where a note fits into the key or chord, and what the balance is here. We should think about the artistic considerations while playing an instrument and as little as possible about the physical and technical. The artistic result we have in our minds dictates what we do technically.

Most of us grow up learning about 75% craft, but that is out of proportion with what it should be. At some point, a fine musician, conductor, artist, teacher, or player makes us click. Morris Secon did that for me when he said, "Dale, you are a wonderful horn player, and you have so much talent you can do anything with the horn. Now, I want to talk to you about singing." For a split second, I was a little bit insulted. First he tells me how wonderful I am, then wants to talk to me about singing. Fortunately, I had heard him play the horn and knew what he could do with a phrase, so I agreed with him about singing.

Technique is largely conditioned reflex. Many students and professionals never learn that to the extent they should. I discovered ten years ago that I somehow came up short in playing the chromatic scale. I had not spent enough time on it as a student and found myself faltering on the technique of a chromatic scale in the piece I was playing. I thought, "This is wrong; I should know this already." For ten or thirty minutes a day I practiced chromatic scales until I learned them. Now I work to play them as musically as possible; I am not concerned about finding the next note. There is a time and a place for compartmentalizing your practice; I tell students to never play a note without meaning or purpose if they want to be a professional.

I don't have regular daily exercises. Some days I begin a rehearsal, although not a concert, without having played at all. The first note I play is on the job. I want to see if I can do it, and of course I can, even though I don't feel the same as if I had warmed up for ten or thirty minutes.

I absolutely must have a nap before some concerts, while for others it isn't necessary. French music calls for a certain playing discipline, as does an hour of Wagner with the Siegfried Call or Immolation Scene. If every other night on a tour I play either *Ein Heldenleben* or the Siegfried Call, I have to rest before performances to maintain sufficient mental and physical energy. We are expected to play like gods when we are on tour, especially when we play in big European cities.

I play by sound. The physical feeling is not a primary criterion, but how I sound is. If I am going to play a major work, I pace myself carefully. When I warm up, I think in terms of quality tones; I play everything from staccato to long notes, thinking primarily of quality. I rarely go through routines or rote. Whatever note, length, or volume I play, it has to have quality. I don't play long tones, I don't play short tones, I play quality tones.

Jacobs says a way to practice getting the center of a note is to start out by just getting a note, without accuracy being too important. Once you get the note, then think in terms of quality, roundness, thickness, thinness, or whatever you want. Don't worry about the ending of the note but that middle section of the note. I practice the lengths of notes that are in the pieces that I am playing.

I practice and teach the ability to start a long tone or play staccato without tonguing. Tonguing is the biggest problem in playing staccato, so eliminate it. Don't tongue, go "phooh." Do it very short, a little longer, whatever. It is analogous to how string players bow. They can play a spiccato by bouncing the bow off the string, or they can play staccato on the string. In a leadership position, I set the pace; if my section does not play the kind of staccato that I want, I will tell them, "Let's not

play quite so clipped. Don't cut off the note with your tongue." It may not sound that much different out in the audience, but it sounds better close up.

Let a note ring, however long, rather than cause it to ring. To play "tah" is one kind of sound and may be used in certain situations, but "taaahh..." sounds so much better. What technique to use is dictated by the desired effect. If I hear anybody else in the orchestra play an effect that I like better, I'll imitate that, and vice versa. I'll make mine more pointed if I don't like what I hear.

Sometimes I use vowels in teaching and performing, but not to a fault; I don't do anything all the time. I may get on a kick and talk to students about the importance of the personality and the emotion of playing. We have a special calling in that playing gives us great joy because it pleases other people. We should produce as many colors in our sound as a painter uses. I don't mean someone like Rembrandt, who used mostly dark colors, but the French Impressionists who planned colors so carefully. I don't think they just slopped paint on a canvas and it came out the way they wanted it; you can't look at Monet and think that. Whatever might help us accomplish a certain color or effect we should try. At times I will make a suggestion or a guess to help a student, but I don't know how much tension they have in their lips, how much air comes across, and whether their tongue is up too high. I certainly don't want them thinking about those things to an extent that could be detrimental, so I might suggest, "... lower your tongue a little bit, say a little bit more "Oh" or "Ah". Let's see what that does to your sound." More often I say to them, "Relax your face just a little. Put the mouthpiece up just a little bit firmer. Let the air come through slightly more relaxed lips, rather than tense lips." Tension equals tense sound, white sound as they call it in the voice world.

My students will never know how much I have learned from them. I have heard students play a phrase or scale for me in the first couple of lessons, and I was dumbfounded at the beautiful sound they got. They may not have realized how beautiful their sound was or that their teacher would imitate their sound. It is not always possible for my lips to do what theirs do, but it doesn't mean I'm not going to try. Often high school students don't try to play pretty tones; they just play notes with tones, sounds, and effects that are grating. Students should try to play a lovely legato, beautiful slurs, and even rhythmic scales. Most students do not play in rhythm or in tune.

Playing melodies and tunes on the mouthpiece will help. I just got a book by Phil Collins with melodies from the repertoire; some are horn melodies, some are originally voice or string melodies, but they are melodies and we play them. I use the Concone books too, for melodies; I want to hear how students turn a phrase. I also suggest singing and playing melodies on the mouthpiece, then on the instrument. This is good advice for all instruments.

Many students hear that the horn is the most difficult instrument while others say it is not any harder than a tuba, guitar, bassoon, or flute. All instruments are difficult, and they are all easy; it depends on who is playing them. A major goal in playing is to make the audience feel at ease and comfortable. I want them to say to themselves, "He likes what he's doing, he enjoys what he's doing."

To be professional takes talent, drive, motivation, single-mindedness of purpose, tunnel vision, and compulsion. It takes excellent schooling, the best that one can get. It is rare that those who are self-taught become professional musicians because they lack discipline, whether tonal, intonational, or personal. Even with excellent education, it is a matter of having the good luck to be at the right place at the right time. All these together still are no guarantee of success, because you have to play an audition well.

Preparation for an audition is a major ingredient in being able to play an audition at a given moment, the first time through, just as in concerts there is no chance to stop and play the solo again. The concept of playing something without stopping is foreign to many students who, whenever they make a mistake, grunt, frown, roll their eyes, or quit playing. It is extremely important to break that habit. Organize practicing to fix this problem; play for an hour without stopping for anything. Play right on through no matter what. Then play for another thirty minutes, and stop for everything that is wrong.

Concentration can overcome nervousness. Rather than think about whether you are going to miss a note, or what people think, try to get rid of the what ifs. Think about tone, line, effect, and the artistic purpose. I heard a fellow play a solo today, and I said, "Imitate me; I'm going to do something a little different." I used a lot of vibrato. He had to think about how to create the vibrato and that kept him from thinking about missing notes or getting through the solo. An instrument is a powerful stimulus; once it comes in front of your face, all the habits, good or bad, that you have will appear. You try to replace those habits, but you don't get rid of them. They are still in your brain, but you cover them with better habits, thought processes, concentration, and different ways of doing things. Instead of playing straight tones all the time, play with a vibrato. Play a melody on a mouthpiece. Do anything you can to make your thinking artistic rather than technical. Concentrate on playing phrases; plan a sequence of phrases. When you can do that well, you will be able to play despite little things that might go wrong.

There are people who audition well, but they cannot play with an ensemble. Others do poorly in auditions but play well in an orchestra. Nobody plays perfectly, only as perfectly as the concept in his head. I try to mirror what is in my brain as closely as I can. This notion is difficult for some students.

Sometimes teachers do not place enough emphasis on music and good sound but let students get by with unpleasant sounds. If teachers are not able to tell students what to do to improve their sound, they should tell them to imitate recordings. A good band or orchestra director will have a stereo sound system in the band room and will talk about music. The director should point out any important characteristics in an artist's playing that might help students. Many students assume that playing well takes a great deal of force and effort; point out that there is no pressing or strain in the sound of the artist on the recording. Playing should sound effortless, however you get to that point; technique is normally the means.

A student may have artistic direction, talent, imagination, and inspiration. Others have talent to varying degrees, and the proof is how they sound; sound is everything. I never tell students they should quit. That is too traumatic, and it is not necessary to say it in so many words. Students should come to their own conclusions about whether they can make it. I have had students who I thought had only a small chance of ever playing professionally, but they grew and matured. I was too young and shortsighted to recognize what their real talents were, and they proved me wrong.

In my philosophy artistry is first, tone is primary; the most important things are the line, the effect, the artistic side. Then comes the technique. I set these priorities with my students in the first lesson, so that when we talk about the craft, it doesn't get out of proportion. How large the cavity, where the tongue touches, hand positions; these are important but they are not the most essential criteria. I will talk about craft, but only in balance with the art form. □

Prior to joining the Chicago Symphony Orchestra in 1966, principal hornist Dale Clevenger played with the American Symphony Orchestra and the Kansas City Philharmonic. He is an associate professor of horn at Northwestern University, where he has taught for 20 years.

The Miracle of Music

by Alfred Reed

Despite all of our scientific discoveries, investigations, and achievements during the past 250 years, we are still not certain just why we hear and react to music. A psychologist recently said that the real miracle is not that seven different persons hearing the same piece may come up with seven different reactions to it, but that there is any reaction at all. From the purely physical point of view, music is nothing but sound of a certain type, and sound is nothing but air in motion.

Regardless of time and style, though, music as an art exists only in the psychological reactions engendered in the human mind. When waves of air set in motion by certain kinds of events impinge upon the ear, electrical and chemical events occur in the brain.

This is about all we can say with certainty about the entire process. While animals also perceive musical sounds, we have no evidence that any animal mind can organize such sounds into extended, continuous, or even meaningful patterns.

The human mind is a super computer with a wide range of choices in stored information. Just as a computer receives, stores, and then retrieves information before it can operate, so too the human mind first receives, remembers, and then retrieves information before it produces those physical and psychological reactions that constitute the art of music. Our minds receive this necessary information through our ears, which convert the physical energy of the air waves into electrical signals sent along the auditory nerve system to the brain. Once the electrical signals arrive at the brain, they are combined in sound patterns of different pitches, colors, directions, and intensities, which the brain then recognizes and responds to.

After all these complex physical and chemical processes take place, the miracle occurs: those physiological and psychological reactions set in, which we call the art of music. We may suddenly feel warm or cold; our heartbeat, blood pressure, pulse, and even metabolism may change. We may feel love or hatred, become happy or depressed, or experience various forms and combinations of other feelings.

We don't know why this happens, just that it does. No one has the slightest idea why air in motion should cause us to think of love and why the same music doesn't produce the same responses in other people, or why it produces no reactions in some listeners and such strong feelings in others. We haven't the slightest hint as yet as to the reason.

We know very little that has to do with our emotional response to music as an art, but we are learning slowly as we probe deeper into that marvelous and awe-inspiring organ, the human brain. Music as an art exists precisely in those complex physiological and psychological reactions that produce patterns of sound by the brain as it organizes and continues separate notes. The wonder of music is not that we can hear separate sounds but in how the mind combines them into coherent musical passages. This applies to all music produced throughout history, from a three-minute rock tune to a one-hour symphony.

So where does this leave us? If this whole process is not a miracle, then I don't know of any better word to describe it or man's laborious search to understand his existence on God's green earth. □

Currently Chairman of the Department of Music Media and Industry at the University of Miami in Coral Gables, Florida, composer Alfred Reed has written 300 published works, 63 of which were commissioned.

Intonation for the Band Conductor

Mark Hindsley

The title of this article has certain implications. First, I shall be writing not only for but also as a band conductor, not as a performer, studio teacher, retailer, manufacturer, or scientist; I may not agree at all times with other groups; I may not even be in agreement with other band conductors. Second, I shall be writing on band intonation, whose elements may or may not all be in common with those of other instrumental, or choral, ensembles.

The pitches of the tones in our modern scale of 12 tones in one octave, or the way the scales are "tempered," furnish the main if not the full criteria for what we call intonation. The pitch of a tone is determined usually by the number of vibrations in a period of time — like the second. I say "usually" because under certain conditions there may be a change of pitch and vibration frequency between the source of the sound and the person who hears it.

There are scales of three different and well-established temperaments with which we should be concerned:

The Just Scale

The *just* scale is based on nature's harmonic pattern of the open tube or the stretched string. With the fundamental as the first tone of the pattern or series, the second tone is an octave higher, produced by vibrations twice as fast, or with a ratio of 2:1, the simplest ratio. The third tone adds a perfect fifth, with a ratio of 3:2. As we proceed

Mark Hindsley served as Director of Bands at the University of Illinois from 1948 until his retirement in 1970. He is now devoting his time to guest conducting, adjudicating, teaching, writing, and editing. He has written six books on instrumental music education and has contributed articles to numerous national magazines.

upward the intervals and ratios become consecutively smaller until the half-step in the diatonic scale has a ratio of 16:15.

From the just scale and its primary ratios are derived the so-called consonant intervals of the perfect fifth and fourth, and the major and minor third and sixth. However, within this scale some of these intervals do not have the primary ratios cited, therefore the scale cannot be completely depended upon for consistent consonance. To be more specific, within the diatonic form of the just major scale (two whole steps and a half-step, three whole steps and a half-step) the perfect and consonant fifths are *C-G, E-B, F-C, G-D,* and *A-E,* but *D-A* is an imperfect, contracted, and non-consonant fifth. It so happens that all the major thirds in this scale (*C-E, F-A,* and *G-B*) are equal and consonant. The minor thirds *E-G, A-C,* and *B-D* are equal and consonant, but *D-F* is contracted and non-consonant. (The inverted fifths and thirds become fourths and sixths and have the same consonant or non-consonant properties.)

Although the two minor seconds, *E-F* and *B-C,* and their inverted major sevenths are equal, the major seconds and minor sevenths come in two sizes: *C-D, F-G,* and *A-B* are larger than *D-E* and *G-A,* with the reverse situation in the inverted sevenths. A study of the chromatic and enharmonic tones would show more inequalities and inconsistencies. The just-tempered scale, then, may be considered as *most valuable* though somewhat unreliable harmonically, and as *quite erratic* melodically.

The Pythagorean Scale

The *Pythagorean* scale is a "synthetic" scale, featuring perfect and consonant fifths and fourths throughout, diatonically and chromatically. None of the major or minor thirds or sixths are consonant from the ideal, simple ratio standpoint, but they, along with the major and minor seconds and sevenths, are all equal to each other. The equalities of the diatonic intervals, in contrast to those of the just scale, foretell the evenness of the Pythagorean temperament melodically. All the tones may move adjacently either way, up or down, with equal "gravitation."

Another feature of the Pythagorean scale is its placement of the chromatic tones; the sharped tones are placed "off-center" toward the next higher tones on the way up, and the flatted tones are placed equally off-center toward the next lower tones on the way down. (This contrasts greatly with the just scale, where the "sharps" are all flatter than the "flats," and the "flats" are all sharper than the "sharps"). The Pythagorean chromatics are thus all "gravitational" in their natural directions. And even the natural half-step diatonic intervals *E-F* and *B-C* are closer than in the other scales, making the *E* and *B* quite proper "leading tones" to *F* and *C.*

The Pythagorean scale, then, may be considered as *valuable, consistent,* and *reliable* melodically, but not one on which we can rely or can approve harmonically.

The Equal-Tempered Scale

The *equal-tempered* scale is also a "synthetic" scale, dividing an octave into 12 equal half-step intervals and eliminating unequal enharmonics ($C\sharp$ has the same pitch as $D\flat$, $D\sharp$ the same as $E\flat$, etc.). This scale long ago became a technical necessity for keyboard and mallet instruments, to make multi-key, modulatory, and innovative harmonic performance possible and practical. This scale makes it possible to play equally in tune or out of tune in all keys. In other words, it is very frankly a compromise temperament, both melodically and harmonically.

From the description I have given of these three differently tempered scales, a broad statement may be made that the *Pythagorean* **scale should be used** *melodically,* **and the consonant, simple ratio portion of the** *just* **scale should be used** *harmonically.* **Actually it is** theoretically possible for singers and for string and trombone players to do just that. As we have noted, however, this combination is impossible for keyboard and mallet players; it is also a practical impossibility for players of wind instruments other than the trombone, for it would involve humoring the pitch of each tone in the diatonic major and minor scales over a range of 33⅓ "cents" (one-third of a half-step or semitone), and in the chromatic scales over a range of 74.3 cents (almost three-fourths of a half step). These extreme variations ordinarily cannot be made in many wind instruments without considerable loss of tone quality and/or control.

It is my conclusion that we should try to have our bands play in the combination of the just and Pythagorean temperaments. Theoretically and for practicality, wind instruments should be tuned to equal temperament in manufacture and adjustment; in their playing we should go as far as possible toward the tone pitches of the other temperaments. We should prefer the Pythagorean scale for *melodic* lines, but at the very worst may have to accept the *equal* scale. We should prefer the consonant, simple ratio relationships of the just scale *harmonically*, but at the very worst we may have to accept the harmonic relationships again of the *equal* scale.

I say we *should* prefer the combination of the just and Pythagorean, but I have found that a majority of band conductors and graduate college band students actually prefer the equal temperament, more so melodically than harmon-

ically. This reveals our dominant "ear-conditioning" by the piano and mallet and wind instruments. Not only have these instruments affected our hearing within the short range of an octave scale and a few close chords, but they have affected our hearing in the long range from octave to octave within the normal six or seven octaves in which we "operate." And for many players it may be apparent that the scales they play (and evidently prefer) do not fall within any of the three temperaments or combinations of temperaments which I have described.

Piano and Organ Tuning

I had been aware for some time that pianos are not tuned "straight up and down" in octaves, that the top tones on the piano are relatively much sharper than the middle tones, and the lower tones much flatter. I accepted as fact what I had heard along our musical grapevines, that the human ear expects sharpness in the high register and flatness in the low register. I learned, however, or was or became aware, that the organ was not tuned in any such manner, rather that it was indeed tuned straight up and down. When we purchased a transistorized electric organ in which every tone could be tuned separately — rather than in perfect octaves — I decided to try an experiment. After having our piano freshly tuned, I tuned the organ precisely to the piano. Although the piano sounded fine to me, take my word for it that the intonation of the organ was about as atrocious as you can ever expect to hear.

It was then that I telephoned our university piano tuner and technician and asked him the perfectly simple(!) question, "How do you tune a piano?" He replied, "Which piano?" He continued that no two pianos were necessarily alike, although certain makes and models had tendencies which could be anticipated. (How like our wind instruments after all, I thought.) He went on to say that it was his practice to "set the temperament" in an octave near the middle of the piano. Using a stroboscope (the portable "Strobotuner"), he then worked upward and downward in octaves, *not* necessarily to an

exact octave, but to the *first overtone* of the lower octave, which more often than not is *not* the same. (The "bands" of the stroboscope make it possible to identify at least part of the overtone series.) Tuning to the first overtone makes for reinforcement of sonority and resonance, reducing conflicts among frequencies of the fundamental and the harmonics above. It also points out the curious and perhaps lamentable fact that (intentionally or unintentionally) the piano as now built (and very likely as it always has been built) produces imperfect harmonics, by nature's standard, in the upper and lower registers. Whether pianos could be built to produce perfect harmonic series I do not know, but I suspect that if such pianos were to be built, few of today's pianists would accept them. I am trying to make the point that to a great extent, in wind instruments as in pianos, we may become "slaves" to the instruments we play, both in what we accept as being in tune, and in how much we can do, or are willing to do, to change their intonation for the better.

String Instrument Tuning

I had been aware also that of the string instruments, the violins, violas, and cellos tuned in perfect fifths, and that perfect fifths were two cents sharper than fifths in equal temperament, thus causing a "stretch" of six cents from the lowest string to the highest, or vice versa, or almost four cents an octave. For some time I considered this a valid reason for wind instruments becoming sharper as they play higher, and flatter as they play lower. I did not take into account that the string bass tunes in fourths rather than fifths, with exactly the opposite results from the other strings, a *contraction* of six cents from high to low string. How all the strings got along in their overlapping registers did not bother me. Nor did I take into account that in the overlapping registers of wind instruments what was the low register in one could also be the upper register of another, thus making unisons quite impossible, if a policy of "stretching" were followed along with customary tuning procedures. *Customary tuning procedures indeed*! It finally occurred to me, or dawned on me, that the cellos and string basses *did not* stretch the *octaves* when tuning their *A*'s one and three octaves below the common *A* of the violins and violas. And when the strings use harmonic tones in their performances I do not think their instruments are so imperfect that those harmonics are stretched as they are in the piano. So I concluded that *if* strings play sharper, and singers sing sharper as they go higher, it is because they *want to*, rather than because of any characteristic or deficiency of their instruments and voices — and they are *out of tune* whether they know it or not.

By recording the pure tones of oscillators I have found that most band conductors and graduate band students can tolerate out-of-tuneness in open octaves to the extent of two cents, but beginning at three cents the sound is objectionable. (Incidentally, in unisons, the tolerance was found to be one cent with two cents objectionable.) These tolerances are considerably lower than the four and six cents I have read elsewhere as being tolerable, even acceptable. If only band conductors were able to demand and secure these close one and two cent tolerances with the instruments of the band!

I have heard about great orchestra conductors who reportedly have had to ask their groups *not* to play so well in tune, because it made the music so gray, so lifeless. I believe I have heard much music played perfectly in tune, but never have I had the experience of hearing music so well in tune that I could complain about it. There are other ways of making music colorful and alive than playing it out of tune.

Some of our colleagues belittle the use of electronic devices to measure and teach intonation, who would possibly decry all this folderol about temperaments and scales and cents, and who would say so smugly, "all that matters is the ear." *To be sure*, the ear is the final authority, but I have learned not to fully trust anyone's ear, least of all my own. *To be sure*, the ear *can* and *must* be trained, and one of the good (maybe one of the best) ways is through the eyes

looking at a stroboscope while the ear is listening — with proper interpretation and in the light of an understanding of what intonation is all about.

Part II

The stroboscope has been invaluable to us in the work we have done in connection with the second of the three objectives stated earlier: selecting and modifying instruments to make good intonation *possible* and relatively *easy* to achieve. We have taken for granted that wind instruments should respond naturally and accurately to the readings of the equal-tempered stroboscope, and that there is a certain point of focus of each tone which is the proper point of departure from which to go up or down to meet the requirements of the other temperaments and other performance exigencies. (I have also taken for granted that everyone is acquainted with the stroboscope, and no doubt its universal and exclusive trade name in our field, the "Stroboconn.")

Now it is time for me to start an "inventory" of what we have done at the University of Illinois in the matter of selection and modification of instruments.

Flutes, piccolos, oboes and English Horns

We did not have to select or purchase any flutes or oboes, for the students' own first-line instruments proved entirely capable of being played in tune when kept in proper adjustment. I will have more to say about tuning procedures and tone production later. We have had one beautiful and beautifully in tune *C* piccolo for Concert Band use for close to 50 years. We did purchase a group of *C* piccolos for marching band and supplementary concert use when the changeover from *D* to *C* instruments was being completed in published music. We could not afford, or did not wish to invest in a large group of first-line instruments, so all we could do was choose the least sharp and the most even scale of the second-line piccolos. We had occasion to purchase English horns, and were successful in securing very fine and very satisfactory instruments.

Bassoons

We objected to three main faults of the bassoon: the frequent unevenness of the scale, the sharpness in the register below the bass staff, and the sharpness at the change of register with the "whisper" key, particularly the *G* fourth space. We had the good fortune of being able to work with Hugo Fox at South Whitley, Indiana, when he was in the early stages of making the instruments that bear his name. With a few trips to his then small factory, at first taking along our own Stroboconn at his request, Mr. Fox tuned an instrument which became a model for the set we purchased and for his entire production, and which removed quite successfully the first two objections: the unevenness of scale and the sharp low register. The sharpness of the middle *G* could not easily be corrected because with the same fingering, except for the whisper key, the lower *G* was in tune, and the instrument simply overblew sharp in the octave above. My amateur solution to this problem was to add a key mechanism which would reduce the clearance of the pad over the low *F* hole sufficiently to bring the middle *G* in tune, merely by straightening the normally curved third finger of the right hand. I installed this key on the set of instruments we purchased, and had every reason to believe it was a practical and successful improvement and solution. However, my amateur mechanical work was not impeccable, some of it fell apart, and I was guilty of neglecting to follow through on this modification in a professional manner. Then, in our affluent society more and more of our players were bringing in their own Foxes and Heckels which they wished to play, so we have lived with the sharp *G*, always exhorting the players to use another key already on the instrument, and another finger, to maybe bring the pitch down.

Contrabassoons

We had no occasion to replace the one instrument in our inventory, and with proper attention to adjustment it has been adequate.

Saxophones

We found that most saxophones were quite sharp above the treble staff when played with the rather firm embouchure needed for a suitable concert-type, ensemble tone. We were successful in being able to find and purchase a set of instruments without that fault. Then, by adding strips or layers of cork to the upper curves of the tone holes that produced sharpness in both the first and second octaves, we minimized our problems still further. The octaves D-D and A-A were still often quite troublesome, with the lower tones flat and the upper sharp, and we tried to compensate with auxiliary fingerings. More recently we found alto saxophones that are quite satisfactory without much adjustment or use of auxiliary fingerings, but the tenors and baritones are still somewhat inconsistent and unreliable.

I am greatly disappointed that we have not been able to completely solve at least the major intonation problems of the saxophone, and that I have had few ideas to help. My impression is that this instrument has been victimized by jazz players, whose loose embouchures and wide vibratos paradoxically make good intonation more nearly possible and cover up many imperfections.

Bb soprano clarinets

I have saved the clarinets until the last of the woodwind family because of their particularly unique and complicated problems. Soon after acquiring a Stroboconn, I began testing the instruments and players of the Concert Band. Incidentally, we had been using $A = 442$ as our tuning pitch prior to this time. When I found that several fine clarinet players had difficulty reaching even $A = 440$, we changed to $A = 440$ as a tuning standard and held it there from then on. But the tests I made revealed other unexpected inconsistencies among instruments and players, inconsistencies so great we felt something drastic had to be done. We were fortunate to be granted a series of appropriations that made it possible to purchase instruments to equip most of the sections of the Concert Band, including the clarinets (and excluding the flutes and oboes, which we felt it unnecessary to purchase because of reasons previously given). The great adventure of selecting and modifying and using these in-

struments (the clarinets) was on.

What we looked for in clarinets basically was an instrument which was in tune, or could be made to be in tune, in the low or chalumeau register (low E to first space F), and which overblew exactly an equal-tempered 12th in the upper or clarion register (B third line to C above the staff). Neither of these characteristics was easy to find; most clarinets were either sharp in the middle of the chalumeau register or flat in the middle of the clarion register; most were also sharp, quite sharp, at the top of the clarion register for almost all our players. We were glad to settle for an instrument that was still somewhat sharp in the middle of the chalumeau register, but really well in tune from approximately D fourth line to A above the staff, a part of the clarion register which is not affected by the size of the register hole or the clearance of its pad. We could take care of the 15 cents average sharpness at the top of the clarion register by reducing the size of the register hole with thin aluminum tube inserts of different lengths, although this would ruin (flatten) the thumb B♭ in the throat register (third line); when these inserts caused flatness in the lower tones of the clarion register, we could make a correction by boring a small hole in the bell (usually less than a quarter-inch in diameter), at the approximate point of the next imaginary tone hole (about one and three-eighths inches from the top of the bell), although this would also sharpen the bottom of the chalumeau register, except B♭, by taping up the individual holes and/or adjusting the pad clearances. To restore the thumb B♭, we installed the S-K (Stubbins-Kasper) mechanism with its supplementary B♭ tone hole. The middle of the chalumeau register had to be lipped down or brought down by the low F key or by pulling the middle joint in isolated passages using the errant tones. For the high or altissimo register (above high C), created by the troublesome fifth harmonic which we shall discuss more fully in the brass instruments, we could only pray and try out some new fingerings.

Twenty or more years ago it was difficult to find a clarinet that met the two basic require-

ments: a good chalumeau register and a good middle clarion register. We found it not quite as difficult when we changed some of our instruments about five years later, and others just a few years ago. I would hope it is not difficult at all today, but I still have doubts.

Without question the clarinet is our most inflexible instrument from the standpoint of intonation, without undue sacrifice of tone quality. One of the reasons is that the best tone quality is found near the top of the possible pitch variation; it is difficult to play much sharper than this optimum point, and playing much lower soon destroys quality. It might be that the fact the clarinet is the only one of our wind instruments that acts as a closed tube (overblowing only to the odd-numbered harmonics) is a factor in this inflexibility. Since players differ from each other in intonation even when using the same equipment throughout and producing equally good tone quality, we must find some mechanical flexibility to compensate for these differences. Even individual players change from time to time and need to make adjustments in their instruments. The mouthpiece, the reed, and the barrel are all interchangeable and may be experimented with. The primary need in flexibility, however, is in the ability to control the overblowing of the twelfth. To do this we must disconnect, or divorce as much as possible, the register hole from the thumb B♭ hole, so that the register hole can be changed in size as desired. (We have done this recently with interchangeable tubes threaded on the outside to insert into the bore of the instrument with the aid of a socket wrench.

After all, what is so sacred about using the same tone hole to make a thumb B♭ and as a vent to facilitate overblowing to the 12th. This hole is not located far enough down on the instrument for a properly placed B♭ and is too small for good tone quality on this tone and for stable intonation. Isn't the correct overblowing pattern more important than this single, chromatically fingered throat tone? It really isn't necessary to choose, and we can have both good overblowing and a good thumb B♭ by installing a mechanism such as the S-K, which as previously noted adds a completely new, properly placed and sized hole for a completely independent $B\flat$. Perhaps still other mechanisms and/or fingerings could be invented which would be better than what we now have.

It should be repeated here that when we reduce the size of the register hole to bring down the pitch of the top of the clarion register, we must be prepared to make a compensating adjustment at the bell to raise the pitch of the clarion tones affected there, and then to lip the very lowest tones in the chalumeau register downward, if necessary, while playing.

For these past many years it has been our practice to "fit" our clarinets to the individual players, or vice versa, much the same idea as fitting a person with eye glasses. As a player changed, his instrument could be adjusted or he might benefit from still another instrument. It has required a lot of work and patience, but the results have been most rewarding. Here is a good example of making all the mechanical adjustments possible before expecting human adjustments; of trying to let the player by the *master* of his instrument rather than its *slave*.

E$\flat$ soprano and alto clarinets

We used these instruments only when absolutely necessary. The soprano $E\flat$ was treated as a solo instrument, and we were able to find satisfactory combinations of instrument and player. We used the alto clarinets both as solo and section instruments on occasion, and actually were able to find and purchase instruments more nearly perfect in intonation than any others in the clarinet family. Our only problems came when we tried to mix these beautiful instruments with other makes and models of lesser stature.

Bass clarinets

The bass clarinets we chose were in tune in the valuable chalumeau register only when we pulled them rather extremely in the middle and at the bell and doctored up a few tone holes. The manufacturer made permanent extensions at these two joints in our complete set and they have worked out well. The clarion register has been difficult to control, and is not

too reliable in intonation, so we have avoided the use of these instruments in sensitive spots above the throat register as much as possible.

Contrabass clarinets (E$\flat$ and B$\flat$)

Selection has not been a problem here, and the instruments have required only routine maintenance and adjustment. Again, we have considered these instruments of primary value only in their lower registers.

Cornets and Trumpets

When discussing the just-tempered scale (Part I), I may have written rather glibly about nature's harmonic series and the consonant nature of the tones derived from its simplest ratios. I have also discussed the non-conformist piano, and various departures from the "straight and narrow" by some of the woodwinds, which normally employ only from three to five of the long series of harmonics. It would seem that Mother Nature herself may not always be perfect, and when combined with human nature there is never an end to imperfection. Pity then the poor brass instruments, which have to contend with up to 12 or more tones of the harmonic series. Think what human nature can do with all those tones to play with! On a three-valve instrument this counts up to some 84 tones to work with, twice as many as are needed in a three and one-half octave range. There are even more in a four- or five-valve instrument or a double horn with its two sets of valve slides. How can all these tones possibly be sorted out?

Really, it doesn't have to be as bad as I have made it appear, and seldom is, but the combination of harmonics and valves makes a formidable team which can be wonderful . . . or terrible. Let's review the harmonic series of the open tones of the cornet and trumpet: fundamental, octave, perfect fifth, perfect fourth, major third, minor third, an un-usable out-of-key seventh harmonic, a third octave, a large major second, a small major second, an un-usable eleventh harmonic, and a twelfth harmonic an octave above the sixth. It is possible for master craftsmen to reproduce this series

exactly, and they are sometimes allowed to do it. They may also reproduce the series quite faithfully when the valves and valve slides are added, even with the handicap of only one bell. The two "flies in the ointment" are the fifth and tenth tones in the series. Although in tune harmonically when they appear as major or minor thirds or sixths in a chord in the key of the particular harmonic series, they are quite flat in the Pythagorean and equal-tempered scales. For this reason, neither the 5th nor the 10th tones are satisfactory, melodically, in *any* key. Neither are they acceptable, harmonically, in *most* of the keys. In the simplest example, the written E, fourth space, played "open," is in tune when it is combined with a "just" C and a just G in a major chord, but it is badly flat as a fifth in a chord based on an equal-tempered or Pythagorean A (15.6 and 21.5 cents).

It is the rare instrument maker who is content *not* to tinker with this fifth harmonic. And by means which are largely beyond my understanding he is able to bring one of these tones, the open tone for example, in tune as an equal-tempered tone, without affecting the other tones in the series. However — and here is the "rub" — I never have found any instrument in which the fifth harmonic of the open tone had been "corrected" and in which the fifth harmonic of the first or second or third valve tone could also be corrected without displacing at least one other tone in the series. Usually when the fifth harmonic is raised, it also raises the sixth harmonic and perhaps lowers the third, both of which originally should have been in tune in all the temperaments (a bare two cents sharp as an interval of a slightly imperfect fifth in equal temperament). And usually those who attempt these "corrections" do so with the philosophy that they are making certain tones "a little sharp" in order that others will be only "a little flat." In other words, instead of one tone out of tune for each such correction, there are apt to be two or three or more. Such is the price of compromise.

Now come the problems of the valves and valve slides. The second valve may lower each open tone one half-step and the first valve may lower each open tone one whole step, but the second valve slide in that case is not long enough to lower the first valve tone a half-step, nor is the first valve slide long enough to lower the second valve tone a whole step. Again the urge to compromise asserts itself. Again a simple example: Let us suppose that both the first and second valve slides are lengthened just a bit so that their separate tones will be only "a little flat" and their combination tone only "a little sharp." And let us suppose that the third valve slide, which is said to lower the open tone one and one-half steps, is made long enough so that its combination with the second valve is only "a little flat" and its combination with the first valve is "not as bad as you otherwise might think" and the combination of all three valves is a "lost cause anyway."

In the instruments available to us there are many variations of harmonic patterns and valve slide lengths with all sorts of intonation results, almost all committed to compromise in a great majority of the tones. It was my feeling that it would be better to select and modify an instrument which would have the greatest possible number of tones in tune in equal temperament, and then by other mechanical means make it possible to play the remaining tones in tune by providing the right lengths of tubing.

We found an instrument, both a cornet and a trumpet, in which the harmonic series was nearly perfect in both open and valve tones, with a flat fifth harmonic throughout. The second valve slide was of exact length to lower the open tone one half-step. The first valve slide was short enough to play the fourth line D in tune, but all the other first valve tones were sharp, so we pulled this slide some 3/16 inch. The third valve slide was of the length required to play the two-three valve combination in tune; we shortened it to make it play exactly one and one-half steps below the open tone, and took a 3/16 length of what we had removed to add to the first valve slide so the latter could not be

made sharp in its basic series. We now had an instrument on which 16 of the 25 tones in the two octaves C-C could be played in tune with open or single valve tones (C, E, F, F#, G, A, B♭, B, C, F, F#, G, A, B♭, B, C). By using the ring on the third valve slide we had the means of achieving the right tube length and good intonation for five more tones (low C#, D, D#, and the two G#'s). To raise the pitch of the four remaining fifth harmonic tones C#, D, D# and E near the top of the staff with normal fingerings, we put a ring on, or connected to, the main tuning slide which permitted closing this slide sufficiently with the thumb to bring these tones into proper pitch. And all this without compromise!

In addition, the main tuning slide was equipped with double-acting springs which permitted the player to push or pull the slide either way while playing, to augment what he might or might not do in humoring the tone, without loss of control or quality. With these arrangements it put all the responsibility for playing in tune on the player, for the instrument was fully capable of it. This was another step in our crusade to let the player become the *master* of his instrument instead of its *slave*.

Most cornets and trumpets are now normally equipped with a ring on the third valve slide to permit the slide's extension when it is used with the first or second valve or both. The moving of this slide should become a part of the regular fingering of the instrument from the beginning of instruction, when the duration of the tones in question is sufficient to make such slide adjustment possible and practical. I am familiar with the trigger which also extends the first valve slide, and which is often used instead of, or in addition to, the third valve slide ring. I am also aware of the ring or "saddle" on the first valve slide, which permits sensitive manipulation either way from a slightly extended position. However, the double-acting main tuning slide does all the first valve trigger or ring or saddle can do and far, far more. This main tuning slide, though, cannot be operated over a sufficient length to permit its

substitution for the third valve slide extension.

After some 20 years experience with it, the instrument I have described, with normal harmonic series, precisely and individually tuned valves, and movable third and main tuning slides, is still the "one for me." Many experts can and do play quite satisfactorily in tune with other instruments, but with "my" instrument even these highly talented performers could do it more easily . . . and the rest of us mortals need all the help we can get to play in tune.

Euphoniums

At first we could find no euphonium without a decidedly sharp sixth harmonic, but we took the best we could find and modified it along the same lines as described for the cornet and trumpet. Later we found an instrument somewhat better in tune, and which was equipped with "compensating valves." We chose the three-valve model (extra tube length is added to all tones using the third valve when that third valve is used in combination with either or both the other valves). The manufacturer was most cooperative in altering the lengths of some of the slides to our specifications; he adopted these measurements as standard for regular production; we found our intonation improved, with less effort on the part of the player.

Our players today prefer the four-valve euphonium with compensating valves (and with bell-up rather than bell-front). The fourth valve does indeed help correct a few tones, but does not compensate in valve combinations without the fourth valve. The value of the extra range provided by the fourth valve is questionable. I have an idea that the fourth valve is as much a status symbol as anything else (on the tuba as well). This is one of our difficult problems in intonation: the make of the instrument, and its accoutrements or lack of them, often become more important to the player than intonation. Only a thin line separates an American-made from a foreign-made instrument in either direction, a *status symbol* from a *gadget*. And when a player thinks one instrument is better than another, it usually is — for him, and for his purposes and standards. It is our job to try to educate him, to convince him that playing out of tune as an individual or virtuoso soloist is really as bad as playing out of tune in an ensemble.

There are now euphoniums with good basic harmonic series, four valves, and movable tuning slides. We purchased some of them, and considered them near-perfect instruments. Now if we could add the third valve compensating feature they indeed would become super-perfect instruments.

Tubas (Double B♭ Only)

Our solution to good intonation in the tubas was quite similar to, and actually preceded, that of the euphoniums. We selected a three-valve compensating instrument with a remarkably good harmonic pattern. The manufacturer changed the length of the main tuning slide, the valve slides, and one of the compensating loops according to our findings, and adopted these specifications for future production. With a minimum use of alternate fingerings we found the instrument remarkably in tune, and our section one of the most dependable for intonation in the band. However, the tuba majors came to prefer a larger bore four-valve instrument which became available. It was our decision to change to this latter instrument, for it was indeed a fine one — in tone quality, response, and potentially in intonation. The students liked to play it better, and undoubtedly they felt a rise in their status (besides having four valves it was also bell-up rather than bell-front), but we had more intonation problems within the section, as well as between the tubas and other instruments, than we had with the former set of instruments.

Horns

We did little with the horns except to select two makes and models which were entirely satisfactory from an intonation standpoint. Some of them required shortening of one of the main tuning slides, and all of them needed critical internal tuning by pulling all the valve slides and keeping them so pulled. Still, the apex of status swung back and forth between the two makes, and both suffered from competition with other makes and models not as well in tune but endorsed by and bearing the names of horn heroes. The heroes no doubt play or have played their horns perfectly, but the students do not do as well.

Trombones

Again we did nothing here except to select instruments for size of bore and desirable tone quality and response. We did not consider the harmonic pattern of particular importance in the trombone because the players could always find the slide position for the right tube length for any tone. We were disappointed, however, in two ways: (1) all the trombones, the tenors at least, were sharp in some of the sixth harmonics of the series, a result of making the instruments with essentially corrected fifth harmonics; and (2) the players were reluctant to bring down these sharp tones (high E♭, E and F) to proper pitch by extending the slide an inch or so from the positions of the octaves below. I believe I would prefer an instrument with an in-tune sixth harmonic and a flat fifth; it might be easier to teach the players to shorten the positions for B, C and C♯ above the staff and use fourth position for D. The player would always prefer to sharpen rather than flatten the tone. He has the means to do both on every tone on his instrument except the low B♭, which, without the now common F attachment, he can only flatten. If he does not play in tune, it is solely because he does not recognize in-tuneness.

Mallets

We soon had our celeste and chimes retuned from A = 442 to A = 440. Later I personally retuned the celeste to achieve a straight up and down pattern, rather than the maker-tuner's pattern of "stretching" (somewhat matching the piano). We found in our inventory a set of wonderful, thick steel bells which had not been used at least for a long time, apparently because they were tuned to A = 440 in a straight up and down pattern — just what we wanted! Within the past few years we purchased a new celeste, xylophone and marimba, after with great pleasure and satisfaction finding them in tune with themselves and with each other at A = 440. We now had no difficulty in matching pitches between and among winds and mallets and harp.

Part III

In 1954 I prepared a series of "tuning guides" for wind instruments, and had them affixed inside the concert folios for ready reference and study by all band members. In the early 1960's they were incorporated in a book by Ralph Pottle, who also published the tuning guides separately in card form.* The gratifying sale of the book and of the guides, through several printings, has indicated the general desire of conductors and teachers to really get hold of the intonation problem and to do something about it. And I honestly believe that more bands play better in tune now than 10 or 15 years ago.

The tuning guides deal primarily with "mechanical" tuning, i.e., with adjustment of joints and slides. They assume and/or encourage the careful selection and any necessary modification of the instrument. Also, it is explained that in many of the instruments most of the joints and slides can be rather permanently set on an individual basis, their setting tested by experience, and only then adjusted further. Tuning by and for the band ensemble can thus be limited almost entirely to a single tone for each instrument. For the woodwinds this tone should be one at or near the "top" of the instrument (near the mouthpiece), where changing the length of tubing causes the greatest change in pitch. (Tuning the clarinet to third space C at the barrel or mouthpiece is an extreme example of *unintelligent* tuning, but one which unfortunately has not yet been stamped out.) For the brasses the tone should be the key tone of the instrument near the middle of its register. Concert B♭ is used for the flutes, all the E♭ clarinets, tenor saxophone, and all the B♭ brasses; concert F is used

*Editor's note: Both the book *Tuning the School Band and Orchestra*, and the guides are available from Ralph Pottle, 407 N. Magnolia St., Hammond, La. 70401.

for bassoons and horns, and concert E♭ is used for all the B♭ clarinets and E♭ saxophones.

At Illinois we encouraged tuning to these tones by attaching a tuning bar of the right pitch to a chair at each desk of players. We frequently sounded the tuning tones and various other tones of oscillators provided by the Petersen Chromatic Tuner over a range of five octaves. We also made available a Stroboconn and a Petersen Tuner for individual reference between rehearsals. And we used to a limited extent a remarkable and rather new electronic instrument called the Johnson Intonation Trainer. This is a keyboard instrument having two scales: one tuned permanently to equal temperament, and the other susceptible to tuning each tone and its octaves through a wide pitch range by turning a set of knobs. The Johnson Intonation Trainer provides a ready and accurate way of studying and demonstrating temperaments, melodically and harmonically. Ideally its use should be extended to the individual and to small groups of players and classes. The instrument can make an effective contribution to proper ear training.

We have had still another device to test instruments and their players and to develop sensitivity to pitch in unisons, octaves, and primary chord intervals. We recorded our electric organ in octaves, in equal temperament, in the first phrase of the melody of the Doxology in all twelve keys. We wrote out this phrase for each instrument in such a way that every tone in the normal register is represented. In one third of the keys the instrument plays in unison or in octaves with the recording, in another third it plays in one harmonization of the melody, and in the final third in a different harmonization. We called this set-up our "Intonation Doctorology," and let me assure you that it really "separates the men from the boys" in the instrument-player combination, and does indeed "doctor up" intonation.

Some Examples of Tuning/Playing Problems and Solutions

It is typical for many flutists, especially the younger ones, to keep the headjoint all or nearly all the way in, and then possibly to blow down to tune. I say "possibly" be-cause many of them have been conditioned to hear and to tune sharp to the tuning tone. But if they have blown down in tuning, when they start to play in ensemble they will revert to their sharpness. Some of this is no doubt in self defense, because of the usual sharpness of so many clarinet players in the upper register.

Because of the unusual perfection of the flute as an instrument, I have found a device which has produced quite good results. It is to use the fingering of the low E♭ to produce the harmonic B♭ above the staff. This harmonic tone is not so susceptible to humoring as is the tone with the regular fingering (again especially with the younger student), so I ask the player to adjust the headjoint until the harmonic tone is in tune, and see that the headjoint is pulled far enough to make this possible. Then I ask the player to produce the same pitch with the regular fingering. This procedure achieves, to a remarkable degree, two results: (1) tuning the instrument mechanically, and (2) stabilizing the direction of air through the embouchure and into the blowhole for optimum tone production. It is possible to play the flute well in tune through three octaves.

Oboe players have a tendency to take too much reed in the mouth, which results in (1) uneven intonation at the change of octave around third space C, (2) flatness in the low octave, and (3) sharpness in the second octave.

Bassoons and E♭ saxophones can be very far out of tune when the conventional B♭ concert pitch is used as a tuning tone.

The best tuning on the B♭ soprano clarinet is achieved when we tune to the thumb F (concert E♭), change register tubes so that this F will overblow a perfect 12th to an in-tune high C, then tune the middle joint just above the staff, and tune the bell to B third line, if necessary boring a hole in the bell to correct flatness caused by reducing the size of the register hole. It is then possible for the performer to play this instrument well in tune throughout its normal register.

Every one of the above examples can be convincingly demonstrated by tape recordings we have made.

Clarinet Section Tuning Experiment

I once asked the whole soprano clarinet section to keep their instruments closed at the middle and at the bell and to tune with the barrel to third space C (concert B♭), which, as I have said, is what is still being done in so many bands. I then had my section play a harmonized chorale. I may say that I was surprised at how well they played with this tuning, and for a few moments wondered if the more complicated tuning I had been prescribing was all that worthwhile. However, I then asked the players to tune to the thumb F (almost all of them had to change the prior adjustment of the barrel to do this), then to G above the staff (more than two-thirds of them found it necessary to pull at the bell). When we repeated the chorale with the new tuning, the difference was amazing. The experience was dramatic proof and reaffirmation to both players and conductor of the worthwhileness of detailed and exacting mechanical tuning. It also served to remind us that we could be lulled into accepting a standard of intonation considerably less than perfect, considerably less than the best.

I can tell you of a still more contrasting "before and after" experience. One September we accepted eight new soprano clarinet players into the Concert Band. Six of them were freshmen, one a sophomore, and the other a graduate student. All of them had been first chair players in their high school bands, and all but one brought in their own first-line instruments. I called them together to test them and their instruments on intonation. I asked them to tune to B♭ concert without further instruction or comment, then we played and recorded a scale and two four-part chorales. In this case, the intonation was surprisingly atrocious, even worse than I could have anticipated. Then began the process of choosing and adapting for each of the players an appropriate instrument from our set, on a tentative basis at this meeting, with a somewhat more detailed — yet still incomplete — checkup in the following few days. At the beginning of the next band rehearsal, without time for warm-up, I asked the eight players with their new instruments to sit in the front row. We tuned to the thumb F only, then repeated and recorded the scale and the two chorales. The improvement was almost unbelievable. Though the intonation was not perfect, the potential for perfection was already there.

Arthur Williams, former band conductor at Oberlin and a brass specialist and expert, has written, "In the hands of a brass player who has learned how to listen skillfully and appreciate varying degrees of sharpness and flatness, the mechanisms which permit this player to *sharp* or *flat* any tone that he can sound so as to play it in tune with any other instrument and still play a tone which is resonantly centered as to quality [this] is the *mechanism we must eventually all learn how to use and accept.*"

I also quote the tuba virtuoso and professor at Indiana University, the late William Bell. "Having found an instrument with good open tones and one on which the first, third and fourth valves can be manipulated with the left hand, there should be no excuse for playing any note out of tune."

This concept of "tuning while you play," which string players and singers and trombone players already can do, is one which is readily adaptable to valve brass instruments and its practicability proven. So many players say they can play their instruments in tune by lipping only. There may be some merit in conquering the intonation on an imperfect valve brass instrument without slide manipulation, like the merit in climbing a mountain because it is there. However, the ultimate goals are to achieve perfect intonation and to get to the top of the mountain, and there is no more sense in depriving the brass or other wind player of valuable tools on his instrument than there is in depriving the mountain climber of rope, axe, and piton.

By way of approaching a conclusion, I wish to quote a few pertinent sentences from the rather short chapter on intonation from the book, *The Art of Oboe Playing*, by Robert Sprenkle and David Ledet.[1] This chapter is so fine a presentation of general intonation fact and philosophy that, with the publisher's permission, I had it duplicated and distributed to the concert folios of our bands for study and reference. I quote: "Powerful disruptive forces result from the divergent tendencies of various musical instruments . . . The use of an accurate, impartial device like the Stroboconn is perfect for measuring the extent of these divergences. This information, to be useful, must be properly interpreted in an unemotional and objective way which is only possible in an atmosphere of mutual respect and cooperation . . . Ensemble playing is a democratic process, and the pitch problem can only be solved by sharing it . . . The mistaken idea that being sharp will provide brilliance to the tone is a cheap way of taking advantage of other players, because sharpness is a comparative condition and can exist only when someone else is flat . . . Some musicians prefer the Pythagorean tuning, some the 'just' intonation, and others the 'tempered' scale. We probably use them all at different times and in different passages, but only the 'just' intonation will tune vertically through chords. In any case, the differences in these systems of tuning are less than the errors that usually offend our ears because of carelessness. Learning to play in tune is a complicated process, requiring sensitivity, control, and understanding."

Conclusion

The wind and percussion instruments that are available for our use in bands surely have benefitted from the technological period in which we are living. The finest tone quality and the greatest facility are readily available to our bandsmen. However, many problems of intonation remain. These are handicaps to the player who is challenged to overcome them by a combination of physical, mental, and musical effort. There would seem to be an alliance of inability and resistance in the matter of building into some of the instruments good basic intonation properties. There is a tendency on the part of nearly all concerned to accept undesirable tendencies as "handicaps to be lived with forever" instead of "problems to be solved." In so many cases, response and facility are considered before and above intonation; and much of the time "response" is apt to be measured in terms of "brilliance," which often is only "sharpness." When one instrument is not as sharp on some tones as another, the first instrument is often pronounced "stuffy." Until we are able to convince ourselves, our own players, and the manufacturers that we do not want sharpness, or flatness either for that matter, we will continue to have instruments that are unnecessarily difficult, if not impossible, to play in tune. Knowing the characteristics of so many deficient instruments, I marvel at how well in tune some bands play, and deplore and sympathize with others that play badly out of tune. Instruments built with more intonation accuracy and standardization would make it *easier* for the good bands to play in tune, and more nearly *possible* for the others. Certainly technology will provide this for us, if we will recognize the problems and agree on what we want. I do not wish to put too much blame on the instrument makers, for no doubt they are responding in large measure to what we will accept. I believe we ourselves are the key to better intonation in instruments, individual players and organizations. What we hear, what we learn, what we know, what we teach can make the big difference in band intonation. I hope this series of articles has made some contribution to that end. ∎

February, 1966

Intonation

RALPH G. LAYCOCK

"Your last note is almost higher than I can match, would you mind lowering it a little?" And then the members of the woodwind quintet tried the final chord again, this time to everyone's satisfaction. The occasion was the rehearsal of the quintet made up of first chair men of the Philadelphia Orchestra just prior to their recital in Utah several years ago. Significantly, there had been no discussion of who was correct—they just wanted to be sure that they would be able to tune to each other satisfactorily in the coming concert. That was evidently more important to them than being "right" in any "tempered" or any other arbitrarily-selected "scale."

If any one aspect of good ensemble can be called democratic, in that a consensus of opinion is apt to be correct, intonation may well be said to be that factor. For no-one can take the attitude that he is always right. Even if his pitch is theoretically closer to correct than is anyone else's if he is not in tune with them, *he is wrong*! And this is true even if he is the person who gave the pitch to which the group tuned only thirty seconds ago! That the organization may need some training and practice in constantly maintaining a satisfactory pitch level may be true, but at any given moment the person who is not "with" the going pitch cannot be considered to be in tune.

Achieving intonation is a battle that we can never quite win, but one that we must certainly never quit fighting. Laying aside any scholarly discussion, good intonation is attained when the pitches of all related musical tones of fixed frequency (excluding non-tuned sounds) are such that they combine in a manner agreeable to the sensitive (sensitized!) ear; in our case, the ear attuned to sounds related to each other in the relatively simple mathematical ratios most common to music of the western hemisphere. Both vertical (harmonic) and horizontal (melodic) relationships are significant, but those tones sounding simultaneously may well be heard as being more obviously in- or out-of-tune because of presence of induced pulsations or "beats" set up by any interval other than a perfectly tuned perfect unison. In practical music-making, imperfectly tuned unisons, fourths, fifths, and octaves are almost always considered undesirable; in part because the beats so caused are quite audible. Other intervals being more subject to personal preference ("low" vs. "high" thirds, sevenths, etc.), let us stay, for now, with those on which most musicians can agree that the intonation improves as the "beats" become slower and fewer, and the interval is literally "perfect" when "beats" are entirely absent. We will also avoid bringing in "difference tones" for the present.

Indeed, there are enough difficulties in achieving the most basic and most obvious aspect of intonation, the elimination of beats in the perfect intervals, to at times almost frighten us into taking "the better part of valour" and vacating the field entirely in this never-ending war. Though future articles will deal more specifically with some of the following matters, a brief listing of some of the difficulties to be overcome may be helpful in drawing up our plan of attack:

(1) "Environmental" problems—pitch level of the organization (or lack of one), temperature, humidity, draftiness, acoustical properties of the room, and even such things as wrong notes in the parts.

(2) Faults of instruments—slipping pegs, false strings, wolf tones, notes "built out-of-tune," faulty adjustment, improper reeds and/or mouthpieces, foreign matter (or object!) in the instrument, sluggish key action, dents, leaks, wrong French horn slides, and (still occasionally) "high-pitched" or other "wrong-pitched" instruments.

(3) Faults of players—the list is endless, but may perhaps be summed up in several main categories—lack of awareness of the sound and value of good intonation, failure to control instrument properly due to unfamiliarity with its deficiencies or being too fully occupied with other problems, and inattention resulting in out-of-tune playing even though they know and can do better.

(4) Faults of conductors—insensitivity to good intonation (or rather to bad "outoftonation"), inability to teach intonation, and a fatalistic attitude about it ("after all, they're only kids").

I am convinced that *no* group of youngsters can possibly play well in tune without their instructor's constant sympathetic (and at times *unsympathetic*) and knowledgeable attention to securing good intonation. But I am equally convinced that, given proper guidance and incentive, most young people can greatly improve their ability to play in tune and rather quickly at that! The key, as always, is good leadership, a combination of sensitivity to intonation, knowledge of techniques of instilling this same sensitivity in the students, and the will to keep at it eternally.

There are, however, a number of well-known clichés about intonation which provide a convenient excuse for those who for one reason or another fail to achieve satisfactory results. May I attempt to rebut them?

Wind instruments, other than trombones, are built with a "tempered" scale, and are consequently played in "tempered" intonation.

They are not, and cannot be, built perfectly in tune with the tempered scale. As a goal it is commendable because it attempts to bring every note within "bending" distance of its proper pitch in *any* musical context. Let it be admitted that in fast passages little or no attempt can be made to humor every individual note, but when a note lasts long enough to be recognized by the sensitive ear as being satisfactory or unsatisfactory in pitch, it is long enough to warrant special effort by the performer to place it correctly. No conscientious wind player is content to use the pitch that just happens to be "natural" to his instrument, but is constantly concerned with the pitch that he should be playing and is doing all he can to humor his notes to match those being sounded by others. Because each type of instrument (and even individual samples of the same type), has different "bad" notes than every other, there is a constant give-and-take in a well-trained group that is demonstrated by satisfactory over-all intonation. And musicians in such a group find it easier to tell when they are in tune *when they are in tune*, rather than being two, three, four and one-quarter, or any other arbitrary number of vibrations sharp or flat, as would be demanded by the "tempered" scale, "well-" or otherwise.

Strings and trombones are the only instruments that can be played perfectly in tune.
The placement of the finger on the string and the positioning of the slide give these instruments great leeway in the pitch level of all but one note on each instrument. But this is a liability as well as an advantage since it takes the greatest virtuosity to perform fast passage work accurately. (If you doubt it, select a very demanding passage in a tape or record of even a famous violinist and play it at half-speed—you may find that your ear has accepted, at full speed, imperfections in pitch that it quickly rejects at the slower, more revealing tempo. And passages that are impossible on the slide trombone can be played fairly well in tune on the valved instrument.) In fact, the normal wind instruments, with their ready-made fingerings, are able to play certain types of passages (fast scales, for instance) more accurately than their more flexible-pitched cousins—they were at least "tuned at the factory," which is more than the players of strings and trombones can ever claim. So far as I am concerned,

when individual instruments are considered, this skirmish is about a stand-off. The advantage that strings are often credited with owes part of its support to the beautiful intonation possible in slow music and to the fact that in an orchestra they are heard *en masse,* and the resulting fusion of sound minimizes individual discrepancies, errors which cannot be masked in the orchestral winds because they are acting in the capacity of solo voices.

He can't play in tune because he has a tin ear.
Though this is one of the most damning things that can be said about a mature person who has his instrument otherwise under satisfactory control, it cannot be said with finality about a younger person, and in this group I certainly include college students. (It is a sad fact that many of them have had little opportunity to develop such sensitivity. I once had a freshman clarinetist who tuned consistently about five vibrations sharp to the others around him. When quizzed about it, he stated that he did so because that was the way they had always tuned at home. But when convinced that the absence of such beats indicated real intonation he could, within a couple of weeks, match pitch very rapidly and accurately.) In fact, I sincerely believe that my own sensitivity has improved significantly since my undergraduate days and would not deny the possibility of that same development to anyone of any age who earnestly desires to improve both his own and his group's sense of intonation. Intensive work with it sharpens one's discrimination in the same way that one can learn to listen more critically for tone quality, balance, or any other musical element. For most of us, it is still ninety-nine per cent perspiration!

Playing chorales is an excellent way to improve intonation.
Playing chorales *is* an excellent way of improving intonation if a real intonation-teaching technique is used. Playing any piece is (and should be!) an excellent way of improving intonation if a real intonation-teaching technique is used. Simple chorales and chorale-like pieces, (in which the parts move

by step and small intervals in primarily diatonic harmony and in largely identical rhythmic values) provide an especially fertile field for training in pitch sensitivity if adequate time and effort are spent on each individual chord to accomplish the task, then they are fitted together carefully so that each one retains its good intonation when the piece is played through in a steady tempo. To merely "play through" a chorale because it is "good for you" is a total waste of time for the organization that does not already have a keen sensitivity built up through much earnest endeavour!

Tuning to one note is useless.
Though this alone will not make an organization play in tune, it is certainly far better than nothing at all. If the tuning note is not left until it is properly tuned, and everyone can tell that it is so tuned, they have gained a certain amount of sensitivity in the process. And the more important advantage is that they are now close enough to a uniform level that, given the opportunity to find the exact pitch needed throughout the coming rehearsal or concert, they *can* humor their instruments far enough to be successful. It is not unlike tuning a TV set; one must be tuned to the correct channel before the "Fine Tuning" adjustment can be of any help.

In summary, achieving good intonation is a task that no conductor can ever hope to accomplish through his own efforts alone. Nor is it possible for the players, even though they may individually have a well-developed sense of pitch, to arrive at the goal of good intonation by themselves. But as everyone learns and accepts his own share of responsibility for the final outcome, the improvement attained allows stronger light to be focused on the formerly murky interior, and continued effort can result in intonation that can be one of the truly beautiful aspects of the group's performance.

And even if total victory is to be forever denied us, we can at least be assured that continued effort and eternal vigilance will effectively take care of the "border incidents" that are bound to occur.

Nowhere High School,
Nowhere, N.W.

Dear Mr. Laycock:
You will never know the furor you've raised around here for the past three months. It started with the kids smuggling in those articles and passing them around and went on for two months before I intercepted one in band one day. Was I furious! You should have seen the letter my wife made me burn! But things really blew apart during the dress rehearsal for the Christmas concert. The band kept rushing, of all things, the march we had used all fall for our halftime entrance, and finally the first cornetist asked me if perhaps it could be partly *my* fault. Highly indignant, I shouted, "Why don't you do it yourselves?" and stormed down the aisle toward my office. Well, some brave drummer thumped out a roll-off, and they did it themselves, and in perfect tempo! I was pretty shocked, but after I cooled off I realized that I had been seriously underestimating them. So I've tried one or two new tricks; I'm putting more of the responsibility on them, and I find that I can relax and really listen for perhaps the first time. Generally this is helpful and we are really shaping up, but one thing is throwing me—I can hear how bad the intonation really is!

So, I have been trying to read up on it, but so far am just getting more confused. I used to think there were two kinds, good and bad, but now find that there are at least three kinds of good intonation —equal tempered, just, and Pythagorean. I guess they are all good; each has champions who claim that the others are impossible. I could quote them but I'm sure you know what I mean.

So, which is the best? And how do I start getting it?
Desperately,
Gettin N. Phast
Dir. of Bands,
Nowhere High School

Dear Mr. Phast:
May I tell you how sincerely I admire you for your willingness to try new ideas. And whether or not they all work is not important, some will feel right to you and will assist you in your earnest desire to give your students the best that is in you. (Some day I'll tell how I was taught to keep my head out of the score.)

Now for your problem, and mine —intonation.

Nothing is as elusive as intonation—"here today and gone tomorrow." Even on a concert one piece may be well in tune but another, equally well-rehearsed, devastatingly out of tune, due to nothing more mysterious than a rise in temperature on stage or to players' fatigue as the evening progresses. (A combination of both can be catastrophic.) Nothing, during actual performance, is less subject to the conductor's direct control; it should have been taken care of during the weeks and months before the concert.

As for your first question, "Which is the best?" I confess that I do not have an unequivocal answer. If I, for the price of a tuning job on a piano, could have an orchestra or band that played as well in tune as that "equal-tempered" instrument I would be first in line with cash on the barrelhead. But good intonation cannot be bought for any price except that of constant, knowledgeable, and sensitive attention to it, and if the price at times seems high, we must realize that we are also getting sonority, blend, beauty of tone, transparency of texture, and other valuable musical attributes.

I doubt that *any* organization could decide to use one of the three "scales" and stick exclusively to it. Intonation must literally be "played by ear" as you go along, and the group that displays the most give and take is the group that plays best in tune. For we must remember that the rigid system of "equal-temperament" is a fairly recent invention, and finds its best use on keyboard and other such instruments that can be tuned very precisely to that (or any other) scale, but cannot be instantly retuned for different needs. We can see but cannot hear "cents," and a player could set a stroboscope in front of himself in band and play every note right in tune with it but be miserably out of tune with his fellows. The strobe is a marvelous instrument for the researcher and the instrument manufacturer, and it is equally a blessing to the performer when it informs him of problems which he may have been unaware or indifferent to, but it cannot develop auditory sensitivity to *real* intonation. You may use it to great advantage in your music program, but do not abdicate your responsibility for the final product to *any* machine.

Which intonation is best? It depends on the context of each measure and is often a compromise. Indeed, the solution might conceivably be different in successive playings and still be right. Confusing? So too it must be to the athletic teams who find that even though they have a play down pat, it must be adjusted on the spur of the moment nearly every time they run it. But they do not win without certain basic plays and options that have been made letter perfect. Nor does a musical organization play in tune without an intimate knowledge of the proper relationship of each note to its neighbors, a knowledge gained through slow and careful work. You might as well hope that a marching band could take one look at the charts of a new show then go out and do it perfectly the first time as to expect a concert band to play any piece in tune without knowing how it should sound. And strings have a greater problem than winds, especially in the higher positions.

The reason that mature groups can play well in tune while sight-reading is that they are made up of performers who can "hear with their eyes" and so usually know the sound of a note before they are required to produce it.

Now for your second question, "How do I start getting it?" I think you will concede that it is just a little difficult to teach intonation by correspondence, but perhaps I can give you a few things to try.

First of all, may I suggest that you spend some time with (and acquire for your department if possible) one of these new "variable-pitch" electronic intonation devices, several makes of which are just now coming on to the market. (Not that I don't think you can "hear." The fact that you are so concerned about your group's intonation encourages me in that respect.) I recommend it just to boost your confidence in your ability to set up a perfect fifth that is demonstrably perfect, a major triad that is a major triad, etc., before you start going out on limbs telling your students that they are sharp or flat. Then I suggest that you go to work both on individual and ensemble intonation, beginning with a demonstration of "beats" and their elimination.

With a variable-pitch device or with normal instruments or both, demonstrate something like the following:

Have two trombonists (rehearsed if necessary) stand where all can watch their slides and have them play A3 perfectly in tune. Then have one gradually move his slide outward (downward) as you point out the beats, the pulsations that speed up as he moves the slide down. Let him return to a perfect unison and then move upward, producing faster beats again as he moves continually higher. (The moving slide gives visual confirmation of the change of pitch.) The groans of those students who are sensitive will quickly indoctrinate many to whom beats have not previously seemed undesirable. A similar demonstration by two clarinetists playing high C5, one of whom varies his pitch by raising and lowering his jaw, will be even more startling, beat-wise, and should be a clincher for most of those who have been as yet undecided about the whole thing. But you may have a few who will take even more

work before they recognize beats and realize their implications in tuning. Stick with them.

All players should spend time in pairs, preferably on like instruments, practicing eliminating beats from unison notes. As information on methods of humoring are readily available in many text and method books, I do not propose to go into it much at this time. The procedure is as follows: after careful tuning of the "tuning note" and adjustment of the instruments to each other thereby, one player, designated as the *leader*, holds a steady tone on a specified note while the other, the *follower*, attempts to eliminate all beats by humoring up or down in pitch without changing the over-all tuning of his instrument if possible. It is important that someone, and it can be one of the players if capable, be present to disapprove or to warmly approve the results being obtained. Then they should reverse roles so that each realizes the responsibility of matching the pitch set up for him. A valuable variation on this is for the leader, after being found, to repeat the note but at a significantly different pitch, by humoring it, altering the fingering, etc., so that the follower is obliged to really search for the pitch. This eliminates any "chance" good intonation and makes it certain that they are indeed finding each other. It must be realized that the beats will not entirely disappear unless each player is producing an absolutely steady pitch without waver and without intentional vibrato. Such practice will not hurt their tone, either!

As they gain proficiency in matching unisons through the entire working range of their instruments, they will probably find that some notes are noticeably more difficult to tune than are others. It is here that the stroboscope can be of real help, for by its aid they can begin to learn the failings of their (wind) instrument and of their embouchure, etc. If a student cannot produce the same pitch, as seen on the strobe, consistently, he is manifestly unable to tune perfectly to another instrument and must develop a more trustworthy approach to his own before he can solve the more difficult problems of intonation. But, in spite of satisfactory

work in this regard, there will still be discrepancies which must be attributed to the instrument and the player must overcome them, by repair or adjustment if possible, by humoring if necessary.

Armed now with some information about their instruments, their embouchures, etc., the pair of students may now move on to octave studies. Starting at the unison, one then moves to the octave above or below, tuning it to the original note still being held by the other player. When he locks it in place, the other player may then move to the same note and tune to it in like fashion, thus:

This is a real problem on the "bad" notes of most instruments and can be quite an eye-opener to those who thought that you just push the button and the note comes out. For variety, they can start an octave apart and change simultaneously to the other octave, attempting to reproduce exactly the pitch that the other has just left, thus:

These latter two versions are especially valuable in matching notes that are particularly out-of-tune and those that are at the extremes of range, where a unison might be tuned together, but tuned *out-of-tune* together.

Many youngsters have gone this far but failed to realize that other **intervals can be just as badly out of tune as the unison and the octave, but they are likewise just as easy to correct by listening for beats. Perfect fourths and fifths respond in the same manner. When perfectly tuned they seem almost to blend into one sound as do the unison and octave. The same exercises as above are equally useful in helping students to tune them exactly and immediately.**

During this careful tuning they may have become aware of still other pitches being produced, very quietly but consistently, by the intervals on which they are working. And they may have noted that when the interval itself is well in tune, the "combination tones" are perfectly consonant with them in the following relationships:

These combination tones become very valuable as the tuning project is extended to thirds and sixths, for the intervals themselves do not produce the beats that are so helpful in the perfect intervals. In this situation the combination tone is consonant with the interval actually being sounded only when that interval is perfectly in tune according to the just scale.

In the following examples the small quarter notes are the combination tones being produced by the whole notes which are actually being sounded. When the players can hear and tune these smaller notes accurately, they can be sure that their upper notes are in tune and gradually learn to gauge the interval itself without having to rely on the combination tones as a guide. It should be obvious that only in a very quiet room will these quiet combination tones be audible.

Having become aware of the proper relationships between members of a two-note interval, the next step is for three persons to sustain three-note chords, checking the pitch of the individual intervals as necessary to ensure satisfactory over-all intonation. Gradually, the students will learn the composite sound of the entire chord and will be able to transfer this "memory" to other similar constructions in other keys and contexts.

Again let me stress that at least one sensitive person be in attendance to guide the hearing of the inexperienced player and to accept nothing but his best. This is the crux of the whole matter—the student's search for intonation will be no more successful than the standards set and maintained by the person into whose hands his training is entrusted, for it is he who decides what time and effort are necessary to accomplish his desires in this area, as in all other areas of musical endeavour.

Though detailed discussion of techniques of obtaining good intonation in the ensemble will have to be left to another time, the above exercises can be adapted for use in the full rehearsal as they are

needed to make the individual student aware of his responsibility in the total picture. And the same careful listening to and checking of intonation of chords, melodies, contrapuntal lines, etc., done slowly enough (much of the time without rhythmic pulse, just note for note) so that the students can find the exact pitch needed to put them in tune with the rest of the group, is haste enough. Not that the achievement of satisfactory intonation will forever be a long-drawn-out process. When they become accustomed to tuning constantly they will take care of a good proportion of the problems with only a minimum of help from the director, and only the particularly difficult spots will need specific work as such. But they will need reminding and help, and it must come from a person whose judgment they trust, whose judgment they *can trust*, or any improvement will be lost within a few rehearsals. For it is a cooperative thing; the director cannot be blessed with **good intonation unless the players provide it,** and they cannot provide it unless he gives them opportunity to "find" themselves any time it becomes apparent that they are not sure what their pitch should be. But together, they can scale the heights! ∎

Intonation in String Playing

Jack M. Pernecky

I T IS THE TEACHER'S RESPONSIBIL-ity to help his students develop good intonation. To place the fingers haphazardly on the strings or to accept a close proximity of proper finger placement is not good enough. One needs to guide the student in securing a firm understanding of the physical, aural, and visual concepts

necessary for playing in tune.

The teacher should decide upon methods that will best implement his own teaching philosophy. If the teacher does not believe in a particular organized approach then his effectiveness in using this approach will be negligible. A sincere effort by the teacher to try to find ways

to help his students play in tune will usually produce effective results. There must be definite approaches that are easy to explain to the student, easy to use by the student, and which successfully solve the problem of playing in tune.

Listed below are some suggested approaches to securing good intonation:

Finger Patterns

In each key, establish a system of finger measurements or relationships for the left four fingers. The fingers will develop a "feel" of where they are placed on the fingerboard and the space measurement of whole and half steps in each key.

For example, during the very first violin lessons the beginning student learns to "set" the four fingers in the first tonal pattern. If the method book uses the D major approach, the first finger is "set" about 1¼ inches from the nut on a full size violin; the measurement between the first and second fingers is a whole step or about 1¼ inches; the measurement between the second and third fingers is a half-step and the fingers are adjacent; the measurement between the third and fourth fingers is a whole step or about 1 inch. The same procedure can be used in locating and "setting" the fingers in this key on the other string instruments.

Employ a silent finger exercise using all four fingers, then pluck these tones in half or whole note rhythms repeatedly making sure that the fingers are placed in their proper positions (Fig. 1). The fingers should be kept in place wherever possible.

Fig. 1

Violin:

This tonal pattern should be practiced many times a day in order to "set" the four fingers and the hand in their proper places. The left hand must be shaped properly so that the fingers may fall in their proper places in a curved manner.

The immediate placement and use of all four fingers is strongly advocated. Beginners can learn to use all fingers from the very start. There are many advantages in this procedure. (1) It immediately forms the first finger pattern in the key of D major. The first half of the scale is created. (2) The finger measurements for the major and minor intervals are established. This impresses upon the student the significance of half- and whole-step relationships in the key. (3) All fingers must be curved. In order to make this possible, the left elbow and hand must be in proper playing position. The

elbow is well under the violin and viola. The palm of the left hand must not touch the neck, but should be placed to the right of the fingerboard so that the fingers can "fall" from the knuckles. The line of the knuckles is parallel to the fingerboard on the cello and bass. (4) It also helps to place the left thumb in the correct position in relation to the other fingers. (5) Simple tunes can be learned immediately with these five tones.

Why delay the use of all four fingers? The conventional method of introducing one finger at a time over a period of several weeks is merely delaying the progress of the student. He can play tunes using the four fingers in the second or third lesson. They could be played in pizzicato style while the bow grip and bowing action are being developed on the open strings.

As the student expands into the second half of the D major scale he finds the measurements of this part of the scale the same as those in the first half of the scale.

As the student learns new keys, he learns new patterns of note relationships. He "sets" his fingers in the half- and whole-step framework of the new key and scale on each string. As new scales are learned old scales should be reviewed in order to retain and solidify old patterns.

Playing in Tune

Ear training is necessary so that the student can recognize whether he is playing in or out of tune.

How does the teacher train the ear of his student? One of the best ways is by the rote system of learning. That is, having the student imitate as accurately as possible the melody, rhythm, tempo, left hand position, etc., played by the teacher. The student is not concerned with reading music, learning a rhythm system, etc. These early songs can be learned by playing pizzicato. Meanwhile, the bow grip and bowing action can be practiced on the open strings. Incidently, various rhythms may be used to develop bowing agility on the open strings.

The teacher can present these simple rote songs in various ways. All three approaches may be used. (A) The teacher plays the song or exercise on the instrument. Pitch, melody, finger placement and meas-

urement, posture, hand position, pizzicato playing or bowing, and rhythms are observed. This procedure serves as a direct model for seeing and hearing the total picture.

(B) The teacher tunes the instrument to the piano and then plays the song and exercise on the piano, being very explicit as to style and rhythm. The student taps his foot while the teacher plays. The younger player "sets" his left hand and fingers and imitates the tones he hears from the piano. Short two or four measure phrases should be used. The teacher should not play along with the student as this may make the student dependent upon the piano rather than on his own ear in creating correct pitches. This approach is similar to the one used by the elementary vocal teacher who teaches songs by rote. Pupils learn melody, rhythm, and words in this manner.

(C) An excellent procedure when learning pitches and rhythms is to have the student sing the melody. Generally speaking, the student who can sing the tune can play it easier and more accurately on his instrument. The teacher introduces the song by singing it and then plays it on the piano or on an instrument.

Mechanical Devices

Developing the ear to hear the proper pitches can be helpful with the use of mechanical devices. The student can see where he needs to place his fingers. By constantly placing his fingers on markers he develops pitch recognition and accurate finger placement. This, done over a period of several weeks, will greatly assist ear training, finger measurement, and placement.

A narrow strip of gummed tape or a paper star can serve as a marker. If the key of D major is used the marker is placed across the fingerboard designating where the first finger would be placed.

This method of ear training is less tedious than the ones mentioned previously. This is training the eyes so that they see the proper placement of the fingers—"The eyes train the ears." Many teachers believe that the use of markers deters the development of the ear. But many students benefit greatly from this system. This approach is easier and more effective for many students. However, the young string player must be aware of hearing good intonation even with these aids. Singing the tune or exercise is also recommended when using markers. The markers should serve as a guide for playing on pitch and not as a substitute for the ear.

Markers are particularly effective in string class work. The teacher can see that the students are playing in tune. The student (who generally cannot hear himself very well in group work) can see where his fingers should be placed.

All of these methods can be used simultaneously. That is, the markers, rote teaching, and singing can be used interchangeably when teaching the beginner. Even before he begins to learn theory and the many aspects of note-reading the student begins to play short tunes or exercises. Pizzicato playing could be used for the tunes, and the bow can be used to play various rhythms, developing bowing actions on the open strings.

Different Patterns

The student should become aware of the changes in finger patterns or measurements (the different locations of half and whole steps in each key) as he progresses from key to key. The establishment of good intonation in each key is accomplished by accurate placement of the fingers.

After the D major pattern is successfully accomplished, the next key could be C major. This new key creates a second pattern with different measurements.

The following procedures might be used to help locate and establish good intonation in the new key: Locate similar half and whole steps between the familiar D major key and the new C major key; locate the half and whole steps in the new key.

The only difference on the violin and viola is the location of the second finger which is placed adjacent to the first finger. Care must be taken so as not to lower the third and fourth fingers when the second is lowered.

The cello merely requires using the second finger for the F♮ instead of the third finger F♯. The string bass uses the second finger for F♮ instead of the fourth finger for F♯.

Knowing the measurements in each key and the similarities and differences will help locate correct finger patterns.

A silent finger exercise (Fig. 2) will facilitate this adjustment of the second finger.

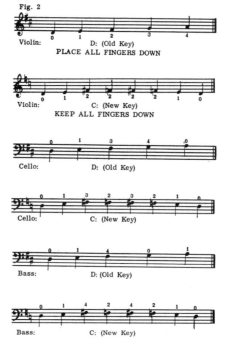

Fig. 2

The same procedure may be applied when learning new finger measurements in other keys.

Proper finger measurements also aid intonation by locating pitches that are not adjacent to each other. For instance, when progressing from the first finger to the third on the violin, place the second finger down with the third finger (one half-step apart). Keep the first finger down. The second finger helps to locate the distance between the first and third fingers. Three fingers are down so in a descending passage the fingers are in place. This is significant in that it helps to increase general technical facility. The fingers are always

in place ready to move quickly and accurately.

Octave Pitch Markings

Another approach to assist the student to establish good intonation is to have the teacher play exactly what the student is to play but an octave higher.

The student should keep his fingers flexible in order to make adjustments quickly to blend with the pitches of his teacher. The young player has a tangible pitch to match. If the teacher plays in unison with the student, it is more difficult to hear and match. As the student becomes accurate with octave pitch matching, he can then try to blend his tones with those of the teacher a third or a sixth apart.

This type of approach gives the student a greater challenge in ear training and proper pitch adjustment and placement.

Bow Pressure

Too much bow pressure on the strings generally will cause intonation problems. Tones become flat in pitch when an excessive amount of weight is placed on the strings, especially in a slow tempo. Even short, accented tones with too much pressure on the string will flatten the pitch. The strings must vibrate freely in all tempos and in all types of bowing to produce a vibrant tone. The weight exerted by the bow on the strings must be in proportion to the tempo and type of bowing.

Oftentimes poor concentration leads to poor intonation. Practice without serious thought will lead to improper finger placement and measurements. The teacher should encourage his students to be alert at all times to proper pitch production.

Slow and thoughtful practice is a necessity, especially when new problems are encountered. By practicing slowly and in rhythm the young player possesses more control over his movements.

Tuning the Woodwinds

George Waln

THE IMPLICATIONS IN THE PHRASE, "Tuning the Woodwinds," are important to all instrumentalists. In the performance of music, whether it be by one or one hundred players, satisfying results depend upon good intonation. Each component part of fine playing is obviously important —tone, phrasing, articulation, etc.— but no matter how beautiful the tone, the ensemble sound will be agreeable only with "in-tune" playing.

With the great differences in the woodwinds, in both construction and methods of tone production, almost insurmountable problems stand in the way of good intonation within the sections in bands, orchestras, and small ensembles. Before one can cope with these problems he must first have a thorough understanding of them.

Problems

What are some of these problems?

There are imperfections in construction in the instruments themselves, although in general, the manufacturers are doing a magnificent job. The acoustical laws of pitch on various woodwinds actually defy the building of the perfect instrument. From the maker's point of view it is a matter of compromise within the commonly fingered octaves or registers.

Improperly made mouthpieces and reeds cause great variance in the pitches. In both pitch and tone quality the differences between a fine mouthpiece and one that is improperly made are amazing.

One concrete suggestion for tuning the woodwinds is to use a common make and a common facing mouthpiece in the clarinet section. The American style of playing leans toward a medium tip opening and a medium length of lay.

Pitch on the woodwinds is affected by temperature changes. That is to say, the pitch produced by a cold instrument in a cold temperature will sound lower than when played by a warm instrument in warm temperature. A flute playing middle C in a temperature rise from 32 to 98 degrees will rise approximately one-half step.

Humidity, too, affects the pitch on all woodwinds. Humid air will cause lower pitch than dry air, because damp air is heavier and has a greater density than dry air, and slows the vibrations of any given note. Similarly, thin air in high altitudes offers less resistance to vibrating columns and encourages higher pitch.

In consideration of this temperature factor, another positive suggestion can be made which will help in tuning the woodwinds. Warm the instruments before formal tuning, and try to keep them warm while performing in concert or rehearsal.

The pitch problem is aggravated still further by the fact that the metal instruments—flute, piccolo, brasses —warm more quickly from exposure to the warm breath than do the instruments made of wood. In like manner, the metal instruments will cool more quickly than those made of wood. Further, the upper portion of the instruments, the portion nearest the warm breath, will warm first and will raise the notes in that part of the instrument to a greater extent than those produced by the longer tubing—the clarinet throat tones, for example.

Specific Problems

Playing in even temperature and on evenly warmed instruments will greatly aid in acquiring proper intonation.

Each player must learn how best to tune his own instrument.

With the flute there is a definite limit as to how far the head joint can be pulled to avoid upsetting the proportions between the tone holes. Sometimes the corked end may be lengthened slightly beyond the prescribed $^{11}\!/_{16}$ of an inch as an aid to lowering the sharp high notes. The head joint must be properly angled to fit the control of the player's embouchure.

The tuning of the oboe is done basically by the cut and length of the reed. Even a very little pulling of the reed will cause flat, squawky low notes.

Two or three bocals of different lengths are an aid in tuning the bassoon. But, like the oboe, the style and cut of the reed are most important, both in tuning and in over-all pitch. Thinning the reed farther away from the tip will lower the pitch on both the bassoon and oboe.

The pitch of the saxophone is, of course, mechanically altered by pushing or pulling the mouthpiece on the corked neck.

The clarinet has more possibilities for mechanical tuning by being able to pull not only at the barrel, but also at the middle joint and bell. To avoid sharp throat tones the place to start the tuning process is open "G." Normally, the Bb clarinet is made with the expectation that some pulling at the barrel will be needed. This is so that in cold temperatures the player will have some leeway to avoid playing flat.

After the throat tones are tuned with the barrel adjustment, the basic tuning is accomplished. It is not unusual, however, to find it necessary to pull at the middle joint to lower notes in the clarion register between C and G, or in the chalumeau register between low E and low C. At times the pulling of the bell will be helpful in lowering low E and its twelfth above.

The large clarinets have similar problems in the mechanical aspects of tuning. Because of their length the amount of pulling at the neck or mouthpiece will be much greater to affect a pitch change than with the B♭ clarinet.

Pitch Tendencies

Each player must overcome the faulty pitch tendencies of his own instrument. Even with a fine instrument, a good mouthpiece, and a good reed, the above tuning and temperature factors must be understood, but they are far from the whole story for playing in tune. The player must now play in tune, "not just finger and blow!" There is much "give and take" to playing in tune, with a good pitch blend, in a section of woodwinds. It involves several basic factors:

(A) One must listen carefully as he plays and must be discriminating enough in his hearing to know when he is in tune.

(B) He must possess a controlled, flexible embouchure, and adequate diaphragm support, to favor his pitch up or down. Favoring is impossible without the breath to back up the embouchure.

(C) One must know the faulty pitch tendencies of his instrument and anticipate and correct these faults as he plays.

A few faulty pitch tendencies, common to the respective woodwinds, which must be understood and corrected, are these: The flute tends to be sharp in crescendos and flat in diminuendos; The clarinet tends to be exactly opposite the flute; The flute blows flat in its lowest four or five notes, on E5, and in "pp" playing or phrase-end taperings; The flute tends to be sharp on C5 and C♯5, and sharp on several notes in the high register. The oboe tends to be flat on the lowest four notes, and tends to be pinched sharp in the middle register in the area of G4 up to C5. The bassoon tends to be sharp on the lowest C, C♯, D, E♭, and on the F♯ and G in the upper two octaves. The clarinet has sharp tendencies in the low register from low G up to D, also on high B, C, C♯. The high notes are variable depending upon embouchure, breath, and fingerings. The tendency is to play higher on soft passages, the opposite of the flute. On the saxophone the lowest four notes are difficult and often flat while the upper middle register plays sharp, particularly on the alto.

Must Compensate

There must be some compensation made for these and other tendencies. Manufacturers have attempted to improve the intonation of woodwind instruments in various ways: by extending and shortening barrels on clarinets and crook joints on bassoons; changing the size and shape of holes and bore; altering the shape of mouthpieces; and adding mechanisms to assist the player. In spite of notable improvements the woodwinds still possess their own pitch idiosyncrasies.

By using a stroboscope one can see these idiosyncrasies. If wisely used this is of immeasurable help in pitch correction. Frequently the instrument is blamed when the fault comes from too much biting and pinching in the embouchure. To be able to see the result of this pinching is one of the most effective ways to correct it.

Summary

The factors most needed for playing in tune are: (1) Good equipment; (2) Knowing the relationships of temperature and tuning; (3) Knowing the pitch idiosyncrasies of your own instrument; (4) Listening as you play. Favoring is accomplished only by a working combination of a developed embouchure and solid breath support; (5) In group tuning, using materials which expose the various instruments in their faultiest pitch areas to encourage favoring and discriminate listening.

September, 1967

Upper Register Intonation

Ralph Laycock

Poor intonation seems to be much more obvious and objectionable in the upper register of the band than in the lower, and unfortunately there seem to be several reasons both for its existence and for the difficulty of clearing it up.

In order to compare the severity of the problem in the lower and in the upper register, let us first suppose that two trombonists, playing their low A, find themselves to be *one* vibration per second out of tune. Though this amounts to approximately ⅛ of a half-step, it is still relatively unobtrusive because of the slow pulsation of the audible beat produced. But now let us listen to two flutists who, playing their high A, four octaves higher, are *proportionately* the same distance out of tune, (approximately ⅛ of a half-step). Because the speed of vibration doubles with each octave rise in pitch, their notes will be fighting each other at the painful rate of *16* beats per second. This is not to say that it is 16 times as hard to play in tune in the extreme upper register, but it may give some idea of the great amount of care that this problem deserves. If "necessity is the mother of attention," the needs here should certainly stir up some action, and the players of the upper-register instruments will, given help and opportunity, go a long way toward solving their intonation problems if for no other reason than self-defense.

In a home-made "intonation sensitivity test" I administered to my own band here several years ago, it may not have been entirely happenstance that the flute and trombone sections scored significantly better than any other sections, possibly because the former had been so constantly under pressure to make the minutely accurate judgments pointed out above, and because the latter, having no buttons to push, could not be satisfied that they had produced a real "note" until they had listened to and checked each one. Of course, it could have been just the personnel that year, but it really *did* occur.

It is not enough to sympathize with the upper winds about their problem, we have to help them overcome it. Perhaps a discussion of some of the contributing factors and their solutions will be helpful.

Embouchure

Among the many physical problems that must be worked out, one of the most urgent is assuredly embouchure control. For instance, in the example cited above, the trombonists are in a very comfortable register, and with even the slightest degree of control, should easily humor far enough up or down, even without moving the slide, to eliminate the one beat per second that separates them. But the flutists, playing near the top of their range, may well be straining to get their notes even to sound, consequently being much too occupied with this alone to be able to deliberately alter the pitch for purposes of tuning. In order to accomplish this latter, there is no substitute for careful training in embouchure adjustment and control, both for change of register and for humoring the pitch of any given note.

One common fault is that the student flutist stretches the lips (as in smiling) when reaching for high notes, causing severe sharping and a shrill tone which only adds to the unpleasant effect. Normally the lips (especially the lower lip) are "pouted" further forward, without bunching, thereby producing more support for the high register and resulting in both truer pitch and better tone quality. Another difficulty is the dependence on too much additional breath pressure, which not only makes the high notes speak, but also forces them sharp as well. With proper embouchure adjustment and good breath *support,* the actual breath

pressure may be relaxed somewhat, to good effect.

By contrast, the clarinet, even with a reed of suitable strength, may fall badly flat in pitch unless the embouchure is adjusted by pushing the lower jaw *slightly* forward and up as the player ascends through the clarion and on into the altissimo register. At the same time, particularly in quiet passages, he may raise the tongue toward an *ee* position as necessary for added security. The alternative, using a still stiffer reed, may lead to other problems of control, tone quality, and intonation.

And so, looking at the contrary tendencies of two of the most important high woodwinds, it should be obvious that systematic attention to embouchure control is needed if they are ever to get together. The following experiments with octave skips should quickly point out the need for pin-point accuracy in moving from one note to another. Two players should tune their instruments until there are no beats as they hold a unison note in the mid-range; then, while one continues to hold this note at exactly the same pitch, the other skips up an octave into the high register, tuning the upper note carefully with the octave being sustained below it. In repetitions of the above, the player who changes notes should attempt to tune perfectly immediately upon moving to the upper note, being guided by his memory of embouchure change that proved successful in earlier tries. A visual demonstration can also be very effective if the student, after adjusting a mid-range note perfectly with a "strobe," will again move up an octave, checking the pitch visually instead of aurally.

Repeated tries should be more successful, due, again, to the player's becoming aware of the exact shift in embouchure that is required. Either test should demonstrate both the desirability and the difficulty of playing perfectly in tune in the upper octave. (The complications caused by intonation problems **built into the instrument itself may make it very difficult to tune perfectly on some notes. This is another matter.**)

Hearing

Though it should go almost without saying, the students' sense of pitch discrimination must be developed through all possible means. I have found it fascinating to work with some of the electronic trainers now on the market; the two I am most familiar with are rather different in scope and design. The Johnson Intonation Trainer, (E. F. Johnson Co., Waseca, Minn.) is a deluxe instrument with a three-octave keyboard, a "reference" chromatic tempered scale, and a tuneable chromatic scale that can be set up to demonstrate both melodic and harmonic progressions in any desired tuning "temperament." The Peterson Multi-Tuner, (Pearce Music Co., Salt Lake City, Utah) is a simple and compact device that will produce up to four tuneable sounds, each with an individual volume control and a continuously variable range of several octaves, suitable for setting up intervals and chords for experimenting with balance and intonation. These or any of the others currently available have the advantage of not requiring the student's involvement in the actual production of the sound, so he can concentrate entirely on listening and adjusting, tuning and mis-tuning at his own leisure, without the limitation of breath, bow, or embouchure that can make it a problem to experiment at length using his fellow musicians.

But control of the embouchure is not enough to do the whole job. Even after every student has developed his embouchure to the point where he is getting precisely the pitch "built into" his instrument, there are many problems still to solve. Without this first major step, though, any hope of achieving satisfactory intonation is vain, for the final solution is based on the ability to produce the desired pitch consistently time after time. There is plenty of work to be done by each and every student in acquiring the degree of control of his embouchure that will make further progress possible. Without excellent embouchure control the outcome is little more predictable than throwing dice.

PART II

Continuing our discussion of the problems of achieving satisfactory intonation in the high register of the band, several rather general statements seem to be in order:

1. Even after the student is able, when given sufficient time, to produce the same pitch on successive attacks or slurs, he may find it very difficult to do as well in rehearsal or concert, due to nervousness. The consequent "paralysis" may make him unable even to think about such delicate adjustments, and even if he is successful in doing this much, it may prevent him from actually manipulating his muscles successfully. For this reason, deliberate and adequate practice of the various means of controlling intonation must be made a part of his regular routine and of rehearsal procedures. With poise and self-confidence thus built up, he will still be able to try for "more than the notes" when under pressure.

2. Familiarity breeds familiarity —his practice must also include systematic development of technique in the high resister. Most fine performers practice technical studies and scales well above the normal range so that they will not be frightened by the notes they meet in public.

3. Keeping up with the brasses— if, for instance, the flutes are seated immediately in front of loud, high brasses, they may seriously overblow in the futile attempt to keep up with them in volume (killing their tone, incidentally, in the process), which results in their forcing their pitch noticeably above that to which they "tuned," probably at mezzo-forte volume. And, no matter where they are seated, they may, in any big climax, allow themselves to become similarly overextended.

4. Instrument adjustment and condition—

a. The tuning adjustment may change due to slippage. For example, loose joints on a clar-

Ralph Laycock is director of bands and orchestra at Brigham Young University in Provo, Utah. He holds the bachelor's and master's degrees from BYU and Juilliard School of Music and is currently engaged in doctoral study in the area of music education. He has often appeared as guest conductor in the northwest states.

inet or a too small neck cork on a saxophone may allow the instrument to change length during the playing period, causing much discomfort to the player who has not realized why he is having more trouble than usual playing in tune. Similar problems can occur on any woodwind or brass instrument.

b. Gradual change of position of the stopper ("cork") in the flute or piccolo head-joint can cause real trouble. Due to the tendency of the screw-end to loosen during playing, the student often tightens it at least a fraction of a turn beyond its former position in order to keep it snug. This action, repeated many times, causes the instrument to play flat, particularly in the upper register. I well remember the new world that opened up for a young piccolo player when the stopper was brought back to its proper position. Not only was the pitch brought up nearly a half-step so that she was comfortably in tune, but the improvement in response and tone quality made her, instantly, a valued member of the organization, rather than the little girl who always played flat.

c. Other adjustments and repairs, dealt with in countless books, repair manuals, etc., are important for many reasons, including that of making them easier to play in tune.

But there is still a major problem, one that cannot be wished or even engineered away, and one that must be solved every time a wind instrument is played. Wind instruments cannot (for the present, at least) be built perfectly in tune with *any* scale. Consequently each manufacturer (and the more conscientious ones are guided by scientific research and/or the opinions of respected performing musicians) makes what seem to him to be the most satisfactory compromises, and these choices are dictated by the playability, the selling price, the probable degree of sophistication of the buyer, among other considerations. From there on, it is strictly the obligation of the performer to find and compensate for the deficiencies of his instrument as best he can. The more intelligently he goes about it, the more successful he will be.

Below is a chart showing the pitch tendencies of various notes on some of the upper winds. Following are a few suggestions for possible solutions to some of the most glaring problems. While *not* intended to be either complete or

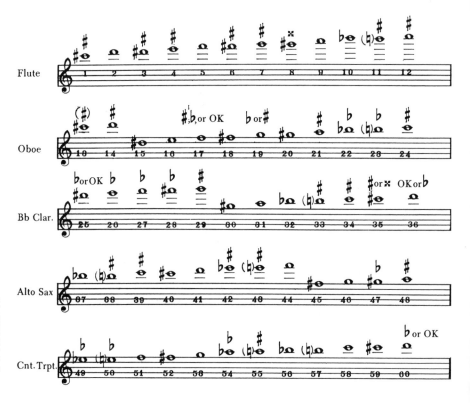

498

able to solve a particular problem on a specific instrument, it is hoped that this guide will serve to open up the subject for further (and never-ending) investigation for those to whom it may not be "old stuff." Each vertical column represents some octave of a given concert pitch note. A comparison of the different problems encountered by the various instruments which might be found playing such a note together should reveal some of the reasons for poor intonation in the upper register and the consequent need for extensive work.

The comments below refer to the numbered notes above. If a note is shown above as having a specific problem, but no suggestion is given below, the normal solution is to "humor" it, using any method appropriate to the instrument.

1. "Humor" down; avoiding blowing harder than necessary.

4. Is complicated by the fact that the left third finger opens *two* holes, making the note comparatively difficult for the less-experienced player to play securely. So, having missed it many times through setting his embouchure too "low," the student often subconsciously sets unnecessarily "high," thus forcing it to be quite sharp. Accurate embouchure setting (which involves "pouting" the lips slightly forward) should make it possible to play this note satisfactorily in normal situations, but for delicate playing, two variations of the normal fingering are available: (a) Remove the right fourth finger—note is more secure, lower in pitch. (b) Lean right second finger to left, opening first trill key —makes note much more secure especially in pianissimo. Also allows player to "flat" the note with less danger of losing it.

6. Is complicated in same manner as 4 above. For special purposes: (a) Using right fourth finger, depress low C♯ key instead of E♭—adds stability and allows the player to "flat" the note more successfully. (b) Use right second

finger rather than third *in an emergency* to "flat" the note, at the expense of tone quality.

8. This extremely sharp note can be stabilized by adding the right second and third fingers. It can then be "flatted" without as much fear of losing it.

13. If sharp, use half-hole instead of leaving first finger off entirely.

17. "Student" instruments without the F resonance key need to have the E♭ key (either right or left) added to the forked fingering.

21. Is unstable in pitch, as are the next several above it, due to the shortness of the tube in use. These notes are particularly dependent on a good embouchure and well-adjusted reed for satisfactory pitch. Fingering aids are: (a) Add right second finger to help stabilize the pitch. (b) For a long quiet note, use harmonic fingering (like low D but with added second octave key). B♭, B♮ and C can be similarly built on E♭, E, and F respectively, with the same octave key.

25. The elementary fingering, employing the right second finger and the E♭ key, is hopelessly flat, useable only for the D♭-E♭ trill and trill-like passages. Instead, use either: (a) left hand same, right hand as for chromatic, B-F♯ and E♭ key; (b) left hand same, right third finger and E♭ key

27. For better response and pitch (and slurs up to it), use fingering like fourth line D with added left hand C♯-G♯ key, when time permits.

28. Standard fingering is quite flat. Use fingering like fourth space E with added left hand C♯-G♯ key.

29. Half-hole left hand first finger on regular fingering, or use first and third of each hand with added E♭ key. (Several fingerings are available; try them.)

35. Half-hole if time permits. Many students generalize that "everything above high C should have the E♭ key added." C♯ *must not;* it makes it badly sharp.

36. High D and above almost always *must* employ the E♭ key.

D is flat without it.

48. Because it lies at the low end of the notes produced with the help of the upper octave key hole, A is out of proportion. It is sometimes helpful to use the right second finger to lower it.

55. As they approach the high register, they push sharp. Often the third valve alone gives better results, as it is built a trifle lower in pitch than the combined first and second. It may well give added confidence. I have even seen the second used alone, though rarely, as it *should* be quite badly flat.

59. Many students use the fingering proper to the lower octave (first and second valves), not realizing that response and tone are better if the second only is used. (Compare with French horn in F one octave lower on staff, but playing the same partial.)

60. This note is better in tune when played open (the proper fingering). Response and tone are likewise better. The first valve may be useful in passage work where a valve change will help security.

As each student learns how and how much to compensate for his instrument's problems, he is doing his part to help eliminate the gross errors of intonation. The finer adjustments will always have to take time and effort if really superior results are desired, but they can only be given attention after the major problems have been solved. Many successful teachers find that this stage comes about sooner if they have their students mark, with arrows pointing up or down, the notes that usually have to be humored or corrected, until such correction is almost automatic and becomes a part of the students' performance. As each does his part to clear the air, it becomes all the more obvious what remains to be done, and the progress may almost seem to speed up as a general rule, though set-backs are not unknown(!). But rest content that, when satisfactory intonation is achieved in the upper register, you will all know it, and eveyone concerned, players and audience alike, will appreciate it! ∎

Improving Orchestral Performance
Intonation and Pitch Discrimination

Robert H. Klotman

CORRECTING FAULTY intonation is one of the major concerns when working for improved orchestral performance. This emphasis is of utmost importance since intonation not only affects the purity of tone, but because it impinges on the clarity and effectiveness of the musical performance. Many teachers dismiss the problem by placing the entire responsibility on the students—either they can or they cannot hear. This premise, however, is not entirely true because many students do not know *how* to hear, and directors can help students hear better by teaching them critical listening.

Pitch Awareness

Good intonation is essentially a problem of awareness and comprehension. The precise problem is how to arouse this awareness and provide the necessary comprehension that will enable a student to rely on his own ear for regulating pitch. Some directors utilize electronic devices which visualize for students pitch variances that they have difficulty in hearing. As a preliminary step toward arousing awareness of pitch discrepancy, this procedure has merit. However, since the adjustment is done by individual notes, one cannot rely on it for a musical sequence.

Another effective method for improving intonation is to call attention to the beats which are produced by variances when playing in unison. By selecting significant passages from the literature being performed, much can be done to ameliorate intonation thru the practice of refining those beats caused by the imperfect unisons.

The most common practice among directors is to make frequent stops, checking the pitch of individual players in relation to the chord struc-

ture. Peculiarly enough, however, unless one is playing a very slow, sustained passage, pitch adjustments in actual ensemble performance are not made chordally but melodically. James F. Nickerson in a report, "Intonations of Solo and Ensemble Performance of the Same Melody," which appeared in the November, 1949, issue of the *Journal of the Acoustical Society of America*, scientifically substantiated this theory of melodic listening.

After analyzing, electronically, several performances of Haydn's *Emperor Variations* by different professional string quartets, Mr. Nickerson concluded that "melodic movement deserves and receives much more attention than harmonic blend to achieve satisfying results." There is no denying, however, that where chordal structure is essential to the thematic content performers do listen harmonically as well as melodically. Mr. Nickerson merely establishes that the melodic content is the dominating influence when making pitch adjustments, and unlike the piano which is tuned according to the "tempered-scale," he states that string instruments, in performance, are governed by the Pythagorean scale. This scale derives its tones from the 5th, the interval by which string instruments are tuned.

Scale Intonation

Realizing that intonation difficulties are essentially scale-wise problems, one must then proceed to prove to students that contrary to the obvious tempered scale of the piano, the pitch of a note varies according to its relationship within a scale. Thus, in the utilization of melodic or scale-wise corrections, all whole steps and half steps are not equidistant. For example, the whole step between the second and third notes of a major

Robert H. Klotman is a past member of the Cleveland Philharmonic Orchestra and is now performing with the Friends of Music Chamber Ensemble. He holds a Bachelor of Science degree from Ohio Northern University, a Master of Arts from Western Reserve University, and a Doctor of Education from Teachers College of Columbia University. He teaches music at the Cleveland Heights (Ohio) High School.

scale is not as large as the whole step between the sixth and seventh notes of that scale. This, conversely, causes the half step between the seventh and eighth notes of the scale to be smaller than the half step between the third and fourth notes of the same scale and produces the raised effect of the leading tone. Another consideration is that the third of the Pythagorean scale is somewhat larger than the third of the tempered and just scales.

A demonstration of this theory of adjusting notes according to their scale relationship is to tune violin strings G, D, and A to perfect 5ths. In order to make your experiment more effective seek agreement among several students. Begin a D major scale on the open D string and stop on the second note ("E"—first finger on the D string). Without moving the finger play a double-stop with the open A string.

One will find that in order to obtain a perfect 4th, he will have to raise the pitch of E a few vibrations. Once the E is adjusted, play a double-stop with the open G string without moving the first finger. It is then discovered that in order to obtain a harmonious 6th it is necessary to return the finger almost to its original position. This is a practical demonstration of how the *same* note can change its pitch in relation to the various chords and scales. The note E is first "re" in the scale of D, next "sol" when played with the fixed A string, and finally "la" in the scale of G. In each instance it requires slight adjustments. It is true that the adjustments are made harmonic-

ally, but the point proved is that the same note can move in various settings.

Once students accept the theory that the same note can vary according to its position in each scale, a psychological block created by the tempered scale of the piano has been overcome. One may then select for study meaningful scale-wise passages from material being performed.

Since the third is most affected in the Pythagorean scale (it is slightly higher), the orchestra can work for comprehension and pitch adjustment by performing a variety of scales in thirds. Part of the orchestra starts playing the scale and the remaining members of the organization begin the scale when the first group has reached the third note. This creates a scale of consecutive thirds and

offers additional opportunities for study of the Pythagorean scale.

When appropriate, one can arouse considerable interest in scale performance by playing the neglected whole tone scale beginning on Bb. Students regard this scale as a curiosity, and it becomes a challenge that leads to further ear development.

Once members of the orchestra become aware of pitch discrepancies and begin to listen, they actually find it easier to play "in tune" rather than "out of tune." With proper emphasis intonation can be improved. It is the director's responsibility to arouse a desire on the part of the individual performer to improve his own pitch perception. Improved pitch enhances the beauty of tone and results in a more pleasurable performance.

April, 1957

Band Intonation and Tonality

Walter Beeler

Walter Beeler is Professor of Music and Director of Bands at Ithaca College, Ithaca, New York. He is a member of the American Bandmasters' Association and is on the Board of the New York State School Music Association. He has numerous music publications to his credit and has been active in clinic and adjudication work in many states.

SEVERAL YEARS ago, while I was engaged in supervising cadet teachers an incident occurred which should have taught me much more than it did at the time. A group of struggling violinists managed to play all of *America* without realizing that they should know the melody. The editor of the book had for some reason failed to use the title. These violinists were extremely young and painfully new to the art. It was obvious that they were so engaged in technical problems that they had no time for listening. They were putting down fingers and moving a bow, note by note.

Universal Problem

It has occurred to me only in recent years that many performers below the professional level are doing the same thing, to a degree. To the extent that any player is *aware* of his instrument, it is not likely that he

is listening critically to the resultant sound. Players *believe* that they hear what they produce, but when they are asked to hum or to sing the sound and then play it, they will alter the tone. The second sound is invariably an improvement over the original.

A surprising percentage (almost all) of those who participate in instrumental music have reasonably good pitch discrimination. However, in listening to average amateur groups one would not be inclined to accept the group's intonation and tonality as evidence of this. The fair test is to have the group sing rather than play, for in singing the group is utilizing its sense of pitch to the fullest degree. Most bands can sing a chord quite well in tune, but very few groups are able to play a chord that is completely satisfactory. Most instrumentalists are not producing tones that are *first heard* and are then dictated to the instrument.

Of course all beginners trust their instruments. If G is fingered with valves one and two, it is thus played, and the subject is closed. However the habit does not end with the beginning stage. Players on the college level continue to do the same thing, to a lesser degree. All directors exort their players to listen. They are asked to listen to others, and to achieve tonality by this means. Listening is not enough. The player may listen to others, then to his own instrument; but if each is listening to an *instrument* rather than to the pitch that his ear would require him to hum, the result will still be artificial.

It is a rare playing organization that achieves tonality that can be produced by a fine choir. Perhaps such a condition is not possible, but by using the device whereby the choir obtains its sense of pitch security much can be accomplished in instrumental groups.

Concentrate on Sound

The ideal situation would be one in which all performers were so accomplished that they could in fact forget that they were playing instruments. This utopia will never be reached, but players can be trained to direct their attention away from the mechanics of their horns. Most players unconsciously feel a moral obligation to keep the thought directed to the instrument. Of course

not thinking about the instrument is a negative procedure and has little merit. Concentrating on the inner sound is a positive action, and it is capable of development. If a director has twenty-five chords played, then sung, then played, an attitude toward listening will develop. Rather than wasting time, as it might appear, this device will save hours of effort usually devoted to general tuning.

Too often *tuning* can be confused with *tonality*. Tuning a band on a single note is fine, but it accomplishes very little. It may even tend to make players careless beyond that point.

Tonality, or key sense, begins where tuning leaves off. When band members are *in tune* it is nothing more than assurance that they may then be able to pull their instruments the rest of the way to the proper pitch needed for a particular chord. The distance that the instrument must be coaxed varies greatly with the chord to be played and the idiosyncracies of the individual players. The important consideration is that the player hears the pitch that he wants and obliges his instrument to play it. If he does not take this step the instrument is playing him.

Values of Singing

The value of singing on an instrument is not confined to pitch discrimination. Phrasing and general musicianship can be greatly improved if the player will follow his

natural vocal tendencies. It is suggested that the reader ask any student to sing and to play *America*. He can note the wide discrepancy between the two styles. Oddly enough, however, the student will rarely be aware that the two styles vary greatly in maturity. The singing is based on feeling—the playing is grounded in mechanics.

The student is not entirely to blame for his indifference as to the musicality of his performance. Rarely is he asked to do anything really creative. We as directors are much more inclined to force directions on the student than we are to draw out his best efforts. This is natural, for we are to lead and he is to follow. The trouble is that the inner student can sleep thru it all. He is asked only to play back a version of what his director hears. The thing that the student hears isn't asked for, so he doesn't have to summon up his innate musicianship. The facial expressions of the players in rehearsals will usually be an indication of whether they are participating or obeying. Most rehearsals consist of the participation of one person and the obedience of the others.

Most directors sing their instructions, no matter how bad their voices. They feel they can in this way give expression to their inner feelings about the interpretation of the music. Their voices convey the best that they can hear. If it works for the teacher, why not for the student?

February, 1954

PLAY IN TUNE

THOMAS F. WELSH

T**HE** S**TROBOCONN IS A STROBO-** scope, an electronic instrument that shows pitch visually. It is widely used by music instrument manufacturers and professional musicians as well as by schools.

Thomas F. Welsh, who makes the initial presentation, is employed by C. G. Conn, Ltd., manufacturer of the instrument. The I**NSTRUMENTALIST** usually adheres strictly to the policy of excluding advertising opinion from its editorial columns, striving to remain objective in regard to products that are advertised within its pages. However, it is making an exception in

the case of the Stroboconn because of its very special and practical uses in education and because there are no competitors for sale of this useful instrument.   —*The Editors*

"P**LAY IN TUNE**" is a phrase in musical vernacular, most often spoken in exasperation. The good and proper intonation of bands and orchestras and of individual performers has been a fountainhead of perplexity to bandmasters, composers and arrangers since the beginning of organized sound.

Although increased attention and

investigation are being given to this important but elusive element, responsibility for its development and perfection in school bands and orchestras still falls on the director. Because musical pitch is so intangible and difficult to express in "word pictures," its relationship to good performance is seldom easily visualized by students. As a result, most directors find themselves spending a disproportionate amount of time analyzing and correcting the causes of faulty pitch.

It has long since been conceded that there is no way of getting around the need for this analysis and correction; it must be done if intonation is to be perfected. In an electronic pitch-measuring device called the Stroboconn there is a way to get around much of the time-consuming effort that these problems require. The Stroboconn brings intonation "out into the light" and clarifies for the student many of the questions surrounding it. Originally perfected for testing the intonation of newly manufactured instruments, today the Stroboconn is an important teaching aid dealing directly and effectively with the intonation problem.

The Stroboconn measures musical tones to an accuracy of 1/100th of a semitone. A tone presented to its microphone appears as a visual pattern which shows immediately whether the tone is sharp, flat or in tune with the Equally Tempered scale based on A=440. All the factors that influence pitch—vibrato, embouchure, blowing, slide positioning, etc. —can be analyzed from this pattern. Too, the exact degree of sharpness or flatness may be measured in units of 1/100th of a semitone simply by regulating a pointer on the face of the instrument. The Stroboconn's range covers that of the piano keyboard.

Visual Guidance

Playing before the Stroboconn, a student is able to see his pitch errors. He hears only the tones of his own instrument and soon learns how each should sound when played in tune. What he learns by visual and muscular coordination with the Stroboconn becomes more firmly implanted in his memory; his learning is more easily retained through this objective approach, and ear training is thereby improved. Adjustments made in embouchure, breath control, etc., to produce a stationary Stroboconn pattern become habitual with the player because he can see the effect of these changes on his tone. Thus, the Stroboconn helps develop good habits in these important areas. It also helps the player learn the tuning adjustments that must be made on each instrument to bring it in tune with itself. Chords, unisons or difficult passages for ensemble work, as well, can be checked and practiced with the Stroboconn since it will measure two or more tones simultaneously.

All this, besides developing good mechanical habits and intonation in the areas concerned, helps tremendously to create a consciousness of pitch. Important, too, is the fact that the director is greatly relieved of much individual supervision. The Stroboconn takes over as "listener." Because it can be operated by students, a schedule can be set up with each player required to spend a specified time with the instrument each day or week. To further relieve the director, responsibility for seeing that this is carried out can be delegated to section leaders.

Most bandmasters carry this plan a step further by utilizing a system of performance charts showing sharp and flat deviations from perfect pitch as measured by the Stroboconn. These are prepared by the students themselves in groups of two or three, the player facing away from the instrument to prevent visual correction and a co-worker taking measurements and recording them on a chart.

Not a Crutch

While the Stroboconn is immeasurably helpful in developing good intonation, it is not intended as a crutch to be relied upon permanently. Rather, it is a means to an end, an "x-ray" machine that helps locate, treat and overcome faulty intonation habits. Requiring the player to face away from the Stroboconn during tests, as mentioned above, will help preclude the possibility of its becoming a crutch and will aid in transferring the learning to the player's ear.

The deviations from perfect pitch shown on these charts give the director the means of following each student's progress without personal checking. This plan has other advantages, too. It presents a definite goal for the student to reach for and introduces an element of competition with other players, further stimulating the desire to improve. Here, again, first-chair players can be responsible for administration of chart preparation.

Students cannot argue with a scientific instrument like the Stroboconn. It is actually a director's "assistant" that judges pitch impartially and accurately, at the same time saving time and work for the director.

THE IMPORTANCE OF BEING RHYTHMIC

Paul Creston

"Rhythm, in music, is the organization of duration in ordered movement."—One of America's eminent composers discusses the principles of rhythm and the rhythmic structure of music.

RHYTHM, AS A TOPIC OF DISCUSsion, is in a more lamentable position than the weather. As Mark Twain remarked, concerning the weather: "Everyone talks about it but no one does anything about it." As to the subject of rhythm in music, practically no one even talks about it. We are dealing now not with performer's but with composer's rhythm, that is, the principles of rhythm or the rhythmic structure of music.

About twenty years ago I came to the realization that there was an abysmal gap in music education. In technical analyses of musical masterpieces, theorists were preoccupied mainly with thematic material, harmonic logic, and formal structure, while the rhythmic element was completely ignored. In every school where music composition was part of the curricula, the courses included harmony, counterpoint, melody, and form, while the subject of rhythm was conspicuously absent. Even those outstanding composers who turned to teaching considered rhythm either as an unwanted stepchild or as a pale shadow of poetic meter. Paul Hindemith's apology for the omission of rhythmic study betrayed an all-too-prevalent intellectual lethargy in the matter, for he wrote in his *Craft of Musical Composition*: ". . . all questions of rhythm, as well as the formal characteristics of composition which spring from it, are still so largely unexplained that it seems impossible at the present time to include rhythm as an integral part of a system of teaching the craft of composition." As a composer, Hindemith need not concern himself with explanations, but as a teacher it is his duty to seek and find them.

With this realization was born my desire to write *Principles of Rhythm*, a text book which would explain and coordinate rhythmic theories in order to assist the student composer in understanding and applying these principles. However, the book need not be limited to students of composition. Just as knowledge of harmony and form clarify interpretation for the artist or teacher, so will the correct concept of the rhythmic structure of a composition aid in the explanation and execution of a work. Moreover, since there cannot be melody, harmony, or form without rhythm, a complete conception of a composition's structure is impossible without consideration of the rhythmic element.

Confused Definitions

The negligence in rhythmic matters was instigated from the start by the confusion in definitions. Here is a sampling of these definitions from the 18th century to the present:

1. "Rhythm is that property or quality by which the cadences of every kind of movement are regulated and determined."—Thomas Busby.

2. "A particular arrangement of the alternately strong and weak sounds of a musical progression whereby, at regular or irregular intervals—that is, every two, three, four or more bars—one sound of the progression (which the preceding sounds cause the ear to desire) con-

veys to the aural sense a feeling of rest, and the effect of a stop or close more or less complete."—Matthis Lussy.

3. "We shall call the constant measure by which the measurement of time is made—Metre; the kind of motion in that measure—Rhythm."—Moritz Hauptmann.

4. "Rhythm . . . is time, pace, metre, and other things rolled into one, and it is not surprising that it has been used to name each of them singly."—Grove's Dictionary.

5. "Rhythm refers to the beat of the music—the time element."—Sidney A. Reeve.

6. "Rhythm is engendered by the motion of the musical picture, and manifests itself in the association of differing time values."—Percy Goetschius.

7. "The disposition of melody or harmony, in respect of time or measure is termed rhythm."—John Callcott.

8. "Rhythm is order and proportion in space and time."—Vincent d'Indy.

9. "Musical rhythm . . . bases itself upon the regular heart-beat of a uniform time-unit, and derives its satisfaction from the many and subtle combinations of pulse-groupings that can be developed upon this, and from the increasingly varied means for their expression."—George Gow.

16. "The term Rhythm is constantly erroneously applied. It has only one true meaning—the number of bars in a phrase."—G. Egerton Lowe. This last definition is probably the epitome of intellectual egotism.

Historical Concepts

Further research, however, will uncover concepts which begin to throw some light on this confusing mystery. In fact, the further back we go in history, the clearer the concept becomes, as some of the following definitions will reveal: 1. "Rhythm is ordered movement."—Plato. 2. "Rhythm is an ensemble of accents disposed according to a certain order."—Aristides Quintillianus—c. 100 A.D. 3. "Rhythm is the art of well-ordered movement."—St. Augustine. 4. "Musical rhythm is the organization of sonorous movement."—Ph. Biton. 5. "The nature of rhythm may be defined as the periodic quality, regular or irregular, of all movement."—Margaret H. Glyn.

6. "Rhythm, in music, is the organization of duration."—Maurice Emmanuel.

There are two basic causes of confusion in rhythmic theory and practice: concept and notation. Perhaps I should say: concept and/or notation. For even when the concept is clear and correct, the composer who thoroughly understands intuitively the true nature of rhythm is saddled with an inconsistent and imperfect system of rhythmic notation, and the teacher similarly endowed cannot successfully decipher it. The solution of the problem is not to invent a new system (a new system rarely improves one that has evolved), but to realize the shortcomings of the established one and to compensate for them. Is it a wonder that errors of rhythmic notation are found in the works of such masters as Beethoven, Wagner, Brahms, Ravel, Bartok, Stravinsky, et al? We should not even consider the medieval composers, for in those days every copyist had his own system of rhythmic notation.

Practical Definition

Let us begin with the true concept of rhythm. If we combine Maurice Emmanuel's definition of musical rhythm with that of Plato's for rhythm in general, we can formulate one which will prove most practical. This definition is: *Rhythm, in music, is the organization of duration in ordered movement.* The value of this definition is its comprehensiveness, for it is applicable to an entire composition as well as a single measure. *Duration* itself is not *rhythm*. A tone sustained indefinitely does not create rhythm: it must be divided into units, must be "organized," to be rhythmic. Were it not for equinoxes, for the division into nights and days or for the division into four seasons, the earth's journey around the sun would be merely duration and not a rhythm.

Applying this concept to music, we have the duration of an entire composition organized into units of measures, phrases, periods, and sections. This gives us the first element of rhythm: *meter*. To achieve "ordered movement," the second element comes into being: *pace*, commonly termed "tempo." Applicable to music specifically, the third and fourth elements: *accent* and *pattern*, are present. The four elements of rhythm, therefore, are: meter, pace, accent, and pattern. To change any one of these elements is to change the rhythm and to describe any rhythm by less than these would result in an inaccurate and incomplete description. In other words, to say that a piece is fast or slow, or that it is in 2/4 or 3/4 meter, is not sufficient identification.

Following are definitions and explanations of the four elements of rhythm:

I. METER is the grouping of pulses within a single measure or within a frame of two or more measures. It is commonly termed "time": 2/4 time, 3/4 time, etc. "Pulse" is commonly called "beat" but this latter term is now reserved for the actual rhythmic beat when it does not coincide with the metrical pulse. For example, a piece in 3/4 meter would be in 3 pulses to a measure; but if the actual rhythmic beat is:

Ex. 1

it would be in 2 *beats*. This particular rhythm, termed the "hemiola," is derived by a regrouping of the units in a measure; that is, the 6 eighth notes of 3/4 which are normally in 3 groups of 2 eighth notes are rearranged into 2 groups of 3 eighth notes. Meter is a grouping within a frame of two or more measures when an entire measure constitutes a pulse, as in Beethoven's scherzo movement from the 9th Symphony:

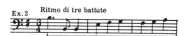

Ex. 2 Ritmo di tre battute

II. PACE is the rate at which the pulses of a meter occur, noted in music by a metronome mark or such terms as allegro, adagio, etc. It is commonly referred to as tempo, a term as equivocal as time for meter. (Tempo, in Italian, has at least five different meanings: time, duration, pace, meter, and movement.)

III. ACCENT is that element of rhythm which makes prominent, or emphasizes, a pulse or beat. Usually, only two types of accent are mentioned, dynamic and agogic, but there are at least *eight* types. These eight types are: *Dynamic* (a qualitative accent), by means of tone intensity, that is, the accented note is played louder than those following it. *Agogic* (a quantitative accent), by

means of tone quantity, that is, the accented note longer than the following and/or preceding one. *Metric*, by sounding the particular metrical grouping, usually aided harmonically by grouping the harmonic changes according to the pulses.

Harmonic, by means of a dissonance on the accented pulse or beat. *Weight*, by means of a larger volume of sound (in terms of *mass*, not dynamics) at the accented point. In other words, if an entire chord is sounded on one pulse and only single notes on the others, a weight accent results. *Pitch*, the highest or lowest note of a group has the value of an accent. The traditional accompaniment for a waltz is one example of a pitch accent, with the bass tone as the accent. An ascending or descending run is another example, with the lowest or highest note having the value of an accent. *Pattern*, as the term implies, exists in a repeated figure of characteristic contour. *Embellished*, by means of any form of embellishment: appoggiatura, acciaccatura, mordent, trill, etc.

IV. PATTERN, as an element of rhythm, is the subdivision of a pulse, beat or group of pulses or beats, into smaller units. Taking a quarter note as the pulse or beat, this can be subdivided into numerous patterns, such as:

Ex. 3

Rhythmic Structures

The organization of duration in ordered movement is ultimately accomplished by five different plans termed rhythmic structures. These structures are: First, *regular subdivision*; second, *irregular subdivision*; third, *overlapping*; fourth, *regular subdivision overlapping*; fifth, *irregular subdivision overlapping*. The applications and ramifications of these structures cannot be discussed in detail. They will, however, be briefly explained and illustrated.

Regular subdivision is the organization of a measure into equal beats, that is, beats of equal duration. In a sense meter itself is one form of the first structure when pulses are considered as rhythmic beats. But the real application of this principle is in rhythms in which the pulses and beats do not coincide. For example, 2 beats against 3 pulses in

3/4 (the hemiola) as already mentioned. The hemiola is found in the music of Greece, Arabia, Western civilization since the 16th Century, and in several South American dances such as the *bambuco* of Colombia, the *pasillo* of Ecuador and the *cueca* of Chile. The Chopin *Waltz in A♭* is an illustration:

Ex. 4 2 beats

3 pulses

Irregular subdivision is the organization of a measure into *unequal* beats, that is, beats of differing duration. This structure is found in the music of Greece, China, India, and our own music from medieval times to the present. The most common form is the 3 + 3 + 2 as found in the Cuban rumba.

Ex. 5   3 + 3 + 2

Overlapping, in rhythm, is the extension of a phrase rhythm beyond the bar line. This was common practice in the 16th Century and has been revived in the 20th Century but in the form of multimeters or changing meters. In this structure, the barline is ignored and the pulses are grouped in various sizes. What results is a multimeter, but without changing the initial metric notation.

Ex. 6   5/4   4/4   2/4   3/4

Regular Subdivision Overlapping is a combination of the first (regular subdivision) and the third (overlapping) structures. It is the organization of a group of measures into equal beats overlapping the barline. To be the fourth structure, however, the overlapping grouping must be a repeated pattern.

Ex. 7   3x2 or 3/2

Irregular Subdivision Overlapping is the organization of a group of measures into unequal beats overlapping the barline. This must also be a repeated pattern.

505

Although only one illustration is given for each structure, it must be borne in mind that each structure is applicable to all meters and that many forms are available. The scope of this article does not permit full discussion of all the forms and patterns available in each structure. Moreover, we cannot even briefly mention such principles as: multimeters, multirhythms, polymeters, polyrhythms, compositional rubato, miscellaneous devices, basic patterns, and rhythmic forms.

Understanding Valuable

It was mentioned that a knowledge of rhythmic principles is valuable to the performer and teacher as well as the composer. Why? The performer, even with an intuitive grasp of rhythm, will be aided immeasurably in interpreting the notation of complex rhythms, especially when the

notation is incorrect, equivocal, or unprecise. For example, the following notation of 3 beats against 4 pulses is common:

At a fast pace there would be no problem of execution. But if it were at a slow pace, the performer would have to reconstruct the rhythm mentally in the form in which it originated:

Try it at the piano and see how simple it is to play 3 beats against 4 pulses in even the slowest possible pace.

Piano teachers have difficulty in simplifying for the pupil the following rhythm found in Chopin's *Waltz in D♭*: 4 beats against 3 pulses.

By writing it according to its origin, the pupil is enabled to practice it as slowly as desired.

Even some of the most accomplished musicians have difficulty in translating certain rhythms in Bartok, Ravel, Stravinsky, and other composers of similar stature, because of equivocal or ambiguous notation. (This is not intended as a criticism of these composers' rhythmic sense —which is impeccable—but of the unclear notation employed by them.) A knowledge of rhythmic principles is invaluable to the performer in such cases. It corrects equivocal notation, clarifies the rhythmic concept, and simplifies execution not only of complex rhythms but even, at times, of rhythms not so complex.

August, 1966

TEACHING RHYTHM

MERLE J. ISAAC

Rhythm is one of the most essential elements of instrumental music, possibly being even more basic than melody or harmony. Much of the music that we love best, from popular dance tunes to symphonies, is decidedly rhythmic. Even slow, sustained melodies often have rhythmic accompaniments.

Rhythm may be heard. It may be felt. At the ballet, it may be seen. In its simplest form, rhythm

Merle J. Isaac is vice-president of the NSOA, vice-president of the Illinois unit of ASTA, and a member of the board of directors of VanderCook College of Music (Chicago). He taught and served as a principal in the Chicago school system and now devotes his time to composing and arranging materials for school bands and orchestras. This article is an excerpt from the forward of his recently-published book, Syncopating Strings. (New York, Carl Fischer, Inc., 1966)

appeals to our muscles: it makes us want to march or to dance, though our response is usually limited to tapping our fingers or moving our toes.

For the most part, young musicians play the right notes with reasonable accuracy as to time values. Yet, too frequently, the playing lacks rhythm. To produce rhythmic music, it is necessary to do more than play the right notes and count correctly. Some notes must be played louder and some softer. Some must be given their full value, while others should be shortened (and small rests placed after them).

Generally, when playing music of a rhythmic nature, one should stress the first note of each measure, though this must not be over-

done or done in a jerky manner. (Sometimes the best way to stress the first note is to play the others more softly.) In syncopated music, the stress or accent may be moved from the first note in the measure to a syncopated note. In fact, the term syncopation has been defined as "misplaced accent," even though syncopated notes are not always accented. Two questions thus present themselves, two questions that every musician must recognize and answer to the best of his ability: (1) *Which note* in the measure should receive the accent or stress? and (2) *How much* stress should this note receive?

On a string instrument, rhythm and bowing are closely related. Some rhythm patterns are easy and effective when played with

506

one type of bowing, but awkward and ineffective when played with other bowings. Students should learn, by various means, how the different rhythm patterns look and sound and how they are bowed.

When selecting music for a school orchestra, it is wise to notice whether or not the string parts are bowed and fingered adequately. If the parts are not marked satisfactorily (or not marked at all) the director should see that they are bowed carefully *before the first rehearsal.* After young string players have learned a piece or a passage with one bowing, it is very difficult and time consuming to get them to change. Especially, bowings should not be worked out in rehearsals of the full orchestra causing the wind players to sit idle for extended periods. Students may lose interest in the orchestra because of this.

There is more to playing rhythmically than making some tones loud and some soft. In rhythmic music, many of the tones must be separated from each other. The style is marcato, rather than legato. We must be concerned with "the proportion of sound to silence, often not indicated at all by the nota-

tion." (Conductor's Corner, *The Instrumentalist,* P. 73, Dec., 1965)

Rhythm, one of the essential elements of music, is the foundation of good performance and musicianship.

Teaching Rhythm to String Players

Rhythms can be taught effectively on string instruments by using a rote method at first and adding the reading of rhythm patterns afterward.

1. Select a rhythm pattern (time figure) in the music to be learned, one with which the students may not be familiar and which may present a problem.
2. Write this rhythm pattern on the board without using a staff.
3. Have the students say the rhythm several times using nonsense syllables (such as pum-da-pum-paah) or words that fit the rhythm (such as co-coa-nut pie), exaggerating the accent.
4. Play the pattern several times on an open string, *pizzicato.*
5. Play the pattern several times on an open string, *arco,* using suitable bowing. (The bowing is important.)
6. Play the pattern on each de-

gree of a one-octave scale, up and down, always with marked rhythm.
7. Have the students find the rhythm pattern in the printed music.
8. Play the pattern as written (with fingering), *pizzicato* at first.
9. Play the entire passage containing the rhythm pattern.
10. Rehearse, emphasizing rhythm, dynamics, and style.

Students should learn many rhythm patterns in this manner. Then, when the patterns are met in printed music, they will be recognized rather than analyzed. When the problems of note reading require less attention, players are able to give more attention to the problems of interpretation.

The musician's major concern must be with making music, not with reading notation. The silent notes on the paper need to be vitalized, brought to life, so that they may bring pleasure and inspriation to all who listen. The imaginations of young players may be stimulated by the thought that it is not enough to have the notes *walk* across the stage: *they must sing and dance!* ■

Any Rhythm Problems?

DANIEL KOHUT

Rhythm is probably the greatest single problem confronting the instrumental beginner. Lack of sight-reading ability on the part of advanced students can frequently be blamed to a large degree upon difficulty in rhythmic reading. No single, ideal approach appears to exist in solving the problem. Rote teaching, mathematical analysis,

Daniel Kohut received the Bachelor's degree at North Texas State University and the Master's degree at the Eastman School of Music. He has taught in the Brighton, New York, Public Schools, and at Arkansas Tech. He currently is teaching in the Penfield, New York, Public Schools while working toward the doctorate degree at the Eastman School.

clapping, tapping the foot, etc. are all effective and each can be employed. Tapping the foot as a rhythmic teaching device has been criticized by some educators and has been somewhat neglected in writings on the subject. Special emphasis will be given to this area in this article. Certainly most of what is due to be stated in these lines is common knowledge to most experienced teachers. It is hoped, however, that younger teachers and those preparing to enter the profession may find these ideas helpful, and that the oldsters may find at least one new approach which is worthy of trial.

Authorities on etiquette tell us that it is in poor taste for an individual to tap his foot while listening to music. Most music educators will agree that foot-tappers on a concert stage present a poor appearance. Experience with young beginners, however, has shown that development of a physical feeling for the beat, its divisions and subdivisions, is a practical and efficient teaching tool. Once the need for foot-tapping ceases to exist, it should be discarded like any other "crutch." There may be some youngsters who will never receive any benefit from its use and some few who do not need this crutch, but these students appear to be in the small minority.

Understanding Time Relationships

It is important that the student knows that in four-four time, for example, the whole note gets four beats, the half note gets two beats, and the quarter note gets one beat. What is still more important is that the student understands and feels the functional time relationships between these rhythmic note values. Using the foot to establish a steady beat, the student should play a series of whole notes followed by a series of half notes. This is done without music. Special attention is aimed toward being certain that the speed of the beat remains the same. Once these note values are performed accurately in separate series, they should be mixed, i.e. a measure of half notes followed by a whole note. Quarter notes should be practiced along at first and later related to the whole and half notes in the same manner. The chosen is arbitrary, although it is frequently easiest to use either the tuning note or the first note that they learned in their method book.

Divisions and Subdivisions of the Beat

Few students will find any great difficulty with the longer note values mentioned earlier. Real problems actually begin with divisions and subdivisions of the beat. (In common time with a quarter note unit, eighth notes are *divisions* and sixteenth notes are referred to as *subdivisions*.) Eighth notes, when first introduced, can be best related to the quarter note as shown below. Whole and half notes should be mixed in later for more complete understanding.

The student should be instructed that the quarter note gets one beat, the eighth note gets half a beat, and that eighth notes are twice as fast as quarters. *The speed of the foot tap must remain the same; the speed of the notes is the variable factor.*

The above concept can be used with other equal subdivisions such as eighth-note triplets and sixteenth-note quadruplets. An extra device to help make these rhythmic note-

values more meaningful is the use of three and four-syllable words as follows:

The choice of words is purely arbitrary as long as the correct number of syllables is present. Children tend to accept the words used more readily if they have local significance. Be sure to mix these new note values with those which are already well-known by the student.

Unequal Subdivisions

Unequal subdivisions are much more difficult to comprehend. Use of the tie as shown in the examples below helps relate the new rhythmic figure to equal subdivisions which the student already understands.

Syncopation problems can be worked out in a similar fashion.

The dotted-eighth and sixteenth figure is often played incorrectly both in terms of rhythm and musical interpretation. Three possible pedagogical explanations are given below.

Use of ties connecting equal subdivisions

Think of the sixteenth note as "going with" the note *after* it rather than the note which comes *before*.

Stop the tone with the breath on the up-beat in order to delay the sixteenth.

I am sure that teaching the quarter-note triplet has presented a special dilemma to many of us. One of my first teachers, Mr. Russell McKiski, who still teaches in that fine state of Texas, must receive credit for introducing me to this technique. While this problem of dividing two beats into three equal parts can be and is frequently taught by rote, a more clear, mathematical analysis can prove to be valuable. Let us use six-eight time as a means toward that end.

The student should practice in slow six-eight time at first, then gradually increase his speed until he is playing two beats per measure. The final result should be the desired one—three equal notes in the span of two beats.

Rhythm Problems of the Advanced Student

Does study of rhythm cease once the student passes the elementary and intermediate levels of study? Certainly not. The metronome should become as much a part of the player's basic equipment as his mouthpiece or bow. As the advanced student begins to show evidence of some real technique on his instrument he should also learn to play with control at any given tempo with a precise, steady beat. The metronome can serve as the student's closest friend in his struggle for mastery in these areas. It is also important that the student be aware of some of the human tendencies toward error in such patterns as those shown below.

In the first two examples the note following the tie is frequently played late due to hesitation on the part of the player. Some teachers use a tenuto symbol or possibly an arrow to indicate that the player should *think of* anticipating this note. The principle here, the same as with the elementary rhythms discussed earlier, still involves accurate subdivision of the beat. The third example is sometimes played with the eighth notes sounding much like sixteenth notes. When this occurs the eighth notes tend to sound rhythmic rather than melodic. The listener becomes aware of the rhythmic aspect of the music at the expense of the melodic line. The true aesthetic intention of the composer is, therefore, frequently lost. But here we begin to get into matters of interpretation which is another subject in itself.

Conclusion

The student should understand that "the *correct note* (pitch) played at the *wrong time* is in reality the wrong note." Using this as a starting point, further arguments for good rhythm can be emphasized as needed. From a pedagogical standpoint acquiring good rhythm is understanding it, working toward a physical feeling for it, and finally, through repeated drill, developing an almost automatic response to complete rhythmic patterns.

As for sight-reading proficiency, perhaps the most important element for success is application of the Pestalozian concept of "learn to do by doing." There has been some speculation in the assumption that the higher I.Q. a student possesses, the better his potential for superior sight-reading ability. On the other hand it seems logical to believe that such a talent must be developed through a proven system of pedagogy and applied through repeated drill and sight-reading experience. Nevertheless, here is hoping rhythmic success to you in your teaching and to your students in their performance, regardless of what your system happens to be.

February · April, 1969

Introducing Contemporary Rhythms

Ralph Laycock

Many conductors have been reluctant to move into one of the most exciting and accessible aspects of contemporary music, music employing meters such as 5/4, 5/8, 7/8, etc., either as the meter signature of a large section of a piece, or, and this can be even more challenging, when intermingled with each other and/or the more conventional meters. The rewards for the sound teaching of such rhythms far transcend the ability to perform such a piece *per se*. The interest generated among the students, the attention to rhythmic detail demanded, and the heightened respect for constant counting in all musical performance can be most valuable in the growth of any music organization.

Unfortunately, most pieces written in this vein seem to presuppose intimate acquaintance with these rhythmic devices, and consequently can be very difficult to teach to a group not already "in the know." However, the resourceful director can originate unison exercises which will put everyone to work (himself included, if necessary), learning how to handle such complexities; only when he feels that everyone will have a fair chance of doing an acceptable job on their own part, will he lead them slowly and carefully into the unfamiliar

Ralph Laycock is director of orchestras at Brigham Young University in Provo, Utah. He holds a B.A. degree from BYU and an M.S. in orchestral conducting from Juilliard. He has also completed course work toward a D.M.A. in conducting from USC.

territory itself. This article and my next one will deal with some possible ways of providing the students with sufficient background to successfully negotiate the difficulties in such compositions.

Prerequisite

It must be understook at the outset that the group *must be* or *must become* adept at counting the more traditional patterns employing notes of the smallest value to be encountered in the piece in question, for to attempt to teach such music "by rote" can only lead to utter frustration for everyone. It is not our purpose to go into such procedures here; this much rhythmic discipline must be taken for granted.

General Exercises

We must assume that a composer who has chosen such a rhythmic idiom has done so because it conveys something that could not be accomplished through any other means. Consequently, it *must* be made to flow in perfect rhythm, otherwise it can only destroy rather than enhance the musical message he has conceived. I have found the following exercises to be very beneficial to conductor and performer alike; when repeated as needed over a period of days or weeks, they become second nature to everyone. The conductor, who must be the most secure of all, can grow along with the students, solving his problem of acquiring a beat

that is meaningful and automatic while they are acquiring technical command of their instruments, and while *all* are acquiring the rhythmic feeling and mental and physical co-ordination necessary for a successful encounter with such a piece.

Because it is the simplest and most popular of the asymmetric meters, the five-pulse measure seems to be the logical one with which to begin.

Everyone, including the conductor, should count aloud, accenting, in *a*, the first and third, and in *b*, the first and fourth beats as indicated. After the students have become secure in counting both versions, the conductor should vary his pattern from one to the other so that the students have to watch his beat carefully in order to know which beats to accent. It would be helpful to point out to them that the conducting pattern is formed of two unequal "halves." After the first (down) beat, the baton works to the left until it is time to begin the second half, for which the strong movement to the right, with its natural feeling of accent, is used. Then the baton works its way out from the center until it is time for the up beat.

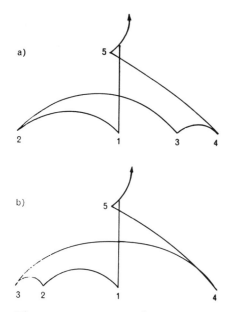

a)

b)

a.

b.

etc.

etc.

Thus, paying particular attention to the two most important gestures, they are not so apt to get bogged down in the details of the total pattern. (Nor, for that matter, is the inexperienced conductor.)

I would stress the importance of accenting the desired, and only the desired, beats. Everyone must arrive at the point where this is second nature so that when they encounter faster tempos they conceive the units in groups of twos or threes and *not* as individual pulses. Clapping the hands together on the accented beats can be very helpful not only in acquiring this feeling for groups but in aiding the conductor to see how thoroughly the students have acquired this concept.

a) $\frac{5}{4}$ etc.
(sung) 1 2 3 4 5 1 2 3 4 5

b) $\frac{5}{4}$ etc
(sung) 1 2 3 4 5 1 2 3 4 5

This exercise is similar to the first, but sung beginning on *do* in *C* major, as a preliminary study to the next example. Again, the conductor should vary the pattern, and, by watching the animation with which they accept their words and/or hand-clapping, make sure that the students acquire the ability to change instantly to the pattern he is conducting. (Also to make sure that he can conduct, without hesitation, either pattern he chooses.)

This is similar to the second, except that it is played on instruments. At first, the most familiar scale should be used, but it can be useful in helping the students acquire facility in any scale desired, (including the one or ones needed in the piece to be practiced later). The use of such rhythms strengthens their rhythmic sense at the same time they are strengthening the technical command of their instruments, and, repeated daily, can help make their playing more secure on both counts. Preferably, it should be done without music so that they can watch carefully for changes of accent dictated by the conductor as above. If you have not used such rhythms previously, I am sure you will be surprised at the speed with which youngsters catch

on. Most of the difficulties of performing such rhythms exist primarily in the mind of the conductor!

At first, string players should play all accents down bow, so that they become that much more accustomed to responding physically to the natural accent of the pattern, thus:

(a) ⊓ V ⊓ V V   (b) ⊓ V V ⊓ V

For the same reason, percussionists not on a mallet instrument should, for a while, make all accents in one hand, then in the other, thus:

(a) L̇ R L̇ R R and Ṙ L Ṙ L L

(b) L̇ R R L̇ R and Ṙ L L Ṙ L

They should not be allowed to sit this out because they do not have different pitches to play.

a.

b.

etc.

etc.

The use of such rhythmic figures comes most characteristically (and most challengingly) in music whose animation is such that these figures cause a real "bumping" of the listeners' natural rhythmic sense. Consequently, the tempos are such (even if written in quarter notes) that the conductor cannot effectively show each pulse of a five-beat measure, and an entirely different conducting pattern becomes necessary. This, also, must become entirely automatic both for the conductor to manipulate and for the performers to "read."

The solution is to adopt a modified two-beat pattern, modified because one of the beats contains a group of three small pulses as against a group of only two in the other beat. One effective way of indicating which is the longer beat is to slow down the speed of its rebound so that the baton spends the additional time still moving up-

ward, thus showing that it is not yet time for the next beat. This is particularly helpful in mixed meters where it serves as a brake to those who might otherwise be tempted to anticipate the following beat. Another manner of conducting such a measure (but which, to my mind, is less successful than that above because it fails to warn of the extra time that must elapse), is that in which both rebounds come immediately to the top, the baton then stopping and waiting for the next beat. In this latter method, even the alert player can be caught off-guard unless he has had time to learn the music very thoroughly.

So let us leave this happy group practicing *all* of their scales in both versions and with various articulations for the next month, by which time they should be thoroughly prepared for the next step. ∎

—— PART II ——

Last month several general exercises were suggested as being helpful in making the students acquainted with asymmetric rhythms and both the players and conductor at home in performing them. With these as background, here are some exercises developed for specific pieces, presented in the hope that they will provide a springboard for your own imagination to assist in solving problems in repertoire you would like to perform.

Allegro con grazia

The second movement of *Symphony No. 6* by Tchaikovsky is available in standard editions for orchestra, and transcribed by V. F. Safranek, from Carl Fischer, for band. Inasmuch as the orchestra is in *D* major and the band in *D♭* major, the key signature has been left for you to supply mentally. When rehearsed slowly, the examples should be conducted in five, employing the *one two three* four five pattern, but at performance tempo a modified two-beat pattern, consisting of a short followed by a long beat, should be sufficient, and is certainly more in character with the music than five fast beats per measure, which would entirely destroy the grace and charm of the piece. It may be worth pointing out that a conductor when first trying to use such a two-beat pattern may feel that he is not helping the group enough, especially during the long beat, but if the players cannot maintain the tempo it is proof that they do not yet feel secure rhythmically, and that more learning is needed.

It is suggested that the following exercises be written on the board the first time they are presented, in one octave only and in one key only, so that the students get to see what they are practicing. Subsequently, though, they should be sung by the instructor only. If the players are used to playing scales and the previously mentioned variations of them, they should have no trouble picking up these patterns.

Example I

This should present no difficulties, as it is one of the general exercises suggested last month as preliminary study in such rhythms.

Example II

The addition of the triplets in the third beat turns it into one of the figures used in the movement itself. Be sure that the triplets are neither rushed nor attacked too roughly.

Example III

Must be played neatly and lightly, as in the symphony itself. Do not overlook the dynamic indications.

Example IV

Perhaps a quick review of Example I might precede this, just to reinforce the fact that these are twice as fast. Though accents might be helpful at first on beats *one* and *three*, the scale should eventually go securely without any undue accent.

Example VI

doo - dle doo - dle doo-dle doo-dle doo - dle

A legato-tenuto feeling is proper here. Be particularly careful that the eighth note is not too insignificant.

With the training above, and a few moments during which the players can search their own parts for similar figures, think through such rhythms as have not been already examined, and solve problems of technique, they should be able to do a successful run-through of the entire movement, especially if a cautious tempo is set. I am sure that their success will spur them on to the additional work and polishing necessary for an authoritative reading of this elegant number.

Take Five

This delightful little tune by Paul Desmond, arranged by Paul Yoder and distributed by Hansen, is actually quite challenging for two reasons. One is the jazz feeling, wherein successive eighth notes are slightly uneven, the one *on* the beat being slightly longer than a true eighth note, and the one following it slightly shorter than a true eighth note, (but *not* as uneven as a quarter-eighth triplet,

often used to "explain" jazz). Other facets of the jazz idiom include the fact that normally the first eighth is also a little louder than the second, and that stray accents may be thrown in to avoid this becoming too monotonous. The other problem

511

is the accompaniment figure—so easy for one person to perform neatly and crisply on the piano, and so difficult to make "swing" when divided up among a number of wind players.

Attacking the first problem may also help to solve the second.

a. Sing to *doodle,* as shown, let-

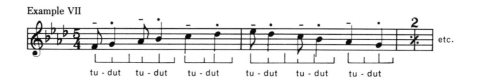

Example V

ting the word cause the notes to be slightly unequal both as to rhythm and volume as explained above, ("doo-" louder, longer; "-dle"—

shorter, quieter). A "leader-follower" routine wherein the conductor sings the pattern for two measures and is then answered by

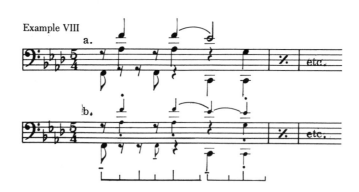

Example VII

tu - dut   tu - dut   tu - dut   tu - dut   tu - dut   tu - dut

Example VIII

a.

b.

the group for two measures can be very helpful in establishing the subtleties of the idiom. When it becomes secure, odd accents can be introduced, as for instance the one shown on the highest note, where a

breath accent, not a more sharply tongued one, serves to give that note the emphasis it needs. For experience, accenting all of the off-beat notes in the same manner, can help make the students aware of the importance of a flexible breath supply, the use of which is imperative in jazz-oriented music.

b. Play the exercise in similar fashion with light tongue and emphatic breath in the manner spoken of above. This should provide the players with a rudimentary knowledge of "swing" jazz feeling, so that they can listen more intelligently to expert performers and realize what they do beyond (far beyond) this to achieve their individuality of expression.

In deciding whether to work out

the melody or the accompaniment first, my vote goes for the latter because it is divided up among so many people that it is difficult for them to conceive it as a whole. Consequently the next exercise is designed to give them this unity of concept.

a. Sing the exercise using the syllables shown. Be sure that the students realize precisely how long each note is to sound; those with the dash continue to sound until the next note is tongued; those with the dot are cut *quite* short, even shorter than a full-sounding eighth. Thus, the long eighth notes are actually longer than the short quarter notes! Even they are different lengths because the first eighth, being *on* the beat, lasts for over half a beat, and the second, after the beat, does not begin until the beat is more than half finished, as shown by the "ruler" underneath the notes. Furthermore, through the use of flexible breath pressure, those notes with large heads are *louder* than those with small heads.

b. Play the exercise using breath accents and light tongue. It will probably be more difficult to make

the pattern sound idiomatic when played than it did when sung because of the slow response of some of the lower instruments. Work for immediate, slightly accented attacks, (*à la* piano) to avoid sluggishness, but do not allow too-pronounced attacks to rob the figure of subtlety. It should not be considered conquered until the flavor can be maintained when all are playing no louder than *piano,* in order that the melody can be heard easily without forcing.

In letter b. an attempt has been made to show the interpretation of the accompaniment figure which is written as at a. Rehearsal of the printed part should be more meaningful with the background the students should now have in both rhythmic and dynamic alterations not shown (and impossible to show precisely) in either the score or the "realization" in version b. above. (One thing is certain, though, without such subtleties the piece is best left alone.) Perhaps the best way of solving the problems is to repeat the first measure many times, with interruptions by the conductor for further instruc-

512

tion, singing, etc., so as to clarify everything for everyone. Those not playing should sing so that they too are becoming more acclimatized to the nuances involved and will be able to handle them, and the rest of the piece, more adeptly when their turn comes.

More difficult technically, but easier to understand because it is "more of a piece," the melody should partake of the unevenness

Example IX

of rhythm and volume learned in Ex. VI, and a brief re-run of that example might well precede detailed work on the melodic line. In Ex. VII the addition of slight breath accents as shown helps to give the melody shape and to avoid the deadly monotony that would set in if it jogged along always in the exact same vein. A creative soloist could add other details that would also help keep it sounding fresh. (In fact, we recorded portions of the accompaniment and let our jazz men work out with it on their own time, then, by repeating these sections with the written melody omitted, gave them "ad lib" solos which they carried off very well.)

One more subtle but worthwhile

Example X

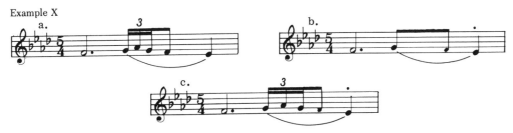

effect is the proper treatment of the measure shown as written at a., and as played at c. Because the triplets are decorative only, the skeleton might be shown as at b., and the measure rehearsed in this fashion until thoroughly understood, with the G eighth note being longer and louder than the F eighth note. When the triplets are added again, it will be seen that they should take a little more time than their written value indicates, because they occupy the space of a "long" eighth note, not a true eighth.

In slow rehearsal, the conductor should use a *one* two three *four* five pattern, but at performance speed (up to ♩ = 168), a modified two-beat pattern, with the long beat first, is to be preferred. Because of the intense rhythmic feel, one might find it helpful to go down snappily on *one*, coast quietly through two, and make a crisp rebound stroke upward and to the right on three, which would show that *four* is imminent. *Four* would then come diagonally down, rather animatedly, and five would move crisply up without delay to alert the players to the coming downbeat, *one*.

For a piece of this nature, my personal preference leans strongly toward making the greater part of the conducting gestures with the wrist, the fore-arm moving casually to the right and a little upward during beat two and somewhat more animatedly back to its starting point during *four*. Any look of awkwardness or heaviness is to be entirely avoided, not only for its effect on the audience, visually, but for its stultifying effect on the performance itself.

Next month: Mixed meters. ■

──────── **Part III** ────────

When a group can play 5/8 meter securely, it is ready to move on to the most fascinating and challenging of the contemporary rhythmic variants—mixed meters. At the present time the eighth note is most often chosen as the smallest rhythmic unit, just as it is in 5/8 time, and the larger (pulse) units are still made up of either two or three eighths (the short and long beats of 5/8 time), or their rhythmic equivalents. The main difference is that in mixed meters these long and short beats do not follow each other in an unchanging pattern as they usually do in 5/8 meter.

Even though the pulse is irregular, much of this type of music, on intimate acquaintance, comes to life with a logical and even inevitable rhythmic feeling that goes a long way toward making the performance much more "solid" than would seem possible at first glance. However, this can happen only if both the conductor and the performers thoroughly understand and feel the rhythmic accentuation as desired by the composer.

The following passage of eighth notes (Exercise 1), has no recognizable rhythmic feel until it has been "organized" into accented and unaccented sounds, as shown in Exercises 2 and 3. These accents determine the length of each measure (from down-beat to downbeat) and the meter signature that must consequently be affixed to each, *and not the reverse.*

513

Exercise No. 1

Exercise No. 2

Exercise No. 3

Exercise No. 4

Because such rhythmic displacements produce their most telling effects when the tempo is fairly rapid, some compromises in the writing thereof have come to be accepted, and even necessary. Note, for instance, that in the third measure of No. 3 the notes have not been grouped as we would expect 6/8 meter to be because that would be contrary to the desired effect—three groups of two notes each. Consequently, it is customary to use 2/4 in place of 4/8. 3/4 in place of 6/8, etc., when there are an even number of eighth values in the measure, *and they are to be grouped as pairs.* Thus, Exercise 3 would more normally be written as at Exercise 4, and the metric relationship would either be expressed, that "the eighth note remains constant," or implied through notation:

$$(\; = \;)$$

General Exercises

As with asymmetrical rhythms previously discussed, the most efficient way to prepare a group to rehearse a piece containing mixed rhythms is to work on exercises that get the point across to everyone at the same time. For this purpose, exercises similar to the following, written on the chalkboard and counted aloud, should prove helpful.

Exercise No. 5a

count 1 2 3 4 1 2 3

5b

count 1 & 2 & 1 & a

Exercise No. 6

count 1 & 2 & 1 & 2 & a

Exercise No. 7

1 & 1 & a 1 & 2 &

1 & 2 & a 1 & 2 & 3 &

1 & a 2 & 1 & a 2 & a

In order to use No. 7, it should be written on the board with spaces between the individual patterns so that, while the students are counting one pattern, the teacher can point to another, then, on signal, have the students change to the new pattern without losing stride. As they become more proficient, the tempo can be increased and the changes made after fewer repetitions.

Exercise No. 8

Less often seen, but subject to greater variety of rhythmic organization within the measure, the patterns shown in Exercise 8 above provide still greater challenge if the group wishes to explore such territory.

Specific Exercises

Rhythmic patterns similar to those above can be extracted from the composition to be rehearsed and written on the board for drill (Exercise 9A). As the basic pulse becomes more familiar, the inclusion of the actual rhythmic elements (Exercise 9b) will make for more meaningful study with greater transfer value.

Exercise No. 9a

9b

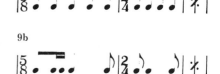

Exercise 10, Donald White, *Miniature Set for Band*, first movement, measure 74

514

Exercise No. 8

Less often seen, but subject to greater variety of rhythmic organization within the measure, the patterns shown in Exercise 8 above provide still greater challenge if the group wishes to explore such territory.

Specific Exercises

Rhythmic patterns similar to those above can be extracted from the composition to be rehearsed and written on the board for drill (Exercise 9A). As the basic pulse becomes more familiar, the inclusion of the actual rhythmic elements (Exercise 9b) will make for more meaningful study with greater transfer value.

Exercise No. 9a

9b

Exercise 10, Donald White, *Miniature Set for Band*, first movement, measure 74

Exercise No. 10

In Exercise 10, above, line c is an extraction of the rhythmic values written for the instruments in the score above it. Written out on the board, it should be counted aloud until everyone understands and can execute it accurately.

Exercise 11

While referring to his own printed part before him, every person should count it aloud, *whether he actually has notes or not,* for it can be very difficult to count rests in mixed meters, particularly in a piece such as this where the rests do not accurately reflect the actual elapsed time. (Notice that whole

rests are used to indicate rests of two beats, and rests of only three eighths duration.) It may well be more difficult to keep one's place through the rests and to come in confidently and exactly on time than to "play on through" once one has made a successful entrance. So *insist* that everyone count audibly through *both notes and rests,* with perhaps a little more stress on the notes in order to demonstrate that they are in the correct place.

Exercise 12

The students should play the passage as written, counting aloud

whenever their vocal apparatus is not otherwise engaged. When they can play it as securely without being conducted as they can while being conducted, they can feel that they are really on the way.

As the students gain confidence in their ability to count such music, through doing a good deal of it, step No. 10 should become superfluous. Indeed, the ability to solve one's own problems as in No. 11 should be the goal of every student so that he can eventually sightread music of this type as well as he can music of more traditional rhythmic organization.

Exercise No. 13a

515

Exercise 13

Mixed meters, being a contemporary compositional device, are often found in association with pitches that themselves pose serious problems to the inexperienced student. This is especially so in atonal, 12-tone (serial), or experimental music wherein the traditional pitch relationships have been deliberately avoided, and the presence of numerous unrelated accidentals and unfamiliar rhythmic patterns may seem, together, an insurmountable obstacle. Again, the solution is simplification.

In preparation for our first reading of the finale of the *Third Symphony* by Merrill Bradshaw, composer-in-residence at Brigham Young University, I dittoed a page

of exercises similar to those shown in this and the preceding articles, and also included rhythmic extractions of some of the more complicated melodic fragments (shown below) along with the original passage shown in Exercise 13, above.

The elimination of the problem of reading and fingering the difficult melodic intervals through the process of simplifying them down to two different pitches (I believe we used *C* and *D* concert), made it possible to work immediately on precise rhythm, articulation and/or bowing, and style. This advance drill proved its worth by turning what could have been a very depressing first reading into a "triumph" when we read the movement through slowly without breaking down in even the most

complex portions. In fact, the players were exuberant at the finish! With that for a starter, they felt that it held no real fears for them and that adequate rehearsal would take care of the intricate details, and they were right!

There is an old Eastern saying, something like this, "If you wish to eat an elephant, you must first cut it up into small pieces." Similar dissection of the problems involved in the performance of music employing contemporary rhythms is equally necessary, for only then can the solving of each small problem be undertaken successfully. When the problems have all been solved, and the piece has been put back together, and has come excitingly to life, that is living, 20th century style! ∎

February, 1967

TEACHING SYNCOPATION

Harry Jenkins

The *Harvard Dictionary of Music* defines syncopation as any "deliberate upsetting of the normal pulse or meter, accent, and rhythm." It further states that our system calls for the grouping of equal beats into groups of two and three with a regular accent on the first beat of each group. Thus, any deviation or shift in accent is felt to be abnormal. This so-called abnormality brings us to the matter of syncopation.

Seeing Figures

When students begin to see confusing syncopated figures, with odd off-beat accents, they become confused by the notation. Perhaps it is because modern notation sometimes (for the reason of attractiveness or music writing economy) seems confusing. Syncopated figures need to be "broken down" mentally in order to be understood fully. Teachers must try to be empathetic, to put themselves in the place of a beginning student who is confronted with this material for

the first time. Here are some common figures:

1. What he sees:

What he must visualize:

2. What he sees:

What he must visualize:

3. What he sees:

What he must visualize:

4. What he sees:

What he must visualize:

Unusual Figures

Here are some unusual rhythmic figures. Let us see how they can be "broken down."

1 Notated

Broken down

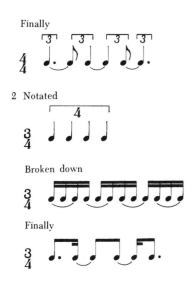

Finally

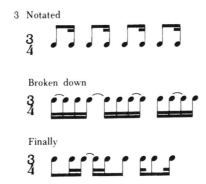

3 Notated

Broken down

Finally

In Conclusion

Students must know *how* to divide and break down various rhythms. They should know where the various beats fall, the downbeats and the upbeats.

They generally need more exercises than are provided in the method books. The teacher, therefore, should seek all available materials. Dance music, in particular, can be a very effective tool since it is full of syncopated figures, and will really motivate the students.

Proper preparation is very important to enable students to grasp syncopation. Syncopation proves troublesome only because the students lack this preparation. ∎

Harry Jenkins is a teacher in the New York City public school system. He has played in the Indianapolis and New Orleans Symphonies.

April, 1966

Balance

RALPH G. LAYCOCK

"But my part says *forte*." How often does a young instrumentalist attempt to justify his actions by quoting some supposedly precise dynamic marking on his music even though he may have neither heard the over-all sound nor realized the relative importance of his own part in it. Or he may have been conscientiously working under the mistaken assumption that if his volume exactly matched that of each other instrument he was properly "balanced."

In concert performance, proper balance is most often the result of the proper degree of *imbalance,* the goal being to ensure that each musical idea is given prominence in proportion to its importance. Thus, in even a relatively simple march, there may be several levels of volume simultaneously in effect, ranging downward in approximately the following orders: melody, counter-melody and/or obbligato, harmony to the melody, bass, afterbeats, snare drum, cymbal, bass drum, with the latter being more felt than actually heard.

To fail to recognize and achieve good balance is, in effect, to admit to the audience, "Here is a great big tangle of sounds. We are sorry, but we weren't able to straighten them out. You are welcome to try to sort them out as rapidly as they come to you. If you can, we're sure that you will enjoy the piece. Good luck!" But little chance the auditors have. If it has not been accomplished in all of the rehearsals, how can they be expected to do it in one quick hearing of music that may be entirely strange to them in the first place.

By contrast, the group which has been competently coached will, in the manner of thoroughly experienced guides, take the audience on an enchanting tour of the music, bringing to their attention every beautiful thought and interesting shading therein. And who is the chief guide? As always, the conductor. And, as usual, he has problems!

Problem of Ascertaining What the Balance Should Be at any Given Moment

I. The Score

A. Most scores indicate only a general volume, all instruments being marked identically.

B. Those that do differentiate may or may not take into account each instrument's dynamic range, so personal judgement will still be needed to assess their proper relative volume. For instance, does *forte* for middle-register flute specify the same amount of sound as does *forte* for trumpet at the same pitch?

C. Few scores indicate the appropriate number of performers needed per section. Recordings of Bartók's *Rumanian Folk Dances* for small orchestra often sport a full symphony string section, which, much of the time, in at least one instance, almost completely obliterates the few winds.

D. Maturity and personality of the individual performers (of real significance in school situations) cannot be taken into account. Even the very presence of a particular instrument cannot be taken for granted.

E. Some instruments may not be specifically indicated—e.g., in baroque music, the "realizing" of the figured bass, the presence of an additional instrument on the bass line, the doubling of string parts by oboes, etc.

II. The Musical Meaning

A. Which is (are) the most important musical idea(s)? For example, in a "variation," how should the repeated theme be balanced with the new ornamentation that comprises the variation technique? In contrapuntal music which are the most significant ideas? (I was once chided by a violinist for not allowing the first violins full reign to sing their "wonderful melody" at the beginning of the Couperin-Milhaud "Overture to La Sultane," as her former director had done.) But the main theme is in the lowest instruments and must be heard and identified as such so that its immediate repetition in the higher voices will also be heard and recognized as such. Her "wonderful melody" is nothing more than the editor's realization of the figured bass as provided in the "complete edition," and was neither composed nor ever heard by Couperin.

B. Has it been well-scored, or do "fillers" really obscure the important ideas? (And here the conductor's knowledge of scoring, counterpoint, etc. is really needed.)

C. What are the authentic performance practices? Would not the small, balanced chorus and orchestra employed by Handel give a more authentic performance than the mammoth unbalanced groups often used? (My recent experience with such a performance of *Messiah* leads me to answer with a resounding *yes!*)

Problem of Achieving the Balance Once It Has Been Decided

I. Physical factors

A. Acoustics of rehearsal room.

B. Seating, both as it refers to placement of instruments in the seating plan and to numbers of players in sections. (And as to the latter, it is often wise to use more "2nds" than "1sts," more "3rds" than "2nds," etc., for two reasons. First, more of the better players are needed on the most difficult parts, so those on the lower parts are relatively weaker players, and second, the lower tessitura makes it more difficult to really "project" without forming bad habits. Seating at least one of the better players in each section helps both because of his own contribution and also because the weaker players can take confidence from him and play more authoritatively themselves.)

C. I n s t r u m e n t s—calibre, type (trumpets vs. cornets, etc.)

II. Personal factors

A. Lack of understanding of music by players—they do not have a full score (which some conductors seem to forget), and must be helped to a full understanding of the music.

B. Performers who, for one reason or another, do not listen as they should.

C. Inability to produce mature

sound, especially in extreme registers, and with it, inability to play either a very full or a very quiet sound.

D. "Extroverts" playing powerful instruments.

E. Dependence on a few secure players to carry the group even when their parts are not important.

F. Nervousness and consequent lack of projection.

G. Type of tone—"buzzy" saxophone, strident trumpet, flabby high clarinets, unneccesary open strings, etc., can make balance impossible to achieve.

H. Flexibility of tone quality—a subject of great importance to the obtaining of proper balance, and one that is not always sufficiently recognized. I will expand on it in a future article, but briefly, a brilliant tone *seems* louder than it is, a mellow tone *seems* quieter than it is, and performers often inadvertently use the one when the other would be more helpful in achieving both balance and appropriate emotional feeling.

Problem of Teaching Balance

As with every other aspect of musical performance, the conductor will achieve better balance, and that more quickly, if he *teaches* his individual players to be aware of and to work constantly for this most valuable goal. The leader who does no more than tell his players, "You are too loud," "you aren't loud enough," etc., will, like the one who teaches rhythm by rote, have to do this with nearly every measure of every piece that is ever rehearsed. But there are many things common to various musical compositions, and as players are taught to recognize them they will, on their own, solve many of the more obvious problems and will be more ready and able to accept their instructor's counsel when needed. Good balance involves hundreds of individual judgements both as to what is needed at each instant, and as to how one must handle his instrument in order to produce exactly what is desired. And this ability to so judge must be built up over a long period of time. Though it is not at all as simple, step-wise or immediate, as might seem to be inferred below, the gradual expansion of the students' (and even the instructor's) hearing can be guided in somewhat the following manner:

The first step must be that of learning to produce a sound exactly equal to that of one's neighbor(s). So, with the entire group listening, have the first and second chair players of a small section (for instance the first two cornets) each play the same note (e.g., tuning C) individually and help them (perhaps with suggestions from their class-mates) to match tone, pitch, and volume as exactly as possible. Then match the second and third chair players in similar fashion, and continue to the end of the section in like pairs, so that each has a chance to feel and hear the sensation of matching his neighbor exactly, or at least, as closely as he is able to. Then have the entire section play simultaneously, with each person trying to match perfectly those on either side of him. If and when it arrives (after further coaching if necessary), point out the blended and united "ensemble sound" that emerges. Repetition of the experiment, perhaps with a different type of instrument, can help reinforce the experience. Subsequently, much work, preferably in sectionals and/or in individual pairs, will be very helpful in both assisting students to gain greater control of their instruments and in learning to listen carefully for balance.

The next step is to balance like instruments in harmony. Again in full rehearsal, use cornets, clarinets, or triply-divided violins, etc. to demonstrate.

Let us suppose we are again using cornets. Tune carefully, then have the 3rds balance, as above, the written *F*. Next, the 2nds on *A*, and the 1sts on the upper *C*, with comments solicited from the entire organization as to what is wrong and how to correct it. Then have all three notes played simultaneously and adjusted as needed. When it "locks in," take the opportunity to point out the beauty and richness of the composite sound that is heard in a well-balanced and well-tuned group. And may I point out that the effect will be equally apparent at any level of maturity—the unanimity of tone and pitch and the equality of volume will make just as much of an improvement in the total sound of younger players as in that of their older brothers and sisters. And *any* group of players is thrilled when they hear themselves, or their peers, really sound fine. The incentive it gives them to strive to sound like that at all times is worth any amount of effort it takes to reach that level for the first time, and for the many times it must be regained in subsequent practice on the same specific goal.

Now they are ready to be put together in complete families and to learn to take into account the very real differences in sound that exist between members of even the same family. Again demonstrating with the brass, choose a triad the notes of which are distributed through the middle range of each section (a triad selected from any appropriate measure in a piece under rehearsal could be used). After tuning and balancing the notes played by each section, as above, have them each play in turn—cornets, trumpets, horns, trombones, baritones, basses, and, with the help of the class, attempt to get equal projection from each group. When successful, have all sections play together, doing the final adjusting as needed. Both they and the remainder of the group should listen intently to the sonorous result obtained, and those playing should individually check their effort and sound against the total as they hear it, so that they may gain the ability to estimate their sound relative to the whole. *It is this individual responsibility for the final results that makes it possible to get something done about the problems of balance.* Unless each player is both anxious and competent to go much farther than half-way, the fight for balance is a lost cause! In the above chord, they will find that certain instruments must be played relatively louder to match the others and that some must be played softer than "normal" so as not to overpower the others. This can be brought out more clearly by having trumpets match horns, cornets play with trombones, etc. and inviting comments from those not playing at the moment. It should quickly become obvious that the type of sound has an effect on its apparent loudness, and also that certain instruments have to be definitely "managed" in order to balance when in mixed company.

Similar experiments with the oth-er major families will turn up other discrepancies in their tonal intensity (oboes and piccolo may seem loud, violas quiet, etc.) and should drive home the point that constant listening and awareness of what is going on in the music is absolutely essential to good balance, even the "equal" balance we have been working with.

Experiments involving the use of notes in the more extreme registers of the instruments will point up still other problems, some of which may be unsurmountable at the present state of maturity.

The next and final step in achieving "equal" balance (but only the beginning of developing the varied balance necessary in actual music-making), is to build a balanced tutti by having each family play a particular chord in turn, balancing it both internally and in total with the other "families" of the organization. And particularly in this case, the podium is *not* the best place from which to judge the success of the project. It is much preferable (and for a really well-balanced concert, indispensable), to do this in the concert hall or other large area so that the conductor may move away from the group and hear it as the audience will. And his own sense of judgment will be enhanced if he will then quickly return to the podium and have the group play exactly as he has just balanced them from out front. He will more clearly realize the difference between the apparent balance at his post and that at the audience's seats and will learn more exactly how to estimate what he should hear in order for it to be properly balanced for the listeners.

Though detailed discussion of "unbalanced balance" must be left for another time, it should be apparent that it is but a logical and refined extension of the training so far outlined. If each player listens intently to everyone else and controls his own playing adequately, it is not hard to convince him of the need for various levels of sonority in order to highlight the important musical ideas they unfold. "If you can't hear the melody, you are too loud." How often have we heard and used that handy expression in the attempt to secure better balance. But how inadequate it

really is to solve our problems! For changes made in only the dynamic level of the various members or sections of a group cannot achieve balance without sacrificing a good portion of the vitality of the music. Without careful attention to the production of appropriate tone quality, a convincing musical representation is impossible.

As we explore this too-often neglected topic, let us first point out a few things about tone itself.
1. There are natural changes in the tone quality of every instrument, dependent on:
a. Register—the normal tone of any instrument gradually changes from relatively dark to relatively bright as one plays from its lowest register to its highest, somewhat as does that of the piano. And in most cases, the carrying power increases as one ascends. (The consequent need to use more players on lower voices of like instruments was mentioned last month.)
b. Volume—the tone of most instruments changes from dark (or even dull) to bright as the dynamic level is raised from very soft to very loud.
2. We become accustomed to these changes, perhaps even subconsciously, and accept them as part of the normal tone of the instrument. Particularly in (b) above, *we tend to relate the type of tone being produced to the volume at which such a sound is the normal one, irrespective of the actual "decibels" involved.* An example taken from the popular recording field may serve to illustrate the point. In listening to a recording of a "big band" supporting a vocalist in a super-charged arrangement, we are made very aware of the fact that the brass are blowing their background rhythmic figures at a solid, even sometimes a screaming, double *forte*. But they are not coming through the loudspeaker that loudly. The total sound of eight or more of them is less than that of the single voice, and were it not so, the voice would be, at best, very ineffective, and at worst, completely inaudible. What, then, gives us the impression of the brass men's great effort? It is the tone quality, the biting incisiveness that comes through even at the low recorded level and keeps the performance keyed up emotionally in a way that

a real *piano* or *pianissimo* sound would utterly fail to do. (Incidentally, one of the very real problems in a live performance of such music, as perhaps in a "musical," is that of getting the required animation in the instruments without completely drowning out the singer.)

3. A single "ideal" tone quality for any given instrument *does not exist*. It is conceivable that there may be an ideal "average" or "normal" tone quality, but I seriously doubt that, even in spite of all the research and opinion-sampling currently going on, any such sound will ever be agreed upon. However, even if it were, that *one* sound would be manifestly inadequate to express all of the valid emotions inherent in music written for any given instrument.

4. The mature instrumentalist cultivates a variety of tone colors and intensities and varies his tone even from moment to moment as is called for by the music. As proof of this, think of the many different means whereby this can be accomplished. They range from mechanical methods such as mutes, special purpose strings, mouthpieces, and even instruments, through such playing techniques as special fingerings, choice of positions, embouchure control, bowing techniques, choice of "attack," manner of striking percussion instruments, choice of mallets, etc.

It should be obvious, then, that tone quality has a great bearing on the proper rendition of the *music* hinted at by the *notes* of the score. And it should be equally obvious that no instrument should be limited to any *one* type of sound, (as its namesake on the organ is limited), but that its tone should be varied as necessary to project the desired musical feeling.

But what is not so obvious is the part that judicious choice of tone quality can play in achieving balance. In the example given above, expert engineering takes care of the problems of balance, but in a live concert they must be solved by the participants themselves, and the conductor must serve as the "engineer." (Indeed, it may be that our concept of what is appropriate in the concert hall may be unduly influenced, if we are not aware of it, by our becoming accustomed to recordings which may have had more "working over" than a live performance can or should even attempt to duplicate.)

But the usual fault in live performance is that too little attempt is made to secure adequate differentiation in the various parts being sounded, particularly in the matter of tone quality. The following graph is a crude attempt to relate the normal relationship between volume and tone quality, (see 1 (b).

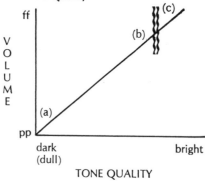

GRAPH NO. 1

Normal Relationship between Volume and Tone Quality

Note that at *pp* volume the tone is comparatively dark, (letter **a**), tending even toward dullness, and that as the volume increases, the tone gradually becomes more and more brilliant, the upper limit of respectability being reached, (at **b**) just before the sound becomes too raucous, too bright, too scratchy, too blatty, or, in short, *too uncontrolled to be useable,* (letter **c**).

However, in the case of the immature player with little control over the sound he produces, the graph will look more like this:

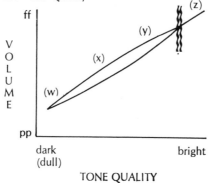

GRAPH NO. 2

Beginner's Relationship between Volume and Tone Quality

Because of his lack of control, his quietest sound, **w**, is neither very soft nor very dark, his loudest useable sound is not really very forceful, and he loses control, **z**, at a rather moderate total volume. Thus, if he is allowed, or requested, to produce a "real double *forte,*" he is apt to display a sound that has neither quality nor stability, but is just "loud." And when control is lost, musicality disappears.

By comparison, the mature player, having learned to control his sound well, has, graph-wise, a large area of ineffective tonal variety at his disposal.

GRAPH NO. 3

Mature Player's Relationship between Volume and Tone Quality

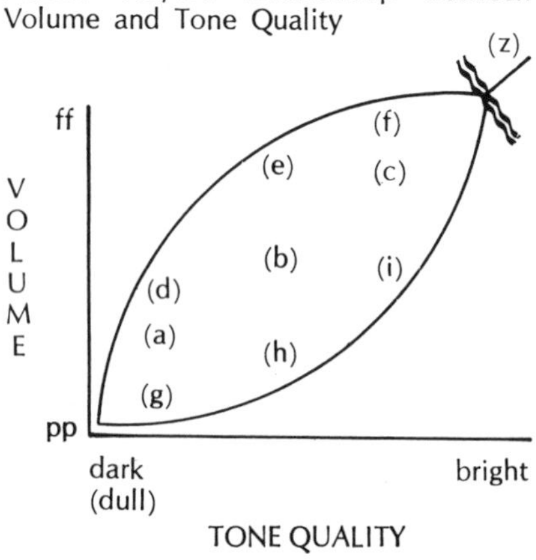

Areas **a, b,** and **c** represent the "natural" tone of his instrument. **D, e,** and **f** show his ability to play relatively "darker" than the volume itself would call for, thus seeming more relaxed than normal. **G, h,** and **i** indicate his ability to play with a brighter than normal tone, thus sounding more animated than the absolute volume would produce. **Z,** as usual, is "out-of-bounds."

Sensitivity to the expressive value of tone quality and knowledge of this auditory effect can be very helpful in achieving the most musical rendition of any piece from an unaccompanied solo up to, and especially in, music written for the most complex mixed instrumental and vocal ensemble. Balance in ensemble performance can only be obtained by:

1. Searching out the meaning of every part of the texture and the tone quality appropriate to express that meaning;

2. Determining the relative importance of these various parts at each moment;

3. Adjusting all parts to each other so as to give due prominence to each. Here it is a matter of making the practical match the ideal as closely as possible in the particular group, the main concern being always to bring out the spirit rather than only the letter of the score.

Perhaps a few examples will give a hint as to the limitless variety of problems of balance, and their solution, in this complex and intriguing aspect of conducting:

1. A quiet, introspective clarinet solo with sustained string accompaniment, both of which are marked *pianissimo*--if taken literally, the soloist may sound ineffective. But if he will deliberately darken his tone and project a little more, (by thinking "oh," bunching the lip a trifle and perhaps dropping the jaw a tiny bit, and adding a little extra breath pressure), he can play with a little more actual sound (as at **d** in graph #3), but still produce a relaxed and calm tone quality. And if, in addition to his fuller but still *quiet-sounding* tone, the strings can be urged, (and it usually takes urging), to bow toward the fingerboard using less hair and avoiding the frog, and perhaps even counter-balancing the weight of the bow a little with their little finger, their sound will be transparent rather than thick, and the clarinetist will have no trouble putting the message across without having to resort to an inappropriate "demanding" sound.

2. The band's woodwinds are to be heard in a broad cantabile, but the brasses are to interject tight rhythmic figures—the necessity of "keeping under" the woodwinds might easily lead the brasses to play with a dull tone incapable of expressing the animation called for. So the woodwinds should play with a large but somewhat dark "singing" tone, (area **e** of graph #3), and the brasses, by tonguing somewhat as in the syllable "tat-tat" and rather low on their upper teeth, forming the embouchure *slightly* toward a smile rather than a definite pucker, and keeping a firm air-column but *not* blowing particularly hard, should be able to produce the necessary "snap" (area **h** on graph #3), without overshadowing the main melodic element being heard in the woodwinds.

This principle is employed constantly in any fine ensemble of any size, and is just as important for proper balance in an unaccompanied contrapuntal duo (where the upper voice is not always the main one), as in more complicated music. The experienced player uses it so constantly that he may be hardly aware of it as a conscious physical act, adjusting almost automatically to fit the musical needs at every moment. I have often thought how instructive it would be if it were possible to record only one instrument of a fine woodwind quintet or string quartet during an actual performance and then to compare the constant variety of tone and volume of his playing with the relatively simple printed part from which he had read. Nothing could more dramatically demonstrate the skill and judgment necessary to fit smoothly and musically into a group.

Like every other aspect of performance, this one must be taught at first in a simple setting (the type of scoring in which everyone has a turn playing the melody is wonderful for this), and in more complex music by taking every measure apart, if need be, to show the how and the why of its use. (After all, the students do not have a full score to look at, but must be able to hear the full score if the performance is to be done with understanding.) But like other facets of performance, it too will become more familiar and easier to achieve with constant attention. Though "If you can't hear . . .," is perhaps a satisfactory guide for a beginning group playing homophonic music, it is entirely inadequate to develop the degree of subtlety demanded in the works of composers whose musical genius has led them to express several musical thoughts at the same time, some of which may even be contradictory in nature. It has been said that in no other art can the simultaneous expression of so many different ideas be understandably carried on, but it is only the expertly-balanced group that can do justice to a composer who has succeeded in getting such a complex creation down on paper in even the very incomplete and imperfect system of notation we are obliged to use.

A keen imagination, a knowledge of available tone colors and how to produce them, and the fine judgment necessary to establish the proper inter-relationships between *every* part of the musical texture will go a long way toward re-creating the full bloom of the music that we find pressed flat and lifeless between the covers of the score. ■

Concerto for Conductor and Unbalanced Orchestra

Donn Laurence Mills

Early in my career as a conductor I remember feeling somehow cheated if the group before me was poorly balanced or lacking in the needed instrumentation. I continually looked for bigger forces to command, for that Utopia where all chairs would be filled with competent players, eager to be led to the heights of artistic satisfaction.

Sound familiar? Enough of my intimate colleagues have voiced the same thoughts to make me realize that many young conductors probably share this common longing. Perhaps our attitudes are to be expected. As students we were encouraged to reach for the stars, and after all, young musicians tend to see only the glamour of the professional music world beckoning to them like a siren on the rocks. We studied our scores, hearing the smooth, well-balanced sound of a Chicago Symphony, not the struggling, asthmatic efforts of a school orchestra. And then reality struck! We took a position with a 30-piece school or community orchestra, and those dreams were lost in frustration and disillusionment.

There are several typical reactions to this situation. Some directors plow through the pages of a score, conducting as though they were indeed facing a great orchestra. They simply ignore what it really sounds like, indulging their private "Walter Mitty" fantasies . . . and they often put on a heck of a show on the podium! Others prefer to "take it out" on the players through barbed criticism and sarcasm. Such conductors let it be known that they resent working with a less-than-perfect ensemble. They see themselves as unfortunate victims of a cruel fate, who have a right to be nasty because their orchestras don't deserve them (well, at least they're right about the last part).

Then there is the martyr's approach. Throughout the rehearsal these conductors lament, "If only we had more violins, oboes, horns, basses, etc., it would sound good." This attitude passes along the conductor's personal sense of disappointment to everyone in the orchestra and eventually generates despondency and a sense of hopelessness among the players. The group feels defeated . . . and they play like losers.

But now and then one encounters a conductor who sees a "hopeless" situation as a challenge and approaches the problem with enthusiasm. For these imaginative men and women, music doesn't make *them*, they make *music*! Sure, it's more exhilarating to lead a fine professional orchestra. The musical rewards are built-in. But there are also rewards in taking a feeble, unbalanced ensemble and creating with it something musically worthwhile. And in good conscience, we *do* want the members of our orchestras to have satisfying experiences. It's not their fault that instruments are missing. So we must do the best we can with what we have, no matter how scrappy and illogical our instrumentation may be. Even poor instrumentation can be made to sound good.

Seating

As conformists (and competitors) we want our groups to at least *look* like the big time, so we seat them in the conventional 19th-century orchestra tradition. Yet this standard formation often puts the unbalanced group at an even greater disadvantage. Second violins are strung out so that they sit somewhere in the vicinity of the horns or percussion, the brass face forward so that their sounds strike the audience (and the backs of the heads of most of the orchestra's

Donn Laurence Mills, a graduate of Northwestern University and the Eastman School of Music, combines a professional conducting career with active involvement in many phases of music education. He is the American educational director for the Yamaha Music Foundation of Tokyo, where he is responsible for the development of creativity and instrumental programs in the U.S. From 1965-1973 he served as director of orchestral activities at the University of Oklahoma. He has been the music director-conductor of the Royal Winnipeg Ballet of Canada, the Charleston (S.C.) Symphony, and has guest conducted major symphonies throughout the world. A well-known clinician for All-State Orchestras, he is also a published composer and author.

mid-section) with full force. Our semicircles look great in the annual photograph, but the actual sound can be garbled and most players cannot hear themselves, or anyone else, very well. What a difference when we seat a small string section in a semicircle around the podium, each member facing forward! Woodwinds also benefit from curved seating patterns rather than the usual platoon-style rows, and brass will not be so overpowering if placed at the sides of the orchestra, facing inward. These seating arrangements will greatly aid the players in relating to one another and in hearing themselves. Also, smaller sections won't feel so intimidated.

For example, let's say you have 6 violins, 1 viola, 3 cellos, 2 basses, 2 flutes, 1 oboe, 2 clarinets, 1 bassoon, 2 horns, 4 trumpets, 3 trombones, piano, and full percussion. To make the group sound good try an arrangement like this:

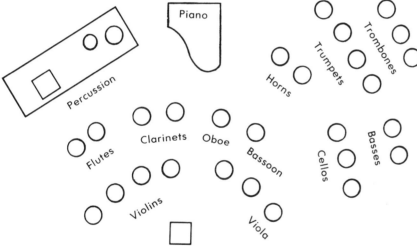

Depending upon the relative strengths and weaknesses of your players, there are several possible arrangements to try.

Doublings and Substitutions

You can double weak parts effectively with other instruments, without losing the intrinsic character of the orchestration. Some possibilities are:

Flutes
Trumpet with cup mute
Sopranino (E-flat) clarinet, played *pianissimo*

Oboes
Trumpet with straight or shastock mute
Solo violin or viola, perhaps *con sordino*
Sopranino clarinet

Soprano saxophone
Guitar

Clarinets
Soprano saxophone
Violas
Trumpet with shastock or cup mute

Bassoons
Trombone with solo-tone mute
Cellos
Tenor saxophone
Three clarinets in unison, in low register
Euphonium or upper-register tuba, played *piano*
Bass clarinet
Horns in lower register, played slightly staccato and *pianissimo*

Horns
Trumpets played into stands or with hat mute
Trombones with hat mute
Cellos, especially if they divide, arco and pizzicato, to resemble tonguing attack
Clarinets behind a baffle or into a box
Bass clarinet
English horn
Saxophones playing *pianissimo*, without vibrato

Trumpets
(Though it's unlikely that you'll ever need a substitute for this popular instrument!)
Oboe, preferably two in unison
Clarinet and oboe doubled
Soprano saxophone
Viola in upper register
English horn in upper register, played staccato

Trombones
Cellos
Bass clarinet
Euphonium
Bassoon, preferably doubled

String basses, dividing arco and pizzicato
Horn in lower register, played slightly open

Tuba
String bass
Two bassoons in unison
Contrabassoon or contrabass clarinet
Baritone or bass saxophone
Piano playing octaves at bottom of keyboard

Violins
Any woodwind instrument, phrased and articulated to correspond with the printed violin bowings
Trumpet, legato with straight or harmon mute

Violas
Two or three clarinets, in middle or low register
Trombone in shastock mute
Horn stopped or muted
Alto saxophone played *pianissimo*

Cellos
Euphonium
Trombone with cup or hat mute
Bassoon, preferably two in unison, playing *piano* and legato
Bass clarinet, preferably two

Basses
Tuba, possibly with mute
Bassoon, preferably two or three in unison or doubled with bass clarinet
Contrabassoon or contrabass clarinet played staccato
Bass trombone with cup or hat mute
Piano playing octaves in lowest register

Harp
Autoharp
Piano with pedal down, played *piano*
Marimba
Clarinets, *pianissimo*, doubled with pizzicato in strings
Guitar
Bass clarinet, marcato, doubled with pizzicato in cellos
Piccolo, played *piano* and staccato in lower or middle register, doubled with bells, played with very soft mallets

The important thing to remember when doubling and substituting instruments is that the effect results as much from the *dynamic level and style of playing* as from the actual instruments used.

Choosing Music

Much of our traditional orchestra music gives "the hard stuff" to the higher instruments, while other members of the group accompany with simple chords or afterbeats. The poor first violins work themselves into a lather while the lower strings and winds huff and puff on dull, uninteresting harmonic figures. Pieces which have long, simple melodic lines on top and put more active harmonies and rhythmic patterns underneath are harder to find but they enable student orchestras to sound better. Ron Nelson's *Jubilee* and Ippolitov-Ivanov's *Procession of the Sardar* are two good examples of such pieces. The brass parts supply wonderful rhythmic underpinning, the woodwinds function as fillers, doublers or soloists, while the strings perform easy, soaring melodies and sound great.

Rewriting String Parts

Since most of the music we play originated before wind instruments became such versatile orchestra members, we find ourselves severely taxing the strings much of the time, while allowing the winds to develop dry rot. Traditionally, demands on string players are heavy, and few student string sections have the technical ability to fully meet the challenge. It takes a bit of work, but the smart director can alleviate this problem. Passages can be rewritten so that the strings play in unison or octave sustained notes while the winds take care of the harmony and counterpoint. Let the winds do more of the tough virtuoso work while the strings sustain the harmonic base, if your players' techniques call for it. The charts of today's pop songs and film scores demonstrate how effective easy string parts can be. It is better to have less flourish and more solidarity than a ragged, failure-prone string section trying to play beyond their capabilities. Give the poor kids a chance to sound good once in a while!

Even very young string players sound good playing pizzicato. Rearrange some passages so that solo wind instruments or sections play legato while the strings play pizzicato and you'll clean up many messy problems. Bowed repeated notes (♫♫♫ ♫ ♫ ♫♫ ♩) are easy, and sound a lot more "virtuosic" than they really are.

Better Use of Brass

Brass players *can* play softly, yet we seldom take full advantage of this stunning effect in our school orchestras. Look for places to add sustained *pianissimo* brass chords, especially in low registers where the sound is rich and won't cover up the thinner strings. Crisp brass articulation (good staccato) will allow the string quality to come through, while sluggish attacks obliterate everything and cause the orchestral texture to be heavy and dull. For more subtle color changes, trumpets and trombones can play into their stands.

The "Wire Band"

Nothing hurts the orchestra director quite so much as the comment, "Sounds like a band." But anemic strings are all but lost when challenged by a full wind section accustomed to the loud dynamics they play in the school band. Since band arrangers have done so well by pilfering orchestral literature, why shouldn't orchestra directors go to good band literature for their repertoire? Band pieces are less "linear," are generally less difficult, and usually transcribe nicely. Besides, much of it is good music. The winds would then have enough to play and the strings could play enhancing parts full of unison and pizzicato passages, in lower, safer, richer ranges. The resulting sound is full, flattering, and quite "orchestral."

Percussion Color

How sad it is that we neglect those eager supernumeraries of the orchestra — our percussion players! We wouldn't feel that percussionists are "extras" if we understood and utilized the many colors they can bring to the orchestra. Adding bell tones, mallet passages (played *piano* or *pianissimo*), batterie accents, reinforcing melodic accents with the incredible variety of instruments and beaters available — or even using the wonderful sounds you can make from junk — all contribute to the color spectrum of your ensemble. If you have a scarcity of the usual "color" instruments (oboe, English horn, bass clarinet, viola, harp, etc.), make up for them through the use of colorpercussion. It can be just as effective.

Piano and Organ

The piano is usually looked upon as an orchestral "cop-out," a last resort to fill out the harmony or replace missing parts. Well, it *is* a cop-out if the pianist continually plays a drab *mezzo-forte*, semi-legato, without giving a thought to the varied color possibilities on the instrument. Imaginative use of pedals, different articulations, and exploration of double and triple octaves are but three very obvious nuances available. When doubling a line in the orchestra, the pianist should strive for interesting sounds to complement, rather than intrude upon, the orchestral texture. Plucking the strings with the fingers for certain notes can highlight a passage the way a harp can, and depressing the sostenuto pedal can serve as an acoustical reinforcer for the entire orchestral sound.

The electronic organ is widely advertised as a "synthetic orchestra," and while we may still hear vast differences between the real thing and an organ stop, there are some interesting combinations possible that can enhance the orchestral texture. Carefully controlled use of an organ can inobtrusively round-out the sound of the orchestra and add thrilling new colors, expecially at climax points. Again, watch the dynamic levels — the organ needn't remind you of the Easter service at St. Patrick's Cathedral!

Amplification

Never, you say? Not kosher? What about professional recording studios? They make excellent use of microphones, not just to increase the amplitude of sound, but to create fine balance and texture, and even add reverberation. In fact, miking and mixing can even produce some sounds that are not possible with ordinary doubling. There are so many fantastic electronic devices available today that we owe it to ourselves and our players to investigate every possibility. Better amplifiers don't distort; they have superb quality, can help improve balance, and can produce some beautiful effects by feeding the source through mixing channels. Contact mikes are available for all instruments and synthesizers can imitate many instruments with uncanny realism as well as produce new and exciting sounds of their own. Let's not overlook these technological possibilities for school groups.

Imaginative directors of course will think of many additional ways to make their groups sound better. The instrumentation that you have been complaining about is really not as much of a stumbling block as you may think. What *is* important is planning it so your group is capable of sounding good — even *before* they start to play! ∎

April, 1956

Tone Quality in the Concert Band

How to improve the sound of the band.

Nilo W. Hovey

ELEMENTS which make up a satisfying and effective exhibition of musical skill are numerous and complex. but probably none could be considered more important than intonation and tone quality. These two items. incidentally. are interrelated to a significant degree.

A good quality of ensemble tone is impossible without good intonation. and likewise. good intonation seems to require a characteristic tone from the various instruments. Possibly it would be more accurate to state that factors which contribute to a poor tone—such as improper embouchure and breath support. faulty reeds and mouthpieces—will also affect intonation adversely. Much has been written about intonation, but information regarding *ensemble tone* is seldom seen.

Two principal problems confront the band director who is striving for a better tone quality in his organization. viz., to improve the tone quality of the individuals of which the group is constituted, and to improve the ensemble tone itself. Since band tone quality is our main consideration here. we shall dismiss the first problem with the statement that essential components of a good individual tone are proper concept. physical aptitude, and good equipment.

Components of Good Ensemble Tone

On first thought, it would seem that an organization in which all individuals produce a good quality of tone would necessarily produce a good ensemble tone, but this is not the case. At this point the rehearsal techniques of the director assume major importance; he must blend the various colors at his command in such a way that the composer's ideas are carried out faithfully and that the final result is pleasing to hear. Moreover, he must be persistent and consistent so that the production of a fine ensemble tone becomes a habit with his organization.

How would you describe a good band tone? What words will serve to draw a mental picture of the ensemble tone you are trying to produce? To me, a good band tone must possess the following characteristics: (1) clarity—not "muddy," (2) compactness—no tendency to "spread," (3) sonority—a richness produced by "bottom to top" sound, and (4) resonance—live and buoyant, not "dead."

Other characteristics of a good band tone include a constancy of color as the volume level is changed. Why do some bands sound like a woodwind quintet in *pianissimo* and a drum and bugle corps in *fortissimo*? The answer is obvious: some students make no allowance for the difference in dynamic possibilities of the various sections. To them, *ff* means that *everyone* plays his loudest! But actually, the composer's desire was merely that the total dynamic output at that point should be at a *relatively* high level. He doesn't ask us to ignore blend and tonal balance.

Achieving Better Tone

Now. what can we do about this ensemble sound? Two of the most productive techniques are. (1) get a proper balance of volume among the players of each section, and (2) get a proper blend among the sections. The organization should sound as a unit—a single instrument. The individual must temper his tonal output according to the requirements of his section; the section must temper its total output according to the dictates of the director. who, in turn, must analyze the composer's intent.

The composer's intent is important, for it justifies contrast in color and the predominance of a particular section when the occasion demands. The idea that soprano brass must *always* be subdued is erroneous. There are times when cornets (trumpets) should cut through the ensemble to convey the desired effect. Then there are times when homogeneity among sections is most effective. Few bands use this effect advantageously.

The director who controls volume and color independently has achieved something that will contribute greatly to the sound of his band. A dark color should be possible at any volume level, so should brilliance. A *crescendo* should be possible without a change in color, so should a *diminuendo*. Is a dark color in loud passages impossible? No, nor is a bright color in soft passages.

In developing a good band tone, it is imperative that every student becomes fully aware of his contribution to the total tonal result of the band at any volume level and in any combination of colors. To do this, he must hear his own part in relation to other parts. In short, one word of advice by the director, conscientiously observed by the student, will produce results. That word is LISTEN.

Nilo W. Hovey is Director of Bands at Jordan Conservatory of Butler University in Indianapolis. He is President of the Indiana Bandmasters' Association and is a member of the American Bandmasters' Association and the College Band Directors' National Association. He is the author of many instrumental methods, and other publications include "The Administration of School Instrumental Music" and "The Selmer Band Manual."

Orchestra Tone Quality

Donn Laurence Mills

If you listed orchestral virtues in order of importance what would you place at the top of the list? Intonation, accurate rhythm, or technique? To be sure, these are important qualities, but if the overall quality of sound is unattractive, not even good intonation and dazzling technique can save the performance. Thanks to radio, television, and recordings audiences recognize good professional sound, and they expect to hear that same sound from your orchestra. Lips curl and noses wrinkle when they don't hear it.

In researching orchestra tone quality, I discovered that school orchestra directors enjoy hearing the same good sounds as everyone else, but they are often mysteriously stricken with aural astigmatism when they conduct their groups. They apparently overlook wretched sound like a stage mother overlooks a daughter's clumsiness. Forced playing, using inferior instruments and performing carelessly and insensitively, may account for some of the poor sound. But students who don't know how to get good sounds produce poor tone. Many private teachers stress tone and can demonstrate what they mean, but what about those students who don't take private lessons? How can a conductor make his players aware of tonal beauty and variety, not only of individual instruments, but of

the ensemble as well? These students need appropriate models.

To begin, a conductor can "talk sound" as part of his regular routine. Of course, he must have a clear concept of the sound he wants before he can describe it to students. It's no accident that certain orchestras achieve a distinctive sound, or that various conductors can get different sounds from the same orchestra. Bernstein seeks drama; Ormandy, richness; Stokowski, delicacy; Toscanini and Szell, clarity; Mehta, excitement; Solti, flow; Giulini, refinement; Von Karajan, definition and focus; Rostropovitch, exhuberance; Bolt, tautness. These maestros deftly change their orchestras' tonal colors through verbal description, singing, stick technique, and close musical rapport with their players. Many school orchestra directors teach the same concepts to their students just as effectively because they know the sounds they want to hear and persist until they get them.

Perhaps you saw the recent television documentary, "Alexander's Bachtime Band," which featured Alexander Schneider and a student orchestra in New York. Most of the rehearsal time was spent on style, nuance, and sound, not on intonation, rhythm, or technique. Miraculously, those other problems vanished as the quality of sound improved. The players were obviously thrilled to get into the soul of the music, and their performance sounded most professional. Their thinking "tone" did it.

Even if a conductor is tone-

conscious and determined, there are still obstacles to overcome. For instance, a conductor can be responsible unwittingly for poor tone quality through his own conducting habits. A steady non-espressivo conducting style causes non-espressivo playing, and a choppy, nervous beat yields a mechanical, shallow performance. Players often subconsciously emulate their conductor's style.

Volume. Because it's easier to play loudly than softly, students may choose the easier way. But the only sound possible in loud playing is a husky, ear-wearying roar, perhaps brilliant for a time, but boring. Subtlety and flexibility are paralyzed by sheer physical effort. Amplified rock groups may be responsible for the youthful notion that loud equals exciting, but loud playing isn't always artistic playing and that's what we're after. Timbre and dynamics are inseparable, and orchestral exercises that combine dynamic and tone control (sustained chords, particularly) improve an orchestra's tone as well as increase it's ability to vary dynamics tastefully.

Vibrato. Playing a smooth vibrato is difficult, but teaching it mustn't be delayed. I've met teachers who introduce vibrato during the first lessons as part of the basic technique of sounding good. I believe teaching vibrato early is a fine idea. In addition, students should become familiar with the many variations between non-vibrato and too much vibrato, and they should be taught how to match vibrato speeds within their sections. Practicing these simple

Donn Laurence Mills is the NSOA contributing editor. He holds music degrees from Northwestern University and Eastman School of Music. A conductor and music educator, he is also the American educational director for the Yamaha Music Foundation of Tokyo.

three-note patterns can help your students match vibrato speeds.

Attacks and releases. Ragged attacks blur an initial atttack and delay it's true timbre by a micro-second or two. Anticipation and disregard for what was just played cause sloppy releases. Bad releases destroy the preceding sound and linger to spoil the sounds to come. Students need to know the when and how of releasing, and practicing this steady quarter-note pattern can help.

When your group can play attacks and releases artistically, you can apply tonal variations to the exercise. But accents must never distort or overload the timbre, and staccato must still be played with good tonal quality.

Range. We usually warm up in the comfortable mid-range, ignoring the treacherous top and bottom ranges, so the middle range of our music sounds good while the high and low passages are often strident and uncomfortable. Play some whole- and half-note exercises in the high, middle, and low ranges, and strive for tonal sensitivity even when the going is tough. Practicing this way is especially important for winds.

Technical Considerations. The pressure and stroke of the bow, finger pressure against the fingerboard, and the grip of the instrument contribute to tonal quality. Posture counts, too, and so does a horn player's right hand position or a percussionist's wrist action.

Students also need to be told what to do to get a better sound, and this usually involves technique, not concept. The conductor must tell a player the information he needs to do the job, poetic description won't help. Words like hard, brittle, lush, fat, thin, thick, edgy, round, full, dark, sensuous, cloudy, and bright may be understood, but they don't give the player the physical means to produce the correct sound. Give your players technical solutions to interpretive problems by translating lofty artistic concepts into practical terms. After students know how to get the desired sound, verbal images may help to achieve your interpretive direction.

Rushing. Like bad releases, nervous anticipation and excitement cause rushing, which pulls, squeezes, and eventually ruins tone. A conductor's frantic command, "Don't rush," has little effect because rushing is guided emotionally; it is not controlled physically or intellectually. Rushing is a beast that must be tamed with podium skills. Drag the beat, pull your players back, and impose your will of tempo. Use a different beat pattern or rehearse by phrases, but don't try to "beat" players into submission with cracks of the baton.

Acoustics. Your orchestra will never sound like the marvellously resonant Concertgebouw Orchestra in a dry, brittle room. For many years I worked in a rehearsal room that absorbed tone like a paper towel, and the concert hall wasn't much better. During rehearsals the orchestra sounded porous and weak, but on tour the orchestra was glorious; the players perked up, played better, and were thrilled by their own sounds. If your rehearsal room absorbs much sound, try practicing elsewhere, perhaps another room in the school, a church, ballroom, or auditorium. Record your group performing in a room that complements the orchestra's sound, and review the tapes. The improved sound will inspire everyone to try harder.

Chord-tone sensitivity. Chamber musicians sweeten thirds and sevenths and cool fifths, and they intensify dissonances and fatten tonics. You can teach these professional devices to your students by practicing V-I cadences. They contain all the material you need to teach chord-tone sensitivity. Select these cadences from music you are already rehearsing.

Variety. A wonderful piece by Elliott Carter contains only one pitch throughout, yet it is dramatic from start to finish because of kaleidoscopic changes in tone color and dynamics. There are hundreds of ways to shade and color a tone, and you can uncover many hidden hues and textures if you play long tones as an organist changes stops. Put students in teams and encourage them to practice "sound seeking", one group matching the sounds of another. Orchestrating a pitch by adding, eliminating, or combining instruments is another fascinating lesson in achieving tonal variety.

Tone quality is one of an orchestra's most important artistic resources, but it's not a luxury; it's a fundamental to good playing, achieved by working diligently. Training students to listen for tone may not suddenly transform your orchestra into a major symphony, but at least you'll be pursuing similar goals. ■

Jazz; Ensembles & Guiding Students

WHY "WING IT"?

by John F. Maltester

Having traveled to schools around the nation, I've discovered that the word has really not gotten out. There are still too many educators who treat jazz as an obscure language and too few who know how to teach jazz. Perhaps you are one of many educators who feels uncomfortable teaching jazz. "Why begin a jazz band?" you say. Well, why not? The demands of instrumentation and musicianship allow students to develop technical, mental, musical, and creative aspects of music faster than any other organized presentation. Putting a jazz band together is not easy, but it can be done even with limited resources.

Organizing a Jazz Band

The instrumentation of a jazz band may vary depending on the students available, instruments, and music. Do not shy away from using euphoniums or saxophones on trombone parts, electric piano for the bass part, or any other substitute that gets the part played. During auditions, do not use improvisation if it discourages students from enrolling.

If you are fortunate enough to have full instrumentation, then you have the dilemma of chair placement. Basically, you need to find a lead trumpet, a drummer, and a lead alto player. You can then build a good band around these players. There are several placement considerations. First, take a look at the strengths of the sax section and place the students in order with the strongest player on lead alto, the second to the strongest on lead tenor, and the third to the strongest on the bari part. If possible, let two players share the lead trumpet chair.

Successful jazz educators have learned to select literature and place personnel to showcase a group's strengths while hiding its weaknesses. Working on the weaknesses is as important as hiding them, otherwise they will always be there.

The group's image is important and fragile. As a director your job is to select music and look for performance opportunities that will have a positive effect on the development of the group. When selecting a program, ask yourself, "Would I want to be in the position I am placing the students in?" Such a consideration will help to avoid many pitfalls.

The Psychology of Rehearsal Procedures

The first consideration in any rehearsal is discipline. Without discipline you will have a disorganized jam session. The progress of the rehearsal depends on your ability to organize, the band's discipline, and the common goal of always displaying the best musicianship possible. Because the music often dictates a "relaxed" situation, the jazz band rehearsal atmosphere should be even more disciplined than a concert band rehearsal. If you demand that students be quiet, have good posture, and show the proper level of concentration in concert band rehearsals, then you should require even more in your jazz rehearsals. If your concert band members are not allowed to wear funny hats in rehearsal, then don't allow this practice in jazz band. It detracts from the atmosphere necessary for good rehearsals.

Encouraging students is critical in a jazz ensemble, but you must always encourage "with a strong stick." The egos of most young musicians fall into two categories: many better players think they are "the answer to jazz," while the less experienced ones always take comments personally. The truth is that the better jazz bands have developed a sense of controlled aggressiveness and a collective ego that is strong enough to take criticism, yet sensible enough to continue to listen and learn from all comments directed toward their performance.

Pace your rehearsal time so that you mix more difficult concepts with those that are easily grasped. Do not belabor a concept if it is not immediately understood. Remember that teaching jazz is like teaching a foreign language. You could not learn French in a week, so do not expect your band to "swing" in five days.

Because every director has a different personality, every approach to rehearsing the jazz band will be a bit different. Some directors can use peer pressure to the group's benefit. If you are able to do this, then do it. Good teacher-student relationships are always important in music, but in jazz they are imperative. There is a delicate balance between aggressiveness and the frustrations associated with experiencing creativity. Coupled with the immediate contact of a one-on-a-part situation, the director often feels like he needs a degree in psychology to keep things moving in a forward direction.

A word about the "winning" syndrome is always necessary. Those directors who thrive on competition and trophies often end up in the middle of a train wreck. Most jazz festival formats encourage competition, but your program will become shortsighted if you center your band's existence around winning. The only competition students need is the competition of always playing their best every time they pick up the instruments. This outlook generates the need to play better at each performance. It is a concept that ensures the proper mental attitude so necessary for continuous musical growth and development. Directors who push for competition with other groups often have rehearsals that are either very good or very poor because the director's goal is not always the same as the students'. Conversely, the band that always tries to better its own performance quickly focuses on the task of each rehearsal and develops in a consistent manner.

When selecting music, avoid imposing your views on the students. Let your players discover what is easy or hard, good or poor by using their own standards. Students are much smarter than we give them credit for. Too often I have heard directors tell groups, "this new music is difficult," or "this isn't a very good chart," or "you've already played some of this arranger's works, so you probably will be bored with it." Good music by good composers and arrangers is only boring when it's played poorly. You will need to consider the psychology of everything that goes on in a rehearsal. Those who do will find that their groups progress and prosper both musically and personally.

Rehearsal Techniques

Always have an outline, written or in your head, of what you want to accomplish at each rehearsal. Your schedule considerations should include improvisation, rehearsing spots in music, jazz history, style, listening, theory, and sight-reading.

Always remember to pace the brass section because of endurance considerations, and never forget that enthusiasm and discipline are necessary aspects of the well-run rehearsal.

Sectionals are important in the development of a jazz ensemble. If you do not have enough class time for sectionals, then have section leaders set up off-campus rehearsals. These meetings can rotate from house to house, include refreshments, and actually become one of the important social functions that all groups need. The section leader is responsible for running the sectional, not the director. Asking the section leader to develop an outline of what is to be accomplished will help this student understand the responsibilities of leadership.

The chain of command in a jazz ensemble begins with the director, then passes to the lead trumpet, and then to the drummer. The director, of course, must take all responsibility for the group, so his decisions are crucial and provide the final word. The lead trumpeter is responsible for establishing all ensemble phrasing, articulation, and any other aspect of playing such as dynamics, lengths of drops, and so on. The drummer is responsible for setting up all ensemble entrances, relating to and supporting soloists, contouring rhythm section dynamics, and establishing a good stylistic feel upon which the ensemble can build.

Try dividing the rehearsal time into four segments. The warm-up should include scales, improvisation, and *tuning*. Tune the jazz ensemble as carefully as you would tune any other group. The players must tune at the same dynamic level they

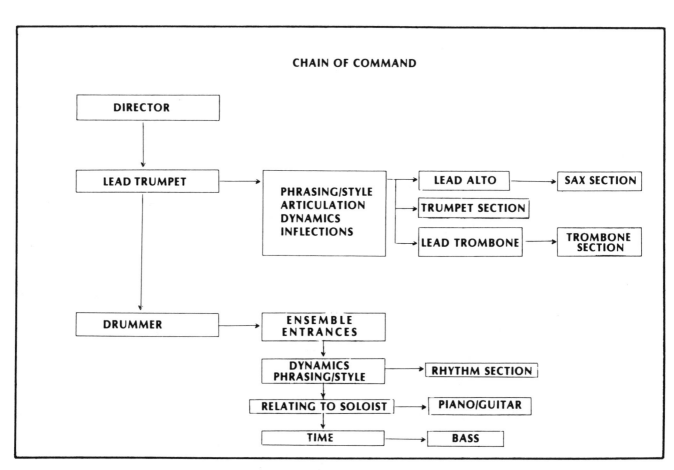

will be asked to play. Make the first selection the "potatoes" of the rehearsal. This should be a spirited tune, one that the band plays well. The "meat" of the rehearsal should be the task of the day, keeping in mind that rehearsing difficult sections is more important than playing straight through the chart. The "dessert" follows — a tune the band likes and plays well.

Your moods will dictate the quality of the rehearsal. Do your rehearsing your own way, because the most comfortable way is the best way. Keep the band members on their toes by not letting them get lax in an attempt to relax. Posture, pitch, and intensity must be a concern throughout the rehearsal. If improvisation is new to you, practice along with the band members — they won't mind.

Rehearsals should include periodic listening. Give some thought as to when to have students hear a recording of a chart they are performing, and make sure students know what to listen for. They should be concerned with phrasing, articulation, kicks, balance, intensity, and so on, not just the "hot" solos. Be sure your players realize the "road syndrome" of professional recordings. This phenomenon occurs because over the period of a lengthy tour, and before the recording session, the band often molds the tune to the personality of the personnel, including different articulations, added inflections, and even some rhythmic changes. When the recording is made, you often get the "road" version. Explain this fact to the students so they do not decide the music, or the recorded group, is incorrect.

The seating of the band is very important. As a general rule, lead players should always be in the middle of the sections and lined up so they can hear each other. Most band setups are too spread apart so the players farthest away from the rhythm section cannot hear "time." The bari sax and bass trombone should be on the same side of the band. The bass player should be able to see and hear the hi-hat. The pianist and guitarist should have eye contact for comping patterns, etc. Set up the band so its strengths are spread out. Do not use a new setup if the players have a difficult time functioning as an ensemble.

Improvisation

If your teaching situation allows room for improvisation, do it. You can involve string players, concert band members, and vocalists as well as the jazz students. There are so many teaching aids available that ignorance or lack of experience is no excuse.

If you can fit improvisation into your ensemble rehearsal time, do it every day. Everyone should play anything at first and then become more selective as the inhibitions fade away. Start with simple ideas, keeping in mind that a few good notes are better than many wrong ones. Relate the scale forms to major scales for easy construction. Do not allow students to play only blues scales. These scales are useful in getting the younger students to play "jazz" sounds, however these musicians easily fall into the false security of thinking that blues scales will suffice as enough knowledge for jazz improvisation. Take the time to play many

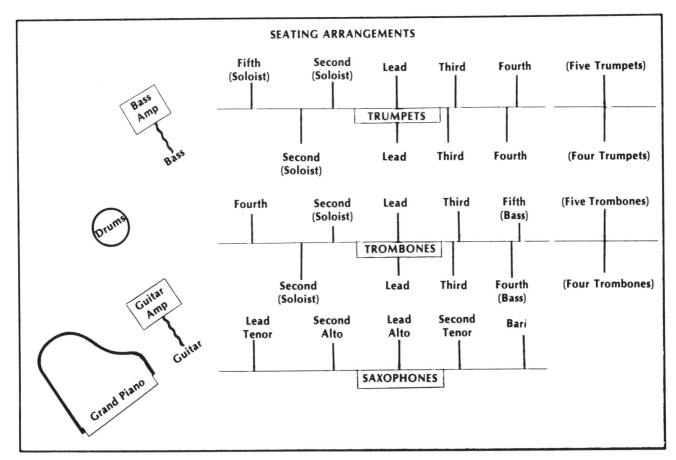

533

recorded examples so your students know what they are working towards.

Singing and writing are as important as playing. Have the class "scat sing" and write solo, and bass lines, so the students will have to think of correct pitches and rhythms. Encourage jam sessions!

Improvisation is the most insecure part of performance for most students. The director can ease any anxieties by approaching it with a serious and disciplined view. Impress upon students that although playing wrong notes will not bring the end of the world, wrong notes are still wrong notes. If played within the learning process, wrong notes are okay. However, they are not acceptable if the student is not making a sincere effort to be creative and expressive.

One of the most important aspects of jazz, and all music, is the ability to hear the tonal makeup of the appropriate sounds. One exercise that helps students and teachers to hear better consists of playing a major scale as the "parent scale," and then playing the basic scale forms found in jazz. These scale forms include the dorian, lydian, dominant, and blues scale. This exercise helps the students hear basic scale forms related to the major tonality, as well as aiding them in realizing scale and pitch relationships.

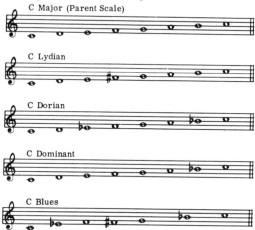

A Jazz Educator's Source Book

One problem that all jazz educators confront is the over abundance of materials. Having so much available is actually more confusing, at times, than it is helpful. One outstanding compilation of information is *A Comprehensive Guide to Jazz Ensemble Literature* by Roger Rickson. This book contains almost 1,000 jazz ensemble chart listings, director aids, students aids, books, methods, improvisational aids, jazz history bibliography, and a big band combo discography. It is available from Roger Rickson, 1015 West Rancho Road, Corona, California and costs $20 per copy, plus $1.50 for packing and shipping. I highly recommend that educators obtain this publication as a major source book for their programs. Although there are other books available, few include information that has been reviewed, and none are more comprehensive.

Other fine books that deal with the basics of organizing, rehearsing, and directing a jazz band are available. Three of the better books are Rick Lawn's *The Jazz Ensemble Director's Manual* (Barnhouse), Hal Sherman's *Techniques and Materials for Stage Band* (Jenson), and the *Complete Guide to Instrumental Jazz Instruction: Techniques for Developing a Successful School Jazz Program* (Parker) by John Kuzmich and Lee Bash.

Jazz and the "Other" Band

Band directors generally put in more hours, both in and out of school, to develop good programs — programs they can be proud of. From a psychological view, the programs we develop are more than a display of talents: they are an extension of our egos and our entire beings. Knowing this, it is difficult to understand why music educators study and listen to music for concert band, marching band, and orchestra, and then turn around and attempt to "wing it" when developing the jazz band.

Jazz is no different from any other form of music. It can be learned, and it can be taught. There is no easy way to develop jazz groups, but with a bit of study, the director who is uncomfortable with teaching jazz, will soon find ways to adapt his personality and talents for a successful approach. ∎

John F. Maltester is the coordinator of performing arts at Los Medanos College in Pittsburgh, California where he has had award-winning ensembles for many years. He was the president of the California chapter of the National Association of Jazz Educators for five years and is now the N.A.J.E. Western Division Coordinator.

Introducing Jazz Improvising

by Arthur Woodbury

The prospect of playing music without seeing written notes has frightened more than one student into complete silence. Thereafter, feelings of inferiority and face-saving rationalizations effectively bar them from any further contact with this special kind of music. "I'm not that kind of musician" or "Jazz music doesn't interest me" are the usual comments.

The combination of fear and avoidance is, unfortunately, all too common. Even though the student may not become a jazz performer or use improvisation as an important tool in his own profession, having some expertise in the area is an important part of becoming a knowledgeable musician. The ability to improvise is not the exclusive province of a talented few; teaching techniques exist that can bring this esteem-building skill within reach of all music students. For teachers, knowledge in the area is becoming mandatory in order to be of service to their students.

Usually the teacher's primary concern is how to get the student to try in the first place. In many ways it is like learning how to swim; to learn you must get into the water. A degree of success in the beginning stages of improvisation eliminates much of the fear of this undertaking and puts the first big hurdle behind the student.

Begin with the Blues

The blues style offers students a good starting place for learning to improvise. It is a familiar style that makes few technical demands on the performer; it is easy to hear, relates directly to what is on the radio every day (much of rock and roll is blues related), and from the teacher's vantage point, it is easy to teach.

The Nature of the Blues

An earthy style of music, the blues is organized in 12-bar patterns with progressions that contain inflected "blue" notes that do not seem to be a part of the equal tempered scale. The blues is more of a chord progression than any particular melody; it can be filled with anything as long as the notes stay in style. Improvisation is an important, if not the central part of the music.

Contrary to its reputation as slow and desolate music, the blues is designed to "deliver one from the blues." It is a catharsis, a means of escaping from the pressures of society. The blues can be performed in all types of tempos and styles — fast, medium, slow, sad, facetious, cynical, happy, philosophical, even funny. Of course, these styles came about primarily because of vocal considerations, but instrumental performance reflects the same attitudes and modes of expression. Graphic portrayals, both musically and physically, are not uncommon.

12-Bar Blues Pattern

We first need to become familiar with the basic 12-bar blues pattern, which is probably the most popular basic blues chord progression; certainly it was popular in the 1920s and 1930s.

1920s-30s Basic Blues Pattern (Ionian Version)

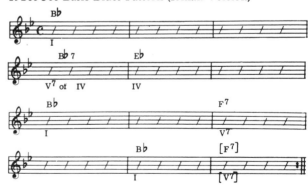

Be-Bop Blues Pattern

Once we are comfortable with the basic 12-bar blues pattern, the next step is to concentrate on a slightly newer version of the blues, one that came into favor during the be-bop days of the 1940s.

1940s Be-Bop Blues Pattern (Mixolydian Version)

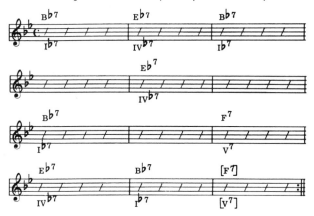

This 1940s be-bop version of the blues is similar to all 12-bar blues patterns because it relies on the three primary chords of the key: the tonic (I), the subdominant (IV), and the dominant (V). The usual blues pattern follows a tonic-subdominant-tonic-dominant-tonic chord progression, as in the first example. The 1940s be-bop pattern varies slightly from the older progression but is recognizable as the same general outline. The use of the Mixolydian scale, while inferred in the older style, is more pronounced in the newer style. This means that the flatted seventh degree of the tonic scale, occasionally used over the top of the older 1920s Ionian mode (major scale) version of the blues, has become a more common feature in the newer 1940s version. Consequently, the newer version is more apt to be Mixolydian (flatted seventh) than Ionian (major seventh). This 1940s Mixolydian version of the blues provides a good starting point for learning to improvise.

Jazz Blues Scale in B♭ (Minor Pentatonic Scale)

Blues Scale

Just as jazz musicians often fall back on the blues scale during a blues improvisation, students can start to improvise using the blues scale exclusively and still stay within the blues tradition.

The blues scale has unique properties that eliminate the usual harmonic and melodic hazards of chord tones and non-chord tones. Whatever the student plays, as long as it is the blues scale in B♭, sounds right. This freedom from

wrong notes is a big plus; it allows the student to fulfill improvisatory fancies without worrying about enthusiasm-blunting clams (mistakes).

I have presented the blues scale (really a minor pentatonic scale) in its descending form because of the tendency for scale members to resolve downward. Of course ascending blues scales are used, but there is a feeling that these swim upstream. The descending form sounds more comfortable and conclusive. For instance, it is typical for the flatted third of the scale (D♭) to resolve down a minor third to the tonic (B♭) and the flatted seventh (A♭) to resolve down a minor third to the dominant (F). The other notes of the scale have this same tendency to resolve downward.

Mixing Major and Minor

By imposing this blues scale over the 1940s bebop (Mixolydian) version of the blues, the soloist plays in minor, while the accompaniment stays in major. Modal mixtures (major and minor played simultaneously) are common in the blues.

Blues Scale Over 1940s Blues Pattern

Freezing our beginning players into the minor blues scale with the accompaniment staying in major reduces many technical demands. In blues, whenever the blues scale is used by the soloist, there is a tendency for this minor pentatonic scale to want to stay in one position and not move. (There are exceptions to this statement, but generally speaking, the observation is true.) The interesting result is that the chords change, but the scale does not. All the student really needs to play an entire solo are the five notes in the minor pentatonic blues scale.

In the post-war 1940s, however, a new note

Arthur Woodbury is associate professor of music at the University of South Florida in Tampa. He is a former associate editor of the magazine, Source, Music of the Avant Garde *and has written numerous articles about new music.*

was added to the blues scale. This note had appeared in blues music before, but the be-bop style adopted it as an identifying trademark. This is the flatted fifth which we will add to conform to common practice. The be-bop musicians took the basic five-note minor pentatonic blues scale and made it into a six-note scale. Three of these notes, the ones most often altered by inflections, have become known as blue notes and are circled in the next example for easy identification:

Modified Six-Note Blues Scale with Circled Blue Notes

Because students will begin to improvise using this modified six-note blues scale only, it is a good idea to have them practice this scale until it comes easily. Of course, the scale will have to be transposed for different instruments. While transposing can be confusing for students, the skill is a part of being a jazz musician and should be learned. All players with B♭ instruments will transpose up a major second (notes, key signature, chord symbols); players with E♭ instruments will transpose up a major sixth; and all other jazz instruments can use the notes that are written here. A clef transposition may be necessary for some instruments.

First Exercise

The following exercise, designed for beginning students, is a 1940s-style blues solo (three choruses) as it might have been played by any typical be-bop musician of the time. Only the notes of the six-note blues scale are used. The exercise will acquaint beginners with the blues idiom and demonstrate the heavy blues sound that results from strictly adhering to this modified minor pentatonic scale (with flatted fifth). Although it does not involve real improvising, the exercise will give students an idea of what it feels like to play improvised passages.

I suggest recording the chord progression in the 1940s be-bop blues pattern to accompany the students for this exercise. A rhythm section made up of piano, bass, and drums is usually available in most schools. Plan on taping 15 to 20 choruses of the chord progression, at MM ♩= 100. The background should be rhythmic, but neutral. Use quality cassettes and tape recorders so that the playback will be on pitch.

Notations for inflections are indicated as follows:

⌣ for a bend
⌢ for an inverted bend
⌐ for a drop
⌐ for a scoop
⌐ for a sag

Use a combination of these when the situation calls for it.

Some students will have to transpose the 1940s be-bop blues solo before playing with a taped rhythm section which could also involve an octave transposition to put the part in a comfortable range. In addition, all students will have to be coached on how to play jazz eighth-note rhythms, which have a lazy, rolled sound that just borders on compound meter.

1940s Be-Bop Blues Solo

Practice Tips

This written-out solo, while not difficult, presents some technical problems. It will take individual practice and rehearsal time with the taped rhythm section before the solo becomes familiar. Perhaps a dub of the rhythm section tape could be made for each student for home practice. Later, the written solo can be used as a head, a unison ensemble part played by everyone at the beginning and end of the composition. The improvised solos can then be sandwiched in between these two sections, the usual playing format in jazz.

Building Blocks

A motive is defined as "a short, distinctive melodic fragment that is also easily recognizable as a rhythmic pattern." Motives are repeated in some form throughout a composition, thereby strengthening their importance. They are not usually repeated literally – sometimes shortened, sometimes extended, sometimes varied, sometimes inverted, sometimes repeated as just a rhythmic pattern. Almost any recognizable variation of the original idea (either melodic or rhythmic) qualifies the fragment as a derivative of the motive. Other melodic fragments that are not either obvious or repeated systematically, but do occur as a matter of course in music, are usually referred to as figures.

Motives, the building blocks of an improvisation, should be thoroughly studied by the student. Related projects, such as taking blues motives from recordings, inventing new motives, playing each other's motives, discussing the relative merits of these motives, and so on, are all worthwhile activities.

Exercise with Tape

For proof of the blues scale's infallibility and the complete freedom from wrong notes that it offers, I suggest the following exercises be performed with the rhythm section tape. This way, students can be gradually weaned from written notes so that improvising occurs naturally, almost imperceptibly.

• Ask students to extract any motive or idea from the written solo and play it anywhere in the progression. Some of the more important motives are bracketed for easy identification. The others, some only possible as motives, are there for students to find.

• Ask students to play some of the bracketed motives anywhere in the progression and to change the rhythmic pattern. They can even play the motives backwards. By now the infallibility of the blues scale should be apparent to everyone.

• Have students invent their own motives spontaneously while the taped rhythm section is playing, using only the six notes of the modified blues scale. No matter how simple or complicated the rhythm is, it is practically impossible to play a wrong note. Occasionally you will hear a mistake which usually turns out to be a note outside the modified blues scale that the student was trying to use.

When this happens it is enough to point out these notes and tell students you will discuss how to handle them later. For beginning students, I have two cautions: 1) do not attempt to play any additional notes other than the six indicated in the modified blues scale until they

learn how to handle them; and 2) when playing the flatted fifth, resolve it either up or down by a half step.

This process of gradually playing improvised music usually takes place without comment from the student. The change from written notes to unwritten ones seems like a natural progression of events. Students are usually ecstatic about the fact that they can sound so right and are playing in style from the very beginning. The next step is to extend these motives to create a feeling of unity over a longer period of time. Improvisation games can be used to teach this. They provide a natural musical situation where these skills can be easily learned.

Melodic Extension

The basic game is statement and response. This, plus the many variations of the game, can be used to teach the concepts of melodic extension. The first game goes like this: arrange the sequence of students playing the game in a specific order, put on the tape of the rhythm section, and indicate to the first student to play a two-measure motive of his own choice. Two measures are easy for everyone to keep track of without counting and allows sufficient time for playing the motive. In the succeeding two bars, ask the second student to try and imitate the first student's motive. It should be understood in advance that it is not important or even desirable to exactly duplicate the two bars. In fact it soon becomes apparent to the students that even partially duplicating the music's rhythm and contour is all they need for a coherent extension of the melodic material. Duplicating pitch is not as important as one might expect it to be.

In the next block of two measures ask the third student to invent a new motive, and then ask the fourth student to try and imitate this motive during the next two measures. This continues on around the room with students taking over for themselves. Coaching students that the six-note modified blues scale contains the only eligible notes is sometimes a good idea.

Many variations of this game are possible. For example, agree in advance to invert the motive during the response. Again, an approximation of the rhythm and inversion, or even a partial approximation of these, is all that is needed.

Another common occurrence in jazz is for contrasting material to be presented in the response, as a consequent that is also related to the blues style. To ensure that the contrasting material does serve as an appropriate response, ask the following questions: did the response actually comment on or add to the motive? Does it serve as a logical consequent to the preceding idea? Does it seem to fit into the general context? Ask students to discuss these questions. There are countless ways to present a response. The students should not find this to be a difficult problem as long as the response stays in style.

Versions of the Game

The three major versions of the game are: 1) the original game of duplication in the response, which most likely contains variations of the motive; 2) inversion in the response, also likely to include variations; and 3) contrasting material as a response. More variations of the game are possible, but these three are the most useful.

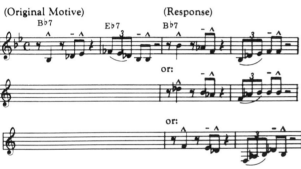

Inversion in the Response

Contrast in the Response

Each version of the game should be studied and mastered separately before mixing the responses is allowed.

Give the student freedom in these early attempts at improvisation. The only guidelines should be to accomplish the goals of the game and use only the modified blues scale. At first this calls for a certain amount of acceptance on everybody's part; improvement will occur rapidly with positive coaching. Jazz improvisation is spontaneous expression. There should be a balance between knowing the modified blues scale and the different kinds of responses and just letting things happen. This balance will differ from student to student.

As students progress, a certain squareness in their phrasing often becomes noticeable. This can be remedied by shortening the response (truncation): leaving off the ending notes, taking out the middle notes, or leaving off the beginning of the motive during the response. Of course, this applies only when attempting to duplicate or invert motives in the response; it does not apply when using contrasting responses.

Another way to combat squareness in phrasing is to extend the motive during the response, although the addition of only a few notes is possible because of the two-bar time slot. Truncating or extending the motive in the response helps to counteract blocklike phrasing, generate more interest in the phrase, and, at the same time, provide an appropriate response. The next example illustrates how this can be accomplished.

Truncation in the Response

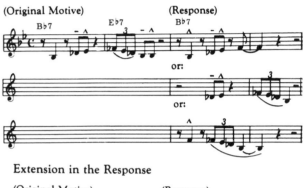

Extension in the Response

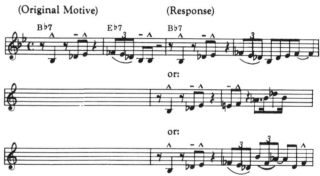

Further variations can be made by shortening the increments of time to a one-bar statement and one-bar response.

When the time comes to lengthen the improvisation segments to four bars, I suggest having each student take on both statement and response. This is like having a conversation with yourself. The student who follows in the next four-bar increment should try in some way to comment on the preceding four bars to ensure continuity.

Autonomy as an Improviser

At this point the student is close to achieving autonomy as an improviser. The game of statement and response automatically sets up an antecedent-consequent result, which is the basis for extending melodic material in all music. This game creates a natural situation that requires players to be sensitive to their musical surroundings and to make personal responses to it. Accomplishing this goal makes the entire project worth the student's effort.

There are two ways that jazz musicians can organize their improvisation. Some players try to keep track of the original motives (ideas) that occur at the beginning of the composition and develop them as they proceed. This is a classical concept. It is more common, however, for the improviser to live from moment to moment. A motive is presented, developed for a short while, abandoned, a new motive presented, possibly abandoned immediately, another new one presented, developed, another new motive, and so on. This is the through-composed approach. Both methods are viable. While the classical approach has followers who can construct highly organized improvisations, the through-composed course is followed by the majority of jazz players. This is the approach described in the statement and response game. It is certainly the easiest course for the beginning student to follow, and I recommend it.

With a little practice developing four-bar statements into full choruses, students should be ready to go into rehearsal with a performance in mind. The following performing format is suggested:

• Ensemble playing of the head (1940s Be-Bop Blues Solo)
• Individual solos (24 or 36 bars each)

• Trading four-bar (or two-bar) phrases among the students
• Ensemble playing of the head (Be-Bop Blues Solo) to a predetermined chord

I usually bring in a rhythm section for this event, and after a little rehearsal students should be ready for a performance.

Students can learn to improvise on their own in a few lessons if they know the blues scale and learn the techniques of statement and response to help them organize and extend the material. The jazz format of head/individual solos/trading four-bar phrases/head out accomplishes the goal of overall organization.

The entire project, from first lesson to first improvisation, can be fun for students and produce immediate musical rewards. The knowledge they gain will give them confidence to thwart the mystery and fear so many students have of improvisation.

Of course there is much more to jazz improvisation than a 12-bar blues chorus and using the blues scale, but the goal of learning these basic improvisation skills should help pave the way for further exploration. Certainly students should now be able to approach the challenge without fear of the unknown. Jazz improvisation should be a familiar experience to all our music students. Not only will they have fun doing it, at the same time they will become better musicians for learning it. ∎

October, 1986

Achieving That Elusive "Big-Band Sound"

BY JAMES WARRICK

Every jazz ensemble director wants his group to produce the rich, vibrant sound that professional jazz bands achieve. Hearing that sound in your mind's ear and not hearing it produced by your ensemble, though, can be a frustrating experience. What follows are proven techniques that can be used to create that elusive big-band sound.

Establish the desired sound in every player's ear. Many young players have never even heard a jazz ensemble when they sit down for their first rehearsal, so take some time to play recordings of ensembles that demonstrate the way you want your group to sound. Much of the music published today has professionally recorded demonstration albums available that you can play for your students.

The time your ensemble spends listening may have a more lasting positive effect than the same amount of time used to work out wrong notes your students could fix on their own outside of class. Of course there will be no time to listen to recordings if you plan too many concerts too close together or schedule an overabundance of music to learn.

Sponsoring in-school performances by high school, college, or professional bands that produce the sound you wish your group to emulate can serve two purposes: all of your students can hear a live tonal quality not often present in recordings, and everyone will have the chance to listen to how more experienced players sound in your concert hall or rehearsal room. If possible, have the guest ensemble use your group's sound system, drumset, or guitar amplifiers. This will demonstrate to everyone whether the acoustics of the room actually are a factor in creating an undesirable ensemble sound.

Be realistic in your musical choices and your expectations of the ensemble. All too often directors make the mistake of selecting literature that is manageable only by older, more seasoned performers, then find fault with the less-than-mature sound of the tape made at the final concert. An eighth-grade trumpet player does not sound like a junior in high school, and a senior in high school does not sound the same as a college graduate student. Many young players today have the technical facility to play the notes, but the sound of a high school jazz ensemble will not likely have the sound characteristics of a college or professional group. Carefully select arrangements that will highlight your ensemble's assets, not their weaknesses.

Use visual aids to demonstrate your goals. To show the internal balance within the ensemble, draw three pyramids on the blackboard representing each of the wind sections.

Each section needs to maintain the internal balance shown in these pyramids with the overall blend and balance of the rhythm section acting as the base. When a section performs independently in non-unison passages, the players have to produce that pyramid by supporting their own particular lead player, even for only a few beats. When the entire ensemble performs, however, each section has to contribute to the pyramid, with the lead trumpet as the apex.

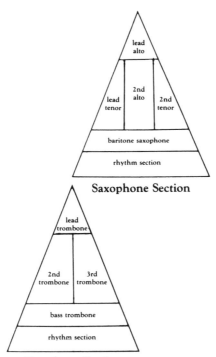

Saxophone Section

Trombone Section

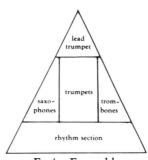

Entire Ensemble

This format gives everyone in the ensemble the same focal point and relieves the lead trumpet player from playing beyond his dynamic capacity. Such a concept is especially important when the lead player is concerned with endurance.

Begin by establishing balance in the rhythm section. A recording engineer works first to achieve balance and tonal equalization in the rhythm section before adding the other instruments. As you listen to the balance of your rhythm section, ask yourself the questions that go through the mind of an engineer:
• Is the bass drum too loud (or soft)? the snare? the ride cymbal?
• Is the drummer exerting enough pressure with the foot on the hi-hat cymbals to produce a tight, clean "chick"?
• Are the drums tuned like those on the recordings you are

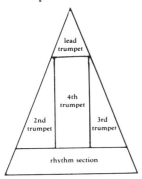

Trumpet Section

trying to emulate? Many school drummers use drumsets that are tuned more for rock than jazz. Consider hiring a professional jazz drummer to tune your school's drumset if you are unsure how to achieve the sound you desire.
• Can you hear specific notes out of the bass amp, or is the sound one low rumble? Experiment with different settings of the tone controls and require your bassist and guitarist to write down those settings for that piece of music. Also ask them to try playing the strings at different locations in relation to the pickups. Small guitar equalizers are rather inexpensive and can make any bass or amplifier sound cleaner.
• Are the guitarist and pianist both playing the same type of comp patterns, with the same type of chord voicings, in the same range, at the same time? This homogeneity creates a bland, muddy texture.

Teach rhythmic stability. Members of professional big bands have a keen sense of keeping time. To teach young players how to play in a steady tempo, regularly use a metronome or drum machine during rehearsals. Small, inexpensive electronic metronomes made with output jacks that connect to an amplifer or headphones can be worn by members of the rhythm section during portions of a rehearsal. While at first the headphones may interfere with the rehearsal, eventually students take them for granted. It is not at all uncommon for professional musicians to perform with a click track in recording studios. These players know how to ignore the click so it doesn't get in the way of their playing. Schools might be wise to purchase a drum machine for members of the rhythm section to use during home practice or to have available on that unfortunate day when the drummer is absent.

Tune first. It is not a waste of time to tune, both before and during rehearsals. What's more, a chord played in tune sounds fuller and more resonant than an out-of-tune chord played loudly. Your ensemble will never achieve that elusive, professional sound unless everyone plays in tune.

Make sure you provide the guitarists with enough time to tune as carefully as the wind instruments. Electronic tuning devices are great for these string instruments, but only if they are properly calibrated and powered at full strength. Small electronic tuners are so inexpensive today that directors would be wise to purchase one or two for students to check out to use at home, as they would a library book. Tuners can be a boon to brass players who need to learn the degree to which a mute placed in the bell affects intonation.

Short of electronic sound reinforcement, there is little that young saxophonists can do to compete with the brass section without playing out of tune. The major contribution of the sax section should be to add color and texture to the ensemble's blend, not volume. The mental attitude of the saxophonists needs to be one of control at all times, with special thought directed toward playing in tune.

Be wary of doubling parts. Do not double parts and expect the result to sound like one player. It may be uncomfortable to tell an extra player to sit out for one composition, but if two players share a part it is impractical to expect perfect intonation and balance.

Direct the brass bells toward the audience. Every marching band director knows that brass instruments produce a directional sound. Achieving proper direction of the bells over the music stands and toward the audience for brass players is perhaps the easiest way to achieve an immediate improvement in a jazz ensemble's overall sound. If this is not done, the tonguing, which creates the clean, precise sound associated with professional ensembles, is lost to the floor or the backs of the saxophonists.

Be resourceful during problem years. There are certain times in every ensemble when incomplete instrumentation creates problems. Many times there are other students in the department who are willing to help out. Before you omit a fourth trombone part due to a shortage of players, consider using a second baritone saxophone, a tuba, or even a bassoon. Certain compositions lend themselves to the addition of a French horn to double unison saxophone lines or assist a weak lead trombonist. A vibraphonist can be an asset when the lead trumpet needs help.

Assess the instruments used by ensemble members. New students may not have had quality musical training or proper individualized attention prior to joining your group. Often, too, students struggle with poor-quality instruments, mouthpieces, and reeds that would make a good performance impossible even for a consummate professional. Make sure to take time to evaluate the equipment of each of your students, especially those who do not study privately. If you do not feel confident in certain areas, consider bringing in a clinician for a day to help.

A notable aspect of the Stan Kenton Band was the consistency in the drum sound over the years, despite personnel changes. This was partly because Kenton owned the cymbals and required each of the drummers to use them. If you are serious about your jazz programs, consider purchasing a hand-picked ride cymbal and a pair of precise sounding hi-hat cymbals.

Avoid the overuse of sound amplification equipment. Too often a jazz ensemble sounds completely different on stage than it does to the audience because the sound system is used incorrectly. The use of too many microphones creates more variables and increases the potential for problems with balance. In most cases, less amplification is better. The Woody Herman Thundering Herd performs using only three microphones.

Treat sound engineering as an art; it should not be the hobby of a poorly trained student. Require your sound reinforcement engineer to listen to professional recordings of the music already performed by the group being amplified, or at least to quality recordings of professional big bands. It is critical that the engineer realize the primary sound source should be produced by the acoustic instruments on stage, not the public address speakers. He should use the sound system to fill in only the sections or individuals that cannot otherwise be heard. It is absurd to take the beautiful natural overtones and harmonics created on thousands of dollars of quality musical instruments performed by young people who have spent thousands of hours working on the art of performance and have the music crushed, condensed, and amplified through an improperly equalized public address system with its inherent distortion qualities using inexpensive amplifiers, microphones, and speakers.

Develop soloists. Regardless of how good a jazz ensemble sounds, it needs to have soloists to receive attention. While some directors inherit soloists who have developed naturally, most of us have to train students to improvise. I conclude that two axioms exist regarding improvisation: Axiom one — there is no alternative to learning the theory associated with chords and scales. (Students who rely only on their ears without learning chord and scale construction have a limited existence as jazz improvisers. Thousands of albums, books, and other publications are available to assist educators in the process of imparting the knowledge necessary to know what to play in almost any given solo.) Axiom two — there is no alternative to listening to recordings of proficient jazz soloists to develop a jazz language. (Too many young players are expected to stand up and solo with little or no exposure to the musicians who have gone before them. Directors who create record libraries of jazz soloists and make them available to jazz students will have the investment fruitfully returned in better solos.)

Special activities can help generate extra enthusiasm. Consider hiring a local college or professional jazz ensemble director to work with your ensemble for one or two rehearsals. Someone listening with a fresh perspective will be able to point out problem areas to which your ensemble has become accustomed. Even if a guest repeats what you have been telling your students, they will listen to him as an expert and give his statements more credence.

Another change of perspective can be gained by taking the ensemble to perform in a jazz festival. The established jazz educators who judge these festivals know how to communicate positively with young players. Students can evaluate themselves, too, so take the time to make recordings of your ensemble and to have your students listen to these recordings in an environment just as intense as your most important rehearsal.

Finally, do not be afraid to ask your students what they think about the music you are giving them to perform. If you find you are on a completely different wavelength, it may be time for you to buy a few more records, attend a few more jazz concerts, and write a few more publishing companies for demo albums.

Nowhere else in the world do young people perform jazz music at as high a standard as in America's schools. Likewise, nowhere else do music educators have the resources available to them to cultivate even higher quality musical performances. As audiences grow more demanding, so should the desire of the ensemble director to have a group that sounds like the pros. ■

James Warrick is director of jazz studies at New Trier High School in Winnetka, Illinois. He regularly reviews new jazz publications for the New Music Review section of The Instrumentalist *and is the newly appointed National Jazz Curriculum Chairman for the National Association of Jazz Educators.*

July, 1985

That Elusive Element: Swing

by David Liebman

When Duke Ellington wrote "It don't mean a thing if it ain't got that swing," he was evoking one of the main prerequisites of great jazz, if not the most important element. "Does it swing?" remains the essential question, and an experienced listener can answer it immediately. The ability to hear — and for musicians, to play — swing can be developed, although some people seem to sense it instinctively. To gain a clear perception of how swing works, it's useful to break swing down into its basic elements.

What Is Swing?

All forms of jazz have their own definitions of swing. For example, Charlie Parker and John Coltrane both swing, but in different ways. Once we understand the musicians' goals in each context we can discuss what sounds swinging. From here on, explanations and judgments are subjective; one musician's idea of swing may sound stiff to another.

Although there is no one way to define swing, a quality of swing common to all periods of jazz is a feeling of looseness and flexibility of the beat. The point is not to metronomically mark off the pulse, which produces a rigid playing style; one of the most subtle effects in jazz is to play around with the beat, staying loose instead of rigidly keeping time. This, by the way, distinguishes jazz from most dance and folk music, for the very context of dance means to put one's feet on the ground in a regulated manner.

The mathematics of swing are that one quarter note becomes equivalent to a triplet. By leaving the middle note out, the player achieves a feeling similar to that of a dotted eighth followed by a loose sixteenth. In jazz, all eighth notes are interpreted in this syncopated manner. It is crucial for the performer or listener to be able to recognize the syncopated rhythm of swing.

Realizing Swing: Hearing

Hearing swing requires the listener or performer to:

1. Understand the general context of the music and the specific considerations of the style in question. For example, in jazz, one of the differences between Charlie Parker's music and John Coltrane's has to do with Coltrane's generally looser approach to the pulse, which is indicative of that period in jazz history.

2. Direct his attention, first of all, to the relationship between the "time-keeping" cymbal

543

beats of the drummer and the placement of the bass line. In bebop jazz, for example, the bass is usually in sync with the cymbal, whereas in free jazz, the idea is to work off of each other — sometimes together, sometimes not. Once the rhythm section feels good and is swinging, the lead player or players is responsible for gliding over and under the basic drum-bass cushion.

3. Remember that swing is intuitive, subjective, and physical. Other aspects of music call for the intellect (ideas of melody, harmony, and so on) or the emotion (expression). Nothing, of course, is cut and dried, but swing should feel good in a sensual, physical sense.

How to Practice the Factors Influencing Swing

Remember that none of the elements listed below exist alone. They affect each other dramatically, but for clarity, I will distinguish between them.

1. Placement of the Beat

In jazz talk, you often hear phrases like "on top, bottom, middle of the beat." The actual metronomic pulse is usually decided upon loosely in the count-off of the tune, but the musician chooses where to place each beat. As mentioned earlier, flexibility of the beat is important. The artist uses anticipation (on top), delay (on the bottom), or dead accuracy (in the middle) to express his ideas. He constantly considers the expressive possibilities of these different placements of the beat.

Of course, because there is no conductor or metronome as such in jazz when performed, the musicians' differing interpretations of where the beat should lie can result in tension. One of the best examples of creative tension in the rhythm section was the Miles Davis band of the mid-1960s with Herbie Hancock (piano), Tony Williams (drums), and Ron Carter (bass). For a great part of their recorded music, there was a tendency for Tony Williams to be slightly on top of the beat in relation to the bass and piano. He did it so well that in effect, he has the patent on that interpretation of time; every drummer playing now must be aware of Tony's approach. On the opposite side of Miles' band was John Coltrane's rhythm team of McCoy Tyner (piano), Jimmy Garrison (bass), and Elvin Jones (drums), which seemed to have a common behind-the-beat vision of time, especially at slower tempos.

Practice

First, the student should learn to play scales, intervals, jazz lines, and so on, with the metronome acting as the second and fourth beat. This is very difficult to do; the tendency is to make the first and third beats strong. The eighth notes should have a dotted feel and a specific articulation, which will be covered under the next subheading. The goal is to place the beat accurately, internalizing the pulse so that one need not think about rushing or dragging while playing.

544

Once the beat feels solid at all tempos, the student can try a line or pattern along with the metronome, purposely trying to play either on top or on the bottom of the beat. He should go back and forth between these extremes as well as playing in the middle for accuracy, alternating repeatedly. The student should tape himself and listen to see whether he executed the lines convincingly.

One note about the metronome: it is for practice only. Using it will instill a steady sense of the beat, but rigidly metronomic performance is not the goal.

2. Articulation-Dynamics

These considerations depend on tempos. A fast tempo, for example, usually connotes an even, legato approach, whether it is achieved by tonguing, striking keys or drums, or plucking strings. In the hands of great musicians, though, no rigid lines apply. The whole range of attacks, from very legato and slurred to staccato and percussive, can be used in combination with double pianissimo to double fortissimo dynamics.

Miles Davis

Swing

Bebop . . . uses a lot of half steps, while modal and fusion jazz employ more fourths; and the avant-garde features wide intervals as its common fare.

"Ghost" (swallowed) notes are often used to create the impression of a sudden drop in dynamics and a relaxation of articulation.

Dynamics are often neglected by the rapid, fast-note improviser. Dexter Gordon and Hank Mobley are great examples of a legato articulation usually coupled with behind-the-beat placement. On tenor saxophone, Johnny Griffin has a very active and percussive articulation. To my mind, Sonny Rollins reflects the greatest variety and flexibility of dynamics and articulations in jazz. Wayne Shorter has evolved different articulations compatible with three distinct stages of his career: as a member of Art Blakey's Jazz Messengers in the early '50s; playing with Miles Davis; and finally, as a member of Weather Report.

Practice

Transcribing and playing along with a solo, matching its articulation, beat placement, and dynamics exactly, is the best way to practice these factors. Every improviser inevitably filters what he imitates through his own personality. Optimally, the result is an individual approach. Next to the personal characteristics of one's own sound, the factors of articulation and dynamics are most important in developing an individual sound. Learning about the qualities of the music performed by earlier jazz players is a good way to acquire the grounding necessary for valid swing, no matter what style is desired.

At first play the scales and lines in subheading number one in a tongued-slurred fashion, or its equivalent on other instruments. Then mix up the articulations and try beginning the lines on upbeats and different downbeats rather than always on the first beat. This teaches flexibility and the ability to make up the articulation while going along in the music. For dynamics, practicing a line at all volume levels and mixing the extremes in the course of one line will be helpful.

3. Interval Choices

This factor is closely tied to style and content. Bebop, for example, uses a lot of half steps, while modal and fusion jazz employ more fourths; and the avant-garde features wide intervals as its common fare. The choice of wide or close intervals serves as a stylistic dividing line.

To most instrumentalists, wide intervals such as the major seventh call for an abrupt, broken articulation to enhance the jagged effect of the line. Closer intervals, on the other hand, are considered more conducive to smooth articulation and softer dynamics. Remember, though, nothing is this rigidly defined; one could certainly play a jagged line smoothly and softly. I am generalizing for the sake of clarity.

Another element in interval choice is the direction of the line. In bebop, for example, there is a tendency to accent the higher note in an ascending line if a leap upward is involved. A downward leap often finds the bottom notes emphasized. For bebop intervals, Charlie Parker is the prime example. In modalism the pentatonics of McCoy Tyner are representative; and for the avant-garde, Anthony Braxton exemplifies the use of wide intervals.

Practice

The choice of intervals is an analytical element. A musician should realize the effects of different interval choices on his articulation, dynamics, and beat placement. He might try to develop a mixture of elements by practicing, for example, wide intervals at a pianissimo level with smooth articulations. Once again, analyzing written solos is quite helpful. The choices of intervals, as of the other elements, is directed towards the goal of finer and clearer expression.

4. Rhythms

Upbeats are important in terms of one beat, as well as in the common $\frac{4}{4}$ meter. They are what give jazz a lilt and relaxed feeling completely different from the heavy, downbeat feeling of marching music. In the basic dotted eighth-sixteenth feel of jazz, there is usually a push or accent on the upbeat. Another crucial element is the timing of the sixteenth notes. The space between the dotted eighth and the sixteenth is open to a variety of interpretations; either anticipation or delay can be used. The type of articulation chosen for the sixteenth will also affect the result.

In playing jazz, drummers must have the ability to understate the first beat of a new phrase, playing what I call a "light one." Nothing is more frustrating than a drummer who accents

Philly Jo Jones

the first beat of every four- or eight-bar phrase with his cymbal, snare, and — especially — bass drum. Of course, every so often a definite one is needed, especially if the improvisers are really inspired and are making sectional distinctions more subtle than usual. An important device here is to try and feel the "and" of the fourth beat prior to the one. This gradually begins to loosen the upcoming first beat, and if mixed with the feeling of the one a little later, phrasing will benefit.

Practice

In doing scales and lines (as in the earlier exercises) with an even tongue-slur, dotted feel, attempt to vary the space between the dotted eighth and sixteenth. See how it feels to play the rhythm with a long and then a short space. Learn how to snap your fingers at first on two and four in the bar; then only two; followed by only four; and finally, the and of two and four. Be able to choose any eighth note in ⁴⁄₄ time and mark off that beat only once per bar. Again, use the metronome for helping in this exercise.

5. Evenness

When I say "playing even," I mean as opposed to jerky. An even flow creates a smooth, settled feeling with eighth notes, especially. It is in the playing of eighth notes where one's time-feel is most evident. By evenness, I don't mean one shouldn't mix up wide intervals and staccato notes, which tends to create a jagged feel. I mean that given all the desired flexibility of the beat that I have been alluding to, placement of time-feel and rhythms is still even enough to result in an overall smooth effect. Miles Davis is a great example of an improviser who uses staccato rhythms and legato lines to achieve an overall effect of smoothness. His use of long periods of upbeats without resolving to a downbeat is worth notice. All these devices still sound smoothly played.

Practice

Evenness has to do with relaxation in a very

physical sense. Musicians should try not to move their bodies more than is necessary when playing or even listening. See if you can feel time with just slightly moving one finger instead of the whole leg. Internalize the time as much as possible. Another clue is to feel a unit of bars, be it four or eight, as a whole instead of each beat separately. You might begin by marking off each bar at first, then two, four, and finally eight bars. This is especially helpful for fast tempos. It gives the player a sense of directing his energy towards a rhythmic goal some bars later instead of concentrating on each step along the way. The quarter notes lose their individual importance and overall phrasing through the bar lines becomes easier.

6. Instruments

Technical considerations vary, of course, but the improviser should feel that what he plays is not limited by his technique. It may be easier to tongue smoothly in one range than another or to create a staccato effect. As much as possible, an instrumentalist has to correct any technical weaknesses he perceives. It has always been understood that a jazz player is a virtuoso on his instrument; consider, for example, Coltrane, Freddie Hubbard, or Jack DeJohnette. I think that classical study books and instruction on the instrument are both useful. For most of us there usually is an easier way to do things; all we need is to be shown the method. Listening objectively to your own playing and noticing technical weaknesses is a key here.

A musician's sense of time is fundamental to his artistic expressiveness. This is true in all kinds of music. It represents the frame of the picture, without which there is something less than a unified whole. In jazz, the musician's feeling of swing is the lifeblood of the music. There is no one way to do it; everyone has his own idiosyncratic manner of swinging. Besides the musical elements, swing is concerned with an artist's philosophy and personality in the broadest sense. The musician is telling the listener how he feels on a very intuitive and personal level. Fine playing does not lie. It reflects the deepest, most intuitive part of a musician's soul.

The act of learning how to swing only goes so far. Through analytical listening, accurate imitation, experience through trial and error, and one's own objective evaluations, a musician can develop a good sense of swing. To personalize it, though, a person must look inward and be ready to experience life on a deep level. ∎

Saxophonist David Liebman has performed with Miles Davis, Elvin Jones, Chick Corea, and most recently, his own group on the recording Quest. *Since 1973 he has consistently placed high in polls by* Downbeat, Jazz Forum, *and* Swing Journal. *As well as performing, Liebman is active as a clinician and lecturer.*

Where's the Groove?

By Lee Bash

Nothing is as essential to a jazz performance — whether by a combo, a vocalist, or a big band — as the ability to play "in the groove." This steady sense of pulse eludes many ensembles. In fact, as a jazz festival adjudicator, the question I most often hear among my colleagues is "where's the groove?"

Maintaining a good jazz groove calls, first of all, for attention to the beat or pulse. Different tempos and styles can alter the sense of what's happening to the pulse. Paying attention to these changes is what produces a good groove.

For students, developing a focused approach to listening is the first step toward understanding how to play in the groove. Because a jazz chart provides only a rough blueprint for the player, an appreciation of the techniques and subtleties that characterize the rhythmic essence of jazz can be gained only through careful, systematic listening.

Recordings of Count Basie's rhythm section provide a solid example of a group that stayed together, kept steady time, and generally contributed to the body of music known as jazz. Dozens of Basie's big-band and combo recordings are available today. You could pick up practically any one of them and gain insight. You may want to select one album to demonstrate the big-band setting and another to show the combo; for the most part, though, you will observe the same phenomenon regardless of the ensemble. If you're eager to select a single album, I would recommend the exceptional *Warm Breeze* recording (Pablo D2312131).

The first time you listen with your students, you should focus almost exclusively on the rhythm section. First, point out that Basie's rhythm section never gets in the way of the rest of the group. Often their performance is so understated and simplified that you have to listen intently to know they are playing; yet all the while they provide a consistent, solid foundation that puts the band at ease. The rhythm section truly illustrates the principle that less is more.

As you listen to Basie's rhythm section play at different tempos in various performances, you should notice that the players' reactions depend on the specific conditions. When Basie plays a slow tempo, the rhythm section seems to delay the beat ever so slightly. This laid-back, behind-the-beat style should not be confused with dragging the tempo. The tempo remains constant, but the beat seems to be pulled between the band and the rhythm section, each playing on slightly different parts of the beat (the band more on the beat, and the rhythm section slightly behind). This helps create a sense of tension for a tempo that otherwise would seem listless and perhaps even uninteresting.

When young bands perform Basie's charts or other pieces at a slow, relaxed tempo, they often fail to match the light, unhurried sound of the Count's band. Achieving the subtle dualism of the beat characteristic of Basie's group is undoubtedly demanding; but the alternative is to give a slow, boring performance that loses the audience. Some groups that try to replicate the delayed feeling of Basie's rhythm section only end up playing progressively slower throughout the piece. This unmusical approach results in the band sounding (and indeed often feeling) tired.

At a moderate tempo ($\mathbf{J}$=120-180) the Basie rhythm section aligns itself more with the beat, along with the rest of the ensemble. Here again, there is always a strong sense of the rhythm section performing as a unit to obtain a solid groove. Most of this sense of solidarity results from each member of the rhythm section being concerned with complementing what the other members of the section are playing. The rest is achieved through a sensitivity to the metric sense and overall mood of the music. Although Basie's rhythm section may move the feel of where the beat is, according to the tempo, concern for playing as a unit and an ever-present sensitivity to time is what ultimately characterizes Baise's playing as being in the groove.

In up-tempo pieces, Basie's rhythm section functions in a manner almost opposite from the way it approaches a slower tempo. At the faster tempo the pulse appears to be slightly ahead of the actual beat, giving the music drive and intensity, yet the actual tempo is always solid and never feels rushed. In brighter tempos they play lightly, never hammering away at the beat. Even at blistering tempos, the rhythm section never intrudes, exhibiting a sense of restraint. When the drummer, pianist, bassist, or guitarist is even momentarily prominent, it is to complement and spotlight the other players. Overall, the rhythm section is responsible for maintaining control and reserve, providing the wind players a secure foundation from which they can perform at their peak.

Basie's soloists also carry on a solid sense of pulse that is especially prominent in the solo break, a favorite device of Basie's. During this event the entire band, including the rhythm section, stops while the soloist plays two, four, or more measures alone. When such a break occurs, the sense of time is always particularly strong, and the soloist sustains this sense so that when the rhythm section (or the entire band) comes back in, it does so solidly, helping to produce a strong sensation of rhythm in the listener.

Now that your students have heard how crucial the rhythm section is to obtaining a solid groove, you can begin teaching traditional techniques and precepts of jazz comping. Rhythmically speaking, everything begins with the drummer. To help your drummer develop a good swing groove, have him begin by keeping time with the hi-hat cymbal only on the second and fourth beats of the measure. Each time the cymbal closes there should be a clear, distinctive "chick" sound. Once the player can maintain this pattern he should add the ride cymbal in a typical swing pattern that, when combined with the hi-hat, would look like this:

Only after your drummer can play this pattern securely should he gradually add the entire drumset, using the left hand and bass pedal. This is usually the time that young drummers create problems that interfere with setting a groove. Encourage the player to restrain the left hand, making sure that it doesn't interfere with the swing feel. In addition, the bass pedal should be kept light, providing a delicate sense of pulse.

The bass player may well have the most critical role of any single member of the group. He has the responsibility for providing the harmonic foundation while scrupulously maintaining a sense of time. The difficulty of the role is compounded by the need for the bassist to play with taste and mature musicianship. It's little wonder that many young bands have problems keeping a groove when a single player is so vital to the ensemble.

To help your bassist achieve a solid groove technique, have him first concentrate on keeping time with a legato sound. He should strive for a relaxed approach, using a fluid articulation and avoiding a ragged quality. Even a young player can learn to observe the difference between major and minor qualities in chords. This is a big problem for young, inexperienced bassists; and it can really work against the effectiveness of an ensemble. Bass lines should, as a rule, use the root or fifth of the chord on the first and third beats of the measure. The second and fourth beats may use passing tones, but repeated tones should be avoided.

At the same time the bassist should be sensitive to the pulse of the music. An inexperienced bass player should work hard to maintain a metronomically even beat. Once that is secure, have him begin to emphasize the second and fourth beats when playing swing figures. Once he can provide a walking bass that maintains strict rhythm, using the proper notes within the harmonic structure and making the appropriate changes, he has mastered the basics. Now encourage him to add chromatic tones a half-step above or below a new chord change on the fourth beat of the preceding measure, using the new chord to help accent the progression.

I'd like to add an admittedly biased view about jazz basses. In some circumstances the use of the electric bass guitar is appropriate and even desirable. In school jazz programs, though, this instrument has been used in situations beyond these acceptable settings. The rationale for this, of course, is always that student interest does not go beyond learning the electric bass guitar. This is no justification for failing to encourage students to master the acoustic bass as well. The process is no more dramatic or demanding than the common transition from clarinet to saxophone.

Today's professional acoustic jazz bassists perform music that would have been considered impossible for the instrument just a few years ago. A student bass player needs to have as comprehensive an understanding of all facets of bass playing as possible. In addition, jazz performance requires the appropriate use of the right instrument under the right circumstances to satisfy the aesthetic demands of the music. Certainly in the case of traditional swinging jazz the acoustic bass contributes significantly to the overall groove feel. Everyone in the group will benefit if you can convince your bass students how important it is to master the acoustic bass.

Once you are satisfied that the drummer and the bassist can work together as a unit that maintains a solid beat, you are ready to bring your pianist into the picture. Student pianists often are confused when they first perform jazz.

This usually stems from a general lack of formal preparation and a disparity between the music they have studied and what is expected of them in the jazz ensemble. Having the pianist proceed slowly in a system that gradually builds technique in a logical sequence of levels will enable the player to develop skill and confidence and allow him to perform with the ensemble at all stages of progress.

The first step of jazz comping is to develop facility at playing simple two-measure rhythmic patterns in octaves. Unquestionably, the key word here is "simple" and you should make certain from the outset that your pianist avoids playing too busily. The pianist should strive to leave open spaces in the voicing in the same manner as Count Basie. This way, piano lines will not interfere with the melodic lines played by the soloist.

The following rhythm patterns are recommended to help guide your pianist through the initial stages. Remember, at the beginning the pianist should only use octaves with these patterns.

Piano Comping Rhythms

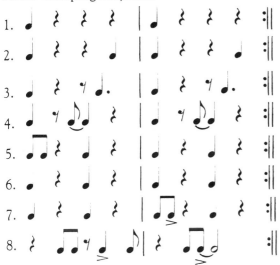

After your pianist is able to use these rhythm patterns naturally and creatively within the context of the music, have him harmonize them in block-chord voicings. The following sequence represents one possible approach.

▶ Start with root position chords, playing only these until progressions are smooth and comfortable.
▶ Progress to inversions.
▶ Begin using common-tone chord progressions. The pianist should be concerned about repeating common tones between chords in the progression. Be sure that chord changes fall on the first beat of the measure whenever appropriate.

▶ Now begin using open voicings in the left hand (with fifths, fourths, sevenths, or octaves) and closed voicings in the right hand

(seconds, ninths, thirds, and so on). Avoid playing roots.

Other approaches to piano voicing are available, most notably Jimmy Amadie's *Harmonic Foundation for Jazz & Popular Music*.

In traditional jazz settings, the guitar is optional. Of course, if your group performs many jazz-rock or funk tunes, the guitar becomes more important. No matter what the style considerations, it is vital that the guitar not interfere with the piano. The entire rhythm section should always listen carefully to ensure that this never happens. If you do use a guitar, make sure that the rest of the rhythm section is already performing in a tight groove before making these suggestions to the guitarist.

First, have the guitarist set the amplifier volume level on low so that it resembles an acoustic guitar. (This may be the most difficult task you encounter.) The guitarist should avoid using barré chords (which use open strings and an all-six-string strum). Two-note voicings are particularly effective when they make use of the third, sixth, or seventh in the chord. Finally, in swing charts, your guitarist should comp on all four beats, playing quarter notes with light accents on the second and fourth beats (thus providing an extra emphasis to what the bass and hi-hat are performing).

If you can persuade everyone in your rhythm section to listen to models of individuals and rhythm sections to better understand his own function within the ensemble, you will have taken a big step towards helping your group play in a jazz groove. Furthermore, if you can get your rhythm section to concentrate on the basics outlined here, you will find that achieving a groove performance is that much easier.

Every member of your ensemble should listen to each other so the group plays together as a unit. The first step is for each player to assume that he is wrong and adjust to the rest of the group. Each player should compromise rhythmically and melodically to conform with the others in the ensemble. This means, of course, that members recognize and agree upon the musical objective for each piece. Impress upon them that they need to continue to listen and adjust throughout the performance.

Adjusting to others calls for good communication, whether through eye contact or body movement. The following example demonstrates how this process evolves from the first reading to a performance before an audience.

Assume that you have selected a new swing chart for your jazz group. First, the group should read through the chart and work mainly on perfecting the technical details, simultaneously listening carefully to gain an overall feel for the composition. When your ensemble can accurately play all the rhythm patterns, accidentals, and key changes, along with the indicated articulations and dynamics, you can progress to the next challenge.

Identify the elements of the performance that contribute most significantly toward providing a jazz feel. These might include a shout chorus, a tempo change, a saxophone or trumpet feature, or a specific mood change. Anything that gives the music a distinctive character should help you in your decision, and your main objective should be to exploit this special character.

This is the logical time to bring a recording to your rehearsal to demonstrate your rhythmic objectives. Rather than having your group mimic a famous recording of the work you are rehearsing, have them listen to a recording of another composition that demonstrates the same feeling of a groove. This way, students can learn general concepts and apply them to the chart you are rehearsing.

During the same period, the rhythm section should play at a low volume level. When this doesn't happen, the result is rhythm players who don't play logically or with any comprehension of the piece. If the rhythm section doesn't take the time to listen to how the piece is constructed and how they should consequently interact, their playing may be inappropriate to the piece, neither complementing the band nor supporting the groove. When that happens, it is difficult to obtain a good groove feel within the ensemble. Only after the rhythm section fully understands how the piece is constructed with respect to form, contour, and general feel, can they begin to expand their parts. At any time, a rhythm player should be able to justify what he is playing based upon the construction of the chart.

The next step in the procedure is probably the most dramatic for many conductors because it departs so drastically from traditional conducting strategies. You should now experiment with the various elements of the piece so that you highlight your ensemble's strengths. This may mean changing the form, adding or subtracting a chorus, altering dynamic levels, or taking a different tempo. Each ensemble has its own personality; any director who inflexibly forces a group to play a chart as written when the group naturally expresses the work differently is work-

ing outside the jazz tradition and creating unnecessary problems for the group. What's more, the piece probably will never work well in performance. Part of setting a groove involves an emotional, expressive element. Balancing emotion with technique is a matter of taste; but both must go into the performance. It is this balance that makes jazz distinctive and appealing to contemporary audiences.

Once the technical problems have been solved and the director has adjusted the chart to suit his players, the rhythm players should open up their performance. Always concentrating on the groove, these players should have more freedom in their role as the section most responsible for the groove. As the core of the jazz ensemble, the rhythm section and the groove they set will dictate the overall impact that the ensemble makes.

There is no guarantee that an ensemble will win additional trophies at jazz festivals if you follow these procedures, but they will receive more compliments from audiences and develop higher self-esteem about their playing. Playing in the groove can't magically solve all problems, but it is fundamental to creating an authentic performance. By following Count Basie's example, your students can learn to listen and play together as a unit that shows taste and style and — most important — that stays in the groove. ■

Author's note: The following are useful jazz references.

Gold, Robert S. Jazz Lexicon: An A-Z Dictionary of Jazz Terms in the Vivid Idiom of America's Most Successful Non-Conformist Minority. *New York: Knopf, 1964.*

Gridley, Mark C. Jazz Styles. *Englewood Cliffs, New Jersey: Prentice-Hall, second edition, 1985.*

Amadie, Jimmy. Harmonic Foundation for Jazz & Popular Music. *Bala Cynwyd, Pennsylvania: Thorton Publications, 1979.*

Lee Bash is chairman of the music department and Director of Jazz Studies at Bellarmine College in Louisville, Kentucky. He is Associate Editor of the Jazz Educators Journal *and has co-authored the* Complete Guide to Instrumental Jazz Instruction *with John Kuzmich. He received his Ph.D. in music education from the University of Buffalo and is on the National Advisory Board for the National Association of Jazz Educators.*

Thoughts on Directing a Jazz Ensemble

BY BOB MINTZER

uring the last decade I have had the pleasure of playing with several of the great big bands, symphony orchestras, my own bands, and a variety of smaller ensembles in the jazz, rock, and orchestral idioms. Working with people like Thad Jones, Buddy Rich, Louie Bellson, Zubin Mehta, Lorin Maazel, and the myriad of seasoned musicians one encounters in the New York music scene has enabled me to observe the conducting prowess of some of the best band leaders and conductors around. In fact, much of my on-the-job-training has involved watching the rehearsal and performance techniques of these leaders and trying to incorporate what they were doing into my musical conception. What interests me most is the fact that different leaders set the tone of their ensembles in drastically different ways. For example, Buddy Rich ran a tight ship and demanded consistent, razor-sharp perfection. Thad Jones and Mel Lewis were more relaxed about such things, as was their music.

As a clinician at both the high school and college levels I have been able to observe the relationship between various school ensembles and their respective directors. In the beginning I found myself wondering to what extent the directors shaped the sound and feeling of the ensemble. In most cases I found that they controlled it quite a lot. The level of involvement and research on the part of the directors had much to do with the playing levels of the bands. The better directors obviously had rehearsed their bands thoroughly; they also took an active role in the performances. They selected well-balanced programs that were sensitive to the his-

tory of big band music. Other directors needed to think more along these lines.

At a performance of the Thad Jones-Mel Lewis Orchestra, it was hard not to feel the powerful presence of Thad in front of the band. He shaped and molded the music (much of which he wrote) in a deliberate yet spontaneous way, often changing the arrangement during a performance. Thad's hand motions seemed to magically draw musical phrases out of the band. Loud, soft, intense, and gentle passages were accompanied by gestures that looked exactly like the music sounded.

Another case in point is Lorin Maazel, under whom I played. Maazel is a powerful, ultra-confident conductor who lives and breathes every note of a score and is clear in his interpretation of a piece. His deliberate rehearsal technique allowed the orchestra to briefly deal with trouble spots and quickly organize the piece into a sensible whole.

How might these examples apply to the situation of the director of a student jazz band? It is not necessary to memorize every note of a Sammy Nestico chart, but it is crucial that the director take the time to acquaint himself and the ensemble with the history of the music and to have a working knowledge of how it should be played. It helps to have a library of big band recordings by such people as Duke Ellington, Count Basie, Stan Kenton, Woody Herman, Buddy Rich, and the Thad Jones-Mel Lewis team. Without the sound of a big band in your head, it is difficult to lead or play in one. We learn to play jazz music through osmosis, which occurs during listening to records and live music.

The logical first step toward preparing a piece of music with a student group is to get a recording and score of the tune you wish to do and listen carefully for style, groove, tempo, and attitude. Listen several times and consider how you might interact with the ensemble as a conductor. Moving your arms and body to the rhythms of the music can help shape a chart, both in terms of dynamics and intensity. In addition, younger students benefit from someone standing in front of the band, moving to the music in a way that reflects the feel of the chart. They get to see how to move to the groove, something they frequent-

---

Saxophonist Bob Mintzer leads and composes for the Bob Mintzer Big Band, members of which have included Peter Erskine, Mike and Randy Brecker, Don Grolnick, and Dave Sanborn. Mintzer has been associated with jazz, pop, and classical groups including the Thad Jones-Mel Lewis Big Band, the Bee Gees, the New York Philharmonic, and the American Ballet Theatre. His saxophone playing can be heard on The Cosby Show *and* As the World Turns. *As a composer-soloist-clinician Mintzer has visited colleges and high schools throughout the United States. Kendor Music Company publishes the Bob Mintzer Series of big band arrangements.*

ly neglect because of the concentration it takes to deal with the technical aspects of playing. As was the case with the Thad Jones band, the band director who actively conducts his ensemble will get more out of the band.

Good rehearsal techniques can help students develop the skills to play in an ensemble, including learning as a group to prepare music for a performance. I like to take difficult spots in a chart and dissect them, slowing down the tempo and having the musicians play the melody and accompaniment one at a time, so that everyone has a clear idea of what's going on. It is essential that everyone know who is playing the primary melodic material and who is playing the accompaniment.

When things begin to gel rhythmically, I start to work on blend and phrasing. A good thing to do is to take a tutti passage for the brass and have them play without the rhythm section at a tempo much slower than the marked tempo. You can even begin with the first chord alone. See to it that everyone is aware of who is playing the lead voice and remind the students that if anyone can't hear that person, they should know that they are playing too loudly. Try to tune and balance the first chord until you can hear the chord ring; you will know when it is right. You may need to stop several times in a piece to do this when intonation and balances seem wrong. Once the blend is right, take a short phrase and have the band play, listening so they hear how it should sound. Make sure everyone is playing under the lead voice and that they are phrasing with the lead player.

The next major consideration is dynamics. I generally ask the band members if they think there is enough dynamic variety in the piece we are working on. For whatever reason things seem to get too loud and too fast in a lot of big band music. One thing you can do is to go over the chart and mark dynamics so that they build logically over the duration of the piece. Decide where the climax is and how to bring the dynamic down after the climax or down and then up again, depending on the particular piece.

Once this is determined, rehearse a loud section of the piece until it sounds full and strong but not overblown. Then take a soft passage and have the band play as quietly as it can without losing the intensity of the line. By doing this you will be able to explore the full range of dynamic variety available to the band. Individual players can work on this on their respective instruments as well so that they get an idea of the full capabilities of their instrument.

Another thing I like to do is to add surprise dynamic changes in crucial places. A subito piano strategically placed can be most effective. In my own big band charts I try to have loud sections followed abruptly by soft passages to create a sense of contrast and drama. Dynamic changes in music act as guideposts for listeners, as well as

to give the music a sense of motion.

One last technique that is useful is to have the dynamic level change with the shape of the line. For example, if a line ascends, the natural thing to do dynamically is to make a crescendo, and if the line descends, to make a decrescendo. This adds a nice shape and flavor to what might previously have been a monotonous piece of music.

Although much of what I have discussed thus far is not much more than a basic orchestral rehearsal technique, I feel that these ingredients frequently are overlooked with big band music. In this loud world of ours it is terribly important that we teach young musicians how to play with well-chosen dynamics and style. Rhythm sections don't have to bash all the time. The band can come down to a mezzo piano at the beginning of a solo, thus enabling the soloist to more effectively build the solo. The element of surprise and wit is far more powerful than volume and brute force.

In dealing with dynamics and phrasing, involve the band members with interpretive decisions. The lead players in particular should become accustomed to deciding on a way to play a phrase and then conveying it to the other band members. These discussions will make for a band that works well together as a team. In my big band in New York there is often background chatter going on concerning dynamics, phrasing, and length of notes.

Sectionals are also a good way to promote student participation in the music. They allow each group of instrumentalists to deal with blend, intonation, time problems, and phrasing in a concentrated and exposed way that is not possible with the full band present. Here section leaders can explain correct phrasing, and this is a good time for listening to recordings of the music being played to check on interpretation, style, and feel. Rhythm section players, in particular, should listen to the recording together so that they may get the appropriate groove and feel going. Whenever I play with a college or high school band I send ahead tapes of my records so that the band members can get the sound of my music in their heads. This works better than anything I can put into words as far as getting them ready to play.

A director who understands the workings and the language of the rhythm section can be a tremendous asset to the band. Frequently a student rhythm section will not get the proper feel of a tune because of a lack of correct interaction. For example, on a swing tune the bass player should walk (playing quarter notes) in sync with the drummer's ride cymbal (also playing quarter notes). On samba and rock feels the bass player should play a rhythm similar to that which the drummer plays on the bass drum. Once students become aware of these things they are able to hook up properly and play together more sympathetically.

If the band director has a working knowledge of the individual instruments in the rhythm section he can deal with other problems, such as showing the drummer the proper beat for a given tune; having the bass player walk in a legato, connected fashion, thus making for a more driving bass line; helping the piano player find good chord voicings and a rhythmically supportive style; and having the rhythm section play with a good steady pulse that doesn't get in the way of the groove. I recommend that all rhythm players practice with a metronome or click track to ensure even, consistent playing.

It is also a good idea for band directors, writers, and players to learn how to play the piano, bass, and drums so that they have some idea of how to converse in rhythm section language. The best way to learn to play rhythm section instruments is to listen to records, paying careful attention to what each rhythm player is doing.

Working on improvisation, playing in the style of individual well-known players, and getting a good sound on each instrument are other important aspects of playing in a jazz ensemble that have not been covered here. It is true that any ensemble is only as good as its individual members. A weak trumpet section or a tentative drummer will certainly throw a wrench in the works, but good rehearsal techniques will help a band to play up to its full potential. If directors of school jazz bands would use their ensembles as vehicles for correct ensemble playing, dynamics, phrasing, and general musicianship the way orchestra directors do, students would benefit greatly. Things are tough out here on the street now, and the survivors are those who can adapt to a variety of musical settings. We should train musicians in the art of playing with others in a multitude of styles, beginning at as early an age as possible. This is important not only for the well-being of future musicians, but also in ensuring the integrity and development of live music.   □

Setting Goals for Jazz Education

An Interview with Harry Miedema

BY GEORGE WEIMER

Harry Miedema speaks in a casual manner common to jazz musicians but unique among the faculty at the University of Indianapolis, where he has taught saxophone, directed the jazz ensemble, and taught classes in jazz pedagogy and woodwind methods. His wit and style belie his formal music education (he holds a Bachelor of Music Education and a Master of Music from Indiana University) and uncommon insight into music curriculum development and jazz instruction. Students often comment on his demanding approach and their tremendous respect for his musicianship.

Is the popularity of big swing bands in high schools good?

Yes, it's good in high schools and for one reason. I'm a free-lance musi-

George Weimer is Professor of Music at the University of Indianapolis, where he conducts the Concert Band and Pep Band and teaches instrumental music education, conducting, and trumpet.

cian; when I get called, it's to sight-read somebody's music, and I have to know in what style to play it. If it hadn't been for big bands, I wouldn't know how to play half the music I do. Improvisation is difficult to teach in high school; but you can keep a student interested and teach him something about jazz style and improvisation through big bands.

I don't think a goal for high school should be to develop great players, because high school students don't know if they want to be great players or great anythings. Still, you can maintain a student's interest so that as he matures and goes to college he has a rational basis on which to decide what he wants to do.

What are proper objectives for jazz study at all levels of instruction? Should they be vocational goals to produce professional players or should they produce listeners and audiences?

One goal for colleges is to make professional-quality players. The odds of a student becoming a professional jazz musician are probably the same as becoming a professional football player for the thousands of kids who start playing football. You have to have a young person who is committed to doing what it takes to do that.

One of the things that I've told the musicians I've seen for four years in the jazz ensemble at the University of Indianapolis is that music is an absolute, just like many things in life. Whether it's art or professional athletics, each has things it asks of you. If you're willing to give it, in return it will give you intense rewards. Not monetary rewards perhaps, but that's not important. Jazz will give you so much fun playing, it's ridiculous. It's not going to meet you halfway, though, so you've got to have a student who's willing to make that kind of commitment. The thing that really drags me about students is when they don't want to expend energy to do anything. I don't care if you don't want to play saxophone; want to do something else, then.

Making a professional player is just one part of jazz education. It's also good to show a player the intricacies of this as an art so that the rest of his life he can spend a few of his entertainment dollars on jazz. It's not horrible, either, if along the way somebody's mom and dad are compelled to listen to something that maybe they hadn't listened to before. All of those things act to keep the art going. I think they are equally important.

You teach a class in jazz studies at the University of Indianapolis. What is your opinion of the quality and availability of jazz instructional texts and histories compared with texts on other styles of classical music?

I'm not happy with most jazz texts. I think it would be fairer to compare contemporary jazz with other 20th-century music rather than older classical music. There are probably people who still don't understand Philip Glass. Maybe 20 years from now it will dawn on all of us what he was trying to do. I don't think you can decide that right now. When Ornette Coleman came out with his group in 1959 people were ready to throw bombs at him. Today as we look back at it, it was one of the greatest events in jazz history. He started a track that nobody else had started.

Can you recommend a text for jazz study in high school or college classes?

The one I use at the university, *Jazz Styles: History and Analysis* by Mark C. Gridley, is good. A good book for the high school level is *Listening to Jazz* by Jerry Coker. It covers almost no history; instead, it explains to the reader the elements of jazz and what we should listen for in the music. It uses everyday language aimed at the non-musician; it is a good, well-written book.

Folks like Wynton Marsalis who can cross over between classical and jazz well are few and far between. Should we expect to be able to train young professional players to be artists in both styles?

It's possible in the same sense that it's possible for Bo Jackson to play baseball and football. I think you'd reach a point at the top of any profession where you would ask, "Am I going to be the best at this?" It's not impossible, but there aren't many people who are going to do it or have the inclination to do it. Wynton is a unique cat.

Would you advise most young players to specialize in one style of music or the other?

No, I wouldn't. I would never try to tell anybody what to do. If somebody's interested in something, then let's sit down and learn how it goes. Sooner or later they can figure out what they want to do based on what they've learned.

Is the development of technique the ultimate aim of jazz education?

That depends on the teacher, but I'd compare that with painting. Do you suppose that if you were to compare Van Gogh, Whistler, and Matisse, one of them would have more technique than the others? I think that you need a technical knowledge of the music; you don't necessarily have to have dazzling technique to display that technical knowledge. To make things technically right you don't have to do it in eight notes; you can do it in four and still make an artistic statement. Now having said that, contemporary jazz is about as technical as you can get.

How young should you start working to develop a jazz technique?

Whenever the interest is there. As early as possible, develop the philosophy of jazz music through whatever means are available, so that as the student becomes more interested in practicing and developing technique, he's already thinking artistically about how to use it. When Maynard was big in the 1950s and 60s, and played higher than dogs can hear, he screwed up many young trumpet players. It was their own fault, because they didn't see that was merely an expression; his playing high notes wasn't the pinnacle of his artistic career, it was only something that helped express what he had to say. So what you want to do is to get a student to understand what a hot phrase is. If he can play a hot phrase in quarter notes, fine. Then as he listens more, maybe it'll get into him that he wants to play a hot phrase in eighth notes and he'll have to practice to do it.

Should training start in middle school?

Certainly. When I was teaching in the summers up at Shell Lake in Wisconsin, there was one junior high band from St. Paul, Minnesota that used to send kids over there. Whoever that band director was — I never met him but I wish I had — his junior high school players all put air through their horns. Their attitude was, "If I miss a note, so what. Here I go." Whoom! They all sounded pretty good. If they had to play a solo, they'd stand up and play it. It may have been technically flawed, but what's more important? You can straighten out the technical stuff. You can't always teach young players to put more air through the horn and get a nice sound. That was great; I loved it.

In your opinion, what is the current state of affairs in jazz education in the public schools and colleges?

I think you need to distinguish between colleges that purport to teach mainly music educators and those that don't care who they are teaching. These are the schools that say, "Come on in and learn how to do this, and go out and use it however you want to, play or teach or whatever." The latter type of college includes schools like the University of North Texas, Eastman, and Indiana University. Those schools all have valid things that they do, though I don't agree with some of them. That's what makes them different, and you need to understand that before you attend one of them. Of the other schools, I think they are getting it together. There are still too few teachers who have sat down and dealt with jazz as a music with a philosophy. They haven't thought about how it might be different from classical music, so that they can intelligently teach others to go out and teach it. If that sounds like a knock, I guess it is. This is a shortcoming in some colleges, and it's easy to fix. It takes somebody who wants to go out and fix it.

Getting down to high school, it's similar to what I said about some colleges. High school teachers, by and large, are taxed with too many things to learn in college. At some point they need to continue their education, as everyone does. That's the single biggest thing that's weird in high schools; a lot of teachers don't know anything about jazz. They open up a big band score, because it's time for big band, and they look at it the same way they look at a Sousa score. If it says this note is short, then that's the one they make short, whether it's right or wrong.

There are certain aspects in writing high school charts that are fundamentally not right, but you have to know that. For instance, most high school drum parts in jazz band charts tell the drummer to play the bass drum with the foot all four beats of the measure. There couldn't be a dumber thing to tell a player. If that's what it says and you don't know any better, that's what you do. That's a swing era thing, so in a big band in the swing era, a drummer would do it. You wouldn't do it in a big band now. People just keep writing the drum part like that because they think the drummer never looks at it anyway.

I don't like criticizing, but I think if you're a teacher or a doctor or anything else, you have to keep abreast of changes, or you get left in the dust. If you are a music teacher who attended a college where you didn't learn anything about it, it's not too late to learn, and it's important, especially if you're in a position where you're shaping other people's attitudes and abilities. I think that sometimes people fall short only from lack of energy, and it's hard for me to knock that because sometimes I don't have that kind of energy either.

What are you attempting with the jazz program at the University of Indianapolis?

I try to teach everyone something about improvising technically, something about jazz history, and something about jazz styles. For instance, one student in the class was asking me, "How do you know which notes are short and which are long?" Well, that's style, and over time you've got to say something about style, because that's something the student will have to do in front of a group. The only thing I don't do is talk about those things from the standpoint of education. I don't say, "This is so you can go out and teach it." I much prefer, "Let's learn how to do this, and then you'll know how to go out and teach it."

We shape a philosophy of music and then fill in the technical parts of it. Part of that philosophy is that music should be as much fun as we can make it. It's always been fun for me. When we first started having a small group at school, we were going to have fun with it, even if I had to explain what fun was. There's a lot of freedom involved in a jazz group. Students have to get used to the fact that I'm not going to point every time something should happen. I'm not going to tell you how long to play your solo. In the middle of a number I might go to somebody in the rhythm

section and say, "Don't play this chorus. Just let the bass player play." Those are aspects of jazz music that are radically different from classical music. You have to get used to them so you can appreciate the fun you can have with them. It's the fun part that makes you want to do it again.

You have an approach to your school jazz ensemble that allows a new player to come into the group while the more advanced players keep going. How does that work?

The new person has to accept that he's going to have to spend some time learning what's going on. Students can participate from the beginning, but their participation is going to be limited by their knowledge. As far as instrumentation goes, as long as I have a rhythm section, anything else is workable.

Do you have any other advice about jazz education?

The two most important aspects of any music are time and sound. There's a pamphlet that Dave Liebman gave out when he was doing clinics. In it he paraphrased a line of a Duke Ellington tune that says, "It don't mean a thing if it ain't got that swing," which is a true statement about time; but Liebman said, "It ain't worth a bone if it ain't got that tone." That's equally true. Those students from the junior high school in Minnesota learned the importance of sound from the beginning.

You produce sound on any instrument by expending energy. If you don't put enough air through the horn, you don't get the sound. The air is the thing that you manage so you can shape sound and articulation. Those young players from Minnesota, man, they all stood up and went "whewwww," like that. Their sound may not be the greatest, but it's potentially great. They had something to work with. That's important.

Then there's the whole concept of time. If you listen to various jazz players play a whole note, they all pretty much sound the same; any whole note sounds the same on any instrument. It's how you articulate notes, the kind of vibrato you use and how you release notes. That's what makes people sound different.

I also talk about those physical things that we can do to allow an instrument to produce a sound. I don't think that you make any instrument sound; I think you allow it to. I'm not

a heavy scientific cat, but I do examine the laws of physics and try not to break them when playing. Those who do are going to get in the way of the saxophone being allowed to play.

How would you advise a young teacher or an aspiring music educator to prepare to be an effective jazz teacher?

I'd try to read as much about jazz as I could, and the best author to read is Jerry Coker. He writes in an easy-to-read style while giving you technical information. Another author who has done more for jazz education than anyone else in this country is Jamey Aebersold, in New Albany, Indiana.

Aside from that, one of the best things that you can do is to listen. The first thing students say after being told to go listen to some jazz records is, "What records do I listen to?" Instead of launching into a discussion of what they should listen to, I say, "Just go out and buy some records. If you don't like them, don't listen to them anymore. If you do, look and see who's on them and buy some more of their records." There are about 1,500 records sitting over there [points to a cabinet across the room] and a lot of them are awful; but I didn't know that till I bought them. Some of them are by artists I like, but the records are terrible. Some of them are by artists we will never hear of again, but they are good records. You never know until you buy them and listen to them.

In the Army I studied saxophone with Joe Allard. One of the things he taught me was that nothing you do ever wastes your time. If some way of tonguing is not the best way, but there is someone who actually does it and sounds all right, how are you going to know if it's good for you unless you try it? That takes a heavy investment in time. If I know ahead of time it's not going to be what I want, fine, I won't waste my time doing it; but if it's possible that it is what I want, I'm going to have to go ahead and take the time to find out. It's the same thing with listening; I know some good and bad players because I've heard that they're good or bad players.

What would you advise a student to look for in a college music program?

I would look for faculty members who are understanding and have the student's interests at heart. Then I'd look for the college that has a good ensemble experience, which I think the University of Indianapolis has. In fact, I think the ensemble experience is better here than at colleges that have just big bands, because big bands by their nature don't allow you to learn as much about improvising and some other aspects of jazz as our ensembles do. Finally, I'd look for a college that has the backup that it takes to give me what I want, a library and recordings to listen to, and those things that allow me to study as far into a topic as I want to go.

You've also said there's something to be

said for accomplishing a goal, for achieving something and getting pleasure from doing it.

There was an article about Barry Krauss, the linebacker for the Indianapolis Colts, last December in the paper. Barry struggled through his entire career playing for a losing team, and then he had a knee problem and had surgery. After the game when they clinched the division playoff he said, "It's great. It's just like life: you can never give up. I know I'm going to walk a little funny 20 years from now,

but it's worth it." He spent his life's work in that endeavor, and he got the reward that everybody wants. Well, luckily in jazz you don't have to pay that physical price. I think in music it's easier; if you work hard, you can get it without having to be on a winning team. It's the same way in life. You can never give up. That's the whole key isn't it? You learn how to work toward something so you can apply that to other aspects of your life. You can become a disciplined person in terms of all your goals, not just those in music. □

April, 1988

Bringing Jazz to the Middle School

BY CHARLES HOLMES

Jazz ensembles have been part of the curriculum in middle schools for some time now, and their benefits are clear. Having a jazz ensemble can help you promote your entire band program and reach new students. The improvisation that is part of jazz encourages a high degree of creativity within an otherwise structured class. The complexity of the music for jazz ensemble can help to sharpen individual and group skills, raising the performance level

not only of the jazz ensemble, but also of the other ensembles in which the students participate. Finally, jazz ensembles give students who

---

Charles Holmes has been a middle school band director for 9 years and has over 20 years' experience as a professional jazz drummer. He holds bachelor's and master's degrees from the University of Wisconsin-Milwaukee and did graduate studies in music theory and composition at the Wisconsin Conservatory of Music.

Photo courtesy University of Miami

would not normally participate in the school music program — keyboard, electric bass, and guitar players, for example — a chance to perform in a structured group.

One warning though: don't let your concert band suffer as a result of your efforts with your jazz ensemble. One way to ensure quality in both groups is to require concert band membership of all jazz ensemble wind players. To avoid scheduling conflicts, consider holding rehearsals before or after school.

When choosing selections for your jazz ensemble, try to expose the students to as many different styles of music as possible. Include swing, rock, and blues along with any other pop-influenced forms of jazz you may want to perform. You may want to try your hand at writing some charts for your jazz ensemble if you have good skills as a composer or arranger. Students love to play charts that are written especially for them. Such performances also make a hit with parents, school administrators, and teaching colleagues.

Swing charts should definitely be a part of your jazz ensemble repertoire. Otherwise, you will have a rock ensemble instead of a jazz ensemble. Middle school students can learn to play swing charts well, and they seem to enjoy playing them a great deal once they are exposed to them.

When teaching swing charts, your interpretation of eighth note rhythms is important.

example 1

example 2

example 3

The eighth notes in example 1 should rhythmically be played like example 2. This gives the music its swing sound and feeling. When teaching this concept to your students, you may want to use example 3 instead of example 2. Many middle school students have a problem with triplet rhythms. Although 2 and 3 are distinctly different, they are close enough in sound that 3, which the students understand better, can be used to teach the concept.

Most jazz ensemble charts have places in them where solos can be taken, but the average middle school student doesn't know how to improvise. In many charts written for beginning or intermediate level students, the composer will alleviate this problem for you by writing in the solos. If you wish to perform a chart that doesn't have solos written in, you will have to write them in yourself.

Often the modes needed to improvise are written in the chart. You can get ideas from records if you don't have improvisation skills yourself. The main idea is to keep it simple yet still be effective.

The standard instrumentation for jazz ensembles is trumpets, trombones, saxophones, and rhythm section. To give everyone a chance to play, you may want to set up a second band for those students who don't make the top group and those students who don't play traditional jazz ensemble instruments. B♭ clarinets can play trumpet parts. Baritone horns can play trombone parts. Bassoons can play trombone parts. Alto and bass clarinets can play alto and tenor saxophone parts, respectively.

The way you seat the wind players in a middle school jazz ensemble is crucial. Even though as a group the wind players are likely to be your best musicians, their ability will vary. Often these students are used to playing two or three on a part. They are not used to holding down a part by themselves. If you put all of your best musicians on one side of the section, most of the sound is going to come from that side. Hence, you are going to be faced with a balance problem. The way your winds are seated can help alleviate this problem.

Seat your first trumpet on one side of the section and your second trumpet on the other side of the section. Place your third and fourth trumpets between them. Do the same thing with your trombones. If your fourth trombone has a weak low register, you may never hear the roots of chords. Moving your second trombone to fourth and moving your third and fourth trombones to second and third, respectively, will help solve this problem. You can also use a tuba to help with the fourth trombone part. When seating saxophones, place the baritone at one end of the section and the tenors at the other. Place alto saxophones between them. Encourage the baritone player to develop the low register if it is a problem. Baritone saxophone and fourth trombone often play chord roots together in jazz ensemble music.

Intonation is a serious problem with students at this age level. Still, there are some things you can do to help your horns blend better. Take the time to tune up individually at the start of each rehearsal. This is important, as it helps the student to concentrate on playing in tune. An intonation exercise can be helpful as well. I like to have my students slowly play each pitch of a concert B♭ major scale. As we play each pitch, we listen to each other and try to blend.

Tuning up individually will help your saxophones and trumpets to play in tune, but not so with your trombones. When time permits, I play trombone parts on the piano. It helps the trombone section to hear the pitches accurately and adjust their slides accordingly.

Developing a strong rhythm section is of the utmost importance. Drummers are the ones who put the drive into whatever you're playing. They must learn to work as individual musicians, as part of the rhythm section, and as part of the ensemble as a whole. The amount of talent and musicianship present will be the determining factor as to how good your rhythm section will be.

There is a heavy emphasis on percussion in contemporary pop music. Instead of having only one drummer in the jazz ensemble, you may want to have two or three drummers form a percussion section. The extra drummers can help out by playing congas, bongos, cowbell, and other percussion instruments when they're not taking a turn on the drum set. This will help add to the quality of your sound.

If you have some experience at playing rhythm instruments (drums, piano, electric bass, and guitar) it often helps students for you to demonstrate the rhythm patterns you want them to play. A good way to teach difficult syncopated rhythms is to place them on the blackboard. Write the count for the rhythm underneath it and have the students practice clapping and counting out the rhythm.

Many times bass, guitar, and piano parts will be written out in chord symbol notation. Guitar players will usually have no problem with such parts, because they are used to them, but young and inexperienced bass and piano players often become frustrated by such parts because of their inexperience at improvisation. You can simplify their parts for them by writing out the notes and the chords in the rhythmic patterns that you want them to play.

Whenever you can, play along. Demonstrating the part yourself helps students hear the style you're after, and it gives them a chance to see your skills. They will begin to see you as a genuine musician, and not just as a music teacher.

Perform often, but don't overdo it. The idea is to keep up enthusiasm for your ensemble in your school and community without overselling it. It should always be a special treat for your school when the jazz ensemble performs. At my school, jazz ensemble members are accorded the highest social status among their peers. Play, but always keep your audience wanting more.

If there are jazz festivals or competitions in your area, attend them. You can take an inservice day and go alone or take your jazz ensemble along and make it a field trip. You don't have to go as a competitor. It can be quite educational for you and your students just to see and hear some good bands. Always take along a note pad and write down some ideas about what you saw and heard.

Listening, whether to live performances or recordings, is crucial for young jazz students. Middle school students normally listen to a lot of rock music, through records, tapes, the radio, and concerts. Encourage your students to start listening to jazz. Through listening, they can familiarize themselves with jazz rhythms, concepts, and styles of performance, while broadening their musical taste.

I often play jazz on the classroom stereo for the students when they enter the room at the beginning of the class period and while they pack up after rehearsal. It's my way of encouraging them to listen. For recordings, I use whatever is available from my personal library or the school library; in addition, I let the students bring in recordings from home.

Encourage your students to study jazz privately, along with classical lessons. During class time, take advantage of jazz clinicians in the area. Often for a reasonable fee they will come in and do clinics on jazz history, theory, style, and improvisation. Many clinicians are competent band directors with teaching certificates. If you are a novice jazz educator, keep your ears open. You could learn a lot.

The last idea for making the ensemble more successful relates to how you can help yourself be more effective. If you have not done so, take some courses on jazz history and theory at a local college. I did this at a nearby conservatory and it really paid big dividends. Jazz theory is quite different from classical, and it helps to understand the differences. History courses will help you learn about various styles and performance techniques, information that you can pass on to your students.

If you are unable to take classes, there are many helpful books to consult. The two books recommended here are not brand new, but I use them because they are still excellent. On the theory side there is Jerry Coker's *Improvising Jazz* (Prentice Hall: Englewood Cliffs, New Jersey, 1964). An excellent jazz history book is Richard T. Dasher's *Black American Music* (J. Weston Walch: Portland, Maine, 1974). For more information on books and learning materials, contact the National Association of Jazz Educators, P.O. Box 724, Manhattan, Kansas or the National Jazz Service Organization, 1201 Pennsylvania Avenue, N.W., Suite 720, Washington, D.C. □

Jazz Improvisation — The Weak Link

David Baker

As I travel around the country as a clinician and/or judge for many jazz festivals, I hear highly competent, well rehearsed, swinging groups. They understand the style of the music; they play the right notes; in short, everything is happening right — until the improvised solos! Then, suddenly it's "amateur night." This criticism maintains whether the festival is junior high school, high school or college.

In this enlightened age, I think that most people involved even peripherally with jazz in education will admit that improvisation is the *sine qua non* of jazz. If most teachers are aware of this, then why the abysmal state of affairs *vis-à-vis* the young improvising jazz player?

It seems that two basic problems exist. First, the myth "either you got it or you ain't" has been used as an excuse for *not* teaching students how to improvise in the jazz idiom.

While it certainly is impossible to produce an improvising giant from an untalented and/or incompetent player, it *is* possible to teach improvisation.

The second basic problem is fear and ignorance on the part of the teacher. Many times the teacher's only qualification for leading the jazz band is a love for jazz — adequate as a pre-requisite for learning, but insufficient for teaching others.

But no longer is the teacher who would work in the jazz areas left solely to his own devices. In recent years, with the inroads made by jazz into *Academia*, numerous methods and analytic studies of one kind or another have appeared to aid both student and teacher.

These aids include: *Music Minus One* records; regular instructional columns in periodicals (*Downbeat Jazz Workshop*); clinics dealing with virtually every aspect of Jazz including improvisation; countless pamphlets ("How to Improvise," N.A.J.E.); as well as many books on improvisation (*Improvising Jazz* by Jerry Coker; *A New Approach to Improvisation* by Jamey Aebersold; and my book, *Jazz Improvisation*).

What all of these sources have in common is the firm belief that jazz improvisation can and should be taught, and that the teaching of it is about 90% organization.

The following material represents my approach to the teaching of the basics of jazz improvisation. Information for determining chord categories:

Chord Types	Abbreviations
Major — 1,3,5,7,9, etc.	Maj., Ma., M.
Minor — 1,♭3,5,♭7,9,etc.	min., mi., m., —
Dominant — 1,3,5,♭7,9,etc.	7,9,11,13, etc.
Diminished — 1,♭3,♭5,6(♭♭7)	Dim, °
Augmented — 1,3,♯5	Aug, +
Half Diminished — 1,♭3,♭5,♭7	∅ or min 7th (♭5)

Alterations and additions are made according to the key of the bottom note.

Chord Categories

- I — all major type chords (C, C6, etc.) — all chords with major in the title.
- II — all minor type chords (minor in the title) including the ∅7.
- V — any dominant 7th chord (letter plus a number, 7, 9, etc, other than 6).
- Anything other than major or minor type.
- Special V chord types.
- Augmented chords equal the dominant 7th of the same name (C+ = C7). Diminished chords are usually derived from the dominant 7th a major third below the root of the diminished chord. (C∅7 is derived from A♭7):

$$C^{\emptyset}7 = \quad C\ E♭\ G♭\ B♭$$
$$\downarrow\ \downarrow\ \downarrow$$
$$A♭7 = \quad A♭\ C\ E♭\ G♭$$

Scales and Chords

The playing of jazz presupposes a certain skill with scales and chords. In practicing scales and chords observe the following general rule:

All scales should be practiced starting on the lowest note on the instrument contained in that scale.

For instance, if the lowest note on the instrument is an F♯ (as in written music for the B♭ trumpet), and the A major scale is being played, start on the note F♯ and play F♯, G♯, A, B, C♯, etc. If playing a C scale, start on the note G, playing G, A, B, C, etc. Play the scales and chords as high as (comfortably) possible.

The jazz player should always be prepared to draw on everything he knows, from any source, concerning scales and chords. He should commit to memory the many scales and chord exercises from such books as Arban, Klosé, Hanon, Czerny, Simandl, *The Universal Method*, and other diverse sources. The jazz player should work diligently toward the acquisition of equal skill and facility in all keys. In all exercises he should vary rhythm, meter, tempo and tessitura.

So that the practice of the scales and chords may follow some order, they should be played moving around the key circle in perfect fourths. Always work clockwise back to the point of origination, as follows: C — F — B♭ — E♭ — A♭ — D♭ — G♭ — B — E — A D — G — C.

An Approach to Improvising on Tunes

There are three basic tune types found in jazz up through the post bebop era (circa 1956):

David N. Baker is head of the jazz studies program at Indiana University. He has toured the United States and Europe with his own ensembles and as a key sideman with Wes Montgomery, Quincy Jones, Maynard Ferguson, Lionel Hampton, and others. His non-jazz compositions are in the repertoires of János Starker, the Berkshire String Quartet, and Josef Gingold.

1. Vertical tunes — those which are essentially concerned with chords or vertical alignments ("Tune Up," "Giant Steps").

2. Horizontal tunes — those which have few chord changes or compositions in which the chord changes move very slowly ("So What," "Maiden Voyage").

3. Combination of vertical and horizontal ("Speak Low," "Dear Old Stockholm," and the blues).

We may also approach any composition in a number of ways. Three of them follow:

a. A scalar approach where we reduce each chord or series of chords to basic scale colors. This is essentially the direction pointed to in George Russell's *The Lydian Concept of Tonal Organization*. In this approach we are less concerned with outlining the particular chords than with presenting a scale or mode that would sound the key area implied by the chords.

b. In the second approach the player articulates each chord. He might simply use arpeggios and seventh chords in a rhythm of his own choosing or he might use what I have labeled *root oriented patterns*, such as 1-2-1-2, or 1-2-3-1, or 1-2-3-5, etc. In a progression they would translate to the following:

Cmi7 /	F7 / |	Bb / / /
1 - 2 - 1 - 2,	1 - 2 - 1 - 2,	1 - 2 - 1 - 2
C - D - C - D,	F - G - F - G,	Bb - C - Bb - C
1 - 2 - 3 - 1,	1 - 2 - 3 - 1,	1 - 2 - 3 - 1
C - D - Eb - C,	F - G - A - F,	Bb - C - D - Bb
1 - 2 - 3 - 5,	1 - 2 - 3 - 5,	1 - 2 - 3 - 5
C - D - Eb - G,	F - G - A - C,	Bb - C - D - F

c. A third approach involves the use of patterns either predetermined or spontaneously conceived. This approach is favored by many post bebop players.

No one of the above approaches is used to the exclusion of the others. In fact, with most players, all three are employed in the course of a single solo. There are many factors which seem to dictate the choice of one as opposed to another at any particular time.

If a tune is extremely *vertical*, some combination of all three seems to work best, according to the player's point of view. If the player wishes to minimize the vertical aspects of the composition, he might do so by using scales. If he wishes to reinforce the vertical aspects he might choose to articulate each chord by using triads, sevenths, ninths, etc. If he chooses to walk a middle ground he might use scales, patterns and arpeggios.

If a tune is extremely *horizontal*, the scalar approach seems to be imperative. When the harmony is static (i.e., when the changes move slowly) there must be some sort of melodic or rhythmic motion. If we run the chord using arpeggios and seventh chords, the material is too sparse to give the song much forward thrust. The same problems exist if we use the root oriented figurations or II-V7 patterns.*

If it is a combination tune, the player might use all three approaches. For instance, he might use II-V7 patterns on the changes that last one or two measures, root-oriented patterns on changes that last two beats and scales on changes that last two measures or more. Many of the finest jazz players use this scheme in some modified form.

* Fm7-Bb7 in the key of Eb. The II(Fm7) is substituted for part of the V7 (Bb7).

Improvisation Exercises (see next page)

Tune I is essentially vertical but with attributes of both the vertical and horizontal.

1. Memorize the changes. (CM7 ////\|////\|Fmi7///\|Bb7///\|CM7/// \| ////\|\|)
2. Play the changes using the root oriented patterns.

This approach teaches the player to hear roots of chords and provides him a way of marking off the bars of a composition. In the initial stages, mostly eighth notes should be used. In the first exercises we omit the fourth degree of the scale because it breaks down the tonal structure. The player should make as much music as possible by variations of rhythm, transposition of octaves, inversions of chords, repetitions, etc.

After working with examples I-a through g, players should add the "excitement" devices (growl, shake, dynamics, etc.).

I-a. On the major chords simply run the major scale (C Major 7 = C major scale) in eighth notes against the chord.

I-b. Different forms of the major scale — i.e., triplets and perhaps 1-2-3-4, 1-2-3-1, or II-V7.

I-c. Different forms of the major scale — i.e., broken thirds, perhaps 1-3-5-3.

I-d. Complete seventh chords.

I-e. Ninth chords.

I-f. Try different inversions of chords.

I-g. Try different resolutions of II to V.

As skill increases, the player must start adding non-chord tones to the improvisation.

I-h. Non-chord tones may simply be leading tones to the roots of the chord being approached.

I-i. The composition should be practiced varying the meter, tempo, dynamics, register, etc.

The Horizontal Approach
Relationship of Chords to the Major Scale:

• I — Major chords = Major scales of the same name. C Major seventh = C scale.

• II — Minor seventh chords = Major scales a whole step below the root of the chord. Dmi7 = C major scale.

• V — Dominant seventh chords = the major scale of the chord of resolution or the scale a perfect fourth above the root of the chord. G7 = C major scale.

• ∅7 — Half diminished seventh chords take the major scale one half step above the root of the chord. C∅7 = Db major scale.

It's important to think in terms of constant modulation — key signature is not necessarily indicative of the scale areas included in a tune. All II-V7 progressions represent different key areas: C major = Dmi7G7; D major = Emi7 A 7.

I-j. Using the major scale to color all chords. Measures 1 and 2 — C major scale (major scale of the same name.) Measures 3 and 4 — Eb scale (both Fmi7 and Bb7 belong to the key of Eb.)

I-k. Variation — It is also possible to think in terms of starting the major scales on the roots of the chords involved. Fmi7 = Eb scale; but start the scale on the note F; result — an F dorian scale, or notes F-G-Ab-Bb-C-D-Eb-F. Bb7 = Eb or the scale starting on Bb = Bb mixolydian scale, or notes Bb-C-D-Eb-F-G-Ab-Bb.

A third possibility is a combination of the first two.

Improvisation Exercises

Tune I

Scales and Chords

Non-Chord Tones

Scales Used to Color All Chords

Tune II

"Tune II" is a horizontal composition and demands a scalar treatment. If the player should decide to realize each of the minor seventh chords with a major scale he would have a C major scale for eight measures, an E♭ major scale for eight measures and a D major scale for eight measures.

II-a. He might use any pattern or motif that conforms to a major scale — for example, "Twinkle, Twinkle Little Star," "In a Country Garden," or "Joy to the World."

II-b. The perceptive player will notice very quickly that despite the scalar approach, chords and arpeggios are still possible and desirable. For instance, the C major scale which colors the Dmi7 chord contains seven different triads; seventh, ninth, eleventh chords, etc.; C Major7, Dmi7, Emi7, F Major7, G7, Ami7, B⌀7. Any one of the chords when played in a scalar context will fit against the Dmi7 chord. This same technique will be employed in dealing with other scale choices as the player becomes more proficient.

Tune III

Tune III is a combination of horizontal and vertical aspects.

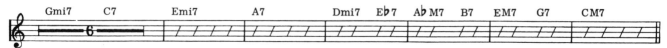

III-a. Notice the selection of scales, chords, root-oriented and II-V7 patterns.

III-b. Another possibility.

Suggested Reading

Improvising Jazz by Jerry Coker
A New Approach to Improvisation by Jamey Aebersold
Jazz Improvising Series by John Mehegan

Suggested Listening

Giant Steps (vertical) by John Coltrane. AT 1321 (Coltrane plays root oriented patterns on "Giant Steps" and "Spiral." 1-2-1-2, 1-2-3-5, 1-3-5-3, etc.)

George Russell at the Five Spot by George Russell. DL 9220 (vertical — "Moments Notice" by John Coltrane; trombone solo by Dave Baker — essentially pattern and chord running)

> For a comprehensive method of study for all players, see *Jazz Improvisation* by David Baker, published by **down beat**.

Kind of Blue by Miles Davis. CS 8163 (Horizontal — "So What." Miles' solo is based on the major scale color — actually the dorian scale — major scale starting on the second degree. Listen to the complete solo; Miles never once violated the major scale color.)

A Touch of Satin by J.J. Johnson. CL 1737 (combination — "Satin Doll" — J.J. plays II-V7 patterns, root-oriented runs and scales — major and diminished.) ∎

University of Alabama Jazz Ensemble

Developing Jazz Band Articulation

BY BRUCE DALBY

The young wind instrumentalist playing jazz for the first time needs to develop techniques that he probably has not learned as a member of a secondary school band program. Most of the adaptations he must make are in the area of articulation, where jazz and symphonic technique differ most. Young jazz bands will benefit from the use of drill material designed to facilitate the development of proper jazz articulation. Following is a list of some of the differences between jazz and symphonic articulation, with some exercises the director can use to develop good jazz articulation in a group setting.

Extensive use of legato tonguing

Even relatively advanced young players will need to improve their legato tonguing in order to play jazz passages in the proper style. Start by having your group play repeated legato patterns

---

Bruce Dalby has 10 years of experience as a high school band director in Idaho and New Mexico. He is currently a doctoral student in music education at the University of Illinois.

on the same pitch. For instance, play scales using this figure on each note:

Emphasize that there should be absolutely no break between notes. The tongue merely touches the airstream without stopping it. Trombonists will probably need a great deal of practice at this. The task is complicated for them because of the obvious difficulty of coordinating legato tonguing with the movement of the slide. Most advanced trombonists try to get around this difficulty by using natural slurs whenever possible and by emulating the sound of the natural slur when they do have to use the tongue.

You will probably be teaching swing rhythm at this time, so practice the above exercise with uneven as well as even eighth notes. Then play various scale exercises in legato style. The scales you use in concert band might provide a good starting place. Practice them in straight and swing eighth notes and practice a range of an octave and a half or more instead of just an octave. Play scales in thirds:

University of Minnesota Jazz Ensemble

Play extended patterns that start on various degrees of the scale:

Continue in the same fashion up to step 5 of the key, then work backwards to the tonic.

Do this extended scale exercise in the key of B♭ concert, then A♭. Although these keys require saxophone players to go into their extreme registers, they work well for most young brass players, who are more likely to have trouble with extended ranges. When the group is ready, do the same exercise in the keys of C and F. With practice they should be able to handle D♭, G♭, and others. Again, be sure to vary the use of straight and swing rhythm. (A further benefit of this exercise is that it can serve as point of departure for a discussion of modes.)

Design other patterns and exercises that fit your own style of teaching and that address particular deficiencies in your group. If possible, all of these patterns should be played by memory, which makes it easier for the student to concentrate on the sounds he is producing.

Extensive use of displaced accents

Jazz playing involves considerable use of accents on downbeats as well as upbeats, but young players have the most difficulty accenting upbeats and need specific practice on this. At first it is enough for the student to know that an accented note is simply louder than an unaccented note. Practice the extended scale exercise with accents on each offbeat:

Although jazz playing does not often require such extreme treatment of accents, young players need a great deal of practice to learn how to control accent location and these exercises provide plenty of repetition. Play them slowly at first, then increase speed as skill improves. Emphasize a smooth, connected legato style, with no break between notes.

When the group becomes fairly proficient at this, make up other accent patterns to play on the scale exercises. For instance, you might play a scale pattern like this:

Have students suggest their own accent patterns. Create various articulation patterns to be used with familiar arpeggio exercises.

Greater use of very forceful articulation

The attack assumes more prominence in jazz ensemble playing and is often greatly emphasized in relationship to the actual body of the note. Students need to develop forceful marcato attacks with control and accuracy. They should also understand that jazz accents are usually treated differently from symphonic accents in that the release of air is more immediately explosive. In other words, full air pressure is applied behind the tongue prior to the attack and escapes with maximum force at the instant the tongue moves. In a symphonic accent there is an almost imperceptible delay between the moment of tongue release and the primary impulse of breath pressure, almost as if in saying "ta-hah," but extremely compressed in time. (We are not talking here about the proverbial pear-shaped tone or the "too-wah" that immature players sometimes produce.) While this distinction is small it is important; young players should listen to live or recorded models of both styles of accent properly executed. The teacher should also insist that each accent style be applied only in the correct context.

In addition, note endings are often more abrupt in jazz playing. Many notes may actually be stopped with the tongue (as in "dut" or "tut"), a practice which is rarely called for in good symphonic playing.

Pronounced differentiation between full and short note values

Young players will often have trouble making short notes short enough, a sure recipe for difficulty in cleaning up ensemble passages. Use exercise patterns that require a lot of repetition of the syllables "tah-dut" (or "doo-dot" or whatever works for you). For example:

(straight 8th notes)

or:

(straight 8th notes)

Play II-V-I arpeggio patterns like this:

(swing 8ths)

Emphasize that the difference in length of adjacent long and short notes should be exaggerated. Players should also beware of situations in some rock and funk tunes where the typical swing pairing of long-short is reversed:

instead of

Articulation markings are not always played as written

Even in modern editions, which are usually well marked, the player must be wary of how a given articulation marking is really meant to be played. This is particularly true of slur markings. Many slurred passages, especially at slow or moderate tempos, should actually be played with legato tongue. On the other hand, some passages (usually fast ones) marked without slur need to be played slurred. Unfortunately, there is not always an easy answer to the question of which treatment is preferable. The director often has to rely on personal judgment born of experience.

Sometimes a passage is too fast to legato tongue each note, but lacks drive and rhythmic vitality if every note is slurred. A good solution is to slur pairs of notes across the downbeat:

Many players find this a useful way to master a tough passage without making it sound stiff or forced. It is only a starting point, however, and won't work for all fast passages. In practice, the tongue is usually applied on the accented notes, which normally occur at the high points of a figure's contour. This may require slurred groupings ranging in length from two to four or more notes.

Ensemble precision will be enhanced if all members of each section tongue and slur in the same fashion. When the director or section leader decides how to articulate a questionable passage, section members should write in the slurring pattern on their parts to ensure uniformity.

Exercises such as these are only one way of working toward improvement of articulation. Appropriate concepts need to be emphasized during all phases of the rehearsal, not just during the warm-up. While some inexperienced groups may need to spend substantial time on exercise material, the majority of precious rehearsal time should be spent playing jazz literature so that ensemble, reading, and improvisation skills can be emphasized.

Devoting some time to drill material is defensible, however, when one considers that most secondary school jazz bands are not blessed with players who are stylistically mature when they enter the group. Their directors are instead confronted each year with an ensemble comprising students of widely varying abilities, from experienced seniors to freshmen beginners. For them, five to seven minutes a day spent on systematic development of articulation technique in a group setting can work wonders toward the achievement of a tight, consistent ensemble sound. □

565

Ensemble Playing

Ensemble playing is one of the greatest rewards of instrumental music. You are important; you cannot be covered, or your sound hidden. You stand on your own, with your musical friends needing you as much as you need them. As you progress with your ensemble playing, you become a better listener as well as a better performer. All your other musical groups — bands and orchestras — benefit from that experience; but, most of all, ensemble playing introduces you to a new world of musical enjoyment that means equal participation.

Music is different from all other art forms because the sound is more important than what is seen. Your tone should be free-flowing, sitting on the air column with ease; it should be round, well-focused, and able to blend with the ensemble. Listen and concern yourself with the best sound that you can make.

You are an equal part of a small group, not more — not less. Balance your sound by listening to the others. At times you will have the melody and your friends will support you. Other times will require that you support your partners. This is done by listening and balancing your part in an equal but changeable relation to the whole sound.

Equality has its foundation in relationships with others. So does tuning. You should listen all around you, but especially to your foundation, the tuba or the lowest instrument playing at the time. If you are the tuba player, be careful to play each note in tune, to provide a consistent foundation for the others. Before you begin, tune your instruments together on a concert B♭. Then, play the last chord of the piece and fit into that chord. Your note will have a proper place that helps the chord shine. The secret is careful listening in a musical relationship with your friends.

Individual Warm-ups
Tuba: The first thing I do is play a long, single note on the mouthpiece to loosen up the lips and find the pitch through the middle of the air column. Then, try a simple four-note mouthpiece warm-up for a minute or two:

Then, play a scale, again on the mouthpiece, making the pitches really in tune with each other.

The tuba player should not try to match the players of smaller instruments insofar as breath phrases. Don't try to make a long phrase. As soon as you're out of air, take a breath. There is no award for duration. It is important to take a deep breath and get rid of it. A nice big buzz. As soon as you are out of air, even for two quarter notes, take another breath.

The warm-up does not have to start when you are in a room with your instrument. Carry the mouthpiece around with you during the day. It's great fun on a school bus.
Trombone: You can do a similar warm-up on the trombone. Try to start with the pitch. It's important to hear the pitch in your head and relate it to the embouchure. Remember, when you're warming up, you're working not only on your lip and facial muscles, but also the breathing muscles. Take a lot of air in. F3 is a good note to start on. Use your trombone to find that note, then work on the mouthpiece only. You can play any melody line you like. Then match your pitches to the instrument, usually just long tones, similar to what the scales are.
Horn: First find the pitch on your horn and then use the mouthpiece to do patterns, breathing as often as necessary, using lots of air. Then go to the horn after your lip feels as though it's responding and play a pattern such as this:

Use all the various fingering combinations, starting with an open F horn, then second valve, first valve, first and second, second and third, first and third, and first, second and third in those same patterns. Make sure that your hand does not close off the bell; otherwise you'll be tuning to a false pitch. The hand position should be as open as possible in order to give a good clear sound and not change the pitch.

Trumpet: In order to get the trumpet to sound properly, a good sound on the mouthpiece is necessary. Then the sound on the instrument will also be clear. So train your ear in pitch and try to get the best tone you can.

Play a scale pattern in a relaxed way, using lots of air and varying the dynamics. If you can only play loudly, try to get the vibration going in the mouthpiece and play softly down and up. Make a sound like a fire siren, but slowly.

Here is another mouthpiece exercise that sums up the others: using your mouthpiece, start on a concert Bb (C on a trumpet, F on a French horn), play up a fifth:

Then move up one note and repeat the exercise. Keep moving the bottom note up until you are at the fifth note in your beginning scale. Then you have enough notes to play a whole octave, plus one note, on your mouthpiece. Do this in eighth notes when you can, with definite pitches, recognizable as a scale:

Ensemble Warm-ups

Have the ensemble play a piece on only the mouthpieces. Make the pitches true. You eliminate many instrumental problems and can concentrate on tone and intonation.

If you have a rhythmic problem, work it out on your mouthpiece, individually or as a group. We do it all the time.

Buzz the mouthpiece and play two or three more bars just on the mouthpiece, and then back on the horn. You will hear a change in the sound; it will be richer and fuller. Sing your parts with the group to help in tuning; then back to the horn. The pitch, everything, is established right there, right at the mouthpiece. The instrument simply reflects the sound we're making; it amplifies it. The embouchure (your whole face) with your mouthpiece, and your ear — that's what is really important.

Breathing

It is important to sit away from the back of the chair. Sit up, don't sit down. You should sit straight, but not rigidly straight. Lean forward just a little, take a deep breath and then, very easily, blow it out through your mouthpiece.

You should think that you are being held up by a hair from the top of your head — an im-aginary hand is holding you up as you sit lightly on that chair.

Breathe in — a full breath. Not only is the chest expanding as the lungs fill up with air, there may even be expansion and movement of the sides and back. Now breathe in and out slowly with the other members of the group, listening to them, and breathing together. The group that breathes together plays together. Now we have everyone breathing together, expanding and supporting the tone. With your eyes closed you should be able to hear and sense the other members of the group who are about to play a note, so that the attack is together — with the air support together. Breathe in through the sides of your mouth and blow out through the mouthpiece.

Think of the air column — not as the beam from a flashlight broadening drastically as it lengthens — but as a laser beam, focused, firm, and alive. Keep your shoulders down, expand the lungs and rib cage as the air comes in. The diaphragm drops, the ribs expand out, and the air is then supported and expelled as if your chest were a giant bellows.

If you are in doubt as to the muscles to be used for breathing, watch your cat or dog while it is sleeping. Expansion in the lower chest cavity is obvious. We've never seen a dog raise his shoulders while taking in air — so don't you. It only decreases the air capacity, tightens the throat muscles, and allows no support for the air. Besides, it looks funny!

Tonguing

Simply say ten times: "The tip of the tongue to the top."

Tonguing is the articulation of notes, defining the beginning and attack. After saying the line above, follow your tongue to the place on the hard palate above the front teeth. Use that spot and say "ta." This basic tonguing will suffice and give a clear presentation.

The simple but important exercise of practicing, "ta, ta, ta," can be accomplished while riding on a bus, sitting in a waiting room, or reading a book. Concentrate on only the tip of your tongue contacting the palate. When rehearsing with your mouthpiece, make sure your tongue stays in the correct place and does not move down between your teeth. You're on your way to clean, bright articulation.

A Few Words on Scales

Always practice the scale of the particular piece you're working on. Play the scale as musically as you can, producing your best tone. Variations of rhythm, volume, and breathing will help.

Fugue in E♭ by J.S. Bach

The word "fugue" in French means flight. This suggests that the opening part presents the melody (subject) and then flies before the following voices as they present the subject. Counterpoint, the interweaving of melodies, is the basis of all imitation, and ultimately, the fugue. Now, if you really want to understand this, learn the Fugue in E♭ by Bach; it is an undeveloped fugue. Why not start with all the players playing the first two bars of their own part at the same time, forgetting preceding rests:

Now you have the subject (melody). Then learn the last seven bars together. Now, start at the pick-up to bar 13. When that is in place, start at the beginning and put all the pieces together. Whenever you have the subject, you become the dominant part, and the other players support you; otherwise, you support the subject presented by the others. The climax of the piece is the tuba entry leading to the conclusion of the fugue.

A key point in preparing a fugue is the essential equality of the performance of the fugue subject. Your next problem: the countersubject should support but not dominate the subject. Originally for keyboard, this simple fugue should sing itself along at a good pace, with the subject being passed from one player to another like a double reverse in football.

A good example of a more complex fugue is to be found on our records: *Fugue in G Minor* (Little) by Bach. When you listen to that recording, see if we keep the subject in mind and always in front of you. Have fun! ■

The Canadian Brass at Lincoln Center, summer 1984

THE CANADIAN BRASS
Discography

Royal Fanfare — Canadian Brass: Vanguard VSD 71254

Canadian Brass in Paris: Vanguard VSD 71253

Canadian Brass Rag-Ma-Tazz: Vanguard VSD 79420

The Pucker and Valve Society Band: Attic Records, Ltd. LAT 1030

Canadian Brass (Direct-to-Disc): Umbrella Records UMB DD5

Ain't Misbehavin' and other Fats Waller Hits: RCA XRL1-5030

Mostly Fats: XRL1-3212

Touch of Brass: Moss Music Group MSG 1123

Unexplored Territory: Moss Music Group MMG 1119

The Pachelbel Canon: RCA ARL1-3554

The Village Band (Digital): RCA ARC1-4436

The Canadian Brass — Greatest Hits: RCA ARL1-4733

Christmas with the Canadian Brass: RCA ARL1-4132

High, Bright, Light, and Clear: RCA ARC1-4574

Champions: CBS FM-37797

Brass in Berlin (Digital): CBS IM-39035

5. Fugue in E♭

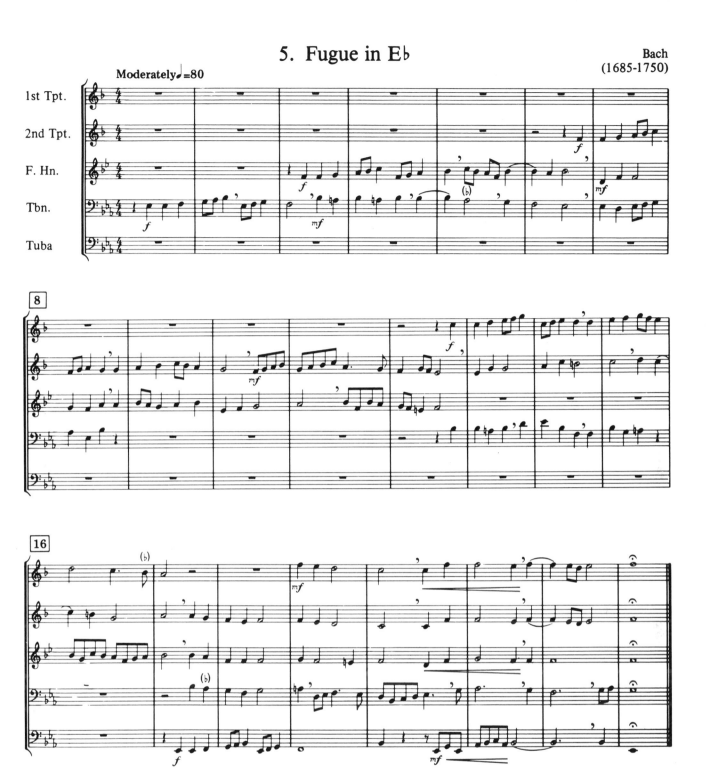

Editor's Note: These comments on playing are reprinted by permission from *The Canadian Brass Book of Easy Quintets* (Volume I of The Canadian Brass Educational Series published by Gordon V. Thompson Music, 29 Birch Avenue, Toronto, Ontario, Canada and distributed by G. Schirmer in the United States.) There are two volumes of quintets now in print; each volume is available with score, parts, and a cassette of The Canadian Brass performing each piece.

SECTIONAL REHEARSALS MAKE THE DIFFERENCE

Gene Lacy

The secondary school instrumental director is very busy with the many concerts his group is expected to perform and in trying to produce the optimum results expected at each public performance. How is he to do this in the scheduled rehearsal time? The answer is quite simple: he cannot. Even for students who study privately, much of the literature is demanding enough to require training *outside* the regular rehearsal period, in smaller homogenous groups. Under the pressures of preparation for performance "there is little time left for actual technique teaching. Of course, much technique may be taught through the music, but a faster development of the . . . player is accomplished through homogenous technique classes."[1]

These sectional rehearsals, perhaps more properly called sectional practices, may involve various activities. They may deal with difficult problems in the current concert repertoire; they could—and perhaps should—also be involved with perfecting a given technique such as vibrato, bowing studies, or position shifting practice for strings, triple-tonguing for brass, upper register fingerings for the woodwinds, or rudimental drill for the percussionists. These extra practices affect the performing group in a direct and positive way. After a relatively short time the director will notice a more solid sound, and better ensemble precision in passages which previously sounded somewhat shaky. The overall group will benefit from these outside practice periods.

We should not forget the benefits to be gained by the individual student. How often do we short-change the interested student when he asks for help in bowing or fingering a particular passage? Here is where we can put into actual practice the goal of meeting the needs of the *individual* student. Here in the section practice "the pupil has the chance to seek help and to receive it."[2] Actual experimentation can take place here with more or less equal interaction between students and teacher. A certain fingering might be attempted (previously arrived at by the teacher), and the students might try their own. From this a conglomerate fingering might be derived using the teacher's model as a point of departure and arriving at a fingering more or less suitable to all. This is how learning takes place, after all, in the acceptance and rejection of ideas in a pragmatic way. In other words, we try it and if it does not work, we try something else. This trial and error method may seem time-consuming, but if we are to educate, it is a necessary expenditure of time. This is how student leaders are developed in instrumental groups. When the director forces his ideas onto the students as the only way to do it, only "followers" will result—a situation which is only too common. Also, if the students feel that the section meeting is *their* time to discuss and try approaches to problems which occur in the music, they will be more likely to view this meeting in a more positive way.

This brings us to a very important point: what is the motivation for the students to attend these meetings? Of course, ideally, the student comes because he is so eager that he allows nothing to come between him and this valuable outside practice session. This is what we should all work toward, but being realistic, there will be those who do not respond to this approach. Some will regard it as an infringement on their time and will be a little resentful of the outside practice session. Obviously we wish to reach as many of our students as possible, and one weak player in any section cannot help but detract from the total effort. Also, this student might receive some good from these sessions, even though he may not realize this, and for this reason we are actually doing the recalcitrant student a personal favor by requiring attendance. The morale of the section will also be affected adversely if certain members are often absent. Therefore we need some leverage, to be sure that all members of the group are present at each rehearsal. Different directors will have different means of accomplishing this. Some will call the parent if a student is missing to ascertain the reason, and to be sure the parent is aware that such an outside meeting is taking place regularly, and that his child *is* expected to be present. Others allow the grade to be affected in some way, possibly giving playing tests at the end of the meeting, and allowing these grades to count toward the final grade of that particular grading period. One writer has said "the sectional rehearsal lends itself to the evaluation and grading of individual pupils."[3] This could very well be the answer to the charge leveled at many a music director that he could not possibly give a reasonable grade to

Gene Lacy is engaged in doctoral study at North Texas State University in Denton and is teaching on an assistantship in music theory. He has taught strings in the Lubbock, Texas public schools and has been principal double bassist in the Lubbock Symphony Orchestra for several years. He has written numerous articles on the double bass.

each student merely on the basis of his performance in a large ensemble. In the outside section meeting we can become better acquainted with the ability of *each* student, and in this way arrive at a more accurate estimate at grading time.

The benefits to be gained by the director from the section practice have been touched on but slightly; there are many ways this period can aid him. Becoming better acquainted with the abilities and limitations of the students has already been mentioned; this section practice might also aid the director in his knowledge of the music, virtually from the inside out. "The inexperienced conductor finds the sectional rehearsal an aid to him in mastering the musical score . . ."[4] It is one thing to look at a score and imagine that a particular passage is rather difficult for clarinet because of awkward fingerings, and quite another to have this knowledge securely tucked away in one's consciousness as a fact. This is where experience is at a premium. The conductor who has had the opportunity to come across many situations which occur in musical scores, and to experience the players' reactions to them, has a definite advantage over the young, inexperienced conductor, regardless of how talented the latter may be. Here sectional practices may be a definite asset to the young director. Another way they could prove valuable to the director is in the way his group performs in public. We are judged by the way our groups are received by a number of different publics. The parents are probably our most immediate critics, but few of them are going to be capable of rendering a musically sound appraisal of what they hear. It sounds good to them primarily because their child is a member. Other publics may not be so charitable. Other directors, either acting as interested observers or as adjudicators at contests or competition-festivals, can render more accurate and telling judgements of our efforts. The section rehearsal can be the difference between the average performance and the really fine, polished presentation.

Actual content of the section practice seems to be a matter for some controversy. The director's own personality will enter the picture here, naturally. His philosophy will also have a bearing on whether he uses technical studies (from method books or of the rote variety), actual concert music, or both. Most directors seem to favor a reasonable balance between current concert music and technical studies. When technical studies are used a certain amount of rote materials will be used—usually during the warm-up portion of the practice session—and a certain amount of these studies will come from selected method books. Many directors choose to allot the section practices which occur in the fall of the year to technical exercises, depending on the weaknesses of the particular section. Then, as the competition, festival, or spring concert approaches, passages from the concert music are used for drill and/or playing tests. Meyer Cahn has said, "Difficult and important passages can be rehearsed into perfection. It is here, in the smaller group, that sectional balance and precision . . . can be developed."[5] Another writer favors using the section practice in a different way: "The major portion of the time [in section rehearsals] is not spent on orchestra music, but on the actual teaching of positions, vibrato, etc."[6] As was stated earlier, it seems to depend on the personality and philosophy of the director. A balanced approach seems more commonly favored and would appear to be more reasonable.

The lack of time can be a very important factor for many directors in the matter of allowing rehearsal time outside the school day for small homogenous groups. The director who has both band and orchestra may find himself not only short of time, but actually too physically exhausted to even consider spending additional time outside the regular schedule for these smaller units, especially during the football season. In this situation "it is often satisfactory to put capable student directors to work training the sections."[7] This would probably only be practicable in the high school grades, however, and then it would be wise to consider using very mature juniors or seniors as student directors. This would be advantageous to the student helper involved, also. He could see the problems involved in working with a group of students, and this would probably serve to make him more cooperative when the director is in charge. This experience could also help the assistant's musicianship as well as his ability to get along with other students and his leadership abilities.

It is hoped that a strong case has been presented here toward scheduling outside section rehearsals for the secondary instrumental organization. There are so many mutual benefits to be gained for the student, the director, and the organization collectively that it is difficult to see any further justification for putting off these practices. The directors who include the section practice as part of their programs will find, as this writer has, that it is mainly a matter of making these sessions a *habit*. Once the student begins to realize these sessions are advantageous to himself and that the organization is benefiting, he will usually be more than anxious to spend the additional time each week in this very valuable adjunct to the successful instrumental program.

[1]Cluck, Nancy, "Sectional Rehearsals for Strings in the High School", *String Newsletter*. Dallas, Texas: Southern Methodist University, Fall, 1967. p. 1
[2]Sur, William R., and Chas. F. Schuller, *Music Education For Teenagers*, New York: Harper and Brothers, 1958. p. 229
[3]*Ibid.*
[4]*Ibid.*
[5]Cahn, Meyer M., *The Instrumentalist's Handbook and Dictionary.* San Francisco, Calif.: Forman Publishing Co., 1958. p. 2
[6]Cluck, Nancy, *Op. Cit.*
[7]Ward, Slyvan D., *The Instrumental Director's Handbook.* Chicago: Rubank, Incorporated, 1940. p. 29 ∎

The Sectional

Donn Laurence Mills

First I heard a faint groan, followed by a ripple of disappointment. It hadn't been a particularly good rehearsal and I'd called for a sectional. Suddenly I felt unpopular. As the conductor of a non-professional group, I knew a sectional would be the most efficient way to get certain problems corrected, yet I also realized that students and amateurs thrive on the thrill of a full orchestra sound. When divided into small groups, they miss the feeling of being part of a complete organization. I suppose it's similar to a committee and a general meeting (you always know that big action will take place when everyone's there to vote). My conductor's indignation soon gave way to understanding, however, when I recalled my own student days. Perhaps you, too, remember some boring sessions devoted to getting the notes. They weren't much fun. It seemed an unmusical exercise at best, a punitive substitute for neglected home practice.

Professional players are expected to play all the notes in tune. They come to a rehearsal prepared. Students and amateurs usually don't practice their parts much outside the rehearsal, or if they do, they often need to be taught how to practice. Because students are probably unfamiliar with both the score and stylistic practice, each rehearsal is a trial and error process aimed at educating ears and fingers simultaneously.

Some of our fellow conductors look upon the sectional only as an extra rehearsal, turning it over to an inexperienced assistant or approached with resolute boredom. Repeated technical drill and disregard for the emotionality of the music are all too common. Well shame on us! A sectional can be an exciting, rewarding experience for conductor and player alike if built into the master schedule as part of the orchestra's normal routine, not just once before a concert, but frequently, maybe one of every four rehearsals.

During full orchestra rehearsals, the score itself dictates rehearsal procedure. In a sectional, the conductor must deal with instrumental techniques and the peculiarities of orchestration on a microscopic scale. Just laboring through a piece accomplishes little. Sectionals must have specific goals. Because a sectional allows for more detail, the conductor can work with subtleties like shading and balance, tone color (using bow placement to change the sound, producing thin or thick tones, articulation, types of vibrato, etc.), as well as dynamics and intonation. It's a chance to pay attention to inner parts, noting voice leading and the little melodic details which are often overlooked. The conductor can teach finer points of artistic performance, explain cues, and assess his players' strengths and weaknesses. What an opportunity to listen and to evoke section pride.

There are many types of sectionals to consider. One time you may schedule only flutes, and concern yourself with blend, intonation in unison passages, tone coloration, or technical matters. Another time all of the woodwinds may meet so questions of doubling, balance, dynamics, phrasing, and style can be settled. In more complex scores, mixed groups can be brought together so players understand how their parts fit together. Chamber music sessions (one on a part) help to acquaint players with contrapuntal lines and cues. Even having random, unrelated parts together can be instructive for the player who has blinders on his ears during full orchestra sessions. In fact, a good conductor should be able to accomplish something worthwhile with any combination of parts. He needn't wait for the ideal instrumentation before getting down to work.

Handling sectionals requires a thorough knowledge of instrumental playing techniques and characteristics. Unfortunately, many student and assistant conductors lack that knowledge and experience. If the regular conductor assigns an assistant, by necessity or "for the experience," there should be a briefing ahead of time to discuss objectives and a de-briefing afterward to review the accomplishments. This not only helps the assistant, but assures the players that the rehearsal is not an improvisation or merely a learning experience

Donn Laurence Mills represents the National School Orchestra Association as our Contributing Editor for the Orchestra Clinic. He holds music degrees from Northwestern University and Eastman School of Music. A conductor and music educator, he is also the American educational director for the Yamaha Music Foundation of Tokyo and editor of the N.S.O.A. Bulletin.

Each member of the N.S.O.A. receives a subscription to The Instrumentalist. *For other membership benefits, current cost, and an application blank, write to James H. Godfrey, President, 330 Bellevue Drive, Bowling Green, Kentucky.*

for the novice conductor.

I've found that more is accomplished by working carefully through a small part of a piece than if the entire score is read through. Studying a segment of the music in depth provides an all-too-rare experience in perfection. It is especially valuable for those who don't study or perform advanced solo literature but confine their musical experiences to large ensembles. Well-marked parts take on personal significance to a player, and the sectional provides the time to write in all kinds of memoranda which payoff dramatically in the full orchestra.

The N.S.O.A. historian and mentor, Merle Isaac, is often quoted as saying, "It's not getting the right notes, but getting the notes right that counts." There are many ways to get those notes "right," of course, yet we seldom have time to explore far beneath the surface during full orchestra rehearsals. Sectionals give us the opportunity to plunge deeply into that ocean of notes and come up with countless buried treasures. ∎

June, 1963

Rehearsing the Woodwinds

James Thornton

James Thornton is professor of woodwinds, chamber music, and theory at the University of New Mexico in Albuquerque. He is a graduate of the Cincinnati Conservatory of Music and the University of New Mexico. In addition to his teaching duties, Mr. Thornton is a professional bassoonist. He has written a woodwind text and a number of works for woodwind choir.

WHEN THE WOODWIND SECTIONS of the band are brought together for rehearsal they should have an opportunity to play music written for the woodwind choir as well as the band parts and study books. All the elements of tuning, style, pitch reference, mixtures of colors, tone weights, articulations, various styles of tonguing, musical phrasing, good sound, and ensemble can be learned in the woodwind family context. The conductor, ensemble director, and the applied music teacher should examine and refine the various aspects of woodwind playing and teach these techniques to the players.

Piccolo and Flute

Student piccolo players should hear the high frequencies and be able to exploit the solo capabilities of the instrument. Since the piccolo can affect the intonation of the woodwind section, it should be tuned first with the flutes, and then with the unlike instruments playing the same voice. Use the "small flute" concept, but use vibrato only in espressivo style solos.

Pitch problems are magnified in the flute's high register. In addition to tone distortion caused by poor aperture, many students do not hear accurately in this high register. Although individual players may not hear themselves in loud passages, they should not try to match the volume of the clarinets and brasses.

The use of several E♭ soprano flutes on the troublesome high parts will help to prevent intonation problems. Use two alto flutes in large sections to solve the problem of low register projection. Tune the flute section first to itself, then to the clarinets. The flute-cornet-trumpet unison may cause intonation problems. Phrases employing this unison should be rehearsed carefully to check the intonation.

Clarinets

One E♭ soprano clarinet may be used to effect a good line in the altissimo register when the B♭ clarinet part is too high. It should fit in the pitch line established by the flute-clarinet combination and blend with their tone quality. This instrument is useful as a solo instrument, and in combination with the E♭ soprano flutes and soprano saxophones.

The size of the B♭ soprano clarinet section makes tonal focus an important consideration. Poor embouchure and blowing may cause a faulty clarinet tone and distort the full band sound. Tongue placement and embouchure formation will also influence the pureness of the tone. Clarinets should establish the pitch line for the soprano reeds. When clarinets have chord factors in more than one register, they should watch the pitch, blend, and balance carefully.

The alto clarinet blends well with the third clarinets, other alto voices, and with the other low reeds. Since modern instruments have incorporated so many mechanical improvements, they may be used in sufficient quantity to be effective.

Use at least four bass clarinets in a large woodwind section. Keep the instruments in good adjustment and tune the lower octave very carefully.

The bass line needs accurate pitch to form a sound foundation for the chord, and the other bass reeds tune to the bass clarinets. To obtain a more mellow sound in the bass reeds, omit the bassoons. Similarly, omit the bass clarinets to eliminate the mellowness in the bass tone.

Parts for the contra-alto and contrabass clarinets require careful editing. The practice of using the tuba part does not always furnish the woodwinds with a satisfactory bass line. The extreme low tones are not satisfactory for articulated patterns in a fast tempo.

Saxophones

One saxophone player should be trained to play the soprano, transposing where necessary. Care must be taken to prevent the tenor from dominating the other tenor voiced reeds. Usually three bassoons will be required to balance the weight of one tenor saxophone.

Intonation in the saxophone section requires careful ear training for the players. Refined vibrato should be developed. Articulation should be executed carefully, listening for a good sound. Staccato, in particular, generally is neither short nor light enough in the saxophone section.

Double Reeds

Treat the oboe as both a solo and a color instrument. It will add edge to the mellowness of the other soprano reeds, and should tune with the clarinets and flutes. The oboe does not tune a clear unison with cornets and trumpets. Unison oboe timbre is not satisfactory except for effects, and is extremely difficult to tune. The second oboe part often is written too low, so the player should learn to transpose the music for the alto oboe (English horn).

The alto oboe mixes well with all alto instruments and adds an edge to the clarinets in the alto voice. It may be used as a solo instrument or with the oboes and bassoons to provide a double reed choir.

Six bassoons are needed in a large woodwind section. They add an edge to the tenor and bass reeds and are effective in octaves. Player interest can be maintained with more solo passages in band. The player should develop a dry staccato style.

The tendency to use more oboes than bassoons in the section is unrealistic. Two oboes, with one doubling on alto oboe, should be sufficient, while two bassoons should be ample for the small woodwind section.

Utility Instruments

Skilled players may be trained to double the piccolo, E♭ soprano flute, alto flute, E♭ soprano clarinet, soprano saxophone, and alto oboe parts. These instruments are useful adjuncts to the regular woodwind voices in addition to providing solo colors. Transposition may be necessary when no part is provided for the instrument, but should pose no great problems for the interested players. Since the soprano instruments in the group can cause serious pitch and tonal problems, select students who hear accurately.

Tuning

Use the clarinets as the tuning reference in each voice except the alto. The alto saxophones should be used for the alto line reference. Develop a program of ear training incorporating melodic and chordal tuning. Poor pitch in the upper reeds will cause tone distortion to the entire section. Tune unlike instruments after the individual sections. Select players for the extremely high and low pitches who are able to hear the pitch differences there.

All woodwind players should be able to play crescendo and diminuendo without altering the pitch; each should know the pitch tendencies of his instrument and be able to adjust to the ensemble pitch line.

Cadences, in particular, require accurate pitch so the chords will be in tune. Correct tuning of chords can be taught thru the voice leading in the cadence.

Style

The woodwinds can produce a great variety of styles and colors. Their full potential has seldom been used in existing materials for the band and the reed choirs. The possibility of great technical dexterity, and limitless sound and color combinations, invite creative writing and playing.

Most reed players need to develop the light staccato in the leggerio style. Groups generally play too short and dry in this style. The detaché is a subtlety frequently overlooked; legato tonguing another. Generally, the reeds can lengthen and lighten tones in articulated patterns.

The dynamic range of the reeds should be extended toward the softs to create the illusion of greater dynamic scope. Great care is needed in the fortissimo to prevent tone distortion. The technical fluency of the woodwinds should be capitalized upon.

Tone quality may be developed thru group work. A good vibrato is important to the singing line and will add color to the section. It will increase the projection of the woodwinds. Tonal focus can be improved thru tongue placement.

Attacks and Releases

Articulations from extreme legato to the most forceful marcato should be developed with good tone in all sections. Since tone length is so important in the consideration of sound and style, develop firm breath support to sustain good tone in all articulated patterns. Consider tone weight, punctuation, and flexibility, emphasizing the rhythmic scheme. Avoid fast articulations in the extremely low registers. Consider release as important as attack.

Bring out the drama of the music by stressing the dynamic contour. Develop leader-follower relationships in each section. Time is an portant factor in ensemble development, and groups do not play together well until they have spent some time doing so.

SMALL ENSEMBLE TRAINING—A NECESSITY

George Seltzer

It has been said that the woodwinds form the "heart" of the orchestra. The same comment may be applied to their importance in the concert band. Not only must woodwind performers be soloists in their own right, but they must also be able to play within the ensemble of their peers in the woodwind section, and with the full organization as well.

There are certain skills necessary to perfect this "playing together" which are extremely difficult (if not impossible) to teach in a private lesson no matter how excellent the instructor. What are these skills and how can they be mastered by the woodwind performer?

Ensemble skills fall into the general categories of intonation, dynamic balance, balance of tone quality, articulation, and ensemble attacks and releases—and they can be best and most quickly learned through playing in small, supervised ensembles.

Discrepancies in intonation within the small woodwind ensemble (i.e., usually three to five players) are perhaps the most readily discernible problem for both performer and listener. It is not enough that each player be aware of the intonation faults of his own instrument—although this in itself is of course a major factor. It is also of vital importance that he know in purely practical terms the acoustical deficiencies of all the other instruments in the ensemble. The clarinetist should know, that, without conscious adjustment, it is "natural" for his instrument to drop in pitch at higher dynamic levels, while the flute will rise in pitch under the same conditions—and that the reverse is also true. The oboist must know that his instrument will tend to be flat in his lowest fourth of its range (as will the flute), while the clarinet tends to be sharp in the lowest part of its range. The tendency of the G and $F\#$ of the bassoon to be sharp should be recognized not only by the bassoonist but by all other members of the group. In short, training in small ensembles will make each player aware of acoustical problems common to his own and other woodwinds, as well as the personal idiosyncracies of the particular instruments owned by the members of the ensemble. This applies to groups of like instruments (i.e., clarinet quartet) as well as groups of mixed instruments (i.e., woodwind quintet).

Good dynamic balance is equally difficult to achieve whether we are concerned with groups of like or mixed instruments. Again, we are concerned with acoustical principles in terms of musical practicality. What is practical (or even possible) in terms of loud and soft is relative not only to the period and style of the music but also to the comparative limitations of the individual instruments. All the other players must be as aware as the oboist of the difficulty of playing a pianissimo low C on that instrument. All should be aware of the relatively large dynamic range of the clarinet or of the difficulty encountered by the French hornist in playing very softly in extended passages in his higher range. The experience gained in this area of small ensemble training will not only enhance the individual's competence in ensemble performance but should also give him a greater understanding and command of his own instrument.

Balance of tone quality is perhaps a more subtle achievement in good ensemble performance. The questions of type and amount of vibrato (or the lack of it), the particular range of the instruments and the particular qualities of tone associated with these various ranges, and the number and variety of instruments involved in the musical passage, are only a few of the many aspects of this problem. Here again, small ensemble training appears to be the most practical method for attaining this goal.

Ensemble articulation involves a consensus of opinion regarding the various degrees of silence between notes. This in turn involves the various types of tongue strokes available to each performer and the effect of these strokes used together. For example, consider a passage of repeated eighth notes followed by eighth rests in medium tempo, common time. Since musical principles supercede all else, the desired musical effect will condition the use of tongue-stroke syllables such as "tut," "dud," "tu," "du," etc. It is conceivable that the best musical effect will be achieved by mixtures of these tongue strokes depending on the instruments and ranges. In rapid articulated passages it is possible for other performers to "cover" purposely one of their number to help all of them create the better musical result. The experience gained in the small ensemble enables the performer to become aware of this problem and is far superior to a simple verbal discussion.

George Seltzer is currently on the faculty of the School of Fine Arts of Miami University. He received the B.M., M.M., and D.M.A. degrees from the Eastman School of Music and has performed in chamber music ensembles throughout the Eastern states.

Attacks and releases of notes are an obvious problem in ensemble performance. Each player must know how difficult (or easy) that particular entrance is for each member of the group. He must know what combined dynamic level and intonation level is best for a musical result. Since woodwinds do not share the continuing vibrations present in the sound boxes of the strings, they must be extremely cautious in release of notes. Just how long should the edge tone, or reed, or lips vibrate? Just how long should the ensemble sound continue?

It should be obvious from the foregoing discussion that these "ensemble skills" are readily transferable from the small ensemble to the orchestra or band. Indeed, without these skills, even an unusually talented woodwind performer is severely handicapped in the larger ensemble and his individual efforts may be wasted musically.

Worse still, in terms of musical waste, is the not uncommon situation of one or two woodwind performers, unskilled in ensemble playing, detracting from the good ensemble playing surrounding

them and creating a musical morass.

In view of the dearth of an extensive quantity of good music written for woodwind ensemble—especially as contrasted with the quantity of great music available for strings—it seems advisable to consider small ensemble training for the woodwind performer a means to an end rather than an end in itself. The goal should be the training of a performer well versed in ensemble skills, so that he may readily take his rightful place as a soloist within the "heart" of the orchestra or band. ■

November, 1983

Preparing an Ensemble for Contest

Robert Klotman

Here are eight steps that conductors can use to prepare an ensemble for a successful contest performance. To illustrate these ideas, I refer to my intermediate-level piece for string quartet, the *Herald Quartet* (Belwin-Mills), that is an arrangement of an unaccompanied violin duet by Charles Dancla.

1. *Assess the group's playing ability and select appropriate music for them to perform.* This step, a seemingly simple one, can make the difference between an excellent performance or a poor one. Too many performances are spoiled when the level of music is beyond the players' abilities. Select material whose parts contain the different technical demands that will be appropriate for the students in the group. It is essential, however,

Robert Klotman represents the American String Teachers Association as our Contributing Editor for the String Clinic. He is Professor of Music at Indiana University, a former president of M.E.N.C. and A.S.T.A., and has taught at all levels of string education from elementary through college.

for the director to use music that each ensemble member can play technically as well as understand musically.

2. *Review the program notes; scan the piece for style, tempos, and dynamics.* I have frequently heard the *Herald Quartet* performed incorrectly in spite of the program notes which state: "The work is written in the early Romantic style; it may be performed in the same manner as a Schubert quartet." I suggest listening to recordings of Schubert quartets, especially the first movements. The melodies sing, while the accompaniments dance in the background. This image helps set the tone for preparing the work.

3. *Sight-read through the piece.* The musicians should play through the work in its entirety at the desired tempo, $\downarrow = 126$. This first reading acquaints the players with the music; missed notes or overlooked dynamics are not important. To help study the composition, each ensemble member should take a turn playing his part from the conductor's full score to see his music in re-

lation to the other parts. That way each player learns the music by both observing and hearing the different lines.

4. *Point out musical form.* Begin these first few rehearsals by breaking the piece into sections and pointing them out to your students so they can begin to recognize musical forms. The 16-measure introduction to the *Herald Quartet* can help ear training because it contains a series of scales and modulations. Beginning in the key of G, the opening unison arpeggio provides teachers with an excellent opportunity to work on slow scale practice and precise intonation (see example 1).

The music quickly modulates to the key of D. The material five measures before letter A, in this new tonal area, offers a second place to practice unison scales as well as scales in thirds.

5. *Practice slowly.* Start working on each section individually. By practicing slowly and listening for intonation, students become aware of the pitch relationships between intervals. For example, the introduction of the

Herald Quartet ends on the tonic chord in the key of A. To accomplish this modulation smoothly, the cellist should raise the leading tone in the key of A to emphasize the tension in a diminished chord. (For more information see the article "Teaching Intonation" in the April 1981 issue of *The Instrumentalist.*)

I often hear chords in the accompaniment of the introduction played too long and with too much bow. They should be played as short, staccato strokes and should not go beyond the middle of the bow. In order to establish the opening key of C, practice the modulation to the key of D in a slow sustained manner, with the melody played as slow as ♩=64 (about half the suggested tempo) to be sure the performers hear the tonal changes as they occur. When played as written, these chords are short, with silences in between. Although measures five to eight are written ♩♪, practice each quarter note as though it were a whole note. Once the intonation is acceptable, perform the music as written.

6. *Exaggerate dynamics.* Rehearse the introduction with exaggerated dynamics. The piano level in the accompaniment should be played pianissimo, and the mezzo forte almost forte. As the quartet is learned, the dynamics will be adjusted. Because young musicians have more difficulty playing softly, having them exaggerate the piano effects makes it easier to play slightly louder when necessary. Furthermore, if the piano is very soft, there is more room to make a crescendo when one is required.

After practicing slowly and listening to be sure the scales and modulations are in tune, the ensemble can then increase the tempo of the introduction gradually until it reaches ♩=126. At this point directors should be certain the music is performed in the appropriate style, which could be either marcato or spiccato, but certainly not legato.

The exposition begins in the key of D. The melody in the first violin part is played dolce and legato while chords in the accom-

Example 1   [1-4]

1st Violin

2nd Violin

Viola

3rd Violin (in absence of Viola)

Cello

Bass (optional)

Herald Quartet, *Belwin-Mills,* © *1960; used by permission.*

Example 2 [25-28]

Example 3 [54-57]

Example 4

1st Violin

2nd Violin

Viola

3rd Violin in absence of Viola

Cello

Bass (optional)

Example 5 [42-45]

Example 6 [65-67]

paniment are performed with a slight separation between each quarter note. It's best to exaggerate the decrescendo at the end of each of the four measures to round out the phrases. The eighth notes with dots are played spiccato. Again, practice the entire section at half the tempo to tune all of the chords (letter A to letter B), and continue to exaggerate the dynamics. Bring out the dynamic contrast as the melody moves from one instrument to another in this section (see example 2).

7. *Trade off melodic sequences.* The development section begins with a tonal variation of the unison in the introduction. After two four-measure phrases a game of hot potato follows. It is played with a fragment of the principal theme. The first violin begins the statement, then tosses it to the cello, who passes it to the viola, who hands it to the second violin. As a rehearsal exercise, have each instrument play only when the melody appears and see if the performers can keep the sequences going without a break in the musical phrase. This type of practice helps eliminate the fragmented feeling that can occur when the performers think only of their own two measures (see example 3).

Even though the score indicates spiccato eighth notes, I still hear quartets perform the accompaniment in a legato fashion. Be certain the development remains in the style established in the exposition.

The recapitulation is almost the exact duplicate of the exposition except that it is in the key of G. Practice it exactly as suggested for the exposition.

The work closes with a 12-measure coda. Intonation in this section will be a major concern during rehearsals. There are several accidentals that should be carefully worked out, especially the half-steps that require left-hand finger adjustments. The sixths and thirds between the cello and the first violin need to be tuned carefully. Even though the cello is playing ♩ ♪ ♩ ♪ and the first violin is playing 𝅝, have these two instruments play half notes very slowly until everyone is satisfied with the pitch, then play it in the correct tempo. This is the type of rehearsing that will improve intonation. The first violin closes the work with a series of arpeggios against a tonic and dominant harmonic accompaniment. I suggest rehearsing this portion of the music slowly with the accompaniment played ♩♪ = ♪ until the pitches are accurate (see example 4).

8. *Play through the entire piece.* With this preliminary work complete, set the metronome at ♩ = 126 and have the ensemble play through the entire quartet, emphasizing dynamics and rounded phrases. The players should listen for key climaxes. The first one occurs at the end of the introduction; and the next one, a soft dramatic climax, occurs in the form of a cadence with expressive dynamic effects at the end of the exposition (see example 5).

A secondary climax occurs at the close of the development in the form of an ascending scale that builds in dynamics as instruments are added (see example 6). The final climax occurs at the end of the composition with full down bow chords in the key of G, re-establishing the opening tonality.

Once your ensemble has followed each step in rehearsing this or any composition, they may disregard the metronome and make music by taking liberties, but without destroying the basic character and style of the piece. When the difficult work of rehearsing is complete, the ensemble can play for the pleasure it derives from performing beautiful music well. This is the real value in preparing a selection for a contest or concert. ∎

May, 1976

Seating Arrangements for Concert Band

Mark H. Hindsley

More than a dozen varieties of instruments make up today's concert band. Each instrument has its own timbre and its own dynamic range, giving us a very large and complex assortment to work with. By using our tonal forces well, balancing and unbalancing them in an almost infinite number of combinations, weaving patterns of color and sonority throughout the widest spectrum, we can contribute to the realization of the concert band's potential as a serious and distinctive medium of musical expression.

The seating plan of the organization can help or hinder all of our efforts toward this end, since it has such an important effect on what the conductor hears, what the band hears . . . and what the majority of the audience hears in the average concert hall.

The conductor will wish to hear the music at its very best, and should do all he can to insure that the audience will hear it at an even higher degree of artistic satisfaction. Though only the few players nearest the conductor will be able to share in this optimum condition, all players will be able to play at their best and enjoy it most in proportion to how well they can hear themselves, their closest neighbors, the rest of their section, and the other sections of the band.

A number of other background factors should be considered.

1. *Balance is the element of performance most affected by seating.* All other elements (tone, intonation, precision, interpretation, etc.) are affected by seating, insofar as the ability to hear and control what goes on is concerned, but seating is particularly critical to the element of balance.

2. *Softer instruments need help.* They can be heard, regardless of the seating arrangement, when they play alone or with a sufficiently subdued or differing tonal background. However, they may be covered completely in ensemble playing, even at middle and low dynamic levels. It is essential that these instruments of lesser dynamic range be given an advantage in seating and that the strongest instruments be given a disadvantage.

3. *Consider the directional properties of sound.* Almost all wind instruments sound strongest when the player faces the listener. Exceptions are the French horn, and the bell-up euphonium and tuba.

4. *Intensity of sound varies in proportion to the distance traveled.* The conductor should have close at hand the least intense instruments: the flutes, oboes, bassoons and to a lesser extent the clarinets, so they will come to him in good balance. All instruments across the front of the band will have favorable access to the audience.

5. *Sound may be partially reflected or absorbed by other players.* Risers may be used to elevate certain players, alleviating some of the reflection and absorption, thus securing better projection and balance. (This perhaps explains why many people prefer balcony seats for concerts: less sight and sound obstruction.)

6. *No seating arrangement is a sure-fire formula or a cure-all for problems of balance.* This will always be determined by the conductor and the players, even to the extent that handicaps imposed by the seating plan may be completely overcome.

7. *It is probably impossible to devise a perfect seating plan.* Yet we should try, even though we may have to sacrifice, compromise, and accept some situations less satisfactory than others for the sake of the overall result.

Woodwinds

In an "ideal" concert band instrumentation of some 92 players, my first consideration is the placement of a 12-piece flute section, the top of a "homogeneous" woodwind choir, which also includes the clarinet family and the string basses. (The flutes now have no wood and the string basses have no wind, but they blend extremely well with the clarinets anyhow.) Because the flutes need a dynamic advantage, and sound strongest when facing the listener, we might put them in front of the conductor in two rows of six or three rows of four. However, we must consider how much sound we would lose (distance to the audience), and whether the conductor would hear them proportionately louder, out of balance with other instruments and sections. Also, in this position they might be occupying a disproportionate amount of "real estate" that would be more valuable for other instruments. An alternate proposal is to seat them along the front in three rows of four. Since the playing position of the flute is toward the right and slightly downward, they will sound stronger to the audience if placed on the left side of the conductor than on his right, even though the conductor might hear them equally on either side. Thus, my decision is for the left side front.

My next decision is whether I prefer to keep the woodwind choir together on one side or spread them all the way across the front. Spreading them out would give them best access to the audience but it might mean placing all the soprano clarinets on the right side, and the lower clarinets and string basses on the left with the flutes. For me this formation would be too wide for its depth, resulting in many problems of precision for the group, and reducing its general effectiveness as a choir. The best choir arrangement — one that gives the flutes the dynamic advantage they need and leaves the clarinets in a good position — is to seat the clarinet family on the left and mostly inside of the flutes: two string basses on the far left corner (where they will point to most of the audience), two contrabass clarinets in the back row inside them, four bass clarinets next in the two back rows, followed by twenty-four B♭ soprano clarinets reaching from near the front all the way through the back row. Another advantage of this plan is that the highly important clarinet family, playing a high percentage of the time, will be well under the watchful eye and baton of the conductor, where their technical work can be steadied by what they see and hear.

Of the remaining woodwinds, the "color" instruments, the two oboes and one English horn are most in need of advantage, so they are placed in the three chairs at the front on the conductor's right. I would like them closer to the flutes, but the remaining chairs in the first row must be reserved for the four bassoons, whose playing on the outside would not be as appropriate as that of the oboes. I would prefer only

two bassoons in the first row, but there is not enough room in the second row since the quartet of saxophones (two altos, tenor, and baritone) will be seated in the second row adjacent to the first row of clarinets.

The fifty-five woodwinds (including string basses) are now all in place, almost all of them on the conductor's left, and all seated contiguously. Each player should be able to give a good account of himself in his position.

Brass

Once seating for the woodwind choir has been determined, it will not be difficult to place the brass in the remaining area. The four tubas will go in the back row near the center (continuing from the clarinets) and the four euphoniums immediately in front of the tubas. Since the tubas are the principal bass instruments of the band and the euphoniums play almost as much with the woodwinds as with the other brasses, both of these sections deserve central positions. And even if they are bell-front instruments their upward directional dark tones will not pose too much of a balance problem. Six trombones, their modern large bore cylindrical tubing providing a mellow enough tone in their medium and lower registers to fit well with the more conical instruments as well as enough brilliance to pair with the trumpets, will continue from the tubas in the back row, and the seven cornets will continue from the euphoniums in the row ahead. The intensely directional cornets and trombones will thus point principally across the band rather than at the audience, minimizing their extra dynamic advantage for the audience if not the conductor. This "homogeneous" brass choir is seated compactly in two rows, and like the woodwind choir will be able to function well in its location.

Of the brass "color" instruments, four trumpets will continue from the trombones in the back row on the right, their bells also pointing across rather than to the front, but with an outside position advantage. (It should be noted that cornets, trumpets and trombones do not play directly into any lighter woodwinds in a row immediately in front of them; and obviously woodwinds will play better without heavier sounds in their ears.) The five horns will fit into the only remaining space, second row right, connecting up with the saxophones. This is really an excellent position for them — fronting the other brasses with their bells away from the audience, and completing the instrumentation of the standard woodwind quintet within the first two rows.

Percussion

The winds of my suggested 92-piece unit are well contained within four semi-circular rows. With these rows completely filled, the percussion must be located beyond. My personal preference is to place them on the right, behind the brasses. The timpani should start immediately at the end of the tubas (in the area behind and to the right); they should be followed in succession by the hand cymbals, bass drum, snare drum, the mallet instruments and other traps. It is wise for the bells, triangle, and other lighter-toned instruments to be played near the front of the formation so that they can be heard more easily by the

During Mark H. Hindsley's long career in music, he has been Director of Instrumental Music for the schools in Cleveland Heights, Ohio, and Director and Conductor of Bands and Professor of Music at the University of Illinois. He is also a recording artist and a published author. Since retirement he has been an active guest conductor, adjudicator, and clinician.

It is quite unlikely that any band will ever have exactly the instrumentation discussed and illustrated here. Variations in instrumentation will call for variations in seating, but the principles and philosophy should still apply.

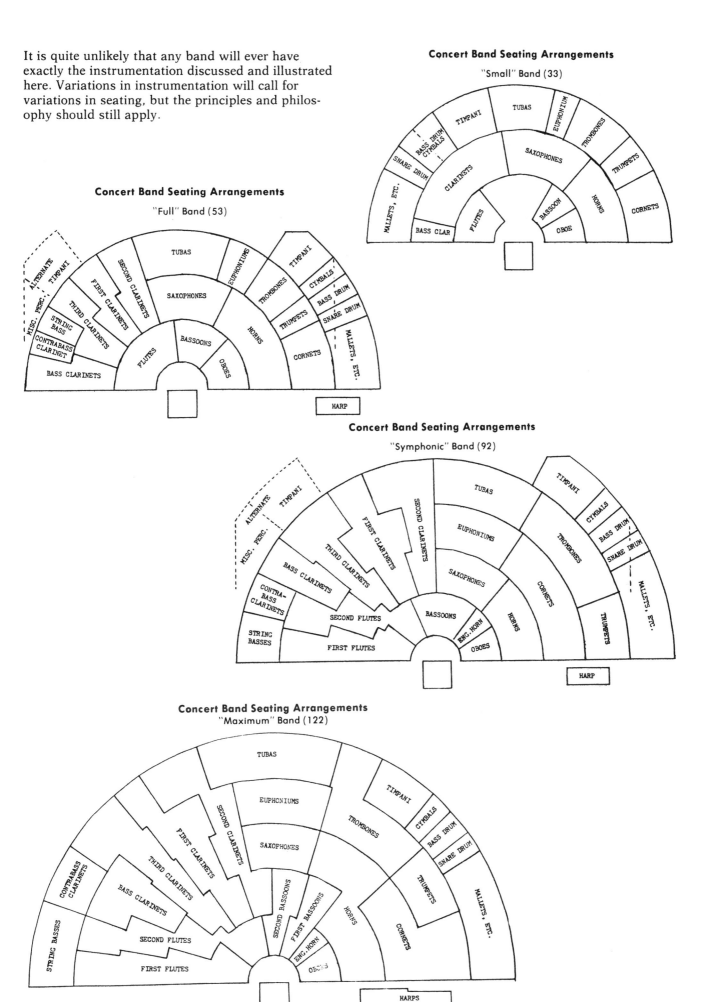

Concert Band Seating Arrangements

"Small" Band (33)

Concert Band Seating Arrangements

"Full" Band (53)

Concert Band Seating Arrangements

"Symphonic" Band (92)

Concert Band Seating Arrangements

"Maximum" Band (122)

audience. If there is not sufficient space to place all the percussion on the right, it may be necessary to place the timpani and possibly some of the smaller accessories on the left behind the clarinets (who will just have to learn to live with their back-door neighbors!).

The harp needs as much dynamic advantage as possible and should be located in front of the semi-circular formation on the right, close enough to the conductor so that he can hear it well. Whether it is on the right or left will make no difference to the audience, but it is best if the harpist's head is in front of rather than in back of the instrument.

Additional Considerations

After locating all the instruments of the band by sections, there is still the determination of seating by parts within the sections. For the audience it is best to have only "first" parts along the front. For the conductor, it is best to have an equal distribution in each row of all parts for instruments seated in that row so that they will all come to him with the same dynamic advantage and with the best opportunity to create a good balance.

The six first flutes should be seated in the three outside desks along the left front, with three desks of second flutes inside them. There should be a desk each of first, second, and third clarinets in the second row, and the parts should be divided as evenly as possible in the next rows (two players per desk). All the other sections with multiple parts are already seated in the same row; they should have an equal number of players on each part except for first cornets and first horn, where an extra player each is provided to relieve the embouchure of the first chair. (For the sake of balance it is seldom advisable for both first horns or all three first cornets to be playing at the same time.)

The following points of detail and refinement in seating may also be of interest.

1. The first flute player who doubles piccolo should be seated on the outside of the second row.

2. If the eight first clarinets are seated in the center of the section, between the eight third clarinets on the conductor's left and the eight second clarinets on his right, then the firsts can exert maximum leadership and control.

3. Recommended saxophone order is, from left to right, second alto, first alto, tenor and baritone. This places the first alto leader of the section in the best position of leadership.

4. The horns should be ordered first to fourth from right to left because the directional sound gives the first horn the best influence in that position and only the first horn should be on the outside of the formation.

5. The order of oboes, bassoons, cornets, trumpets and trombones should also be from right to left.

6. The first chair players of first and second bassoons, first and second trumpets, and first and second trombones should be seated together on the inside of their sections. This will provide the most effective ensemble particularly when the scoring calls for only one on a part. (Clarinets and cornets are not included in this plan because the best scoring will call for one desk divisi when only two instruments are to play.)

7. First chair euphonium and tuba players should be seated near the center rather than at the end of their sections.

8. Should there ever be more than four horns (plus the assistant first) in the instrumentation, the excess should be seated separately from the principal quartet to permit the most balanced and refined playing in this section. (This plan might also be considered for cornets and trombones.)

Physical Set-up

The center of the conductor's podium should be the focus of the whole set-up. All chairs should exactly face the conductor. The radius of the first row should be at least 7-1/2' — less will increase the effect of a front row "screen" and disturb the conductor's "aural perspective" of the band as a whole. The radius of the succeeding rows should be increased by up to 4'9", allowing plenty of room to play, hear, and be comfortable. The conductor's podium should be even with the front edge of the formation; no player should ever be even with or behind the conductor, except perhaps the harpist who is placed slightly in front of the formation. (It is advisable to mark the floor of the rehearsal room as a guide for regular placement of chairs and stands.)

The players should be instructed to adjust the height of their music stands so that looking over them they will be able to see no lower than the top of the conductor's stand or waist line (normally the lowest point of his conducting movements). They must be able to see this much, but if they can see more, their stands are too low and they will have problems in seeing both the music and the conductor at the same time. When two persons play from the same music stand, the stand should be precisely in the middle of the space between the chairs so that each person has the same chance to see the conductor over the music.

If risers are used, the eye level of the players in the last row should be no higher than the eyes of the conductor. Otherwise, these players will have to look and play downward. Ordinarily the first two rows need no elevation, and remaining rows need no more than six inches each. On the concert stage, risers can generally be omitted from the sides of the formation for the first six or seven chairs.

Personal Objections

I recall the story about a young man who was building a new house for his family. As work progressed, he had the usual number of visitors and "inspectors," and could not help but hear their remarks, some of them derogatory. At last he put up a sign which read, "We don't like *your* house either." I include this story because now I want to list several things I don't like about many of the concert band seating arrangements I have experienced as a concert-goer and adjudicator. I say this even though some of these arrangements have produced some of the most exquisite music I have ever heard. Of course, I wonder how they did it — and I can only believe that if *my* arrangement had been used, the music would have been even better!

Flutes occupying the entire first row may be beautiful, but they set up too much of a massed sound screen before the rest of the band, and the conductor will hear them out of balance. If the flutes are on the right side of the conductor, half of them practically turn their backs on the audience and all of them point their instruments away from the audience. In addition, it is difficult to hear them in the full ensemble unless they are playing something up high by themselves. Even worse, with brasses blowing into their ears, it will often be difficult for the flutes to hear themselves, tempting them to force their tones sharp and inclining them toward shrillness.

I don't like the oboes and bassoons hidden away in the interior of the band, they (like the discouraging word in "Home on the Range") are seldom heard — unless they are soloists or the instrumentation is very thin. I sympathize with the author of a recent article, "The Bored Band Bassoonist," who complained that bassoons in the concert band are not given enough independent and interesting parts, and when they do have good parts they can't be heard because of where they are sitting.

As a conductor I don't like clarinets in the front row. The clarinets make up the largest and perhaps most basic section of the concert band. The first chair player is the concertmaster and he and his colleagues carry the leadership of the whole band on their shoulders. I want them to take on that leadership role — but from the second row where they will not overbalance the flutes, oboes and bassoons. In addition, if the first clarinets are grouped together in front of the similarly grouped seconds and thirds, I will hear very little of the latter. Each of the three groups might play wonderfully together, but they will be inclined to forget who else is around; and I doubt if they would be able to adequately contribute to and enjoy the thrill of close harmonies and harmonic balance.

All instruments across the front of the band will have favorable access to the audience.

It is surprising how many conductors give the advantages of direction and elevation to the already strongest instruments of the band by placing cornets and trumpets in the center of the band on risers, who are playing right into the audience. When the listeners can look right into the bells of these instruments, the sound is usually too bright and far too dominant. Save this kind of sound for special effects — such as the brilliant finale of *The Stars and Stripes Forever*, when these instruments often line up across the front of the stage or rise in their seats to truly electrify their listeners.

I do not like the placement of cornets and trumpets on one side of the band and trombones on the other. Members of the audience sitting on one side of the auditorium will hear these instruments unequally. And it will be more difficult for the conductor to secure choir balance, intonation, blend, and precision in a spread out formation than in one that is more compact.

Consider the directional properties of sound...

I also object to horns on the conductor's left with bells facing the audience. With the players' hands in the bells this is not as much a matter of dynamics as tone quality. Neither do I see any reason for reversing or otherwise changing the traditional order of first to fourth from the conductor's right.

Sometimes the heavier percussion instruments — timpani, bass drum, snare drum, or cymbals — are placed at the front edge of the seating formation, where they are inevitably too strong. It is also not a good idea to spread them across the back of the band since the necessary movements of the players can become distracting to the audience.

Finally, some directors have a predilection for dance band style seating in long, almost straight rows across the stage — even though this arrangement prohibits players from focusing on both the music and the conductor at the same time. And should two players be using the same music stand and if the stand is placed between them and in line with the conductor, the outside player might well need binoculars to read the music!

Just the Top of It

Like the first time ocean-crosser who exclaimed, "What a lot of water" — only to be told, "That's nothing. All you're seeing is the top of it!," I believe that seating may be one of those many things *beneath the surface* which are involved in bringing a band to a high level of artistic performance.

My presentation has been intentionally fervent and I hope, to a proper extent, persuasive. Surely I have left little doubt about my likes and dislikes. Let me ask some final questions. Can you (or do you want to) hear any woodwinds in the playing of a military march, or are you satisfied to hear only brass and percussion? Can you (or do you want to) hear the flutes when they are playing in unison with the clarinets? Can you (or do you want to) hear the tonal coloring of the flutes, oboes and bassoons in the full ensemble — at least in the middle dynamic range? Would you like to allow these things to happen rather naturally? If so, you will want to give serious consideration to the concert band seating arrangement I have proposed and have proven in my own experience. ■

Some Considerations in

Band Seating Arrangements

Al G. Wright

THERE ARE ALMOST as many different band seating setups as there are different band directors. Each of us has his own peculiar way to seat the instruments in the band. This individualism is a good thing because it prevents our bands from becoming stereotyped and helps each director to develop a "sound" that is pleasing and unique to his own wishes.

However, each of us should periodically review the reasons on which we base our own particular seating plan. Instrument placement will not only have a considerable effect on the way the band will "sound" but will also affect our rehearsal procedures.

Fundamental Considerations

A number of basic principles should be considered:

(1) All instruments should be placed so that the player is facing directly toward the conductor. The music stand should be in as straight a line of sight between the player and the conductor as is possible.

(2) Like instruments must be seated together. The large sectional groupings (reeds, brass, percussion) should be blocked out first. Then the

separate sections are grouped within the large block. Thus, all the clarinets are in one place, cornets in another, trombones in another, and so on. Within the sections the players are usually seated according to the part they play (1st, 2nd, 3rd).

(3) A better ensemble will result if the "lead" or "first chair" players of the several sections are seated close enough together so that they can hear and see each other.

(4) The grouping of the instruments (clarinet, cornet, etc.) within the larger sections (brass, woodwind, percussion) is important. However, there is considerable latitude for variation here.

(5) The appearance of the band is also an important consideration. This indicates that the setup must fit both the rehearsal room and the stage on which the band customarily performs publicly. Bands rehearsing in a wide but not very deep area (a rectangular room) would use a setup which would spread the band to the director's left and right. Groups rehearsing in a deeper area (square room) would bring the sides of the band closer to the director but would

extend the players in front of the director closer to the back of the room. A room one and one-half times as wide as it is deep is the most desirable proportion and will accommodate a very effective setup or seating arrangement.

(6) Bands using risers (elevations) will be able to establish a more effective setup than those that do not. Risers are a very important contribution to the "sound." In particular, risers help the brass section since they allow each of the instruments in the brass section to be heard equally well, rather than having those in back muffled by the ones seated in front of them. This makes for a better ensemble and a more balanced sonority.

Since the sound of the woodwinds is not as directional, seating them on risers is not too important. Woodwinds, then, are usually seated on the floor (in front of the risers). The use of risers has an additional advantage —that of making it easier for all players to see equally well thus enabling them to follow the conductor more closely.

Purdue Arrangement

With the above considerations in mind I would like to discuss a setup I have used for many years (see Fig. 1).

This seating plan assumes that risers are available. However, it has been found to be as effective as other setups when no risers were available. The following features will be noted:

(1) The soprano woodwinds are grouped to the conductor's left, the double reeds and deep reeds are to the conductor's right, and all brass are directly in front of him. This massing of the primary sections of the band makes for a strong feeling of ensemble within the band's major divisions and provides the first step in developing full tonal sonorities within these sections.

(2) In the deep reed and double reed sections the 1st oboe is seated directly in front of the 1st bassoon,

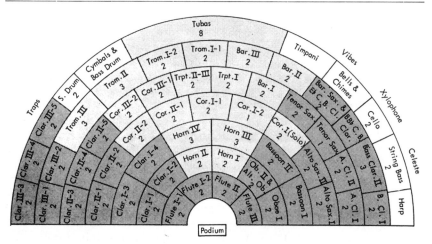

Figure I—The seating arrangement of the Purdue University Concert Band, Al G. Wright, Director. The Roman numeral refers to the part, the number following the numeral indicates the stand; and the number underneath refers to the number of players on that stand. The lightly shaded area encompasses the brass instruments, while the darker shading indicates the woodwinds.

University of Michigan Band

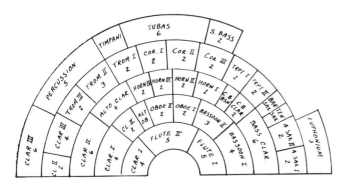

Comments by Director William D. Revelli: "Why I prefer this seating arrangement would be too long a story to discuss. Briefly, I prefer it simply because it places the instruments in a locale which I believe makes for the best response, balance, and ensemble."

University of Colorado Band

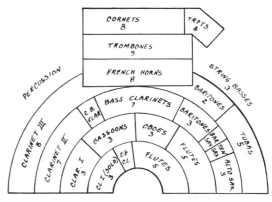

Comments by Director Hugh E. McMillen: "The reason for this particular setup is an entirely functional one—this is the way our band sounds best from the standpoint of balance, precision, and blend on the stage of our auditorium."

and both of these players are seated facing directly across from the 1st clarinet and 1st flute. These four important 1st-chair woodwind players are able both to hear and to see each other easily, resulting in better ensemble playing in the solo woodwind passages.

(3) All brass players face in the same general direction, which is directly forward. The French horns (because their bells turn to the back) are placed in front of the other brasses where they will be heard to better advantage.

Note that the 1st-chair players of the several brass sub-sections are seated within a few feet of each other. The 1st horn, the 1st cornet, the 1st trumpet, the 1st trombone, the 1st bass, and the 1st baritone are all seated reasonably close to each other.

With the contemporary composers today writing so much in "block"

style and constantly using the full sonorities of the reed and brass sections it is becoming increasingly important that we maintain a homogeneity of seating within these large sections. The brass seating shown in Fig. 1 is an illustration of this "block" seating. Attacks and releases require less rehearsal, tonal balance is more quickly obtained, and the intricate rhythmic figures found in many contemporary compositions respond more quickly to rehearsal and are played with greater security and solidity.

(4) The percussion section is placed in the "traditional" position at the back of the band. It is split with "pitched" percussion (timpani, chimes, bells, vibes, xylophones, etc.) on one side of the band and the "rhythmic" percussion (snare drum, bass drum, cymbal, traps) on the other side. The timpani's position

close to the 1st bass makes it easy for the player to obtain pitch constantly during rehearsal or concert.

Any director who has visited the percussion section while the band is playing (try some peripatetic rehearsals, they're ear-openers) will immediately realize that this section is undoubtedly in the very worst position since it is almost impossible for the drummers to "hear" in the back of the band. It is also difficult to "catch" the conductor's beat with the eye since he is so far away. However, as long as the percussionists remain standing while playing (and the mobility required of the player to move from one instrument to another during the playing of a number almost predetermines this) the percussionists will be relegated to the back of the band.

H. E. Nutt (Head of the Vander-

Seating arrangements must sometimes be modified for concert presentation. A comparison of the instrument placing in this picture of the Purdue Band with the seating chart (Fig. 1) indicates that most of the instruments retained their approximate position in the ensemble. However, because of the stage dimensions the band has been spread sideways to the conductor's left and right and the tubas brought closer to the conductor making a shallower setup.

U.C.L.A. Band

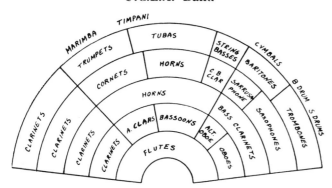

Comments by Director Clarence Sawhill: "This is much like the plan Mr. Harding used at Illinois. Our feeling is that the brass voice coming from the back of the stage, thru the reed section, gives the color of ensemble tone that we are striving for. The tone comes to a focal point in front of the conductor. Our seating plan varies some depending upon the type of music being played, but the above is the one most generally used."

Eastman Symphonic Wind Ensemble

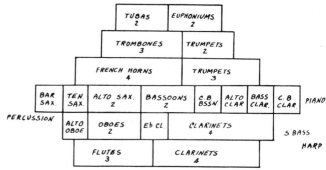

Comments by Director Frederick Fennell: "All seatings are a compromise but this one compromises our wishes the least. It is based upon the simple desire to allow the instruments to project themselves with ease and to produce a uniform sound by generating it from a common direction, directly forward . . . I prefer to play on the flat but vision requires that the back two rows be raised . . . This set has undergone almost no re-arrangement in the past six years."

cook College of Music in Chicago) has long advocated that percussionists play from a seated position. Perhaps he has something here. How much a band's precision and rhythm would be improved with the percussion section playing *in* the band rather than *behind* it!

(5) In most bands (except perhaps the finest professional groups) the membership is made up of players of varying proficiency. The band's seating arrangement must take into consideration these variations of player strength. I have always felt that it is important to distribute the stronger players among all the parts so that all of the voices are covered (rather than all of the best players on first parts and all of the poorer players on the other parts). However, we must also realize that because of the range and technical demands as well as the incidental solos often encountered in the first parts, these top voices must be covered by one or more fine players.

In the French horn section the players must be rated as either "high horn" or "low horn" (depending upon the player's lip tessitura or "best range"). The "high horns" are seated on the 1st and 3rd parts and the "low horns" on the 2nd and 4th parts. Many directors, however, seat the horns successively rangewise from 1st down to 4th.

The setup discussed in this article presumes a full double reed and a large deep reed section which is not found in some bands. Bands having a shortage in these sections often maintain larger saxophone and flute sections to compensate. These extra flutes and saxophones can be seated to the director's right to fill the area ordinarily taken up by full double and deep reed sections.

Experiment

In closing, the reader is urged to experiment with his band seating. For a real eye-opener (ear-opener) seat the clarinets "backwards," i.e., 3rd clarinets in front and the 1sts in back. Or try seating them "violin style" with all the 1sts down the outside of the band.

For just one rehearsal bring the drums down front by the 1st clarinets. Not only will the rhythm improve without rehearsal but, also, the drummers will realize very quickly that they have been playing too loud most of the time. An occasional change in rehearsal seating will make the players more conscious of the importance of listening to the other fellow while playing.

Oklahoma City University Band

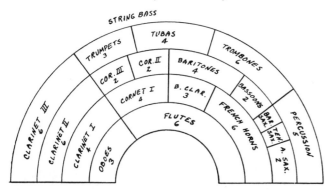

Comments by Director James Neilson: "The seating arrangement . . . is designed to make maximum use of the acoustical conditions which prevail in the School of Music auditorium. The reverberant count in the auditorium is about '2' . . . I wish to make it plain that this seating arrangement is subject to change whenever and wherever I find acoustical conditions that make a change necessary . . . On our stage we have three level risers, and we use the first and third for the back two rows."

University of Florida Band

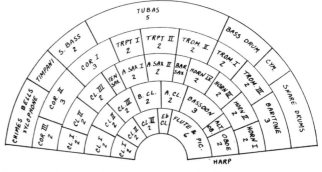

Comments by Director Harold B. Bachman: "This arrangement is the one we are currently using. I say 'currently' because I find that we must readjust from time to time as the size and strength of the various sections of the band change. Also certain changes must occasionally be made to conform to the dimensions of the various stages where we play . . . We have the 1st stand of each of the three Bb clarinet parts in the front row; and we seat saxophones, cornets, trumpets, and trombones with the 1st or leading part in the center of each section."

Something New in Band Seating Plans

C. B. RIGHTER

Most band directors have been dissatisfied with the old seating plans which were inherited from the Silver Cornet Band era, but few have attempted to do anything to correct the situation.

Some small bands still use cornets and trombones on the right and woodwinds on the left, but the larger symphonic groups have generally followed the newer pattern of clarinets on the left and other woodwinds on the right. There still seems to be no accepted plan for the disposition of the brasses. The horns are usually buried in the center of the band, with the trombones on the far right and the cornets and trumpets at the left rear or in the center behind the horns.

Very definite criticisms can be leveled at most of the seating plans which are now accepted as standard. Specifically, with the trombones on the far right and the cornets center or left-center toward the back of the band, the tonal balance between these important brass sections leaves much to be desired. An even greater loss results from the placement of the horns in the center of the band midway back. In this position the horns become almost completely submerged, partly due to the fact that their tone blends too easily with that of other instruments, but chiefly because their bells are directed downward and back in such a manner that the tone is actually lost to the listener.

The same loss of tone because of the *direction* in which it is projected applies to the flutes when they are placed on the right of the director. The flute tone is weak in any case, but when it is thrown toward the back of the band the result is quite hopeless. Moreover, the practice of placing oboes, flutes, and bassoons on the outside at the right makes it difficult for these instruments to hear one another and hence to achieve a proper blend and balance.

Faults of Old Systems

The writer has experimented with many different seatings over a period of several years and has been dissatisfied with all of those in common use. The three chief weaknesses seemed to be, in order: 1. Lack of flute tone; 2. The "covering" of the horns, especially in solo passages; 3. Poor balance between cornets and trombones, with too much cornet tone when the cornets were partly facing the audience.

To correct this situation it seemed essential to have the flutes and the horns on the conductor's *left* in order that full advantage might be taken of the directional characteristics of these instruments. This move dictated a radical change in the location of the clarinets, but there seemed to be no valid reason for always having the clarinets on the left. The placement of the cornets on the extreme left seemed quite logical for two reasons: 1. They would balance the trombones by being in an exactly corresponding position; 2. They would not be blowing directly into the audience. A possible weak-

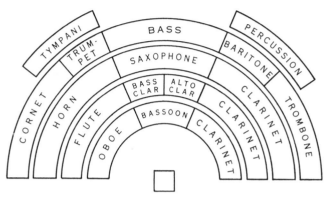

Flutes, horns and cornets belong on the conductor's left; the "color" sections should be grouped in the center.

ness was suggested, namely, that the distance between these lead brass sections might make it difficult for them to keep together. As is often the case, however, actual practice disproves preconceived theories. With the trombones and cornets at the extreme right and left of the director, these sections are able to hear one another without difficulty, and they seem to gain in independence and clarity, without any loss to the general balance of tone.

Obvious Advantages of New Grouping

The chief gain from this new seating plan, beyond those which suggested its use, is that the "color" sections of the band (clarinet, oboe, flute, bassoon, horn, alto and bass clarinets) are all fairly well concentrated in the center of the band where they can hear one another and be heard by the audience. A secondary advantage is that the saxophones are near enough to the "color" group to contribute to it when occasion demands, but are also well-located to give a solid harmonic and melodic basis to the musical structure.

It should perhaps be said that this placing of the horns will not be wholly satisfactory for a band which plays music calling principally for harmonic "afterbeats" in the horn parts. When such parts do occur, they must be handled with discretion; but where the horn parts are essentially melodic, this arrangement is ideal.

The new plan outlined herein is being used for the second season by the University of Iowa Concert Band and, on the basis of this test, it has proved to be far more satisfactory from every standpoint than any of the many seating plans which have been used in the past. Other directors are urged to use it on an experimental basis. If weaknesses which have not thus far become apparent should fail to materialize under a broader use of the plan, it seems reasonable to predict that the new method of seating may eventually gain common acceptance, at least among the larger bands.

SEATING THE BAND OUT-OF-DOORS

Leonard Smith

The placement of the various instruments in the band should be a matter of prime concern. I believe it is even more critical in open air concerts than when playing within the confines of an auditorium; the sound in the auditorium is at least somewhat contained in a given area.

In discussing how I seat my band, I will explain and justify my reasons. I will also comment on some practices which, in my opinion, ought to be avoided.

It would be well to examine a popular seating arrangement, the one with the clarinets on the left of the conductor and the cornets on the right. This so-called "traditional" seating plan was possibly well founded; years ago, it was probably the expedient thing to have the most persuasive or strongest melody parts close at hand for the conductor. In this way, he could even convey supplemental oral instructions or indications to these key players successfully when they were right under his baton. In small bands of 20 players or so, who played without much, if any, rehearsal, this seating arrangement could be a great asset for the entire band. However, I don't think we can justify this seating arrangement on those grounds *today*, and I am frankly quite amazed to see it still employed so frequently—not only out-of-doors, but inside as well.

Surely, a walk into the audience area by the conductor, while his assistant takes over, would serve to convince him that an adequate tonal balance is simply not possible under these circumstances.

But perhaps it is sentiment which rules in some cases today: "This is the way Sousa seated his band, and if it was good enough for him, it's good enough for me!"

I choose to believe that Mr. Sousa seated his band for very cogent reasons of his own. Herbert L. Clarke and Frank Simon were star attractions. Seated up front, they could be *seen* as well as heard. Likewise, trombone soloist Arthur Pryor, when stage dimensions made it practical, was also seated at the front of the stage. Further, this seating arrangement made it highly convenient for the cornets and trombones to march out and line up across the stage for the *Stars and Stripes Forever,* a regular feature of all Sousa Band concerts.

We must take into consideration also the fact that risers were not used in those days. Consequently, very little of the personnel of any music organization could be seen from the audience, except from the balconies when playing in theatres or the like. Lastly and most important, the greatest attraction of the Sousa Band was

Leonard Smith, well-known as a composer, conductor, and cornet virtuoso, has been conductor of the Detroit Concert Band since 1946. He has appeared throughout the country as a guest conductor and soloist and has also been guest lecturer at leading colleges and universities. In addition to their annual eight-week summer series of performances, the Detroit Band broadcasts a one-hour radio program every Saturday evening.

Mr. Sousa himself and his marches. How he chose to seat the band was primarily a matter of *showmanship* on his part.

If our primary concern is to provide for the possibility of a balanced tone of the band, in the aggregate, then the seating of the brass players must be taken into account for the obvious fact that their instruments are *directional* in sound. By contrast, the sound of the woodwinds emenates from the tone holes; thus the sound of these instruments is non-directional.

Placing cornets, trumpets, and trombones so that their tones are directed across the band, to the opposite side of the stage simply means that a large portion of the audience will be hearing a deflected and/or muffled tone from these instruments.

Although the French horn is genetically a brass instrument, I regard it as a member of the woodwind family in my seating arrangement because the tone of this instrument is intentionally non-directional. If the French horn were to be played with open bell, with a directional sound, then I could see logic in redesigning it to allow for this circumstance, just as other instruments have undergone such a metamorphosis. Or, if "afterbeats" are the problem, it's a simple, if tedious, process to re-arrange the music and take advantage of the trombones and/or 2nd and 3rd cornets to solve this. Incidentally, I have done this in the trios of many of my marches, *Jurisprudence, Horns-a-Plenty,* and others. Although much printed music for band demands it, I frankly don't think the mission of the French horn is playing afterbeats! Certainly the ineluctable charm and elegance of the French horn tone is its very diffusion of sound, made possible by the hand in the bell. For that reason alone, it is essential that we regard it as a woodwind in seating arrangements.

I prefer to seat my band with the non-directional instruments up toward the front of the stage, and across the entire width of the stage, on two risers. With the directional-toned instruments above and behind them, in a slightly semi-circular row facing the audience, the sound of the brass instruments then *fuses* with the woodwinds and offers the *possibility* of an excellent blend of sound.

I will refer the reader to the accompanying chart. If, for example, all the clarinets were to play the same tone, it would be heard as completely balanced tonally, equally distributed, and coming to the audience's ear from across the entire stage. Since the oboes possess a more delicate tone, they are placed up front and near the center so they can more easily radiate clarity. The saxophones are ranked with the horns, in the area of the bassoons and alto and bass clarinets, on risers. The flutes face the audience and their tone is welded into this total woodwind sound.

The placement of the various instruments is of crucial importance in providing a balanced tone

I recommend that each director test this in order to be thoroughly convinced and satisfied. The experiment with this portion of the ensemble should be made at the various dynamic levels to further confirm the practicality of such seating.

As I have noted, the tones of the brass instruments are directional. Therefore, I regard it as being completely illogical today to place these instruments in any other direction than toward the audience. The brasses, when placed on risers, a step above the woodwinds who are immediately in front of them, unite with the woodwinds in a focused sound and the audience hears a coalescence of that sound.

As a further experiment, test this brass seating with a chorale and observe the ease with which the players *themselves* are able to come to agreement in balance of tone, intonation, attack, and general precision—quite contrary to what might be expected. And you, as the conductor, can hear this composite sound and can make the slightest adjustments not only with authority but with confidence, knowing that you are hearing their blend of tone just as the audience will hear it.

Baritones, especially those with the upright bells can, if necessary, be placed behind the trombones, for their tone is especially penetrating. I choose to place the tubas on risers, just right of center stage only for the reason that complete center placement at the rear of the stage sometimes involves a backlash of tone which is distracting to the tuba players. The percussion is placed in two corresponding locations on the left side.

A further examination of this seating arrangement reveals that many of the first chair players are in proximity to each other. (These players are indicated on the chart by solid dots.) First chair clarinet, flute, and oboe are seated almost as close to one another as they are in quintet! The first chair horn, saxophone, cornet, trombone, and tuba players are all grouped together. This obviously constitutes another factor in developing and maintaining ensemble precision. Also, the tenor-voiced instruments, which frequently perform together, are grouped in a concentrated area so that they too can perform with greater compatibility.

In the case of large bands of 125-175 players, I would prefer to retain this same general seating plan even if it means double rows of brasses. I much prefer this to the long single line of trombones, for instance, which swings from center rear all the way around to the front of the stage on the conductor's right. Such groupings usually have a tendency to become unwieldly.

Lastly, from the audience's *visual* standpoint, the band presented in this manner creates its own fascination. Those instruments most easily and frequently recognized and identified by sound can also be seen just as easily. And on those occasions when you want the cornets, trumpets, and trombones to rise, as on the last trios of some marches, the sight and sound are both highly effective. The golden edge to the tone quality of the brasses coming over the band in this manner never fails to remind me of the delightful way a French woman described the final trio of *Stars and Stripes Forever:* ". . . like the American Eagle shooting arrows into the Aurora Borealis." ∎

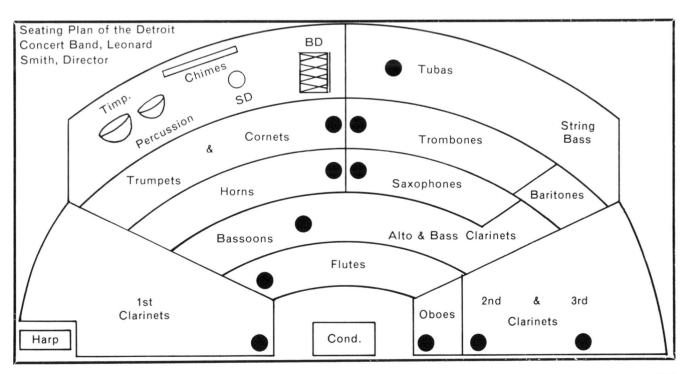

Seating Plan of the Detroit Concert Band, Leonard Smith, Director

The String Choir—
A Small Orchestra Seating Plan

Paul L. Paradise

Paul L. Paradise is String Instructor and Conductor of the Boston Public School Symphony Orchestra and Director of the string program in the Needham, Massachusetts, Public Schools. He is also a charter member of NSOA.

U NLESS A SCHOOL orchestra conductor has a large school enrollment to draw upon or directs a combined school group or youth orchestra, chances are that his orchestra's string section will be relatively small and will sound weak. It is seldom that one hears the strings as a dominant part of a small school orchestra.

New Seating Plan

The problem arises of how to seat a group of 8-18 violins, 2-5 cellos, 2-4 violas, and probably one string bass. Using the standard seating plan, the strings in this small proportion have difficulty penetrating thru even the minimum brass and woodwind sections.

The "string choir" orchestra seating plan (see diagram) can serve to improve this situation. By applying the structure of the vocal choir you can revitalize your orchestra's sound. If you arrange the string section in a semicircle across the breadth of the stage in one or two rows (if you have that many), you will establish a wall of string sound that even a *fortissimo* of brasses and woodwinds cannot completely drown out.

Advantages

With this seating plan, bowing and technical problems are laid out right in front of the conductor, making them easy to correct. Each orchestra member has a good view of the conductor. You may have a concertmaster if you wish, but it is not essential. In this way your first and second violins (Violins A and B preferably) have less demarcation, and strong players will not balk at playing violin B first row in preference to playing violin A second row. Too often violins A overbalance violins B so that their part is completely subordinate in the total sound.

The string choir has considerable flexibility in its seating arrangement. Any combination of strong players or sections at the extremities of the arc helps to unite the string body and solidify the sound. This seating plan works well with any number less than standard or near the standard number required for a symphony orchestra, and best with the small school group.

The main difference between this seating plan and the traditional one is that the strings are united in a concave instead of a horizontal wall of sound. With the latter, the distance between the last stand of each section is so far apart that the strings cannot project as strong a sound as when there is an arc of strings all facing the audience. With the string choir arrangement the instruments are directed toward the audience for a unified timbre; in the standard arrangement the section on the conductor's right is muffled because the instruments are turned in toward the orchestra.

The visual factor should not be overlooked. With the string choir seating plan everyone is seen full face, which gives the appearance of a television studio orchestra and a sound that is larger than one would expect from the actual size of the group.

This seating plan accomplishes what was previously impossible with a limited number of string players, and it is certainly worth a try.

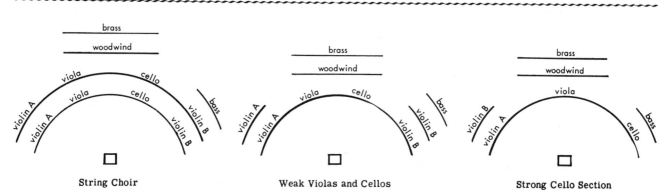

String Choir   Weak Violas and Cellos   Strong Cello Section

Placing the Strings

Is there such a thing as an ideal seating plan
that the orchestra string section should adopt?

TRAUGOTT ROHNER

THE TRADITIONAL manner of seating string sections is to place the first violins to the director's left, the second violins to the right, the violas to the right of center, the cellos to the left of center, and the basses directly behind the cellos. (See illustration.)

This placement is used by some professional conductors, such as Toscanini and Bruno Walter, and by some conductors of school orchestras. Whether it or some other seating plan is used, it is important for every conductor to consider carefully the advantages and disadvantages of each plan. It is even quite possible that there is no one ideal seating plan but that each may be suited to certain particular circumstances. Let us, therefore, enumerate the major factors involved in the placing of the string section.

1. Balance. It is highly desirable that the string choir sound balanced to the audience in front of the stage rather than to one listening backstage. Since the sounds from all stringed instruments come forth through the "F" holes, the direction in which the "F" holes are pointed has much to do with the volume and the balance of the string section.

2. Proximity. When the music of two or more sections is similar, it is desirable to place these sections as near as possible to each other. For example, in most of the music of the early classics the first and second violin parts move together; the same cooperation is found even more frequently in the cello-bass parts. It is in such cases especially that the two

violin sections and the cello-bass sections should be placed very close together. In much of the modern music this is, of course, not true.

3. Appearance. A balanced appearance is desirable if other factors are equal. Maximum uniformity dictates that the traditional manner of seating be followed with the exception that the basses are placed at the center back.

The three points already mentioned are the major ones. Let us consider them as well as a few additional suggestions.

Placing the basses at the center back of the stage not only looks well, but the back wall helps to reflect the important bass parts into the orchestra as well as out to the audience. Everyone will agree that it is desirable for all players to hear the bass part.

Right Side Weak

The location that is weakest in volume is the one to the director's right because here the violins or violas are projecting their tone to the back of the stage instead of to the audience. Even the cellos suffer to some extent if placed here because they, too, project some of their tone into the orchestra. Obviously, the basses cannot be placed here.

Thus, the section which suffers least from the weak location, the cello, is the one to be placed to the right. If the cello section is very weak, it may be seated to the left or right of center front. Of course, one should not forget that most players like to be placed on the outside or to the right of the director since these are the most prominent locations. Some prospective cellists may even be "sold" on the instrument because of its prominence on stage.

Reasons for placing second violins inside first violins are numerous, especially in the case of school orchestras. Most orchestra music is written so that the first and second violin parts are closely associated in structure and rhythm. To achieve a cohesive whole they should be placed near each other.

Violins Together

Band directors rarely divide their clarinet sections by placing them on both sides of the front of the stage; neither should orchestra directors divide violins. Furthermore, most school orchestras have more young and inexperienced players in second violins than in any other section. It is desirable not to isolate them or to place them too prominently; they will play much better and with greater confidence inside the first violins, and the tones of their instruments will be projected much better.

The second violins will learn much from the better first violins. Bowing techniques can be picked up to a considerable extent by association. Finally, the director will find that he will have much less worry and will have to spend much less time with the seconds when they are placed inside the firsts.

Just as the right side of the stage is weaker for violins and violas, so in contrast the left side is stronger. The first violins have this spot by force of tradition, appearance, and importance.

In most school orchestras the viola section is weak. It might be encouraged by being given more prominence. Perhaps the director cannot give it the violins' traditional space, but he might feature it by having the players stand in front of the orchestra or even by their chairs. If composers and arrangers of music would make the orchestra viola parts stronger and more interesting, the instrument might attract more performers.

One Basic Plan

Several good arguments could be set forth for arranging the strings according to the type of music which is being played. But since it is not quite practical to shift positions for each different number, it is better to stick to one basic plan or at least to reserve the shifting of sections to intermission time. The director, however, may still feature a section by lining the players across the front of the stage.

As a whole and in the light of all the arguments, it appears that the following placement of the string section has a maximum of benefits, at least for the school orchestra, and a minimum of faults.

A strong and dependable bass section may be placed directly in the center back rather than to the right, as indicated in the above illustration.

If any director is skeptical about placing the second violins next to the first violins, the writer encourages him to try this set-up for about eight or ten rehearsals. In the final analysis, of course, a superior orchestra will outplay an inferior one regardless of the seating arrangement used. But within the same framework, with all other things being equal, there is a marked difference in the results of the various seating plans.

August, 1984

Placing the Horns
Thoughts and Opinions from Seven Directors

David L. Martin

Music educators and conductors agree that the placing of the French horn section is more difficult than the placement of other instrumental groups. This section requires special consideration because in many scores, the horns serve as an orchestrational bridge between the woodwinds and brass. Constructed as a reflecting instrument, the horn's bell points away from the audience so the instrument's sound is heard as it reflects off a different surface rather than being heard directly as are other instruments. Furthermore, various scoring systems suggest placing the horns in such locations as near the saxophones, the lower brass, or the double reeds. For these reasons, the placement of the French horn section deserves special thought. In order to clarify this issue, I contacted seven prominent band directors and conductors from various sections of the country and asked them to share their ideas on placing the horn section.

Three Distinct Practices

In comparing the responses of these seven conductors, three distinct practices emerged:
• Placing the horns in the center of the ensemble
• Placing the horns away from the center to give them prominence
• An experimental approach — finding the best placement with respect to the program being performed and the concert hall being used

David L. Martin received his bachelors degree from Rutgers University and his masters degree in music education at Northwestern University.

All seven conductors preferred to seat their horn sections in a straight line, with the principal player to the section's left (the conductor's right), unless a specific composition dictated a different arrangement.

Robert Winslow, director of bands at North Texas State University, is among those who prefer seating the horns in the center of the band. He places the horns slightly to the rear of the center and close to the tuba section. Winslow states, "I find the band can produce a darker, more resonant ensemble timbre with better intonation if this group is located near the center . . . where they can serve as a core." Close to this core, Winslow places the low reeds, bassoons, bass clarinets, contrabassoons, and baritone sax. This, he says, "solidifies the intonation level and allows me to successfully place most any soprano sound on top of it." Winslow adds that the straight line set-up seems to be counterproductive in works requiring multiple horns (eight or more). In this case he uses a block arrangement, seating the first and second players in front and the third and fourth players immediately behind them.

Another advocate of this type of seating is **John P. Paynter,** director of bands at the Northwestern University School of Music and conductor of the Northshore Concert Band. Paynter believes that because the horns are scored as a bridge between the woodwinds and the brass, they should be placed between the two. He seats the horns in a straight line immediately in front of the brass and behind the woodwinds.

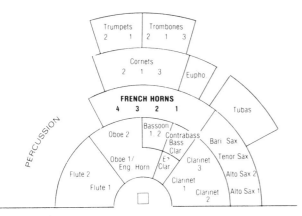

JOHN P. PAYNTER
Northwestern University

Trumpets 2 1 2 Trombones 1 3

Cornets 2 1 3 Eupho

FRENCH HORNS 4 3 2 1 Tubas

PERCUSSION

Oboe 2 Bassoon 1, 2 Contrabass Bass Clar Bari Sax

Oboe 1/ Eng. Horn E♭ Clarinet 3 Tenor Sax

Flute 2 Clar Clarinet 1 Alto Sax 2

Flute 1 Clarinet 2 Alto Sax 1

This arrangement, he adds, "also aids in blend and intonation within the ensemble." When questioned about other formations where the horns are seated away from the center, Paynter notes that "there is no purpose other than appearance...the group doesn't hear or relate well." In closing, Paynter emphasized the importance of asking players what they think about the seating, as well as being willing to experiment to achieve better results.

James Croft, director of bands at Florida State University, also prefers placing horns in the middle of the ensemble. Croft, who is a horn player himself, says that, "the horn has a quality that is most complementary to all winds in terms of timbre, and is most effective when placed so that all benefit from its wonderfully enhancing quality." In regard to placing horns away from the center, Croft adds, "I abhore placing the horns on the left side (on the outside) of the conductor because none of the benefits are available." He also sees no advantage to placing the horns on the conductor's right, "although the instruments have less of a cutting edge from this side."

Another proponent of the center placement idea is **Harry Begian,** recently retired director of bands at the University of Illinois. Begian places the horns in the center of the band, directly in front of the tubas and to the right of the trumpets, just behind the saxophones.

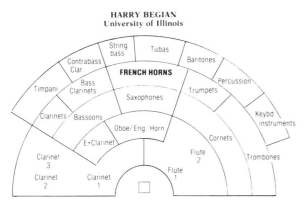

HARRY BEGIAN
University of Illinois

String bass Tubas Baritones

Contrabass Clar **FRENCH HORNS**

Bass Clarinets Percussion

Timpani Trumpets

Clarinets Saxophones Keybd instruments

Bassoons

Oboe/Eng. Horn

E♭ Clarinet Cornets

Clarinet 3 Flute 2 Trombones

Clarinet 2 Clarinet 1 Flute 1

His reason for placing the horns here is their closeness to the tubas, "with whom they usually form the harmonic basis for most music played." In addition Begian notes that this position complements the horns' prominent harmonic function; he places the section near the saxophones, with

whom they are often paired on both lyrical lines and countermelodies. He also sees no reason to place the horns away from center or in other "acoustically strange places."

In contrast to these ideas, **Richard E. Strange,** director of bands at Arizona State University places his horn section to the conductor's extreme right, directly behind the saxophones and to the left of the trombone section.

RICHARD E. STRANGE
Arizona State University

PERCUSSION

Euphoniums Trombones 3 2 1

Tubas

Contrabass Clar Cornets 3 2 1 Trumpets 1 2 4

Piano Alto Clarinet E♭ Clarinet Bass Clarinet Bassoon 1 2 Contrabassn. Baritone Sax 3 **FRENCH HORNS**

Clarinet 3 English Horn Piccolo Flute 2 Tenor Sax 2 2

Clarinet 2 Clarinet 1 Oboe 2 Flute 1 Alto Sax 1 1

Strange prefers this position because the horns are "featured and out front," and are near the saxophone and trombone sections, with whom they are frequently scored. He was also careful to note other reasons for the location: "I do not seat the horns in front of the trumpet section as is done in many bands, because the trumpet tonguing can be felt 'hitting' the French horn embouchure when the trumpet bell is aimed at the French horn bell." To illustrate his point Strange suggests having a trumpet player play a *staccato* note behind a French horn player.

Scott Whitener, director of bands at Rutgers University, echos the non-center placement idea. Although Whitener advocates being flexible and experimenting with seating arrangements, his most recent seating plans place the horns to the left of center, in front of the percussion section and to the left of the trumpet section. According to Whitener, the worst place for the horns is in the center of the band, in front of the trumpets and trombones because "the result is a very muffled horn sound. What is most important is that the horns are clear of bodies. The horns must sound!" Emphasizing flexibility, Whitener adds that the conductor must always be willing to experiment, and should avoid sticking to a single set-up. A rule-of-thumb that he suggests is, "Do what works best with your group in your hall." He also adds, "it is just as important for the horn players to be able to hear (ask them if they can), as it is to hear the horn players."

Whitener's comments are unique among this group of conductors because he was the only one who addressed the horn's unique quality as a reflecting instrument, and was one of two to mention the player's ability to hear as important to seating. Both are important considerations when placing a horn section.

Frank Battisti, conductor of the wind ensemble at the New England Conservatory of Music was the final conductor questioned. He also advocates the importance of being flexible and experimenting with seating arrangements: "My approach to seating plans in general is very flexible. I like to experiment and try to come up with a plan that provides for the best projection of the music, makes the players feel comfortable, and allows them to hear what they have to hear with clarity. When I move to a new concert location, I often change seating plans for a piece if I feel my objectives are not possible in the seating plan I am using."

Although this small collection of ideas is not intended to be an exhaustive survey, it may provide a variety of ideas to help the school band or orchestra conductor examine his own methods. Here is a summary of what I found.

Placing the horns in the center of the ensemble benefits blend and balance. However, horn players positioned in front of the trumpets may find it difficult to hear other members of the ensemble, as well as other members of the section. This location may also present a projection problem (though it may only be imagined) because the horn player usually feels that he must work hard to be heard, even though the sound may be carrying into the hall with relative ease.

Placing the horns away from the center, on the other hand, is excellent especially if you want a clear, distinctive horn sound. Players often think it is easier to play in this position because they feel as though they don't have to work as hard in order to be heard. Balance and blend may be more of a problem because of the distances involved, but it's easier for horn players to hear without trumpeters blowing close behind.

The horn, as a reflecting instrument, does seem to require special consideration. Regardless of the seating arrangement you currently use, I hope this collection of ideas will encourage you to consider other possibilities that may help improve the sound of your horn section and your ensemble in general. ■

December, 1987

Pull the Switch
for a Better Band

BY D. SCOTT LOOSE

As a teacher I am always on the lookout for ideas that will help my students to improve and to appreciate the efforts of their fellow band members. At Lampeter-Strasburg High School my colleagues and I have found a way to do this, with the unexpected side benefit of improving students' writing skills and awareness of the teacher's job.

The idea first occurred to me during a break at summer band camp when I saw some students trying to play each other's instruments. I immediately flashed back to my college instrumental methods classes and the fun we had learning other instruments. Why not do it as an organized project with the entire band? The more I thought about it, the more the benefits listed above oc-

D. Scott Loose is director of instrumental music at Lampeter-Strasburg High School in Lampeter, Pennsylvania. He holds a bachelor's degree from Wittenberg University and a master's from West Chester University.

curred to me. I decided to save this experiment until the February doldrums invariably set in.

The first order of business was to buy several cans of spray mouthpiece disinfectant. I then contacted our elementary band director, explained my idea to him and got his recommendation on a suitable band piece to use. We decided on "The Blue Rock" by Dale Lauder, because we wanted a piece that the players would remember from their elementary band days and one that would turn the spotlight on each section for a while. Ranges of the instruments were a primary concern, along with interesting percussion.

To try this with your group, divide the band in half, separate the brass and woodwinds, then divide the percussion between them to balance the numbers. Write the names of the brass or the woodwind half of the band on slips of paper and put them into a hat. At the end of the last rehearsal, the week before you

want to do the switch, have the other half pick names. Let a percussionist go first, and have him pick again if he gets another percussionist. The pairs can then introduce themselves and discuss the plan for the next week. Pass out the band piece so that they can see what they will have to teach. I also recommend passing out soft reeds so that clarinets and saxes will be able to produce a sound the first day.

Have each student teach his partner a concert B♭ tuning scale and anything else they need to play the piece. Percussion players should teach simple rudiments and have their partners play a wide variety of instruments and accessories. The teachers can use a variety of materials ranging from old method books to manuscript charts.

Warning: The cacophony of squeaks, squawks, and honks can be deafening in the confines of the band room. It is best if the pairs can spread out over several areas surrounding the music room. As the director, I tried to keep my nose out of the teaching and let the students experiment. When asked, I discussed possibilities and tried to have them discover solutions themselves.

The schedule we followed was to use the first period concentrating on only one instrument, the following rehearsal the other. The third rehearsal was spent one-third on one instrument, one-third the other, and one-third reading through the ensemble piece together. We continued doing this once a week until the concert, when we performed the piece to a standing ovation.

The final part of this experience was a written assignment to be turned in by each student one week after the concert. It consisted of two essays in response to the following questions: What did you learn about your own instrument from this experience? What did you learn about the other person's instrument from this experience?

I can guarantee responses that will "charge your battery" for the rest of the year. Everyone benefits from "Pulling the Switch!"

Students Respond

What I Learned About My Instrument

I learned some things about cornet that help me sympathize with our first teacher. It's hard to explain to someone who knows nothing about the cornet how to make a good sound; and getting a sound out was the beginning of a whole bunch of questions that I couldn't answer. I don't really think about buzzing my lips any more, or trying

to blow a steady stream of air through the horn. I couldn't think of what to, tell Mark to explain how to make a high note while pushing down the same valves as for a low note. The whole experience brought me back to some fundamentals of cornet playing.

While practicing for my playing exams recently, I thought back to some of the things I told Mark about how to improve his tone, such as a steady flow of air, getting higher notes by tightening the lips from "ah" to "oh" to "ee," and pressing the valves correctly. I reminded myself of the proper way to hold my instrument and of good posture, which through time had deteriorated into bad habits. I learned how frustrating it must be for a teacher to give advice on how to improve when he can't figure out what the student is doing wrong.

What I Learned About Mark's Instrument

Most of all I learned that woodwinds aren't as loud as brass. It was frustrating to be blowing hard and hardly be heard. It helped me to appreciate my instrument, because the trumpet part seems a little more important to me than a part that can't be heard. But a nice thing about the woodwinds is that your lips don't hurt as much, so you can play longer than you can when you start to play a brass instrument. I also like the fact that a saxophone has a different fingering for each note, which makes it easier to go higher or lower. It was hard, learning to listen for such a different tone than trumpet and for a harmony part instead of the melody. I like playing the melody better, but until I played the sax, I never thought about what it was like not to play melody.

One of the most difficult things about playing the baritone saxophone is holding it so that your fingers can reach the right keys. I kept putting the wrong fingers on the keys. I'd rather have just three valves and adjust my lips!
— Missy Grimm

Other Selected Comments
As a future music teacher, I got my first taste of what life is like on the other side. Although it was challenging, I'm sure this is what I want to do.
— Senior Woodwind

I used to get mad when the director let the brass players rest and made the rest of us play. Now I understand how tired and sore their lips can get, and I only played a half hour. I can imagine what they feel like after a two-hour marching band rehearsal.
— Junior Woodwind

How do woodwind players remember all those fingerings? My fingers didn't want to cover the holes. If I had started on clarinet, it would be a lamp by now.
— Senior Brass

I took for granted how difficult it is to play my instrument. Now I realize how far I've come in six years, and I feel really good about myself; I do have a special talent.
— Sophomore Woodwind

I never realized how much patience it takes to teach someone to play an instrument. It was very frustrating trying to tell someone how to do something I do without thinking.
— Senior Brass

I used to get mad when the drummers would beat on everything in sight. But when I got a pair of sticks in my hands, the same disease struck me. I wonder if there is a cure.
— Junior Woodwind

□

So You're Putting On a Musical?

BY KIM TRYTTEN

It's 7:58 p.m. and over your headset you hear the technical director:
"One-minute warning. House lights ready to come down.
Stage manager ready? House lights at one-half.
Orchestra ready? House at one-quarter.
Let's put this one in the bag."

Months of preparation and rehearsals will soon come to bear. Are you ready? Could you have been better prepared? The following ideas may be of help in the care and feeding of an orchestra for the musical you are preparing.

Selecting the Musical

Unless you are the director of the New York City School for the Performing Arts, you may have to relinquish your dream of doing *West Side Story*, or any number of other musicals that may be over the heads of your musicians. Reviewing the score for these rental musicals is only partially revealing, because they give only sketchy details as to what is actually written for your first trumpet, flute, clarinet, or cello. Full scores, needless to say, are unavailable, and the piano/conductor score does not give a full accounting of ranges and the relative difficulty of parts.

Try to find out who in your area has performed the show and pick their brains as to instrumentation, ranges, and difficulty of the music. As the orchestra director you should have some input in selecting the musical, and ideally this includes a veto.

Scheduling

Those in charge of the show need to sit down and schedule all rehearsals, makeup calls, set construction days, and other details well in advance. The orchestra and vocal directors should schedule several rehearsals, combining the orchestra and soloists at least two weeks before the production comes together on stage. There is no sense in wasting the time of the technical crew, chorus members, and others to work out material on stage that should have been accomplished in rehearsal.

To give yourselves the practice of an extra dress rehearsal, arrange a free performance for an area grade school, service club meeting, or senior citizens' organization. The entire cast benefits from performing before an audience without the pressure on opening night. Be aware that another performance may increase the royalties you pay to rent the musical, so check your contract before making such an offer.

Do your best to avoid scheduling the musical on a date that would conflict with other events in your area; don't make the mistake of having your show on the opening night of the county fair, or you may come in a distant second to tractor-pulls and cucumber judging. Consider church, school, and civic schedules to increase the chances of a well-attended show.

Recruiting Players

A few weeks before the first rehearsal announce the dates of the musical; plant the seed and allow it to germinate before you start asking people to play. This will give interested singers and orchestra musicians some time to think about it, as well as give you the chance to talk to those who participated last year. To create interest, post a few pages of manuscript from a rehearsal book in the music room and show a videotape of the musical. Generate as much interest as possible, and you'll have better luck finding players.

One week after the general announcement start meeting individually with prospective players and ask if they would like to participate. Students respond readily when they are approached this way: "Mary, I'd like you to play oboe in the musical. I think you will enjoy the challenge, and it will be a valuable experience. Here is a schedule to look at; think about it and I'll talk to you again in a few days." The simple announcement of a sign-up sheet for an orchestra often is not sufficient to garner the players you need.

Kim T. Trytten is Director of Bands in the North College Hill City School District in Cincinnati, Ohio. A native of Iowa who for eight years has taught all levels of general and instrumental music, Trytten holds a B.M.E. from the University of Northern Iowa and an M.M. from the University of Cincinnati. He has appeared as euphonium soloist, guest conductor, and clinician with high school and university bands in Iowa, Michigan, and Ohio.

In producing a community show contact area band directors, conductors of community bands, church music directors, instrument and sheet music dealers, the local university music department, and anyone else who might supply you with the names of musicians. You will be surprised at how many of these people still play and would like to participate. Be sure to tell the musicians whether you are asking them to volunteer their talents or what they will be paid, so no misunderstandings will arise later. Few situations are more embarrassing than when your first violinist or accompanist waits for you after the last show and gives you that look that says, "I'm waiting for my check, Mr. Jones."

An ace pianist can be particularly valuable to the quality of a musical production; my advice is to hire a good one if your budget allows. He is the person who will work with the soloists and come to know them. If the accompanist is also a member of the pit orchestra, he is in the position to fill in parts, should they become too difficult or if there is a communication problem during the course of a musical number. Often, the piano score has minor discrepancies, such as inconsistent numberings or letterings in the parts or incorrect key signatures. It is imperative to compare the director's score page by page, with the accompanist's book to be sure they are the same.

Players' Books

The musicians' parts are generally rented for one or two months. It is possible to obtain additional parts or extend the rental period, though the result is often a higher fee. A copy of a score and script are usually accompanied by a list of instrumentation that typically looks like this, depending on the musical chosen:

Reed I	Trumpet I	Violin I + II
Reed II	Trumpet II + III	Violin I + II
Reed III	Horn I + II	Cello
Reed IV	Trombone I	Bass
Reed V	Trombone II	Percussion

The combinations of instruments vary. Reed I may be flute and piccolo; Reed II may be oboe and English horn; Reed III may be E♭, B♭, and bass clarinets; Reed IV may be alto sax or bassoon; and Reed V may be tenor and bass saxophones.

A professional musician would have no problem playing E♭, B♭, and bass clarinets and probably owns them all. With high school or community musicians you may not have any French horns, or perhaps there are no string players available in your area. Older musicals (*The Music Man*) call for such seldom-used instruments as the bass sax; others such as *Fiddler on the Roof*,

call for accordion, English horn, and acoustic guitar. Still others (*Godspell, Bye, Bye Birdie*) require a battery of electric and bass guitars.

Don't panic; there are a variety of ways to get around these problems if you use a little daring spiced with creativity. Though flutes never will sound like violins, they are an acceptable substitute in a pinch. Your tuba player can perform string bass parts, though purists may choke at such an idea.

A capable baritone player can cover parts for everything from cello, electric bass, and trombone. Bass clef baritone players can read from E♭ alto saxophone parts quite easily by mentally changing the treble clef to bass clef, and then adding either three flats to an already existing flat key signature, or subtracting three sharps from an existing sharp key signature.

Here's a closer look at the process. To read from the following alto saxophone part written in one flat, a baritone hornist mentally reads bass clef and adds three flats to the key signature:

The baritone hornist reads B♭s as D♭s; any sharps added to F, G, or C would result in the hornist playing A♮, B♮, or E♮.

To read from an alto sax part written in two sharps, the baritone hornist subtracts three sharps and plays a key signature of one flat:

In the new key, F♯s and C♯s would become A♭s and E♭s for the players. Your bass clef baritone player can also transpose French horn parts using a similar approach.

If your bass clef baritone player also reads treble clef, other possibilities open up for covering tenor sax, trumpet, and some clarinet parts. Some of the best experiences for my students have come at a time when they have helped by rewriting parts, learning to transpose at the octave.

If you can determine that the percussion book includes all mallet percussion (bells, xylophone, chimes, vibraphone, etc.), then for convenience's sake, order an extra book for your players. You may also want to order extra books when players share parts, as in the case of Trumpet II

+ III or Horn I + II. That extra book will be of great help in allowing your players to have their own music to take home and practice.

Score and Script Study

A week before rehearsals begin get together with the show director and go through the entire musical on the piano, agreeing on tempo, dynamics, style, chorus phrasing, rubatos, and cuts. No doubt you have seen two directors arguing over style and tempos in front of cast members. This is unprofessional and can be avoided by talking through the show beforehand. Pay particular attention to dance sequences, because the orchestral parts for these sections are usually considerably more difficult. Make decisions early as to cuts and segues.

As the music director you should know the score so well that there is no confusion as to roadmaps, style, vamps, and key signatures and how they relate to bowings, trill fingerings, and articulations.

Mark the script book so that you can follow the action of the show and cue the music. Nothing is worse than realizing that the entire cast and chorus, technical crew, and director's staff have been waiting for music to begin for the past 30 seconds. You're bound to be hearing, "Mr. Jones! Where's the orchestra?"

One cannot expect orchestra members to be on their toes for every second of a two-and-one-half hour show, with all the sections of dialogue that separate the musical numbers. Try this idea: each time the orchestra finishes playing, turn off your music stand light. This means that players can relax, look over the music for the next scene change, or visit quietly. Thirty seconds before the next orchestra entrance, switch on your music stand light, indicating to orchestra members that they should gear up to play. This works well, though it puts the responsibility on you to stay alert.

Agreements and Contracts

Because the music rental company will hold you responsible for the score and part books, have each player sign an agreement when he checks out his music to acknowledge receipt of the music and the cost if he loses or damages it.

A performance contract is an effective way to state objectives and outline acceptable behavior during rehearsals and performances. It also lets parents know dates and times of rehearsals. Tailor the contract to include topics such as attendance at rehearsals and performances, planned absences from rehearsals, and guidelines for allowing friends and parents to attend rehearsals. The contract should cover topics such as having food or beverages in the pit area, handling props, and participating in activities on stage that could injure someone.

Once your players know the music, practice adjusting and improvising for the mistakes and delays that will arise during a performance. You may have attended a show and witnessed the confusion that occurs when a singer misses an entrance; the song may plod on for 200 measures with the orchestra and vocalist several bars apart. Be ready to deal with such an occurrence.

Technical Planning

If the orchestra will be located in a pit, you are in luck; but there are still concerns. If the walls and floor of the pit are brick or concrete, the music may overpower the singers. Carpeting the area, including the walls, will reduce volume and improve balance between the orchestra and vocalists. If carpeting is not within your budget, borrowed army blankets or heavy curtainlike materials will do the job nicely.

When no pit is available, arrange the orchestra on the floor in front of the stage. Use flats to hide the orchestra from the audience if you desire. The flats can double as scenery flats. If the house seats are situated too close to the stage or

Courtesy Kim Trysten

Break time for pit musicians

598

The Musical Language of Broadway Shows

Attaca subito – The next section or musical number will follow without pause or break.

Col tpts voce – The trumpets will play the same part as the singers. Music for the violins may state "col ww," meaning the woodwinds play the same parts.

8va or 8ve – The part is to be played at the octave.

Recit. – The vocal solo should be rendered in a free rhythmic manner. The conductor and orchestra will follow.

Rep. ad lib. – Repeat with freedom. See *vamp, safety.*

Segue – The performer should continue to the next song or movement without any pause or break.

Sim. – Continue in the same way, usually in regard to bowings or articulations. *Simile.*

Tacet – Found in some instruments' parts to indicate that there is no music written for that part. The term is sometimes written in the parts for the entire ensemble.

Tutti – An entire section or the remainder of the orchestra should enter playing.

Vamp, safety – One to four measures of repeated accompaniment, usually simple chords and rhythms scored between short bits of dialogue or action in a musical number. The conductor cues the end of the vamp simultaneously with the continuation of the vocal number.

– A one-measure repeat of the preceding measure.

– A two measure repeat of the preceding two measures. Players may also encounter repeats of three and four measures.

– Caesura or "railroad tracks" indicate an abrupt stop in the music. Dialogue or music may follow.

– V.S. designates *volti subito* or turn quickly. The symbol appears at the end of a page and means the music continues over the page turn.

– Div. is the abbreviation for divisi. Used in the first violin part, for example, it indicates these players are divided into two parts for playing passages in thirds, sixths, or some other harmony.

---

if seating is limited, arrange the orchestra behind the stage curtain or at the rear of the stage area. The orchestra faces the back wall while the conductor faces the audience, and curtain hides the orchestra from the cast and audience.

There are other questions to ask. Will you have stand lights, extra bulbs, and multi-plug extension cords? If the house is dark during the show, you will need these items because stage lighting alone will not be sufficient to illuminate the players' music. In exchange for a few inches of advertsing space in your program, your music dealer might just lend you all that you would need.

Will you have a headphone linking you with the technical director and the lighting manager, sound technician, and stage manager? These systems can save the show. During one performance of our spring musical, the music had started and vocal cues were fast approaching when the technical director encountered a major problem occurring in the wings of the stage. In a matter of seconds the stage manager relayed the problem to the technical director, who asked me to delay the vocal entrance. The orchestra responded when I indicated a hastily inserted eight-bar vamp into the music. The technical crew corrected the problem, and the show went on without anyone the wiser.

Sometimes the conductor has difficulty hearing vocalists. If feasible, have a monitor, such as an audio speaker, in the pit or behind stage.

During the week before the show, as all the musical and technical elements come together, keep yourself and your orchestra armed with pencils for the inevitable fine tuning. There will be places where vamps become a set number of measures, where music for scene changes will need to be extended, and where overture, entr'acte, and music for curtain calls will need to be adjusted.

Don't be afraid to try the unconventional. Adapt, rearrange, adjust, and replace as necessary. Above all, have fun. Producing a successful musical can be the highlight of the year for your instrumentalists, and you.

Directing a Musical Show

Mario F. Oneglia

The production of a Broadway-type musical show has become a regular part of the annual schedule of many schools — indeed, it has literally "taken over" in some places, with directors and students spending a great deal of time and effort on the project. Since band and orchestra directors are usually asked to lend their expertise, we have the opportunity to guide these entertainment productions into a meaningful learning experience for our students.

A show can act as a valuable educational project involving an integration of the dramatic, musical, and visual arts. Not only do students and faculty from these artistic areas come together in producing a show, but there is ample opportunity to involve those in business education and the industrial arts in such practical matters as publicity, ticket sales, and the building of scenery and props.

This interdisciplinary aspect calls for a great deal of preliminary planning and a willingness to compromise on the part of all the participants. Planning committees made up of students, faculty, and administrators should be set up to deal with questions such as the reasons for giving a musical, how a particular musical

Mario F. Oneglia holds degrees from the Manhattan School of Music and Columbia University. He has taught public school music in Long Island and is currently Associate Professor of Music at Montclair State College (Upper Montclair, New Jersey) where he conducts the college orchestra. He has performed in many broadway theaters and has conducted a number of off-broadway and college show productions.

must meet several criteria, and what shows are possible in a particular situation. A shows committee, charged with the responsibility for communication with publishers and the procurement of sample study scores and recordings will also be needed to assist the planning committee in making a final choice.

Here are some criteria which might be used in choosing a show: the show should have the possibility of "mass involvement"; it should have a book or story plot by a master writer (Shaw, Shakespeare, Isherwood, and Runyon are examples); it should have lots of tunes or memorable melodies (don't pick a "one-tune-show"); the story should contain some degree of universality; and it should provide opportunities for actors, singers, and dancers to work in both bit or solo capacities as well as in group situations. Admittedly, few shows meet all of these guidelines, but an agreement on standards for selection will help the work of both the planning and shows committees.

Types of Shows

The three general types of musical shows could be classified as the review, the musical comedy, and the music drama. In the review, a loosely knit series of songs, comic bits, pantomimes, dances, or choral selections are presented without much more unity than an underlying theme such as patriotism. Often, this type of show will have no binding thread running through it at all and will simply be a series of separate acts (vaudeville). The musical comedy has a story ("a book show") in which the emphasis is on reparteè, two or more items are checked, this interpretation is open to question, and remedial action should be undertaken immediately.

☐ The normal attack was not used in the appropriate places. In this attack the note is addressed without delay and played without dynamic modification. There may or may not be separation between successive notes.

☐ The legato attack was not used in the appropriate places. This is a smooth attack usually pronounced with a relaxed tongue (but never a relaxed embouchure). The correct use of the legato attack makes it possible to interpret lyrical passages smoothly and in a singing style.

☐ The attack by impact was not used in the appropriate places. Here, the note is addressed without delay at a point somewhat above the prevailing dynamic. There is a slight diminuendo to the end of the note. Note-spacing is implied and should exist.

☐ The attack by delayed impact was not used properly. The note should be addressed slightly after the ictus of the beat at a point somewhat below the prevailing dynamic. There is a slight crescendo to the end of the note. This is a useful style to employ when three or more successive chordal accents occur in highly dramatic music. Note-spacing is implied and should exist.

☐ Staccato pronunciation in this interpretation was often at odds with the style and mood of the music. Remember that staccato means "detached" (not "short"). The detachment may be slight or longer — depending upon the style of the music and the context in which the passage appears.

☐ Attacks and releases were not articulated precisely — the result of a vague beat pattern. Your conducting technique needs improvement in this area.

☐ The rhythmic design of slurred patterns was not always made clear. Check the score to determine why slurred passages occur and what kind of rhythmic propulsion should then take place. As a general rule, except when smooth passage work is desired, the first note in a slurred pattern should be accented slightly or, if a hemiola exists, a little more forcefully.

☐ Rhythmic propulsion was not taut and rhythmic vitality was lacking. Since rhythm functions in combination with harmony to bring tension and release to music, it is imperative to maintain rhythmic balance and tension at all times.

Intonation

Faulty intonation is generally the result of:

☐ Players entering the phrase with relaxed embouchures (causing flatness), tightening the embouchure during the phrase (bringing overall pitch up to acceptable levels), and anticipating the taking of the next breath by relaxing the embouchure again. These devastatingly bad habits make it impossible to achieve an acceptable overall tuning.

☐ Upper woodwind and brass players pinching the embouchure during fortissimo tutti playing. This causes considerable sharpness in "lead" parts.

☐ The bad habit in all sections (but especially in inner voice parts) of relaxing the embouchure when playing softer passages. This causes considerable flatness.

☐ Failure to support long tones with sufficient intensity of breath pressure throughout the duration of the tone (especially in larger bore instruments). Considerable flatness resulted as these longer notes came to an end.

☐ The overall tuning center in this band being higher than the customary A440-442. This high pitch center cannot be maintained by many instruments used in this band. Why not bring the overall tuning down to more acceptable levels?

☐ The existence of more than one pitch center in the tutti ensemble of this band, a fact that made it impossible to evaluate intonation meaningfully. May I suggest a way toward improvement in this area? Play unisonal sustained tones in middle ranges for five minutes each day, utilizing descending scales only. Students will find it much easier to come to an understanding and appreciation of subtle pitch difference during the playing or singing of descending scales.

Timbre

The quality and purity of ensemble sonority is a most important factor when an adjudicator makes a "rating" evaluation of an interpretation. All instruments, from tubas up to piccolos, should produce all notes as "singing tones" — no matter what their duration or at what pitch level they occur. This is as true when playing a Sousa march as when playing a Bach chorale. When individual players or sections in a band neglect to produce "singing tones," ensemble intonation, balance, and sonority suffer grievously and, as a consequence, it is impossible to secure a convincing interpretation.

☐ The ensemble sonority was harsh and strident due to overblowing and inferior embouchure placement. This was especially true in the following sections:

☐ The overall ensemble sonority lacked lustre, vitality and character. This band should go on a daily diet (at least 10 minutes per day) of ensemble sustained tone practice, concentrating on producing a beautiful ensemble tone and maintaining an acceptable overall tonal balance.

☐ Certain sections overpowered all others in tutti sonorities. This was especially true in the following sections:

☐ Certain solo passages were not played authoritatively, due, no doubt, to nervousness on the part of the soloist. This was especially true at:

Additional experience will take care of this matter. ■

The Art of Accompanying Student Soloists

Shirley Mullins

Finding good accompanists for solo and ensemble contests, recitals, and other music programs is a common problem for most school music directors.

Piano teachers are an obvious first choice as accompanists, but frequently they have heavy teaching schedules on Saturdays, when most contests occur. They may be more available for recitals that are held during the evenings or on Sundays. Many teachers are happy to help and appreciate being asked. Even if they are unable to participate, they may be able to give you the names of other pianists in your town.

Asking your students if either of their parents plays the piano may reveal several interested adults who would be delighted to accompany. While they may wish to avoid working with their own child (it doesn't always work out), many parents are willing to play for other students. You should also encourage the advanced piano students in your school to accompany younger students.

If you play the piano, you might consider accompanying some of the students yourself. Although my primary responsibility is leading our high school orchestra, I accompany dozens of students every year. My reasons include the following:

• It's fun.
• You get to know the students on a one-to-one basis.
• You see the students grow from one year to the next.
• You learn ideas from different private teachers.
• You share the excitement of the performance with the student.
• You learn new music and the styles of new composers.
• It keeps you practicing the piano.
• It helps you improve your sight-reading skills.

Shirley Strohm Mullins is an orchestra director at the Yellow Springs High School in Ohio. She is a graduate of the University of Iowa and gives workshops on orchestra development.

Tricks of the Trade

We all want to avoid poor performances. Advise your accompanists that they do not have to play every note on the printed page, and remind them that the soloist, even an 11-year-old violinist, is the artist who must be followed at all costs. In the excitement of performances, young musicians may drop or add beats, forget repeats and rests, come in early or late, and jump back or ahead, especially if they are playing from memory. Accompanying beginning students is always an adventure.

Here are some suggestions for pianists with fair to adequate technique but who have very little practice time:

• Remember that the two skills which most quickly abandon "week-end" pianists are independence of the hands and the geography of the keyboard. First of all, play straight through each piece once and mark the trouble spots. Mark accidentals, division of hands, and key and time changes. Your motor memory won't help very much because there won't be enough time for repetitive practice.

• Always make a cut in the opening tutti of a concerto unless it is already quite short. Piano reductions are frequently unpianistic and difficult, and your practice time is better spent elsewhere. Also, make cuts in long piano solo passages, but be sure the resulting harmonic progressions make musical sense.

• Leave out trills and other ornaments if they cause trouble.

• Memorize short difficult spots so you can look at the keyboard.

• Mark spots where the soloist has trouble so you will be prepared for anything.

• Check different editions. Piano parts vary tremendously, especially with Baroque works.

• Watch out for contrary motion patterns in both hands and simplify them if possible.

• Fake whenever necessary to keep the beat steady.

• Keep your eyes moving ahead; disaster may be lurking just around the corner. Don't worry about the notes you've missed.

• Bring out the important melodic lines, letting other things go if necessary. A clearly marked

score is absolutely necessary. Use a multi-colored pen to clarify repeats, endings, codas, and other tricky spots so your eye spots them immediately. Write in crucial fingerings.

• Cut out octaves and just play single notes, especially in rapid passages in the left hand.

• Watch out for difficult passages following a rapid page turn and be prepared. (A good idea is to memorize the measures just before and after the end of a page.)

Remember that the accompanist's job is to assist the soloist in every way. Avoiding wrong notes is important, but the primary concern of the pianist should be to support and enhance the performance of the student musician.

Adequate Rehearsals

The soloist and the pianist must have adequate rehearsal time together. Many ensemble problems occur because the soloist is confused by the piano rhythms and harmonies. For instance, students often overlook rests when practicing alone so they are not prepared to play at the correct time with the accompanist. Another common problem is carelessness with dotted rhythms. For example, students often play ♪. ♪ and ♪♪ as ♪³♪ and ♪², which only become more confused when the piano part is added.

A somewhat red-faced ninth-grade horn player appeared after school on the day before the solo contest. He had asked me weeks before if I would accompany him and I willingly agreed. I hadn't seen or heard from him since that conversation. To make a long story short, he played his own part passably well; but the moment the piano was added, the music was a disaster. The piano part was filled with triplets against the soloist's duples, which were somewhat shaky in the first place. After a half-hour rehearsal, the soloist decided (with his teacher's support), to cancel the performance. It was disappointing, but not as shattering as the inevitable III or IV rating that would certainly have been awarded. You can bet this particular soloist will be the first to sign up for rehearsal time next year.

Enhancing Musicianship

A good accompanist can greatly enhance the performance of a young student. Working with an accompanist gives the student the opportunity to respond to someone else's musicianship. The young instrumentalist does not have this experience when he is practicing alone. The best situation occurs when the private teacher or

school director can work with the student and the accompanist together. The teacher can help to establish the desired tempo and point out mistakes in notes or rhythms. If the director is unable to attend rehearsals, the accompanist must help the student soloist correct mistakes. Most soloists appreciate help and suggestions.

Performance Procedures

The pianist should advise a young soloist of the following procedures:

• The student plays the tuning note (mutually agreed upon in advance for each instrument), stops, then the pianist plays the note. The student listens and adjusts (with the teacher's help if necessary). This procedure is repeated. The student should nod or smile at the accompanist to indicate readiness to begin.

• The soloist should correct the tempo if it is too fast or too slow. It is the accompanist's job to follow such changes. The soloist should not stay with an uncomfortable tempo.

• The soloist should let missed notes go, not go back to make corrections. It is hard for the accompanist to find the exact spot in the piano part and the soloist may still miss the notes the second time.

• If the soloist is playing from memory and the memory slips, both performers should keep going. The muscles may be able to recall what the mind has forgotten. If the pianist keeps playing, the soloist will usually hear something familiar in the piano part and will be able to jump back in.

• In case of a complete breakdown, the soloist should clearly say, "Measure 58" or "Letter B" and continue as if nothing had happened. There is no need for an extended conversation regarding the relative merits of starting at "A" or "B."

• Count rest measures carefully. There is nothing worse than being unsure of an entrance.

• It is not necessary for the soloist to acknowledge the accompanist at a contest. At a recital, it is always appropriate to ask the pianist to stand and share in the applause.

Follow the customs of the community when deciding whether or not to pay an accompanist. Some pianists accompany as part of their earned income and will immediately state how much they charge. The students (and parents) can decide whether or not they can afford to have a professional accompanist. Many pianists who are not professional teachers or performers are willing to accompany free of charge because they also gain something from the experience. The instrumentalist and teacher should be sure to let the pianist know how much the time and effort are appreciated. A gift, along with a note of thanks, is appropriate if you do not pay the accompanist. When next year rolls around, pianists will remember the student who did not even bother to say, "Thank you."

Explore your community and schools for potential pianists for contests and recitals. Your students, the pianists themselves, and of course you, the busy school conductor, will all reap the benefits of a strong team of accompanists. ■

A Vehicle
For Sharing

Shirley Strohm Mullins

"Just talk about your philosophy of education, or anything else you want to share," the voice on the phone pleaded. "It's very informal and it only takes an hour. Won't you, please?"

That's how I came to speak to the Unitarian fellowship on my views about music and sharing. Much to my surprise people were genuinely interested in the topic, making the discussion period animated and extending it beyond the allotted time. Since giving that informal talk two years ago, the concept of sharing through music, i.e., community service, has remained in my thoughts.

By community service, I mean taking music to the people, whether it is through a program called Outreach, Run Outs, Concerts in the Park, or simply playing for friends. Music, along with all the arts, is meant to be shared. The audience's response — the laughter, the applause — is the artist's life blood. As performers, we all need it. However, to reach the concert stage, recital hall, or art gallery, people must travel — a simple act for some, that is impossible for many. If musicians want to touch lives in different ways, sometimes they must go to the people instead.

Music, especially, is an art form we can all share with others, regardless of our age or ability. Many people have the mistaken idea that there are two

---

Shirley Strohm Mullins, a string specialist and orchestra director at Yellow Springs (Ohio) High School, also teaches string methods classes at Central State University and Cedarville College in Ohio. She is a graduate of the University of Iowa.

types of musicians — professional and amateur — and that only the professionals should perform. That's utter nonsense, of course, as most of you know. If you sing in a community or church choir or accompany a child soloist, you are a performer. It's just a matter of degree of competency, not an "either or" situation. No one enjoys hearing a performance that is full of wrong notes, incorrect rhythms, and awkward memory slips. On the other hand, a simple melody played well, with obvious enjoyment and confidence, is a joy for all.

Many of us have seen performances where the musicians looked and acted like grim death. As members of the audience, we could hardly wait until the soloists were finished; and *they* could hardly wait until they were finished. Players usually avoid the agony of such an experience for a long time. That is not the kind of performance I advocate. Instead, I picture performances where children, adults, professionals, and amateurs, get up and give of themselves. The person playing or singing enjoys it, and the person listening enjoys it. The performance is not painful for anyone. It's sharing something special.

Self Esteem

What's involved in a public performance beyond the event itself? What does it mean to the people who participate? The answers reflect the concept of self worth and self esteem. It's true that through performance you share something with other people, but you also do something for yourself. You think "I can do this, I'm a part of something special." It's an extraordinary experience to have people come up after a concert and thank you for the music because it was so beautiful. It's also a very self-centered and self-satisfying feeling. Everyone might not admit it, but I admit it freely. Coming out on stage, I love feeling the excitement and seeing the faces in the audience. It gives me great joy. That's the main reason I continue to give public concerts. The performing part of my life would be the easiest thing to give up because the time commitment for practicing and performing is time that could probably be spent on more practical things. However, I would rob myself of a great source of pleasure.

Recently the elementary orchestra performed at a Shakespearean festival in the village. The children sometimes pretend that these informal concerts at community functions aren't all that important. Actually, however, these young musicians get a big kick out of being asked to play. They like getting that recognition. After a performance, people stop the students on the street and say, "You were really good at the festival." The players' faces light up; they receive as much reward as the audience does. Honestly, I would say more.

Performance, the Motivator

Public school music teachers have a great opportunity to bring the arts to their communities. In a typical school program, there may be two or three big concerts during the year. Many directors

---

"Come Whenever You Want To"

A small group of children was about to play for a gathering of senior citizens at their monthly birthday party. "That's my granddaughter. That's my Ellen," said a strident voice as it cut through our tuning. "Hi, Grandma," a little girl responded. Ellen smiled and with her classmate, Holly, started playing *Oh, How Lovely is the Evening*, as the others joined in the round. The ladies stopped knitting and talking. They watched the children and began nodding and moving to the gentle beat. One by one, the young musicians announced their songs. "Now we'll play *Our School March*," Jason boomed out as Rachel giggled. (He had been told to speak loudly and clearly because some of the guests were hard of hearing.)

After the short concert, the children were treated to punch and cookies, praise, and thank yous. "When can we come again?" young Brendan asked. "Whenever you want to," was the spontaneous reply.

---

don't want to be bothered with anything beyond those commitments. That's understandable because preparing the students and making all the necessary arrangements can be time consuming. For example, parents may be needed to drive students, move equipment, set up chairs, or help chaperone. Any time you see amateur musicians playing anywhere, you can be sure there has been a lot of work behind the scenes. Extra performances can be a real burden and a drain on the director's time and energy. When the calls come from the Kiwanis Club or the library association, it's much easier to just say "No, that's not a part of our program," than to accept such a commitment.

Public performance, however, is a great motivator. To minimize your own work load, I suggest that you plan ahead. Allow small ensembles to practice during a large group rehearsal. When the students feel they are ready to perform publicly, listen to them and give suggestions for improvement. When a call comes requesting the concert band, orchestra, or jazz band, offer the small ensemble instead. This will save you a tremendous amount of time, as well as such problems as transporting 60-75 students and their equipment. You are still honoring the organization's request without pulling a large number of students out of class.

Small ensembles of instrumentalists and vocalists from my school perform frequently for community events including the sidewalk sale, school festival, peace marches and rallies, church services, funerals, and weddings. The list is endless and changes constantly. Sometimes the students are paid a fee or the performers may ask for a donation to help fund a specific project. Often, however, the students play just for the fun of it, being only slightly aware that they are doing a community service.

Building Group Pride

As part of the public music program, the orchestra frequently takes field trips and gives informal concerts. For example, we have played at the Four Oaks School (for special and handicapped children), Greene County Home, Friends Day Care Center, and the Women's Reformatory at Marysville, Ohio. The students think that the main reason for going places is to have a holiday, because it is fun and exciting to do these special things, especially for the elementary and junior high students. The real reason, however, is my interest in bringing music to people who wouldn't normally come to our public concerts.

These field trips build group identity and pride:

"Remember when we played at the County Home and the cows were mooing, and the wind blew our music away, and we had to chase it? Remember that?"

"Yeah, I remember. It was funny."

"After we play at the Children's Hospital, we'll head for McDonalds."

"All right."

Performing builds self worth and self esteem.

"Can you come back — soon? You were good."

"Can I touch your cello?"

"Do you like playing for us?"

"Sure. It was fun. Besides, we got out of school."

Community Service Benefits

Community service excursions provide the students with many benefits that have nothing to do with music. When the orchestra played at a women's reformatory, we learned something about living in an institution. On the way home, the children talked about the grim life in such a system. For example, some women in the laundry had worked twice as fast as usual so they could finish their jobs on time for the concert. However they weren't allowed to come, because a rule said they had to work until it was exactly 12:00 P.M. There was no provision for an exception to the rule.

Before we left the grounds, a prison guard went through the school bus looking under every seat, just in case someone was trying to escape. The students were surprised because no one had thought of that possibility. A young man, the prison's recreation director, told us about attitudes towards prisoners. "The women in this reformatory have made some mistakes, and they are paying for their mistakes. Prisoners shouldn't have to pay forever; but in some places, that is what happens. These people need our help and understanding." The children learned a great deal from that brief visit.

Field Trips

When given adequate information and enough time, principals are often open to musical groups going on field trips that involve community functions. I suggest that you put a request in writing by developing a brief outline that lists all the details of the event. Be sure to include what, when, where, who, and why — especially, why. There is a public relations value to community service that administrators appreciate. Use this awareness to your advantage. Classroom teachers and administrators need plenty of advance notice, at least two weeks for teachers and considerably more for the principal, depending on the type of activity. Also, don't abuse these opportunities for students by requesting too many school time performances. Choose field trips wisely.

Performance Motivates

To a certain extent, most music students play and practice regularly. However, if you schedule a concert, contest, recital, or performance field trip, suddenly young musicians practice with more enthusiasm. I know this from my own experiences and you probably do, too. When young players know that they are going to get up in front of people, they don't want to make fools of themselves. They want to do well.

The school's music faculty stresses going to contests and competitions, and auditioning for anything that comes along, as well as our informal appearances. I'm constantly saying "The concert (recital, play) is coming up. We'd better get moving or we won't be ready in time."

Only the Best?

Music teachers often have the mistaken idea that only "the cream of the crop" should perform in public. This concept is limiting because the top students are often self-motivated and already committed to practicing. The student who holds the last chair in the second violin section also needs the experience of performing; and besides, his family and friends would be proud to see him on stage, too. Involve as many children in as many different ways as you possibly can, without lowering your performance standards. Your entire program will benefit from this all-encompassing philosophy.

Some Personal Sharing

My own training and background supports this theory of sharing. Both of my parents loved music. As a youngster, I remember listening to the radio a lot. Every morning I woke up to the Polka Party, with its driving beat, and every night the next door neighbor would pump her player piano, which naturally never missed a beat. In spite of my mother's inability to sing on pitch, she sang hymns at church and enjoyed going to concerts throughout her lifetime. To broaden my musical interests, she would take me to Chicago, about 180 miles from our home in Iowa, to hear recitals at De Paul University. We had a free railroad pass and she took great advantage of that opportunity for travel. It never occurred to me that it was unusual to travel that far to hear a student recital; it seemed perfectly natural.

There were eight children in my family and everyone played a musical instrument. An attitude of participation and sharing, whether it was in athletics, scouts, church, or music, was imbedded at an early age. My sister Alyce, four years my senior, and I shared a childhood of piano lessons, musicales, and recitals. Paul, the next oldest child, played the tuba in the marching band. His ompahs, my brother Barney's cymbal crashes, and

Playing for others builds group identity and pride.

Lloyd's trumpet playing made our household a busy and noisy place. The two oldest boys, Frank and Abe, played in the drum and bugle corps, looking smart in their white pants and gold capes. The family joke was that Mom tried music on all eight kids and hit the jackpot with the youngest. The atmosphere in which I grew up certainly explains my understanding of performance as a means of sharing. It also explains why I encourage all students to share their musical skills.

Today, our daughter, Amy, typifies students who pass through the music program at Yellow Springs High School. She is a senior at Indiana University in Bloomington, and plans to be a social studies teacher. As a hobby Amy takes her cello on the bus to perform for the senior citizens' home, the children's center, and wherever people want to hear her music. She gets other students who can play instruments to join her. They get great pleasure from sharing their love of music with others. Her last word from Bloomington was that she bought a "hook-up" for her cello and was playing in a rock band.

Performing develops our students as well as our own self-esteem. Sharing concerts and field trips gives a sense of group pride and identity. Educators broaden their own experiences as well as those of their students by taking music to people who can't come to school programs. Performing motivates students to practice and strengthens their interest as well as that of their parents. Performance is a great vehicle for sharing in the life of your community. Use it with love and joy.

607

STAGE FRIGHT? NEVER!

Mental Attitudes for a Successful Performance

Randall G. Reyman

Nerves, stage fright, performance anxiety, jitters — though the labels are many, this single problem has long plagued musicians, amateurs and professionals alike. Don't despair, help is on the way. Here are some practical mental techniques — attitudes — designed to make that life-threatening performance a little less frightening and perhaps even enjoyable and fun.

Feel free to mix any of these attitudes, or add other ideas. The object is to find the things that work best for you. To make these approaches part of a performance, read them often and memorize the accompanying catch phrases. Repeating the phrases during a performance will help you keep calm and maintain composure.

The Proper Perspective

Musicians can create anxiety by placing too much importance on a performance. To put an upcoming performance in its proper perspective, ask yourself the following questions:

What will be the consequences if the performance is a success? A failure?

Who will remember the performance in one week's time?

In one month's time?

A year's time?

Will the performance change the course of history?

To take the performance less seriously, think about an upcoming activity that will take place right after you've played. The performance will then seem secondary — simply a job that needs to be completed before the anticipated purely-enjoyable activity.

Memorize the following sentences and repeat them during the performance:

Success or failure will not significantly change my life.

No matter what the outcome, my friends will still like me; loved ones will still love me.

This performance is really not so important, so I will enjoy it.

Randall G. Reyman teaches trumpet and jazz studies at Millikin University in Decatur, Illinois. He holds degrees from the University of Northern Iowa and the University of Illinois, and is pursuing a Ph.D. at North Texas State University.

Success or failure will not change the course of history.

The "Why" Of It All

Why do you perform? Players whose goal is to impress the audience may be asking for trouble. When the curtain goes up it's easy to suddenly doubt your ability to please everyone there. That's when anxiety and tension intrude into the performance. The person who performs to please himself, however, minimizes performance anxiety by thinking only of what he is doing, and finds the presence of an audience has less control over thoughts and actions.

Consider also the amount of preparation invested in a performance. It's simply unfair to allow anxiety to take control, overriding hard work and resulting in an unsatisfactory performance. Catch phrases:

I will perform for my own enjoyment.

Whatever the audience thinks does not matter.

I am performing for myself.

It is not fair to allow anxiety to affect my performance.

Do Your Best, But Expect Less

Many performers expect too much of themselves. A musician who attains a high degree of excellence during practice sessions should expect to make more mistakes than usual when going before an audience. When performers resign themselves to the fact that they play at about 70-80% of their ability during a public performance, any self-imposed pressure to perform perfectly is reduced. The result is better-than-expected playing. In other words, by expecting less, you may end up with a better performance than otherwise thought possible.

Being able to forgive yourself for mistakes is important. As soon as you make one, forget it; don't worry about it. Tell yourself the mistake is history, and nothing can change it. Try to adopt a less critical attitude about a performance, letting yourself perform automatically, whether there is a mistake or not.

It's important to remember that you are an individual. Because you are not like anyone else, don't try to play like anyone else. Everyone has performance limitations, so be satisfied with your own. By constantly comparing your performance with an unreasonable standard, you will continue to be disappointed and frustrated. You can only do as well as you can do, no better. Accept this reality, and your performance will be much more enjoyable and satisfying.

Catch phrases:
I will forgive myself for making mistakes.
Mistakes will happen; I expect it.
I expect to perform at about 75% of my potential.
Nobody's perfect; I don't expect to perform perfectly.

Performer vs. Audience

Musicians often think of the audience as the enemy. Instead, convince yourself that you and the audience are on the same side. Many people in the audience imagine themselves on stage and want you to do well. They become uncomfortable if you are obviously suffering from stage fright.

Catch phrase:
The audience is not hostile.
We are in this together; the audience is on my side.
The audience and I are after the same goal.
Relax.

Performer vs. Audience?

The "Knock 'Em Dead" Approach

Performers often feel confidence sag just before going on stage. To change this attitude convince yourself that you're going to "knock 'em dead" with a magnificent performance. Take the attitude that the audience is privileged to hear you play; don't even consider that you may be wasting their time.

Catch phrases:
This performance will be great.
I am ready for this performance, both mentally and physically.
This performance cannot be anything except magnificent.
Knock 'em dead.

The problem with this approach is that it's effect continues only as long as the performance is error free. When mistakes occur, the performance ceases to be magnificent and confidence can wane. The "knock 'em dead" approach works best if the performer has a backup attitude in reserve should things begin to go badly.

The Fate/Religion Approach

Many performers find they can eliminate excessive nervousness during a performance by placing the responsibility for its success or failure in the hands of fate or religion. By believing that whatever happens is meant to happen, the musician relinquishes any personal responsibility for his efforts. He becomes more relaxed because the performance is being controlled by an outside entity.

Catch phrases:
Whatever happens is meant to happen, I am not responsible for the outcome.
I have prepared for this performance, but the performance itself is out of my hands.

The "I'm Rampal" Approach

Imagining yourself as a well-known artist, one whom you admire, is another attitude that is successful with musicians. A trumpeter might imagine himself as Maurice André, a flutist as Jean-Pierre Rampal. By pretending to be a specific, accomplished player, you take on the confidence of that performer. Any doubts about being prepared or a lack of playing ability are less likely to occur because the artist whose role you are imagining always performs at a consistently high level of excellence.

Imagination is also useful in preparing for a performance. When practicing, imagine yourself in front of a critical audience. Go through the motions of walking on stage, bowing, adjusting your instrument, cuing your pianist, and performing. Try to experience the feelings of tension that accompany a public performance, and then attempt to control them by using these attitude techniques. By practicing in this fashion, the actual performance will not seem so traumatic because of the many times you've performed under those conditions in your imagination.

Imagine yourself as a well-known performer.

The Auto-Pilot Approach

The key to many of these attitudes is the ability to relax and let the performance happen. As a musician, however, you cannot *force* yourself to relax; you need to *let* yourself relax. This is easier said than done when under the watchful eye of an audience.

To relax during a performance, try the auto-pilot approach. Use the idea borrowed from a mechanism that keeps an airplane on a pre-set course and automatically corrects any deviations, allowing the pilot and passengers to relax and enjoy the ride.

Musicians who are fully prepared should be able to simply let the performance happen and enjoy the entire experience. Imagine that you have an auto-pilot mechanism on your body. When you walk on stage and take your position, engage the auto-pilot switch, literally. The physical action will strengthen the mental image. By engaging the auto-pilot you give up control of the performance to a device that is automatic and nonjudgmental. Because you are no longer responsible for the performance, you can relax and enjoy the music. Try to remember that an airplane's auto-pilot does not have anxiety attacks over errors; the mechanism simply corrects the heading and continues on. In a performance, the musician needs to do the same. A mistake is not a signal of impending doom, but rather should be viewed as a minor error of little consequence. Let your auto-pilot bring the performance back on course.

During a performance, it may be helpful to re-engage the switch occasionally to maintain a strong image of the auto-pilot mechanism. The stronger and clearer the image, the more trust you will have in the approach. A musician who uses this attitude effectively may at times have the impression that he is not the performer, but rather a member of the audience. This approach seems to separate the thinking part of the mind — with its judgments, tensions, and anxieties — from the automatic reflexes of the body, which are programmed through diligent practice.

Relax and enjoy the ride.

Action vs. Results

Musicians in front of an audience often feel that they must exert complete control over every part of the performance, just as athletes attempt to have conscious control over every muscle used for a specific action. Of course, this is not how the body works. If a person had conscious control over all the muscles that enable him to walk, he would not be able to take one step. Success at walking, talking, grasping, etc. is due to automatic reflexes that are acquired through practice. All an individual needs do is think of a particular action, and the body does what is necessary to accommodate that thought.

Musicians should operate the same way. During a public appearance, a carefully prepared instrumentalist needs to concentrate on the desired result of the performance, rather than the specific required actions. Just as the baseball player should think of where he wants the ball to go (not the muscles needed to get it there), the trumpeter should concentrate on the kind of sound he wants from the instrument (not the control of the facial muscles).

More Ideas

Here are some additional techniques that can help to keep performance anxiety to a minimum.

• Perform as much as possible. Repeated exposure to performance situations provides the opportunity to learn to cope with the accompanying tensions.

• If possible, practice in the same place in which the performance is to take place. Surroundings that are familiar will make you feel more comfortable.

• Sight-read completely new music in the few minutes preceding a public appearance. The required concentration clears the mind of any anxieties incurred from anticipating the performance.

• Concentrating on breathing is one of the best ways to relax. Tension inhibits the breathing process and therefore reduces the oxygen intake that is essential to effective concentration. Before and during the performance, take deep rhythmic breaths to relax the body and clear the mind.

• Reduce the symptoms of performance anxiety, such as dryness in the mouth or trembling, by exaggerating the intruding sensation rather than fighting it. For example, a musician who experiences a dry mouth during a performance should concentrate on making his mouth as dry as possible. By intensifying the condition, it will often subside to a tolerable level.

Some Final Thoughts

Remember that adequate preparation comes first. Through diligent practice, musicians should work toward performing the music automatically, without hesitating at difficult passages or missing tricky notes. Preparation builds confidence; a lack of preparation breeds doubts about a performance and results in inconsistent playing.

Once this solid base is established, try using these performance attitudes to control your emotions. Make the audience your friend or switch on the auto-pilot to relax and enjoy the performance. Whether the problem is nerves, stage fright, performance anxiety, or jitters, never let it bother you. ■

Overcoming
AUDITION
Jitters

BY RUTH LUPUL

Editor's Note: During the Fifth Annual Summer In-stitute of the Los Angeles Philharmonic, members of the orchestra spoke to a group of advanced music stu-dents about the pitfalls of auditioning and the reali-ties of planning a musical career. The enlightening comments presented here are based on the advice of the panel members pictured below, from left to right: Tamara Chernyak, Boyde Hood, Janet Ferguson, Daniel Rothmuller, Ralph Sauer, Herbert "Sonny" Ausman, and Jeffrey Reynolds.

I n the words of Jeff Reynolds, bass trom-bonist of the Los Angeles Philharmonic, "The only way to get into a professional symphony orchestra is to audition for it." Reynolds and the other panelists at the orches-tra's summer institute agree that auditions, nerve-racking as they can be, do demonstrate a player's skill under pressure as nothing else can. Being prepared, the panelists agree, is the key to successful auditioning.

"It's like preparing for a concert," says Daniel Rothmuller, associate principal cellist. "You have between 5 and 15 minutes to convince someone about your playing. In a concert you can start off slowly, not so in an audition. You'll never not be nervous. The depth of preparation has

everything to do with overcoming the pressures."

Being prepared involves everything from build-ing repertoire to taping a performance, from se-lecting tempos to warming up, from choosing au-dition attire to staying away from competitors at the audition. It involves maintaining poise after a mistake and even the need to practice sight-reading. The suggestions these panelists offered came from their experiences in auditioning, and for some, from serving on the Philharmonic's au-dition committee.

The musicians' advice to aspiring orchestral players includes a recommendation to learn all the selections on an orchestra's official audition list, because each piece is fair game. "The audi-tion committee may even ask for more," says Rothmuller, who speaks with authority as a member of his orchestra's committee. Applicants should practice sight-reading, too. Tamara Cher-nyak, first violinist, says that some orchestras, notably the Cleveland Orchestra, ask their hopefuls to do just that.

Rothmuller advises getting the scores for all the listed music and copying them if necessary. "Learn the standard repertoire for your instru-ment," he suggests, "because not every orchestra publishes an audition list."

Courtesy Los Angeles Philharmonic/All photos by Robert Millard

Being a superb solo player is only the first step in the audition process. Then comes submitting screening tapes to the audition committee, which is a standard application procedure. Janet Ferguson, principal flutist, says, "Do it a month before the audition. Your tape has to be really fine. The committee members sit there listening to one tape after the next; they focus on the music and certainly hear any wrong notes. The tape should be note-perfect and a good representation of how well you can play. If you are ready to audition, the first tape you make is usually the best."

Herbert "Sonny" Ausman

Trombonist Sonny Ausman is also a recording specialist. He believes a professional is the best person to handle the technical difficulties of producing a high-quality audition tape. He suggests that anyone who makes a tape himself should use an omnimicrophone, which collects sound from all sides. A model such as the AKG 451, which costs about $200, is a good general-use microphone. Ausman explains, "Recording compresses dynamic range, so the performer should compensate by exaggerating dynamic contrasts. High frequencies tend to be cut off in recording on cassette tapes. To compensate for the noise level of cassette tapes, boost the level a bit on softer excerpts."

Whether to splice or not to splice the audition tape is a controversial question. "It's been done," says Ausman, "but it doesn't really show what the player can do." Ralph Sauer, principal trombonist and panel moderator, thinks that not splicing out a wrong note may give the audition committee the impression that the applicant didn't hear it. A further suggestion from Sauer is

to count out rests of two measures or less. Sauer says that "all selections should be recorded in the same environment, keeping them together on one master tape. All players should record the top 20 for their instrument."

Tempos pose another difficult decision for the performer preparing a tape. Most of the panelists recommend choosing a middle-of-the-road tempo, neither unusually fast nor remarkably slow. They agree that the tempo markings on the listed selections are good rules of thumb, but Jeff Reynolds is quick to qualify this statement with the observation that audition committees may supply parts without editorial markings of tempos or other corrections.

Tamara Chernyak notes that conductors are individualistic about tempo preferences. "Different conductors, Mehta and Giulini, for instance, can finish the same selection three to four minutes apart. You should listen to recordings of the orchestra you want to play for."

Once the tapes are sent off and the audition scheduled, there are more hurdles. During the audition, the problem of tempo resurfaces. Sauer advises auditioners to play at a medium speed when taping as well as at the audition. "Be adaptable," he says, "give your best interpretation and show the conductor that you can change tempos. Flexibility appeals to conductors."

Janet Ferguson

Some other common audition hazards concern intonation and rhythm, which suffer under pressure. "The bass player may find his instrument sounding sharp," Reynolds offers, "while the wind player may hear his instrument sounding flat. Furthermore, mistakes sometimes occur.

Tamara Chernyak

Sometimes you'll be asked to play the passage again, because the committee really does want to hear you play well." If you do make a mistake, the panelists advise just taking the attitude that it's the first time you ever missed that passage.

Selecting a solo piece for the audition has its pitfalls, too. Rothmuller urges auditioners to select pieces they know best rather than the most impressive ones in their instrument's repertoire. Sauer favors music that shows contrast; he warns that auditioners may be asked either to play the entire selection or begin arbitrarily at any section of the music.

Audition-day nerves are a common complaint that everyone on the panel admits to having. Chernyak recalls that it made her nervous even to think about the 7 auditions she played in one year in the United States and the 14 others she performed before that in Russia. "Extreme numbness" are the words Reynolds uses to describe his feelings about audition day. Rothmuller's story about Joseph Gingold further exemplifies the common problem. A very nervous student of the well-known concertmaster was about to audition for George Szell, not an easy conductor to please. Gingold decided the student needed an emotional warmup for the audition and hit upon an appropriate strategy. Gingold had the student run up four flights of stairs, stand on a chair, and play a Mozart symphony. When the student finished, Gingold said, "That's how it's going to feel."

As a more practical warmup suggestion, Rothmuller advises getting rest, if possible, between stages of the audition. Reynolds and trumpet player Boyde Hood warn against negative reac-

tions. "Everyone there is going to sound better than you think you do," states Hood. "While you are waiting for your turn, get away from the mob. Don't be too sensitive about what you do. Audition day is always a long day."

Sauer suggests, "Try to simulate the experience as much as possible. Walk into the hall if you can. Practice behind a screen if you know that's what you'll be doing at the audition." Ferguson says, "Get your friends to watch you. Play in a strange hall without a warmup, just cold. Switch pieces and styles. You'll have to during the audition, so practice that way. You need to be able to change mood and expression quickly. It's like a condensed concert."

A successful audition isn't the end of the line. "If you do get the job," Chernyak says, "don't stop practicing. You may want a better one or you may want to advance in your section. If you're lucky, the next audition may be better for you." Ferguson agrees. "Usually it takes a lot of auditions before you get the job. Don't put pressure on yourself by thinking 'I just have to have that job.' Take a temperate view of each audition. Give yourself time and space to grow. When I was ready, I got the job."

Jeffrey Reynolds

That temperate view of auditions seems very good advice. Along with in-depth preparation, it can be the secret of success. ■

Ruth Lupul is a writer living in Northridge, California. She teaches business communication at California State University and plays piano for pleasure.

Those interested in applying to the 1987 Los Angeles Philharmonic Institute may do so by writing Amy Iwano, 135 North Grand Avenue, Los Angeles, California, or telephoning (213) 972-0702.

How to Practice Effectively

Larry Combs

As a busy professional, I have limited time to practice, so I have organized my practicing so that it is rewarding and effective. Through a process of trial and error, most accomplished players arrive at their own techniques for effective practice. Some of these may be helpful to younger students, accomplished young players, and even experienced teachers.

There are two questions students ask most often in regard to practicing: "How much should I practice, and how should I practice?" Quite a few factors determine the ideal length of daily practice routines. Perhaps the most important of these is physical conditioning — for wind and brass players particularly, that of the musculature and respiratory system.

As in any form of muscular activity, increased endurance is built up over a period of time. For beginning players, or more experienced ones who have had a long absence from the instrument, shorter practice sessions (15-20 minutes at a time) repeated throughout the day are preferable to a single, longer practice session.

The serious instrumentalist, whose playing is changing and developing, should devote two to four hours daily to thoughtful, organized work, in addition to the playing done in rehearsals and performances.

For all musicians practice time should be a period of intense concentration, devoted to the idea of working out rather than playing through the music. The practice room should be private and quiet, without distractions of T.V., stereo, or other people. The room itself should not be dead in sound, which is discouraging, or so live that the sound is too enhanced.

Often the practice session is most beneficial when the player reserves a certain time of day to work. Usually a practice session at the end of the day, when you are mentally and physically fatigued, is fruitless. You should also be aware of reaching points of diminishing return, and at that time take a break of sufficient length to revive mind and body.

Good Practice Habits

A major factor in sustaining your best playing for a longer period of time is to develop efficiency in your playing. Negative habits formed over the years can cause greater exertion than is necessary. Incorrect, inefficient breathing; undue tension in the hands, arms, or neck; and poor posture, for example, can restrict the amount of effective practice time. One of the goals for each practice session can be to replace gradually some of these negative habits with more efficient habits.

When beginning the practice routine have a well-organized idea of how to utilize best the time that is available. It is not necessary to follow any sort of rigid pattern, such as 30 minutes of scales, 30 minutes of long tones, 30 minutes of articulation studies, although just such a regime may be advantageous to certain students at certain periods in their development. Especially when immersed in preparing for a performance or lesson for which the preparation is expected to yield a more or less "finished product," some thought into the overall goal of each practice session is valuable.

I like to begin with a few minutes of easy playing that avoid any extremes of the instrument, especially *fortissimo*, very high register, or very fast playing. Concentrate on the quality of the sound, proper flow of the wind, response of the reed or embouchure, and continuity or homogeneity of sound without becoming involved in reading notes or articulations. On most instruments this is accomplished best with long sustained tones.

For this warm-up I use a simple pattern of sustaining one of the fundamental low register tones (for example C4) for four slow counts, followed by the corresponding upper-register tone with the same fingering (adding the register key), in this case G4. Try to make this connection as seamless as possible, with a sensation of gradually gathering wind speed during the low note into the upper note, and coordinating the increased wind flow with a very slight increase of muscle tone in the upper lip downward around the upper curvature of the upper surface of the mouthpiece.

I make the crescendo joining the two tones a rather subtle one, say *piano* to *mezzo piano*, and then continue without any break or breath with a descending major triad based on these tones, in this case C major. This is held for two counts for each note ending on the starting tone, held for as long as the breath lasts. The breathing should be full, not forced or pushed.

Then, vary this by using different low register starting notes, perhaps expanding chromatically upwards or downwards until all the fundamental tones and corresponding twelfths are used. Note that this warm-up does not extend into the *altissimo* register at all, and need not go dynamically past *mezzo piano* which at this point in the practice routine is just as well.

The metronome can be used to great advantage in this routine. I suggest starting with a tempo of ♩ = 72 and over a period of time *decreasing* the tempo. The slower the tempo, the more taxing the exercise.

A corresponding pattern could be practiced on any instrument for the purpose of developing evenness in playing throughout the range of the instrument. Each musician's goal is a homogeneous sound — without breaks at register points, or at shifts in hand position for the strings.

The Value of Scales

The next item in the practice agenda could be organized scale material. Again, practicing scale patterns from memory to eliminate reading will allow you to concentrate on evenness, quality of sound, and steadiness of pulse. I practice a two and a half octave pattern in all keys, with a variety of articulations, in both duple and triple rhythmic patterns.

Each instrument has its own books of scale studies; some of the most popular for clarinet are Baermann, Jettel, Klosé, and Stark. Each has its own manner of laying out the studies (including scales in 3rds, 4ths, 5ths, major and minor, arpeggios, and so on); therefore all are of some value. Perhaps the most concise for clarinet is the two-page presentation of all the major and harmonic minor scales organized in the cycle of fifths, found in the Klosé clarinet method.

Why is this area of practice so critical? In much conventionally notated music, scales and arpeggios and fragments of them are the basic building blocks of melodic structure, and having these ingrained into finger patterns in a habitual way makes great facility possible. This is especially true when the patterns have been worked out slowly and with a great deal of accuracy.

Having scale and arpeggio patterns well in hand can mean a tremendous improvement in sight-reading ability, because instant recognition and reproduction of rapid material is dependent on the eye's ability to take in groups of notes and to immediately translate them into a "message unit" to the fingers, tongue, and wind.

The importance of diligent scale practice in developing an even and homogeneous tone quality should not be overlooked. Each instrument has its own particular problems in this respect. The clarinet has a particularly difficult situation due to the different sounds of the different registers. The player must make certain adjustments in embouchure flex, wind flow, and tongue position to compensate. Because these adjustments should become second nature, slow scale and arpeggio practice with very critical listening can be most helpful.

Approaching Etudes

Etudes comprise a large body of works written specifically for practice and study, as opposed to public performance. These works cover a wide variety of styles, difficulty, and musical interest. Perhaps the most important consideration when beginning to work on an etude is determining the primary purpose of the study. Most of the traditionally used etudes will fall into two divisions: those intended mostly for practice in developing basic execution, and those mainly concerned with style, phrasing, and tone development. Of course, both elements will be present in all etudes, but their composers generally have a specific purpose in mind.

In a typical etude some of the problems presented might be:
• Rapid articulation
• Accuracy in reading mixed articulations (detached & slurred)
• Maintenance of pulse
• Matching tonal quality between articulated and slurred playing
• Matching timbre in various registers

It may be fun at first to try to sightread straight through an etude in the proper indicated tempo and it's also good sightreading practice. But after reading it through you must begin to refine your approach. It's important to insure that:
• Steadiness of pulse is maintained
• Initial practice is done at a very slow tempo, never quicker than seems easy and accessible
• Tempo is increased only gradually, to the point where certain difficulties begin to become apparent

"The study of solo works, chamber music, and the large ensemble repertoire is where the care taken in building the fundamentals begins to pay off."

At this point it becomes important to again *decrease* the metronome tempo, then try to identify and isolate whatever is causing the particular difficulty. You must learn methods to single out and overcome the difficulties you encounter.

When learning an etude on a single line instrument such as a trumpet, clarinet, or flute, the musician should first analyze and understand the musical elements of the piece: form, key, and tonal progressions. Some difficult passages become easier once your ear clearly hears the harmonic structure of the piece. It's often a good idea to write out a chordal accompaniment to an etude.

Slowly, but Surely

It is important to practice slowly and to avoid continued unsuccessful repetitions of a problem passage. Find a tempo in which the passage seems easy and work gradually toward a faster tempo. Do not waste time continuing to practice less difficult portions in too slow a tempo, but rather isolate the more difficult passages for detailed attention. Continue to work on these trouble spots until they can be played easily in a tempo that is comfortable for the entire etude.

Passages that present stumbling blocks require our imagination in devising ways of working toward playing them comfortably. Usually, rapid detached or legato passages can be made to feel more solid rhythmically if the organization of the notes is thought of as being across the beats rather than on the beat. Another way to practice passages of this sort is to actually alter the rhythm into various patterns.

When encountering ornaments such as trills, grace notes, and turns, it's helpful initially to assign specific rhythms to the ornaments, practicing slowly and precisely, before incorporating them into the entire passage.

It's important when practicing in small units that the unit itself makes sense musically, and is a complete phrase. Then, repetitive practice with the metronome can make rhythmic sense, and gradually moving the tempo up can simplify learning the passage.

Phrasing

Often more attention is focused on practicing technically difficult material rather than slow melodic playing. Because execution of the notes themselves in slower etudes offers no particular problems, often little time is allotted for this type of practice. This is an unfortunate omission. Part of the time given to etude practice should be reserved for slower melodic playing. Gains in musical understanding and awareness of line and shape and the communication of playing, along with the development of tone quality in legato are all products of thoughtful practice of melodic material.

First try to determine the length and overall shape of each phrase, and then find the focal point of intensity of each phrase.

All the qualities developed in melodic practice will also be applicable to faster, technical playing, and will greatly enhance all of your playing. The two basic types of etude work are dependent on one another and will lead you to becoming equipped to deal with all musical situations. The successful performer on any instrument is the one who is able to balance and blend technique and style.

The study of solo works, chamber music, and the large ensemble repertoire is where the care taken in building the fundamentals begins to pay off. In this area we also have the added responsibility of knowing and understanding the context in which one's individual part fits into the whole. Good musicianship requires a thorough understanding of the music, before approaching the individual instruments.

An understanding of form, thematic materials, development, key and chordal relationships will enable all musicians to approach their own literature with the knowledge and conviction required for a successful performance. For many instrumentalists this "pre-practice" will necessitate a study of the accompaniment to a solo piece or the score of an ensemble work.

In summary, some of the facets of playing needed to achieve the virtuosity required for a convincing performance include: 1. natural efficient tone production, which yields a clear, attractive sound, free of distortion; 2. precise even technique, finger action, developed with slow, diligent scale practice; 3. light, clear, natural sounding articulation and the development of a range of length and intensity of articulation, to fit various styles; 4. the ability to project a sense of shape, line, and color, so that your playing has a natural, human quality.

If a day's practice routine yields advances in just one of these areas, the practice session can be tremendously gratifying. If all of these elements are held up as goals, every practice session will be interesting, stimulating, and downright fun. ■

Being Your Own Teacher

by Roger Bobo

The time you take to study a musical instrument falls into three categories: ensembles, private lessons, and private practice time. Ensembles are led by a conductor or a coach, or are simply a collective effort of the players. Private lessons are periodic sessions with a teacher, meant to keep your course of study progressing in a good direction.

Private practice is the time for you to exercise and study the information received from the rest of your musical life. It is the time to develop instrumental self-confidence, security, and musical thought. It is also a time that can be wasted or even be destructive if not carried out with thought and planning. Practice is the art of being your own teacher.

Photo courtesy Lewis H. Strouse/Ball State University

Roger Bobo has played in the Los Angeles Philharmonic for 23 years and with the Concertgebouw Orchestra of Amsterdam for two years. He also performed with the Rochester Philharmonic for six years. In 1961 Bobo gave New York City's first tuba recital in Carnegie Hall. A soloist throughout the U.S., Canada, Japan, and Europe, Bobo will take a sabbatical beginning in September 1989 to lecture and perform in Europe.

Enthusiasm and eagerness are essential forces in musical study, but alone they are not enough. Without thought and organization in the practice room, enthusiasm and eagerness can become destructive forces. How often have you missed a note, then stopped for an instant and without even taking a new breath, continued the passage from the missed note? The next time the passage is played, you probably missed the same note and tried to correct it the same way.

This is study by erosion. You may hope that if you get through a difficult lick enough times it will finally wear down and be correct; but this is not the way it works.

Many students have unsuccessful practice sessions because they fail to isolate their problems. When you miss a note, ask yourself whether it was because of poor fingering, embouchure fatigue, breathing, ear training, tonguing, intervals, or lack of concentration. Where, exactly, did the problem occur? What's the best way to correct it?

Without a breathing plan, it is easy to waste an enormous amount of practice time. Take the time to realistically mark the breaths in the music. You can always make changes later, but start with a plan.

Ear training deserves far more emphasis than it usually gets. It is better not to have the instru-

ment in hand so that you don't let it do your thinking. You can practice ear training at the piano or by singing. More difficult ear-training problems can be played on a piano and recorded on cassette, then listened to at another time — while driving a car, for example. If the passage is difficult to hear because of large and perhaps atonal intervals, make the exercise easier by diminishing all the intervals to midrange, so that no interval is larger than a tritone.

When particularly awkward fingerings seem to be the cause of difficulty, try practicing the fingerings alone at a very slow speed, gradually increasing speed without blowing into the instrument.

When working in the high register, balance the high-register practice with at least an equal amount of work in the low register. This will keep the low register strong and give far more control and beauty at the top. It's exactly the same for fortissimo playing. Balance time spent on fortissimo with at least an equal amount on pianissimo. This will keep the pianissimo in good shape and lend more control and beauty to the fortissimo. Practicing this can save you an enormous amount of unnecessary embouchure fatigue.

Many intelligent students become bored when learning a musically simple but technically difficult study. Out of boredom they quickly learn the study just well enough, but lack the perseverance and wisdom to continue the kinetic training necessary to truly finish the study.

Impatience is the number one enemy of art. The passages that don't come fast, the concerto that won't flow, anything we work on that doesn't sound up to the standard of our mind's ear — these are the breeding grounds for impatience, and for turning on yourself for not being good enough.

Consider the baby taking his first steps. When the baby falls after one or two steps do we spank him for not being good enough? No. We celebrate his progress and continue working with him. Within a year the baby can walk effortlessly.

The points mentioned above cover only a few of the most overlooked practice problems. A good teacher is a balance of patience, perseverance, knowledge, and wisdom. He needs always to be on the alert to locate and correct problems.

The kind of teachers you are to yourself can determine the kind of player you become. Practice time should be organized, analytical, progressive — and fun. If we are good teachers to ourselves, we will become good teachers for others.

To be a musician is a great gift.

Use it well.
□

Mental Practice Techniques

BY STEWART L. ROSS

Almost daily I overhear music students brag to one another about the number of hours they practice. Their criterion for success seems to be not what they accomplish during the time, but how many hours and minutes they log. Musicians are not the only ones who emphasize repetition during practice. In almost every educational field, be it sports or vocational tasks, the primary way to evaluate success rests on the length of time spent in practice.

Mental practice is one technique rarely used by student musicians. A self-teaching method, the approach involves imagining the physical movements associated with musical skills without physically moving the arms, fingers, or embouchure. It requires relaxation, the ability to recognize cues, and the repeated use of a mental model. The idea may seem abstract at first, but it has many practical uses.

Examples of mental practice include the bowler who imagines the motions of throwing a spare while waiting for his ball to be returned, and the instrumentalist who prepares for an entrance by mentally playing a passage several times without any physical movements or sounds. In her book, *A Soprano on Her Head*, Eloise Ristad describes how she applies mental practice to the piano:

"...I sense in advance exactly how the keys will feel under my hands on the keyboard, how the black keys and the white keys create a pattern under my fingers, how the stretches and contractions of my hands feel, and the sensations in my fingertips as they play...I simply play the passage mentally, feeling all those tiny muscle impulses....My internal rehearsal is different from playing a passage silently on the piano. It is not the same as just remembering what the notes are, because of that distinct sensation in the muscles...."

Bruce Jenner, the winner of the Decathlon in the 1976 Olympics, erected a hurdle in his living room during his years of training, so that when he lay on the couch he could look at the hurdle and mentally jump over it. Jenner claims that it helped his performance. Musicians who mentally rehearse their skills by imagining a physical performance tend to improve, too. Unfortunately, so many musicians are used to using maximum physical efforts for minimum efficiency that mental practice techniques sound too good to be true. As Ristad suggests, the use of mental practice "seems to conflict with all we know about hard work and discipline and struggle. It seems almost easier to use a list of painful practice techniques and go on a high-powered, muscle-punishing binge of practicing."

Try this short experiment to see how mental practice can work in a practical way. Set a wastebasket about 12 feet from where you sit; take a few sheets of paper and crush them into small paper balls. Now throw them into the wastebasket, one at a time.

No doubt you began by simply looking at the opening of the wastebasket and throwing the paper balls as best you could without concentrating on the speed, height, or distance of the throw. When a paper ball landed on the floor, you probably made slight adjustments for speed, or height, or distance in order to get the ball into the wastebasket.

Next try the same process, except throw the paper balls mentally, without physical motions, using the following instructions as a guide:

1. Imagine a perfect toss into the middle of the wastebasket each time you are about to throw.

2. As you throw the paper ball, try to see and feel the backswing and forward motion of your arm and hand. Try to feel the muscles as they tense and relax.

3. Imagine the ball in the air; watch its flight.

4. After each mental throw, imagine any adjustments in your arm motion and aim, which will give you a more accurate throw.

When you have completed the mental tosses, again attempt a few physical throws. If you are like most people, you will feel more confident about your ability to throw accurately and will have improved your chances through concentrated practice.

Now try to use mental practice in a musical context. Select a new piece of music and play it through on your instrument. Next put the instrument aside and attempt to perform the same exercise using mental practice instead; do not make any physical movements. Follow these principles:

1. Relax, try to feel as comfortable as possible in your chair. You are to mentally play the excerpt.

2. Use any tempo you wish but try to keep the pulse steady to the end. Do not stop or go back and repeat any notes.

3. Try to hear each pitch (do not vocalize) and try to feel the movements of your embouchure (do not move your lips). Try to feel the movements of your fingers as you move the instrument's valves, keys, or slide for each note. It is important that you concentrate.

After mentally practicing the music a few times, attempt to play it with the instrument. If you concentrated and followed the instructions you probably noticed an improvement from the first performance. While mentally practicing you were able to focus on some of the cognitive aspects of the music that you missed the first time: alternate fingerings/positions, incorrect overtones, dynamic nuances, or phrasing. Furthermore, you did not have to think about tone quality, breathing, poor attacks, or any of the myriad technical problems of a real performance.

A variation of this format that helps some players is to move the valves, keys, or slide of the instrument as you mentally practice. In this way the player receives some sense of muscle movement, although it may cause problems with focusing on the more cognitive aspects of performance.

Once you have mastered the technique of mentally practicing, try to use it with music you have been studying. Remember that it is important to combine physical and mental trials during rehearsals. If you were to use only mental practice, you would soon lose any feedback as to the actual sound of the performance. If you were to use only physical practice, the improved level of concentration might be lost.

In my own teaching and performance, I often use mental practice techniques, usually with good results. I first experimented with a type of mental rehearsal as an undergraduate student when I played with a community orchestra. As a trombonist, I soon realized that I was counting rests much more than I was actually playing my instrument, which became a problem. Not only did I begin having trouble concentrating but I found that when I did begin to play, things did not go well for the first couple of measures.

Instinctively, I began to mentally play my next entrance during the long rests. I would look at the notes and try to feel the embouchure and slide movements as I mentally played the passage. I was also able to decide which positions I would use when alternate positions were available. The only drawback to this mental rehearsal was the problem of losing my place during the rests. However, with the use of orchestra cues and others in the section counting, this was rarely a concern, especially after the first rehearsal.

To my amazement my playing improved to the point where I no longer was nervous about that next passage and even the first measures sounded as sure and clean as the rest of the music. Better yet, I began to enjoy what had been boring rehearsals because I was concentrating even during those long rests. I was accomplishing something when so many others were fooling around, talking, or sleeping with their eyes open.

As a conductor, I have used mental practice since my first college score study assignment. When reviewing music, most band or orchestra directors either play the parts on a keyboard instrument or mentally recreate them in their minds. Certainly, every successful conductor has spent many hours with a score, mentally creating a perfect performance that can be used as a comparison to the music the group actually plays.

In a practical way, mental practice can aid the school director during daily rehearsals. Typically, the first few minutes of a rehearsal are the most difficult because students have just started to think about music. To help students prepare for the rehearsal I have them mentally rehearse the first phrase or two of a composition. (The students already know how to use this technique.) The benefits of mental practice are many: The room becomes completely quiet; students begin the process of imagining fingerings or embouchure movements and become immersed in the rehearsal. Not having the instrument available forces them to a high level of concentration. When the students do begin to play, they are prepared for what is about to happen. This is not unlike what

Suggested Reading

Bryant J. Cratty, *Movement Behavior and Motor Learning*, Lea and Febiger, 1967.

Eloise Ristad, *A Soprano on Her Head*, Real People Press, 1982.

Stewart L. Ross, "The Effectiveness of Mental Practice in Improving the Performance of College Trombonists," *Journal of Research in Music Education*, Winter 1985.

Robert N. Singer, *The Learning of Motor Skills*, Macmillan Publishing Company, 1982.

Robert Sommer, *The Mind's Eye*, Delacorte Press, 1978.

Readers should also review the article, "Inner Game of Music," by Barry Green in the January 1982 issue of The Instrumentalist *as well as a chapter from Green's book of the same title, reprinted in the March 1986 issue.*

any good conductor does before bringing down the baton: he mentally prepares the first few measures so the correct tempo, dynamics, and physical motions are imparted on the all important downbeat. If it works for the conductor, why not teach this same technique to the players?

I find that many university students do not use their practice time wisely. They often come to lessons in a tense state, nervous about the performance they are about to give. In order to alleviate some of this pressure, I ask the student to mentally play the first line of the etude or solo. This mental preparation usually has a calming effect, giving the student some added confidence for the upcoming performance. Most important, by presenting and refining this practice technique during lessons, the student is better able to adapt it to practice sessions during the week. When the lip gets tired, the mind can take over. In this way, time that might otherwise be spent getting a drink of water or talking to a friend can be used to improve performance.

Fortunately, there is more than one blueprint for teaching and learning to play music. Physical practice will continue to play a major role in practice sessions because it is the only way to develop and condition the muscles. Nevertheless, traditional practice techniques that rely only on the physical components of performance can be enhanced with mental practice. The combination of these techniques can lead to more efficient and improved learning while enabling the performer to rehearse more frequently, even when the instrument is unavailable. ■

Stewart L. Ross is Associate Professor of Music and Director of Bands at Mankato (Minnesota) State University. He holds music degrees from Lawrence University and Northwestern University, where he received a Ph.D. in music education.

November, 1987

Help Your Child Learn to Practice

BY BARBARA PRENTICE

Editor's Note: Parents often wonder how they can help their children with their practice sessions. Here are some suggestions. Copy this page and pass it out to parents at your next parents' night or band booster meeting.

Before school started last year my eight-year-old son could hardly wait for Day One. He counted his pencils over and over as he put things in and took them out of his backpack. I knew his sense of excitement because I see it every year in my students.

As parents, you can stimulate this kind of excitement about school by helping your child learn practice techniques. Playing an instrument develops more than musical skills. It also teaches children how to plan time and set goals. By showing your child how to get organized for practice sessions, you will be helping him develop skills that will carry over into other academic subjects.

Naturally, your child will need the right supplies, but parents soon catch on to the difference between wants and needs. You don't need an expensive inventory, but do keep a backup supply of items such as reeds, oil, cleaning supplies, and music. A metronome and a folding music stand are useful for at-home practice.

Along with the right supplies, a child needs something to help him get those things to and from school. Tote bags, backpacks, or duffle bags will help a child "get it all together." At home designate a launch/landing pad where your child can set down his belongings upon arrival and gather items before departure. The mechanical activity of putting his own name on everything will help your child keep track of things.

Get to know your child's band director. Go to parents' meetings and band booster meetings. Be aware of assigned tryout materials and audition dates so that you can give support at home.

Create an environment where practicing is easy:

• Set aside a place for practice. For some it's in the den by the piano; other kids have a practice area in their own bedrooms. Check for adequate lighting, ventilation, and temperature.
• Schedule a regular time for practice. Mornings are a good alternative to busy afternoon schedules.
• Control the T.V. or put it in another room so that it does not tempt your child to neglect prac-

621

ticing.

• Participate in the practice sessions. My neighbor sat in on her son's private lessons and coached him each day in his practice, reminding him of his private teacher's suggestions and rehearsal hints. That boy made All-State every year he auditioned.

• Set up a supportive environment for your child. Encourage his practice, and don't hound him to stop because you want peace and quiet. Never use practice as punishment.

Parental responsibilities include patience in repeatedly reminding your child, "It's time to practice," and offering encouragement when the going gets tough. Some things are easy to learn; others require intensive and repeated practice. Parents should show imagination in creating a musical atmosphere at home, whether by playing recordings, performing together in family ensembles, or watching musical programs on public television.

Even if you are not a trained musician or teacher, you can give your budding trumpeter or trombonist help in his practice sessions. Remind him to work on new music first, adding to his repertoire of solo pieces and exercises. If you keep hearing the same sour notes, suggest practicing in short sections. Recommend isolating the problems — a few notes or measures — and working those out slowly.

Remember the axiom computer experts use: "Garbage in, garbage out." Check the notes carefully to see that the child is reading them accurately. No rewriting or composing is allowed.

No beginner plays his instrument beautifully. Even Doc Severinsen once probably sounded like your sixth grader, so be patient. Expect only gradual improvement; praise work well done.

Parents should have the firmness to insist upon what they know is best in the long run, regardless of the frequency, length, and volume of the resistance.

Just as a good academic student develops a system for keeping track of assignments, class handouts, and notes, a good music student learns to pace practice throughout the week instead of rushing madly to learn the music at 10 P.M. the night before tryouts. Organization is the key. Give your child that key, and he can unlock the joys of music and the satisfaction of future accomplishments. □

Barbara Prentice is Director of Bands at Boles Junior High School in Arlington, Texas and a Contributing Editor of The Instrumentalist. She holds degrees from Texas Tech and North Texas State University.

James Van Develde

Twenty Reasons
Students Don't Practice

1. "My horn's no good. I need a new one."

2. "I don't have a music stand at home."

3. "My sister hollers at me to stop the noise."

4. "I'll never be as good as my brother."

5. "We don't have any playing test coming up in the near future."

6. "The band concert isn't for another three weeks."

7. "I got a B on my report card last time, and I didn't practice much."

8. "We've done six performances in five weeks. I'm tired of practicing."

9. "It's no fun practicing alone."

10. "I'm too busy with (a) sports, (b) work, (c) studies, (d) cheerleading, (e) etc."

11. "This baritone is too heavy to carry home every night."

12. "My baritone takes up a seat on the bus, and the bus driver gets mad."

13. "No matter how much I practice, I never get any better."

14. "I wanted to play French horn — not cornet."

15. "I get tired after I've practiced for 15 minutes."

16. "I don't like the music we're rehearsing."

17. "The music we're practicing for the concert is so hard. I'll never get it."

18. "The music we're practicing for the concert is so easy. I had it the first day we read it."

19. "I'm the only oboe player and nobody hears me anyway."

20. "I'm bored with the materials I've got at home. I can play them all."

Conversations with students in the 5th through 12th grades have produced a list of 20 reasons why they haven't practiced. While many may appear to be shallow and superficial, let's assume that the students are being truthful, and try to diagnose their ailments. I'm sure you have heard many of the same reasons from your students and perhaps have already developed successful solutions or will think of others as you read the reasons. I've offered a few of my own suggestions for motivation.

1-4. A phone call to the parents might shed some light on the situation and provide a simple solution.

5-6. If the student is motivated by public performance, create some. Have high school musicians prepare and present solo and ensemble concerts for the junior high bandsmen, and have the junior high students do the same for the 5th or 6th grade musicians. All will profit from the experience.

7. This response may reflect a low level of aspiration. Check on the student's academic standing in other subject areas; the "B" in band may be the student's best grade for that marking period. Or, is it possible there is something in your grading system that is encouraging mediocrity?

8. While one student thrives on public performance pressure, another can be defeated by it. Occasional evaluation of the performance calendar from both standpoints is a good idea.

9. Ensembles, Music Minus One records, the Laureate Series Contest Solos, and the Master Solos (cassette tape) are all ways of practicing and avoiding the "solitary confinement" feeling at the same time. In addition, I have tape recorded the band in rehearsal and loaned the tape to a student so he could practice his part with the tape. This procedure has been especially successful with the stage band.

10. Budgeting time properly can be a headache for adults, and for the typical youngster it is next to impossible. Try taking some of your own valuable time to chaperone a school dance, attend a junior high track meet, basketball game, or any event that involves some of your band members in a non-musical role. The point is that if the director can find time to attend events in which the student is interested, maybe the student will make more of an effort to find time for the director's interests.

11-12. Is there an extra baritone in the inventory the student could keep at home?

13. Try playing a tape of a concert in which the student participated as a 5th or 6th grader. It will go a long way toward dispelling the notion that "I never get any better."

14. Try him on French horn.

15. Check into the student's warm-up routine. If one exists at all, chances are it is incorrect.

James Van Develde is the band director in the Frankenmuth, Michigan schools.

16-18. Maybe the director should take a look at his folio. Does it reflect a balanced diet of music? Is there something in it that will allow a less talented student to feel successful? Is there also something in it that will challenge the more talented student?

19. Involvement in an ensemble might be the answer, or you could assign an oboe solo, or look for a band piece in which oboe passages are more exposed. Another possibility is to demonstrate the importance of the oboe to the timbre of the woodwind section of the band by recording a passage in which the oboe is present and doubling the flute part an octave lower. Then record the same passage with the oboe absent and compare the two.

20. This problem is easily solved if the band library is adequate, or if a local music store carries a plentiful selection of materials for all instruments. Frequently, however, the student does not realize the capacity of a simple exercise. Variations based on dynamics, articulation, tempo, and rhythm can give new life to an old etude. A little guidance by the director, a little imagination by the student, and a goal for each variation can bring a fresh challenge to the "I can play it all" material. ∎

Our October issue contained other prescriptions to help motivate students. See "Rx for the Practicing Blahs," pages 19-21.

The Metronome Has Us Beat!

BY GARY KARR

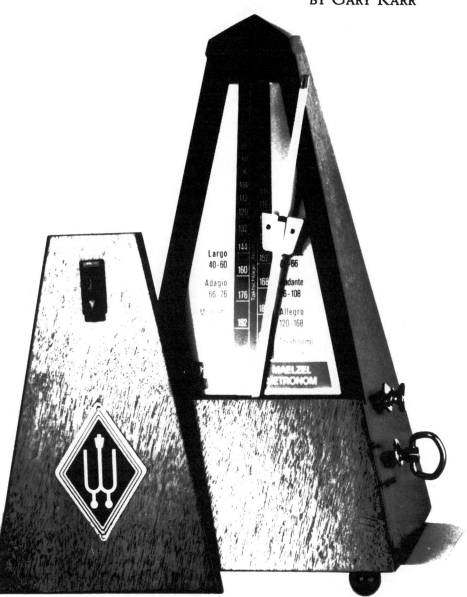

My biggest complaint with modern metronomes is the number 40. Why is 40 still the slowest speed? In the old days before electricity 40 divisions per minute made sense, because the wind-up pendulum type metronome couldn't beat more slowly without stopping. Today, though, especially with the incredibly accurate assistance of quartz, it seems an unforgivable oversight that most metronomes still use 40 beats per minute as the longest division of time. The fact that this has not been questioned signals the general lack of understanding as to the best way to work with a metronome. Because musicians rarely point the indicator to the slower numbers, manufacturers have never built slower metronomes. As a long-time devotee of the ultra-slow metronome, it seems to me almost unbelievable that any musician would even consider practicing with a fast beat. This is not only an abysmal misuse of the metronome, it's asking for real trouble.

Any setting faster than 80 should be used with great caution. It can cause the shakes, a bad case of nerves, exasperating humiliation, poor intonation, and worst of all, a general weakening of any kind of rhythmic concept. A fast setting can be used, however, to corroborate the composer's metronomic marking or to compromise on the tempo when there's no other choice.

In the case of the composer's indications, it has often been my experience in commissioning compositions that the published metronome markings are usually wrong. Usually they are too fast. For reasons that escape me it

Depending on how the metronome is used, it can be a musician's best friend or worst enemy. Unfortunately, as a powerful learning aid the metronome has been grossly misunderstood for years. Since its inception during Beethoven's time, it has been the cause of untold grief and humiliation for countless numbers of musicians who have tried in vain to use it effectively. Even with 20th-cen-

tury improvements such as electricity, the transistor, and quartz, the present-day metronome is still one of the most misused and primitively conceived tools of the musical trade. Knowing what an invaluable device it can be, I feel compelled to draw attention to a few points that I hope will excite a response that will ultimately put pressure on metronome manufacturers to make a more useful metronome.

seems that most composers designate an inaccurate metronomic measure which, when assiduously followed, often yields too rapid a tempo. This published flaw has been confirmed by many composers I contacted; I wish I also had validation from the dead ones.

I'm sure that trying to solve this frequently encountered problem has caused a lot of aggravation. I wish there were a simple solution to this enigma, but I'm afraid each case has to be judged on an individual basis. Apart from deciphering composers' intentions, the metronome can be useful as an aid during practice, but until metronomes are produced that divide the minute into fewer than 40 subdivisions, the benefits of working with a metronome will continue to be minimal.

A number of years ago I became fascinated with a notion that one charismatic quality of some of the exciting older performers was an innate perception of duration. To test this idea I had a metronome built that started from one beat per minute and I then collected recordings of my favorite past artists, such as Pablo Casals, Wanda Landowska, and Fritz Kreisler. I set my special metronome at very slow speeds (below 20) while listening to these performances and to my utter amazement and delight what had seemed to be free rhythmic interpretations filled with Romantic rubati were, in fact, metronomically accurate performances. What seemed to be freedom of phrasing was actually held together by a rigid framework of predictable and regular equal durations. It just happened that these specific equal durations occurred every four or eight measures. In other words, the metronome clicked precisely at the beginning or middle of each phrase. What an idea!

If this discovery were applied to practicing it would set up a challenge never before faced by musicians. Instead of subdividing every ¼ measure into two or four equal units, the metronome could be set slow enough to click only at the beginning of the measure or even on the first beat of every other measure. In other words, if the metronome marking in ¼ time were ♩=80, then instead of setting it at 80 to beat four times each measure, it could be set at 40 to beat twice per measure or at 20 to beat once per measure or at 10 to beat once every other measure.

As a result, for the first time since I became preoccupied with practicing with the metronome, it became an invaluable assistant in helping to strengthen my sense of duration. That, to me, is what a metronome should do – strengthen duration directly and rhythm indirectly. Good rhythm depends upon the player's sensitivity to duration. The more one subdivides a given duration into smaller units (for example, four or eight beats per   measure instead of one or two beats per measure) the weaker will be one's comprehension of rhythm. Subdividing is only useful in academically analyzing a difficult rhythm. Apart from that I regard subdivision as one of the primary enemies of good phrasing and musicality.

Solo bassist Gary Karr has made more than 20 recordings and has been a featured soloist with the Berlin Philharmonic, the New York Philharmonic, the Chicago Symphony, and others. He teaches bass at Yale University and the University of Hartford.

Another benefit derived from practicing with a slow metronome is better intonation. The slower beat and longer durations give the musician a sense of relaxed time in which to find the desired note. Unnecessary subdivisions cause tension that impairs intonation. Good intonation is strengthened by one's ability to think ahead. With longer durations this process is easier and results in greater accuracy.

Although technical development on an instrument is difficult to judge on a day-to-day basis there is no more tangible way of measuring and fostering progress than with a metronome. Used properly it can do wonders. Most important, it has the power of fighting impetuousness by forcing the player to practice slowly. The process of improvement happens gradually, and the metronome is especially useful in developing an appreciation for that fact. Accuracy and clarity can be helped enormously by systematic use of the slow metronome. By the word "systematic" I mean keeping a daily written record of the metronomic settings used with specific musical compositions. By observing this approach, one can increase the tempo by a click or more per day (depending on the number of times you are willing to play through the composition). Although this process seems excessively slow, the written daily record is a friendly reminder that, yes, you are indeed making progress. After several days you will be amazed at your technical development. The metronome used in this systematic way does actually save time and encourages thoughtful and intelligent practice.

Do not let the metronome intimidate you. Use it wisely and the metronome won't beat you down. Join my campaign to encourage metronome manufacturers to ease up on their numbers. Let's get manufacturers to produce metronomes that play below 40. In the meantime, I wonder what makes the metronome manufacturers tick! □

The Magic of Scales

Ed Solomon

Every occupation has its tools of the trade: the mathematician has his multiplication tables, the chemist has his valence tables and atomic weights, the carpenter his hammer and saw, and the musician his scales. However, teaching scales is too often left to chance. Memorizing the names of the notes, the key signatures, and the fingerings require long hours of practice before competency is achieved. The treatment of half step and whole step relationships is often left until theory class or mentioned only in a scale building explanation with no later follow-through. The priority set on scale development varies widely from band to band. In some groups scales are stressed to the exclusion of other fundamentals. It is an accomplishment to be able to play 12 major scales in under two minutes, but not if the principles of tonality are ignored or misunderstood when a new piece of music is assigned.

Scale development can be a systematic learning process involving an understanding of tonality, key signatures, and half step relationships. My approach to teaching scales is for the very young student who cannot read six flats in the key signature and remember which note is involved when they try to play them. My method is based on the half scale concept or "tetrachord plus one." While not new by any means, this approach establishes tonality in the framework of five notes and is well within the technical scope and grasp of most young students. Incorporated into a warm-up procedure, a new half scale can be learned daily and repeated enough times to establish the fingerings, names of notes, and most important, the key center, with strong emphasis on tonic and dominant. A simple I-V-I accompaniment at the piano helps establish tonality, and the use of various articulation devices helps prevent boredom. Once the fingering pattern is learned, concentration on the articulation actually seems to let the student stop worrying about the fingers, and technique develops as a normal consequence.

I use the tetrachord approach with my beginners and intermediate students as soon as the class has reached that very first scale in the method book. The idea of the common tone (the last note in the half scale being the first note of the next scale) and the 1-9-1 form establish the basis for the circle of fifths, construction of major scales, and development of technical skills. The 1-9-1 form, incidently, is excellent for harmonic

Ed Solomon, on the music staff of the New Braunfels Public Schools (Texas), holds a master's degree from North Texas State University. He is active as a clinician, adjudicator, and composer of solo and ensemble literature. Solomon has performed with the San Antonio Symphony and in local theater productions.

listening. For example, have the brasses start on 1 and then have the woodwinds begin when the brasses reach the 3rd. The resulting parallel thirds are good listening and tuning devices. The inclusion of the low seventh tone (1-9-1-7-1) provides a base for extended harmonic treatment or experimental listening. It is also a good reinforcement for learning the 7-8 half step that is often missed within an exercise or study.

Begin with the C major scale by numbering the notes 1-8, showing the notes on a keyboard (piano, mock-up, or drawing). Discover and identify the enharmonic notes and the natural half steps E-F and B-C. I tell my students, "We won't worry about learning a whole scale for now, just half of it." It's funny how most students are willing to do half the work if they think they are getting out of doing something more difficult.

Using the two natural half scales (CDEFG and GABCD), the students learn that there is a half step between steps 3 and 4. (I don't say anything about the half step between 7 and 8 because in actuality, 3 and 4 become 7 and 8 when the next half scale is learned.) Point out that the first note of the half scale gives its name to the scale and the key signature. Even though the half scale does not contain all the notes of the key signature it is wise to establish their number and location on the staff in relation to the key name.

Visual Aids

I ask the students to write down the famous or infamous locators:

• For sharp keys the last sharp is always the seventh tone and the next note is the key note.

• For flat keys, look at the next to the last flat or count down four from the last flat to find the key note.

• When adding flats to the key signature, the new flat is always the fourth note of the scale.

The following visual aid is also helpful in remembering the key names and the key signatures:

0	1	2	3	4	5	6	7	
	F	Bb	Eb	Ab	Db	Gb	Cb	flats
C								
	G	D	A	E	B	F♯	C♯	sharps

Just for fun I use silly sentences to help students remember the key order: "**F**at **B**ull **E**lephants **A**lways **D**rive **G**reen **C**ars;" and "**C**ats **G**o **D**own **A**lleys **E**ating **B**ird **F**eathers **C**arefully." These nonsense gimmicks may seem superfluous, but it is necessary to use several approaches to teach the same fundamental as not every student will learn the same way.

I use a handout sheet (see example 1) and a chart (see example 2) as a ready reference for the half scale concept. These sheets provide the following information in one compact package.

- major half scales presented in letter names to be performed as 123454321
- all common tones (5) circled
- the two half scales making up each major scale
- scales numbered according to the particular instruments
- number of sharps or flats in each key signature
- chromatic sequence of half scales

Suggested Drills

I use the following drills to reinforce scale development:

- using only the half step 3-4, progress chromatically through the 12 keys.
- introduce the minor tonality by mentally lowering the third
- combine half scales and play 12345678987654321
- have the flutes play the key note while everyone sings "123454321" and fingers the keys
- have each section say the note names while fingering the keys
- play through the half scale slowly, popping the fingers on the keys and increasing the speed with subsequent repetitions, and then move chromatically to the next half scale
- follow the same procedure as above but move through the circle of fifths.

Testing

Testing is done individually or within sections, using one half scale per week with beginners and six half scales for a major test. To create a challenge situation I have one student play a half scale and the next student begin on the common tone and play the next half scale. The challenge can be played within sections.

Purists may complain that my approach is based on rote teaching rather than note reading, but I maintain that the mental preparation of learning the names and fingerings will have more residual effect in the early years than reading notes. Spend some time with the two charts I've devised and experiment with your own group. You'll find the results well worth the effort. ∎

Example 2

	Key Signature	Keynote 1	2	3	4	Common Note 5	Half Scales	Needed
C	2b	Bb	C	D	Eb	F	Bb	F
	5#	B	C#	D#	E	F#	B	F#
Bb	0	C	D	E	F	G	C	G
	5b	Db	Eb	F	Gb	Ab	Db	Ab
	2#	D	E	F#	G	A	D	A
	3b	Eb	F	G	Ab	Bb	Eb	Bb
	4#	E	F#	G#	A	B	E	B
F	1b	F	G	A	Bb	C	F	C
	6b	Gb	Ab	Bb	Cb	Db	Gb	Db
Eb	1#	G	A	B	C	D	G	D
	4b	Ab	Bb	C	Db	Eb	Ab	Eb
	3#	A	B	C#	D	E	A	E

- Full scale form 12345678987654321.
- 5 and 9 are common tones from the two half scales used to make major scale.
- Read horizontally for major half scale development.
- Read vertically (top to bottom) for chromatic development.
- Lower the third tone (horizontally) for minor half scales.

Example 1

INSTRUMENT Scale number		Concert Instruments		Bb Instruments			F Instruments		Eb Instruments		
Common Tone	5	F	F#	G	Ab	A	Bb	B	C	Db	D	Eb	E
	4	Eb	E	F	Gb	G	Ab	A	Bb	Cb	C	Db	D
	3	D	D#	E	F	F#	G	G#	A	Bb	B	C	C#
	2	C	C#	D	Eb	E	F	F#	G	Ab	A	Bb	B
Key Note	1	Bb	B	C	Db	D	Eb	E	F	Gb	G	Ab	A
Key Signature		2b	5#	0	5b	2#	3b	4#	1b	6b	1#	4b	3#

Two half scales	F	F#/Gb	G	Ab	A	Bb	B	C	Db	D	Eb	E
make complete scale	Bb	B	C	Db	D	Eb	E	F	Gb	G	Ab	A

December, 1983

A Medical / Musical Analysis

The Dynamics Of Breathing
by Kevin Kelly

with Arnold Jacobs and David Cugell, M.D.

Arnold Jacobs is principal tubist of the Chicago Symphony Orchestra, where he has been a member since 1944. At the age of 15 he became a student at Philadelphia's Curtis Institute of Music and went on to play with the Indianapolis and Pittsburgh Symphonies. He toured with Leopold Stokowski and the All-American Youth Orchestra before joining the Chicago Symphony Orchestra. Jacobs, who is sought by students and professionals alike for his approach to wind instrument playing has made talks at many gatherings and provided the 1982 Mid-West National Band and Orchestra Clinic with his presentation "Motivational and Respiratory Factors in Wind Instrument Playing."

David W. Cugell, M.D. is head of the pulmonary function laboratory at Northwestern Memorial Hospital in Chicago and has been a member of the faculty at the Northwestern University Medical School since 1955. A graduate of Yale University and the State University of New York School of Medicine in Brooklyn, Cugell is president of the Chicago Lung Association and their representative/director for the American Lung Association. He was awarded the 1983 Chicago Lung Association medal. A musician as well as a physician, Cugell played clarinet and saxophone through college where he was a member of the marching band.

At some time every student of a wind instrument is instructed in the "correct" method of breathing. If he studies with two or three different teachers, he probably learns two or three different methods, all presumably correct. I studied with six horn teachers and learned five breathing methods, each slightly different and none especially helpful.

The problem is two-fold. First, few teachers fully understand how the body regulates breathing, let alone how the breath is used in wind instrument playing. Second, those who have at least a partial understanding teach it in the wrong way, through attention to anatomy. The teacher's incomplete understanding is conveyed to the student, who becomes confused, disillusioned, perhaps even immobilized. The standard "art of playing" books for each instrument help little, because few are coherent on the subject and even fewer agree with any other text.

628

In an attempt to understand this problem, I conferred with two noted authorities on the subject of breathing: Dr. David W. Cugell, Bazley Professor of Pulmonary Diseases at the Northwestern University Medical School in Chicago, who also heads the Pulmonary Function Laboratory at Northwestern Memorial Hospital; and Arnold Jacobs, principal tubist of the Chicago Symphony Orchestra and a world-renowned teacher, who is sought by students and professionals on all wind instruments, primarily for his approach to the psychology of breathing.

Wind instrument players are concerned with the creation and maintenance of a moving column of air, which is the responsibility of the respiratory muscles alone. Many of the muscles of the abdomen and chest, and some in the neck, are involved in moving air in and out of the lungs. The diaphragm is the one most frequently mentioned in connection with wind instrument playing and the one least understood by wind players. It is popularly considered a main element in the concept of breath "support" — we are often told to support the tone from the diaphragm — as if the diaphragm were active in expiration (blowing air out). It is not.

"The diaphragm is a muscle of inspiration (taking air in)," Cugell says. "Located around and above the abdomen (see example 1), it is unique among the muscles of the body in that it contracts not from one end to the other, as the muscles in your arm, leg, or back would, but in a circular fashion, so that a contraction of the diaphragm will reduce its size while flattening it out. The diaphragm is connected to the lower ribs in such a manner that when it contracts it moves downward. It's one muscle, but like all muscles it's made up of multiple fibers that contract synchronously. When it contracts, the effect is to push it downward.

"The active part of breathing is the inspiratory portion. In order to move air into the chest and expand the lungs, an active muscle effort is required, and that means contraction of the diaphragm. Now you can produce a little bit of breathing by contracting other muscles, such as the strap muscles in the neck. You see someone complete a hundred-yard dash, they're gasping and tugging with their neck muscles as well as with their diaphragm, but that's the agonal gasp of the subject who is in extremes of physical activity, which is not the case when you're playing a musical instrument. You may need to breathe in a hurry or you may need a big breath, but coordinated and planned breathing is not assisted by contracting some of these other muscles, which contribute relatively little in comparison with what a healthy diaphragm can do."

Cugell points out that the diaphragm functions only to assist taking the air in. "It's the other muscles, particularly in the chest area and the ab-

domen, that we use to exhale and that collectively develop the air pressure you need to play.

"A man in England did a nice little study in which he had a number of trained singers stand in front of a fluoroscope (an instrument used to examine the interior of a body) and told them to sustain a note with the breath coming from the diaphragm in whatever manner they were trained. Then he repeated the process and had the singers breathe in a manner which was quite incorrect, without using the diaphragm in the way in which they had been instructed. The fluoroscope showed no difference whatsoever in the activity of the diaphragm under these two circumstances. This is really not surprising, because the diaphragm accounts for 90% of all breathing and you cannot control or change the proportion of your breathing that is contributed by it (or by a few other muscles, whose contribution is relatively small).

"Now what I suspect is happening is that when someone sustains a high C in a proper way 'using the diaphragm' — as opposed to someone who does it improperly — it has not really anything to do with the diaphragm. It has to do with how the person contracts other muscles in the abdomen and chest. This information has been transferred in the lingo of singers and wind instrument players to assume that this exhaling is accomplished with the diaphragm, when in fact it is done by contracting other muscles.

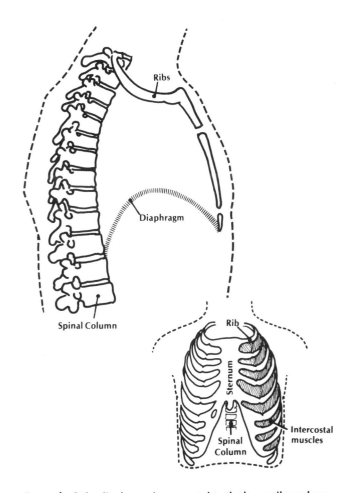

Example 1 The diaphragm is connected to the lower ribs and contracts in a circular fashion as it moves downward.

Kevin Kelly is completing degrees in music criticism and English writing at Northwestern University, where he has played horn in the major wind performance ensembles.

There are two overlapping layers of muscles between the ribs, called the intercostal muscles; some contract during inspiration and some contract during expiration. If I inhale in a hurry and I want to stop at a certain point, before I actually stop, the muscles which move the chest in the opposite direction begin to work. It is this interplay of the muscles that move things in opposite directions which provides the fine control."

The late Professor, Arend Bouhuys, of the Yale University School of Medicine to whom Cugell referred to frequently in our discussions, offers a good illustration of how the breathing-in and breathing-out muscles cooperate in wind playing:

"The diaphragm is a muscle of inspiration (taking air in)...it is not active in expiration (blowing air out)"

The respiratory muscles help to generate most of the energy that goes into playing a horn. They act on the chest, which is for our purposes an elastic bellows. When the chest (that is, the lungs in it) is full of air, the chest tends to collapse as it relaxes. Just try for yourself: inhale as far as you can, relax all muscles, and you exhale with a sigh. Now try the opposite, which is more difficult to do: breathe about as far as you can. Now relax all muscles, and the air flows in. The resting position of the chest bellows is somewhere in between, roughly in the middle of the volume excursion range of the chest. The respiratory muscles have to work with or against these elastic forces, depending on what the chest volume is and what pressure we need to play the horn.

If we first want to breathe out slowly with very little pressure, after breathing in as far as possible we must use considerable inspiratory force to keep the air from going out with a sign. Again, try for yourself. Breathe in deeply, and let go very slowly. You have to 'brake' your exhaling, using inspiratory muscles to hold back, to keep the chest volume from decreasing too rapidly because of its own elasticity. When you continue, you reach a point where you are relaxed. Now you continue to breathe out slowly, and you find that you now have to push with expiratory muscles to move the air out at the same slow rate. (Arend Bouhuys, "Physiology and Musical Instruments." Reprinted by permission from *Nature*, volume 221, number 5187, page 1200. Copyright ©1969, Macmillan Journals, Ltd.)

The amount of control the wind instrument player has over this procedure is limited by what is called the pressure-volume diagram of the chest (example 2), which says that greater pressure is required to move air at volumes below the resting lung volume than at volumes above the resting point. As Cugell explained it, "In the lung the pressure-volume relationship is linear over the midrange — that is, I get equal volume increments for equal pressure increments. Once I reach the elastic limit, no matter how much pressure I apply, I don't get any more volume.

Example 2

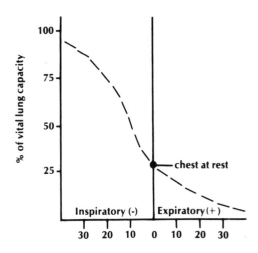

Muscle Force (pressure on lungs)

During slow release of a breath, inspiratory muscles (*not* including the diaphragm) keep chest high. Below the chest resting point, expiratory muscles further reduce lung size as moving the air becomes more difficult.

"With no conscious effort to facilitate things, the pressure is greatest when the lungs are largest. Similarly, when the lungs are largest, the conscious contraction of the muscles produces the highest pressures. Active expiratory effort is, of course, needed whenever the required mouth pressure for the instrument is higher than the relaxation pressure at the prevailing lung volume. As the lungs get smaller, they are no longer going to contract and generate pressures on their own. You have to do it by squeezing with the muscles.

"For example, if you inflate the lungs to their absolute maximum and then play a high C on the trumpet at maximum volume, you haven't used much air, but the volume of air in the chest is reduced considerably because you've had to squeeze so much. You compress the air in the chest just as much as the air in the mouth. Whether you have an instrument that has a low pressure, for which you're going to need a high air flow to get a large sound volume, or you're playing an instrument that has a low flow at enormous pressure (one that uses a small mouthpiece) the effort required of the player is essentially the same. In other words, you've got to squeeze with the muscles to generate either a high flow or a high pressure.

"The vast difference is that if you don't need much pressure you can play with the entire usable portion of the lung volume. However, if you need a lot of pressure you can only use a small portion of the lung capacity because when the lungs are partially empty it's not possible to generate the pressure, as shown in example 2. You can generate the maximum pressures when the lungs are full, and you want to do that to play a loud, high note; but after you've exhaled some air the lungs are smaller and then it's not possible to sustain as high a pressure. So there is a limited period of time when a player has both the volume and the pressures to produce the sound. On the other hand, the time during which an oboist can sustain a note is not limited so much by the air pressure and air flow requirements of the instrument as by his breath-holding time. If you don't need much pressure and you don't need much flow, then you've got all day; but there's only so long you can hold on before you've got to breathe again."

The point that Cugell insisted upon throughout our discussions is that, given all the facts of breathing anatomy, each player will discover the practical applications for himself: "I'm a firm believer in the capacity of the organism to minimize the burden of the work it has to achieve. In other words, there are studies that show whatever breathing pattern people assume generally represents the minimum amount of work that is required to produce the necessary amount of breathing.

"For example, people with a certain kind of lung disease breathe with a large breath relatively slowly. When making objective measurements of the work of breathing — and by that I mean the pressure, the volume, the physical parameters of work — you will find that if you change their breathing so that they are breathing with a smaller volume more frequently, which would net out to the same amount of breathing, the work required is larger. A patient who has the kind of lung disease that makes the lung stiff may adopt a breathing pattern of panting. He does that because it takes a lot of work to distend a stiff lung. The patient can breathe the necessary amount if he breathes quickly and at small volumes. If you tell him, 'Gee, you're breathing all wrong. Try taking a big breath and breathe less frequently, you'll get the same amount of breathing for it,' he'll say, 'Well I tried it and I didn't like it,' because he had to work so hard to expand the stiff lung.

"My point is that the compensatory pattern of breathing that people spontaneously adopt will represent the minimum work that is required, and it is probably incorrect to impose a different pattern. I think a person playing a wind instrument fits into the same category. If he's got to grab a breath between two passages, he's going to do it in a way that's best for him; I doubt that there would be any purpose in imposing a different pattern. If the player did it once and ran out of air, the next time he's going to breathe a little more because he knows he has to."

Furthermore, the particular breathing pattern a person adopts is no indication of his quality as a wind instrument player. Cugell says, "If you compare the breathing patterns of you and me or anybody else, they would all be different, but there would be no way to categorize that as saying 'normal' or 'abnormal' or 'this one's old' or 'this one's young.' There's nothing characteristic about breathing that can be defined as representing gradations of normality. That being the case, it's not surprising that if four people play the same music, they're going to breathe a little differently, because they breathe differently when they're not playing music."

He referred to the *Nature* article, where Bouhuys tested four flutists playing Debussy's *Syrinx*. One of these men was first chair in the Concertgebouw Orchestra of Amsterdam, one was a good amateur, and two were young professionals. Recordings from a pneumograph (an instrument designed to measure chest movement during respiration) showed four slightly divergent readings within the same general pattern, with slight tempo fluctuations. With the exception of one man, who had a slightly smaller lung capacity and took one extra breath, the performers adhered to the phrase-breath markings in the music. This test showed to what extent the music determines a player's breathing pattern. "So if we subscribe to the concept, with respect to instrument playing, that we will spontaneously assume the most efficient and effective pattern," says Cugell, "then it certainly makes good sense not to concern yourself with it so you can concentrate on all the other aspects of your playing."

Anatomy and Psychology

Arnold Jacobs bases his teaching on all these other aspects of sound and phrase — the "products" of music. He makes the distinction between anatomy and function through what he calls the "computer activity of the brain," separate from the "thinking part of the brain."

"When you go to the product of whatever you're trying to accomplish, you'll find the physical action required to do it is based in the computer activity of the brain. In other words the conscious levels of the brain, where volitional thought takes place, handle the product. Another level of the brain, the thinking part, will handle motor impulses carried by nerves throughout the body. The firing up of the systems is handled at subconscious levels, just like the ability to walk or to talk or to run. The muscle activity will result from what you're trying to accomplish. With all machines there is a set of controls, like an automobile, which has complex machinery under the hood but simple controls in the driver's compartment. There's nothing as complex on this planet as the human being; but man has magnificent controls, and he goes through this control system.

"A teacher should always try for the simple answers that bring about proper motor response"

"By this I mean that there are divisions in the brain that are going to control all sorts of physical functions — cutting up food, bringing it to the mouth and chewing it, handling the body for sleep at night, or even going insane. The thinking part of the brain is free to cope with life around us, it does not have to cope with life within us. It's with the thinking part of the brain that we begin to establish what we want in the way of product.

"This, of course, is what players are up against;

in music so often a teacher makes the mistake of altering the machine activity rather than altering the product or what he wants accomplished. The instructor is giving machine methods of how to do it, and people can't work that way. None of us can. We have to look for the easy answer all the time. It is so simple. If you want a lot of breath, just take a lot of air. Don't worry about where it goes. If you want to blow, just blow. With students a teacher

---

"...not to correct what's wrong, but to establish what should be right"

---

should always try for the simple answers that bring about proper motor response. That idea belongs not in the realm of anatomy but in psychology."

The answer that Jacobs introduces students to is what he calls the "phenomenon of wind" — the idea of air blowing out through the instrument to prevent pressures from building up inside the lungs. Most students who come to Jacob have acquired the habits of thinking about air pressure instead of air in motion. Because these habits are difficult to break, he uses psychology to create new habits, to get students to use their muscles for the proper function.

The respiratory muscles are involved in three ways. One is respiration, the single complete act of breathing in and out. The second has to do with pelvic pressures when the upper end of the airway is closed, forcing pressure downward for such events as defecation and childbirth. The third has to do with the isometrics of physical function, the kind of static muscle tightening involved in weightlifting and wrestling.

"A musician has to make sure that he is using the right approach when playing an instrument," Jacobs says. "He doesn't want the one that immobilizes, he doesn't want the one that creates great isometric contractions that have no movement potential. Because a continuous flow of air requires movement, the player should go to respiration.

"The human brain is responsible for conditioned responses to stimuli or reflex responses to stimuli in everybody, musicians or non-musicians. These are non-respiratory functions. In respiration a bellows action occurs in the muscles. We take air in and we blow air out by the phenomena of enlargement and reduction. It becomes simple when you think of movements of air. Whether it's from the diaphragm descending or the rib cage ascending, there has to be enlargement to lower air pressure internally below atmospheric pressure so air will move into the lungs. The same thing happens as you reduce the size — the air pressure increases as you move out. That's how we blow; it's how we breathe.

Move Air As Wind

"The psychology of blowing is always to blow

outward, to work with wind rather than air pressure. The psychology of it is important. Take your hand, hold it at a distance and blow onto it. Now where the air lands is the area to concentrate on. Some teachers will have the player blow through the instrument or through the far wall. It doesn't matter what the technique is to motivate a student; the psychology of it is to move air as wind, not air pressure.

"With wind there is always air pressure. With air pressure, there is not always wind. If you just concentrate on the air pressure — which can happen in any body cavity — the danger is that you may have stimulated the Valsalva maneuver (in which you try to breathe out with your mouth and nose shut) or the pelvic pressure syndrome, or the isometrics, which do not involve movements of air.

"But an instructor is never going to get this idea across by telling students to push with this muscle or that muscle. I get them to blow. Away from the instrument I let them observe their body. I use special equipment or I may have students blow up balloons or blow out matches, and then show how quantities can be taken from any part of the thorax (the body area between the neck and the abdomen). In other words we go through a certain amount of perspective training away from music to become acquainted with the body, so that the studies of air in life are involved."

The confusion of many teachers about both the role of the diaphragm and the idea of abdominal "support" of air is largely responsible for many students' preoccupation with the kind of pressures resulting from misdirected muscular tensions.

"First of all, the term 'support' raises questions in itself. Many people make the mistake of assuming the muscle contraction is what gives support. The blowing of the breath should be the support, not tension in the muscles of the body, but the movement of air as required by the embouchure or the reed.

"You go into the mechanics of movement and confusion arises; it's a cause and effect relationship. When a player blows, the body undergoes certain changes. There will be increasing palpable tensions that can be felt just by touching a person. Toward the end of a breath, there will be a certain number of fibers that are stimulated. There will be increasing motor activity in order to get the air out, and this varies according to the length of the phrase and the amount of air in the lungs originally; but 'support' is never 'tight muscles,' whether you're silent or blowing, or in a *diminuendo* or *crescendo*. In other words it's simply a static, constant, isometric type of contraction that so many people call support. This is not support at all.

"I can explain it from different points of view. Do it this way: your diaphragm is like the floor, a movable partition between the thoracic and the abdominal cavities. Now if you were to build up considerable air pressure with a loose abdomen and a loose diaphragm, the air would simply move the floor downward. Instead of air coming out, as the player builds pressure it would simply lower the floor. So by thinking of support as something that will hold the diaphragm in the upper position, you could conceivably see abdominal tension as building pressure beneath the floor. You keep that in a fixed position while building up high pressure through the rib activity to have expulsion of breath based on this pressure. I can't conceive of it this way, but I know that many teachers think this way. This is not, to me, support.

"Support is always a reduction phenomenon. Wherever the player is going to build pressure, according to Boyle's Law, he is going to have a reduced chamber. Now the chamber can be reduced anywhere it is enlarged. It gets bigger when you take air in, it gets smaller when you move air out. When you blow, the brain will deactivate the diaphragm, normally. Expiratory function will normally deactivate inspiratory function. If you are using air to create pelvic pressures, the diaphragm will not deactivate — it will remain stimulated. Abdominal muscles that would normally be expiratory will start contracting, and there will be a closure at the throat or the tongue or the lips which causes the air pressure to bear down on a downward-contracting diaphragm to increase the pelvic pressure for expulsion of fecal matter. Of course, to bypass this we have to have a blowing phenomenon that is different. You see, you have to form a new habit, and a new habit does not come

". . . you don't worry about the function. You worry about the sound"

right away. A new habit takes time to reach the subconscious level."

Jacobs uses a wide variety of non-musical exercises to get players to feel and hear the difference between blowing air out freely and blowing out in a choked manner that results in tight chest and abdominal muscles. For example, blow onto the back of the hand using a tight hissing sound through your teeth, as loud as possible. You will feel very little air. By blowing out freely onto the hand, you feel a considerable amount of air under low pressure. The hiss is under high pressure, but there is little quantity. By closing the lips in the midst of the hiss and then releasing the sound explosively, you will have felt considerable pressure behind the lips and also behind the tongue. As soon as you open the lips, you have an immediate shortage of air.

"We see these closures in students all the time," Jacobs says, "coming from a sibilant 's' (the hissing sound) or at the back of the tongue, and even some where the larynx and epiglottis start to come together. If I have a student whose tongue is blocking the air, allowing very little air movement but at high pressure, I immediately encourage using the open vowel form such as 'oh' or 'ah.' All through life you have language; language involves the tongue. Over the years you have built up reflex response for shape that is very powerful. You hear

a trumpet or a bassoon, but it sounds like a singer with a voice like that singing 'oh.' Listen for that sound and the tongue shape is correct. This pertains to any need to open up the airway."

Following one of Jacobs' recent master classes at Northwestern University, a woman asked how to help a bassoon student who lets the air get "like a brick wall" — constricted and tense — which apparently resulted in quite a horrible sound.

"First of all," he said, "get her away from the bassoon. You don't have to use the reed; just put something in her mouth. Have the student start blowing or start blowing against something in order to see that the air will do something where it lands. The importance of this approach is not to correct what's wrong, but to establish what should be right.

"I would give her a couple of straws and have her blow at the pages of a book and watch what happens on the other side. Have her blow at some matches or blow up a weak balloon, but always with the thought of becoming acquainted with air, rather than air pressure. Studying childbirth and coughing gives the picture of what air pressure will do. However, when you study a burn and cool it by blowing on the hand, or when you're doing what I used to do, blow peas at people with a pea shooter, then you get a different picture of what air will do."

The woman pointed out that this particular student was a singer who had played the bassoon for only a year. "Don't singers have to use a lot of air?" she asked.

"No, it's just the opposite," Jacobs said. "Singers use less air than anybody. Their reed is at the throat, and as a result they have to keep a fairly sizable pressure at the laryngeal region. The student is using the technique of singing on the bassoon. Now compared to singing, bassoon playing will seem like a large volume of air is in transit. It's important to recognize that she has habits already formed.

"Start mechanical movements without the instrument so the student experiences change in the abdominal-diaphragmatic relationship. Deliberately have her create massive motions in the abdominal region, sucking the belly in, forcing it out, pushing it up and down — this is the region where she's been stabilized. Now deliberately destabilize it. Start the muscle activity of change in front of a mirror so the senses work together to strengthen each other. Don't tie it into music, though, or else she'll have to fight her own habits.

"Then tie in the movements of air by using motion — every day — blowing out matches, taking in lots of air and enlarging. Allow a few weeks, where she has to be practicing this every day. In the abdominal region where the student was stable, she will begin to establish motility of function. It has to be recognized in this manner before you apply it to the bassoon. Then you do it with just some reed squawks, but with exaggeration.

"Exaggeration is one of the important tools. Doing things just right is not what you want. The recognition is not there. So you overchange. You're not doing it with the music, so there's no damage.

Then when you get to the bassoon, you don't worry about the body change, but you go to the study of air.

"It is natural for the lungs to get smaller as you use up air. The bassoon student has made it unnatural. As a teacher, you go through a program to get her back to what is natural. As soon as this process starts, she begins to use air as wind to deactivate the diaphragm. There can be no stiffness in the anterior abdominal wall without the antagonist, which is the diaphragm. The brain will deactivate this action, and as the diaphragm comes up, you'll find the student is able to blow against the reed, where the wind belongs. If you tell her to do these things based on intelligence, she will understand, but she can't communicate it to her body. The wind becomes the body's signal for change.

It's the Tone

"But wind is finally only a minor part. Tone production is the major. You use the wind as fuel. With a wind instrument, the horn resonates sound waves; it's reacting to sound and amplifying it according to acoustical properties. Our air isn't used to fill an instrument. It's used by the embouchure as energy so the lips vibrate.

"So players certainly shouldn't worry about the air, but about the quality of tone. When you get the tone, you will have all the requirements of tone at the subconscious levels. The blowing is an incidental part; the tone doesn't exist without the

---

"... introduce students to the 'phenomenon of wind.'"

---

blowing, but the blowing can exist without the tone. As an artist you go for the product — the product is sound and phrase and all the emotions in music — you use thought processes that stimulate motor function, but you don't worry about the function. You worry about the sound. You will use the breath as needed. You will do it primarily without awareness of air. The air should be used freely — waste it, do anything you want. A player's awareness is of the communication of sound to whoever he is talking to.

"This is true of any wind instrument. You teach expertise in phrase and the study of dynamics. As the sound production becomes more efficient, which it will, you'll find that you use the breath with greater and greater ease. I'm an old man, but I can still function quite well in playing a brass instrument, because my lips respond quite readily to my thoughts. Moving air under pressure is required for my lips to vibrate, but those lips are not trying to resist the air. They're trying to vibrate based on the thoughts coming from my brain in terms of sounds."

There are, of course, many ways students and professionals have of inhibiting their ability to express sound freely. Probably the most common is

poor posture. "Posture is very important," Jacobs acknowledges. "We're structured so that the maximal use of air comes in the standing posture, as if you would run or fight for your life. Standing offers the greatest ability to move large volumes of air in and out of the lungs. The closer you get to the supine, the poorer it becomes.

"If you think of the respiratory system, it should be thought of not as one bellows, but as a series of segmented bellows, depending on your posture. When lying on your back on the floor, you'll find there is little ability to use chest breathing. You will have a marvelous use of diaphragmatic breathing, which is more than enough to sustain life; but the diaphragm isolated from the rest of the rib cage provides a rather small breath. There is no such thing as a full breath without the use of the sternum (the compound ventral bone and cartilage that supports the ribs). If I lean back on the chair and reach over my head, the motion pulls the rib cage up, which is already in the expanded position. That means I can't use it for breathing in or out. If I bend forward over my belly, pressure in the abdominal region under the diaphragm is such that I have great difficulty using diaphragmatic function.

"If you need large volumes of air, you will use the entire respiratory system. If you're playing an instrument that doesn't require much air, you're never going to use a full breath; however you should be able to. Performers have to take sufficient air in to be able to complete phrases. This involves taking in quantities of air based on judgments of how much air will be left at the end of a phrase.

"Standing while seated is the best posture because players have the greatest ability to move air in and out of the lungs. However, if you are breathing with comfort, the posture doesn't have to be that way. As long as you are in the upright position, you should have more than enough air. If you're a large person with large lung reserves, posture is not that important; however, people who have small lung volumes must stay upright and make use of whatever nature gave them." (We come back to the point that Cugell made earlier: the body will adopt the most comfortable and effective means of performing whatever task it is given to do.)

"In this art form," Jacobs concludes, "we are dealing in sound. Respiration is made too much of. We need sufficient quantities of fuel that we can use easily — as I say, waste it, it's free — but don't make a big deal out of it. We don't start anything with skill; skill is developed over a period of time in spite of yourself. We have to recognize what we're trying to accomplish; the orders that come from the various parts of the brain must be based on the sound of the instrument. We have to make sure that we don't take the level of the brain at which we have volitional thought and try to take charge of the human machine through its individual components. We can't handle it. You've got to get out of the way and allow your body to function for you. The point is to try to sound great when you play." ∎

January, 1982

Inner Game of Music

Barry Green

Many sports-minded musicians reading Timothy Gallwey's first book, *The Inner Game of Tennis,* were quick to recognize the abundance of useful suggestions that apply to music — quieting the mind, combating nervousness, improving concentration, and increasing one's awareness. Now Gallwey is helping people in many professions to overcome mental obstacles so they can better perform, learn, and enjoy. I started out a skeptic, but am now music consultant for the Inner Game Corporation.

My brother, Jerry, introduced me to Gallwey's principles through the book, *Inner Skiing.* We both began to ski two years ago and even though I am the younger brother, I have always been stronger and more physically coordinated. I took an extensive series of skiing lessons in order to satisfy my desire to learn quickly. A year later we met at a California ski resort and I was amazed that in the same amount of time my brother had learned to ski more courageously, faster, and with more joy than I had. In consoling my deflated ego, he told me I looked paralyzed by too many instructions. In each turn my mind resonated with echoes of my teachers' commands: "Put your weight on your downhill ski." "Carve the turn with the front edge of your uphill ski." "Don't lean back." "Bend your knees, sit up and keep your shoulders straight." "Keep your hands in front of your body." After giving me Gallwey's book he told me to forget all of my lessons and just start by "feeling the mountain and enjoying skiing." I was skeptical and reluctant to subscribe to this unfamiliar, undefined and (to my thinking) "pop California philosophy." Out of respect for Jerry, I read *Inner Skiing* and was amazed at its depth and practicality. It not only completely transformed my skiing, but also gave me invaluable insights into my profession of teaching and learning music — without complicated instructions. The book dealt with combating fear, learning to concentrate, and performing at one's full potential.

At the time I was on a sabbatical leave from the University of Cincinnati and the Cincinnati Symphony and was teaching double bass at Indiana University. With my bass students I began to experiment with applying Gallwey's techniques to change habits through increased awareness.

o o o o o o o o o

Barry Green is principal bassist of the Cincinnati Symphony and adjunct professor of double bass at the University of Cincinnati, College-Conservatory of Music. He is also executive director of the International Society of Bassists.

Thinking I had made an exclusive discovery, I soon learned that the horn teacher (Robert Elworthy) had written an article on inner horn playing (using Inner Game principles) and that many musicians were applying the same techniques to music. After reading *The Inner Game of Tennis* and *The Inner Game of Golf* and greatly improving my own tennis and golf games, I called Tim Gallwey to ask how I could further apply the Inner Game to music. He invited me to participate in training sessions he was conducting for health practitioners. His method was to coach them on tennis in the Inner Game mode, so they could apply the same principles to their field. My challenge was to make the same comparisons and applications to music.

Although I am a better than average tennis player, I began my lesson with a typical case of nervousness, wanting to make a positive impression on Tim Gallwey, "the celebrated sports guru." Even though I studied his books I was a victim of the infamous mental game Tim says we all play between "Self I" and "Self II." Self I refers to the personality that is always passing judgment, giving instructions, interfering with the present, casting doubts, and wanting to remain in control of the situation. Self I told me, "You better make a good impression or Tim will think you are a lousy tennis player *and* bass player." "Be careful to hit the ball well." "Make sure your shirt is tucked in." "Pretend you know what you are doing, so he will respect your accomplishments." (I remember a similar conversation before a recent bass concert. "I'm nervous," Self I would say, "My bow is shaking." "I think I'm going to have a memory slip." "I feel sick to my stomach." "I hope I look good." "What about my reputation if I goof up?") Tim hit some tennis balls my way, not acknowledging my nervousness or desire to make a good impression. He cleverly moved my attention off myself by telling me to watch the seams of the ball, listen to the sound as it hit my racket, and notice the feeling of the swing and the resistance of the racket. I soon became so engrossed in watching, hearing, and feeling that I forgot my usual fears about whether or not my shots were going in the court. Self I was suddenly quiet, giving Self II a chance to emerge. Self II, the body and brain, learns from the actual experience — its sights, sounds, feelings, and understanding of the performance. Self II deals with the actions and perceptions of the present moment with no wandering of the mind into the past or future. Self II excludes the personal ego and self-doubts. It seemed as if I was playing "out of my mind" and everything was easily falling into place. I recalled a similar experience in playing my bass. Gallwey calls this state, "relaxed concentration," and maintains that it is the "master skill" essential to excellence in any pursuit. If only I could find a way to recreate this state with consistency and control — to learn, enjoy, and perform at my full potential every time I walk on stage or the sports field, I could revolutionize the quality of my life as well as my music.

Tim showed me how this brilliant process solves all kinds of problems. First he asked me, "What do you want to change about your tennis stroke?" I told him, "My forearm feels out of control." He was helping me to establish a goal. When teaching a music lesson, similarly begin by asking the student what he would like to fix, change or accomplish. Amazingly, students know what needs to be done. Once the goal is clearly defined (the forehand stroke or the intonation of a particular passage), proceed with an awareness process by

"I soon became so engrossed in watching, hearing, and feeling that I forgot my usual fears..."

having the student focus on what is happening at the moment. In the case of my forehand, Tim had me hit several balls, and locate exactly when my forearm felt awkward and what felt awkward about the motion. In music, have the student find exactly where the intonation is faulty by locating which notes are flat or sharp. After hearing the reality of the present situation, changes will occur naturally along the lines of our pre-established goals. Looking more closely at my tennis arm, I discovered an uneven motion in my elbow precisely before I hit the ball. I learned that if my elbow was stabilized just before I hit the ball, the motion became smooth. Tim then put a number 5 on my present elbow motion. The number 1 would represent no excess motion and 10 would be an extreme elbow motion. As I hit the ball, I was to tell him the number that corresponded to the movement of my elbow without judging myself or trying to control my stroke. The first ball was a 5, then a 3, then a 2, and then a 7, then a 2, and finally a 1. Using the numbers focused my sensitivity and awareness of the motions of my elbow which assisted me in allowing Self II to make the necessary adjustments toward my goal.

Using the same principle I began instructing my bass students to pay attention to their elbow, when shifting over the neck of the instrument caused them to play flat. Many students discovered by themselves that if the elbow is raised before the shift, the notes will not be flat, and through that awareness, the change was made automatically. In Florida during one of my first Inner Game lectures, I tried an experiment with a pianist. The student wanted to know how to make the piano sing like a string instrument. She played a series of chords and asked me to help her find ways to sustain the sound. Not knowing how to play the piano, I had no idea what instructions to give her, so I used the Inner Game process and asked her to give me an idea of how she would like it to sound. She replied, "If I could show you how I want it then I would not be asking you how to play it." We laughed. I suggested to her that on a scale from 1 to 10, she state how she was presently sustaining the chords. She replied, "About 4." I asked, "Could you sustain them less — in the opposite direction from the way you want to improve — to a 3?" She reluctantly demonstrated how she didn't want them to sound, and then evaluated her performance at a 2. Then I asked, "Without trying to make a high score, could you sustain a level of 5?" I knew it was only one degree more than where she began. This did not appear difficult for her as she played the passage. She surprised herself and gave her performance an 8. She was amazed that she almost completely solved her problem. I asked her what she had found different between the performance that was a 2 and the one that was an 8. Her response, after thinking carefully, was a list of technical changes sounding like, "I kept the weight of my arms into the keyboard...relaxed my shoulders, and my pedal motion was quicker and more precise...heard the music in my head." I pointed out to her that after establishing clear goals, all she had done was to become aware of the present without passing judgments. Then she began to move naturally toward her goal without having to "try" to produce all the individual changes that had taken place.

Tim further explained the learning process through using a model triangle to illustrate how will, awareness, and trust skills are developed to increase "relaxed concentration."

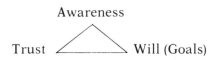

After establishing a goal (will) of what needs to be changed, we increase our awareness of "what is"

without judging or trying to change it, by using our senses of sound, feeling, sight, and our mental perception. We are able to begin to trust the wisdom of the body and brain through exercises designed to allow us to rely on Self II to learn and perform. This enables us to keep our mind in the present, maintaining our concentration and confidence without being distracted by doubts and fears of the past or future.

I was excited to find a process that I could use to change my behavior. I had always found it difficult to concentrate while playing the bass in a large ensemble (band or orchestra). By applying the Inner Game triangle whenever my concentration lapsed, I was able to meet my goal of becoming more involved in the music. I used my awareness skills and began listening to how my bass part fit into the ensemble, how it worked by itself, and how it blended with the bass section. I used my eyes to see how well I could watch the conductor while seeing my music and myself playing the bass. I enjoyed the physical feeling of the resistance of the bow and the vibrations of my bass. Finally, I used my mind to understand the music I was playing. I thought about how my part was written to portray the rhythm, the harmony, the melody, and the meaning of the music. I soon became able to recognize when Self I began to interfere by thinking in the past or future. I was aware when Self I told me, "I'm looking at the clock," that "I should decide what I am going to eat for dinner," or "I wonder if the conductor just heard the mistake I made." I allowed Self I to exist but at the same time gently guided my attention to the music, my bass, the sights, sounds, feelings, and meanings of the music I was playing. I found myself so busy and involved in the rehearsal that I rarely had the opportunity to lose my concentration.

My tennis lesson continued as I let go of my initial self-consciousness. Tim explained, "We are going to shoot a make-believe film of you playing tennis but the camera will never show where your ball lands. Don't worry about the accuracy of your shots. Just enjoy swinging and assume the role of your favorite tennis player." I decided to "become" Bjorn Bjorg because he impressed me as being in complete control of himself. Without conscious effort, my strokes became smooth, my footwork coordinated, and my level of enjoyment soared. The funny thing was that my shots were amazingly accurate even though I was not trying to hit them in the court.

In Canada I used this same technique during a demonstration of the use of role playing in music. I told a violinist that we were going to film a make-believe movie of her playing the violin; however, her sound would be replaced by a recording of her favorite violinist. She should play without worrying about making mistakes, poor intonation, or phrasing. Her job was to imitate the appropriate visual qualities and spirit of the music. She chose to imitate Arthur Grumyo because she said his performance of the Mozart concerto was like the quality of spring and sunshine. She assumed a proud and confident posture while her playing was immediately light, free, and accurate. The shift into her ideal mode was a movement into her Self II — playing in the present, expressing the realities of her experience with the sound of spring and the qualities of sunshine that gave meaning to her music. Because her performance was being dubbed by her idol, Grumyo, Self I had no opportunity to distract, interfere, or criticize her own playing.

My tennis lesson was concluded on a similar note. Role playing Bjorg, I was exuberant and no longer concerned about making a good impression with Tim. Self II led my concentration into the process of discovery, through awareness, trust and will. Later, in pondering how effortlessly I learned, I realized that Tim gave no instructions on how to swing the racket, where to place my feet or position my body. Through Tim's questions, I established my goals, pointing my attention to the areas I felt needed to change. Instead of focusing on how I was doing, my mind was busy on the experience of playing — increasing my awareness of the present and establishing goals so changes became effortless and easy.

As a teacher, I had some initial apprehension that this process would sometimes be time-consuming, but I've found I can help my students learn to listen and establish goals by providing them with quick alternatives. For example, if I hear bad intonation, instead of stating, "You are out of tune," I ask, "Is the B sharp or flat?" The student listens and decides, "I believe it is flat," thus becoming involved in the learning process, and heightening his ability to hear and discriminate intonation. The Inner Game teacher guides the students' attention toward making choices, establishing goals, and assuming responsibility for changes. Serving as a guide or coach does not bruise student egos but enhances their confidence and eliminates a dependency on the teacher for all the answers.

Of course, this is only a brief introduction to the possibilities of playing and winning the Inner Game in music teaching and performance. I've found that learning the inner skills of awareness, will, and trust is a process that requires patience and commitment, but one which is well worth the effort involved. I see that it is possible to overcome mental obstacles and free myself and others to perform, learn, and enjoy to our fullest potential. ■

○ ○ ○ ○ ○ ○ ○ ○ ○

The American String Teachers Association (A.S.T.A.) will sponsor Timothy Gallwey and Barry Green in a lecture-demonstration at this year's M.E.N.C. convention on February 12th in San Antonio, Texas. Green will also present an Inner Game lecture at the M.T.N.A. national convention on March 21-22 in Kansas City, Kansas.

Readers who are interested in sharing experiences in applying Inner Game techniques to music, learning about a teacher's conference in the spring of 1982, or being included on a mailing list of Inner Game activities, should write to Barry Green at 3449 Lyleburn Place, Cincinnati, Ohio.

The Inner Game of Music

by Barry Green

This is the first book written about the Inner Game principles of "natural learning" that applies this methodology to a subject matter outside the area of sports. I am pleased that this should be the case for several reasons, since sports and music share similarities that are relevant within a learning context.

People "play" sports and "play" music, yet both involve hard work and discipline. Both are forms of self-expression which require a balance of spontaneity and structure, technique, and inspiration. Both demand a degree of mastery over the human body, and yield immediately apparent results which can give timely feedback to the performer. Since both sports and music are commonly performed in front of an audience, they also provide an opportunity for sharing the enjoyment of excellence, as well as the experience of pressures, fears, and the excitement of ego involvement.

The primary discovery of the Inner Game is that, especially in our culture of achievement-oriented activities, human beings significantly get in their own way. The point of the Inner Game of sports or music is always the same — to reduce mental interferences that inhibit the full expression of human potential. What this book offers is a way to acknowledge and overcome these obstacles in order to bring a new quality to the experience and learning of music.

I found that much of the self-interference in the practice of sports originated in the way they were taught. The Inner Game sports books presented a radically different approach to learning. Techniques for heightened performance were successfully conveyed, without the normal frustrations and self-judgments that tend to

take the joy out of learning and playing the game. In *The Inner Game of Music* Barry Green has translated these methods in a way that promises to bring new life and learning possibilities to this field of endeavor.

Since the success of *The Inner Game of Tennis* in the mid-seventies, many people have approached me to co-author Inner Game books on a variety of subjects. Barry was excited by the results he had achieved with *Inner Skiing*, and wanted to write a book applying the methodology to music. "You know, Tim," he exclaimed to me, "I could write a book on the Inner Game of music, almost by just changing a few key words in any of your other books. It's all the same magic; it will work anywhere!"

I'd often thought about the possibility of cranking out simple "translations" of the Inner Game into different fields. But I felt it was important for Inner Game methods to be re-created to reflect the unique and special aspects of a particular subject. I asked, "Barry, how would you like to take two or three years and explore the possibilities that the Inner Game might bring to the field of music? Explore them in your playing with the symphony, and with your students, develop methods and new techniques, and then refine them when you have some experience in using them. Then, when there is sufficient evidence that the technology is feasible and workable, we might think about doing a book to share what we have learned with others."

What distinguished Barry Green is that he accepted this challenge, and didn't speak to me about writing a book for nearly three years. During this time he did literally thousands of hours of research and experimentation with his own performances and in his teaching. Barry's commitment to making a difference in the way music is learned takes this book out of the

realm of clever theory. It is a book that succeeds as a practical guide for improving the quality of music experience.

— Timothy Gallwey

Playing Together

One of the hardest things to do in an ensemble is to play together. I have found it very helpful to focus on another voice, whether I'm playing the melody, a countermelody, or an accompaniment figure. I find it is natural when I'm playing a secondary part to let my mind "sing along" with the main melody.

When you're playing the melody, you can make up a duet with yourself. When another instrument is playing a part that relates naturally to your own, you can "internalize" its part while playing yours. You don't have to memorize the other part to do this; just allow your inner voice to ride the line, and sense how it fits in with your own part.

This technique increases your awareness of the rhythm, volume, tone, counterpoints, and harmonies of the entire piece. It helps you play along with others in tune and with accurate rhythm, and it also makes you feel more a part of the overall musical effect. I don't feel as isolated and overwhelmed in larger ensembles as I used to, and I find that orchestral playing can be as challenging and exciting as playing in a chamber ensemble of five or six players.

I encourage you to experiment with "singing along" in your next ensemble rehearsal and to notice any difference in your own awareness and how this can affect your playing.

Exercise: Playing Together

When you are playing or singing in an ensemble, allow yourself to sing along in this way with another part. You will find this increases your musical feedback and that you will be able to play your own part with more accuracy, sensitivity, and meaning than before.

Let's take an example from this excerpt from Beethoven's Fifth Symphony, second movement, *Andante con moto*. Since you can't be all the instruments in a string section at one time, you'll need to grasp the general principles from this example and then apply them in real rehearsal with your ensemble.

1. Suppose you're playing the cello part. In the beginning you play the melody in unison with the violas. Sing the melody as you play, and see whether you're with the rest of the section.

2. Repeat the exercise, this time playing the melody and singing along with the bass pizzicato. Does this affect your rhythmic accuracy? Does it enhance your understanding of the harmony?

3. Now imagine you are the basses playing pizzicato. Sing the melody in the violas and cellos to yourself as you play the bass rhythm. When you sing the first two pickup notes to yourself, is it easier for you to know when to play your downbeat? How does singing the 32nd-notes in the melody affect the way you phrase the eighth notes? Does following the melody create any overall phrasing for your pizzicato? Do you notice any subtle changes in the dynamics when you follow the melody in this way?

4. Now look at the second phrase of the Beethoven:

5. If you play the cello line (viola, cello, and bass together), sing along with the violins who are carrying the melody.

6. Notice your ability to play together with the other instruments in your section after you sing the three violin notes that precede your entrance.

7. In the second measure, can you feel all the instruments playing together on the downbeat after the 16th-note pickups in the preceding measure?

8. Pay attention to your volume, so that you can still hear and follow the melody over your own part.

9. Does your awareness that all the instruments are moving into crescendo together affect the volume at which you play? Notice whether your crescendo covers up

the melody.

10. How does the information you receive by singing along with another part in your head relate to the cues you're receiving from the conductor? Are the conductor's cues more meaningful and relevant to your part?

Here are some other awareness exercises that can help you integrate your sound into that of the ensemble. Notice how your sight, sound, feeling, and understanding can increase your feedback from other parts of the ensemble and thus help you in your own interpretation and performance.

Exercise: Visual Awareness

1. Notice which musical voices (melody, inner voice, rhythm, countermelody, bass line, etc.) the conductor is gesturing toward.

2. Watch and notice how the conductor's facial expression, hands, body, and baton reflect the meaning the conductor wants to draw from the particular voice he's conducting.

3. Notice how the bow directions, bow placement, articulations, and attacks reflect the sound quality and the intensity of the music.

4. Watch the physical movements of the other members of your section as they prepare for an entrance.

5. With your eyes a little out of focus, see how many different aspects of the performance you can watch without focusing on one

particular object. Your music? Yourself, your posture and handling of your instrument? The conductor? The performance space? The stand? The colleagues in your own section?

6. Notice when your visual attention is drawn specifically to one of these areas.

Exercise: Sound Awareness

1. Listen for the ways in which your part reflects the meaning, nuances, colors, character, and other emotional and expressive elements in the music.

2. Hear how your instrument is blending in with the person next to you, with the section as a whole, and with the other instruments who are playing the same or related parts.

3. Notice the blend, volume, contrast, and rhythmic interplay of any two voices (bass and tenor, soprano and second soprano, rhythm and melody, etc.).

4. Sing along (in your head) with a part that complements your own.

5. Be aware of the pitch of the other instruments that are closest to your own range. Follow the intervals created by the two voices — the octaves, thirds, unisons, dissonances, and consonances.

6. Listen for the voice that has the closest rhythmic interplay with your own. Notice if you are playing with these instruments or if your pulse is ahead of or behind them.

March, 1992

7. Notice whether your attacks and releases are ahead of, with, or behind the rest of your section.

8. When you're playing an accompaniment figure, play at a volume that still allows you to hear the more important voices in another part of the orchestra. (In the Beethoven example given earlier, the basses would play at a piano level so they could still hear the violas and cellos carrying the melody.)

Exercise: Feeling Awareness

1. Notice any feelings of resistance or tension in your hands, arms, body, or voice as you play or sing.

2. Because you cannot always hear other voices that are playing similar parts to your own, examine how much feedback your body can give you with regard to pitch and rhythmic accuracy, and the balance and meaning of the music.

3. Notice the feelings that are expressed in the music by your instrument, the other voices, and the entire ensemble.

4. Notice how these feelings are reflected in your own body as you perform. Where in your body do you feel the different emotions and musical vibrations?

Exercise: Knowing Awareness

1. Pay attention to the personal background of the composer, the history of the work, and the time in which the piece was written. How can you reflect this knowledge in your own playing?

2. Let your awareness of the form, style, and construction of the piece illuminate the significance of your own part. How does your part fit into the introduction? Into thematic statements? The development? Recaps? The coda? The ending?

3. Notice the meaning of the specific sounds in your part and the way in which your part relates to the complete texture in terms of emotional quality, story line, static sounds, transitional material, etc.

4. Be aware of the function your particular voice has in relationship to the texture of the music as a whole. Are you playing the melody, the rhythm, an inner voice? What does your voice add to the texture and color?

You can select from among these exercises, or invent your own means of focusing your awareness on your own part, the parts that interact with yours, and the entire ensemble. These exercises will help you to feel more fully involved in your playing in larger and smaller groups, add color and precision to your performance, add to your experience and enjoyment of the music you are playing, and hopefully, bring back some more of that musical magic that can turn ensemble playing from something you take for granted into a challenge and a delight. ∎

Music's Inner Game

by Barry Green

Tennis professional Timothy Gallwey developed a method of mental exercises, known as the inner game, as a result of his observing how the best coaches worked, how coaching styles sometimes helped or hindered students, and how a student's thought processes affect tennis play. His study of mental interference led Gallwey to question his teaching, when he discovered strategies that the best coaches and tournament players used.

The method of the inner game is based on teaching a student to do what comes naturally, and how to avoid references to specific pitfalls and habits acquired from primary school and beyond. In this sense the method is not a new technique, but follows naturally from what is the best, most natural, easiest, and most graceful way to play.

Tim Gallwey wrote *The Inner Game of Tennis* to express his insights, and the success of this first book led to books on skiing and golf. While the method is not a technique, it is a natural approach codified that consists of a number of mental exercises and techniques of control that can improve playing music, golf, or whatever.

As principal bassist with the Cincinnati Symphony for the past 24 years, a university professor, and parent of young musicians, I developed this method as the most natural and effective way for teacher and student or conductor and ensemble to work together. It suggests a style of rehearsal and performance that involves everyone in the ensemble and allows the conductor and musicians to recreate a composer's score efficiently and effectively. This way no one will be plagued by boredom, pressure to achieve results, intimidation, confusion, or the mechanical reading of rhythms and notes; the emphasis is entirely on the music.

I have played under conductors who ran rehearsals that are consistent with the approach, but who have never heard of the method. These conductors are among the best in the business, and we should follow their example because they have discovered what is most natural and works best. Without formulating their discoveries in this particular way, they too have been using the method. We can all take greater advantage of these natural and inherently successful styles of rehearsal. Using a structured and codified approach to fine tune a rehearsal, as if the rehearsal itself were an instrument, is the secret of playing with ensembles.

Consider the curious little word *try*. Only three letters long, it trips off the tongue easily. We may scarcely be aware we're using it, but that little word implies that something we are doing is difficult and requires special effort. When we hear that word, we often translate the extra effort directly into body tension. We tense a wrist muscle as we try a difficult passage, adding the difficulty of a tense wrist to other problems. Along with tense muscles, we close down our senses ("When I try too hard, I find myself squeezing my eyes shut . . .").

When we have tried our best, we evaluate the effort on the basis of whether we succeeded or failed. If we succeeded, we probably want to repeat our success. If we failed, we try even harder and begin another cycle of effort that often continues until we fail. These successes and failures add up to an exhausting and unnecessary struggle with ourselves that has little to do with making music.

Avoid using the word *try* in teaching. It's not impossible, and you will discover such phrases as "play it again," "notice if you were . . . ," "now I want you to repeat the passage," or "see if you can . . . ." The first step is to notice how often you use the word *try*. Just being aware of that will make it easier to find other ways to express what you intend to say; just don't try too hard.

Following inner game guidelines may change the way you rehearse and teach, but members of your ensemble may be reluctant to change their ways. Even though you give instructions, you need enthusiastic participation from the ensemble.

Since I began working with this system, I have observed a number of public school and professional ensembles and noticed significant differences in both rehearsals and concerts at all levels of competence. These are not the natural differences between ensembles at varying levels of competence, but differences in musical expression that can exist at any difficulty and age level. The Suzuki approach, for example, allows young musicians to sing with their instruments, have fun, make music, and reach their audience at an amazingly early age.

Regardless of the age or level of the ensemble, the more successful groups go about their playing in a qualitatively different way from those who are struggling. Specifically, I have noticed that in many ensembles most problems can be traced to the printed page.

When reading our parts, we are in effect reading musical instructions while we play music, similar to reading a road map while driving. If you wanted to ride a bicycle or drive a car in a strange city, you would probably first study your map; if you got lost, you might pull over to look at your map and find out where you were before going any farther. You certainly wouldn't try to drive an unfamiliar freeway system while gazing at the map.

This analogy applies to music, yet as musicians, many of us have become adept at following a complicated music map with our eyes, carrying out instructions for notes, rhythms, dynamics, articulations, expressions, tempo cues, fingerings, bowings, and breath markings, while attempting to play accurately, follow the conductor, and make music.

Players may even hear an inner voice saying, "Get the notes right, watch those rhythms, follow the beat, no mistakes please, now smile, play your best so we can get a number one rating." This is much like having a back-seat driver.

The ensembles that struggle are usually the same ones that appear to follow a musical map in reading their parts. These students and colleagues say, "The music is on the page. All I have to do is play the right notes in the right place and wait to be told if I'm right or wrong, too loud or soft,

early or late."

Compare this type of performance to that of the great ensembles (at any age level) that know the music. These musicians are not reading; rather, they are feeling the music and have a sense of spontaneity. Both conductor and musicians are involved in the whole sound as they recreate the composer's intentions. Through their understanding they express the character of the piece. The music isn't written in black and white notes on the page; it is inside the musicians and they are able to communicate it.

Many ensembles eventually reach this level by concert time, after many rehearsals and any amount of blood, sweat, and anxiety. Yet if we take care of these aspects of the music at the beginning, we can make the best use of rehearsal time, and the players can reach their potential.

When we play tennis or golf or football, there's an opponent — the other team, and other players. We measure our success by how we compare with this opponent, and in many sports, though not in golf, this opponent or opposing team will actively try to make life difficult for us. When we play against this outer opponent, the skills we use are the skills most coaches cultivate: a strong serve or drive, which in music may be the rapid fingering of an arpeggio.

The inner game, by contrast, is played against a different opponent, the inner opponent, who lives inside the player. It is the part of you that doubts, evaluates, judges, disapproves, exhorts, and flusters you. It is usually not a single opponent, but a team of inner voices. When you lose against this invisible, internal opponent, it seriously interferes with your performance in the outer game.

In terms of music, the outer game involves following instructions properly and playing the correct notes. The goal is to play well or to win the competition. There is nothing wrong with those goals, and the inner game approach doesn't mean giving up playing the outer game or winning. However, any pressure to play well or win a competition strengthens our inner game opponent and makes our goals harder to achieve.

When we are free of voices of doubt, judgment, and confusion, we can listen to and feel the music and understand the function of our parts within the ensemble. By developing the three inner game skills of awareness, will, and trust, we can make a deeper contact with the music.

First, awareness means the players are in touch with what is happening in the music. If a teacher or conductor suggests something a player does is right or wrong, good or bad, he is judging the player, not making him aware of the music. By assessing performance without making the player aware of his part in the music, the teacher or conductor joins the player's inner opposing team.

Awareness exercises simply put musicians in touch with some part of what they can see, hear, feel, or understand about the music. These exercises deal with sights, sounds, feelings, and musical understanding. When a conductor asks the flutes to play softly enough to still hear the strings, this is an awareness instruction concerning sound. It encourages each musician to be aware of his own dynamic level and to participate in the sound of the entire ensemble. Using superficially similar instructions, such as telling flutes they are too loud because you can't hear the strings, involves a judgment.

Take, for example, the opening of Ravel's *Daphnis et Chloe* in which the flutes play a passage of sixty-fourth notes in the low to middle registers. Many flutists panic at the sight of so much black ink on the page. However, being aware of how the flute part fits into the entire score makes it easier to play. The flute line only adds a murmuring effect to the music. When the player is aware of how softly he should play to produce the effect, the fingering becomes effortless.

Next, using the skill of will helps create direction and intensity in the music. This involves knowing what to do, then doing it the way it is supposed to be done. Our bodies and minds strive to do what is best and what works most naturally. This natural process creates a bond between the player and the music, and will exercises strengthen this bond.

Typically, will exercises deal with musical interpretation or how the music should sound. They focus on what needs to be accomplished musically and call forth the commitment that is needed to do it. Besides using will for musical interpretation, it can be used for non-judgmental technical instructions. It is primarily the conductor's responsibility to communicate this musical interpretation to the musicians: "This allegro needs to move faster and build excitement to the coda."

Closely linked to interpretation is the question of how one should play the piece on a particular instrument. Using will exercises, such instructions as, "Flutes, play in the third register and use a hard articulation" will improve performance. In some ensembles fellow musicians or the principal players can give assistance like this, while other players will need help from their conductors or teachers.

When a player has trouble interpreting and performing an unusual rhythmic notation, instead of avoiding or omitting it, he can use the skill of will to understand how it should sound, when the same figure is played by another instrument. Using a different articulation, such as the clarinet's *du* instead of the flute's *tu* can facilitate the passage. Problems in blending can be eliminated by realizing the significance of a pitch within the overall harmonic scheme. When a part includes a difficult fingering, instead of playing it unevenly or succumbing to its technical difficulty, a player using the skill of will can find and use an alternate fingering.

The final category of trust deals with what musicians ultimately express when they play. When the notes, rhythms, pitches, and technique are clearly understood through will, trust skills allow you to transform this understanding into musical expression. This involves trusting the energy of the music and flowing with its excitement, beauty, love, grief, or precision; sensing that the music evokes thoughts of a forest, an ocean, a festival, an explosion, or stillness. When musicians give in to these aspects of the music, they transcend the merely technical level of playing and feel the composer's inspiration.

By developing awareness, will, and trust skills, you will enjoy increased focus on the music and less interference from judgments by inner voices. Technical problems will seemingly solve themselves without any overt attention to them. The enthusiasm of individual players builds and is infectious within an ensemble.

You will notice a change in students' attitudes. Instead of rehearsals or lessons that are marathons in reading notes and rhythms or following instructions, you may experience higher levels of playing that are more like chamber music.

As I travel across the country conducting clinics, musicians have many questions regarding how the inner game can improve their playing. I have included several of these questions to illustrate how inner game concepts can be applied to musical challenges.

When I play a difficult piece I have problems and lose my confidence. I think about it being difficult and I know I will stumble and make mistakes. As a result, when I get to a tricky passage, I either slow it down or mess it up. My teacher has told me to trust myself because I know the notes. What else can I do?

There is a big difference between blind trust and trusting what is trustworthy. The critical question you should ask yourself is where your attention should be when you get to those fast notes. Your problem is that your attention and energy are in many places. What works for your teacher, or even yourself in practice, may not work during a performance. Under the most difficult conditions, what works best is often the least likely choice.

An example of this is the experience of learning to ride a bicycle. Do you remember the feeling of traveling fast over a smooth surface and then suddenly hitting rough, bumpy gravel? The same feeling happens when skiing smoothly downhill and then encountering bumpy snow or small moguls, or running down a hill with rocks or other obstacles. In each of these situations or in playing a Bach sonata, the natural instinct is to slow down, and protect oneself from getting hurt (or making a mistake). If it is impossible to slow down sufficiently because the speed is too fast, chances are you will stumble and fall. Yet the last thing one thinks of doing is aggressively going into the hazardous spot.

When riding a bicycle over rough terrain, the best way to maintain control is to relax. Tension makes us feel heavier and inhibits our ability to respond instinctively. Occasionally the body can negotiate quickly and more naturally without conscious effort.

There is a big difference between believing or hoping something will work and using what works best for you. Sometimes it is better to trust the feeling of calmness or beauty. At other times the most musical playing comes from being reckless, playful, or vivacious. When going down a hill, trust your feet to balance and carry you. In music trust your fingers to move by themselves without mentally directing them to be too cautious. Trust the numerical tempo marking, but also trust the feeling or character implied by the marking.[1]

Explore what is the most trustworthy way to bring life to the music. Practice the section in a variety of ways, and be certain that your body knows the notes well enough to play without reading the music. Then experiment by playing the passage in many different ways. Trust the steady beating of the metronome, and trust yourself to play the piece without making any mistakes. Let go of the need for accuracy so you can play with vitality and energy. Play with reckless abandon, and permit yourself to make mistakes. Play again and concentrate on a feeling of excitement. Another time let your fingers go wild. Of all these ways to play, decide which comes closest to being the sound you want.

Once you have concluded what sounds best, when you play that same passage again, return to what works. Trust the most trustworthy version. Don't return to the cautious, tentative feelings that never sounded right. By drawing from the most appropriate feeling, energy, quality, or experience, you can recreate the best sound every time. It may be a little scary, but it is more trustworthy.

I have been successful in small competitions, seating auditions for school ensembles, and even regional state auditions. However, when I audition for All-State or large summer music festivals I do not play my best. Auditioning for a prestigious music school will be impossible. How can I block out this pressure and succeed?

It sounds as though you play well for low risk auditions, but when you feel pressure to succeed you don't play as well. Succeeding in auditions has absolutely nothing to do with performing the music correctly. Perhaps the thought of being successful is preventing you from performing your best. One way to deal with this problem is to neutralize your need to succeed. Do this by giving yourself permission to fail. Do not focus on the result of your performance; rather, concentrate on playing the music. This is the purpose of performing in the first place, so it is a worthy effort.

The need to succeed or win in competition is commonly dramatized in sports. When the game is on the line, players who feel pressure to be heroes, make the shot, score the touchdown, hit the home run, or make the goal often fail. Yet a world-class athlete who

¹From "Techniques of Trust" from *Inner Game of Music* by Barry Green with W. Timothy Gallwey, published by Doubleday, 1986.

is successful under the pressure of competition has uncanny mental concentration.

Focus on the basics of fundamental technique: breath support, tone, accurate rhythm, dynamics, and interpretation. Concentrating on the task of playing the music as it should sound is demanding; don't add the pressure of winning to making music.

While concentrating on making music without pressure of winning, consider strengthening your commitment to the music. One of the three primary skills of the inner game is the skill of will, but will or commitment by itself is meaningless. Will is like a strong glue that cements the player inseparably to the music.

Believe the best professionals in sports and music. If you become distracted in your playing by thinking about winning, it will take away from performance. Know your stuff, and glue yourself to the music. Then relax and enjoy just doing it.

This is the time of year for seating auditions in our band. I know I play much better than my competition, and in rehearsals and concerts I play well. Every time I play a seating audition, though, I see the judges in front of me and lose my concentration. All I can think of is, "How can I get my fingers to stop shaking?" My tone is nervous; I make stupid mistakes I never made before and know I will not make the first chair. What can I do to play the way I know I am capable of playing and skip the horrors of auditions?

The problem is that you are playing an audition and not playing the music. Your best auditions are not auditions. Consider what you are thinking when you play in rehearsal. Perhaps you hear the other instruments playing when you play your part; you may hear the others in your section. When playing in the band, you probably try to play in tune, blend with your colleagues, and enjoy the music.

If your function is different when playing your audition – if your purpose is now to win the first chair – you have changed your attitude and purpose in playing. No longer are you trying to blend, play with your section, and enjoy the music, but you are trying to do all that as well as win the chair, stop the shaking hands, avoid mistakes, and impress your teachers. You can only do so many things at once. Taking on all these outer games makes your task twice as difficult as the music demands. Here are two different suggestions for dealing with this problem; explore one or the other

but not both at the same time.

As a means of silencing the voice in your head instead of listening to these concerns, doubts, and fears of doom and gloom, replace those with the sound of your instrument. Every time you hear your inner voice talking, listen to your tone. It is difficult to hear two things at once, so listening to your sound will put you in touch with the music. That may attract your interest and help you hear what you are doing. When you hear your musical voice, you are in a better position to make adjustments to your playing. This uses the inner game concentration skill of awareness (of sound) to silence the distracting voice.

Apart from listening to your sound, you can explore the use of imagery to change the hostile, unnatural setting of the audition to a friendly imaginary rehearsal where you play your best. If you are playing in an empty band room with two teachers sitting in front at a desk, pen and paper in hand, you can instead transform your imaginary playing position to your favorite seat in the band. Imagine your colleagues around you playing their parts; the room is full, the teachers are now part of the flute section and following the conductor. Instead of hearing your music as a solo piece, listen in your imagination for the other instruments in your section so that you hear the sound of the entire band as you play. If you are playing a solo piece that you only play in your home, then transform the setting of the cold room into the friendly confines of your practice space, where you are comfortable and confident. Play as if you are at home; the chairs in front of you are now your living room window, the teachers are sitting where your couch rests under your favorite picture.

The extent to which you believe in what you are doing by focusing on one of these two techniques will determine your success. If you focus 50% on the technique, 25% on worry about the judges, and 25% on worry about the technique working, then you pollute the exercise and will be less successful. However, if you can completely block out the distractions and focus your attention 100% on the musical sound or friendly playing environment, then you will be safe and the music will flow. Trust what works for the music, repeat a technique not for the purpose of repeating a success, but just to put you back in touch with the music; then just let it happen. □

643

Jazz Rehearsal Techniques

by Charles L. Booker, Jr.

Jazz has its own history, traditions, composers, leaders, conductors, and soloists, and the father of modern jazz bands was Fletcher Henderson. While performing at the Roseland Ballroom in 1923, he felt his band needed a hot jazz soloist, so he sent for Louis Armstrong, who was performing in Chicago with King Oliver's Creole Jazz Band. Armstrong joined Henderson's band in New York for nine months in 1924, and his rhythmic ideas, the basis of his swing style solos, had a sensational effect on the Henderson band, especially its arranger and composer, Don Redman. Redman and Henderson laid the foundation of the modern jazz band after Armstrong's visit, and by the mid 1930s, the exciting jazz band arrangements and compositions of Fletcher Henderson and Duke Ellington, and the hard swinging riff bands of Bennie Moten and Count Basie, set the stage for the wide popularity of the big bands of the 1935-45 swing era.

Benny Goodman described Henderson's arranging style as using an ensemble passage, or section of the band, in a unison melodic line in much the same way a soloist would play while improvising. Goodman felt that in all aspects Henderson's ideas were "far ahead of anybody else's at the time" and that by 1934 the instrumentation for large bands became standardized with five brass, four saxes, and four rhythm, whereas ten was the previous limit for even a large orchestra. By late 1934 Goodman had 36 Fletcher Henderson arrangements according to Marshall Stearns in *The Story of Jazz*.

By the mid 1940s jazz band instrumentation was much as it is today with a four piece rhythm section (piano, bass, drums, and guitar), five saxophones (two altos, two tenors, and baritone), four trombones (three tenors and one bass), and four or five trumpets.

Over the years compositions have developed with more dissonant harmony, larger forms, complex meters, and a combination of styles. Soloists have led the way by making innovative advances in improvisation and jazz bands have followed the lead; assimilating complex arrangements with soloists bringing about a new and higher level of musical performance.

As in classical music, articulation is important in defining jazz styles. Articulation in the performance of Mozart's music is quite different from that used in Mahler; likewise, the bands of Fletcher Henderson and Stan Kenton articulate the same phrase differently. Generally, jazz performers use the legato syllable "du" instead of "tu". Many young players not only use an attack that is too staccato, but fail to master the $\frac{12}{8}$ or triplet swing feel. Eighth notes in jazz are played differently depending on style, tempo, and era of the composition. The last note in a phrase of running eighth notes is normally short, but the length depends on the tempo. An example of swing eighth notes is the following:

Latin music, rock, and ballads are usually performed with even eighth notes, but swing ballads and slow blues charts are played with a $\frac{12}{8}$ or triplet feel. When arrangers do not indicate straight eighths or swing, familiarity with jazz styles and rhythmic figures helps determine which to use.

Rhythm sections are often the weakest link in jazz bands because the piano, guitar, and bass parts can be little more than a sketch with chord symbols and slashed lines. When parts provide so little information, rhythm sections of inexperienced musicians can sound chaotic. Each member of the section should know his function, within his section, and within the band. While projecting energy to the band and audience, rhythm sections should be precise, but not stiff; together, yet loose.

In setting the rhythmic pulse and basic interpretation of style, the drummer should not play too loud or develop too complicated rhythms. Working closely with the bassist to establish a steady tempo, he should study the score or brass parts to locate the ensemble sections.

The bassist is the anchor of the band, outlining the chord structure and adding to the pulse. He should sit next to the drummer's hi-hat and listen

Chief Warrant Officer Charles Booker, Jr. is the director of the Jazz Ambassadors of the United States Army Field Band, the official touring jazz band of the U.S. Army. He studied with jazz composer Hank Levy and has published works with Kendor Music.

Seating Arrangement

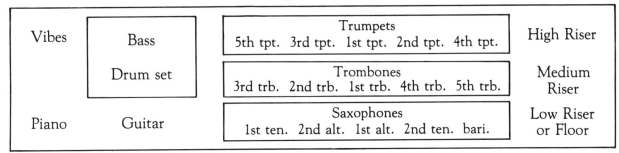

Vibes	Bass	Trumpets 5th tpt. 3rd tpt. 1st tpt. 2nd tpt. 4th tpt.	High Riser
	Drum set	Trombones 3rd trb. 2nd trb. 1st trb. 4th trb. 5th trb.	Medium Riser
Piano	Guitar	Saxophones 1st ten. 2nd alt. 1st alt. 2nd ten. bari.	Low Riser or Floor

to the accent on two and four; they should become a cohesive rhythmic unit.

The pianist plays rhythmic fills as needed and should use the music only as a guide, not necessarily playing everything written on the page and omitting monotonous or busy portions. During ensemble sections he should listen carefully and add only a note, figure, or ornament that furthers the composer's intent. The master of this technique was Count Basie.

The guitarist shares responsibility with the pianist for playing chords. On a swing piece he often plays four beats to the bar using two to four strings and no bar chords. Freddie Green of the Basie Orchestra was famous for this style of playing. The guitarist and the pianist should decide ahead of time who will accompany behind the soloist; too many layers of rhythmic figures will convey an unsettling, busy effect to the soloist and audience.

The seating arrangement of any musical ensemble affects the balance, blend, and cohesion. The majority of bands use one seating arrangement which has evolved from the jazz bands of the 1920s through the swing era to today.

This set-up aligns the lead players in the middle of the section for cohesion and consistent interpretation across the band. Section players should match the lead player's interpretation, sound, and articulation, playing, and breathing.

This seating puts the saxes close to the audience, keeps the bassist near the hi-hat, and groups the guitar and piano. The jazz soloists, usually the 5th trumpet, 3rd trombone, and 1st tenor saxophone are next to the rhythm section and will hear the chord progressions and sense the reaction of the rhythm section to their improvisation. The inspiration that soloists derive from this interplay creates an essential element of jazz, the excitement of improvisation.

Bands should be as close to the front of the stage as possible leaving room for the conductor and soloists to move easily to the front. For the best projection of sound brasses should keep the bells of their instruments above the stands, and saxes should stand for solos and soli sections.

Many conductors prefer the trumpets to stand when playing. This brightens the band's sound, and if they stand on a riser, the trombones should stand on the stage.

For enhanced visual effect put the bassist and drummer on a riser at the level of the trombones with the pianist and guitarist at stage level. The bassist, guitarist, and any electronic keyboard should raise their amplifiers to waist level to hear the on-stage volume. Many rhythm sections play at one dynamic level, while the rest of the band observes all dynamics, destroying the balance.

Some directors involve more youngsters in the jazz band program by having more than one person on a part. Because each instrument plays a different harmonic part, too much emphasis on any one part diminishes balance and intonation. A better idea is rotating musicians between pieces, giving each student a chance to play while preserving balance.

In *Jazz - Its Evolution and Essence* André Hodeir writes that "Swing is a certain way of making the rhythm come to life...it would really be impossible to overemphasize the fact that swing is an essentially rhythmic phenomenon." In swing a steady tempo from the rhythm section, with accents on two and four on the drummer's hi-hat, conveys the beat and where the notes should be placed. No matter what the figure or melodic line, placing the syncopated notes on the last third of the beat creates the swing effect.

Jazz bands should feel and sound relaxed while performing. Hodeir writes, "Relaxation plays an essential role in the production of swing. It is what gives the rhythm section's pulsation the bounce that characterizes swing; it is what makes it possible for the soloist to get everything in the right place without seeming to try." Many musicians play in the correct tempo, with proper phrasing and note placement, but cannot relax enough to swing. Some bands try to play so perfectly that the elements of excitement and drive are missing from the performance. Precision is important, but not at the expense of swing.

Good conductors need the skills and knowledge of theory, score analysis, and music history to develop a jazz band into an excellent performing ensemble. Some conductors are familiar with different jazz styles but fail to develop improvisation in rehearsals, and a few never teach improvisation which is the very essence of jazz. Without jazz solos, the audience might as well be listening to a concert band playing in different jazz styles.

In improvising a soloist chooses fragments of the melody and creates variations on it; the more modern the style, the less improvisation is based on the original theme. Soloists today create themes, paraphrasing above the chord progression, and understanding the relationship between melody and harmony. They introduce new notes, rests, embellishments, rhythms, and articulations.

Technical competence and the idiosyncrasies of the instrument are the only limitations to improvising. Soloists inherit musical tradition and develop their own style by practicing, transcribing solos, and imitating others. Each performance is the culmination of years of study, practice, and listening. Jazz musicians may refer to someone sounding like Parker or a comping style like Hines; Wynton Marsalis would not sound as he does if there had been no Roy Eldridge.

Jazz solos should have focus and continuity of thought, with the mood and style of the piece being a prime consideration. Practicing solos avoids monotony, lack of direction, and phrases haphazardly thrown together. Do not work out the solos with paper and pen, but study the melodic and harmonic content and develop solos in either solitary practice or jam sessions. Decide ahead of time what figure, motif, or device to begin with, when to move on, where to recap or summarize, and how to end. Planning out solos increases continuity and smooth presentation of musical ideas, but planning should not take the place of improvisation. The same secure, routine solo performed many times is not improvisation but a written cadenza.

Jim Snidero, a jazz saxophonist living in New York City, stated that dedicated jazz soloists should memorize one piece of music a week by writing a song in a music notebook, learning the melody on their instrument, playing the chord progression from memory on the piano, and listening to recordings by different artists, transcribing at least one improvised solo and memorizing it in a different key. Snidero does not encourage buying and memorizing published, transcribed solos but believes it is crucial that musicians learn improvised solos in context, from a recording to understand the soloist's ideas and hear how other musicians from the group added to or inspired him.

Jazz is a young art form, and its evolution can be fully documented through recordings and music manuscripts. There's no way to know how the music of Mozart or Beethoven sounded when originally performed, but that is not the case with jazz. Through recordings it is possible to listen and study the original performances of Louis Armstrong's *Gut Bucket Blues*, Duke Ellington's *Mood Indigo* or Fletcher Henderson's *Wrappin' It Up*. Many books document the evolution of jazz, but little is written about the responsibilities of jazz band conductors because the position is a fairly new concept developed by music educators. Jazz conductors rarely direct an entire piece during a performance; most direction and guidance is given during rehearsals.

Jazz conductors should consider whether music is suitable for an audience and written within the band's capabilities. The conductor should know the purpose of the concert, age group of the audience, and what type of music they expect to hear, selecting music for both entertainment and enrichment.

Much music published today is taken from recordings of bands in Los Angeles and New York. Some conductors purchase these compositions and discover after much frustration that the band is incapable of performing them. Conductors should challenge and develop a jazz band, but not expose weaknesses to audiences. When young trumpet players struggle with high notes, sax players scuffle through soli, and rhythm sections are unable to maintain fast tempos or are panicked by complex meters, the problems leave no time to swing.

Before rehearsing the music selected, the conductor should learn the scores. There is more to conducting a jazz band than just counting off the tempo and sight-reading. Read the score as you would a book, from beginning to end without stopping. Most of the time the first page tells who wrote the piece, if it is a transcription, new arrangement, or original composition, whether standard instrumentation is used, and what the style and tempo are. Make a note of section solis, solos, repeats, modulations, unison figures, signs, and codas. With an understanding of the form, go to the piano and play through the chord progressions, melodies, countermelodies, and sections for improvisation. Use a pencil to mark where phrases begin, end, and overlap, noting dynamics and compositional techniques. Most jazz compositions are variations of a 12 bar blues, 32 bar song in ABAC or AABA form, or theme and variations. Jazz composers often use chord progressions of popular songs, but with a new melody; Duke Ellington used the chord progression from *I Got Rhythm* for *Cottontail*.

When the musical details and composer's intent are clear, find an original recording of the piece. Using the score and a pencil, listen to the recording, noting all the differences between the written music and the performance. Try listening to recordings of the same piece from various time periods. Scores and parts sometimes differ and have evolved. Duke Ellington's 1937 recording of *East St. Louis Toodle-oo*, is very different from the 1927 version. The published scores of the Count Basie orchestra were much different than actual performances, and Thad Jones' compositions were first recorded, then published. Listen to the ensemble or soli sections for nuances not found in the score but keep in mind that bands should strive to develop a personal style. As long as it is true to the composer's overall intent, every performance should be a new experience, not a perfect imitation of the original.

Successful performances are the result of rehearsal time with prepared conductors. I suggest breaking rehearsals into four segments, beginning with scales, sight-reading, and improvisation. Write out the circle of fifths on the blackboard. While the drummer establishes a medium swing tempo, have the band play major scales in swing eighth notes; separate each scale by a measure of rest but have the drums continue. Use this exercise in every rehearsal working in all forms of minor scales as well.

Sight-reading material should be placed in an established sight-reading folder and be music that helps solve ensemble, section, and individual problems in style, time, swing, blend, balance, and improvisation. Don't pick music that is technically difficult; you want to get past the notes and develop musicianship. Use just the rhythm section to open up a section in a sight reading piece for improvising. With the riff-band concept, trumpets, trombones, and saxophones can create harmonized riffs and call-response patterns. After sight-reading, continue by reviewing a piece recently learned and needing review but devote most rehearsal time to working on difficult sections of new music. Play a recording and have students match the style and nuances they hear, and even borrow ideas from the improvisations. Finish the rehearsal with a chart the band already knows, enjoys playing, and plays well.

Set aside time for jam sessions and encourage students to memorize bop tunes in unison. By learning the standard jazz format of head (exposition), individual solos (variations), trading fours (switching soloists every four bars, including the drummer as a soloist), head again (recapitulation), and then out (coda), improvisation technique will improve dramatically, making jazz band performances more exciting.

Conductors should learn to compromise between conducting too much and not conducting enough. For visual effect or musical emphasis enhance the performance by directing part of a section. In a soft ballad, conduct the exposition, high point, and last eight bars or coda and any holds, ritards, or changes in tempo. Never leave the stage; conductors are part of the performance and can inspire intensity from the bands, or prompt the audience to acknowledge the soloists.

Conductors who stand in front of the band beating time during a swing piece only interfere with the feel, and the band will never swing. Swing is felt and achieved by the performers, not the conductor. Young bands initially need help to keep time but will gradually gain confidence in their ability to swing. Through the efforts of music educators, big band music is alive and well. With interest and involvement at a high level, the future is bright for this original American art form.

References for a library might include *The Story of Jazz* by Marshall Stearns; *Bird Lives* by Ross Russell; *Jazz, A History* by Frank Tirro; *Music I My Mistress* by Duke Ellington; *Jazz Styles: History and Analysis*, Fourth Edition by Mark Gridley; *Inside The Score* by Ray Wright; *The Big Bands* by George Simon; *Jazz Masters of New Orleans* by Martin Williams; *Early Jazz and the Swing Era* by Gunther Schuller; *Good Morning Blues: The Autobiography of Count Basie* as told by Albert Murray; and *Duke Ellington, Benny Goodman, and the Swing Era* and *Louis Armstrong, An American Genius* by James Collier.

March, 1990

Thoughts on Jazz Education
An Interview with Rich Matteson
by Harvey Phillips

Rich Matteson is a legend among brass players and respected by his peers as a dedicated and effective jazz music educator. This was not always so. For years Rich was one of the best-kept secrets in jazz.

When I first heard Rich Matteson perform in a jazz club in Chicago in the late sixties I could not believe I had not heard of him before; he blew me away. I was embarrassed. After all, I had been an active professional tubist for 20 years and here was this incredible jazz euphonium player. The obscure status that went along with Rich's confinement to jazz clubs in Las Vegas and elsewhere was changed *when he became a jazz clinician and teacher.*

Extended contact with Rich in brass conferences and festivals here and abroad has been so musically rewarding that in 1975 it prompted us to form the Matteson-Phillips TubaJazz Consort. Rich is no stranger to me anymore, but I continue to be inspired by his playing, impressed by his dedication to music education and stimulated by his observations and metaphors: "In the training of young musicians, we need to bring about a better balance of 'higher' and 'hire' education." It is something to think about. Thanks, Rich.

— Harvey Phillips

What problems confront jazz music educators today?

Many colleges insufficiently prepare teachers for a life in public school music. They try to cover most of the bases, but they usually don't cover the base called jazz education. Most high schools now have a jazz band. No music education program would send a graduate out to teach without performing and conducting experience. It would not send someone out to lead a school's marching band without marching band experience; but colleges frequently send people to teach jazz band who have had no experience in the care and feeding of a jazz band. They don't know how to teach improvisation or even how to select music. Most colleges don't offer any courses on that, so the new band director has to learn on the job, using trial and error, creating a bad situation for all. The college didn't train him because it didn't think jazz education is worthwhile.

I'll never forget the first day I walked into class at the University of North Texas to teach improv. The class was 50 minutes long and there were 43 students. I looked them over and thought, "I have two complete jazz bands in here, I have so many kids!" Each kid would have time to play for less than a minute, then if I stopped to correct him, it would be chaotic. I knew that wouldn't work, so I broke it down into 12-15 kids in a class.

Colleges don't consider jazz music a valid art form. Many colleges have jazz bands because that helps them recruit, but they don't offer courses in jazz for those students. A college may have several hundred music students; over the course of four years, maybe forty of them get jazz experience; the rest leave school without any.

Do you feel that changes are being made to improve that situation?

Some schools are starting to make changes, but most schools are still fighting change. Many educators simply refuse to accord jazz the respect it deserves. For example, the University of North Texas has an incredible jazz program. The classical students who go to U.N.T. and become band directors graduate without taking any courses in teaching jazz band. No student who is going to be a band director should be allowed to graduate without concert band, marching band, and jazz band training. In all probability all three groups will cross their desks at one time or another.

So you're saying that we're really not preparing our music educators adequately in many instances to deal with today's music programs?

Harvey Phillips is Distinguished Professor of Music at Indiana University and Executive Editor of The Instrumentalist.

That is correct. Now, don't misunderstand; I am not finding fault with the existing training in classical music and even in marching band. That's always been pretty thorough, but jazz should be added. I'm not talking about replacing; I'm talking about adding. High school students want to have just as good a jazz band as they do a concert band. Some jazz bands play badly because the teacher hasn't had training. We would never permit our concert bands to perform at that level; yet, because it's jazz, it's good enough. That's what's wrong.

Of course, the fact is that the music business changes. Some people say we have to learn to live with that; I say we have to learn to work with that. I think one of the greatest tragedies is when a kid who is a marvelous player gets out of school and then has the privilege of sitting around waiting for someone to die so that he and 235 others can audition for that job. Nobody ever says to kids, "I'm going to train you how to earn a living before that guy dies."

The music business is difficult enough to earn a living at, but many times schools turn out musicians who are not competent in all styles of music. There are fewer than 30 symphony orchestras in the U.S. where a player can earn a full-time living performing on his instrument. If musicians learned the art of improvisation and reading jazz and commercial music, they would have a better chance at survival. Let's face it, you never know what kind of job you'll be asked to do when the phone rings.

When did you first realize the necessity of a music education?

After I got out of service and went on the road with a group I got quite an education. There wasn't the captive audience we had at the Army base, where you play at the enlisted men's club, and all these guys listen to you and clap. The truth is, they have no money and no place else to go. When you go out on the road and you play the same music, those people have a choice; they have money in their pockets, so they can leave if they want to. We were just awful; we were in no way prepared to be professional players. We thought we were; but it took me only a couple of weeks to figure out, "Hey, man, you're in trouble. You need to get an education." So I went back to Rock Island, Illinois. I told my dad I wanted to go to college. He was happy, and he said, "Well, what do you want to do?" I said I wanted to get a degree in music and he said, "Fine. I think you should go to the University of Iowa."

Did the University of Iowa have a stage band or any kind of jazz band?

No, in fact I was somewhat ostracized by some teachers because I played professionally on weekends. The brass teacher, William Gower, understood and didn't mind as long as I had my lesson prepared. If I didn't have the lesson prepared, I paid dearly. My theory teacher understood, too, but there were teachers who were against any sort of jazz education or playing. Back then, jazz education hadn't become popular yet. Well, it had at U.N.T., but I didn't know it then. I got the nickname Downbeat because I played all the time.

What other playing and learning experiences did you have outside of college?

My stint in the Army turned into a wonderful opportunity. Playing in the 179th Army Band was a very good experience for me because I ended up writing for the jazz band. I had never written for a big jazz band, but I have good ears. They made me a corporal, and I started writing charts for their dance band (what we call a jazz band). It was great. I worked on something for the jazz band and if they liked it, they rehearsed it. If it was wrong I'd take it back upstairs to my room with a piano and work on it some more.

Kids now have learned to look at college the way mom looks at the grocery store. Mom has the choice of five different supermarkets and goes to the one that gives her the best value for her money. That's what kids are now doing; they look at colleges and say "Hey, which one will give me the best value for me and my future family? So, we have to offer courses that are practical if colleges are to survive.

Do you foresee changes in professional music opportunities for young people who leave our universities and conservatories with advanced musical training? We know that it will be difficult to generate more symphony orchestras, yet we turn out more wonderful musicians all the time. How can they find employment in their chosen field?

In one way you are really talking about marketing, kids learning to sell what they can do. I learned about marketing in Vegas. You may want to play jazz but many times you have to find a way to get away with playing jazz. I can remember when the Bossa Nova became popular. If we played a straight jazz tune people didn't buy it, but if we put a bossa nova beat behind it, they thought it was lovely. I remember playing some Duke Ellington tunes with a bossa nova beat and the people thought it was wonderful. The only thing we changed was the beat but it helped us to sell our performance.

Other times we'd do a piece of comedy that was dumb, yet when we got the audience to laugh, we could play anything we wanted for five minutes and they'd buy it.

I'm not saying that musicians should play

bossa nova or do comedy, only that if you can find some sort of hook to get people to listen, they will then absorb something from your performance and you will have picked up a few more believers. So, marketing is important.

What do you believe can be done to improve or attract more public support for music programs in the schools? Some schools around the country that had good music programs have cut them entirely. What can we do to reverse that trend?

Here I'm going to raise some eyebrows. I think that students are not into the classics and jazz because of radio and television. You turn on the radio; you don't hear concert band music. You turn on the radio; you don't hear jazz band literature. You turn on the radio; you don't hear opera or symphonic literature. If you let your children stay up until four in the morning they might hear some classical music or some good jazz. During the run of the day, they all play the same thing: today's rock, today's pop, soft rock, fusion. That's played on and on; that's what the kids identify with.

One of the proofs of this is the problems you have getting kids to start on clarinet or trombone. Kids all want to play saxophone because they want to emulate what they've seen and heard. When you go to Europe, where good music is played, the kids love it, are familiar with it, and identify with it. They're ready to study it; they look forward to studying it. If you go to Sweden or Norway and look at the paper, you can see by the radio schedules that classical music is played all the time, so that's what they listen to. Over here you have 15 radio stations and they're all copycats.

It used to be that you could hear some classical music on F.M. In many places now you won't find it on the dial no matter how badly you want to listen to it.

This is the case even with public radio stations.

Absolutely. You know how they say, "You can't make any money with jazz." That just can't be. What happened when the first C.D.s came out? They went back and made C.D.s of all the jazz masters. Because they knew they would not sell? No, because they knew they would sell. They didn't make those C.D.s to stock in a warehouse. They made them to sell. Now you can buy all that music on C.D.s and it does sell.

The radio stations deserve a large part of the blame. We talk about how teachers need to spend more time playing records with the kids in school, and that's fine; but that doesn't come across with the magic of radio. It's the real thing when it comes across radio or T.V. One program a month or one program a week won't do it. Those stations are guilty of changing our cultural taste. They have so much power, so much influence.

I find that if you expose young kids to jazz, they love it. I expect approximately 200 grade school kids to come to a rehearsal in 2 weeks (we did this last year). A school called and asked if their kids could come up to hear the band. I agreed, kids came up and there were so many that I had them sit between the trombone players. The room was just covered with kids. We started to play a shuffle, and I showed the kids how to clap their hands on 2 and 4. I had all of those grade school kids laughing and hollering and clapping their hands on 2 and 4, some of them getting up and hopping around. They had an absolute ball. They loved the jazz. I asked, "Did you ever hear this before?" "No." "Do you like it?" "Yeah." It was exciting to them.

So, what we've come down to, with the attitude of broadcasting stations, is that the only place you can hear and appreciate as a public audience the music that's being taught in our schools, be it jazz or classical, is in the schools.

That's right. We can't say that every radio station is guilty of this, but most of them are. I'm not saying, "Take all rock off the air." Have you ever driven along in your car with the radio on, playing some tune; you can't stand it, it's just not your taste and you push a button, get another station, and it's playing the same tune? It happens all the time. They say, "If we play any other kind of music, nobody will listen to us." I won't say that jazz will become the hottest thing in town, but I think that broadcast stations have an obligation to help with the cultures; that's an obligation that goes along with being given air rights.

I was dumbfounded the first time I went to Sweden and heard what was playing on the radio and at my first public performance in Sweden, when I announced to the people that I would play something by Duke Ellington. The crowd rose to its feet and gave me a standing ovation before I even started. It shook me as nothing ever has on stage. Afterwards I asked why this happened. "Don't you know about Duke in Sweden?" they asked me. He toured there many times and was always smart enough to add a couple Swedish musicians. He is played on Swedish radio all the time. When I went back the next time I did a jazz show on network TV called "Tomorrow is Saturday." Ten and a half million people watched that show. I played Ellington tunes; I'm not dumb.

The next morning as I walked around downtown Stockholm, an elderly couple stopped me. The woman said, "We saw you on television last night." I'm not used to that. I said, "Well, yes." "You played Duke Ellington. Did you know

Duke Ellington?" she asked. "Yes," I said, "but not in the way you mean. All musicians were familiar with Ellington, but I didn't write him letters and he didn't call me on the phone just to pass the time of day." She asked again if I knew Duke Ellington, and I explained again that I was not one of his personal friends. She said that I must know him because we were both jazz musicians. "Okay, I know Duke Ellington." "Well, how is his sister? She has been very sick." "Sister?" I didn't know anything about his family. "Well, he has a sister, and we've heard that she has been very sick." '

I was really embarrassed by this so when I got back home I finally found out from Milt Hinton that Ellington had a sister who had been quite ill but was recovering. This was an incredible lesson to me. If you can get radio stations to broadcast good music this is the kind of interest it will generate.

How can we persuade radio stations to change?

My answer to this is another question. I know that whenever people get together and make demands as a group, they can be successful. I wonder if it would be possible for the band directors in small towns to say to the local public radio stations, "For the sake of educating ourselves and our students, we demand that you play classical music and jazz"?

How can schools teach and generate more public audiences for the kind of music that we espouse? How can we reach the public if radio isn't going to help us?

Just as Mohammed went to the mountain, you have to take your band out and play. There's a place called Jack's Landing here in town; our bands go there to play for various things. Still, that doesn't guarantee more exposure, because sometimes the only people who come to hear the band are the parents of the kids, and not all of them come. I've found that if you can get some of the townspeople who are at the top of the financial heap to support you by coming, then they start talking about it, and it becomes the in thing to do.

Perhaps we need some courses in marketing for music educators?

Absolutely. I explained earlier how I learned to market myself. Selling your product is a course that schools should offer. That old saying "Mohammed went to the mountain" means you can't sit there in the school and expect the kids to show up; you have to go out and get them. Speaking of ways to sell a band, I remember a guy in Cedar Rapids who was clever. He found out that the number one sportscaster in town used to play trombone, so he threw a big concert at the college and this sportscaster came up and did all the announcing. Of course it was all over the radio that this sports announcer would be there and would get his trombone out and play. Everybody came to see that. What the director didn't tell the audience was that when it was time to perform, the trombones would wear basketball outfits, basketball shoes, and basketball shirts with the letter I. They stood in a line and played and it brought the house down. I think that was a stroke of genius.

So, in music education course curricula we're missing jazz studies, or the studies of American music, and we're missing a course in public relations and marketing.

Yes, for all music, not just jazz, and I think that sometimes we get too formal. A player practices and practices to get to the level that he can play in front of an audience. When he finishes, his bowing (if he bows at all) or his nodding is very stiff, with no warmth. Why play in the first place? You might as well stay home and play in your closet if it didn't mean that much to you. That audience had the choice of many things to do that day, but instead decided they would go listen to this band or this person play. When they applaud they are saying, "Thank you for playing for me." We need to teach kids how to accept applause and show the audience gratitude. Sometimes in concert band and symphony performances the first ones out to the parking lot afterward are the symphony members. They don't stay around to talk to people, to share. That's all part of selling.

In 1986 you made a major change in your career by becoming the Koger Distinguished Professor of American Music at the University of North Florida. How did this come about?

I was asked to come down to Jacksonville for a concert with the St. John's River City Brass Band. Ira Koger, head of Koger Industries, had started and financed a brass band here that played traditional brass band music. Koger suggested that the band should play some jazz, and somehow they located my name and asked me to perform. When I played with that brass band and Koger asked me if I would come back the following October 1985 to play with that same brass band in the Jacksonville Jazz Festival, I agreed.

I came back and played in the Jazz Festival, and he invited me aboard his yacht. I was

surprised when he said to me, "All right, Matteson, what would it take to get you to move here?" I just looked at him, dumbfounded. I said "What do you mean, move here?" He said, "Move here. They don't need you at North Texas; we need you down here. Would you move here?" I looked at him and said "Mr. Koger, you're having a party. I don't think this is the time to talk business. Can I think about this and submit a proposal to you?" He said, "Sure." I spent two or three months preparing a proposal. I really didn't submit a proposal about a school of music; I told him that I was happy in jazz education and didn't know what he had in mind. Whatever happened, I knew I wanted to stay in jazz education: I must both play and teach to be happy; one or the other alone doesn't cut it. The next thing I knew, he had spoken to the president of the University of North Florida, who called me and said "You don't know me; but I know all about you. I've checked you out with some people I know in teaching. I think you'd better catch the next plane down here so we can talk, because you're going to be here next fall." One thing led to another. He and Koger wanted me to form the School of American Music Studies, starting with jazz because it would be the most obvious draw. We wanted to add other American music too — opera, American theater, gospel, country and western, rock - everything. For now, it's jazz and it will be that way for a while, because it takes time to get things going. Koger is a very influential man and a very dedicated man to the arts. I was happy at North Texas and planned to teach there until I retired, but I was offered an opportunity to start a whole new program of jazz studies. I just couldn't say no to that incredible opportunity.

It was one of those lightning bolts of opportunity, but also a challenge.

Yes, a tremendous challenge. I believe that this is the right thing to do, and I have support. For some reason I have been allowed to be involved in jazz education for the last 21 years, teaching kids about jazz and performing jazz. So, for 21 years now I have made my living doing exactly what I wanted to do. I can't even think about doing anything else. The opportunities that have been presented to me in working with these beautiful young players is just incredible. I am grateful to music education for that opportunity. □

Tailoring the Teaching
of Improvisation

by Phil Wilson

I wonder what some of the jazz giants would think if they could see the fuss made over their art form in 1989. Can you picture a young Bill Basie as a freshman pianist at Berklee College or Fats Waller and Art Tatum being told to not drag their thumbs during descending arpeggios? How about a young Louis Armstrong playing in the Storyville district of New Orleans to save up enough money for his first year at the University of North Texas, Benny Goodman shedding his II-V's at Northern Illinois University, or Cat Anderson checking out the hemispheres of the brain and their relationship to playing good jazz? Hard to fathom. Nevertheless, the art form these pioneers fathered is now a major part of the music education curriculum all over the world.

Truly top-notch players, such as the late pianist Bill Evans, are satisfying emotionally, melodically, rhythmically, and intellectually. Evans's playing was the coupling of imagination with complete proficiency on the instrument. Without this technical command, the imaginative aspect of his music would never have been completely revealed.

Most students develop to different degrees in these areas. Generally they focus their playing and practicing to reinforce their attributes while neglecting their deficiencies. It is the job of the teacher to recognize and bring to the fore these problem areas, otherwise the student will remain limited and never realize his full potential.

The three common types of students I have worked with the last 24 years are the natural, the intellectual, and the rhythmically oriented musician. The natural student has excellent basic instincts for improvisation and at an early age is able to impress the listener on many levels, but he may lack rudimentary skills such as how to arpeggiate chords or even read music.

The intellectual plays correct notes in the chords but can't seem to find the right place to put them. His solos usually lack emotion. Many orchestrally trained musicians find themselves in this category when they first attempt to play jazz. Part of this is due to their training in European music, which has a simpler rhythmic content than most forms of jazz.

People of African, Caribbean, or Latin American background often, but by no means exclusively, show up in the third category, the rhyth-

mically oriented. Rhythm as it is used in their cultures deserves as much study as the melodic and harmonic practices in European music. Jazz is, after all, the blending together of these different musical approaches.

Picture a drummer who picks up a set of mallets and begins to play on the vibraphone, just hitting the bells randomly, not knowing what notes to play, but with an excellent time feel. He may sound impressive, but only until the listener realizes there is little melodic organization.

Often the natural player who improvises effortlessly on almost any tune has a major lack of initiative. He doesn't read music, so he can't support himself by playing regular gigs where he could be learning standard tunes or the musical traditions of other cultures. Nor does he build endurance and power by playing circus jobs. Likewise, he doesn't understand the value of learning chords and harmony in order to raise his level of playing. Having been able to impress at an early age, he doesn't feel the need to develop discipline and proper practice habits.

How do you trick a natural into learning the rudiments of his trade? Try directing him to group situations where even though he is recognized for his solo abilities, playing his part in the ensemble is more important. This will put him in a sink-or-swim situation that makes him come to his senses. I have lost some students doing this, but nobody said teaching was a popularity contest.

Another approach is to have the student transcribe the work of his favorite soloists. An assignment to notate some familiar solos usually interests the natural player. Monitor the whole process carefully, though. If the solo is too difficult, the exercise may become a huge turn-off.

I play with all my students and find the Jamey Aebersold play-along records a most useful teaching tool. Choose a selection that the natural student really likes. He may be able to play some of the tunes by ear. Play the heads as presented in the book, insisting on absolute concentration on the printed note. As time and a lot of practice go by, the student should begin to correlate the eye with the ear. This is the begin-

---

In addition to making numerous recordings and solo appearances, jazz trombonist Phil Wilson has taught at Boston's Berklee College of Music for the past 24 years.

ning. As the student shows progress, find some two-part music you can play together. Bach has a way of turning on the natural player, even today.

The intellectual type often has a reasonable ability to arpeggiate chords. While he may be well-versed in the classics of the European tradition, rhythmic training is needed, not in the sense of playing a string of baroque eighth notes, but experiencing the flow and hypnotic qualities of rhythm as it is used in the African musical tradition.

With this kind of student I will start with a bossa nova or simple rock tune because of the straight eighth-note feel, which is similar to the straight eighth-note feel of the baroque music of Bach that is familiar to many intellectually oriented musicians. Jamey Aebersold's play-along record called Bossa Novas, Vol. #31 is excellent for the more harmonically advanced. Beginners do well with Sonny Rollins's *St. Thomas* (on Aebersold #8) because of the tune's simple harmonic structure.

Following a few months of weekly lessons in this manner, I will introduce a highly rhythmic bebop tune. For the more capable student Charlie Parker's *Billie's Bounce* works well; for the less advanced I use *Now's the Time*. I accompany the student on the piano using a half-time rock feel, thus maintaining the straight eighth-notes he finds so comfortable. When he is proficient with both the song and chords, I then use the jazz rhythm section record to accompany him. The swinging jazz feel will be hard to deny after all that straight eighth-note music.

If students try the above and still find the swing feel elusive, I have them practice arpeggios, scales, then tunes with the metronome clicking on two and four, instead of the more usual one and three. This takes some patience but has been rewarding to many. Try playing the first movement of Bach's *Concerto in E♭ for Two Violins* with the metronome on two and four. It isn't long before you experience the feeling of swing. As the intellectual student grows rhythmically, I have him transcribe solos using

mid-thirties Lester Young recordings or almost any Clifford Brown recording as models, if only for their harmonic and rhythmic clarity.

The third type, the rhythmically oriented person, must connect his rhythmic abilities to melody and harmony. One method of achieving this end is made possible by what Clark Terry calls "the theory of melodic drums." As a child, did you ever play the musical game where one person beats out the melody of a song on a table while the others try to guess the song title — songs like *When the Saints Go Marching In, Silent Night,* or *Havah Nagilah.*

Have your rhythmically oriented student beat the melody to a simple song. If he is more advanced, try some of the bebop tunes of the forties, such as Parker's *Billie's Bounce*. These melodies are so rhythmic, students can readily get into the groove. For most people this is easy and fun.

Now take this musician to the vibes and have him beat out the melody. Colored stickers on the bells will help the novice become acquainted with the keyboard. If an instrument resembling a vibraphone is not available, have the student beat out the melody on the piano, using one finger on each hand. Eventually this should lead the rhythmically oriented student to a basic understanding of melodic and harmonic principles. Once he has some working knowledge of the chromatic scale, then introduce the basic rules of diatonic harmony, eventually leading to the formation and memorization of chords.

When I refer to memorization of chords I mean the following: major, minor, augmented, and diminished triads including X^6, $X\text{-}6$, $X\vartriangle 7$, X^7, $X^7(\text{sus}4)$, $X+7$, $X\text{-}7$, $X\text{-}7(♭5)$, and finally $X^\circ 7$. "X" refers to the letter name of the chord. A student should have these down in all keys up to seven flats and seven sharps.

The needs of these three types of students are different yet similar. Everything depends on their inborn instincts. Life would be easy if everyone fit clearly into one of these categories or another, but this is not the case. Most students are a combination of these three types and teaching them calls for flexibility and intuition. □

The Three Types of Jazz Improvisers

Type of Student	Harmony	Melody	Rhythm	Control of Instrument	Emotional Content	Reading
Natural	Low	High	High	Low	High	Low
Intellectual	High	Low	Low	High	Low	High
Rhythmic	Low	Low	High	Low	High	Low

Most students are a mixture of the above characteristics.

note Latin feel. Likewise, discourage young improvisers from using too much tongue when they solo in a Latin-feel tune. When playing a Latin pattern the bass player should just play:

Use a bossa nova beat in the rhythm section when teaching a straight eighth-note style; this creates a good opportunity to expose the drummer to a new hand/foot coordination.

Experiment with the following ideas as soon as the students are comfortable with their scale sheets.

• While the rhythm section comps, play each scale line twice followed by 16 measures with everyone improvising. Move to the next scale and repeat the process. The aural chaos that results from group improvisation will only seem uncomfortable to the director; young students don't mind. In fact, this may be the only way to get your shy students to begin improvising.

• As the rhythm section plays the comping patterns, skip around the scale sheet, shouting out a new scale number just before starting each new line. You might write the scale numbers on the blackboard and point to the next desired scale.

• Give the rhythm section a predetermined order of chords to play. Have the ensemble members see who can be the first to identify which scale would fit with the chords the rhythm section is playing by singing or joining in on their instrument. Cue the rhythm section to proceed to a different chord only after everyone in the ensemble is playing or singing the correct scale. This teaches students the concept of playing what they hear in their mind's ear, which is the whole idea of improvisation.

• Give the students instructions such as, "Rest on the third note of the pattern" (example A); or "the fifth and sixth note" (example B); or "hold the fourth note for two eighth-note val-

ues" (example C). This will show the students how to create simple melodies, which they will eventually do intuitively.

Example A: (Bb Maj 7)/(C min 7)

Example B: (D Maj 7)/(E min 7)

Example C: (Ab Maj 7)/(Bb min 7)

• Have the students select one of the pitches on counts 1, 2, 3, or 4 (for the major chords), or the upbeats (for the minor chords), and play them as whole notes. This is the first step in teaching chord structure to the students.
• After the students know the root, 3rd, 5th, and 7th of a chord, have them play a scale degree in whole notes based on where they sit in their section. (Lead players will play the 7th, second parts play the 3rd, third parts play the 5th, and fourth part players play the root.) This will allow you to create background harmonies to accompany the soloist's riffs. Interchange and combine different voice parts to teach concepts of timbres and arranging.
• Have the students write their own combinations of scale numbers on the blackboard for everyone to play, or draw a series of scale numbers out of a

hat. This is the first step in teaching the concept of chord changes. For the rhythm section you might refer to "No. 3 Major " or "No. 3 Minor."
• Select logical groups of scale/chord numbers and write them on the board for everyone to play. For example, with a Latin feel, play no. 3 Minor (8 bars); no. 6 Major (4 bars); no. 5 Major (4 bars); no. 6 Major (4 bars); no. 5 Major (4 bars). These are the chord changes to Little Sunflower, a standard tune for combos written by Chuck Mangione. Using line numbers for the scales and chords allows students to relax and think in their own key rather than constantly having to transpose from the concert key.
• Play a line with a Latin feel, followed by the same line with a swing feel. It is important for rhythm section players to have an opportunity to practice this shift since many jazz tunes such as Night in Tunisia or On Green Dolphin Street use this effect.
• When it is time for a written test, just hand out a scale sheet with the notes and accidentals deleted. Ask the students to write in the scales from memory.

Have young students limit their improvised melodies to a one-measure phrase followed by a measure's rest, then a two-measure phrase followed by two measures' rest. This may seem like a long time to rest, but it gives a young player a chance to listen to the rhythm section and think about what he will play next. This limitation also forces young students to use space in their solos — a technique their future audiences will appreciate.

Some teachers do not advocate using a scale approach because they feel it limits creativity. While this might be true for more advanced improvisers, beginners need all the tools and suggestions they can get. The most beneficial use of a scale approach to teaching beginners how to improvise is that it helps the students become confident enough to make up their own melodies using the scales they have learned. However they must learn that scales are only the building blocks. Their improvised melodies are the real music. □

Explicit Jazz Notation

by Jeff Jarvis

Before editors and proofreaders get to the manuscript of a best-selling novelist, the copy often contains spelling errors, run-on sentences, and misplaced modifiers. Similar errors occur when musical writers communicate with notes. Fluency in any language depends on following principles that give clarity to the information.

After hearing an unsatisfying performance of his music a composer may blame the musicians and conductor for reading mistakes and misinterpretations, although they may be blameless. Musical effectiveness depends on the intelligence of the music, the abilities of the performers, and the legibility of the music. Handing conductors and musicians music that is sketchy, inaccurate, or difficult to read greatly reduces the chance of a good performance. Some manuscripts reflect a lack of awareness of notation fundamentals, and others show liberties with the rules.

Not every writer has the time or ability to autograph perfect elliptical noteheads or straight stems that are exactly three and a half staff spaces high. However, with planning and attention to detail, writers can produce manuscripts that are readable and accurate, giving the music a better chance of being performed correctly.

A word of caution: a growing number of writers purchase computerized desktop music publishing gear, reasoning that the equipment will make their manuscripts legible. Unfortunately, writers who once produced messy hand-written manuscripts usually generate messy manuscripts with their laser printers. Regardless of the method, writers should learn and follow the accepted rules of notation.

Visual appeal is lost when a composer clutters a page with written instructions, rather than trying to impart information in a thorough, efficient manner. Too many words above or below the staff make the page look busy, and the busier the page, the more the reader will miss or ignore. The following style marking, for example, is certain to confuse the player and cause vertical spacing problems that contribute to a cluttered look:

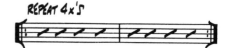

Take care to avoid directions that may be interpreted in more than one way.

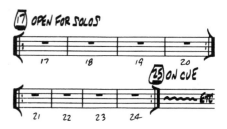

One musician might play this example four times, but another might play it once and then repeat it four times. By removing the word "repeat," the direction is less confusing.

At first glance, the notation in the next example suggests bars 17-20 are the open repeat.

In actuality, you play bars 17-20 twice, then play bars 21-24 twice before repeating back to measure 17 for additional choruses. Placing a repeat within a repeat is bound to cause trouble. When in doubt, write it out. It takes

Jeff Jarvis, vice-president of the editorial department at Kendor Music, is a composer and Yamaha trumpet artist. He serves on the advisory council of the International Association of Jazz Educators, and his recordings as a solo artist are on the Optimism label.

Educator Jamey Aebersold improvises at a jazz clinic.

less time to notate the music than to explain it during rehearsals.

The symbols for Segno 𝄌 and To Coda ⊕ are frequently misused in notation. The D.S. (dal segno) directs players to return to the segno; and the To Coda sign advances the player to the coda, indicated by the word Coda. Variation can provide superfluous information or misdirect the reader.

Correct   Incorrect

D.S.Al ⊕   D.S.Al Coda, 𝄌 Al ⊕

         ⊕   To Coda, To ⊕ ,

         To ⊕ Coda

Coda ⊕ , ⊕ Coda

There is no need to direct the player to D.S. more than once.

The purpose of chord symbols and other forms of musical shorthand is to convey information in a compact, efficient manner. When writers invent their own symbols, rhythm section players and jazz soloists have to decode them, and misspellings result.

Cᴍᴀ⁷..C△, C△⁷, Cᴍᴀᴊ⁷, C⁷ etc.

To minimize confusion, consult a handbook titled *Standardized Chord Symbol Notation* by Carl Brandt and Clinton Roemer, which shows clear, descriptive chord spellings in proper configurations.

Chord symbols should always appear above the staff. If you use a grand staff on a keyboard part, symbols go above the treble clef staff, not between the staves.

Correct

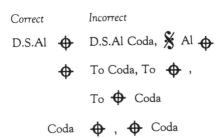

Incorrect

Many musicians persist in using the terms slur and tie interchangeably. A tie connects two neighboring notes of the same pitch, uniting their time

value; a slur embraces notes of different pitch to indicate legato phrasing with no break between notes.

Correct

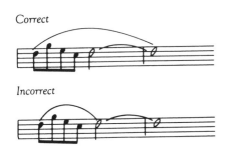

Incorrect

Slurs and ties should extend from notehead to notehead without touching them. Ties used in single part music curve in the opposite direction of the stems; slurs normally go with the noteheads. If stems go in both directions, the majority rules. In the event of an equal number of both stem directions, the slur goes above.

Articulation markings specify a note's attack, length, or emphasis; and though the interpretation of these symbols is not absolute, writers can ensure that musicians observe them in some fashion by regulating their frequency. Underuse of articulation leaves players to interpret the music as they see fit.

Overarticulating music results in superfluous information and clutter, which irritates musicians. When writing for developing players, frequent use of articulation is acceptable.

Here is a properly articulated phrase.

When you use dynamic markings, be aware of their effects. Most writers

indicate such stationary dynamics as *mf* properly, but are vague about changes in dynamic level. A crescendo wedge should communicate your intention clearly, including the start and end of the crescendo.

Correct

Incorrect

In the example below written dynamics give the level of volume from start to finish. Unless you wish the performers to remain at the ending dynamic, indicate a return to the original volume.

Be sure to beam notes to facilitate reading. The lower example might be read as a triplet; the one on top is more concise.

Correct

Incorrect

Here you can see the middle of the bar, which makes subdividing the beats easier.

Correct

Incorrect

Providing literal notations for a swing eighth note feel can yield a rigid, forced sound; using the dotted eighth and sixteenth ♪. ♪ as a substitute is also not advisable because a literal interpretation is not accurate.

Incorrect

Instead, offering an explanation of swing eighth notes as part of the style marking helps when writing for younger players or musicians who normally do not play jazz. Indicate swing eighth notes as regular eighth notes.

Correct

Placing accessory numerals in an incorrect position can make figures difficult to read; eliminate unnecessary brackets and place the numerals with the beams, allowing readers to better determine notehead placement.

Correct

Incorrect

For note groupings covering a long time span, use a straight bracket.

To indicate intervals of a second in note clusters on keyboard parts, place the higher note on the right side of the stem and the lower note on the left regardless of stem direction. This rule also applies to clusters involving ledger lines. In the case of a cluster of whole notes, arrange the configuration as if a stem were present.

Correct

Incorrect

Using rehearsal numbers is preferable to rehearsal letters. Once all the measures in the score are numbered, place a boxed location number at each appropriate section in the music. This provides easy-to-locate reference points for conductors and musicians. It is not necessary to use double barlines at every rehearsal number because they signal the end of a section of music or precede a change in meter or key signature.

There are dozens of devices composers use to save time during the scoring or preparation process, but devices that save work for the writer often add work for someone else later. Unless the score is for only the writer, take care to eliminate shorthand that could be misunderstood.

Many writers use "copybacks" to shortcut notation: professional copyists refer to previously written material when copying these Come Sopra (as before) measures.

When using copybacks, verify that the beginning and end of the Come Sopra section matches the adjacent measures. If you turned back in the score and found that measure 26 was a whole rest, that measure would not line up with the fourth bar because of the continuation of a slurred figure.

The overuse of single repeat bars ✗ invites error through miscounting. Multiple repeat bars are even more risky.

Keyboard voicings are sometimes abbreviated.

Though keyboardists are accustomed to these abbreviations, horn players are not, so this notation is not recommended for horn parts.

As a music editor I have noticed that few jazz writers devote the same

attention to writing rhythm parts as they do to horn parts. Many rhythm parts appear to be afterthoughts rather than an integral part of the creative process. When writing for experienced players, composers walk a fine line between giving too much information and not giving enough. The notation in the next example is likely to limit the creative input of the better players; however, if younger, less experienced groups are performing the music, notate a detailed part, as long as chord symbols are provided as well to give stronger players the option of performing the part as is or ad. lib. Because young players interpret notated rhythm parts literally, writers should devote sufficient time to their preparation.

Sketchy rhythm parts place a burden on rhythm sections, and writers should be prepared to accept any interpretation. On the other hand, a thoughtful balance of specific notation and space allows experienced players to comp or improvise their parts.

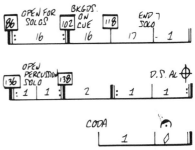

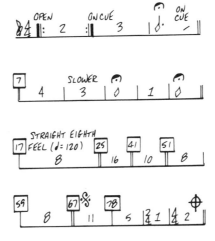

Those who compose, arrange, or prepare music should check the accuracy of their work before submitting it to performers, publishers, or contests. Recognizing the importance of proofreading allows conductors and musicians to spend valuable rehearsal time learning the music rather than fixing it.

Proofreading is a methodical rather than a creative task, so once a score is finished, study each page for the following details:
• bar numbers at the bottom of the page.
• empty measures in any of the parts.
• consistent use of dynamics and articulations between instrument choirs.
• chord changes in the rhythm parts in agreement with ensemble voicings.
• correct key signatures in every part on every page.

• instrument or mute changes.
• missing beats in any of the parts.
• too many directions.

Once you are satisfied that the score is reasonably clean, copy the parts. Then, the next phase of the proofreading process begins. Check each part against the score for wrong notes, accidentals, and omissions. Next, make a diagram of the score that shows style and metronome markings; key signatures in concert pitch; time signatures; rehearsal numbers; the number of measures between each rehearsal number; tempos (including accel., rit., and fermatas); repeats, first and second endings; D.S., D.C., ⊕, coda, and fine information; and special information such as "play second time only."

Once the diagram is complete, check parts against it. During this step you are likely to find errors that were overlooked during the initial check through when you were concerned with locating note mistakes. Finally check similar parts against each other (1st alto and 2nd alto) for consistent articulation, dynamics, and unisons. Then count the beats in every bar on all parts.

Whether you use this system or another one, be sure to go over the music several times, focusing attention on different types of information each time. If an error or two pops up at the first reading, don't be discouraged. You can proofread a work 10 times and still find discrepancies. The idea is to try to prepare music that is accurate, legible, and professional. Don't wait for compliments on your accurate and meticulous editing though: nobody seems to notice when you do a good job; they only notice when you don't. □

August, 1990

The Fewest Words Possible In Ensemble Rehearsals

by Sam Pilafian

The one important thing that members of every aspiring chamber music group should understand is that if they don't rehearse well, they will not play well. For years the Empire Brass rehearsed several nights a week above a Boston paint store. Taping every session, we would finish at 2 a.m. and stay for another hour to listen to the tapes. During that time three Empire Brass members played in the Boston Symphony Orchestra, and I commuted regularly between Boston and New

than a hundred trips in one year. We were young enough then to maintain a rehearsal schedule of intensive late-night sessions, which became a major building block of the group.
block of the group.

During those years of struggle we came up with the idea of teaching the next generation of chamber brass musicians so they could move ahead more quickly. Thus, we started a Boston University Tanglewood program, which is similar to having a lit-

tle league, and in doing this we learned to explain to others just how brass quintet music works. Much of what we teach, the Empire Brass never did because we never had to; we were five people lucky enough to have had good teachers and a natural feeling for imitating one another's phrasing. There were frustrating times when we first tried to teach phrasing and tonguing, or how we played staccato; we never thought of how we did these things, but we had to figure out how to teach them to young players.

Every chamber ensemble needs one basic ground rule: everybody has to know his part. This is the simplest thing in the world; but if one player hasn't done the homework, you cannot have a chamber music rehearsal. Instead it will be four players watching one struggle with his part instead of five working on intonation, phrasing, and accompaniment. Real chamber music rehearsals happen only when each player walks in prepared.

Too many groups rehearse with their mouths instead of their instruments. When a group talks too much about the way to play things, a lot of animosities build up; someone usually feels that he never gets his way. More important, when a group is talking, it is not making music. One of the best rehearsal rules the members of the Empire Brass established was more play, less talk. Until we agreed to say things in the fewest words possible, our rehearsals sometimes came close to fistfights. When two of our members voice differing views on how something should be played, we try it both ways and then vote on it. One good thing about a brass quintet: it has five players and there is never a tie vote.

Over the years we learned that nobody gets his way all the time. Sometimes you make a suggestion that the group adopts and later wish you hadn't. That doesn't matter, but what does is that the group agrees on one interpretation.

It was a big deal for us to record our early rehearsals; this was before the Sony Walkman and high-quality cassette recorders. Most recording equipment didn't reproduce the sound of brass instruments very well, but John Newton, an amateur recording enthusiast who went on to become a well-known engineer, helped us out, and his tapes became our teacher.

Recording rehearsals is something every serious brass quintet should do. Many times I thought I had played something perfectly only to find out an hour later when I listened to the tape that I lagged behind the rest of the group like a dead dog. You don't need a teacher to tell you things like this; all you need is a good quality tape recorder and a pair of headphones or speakers to learn the painful lesson of life as a brass player: half the time you don't really hear what's coming out of the bell; it's not how you feel but how you sound that is important.

A conductorless group has to have members who agree on subdividing the basic rhythm and it should be an eighth or even a sixteenth note subdivision. This is why metronomes that divide the beat have become useful chamber music tools. Using one of these, you can set up a Renaissance dance with the necessary subdivisions going on. Alternate playing with the metronome and without it, and after awhile you'll be able to hear all those subdivisions in your head.

We often ask one member of a student group to play four bars of a solo phrase, then have another pick it up for the next four bars, with each remaining member in turn until they finish the phrase. Then we ask, "Did everyone play the phrase the same way? What was different?" This requires them to think about the subtle differences in playing and teaches everyone to listen more carefully.

The more we taught and shared, the more we learned. When we coached student groups and closely examined what went into a performance, we began to define just what it takes to be a brass quintet. Sometimes we go so far as to have student groups play in the dark to see if they can start and cut off by breathing together and listening intently to each other while playing. There are two things every brass quintet should have: radar and a good group breath. We also ask students to play duets so when they go back to their quintet, they have a better feel for one another's playing. The same is true of high school musicians who play chamber music. When they go back to concert band they have a heightened awareness of phrasing, intonation, and rhythm. Conductors love to have players with chamber music experience in their ensembles.

Another good exercise involves relative tuning drills: one student sounds a note and another plays a scale against it. Then they reverse the procedure so that each person learns to play against another musician's pitches, at the same time developing the ability to play his instrument in tune with itself. This drill works with an electric tuner too. Set the tuner on audible and select the pitch, then play a major scale beginning on that note and listen to how in tune your intervals sound when played against the drone.

The Empire Brass began as a student group at Tanglewood, and our first rehearsals were riotous occasions. We even got together on our own in addition to the regular Tanglewood rehearsals because playing together was so much fun. At that time I was 20 and Rolf Smedvig, our first trumpet, was a freshman in college. Our first model was the New York Brass Quintet, which was the first brass group that any of us listened to and it had a successful sound. Later we found the Philip Jones Brass Ensemble recordings, but it wasn't until we came across a recording of the Chicago Symphony Brass Quintet from the early 1950s that we found what we were looking for. We wanted to play chamber music using orchestral tone production.

Sam Pilafian is a founding member of the Empire Brass and teaches at Boston University.

For us, that recording of the Chicago Symphony Brass Quintet was a declaration of independence. Here were orchestral players who didn't change their sounds to play chamber music.

Another group that influenced us was the King's Singers. Sometimes when they perform Thomas Tallis they hit a chord and become one, completely losing their identity as individuals. This is what I call meltdown: five players producing one sound that is different from the five sounds that make it up. This is the signature of the Empire Brass and something all brass quintets should strive for, but it can only occur when all the rungs of the ladder are in place: the sound of the trumpets fits into the sound of the horn, which fits into the sound of the trombone, which in turn fits into the sound of the tuba. For the Empire Brass, meltdown was there from the start. To have everything align and click like that when a group sits down is rare. Even though we were quite young at the time, we knew that something like this was hard to find and did everything from that day forward to keep it.

The only way to achieve meltdown is to spend time learning each other's playing, and the best way to do this is in sectional rehearsals. As in band, sectionals count, but for some reason many quintets never think of having only two of their players rehearse together. In the Empire Brass the horn player stands at one end of the group while I sit at the other, but because we play duets together and work on our quintet music in sectional rehearsals, we have a built-in musical radar for one another.

If you can get your first trumpet and tuba, the two outside voices, to agree on note length and tempos, the whole group will benefit. If the two trumpets learn everything they can about each other's playing, they will sound as one when they have to. Try sectional rehearsals in different combinations of twos then threes before putting the whole group together. Another way to learn about each other's playing is to rehearse chorales and simple early music. We started our group with the ideas that we would primarily rehearse and play contemporary music, but it was those countless hours we spent working on simple early music that gave us what we have today.

If you are in a quintet that is serious about improving, use a coach, though not necessarily a coach who is a brass player, just any good musician. We used a number of string players from the Boston Symphony and found that we learned a great deal from a non-brass-playing coach because he isn't sympathetic to our breathing and technical problems. It is only the

musical results that interest him, not the way in which we obtain them. Once we recorded one of Victor Ewald's symphonies for brass quintet and used a B.S.O. string player to prepare us for the recording. He was Russian and went berserk when we first played for him. "You are so American; you sound so American." He proceeded to tell us a story about a little barefoot girl playing among the giant trees of the Russian forest, and his closing line was, "she's not making as much noise as you do when you tongue." He viewed this piece from a completely different standpoint and even had us change where the accents occurred in each bar. It was because of our Russian coaches that we became enamored with the idea of intense rhythm and emotional involvement in our music making. We try to exaggerate everything — really strong marcatos and short staccatos — so they communicate 300 feet to the back of the hall.

When we rehearse we know exactly what we will work on because we plan our rehearsal time well in advance and never ask the questions that you hear so often in student groups, "What do you want to work on today?" They get together, read through pieces, perhaps work on a few difficult passages, and call that a rehearsal. The Empire Brass has different types of rehearsals, including regular reading rehearsals in which we play through literature looking for pieces we might perform. Once we select a piece we schedule it on a series of technical rehearsals and take it completely apart, reducing it to its basic building blocks, then put it back together. In these rehearsals we use all the techniques a player would use when practicing alone. We stop and fix, play through sections of the piece first with a metronome and then without, always treating the ensemble as if it were a single individual.

In a dress rehearsal we play it straight down without stopping, then talk about what went wrong. Student groups stop at this point in their concert preparations, but we go far beyond. Many times a group becomes used to taking long breaks between pieces to discuss the performance, but in a concert you don't have the luxury of several minutes between pieces to rest. We prepare for this by dress rehearsing the entire concert, playing one selection after another just as we would on stage. We pause at intermission, talk about what went wrong during the first half, then after the allotted intermission we play through the remaining program. This preparation gives us the mental and physical endurance to play difficult passages as they occur in the program, and this intensity only heightens our concentration.   □

Auditioning With Finesse

by Ellen Rose

Taking auditions is a challenge to any musician seeking an orchestral career, and knowing how to prepare well in a limited time can mean the difference between giving an outstanding performance and a mediocre one. Good organization and time management, knowing how to practice, and mental readiness are integral parts of preparation.

Working under a deadline, you will be more relaxed and better prepared if you have all of the music thoroughly learned a month before the audition date. Organize practice time for all pieces, not leaving one excerpt or piece to prepare at the last minute. Divide excerpts and solos into those you know well, those you know partially, and those you have never prepared. Every day practice a group of excerpts from each category, quickly reworking the familiar ones and focusing on the difficult excerpts. When practicing on the next grouping, keep up the first group but spend less time on it. Circulate through the excerpts until you have practiced them all, marking the most difficult passages and working on these spots daily. As the audition date gets closer, play through these often.

Use audio and visual aids to monitor your work: tape and play back entire excerpts and also single phrases. Listen to a small section and practice it to get the sound, intonation, articulation, and phrasing that you want. Record it again and decide if you are satisfied. This process is time-consuming but productive. Because rhythm is important, practice with a metronome some but try to develop an internal beat.

Photographing yourself with a video camera is beneficial, but a full-length mirror in the practice room is an inexpensive though less effective substitute. String players should verify if bowing is straight or veering off course and affecting tone. Watch your physical movements to ascertain if they enhance your sound, articulation, and phrasing, or work against it. Verify that during spiccato passages the instrument is stable and the bow drops from a consistent height.

Listening to recordings of orchestral excerpts enhances your performance. It is not sufficient just to play an excerpt well; play as though you are on stage with an orchestra. Using earphones, play along with the recording to get a sense of vitality, phrasing, and musical scope that practicing the excerpt out of context cannot yield. Successful contestants play and sound as though they hear an orchestra surrounding them.

If sightreading is required in the audition, set aside time each day to develop sightreading with accuracy and ease. Two techniques will improve sightreading: open the book of excerpts to a different page each day and sightread it with a metronome, never stopping or missing a beat. You will miss many notes in the beginning, but gradually you will learn to look ahead, a necessary skill for good sightreading. A second technique is having a friend hold an index card on the measure you are playing, forcing you to look ahead; this trains your eyes to see notes in groups and clusters and eventually the tendency to focus on one note at a time lessens.

To master a tricky passage, diagnose the main difficulty, whether it is a right hand problem, a left hand problem, or a combination, then practice it by making the passage even trickier: in a rapid sixteenth note passage, instead of practicing down-up-down-up, practice up-down-up-down. Make up different patterns of slurs and rhythms, or play the passage on the correct open strings without the left hand. Play a legato passage four times more slowly, then two times, but use the same bowings and dynamics as in the normal tempo. In Mahler's "Adagio" from *Symphony No. 10*, play the opening phrase twice as softly at one quarter-tempo, then half-tempo. Jazz up a passage, playing it faster and with different dynamics. Having fun and experimenting with your work creates mental and physical flexibility while enlivening your practicing.

Playing excerpts in a technically perfect manner with correct dynamics and intonation is not enough. While polishing a piece technically, throw yourself into the music in the mood the composer indicated. Technical problems often become easier when you approach the piece from the standpoint of the emotion in the music; play an exciting or moving passage with passion, a melancholy one with sadness, and a buoyant one with delight in your heart. Don't hold back; play with feeling and conviction.

The more you play passages from memory, the more refined they will be. Memorize the fingerings so you will be prepared if you cannot use your copies of the music. If the excerpt list gives measure numbers, concentrate practice on these areas, but a committee may ask for passages not on the list. Cover all bases by learning the entire excerpt as thoroughly as time permits.

Practice tempos by arranging excerpts in a contrasting order; work from *Roman Carnival Overture* to *Midsummer Night's Dream* and then Mahler's 10th Symphony. Take time between excerpts to concentrate on the new tempo. The audition may switch from a legato passage to a spiccato passage and this practice will help.

Aim for your best performance the first time through each excerpt because you will have only one chance to play an excerpt at an audition; it is not realistic to give yourself two or three chances to play it well during practice. Learn to trust your automatic responses when playing. The intellect is too slow to move fingers and the bow; so leave that job to the part of your brain that takes care of automatic movement, such as walking or driving a car. Your hands will play better if you do not interfere by thinking too much. Instead, focus your mind on the musical interpretation you desire.

Play audition material for friends even before it is polished. As the audition nears, play for several groups of people. Auditions are heard by a group, and it is a different experience from playing for one person. To develop suitable dynamic ranges, play at least once in a large hall. Your sound at its largest should fill the hall, while your smallest pianissimo is confident and audible.

If you are currently not taking lessons, find an experienced orchestral player to be your mentor. A coach can hear you in a way that you cannot hear yourself, and will hear flaws in articulation or style that might prevent you from reaching the finals.

Mental preparation is as important as practicing. When you decide to take a particular audition, make a firm commitment to see it through from start to finish. Don't audition because it is nearby or convenient; if you cannot present your best work, you do yourself a disservice. An audition is a chance to play at your best and build your reputation. Motivate yourself mentally from the start; be encouraging and give yourself praise for good practice sessions. Be aware of any voices of fear in your head and deal with them as they arise, and convince yourself that you deserve to play an excellent audition.

Have a positive attitude towards the excerpts. If you dread playing a particular passage, modify your attitude by affirming that you like the excerpt, that you play it well, and that you are glad the committee wants you to play it. Imprint this attitude in your mind and repeat these affirmations silently when the proctor asks you to play the passage.

It is important to train yourself not to react to mistakes, and above all, do not stop. Let the mistake pass from your mind and continue playing; fixation on a mistake will undermine concentration. Focus on the present moment and on what is to come. Beware of taking the audition too seriously. Have fun while preparing, or the job becomes stale and feels like drudgery. Regard the audition as a personal challenge and a chance to improve your artistry, and be sure to schedule time for diversions you enjoy.

Because so much of making music is mental, you can practice without your instrument. With a metronome, a 440 pitch, and an easy chair, spend time each day practicing mentally. Hear the correct pitches in your mind and see yourself bowing, fingering, and playing with full musical expression.

In the early stages of preparation, devote the greatest amount of time to learning the repertoire. As the audition nears, spend more time practicing mentally and less on physical practice. Imagine yourself going through the audition easily and successfully. Walk yourself through the entire audition, from arrival at the hall through the complete performance. Stop when you experience anxiety and retrace to the point when you began to feel uncomfortable, and repeat the scene in your mind until you can walk through the uncomfortable moment with ease and confidence.

You are in physical training on the fingerboard; get your entire body in shape to develop stamina and mental clarity. Develop an "I can do it" attitude by reading inspiring success stories or watching films about people who reach great heights. During periods of performance anxiety, keep performing in order to deal with the problem.

Arrive at the audition city one day early to rest and be fresh for the next day. Because your goal is to focus on the task ahead, it is best not to stay with friends or relatives. Children, cats, dogs, and well-meaning friends will distract you; the money spent on a hotel will be well-invested in your goal. Choose a hotel near the audition site, so if there is a delay in the audition schedule you can return to the hotel for rest or practice.

Your imagined backstage procedures may have little basis in reality. The fewer expectations you

---

Ellen Rose is principal violist of the Dallas Symphony Orchestra, the Dallas Bach Society, and the Aspen Festival Orchestra. A professor of viola at Southern Methodist University, she is a graduate of The Juilliard School, and a recipient of Aspen and Tanglewood fellowships. Though the author addresses string players, the information she offers is universal and will benefit all musicians preparing to take an audition.

have, the more you can adjust to events withough being thrown off course. You cannot control the way a personnel manager organizes the audition, but you have control over your mental attitude toward these events. Bring along a tape recorder and earphones so you can listen to your favorite performers or whatever inspires and relaxes you.

Once you are backstage it is too late to practive, because frantic last-minute attempts would only waste your energy. Warm up quietly, check a few passages, then mentally collect

yourself and five it over to the fates. Though your mental preparation and practicing is in your power, the decision by the committee is not. Don't go in to your audition with the idea of having to win; go in only with the desire to play your best. Competing against your own highest standards is better than competing against other players. Once you are onstage, take your time between pieces and excerpts. Do not start an excerpt until the tempo is firmly in your mind, and do not let the proctor or committee rush you. You determine your pace;

the committee can wait until you start.

Being asked to repeat a passage is a positive sign. The committee may hear that you are nervous and know that you could play it better. They are giving you a second chance; take it. Be delighted to play any excerpt requested, and remind yourself how well you play it. Mentally let go of any mistakes, and fill the hall with sound. Enjoy hearing yourself play. You can have a good audition because good luck happens when preparation meets opportunity. □

July, 1990

Sascha Gorodnitzki on Music

Sascha Gorodnitzki joined the piano faculty of the Juilliard School in 1935 and taught there until his death in 1986. When appointed president of Juilliard in 1963, the late Peter Mennin asked his old friend Gorodnitzki to deliver the first convocation address at the opening of the new school year knowing that he and Gorodnitzki shared many of the same ideas on education, art, and life.

Throughout the summer of 1963, Gorodnitzki worked on the speech at his country home on Long Island, painstakingly researching the quotations for accuracy. The result is a timeless treatise that is just as relevant today as it was 25 years ago.
— *Dolores Fredrickson*

When President Mennin first approached me about speaking today, I recalled what my friend John Erskine, who was once president of this school, had said in a book he wrote: "Musicians are notoriously inarticulate about what concerns them most. I tremble for their art whenever they take to writing or public speaking about it."

With this in mind you would think that I would not be here, but my situation was a bit like that of Philip Hale. Mr. Hale was a famous music critic in Boston who made no secret of his aversion to the music of Brahms. "Someone," he argued, "someone should request manager Ellis to have a special door built in Symphony Hall, with a sign over it in large red

letters: Emergency Exit in case of Brahms." Now, there should be some emergency exit in case of being asked to speak at convocation, but like Mr. Hale I could not find one.

The convocation of our school each year is important, however, because it is one of the few times during the school year when all of us gather together who will carry the responsibility of music into the future. It is with the handful of us and our counterparts in the principal music schools of the world that the continuation of music rests. Not all of you will be leaders of your generation in channeling this continuous flow of the musical art, but all of you who complete your studies here will contribute to it.

You have come to a school which is, in its best sense, a professional school. The aspirations fostered here are for the highest levels of artistry. You are encouraged at Juilliard to preserve the idealistic view of the musical art and to develop cultivated minds as well as significant musical skills.

Naturally, as a performer, I am intimately acquainted with the hours of practice necessary for you to grow in your musical abilities here at Juilliard, but I also feel the hours you spend at your academic studies are of utmost value. In this respect today's Juilliard School of Music is better able to equip you for your future life on leaving its walls than was the conventional conservatory of old. You can avail yourselves of courses in literature, sociology, history, and receive the guidance

of specialists in their fields as you also receive your training in music from performers and composers of acknowledged excellence. This is an advantage not enjoyed even by those of us who attended the old Juilliard Graduate School.

I remember we students gave a show affectionately spoofing the school, the administration and faculty...in the early 1930s at the beginning of the Great Depression. I was President of the Student Council at the time and was selected to represent a typical Juilliard graduate of the year who was just out of school making his way in the world. As the curtain went up, there I was — selling apples in front of the entrance to Juilliard. On stage came a boy named Marcus Gordon, who was cast in the role of a brash, new applicant for admission. When he saw me he demanded, "Say, is this the Juilliard School?" I pointed to the large lettering on the building. "Can't you read?" "No," he answered shrugging. "I spend all my time practicing the piano."

Among the endowments you as students will need, I would specify first the capacity for work. This would seem too obvious to be worth mentioning except for the fact that the utterances of every great artist, every great performer, and every great composer emphasize it. When someone sought from Bach an explanation of his genius, Bach is said to have replied in a tart understatement, "I worked hard." The notebooks of Beethoven are evidence of how hard genius does work; he has left a clear record from the first sketchy notations through the numerous revisions and finally the finished score that seems so inevitable and inspired. When the incomparable Nijinsky astounded Paris audiences with his famous high leap, to how many did it occur that there were fifty thousand practice leaps before it?

There is good reason why the best artists in any field do not live dissipated or disorganized lives any more than do the best surgeons or best nuclear physicists. The successful practice of any art is a demanding, wearing, daily discipline, which makes hard demands on physical and emotional fitness. It is a lonely affair. Few human beings have the cold courage required day after day, without a boss to tell them what to do and without colleagues to sustain them into continued production. Many would-be artists cannot stand the discipline, and they fall apart.

One who did not fall apart was Rachmaninoff, to my mind, the greatest pianist of recent memory. He was an exile from Russia in 1918 at the age of 45 and was suddenly faced with the need to transform himself from a composer-conductor-pianist into a virtuoso pianist in order to support his family. Twelve months he worked in solitude overhauling his technique and building a new repertory. In 1922 after tours in America and Europe he writes, "For four years now, I practice, practice, and play many concerts. I make some progress, but actually the more I play, the more clearly do I see my inadequacies. If I ever learn this business thoroughly, it may be on the eve of my death. In the past when I composed, I suffered because I was composing poorly, and now because I play poorly. Inside I feel some assurance that I can better both the one and the other. This keeps me alive!"

So closely allied is the capacity for work to achievement in the arts that talent has sometimes been defined as "an insect-like persistence." This is, of course, as much an over-simplification as George Balanchine's amusing reply to the question, "How do you recognize talent?" "Let me put it this way," Balanchine said. "You have a stable of horses. You give them all the same training. One horse runs faster. He has talent." Perhaps the Chinese proverb puts it best: A gem is not polished without rubbing.

Next, I hope you have the capacity to learn, or more to the point, the inclination to learn. This may sound incongruous, but the pupil unwilling to be taught must have been with us a long, long time — in the first century B.C., Epictetus, the Greek Stoic, maintained, "It is impossible for anyone to begin to learn what he already thinks he knows."

It takes years of work to understand and think out problems in music, and yet you are here to benefit from the understanding your teachers have gained through their years of study and experience in living with the music. The painter Whistler once confessed that it took him only two days to do a picture — one day to do the work and another to finish it. "That was the labor for which you asked two hundred guineas?" the buyer protested. "No," said Whistler, "it was for the knowledge gained through a lifetime." Whistler also had a rebellious pupil who grumbled in response to a criticism, "I am sure I just paint what I see." "Ah!" said Whistler, "but the shock will come when you see what you paint."

There is one learning device that is dangerous, however, and I will explain why. When I was a boy and student, there were not many recordings available, and we were influenced mainly by our teachers and the artists we heard in public halls. The great artists left impressions which in many cases had a profound effect on our own work, but today, nearly everything has been recorded, and the young student, upon being given a new assignment, too often rushes to the record library, listens repeatedly to a performance of his new piece, and literally copies it. This, I feel, is a serious mistake. It is not only sheer imitation, but plagiarism.

The student may ask, "Isn't it the same as following my teacher's interpretation?" Not at all. The teacher analyzes and gives reasons for his interpretation, thus developing the intellect, resources, and knowledge of the student. This is the way in which the teacher seeks to develop a student to the point where he can walk alone.

I do not wish completely to deny the value of listening to recordings. A student can derive great benefit from hearing records if he first makes a serious attempt to grapple with the problems of interpretation and the art of making the music effective. After this first step he could then compare his performance with that of an artist he admires and could then even incorporate, occasionally, what he might consider to be a better idea.

This brings me to a subject that troubles many students: tradition. A wag once said that tradition is the last bad performance. Perhaps we could define it as an expression and line of interpretation established by great performers of the past. In exceptional cases an artist of the highest talent and skill will sometimes disregard tradition, but for the most part great artists do not depart radically from the accepted. They know that personality can make the music flower and come alive. Yet in all cases these performers have had their own ideas enriched by the studies of their predecessors.

The celebrated singer-actor Chaliapin, who was noted for his interpretive innovations, reminds us that he always kept in mind the lessons learned from his predecessors. Moreover, anything of his own that he appeared to add to an interpretation was for the sole purpose of rendering more faithfully the spirit and character of the work itself.

Do not infer from this that I suggest any of you be hidebound by tradition, but you must be aware of it in order to make any intelligent departure from it; and if you have something to say, you can usually say it within the boundaries of the composer's indications.

I would suggest from experience, which is a great teacher in practical matters, that the young soloist be wary of radical departures when performing with orchestra. Usually there is only one rehearsal. You can get some real shocks, such as having to play without any rehearsal at all. This has happened to me more than once.

Several years ago I was on tour with Fritz Reiner and the Pittsburgh Symphony doing the Tchaikovsky Concerto. One evening toward the end of the tour, I arrived at the hall about 9:30 because my concerto was last on the program. The manager, Edward Spector, stopped me in the wings. "I have news for you, Sascha, Reiner is ill." I must confess that my first concern was not for Reiner's health. "Who's going to conduct?" "Bakaleinikov." "We haven't rehearsed." "Oh, have a little talk with him during intermission."

The very next season the reverse occurred when I was to play with Erich Leinsdorf. He was ill at rehearsal so we met for the first time just before the concert. I remember that we discussed what we were to do while he was in his dressing room putting on his tie. I do not wish any of you such surprises, but it is well to be ready for them. They do happen.

One of the things students seem to worry about during their school years is that their own personalities may be submerged or smothered, or conversely, that they are not able to project a strong individual personality. Because every student is an original, unique human being he already has or has not the qualities that will excite or attract audiences and will create the magic that is music. Personality cannot be developed consciously. Personality also cannot be buried. This is true for both composers and performers. I think of two composers to illustrate what I mean.

Edvard Grieg is today considered a minor poet, but what he said of his studies at the Leipzig Conservatory is pertinent here: "I had great teachers, Hauptmann, Richter, Reinecke, and Moscheles. They put me into a straitjacket that was irksome but obviously necessary, for my untamed Norwegian temperament was badly in need of such discipline." The straitjacket did not destroy Grieg's Norwegian individuality.

On the other hand Prokofiev tells of showing a youthful symphony to his teacher, Taneyev. "Pretty well, my boy. You are mastering the form rapidly. Of course, you have to develop more interesting harmony. Most of this is tonic, dominant, and subdominant." Eleven years later Prokofiev brought one of his new scores to Taneyev. "My dear boy, this is terrible. What do you call this? And why that?"

"Master," Prokofiev said, "please remember what you said to me when I brought my G Major Symphony. It was only tonic, dominant, and subdominant." "God in heaven," Taneyev shouted, "am I responsible for this?"

Your personality will emerge; it cannot be nullified. What should be of concern to a student is his growth, the kind of growth that leads to independence. This growth comes about in two ways: one, as you develop mastery of the materials of expression; and two, as you develop as a person — your intellect, imagination, and capacity to feel and to communicate. It must be a simultaneous development since one is indelibly wedded to the other. Mastery of the technical side of performance is highly important, for there must be no physical obstacles to bar full expression. Communication is the ultimate goal. Without communication, a performance is a failure.

The portrait artist paints the face so that we can understand what is going on in the mind. The musical artist must reveal what went on in the mind of the composer and what is going on in his own mind as well.

Much has been written and discussed these days about the plight of the young artist, the difficulties of the musical career, and the fact that so few musicians ever get rich in our affluent society, but we seldom hear anything about how lucky the musician is to be a musician, or anything about his joys and satisfactions. These, I can assure you from experience, are very great.

It is fairly commonplace to hear of the harassed executive who asks himself, why am I doing this? What is it all about? These are questions I never hear musicians or artists ask. I never hear them wishing they had chosen to do something else. Not that musicians do not complain — they are among the greatest complainers in the world; but they do not say, what is it all about, because like the painters and poets they think they know. The artist has a deep conviction that he is in

touch with reality, and furthermore, the reality that the artist perceives is always more orderly than the real world. The artist must organize his vision into a form that has order and discipline for himself and also for others if he is to attract an audience. This is one reason why artists are among the sanest members of society.

Another is that the artist is doing what he wants to do, and what he wants to do is both creative and personal. He has identity with his work, and in that direction lies sanity. Many of man's emotional troubles in our times stem from doing impersonal, uncreative work which is in no way identified with the man who performs it.

The artist, on the other hand, more often than not decides what he is going to do, does it by himself, and judges his own achievement. His guide is an ideal of perfection that lasts throughout his life.

I think of a man like Casals, in his 80s, who still exudes a fresh enthusiasm and love of his work. A friend of mine was invited by Casals to attend his master classes in Puerto Rico. When he arrived, Casals was giving a lesson to a young woman. After a few minutes of rather pallid cello playing, he stopped her and said, "Young lady, I don't ask a question like this very often, but how old are you?" "I'm 22." "You know how old I am? I'm 82, but you play like 82, and I play like 22!"

We can agree, I think, that all creativity takes place in a mood of excitement and delight. There is even something akin to play in all creation. At any rate, let us never forget the joys we reap from our learning and labor in music.

In Rachmaninoff's words, "Music is enough for a whole lifetime, but a lifetime is not enough for music." □

Repertoire

Standards of Excellence
for Band Repertoire

by Harry Begian

There is growing concern among band conductors that the school band movement is in a general decline; some say it is at a crossroads. Various band associations have shown their concern by producing philosophical position papers in an effort to reverse this trend. The American Bandmasters Association issued "The American School Band Program of the Future" which addresses the position of music education and bands as an artistic function with the concert band as its central focus. Two concerns expressed are the study and performance of great artistic literature from all periods of western history, and the evaluation of artistic musical expression. Both areas are lacking in many school band programs. School bands that study and perform music of limited substance cannot do anything good for young musicians and may eventually turn students away from band. The study and performance of good music is what attracts students to a band program. Conductors who play only the best music with their bands rarely have a dropout problem. By learning about the expressive qualities inherent in good band music, conductors can impart the joy of music-making to their students.

Because I feel strongly that the music we play affects the quality and success of music programs, I agreed to coordinate the compilation of a list of outstanding band repertoire for grade levels 3, 4, and 5. The listings represent the

evaluations of seven outstanding conductors who have directed school band programs during their careers.

Band conductors teach to bring the best in music to their students and to introduce them to quality of musical expressiveness. We cannot achieve these goals by playing music for fun, but only through a serious approach that can prove there is much more to playing quality music — there is joy. Participation in band, orchestra, or choir is one of the few places in a public school where students can experience such joy.

No listing of band works can be absolutely comprehensive, and this list surely misses works that some will believe should have been included; we trust that directors will communicate their suggestions for amendments to the lists.

Student musicians and general concert audiences can distinguish between good and bad music; they also can tell whether that music is played well or poorly. Last May at the Smoky Mountain Band Festival, the Joliet Township High School Band directed by Theodore Lega performed Elgar's *Enigma Variations*. Filled to capacity with student musicians and their parents, the auditorium remained quiet as the audience listened intently. At the completion of Elgar's work, the audience gave the band and conductor a thunderous and prolonged ovation. It was clear that the audience of students and parents realized they had just heard an exceptionally fine performance of great music by a well-trained band. That high level of playing was brought about by the skilled training and teaching of the conductor. The old cliché came to mind once again: a band is no better than its conductor and is a reflection of what he is and thinks musically. The performance also showed how thoroughly he knew the music and that he trained and motivated his players to give their musical best. This performance was proof that many high school and college band programs can improve when guided by conductors of talent who choose good music and train their

---

Harry Begian has appeared as a conductor, adjudicator, and lecturer in the United States, Canada, and Australia and is Director Emeritus of the University of Illinois Bands.

Selected Grade 3 Literature

Johann S. Bach	*If Thou Be Near*	arr. Moehlmann, Fox	3
	Jesu, Joy of Man's Desiring	arr. Leidzen, Carl Fischer	3
	Komm Süsser Tod	arr. Leidzen, Carl Fischer	3
	Prelude and Fugue in D Minor	arr. Moehlmann, FitzSimons	3
	Prelude and Fugue in G Minor	arr. Moehlmann, Remick	3
Johannes Brahms	*Blessed Are They*	arr. Buehlman, Ludwig	3
Elliott Carter	*Overture for Winds*	Bourne	3
Frank Erickson	*Toccata for Band*	Bourne	3
Francois-Joseph Gossec	*Military Symphony in F*	arr. Townsend, Presser	3
Percy Grainger	*Ye Banks and Braes o' Bonnie Doon*	Schirmer	3
Clare Grundman	*American Folk Rhapsody (Nos. 1,2,3,4)*	Boosey & Hawkes	3
	Fantasy on American Sailing Songs	Boosey & Hawkes	3
	Hebrides Suite	Boosey & Hawkes	3
	Irish Rhapsody	Boosey & Hawkes	3
William Latham	*Court Festival*	Summy	3
Jules Massenet	*"Meditation" from Thais*	arr. Harding, Kjos	3-4
W. Francis McBeth	*Chant and Jubilo*	Southern	3
	Kaddish	Southern	3-4
W.A. Mozart	*Il Rè pastore Overture, K. 208*	arr. Barnes, Ludwig	3
Claude T. Smith	*God of Our Fathers*	Wingert-Jones	3-4
Richard Strauss	*Allerseelen*	arr. Davis, Ludwig	3
Hugh Stuart	*Three Ayres from Gloucester*	Shawnee	3
R. Vaughan Williams	*Flourish for Wind Band*	Oxford	3
	Rhosymedre	arr. Beeler, Galaxy	3
	Sea Songs		3
Giuseppe Verdi	*Prelude to Act I, La Traviata*	arr. Falcone, Kjos	3

students to play it. Other conductors through hard work, musicianship, and sensitivity to real music can present the best band music to their musicians and train them to play it with sincerity and conviction. If other band conductors would follow this example, recruiting and retaining players would not be a problem. A serious approach to music-teaching and performance with conviction gets through to young people now as it did in the past; students will give their best when playing quality music.

Achieving a successful band program has never been an easy task, but if we are serious enough to teach our young players the best kinds of music instead of the musical nonentities that so many bands play today, it is possible. The most common excuse for the poor quality of music played by school bands is that it is what publishers market. Publishing firms like other businesses produce commodities that are saleable. A successful business will produce what its customers want or the business fails, and publishers should not be blamed for the low quality of some of the music they market. Those of us who purchase bad music and foist it on young musicians should take the blame.

If music is not worthwhile, then don't buy or perform it; instead study good band music, such as that listed here or some of the many other fine works that are available for grade levels 3, 4, and 5. The panel does not claim that these listings are complete, but they feel the pieces are worthy of the time spent in performance and rehearsal. The panel chose works as worthy of being played by school bands. The panel concentrated on grade levels 3 through 5 because groups of this degree of ability can develop the musicality of a work, and directors of grade 6 bands generally know all of the available literature. In future issues we will review briefly the pieces on the list and include program notes for use by directors.

The music review panel that selected the works in the listings are Thomas Dvorak, University of Wisconsin – Milwaukee; Charles Hills, formerly of the Ann Arbor Public Schools; Richard Suddendorf, Western Michigan University; Myron Welch, University of Iowa; Frank Wickes, Louisiana State University; Victor Zajec, VanderCook College of Music; Harry Begian, formerly Director of Bands, University of Illinois. □

The following are comments on quality literature that appeared in past issues of The Instrumentalist.

"An objective for the members of our concert bands is the development of a lasting appreciation for fine music. This may be gained from the study of existing standard works and transcriptions for the band, as well as the wealth of contemporary original works, which are each year being added to the literature of the band....Appreciation for fine music is heightened by an understanding of how music is made and how difficult perfection really is."

– Frank A. Piersol, April 1959

Selected Grade 4 Literature

Malcolm Arnold	*English Dances*	arr. Johnstone, Belwin	4
	Four Cornish Dances	arr. Marciniak, Carl Fischer	4
	Prelude, Siciliano, and Rondo	arr. Paynter, Carl Fischer	4
Johann S. Bach	*Fantasia in G*	arr. Leist-Goldman, Mercury	4
Leonard Bernstein	*Selections from West Side Story*	arr. Duthoit, Schirmer	4-5
Houston Bright	*Prelude and Fugue in F Minor*	Shawnee	4
Charles Catel	*Overture in C*	Presser	4
John Barnes Chance	*Elegy*	Boosey & Hawkes	4
	Variations on a Korean Folk Song	Boosey & Hawkes	4
Elliot Del Borgo	*Do Not Go Gentle Into That Good Night*	Shawnee	4
Norman Dello Joio	*Scenes from The Louvre*	Marks	4
Arthur Frackenpohl	*American Folk Song Suite*	Shawnee	4
Girolamo Frescobaldi	*Toccata*	arr. Slocum, Belwin	4
Vittorio Giannini	*Fantasia for Band*	F. Colombo	4
Reinhold Glière	*Russian Sailors' Dance*	arr. Leidzen, Carl Fischer	4
Francois-Joseph Gossec	*Classic Overture in C*	arr. Liest, Mercury	4
Percy Grainger	*Handel in the Strand*	arr. Goldman, Carl Fischer	4
	Irish Tune from County Derry	arr. Kent, Carl Fischer	4
	Shepherd's Hey	Schirmer	4
Howard Hanson	*Chorale and Alleluia*	Carl Fischer	4
Gustav Holst	*Suite No. 1 in Eb*	Boosey & Hawkes	4
Anthony Iannaccone	*After a Gentle Rain*	Shawnee	4-5
Gordon Jacob	*An Original Suite*	Boosey & Hawkes	4
	William Byrd Suite	Boosey & Hawkes	4
Robert Jager	*Third Suite*	Volkwein	4
William Latham	*Three Chorale Preludes*	Summy	4
Martin Mailman	*Liturgical Music*	Belwin	4
Robert Margolis	*Color*	Manhattan Beach	4
W. Francis McBeth	*Beowulf*	Southern	4
Vincent Persichetti	*Chorale Prelude: So Pure the Star*	Elkan-Vogel	4
	Pageant	Carl Fischer	4
	Psalm for Band	Elkan-Vogel	4
Alfred Reed	*A Festival Prelude*	Marks	4
Gioacchino Rossini	*Italian in Algiers Overture*	arr. Cailliet, Fox	4
William Schuman	*When Jesus Wept*	Schirmer	4
Dmitri Shostakovich	*Folk Dances*	arr. Reynolds, Carl Fischer	4
Claude T. Smith	*Emperata Overture*	Wingert-Jones	4
	Eternal Father, Strong to Save	Wingert-Jones	4-5
Franz von Suppé	*Poet and Peasant Overture*	arr. Safranek, Carl Fischer	4
Terig Tucci	*Lola Flores*	arr. Krance, Marks	4
R. Vaughan Williams	*English Folk Song Suite*	Boosey & Hawkes	4
Richard Wagner	*Liebestod*	arr. Bainum, Kjos	4
	Trauersinfonie	arr. Leidzen, AMP	4
John Zdechlik	*Chorale and Shaker Dance*	Kjos	4

Selected Grade 5 Literature

Malcolm Arnold	*Four Scottish Dances*	arr. Paynter, Carl Fischer	5
Warren Benson	*The Solitary Dancer*	MCA	5
Hector Berlioz	*Roman Carnival Overture*	arr. Godfrey, Chappell	5+
Leonard Bernstein	*Overture to Candide*	arr. Beeler, Schirmer	5
	Slava!	arr. Grundman, Boosey & H.	5+
Mark Camphouse	*Elegy*	TRN	5
John Barnes Chance	*Blue Lake Overture*	Boosey & Hawkes	5
	Incantation and Dance	Boosey & Hawkes	5
Aaron Copland	*A Lincoln Portrait*	arr. Beeler, Boosey & Hawkes	5
Camille De Nardis	*Universal Judgment*	arr. Cafarella, Carl Fischer	5
Norman Dello Joio	*Variants on a Medieval Tune*	Marks	5
Umberto Giordano	*Andrea Chenier Selections*	arr. Richards, Kalmus	5
Percy Grainger	*Colonial Song*	Carl Fischer	5
	Hill Song No. 2	TRN	5+
Paul Hindemith	*March from Symphonic Metamorphosis*	arr. Wilson, Belwin	5
Gustav Holst	*Second Suite in F (Revised)*	Boosey & Hawkes	5
Charles Ives	*Variations on "America"*	Schuman-Rhoads, Presser	5
Gordon Jacob	*Music for a Festival*	Boosey & Hawkes	5
Joseph Jenkins	*An American Overture*	Presser	5
Vassili Kalinnikov	*Symphony No. 1 in G Minor, Finale*	arr. Bainum, EMS	5
Timothy Mahr	*Fantasia in G*	Kjos	5
Felix Mendelssohn	*Overture for Band, Op. 24*	arr. Griessle, Schirmer	5
Peter Mennin	*Canzona*	Carl Fischer	5
Darius Milhaud	*Suite française*	MCA	5
W.A. Mozart	*The Marriage of Figaro*	arr. Slocum, Belwin	5
Vaclav Nelhybel	*Symphonic Movement*	Belwin	5
Roger Nixon	*Fiesta del Pacifico*	Boosey & Hawkes	5
Carl Orff	*Carmina Burana*	arr. Krance, AMP	5
Vincent Persichetti	*Divertimento for Band*	Presser	5
	Symphony for Band	Elkan-Vogel	5
Alfred Reed	*Armenian Dances, Part One*	Fox	5
	Armenian Dances, Part Two	Barnhouse	5
	Russian Christmas Music	Fox	5
N. Rimsky-Korsakov	*Procession of the Nobles*	arr. Leidzen, Carl Fischer	5
William Schuman	*Chester Overture*	Presser	5
	George Washington Bridge	Schirmer	5
Dmitri Shostakovich	*Festive Overture*	arr. Hunsberger, MCA	5
Kenneth Snoeck	*Scaramouche, Symphony No. 3*	Shawnee	5
Fisher Tull	*Sketches on a Tudor Psalm*	Boosey & Hawkes	5
Joaquin Turina	*Procession du Rocio*	arr. Reed, F. Colombo	5
R. Vaughan Williams	*Toccata Marziale*	Boosey & Hawkes	5
Richard Wagner	*Elsa's Procession to the Cathedral*	arr. Cailliet, W-7	5
Jaromir Weinberger	*Polka and Fugue from Schwanda*	arr. Bainum, AMP	5
Clifton Williams	*Symphonic Dance No. 3, Fiesta*	Fox	5
Haydn Wood	*Mannin Veen*	Belwin	5
Gregory Youtz	*Scherzo for a Bitter Moon*	TRN	5

"There are fads in music, as there are in everything else, but I think one constant is concert music, and it should be stressed. Concert music will always be part of our musical heritage." — Arnold Gabriel, October 1981

"In choosing literature for performance, the musical quality of the works should be the primary consideration. While style, technical challenge, audience and performer appeal, and educational value are important considerations, none will be well served if the music does not measure up to high standards of quality. Both conductor and performers need to live with a piece for a long time during the intensive preparation period before a performance. If the music is shallow and poorly constructed, the task becomes less interesting and little growth occurs. Conversely, a solidly composed piece allows for new discoveries and challenges as it is rehearsed and analyzed over a lengthy period of time. Fine music seems to become more interesting with greater exposure, no matter what level of technical difficulty."

— Elliot Del Borgo, November 1988

"We started late with the band, and have a lot of ground to make up...Those interested in the band have done a good job of encouraging talented people to write original compositions and arrangements for band."

— John Paynter, July 1979

"We have an educational job to perform in seeing to it that our students become familiar with worthwhile music of the past. The fact the teacher may be a little tired of the old music and may pine for something new to freshen his own tastes does not relieve him from the responsibility of presenting the great music of the masters to his students." — James C. Harper, June 1957

March, 1992

Assessing the Wind Ensemble

by W. Francis McBeth

In 1981 I received a letter from a music professor asking about the conflict between concert bands and wind ensembles:

> I am currently involved in a dissertation which might be of mutual interest. The title is The History and Development of the Wind Ensemble. (A colleague) has been of great assistance in my work, and suggested that I contact prominent composers in order to document opinion and philosophy concerning the wind ensemble movement.
>
> As you are aware, a controversy exists concerning a potential threat to the nation's concert band programs by the wind ensemble movement. Furthermore, the vast majority of concert band repertory has been accused of banality and commercialism. The repertory for the wind ensemble, on the other hand, appears to be conceived from an artistic, aesthetic viewpoint. Many composers have avoided the wind band medium entirely, while others have contributed to the concert band, wind ensemble, or both.
>
> I feel that your views concerning this topic and your philosophy of writing for and the future development of the wind ensemble in America's colleges is vital to this study. It has been stated that the future of the medium is in the hands of the composer.

I replied with the following letter, which I believe is as correct today as when I wrote it:

I thought that I was aware of all the trends, movements, and even gossip, but you state that some have said "a controversy exists concerning a potential threat to the nation's concert band programs by the wind ensemble movement." I have done more than thirty-five out-of-state concerts

per year for the past eighteen years and I have never heard this "controversy" mentioned. It must exist somewhere, however, or you wouldn't have mentioned it. It is a fear that no one should worry about.

No viable medium has ever replaced another — it just adds to the whole of musical expression. If any musical ensemble should be a threat to the concert band program, it should be the orchestra — with 300 years of repertory behind them, orchestral programs should be blowing band programs off the face of the earth. Why is this not happening? Because no viable medium replaces another, but adds to the total of all musical experience.

The next comment that you report is extremely interesting and opens up a musical Pandora's box, letting loose everything from true concern to snobbery — the statement, "The vast majority of concert band repertory has been accused of banality and commercialism."

This accusation reflects a motivation that is highly suspect, demonstrating a lack of knowledge of the roles of school band programs in the United States. The school band programs (junior high, high school, and college) represent about ninety-nine percent of all band programs in this country. No musical medium in the history of music has ever been required to wear as many hats as the

W. Francis McBeth is professor of music, chairman of the theory/composition department, and resident composer at Ouachita University in Arkadelphia, Arkansas. His education was received from Harding Simmons University, The University of Texas, and the Eastman School of Music.

band. Choral programs would be next. The public school band program is required to be successful in four areas; college programs serve the latter three functions. You are as aware of these areas as I am, but let me state them for continuity.

Area One: The training of beginning and intermediate players. The public schools must train their players to play from scratch. Obviously, this is not done and cannot be done with masterpieces of wind literature. To list the literature used to accomplish this purpose as "banal and commercial" is to miss the point. They are training pieces, pedagogical efforts — nothing to do with wind repertory.

Area Two: Football, basketball, and pep rallies. School and college bands derive much of their financial support because they are willing to go into show business part time. No matter how you slice it, the majority of English horns, contrabass clarinets, sets of *Lincolnshire Posey*, etc., are purchased with money set aside for ensembles because they will also appear at sporting events to entertain the crowd. Cut this out and in ninety percent of all high schools and colleges three-fourths of the budget will vanish. I can name dates, places, and schools where it has happened.

Area Three: The Stage Band. Its function and existence are important to the retention of many players who later get serious. From Clifton Williams to John Barnes Chance to myself, our introduction to composition came as the result of arranging for our high school or college stage bands. Many great wind performers were kept in the programs during their salad days by the stage band program, only to go on to greater musical interests and goals in later adolescence.

Area Four: The concert band program. There is no need to discuss this except to state that this is the only area in which repertory should be judged. Let us only speak of banality and commercialism in this area.

Now let us re-examine your statement that ". . . the vast majority of concert band repertory has been accused of banality and commercialism." Let us subtract all of the music written and published for areas one, two, and three. After this subtraction what is left is the literature written for serious wind performance, and I daresay this constitutes about ten percent or less of the band music published each year. These are the only publications that can be accused of banality and commercialism in comparison to wind ensemble publications. If these publications are closely examined (and let's look at only the past twenty-five years) it is unbelievable how many brilliant works for band have appeared in such a short period of time.

By way of comparison, it is instructive to note that the percentage of poor works (in the band category — area four) isn't nearly as high as in the choral publications of the past twenty-five years.

Let us turn now to the statement, "The repertory for the wind ensemble, on the other hand, appears to be conceived from an artistic, aesthetic viewpoint." I feel that a statement such as this about any musical ensemble is pretentious and smacks of snobbery.

When Frederick Fennell created the wind ensemble and chose the name, he performed one of the most ingenious acts of the 20th century. Fennell saw into the future. He saw a coming repertory for the winds. He was well aware that the name band was a four-letter word to many serious musicians. He wanted to present serious wind literature to audiences, but realized that the term band was an albatross around the neck of many people because of the past. Every wind conductor in the United States is indebted to Frederick Fennell, more than any other man, for improving our status with the serious music community.

What he did was a stroke of genius. History will be very kind to Fred. I guess you sense my affection for him both personally and professionally.

It was never his intention, in my opinion, to replace the band, but to add another dimension to it. Fred conducted the Eastman Chamber Orchestra each summer and the concerts were just superb, a highlight of my summers for many years, but he wasn't attempting to replace the full symphony orchestra. He was again showing a wonderful addition to our musical experience.

Now let's get to the matter of literature. I can match you four or more band masterpieces to each one wind ensemble masterpiece. Does this mean that the band is superior to the wind ensemble? No, it simply means the band is older. I can match you fifty or sixty orchestra masterpieces to each one band masterpiece — because the orchestra is much older. I can match you fifty to one in violin to French horn masterpieces, and so on.

If you were to ask me what musical ensemble has the highest percentage of works "conceived from an artistic, aesthetic viewpoint," the answer would be the string quartet, and I'm quoting Dr. Eugene Selhorst. Does this mean that it has a repertory superior to that of the orchestra? Of course not, only a more narrow role. This also doesn't mean that all serious music for the string quartet is great music, which brings us to an interesting phenomenon that I have observed with too many wind ensemble works and conductors. This phenomenon is the strange concept that any work for wind ensemble that is a grade 5 or above is considered a great work. It would be bad manners and show a lack of breeding to name specific works here. Bernard Rogers said many times, "There is no such thing as good or bad music — there is only honest or dishonest music." It took me years to understand this. I now could write a dissertation on the validity of that statement.

One last point to show the futility of the debate over which repertory is superior can be seen in this hypothetical question. Can anyone name the wind ensemble literature that has been written to train young wind ensemble players who are in the fifth grade? When anyone can do that, then I will discuss the aesthetic difference between the complete band literature and the complete wind ensemble literature. I am very pro wind ensemble, but I am very anti snobbishness. History will settle all these questions.

Now let us discuss the real problem that affects both the band and wind ensemble at the artistic and aesthetic level the ability of the conductors of wind music.

Fred Fennell and I are the only two band conductors I am aware of who have also been conductors of professional symphony orchestras with budgets of over a half million dollars. I state half a million to distinguish these or-chestras from urban or community orchestras. There are others capable of this who haven't had the opportunity, but you can just about count them on one hand James Neilson, William Revelli, William Santelmann, to name a few of our elder colleagues. The conductors of bands have done a superhuman job in organiza-tion and pedagogy, producing the greatest wind players in the world, both in numbers and in ability. The wind literature has accrued more great works in a short amount of time than any repertory in history. It is the podium alone that is our Achilles heel at this point in our history; it is our most serious problem. Masterpieces of any medium become banal in the hands of amateurs.

Please forgive me for responding at such length, but I felt it important to do so by the content of your letter and the importance of your work.

November, 1989

Don't Lose Your Audience

An interview with Robert Phillips of the Indianapolis Symphonic Band

by George Weimer

The Indianapolis Symphonic Band is a non-profit community band that gives musicians ranging from middle school students to adults a chance to perform. Less ex-perienced players are invited to join, and seating them next to seasoned veterans gives them the chance to improve.

The 75-member ensemble performs music from traditional orchestral transcriptions and original band compositions to show tunes and popular favorites. Numerous small ensembles, including a jazz band and woodwind and brass ensembles, also play separately from the group. Summer concerts by the band draw crowds of more than 1,000 people to each performance.

Robert Phillips, the band's founder, was born in 1913 and graduated from Purdue University with a degree in chemical engineering. He worked for chemical and pharmaceutical com-panies and has served as a volunteer tutor in the Indianapolis Public Schools.

How did you get involved with music in the first place?

I never studied an instrument formally. I took lessons when I was 10 to 12 years old from Ed-ward Meretzki Upton, a harmony and theory teacher who commuted to Chicago from Toron-to. He said, "If you know what you are doing, any fool with eyes and fingers can learn to play later." I learned a thorough background in theory from him; it was all he taught. He would play a progression, including modulations, in class; we couldn't see the keyboard. He would say, "Here is where we begin; where do we end? Get it right the first time you hear it." He believed theory is something you don't get out of a textbook.

I was drafted as a string bass player in high school because I was tall enough. I had excellent high school music teachers in orchestra; and I picked up jazz and classical piano using my ear training background. After high school I went on the road playing string bass with jazz bands. Later I started with a string quartet in my front room and teaching blossomed from that. I bought the music and served as a coach.

In 1945 Sandor Kallai, an Indianapolis Sym-phony French hornist, decided he wanted his students to get some playing experience. He asked if I could contribute some of the students I coached in brass, woodwind, and string

George Weimer is a professor of music at the University of Indianapolis, where he is director of bands and teaches instrumental music education, conducting, and trumpet.

ensembles to play in a group. He did the organizing and conducting, and provided the music that formed the core of the present library. He was a fine musician and conductor but left Indianapolis to play in Kansas City; the library and the students remained and I took over the group.

Who were your musical heroes when you were young?

That's a hard question, but I would say Victor Herbert, John Philip Sousa, and Alfred Wallenstein. Victor Herbert raises some eyebrows today; his music is dated, but I play it once in a while as a curiosity. As composers neither Herbert nor Sousa were afraid of melody and simple structure. Today the world is full of college instructors who think they are saving the musical world. Half of their job should be to please the public, not play down to it. Some pieces I play because the band likes them; some because I like them; some for educational purposes, but not many. If I find a good march, I'm much more likely to play it than a high-toned and expensive-sounding piece. The audience reacts to Viennese waltzes and good marches. We also play some of the not-so-usual repertoire, including such fine marches as Sousa's *Daughters of Texas*, *Kansas Wildcats*, and *Bullets and Bayonets*. Karl King's *Melody Shop* is also excellent; Fred Jewell marches are good. Our audience enjoys Broadway musicals and hymn tune settings, such as *God of our Fathers* by Thomas Knox. We have good luck with *paso dobles*: I could mention *Pepito Greus* by Pascual Perez Chovi, and *Espana Cani* by Pascual Marquina.

What contributions do you think the Indianapolis Symphonic band makes to the community?

It gives good players who have graduated from high school a chance to play.

What is your secret for motivating players and why do they keep coming back?

Because we challenge them. We seldom repeat literature, and we give them good music. The selctions are not always heavy, intellectual stuff, but they are always good. We run a structured program. If a kid stays for four years he will have played all styles and periods.

No one in the band is paid. Why does this work? I know few other community bands that can keep unpaid players.

They are not offering the right bait. Members should enjoy playing and having good people around them. I've never asked to be paid, and we've never had paid players.

How are new players brought into the band?

In addition to publicized open auditions, new players are brought in by band members, some are their school or private students. Some music

teachers come to hear music they can perform with their high school groups. They could fill a notebook with pieces they can play and build an excellent repertoire. Some directors borrow pieces from our library to use with their school bands. When we play our annual concerts in high schools, we ask the best players from their band to play and invite them to continue if they are good enough.

It is left to the section leader's discretion whether a student is invited back. I seldom turn anyone down. We joke that we have engraved certificates for players: first year in the band, and last year in the band. It's not completely a joke, and on two occasions we got rid of people using the certificate. I once had an older fellow who wouldn't take the hint until I stopped during a rehearsal and said, "I checked the score and can't find a part for barking dog." He got the message.

If you could give one piece of advice to band directors, what would it be?

Don't play junk! I won't say I won't play rock 'n 'roll; I play it only once. Some of it is good, but I'm not going to perpetuate it. I'm not impressed by a piece just because it's got a big name. Some directors, particularly college directors, ask why we don't play more standard repertoire. The reason is simple; it doesn't deserve playing. The audience doesn't care what is standard repertoire.

How do you feel about the way most directors program their concerts?

It's a mutual admiration society. "I'll play your piece, and you'll play mine and we'll tell everybody how marvelous they are," but you

676

know in your heart they're not.

Are you talking about large high school and college bands?

Yes; the quality of much of the music is not what it should be. It is technically difficult but not musically rewarding. James Curnow, Francis McBeth, Elliott Del Borgo, Norman Dello Joio, and Clifton Williams are outside of that mess. These composers and a few others have something to say. I have strong feelings about composers making statements and not just dragging their feet. A lot of the feeling for what is good literature is shared by the band. They rebel every once in a while, and I have to go with them. If the band actively doesn't like a piece (sometimes out of ignorance, but not very often) I can't get a decent performance. They are good judges of the real value of what's being played. Some popular music is not of high quality, but we will play it once. I can tell what they like by how they sound. If they like it, they really dig their toenails into it and make it sound.

What are some of your ideas concerning concert programming?

Don't be afraid to program something like "Santa Lucia," which is two choruses of the melody in thirds. It's just a sweet, easy folk song that the band first thought to be too simple. What's wrong with simple? Some directors forget that there has to be a melody and a logical structure for the audience.

Do you take the audience into consideration when you plan a program?

Absolutely; aren't they part of the program? At least half of the music on a program should be recognizable to the concertgoer. We present a carefully balanced mixture of concert selections. If you sit through one of my concerts, you hear a variety of different styles and approaches. We try hard to play music authentically, in the style that it was written. We have a formula for every concert: march, *paso doble*, overture, a familiar symphonic piece (including ballet and opera), a modern piece or two, a recognizable waltz or a polka, something sacred, a baroque or classical piece, and at least one popular or jazz selection. We always end with a march.

How much new literature would you program for a concert?

One-third of a concert at the most. I'm not trying to destroy modern composers. I play their music as much as I can without losing my audience and my band.

I particularly like *Elegy for a Young American* by Ronald LoPresti (liked by the band as well), *Canticle for the Creatures* by James Curnow, and

Do Not Go Gentle Into That Good Night by Elliott Del Borgo.

In searching for good band music you have visited many other countries. What have you found?

I have located some early Ricordi transcriptions for Italian band with all the high clarinets and $A^\flat$ soprano saxophone. These pieces are now a part of the band's library, and they are worth playing.

What sources of band music are not commonly known to directors? Where could they go to find more good music?

The German publishers have a lot of stuff that's not known. Arnold Simon in West Germany is a broker for most European publishers. Alphonse Leduc of Paris now has an American outlet. I like the band publications of Molenaar's from Holland, Musica Mundana also in Holland, Carl Gehrmans in Sweden, and Fest-Musik-Haus, which has an outlet in Texas.

What guiding philosophy has contributed to your success?

Basically it is knowing how to program and having a sense of when we are losing the audience. Once during a four-movement ballet suite, I stopped conducting after two-and-one-half movements. Even though my back was to the audience I could hear and feel the restlessness. We could have continued, but doing so would have been a disfavor to the music business. If you are making people restless, why do you exist? Some of the band members accused me of ruining the piece by ending it where I did. "No," I said, "We ruined it by playing it in the first place."

How is the band financed?

We get most of our money from private contributions, and the shopping center where we perform most of our concerts pays us a fee to play there. We use some of the money to provide college scholarships for our best high school players. Scholarships are awarded on playing ability only, and the money may be used in any way the student decides. We generally award three or four scholarships a year, each of $100-$150. We hope to be able to increase the amount of each award in the future. The rest of the money is used to purchase music.

At each concert we invite the audience to complete a comment card if they want to be added to our mailing list. The board uses the list to advertise concerts and to ask for an annual contribution.

What is the band's concert schedule?

The band plays seven summer concerts and a

couple of concerts at Indianapolis high schools.

The band provides instruments for students who can't afford their own. How do you obtain those instruments and match them to students?

Band members donate them, and I do the matching. Until recently I was an unpaid tutor in the Indianapolis Public Schools. When I find a kid with talent and no horn, we lend him one. The kid gets to keep the horn as long as he needs it. They may not be pretty instruments, but they play well.

What are your hopes for the future of the Indianapolis Symphonic Band?

Our future rests on our ability to get good high school kids in the band, and unfortunately many local band directors are not cooperating with us. Whether they think I'm a threat, I don't know, but some of this revolves around marching band. Some directors think that I steal from their time to bring kids to rehearsals in the evening. We rehearse too late for some high school players. We try to let the school kids leave at intermission, halfway through the rehearsal, so they can do their homework.

What is the future of the concert band in schools?

It's dead. Look back at the last 10 years and see what school concert bands have become. Many have declined in enrollment and few are still viable. One of the problems is marching band. Teachers require the best players to be at every marching rehearsal because they teach the other kids the notes. That's wrong. As part of their educations student musicians need to sit beside fine adult players some of the time.

Do you think there is a proper balance in school programs with concert band, jazz band, and marching band?

No. School programs are top heavy in marching. By the time marching season is over, you have to rebuild the kid's attitude and lip. If I were involved under the present system, I would quit. I would have a good pep band of people who wanted to play in a pep band and were enthusiastic about it. I would have a short marching season. If other directors want trophies, I would let them compete; but I'm incapable of

running a marching band, and that colors my judgment. I don't have a degree in pageantry.

Is contest competition healthy for high school students?

To some extent, yes, but then students stop learning when it eventually becomes nothing but competition. I came up through contests, but my high school band director would prepare only the week before the contest. We'd rehearse the music we were going to play, then after the competition we'd never play it again. My director's philosophy was that we would get all the discipline and all the musical value we needed from marching band in one week. I agree with him. There's too much good music that needs playing and kids should be able to play in several different styles, not just marching band.

What are those styles?

When a student finishes high school he should have played eight overtures; know the different styles of marches: German, English, French, circus, gallops, and processionals; and of course know some opera and ballet selections. He should be familiar with baroque and classical pieces and be fluent in jazz and pop styles. Kids should be able to improvise, although improvising isn't for everybody. After four years in a high school band a player should be able to play everything you hand him and be able to sight-read decently too.

How important is sight-reading?

It's very important, otherwise you waste rehearsal time. Half of every lesson or a quarter of a rehearsal should be spent sight-reading. This should start in the fifth grade. When the band plays at high schools, we invite talented players from the school to join us for rehearsals and the performance. Unfortunately we leave it to the school director to decide which students play with us, and some recommend people who do not read music well. Many directors are insensitive to how poorly their kids read. Most high school bands sight-read so little at rehearsals that the directors never notice which kids can read and which kids can't.

As director of the Indianapolis Symphonic Band what do you feel is your greatest success?

It's the number of players who have stayed with us for a long time. Some have played with us for 35 and 40 years.

What has been your greatest inspiration?

To see some of our young musicians go on to major performing careers while others who would never have played after high school are still playing and enjoying it. ☐

Perceiving Music

Personal Evaluation of Quality in Music

by W. Francis McBeth

By what process does a person evaluate the artistic merits of a creative work? How do you decide the quality of a painting, of a play, of a novel, of a musical composition? How does one evaluate anything? People evaluate by what they perceive something is supposed to be. Let me repeat, people evaluate by what they perceive something is supposed to be.

The problem is that all people believe that their perception is correct; this is human nature, while history usually proves the majority of perceptions to be incorrect. What genetic, environmental, Freudian, parental, geographic, religious, or prejudicial factors control our likes and dislikes?

Our perceptions dictate not only our process of evaluation, but our course of action. The Nazi geo-politicians and Stalin perceived the world in terms of labor and raw materials and this demanded territory. Gorbachev perceives the world as "markets are more valuable than territory, information more powerful than military hardware." These two diverse perceptions of the metaphysics of global power will dictate diverse directions and methods. Schweitzer viewed the world as a challenge to reduce human suffering. Teilhard de Chardin viewed the world as a struggle between the forces of good and evil. Individual perceptions dictate diverse responses.

How do you perceive music; what do you want to be? Schenker said that there are two kinds of people in the world, those who like good music and those who don't. He said that the difference between the two groups is that those who like good music can hear polyphony and those who don't cannot. He added that for those who can't hear polyphony, music can never be anything more than a song, a dance, or a march. After years of listening and thinking, I believe his thesis has some merit.

If we assume that most professional musicians fit into the first category, this raises the question of how musicians perceive or evaluate quality in good music, or as I prefer, music with artistic intent. One of my lifelong cohorts, Dr. George Keck, asked me years ago how I decided the level of quality in a composition. It was an excellent question because it forced me to think through and put into words what I, by ear and instinct, advised my students every day in my composition classes.

I think that there are two constants in all great music: *direction* and *originality*. Direction is always evident in great music; lesser efforts always wander. Great music is never a succession of acceptable progressions but a journey of sound to somewhere.

Music was the last of the fine arts to become art, much later than painting and sculpture, and it didn't become an art until the invention or discovery of motivic development.

Beethoven was the first to reach its potential summit; he was the master of "going somewhere." In a Beethoven symphony by score page 12 listeners know that we are on our way and know when we get there, and the trip was sublime. The worst musical experience is to just float in a still pond of sound. Beethoven was the first to combine direction with, as Furtwangler called it, a "sense of the catastrophic" — what a powerful aural experiment.

Now to the second constant or yardstick, originality. I use the word originality, Bernard Rogers always used the word honesty. In fact

W. Francis McBeth is professor of music, resident composer, and chairman of the theory-composition department at Ouachita University, Arkadelphia, Arkansas, and has written extensively for band, orchestra, and chamber ensembles. He is a former conductor of the Arkansas Symphony at Little Rock and has conducted extensively in the United States and abroad. McBeth's formal education is from Hardin-Simmons University, the University of Texas, and the Eastman School of Music.

Rogers never spoke of good or bad, but of honest and dishonest music. He seemed to classify all original music, whether one liked it or not, as honest music and music that was not original (rewrites of other composers' originality) as dishonest.

I cannot abide the music of the Grand Ole Opry types with their fake cowboy hats and sequins; but the real country music of Stone County, Arkansas, written and played by people in old overalls on instruments that they built, is absolutely wonderful. Honest or dishonest, that's the yardstick. How about the four boys from Liverpool who sang in an Alabama accent and stole everything original from Little Richard — honest or dishonest?

W. Francis McBeth with Howard Hanson

In evaluating music, and new music in particular, as to originality, the process always brings us to style. Personal style is the single most sought after and hoped for ingredient in art by an artist. Style is that special ingredient that distinguishes a work as belonging to a specific artist. Few aspiring artists ever achieve a personal style, but almost all successful ones do.

What constitutes personal style? When an artist creates elements in his art that are expressly his own, be it thumb prints or slips of the chisel, and these elements are always recognized as related to that artist, a personal style has been created. An artist can have a personal style without being successful, but almost no artist has been successful without one (the "almost" takes care of such composers as Bruch, Capputzzi, and Herbert L. Clark, whose successes were not in composition but in concertant or virtuoso performance writing).

Poor Mussorgsky; Rimsky kept "correcting" the rough-edged composer's work, but each decade since, Mussorgsky's star rises higher and higher than Rimsky's — why? Originality. It always wins out in the end; I say the end because it is usually not so in the present. I witnessed a standing ovation a year ago for a difficult new work at a major new music convention that was a rewrite of Mahler's 5th and 8th Symphonies. Why the standing ovation? In evaluating the quality of the composition the majority in attendance preferred familiarity over originality. Creation and re-creation are two entirely different activities.

Re-creation is always more readily accepted than creation. The best work that year was not performed at the convention; and if it had been, it would not have had the acceptance that the Mahler re-write received. This does not bother me at all; it has always been this way. Eduard Hanslick, the major European critic of the time, loved Meyerbeer and hated Beethoven.

One of our well-known conductors asked in an article about eight years ago, "Where are the young march composers?" (I assume to challenge Sousa and King). That is the same as saying, where are the young men who will fly the Atlantic alone in a single engine plane. The answer is, it won't ever happen again; it has already been done. One cannot re-invent the light bulb. My like question would be, where are the young composers who will write great new Protestant hymns? The answer to my own question is, it has already been done and can't be done again in that form. If new marches and hymns are written, they cannot be in the style, form, melodic and harmonic usage of the old standards and still be creative work.

Creativity and difference are not synonymous; just being different or strange does not constitute artistic creativity. Originality does not create art, but art cannot be created without originality. Being different is the easiest thing in the world, but creating something new and viable is difficult and is an entirely different process. How do we evaluate viable or successful music? What causes music to be successful?

Most unsuccessful music results from a composer who writes notes on paper before the idea for the work is formulated. Why would one do this? For many reasons: a pressing deadline on a commission, a class assignment, or the desire to have written a piece, but the result is scotch-taping one measure to the next. This never works because music must be conceived before the act of setting it to notes. The reverse is almost always the method used by students and amateurs. Notes come last, ideas are first or the music will be completely lacking in direction. A composer must know how a composition will end before he can write the beginning.

I have discussed the process to help you understand the mechanics, but your personal evaluation of quality in music must go beyond mechanics. It must be rooted in your ability to sense direction and originality, framed in expert craft. No one element can stand alone. □

Repertoire

for
Wind Conductors

Donald R. Hunsberger

This article is based on a clinic-session on wind repertoire and programming presented by the author at the Eighth National Wind Ensemble Conference, in February 1977 at Northern Illinois University. It was prepared for publication in this issue of *The Instrumentalist* as a preface to the papers to be presented at the Eastman Wind Ensemble Festival Symposium, October 7-8, 1977 at the Eastman School of Music.

During the quarter century since the first concert of the innovative Eastman Wind Ensemble (February 8, 1953) significant advancements in repertoire and performance procedures have been made, establishing solid musical directions for the future of wind music.

The second wind conductor has come of age and may stand erect among ensemble leaders of all genre. His place has been established by the ever-increasing

Donald R. Hunsberger, conductor of the Eastman Wind Ensemble, is co-chairman of the Conducting and Ensemble Department at the Eastman School of Music. He also serves as executive secretary of the National Center for the Symphonic Wind Ensemble which he founded at Eastman in 1973.

credibility of contemporary wind repertoire and by programming concepts concerned with *what music is performed* rather than with reaching out for acceptance on the level of the lowest common denominator.

No longer do wind conductors rely upon orchestral transcriptions or light-headed occasional music for the staples of contemporary programs, and no longer are they bound to the safe, yet tone-color-restricting military band journal school of wind scoring with its multiplicity of cross-cueing techniques designed to protect the empty inner-chair voice, and in turn, inhibiting that voice's growth when present.

The goal of the wind conductor is still the same as it has been the past half-century: original composition indigenous to the medium on the same musical standard employed for other performance media. Today the goal is not quite so inaccessible, for composers of international stature now examine the wind band as a flexible instrumentation ensemble dedicated to serious performance practices rather than as an organization that would play any material anywhere at any time. The higher the level of self-respect a conductor engenders toward his ensemble and its repertoire, the more serious a view will be undertaken by the world's foremost composers.

681

To insure progress during the next quarter century, the wind conductor must continue to develop and maintain a personal image as a serious performing musician — one who specializes in wind instrument repertoire and performance. Far too often, the crowning achievement in a director's career is his successful administration and maintenance of an ensemble or group of ensembles. This activity, frequently recognized by administrators and governing boards as the primary function of a band director, should be of secondary importance; primary attention should be directed toward music itself and the composer-creator.

It is the personal obligation of each serious wind conductor and teacher to assess his own abilities to provide continuous growth and to discover *that musical repertoire* whose contribution will be valid. Through such an assessment, the conductor should discern a personal *basic repertoire* which will form the cornerstone of his commitment to serious music. Secondly, a *philosophy of programming* should be established through which the conductor transmits his personal standards, and projects music by important composers.

Let us first examine basic criteria of *programming philosophy* to determine what we are searching for in substantial wind composition. Over the past two-and-one-half decades, two principal repertoires have emerged, each differing in size and purpose. The larger of these two groups of literature might well be described as *educational instrumental ensemble music*, that is, music written for young, developing performers, frequently with technical limitations considered, and with compositional and scoring techniques employed that retain the positive characteristics of the English military band and its American symphonic band counterpart. The other repertoire employs flexible instrumentation as desired by the composer, with primary emphasis placed upon the individual performer rather than upon the larger massed section. The composer is directly responsible for all weights and balances of each individual voice (thus separating instrumentation from personnel assignment), and is free to write without restrictions of technical difficulty, interpretative demands, duration, or immediate audience accessibility. A few works from the large ensemble repertoire also fulfill this description of serious concert works, and are not typical of the majority of educational ensemble compositions. The smaller ensemble style develops the individual performer, espouses clarity and balancing of inner voice lines, and reflects the orchestral concept of instrumental performance. It bears the title of wind ensemble, wind orchestra, orchestra wind section, or wind symphony, among others, and while it is always dangerous to affix labels to creative endeavors, these designations illustrate its affinity for the orchestral style of performance, and may be traced back to their origins in the classical period orchestra of the eighteenth century.

Programming is one of the most difficult tasks for any conductor, and especially wind conductors, as they do not possess an enormous literature of serious works of substantial duration. The orchestral conductor may easily fill an average program of 75 minutes with only three works: an overture or suite, a concerto, and a symphony. Thus, wind conductors must consider all the ramifications of each work programmed, especially since most have not stood the test of time as have the bulk of the standard orchestral repertoire. The following criteria may be of assistance in establishing a *philosophy of programming*:

• The *art of programming* is the outward vestige of a conductor's *evaluation* of the current status of the performing arts, and in this instance, the assessment of current standards guiding the wind band and its repertoire.

• It is a public indication of the *respect* he holds for his ensemble, its *obligation* to the furtherance of the performing arts, and that *music* to which he requires the performers to devote their time and energies — musical, mental, physical, and emotional.

• It represents his *concept* of the audience he serves ' or wishes to attract to hear his ensemble perform the music deemed valid.

• It represents his *joy in life* found through performance of music which makes a substantive contribution to the welfare of all involved, and provides an artistic validity without compromise.

Once a conductor feels secure in his estimation of value structures, attention must be focused upon *what music* is to be performed and for what purpose. I find it helpful to make a list of primary landmark repertoire that is valid for concert or educational use.

This past February, at the Eighth National Symphonic Wind Ensemble Conference held at Northern Illinois University, I distributed a list of 99 basic wind repertoire compositions to those in attendance during a discussion session concerned with repertoire development and programming techniques. This list was the distillation of many larger lists beginning with the fantastic collection, *Wind Ensemble Repertoire*, compiled under the direction of H. Robert Reynolds, and distributed by the University of Wisconsin Band Department. The listing distributed at Northern Illinois carried an accompanying challenge: "If you find any works that should not be contained in such a primary compilation, replace them with works of your own choice." The entire procedure was obviously a simple, straightforward process to force the conductors to consider seriously every composition on its own merit against a musical standard that does not stop at the boundaries limiting traditional wind band repertoire, but rather is compatible with a repertoire standard that applies to *all* instrumental composition.

I shall start from an even smaller listing — that of ten hallmark original compositions drawn from the total repertoire — to be followed by a second ten, etc. The works are selected solely on musical merit without regard to size or distribution of parts. I sincerely hope that this listing will stimulate an evaluation of each conductor's own basic repertoire, and strengthen his belief in those works of magnitude. The works are presented in alphabetical order by composer.

Sinfonietta for Concert Band   Ingolf Dahl
Serenade   Antonin Dvorak
Lincolnshire Posy   Percy Grainger

Symphony in Bb	Paul Hindemith
Music for Prague 1968	Karel Husa
Suite Francaise	Darius Milhaud
Serenade in Bb	W.A. Mozart
Symphony No. 6 for Band	Vincent Persichetti
Theme and Variations	Arnold Schoenberg
Symphonies of Wind Instruments	Igor Stravinsky

If every conductor (and his ensemble) were familiar with each of these works to the greatest detail possible, he would possess a broad view of comparative compositional techniques. To provide the stimulus so necessary for continual growth, it is absolutely essential for serious conductors to invest time and energies studying material that is above and beyond their current capabilities. One of the most frequent dehabilitating factors in secondary school instrumental programs is the lack of growth stimulation generated by the ensemble to continually urge the conductor to maintain a professional development; thus there must be a self-generative desire on the conductor's part to learn and constantly broaden his thought patterns and modes of learning.

A second list of ten might include the following: (again in alphabetical order by composer).

The Leaves Are Falling	Warren Benson
Outdoor Overture	Aaron Copland
Chorale and Alleluia	Howard Hanson
Hammersmith	Gustav Holst
Canzona	Peter Mennin
Et Expecto Resurrectionem Mortuorum	Oliver Messiaen
Masquerade	Vincent Persichetti
La Fiesta Mexicana	H. Owen Reed
Serenade	Richard Strauss
Octet for Wind Instruments	Igor Stravinsky

As each list must, by its own definitions, reflect the personal prejudices and biases of the compiler, each conductor's list will be different. *Criteria for evaluation* are of considerable importance in the selection process, and are major areas that merit constant improvement. Next is a listing of works that may be considered potential additions to a basic landmark repertoire; again, the list is alphabetical by composer.

King Lear	David Amram
Concerto for Flute and Wind Orchestra	Henk Badings
Designs, Images and Textures	Leslie Bassett
Symphony for Drums and Wind Orchestra	Warren Benson
Kammerkonzert for Violin, Piano and 13 Winds	Alban Berg
Fanfare for the Common Man	Aaron Copland
Celebration Overture	Paul Creston
Variants on a Medieval Tune	Norman Dello Joio
Sacrae Symphoniae (1597) (1615)	Giovanni Gabrieli
Symphony No. 3	Vittorio Giannini
Symphony for Band (West Point)	Morton Gould
Music for the Royal Fireworks	G.F. Handel
Dies Natalis	Howard Hanson
Symphony No. 4	Alan Hovhaness
Suite in Eb	Gustav Holst
Suite in F	Gustav Holst
Apotheosis of This Earth	Karel Husa
Music for a Festival	Gordon Jacob

William Byrd Suite	Gordon Jacob
Miroirs	Rudolph Kelterborn
Suite from the Good Soldier Schweik	Robert Kurka
Concerto for Wind Orchestra	Nicolai Lopatnikoff
Seventh Seal	W. Francis McBeth
Liturgical Music	Martin Mailman
Music with Sculpture	Toshiro Mayuzumi
Serenade in Eb	W.A. Mozart
Serenade in C Minor	W.A. Mozart
Trittico	Vaclav Nehlybel
Pittsburgh Overture	Krzysztof Penderecki
Parable	Vincent Persichetti
Suite Francaise	Francis Poulenc
Scenes	Verne Reynolds
Adagio for Wind Orchestra	Joachin Rodrigo
Three Japanese Dances	Bernard Rogers
Symphony for Brass and Percussion	Gunther Schuller
New England Triptych	William Schuman
Be Glad Then America	
When Jesus Wept	
Chester	
Concerto for Piano and Wind Orchestra	Igor Stravinsky
Histoire du Soldat	Igor Stravinsky
Octandre	Edgar Varese
Trauersinfonie	Richard Wagner
Three Penny Opera Suite	Kurt Weill
Fanfare and Allegro	Clifton Williams
Toccata Marziale	Ralph Vaughan Williams

Many questions will arise from a selective process such as this:

1) What standards of excellence does one apply to such decisions? Where do you develop such standards? How do you evaluate or separate emotional response from intellectual appreciation of technical prowess?

2) How does one evaluate proportional or aleatoric composition? Is it all skill or is there an emotional area to be investigated?

3) How do you evaluate a single composition from a composer, i.e. Mennin's *Canzona* versus individual works from a prolific composer written over periods of development and experimentation?

4) How do you compare established works such as the Holst Suites with newer, relatively untested compositions?

The selective process must provide answers to these basic questions, plus the myriads of other considerations contained in measurements of excellence; and, every conductor must establish a personal system for evaluation. Each musical thought must be examined and retained or rejected, and the standard of evaluation must be one that is valid for all music — not just wind music.

We all must strive for more finely-honed performance practices, more honest, uncompromising literature for our ensembles, and more depth in the thoughts and actions of serious wind conductors. We are what we honestly believe ourselves to be, and our wind bands are a direct result of the seriousness with which we approach our art. Let us continue to grow through reflection, self-determination, and the development of the finest wind literature possible. ■

College
Band
Repertoire

Acton Ostling, Jr.

From 1973-1978 I conducted a doctoral study at the University of Iowa to evaluate band literature solely on the basis of serious artistic merit. The intent was to establish a basic or "standard" repertoire for the wind band.

The problem posed by the study required (1) the development of an appropriate ensemble definition, and criteria for types of compositions to be evaluated, (2) a list of criteria for judging compositions in terms of serious artistic merit, (3) a collection of titles and a procedure for selecting evaluators, and (4) developing a rating scale for use in determining musical quality.

Wind band compositions were defined as those scored for at least ten wind instruments, excluding percussion; written for a mixed rather than homogenous ensemble; and requiring a conductor to perform. Thus, the study evaluated compositions such as the Mozart *Divertimenti* for ten wind instruments, on up to those written for standard band instrumentation. The compositions considered were either original works, transcriptions of compositions written before 1750, or transcriptions of 20th-century compositions. The justification for including some transcriptions, rather than limiting the list to original compositions, was that the standard repertoire for symphony orchestra also includes transcriptions of music written for other types of ensembles or for the keyboard. Music prior to 1750 was often written for the musical line rather than the sound of specific instruments; therefore, it transfers well to other mediums. However, transcriptions of music written between 1750 and 1900 were excluded because orchestra music from the Classic and Romantic periods requires a large and complete string ensemble foundation, and its unique sonority and lyricism is considered essential when one is considering artistic merit alone. (Valid educational reasons for the use of such transcriptions abound, but were not the concern of this study.) As string writing became more percussive in 20th-century orchestral scores, it became possible to transcribe such music for ensembles of wind and percussion instruments.

Collection of Titles

The first step in compiling the compositions was to develop a select list for use as a model in obtaining recommendations from other conductors for compositions of like quality. Frederick Fennell, who was in Iowa City during the beginning stages of the model list, gave invaluable assistance in developing an initial model. The major source for titles other than those included in the model list was the publication headed by H. Robert Reynolds, *Wind Ensemble Literature,* second edition, published in 1975 by the University of Wisconsin Bands.

Criteria for Evaluation

These criteria were developed from three sources: (1) texts on music theory and orchestration, (2) other literature in books, journals, dissertations, and magazine articles, and (3) personal discussions with eminent conductors concerning their own criteria for judging musical quality.

Basic principles were developed to evaluate the quality of the compositions. Some of the areas covered by these principles were balance between repetition and contrast, musical form, craftsmanship in orchestration, consistent quality and style, and imaginative development. Compositions were not chosen on the basis of their historical importance or pedagogical usefulness. The final collection of titles to be evaluated according to these criteria were 1,481.

Acton Ostling, Jr., is director of bands at the University of Louisville in Kentucky.

The Evaluators

Evaluators for the study were chosen by surveying 312 band conductors at colleges and universities having 15 or more full-time faculty members in music. Those surveyed were asked to nominate 10 wind band conductors who sought out and consistently programmed music of artistic merit, and whose evaluation of the literature would be most respected. Twenty evaluators were selected: Frank Battisti, New England Conservatory of Music; Harry Begian, University of Illinois; Frank Bencriscutto, University of Minnesota; Paul Bryan, Duke University; Frederick Ebbs, Indiana University; Frederick Fennell, University of Miami; Charles Gallagher, University of Maryland; Robert Gray, University of Illinois; Donald Hunsberger, Eastman School of Music; Donald McGinnis, Ohio State University; James Matthews, University of Houston; Kenneth Moore, Oberlin Conservatory of Music; James Neilson, G. Leblanc Educational Department; John Paynter, Northwestern University; William D. Revelli, University of Michigan Emeritus; H. Robert Reynolds, University of Michigan; Richard Strange, Arizona State University; Robert Vagner, University of Oregon; David Whitwell, California State University-Northridge; Keith Wilson, Yale University.

Compositions	A	B	C	D	E
Adler, *Festive Prelude.*	x	5	x	NA	NA
Bach-Goldman-Leist, *Fantasia in G Major*	4	x	x	4	4
Bach-Holst, *Fugue a la Gigue.*	x	6	x	x	x
Bach-Falcone, *Passacaglia and Fugue in C Minor.*	6	x	x	NA	6
Bassett, *Designs, Images and Textures.*	6	x	x	6	6
Bennett, *Suite of Old American Dances.*	6	6	6	6	6
Bennett, *Symphonic Songs.*	6	6	x	6	6
Benson, *The Leaves are Falling.*	5	6	x	NA	4
Benson, *The Solitary Dancer.*	5	6	x	NA	4
Bergsma, *March with Trumpets.*	x	x	6	x	x
Bernstein-Beeler, *Candide: Overture.*	6	6	6	6	6
Chance, *Symphony No. 2.*	NA	NA	6	NA	NA
Copland, *Emblems.*	6	6	x	6	6
Copland, *An Outdoor Overture.*	6	6	x	6	6
Creston, *Celebration Overture.*	6	x	x	6	6
Dahl, *Sinfonietta for Band.*	6	x	x	NA	6
Dello Joio, *Variants on a Mediaeval Tune.*	6	6	x	6	6
Fischer-Wilson, *Le Journal du Printemps.*	x	5	x	5	5
DeLone, *Symphony No. 1: Introduction and Allegro.*	x	x	x	6	6
Giannini, *Praeludium and Allegro.*	6	6	x	6	6
Giannini, *Variations and Fugue.*	6	6	x	x	6
Grainger, *Colonial Song.*	5	5	x	x	x
Grainger, *Hill Song No. 2*	6	6	x	5	5
Grainger, *Irish Tune and Shepherd's Hey*	5	5	5	4	4
Grainger, *Lincolnshire Posy.*	6	6	6	6	6
Hanson, *Chorale and Alleluia.*	5	5	5	5	5
Hartley, *Sinfonia No. 4.*	x	6	x	x	5
Hindemith-Wilson, *Symphonic Metamorphosis: March.*	5	x	x	NA	NA
Hindemith, *Symphony in Bb*	6	6	x	6	6
Holst, *Hammersmith.*	6	6	x	6	6
Holst, *Suite No. 1 in Eb*	5	5	5	5	4
Holst, *Suite No. 2 in F.*	5	6	5	5	5

Compositions	A	B	C	D	E
Husa, *Apotheosis of this Earth.*	6	x	x	NA	NA
Husa, *Concerto for Percussion.*	6	x	x	NA	NA
Husa, *Music for Prague 1968.*	6	6	x	NA	6
Ives-Sinclair, "Country Band" *March.*	x	6	x	NA	NA
Ives-Schuman-Rhoads, *Variations on "America."*	6	6	6	NA	4
Jacob, *Music for a Festival.*	6	x	x	6	6
Jacob, *William Byrd Suite.*	6	6	6	5	5
Mendelssohn-Creissle, *Overture for Band.*	6	6	6	5	5
Mennin, *Canzona.*	6	6	6	5	5
Milhaud, *Suite Francaise.*	6	6	x	6	6
Nelhybel, *Trittico.*	6	6	6	6	6
Nelhybel, *Two Symphonic Movements.*	6	6	x	NA	NA
Persichetti, *Divertimento for Band.*	6	6	x	6	6
Persichetti, *Masquerade for Band.*	6	6	x	6	6
Persichetti, *Psalm for Band.*	5	6	x	5	5
Persichetti, *So Pure the Star.*	4	6	x	4	4
Persichetti, *Symphony No. 6.*	6	6	6	6	6
Persichetti, *Turn Not Thy Face.*	x	x	x	NA	3
Piston, *Tunbridge Fair.*	6	x	x	x	5
Reed, *La Fiesta Mexicana.*	6	6	6	6	6
Reynolds, *Scenes.*	6	x	x	NA	NA
Rhodes, *Three Pieces for Band.*	6	x	x	NA	4
Rogers, *Three Japanese Dances.*	6	x	x	x	x
Schmitt, *Dionysiaques.*	x	x	x	6	6
Schoenberg, *Theme and Variations.*	6	x	6	6	6
Schuller, *Diptych.*	6	x	x	NA	NA
Schuller, *Meditation.*	x	x	x	6	6
Schuman, *George Washington Bridge.*	6	x	6	6	5
Schuman, *Chester Overture.*	6	6	6	6	5
Schuman, *When Jesus Wept.*	x	5	x	4	4
Shostakovich-Hunsberger, *Festive Overture.*	6	6	x	5	5
Vaughan Williams, *Folk Song Suite.*	5	5	5	4	4
Vaughan Williams, *Sea Songs.*	x	x	5	x	x
Vaughan Williams, *Toccata Marziale.*	6	6	x	6	6
Wagner-Leidzen, *Trauersinfonie.*	5	5	x	4	4

A - 1976-78 Virginia Band and Orchestra Directors Association Manual

B - 1975 New York State School Music Association Manual

C - 1978 North Carolina Band List

D - 1967 Maryland Band Directors Association List

E - 1971 Music Educators National Conference List

NA - indicates composition not available at time list was issued.

The Rating Scale

Each evaluator was sent the list of 1,481 compositions and asked to judge whether the piece belonged on a list of compositions of "serious artistic merit," considering only those pieces he knew. The rating scale included the following levels: (1) strongly disagree, (2) disagree, (3) undecided, (4) agree, and (5) strongly agree. A total number of points was determined for each composition by adding the numerical ratings received. The total was then converted into a percentage of the maximum points possible. Compositions considered to have met the criteria received at least 80% of the possible points from evaluators familiar with the composition (80% is equal to all ratings of "4" — agree for any given work). In all, 314 compositions met the criteria, including 158 compositions using a standard band instrumentation.

Competition-Festival Music

Band competition-festival lists from several states and from the Music Educators National Conference (MENC), represent the major previous attempts to judge the quality of wind band music. These lists in most instances were not highly selective, but they were attempts at considering the quality of compositions appropriate for the amount of time school music organizations devote to contest-festival music.

My study was concerned with music suitable for college and university ensembles, whereas the state band lists and MENC lists cover high school and junior high school band music. However, there is some overlapping of material.

The 158 band compositions that appear on the "serious artistic merit" list would seem to represent first choices of literature for those high school bands able to perform the works, at least given that repertoire available through 1976 (the stopping point for literature evaluated in the study).

The following table shows the compositions from the study which also appear on the 1971 MENC list, on state and band lists in New York, Virginia, North Carolina, and Maryland. The difficulty levels on each list are also indicated. Of the nearly 90 compositions judged to be of serious artistic merit but not appearing on any of the competition music lists, almost all fall into one of these categories: they were in manuscript form and not published at the time; they were available on rental only at the time; or they were concertos for various solo instruments. Only four published works were not included: *Elegy* by John Barnes Chance, *Lincoln Portrait* by Copland, *Parable* by Persichetti, and *Study in Textures* by Gunther Schuller.

The Virginia Band and Orchestra Directors Association (VBODA) Manual does not define the levels of difficulty, but it does give the following information concerning the selection of the material: "The purpose of this Manual is to give as broad a selection as possible of the various publications for each category. The music lists in the Manual, however, are not intended to be a compilation of all published materials available." The VBODA band list is the largest of such selective lists.

The New York State School Music Association's plan of classification was first presented in 1938. The plan chooses music appropriate for the amount of rehearsal time given to competition-festival music. These pieces are classified according to six difficulty levels and directors are free to choose the music and difficulty that best suits their performing group. The NYSSMA Manual does not give information on the criteria for selecting the music.

The North Carolina Band List seems to be a selective list that falls somewhere between larger selective lists and special state contest lists which give only four or five titles at each level for any given year. The smaller size of the North Carolina Band List might indicate that it is more selective than other lists. However, when one identifies missing compositions which are commonly known to the profession, this does not seem to be the case. There is no information given concerning the selection process.

The Maryland Band Directors Association (MBDA), with assistance from the University of Maryland music faculty, produced its first list in 1963. This project attempted to produce a more selective band list for competition-festivals than had previously been published, to correct an inflation in the grade levels of difficulty through the years in some other lists — an effect which produced extreme variations in the difficulty of grade 6 listings. The MBDA list indicated that it was for competition-festivals only and was not to be considered a comprehensive source.

In 1971 a selective music list was issued for band, orchestra, and string orchestra by MENC, prepared by its associated organizations. A committee from CBDNA prepared the band list using the 1967 MBDA list as a guide. The list was also intended only for competition-festivals although no preface describes the intent of the list or the process of selection. ∎

SELECTED BIBLIOGRAPHY

Bernstein, Leonard, *The Unanswered Question: Six Talks at Harvard*, The Charles Eliot Norton Lectures, 1973, Harvard University Press, 1976.

Carse, Adam, *The Orchestra in the XVIIIth Century*, Cambridge, England, W. Heffer and Sons, 1940.

Cooper, Paul, *Perspective in Music Theory*, Dodd, Mead and Co., 1973.

Fennell, Frederick, *Time and the Winds*, Leblanc Publications, 1954.

Goldman, Richard Franko, *The Wind Band: Its Literature and Technique*, Allyn and Bacon, 1961.

The Instrumentalist, "The Best in Band Music," August, 1958.

Meyer, Leonard B, "Some Remarks on Value and Greatness in Music," *Journal of Aesthetics and Art Criticism* 17, June 1959.

Reynolds, H. Robert, Eugene Corporon, Stanley DeRusha, Robert Grechesky, and Alan McMurray. *Wind Ensemble Literature*, 2nd ed. University of Wisconsin Bands, 1975.

Riemer, Bennett, "Leonard Meyer's Theory of Value and Greatness in Music," *Journal of Research in Music Education* 10, Fall 1962.

Rogers, Bernard, *The Art of Orchestration*, Appleton-Century Crofts, 1951.

Sessions, Roger, *Questions About Music*, Harvard University Press, 1970.

Thomson, Virgil, *The Art of Judging Music*, A.A. Knopf, 1948.

Whitcomb, Manley, "What is a Band — When?" *Book of Proceedings from the Fifteenth National Conference*, College Band Directors National Association, 1969, Section I.

Whitwell, David, *A New History of Wind Music*, The Instrumentalist Co., 1972.

Whitwell, David, "Three Crises in Band Repertoire," *The Instrumentalist*, March 1965.

November, 1988

Selecting Quality Literature for Bands and Orchestras

BY ELLIOT A. DEL BORGO

I will begin by clearly stating that I am not a disinterested observer. As a composer for instrumental groups of varying levels of development it has been and is my goal to extend Paul Hindemith's idea of *Gebrauchsmusik* — music in contemporary style for use by all musicians — to today's performers. As a conductor and music teacher my concern is the aesthetic and technical growth of young players, which can be accomplished by performing carefully selected literature that reflects the long line of musical and artistic development representing the best of Western — and now global — artistic thought.

In choosing literature for performance, the musical quality of the works should be the primary consideration. While style, technical challenge, audience and performer appeal, and educational value are important considerations, none will be well served if the music does not measure up to high standards of quality. Both conductor and performers need to live with a piece for a long time during the intensive preparation period before a performance. If the music is shallow and poorly constructed, the task becomes less interesting and little growth occurs. Conversely, a solidly composed piece allows for new discoveries and challenges as it is rehearsed and analyzed over a lengthy period of time. Fine music seems to become more interesting with greater exposure, no matter what the level of technical difficulty.

Musical quality is a most difficult factor to quantify. An airtight definition of true and lasting excellence in this area has eluded aestheticians and critics for centuries. Musical taste is one element of musical quality, though taste is a changing and personal factor. Still, it is possible to make some objective judgments, for example, about how the composer manipulates the various musical parameters. Solid craftsmanship usually will be apparent whether a work is to your taste or not.

Elliot A. Del Borgo is a professor of music at the Crane School of Music, where he has held teaching and administrative positions since 1966. An award-winning member of A.S.C.A.P., he is a consultant, clinician, lecturer, and adjudicator. Del Borgo holds degrees from the State University of New York, Temple University, and the Philadelphia Conservatory, where he studied theory and composition with Vincent Persichetti and trumpet with Gilbert Johnson.

Variety is an important aspect of any composition because it keeps students involved. How well a composer balances variety and repetition to bind together the elements of a composition can be a good indicator of quality. Western music has a long tradition of fine composers who have shown their skill through the interesting, clever, and creative manipulation of their basic musical ideas. Look for variety in certain key areas:

Melodic material. Check to see whether there is variety in the placement of primary melodic material. A piece dominated by flutes may be appealing to the flute section, but the music may not be very interesting for the rest of the band. Melodic material that is shared with the middle and lower voices can increase the impact of the work. Also note whether the piece contains melodies of varied character. Using both instrumental and vocally oriented melodic lines places different demands on performers and increases interest for the listener.

Diverse timbres. Review the score, looking for a variety of instrumental colors. Bands and orchestras offer a rich palette of timbres. The composer's use of individual colors and interesting blends is critical to successful orchestration.

Balanced material. See if you can easily discern and balance background and foreground material. Ask yourself whether the composer has provided interesting and appropriate backgrounds and if they change in a logical manner.

Interesting textures. There should be a variety of textures in the work. Polyphonic textures are interesting to perform and give a piece a higher level of sophistication, while homophonic textures are somewhat clearer to the audience. Even sections of monophonic texture can be used to excellent effect. The interplay of textural variety is an important musical element and should be a prime factor in determining the suitability of a piece.

Contrast is a key element of the composer's craft. Juxtaposing contrasting ideas heightens the effect they would have individually. A solidly written composition will contain contrast, particularly in the following areas:

Dynamics. Here is one of the oldest and most effective means of creating contrast. When reviewing a score, carefully note indications of dynamic levels and types of change, such as sudden fortissimos, gradual decrescendos, and crescendos created by adding instruments. Consider how the percussion section is used to enhance dynamic contrast within the piece.

Rhythmic material. A solid and well-crafted piece should contain more than predictable rhythmic patterns. The music should exhibit a lively vitality that gives it an exciting propulsion and sense of momentum. Slow sections should afford the opportunity for careful use of rubato at important points within the phrase and at cadences.

Tempo. If the length and type of piece allow, contrasts in tempo can provide relief and interest as well as serve as an important structural element. Look to see whether slight gradations of tempo are carefully marked and if they are appropriate to the overall phrasing of the section.

Instrumentation. Look for contrast in the use of woodwinds versus brass or strings versus winds. Sectional writing provides differing timbres as well as as opportunity for players to rest.

Mode and key. Note the overall harmonic scheme of the piece. Most well-written tonal or neo-tonal pieces have a definite and logical progression of key centers, somewhat like a progression of chords, which is an important part of musical structure. The change from major to minor in tonal pieces or a striking modulation can give a work a strong individual flavor. Attention to these matters shows the composer's

thought and care in forming the macro-structure of the piece and produces a genuine sense of purpose and direction.

Musical interest lies in the ear of the beholder, and no two musicians think exactly alike. Because our musical judgments are the product of a great variety of influences, there is room for varied responses to any composition. Nonetheless, it is possible to objectively consider aspects of it, such as:

Fresh ideas. Ask yourself whether the piece has a unique sound that is reminiscent of other works by the composer. The selection should have a musical personality of its own.

Harmonic material. Do the harmonies reflect an inventive scheme that uses tension and release with clearly defined cadence points? Given the wide latitude afforded contemporary writers, it is reasonable to expect interesting and varied harmonic material that will enrich and extend students' concepts of the harmonic element in music.

Dramatic Shape. The overall design of the work should include carefully placed high points and a logical approach to these points. The elements of contrast, discussed earlier, are an integral part of writing a piece that has an effective rise and fall of dramatic line.

Coherent ideas. A logical unfolding of musical thoughts results when ideas are coherently planned; Aaron Copland calls this unfolding the long line in a work. An important question to consider is whether repeats are essential. For example, does a D.C. or D.S. represent an important balancing of ideas, or does it simply lengthen the composition?

Natural transitions. Be aware of the use of transitional passages and how they are scored. Specifically note the smoothness and naturalness of these passages as the work moves from section to section.

It is the combination of all these elements that gives a composition its aesthetic impact, though it is extremely difficult to quantify this aspect of any musical composition. What the band or orchestra director can do is to determine whether the results of the composer's effort to work with these elements has led to a piece that has a musical meaning to whether the piece is simply an exercise in note-spinning. At the very least, careful attention to the parts will give better insight into the value of the whole.

When planning a program be sure that the composers represented are a good sampling of the best of the musical art for the type of ensembles. The serious and committed conductor will take the time to make an informed judgment as to the musical value of the works he has selected for performance; he will not play poorly written music. Excellent educational pieces for young musicians lay the groundwork for fine performances of masterworks later on.

Band or Wind Ensemble

An Important Distinction

Elliot A. Del Borgo

All levels of instrumental music, from junior high school to college and professional groups, show a striking lack of agreement as to what constitutes a wind ensemble or band. Even the rich profusion of titles — symphonic band, wind symphony, symphonic wind ensemble, concert band, symphonic winds — suggests a considerable degree of freedom in our conception of what wind groups are and how they should function. There appears to be a strong need to consider the important differences between bands and wind ensembles in terms of educational goals, the variety of available literature, performance requirements, and the impact on composers and arrangers.

Because music represents a unique way to develop a person's way of feeling and knowing, the primary goal of all ensemble programs should be a rich, varied, and satisfying musical experience for everyone involved. This rather broad goal has within it some critical aspects that need to be met by all of the musical activities that comprise a well-balanced performance program. Essentially, instrumental ensembles should help develop aesthetic sensibility, a high degree of performance accuracy, and refined skills, as well as expose players to a wide variety of literature and musical styles that offer understanding and appreciation of the art through personal experience. Both the band and wind ensemble are capable of accomplishing every aspect of the basic goal; the question appears to be when to use each group for maximum benefit.

The essential difference between these two groups is simply one of size. When a wind ensemble becomes too large or a symphonic band too small, the idiosyncrasies of each group are lost and thus the musical capabilities of each fall short of expectations.

The wind ensemble should provide a chamber-music concept of clarity of line and texture with the type of response between players that only smallness can afford. Timbres should be sharply defined and an intimacy of musical purpose readily apparent. While control and precision are goals of ensembles of any size, the wind ensemble should greatly heighten these aspects of performance. The lean, crisp approach has a particular value in an intellectual, almost classical restraint that it brings to the performance of certain works.

The wind ensemble should also offer flexible instrumentation to allow for stylistic accuracy in the performance of the wind music by composers such as Mozart, Strauss, Stravinsky, and Varèse.

Can the wind ensemble also perform works scored for full band? Yes, but only if the pieces are chosen with the purpose of using the concepts indicated earlier and if the works themselves have characteristics that do not require the resources of a symphonic band to make their full impact. A

Elliot A. Del Borgo holds degrees from the State University of New York, Temple University and the Philadelphia Conservatory where he studied theory and composition with Vincent Persichetti and trumpet with Gilbert Johnson. He is professor of music at the Crane School of Music and a widely known conductor and composer.

work like Hindemith's *Symphony in B♭* has a musical character that makes it ideal for wind ensemble because its linear and timbral aspects are greatly enhanced by a smaller number of players. Thus the wind ensemble conductor has an opportunity to provide a great deal of variety in programming because a concert can offer a variety of styles with tonal combinations ranging from an octet to the full complement of players.

The symphonic band has quite a different sound and role. Its make-up and size should reflect this difference and enhance the literature chosen for performance. The greater number of players should produce a full, rich sonority that has a visceral, romantic quality. A symphonic band must be capable of producing massive blocks of sound, at a *forte* and *pianissimo* level, that is truly exciting when created by many players. When appropriate, an organ-like blending of colors — as in some of the Bach transcriptions — can be a genuine musical treat. This is most certainly a large-scale approach to music, and the sheer power of sound to move one's emotions is an important consideration. The performer's goal should be whole sections of players working together to produce the desired effect. Because the actual make-up of the band is unlikely to change during a program, the conductor must achieve variety by carefully selecting music of different periods and idioms to illustrate the great sonic versatility of the band. While the smaller, more intimate, wind ensemble seeks to project chamber-like detail, the symphonic band draws its images in broad strokes.

Considerations of balance, instrumentation, tone quality, and even the physical set-up are also important in the distinction between symphonic bands and wind ensembles. A true wind ensemble may employ 35-40 players, while the full complement of a symphonic band may be 80-95, depending on the conductor's preference for differing combinations of particular instruments. Balance of sound — most notably between woodwinds and brass — is a critical point to consider. Many wind ensembles tend to be brass dominated. The one-on-a-part concept leaves the flutes and clarinets in a very precarious position and is most likely the reason why conductors decide to double these parts. The danger of losing the unique effect of a true wind ensemble occurs when too much doubling is employed and the group in fact becomes a small symphonic band. The solution appears to lie in keeping the brass section relatively small (one on a part, if practical) and encouraging an orchestral concept of playing that looks toward the focus and projection of a clean, crisp sound. Percussion should be treated in a similar manner, with playing tailored to the amount of wind sound used in each piece.

The balance problems within the symphonic band tend to be the reverse of those faced by the wind ensemble. Many bands are top-heavy and tend toward a strident tone quality that results from too many players in the upper part of the sound spectrum. Because higher ranges tend to project more, it is prudent to use fewer players on first parts and more on second and third parts. This arrangement, when used throughout the band, allows for a more even plane of sound and avoids the harshness that can detract from the beauty of tone the full band can produce. Also, because conductors usually assign stronger players to lead parts, the larger numbers on the lower parts will contribute to better balance. Unfortunately, alto and bass clarinet parts are generally assigned to only one or two players, even in a large band — an arrangement that is as unsatisfactory as having only two violas and two cellos in a symphony orchestra. A full section (four to six) of alto and bass clarinets would fill this portion of the sound spectrum and contribute a darker, more mellow quality to the band sound. The implication for composers and arrangers is quite obvious. If real alto and bass clarinet sections are available, scoring for the woodwinds takes on a significantly different dimension. As of now, it is difficult to entrust a critical line or chord member to just the alto clarinet because writers cannot be sure of its weight in the band.

The relative size of the band and wind ensemble also has a bearing on the physical set-up of each group. Any seating plan should be designed to allow players to hear each other easily for precise ensemble and accurate intonation. Using a front-facing plan with a wind ensemble that is large tends to stretch the sections across the stage and makes hearing more difficult than it needs to be for the players. The playing and blend of sound would improve if a more traditional band seating plan of concentric half-circles were employed. There is not much to be gained and a great deal to be lost by setting up a band to look like a wind ensemble.

To gain the greatest musical and educational benefit from both bands and wind ensembles, conductors should maintain a clear distinction between the two groups. The wind ensemble should not grow beyond reasonable size, and a symphonic band should not be shrunk to proportions that rob it of its true sonority. Each group should program appropriate literature that is well suited to the musical capabilities of the forces available. Our players need the experience of playing in both types of ensembles, and we should strive to maintain the viability and integrity of each. In doing so, the vast body of wind literature can be well served and our students and audiences can appreciate varied programs of interesting music. ■

September, 1990

Some Thoughts on Band Instrumentation

Wind Ensembles and Concert Bands

by Alfred Reed

To many people the wind ensemble is nothing more than a small or reduced concert band; to paraphrase Shakespeare: *"What's in a name! That which we call a band By 'any other name would sound the same."* However, it is my conviction, based on 30 years' experience as a composer and conductor, that there are differences between these two groups other than overall size and numbers of participating instruments. While these differences may not be major, they do exist and concern all of us whose careers center around wind music.

In his pamphlet, "Time and the Winds," Frederick Fennell traced the background and development of serious music for winds leading up to his establishing the Eastman Wind Ensemble 38 years ago. His choice of a name for this new group convinced some that the wind ensemble is nothing but a small band, that it never was anything else, and never will be anything else, regardless of what anyone might claim.

My object in setting down these thoughts on this subject is to ascertain whether there are any objective differences in sound between the concert band and wind ensemble and if there are, to what degree they exist, to what purely musical uses they may be put, and whether they should be put to such uses. Although I prefer the term wind orchestra to wind ensemble, it is not what a thing is called but what it is, as Shakespeare so aptly reminds us. In music what ultimately matters is not what it is called, but how it sounds.

While no two people hear a sound in exactly the same way, and therefore cannot react to it the same way, differences between listeners are relatively small; and there are minor differences in people's abilities to discriminate between different degrees of differences. If we accept the fact that people hear the same thing differently, then we should further accept that the line between a first-class concert band and a first-class wind ensemble for some may fade away altogether.

In 1955 I published a pamphlet in the Leblanc Educational Series called "The Balanced Clarinet Choir," and proposed rounding out and completing the clarinet choir, both as the basic tone color of the band and as a separate performing group, by adding a true contrabass clarinet, and that we redistribute the performers on each instrument in the choir to obtain the same balanced, overall sound as exists in the string choir of the orchestra. While both the orchestra and the band began as ensembles, the orchestra quickly graduated from this status to a basic pattern of organization that has never really changed, from the 35-piece group that performed Haydn's and Mozart's symphonies, to the 125-piece group that performed Wagner, Strauss, Mahler, and Stravinsky. Through those years the band had remained an ensemble: a grouping of instruments in differing proportions, its exact instrumentation varying from town to town, group to group, occasion to occasion, and even director to director. The word ensemble came to mean a group of no fixed size or instrumentation, except what a composer might call for in any one piece. Size, though, is not the most important matter, nor is a general instrumentation.

Currently Chairman of the Department of Music Media and Industry at the University of Miami in Coral Gables, Florida, composer Alfred Reed has written 300 published works, 63 of which were commissioned. In addition to composing, teaching, and editing, Reed is the principal guest conductor of the Tokyo Kosei Wind Orchestra with whom he has recorded nine albums.

Editor's Note: This article is adapted from a chapter of the forthcoming Heritage Encyclopedia of the Band *by William H. Rehrig and edited by Paul E. Bierly, which will be published in 1991. The article is also a preliminary study for Alfred Reed's projected book on scoring for the modern wind orchestra.*

The symphony orchestra, for which some of the greatest music written during the past 200 years has been conceived, is not just a group of 35, 85, or 125 performers, nor is it just a collection of string, woodwind, brass, and percussion instruments in varying numbers and colors. What caused the modern orchestra to graduate from its former ensemble status, where it remained through the lifetime of J.S. Bach, was the adoption of the string choir as the basic tone color of the group and the contrasting of this basic tone color with those of the winds and brasses, the latter with only one player to each line or part. This principle has remained, with a few experimental exceptions, as the organizational pattern for all orchestras, regardless of size, since then.

Winds and brasses have one to a part for two reasons: each and all of the wind and brass instruments can drown out any single department of strings and even all of them together; and there is the matter of the brilliancy (not volume or sonority) of individual wind/brass colors when playing solo rather than soli.

Do not confuse brilliancy with volume (loudness) or sonority (weight or amplitude of tone color) as many people unfortunately do. As a matter of fact the question, "How can you get an orchestra or band to play brilliantly when playing very softly?" staggers them. Some would unhesitatingly regard it as a contradiction in terms: there simply ain't no such thing, they would say in return. Brilliancy is a quality of tone color, not volume or sonority, and is the result of a fine performer producing a tone not only of pure quality but also rich in overtones.

If we ask two trumpet players to play the same single note in unison, they will not only play exactly the same pitch at the same volume, but they will also have to match their tones to one another. This is the secret of good section playing: the evenness of tone color. Regardless of how carefully the two trumpets match their tones, they cannot match each other's upper harmonic partials that their fundamental tones produce. This lessens the brilliancy of their overall sound. Thus, two trumpets, while sounding more sonorous (powerful) than one, will never sound as brilliant.

The shape of sound waves is similar to that of water waves. Like water waves, sound waves have a high point (crest) and a low point (trough). If two waves are produced at the same time and can be made to match perfectly, dovetailing one into the other, crest to crest and trough to trough, they would so amplify each other. If they do not match and are out of phase, crest to trough or trough to crest, the result is not merely little or no enhancement but actually a dampening of the overall sound. This causes a loss of brilliancy in their resulting combined sound.

If two players of the same instrument cannot match their overtones, how much more difficult is it when the two instruments are not the same? The harmonic profiles of the trumpet and clarinet tones are quite different, yet we have different instruments to blend or contrast in our instrumental writing. It is the harmonic shape (fundamental plus overtones, and the relative strength of each) that causes a trumpet to sound different than a clarinet, and both of these different than a violin. The materials of which an instrument is made, and the particular manner in which the air inside it or around it is set in motion and the tone sustained, produce its individual harmonic shape.

Whether it be 35 players or 135, the basic principle of organization of the orchestra has not changed: it is a group of solo winds, brass and percussion, contrasted by a basic tone color provided by a soli group of strings in which we sacrifice the individual tone color of each violin, viola, and cello to get the needed weight and volume (sonority) necessary to balance even four or six winds, let alone 33 or 38. We accept this trade-off in even the early, small Haydn-Mozart orchestra, to say nothing of the Strauss-Mahler-Stravinsky behemoths simply because the combined range, dexterity, expressiveness, and tonal cohesion of string instruments is second to none. No other group, be it single-reed, double-reed, brass, or any other can equal the strings in this overall achievement.

I therefore propose that in the wind ensemble we use this same basic principle or organization:

the adoption of a single basic tone color with the others grouped around it, and contrasted with it, on the basis of one to a part. A stabilized instrumentation, together with the same brilliancy of sound and dexterity of tone production which have characterized the orchestra, might be similarly productive for the wind ensemble. It will also offer the serious composer the same opportunity of being in complete control of his instrumentation as he has been with the orchestra. This is the primary reason why more writers of symphonic music during the past 75 years have not produced more for the large wind group. Throughout history composers have written for what is available, and the band certainly has been available at least as long as the orchestra.

From the composer's viewpoint the problem is that band instrumentation has always been so fluid and so inconsistent that it varies from city to city, from group to group, and from director to director, that the composer could never be certain that his balances, blends, contrasts, and doublings would sound as he intended.

If the orchestra had varied as much as the band, exactly the same thing could and would have been said of the composer and the orchestra, too. This has not happened because it was circumvented nearly 200 years ago by the music directors of the various dukes, counts, and kings in the daily course of work who had the advantage of having fewer players to contend with in the development of the orchestra's instrumentation.

The band's instrumentation developed as a result of the demand for volume and carrying power for military duties. This resulted in a basically brass instrumentation with secondary woodwind enhancement and a striving for a homogeneous musical texture with the entire group playing most, if not all, of the time.

This is certainly understandable, but when the military marching band became the so-called concert band and moved indoors to the orchestra's domain, trouble inevitably began.

First, as someone once said, a concert band is not, and should not be, a marching band playing sitting down, especially when it plays indoors. Most of the time the concert band is too large and produces too heavy and ponderous a sound indoors. The finer the acoustical framework in which a band performs, the more difficult it becomes to produce the lightness, flexibility, and variety of sound that we take for granted in an orchestra of similar size.

The kind of writing and texture that helps ensure a successful sound outdoors can be deadly indoors. I refer to the homogeneous texture produced by the whole group playing almost all of the time, or as some directors call it, "the big, round sound," which is neutral in color and lacking one of the necessities in all art: variety. Without variety of color and texture

even the greatest music would have a hard time maintaining the listener's interest. One has only to think of the mostly unvarying sound of Schumann's orchestral music to appreciate the importance of variety of instrumental texture in any piece longer than a few minutes playing time. Variety is precisely what the big, round sound cannot have or offer.

If even Schumann sounds somewhat monotonous today, what shall we say of the hundreds of made-to-order band pieces that appear regularly? We should wean players from these safe pieces, with their frequent doubling of parts with no exposed lines, as soon as possible.

When we compare the wind ensemble with the larger concert band, we are measuring a select group of above-average players against what is usually an average to below-average group in performing ability. If we restrict wind ensemble membership to the best players, and open the concert band to a far greater range of performing abilities, then such a comparison is unfair to the larger group. What we really need is a head-to-head comparison between a first-rate, professional wind ensemble and a first-rate professional concert band, with top players on every chair and with both groups playing the same music.

There is one real difference between the concert band and the wind ensemble, and this has to do with the basic concept of a floating instrumentation to play any work for winds that requires a conductor for effective performance: from the two Mozart Octets, in Eb major and C minor (calling for 2 oboes, 2 clarinets, 2 horns, and 2 bassoons), up to and including the Hindemith *Symphony for Band* with its full instrumentation. Frederick Fennell originally conceived the Eastman Wind Ensemble as just that: a group of 8 to 50 players, depending on the music to be played, but retaining the brilliance of the orchestra's wind section.

Thus the full instrumentation of the wind ensemble is based on the same principle of organization as that of the orchestra: a single, basic tone color, complete and balanced throughout its register (in this case the single-reed tone of the full clarinet family) with all of the other tone colors employed, as in the traditional orchestra, but with one player to a part, for maximum brilliancy. The only exceptions will be the Bb soprano clarinets, where there will be two players to each part for the sake of balance, and two baritones and two tubas, for the same reason, and for divisi passages.

With this instrumentation accepted by and adhered to by conductors, the specific choice of instrumentation of any piece of music, from eight players to the full instrumental group, will return to the composer, where it belongs. He then can calculate his instrumental combinations and balances, and have the assurance that each performance of his work will sound much the same, with only differences in players' abilities and conductors' interpretations to contend with.

The direct result of this continued assurance for the composer will be a repertoire of works for winds that will make use of the combinations of colors inherent in a balanced and fully integrated grouping of these instruments. Many new sounds will have a chance to be heard; for many listeners for the first time. This will lay to rest the general band sound, an absolute necessity in the creation of longer and major works for the winds. This was also the case of the developing orchestra over 150 years ago.

The variety and contrasts that will emerge from this standardization will startle a good many people – not the least of whom will be band directors who will feel that the rich, mellow, rounded sonority has robbed the wind orchestra of its inherent brilliance and liquidity of tone, and also needlessly hampered its potential flexibility and clarity of sound.

The wind ensemble is not the second coming; it is not even the first. It is not and should not be regarded as a threat to the concert or symphonic band, and most certainly not that of the orchestra. The wind orchestra cannot possibly replace or supplant the traditional orchestra; it can only be the opposite side of the coin bearing the inscription: Large-Scale Serious Instrumental Music. The concert/symphonic band has its own place, its own claim to attention and its own audience, and will continue as long as the demand for its services continues. All that the concept of the wind ensemble represents is the carrying-over and application of an organizational principle developed over two centuries, from the traditional orchestra to the relatively new concept of an orchestra of winds, brass, and percussion. To composers it offers it the same promise as it has to all of the writers of orchestral music during this same period, which has resulted in the most successful and artistically laudable form of instrumental music yet achieved.

Practicing this principle will give the composer two fully integrated and fully controlled instrumentations to dream about and write for. The conductor will no longer have to rewrite a work in order to make it playable with whatever instrumentation he may have.

If the wind ensemble does not represent a threat to the concert or symphonic band, or the orchestra, it does represent competition for the same audience, but such competition has always existed throughout the history of music. Ultimately, the wind ensemble amounts to a relatively new form, another development in the long history of instrumental music. □

January, 1992

Choosing Literature for Young Bands

by Quincy Hilliard

In selecting literature for elementary bands, directors face the difficulties of both the technical limitations of these groups and the sheer quantities of new publications produced each year. There are almost three times as many titles published for young band as there are for grades three and above, resulting in a rapid turnover of music and repertoire lists that are soon outdated.

Some directors view elementary music as a collection of quick and easy tunes to be played once and filed away forever, while the primary teaching tool is a method book. This attitude causes many in our profession to frown upon the repertoire and the composers of young band music. It is wrong to believe students can learn all skills and concepts from a method book, which is merely an outline of the skills students should learn.

A practical solution to this problem is selecting music that teaches specific concepts and skills. By making a direct correlation between what the student is learning in a method book and what is in the music, the music gives more meaning to the method book.

Most method books for first year students focus on elementary counting and learning notes rather than proper breathing techniques or long tones. Teaching students proper breathing techniques and correct embouchures by stressing long tones is the foundation of good tone quality on any instrument. Intonation problems decrease rapidly once students learn these skills.

An effective composition for teaching proper breathing is Crusaders' Hymn, arranged by

Quincy Hilliard teaches at the University of Southwestern Louisiana in Lafayette; he is a composer and clinician for Carl Fischer and Boosey and Hawkes music publishers.

Andrew Balent, which has easily identifiable phrasing.

At letter A there are breath marks every four measures. Students should breathe rhythmically through the first four measures, using correct techniques without instruments, at the tempo indicated (♩=100). After the band can play the piece with proper breathing, slow the tempo to ♩=90, ♩=80, ♩=72, ♩=60, while students continue to play four-measure phrases in one breath. Too often directors emphasize melodic phrasing more than harmonic phrasing, the supporting material with implied breath marks behind the melody which comprises the chord structure of a piece. Sometimes a harmonic phrase has a particular style with implied breath marks that could be two, three, four, or even five measures long. In *Crusaders' Hymn* the horns, lower woodwinds, and brass should complete the four measure harmonic phrase before breathing. This piece is a versatile work that can be used as a breathing exercise with students practicing breathing through the entire piece with instruments in playing position but without producing a sound. It can also be used as a warm-up chorale to develop balance and blend in middle and high school bands, or it can be used to check sectional intonation in high school bands.

Counting for wind players in the first year is limited to 𝅝, ♩., ♩, ♪, ♫, and corresponding rests while percussion players advance to sixteenth notes, but it should include any combination of these notes in eighth note patterns: ♫♫ ♩, ♩. ♫, and ♩ ♫ ♩. Kenneth Henderson's *March of the Cyclops* is an example of elementary counting.

The rhythms in the flute melody line are within the ability of first year students, but by avoiding boring repetition the composer kept the part interesting.

Grade one music should include eighth note rhythms in patterns that are not technically complicated. It helps students if the director writes the frequently used patterns on the board

and uses them in clapping and training exercises. *Festival Overture* by Paul Halliday is excellent for introducing students to eighth notes because the eighth notes are introduced in patterns.

Emphasizing long tones develops young embouchures, tone quality, and intonation. If appropriate literature is selected, a director can also evaluate the student's breathing techniques. *Spring Song* by Jerry Nowak emphasizes *legato* phrasing and provides the opportunity to sustain pitches. Because the opening measures incorporate long tones and harmonic phrasing, the director can teach the importance of breathing correctly and show how it relates to developing a beautiful, focused tone.

Some secondary elements directors should consider in selecting music are scoring, range, key signature, style, percussion parts, and structural elements.

Scoring adds textural variety in young band music. Early works for young band are usually written in block style: woodwinds or brass play, then the entire band plays with the same rhythms without contrapuntal movement or variety of texture. Block writing provides good counting exercise but not interesting textural colors, but is a good way to introduce the

	Intro	A	B	C
Melody	Trumpets	Clarinets	Clarinets	Upper Woodwinds, Trumpets, Horns
Countermelody or Harmony		Flute & Bells (2nd Time)	Flute & Bells	Lower Woodwinds & Brass

D	E	F	G	H
Lower Woodwinds & Brass, Horns	Low Woodwinds & Brass, Horns	Trumpets	Trumpets & Alto Saxophone	Flutes, Clarinets, Trumpets
Flutes, Clarinets, Alto Saxophones & Trumpets	Flutes, Clarinets, Alto Saxophones & Trumpets	Flutes, Clarinets, Bells	Flute & Bells	Low Woodwinds & Brass, Horns

concept of playing together; it should be avoided at later stages. A good piece has a variety of textural colors in different melodic color combinations: flute and saxophone, saxophone and clarinet, saxophone and trumpet, trumpet and clarinet, flute and trumpet, saxophone, trumpet, and flute, clarinets in the low register and baritone, and tuba, trombone, baritone, and clarinets in the low register. A piece becomes more interesting with variety especially if every instrument has the opportunity to play the melody. The diagram above shows the textural colors used in a piece of mine, *Eagle Command March*.

Every instrument plays the melody and the textural variety makes interesting color combinations. Too often the lower instruments have boring parts with only half and whole notes, and the players never feel as though they are an integral part of the ensemble. By playing the melody, lower instruments have an interesting and more difficult part.

Look for full or complete chord structures throughout a piece to enhance the sound of the band. Chords in young band music are usually triads and sevenths. In a triad the root and third should be present even if the fifth is omitted; in the seventh chord, the root, third, and seventh should be present. Because

composers score grade one music for bands with minimum skills, doubling all parts is a necessity. Incomplete chords detract from the full sound of a piece, giving it an empty, open quality. The condensed score version of *Eagle Command March*, shows the complete chord structures.

To avoid range problems in easier grade one material, the clarinets usually play below the register break while in more advanced material only the first clarinet crosses the break. Instrumental ranges should cover an octave or twelfth and avoid the following notes because of intonation or technical problems: low C♯ on all saxophones, C♯ and A♭ on trumpet, and B, D♭, and G♭ on trombone, baritone, and tuba.

Method books emphasize the keys of F, B♭, and E♭ and grade one level music usually correlates. All the accidentals relate to the three keys so students do not have to learn new notes. Anne McGinty's work *The Challenger* is written in the key of F, but the composer sometimes writes a seventh chord which includes the E♭; when the key changes to B♭, the composer writes harmonies that include A♭ in the chord. In both cases the accidentals are notes that students know from common key signatures.

Other accidentals are acceptable if they do not present awkward fingering problems. Key signatures are a problem for beginners, and students need reminders when accidentals are present.

Grade one music format is usually monothematic because it cannot be lengthy. Works limited to 40-60 measures of 𝄴, 50-70 measures in 𝄲, and 60-80 measures in 𝄴, take the playing time of young embouchures into consideration.

Short and frequent rests throughout a piece are desirable. Overture format, ABA, at this level is too long and stressful for young players; marches, ballads, and novelty works are preferable.

A grade one band can play *marcato* and *legato* styles emphasized with the syllables of *di* for *marcato* and *doo* for *legato*. Marches are an excellent way to teach the *marcato* style and a ballad or chorale is suitable for *legato* style. When teaching *legato*, avoid technical passages so students can concentrate on breathing and tone production.

Percussion parts in good literature are interesting, blend with the work, and add to the textural colors. Directors should look for parts that include triangle, bells, woodblock, and such special effects as tambourine played on the snare drum in addition to snare and bass drums, and cymbals. Usually a grade one piece has three or four percussion parts including bells; sometimes composers write a non-melodic part for one player using two instruments, which makes it possible for a small percussion section to cover more instruments. For example, a student can play a tambourine and triangle part if he is given time to change instruments.

The structural elements that make up the framework of a grade one piece of music should include melodic content, harmonic structure, rhythmic content, texture, and teaching concepts. In a quality grade one work all of these elements should form one conceptual idea resulting in an interesting composition that provides an enjoyable learning experience for students and directors. Quality literature should aid directors in teaching the fundamentals. There should be a direct correlation between the quality of the literature and the performance skills the student learns. Successful young band literature should stand alone and not invite comparison to advanced literature. Young band music may have the same characteristics as advanced music, but its purpose is to teach. □

Breathing and Emphasis on Long Tones
A Song To Remember, Paul Halliday; Boosey & Hawkes.
Athanum Ridge, Jim Eggebration; Kjos.
Crusaders' Hymn, Andrew Balent; Carl Fischer.
Spring Song, Jerry Nowak; Boosey & Hawkes.
Ten Chorales for Beginning and Intermediate Band, Quincy Hilliard; Kjos.
Elementary Counting
Chesapeake March, Quincy Hilliard and Chuck Elledge; Kjos.
Festive Overture, Paul Halliday; Boosey & Hawkes.
Lexington March, John Edmondson; Queenwood.
Liberty Bell Overture, Bruce Pearson; Kjos.
March of the Cyclops, Kenneth Henderson, Carl Fischer.
Trumpets In Command, David Gorham; Wingert-Jones.
Two Sunset Sketches, Feldstein/O'Reilly; Alfred.

Music With a Purpose

by Quincy Hilliard

After students learn the basic skills for playing an instrument, middle school directors should select music that emphasizes breathing, intonation, and counting. At this stage students cope with some challenges in the areas of interpretation and expression.

Directors should select music that will emphasize tone quality, such as John Kinyon's *Londonderry*

Londonderry Ballad

Ballad. In this and other pieces tone quality will depend on correct breathing techniques and embouchure flexibility to play the long notes that develop good tone production.

Tone quality and intonation are closely related skills; when directors emphasize tone production, many intonation problems disappear. The central issue in improving intonation is for students to listen to the sounds they produce and to develop the ability to identify and correct errors on their own. This is one of the most important skills a director can teach to middle school music students.

Slow ballads and chorales are excellent for working on intonation, but many directors fear programming these because they highlight deficien-

Quincy C. Hilliard teaches at the University of Southwestern Louisiana in Lafayette; he is a composer and clinician for Carl Fischer and Boosey & Hawkes music publishers.

cies in the band. However, by using a slow piece as a warm-up, students will concentrate on breathing and embouchure formation each day. A director's trepidation about performing slow pieces will fade as students improve in legato playing. Ed Huckeby's *Blue Lake Reflection* has legato playing in exposed woodwind octaves that sharpens students' abilities to listen and adjust intonation.

By middle school students should be able to subdivide quarter and eighth notes. *Windridge* by David Myers is a recent work with many opportunities for teaching beat division, perhaps by writing the lower brass parts on the board as a rhythmic exercise for the entire band.

Windridge

In choosing pieces avoid block scoring and choose those with independent contrapuntal lines, such as those with melody versus countermelody with accompaniment, to teach students to count and be responsible for their parts instead of just playing along with the group. Contrapuntal scoring is interesting and gives the band a more mature sound. In Leroy Osmond's *Hebrew Folk Song Suite* the melody is in the upper woodwinds and cornets, the countermelody is in the alto and tenor saxes, and the accompaniment is in the lower brasses and woodwinds.

Hebrew Folk Song Suite

Short solos are possible if they are not technically difficult and are written in a comfortable range. Solos for flute, clarinet, alto sax, and trumpet are the most common. Limiting ranges to an octave is good for second and third clarinets, trumpet, and trombones because these are often played by less advanced students.

By middle school, students should have learned the scales and can move on to an expanded variety of works, including those with occasional accidentals, such as David Holsinger's *The Cluster, Fluster, Buster March* and John Edmondson's *Catalina for Winds*. Avoid works with frequent meter or key changes and select pieces within the keys of F, Bb, Eb, Ab, and ¾, ⅜, ¼, and simple § meters. The following chart shows rhythmic patterns students should learn at this level.

Duple

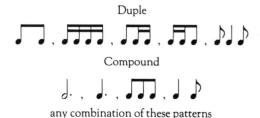

Compound

any combination of these patterns

Most works for middle school bands are written in an overture ABA format with an occasional fanfare followed by an overture or suites with several movements. In my piece, *Korean Festival*, I use the theme and variation format instead of the traditional ABA format. The diagram shows the changes in tempo and style from one variation to the next.

Examine the structural elements of harmony, manipulation of melody, rhythm, form, and texture when selecting music. The more elements a composer uses, the stronger the work. Weak pieces emphasize melody and harmony, relegating rhythm, texture, and form to minor roles.

Good literature will also test interpretation and expression, but if it is too tightly woven all performances tend to sound alike. An effective score should be flexible enough to produce many interpretations.

Most middle school bands can play legato and marcato; *Creed* by William Himes will teach several types of articulation and style.

In composing I try to involve the percussion as much as possible without over writing because an entire work based on an ostinato rhythm in the percussion section, for example, produces a superficial, one-dimensional design. Percussion writing should capture the imagination of young percussionists; too often their parts are boring and without focus. In *Korean Festival*, a variety of percussion instruments spark the students' interest, but at no given time are all parts played simultaneously because that would create a scoring imbalance.

Korean Festival

	Intro	Theme	Var. 1	Var. 2	Var. 3	Coda
Tempo	Allegro	Andante	Andante	Allegro	Andante	Allegro
Style	Marcato	Lyrical	Legato	Marcato	Chorale	Marcato

Korean Festival

Such special effects as playing the tambourine with snare sticks or a coin rake on a cymbal enhance the overall color of a piece and make the percussion parts more interesting. At this level the timpani part should be optional or limited to two notes to avoid pitch change within a piece.

More new concepts are taught at the middle school level than at any other time in a student's musical training. Before entering high school, students should have good tone quality, be able to make intonation adjustments, and subdivide beats. Good literature can teach these concepts, which are the foundation for becoming a good musician. □

Suggested Repertoire
Tone Quality and Intonation

Londonderry Ballad, John Kinyon; Alfred.
Blue Lake Reflection, Ed Huckeby; Barnhouse.
Air for Winds, John Edmondson; Southern.
A Childhood Hymn, David Holsinger; Wingert-Jones.

Counting (Subdivision)

Mission Creek, Jared Spears; Barnhouse.
Crossgate, James Barnes; Southern.
Windridge, David Myers; Boosey & Hawkes.
Creed, William Hinds; Kjos.
Brookpark Overture, James Swearingen; Barnhouse.

Style and Character

Spiritus, David Shaffer; Barnhouse.
Creed, William Hines; Kjos.
Sundance, Quincy Hilliard; Southern.
Korean Festival, Quincy Hilliard; Southern.
Hebrew Folk Song Suite, Leroy Osmon; TRN Music Publishers.

April, 1972

The Band Sound
of Vincent Persichetti

William Workinger

In the ever-accelerating search for new compositional ideas and techniques, Vincent Persichetti has already become an almost "historic" figure as a composer for band. Throughout the 1950's and 1960's he was probably the most active, influential, and well-known composer for that medium, answering nearly a score of commissions from high school, college, and professional groups with a uniformly high caliber of works:

Divertimento, Op. 42 (c. 1951), Ditson.
 (the Goldman Band)
Psalm, Op. 53 (c. 1954), Elkan-Vogel.
 (Pi Kappa Omicron of University of Louisville, Ky.)
Pageant, Op. 59 (c. 1954), Carl Fischer.
 (American Bandmasters Association)
Symphony, Op. 69 (c. 1958), Elkan-Vogel.
 (Washington University, St. Louis)
Serenade, Op. 85 (c. 1961), Elkan-Vogel.
 (Ithaca High School Band, New York)
Bagatelles, Op. 87 (c. 1962), Elkan-Vogel.
 (Dartmouth College, New Hampshire)
Chorale Prelude: So Pure the Star, Op. 91 (c. 1963), Elkan-Vogel.
 (Duke University, North Carolina)

Masquerade, Op. 102 (c. 1966), Elkan-Vogel.
 (Baldwin-Wallace Conservatory, Ohio)
Chorale Prelude: Turn Not Thy Face, Op. 105 (c. 1968), Elkan-Vogel.
 (Ithaca High School Band)

Because of the impact of this body of literature, Persichetti's influence is evident in much of the band music of the present decade.

An eclectic and rather conservative composer, Persichetti consolidated rather than innovated compositional and scoring techniques and, in doing so, he drew widely on the developments of the first half of the twentieth century (which are summarized in his book, *Twentieth Century Harmony*, W.W. Norton & Co., 1961). Before turning to the band, Persichetti had already composed in a great variety of musical mediums. How, then, did he think of the band as a sound resource? In discussing the *Symphony for Band*, Richard Franko Goldman states:

> In its way, it represents how greatly the concept of band sound and texture has changed in recent years. In general Persichetti's score is spare in texture, with carefully calculated balances, and an important (and subtle) role assigned to the percussion.[1]

To amplify and develop this idea further, I selected for study certain measurable aspects of the scoring of the 9 works listed above. These include (1) instrument usage, (2) doubling, (3) scoring groups, (4) thickness and thinness, and (5) division of parts.

Usage

Persichetti's band consists of stable woodwind and brass sections and a fluctuating percussion group. His standard instrumentation is listed below, along with the percentage of playing time of each instrument for all nine works.[2] For percussion, the number of works in which the instrument is scored is given. The over-all figure for usage of all instruments in all works is 34% — just one-third of completely full scoring.

Brass

Cornets I-II-III, 40%
Trumpets I-II, 24%
French horns I-II-III-IV, 51%
Euphonium or Baritone, 44%
Trombones I-II-III, 34%
Tuba, 31%

Woodwind

Piccolo, 28%
Flute I-II, 51%
Oboe I-II, 45%
(English horn used in one movement of *Divertimento*)
E♭ Clarinet (8 works), 37%
B♭ Clarinet I-II-III, 70%
Alto Clarinet, 52%
Bass Clarinet, 50%

Contra-bass Clarinet (4 works) 24%
Alto sax I-II, 50%
Tenor sax, 41%
Baritone sax, 32%

Percussion

Bass drum, 9
Cymbal, 9
Snare drum, 7
Timpani, 7
Tenor (or alto) drum, 7
Xylophone, 4
Tambourine, 4
Woodblock, 3
Triangle, 3
Additional traps, 1
Glockenspiel, 1

The clarinet sound (B♭, alto, and bass) is the basic timbre of the writing. The other most important instruments in terms of usage are flute, French horn, alto saxophone, and double reeds — a heavy woodwind emphasis. Generally the instruments scored the least are those with extreme high or low ranges. The very important effects of the percussion section result from the contrast between tuned and untuned drums in opposing groups (i.e., timpani vs. bass, alto and tenor drums). The thematic significance of such writing is shown in this characteristic excerpt from the beginning of the fourth movement of *Bagatelles*, using snare drum (snares off), tenor drum, and bass drum to "state" a theme.

**Thematic percussion statement
from Bagatelles, IV**

© copyright 1961 by Elkan-Vogel, Inc., used by permission

Doubling

There is heavy doubling in these scores — a somewhat surprising finding, considering the light texture of most of the music and the complex chordal structure of which Persichetti is so fond. The heaviest doubling occurs in the low woodwinds, particularly with low clarinets and saxophones. The high woodwinds exhibit less doubling (except for the E♭ clarinet), and the brass show the least. One obvious reason for this pattern is that woodwind voices outnumber brass (in scoring as well as number of instruments). In addition, the ability for sound projection increases from low woodwinds to high woodwinds to brass; thus doubling becomes one means of achieving balance among these three groups. Finally, the strong tradition of doubling in band music for outdoor performance cannot be overlooked, as its vestige remains in Persichetti's work.

One striking facet of his original approach to doubling is his use of large blocks of *high* woodwinds in fast, unison, melodic passages. Persichetti himself has noted, "Much use is made of unison texture in twentieth-century composition; it has significant formal and coloristic functions."[3] *Divertimento*, *Psalm*, and *Pageant* abound in this type of scoring. Its use declines in later works but returns in *Masquerade*. Finally, no wind instrument is doubled, at least in some of its voices, for less than half its playing time, and most of them considerably more.

Scoring Groups

In combining instruments, Persichetti has experimented with and exploited countless combinations and colors. One-third of all his band writing is scored for an infinite number of woodwind-brass-percussion mixtures. *Bagatelles* shows many examples of these interesting sonorities, which fully integrate the percussion with the brass and woodwinds. In the fourth movement of *Symphony*, which presents virtually a catalogue of Persichetti's scoring groups, there is an interesting study in extremes. In measures 142-156, high woodwinds (piccolo, flute, and E♭ clarinet) and low brasses (trombones and tuba) are joined by percussion background — the tuba has the melody.

Another third of all the writing consists of woodwind-brass mixtures. "Song," "Dance," and "Soliloquy" from *Divertimento* as well as *So Pure the Star* emphasize these groups. Woodwinds alone are used in only about one-tenth of the nine compositions. Notable examples of this scoring appear in several variations of *Masquerade* and the second and third movements of *Bagatelles*.

Though small in quantity, woodwind-percussion groups are used with great originality by Persichetti. In Variation III of *Masquerade* (measures 31-42), flute and piccolo are set against four percussion lines — xylophone, woodblock, and the rims of snare and bass drums. In Variation IV, sandpaper blocks, woodblock, tom-tom played with fingers, snare drum and cymbals played with brushes, join the upper woodwinds in exotic sound patterns. Variation VIII also exhibits woodwinds, high in range and fast in tempo, with splashes

1. Richard Franko Goldman, *The Wind Band* (Boston: Allyn & Bacon, Inc., 1961), p. 239.

2. All percentages and figures mentioned in the article were arrived at by exhaustive research using accepted statistical procedures which are not defined here.

3. Vincent Persichetti, *Twentieth-Century Harmony* (New York: W.W. Norton & Co., Inc., 1961) p. 243.

of color from triangle, tambourine, cymbals, drums, and glockenspiel. In the opening of the fourth movement of *Symphony* the theme is stated by a woodwind-percussion ensemble, and later (measures 148-181) staccato chords by clarinets, saxophones, and bassoons are augmented by delicate wisps of percussion sound — sizzle cymbal with brushes, wire brushes on timpani, bass drum on the rim, etc. Finally, in this category, *Turn Not Thy Face* opens with a flute solo, joined by low register clarinets over timpani or bass drum rolls.

> "... one of the first composers to successfully use the variety, flexibility, and infinite colors of the band to reflect a first-rate musical imagination."

Small amounts of writing for brass alone appear, chiefly in *Pageant* and *Psalm* and usually in short phrases in choir-contrasting passages. Occasionally the brass is further subdivided into smaller ensembles for more subtle color changes.

In *Pageant* and especially in *Symphony* (I and IV) brass-percussion writing is prominent in stating thematic material but it is found very little in the other works.

Although percussion is extremely important in Persichetti's works, it seldom sounds alone. A favorite device is a quasi-thematic percussion statement at the opening of a work or movement. It may include xylophone and pitched or un-pitched drums combined with some brasses or woodwinds. Such beginning passages occur in *Divertimento* (VI), *Pageant* ("fast" section), *Symphony* (Adagio of I, Allegro of I), *Bagatelles* (II and IV), *Masquerade*, and *Turn Not Thy Face*.

Like-instrument writing (with only one instrument or section sounding) occurs for at least a small period of time in every work. The clarinet and French horn are by far the most often used in this way. They each have sectional-solo passages in eight of the nine works. The openings of *Psalm* and *Pageant* are examples. In *Masquerade*, Persichetti uses short cadenza-like passages on numerous instruments as connecting links between variations.

Most of the above categories are found in each work. Persichetti has achieved constant color-interest, and his shifting scoring groups — with few tutti or monochromatic combinations — are not subservient to the musical content, but part of it.

Score Thickness

If all instruments play all of the time, there would be little variation in color. There are, instead, far greater possibilities for contrast with a thinner texture. This is clearly shown by Persichetti's scoring. *One-fifth* of all the writing in the nine works is for five voices or less; *half* is for ten voices or less and *three-quarters* of the works are for fifteen voices or less. This means that Persichetti is treating the band essentially as a small en-semble with limitless color potential. He does use occasional extremes for dramatic effect, as in the final seven measures of *Masquerade* where upwards of thirty-five voices sound all twelve pitches simultaneously, contrasting with earlier unaccompanied solo-writing in the same work; or in "Dance" from *Divertimento* when more than twenty brass and woodwind voices break off abruptly to let a single trumpet voice sound. He varies thickness constantly and it becomes inextricably bound to color, as well as to musical content.

Division of Parts

Because of the standardized layout of the band score, it is common to think of those voice divisions as the normal ones — flutes in two parts, clarinets in three, horns in four, etc. Persichetti's scoring deviates somewhat from this standard. Flutes are written in a single voice for more than two-thirds of their playing time. Oboe, cornet, and French horn (surprisingly) also have over half of their scoring in a single voice, accomplished either by unisons among the different "parts" or by omitting the bottom voices. Bassoons and alto saxophones are written in two parts only slightly more often than in one. But trumpets and trombones are written mostly in their expected two and three-part voicing. Also notable is Persichetti's tendency to write a divided tuba part in fifths; this occurs somewhere in every work except *So Pure the Star*.

The Bb clarinets exhibit the most versatile treatment of division. While three-part writing predominates, there are sizable areas of unison and two-part scoring. In "Nocturne" from *Serenade*, Persichetti divides the clarinets into five parts briefly near the end. In the first movement of *Bagatelles*, he sounds the theme in unison clarinets, then, in measures 15 and 16, in *six* parts; the sound contrast is extremely fresh and original.

Bb clarinets and the theme of Bagatelles

© *copyright 1961 by Elkan-Vogel, Inc., used by permission*

701

In the fourth movement of *Bagatelles*, in the course of eighty measures, the voicing of the Bb clarinets shifts fifteen times. *Masquerade* also abounds in unique examples of Bb clarinet scoring. There are sections in two, five, six, seven and even nine divisions. The first nine-part writing occurs in Variation I within a dense passage of chromatic, polyphonic woodwinds. Crisp nine-part chords (with percussion) also bridge Variations II and III. In Variation IV, clarinet choir, flute, and percussion (played by fingers or brushes) whisper in intense, eight-voice, syncopated rhythms, with clarinets in five voices. The most original scoring occurs near the end of Variation VII. After a climactic section of passage work in the high woodwinds supported by brass chords, the clarinets, saxophones, and double reeds be-gin a descending chromatic scale, each stopping on a different pitch in reverse-pyramid fashion. Here, Bb clarinets are in seven parts.

All of these dimensions of scoring become an integrated part of the content of these originally conceived band works, not merely a container for abstract musical ideas. Vincent Persichetti is one of the first composers to successfully use the variety, flexibility, and infinite colors of the band to reflect a first-rate musical imagination. ∎

William Workinger is teacher of instrumental music and music theory at Bloomfield (New Jersey) High School. He holds the Ed.D degree in Music Education from New York University.

August, 1973

The Wind Music of Charles Ives

Frank Battisti/Donald Hunsberger

Early in the 1972-73 school year, I presented a concert of Ives' works for wind instruments and wind band. We grouped the three ensembles necessary to perform these works on the stage all at the same time. Some of the pieces are very short (one is 22 measures long) and I walked from group to group so that the "time lag" would be eliminated between numbers and the pieces (all employing different instrumentation) could be performed in consecutive sequence (similar to the performance of a "suite" of pieces). As a result of the preparation for this concert, I became very interested in Ives; and although I am no authority on him, I would like to share some of the music and information I uncovered.

From his early childhood, Ives was in direct contact with New England town bands; his father was a bandmaster and had a band in the Civil War which was reputed to be one of the finer bands in the Union Army. Charles played the drums and the cornet in his father's town band and was also involved in theatre bands. He had a great respect and love for what we now call "American traditions" and the town band was certainly an American institution. His father saw to it that the young Charles had a very solid back-

Donald Hunsberger is Associate Professor of Music at The Eastman School of Music where he conducts the Eastman Wind Ensemble and the Eastman Symphony Band.

Frank L. Battisti is Conductor of Wind Ensembles and Chairman of the Music Education Department at the New England Conservatory of Music. He was previously Director of Bands at Ithaca High School where he inaugurated a commissioning works project in 1958. Within 9 years, 214 works for band were commissioned from such well known composers as Karel Husa and Walter Hartley

Editor's Note: This article was excerpted and edited by Donald Hunsberger from a lecture/demonstration presented by Frank Battisti at the Fourth Annual Wind Ensemble Conference, The University of Wisconsin — Madison, April 26, 1973.

ground in musicianship — piano, violin, cornet and snare drum, with lessons in counterpoint and sight-reading. His listening included country fiddlers, Puritan hymns, revival hymns at camp meetings, romantically-harmonized hymns in fashionable parishes, popular tunes, minstrel tunes, Stephen Foster, delicate sentimental drawing-room ballads, and the music of Handel, Bach, and Beethoven played by father and his friends on weird combinations of instruments. This environment is reflected in his music via his "quotations" of many of the tunes he came into contact with in his various social experiences. He seldom quoted things exactly, but he doesn't go the the abstract route, either. Some of his other musical techniques included the use of polytonality, polyrhythmic devices, 12-note rows (he wrote things called *Tone Roads* which were really serial pieces), micro-tones, quarter-tone music... and he used these techniques long before they were "discovered" and established.

The following works represent some of the compositions he wrote between the ages of 18 and 47. They are fun pieces but they offer an opportunity to see Charles Ives in a different perspective and gain some insight into his work.

Intercollegiate March

This piece was written by Ives in 1892 and is his first published work. He refers to this particular march in a note written on the back of one of his Ives American Insurance Calendars*: "*Intercollegiate March* 1895. New Haven Band, Washington Marine Band, McKinley Inauguration 1897, published by Pepper and Company, Philadelphia." This then was a march played in the inauguration of 1897.

March Omega Lambda Chi

Written in 1896, this march contains the air "Omega Lambda Chi" (tune = "Sailing, Sailing") and includes some unusual (for the first time) compositional features. As with the *Intercollegiate March*, Ives was still a student at Yale and used fraternity-university tunes.

Country Band March

Ives composed this work at the age of 29. It has recently been arranged by James Sinclair, a graduate student at Yale. In a letter to me Jim made the following comments:

I am convinced that the *Country Band March*, regardless of the strengths or weaknesses of my arrangement, is the most important and representative of Ives' works that could be done in the band medium. It is important to note that while the *Country Band March* is a "march" by name, it is really about an aspect of New England

*Ives made a handsome living from the insurance business, and composed as a hobby.

life, or American life, if you will — the country band. It is about *what*, and more *how*, a country band played, or played at, those many tunes they loved. In the *Country Band March*, Ives quotes *Arkansas Traveler, Battle Cry of Freedom, British Grenadiers, The Girl I Left Behind, London Bridge, Marching Through Georgia, Massa's in de Cold, Cold Ground, My Old Kentucky Home, Violets, May Day Waltz, Yankee Doodle*, and *Semper Fidelis*. There is rarely anything straightforward about these quotations; they are subjected to the now famous Ives technique of poly-everything. The result is just the right mixture of confusion, off-beatness, and the go-get-'em attitude that expressed the phenomenon of the country band, a thing that Ives must have dearly loved...The original medium of the march was the theatre orchestra, but not surprising, Ives often referred to it (in his Memos) as "brass band stuff." Much of the material from *Country Band March* is familiar to us in its later use for "Putnam's Camp" of *Three Places in New England*, but *Country Band March* is truly itself a masterpiece.

Calcium Light Night

Calcium Light Night was probably begun while Ives was at Yale and was completed in 1907 (four years after *Country Band March*). The following year, Ives noted that this work was concerned with an "evocation of the torchlight parades at the time of student society elections."[1] The work uses familiar, borrowed tunes and, in addition, exemplifies the use of the "percussion piano" technique. Ives made the following comments on this technique in which drum parts are played on the piano.

When I was a boy, I played in my father's brass band, usually one of the drums...In practising the drum parts on the piano (not on the drum — neighbours' requests), I remember getting tired of using the tonic and dominant and subdominant triads, and Doh and Soh etc. in the bass. So [I] got to trying out sets of notes to go with or take-off the drums — for the snare drum, right-hand notes usually closer together — and for the bass drum, wider chords. They had little to do with the harmony of the piece, and were used only as sound-combinations as such. For the explosive notes or heavy accents in either drum, the fist or flat of the hand was sometimes used, usually longer groups in the right hand than left hand... sometimes, when practising with others or in the school orchestra, I would play drum parts on the piano, and I noticed that it didn't seem to bother the other players — if I would keep away from triads etc., that suggested a key. A popular chord in the right hand was Doh#-Me-Soh-Doh♮, sometimes a Ray# on top, or Doh-Me-Soh-Ti, and one with two white notes with thumb, having the little finger run into a 7th or octave-and-semitone over the lower thumb note. The left hand often would take two black notes on top with thumb, and run down the rest on white or mixed.[2]

1. John Kirkpatrick (ed.), *Charles E. Ives Memos* (New York: W.W. Norton & Co., Inc. 1972), p. 266.
2. *Ibid.*, pp. 42-43.

The See'r

This extremely short piece is only 38 measures long. One of Ives' *114 Songs*, it was sketched in 1906 and was arranged by Ives for a combination of wind instruments (clarinet, cornet, and alto horn), piano, and drum (1913?). Ives was actually a very practical composer concerning the use of various instruments in his music, indicating what instruments might be substituted if his first choice was not available. In this case, the alto horn part may be performed by French horn, trombone, or tenor saxophone.

Ann Street

This composition, written in 1921, was inspired by a poem by Maurice Morris about a short street in lower Manhattan that runs off of Broadway. According to Gunther Schuller (who has written an arrangement of this work), "All Ives really did was to tear two pages of *Ann Street* from his collection of *114 Songs* and annotate them with indications toward rescoring for trumpet, flute, trombone, and piano." Schuller has added a few glockenspiel notes and a cup mute to the trumpet at the end.

A Final Word From Ives

Finally, I would like to quote some Charles Ives philosophy. This was written by Ives in the early 1930's.

My business experience revealed life to me in many aspects that I might otherwise have missed. In it one sees tragedy, nobility, meanness, high aims, low aims, brave hopes, faint hopes, great ideals, no ideals, and one is able to watch these work inevitable destiny. And it has seemed to me that the finer sides of these traits were not only in the majority but in the ascendancy. I have seen men fight honorably and to a finish, solely for a matter of conviction or of principle — and where expediency, probably loss of business, prestige, or position had no part and threats no effect. It is my impression that there is more open-mindedness and willingness to examine carefully the premises underlying a new or unfamiliar thing, before condemning it, in the world of business than in the world of music. It is not even uncommon in business intercourse to sense a reflection of a philosophy — a depth of something fine — akin to a strong beauty in art. To assume that business is a material process, and only that, is to undervalue the average mind and heart. To an insurance man there is an "average man" and he is humanity. I have experienced a great fullness of life in business. The fabric of existence weaves itself whole. You cannot set an art off in the corner and hope for it to have a vitality, reality, and substance. There can be nothing "exclusive" about a substantial art. It comes directly out of the heart of experience of life and thinking about life and living life. My work in music helped my business and my work in business helped my music.[3]

---

3. Henry Bellamann, "Charles Ives: The Man and His Music," *Musical Quarterly*, Vol. XIX (1933), 47-48.

Ives' Wind Music[4]

Existing Band Pieces

March No. 5 or *Intercollegiate March* (1892). The first published work by Ives. Pepper & Co., 1896.

March in F and C "Omega Lambda Chi" (1896). Not published.

Band Arrangements

A Son of a Gambolier (1892-95). From the *114 Songs* (where it is marked by Ives as a brass band march), arranged by Jonathan Elkus for band. Peer, 1962.

Variations on America (1891). Arranged by Schuman-William Rhoads. Merion Music (Presser), 1968.

Country Band March (1903). Arranged by James Sinclair, 1973.

Symphony No. 2 (1899). Last movement arranged for band by James Sinclair, 1972.

Wind Ensemble Pieces

From the Steeples and the Mountains (1901). For bells (or chimes or two pianos), trumpet and trombone. Peer, 1965.

Chromâtimelôdtune (1909-1919, 1913?). Subtitled "Ear Study," Ives' manuscript indicates his intended instrumentation to be for E♭ cornet, B♭ cornet, trombone, tuba, and piano. Gunther Schuller has reconstructed and completed the piece for chamber orchestra. The chamber orchestra arrangement has been published by MJQ Music, Inc., 1963.

The See'r (1907?). From *Set No. 4* for clarinet, cornet (or trumpet or French horn ad lib) piano, alto horn (or French horn, trombone or tenor saxophone) and snare and bass drum. Not published.

Over the Pavements (1906). A scherzo for piccolo, clarinet, bassoon (or saxophone), trumpet, 3 trombones, cymbals, bass drum, and piano. Peer, 1954.

Calcium Light Night (1907?). For piccolo, oboe, clarinet, bassoon, trumpet, trombone, snare drum, and piano(s). Uses fraternity songs of Psi Upsilon and Delta Kappa Epsilon. Edited by Henry Cowell. Presser (rental).

Wind Ensemble Arrangements

Ann Street (1922). Arranged by Gunther Schuller, from *Set No. 6*, for trumpet, flute, trombone, piano, and glockenspiel (196-).

Pieces for Voice(s) with Wind Accompaniment

Song for a Harvest Season (1894). Voice, cornet, trombone, basso (bass trombone or tuba), or organ (two manuals and pedals). Published as Volume 7, Number 1 of *New Music*. Merion Music (Presser), 1933.

The Circus Band (1894). Ives (in his *114 Songs*) labeled this piece "brass band march." It has been arranged as a song for voice and piano, for mixed chorus and orchestra, and for mixed chorus and band (Jonathan Elkus).

Three Harvest Home Chorales (1898-1902). For mixed chorus and piano *or* organ *or* brass, organ and percussion. Edited by Henry Cowell. Mercury, 1949.

December (1912-1913). For unison men's chorus accompanied by piccolo, 2 clarinets, 2 horns, 3 trumpets, 3 trombones and tuba. Peer, 1963.

---

4. The source for the publisher names and dates of publication for the works listed here was Dominque-René de Lerma, *Charles Edward Ives, 1874-1954: A Bibliography of His Music* (Kent, Ohio: Kent State University Press, 1970).

Ives for Band

Keith Brion, James Sinclair, and Jonathan Elkus

Something wonderful has happened! American school and college bands can now perform the "red-blooded" music of America's greatest composer, Charles Ives, a composer who really loved bands. The Charles Ives celebration which centers on Ives' 100th birthday, October 20, 1974, has stimulated the publication of Ives' extant original band music as well as band arrangements of many of his most representative compositions. The music ranges from the charming American simplicity of his early band music, to the later more sophisticated polytonal and polyrhythmic works such as *Country Band March*. This article presents a listing and general description of both published works and those in preparation. Conductors, performers and audiences will have a lot of fun, excitement, and enjoyment with this delightful and *very* American band music.

Original Band Music

Ives' original band music was first conceived for the Danbury, Connecticut town band. Young Charles often played the drum parts while his father George conducted and played cornet. The instrumentation of the Danbury Band was full by existing standards: 1 piccolo, 3-5 clarinets, 1 tenor saxophone, 3-5 cornets, 3 alto horns, 3 trombones, 2 baritones, 2 bass horns and 3 percussion. While much of Ives' original band music has been lost, we hope that parts for the missing Ives band pieces may yet be found in some forgotten trunk. All of the surviving original band music was composed by Ives between his eleventh and twentieth years.

March: Intercollegiate (1892). Edited and arranged with additional parts for modern band by Keith Brion, 1965 (source: the 16 printed band parts (1896) and Ives' MSS). South Hackensack, N.J.: Joseph Boonin, Inc., 1973. This is a 6/8 march using the air "Annie Lisle" (the Cornell Alma Mater). It is a nearly-conventional 19th century march, but the air has an altered rhythm and the trio modulation is C to A♭! Duration 3:00. Grade IV.

March: Omega Lambda Chi (1896). Edited and arranged with additional parts for modern bands by Keith Brion. 1964 (source: Ives' MS band score). New York, N.Y.: Associated Music Publishers, 1974. Another 6/8 march, this one introduces the air "Omega Lambda Chi" ("Sailing, Sailing"). It is a robust 19th century march with a 32-bar second strain and a 32-bar trio. The trio opens with a floating horn solo. Duration 2:55. Grade IV.

Lost Original Band Music

A number of Ives' works for band are known to be lost. These include "Schoolboy March" (1886), "Holiday Quickstep" (1887), "Slow March on 'Adeste Fidelis'" (1886 or 1887), "Fantasia on 'Jerusalem the Golden'" (1888), "A Son of a Gambolier" (1892), "The Circus Band" (1894), "Overture: Town Gown and State" (1896), "March for Dewey Day" (1899),

and "Runaway Horse on Main Street" (1905). However, some of these exist in other versions, which have been used as the basis of new arrangements.

Variations on "Jerusalem the Golden" (1888-1889). Setting for brass band or brass quintet and concert band by Keith Brion, 1972 (source: Ives' MS, probably for organ). New York, N.Y.: Associated Music Publishers, 1974. This setting of these beautiful hymnic variations contrasts a spatially separated solo cornet and brass ensemble with a modern concert band. Duration 3:00. Grade III (solos, Grade V).

A Son of a Gambolier (1892). Transcribed by Jonathan Elkus, 1961 (source: Peer edition of Ives' version for voice and piano). New York, N.Y.: Peer International Corp., 1962. This jaunty 6/8 march has been provided with a colorful concert orchestration. The tune is familiar today as "Ramblin' Wreck from Georgia Tech." Duration 3:30. Grade IV.

The Circus Band (1894). Transcribed for band with optional mixed chorus by Jonathan Elkus, 1968 (source: Peer edition of the chamber orchestra version by George F. Roberts and Ives' version for voice and piano). New York, N.Y.: Peer International Corp., 1971. One of Ives' finest marches, it is enlived by the use of ragged rhythms. Duration 2:30. Grade IV.

Band-Influenced Works

Ives' fascination with the tradition of bands in Danbury is apparent in a great deal of his musical output. Apart from the original works for band, there is a diverse body of music inspired by, or clearly based on, the band experience. These include (1) "band-like" works, which display band forms and typical musical styles of the late 19th century; and (2) "brass band stuff," a term used by Ives to refer to one of his favorite compositional stunts — imitating or parodying the actual playing style of the town band.

Ives composed a raft of "band-like" works which are notable for their youthful freshness and infectious enthusiasm. Among these are at least 10 marches for piano, many of which Ives also worked out for theater orchestra or brass band. These marches are all early works. The "band-like" category also includes some of the larger works, such as the *Second Symphony* with its roaring finale using "Columbia, the Gem of the Ocean."

Keith Brion is Director of Bands at Yale University. Previously, he was Supervisor of Music in the Caldwell-West Caldwell, New Jersey Schools and Music Director of the North Jersey Wind Symphony.

James B. Sinclair is an assistant to John Kirkpatrick at the Yale University Ives Collection, Assistant to the Director of the Yale Bands, and an editor of orchestral works for the Ives Society.

Jonathan Elkus, conductor of the Lehigh University concert and marching bands from 1957-1973, is currently engaged in free-lance editing, lecturing, composing and conducting.

After leaving Yale in 1898, Ives lost his close contact with brass bands, and he soon began composing his "band stuff," mainly as small pieces for theater orchestra. These attempts to set down the *real* sounds from the town square or local "opera" house led him to forge important developments in 20th century music. (How could a composer imitate colliding

---

Ives Centennial Concerts

The Yale University Band, conducted by Keith Brion, James Sinclair and Jonathan Elkus, will present many of these Ives works in free public concerts for the Ives Centennial in New Haven, Connecticut (October 20, 1974), Kennedy Center, Washington, D.C. (March 8 and 22, 1975), Miami, Florida (March 14 and 17), and Hilton Head, South Carolina (March 19, 1975).

---

marching bands without incidently developing polytonality, poly-meter, "poly-everything"?!) In the monumental Fourth Symphony, the second movement (the "Comedy") presents an exceptionally vivid picture of Ives' band experience.

1. "Band-Like" Works

Decoration Day. Transcribed by Jonathan Elkus, 1974 (source: Peer edition of the orchestral score). To be published by Peer International Corp. At once a reverent and joyous tone picture of a holiday as observed by 19th century New Englanders, this work includes a lengthy qote of D.W. Reeves' "Second Regiment" March. Duration 8:40. Grade V.

Finale from the Second Symphony. Transcribed by Jonathan Elkus, 1973 (source: Southern edition of the orchestra score with editing from Ives' MSS). New York, N.Y.: Southern Music Publishing Co., Inc., 1974. This is one of Ives' most popular orchestral works. The finale features numerous popular American tunes, and the ending ("Columbia, Gem of the Ocean") is quite a rouser. Duration 11:00. Grade V.

2. "Band Stuff"

Country Band March (1903). Transcribed by James B. Sinclair, 1972 (source: Sinclair's edition of Ives' score-sketch for theater orchestra). Bryn Mawr, Pa.: Merion Music (Presser), 1974. An Ives masterpiece, this is both a great concert march and a riotous picture of a 19th century band. Later this material became part of "Putnam's Camp" in *Three Places in New England*. Duration 4:00. Grade V.

Overture and March: "1776" (1904?). Transcribed by James B. Sinclair, 1973 (source: Sinclair's edition of Ives' score-sketch for theater orchestra). To be published by Merion Music (Presser). The middle section is a humerous portrayal of cornets with their A and B♭ shanks mixed up! The result is a wild sound that goes over well. This material was also used later in "Putnam's Camp." Duration 2:50. Grade IV-V.

They Are There! — *A War Song March* (with optional unison chorus) (1917, 1942). Transcribed by James B. Sinclair, 1973 (source: Peer edition of orchestra-chorus score with editing from Ives' MSS). To be published by Peer International Corp. Patriotism screams forth in multi-sounds. "Wrong notes are right" and high spirits prevail. Duration 2:45. Grade IV-V.

Transcriptions

Transcriptions of orchestral, keyboard, and vocal music have long been a mainstay of the international band repertory. Most transcriptions for band have been the work of experienced band conductors who have transcribed pieces which they felt would be particularly appropriate to their own band and appealing to their audiences. It would be difficult to overestimate the exposure that distinguished musical works of almost every genre have received and continue to receive through band performances. With respect to Ives' repertory, band transcriptions are particularly appropriate. When one recalls Ives' own personal experience with bands and the importance of bands in his musical upbringing, it is not at all surprising that even the most contemplative moments of Ives' music turn out in transcription to be idiomatic band music of the most expressive kind.

The Alcotts (1912-1914). Transcribed by Richard E. Thurston, 1968 (source: Associated edition of the *Concord Sonata* for piano, third movement). New York. N.Y.: Associated Music Publishers, 1972. This is an advanced, lyric work with moments of powerful expression. Duration 4:40. Grade V.

Concord Village. Freely transcribed by Maurice Gardner, 1969 (source: *Concord Sonata*, third movement). New York, N.Y.: Staff Music Publ. Co., 1970.

Hymn (1904). Transcribed by James B. Sinclair, 1972 (source: Peer edition of the string quintet version). To be published by Peer International Corp. An expressive treatment of two hymn tunes. Duration 3:00. Grade III.

Fugue from String Quartet No. 1 (1896). Transcribed by James B. Sinclair, 1972 (source: Peer edition of the quartet score with editing from Ives' MSS). To be published by Peer International Corp. Based on hymn tunes, this piece is charcterized by flowing counterpoint and beautiful lines. This material also appears in the slow movement of the *Fourth Symphony*. Duration 6:00. Grade III-IV.

Old Home Days — *Suite for Band*. Transcribed by Jonathan Elkus, 1974 (source: Peer editions of songs by Ives for voice and piano, including (1) *Waltz*, (2) *The Collection*, (3) *Slow March*, (4) *Memories* ("Very Pleasant," "Rather Sad"), and (5) *Religion*. To be published by Peer International Corp. A charming collection from Ives' many songs. Not difficult but fine music. Duration 7:00. Grade III.

Variations on "America" (1891). Transcribed by William E. Rhoads, 1967 (source: arrangement for orchestra by William Schuman of Ives' work for organ). Bryn Mawr, Pa.: Merion Music (Presser), 1968. The variations are a parody of the popular 19th century style. This brilliant concert piece has become a standard in the repertoire. Duration 7:20. Grade V.

Ives-Derived Works

Perhaps some of the most significant contributions to band music will turn out to be works by later composers who have been inspired by both the letter and the spirit of Ives' music. The "spatial" works for large wind and percussion groups by Henry Brant are already familiar to many players. Among the Ives-inspired works for band should be mentioned David Borden's *Variations on America by Charles Ives as heard on the Jingle Jangle Morning in Emerson Playground by You, and the Signers of the U.S. Constitution (and who knows, maybe the FBI)* for band and prepared tape, and Robert Moran's *Hallelujah, a Joyous Phenomenon with Fanfares* for marching bands, drum and bugle corps, church choirs, etc.

"You cannot set an art off in a corner," wrote Ives, "and expect it to have vitality, reality and substance." And for Ives it was band music and "band stuff" that constituted the vitality, reality, and substance of so much of his music. ■

Young Band Music: What To Look For

Lloyd Conley

Finding good new music for young bands can be perplexing for every director. Having faced the problem for many years both as teacher and composer/arranger, I know that the solution is not easy. Guided by promotional materials, suggestions from colleagues, dealers' lists, and just plain hunch, most of us order some new music and hope we will find enough suitable for our scheduled performances.

Such factors as title, grade, length, price, and composer/arranger are worth considering, but to select music intelligently we really must hear it and examine the score and parts. For this reason, sound sheets and recordings accompanied by sample scores are a real help, particularly if they include the entire composition.

Regardless of what aids are used, each individual must determine his own criteria for choosing music. Listed below are the elements I consider important for young bands (Grades I and II), although many of the criteria apply equally well to music of all difficulty levels.

Key Signatures

E♭ concert is probably the easiest key for young bandsmen because its scale includes more tones that young players learn first (A♭ and E♭ in particular). Also, the keys of B♭ and F concert are considered acceptable for even the easiest band music. Moving beyond these three keys increases the problems, but I believe the problems are highly over-rated. For example, fingerings for the pitch D♭ (concert) are not particularly difficult for most instruments, yet intelligent use of that one tone adds the key of A♭ to the repertoire and expands the tonal pallet considerably. In a similar manner, B natural (concert) opens the door to the key of C concert, although that tone is not as easily handled as D . Low C♯ on cornets, trumpets, and treble clef baritones; low B natural on trombones, baritones, and tubas; and low C♯ on tenor saxes are all troublesome for young performers (and often older ones); however, knowledgeable writers can and do avoid these tones and still use the keys successfully. Even the key of D♭ can be used sparingly if the composer/arranger avoids difficult fingerings and awkward voice leading.

Lloyd Conley, a 28-year veteran of directing school bands, has over 200 band compositions and arrangements published by 5 different companies.

I look for materials that use keys other than F, B♭, and E♭, while watching for writing that may cause unnecessary problems for young musicians. Remembering to use the key signatures can be a real problem for beginners, so I also like judicious use of reminder accidentals.

Time Signatures

Because the quarter note is usually the first beat unit taught, time signatures of $\frac{2}{4}$, $\frac{3}{4}$, and $\frac{4}{4}$ are always appropriate and safe. Even $\frac{6}{4}$ presents little problem for youngsters and is used in many methods. ¢ and $\frac{6}{8}$ are certainly appropriate at grade II level, but must be used sensibly by writers.

I recommend you look for music using $\frac{5}{4}$ and $\frac{7}{4}$, but hasten to add that you will find very little. Both of these meters are merely combinations of 2s and 3s and are suitable for grade II music if handled properly. They feel and sound different and are unusual, requiring careful concentration in performance; but easy music with limited use of $\frac{5}{4}$ and $\frac{7}{4}$ can be written and we writers do a disservice to the profession by not writing such music. Of course, publishers must be willing to take a chance on innovative material, and ultimately it is the purchaser — the band director — who will determine by his response whether such pieces will be made available to him or not.

There are easy materials already available that require students to move freely between simple time signatures:

Music with mixed time signatures is interesting for students, adds variety to rehearsals and performances, and prepares students for the complex rhythms they will face later. However it is questionable to expect young musicians to handle mixed time signatures where the unit of beat changes:

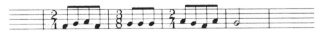

Rhythms

It is probably not possible to prepare a list of rhythm patterns that are "appropriate" for any given grade of music because it is much more important how a particular rhythm pattern is used — whether it fits naturally into the music, lays well on the instruments involved, is used at a workable range, and balanced with other technical requirements. Normally ¢ and § are not used for grade I music but that is not to say that these time signatures and the rhythms they incorporate can't be taught successfully at that level by an astute teacher. Common sense will dictate what is acceptable for your group, but don't forsake the need to challenge students sensibly.

Ranges

Directors usually watch carefully for demanding high ranges and (to a lesser degree) very low ranges, and well they should. To require excessively high tones can destroy young embouchures. On the other hand, growth demands challenge and the director must present these challenges to the students. Therefore, don't pass over an otherwise good piece of music because of a few high notes. One talented student might be taught to get the high notes while others in the section can be assigned appropriate lower tones. You can also use that good piece of music by giving the troublesome tone to a different instrument. . . sometimes. Flutes can cover high clarinet notes, clarinets can play high trumpet notes, and the horns can easily play high trombone and baritone notes. Saxes are very versatile, and thus useful in this role. In making substitutions it is important to notice how the problem tone is approached and how the substitution would affect the over-all scheme of things. It is fair to add that while it can be very workable, a substitution is rarely as good as the original.

Counterpoint

Getting away from the unison writing of beginning methods as early as possible is one of the secrets of moving students toward part independence. The insecure feeling that results from playing rhythms and pitches different from players around you is normal, but it must be overcome if students are to develop properly and enjoy the variety that counterpoint brings to music. The sooner the better, so look for music that uses counterpoint. Fear that it will result in greater student insecurity or lack of interest is unfounded. Persistent effort is required by all but once students understand the purpose and importance of this basic element of good music they will not only handle it effectively but will relish it. The variety and genuine musicality resulting from the greater use of counterpoint will increase student interest, to say nothing of your own.

Instrumentation

The wide divergence of philosophy, method, numbers, and equipment in school music departments results in a similar divergence in band instrumentation. Therefore, variety and versatility in the instrumentation of young band music is necessary to meet the problem. Published music runs the gamut from full instrumentation with no doubled parts to very basic instrumentation with many doubles. Obviously, it is more interesting for players and more musically satisfying for everyone when there is full instrumentation with parts written specifically for each instrument; it certainly allows the writer more latitude. But perhaps most young bands are not so well blessed and must subsist with no bass, no horn, weak low

brass, an abundance of flutes, etc. Publishers have sought to produce materials that can be used effectively by such groups, and have been very successfull by printing a variety of doubled parts, all of which have certain drawbacks. Doubling alto sax and horn, for instance, leaves a very limited range that is useable for both instruments, particularly in grade I materials. The tenor sax/baritone T.C. combination is similar although somewhat better. Other doublings are more kind to writers and performers: oboe/2nd flute and baritone/bassoon, for example. The use of divisi and tacet can add variety if the director makes sure that students are following the writer's directions.

Prudence demands that you look for an instrumentation structure that best suits your band, and hope to find the kinds of materials that you want and need. Remember, however, that a little ingenuity by the director will go a long way toward making a piece workable with a lop-sided instrumentation. Thinning texture, strengthening some tones, and substituting instruments often can do much to make a piece usable. Color and authenticity will be partially lost, but if the editing is done with musical taste and in the interest of good performance, writers and publishers are not likely to object.

Check the number of parts included in the band set. If there aren't enough you can buy extra parts (considered a bother by some publishers and dealers) or an extra set. Copying parts is against the law and thus not an available alternative. Also watch for parts printed back-to-back, and for poorly planned page turns — a rare problem in that most young band music is printed on single pages.

Scores

A full score is desirable for any musical organization. I cannot accept the concept that young band music does not require a full score; indeed it is often more important for inexperienced players than for mature groups. Because of cost, few young band materials include full score. The usual alternative is a semi-full score of six to ten staves; and unfortunately condensed scores are still used occasionally.

Be sure enough detail is included in any score to make it sufficiently informative and easy to use. Look for specific instrument labels, clearly marked cues, proper spacing, bar lines broken between major sections, instrumentation indications on each page, metronome markings, and performance time.

Texture

Probably every young (and old) band has a few players who are content just to be part of the group, never really caring if they are heard and often afraid that they might be. However, most students do want to be heard and should be given the opportunity. They will grow from the experience and become better and more self-sufficient players.

Seek music that offers sections and individuals a chance to be heard. The colorless sound that results from the overuse of materials that are "full and safe" is well known. To use such music exclusively is to insult students' intelligence and performance potential and to rob them of the joys of playing really good music. It is normal for young students to hesitate when first encountering a solo or thin texture but usually they will accept the challenge and go to work once they grasp its purpose and meaning in the music. Stronger players and much more interesting performances will result.

Use discretion and select materials with a reasonable balance between thick and thin textures, between tutti and solo. Consider musical coherence as well as practical concerns for the group's relative strengths and weaknesses, and experiment with textures to find ways to make music more colorful and interesting.

Scoring Techniques

The limitations of key, range, rhythms and dynamics, plus the allowance for inadequate instrumentation all lead to a tendency toward sameness in easy band music. Such techniques as block scoring, grouping by range, and using the brass and woodwind as undivided families are common. Some publications group all trombones, baritones, tenor/baritone sax, bass clarinet, bassoon and tuba on a single, bass-oriented part. There are good arguments against such an approach but if one has a very poorly instrumented group it is an obvious answer to the search for usable materials. Given reasonable instrumentation, however, it is better to look for music that offers a greater variety of parts, thereby allowing for more sophistication in harmonic content and greater tone color possibilities. Characteristics noted in the paragraph on texture are an integral part of scoring techniques; however, for some purposes (pop concert, pep band, variety show) less sophisticated scoring techniques may be desirable.

Characteristics of Good Music

In some ways it is more difficult to write good music for young musicians than for more mature players, but it is certainly being done. Therefore it is imperative for directors to consider such items as form, melody, harmonic content, counterpoint, voice-leading, and general over-all musical content when seeking out good young band music. It is the director's responsibility to put serious effort into finding the very best that is available at any given grade level. Even pop tunes and novelties can be handled so they have substance for the musician. Options and tastes vary and we won't all agree, but the earmarks of good music are evident if we look for them.

Publishers Practices

Despite the advantages of full scores, there are still directors who shy away from them. Learn to use a full score, look for music that has them, and encourage publishers to provide more full scores by buying them when they are available.

Although the percussion line on the conductor's score can include more than one instrument, separate lines are desirable. Crowding may be necessary on the score, but students' parts should be spread out as much as is practical. Generally two different instruments on a single part is enough,

although often a third instrument is used so sparingly that a separate part would not be practical.

Good proofing is absolutely essential. There is probably no aspect of publication that is more tedious, but none is more important. Even though publishers work very hard to avoid mistakes, a few do get by. If you encounter them, let the publishers know. Some errors will show up in a reading session but many will be found only through thorough rehearsing, because it is virtually impossible to detect certain types of errors by visual scanning — particularly true in cases where score and parts don't agree. Should you find errors repeatedly in the music of a publisher it is just good common sense to avoid publications from that company.

You won't find it very often any more, but watch for printing that is hard to read. Small notes, improperly or carelessly placed notes, crowded measures, poorly planned page turns, unclear printing, and unusual page sizes are all factors that contribute to poor reading and add to the director's problems. Again, tell the publisher. The publishing industry gives high priority to quality production of the music they choose to print and they will react to constructive criticism. Failing that, avoid music from companies that consistently display poor publication practices.

Look and Listen

Take care to select music that is neither too easy nor too difficult for the band; either extreme could diminish the effectiveness of your teaching. It is easy to underestimate the abilities of students and keep them playing trite, immature materials long after they have grown enough to accept more of a challenge. Music that is too difficult can also be discouraging if the students cannot handle the ranges, rhythms, or mature musical concept that the piece demands. Between the two extremes is a somewhat limited selection of music that is just right for your band. Given all the desirable characteristics of good music and all the limitations of a young organization, the director is often faced with a formidable task when he looks for the right material, especially if there is the additional restriction of a search for a certain style of music. The resulting performance can be bland at one extreme and very ragged at the other. Challenge is necessary but so is the relaxation that comes from playing something lighter and easier. How to achieve a balance is up to the sensitivity and expertise of each director.

The key words are look and listen. Take time to look at and listen to as much material as possible, bearing in mind the many positive and negative factors that can be found as well as the peculiarities of your own situation. Consider the potential uses of the music for your band, both as performance selections and as educational material that will further the learning process. You must know your students well in order to be able to apply these criteria in an intelligent and effective manner. You won't be right 100% of the time, but the odds are that you'll be right more often than wrong, and as a result your program will improve.   ■

Selecting Music for Young Bands

BY BARBARA PRENTICE

Every fall the same situation arises. The other teachers in your building are assigned teaching materials by the state textbook adoption committee. As the music teacher or band director, though, you face the task, the challenge, and the freedom of selecting the subject matter for each performance class. This option carries with it a great responsibility, for the musical growth of your students depends on your selection of worthy repertoire.

Zoltan Kodaly once said, "Children should be taught with only the most musically valuable material. For the young, only the best is good enough. They should be led to masterpieces by means of masterpieces."

Kodaly didn't have an $800 yearly music budget or a junior high band for which to purchase. You do — or you have similar limits. Just how do you sift out the masterpieces from the stacks of new publications at the local music store? How can you be certain that you're spending your money wisely? Are there some specific rules, some criteria you can follow to help you make intelligent choices?

When I started teaching band 20 years ago, a limited amount of literature was available for young bands; I simply bought whatever was on the shelf. Luckily, that situation has changed. In recent years, a large number of composers and arrangers have begun writing specifically for young, inexperienced bands and for bands with incomplete instrumentation. Although some of this music is of high quality, much of it lacks substance, historical value, or aesthetic worth.

Asking yourself the following questions will help you appraise literature you are considering adding to your music library.

Does the composition fit my ensemble?

There are two possible answers to this question. One is to choose music that features already strong players; the other is to select a work that challenges weak players (or sections) to improve their skills. Although I wouldn't suggest choosing music that shows up your weaknesses to play at a contest or festival, selecting pieces that build players will strengthen your band program in day-to-day rehearsals.

Look for solo and soli sections to see whether they're written for your strong or weak players and sections. Check the number of percussion parts and note whether there are mallet parts. Does the piece have essential oboe or bassoon parts for which you have no players? Did your entire French horn section just switch over from cornet? Check to see whether the piece has four independent horn parts or whether there are two that are doubled elsewhere.

Can I teach and conduct this piece?

Young directors new to the teaching field and fresh from a university band may feel that they really know the Hindemith Symphony, but few members of public school bands, especially young bands, could understand and appreciate that work. Be realistic about your own teaching and conducting abilities. Also remember that often young players are technically advanced enough to handle the rhythm and technique needed for a particular piece but lack the musical maturity to understand it. You must be careful to match the maturity level of the band to the music.

Does the selection show musicianship and expression as well as technique?

Too often, music is judged good if it has lots of notes — especially fast notes. Richard Floyd, director of music activities for the Texas University Interscholastic League, which sponsors contests statewide, warns, "Avoid the pitfall of confusing technical achievement [this is the hardest piece the Marina Junior High Band has ever played] with comprehensive musical experience."

Will the composition be musically

satisfying?

Mark Twain once said, "We often feel sad in the presence of music without words; and often more than that in the presence of music without music." Our job is making music, and that should remain our primary goal. Frequently I select music from the masters of the classical or baroque eras because I can teach my young charges a great deal about style and music history with these pieces. Although they weren't written for our medium, music by Bach, Brahms, Beethoven, Mozart, and innumerable others has passed the test of time. I disagree with the idea of playing extremely watered-down versions of great music; but I do believe that one of our responsibilities is to make our students aware of their rich heritage of music and to help them become more educated listeners. I think we can teach more than the mere melodies of Brahms or Tchaikovsky; we can instill a deep appreciation for serious music.

Will the students enjoy studying the composition?

Although I give this less consideration than the other criteria I use in selecting band literature, I believe students are more likely to practice something they enjoy playing.

Now that you've answered these questions, what else can you look for to ensure that the music you buy will fit your band, be worth the money, and be usable for a sustained period of time?

James Sudduth, director of bands at Texas Tech University, says that when he first looks at a score, he just glances at it, rather as one would flip through a magazine. If he sees anything interesting, he stops to read in depth. Although he confesses to intuitively discovering masterpieces on the shelves, he also offers this concrete suggestion: know your composer or arranger. If you know that one writer uses colorful lines, imaginative scoring, rhythmic excitement, and gor-geous melodies, then you can almost always be assured of a good piece when his name is attached to it. Sudduth also suggests that you sing through the lines, studying the score carefully so that you are not surprised when you look at it later.

Check the ranges of individual parts and the independence of lines. To check the latter, Donna Strain, who has directed successful junior high programs in Oklahoma and Texas, uses these rules of thumb: For beginners — 1 clarinet part, 1 cornet part, 1 low brass part (unison trombone, baritone, tuba). For second-year players — 2-part division in clarinet and cornet. For third-year players — 3-way division in clarinet, cornet, and trombone, with separate, independent baritone and/or tuba parts.

Each publisher has several series designed especially for young bands. The criteria for each series varies, with different limits on instrumentation, ranges, keys, rhythmic complexity, and division of parts. Noted composer/arranger John Edmondson has compiled a brochure entitled "Instrumentation: the Key to Selecting Music for Smaller Groups," which lists 32 different series from 14 publishers who specialize in music for young bands. His research indicates which parts are essential, which add fullness but are optional, and which are doubled in other voices.

On the clarinet parts, Edmondson has indicated whether the part stays below the break or is an optional part with some notes above the break. He also marks low voices as divided or unison (an octave bass line that would give you a complete ensemble sound with only one voice present). Edmondson points out that many band directors don't know the differences between the various young band series and thus often buy a simpler arrangement than their bands need. Directors armed with the information included in his brochure can make intelligent choices in selecting their music.

Tonality is another major consideration. For my younger players I try to stay within the range of one to four flats (concert pitch). Usually my third-year players can handle one sharp through five flats. I select music in major and minor tonalities as well as pieces written with modal melodies. In addition, because I'm working with inexperienced young players, I search the score and make notes of interpretive markings and terms that will require explanation.

Rhythmic intricacy and scoring play a part in my decision. Because my students regularly work with such rhythm studies as *14 Weeks to a Better Band* and the 35mm slides that are available with *Division of Beat*, they do fairly well with standard concert rhythms; but the modern rhythms in the pop tunes invariably throw them for a loop. A far greater problem than intricate rhythms, though, is that of transparency in a piece. A large number of players on the same part gives the students courage and a certain amount of stability, while solo sections or soli sections with thin background can be treacherous for inexperienced players.

Some pieces have built-in rehearsal problems. Parts with more rests than notes fall into this category. Slow tone poems that have little written for the percussion section (the notorious troublemakers) spell difficulty for a middle school or junior high band. Fortunately, many of today's band composers who write grade 1 and 2 pieces include interesting parts for all sections. The talented writers are able to vary texture and timbre without extensive rests for any one section. I select music to develop beauty, blend, and balance in the band's tone as well as self-restraint among the percussionists. Many wonderful studies for phrasing and improving tone quality, blend, and balance exist in band transcriptions of the great choral works.

Here's a list of composers and arrangers whose past work has proven to be musical, well scored for young bands, interesting, and challenging. These are my personal favorites, names I can trust to be good choices when I go to buy music for my groups. Some of them write in both concert and pop categories, but I have included the names in only one.

Concert Arrangers
John Edmondson
Frank Erickson
James Ployhar
John Kinyon
James Swearingen
Claude T. Smith
Clare Grundman
Francis McBeth
Paul Yoder
Charles Richard Spinney
Andrew Balent
Phillip Gordon
Anne McGinty
Leland Forsblad

Pop and Football Music Arrangers
Paul Cook
Bob Lowden
Jerry Nowak
Bill Holcombe
Larry Norred
Eric Osterling
Bob Cotter
Jim Curnow
Jay Chattaway
Andy Clark
Ken Harris

After answering all the questions listed here, what types of music do I choose? Marches, overtures, folk tunes, contemporary works, tone poems, patriotic music, and numbers written for specific occasions such as Christmas or graduation.

Marches are the band's heritage, and they should be presented at every public performance. Marches for every taste — street marches, concert marches, paso dobles, and marches featuring folk tunes or the flavor of other countries — are available in varying degrees of difficulty. There are a large number of grade 2 Karl King street marches, containing excellent training material, that are in danger of becoming extinct. If there is no call for these marches, or ones of their type at the music stores, we run the risk that publishers will discontinue printing them and an important part of our band history will be lost to future generations of bandsmen.

Overtures, old standards like those written by Buchtel and Olivadoti, serve as excellent sight-reading material because of the numerous changes of style, key, time, and tempo. (A word of caution: Young bands often don't sound their best on these works because of the voicing, particularly in the clarinets.) Contemporary overtures usually change style and tempo, but the pieces aimed at younger bands have as wide a variety of key signatures as the classics. Some contemporary composers write in mixed meters even on grade 2 and grade 3 levels, and others write excellent material for training young bands to hear contemporary harmonies and even to learn some aleatoric skills.

Pop music (which comprises a large percentage of what's available on today's market), scores from Broadway musicals, and arrangements of television themes all make good program selections for young bands. Pop music appeals to youngsters, and the musicals and television themes, with their familiar melodies, are often audience favorites. Be forewarned that much misplaying of rhythms occurs in the simplified arrangements of pop or rock charts. My students tend to play their favorite tunes the way they've heard them on the radio or MTV, rather than playing the actual written notation, and often they are disappointed in the band arrangements because they sound so different from the original instrumentation.

Another area you might consider for program material is special feature numbers. Consider showcasing talented members of your ensemble performing with band accompaniment or inviting a guest artist, perhaps a teacher/performer from a nearby university, to solo with your group. Cornet trios, flute ensembles, and trombone quartets, as well as features for the ever-popular Dixieland group are all available.

One category of music I feel quite strongly about presenting to the public is patriotic music. Stirring medleys of Civil War tunes or armed service songs, marching songs such as the *Marine's Hymn* (including arrangements with narration) are available along with arrangements of the folk music of America. From the youngest player to the most advanced musician, everyone should experience playing the music that is characteristically American.

"Why do they call it a Christmas Concert? There is not *one* Christmas carol or holiday song on the program," my former high school band director once said in dismay. Because of the loud outcries from some members of the community, many bands refrain from playing religious music — either Christmas or Chanukah selections — on their winter concerts. There is much secular holiday music available if yours is such a community. Only you can be the judge of what is appropriate for your band and your audience, but if you call it a Christmas Concert, don't disappoint your audience by playing nothing seasonal.

The final category is what a friend of mind calls "educational pieces," those written specifically for teaching purposes. Many are formula pieces, merely catchy tunes supported by endless ostinatos. Students can learn much about reading, style, and rhythm from such pieces, and they can build technical facility, but be certain that your repertoire contains more than just this kind of music. Select compositions that require a little study and reflection on the part of both director and students — that is, music of substance and quality that will last.

Barbara Prentice is director of bands at Gunn Junior High School in Arlington, Texas. She holds degrees from Texas Tech University and North Texas State University.

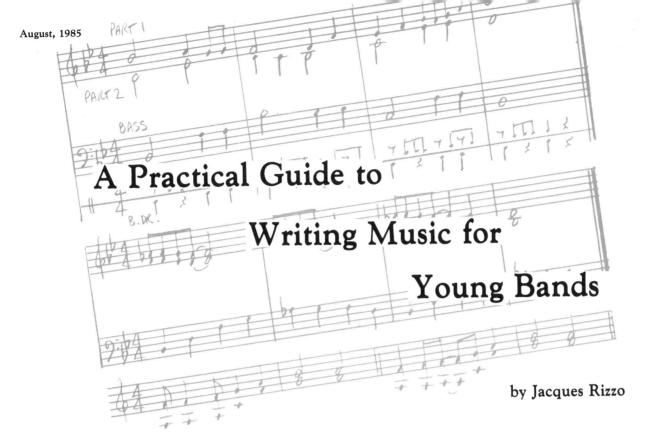

A Practical Guide to

Writing Music for

Young Bands

by Jacques Rizzo

Arrangers and composers generally agree that the real challenge in writing for young bands is tailoring their musical ideas to the young musicians' abilities. This does not mean music that the aesthetic content of the music need be limited – great composers from Bach to Bartók have written easy yet masterful works for students. A good understanding of young instrumentalists' abilities is essential if the music is to play well. Following are some detailed guidelines and suggestions for writing young band arrangements.

Grade One Bands

A typical elementary school has 15 to 20 students (fourth and fifth graders) in the band. The students perform grade one music, arranged for those with one or two years of playing experience. A well-balanced instrumentation might contain 4-5 flutes, 4-5 clarinets, 1-2 alto saxophones, 4-5 trumpets, 1-2 trombones and/or baritone horns, and 1-2 percussion. This type of ensemble prompted John Kinyon to arrange music in an abbreviated-score format including flute, first and second clarinets, alto saxophone, first and second trumpets, low brass and woodwinds on the same bass line, and percussion. When writing for this instrumentation, the arranger considers all other instruments as optional, and cues important lines in each of the basic ensemble parts.

In some instances band directors combine several elementary schools for concerts, allowing for a larger group and, in many cases, a more varied instrumentation which might include tenor and baritone saxophone, bass clarinet, French horn, and tuba. A more complete instrumentation such as this is often found in larger city or district-wide schools.

Many more elementary schools have an unbalanced instrumentation – 6 flutes, 3 clarinets, 5 trumpets, and 2 percussion, for example, with alto saxophone and bass clef instruments absent. Because these ensembles also vary in instrumentation from year to year, the composer who writes for them can arrange music for two-, three-, and four-part treble ensembles, assigning each instrument to all the ensemble parts, with optional bass and percussion parts. This gives the teacher freedom to consider the best balance for his particular group before assigning parts to the students. Several folios of this type are currently published.

Grade Two Bands

The middle school band is usually several times larger than the grade school band because its members come from several elementary schools within a district. These students are typically sixth, seventh, and eighth graders who are capa-

Ed. Note: In this article, pitches are referred to by the letter name of the note plus the number of the octave. For example, A (440), which appears in the fourth octave, is called A4.

Jacques Rizzo has taught instrumental music in both elementary and secondary schools in New Jersey for more than 25 years. His publications include educational arrangements for elementary, junior high, and senior high school band and orchestra, as well as transcriptions of classical composers and editions of popular songs and Broadway show tunes.

Writing Music

"Many more elementary schools have an unbalanced instrumentation — 6 flutes, 3 clarinets, 5 trumpets, and 2 percussion."

ble of performing grade two music. Many middle schools have two or more bands that are divided by grade level (a sixth grade band and a combined seventh and eighth grade band) or by ability (an intermediate and an advanced band).

In middle schools directors often transfer students from a beginning instrument to one that the band needs to improve its instrumentation (a flutist may be transferred to oboe, for example). In addition to the instruments found in the grade school band, the middle school almost always has a tenor saxophone, trombones, and baritone horn. Bass clarinet, baritone saxophone, and tuba are also more likely to be present in middle school bands, but cannot always be relied upon. Although students playing oboes and French horns are present in some bands, alto clarinet and bassoon players are found more rarely.

Because of both the large number of flutes and alto saxophones in the band and the difference in the players' skill, arrangers usually divide these sections into two parts. The clarinets can be divided into three parts, although the sections may not be as large as desired. The trumpets divide into three parts and trombones into two parts, provided that the parts have the same rhythm patterns, are not too dissonant, and do not move quickly.

Charts of Available Notes

The charts on the following pages show the notes that are available to arrangers for music at grade levels one and two. These notes are transposed for the various instruments; they are not at concert pitch. The notes on the chart with ranges for grade one are those that most students will know at the end of their first year of study. The chart for grade two players extends the ranges of the first chart and includes more accidentals. You may use accidentals in the grade two chart in grade one music as long as they lie within the grade one range; however, keep in mind that the tones on the grade one chart will provide a sufficient challenge for many students.

Note that the accidentals are written as students would know them; enharmonic notation would be confusing to most young musicians. For example, most first year trumpeters have no trouble playing B♭, but have yet to learn that this note is also written as A♯.

Music arranged at the grade one "plus" level might extend the grade one ranges slightly and include a few more accidentals. Music that is grade

two "plus" might contain the solid note heads (described in the key) used more freely.

Special Considerations for Each Instrument
Flute

Flute is a popular instrument and young bands are likely to have as many of them as clarinets or trumpets. The lowest register below C5 is weak, and solos scored in this area should have a very light background. As the instrument's range ascends, the tone becomes stronger and notes above G5 project well. Grade one players have some difficulty with fast passages alternating between C5 and D5.

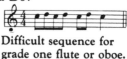

Difficult sequence for
grade one flute or oboe.

Grade two players have usually overcome this fingering difficulty. There are few other restrictions in scoring for flute. The F5-G5 trill is easy to play and may be written for grade one students. Grade two students can perform most trills within their range.

Flutes may be scored soli with low register clarinets and/or a light percussion rhythm pattern in the background. More often, they double the melody in the brass or woodwinds an octave higher.

Oboe

Few grade one bands have an oboe; however, more and more grade two bands have oboists who, given a fairly good reed, add a valuable tone color to the ensemble. Because most band directors place their better students on oboe, these players can usually be relied upon for short solos, provided they are cued in another instrument. Because young oboists usually do not have a well-developed embouchure, however, scoring many rests (about half the number of the total measures in a piece) will ensure better tone quality and intonation.

The best scoring for oboe lies within the range shown on the grade one chart: F4 to G5; beginning students have difficulty playing low notes with good tone quality and often have intonation problems above G5. Playing over the break, C5 to D5, is not as difficult as on flute or clarinet, but at the grade one level it's best to avoid fast passages alternating between these two notes, just as in the example for flute. Most oboists at the grade two level have not mastered the left hand E♭ fingering, so avoid scoring rapid scale work and trills involv-

Writing Music

Available Notes for Grade One Bands

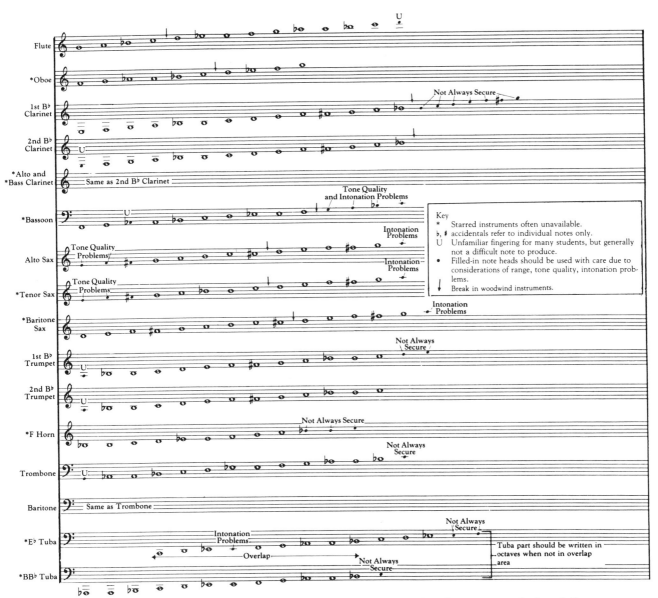

Jacques Rizzo originally prepared these charts to help the arranging staff at Carl Fischer, Inc., create the Sounds Spectacular Series for Young Band. *The material is reprinted here with permission from the company.*

ing Db5 to Eb5 if possible. Most students at this level can play all other trills within their range.

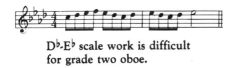

Db-Eb scale work is difficult for grade two oboe.

It is a good idea to score beginning oboe parts almost exclusively on melody or countermelody (as opposed to inside harmonies) because the tone produced by players at this level is often too strong to blend into a harmonic background. Because the breaks on oboe and clarinet occur at different points, scoring the oboe in unison with clarinets will often help smooth the transition in crossing the break from the low to high registers.

Clarinet

Clarinets are the workhorses of young bands. Because of their comparatively wide range, they can perform a variety of functions admirably — a melody in the chalumeau or middle register, soft background parts, doublings in the soprano, alto, or tenor range. Unfortunately, the clarinet has lost some of its past popularity and, as a result, clarinet sections in many elementary school bands are smaller than those of a generation ago. For this reason, it is better to score only two clarinet parts in music for grade one bands. The larger middle school bands can usually support a division of the clarinet section into three parts.

The best scoring for first-year clarinet parts lies within the instrument's lower register, from E3 to Bb4, because the embouchures of most young

Available Notes for Grade Two Bands

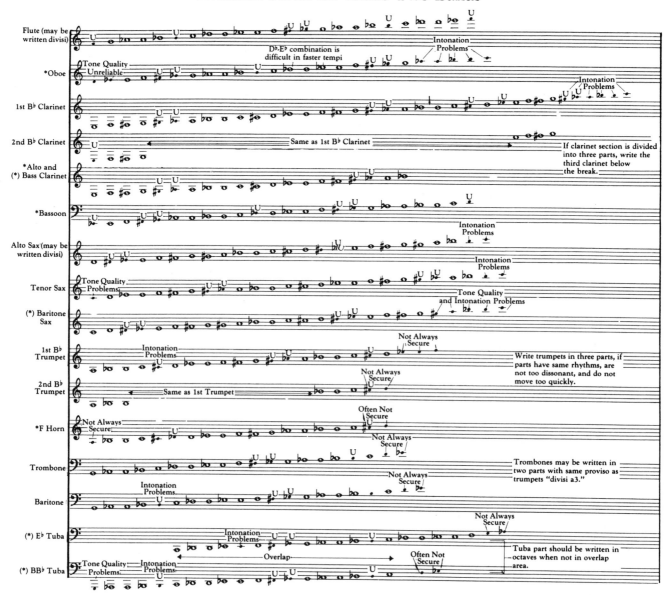

(*) *Although starred, bass clarinet, baritone saxophone, and tuba are more likely to be available in grade two bands.*

players are not well-developed enough to ensure good tone quality or intonation in the upper register. In arranging grade one publications, several composers presently keep both first and second clarinet parts below the break, which is a good practice. When scoring in the upper register, avoid ascending passages that cross the break, A4 to B4 or Bb4 to C5, in all but the slowest tempi.

**Ascending passages over the break
are difficult for grade one clarinets.**

Players at the grade two level have embouchures developed sufficiently to produce fairly well-con-

trolled tones up to G5. Although most students can play notes above this pitch, their tone is often strident and suffers from intonation problems; it is better to assign these notes to the flutes. Grade two players can also negotiate ascending passages over the break with some degree of fluency as long as the notes are tongued and not slurred. Descending passages over the break offer far fewer problems and may be written freely.

The B3 to C4 and Bb3 to C4 trills are practical for grade one players. Grade two players can perform most trills within their range, but those involving the little finger of either hand are more difficult to play as quickly as other trills and should be avoided if possible. These little finger trills include those on E3, F3, F#3, G#3, B4, C5, C#5, and Eb5.

Writing Music

Alto and Bass Clarinet

Alto clarinets are rarely found in bands that play grade one and two music. Bass clarinets are more plentiful, but do not rely on their presence, especially in grade one bands. The bass clarinet provides a full, rich bass voice for the woodwind section. However, confine any scoring for either instrument to the lower register.

Alto Saxophone

Alto saxophones are usually present in both grade one and grade two bands. Because the saxophone's tone is quite full and a sufficient number of players is usually present, you can write divided alto saxophone parts for bands at the grade two level.

For grade one bands, the single alto saxophone part blends well with both woodwind and brass sections. It can double the melody in divided clarinet parts to give strength to a small clarinet section, or it can double the melody in the trumpets to add pitch security. In three-part chords scored for trumpets *divisi* and alto saxophone, score the alto saxophone as the lowest voice. In three-part chords scored for clarinets *divisi* and alto saxophone, use the alto saxophone as the middle voice, allowing the lower clarinet part to remain below the break.

Scoring for alto saxophone with divisi trumpets or clarinets.

As with the oboe part, scoring the alto saxophone in unison with clarinets crossing the break helps to smooth the transition from low to high register in the clarinets; however, take care not to write the saxophone too high.

Young players often find it difficult to control the saxophone's lower tones and, although suitable in *forte* passages, these notes should not be written at softer dynamic levels. The instrument's upper tones present intonation problems and are best avoided. The break on the saxophone does not present as great a problem as it does on the clarinet, and except for rapid alternating notes between C5 and D5 in grade one music, you need not give it much consideration. Players at the grade one level can perform the trills B4-C5, C5-C♯5, F4-G4, and F♯4-G4. Grade two players can perform most trills within their range.

Tenor Saxophone

All remarks about the alto saxophone also apply to the tenor saxophone. For music in which all low brass and woodwind instruments are scored on the same line, arrangers often score the tenor saxophone in unison with the trombone and baritone horn on the tenor saxophone's low D4 and C4. Because beginning players usually have difficulty controlling these notes, you're better off to avoid this practice. Instead, double the tenor saxophone with a higher part — clarinet 2, trumpet 2, alto saxophone, or French horn.

Baritone Saxophone

Contrary to the tendencies of the alto and tenor saxophone, the baritone saxophone speaks easily on the lower tones. However, avoid C4 with grade one players because their fingers are usually too short to reach the required key.

Brass Instruments

Arrangers should certainly use the upper tones (solid note heads on the chart) on all brass instruments, but because these tones are more difficult to produce, do not approach them by skips greater than a fourth. Avoid writing any parts in the upper range of a brass instrument for lengthy periods, because players are likely to tire and produce lower, incorrect partials.

Because students are unfamiliar with the 1-2-3 valve combination, it presents intonation problems on the following valved brass instruments: trumpet-C♯4, baritone horn-B2, E♭ tuba-E2, and BB♭ tuba-B1. On the other hand, even though most texts cite the 1-3 valve combination as offering intonation problems, students are quite familiar with it and arrangers should use the combination freely.

The rapid alternation of the second valve with the first and third valve combination is difficult, so avoid it if possible, especially at the grade one level. This occurs between D4 and F♯4 or B3 on trumpet, C3 and E3 or A2 on baritone horn, F2 and A2 or D2 on E♭ tuba, and C2 and E2 or A1 on BB♭ tuba.

Do not write the note B2 for grade one and two trombonists because the students' right arms are usually not long enough to reach seventh position.

Descending skips are easier than ascending skips on all brass instruments. It's best to avoid skips that are greater than the distance between the overtone partials in grade one music, and even in

Writing Music

grade two music they should be treated carefully. The French horn is more difficult to play than the other brass instruments because its construction places these partials in closer proximity. Voice notes carefully in the instrument's best range and avoid skips larger than a third.

The overlap cited in the range chart for the Eb/BBb tuba parts refers to that portion of the bass part that need not be written in octaves. When changing from octaves to unison and vice versa, good voice leading in both parts should be the predominant factor in any scoring decisions. If possible, avoid skips of a seventh.

On the charts, the parts for baritone horn are written in bass clef. The same range (transposed) and comments would apply to treble clef baritone horn. It should be noted that the majority of younger players read treble clef parts because they have transferred from trumpet, which has the same fingering. The trumpet and Eb tuba fingerings are also similar; however, in this instance, the student fingers the part as though it were written in treble clef (changing the key signature) although the part is written in bass clef.

Percussion

Bands at the grade one level usually have a snare drum, bass drum, crash cymbals, and common traps such as triangle, tambourine, wood block, and often bells. Grade two bands would additionally have a suspended cymbal, and perhaps a dance drum set with tom toms and hi-hat cymbals, as well as two timpani (the later are not found as often and should be considered optional and cued in other instruments).

Bass Line

Arrangers compensate for limited numbers of low brass and woodwind instruments in beginning bands by doubling the bass part in other instruments to ensure its presence in performance. Scoring all low brass and woodwind instruments on the bass line as a solution to this problem has already been discussed.

One publisher solves the problem with a convertible bass line, a bass line written in concert key with a range from B1 to G3, allowing it to be played by baritone horn, trombone, bassoon, bass guitar, or synthesizer. The latter two instruments, although far from being in common use, are used more frequently in elementary and middle school bands as either a substitute for the tuba or to strengthen it.

Works containing a low brass and woodwind unison already have this part present as the baritone bass clef/trombone part. However, in works not written in this manner, the convertible bass line gives players on the baritone horn, trombone, and bassoon the option of playing either the convertible part or the part they would normally play in traditional scoring. With the usual amount of doubling among these instruments (alto and bass clarinet, bassoon, tenor and baritone saxophone, trombone, baritone horn, and tuba), you can construct a much more sonorous and colorful arrangement, yet bands with incomplete instrumentation can also play the arrangement because some instruments can perform the convertible bass part.

Rhythmic Complexity

The rhythmic considerations to observe when writing for young bands fall into two categories — the complexity of individual rhythmic patterns and the number of separate rhythmic patterns that occur simultaneously in the various parts.

Grade one students are familiar with $\frac{3}{4}$, $\frac{2}{4}$, and $\frac{4}{4}$ signatures. Faster tempi are often labeled $\frac{2}{4}$ or ¢. Students initially study the music in $\frac{4}{4}$ meter; as they master it, the director gradually increases the tempo until students are playing in *alla breve*. Slow $\frac{3}{8}$ and $\frac{6}{8}$ are possible, but confusing to students; the music is better written $\frac{3}{4}$. It's best to avoid fast $\frac{6}{8}$.

Rhythm patterns using whole, dotted half, half, and quarter notes are familiar to grade one students, and easy eighth-note and dotted quarter-eighth note patterns may also be included. Drummers are usually more rhythmically advanced and, in addition to these note values, they enjoy playing easy 16th-note patterns, especially if one- or two-measure patterns repeat many times.

Easy, repetitive 16th-note rhythm for snare drum.

Long rolls are possible, but because first year students often have little control of the rebound strokes that rolls require, rolls often sound uneven and bumpy. I suggest avoiding measured rolls at this stage.

You may also include more difficult rhythm patterns that involve easy, catchy syncopations that repeat several times in grade one pieces. Directors usually teach these patterns by rote with few, if any, students actually reading the notes.

"...music teachers will find that students become quite enthusiastic over a piece their director has written 'just for them'."

Easy, catchy syncopation repeated several times for grade one band.

Different rhythm patterns occurring simultaneously should be quite uncomplicated in grade one music. Two different rhythmic patterns, in addition to sustained whole note backgrounds, bass lines, and a percussion part, are about the limit.

Extent of rhythmic complexity for grade one band.

Easy rounds are an exception, and students can usually play these with three or four separate parts.

Easy four-part round for grade one band.

In grade one music, handle voicings for dissonant structures with care, using a stepwise approach if possible. These dissonances are easier for woodwinds than brass, because students on brass often play higher or lower partials if they cannot hear the note in their heads before they play it. Dissonances for brass instruments are best written in the players' most comfortable range.

Dissonant structure for grade one players.

Grade two students explore the same note values as grade one students. However, you can use slightly more complicated structures that involve syncopations, which may contain ties and/or rests. If the melodies are tuneful and repeat several times, they will be easier for students to play.

Syncopations for grade two band.

Use simple 16th-note patterns on the same note if the tempo is not too fast.

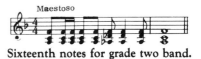

Sixteenth notes for grade two band.

You may use slow $\frac{6}{8}$ patterns involving dotted-half, dotted-quarter, quarter, and eighth notes. Fast $\frac{6}{8}$ time, if not too complicated, may also be included, but keep rhythms with several consecutive eighth notes on the same tone.

Fast $\frac{6}{8}$ for grade two band.

Phrasing

Most grade one students find a challenge in playing a two-measure phrase in $\frac{4}{4}$ time in one breath. For most grade two students, the challenge changes to a four-measure phrase played in one breath. At this level the arranger can compensate for the students' short phrases through use of sustained background notes and counterlines that overlap with the melody.

Although I originally developed this information for Carl Fischer, Inc. as a guide for arrangers and composers preparing works for young bands (grade levels one and two), I hope it will encourage band directors in elementary and intermediate schools to write for their own ensembles. In addition to an experience that is both rewarding and instructive, music teachers will find that students become quite enthusiastic over a piece their director has written "just for them." For some students the experience and the music will remain with them throughout their lives. ■

Scoring for Beginning Bands

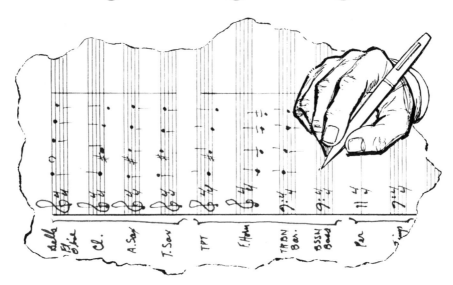

John Kinyon

Can your first cornets negotiate E5? Have the second clarinets learned to cross the break? Can the trombones reach seventh (or even sixth) position? Can the snare drummers execute five-stroke rolls?

Because you are so familiar with the strengths and weaknesses of your own group, you are in a unique position to write practical and playable arrangements that will give your students the opportunity to produce a cohesive musical sound. If you have the time, talent, and disposition to experiment, the rewards can be considerable. Remember that while it is tempting to write "safe" arrangements that can be performed with a minimum of rehearsal time and effort, it is also possible to write music that will progressively challenge students and help them to improve their skills.

Scoring for beginning bands is different from arranging for more experienced groups and requires special insight into the musical interests and capabilities of children. The arranger should use his skill and inventiveness to compensate for the musical and technical limitations at the elementary level.

Basic Guidelines

One of the first considerations in arranging for beginning ensembles is the choice of material. Unless the arranger has legal access to copyrighted music, the choice is limited either to music in the public domain or original works. Because young students prefer to play familiar melodic lines and there is an abundance of such

---

John Kinyon is a composer, arranger, conductor, and clinician who teaches at the University of Miami in Coral Gables, Florida. He began his composing and arranging career 40 years ago (when he was an elementary school band director) by writing tailor-made arrangements for his own group.

material, most published elementary band music is derived from the public domain.

The second consideration is the length and form of the song to be arranged. The typical 32-bar A-A-B-A form, for example, is ideal because it gives the arranger plenty of room for statement and development plus the added advantage of a contrasting section. Another consideration is the range of the basic tune; beginning ranges, especially for brasses, may be limited to not much more than an octave.

The character of the song is also important. Does it involve a lot of chromaticism, awkward leaps, or intricate rhythms? Among beginners all these musical matters are practically impossible to overcome. A simple, singable melody in a moderate tempo is best.

Once a suitable tune or medley of songs has been selected, the arranger will do well to carry it around in his head for a time, consciously mulling over its possibilities as well as letting it ride on streams of imagination. This creative process cannot be forced; you must allow it to happen. From this musical imagining, the style, shape, and substance of the arrangement-to-be emerges.

Of course, there are many practical considerations with which this process of imagination must be tempered. In writing for the beginning level of musical development, playability is the chief concern. What is the best range and key for the clarinets here or the cornets there? Considering the rehearsal time available and the attention span of the young students, how long should the arrangement be? (In arranging for beginning band publication, the consideration of musical length very often boils down to whether the individual parts can be printed on one side of a page.) How can all the parts be kept interesting and challenging, yet not exceed the capabilities of the students? Once these questions of playability are answered and the structure, scope, and plot of the arrangement are firmly in mind, you are ready to write your ideas.

To illustrate these arranging considerations, here are a few workable keys, ranges, and musical ideas for an arrangement of "Twinkle, Twinkle, Little Star."

Original version

Unison cornets

Harmonized cornets

Clarinets at the octave

Unison clarinets in the chalumeau register

Harmonized clarinets

Unison low brass and woodwinds

Flute and clarinets (concert pitch)

Cornets, alto sax and trombone (concert pitch)

Simple variation on theme

Imitation

Change of mode

Each of these musical ideas and scoring possibilities suits the range and technical ability of beginning band students. They could be developed and incorporated into a full-length arrangement, which would be interesting to the students and easily playable.

Meter, Rhythms, and Other Considerations

Common sense dictates that the challenges of rhythmic reading should parallel the level of the students' lesson material. Tunes originally in $\frac{6}{8}$ and $\frac{6}{8}$ can often be changed to $\frac{3}{4}$ and $\frac{6}{4}$ without losing their essential characters. Rhythmic figures can also be modified to the level of students' reading and execution skills. For instance, the figure could be altered to in the opening notes of the folksong "Clementine."

Here is another modification device illustrated with "Dixie." The common version, usually notated

can be changed to

For beginning band students the advantages of the second version include easier comprehension of the rhythms as well as a more exact feeling of the beat. However, if you're teaching sixteenth-note patterns, the first version is preferable. Rhythm and meter changes can make reading and playing easier for young performers, but all such modifications should be governed by your musical taste and the students' abilities.

Full or Condensed Score

You can hone your elementary band arranging skills by studying the following excerpts of a six-line, transposed score from Alfred's Mini-Score Series for Young Bands. Only the essential instrumentation is shown on the score and you may wish to model your score after this one's instrumentation. Optional (doubled) parts, which come in the set of published music but are not vital to the arrangement, are oboe, bassoon, alto clarinet, bass clarinet, tenor saxophone, baritone saxophone, French horn, and tuba. All the low woodwinds and low brasses repeat the same bass line, thus giving strength to the section that in most elementary bands is smallest.

Choose the scoring format which best suits your own instrumentation. Your own score may look something like this Pinafore score, or perhaps your band will accommodate a more full instrumentation with three clarinet and three cornet parts, or two trombone/baritone parts.

The most subtle considerations beyond the obvious factors of range, rhythm, and meter are those intuitive scoring practices that can be developed only through experience in teaching beginning bands. As you analyze this, or any beginning band score, observe the arranging devices that influence the musical rendition of the arrangement and the students' playing enjoyment.

• Measure 1 and continuing: the flute part is not doubled with the clarinet part, thus ensuring that it can be heard by the flutists and the conductor.

• Measures 3-4 and 5-6 and continuing: the first and second cornets alternate on the melody, giving the less experienced players their own musical identity.

• Measure 37 and continuing: here is a good opportunity to break that "elementary band beat," to change style and pace, and to teach rubato. Notice that the second clarinets are required to count and make their entrance independently of the firsts, giving the seconds an added sense of musical responsibility.

• Measures 11 and 15: the first clarinet melody part is slightly modified on the first and second beats to eliminate the possibility of fumbling over a quick register change; the true melody is retained in the second clarinet and alto sax parts. Notice also that the flutes in this passage are scored to require a slower technique than the clarinets.

Music reproduced with permission of the publisher.

• Measure 53 and continuing: flutes and unison clarinets are scored in octaves until measure 61, where a two-octave expansion is easily within the range of the performers.

• Measure 69 and continuing: here the essence of the first section is recaptured by the staccato accompaniment. The strong but simple melody builds to a final climax by adding layers of instruments at the octave; first the cornets, then the first clarinets, and finally the flutes, all in a long crescendo.

Rx for the Block-Chord Blahs

Chorale-type arrangements are excellent for certain teaching purposes, but a few decades ago they were the only kinds available for beginning bands. A steady diet of tutti playing leads to the block-chord blahs. Instead, give your students music with exciting parts and exposed sections through which each player will learn musical responsibility. Offer your students arrangements and compositions that encourage elegant phrasing and expression. Furthermore, give them music in which all melodic, harmonic, and rhythmic components are scored so that your beginning ensemble will sound musical no matter what the instrumentation, balance of parts, or musical maturity of the students may be.

Whether you select published arrangements or write your own, choosing concert materials judiciously can greatly help your students develop their technique and musical understanding. ■

The ABC's of Elementary Band Arranging

The limitations of beginners' ranges are the salient considerations of scoring for elementary band. Here are suggested ranges for the basic band instruments with tips on their uses in arranging.

Flutes

Flute players in the beginning stages of ensemble playing, confronted with fingering B♭, E♭, and A♭ as well as manipulating the break between registers, cannot be expected to be quite as flexible as clarinet players. Indeed, for some flute players, coaxing a consistent tone from the instrument may still be a problem. Remember also that flute lines scored in unison with clarinets will be obliterated. This discourages young flutists who need to hear themselves. Although the lowest register of the flute can be beautiful in solo passages, for all practical purposes avoid using it in beginning band scoring.

Clarinets

Although the more experienced clarinetists can usually play and stay in tune up to B♭5 or even C6 the less experienced must often be confined to playing below the break in their initial band participation. However, the use of unison soli clarinets in the chalumeau register can be very effective. Because the clarinet overblows a twelfth, the range of the beginning clarinet section is quite extended, offering the arranger opportunities for writing first and second parts at the octave, or in sixths or tenths.

Alto Saxophones

The alto sax is not only a solid sounding solo voice, but it also serves well as a middle voice in both woodwind and brass sectional scoring. The tone can become very heavy in the lowest register and may tend to cover any other instrument with which it is doubled. This can be either an advantage or disadvantage, depending on the other instrument.

Cornets or Trumpets

First-part players can be expected to play to D5 with confidence, and perhaps higher depending on the individual. Second-part players generally are more limited in both range and flexibility. Occasional rests in cornet scoring are usually welcome because the players' endurance may be limited at this stage of embouchure and breath development.

Trombones

Because of the slide technique involved, the trombone may be considered a "slow" instrument in the beginning band. Avoid passages requiring extremely rapid slide manipulation. Notes in seventh position, such as B2 should also be avoided. Young trombonists do deserve an occasional melodic line or countermelody, and they should not be continually relegated to uninteresting accompaniment parts.

Percussion

While the wind instruments are generally limited to eighth-note patterns in beginning band music, snare drummers should be capable of sixteenth-note patterns plus flams and basic rolls. The variety of percussion instruments should not be overlooked by arrangers of beginning band music. Snare drum (both with snares on and snares off), bass drum, triangle, woodblock, bells, claves, tambourines, maracas, and cymbals are commonly available accessories. Even pre-tuned timpani can be used effectively. Percussion parts should be equally as interesting as the wind parts.

The Instrumentalist's Basic Library

We asked experienced school band and orchestra directors for their recommendations of the compositions that should be in every school band or orchestra library in the country and studied at least once during a student's time in the organization. They were asked to select the best literature for students, the musical equivalents of Shakespeare's plays, Hemingway's short stories, or Frost's poetry. We further described the pieces we were looking for by quoting Frederick Fennell as he began his series for us on basic repertory:

"I will concentrate on *good* music — indestructible masterpieces for band that have survived the ravages of time and many an inept conductor, as well as newer works of quality that seem destined for longevity. All will be pieces that have rewarded me for the time I have spent with them, compositions which I would not want to live without."

Each piece is graded according to the system used for many years in our new music reviews:

I - mainly for first-year instrumentalists
II - for those definitely beyond the beginning stages
III - for those who have acquired some technique
IV - for more advanced instrumentalists
V - mostly for college players
VI - for the skilled professional

There are five categories in the list: (1) Junior High School Band, (2) High School Band, (3) High School Jazz Band, (4) Junior High School Orchestra (full and string), (5) High School Orchestra.

Because each conductor undoubtedly has a personal list of high quality compositions, we expect there will be those who will disagree with these selections. As always, we encourage your response.

High School Orchestra

Composition	Grade
Bach, *Brandenburg Concerto #3 (Kalmus or AMP)*	V
Bach[Caillet, *Fugue in G minor ("The Little") (Fischer)*	V
Beethoven/Sopkin, *Egmont Overture (Fischer)*	V
Beethoven, *Symphony #1 (Kalmus or AMP)*	VI
Beethoven, *Symphony #5 (Breitkopf or Kalmus)*	VI
Bizet, *Carmen Suite, No. 1 (Kalmus)*	IV
Bizet, *L'Arlessiene, Suite No. 2 (Peters or Kalmus)*	V
Britten, *Simple Symphony (Oxford)*	V
Copland, *Hoedown from "Rodeo" (Boosey & Hawkes)*	V
Copland, *An Outdoor Overture (Boosey & Hawkes)*	V
Daniels, *Festique (Ludwig)*	III
Dvorak/Roberts, *Symphony #5 (Fischer)*	VI
Dvorak, *Slavonic Dances Opus 46 (Boosey & Hawkes)*	VI
Dvorak/Isaac, *Slavonic Dances Opus 46 (Carl Fischer)*	III
Frescobaldi/Kindler, *Toccata in D minor (Belwin-Mills)*	IV
Gliere/Isaac, *Russian Sailors' Dance (Fischer)*	IV
Gluck, *Iphegenia en Aulis (Kalmus or Fischer)*	IV-V
Grieg, *Peer Gynt, Suite No. 1 (4th mvt.) (Fischer, Kalmus, or Peters)*	V
Handel/Johnson, *Music from "The Royal Fireworks" (Kjos)*	IV-V
Handel/Harty, *Water Music (Chappell)*	VI
Haydn/Isaac, *London Symphony, first mvt. (Belwin-Mills)*	III
Holst, *St. Paul's Suite (Schirmer)*	IV
Moussorgsky/Reibold, *Great Gate of Kiev from "Pictures at an Exhibition" (H.T. FitzSimons)*	III
Moussorgsky/Sopkin, *A Night on Bald Mountain (Kalmus or Fischer)*	V
Mozart, *Eine Kleine Nachtmusik (Fischer, Kalmus, or Peters)*	IV
Mozart, *Sym. No. 40 (Fischer, Kalmus, or Peters)*	VI
Nelhybel, *Movement for Orchestra (Colombo)*	IV
Nelhybel, *Music for Orchestra (Colombo)*	IV
Nelson, *Jubilee (Boosey & Hawkes)*	IV
Offenbach/Isaac, *Ballet Parisien (Carl Fischer)*	III
Schubert, *Rosamunde Overture (Peters or Kalmus)*	V
Schubert/Dasch, *Sym. No. 8 ("The Unfinished") (Peters, Fischer, or Kalmus)*	V
Sibelius, *Finlandia (Fischer or Kalmus)*	IV
Vivaldi, *Concerto Grosso in D minor, Opus 3 (Peters, Belwin-Mills, Etling)*	IV

High School Band

Composition	Grade
Arnold/Johnstone, *English Dances* (Lengnick)	V
Arnold/Paynter, *Four Scottish Dances* (Fischer)	V
Bennett, *Suite of Old American Dances* (Chappell)	V
Bernstein/Beeler, *Overture to Candide* (Schirmer)	IV-V
Chance, *Incantation & Dance* (Boosey & Hawkes)	V
Chance, *Var. on a Korean Folk Song* (Boosey & Hawkes)	IV-V
Copland, *Emblems* (Boosey & Hawkes)	V
Dahl, *Sinfonietta for Concert Band* (Broude)	VI
Dello Joio, *Variants on a Medieval Tune* (Marks)	VI
Grainger/Kent, *Irish Tune from County Derry* (Fischer)	III
Grainger, *Lincolnshire Posy* (Schirmer)	V
Hanson, *Chorale and Alleluia* (Fischer)	IV
Hindemith, *Symphony in B-Flat* (Schott)	VI
Holst, *Suite No. 1 in E-Flat* (Boosey & Hawkes)	IV
Holst, *Suite No. 2 in F* (Boosey & Hawkes)	IV
Husa, *Music for Prague* (Associated)	V-VI
Jacob, *An Original Suite* (Boosey & Hawkes)	V
Jenkins, *American Overture for Band* (Presser)	V
Makris/Bader, *Aegean Festival Overture* (Galaxy)	V-VI
Milhaud, *Suite Francaise* (Leeds)	IV
Persichetti, *Divertimento for Band* (Elkan-Vogel)	V
Persichetti, *Pageant, Opus 59* (Fischer)	IV
Persichetti, *Symphony for Band* (Elkan-Vogel)	V
Reed, *Russian Christmas Music* (Sam Fox)	V
Reed, *La Fiesta Mexicana* (Belwin-Mills)	VI
Schoenberg, *Theme & Variations, Opus 43A* (Schirmer)	V
Schuman, *Chester Overture for Band* (Presser)	IV-V
Schuman, *George Washington Bridge* (Schirmer)	V
Shostakovich/Hunsberger, *Festive Overture* (Leeds)	IV-V
Sousa, *Stars and Stripes Forever* (Fischer, Boosey & Hawkes)	IV
Vaughan-Williams, *English Folk Song Suite* (Boosey & Hawkes)	IV
Vaughan-Williams, *Toccata Marziale* (Boosey & Hawkes)	V
Wagner/Leidzen, *Trauersinfonie* (Associated)	III
Williams, *Fanfare and Allegro* (Summy-Birchard)	V
Zdechlik, *Chorale and Shaker Dance* (Kjos)	IV

High School Jazz Band

Composition	Grade
Akiyoshi, *Quadrille Anyone* (Kendor)	V
Burns, *Early Autumn* (Hal Leonard)	III
Ellington/Foster, *In a Mellow Tone* (Big 3)	IV
Ellis, *Final Analysis* (Ellis Ent.)	V
Garland, *In the Mood* (Shapiro, Bernstein)	IV
Green/Paich, *Body and Soul* (Warner Bros.)	V
Hefti, *Cute* (Hefti Music)	IV
Hefti, *The Kid From Red Bank* (Cimino)	III
Hefti, *Li'l Darlin'* (Hefti Music)	III
Herman/Bishop, *Woodchopper's Ball* (Hal Leonard)	V
arr. Hooper, *On Green Dolphin Street* (Creative World)	V
Jones, *Ahunk Ahunk* (Kendor)	V
Jones, *A Child Is Born* (Kendor)	IV-V
Jones, *Don't Get Sassey* (Kendor)	V
Jones, *Kids Are Pretty People* (Kendor)	V
Jones, *Us* (Kendor)	IV-V
King/Stapleton, *Corazon* (Hal Leonard)	IV-V
Johnson, *La Fiesta* (Creative World)	V-VI
arr. Maiden, *A Little Minor Booze* (Creative World)	IV-V
Mays, *Sir Gawain and the Green Knight* (Creative World)	V
Menza, *Groovin' Hard* (Hal Leonard)	V
Nestico, *Front Burner* (Hal Leonard)	V
Nestico, *Magic Flea* (Kendor)	IV-V
Nestico, *The Queen Bee* (Kendor)	IV-V
Nestico, *Quincy and the Count* (Studio P/R)	III-IV
Nestico, *Tribute to the Duke* (Hal Leonard)	III-IV
Nestico, *Wind Machine* (Hal Leonard)	V
Nordal, *Oregon* (Barnhouse)	V-VI
Nordal, *Suncatchers* (Barnhouse)	IV-V
Steinberg, *Nice and Juicy* (Creative World)	V
Taylor, *You Too* (Wm. Allen)	III
Van Heusen/Barton, *Here's That Rainy Day* (Creative World)	IV
Webb/Barton, *MacArthur Park* (Warner Bros.)	V
Williams, *Threshold* (Mission Music)	VI
Wright, *Torock* (Steve Wright)	III-IV

Junior High School Full Orchestra

Composition	Grade
Bartok/McKay, Weeks, *Five Pieces for Younger Orchestra* (Warner Bros.)	II
Beethoven/Woodhouse, *Finale, Sym. #5* (Boosey & Hawkes)	III
Brown, *Hebraic Sketch* (Pro Art)	II
Grundman, *Two Sketches for Orchestra* (Boosey & Hawkes)	III
Haydn/Isaac, *Andante, Sym. in G Major* (Fischer)	II
Isaac, *Apollo Suite* (Etling)	II
Mussorgsky/Isaac, *Hopak from "Fair at Sorochinsk"* (Belwin-Mills)	III
Tschaikowsky/Herfurth, *Marche Slave* (Fischer)	III
Tschaikowsky/Isaac, *Russian Chorale and Overture* (Fischer)	III

Junior High School String Orchestra

Composition	Grade
Anderson, *Plink, Plank, Plunk* (Belwin-Mills)	III
Bach/Isaac, *Brandenburg Concerto #3* (Etling)	III
Corelli/Müller, *Adagio and Allegro* (Ludwig)	II
Handel/Isaac, *Harmonious Blacksmith* (Etling)	II
arr. Isaac, *Early American Suite* (Etling)	III
Kriechbaum, *Petite Tango* (Etling)	II
Mozart/Johnson, *Dance Suite* (Kjos)	II
Nelhybel, *Passacaglia* (Colombo)	III
Piccini/Scarmolin, *The Good Daughters Overture* (Ludwig)	III
Pleyer/Halen, *Suite in C* (Southern)	II
Rameau/Gordon, *Village Dance* (Kendor)	II
Stamitz/Green, *Sinfonia in D* (Fischer)	II
Washburn, *Suite for Strings* (Oxford)	III

Junior High School Band

Composition	Grade
Bach/Moehlmann, *Prelude and Fugue in D minor* (FitzSimons)	III
Bach/Moehlmann, *Prelude and Fugue in G minor* (Remick)	III
Bohm/Spinney, *Still Die Nacht* (Byron-Douglas)	II
Carter, *Overture For Winds* (Bourne)	III
Brahms/Buehlman, *Blessed Are They* (Ludwig)	III
Delle Cese, *Little English Girl* (Pagani)	IV
Erickson, *Air for Band* (Bourne)	II
Erickson, *Toccata for Band* (Bourne)	III
Giovanini/Robinson, *Chorale & Capriccio* (Sam Fox)	IV
Giovanini/Robinson, *Overture in B-Flat* (Sam Fox)	IV
Grainger, *Irish Tune from County Derry* (Fischer)	III
Jacobs, *William Byrd Suite* (Boosey & Hawkes)	IV
Kistler/Barr, *Kunihild, Prelude to Act 3* (Ludwig)	III
Massanet/Á.A. Harding, *Meditation from "Thais"* (Kjos)	III
McBeth, *Canto* (Southern)	II
McBeth, *Chant and Jubilo* (Southern)	III
McBeth, *Masque* (Southern)	IV-V
Mozart/Buehlman, *Ave Verum Corpus* (Ludwig)	III
Nelhybel, *Festivo* (Colombo)	III
Offenbach/Isaac, *Ballet Parisien* (Fischer)	III
Reed, *A Jubilant Overture* (Barnhouse)	IV
Reinecke/Osterling, *King Manfred, Prelude to Act V* (Ludwig)	III
Smith, *Emperata Overture* (Wingert Jones)	IV
Strauss/Davis, *Zueignung (Dedication)* (Ludwig)	IV
Stuart, *Three Ayres from Glouchester* (Shawnee)	II
Vaughn-Williams, *Sea Songs* (Boosey & Hawkes)	III
Zdechlik, *Psalm 46* (Schmitt)	III

Practical Re-scoring Tips

Lida Oliver Beasley and Rule Beasley

Some ten years ago when I was getting my junior high concert band ready for a festival appearance, things were going along reasonably well. The students had their notes learned and were playing together nicely with good pitch and tone. But I was, as usual, looking for some way to pull a better sound out of the group. A visitor to the rehearsal one day, Sam Trickey, then a faculty member at North Texas State University, surprised me with the following statement: "Your group is shaping up pretty well, but now it's time to begin re-scoring." "Beg your pardon?" "Re-scoring . . . (pause) . . . you know, you have to rewrite certain passages to improve your balance, blend, and technical clarity." I stared into space for a while trying to grasp this idea, for I must truthfully say that the notion was brand new to me. After a few days I began to experiment with shifting parts, relocating octaves, deleting players here and there and reinforcing this passage and that, until to my delight the missing something in our sound began to appear. Since that time, I have used this procedure without exception every time a group is being prepared for a festival or public concert.

L.B.

Music for school bands and orchestras is scored for an ideal ensemble, every section having the optimum number of instruments with strong players on every part. Few school groups ever realize this ideal situation because of the rotation of students in and out of the performing groups every year. The answer to the lack of perfect instrumentation is to adapt the score to your group and furthermore, for you to do the adapting, because no one knows better than you the strengths and weaknesses of your own ensemble.

Improving Balance

The most obvious problem is one of tonal balance. If a note or a passage is heard too prominently, take players off the part, which may be doubled throughout the group, until the desired balance is achieved. The deletion of one player could be sufficient, but it might take several. It's easy enough to have students write "tacet" on their parts during rehearsal, or to write some kind of personal memo in the music — "Don't play here."

If a passage does not come through as prominently as desired, players who are resting at the moment can be added. The re-scoring suggestions which follow have been on our standby list of useful possibilities for some time.

Lida Oliver Beasley teaches junior high band and orchestra in Santa Monica, California. She attended North Texas State University and the University of Illinois.

Rule Beasley is instructor of music theory at Santa Monica College and is a freelance bassoonist in the Los Angeles area. He received his musical training at The Juilliard School, Southern Methodist University, and the University of Illinois.

Put trombones on horn parts:

Example 1
from *Stateside March*, by Richard Fote (Kendor Music, Inc.)

Re-scored version:

In the above case cut-out strips of manuscript paper containing the new notes were given to the trombone players to tape onto their music.

Put bassoons on horn parts:

Example 2
from *Jaws*, by John Williams, arr. Cacavas (Duchess Music Corp.)

Re-scored version:

The Db's given up by the bassoons in order for them to be added to the horns were already adequately covered by the cellos, double basses, and bass clarinet.

Put alto saxophones on horn parts
(or saxophones combined with one or two bassoons):

Example 3
from *Jaws*, by John Williams, arr. Cacavas (Duchess Music Corp.)

Re-scored version

As in the previous example, the original bassoon part was already doubled by other instruments.

Put cornets on horn parts:
Example 4
from *Prelude and Fugue*, by J.S. Bach, trans. Moehlman (Remick Music Corp.)

Re-scored version:

Notice that the cornets play into the stand to emulate the distant effect of the horn tone.

Other Balance Suggestions:
• Put bass clarinet and/or contrabass clarinet on tuba parts when the line is particularly important and the section understaffed.
• When the 1st clarinets are *divisi*, add sufficient 2nd clarinets to the 1st clarinet notes to bring the chords into perfect balance.
• Put euphonium on tenor saxophone and/or bassoon parts.
• Strengthen bassoon lines with the bass clarinet.
• Strengthen cello lines with the bassoons.
• Add bassoon(s) to tenor saxophone or baritone saxophone parts.

In the following situation the understaffed clarinet section encountered a passage which needed a greater sense of climax, so 2nd and 3rd cornets were added (the 1st cornet was unavailable at this point):

Example 5
from *Essay for Band*, by Brent Heisinger (Shawnee Press, Inc.)

Re-scored version:

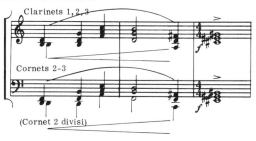

If certain middle-range string parts require added weight in order to compete against heavy scoring elsewhere in the ensemble, reinforce with trombones as follows:

Example 6
from *Jaws*, by John Williams, arr. Cacavas (Duchess Music Corp.)

Re-scored version:

Technical Clarity

Practically all the suggestions listed above with reference to balance problems can be used to solve problems arising from lack of technique. A flute, clarinet, or alto sax can be substituted for a weak oboe soloist; the weak half of a cello section can be taken off a formidable part and placed on the double-bass part, leaving the strong half in charge of the *soli*. In string ensembles weak violas can be assisted by violins or by cellos, depending on ranges and availabilities.

A clarity problem that appears in orchestral music is the frequent lack of attention given to matching the articulations of wind parts to those of the string parts. In such cases re-editing is very helpful. In the example below, after considerable trial and experimentation during rehearsals, we discovered that a significant gain in clarity and precision resulted from re-writing the flute slurring to match that of the violins exactly:

Example 7
from *Carillon*, Georges Bizet, arr. David Stone (Boosey & Hawkes)

Re-edited version:

Re-scoring for Intonation Reasons

When you are involved in the universal struggle to improve intonation, consider re-scoring. These solutions have been performed and were proven to be workable and effective.

• When a flute passage is in the difficult third octave continuously, have the less reliable players (one half or more of the section if necessary) play down one octave.

• If your alto saxophonist cannot get D5 and E5 in tune or has intonation problems on A5 and above, try a tacet for that player and put one or more clarinets on the part.

• In the passage below we encountered pitch discrepancies between the clarinet section and the euphonium which doubled the line an octave lower:

Guide to Notation
Pitches are referred to by the letter name plus the number of the octave. A (440), which appears in the 4th octave, is called A4.

728

Example 8
from *Chant and Jubilo*, by Francis McBeth (Southern Music Co.)

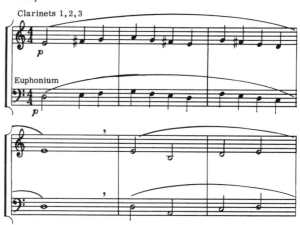

The clarinet written Es are characteristically flat whereas euphonium written Ds (the same concert pitch an octave lower) are most often sharp. The clarinet A in the infamous throat register tends to be very sharp whereas the same concert pitch an octave lower in the euphonium (written G) is most often flat. The problem was solved by taking the euphonium out altogether and giving the part to the bass clarinet. A beneficial side result of this substitution was a more confident overall band sound, as young euphonium players can rarely play softly enough in this passage. The slur from D3 (sharp in pitch) down to A2 (usually flat in pitch) and then back up to C3 (sharp again) is particularly formidable within a *piano*.

• Many times a horn part involving notes written above C5 will offer pitch problems. Because cornets are more stable in pitch in that register, substitute them for the horn if they are available. The cornets should play bell-into-stand and at one dynamic-level lower.

• If your bassoons are struggling to stay in tune, try adding bass clarinet(s) to the line, in unison. We have found that the timbre of the bass clarinet tends to smooth over rough spots and adds body and warmth to the sound.

• In a given clarinet unison line involving the throat tones, if some players are doing well and others aren't, look for another musical line in the ensemble for the weaker players to play.

Example 9
from *Prelude and Fugue*, by J.S. Bach, trans. Moehlman (Remick Music Corp.)

Re-scored version:

The 3rd clarinets were taken out of the unison and put on the bass clarinet part. Don't be disturbed by the last D in the 3rd clarinets. This sudden vaulting out of the proper octave necessitated by range limitations and normally discouraged by good orchestration procedure will not rock the boat in this specific instance, because the bass clarinet line is considerably reinforced by horns, trombones and the baritone saxophone. In other words, the 3rd clarinets will be very much in the background here.

Interpretive Considerations

Our final re-scoring suggestions involve a more subjective and intangible set of circumstances, namely the areas of musical style, sonority, expressiveness and interpretation, all very much matters of individual taste and therefore centered around the personality and predispositions of the director. Most of these changes involve editing, adding or deleting slurs, adjusting articulations, etc., rather than shifting of parts, although once in a while notes are changed for some specific purpose.

In the following unison passage we felt a sudden loss of melodic continuity when the alto saxophones were pulled off of a thematic line before it had reached its logical conclusion:

Example 10
from *Essay for Band*, by Brent Heisinger (Shawnee Press, Inc.)

So we let them continue the theme. The chord tones which they were to have played in the third and fourth bars were already adequately covered by trombones, horns, and low clarinets:

Re-scored version:

For the sake of sonority, durational values are occasionally lengthened so that ⁴₄ might be changed to ⁴₄ in order to avoid conspicuous gaps in the texture or to connect blocks of sound more effectively. A word of caution: never extend rhythmic values except when the harmony is the same all the way up and down the score. Overlays of harmony, if used at all, are at the discretion of the composer, not the conductor.

A final example illustrates a gain in fullness achieved by the addition of octave doublings and the addition of certain instruments to broaden the sound. This can be a risky technique and shouldn't be applied indiscriminately, but in this case there was a gain in textural richness:

Example 11
from *Concertino for Tuba and Band*, by Frank Bencriscutto (Shawnee Press, Inc.)

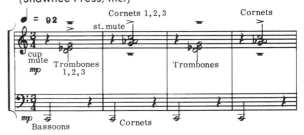

Re-scored version:

A band or orchestra score is not immutable, or "etched in stone" as the saying goes. The director is in an excellent position to make certain appropriate changes in the printed parts because no one else knows his group as well as he does. Few arrangers, transcribers, or composers have as much of an opportunity to experiment with combinations of sounds they might like, because they do not have a full-time performing group at their disposal every day. There may be an initial reluctance to make changes. But once a few re-scoring experiments prove successful, the stage is set for many good sounds not achievable by any other approach. ∎

Commissioning Music for Your Band

Carl Rohleder

Commission a leading composer for as little as $500? Yes, from the profits of a Saturday afternoon doughnut sale you can provide your students, parents, and community with an enjoyable and memorable musical experience. A director from the foothills of North Carolina tells how his band has commissioned three composers in the past three years, and offers his advice for others who want to give it a try.

Jared Spears conducts the premiere of "Ritual and Capriccio"

When fellow conductors hear of my commissions, their reaction is usually, "What a great idea. I've always wanted to do that myself." Although the idea is in the back of my colleague's minds, most assume that musical groups that commission works are on the university level, have fantastic reputations, or are endowed with unlimited funds. This belief has its roots in the history of commissions dating from the 17th and 18th century patronage system to the present-day establishment of grants and fellowships by large foundations. On the contrary, commissioning is an opportunity available to almost every school program.

The reasons for commissioning go beyond the obvious musical value and the added recognition your group will receive. As directors, we should be interested in building our literature, and by commissioning you will be helping to keep good music in our libraries, and in a small way, to shape the literature of our medium.

First Commission

Securing a commission can be as easy as picking up the phone or writing a letter. My first contract came about through a stroke of luck in 1978. I had written to Francis McBeth asking him about commissioning procedures. (I figured that if anyone could answer my questions, he could.) In his reply McBeth suggested hiring a well-known composer

rather than someone who was lesser known because not only are most composers' rates comparable, but a well-known composer could get the piece published. I also learned that most composers are not booked far in advance. Although McBeth is one of a few composers in great demand, I had written to him at an opportune time. He had just written *Canto* for the Japanese National Contest. Band directors were enthusiastic about the work and had encouraged him to compose another piece at the same level (grade 2). So he had set a few months aside for the project and was waiting for a commission when I wrote. *Cavata* was premiered by our ninth grade band in May 1979.

More to Follow

In the Fall of 1979 we commissioned a second piece, *Ritual and Capriccio* by Jared Spears. Because of the need for quality junior high band music we decided that the piece should again be at the grade 2 or 3 level. (Composers and publishers are also pleased when music is written at this level simply because more bands can play it.) In com-

Carl Rohleder is Director of Bands at Burns Junior and Senior High Schools in Lawndale, North Carolina. He received degrees from Mars Hill (North Carolina) College, and East Carolina University.

missioning a piece a director can suggest the grade level and length for a piece, and point out strengths and weaknesses within the premiering group without hampering a composer's creativity.

The musical highlight of that year was in May when Spears came to our school and conducted the premiere of his piece. Misconceptions among students were dispelled when they found out that composers are real people, not just names on pages of music. A composer once told me a student told him "I thought all composers were old...or dead."

Some composers charge a nominal fee for conducting a premiere, while others will ask only for expenses. The experience of performing under the composer's baton cannot be assessed a dollar value, however, and will be remembered by your students for the rest of their lives.

Our most recent commission, *Images of Aura Lee* by John Zdechlik, was premiered by our high school band, again with the composer conducting. The band held cheese and sausage sales for three days to cover the commissioning fee, and our booster club took care of traveling expenses. Zdechlik conducted two rehearsals before the concert, which proved adequate because the band was prepared and no major changes were needed in the piece.

If you are considering a commission and would like the composer to conduct your group, you may be feeling some apprehension: Aren't these composers used to conducting only the finest bands and orchestras in the country? Won't they be offended when they hear my "average" group play their music? Will they ever accept a commission from us? Admittedly, these thoughts crossed our

minds, but I assure you that composers consider it an honor to be commissioned and, with few exceptions, will also feel honored to conduct at your school.

Costs

The cost of a commission increases with the piece's length and difficulty. One formula is to double the price for each grade level: grade 2 — $500; grade 3 — $1,000; grade 4 — $2,000; etc. An even more commmon method is to set an increment (say $250) for each level: grade 2 — $500; grade 3 — $750; etc.

A few composers determine their fees by length. Generally, $100 for each minute of written music is standard; but this, too, may vary according to the style and character of the piece. A slow piece with half and whole notes would last longer than a faster piece with many sixteenth notes, but would take much less time to copy, and therefore cost less.

Some composers have a separate rate for major works, including symphonies or similar works of difficulty and length. These fees may go as high as $8-$10,000.

Commissioning fees will vary from composer to composer as much as their composition styles do, so consider these figures as just a general guide. I suggest setting your budget first, then begin shopping around.

Rights and Guarantees

Certain rights and guarantees come with each commission package to protect both you and the composer:

• When the piece is completed, the composer will send you, in manuscript, a full score and set of parts. Some composers leave the job of copying individual parts to you. (This is very time-consuming, so schedule rehearsal time and the premiere date accordingly.) Most composers prefer to copy individual parts because it allows them to correct errors in the score.

• Most composers and their publishers will guarantee you, the commissioner, the premiere performance if it occurs within three or four months after you receive the manuscript. If you wait any longer, the piece could already be on the market with half the schools in the country playing it.

• If the piece is published, the name of the commissioning organization and its director will appear somewhere on the piece, usually on the title page of the score and sometimes on each part.

• The composer or publisher holds all rights to the music itself. You will not be involved in any aspect of publication, marketing, sales, or royalties.

To be sure that these rights and guarantees are understood, you may want to draw up a contract to be signed by the composer and commissioning party. (See sample contract.)

Now is the time to contact your favorite composer and discuss a commission. If you act soon, your band or orchestra could be premiering a new work at your Spring concert. ∎

Contract of Commission

It is agreed that the Burns Senior High School Band, Carl Rohleder and Dawn Taylor - conductors, has engaged _____ (composer) for the purpose of composing a musical composition (concert work) expressly for the above commissioning party at the commissioning price of _____ dollars to be delivered by _____.

The commissioning party receives the right of premiere performance, and in case of publication, the commissioning party's name and premiering ensemble will appear on the first page of the condensed and full scores on all printings.

The composer retains all rights and privileges beyond the aforementioned.

Payment will be due within _____ days of delivery of work.

_____   _____
Authorized representative of   Date
commissioning party

_____   _____
Composer   Date

(courtesy of Jared Spears)

Let Us Not Forget the Outstanding Band Literature of Yesterday

Leonard Falcone

Many college band conductors are becoming increasingly concerned with the over-emphasis which some bands are placing on modern and contemporary music. In some cases, almost no music from the standard band literature is being played. The explanations offered by the conductors of these bands run something like this: the band is not a satisfactory medium to perform orchestral literature; music written especially for band sounds better than transcriptions; if the band is to have a literature of its own, then bands should give preference to original band compositions. Another reason given is that the standard band literature is old fashioned and no longer worthy of being played by our fine college bands. There is a certain degree of truth in these statements. However, the main point involved here has nothing to do with these opinions.

There is no disagreement on the need to enlarge the list of original band compositions. We have been doing this for quite some time. Many efforts have been made to encourage competent composers to write for band. Some of our schools and professional organizations have commissioned new band compositions. As a result we now have a considerable list of significant band music written by such eminent composers as Aaron Copland, Norman Dello Joio, Vittorio Giannini, Morton Gould, Paul Hindemith, Alan Hovhaness, Vaclav Nelhybel, Vincent Persichetti, H. Owen Reed, Gunther Schuller, William Schuman, Clifton Williams, and others. It is most gratifying to have such respected composers writing for our bands. Certainly if we are to continue to encourage serious composers to write for band, it behooves us to play their music.

However, there are two main points which concern and disturb most band conductors in the current over-emphasis on modern music and the exclusion of the standard band literature in some of our band programs. One point is the *imbalance* of the programs; the other is that we ask our students to study and perform a type of repertoire that is slanted or one-sided.

The essence of good programming is balance. A well-balanced program has a wide variety of types of music. By all means, our repertoires should include contemporary band music. But from the standpoint of the listening audience and performers, is it wise and desirable to make our programs *entirely* of modern music? This would be akin to asking people to eat the same food for breakfast, lunch, and dinner for several days. Even the most succulent steak has to be accompanied by a variety of other foods to provide a balanced meal. So it is with music. It is very tiring to listen to an entire program of modern music; like the music of any one period in music history, it has a certain degree of sameness. The excessive use of percussive and rhythmical effects in some modern music can be quite monotonous to the listeners. I have heard people say that too much modern music makes them nervous. (Recently a well-known university band, in announcing its annual band clinic, stressed that no contemporary or modern music would be played. The inference here is obvious. Most band conductors have become satiated with modern music and might not attend the clinic if they were to be "treated" to another over-dose of contemporary music.) It would seem sensible, then, in constructing our programs, that due consideration be given to balancing the old music with the new—thereby offering a variety of styles and types of music that will appeal to the listeners and musicians alike.

Is the band not a satisfactory medium to perform orchestral transcriptions? Not all transcriptions nor all orchestra music sounds satisfactory with band. There are, however, many excellent transcriptions that fit the band exceedingly well. The success of some transcriptions depends on the good taste of the conductor. There is no denying that a large amount of the music of Bach, Tschaikowsky, and Wagner and many of the overtures of Verdi, von Weber, Rossini, Beethoven, Mozart, and others are most effective with band. If good transcriptions are selected carefully and played artistically, there is no valid reason why bands should not play them.

Since some of the greatest and most effective band music is found in the standard literature, to exclude this music from our repertoire would, in effect, close the door on an important phase of our bands' musical heritage. But perhaps a more compelling justification is that our band students deserve the opportunity to study and perform the outstanding band literature and transcriptions of yesterday. It would be wrong to deny them the background and knowledge of these great works.

The main function of our bands is to attain as high a degree of technical proficiency and musical artistry as possible, and to study and perform a wide variety of good music encompassing both the modern and standard literature. The key point here is *balance* between the old and the new music. Indeed, we must continue to encourage serious composers to write for band and we must make sure that our bands play their music; but in selecting our repertoires, let us strive for balance and variety. Above all, *let us not forget the outstanding band literature of yesterday!* ∎

Leonard Falcone is professor of music and director of bands at Michigan State University. He began his music career in Italy and came to the U.S. in 1915. Professor Falcone attended the University of Michigan, graduating as a violinist from the School of Music. In 1927 he joined the faculty at Michigan State and since that time has distinguished himself as a conductor, adjudicator, and clinician. In addition to his teaching and conducting duties he has written for numerous music journals. He is also one of the outstanding euphonium artists in the United States.

Why Not More Conductors Scores?

Our survey shows nearly all band directors want full scores. We can put the blame
on the publisher if we like, but let's be sure it doesn't boomerang.

Reported by Traugott Rohner

Exactly 93.5% of the directors voting *want and will pay for full scores of all numbers for band* except standard marches and novelties. Yet there still continues a stream of ineffective, inadequate, and unwanted condensed scores, and 'lead' sheets!"[1] Why, then do publishers not print more full band scores?

It is not necessary to enumerate the many advantages of a full score. Actually, we should have a *full* score for *all* band, orchestra, and ensemble music. Rehearsal efficiency is at the core of the arguments in favor of this.

A major argument against printing full scores is the expense. There are as many notes in a full score as on all the separate parts combined. But, we counter, "the directors will pay for full scores." Don't the publishers read our magazines? Are they not aware of our requests? Why is it that we do not have at least more scores for concert band numbers? What is the prospect for the future? What do the publishers say?

The Publishers Speak

A letter was sent to the leading publishers of band music requesting facts, figures, and ideas in answer to some of the above questions. The publishers were assured that their identities would not be revealed. The answers they submitted are revealing.

Publisher A: "It has been my experience that a very small percentage of band directors ask for or can use full scores. Part of the cause may be attributed to the fact that we have not published scores in full instrumental form, and part due to the fact that these people have not the background for this type of material, as yet.

"With the coming generation of conductors, however, I am sure that this is going to be changed. Our demand for full scores now comes from the teacher training institutions, and from the seasoned musicians of advanced training. When the demand is great enough that the added cost of production is cared for, the full scores will be printed."

Publisher B: "...we have found that, at the most, one full score will be ordered to every ten full or symphonic band copies, and in many instances the average is a great deal lower. For example, on (a favorite concert number listed by name) the average sale of band copies amounts to several hundred a year over the last fifteen years, whereas, the full score sold from ten to fifteen copies per year."

Don't Pay the Cost

Publisher C: "I am sure that every publisher wishes, as we do, that '93.5% of the directors want and will pay for full scores....' As you probably know, (company name) was the first publisher to issue full scores for band. I can tell you in all honesty that not one of them has ever sold enough copies to pay for the cost of publication. I don't believe that any Class A band number ever had a greater sale than _____, (yet) I learned only recently that the first edition of the full score was never sold out."

Publisher D: "I have taken a little time to go over the stock of numbers having full scores and have arrived at a figure approximating four full scores (sold) to every ten copies. This is a general average of all numbers having full scores and while some of them run 50%, none will sell more than that."

Publisher E: "I have your interesting letter...on the subject of full band scores. It proved more interesting to us in view of the fact that we have recently announced a policy whereby we will provide a full score for every band number published in the future by this company.

Can't Read Full Scores!?

"I feel at the present time the full score position is treated differently by two classes of directors. On one hand there is the band leader who has come out of school, let us say within the last ten years. We find these men to be definitely full score conscious and prefer to buy music that is available in this way. On the other hand, the greater majority of those directors who might be classified as the veterans of teaching do not have any particular desire to buy full scores for the simple reason that they cannot read them or they do not know how valuable they can be to them."

Publisher F: "Based on our sales covering the last six months of 1947 of the band numbers which include full score, the percentage of sales of full scores is from 14 to 25% of full band sets. In the case of one number, the percentage was 52%, but this was one of the required contest numbers."

Publisher G: "The results I got were rather astounding to me, as I am sure they will be to you. On a work line (a great band favorite) of which we sold several thousand sets, the percentage scores of full scores never amounted to more than one such score to a hundred sets. I, for one, have always liked the idea of issuing full scores since I have felt the band should be on a par with the orchestra."

Publisher H: "I acknowledge receipt of your letter and all I can say is, congratulations — you certainly are on the job and on the beam.

"About ten years ago, I don't think it's any longer, the full score panic broke loose; and when I say panic, I mean that at meetings of bandmasters and clinics conducted by college bands, the full score debate broke out with tremendous force; everybody wanted full scores, if for no other reason than to create an atmosphere of letting the world know that everybody wanted them, could read them, and was going to buy them. However, exactly the opposite happened — and again I am referring to ten years ago. Today, conditions have changed."

Publisher H now sells a symphonic band copy with a full and condensed score for only 75¢ more than the same without the full score, thus encouraging the sale of full scores.

Conclusions

The publishers do listen to what we have to say; they are our friends. They will print anything that will sell but they cannot afford to print scores which we will not buy. As more directors are being trained to use full band scores, the demand is increasing so that the day will arrive when all band music will have full scores.

Could it be possible that a good deal of the blame for the scarcity of full scores belongs to us? Do YOU request a full score for every number you buy? Apparently not 93.5% of you. How else can one justify the "93.5%" figure against those given by the publishers? (The "93.5%" figure is accurate, representing 600 band directors selected at random. Their signatures are attached to the questionnaires on file.) Similarly, the quotations from the publishers are on file. Perhaps some of us will vote "YES" to a question concerning full scores, but forget to request a score for EACH number we buy? Every request and every purchase is a real vote FOR the full score, while every omission is a vote AGAINST it.

[1]"600 Directors Can't Be Wrong!" by Chester Travelstead, page 5 of the November-December, 1947, issue of The Instrumentalist.

October, 1989

My View of
the Wind Repertoire

by Frank Battisti

Part I (1900-59)

The 20th century has witnessed the development of a significant body of literature for the wind band and wind ensemble. In the era since the end of World War II (1945) the vast amount of this literature has been written by some of the most important composers in the United States and throughout the world. To put post-World War II events into context, let's first look back to the turning of the century.

Gustav Holst composed the first important work of the 20th century for wind band in 1909. His *First Suite in E♭ for Military Band* is the cornerstone of the wind band repertoire and a first-rate piece both in content and craftsmanship and is probably the most frequently played composition in the wind band repertoire. Holst turned to the band medium again in 1911 and 1931, composing the *Second Suite in F* and *Hammersmith*, respectively. Fellow English composers Ralph Vaughan Williams and Gordon Jacob also wrote five excellent pieces for the wind band in the 1920s. Three of these pieces, the *Folk Song Suite* and *Toccata Marziale* by

Vaughan Williams and the *William Byrd Suite* by Jacob are now established as part of the wind band's basic repertoire.

Percy Grainger, an Englishman transplanted from Australia, composed his masterpiece for band, *Lincolnshire Posy*, in 1937. In the period from 1918-39 he also created many beautiful British folk music settings for band, including *Irish Tune from County Derry, Shepherd's Hey,* and *Molly on the Shore.*

American bandmasters and composers John Philip Sousa, Henry Fillmore, and Karl King composed some of their greatest marches for the wind band during the first part of this century. European composers also wrote works for the wind band during the first half of the 20th century. Florent Schmitt composed his elaborate, romantic, and brilliantly orchestrated work *Dionysiaques* in 1925 for the Garde Republicaine Band of France. A variety of works were produced by Ottorino Respighi (*Huntingtower Overture* — 1932), Nikolai Miaskovsky (*Symphony No. 19, Op. 46* — 1939), Sergei Prokofiev (*Athletic*

Festival March – 1937 and March, Op. 99 – 1943), and Arthur Honegger (*The March on the Bastille* – 1937).

In the United States, William Schuman composed his first piece for band, *Newsreel*, in 1941. Schoenberg created his uncompromising and tonal *Theme and Variations, Op. 43a* in 1943; Copland made a wind band version of his *An Outdoor Overture* in 1941; and Alfred Reed composed the *Russian Christmas Music* in 1944. Other American composers writing pieces in the early 1940s were Samuel Barber, Henry Cowell, and Paul Creston.

During this same period (1900-1944), many important world composers wrote works for woodwind, brass, and percussion instruments but did not yet use the set instrumentation associated with the wind band.

Stravinsky composed three important neoclassical works, *Symphonies of Wind Instruments* (1920), *Octet* (1922-23), and *Concerto for Piano and Wind Instruments* (1923-24). Edgar Varèse created four unique and revolutionary pieces: *Octandre* (1923), followed by *Hyperprism* (1924), *Integrales* (1926), and the masterpiece for percussion ensemble, *Ionisation* (1931). Kurt Weill composed the excellent but seldom performed *Concerto for Violin and Wind Orchestra* in 1924 and the *Kleine Dreigroschenmusik* in 1929. English composer William Walton, using verses by Edith Sitwell, produced *Façade* (1923), and Canadian composer Colin McPhee contributed the *Concerto for Piano and Wind Octet* in 1928. In 1925 Ernst Krenek composed his *Symphony No. 4, Op. 34*, and Berg contributed his monumental *Kammerkonzert for Violin, Piano and 13 Winds.* Charles Ives composed two pieces for small wind ensembles: *Scherzo: Over the Pavements* (1906) and *Calcium Light Night* in 1936. Grainger composed his unusually orchestrated *Hill Song No. 1* (2 piccolos, 6 oboes, 6 English horns, 6 bassoons, 1 contrabassoon) in 1900 and *Hill Song No. 2* in 1907. French compositions for the wind ensemble were Darius Milhaud's *Dixtour (Little Symphony No. 5, 1922)* and Poulenc's *Suite Française* (1935). Hindemith contributed two pieces, the *Konzertmusik for Wind Orchestra* (1926) and the *Konzertmusik für Klavier, Blechblaser und Harfen, Op. 49* (1930). Other important composers writing for the wind ensemble from 1900-1944 included Georges Enesco, Ernest Toch, Vincent Persichetti, Charles Koechlin, Richard Strauss, and Anton Webern. Each of these pieces is of high musical quality and many are now considered masterpieces of the 20th century.

In 1945 wind bands had only a small number of good original works to perform. The repertoire used by bands at this time still consisted mainly of transcribed works, arrangements, and marches. It seems that most band directors were

not interested in playing original wind band literature or in trying to motivate the great composers to write for their medium. Edwin Franko Goldman, the founder and conductor of New York City's famous Goldman Band, was one band director who was interested in original wind band music and tried to create a new kind of concert wind band, one very different from the Sousa-style professional bands that flourished until the 1930s. In fact, in 1920 Goldman inaugurated the first American competition for major band works. He consistently tried to persuade the leading composers of the day to take an interest in the wind band. On July 21, 1942, the Goldman Band presented the first complete program of works composed for the wind band. The program included works by Leo Sowerby, Morton Gould, Creston, Schuman, Holst, Cowell, Grainger, Vaughan Williams, and others. Measured by today's standards, this was not a great program; but it was a significant and historical program in the development of the wind ensemble's repertoire.

A look at the instrumentation of four important bands in the United States in 1946 gives perspective on the developments in the period from 1945-1959.

Except for the Goldman Band, which numbered 60 players, the other three bands were large ensembles with 81-100 players. The music selected to be played by these ensembles had to be pieces that fit the dimensions of their large instrumentation. At this time few of the pieces composed specifically for instrumentations of woodwinds, brass, and percussion by composers such as Stravinsky, Varèse, Krenek, and

---

Frank Battisti is conductor of the Wind Ensemble at the New England Conservatory in Boston, Massachusetts. A recognized authority on wind literature, he has conducted wind ensembles and bands for over 30 years. He is Past-President of the College Band Directors National Association, founder of the National Wind Ensemble Conference, and a member of the Standard Music Award Panel for A.S.C.A.P. He is a contributor to many journals and magazines, and in 1986 was a Visiting Fellow at Clare Hall College, Cambridge University, England.

The Goldman Band*

1 piccolo
3 flutes (all doubling on piccolo)
2 oboes (2nd doubling on English horn)
1 E♭ clarinet
19 B♭ clarinets (1st, 2nd, 3rd)
1 bass clarinet
2 bassoons
1 alto saxophone
1 tenor saxophone
1 baritone saxophone
4 cornets
3 trumpets
4 horns in F
6 trombones (4 tenor, 2 bass)
2 euphoniums
4 tubas
1 string bass
1 harp
3 percussion
Total: 60 players

United States Air Force Band*

6 flutes (all doubling on piccolo)
3 oboes (one doubling on English horn)
1 E♭ clarinet
14 B♭ clarinets
1 alto clarinet
1 bass clarinet
5 saxophones (2 alto, 2 tenor, 1 baritone)
4 bassoons (one doubling on contrabassoon and one on bass sarrusophone)
11 cornets & trumpets
8 horns in F
6 trombones (4 tenor, 2 bass)
3 baritones
4 tubas
4 violoncellos
4 string basses
6 percussion
Total: 81 players

Lenoir (NC) High School Band*

6 flutes in C
2 flutes in E♭
2 oboes
24 B♭ clarinets (4 solo, 5 1st, 9 2nd, 6 3rd)
2 alto clarinets
3 bass clarinets
3 bassoons
4 alto saxophones
1 tenor saxophone
1 baritone saxophone
12 cornets or trumpets (4 each on 1st, 2nd, and 3rd parts)
7 horns
4 baritones
4 trombones
4 tubas
6 percussion
Total: 85 players

University of Michigan Band*

8 to 10 flutes
2 to 4 oboes (English horn)
24 to 28 B♭ clarinets
3 alto clarinets
3 bass clarinets
3 to 4 bassoons
5 to 6 saxophones (alto, tenor & baritone)
6 to 8 cornets
2 trumpets
6 to 8 French horns
4 baritones or euphoniums
6 trombones
6 tubas
2 string basses
1 or 2 harps
4 to 6 percussion
E♭ clarinet and 2 flugel horns are occasionally added
Total: About 100 players

*Information is excerpted from *The Concert Band* by Richard Franko Goldman.

Hindemith were played and performed by wind bands on their concert programs.

An examination of mid-1940s programs shows that the large majority of pieces performed were transcriptions.

A typical program* presented by the Goldman Band (on the Mall in Central Park, New York), under the direction of Edwin Franko Goldman:

Grand March, "America"..................Goldman
Suite from "The Water Music"..........G.F. Handel
An Outdoor Overture....................Copland
   (arranged by the composer)
First Suite for Band, in E♭ ....Holst
Finale from "The New World Symphony".....Dvorak
Festal March........................Philip James
Fantasie for Cornet Solo...............Del Staigers
Russian Dance from "Petrouchka".........Stravinsky
"Lads of Wamphray"......................Grainger
March, "Anniversary"....................Goldman
Waltz, "Liebeslieder"...............Johann Strauss

A typical program* presented by the University of Michigan Concert Band for its appearances at the Hill Auditorium in Ann Arbor, conducted by Dr. William Revelli:

Overture, "Il Matrimonio Segreto"..........Cimarosa
Prelude to Act I, "Lohengrin"................Wagner
Bravada, Paso Doble.......................Curzon
Trombone Solo............................Pryor
Frühlingstimmen Waltzes...........Johann Strauss
Rhythms of Rio...........................Bennett
Capriccio Italien.....................Tchaikovsky
Three Chorales............................Bach
March, "Varsity".........................Moore
Mannin Veen......................Haydn Wood
Stars and Stripes Forever....................Sousa
The Yellow and Blue (University of Michigan school song)

A typical program* presented by the United States Army Air Forces Band while the band was on tour in Canada, conducted by Captain George S. Howard:

Il Guarany Overture......................Gomez
Pavanne ....Gould
Trombone Solo............................Pryor
Dance of the Amazons.....................Liadov
Horn and Flute Duet: Serenade.................Titl
Finale from Symphony No. 4..........Tchaikovsky
Melody of Popular Airs
Polka from "The Golden Age".........Shostakovich
Russian Sailors Dance.....................Glière
Saxophone Solo..........................Coates
Waltz: Voices of Spring....................Strauss
Vocal Solo, "Danny Deever".............Damrosch
Rhapsody in Blue.......................Gershwin

A typical program* given by the High School Band of Lenoir, North Carolina, James C. Harper, director:

Symphonic March . . . . Mancini
Elsa's Procession to the Cathedral, from
    "Lohengrin" . . . . Wagner
The Sorcerer's Apprentice . . . . Dukas
Entrance of the Bojaren . . . . Halvorsen
Southern Roses Waltz . . . . Strauss
Il Guarany Overture . . . . Gomez
Ballet Suite, "La Source" . . . . Delibes
Tannhauser March . . . . Wagner
Woodwind Ensemble, "Ballet
    Egyptien" . . . . Luigini-Holmes
Overture to "Merry Wives of Windsor" . . . . Nicolai

Many of the works in the wind band repertoire at this time were short, which made it necessary to include a large number of pieces to create a full-length program. The average number of works on the programs shown above is 11.5. The band repertoire in the mid-1940s needed more good original works and more pieces that were longer in length. Few of the major pieces to be found in the wind band's repertoire, such as the Schoenberg *Theme and Variations, Op. 43a*, were being programmed very often. This interesting and musically rich work was thought to be too challenging for the band audiences of this era.

Many of the published band works, both original and transcriptions, came only with condensed scores. In quick-step sized march publications, the conductor's sheet often consisted of a solo cornet part with the accompaniment sketched in around the melody line. For a conductor to thoroughly study a composition, a full score is essential; but many conductors were forced to conduct pieces without complete score information. This hindered the performance of works that were new and often more complex than the traditional pieces found in the repertoire of this era.

In his 1946 book titled *The Concert Band* Richard Franko Goldman states, "I believe that the future importance of bands as concert organizations depends on the cultivation of a special repertory, embracing the few traditional forms, such as the march, and the new special literature which alone can give musical meaning to band programs." William D. Revelli, conductor of the University of Michigan Band, in an address to the 1946 College Band Directors National Association Conference said, "We band leaders in colleges and universities must devise ways and means of motivating our better composers to give us masterpieces of original music."

The need for more new original literature was similarly being recognized and preached by other leaders of the wind band movement, who urged all band directors and conductors to commission the best composers to write works for the wind band.

Between 1945 and 1959 the number of original pieces for the wind band and wind ensemble increased considerably. Pieces composed for the wind band included Milhaud, *Suite Francaise* (1945) and *West Point Symphony* (1957); Gould, *Ballad for Band* (1946) and *Symphony for Band* (West Point) (1952); H. Owen Reed, *La Fiesta Mexicana* (1949); Thomson, *A Solemn Music* (1949); Robert Russell Bennett, *Suite of Old American Dances* (1950) and *Symphonic Songs* (1957); Walter Piston, *Tunbridge Fair* (1950); Hindemith, *Symphony in B♭* (1951); Peter Mennin, *Canzona* (1951); Vincent Persichetti, *Divertimento for Band* (1949-50), *Psalm for Band* (1951), *Pageant* (1953), and *Symphony No. 6 for Band, Op. 69* (1956); Schuman, *George Washington Bridge* (1951); Howard Hanson, *Chorale and Alleluia* (1954); Creston, *Celebration Overture* (1955); Clifton Williams, *Fanfare and Allegro* (1956) and *Symphonic Suite* (1957); William Bergsma, *March with Trumpets* (1957); Vittorio Giannini, *Symphony No. 3* (1959).

Besides these original works, composers made transcriptions of their orchestral works, such as *Variations of a Shaker Melody* by Copland, *Three Japanese Dances* by Bernard Rogers, and *When Jesus Wept* and *Chester* by Schuman.

Space does not permit the listing of all the works composed for the wind band between 1945-59, but an examination of the names of composers listed above shows that many of the more important composers of the era created works for the wind band during the period between 1945-59. Even though there are a number of short pieces on this list, there were longer multi-movement pieces, such as the *Suite Française* by Milhaud, *Symphony in B♭* by Hindemith, *Symphony No. 6* by Persichetti, *Suite of Old American Dances* by Robert Russell Bennett, and *La Fiesta Mexicana* by H. Owen Reed. All of these works have become part of the basic repertoire of the wind band.

Persichetti's contribution to wind band literature in the 1950s was significant because he was a respected composer who saw the potential of the wind band and enthusiastically embraced it by composing four excellent works for it from 1949-56. Persichetti's music was spare; he made well-calculated assignments of instruments to achieve clear colors and textures. He seldom scored for full wind band and his innovative use of percussion instruments added a new textural fabric to the wind band sound. In the 1964 autumn issue of *The Journal of Band Research* he wrote, "Band music is virtually the only kind of music in America today (outside the pop field) which can be introduced, accepted, put to immediate wide use, and become a staple of the literature in a short time." His pieces did just that: they immediately became part of the basic repertoire of the wind band.

Various national organizations and individual college, university, and high school bands began to commission works. From 1949-59 Richard Franko Goldman, working first with the League of Composers and later with the American Bandmasters Association, commissioned nine of the band works listed above.

Composers also created works for the wind ensemble during this period. They included Richard Strauss, *Symphony for Winds* (1945); Hindemith, *Septett für Blasinstrumente* (1948); Willem van Otterloo, *Symphonietta for Wind Instruments* (1948); Bernstein, *Prelude, Fugue and Riffs* (1949); Ingolf Dahl, *Concerto for Saxophone and Wind Orchestra* (1949, revised 1953); Schuller, *Symphony for Brass and Percussion, Op. 16* (1949-50); Wallingford Riegger, *Music for Brass Choir* (1949); Varèse, *Deserts* (1954); Easley Blackwood, *Chamber Symphony No. 2* (1955); Olivier Messiaen, *Oiseaux Exotiques* (1955-56); Robert Kurka, *The Good Soldier Schweik Suite, Op. 22* (1956); Ned Rorem, *Sinfonia* (1956-57); Alan Hovhannes, *Symphony No. 4* (1958); Peter Maxwell Davies, *St. Michael Sonata* (1959).

Stravinsky revised three works composed in the 1920s: the *Symphonies of Wind Instruments* in 1947, the *Concerto for Piano and Wind Instruments* in 1950, and the *Octet* in 1952.

Another event that took place in September 1952 had a profound effect on the wind band and wind ensemble and its literature: Frederick Fennell organized the Eastman Wind Ensemble, a group of woodwind, brass, and percussion players that had a maximum of 45 players.

The instrumentation of the 1952 Eastman Wind Ensemble was as follows:

Reeds
2 flutes and piccolo
2 oboes and English horn
2 bassoons and contrabassoon
1 E$^\flat$ clarinet
8 B$^\flat$ clarinets or A clarinet
   (divided as demanded by composer)
2 alto saxophones
1 tenor saxophone
1 baritone saxophone

Brass
3 cornets in B$^\flat$ or 5 trumpets in B$^\flat$
2 trumpets in B$^\flat$
4 horns
3 trombones
2 euphoniums
1 B$^\flat$ tuba
1 BB$^\flat$ tuba or 2 BB$^\flat$ tubas if desired
Other instruments — percussion, harp, celesta, piano, organ, harpsichord, solo string instruments, and choral forces as desired

Fennell's formula for creating programs for the Eastman Wind Ensemble was one-third of the music for woodwinds, one-third for brass, and one-third for the reed-brass-percussion combination. The first concert of the Eastman Wind Ensemble was a perfect example of his approach to the use of wind band and wind ensemble literature. Works on the inaugural concert of the Eastman Wind Ensemble were Mozart's *Serenade No. 10 in B$^\flat$, K. 361*; Riegger's *Nonet for Brass*, and Hindemith's *Symphony in B$^\flat$*.

Fennell's concerts consisted of performances of the best literature for the full wind band and wind ensemble along with works from the excellent literature available for wind ensembles of selected instrumentation. The 22 Eastman Wind Ensemble Mercury recordings produced under Fennell's direction are evidence of the body of excellent literature for various sizes of wind ensembles available at this time. All but two of the recordings contained works written specifically for wind band or wind ensemble.

Frank Battisti

Fennell's philosophy of programming and superb recordings had a profound influence on band directors and conductors. Hearing the excellent recordings of original works by Hindemith, Schoenberg, Stravinsky, Holst, and Persichetti inspired these band directors and soon many of these works were appearing on their concert programs. The line separating the use of works for full wind band and selected instruments wind ensemble literature began to gradually melt away.

Fennell urged composers to write for the wind ensemble and promised them caring and excellent performances of their works. The Eastman Wind Ensemble recordings made it possible for people to hear and become familiar with many of the excellent original works for the wind band and wind ensemble.

As a young high school band director in central New York in the mid-1950s, I can attest to the powerful influence of Fennell and the Eastman Wind Ensemble. This model was a key factor in my decision to make a deep commitment to commissioning music from important composers for the high school band. Fennell advised me on composers to commission and was a continuing source of support. The result was that from 1955-67 the Ithaca High School Band commissioned over 20 works for band from many of America's most distinguished and important composers including Vincent Persichetti, Karel Husa, Warren Benson, Leslie Bassett, Robert Ward, Walter Harley, Barney Child, and Alec Wilder.

One cannot leave the 1950s without mentioning the American Wind Symphony Orchestra. Conceived and created by Robert Boudreau in 1957, this group of 45-50 young woodwind, brass, and percussion players came from universities and conservatories all over the United States. Later Boudreau auditioned and recruited players from around the world. The American Wind Symphony Orchestra presented concerts in Pittsburgh, its home base, as well as up and down the waterways of the eastern and central part of the country. Boudreau emphasized 20th century music in the ensemble's repertoire instead of popular or light music. He also embarked on a huge commissioning project, inviting composers from around the world to write for the ensemble. These works have broadened the international dimensions of the repertoire for the wind ensemble.

Another important event having an effect on wind band and wind ensemble literature occurred in 1957 when the Ford Foundation began to examine the relationship between the arts and American society. Composer Norman Dello Joio suggested that a program be initiated involving composers and the public school music programs. His idea resulted in the Young Composers Project, founded in 1959. This project placed composers under 35 years of age in public schools to write music for school ensembles. As a result of this, a large body of contemporary music, including wind band repertoire, was created for school age musicians. The project was administered first by the National Music Council and then by the M.E.N.C. from 1962-68, and by 1968, 46 composers had been placed in public school systems. Some of the young composers participating in this program were Stephen Albert, Donald Erb, Arthur Frackenpohl, Charles Fussell, Peter Schickele, and Philip Glass. This project made many high school wind band directors much more receptive to original contemporary wind band and wind ensemble music.

In 1954 Leblanc published Frederick Fennell's book, *Time and the Winds*, which is a short history on the use of wind instruments in the literature of the orchestra, band, and wind ensemble. It was an important contribution because it provided all wind band and wind ensemble conductors with the knowledge of their literature, heritage, and history.

By 1959 these Pulitzer Prize winners in music had composed at least one piece for wind band, wind orchestra, or wind ensemble: William Schuman, Howard Hanson, Aaron Copland, Leo Sowerby, Charles Ives, Walter Piston, Virgil Thomson, Douglas Moore, Quincy Porter, Ernst Toch, and Samuel Barber.

In spite of the increased number of original wind band and wind ensemble works available and the exposure this literature was receiving, transcriptions were still the predominant music being programmed by wind bands in the United States.

In August 1958 *The Instrumentalist* published a listing of "The Best in Band Music." Thirty-one of the magazines's guest columnists, who were all among the leading bandmasters of the time, selected what they considered "the finest selections available for performance by band." Of the 118 compositions listed, 67 (over 57%) were transcriptions. The nine top-rated compositions follow; six were original works for wind band: Holst, *First Suite in E$^\flat$* ; Vaughan Williams, *Folk Song Suite*; Wagner/Cailliet, *Elsa's Procession to the Cathedral*; Hanson, *Chorale and Alleluia*; Holst, *Second Suite in F*; Fauchet/Gillette, *Symphony in B$^\flat$* ; Milhaud, *Suite Française*; Bennett, *Suite of Old American Dances*; Bach/Leidzen, *Toccata and Fugue in D Minor*.

It is especially interesting that few marches were included in the 118 pieces on this list, and none of them was a Sousa march. In a letter to the magazine following publication of this listing Gabriel Kosakoff of the High School of Music and Art in New York City wrote, "Since, apparently, there is not an overabundance of good origianl band music, it is up to us, the band leaders, to do something about it. I am encouraged by the organizations and schools commissioning original band works, and the bandmasters who enable composers to have a hearing of their compositions...Let's all band together, and plan at least one entire program this season of original band music."

The period from 1945 59 was exciting in the evolution of the wind band and wind ensemble and its literature. Many new and interesting works were being composed and performed; and older, neglected original compositions were being revived. Conductors began to look for better quality music to perform and some organizations, individuals, and ensembles became involved in expanding the literature by commissioning and encouraging composers to write music for them.

Note: The literature dealt with in this article (and the two to follow) are works for the wind band or wind ensemble; woodwinds, brass, and percussion instruments plus piano, keyboards, harp, and string bass. Some works for solo woodwind, brass, percussion, piano, and string instruments with wind band or wind ensemble are included. This series of articles does not include works for solo voices or choral groups. ∎

Part II (1960-74)

By 1960 there was an increasing amount of original literature written and published for the wind ensemble, but it had not become a significant part of the repertoire. I am using the term literature to mean the entire body of music and the term repertoire to mean that portion of the literature actually being performed. Some of the band programs performed between 1954 and 1959 reflect this situation.

These programs contain many transcriptions and light music selections and represent school and military band concert programming of the period. Transcriptions were a significant part of the repertoire; in 1958 *The Instrumentalist* selected the following as among the best in band music: Bach/Leidzen, *Jesu, Joy of Man's Desiring,* and *Komm Susser Todd*; Bach/Moehlmann, *Prelude & Fugue in G minor*; Bach/Leidzen, *Toccata and Fugue in D minor*; Berlioz/Henning, *Beatrice and Benedict Overture*; Couperin/Milhaud, *Overture and Allegro (La Sultane)*; Korsakoff/Leidzen, *Procession of the Nobles*; Shostakovich/Righter, *Finale to Symphony No. 5*;

Wagner/Cailliet, *Elsa's Procession to the Cathedral,* and *Siegfried's Rhine Journey*; and Weinberger/Bainum, *Polka and Fugue from Schwanda.*

By the 1960s individual conductors and band associations had succeeded in stimulating important composers to write works for the wind ensemble, but to sustain this development it was essential for these original works to become the core of the performance repertoire. The Eastman Wind Ensemble recordings continued to be influential in introducing many of these new works.

The formation of the Netherlands Wind Ensemble in 1960 also helped expose the growing wind literature. Composed of musicians from the best orchestras in the Netherlands and led by Edo de Waart, the group received international recognition for its series of outstanding recordings. On the ensemble's tours in this country, it gave many concerts on university campuses, performing standard 18th and 19th century literature along with contemporary pieces.

As the enthusiasm for original and new music grew, more organizations and foundations commissioned new works. In a report to the 1967 College Band Directors National Association Conference on Commissioning, Paul Bryan, conductor of the Duke University Wind Ensemble said,

> "Several of the band associations, notably the C.B.D.N.A. and A.B.A., have been very influential. The band fraternities, especially Kappa Kappa Psi, have provided several commissions. The efforts of the Ithaca High School Band have been abetted by several other localized secondary school groups....There is a tradition whereby composers are actively encouraged to write for band and that it is in a healthy and advancing stage of development....The results of our efforts will determine whether the great composers will take us seriously or not. Not our technical proficiency but the make-up of our serious programs will persuade our colleagues in the musical world to recognize us as peers.... Only by considering ourselves primarily as artists rather than showmen, as musicians rather than band directors, can we properly fulfill our mission."

Who were the composers being commissioned? In 1962 Norman Dello Joio wrote *Variants on a Mediaeval Tune* for Duke University. The Greensboro, North Carolina High School Band, with assistance from the Benjamin Restful Music Foundation, commissioned Gunther Schuller to write *Meditation,* which was premiered at the 1963 A.B.A. convention with the composer conducting. In 1963 Kappa Gamma Psi commissioned Warren Benson to write *The Leaves Are Falling,* which was premiered in 1964 by the Eastman Wind Ensemble conducted by Clyde Roller. Pulitzer Prize-winning composer Leslie

Bassett composed his first piece for band, *Designs, Images and Textures*, in 1966 on a commission from the Ithaca High School Band. In 1968 Karel Husa composed his powerful *Music for Prague* on a commission from Ithaca College.

All of these composers derived techniques from contemporary orchestral practices. They introduced changes in composition and orchestration that became evident when compared with traditional transcriptions and military band scoring techniques. For example, they scored with an exact instrumentation in mind, achieving new and varied textures and colors. There was clarity of part writing and little doubling. Each of these pieces represented unique, expressive creations for the wind band.

Vincent Persichetti continued to compose works for this medium, writing *Bagatelles for Band* (1962), *Masquerade* (1965), and *Parable IX* (1972). On a 1964 commission from C.B.D.N.A. Aaron Copland wrote *Emblems*, his first original composition for wind band. Other composers writing important pieces during this period were Ingolf Dahl, Samuel Adler, Donald Erb, Ross Lee Finney, Morton Gould, George Rochberg, William Albright, Martin Mailman, Walter Hartley, Howard Hanson, Roger Nixon, Alfred Reed, Fisher Tull, Vaclav Nelhybel, Ron Nelson, Ron Lo Presti, Robert Jager, Francis McBeth, and John Barnes Chance.

Sample Programs from the 1950s

University of Michigan Symphony Band, William D. Revelli, Conductor, March 28, 1954

"M" Signature...............................Bilik
Prelude and Fugue in D minor.................Bach
Overture to "Anacreon".................Cherubini
Andante et Scherzo (cornet solo)............Barat
Siegfried's Rhine Journey from
    "Gotterdamerung"....................Wagner
    Intermission
Symphony in B ....Hindemith
Cambodian Suite........................Varman
Tribute to Sousa........................Sousa

Ithaca College Band, Walter Beeler, Conductor, March 7, 1954

Overture — The Italian in Algiers...........Rossini
The Hidden Fortress......................Donato
Ballet Parisien.........................Offenbach
Flute Cocktail..........................Simeone
Selections from "The King and I".Rogers-Hammerstein
Quadrille from "Can Can"..................Porter
Transylvania Fanfare.....................Benson

United States Air Force Concert Band, Holy Cross College, June 20, 1954

Introduction to the Third Act of "Lohengrin"..Wagner
Sempre Fidelis March.....................Sousa

La Calunnia a un Venticello (Barber of Seville)
    (Vocal Baritone solo)..................Rossini
Fandango .... Perkins/Werle
Chicken Reel..........................Anderson
Exekiel Saw the Wheel (arr. Genuchi)
Tenebrae Factarae Sunt (Palestrina)
Whiffenpoof Song (arr. Werle)
With a Song in My Heart (arr. Werle)
...................The Singing Sergeants
Fire Dance......................DeFalla/Kepner
Fantastic Rhapsody (Accordian solo)....Deiro/Lesser
In Malaga (Third Movement)................Curson
E Lucevan Le Stelle (Vocal Tenor solo)..Puccini/Werle
Stars and Stripes Forever....................Sousa
Armed Forces Medley...................Cray (arr.)

University of Michigan Symphony Band, William D. Revelli, Conductor, January 8, 1959

Manzoni Requiem (Excerpts).................Verdi
Concerto for Clarinet (Finale)..............Tomasi
Denneriana (Clarinet Solo)..................Bloch
Jubilation ....Ward
Symphonic Songs for Band.................Bennett
    Intermission
Marche Hongroise from "The Damnation
    of Faust"............................Berlioz
Portraits from the Bible.....................Work
Dramatic Essay for Trumpet and Band.......Williams
Symphony No. 1 (Finale)................Kalinnikov
Silver Anniversary March.....................Yoder

The avant-garde movement, which started around 1950, reached the wind band and wind ensemble world in the 1960s. Gould entered this new arena in 1963 with *Prisms*. The University of Houston Band performed Arthur Jordan's *Interpolations* in 1965, and Barney Childs composed an aleatory piece called *Six Events for Fifty-Eight Players* for the Ithaca High School Band in 1965. Lukas Foss, William Albright, Krzysztof Penderecki, Donald Erb, Herbert Bielawa, David Bordon, John Pennington, and others also composed avant-garde pieces for the wind band and wind ensemble during this era. Bielawa, Bordon, and Pennington wrote works for high school bands under the auspices of the M.E.N.C. Young Composers in Residence Project. Unfortunately, many of the works of lesser-known composers during this period did not receive second and third performances and had little impact on the developing repertoire.

Karl Holvik of Northern Iowa College conducted a survey of C.B.D.N.A. members in 1965. Hundreds of colleagues answered his question, "Is there an emerging band repertoire?" by sending him copies of their concert programs from 1961 to 1966. Holvik then compiled a list of all the pieces performed and identified 234 different works. Of these, 136 were original pieces for the wind band, 98 were transcriptions, and 21 of the top 30 pieces were original band works: Giannini, *Symphony No. 3*; Sousa, *Stars and Stripes Forever*; Dello Joio, *Variants on a*

Mediaeval Tune; Schuman, *Chester*; H.O. Reed, *La Fiesta Mexicana*; Persichetti, *Symphony No. 6*; Bernstein/Duthoit, *West Side Story*; Grainger, *Irish Tune from County Derry*; Sousa, *Fairest of the Fair*; C. Williams, *Festival*; Jacob, *William Byrd Suite*; Hansen/Bainum, *Valdres March*; Mendelssohn/Grissle, *Overture for Band*; Wagner/Cailliet, *Elsa's Procession to the Cathedral*; R.R. Bennett, *Suite of Old American Dances*; J.B. Chance, *Incantation and Dance*; Korsakov/Leidzen, *Procession of the Nobles*; Shostakovich/Hunsberger, *Festive Overture*; Creston, *Prelude and Dance*; Holst, *Second Suite in F*; Milhaud, *Suite Française*; Grainger, *Lincolnshire Posy*; Tucci/Hunsberger, *La Bamba de Vera Cruz*; Creston, *Celebration Overture, Op. 61*; Holst, *First Suite in E♭*; A. Reed, *A Festival Prelude*; Hanson, *Chorale and Alleluia*; Rogers/R.R. Bennett, *The Sound of Music*; Turina/A. Reed, *La Procession da Rocio*.

The three programs presented at the 1967 C.B.D.N.A. Conference reveal that most of the repertoire on these concerts were original works.

Ithaca College Concert Band, Walter Beeler, Conductor, February 8, 1967

Overture to Colas Breugnon . . . . Kabalevsky/Beeler
Symphony No. 1 for Band . . . . Harry
Prisms . . . . Gould
Concerto for Saxophone . . . . Hartley
Transylvania Fanfare . . . . Benson

University of Michigan Symphony Band, William D. Revelli, Conductor, February 8, 1967

Symphony in B♭ . . . . Hindemith
Designs, Images and Textures . . . . Bassett
Concerto for Symphonic Band (First
    Movement) . . . . Corina
Two Marches for The Sultan
    Abdul Medjid . . . . Donizetti/Goldman
Trittico . . . . Nelhybel
March, Pride of the Wolverines . . . . Sousa

Ohio State University Concert Band, Donald E. McGinnis, Conductor, February 10, 1967

Overture to "The School for Scandal" . Barber/Hudson
Etude for Symphonic Wind Band . . . . Johnson
Five Fold Songs for Soprano and Band
    (No. 2 & 3) . . . . Gilmore
Liturgical Music for Band, Op. 33 . . . . Mailman
Symphony for Band (Movements 2, 3, 4) . . . . . . Polster
The ballet from The Perfect Fool,
    Op. 39 . . . . Holst/Harpham

A small number of transcriptions made between 1960-74 have achieved an important position in the wind band repertoire:
Arnold/Paynter, *Four Scottish Dances*;
Bernstein/Beeler, *Overture to Candide*;
Copland/Copland, *The Red Pony*;
Grainger/Goldman, *Handel in the Strand*;
Grainger/Goldman, *The Sussex Mummer's Christ-*

mas Carol; Ives/Elkus, *Old Home Days (Suite for Band)*; Ives/Schuman/Rhodes, *Variations on America*; Kennan/Kennan, *Night Soliloquy*.

During this period some of the larger university band programs with concert or symphonic bands added a wind ensemble. Directors in other colleges and universities adopted the flexible instrumentation approach to programming. In some schools nothing changed; these directors continued to perform only repertoire that conformed to the entire instrumentation of their ensembles.

In addition to composing excellent pieces for the basic wind band instrumentation, many composers scored their works for modified instrumental groupings. The American Wind Symphony Orchestra commissioned and premiered pieces composed by David Amram, George Auric, Henk Badings, Warren Benson, Elmer Bernstein, Eugene Bozza, Henry Brant, Chou Wen-Chung, Lubos Fiser, Alan Hovahaness, George Kleinsinger, Ron de Leeuw, Krzysztof Penderecki, Ivan Lopatnikof, Ivana Loudova, Toshiro Mayuzumi, Colin McPhee, Quincy Porter, Joaquin Rodrigo, Bernard Rogers, Ned Rorem, Carlos Surinach and Hector Villa-Lobos.

Other composers writing pieces for the wind ensemble included: G. Binkerd, *Noble Numbers* (1973); E. Bozza, *Children's March* (1964); A. Bush, *Scherzo, Op. 68* (1969); A. Etler, *Concerto for Clarinet with Chamber Ensemble* (1962); L. Foss, *Music for 24 Winds* (1966); B. Jolas, *Lassus Ricercare* (1970); R. Kelterborn, *Miroirs* (1966); O. Knussen, *Chorale* (1972); E. Maconchy, *Music for Brass and Woodwinds* (1963); O. Messiaen, *Colors of the Celestial City* (1963), and *Et Exspecto Ressurectioneni Mortuorum* (1964); V. Reynolds, *Scenes* (1977); R. Selig, *Pometacomet, 1676* (1974); E. Stokes, *Continental Harp and Band Report* (1974); B. Tischenko, *Music for Cello and Wind Orchestra* (1963); I. Zenakis, *Akrata* (1965).

Most performances of this repertoire involved renting the score and parts. Many band directors overlooked this rental music, so many fine pieces were rarely performed.

The following programs are good examples of concerts combining selectively orchestrated pieces and works for the full wind band:

Hartt Symphonic Wind Ensemble, Donald Mattran, Conductor, March 18, 1969

Suite for 13 Wind Instruments, Op. 4 . . . . Strauss
Chimaera for Cello and Wind Ensemble . . . . Franchetti
Interferences II . . . . Lanza
Music for Prague, 1968 . . . . Husa

San Fernando Valley State College Symphonic Wind Ensemble, David Whitwell, Conductor, November 20 & 21, 1970

"Echo" Partita, for two wind ensembles . . . . . Triebensee
Alarms . . . . Mailman
Lincolnshire Posy . . . . Grainger

Music for a Temple of the Night..............Salieri
Concerto for Wind Orchestra, Op. 53....Orrego-Salas
Symphony in B♭......................Hindemith

New England Conservatory Wind Ensemble, Frank L. Battisti, Conductor, November 18, 1971

Concerto Grosso a Quattro Chori...........Stolzel
Serenade in D minor, Op. 44...............Dvorak
Sonata XIX a 15.........................Gabrieli
Octet for Wind Instruments.............Stravinsky
Music for Prague, 1968......................Husa

In contrast to the kind of program presented by these ensembles was the mixed bag approach to programming. A symphony by Persichetti or Hindemith might be followed with a Leroy Anderson piece and a medley of tunes from a Broadway musical. The format of these concerts often resembled that of a variety show. Unlike many orchestra concertgoers, who tend to be more interested in the music itself, it seemed that the public often attended band concerts to be entertained.

By 1970 many conductors of college wind bands and ensembles wanted to move their groups away from entertainment and squarely into the mainstream of serious music. In a letter published in the October 1970 issue of *The Instrumentalist*, H. Robert Reynolds, then director of bands at the University of Wisconsin wrote, "many of us....are working (and I believe succeeding) to help shift the role of the university band from a provider of 'situational' music to a medium primarily for the performance of music of aesthetic worth."

In 1973 the C.B.D.N.A. *List of Recommended Published Band Music* included 318 original works of various styles, all but four of which were for standard concert wind band instrumentation. That so many excellent works for modified instrumentation would be omitted from a recommended repertoire by such a prestigious association is surprising.

During the 1970s concert programs included more premiere performances of recently composed original works for the wind band and wind ensemble. Workshops and seminars offered opportunities for conductors to improve their skills and study new literature. Composers were often invited to conference sessions to discuss their works. At the first National Wind Ensemble Conference held at the New England Conservatory in 1970, for example, the conference focused primarily on literature. Hosted by Frank Battisti, the three-day event featured readings, rehearsal sessions, and panel discussions. Bassett, Benson, and Husa lectured on their works. Frederick Fennell, Robert Boudreau, and Donald Hunsberger conducted numerous new pieces, and Robert Moog demonstrated his invention, the Moog Synthesizer.

National Wind Ensemble conferences from 1970 through 1977 were gatherings of composers, conductors, and publishers interested in promoting the evolving literature. Many new pieces received exposure at these conferences and were subsequently performed throughout the country. An outgrowth of these conferences was the formation of the National Center for the Symphonic Wind Ensemble, established at the Eastman School of Music. Under Donald Hunsberger's direction the Center is dedicated to the collection, dissemination, and documentation of wind band and wind ensemble scores, recordings, and reference materials.

Beginning in the late 1960s historian/conductor David Whitwell wrote a series of articles dealing primarily with the wind music of composers from the 17th to the 20th century. *The Instrumentalist* magazine published these individual articles and in 1980 compiled them into a single volume titled, *A New History of Wind Music*. Whitwell's research led to the discovery of many previously unknown works (particularly from the classical period) that are now distributed through the Wind Instruments New Dawn Society (W.I.N.D.S.).

Through the 1950s the repertoire performed by the best collegiate wind bands and wind ensembles in the U.S. was also performed by good high school bands. The excellent performances of the literature by university and conservatory ensembles served as models and influenced the musical development of the school band movement. Unfortunately, many pieces commissioned from the 1960s to the present are beyond the technical capabilities, instrumental resources, and musical maturity of high school bands; they can be performed only by the finest college and conservatory ensembles. Today, college ensembles perform a completely different repertoire than do high school bands. The following list includes sample programs from the 1973 C.B.D.N.A. National Conference.

University of Michigan Symphonic Wind Ensemble, Harry McTerry, Conductor, December 9, 1973

Serenade No. 10, K. 361....................Mozart
Intermission
Concerto for Trumpet......................Haydn
The Solitary Dancer........................Benson
Three Satirical Marches, Op. 44.............Krenek
La Fiesta Mexicana.........................Reed

Northwestern University Symphonic Wind Ensemble, John P. Paynter, Conductor, C.B.D.N.A. Conference – January 11, 1973. "A concert of original manuscript compositions for band"

Symphonic Variations for Wind Ensemble.....Haigh
Sketches on a Tudor Psalm...................Tull
"Scaramouch" – Symphony No. 3...........Snoeck
"Triptihon" for Symphonic Band..........Vojnovich
Prelude and Variations on
    "Gone is My Mistress"..................Sclater
Propagula ....Linn

University of Redlands Wind Symphony, James Jorgenson, Conductor, January 12, 1973

Overture to "Russian and Ludmilla"..Glinka/Hindsley
Symphony in B♭ ....Hindemith
Interlude and Solo, for Wind Symphony
    and Clarinet......................Childs
Suite No. 2 for Winds....................Browne
The Solitary Dancer....................Benson
American Epic............................Peck

The two programs listed below also demonstrate the shift away from transcriptions to the use of original works on concerts during the mid 1970s.

Representative Programs from the mid-70s

Massachusetts Youth Wind Ensemble, Frank L. Battisti, Conductor, November 23, 1974

Procession of the Nobles...Rimsky-Korsakov/Leidzen
Supposes: Imago Mundi (1979)...............Child
Theme and Variations for Brass Choir......Reynolds
Suite in B♭, Op. 4.........................Strauss
Symphony No. 6, Op. 69................Persichetti

University of Michigan Symphony Band, George Cavender, Conductor, February 24, 1974

Symphony for Band.......................Gould
The Leaves are Falling....................Benson
Concertpiece No. 2 (Clarinet)......Mendelssohn/Gee
March for Concert Band..................Walton
        Intermission
Scaramouch, Symphony No. 3..............Snoeck
First Solo de Concours (Oboe).........Colin/Marco
Sinfonia Sacra..........................Werle

By 1974 Benson, Dello Joio, Husa, Schuller, and Bassett had written numerous works for the wind band and wind ensemble. The continued commitment of these five composers started a trend toward high-quality pieces. Because of them and other contemporary composers the literature expanded and new compositional techniques and styles (including serial, avant-garde, electronic sounds, mixed media) found their way into the literature of the wind band and wind ensemble. These were exciting years of growth for both wind ensembles and wind bands.

Part III (1975-89)

Wind band conductors' horizons expanded with the commissioning and performance of works by world-class composers in the years 1975-89. Their association with musicians outside of the band world sometimes resulted in the commissioning of a composer who had not previously written for wind ensemble. Now, instead of being told what to write and what instrumentation to use, composers were urged to write what they wanted using the instrumentation they needed. Often, the

finished works deviated from the standard wind band instrumentation. The goal of commissioning shifted to producing works that would add to the great literature of music, not only to the literature for winds.

During this period four Pulitzer Prize winners in music — Michael Colgrass, Mario Davidovsky, Joseph Schwantner, and Ellen Taaffe Zwilich — composed their first works for the wind ensemble. Davidovsky's Consorts was commissioned by the College Band Directors National Association and premiered at the group's national conference in Ann Arbor, Michigan in 1981. Michael Colgrass composed the Winds of Nagual in 1985 on a commission for the New England Conservatory Wind Ensemble. This piece received much recognition and won the 1985 Sudler International Wind Band Composition Prize, the National Band Association's Best Composition Award, and the prestigious Barlow Award. Considering that the second and third prizes in the 1985 Sudler International Wind Band Composition went to Gunther Schuller for his Symphony No. 3 and Leslie Bassett for the Concerto Grosso for Brass Quintet, Winds, and Percussion, it seems clear that music of the highest quality level was being written for the wind medium in the 1980s.

Joseph Schwantner, the 1979 Pulitzer Prize winner, composed ...and the mountains rising nowhere... for the Eastman Wind Ensemble in 1977 and a companion piece, From a Dark Millennium in 1980. In 1987 the wind band version of Colgrass's Pulitzer Prize-winning composition Déjà Vu for percussion and orchestra was premiered at the C.B.D.N.A. National Conference. The 1983 Pulitzer Prize winner, Ellen Taaffe Zwilich, was commissioned by Florida State University to compose a piece for its symphonic band. Her Symphony for Winds was premiered at the 1989 American Bandmasters Association National Convention in Tallahassee, Florida.

Continuing to write works for the wind band and wind ensemble were Bassett and Schuller as well as Warren Benson and Karel Husa. Bassett composed Sounds, Shapes, and Symbols (1977), Concerto Grosso for Brass Quintet, Winds, and Percussion (1983), and Colors and Contours (1984). Among the works written by Benson during this time were Symphony II — Lost Songs (1983), Wings (1984), and Dawn's Early Light (1987).

Husa, responding to an Ithaca College Walter Beeler Commission, composed a work for high school band, Al Fresco, in 1975. He also composed Concerto for Wind Ensemble (1982), which won the 1983 Sudler International Wind Band Composition Award, Concerto for Piano and Winds (1984), and the Smetana Fanfare (1984).

Schuller's new pieces composed during this era were Eine Kleine Posaunemusik (1980), Symphony No. 3 (In Praise of Winds) (1981), and On Winged Flight: A Divertimento for Band (1989).

Other composers around the world wrote works for the wind band and wind ensemble between 1975-89: Howard Hanson, *Laude* (1975); Syd Hodkinson, *Stone Images* (1975); Edward Gregson, *Metamorphosis* (1975); Ivana Loudova, *Hymnos* (1975); Henry Brant, *American Debate* (1977); John Corigliano, *Gazebo Dances* (1978); Ross Lee Finney, *Skating on the Sheyenne* (1978); Alec Wilder, *Serenade for Winds* (1979); Daniel Pinkham, *Serenades for Trumpet and Wind Ensemble* (1979); William Kraft, *Dialogues and Entertainments* (1981); Ernst Krenek, *Dream Sequence, Op. 224* (1981); Karlheinz Stockhausen, *Lucifer's Tanz* (1984); Joseph Horovitz, *Bacchus on Blue Ridge* (1985); Vincent Persichetti, *Chorale Prelude: A God Unseen* (1985); John Harbison, *Music for 18 Winds* (1986); Richard Rodney Bennett, *Morning Music* (1987); and William Thomas McKinley, *Symphony for Winds* (1988).

Other composers continuing to create works for the wind band or wind ensemble included Alfred Reed, *Armenian Dances — Part II* (1975); Ron Nelson, *Medieval Suite* (1983) and *Aspen Jubilee* (1986); Verne Reynolds, *Scenes Revisited* (1976); Samuel Adler, *Double Visions* (1987); and Martin Mailman, whose *For Precious Friends Hid in Death's Dateless Night* (1989) received the 1989 A.B.A. Ostwald Award.

Composers writing their first works for the wind band/ensemble included Louis Chobanian, *The Id* (1975); Eric Stokes, *The Continental Harp and Band Report* (1975); Nicholas Thorne, *Adagio Music* (1981); David Maslanka, *A Child's Garden of Dreams* (1981); Rodney Rogers, *Prevailing Winds* (1983); Guy Woofenden, *Gallimaufry* (1983); Philip Wilby, *Firestar* (1983); Ronald Perera, *Chamber Concerto for Brass Quintet, 9 Winds, Piano and Percussion* (1984); Robert Rodriguez, *The Seven Deadly Sins* (1984); Dana Wilson, *Piece of Mind* (First Prize winner of the 1987 Sudler International Wind Band Composition Competition); Michael Ball, *Omaggio* (1987); Jochem Slothouwer, *Concert Variations for Piano and Band* (1987); and Tristan Keuris, *Catena* (1989).

Many organizations, schools, foundations, and individuals had become active in commissioning works. The American Bandmasters Association, National Band Association, and the Louis Sudler Foundation awarded prizes to composers who wrote for wind band or wind ensemble. By 1989, Robert Boudreau and the American Waterways Wind Orchestra had commissioned and premiered 350 works by composers from around the world.

The 1981 formation of the World Association of Symphonic Bands and Ensembles (W.A.S.B.E.) both increased and improved communication among wind band conductors, composers, and publishers throughout the world, generating more works for the wind medium by composers from other countries. The United Kingdom is a prime example of new and re-newed composer activity regarding the wind band. Excellent works by Richard Rodney Bennett, Michael Ball, Philip Wilby, Guy Woofenden, Alan Bush, Joseph Horovitz, Edward Gregson, and other composers from the U.K. are often performed by wind bands and ensembles throughout the world. The international dimensions of the repertoire have broadened as composers from other countries have contributed new works.

Transcriptions remain a part of wind band and wind ensemble repertoire. One of the best works composed during this period was William Schuman's *Be Glad Then America* in 1975. This wind band version of the first movement of *New England Triptych* made it possible for wind bands to perform Schuman's complete work. (Wind band versions of the last two movements, *When Jesus Wept* and *Chester*, were already available.) Other transcriptions were: Michael Colgrass, *Déjà Vu* (1987); David Amram, *Ode to Lord Buckley* (1981); Jan Sweelinck/Ramon Ricker, *Mein Junges Leben Hat Ein End* (1975); Jan Sweelinck/David Noon, *Variations* (1981); Jan Sweelinck/Michael Walters, *Ballo del granduca* (1983); Charles Ives/Jonathan Elkus, *Decoration Day* (1978); John Adams/Larry Odum, *Short Ride in a Fast Machine* (1988); Jules Massenet/Verne Reynolds, *Le Cid* ballet music (1984).

With ensembles devoting their performance time to the many new works being written, the older works in the repertoire were neglected, generating a perception that there was no standard repertoire for the band or wind ensemble. Many directors in this era have sought to change this perception by defining a basic repertoire and frequently performing it.

Acton Ostling, Jr. attempted to define a basic repertoire of serious artistic merit for the collegiate wind band and ensemble through a doctoral research project undertaken at the University of Iowa from 1973-78. He selected for evaluation works scored for at least ten wind instruments and a conductor. They could either be original works or transcriptions of works composed before 1750, or else transcriptions of 20th century works. Ostling developed the criteria for selecting the compositions and then chose 1,481 works for evaluation.

He selected evaluators for his study by surveying 312 conductors from all over the country. He asked those he surveyed to nominate ten wind band conductors who sought out and consistently programmed music of artistic merit and whose evaluation of the literature would be respected. The 20 evaluators were Frank Battisti, New England Conservatory; Harry Begian, University of Illinois; Frank Bencriscutto, University of Minnesota; Paul Bryan, Duke University; Frederick Ebbs, Indiana University; Frederick Fennell, University of Miami; Charles Gallagher, University of Maryland; Robert Gray, University of Illinois; Donald Hunsberger,

Eastman School of Music; Donald McGinnis, Ohio State University; James Matthews, University of Houston; Kenneth Moore, Oberlin Conservatory of Music; James Nielson, G. Leblanc Corporation, Educational Department; John Paynter, Northwestern University; H. Robert Reynolds, University of Michigan; William D. Revelli, University of Michigan (emeritus); Richard Strange, Arizona State University; Robert Wagner, University of Oregon; David Whitwell, California State University at Northridge; and Keith Wilson, Yale University.

Ostling sent each of the evaluators a list of the 1,481 compositions and asked them to judge the artistic merit of each work. Of the 314 compositions selected, 158 were compositions for the standard wind band instrumentation and 156 were scored for wind ensemble.

The 24 works receiving the complete endorsement of every evaluator were all original works. They were: Berg, *Chamber Concerto, Op. 8*; Copland, *Fanfare for the Common Man*; Dahl, *Sinfonietta for Band*; Dukas, *La Peri: Fanfare*; Dvorak, *Serenade in D Minor, Op. 44*; Grainger, *Lincolnshire Posy*; Handel/Baines/Mackerras, *Music for the Royal Fireworks*; Hindemith, *Symphony in B♭*; Holst, *Suite No. 1 in E♭*, and *Hammersmith*; Husa, *Music for Prague, 1968*, and *Apotheosis of this Earth*; Milhaud, *Suite Francaise*; Mozart, *Serenade No. 10, K. 361*; Persichetti, *Symphony No. 6*; Schoenberg, *Theme and Variations, Op. 43a*; Schuller, *Symphony for Brass and Percussion, Op. 16*; Schuman, *New England Triptych*; Strauss, *Serenade, Op. 7*; Stravinsky, *Octet, Symphonies of Wind Instruments*, and *Concerto for Piano and Wind Instruments*; Vaughan Williams, *Toccata Marziale*.

Robert Hornyak of the Cincinnati Conservatory of Music also conducted a research project dealing with the wind band and wind ensemble repertoire. In 1983, Hornyak issued a preliminary report, *The Repertoire of the College University and University Band: 1975-1982*, detailing the most frequently performed pieces during that period. He based his report on data obtained from the study of hundreds of wind band and wind ensemble programs performed at four-year colleges or universities offering bachelor's, master's, and doctoral degrees in music. He reported that the most performed works were Shostakovich/ Hunsberger, *Festive Overture*; Grainger, *Lincolnshire Posy*; Holst, *Suite No. 1 in E♭*; Sousa, *Stars and Stripes Forever*; Grainger, *Irish Tune from County Derry*; Holst, *Suite No. 2 in F*; H.O. Reed, *La Fiesta Mexicana*; Vaughan Williams, *Folk Song Suite*; R. Russell Bennett, *Suite of Old American Dances*; Milhaud, *Suite Française*; Vaughan Williams, *Toccata Marziale*; Jenkins, *American Overture*; Hindemith, *Symphony in B♭*; Wagner/Cailliet, *Elsa's Procession to the Cathedral*; Persichetti, *Symphony No. 6*; Jacob, *William Byrd Suite*; Chance, *Incantation and Dance* and *Variations on a Korean Folk Song*;

Bernstein/Beeler, *Overture to Candide*; Sousa, *Fairest of the Fair*; Grainger, *Shepherd's Hey*; Ives/Schuman/Rhodes, *Variations on "America"*; Arnold/Paynter, *Four Scottish Dances*; and Jacob, *An Original Suite*.

This list comprises 20 original works and five transcriptions. For various reasons, over 50% of the repertoire in the Ostling study identified as worthy of serious artistic merit was not being performed by college wind groups. Compared with the Ostling repertoire, the works Hornyak chose were technically less demanding, shorter, and generally lighter in character. Absent from Hornyak's performance repertoire list were Berg's *Chamber Concert, Op. 8*; Mozart's *Serenade No. 10*; Stravinsky's *Octet, Symphonies of Wind Instruments*, and *Concerto for Piano and Wind Instruments*; Husa's *Music for Prague, 1968*, and *Apotheosis of this Earth*; Dahl's *Sinfonietta*; Holst's *Hammersmith*; Schuller's *Symphony for Brass and Percussion, Op. 16*; Strauss's *Serenade No. 7*; Dvorak's *Serenade Op. 44*; and Handel's *Music for the Royal Fireworks*: all masterpieces of the wind literature.

Frederick Fennell provided valuable information about conducting compositions for the wind band in his "Basic Band Repertoire" series of articles, which appeared in both *The Instrumentalist* and *B.D. Guide* from the 1970s to the present. Throughout his career, Fennell has actively promoted and conducted these works because he believes they should be recognized as the basic repertoire of the wind band medium.

The C.B.D.N.A. Journal, inaugurated in 1985, also provides valuable information on the wind band and ensemble repertoire. This journal publishes articles by composers, conductors, historians, and theorists on important works. It also prints interviews with composers as well as important lectures and papers on wind literature presented at various national and international wind band and wind ensemble conferences.

In 1981 National Public Radio aired a series of 13 one-hour concert programs featuring music for the wind band and wind ensemble. Titled *Windworks*, the series was hosted by Fred Calland with commentary by Frederick Fennell. Broadcast over a national network of more than 80 stations, the programs presented a cross-section of wind repertoire from the 16th to the 20th centuries.

This series provided radio audiences an opportunity to hear for the first time many original works performed by some of the finest wind ensembles and concert bands in the country. *Windworks* was probably the first nationally broadcast series to focus on original music for winds. When asked what he thought was the most important contribution of *Windworks*, Frederick Fennell replied, "I hope it will encourage people to listen to music for winds in a different way than they have before. For some people *Windworks* will open a window on a new music world."

It is unfortunate that there are not more programs such as *Windworks* and that there is no longer a steady release of commercial recordings such as those made by the Fennell-era Eastman Wind Ensemble and Netherlands Wind Ensemble recordings. Commercial recordings and radio broadcasts are essential to expose and promote this music to the listening public.

To gain perspective on the changes in repertoire since 1946, compare the following three programs given in that year with those presented between 1977 and 1989:

A typical program* presented by the Goldman Band (on the Mall in Central Park, New York), under the direction of Edwin Franko Goldman:

Grand March, "America"................Goldman
Suite from "The Water Music"..........G.F. Handel
An Outdoor Overture...................Copland
   (arranged by the composer)
First Suite for Band, in E♭ ....Holst
Finale from "The New World Symphony".....Dvorak
Festal March.........................Philip James
Fantasie for Cornet Solo...............Del Staigers
Russian Dance from "Petrouchka".........Stravinsky
"Lads of Wamphray".......................Grainger
March, "Anniversary"....................Goldman
Waltz, "Liebeslieder"................Johann Strauss

A typical program* presented by the University of Michigan Concert Band at the Hill Auditorium in Ann Arbor, conducted by Dr. William Revelli.

Overture, "Il Matrimonio Segreto".........Cimarosa

Prelude to Act I, "Lohengrin"...............Wagner
Bravada, Paso Doble.......................Curzon
Trombone Solo.............................Pryor
Frühlingstimmen Waltzes...........Johann Strauss
Rhythms of Rio............................Bennett
Capriccio Italien.....................Tchaikovsky
Three Chorales............................Bach
March, "Varsity".........................Moore
Mannin Veen.....................Haydn Wood
Stars and Stripes Forever....................Sousa
The Yellow and Blue (University of Michigan school
   song)

A typical program* presented by the United States Army Air Forces Band while the band was on tour in Canada, conducted by Captain George S. Howard:

Il Guarany Overture.......................Gomez
Pavanne .... Gould
Trombone Solo............................Pryor
Dance of the Amazons.....................Liadov
Horn and Flute Duet: Serenade.................Titl
Finale from Symphony No. 4..........Tchaikovsky
Melody of Popular Airs
Polka from "The Golden Age".........Shostakovich
Russian Sailors Dance......................Glière
Saxophone Solo...........................Coates
Waltz: Voices of Spring....................Strauss
Vocal Solo, "Danny Deever".............Damrosch
Rhapsody in Blue.......................Gershwin

Eastman Wind Ensemble, Donald Hunsberger, Conductor, February 28, 1977.

Hill Song No. 2...........................Grainger
Music with Sculpture......................Mayazumi
Evosträta ....Foley
...and the mountains rising nowhere.........Schwantner
La Fiesta Mexicana......................H.O. Reed

Northern Colorado University Wind Ensemble, Eugene Corporon, Conductor, April 11, 1980

Hammersmith, Op. 52.......................Holst
Trauersinfonie............................Wagner
Colloquy.................................Goldstein
Kleine Blasmusik, Op. 70a..................Krenek
Three Japanese Dances....................Rogers

University of Michigan Wind Ensemble, H. Robert Reynolds, Conductor, November 1, 1981.

A Flourish for a Festive Occasion.............Pinkham
Divertissement, Op. 36.....................Bernard
The Bear and the Nightingale...............Bertoni
Partita for Brass.........................Merilainen
Concerto for Wind Orchestra...............Lopatnikoff

Goldman Band, Ainslee Cox, Conductor, July 6, 1983.

Overture and March........................Boyce
Overture for Band, Op. 24................Mendelssohn
Kol Nidrei...............................Bruch
Concerto for Trumpet and Band...............Whitney
Hunting Polka............................Strauss
Balance All and Swing Partners.............Sousa

March, "Sesquicentennial"	Sousa
Hill Song No. 2	Grainger
Ye Banks and Braes O'Bonnie Doon	Grainger
Suite of Old American Dances	Bennett
Pan-America	Herbert
Victor Herbert Favorites	Herbert

New England Conservatory Wind Ensemble, Frank L. Battisti, Conductor, November 13, 1985.

Octet for Wind Instruments	Stravinsky
Music for Brass and Woodwinds (1966)	Maconchy
Serenade in D, Op. 44	Dvorak
Slavonic Dances, Op. 72 Nos. 1 and 7	Dvorak
Chamber Concerto for Brass Quintet, 9 Winds, Piano, Percussion (1984)	Perera
Sounds, Shapes and Symbols (1977)	Bassett

United States Air Force Band, Lt. Col. James M. Bankhead, Commander and Conductor, July 25, 1987

Overture for Band	Heins
Winds of Nagual	Colgrass
Quintessence	Kraft
Dawn's Early Light	Benson
Hands Across the Sea	Sousa
Medea's Dance of Vengeance	Barber/Bader

There was a great change in the repertoire from 1946 to 1989. The works on the 1977-89 programs are generally longer and the instrumentation varies from piece to piece. The exception to this is the Goldman Band program on July 6, 1983, at which all works were in the content and style of the Goldman Band in 1946.

As I look over the list of works that I have identified in this article, I feel that the overall quality is very good — and in many instances exceptional. Some of these works are representative of the best music ever created by the composer. Many of the greatest composers in the world are included on this list. However, many important composers have never written a work for the wind band or wind ensemble. Composers whom we should commission immediately are Leonard Bernstein, John Cage, Gian Carlo Menotti, Elliott Carter, Pierre Boulez, and Michael Tippett. I wonder if anyone attempted to commission a work from Benjamin Britten or Roger Sessions when they were alive.

Today directors can approach wind band literature with assurance that it will continue to thrive. Because of the renewed interst in commissioning and performing there is no longer a lack of high-quality literature. However, we need to clarify a basic repertoire by regularly performing the best works from the literature, and we should continue to expand on the tradition of commissioning works that began in this century. As a medium of musical expression, the wind band and wind ensemble repertoire is worthy of the finest efforts of our great composers.☐

November, 1991

Selected Elementary Band Literature

by Daniel Kohut and Karen Mohr-Sheahan

Knowing concert literature is a prime requisite to being a first-rate instrumental teacher. Nowhere is this more important than at the elementary level, yet finding suitable literature for grade school musicians is never easy. Ordering a work classified as Grade 1 only to discover later that it is really Grade 2 is frustrating. Equally annoying is finding a slow legato work listed in Grade 2, presumably because of its easy rhythms and playing range, yet its tonal, intonational, and expressive demands place it in Grade 3, or even Grade 4. There is also a preponderence of synthetic music, written specifically for public school use as training literature. It is questionable whether these works merit valuable

rehearsal time if they are not good enough musically to be programmed on a concert.

Probably the best way to learn grade school band literature is to thoroughly research the medium, but at best this is still time-consuming, and beginning teachers seldom find the time and energy to investigate publications. If they did, they would discover much literature that is lacking in musical and educational merit because publishers mainly publish music that sells. If it doesn't sell, they stop publishing it. Consequently, school music directors are the primary influence on the quality of literature available to us.

After many years of researching, rehearsing, and programming extensive

amounts of elementary band literature, we recommend the following selected list with regard to its musical quality and grade of difficulty. Grade ½ is intended for the beginning band's first concert; grade 1 is for first-year players; grade 2 is for second-and some third-year players.

Grade ½

Fanfare March by Frank Erickson (Belwin-Mills). An easy piece for the first concert, it makes the band sound full.

March for a Fat Cat by W. Littell (Wm. Allen). This is a first concert piece that young students enjoy.

Grade 1

Three Folk Songs by Bartok (arr. Anne McGinty, Hal Leonard). This well-arranged delightful work is a challenging grade 1.

Hymn to Joy by Beethoven (arr. K. Henderson, Pro-Art).

Trumpet Voluntary by Clarke (arr. John Kinyon, Alfred).

Bells of Winter by F. Erickson (Belwin-Mills). From the *Away We Go* collection, this piece is easy, fun, and full-sounding. It is perfect for the first winter concert.

Knights of the Round Table by F. Erickson (Columbia Pictures).

Rockin' Christmas by Saul Feldstein (Alfred). An arrangement of *Jingle Bells* in rock style, this piece is well-liked by players and audiences.

Six Episodes by Kabalevsky (arr. Seikmann, M.C.A.). Probably the best work available in Grade 1, it is easy to play and makes a first-year band sound good.

Air and Dance by J. Kinyon (Alfred). The Air is a particularly good composition for this level.

Flurry for Winds and Percussion by John Kinyon (Alfred). This is one of John Kinyon's best works for elementary band. It is a Grade 1+.

Marche Fantastique by John Kinyon (Alfred).

A Round of Peace by John Kinyon (Alfred).

Royal March by John Kinyon (Alfred). This work and *Six Episodes* are two of the easiest Grade 1 works. Both are perfect for the first-year spring concert.

Chorale and Canon by Anne McGinty (Hal Leonard). A well-scored, well-written piece, this is an advanced Grade 1 work.

Prelude to a Festival by Anne McGinty (Hal Leonard).

Chester by Eric Osterling (Jenson).

Modal March by T. Tyra (Barnhouse).

Rock One by G. Vitale (Wm. Allen).

Grade 2

Pachelbel's Canon (arr. A. Balent, Warner Bros.). A great opportunity for a young band to learn a classic work and develop the ability to sus-

tain a good tone.

Three Pieces from "For Children" by Bartok (arr. J. Finlayson, Boosey & Hawkes).

The Original Thirteen by Billings (arr. J. Ployhar, Belwin-Mills).

Allegro by J. Chattaway (Wm. Allen).

Fanfare by J. Chattaway (Wm. Allen). This work is highly recommended; it makes the group sound more advanced than Grade 2.

Rodeo by J. Chattaway (Wm. Allen).

Starship One by J. Chattaway (Wm. Allen).

Sunride by J. Chattaway (Wm. Allen).

Lyric Essay by D. Coakley (E.C. Kirby). This work and the *Songs for the Morning Band* are challenging for Grade 2. Both are excellent short works by a Canadian composer.

Songs for the Morning Band by D. Coakley (E.C. Kirby).

Modal Song and Dance by E. Del Borgo (Wm. Allen).

Amazing Grace by J. Edmondson (Hanson).

American Folk Fantasy by J. Edmondson (Boosey).

Pride of the Corps by J. Edmondson (Hal Leonard).

Three Scottish Folk Songs by J. Edmondson (Birch Island). The songs include "Will Ye No' Come Back Again?," "Turn Ye to Me," and "Charlie is My Darling."

Citadel March by F. Erickson (Columbia).

Symphonette by F. Erickson (Bourne). This is one of his earliest and best works for young band.

American Medley by S. Feldstein and J. O'Reilly (Alfred).

Break it Up! by R. Gingery (Wm. Allen).

Discovery by R. Gingery (Wm. Allen).

Espana by R. Gingery (Wm. Allen).

Main Street Blues by R. Gingery (Wm. Allen).

Mini-Suite by M. Gould (Chappell). A fine work by a good composer.

Little Suite for Band by C. Grundman (Boosey). Highly recommended, this

impressive-sounding piece is not difficult to play.

Triumphant Festival from "Royal Fireworks" by Handel (arr. J. Kinyon, Alfred).

Belmont Overture by R. Hermann (Jenson).

Clarinet Promenade by William Holcombe (Wm. Allen).

Three Songs of Colonial America by L. Jackson (Warner Bros.).

A Suffolk Celebration by J. Kinyon (Alfred).

Bach Fugue by J. Kinyon (Alfred). Players learn to concentrate on performing independently in the context of a masterpiece of music.

Fanfare, Ode and Festival by B. Margolis (Manhattan Beach). These delightful early transcriptions are challenging for this level.

Canto by W.F. McBeth (Southern).

Discovery Overture by A. McGinty (Hal Leonard). This is an expressive, full-sounding yet easy work.

Advance Guard March by J. Nowak (Wm. Allen).

March of the Irish Guard by J. Ployhar (Carl Fischer).

William Tell Overture by Rossini (arr. A. Balent, Carl Fischer).

Forest Park Overture by J. Spears (Barnhouse). A challenging but good work. Grade 2+.

Brookpark Overture by John Swearingen (Barnhouse).

Brookside Overture by J. Taylor (Wm. Allen).

Entrada by J. Taylor (Wm. Allen).

Street Dance by J. Taylor (Wm. Allen).

Concerto for Band and Pots and Pans by N. Ward (Columbia Pictures). This novelty piece is fun to play. □

Daniel Kohut teaches at the University of Illinois and has written three books on instrumental pedagogy and conducting.

Karen Mohr-Sheahan is a graduate student at the University of Illinois and was an elementary and junior high band director for 10 years.

How A Composer Works

by Alfred Reed

Every composer throughout history has been asked at one time or another just how he works, what he does in order to create a musical work, where his inspiration comes from, and how he captures his ideas as they flow through his mind.

We ask the same questions of artists, sculptors, and photographers; but the questions have to do with seeing rather than hearing. The desire to know how a creative artist works is basically the same regardless of the art involved.

I often reply to this query by asking the questioner to tell me just how he for example, writes a letter to a friend. This response usually surprises the questioner, who evidently cannot believe that the two operations have anything in common. "Anyone can write a letter," he will say, "but only a few people can compose music, especially music of a symphonic nature." Despite the obvious differences between writing a letter and writing a piece of music, the two processes are the same.

In order to write a letter you should first have something to communicate to another person. You should be able to say what you wish to communicate in the simplest and clearest possible manner, so that the person reading the letter understands what you are trying to tell him; and then you go ahead and write it.

This may seem too obvious, but before the first note is written down, all three of these basic factors have to exist. You may have the most wonderful ideas in the world chasing themselves around in your head, but if you cannot draw them out in a way other people can see, hear, or read them, then what good are these ideas to anyone other than yourself? Unheard melodies, unread words, and unseen pictures do not benefit anyone else in the world if they only exist in the creator's mind.

Every creative artist feels the need to communicate what he thinks, feels, sees, or hears in his mind. This is the basis of all art, no matter what form it takes. In the letter, as in the novel, the poem, or the play, the author expresses ideas in words; in music composers express them in tones represented by symbols called notes. Whether an artist uses words or tones, the principles of construction remain the same: unity, variety, contrast, balance, and logical structure are the building blocks with which the creator has to work if his resulting patterns and forms are to have any chance of being understood by his readers or listeners.

It is interesting to observe that almost all composers, no matter what their time and place, seem to have worked in much the same way. I refer to so-called serious or concert music, not just simple songs. First they will make a preliminary sketch, on one or two lines at most, to put down the basic ideas as they occur. There is no time to develop them at this point; if you stop to work them out at the time they occur, you will lose those fleeting moments of inspiration when the ideas seem to flow of their own accord. Once these fragmentary ideas depart without having been notated, written down in some permanent form, they are gone forever.

With the accumulated pages of sketches, full of disjointed and unconnected fragments of musical themes, the composer will next begin to develop the basic material. He works out the basic design to produce a final musical structure; he cuts and pastes together the bits and pieces of musical material just as a tailor cuts and sews a dress or suit from pieces of material to make a complete garment. It is here that the highest form of musical craftsmanship comes into play; here the composer's true originality shines forth, even more so than in the flashes of inspiration that produced the original bits and pieces of his themes. Here he hammers out the basic, purely musical texture of his piece.

He rewrites and revises until he feels that every last note is in place and any further additions, deletions, or changes would in some way or other harm the design, the patterns, the logical flow of ideas. Only at this point can one say that the work is truly on paper. It has emerged from its creator's mind and is almost ready to give to the world.

The final step is the writing of the full score if it is an instrumental piece, or the final copy of a vocal work in a piano and vocal score. For an instrumental piece this involves writing each instrumental part in the score. Here the composer enters on a new, although closely related task. He usually does not make any changes in his basic musical texture at this point, aside from such minor matters as devising the best grouping of notes in a

Since 1966 Alfred Reed has been Professor of Music in Theory-Composition and Music Education at The University of Miami School of Music, where he introduced a music merchandising program.

harp arpeggio, for instance, or in the lay-outs of individual chords. He concerns himself almost exclusively with color, how individual notes and lines will sound through the instrumental voices he has chosen. He takes into account the relative importance of each line for the listener, sometimes even single chords, so that the musical ideas flow logically and naturally from one point to another, and the listener can follow them. If there is a main melodic line with an accompanying countermelodic line, then the composer should make certain that the main melodic line stands out clearly from the countermelody, or the listener may become confused. He should make certain that the accompaniment never obliterates the melody it underlies and that he has written for each instrument in a way that makes the part as easy to play as possible, so that the player can center his attention on expressive phrasing rather than on the technical aspects.

There are many technical matters that the writer of music, as well as the writer of English or Japanese concerns himself with, in order for the reader or listener to follow his ideas without difficulty, and so following, grasp and understand them so that he can respond to them in a way that all creative artists hope the majority of those experiencing their works will respond: gladly, joyously, and with uplifting of the human spirit. This comes from the sharing of thoughts and ideas through the medium of words, tones, or pictures that constitutes what we call a work of art. □

Band Directors' Report Card: Rate Your Repertoire

BY GERALD WELKER

Listed below are 25 of the best-known and most frequently played pieces from the repertoire for high school and college bands. Although this list could justifiably include 100 or more titles, this is a sampling of works — some old, some new, some short, some long, some simple, some complex — that should be a part of the well-prepared band director's repertoire.

☐ Arnold — *Four Scottish Dances*

☐ Bennett — *Suite of Old American Dances*

☐ Chance — *Incantation and Dance*

☐ Del Borgo — *Music for Winds and Percussion*

☐ Dello Joio — *Variants on a Medieval Tune*

☐ Erickson — *Toccata for Band*

☐ Giannini — *Symphony No. 3*

☐ Gould — *American Salute*

☐ Grainger — *Lincolnshire Posy*

☐ Hindemith — *Symphony in B♭*

☐ Holst — *First Suite in E♭*

☐ Husa — *Music for Prague, 1968*

☐ Jacob — *William Byrd Suite*

☐ McBeth — *Drammatico*

☐ Milhaud — *Suite Française*

☐ Nelhybel — *Festivo*

☐ Persichetti — *Pageant*

☐ Reed — *A Festival Prelude*

☐ Schuman — *Chester Overture*

☐ Shostakovich — *Festive Overture*

☐ Smith — *Emperata Overture*

☐ Vaughan Williams — *English Folk Song Suite*

☐ Wagner — *Elsa's Procession to the Cathedral*

☐ Walton — *Crown Imperial*

☐ Williams — *Caccia and Chorale*

Whether you want to increase your knowledge or maintain an already strong command of the literature, an organized, consistent approach is best. Initially, we should accept the fact that we need to know the literature — not just the pieces we perform in public with our own bands, but most of the important band compositions. We have some unique problems to face, however. Quality band music has been composed for over 100 years and yet this music is not recorded or written about as frequently or voluminously as orchestral, choral, or chamber music. The dozens of exciting, rewarding new works being published each year add to the challenge of keeping up to date in band literature. Here is a four-way plan for becoming more literate in literature.

Read

Study major periodicals in instrumental music education thoroughly, looking for band music reviews, analytical articles, and advertisements. Make notes for your own band literature notebook.

Purchase your own copies of the latest editions of *Band Music Guide* (published by The Instrumentalist Company), Frederick Fennell's informative and insightful *Basic Band Repertory* pamphlets, *Wind Ensemble/Band Repertoire* by David Wallace and Eugene Corporon (available from the University of Northern Colorado), Smith and Stoutamire's *Band Music Notes*, and Norman Smith's new companion volume, *March Music Notes*.

Gerald L. Welker, Director of Bands and Professor of Music at the University of Alabama, is the founding conductor of the wind ensemble at the University. He holds degrees in music education, music literature, and performance from the Eastman School of Music.

Give yourself:

4 points — if you have conducted the piece in rehearsal or public performance

3 points — if you have performed it as a player or heard other bands play it but not conducted it yourself

2 points — if you have only heard a recording or perused the score

1 point — if you know of the composer and title but have had no other contact with the work

0 points — if you have no knowledge of the piece

Bonus Points — Add 1 point for each year under 10 that you have taught.

Your Repertoire Rating

85-100 — *Superior*
(You are extremely knowledgeable and well-versed in band literature.)

70-84 — *Excellent*
(You have a good, solid acquaintance with band music.)

55-69 — *Fair*
(There are some real weaknesses in your repertoire.)

0-54 — *Poor*
(You need to take some dramatic steps to improve your knowledge of band music.)

Listen

Attend concerts given by other high school and college bands. Make notes on pieces with which you were not well acquainted. Keep programs from these concerts or develop a computer file of the works played. Make notes on all the pieces you did not know. Many times, something will not strike you positively on first hearing, but will become a real favorite when you return to it. We have a responsibility to know more than just a small group of favorite pieces.

Obtain every band recording — disc, LP, or tape — that you can find. There are commercial recordings of fine ensembles (such as groups at Eastman and the University of Michigan, the Cleveland Winds, and the Tokyo Kosei Wind Orchestra), which every director should own; however, many tapes and records of other groups also feature standard and new band repertoire.

Golden Crest, an independent recording company, has produced many fine band albums, including its Authenticated Composer Series. Major annual clinics and conventions such as C.B.D.N.A., A.B.A., N.B.A., and Mid-West International Band and Orchestra Clinic all produce superb recordings. Likewise, high school honor bands and all-state festivals are a valuable source of tapes and records.

Discuss

Music educators' conventions, honor bands, and other festivals provide fine opportunities to talk with band colleagues about literature, new and old. A number of the music dealers around the country, especially in the major markets, have specialists in band music who know a great deal about the band repertoire, especially newer works, and can provide valuable insights and access.

Composers can be a direct and helpful source of information regarding their music. Many are willing, and even eager, to talk with conductors about style, content, and rehearsal approaches. Many of the better-known composers of band music are on the faculties of American universities and can easily be located through college directories.

Study

Scores can be obtained separately, without sets of parts, for all band pieces. They are perhaps the most direct and valuable access to compositions. I suggest that all band conductors compile and maintain an indexed catalog of personal copies of full scores to the major works in the repertoire. Study them carefully and frequently, with and without performance recordings.

Divide repertoire into study units. For example, spend your study time for one month on the Holst *Suites*, the band works of Persichetti, or the Wagner transcriptions. Groupings like this help to organize thoughts, focus learning, and move away from the staggering task of learning the band repertoire in its entirety.

Try this four-part plan of repertoire building beginning with the "Rate Your Repertoire" selections you did not know; then, set up other units of study for a period of six months. You will find that your insight into the band repertoire will improve significantly. □

October, 1991

Divergent Music Lists

by Kurt Saville

For years directors have struggled to choose good music for school bands. As early as 1945, C.B. Righter wrote, "When Diogenes took his lantern in hand and set forth in quest of an honest man, he faced no more difficult task than does the conductor of a school band or orchestra when he searches for material suitable to a concert performance." Because the music selected becomes the textbook and the curriculum for students, many directors turn to graded music lists to identify literature of merit. There is no shortage of graded music lists, as many states and band organizations have compiled them. Unfortunately there is also an abundance of definitions and difficulty levels in these lists.

The graded music lists of many state music associations are used by directors to select festival music, and lists outline compositions appropriate for each grade level. A survey of state music associations showed twenty-two state music lists, and ten states that had no lists but suggested using another list. Only four states suggested a list in addition to their published list. Eleven of the states did not use a state list or suggest using any other.

The states using graded band music lists are Alabama, Arkansas, eastern Washington, Florida, Idaho, Indiana,

Kentucky, Michigan, Minnesota, Mississippi, New York, North Carolina, North Dakota, Ohio, Oklahoma, Oregon, South Carolina, southern California, Texas, West Virginia, and Wisconsin. Alaska and Tennessee endorse The Selective List for Bands. Arizona and Virginia use the *Directors Guide to Festival and Contest Music*.

Directors face a multitude of grading standards in the lists, because they vary from having ten grading levels in Michigan to two levels in North Dakota.

Besides differences in the number of categories, some lists use different definitions of difficulty within the same number of grade levels.

Comparison of the New York State School Music Association and the National Band Association Lists (only key words are included).

Difficulty
Level

1 (N.B.A.) grade school
  (N.Y.) newly organized or
    elementary groups

2 (N.B.A.) advanced grade
    school, good jr. high
    bands
  (N.Y.) advanced elementary
    or middle school with
    some experience

3 (N.B.A.) good high school
  (N.Y.) advanced middle/jr.
    high or 2nd h.s.

4 (N.B.A.) advanced h.s. wind
    ensembles
  (N.Y.) jr. high and average
    h.s.

5 (N.B.A.) advanced h.s. and
    college
  (N.Y.) more advanced h.s.

6 (N.B.A.) college and profes-
    sional
  (N.Y.) mature groups

In levels three and four the differences in the definitions of the difficulties are most divergent even though both lists use six levels. Such differences in standards can cause confusion and error in choosing literature.

It is not possible to determine the difficulty of any musical selection without understanding the rating system used. A selection graded level 3 on one list may not be a grade 3 on another list. In reviewing nine lists with six grade levels, I found that only 30% of the ratings were the same. Of the pieces, 46% had different grades on at least two lists, and 17% had ratings which varied by a minimum of two levels.

Despite these problems graded band lists are important in choosing music for an ensemble along with the advice of seasoned directors who have pre-

pared and performed many works. Graded music lists can improve the odds of finding good music to build a library, particularly by identifying the grade level assigned by a list to pieces you have performed and identifying other titles rated similarly.

New music presents a challenge because the ratings of music publishers vary greatly. Look in educational journals for new music reviews by directors experienced in determining difficulty levels.

Grading Systems Comparison

Degree of Difficulty

State	Easy		To			Hard
10 Levels (5 H.S., 5 Jr. H.S.)						
Michigan (H.S.)	D	C	B	A		AA
Jr. H.S.	D	C	B	A		AA
7 Levels						
Alabama	D	C	CC	B	BB	A	AA
Florida	1	2	3	4	5	6	7
6 Levels						
Idaho	1	2	3	4	5	6
Indiana	1 Jr.	2 Jr.	3 Jr.	1 Sn.	2 Sn.	3 Sn.
N.B.A.	–	2	3	4	5	6
North Carolina	–	2	3	4	5	6
New York	1	2	3	4	5	6
South Carolina	1	2	3	4	5	6
Virginia	1	2	3	4	5	6
Washington	1	2	3	4	5	6
West Virginia	1	2	3	4	5	6
5 Levels						
Arkansas	–	2	3	4	5
Oregon	1	2	3	4	5
Oklahoma	A	AA	AAA	AAAA	AAAAA
Texas	A&C	AA&CC	AAA&CCC	AAAA	AAAAA
4 Levels						
Ohio	1	2	3	4
Wisconsin	D	C	B	A
3 Levels						
Minnesota	3	2	1
2 Levels						
North Dakota	Medium					Difficult

Repertoire lists may be compiled with different objectives. Some, such as the *Band Music Guide*, include all literature while others include only works of artistic merit, such as *Blue-* *print for Band* (Garogale), *College Band Repertoire* (Ostling), *Repertoire for Today's Schools* (Hunsberger), and *Selective Music List for Bands*. Some delineate standard literature for band (*Basic* *Band Repertoire*, Fennell), while others represent music for a select size or type of ensemble (*Wind Ensemble Literature*, Reynolds and *Young Band Music: What to Look For* Conley). □

Music Reviews Revisited

Since *The Instrumentalist* first printed reviews of new music for bands and orchestras in September 1954, it has adhered to consistent difficulty levels. Despite minor improvements in the wording of the definitions of the levels, the only substantive change occurred in September 1968, when grade 5, which included "music for college or professional players" was divided into levels with a new level 6

"for the skilled professional."

When articles were received on subjects dealing with lists of repertoire they were sent back to authors for revisions if the difficulty levels were inconsistent with the new music review standards. Without checking each article over that period of years, we suspect that a few slipped past us using other standards. As the current article indicates, many organizations did not follow our lead, although

many did.

An additional perspective on music reviews is that in 1984 we tried to review almost all new music received although reviewers had the option to skip reviews of so little merit as not to be worth the space. In recent years reviewers have indicated highly recommended music with a checkmark and potential additions to the permanent repertoire as reviewer's choices.

November, 1990

Survey of Band Repertoire

by Brian Hughes

It is discouraging to hear of staff and budget cuts in school music programs, and even in Iowa highly respected programs are being trimmed. There is a decline in the overall quality of education: average test scores are declining, literacy is faltering, and tenth graders don't know when the Civil War was fought. Many school administrators are examining their curricula, and music teachers are especially accountable for their work. If music programs cannot be justified, they may be eliminated.

Music educators should question what they teach and how they teach it, and whether they prepare students for the next contest or teach them music. In particular I am concerned about whether the literature that our ensembles play develops a complete musical background for students. In an attempt to reach audiences, many directors have become misguided by performances and competitions, and have lost sight of our musical heritage. We should ask ourselves what our students ought to know, and whether the repertoire is fulfilling this need; we should consider a more effective method of music selection and develop a master plan for choosing music.

To this end Randall Aitchison, former conductor at Forest City (Iowa) High School, and I devised a survey for high school wind conductors. We discovered that our concern for the quality and depth of high school band music is pervasive; many directors agree that students should play the best music available. Best, of course, is a relative term; what is best for the Pioneer Wind Symphony of Alleman High School will not be best for the Smallville Concert Band. However, each group deserves to learn the highest quality music we can offer.

Our survey offered a diverse list of 50 original works, ranging from Louis Jadin's *Symphony for Band* (1794) to pieces of the past decade and asked conductors whether a work was familiar, if they had performed it, and whether they owned a score or recording.

John Barnes Chance's *Incantation and Dance*, Percy Grainger's *Lincolnshire Posy*, Gustav Holst's *Suite in E♭*, and Alfred Reed's *Russian Christmas Music* were familiar to all respondents. Holst's and Reed's work also were in the five most performed pieces along with John Philip Sousa's *Liberty Bell*, W. Francis McBeth's *Kaddish*, and

Robert Russell Bennett's *Suite of Old American Dances*. The least familiar works were the contemporary compositions.

In a significant portion of the survey conductors articulated their core repertoire, implying that there is a body of literature that they believe students should study. Holst's *Suite in E♭* and *Suite in F*, Vaughan Williams's *English Folk Song Suite*, Grainger's *Lincolnshire Posy* and *Irish Tune From County Derry*, Reed's *Russian Christmas Music*, Sousa's *Stars and Stripes Forever*, and Zdechlik's *Chorale and Shaker Dance* were cited on at least 5 responses and the two Holst *Suites* received 12 and 15 responses each. Interestingly, the composers conductors played most in the division I bands at Iowa's High School Music Association contests in 1988-89, Claude T. Smith and James Swearingen, did not appear on the survey's must-play list. Apparently there is a disparity between what we say is significant and what we choose to perform.

To ensure the survival of the concert band, universities should offer studies in contemporary compositions for junior high and high school winds and percussion. Promoting scores and recordings of these works is an excellent starting point. Schools could join together to make scores and parts of out-of-print music available to one another.

Having identified significant band repertoire, it is up to everyone in the field to perform it. Conductors complain about the poor selection of music; however, publishers print according to the demand, so we need to be willing to buy and perform good literature.

Conductors should also study significant literature beyond the material they prepare for the next concert. To be proficient educators, we should be familiar with the important band literature. Although directors may argue that their schedules are too full for extra study, we ought to establish priorities to maintain our growth and establish a core of required compositions so students will learn the important compositions and transcriptions for band. In reviewing the works in your core repertoire, it is important to study one work of Elliot Del Borgo, for example, but certainly a student need not play them all, just as it is not necessary to perform both Holst Suites. To provide students with a substantial musical education, treat band as an academic course. A core curriculum should be similar to those established in other subjects. Consider band in a sequence of 16 quarters with each quarter adding to a student's musical development.

Unlike other teachers, conductors contend with such utilitarian aspects as marching band and pep band. Question the value of these tasks to music: no other school department spends such a disproportionate amount of time supporting civic events. Music should be viewed in the perspective of a course of study that makes it a valued part of the curriculum, not the handmaiden to athletic teams and civic organizations.

We should encourage prominent composers to write for band so that a musician like Carl Orff does not retire before composing for winds and percussion. Commissioning such composers is an appropriate project for the Music Educators National Conference, National Band Association, and the American School Band Directors Association. These organizations can make lasting contributions to our culture.

There is a rich heritage of literature written or transcribed for bands, and the future of the American school band movement will be less bleak if we design the band curriculum around these compositions.

Survey of Band Directors

Iowa high school band directors responded to the following statements regarding 50 works (some major composers were not included):

- Familiar (F). I know this work, either because I have performed or heard it.
- Performance (P). I have performed this work with an ensemble.
- Study (St). I have not performed the work, but I have studied the score.
- Score (Sc). I own a score to this work.
- Recording (R). I own a recording of this work.

All numbers are percentages of the responses to the survey. The compositions are listed beginning with the most familiar first.

Holst *Suite in Eb*, 98F, 76P, 80St, 54Sc, 66R

Reed *Russian Christmas Music*, 98F, 63P, 56St, 39Sc, 51R

Chance *Incantation and Dance*, 98F, 44P, 44St, 34Sc, 39R

Grainger *Lincolnshire Posy*, 98F, 41P, 56St, 39Sc, 56R

Sousa *Liberty Bell*, 95F, 68P, 49St, 37Sc, 44R

Dello Joio *Scenes from the Louvre*, 90F, 41P, 39St, 27Sc, 37R

McBeth *Kaddish*, 87F, 46P, 34St, 24Sc, 39R

Persichetti *Pageant*, 87F, 39P, 37St, 29Sc, 29R

Bennett *Suite of Old American Dances*, 85F, 46P, 44St, 32Sc, 44R

Hindemith *Symphony*, 85F, 10P, 21St, 7Sc, 24R

Nelhybel *Chorale*, 83F, 41P, 39St, 32Sc, 21R

Williams, C. *Symphonic Suite*, 83F, 41P, 44St, 34Sc, 37R

Grundman *Fantasy on American Sailing Songs*, 83F, 34P, 32St, 21Sc, 12R

Jacob *William Byrd Suite*, 80F, 37P, 37St, 24Sc, 39R

Vaughan Williams *Toccata Marziale*, 78F, 29P, 27St, 21Sc, 41R

Milhaud *Suite Francaise*, 73F, 27P, 29St, 15Sc, 24R

Wagner *Trauersinfonie*, 71P, 32P, 24St, 20Sc, 34R

Gould *Symphony for Band*, 68F, 15P, 21St, 17Sc, 21R

Mennin *Canzona*, 63F, 34P, 34St, 24Sc, 29R

Beethoven *Military March in D*, 63F, 2P, 10St, 2Sc, 12R

Husa *Apotheosis of this Earth*, 63F, 2P, 7St, 5Sc, 7R

Ives *Circus Band March*, 61F, 10P, 21St, 5Sc, 7R

Schuman *New England Tryptich*, 61F, 10P, 12St, 7Sc, 17R

Dahl *Sinfonietta*, 59F, 15P, 10St, 7Sc, 12R

Stravinsky *Symphonies for Wind Instruments*, 59F, 5P, 10St, 10Sc, 12R

Barber *Commando March*, 54F, 15P, 15St, 12Sc, 21R

Berlioz *Symphonie funebre et triomphale*, 54F, 2P, 5St, 2Sc, 5R

Schönberg *Theme and Variations*, 54F, 0P, 7St, 5Sc, 12R

Creston *Legend*, 51F, 7P, 12St, 10Sc, 5R

Nelson *Medieval Suite*, 49F, 5P, 5St, 7Sc, 12R

Alford *Vanished Army*, 46F, 24P, 15St, 15Sc, 10R

Prokofiev *March, Op. 99*, 44F, 21P, 17St, 10Sc, 15R

Erickson *First Symphony*, 44F, 15P, 21St, 12Sc, 12R

Hanson *Dies Natalis*, 41F, 12P, 20St, 12Sc, 10R

Benson *The Leaves are Falling*, 41F, 5P, 5St, 5Sc, 5R

Copland *Emblems*, 39F, 5P, 10St, 5Sc, 7R

Hovhanness *Symphony No. 4*, 39F, 2P, 2St, 5Sc, 7R

Bassett *Designs, Images and Textures*, 37F, 2P, 12St, 7Sc, 10R

Adler *A Little Night and Day Music*, 37F, 0P, 7St, 5Sc, 5R

Schuller *Meditation*, 29F, 5P, 2St, 2Sc, 2R

Piston *Tunbridge Fair*, 24F, 2P, 5St, 2Sc, 10R

Hartley *Sinfonia IV*, 21F, 0P, 2St, 2Sc, 2R

Broege *Sinfonia VI*, 20F, 5P, 5St, 2Sc, 2R

Schwanter *From a Dark Millenium*, 20F, 2P, 5St, 0Sc, 2R

Thompson *A Solemn Music*, 20F, 2P, 2St, 2Sc, 2R

Jadin *Symphonie for Band*, 17F, 7P, 5St, 2Sc, 2R

Colgrass *Winds of Nagual*, 17F, 0P, 0St, 2Sc, 2R

Cowell *Shoonthree*, 10F, 5P, 7St, 5Sc, 7R

Badings *Transition*, 7F, 0P, 0St, 0Sc, 2R

Hodkinson *Tower*, 2F, 0P, 0St, 0Sc, 0R

1. Do you have a core curriculum?
Yes: 32; No: 44; No response: 24.

2. Name 10 pieces all of your students shall study or perform during their high school years.

(37) Gustav Holst *Suite in E♭*; (29) Gustav Holst *Suite in F*, Ralph Vaughan Williams *English Folk Song Suite*; (17) Percy Aldridge Grainger *Lincolnshire Posy*, Alfred Reed *Russian Christmas Music*; (15) John Philip Sousa *Stars and Stripes Forever*, John Zdechlik *Chorale and Shaker Dance*; (12) Percy Aldridge Grainger *Irish Tune from County Derry*; (10) John Barnes Chance *Variations of a Korean Folk Song*, Frank Erickson *Air for Band*.

3. List 5 contemporary composers for winds and percussion.

(32) Alfred Reed; (29) W. Francis McBeth; (20) Eliot Del Borgo; (17) Frank Erickson, Vaclav Nelhybel, Claude T. Smith; (12) Karel Husa, Ron Nelson, John Zdechlik; (10) Timothy Broege, Vincent Persichetti, Jared Spears.

4. What major works for winds and percussion will you be studying this year?

(12) Gustav Holst *Suite in E♭*; (07) Robert Jager *Third Suite*, John Zdechlik *Chorale and Shaker Dance*; (05) John Barnes Chance *Incantation and Dance*, Frank Erickson *Air for Band*, Cesar Giovaninni *Overture in B♭*, Gustav Holst *Suite in F*, Darius Milhaud *Suite Francaise*, Ralph Vaughan Williams *English Folk Song Suite*.

5. Here is a list of significant contemporary composers who have made little or no contribution to high school band repertoire. If an organization commissioned a new work for high school band, rank (1 being high) these composers in order of your preference.

1. Husa, Karel (1.75); 2. Colgrass, Michael (3.88); 3. Adams, John (4.0); 4. Foss, Lukas (4.02); 5. Babbitt, Milton (4.27); 6. Stockhausen, Karlheinz (5.47); 7. Davies, Peter Maxwell (5.66); 8. Rorem, Ned (6.01); 9. Musgrave, Thea (7.1); 10. Wuorinen, Charles (7.96); 11. Argento, Dominick (8.1); 12. Harbison, John (9.0).

6. List at least 5 recordings you own (excluding publisher's promotions) of significant band works.

(21) *Cleveland Symphonic Winds* (Fennell); (12) *British Band Classics* (Fennell); (10) *Lincolnshire Posy* (Eastman-Fennell); (07) *Educational Record Reference Library* (Belwin), *Wagner for Band* (Fennell); *Stars and Stripes Forever* (Eastman-Fennell); *American Concert Band Masterpieces* (Eastman-Fennell); *McBeth conducts McBeth*.

7. Size of band program (average) 87 players. Educational background: B.A. 17; M.A. 44; No response 39. Degree-granting institutions represented: Bemidji State, Drake University, Iowa State University, Northeast Missouri State University, Northern Arizona University, Northwestern College, Northwestern University, Parsons College, Southeast Missouri State University, South Dakota State University, University of California, Los Angeles, University of Iowa, University of Minnesota, University of Northern Colorado, University of North Dakota, University of Northern Iowa, Wartburg College, William Penn College.

Brian Hughes, director of bands at Alleman High School in Rock Island, Illinois, is a master's candidate in the music education program at the University of Northern Iowa.

Improving Band Literature

by Peter Schmalz

"T he Friendly Advice," article in the July issue prodded directors, publishers, and music store owners to reflect on the products and services they offer each other. The article highlights the dearth of good band literature, and even casual conversation at conventions includes complaints about the lack of good new music, but because people assume that everyone knows good literature when he hears it, remarks such as these seldom include a definition of it. A closer examination reveals that band directors really don't agree in their judgments about quality, but do agree that there is a problem, especially with grade III and IV music.

Suggestions for Band Directors

My personal perspective reflects more than a little nostalgia. When I began teaching 21 years ago there was tremendous excitement about new music as publishers annually issued numerous grade III and IV pieces. Some of this music was simply well written, some was by composers already established as producers of significant band music, and some was by unheard-of composers. Leading students into this literature was one of my chief reasons for going to work each day.

In the intervening years publishers' production costs rose dramatically and today many publishers avoid risky literature and unknown composers. However, publishers produce what band directors consume, and each year new pieces appear that exhibit that elusive quality that we seek.

To find them make use of publishers' free tapes and scores, and look beyond the practical playing considerations. Interesting literature contains musical richness and depth, contrast, elements of surprise and drama, sensitivity, thematic development, rhythmic energy, excellent orchestration, counterpoint, and satisfying form. As you listen to and read scores consider

Peter Schmalz is director of bands at West High School in Oshkosh, Wisconsin, and is a composer and publisher of band music.

whether the music is merely functional or if you will eagerly conduct it ten years from now. If you are convinced of the music's worth and are an enthusiastic conductor, be confident that students will come to appreciate the selection over time.

Planning next year's program is best done during the summer. Identify concert themes, if you plan programs that way, or establish a quota of old and new music to achieve balance throughout the year. By setting limits on new music you will consider purchases more carefully. With planning you can avoid desperate searches through the band library three weeks before a concert or performing a work solely because it matches students' playing abilities.

For the last decade band directors have tried to identify a basic band repertoire. Lists of good music are useful, but the established band repertoire consists of only several dozen great pieces. Directors cannot afford the ease of dwelling only in the safe haven of basic repertoire, but should go beyond this.

Some directors focus on the band contest for an entire year, but for others band competitions are nonexistent. If you play in competitions, make sure that the contest pieces you choose are of the highest level and play important works whether a contest requires them or not. Today, a band that plays only two or three serious pieces in nine months is untenable educationally. If you find conductors who share your passion for good band literature, exchange the names of promising pieces with them on a regular basis. Through time you can purchase new music solely on a colleague's recommendations.

Focusing on the music of one or two composers each year will give you and your band an opportunity for an in-depth study of a respected musician's music. Choose your composers with care: some have written the same piece several times over and used different titles. Try to program one piece of a chosen composer at each concert, or alternate a contemporary composer with one from the past.

There are people who write good music for band who would consider a residency at your school, if you are willing to pay their expenses and a fee for their services. Either present an entire program of their works or feature several pieces at a regular concert. A project like this offers an exciting way to contribute to the growth of band literature.

This year I discovered *The Forest of Arden* by English composer George Lloyd. Impressed by his boldness, lyricism, and orchestration, I decided to track down this new piece and found that I could only obtain the work directly from the publisher (R. Smith, London) at an outrageous price. Nevertheless, I convinced the school purchasing agent to place the order in pounds sterling. The experience of learning and performing this music was worth the detective work.

Although negative responses to new works fill music history, school music educators cannot afford negative reactions to programming too often, but serious involvement in this art dictates that we should take risks with new music. If a work communicates in a powerful way, it will overcome initial student resistance. Having only one chance to hear the piece, the audience may find a challenging work confusing. Consider programming a new piece twice on the same concert or explain it by having students play examples of themes and countermelodies before performing it.

Come back to a good piece in four or five years. To expand the basic repertoire conductors should play and replay good new music.

Students should understand that challenging music requires a long-term commitment, a difficult prospect in this age of instant gratification. I try to convince youngsters that it is exciting to be an active participant in a growing culture. If they expect to play high-quality music in band, their enthusiasm for new music will follow. Work on developing pride in artistic experience rather than in competitive accomplishments, and convince them that while this may be difficult work, it has long-lasting benefits.

One way to have enough time for finding and rehearsing new music is to reduce the number of hours spent playing and rehearsing for school and civic functions. Play the same music at each graduation, and rotate a few pieces in the pep band folder, carrying the bulk of music over from year to year. Cut down the number of events at which you perform and spend this time with significant literature.

Remember that your dollars speak more powerfully to publishers than your complaints. Consider redesigning your budget to allow the purchase of more concert band music, and less for marching band, pep band, and jazz band.

To encourage publishers to produce good literature, don't abuse the copyright law by photocopying music. By saving a few dollars in the long run you only benefit the photocopy machine manufacturers. Publishers lose profits, which they need to produce new music, composers lose royalties and the incentive to create new works, and directors suffer from the lack of good literature to rehearse and perform with their students. □

Trends in Contemporary Band Music

The band's full musical potential remains unrealized

Bernard Fitzgerald

THE COLLEGE Band Directors National Association and the American Bandmasters Association have been directly responsible for many recent contemporary compositions for band, both thru officially commissioning new works and encouragement provided by individual members of these organizations. The ABA annually sponsors the Ostwald Band Composition Award, and the CBDNA has sponsored band composition awards in 1956 and 1960. Richard Franko Goldman commissions a new band work each year in memory of his father, the founder of the Goldman Band. The late Edwin Franko Goldman was personally responsible for many commissions and performances of new band compositions, and his untiring efforts in behalf of bands and band literature resulted in the creation of many important additions to the band repertory. An increasing number of colleges and universities have also undertaken the commissioning of works by major composers.

During the past two decades a growing number of distinguished American composers have contributed significant original compositions to the repertory of the symphonic band. Works of major importance include the symphonies by Paul Hindemith, Morton Gould, Vincent Persichetti and Vittorio Gianinni, and the commissioned compositions by Howard Hanson and Paul Creston. These and other compositions by Peter Mennin, Darius Milhaud, Walter Piston, William Schuman, Owen Reed, and numerous other important composers constitute a distinctive contribution to contemporary music that is vitally important to the development of the band repertory. In addition, many college faculty and student composers have written original band compositions that deserve a permanent place in the band repertory.

The works by contemporary composers encompass varied concepts as to the instrumentation of the band

Bernard Fitzgerald, Head of the Department of Music, University of Kentucky, is a graduate of Oberlin Conservatory and Jordan College of Music. He has taught at Jordan College, Kansas State Teachers College, Hendrix College, and the Universities of Idaho and Texas. Fitzgerald is a past president of the CBDNA. In addition to teaching, he is widely known for his original compositions and numerous transcriptions for brass solos and ensembles. From 1946 to 1953 he conducted the Brass Clinic department for "The Instrumentalist."

with adaptation to the individual style and technique of the composer. This is both understandable and justifiable since creative inspiration does not thrive when hampered by restrictive limitations. The divergence of opinion, however, as to the specific instruments and the number of performers in a symphonic band is just as haphazard as the instrumentations of the bands that may range from 40-120 players. This represents conflicting concepts of instrumental balance and possibly reflects the personal preference of the conductor or is determined by the number and ability of available performers.

Lack of Standards

Although composers and publishers, in general, follow the instrumentation recommended by the ABA in regard to the numbers of parts published, American bands have not evolved or maintained a standardized instrumentation. The composer is understandably confused regarding the instrumentation of the concert or symphonic band, for the personnel may vary from 40-120 performers and include the following extremes: 3-18 flutes; a complete clarinet choir from E♭ soprano to BB♭ contra-bass, or B♭ clarinets plus one or two bass clarinets; a quartet of saxophones or an assorted combination of 10 players assigned to perform the same basic four parts; cornets and trumpets used indiscriminately, varying in number from 6-15 and assigned to play five or six different parts. These inconsistencies represent major obstacles to the composer, since performances even by superior bands sound radically different due to the divergence in instrumentation, personnel, and the ratios of the woodwind, brass, and percussion sections.

The instrumental distribution may attain such absurdities of imbalance as 24 B♭ clarinets and 2 bass clarinets, or 6 French horns versus 22 cornets and trombones. The skilled conductor considers such extremes impossible from an artistic point of view, yet composers frequently hear their musical concepts grossly distorted as the result of instrumental imbalance.

Since composers receive much of their training in orchestral scoring, they are accustomed to writing for an ensemble in which the basic instrumentation and sonority ratios are well established. Although individual preference may be expressed for the sound of certain professional orchestras in comparison to others of equal excellence, these organizations obviously are composed of the same basic instrumentation, perform the same orchestrations, and are capable of achieving comparable tonal textures, sonorities, and balance, subject only to the limitations of the personnel and the artistry and skill of the conductor.

Composers may justifiably expect that performances by competent bands attain comparable sonority and instrumental balance, at least to the point that the basic tonal sonorities conceived by the composer are not altered radically. Thus, it is imperative that the instrumentation of the band be stabilized with respect to the basic ratios, weights, and balances of the various sections as related to the total instrumental sonority. Composers are handicapped by the absence of a standard instrumentation and balance and must continue to compromise until these factors are definitely established. The band has a potential flexibility to achieve a wide range of sonorities and textures, adaptable to the performances of music of different styles just as the orchestra is capable of utilizing its basic instrumentation in the performance of compositions from the classic, romantic, and contemporary periods. The realization of this artistic goal is an absolute necessity if the band is to attain a versatility of expression comparable to the orchestra.

Experiments Needed

Although recent contemporary compositions for the band contain some innovations in scoring techniques, experimentation has been limited to a relatively few composers having a more imaginative approach toward the instrumental colors of the modern concert band. In view of recent trends, it is important that the composer be encouraged to explore further the tonal resources of the band to avoid limiting the band to a relatively small number of scoring effects and devices. New concepts in sonority and scoring are necessary for an emerging musical medium, although many composers appear content to follow the general pattern of a few original band compositions resulting in the overuse of some scoring techniques.

While it is apparent that contemporary music for band includes some exploratory and experimental compositions, it is also evident that composers are motivated by a genuine interest in the band as a concert medium. Experimentation, inevitably a part of the process of musical evolution, must both precede and accompany musical progress if the composer is to find the means for expressing his ideas. The absence of an established repertory by major

composers of the past means facility and skill in scoring can be acquired only thru experience and experiment, not by dependence on the techniques of earlier composers.

Trends to Avoid

Examination of manuscript band scores submitted for contemporary music festivals and competitions reveals the following trends and techniques that, if employed exclusively, will ultimately restrict the musical potential of the symphonic band.

Emphasis on massive sonorities. Many composers tend to exploit the large tonal masses of the band almost exclusively. Although the sonorities of *tutti* scoring are often skillfully employed, one of the major needs is a fuller realization of the potential of the band with regard to tonal coloring, utilizing the available instrumentation in both independent and tutti scoring.

Thick harmonic texture, particularly in scoring for the tenor and bass instruments. The preponderance and tonal weight of instruments in the lower range frequently cause complex rhythmic and tonal textures to lose clarity and definition. The heavy, massed texture lacks sufficient upper harmonics to achieve linear and rhythmic clarity. A careful analysis of the tonal weight and balance of the respective sections is necessary and may require a reduction in the number of parts employed.

Limited use of the contrasting tonal colors of the bright and mellow brass instruments. The lack of distinction in scoring for cornets and trumpets reflects this problem, a situation often resulting from the indiscriminate use of these instruments by the conductor. Just as important, however, many so-called cornets are often slightly modified trumpets and when used with a small mouthpiece present tonal characteristics which closely approximate those of the trumpet.

Stress on the percussive style of writing for the brass section. This leads to a corresponding neglect of the lyrical and more subtle expressive qualities of the brass instruments.

Unsatisfactory distribution of dissonances. The distribution of extreme dissonances requires particular care, especially if instruments in the high register are assigned parts of secondary importance. This is particularly

obvious when the clarinet, oboe, or trumpet has such a role in the upper range.

Absence of contrasting textures, an important point in scoring to avoid when the principal solo instruments are assigned an appropriate role in solo or small ensemble passages.

Overscoring for the percussion section. Although a few composers have effectively explored the importance of the percussion instruments as a choir, many scores indicate little or no restraint with respect to dynamics or selective use of those instruments to enhance rather than dominate the ensemble sonority.

Scoring of instruments in undesirable registers. Some band scores fail to attain the effect intended by the composer because of the use of instrumental registers that are not conducive to satisfactory sonority, tone quality, or intonation. This usually involves either the extremely high or low register of an instrument.

A marked tendency to build compositions on brief motives or fragmentary melodic ideas. This approach frequently produces music lacking in continuity and sustained interest, and the score may often be constructed upon a limited number of rhythmic patterns that do not provide sufficient rhythmic contrast.

Emphasis upon short compositions, or suites of several brief movements, usually not more than six minutes in length. Compositions in the larger forms are essential to the musical development of the band repertory.

While varying concepts of instrumentation or modifications with appropriate adaptation to the individual style of the composer are desirable, these trends give composers evidence they may falsely assume represents the ultimate potential of the band. It may be argued that the predominance of these concepts proves contemporary band music reflects those characteristics that are representative of contemporary music in general.

Although this may be true, the full musical potential of the band is yet to be realized, and inevitably its significant repertory must come from contemporary composers. Conductors must continue to present artistic performances of contemporary music if the interest of the composer in band music is to be sustained and encouraged.

May, 1987

Arrangements for School and Youth Orchestras

BY PAUL H. KIRBY

The use of simplified arrangements of symphonic repertoire has stimulated long discussions and occasionally heated debates. Opinions range from approval to aversion. In my opinion, good arrangements have their place; in fact, they are indispensable in certain situations. The type of ensemble involved and the musical experience desired should influence the choice of arrangement. I find it helpful to divide arrangements into categories.

The first category consists of music originally composed for instruments other than the full orchestra, usually transcribed for performance by professional orchestras. For that reason the musical quality is normally quite high, but the difficulty of the scores often makes them impractical for school and youth orchestras. Examples include Ravel's orchestration of Mussorgsky's *Pictures at an Exhibition* and Stokowski's transcription of Bach's *Toccata and Fugue in D Minor.*

Category II comprises editions of original orchestral works for which the editor has provided performance suggestions without fundamentally changing the composition. The Carl Fischer edition of Mussorgsky's *Night on Bald Mountain* is an example. Common editorial decisions include bowings, fingerings, phrasing indications, dynamics, changes in instrumentation, and even transpositions. Because they are adaptations of standard symphonic works, these editions are often good choices for youth or

school orchestras. In evaluating them, however, the conductor should consider what changes the editor may have made, and what effect these changes may have on performance. The edition should be compared with the original score to determine whether the alterations facilitate performance without altering the musical style or structure of the work. For instance, Winter's (Boosey & Hawkes) introduction of trombones and clarinets to Haydn's Symphony No. 7 (really no. 97) allows the entire wind section of the orchestra to participate in the performance without compromising the character of the work; the same might be said of George Dasch's judicious addition of tuba to Schubert's *Unfinished Symphony* (Carl Fischer). On the other hand, I take issue with Isaacs's addition of percussion to Gluck's Overture to *Iphigenia in Aulis,* because it creates a serious clash of styles.

Like the second, Category III consists of performing edition/arrangements, but ones that stem from a need to recast works for the modern orchestra. This might include original orchestrations that, while not difficult in the usual sense, present peculiar problems of instrumentation. For example, Handel's *Music for the Royal Fireworks* is technically feasible for advanced high school orchestras but contains clarion trumpet parts impractical for most high school trumpeters. Other works in this category are transcriptions originally intended for professional orchestras that have found their way into the

school and youth orchestra repertoire, such as Calliet's arrangement of Bach's "Sheep May Safely Graze."

In Category IV are arrangements of standard orchestral works that have been simplified to make them accessible to school, youth, or community orchestras. The basic structure of the original work is preserved with only minor cuts, if any, so that the work retains its identity. Isaac's arrangement of the "Berceuse and Finale" from Stravinsky's *Firebird Suite* (Belwin Mills) is a good example. If well done, such arrangements are valuable to school, youth, or community orchestras for which the original is too difficult. Keep in mind, however, that orchestras advanced enough to play the most challenging arrangements in this category can often manage worthwhile original compositions.

To Category V belong simple arrangements of excerpts from larger works. Often a tune or two from the original is recognizable, as in *Themes from The Creation* (Haydn/Forsblad/Leonard). In some cases sections of the original composition are retained with substantial reworking, as in *Romeo and Juliet* (Tchaikovsky/Muller/Kjos). The arrangements in this category must be judged as compositions in themselves, for that is what they are, substantially. While there is some value in familiarizing students with famous tunes, the form and structure of the music constitutes much of its substance; therefore, performing an arrangement that seriously alters that is tantamount to performing another piece with similar melodies. An extreme example can be found in the various simple arrangements of the *Ode to Joy* performed by many elementary and junior high orchestras. Beyond the use of the familiar melody, they bear little resemblance to the finale of Beethoven's Ninth.

Although I am not categorically opposed to all such arrangements, I believe adaptations that substantially recast the music should be evaluated as new compositions on their own merits and compared with original easy works when selecting music for a young orchestra. While the easier arrangements in this category are often useful for young orchestras, I prefer to avoid the more difficult ones, as there are usually better alternatives for programs.

Of course, this system of categorization is subject to interpretation, and there may be some overlap. While most arrangements can be easily categorized, a few may fall into the cracks. Generally, those most useful to school and youth orchestras tend to belong to categories II, III, and IV because the transcriptions from the first category are usually too difficult and the arrangements from category V often represent substantial alterations from the original scores.

The following annotated list of arrangements from groups III and IV may be helpful to less-experienced directors in choosing appropriate music for their ensembles. Veteran directors may find it useful to compare their own favorites with mine. Category II was not included because these editions differ only slightly from the original scores. Bear in mind that only western art music has been considered and that the commercial availability of the editions was not a factor in choosing works for the checklist.

Category III: Classics Recast for the Modern Orchestra.

Bach/Calliet/Boosey & Hawkes: *Little Fugue in G Minor* — This effective orchestration of J.S. Bach's organ fugue contains sufficient cross-cuing to make it playable by orchestras with incomplete instrumentation. The original key and structure have been preserved, and enough filler has been added to create an expansive sound. Though not particularly easy, it is playable by most youth orchestras, especially if additional bowing and editing is provided by the conductor.

Bach/Calliet/Boosey & Hawkes: "Sheep May Safely Graze" — This aria for soprano, two flutes, and continuo has been colorfully orchestrated. For a long time I suspected that Calliet had composed the introduction himself, because I had never seen it in any of the numerous choral settings. It turns out that Calliet adapted the introduction from the recitative that immediately precedes the aria in the cantata, a fact that might affect the performance style of the introduction.

Bach/Luck/Luck: "Jesu, Joy of Man's Desiring" — This fine straightforward arrangement of a movement from Cantata No. 147 was originally scored for SATB chorus, trumpet (doubling the soprano line), strings, and continuo. In this version, the brass assumes the role of the chorus.

Bach/Ormandy/Boosey & Hawkes: *Wachet auf* — Ormandy has in effect made a new realization of the tenor chorale from Bach's Cantata No. 140. He has maintained the melody and bass line throughout, and provided a full orchestration, complete with phrase markings. The original version calls for tenor soli, unison violin and viola, and continuo.

Frescobaldi/Kindler/Belwin Mills: *Toccata* — In spite of the fact that the work is not really by Frescobaldi, or even Kindler, it is a delightful arrangement.

Handel/Baines and Mackerras/Oxford: *Music for the Royal Fireworks* — This edition/arrangement might belong to Category II except for its simplified B♭ trumpet parts and optional parts for flutes, clarinets, and trombones not found in the original. It requires extended high-tessitura playing from the principal trumpet and horn. The edition is playable by winds alone or by the full orchestra.

Handel/Kindler/Belwin Mills: Prelude and Fugue in D Minor — In this free adaptation of the first two movements of the Concerto Grosso, op. 3, no. 5, originally scored for two oboes, strings, and continuo, certain passages have been extended and a cadenza added at the end. Material from the prelude is recapitulated at the end of the fugue, but this is not stylistically offensive. The editor's interpretation of the dotted rhythms in the prelude is questionable; nevertheless, the arrangement is worthy of performance.

Monteverdi/Peress/G. Schirmer: Toccata and Ritornello from *Orfeo* — Because this arrangement is not specifically directed at younger orchestras, the score is not simplified. The editor has, however, done considerable reorchestration, excerpting, and transposition. Only the principal bassoon has an extremely demanding part characterized by very high tessitura, and rewriting it for another instrument would make the arrangement practical for most youth orchestras.

Vaughan-Williams/Greaves/Oxford: *Rhosymedre* — This setting for small orchestra of a lovely Welsh hymn tune is not difficult, but it requires a rich string sound, especially from the violas.

Vaughan-Williams/Greaves/Oxford: *Fantasia on Greensleeves* — Greaves's setting combines the familiar tune with another English folk song, "Lovely Joan," to create a ternary form. It is attractively scored for two flutes, strings, and harp (for which piano or guitar can substitute).

Vaughan-Williams/Rosenberg/Fischer: *Sine Nomine* — This arrangement of the hymn "For All the Saints" makes a fine processional. An optional choral score is provided for concert use.

Category IV: Simplified Standard Works

Bizet/Stone/Boosey & Hawkes: *Farandole* — This arrangement is suitable for a young orchestra that has trouble with the 16th-note figures at the end of the *L'Arlesienne Suite No. 2,* from which it is excerpted. These passages and similar ones have been eliminated, and some of the ornaments have been simplified. A good youth or high school orchestra should opt for the original score.

Brahms/Boss and Page/Ditson: *Hungarian Dance No. 5* — The entire piece has been transposed up a half-step to G minor, some figuration has been simplified, and some of the high passages have been lowered an octave to make this original piano piece playable by the young orchestra.

Britten/Stone/Boosey & Hawkes: Courtly Dances from *Gloriana:* This outstanding arrangement of excellent, rarely heard music is not easy but well worth the effort. The reduced orchestration maintains the original structure with the exception of one movement, the galliard, which has been omitted. Though thoroughly cross-cued for performance without winds, I do not recommend that, because the original orchestration is heavily weighted with wind color and very adventurous in the use of flat keys.

Debussy/Isaac/Fischer: "En Bateau" and "Ballet" from *Petite Suite* — Available separately, these movements are transcribed from a suite for two pianos previously orchestrated by Henri Büsser. Some of the passage work has been simplified, and cross-cuing is provided. While harp parts are included in both excerpts, the harp is essential only for "En Bateau." The more advanced orchestra might prefer the Büsser orchestration, while the more elementary one might consider David Stone's simpler arrangement of "Ballet."

Fauré/Gearhart/Shawnee: *Pavane* — A fine piece of music, this work was originally scored for optional SATB chorus and orchestra. Gearhart has reduced the paired winds by eliminating one oboe, one bassoon, and one horn, while adding trumpet, bass trombone, and optional harp. Other alterations include transposition up a half-step to G

minor, considerable reorchestration, and substantial changes in musical content in the middle section. This arrangement is especially suitable for school orchestras with developing harp players. Apart from the key of F♯ minor, however, the original version is not much more difficult, and advanced orchestras should opt for it, especially if choral involvement is possible. The French text is an innocuous account of a flirtatious encounter in the dance.

Fauré/Stone/Boosey & Hawkes: *Sicilienne* — While structural integrity has been maintained and there is relatively little simplification, there are considerable changes in orchestration in this arrangement. Two trumpets, trombone, and percussion have been added to the original, and cues have been put into the string parts to accommodate the absence of harp. Orchestras with a good harpist should opt for the original version.

Gliere/Isaac/Fischer: *Russian Sailor's Dance* — A classic among arrangements, this has been performed by numerous junior and senior high orchestras and is very popular among students. Most of the structure is maintained, although the original seventh variation is omitted, as are four measures of the coda. The difficult viola passages in the fourth variation (no. 6 in the arrangement) have been reassigned to the first violins and their original octave figurations omitted. More advanced orchestras may want to try the original, which is pitched a step higher and employs more percussion.

Handel/Stone/Oxford: *Water Music Suites I & II* — While these are good arrangements, they are not especially easy, and more detailed bowing indications are needed for a clean performance. Only the trio section of the second movement of the first suite is used; otherwise, the original structure of both suites is preserved. Da capos are freely realized and there are some changes in orchestration.

Haydn/Stone/Boosey & Hawkes: *Divertimento* — Though

adapted from the *St. Anthony Divertimento* for winds, this is a good piece to introduce the 18th-century style of bowing and phrasing to string students. The three final movements — Chorale, Minuet, and Rondo — have been transposed and rescored for high school or advanced junior high orchestra.

Mozart/Muller/Kjos: Overture to *Il Re Pastore* — This arrangement provides a good opportunity to teach young players late 18th-century orchestral bowing technique. The editor preserves the structure of the overture up to measure 100 then introduces a concert ending, because the original leads directly into the first scene of the opera. There is much simplification, including deletion of some syncopated figures and higher octaves that should not be out of reach for many youth orchestras. In fact, most orchestras that can play this arrangement could probably play the original version, which is available with a similar concert ending.

Mussorgsky/Reibold/Fitzsimmons: "The Great Gate of Kiev" — The finale from *Pictures at an Exhibition* is a majestic work for school orchestras; and while Ravel's famous orchestration is clearly superior in color and flair, it is also much more difficult than this practical edition for orchestra, including three-part violins and alto and tenor saxophones. The original key and structure have been preserved in spite of some condensing in the middle section. These liberties are no greater than those Ravel took and do not detract from the arrangement.

Mussorgsky/Stone/Boosey & Hawkes: *Gopak* — Stone has made a practical, useful arrangement of a good tune, although he has simplified it some and made minor structural changes. While the original is not a great deal more difficult, it requires complete instrumentation.

Offenbach/Isaac/Fischer: *Ballet Parisien* — This suite is a pastiche of selections from several different operettas. Unfortunately, no full score is published; nevertheless, it is delightful music presented in a practical arrangement for young orchestras.

Prokofiev/Isaac/Fischer: *Romeo and Juliet* — Two excerpts from the famous ballet, "Masks" and "Montagues and Capulets," are presented in their original keys without significant structural alteration. Various changes in octave, orchestration, and figuration — plus the elimination of one modulation — were made to render these difficult movements accessible to the young orchestra.

Prokofiev/Isaac/Fischer: *Troika* — Without changing the key or structure, the editor has made a difficult piece easier by simplifying the more awkward passagework and providing transposed parts and cross-cuing.

Purcell/Rafter/Bosworth: *Suite No. 1 in D Major* — Adapted from the fifth harpsichord suite, this is a similar arrangement to the *Water Music Suite*. Certain movements have been omitted and others reordered. Minor liberties are taken with rhythmic and melodic figures, and some implied harmonies and ornamentation are written out. The advanced high school or youth orchestra should probably opt for original suites and concertos from the period.

Rossini/Isaac/Wynn: Overture to *The Barber of Seville* — Although the structure is preserved, there is considerable simplification of difficult passagework, notably the first eight measures of the coda. Only the most difficult passages have been altered, however, so this is by no means an easy arrangement. The editor has added percussion, which, except for the bells, does not disturb the spirit of the composition. To the original wind section, Isaac has added bass clarinet, third and fourth horns, and tuba.

Saint-Saëns/Isaac/Fischer: *French Military March* — The original structure is preserved except for the omission of one section and the transposition of another up a half-step. There is some simplification and reorchestration as well. The original, which appears as the final movement from the *Suite Algérienne*, is not a great deal more difficult, but it requires four each of horns and trumpets.

Schubert/Stone/Boosey & Hawkes: *Rosamunde* Ballet Music No. 2 — Though structurally intact, this arrangement alters the orchestration and simplifies some of the figuration. The original, though generally not much more difficult, calls for two horns in G and two clarinets in C. This arrangement is preferable to the one published by Ditson, because the latter is incomplete.

Shostakovich/Isaac/Fischer: *Polka* — While excellent and useful, this arrangement lacks a full score. Structural integrity is maintained, but the time signature is altered.

Stravinsky/Isaac/Belwin Mills: "Berceuse and Finale" from *The Firebird Suite* — In this classic of the arrangement repertoire, Isaac has preserved the structure and spirit of the original while simplifying many of its more difficult aspects. Finger tremolos have been replaced by bowed ones, and rapid figures have been made easier. The keys have been raised a half-tone, except for one passage left in the original key, which alters the original modulation sequence. Cross-cuing has been provided along with transposed parts for Bb trumpets. Some high school orchestras can play the original, which is superior in coloration, but the arrangement is an excellent alternative for those that cannot.

Verdi/Stone/Boosey & Hawkes: Grand March from *Aïda* — The key has been changed from Eb to D, and the form freely adapted. The original, which appears in Act II of the opera, calls for orchestra, chorus, soloists, and stage band. This well-conceived arrangement will help a moderately good orchestra sound excellent with minimal rehearsal.

Wagner/Weaver/Belwin Mills: Introduction to Act III of *Lohengrin* — This arrangement follows the original structure, although substantial orchestrational changes occur in the middle section. Note that the score calls for first, second, and third violins (each with an independent part not duplicated by the violas) plus optional advanced violin. On the whole, it is a good arrangement that sounds fine with a large string section, and it is somewhat easier than the original.

Walton/Stone/Oxford: *Crown Imperial* — Bar for bar, this arrangement matches the Oxford score of Walton's march. Because not all the difficult passages have been simplified, it should still provide a challenge to most school orchestras. Instrumentation has been considerably reduced in the arrangement, which is available for purchase, while the original must be rented.

While school and youth orchestras should strive to perform original works by the masters whenever feasible, most will find it more practical to perform a mixed repertoire of original works and arrangements. Fortunately, there are many fine works in both categories that are accessible to young players. I hope that this article provides some useful suggestions for a repertoire of musical arrangements. ∎

Paul H. Kirby is conductor of the Houston Youth Symphony and director of the orchestra at Iowa State University. He holds degrees from the University of Michigan, Michigan State University, and Rice University and has studied at the Mozarteum in Salzburg.

December, 1980

Standard
19th-Century Repertoire
for School Orchestra

Donn Laurence Mills

Those of us whose education has been steeped in standard symphonic repertoire are naturally eager to introduce our students to major works. The difficulties and instrumental requirements of 19th-century orchestral music, however, usually cause us to pass it by in favor of the safer Baroque, easy Classical, conservative contemporary pieces, and simplified arrangements.

Before giving up entirely on the very heart of symphonic literature, we should take a closer look at some of the masterpieces to see what can be played by a good school orchestra.

Looking over the field, there are three categories to consider: The Symphonists, The Colorists, and Stage Composers.

SYMPHONISTS
Beethoven
Overtures. While some parts are easy, there are always a few sticky passages. Good cellos are essential. *Egmont* is certainly the most likely candidate, and *King Stephen* (a decidedly minor work) is also playable. Two trickier, but possible, works are *Coriolan* and *Fidelio*.

Symphonies. All are difficult in their entirety, but movement-by-movement there are possibilities: Symphony No. 1, movements one and two; Symphony No. 2, fourth movement (a delightful rondo); Symphony No. 3, movements one and four; Symphony No. 4, second movement (although it will take good

control and woodwinds); Symphony No. 5, movements one and four; Symphony No. 6, first movement; Symphony No. 7, second movement; Symphony No. 8, movements one and two; Symphony No. 9, "Ode To Joy" (has divisi-à-4 violas and awkward triplet figures).

Also worth mentioning is a charming symphony attributed to Beethoven, known as the "Zero Symphony." Although more in the Classical style, it's easy enough and worthwhile. It's usually listed as Beethoven's "Jena Symphony." All movements can be played by relatively inexperienced players.

Schubert
Marche Militaire is good, as is the *Rosamunde Overture* and *Ballet Music.*

Of the symphonies the following movements can be used: Symphony No. 4, "Tragic", second movement (but Ab major might cause problems); Symphony No. 5, all movements are beautiful and playable, requires sensitivity; Symphony No. 8, "Unfinished", first movement.

Schumann
All of his music is risky. Some possibilities might be the Finale of the 2nd Symphony (if you're brave), the first movement of the 3rd "Rhenish" Symphony, and the fourth movement of the Fourth Symphony (though it's thorny with dotted-eighth-sixteenth figures).

Brahms
Both overtures are possible and certainly worthwhile, but the violins are high; and the German Requiem is not overly difficult. *Serenade No. 1 in D, op. 11* is pleasant and possible with good horns.

As for the symphonies, you need a solid orchestra with plenty of depth in all departments, but if you want to try them, the least fearsome are: Symphony No. 1, third movement; Symphony No. 2, third movement; Symphony No. 3, out of the question; Symphony No. 4, third movement and possibly the chaconne Finale.

Tchaikowsky
Unfortunately Tchaikowsky demands independent string sections to play his characteristic scale figures. The seconds and violas need plenty of technique and must be in the upper positions. Cellos also need advanced technique. Tchaikowsky scores for good high school orchestras can be found, however. The ballet scores yield many gems that are often not the overly familiar tunes, either. Character dances such as the *Grandfather Dance*

Donn Laurence Mills is the NSOA contributing editor. He holds music degrees from Northwestern University and Eastman School of Music. A conductor and music educator, he is also the American educational director for the Yamaha Music Foundation of Tokyo.

from "Nutcracker" or the *White Swan Waltz* from "Swan Lake" are relatively easy. *Capriccio Italien* and *Marche Slav* are reasonable. Your winds would probably enjoy the challenges of *"1812"* and *Romeo and Juliet,* but without strong seconds and cellos, as well as six or eight-deep quality in the firsts, it would be a mistake to tackle those scores in their original versions. *Suites No. 1 and 3* have good sections such as "March Miniature" and "Gavotte" from No. 1 and the "Theme and Variations" from No. 3.

The symphonies include the following: Symphony No. 1, second movement, fourth perhaps; Symphony No. 2, first movement; Symphony No. 3, second and fifth movements; Symphony No. 4, second and fourth movements; Symphony No. 5, fourth movement; Symphony No. 6, not recommended.

Dvorak

There are 16 *Slavonic Dances* to choose from (op. 46 and op. 72). Usually you have to purchase the set to get the one you want, and most of these are difficult. Violins need 7th position and violas and 2nds noodle a lot. The ones best suited for a student orchestra would be 1, 3, 4, 6, 7, 8, 10, 11. There are many interesting tone poems and overtures by Dvorak, but generally they present formidable hurdles, especially for inner parts.

The symphonies include: Symphony No. 5 in E minor, all movements are possible providing you have strong, plentiful violas; Symphony No. 7 in D minor, second movement; Symphony No. 8 in G major, fourth movement.

Mendelssohn

Fingal's Cave and *Ruy Blas* are fun, although some passage work is awkward. Of the symphonies, the likeliest are: Symphony No. 1, op. 11, first movement; Symphony No. 3, "Scottish," second movement; Symphony No. 4, "Italian," second movement; Symphony No. 5, "Reformation," first and second movements.

Mahler

Better left to the pros, however the *Adagietto* from the 5th Symphony for harp and strings works if you have enough strings and players with vibratos.

Bruckner

Too enigmatic for student orchestras.

Sibelius

A musical gold mine, but repetitiveness soon becomes boring. *Finlandia* and *Karelia* are old school orchestra favorites; *Valse Triste* and *Pelleas and Melisande,* maybe.

Of the symphonies, you might consider: Symphony No. 1, second movement, Andante; Symphony No. 2, fourth movement; Symphony No. 5, first movement (but sophisticated and a bit tedious to rehearse). The other symphonies are too problematical and treacherous for youngsters.

Kallinikov

Some conductors are reporting success with a little-known First Symphony by Vassili Kallinikov (1866-1901).

The works by the colorists and stage composers of the romantic century require stylistic understanding and deft rehearsal schemes to make the pieces sound convincing.

COLORISTS

Wagner

Some considerations might be: *Adagio for Clarinet and Strings, Prelude to Act III-Lohengrin, Prelude to Die Meistersingers, Good Friday Spell from "Parsifal," Overture to Rienzi.* Wagner demands full instrumentation and bold playing, so programming his music means you have a lot of confidence in the ability and persistence of your players.

Mussorgsky

Gopak from the Fair at Sorochinsk, Night on Bald Mountain (yes, *very* possible), *Kovantchina: Persian Dance, Entr'act.* The Ravel orchestration of *Pictures at an Exhibition* has a number of playable sections, but it's an ex-pensive rental and other arrangements of the easier parts serve as well.

Rimsky-Korsakov

Dubinushka, op. 62 (easy and glorious); *Introduction and Wedding March,* "Le Coq D'or"; *Russian Easter Overture* (needs good soloists); *Capriccio Espagnol* (must have excellent concertmaster, fine cellos and advanced winds); *Scheherazade,* movements two and three; *Cortege from Mlada* (a brass player's dream).

Borodin

Steppes of Central Asia (delicate, but easy); *Prince Igor: Overture and Polovetsian Dances; Symphony No. 2,* first movement (with good cellos); *Nocturne,* from string quartet (if you have a good group of strings they might do well with this music).

Berlioz

Damnation of Faust, Hungarian March and Dance of Sylphs; *Symphonie Fantastique,* movements four and five. The overtures and descriptive works are too difficult.

Liszt

None of his music is easy, not because of his virtuoso writing skill, but because he was not a good orchestrator. *Hungarian Rhapsodies* (No. 2 especially); *Les Preludes* (programmed a lot in the past, but it's a lot of work to master the arpeggio passages). Such works as Prometheus, Tasso, Orpheus, Mazeppa, Faust, etc. are probably not worth the effort.

Grieg

Lyric Suite, op. 54 (nice and practical); *Peer Gynt Suites* (warhorses, but deservedly so); *Holberg Suite,* first and second movements (strings only); *Sigurd Jorsalfar,* op. 56, Introduction, Intermezzo, and March; *Two Elegiac Melodies* (strings). The piano concerto is not too difficult if you have a few good cellists.

Smetana

Dances from "The Bartered Bride" (winners); *Ma Vlast Cycle,*

"My Fatherland," Blanik No. 6, Bohemia's Meadows and Forests No. 4, Vysherad No. 1 (requires harp).

Franck

Symphony in D minor. With the proper instrumentation this can be successful for student groups. The tone poems are too tough.

Saint-Saens

Carnival of the Animals (limited orchestration, some parts require skill, but altogether not bad); *La Princess Jaune Overture,* Op. 30; *Suite Algerienne,* (the March especially); *Danse Macabre,* (some cuts might be necessary); *Symphony No. 3,* "Organ," sounds and looks easy, but isn't. *Phaeton* and *Omphale's Spinning Wheel* are difficult. There are lesser works — *Henry VIII, A Night In Lisbon, Orient and Occident March* — that are not too difficult, but are not among the composer's best.

Richard Strauss

While this music is usually too demanding for students, there are three possibilities: *Death and Transfiguration* (need independent strings who can get around well in high positions); *Horn Concerto,* op. 11; *Till Eulenspiegel* (if you have the horns, E♭ clarinet, and good 1st violins) I have heard this played well by amateur and better-than-average student groups. All those other tempting scores like *Don Juan, Ein Heldenleben, Thus Spake Zarathustra,* and *Dance of the Seven Veils* are out-of-reach. Your winds might like a crack at the E♭ *Serenade,* and there are a couple of successful arrangements of the *Rosenkavalier Waltzes* available.

STAGE COMPOSERS
Rossini

The overtures are truly hard. Like Mozart, nothing can be swept under the stand. The easiest of the lot are: *Barber of Seville, Semiramide, Il Signor Bruschino.* The *William Tell Ballet Music* is possible and entertaining. The *Sonatas for Strings* (six in all) are corny, but within reach. There are no viola parts.

Weber

These overtures could be considered: *Jubel, Oberon, Invitation to the Dance. Euryanthe* and *Der Freischutz* are more difficult, but could be done if you're determined enough.

Delibes

There are excellent dances and scenes from *Coppelia, Sylvia,* and *La Source* as well as *Le Roi S'amuse* to be considered. Listen to a complete recording and select your favorites. Most are straightforward with much of the work centered in the first violin. Some re-writing is advised.

Glinka

Russlan and Ludmilla Overture is rapid, but lays well and is popular with kids. *Kamarinskaya* (Wedding Song and Dance) is a possibility.

Verdi

Sicilian Vespers Overture, Aida Ballet Music, Prelude to Act I of La Traviata.

Massenet

Le Cid Suite, Scenes Pittoresques, Scenes Napolitains, Scenes Alsaciennes, Prelude to Werther. Probably none of these suites is good from beginning to end so you may need to pick and choose, but there are good program numbers among the ruins.

Nicolai

Merry Wives of Windsor Overture (a merry romp indeed).

Bizet

L'Arlessienne Suites I and II, Carmen Suites I and II, some of *Jeux D'Enfants,* op. 22, *Overture to "The Pearlfishers."* The *Symphony in C* looks easy, but is full of intonation problems and awkward string crossings.

Humperdinck

Prelude and Dream Pantomime from Hansel and Gretel.

Gounod

Faust Ballet Music.

Granados

Intermezzo from "Goyescas."

Offenbach

Overture to Orpheus in the Underworld.

VonSuppe

Not always easy, but fun if you don't take him seriously. *Pique Dame, Beautiful Galatea, Light Cavalry, Poet and Peasant.*

J. Strauss

Polkas, marches, galops and waltzes offer a wealth of good programming material for any orchestra. The 1st violin parts usually carry the weight with 2nds and violas providing mostly harmonic and rhythmic background. The two big overtures, *Die Fledermaus* and *Gypsy Baron,* are tricky in spite of their tunefulness.

Unfortunately all major works require subtlety and clarity to bring them off well, so it's easy to become discouraged when your orchestra doesn't even come close to your favorite orchestra recording. To avoid the frustration, I've found it best to rehearse such critical works a little at a time until the technical problems are solved. Take a passage or two at each rehearsal and work the socks off it. Let the kids hear a recording of the piece and impress them with the challenges, but don't let them lose heart.

This era of orchestration requires divisi and independent string groups. There are broken chord figures and arpeggios to contend with as well as delicate woodwind passages and stylistic characteristics which students can't comprehend until they're taught by someone like you. If your top players are fine, but the rest can't get out of 1st position, you should stay with arrangements and do them well. But if you have sufficient instrumentation and strength, program a standard work or two and give it all you've got. It may never sound as full as those simple homophonic arrangements, but you will be getting a little closer to the real thing — the music that sold you on orchestra in the first place. ∎

Arranging for the Elementary Orchestra

Robert Bauernschmidt

In arranging for the elementary school orchestra the arranger is apt to encounter certain problems peculiar to this grade level, problems which are not disposed of by any single solution but which he must grapple with constantly as he attempts to provide a worthwhile arrangement for elementary school use.

As an approach to the main problem, first consider this: the orchestral arranger who arranges for the general market at the elementary school level is never quite sure of the exact instrumentation of the groups for which he is arranging. Instrumentation and player ability vary widely at this level. In order to be assured of getting the essentials into the arrangement, the arranger must concentrate first on the more popular instruments of the school orchestra. When he adds the other instruments to the score individual tone quality and clarity of line are often lost, due to excessive doubling. Contrast of color and orchestral variety give way to the somewhat neutral sound of all available instruments playing constantly throughout the arrangement.

The main problem, then, is derived from the foregoing paragraph: How can the arranger present a practical arrangement for general use without sacrificing clarity of line, transparency, variety of orchestral color, and the other desirable elements of a good arrangement?

Limited vs. General Use Orchestrations

There seem to be two reasonable approaches to this problem. Either the arranger can arrange for the exact instrumentation he wants and limit the use of his arrangement to those orchestras which contain his instrumentation, or he can write parts for all instruments with directions in the score to omit certain lines when unwanted doubling occurs. The second approach seems more practical in that it makes the arrangement adaptable to more groups by giving the director an opportunity to select an instrumentation applicable to his own group.

Scoring for Flexible Instrumentation

If, for example, the arranger wants to write a certain passage as an oboe solo with string background, why shouldn't the solo appear in the flute and clarinet parts as well? In the event that the oboe is found lacking in a particular school orchestra, the solo can then be played as a bona fide clarinet or flute solo. Care must be taken to rearrange the solo to suit the ranges and technical aspects of these other instruments so that it will not be thought of as a "misplaced" or "second best" oboe solo. Giving the director this choice of instrumentation will tend to make a more practical arrangement without sacrificing clarity of line, variety of orchestral color, etc. It will also make solo experience available to more players (if they all take turns playing it at rehearsals) and allow the director to choose the best soloist for performance. Directions for these choices should appear in the score, of course.

Although the above procedure is often taken care of by cues, an over-abundance of cues is sometimes confusing to the young player and is likely to make the part seem less important when the player is called upon to play the cued part. If the arranger will write parts for all the instruments, with directions in the score to help the director dispose of excessive doublings and choose an instrumentation to fit his particular group, the result certainly should be better than the dull tutti sound of all instruments playing constantly.

Assuming the arranger has a piece of music of aesthetic and educational value to arrange, he must then consider two additional problems in providing a good orchestration for elementary school use.

Producing an Adequate Bass Line

The first problem — one which confronts both the arranger and the director—is that of producing a good and adequate bass line, of getting depth into the elementary orchestration. The reasons for the lack of a good bass line in many orchestras are obvious enough. The young student seldom purchases his own cello or bass. Smaller schools with limited budgets usually begin their purchasing program with the smaller, less expensive instruments. Even when the instrumental inventory is considered complete, the bass instruments are likely to number no more than one or two cellos and perhaps a string bass. Since there are usually so few players starting on these instruments, the director is fortunate if he has more than one strong player at a time on any one of them. The larger instruments are awkward to transport back and forth from home to school, especially in rural areas. This makes home practice more difficult. The arranger must be aware of these difficulties and attempt to strengthen the bass line by other means.

In my opinion, the bass line has been rendered ineffective too often in many arrangements simply by dividing the cello and bass parts into two dissimilar lines. While it must be conceded that the cello can be very effective on a part other than the bass line, it seems an unnecessary waste to use it as "fill in" harmony in its open A range. The cello is not "the baritone horn of the orchestra" as one might conclude after hearing the cello parts of certain elementary orchestrations.

Robert Bauernschmidt is director of the Reedley City (Cal.) junior and senior high school orchestras and also serves on the staff of the Kings Canyon Unified School District. At the schools he directs a string training program and a newly formed summer youth orchestra. He received his M.A. from Fresno State College.

It is the bass of the string family and should be given this role, especially in the elementary orchestra where a strong bass line very often is lacking. The double bass part, then, should double the cello part as the name implies. This doubling of the bass line becomes all the more important when the players on the part number only two or three.

In addition, the arranger has several other means of strengthening the bass line. The trombone can be brought down from its tenor register, where it is often found, to reinforce the bass line when such a procedure is practical. A second French horn can sometimes help in the upper bass range. It does not hurt to include a bassoon part, in the possibility that one might be included in some elementary orchestras. Obviously the bassoon is well-suited to a bass function. The clarinets, of which most school orchestras have a surplus, can be used to good effect down to the range of the open D on the cello. Most young clarinet students can produce an acceptable tone in this register and thus not only add depth to the orchestra but help the overall orchestral sound. The use of a bass clarinet part might also be considered. It is very possible that a bass clarinet player would be easier to come by in the typical elementary situation than a bassoon player. The piano, too, can play an important part in giving aid to a weak bass line, especially if it is given an essential part of the arrangement rather than a haphazard accompanying part, as is so often the case. Finally, the arranger should consider the use of the timpani at all dynamic levels in the orchestration as a simple but limited means of helping the bass line.

Transparency and Variety Tone Color

The second problem with which the arranger is faced is that of providing transparency and variety of orchestral color in the upper voices of the orchestra. It is in this range that an over-abundance of the more popular instruments are usually found. In contrast to the first problem, the problem here is to keep the score from becoming too thick, heavy, and dull. When all the instruments play constantly throughout an arrangement, with several different instruments on each line, the orchestration is sometimes referred to as "safe." This type of orchestration enables instrumental groups of varied instrumentations to use the same arrangement, but transparency and orchestral color are apt to be sacrificed when the "safety" is provided in the score by immoderate doublings.

While the doubling process may serve well to strengthen an otherwise feeble bass line, this same process should be used with discretion when applied to the upper voices of the orchestra. When excessive doubling occurs here, the result is too often the "safe" but dull tutti from beginning to end. Woodwind quality and

color are the first to be lost in the deluge of sound. This "safe tutti" type of arranging is very often a result of ineffective scoring in the woodwinds themselves. When they are used effectively in the score, orchestral color, transparency, and clarity of line will replace the monotonous tutti. These instruments too often are assigned only the prosaic task of reinforcing or doubling other lines; they are used merely to add to the general mass of sound, to add "safety" to the arrangement. Rarely are they given independent parts with light accompaniment, which allow the individual woodwind colors to shine through the orchestration.

How often is the pure flute or clarinet tone heard in a solo capacity with light string accompaniment? Yet these instruments, unlike the bass instruments, certainly are among the more popular instruments of the elementary school orchestra, and it is not likely that the arranger is unduly jeopardizing the "safety" of his arrangement by scoring lightly for the sake of the woodwinds.

Discounting the double reed instruments, which are less frequently found in elementary school groups, a variety of possibilities still remain for providing the orchestration with effective woodwind parts by using only flutes and clarinets. Solos, duets composed of like or mixed instruments, mixed combinations of trios and quartets are all fairly reliable possibilities which should be considered by the arranger. The quartet combination might be arranged in such a way that a duet or trio could be extracted from the score when a particular instrumentation does not provide the quartet.

In reference to the double reeds, the arranger certainly should not avoid giving them their essential role in the woodwind section. It would be wise, however, to provide adequate cues or alternate parts for these lines, since the double reeds are less frequently found in the elementary orchestra.

Good Quality Music Essential

Finally, it would seem axiomatic that to produce a worthwhile orchestra arrangement for elementary school use the arranger must have at hand a piece of music of good quality to arrange. Young players, when properly motivated, seem to work harder and maintain interest over longer periods of time when working with something they consider worthwhile and important. The arranger, in a sense, is providing the "text books" for these young players to be used in the music education process. He most certainly should be concerned with the educational as well as the aesthetic value of these "texts." If the arranger of elementary school orchestra music will consider himself a contributing member of the total music education program, he is not likely to deviate from his responsibility of providing worthwhile and suitable arrangements. ■

Orchestrations of Handel's *Messiah*

Harold Geerdes

The 1977 performance of "Messiah" by the Calvin College Oratorio Society, Harold Geerdes conducting, in the George Welsh Civic Auditorium in Grand Rapids, Michigan.

As the Christmas season approaches with its many performances of Handel's *Messiah,* orchestra directors are faced with important decisions regarding the edition and instrumentation to be used. Unlike most major compositions, *Messiah* was not put down once and for all in a single version but was adapted and changed as Handel saw fit for each of the performances he conducted. In addition, Mozart did a major revision based on an inaccurate copy of the original score and thereby perpetuated many details which are questionable.

The first performance (in Dublin, 1742) featured a chorus of 20 men and boys with 5 soloists and an orchestra of 33. In addition to strings, the orchestra consisted of 4 oboes, 4 bassoons, 2 trumpets, timpani, harpsichord, and organ. Basically, this was the same instrumentation Handel used in subsequent performances, although sometimes he added 2 French horns and a few more strings.

Handel played the harpsichord for the 36 performances he conducted between 1742 and his death in 1759. The relatively large number of double reeds in

Harold Geerdes is associate professor of music at Calvin College in Grand Rapids, Michigan, where he has conducted the Calvin College Oratorio Society for the past 12 years. Prior to that, he prepared the orchestra and played as its concertmaster for 20 years. He has been involved in some phase of performing or conducting Messiah *each year since his high school days, and has made it a subject of special interest and study.*

his orchestra (twice that used today) was necessary because of the thinner sound of the Baroque instruments. The trumpets were small bore and pitched in the key of C or D. The brass and percussion were called on only for the big, climactic choruses, to add brilliance and color. In performances during Handel's time, the trumpets and percussion were withheld until the 17th number, "Glory to God," and were used only for this chorus, the "Hallelujah" (No. 44), and "Worthy Is the Lamb, Amen" (No. 53), and for a single bass aria, "The Trumpet Shall Sound."

The Baron van Swieten, wealthy diplomat and patron of the arts, commissioned Mozart to arrange and re-orchestrate four Handel oratorios (including *Messiah*) for performances at his concerts in the Schwartzenberg Palace in 1788-1790. Mozart's revamped score, based on a copy of the original which was not itself free of errors, included some minor alterations in the violin and viola parts but added 2 flutes, 2 clarinets, 2 French horns, and 3 trombones to the orchestra. The original oboe and bassoon parts were retained and given their own staves in the score rather than being indicated as doublings of chorus parts. This enlargement of the orchestra in the style of the late Classical period (only two years before Mozart's death; he never saw the published score) altered the Baroque character of the work. Much of the accompaniment became thick and heavy in contrast to Handel's transparent, clear scoring (see figure 1). Nevertheless, this orchestration (further disfigured by Johann Hiller and others) was used in countless performances and helped spread

769

Figure 1. Facsimile of Handel's original manuscript showing the opening bars of the "Hallelujah Chorus." The top score calls for 2 trumpets, probably in C since the parts are not transposed. The second score is the timpani, followed by first violin, second violin and viola, the four chorus parts (note the use of the alto clef for altos and the tenor clef for tenors) and basso continuo, which was to be played by the cellos, bass viols, and bassoons. Handel used an organ with performances but never wrote out an organ part. Edited by Chrysander and published in Hamburg in 1892. Available from Da Capo Press, 227 W. 17th St., New York, N.Y.

the fame of *Messiah* throughout Western Europe and the United States.

In 1902 the English musicologist Ebenezer Prout issued another edition which corrected errors in the Mozart score but kept its instrumentation. "While Handel's text has been scrupulously respected," said Prout, "no attempt has been made to preserve his orchestral colouring." This edition was republished later in the United States and has been most widely used here during the past half century.

In recent years various conductors have gone back to an original Handel version, eliminating the added instruments, using smaller choruses, and encouraging vocal soloists to embellish the vocal lines in the arias according to the practice in Handel's time. If Handel had settled on a single, definitive version of the work and given it his blessing, the choice of which edition to use would be much simpler. However, changing circumstances of performances and soloists made constant revisions of the score expedient. For the modern conductor as well, the choice of edition can be made according to its suitability for a particular performance.

I would recommend that the school or amateur orchestra use the Prout edition, modified if necessary.

Nº 44. CHORUS. HALLELUJAH.

Figure 2. The 1902 Prout Edition based on the original scores and incorporating many of the Mozart revisions. Trombones are added as well as a pipe organ. The trombones were Prout's idea and he added them wherever the brass played. This edition has piano and organ parts and can be used with the Schirmer vocal score.

It incorporates the basic Handel instrumentation with the best of Mozart's additions and few of his errors. It is easily obtainable and is particularly useful if no organ is available because the woodwind parts include cues for clarinets and bassoons which may be substituted for organ in crucial accompaniments.

A copy of Handel's score or a good contemporary edition such as Mann (see figure 3) or Shaw is absolutely essential in making instrumentation decisions. Compare the Prout or Mozart editions carefully with the original and use only the added parts which will enhance your performance. For example, I always leave out the three trombone parts in both these editions. However, if the orchestra or chorus was a little weak

---

Messiah a Last Resort?

If George Frideric Handel hadn't gone broke producing expensive and sophisticated Italian operas, the world might never have had the *Messiah*, one of the best-loved pieces of classical music of all time.

Six box office records discovered in the Harvard University Library leave no doubt about the seriousness of Handel's financial problems in the 1720s and '30s that eventually led him to try a new musical genre of which *Messiah* was representative.

Covered with doodles and columns of figures, the records are from six nights of performances by Handel's opera company in 1732-34. They were discovered by Robert D. Hume, professor of English at The Pennsylvania State University, and Judith Milhous, assistant professor of theatre history at the University of Iowa.

The find makes it possible for historians to substantiate events that led Handel from the Italian operas he had been writing to the more popular English oratorios, like *Messiah*.

"The find was entirely accidental," Hume says, noting that he and Milhous had originally gone to Harvard to catalogue some of the Coke Papers, a collection of manuscripts concerned with the late 17th- and 18th century theatre in England. The records from Handel's company showed up in the scrapbook containing that collection, although the Coke manuscripts deal with an earlier period.

The six documents were all handwritten. Five of them show that Handel's operas were playing to very small audiences. The sixth, the only sold-out house, celebrated a royal wedding.

"He must have been losing his shirt," Hume says. "For a while, he had a whopping subsidy from the King and he took in a lot of money, but he spent tremendous sums on each production. He hired well-known singers from the Continent at high prices and had fantastic sets and costumes; it was all spangles and gold and brocades."

According to Hume, audiences were small, not because Handel wasn't appreciated, but because he was producing Italian operas, which were declining in popularity in London. Far more popular were the lighter oratorios, performed in English, that he began to write after he was forced to seek a medium that would draw larger crowds. He was in his fifties when he made the change.

Says Hume, "You can imagine how he felt, night after night, watching the audience arrive and knowing he wasn't breaking even. Lots of books have been written about Handel and his work, but I felt I understood his difficulties better from these six slips of paper than from anything I've read."

and would benefit from the addition of trombones, I would not hesitate to use them. I sympathize completely with the historian or musicologist who strives to authenticate each detail, but I want my presentation to be the strongest possible in my particular situation, just as Handel did. Strive for clarity and openness of texture, and don't use all the players just because they are available. Remember that the only winds Handel used were trumpets and double reeds.

Figure 3. The score of the 1961 critical edition by Alfred Mann, published by the Rutgers University Press, which is based on the latest and most authoritative source material and is true to the original Handel score. Oboes I and II double the chorus soprano line, as indicated in the Coram score, copied from Handel's performance material. The "senza rip." indicated for the first 3-1/2 bars for the strings meant "without ripieno" or without the full orchestra, using only a small "concertino" group as in the Baroque concerto grosso. The full orchestra enters at the "con rip." sign. Available from J.J. Fischer & Bros., Glen Rock, New Jersey.

Messiah Recordings

Here is a sampling of the fine Messiah recordings available.

• Argo D183D 3 with the Academy of St. Martin-in-the-Fields, Neville Marriner conducting
• Columbia M2S-603 with the New York Philharmonic, Westminster Chorus, Leonard Bernstein conducting
• Columbia M2S-607 with the Philadelphia Orchestra, Mormon Tabernacle Choir, Eugene Ormandy conducting
• Deutsche Grammophon DG 2709 045 with the John Alldis Choir, London Philharmonic Orchestra, Karl Richter conducting
• Erato STLU 70421/3 (also RCA CRL 3-1426 and Musical Heritage Society MHS 3273/5) with the English Chamber Orchestra and Chorus, Raymond Leppard conducting
• Harmonia Mundi SLS 774 (also Angel S 3705) with the Ambrosian Singers, English Chamber Orchestra, Charles Mackerras conducting
• London 1329 with the London Symphony and Chorus, Adrian Boult conducting
• Philips 6703 001 with the London Symphony and Chorus, Colin Davis conducting

---

What to do about the piano accompaniment is also a question. The piano part in the chorus book is a reduction of the full orchestra score and, because it doubles the orchestra parts, it should not be used in performance. Although much of it is very playable for rehearsal, certain choruses are very difficult unless the pianist makes discrete omissions. Octaves and parallel thirds may often be simplified by playing single notes, as in parts of No. 26 "All We Like Sheep" and No. 53 "Worthy Is the Lamb," for example. The reworking of the piano part found in the choral book for the Watkins Shaw edition would be helpful to rehearsal pianists.

Messiah has survived countless bad performances in over 200 years, but the underlying quality of the text and the music is such that no matter how it is presented its strength comes through. The sound of Handel's all-male chorus and his orchestra with 40% of the players on oboes and bassoons would be unrecognizable to our ears, and contemporary performance should not attempt to reproduce it. The orchestra director should choose his accompaniment wisely and carefully, so that this marvelous work makes its maximum impact on any audience which hears it. ∎

The full score and orchestra parts for *Messiah* currently available from the publishers are the following:

Urtext (Original) edition (Peters) Includes parts for organ and for harpsichord.

Mozart edition (Bärenreiter) The beautifully engraved 1961 printing of Mozart's score as he revised and supplemented the Handel orchestration. Includes organ. The clarino parts are for D trumpets. Mozart added three trombones, but only in the first 24 bars of the Overture, and in the chorus "Since By Man Came Death."

Prout edition See figure 2.

Coopersmith edition (Carl Fischer) A 1946 edition by an American musicologist which sparked the interest in the original edition.

Watkins Shaw edition (Novello) Published in 1965, this edition is true to the original source material. The oboe parts, which double the sopranos and altos, are written on separate staves. Chorus parts are written in treble and bass clef.

Kalmus edition The full score gives the original Handel orchestra parts on the bottom ten staves. The Mozart revisions of the Handel trumpet and timpani parts are included, plus the parts he added for flutes, clarinets, and French horns. The oboe and bassoon parts are written out (these parts were implied in the original score, since custom dictated doubling of the violin parts by the oboes and of the bass parts by the bassoons).

Alfred Mann edition See figure 3.

Note: The Urtext edition, Mozart edition, and Prout edition are available for rental or purchase from Broude Brothers Ltd., 56 E. 45th St., New York, New York, or from Luck's Music Library, 15701 E. Warren St., Detroit, Michigan.

November, 1988

The Influence of Jazz on the History and Development of Concert Music

by Gunther Schuller

The Influence of Jazz on the History and Development of Concert Music by Gunther Schuller was prepared for National Jazz Service Organization and presented at the national conference called New Perspectives on Jazz held September, 1986 at Wingspread, the Conference Center of The Johnson Foundation in Racine, Wisconsin.

In its unedited form this paper is part of a publication, New Perspectives on Jazz, that reports on the conference and is included in this issue of The Instrumentalist with the written permission of National Jazz Service Organization.

The relationship between jazz and classical "concert music," as the lecture title calls it, has always been both profound and fragile and frequently confusing and misinterpreted. "Profound" because certain aspects of the European classical tradition, particularly its harmony and to some extent its melodic, rhythmic, and instrumental traditions, were from the outset fundamental and inextricable parts of the evolution of jazz as a distinct musical language. That is, of course, not to deny its even more crucial relationship to West African musical forms and traditions.

"Fragile" because throughout most of jazz's now more or less 100-year history, classical music and jazz have been rejecting each other, misinterpreting each other, mistrusting each other, and frequently skimming off the top elements and concepts indigenous to both traditions in ways that can only be described as superficial. "Confusing and misinterpreted" because of ignorance and prejudice on both sides — although I hasten to add that in the realm of prejudice, classical music and musicians have the longer and sadder history.

In these relatively few words, I believe I have staked out the territory, the frame of reference, in which our discussion on the influence of jazz on the history and development of concert music must take place; but to lay out the territory is not yet to define the territory. We must take care of that detail before we tackle the larger question of jazz's influence on classical music.

First, let us dispose of some annoying questions of terminology and mythology. The language with which we describe these two musics is inaccurate and confusing. The word "jazz" is

A native New Yorker born in 1925, Gunther Schuller is widely regarded as one of the music world's most eloquent advocates of the musical arts. His expertise extends from his work as a composer and conductor to his work as an educator and administrator. At age 16 Gunther Schuller was already playing in the New York Philharmonic under Arturo Toscanini and in the Ballet Theatre Orchestra under Antal Dorati. At 17 he was appointed principal French hornist of the Cincinnati Symphony, where he appeared as soloist the following season in his own Horn Concerto. By the age of 19 he was playing with the Metropolitan Opera Orchestra. He remained there as solo hornist until 1959, when he resigned to devote all of his time to composing.

Leading arts organizations and performers have commissioned Schuller to compose. Recent commissions include works for the orchestras of Berlin, Dayton, and New York, in addition to the Naumburg Foundation. As a conductor, Schuller travels to Europe annually for guest appearances with orchestras including the Berlin Philharmonic and B.B.C. Symphony; in the United States he has directed the symphony orchestras of Boston, Chicago, New York, Philadelphia, Cleveland, Detroit, and Pittsburgh, to name just a few, and serves as Music Director of the Festival at Sandpoint.

A strong proponent of contemporary music, Gunther Schuller was responsible for "Twentieth Century Innovations," a series of concerts presented by Carnegie Hall from 1963-65. He is credited for the popular ragtime revival of the 1970s, having introduced the New England Conservatory Ragtime Ensemble in the premiere of his re-orchestration of the long-lost works by Scott Joplin known as the Red Back Book. A former head of the composition department at the Berkshire Music Center at Tanglewood, he also served from 1967-77 as President of the New England Conservatory of Music. Gunther Schuller is the author of four books, the latest of which, a compendium of his published essays and articles titled Musings, received the Sonneck Society's 1988 Irving Lowens Award for a distinguished published contribution to American music. Recently Schuller was selected as first occupant of the "Elise L. Stoeger Composer's Chair" by the Lincoln Center Chamber Music Society.

and was an indignity that most thinking individuals by now reject as a proper name for America's one truly indigenous musical art form. It persists, of course, both by traditional long-term usage and for lack of a handy or more appropriate term.

"Classical" and "concert music" are also inaccurate and severely limiting terms. Even within the realm of so-called classical music, the term is used differently by its own practitioners. Some use the term generically to describe all music that comes out of the Western art tradition, a definition that leaves folk, popular, ethnic, or vernacular European musical traditions in terminological limbo. Historians and musicologists limit the term classical to a specific period in European musical history, the years roughly between 1750 and 1825.

To add further confusion to the semantic muddle, many jazz writers and critics have lately begun to call jazz "America's classical music" while others refer to the 1930s, the Swing Era, as the classical period in jazz. Those who apply the term classical to jazz or to some of its developments, are undoubtedly well-meaning, though misguided. Their thinking is based on the most ancient of myths: In order to gain acceptance in our society and musical culture, jazz needs the approbation of borrowed European aesthetic terminology. Jazz is its own self-defining musical art form. It does not or would not, in a world of justice and understanding, need to defend its pedigree or its right of existence in terms other than its own.

"Concert music" is an even more confusing and limiting term. On the one hand, not all classical Western music is concert music performed in concert. Nor can it be said that jazz is not played in concerts. Benny Goodman's 1938 Carnegie Hall concert, Duke Ellington's years of Carnegie appearances, and Norman Granz's *Jazz at the Philharmonic* took care of that syndrome a long time ago.

Let us gratefully note, however, that we have at least finally done away with the term serious music — as if jazz were an unserious music — and that the rest of the musical field has not done much better with terminology. For example, "popular music" (in which jazz is often included) means to some people, music which has attained popular success, with the emphasis on success and the further emphasis on financial success. To others popular music means music of the people, by the people, for the people, something akin to folk music. But does folk music still really exist? Indeed, are there any folk left in this world of instant electronic communication, in which the isolation that used to spawn folkloric, ethnic, regional, and national traditions has all but disappeared? Today's so-called folk

music is a synthetic, inauthentic product primarily conceived in the Brill building and in Nashville recording studios.

That is why the term vernacular music is more appropriate. At least it is a more harmless term, avoiding all the complex implications of popularity or of authenticity. By the same token, names like rock music and Third Stream also have the virtue of a modicum of descriptive accuracy. They at least say more or less what they are and in themselves do not cause confusion — which is not to say, alas, that they are not often misunderstood and misinterpreted.

This imperfect terminology makes the task of defining what we are talking about all the more difficult. Even the terms improvised music and black music for jazz are inadequate, because not all jazz is improvised, and many other musics besides jazz are improvised. Not all jazz is black, either, although clearly its origin is black, its essence is black, and all of its major creative thrusts have come from black musicians.

As for the aforementioned question of myths — and for purpose of this discussion, I would like to single out only one of the many myths surrounding jazz — jazz always seems to have to measure and defend itself against the prevailing white, essentially European establishments and concepts of music. If we are going to discuss the influence of jazz on the history and development of concert music, that is, classical music, then I for one can only carry on that discussion in terms of artistic and social equality. Jazz is a music as capable of greatness as any other musical tradition. Jazz can claim its own venerable traditions and distinctive artistic accomplishments. It can even be argued that jazz and its derivatives have exerted a more powerful, penetrating, worldwide influence than any other music in human history. The fact that jazz is loved, understood, studied, and taken seriously everywhere in the world except in the land of its origin is, of course a tragic reality. This is a reality that many of us,including the National Jazz Service Organization, hope to amend.

The sad truth is that jazz is one of America's most neglected musics, particularly in its more modern and advanced manifestations. If the average American recognizes the existence of jazz at all, he is likely to think of the music called Dixieland, or even worse, such pallid commercial derivatives of jazz as the music of Lawrence Welk or Guy Lombardo. Even in more enlightened circles jazz is reluctantly accepted in patronizing condescension as mere functional music, for dancing, for example; a mere entertainment music with its creative, artistic, and aesthetic merits ignored.

I do not wish to imply that functional music is a demeaning category of music. The adjective "mere" is added by those who see jazz only as a commercial, usable, buyable, exploitable entertainment commodity. Indeed in its earlier history and development from a true black folk music through a nationally popular entertainment music to a world art music, jazz was indeed primarily a dance music and proud of it. It derived much of its strength and sustenance from being a dance music. But jazz has long ago moved beyond the realm of dance and entertainment functions, those being limitations not inherent to the deeper nature of jazz.

The patronization of jazz has its origins in its social history. For deep-rooted social, political, and economic reasons, jazz was born on the wrong side of the tracks as far as the prevailing white-dominated society was concerned. The fact that society imposed the very conditions that did not permit jazz to be born on the right side of the tracks did not occur to those who condemned jazz for what they perceived as its lowly and unacceptable origins. Ignoring the realities of poverty, illiteracy, and prejudice made it easier to denigrate and ignore the music. Alas, this vicious circle has not been entirely broken even to this day.

How all the more glorious it is that the music we call jazz has triumphed over all these trials and tribulations and vicissitudes, whether it be its humble birth, its rejection by its own homeland, or its near demise in the 1970s at the hands of rock and roll, ironically one of its own ungrateful and greedy offspring. In fact it would not be difficult for a social historian to argue that much of jazz's strength and persistence derives from its constant battle with opposition and neglect, and its constant confrontation with impossible odds. Indeed, its very birth and existence derives from its creators' deprived place in our history and society. What an irony in all this!

When the question is put as to the influence of jazz and classical music upon each other, it was often asked in the past with the automatic implication that jazz is a music that needs to justify itself and be measured *vis-à-vis* classical music. Twenty-five years ago, when controversy raged over the concept and name of Third Stream, the assumption on both sides was that the idea behind Third Stream was to bring jazz up to the level of classical music, that jazz somehow needed infusion from the classical side to be a music that could be taken seriously. I can vouch for the fact that that was not what I intended when I coined the Third Stream idea. The arguments were symptomatic of the unease that existed on both sides: that somehow each music would be contaminated by contact with the other.

The conservatives on the jazz side wanted to preserve jazz from further musical and technical advances: bebop and modern jazz, according to them, had already done enough damage along those lines. Jazz progressives, on the other hand, wanted to preserve jazz from what they called the further intellectualization and academicization of jazz, robbing it — so they alleged — of its freedom and spontaneity. The special irony in this was that many of these self-styled progressives had almost driven jazz to the brink of atrophy by their virtual elimination of improvisation.

On the other side, classical composers, critics, pundits, and purists saw the contact with jazz not so much as dangerous as irrelevant and beneath classical music's dignity. That attitude harked back to that old bromide held by many in the classical field: "Jazz is all right in its place, but what is it doing in Symphony Hall?"

The storm raised by the concept of Third Stream was but one brief cloudburst in a long, ongoing history of coexistence and cross-fertilization between jazz music and concert music. Contrary to its adversaries' claims, Third Stream was not touted as something new, nor as some panacea to contemporary music's problems, and least of all as a musical form that was going to replace both jazz and classical music. The idea embedded in the basic philosophy of Third Stream was its concept of an offspring begotten from the marriage of two equal mainstreams — and I emphasize the word equal. These two musics could also be left to continue to develop in their own organic ways without benefit of further fusion if they so chose; that is to remain discrete and distinct. Today the Third Stream is but one approach by which the two musics can find and meet each other on common ground.

The history of cross-fertilization goes back to the very beginnings of jazz. To the extent that African musical traditions were allowed to survive in America through slavery and the early decades of emancipation, and begin to merge and integrate with the European musical tradition, some rare individuals on the classical side, with their ears to the ground, began to take note of what was emerging in Black and Indian folklore. The most famous and influential of these were Antonin Dvorak and Charles Ives, Dvorak urging his American students and colleagues to use native folk or popular materials of their music; and Ives actually borrowing and incorporating the rhythms and new spirit of black ragtime in his works as early as 1901. It is interesting to envision Jelly Roll Morton listening to opera and other classical music in the French Opera House in New Orleans and to the brass and woodwind bands that played in the parks and on the riverboats in those days, and Ives, 1500 miles away, listening to ragtime orchestras in the Globe Theatre in New Haven or in other places of entertainment in New York and Danbury.

In Denver black violinist George Morrison was studying classical music, even taking lessons from the renowned Fritz Kreisler while working as a musician in Denver honky tonks; at almost the same time, one of his teachers, Wilberforce Whiteman (who also taught Andy Kirk and Mary Colston the fundamentals of music) was sympathetically listening to the emerging music of jazz, encouraging his son, Paul, to enter that field rather than play viola in the Denver Symphony.

Picture Scott Joplin composing his great classic rags, borrowing the basic ragtime form from John Philip Sousa's marches and learning proper harmony and theory from other classical sources, then Sousa returning the compliment by taking ragtime to Europe as early as 1900 and frequently defending it to its legions of detractors. Indeed it was Sousa who first brought ragtime to the attention of composers like Debussy and Satie. Following later were James Europe's recordings and performances (particularly with his Hell Fighter's Band) and Will Marion Cook's Southern Syncopated Orchestra, a group that toured Europe in 1919 and drew the first intelligent criticism of what might legitimately be called jazz from the young Swiss musician, Ernest Ansermet, a close friend of Stravinsky.

By the late teens of the century, when ragtime was just being transformed into jazz, Stravinsky had written several ragtime pieces: a short dance sequence in *Histoire du Soldat*, a piano piece, and a work called *Ragtime* for 11 instruments, featuring the unjazz-like Hungarian national instrument, the cymbalom. While Debussy's, Satie's and Ive's works easily captured the style and essential characteristics of ragtime, Stravinsky's barely did. At time Stravinsky's early jazz pieces are almost as remote from ragtime as his *Ebony Concerto* of 1943 is from jazz; but remoteness from their avowed source does not necessarily make them works of lesser creativity or of lessser skill and quality. I do not think it was a matter of incompetence in adopting the new American style, but rather one of choice. Stravinsky seems to have been unwilling to relinquish as much of himself and his then

rather acerbic, sparse musical language as were Debussy and Satie of theirs.

Indeed, more than any other, Stravinsky's jazz and ragtime works raise the question of how one should evaluate the artistic merit of such hybrid efforts. Are we to evaluate them by their stylistic authenticity to the sources they claim to have been inspired by, or are we to evaluate them on their own terms and merits as finite works, regardless of stylistic pedigrees? In other words, how important is the ragginess of Stravinsky's *Ragtime* or the jazziness of his *Ebony Concerto*? It is the same question that folklorists might have asked Mozart regarding the authenticity of the menuets in his symphonies, or of Bach's sarabandes in his suites. It is still the central question when we encounter works announcing that they are based, to some extent, on a popular or vernacular style.

Though we tend nowadays to accept the integrity and unity of Bartók's use of Hungarian and Roumanian folk material, I can well imagine that 50 years ago aficionados of Hungarian folk and dance music could relate more positively to Bartók's simpler folk-influenced works than they could, say, to his complex, harshly dissonant *Miraculous Mandarin* ballet music. Conversely, I can also imagine that in those early days certain Balkan ethnomusicological purists must have resented the intrusion of atonal and modern harmonics into the private domain of their folkloric territory. The question arises time and time again when we confront jazz-influenced classical works (as well as those on the jazz side that borrowed elements from the classical field).

With the mention of Stravinsky's works, we had arrived at a time coincident with the very beginnings of jazz. As jazz and blues, suddenly widely disseminated through recordings, spread like wildfire, composers everywhere began to be captivated by jazz and its novel sounds. Some of the more important composers who were attracted to the upstart mavericks from the wrong side of the tracks included, in this country, John Alden Carpenter, George Gershwin, Aaron Copland, and Louis Gruenberg; and in Europe, Darius Milhaud, Maurice Ravel, Arthur Honegger, Georges Auric, William Walton, Alfredo Casella, Paul Hindemith, Ernst Krenek, Kurt Weill, and Boris Blacher, to name some. Very few of them, however, captured the

true spirit of jazz, or even wanted to. There is a good reason for that; very few of them ever heard true jazz. Most of them heard the more commercial trivializations of jazz, as purveyed on popular recordings or as heard in transplanted dance orchestras — with their token "hot" musicians playing an occasional "hot" chorus — in the finer hotels of Paris, Berlin, and London. They did not hear the Hot Five recordings of Louis Armstrong, the early recordings of Ellington and Henderson, the Savoy Bearcats, or Charlie Johnson's Paradise Band.

What all of those composers, with one exception, failed to hear and see was that true jazz was an essentially improvised, spontaneously created music. For example, Aaron Copland for one, admitted years after the fact that he was exclusively interested in the jaunty, perky, syncopated rhythms of jazz; its fascinating sounds and timbres; its newfangled brass mutes; and its effects (like the trombone glissando, the growl, and so on). The fact that these rhythms and effects were the result of a confrontation between divergent cultures and musical traditions seems to have held very little interest for Copland and his contemporaries.

The one exception was Darius Milhaud, who did hear true authentic black jazz in 1922 in Harlem and in Georgia. While on a United States visit to conduct the Philadelphia Orchestra at the invitation of Leopold Stokowski, friends took him to hear "le jazz hot" in Harlem. He also brought back to France a stack of records he bought in Harlem, mostly on the Black Swan and Gennett labels (in those days called race records) of artists such as Fletcher Henderson, Ethel Waters, King Oliver, and the New Orleans Rhythm Kings. The result of his encounter with real jazz was his 1923 *Creation Du Monde* (Creation of the World), a work that, without relinquishing any aspect of Milhaud's own already well-formed bitonal and polytonal style, captures the spirit and freedom of spontaneity, and the polymetric, polyphonic essence of early jazz more than any other classical work known to me.

How close Milhaud came to capturing the spirit, sound, and excitement of early jazz can be gained by comparing certain excerpts from *The Creation of the World* (the Fugue, for example) with excerpts from the Original Dixieland Jazz Band's *Livery Stable Blues*, a 1917 recording that all European intellectuals knew by 1920 and live performances of which many had heard on the Original Dixieland Jazz Band's

1918 European tour.

My point about Milhaud's identification with black jazz is not weakened by the fact that the Original Dixieland Jazz Band was a white band. First, it was a band that seriously tried to emulate its black New Orleans counterparts. Second, the Original Dixieland Jazz Band did feature a particularly abandoned, raucous, almost uncultivated boisterousness that must have appealed to a sophisticated, rebellious Parisian like Milhaud. Third, I suspect that the Gennett and Black Swan recordings Milhaud bought were of such poor technical quality, as compared to the state-of-the-art Victor recordings, that the Original Dixieland Jazz Band's record served as a much more accessible and audible model to emulate.

By the early 1930s, the novelty of jazz had begun to wear off for European and American composers. Its attraction as a source of inspiration, even in a superficial sense, had begun to wane, especially in the face of the extraordinary advances taking place harmonically, rhythmically, structurally, technically — in short, linguistically — in contemporary music. Against Schoenberg's freely atonal works of the teens and '20s, and his 12-tone works of the late '20s; against Stravinsky's highly sophisticated neoclassicism of the '20s and '30s; against the experiments of the Antheils, the Ornsteins, the Sorabjis, the Henry Cowells; against the Young Turks in Europe like Igor Markevitch, Webern, and Berg; and against Shostakovitch and Prokofiev in Russia, jazz of the late '20s and early '30s began to seem rather primitive, limited, repetitious, and devoid of radical invention to classical composers. The last major works of the era that reflected the earlier fascination with jazz were Louis Gruenberg's *Jazz Suite for Orchestra* of 1930, Ravel's two piano concertos, and Honegger's 1930 concertos for cello and for piano.

It is amazing that all those composers did not hear or listen to Ellington's *Mood Indigo*, *Daybreak Express*, or *Creole Rhapsody*; Fletcher Henderson's *King Porter Stomp* or *Queer Notions*; Bennie Moten's *Toby* and *Prince of Wails*; Chick Webb's *Dog Bottom*; Jimmy Lunceford's *Jazznocracy*; or even the Casa Loma's *Casa Loma Stomp*. In effect, they shut off the jazz spigot and the result was a long dry spell for the compositional influence of jazz on classical music. It was a dry spell that continued well into the late 1940s.

Interestingly enough the fascination with and attraction to jazz began to be felt in an entirely different realm, that of instrumental technique, especially brass and wind. To the utter amazement of conservatory-trained classical musicians, the mostly untutored jazz musicians had, out of their own resources, energies, and instincts taken instruments such as the trumpet, the trombone, the clarinet, and especially the saxophone, and enormously expanded their technical and expressive boundaries. Louis Armstrong and Jabbo Smith, Rex Stewart, and Cootie Williams could do on their trumpets and cornets what no symphony trumpet player could even dream of doing, let alone carry out, certainly not in spontaneous improvisations. Lawrence Brown, Jimmy Harrison, "Tricky Sam" Nanton, Tommy Dorsey, and Jack Teagarden could perform on their trombones feats of dexterity and agility, endurance, and expressive versatility that no trombonist in the New York or Berlin Philharmonics could imagine, let alone duplicate. I won't mention what happened to the clarinet with Benny Goodman and Jimmy Noone; to the saxophone with Coleman Hawkins and Ben Webster; and to percussion with Chick Webb, Gene Krupa, and Sid Catlett.

In the realm of brass instrumental range, jazz musicians led the way and broke all existing boundaries. Schoenberg wrote one high E♭ for trumpet in his *Orchestra Variations* of 1928 (and he made that optional), and Stravinsky wrote one in 1913 in his *Rite of Spring* (but that was for the smaller, narrow-bored, newly invented piccolo trumpet); but when Louis Armstrong started hitting high Fs regularly in the early 1930s — one night in Paris in 1933 he played 70 successive high Cs in one song — it was hard for classical players to argue that such high notes couldn't be played on the trumpet. They could no longer ignore the reality of Armstrong's awesome achievement and justify their indolence by the fact that trumpet exercise books contained no high Fs.

The same was true for the trombone; Trummy Young's and Jack Jenney's mid-1930s high Fs, played with consummate ease and used for expressive, not pyrotechnical purposes, led eventually to the extraordinary exploits of trombonists Bill Harris, Urbie Green, Bill Watrous, Jimmy Cleveland, and Curtis Fuller.

Combine these advances with the invention and expressive use of the cup mute, the Harmon mute, the megaphone mute, and the bathroom plunger in an evolution of an entirely new sound spectrum for the saxophone by Coleman Hawkins, Lester Young, Johnny Hodges, John Coltrane, and Ornette Coleman, and you begin to gain a glimpse of similar technical and expressive extensions jazz players have brought to their instruments and to music.

Through the decades, the extraordinary advances made by jazz players have gradually trickled down to the classical field. While most classical players still cannot cope with the full extent of the jazz players' self-created demands, there is at least now a wide-eyed respect for jazz players and a dramatic expansion of the technical skills of classical wind players and percussionists. The days when Dizzy Gillespie's high-flying trumpet parts could only be played by classical *flutists* are finally gone.

Paradoxically, it was the expanded skills of American brass and woodwind players that brought composers back to jazz in the mid- and late 1940s, a development that continues to grow. Whether in some of the works of Leonard Bernstein, Gunther Schuller, William Russo, Alec Wilder, Hall Overton, Bill Smith, Andre Hodeir, David Baker, Anthony Davis, or James Newton, the integration of jazz styles and jazz techniques led eventually in recent years to a true synthesis of styles and musical concepts. Boundaries between jazz and classical music are often so blurred as to be no longer discernible. The avant-garde in both fields have met, embraced, and fructified in ways that defy labeling and categorizing, one hopes precluding the terminological confusion I spoke of earlier. The distance (in broad linguistic terms) in the pianism of a Cecil Taylor or a Ran Blake and the pianism of an Elliott Carter or a Milton Babbitt is not all that great. The recent scores of Bob Brookmeyer or Carla Bley are not all that different from countless scores of the European and American classical avant-garde. Who is to say whether the music of James Newton, Anthony Davis, Anthony Braxton, Leo Smith, and David Baker belongs in the classical or jazz field?

This brings us right back to the question raised by the early Stravinsky and Milhaud works, a question that is still with us today: By what criteria shall we evaluate such works? Is it on their intrinsic values as compositions, regardless of their stylistic persuasion? How much does the thoroughness of fusion and the quality of the elements being fused enter into an evaluation of the work under consideration?

These are difficult questions. In the arts no absolute, completely objective, finite, demonstrable judgments are possible. At best all we have is presumably enlightened, informed, well-considered opinions in which we can hope that stylistic preconceptions and prejudgments will be largely absent. Still, there are two ways to answer those questions. The first is to judge the work on its own merits, based on its own purported intentions as far as we can know them as indicated by the composer (or improvisor) or from a thorough study of the work itself. Second, and perhaps even more important, are the factors of performance quality and authenticity. This is especially true when improvisation or any specific, easily recognizable stylistic element is involved. Many times works that represent stylistic cross-breeding have been unfairly criticized for compositional and conceptual flaws when in fact it was their performances that were crucially flawed. Many a time Milhaud's *Creation du Monde* has been criticized by jazz critics because it didn't swing, because its jazz elements didn't sound spontaneous. In Milhaud's first recording of the work in the late 1920s, played by French non-jazz studio musicians, of course it didn't swing; it couldn't have. Those musicians couldn't play jazz, nor could real jazz musicians of that time have read and performed that score. Today, 60 years later, any number of musicians can render authentically all aspects of that great work, at least in the 17-piece chamber version.

Similarly, Stravinsky's *Ebony Concerto* could not be played correctly and authentically by the Woody Herman band at its premiere in 1943, and yet the work was roundly condemned by classical critics who could not recognize that the performers fell short of the task. In that instance the jazz critics also were disappointed, because they could not comprehend the non-jazz elements and character of the work. Nor could those critics hear that the musicians in Herman's band, dealing with a difficult, completely written-out score, were unable to do justice to the jazz elements it did contain.

No hybrid work should be judged until it has been performed authentically, giving the work its full due as required by the stylistic amalgams contained therein. Only then can one deal somewhat objectively with the work as a whole. The degree to which a work respects the stylistic components it proposes to merge is less important than the imagination or creativity with which those elements are fused. It is the newness, the originality that results from the fusion that counts, not mere novelty or experimentation for experimentation's sake.

It seems to me quite irrelevant whether a jazz-influenced work makes use of this or that style of jazz or this or that classical concept or technique. It does matter that what takes place is a true fusion, not some superficial overlay of one part of the amalgam on the other, a mere veneer. Some new, heretofore unattainable creative result should evolve from this marriage. That, by the way, happens also to have been the underlying concept of Third Stream as I originally envisioned it.

By such criteria, the degree to which a jazz-influenced or Third Stream work succeeds or fails is not measurable by the degree to which the composer or creators succeed to fully represent the various stylistic elements. It is rather the degree to which a work brings forth a new creative entity, never heard of before, that counts. To the extent that one element inspires, informs, and fructifies the other, it makes the work more successful artistically, regardless of its stylistic pedigree.

Seen from this viewpoint, the influence of jazz on certain composers, on certain 20th-century works, and on certain developments in contemporary music has been, on the whole, positive and benign, at the very least, instructive. A rich body of work now exists that could not have been written without the benefit of jazz, a body of work that represents one important direction the synthesis of various elements, styles, and languages has taken in our century. To me, as an American, it is one of the most fasci-

nating and relevant syntheses to occur in our time, although to a Hungarian national, Bartók's work with Hungarian folk music might seem more important and more relevant.

Such are the variations possible in our present-day musical environment, where the world's music, in all their myriad disparateness, come closer together. The results, I suppose, in some far away future time will be the ultimate grand syntheses, where all musics co-exist peacefully and even cohabit fruitfully. The entire history of music, particularly European music, is, like the genetic process itself, a prolonged history of musical intermarriage, acculturation, crossbreeding, fusing, and new symbiotic relationships, always subject to further renewal and genetic regeneration.

What we have witnessed thus far in the influence of jazz upon classical music is but a small flick on the larger screen of history, and we have just arrived at one of the many new beginnings. The energizing force of jazz has already contributed very much, but I am certain there is much more to come. ☐

Is Jazz Popular Music?

by Mark C. Gridley

Classifying types of music is always a knotty proposition, and the question of how to categorize jazz is no exception. Musicologists may accept a definition of jazz as improvised instrumental music that elicits a swing feeling, but they disagree on how to classify it. Most don't want it to be given the label of classical music, "serious" music, or art music. A few give jazz its own category, and some place it with folk music. Most toss it in with popular music. Many educators and school administrators follow suit. These attitudes have a direct bearing on how jazz is presented in school music programs, so it is important to look at how jazz and popular music compare.

Audience. By definition, the word popular means that many people like something. If selling a million copies is a relatively well-accepted indication of being popular, then jazz does not meet the standard. Fewer than a couple dozen jazz records have ever sold anywhere near a million copies, and jazz traditionally has held only about a three percent share of the record market. The term popular music can be especially misleading for distinguishing jazz from classical music, because over-the-counter sales of classical records currently outnumber jazz sales by about two to one. By those numbers, classical music is more popular than jazz. Actually, jazz and classical sales together account for less than 12 percent of record and tape sales, thereby demonstrating that neither is truly popular.

Training. Neither jazz musicians nor their fans have ever been typical of the American public. A central theme that emerges from jazz musicians' biographies is that these musicians rarely represented the social class or neighborhood norms of their childhood. Many jazz players have been members of an educated elite. Even the earliest players had formal instruction, at least in techniques of playing their instruments. Frequently they also had instruction in theory, harmony, and composition. The training was often in tutorial format rather than in a conservatory setting, but it was not the trial-and-error blundering that many historians and many current teachers believe it to be. Many of the earliest jazz musicians undertook study of Euro-

pean art music before learning jazz improvisation. Pianist James P. Johnson studied under Bruno Giannini. Clarinetist Benny Goodman studied under Franz Shoepp. Saxophonist Coleman Hawkins began on cello. Both New Orleans trumpeter Freddie Keppard and Chicago clarinetist Frank Teschemacher began on violin. Saxophonist Stan Getz played bassoon and attended the New York High School for the Performing Arts.

Besides studying privately, many famous black bandleaders of the 1930s — Fletcher Henderson, Jimmie Lunceford, Don Redman, Teddy Wilson, to name just a few — also had at least some college education. Keeping in mind how rare college attendance was at that time for anyone, we can appreciate how elite the jazz musician was. We should not forget that later jazz musicians also have had college or conservatory training. In other words, jazz musicians have not usually been average people — street musicians like blues singers and folk musicians. Formal training by a few of today's top jazz improvisers includes study at New England Conservatory (pianist Cecil Taylor), North Texas State University (bassist Marc Johnson), Indiana University (saxophonist Michael Brecker), Northwestern University (bassist Rufus Reid), and Juilliard (pianist Roland Hanna), not to mention the many who have studied at Berklee College.

A disproportionate amount of publicity has been given to famous exceptions to the rule of extensive training that jazz musicians must undergo to become competent. This has perpetuated a myth of the intuitive genius or noble savage. True, there are exceptions, trumpeter Louis Armstrong for one. But usually these exceptions are players who could read music yet somehow found themselves labeled as backward because the writers of jazz history believed they could not. The confusion may have arisen because among musicians it is often said that someone who is not a sharp sight-reader "cannot read." Though musicians know what this means, the lay person or historian often takes the expression literally. They may assume that Armstrong lacked basic technical skill and was an untutored genius. In fact, Armstrong studied under Peter Davis and David Jones, and musicians generally recognize Armstrong as being among the most technically skilled of jazz trumpet improvisers. He did understand chord progressions and he could read music, although he was not a sharp sight-reader.

Defining terms. In the 1920s the word jazz was used to denote popular music as a whole, and almost every kind of lively American music. Historian Mary Herron Dupree has pointed out Hugo Riesenfeld's observation (in his article "New Forms for Old Noises," *League of Composers Review [Modern Music]*, June 1924) that what often was called jazz in 1924 was really just "popular syncopated music." One example was the fox trot. According to this broad use of the term, even Guy Lombardo could be said to have played jazz. In fact, at the time he emigrated to the United States, that is exactly what he did consider his music to be, according to personal communication with George West, former trombonist with the Lombardo band. In the case of the Al Jolson movie about a vaudeville singer, *The Jazz Singer*, neither the original movie nor its recent remake starring Neil Diamond had anything to do with jazz.

In the August 1933 issue of *Fortune* Wilder Hobson noted that, "To some it means the whole cocktail-swilling deportment of the post-War era. To others it suggests loud and rowdy dance music. Many people go so far as to divide all music into 'jazz' and 'classical.' By 'classical,' they mean any music which sounds reasonably serious, be it 'Hearts and Flowers' or Bach's 'B-Minor Mass,' while their use of 'jazz' includes both Duke Ellington's Afric [sic] brass and Rudy Vallee crooning, 'I'm a Dreamer, Aren't We All?'...But Duke Ellington bears just about as much relation to Vallee as the 'B-Minor Mass' to 'Hearts and Flowers'...Ellington's music is jazz."

The confusion of jazz with pop that existed in Wilder Hobson's era still exists today. Recently the program director for a National Public Radio station remarked to me that the mission of his station was "to serve the unmet needs of the community's radio audience," so he was surveying his listenership regarding increasing jazz programming. Some of his classical subscribers responded, "We don't need any more jazz. We already have plenty on the other stations in town." Then the director explained to me that actually there was no jazz on any competing stations. It was all rock, but some of his classical listeners made no distinction between jazz and rock. To them the entire output of the competing stations was jazz.

The moral of the story is, don't assume that anyone understands the differences between jazz and pop. If you run into resistance establishing a jazz curriculum or in trying to obtain funding for a jazz concert series, remember that those who hold the purse strings might be withholding the money only because they are confused about what jazz is and because they see the music as so commercially successful and plentiful that it does not need their patronage. They may also see it as not warranting study because pop music by definition is not serious.

You may be able to solve this problem by playing for these people some of the most serious jazz you can lay your hands on: almost anything by Lennie Tristano, Charlie Parker (except his recordings with orchestra), or the Modern Jazz Quartet. You also need to explain jazz improvisation, and throw in a bit of history about the analogous tradition for extemporizing that exists in classical music. (Famous improvisers include Bach, Liszt, Beethoven, and Chopin.) Also point out that almost all Baroque performers were required to improvise.

Emphasize that jazz improvising is serious business that requires high-level skills as well as outstanding creativity. Explain that to improvise is to simultaneously compose and perform. After you have said all this, let it sink in for a while. I have been in your shoes many times in the past 30 years, and my experience is that such a realization is a profound idea for non-jazz people in particular, and non-musicians in general. After it sinks in, be certain to mention that improvisers have to have their wits about them at all times during every performance, or else they cannot keep track of continuously changing harmonies and the creative requirements placed upon them for continuity, originality, swing feeling, and ensemble cohesion.

Append to your discussion a disclaimer about commercial packaging for some jazz improvisation that can frequently mislead people. In pop jazz-rock and pop big band arrangements, the improvisation is often obscured by "light" music. Be prepared to draw distinctions between the output of Glenn Miller, which was glossy dance music ("sweet band" was the category musicians used for it), and that of Count Basie, which prominently displayed high-level jazz improvisation.

Better yet, play records by John Coltrane (*Giant Steps*), the Modern Jazz Quartet, and Dave Brubeck, all of whom are well-trained composer-performers. (When you play examples, use compositions by the players, not pop tunes.) Or take listeners to hear the best national act that comes to town. Be sure it is a combo and that the musicians perform in a concert hall, not a bar. Many non-jazz people will not be able to distinguish a concert jazz big band from a dance band, nor will they be able to distinguish serious music presented in a bar from pop music presented in the same setting.

Vernacular music. The labeling confusion that began in the 1920s might stem from jazz being seen as part of a larger group of styles that H. Wiley Hitchcock in his *Music in the United States* calls vernacular music: "a body of music more plebian (than that of a 'cultivated tradition'), native, not approached selfconsciously but simply grown into as one grows into one's vernacular tongue; music understood and appreciated simply for its utilitarian or entertainment value." Taking this idea one step further, vernacular music is different from Hitchcock's concept of "the cultivated tradition" (classical music) because the latter is "...to be approached with some effort, and to be appreciated for its edification, its moral, spiritual, or esthetic values."

From teaching music appreciation courses, I can vouch that jazz requires the same degree of attention that classical music requires of its listeners. And jazz brings similar esthetic and intellectual rewards to its listeners. (Watch the audience at a jazz concert, or observe jazz listeners when you have invited them to your home to listen to records.) It is not legitimate to say that jazz, like vernacular music, is usually "appreciated simply for its utilitarian...value." By Hitchcock's definition, much jazz fits the cultivated tradition, not the vernacular one.

Some of the confusion over whether jazz is popular (vernacular) music may stem from the fact that jazz sometimes serves as informal dance music as well as accompaniment for stage shows and ballets — as does classical music. Many people still think of Duke Ellington as the leader of a dance band, not a composer of serious concert works that incorporated original jazz improvisations, yet he was both. Most people probably associate Louis Armstrong more with singing "Hello, Dolly" than with developing a style of jazz trumpet improvisation that influenced generations of jazz musicians.

People who define jazz as "the music of the big band era" are likely to confuse jazz with popular music if they do not realize that most of the dance music produced during that period was just swinging band music, not improvised jazz, though many jazz musicians were employed in the big bands to play ensemble parts and occasionally were given solo spots. We can appreciate that era's distinction between jazz and pop better when we read accounts of jazz musicians' lives during that period. In these accounts a common theme is the practice of searching for after-hours clubs in which to improvise jazz after the dance jobs were over — and there was no longer any requirement for the musicians to serve as accompanists for commercial singers and stage shows.

Perhaps it would be easier to understand distinctions between art music and pop music if we considered that most jazz musicians are sufficiently versatile to perform several different types of music, some being necessary for earning a living, others for creating art. Sometimes the types overlap, but often they don't. Usually the musicians themselves draw clear distinctions between the types of music they play. For instance, Los Angeles trumpeter Conte Candoli often plays a few hours with Johnny Carson's *The Tonight Show* orchestra, which is essentially a pit band for the variety show. Then he proceeds to a much lower-paying engagement in a night club where he will be required to improvise jazz solos, knowing that this product is serious music requiring on-the-spot creativity, drawing upon all the instrumental proficiency and knowledge of compositional rules he can tap.

Here are some other examples. At one time or another during his career, jazz violinist Joe Venuti played in the string section of the Detroit Symphony Orchestra as well as in the dance band of Paul Whiteman and the jazz band of Bix Beiderbecke. Modern jazz bassists Richard Davis and Ron Carter have also derived their livelihoods from a similar distribution of affiliations. The situations of these players is typical, not unusual. The point is that an association of jazz musicians with popular music should not be used to mistake jazz itself for popular music. That makes no more sense than calling a performance by the Los Angeles Philharmonic anything less than serious music simply because members of the orchestra also earn portions of their livelihood by recording movie music in Hollywood.

Motivation. Naturally there are differences in the audiences who listen to the various types of music jazz musicians provide. One way to further distinguish jazz from popular music is to show what audience the creator of the two varieties of music has in mind. Much jazz improvisation is created primarily for the emotional and intellectual satisfaction of the player, though, so it has no intended audience, in the sense that some musicians market their product for Top 40 or easy listening categories. There is no question that most jazz artists would be pleased to learn that someone besides themselves appreciated their work. Yet most jazz players improvise to the best of their abilities, trying to be as original as they can be, and then leave it at that. For instance, when the Dave Brubeck Quartet became popular in the 1950s playing improvised jazz, the group's success was not a result of selling out; the musicians did not intentionally water down their music. They played what they liked to play, and it just happened to please many people.

While popular music is utilitarian in the sense that it is made specifically for the market rather than being almost exclusively an indulgence of the players, jazz usually exists more for the pleasure of the musicians themselves, who oftentimes are happy to have a gig that pays any amount sufficient to bring their band together. In striking contrast to pop musicians, some jazz musicians comment that audiences constitute a distraction. Among many jazz players it is considered virtuous to remain uncompromising and ignore the wishes of the audience. In fact, few jazz groups take requests. For these performers, as for players of art music down through the ages, the popularity of their music is incidental to the act of creation, not central to it.

The situation in popular music is quite different. Much of the music is tailor-made for particular audiences, and underlying the preparation of new works are extensive studies of what sells. In fact, soon after any "new sound" captures public attention, hundreds of imitations are rushed to the marketplace. For much of popular music, then, the motivation lies outside the creator, because the reason for creating is to reach the audience, not simply to please himself. In the book *Yesterdays: Popular Song in America*, Charles Hamm states that one criterion for defining the term popular song is that it is "composed and marketed with the goal of financial gain."

A fair number of the Las Vegas, Hollywood, and Motown stars with whom I have performed place great stock in crowd reaction. Frequently they measure their success not by their own assessments of the artistic creativity of their performances but rather by the intensity of applause and the record sales. (We must remember that the creativity in floor shows by pop acts is tapped primarily when the show is being conceived and rehearsed, whereas little occurs in the countless performances of set routines. For the most part, pop music is packaged and reproduced, whereas jazz is created on the spot, fresh for each performance.) All of the above is not to say that jazz musicians all play exactly the way they wish all the time, only that the compromises they make do not come close to those made by creators of popular music, for whom marketing is the chief impetus.

Market segmentation. Jazz critic Martin Williams has said that jazz competes with popular music for the same audience. He is correct as far as nightclubs, bars, and discotheques are concerned; jazz performers often lose out to pop performers when competing for these gigs. Yet there is another side to the issue. Popular music radio stations rarely program any jazz, but National Public Radio affiliates frequently program it, along with other non-popular styles such as folk and classical music and foreign language music that attract a small audience. Furthermore, a 1985 Arbitron survey of 3,000 people who listen to jazz on an N.P.R. affiliate showed that 77 percent of them also tuned into broadcasts of classical music; and a National Jazz Service Organization report published in September 1986 showed that of people who attended jazz performances, 34 percent also attend classical or chamber music performances and 41 percent also attend operas. In other words, in some ways, jazz competes with classical music — not popular.

References and Suggested Reading

The NPR Audience 1981, David Giovannoni, Effie Metropoulos, Evelyn Jones, National Public Radio, 2025 M Street N.W., Washington, D.C., 1982

Jazz Styles: History and Analysis, 2nd edition, Mark C. Gridley, Prentice-Hall, 1985.

"Why Have Bop Combos Been Less Popular Than Swing Big Bands?" Gridley, in *Popular Music and Society*, Vol. 9, No. 4, pages 41-46, 1984.

"How Do Cognitive Processes Differ by Level of Jazz Fanaticism?" Gridley, in Melanie Wallendorf and Paul Anderson (Eds.) *Advances in Consumer Research*, Vol. 14, Association for Consumer Research, Brigham Young University, Provo, Utah, 1987.

Yesterdays: Popular Song in America, Charles Hamm, W.W. Norton, 1979.

Music in the U.S.: An Historical Introduction, 2nd edition, H. Wiley Hitchcock, Prentice-Hall, 1974.

"Patterns of Relationships Among Esthetic Preferences and General Customer Characteristics: An Application of Multidimensionally Scaled Correlations to Mapping the Market for Music," Morris B. Holbrook and Douglas V. Holloway, Columbia University School of Business, working paper, November 10, 1978.

"Marketing Strategy and the Structure of Aggregate Segment-Specific, and Differential Preferences," Holbrook and Holloway, *Journal of Marketing*, Vol. 48, pages 62-67, 1984.

The American Jazz Music Audience, Harold Horowitz, National Jazz Service Organization, 1201 Pennsylvania Avenue N.W., Suite 720, Washington, D.C.

Listen, 3rd edition, Joseph Kerman, pages 485-6, Worth Publishers, New York, 1980.

Inside the Recording Industry: A Statistical Review, pages 1-25, Recording Industry Association of America, 888 Seventh Avenue, 9th floor, New York, New York, 1985.

Pop Memories 1890-1954: The History of American Popular Music, Joel Whitburn, Record Research Inc., P.O. Box 200, Menomonee Falls, Wisconsin, 1986.

Top Pop Albums 1955-85, Whitburn, see above publisher.

Studies by Morris B. Holbrook showed that jazz fans who view jazz as serious music tend also to listen to classical music. Those who view jazz as party music and dance music often also listen to pop. Furthermore, the particular jazz artists liked by those two different slices of the jazz audience differ: the jazz fans who did not view jazz as seriously listed favorites such as Chuck Mangione and Bob James, whereas the other slice of fans listed Thelonious Monk and John Coltrane as favorites. What this data shows is the same pattern that H. Wiley Hitchcock isolated in his distinction between vernacular and cultivated traditions. Those who like pop music and view jazz as utilitarian tend to like pop jazz. Those who like classical music and feel jazz serves esthetic, intellectual functions tend to like serious jazz.

Only after extensive market surveys will we know how many jazz fans listen more to rock than to classical music. It may be inaccurate, though, to classify jazz with popular music on the assumption that jazz draws its listeners from popular music's audience. If we classify jazz according to where it draws its listeners (as far as we can tell from the information now available) jazz lies closer to art music.

Conclusion. Now we can answer a number of questions concerning the status of jazz. Does jazz qualify as popular music if popular means that something is liked by a relatively large portion of the population? No, because most people do not like jazz. It also does not qualify as popular music, if you define popular as meaning "of the common people," because most jazz musicians are not ordinary people. They reflect a specially trained elite. Because the term "jazz" was once

applied so loosely that it denoted popular music in general, confusion continues today, even now that the term has a much narrower meaning.

Is some jazz popular music in the sense that it is vernacular music because it is approached unselfconsciously and is utilitarian in the sense that it has been used as dance music, film music, and party music? Yes, but much jazz fits none of these qualifications and better fits the "cultivated tradition" label because it is appreciated primarily for its esthetic and intellectual rewards, and is approached with some effort. Can we call jazz popular music because it competes with rock for its audience? Yes, in some cases, but no in others, because most jazz listeners divide their listening time more with classical music than with popular music.

To answer the question of whether jazz is popular music, we can simply say that much jazz fails to qualify as popular music by any definition. It lies within the cultivated tradition and warrants the label of art music. Even if new research were to show that a significant slice of jazz really is pop music used for utilitarian purposes and does compete with other pop music, it would be wrong to let this undermine our efforts to have more intellectual jazz taken seriously and taught in our schools as art music. After all, these discussions and definitions are only a means to bring about the most important end: teaching and playing the music itself.

Mark C. Gridley is a free-lance jazz flutist/saxophonist and educator. He has written a widely used introduction to jazz for high school and college students, Jazz Styles: History and Analysis (*Prentice-Hall, 1985*), *reviewed in the August 1986 issue of* The Instrumentalist.

December, 1977

Sousa Marches: The Arranged Versions

Ron Cowherd

As part of a study to gain a better understanding of arranging techniques used in school band music, I examined a representative sample of the 47 original Sousa marches available in published form, as well as the 74 arrangements and editions of the originals. The following originals and arrangements were used in the study.

Basic elements were examined, including melody, countermelody, rhythm, harmony, form, key, range, instrumentation, accompaniment, percussion, and interpretation.

Ron Cowherd has taught instrumental music for 11 years and is presently teaching in the Ballard County (Kentucky) schools. He holds degrees from Murray State University and from Indiana University.

Of the five arrangers involved, three (Yoder, Lang and Buchtel) did not alter the Sousa melodies, but all of the arrangers tended to spread their instruments equally among the different functions while Sousa scored particularly heavily on melody and countermelody, lighter on harmony and accompaniment. The most frequent alteration found in the melodic line was due to the simplification of the rhythm (see example 1-5). In one instance a slight modification of the melodic line occurred, changing an arpeggio into a diatonic figure, and reducing the melodic range span from a tenth to a fifth (see example 6). One alteration of melody was possibly unintentional: a flat was deleted from the melodic line which in turn modified the harmonic structure (see example 7).

Composition Composer-Arranger	Publisher	Date
The Stars and Stripes Forever		
John Philip Sousa	John Church	1897
Sousa-H.L. Walters	Rubank	1953
Sousa-Paul Yoder	C. Fischer	1953
Sousa-F.L. Buchtel	Kjos	1953
Semper Fidelis		
John Philip Sousa	C. Fischer	1888
Sousa-Paul Yoder	C. Fischer	1945
Sousa-Philip Lang	Mills	1946
Sousa-J.A. Scott	Rubank	1948
Washington Post		
John Philip Sousa	C. Fischer	1889
Sousa-Philip Lang	Mills	1945
Sousa-Paul Yoder	C. Fischer	1946
High School Cadets		
John Philip Sousa	C. Fischer	1890
Sousa-F.L. Buchtel	Kjos	1948
Sousa-J.A. Scott	Rubank	1948

Arrangers altered countermelody, using three different approaches: deletion, modification, and addition. In five arrangements (Walters, Buchtel and Scott) only the original Sousa cornet parts were used, thus eliminating the trumpet flourishes of the original version. This loss is seen in example 8. Countermelodies of the arranged versions were often modified, but not so much for the purpose of simplification. Eight instances of modification were found involving a total of 127 measures of the arranged versions (see example 9-16).

Alterations of Melody

Example 1 *The Stars and Stripes Forever*
Sousa original

Walters arrangement (measure 7)

Example 2 *The Stars and Stripes Forever*
Sousa original

Walters arrangement (measure 11)

Example 3 *The Stars and Stripes Forever*
Sousa original

Walters arrangement (measures 13-)

Example 4 *The Stars and Stripes Forever*
Sousa original

Walters arrangement (measures 70-)

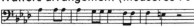

Example 5 *Semper Fidelis*
Sousa original

Scott arrangement (measure 1)

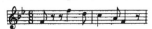

Example 6 *The Stars and Stripes Forever*
Sousa original

Walters arrangement (measures 79-)

Example 7 *High School Cadets*
Sousa original

Scott arrangement (measure 30)

Example 8 *Semper Fidelis*
Sousa original (measures 83-)

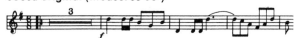

Example 9 *The Stars and Stripes Forever*
Sousa original

Yoder arrangement (measures 15-)

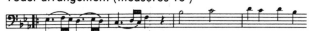

Example 10 *Semper Fidelis*
Sousa original

Yoder arrangement (measures 9-)

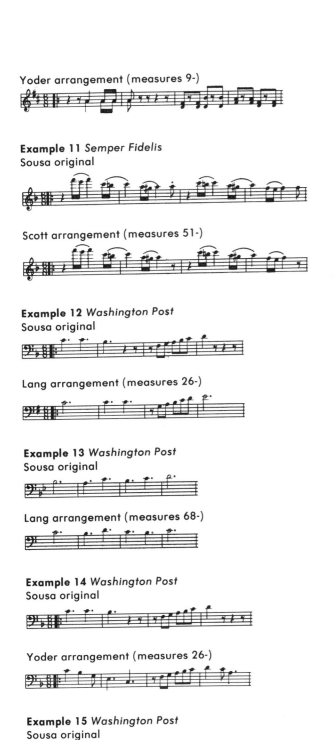

Example 11 *Semper Fidelis*
Sousa original

Scott arrangement (measures 51-)

Example 12 *Washington Post*
Sousa original

Lang arrangement (measures 26-)

Example 13 *Washington Post*
Sousa original

Lang arrangement (measures 68-)

Example 14 *Washington Post*
Sousa original

Yoder arrangement (measures 26-)

Example 15 *Washington Post*
Sousa original

Yoder arrangement (measures 69-)

Example 16 *High School Cadets*
Sousa original

Scott arrangement (measures 68-)

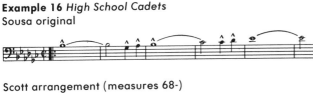

Additions of Countermelody

Example 17 *The Stars and Stripes Forever*
Walters arrangement (measures 5-)

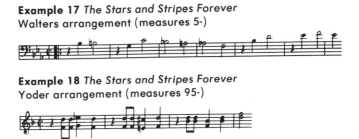

Example 18 *The Stars and Stripes Forever*
Yoder arrangement (measures 95-)

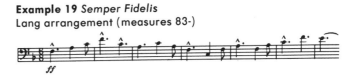

Example 19 *Semper Fidelis*
Lang arrangement (measures 83-)

Example 20 *Semper Fidelis*
Scott arrangement (measures 9-)

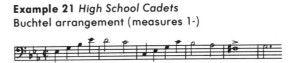

Example 21 *High School Cadets*
Buchtel arrangement (measures 1-)

By far the most frequent alteration was the addition of newly created material, 17 instances involving a total of 254 measures. Sousa did not include a countermelody in every strain, but the arrangers were more apt to do so. Countermelody added by arrangers is shown in examples 17-21. Other additions have been made as follows:

> *The Stars and Stripes Forever*
> Walters, measures 22-38
> Yoder, measures 39-70
> *Semper Fidelis*
> Yoder, measures 9-21
> Yoder, measures 26-42
> Lang, measures 9-21
> Scott, measures 26-42
> *Washington Post*
> Lang, measures 44-50
> *High School Cadets*
> Buchtel, measures 9-33
> Buchtel, measures 34-50
> Buchtel, measures 51-65
> Scott, measures 9-33
> Scott, measures 34-50

Only one instance was found in which the form of the original Sousa march has been altered. Harold L. Walters in his arrangement of *The Stars and Stripes Forever* chose to delete measures 78-85 (eight measures of the interlude) of the original composition. The only apparent explanation for this alteration is perhaps a desire for brevity.

Four instances of key alteration were found in the

arranged versions. In one case (*Semper Fidelis*, Scott), only the key of the march section is altered, thus creating a modulation to the dominant key in the trio rather than to the subdominant as is customary. The Scott version of *High School Cadets* is lowered a minor third, apparently to ease upper range requirements. Other key changes are designed to simplify the key signature.

In practically all cases, the Sousa version requires the widest tessitura. Out of 86 examples, only 8 instances were found in which the tessitura was wider in the arranged versions, 5 above and 8 below. The most extensive deviation occurred in woodwind parts (bassoon, alto clarinet, flute, E♭ clarinet, and B♭ clarinet).

The original Sousa sets include parts for English horn and bass saxophone. These are deleted in the arrangements. Walters, Buchtel, and Scott also chose not to include trumpet parts. Other instruments not frequently used by the arrangers in these four marches but included in the Sousa editions are 2nd flute, 2nd oboe, bass saxophone, and string bass. Yoder added a BB♭ contrabass clarinet part to *Semper Fidelis* and *Washington Post*.

The rhythmic structure of the accompaniment elements in the arrangements was greatly modified from the Sousa originals. The arrangers used Sousa's rhythm patterns in 558 measures, with their own patterns appearing in 270 measures. In both original and arranged versions the French horn section carries the major responsibility for the accompaniment harmony while the tuba and the string bass supply the bass line. However, Sousa employs cornets and bassoons for additional accompaniment support while the arrangers generally rely on the saxophone and trombone sections for this purpose.

Percussion modifications are generally for simplification. Basic unembellished rhythmic patterns are used in the percussion parts of Buchtel and Walters, with a lesser degree of simplification evident among the remaining arrangers, although there is a tendency to minimize the use of the roll and flam.

Interpretation

The original published versions of Sousa marches are probably not entirely accurate as to interpretation. Former Sousa musicians recall that when a newly composed manuscript was submitted to the publisher, "nothing but the notes reached the printed page."[1] August Helmeke, drummer for 22 years under Sousa, has explained that Sousa "refrained from writing in accents because he didn't want any other band to play his marches the way he did."[2] Nevertheless, the four published original Sousa versions investigated in this study do contain performance instructions, the authenticity of which we may assume is doubtful. Therefore, no direct comparison was made with the arranged versions. However, the following observations may be helpful.

1. Dynamic indications vary very little between the original and arranged versions; however, crescendo and decrescendo markings are absent in some editions.

2. There is a general lack of discipline in regard to sforzando piano (*sfp*) indications. Accents are frequently used in their place.

3. Articulations are often omitted.

4. There is a greater tendency to delete interpretive markings than to add them. Without a doubt, the Sousa revival during the 1950s has greatly influenced the consciences of band directors and arrangers alike concerning the proper interpretation of Sousa marches. Arrangements written after 1950 often include interpretive markings reflecting the suggestions of former Sousa bandsmen. The roster of these players, although shrinking, could still provide an authoritative source for a careful researcher.

Conclusions

The arrangers represented in this study have taken the original Sousa melody, countermelody, harmony, instrumentation, and form as a point of departure for the production of a playable piece of music for amateur musicians. Upon this foundation they have built their own structure, slightly less demanding than the original Sousa version, but generally complying with the intentions of the composer. The most extensive alterations for purposes of simplification have taken place in the instrumental ranges, key signatures, accompaniment rhythms and percussion parts. We may assume that these elements are of primary consideration to the arranger who is writing for the school band. The most significant and possibly unjustified alteration has been the addition of newly composed material as counterpoint where Sousa used none. It is my opinion that the few modifications of melody and the various insertions of additional countermelody are questionable, and neither serve the original intentions of Sousa nor contribute to the playability of the arrangement.

For those conductors who wish to play Sousa marches I recommend the revised editions of the original published versions. They are by far the most authentic.

The following books and magazine articles can provide additional information, including a discussion of proper interpretation.

Band Music Guide. The Instrumentalist Co., Evanston, Ill., 1975, 361 pp.

Dvorak, Raymond Francis, *The Band on Parade*, Carl Fischer, New York, 1937, 115 pp.

Evenson, E. Orville, "The March Style of Sousa," *The Instrumentalist*, November 1954, p. 48.

Goldman, Richard Franko, *The Concert Band*, Rinehart & Company, Inc., New York, 1946, 245 pp.

Goldman, Richard Franko, *The Wind Band*, Allyn and Bacon, Inc., Boston, 1961, 286 pp.

Harlow, Lewis A., "The Stars and Stripes Forever," *The Instrumentalist*, December 1964, p. 53.

Helmecke, August, "Why the Accents Weren't Written in . . .", *The Instrumentalist*, March-April 1951, p. 15.

Reynolds, George E., "Sousa", *The Instrumentalist*, March-April 1951, p. 12.

Sousa, John Philip, *Marching Along*, Hale, Cushman and Flint, Boston, 1928. ∎

1. G.E. Reynolds. "Sousa". *The Instrumentalist*. March-April 1951, p. 12.

2. A. Helmecke. "Why the Accents Weren't Written in . . ." *The Instrumentalist*. March-April 1951, p. 15.

Sousa Works in Print

To help you locate works by John Philip Sousa currently available and in print, we have compiled a list based on information given us by publishers. The works were neither examined nor graded by us. The list includes the following information: title, publisher, and price; the editor/arranger and type of ensemble — marching band, concert band, or orchestra — are listed when known.

Across the Danube March - Kalmus (mb, $7.50)

Ancient and Honorable Artillery Company March - Kalmus (mb, $7.50)

Atlantic City Pageant March - Kalmus (mb, $7.50)

Beau Ideal March - Alfred (Gore, cb, $30); Carl Fischer (mb, $15); Kalmus (orch, $12; mb, $6)

Belle of Chicago March - Alfred (Gore, cb, $30); Boosey & Hawkes (mb, $18); Carl Fischer (mb, $10); Kalmus (orch, $12; mb, $7); Shawnee (Gray, low brass quartet, $6)

Ben Bolt March - Kalmus (mb, $7)

Black Horse Troop March - Sam Fox (Fennell, cb, $25); Kalmus (mb, $7.50)

Bonnie Annie Laurie March - Kalmus (mb, $6)

Bride Elect March - Kalmus (orch, $10; mb, $7); Presser (mb, $7.50)

Bride Elect Selections - Kalmus (cb, $27)

Chantyman's March - Kalmus (mb, $7)

Charlatan March - Kalmus (orch, $10; mb, $7)

Charlatan Waltzes - Kalmus (cb, $27)

Colonial Dames Waltzes - Kalmus (cb, $10)

Comrades of the Legion March - Kalmus (mb, $7.50)

Coquette (Characteristic Dance) - Kalmus (cb, $17.50)

Corcoran Cadets March - Carl Fischer (mb, $15); Kalmus (mb, $7)

Crusader March - Carl Fischer (mb, $15); Kalmus (orch, $10; mb, $6)

Diplomat March - Kalmus (orch, $10; mb, $6)

Directorate March - Kalmus (orch, $12; mb, $7); Presser (mb, $7.50)

El Capitan March - Barnhouse (Contorno, cb, $20); Belwin (Gore, cb, $35); Boosey & Hawkes (mb, $24); Hindsley (cb, $13); Kalmus (orch, $10; mb, $6); Musicians Publications (Holcombe, cb, $25); Presser (Helmecke, mb, $10); Rubank (Walters, $10)

El Capitan Waltzes - Kalmus (cb, $27)

Fairest of the Fair March - Kalmus (mb, $7.50); Musicians Publications (Holcombe, cb, $25); Presser (mb, $10; Fennell, cb, $20)

Free Lance March - Jenson (Revelli, cb, $40); Kalmus (orch, $10; mb, $6); Presser (Goldman, mb, $18)

Funeral March - The Honored Dead - Kalmus (mb, $8)

Gallant Seventh March - Sam Fox (Fennell, cb, $25); Kalmus (mb, $7.50)

Gladiator March - Carl Fischer (mb, $10); Kalmus (orch, $12; mb, $7); Musicians Publications (Holcombe, cb, $25)

Globe and Eagle March - Kalmus (mb, $7.50)

Glory of the Yankee Navy - Kalmus (mb, $7); Presser (Fennell, cb, $27.50)

Guide Right March - Carl Fischer (mb, $15); Kalmus (mb, $6)

Hail to the Spirit of Liberty March - Kalmus (orch, $10; mb, $7)

Hands Across the Sea March - Barnhouse (cb, $15); Kalmus (orch, $10; mb, $6); Presser (mb, $10; Fennell, cb, $27.50)

High School Cadets March - Barnhouse (cb, $14); Belwin (Gore, cb, $30); Carl Fischer (Yoder, mb, $10); Jenson (Norred, mb, $20); Kalmus (orch, $15; mb, $6); Rubank (Scott, $10); Wynn ($12)

Imperial Edward March - Kalmus (Salabert, orch, $11; mb, $8)

International Congress - Kalmus (cb, $60)

Invincible Eagle March - Kalmus (orch, $8; mb, $6); Presser (mb, $10)

Jack Tar March - Kalmus (orch, $10; mb, $10)

King Cotton March - Belwin (Gore, $30); Boosey & Hawkes (mb, $26); Carl Fischer (Yoder, mb, $10); Hindsley (cb, $13.50); Kalmus, (orch, $15; mb, $6); Musicians Publications (Holcombe, cb, $25); Presser (mb, $7.50; Fennell, cb, $27.50); Rubank (Walters, $10); Wynn (mb, $8)

La Reine de la Mer Waltzes - Kalmus (cb, $28)

Liberty Bell March - Boosey & Hawkes (Winter, mb, $20); Carl Fischer (Yoder, mb, $10); Jenson (Revelli, cb, $40; Osterling, cb, $20); Kalmus (Winter, orch, $18; mb, $6); Hal Leonard (Brion, cb, $45); Musicians Publications (Holcombe, cb, $25); Presser (cb, $10); Rubank (Walters, $10)

Looking Upward Suite - Kalmus ("By the Light of the Polar Star" - cb, $30; "Beneath the Southern Cross" - cb, $30; "Mars and Venus" - cb, $32.50)

Loyal Legion March - Kalmus (mb, $8)

Man Behind the Gun March - Kalmus (orch, $10; mb, $7)

Manhattan Beach March - Barnhouse (Contorno, cb, $18); Carl Fischer (Yoder, mb, $10); Hindsley (cb, $18); Kalmus (orch, $12; mb, $7); Musicians Publications (Holcombe, cb, $25); Presser (mb, $10; Fennell, cb, $27.50); Rubank (Walters, $10)

Mikado March - Kalmus (mb, $7)

Minnesota March - Sam Fox (Fennell, cb, $25)

Mother Goose March - Kalmus (mb, $7.50)

Mother Hubbard March - Kalmus (mb, $7.50)

National Fencibles March - Carl Fischer (mb, $15); Kalmus (orch, $12; mb, $7)

National Game March - Kalmus (mb, $7.50)

New Mexico March - Sam Fox (Fennell, cb, $25)

Nobles of the Mystic Shrine March - Sam Fox (Fennell, cb, $25; mb, $15)

Occidental March - Carl Fischer (mb, $15); Kalmus (mb, $6)

On Parade March (The Lion Tamer) - Alfred (Gore, cb, $30); Kalmus (orch, $12; mb, $7)

On the Tramp March - Bourne (Gore, cb, $25.50); Carl Fischer (Lake, mb, $15); Kalmus (Lake, mb, $7)

Our Flirtation March - Carl Fischer (mb, $15); Kalmus (orch, $12; mb, $6)

Pathfinder of Panama March - Presser (Dvorak, mb, $7.50)

Picadore March - Kalmus (orch, $12; mb, $7)

Powhatan's Daughter March - Kalmus (orch, $12)

Presidential Polonaise - Kalmus (orch, $12; cb, $20)

Pride of the Wolverines March - Sam Fox (Fennell, cb, $25; mb, $15)

Revival March - Kalmus (mb, $7)

Riders for the Flag March - Sam Fox (Fennell, cb, $25)

Rifle Regiment March - Barnhouse (Contorno, cb, $23); Carl Fischer (mb, $10); Kalmus (mb, $6)

Right-Forward March - Kalmus (mb, $7)

Right-Left March - Kalmus (mb, $7)

Royal Welch Fusiliers March - Presser (mb, $7.50)

Sabre and Spurs March - Sam Fox (Fennell, cb, $25)

Semper Fidelis March - Belwin (Gore, cb, $35); Boosey & Hawkes (mb, $26); Carl Fischer (Yoder, mb, $10); Hindsley (cb, $13); Jenson Osterling, cb, $20); Kalmus (orch, $12, mb, $6); Musicians Publications (Holcombe, cb, $25); Rubank (Scott, $10; Walters, for Dixieland band, $10)

Sesqui-Centennial Exposition March - Kalmus (mb, $7.50)

Sound Off March - Carl Fischer (mb, $10); Kalmus (orch, $12; mb, $6)

Star Spangled Banner (Sousa arrangement) - G. Schirmer (Damrosch, cb, $18)

Stars and Stripes Forever March - Belwin (Gore, cb, $35); Boosey & Hawkes (mb, $18); Carl Fischer (Yoder, mb, $10); Hindsley (cb, $18); Jenson (Balent, mb, $20; Higgins, mb, $30; Bocook, mb, $30); Kalmus (orch, $9; mb, $7.50); Hal Leonard (Brion, cb, $45); Musicians Publications (Holcombe, cb, $25); Presser (mb, $10); Rubank (Walters, $10); Shawnee (Hartzell, cb, $20)

Tally-Ho Overture - Kalmus (Claus, cb, $28)

Three Quotations Suite - Kalmus ("The King of France" - orch, $8; cb, $25; "I, Too, Was Born in Arcadia" - orch, $8; cb, $12; "In Darkest Africa" orch, $8; cb, $10)

Thunderer March - Barnhouse (cb, $14); Boosey & Hawkes ($18); Carl Fischer (Yoder, mb, $10); Jenson (Norred, mb, $20; Jurrens, cb, $40); Kalmus (orch, $12; mb, $6); Musicians Publications (Holcombe/Rothrock, $25); Rubank (Scott, $10)

Transit of Venus March - Kalmus (mb, $7.50)

U.S. Field Artillery March - Carl Fischer (Akers, mb, $10; Lake, mb, $10)

University of Nebraska March - Kalmus (mb, $7.50)

George Washington Bicentennial March - Sam Fox (Fennell, cb, $25)

Washington Post March - Boosey & Hawkes (Winter, $18); Carl Fischer (Fennell, cb, $35; Yoder, mb, $10); Jenson (Osterling, cb, $20); Kalmus (orch, $10; mb, $6); Musicians Publications (Holcombe, cb, $25); Rubank (Scott, $10); Wynn ($12)

White Rose March - Jenson (Gore, cb, $40)

Wings of Victory March - Sam Fox (Fennell, cb, $25)

Wolverine March - Kalmus (mb, $7)

Yorktown's Centennial March (Sen-Sen) - Kalmus (mb, $8); Southern Music (Jurrens, cb, $35)

Collections and arrangements containing Sousa's works:

March King, arr. Lee. Wynn Music, $12. Contains "King Cotton," "Semper Fidelis," "Liberty Bell."

Sousa! arr. Barker. Jenson, $55. Concert band.

Sousa! arr. Higgins. Jenson, $40. Marching band.

A Sousa Celebration, Middendorf/Martino. Bourne, $44. Concert band. Original melodies following Sousa's ideas without using his exact notes.

Sousa Medley. Wynn, $12. Contains "El Capitan," "Thunderer," "Stars and Stripes."

Sousa on Parade. Palmer/Wright. Paxton/Novello (Presser). Arrangement for British brass band.

Sousa the March King, arr. Tatgenhorst. Presser, $7.50.

Sousa's Famous Marches, arr. Laudenslager. Presser, $3.95 conductor, $1.50 parts. Folio containing 12 marches.

Sousa's Favorite March Book. Carl Fischer, $7.50 conductor, $1.95 parts. Folios.

Sousa's/Yoder March Book. Carl Fischer, $6 conductor, $1.95 parts. Folios. ∎

Interviews/Profiles

∽∽∽∽∽

Revelli
The Most Determined Director

An Interview with William D. Revelli

by Harvey Phillips

Most directors know the story of William D. Revelli, from his starting a band from scratch in a small Indiana town and establishing an outstanding high school program, then bringing to a major university his personal standards of excellence and professionalism. Before his arrival there, students smoked in rehearsals and the band's music library consisted of *The Victors*, *The Yellow and Blue*, and little else. Revelli stayed at the university until his retirement, and today is regarded as the dean of American band directors.

There is more to the story, though. Revelli worked rigorously to achieve excellence: he taught solfege to junior high students and required them to sing every note of their band music; he took 10 years of lessons with Chicago Symphony members just so he could demonstrate good tone to his pupils. This is the other side of his story.

What were your primary musical influences and what opportunities were available to you?

My first musical influence was my dad who developed a great love for opera growing up in Milan. He regularly attended La Scala and as an adult owned the old Victor recordings which had terrible fidelity but contained the voices of Caruso and greats of the time. My mother loved music, too.

While growing up I became infatuated with music because of Dad's influence. He was in the theater business, and gave me a violin for Christmas and signed me up with an itinerant teacher who came once a week to our little town of Panama, Illinois. The teacher was a delightful man; I owe a lot to him because he motivated me, but his influence in developing my musicianship was nil. He couldn't play any instrument. After four lessons with him Dad sent me to St. Louis to study with Dominic Sarli, who was a violinist in the St. Louis Symphony Orchestra. Because he could only teach me on Sunday mornings, I got up at 4:15 a.m. and caught the 5:15 train to St. Louis, and returned at 10:30 p.m. That was the beginning of my musical career.

Sarli was a wonderful man and a fine teacher who motivated me and did a good job teaching fundamentals. He recommended that I go to Chicago Musical College to study with Leon Sametini, who had a worldwide reputation as a concert violinist and teacher. Upon finishing high school I went to Chicago Musical College and graduated from there; after which I played professionally in Chicago movie theaters. At that time orchestras accompanied silent movies in the larger theaters, but when movies with sound made their debut, theater musicians lost their jobs. To earn a living I gave private lessons and soon discovered that teaching was my greatest love. I finished a music education degree at Columbia School of Music in Chicago because a performance degree did not permit me to teach in public schools; in one year I completed the entire course and received my music education degree. I applied for several jobs but didn't get any.

Finally a job in Hobart, Indiana opened up, but I had never been in Hobart, and didn't know anything about it. That job was a Godsend to me; I look back now and feel the good Lord was looking down on me. I have had only two positions in my lifetime: one was Hobart, the other was the University of Michigan. In both places I started from scratch. Hobart had only three music students in the whole school system: Eba Sandstrum played the violin and studied in Chicago; Nick Cavarillo, a clarinetist; and Margery Lutz the pianist for the choir. Those were the only students in that school system who played an instrument, and I was supervisor of music, or what we would today call a coordinator of public school music. I never knew what the title meant because I never had anyone to supervise, only myself.

After three weeks of school, I had the itch to start an instrumental program. I was the music man of the community; because there were no instrumental groups, my day was spent teaching music to kids from the kindergarten on up. I took my violin to class and played while they sang. I taught grade school music, junior high chorus, high school chorus, mixed chorus, madrigal club, the whole works from 8 a.m. until 4 p.m. After four or five weeks of this I asked Guy Dickey, superintendent of schools, for permission to organize an instrumental program in the Hobart schools. He thought it would be wonderful if I had four or five students to play at the basketball games; that was his concept of music education. He was a wonderful man, just was not aware of what a music education program could be. He supported my efforts and gave me permission to start but informed me that there was no place to rehearse, no time to rehearse, and no budget; but I had what I asked

for, permission to start an instrumental program. There were fewer than a hundred students in the high school, so I recruited from the junior high and began instrumental classes starting in fourth grade. My band met at 7:00 a.m. in the chemistry room, where we moved equipment out and put down music stands and chairs; each student had a responsibility. After four weeks we could do that in a minute, wasting less time than programs with all the facilities.

We had no budget, so instruments came out of attics, some having been there since the Civil War. I started instrumental classes in fourth grade, but only on clarinet, cornet, violin, and piano. The band consisted of junior high and senior high students, and because we met at 7:00 we had no conflict with other classes. There were 22 people at the first rehearsal and we had a good balance, with all instruments represented except the double reeds.

How did you establish a balanced band?

I consulted privately with parents before their child entered the program. I had physical and musical tests, which I still believe in, but I chose the instrument for the child. If the father had played trombone and his son could adapt to the instrument in the attic, that's the way it came out. This was the beginning of the Hobart School instrumental program and the first band mother's club in the United States. I don't think there were any band parent's clubs before that.

It must have taken the complete support of the school, parents, and students to get such a program underway.

The administration was wonderful. There were no scheduling conflicts because the band practiced before school began, so there was no reason for academic teachers to be concerned. Guy Dickey supported me all the way through, and the principal of the junior high was equally interested; parents were marvelous and the kids were super. It was not as difficult as it might seem.

When did you present your first concert?

We started rehearsals in the latter week of September, and our first public appearance was not in concert, but at a basketball game. We weren't ready to play anything; I had to mark fingerings above the notes because many students had not yet learned to read notes without fingerings. We played *Military Escort* until it was coming out of our ears. We played the introduction, the first strain and put a tonic chord on the end of it and repeated it three times; that was our first piece. We then played

Harvey Phillips is Executive editor of The Instrumentalist *and Distinguished Professor of Music at Indiana University.*

the introduction, the first strain, then the second strain and put a tonic on that. That was our second piece. Next we played the introduction, first and second strain and the trio. That was our third piece. Then we'd play the breakup strain and go back. We had a whole repertoire in the same piece and played it about nine times.

The gym was the only place we could give a concert, but the basketball coach thought that people walking on the gym floor might ruin it. We had bleachers, but you wouldn't want to play a concert that way, so the band mothers gave a couple of chicken dinners and had enough money to buy a tarp to protect the gym floor. Later they put up a stage. I can't think of anyone who began an instrumental program with as many obstacles: we had no place to rehearse, no program, no budget, no place to give concerts, and no tradition, although there are some traditions that I wouldn't want to inherit. Nevertheless, this was the beginning of the Hobart Band, and most people don't realize that we also had a good orchestra and a choir that won first-place in the district festival. The program was not just band, although you must remember that in those days there were no national orchestra contests.

Hobart is now famous among music educators and band directors for the music education program you established there, but when did you feel the program had substance?

From the beginning I was happy with the tremendous enthusiasm of the students and support of the faculty, administration, and parents. In my 10 years there only three students dropped out of band. That is hard to believe today.

I can't tell you how many times I visited a student's home to motivate a child and revive waning interest. I made telephone calls, wrote letters to parents; I did not just open the rehearsal room and have a rehearsal. It was a day and night job with sectional rehearsals after school and individual lessons at night. Anyone in Hobart could tell you that the daily schedule of Revelli was 7 to 11. We had musical clubs, recitals, Sunday afternoon vesper concerts, and I was enthusiastic and loved every moment from the day I started.

The real evidence of what we were doing from a musical standpoint came in 1929, when we won the first state contest in Bloomington. In those days there was no divisional rating, it was all by rank: only one first place, one second, one third. If you were first or second place, you were eligible for the national band contest. When we won this state contest in Bloomington, it was the first time Hobart had ever won anything;

the people were ecstatic. We took a train from Indianapolis to Gary, arriving at 2 a.m. Everyone came from Hobart to meet us, and I can still hear their automobile horns honking, waking everybody up and telling the whole population of Lake County that Hobart had come back from Bloomington with the first place trophy.

That was a great moment, not because we won but because the band had played beautifully. The national contest was held in Denver, and specified a warm-up march, a required selection, and then you went directly to sightreading three numbers. The biggest obstacles for us were getting the money for the trip to Denver and meeting the instrumentation required by the National Bureau for the Advancement of Music. Every band had to have that instrumentation or take a penalty of 1/2 point for every instrument less than 8 flutes, 1 interchangeable on piccolo; 2 oboes (if the score called for English horn, you could substitute but take a 1/2 point penalty); 2 bassoons; 2 E♭ soprano clarinets; 24 B♭ clarinets; 2 altos and 2 bass (the contra had not come into existence yet); 4 saxophones, 2 altos, tenor and baritone. The brass requirements were 6 cornets, 2 trumpets, 2 flugelhorns, 6 French horns, 5 trombones of which the 5th must be bass, 3 euphoniums, 6 tubas of which 3 were to be E♭s, and 4 percussion.

When we played our first national contest in Denver, John Philip Sousa, Edwin Franko, Goldman, A.A. Harding, Frank Simon, Arthur Pryor, and a couple of others judged us; those seven judges were the giants of the day. Our best possible grade, if we had played a perfect performance, was 86; I had only 8 clarinets, 1 oboe, 1 bassoon, 3 horns, 3 flutes. What made it more difficult was the required *Two Oriental Sketches* by Cecil Burley. How do you play oriental music without an oboe and a bassoon? We did it by muting the cornet as a substitute for the oboe, and I still have the comments of Sousa, Harding, and Goldman. We came out with a grade of 85.4 out of a possible 86, losing .6 of a point in the required performance and sightreading.

We made the finals and had to play again. They averaged finals with preliminaries and sightreading, so it wasn't one performance; there were three. We came out second, even with less than the required instrumentation. To get there we traveled by train and slept in the yards in Denver. The mothers wanted the band to look beautiful, so they washed all the white trousers and hung them on trees around the Denver railroad yards. Soot from a train ruined them; we had to wash them again at midnight.

When we returned from that contest we had $4,000 left over and $4,000 in 1925 could buy a lot of instruments. I bought two oboes, two Heckel bassoons, four French horns, two euphoniums, three tubas, a timpani, and a baritone saxophone, which was everything we needed to complete our instrumentation.

The fruits of my grade school program of small classes became apparent when I had a 60-piece junior high school band. With four cornets, four clarinets, four violins, piano, and percussion the sessions were like private lessons. We were in no hurry, and I had everyone singing solfège. Harold Bachman first heard my band when we were rehearsing *El Capitan*, taking it in a slow six instead of two, and the kids sang every note instead of playing their parts. Bachman wrote an article on my rehearsal techniques after seeing that.

I have never been enthusiastic about putting beginners in full band and prefer small beginning classes to avoid the hazards of poor embouchures, hand positions, and other problems. I had a wonderful junior high band of 80 players by the time I left. It walked off with first place in the Indiana contest every year.

Being a violinist, how did you learn so much about wind instruments?

I studied clarinet and cornet for a year, but when it came to flute, trombone, tuba, French horn, saxophone, and percussion I knew nothing. I had fingering charts all over my room; it was the blind leading the blind. I didn't know the flute embouchure, so after one of my weekly cornet lessons with Hale E. VanderCook I said, "I feel terrible. I'm teaching a high school band, and I feel incompetent. I don't know the instruments and I've got to do something about it, but what? I don't know what to tell them."

That wise old man said, "If I were to describe a rose to you, I could describe its shape, its size, its color; I could draw you a picture of one, show you a photo of one, and you'd have a good idea of what a rose looks like. If I spoke into eternity, though, I never could describe its fragrance. That's how important it is to study these instruments. You're the music man in Hobart, and you're the only one who they will hear tone from, and they have to hear that tone. Just produce a lovely tone; you don't have to be a great player, but produce a lovely tone and know the proper techniques. Get a fine teacher; don't go to anyone second-rate but go to the best there is." That was on Tuesday night; on Thursday night I had my first lesson with Ernie Liegl, first flutist with the Chicago Symphony in the basement of Orchestra Hall. For 10 years I studied there every Thursday, then went up to hear a concert afterwards. After Liegl I studied with Albert Barthel on oboe, followed by bassoon lessons with Hugo Fox, then Max Pottag, who was second horn and a fine teacher. I studied percussion technique with Bill Ludwig Sr. who was in the orchestra at the time. It was this learning process that was instrumental in my getting the job at Michigan.

Are today's instrumental techniques classes comparable to private study of the various instruments?

As far as I'm concerned, private study is the way to learn. I already had a degree in performance and in music education, but my music education degree provided me with no knowledge of the instruments. You can graduate with a music education degree from any university and never know a thing about some of the instruments. You won't know the fingering of the bassoon, you will never have it to your lips, never play a note on the oboe, tuba, trombone, or French horn, yet you will graduate and conduct a beginning class of students that have never heard a note on those instruments.

There are band directors who never held a timpani or bass drum stick or played a cymbal. This is a quack way of teaching; it is not the proper approach. Today many students study privately, but many don't. Band directors should get enough fundamental training to produce a fine sound on each instrument. There are students in isolated little towns who never hear a good sound because their teacher can't produce one.

Today the music education program has taken second place in the minds and interests of many universities. They are defeating their own purpose, because public school music is the cradle of it all. If universities want fine students, they have to question where they will come from. If a public school music student is well-trained, his performance ability at the college level will be better than if he were poorly trained. The music education programs in most universities are not strong instrumentally. They neglect the fundamental training that is essential on all instruments for a successful career in conducting in public schools. □

Learning from William Revelli

by Jerry Bilik

On February 12, several dozen loyal friends, students, and colleagues gathered to honor William D. Revelli on the occasion of his 90th birthday, which I attended as a member of all three categories. For those who do not know this magnificent maestro, he probably exists in one of several imaginary roles: an awesome guest conductor scaring the daylights out of students in an all-state band; a near deity described in nostalgic terms by loyal students; or an old fuddy-duddy wasting valuable rehearsal time with obscure details.

My first encounter with him took place in the fall of my first semester at the University of Michigan when Revelli, who wanted to know everyone in his band, personally auditioned each applicant. Being a brash New Yorker and a loud trombonist, I decided to demonstrate the kind of playing we could produce in the Empire State. Not knowing anything about this slightly rotund gentleman, I took a huge gulp of air and let it fly, when Revelli quickly admonished, "Do you like that tone?" After what seemed like an eternity, I staggered out of his office, muttering incoherently and wondering about majoring in animal husbandry instead. Somehow I managed to squeeze in as 17th of the 18 trombones, and two days later in Harris Hall we played *The Victors* with a sound I had never heard before. It sent chills throughout my body, and ever since I have tried to recreate this sound. Sometimes I have come close, but it has always remained the elusive, magical, and mysterious sound of pure music.

In the late 1930s America emerged from a major depression determined to grow into a sophisticated political and economic society. It was a time of great national and regional pride, and communities actively supported their educational institutions so children could learn to deal with the new world and bring about the wonderful future everyone sought. This mood encouraged a generation of brilliant and dedicated educators, which in music included Austin Harding at Illinois, William Knuth in California, Joe Maddy in Minnesota and Interlochen, and Paul Van Bodengraven in New York. Viewed today it is difficult to comprehend the extent of their idealism. They approached their jobs with an almost religious fervor; to them music was a sublime vehicle to excite, inspire, and motivate a quest for perfection. It

was a means to stretch students beyond their imagined limits to the highest levels of skill and concentration. Because music only comes alive when played, it was their job to make music and to make it beautiful in order for it to be appreciated.

Revelli and such contemporaries as Mark Hindsley, Robert Hawkins, Clarence Sawhill, and Elizabeth Green were driven by the desire to bring the joy of fine music-making to as many youngsters as possible. While they were demanding perfectionists with college groups, they also travelled tirelessly to promote music programs at all levels. They believed every child could gain pride, sensitivity, confidence, and respect for others and themselves through music.

As for me, after just making the symphonic band my first year, I wondered if I had made yet another mistake; the rehearsals were sheer agony as we played pieces one note at a time, going through every player in a section to achieve the right attack and spending 15 minutes on a single cymbal crash. When it was the trombone's turn on the firing line, we felt terror. When someone missed a note, there was a feeling of suspended animation as the player waited for the dreaded, "Did you like that?" or the satirical imitation of producing a simple, sustained tone. As freshmen we could not understand the process at all until, we finally gave a concert, and the music came out as if someone else were playing it; it was lush and sonorous, with shimmering beauty and rolling dynamics. I realized much later that this was the education and growth Revelli and his contemporaries sought to impart.

Despite some very close calls including almost being thrown out of rehearsal, I survived and made it to the second year. In marching band Revelli asked if any students wanted to try their hand at arranging, and I immediately volunteered; I was so far down in the trombone section that Revelli thought I was someone else.

Jerry Bilik served as musical coordinator and arranger for the Oscars, Emmys, Grammys, People's Choice, and Golden Globes and received A.S.C.A.P.'s Annual Composers Award. He was the story-writer, arranger, composer, sound producer, and theatrical director for Irvin Feld and Kenneth Feld Productions, Inc. for ten years and served on the faculty of the University of Michigan School of Music.

I timidly entered his office, and in a moment of weakness he gave me a chance. The result of this daring endeavor was the beginning of a new relationship that took root in the fall of 1952 and to this day remains one of mutual affection and respect. Like anything of value it grew slowly and sometimes painfully; he responded to every submitted score with "why this?," "why not this?," "too low," "too high," "too thick," or "too thin." Hardest of all was the fact that his criticisms or suggestions were always correct. This incredible perception came from the intensity with which Revelli approached music and teaching. There were no casual glances at a score, only precise scrutiny. It was part of his dedication to perfection; nothing more, nothing less.

There was another factor of equal importance in Revelli's analysis of a score. He could tell how a piece would sound by examining the score, and he had an absolute concept of what the sonority of a band should be: full, rich, balanced, and sometimes mighty in scope. It should be deep, wide, and shimmering with beauty, never brittle or painful. Each player contributed by performing in tempo with pure, controlled tone supported and properly generated from *ppp* to *fff*. This quest applied not only to the concert band, but to the marching band as well. I remember standing outside on the practice field one November, shivering in an icy rainstorm while that madman went down the trumpet section one by one checking tone. If you ever heard the Michigan Band play in those days you know why 100,000 fans roared and screamed in response to such over-powering sonority and why certain works sounded so beautiful the crowd rose to its feet.

As my arranging developed I tried to figure out how to achieve the fullness of sound that Revelli diligently pursued. The secret, which I happily share with others, is simplicity: exploit the basic tenets of music with clear flowing melodies, properly balanced triadic harmonies, melodically functional contrapuntal bass and interior obbligatos, and no interference (music does not live by drums alone). Directors can experience the thrill of full sonority and musicality outdoors, regardless of ensemble size or instrumentation, by learning and following Revelli's principles and altering scores and rewriting parts to make them musical while dedicating yourself to achieving a musical performance from every member of the band.

For Revelli and his colleagues the music came first, whether in concert or a rehearsal or in scoring and programming. He selected works to teach us something important about music and never chose music merely to show off. When his band recorded on Vanguard in the 1960s, the word on the street, entirely untrue, was that there were professional ringers laced throughout the band. In fact, if ordinary students could not achieve near-perfection, Revelli and his cohorts would have considered themselves frauds and failures. The only measure of success came from students' growth and development.

As to the distinctive sonority of his bands, Revelli achieved a depth and warmth of sound primarily by blending multiple players on a single line. This is the fundamental concept of orchestral and choral music: individuals working in unison to achieve a higher purpose. The purpose of large ensembles was educational as well as musical. These pioneering conductors were committed to providing the best experience for the largest number of students and never considered skimming off the finest players to form elite ensembles. If a student merited special attention, they programmed a concerto or a solo, but the unselfish objective of education was always the guiding operative.

I have been chagrined by band directors who are lured by the so called purity and finesse of

wind ensembles while relegating the less talented youngsters to a secondary or training band. Some of the rationalizations I have heard from directors are that students who do not make the wind ensemble will be motivated to try harder, that the administration counts on the group to win contests and the director cannot take a chance, or that directors cannot get a large band together. Some directors may think students of the 1930s did not work hard, but Revelli's band at Hobart High School did not meet at noon in an air-conditioned, sound-proofed, multi-tiered, music room; it met at 7 a.m., started with 12 students, and grew with his cajoling and inspiration. The issue is not the size of an ensemble, or if a director with a new or decimated program has a minuscule ensemble of ridiculous instrumentation, the point is to figure out where to go from there, and to achieve it.

The more I see and hear, the more I feel that the concept of wind ensembles, despite their purported educational and artistic credentials, has unwittingly served as the perfect cop-out for educators who are either unwilling or unable to do what they were hired to do: teach. As a result, the field of music education has been sapped of its inherent strength by those who turned away from the precept of education for all to encouraging only the elite. These are difficult times, and to survive many directors perform feats of super-human energy, courage, and endurance. Education is not intended for the comfort of or praise for the teacher but to help students grow. People who believe in that will join the struggle no matter what the odds.

Revelli and his colleagues believed this as did their first generation of students, which included Fred Ebbs and Harry Begian. The more people they could introduce to the joy, sweat, and strain of music making, the more potential first-class citizens they could develop. I grieve when I observe how the example of their energy and enthusiasm is eroded by teachers who try to impress others with gold medals, virtuoso performances, and an erudite, proper repertoire. Music is not an olympic event, even though contest organizers do their best to convince directors and administrators it ought to be.

In an era of shrinking budgets and cancelled programs, directors should market and promote bands. For some musicians any pandering to sell their program is distasteful, but as a music educator it is not your feelings alone that should be considered but the tremendous benefits music education can bring to worried, hassled, frightened, old-too-soon youngsters. All you have to do is be the vehicle and let the music do the work. To survive, do as Revelli and the musical pioneers did: open your programs and reach out. Contact anybody who cares about children: parents, police, and ministers and enlist them in a down-and-dirty fight to sell the incredible benefits a music program offers. Try to understand the benefits should not be for you but for the students and try to keep going after the inevitable bitter defeats and disappointments. Even if you reach just a few children, you will discover a satisfaction that far surpasses winning a gold medal.

This approach represents true education and is something I can speak of with intimate knowledge. If William D. Revelli had used his top students at Michigan to form an exclusive ensemble, I do not know where the rest of us would be now. Some of these average students emerged from his sessions and carried on the true aims of music education in different ways and places: I through writing, some at bigshot colleges, and others at podunk junior highs. Each in his way uses the art of performing music to bring growth, learning, and a sense of pride to youngsters.

As a young student hanging by a fragile thread, I noticed from time to time that Revelli diverted his attention from his star players to me, a jerky trombonist learning to write arrangements. I would never be a great performer, but despite my contrary inclinations I actually began practicing. I couldn't stand the humiliation when he went down the section, and I began to feel guilty about not doing my part for the band or the music. By the time I graduated and finished with the West Point Band, I had improved enough to get professional symphonic jobs. I am especially grateful for his being creatively honest and his genuine affection as he guided me in learning composition; as I ventured out into life these helped me move forward. Every time I complete a score, whether it's a seven-minute production or a four-bar bridge-cue, I can still see that slightly rotund gentleman peering over my shoulders and scrutinizing the score with "why this," "too high," "too low," and "do you really like that?". ☐

Balanced Programs and Tarnished Trophies

An Interview with James Croft

by John Thomson

James Croft is director of bands at Florida State University in Tallahassee and a past president of the National Band Association. With forty years of teaching experience, he shows his views on music education in a recent interview.

What advice would you give on balancing marching with other components of a music program?

I eliminated marching from my program in Oshkosh, and have told a number of people that this was a mistake. It seemed like the right thing to do at the time, but since then I have seen wonderful social influences emerge out of marching bands in schools that maintain a balance between concert and marching activities that my program didn't have.

I like the concept of learning one show before school begins. If you have a wonderful drill, just alter the music so that you can work on the music and not have to keep pounding away at new drills. I am very negative about competitive marching bands.

How would you counsel new music teachers concerning competitions?

Do not compete. Alfie Kohn's book *No Contest* places into a niche the concepts of cooperation and competition. I think that competition ultimately benefits the king of the jungle; the winner becomes richer. They also burn out and go into something other than music because in competing they lose sight of the only reason for teaching music, which is to inspire kids.

Do you feel as strongly about concert band competitions?

Yes. I sought competition when I was young, mostly because when we're young we want someone to tell us, "You have a division one band here." Interestingly enough I've never received anything but a one rating. In my first year of teaching in Traer, Iowa I was lucky to have a half-dozen kids in the small band who had been wonderfully taught and were fine musicians. With thirty students we played the *Trauersinfonie* by Wagner, Prelude and Fugue in G minor, and a march, and were musical enough to persuade two of the judges to give us a one and the third judge to give us a one minus.

From then on I never received anything but ones, but after awhile I realized that it didn't mean anything. What does a string of 39 straight years of division one ratings mean? Does that become the motivating reason for our being? It has nothing to do with it.

What is the motivating reason?

The only real motivation ever is how music affects your head and heart. To what dimension of the human spirit does music making add? If something doesn't happen to you, the ensemble, and the audience, you should reassess.

What advice would you give concerning chamber ensembles and jazz ensembles?

I am very enthusiastic about jazz ensembles, even though I'm not good at it. I've come from such another era that I am not current and never really have been. I recognize the intrinsic value and improvisational values of jazz programs. I think much of what we masquerade as improvisation should be counted as prepared music. There is the concept of inappropriate approval in education and learning that is disrespectful of real learning. Much of what we hear in jazz programs, particularly applauding for mediocre solos, doesn't have anything to do with the music. A jazz ensemble should be a part of the program, but if a teacher feels uncomfortable with improvisation or cannot teach it, at least he can teach style.

Chamber ensembles were very important, although not just for contests. We always tried to get ensembles going early in the year and encouraged activities. The more quartets, quintets, and choirs that we could organize the better off we were. The chamber program became our marching band in a sense, a way for students to participate in another group. At Florida State we require that every freshman and sophomore play in a quartet or quintet. They can march or perform in other ensembles, but they have to be in a quartet or quintet during first semester. This change has had a dramatic effect on our program.

How frequently and at what occasions should school groups perform?

Students should probably perform several times a semester to share what they have learned. In developing performance etiquette and knowing how to behave when performing, students will learn the importance of projecting when making music.

Unfortunately it seems that the smaller the school, the greater the number of services music programs are expected to provide for the community and at athletic events. That's tragic and reprehensible. It makes teaching music impossible and I feel desperately sorry for directors and bands caught up in this.

Are you talking about excessive pep band appearances and parades?

Oh yes; pep bands have to be available for every football, basketball, and volleyball game. There should be regulatory agencies in every state that say you just simply cannot have excessive public performances – once a week at the outside and that's it. More would be exploiting those kids, especially at smaller schools. Larger schools just split up to form several twenty-piece pep bands.

Recognize that the community will tend to exploit the band program and expect it to be available for the opening of every Winn-Dixie. Develop a clear policy with your board and administration that certain services cannot be provided because they are inappropriate to education and policy.

As we hear so much about budget and scheduling constraints, how can teachers make the school board and administrators understand the value of school music?

The first thing to do is to make sure that administrators sit in on your rehearsals. Don't just invite them, but say, "I want you to hear this and to see the learning that occurs." I think that is the most convincing step to take if you are a good teacher. If your band has the chops, get them down there and invite members of your school board. On band parents' night, make sure there is a board member or two there and demonstrate the learning that goes on in rehearsals.

I had the same high school principal for seventeen years in Oshkosh and periodically he brought his work down to the band room, and did the same with the choir and the orchestra. He just sat back there, and once in awhile he would stop and say, "Kids, I hope you know how fortunate you are, what a joyful experience this must be." He never missed a concert and was so complimentary. The superintendent of schools was the same way.

You have enjoyed support from administrators, but not everyone has this luxury. Aside from inviting them to rehearsals, what other actions build support?

Make sure you are friendly with colleagues. Very often we think of ourselves as separate from the rest of the faculty because the band room is often physically isolated from the rest of the school. There is a professional isolation if we don't talk with our colleagues except when we send students late to their classes.

What would you tell an administrator who has never experienced the thrill of playing in an ensemble?

Ask administrators if they have heard of important musicians such as Beethoven. Then ask them in a friendly way to identify who won the Heisman trophy in 1954, or any year. The sports heroes have been forgotten but important musical works survive. In the hierarchy of what is really important, students should be familiar with their cultural heritage. What does that better than the fine arts and the humanities? Public schools do not exist as trade schools if general education is our goal. The worst thing we can do is to confront people who have not experienced being in an ensemble. Many of my closest friends in school were coaches, and I understand how they become absorbed in their sports. I realize that they might not be as interested in my work because they haven't had the same experience. With administrators you should build friendships so they will have confidence in you. This means that you can't stay there for one or two years and then leave. You have to build credibility for two or three years before they will have confidence in you.

What are some tips for young teachers as they arrive at their first job?

Establish that you care about your students; they have to know that. Bob Reynolds once said the mark of a great teacher is a passion for music, and a passion for people. Kids need to perceive that you have an uninhibited passion

John Thomson is director of bands at New Trier High School in Winnetka, Illinois and a Contributing Editor to The Instrumentalist.

for music. It is almost impossible for you to dislike someone if they like you. Kids sense when you don't like them. You have to make it clear that you will not tolerate inappropriate behavior.

What trends in our profession do you find encouraging?

There is more good music available to bands than ever. It's not being played, but there is more quality literature than ever before. Unfortunately much of it is on rental or is too hard to perform. The sophistication of wind literature for able groups is unprecedented. We've never had players comparable to those of today, although I don't think we're as deep right now as we were. When I talked with Frances McBeth about flute players twenty years ago he said, "Out in West Texas you can kick over a rock and find a kid who wants to play the Chaminade and the Nielsen." I don't see the same level of flute playing today; I see more of them but not the same depth of player.

Clarinets are another issue. The best players are better than ever because of improved instruments and teaching, but we see fewer and fewer of them. We have some wonderful oboe, bassoon, and horn players, but I am concerned about the edginess of trombone and trumpet sound as a result of far too much fifty yard line paint peeling. It actually becomes abusive; there aren't enough kids on the field so we try to make up for it by just overblowing. Tubas also overblow, but there are better tuba players than we've ever had and better saxophone players, although there are too many of them in our bands.

What other positive trends do you see?

I see improved conductors emerging because many young conductors are less mechanical and more expressive, and as a result they probably teach better.

What trends concern you?

I think competitions running all year round are a sick part of music education. I think it is a malady because I recognize the function of the winter guard. I'm sure that many people think it is a wonderful activity, but it hasn't anything to do with the music program. If kids twirl flags year round instead of playing music in a band, that is a mistake. We are seeing the emergence of year-round drum lines that perform at basketball games and become a separate entertainment component. However, as the drum line becomes entertainment, it is activities-oriented not arts-oriented. We should not try to sell it as a curricular activity because it doesn't offer anything that can be defended. It should be outside the school day because these things will develop into competition and will eventually

hurt a lot of kids in the process. If there is one thing at this point in my life that I cannot support, it is a heavy measure of competition. I am not going to completely divest myself and say that there is not a place for evaluation, but it is suspect. The guy who comes home from a parade with a 56.8 and a five foot trophy confirms his values and the community's opinion. His perception of the band is trophies, but the only worthwhile trophies are kids whom have been touched in an important way as a human being, a musician, or combination of both – these are your trophies.

In a four-year high school career, what works should students play?

Rather than specific things, I think that there should be generic experiences students should have. It is great if students can play the *Toccata and Fugue,* but they should first experience Bach. They should recognize the textural design of contrapuntal music. I'm not going to say they should play only Moehlman's arrangements or John Paynter's arrangements, but they should experience transcriptions that adapt well to wind sonorities, avoiding those that do not. For the most part we should not play transcriptions of music from the 18th century because they are inappropriate literature. We can play music from the French Revolution, which is important historically and we can learn those same classic designs and structure. I think students should have this experience. If we can play *Elsa* we can play romantic pieces that are scored for wind sonorities. Students should have a liberal experience with folk music because there is nothing that touches either the heart or the toe quite like its reservoir of wonderful melody and adapts well to variations. *Lincolnshire Posy* is an incredibly imaginative use of folk music. In our heritage we should have experiences with jazz techniques, which often do not adapt well to large ensembles, so we shouldn't play a lot of them. Broadway has produced important music that students should play, and they should experience the vitality and joy of different kinds of marches because they are the band's heritage. Finally, directors should give students experience with 20th-century music, which requires a lot of a conductor.

Is there a topic you would like to address that we omitted?

This is my fortieth year teaching, and I can count on one hand the days I did not eagerly look forward to my work. I have difficulty understanding people who stay in this business when they are unhappy; I wish they'd get out so they don't infect kids who might find the magic that takes place in rehearsal and concerts. They should make way for a teacher who is excited about music and kids. □

Harry Begian
Speaks From Experience

by James Hile

Harry Begian holds degrees from Wayne State University and the University of Michigan. Director Emeritus of the University of Illinois Bands, Begian has appeared as a conductor, adjudicator, and lecturer in the United States, Canada, and Australia. In the March 1990 issue we presented his article, "The Conductor's Responsibilities," which focused on programming music.

How did you learn to conduct?

I learned the most by observing symphony orchestra conductors in rehearsal. As a youngster I slipped into rehearsals of the Detroit Symphony unbeknownst to the stage manager, and sat in the darkened auditorium listening to such high-caliber conductors as Fritz Reiner, Eugene Ormandy, and Leopold Stokowski work with the symphony week after week. This was at a time when the Ford Motor Company hired the Detroit Symphony to perform on a series of N.B.C. broadcasts heard all over the country. To me that was the greatest musical experience I could imagine, and at an early age I saw how the big boys did it. They impressed me not only with their conducting technique but with the momentum of their rehearsals and how much they accomplished in a certain amount of time. To professionals, time is money. I latched onto this idea and carried it over into my work in the schools and universities. I always felt that I wasn't there to preach but to conduct and teach.

What experiences in listening to orchestras made a lasting impression on you?

The summer I spent at Tanglewood was one of the greatest musical experiences of my life. For six weeks I heard the Boston Symphony in rehearsal with Serge Koussevitzky and at times with Leonard Bernstein. Hearing the fine performances and participating in a chorus conducted by Robert Shaw were important influences on me. The thing I will never forget about Shaw is how he worked the hardest of anyone in the production of a piece of music.

Five minutes into the rehearsal he was dripping with sweat. You couldn't sing in the chorus at Tanglewood under Shaw and not get involved; that was an important thing to learn and something my colleagues don't know about. They are so detached from the music making process that they could rehearse in a white shirt and tie, and after an hour and a half have nary a trickle of sweat on them. Not that sweat makes a good rehearsal, but involvement does.

What made you decide to become a band director instead of a symphony orchestra conductor?

When I was about 15 years old I decided to take the band route instead of the orchestral because I believed there was no chance with the orchestra for someone with my economic and educational background. I was not able to study privately until I went to college.

When I heard the sound of a good university band, like Revelli's University of Michigan band, I thought this kind of group had a future. In it I heard refined musical sounds produced by technically capable students who could play just about anything written.

What are your views on today's band music?

Most of today's band music is educational music written for the junior high or lower high school level. There's a place and a need for it, but I question why band directors hold it up as good music; it is functional music. Unfortunately, there isn't enough quality music to keep a fine university band afloat. So much of the music that my colleagues play and propogate in the name of new, contemporary, or original music for band or wind band is not worthy of public performance. If conductors wish to oblige composers by playing this music in rehearsals, that's one thing, but foisting it on an audience is

James Hile, director of bands at the University of North Carolina - Chapel Hill, earned a master's degree at the University of Illinois and is currently completing the doctoral program there.

another. They chase away the audience by performing bad or insincere music. If people can't relate to the music, they won't come to the concerts. This doesn't mean you have to play junk; it just means you should play something audiences can relate to.

How do you respond to the statement that music offers experiences unavailable in any other way?

This is true. If we can't show or present expressive qualities of music then we've really done nothing with it. This happens in too many cases at all levels of performance where players aren't confronting music that has any expressive qualities; they never come to grips with the most important thing music has to say.

You often talk about the joy of music as compared to the fun of music.

Participating in musical activities just for the fun of it isn't enough. There's something more to be gained from music participation than just fun and games, and that is joy. When you play or sing music to the best of your ability and give expresive elements to it, that is the joy of music; you can only approach it through serious music making.

Is your concern that composers are not writing quality music?

The problem is more serious than that. I don't think you could name four people on the scene now who can write a first-class work for band. I just don't think there are composers like that. I came into this field because I believed in the expressive qualities of wind instruments and the future of the symphonic band. Today's composers are writing little music for the level of ensembles that I have conducted.

How then can we encourage composers of the highest echelon to write for band?

I thought at one time that just by asking the better composers they would willingly write for band. It's not like the symphony orchestra, where a composer has to fall on his knees to get his work played. There are hundreds of bands capable of playing anything a composer could write. Still, the top composers do not write for the band. So we will have to pay them and pay them a big price for their work.

What ingredients should a significant concert band piece have?

It should have a solid structural basis, starting somewhere, ending somewhere, while following some sort of logical procedure that we can discern with the ear or through score study. I also think it should have a melodic element that the listener can hang on to, maybe not the same melodic writing as in a 19th-century operatic aria, but perhaps melodies like Hindemith used, based on fourths instead of triads. Texturally,

there has to be something of interest for the ear. It can't be all blocks of sound. A piece for band should have light textures to contrast the heavier, darker textures and there should be good harmonic or contrapuntal interest. There has to be developmental interest, and anyone who can't handle a variation form is not much of a composer. The reason we categorize Beethoven as a great composer is primarily for what he did structurally and developmentally. He could take a germ idea of just three or four notes and expand it into a symphony. His Fifth Symphony is a perfect example of this.

The way a composer uses rhythms and rhythmic play helps to make a composition effective. Finally, there has to be expressiveness in this music. If it doesn't have anything of expressive worth to it, then it is a questionable piece. These are the elements that make for a good work.

Does contemporary music fail in any of these areas?

The approach to melodic procedure is just too far gone in contemporary music. It is as though composers avoid melodic writing at any cost. They give too much play to the rhythmic aspects of the music, as if they believe that the more complicated the piece is rhythmically, the better it is. I don't believe this; complication does not add to the worth of anything, whether it's a speech, a piece of writing, or a piece of music. To uncomplicate music is the harder thing to do.

Most modern music has little emotional content. I don't hear it or see it in the scores. Too much of today's music focuses on extremes of range, extremes of articulation, and extremes of rhythmic complexity. The only thing modern composers stick with is structure. In fact, their structures are so premeditated they are almost like a map.

The last 35 or 40 years represent a new band period from which conductors and educators should distill the things that are good. There should be a contemporary piece on every university band concert, but it should be well chosen.

What about the older band music?

The band medium has some original music from the past, but not all of it is of high quality. Some of the music written in the 1940s should be played, including the great corpus of march compositions. Audiences love marches, and they also enjoy good transcriptions, as well as a good soloist with band accompaniment. There are some transcribed arias that can be played as sensitively with a band accompanying them as they can with an orchestra. Some transcriptions of solo works with orchestral accompaniment come off beautifully if you play them with the right size ensemble. It is a terrible mistake to play the accompaniment of a Weber clarinet concerto with a full-sized concert band. That isn't the size ensemble that Weber wrote for. It sounds better when played by a scaled-down group of 45 to 50 winds. The same is true for the Haydn Trumpet Concerto. The printed edition sounds right only after I go back to the orchestral score and rewrite the horn, oboe, trumpet, and timpani parts. Instead of treating it as a band piece, I try to get it more like the original, and a 45-piece wind ensemble is the most effective equivalent. This size group makes an excellent accompanying ensemble for music of the 17th, 18th, and early 19th centuries. Playing the Haydn accompaniment with a full-size concert band is similar to an orchestra of the romantic period playing baroque or classical music; it doesn't work. Orchestra people know this, but band people have taken a long time to catch on.

Should conductors go back to the original score?

Definitely, because some of the earlier transcribers wrote for the size bands that existed in their time. For instance, many scores transcribed for Carl Fischer were intended for a military band of 30 pieces, which might have had one oboe, one flute, and no bassoon. That picture changed by the 1930s and 1940s when additional flutes gave the band a full-sounding soprano section. Those same bands often played transcriptions written on the premise that they could be performed by groups numbering six or sixty. It took me some time to figure out that this was nonsense. It was only after I went back to the original orchestral score, found what the composer initially intended, then rescored some of the transcribed parts that these pieces made sense to me.

How do you feel about the wind ensemble versus the full symphonic band?

The wind ensemble is the answer for the small school that cannot field a full band. It is ideal for performing Mozart, or the light works of Richard Strauss, but it should not play music of reputable composers written for larger bands. For example, I don't care to hear the Hindemith *Symphony* or the *Theme and Variations, Opus 43*A of Schoenberg played by a wind ensemble. The performance isn't comparable to a good concert or symphonic band. Although a wind ensemble can play with an exactitude of rhythm, finer intonation, and all those things obtained from better players, it rarely does. Most wind ensembles never approach the tonal colors, the balances, and the expressive sound of the concert or symphonic band.

What then is the place of the wind ensemble in our educational system?

The only kind of wind ensemble I want to hear for my listening pleasure is one that exhibits the highest quality, with players who perform accurately and cleanly on a high level of musical expression. Few wind ensembles can meet these standards. The Netherlands Wind Ensemble is one such group. I enjoy their recordings tremendously, but to expect this level of playing from a high school group is unrealistic. For me the finest kind of ensemble playing is the string quartet with four equal partners. Each is responsible for delivering a part without error or scratches. The smaller the group the more skilled the players have to be, and most high schools do not have such players. In my 40 years of hearing and directing wind ensembles, I've felt them to be superior only when playing works for small groups, such as the Strauss serenades, divertimentos and cassations, and the Richard Strauss and Dvorak pieces for a particular size group.

If you could establish the ideal band program, would the wind ensemble be part of it?

Yes, because there is a body of music written for it. The University of Illinois didn't allow me to have a wind ensemble when I was there; I wanted it to be part of the band program but my predecessor refused to have one and it was something I could not touch. Had it been part of the band program, then I would have conducted it.

Should the wind ensemble function as a smaller segment of the larger band?

Yes, in the large band you have all the ingredients of the wind ensemble. When you aim for the contrast in textures and colors and want to narrow the sound to four players, the four players are there just as they are in the wind ensemble. You have one on a part when necessary for contrast or when the composer asks for it.

On the other hand the wind ensemble can never approximate the sound of the symphonic band. People like A.A. Harding, one of my predecessors at the University of Illinois, promoted an instrumentation for the large band as an offshoot of the symphony orchestra of his time, the 102-piece orchestra of Strauss and Mahler. Attempting to find different voices for contrasting elements in that instrumentation, Harding tried all kinds of instruments. Some he kept, like the contrabass clarinet; some he discarded. The alto clarinet didn't do anything for the sound of the band, but the contrabass and bass clarinets had value.

Such directors as Harding, Revelli, Bainum, and Hindsley, the people of the generation before me, evolved the instrumentation of the concert band. I believed in that sound; I was convinced by those instruments. I still am, although I had grave doubts about it for a long time during the 1970s. I've come back to this notion: if it is a band, I know what instruments it should contain and how it should sound. I don't have the same sense about the wind ensemble. You often speak of the pendulum swinging back and forth; this is an example.

The wind ensemble represents a reversion in size and color. We've performed with wind ensembles now for over 40 years, and they are the ideal medium for playing a certain type of music, but the concept has not sold to either public high school band directors around this country or to audiences. I believe there are two reasons why: the wind ensemble lacks tonal colors; and philosophically, it doesn't work in the public high school. I don't think it's right to tell players, "No, I'm keeping one player on a part no matter what." We are there to teach music through bands; but to exclude some students is not the way to do it. The M.E.N.C. and other music organizations should have objected to this kind of exclusivity immediately. It has created a self-pronounced elite in the band world. What used to be a strong fraternity among musicians has now splintered.

Today band directors can go in any one of four directions: the traditionalists, such as concert or symphonic band; the wind ensemble; the marching band; the jazz band. Band directors have become specialists in one of these areas, and they won't look to the left or to the right. At conventions it is rare to see a director of one classification having any discourse with one from another. Marching band directors stick

to themselves, as do concert band and jazz band directors. Wind ensemble conductors are unapproachable. This is one of the unfortunate by-products of the last 30 or 40 years of development.

At this point in your career, what do you regard as the purpose of the band in the public schools?

The purpose is to bring quality music that can be played on any level to students. If a conductor chooses wisely, he can present selections that introduce students and players to the expressive qualities in music. As Charles Leonard would say, if music education can't show players the expressive qualities of good music, then it has no place in the public schools.

Harry Begian, 1970

Many people think the marching band has become the dominant force in public school education. How do you feel about this?

Marching band is an adjunct function that has grown to be overly important in band programs around the country. It has gone hand-in-hand with the development of the athletic consciousness in the professional and school level. This is unfortunate because it has been detrimental to the musical qualities of bands and also to the retention of quality players.

Can you talk about some of the detrimental things?

Because marching bands don't require clarinets, flutes, French horns, and double reeds in large quantities as concert bands do, we've found fewer people on these instruments in the last 10 or 12 years because they are not participants in the marching band. We see that, and we also see a lowering of the playing level on certain instruments because of marching bands. The arrangements played in the marching band for the most part are simple and can be learned in a brief amount of time. They make no great technical or musical demands on the players. The emphasis is more on marching and the drill aspects and not the music. Therefore, a person can go through high school as a flutist and come out a much less proficient flutist than he would have 20 years ago. So we are getting fewer players of lesser quality on certain instruments than in the past. This is noticeable particularly on flute and clarinet; at one time there were hundreds and hundreds of flute players around the country in various types of bands. The playing level on the flute has dropped in the last 10-15 years, and the same has happened on the clarinet and the double reeds. I think this is principally because of the marching band movement as it is now as well as the type of music played.

Most marching band people say that they are raising the standards of excellence for the marching band through competitions. How do you react to that?

As a young band director, I believed that competitions and festivals were good for public school bands and orchestras. As time went by I changed my opinion about the competitive idea completely. The only kind of competition for musicians is the competition that one has with himself and his abilities to recreate music with his players.

Is there anything in the course of your career that changed your way of thinking like that, or was that just evolved over time?

My opinion has changed because of adjudicating at contests. As the years went by I saw the same bands and the same conductors learning nothing from their experiences. They did not improve intonation, rhythm, balance, or the things you look for over and over again on those rating sheets. I figured these competitions weren't doing what they're supposed to or that the conductor and his students weren't listening to the other bands. Instead they worked on three or four pieces for half a year. The notion that we've got to be number one, and we've got to be the winners in a competitive situation is stupid. The competitions sound more and more like offshoots of athletic departments, not educational institutions.

Often directors talk about the dropout rate connected with the marching or concert band. How do you feel about that?

Students everywhere want to be a part of anything that's great, whether it's a concert band or a marching band. If they play in a marching band, and it's a great marching band, there won't be much of a dropout problem. The same holds true in the concert area. You can't keep better players in a concert band if it's not a great group. If the group does not meet the needs or demands of the students, then you have a dropout problem. I'm not boasting, but I never had a dropout problem in any school I've taught in. In high school, my problem was one of inclusion, not exclusion. I had to create one band after another because the students respected what they were hearing and they wanted to participate in band activities. If they had any preparation before they came to high school they wanted to play in one of the bands. So I had four bands at one time.

It was the same thing when I went to Wayne State, where I inherited a university band that had dwindled down to 45 players. By the time I left Wayne State after three years to go to Michigan State I had two bands with about 80 pieces each. When I got to Michigan State I had to create still another band in addition to what was already there. Three years later when I took the Illinois job I inherited two large bands; after a few years the students flocked to those bands and we had two symphonic bands, three concert bands, and the marching band grew to be over 300, and finally we added a brass band. I think my success was due to the fact that I was able to work with fine young people who wanted to make music. As their teacher I worked to produce a good-sounding and good-performing band, which attracted other students. The other reason was that we didn't play any trash; we played the best music that we could play. The ultimate success hinged on the fact that I never complained, particularly to high school students, that this was a hard piece of music. I just said here is a piece of music I think you will enjoy, we're going to play it.

Do you think we could help solve the dropout problem by providing quality music?

Give students an experience performing good literature and there won't be a dropout problem. That experience doesn't come from an undisciplined atmosphere at rehearsals. It comes from a disciplined, sincere, honest approach to music.

I read an article the other day that said the future of the concert band is dead. How do you react to that?

I don't believe that. I referred earlier to the pendulum effect in American life where sometimes we go to one extreme and then go back the other way years later. I now see a swing back from 30 or 40 years of concentration on wind ensembles. As I go around the country I see more and more people returning to the concert band. I don't think the concert band is dying, but some directors have become concert band specialists. We need directors who embrace the concert band, wind ensemble, marching, and jazz band. United, the band movement will continue to grow and develop. ☐

Band Music and the Paper-Plate Mentality

An Interview with W. Francis McBeth

by Roger Rocco

Whether composing, conducting, or teaching W. Francis McBeth is devoted to music. In a generation that serialized and codified, McBeth followed his convictions and wrote music that touches the listener. His observations are fresh — "Alban Berg was good because he cheated," — and his perspectives are entirely his own.

What is your view of music education today?

Instrumental pedagogy hit its zenith in the late 1970s, when we had high school bands playing better than turn-of-the-century professionals. In the 1980s the level of performance topped off; and judging by the all-states I have conducted in the last few years, it has taken a slight downturn.

This is not because directors are not doing as well, but because of factions and problems within the public school system. Public schools in much of America are in such disarray and the attempt to correct them has caused such confusion as to priorities that music education has been set back. Our problem now is justifying music programs and convincing administrators that music is not an extracurricular activity. Music in the Texas schools has been hurt because of the H. Ross Perot bill, which was dubbed "no pass, no play." This bill was an honest attempt to require academic achievement before students participate in extracurricular activities. Its disastrous effect on music education was a result of the Texas legislature thinking that music was extracurricular: they only observed bands at football games, and it seemed logical to them to categorize bands with pom-pon squads. If a first chair clarinet player failed one course and made A's in all others, he could not perform at contest with the band. If music is extracurricular, then Harvard University has an entire school of extracurricular activity. Music is one of the oldest courses of study in the world and is just as important as mathematics for a junior high school student.

Another major concern on the horizon is the track system, which is already being implemented in California, whereby the school year is divided into four tracks (periods of time) with students choosing three tracks or portions of the year for schooling. This system staggers students to get 12-month usage from buildings and uses only three-fourths as many teachers. Both three-track and four-track systems are being implemented, but under either, all of the students are never in school at the same time. This is a great concept for industrial management, but disastrous for ensemble music programs.

In the last decade the number of upper-level students has seriously declined in summer study projects. Students now have more options than just going to band camp in the summer, and most summer camps have lost junior and senior students. Many camps I have worked with over a period of thirty years are just a shadow of themselves in performance ability because of a lack of older players. This does not stem from an absence of interest in older students but from a myriad of options. I worked at a camp several summers ago and three wonderful players I expected to be there were not. I inquired about them and found that they were in Paris with the French Club. Add to this those who are trying to pay for a car and you see what has caused the problem. This lack of summer study will show up down the road. Before the proliferation of women's sports, females had few choices. It was either the pom-pon squad or the band and they were certainly smart enough to see which to choose of these two. Now women's sports have cut into instrumental music.

Do you think we can turn this situation around?

One challenge is to educate administrators on the importance of music study, but retaining more junior high players may be even more important. In this day of slick commercial music, the musical experience has got to be more exciting than much of it is today.

W. Francis McBeth is professor of music and chairman of the theory/composition department and resident composer at Ouachita University in Arkadelphia, Arkansas. His education was received from Harding Simmons University, The University of Texas, and the Eastman School of Music.

I think we would be shocked if we knew students' reactions to much of the music that is played: they are really quite bored with it, and I don't blame them. Too many directors choose music neither they nor the students really like. It's chosen because it fits a minimum instrumentation or shows off a few skilled players at contest.

When my son was in junior high school his band played a concert of canned rock, which the kids loved; marches, which they thought were all right; and folk song suites, which bored them but which parents thought they should appreciate. It was that night I decided to write *Canto* with its clapping and wood clackers. If composers do not write some exciting concert music for junior high students, we will lose them.

It is important to show young players that concert music can be more exciting than pop by our choice of literature. There are wonderful junior high works not played any more, such as Clifton Williams' *Arioso*, which is easy, wonderful and 20th-century.

Few composers have taught kids. In my educational music I try to write real music with contemporary devices while still considering each instrument and fingering. In *Chant and Jubilo*, for instance, the trombone ostinato does not require moving the slide, and the fast trumpet passage in *Masque* involves the movement of only one finger; by transposing *Masque* up or down one step, you triple its difficulty.

I think many composers take the wrong approach to junior high music. They feel that simple rhythms and conservative registers constitute approachable music. The direction should be writing more musically challenging music but tailoring it to the ease of fingerings and the characteristics of each instrument: in other words, simplicity of mechanics as opposed to simple music. This is the difference also between Tchaikovsky and Prokofiev; Prokofiev wrote at the piano and then scored the music, which is very hard to play. When Tchaikovsky wrote, he wrote for each instrument and knew what that instrument could do. Some years ago I conducted the Prokofiev *Third Piano Concerto* and the Tchaikovsky *Fifth Symphony* on adjacent concerts with the Arkansas Symphony. The beginning of the Prokofiev had simple rhythms – quarters, eighths, halves – but was very difficult to play. With the Tchaikovsky the first reading sounded like we had worked on it a week because when Tchaikovsky wrote for the clarinet he wrote for the clarinet and for the trombone he wrote for the trombone. Young players don't need simple music; they need more complicated music that entails simple mechanics.

What is your approach to the rehearsal?

Everyone knows that a thoughtful plan for the 50 minutes is imperative. It can't just be a happening. The worst possible plan, which so many do, is to warm the band up for ten minutes. Ten minutes is twenty percent of your rehearsal time. Perhaps this is just personal with me because I never needed that much warmup, and never walked into a rehearsal that I was not already warmed up, and no conductor can warm me up as well as I can by myself. I have played in bands where my lip was almost shot after the warmup. I was a running back on a championship football team in Texas, and it always took me five minutes of the first quarter to recover from the pre-game warmup. Fortunately, coaches have learned better. A ten-minute warmup is extremely boring; why spend the first twenty percent of the rehearsal in sheer boredom when it is not necessary? I am not saying nothing is to be done, but much much less is necessary.

I plan rehearsals so I know what I will end with because I don't want the bell ringing while working with only two players on a duet as the rest of the band sits for six minutes. This would leave a bad taste in their mouths; and I want to end big with everybody participating. I have also quit working a passage that needed more time because too many people were sitting for an extended time. I force myself to rehearse as fast as possible and limit talking to the fewest words necessary to achieve what I want. Rehearse the sections that need rehearsal, skip those that don't.

One of my favorite stories happened to my son. After a public school concert we discussed a particular work they played, and I said the first half was excellent and the second half was terrible. How could that be? My son said, "You know, Dad, the spot where it got bad is the place where the bell rang every day."

807

How do you feel about today's band literature?

I am not pleased with much of the present literature, and I'm not speaking about the obviously poor music. The poor will be with us always. I am speaking of the music of the 1980s that so many classify as quality literature. Much of it is Broadway show music at a beastly difficult performance level. Maybe it's a natural reaction to so much truly ugly music of the 1960s and 70s. Honneger, in his book, *I Am a Composer*, said he feared "the drinking of all this carbolic acid" would lead to "the drinking of syrup." He was probably right. The world got so tired of the ugly, overly dissonant music that I fear the pendulum has swung too far the other way. When undergraduate composition students snicker at a major band composition winner (jazz ostinato with a major major 7th chord) while many bandmasters try to deify the piece, it's not a good sign. Enough of the negative; the beginning was so exciting.

When Clifton Williams won the first Ostwald competition in 1956 for *Fanfare and Allegro*, band music was getting exciting. Williams promoted band music with a missionary zeal. At his annual Southwestern Symposium at the University of Texas he would alternate bringing in Vincent Persichetti and Paul Creston because they were the major composers with true band interest in those days. John Barnes Chance and I were students at the University of Texas during that time, and we wrote mainly for orchestra. Williams convinced us, and I should include Larry Weiner, of the necessity of writing for band. One noon at an Austin restaurant,

Williams said, "The orchestra is the Cadillac; I know that, but they don't want you. They don't want anything past Debussy and truly dislike 20th-century music. The winds are where you want to go because they want new music. They are ripe for it because they don't have a repertoire. They've about folk-song suited themselves out of business."

Then came Barney's *Incantation and Dance*, more Persichetti, then Martin Mailman's *Liturgical Music* and the *Geometrics Series*, a few things of Lo Presti, then Claude Smith's *Incidental Suite*. You notice I left myself out of this period because of Southern modesty. Hanson, Schuman, Mennin and others were seeing the possibilities of wind music. The biggest spurt in the literature came from Nelhybel — a real European into the fray. His *Symphonic Movement* and *Requiem* are two of the very best works ever written for band. I use the *Symphony Movement* each year to teach my students the art of organic growth. What an exciting time for us, and it lasted well into the 1970s.

I don't hear much of this music played today except for Chance.

You will in the future; the repertoire has not solidified, but it will. We are still in our paper plate period — using a piece once and throwing it away — but that will change. History will change it, and history will determine our repertoire, not the compilation of lists today.

What music did you have in mind when you spoke of ugly music?

Some of the experimental music that we were afraid to challenge and almost all of the twelve-tone music. I am thrilled to have lived long enough to see twelve-tone music vanish. What a wonderful time, the Russians embracing Capitalism, the Berlin wall is down, and serial music has just gone away. Are these not causes for rejoicing?

The twelve-toners tried to lower music to the level of science. The dodecaphonic period lasted as long as the classical period, and what do we have to show for it? You can count them on one hand. Alban Berg was good because he cheated. He said, "I still want to use my ears." It was tough on students at many schools in those days; if you wanted to make an A in composition, you had to turn in a piece where in the stretto, retrograde, inversion and augmentation, every third note formed a recipe for kidney pie, and if you held the score up to an incandescent bulb, it formed the outline of Sandra Dee. Fortunately, we are trying to return to music that touches the soul instead of perplexing the brain.

What would you suggest to encourage good literature or improve it?

The composition contest was a great help to get the process started, but it has now run its course. Composers now know of the winds as a viable medium. The contest of today gives awards to the best piece sent in that year, but most professionals do not enter contests, and the contest money should be rechanneled to commissions. As far as I know Roger Sessions never wrote a band piece. *Lincolnshire Posey* was a commission, not a contest winner.

How do you learn a score?

I put all that I do or have learned to do in an article in the May 1990 issue of *The Instrumentalist*, but let me give a short capsule of my approach.

Most books and articles on score study insist that you first learn the form, but I say that that has never helped me. You don't have to know the form of a poem before you understand it or memorize it. Every architectural structure is different, every sonata allegro is unique in time and number of measures. It is not the form that is to be remembered but the sequence of events. I memorize a piece first, then the form is obvious to me. As I tell my theory students, memory can only be achieved by repetition. I physically conduct through a score that I am learning, while singing it to myself. When I get lost in memory, I then refer to the score and start over, always from memory.

A composer has a problem that others don't have when conducting his own music. I almost always use a score on my own music because my brain can jump to another of my own pieces because of the similarity of a certain section. I once, from memory, took the *Kaddish* ending on *Grace Praeludium*. Thank goodness the timpani player wasn't watching. □

From the Podium

A Conversation with Donald E. McGinnis and Mark Kelly

by ROGER ROCCO

Experience is the best teacher, and two veteran teachers whose careers with college bands are legendary, Don McGinnis and Mark Kelly, discuss their years on the podium and thoughts on the art of teaching.

Roger Rocco: In preparing for rehearsals, what plans do you have to use the time effectively?

Mark S. Kelly: At rehearsals I am never the last person to enter the band room but wait on the podium saying, "C'mon, clock, come on." I never start a rehearsal late; if we are scheduled to start at 3:30, when the clock hits 3:30, boom, we're off.

Every time I go into a rehearsal I know exactly how many minutes I will spend on each tune. I use my watch because if I didn't, I would probably lose track of things. I pace myself, and I pace rehearsals. If I have four pieces at various levels of difficulty, I would not start or end with the toughest. I don't subscribe to the view that kids should leave the room singing and happy. Sometimes I would rather they leave concerned.

I don't tape the first day of rehearsals because I can remember where the problems are for a few days without being reminded by a tape recorder. After a rehearsal I think about what happened. The secret to efficient rehearsing is to plan your work and work your plan. This is one of the hardest things for student teachers to learn. They may plan their work, but they don't know how to work their plan. One of the big things about a rehearsal is what you do after it is over. I sit in my office with my yellow note pad and recall all the things that went wrong.

When we get closer to a concert, I throw on the tape recorder in my band library at night and sit there with my yellow note pad and headphones, feeling unhappy. I make notations; I am my own adjudicator. In rehearsal I may have been oblivious to the timpani while concentrating on other things, but with the tape I notice that the timpani didn't come in. Some directors don't need a tape recorder, but that's what works for me.

Don McGinnis: I am either the victim or beneficiary of short rehearsals. Some conductors

Roger Rocco was principal tubist with the Honolulu and Seattle Symphony Orchestras and is director of bands at VanderCook College of Music.

have an hour to an hour-and-a-half daily, but at Ohio State we had 48-minute periods. I planned how much time to warm up and how I would do it, so we usually warmed up within the music. In preparing a score I not only studied the form, instrumentation, and technical difficulties, but I also planned where to start the music to benefit the entire band without being a drain on the brass players.

If my clarinet were here with a good reed, I could pick it up and play for an hour without hurting my lip. Among woodwind players, only the double reeds have fatigue problems. Clarinets, saxophones, lower reeds, and flutes can play without warming up and have no particular strain on their anatomy. I would never start with the high range for any instrument or by hacking away at a spot that required high trumpets, pedal tones in the tubas, or high ranges in clarinets or flutes because players would start pinching. I take these things into consideration and plan my strategy.

Before studying the score I look at individual parts. I don't study each for an hour, but I know by looking at the first cornet part or first trumpet part or first clarinet part what the problems will be.

Mark S. Kelly

How regularly do you use warm-up routines?
Kelly: I like to use a warm-up based on what we will play at the next concert. I always rehearse with the idea that if Fred Ebbs or Jim Nielson walked into the room, he would say "you're doing a good job" rather than "Kelly, why are you doing that?"

I am a competitive guy and like to get to the heart of a thing quickly. You can use a book such as Jim Curnow's, which is S.A.T.B., to play a scale in unison or a scale with the soprano and alto in the top part, tenor and bass in the bottom octave, or you can play in four-part harmony. Early in the school year I spend quite a bit of time with that book at the start of each rehearsal because I want everybody to figure out what part he plays in this year's band. This year's French horns have to realize that to fit into this year's band they should play and think in a certain way; and it should be the same if it were a middle school, high school, or college band. I want bassoons, bass clarinets, tenor saxophones, the second alto, the third clarinets, and third cornets to realize they all play in the same range. These days a clarinet section can meet in a phone booth, but you need an exhibition hall for the sax section. I tell them there are other instruments than saxes and hope they realize what part they play in the sandwich.

I can get insensitive quickly when somebody plays loudly with five other people on the same

note. I tell students who play too loudly that when they play their note the train is already moving. I want them to add to the sonority, not wipe it out. I am not interested in hearing "that's a great French horn section" or "those trombones really did it." It is the sound that comes from the whole band that matters. Too often it is not a homogenized sound but is heterogenous.

Curnow's book develops blend and keeps it from being bland. If I were to listen to a high school band for 30 minutes, other than right and wrong notes and right and wrong rhythms I would listen for variety of timbre, blend, and balance. I like a variety of tone colors in bands; I hate bland bands, which are like biting into a sandwich with no meat. I want sonorities.

Donald E. McGinnis was director of university bands and taught clarinet and flute at Ohio State University from 1941 until his retirement in 1979. During World War II he was the clarinet soloist with a Navy musical unit that also featured Adolph Herseth as solo cornetist.

Mark S. Kelly is director of bands and professor of music education at Bowling Green State University. He has received a bachelor of arts and master of arts degrees from the University of Iowa. In 1984 he received the Citation of Excellence from the National Band Association.

What should be foremost in a conductor's mind when beginning a rehearsal?

McGinnis: I don't care whether it is a grade school band, junior high, high school, or the best university band in the country, you cannot work if you do not have discipline. If you don't have discipline in your life, you are not going anywhere. By discipline I don't mean coercion or frightening students half to death so they are on the edges of their chairs; they should be inspired by you and know that you mean business.

Kelly: The ensemble should respect a conductor as the person who says, "I am the chief, and all the rest of you guys are Indians. There can only be one chief, and that's me." You're either going to do something for a teacher because you fear him, like him, or respect him. I've played for conductors I didn't particularly like, but they didn't have to tell me twice how to play a part. I respected them. You want players to work through a rehearsal and be glad you didn't notice them. I tell students to go into a rehearsal and dare the conductor to find fault with them. A conductor should train an ensemble to respond to him. There are many antiseptic conductors with bands that may play well and have good tone, but they sure don't get to me.

High school directors should realize that they are the music man in their community. If it were

McGinnis (1970s)

not for them, many towns would have no instrumental music. I was the only director in a small town, and people came to me with band and instrument problems because there wasn't anyone else. When you teach at a university, you're just a little cog in the big wheel. College students have studio teachers, history teachers, theory teachers, and advisors. They are with you only part of the time. I have told high school kids that it is okay to read a physics book for five minutes while I work with the clarinets. I tried to instill in them that I care about them and I am not such a bad guy off the podium.

Is it possible to balance marching band with concert band?

McGinnis: I don't feel qualified to answer that question. In my fifth year at Oberlin Conservatory I was selected to conduct a high school band. It was fun and I enjoyed it. The high school had a marching band, but most of the emphasis was on concert band, which is typical in a small town that has a big conservatory like Oberlin. When I graduated, I was named instructor at Ohio State University and became assistant director of bands and worked with marching and concert bands. At Ohio State marching band is an expansive program that started with Eugene Weigel in the early 1930s when he was brought from Cleveland to direct the marching band. He made it into an all-brass band. The marching and concert bands there complement each other. Those who spend a lot of time with marching band do so only during the autumn quarter. Because they memorize all the music, they rehearse two hours a day, probably the longest rehearsal of any marching band in the country. Now as few as 10 to 15% of the players in the marching band are music majors.

What qualities do you look for in students?

McGinnis: When I accept a clarinet or a flute student, I don't accept him because of talent or previous skill or anything like that. I accept him because of the interest he shows in studying. I also take into account the interest of his parents and the interest of his band director in having students study with me. If an eighth or ninth grader will guarantee me a minimum of half an hour a day of practice time, then we can go places. By the time the students get through those first four or five years of private study, they should be accomplished in phrasing, musicianship, rhythm, sound, tone, intonation, and have all of those things in a balanced form. It is incredible what can happen with a minimal amount of practice, with a teacher who can define the fundamentals and analyze what's

811

wrong with the embouchure or why the throat is tight or if the breathing is adequate and why they can't finger tones well with the right hand because it gets cramped. All of these things should be examined in each lesson. I call this the nurturing process. We nurture kids along gradually; you can't slap them down every time they do something wrong. Young students should be told when things are not right and encouraged to change them.

How do you teach tuning to students who have never worked on intonation before?
Kelly: Intonation starts with tone, and tone is dependent on the way a student sits in the chair. Students have to hold the horn properly, breathe correctly, the mouthpiece has to fit the barrel, the reed has to fit the mouthpiece, and they should have a proper conception of sound. I sometimes wonder what kids listen to as an example for their instrument's tone. I suggest that students have an opportunity to listen to a recording of a good tone for their instrument. Tuning starts with a concept of tone.

How do you feel about the current direction of music education?
McGinnis: As I view high school bands, it scares me because there are directors whose primary interest is marching band, but I'm almost as scared of the jazz ensemble. If the concert band program and performance program for young people is not the hub of the wheel, I think there is something wrong. If everything centers around marching band or jazz band, then the students involved will lose.

I certainly was not a big name in the jazz ensemble field, but I played in a jazz band four of my five years at Oberlin. My first year I played lead alto in what we called the Mickey Mouse band, which was a way I could make money. For the next three years I played tenor in the top big band and considered it to be one of the greatest things that happened to me. Along with everything else, I played principal clarinet in the symphony orchestra, the band, and the top woodwind quintet. I did not play in marching band because I didn't have the time. Everything should migrate to the central idea of good performance, whether it is good band performance or good orchestra performance.

Anything worth doing should be done outstandingly well. That is my philosophy of music education. I'm a music educator from way back even though I have emphasized performing and

conducting in my career and had great opportunities in performance. I am grateful to have gone through Oberlin at a time there was a great man in charge of music education, Karl Gehrkens. He wrote some fine books and is one of the founders of music education in America. He had a tremendous influence on all of us.

There is a disturbing trend in music schools these days that I find is dishonest. Many schools are moving toward high-level performance with the attitude that the school doesn't exist for the students but the students exist for the great conductor at the university. The students are there to satisfy his need to conduct an ensemble. Do you see this?

McGinnis: Any number of the big university programs have gone overboard with performance. I am balancing on a fine line because I still consider myself an excellent performer who loves performing. I have had excellent opportunities to play under some of the world's greatest musicians, and those opportunities don't occur unless you play well enough to be in an atmosphere like that, but I keep coming back to the fact that schools have gone too far in the field of performance. The average person coming out of Oberlin, Juilliard, or Eastman these days thinks of teaching music but only until "I can get the principal trumpet job when Herseth retires from the Chicago Symphony, otherwise I'd rather do something else than be in music." Teaching is only a means to an end for them, and I'm not sure people who graduate from these schools will be devoted teachers. They are certainly wonderful musicians and often great performers, but most of them would like to have a good college teaching job if they couldn't find a good playing position. Many schools have gotten away from the idea that their principal mission is to train teachers. Instead they train performers. These days 350 tuba players will line up for a job in the Chicago Symphony.

Both of you have spent your lives in music education. What do you consider rewarding?

McGinnis: When you teach kids you should remember that they need encouragement. Helping them accomplish something is gratifying.
Kelly: When you start a fifth grade kid on cornet after school in the choral room and later take him to the Midwest stage in Chicago, you have had a lot to do with that youngster and have become close to him. That's rewarding.

Obsessed with Excellence

An Interview with Frank Battisti
by Tom Everett

Frank Battisti has conducted bands and wind ensembles for 30 years and currently leads the wind ensemble at the New England Conservatory. As a band director at Ithaca High School in Ithaca, New York, he commissioned many pieces that are now mainstays of the wind literature. He is a past president of the College Band Directors National Conference and founder of the National Wind Ensemble Conference.

Much of what you performed in your high school teaching days was contemporary literature. What are the advantages and challenges of using contemporary music, particularly music using techniques and non-harmonic language with which students and audiences have little experience?

Avant-garde compositions introduce students to new ways of making music and make them listen to and think about the elements of composition. In performing traditionally notated music, they can play in the right places and fit in; but if they work on a piece in which they are essentially composers, they have to know something about composition. You can get through a traditional piece without knowing anything about how a composer composes, but to play something reasonable in an aleatoric piece, a student

has to listen differently, not to hear if he's in tune but to know if what he plays relates to the rest of the composition. Involving students in avant-garde music makes them aware of a musical composition in ways that performing traditional pieces does not.

There are a lot of pieces that many of us consider staples of literature today that did not exist in 1955 when you took over the direction of the Ithaca High School Band. What kinds of literature and pieces do you remember performing your first few years with the band?

After the first concert I thought the band had done a wonderful job. Warren Benson, one of my college teachers, was complimentary about the performance but asked me why I played that funny music. I had worked hard to produce a fantastic performance, and then someone questioned the quality of the music. When I look at that program now, I think it is funny too. Benson's question didn't make me feel particularly good, but it made me think about my criteria and gave me an awareness of the lack of good quality literature for high school bands.

I wanted to do something to upgrade and enrich this literature. This was the basis for our high school commissioning project, the first of which was awarded to Warren Benson.

Being a high school band director in Ithaca offered possibilities not found in most places. In addition to Benson there was Karel Husa, who taught nearby at Cornell; and 90 miles away in Rochester, Fred Fennell had ideas that profoundly influenced me and my students.

From 1955 until I left in 1967 the Ithaca High School band attended every concert performed by the Eastman Wind Ensemble. We traveled by bus to Rochester, and Fennell often got on our bus after a concert and talked to the students. It was fantastic that they could meet and be inspired by someone like him. The great thing about those years was that the Eastman Wind Ensemble recorded music that a good high school band could play. Every band director in

Currently the band director at Harvard University, Tom Everett is a graduate of Ithaca College and founder of the International Trombone Association.

the United States could pick up the latest Mercury release and hear a great performance of the literature that they were working on. We no longer have a model like that because, while we still enjoy performing the literature of the 1950s and 1960s, college and university bands now play sophisticated pieces beyond the abilities of most high school bands in this country. Now we have two different streams: high school band literature and the sophisticated university and professional literature, but a model for high school band directors to emulate is not there anymore. No one would deny that Gunther Schuller is a significant composer, but when was the last time that a high school band commissioned him to write a piece? We could ask the same question concerning Warren Benson or Leslie Bassett.

In the 1950s and 1960s I had no trouble as a high school band director finding a model because I could listen to the Eastman Wind Ensemble. Other great bands then were the Ithaca College and the University of Michigan bands. I brought both groups to Ithaca to play concerts for my students, but it is very difficult to get those groups into your high school now. They inspired directors of the 1950s and 1960s to learn and perform the literature, and we got excited about it.

Did you go from being a college student right into the teaching position with the Ithaca public schools?

In my second semester of my senior year at Ithaca College Jack Graves, my high school band director, moved up to vice principal of Ithaca High School. They needed someone to teach private lessons and offered me a 5/6 time position while I was still a student. I had a teaching position but I didn't have the responsibility of performing groups. All I did those first two years was teach; there's no better way to start in this profession. I didn't have the responsibility of concert performances or any of the headaches of running a high school band. Instead I learned how to be a good teacher. During those years I studied minor instruments three at a time. I learned to make oboe and bassoon reeds and acquired other skills, but if I had a full-time directing job, I would never have had time to learn those things. After two years the school gave me a full-time position, and by then I was ready for it. Twenty-five years ago there were better teachers and better teaching in public schools. Today we are not as rigorous in demanding knowledge and skills on instruments as we were then.

When did you decide to pursue conducting instead of trumpet playing?

I never was passionate about being a great trumpet player, but I was passionate about music and started buying scores in high school. I was more interested in the music than in the playing: I wanted to deal more with all of music instead of being just a player on a part, but the trumpet gave me the opportunity to learn something about making music from the inside. When I went to college I sang in the choir and studied viola so I could play in the orchestra by the time I was a senior; I chose conducting because it allowed me to deal with the complete picture.

Was there music in your home?

In those years there was more music in homes; my sister and I took piano lessons, and every Friday our two-room country school offered general music. We played any time that we had company and even had a little neighborhood orchestra in which adults and children played together on Sunday nights; it was terrific.

During your high school years were there any national conductors or performers that influenced or inspired you?

I was in high school from 1946 to 1949, the years right after the Second World War. Many G.I.'s who had played in the service bands came back to Ithaca College; I remember their fabulous concerts at DeWitt Park and thinking how great they were. That was an important influence on me.

Colleagues and students often marvel at your sense of organization. Did you inherit that from your parents?

My father and mother provided order and discipline; our home was one in which you put things away. We did not have a lot, but everything had its place. My upbringing made me appreciate every opportunity.

My father, who had numerous jobs and finally became a building superintendent at a savings bank, cared a great deal about his family. He enjoyed life, lived to be 93 years old, and never worried about anything. I did not inherit that from him; my mother worried and so do I.

What were your main interests as a student?

I liked journalism and I worked for the school newspaper. I wasn't involved in athletics, but I love sports. Cornell had great football teams in the late 1930s, and I went to a neighbor's house every Saturday afternoon to listen to the games with him. Ithaca was a community with many things to do and a wonderful place to grow up.

What else influenced you?

Some of my interest in music stems from a neighbor across the street who played trumpet; anything he did, I wanted to imitate. In high school we had a good orchestra and band for the time, and the conductors were an inspiration to me; I sensed that they derived something special from teaching.

Did you play any contemporary literature as a high school student?

No, the things we played in high school were traditional and nothing you could call contemporary music.

What was it like being a music major at Ithaca College in the early 1950s?

Ithaca College was a wonderful environment with a tradition of training excellent teachers. Many music teachers in New York state were trained at Ithaca by Walt Beeler. I studied with a terrific theory teacher named Lynn Bogart for all four years. Everybody in school was in the chorus. I'm not sure we always sang the best, but it was an opportunity to learn a lot of literature I would not have known otherwise:

Mendelssohn's *Elijah*, Handel's *Messiah*, and Mozart's *Requiem*. The men and women I graduated with wanted to have the best high school band or chorus they could. We were obsessed with the idea of excellence. Such teachers as Don Wells and Ferdinand Pranzatelli, the orchestra conductor, helped establish my standards of excellence and values. I am fortunate to have had that quality of education; it has served me well.

What goals are still left there for you to tackle?

The only thing I want to do is to continue to grow and to learn. I want to share things with people and commission composers to write music for the wind band or wind ensemble. I want to write more and continue with exactly what I'm doing because I feel as committed, as passionate, and as energetic now as I ever have. □

January, 1981

Frank L. Battisti: The Role of the Conductor/Educator

An Interview by Denis W. Winter

How did you develop the outstanding program at Ithaca High School?

We didn't have a lot of money for anything, and a very limited amount of time to rehearse, so it was a matter of gradually trying to improve the teaching, increasing the amount of time we had on the schedule, and getting more money to buy the things we needed. I think the first thing I did was work very hard myself and ask the kids to do the same so we could achieve a high level of quality. As a result, the kids developed pride, and the community became aware of the band — it sounded better in concert and looked better on the march. Then it was a matter of winning more time in the school day from the administration. At first we had three rehearsals a week in the fall semester and two in the spring. When we could have band every single day on school time, that was a big step.

Also I tried to make students aware of music's place in history and its relationship to other arts. In the hallway in front of my office, I put up reproductions of paintings and architecture from the same period as the music we were then studying.

I wanted the students to understand the parallel between music and the other arts.

Gradually I tried to establish awareness of music as an art, rather than just as an activity. One way was to bring very good players and com-

petent conductors into the schools.

In the mid-1950s the wind ensemble at Eastman was beginning to form, and Frederick Fennell brought an exciting dimension to wind playing, both as a personality and as a conductor. I began to expose my students to the Eastman Wind Ensemble recordings, took them to Rochester to hear the group live in concert, and invited Fred to come to Ithaca, which he always did, usually on the day before Memorial Day. I would get the students out of classes for the whole day and we would play 15 or 20 pieces with Fred which we had already rehearsed rather well. We did not play a concert. There was no pressure to prepare five pieces for an audience. We just enjoyed the day, playing pieces that ranged from Mozart Serenades to full band compositions and gaining the knowledge he had of them. We also recommended that the students go to concerts at Ithaca College and Cornell; and whenever orchestras or ensembles came into town for concerts we tried to get their members to come to Ithaca High School to work with our students, give clinics, or to conduct the band.

As the students became more aware of musicians and excited about what they heard and saw, they developed a desire to be more like what they

Denis W. Winter teaches at the University of Central Arkansas in Conway.

heard and saw. The excitement was transferred into hard work, more kids being interested in studying privately, greater awareness of expression and creativity. As they developed more and more skills, they had more appreciation for creativity, increased interest and enthusiasm to develop more skills. . .and the cycle continued.

How did the commissioning project evolve?

I became the director of the high school band in 1955 and I think we commissioned our first work in 1957. It went to Warren Benson, a logical choice because he was then teaching at Ithaca [now at Eastman], and I was working with him. The piece was *Night Song* for concert band. We continued to commission works until I left Ithaca in 1967. This program brought composers into direct contact with the students, and they built up tremendous anticipation for the arrival of a new piece, and of course they worked very hard in trying to mount a first performance because they felt a great responsibility to give this piece the best performance they could. Wanting to satisfy the demands of the commissioned composer gradually led to a requirement that every student in the high school band had to write an original piece for his own instrument. When I first announced that idea, some kids were reluctant, but gradually they all participated and became enthusiastic. The project gave them great insight into the creative process, and established an appreciation for the creator and the creative act. It also developed a certain amount of integrity and moral responsibility toward other people's music, because the students realized how important other people were in the mounting of their own compositions. And of course it contributed tremendously to the overall plan of helping students become more sensitive to music and more excited by it.

How were these commissions financed?

Every cent — including the money it cost to copy and reproduce the parts and to bring the composer to Ithaca — was raised by the students. The parents and other members of the community were willing to contribute to the commissioning fund, but the students refused their help. They wanted the composer to know that this money was a result of their commitment to the project, and they went out and raised literally thousands and thousands of dollars to make this possible. The composers were very impressed that kids were willing to go out and paint houses, sell chicken barbecue, and all kinds of other things to raise money for this kind of activity.

How long did it take before you felt the program had reached a musical apex and there was pride in the group?

I can't remember, although I know it was not in the first, second, third, or fourth year. I know it was quite a way down the road. When I first started teaching, someone (I don't remember who) told me that to create something that you could be proud of you'd better plan to stay someplace for a number of years — that person said 15. I think that most great high school situations are developed by someone who has the necessary commitment and dedication. It is not done quickly and it is not done through gimmicks. It is done by developing a plan and then having the patience and dedication to implement it. And it seems to me the plan should be based upon the foundation that music is part of the arts program in the school, and the arts program in the school is aesthetic in nature. The director must make sure that the activities developed and the strategies used are basically art-oriented — students being helped to develop good musical skills, good musical knowledge, good attitudes, appreciation for good music and for good performance.

How did you react to competition?

The system that I taught in did not believe that music should be a competitive experience. There were standards we were trying to help the kids recognize and achieve, and we believed that evaluation is very important; but you can have evaluation without ranking. They are not the same. We were in the business of evaluating students, of setting standards, trying to motivate students, of setting standards, of trying to motivate students to achieve. We were not in the business of educating students to think they had to beat someone else out in order to be good.

During this period at Ithaca, how did your conducting technique evolve?

I had the opportunity to observe many conductors — the various guests we brought in for the high school band, and also those who conducted the many concerts I went to. (I'm not just talking about band concerts, but all kinds — orchestra, choral.) As I observed these people at work, I became more and more aware of the liabilities I had as a conductor. I saw what other conductors could achieve with my band, and the things they could get students to do as a result of their professional conducting technique and facility. I realized then that what I had was a very primitive, basic conducting technique; and I knew I had to do something about growing as a conductor. My evolution has been mainly a result of observation and asking for help from those who came in to conduct my band, plus later trying to define and refine what conducting is made of, to find out what can be taught and what things have to be left to experience.

You were invited to New England Conservatory to establish a permanent wind ensemble. How does one go about developing such a program?

Before I came to the Conservatory in 1969 they had been doing some wind ensemble programs — concerts were scheduled and two weeks of rehearsals were devoted to preparation — but there was no ongoing wind ensemble as such. Gunther Schuller and Harvey Phillips [President and Assistant] believed that the Conservatory should have as broad a program in music as possible, so a decision was made to start a full-time wind ensemble. As we all know, Gunther Schuller is a very

Photo by Bruce Nolan

broad-based kind of universal music exponent, and he feels that good music of all styles is very important. He believed that in 1969 it was time the Conservatory recognized the fact that the wind ensemble had come of age and was part of the music-making of our time. For me, it meant the creation of an ensemble that would expose Conservatory students, most of whom want to get jobs in orchestras, to the body of literature that orchestral wind players ought to know. I also felt we should play significant music for winds, brass, and percussion instruments, so students would know, understand, and perform the pieces they would encounter as professional wind players.

So this is when you felt it necessary to take on the works of Varèse and Stravinsky. It must have been completely different from the things that you had done before.

Absolutely, and it demanded that I grow in my ability to deal with new music. I don't mean "new" in the sense that it was written five minutes ago, but literature that I had not done before. Because a lot of this music demanded things of me as a conductor that had not been demanded before, it also meant I had to grow technically.

Let's say that you just elected to do Varèse's, Octandre. *How would you approach the score and what would be your method of study?*

The method of approaching a Varèse piece is not much different than any other. The first thing is extensive study, putting the piece under a microscope, just like in a laboratory, to find out what it's made of and how it has been brought together. A thorough examination includes analysis from a thematic and harmonic point of view, dealing with the linear and horizontal aspects of the music, examining the orchestration, understanding the technique of development. All details of the piece have to be discovered, and then assimilated by the conductor.

Once the conductor knows the piece, he must deal with the actual mounting of it, the rehearsal.

Of course, the conductor must be able to execute what is needed (changes in tempo, shifts of meter, subdivisions) to gain the precision demanded in the score. For me, it is essential to plot rehearsal strategy so students play with an awareness of how what they're doing relates to the moment and also to the large structure of the piece. I think it is very important to carry out a rehearsal not just in the sense of mounting the piece, as one might do if it were a professional performance, but to bring an understanding of the piece to the players.

How do you map out the time that you spend studying a score so that you feel ready when you first have to rehearse it?

It's possible to cram most of the activity of learning a score into a concise number of hours, but I'm not sure that is the best way to learn it. I do a lot of my score study during the summer for pieces I'll do in the next school year. I don't try to get through everything in a certain amount of time, but study on an ongoing daily basis. I learn a score slowly, and this method allows me time to think about what I'm doing — kind of cooking the goose in a nice slow way. I feel the knowledge is assimilated better this way, and I like to start early enough so I can enjoy the process of reading what I'm doing, of evaluating, of spending as much time as I want to analyzing any detail I might discover. If there is a vertical texture that I'm dealing with, I might want to draw a little piano clef at the bottom of the score and put all the notes in so I can see them more clearly in my own mind.

I use two scores often, one for reading and the other for performance, because in the process of analyzing a score it becomes very cluttered with my notes, so I prepare another for performance.

Do you solfege the parts or use a piano?

I use both, but I don't think the means are quite as important as the end. One should not be reluctant to use whatever is desired or needed.

How about recordings?

I think it's dangerous to use recordings to learn a piece because we are such great imitators of what we hear; however recordings become valuable once you have learned a score. At that stage you have your own image of the piece and the recording becomes something to bounce off, an opportunity to compare your interpretation with another.

Most music education majors come out of college with a minimal amount of conducting experience, and little instruction. Yet this is their primary duty. How does one go about improving conducting technique?

Many music educators have never clarified in their own mind what their responsibilities are, and have never established what students should do as players in order to function as part of the musical ensemble. They mainly come to doing whatever they do almost by chance. Directors must have the dedication, and the perseverance, and the willingness to help students develop those habits that make them good ensemble players. For example, if we tell the student that he should always watch the conductor, then give a downbeat when he is not watching, we are subverting our teaching. If we did not give the first downbeat until everyone is looking at us, and insisted on that every single time, each student would gradually develop a habit of looking at us. Of course, if I am telling the student to constantly watch me, there better be a good reason for him to do it. If you're up there with your beat always in the same style, and you are not communicating precisely what you want, then the student has no reason to look at you. If you want a staccato note, you have to make the conducting pattern look like you want detached articulation. If you want it soft, the pattern has to take on another dimension. You must try to have in your conducting technique the precision of articulation that you would have on your instrument.

The school conductor must be aware that he has a dual function when he stands in front of a group: teacher and conductor, and he must decide very carefully which is which, because you might do things as a teacher that you should never do as a conductor.

Can you give some examples?

As a teacher you might have to count off into a downbeat, but a conductor who does that negates the reason for the player to look at the downbeat. If you use a podium, I think it's a good idea to step off of it when you are a teacher — drilling things,

Photo by Bruce Nolan

or helping students solve problems in the music. Then when you step on the podium the players know you are a conductor. That means you have to act like a conductor, and continue to grow. If a student is in your band for three years, he ought to see growth in you just as you are expecting it in him. The best way for us to teach students is by our example, and students should see that growth is something one pursues at every stage of life.

Then you are very careful not to compromise your conducting for your teaching.

Absolutely. That is a very serious thing to do and a thing that many school conductors get trapped into. They do not define the two different positions and before long it all kind of becomes one, and they subvert themselves as a conductor. If we graduate from our music education curriculum with only primitive conducting technique, we obviously have to do something about it. Unless we do, the students may be looking, but we cannot communicate what we want through conducting technique, and so have to stop and try to explain in words what we want. That's not conducting. Conducting is being able to clearly demonstrate, minimizing the need to stop and tell people what you want. The ensemble player should have the playing skills to be able to respond to what he sees, thereby creating a situation where the conductor gives, the players see, and the music is affected.

What do you look for in good performers?

Ultra sensitivity, the ability to perceive the smallest deviation. If the student is very sensitive to the subdivision of the beat, he will be able to perceive the slightest imperfection in a series of four even quarter notes, for example, and will be able to correct a small flaw in that passage. The ultimate issue in playing is hearing and listening. Technical facility and good basic musicianship skills allow complete concentration on listening to what is being produced. Students must be taught all of these things so that one can finally arrive at making music and concentrate totally on expression.

So, it is clear that you make a distinct difference between the conductor and the conductor-educator.

Yes, I see myself as a conductor functioning in an educational environment, where it is not just a matter of mounting a concert, it's a matter of teaching students ensemble skills. I see my job as rehearsing pieces in a way that allows me to pursue the most expressive performances I can create, while at the same time helping students to know the entire piece as well as their parts, and to gain more insight as to how they function in an ensemble than they had when they started to play the piece. Also, I think that after we have mounted a piece, it is to our advantage to play it more than once. The performance experience is unique and students should have several opportunities to deal with a piece in public.

Let's examine one of your programs and investigate how you selected the music.

It seems to me that there is something in common between Gabrieli and Varèse and the idea of mixing them — a Gabrieli piece and then two Varèse pieces, and then another Gabrieli — is to put Varèse in a position where the listeners might see them in a different light. They also might see Gabrieli differently, because in my way of thinking there is some commonness.

They are both innovators.

It is not only that. I'm looking at the pieces directly, not at the men, but both these men looked at sound as being very important. Gabrieli was very aware of the acoustics of space. All of Varèse's music is dealing with acoustical problems, and acoustical possibilities. I'm not telling the audience to listen for these things, I'm just presenting them together in the hopes that someone may be able to see each piece in a way they may not have seen before.

It's unusual to see Gabrieli in the middle of a program.

Yes, and also I think that it's not traditional to see Gabrieli and Varèse back to back; but to me that makes sense. The Stravinsky, which follows it — L'Histoire — is a wonderful piece, and the Ives piece is like a little encore. Rather than use a traditional march here, I chose to do an Ives march simply because it would probably be a new listening experience for the audience.

The Schoenberg *Theme and Variations* was included because it was the 100th anniversary of the birth of Schoenberg, and I felt we should honor that fact. I like to include a solo piece, because it adds a varied dimension for the audience. The Hindemith, Stravinsky, and the Varèse *Intégrales* were all written within ten years of each other, so there is a 1920-30 common relationship, and it's a chance to get a glimpse of three different kinds of pieces, all composed in roughly the same era. Also, we have a full wind band piece, one for orchestral wind section, a brass ensemble piece of Gabrieli, the Varèse *Density* for solo flute, then the *Intégrales* which we played with a small wind orchestra with percussion players, then we go back to a Gabrieli piece which is for a small brass ensemble, then the Stravinsky *L'Histoire* which is a chamber ensemble piece, and then the Charles Ives *March* for small pit orchestra. There is a variety of music and kinds of ensembles. To me as a listener, that makes the program more enjoyable than hearing the same thing coming at me for the whole program. Variety is important.

What are your thoughts about programming the standard wind band literature?

I think that if we are ever going to cultivate an audience that appreciates this body of literature, we have to play the standard pieces from it many times over. If we help people identify these pieces, and they begin to understand them and enjoy them, then when you program the Stravinsky

Octet, for example, people will see it's on the program and will come to hear the piece. Most people go to orchestra programs to hear the piece that is being played. Most people go to band programs to hear the band. We have not done a good job of helping the public know the basic repertoire of our medium. I try to include standard repertoire and also things that are new. They might be old pieces, but new in the sense that they have not been programmed very often. And for me personally, if I want to grow as a conductor, I must continually put pieces on the program that I have **never conducted before.**

Please tell us about your research and how it has affected your conducting.

I have an ongoing curiosity for the literature that is part of the heritage I work in, and I never felt I could get the clarity I wanted in pieces such as the Holst *Suites* and *Hammersmith*, and Vaughan Williams' *Toccata Marziale*, all part of the traditional wind band repertoire. This concern led me to try to discover something about the published versions by examining the original manuscripts. It would seem to me that this would be true of any music: going back to the composer's original score might develop insights, and lead to discoveries that would be significant in developing one's interpretation of those pieces. That's what led to my examination of those original scores and mounting performances here in their urtext version, which gave me insight that carries over when I conduct these pieces in other environments, when I'm using the published versions.

Over the course of years, through various editions and printings, things can be added, changed, left out — some by intention, some by neglect — so it is wise for us to constantly be slightly suspicious of what we get and to look at the most original source we can.

Many public school band directors become frustrated, finding that they must be promoters, fund-raisers, and develop many other non-musical talents to do their jobs. Do you have comments on this problem?

It seems to me that a music educator must decide what music education should be. In a lot of places it doesn't fit into the curriculum, and that is a serious problem because as long as it is on the fringe, then music teachers are probably going to have to deal with administrators from the perimeter. If we believe that music is one of the "back-to-basics" of education, then we must know what makes it basic. And the band director has to be very careful he does not find himself involved in a program where most of his efforts are devoted to fund-raising and all those other things you were talking about, because our activities affect who we are, change our attitudes, and order our priorities. A music teacher who is raising money and dealing with non-musical activities 75% of the time is going to be frustrated. Musicians need the fulfillment of working with music. The music teaching establishment — those who actually work in the schools or who train others to do so must realize that they have the capacity to do something about their programs by clearly defining what those programs are. Programs have become whatever the community has come to think the program is, affected by how courageous the music teacher might be in confronting the realism of the present program as against the ideal or the goals of an arts-oriented music curriculum. I think that's the issue. I believe what is needed in most places is for the band director to think of himself first as a musician, then realize that as a musician he has a responsibility to art; having accepted a responsibility to his art, it then becomes clear that he has a responsibility to his students to make sure what they are getting in the program is art. He must believe that his job is not to direct activities, but to help kids develop skills in a subject, and to establish attitudes of understanding that will result in life-long appreciation for the art. ■

Battisti as Executive

Frank Battisti is the current president of the College Band Directors National Association. Their 21st National Conference will be held at the University of Michigan in Ann Arbor February 11-14. The program will include premiere performances of new pieces by Gunther Schuller, Mario Davidovsky, William Kraft, and Verne Reynolds.

Battisti is also chairman of The International Conference for Symphonic Bands and Wind Ensembles to be held July 20-26 in Manchester, England. The conference is the result of many years of thought by Battisti and others, and a number of organizations are cooperating in its planning. Additional information can be secured from William Johnson at California Polytechnic State University in San Luis Obispo, California.

Concert Hall at the Royal Northern College of Music, site of the International Conference in Manchester, England.

An Interview with Arnald Gabriel

Kenneth L. Neidig

It is Monday morning and the concert band at the University of Kansas Midwestern Music Camp has been rehearsing since 7:55. At 8:35 Arnald Gabriel is introduced. The full-bird colonel, conductor-commander of the United States Air Force Band, is spending leave time ("vacation" to non-military types) doing what he does almost every day of the year. It's a way of life and he seems to thrive on it. Today he's working with high school students whose skills are far less advanced than his Air Force professionals. He adapts easily to the different level, but does not compromise in his relentless pursuit of excellence. From the very beginning, the students see a dynamic and dedicated musician who is not going to waste his time or theirs. Within the first 12 minutes he has heard each person play individually; adjusted the pitch downward from the all-the-way-in level of many bands; simultaneously worked on intonation, balance, and blend with a chord-member assignment plan ("all 1st trumpets on C, 2nds on E, 3rds on G," etc.); and set up a routine that will be refined throughout the week leading to a Saturday concert.

At 8:47 he calls up Russian Sailor's Dance *and works hard to get everything right, both technically and musically. He does not use a score, but it is clear that he knows every note and nuance in every measure of every part. Some players left behind by his rapid-fire instructions try to get help from a stand partner and are told, "If you have a question, please direct it to the podium." His manner is polite, yet firm. There are neither tantrums nor sermons, and only those who have not yet learned to concentrate receive an unfriendly look. The percussion players are asked, "Do you have to sit down when you're not playing? It takes 10 seconds for you to get back to your instruments, and we can't afford to lose that time."*

Gradually the students get the message, and by 9:20 they have played from the beginning up to letter H with precise articulation in a musical style that seemed out of reach 33 minutes earlier. Those 85 bars are nearly ready for performance, and the rehearsal ends on time.

A symphonic band rehearsal follows, where the subject is Jericho *and the players are more advanced; but the approach is basically the same — energetic, efficient, friendly (but no jokes), with the fun and satisfaction growing out of accomplishment.*

The Colonel gets in a few miles of running before we meet to enjoy informal lunchtime conversation, then move to Bob Foster's Jayhawk Band office to record a formal interview before still another rehearsal, this time with the camp orchestra.

If I were a hypnotist and could take you back to the first time you ever heard any music, could we find a time when you said, "This is it; I must do this the rest of my life."? Is there a magic moment?

Yes, there really is a moment that I recall very vividly. I must have been five or six years old. I came from a very small Italian neighborhood [Cortland, New York], and in a basement of a Catholic church they were doing the *Cavalleria Rusticana*. It was a touring organization, I think, probably out of Syracuse. I have other vivid memories about how bad the makeup and the lighting were; but, when they did the "Intermezzo" and they used strings, it was the most gorgeous sound that I had ever heard. I was so enchanted, and I thought probably the most important thing that I could ever do would be to make other people feel the way I was feeling at that moment. It really touched me very deeply. I was just transcended. You know, even a kid of five or six has insecurities and stresses, but that music just transported me, made me feel relaxed and completely divorced from any worldly concerns. To this day it is my favorite piece of music.

One day my wife, then a staff announcer on W.G.M.S. (good music station in Washington) called and asked, "How do you feel?" and I said I was really down in the dumps about something, and she said "turn on the radio." She was playing that piece. When she said "Don't you like that?" I replied "like it...do you know what that piece means to me?" She has an uncanny ability — claims she's a Bohemian witch — and some of the communications we've had have been almost eerie.

Do you have any other memories of your early years?

My dad listened to the Metropolitan Opera every Saturday on the radio, the Texaco broadcasts, and I remember that made a deep impression on me. Also, I was only eight or nine when I heard my older brother practice piano all the time. I just sat on the bench and watched the music go by, and was fascinated by it. Of course we didn't have much money in those days, during the depression. One boy was already taking music lessons, so I waited a couple of years until I was about 10 or 11 before I started to play the flute.

Your choice?

I don't know how that came about, but somehow it was decided that I would play the flute. I went to Syracuse and took lessons from a gentleman named George Hambrecht, whose son became quite a flutist, and is now principal with the Cincinnati Symphony.

Did you play in your school band?

Yes, up through high school and also in the town band, which was quite good. It was conducted by Frank Crisara, whose son Ray went on to become quite a musician — Metropolitan Opera Orchestra at age 19, and then he played with Toscanini and the N.B.C. Symphony for over 20 years.

Was it obvious to everyone that you really had something special?

Well it wasn't to me, but apparently my high school band director thought so. I was working in the canning factory after coming back from World War II and had no idea that I could become a professional musician. You can imagine what three years in the infantry do to a young man's mind. I was bitter, to be perfectly honest about it, and I thought at that time there was no way I could compete with those musicians who had played in the military bands, or those students who were graduating from high school and going directly on to college. My high school band director, Burton Stanley, said I really ought to go to college; but I told him, "No, I'm working here at the canning factory, and I just can't compete — I've not been on the books academically, or on my horn musically." Well, he simply went to Ithaca, paid my matriculation fee, and talked to Walter Beeler who agreed to accept me without audition. So when he did that, I practiced religiously. I even took my instrument along to the canning factory.

I can't prove this, but I think Burt Stanley told them, "Here's a guy who has a lot of ability and a lot of ambition, but what he really needs is a challenge." They put me on the first student recital (the first day of October), plus the University band audition. I think I was the only freshman to make a first chair. I'm not sure that I played the best, but I think they just did that knowing that I had this ambition — and perhaps talent — that needed a challenge. Burton Stanley had asked me to try it for one semester to see how I liked it, and it went pretty well.

Was there ever any problem recognizing your talent or was it obvious? I'm thinking that there are many band directors who may have an Arnold Gabriel sitting in their flute section today. How do you recognize talent and help it grow?

Well, I don't know quite how to answer, except to say he recognized that before my unhappiness with what happened in the war, I was a productive musician and cared about what I was doing. Oftentimes if you take an angry young man (and that's what I was) and challenge the bitterness, you can turn it around.

There are lots of angry young men today...

Exactly. I have promoted people who have been unhappy with the way they've found things, and now some of them are running my organization. They were right, they had a reason to be unhappy, and I channeled that unhappiness, just as Burton Stanley did with me.

So a good band director has to be a good psychologist and student of human nature?

I don't think there's any question about that. To be a good band director, first of all you have to like people, be able to see the best in them, and know how to bring it out. I don't care if you have memorized every score ever written, and can

analyze every technical detail. A tremendous wealth of knowledge and musicianship is important; but there are lesser musicians lacking that knowledge who do a great job just because they have the ability to inspire others.

Band directors tell stories about you — your conducting ability, your sensitivity. They say you have a photographic memory.

Well I don't.

But there's something special there...

There is a lot of hard work. I think I have a good memory, but I don't think it's unusual. I guess I have a little higher than average I.Q., but I don't think it's unusual either. I believe that most people regularly work with only a fraction — say 60% — of their available mental capability, and maybe I'm able to work with about 65%.

I think people should challenge themselves more. They'd be surprised at the kinds of things they can do.

When I first look at a score, I try to see the large picture, similar to an architect who can look at a blue print and see the finished product at one glance. It's a little more difficult for a conductor because there are so many pages; but you should be able to see the high points and positions of repose, then block it out in large hunks in your mind, so that everything doesn't sound similar. After that you look at details. Every measure says something, every measure goes somewhere or comes from somewhere, and there is something musical to be brought out from every note in every measure.

Just to test the mental retention of a conducting clinic audience, I'll sometimes say, "Measure 137 is the high point. Measures 1-4 and 153-155 are the positions of repose. After the introduction, we do a first statement with three phrases, the third of which is augmented." Already I've lost some people, but I'll go on — "the second statement is so and so, and the third statement is so and so...," and some people are still with me. Then I take it down to the next level, saying, "Having blocked out that much, the next consideration is so and so," and slowly you start to lose people. It's their ability to concentrate and retain, of course, that needs the challenge. After bringing it down to the phrases, then you get down to the measure, and inside the measure you get through the articulation, then...

You haven't always been able to do this.

No, I forget when it started, about 12 or 13 years ago, near as I can estimate. I was doing an all-state, I don't even remember what state, and found myself looking down less and less, so finally I said if I don't really need the music that much, maybe I can retain the whole score. But memorizing the score is immaterial, the fact that you prepare it properly is important. Before you mount the podium you should have that score in your head, absolutely at your command. Not using a score with student bands allows you to work faster and more efficiently. When you stop and want to start

Every second counts

at a certain measure or rehearsal letter, you can recall it instantly without turning pages. Also, there is constant eye contact. The moment you look down in that score and start turning pages, you've lost part of your band.

When you first started memorizing scores were there training devices you used to develop a longer retention span, or did it just evolve naturally?

I think it evolved naturally; obviously there are processes of association you use that sometimes work. Some of them sound awfully unsophisticated. I'm trying to think of one that would be particularly relevant. In *Emperata Overture* letter E is the exposition. That's easy to remember. At letter F there's a flute solo. You can use things of that nature as pegs for rehearsal letters and numbers. These associations are now coming back to me. In the *Variations on America* (Charles Ives), the F section is where all of the woodwinds are playing grace notes that sound like flams. That's how I remember that variation. It sounds unsophisticated, but it is a crutch, a device, a peg upon which to hang that memory. After you have learned the piece thoroughly you don't need those crutches anymore.

I can just hear band directors out there saying, "That Gabriel, he's a genius or something, I can never do anything like that..."

Oh yes they can. Absolutely.

O.K., let's talk about how they can.

I never really teach people to memorize a score; I teach them to prepare the score thoroughly. And if they have prepared it adequately, they probably can do much of it from memory. That's the whole point. I don't think they really delve into the score as thoroughly as they should. Most high school

band directors are concerned with so many other kinds of activities — stage band, and marching band, which is very time consuming — so they don't have a lot of time to learn the score perhaps as thoroughly as they should. Even so, I think if they would tax themselves they would find their abilities to be far greater than they think they are. It really isn't all that easy for me, because I have to sit down and work at it. I mean work, work, work, work.

It's clear to me that you're learning every day. What have you learned lately?

You can't ever rest on your past laurels. You always have to prepare a new score and find something new and exciting in your life, and that's what I'm learning all the time.

Also, the longer I'm in music, the more I use words such as "ponderous," "dainty," or "sonorous" in rehearsal, rather than technical terms such as "loud," "soft," "short," or "long." Those are so academic and so undescriptive, and I'm beginning to think that the emotional content of music is more important.

The older I get the more I realize that you don't have to be a tyrant. If you're secure with your art and your profession, it's unnecessary to talk down to anybody, or to berate, or to raise your voice. If I do, it's only because they're being unattentive or something of that sort, it's not related to our ability to make music together. We conductors have to realize that we are not the most important elements. The composer is, the truth that is in the score. We are just the re-creators. The performing organization and conductor together make the music, and there has to be mutual respect and admiration. I admire my groups, and I hope that they have respect for the knowledge I have of the score. By working together we can re-create the work.

I don't use a baton. It has become smaller and less important since Lully hit himself in the foot, developed gangrene and died. That made him stop pounding on the floor. But it still seems to me that too many conductors use the baton as a symbol of authority, and I don't think we need that. I believe a baton invokes a certain fear, and there should be no fear in making music; there should be respect. We should get away from the stick, which seems to be that symbol of the kind of authority that people resent.

That's interesting coming from someone who's in the military full time...

I have infinite respect for all of my players, and when we've played a great concert we've done it together.

You have your part and they have theirs.

Absolutely, and I've never conducted a great concert when they haven't played a great concert.

Let's talk about efficiency. Just a few minutes wasted here and there is going to pile up. This morning you told the percussion section "We just can't afford to waste that 10 seconds."

That's right. I think that many conductors do waste an awful lot of time. The more you can get out of the time allotted, the better your concerts are going to be. Much of the delay is because it takes the director so long to find where he wants to start, and it takes the students so long to find it in their music. It takes so long because they're not concentrating. What you saw this morning in my rehearsal is something that I do constantly: when I stop I say we're going to start in the third measure of number 3, and I mean we want to start there NOW.

I noticed that your efficiency eventually transfers to the kids.
Yes, it takes a while. About Wednesday they realize "this guy means what he's saying."

But even here at the beginning of the week, it seemed that students were realizing it. I've seen so many directors who will be most inefficient themselves, act almost lethargic, and then expect the kids to play with a lot of enthusiasm on the edge of their chairs. But you throw yourself into the music, just as you expect the kids to do.
Again it's that trigger response you want, constantly. Then when the concert comes, in the event something ever goes wrong, you can get things corrected very quickly because they're used to that kind of response.

Of course when you know the score absolutely thoroughly you're going to save time because you know exactly what you want. That kind of conductor is like the sculptor who was telling how easy it is to create an elephant: "I just get a huge piece of stone and chip away everything that doesn't look like an elephant." You have to know where you're going, keep your eye on that objective, and just chip away everything that doesn't sound like you want it to sound. If the conductor knows the score, he isn't going to waste any time because he will be very dissatisfied with what he hears, and work quickly to correct it.

But if he's searching along with the kids, then . . .
Then the kids know. Kids are so bright. When the conductor gets lost, he can always blame his stop on a hundred things ("Tubas, you're dragging"), but that isn't why he stopped, and the kids know it.

I think leadership by example is important in all aspects of our life. In the United States Air Force we have certain physical requirements. For example, we're supposed to run a mile and a half in a certain time. I've forgotten what it is for people my age, but I insist on running as fast as the 21-year-old in my band. I think that's leadership by example. If they complain that these requirements are too severe, I tell them "I can do it, and I'm old enough to be your father, almost grandfather."

You're 56 or thereabouts?
That's right, 56, and I run a mile and a half in 14

minutes, which is required of a 21-year-old. I would do it anyway, whether I were in or out of the military, because I firmly believe in it both as a personal discipline and because it does make us healthier animals. We can function better as human beings if we're healthier animals.

You are well known for your intensity, and surely this physical well-being contributes greatly to that.
That's right. There are physical fitness people who have written books on the subject, and say it far more articulately than I can, but I firmly believe that you can think better if you're physically fit. I can see the difference. When I don't work out regularly I feel so guilty and so lethargic, because I'm not working at peak efficiency.

You push yourself pretty hard, don't you?
I don't know whether it's pushing; I do challenge myself. My wife thinks I work too hard; my mother thinks I work too hard; but what's too hard? As I said before, I don't think people work up to their potential. If I were in a deep state of depression, then I would be working too hard. If I had to work six or eight hours in several occupations I could think of I would get bored. Pushing yourself is relative, and I just thrive on this kind of activity. I wouldn't do anything else. I have 33 years military experience and could have retired years ago, but retire to what? Beachcomber? I'm nourishing my own spiritual values and I feel that I'm contributing to other people and that they are contributing to me. How could I be more happy?

Another thing I noticed you doing this morning was the "bite-size-chunks" kind of rehearsal, concentrating only on the first statement in Russian Sailor's Dance. *When conductors do an entire piece it seems to me it sometimes gives the kids a feeling of hopelessness; that they'll never get it all. But at the end of that one rehearsal this morning those kids seemed fairly well convinced it had been great fun.*

Well, I know many fine conductors who do read a piece the whole way; but I think that most of us — students and adults alike — are creatures of habit, and if you start playing that thing badly and no one stops you, you think that's the way it's going to be and you start forming bad habits immediately. I like to do it right, from the beginning, and not only talk about the proper notes, but the proper style as well. I mean nothing is going to get by. They understand the ground rules and know that's the way the rehearsals are going to be. If you read too many passages and let too much get by, I'm afraid those bad habits are going to be formed. They think "O.K., I got by with that." Maybe they didn't even know it was wrong. They must know, and they have to think about every note. You try to work everything at the same time — talking about balances, intonation, style, blend — from the top of the rehearsal. You don't just say "We'll get the notes first, then we'll worry about articulation and dynamics." You don't do that, at least I don't. They know there's only one objective, and that's perfection. Some conductors say first they want to "see if it goes." Anything will go; it depends on your determination to make it go.

You've been critical of the fact that too many bands play with great technical superiority and not much musicianship. Are there ways to teach musicianship?

That's a large step, the difference between a craftsman and an artist. We have a lot of craftsmen who can get all the nuts and bolts done, and academically and technically it's perfect; but the music is just lacking. You know, so many of our academicians are afraid to inject emotion into their music, for fear that we over-emote. In the United States I'm considered to be a fairly emotional conductor, and yet when I go to Europe they think I'm not emotional enough. It's an incredible thing. When I worked with a group in the Netherlands (and there is no finer wind playing in the world), after the first rehearsal I tried to find out how they thought I was doing. They indicated that we had been working an awful lot on notes and could we get into the emotion. I thought I was being very emotional, but then I really cut loose and expressed myself just the way I felt, and they loved it. They are extremely emotional in Europe, but not burlesqued or overdone, nothing of the sort. So often in this country we're too concerned with the technical approach. There are conductors who tune every chord with the Stroboconn, for example. I think that's using a training aid to a dangerous degree, where a musician doesn't listen for himself.

In your tuning routine this morning, you were telling them "sharp" or "flat." You'll refine that, I assume, the rest of the week, and have them doing it themselves.

Absolutely, that's just a starting point. Very often a group just puts their instruments together all the way, not remembering where they were yesterday. Then they're sharp every day and start from there; I tell them to remember where they were yesterday, start there, and then refine every single day.

So you're saying that the way to teach musicianship is to be a musician yourself, and transmit it in every one of those small ways that we all can. But how does one continue to develop musicianship?

I can't really say what's the difference between a craftsman and that step to musicianship.

Does listening do a lot of good?

Yes. I'd try to listen to as many fine groups as you can. It doesn't need to be a band or an orchestra. Go hear a string quartet, or a fine vocalist. Of course opera is the alpha and the omega, because that's everything — staging, costuming, singing, instruments, all the arts — in one giant confluence. When I was leader of the Air Force Band of Europe from 1958-63 there were 43 full-time opera companies in Germany and 3 within 20 kilometers of Wiesbaden, Germany. Because they were state supported, admission was 3 Deutsche marks, then only about 75¢. I went frequently and just watched the conductor and learned a great deal. I love Verdi and Puccini; in particular *La Bohème* and *Tosca*. I could go 10 times a week and not be sick of them, they're just gorgeous, so melodic.

Yes, to develop musicianship you must listen. That's the only way, you can't learn it out of a book. Recently Stanley Drucker [New York Philharmonic principal clarinet] was a guest soloist with the band and my whole clarinet section is better for having listened to him.

Are there any especially good pieces you've found to teach musicianship?

I would suggest that high school directors get all of the Ravel and Debussy recordings they can and follow along with a score to see what several different conductors do with bringing out inner parts. It isn't just block harmony with a melodic line, as unfortunately so many of our band pieces are, where there isn't much room for interpretation. I think impressionistic music does more to bring out sensitivity than any other kind of music I know.

Can you get anything from recordings or is it strictly a live kind of experience?

Live is better, but a record is better than nothing. DiStefano was a great operatic conductor with the St. Cecelia orchestra in Rome, and to listen to that kind of recording, that kind of performance, is just invaluable. When I drive to work in the morning I listen to our good music station. When that sound is in your ear, and you take it with you to the podium, it is hard to be satisfied with anything less. I think if a high school director listened to a fine symphony recording before his rehearsal started — it doesn't matter what composition as long as he hears that sonority, that balance, and that blend — and he takes that sound with him to the podium, he will do his best to produce that sound. Here again you have a concept, a goal toward which you're aiming.

Is there any band music that directors can use to teach this to their kids?

Well, actually, you can get sensitivity from any piece, even a B♭ scale — at an audition you hear a guy warming up in the hall playing a scale and you know whether you're going to take him or not.

What about the atmosphere you play in? If you're sitting in a band playing mechanical things day after day, then aren't you going to develop into a mechanic? It would seem better to be sitting in a band playing music that demands at least some sensitivity in order to come off at all.

The U.S. Air Force Band plays a Bach chorale every morning to start our rehearsal, and I heartily recommend the book. When you play them softly and listen carefully you establish the ground rules for balance and blend, intonation, and sensitivity. I've heard many bands start with a march, and that is counterproductive. Everybody's blowing his brains out, not listening, and not playing sensitively. We start with a Bach chorale, and some people may think that's junior high schoolish. Not at all.

One of the things that really bugs me during a rehearsal is any kind of distraction. I don't mind teachers coming into an all-state band to listen, but I don't want them to distract in any way. I tell the band, "We're in a situation here where many of your teachers and other people will be coming in and going out. Never look at them. Look at the music or look at the conductor." High school directors need to eliminate distractions — cut off school bells in the band room, keep people from moving in and out of the room during rehearsals, try to control traffic or other outside noises, and make sure that the rehearsal room is as quiet as possible, so the students are not distracted. That's the only way to approach anything sensitively.

In the past you've criticized contests. Do you still feel that way?

Yes, they tend to encourage sterile performances because the judges are often looking for a very literal performance of the score, and there's no room for individuality. I think there has to be some license for the conductor to inject his own personality, sensitivity, and musicianship. I'm not suggesting that we change the chords; conductors are not composers. I never do that, but that's not to say I can't change the tempo a little bit, or change the voicing, or change the balance. *Forte* on a band score is meaningless because bands may number from 38 to 138, so what is the proper balance? How many flutes are you writing for — is it 4 or 14? The composer doesn't know. I have 4; most high school bands have 14; so *forte* for flutes is meaningless, and the conductor needs the license to change those dynamics to get the sound he thinks the composer had in mind. You really have to pick the composer's brains. In impressionistic music, for example, there are often several lines going on that must interweave, all of them in proper proportion and balance. You can listen to 4 or 5 great conductors do French impressionistic music, and you will hear different inner voices because that's what each one wants to hear. It's that individuality that a contest robs us of. If you bring out an inner line, the judge may say, "That's not written *forte*, it's written *piano*."

Can you describe what you do when you get a new piece of music?

I open that score and flip the pages until I find areas of tremendous interest — this is going to be a high point, this will be extremely soft. Those are the mile-posts that I want imbedded in my mind. If I figure out that measure 137 is the climax, then I know that the first 136 measures will not be that loud, and I'll try to build that way. If there are problem areas for the band I try to figure out how I will solve those problems before I get on the podium. I lay out the piece in big blocks, noting that the whole first section is 37 measures and has four phrases, for example.

All this is contingent on how much time you have, and how adept you are at score reading. I remember that Dave Brubeck once played a solo with my band. We rehearsed from 1:00 to 2:00 with the concert starting at 3:00. He was so pleased with the rehearsal that he wanted to do an encore. I said, "What encore?" and he sat down and dashed off a lead line. It's now between 2:00 and 3:00 and one of my arrangers is starting on an arrangement. While the concert is going on they passed the music under the chairs and we sight-read it. Not much score preparation there. That's what I mean by the extreme, it depends on how much time you have. When that encore hit my desk, I had to look at that thing real fast — block it, see the tempo changes, check for danger spots.

So you actually did in a few seconds what you would do...

...over a couple of hours. It really wasn't a very difficult piece, but still I had to do it with 4,000 people sitting out there. The wrong place to make a mistake.

Would that be a good game for somebody — not with 4,000 people sitting out there — to grab a score from the library and just do it as quickly as you can?

Absolutely. I couldn't espouse that enough. Festivals used to have sight-reading. Some still do. I think it's a great exercise, because preparing one or two pieces for contest requires a certain kind of a talent and a certain kind of preparation, but I'm not certain that it's music education. If you have taught those kids properly, they can sight-read properly, because that's a part of it. Otherwise they have learned through note-rote. They're not musicians; they're trained ponies. Sight-reading is vital.

We give conducting applicants for Air Force bands a score that they have weeks to prepare. A lot of them do it from memory, and that's commendable. It proves they have studied the score. Then we give them another score that they study for only about an hour, and we see how quick they are and how much innate musicality is there. Sight-reading can be learned like anything else: by doing it. I'd suggest putting out a new piece of music about once a week and make the students scramble, make them think. Have them draw on their complete resources to apply to that very moment.

What trends have you seen in the people coming in for auditions over the 17 years you've been with the band?

The musicianship of the players is better and better, but the conducting applicants are worse and worse.

Why?

I don't know. The kids who come in to play for auditions are well qualified, both technically and musically. Maybe the problem with the conductors is the way they are trained. I remember my introduction to conducting. I think the entire freshman class was in there, and all it really included was sort of a history of conducting. We did no time beating. "Advanced Conducting" was not very involved either; it meant getting up in front of the class and conducting one piece while they sang it, which really doesn't give you a great deal of experience. But then the graduate class that I took with Walter Beeler (I was the only one in the class) was where I first saw the light at the end of the tunnel. That happened when he said, "O.K., this is the way you prepare a score. Here is a pitch, and when I point to the French horn part you sing the French horn part, and when I point here to another part, you sing that part." Well, to be able to transpose quickly into the right key and to know solfege, and to memorize the chord progressions, that was my first insight into what score reading was all about.

I also think that personal initiative has much to do with it. People say, "How do I learn to conduct? Where do I get experience? I can't find an organization to conduct." When I went to college, I conducted a church choir, and a drum and bugle corps. I also had a 40-piece municipal band in Homer, New York, with a weekly concert about six or eight months of the year. I knew they once had a band but hadn't played for 30 or 40 years, so I went to the mayor and asked, "Whatever happened to the band?" The library was still there, and we rounded townspeople up and some high school players. So there was this little kid 21 years old, just out of the Army, and they were saying, "Who is this guy?" I also played dance work with a man named Spiegel Wilcox, who had played with Gene Goldkette, the first R.C.A. recording band in 1925 that included the Dorseys and Bix Beiderbecke and other great musicians. I needed the money from all those jobs, but I didn't realize the vast amount of experience I was also getting. When I graduated from college I had probably conducted more concerts of greater variety than many people do in 10 years.

Can you remember, or will you admit, how bad you were in those days?

I don't know, I guess I was as bad as anybody else who starts out, and I'm sure many of them were very tolerant of me.

Once again, I'm hearing those directors out there who are saying, "Well, that's Gabriel; I don't have that kind of talent." But I'm feeling that maybe Gabriel wasn't always that special.

Well, my high school band director said I had a natural flair for conducting...

O.K., so maybe it was always that way.

That's not to say that I didn't have to sit down and learn scores. I don't care how good or bad you are, you still have to know that score thoroughly. That's what I had to do, and it was a tremendous challenge for me to carry a full college load and prepare all of that material I needed for all of those groups.

You must have been going day and night.

I still am. Well, I believe in the work ethic. I really do.

What about the future?

Well I would like to stay in my job as long as I can. I know there are statutory limitations and that date is February 1985. I think extensions are possible, but one never knows in this business how long one will serve. As long as my health is good and the Air Force wants me to stay, I'll stay, and I'll continue to conduct in public just as long as I think that I'm effective. I hope I'm smart enough to know when I'm not.

What do you want to do musically in the next few years?

I would like to have the opportunity to learn, to memorize, more scores.

What kind of a personal score repertoire do you have now?

Oh, I probably could do 30 or 35 hours from memory, but I would like to make that 100 hours. There are lots of scores I would like to sit down and learn, and have just not had the chance.

I know there are many people in this country, university band directors as well as Air Force conductors, who would like to have my job, and I'll tell you who's going to get it. I don't know his name, but he's going to have a fine concert repertoire. I don't care what he knows about marching band and all the rest of it, but he better know the repertoire! There are fads in music, as there are in everything else, but I think one constant is concert music, and it should be stressed. I know other groups are needed, but it seems to me there's too much emphasis on marching bands and stage bands to the exclusion of concert bands. I'm sorry to say that this emphasis has crept into the military service as well. Some of our bands are nothing but show bands, and concert music has disappeared. We had concert music 200-300 years ago, and we'll have it 200-300 years from now; I'm not sure if we're going to have those other things 200 years from now.

If school band directors really care about what's happening in the profession, if they really care about the musicality of their students, they'll stress concert music and try to place stage bands and marching bands in the proper perspective. Concert music will always be a part of our musical heritage. ∎

Frederick Fennell
Lifetime Listener

BY FREDERICK FENNELL

At a recent press interview an excited young lady asked, "What's it *really* like up there on the podium making all that music?" The question lit up my flashers: "Deny, deny, deny." The denial was for her last four words, ". . .making all that music?" The first eleven, though equally difficult to really answer, do elicit a positive — if highly personal — response. But those four final ones — they may have hung a colleague or two, I fear, inasmuch as it has been my lifetime belief that "up on the podium" I don't make anything; I just try to *listen* and react. When it comes to making music the program to be played is the only thing that a conductor can do alone, and that is done out of the listening experience that covers one's conscious lifetime.

Mine probably began at age six when I became aware of my father and his brothers-in-law playing together as fifers and drummers in our family's fife and drum corps. This was part of the annual day-long celebration of the Fourth of July held at Camp Zeke, which was assembled on the two-and-a-half acres that remained of my grandfather's pioneer farm in what is now southeast Cleveland. Describing my family's pursuit of the study of our country's history through these summer-long assemblies at Camp Zeke is even more difficult than replying to my interviewer's so well-meant question about conducting. May it suffice to say that 66 years later I have not yet recovered from the wonderful sounds of those shrieking fifes and rattling drums. They really got my attention, and later when Father hung a very big drum around my very little neck and told me to "play along," I did what I did by lis-

tening to what was happening around me. There was nothing very different about that, but I knew from then that this was to be my number-one way to learn while staying out of trouble.

But just avoiding problems is hardly fit behavior for a would-be conductor; I ran headlong into a full catalog of them. My first group experiences came at Miles Elementary School just across the street from where Camp Zeke ended. At Miles my days of playing mostly without music ended when I was introduced to the *Bennett Band Book* and the *Fox Orchestra Folio.* Then a very cute girl pianist in my classroom and I were asked to play a march out in the big main corridor for the changing of classes. In addition to noticing her, I discovered that we sounded louder out in that cold-looking open space than when we practiced on the warm, carpeted stage in the auditorium. Acoustics began to be part of my listening life along with *Our Director* and Evelyn Bittner, the pianist. Our romance ended a year later when she refused to learn *El Capitan,* but I'm still chasing acoustics and listening to marches by John Philip Sousa.

Next came my first set of drums as a Christmas present when I was ten. My sister Marjorie and I put together another piano and drums act that we played for parties at the mill where our father worked almost all of his life. Our musical inclinations and nature's priceless gifts of hearing and retention came from him. When my father was our age there were no musical opportunities such as his interest and support made possible for us to enjoy at home and in school. Home included a 1926 state-of-the-art phonograph and cabinet filled with a variety of records, and that phonograph's rewarding instant replay set me on my way to begin learning how to listen to music.

The family library included Arthur Conan Doyle's remarkable *Adventures,* and it was while reading one of Sherlock Holmes' recapitulations of how he solved a case by observation and deductive reasoning that I began to apply the Doyle/Holmes words to discipline to become a true listener. The great detective's companion, Dr. Watson, full of questions when expressing amazement at how Sherlock Holmes had discov-

Frederick Fennell is Music Director of the Tokyo Kosei Wind Orchestra of Japan. During a long and distinguished career at the Eastman School of Music, Fennell was Music Director of the Eastman Opera Theatre and Conductor of the Eastman Chamber Orchestra; he founded the Eastman Wind Ensemble in 1952. Fennell served as Associate Music Director of the Minneapolis Symphony Orchestra, then in 1965 was Conductor of the University of Miami Symphony Orchestra and Wind Ensemble. He received the title Conductor Emeritus in 1980, and has been one of the most provocative, influential, and active conductors of our time.

ered the facts that revealed the criminal, would be chided: "My dear Watson, you see, but you don't observe." So too, the musician who hears but somehow forgets to listen, passes rich opportunities to learn.

High school began in the ninth grade when I went to John Adams. There I met a teacher who would further sharpen my listening habits while introducing me to the ordered study of harmonic practice. John B. Elliot's position on the Adams faculty reflected the unusual commitment of the Cleveland Board of Education to the teaching of music; he was our full-time professional accompanist for everything that happened in school. He also taught a class in theory, counterpoint, form and analysis, and music materials, which functioned in tandem with Amos Wesler's orchestra and band rehearsals; it was no surprise when both ensembles became national champions. For those who could meet his high standards, Elliot's classes were a learning experience I could only wish to pass to others; they were to ease me into the next school in my life.

In my high school freshman year Elliot led us through the most detailed and rewarding examination of the Prelude to *Die Meistersinger*, required music for the Greater Cleveland Contest. I still have that miniature score. From it I began the habit of playing while trying to listen for everything — which in *Meistersinger*, of course, *is* everything. Repeated rehearsals afforded me the chance to isolate instruments. As a challenge I would follow each instrument in a single line of counterpoint or play the game of switching concentration from one to another on call. I had heard a lot of music prior to this but now I was really beginning to LISTEN! — and to think about what I was hearing. *Meistersinger* became my bible of music composition. Elliot's classes, Wesler's rehearsals, and Wagner's music were exciting lessons for a young man.

There were other lessons for those of us in the Cleveland schools at this time; Music Supervisor Russell V. Morgan had worked out a Saturday morning plan of instruction with members of The Cleveland Orchestra and other musicians in the city whereby we could have top teaching for 50¢ a private lesson given in a centrally located school. Cleveland was truly a hotbed of young musical talent in those years. Families who had recently arrived in the United States had produced first-generation children who were to have everything that might have been denied their parents, including the time to practice the violin every day after school. As I participated, I also learned to listen with them.

Listening to the radio was another of my pastimes. One Sunday afternoon in the summer of 1930, I happened to hear a concert broadcast from Interlochen, Michigan played by the National High School Orchestra. It was a shatteringly wonderful experience and I became determined to get to that camp, however impossible it seemed in the second year of the economic depression. Once again the Cleveland schools helped me, this time when I received a booklet about Interlochen from my mentor, Mr. Morgan. When the camp was short on percussion players for the 1931 session, my talented father found the way to get me there. I date my life from those eight weeks spent between the beautiful lakes in the northwestern Michigan woods.

At Interlochen all my listening and studying and practicing were up for grabs. I found myself in company with a stageful of what had to be some of the most outstanding young musicians of that time. The Interlochen Bowl stage, a magic place for so many of us campers, afforded me the next dimensions in my quest for the education I needed to become a conductor. Here I was listening again, with an added ingredient called competition, that dominant element in the world of professional music making. I'm glad I had to face it at this early age when I was just beginning to learn a few things about myself. Fellow percussionists, older and with two summers of camp experiences ahead of me, were way out in front. Listening as I watched them play, I began to close the gap of experience between us.

I was never without a pair of heavy drum sticks under the belt on my blue corduroys, a rubber practice pad in one hip pocket, and a dog-eared miniature score in the other. (I didn't need a pitch-pipe for tuning the kettledrums; I just listened to the one nature had put in my head.) The summer was spent listening and sopping up everything I heard at Interlochen.

Placement of percussion instruments (and especially the kettledrums) in large ensembles offers a panoramic view of the technical command of the conductor as well as all that is happening in the other sections. Usually it is while listening from the rear (where balance is easily disturbed) that percussion players lose touch with what is happening in front of them. The percussion part is a problem, for it rarely tells players anything beyond when to play; even how to play and with what is vague. The good percussionist is thereby obliged to become an acutely tuned listener and to develop retentive habits that account for all that is played. Listening while following the score or a violin or clarinet part is much more informative and rewarding than trying to be an adding machine. Listening to the sonorities of which the percussionist's music is part is the key to balance and the only reliable guide to texture. At camp I had the chance to do this twice daily seven days a week. I had not been there long before my principal concern was to find some way to get back there for my two remaining years of high school.

It was obvious to me from the start that Interlochen is a great separation center. Young men and women there stand at the fork in the road. Camp helps them make the sometimes painful choice: doctor, lawyer, merchant chief — or, for a few, musican. When that field is to be performance, a person had better have a peaceful understanding of the demands. Those who discover that they don't like to rehearse and who find the daily routine of practicing to be a drag will have to go in another direction. Interlochen groups certainly offer a fair shot at the former. Other factors along with the practicing routine probably help lead a camper to a decision. Mine had been made for me; I simply could not have done anything else in joy or with purpose.

It was interesting to discover that first summer that retentive listening saved me a lot of time and that it wasn't just the music I could remember. The visual scene of the trees in the grove, the hour of the day with the morning aroma of the canvas awning in front of the bowl being heated by the sun, the look of a Breitkopf & Härtel music cover, the smell of the pines, the way horn players in front of me barely got the tuning slides back in place to play after dumping water — all these are still indelible memories of the first time I played Brahms' Symphony in C Minor. All these sensory receptions and retentions were stimulated by listening as I heard.

I did make it back to camp the next two summers and was fortunate to add two more disciplines to the experience of performing. The urge to conduct had been fed a bit the first summer when Vladimir Bakalienikoff herded about 50 of us into Grunow Hall for his basic class in baton technique. Knowing that anything beyond that class was strictly daydreaming, I took the only route open to me in 1932 as a potential music leader — the Interlochen course in drum majoring, all 5' 1" of me! Mr. Giddings, Director of Instruction, arranged for me to attend the university class in drum majoring and field tactics offered by Mark H. Hindsley, whose pioneering Cleveland Heights High Marching Band was peerless on the field. His order and logic in teaching those studies were in sharp contrast to the guarded secrets of the twirling baton when I sought some lessons from a counselor at Boys' Camp. The counselor told me that, in the best tradition of the magician, I could keep what I could steal from him — which I did.

Returning home to my final fall at John Adams I found Mr. Wesler open to the idea that I might be the band's drum major. At least and at last I could conduct the band for marching although that square one-two, up-down motion didn't really interest me, even then. My life as a music leader was happening and I have always cherished the way it began; the long road to a podium was to be shortened considerably by events that occurred in the summer and fall of 1932.

It was time to be thinking about a music school, like the one in Rochester, New York where Dr. Howard Hanson was director. We all knew him as annual guest conductor of the National High School Orchestra; and his school had everything I needed, including a generous program of student financial aid. We had talked about it in 1932, but there was no action on my application for admission as late as June of the following year. William F. Ludwig, Jr. became a camper in 1932, and by 1933 we were close friends and sharing the kettledrum stool on a draw lots basis. Bill drew the lot for Dr. Hanson's visit that year. Desperate to make any points with Hanson, I was grateful when Bill offered me his week so that I could play in Hanson's first Interlochen performance of Symphony No. 2, "Romantic." This is probably how I became a percussion major at Eastman that September; Interlochen's fork in the road pointed straight to Rochester, New York.

The discipline I chose for my final high school camp session was composition. Among the pieces I wrote for class was a mildly successful march. I decided at camp, however, that I would neither clutter nor pollute the world with further creative attempts and that I would devote my life to listening and hopefully to conducting the music of others. This, too, was a listening decision made by all that great music from the *National Emblem* to *The Rite of Spring*. Before this abandonment, however, Dr. A.A. Harding had invited me to make my debut as a conductor with the National High School Band leading that summer's march composition at the final concert. A treasured photograph of the occasion reveals all that could possibly be wrong in a very young conductor — except the look on my face.

At Eastman, as at Interlochen, I was free of the usual domestic responsibilities — no trash to take out, no grass to cut, no wood to carry for Grandma Putnam's magic oven (but no pies and cakes, either). Listening was for keeps at Eastman, where amidst the fast pace I was oh-so-grateful for all to which I had been exposed en route.

If memory is born of interest and listening is fed by curiosity, why not pool all of these as we listen to others perform, practice, rehearse, improvise, warm-up and down, wherever and whenever we find them? I was about to learn some of these big lessons if hardly all of the answers. In the next portion of this autobiography, which will be in the December issue, I'll try my best to tell what it has really been like up there on the podium; my 30 years on one at the Eastman School of Music were about to begin. ■

December, 1986

The Eastman Years

Editor's Note: In the October issue Frederick Fennell told us about his early musical training — family gatherings at Camp Zeke, the influence of John Elliot, summers at Interlochen. In this portion of Fennell's autobiography he continues with the story of his years at Eastman and a conducting prize that took him to Salzburg.

I had never seen a real chamber music hall, let alone one as strikingly beautiful as Kilbourn, or a theater as impressive as the one that bore the name of George Eastman. Word was that this genius of industry and finance with an obvious passion for music could not (perhaps to his eternal regret) carry a tune in a basket. Maybe this is why he built and endowed so magnificent a school for the training of those who could. Both of these remarkable halls were to become important rooms in my life. Everything about the Eastman Theatre was impressive — the sheer size, the beautiful murals, the elegant crystal chandelier, the big stage — but the setting was not what struck me then.

What made me stop and pay attention was the sound of that marvelous acoustical chamber, which later was to become so vital a part of the many phonograph recordings that the Eastman Wind Ensemble and I would make there.

The first time I heard the special sound of that theatre I was in it all alone — which I never should have been. Over the years the never-should-have-beens were to mount; but for now they were confined to surreptitious forays into the darkened Eastman Theatre, where in the silence of those ghostly surroundings I could listen to the thoughts in my head.

The preliminaries accomplished, I spent those first weeks at school adding to life's two inevitables, death and taxes, a third called theory — thank you, John Elliot. We music students knew we were in a school of a university where the academics took no secondary place. The parent University of Rochester recently had moved to a beautiful new campus where its College for Men was housed. An aerial photo showed a modest but handsome athletic stadium with high stands on one side. I thought I'd try becoming involved as drum major with whatever football and marching band activities there were. I asked the director of athletics at the River Campus (who also had the challenging responsibility for teaching Eastman's most hilarious class, hygiene) if he could tell me where I might contact the leader of the band for an audition as drum major. His reply that they didn't have either lit up all my youthful flashers and this time the printout was: go, go, go! "How would you like to have a marching band, Dr. Fauver?" I asked. "I can organize and lead one for you." After a silence, which I was fortunate not to break, an unforgettable look of disbelief crossed his face. Two weeks later, however, when several willing sources of energy pooled their resources into a group — many former Interlochen campers joining out of courtesy, other people out of curiosity — Dr. Fauver's look of approval was unhesitating.

It was a pretty good parade — thank you, Mark Hindsley. My career as a band conductor had begun as an Eastman School freshman with no warning of its arrival and no hint of the consequences ahead. While the money I earned put me through school, the audacity of my act put me in touch with kindred souls, and I had a great need for both. The number one kindred soul and critic (I needed that, too) eventually became my wife after a succession of bone-chilling fall Saturday afternoons and all that attends life with the conductor of a marching band. Dorothy Codner didn't much care for bands as she heard them, and some of the time neither did I. Doing what we could about that was to consume much of our life together. A violinist who switched to viola, Dorothy was a year ahead of me in school. I was happy to have found myself through her.

School was tough. In addition to old-fashioned competition came grades, class lessons, studio pressure, practice-room checkers, and house mothers. Eastman had been around for 11 years and Howard Hanson had been its director for almost all of them; there was no doubt of his complete (but benevolent) authority and the students' great admiration for his musical leadership. My little bit of business with Dr. Fauver and the assembling of those never-should-have-been marching Eastmanites (plus men from the college which paid the bills) happened only with his approval.

Eastman's resources reached beyond practice rooms and marble halls into immediate and intimate association with the thriving professional music life of the city of Rochester, located right across the corridor from the school. The professional life was always part of our education, and non-university groups shared the rehearsal and performance facilities so generously provided by Mr. Eastman. The chance to hear our teachers play for keeps under almost every imaginable ensemble circumstance, six days a week, was the ultimate lesson. Furthermore, when it became apparent that the skills our teachers demanded in the studio were the same ones they needed under the pressure in the professional hall, it encouraged all of us to reach beyond what we had thought was our potential. This lesson, together with the immense holdings in the Sibley Music Library, were Eastman's greatest assets.

After the initial success of the band that

marched while it played, some of the players encouraged me to organize one that sat down in a nice, warm room. The University of Rochester Symphony Band played its first concert on January 25, 1935, on campus. It was my debut conducting a concert band. Howard Hanson was present and requested a repeat performance a few weeks later in Kilbourn Hall. When the dust had settled our name was changed to the Eastman School Symphony Band, and we were added to the ensemble curriculum. I was the group's conductor for the next 26 years.

Our percussion teacher and performer par excellence, William G. Street, was a solid supporter of my moves toward conducting. At the same time I was still a percussionist, and I practiced the instruments as though that was all I had to do. I performed in all the school's ensembles, and when I graduated with my class in June 1937, I was Eastman's first percussion major to receive the Performer's Certificate.

Bill Street had taken me into the section of the Rochester Philharmonic a few years before. It was an opportunity of priceless value for a young conductor to be part of a group with such a high level of professional playing and to be in the company of international soloists. There was much for which to listen, and I had scores to everything that I could buy of what was played.

The music director of the Philharmonic was the distinguished Spanish musician and pianist, José Iturbi, who enjoyed the privilege of parking his car in the garage under the main rehearsal room. Hearing sounds from above, he came upstairs unobserved to watch a rehearsal that I was conducting with the band. Some days later, to my complete surprise, he asked me to conduct a portion of the same work, Enesco's *Rumanian Rhapsody*, so that he might go out into the Eastman Theatre to hear the Philharmonic's sound and balance. Hearing the wonderful sound of the Orchestra coming right at me, so well-played and so responsive to whatever I did, was overwhelming. I began to feel what it was like to be up there on the podium "making all that music."

My first employment was not as a conductor but as a kettledrummer with the San Diego Symphony Orchestra. I was hired to play the full 1936 summer season at The Bowl in Balboa Park as part of the California-Pacific International Exposition. Others from Eastman, including two players who had gone to San Diego High School with the conductor, Nino Marcelli, were in the orchestra as well. The cross-country trip in my car, mostly alone, was an education in itself. I'd never seen an ocean, and my first view of the Pacific coming up over the brow of a hill in what is now Camp Pendleton was a sight that has never left me. California was very different from New York; San Diego was charming and beautiful. Rehearsing and playing daily in a good orchestra became another way to expand my knowledge of repertory and learn what worked. Playing from scores and listening for everything was endlessly informative.

That summer Otto Klemperer, conductor of the Los Angeles Philharmonic, offered a cycle of the Beethoven symphonies on Monday nights at the Hollywood Bowl. We San Diego players had the night off, so in company with Norman Herzberg, our first bassoonist and Harold Kurtz, the flutist who had steered us into the San Diego job, I drove to Hollywood to hear performances of those masterworks. Seated on the fringe of the sound in the Bowl I heard things that I still associate with the proper interpretation of this literature. The lack of amplification did not seem to hinder the strength of the music. Klemperer was impressive, not only as a conductor, but also as one so tall that he did not need to use a podium.

One Monday afternoon the San Diego's wind players and I went neither to the bathing cove at LaJolla nor to Klemperer's Beethoven. Instead, John Barrows, our principal hornist, assembled us at his family home, a classic California wooden cottage with ample room and a great sound for chamber music. Among the works to be read was a piece I had not heard, the *Sere-*

nade, Op. 7, by Richard Strauss. I was along as a listener, but when things became a little rocky in the middle section (B minor, *più animato*) Herzberg suggested that I assist the ensemble. The subsequent play-through was the beginning of a long love affair with this charming piece; I had found one of the pivotal scores that would lead me to the Eastman Wind Ensemble. At summer's end Norman and I went to see the Big Trees at Yosemite; at last they were more than just black-and-white photos in a geography book.

School and the marching band season began without Dorothy, who had graduated and returned home to Iowa. In 1935 the University of Rochester had a new young President, and somewhere among the myriad questions asked him was one by a local sports writer as to when the band might get some real uniforms. His casual reply that an amount would be allotted for the fall of 1937 was enough encouragement for me to request a cost quote from Greenville, Illinois. The quote led to drawings and a fitting session for all the men who would return. With the slim assurance of a few devoted alumni that somehow the bill would be paid, I gulped a few times and sent in the order. Two weeks later I hurried off to Iowa to be married.

The automobile trip to San Diego and the 1937 summer season of the San Diego Symphony were our honeymoon. Back in Rochester, the new uniforms had arrived, along with a huge bill. I went to see President Valentine, the bill in my hand and my job on the line. Somehow, and with his appreciation of what the band had been contributing, another never-should-have-been came to pass.

Both Dorothy and I were in graduate school on a very tight budget — hers! We practically lived in Sibley Library, researching our material for dissertations in music theory. *The Orchestral Development of the Kettledrum from Purcell through Beethoven* demanded and got every other minute of my time for two years; the rest of my work went on around it. I became a looker as well as a listener. Research to support the thesis meant that I had to explore all printed scores before Purcell and then patiently to peruse every score in the complete works of Purcell, Bach, Handel, Haydn, Mozart, and Beethoven. Through this survey of a composer's use of the kettledrums I had the chance to observe much beyond that area as well.

School had barely begun that fall of 1937 when a notice appeared on the bulletin board from the Institute for International Education advising that applications for the Salzburg International Prize in Conducting should be completed by the first of October. The Mozarteum in Austria would award the prize the following summer. This was the only prize for a young conductor at the time, but confidence that my training and experience made me eligible was tempered by a realization that conductors of bands sat rather low on the artistic totem pole. I vividly remember dropping that application in the Eastman corridor mailbox and thinking, "Well, who knows?" Howard Hanson, José Iturbi, and Vladimir Bakaleinikoff had agreed to let me list them as sponsors; when time passed with no acknowledgement, I finally ceased to think about it. The mountain of paper on my Sibley study cubicle received all of my attention. On the 28th of February word came that I had been awarded the prize after a jury had secretly visited the darkened Eastman Theatre during a Symphony Band rehearsal.

Dorothy's and my happiness at this great opportunity ended as abruptly as it had begun with the news on March 12th that Hitler had completed the annexation of Austria for the Third Reich. Wanting no gifts from Nazism, I relinquished the prize, and my disappointment was eased when the Mozarteum Academy's summer

plans were cancelled. Dorothy and I were in Iowa for the summer when I received a telegram from Howard Hanson stating that the prize was on again. The State Department requested that I please be in Salzburg by July 10th. Somehow I was, and alone. The sudden change from pastoral Iowa to the busy decks of the German liner *Europa* found me with my nose once again in a German dictionary.

The first night in Salzburg I lodged in a comfortable private home. The score to Mozart's "Jupiter" rested atop a great white down comforter as I read my way into the spirit of my new surroundings. Amid reflections of the family, teachers, and players who had sent me there, sleep was about to claim me when I heard the distant but unmistakable sound of marching boots approaching in a precise crescendo. Then this rude interruption of Mozart and my reverie became the accompaniment to German soldier songs. As the marchers sang and passed, sleep no longer came easily or peacefully. I knew that evening in Mozart's beautiful hometown, as a wonderful time was beginning for me, that things were about to go all wrong for lots of other people; those boots in the night were just an omen of its beginning. ∎

Campers at Interlochen, Fennell and lifetime friend Bill Ludwig pose with William F. Ludwig, Sr., founder and president of the Ludwig Drum Company.

Growing as a Conductor

Salzburg was unlike any place I had seen before, and it started my imagination working overtime. Walking down the streets where Wolfgang Amadeus had gone before, my feet never touched the cobblestones. The Mozarteum Prize that had brought me to the city offered daily seminars in score study together with the usual student postmortems of the previous night's opera or concert and a few brief visits with Wilhelm Furtwängler, the Festival's chief conductor. My day-to-day instruction came from Herbert Albert, chief at the Opera in Stuttgart. Just being that close to the Vienna Philharmonic was a daily lecture in a style of orchestral playing that had helped to set standards for the world. The Mozart orchestra provided playing sessions for the class. On these occasions my Symphony Band podium experience rewarded me with the honors position at our final concert when Albert thought it was appropriate that I should conduct the "Scherzo" and "Finale" of Dvorak's *New World Symphony*.

Studying at the Mozarteum was a pleasant and encouraging confirmation of my musical talents. It provided exposure to a different language, to another culture with its museums, libraries, theaters, and restaurants. Most important of all, however, was the adjustment of my conductorial alignment to include the orchestra. The mere physical act of having proceeded up and down gangplanks that connected the United States to Europe and back again framing brief residence in a name European conservatory certified me as a bona fide conductor. Just to prove the point, I had been back in Rochester for only three weeks when my brothers in Alpha Nu chapter, Phi Mu Alpha Sinfonia Fraternity invited me to become conductor of their superb Little Symphony.

Eastman's growing popularity with ever-better players emerging from the high schools had

Fennell (far left, holding pipe) and associates at the Mozarteum in Salzburg, 1938

swelled the size of Symphony Band to overflowing. I searched for quality transcriptions, and even harder for anything original. Unlike a typical college, university, or conservatory band, we had no uniform, no budget, no officers, no organization — just Dorothy, me, and one vastly underpaid library assistant. The simple words of Director Howard Hanson guided the instrumentation: "...if your applied music is not strings, but an orchestral or band instrument, you will play in Symphony Band."

The result was an ensemble that grew in size because of the popularity of such teachers as Emory Remington and Joseph Mariano whose students in the 1940 Band numbered 14 trombones and baritones, and 14 flutes. The Eastman Theatre stage was filled by an additional 6 oboes, 2 English horns, 4 bassoons and contra, 12 horns, 10 trumpets, 5 tubas, 2 string contrabasses, 2 harps, and 5 percussion; total: 98.

I considered the group to be just an overgrown wind quintet, whose purpose was to provide an additional ensemble experience in basic repertory regardless of how far the music might be wrenched from its original key and orchestration. Style is style; all the elements of nuance and dynamic were there to be achieved as faithfully as possible.

This pursuit was a training course for me that I never could have found elsewhere. I wanted to conduct, and with Symphony Band I was able to start at the beginning — by learning how to rehearse. I'd had the experiences all of us do as we learn to play an instrument in a group, and remembering both the good and the not-so-good of them was a solid base for my beginning hours on the podium. The listening habits I had developed when I was a player were just the training I needed to be conducting this group. Those games I had played at isolating instrumental textures and switching contrapuntal lines were probably what kept me up there on the podium.

I learned all my lessons there on the hot box. In the first years two-thirds of the band were upperclassmen. They met me more than halfway; I just kept things moving so there was no time for problems. I knew that I must always come thoroughly prepared for every aspect of the rehearsal. If anything, I probably came over-prepared at first, but with friendly counseling I gradually learned how to pace my plan as the rehearsal unfolded. There were times, amidst tension and stress, when I had to remind myself that trying to be a conductor had been my idea. Nobody, except my half-frozen

Growing as a conductor included a position directing Interlochen's National High School Band in 1940

marching band friends seeking a nice, warm room had invited me to do this.

I knew that I needed to develop my own technique and in the process, I stood in the shoes of many a famous maestro of my youth. Most of them were comfortable, to a certain extent, but when I began to feel the pinch I knew they weren't my shoes. Remembering what did feel comfortable, I would slip into Toscanini's or Stokowski's for a while. Faculty colleagues, beginning with Dr. Hanson, never hesitated to tell me what was working and what techniques they thought I should get rid of. The criticisms I treasured most were from my wife, Dorothy, who had seen and heard it all.

For the summer of 1939, my master's degree behind me, Joe Maddy invited me to join the faculty at Interlochen as teacher of percussion. Working in the first of the buildings given by the Ludwigs was my final commitment as a percussionist. That summer brought me a close friendship with another man whose absorption with music would bring and keep us together for years. At the time Oscar Zimmerman played on the principal stand of string contrabasses in Arturo Toscanini's N.B.C. Symphony. As an encore to his serious solo bass recital (rare in those days), he asked me to join him in a surprise presentation of Bob Haggart and Ray Baduc's popular novelty for bass and jazz drums, *The Big Noise from Winnetka.* That was the first jazz ever played at Interlochen Bowl and it was a sensation. If I had to draw the double-bar on my career as a percussionist, that was the way to go. "The Big Noise" didn't cause any damage either; the next summer Maddy and Giddings made me conductor of the National High School Band.

Dorothy spent the summer of 1940 as a member of Leopold Stokowski's All American Youth Orchestra, and it served both her and me, for her letters were filled with keen observations of Stokowski's superb technique and his imaginative concepts of orchestral playing. I studied him carefully for several months and his beautiful suede shoes felt very comfortable. Friends who played in the Little Symphony urged me to try to get into Serge Kousse-

vitzky's class at a new summer Music Center called Tanglewood. I relinquished the Interlochen post when he invited me to come in 1942.

My stay at the Berkshire Music Center began with an outdoor reception at which I met my colleagues in the class, Robert Zeller, Walter Hendl, Lukas Foss, and Leonard Bernstein. Lenny was in his third summer there, and from observing as he coached in the open theater, a great career for him seemed inevitable.

Serge Koussevitzky was a remarkable man. His annual visit to Rochester with the Boston Symphony always guaranteed a brilliant and precise performance, and from my vantage point as an usher in the balcony of the Eastman Theatre, his conducting had an air of mystery enhanced with elegance. Koussevitzky's technical approach was almost diametrically opposite that of Toscanini's, whose rapier-like baton left nothing in doubt. Koussevitzky's stick was not much longer than an unsharpened pencil, and it fit the rest of him perfectly. Both he and Toscanini were slight in physical stature, and both of these great men wore superbly tailored clothing that elevated them as they stood on the podium "making all that music." However different Koussevitzky's approach may have been from Toscanini's, they arrived at the same destination: making great music.

"Koussey," as we called him behind his back, was a great teacher. He had the ability to find simple ways for us to develop the resources within each of us. We were not to imitate others, beginning with him. I didn't need to slip into his shoes, because he quickly convinced me that my own fit much better. It was fun to discover myself again. Koussevitzky's English was colorful and highly personal, charged with elements from other languages he spoke. Words were unimportant in the exultation of music that exuded from his every pore. Koussevitzky gave unstintingly of himself, his knowledge, and his experience. He also taught entrance, exit, bowing, dressing, tea drinking, and manners.

Haydn's 88th Symphony in G was my first assignment with orchestra at Tanglewood. The first movement passed without comment; as I began the second Koussevitzky came up to the stand and as the music died he quietly said, "Too slow – remember two things, first to sing it, then to bow it – and always listen to the orchestra." The admonitions were not forgotten.

We got along very well and when Tanglewood resumed after World War II he invited me to be his assistant with the class and to conduct one of the orchestras; unfortunately, Tanglewood was closing down for the duration. Four years previously while I was so busy living Act II of *Der Freischütz* the big decisions leading to the war were being made in Berchtesgaden, not many kilometers down the road from the Mozarteum. Those Salzburg boots in the night had caught up with all of us.

It was no surprise to be turned down by already over-staffed Washington service bands and no disappointment, either, for I wanted to be a fly-boy. They told me to go home; I was an old man – at age 29. One particularly gloomy November morning Hanson called to ask me to meet a man who had a proposition that might interest me. The head of National U.S.O. music stateside had come to Rochester to attend the funeral of composer Nathaniel Dett, composer of *Juba Dance*, who had died on United Service Organization assignment; and on Armistice Day I took my oath to serve the U.S.O. as his replacement. Dorothy had to stay in Rochester because of her orchestra contract.

The trip from Chicago to San Francisco took an incredible five days. Not knowing I had pneumonia, I was shipped south to San Diego. I arrived in Los Angeles in a coma and was car-

ried to the hotel listed on the itinerary in my pocket. When I failed to keep a date with Eastman organist Catherine Crozier Gleason, she called the hotel and I woke up eight days later in the critical ward of Los Angeles County General Hospital with José Iturbi sitting beside the bed. He took care of my release. A huge depression followed, and the only things keeping me on course were a small radio and my miniature score to *Tristan und Isolde*.

After a reunion with Dorothy at Christmas we wound up in San Diego where the U.S.O. had on its hands 76 units of the major services in San Diego County. At once I found myself with armored forces training in the desert. With my ukulele and harmonica I was to lead the G.I.s in community singing. The holes they stared through me made them my toughest audiences, ever.

In San Diego, the great Navy town, that service was my primary concern. At my desk a Captain whose salt-encrusted braid was his identification introduced himself, laid $10,000 on my blotter, and asked if I could find him a piano. The U.S.O. did not accept such funds and by that time there were no pianos at any price. He wanted it for his C.V.E.; the money had come from the bar and soda fountain for the officers who flew from the deck of his carrier. Another such visitor had brought his buglemaster (C.V.E.s were not authorized for musicians); they wanted manuscript paper and band instruments in any state of disrepair. They had some funds with which we wheedled two tired clarinets and so-so cornets from the last store with anything to sell. They took trash from the repair bins, a badly mashed old helicon tuba, and a C melody sax that had been on a top shelf for years. Somehow in the aircraft maintenance shops the musicians made the instruments work and put together a band of 10 players. When they sailed from North Island, their band

played an *Anchors Aweigh* I shall not forget.

Then there were all those wonderful musicians who had enlisted in the bands. I had not been in San Diego very long before Navy Musician Robert Marsteller suggested the great potential of a U.S.O. evening during the week when musicians in service could adjust their pass/liberty time to come and play just for the fun of performing the music they knew before the war. Bob had been one of those marching Eastmanites and he knew how to spread the word around the Navy installations. I found the music in the Clark Collection at the Los Angeles Public Library and got clearance to use the Roosevelt Junior High band room. The first rehearsal was an absolute joy for about 50 players from all services.

We just read the tunes down, one after another, no rehearsing. Missing instruments were quickly covered by doublers. We later turned a vacant Masonic Lodge room into a rehearsal hall with practice rooms, listening booths with records, and a small library of chamber music. When a concert benefiting Russian War Relief was held, José Iturbi volunteered to play the Grieg Concerto. We were a smash. The correct description of my position was: civilian music officer, no rank, pins, stripes, or benefits; but the work gave me access to many places and people that U.S.O. might serve.

Suddenly the war was over and the streets were filled with celebrating people. Back in Rochester, school was already jammed with former students and lots of new faces. It didn't take long to sense that many things had changed. The innocent sequence from high school to college had been interrupted by the war. G.I.s sought to be excused from the band because they'd "...had three years of it!" We had to make the G.I. Bill work to serve those students.

A new item on my agenda was the College Band Directors National Association, which became a necessary seminar on the many post-war problems that musical ensembles faced. Preparation for the annual conferences and my own problems where none had existed before raised serious questions with no easy answers. Out of frustration, I suggested to the wind and percussion faculty that we regroup the players into orchestral wind sections. My associates didn't like that idea, but I did extract from them a promise to clear the one o'clock hour for miscellaneous wind groups.

The Little Symphony appointment, Salzburg, and maturity — together with a lot of just plain listening — had opened my view of wind repertory training for Eastman students. Endless digging in the Sibley stacks revealed fresh treasures waiting to be performed. Our one o'clock rehearsals finally led to a 1951 concert in Kilbourn Hall that engaged almost every wind music major in the school. We played the following works:

Ricercare for Wind Instruments - Willaert
Canzon for Wind Instruments - Scheidt
Motet: Tui Sunt Coeli for Brasses - Lasso
Sonata pian e forte - Gabrieli
Canzon Noni Toni a 12 - Gabrieli
Suite No. 2 for Brass Instruments - Petzel
Three Equale for Trombones - Beethoven
Serenade No. 10 in B♭ for Winds - Mozart
Serenade in E♭ for Winds - R. Strauss
Angels, for Brasses - Ruggles
Symphonies of Wind Instruments - Stravinsky

I included scholarly comments about the music as part of the invitation to attend. The success of this informative departure from customary concerts at school prompted plans for another performance in 1952.

The bottom dropped out when it was discovered in November 1951 that I was seriously infected with hepatitis. Weeks in a hospital were followed by more at home. The only prescription for recovery was absolute rest, a pound of sugar candy with gallons of water daily, and a strict diet. I had not had a real vacation since I was a boy, and meditation wasn't part of those jampacked Eastman days and nights. Because I was under orders to barely move my eyeballs, I decided to make the most of all that time on my back.

The Kilbourn concert had convinced me that we needed a reed, brass, percussion, and keyboard ensemble with a fresh point of view and a name that could start from its own square one. With nothing to do but suck lemon drops, drink water, and stare at the ceiling, I had plenty of time to bounce around my thoughts about this wind group, some of which dated back about 20 years. Recall was easy in all that solitude, so I reached back to conversations with fellow campers, among them one with Sidney Mear, as good a cornet player as any I knew in 1933. Walking back to Boys Camp through the Interlochen woods I had asked him how he liked sitting first chair in such a fine big band with so good a conductor as Dr. Harding. Allowing it to be okay, he had added that one thing bothered him: ". . . anytime I want to put my horn down I can hear 10 other guys playing my part." The 10 would have to go. I wanted a carefully balanced instrumentation capable of performing styles from 16th-century brass music and moderate-sized chamber music to Paul Hindemith's new *Symphony in B♭*.

Using the basic format of the British military band but increasing it to allow for triples among the reeds required for Stravinsky's *Symphonies*, each player would be the soloist his private teacher always taught him to be. I had never met anybody who taught "section clarinet" so we could cut the players to one on a part allowing for divisi. I could hear how clean this sound was going to be, for I knew it from the orchestra; but now I could apply that attitude and its clarity to band music. We would sit in the straight rows of orchestral seating. While we were at it, why not make some reference recordings of the best of the band's music, since none existed?

I was supposed to be at absolute rest, and I was, except for the fact that I had been told of the high fatality rate of people in my condition. What worried me most was that I might forget some of what I had planned before I was well enough to sit up and write it all down. Then Dorothy brought me a notebook into which I wrote what I had bounced off the ceiling about what I had decided to call a wind ensemble. Now I really had to get out of that hospital where the daily blood test called the tune.

One afternoon a concerned Dr. Hanson came to see me. Conversation with him was always inspiring. He was about to leave when he asked if there was anything he could do for me. "Yes, Dr. Hanson, since you ask, there is," I said. "Here in this bed I've had the chance to think through a plan for a new wind group for school, which I hope you'll consider letting me try." I gave him my notes and he sat down to read them. After a while his hand moved involuntarily for the inevitable cigar. When he smiled and began to make those familiar little conducting motions with the still-unwrapped panatela, I knew I had his attention. The Eastman Wind Ensemble played its first rehearsal on September 20, 1952. ∎

Frederick Fennell went on to serve as Associate Music Director of the Minnesota Symphony Orchestra and in 1965 became Conductor of the University of Miami Symphony Orchestra and Wind Ensemble. He is now Music Director of the Tokyo Kosei Wind Orchestra of Japan. With the third part of this series, we bring to a close this portion of Fennell's autobiography, with his promise that he will someday put it all in a book.

Frank Bencriscutto
Raising Standards

BY JAMES WARRICK AND JOHN THOMSON

In the first years after I got my doctor's degree at Eastman I read many books on aesthetics and philosophy. There is so much written about music from early Greece up to contemporary time. We live such a short period of time that I think we ought to know what we're doing and why we're doing it.

In those early years, when a rehearsal didn't go well because students were not "into it" or their egos were consumed with chair placement, I would go home and start to write, asking myself, "Why are we making music?" "How can we reach beyond the superficial?" I think that this questioning has made a tremendous difference in my career and in the results of my groups.

Did this introspection bring you to some truths?

Knowing "truths" is an ever-evolving process. I believe that it is important to share the best that

each of us possesses without intimidation, with a sense of gratitude for what we have to contribute and a sense of humility for having whatever gifts we have. Ideally, the essential purpose of contributing those gifts should be for the well-being of all people so that no person feels less important than any other person. I've never had

---

Editor's Note: Now in his 28th year as the Director of Bands and Jazz Ensembles at the University of Minnesota in Minneapolis, "Dr. Ben," as his students call him, remains active as a saxophonist, arranger, and composer as well as conductor. Amidst his many interests, one of Bencriscutto's greatest concerns is the future of school band programs and their place in the academic curriculum.

James Warrick directs the Jazz Ensemble at New Trier High School in Winnetka, Illinois. He is a Consulting Editor and New Music Reviewer for The Instrumentalist. *John Thomson directs the Wind Ensemble at New Trier High School in Winnetka, Illinois. He is a New Music Reviewer for* The Instrumentalist. *This interview took place at New Trier High School, where Bencriscutto recently served as a Composer/Conductor-in-Residence.*

any difficulty seeing through the surface of individuals and seeing that underneath are some great qualities — desire for self-respect, self-esteem, and love of fellow man. To search for that which is good, just, and beautiful is at the basis of truth.

Feeling this way, why did you become a band director and not a pastor?

Because I think music is more universal than religion; it transcends all differences of creed, race, and politics. When I took the University of Minnesota band to the Soviet Union to represent the United States I came to realize that music is a great force for peace. In our afternoon visits to conservatories in the major cities, my students and the Soviet students performed for each other and had a chance to talk. It struck me then that though the political and religious differences were enormous, the hearts of the individuals were the same. Music transcended all those differences and brought individuals together. We would end our performances embracing and feeling a great sense of warmth — a kind of tie, people with people, standing above all the conflict of politics.

I see music as one of our most effective vehicles to help our society, and that's why I'm so anxious to find out why our music programs are not at the center of the curriculum and why music education isn't more highly respected. These problems have consumed me over the years. How can state and school administrators demand languages in the high school as a criteria for entering college but not respect music as a language when it is, in fact, the most universal language? One of our problems may be that we've been feeding students the candy, the dessert portion, without supplying them with the main part of the meal.

If you were now teaching in a public school program, how would you keep from being cut?

People in our society want something tangible. Society doesn't understand the intangible, and music is an intangible. It doesn't consist of clear-cut contests, as in athletics, where physical body meets physical body with a winner or loser. Music has tried in vain to be an athletic event, in an attempt to give a society that doesn't understand the true nature of music something tangible to relate it to.

Contests can have value if balanced properly and not overdone, but they are really contradictory to what art is all about. Art is not a matter of "I am better than you are." Art is a matter of "one for all and all for one," and "let's do it together," and a contest is the antithesis of that. The last chair clarinetist should have the possibility of having as great an experience as a solo artist. The junior high school student who's trying to produce a beautiful sound achieves beauty in the process of striving for it, even if it's on his level. In this pursuit the student can experience the same positive values that a performer in a symphony orchestra is able to achieve.

Number ratings at contests are an effort to make relative judgments. We are all aware that no one can say a group deserves precisely a 91 or a 93, etc. My personal preference has been for festivals with comments by adjudicators — constructive, encouraging, and positive kinds of comments. If somebody has to judge, we might as well choose people who believe that we have to transcend the system and be helpful to students and directors in the process. Contests should exist to whatever degree they may assist the greater purpose, but it is more important for us to find a way to measure skills and theoretical knowledge and to establish definite goals. We need to have a curriculum of study for music just as for other academic subjects.

Are you saying the ability to measure results is one way to respond to concerns about program cuts or music's status?

Yes, there should be clear expectations and ways of measuring those expectations as far as skills and theory are concerned. We need a progressive course of study with testable goals that students, parents, and administrators understand. We should also seek to ingrain some idea of the aesthetic, philosophic, and humanistic nature of music. You can't have a philosophy class in a band rehearsal because the students don't want it, but if you deal with the human values in a subtle, natural manner, I think pretty soon students become comfortable with these ideas.

How many schools deal with aesthetics or humanistic philosophy as related to the arts? Do they talk about philosophy and its relationship to music? Maybe in one course in four years. That certainly doesn't parallel the amount of time spent dealing with the science and skill of performance. I remember a quotation from Confucius: "If you want to understand the nature of a society or of a people, whether their loves be good or bad, selfish or unselfish — study their music." He was a pretty insightful man.

Our colleges need to consider the humanistic side of music in society. Aristotle said, "It is clear that music affects the human being, affects society; therefore it behooves us to understand and study music more deeply so we can use it in a way that is good." Anything that is powerful can be used for good or for bad purposes. A fire can warm the home or burn it down. I think music is like that, so we need to understand it more than we do.

What difference is that understanding going to make in a ninth-grade band rehearsal? And how can you communicate it subtly?

You could post some quotations about music and its nature on a bulletin board or make them part of your podium vocabulary. I don't think you should thrust these ideas down the students' throats; gradually they will absorb them. Occasionally you could ask the students what the music is saying to them. Perhaps you could be more direct at times and talk about togetherness, teamwork, quality relationships, and awareness of each other. There is no question in my mind that such discussions helped my students to have some peak experiences. This kind of thinking will give greater purpose to the experiences of students in all grades.

I think our students, their parents, and administrators need to see music as being something more precious. Marshall McLuhan compared the average person's understanding of music to natives on some island who wear precious diamonds and pearls around their necks, but don't realize the value of those pearls or diamonds. If students better realized the value of music, I think they would be less superficial, more serious, more dedicated.

Remember the *Tanglewood Report?* Those national personalities (mostly non-musicians) who contributed to it said that music should be at the center of the curriculum and everything should relate to its artistic nature. Yet where is music today? It's almost out of the curriculum!

What indications have you seen that in-depth teaching is crucial right now?

I was in Tennessee recently and heard that state's head of curriculum speak to band directors. He told them, "You must spell out what you intend to accomplish in your band class," and, "It is imperative that you continue your professional growth or eventually you will find yourselves without jobs." He was right; all of us need to learn new skills, new ideas, and not just continue the same patterns without reevaluation.

Support for education went downhill in the 70s. I'm now seeing an upswing and a concern about education with greater financial backing. The question is, will music benefit from this fiscal upswing?

If you could outline an ideal program, what types of organizations would you have and what would be your emphasis and direction?

I'd say that we have to deal with two components: the science of music and the art of music. I'm not sure we've dealt with either in the public schools. We've dealt with the skill of per-

formance, but it's been more like training parrots. You say the words and the parrot says something back to you. You tell them how to play it and they play it that way. We haven't been teaching the language so I don't think we've been necessarily teaching the art or the science.

We should continue to emphasize performance, but to justify our programs, we must also include some basic theory and discussions as to the value of music to society. It need not take more than 20 minutes of rehearsal time per week to teach musical language basics such as scales, modes, triads, 7th chords, chord progressions, intervals, and form, organized in a way that students, parents, and administrators can all understand.

As students absorb the vocabulary and basic theory, they will identify more deeply with the music. Their motivation will naturally improve, creativity will increase, and music will become more vital to them.

I recently returned from doing clinics and guest-conducting in Japan. The Japanese are doing the daily technical drilling we used to do and must do again if we hope to maintain and improve our programs.

What is the relationship of concert band to other groups in a total music program?

As a director who has worked many years with all phases of the band program, I see marching band as a valid and effective entertainment form of music; the jazz area as an important creative component, and concert band as covering all categories — pop, jazz, and classical. I see concert band as the home for everybody: for the people in the jazz ensemble, for the people who go out and march on the field to entertain the audience, for the pep bands and for the individuals who solo.

The concert band is one of the most important mediums of expression in 20th-century America. In a sense, the concert band has evolved as a melting pot of different styles of music. The further we stray from the concert band as the hub of the wheel, then the further we stray from the ideal of the American band program as a significant form of expression, justifiable as the center of the music curriculum. I think it's a tragedy when a school program places the marching band as the primary focus.

Would it be as tragic to have jazz ensemble as the primary focus?

No, not as tragic because if you have a good jazz program, you are dealing with creativity. The members of the jazz ensembles at the University of Minnesota also play in the concert bands. Our emphasis is on jazz with classical tone quality and classical articulation. Jazz is often defined, in part, as improvisation and, as such, it is spontaneous creativity and the seed of expanding perceptions and ideas.

I don't see jazz being taught properly in enough schools. We should be teaching creativity and theory, but in probably 95% of the schools the students don't understand what they're doing. In most jazz ensembles they're playing the charts, but as soon as there is an individual creative opportunity, they don't understand the language. When I travel around the country, I hear few jazz soloists in high schools who show an understanding of harmony or an understanding of where they are, where they are going, and what scales or chords fit in at that moment. Most players don't have awareness of the beauty of developing an idea, creating a motive, and working with that motive in a sense that has unity, evolution, and contrast. Composers sit down and spend months trying to get that unity. A skilled jazz player at times can do it in a second. Jazz can be a marvelous creative vehicle if more time is spent teaching the theory and vocabulary so that students know what they are doing.

Going back to your ideas on competitions, did you ever go through a period in your teaching where you were into getting that score or beating that other band?

Never, but I can't say that I'm a saint. You know there's a great deal of competition everywhere. You want to have a place in society, a place in your profession. You want to be respected; you want to respect yourself. As much as possible I attempt to get my ego out of the way so that I can get into the real purity and chemistry of the experience. Usually when that happens, the results are more apt to achieve inspirational levels.

I suppose my mother was the strongest influence on my feelings on that subject; her whole life was a gift to her family. I was the ninth of ten children including five older brothers, and I looked up to those people and learned humility very quickly. My wife Jean, a professional flutist, has been my sounding board; the countless hours of discussions we have shared have encouraged the crystallization of my philosophies.

In the educational world I felt a strong affinity for Howard Hanson and his outlook on music. He felt music deeply and sincerely; the expression existed without the impurities. Howard Hanson loved life, loved people and believed in the potential of music to cure the ills of humanity. That was his motivation.

Did you become a teacher because you wanted to influence others to think that same way?

That certainly has evolved to become the most significant reason. I believe that if we're not careful, we'll all be separate islands. Playing music helps us to understand that we can fulfill ourselves, both as individuals and as a society. I guess that's probably my central philosophy.

There's a natural tendency for rhythms to click together and a natural tendency for voices to come together in a unison. There's also a natural tendency for every note to express itself as beautifully as possible within a given moment without distorting its relationship to the next note, and to the next note, and to the whole phrase. In the same manner, as individuals, we should seek to fulfill ourselves and yet not distort or deny the opportunity for others to fulfill themselves. We seek to function together so that the ultimate whole can be a symphony of life that can relate to that ideal symphony of sound. That, in a nutshell, is the kind of a philosophy that requires involvement. I'm really bothered by people who "stand on the outside looking in," like spectators watching a game on the field, instead of becoming involved. Too few people get totally involved. While their intellect might be there, their emotions might not be. There are many students who say, "Here's 1,2,3,4- 1,2,3,4," but they're not feeling anything. They are missing the rewards of personal expression. I talk to them about the intellectual, emotional, creative, and physical aspects of involvement. Until those things come together, the music these students create is a fabrication of the real experience.

Is this involvement the reason it is important for you to be a band director in addition to being a composer?

In a sense I have my cake and eat it too. I think composing and conducting are equally important means of expression. Helping young people find themselves, feel good about themselves, or fulfill themselves is tremendously rewarding. The search for and appreciation of that which is beautiful in musical expression can serve as ideals for humanity to follow. We are all partners in that effort.

We've come full circle. What is the first step in elevating band to its rightful academic position?

There is no simple solution. Band, orchestra and choir directors need to come together and discuss this question at length. We should create a national statement with ideas from everybody in our profession who is concerned about our future. Once we had such a statement, it could inspire strength through mutual support, allowing us to contact national school administration organizations and the press at a national level. Who knows what wheels that could set in motion? □

An interview with John Paynter

by Kenneth L. Neidig

John Paynter became a university band director at the age of 21, hand-picked for the prestigious North-western University position. by Glenn Cliffe Bainum, who was the director of bands for the 27 years between 1926 and 1953. Paynter has remained at Northwestern for the past 29 years, but his influence has been felt around the world through personal appearances as adjudicator, clinician, and guest conductor; as the composer or arranger of over 400 works; as the president of professional associations; and as the contributing editor for the new music review section of this magazine.

I asked if he could remember the day he first walked into Northwestern and met Bainum.

Oh yes, I can remember that vividly. I played an audition for him in old Music Hall that we abandoned only two years ago. He opened a sight-reading book, one I still use, and asked me to play. I think the audition lasted all of a minute and a half. He told me I was a "marvelous" clarinet player, and that I was in the band. (I knew at the time he was just being awfully nice, and as years went by I knew it even better.) But the most important thing I remember was that before I left the room he asked me if I knew how to operate a mimeograph machine. I said yes (even though I never had seen one) because I knew from the look on his face that he wanted a mimeograph operator, and he wanted me to say yes. With that he handed me a stencil, one of his intricate marching band maneuvers, and asked me if I would run it. He went back to more auditions, and I suddenly had a job on the band staff. I went to the machine, put the stencil on upside down, and very nearly ruined it completely. The secretary and I spent the rest of the day trying to figure out how to get it cleaned up and make it useful. I don't think he ever found out about the problem.

What did you learn from him?

Oh, my goodness, that would be a book. More than anything else I would have to say musicianship. He was such a marvelous musician, so much better than most people knew that it amazes me even today how much musicality he showed in his writing and in his conducting and in talking about music. The things that he said just off hand about music have become such giant precepts in my own thinking. I don't recall ever hearing him talk about pitch, or saying "flat" or "sharp." I rarely ever heard him say "loud" or "soft";

he talked about shading and flexibility and warmth and nuance. These were words he used over and over again, and I think he achieved all the rest through that device. When his bands played in tune — and they did — and when they played with the right balance, it was all done on the basis of musicianship. He was also a great baton technician, with one of the most unusual and effective batons ever. And from him I learned a great deal about organization, efficiency, integrity, and preparation. I'm not nearly as good at it as he was, but I would have been a lot worse if it were not for him.

How about his human qualities, his personal relationships?

With people he knew well his personality had the normal ups and downs; but he was especially good with the person he knew only as a member of the band, or in an all-state group, or as a student in his class. He had the ability to make these casual acquaintances feel immediately that he knew them more intimately, making them feel needed and treating them in just the right way.

I know Bainum had a tremendous influence on your life. Were there others?

Yes. I grew up in a very small town, Mineral Point, Wisconsin; and a gentleman named John Alderson lived there. He was sort of the Mr. Everything in music: he played cornet and was director of the town band, played violin in the Sunday school orchestra, and was the organist at the church I attended. Every Sunday afternoon he gave me free organ lessons. I'd go to the church and sit for two or three hours with him; he would teach by example, just playing more than anything else. He was also a good composer and an incredible man. In fact when he was in his 70's he slipped on the ice and broke his left wrist and couldn't bend it enough to play the violin any more, so he restrung the instrument the opposite way and learned to play all over again, left-handed.

Adeline Paulsrud and Ruth Wilhelmsen (who became Ruth Paynter when she married a shirt-tail cousin of mine) were both St. Olaf graduates and conducted the school choirs in the St. Olaf tradition. With them I learned sight-singing and the ability to express myself with my voice. They just did not believe in pop music or rinky-dink materials of any kind, so we sang very good things.

I think the turning point for me was when I was in the 9th grade and Bernard Stepner came to town as the band director. After just one year he was drafted, but in that short time he influenced a lot of us; and out of that small class we had nearly 20 people who did well in music.

Being born and raised in a small town was very fortunate for me because it was the kind of setting where there was abolutely no restriction on opportunities. (There were plenty of restrictions on behavior and I view that also as a plus.) If a young person wanted to take part in athletics, music, drama, boy scouts, and church, it wasn't an exception, it was almost the rule. Everyone was able to do everything.

Can you remember your first contact with music?

From the earliest days I can remember I was interested in music. No one ever forced me, it was just a part of what was good in life. There was a piano in the house and the occasional evening when we all sat around and either sang or played or did both. There were three girls and me in the family, and all four children took piano lessons as early as we could. It might have been first or second grade when I started piano, and there were the usual periods of dropping out and coming back to it. We never had a lot of money (my dad was a plumber long before plumbers made much money), but there was always money for music.

My dad played clarinet in the city band, and my mother played the piano quite well. I can remember wanting to play an instrument and my dad bringing me one of his clarinets to try. Very shortly after that he bought me a new clarinet.

Did you play in a school band?

Oh yes, I started in the 5th grade. An advantage of the small town was that you played in the high school band when you were ready; I think I probably got in when I was in the 6th or 7th grade, and played all through school. I also played sports and never marched in a football band before Northwestern because I was on the high school football team.

Why didn't you pursue the sports side at Northwestern?

Because I was so bad. I was successful in high school sports more because of being a little smart than being a gifted athlete. I ended up being the quarterback on the football team and the playmaker guard on the basketball team because I could remember the plays. I couldn't even begin to match the caliber of players at the college level, but I loved sports.

Well you've certainly been successful as a band director. What advice do you have for younger people who are seeking that kind of success?

I've had an awful lot of good luck and nice breaks. There is one thing about myself that seems different from some of the people I've associated with: I seem to change emphasis every four or five years, whereas some people in this profession have had a

particular goal in mind from as long ago as I can remember them, and they have pretty much stayed on that track.

I've worn a lot of different hats in the short time I've been working. For example, the year Mr. Bainum retired I went through a period of real excitement arranging for the band, and turned out a number of rather large pieces. Now only in recent months I'm picking it up again because some things are starting to be published from that group that was done so long ago — the Bach, the transcription of *Night on Bald Mountain,* and a number of others.

Also, I was not the person who pioneered the idea of the wind ensemble but I was one of the very first to devote major interest to it and make it a part of a major university program. In 1956 we started an ensemble group at Northwestern that was separate from the rest of the band. With the wind ensemble I went through a period of time when I spent a great deal of energy and effort uncovering and promoting new band music. We premiered a number of things, in a sense we commissioned them, without funds, by asking composers to write a piece for us in return for our copying the parts for them.

There was a period of time when the marching band had to be foremost in my mind. I was excited about it, worked extremely hard, and was determined to accomplish certain things. Once that goal was achieved, I must say that we have not been terribly innovative since — the formula has continued to work for us very successfully. Oh, maybe we're innovative, but we're not pioneering anymore.

Then there's the time I've been so involved with the Northshore Band and the whole community band movement. There was another period when I did small ensembles: octets, nonets, double quintets.

I don't know, maybe I just can't keep my mind on one thing for long.

When you add these new things you don't necessarily give up the others do you?

No, no, I think we just put the emphasis in one direction, and take the others along. There's never been a period of any longer than a year where I went without arranging something, for instance. So to get back to your question, "What should a young person do?" I'd suggest that he should stay flexible.

To have this good luck you say you've had, doesn't one need a large reservoir of talent? Otherwise you may get the lucky break, but you're going to flop.

Well sure, but I think the talent is something that just an awful lot of people have. I think there are as many truly talented musicians who are not involved in music-making as there are who are busy in music. I think the thing that sets apart leaders in our field are things that are, strictly speaking, not musical at all. Most of the people who succeed in band or orchestra conducting have qualities that would make them reasonably successful in business, or in the sciences, or in the trades.

What are those qualities?

Salesmanship, selling yourself is very important —

selling your ideas, speaking well in public. Self confidence, being convinced that what you're saying on the podium or in the classroom is right — even when you make the mistakes that everyone does who is human — and being able to convince others that you believe what you say. Just sheer energy is important. I'm 50 years old and I'm watching people fall away, changing professions, or going into semi-retirement. My wife and others often ask how long I can continue at the present pace; but I don't feel that it's a particularly fast pace. It's just the way I do things, and it's the way everybody does who is really excited about the band business. They carry a lot of activities at one time and seem to have the energy to bring it off. So energy, good health, and enthusiasm are all important.

Is there any way to keep from burning out? Maybe that's why you keep shifting from one enthusiasm to the other. Is that part of what keeps you going?

Well, I don't know. I think there's some kind of fresh pasture there all the time. I'm the same way with hobbies. I go into each one with such enthusiastic interest and it lasts such a short time that it's almost discouraging sometimes; and yet I will come back with renewed interest. My wife and I do many of those things together. We were avid stamp collectors for about five years, and now it's sort of a dormant hobby. There is always something that has occupied our interest — picture matting, painting, woodworking — and as a consequence neither one of us has ever been bored. If you weren't here tonight I would be busy at something, either as my vocation or avocation, because every night has to be filled with something.

Do you think life is long enough to satisfy all these interests?

I'm sure it isn't. I see so many things I want to do. Maybe that's good. Maybe that's what's nice about the job I have. I don't feel I'm anywhere near finished. There's plenty to do.

Recently I watched you work with individual band directors as a part of the festival conducted by the Northshore Concert Band, and I know you have worked with many directors through the years. Surely some of the same problems come up again and again.

Each teacher and each conductor is really an individual personality, and it's within that personality that the band has either its successes or its problems. Two things often do stand out as general weaknesses. The first is musical — the failure to recognize the things that don't sound like music. A good conductor must be able to hear what is going on, while it is going on, and suggest what to do to change it. So many of our people are well-trained to read the score, and well-trained to lead with a baton; but they are not really well-trained to hear what's going on and change

it. As a consequence some basically unmusical, inflexible, and unnuanced (here I come back to Mr. Bainum's theories) things continue to happen. The other thing is personal. A lot of potentially wonderful teachers aren't doing a very good job because they are too frustrated by all of the mechanical and personal things that can get in the way. A band director must enjoy what he's doing, be head-over-heels in love with it, so he can work around the technical problems and push through to the job of having fun and making music.

Many of our long-time readers may know you best as a reviewer of new music. What do you look for?

Certainly the elements of good music as we've all had them described to us: correctness of approach to writing harmony, counterpoint that makes sense, contrast of textures and varieties of keys and rhythms — that sort of thing. But you can get shot down on that too. I always think of *The Joy of Music*, in which Leonard Bernstein wrote how a Beethoven symphony fails to qualify on all these "rules of good music." I like to see something that allows the solo instruments of the band to be heard and helps to develop the interest of the particularly talented players. Until one has a lot of experience with music, I suspect you look mostly for people you know, the good arrangers who present a consistent challenge. If they say with the first ten measures that a work is grade III, it's grade III in the last ten measures too. And they also make things happen musically, with phrases, and form, and style.

After these many years of looking, how much really good music do you expect to find? Is it a surprise when a good piece comes along?

I don't think it's as big a surprise as it was 10 or 15 years ago. There are more good things all the time, even though there still aren't nearly enough. If I look back on how I have spent my time and look forward to how I'm going to spend it in the future, I think almost everything has to do with the search for good things to perform. And that isn't a pessimistic view at all; it is very optimistic in that we have a much larger repertoire now to choose from than we had a while ago. We started late with the band, and have a lot of ground to make up. Before we have a large and reliable body of wonderful things to play we're going to have to go through things that aren't as good to play in order to find them. Those interested in the band have done a good job of encouraging talented people to write original compositions and arrangements for band. At the university we now have an immense library of music for the band, and I would think that fully 5% of it is substantial music. The difference is that today it's 5% of a much larger body than it was a few years ago. So we're on our way.

You've done a lot of composing and arranging yourself....

I'm a far better arranger than I am a composer. I majored in composition at Northwestern, with both a bachelor's and a master's degree, and it taught me that I shouldn't compose. I've written down a lot of notes, but I don't feel I've composed much that's of lasting value. However, out of it I've become a better analyst of other composers, and maybe a little better score reader, and somewhat skilled as an arranger. I often specify an exact number of players on a part, one of the ways I reflect my background as a composer and conductor. I may have a little more intimate knowledge of what a clarinet section sounds like with two on a stand and one on a stand and four on a stand than the person who is writing but not conducting at the same time. I think you can get a great deal of color contrast by varying the number of players. I also like to include the color instruments, even though I realize that this puts some of the things I arrange out of reach for some bands. Even in a simple little arrangement like *Sarabande and Polka*, I call for soprano sax, English horn, and muted cornet, all playing at the same time. It's quite possible that the first school band we see won't have any of those instruments, but nevertheless I think those are colors we need if we're going to rise above a certain level of performance and expression.

I'm not through writing; it just is going to take a little rearranging of my schedule to do it on a more regular basis again. With the children grown up, married, and gone, it is more fun to be sitting at the table again writing arrangements.

I know the family is very important to you. Weren't you and your wife childhood sweethearts?

Yes, Marietta and I were baptized together. We were born and raised in the same town and went to the same church, the same school. We've always been a close family and we get along very well — we like each other. One of the turning points was the year we lived together in Europe when I was on leave. I saw more of the family in that year than I might have on evenings and weekends for a whole lifetime.

Usually musicians are asked if their children play. I'm sure you get a lot of that, as well as questions about how much parents should push their kids.

I don't know if you should push or you should pull. I think you should influence. Both of our children took piano lessons in the prep piano department at Northwestern, but neither one of them has continued to play the piano. Bruce played oboe, sousaphone in the marching band, and was a member of my band staff at Northwestern. He's now a lawyer in Chicago, and has said many times that learning pride in his work and attention to detail as a member of the band staff was one of the best life preparations he had. Megan teaches first grade in Prospect Heights and plays horn with the Northshore Band.

To say that children should do what they want to do is a great percentage of the problem of society today. To think that the child will naturally take to music any more than he would naturally take to Sunday school or to physical exercise I think is naive. At least

those who do take to it naturally are far outnumbered by those who don't because music takes discipline and no child is ready for that. I'm glad my mother and dad kept pushing me.

How did they do it without turning you against music?

I don't know, except that they were able to convince me of everything they wanted me to do. I had enough trust and faith in them that music was just another thing to be done the same way. That might be the answer, maybe the problem is that when it comes to music, parents try to be different, not the same kind of disciplinarians as when they run everything else that affects the child.

One of the things that's taken you away from home and the family has been the all-state bands, and you've done a tremendous number of them through the years. How should an all-state conductor be treated?

Carefully. I don't believe an all-state conductor is any different from any other kind of guest conductor. A conductor is an artist, and I don't mean that in a snobbish way at all. A person who has spent time perfecting what he does and has presumably spent many hours studying the scores, determining the program, and getting ready psychologically, should be greeted with the same sort of enthusiasm and preparation. And I must say that in more than nine out of ten cases that's exactly what happens. There is someone who greets you at the airport, gets you to your hotel room, takes you to dinner, and makes sure you get to the first meeting. It is only occasionally when the local hosts are perhaps overbusy with the details of organizing the event, that they forget the conductor is a special person. "Special" only in the sense that he controls the destiny of the musicians for the next 48 hours, and that if he is not rested or happy or given the tools with which to work he cannot produce the expected result. I suppose the hidden discourtesy, one that happens more often than it should, is the failure to prepare the students — either to prepare them psychologically to be under the discipline of a gifted conductor or to prepare them on the parts they're going to play. It is sad that from time to time there really is no purpose in the visit of a guest conductor because the parts have not been prepared and there is little or nothing the conductor can do. Though that doesn't happen very often, it happens far too often.

I remember watching you work with the New Mexico All-State Band. One thing you did was to put lyrics to one of the phrases to show them what was going on in the music, assigning characters to the antecedent and the consequent of the phrase. They understood that it was a conversation, and that the melody was being passed around the band. And in the concert the next day, it was coming through, they were making music. How many of those kinds of things do you have? I hate to call them a whole bag of tricks....

Well, that's just what they are — they're tricks, they're gimmicks to make the teaching come across a little easier. Oh, there are hundreds of them I am sure. Not just mine, but hundreds that others are using. I think one of the best short cuts we have is verbalizing or vocalizing, singing the line, using nonsense syllables, or rhythmic sight-singing or the verbalization that you heard me do. Some of the old master teachers used to pick up their cornet or their violin and play it for the students; when I'm on the podium I use my voice to replace the instrument and do the same thing. You can lose them in that process if you stop every third bar and sing something for them. Pretty soon they don't want to hear you sing any more. You have to find as many ways to make a point as you can. I don't think there is anything more dull than saying the same thing the same way over and over again. A common rehearsal technique is to stop and correct, stop and go down the line and have the next person play and the next person. Although I've done my share of that, I always dislike myself in the morning after I've done it because there are so many better ways to teach. I like to teach by example, by singing or saying or playing what I want.

Do you recall any particular things that have worked especially well for you?

I think the most effective single thing I've used in recent years has been my insistence that we tune up and warm up in a particular, structured way. I start with the pitch F (because that's the nastiest of all tones to tune) and then work around it diatonically. The merit of it has not been so much the warm-up and the tune-up that everybody in the room seems to hear, but the fact that it brings the ensemble under total control. Sometimes after over two hours of rehearsing when the band has had a break for 20 minutes and they come back and start dealing with the warm-up and tune-up again, I've had some of the conductors

come in and say, "My goodness, aren't they warm enough by now?" They don't understand that the whole purpose of using it again after the break is to get the break to end in the student's minds and get their attention back to the discipline of the music. If we can get players to listen to each other, to relate their role with the role of everyone else in the room, we can cancel out a lot of the problems that we would normally have to stop and rehearse.

I think sometimes it's good for the conductor to imagine he has an adjudicator's form in front of him with the various categories like tone, intonation, balance. He might spend consecutive rehearsals working on those fundamentals: one day nearly all of the time is devoted to the matter of balance, and another you don't think of anything but tone quality. All the other fundamentals will improve at the same time, but one of the objectives is to get the young people to think of the fundamentals. Every note they play on a given day is subject to scrutiny as to its pitch, the next day as to the beauty of its quality, the next day as to its nuance or shading. Sometimes it's too much to ask for them to remember all of that in one sitting, but you can stress one thing at a time. I've seen conductors work with a two hour period divided into four quarters, like a football game. One quarter they talk about pitch, another about balance. And there are many conductors who talk about many things at one time, without any special emphasis. Of all the things I've used, the warm-up/tune-up has been the most effective because it teaches that we should listen and watch and shows how we relate to those around us.

Is this printed or do you just describe it as you go?

I have it printed out. It's just a little exercise out of the Arbans book with some adjustments that have developed over the years. But the students don't have to read the music and that's very important. Their minds are concentrating completely on the sounds they're producing, the attack they're playing, the pitch they're involved with, the volume they have, the blend they're making. And they can look right straight at you the moment they're doing it. I find some of the most expressive results coming out of those warm-ups because when they are playing a piece later they see my same gesture meaning the same thing in a new role.

When you're rehearsing how do you figure out what to repair and what to leave alone? Are there priorities? We've all seen so many conductors who waste time on things that really don't matter.

Sometimes I think I do too. There are rehearsals when I feel like I've spent the whole time chipping away at things that don't matter. There's no magic formula. To be efficient, the most important thing is to know your people. Obviously you rehearse a group like the Northshore Band that meets once a week for two hours much differently than you would rehearse a university band that meets four hours a week, or a high school band that meets 40 minutes every day. You asked the key question — what do you try to get done and what do you let go? I know the personnel of the Northshore Band so well now that I know that just by uncovering the mistake, the mistake will be corrected. There's no need to go back and prove that you can do it if you've had the opportunity to scowl at somebody when they did it wrong. With a group you don't know as well there has to be a period of time in which you make sure they will make the corrections once you have pointed them out.

But correcting is really not the most efficient way to rehearse. It is best to have in your head the sounds you want and to conduct those sounds right from the start, guiding the performer so the mistake is never made in the first place. That's idealistic, but it certainly is more efficient.

Of course, the most efficient "rehearsal technique" is the score study that precedes the rehearsal. This nit-picking rehearsing you and I have seen is the result of the conductor really not knowing the score. The conductor will spend time pecking away at something he knows is safe because he doesn't know what else to rehearse.

Let's talk about score study. What technique do you use?

My first look at a score is just flipping through, like picking a magazine off the rack to see if you want to buy it. It's the look-through that tells you if you're interested in looking any further. The second time around is where I try to see something of the shape of the piece — the forms, the architecture, the overall design, not the bricks and the screws and the hinges. It's at this point that I need to know something about the instrumentation and its demands — whether it's suitable or worthwhile or perhaps too difficult or too easy. I might also stop long enough to see something of the ingredients, at least the harmonic language or the contrapuntal complexities, but I would not analyze it carefully. Then the next time through I'm starting to look section by section. That's when I do my sight-singing of the score. I really believe that to study a score thoroughly you have to sing every line. I'm not the first one to say this by any means, and I was not taught it at Northwestern, mind you. I just came to it by teaching and by talking with people I think read scores well. It is during this third stage that I do any detailed marking that is necessary. I believe in marking as much as you have to, or as little as you can get by with. The last look is when I do a performance sitting at my desk. Of course I may come back many times after that. I think some of the nicest moments the conductor has is when he digs out a score he thinks he knows and finds out there are many new things to know about it. I think that's fun.

How long does this process take? I know it varies according to the piece, but can you give us some idea?

It's very gratifying and rewarding, but it is not something you can do quickly. Most young conductors delude themselves if they think there are people who can sight sing a score at tempo the first time and hear all the parts. It's mostly hard work and careful study.

Let's assume you've selected a score or you know you're going to perform a work sometime, how long before the first rehearsal do you really get serious about the architecture stage, the sight-singing stage, the conducting-at-the-desk stage?

Well, there have been times and there will be times again when that serious moment is 20 minutes before the rehearsal. That's one of the realities of the college teacher's life. There are times when we simply don't have adequate score preparation time. If we had our druthers, we would start studying a year ahead of a performance and accelerate in the last month.

It's more fun for me to sit and read a score in the evening than it is to read a novel or a magazine, or certainly more fun than to watch a television show. I don't do it nearly as much as I would like, but right now I am studying some scores with no performance date in mind, with at least one all marked and virtually committed to memory. But that's a rarity.

How long did you have with the Messiaen pieces? [Oiseaux Exotiques, Couleurs de la Cite Celeste, and Et Exspecto Resurrectionem Mortuourm by Olivier Messiaen were performed by the wind ensemble at N.U. last year, with the composer present]

I had only a month to study those and I could have used another two or three easily. I would have liked to study them for a period of several years but those performances came up much faster than I expected, so we did them. I'm a very good sight-reader of scores, and I think that is something that one can learn to do. You can learn to sight-read a score just as well as you can read a book. And fluency in reading is a most important asset to anybody who wants to succeed professionally, words or music.

Does score study apply to a grade III piece and a high school director as well as to the Messiaen piece with a university wind ensemble?

I think that's terribly important. The person who believes he shouldn't study as much because the music is easier is not really being fair to the level of the player he controls. Many dull band rehearsals are the result of the director not having studied the score and not knowing what to say to the youngsters about the music. I feel strongly about this. Last December at the Mid-West Clinic I gave a lecture to the Marine band directors and was talking about how important it is to prepare a score. One young officer raised his hand and said, "Well, obviously you have never had to play just reviews over and over again where all you play is a march and all you have is a cornet copy." I really admonished him on this, and said, "If that were my situation and I had all of the labor that you have available, I'd have those marches copied out in full score so I could study them and know what's going on, so I could teach the band to play that march properly." I think there is no excuse for asking the band members to tell you what they have written in their part.

Let's talk about the future. You came into this North-western job a long time ago. Many of your colleagues who have held their jobs for 29 years are now retiring at 65, and you're 50 and not even close. Where do you go from here?

Next Fall I'm going to be much more involved with teaching music education. This is something I haven't done. I don't have a music education degree, and I've never taught in the public schools; but I've had so many experiences with school age children at festivals and contests that I have many ideas I think are worth hearing. It will be another new challenge for me. I am also looking forward to having more time to write, some in words and some in notes. I'd like to try to figure out what it is I'm trying to say and get it said in both areas. Publication is important for me right now, not just financially because it doesn't amount to that much, but it's really gratifying to see these pieces I've been using in manuscript begin to come out in print so others can have them. Once you see the first one it's like popcorn, you can't stop. Just today I found myself saying, "I ought to re-arrange the Bach." It is 25 years old and there are a lot of things I can improve. I thought today as I was playing it how sure I was in 1953 that nobody could do it better than I could and how I had it exactly the way it ought to be, but every year since I've found things I want to change.

What else have you learned about yourself in this past quarter century?

Not enough, I'm afraid. I'm still as pompous as I was when I was 23 years old. You learn your limitations and you also learn that you are very good at certain things. I guess I've learned that many people have been awfully nice to me at the University and in the community band too. The Northshore Band has added a separate dimension to my life. It's taken me places I couldn't have gone otherwise; it's given me opportunities to do music I couldn't do otherwise; and we've reached people through the band that we couldn't reach other ways. It really is a blessing — I don't know how I could express it in any other form. I think that particular community band — the combination of personalities and friendships that have been in it — is better than any kind of a social club or church involvement or any other kind of activity that I might have had to replace it with. It has been a wonderful thing.

This could happen with people all over the country, couldn't it?

Yes, and it's going to. Mity Johnson, a fellow I admire very much [Miles Johnson, St. Olaf], just told me that he started one up in Northfield, Minnesota. He started it as an alumni band, but it's open to any adult who wants to play. Oh, there are so many, they're just springing up all over.

Does the band director who is teaching in a school owe anything to the community?

I think he has a moral obligation to uphold standards of music in the community. The odds are that the band director is one of the three best musicians in town, and he may even be the best. To simply say that he has no responsibility beyond his six or eight hours in the classroom is terribly unfortunate. If he has a special gift that others haven't had bestowed on them he ought to share that, move it into the community, uplift their standards, and lead the way. I get peeved with young band directors who tell me about their town being a "cultural desert" as though they didn't have anything to do with it. I want to say, "Why don't you get a hose in your hand and start to run some water and bring something to fruition there?" I think there is a very definite obligation. It may be in adult education, community music making, a wider involvement in their churches or service clubs, or just in seeing that cultural events come to town.

Well, you certainly seem to enjoy everything you do, but I suspect you'll always be involved somehow in conducting a group.

Yes, I really do enjoy it. You know I've conducted the Waa-Mu show [student Broadway-type musical production] all these years. Not too long ago one of our students was conducting the show chorus and being a bit of a cynic, saying he was glad to take the money for doing it but he wasn't happy in his job. Just as I was standing on the steps ready to go into the pit, he said, "Mr. Paynter, why in the world do you do something as corny as this show when you have so much to do? Why do you want to do it?" And I had to think before I answered, to tell him how much I loved what I was doing; how much fun it was to control a show from the pit, to run the show just as standing on the tower you run the marching band, and standing on the podium you run the concert band. I suppose it's a little bit of an ego trip but it's just such great fun. I love it. ∎

Albert Austin Harding —

A Tribute During the Centennial of His Birth

Almost no one who has spent any portion of his life working with school bands in this country during the past 60 years could have moved with such seeming ease from square one to square two without the achievements of Albert Austin Harding at The University of Illinois during the years 1905 to 1948. His distinguished name and his unprecedented exemplary life-work must be remembered always, but with special emphasis in this centennial year of his birth.

The wide swath he cut across the field of university band activity and organization is a most impressive musical and educational harvest. Any single man in a like discipline has rarely equalled it. The contemporary American bandmaster's heritage was established through the environment that Harding created on the Illinois campus where the modern concert band, gridiron marching band, band clinic, and pursuit of the colorful and sensitive symphonic transcription were among his outstanding contributions; they did not exist before him.

In this centennial year I remember with considerable affection three highly influential Interlochen summers with him in the National High School Band. Much is owed to him in this salute to his imagination, his discipline, his dedicated musical achievements, and his quiet and genuine humility.

Here's to the memory of a great man. *Happy Birthday*, Dr. Harding.

Frederick Fennell

Albert Austin Harding was born in Georgetown, Illinois on February 10, 1880. He began cornet study at age 14 in Paris, Illinois, and subsequently studied baritone horn, trombone, piccolo, and drums. Following graduation from high school, he performed full-time as a professional musician and served as director of the Paris Concert Band. In 1902 at the age of 22, he entered the University of Illinois as an engineering student and received a degree in 1906, continuing his playing throughout college. He was a part-time instructor in the School of Music and became conductor of the University Band in September 1905 at the beginning of his senior year, remaining in the position until his retirement on September 1, 1948. He died December 3, 1958.

A.A. Harding's Assistants

George C. Wilson, now retired as director of the National Music Camp at Interlochen, once served as librarian of the University of Illinois Bands and assisted in the installation of library procedures when Harding assumed leadership of the Interlochen band program. His memories include these thoughts:

To have been one of Albert Austin Harding's "boys" was indeed a unique privilege. His relationship with us was a warm one, and he always found time to share himself and his musical experiences. To him I owe an eternal debt for he was in a real sense my musical father.

He was a humble man of quiet yet powerful dignity, always neat and well-dressed, appearing to be the gentleman he was. He was considerate of others, but demanding in his quest for the best musical response possible. All who were fortunate enough to play under his baton were truly inspired by this great musician. He was a master of beautiful baton control, sensitive to every nuance and challenging each player to produce the finest possible performance.

Under Harding's leadership I developed an exciting love for the richness of the music of Wagner, Ravel, Strauss, Tchaikowsky, Shostakovich, and Kodaly, as well as the great marches of the band repertoire, especially those of John Philip Sousa. Harding was a close personal friend of Sousa and had such admiration and respect for him that it was easily contagious.

Although a member of the University of Illinois Symphony Orchestra (as a violin-viola major) it was in the Concert Band (playing tuba, double-bass, oboe, and English horn) that I was initially introduced to the body of great symphonic literature, through Harding's superb transcriptions. At that time there was very little band music of stature written by our finest composers, so in order to provide his students with good music — and more important, to try to convince composers that the band medium was a worthy one — Harding began to produce transcriptions of the finest symphony orchestra literature.

With a deft touch he set his transcriptions in the fullest and richest wind band colors. His scores abundantly doubled voices and thus embodied the richness of complete choirs throughout the band; for example often using full flute family groupings including piccolo, flutes, alto flute, and occasionally a bass flute part. This extensive use of all the wind band colors available produced a richness of sound that was beautiful and well suited to the romantic music he dealt with most of the time. However, he saw the concert band not as an imitation of the symphony orchestra, but as a strong, singularly powerful statement of the musical message.

Clarence Sawhill, retired director of bands at University of California, Los Angeles, spent ten years (from age 30 to 40) at the University of Illinois working with A.A. Harding.

We had a leader who set a standard which challenged the best that was in each of us. A.A. Harding was a man who did not accept excuses, a man who gave his best, and who expected no less from his co-workers and students. He was a gentleman first, and he was also a scholar, musician, innovator, and administrator whose teaching gave me a background from which I drew ideas, strength, and courage for the past 30 years, and from which I gained an unshakable faith in the importance of our profession on the campuses of our country.

Raymond F. Dvorak, retired director of bands at the University of Wisconsin, spent 16 years with Harding as a student and assistant.

I was fortunate to be in this man's presence. He was a kindly gentleman who never spoke an ill word about anyone, and he had a great influence on my life. He was not a man to order others but he set a good example and expected others to follow. There are many who came under his influence who have followed his example.

Mark H. Hindsley, now retired, assisted Harding, then succeeded him as director of bands at the University of Illinois. He wrote a memorial to A.A. Harding as part of a special committee of the University Senate. The following is an excerpt from that document.

In 1899, Director Harding heard the band of the famous John Philip Sousa for the first time. There is no doubt that this experience was an inspiring one, and was later called upon as the vision of the possibilities of the college band grew upon him. Harding's bands immediately began to take on professional qualities of musicianship and showmanship. With a motto of "Always Something New" he provided musical challenges for his students and stimulating performances for his audiences, in concerts and at athletic events. His musical and scientific mind led him to experiment boldly with innovations in instrumentation, seating arrangements, and band literature. Quickly tiring of the standard published band repertoire he began to make transcriptions of great orchestral music for his own expanding instrumentation. The scope and quantity of these transcriptions became very large during his lifetime, and their quality is a standard for the profession.

Harding's University Bands inevitably attracted favorable attention from other colleges, and were in large measure responsible for one of the most unique latter day developments in education, the rise of the instrumental music program in the public schools. From an annual gathering of Illinois high school band directors to observe rehearsals of the University bands, there grew the famous band clinics. Inaugurated in 1930 by Harding, they soon became official national events, and served further to make the University of Illinois the world's school band capital. Harding-trained graduates spread from coast to coast in their own teaching and performing positions. In hundreds of high schools and in some forty colleges and universities they conducted bands in the Harding image.

Harding tirelessly served the school band movement, as adjudicator and clinician, and perhaps more significantly in the selection of appropriate music for its activities. He lent his support and encouragement through national organizations, in which he immediately became prominent. He was a charter member of the American Bandmasters Association in 1930, became its president in 1937 and honorary president in 1956. He was elected as the first honorary life president of the College Band Directors National Association upon its organization in 1941.

No chronicle of the achievements of Harding could possibly reveal to a satisfactory degree the impact of his personality, his leadership, and his greatness upon his students, his associates, the University, the State, and the Nation. He was truly one who could "walk with kings, nor lose the common touch." His work and his influence were of such dimension and of such nature that they will project far into the future. ∎

The story of Mark Hindsley, who served for many years at the University of Illinois and is one of America's most venerable college band directors, begins near a small town in Indiana. He recalls:

"I lived in the country and went to a country school. My father bought me a third-hand cornet one night and asked a cornet player, who taught in the public schools and was also a good friend, to give me lessons. He charged 25 cents and came to our house. After my third lesson he left for the Navy [World War I], and although my father tried, no other teachers were to be found. No professional musicians lived in our town — the town band director was a mail carrier and he didn't want to teach — but I kept on playing."

This obviously was a determined young man, and one with parental encouragement. His early ensemble experience came from a school orchestra, a school band, Sunday school orchestra, municipal band, and the family orchestra, which consisted of his mother, brother, four cousins, and himself (four violins, cornet, trombone, and piano). The school orchestra ("a creditable one," says Hindsley), was conducted by the school principal, an accomplished pianist and violinist. The school band also had an unusual conductor:

"The band director was a hack driver for the country schools. [A hack was a horse-drawn bus.]

In the winter he did not have to go home to work on the farm during the day, and he asked to form a school band. So we had a band of sorts. We never played anywhere, but we practiced once or twice a week. That was my band experience until I joined the town Sunday school orchestra and the municipal band when I was 12."

At Indiana University Hindsley majored in chemistry; yet his overwhelming interest in music often pushed his studies aside. He played first chair cornet in the band, first trumpet and string bass in the orchestra, and sang in the chorus. In addition he conducted a Sunday school orchestra during his senior year. While still in school he was offered an assistantship in chemistry, but turned it down to become the director of the university's band when its leadership was transferred to R.O.T.C. From then on he was hooked on a career in music. He says, "I got into it and never could get out."

After graduating from Indiana University in 1925 with distinction in chemistry, Hindsley was appointed the official director of the Indiana Band. The band's drillmaster was a military man, Grover Cleveland Cleaver, U.S. Infantry Captain, for whom Hindsley had great admiration, calling him an "exemplary leader." In addition to learning about marching, Hindsley was exposed to "the military demeanor" and "learned what it meant to be a leader, to assume authority and to be secure."

So Cleaver managed the marching and Hindsley handled the music. They were a successful team, but Hindsley felt that the marching band was overemphasized and that excessive practice time was causing too much turnover in personnel.

Mark Hindsley — Distinguished Conductor

May, 1982

Ned C. Deihl

Editor's note:

As we become more familiar with the lives of the outstanding people in our profession, we can recognize certain consistent elements — intelligence, hard work, family interest in music, inspiration provided by individuals or performance groups of high quality, and the good fortune of being a well-prepared person in the right place at the right time.

Sometimes because the outer features are so different we miss the underlying similarities and basic principles. For example, in 1925 Mark Hindsley was already a successful cornet soloist, but he traveled 55 miles to take private lessons from a top level player and teacher. Sound familiar? It's obvious, even though you may have to substitute "trumpet," and "550" miles. Successful people today are still working hard to get even better, although they may be riding on airplanes instead of trains to find those who can help them. Other parallels may be more difficult to recognize.

Perhaps if we could identify all the necessary elements and maintain an atmosphere in which they will grow, we could be assured of a steady supply of people like Mark Hindsley and other leaders.

Surely there is a formula, and it seems logical that a close examination of the lives of outstanding individuals could reveal a pattern for us to follow. It seems a worthy pursuit, even though it does start to sound a little like a spec. sheet for a super robot, more appropriate for 1984 or Brave New World.

Because he was to teach trumpet in addition to directing the band, Hindsley decided to take trumpet lessons. He traveled to Indianapolis, 55 miles away, where he studied with Leslie Peck at the Metropolitan School of Music, now known as the Jordan College of Fine Arts.

This was actually the first private instruction he had, except for those few lessons as a child. He had tried to get cornet lessons one summer during his college days from Sam Williams, father of famed cornet soloist Ernest Williams. Williams, however, was more interested in forming a boys band, and so the lessons didn't materialize.

"Peck started me from scratch, even though I had been a soloist, first chair and all that. He taught me not only trumpet but music — breathing, basic tone, attack. Our material was Arban, of course. We went through a lot of Vandercook solos, too, and worked on interpretation."

As a teacher of Ernest Williams and an opera orchestral player, Peck had been quite a performer in his younger years. Hindsley concedes that "everything I did in my teaching and ensemble performance started with Peck." Peck's teaching was apparently similar to that of Vandercook, and Hindsley admits to being influenced by Vandercook's writings as well. H.E. Nutt of Vandercook College of Music thought he "sounded more like a Vandercook student than many others who had actually been students of Vandercook."

Another point of inspiration for Hindsley was the appearance of the famed Sousa Band in Bloomington, Indiana in the fall of 1925. He had heard many town bands, but none that compared to Sousa's band. Although he heard many other inspirational concerts during these years — the Minnesota Orchestra, Percy Grainger on piano, Paul Whiteman, Bachman's Million Dollar Band, and cornet soloist Bohumir Kryl — Sousa was always the pinnacle for him.

Hindsley, frustrated with Indiana University's lack of support for the music department, moved on to Cleveland where he became the director of instrumental music at Cleveland Heights High School. (One of Hindsley's classmates in chemistry and a baritone player in the Indiana band, Herman Wells, was later to become President of Indiana University and a staunch supporter of its burgeoning School of Music during the 1950s.) Hindsley's time in Cleveland was a period of growth and recognition for him: he developed an outstanding band that won first divisions in national contests; he was inspired by many Cleveland Orchestra concerts; he attended several clinics of the great A.A. Harding of Illinois; and one summer he played in the college division band at Interlochen National Music Camp under the baton of A.A. Harding.

The summer before starting his position in Cleveland, Hindsley had received his first formal conducting training, studying with Victor Grabel at the Sherwood School of Music in Chicago. This experience had given him the chance to apply to an ensemble the musicianship he had learned from Peck. By later attending a summer session at Interlochen, Hindsley not only continued to learn

under Harding but maintained contact with him. Thus it came as no surprise when Harding chose Hindsley as his assistant band director at the University of Illinois.

Hindsley had always admired Harding and the Illinois Band. When he was at Indiana, Hindsley had taken his band to an Illinois-Indiana football game at Urbana. The Illinois marching band sounded to him like a concert band on the field. Harding was a visionary who could foresee and help to shape the future. He had been influenced by Sousa, but yet had developed his own style. Harding was a father figure to Hindsley and a great influence. According to Hindsley the symphonic band at Illinois at that time was undoubtedly the premier concert band in the country.

Hindsley became director of bands at Illinois after Harding's retirement. He wrote numerous first-rate transcriptions for concert band, made a series of recordings of concert band literature, and authored seven books including his latest, *Hindsley on Bands (The Gospel According to Mark)*. His research in the area of intonation is particularly noteworthy. He also served as President of the College Band Directors National Association and as president of the American Bandmasters Association, where he was recognized as an organizer and administrator as well as a conductor. His skills were also recognized and used during World War II: for three years he served as the music officer of the Army Air Forces Training Command and was responsible for some 150 Air Force bands. He was then appointed for two terms as band and orchestra conductor and conducting instructor of the G.I. Biarrity American University in France. When he was released from duty as a lieutenant colonel and returned to Illinois, Hindsley soon accepted the director's baton from Harding and continued the Illinois Band's tradition of leadership among college bands.

After a 45-year career in public school, college, and military music, Mark Hindsley continues to be active in "retirement" as a guest conductor, adjudicator, writer, transcriber, and publisher. He concludes:

"It's been exciting and rewarding to have had a lifetime that's so closely paralleled the development and growth of school bands. Their accomplishments and their levels of musical and technical proficiency have reached almost unbelievable heights. In back of it all is the intrinsic worth and the love of great music. There have been distractions and detours along the way that have hindered the band's development, but the concert band that plays the greatest music of which it is capable will continue to remain on the pedestal where it belongs, flourishing under dedicated leadership." ∎

Ned C. Deihl is a professor of music education at Pennsylvania State University in University Park. This article is based on a dissertation by Glen Yarberry (An Analysis of Five Exemplary College Band Programs) and an interview with the subject.

Malcolm Arnold At 70

by John Swallow

The years following World War II were an exciting period in the history of brass chamber music as thousands of former servicemen filled music schools with help from the G.I. Bill. There were more performers than jobs, and many brass players formed ensembles and sought out composers to write music for them, and over time a substantial amount of new brass chamber music emerged. Robert King's pre-war efforts, particularly in brass transcriptions of early music, were succeeded after the War by Malcolm Arnold's *Quintet*, which along with Eugene Bozza's *Sonatine*, Gunther Schuller's and Alec Wilder's quintets, and Alvin Etler's baudy, atonal, and jazz-influenced work anchored the contemporary brass chamber library of the late 1950s and early 1960s.

Arnold came from an artistic and free-thinking family of modest means. One brother was killed in W.W. II, another committed suicide, and his sister was expelled from art school for appearing nude on a parade float in the 1920s. Arnold fathered an autistic child along the way and has been divorced twice.

In his later life Arnold faced a heart attack and alcoholism with resultant manic depression. He was so ill in 1984 that doctors did not expect him to live more than two years. In 1986 he had a coronary attack accompanied by drastic weight loss, and his doctors doubted he would ever compose again. Arnold stopped drinking almost overnight, and he has since composed twenty-four works. When he is removed from the extraneous problems of daily living, the music just flows. Somehow he maintained the discipline and drive to compose music and enjoy the life that goes with it. He is proud of his success and seems to enjoy the fact that composition in Britain was at one time "the prerogative of people of private income."

Music was part of his family life from the start. His grandfather formed a family string quartet, and his mother gave him a set of trap drums early on. Arnold says he learned rhythm by accompanying her piano playing. Somewhere along the line he picked up a trumpet in an arcade and studied with a Russian immigrant,

who gave him "long lessons" from which he "developed a good embouchure." Soon he played vaudeville at the New Theatre in Northampton and attended the Royal College of Music in London on a scholarship.

Winning the Mendelssohn prize for composition at the Royal College of Music in 1947 marked the end of Arnold's playing career. On the advice of his composition teacher he

John Swallow was a member of the New York Brass Quintet for 25 years and currently teaches at the Yale School of Music and the New England Conservatory.

used the prize money to attend the British School in Rome in the Piazza d'Espagne as a married student with one child.

There is in Arnold, as with so many artists, an empathetic awareness of his audience, yet he says outrageously contradictory things. He moves from the posture of conductor to composer to performer like a chameleon. His anecdotes and comments about conductors, as with most orchestral players, run the gamut from adoration to irreverence: "Let me tell you, the meanest, smallest second fiddle player knows more about music than any conductor."

When conversation turned to Sydney Langston, principal trombonist with Arnold in the London Philharmonic Orchestra, Arnold told an amusing tale. "I knew Sydney very well. He dealt in old cars; actually he dealt in all sorts of things. He played the pea shooter, which was a small-bore English trombone. He would say to me, 'You're good enough not to practice; come out and have a pint.' My response was, 'Not with you, mate. I shan't be able to get to the concert.' I often brought a sandwich to rehearsals and spent an afternoon practicing my difficult bits. You have to if you're a brass player, but not Sydney. When it came time to play, he entered on those chords in *Ruy Blas* on the alto trombone. There wouldn't be a cracked note, and it would be beautifully in tune with everything right on track."

This preoccupation with virtuoso players performing well despite their indulgences is a part of the folklore of mid-century performers, not unlike the lifestyle surrounding the Carnegie Tavern of the late 1940s and 1950s. Of himself as a player, Arnold said, "I wanted to be a great trumpet player. Now all I can say is that I was never fired. I played the Haydn once or twice as a member of the orchestra, but I've never been a distinguished trumpet soloist, just a run-of-the-mill trumpet player."

Arnold wrote twelve works for brass bands because "in England we have the brass band movement, which is the oldest amateur band movement, older than the Salvation Army. All brass bands were originally temperance bands; but if you followed a temperance band after it appeared at Albert Hall, it would stop at the nearest tavern." Arnold discussed conductors: "Fritz Reiner was a bully. In Europe people used to say to me, 'You think you're a principal trumpet player; wait until Fritz Reiner hears you. He'll chuck you out.' I would reply, 'If I see his name coming to conduct, I'll wait, and if he's rude, I'll walk out.' "

Pierre Monteux was a favorite. "He looked like a French waiter. There was no orchestra in Paris good enough for a man of his stature to conduct, and there still isn't. Paris is riddled by the deputy system. There's an old joke about a famous conductor who said to a Parisian musician, 'You're the only person who attended both rehearsals.' He replied, 'It's okay, maestro. I'm not playing the concert. My brother is.' Monteux was a great conductor of Mozart and French Impressionist music, but orchestras have to play more than *'L'apres midi d'un faune.'*"

Pierre Monteux

Conductor Eduard van Beinum was important early in Arnold's composing career. "Van Beinum conducted my first recording, and I adored him. At the London Philharmonic offices, I just walked up to this very handsome gentleman and said, 'Maestro van Beinum, how are you?' When I told him that I was the principal trumpet player of the London Philharmonic Orchestra, all he said was, 'Where can I buy a good bicycle?'

"He was our permanent conductor at the London Philharmonic for as long as his heart allowed him to commute from Amsterdam. We couldn't pay him enough money; nobody could pay van Beinum what he was worth. When we were recording the Beethoven *Pastorale* he said to me, 'I'm going to finish this early and devote the rest of the session to your overture *Beckus, The Dandipratt.*' I was most nervous. He was a viola player, so I said, 'I'd rather you'd play the viola; I'll conduct and we can get someone else to play the trumpet part.' After the first take he just sat there and said, 'Malcolm, ein schlage,' which means a hit in German. Decca later used that pressing as a test record for their high frequency recording.

"Van Beinum died of a heart attack in Liverpool while rehearsing Brahms' Third. I conducted it once and they said, 'That's exactly like van Beinum; too bloody slow.' I replied, 'It's not; it's exactly as Brahms wrote it. Fasten your seatbelts because at the performance it's going to be slower.' "

Arnold is proud and self-conscious about his film scores. "When I was a child I went to the silent pictures with Nanny and my brother. Most of what I saw was trash except for Al Jolson in the *Singing Fool* in which he burst into song, 'When There Are Gray Skies.' It was the first film with sound that I remember.

"I wrote for films to earn a living, but I was careful what I wrote because it would be heard by a huge audience." The score for *The Bridge on the River Kwai* won Arnold an Oscar and brought world-wide recognition. "I'm ashamed to say how many films I've done, but when I started repeating myself and then when it sounded like a Max Steiner score, I gave up. Steiner's tune for *Johnny Belinda* with Jane Wyman was wonderful, and the score for *Treasure of the Sierra Madre* was fabulous."

Writing serious compositions became increasingly important to Arnold after his film writing stage and remains the one constant with him as his health and private life become more circumscribed. He travels the world performing and premiering his newest works with undaunted enthusiasm. Arnold often speaks of writing music for various artists without remuneration. After hearing our records, he wrote to Bob Nagel that he would write a piece for the New York Brass Quintet. One day his first brass quintet just arrived in the mail with no fee attached.

When asked about his concerto for Benny Goodman, Arnold said, "Benny Goodman was a lifelong friend. When I heard he was dead, I just didn't want to live anymore. He often stayed with me in London and was a generous man. I charged him nothing for the second concerto; I'm the fifth son of a shoemaker, and he was the tenth son of a tailor."

Arnold's career has parallels to Gunther Schuller's although their music is dissimilar. Both began as orchestral players: Schuller in Cincinnati and Arnold in London. Each aspired to conduct and compose and was influenced by jazz. Their approach to performers differs. While Schuller was writing the *Eine Kleine Posaunemusik* trombone concerto for me, his father asked why he had written the part so high. His response was that I had sent him a recording that included a high F. "If he can play an F, then surely he can manage F♯," Schuller said. Arnold's approach is to know the player well but not to tax him. Unlike Schuller who pushes our limits, Arnold challenges us in traditional ways and puts us at ease.

Arnold said of Vaughan Williams' Tuba Concerto, "Who could improve on that? Vaughan Williams had the good sense to go to the tuba player of the London Philharmonic and ask him what the tuba can do. The concerto is not too demanding and shows the beautiful sound a tuba can make."

Arnold identifies himself with men as diverse as Beethoven and film composer Max Steiner. Like many artists of his time Arnold became caught up in the pursuit of the romantic and glamourous life. Considering the obstacles he overcame along the way, it is extraordinary what he accomplished. Surely the performance and creation of music were his salvation; he is an example of an artist who retained his sanity through his work.

Malcolm Arnold is refreshingly open and candid in this much too image-conscious world we live in. He seems only to ask us to share his humor, insight, and skill by listening to and enjoying his music. □

Arnold and Paynter

John Paynter's arrangements of Malcolm Arnold's works came about by chance. Paynter and his wife listened nightly to a classical radio station that one evening programmed Arnold's *Four Scottish Dances*. "That sounds like a band piece," Paynter said after first hearing the work.

Determined to arrange it for band, Paynter sent away for the orchestral score. "I went to work arranging it without ever seeking permission," he said. "When I reached the point of copying the parts, I realized that I would be in big trouble if I didn't get an okay from the publisher."

The publisher was Patterson's of London, who granted permission. "We played *Four Scottish Dances* at an M.E.N.C. conference in Chicago, and the owner of Patterson's showed up. He was a delightful old Scotsman, who not only liked the arrangement, but commissioned me to arrange other Arnold pieces."

Paynter's name became so closely linked with Arnold's works that when visiting this country, Arnold dropped in on an all-state band that was rehearsing *Four Scottish Dances* and approached the podium to shake hands with the conductor. "How do you do, Mr. Paynter," he said, thinking the only person who would be conducting a band arrangement of his piece would be Paynter. The conductor gave Arnold the baton and let him put the band through its paces, after which Arnold hurriedly left never realizing that the conductor was not Paynter but Myron Welch.

Arranged by Merle Isaac

by Alexander M. Harley

How would you pay tribute to a person who has devoted the better part of 90 years to music education? The friends and admirers of one such person decided to honor their colleague with a birthday party and reception held at the December 1988 Mid-West International Band and Orchestra Clinic. In this case the friends and admirers included members of the National School Orchestra Association and representatives of several music publishers. Several hundred guests from among the 8,000 people who attended the clinic gathered to thank their special colleague, Merle Isaac, for his music, his arrangements, as well as for his years of service as a distinguished music educator.

I have had the pleasure of knowing Merle since the 1930s, when we were members of the In-and-About Chicago Music Educators Club. By that time he already had worked both as a theater organist and as director of the Marshall High School Orchestra, a 90-piece ensemble that received national recognition.

Merle's name is familiar to most music directors because he has composed or arranged hundreds of published works, making significant contributions to the literature available for school bands and orchestras. As chairman of the music department at Maine Township High School, I often performed his compositions and arrangements with my orchestra. On a number of occasions, Merle served as guest conductor. During those and later years he was a clinician and adjudicator for many clinics and contests as well as conductor at festival concerts.

For his distinguished career in music Merle has been honored by the American Society of Composers, Authors, and Publishers, the American String Teachers Association, the National School Orchestra Association, the VanderCook College of Music Alumni Association, the Tri-M Music Honor Society, and the Mid-West International Band and Orchestra Clinic. He has rightfully become known as the dean of school orchestra arrangers.

In recent years Merle has been a member of the Garden Street String Ensemble, rehearsing weekly in my home with a group of experienced string players. After one recent rehearsal we talked about his career in music and his outlook on music education. He began by telling about his musical experiences as a boy growing up in Chicago.

When I was a boy, I lived in the country and attended a one-room school. Later, my family moved to Chicago, and I had a fourth-grade teacher whose pupils could read music and sing *do-re-mi*. This was all very new to me. My parents sent me to a church organist to learn about the syllables. The organist, however, was also a piano teacher. She gave me piano lessons and let me practice on her piano. Some time later my parents bought a piano, and I took lessons until I graduated from the eighth grade.

In my first year of high school I sang in the glee club, and in my second year I sang a solo part in a production of *H.M.S. Pinafore*. By my third year I wanted to play in the orchestra. They already had a pianist, so I bought a wooden flute from Sears and Roebuck and taught myself to play it. Then, for two years, I was the one and only flutist in the Crane High School Orchestra.

After you graduated from high school, did you continue to study music?

After I graduated from high school, I worked in the office of a printing company, took piano lessons, and practiced in the evenings. Somewhat later, I worked at the Western Electric Company and still kept in practice on the piano and the flute.

Three years after I graduated from high school, I decided to enroll at Crane Junior College. I attended classes in the morning and practiced on a church organ in the afternoon. Some evenings I visited movie theaters and became acquainted with the organists. I learned about the various kinds of music that were used to accompany the silent pictures. I registered with one of the organ companies as a theater organist seeking employment. Then, the day after Christmas, I received a call to report to a theater for work.

(Their organist didn't show up on Christmas Day!)

After a few months at that theater, which had matinees on weekends only, I changed to a theater closer to my home with matinees every day. At that time I began to study organ, harmony, and counterpoint with J. Lewis Browne. I learned the truth of the saying, "We learn by doing."

What was it like to play the organ for the silent pictures?

It was quite an experience. For the serious dramas, one could play excerpts from operas and symphonies. For the comedies, ragtime and jazz were used. Of course, all of the songs that were popular at that time were played. Each feature picture had a cue-sheet that suggested the various kinds of music to be played with the picture, changing every few minutes. When I started to play an accompaniment, I had a variety of pieces on the music rack readily available as needed.

Pictures usually ran two or three days. On the first day of the matinee, I watched the picture and either improvised suitable music or played from memory. Improvising music to accompany a quiet love scene or a lively chase is quite a valuable experience. One had to provide a suitable melody in the right hand, harmony in the left, and a bass in the pedals. Sometimes I would improvise a countermelody in the left hand along with the harmony. I also controlled the swell pedal, making the music loud or soft, and the registration, imitating a flute, oboe, or one of the other instruments. During those years I began to write down some of the improvised music that I found myself playing from time to time.

What did you think when the silent pictures became talking pictures?

In 1927 the silent pictures began to change to talking pictures. I went to see one on my dinner hour and decided that the new talking pictures would be successful, that the theaters would not need live musicians, and that I would have to find another way of making a living.

About this time J. Lewis Browne became director of music for the Chicago Public Schools. He planned to develop the music programs in the schools, and he encouraged me to consider becoming a high school orchestra director. I began to take counterpoint and orchestration lessons from him. I wrote pages and pages of exercises. At one of my lessons he said, "Merle, you are a glutton for work." I also began studying the violin and trumpet with other private teachers at this time.

Then you took the examination for teachers of instrumental music?

All too soon, the Chicago Board of Education announced it would give an examination to certify teachers of instrumental music. There would be a written examination, a directing examination with the Lane High School Orchestra, and examinations in playing the various instruments of the orchestra and band. I took the examination, passed, and on Labor Day received an assignment to the Marshall High School on Chicago's West Side.

For some reason, the previous orchestra director had quit before the end of the year, and the students did not include orchestra in their September class schedules. During my first week at Marshall, I had no students. I went from room to room and announced that there would be orchestra rehearsals for intermediate and advanced players as well as classes for first-year students in playing the cello and the bass.

The advanced orchestra met in two parts. Some of the students could adjust their programs to take orchestra in the morning, while others attended an afternoon rehearsal. After a few weeks we put the two parts together for one rehearsal and gave a concert in the assembly hall. Because a new teacher was on probation

for three months, I continued to work in the theater every evening with matinees on Saturdays and Sundays.

What did you learn when you started to direct the Marshall High School Orchestra?

A number of the violinists were very good; in fact, some later became members of the Chicago Symphony Orchestra. However, there were few players on the other string instruments. The school owned four violas, four cellos, and four basses. Fortunately, there were four bass players. Four members of the second violin section offered to play viola, and four other violinists offered to play cello. I worked with these students after school. The wind and percussion players were members of the Marshall Band who attended orchestra rehearsals twice a week.

I found some published music in the orchestra room, but there was little that I could use. Some was too difficult and some was too easy. Actually, not much of the music published at that time was suitable for school orchestras. I was well acquainted with music that had been arranged for theater orchestras with 10 to 20 professional musicians, but this music was not suitable for school use. The string parts needed editing by teachers who knew their instruments and who knew students. I had to simplify some of the parts and omit others. By selecting, editing, and changing the music to match the abilities and interests of the students, I learned what students could do and what they could not do, and I saw what students like to do and what they don't like to do.

During my first year at Marshall, I realized that I needed to know more about all of the instruments and about teaching students to play them. The orchestra's wind players were the best musicians in the band. However, playing a wind instrument in a band and playing that instrument in an orchestra are not exactly the same. I needed to know more about this.

Fortunately, I had heard about the Vander-Cook College of Music, and I began to spend my Saturdays there. In classes, I learned to play all of the instruments (though not well). I played in the band, and I taught piano. During the week I took private lessons and practiced. Some evenings I attended classes at Lewis Institute (now the Illinois Institute of Technology). In time, I earned degrees at both institutions.

Did you still find time to write music?

Yes, I wrote music because I needed certain kinds of pieces that were not readily available. I wrote a string class method and arranged a number of pieces, which the orchestra played on various programs. For example, the orchestra played daytime concerts at the elementary schools whose graduates came to Marshall. I wrote *Mummers*, a solo for the string bass section, to get students to want to play the string bass.

Once, when I attended a concert given by the Chicago Symphony Orchestra, the entire first violin section stood up and played *Perpetual Motion* by Paganini. I wanted Marshall's first violin section to do something equally spectacular, but the Paganini was much too difficult. A violin teacher suggested *Perpetual Motion* by Böhm. I made an arrangement which the orchestra played at a national contest. H.T. FitzSimons heard the performance and later said that he would like to publish the piece. The Böhm *Perpetual Motion* was my first published arrangement and it is still being played today.

Since that time you have made many other arrangements. What factors do you consider when selecting a piece of music to arrange?

When I select a piece of music to arrange for school use, I ask myself certain questions:

• Is the music copyrighted? If so, permission to use it must be obtained from the copyright owner.

• Are there already some published arrangements of this piece?

• Is the music written in a key suitable for students? If not, could it be transposed to a more playable key?

• Is the music of suitable length for students, neither too long nor too short?

• Will students be able to play the piece?

• Will students like to play the piece?

• Is the music worth learning? Is it educational, enjoyable, and the kind of music that one remembers?

• Will learning this piece develop skills and understandings applicable to other pieces of music?

• Will the teacher be able to teach the students to play this piece within a reasonable amount of rehearsal time?

• Will the music hold the students' interest if it has to be rehearsed over and over for weeks?

• Will audiences enjoy hearing the students play the music?

Considering the answers to all of these questions helps me decide whether to make an arrangement.

After you have selected a piece, how do you go about arranging it for string orchestra?

I usually start by making a pencil sketch on three or four staves. This is especially helpful if the arrangement is to be in a key different from the original. I put the principal melody at the top and the bass, which determines the harmony, at the bottom. Next I add the second vio-

lin part, making it a duet with the first violins. Then, I add the viola part to make three-part harmony in the three upper voices. The cello part may be a countermelody or it may double the bass part.

Then I copy all of the parts into a full score. This score will have five staves for the string parts and two staves for the piano part. I use music paper with 14 staves. Thus, I have a seven-stave score in the upper half of the page, and another in the lower half.

Next, I go over the score several times at the piano, checking the vertical aspects of the music (the harmony) and the horizontal aspects (voice leading, fingerings, and so forth). Then I extract a set of parts, always keeping in mind the fingerings and the bowings, though not writing them down. I have the parts edited by teachers who know their instruments and who know students. Finally I photocopy a set of parts and have the arrangement played. Often the performance of the music suggests that changes should be made, which involves going back to the drawing board. This is when I remember that an eraser is an arranger's best friend. Writing is fun, but re-writing is drudgery.

In an arrangement for full orchestra, how do you keep all of the parts interesting?

All of the parts should be readable, reasonably melodic, and rhythmically interesting. There is some truth in the saying, "If you can't sing it, you can't play it." Of course, what is melodic for the flute and what is melodic for the tuba are not the same.

When I write a trombone part, I try to consider how I would feel if I were a trombonist playing that part. I would not care to have 64 measures of rest. Neither would I care to be playing all of the time, as the strings often do.

Every part should be difficult enough to be challenging, but should not be so difficult as to be discouraging. Each player in the orchestra needs to feel that he is a member of the team and that he is making an essential contribution.

By the way, I tried to explain and illustrate these principles in a book that I wrote several years ago called *Practical Orchestration*, published by Robbins Music.

How important is editing?

Music to be played by school orchestras must be edited. It is of vital importance that the published parts include some bowings, fingerings, valve combinations, and slide positions. Young string players need to be instructed and reminded when to slur and when not to, when and where to shift positions, and whether to use an open string or the fourth finger.

Brass players need to be reminded how to finger some of the notes in the sharp keys because they are more accustomed to playing in flat keys in band. It is just as important to remind woodwind players, but it is difficult, if not impossible, to indicate woodwind fingerings in the parts.

There are times when the orchestra director may wish to change some of the markings in the music. However, a busy director just doesn't have the time to fully edit all of the parts. Skillful editing, by editors who know students, helps the busy orchestra teacher. It is a must!

When you start to make an arrangement, do you know what the grade of difficulty will be?

In an arrangement for string orchestra, the principal melody (usually in the first violin part) determines the overall grade of difficulty for the piece. All of the other parts should be written according to the standard set by the principal melody.

If the first violin part is playable in the first position, the cello part shouldn't include a tenor clef. The second violin part should be less difficult than the first violin part. In works written for professional musicians, however, this is often not the case. Some second violin parts are more difficult and less interesting than the first violin parts.

Many arrangements of music in the standard repertoire are considered to be watered down or seriously compromised. Are there ways of avoiding this problem?

Simplified versions of the classics help both players and audiences become acquainted with the standard orchestral literature. For these arrangements, the parts need to be within the technical and musical capabilities of the students and within the teaching time and capabilities of the teacher. All of the parts have to be readable, playable, interesting, and understandable.

When arranging a well-known classic, the melody and the harmony must not be changed, though the inside voices may be altered to make them easier to play. Sometimes a change of key is advisable. For example, if the original work is in the key of A , many string players would have difficulties playing in that key. By lowering the key a half-step to G, the music becomes much easier for the string players, though not for the winds. Whether in A or G, the music sounds the same to the listeners.

Some slow movements of the classics are written in $\frac{4}{4}$ meter. This requires many eighth notes and sixteenth notes, making the printed music look dark and difficult. When this music is written in $\frac{2}{2}$ meter, it is much easier to read, though it sounds just the same.

Sometimes an arrangement is shorter than the original. For example, a movement of a symphony may consist of several sections: introduction, exposition, development, recapitulation, and coda. When the selection is shortened, ideally all of these sections are shortened proportionately.

An arranger has to study students, instruments, and music to be able to change the notation and the grade of difficulty without changing the beauty and the effectiveness of the music. An arrangement of a well-known classic, even though simplified and abridged, should be just as beautiful and just as musically satisfying as the original.

What kinds of music do students enjoy most and how do they benefit by playing in an orchestra?

Students, as a rule, enjoy playing music that is loud and fast, lively and rhythmic. They don't like to play easy music or slow music. String players like to play fast, but they don't play very loud. Brass players can play loud, but they don't play very fast. A person can enjoy playing an instrument by himself, but it is much more enjoyable to make music as a member of a group.

Since 1923 Alexander M. Harley has had a notable career as a pioneer in the field of music education. In 1936 he and his wife, Frances, founded Modern Music Masters, now known worldwide as Tri-M Music Honor Society for student musicians. In 1986 Harley was the first recipient of M.E.N.C.'s Music Educator of the Year award.

Continued on page 62

Students derive many benefits from playing in an orchestra. The intellectual outcomes include knowledge and understanding about music and musicians, about musical instruments, about how organizations function, and about working with other people to achieve a common goal.

Members of an orchestra experience feelings and emotions through the music they play. They develop interests, attitudes, and appreciations. They learn about teamwork (cooperation) and about accepting responsibilities. They learn to be at the right place at the right time. They learn about life!

Students of instrumental music use fingers, hands, arms, and tongues to develop motor skills needed for fingerings, bowings, and articulations. Schools work to develop the human brain, but neglect to develop the human hand. Without the hand to write, there would be nothing for the brain to read. Playing in an orchestra develops the head, the heart, and the hands. Music is important because it does things for people.

What is the most important responsibility of the director of a school orchestra?

The most important responsibility of any teacher is to further the education of the students. In the case of the teacher who directs a school orchestra, selecting the right music — at the right time — is an important part of this responsibility.

Selecting the right music involves the likes and dislikes of the teacher, the students, the parents, and the community. For the teacher, it involves his own abilities as well as those of his students. To be considered are the purpose, the grade of difficulty, the interest level, the instrumentation, the availability of the music, and the budget.

The purpose of a school orchestra is to provide students with the best musical experiences possible so that they may learn and grow. Students should experience success rather than failure. As music directors, it is our job to guide young people in successful performances and to help them enjoy the kind of music that we enjoy.

It is our job, also, to teach young people that it is more fun to play music than merely to listen to it, and that the better we can play the more fun it is. Simply stated, the more you put into it, the more you get out of it. □

November, 1992

Vincent Persichetti Remembered
Music From Gracious To Gritty

by Donald Morris and Jean Oelrich

When composers think of the band as a huge, supple ensemble of winds and percussion, the obnoxious fat will drain off, and creative ideas will flourish. (Vincent Persichetti)

Advocate for Bands by Donald Morris

On August 14, 1987 the band world lost one of its greatest champions, Vincent Persichetti, a major American composer who wrote works for the New York Philharmonic, the Philadelphia Orchestra, the Juilliard School, and internationally-known chamber ensembles and soloists. He also found time to turn his creative energies to compositions for high school and college bands. Persichetti respected the band medium

and recognized the artistic potential of what many viewed as only a source of popular entertainment.

Five years after his death Vincent Persichetti is remembered as a versatile composer and educator, and one who enthusiastically wrote for bands and wind ensembles. Born in Philadelphia in 1915 Persichetti studied piano, organ, double bass, tuba, theory, and composition as a child. At 11 he helped to support himself by performing as an accompanist, and by 20 he was simultaneously head of the theory department at Combs College, a conducting student of Fritz Reiner at Curtis, and a piano student of Olga Samaroff at the Philadelphia Conservatory. He received a diploma in conducting from Curtis and a doctorate from the Philadelphia Conservatory, where he became chairman of the theory and composition departments. In

1947 he began teaching at Juilliard, becoming chairman of the composition department in 1963. Persichetti was an articulate, witty teacher and speaker, an honorary member of the American Bandmasters Association, and a consultant for Elkan-Vogel Company.

By 1950 Persichetti had a solid reputation as a serious composer in several fields. The Philadelphia Orchestra performed his Third Symphony and *Fables* for narrator and orchestra, Martha Graham commissioned music for the ballet *King Lear*, fine performers played his piano and chamber music, and he had won awards for his *Dance Overture*, the Third Piano Sonata, and the Second String Quartet. He had yet to establish a national reputation and a place among the prominent composers of the day.

With the 1950 premiere of *Divertimento for Band*, Persichetti earned a measure of recognition that previously had eluded him. He became a champion of the band movement, composing repertoire of uncompromising quality.

As a speaker, writer, and subject of interviews, Persichetti often expressed his views on bands and band literature. In *The Wind Band* Richard Goldman referred to a Persichetti letter crediting the eagerness of bands to play his music with making the effort "both spontaneous and worthwhile.... it seems to approach the relation of composer and performer in other, happier centuries." The composer often stated his appreciation for band.

> Performance groups throughout the country are technically and aesthetically ready to play the literature — the chamber literature, not the orchestral works. Among the most active in this country are university chamber ensembles and bands. In contrast to most major symphony orchestra personnel and management — not to mention conductors — chamber groups and bandsmen are happy if a composer writes for their medium, and often set up elaborate commissioning plans for new music.

Many Persichetti works quickly became part of the standard repertoire, especially among college band conductors. The composer's wife, Dorothea, wrote:

> At its first rehearsal, the [*Divertimento for Band*] was asked for and given to the Presser Publishing Company, and it was quickly put to print. There followed performances by most of the elite university bands in the country and by countless other smaller groups. And bands, unlike professional orchestras, keep new works in their repertoire and play them regularly. The composer has conducted it with many groups, heard it played well and poorly by

many others, happened upon it in a band shell in a small town on a summer evening, and met countless youngsters throughout the country who know none of his symphonies but say, "I played the *Divertimento*."

Persichetti considered bands to be worthy of his artistic efforts.

> The concert band is a medium of expression distinct from, but not subordinate to, any other medium. More and more young American composers are turning to it now. You can get lots of things out of a band that you just can't get out of an orchestra.

> I know that composers are often frightened away by the sound of the word "band," because of certain qualities long associated with this medium — rusty trumpets, consumptive flutes, wheezy oboes, disintegrated clarinets, fumbling yet amiable baton wavers, and gum-coated park benches! If you couple these conditions with transfigurations of works originally conceived for orchestra, you create a sound experience that's as nearly excruciating as a sick string quartet playing a dilettante's arrangement of a nineteenth-century piano sonata.

Persichetti saw the band's inherent musical possibilities and recognized that their problems were not inherent ones, but only resulted from how they were used or abused. In a dissertation on Richard Goldman, Noel Lester wrote that Persichetti tried, unsuccessfully, to persuade Goldman to become director of the Juilliard wind ensemble because "he was just the right person to demonstrate that being a serious musician and a band leader were not incompatible."

Donald McGinnis relates the story of attempting to tune the clarinet and oboe unison at measure 82 of the *Psalm for Band*. When the performers could not play in tune together, McGinnis had the oboist leave the note out. He asked Persichetti about this, who said, "I probably should not have written the note for the oboe. I was thinking musically instead of thinking in a certain instance where that particular instrument could no longer make the adjustment to the tone."

Donald Morris, assistant professor of music and director of bands at Charleston Southern University in Charleston, South Carolina, gathered material from his doctoral dissertation, "The Life of Vincent Persichetti, with Emphasis on the Works for Band."

Jean Oelrich interviewed Vincent Persichetti when she was an editor at The Instrumentalist. *She is director of public relations at the Ravinia Festival in Illinois.*

In a 1963 interview with Kenneth Snapp about the *Bagatelles for Band* Persichetti explained that he did not accept commissions unless he had ideas at the time for that ensemble and did not use band ideas for orchestra or vice versa. Snapp asked why many of his band pieces were so short and Persichetti replied,

> Length has nothing to do with quality. I feel that each movement of the *Bagatelles*, for example, is as carefully a worked out musical idea as is a movement from one of my symphonies, and it stands as high in my esteem. I certainly will not add padding to a movement in order to prove its importance.

Parable IX is proof that Persichetti did not write down to bands.

> There are many excellent bands in this country, who play as well as the fine orchestras. My *Parable for Band*, a compendium of musical colorings demanding virtuoso technique and flexible shaping of phrases, has had countless first-rate performances. Every musician is asked to play meaningfully and skillfully, even the second bassoonist and second alto saxophonist — and they do!

Of the fifteen works that Persichetti wrote for band or wind ensemble, only *A Lincoln Address* is a transcription of an orchestral work. Persichetti did not like transcriptions, and while studying piano at the Philadelphia Conservatory, his piano teacher, Madame Olga Samaroff Stokowski, asked him to transcribe a Brahms organ prelude for piano. "I finally told her that I didn't want to get involved with those awful people who make transcriptions." Indeed, the Brahms Prelude and Fugue in A Minor for piano and *A Lincoln Address* for band are the only transcriptions out of 166 compositions in the Persichetti catalog.

In a letter to Hugh Aitken, who had submitted some manuscripts to Elkan-Vogel Company for publication, Persichetti as editor wrote about the company's decision to publish the pieces, including some band transcriptions. His letter stated, "Now, personally, I don't like putting in extra parts as you know. However, this is for the educational market — but of course you remember that I am against transcriptions for band."

Goldman wrote, "Mennin's *Canzona*, Thomson's *A Solemn Music*, and Persichetti's *Divertimento*, for example, sound as if good composers were writing without condescension."

Straight Talk from Vincent Persichetti by Jean Oelrich

Following a lecture at DePaul University on February 14, 1985 Persichetti talked with Jean Oelrich, then on the editorial staff of The Instrumentalist, *and the following comments are from that lecture and interview unless otherwise indicated.*

On Writing for Bands

"You have got to really dig up new music for band. Many band conductors are better than orchestral conductors. The orchestra conductors may not want to try new literature; the orchestra already has the bigger literature."

"Saxophones are a little complicated to write for, but I would not want to omit them, but you have to make the effort. I thought maybe you could get rid of the alto clarinet, but I just finished a band piece (1985) with a lot of solo alto clarinet work in it."

On Becoming a Composer

"When I was eleven, I joined the Junior Federation of Music Clubs Orchestra; I was a pianist. We played Schubert's Unfinished Symphony, which has no piano part; but I was hired to play the parts that were missing, second oboe, clarinet, whatever. It was invaluable experience. I started on organ at that time (11) and played at big churches when I was 16."

"Some composition students today have that kind of experience, but most don't. A lot of them at 17 suddenly want to become composers. Nobody should try to be a composer, maybe a missionary or a lawyer. Why should you want to *be* a composer? You have to want to write music, that

is all. There is no assurance that you will write wonderful stuff or earn a living."

"Never try to be a composer; if you want to write music, that is worth the starving."

"I loved playing the double bass when I was young because I wanted to get the feel of a stringed instrument. I started to play in the orchestra and I became the first bass player of the All-Philadelphia High School Orchestra. I think it is valuable for a composer to play in an orchestra to understand the balance and count the measures. The rests are hard to play. You start to respect those people and to listen, especially in Brahms. If you come in, you're a fake."

On Commissions

"I don't accept a commission until I have an inspiration. Why should I try to write something? I don't need the lunch money; I don't think of myself as a commercial composer. I wrote my first harpsichord sonata in 1950; about two or three years ago I got some good ideas for a second one. If I hear an idea, I don't just hear a tune or a harmony; I hear it in a medium."

On Divertimento

"My first piece, written when I was 14, was for winds because I knew a lot of people who played wind instruments. In 1949 I was in Kansas for a summer, and they gave me a school orchestra. There also was some chamber music and band music, but I had to scrounge around and found that I was writing something. I don't always know what it means. It went chump, chump! ba-da-da-da-da bum! bum! The percussion came in and it had a lot of rhythm. After a couple of weeks I realized the strings weren't coming in. That was my *Divertimento for Band* (op. 42)."

"My earliest works were stimulated by the sound of winds. In 1926 my grade-school chamber group – oboe, horn, and bassoon (the Angelucci brothers), plus soprano sax, violin, and piano – performed arrangements of hotel and symphony music. Then, in 1929, came my Op. 1, *Serenade for Ten Winds* and in 1934 the *Pastoral for Woodwind Quintet*. I'd been composing in a log cabin schoolhouse in El Dorado, Kansas during the summer of 1949, working with some lovely woodwind figures, accentuated by choirs of aggressive brasses and percussion beating. I soon realized the strings weren't going to enter, and my *Divertimento* began taking shape." (Rudy Shackelford)

Origin of Works

"A committee decided they wanted a piece with narrator and orchestra based upon Lincoln's second inaugural. I thought that this is a commission I might want to do and there isn't much time, but since it's my government calling me, I won't say no. I realized I could do something. Ormandy was going to play it with the Philadelphia Orchestra for Nixon's second inauguration in 1972. About three weeks later the score was delivered and parts were made. The committee called back and said they had changed their minds after seeing the text. They had given me the text, but the country was involved with Cambodia, Vietnam, and the words were about bloodshed. . . . The press said the government wasn't treating artists right, and compared it to [censorship in] the Soviet Union, but it wasn't that; they hadn't even seen the score. They changed their minds about the text, but the major orchestras played the *Lincoln Address* anyway."

"Hymnals are fertile ground. . . . 'The ground he called light' section is this:

From this theme the winds play, it grew and grew, and pretty soon the horns came in and the trombones, and it turned out to be my Sixth Symphony."

On Fritz Reiner

"Reiner was not theatrical; he never went in for show like Stokowski. Stokowski got too excited; Reiner underplayed everything, but he had a tremendous technique. If you really studied, Reiner would help you. It was luck to study with one of the great conductors. How good is good?

"He had a favorite in the orchestra, the percussionist. Once at a rehearsal for a broadcast the kid dropped a cymbal. Reiner got so emotional, he expelled the student from school but then called a break. He ran out around the block and when he caught up with the student in the back street, he brought him back, "I'm going to reinstate you in school." Reiner was supposed to be a tough guy, but he really wasn't; he was a softie. He would yell at the flute players in the orchestra if they were being stupid; it irritated him, but he really wanted to help people. I think he didn't want friends.

"Reiner didn't like a lot of the fake conducting. He showed me how you learn, for instance, the scherzo movement of Beethoven's First Symphony in a fake way. He made a draft of it and taught one of the conducting students from this scherzo draft without telling him what the piece was. 'See, you can go one in a bar, ¾ time, with soft beats here, bigger ones here.' He had one of us get up and play the piano, but the conducting student didn't know the score. That is what he called cheating, not really learning. He tried to make a point about conductors who didn't know the score, counting to 20 and making their cue. He was very conscientious. Reiner wasn't much of a pianist, but he could play the chords. He would make the students stop at any time and play the chord at that point."

Dishonest Music

"Dishonest music is writing things that you don't really hear, just something you figured out and calculated. Some people get so put off by band, with all the transpositions and so forth, they are frightened....they sometimes just figure out composing without using their ears, which you can do. It's as if you would learn a craft at the piano and not know a Beethoven phrase."

"Some people force volumes of stuff. It is dishonest, not really hearing it aurally to straighten it up."

On Charles Ives

"I never met Charles Ives, but I sent students to him. He was a funny guy and told one of them, 'Don't shake my hands. You can just touch the end of my cane: shake hands this way.' My student was getting petrified. 'Why are you coming to see me? Is it because you think I am getting famous now?'

'No, no, it is because of your music.'

'What music?' He was just playing with him.

'I love your harmony,' my student said. Ives yelled, 'Get out of here! You keep your hands off my wife!' His wife's name was Harmony. Ives called him back and said, 'Why don't we settle this? Why don't you meet her?' Ives spent the entire day with the student. He just didn't want some fake from

Vincent Persichetti

New York coming to interview him, and he didn't know who the student was."

On Percy Grainger

"Grainger was a good friend of Richard Franko Goldman. He would come to the Goldman band concerts, hear my pieces, and get curious about a young guy writing for band. When Grainger was getting ill, he told me, 'People do that, they get older and they die. It bothers me, so I finally decided I won't recognize them.'"

On Marcel Tabuteau

"When Tabuteau taught at Curtis, he used to take the reeds he didn't like and toss them out the window of his second floor studio. He and the oboe students would watch with glee to see if anyone was walking below at the time."

On Walt Whitman

"Walt Whitman used to come into my grandfather's restaurant bar in Camden, New Jersey long ago. When I was a little boy, I heard stories about my grandfather and his poet friend, Walt Whitman. I was about three years old, so I always dismissed Walt Whitman as part of my grandfather's circle. It wasn't until much later that I realized who he was. I had never read his poetry, though everybody said it was good. One day I was reading *Leaves of Grass* and thought, maybe this guy has something. I got involved and very excited about it, and wrote the cantata, *Celebrations*. I like that work a lot. It is funny how someone can be so important, and yet you ignore him; you have no experience of him. For instance, I didn't know the B Minor Mass of Bach for a long while; I looked at it one day and got to know it, and thought, 'By God, it is a great work.'"

On Composing

"I am a very slow writer. I just write all the time. I write sometimes for a six or seven hour stretch.

"Never try to be a composer; if you really want to write music, that's different. Then it's worth the financial risk, it's worth starving. Early on I had a church job for 18 years. I got so I would improvise and play things like *Rite of Spring* as an anthem.

"I learned from playing the piano that I am a composer. I played various famous themes and found relationships between them, pop music and Chopin. Then I realized I had a disease.

"I have certain composers that I feel close to: certainly Robert Schumann because I like the way he set tenor voices for piano or for orchestra, Honegger, Beethoven because he says more about less rather than saying less about more. If a piece has a lot of wonderful ideas but says nothing about them, that's fine but I don't have time in my life for listening to it. There was a wonderful generation of American composers, an exciting time, when Piston and Roy Harris wrote."

On Composition Style

"My music varies, it goes from gracious to gritty very often. Sometimes it has a lot of serial in it; other pieces have less of that and are more tonal. It's a mixture. I may have had something in 1942 that was more avant-garde, more advanced than something I did this year. It is not a change, but just that you happen to hear a piece that is more avant-garde than tonal. Right next to it might be a piece that is more relaxed; my music is always enigmatic. I have never joined a camp."

To Learn Composition
From Persichetti's *Twentieth Century Harmony*:

"Construct twelve-note chords for full band that punctuate a rapid solo timpani passage.

"Write an allegro section for brasses and feature added-note chords of the sharp variety.

"Write a sarcastically rhythmic passage for string quartet. Feature augmented fourth chords with added notes.

"Harmonize the following first-trumpet melody in six-part brass harmony (three trumpets and three trombones). Use a predominantly polychordal texture with occasional unison relief."

"Although knowledge of materials and technique does not in itself create a personal style, precision in the choice of notes and understanding of harmonic devices are desirable in perfecting a means of expression and in stating a musical idea clearly and consistently.

"Large tertian chords, no matter how many thirds have been added, form only a small portion of the harmonic palette. The multiple tones of eleventh and thirteenth chords add density but reduce suppleness.

"Dynamics are an essential element in composition. Harmonic progression is affected by the degree of dynamic nuance in which it is conceived. A dissonant and restless progression set in a pianissimo context is likely to explode into a subito force of violent polychords, while the same progression in a forte context might find harmonic satisfaction in its overbearing tension and remain in the same harmonic sphere. Highly chromatic chords blend with more harmonic ease in soft passages than in loud."

On Teaching Composition

"I could teach composition students the way I would write, but I don't think that is particularly good. Hindemith did too much of that; he made students write the way he did. I would expose them to music. With bands or orchestras if you hear something you like, you should make it your business to know how that composer got that sound. I make students do that; it saves a lot of time. They can study the orchestration and reduce it, look at it. There could be tremendous things in bands or ensembles that don't hold together to

867

form patterns, but students sit at the keyboard and know they can do this or that. They get ideas and write, but it is hard for them to do it for orchestra and band. How do you get that sound, especially in an orchestra, like the opening of Brahms' Fourth Symphony? It is not just a chordal guitar part. Brahms gets it a certain way.

"It is the students' business to know. You store this information away subconsciously, then have some place to start. No one just writes from nothing. We all have a heritage. Playing in the Michigan band under Revelli taught students better than a book. Listen to records for a certain special sound. You don't copy the sound, you just find out how."

Past and Future

"Works of high caliber are plentiful in the twentieth century. The rich mixture of materials and styles is made up of many ingredients: rhythmic energy, vivid harmonic fabric, melodic color, and fresh linear writing. There are bold statements and delicate embellishments, moments of fancy, and developmental forces that refuse to be bound by a severe formal plan. There are daringly experimental and strongly traditional forces which bring divergent materials together." *(Twentieth Century Harmony)*

"Have you noticed how the standard of band conductors has gone up around the country? It's amazing. I remember driving behind a school bus trying to get to the middle of Arkansas, and I didn't see one student come off the bus without an instrument. One music teacher can do that; he can get students who later become much better conductors than his colleagues were 25 years ago. It's an optimistic time. I think we are getting ready for a rich period at the turn of the century that will combine these things."

"Who of us can write as intensely as Beethoven? We can't do that. The great composers could barely write what they were writing; it's hard. It is not that we are trying to be better or worse; we just happen to be of our time, making sounds that might influence or lead the way for somebody else."

"Music doesn't get better century after century. It's just as meaningful today as at some other time, but it is music of the era. If you go back to the time of Beethoven, Mozart, Haydn, all these gods were a small percentage. The rest were mediocre. We compare every new work to the cream of the past. I don't know how we can help it, but if you happen to hear 20 contemporary works that you think have no meaning, don't be discouraged."

Ideal Instrumentation

Vincent Persichetti joined composers Paul Creston, Morton Gould, Vittorio Giannini, and Philip Lang in a 1960 College Band Directors National Association conference on band repertoire and instrumentation. Along with three publishers and three C.B.D.N.A. representatives, they constructed this scoring list for an ideal band that would have any desired instruments available in any quantity they wished.

The composers admitted slighting E♭ alto clarinets but thought the instrument was essential for a complete clarinet family voicing, along with the E♭ soprano clarinet. They considered the E♭ contrabass clarinet better than a B♭ contrabass because of its excellent upper range. The panelists said that properly balanced saxophones contributed brilliantly to a band; they recommended a balance of one each of soprano, alto, tenor and baritone saxophones, suggesting the addition of the bass saxophone because it has agility and a weighty, warm tone color.

They wanted to distinguish between trumpets and cornets, deplored the practice of doubling cornet parts, and considered the E♭ cornet a good solution for high brass writing. The composers did not like horn sections of more than four players. They recommended using a bass

trombone and not doubling trombones, and also thought the BB♭ tuba the only desirable brass bass, though most bands had too many of them. (Whitwell and Ostling)

1 piccolo (C)	One part for piccolo
6 flute	Two or three parts
2 oboe	First and second parts
1 English horn	Possibly an oboe player doubling
2 bassoon	First and second parts
1 E♭ clarinet	
18 B♭ clarinet	First and second parts
6 E♭ alto clarinet	
3 B♭ bass clarinet	
2 E♭ contrabass clarinet	
1 B♭ soprano saxophone	Straight soprano
1 E♭ alto saxophone	
1 B♭ tenor saxophone	
1 E♭ baritone saxophone	
1 B♭ bass saxophone	
1 E♭ cornet	
3 B♭ cornet	Two parts, three voices
3 B♭ trumpet	Two parts, three voices
4 horn	Four parts
3 trombone	Two parts, three voices
1 bass trombone	
3 euphonium	One or more voices
3 BB♭ tuba	One part
5 percussion	Two parts
73 Total	

Sources

1. Lecture and interview, Vincent Persichetti at DePaul University, February 14, 1985.
2. David Whitwell and Acton Ostling, Jr. *The College and University Band.* M.E.N.C. and College Band Directors National Assn., 1977.
3. Vincent Persichetti. *Twentieth Century Harmony,* 1961.
4. William Workinger, "The Band Sound of Vincent Persichetti," *The Instrumentalist* (April 1973).
5. Rudy Schackelford, *Perspectives of New Music* (1982).
6. Barry Kopetz, "Psalm for Band," *The Instrumentalist* (February 1991).
7. Joe Mullins, "Three Symphonies for Band by American Composers," D.M.Ed. diss., 1967.

Persichetti Band Works

Serenade for Ten Wind Instruments, Op. 1, 1929.

Divertimento, Op. 42 (1950) (The Goldman Band)
Psalm, Op. 53 (1952) (Pi Kappa Omicron, University of Louisville, Kentucky)
Pageant, Op. 59 (1953) (American Bandmasters Association)
Symphony, Op. 69 (1956) (Washington University, St. Louis)
Serenade, Op. 85 (1960) (Ithaca High School Band, New York)
Bagatelles, Op. 87 (1961) (Dartmouth College, New Hampshire)
Chorale Prelude: So Pure the Star, Op. 91 (1962) (Duke University, N.C.)
Masquerade, Op. 102 (1966) (Baldwin-Wallace Conservatory, Ohio)
Chorale Prelude: Turn Not Thy Face, Op. 105 (1967) (Ithaca High School Band)
O Cool is the Valley, Op. 118 on poem by James Joyce (1971) (Ohio Music Educators)
Parable for Band, Op. 121 (1973) (Duke University)
A Lincoln Address, Op. 124A (1972)

April, 1990

Music by Leroy Anderson

by Frederick Fennell

Music by Leroy Anderson. That familiar phrase triggers a wide response inseparably tied to an endless stream of just-the-right titles to go with the-just-right music: *Fiddle-Faddle, The Syncopated Clock, The Typewriter, Sleigh Ride.* Music and words were Leroy Anderson's two disciplines, and several times in his life he wasn't so sure which would claim him; eventually he became fluent in nine languages. In those formative years that led to a career decision, he spent most of his life (1908-75) in and around Cambridge, Massachusetts, where he graduated magna cum laude and Phi Beta Kappa from Harvard in 1929. There he was into it all, playing trombone in the band, string contrabass in the orchestra, and singing in that famous glee club. When the conductor of the Harvard Band left the post for graduate study, Anderson took over the job in his senior year as its drum major, goal post toss-over included. Not resting on that laurel, he began to score traditional Harvard songs and other Ivy League tunes for the band, in ways so convincing that people began to notice the difference and the quality of his work.

It is not all that difficult to imagine what the Harvard music faculty must have thought of their magna cum laude graduate associating himself with the nonsensical trivia of a marching band at a football game, even though it was at Harvard. Anderson doesn't seem to have let it bother him in the slightest; he went right on with the job into graduate school.

Frederick Fennell is in his seventh season as principal conductor of the Tokyo Kosei Windorchestra in Japan. A longtime admirer of Anderson's music, he frequently programs the composer's works on his concerts.

Anderson's subsequent commercial jobs arranging and sometimes playing music for Boston hotels, radio, summer resorts, and a band-on-board boat trip to Scandinavia helped pay the bills while the experiences fed his need to know how and what to score on order. One of his early accounts was Ruby Newman's popular society orchestra. Leroy played and wrote for him in Boston while living in New York, where the experience kept his foot in the door of the music business.

Years ago Harvard Night at the Boston Pops was one of the highlights of the Pops season, which ran seven nights during May and June. Enter Maestro Arthur Fiedler. A sold-out Symphony Hall on a night he conducted was guaranteed. George E. Judd, manager of the Boston Symphony Orchestra and also a member of the class that was to celebrate its 25th anniversary that year, remembered the good sounds he had been hearing lately by the Harvard Band at football games. He requested arrangements of Harvard songs for the orchestra.

Enter Leroy Anderson, who on that important night in his career conducted the Boston Pops Orchestra while Fiedler listened and liked what he heard. Some short time later, at Fiedler's request, Anderson put a little tune for the strings of the Pops Orchestra on the maestro's desk. This time Fiedler liked what he saw. Paired later with its counterpart, *Jazz Legato*, it was *Jazz Pizzicato* that began Leroy Anderson's remarkable career and created the made-in-heaven relationship between him and Arthur Fiedler and the Boston Pops.

Even if things really do come in threes, such an alliance as this is still very rare; this one was incredibly productive for everybody. Enter next the publisher, Mills Music, Inc., and the trio becomes a quartet — composer, conductor, orchestra, and publisher. R.C.A. Victor Records came automatically with the Boston Pops Orchestra, icing a truly delicious commercial cake that probably had not been baked by anybody since John Philip Sousa. Anderson's career had staying power to match its unusual momentum. Soon after Fiedler had discovered Anderson's orchestration facility, the composer began a series of commissions for special arrangements of music from Broadway shows tailored to the Pops Orchestra and its audience. Anderson produced the selections at intervals between composing original works.

Just as his career began to flower, the U.S. Military called on Anderson to serve in World War II. Anderson was assigned to military intelligence and stationed in Iceland, where his fluency in Scandinavian languages took precedence over the music skills he had honed so sharply. Obviously, the two disciplines did not mix; and beside that, Fiedler's belief in Anderson had helped the composer to choose music, not language, as a career. During his time in service, he produced only two compositions, *Promenade* and *The Syncopated Clock*. What would the late, late movie on the TV-to-come have done without that one? Yet though he dammed up the creative stream, putting little down on paper, I suspect that more than a few musical ideas continued to lap over the edge, quietly developing in his head.

Denying attractive offers at the end of the war to sign on with military intelligence, Anderson returned to the life he had left in such high gear. Titles and music began to pour out: *Blue Tango, Chicken Reel, The Irish Suite, Serenata, Belle of the Ball, Bugler's Holiday*. He composed a grand total of 40 pieces, many of them written in Woodbury, Connecticut, where he had settled quietly with his wife Eleanor and family.

Anderson's success didn't just happen; there were reasons. The composer had a classical education in all the facets of music at the hands of distinguished and demanding teachers. His was an unusual talent, fed by curiosity and marked by an unmistakable instinct to do what was uniquely his. Missing no opportunity, he always seemed to possess the ability not just to learn but also to remember and to apply. After his success he remained a shy individual, so I am told, though he guest-conducted widely, matching his interpretations of the Anderson classics on phonograph recordings to those of his illustrious patron.

I never met Leroy Anderson, and we never exchanged letters or calls, but I did know him as he probably wanted to be reached, having recorded all but 2 of his 40 published titles in both his originals for orchestra and the settings for band. Anderson arranged most of the band transcriptions too, scoring them with the same special care that professionals in the orchestral world so admired.

Rehearsal of the Anderson pieces, whether for band or orchestra, takes time, regardless of how familiar they seem; but his deceivingly simple-sounding music was conceived for those who can play. From my own experience at the Pops, with its absolute minimum rehearsal schedule, I remember that these miniature orchestral masterpieces come as close as we can imagine to being — and I say this affectionately — conductor-proof!

As I got to know each new composition over the airwaves, I believe I frequently shared a reaction with others hearing a new piece for the first time, saying to myself, "Oh, yes, I think I know that one." As the music played on, however, I had to say, "I've not heard that, I don't know it or what it is, but I sure do like it;

that *has* to be music by Leroy Anderson." That part of the identity was immediate. He called one of his last compositions, *Golden Years.* Thank you for yours, Leroy Anderson – unique composer, distinguished American.

Anderson's Band Arrangements

Most of Anderson's works were also arranged for concert band – largely by himself. Arthur [Fiedler's] comment was that he didn't farm anything out as a rule, he worked at it. These band versions, of course, made a lot of money for Leroy and his publisher since the performance market in that area is stronger than that in symphonic orchestra. (Just consider the high school and college bands across the country!) Curiously enough, however, there have been very few recordings of his music by bands (even that of Harvard University), at least none well known. This can be accounted for by the fact that professional bands such as the Goldman and Cities Service of America are rare birds today, and they would be the ones likely to make recordings for national distribution. However, perhaps Anderson and Decca missed the boat by not doing at least one album of his most successful pieces with a fine wind band (under Andy's direction, of course).

— *George Wright Briggs*

Highlights from Anderson's Music

Leroy Anderson composed these pieces first for orchestra and later transcribed them for band.

Belle of the Ball - Presser/Filmtrax (orch); CPP/Belwin (band)
Blue Tango - CPP/Belwin (orch and band)
Bugler's Holiday - CPP/Belwin (orch and band)
Chicken Reel - E.F. Kalmus (orch)
Christmas Festival - CPP/Belwin (orch and band)
Clarinet Candy - Woodbury Music (orch and band)
Fiddle-Faddle - CPP/Belwin (orch); Presser/Filmtrax (band)
Forgotten Dreams - E.F. Kalmus (orch and band)
Horse and Buggy - E.F. Kalmus (orch); CPP/Belwin (band)
Irish Suite (complete edition) - Presser/Filmtrax (orch); "Irish Washerwoman" CPP/Belwin (band); "Minstrel Boy" E.F. Kalmus (band); "The Rakes of Mallow" - E.F. Kalmus (band); "The Girl I Left Behind Me" - E.F. Kalmus (band)
Jazz Pizzicato - CPP/Belwin (orch); E.F. Kalmus (band)
Serenata - Presser/Filmtrax (orch); CPP/Belwin (band)
Sleigh Ride - CPP/Belwin (orch and band)
Syncopated Clock - CPP/Belwin (orch and band)
Trumpeter's Lullaby - CPP/Belwin (orch and band)
The Typewriter - CPP/Belwin (orch and band)
The Waltzing Cat - CPP/Belwin (orch); Presser/Filmtrax (band)

Available Recordings

Leroy Anderson Collection; MCA Classics (2 CD set), MCA D2-9815; Leroy Anderson conducting his orchestra.
Syncopated Clock; Pro Arte 264, CD, cassette; Erich Kunzel conducting the Rochester Pops Orchestra.
Classical Jukebox; Pro Arte 414, CD, cassette; Newton Wayland conducting the Rochester Pops Orchestra.
Fiddle Faddle; Vanguard VBD-10016, CD, cassette; Maurice Abravanel conducting the Utah Symphony Orchestra.
Belle of the Ball; Kosei, LP KOR 8412, CD KOCD 2812; Frederick Fennell conducting the Kosei Wind Ensemble.
Serenata; Kosei, LP KOR 8413, CD KOCD 2813; Frederick Fennel conducting the Kosei Wind Ensemble.

For a complete catalog of compositions and recordings write to Woodbury Music Company, P.O. Box 447, Woodbury, Connecticut.

Leroy Anderson with Arthur Fiedler

Anderson on Broadway

Playwright and New York drama critic Walter Kerr remembered working on the musical *Goldilocks*, for which Anderson provided the score, this way:

"Once we got into rehearsal, Leroy was pretty much off in his own department (working with the arranger, watching dances rehearsed, training singers, etc.) while I was in mine (staging the book). In fact, the show itself got too departmentalized during rehearsal and I failed to bring it together early enough to give its elements a smooth fusion before opening. We had other problems (plenty of them) but the fact that I'd gone rusty as a director without realizing it was one of the causes of our mounting mishaps.

"An example of Leroy's total concentration and single-mindedness: At the last preview before opening in Philly, I think it was, we hit one of Those Nights when absolutely everything is fouled up. Platforms didn't slide in on time. The girl who was supposed to ride on the moon couldn't get onto it. Cues were missed. The snowbag in the high grid, which was supposed to be used late in the second act, got fouled on some ropes and began dribbling snowflakes all through the performance, until it was practically empty by the time the snow was actually called for. We were out of our skulls at the mess. Running into Leroy immediately after the performance, Jean said, 'Wasn't that the most awful experience you ever had?' Leroy replied, with intense sobriety, 'It certainly was — that trumpet player must go!'

"He'd been listening to the pit so closely and so exclusively that he hadn't noticed all those other things going wrong. And, I believe, he did get rid of the particular trumpet player who offended him.

"One of the things I'd worried a little about before we asked Leroy to join us on the show was whether he'd be able to work fast enough on changes once we got the show out of town. We'd had a bit more experience of this sort of thing (we should have had more) and knew about what you had to be able to accomplish overnight. But Leroy presumably had always written on his own time, on his own order, and might not be able to turn out new songs as rapidly as they might be needed. Well, I needn't have worried. He was the fastest of the lot. New songs *were* needed, and he'd have them the next morning. Furthermore, they were good. I'm still extremely fond of 'Never Know When to Say When,' which was an overnight job, and absolutely perfect for the spot it was meant to fill. He also turned out 'Give the Little Girl' and the extended group number 'Two Years in the Making' in an incredible hurry. There may have been others, I forget.

"The whole out-of-town period, in Philly and Boston, was a horror as the show got better but never good enough....But the odd thing here is that everyone remained friends. Except for the one performer I mentioned, there weren't any fights. Everybody worked like _____ trying to make something out of the show (I finally ran into George Abbott in Boston, where he had a show of his own but had dropped by to see ours, and he said, 'Walter, you were licked when you devised that storyline' and my guess is that that was the size of it). Winchell kept reporting that Agnes de Mille and I were fighting, and Agnes and I laughed about the item in the aisles as we hurried to restage numbers. Bob Whitehead lost a bundle and we're still close friends. But Leroy may have been the most stable and serene of all. Went about his own business efficiently, responded to *your* requests swiftly, kept cheerful and uncomplaining." □

— *George Wright Briggs*

July, 1990

Karel Husa
Keeping Ties with Tradition

by Frank Battisti

Karel Husa's frequently performed works include three string quartets, the *Concerto for Wind Ensemble, Apotheosis of This Earth*, and the one he conducted for the first time in Prague this year, *Music for Prague 1968*. He is currently completing a fourth string quartet, and pending commissions include a violin concerto for the New York Philharmonic, a chamber work in celebration of the 1991-92 centennial of Ithaca College, and a new work for the Air Force Band.

Born in Prague in 1921, Husa studied at the Prague Conservatory, in Paris with Arthur Honegger and Nadia Boulanger, and has taught at Cornell University and Ithaca College in Ithaca, New York since 1954. For additional background on Husa and his work, see "Karel Husa — Echoing Mankind Through Music" and "*Music for Prague 1968*: An Interpretive Analysis," both of which appeared in *The Instrumentalist*, October 1987.

When did you begin composing music?

When I was about 13 I wrote some little pieces for violin and piano and piano solo. One I called "Spring Song," another one "Lullaby;" the others I don't remember very well. They were really nothing, just tonic and dominant chords, but they gave me the feeling that I would like to write music, and that I didn't forget.

What were the musical influences on your work and growth as a composer in those early years?

Definitely the music of Czech composers — Smetana, Dvořák, Janáček, as well as Suk and Novák — otherwise I didn't know much music.

I played the violin, and mostly I knew composers who were virtuoso violinists. I played a lot of Wieniawski and Kreisler, but I didn't play much Mozart or Beethoven. The Czech Philharmonic played mostly composers of the past and Czech

---

Frank Battisti is conductor of the Wind Ensemble at the New England Conservatory in Boston, Massachusetts. A recognized authority on wind literature, he has conducted wind ensembles and bands for over 30 years. He is Past-President of the College Band Directors National Association, founder of the National Wind Ensemble Conference, and a member of the Standard Music Award Panel for A.S.C.A.P. He is a contributor to many journals and magazines, and in 1986 was a Visiting Fellow at Clare Hall College, Cambridge University, England.

music. Also at that time in Czechoslovakia, French art and music were much admired. Martinu, for instance, studied with Roussel. We admired Debussy and Ravel as we admired impressionism in painting and poetry. So there was close contact between the Czechs and the French.

I also knew a young composer, Jan Rychlik, who was the percussionist in the best jazz group in Czechoslovakia. He was in my class at the Prague Conservatory, although he was several years older. This man knew everything about American jazz. He had scores by Schumann, Barber, Copland, and Ives, as well as American jazz records: Louis Armstrong, Count Basie, and Duke Ellington. He also had recordings of the Bach Brandenburg Concertos, which you couldn't find then. He would take me to his home and play jazz and then a Brandenburg Concerto, and I found both equally exciting. I went every Sunday to hear his group play, and that's how I learned about jazz.

Your early pieces include Sonata for Piano, String Quartet No. 2, Overture for Large Orchestra, *and* Suite for Viola and Piano. *Would you describe the style of those works?*

I was influenced by classical, romantic, and French music, but mostly by Czech composers. I wrote a sinfonietta in 1945-46 while I was in Prague, and then I went to Paris to study. When it was performed in Prague in 1949, some of the critics wrote that with this piece I got worse instead of getting better because they thought I wrote it in Paris. To understand the situation better, Czechoslovakia became a communist country in 1948 and these critics were members of the party, naturally rejecting any influence from the West. They didn't realize that I had already embraced French impressionism before I went to France.

Today you use aleatoric techniques in your music, although writing a completely aleatoric piece doesn't interest you.

I use aleatoric writing only to the extent that I can control it as a conductor or performer; I don't leave a piece completely up to the performer because then it would not be my piece, it would be the performer's piece. I think it's taking a big chance to leave too many things to the performer. During a performance musicians may be nervous, and by accident find interesting things, but the chance is one out of a hundred. A work of art has to be the work of the person who created it. If I do some aleatoric things, they would be in the area of an extended trill, a recitative, or the freedom you find sometimes in jazz, but not beyond that.

You're looking for an added dimension of spontaneity within a controlled situation.

Exactly, and the more I conduct works of this type, the more I think it's better if I leave some freedom for the performer but indicate very specifically what I want.

As a composer do you follow a routine? If you're home and you don't have to go any place for a month, would you compose every day?

I would, from the morning to the evening; that's what I try to do when I am on vacation during the summer. I get up in the morning and am interested only in the piece I'm writing. I am not the type who could compose only for the couple of hours I have free during the day. I become completely absorbed in that one thing. I forget to write letters or make calls; all these things disturb me. I have to concentrate on the music, so I usually compose during the summers. Naturally if I already have the sketches, I can orchestrate during the school year; that's how it usually works.

You sometimes create electronic effects in your music, yet you've never composed anything using electronics.

I never did, although I was very interested in Robert Moog's work. I prefer to write music for performers, but I like to introduce electronic sounds I've heard and put them in regular music. Now, at age 68, I feel I am getting a little too old to learn to compose electronically; time for me is so pressing. I don't think I could learn it in less than two years, and I don't have those two years. Ultimately I'm interested in human performers, because I like the connection between writing the music, putting it on paper, bringing it to a performer, and then making music. It's a feeling that is second to none.

Yet you have found electronic sounds that interest you and have created similar textures and sounds using traditional instruments.

These sounds exist today; it's good to incorporate them because they make my music part of the music of today. I'm grateful to all the people who find these new things. I remember when I was in Paris I was amazed to hear *musique concrète*, a type of recorded sounds, on the radio. I found the sounds fascinating, and that's what I try to put into my music.

Percussion plays an important part in the texture and colors in your music. What is your outlook regarding new sources of sound?

As a violinist I found from looking at orchestral and chamber music scores that composers had already explored the stringed instruments so fantastically. What can we do after Bartók and Berg with stringed instruments? Nearly everything is there already. The same is true to a lesser extent with woodwind instruments. Brasses, though, still have so many possibilities; 50 years ago composers had not explored brass instruments the way they have since. Orchestral sound can be renewed and refreshed by including more sounds from percussion, brass, and some winds; then all members of the orchestra participate more or less equally. It was not fair to have performers study percussion five years and then play in an ensemble and count more measures than they play. That was another concern, but also these sounds are absolutely terrific.

Where did you get your knowledge of percussion instruments? What gave you such an intimate acquaintance with the possibilities?

I studied instrumentation in the conservatory, and in 1945 and 1946 I conducted for the Prague radio, so I thought I knew about percussion. Years later, after a rehearsal of an orchestral piece of mine, a percussionist from Ithaca College who played in the Cornell Orchestra, came to me and said, "You write here for xylophone; what type of stick do you want me to play?" Then he went on to other parts and with that I thought, I'd better learn more about these instruments. So I went to the band room at Cornell and spent two weeks with the percussion instruments and all the various mallets. As I tried to play them, I tried to produce different sounds. Those two weeks were like Liszt's visit to the monastery, because I learned so much. I got so interested in percussion that it became almost an obsession.

When I conducted *Music for Prague* in Prague this past February, the Czech orchestra found my use of percussion and brass in the piece rather unusual. Perhaps I have become Americanized, but here we use the percussion so tremendously and brass playing is on such a fantastic level.

Did orchestra members in Prague have all the necessary equipment to perform your work?

No, I brought some with me. I telephoned the conductor a week before the performance and he said they had only straight mutes; they didn't have Harmons or cup mutes. So I brought Harmons and cups with me for the trombones and trumpets, and they were so delighted, I left the mutes with them.

Were they able to find all the percussion equipment?

In the rehearsals we didn't have a marimba; only in the dress rehearsal in the afternoon did we add a marimba. The vibraphone had only two octaves, C to C, with no F extension. I started to realize how lucky we are here. Prior to going I went to ask Gordon Stout at Ithaca College for a pair of the special sticks for the marimba at the beginning of the aria, because I wasn't sure the Czech player would have them. While I was there I noticed that he had at least eight marimbas; the Czech marimba was the only one in Prague. All these items are rather precious things that you find only in one place, not like here. With the new freedom, I am sure, many of the western instruments will now be bought.

Why is placing the instruments so important in many of your works?

In *Music for Prague* my idea was to spread the percussion wherever possible on the stage and have three different players play the same instrument but of high pitch, medium pitch, and low pitch. I spread them around the wind ensemble or orchestra so that the effect is like bells ringing around the city of Prague. It's an incredible effect. In the *Concerto for Wind Ensemble* I thought it would be interesting for the players, who always sit in the same places, to be separated and hear the music from a different angle. If you are a horn player or trombone player and are always sandwiched between timpani behind you and trumpet in front of you, you always hear the music the same way.

Have you ever thought about writing a piece in which the players were not all on the stage, but placed in different positions around the hall?

I've thought about it; I haven't done it yet, but I would like to. The idea came to me when I conducted the Berlioz *Requiem*, but of course it's over one hundred years old.

When Gabrieli wrote his music, he knew it would be played in St. Mark's, so he could score with some degree of precision. When you write a piece using offstage players, aren't you at the mercy of the performing hall? When you compose are you concerned about the space, which you can't always control?

Yes, that is correct; but the way Berlioz scored his music, it is very effective in many different halls.

There is often a wide gap between present-day composers and their audiences. Can we blame this on the lack of audience exposure to new music, or do you feel that composers themselves need to reconsider the issue of musical expression and communication?

I think it's both. Some audiences do not want to accept new ideas, and some composers think they would belittle themselves if they came closer to the audience and tried to establish a link with them. When I write music I don't think directly about the audience and whether they will accept it or not; I think in terms of what would touch me and how I understand music. When I compose I'm using musical language that is based on what we have from the past. I don't want to break with tradition; at the same time I cannot write music in the language of Beethoven. Yet music is a language, and if we can still use some things from the past, why not? Sometimes I see scores that use new terms or symbols for *pizzicato* or *crescendo* and *decrescendo*. We still have these normal signs and symbols, so why not use them? As a conductor I usually have three rehearsals and then a concert. If we change the vocabulary, it would take so much time to explain what I want to do to the orchestra or band that I would never get to the music. This is also true of the musical content; there are things we still can use.

In terms of language, we continue to use words that we inherit from tradition. We might add new words that explain something in contemporary terms, but we don't completely discard what we have grown to understand and use. It seems to me the same is true in musical composition. An audience comes with a certain background of musical experiences, so it's wise to build on that background, to add things, but not to leave the audience completely afloat, trying to cope with something unlinked to history and tradition.

Yes, and also we have to be aware of differences between audiences. An audience accustomed to only light music would find the *Fourth Symphony* of Beethoven a little exhausting. On the other hand, audiences familiar with classical, romantic, and impressionistic music can even accept Schoenberg and Berg because they still use a language from the past. If the music has a specific content, it can be advanced technically and the public will still understand it. When I was a student in Prague around 1945, I heard Bartók's *String Quartet No. 4*, and it really bewildered me. Here I was, a young composer, and I had heard new things, yet I thought this bordered on not being music.

Today when I listen to that piece, it seems like Beethoven, absolutely classical music, and I wonder how I ever could have thought that this bordered on non-music.

The music doesn't change, but we change.

We accept it after repeated listenings; time soothes the dissonances. Time even soothes the abstraction of Picasso or Braque that 40 years ago looked incredibly sophisticated; today it seems simple.

Of your works for wind band or wind ensemble, is there a favorite? Which of the works would you like to see performed more?

Apotheosis of This Earth is a piece I like very much, and I am a little surprised that it is not played more often. Bands mostly play *Music for Prague 1968*, but the message of the *Apotheosis* is strong, too. In the last two years the piece has received more performances. Technically it is not too difficult, but putting it together is difficult. I would also mention *An American Te Deum* and the *Concerto for Wind Ensemble*. I think the reason the *Concerto for Wind Ensemble* is not

performed more often is a practical one; many conductors express interest, but then they learn that the work is only available on rental. They would prefer to buy the parts, add it to their library, then play it when they wish.

What first interested you in the wind band or wind ensemble?

Although I wrote a wind ensemble piece in Paris for U.N.E.S.C.O., I never heard it, and I don't know where the score and parts are. I am glad you asked this question, because my interest in the wind ensemble is mostly because of you. When you and Don Sinta asked me to write the *Saxophone Concerto*, my first piece for an American band, I was naturally delighted. I was amazed by the quality of bands here in the United States, and I am even more amazed today, when excellent European bands still play traditional marches and transcriptions of famous overtures. It was amazing to me to hear Percy Grainger, Vincent Persichetti, Leslie Bassett, and other composers writing for band.

You're so busy conducting your own works, I was wondering what wind ensemble pieces do you conduct that are not your own?

Mostly I am invited to conduct my own music, but I would love to conduct Grainger, Schoenberg, Hindemith, Persichetti, Bassett, Ross Lee Finney, and even more modern things. I haven't conducted many of them, but I find them exciting.

You are also a wonderful conductor. What do you think are the characteristics and components of effective conducting?

First of all the conductor needs the technique to convey the music with the baton or with his hands. The technique should be so good that one doesn't even notice it. Some may think technique is not so important, but I think it's incredibly important, because you don't have time in rehearsals to explain what you will do with your hands at every moment. It's like playing the piano; you don't spell out fingerings for every single measure.

A second factor is attitude, how well and how efficiently you can work with an ensemble. Whether it's a professional or student ensemble, the problems are the same: we never have enough rehearsal time.

You also should know how to deal with people, and that is not as easy as it sounds. You come to a rehearsal with the best intentions and things may turn out in a way that you hadn't planned. You have to be a juggler of feelings. Technique is very important, and how the conductor deals with the players is very important. You can get a lot from players, or you can appear in front of an ensemble that has so much to offer and get nothing from them. A conductor has to come in front of a group completely prepared. In 15 minutes the performers can say whether the conductor knows the score or not; you cannot fool anybody.

You composed Music for Prague *in August, September, and October 1968. Had you ever thought about composing a piece about Prague before this time?*

Yes, many times, but after I decided I could not return to Prague in 1948, it became a symbol of my youth, of my family, of everything that I dream of but cannot attain. Especially after hearing Mozart's "Prague" Symphony, I always thought I would like to write a piece about Prague that would be beautiful and happy, because my years there were beautiful. I still remember those magnificent days in December, when the stores and vendors in the streets sold Christmas things, and the incredible smell of the city. It was fantastic, yet when I heard the news over the radio in August 1968, it was not a time to write something very happy. I definitely wanted to write something positive at the end, so I left the three notes D, E, and C unresolved; the work would have finished on D if it were tonal music, but I thought the lack of resolution would represent hope at the end.

Are you still going to write a joyous piece about Prague?

Yes, I would love to, and I've been commissioned to write an orchestral *Music for Prague* of the present.

You composed the Concerto for Saxophone and Wind Ensemble *in 1967, but the* Music for Prague *was the first piece in which you explored the complete resources of the concert band. You used the 15th-century religious song, "Ye Warriors of God and His Law," but you also used a number of avant-garde, contemporary techniques, including 12-tone rows. Was this the first piece in which you combined a Czech melody with serial and avant-garde techniques?*

Yes, the combination of new and old intrigued me. It's because of the nature of the composition that it happened that way. When I left Czechoslovakia I went to France and studied with Honegger. When I got to Paris 12-tone writing suddenly exploded; it was the main technique used at that time. I thought it was important for a young composer to learn all the techniques in use, because they are extensions of the language, and every composer can take whatever he wishes to explore. Beethoven and Debussy did the same thing; every composer has somehow extended the language and looked for as many fathers as he could find. So when I came to the United States I explored 12-tone technique. I didn't use it strictly in many of my compositions, but I did use it and liked some of the results.

I included the 15th-century war song in *Music for Prague* for patriotic reasons. I remember in 1939 and 1940 when the country was occupied, the Czech Philharmonic performed works by Smetana and Suk and Dvorak. In one performance of *My Country* by Smetana, the conductor finished the fifth poem, *Tabor*, and tried to start the sixth, but the applause was so incredible that he couldn't go on. The next day the order came that there would be no break between the fifth and sixth poems, although there were breaks between the others. At the next performance the conductor finished *Tabor* and went on, but we couldn't hear anything for five or six minutes. We saw the Czech Philharmonic playing, but there was no sound, only applause. Then the order came forbidding all performances of this piece. In April 1945, one month before the end of the war in Europe, the Czech Philharmonic put it on the program, and a reviewer wrote of the concert, "and we can already sense the beginning of a new era." He didn't say any more than that, but the next morning he was executed by the Nazis. So the music had incredible power, and that's why I put it in, as the most powerful war song we have ever had. Perhaps it should have become the national hymn of Czechoslovakia.

Could you foresee the reception this piece was going to have and the impact it would have on your life?

No, definitely not. It was commissioned by the Ithaca College Concert Band and premiered at the M.E.N.C. convention in 1969. During the program I ended up sitting with people who didn't know who I was. It was amazing that at the end of the piece, immediately the people around me stood up; I didn't stand up immediately, as I was astonished by the reception. Kenneth Snapp, the conductor, signaled me to come to the stage. It was an emotional time for me; I had never before experienced anything so moving. It is satisfying to know that the belief I had in 1968 was not in vain. Life has confirmed that freedom is the supreme thing in man's existence and it's worth fighting for. □

Karel Husa

Musician from Prague

by Harvey Phillips

This June Karel Husa retired from Cornell University, where he had been the Kappa Alpha Professor of Music since 1954. He is currently working on a violin concerto for the New York Philharmonic, an orchestra chorale for the Chicago Symphony, and a wind ensemble piece to honor John Paynter for his 40 years with Northwestern University (it will be presented in 1995 during the school's 100th anniversary). In the future he plans to travel throughout Europe and the United States conducting and giving master classes. Ten years from now he hopes to be "overlooking Cayuga Lake as I am at this moment, pursuing the same things, because writing and making music have been an ideal combination for me."

What are your strongest memories from your teaching?

I have wonderful memories of helping aspiring composers and conducting the student orchestra for 20 years. I remember programming an orchestra concert with the Berg Violin Concerto, but from the beginning it was obvious that the students did not care for it. Once we put it together with Louis Krasner though, it became the most incredible experience for those students, something they have never forgotten and which they still talk about with me 20 or 30 years later. They learned that some things created recently are important and that we cannot write music the way Beethoven or Brahms did, even though they did it so beautifully.

Do you have any unpleasant or bad memories of teaching?

I don't have any bad memories of teaching but there were some disappointments. I remember

rehearsing my *Apotheosis of This Earth* at some school, but I noticed that it was the piece the students least liked. When conducting, you can see the interest or lack of interest, and in despair I told the performers that if they did not want to play it, we would replace it with something they liked. When they voted, only three students raised their hands, so I changed the piece. I think that later the students regretted their decision, but it was too late then. I made this decision because it was my own music; I have never changed other composers' works.

What changes have you experienced in composing?

The biggest change in composing was the decline of the twelve-tone system. In 1946 the twelve-tone system was the accepted technique for composing and every young composer in Europe, and I assume in this country too, was expected to train and write in it. Things became so incredibly rigid and forceful that thousands of composers wrote in this style until the 1970s. The music of composers who did not write in some sort of twelve-tone system was not considered for performance. After the 1970s a change occurred because composers realized twelve-tone was not the only system of composition. Although there are still remnants of it, especially in Europe, composers went to other extremes shifting from the most complicated and intellectual to very simple writing. It was a necessary change which is part of life; at some point people don't accept rigid rules in music, politics, or anything.

Harvey Phillips is Executive Editor of The Instrumentalist *and Distinguished Professor of Music at Indiana University.*

How do you feel about the evolution of concert bands?

The evolution of the concert band is amazing to me. I remember being in Paris when I was given a commission by U.N.E.S.C.O. to write whatever I wished. I decided to write music for amateur bands in Europe, but they were not very good, so my writing for them was simple. I became interested in writing something for a community band, and it was then that U.N.E.S.C.O. told me about the hundreds of bands in the United States that were technically very good. When I came to Ithaca in 1954, they had an excellent band conducted by Walter Beeler. I went to concerts and was amazed by the quality, technical ability, and musicality of Ithaca's band.

In 1969 I began traveling to conventions and saw the evolution and interest of band directors, including Bill Revelli, Frank Battisti, David Whittwell, Bob Reynolds, Frederick Fennell, and Harry Begian. I was impressed by the vitality of these people, who wanted composers to write music for them. I was sure that bands would succeed with people who were as organized and who worked as hard as they did; I think they have. It was a pleasure to write for ensembles that performed my music immediately. Sometimes I wrote orchestral pieces and waited to have them performed but bands played my music right away, not just once but several times.

Having written important chamber works, how do you feel about chamber music, particularly the explosion of brass quintets in recent years?

This is so amazing. When I came to the United States in 1954, there weren't many brass quintets in Europe, and it was rare to hear just a brass quintet concert. A brass quintet would play one work and various combinations of instruments played the others. Composers felt they had to write short pieces for brass instrumentalists because they needed rest and could not play like strings or woodwinds. When I came to this country, I was inspired by a New York Brass Quintet concert of more than an hour and a half where everybody played the whole time. I remember they played modern American works here at Cornell, and I was astonished by all the colors they created with their instruments and mutes; it was a revelation for me.

What changes in music education have you observed over the last 25 years?

Students coming to college now seem more advanced than they were 30 years ago. Technically they are better, they know more, and the teaching can go ahead quickly. I am amazed that my grandchildren at the age of nine know much more than I did when I started on an instrument. One starts sooner with children who go into music, and they somehow seem to know much more than I did. I remember having undergraduate and graduate students thirty years ago who did not know as much as students do today.

As you travel the world to conduct your music, is it easier to bring performance levels higher than they were thirty years ago?

Definitely. It is also easier to raise the level of understanding. When I wrote *Music for Prague 1968*, a friend told me that the piece was so difficult only two or three bands in this country would be able to play it. Now it surprises me when I receive a tape from a high school band in Texas, and it is a terrific performance.

Have there been changes in audiences as well?

Yes, but not as fast as the students. Audiences are still a little behind, and I think the reason is that students hear the music in rehearsals numerous times and get used to it; audiences do not. Things have improved though, because 20 years ago *Apotheosis* was difficult for players to understand, and now even audiences accept it.

How should directors rehearse a piece of music that students have not heard before?

The conductor's attitude is very important; I always found it helped when I had a positive attitude and believed in a piece. I believe the Berg Violin Concerto is good music and have faith that in time students will realize its value. Conductors should be persistent and always present a piece in the most positive way, even if some rehearsals are disappointing. With new music, some rehearsals will not do justice to the music, but with classical music you know it's not the fault of the music. Even so, I would rather play new pieces with students because life is short. I always thought students would continue to play in the future, but many of them leave and go into another profession; even when they are in music, they may not have the opportunity to perform many new compositions.

If they understand what new music is to them, they can transfer it to others. I remember when I was in my last year at the conservatory in Prague, the Hungarian quartet Vegh performed Bartók's Quartet, and I was bewildered because to me it wasn't music. Now, when I listen to it many years later, I recognize that it is very close to Beethoven's Quartet. We have to help young people by explaining what new music is, and letting them play it enough to decide for themselves.

Do you think it's important for a director to share some insights into the composer and the work at the first rehearsal to get students interested and fired up?

Yes, I think it helps, and directors should also explain why a composer did certain things that the students do not understand immediately. Going into the unknown is important and exciting. We cannot always go into the forest and take the path that has been there for a hundred years; especially when you are young, you should go somewhere that everybody said not to. That is always what I like to do. To only play well known pieces makes students tired. In college I have noticed that students sometimes become bored when they play the same repertoire as in high school. If they had a good high school conductor, one who showed them new possibilities and taught them incredible things, they may be disappointed when they get into college and repeat the same things.

Did you use compositional or orchestration method books, or did you generate your own?

I used books and scores that existed, but it was easier for me to teach at Cornell because most of the students who came to me were already graduate students with the basic technique. Teachers guide students through the long history of music and teach the techniques Bach, Beethoven, Debussy, and Stravinsky used. When graduate students come knowing these techniques, they

Photographs © Louis Ouzer

already have some premonition of what they like. Many of them will hate the 12 tone system, but others will like it, and some of them will look to music of the past, while others will be incredibly avant-garde. I let them do whatever they like

because I think there is something in us that inevitably goes the way we have been educated to think, and we don't change too much. There's more evolution in that process than revolution, so I let students compose the way they want. However, if they are too academic or look for the past too much and are afraid of new things, I point them towards new possibilities and make them write something completely new that they have not done before. If, on the other hand, they bring me something incredibly new every time, and I have the impression that it doesn't have roots, or it is not solidly built, I advise them to go back and write a sonata similar to Beethoven's just to learn and try it. When students leave between the ages of 25 to 30, they are still young, and they should know what all the possibilities are so they can choose what they like. Composing is a matter of 30 or 40 years of hard work, like performing. The evolution of a composer and performer is similar because we continue to learn and develop. I would conduct a Dvořák Symphony differently today than 30 years ago, but I would not say that what I did 30 years ago was not good because it might have had something different. Music is written so one can present it many different ways.

Has the world of music made much progress?

I think we have definitely made progress, and I am also optimistic about what we have done in the world. There is no doubt that we have developed and live better than 30 or 40 years ago. I don't think there has been a failure of the teaching or evolution of music, but we could do better.

What problems do you see in the future for musicians?

While we have very able composers, unfortunately the problem is that there are too many and all cannot find positions. The same thing goes for performers, but that is not the fault of teaching. Naturally, we are producing too many musicians, but in a democracy everyone who has talent should get a chance. The problem is also that our society considers music and art mostly as entertainment. When people go to concerts they should expect that there will be something new or something that they can learn from in that concert. It may not be entertainment that they can dance to; it may be heavy, and they should expect that. I recently heard Arthur Miller say he is disappointed that he is asked to write plays to entertain the public, and he does not want to do that. There are a lot of people interested in music, but we have lost a lot of young people to rock music, and that is a problem. It is not a problem of having educated musicians, because we have terrific musicians; the problem is that the world today generally prefers easy and relaxing entertainment. □

Herbert von Karajan
a Great Artist and Conducting Genius

by Maurice Faulkner

During many years of observing top-level conductors in both rehearsal and performance, I have established my own ranking for them and their orchestras. Perhaps the one who has stood out for the longest has been Herbert von Karajan, artistic director of the Berlin Philharmonic, lifetime honorary conductor of the Vienna Philharmonic Orchestra, and the guiding light of the Salzburg Festival, where he began his career as an assistant to Toscanini, my early idol.

Through the years I have heard Karajan perform a number of works in a variety of concert and operatic halls and talked with him at length after rehearsals, attended his symposium on the relationship of the brain to musical performance and listening, enjoyed several conducting competitions that he sponsored in Berlin, and sat through innumerable orchestral competitions, also in Berlin under his patronage. I believe his artistic skill will probably reach its peak within the next year or so as he approaches his 75th birthday.

His recent career has been entwined with two great organizations, the Berlin Philharmonic and the Vienna Philharmonic, and it is with these ensembles that we must judge his contribution to the musical arts. Although personnel changes have had mixed effects on both orchestras over the past three decades, Karajan has put up with them and never remarked publicly about the distress they caused him. He continues to generate the lovely string tone quality for which the Berlin Philharmonic has become noted. According to some of my friends in the orchestra, he works diligently on pitch accuracy among the strings. However, a busy schedule of concerts, operas, recordings, and television appearances makes it impossible for him to give as much attention to other vital details as he might in less demanding circumstances.

My most recent experience with this great orchestra and its genial conductor took place on two evenings in early May (1982) when the organization celebrated its 100th anniversary in the Golden Hall of the famous Musikverein in Vienna, preceding the opening of the Vienna Festival. The 110 musicians performed for sold-out houses two great masterpieces: Mahler's Ninth Symphony on the first concert, and Beethoven's Ninth Symphony on the second. Roaring audiences greeted the appearance on stage of the orchestra members, the concertmaster, and the revered conductor. Karajan, whose health has suffered lately because of a battle with arthritis in his back and right arm, stepped onto the podium carefully with a slight limp, which he tried to disguise. After acknowledging the audience, he turned to his men and, without a score, molded the magnificent sonorities and subtleties of the Mahler with the delicacy and imagination of a great painter working in oils. Every phrase and dynamic nuance was guided by the maestro. His musicians are top professionals, so he seldom had to give entrance cues and could devote his complete attention to the music, bringing each element of structure into its proper perspective as the work moved from climax to climax.

My feeling about the second concert, Beethoven's Ninth, was less complimentary. When Karajan performs classical works, he usually doubles the winds to produce more sonority in the tuttis. To my ears this spoils the nature of classicism — that of the basic string sonority enhanced by a restrained woodwind and brass sound. (I have criticized him in the past for this practice in Mozart and Haydn symphonies, even early Schubert works and Brahms.) Karajan took the Beethoven Ninth and molded it into a Mahler-like texture with eight horns on four parts, four trumpets on two parts, and all woodwind parts doubled. Only the trombonists played one to a part. This method doubles the risk of intonation problems, overwhelms the strings and vocalists in the tuttis, and changes the overall complexion of the work. In the subtle aspects of the score, however, Karajan's interpretation was impeccable — true artistry of the finest standard.

We must not dwell on problems, however, but concentrate instead on the wonderful aspects of the music he has unfolded for us: his Wagner operas, Richard Strauss, Mahler, Bruckner, Debussy, and much more. As I worshiped the deeds of Toscanini in my youth, I now bow down to the great genius of Herbert von Karajan. Truly, I do not believe that the world will enjoy his artistry much longer, as his health may very soon dictate a less-demanding schedule. Therefore, I advise anyone who is interested to make pilgrimages to the musical centers where Karajan will be performing. The Berliners will come to New York in the fall of 1982 and go on to Mexico City in the same tour. Karajan will continue to work at the Salzburg Festival during the summers, July and August, until he can no longer conduct. His annual series in Berlin and his brief tours through Europe with both the Vienna Philharmonic and the Berlin Philharmonic may not extend beyond two years. Thus, I for one intend to spend as much time as I can in his presence during these next few years while he is still on the podium. ∎

Maurice Faulkner, now retired, taught conducting for many years at the University of California, Santa Barbara, and at Columbia University Teachers' College.

Witold Lutoslawski

Witness to 20th Century Music

by Bogdan Gieraczynski

Witold Lutoslawski first attracted public attention in 1937 with his work Symphonic Variations. In 1945 a music publisher asked him to write a cycle of easy piano pieces based on Polish folk songs, and he continued to use Polish folk material in his works culminating in his Concerto for Orchestra in 1954. It wasn't until 1958 that he achieved international recognition through his Funeral Music, a serial work dedicated to the memory of Bela Bartók. Lutoslawski later experimented with controlled aleatory, a technique he still uses, in Jeux Vénitiens composed in 1961. He has received both the Gold Medal of the Royal Philharmonic Society of London, and a Grammy Award for his Symphony No. 3. The 77-year-old composer lives in Warsaw.

Even the most original musical works come from some musical tradition. With what do you connect your music?

Twentieth-century music has split into two streams. One arose from the second Viennese School, from Schoenberg, Webern, and Berg, while the other came from Debussy. There is a widespread belief, cultivated by the heirs of the Viennese School, that Webern combined these two musical currents in his works. I find this idea farfetched. For the time being the two main traditions are still distinct, although it is possible that one day they might unite into one musical amalgam. As for me, I feel a part of the second tradition, that of Debussy.

Yet the work that marked the introduction of your style, Funeral Music, of 1958, is based on the serial technique. How do you account for this?

It is only partially a serial work. Every 20th-century composer is interested in the 12-tone row. I use it in my compositions in a non-tonal way, but my works are not necessarily dodeca-

phonic. However, the methods I worked on for the last few decades have nothing in common with Schoenberg's doctrine, apart from the use of all 12 tones in a relatively limited space; that is all that links me with Schoenberg's technique. It is possible to trace the technique of using all 12 tones in an abbreviated space to the early 18th century. It wasn't Schoenberg's invention! Josef Matthias Hauer came up with a similar theory, but because he wasn't as important a composer as Schoenberg, the significance of his discovery was overshadowed by the fame of his great colleague.

The 12-note scale was used before Schoenberg by composers who employed the tonal system, but not to its greatest capacity. Certain works by Scriabin, or even Strauss and Mahler, who were by no means dodecaphonists, foreshadow the use of the tone row. There's a fugue in Bach's *Well-Tempered Clavier* that proves this is a natural stage in the development of musical thought. It uses all the sounds of the chromatic scale; but it's not a 12-tone work, it's a tonal one.

Can we look forward to the emergence of a new musical convention or tradition?

The 20th century has revealed a wealth of possibilities in sound and the patterning of sound that still haven't been fully exploited. It is probable that a new order or convention for using sound media, something as sweeping as the tonal system, will emerge. The 12-tone system cannot be considered such a convention; in its pure form 12-tone music has already exhausted its inspirational and creative potential. We will have to wait for some kind of classicism to arise in the future. When we consider the vast wealth of musical potential that has been discovered in recent decades, as opposed to the small number of musical works characterized by great and lasting value, my optimism is well founded. Furthermore, the traditional scale with its 12 notes has not yet been fully exploited in terms of harmony; there are many possibilities to be discovered, independent of Schoenberg's 12-tone technique.

When did you first discover that music was your vocation?

At nine years of age I scored a little piano piece; but even before that, I improvised on the piano and realized that it was my fate to compose music. My search for a musical language and my efforts to develop it, which haven't ceased to this day, led me to write many different kinds of pieces over the years. During the period when I worked on the method I wanted to use in future compositions, my temperament wouldn't let me suspend my creative efforts. When Arnold Schoenberg

struggled to crystallize his 12-tone system, he didn't compose at all for eight years, but that kind of voluntary void would be unthinkable for me. For many years I wrote what music I was capable of, not yet being able to compose as I would have liked.

In 1949 your first symphony, a work that summarized all your previous musical experience, was banned in Poland and labeled as formalist. Why was that derogatory term significant in relation to a piece of music?

I never understood what formalist was supposed to mean. To me, it was nothing but typical art official's jargon, useful for persecuting artists who retained some individuality, whose creativity didn't conform to the obligatory socialist realism of that time. In any case my symphony was not performed in Poland for 10 years. After the last performance of the work at the Polish National Philharmonic Hall in 1949, the minister of culture stormed into the conductors' room and in front of a dozen people announced that a composer like me ought to be thrown under the wheels of a streetcar. This was not meant as a joke; he was really furious. While this story sounds anecdotal, it illustrates the artist's situation in Stalinist Poland.

Could you tell me the sources of your compositional inspiration in those days?

I don't suppose a composer ever lived who did not worship great artists in his youth. Copying favorite masters in order to learn their skill is not restricted to painters. In my musical career the works of various composers served as models. The Viennese classics, above all, Beethoven, as an unequalled master of large scale forms in general, and Haydn and Mozart were models. Despite my sincere love for the Brahms symphonies and concertos, they had a negative impact on me. My second symphony and string quartet oppose Brahms's concept of large scale forms as a matter of principle.

Among the Romantics, it is Chopin's work that moves me most deeply, and for me his music is a source of inspiration for my composing imagination. Another master whose work had a constructive influence on me is Albert Roussel. Even in my youth the thought that the riches of the French sound palette created by Debussy, Ravel, and their successors still hadn't been fully explored in large scale forms unsettled me. It was Roussel's *Third Symphony* (1930), that partially fulfilled this ideal. I should also mention that Bartók and Stravinsky's music made an enormous impression on me and every composer of my generation.

The various inspirations and imitations have a place in molding a composer's creative stance, but the time comes when all the outside influences undergo a process of elimination, and there comes a crystallization of the composer's personality, if he has one. For example, the form of my third symphony (1983) is the result of years of listening to music, particularly large-scale forms. Although Beethoven's extraordinary strategy in these forms always fascinated me, and was a supreme lesson in musical architecture, the symphonies before Beethoven, particularly Haydn's, served as my model. I confess that I feel exhausted after a performance of a Brahms symphony, concerto or even a sonata, probably because there are two main movements, the first and the last in each of them.

I searched for other possibilities and finally found a solution in a two-movement, large-scale form in which the first movement prepares for the main one to follow. The first movement attracts and involves, but never fully satisfies the listener. During the first movement the listener expects something more important to happen, and may even grow impatient. This is exactly the situation when the second movement appears and presents the main idea of the work. This distribution of the musical substance over time seems natural and agrees with the psychology of the perception of music. I have composed several works in this form, the most characteristic being my string quartet and second symphony.

What is the origin of aleatorism in your music?

In 1960 I heard a radio broadcast of John Cage's *Concerto for Piano and Orchestra* (1958) and in a flash I realized what potential this method of composing had. Cage's answer to the serialism of the 1950s was to create music entirely opposite to that doctrine, music as a product of chance, hence, the term aleatorism. This method had always been completely alien to me; nevertheless, that one encounter with Cage's music during the radio concert excited my imagination.

A composer can listen to music in two ways: passively, or in an active, creative way, so that the sounds activate his musical imagination. In a composer's imagination the sounds generate images and musical combinations that do not exist at all in the work being performed. That's exactly what happened while I listened to Cage's piece. I suddenly realized how meaningful it would be to instill my music with an element of chance, but in a controlled way. It was a vision of sound, an idea that I began to work on that very moment.

The outcome was music I called controlled aleatorism, limited aleatorism, or textural aleatorism; and I gave the name aleatory counterpoint to this compositional technique. These terms delineate a concept that was previously unknown. When I heard Cage's piano concerto again a few years later, I couldn't find a trace of what had so strongly stirred my imagination, but I have never hid my gratitude toward Cage and for what his work accidentally gave me. In the 1960s Cage asked me to send a rough draft of one of my pieces for reproduction in his book *Notations*. I sent him the full score of *Jeux Vénitiens* (1961), the first work I wrote as a result of listening to his *Concerto for Piano and Orchestra*. This story is an oversimplified picture of that crucial moment in my musical career, but it shows how mysterious and astonishing the sources of inspiration can be.

Jeux Vénitiens, which I wrote in 1961, was my first composition to use elements of the aleatoric technique. It doesn't seem overly innovative, but the consequences for enriching the rhythmic aspect of the composition without increasing the difficulties for its performers, and allowing free, individualized play on the instruments in the orchestra were enormous. It was these elements of aleatory that interested me most of all, because they permitted me a wide vision of sound otherwise impossible to notate.

I'm not interested in elevating chance to the dominant position in composition, or making it an element of surprise in each successive performance of the piece. Because the introduction of chance at a precisely anticipated moment in my compositions is only a means of developing the action, not an aim in itself, the composer is still important.

In my latest work, *Concerto for Piano and Orchestra* (1988), the element of chance appears to a lesser degree than in my other works. As always the principles of organization of pitch, harmony, and melody precisely control it. I explained how this works in an article published in 1969 in the periodical *Melos*. I won't repeat my line of reasoning here, but there is no improvisation in my work. Everything is notated and should be precisely carried out by the performers. There is one fundamental difference between the *ad libitum* sections, which are not conducted, and those which are divided into measures with a given meter. In the former there is no common division of time for all the performers, and each player performs as if he were playing alone and not coordinating with other performers. The result is a special frail texture with rich and whimsical rhythms, quite impossible to achieve in any other way.

All of this is connected with a matter of secondary importance, the means a composer uses to attain his goal. What is this goal? Only music itself can answer this question. Fortunately, it cannot be expressed in words. If a musical composition could be exactly related in words, music would be a completely unnecessary art.

Can you differentiate between inspiration and technique in your works?

Anyone well versed in composition knows that the rational factor dominates in my works. Mine is a deliberate, organized working technique. However, I ascribe fundamental importance to what used to be called inspiration. Although this term is a bit pompous and imprecise, it is irreplaceable in referring to the spiritual state essential to the act of creation: everything authentic in a piece of music is the result of inspiration. That which is usually called compositional technique, as opposed to inspiration, does not even exist;if it did, a work of art could be created without any sort of talent. I have used a style for decades that could go by the name of compositional technique. I accumulate specific, individual components that help in the overall task of organizing sounds, their pitch and their interplay. Everything that makes up compositional technique is a product of inspiration; it arises in the composer's imagination of its own accord, not through intellectual effort. It should intrigue; it should be original enough to make it worth coming back to again and again. The only way to make that kind of discovery, though, is through years of systematic work, sometimes drudgery. When a lady once asked Tchaikovsky if he worked regularly or waited for inspiration, he replied, "My dear lady, I work regularly; inspiration does not come to idlers." This is the crux of the matter: when you wait for inspiration, it doesn't come; but if you work regularly, like Bach or Mozart, then your reward is that something arises in the mind's ear, something attractive that didn't exist a split second before.

What do you think is the fundamental message of music?

I subscribe to an abstract concept of music. The only unambiguous message that music in itself can convey is a musical one. Music is music! Of course, that is not an adequate definition, because music strongly affects human emotions.

Some people interpret music in an extra-musical way. The world of sound alone is not rich enough for them; music alone cannot encompass their idea of music. Less sensitive listeners feel alien in the world of sound; their thoughts escape to a realm of images or feelings that do not exist in a given piece of music. This is a subjective reaction to music, but there are people of greater musical sensitivity, composers for instance, who do not have this anxiety reflex, who confront the sounds directly. They have no need to search for anything beyond the sounds themselves.

Because you view your creative work as an expression of truth through music, you have been unwilling to compromise and public acceptance of you as a composer has come late in your life. Can you explain how music can be truthful or not truthful?

The word "truth" as it applies to a work of art must not be confused with the common understanding of the term. A piece of music is true when it reflects a personal, original, artistic conviction without regard for the consequences. You may wonder whether this position is not utterly egocentric, and whether society needs art created on the basis of such principles. Society needs only such art. A work based on lies, on the abandonment of principles for the sake of pleasing the critics or the public, or to get applause or fame or money, those kinds of works are not only unnecessary, but also harmful. They are not the products of purely artistic motivation.

Paul Sacher, Anne-Sophie Mutter, and Witold Lutoslawski

Do you believe in the permanent and lasting value of your art?

I neither believe nor disbelieve. All I can say is I know from experience that some of my pieces, written decades ago, are still being played. Performers and audiences find some value in them, but this is not one of my overwhelming concerns. What interests me is using all the creative ideas and concepts that I still have, and producing new works. That is what I care about, not the question of the future of my compositions.

What does music mean to you?

That simple question is difficult to answer. Music is of immeasurable importance; it is a need as basic as water and air. I cannot imagine life without music, nor can I imagine the last half-century without composing. I can't give you a full answer. It seems I am not yet ready to have the last word.

Principal Works

Symphonic Variations (1938); *Variations on a Theme of Paganini for Two Pianos* (1941); *Symphony No. 1* (1947); *Concerto for Orchestra* (1954); *Funeral Music for String Orchestra* (1958); *Jeux Vénetiens* (1961); *Three Poems of Henri Michaux for Choir and Orchestra* (1963); *String Quartet* (1964); *Paroles tissées* for tenor and chamber orchestra, text by Jean-François Chabrun (1965); *Symphony No. 2* (1967); *Livre pour Orchestre* (1968); *Concerto for Cello and Orchestra* (1970); *Preludes and Fugue* (1972); *Les espaces du sommeil*, text by Robert Desons (1975); *Sacher Variation* (1975); *Mi-parti for Orchestra* (1976); *Novelette* for orchestra (1979); *Double Concerto for Oboe, Harp, and Orchestra* (1980); *Symphony No. 3* (1983); *Chain 1 for Chamber Orchestra* (1984); *Partita for Violin and Piano* (1984); *Chain 2, Dialogue for Violin and Orchestra* (1985); *Chain 3 for Symphony Orchestra* (1986); *Concerto for Piano and Orchestra* (1988).

Selected Discography

Werke für Orchester (six discs) EMI Electrola 1C 165-03 231/36 Q: *Preludes and Fugue, Symphony No. 1, Symphony No. 2, Concerto for Cello and Orchestra, Livre pour orchestre, Concerto for Orchestra, Funeral Music, Five Songs, Three Poems of Henri Michaux, Paroles tissées, Symphonic Variations, Three Postludes – No. 1, Jeux Vénitiens, Mi-parti*. Halina Lukomska, soprano; Louis Devos, tenor; Roman Jablonski, cello; Cracow Radio Chorus, Wojciech Michniewski; Polish Chamber Orchestra; Polish National Radio Symphony Orchestra, conducted by Witold Lutoslawski. Released 1978. International Record Critics' Award 1979.

Lutoslawski Conducts Lutoslawski Compact Disc Phillips 416 387-2 (also available on LP and MC): *Symphony No. 3, Les espaces du sommeil*. Dietrich Fischer-Dieskau, baritone; Berlin Philharmonic.

Lutoslawski Conducts Lutoslawski Compact Dics Phillips 416 817-2 (also available on LP and MC): *Cello Concerto, Dance Preludes, Concerto for Oboe, Harp, and Chamber Orchestra*. Heinrich Schiff, cello; Heinz Holliger, oboe; Ursula Holliger, harp; Eduard Brunner, clarinet; Symphonie-Orchester des Bayerischen Rundfunks.

Martha Argerich/Nelson Freire Compact Disc Phillips 411 034-2 (also available on LP and MC): Witold Lutoslawski *Variations on a Theme of Paganini for Two Pianos*. Martha Argerich and Nelson Freire.

Lutoslawski Compact Disc CBS M2K 42271 (also available on LP and MC): *Les espaces du sommeil, Symphony No. 3*. John Shirley-Quirk; Los Angeles Philharminic, conducted by Esa-Pekka Salonen.

Lutoslawski Compact Disc EMI CDC 7 49304 2: *Concerto for Cello and Orchestra*. Mstislav Rostropovich, cello; Orchestre de Paris, conducted by Witold Lutoslawski.

20th-Century Classics – Witold Lutoslawski Compact Disc Deutsche Grammophon 423 245-2: *String Quartet. La Salle Quartet.*

Witold Lutoslawski Compact Disc Deutsche Grammophon 423 696-2: *Partita* (version for violin and orchestra), *Chain 2*. Anne-Sophie Mutter, violin; BBC Symphony Orchestra, conducted by Witold Lutoslawski.

Witold Lutoslawski Compact Disc Thorofon CTH 2041: *Chain 2, Jeux Vénitiens, Funeral Music, Little Suite*. Krzysztof Jakowicz, violin; Pomeranian Philharmonic Orchestra, conducted by Takao Ukigaya. □

Andre Previn
A View from Two Continents

BY MICHAEL BUDDS AND EDWARD DOLBASHIAN

*T*he name Andre Previn evokes many images — pianist (both jazz and classical), orchestrator, composer, arranger, music director, conductor. Though Previn currently serves two major orchestras — as Music Director of the Los Angeles Philharmonic and as Principal Conductor of the Royal Philharmonic Orchestra of London — his talents have brought him lifelong recognition in many areas of music.

Born April 6, 1929 in Berlin, Previn was schooled at the Berlin Hochschule für Musik and the Paris Conservatoire. Previn's family moved to Los Angeles in 1939, and while still a teenager Previn began orchestrating films for MGM.

Performing jazz piano, conducting under Pierre Monteux, winning Academy Awards for his arrangements — *Gigi* (1958), *Porgy and Bess* (1959), *Irma la Douce* (1963), and *My Fair Lady* (1964) — and appearing as a concert pianist are some of Previn's early accomplishments.

A conducting debut in 1962 with the St. Louis Symphony pointed the musician's career toward positions at the helm of orchestras, both in Europe and the United States. First, in 1967, the Houston Symphony Orchestra became his home, then the London Symphony Orchestra, followed by the Pittsburgh Symphony Orchestra in 1976. In addition to his current positions in Los Angeles and London, Previn has guest conducted the Berlin Philharmonic numerous times and has been an annual guest conductor at the Vienna Philharmonic for the past 10 years. During a recent visit to the University of Missouri at Columbia, Previn discussed a wide range of musical issues, beginning by comparing programming in the United States to the situation in England.

Andre Previn: Because there are subscription series in America, I can do a program that has a major piece on it that might not be to an audience's liking; there might be fewer subscription people, but the seats are paid for. In England there is no such thing as a subscription series; every concert begins with the sale of one ticket. Therefore, it's much more important to fill the hall. Programs in England tend to be a lot safer. I could never have done the things in England I've done in Los Angeles in the last two years, except during festivals, because that's a different audience. If we do a Tippett symphony or a new American piece or a Dutilleux symphony, that's

taking a tremendous risk in England. In Los Angeles we give a lot of commissions every year; you can't do that in England. Of course I get angry letters. I did two Roger Sessions symphonies last year and I received a lot of hate mail. I'm not messianic about it the way, let's say, Boulez is. He says, "I'm going to educate you people, whether you want it or not." That's fine if you come for two weeks, but it doesn't work if you're the music director.

I have to do a lot of standard works, but they tend to be standard because they're that good. It would bother me if it were what I call the "New World Symphony syndrome" over and over again. I don't have that problem in Los Angeles. It becomes a matter of familiarity. I think if you know a piece well, you automatically like it better. If you could hear out-of-the-way pieces as much as you hear Tchaikovsky Five, you would have fans of these pieces. That's too large-scale a problem for anybody to work with. Last year I programmed a big symphony by Harold Shapero that was about 45 minutes, which by today's standards is huge. I thought it was a great piece. It was the focal point of one of our subscription weeks four times, and I feel so strongly about it that we're going to do it again this year, which is rare. Then I'm going to take it to New York with the orchestra. I have no idea whether people will come two years in a row to hear it, but I thought it was worth trying.

Michael Budds: What kind of approach would you take if you could choose the music you would like to program? Cite some composers or the percentage of music that would be new.

Previn: To be realistic, keeping in mind the responsibilities I have as a music director, I would

---

Michael Budds is a member of the musicology faculty at the University of Missouri at Columbia. He holds a Ph.D. in musicology from the University of Iowa. Budds was a contributor to The New Grove Dictionary of American Music *and wrote the book* Jazz in the Sixties *(The University of Iowa Press).*

Edward Dolbashian is Director of Orchestras at the University of Missouri at Columbia. He studied conducting under Otto Vernon Mueller at Yale and Charles Bruck at the Monteux Conducting School, as well as at Tanglewood and the Blomstedt Institute. He is director of the University Philharmonic and the Missouri Sinfonia, a faculty chamber orchestra.

think that 20% should be unknown music. You see, I think of new music as music that hasn't been heard in that city. It doesn't have to be something that was written last Thursday. It would be nice if one could do early Haydn symphonies, the earlier Dvořák symphonies, or the Brahms serenades instead of the symphonies. I'm not even being arcane. It comes down to this: If you're going to play a new piece of any consequence, then it's important to have Brahms One or Tchaikovsky Four or something standard on the same program.

Budds: You alluded to the difference between English customs and American customs. What are the primary differences between the European orchestral syndrome and the American one?

Previn: Europe is a different situation from England. Every year I work a great deal with the Vienna Philharmonic and also fairly often with the Berlin. (They are so government supported that their finances work on a different kind of level. They all make a lot of money.) The English orchestral musicians are the worst paid in any country in the civilized world. You can almost say they earn half the salary of an American orchestral musician. Therefore, they don't repeat programs and they will often take work that is not good enough for them. American and continental orchestras are under contract, which means, to oversimplify it, that on January 1 the bassoon player knows what he is going to be earning in June. In England, on January 1, the players don't know what they're going to be earning in April or in March, so when something is offered that doesn't look interesting musically, they'll take it because March or April might be a fallow month. It results in a lot of extraneous and, frankly, stupid work that they have to take on. The pay is less, the hours are greater, the work load is greater; but the English orchestras, in terms of spirit and playing expertise, are wonderful.

Next year the Royal Philharmonic Orchestra is going to be the first orchestra in the history of English orchestras to put its players under contract. We're doing it at the worst time possible, because the Arts Council doesn't want to know; the government is the same as the government here in not caring about the arts. We decided that if somebody doesn't give it a shot for a year, which will prove either extremely beneficial or very dangerous, then nobody will ever change the system. The orchestra players got together and voted on it.

Working with various orchestras I've seen that the work ambience in Los Angeles has nothing to do with the work atmosphere in Vienna, and that doesn't with London, and that doesn't with Berlin, and that doesn't with Paris. Yet a hundred or so professional orchestral musicians

preparing a concert is the same the world over. In some places they might wear a suit and in other places they might wear a T-shirt, but the attitude is more or less the same: they all work too hard, too much is expected of them, and they're all very dedicated, because if they weren't they'd do something else. There are easier ways to make a buck. At the same time, they want to get on with it. No lectures, please. No long stories about Beethoven's life at the time. Just do it. I found that works everywhere. Showing off one's peripheral erudition is beside the point, because the performers are there to play and go home. I don't mean that in any way callously, because when it comes time for the performance they put their blood on the floor.

Edward Dolbashian: I know that you worked with Pierre Monteux; and I'm sure that experience gave you some valuable insights into Stravinsky, Debussy, and Ravel, all of whom he had contact with. Unfortunately, that's a rare experience. This lineage from the composer to the conductor is dying out. Would you comment on your experiences in working with Monteux.

Previn: There was absolutely nothing about the orchestra Monteux didn't know. The man was an absolute walking encyclopedia. If you remember the premieres the man did, it was enough to boggle the mind. He was always good with students. He would say, "If it's on the page, let's hear it." As a result, most of his students, certainly myself included, tend to do Debussy, Ravel, and Stravinsky a little slower than is the fashion now. He would tell us, "All those little dots, all that infinite care, let's make sure you hear it." Doing it slowly is not always a popular thing with audiences; it can't be done if you're going for the effect of the whirlwind. Monteux is a real hero of mine; I worship that man.

Dolbashian: I had the good fortune of studying under Charles Bruck at Monteux's school in Maine for six summers. Bruck always would say, "Mr. Monteux said this, this, this; and you won't find it in the score, because he spoke directly to the composer." It seemed like a rare situation.

Previn: Yes, that is impossible now, if you're talking about composers of that ilk. In a miniscule and infinitestimal way I worked with Benjamin Britten and William Walton. A lot of things were passed on directly: "This isn't in the score, but...." There are certain composers of the younger generation whom I work with closely. I'm very fond of the music of John Harbison. I had him as composer-in-residence at Pittsburgh and took him with me when I went to Los Angeles. I've done a great deal of his work and believe in it strongly. I was pleased when he won the Pulitzer Prize last year. He and I are able to work a long time together before a performance, but that's harder and harder to come by.

Dolbashian: It does seem that a music director today needs to ally himself with a composer in order to forward his vision.

Previn: There's another problem. I taught at Tanglewood for about eight years, and now for the last two years I've taught at the Los Angeles Institute, which is also a good school. I found that young conductors often learn a piece from recordings; that's a death trap, because they are learning somebody else's performance. If I'm given a manuscript by some avant-garde composer and there's a tape of it, I want to hear the tape. I'm not proud. However, the student who's preparing for his first "Eroica" by learning it off of a recording is misguided. I think once he's learned the music and has conducted it a few times, he can hear how a major conductor does it if he wants. That's a great plus. In that way recordings are invaluable, but I think it's a mistake to learn something off a record.

Dolbashian: It is possible in this country to go to college and become a conducting major, earn your degrees, and be placed with an orchestra, with neither having played in an orchestra nor having been on stage as a musician making music at some high level. Is this also the case in Europe in conducting study? Is that the way it works?

Previn: I don't think it's much different in Europe. It is true, however, that most conducting students have had either orchestral or chamber music experience, or they have played in an orchestra, for example. It's invaluable. If nothing else, it helps the conductor in dealing with players at a rehearsal. Until you've done it yourself, you don't know what the musicians are capable of, either physically or psychologically. You can drive an orchestra completely crazy if you don't know how the members feel. I've seen some young conductors treat an orchestra as if it were an inanimate object: "Here, play this." It doesn't work. I always tell those people who are supposedly listening to what somebody else is saying that if they play an instrument, keep it up.

I play an enormous amount of chamber music everywhere and maybe five or six times a year perform a concerto and conduct from the keyboard. From the standpoint of actually physically producing the sound, performance is terribly valuable. Orchestral players like the fact that the conductor is going to gamble the same set of nerve ends that they gamble every night. Because, to be blunt about it, if the conductor makes a mistake, and misses a beat, who is going to know? The orchestra knows and you know, but nobody out there, or at least very few,

know. If somebody makes a wrong entrance on a clarinet or enters incorrectly on a trombone, everybody knows and I think players like it when a conductor openly does that kind of gambling.

Budds: What is your attitude toward the cult of the conductor? There's the idea that this is Previn conducting Beethoven and that there's a personal stamp we've come to expect the conductor to put on the music.

Previn: I think it gets dangerous when, for instance, on recordings the conductor's name is in bigger print than the composer's. You can see that often. No, I don't believe in that.

By the same token, I don't believe in an orchestra having a specific sound. Some used to say, for example, that the Philadelphia Orchestra had the "Philadelphia sound." That's impossible. I think the orchestra has to sound exactly the way the music being played dictates. If it can't, then the conductor is bound to be doing a disservice to somebody. As far as conducting is concerned, orchestral literature is just chamber music on a great big scale, and everybody has to drive. I don't like passengers. The conductor does about 75% of his work at rehearsals and then after that he makes sure that it's still happening.

Budds: Tell us about your early experiences with jazz and how the broad view of your musical world affects your role as a conductor and as a musician in general.

Previn: I was never a jazz player 52 weeks a year, but I did a lot of it. If I were to relate that to what I do nowadays, I would say it has given me a different kind of rhythmic impetus. Certain meter variances, ones that go across bar lines, for example, don't seem to bother me. Other than that, I don't think jazz has any direct bearing on what I do now.

Budds: It seems to me that many classically trained musicians are pagebound, absolutely compelled by the page. The idea of putting an ornament on something is not even considered, whereas that problem doesn't exist in jazz. You have a different perspective. I would think that makes a big difference, just in the way you feel about music.

Previn: In the way you feel about it, yes, not necessarily in the execution of it. I know what you mean.

Budds: Which pianists were you especially influenced by? Art Tatum?

Previn: Oh, in that field? You won't find anybody who has ever played jazz who won't say Art Tatum. Nowadays, I tend not to have the chance to hear too many people. So my heroes in that particular genre tend to be the same as they were 25 years ago, which are Tatum and Bill Evans and Oscar Peterson. I still enjoy jazz, but I don't play it anymore, simply because I conduct about 125 concerts a year and when you add to that the rehearsals, the studying, and the travel, and I'm always composing something, you see I don't have a lot of extra time. About 25 years ago I had to decide which areas in my musical work were expendable. I found that jazz was, even though it didn't lessen my admiration of it, and certainly the film work, which I stopped completely. The last time I was in a film studio was 1964. I don't miss it at all, but it was terrific training.

When I made that same point at Tanglewood someone said, "Well, I was offered to do the road company of a Broadway show and of course I didn't do it." I told him, "Well, of course, you're crazy." I believe that as long as there are living, breathing musicians sitting in front of you, who are going to play the way you ask them to play, then you'll benefit from the experience. I said, "If they ask you to do the Ice Capades, do it. Anything. It's better than nothing." Doing film work gave me great ease in orchestrating rapidly. Even though the music was certainly second-rate, and often tenth-rate, it had to be sight-read, rehearsed, and performed in as short a time as possible. It gave me a fairly secure rehearsal technique because I knew the difference between the things that needed rehearsal and the things that, with a good orchestra, would right themselves anyway.

Budds: On the way here, we talked about an issue that you had addressed, apparently at Tanglewood. It's the problem of conductors getting locked into stereotypes, such as the ballet conductor or the opera conductor.

Previn: That's sometimes inadvertent. With so many conductors and players making recordings early in their careers, success with one specific kind of music labels you as an expert. Within the confines of classical record sales, I had big successes early on with Shostakovich and Prokofiev, so everybody said, "That's what he does." Even today that still backfires on me, but it depends entirely on where I happen to be. In Vienna, for instance, where I perform several times a year, someone said to me, "You've done so much Mozart through Strauss, we'd love to have something a little different — some Russian music and some American music." Whereas in the States, if I do Mozart, they say, "That's a little out of Previn's territory, because he's more at home with Rachmaninoff." That's critics' talk and not to be taken seriously.

Dolbashian: I have a question about auditions for young musicians. Often a work like *Don Juan*, which requires a full symphony, can be put together quickly because the players have been practicing the excerpts all their lives and have the entire parts memorized. Do you have a core

Just out of high school, Andre Previn created the musical score for the MGM feature "Sun in the Morning."

of three to five pieces, let's say for violin, that you prefer to hear in an audition that provides a signal as to what the musician is made of?

Previn: Yes, I do. First of all, I never specify the material for auditions without a long session or sessions with the section leader involved. I always feel that the principal in each section is going to know more about the technical secrets than I do. I let him make up the list, which I then either amend or leave as is. I think you're right; the fiddle player who can't perform the beginning of *Don Juan* doesn't exist anymore. By that same token, with conducting auditions, everybody can conduct the end of *The Rite of Spring* by now. Everybody.

Dolbashian: By memory.

Previn: It's the only way. You can't afford to look down. But it doesn't mean all that much. The second violin part in Mozart's 39 is difficult for many other reasons. Schumann Two, the fast movement, is difficult. Every conductor gets his own kind of pet tricks that he wants to do. Generally speaking, however, the section leaders, the principals, do that very well.

Dolbashian: One music director of an orchestra told me that for their violin audition the first thing a player performs after his concerto is Mozart 39, the first violin part, the very first G to E♭. He reasoned that few violinists could correctly place their E♭ above a G in terms of pitch, and then sustain the sound, and then play the dotted rhythm.

Previn: There is also a long E♭ scale. I want to know if the player can do it without making the crescendo, which everyone makes, but which is not written. With violin auditions, which tend to occur more often than any other kind, a lot of things happen. Somebody comes up and plays the most outstanding Paganini caprices in the world but then can't play the Mozart symphony. Some produce the same sound on a Tchaikovsky excerpt as they do for a Haydn symphony. I tend to take that into consideration.

Budds: Changing the subject a bit, what is your perception of the quality of American music education?

Previn: I'm not familiar with the inner workings of Juilliard, Curtis, Indiana, and similar schools, but youth orchestras tend to be so spectacular now that it must be due to American music education. The National Youth Orchestra, the orchestras that visit Tanglewood or the L.A. Institute are technically staggering and absolutely unbelievable. They can play anything. I tend to think that American music education on that level is very good.

On the other hand, the music education system completely lacks the ability to instill some kind of need for music in young people who don't play instruments. Even centuries ago when I was in school, there was a course called Music Appreciation, which, if I hadn't already been on my way to being a professional, would have turned me against music. I think that if students could read even treble clef — anything — their knowledge would unlock many mysteries. With the exception of my youngest child, who shows signs of talent, my other kids don't really play. If they do, they don't play exceptionally. They all need music, though; they all love it. They play tapes in their free time, and they go to concerts because they grew up in that kind of atmosphere. I think that when people get out of school, they should know enough about music to make it a taken-for-granted part of their well being. Isaac Stern once said, "When I play in America, I often feel like I'm a luxury item, aimed at and designed for a specific group of people. When I play in Europe, I think I'm a necessity." That's nicely put.

When I first went to England 20 years ago, going to a concert seemed alien to a lot of young people because it meant blue suits, white shirts, and ties. I gave a whole season of concerts with the orchestra in shirts and sweaters until people started dressing as though they were going to the movies. It worked. I don't always advocate that casualness, because I think there's something to the theatrical nature of an orchestra being dressed for the concert. If students, especially university-age students, can't find a film they want to see on a Saturday night, it would be nice if they automatically checked the newspaper to find out what was going on in the way of concerts. I think the reason they don't is not the price of the tickets; it's because they feel they might be out of place.

Budds: I'm starting to worry about the numerous breakthroughs in technology that have had direct implications on the course of music. The great strides in electronic and synthesized and computerized instruments are eventually going to have a big impact on performers. For example, last fall on television I heard Barbra Streisand accompanied by a lush orchestra. At the end of the concert she introduced her so-called orchestra and it was three or four men playing synthesizers. It was phenomenally good. The sound of the cello was really the sound of the cello.

Previn: Honestly? I'm sorry to hear that.

Budds: Honestly. I presume that the orchestra will always exist as a museum piece, but I would like to think that it will go forward as a vital, alive tradition as well.

Previn: I know what you mean, and of course it's a worry. I'm not a big expert on synthesizers. There, you have to talk to others. In the long run I don't think they'll replace orchestras, not just as museum pieces, because three or four people approximating the sound of a Brahms symphony are never going to make a performance of it. If great music were only the production of the sound, you might have a case. For all I know, maybe synthesizers could do a sensational *Pines of Rome*, but if you're talking about music that is the expression of many individuals making music together, then I don't believe the machine will take the place of the orchestra. I'm clinging to that. There's so much attention paid to sound now.

I'm in the process now of a large-scale recording venture: the nine Beethoven and the four Brahms symphonies. A couple of months ago we did a musically terrific take of one of the Brahms symphonies, but the people from the record company told us, "We heard the clicking of bassoon keys." I said, "So what?" We had to do it again, because the people buying the recordings say, "Ah, what is that?" It goes against the grain for a musician, but on the other hand it's thrilling to hear things so well reproduced. I'm concerned because an entire generation has grown up on phenomenal-sounding recordings and the automatic acceptance of perfection. If you buy a

record by a major artist, there aren't going to be accidents, there aren't going to be mistakes, and nobody's going to rush or play out of tune because it'll have been taken care of. I find that unreal. I've made about eight or ten records with the Vienna Philharmonic. All are live-performance recordings and there are things in them that I'm sure certain record companies would not allow anymore. I can still recall doing them, but some of the records we've made lately I don't remember. I never know which take it is! It's terrific to have records at such a high level of reproduction available to everybody, but sometimes it does come at the expense of the performance and that worries me.

On the other hand, I'm not convinced by the people who perform on original instruments, either. I question the need to play a Beethoven symphony on the instruments of the time, or to make instruments sound the way he might have heard them. It's quite remarkable if you're talking about old music that has not taken a foothold in the symphonic repertoire, but because instruments are more secure now is no reason to negate them. Christopher Hogwood is a nice man, extremely gifted, and perfectly able to take ribbing. The last time we both worked in Boston I said to him, "You know, Chris, the fact that you have to go overtime on rehearsal, just to make sure that everybody plays out of tune, is beyond me." He was sweet about it, and he laughed a lot. It's just a difference of approach.

Just this past summer I was at the Institute in Los Angeles and coached some chamber music. I heard a remarkable group play the Mendelssohn Trio in D Minor, and the cellist made the most beautiful sound. I said to her, "Tomorrow, when you sit in the orchestra (we were in fact doing Brahms Four), you must be looking forward to that slow movement, that big tune." She responded, "I'm looking forward to it because I've been told it's so beautiful." I said, "You've never played it?" She replied, "No." I said, "You've never heard it?" "Not really," she said.

Instead of finding it funny, I thought, how I envy that woman, because she would suddenly have that moment when the literature would spring out at her. The problem is that it's difficult for the likes of us here in this room not to think, "Well, yeah, Brahms Four." I don't mean in its intrinsic value, but in the prospect of doing it again. For that woman, with her capabilities, to come across that music as a revelation would be wonderful. That's what conductors keep striving for. If you have to conduct, yet again, Beethoven Seven or Tchaikovsky Five you do your best to think of it as if you'd never heard it before, which is impossible in many ways. To have that happen for the first time is terrific. □

An Interview with Georg Solti

Kenneth L. Neidig

The combination of Georg Solti (pronounced "Shol-ti") and the Chicago Symphony Orchestra (pronounced *Sine qua non* by *Time* magazine) has been called a most successful "marriage" by many critics. It was consummated at a time when both seemed to be seeking the qualities possessed by the other. Today, six years later, there is an obvious compatibility based on mutual respect that seems to be growing into the deepest love.

This article was prepared from a tape-recorded interview with Maestro Solti in his office at Orchestra Hall, immediately following a Friday afternoon performance of *Decoration Day* (Ives), *Symphony No. 39* (Mozart), and *Symphony No. 2* (Elgar). Gordon Peters, principal percussionist with the symphony and administrator/conductor of the Chicago Civic Orchestra, joined us for part of the interview.

Sir Georg's comments have been adjusted slightly, "translated" from his English — often transposed, rapid-fire, sometimes cryptic but eventually decipherable and always charming, the product of a Hungarian childhood, fifteen years in Munich and Frankfurt, and the extremely productive ten years at Covent Garden that led to his being knighted by Queen Elizabeth.

In transcribing the maestro's very dramatic speech patterns, we were tempted to use musical markings to indicate the *tenuto* often applied to a particularly significant word or syllable, the terraced-dynamics of a repeated phrase, the *accelerando* leading to a climax . . . followed by a tender *sotto voce*. But perhaps the imaginative and musically sensitive reader will hear all of this in the comments that follow.

First, I would like to know about your conducting. What makes a good conductor? What are the qualities? Most of our readers are conducting all the time; what should they strive for?

Well, obviously there are two major ingredients for a conductor. One is talent, the other is experience — 70% talent and 30% experience. Even the most talented youngster will have very grave problems conducting in the beginning — partly technically, partly psychologically. That's natural in dealing with your natural enemy — the orchestra regards you as their enemy. OO-hoo! Why should he teach

Photos on pages 27 and 30 are by Robert M. Lightfoot III. These and many others appear in a new book, The Chicago Symphony Orchestra *.*

me? It's natural. Every child has that feeling. It's a revolt against their parents, the natural revolt against authority. So the conductor must overcome that feeling, and for a young man that is very difficult. All of us suffer a great deal from that problem — a question of age, a question of experience. More experience than age, because the orchestra doesn't reject a younger man. Never. It rejects someone with not enough experience, or who cannot beat properly, or is unclear or talks too much, or stops every time and all that sort of thing. Of course, the major ingredient is the talent.

Let's talk about the "tyrant" vs. the "new" kind of conductor.

Well look, the tyrant was a 19th or early 20th century phenomenon. Mahler and Toscanini were the two prototypes. Of course, now they would not be possible. There is no need for this today: the discipline is very much better, the technical abilities are much higher. Today you can go to a high school orchestra and find that the violins play together in a passage. But that wasn't true in the Vienna Philharmonic in 1904. So this has changed.

Do you think it's necessary to be tyrannical if there is a need for technical improvement?

No, no, no. Now look, our total conception of working together is changed, and we are working with an entirely different attitude today. It has to do with the liberation of the working class, and the rise of the unions. Toscanini threw out one player after another. That wouldn't be possible today; the union would react to the extent that we wouldn't be able to work anymore. That would be the end of it. Now this is all finished. There is this absolutely splendid joke — I think it's very significant because it gives the answer to one of the parts of the question. There was an oboe player in Toscanini's orchestra (the NY Philharmonic, not the NBC) who rode out every storm with complete calm, and he never lost his smile — even after the stormiest experiences. And so somebody asked him, "What is it? How can you smile? How can you take it?" "Oh, it's very simple," he said. "I have $20,000 in the bank." So it was easy — very fine and safe for him. But we have many examples in the past of musicians who just flew around like flies from one orchestra to another, because a tyrant conductor had fired them. That is not possible today; it is not necessary today. The whole situation has changed so much that the tyrant conductor is not needed. We are now working with a *consensus* so to speak. And, I think it is good.

Look, may I give you an example — and Gordon is a witness for what I'm saying. I am starting my sixth season with this orchestra. And I only raised my voice once in six years. It was a recording session — I had to shout and I lost a bit of my temper. But that was rightly so — somebody behaved badly... it doesn't matter. But only once in six seasons! Now what do you want? Isn't that a clear answer that there is no need for a tyrant? And the results are not worse because I'm not shouting.

There are still some school people we know who emulate the tyrant type of conductor.

That is not necessary. It's stupid! Emulate the Toscanini spirit in its true essence — that he lived and breathed the score — all day — that's what young people should emulate, not the shouting. The shouting is wrong, but the knowledge of a score, and the conscious study of the score...

Let's talk about that. How do you approach a score? What do you do?

There are all sorts of ways to learn a score. I'm very slow, I'm a sort of fly walking on the score. I learn tone by tone, up to down, bar by bar, very slow.

GP: *Do you learn by solfege? Learning the instrument pitches one at a time?*

Yes. But I do not sing anything — just inner hearing. Many, many years ago I used to work at the piano, reading the piece and playing it. This is very bad, because a piano is a sort of morphine — it kills your inner hearing. That's no good. The piano gives you a false picture of the orchestra sound. I have no instrument in my major learning place — our summer home in Italy. I do have a little record set there, and from time to time I play my colleagues' records (never my own — I just make them and I don't want to hear it again. But that's natural. I hear that all my colleagues are the same — the colleagues play my records, not their own. That's very natural.) But there are all sorts of ways to learn the score. Years ago I first worked through the music a little bit so I understood a little bit — I had an idea of the structure but no idea of the orchestration yet. Then slowly I would understand more and more, digging it out. Now I start with the digging, and then I build something out of the digging. When I *start* I have no idea of where it will lead. I just read... read...and try (like a printer) to put the letters together to make a word.

In order to have the proper idea I have to read it four times — once slowly, once a little bit faster, once still faster, and then in tempo...when I try to make music of it. And I pace myself. For example, if I have 30 days learning time for *Valkyrie*, I know that I will have to cover 440 pages of score — about 7-8 days for each of the four readings. This is a method which is mainly for opera conductors because of the huge amount of music that you have to learn, but I use the same technique with a symphony. It's a very complicated process. First, I'm reading very carefully — looking at markings, looking at tempos, looking at the metronome, checking everything very carefully. And then I try to make music. First 16 bars...or 30 bars...or two pages — put it together. Once I am on the way to a "harvest" — when I'm making music — I check myself, because very often a conductor has a feeling of absolute tempo but is really rushing, or makes a diminuendo and slows the tempo. I use a metronome to fix a basic tempo and to control myself all the time. Working with a Mozart symphony, for example, I will set the metronome on the table in front of me as I read through the score, conducting — just with one finger, very lightly — to feel the tempo. With the Elgar Symphony there is no need to use the metronome all the time to check what I'm doing, because there is a certain liberty. So check always, so that you control yourself. Never become a slave to the metronome, but do use it as a measurement of your tempo when you are learning the score.

At what point in the process do you mark your scores?

Immediately. I begin during the first reading, when I am studying the harmonization.

Do you do a lot of marking in the scores?

Less than previously. And never with colored pencils. My early scores looked like Renoir paintings. That's hysterical. It's all gone now, I just mark with a soft black pencil that you can easily see...

GP: *Am I right that the score you actually use for performance may not be the one that you studied from initially?*

No, most of the time it is the same score...

GP: *Don't you usually just mark orchestration, cues, ~~meters~~ on the performance score?*

No, no...the score is something like a friend, you know — you get used to it. Maybe it's a dirty score, but that's your friend...

GP: *With your own personalized markings...*

Yes, yes. In the past, there have been certain scores that I have marked up so much during a recording session I just had to get a new copy, but that doesn't happen under normal circumstances, only on recordings where you have to work so quickly. Listening to the play-back you have to make very quick notes — *right in the fever.* So it happens that you ruin your own score.

What qualities do you look for in the orchestra players that you really like to work with?

Obviously what should be, and what I expect from a player, is that he know his instrument and that he has a natural musical talent. Those two things — technique and musical talent. In the group which I

have the honor to lead at this moment, these are *given* conditions. We never have to say, "Use the fourth finger..." or that sort of thing. There's no time. Look, we are working incredibly fast. Last week's program was the Schönberg Variations, Tchaikovsky's 5th, Dutchman Overture — very difficult pieces. Many things (like bowings) are prepared in advance, but even so, we couldn't play programs like that if I had to work out the details with each player. Sometimes I will refer to a certain passage and say, "Maybe you should look at that." You can be sure with my boys that when I say, "Maybe you should look at that," there's no doubt that by the next rehearsal the passage will be taken care of. And you don't need to shout or raise your voice. You just say, "Maybe it would be good if you..."

GP: *What do you look for in players when you audition them?*

The same things, exactly — technical ability and musical sense. And I don't look for the "routine" or the "experience." That's not the thing I'm looking for, because the talented players get it quickly... very quickly. I never had any problem with any people in the orchestra who are talented, but lacked experience. All get it very quickly. Swimming...swimming a year or two, but then they have it.

The player must be a master of his instrument. I am speaking of standards for the Chicago Symphony; I wouldn't judge school orchestra players that way. But standards for that top class orchestra are: technical mastery, sound quality (a very essential point, so that we get neither a rough nor a harsh sound in any group), and musical talent. All together.

GP: *Included there would be a great ability to sight-read, is that correct?*

Yes, but I'm not very keen on that. I don't mind. I almost close an eye for that. If someone has the first three and can't read very well, I take him —

Solti's Score
Beethoven's 8th,
3rd movement

against the advice of committees, whom I sometimes over-rule — simply because *I know!* And I will never let down. There are many youngsters in this orchestra now, and they're all very good — they learn quickly, and they see elder members taking it seriously. This is the point! Once you come in an orchestra and you see that everybody practices, you jolly well immediately take your part home and you work at it, because you will not make a fool of yourself.

How effective is the Civic Orchestra as a training device?

Wonderful, wonderful. I just wish I could have more time with them. That's the only reason that I really wish I could be a permanent resident of Chicago. But I have some plans which Gordon knows about — a conductor competition — again working with an orchestra...really with the youngsters. This is a sadness that when I come here, my schedule is so incredible — like this evening is a Civic Orchestra concert — my wife will go — but after such a long symphony program I just can't go and listen to a concert. I just can't.

Tell me about the conductors' competition — the things you noticed in younger conductors — the strengths, the weaknesses, the things that they might work on improving.

I found a great deal of talent in these young people and I enjoyed the whole competition tremendously, so I want to do it again. Fairly soon. I enjoyed working with them; I enjoyed very much seeing the progress which is possible even in a week. It was very enjoyable. I find a great deal of talent. Most of the problems are, naturally, the inexperience.

You mean that they too might go to an opera job with only one work in their repertoire?*

No, I'm not saying this. Look, that was an exception — an exceptional situation (dare I say an exceptional talent also?). Under normal circumstances, that would not happen, could not happen, and *should not happen*. It's a sheer miracle that I survived. Sheer miracle. So that is not the right way to do it. But go to the opera house? Yes! If he can, I would advise every young conductor to start in the opera house, then come to the symphony. That's the best way to do it.

How about conductors coming out of the orchestra — former players — does that work so well?

It very often does. Very often does, very often not. It's always a question of talent...there is no rule. The major talent questions include the leadership question, namely, "Can you lead an orchestra?" This you cannot learn. This you are born with; you can never learn it. That's the sadness.

You can have a great musical talent, but if you haven't got that feeling of *pulling* — split-second beat-

ing before the music is played — just that split second. Not beating along with or after the orchestra. The sad thing is that you can't learn it. I saw 100 young people in this room and within five minutes — no, actually within two minutes — it was perfectly clear who will never make it. The negative is perfectly clear immediately. The positive — how far these young people will go — is much more difficult to say. That depends on talent, not only musical ability, but also on the industriousness. This is a slave profession. You must work — work, work, work, work. It is nothing else. And of course, if a young man comes to me I don't know how *industrious*, I don't know how *ambitious* he is. But the conducting talent — yes or no — that you can see in two minutes.

Let's talk about those kids that I know you are anxious to get home to see. What plans do you have for their musical future? What would you — as a father — like to see happen to them in the public schools as far as music education goes?

Yes...that's a very good question, a very important question. Let's assume that my children are perfectly normal children, not very musically talented, because if you are talking about a very musical talent, he or she will always make his way. So we don't talk about that. Let's talk about a normal child who has a certain musical background, who has a home in which they are listening to music. Now, what I would like to see in the school where both of my daughters will go is that they will be teaching them to *love* music. And how can you do that? To explain. To play any sort of music — I don't mind playing jazz music also, it does not have to be "high-brow," there's no need for it — it could be anything. *Peter and the Wolf*, Prokofiev, is my favorite piece for my little daughter. She adores it. Just adores it! It doesn't matter *what* you play as long as you have a teacher who from time to time will point out the beauty of certain things — the interesting things, the funny things. It doesn't matter. Just get the child interested to a certain point. Because, if you like music, even if you're not talented, it can enrich your life so incredibly. Nothing in this world can give you so much pleasure as listening to good music. But that must start at an early age — at a very, very, early age. If I were Mayor Daley, I would make a special grant for music, and I would select the best possible people to get music going here. I have told some people that I would be willing to hold a seminar for all the music teachers, to get them together in this house...and I would like to do it very much because here in America the music appreciation is not good enough in the schools. Too little is happening. And that is an essential point that I am missing in America — it's not that I am looking for musicians: I am looking for *human education*. Music teaching must be done with great psychological talent, because if you play something too difficult, the children will not respond. Most of the time I can make my elder daughter (4½) aware of something funny. This is the age when everything must be funny. It doesn't matter. It absolutely doesn't matter — as long as she listens! And this is what I'm aiming for, this is what I'd like to see for every child in this community. Every child. A basic musical education. ∎

---

*Note: After a long period as an opera coach (répétiteur), piano virtuoso Georg Solti was given the opportunity to conduct *The Marriage of Figaro* at the Budapest Opera in 1938. The following year he went to Lucerne to see Toscanini (Solti had been his assistant in Salzburg). Since Hitler had taken over Hungary, the Jewish Solti stayed in Switzerland throughout World War II, but could not conduct because of Swiss work permit laws. After the war, when the U.S. Occupation Forces were looking for conductors with no Nazi connections, they found Solti. He learned *Fidelio* in a hurry (his second opera!), conducted it successfully at the Bavarian State Opera in Munich, and wound up as their musical director.

Giulini: On Preparation, Rehearsal, and Performance Gerald M. Stein

How should a musician approach a score? If you question Carlo Maria Giulini, music director of the Los Angeles Philharmonic, he may first give you an example of how not to do it. In 1945, years before his appointments as music director of La Scala and principal guest conductor of the Chicago Symphony, Giulini was asked to perform Bach's Brandenburg Concerti. He had only recently conducted the first post-liberation concert of Rome's Augusteo Orchestra. Yet he could not accept the new offer. "I said I wasn't ready, that I was too young and inexperienced to play this great music."

The concert promoters were not so easily thwarted. The maestro was asked to set aside his personal feelings so that he might give music's solace to a war-torn and suffering people. The appeal worked, but it was with an attitude of respect if not trepidation that Giulini performed the music — "the do-not-touch approach" as he calls it. By holding the score at arms length he "killed" the music. Moreover, the performance was so personally unsatisfactory that he did not conduct a single note of Bach again for over 20 years.

"It is my fault if I don't understand," Giulini explains. "If I am not convinced of every note, I will wait until I am to perform a piece. When you are dealing with a work of genius, if you don't understand something it is your fault. I don't want to do something just because I can read it." Not surprisingly, Giulini has been criticized for his slowness to take on new repertoire. His response to the charge emphasizes that this is by design. "I always say it is better to be three years too late than three minutes too soon. It took Mozart two days to write the Linz Symphony, but it takes me two weeks to get ready to rehearse it."

Clearly, the maestro doesn't take his commitment to music lightly. Indeed, he might be called a method conductor. The 66-year-old artist articulates his beliefs in a highly stylized English: "An interpreter, in the moment he is involved in a great expression of art, becomes himself the composer. A great actor, in the moment he is playing Iago, has to be Iago. A great interpreter must live with a deep, 100% conviction in what he is doing. No one should misunderstand, no one should

---

Gerald M. Stein, who received his doctorate in clinical psychology from Northwestern University, has been on the faculty of Rutgers and Princeton Universities and is currently the coordinator of Continuing Medical Education as well as associate director of research at Forest Hospital in Des Plaines, Illinois. Stein's commentary on music has been heard over WNIB Radio in Chicago and has appeared in the Chicago Tribune and the Musical Heritage Review.

think we are here for ourselves; we are here to serve the music. But we shouldn't be humble in the moment before we perform."

How then should one prepare for this moment? "After many years I have arrived at this opinion: the composers themselves do not know exactly what they want from their music. They write the music, of course, but the sound is always a mystery. Take Mahler, who was not only a great composer, but also a great conductor. He had an experience of sound, of balance, of everything. Yet he changed the score after the first performance.

"Beethoven, for example, lost contact between the ear and the sound. This didn't affect his imagination because his imagination had no limits; but you see sometimes in the scores that the contact between his image of the sound and the reality of the sound is gone. If you think of the climax of sonority of the Missa Solemnis in the *Agnus Dei*, where all the orchestra is fortissimo — one bassoon is playing. If you had 50 bassoons you still couldn't hear it.

"Music has this problem. We have a note in music with the value of one; we know the quarter note is double the eighth note. But we don't know how much is one. What does a quarter note mean? Nothing. Nothing. Absolutely nothing, because a quarter note can be long, can be short; and what does adagio mean? Piano? Forte?

"You know, Toscanini once told me that he wanted to do the *Four Sacred Pieces* by Verdi. And he had the feeling that at one point he had to do a small ritardando that wasn't written. So he got an appointment with Verdi though he was very young and very afraid of going to this old man. Verdi asked Toscanini to play the piano and when he arrived at this point he did a small rallentando expecting an explosion from Verdi. Nothing happened.

"At the end Verdi said, 'Alright. Good.' So Toscanini said, 'But I did this small rallentando which is not in the score,' and then Verdi became angry. He said, 'We can't write everything — the composer can write a few things, but not everything. The musician has to understand and do it.'"

"This is marvelous and horrible at the same time because of the responsibility. We have to know Beethoven, Brahms, Mozart, Verdi — what they really wanted. For an interpreter everything is hard, nothing is easy."

Giulini has made music from both sides of the podium. In pre-war Rome he moved from last to first viola in the Augusteo Orchestra, playing under such men as Furtwangler, Strauss, Reiner, Monteux, Mengelberg, and Klemperer. His experiences there affected his attitude toward rehearsal. "The contact between a conductor and musicians depends in part on the human per-

sonalities involved. During my first year in the orchestra as twelfth viola, we played the Brahms First Symphony with Bruno Walter. At the end of the performance I had the impression that I played a First Brahms Symphony for twelfth viola solo and orchestra because I was so involved. Walter gave to all the musicians the sense of their making music, of the importance of their playing."

For Giulini this human contact is paramount and explains why he took 18 hours of rehearsal in preparation for his 1978 inaugural concert as Los Angeles' Music Director. "It wasn't just the Beethoven Ninth I worried about. There was more involved. This wasn't just a musical start. I wanted to make human contact with the orchestra, to establish a rapport. We needed to listen together, play together, to work toward achieving a common language."

Still, he is usually content with more limited preparation time. "I prefer rehearsals that are both short and concentrated. I like to work very intensely. When you know what you have to do, it is much better to be rested and fresh for the performance, than to repeat what you already know."

It is for others to explain the means by which Giulini accomplishes his goals within a short rehearsal time. According to Jacques Israelevitch, concertmaster of the St. Louis Symphony, "Some conductors, like Giulini, come with their own material, completely annotated. They know exactly what they want and why . . . and I think it's important for the conductor to pay attention to that sort of thing because it very much changes the sound of the strings."

Dale Clevenger, the Chicago Symphony's principal horn, feels the same way about Giulini's markings: "Giulini does it in very strategic places for very good reasons. Once you play it, you see why he's done that — an orchestration is too heavy for one to hear what's really important so he brings you down. When we're going over a rehearsal he plays it through and if he doesn't hear what he has written he asks, 'Did I write in this?' and if it's there and you didn't do it, then obviously you didn't do enough of it. But he doesn't have to go over the entire piece and tell you every little thing he did.

"Giulini has a very strong opinion, and it's studied and it's reasonable to him why he does things; but sometimes he will come up and admit, frankly, that he doesn't know what to do in this spot. He says, 'I've thought about it, studied it, I don't know, I can't understand it. It says one thing in the score and I've done another thing and nothing seems to work' or 'Let's try it this way tonight and maybe another way tomorrow night.' Once in a while things like this will happen, but 95+% of the time he knows exactly what he wants, exactly the effect."

However sure he is of what he wants, Giulini does not forget Bruno Walter's lesson. Here perhaps, is the key to the admiration he receives from audience and orchestra alike: "I try when I do a rehearsal, not to impose, but to convince. If you do something because it is imposed, you do it another way. So I try to bring out the best from every musician, the best of himself. If it is necessary, I give them, within the limits of the general conception, the freedom of a soloist. If an instrumentalist has to do a solo, if he stays within the character of the interpretation I'm very happy to help him and to give him the possibility to express the best of himself."

On the subject of expressing the best of oneself, only Giulini's music making speaks more eloquently.   ∎

Claudio Abbado
The Human Touch

Jean Oelrich

"I have the greatest respect for musicians. Some conductors may think, 'I am the dictator. The orchestra doesn't matter.' I try to maintain good communication with the musicians. We cooperate in creating the performance."

If there is any secret to Claudio Abbado's successful international conducting career, it must certainly be the warm, sensitive, and very human way he communicates his love for music to an orchestra. Musicians have commented that under his direction they play better than they are normally capable of performing. When asked how he inspires musicians to reach for the highest in themselves, he shrugs modestly and says with a shy smile, "I think the human approach is very important to establish a rapport for a wonderful collaboration with the musicians."

A soft-spoken maestro from Milan, Abbado conducts everything from memory, including complicated contemporary works and Wagnerian operas. This enables him to maintain intense eye contact with musicians throughout a performance. In conversation he reveals that his guiding principles are always "what is best for the music and what will help the player." Freed from the printed score, he has an uncanny knack for intense musical communication almost verging on the extra-sensory. "Sometimes, I can tell if a musician is going to make a mistake a fraction of a second before it happens. For example, I may sense a player is unsure about an entrance and so I try to help." The flexibility to be able to help players at the very moment when they need it most stems from Abbado's heightened awareness of the present moment and his formidable powers of concentration.

A Commitment to Youth

Even in relaxed conversation this intense concentration is immediately apparent. With a riveting gaze he enthusiastically suggested we begin by discussing his active involvement with the European Community Youth Orchestra. Abbado's face lights up when he talks about this superb ensemble of talented young musicians (ages 14 to 23) recruited from 10 Western European countries. In spite of a busy conducting schedule, he sets aside six full weeks every summer to work with the orchestra, rehearsing the musicians on the music for their annual summer tour. He also conducts the ensemble on shorter tours in the spring. His dedication to nurturing tomorrow's talent is so strong that he works without salary. Perhaps Abbado's comitment to this orchestra can be explained with these sentiments expressed by Andreas Papandreou, Prime Minister of Greece, who recently acknowledged the orchestra's success:

The European Community Youth Orchestra does not simply accomplish a very important cultural task, its structure and operation underline a deeper concept: The enthusiasm of youth is the foremost pillar of our expectations for a better world. The language of music, a language without boundaries, always brings a message of peace, friendship, better understanding and communication among nations.

To the young musicians in this orchestra, Abbado brings the unique musical insight that only a world-class conductor can offer. He explained how this fine training orchestra came into existence.

"I had been working with young musicians in Parma for two years, teaching them chamber music. I was invited to conduct the International Youth Orchestra in Aberdeen in 1974. After our concert in London I thought it would be nice to have a European Youth Orchestra composed of all the best young European musicians. So we started auditioning musicians from all over Europe. Now we do something like five or six thousand auditions every year throughout Europe. These musicians are really fantastic. Technically they are good and they have a lot of enthusiasm; that's the best thing."

Obviously their youthful enthusiasm is infectious, because Abbado speaks animatedly of the time he spends working with them for the 10 days before the summer tour. "We get together first at some convention center, usually Courchevel, near Mont Blanc surrounded by the Alps. It's a wonderful place. There is a beautiful hall there for rehearsals, and the restaurants, swimming pool, and hotel are all together. These are incredible young musicians. When they arrive at the first rehearsal, they already know the pieces by heart because we send them the music four months in advance. They have such enthusiasm and discipline that I never have to say one word during rehearsals." Raising his eyebrows in astonishment, he continues, "And you know, after I finish the rehearsal, they stay there to work some more and then play chamber music until midnight or one o'clock in the morning!"

When asked how it is different working with young musicians rather than professionals, he replied, "There are a lot of sectional rehearsals. We invite some of the best teachers from around the world to coach them, such as Lynn Harrell for the cellos, Thomas Brandis, the concertmaster of the Berlin Philharmonic for the violins, David Searcy from La Scala for the percussion section. Every year there are different teachers. In the summer of 1982 we had many of the winds from the Chicago Symphony as coaches — Adolph Herseth for the trumpets, Dale Clevenger for the horns, Ray Still for the oboes.

"Sometimes I rehearse certain spots more carefully, more in depth than I would with a professional orchestra. A professional player in an orchestra knows the standard repertoire, but young musicians are still learning these pieces. When we do the auditions, however, we are looking for the same qualities anyone would expect from a professional musician: musicality, technique, sound, and an understanding of the music.

"But in the end, they are musicians, and they are good musicians! I relate to them the way I do with my children: I remember to always speak with them as people; age is no problem. I receive fantastic letters from these young musicians. There are many good friends now in the orchestra and our relationship is really something special. Many musicians who played with the E.C.Y.O. are already playing now in major orchestras all over Europe, such as the London Symphony or at La Scala." Abbado's recording of the Berlioz *Te Deum* with the E.C.Y.O. testifies to the extraordinary performances he inspires from this talented group of young European students.

Musical Development

For someone who is so concerned about music and today's youth, what are his own musical memories from childhood? "My father was a violinist, my mother played the piano, and in fact, everyone in the house was playing music except my youngest brother who is an architect."

As a schoolboy of eight, Claudio Abbado felt his first aspirations to become a conductor when his older brother took him to a concert at La Scala in Milan, his hometown. The conductor that night, who made such a lasting impression on the young Abbado, was the aging Antonio Guarnieri. "You know how Fritz Reiner conducted with very small gestures? Guarnieri was this kind of conductor, just one finger, no left hand, nothing. The orches-

tra played wonderfully. I heard Debussy's *Nocturnes* for the first time, and I thought, that's something I'd like to do one day. Before that I was not certain; then I was positive. I wrote in my diary, and from that day I decided to be a conductor."

Abbado began studying piano with his mother and later enrolled at the Verdi Conservatory in Milan where one of his teachers was Carlo Maria Giulini, for whom he has nothing but praise. "As a man and as a musician who understood orchestras, Giulini was marvelous, a great human being." After finishing his studies at the conservatory he left for Vienna to study piano with Friedrich Gulda and conducting with Hans Swarowsky.

Under Swarowsky's guidance, Abbado learned many invaluable lessons and began to develop the phenomenal memory that is such an integral part of his conducting style. "Swarowsky felt it was a good method to conduct from memory. If you take Wagner's *Lohengrin*, for instance, you think: 'Oh, my God, it's impossible to study all this by memory.' But then if you start with 16 bars and you study just those 16 bars or 8 bars or even only 4 bars, it becomes possible. I divide the music up into smaller sections, not mathematically but according to the structure of the piece. I always keep in mind the musical arc, such as the introduction to the first theme. When you study architecture you see that there are big arcs and then many smaller arcs. Music is constructed like that; so you study all the small arcs and then you put it together into one larger structure. In a way, memorizing is psychological."

Although he admired Swarowsky's teaching ability, Abbado feels he could never teach conducting. "One of the reasons I don't teach is because a teacher has to examine all aspects of conducting technique to try to understand and to tell the students what they have to do. If I had to analyze something that is natural for me, then maybe it would no longer be natural. I think everything has to be spontaneous."

Surprisingly enough, Abbado doesn't feel that conducting came to him naturally. "I don't think I'm a born conductor. I remember when I was studying in Vienna, Zubin Mehta was a classmate of mine at the Vienna Academy. He was already a fantastic conductor. He was a born conductor, and I was not. No, I had everything inside me, but maybe because I wasn't so extroverted as Zubin, it was more difficult for me. I am introverted, but I knew that there was something inside me that would take off, so I tried to learn how to conduct, how to express myself.

"Swarowsky was a great teacher. He always said to us, 'I am teaching for idiots so I have to teach a thousand different ways. Then you can pick up what is best for you.' One thing he did to develop independence between the left and right hands was to have us play Stravinsky's *Le Sacre du Printemps* on the piano with the left hand while conducting with the other. Then he would have us do the opposite: play with the right hand and conduct with the left.

"It's very important to be able to anticipate what is coming up in the music. On the piano, you may be playing one line, but you must already know what is going on in the next three or four bars. When you're conducting, you need to think ahead so you can give an important upbeat or cue to an instrument."

While studying in Vienna, Abbado eagerly seized opportunities to observe such famous conductors as Klemperer, Walter, and Scherchen in rehearsal. "The Musikverein was closed for rehearsals, but Zubin Mehta and I decided to sing in the chorus. That was the only way to listen to the rehearsal." He wistfully recalled the wonderful performances of his student days in Vienna. "I remember Beethoven's *Missa Solemnis* with Szell, the Brahms *Requiem* with Karajan, Mahler's *Second Symphony* with Krips — a great experience."

Of all the great conductors, who did Abbado idolize when he was growing up? Without any hesitation, he answered emphatically, "Furtwängler. Even though I felt Toscanini was a fantastic conductor, I preferred Furtwängler for all the German repertoire from Schubert and Schumann to Brahms, Wagner, Strauss, and Bruckner. I heard Furtwängler at La Scala, but then I also heard all of his recordings. For me he was really a most profound musician capable of creating incredible tension." Sharing the excitement of past musical memories Abbado continued, "I remember Furt-

wängler walking onstage at La Scala. Already before the music started there was something in the air like electricity. There was some sort of magnetism that he had."

International Success

After exposure to the highest artistic standards of a cultural capitol such as Vienna, Abbado headed for the United States to join the conducting class at Tanglewood in 1958. He was able to conduct at least one piece every week and that summer won the Koussevitzky prize. In 1963 he won the Dimitri Mitropoulos International Conducting Competition in New York. With that award came a year's residence as an assistant conductor of the New York Philharmonic. In the mid-sixties he made an impressive debut at the Salzburg Festival at Herbert von Karajan's invitation. Eventually at age 34 he was invited to become the principal conductor of La Scala in 1968 where he set about building the orchestra and expanding its repertoire to include more contemporary works. Under Abbado's direction La Scala presented several world premieres and major new productions.

Abbado has conducted every major orchestra in the world. After a series of successful concerts with the Vienna Philharmonic in 1971, the members of the orchestra invited him to become their Principal Conductor. In 1979 after eight years as Principal Guest Conductor for the London Symphony its members also elected him as their Principal Conductor. In 1981 Abbado accepted a three-year position as Principal Guest Conductor of the Chicago Symphony. He establishes a personal rapport with all the orchestras he works with regularly and has special feelings for each of them.

"The La Scala Orchestra is different from all the rest because it's really an orchestra that grew up with me. In it there are many friends and musicians who studied with me. There are many pupils from Parma where I taught for two years and also many who studied with my father. So we all know each other. When the Vienna Philharmonic plays Bruckner or Brahms, it is fantastic. The orchestra plays slightly behind the beat and gets a warm, rich sound. The Chicago Symphony has an incredible sense of professionalism. The brass and winds are fantastic, and there are very good cellos and double basses."

A smile plays at the corners of his mouth as Abbado thinks of the London Symphony. "They are a very flexible orchestra with good humor. They learn very fast and there is a good feeling there." When the London Symphony came through Chicago on tour recently more than a few musicians mentioned that "Claudio," as they all call him, is a warm, approachable man whom they enjoy working with and whose musical insight they greatly respect. Both the London Symphony and Vienna Philharmonic are self-administering orchestras and could choose any conductor they wanted. What is it about Abbado that so many musicians prefer working with him over anyone else?

901

Perhaps it is because his understanding of human nature is as comprehensive as his grasp of music. He states simply, "Musicians love to play music. I know that they don't want to listen to conductors talk, talk, talk — so I don't speak much during rehearsals. During a concert you can't talk to the orchestra, so each and every gesture you make is important for the music. Because I don't rely on words so much, musicians become accustomed to watching carefully from the very first rehearsal. This is the reason why I conduct so many scores from memory. I think there is better communication between conductor and musician if there is more eye contact."

Because he doesn't agree with the dictatorial approach to conducting, Abbado encourages feedback from instrumentalists. His refreshing lack of egocentricity stimulates truly creative music-making. With genuine sincerity he states, "My concern is always what is best for the music. Sometimes an idea may come from a musician in the orchestra. If they know better than I, why shouldn't I listen to them? Normally, the conductor knows what is best for the music because he is working from the complete score, but sometimes a musician might know a solo better than I. Good communication and cooperation with the musicians is very important."

Tools of the Trade

Unlike some conductors who specialize in contemporary music or works of certain composers, Abbado is equally at home in the opera house or concert hall, conducting everything from Bach to Berg and beyond. How does he approach a new score that he has never conducted before? "First I try to read it like a book. If necessary, I play it on the piano if parts of it don't already sound in my head. Then I start to study it and analyze the musical structure. Memorization comes later, when I know the piece. Although sometimes I study,

study, study, and it's already memorized. I don't mark very much — just little things, essentials." And as if to illustrate that point he handed me his score to *Lohengrin*. Glancing quickly through the opera, I was amazed to see only a few neat markings at critical points.

A Chicago critic once observed that Claudio Abbado is "a distinguished conductor who speaks softly and wields a powerful stick." Certainly Abbado's laconic rehearsal demeanor belies the panther-like intensity he unleashes in performance. During rehearsals he works quickly and efficiently, making brief, verbal comments only when absolutely necessary. With the objective scrutiny of a Swiss watchmaker sensitively manipulating a delicate mechanism, he touches upon only those aspects of the music requiring adjustment. It is as if in rehearsal he is coolly observing the music-making, whereas in performance he generates electricity and tension by actively participating in it. Perhaps this accounts for his magnetic stage presence and a conducting style marked by a perfect balance between head and heart.

Abbado's interpretations are always distinctive for their fresh transparent sound quality, elegantly sculpted phrases, and startling dynamic contrasts. Even old familiar works sound new and exciting, as if one is hearing them for the first time and the composer's ink is still wet. How does he consistently obtain such exceptional performances expressing the entire range of human emotions?

"I try to focus on the strengths and weaknesses of each orchestra. Here in Chicago there are fantastic brass players, who are very solid and very loud. Sometimes they cover up the strings. So I try to get more sound, a warmer sound from the strings. To do that I think always of bowing. I give them time to play the music so they can have a rich sound, and certain gestures will naturally give a rich sound to the strings. To draw a legato sound from the winds or a staccato sound from the percussion all require different gestures.

"To insure good balance I may say during a rehearsal 'listen to this part, or listen to what is the main important line.' Because they are good musicians, they listen and they play it softer. Sometimes the composer may ask for extreme dynamics. For example, in Rossini's *Semiramide Overture* there is a passage where I ask for *pianissimo*. The music says *sotto voce* so it has to be *sotto voce* — it's less than *pianissimo* — like nothing. I never think about baton technique really. I always think about what is important for the music and how can I make this clear to the musicians."

Yet listeners can't help but be struck by Abbado's expressive baton technique. He doesn't simply beat time cleanly and accurately, he seems to sculpt sound with his baton, varying his gestures with fluid, musical motions to fit the tonal quality he seeks from an orchestra. It's almost as if one could imagine what a composition sounded like just by looking at the way he embodies the music. Musicians who have worked with Abbado have commented on how easy it is to play well under his baton because he so clearly communicates all the musical details in the score with his hands, eyes, and facial expressions. His is almost a chamber music approach to conducting. He believes in collaborating with the musicians, providing them with a precise beat while giving them freedom to play the music together. Orchestra players can relax and express themselves, secure in the conviction that Abbado has all aspects of the performance completely under his control. Given such an agile, flexible conducting style, this master of nonverbal communication can instantly rectify any one of 100 musicians' minute miscalculations.

With the pressures an international career imposes on a conductor, does Abbado ever get nervous? "No, not exactly nervous. Although there is always something I call 'a little crisis' that happens anywhere from months before to only a few days before a performance: I think to myself that I don't know enough, but that makes me study more and more. Then when I'm onstage the evening of the performance, I'm fine. When you know that as a conductor you have to help someone, then you realize that you have to be very sure of yourself if you are going to be able to help them.

"When I conduct an opera there are so many things that could go wrong: the singers have their problems on stage — running out of breath, remembering all their lines — so I have to help the singers. Sometimes I have to conduct differently during a performance than I did at the rehearsal because I may give the singer more time if they need to breathe. I have to be flexible. Then there are the musicians in the pit; I must be able to help them, so I must be very sure of everything. At the beginning of my career I had to really concentrate on the idea that I was helping them. Now it comes naturally."

Claudio Abbado: Discography

Bartok: Concertos Nos. 1 & 2 (Pollini, C.S.O.) DG 2530901

Beethoven: *Prometheus Overture* (Vienna Phil.) LON STS-15495; *Symphony No. 7* (Vienna Phil.) LON STS-15495

Berg: *Altenberg Lieder* (L.S.O.) DG 2543804; *Suite from Lulu* (L.S.O.) DG 2543804; *Three Pieces for Orchestra, Op. 6* (L.S.O.) DG 2543804

Berlioz: *Symphonie Fantastique* (C.S.O.) DG 410895-1GH; *Te Deum* (E.C.Y.O.) DG 2532044

Bizet: *Arlesienne Suites Nos. 1 & 2* (L.S.O.) DG 2531329; *Carmen* (L.S.O.) DG 2709083; Highlights from *Carmen* (L.S.O.) DG 2531171; Preludes to Acts 1-4 from *Carmen* (L.S.O.) DG 2531329

Brahms: *Academic Festival Overture, Symphony No. 4* (L.S.O.) DG 253560; Edition of the Orchestra Works [Vol. 1] (Vienna Phil.) DG 2740275; *Hungarian Dances* [Complete] (Vienna Phil.) DG 2560100

Chopin: *Concerto No. 1 for Piano* (Argerich, L.S.O.) DG 2543524; *Concerto No. 2 for Piano* (Pogorelich, C.S.O.) DG 410507-1GH

Debussy: *Nocturnes* [Complete] (B.S.O.) DG 2530038

Great Film Classics [Vol. 2] (L.S.O.) DG 2535469

Mahler: *Songs from Ruckert* (C.S.O.) DG 2707128; *Symphony No. 1* (C.S.O.) DG 2532020; *Symphony No. 2* (C.S.O.) 2707094; *Symphony No. 3* (Vienna Phil.) DG 2741010; *Symphony No. 4* (Vienna Phil.) DG 2530966; *Symphony No. 5* (C.S.O.) DG 2707128; *Symphony No. 6* (C.S.O.) DG 2707117

Mendelssohn: *Symphony No. 3* (L.S.O.) LON JL-41044; *Symphony No. 4* (L.S.O.) LON JL-41044

Mozart: *Symphony No. 40* (L.S.O.) DG 2531273; *Symphony No. 41* (L.S.O.) DG 2531273

Mussorgsky: Music for Orchestra (L.S.O.) RCA ARLI-3988; *Pictures at an Exhibition* [arr. Ravel] (L.S.O.) DG 2532057

Prokofiev: *Alexander Nevsky* (L.S.O.) DG 2431202; *Concerto Nos. 1 & 2 for Violin* (Mintz, C.S.O.) DG 410524-1GH; *Scythian Suite* (C.S.O.) DG 2530967; Suite from *The Buffoon* (L.S.O.) LON STS-15477; Suite from *Lieutenant Kije* (C.S.O.) DG 2530967; Suite No. 1 from *Romeo and Juliet* (L.S.O.) LON STS-15477

Rachmaninoff: *Concerto No. 2 for Piano, Rhapsody on a Theme of Paganini* (Licad, C.S.O.) CBS 38672

Ravel: *Pavane for a Dead Princess* (B.S.O.) DG 2530038; *Suite No. 2 from Daphnis et Chloe* (B.S.O.) DG 2530038; *La Valse* (L.S.O.) DG 2532057

Rossini: *Barber of Seville* (L.S.O.) DG 2709041; Highlights from *Barber of Seville* (L.S.O.) DG 2437010; *Cinderella* (L.S.O.) DG 2709039; Overtures (L.S.O.) DG 2530559

Scriabin: *Poem of Ecstasy* (B.S.O.) DG 2530037

Stravinsky: *Jeu de Cartes* (L.S.O.) DG 2530537; *Petrouchka* [1911] (L.S.O.) DG 253200010; *Pulcinella* (L.S.O.) DG 2531087; *Rite of Spring* (L.S.O.) DG 2530635; Suite from the *Firebird* [1945] (L.S.O.) DG 2530537

Tchaikovsky: *Romeo and Juliet Overture* (B.S.O.) DG 2530317; *Symphony No. 4* (Vienna Phil.) DG 2530651

Verdi: *Aida* (La Scala) DG 2741014; *Macbeth* (La Scala) DG 2709062; *A Masked Ball* (La Scala) DG 2709062; Highlights from *A Masked Ball* (La Scala) DG 2740251; Opera Choruses (La Scala) DG 2530549; *Simon Boccanegra* (La Scala) DG 2709071

Vivaldi: *The Seasons* (Kremer, L.S.O.) DG 2531287

(Orchestra abbreviations: B.S.O. — Boston Symphony; C.S.O. — Chicago Symphony; La Scala — La Scala Opera Orchestra, Milan; L.S.O. — London Symphony; Vienna Phil. — Vienna Philharmonic)

Advice for Aspiring Conductors

When asked what it takes to be a good conductor, his reply was not surprising considering his respect for the composer's intentions. "I think it is important to know the score, to know the music. You should be able to get inside the music, really love the music, and want to express yourself musically. You can have good technique, but that's not so important. Of course, good technique makes it easier to express your ideas to the orchestra; but sometimes I prefer good musicians who make music, rather than conductors with fantastic technique who have nothing to say. There are many soloists — singers and instrumentalists — who conduct orchestras and make great music even though they don't have great technique. The most important thing is to know the score." But Abbado does concede that ultimately there may be some element of conducting that is simply indefinable.

Abbado not only brings all those elements to a performance but he is also an enormously well-rounded, well-read man with artistic interests outside of music that enrich his conducting. "I think it's very important to know all about music, painting, and literature. For instance, to really understand Mahler you must read German or Austrian literature. You must know the work of Kafka and Kleisst, the poetry of Schiller, the art of Klimt and Kokoschka. The element of fantasy in German art and literature also plays a role in German music.

"Sometimes there is a connection between something I read, or see in a painting, that gives me help with the music. For example, when I conduct *Night on Bald Mountain*, if I didn't think about Gogol, Chekhov, Tolstoy, or Dostoyevsky, there would be many things about Mussorgsky I would never understand. Knowing part of the Russian folklore, not just the music, but the feeling of the Russian people, is a help when I conduct."

Where does he find time for other interests with all the transcontinental travel of a busy conducting schedule? His answer is simple and logical, "When you love something, you find time. That's my philosophy. When I vacation at St. Moritz in Switzerland to go skiing, I bring some books and scores with me. I always find time to go up in the mountains, and I also like sailing very much."

A dedicated musician who mixes work with pleasure, Abbado described taking his scores with him to study when sailing in the ocean outside of Sardinia where he has a summer home. With the dreamy, faraway look of an artist immersed in another world, he painted the scene: "There is only the sound of the sea. Once in awhile a school of dolphins dance by, their movements seem to be choreographed like a ballet — graceful, beautiful, peaceful."

At a time when the world goes by at too dizzying a pace and modern technology seems to be rapidly depersonalizing our lives, we need the human touch of an artist like Claudio Abbado more than ever. ∎

Jean Oelrich, Managing Editor of The Instrumentalist, *is also a faculty member of the American Conservatory of Music and an active orchestral musician in the Chicago area.*

May, 1967

Herbert Von Karajan and the Berlin Philharmonic Orchestra

Maurice Faulkner

Herbert von Karajan, permanent musical director of the Berlin Philharmonic Orchestra, is one of those exciting personalities whose imaginative concepts in music and drama have contributed to his reputation as one of the greatest of modern conductors. When we talked with him about the Berlin Philharmonic, he described it by discussing its key personnel. Each of these musicians has been selected from exhaustive auditions held throughout Europe and, in some cases, in other parts of the world as well. His first oboist, a double-reed genius if there is one anywhere, is a German trained in the Rhineland who uses a German instrument, but with the French conservatory system fingering. The first of his three concertmasters is a Swiss who could take his place on the concert platform as one of the world's great soloists. His principal violist is one of those unusual musicians who can lead a section with such unanimity of sound that it is almost unbelievable and, at the same time, can perform the difficult solo parts of the symphonic repertoire with undisputed artistry.

And so it goes, throughout every section of this magnificent orchestra: artists on every chair; men who sit in the rear of the strings could serve as concertmasters and principals in lesser orchestras. The oboe, flute, bassoon, clarinet, trumpet, horn, and trombone groups have at least two first-chair or solo players in them. We prefer the system where only one man is responsible for the section, but this orchestra is so busy that the solo duties must be shared. Yet the superb qualities of these individuals throughout the orchestra testify to von Karajan's qualitative standards in the selection of his personnel.

Collecting such an ensemble of outstanding musicians is not a difficult problem as long as one has the essential financial backing and can interest the performers in a first-rate musical program. The city of Berlin has produced the money for such an expensive organization and von Karajan's imagination has developed a concert program that keeps the men alive and alert. This year even gives them an opportunity to play opera when the orchestra will inaugurate the Salzburg Easter Festival with a series of Wagner's "Walküre," staged and conducted by von Karajan. They began rehearsals while the orchestra was performing at the summer Salzburg Festival in 1966 and have now reassembled in Berlin to make recordings of the opera for distribution to patrons and for sale. The men look forward eagerly to this project because it enlivens their usual concert season.

The orchestra now stands at a peak of perfection which varies according to the conductor of the moment. It is a peak that can drop rather noticeably when a second-rate time beater mounts the podium. Yet it is an artistic achievement under its permanent maestro and those renowned conductors who have earned their spurs in long careers of competent music-making. I have enjoyed the orchestra's programs in numerous concerts over the past ten years in a variety of concert halls and in myriad national atmospheres—from California to Austria; from Berlin, in their unusual new concert hall, to Switzerland and other way-stations. We have visited it during rehearsals; we have lived in the same *Gasthaus* with some of its musicians and have discussed good and bad concerts, the day after, over breakfast coffee. We have come to admire this orchestra on many occasions, and to criticize it on others. We enjoy von Karajan's interpretations at their best, and decry some of his ideas when they lack integrity and conscience.

This article has been written to describe one of the world's great cultural institutions at a time when it stands at the top. It has also been written to analyze what it is that makes a great orchestra and how that greatness can become tarnished through musical indiscretions and idiosyncracies.

What Are the Essentials For a Great Orchestra?

Putting aside such important considerations as rehearsal halls, equipment, financial support, a cultured public astute enough to want and need orchestral music of quality, and other matters of that type, we deal directly with the major components of a great orchestra: the members of the orchestra and the conductor. As von Karajan has said to us: "A great orchestra must attract great musicians."

One of the problems of combining a select group of outstanding instrumentalists is that of forming such an ensemble of individuals into a self-sacrificing unity for the interpretive concepts necessary when a conductor must demand unanimity of pitch, tone, vibrato, color, and bowing and tonguing styles. So many potentially great orchestras, with expert instrumentalists, fall by the wayside because the individuals within the ensemble will not give in to produce exact pitch, tone quality, etc. Americans have marvelled at the ability of George Szell's Cleveland Orchestra to overcome these difficulties and develop a unified sound that won acclaim from the hard-boiled European critics on its tour during 1965.

If great music is to be performed artistically, what or who can mold the prima donna instrumentalists of an orchestra into the unity demanded? Toscanini, when he established the NBC Orchestra, called upon Rodzinski for that uncomplimentary job. The latter didn't earn the plaudits of his musicians, but when the Italian maestro took over the orchestra following its training stint, the first concert over the air proved that he had chosen a first-rate orchestral trainer for the job. Thus, a great conductor is essential for a great orchestra.

The Berlin Philharmonic Orchestra has not exploded into the limelight overnight. Formed more than 80 years ago by a rebellious group of Berlin musicians who were dissatisfied with their own orchestra, they united themselves with a legal document in which each member together with his assets was liable for the total group and its actions. They drew up a democratic constitution, which is still valid, in which each member is charged with absolute responsibility. This includes all artistic decisions, such as the selection of the chief conductor and the acceptance of new members. In this manner they organized to control their own destinies through a united effort.

The imperial opera and theater in those days were supported by governmental funds, but this new symphonic unit could not develop such assistance and the organization faced many financial crises. Patrons usually turned up to bail them out of such difficulties in time for the orchestra to continue another season. (The history of American orchestras quite often has followed a similar pattern.) The Berlin Philharmonic's accomplishments though, have been tied up with the second major factor in any orchestra's success: a first-rate conductor who can stimulate musicians and audiences alike with his artistic interpretations.

In 1887 the musicians persuaded the gifted and renowned Hans von Bülow to become their leader, and one of his major contributions to the history of the city and the orchestra was the introduction of the new tone poems of Richard Strauss. Von Bülow conducted his last concert on the 13th of March in 1893, and died a year later. Richard Strauss took over the podium in the interim until, on October 14, 1895, Arthur Nikisch began his long tenure at the orchestra's helm and gave it the international reputation which it has held since. Wilhelm Furtwängler took over in 1922 upon the death of the great Nikisch. Other noted conductors etc. were invited to participate in the orchestra's tradition, and Bruno Walter maintained an annual Walter cycle for ten years during the "Golden Twenties." Great musicians who were associated in the development of the orchestra during that era were such important figures as Klemperer, Kleiber, Mitropoulos, and Fried, to mention but a few. Furtwängler's wartime associations made his resumption of the conductorship following the war unpopular, and his early death, just before he was to resume his leadership on a tour to America, ended his regime.

Herbert von Karajan took over the vacated podium for the American tour and returned to Germany as the permanent artistic head for life, elected unanimously by the men. What sort of man is this star of the baton?

Herbert von Karajan

Von Karajan is a small man in stature. He has an attractive physical personality and is especially favored by the feminine contingent in his audiences. He could become a matinee idol if he were in the theater. He makes his decisions with astute understanding of persons and ideas. He is Austrian by birth, coming from Mozart's Salzburg. He trained there at the Mozarteum and then later in the rough-and-tumble of pre-war Viennese and German musical life. He had made a considerable reputation before World War II on the Berlin Philharmonic stage. His wartime activities, in connection with the Nazis, left a mark on his record, but that was alleviated somewhat by his later difficulties with the Nazi authorities because of his marriage.

After the war he returned from Italy, where he had been protected by friends from Nazi reprisals, and began to pick up the pieces of his career. His successes in the theater and the concert hall are too numerous to list here. He reached the pinnacle of operatic fame when he was appointed director of the Vienna *Staatsoper* after superlative service to that institution. That, however, was short-lived because he refused to knuckle under to various demands by unions and other influences concerning the artistic program which he contemplated for that house. He resigned in anger and now gives all his time to the Berlin Philharmonic and his numerous other enterprises—recording, broadcasting, movies, opera, and concert. By any standards he is a wealthy man, owning a Rolls-Royce, a Mercedes-Benz, a Ferrari, an airplane, which he purchased with some of his American tour income from last season, and several houses where he enjoys relaxing.

The personality of such an individual accounts for much of his success in interpreting great music. He is gifted in searching out the underlying ideas in musical drama and in translating them into symbols which his

audiences can understand. Perhaps he approaches abstract music with too much of this flair because he has been criticized for interpreting symphonic materials, which have little programmatic or dramatic basis, in too histrionic a fashion.

We have watched him rehearse Debussy's "La Mer" in hour-long periods when he draws from the subtle colors of the score much more than the usual interpreter hears. We have also followed him into the concert, where the Debussy work was performed, and watched him conduct it, without score, and miss many of the subtleties that had been so carefully rehearsed. When we discussed this with some of the musicians, one cellist indicated that the members of the orchestra would appreciate him conducting with his eyes open "because he has such beautiful, blue eyes!" The tendency to work without a score, especially in concert appearances, is unfortunate because he seldom remembers all of the intricate details of the dynamic patterns. He closes his eyes in such concerts and loses himself in a mystical, musical reminiscence that interferes with his effective baton technique in conveying his ideas to the orchestra.

We recall one rather disastrous Viennese experience with Strauss's "Heldenleben" when he lost contact with the two flutes in an intricate, delicate passage where they needed some sort of a precise indication from him for making their beat changes in a shapely, nuanced duet. There are points of this type in almost every orchestral concert we have heard him conduct. Sometimes his section leaders take the beat into their own hands and cover up for him by indicating changes of tempo and beat to their sections. But these are personal idiosyncracies which mar, but do not damage, the total concert experiences of this gifted conductor.

What von Karajan does for his orchestra that few others can accomplish is to bring this highly sensitive group of individuals into a cohesiveness that builds every sound into a unanimity of color. When the strings are in this mood their tone, from violins to basses, is so unified in pitch and sonority that they play as if they were angelic hosts. He insists upon careful pitches for the strings and works them thoroughly on melodic and harmonic lines which must be played with exactly uniform intonation. He is less careful with the winds and their pitch deviations sometimes are unfortunate, especially when their pitches must be matched by his strings.

When George Szell guest-conducted this organization at the 1966 Salzburg Festival he, too, achieved this finesse in pitch and tone control in a Mozart concert. The orchestra probably achieved one of its greatest heights in that experience. Von Karajan's Berlioz "Symphonie Fantastique" two weeks later with the same orchestra and on the same stage, was effective for its total impression but weak in just those little nuances where effective control of details is important to the orchestral

Maurice Faulkner is Brass Clinic Editor of The Instrumentalist *and professor of music at the University of California at Santa Barbara. He is director of the Brass Choir at the University and has also served as conductor of the All-California High School Symphony Orchestra. Dr. Faulkner is a graduate of Fort Hays Kansas State College and has his master's degree from Columbia University and a Ph.D. from Stanford University. In recent issues he has discussed the music festivals of Europe and Great Britain and performances of the National Theater in Greece.*

musicians. The men themselves recognize the problem of understanding both what his baton implies and what his mind wants. Yet, with his eyes closed, they find it difficult to fit the details together.

But this orchestra needs a man of von Karajan's stature. Recently, in its Philharmonic Hall in Berlin, we heard it again under the baton of a second-rate general music director from one of the German provinces. This conductor was competent in most of his baton maneuvers, but was inadequate in all of the interpretive inspiration needed by a fine orchestra. He worked the Brahms *Third Symphony* with so much sentimentalism that it not only drained the orchestra but overworked the audience and became a boring and trite experience. In such a situation the orchestra could only play with its superb skill and put together a passable result without sensitivity. Undoubtedly the men must have felt they had been through the wringer after such an evening, although we didn't discuss it with them. They left the stage as hurriedly as possible and appeared to be under some duress in the last movement when the perspiring young conductor was swimming through the emotions of a trapeze artist in knocking out the final allegro.

As von Karajan's interests involve him in multiple duties all over the globe he returns fewer times to his orchestra in Berlin. According to recent information he will conduct only 12 concerts there this season. The orchestra loses when its permanent conductor does not appear any more often than that. Guests, in his place, cannot achieve the same results for maintaining a great orchestra's superiority. And if the guests continue to level off at the time-beater standard, this great ensemble will deteriorate, just as a fine piece of machinery disintegrates from lack of expert use.

A great orchestra needs a great conductor who has the authority to demand the finest standards of his instrumentalists. The players may not appreciate such a conductor because of his demands, yet their reputations are made by the successes which they and their orchestra achieve in the realm of great music. And furthermore, their total incomes will become enhanced because of the demands of the public for new recordings and festival appearances of so renowned an orchestra.

Experience has proven, a great conductor needs a great orchestra just as the great orchestra needs the inspiring conductor. Herbert von Karajan and the Berlin Philharmonic are happy mated, but the maestro has other mistresses who attract his glances and his time. If he should return to the orchestra full-time, for a season of at least 30 weeks, we doubt that the Berlin Philharmonic could be surpassed anywhere, even with von Karajan's personal idiosyncracies. But, without him, and with guests for numerous concerts over the year, the great orchestra will disintegrate and turn into a second-rate ensemble. ∎

October, 1985

Erich Leinsdorf Interprets

𝕭𝕬𝕮𝕳

by Dennis Polkow

The 300th anniversary of Johann Sebastian Bach's birth has promoted even more than usual interest in the man most often revered as the greatest musical genius of all time. Performers who specialize in the music of Bach would lead us to believe the problems associated with interpreting Baroque music are so complicated that performers need to be scholars as well as musicians to play it properly. This view leads many musicians who prefer a diverse repertoire to bow to Bach a little more, but to perform him a little less. Often performers are so intimidated by what they think they need to know in order to interpret Bach, that his music seems to be more and more in the hands of Baroque specialists and those who play original instruments.

Erich Leinsdorf does not share this view. For almost 50 years now, Leinsdorf has conducted works of Bach as part of his performing repertoire. Ever since being introduced to Bach as a child prodigy in Vienna in the early part of the century, this music has held a special place in his heart. During his stints as music director of the Cleveland Orchestra, the Rochester Philharmonic, and the Boston Symphony Orchestra, Bach has always been a staple in Leinsdorf's vast repertoire, which in Boston alone included over 429 works by 96 composers. Leinsdorf's amazing diversity and the fact that he does not specialize in the music of any one composer, period, or genre give his opinions on Bach's music a much broader perspective than the Bach specialist. He is as renowned for his international operatic performances as he is for his symphonic performances which extend far beyond the usual Romantic repertoire of so many of his colleagues.

This extensive repertoire is well represented on the numerous recordings he has made over the years.

In the years since relinquishing any formal music position, Leinsdorf has authored two books — *Cadenza: A Musical Career* (Houghton Mifflin, 1976) and *The Composer's Advocate: A Radical Orthodoxy for Musicians* (Yale University Press, 1981). The latter book espouses three simple premises:

1. *Great composers knew what they wanted.*

2. *The interpreter must have the means at his disposal to grasp the composers' intentions.*

3. *Music must be read with knowledge and imagina-*

tion — without necessarily believing every note and word that is printed.

Leinsdorf's unique approach to Bach clearly reflects these premises. He interprets Bach's masterworks in the light of modern conceptions and expresses himself in conversation with the same candid, articulate style so characteristic of his writings.

How do you feel about recent interpretations of Bach?

In recent years I have read with great interest some of the contributions made by musicologists on the newer findings about performing Bach. It upsets me to observe that some of my older colleagues, and even some younger ones, resist adopting these findings particularly in regard to the rhythmic notation of all of the Baroque composers. For instance, I know where in Bach's music to point out that dotted eighths with 16ths have to match a triplet when they are joined. I know exactly which cantata proves this fact 56 times over because an *obbligato* part has triplets and the continuo has the first and third note notated as a dotted eighth and 16th. That's in Cantata No. 70 if anybody wants to look it up. It seems that even the most noncontroversial scholarly findings about Bach have not found universal adoption by today's performers, which is sad.

How did you come to such a comprehensive grasp of Bach's complete repertoire?

In Vienna I studied with a piano teacher who felt that Bach was the beginning and end of all things. By the time I had reached my midteens I had studied in-depth all the keyboard music of Bach. This teacher felt Bach to be very important in learning how to isolate the hands in polyphonic music, which is incomparably difficult. Studying Bach has benefited me enormously in studying scores and conducting orchestral music because the ability to follow and hear more than one voice at a time provides an unparalleled foundation in understanding the great contrast between poly-

Dennis Polkow did his undergraduate and graduate work in theory and composition at DePaul University. He is active in the Chicago area as an arranger and music journalist.

phonic and homophonic music.

When I began to coach with singers at age 15, I became intimately familiar with much of the vocal music of Bach. Later I accompanied a choir in Vienna that was directed by Anton von Webern. Gradually through playing chamber music at home I learned the Duo Sonatas for Violin and Keyboard and through studying the cello I became familiar with the cello parts of most of Bach's instrumental music.

As a conductor, I have performed many of the big Bach pieces: a good number of Cantatas, the two Passions, the *Mass in B Minor*, the *Magnificat*, and the *Christmas Oratorio*. I feel that while probably nobody can claim to know the entire Bach repertoire, I do know a number of Bach's works that make me feel very familiar with the variety of his styles.

How do you feel about performances of Bach's music on original Baroque instruments such as strings with lower tension tuned to low pitch, valveless brass instruments, and so on?

If a performance on original instruments is carried into the wrong environment it becomes counterproductive. Playing on original instruments more or less forces the performance to be given in places that are small. It makes little sense to exhibit the gamba and the flute à bec in halls that seat two or three thousand people. Let us be a little bit simple-minded: music must be heard. If music isn't heard, then it is for the cat.

However, performing Bach on original instruments for 400-500 people in a small hall with good acoustics is fine. So many of our halls, though, are bad acoustically and cannot be compared with anything like the St. Thomas Church in Leipzig where Bach performed or with some of the fine small European halls appropriate for chamber music.

In the authentic instrument interpretations I never use boys for the soli instead of women. For example, in the second cantata of the *Christmas Oratorio* there is an unbelievably gorgeous piece, "Schlaffen mein liebster Jesu." This cradle song for alto has every bit of warm maternal feeling that you could ever conceive of in the last 300 years of music. To have this sung by a piping boy who doesn't know anything doesn't make sense. Bach didn't have anyone else so he had to have a boy singer, but such a youth could not have the imagination of a mother to put the right spirit into the music.

Perhaps people who immerse themselves all their lives in playing antique instruments can be as free on them as a good instrumentalist can be on a modern one. It is very difficult to get modern musicians to play Bach so it doesn't sound either like a typewriter or an incorrect interpretation in the 19th-century tradition. If you can achieve a good performance on modern instruments it will be a better performance that communicates and is well-received by contemporary audiences. The question of authentic instruments, however, distracts from the primary focus which is: can you capture what was in this man's mind?

The ambition to be authentic creates in the end a costume party. My fear is that eventually the life goes out of the music because of the historical trimmings. If this is what people choose then so be it, but I cannot subscribe to it and I don't try. Instead I prefer to incorporate findings regarding Bach performance with the use of modern instruments. I reduce the forces according to a combination of retaining the clarity of the polyphony within the size of the place for the performance. I may use six first violins in one place and only three in another if the hall is smaller. I don't go by any book when it comes to the execution of *appoggiaturas*, ornaments, and so on. I use what I think is entirely my own judgment in these things; I always interpret the *appoggiatura* in a melodic sense.

What approach do you recommend to others when performing Bach?

Allow me to reply with a story. About eight years ago I was on tour with the New York Philharmonic in Japan where my wife and I bought four woodblock prints in an antique shop in Kyoto. We sat around on a podium while the saleslady knelt and bowed frequently — I don't know if she was into aerobics or if it was just courtesy — but then when we had decided on the four prints we wanted, my wife said to her, "What kind of frame would you recommend?" The lady bowed again and again about a half-dozen times and said, "Simple. Simple. Simple. Simple." And that is my recommendation on how to play Bach: "Simple. Simple."

Don't believe that there are rules when they contradict your best imagination. You must let your own imagination be the criterion particularly when it comes to ornaments, to trills, to other things. Studying books can be useful if you know when to throw the book away. I don't write books saying "you must do this." Learn to guess right. Use your imagination; don't perform a melody with hiccup *appoggiaturas*. The *appoggiatura* is a melodic, soft cadential element and not a hiccup.

How do you approach studying a score by Bach?

I try to understand Bach just as I try to understand Berlioz or Debussy. I do believe that one of the essentials is to be familiar with the language of the text, to understand the texts that inspired a composer — this goes for Bach as well as for Brahms. I think it is unacceptable to prepare the *St. Matthew Passion* in isolation without knowing Bach's instrumental works. I believe the same things I've said all along: you must know the composer.

All my life I have had an unsystematic way of

studying music. For instance, if I am preparing to perform the *St. Matthew Passion*, I know that I have performed it enough times over the last 35 years so that I don't have to go through the whole work to find out how it ends. I don't have to know whether the ending is happy or not, or who murdered whom. Instead I will pick out another volume of Bach's works and sit with it for awhile, or play something, or perhaps play a French Suite. By going to different pieces by Bach and browsing through them, I come back to the *St. Matthew Passion* with a lot of new ideas.

What motivates you to perform transcriptions of Bach such as those by Schoenberg and Webern?

Throughout the past 300 years transcriptions have been a way of satisfying public demand for music that has been successful. I think the transcribing of music is a necessary testimony to its success; no one ever transcribed unsuccessful music. We know that Bach took anything and transcribed it: his own works, Vivaldi's works, others' works. There is no reason not to transcribe Bach. I've stated publicly and in print, that I not only don't mind hearing Bach's music played on a Moog synthesizer, but that I also find it quite charming.

Schoenberg's and Webern's transcriptions of Bach interest me because they are musical minds whose interpretations reflect a way of transcribing Bach in contemporary terms that I do not want to withhold from the public. In the six-part *ricercare* (which was never orchestrated by Bach for any specific set of instruments) Webern's version fully brings out a spiritual dimension that even the most assiduous reading of the six-part score on paper will not give you.

On the other hand, Resphighi's transcription of the *Passacaglia in C Minor*, which Toscanini used to perform, is a horror of a piece. Anyone could easily duplicate that kind of transcription with no imagination simply by telling a good copyist: double this, this, and this, and wherever the pedals don't go you play single instruments, and so on. The Schoenberg and Webern transcriptions, however, are rewritings of music; these are real arrangements and transcriptions.

Ultimately I find it most illogical and unfair that the virtuoso solo players can perform transcriptions, but the orchestras cannot. Nobody has ever objected against the most absurd transcriptions for piano and violin as long as they show the performer in his best light. So why not for the orchestras? Bach's works are always for small orchestra; there is no orchestral work by him in the sense of the modern orchestra. Orchestras need good transcriptions.

How would you place Bach in the history of music?

Just as most of the greatest composers are the end of a development, Bach was the crowning glory of the Baroque period. I think I set off Bach better than any other way by describing Vivaldi. Luigi Dallapiccola summed up Vivaldi's work by saying that Vivaldi did not write 637 concertos, he wrote one concerto 637 times; this represents my opinion, too. These secondary Baroque composers achieved popularity because their pattern writing allows the listener to anticipate what comes next in the music. If you take a little nap and wake up later you won't miss anything. Listening to Bach you cannot nap one second without missing something in the music that is never going to come back. I once looked at the first few bars of the second oboe part in the *St. Matthew Passion* and I found roughly 12 different rhythmic patterns in eight bars. Bach's music has a variety and a richness not found in the music of his contemporaries.

Is this why Bach has such a universal appeal?

I do not feel that Bach has a universal appeal. I could fill concert halls with people who would be just as bored by Bach as by any other composer, and if they had the courage would leave after the first three numbers. Bach makes the highest demands on the performer and on the listener.

Could this be the reason why his music was largely unknown by the general public for almost a century after his death?

Contrary to popular belief, Bach was never forgotten; this is a canard. In 1802 the Bach biographer Forkel wrote "He's a national treasure." No one would write this about somebody who's forgotten. This was 52 years after his death. No, he was never forgotten. Bach was and always will be admired and adulated by composers.

Leinsdorf best explains the durability of Bach's great masterpieces over the past three centuries in the following passage from The Composer's Advocate:

"If we look at any score by Bach we find that he trusts almost entirely to the sufficiency of the notes, adding on rare occasions a *piano* or a tempo marking. In this he resembles Shakespeare, who gave few stage directions. But compare a Bach score to one by Schoenberg. The modern composer insisted on specifying even the fingering for harmonics on the string instruments, having no confidence whatever in the performance tradition of his time.... The score with the fewest directives is usually the most resilient because the text itself, free of extra comments, allows for the changes that decades and centuries brought about. These changes are comparable to the changes that take place in the human organism from birth to death. It is not accidental that the passing centuries have brought renewed youth and relevance to the works of Bach and Shakespeare. The architectonic quality of Bach's music in particular reminds us of great buildings and bridges that must sway with the winds and yield to the elements, lest they crack under the strain of too rigid a resistance. Ships and airplanes also must be flexible; and scores that are to survive the ages have some of the same qualities."

Erich Leinsdorf –
The Composer's Advocate

by Kenneth L. Neidig

Erich Leinsdorf is well-known and highly respected in the symphonic and operatic worlds. He has served as a regular conductor at the Metropolitan Opera, Director of the New York City Opera, and Music Director of the Boston Symphony, where in 7 seasons he conducted 429 different works by 96 composers. Since 1969 he has conducted on every continent, and led the world's greatest orchestras at home and on tour as a frequent guest conductor. His vast number of recordings with various orchestras include the complete symphonies of Beethoven, Brahms, and Mozart; the complete operas of Mozart, Wagner, Verdi, Puccini, and Strauss; and a cycle of symphonies and concertos by Prokofiev.

While head of the Berkshire Music Center at Tanglewood he chose students through competitive auditions, instituted a comprehensive scholarship program, and filled Tanglewood each summer with the most promising young American and foreign musicians.

In his book, *The Composer's Advocate* (Yale University Press, 1981), he presents "A Radical Orthodoxy for Musicians," insisting that conductors look to the composer for interpretive direction, rather than depending on the recorded performances of other conductors. The book is filled with examples drawn from the repertoire and rehearsal-performance experiences of a top-level professional; but the principles apply equally well to all levels from the elementary school beginning band or orchestra conductor through junior high, high school, and collect ensemble directors.

The message of chapter one, "Knowing the Score", is "the proven need for fluent literacy," which includes learning to read and play four-part writing in different clefs (Bach's *Art of Fugue*); acquiring a thorough knowledge of Italian, French, English, and German; and studying composition in order to recognize editions of scores that may be correct in a scholarly sense (probably a consensus of elaborate historical research), but contain markings that don't make sense musically.

In chapter two, "Knowing the Composer," Leinsdorf insists that young conductors "devote their highest mental abilities to investigating precisely how the great composers applied their minds to solving musical problems." His first suggested approach is through "Representational music, in which words make explicit the ideas that the composer has tried to express in his music." The Bach *B Minor Mass* yields many examples. Another approach is "to study the ways in which he [the composer being studied] learned from

earlier composers," and Leinsdorf shows Beethoven's probable use of Mozart's *Symphony in E♭*, K. 543 as a model for the "Eroica" Symphony. He also believes, "As interpreters, we should try to absorb fully all the connections, as well as the radical differences, between works." Leinsdorf regrets the narrow specialization of so many musicians and reminds the orchestra conductor that "Up to some undeterminable point in the nineteenth century, instrumental music was an elaboration of vocal music. Mozart was preeminently an opera composer. Let no one forget that fact when playing his concertos or conducting his symphonies." A third approach Leinsdorf suggests is to "Explore in depth works that he [the composer] has revised," including "transcriptions for other groupings or solo instruments." The revisions Beethoven made in the overtures Opus 72 and Opus 72a (*Leonora* No. 2 and No. 3) are discussed. The chapter concludes with "How to Recognize Genius" and the observation that it is elusive but "has one quality beyond debate: the ability to exhilarate the mind and the heart."

Leinsdorf believes that "composers have very clear ideas about how they want their works performed, and they are more likely than anyone else to be correct." His firm conviction is explained and developed in the third chapter, "Knowing What the Composers Wanted." The next chapter, "Knowing Musical Tradition", covers appoggiaturas and other ornaments, triplets and dotted rhythms, alla breve (not "in two" but referring "to the next higher unit as the basis for the phrase and the tempo"), folk and regional traditions, staccato ("No greater diversity can be found in music than in the possible interpretations of this little mark."), and accents.

"Knowing the Right Tempo" (I and II) is the subject of two more chapters that are filled with examples that come from a vast repertoire, yet always carry the recurring theme: study, question, return to the score.

Chapter seven — "Knowing the Conductor's Role" — includes Leinsdorf's "ten admonitions," which are "some suggstions about the practical, daily routine of the profession." Most apply directly to the school band or orchestra conductor, although the extended discussions of each are filled with examples from the professional orchestra and opera world.

"1. Be Prepared. [Learn the score before rehearsal]

2. Work with the librarian. [Edit the parts before rehearsal]

3. Plan rehearsal time. [Some works take longer to prepare]

4. Speak little.

5. Stop seldom.

6. Do not keep musicians idle. [Plan rehearsals so you can excuse unneeded players]

7. Stand to conduct. [Rehearsals should match performance conditions]

8. Understand players and their parts. [Help individuals see musical interconnections]

9. Do not fake. [Don't repeat a section because *you* are uncertain of how to interpret the nuances]

10. Do not delude yourself."[Beware of boasting; knowledge, musicianship, and behavior are what matter]

It is an excellent book — well worth repeated reading and study by every conductor — but it is also discouraging because the author makes it so clear what a tremendous storehouse of knowledge is essential to become a first-rate conductor.

After he had finished a rehearsal as guest conductor of the Chicago Symphony, I met Erich Leinsdorf in his dressing room, referred to the book, and said, "I'm really tempted to summarize it as 'a first rate conductor has to know everything about everything.'"

You are quite right; that is absolutely my feeling.

Can we get some idea, however, of your priorities; it's overwhelming for a lot of people to have to start on a project when they know they must know everything about everything.

Priority number 1 is that the professional study with the composer and not with other performers. This, following the subtitle of the book ["A Radical Orthodoxy for Musicians"] means avoiding contact with the recordings of the works under study, and by implication, also avoiding contact with performances by other people of those works. Naturally, priority number 1 is shared with another priority number 1, which is to study the whole composer, even before tackling any specific work. To put a work into one's mind without having the context of the composer's individuality is impossible. To understand a Beethoven symphony, for example, you must have the cross-references — the string quartets, piano sonatas, piano trios, violin sonatas, the songs, and whatever else. You have to know a whole composer to know when he uses shorthand, when he uses a simplified spelling, when he uses a particular formula nobody else has used. All of this is only possible if you know the whole composer, and not just a piece.

How do you go about doing that?

By studying all the works of all the great composers.

Now that's where overwhelming comes in, isn't it?

Look, I know precisely what is on the minds of people who are going to encounter this, because a very gifted young conductor attended my seminar in Aspen, and one day he said to me, "Yes, the ideas are fine, but the time..." I said, "You have to make the time. Actually in your musical life you don't do much else but study, because the time you spend performing and rehearsing is not nearly as much as the time you spend in preparation."

Is there any realistic way a university can set up a course for conductors that will cause what you're talking about to happen?

I'd like to have one misunderstanding taken out of this conversation. We cannot ever be sure that — even after accumulating all the knowledge — a person will be a conductor, because there is the inherent element of persuasive leadership. They tell me there are leadership schools, and I have great skepticism; but if such a thing can and does exist, I would say that is the place to train conductors. What I have proposed is that without the superior insight, the in-depth study of music, nobody can be a first-rate conductor; that much I will say. I think that by following what I've suggested in the book, everybody can develop methods of getting to know the great composers, which will make them authorities. Now if this authority is combined with a natural ability to persuade, coach, coax, lead other people into a team effort, it could result in success. I say "coach" because it goes right into athletics, where you don't necessarily have to be able to run 900 yards in order to coach a football team, but you do have to know how to get those people to work together.

There is also another misconception about conducting. When I appeared one morning at Interlochen all the students sat there with little batons on their laps. I said "You can throw them away; we don't need batons here. You won't have any chance to use a baton, because a baton is an extension of your body, for greater clarity. It is not at all necessary. It is a convenience, but it has nothing to do with conducting; conducting is a mental process, a psychological process that some people are able to do and others are not."

If I'm a typical school conductor who is faced with all these time problems that your young friend told you about, how can I most wisely spend my time in this pursuit?

By making a program and gaining access to much music. If one does that regularly, instead of reading the newspapers or the other local things which have no bearing or which can be gotten in two words from somebody else, it is surprising what one can accomplish. If one spends three hours of course it's so much the better, but everybody has two hours, I think — maybe an hour in the morning, an hour in the evening. You'd be surprised how much music you can read in an hour because this is not studying note-by-note. And you can learn to read faster, because when you recognize a pattern you can skip. I'm not pedantic and say that you have to know every last piano exercise that Brahms wrote; but the main thrust of his life's work has to be familiar to somebody who wants to do a Brahms symphony.

You say in the book that poetry will always be "one of the best bridges into the land where great music originates." I assume you would have people reading poetry, reading great literature?

In the language. You see, this is where the teaching of notes is so very insufficient, because if you can read notes, you still can't read music; but if you understand the poetry that animated Schubert's lieder and Brahms' lieder, you will thereby have access to the chamber music of Schubert, and to the chamber music and symphonic music of Brahms, and to all sorts of things to which you have no other real access.

You seem to be saying over and over so many times in the book that a conductor must have certain sensitivities, and I read into your idea about poetry that it's not only the specific reference to the work, but it's the developing of a sensitivity...

Oh yes, yes, yes.

...and that poetry with the connotative words, rather than the denotative words, may develop that overall sensitivity.

Well, you have to try to understand the processes by which a composition was made, and if you understand these processes, you will be the better off for it.

Are you consciously sensitive to art works, to the appreciation of beauty wherever you find it, or is this just a part of your personality? Can that be taught?

I think that the connections can be taught, as long as one is not dogmatic about it, of course. For instance, in the book I mentioned Grillparzer, an Austrian dramatist who wrote a poem for the interment of Beethoven; but I would not tell a class that they had to read every drama of Grillparzer while they study Beethoven. That is not meant; but to be aware of certain people and the outlook they had on the same world is important. Another subtitle for the book could be "an attempt to open a lot of windows," from a limited room — the notes. If you open the window, there's the poetry here, there's art there, and there's drama over there; and there's language, of course, above all.

Very nice. How can we preserve all this knowledge? You talk a lot about the performance traditions before 1800, for example the double-dotted quarter and sixteenth. We want to pass that knowledge or I assume it will be lost forever when the people who know it are gone; but how do we do that and avoid simply imitating one's elders (which I know you object to also)?

Here is a place where the teacher of early studies can be very helpful. I think it is very important to not claim that everything one sees printe' must be executed that way. Start with jazz music .o show them that if you play jazz trumpet, this is the way your part looks, and this is the way it sounds. It doesn't look as it sounds. It is the same for the 18th century, and the same for some of the 19th century. There's not too much music where we can take every note literally — only some in the second part of the 19th century and the first part of the 20th century. Now we are into the aleatoric, and have this approximation again. It was the same in the 18th century.

It's amazing that one of the baroque practices — the dotted eighth and sixteenth equaling two thirds of a triplet — is the same in jazz.

Yes, but this is still being challenged. Every time it comes up you have to rewrite it in the parts.

Just a few quick questions and answers before you go: first, would you comment on the autocratic, dictatorial conductor of the past vs. the coordinator of the present? Are those days gone forever? Some of the people in school don't seem to think so.

They're absolutely gone, because the entire economic situation has changed. The autocratic approach is gone, and I say good riddance, because it must be replaced by a real authority, which I stress. The real authority will never be challenged, not from a teacher, not from a conductor, because people do recognize when somebody else knows more than they do.

Another subject: was there ever a time when you said "Music is it, I must do this the rest of my life."?

No. I was sort of sliding into it automatically, without any great philosophic or emotional turmoil.

No magic moment?

No. There was one moment when I switched ambition from being a professional soccer player. I was about 12 or 13 and I think it became clear that for soccer playing I wasn't a good enough runner, and so maybe for music I was a good enough runner.

Today at age 69 you say in the book "an artist remains a student all his life or he ceases to be a true artist."

Yes.

What are you studying today?

Everything.

Is there anything that's really exciting you currently?

Well first of all, I constantly do things I haven't done before. When somebody asks me to do a new commissioned work, I'll look at it and if I find it has merit, I'll study it, and I'll perform it. Whatever I do again for the 100th time I re-examine. I may not pour over the score, but suddenly in the middle of the night, I may wake up — that's one of the reasons why I'm not sleeping very well; too much runs through the head, you know. There is a constant process of re-examination, I'm quite sure. You see, this is the reason for my admonition that there is nothing fixed about music. Everybody should try to find the truth, what the composer wanted. I want nothing more than people who are self-reliant, and in their self-reliance rely on the composer. ■

July, 1980

Observing Eugene Ormandy in Rehearsal

H. Robert Reynolds

Eugene Ormandy has conducted the Philadelphia Orchestra for the past 44 years. Both are celebrating 80th anniversaries this year — the maestro was born on November 18, 1900 and the orchestra gave its first concert just two days earlier. In May Ormandy became Conductor Laureate, which means that he will reduce his concert-conducting load by one-half (to only 50 concerts!) to make way for his selection as successor, 38-year old Ricardo Muti.

During the orchestra's annual residence at the May Festival of the University of Michigan Musical Society, I had an opportunity to observe one of Ormandy's last rehearsals as music director.

I arrived for the rehearsal 30 minutes early and noticed many members of the Philadelphia Orchestra warming up, talking with each other, and generally making ready. By 15 minutes before the rehearsal hour most musicians were on stage; and 10 minutes before the 10:00 a.m. tuning all were there, in or near their chairs. Just before the hour, Ormandy made his way toward the podium in a casual and friendly manner, stopping to talk briefly to various individuals. Precisely on time he stepped onto the podium and began talking to the whole orchestra. A relaxed and congenial atmosphere prevailed, often punctuated by laughter. As the rehearsal began, I had the feeling that I was watching a most compatible family launch into a pleasant and familiar project. On the conductor's stand lay Ormandy's wrist watch

H. Robert Reynolds is director of university bands and chairman of the conducting department at the University of Michigan.

along with the unopened score to Prokofieff's *Classical Symphony.*

The familiar composition came to life and it was clear from the outset that Ormandy had an indepth knowledge of the music. His gestures were mostly passive until he heard sounds he wished to alter; a little more viola here, a strong stress on a certain note there, less intensity in the tone quality, and a nod of approval to sections or individuals. He was not the energy generator but rather the monitor of its flow, the one who adjusted the result until it matched his inner aural image, transferring the printed page to sound with definite shades, densities, and textures. It seemed that with his conducting gestures he was describing a very old friend, and it was clear to me that he relied heavily on intuitive instinct to achieve results. However, the Ormandy instinct is no casual whim of the moment; it is one molded by rehearsals and countless hours of study. He used the score as a reference tool, consulting it occasionally and treating it somewhat as a dictionary to be opened to check spelling or be sure of a definition. It seemed to me that he purposely stayed away from the score for fear it would interrupt his musical instinct for flow and direction. Perhaps he thought that if his eyes were occupied with seeing the music, he would not be able to hear the orchestra as well.

He talked above the orchestra's playing; "diminuendo," "diminuendo *molto*," he said, but he always related his voice quality and volume to the mood of the music.

914

He often focused on individuals and sections, with comments that through 44 years with "his" Philadelphia Orchestra have developed into specifics, hitting the bull's eye of his musical target every time.

The focus of the rehearsal was a little difficult to understand at first because the orchestra obviously knew all of the music so well. Clearing up minor technical problems was far less important than recapturing the overall grasp of a masterwork and performing it with unanimity of concept and purpose. Thus it became a meeting of old musical friends without those awkward moments of reacquaintance.

Occasionally the conductor stepped off the podium to look at a passage on a player's part; but only once did he drill a section of the music, working for precision in a very difficult violin passage. Throughout the entire rehearsal no time was spent learning notes, of course. The maestro assumed each person had taken care of that responsibility on his own, and he was right.

When orchestra members noticed minor inconsistencies they would make corrections themselves. This practice was most apparent in the string section, where the concertmaster or the principal second violinist would suggest a particular bowing to achieve a certain sound and the information would travel quickly back through the section. Much of the success of the rehearsal can be attributed to this kind of internal leadership.

The rehearsal break provided additional insight to the orchestra's success. As many members left the stage, the principal clarinetist moved next to the principal oboist to go over a passage. Neither player had acted on orders from the conductor, further demonstrating that quality of performance in this or any other organization largely depends on the players themselves attending to those things they know are needed. The conductor cannot hear everything.

The rehearsal atmosphere was businesslike and ordered, with a high level of concentration prevailing, yet it was relaxed. All players seemed to know exactly when to concentrate, as well as when to laugh and talk. They seemed to have a col-lective and infallible sense of what was appropriate to the situation and to the mood of the conductor, whose powerful personality pervaded the hall, even when he was not actually on stage. And they are genuinely nice people. For instance, I asked one of the orchestra members who happened to be near me at break time if he knew where I could find an old friend of mine who is in the trumpet section. "Just a minute" he said, "I'll go find him for you." What ever happened to those "aloof" professional musicians we've heard so much about? They certainly aren't in the Philadelphia Orchestra.

This brief experience with Eugene Ormandy and the Philadelphia Orchestra was neither my first nor last attempt to grow personally and professionally from observing top-level talent at work. I considered it a valuable lesson during which I learned, perhaps re-learned, some very important things:

• Rely on musical instinct that has evolved through careful study.

• Learn the sound of the music, not just the graphic details of the score, and develop a vivid aural image so rehearsing goes beyond simply reproducing the correct notes and markings.

• Become completely immersed in the musical and aesthetic atmosphere created by other conductors; it can be more beneficial than being able to list ten new specific rehearsal techniques picked up from them.

• Continue to be stimulated and revitalized by going to rehearsals of the best conductors and ensembles. By being acquainted with higher quality, one strives for higher goals.

And finally, I decided that if Eugene Ormandy can know so many difficult and complex scores so well, I can learn at least a few that well. ■

Eugene Ormandy
With or Without the Baton
The Music's the Thing

by Winthrop P. Tryon

GO BACK to J. Fred Wolle, who made Bethlehem, Pa., famous for its annual performances of Bach's B minor Mass. Wolle directed his unexampled choir without a baton. He was quite an innovator among conductors; and at the same time, he was one of the most conservative musicians of his period. To him Beethoven—no exaggeration to say—represented modernism without particular advance. Take him for his way of beating the time and his refusal to consider anything as having happened in music since the eighteenth century, he would have been regarded as a curiosity, but that his singers surpassed all others in the presentation of Bach.

Then, a little later, consider Leopold Stokowsky, who took a notion all at once to direct the playing of the Philadelphia Orchestra without baton. "What will he do next?" his manager asked in alarm and confusion. But Mr. Stokowsky did not return to the old way; and now his successor, Eugene Ormandy, is found up to the same devices, following in the path which Mr. Stokowsky, in the latter years of his incumbency, struck out.

Something which managers neg-

lected to do for Mr. Stokowsky, they have happily undertaken to do for Mr. Ormandy; and that is to show, through photography, just what conducting an orchestra with both hands free looks like as seen from the viewpoint of the players.

Conductor 'Captured'

It comes from the News Bureau of the Ford Motor Company, in connection with the Ford Sunday Evening Hour on the radio; and it represents all the difference between a back-to silhouette of the conductor, and a real face-to encounter. Here, indeed, we get what we have long wanted. From the audience side, we have been able only to guess at the purport of the conductor's attitudes, and his indications of hands and face.

We could possibly surmise a little from the behavior of the instrumentalists as they responded to his action on the conductor's stand; but now the camera, allowed to wander in candor from side to side and back and forward on the platform, captures expressions we have known nothing about —glance of eye, lift of finger, pursing of mouth, and what not else.

The lens did its work during the informalities of rehearsal, where, after all, most of the work is done; but we have only to put Mr. Ormandy into evening clothes and the story would be the same in real performance. But while we may safely say that the pictures would not be at all the same if Mr. Ormandy's right hand were engaged with the time-beating stick of old, we should not too hastily conclude that the sound and the expression elicited from the orchestra is any better. No; a little piece of wood is not so potent as that, whether present in the conductor's grasp or laid aside. For down to date the conductors who have hung up the highest record of interpretation have been batonists.

Detail of Movement

The open-hand school of conducting remains, then, on trial, Mr. Ormandy being one of its most eminent and successful champions. We may rest certain, too, that every detail of movement in the picture means something to the members of the ensemble being rehearsed.

That uplifted little finger of the left hand could be a signal to the horn player away at the back of the platform. The two hands close together, palms up, may signal a steady choral sonority from the big brasses. The O-shaped right may ask for the delicate outlining of the glance motive in the "Tristan und Isolde" Prelude.

We shall have to ask the artists themselves. But Mr. Ormandy's listeners know that he has a style, and that it is his own. His mood is much on the romantic. His orchestra sings. He himself, while conducting, is a listener, and his is satisfied only with tone that possess charm and that speaks to the heart.

(From the *Christian Science Monitor*. Reprinted by permission.)

September, 1982

Leopold Stokowski
A Centenary Tribute

Michael Gartz

April 18th marked the centenary of Leopold Stokowski. To most people his name was synonymous with that of the Philadelphia Orchestra, which he conducted for some 25 years, developing it into one of the finest virtuoso orchestras in the world. His name was also associated with the Cincinnati Orchestra, the Hollywood Bowl Symphony Orchestra, the New York Philharmonic, and the Houston Symphony. In addition, he was a pioneer in the recording industry. One of his most memorable achievements was his recording of the music to the Walt Disney film, *Fantasia*, which was released in 1938. But a great part of Stokowski's conducting life, which spanned a period of nearly 70 years, was spent with young people, and two of his orchestral posts were geared toward young musicians: the All-American Youth Orchestra, which he formed in 1940, and the American Symphony Orchestra, organized in 1962.

People have often wondered why Stokowski, a conductor accustomed to working with great orchestras such as the Philadelphia, would wish to devote so much of his time to the young, relatively inexperienced musicians found in youth orchestras. The answer is simple: Stokowski always had a passion for young people, finding them more receptive to music than their often staid elders. It was his fervent wish to bring his love of music to these young people, for it was in them that the future of music would ultimately rest. "I live only in the future," Stokowski once said. "One cannot do

Michael Gartz is a student at the Eastman School of Music in Rochester, New York.

anything about the past, one cannot change it. One can change the present — every second of it. And one can change the future, one can create the future, and that is where the interest of life lies." This preoccupation with young people continued throughout his life. When Stokowski was in his 80s, a group of young admirers came to greet him after a concert. He told them, "Whatever you enjoy doing, do it. I like anything that makes for self-

917

expression. Life is changing all the time. We are all looking for the vision of ecstacy of life. I am too."

When his association with the Philadelphia Orchestra was severed Stokowski set about forming the All-American Youth Orchestra. He personally auditioned over 1,000 young musicians from all over the 48 states. In 1941, he took the orchestra on a triumphant tour of North America, all across the United States, into Canada, and southward into Tijuana, Mexico. At about this time, Stokowski made a statement about his work with the new orchestra: "It has always been thought that it takes 20 years to make a symphony orchestra. We made this one in two weeks last July." With the All-American Youth Orchestra he also recorded a series of 17 albums and 16 single discs for Columbia Records. He also organized a second tour, this time to South America. Stokowski had two purposes in mind for these tours: "An inspirational opportunity for our understanding young musicians to come into contact with music lovers at home, but also a proof to the rest of the world that American musical life is a vital aspect of our culture." Plans for a third tour were thwarted by the outbreak of war when many of the players went into military service. Clearly Stokowski reached his goal of creating a youth orchestra geared to professional standards. Critical reviews compared the orchestra favorably to the Philadelphia Orchestra.

Twenty years later, in 1962, the 80-year-old Stokowski created what was to be his last orchestra, the American Symphony, "to afford opportunity to highly gifted musicians regardless of age, sex, or racial origins." Again, it was a group of mostly young people. For the next ten years Stokowski auditioned, trained, performed, and recorded with this orchestra, donating money to it each year and conducting without a fee. Critical reaction was again enthusiastic. It seemed that Stokowski's youthful zest and acumen — he was now in his 80s — was a reaction to making such vital and unique music with his young orchestra. During this period, Stokowski remarked, "Next to music,

young people are the most important thing in my life. Young people enlighten my mind."

With his retirement from the American Symphony in 1972, Stokowski moved back to the place of his birth, England, and continued to conduct and make records until his death at the age of 95 on September 12th, 1977.

In 1973, Stokowski had been invited to work with the International Festival Orchestra. He conducted this group of high-school-aged musicians from all over the world in performances in Aberdeen and London. Fortunately for posterity, a two record set has been issued by Cameo Classics (GOCLP 9007) of their performance of the Tchaikovsky *Fifth Symphony* along with a unique record of the rehearsals. This set allows us to be with Stokowski when he was at work with a youth orchestra and demonstrates the amazing progress that took place from the early rehearsals to the final stupendous performance. The rehearsal begins with the first movement, and Stokowski lets the orchestra play uninterrupted for a while, allowing the musicians to listen to each other and develop a feel for the acoustics. Everything that Stokowski asks them to do at this point is intended to create a feeling of flexibility. His excessive ritards and rhythmic manipulations plainly offer an opportunity for the players to loosen up. Stopping at one point in the first movement, he refers to a particular string passage, "It may be marked down — is it printed downbow? Those printers! Drown the printers! Are we on the river Thames? (Yes!) Is it clean? (No!) It's dirty? Drown them in it just the same!" This exchange shows both Stokowski's sense of humor and his approach to music: he was far more interested in breathing life into music than slavishly following every letter of the score. It is clear that the young musicians were in awe of the 91-year-old maestro, and if they didn't realize just why he was making them bend so much with the music, they were nevertheless willing to follow any of his requests, no matter how unorthodox they might seem. Perhaps the most illuminating incident occurs during the third movement, when there is an unusual outburst from the conductor, "NO! NO! Oboe, fagott — you're playing mechanically! You'll wake up one morning, you'll look in your bed and see that you're not yourself anymore — you're a little machine! What kind of a machine would you like to be?" It was precisely this type of mechanical playing that was so abhorrent to Leopold Stokowski. If he seems to have gone a bit overboard in liberating the players from the printed score on the rehearsal record, one only has to listen to the final performance to see how right he was.

Shortly before his death, Stokowski said, "I have never really done a day's work in my life. I simply make music, and people have always been foolish enough to pay me for it." Nothing could be farther from the truth, of course, for Stokowski is one of those responsible for giving us all a taste of that flexibility without which music cannot survive. This is the living legacy of Leopold Stokowski and we can do him no greater honor than to follow his example. ∎

There is an abundance of youthful talent to insure

Our Musical Culture

Leopold Stokowski

CONTEMPORARY STUDENTS ARE DE-veloping talents, ambitions, and vital energies which, if given opportunity, could create a glorious future for this country in every field. In many cases, although the desire for expression flourishes, the opportunities are not given, and talented students are discouraged and inhibited, and depressed by a sense of insecurity. Obviously, what we need are outlets for these talented young artists and scientists so that their method of earning a living will be a valuable contribution to the national life.

There are conflicting currents in our national life which could cause us trouble and even danger in the future. In the world of politics we have threats of nuclear war; there often is violent dissension between labor and management of great industries; a complete new concept of the relation of our country to all other countries is developing because of rapid travel; racial discrimination is still a serious problem. All these disturbing influences tend to create a state of mental unrest and nervous tension.

One solution for the harmonizing of these conflicting conditions would be a renaissance in all the fine arts, and an increase in the evolution of every branch of science. Also needed is the corresponding development of young men and women trained with the knowledge and faculties to carry out the detailed work necessary to make this new knowledge a significant contribution to our national life. For the future safety of our country, and humanity all over the world, this renaissance in the arts and sciences should be immediate and international.

New Orchestra Formed

When I recently was invited to form the American Symphony Orchestra I believed that not only could we provide good symphonic concerts for the music lovers of New York at prices well within the means of the average family, but also we could include in the orchestra some of the most gifted of the young people I had met in the many cities where I have conducted.

Even tho I had previous experience with the All-American Youth Orchestra, I was amazed to find how many first-class young players there are from the eastern music schools alone. So many, in fact, that we have had to place many fine players on a "waiting list."

This new orchestra is providing an opportunity for about thirty of these brilliant young instrumentalists, without regard to color or sex, to play with about twice as many experienced older musicians.

But while the American Symphony Orchestra is able to provide thirty places for gifted young musicians in New York, what can we as a country do to utilize the great young talent in other areas? In my opinion there are several ways.

First and foremost, civic-minded citizens should organize and sponsor local youth orchestras all over the United States, to be conducted in part, by young conductors.

Next, the repertoires of these new youth orchestras, as well as those of established orchestras, should include the music of talented young composers.

Third, gifted young soloists should be featured whenever possible.

And finally, advanced study projects should be instituted by major symphony orchestras to develop promising American conductors. These projects would develop all the essentials in the art of conducting, emphasizing the basic principles but always careful not to interfere with the personality of the conductor in an effort to assist him to develop the fullest expression of his personality.

Much to be Done

Much has already been done by the great foundations in medicine, the arts, science, and education but more remains to be done, particularly in the music field. The abundance of young musical talent cries for a concrete Youth Program. While this will be costly, several foundations and groups of civic-minded people could make it possible.

We must not fail this new generation of gifted youth, for if we do they will become frustrated, inhibited, disappointed, and discouraged; and the future cultural life of America will be one of decadence. It is our responsibility to see that this does not happen.

We have the talent and wealth to insure the highest levels of culture in this great land. Our future can be glorious or shameful. We must decide and act without delay. The future lies entirely in our hands.

Leopold Stokow-ski was born in London of Polish parents, and has always maintained a flair for internationalism. His early musical studies took place in London, at the Royal College of Music and at Oxford, as well as in Paris, Munich, and Berlin.

His debut as a conductor took place in London in 1908. The following year he came to America as conductor of the Cincinnati Symphony, and stayed to become an American citizen. From 1912 to 1938 Stokowski was Music Director of the Philadelphia Orchestra, which he developed into one of the foremost symphonic groups in the world.

From 1940 to 1942 he organized and conducted the All-American Youth Orchestra. He was co-conductor (1942-43) with the late Arturo Toscanini of the NBC Symphony and with Dimitri Mitropoulos of the New York Philharmonic (1949-50). In between these conductorships he was musical director of the Hollywood Bowl for two seasons.

In his long and distinguished career, Leopold Stokowski has missed few of the major concert halls of the world, and he has also conducted orchestral concerts in many opera houses of Europe and North and South America. In Europe, Mr. Stokowski has performed with virtually all of the chief orchestras.

Mr. Stokowski has maintained a consistent policy of performing new music, both American and European, and is responsible for major debut performances in the United States of works by Mahler, Berg, Schoenberg, Stravinski, Shostakovich, Prokofiev, and others. His own contributions, now in the standard concert repertoire, include orchestral transcriptions of Bach and symphonic syntheses of such works as *Tristan and Isolde, Parsifal,* and *Boris Godunov.* Mr. Stokowski's research and experimentation in acoustics, radio, and recorded sound have led to improvements now accepted as standard in these fields.

Mr. Stokowski recently organized the American Symphony Orchestra in New York City. From 1955 until he began work on the organization of his present orchestra he was music director of the Houston Symphony.

February, 1963

Bruno Walter
The Last of a Great Tradition

George J. Buelow

O N SEPTEMBER 15TH of this year, Bruno Walter will be 85 years old. Age in respect to his career symbolizes much more than just a procession of successes, disappointments, and injustices. 1876, the year of his birth in Berlin, stands squarely in the midst of European music culture's last great romantic flourish. When we consider that Wagner, Brahms, and Bruckner were alive during Walter's childhood and that many musicians active at that time still possessed fresh memories of Mendelssohn and Schumann on the podium, we realize the momentousness of this span in music history. Moreover, Walter was the younger contemporary of Gustav Mahler and Richard Strauss, the last exponents of German romanticism.

Career

Walter was born to a not affluent, Jewish family that bestowed upon him

the blessing of a peaceful, well-adjusted childhood. His father was a bookkeeper, and his mother had sufficient musical training to begin her son in piano lessons. He seriously entertained thoughts of a career as a concert pianist and made his debut with the Berlin Philharmonic at 13. But shortly thereafter, as Walter recalls in his beautiful and moving autobiography[1], he gave up the idea because of the profound effect upon him of an orchestra concert directed by Hans von Bülow:

> *I saw in Bülow's face the flow of inspiration and the concentration of energy. I felt the compelling force of his gestures, noticed the attention and devotion of the players, and was conscious of the expressiveness and precision of their playing. . . . That evening decided my future. Now I knew what I was meant for.*

The next day he began to study scores with a voracious appetite, and soon after attended his first Wagnerian opera, which immediately converted him into an ardent Wagner champion. After considerable self-education and some instruction at the Stern Conservatory, Walter, at 17, obtained his first position, vocal coach for the Cologne Opera. During the year in Cologne, he learned an invaluable lesson: to distrust the superficiality that was so easily substituted for genuine artistry. He found the Cologne Opera an organization producing routine performances that lacked musical enthusiasm and integrity. Walter had a number of opportunities to conduct operas, and because he was naturally gifted he found his tasks surprisingly easy and self-assuring.

> *I succumbed to the allurement of the facility with which routine knows how to smooth the*

rough spots of art and change the works of the masters into theatrical enterprises. I began to be proud of the ease with which I achieved everything asked of me by the leaders of the theater. For it is the atmosphere of theatrical routine that breeds vanity, the professional disease of artists, while the atmosphere in the realm of art calls forth a sense of reverence.

Since self-satisfaction and vanity were so alien to Walter's personality, he soon recovered from the temptations of easy success and began a lifelong devotion "to the removal of the varnish of routine and the consigning to oblivion of the conventional, with the aim of penetrating again to the core of the work itself and of producing it as if it were having its world *première*." In these words, Walter expresses succinctly the most distinguished characteristic of his conducting art: his constant re-evaluation of music and the tireless search for and re-creation of the composer's true musical intentions.

Mahler's Influence

In 1894, Walter joined the coaching staff of the Hamburg Opera. The musical director of this illustrious opera house, in Germany's second largest city, was Gustav Mahler, a giant in German-Austrian music history and, of course, the composer of provocative symphonic music all too little known to this day. Walter became Mahler's disciple, and Mahler's attachment to Walter grew into a close friendship over the many years of their professional association. Walter absorbed Mahler's idealistic approach to conducting, and later, when spending summer holidays at Mahler's home in the Austrian Alps, Walter was the first to hear many

of Mahler's scores played on the piano by the composer.

Walter has written with deep emotion about his friendship with Mahler in more than one book; and to this day he is an ardent champion of Mahler's music and certainly the world's greatest interpreter of the Austrian composer's complex and monumentally-conceived symphonies.

After Hamburg Walter spent a few years in provincial opera houses that exist in such profusion in Central Europe, which make this area the greatest training ground for conductors in the world. At the age of 25 he rejoined his master in Vienna, where Mahler had become the director of the Vienna Opera.

Munich and After

Walter worked with Mahler until a permanent rupture of Mahler's relations with the opera house management led to his resignation. In 1913 Walter accepted the significant post of General Musical Director of Bavaria and artistic head of the Munich Opera. For the next ten years he led one of the most brilliant and musically outstanding opera companies to be found anywhere in Europe. In 1929 he was named successor to Wilhelm Furtwängler, director of the Leipzig Gewandhaus Orchestra. Walter, who had never taken the slightest interest in politics, soon found himself the victim of the political cancer eroding rapidly into the heart of German life — Naziism. After Hitler was elected in 1933 and this evil madness became German national policy, Walter was coerced to abandon the Leipzig Orchestra because he was a non-Aryan.

Fleeing with his family to Austria, Walter spent five years building the Viennese and Salzburg musical forces in the unreal political world of the Thirties. Hardly established, he again was compelled to break musical and

George Buelow, pianist, musicologist, composer, received both his Bachelor's and Master's degrees from the Chicago Musical College. At present he is completing his Ph.D. at New York University. In 1954 he was awarded a Fulbright Scholarship enabling him to study for a year at the Hamburg (Germany) University. He is Associate Editor of *The Instrumentalist.*

personal ties when Germany engulfed Austria. He moved to France, which promptly made him an honorary citizen, but in November, 1939, with all of Europe aflame with war, Walter came to the United States — which he had visited several times in previous years. He remains in this country as one of our most distinguished citizens. For a number of years he was regular guest conductor of the New York Philharmonic and the Metropolitan Opera. In more recent times, he moved to Beverly Hills, California, to live with his daughter; today he conducts less frequently and only for the recording engineers of Columbia Records.

Greatness

Temperamentally a quiet, unassuming man, idealistic and in love with the music of Wagner and Brahms from childhood, Walter fol-

lowed what seems to have been a preordained pattern assuring the fullest development of his talents. When he moved to Vienna, he tells how it felt as if he had not discovered that city but "re-discovered" it — the home of Beethoven, Schubert, Brahms, and Johann Strauss, Jr. Essentially Walter is a true Viennese. What does this mean? It is as difficult to explain as the German word *Gemütlichkeit*, which is a basic ingredient of Viennese life. The inhabitants of Vienna have a great propensity for enjoying life; they like to sit in coffee houses and watch the world and talk about it; they have a sentimentality toward nature and a heart that skips a beat each time they hear a waltz melody. The world is beautiful to the Viennese despite the worst tragedies they may experience.

The career of Bruno Walter extends a great line of conductors: Bülow, Nikisch, and Mahler. More than likely, Walter brings this line to an end, since the world no longer seems to possess the necessary elements to produce another. Unlike the Bülow — Nikisch — Mahler tradition, which is lost to us, we will have preserved at least a small part of Walter's art on records. The achieve-ments of Bruno Walter, if they represent anything, are a noble example of artistic integrity, courage, and devotion to music. Perhaps somewhere a young American or European conductor will find in Walter's recordings the same spark of inspiration that started Walter on his long road of greatness more than three score years ago in Berlin.

[1]Bruno Walter, *Theme and Variations, An Autobiography*, trans. by James A. Galston, New York: Alfred A. Knopf. 1946.

March, 1961

Bruno Walter with his daughter and son-in-law, Mr. and Mrs. Lindt, in front of their home in Beverly Hills, California. (Photos with this article thru the courtesy of Columbia Records, Inc.)

GERARD SCHWARZ:
Thoughts From Both Sides of the Baton

BY HARVEY PHILLIPS

From my first musical acquaintance with Gerard Schwarz in 1965, I have been an ardent admirer of his musicianship and virtuosity as a trumpet player. Gerry came into the New York City freelance scene like a comet. Everyone who heard him was impressed by his personality and his youth. His playing and musicianship were mature beyond his years. In 1974, while serving with Gerry on the faculty of the School for Advanced Musical Studies in Montreux, Switzerland, I played with him in a faculty brass quintet and was again deeply impressed by his musicianship and personality. Having listened many times to his recordings of Herbert L. Clarke solos, I cannot imagine them being played more flawlessly; his performances are definitive. Like his many other admirers, I was distressed to learn he had resigned his position with the New York Philharmonic to pursue conducting as a career. My disappointment was dispelled as I heard more and more about his conducting accomplishments. Now I understand the considerations that influenced his decision. I am excited about the enormous contributions to music he has already made and about those surely yet to come. In my view, Gerry Schwarz has risen to the level of what is known as the complete musician. He is in rare company.

In a recent interview, Schwarz began the conversation by discussing how music programs today contrast with the one he grew up with in Weehawken, New Jersey.

The moment there are financial problems of any kind in an educational system, people say, "Well then, we have to cut the music program." I've received a number of requests from people pleading with me to write a letter to their Board of Education, urging them not to eliminate the music program in their town. In Weehawken, New Jersey, where I grew up, we had an orchestra and a band in elementary school, junior high, and high school. We had music once a week, and we all sang in the chorus. It was the end of that era when music education was part of everyone's life. It was in the mid-1950s, just before the National Science Foundation began to emphasize science and the feeling became that music isn't important any-

more; now we have to learn about science. At that time the National Endowment for the Arts was not interested in education; now it is, thankfully, because music education is crucial. As long as people have the idea that the arts are superfluous in society, we will have a decline in support of the arts.

How old were you when you decided that music was going to be your direction?

I started playing the piano when I was five. It was expected in my family. My parents were from Austria and everybody in the family — my mother, my father, my sisters, and I — all played the piano. It was just part of life. From the time I was five years old I would go to New York Philharmonic concerts, to the Metropolitan Opera, and to the ballet. I was a lucky kid because my parents loved music and the arts, and they took me to all these events. Talk about exposure. I remember what attracted me to the trumpet; it was seeing the movie of *Aïda* when I was seven years old. When I heard that great "Triumphal March" and those trumpets, I thought, boy, that's for me. Then when I was 11 I went to Interlochen in the summer and played trumpet in Sibelius's Second Symphony. I decided that this was what I wanted to do with my life.

I was lucky to have private lessons quite early on. My studies began with Don Benedetti and then I went to Ronnie Anderson until I began studying with William Vacchiano, who was then first trumpet in the New York Philharmonic. He was a wonderful artist. I adored the man and the sound he made; I wanted to be like him, to have that position.

Going to the High School of Performing Arts in New York was phenomenal. I was very involved in jazz; in those days I loved to play jazz. Everybody was here in New York: you could hear them, you could see them, you could play

Harvey Phillips is Executive Editor of The Instrumentalist *and Distinguished Professor of Music at Indiana University. His career as tuba soloist, orchestral player, and chamber musician has spanned over 40 years.*

with them, you could talk to them. We were very lucky.

You mentioned that you were lucky partly because you got in on the music education system when it was still considered of prime importance. At what stage is it now? What's missing in music education today?

What everyone says is that there's no money, and that if we have trouble teaching people to read and write, how can we teach them music? I find that a weak excuse. I don't believe that because one thing is bad something else should be worse. If we're having a problem teaching reading, writing, and spelling, we should work harder at it; but we shouldn't eliminate music. In public schools, especially, interest is much more valuable than money. You don't have to have a music specialist to interest students in music.

Everybody studies Shakespeare in high school, at least I think they still do; I certainly did. How many high school students study Beethoven — the man, the music and the history behind it? Is Shakespeare so much more important to our life than Beethoven?

The language of music seems to be unfamiliar to many people. The great tragedy is that people say, "Tell me about music, explain it to me, use the words, what does it all mean?" but you can't talk about music like that. Music is something a little more special, a little different from that. It's different from art, it's different from poetry, it's different from sculpture, it's different from dance. It is the most profound, deeply felt language that exists.

Do you feel that young students today are given sufficient career guidance in high school and college?

In my opinion, no. I've come in contact with so many kids who really don't understand what they're getting into. They don't understand the responsibilities, the hard work, the discipline that's necessary, and the final results of what they're striving for. Many string players have been led towards a solo career, so they end up dissatisfied as orchestra players rather than being thrilled by the job; but the musical involvement you can get as an orchestral player, and the satisfaction too, can be much greater than being a soloist if you're not taught that being an orchestral player is something less wonderful. If you're a violin soloist you get to play Brahms's violin concerto, but if you're in the orchestra you get to play four symphonies.

Competition winners are put in the position of being important artists in their 20s. You can be talented, but it is very unusual to be an important artist at that age. Instead of having a chance to grow as they should, these players are

forced into performing with the major orchestras of the world at a very young age. It's too much pressure, and few of them survive.

Do you feel that musical sensitivities of young people studying music today would be awakened at an earlier age if they could play chamber music in junior high and high school?

Absolutely. When I auditioned for the American Brass Quintet it was the summer after my senior year in high school, just before I went to Juilliard; I actually joined the group six months later so we had a brass quintet at Juilliard for these six months. When I auditioned I was 17 years old, and I knew all the pieces because I had already played them all with my brass quintet in high school. Playing chamber music was important to my musical growth and development.

You have an opportunity, in all the many areas that you conduct, of coming into contact with outstanding young musicians. How do you feel the level of young musicians today compares with that of 10 years ago or 20 years ago?

Well, we are supposed to say that everyone is better these days; players are the best ever, no one has played as well and the level is extraordinary. You won't hear that from me because I think that something is lacking nowadays, not only in musicianship, but in the attitude toward making music. The attitude is, "Can I play this technically better than the next guy? Am I going to nail every note?" Everybody takes the audition and says, "Listen to me play; I'm going to wow them." Yet it's rare that we hear anybody who is sensitive about what he is doing musically and who is ultimately cooperative about trying to make music at a high level. Maybe people are playing better, but the orchestras are not necessarily sounding better.

Do you think the technical overshadows the aesthetic?

I think so. What I look for is someone who has a beautiful sound and is musically sensitive, who is going to make a contribution to the orchestra, who's going to get along, who's a thinking musician, who cares about music, who wants to be involved in something that is great. That's what I care about.

You can't care about music if you don't care about others.

I agree with that; I really believe that. At the Seattle Symphony we gear our auditions in the direction of finding someone who can make a musical contribution to the ensemble. We're not looking only for the great virtuosos. If someone's a great virtuoso and also can make that contribution, we'll take him or her in a minute, there's no question. Once we were looking for a harpist and the person who won the position didn't necessarily give the best audition, but you could feel what she was doing artistically. I said, "Look, this is for us; this is someone who really has a future in music. She plays well, she cares about it, and she's sensitive." You can't spend your time as a conductor explaining, "No, play it earlier; no, play it later; do this, do that." Yet sometimes I have people around me who don't intuitively know what I am trying to get at. Someone like this harp player just feels it, understands it.

Most students are mesmerized by technique, so when they play something that is technically flawless and you say, "You're not making music," it's difficult for them to accept. Would you agree that we're getting more and more students who are raising the technical standard and we're developing more and more great technical exponents of our symphonic instruments, but that those with truly musical abilities are as rare as ever?

That's exactly right. The great artists on any instrument are always a small minority of people. What makes great orchestral playing is not necessarily the greatest players in the world or the greatest salary in the world, it's the best attitude with good and sensitive musicians. It also takes a conductor who will inspire and lead the musicians. They don't have to like the conductor, but they do have to respect him. This idea that if the conductor is bad, you play badly is bizarre; it's ridiculous. When I look for orchestra players, the most important thing to me is to find someone who is going to cooperate, who is going to try to make music wonderfully.

Do you find this attitude of cooperation among musicians when you program new music? Who are some of the great young composers of today?

I think we have some of the greatest compositional talent that we have had in many years. Composers today write extraordinarily well. I won't name them, because there are so many and I'd hate to leave anybody out, but audiences are starting to really look forward to hearing the premieres of some of the young composers. The climate for new music is created by a conductor. If you do it well, you can create a wonderful environment, but if you just shove new works down people's throats, you create more antagonism than you do converts.

If you believe in what you're doing and you do it well, musicians will have enough respect for you to give you that chance. Unless you're careful, the audiences aren't going to give you that chance. Building interest in new music is something that takes time.

You were also a great success as a trumpet player. When you made the change from playing in an orchestra to being a conductor, how did your life change?

I was a prominent, well-respected trumpet player; and I had worked very hard to develop my ability on the instrument and my reputation. Then all of a sudden as a conductor, I was at the bottom of the ladder, rather than at the top, starting from scratch again. Often people ask, "Why would you give up being a great trumpet player to be a mediocre conductor?" If I had thought I was going to be a mediocre conductor, I wouldn't have started conducting. Even though I can remember being a part of many thrilling concerts when I played with the New York Philharmonic, it wasn't ultimately what I wanted for the rest of my life. That's as simply as I can say it.

Which conductors influenced you?

You learn from the bad ones what not to do and the good ones what to do, and you try to take the best from everybody. The conductors that I was enamored of were not necessarily the ones I played under. When I was a kid, going to the New York Philharmonic and then the Cleveland Orchestra here in New York, I used to go wild over George Szell. I would just marvel at what he was able to do as an artist and how he was able to make that orchestra sound like an instrument, to make it sound like one voice. As a kid I also adored Bernstein, whose performances with the New York Philharmonic truly inspired me.

Working with Stokowski was an inspiration. He was older and was able to get a sound out of the orchestra that was unbelievable, like no one else. He could do things with his hands and his arms as no one could. Somehow he could subdivide into sixteenth notes, and you always knew where he was. One of his trademarks was that he ran through repertoire; he didn't rehearse meticulously. He ran through every piece in the program at every rehearsal, and most of the problems solved themselves as the orchestra became familiar with the music. We were a part of the music making, rather than being taught bar by bar how every piece goes and never experiencing it as a whole.

Once I asked a soloist in a new music concert to come to a rehearsal. He said, "I know the piece. I don't need to come to all these rehearsals." I said, "Yes, you know the piece, but the ensemble doesn't know the piece, and it's important that they know how it goes so they can be a part of the music making, otherwise they are just going to be playing their little notes on the page and they won't know how it relates." I asked him to come to every rehearsal and sing so that they could hear how the piece went. After working out the problems, I started to do more run-throughs, and by the end everyone knew how it all fit together. The genius of Stokowski was to make the musicians comfortable playing music. He was right, and I learned a great deal from him.

If you were to ask what was most important in my preparation as a conductor, I would say the years I played chamber music. It taught me volumes: how to study a score, to rehearse a piece, to get along with my colleagues, to deal with technical problems of balance, intonation, things like that. When I started the Waterloo Music Festival and School 12 years ago, it was structured to be completely based on chamber music. Now we have an orchestra of 85 players, 4 woodwind quintets, 2 brass quintets, and 10 string quartets. I believe that the basis of great playing, whether individual or orchestral playing, comes from chamber music. That is where you give and take, where you learn from others while also playing individually.

When I first went to Juilliard I formed a brass quintet with André Smith, Per Brevig, John Cerminaro and Bob Sirinek, all fine players who now play in orchestras. We had no teacher, and we couldn't get any credit for it. I can't even say that we were encouraged. Brass players studied orchestral excerpts; they didn't play chamber music. When I taught at Juilliard, we fought very hard for a chamber music program, and Per Brevig was instrumental in getting the brass chamber music program started. At Juilliard I even coached woodwind quintets because some of the woodwind players would ask me. Now I meet musicians from all over the world whom I taught at Juilliard. I know for a fact that many conservatories and colleges today don't have structured chamber music programs, with classroom hours for the teachers and credit for the coachings.

Do you feel that as a conductor you can have more influence over the direction that music is taking than you did as a performer or teacher?

If I believe in something as a conductor, I will be able to get those ideas facilitated. As a member of the orchestra it's a little more difficult; still, there were a number of us in the New York Philharmonic who felt we could influence our environment in a positive way. I hope that everyone in the big orchestras feels that way; it's important.

Don't you think we've allowed some of our own representatives to present music as an elitist enjoyment? Aren't there many people who would enjoy music if we could just get them into the concert hall?

There are two separate problems. On the one

Jack Mitchell

hand, elitist is not a bad word. People want to say that elitist means that you are not allowing people to appreciate something. The reality is that if we doubled the size of the classical music audience, we'd still be elite in terms of numbers. There's no way the majority of people in this country, or any country, are ever going to appreciate the arts on the highest level.

On the other hand, there is an absolute barrier that says "unless you are sophisticated, well-educated, probably wealthy, you can't appreciate fine music." Well, that's bizarre. Everyone can appreciate fine music on different levels. It can be important to one's deepest feelings and emotions because there's something in music that can teach us like nothing else.

If you go to a play or hear me talking, you have an impression of what I'm saying with these words because this language is familiar to all of us. Because music is not familiar, you can get from it what you want, which is quite extraordinary. I think one of the major problems we have is that people are insecure about classical music. They don't realize that you can react to it the way you react to popular music. Yes, it may be more sophisticated, but the reaction is the same; it makes you feel something: excited, sad, happy. It makes you think more deeply. It brings you away from the realities of the moment onto a higher plane. It is something special in your life.

Many times people come backstage and say, "I enjoyed the concert a lot but I don't know anything about music," as if they really shouldn't say that they enjoyed it. Now, when I walk down the street and look at a building I want to know something about architecture; I feel that I'll appreciate it more if I know something. Not knowing music is to me an impossibility, because everyone responds to sound. When you turn on the radio or the television, when you walk down a street or you're in an elevator, wherever you are, the air is filled with music. The transition from thinking of music as a constant background to something in the foreground is not a big transition to make.

How do you allow people to know something? You try to teach them. If you don't teach them in the elementary school, junior high, and high school then they will probably never have the opportunity to learn. That's not to say that someone who's a little naive about music can't appreciate it; in some ways they appreciate it more because they don't have any preconceptions. They are influenced by the music rather than by the performance. They hear Mozart rather than a person or group playing Mozart. When trained musicians go to a concert we don't say, "The Beethoven Sonata was phenomenal and this pianist played it well." No, we say, "This pianist played it this way." We're evaluating performers.

With Beethoven symphonies, for example, a number of conductors are doing the supposedly musicologically correct versions with old instruments and metronome markings, and this has been getting a lot of press. A critic can't say, "You know, what Beethoven did in the recapitulation of the first movement was fascinating" because everybody knows what Beethoven did there. Yet if the orchestra plays it on period instruments, then the critic can evaluate it, and review a Beethoven symphony, which is a great honor.

How many critics are there who are really capable of taking on a new work that they've never heard

before? They can't talk about interpretation so they have to talk about the creative entity itself. How many critics truly have the credentials to do that?

I think more of the critics today than I used to. They have a tremendous exposure to a varied musical repertoire, the intelligent ones have a feeling for the pulse of what's going on in music.

To me being a critic means you've got to know music upside down and backwards. You have to know all the pieces, not some of the pieces; you have to have studied them all. You have to be a really first-class musician, and after that you have to also be able to write. It's a very difficult position. I feel there's certainly a place for teaching criticism in our conservatories and in our universities, and many of them do.

I think music criticism is like teaching a conductor. How do you teach a conductor? Do you teach him by showing him how to beat time? The conductor's training is really musical training. You study everything Bartók ever wrote. You sit down and you study it, you learn it, you understand it, you think about it. It's not just how you move your arms. Being a critic is, in a similar sense, not just how you write, even though how you write is important. The real issue is how much you know, how much you have experienced.

What advice would you give to young conductors or young musicians who aspire to a career in music?

There are three basic areas. One is to work very hard and be willing to make the sacrifice to practice and to give it the time. Two, you have to remember why you are involved in music: to be a part of it, and to make an artistic contribution. And three, to have perseverance. If you really believe you have talent and you have something to contribute, then hanging in there when things get tough is as important as anything else.

So often during my work I think, "What a way to make a living! What a great honor and what a thrill it is, and what a privilege for us to play Beethoven and also make a living from it! Musicians say 'play' Beethoven, we don't say 'work' Beethoven. It's even more than play, though; it's something much more important to all of us who do it. □

Henry Mancini
Making Film Score Magic

by Lida Belt Baker

few years ago Henry Mancini returned to his boyhood home in Aliquippa, Pennsylvania for a Henry Mancini Day celebration complete with marching bands and flowery tributes by civic leaders. That evening after the festivities Mancini ran into a former schoolmate who slapped him on the back and exclaimed, "Hank Mancini, you old son-of-a-gun! What are you doing these days?"

What Hank Mancini is doing these days is actively continuing a career of more than 30 years as a composer, arranger, conductor, and instrumentalist. While his exuberant classmate had apparently never made the connection between the Hank Mancini he knew in school and Henry Mancini the composer of the music for more than 70 films and numerous television programs (not to mention such popular standards as "Moon River" and "Days of Wine and Roses"), it is difficult to imagine a T.V. watcher or moviegoer in America who is unfamiliar with Mancini's music. Consider too the multitudes who attend his concerts and listen to his recordings, as well as those who hear his music in a variety of other circumstances — on the radio, at their children's band concerts, in restaurants and nightclubs, on airplanes (Delta is currently featuring an hour-long concert of his music as one of its in-flight entertainment choices), on music boxes, and even on video games. It is evident that the music of Henry Mancini is known to millions.

The recipient of countless honors and awards, including 16 Academy Award nominations, 4 Oscars, 65 Grammy nominations (more than any other musician), 20 Grammys, and 7 Gold Records, he is truly a giant in the popular music field.

Tonight Mancini will be appearing in Bloomington, Indiana, where, as composer-arranger-conductor-pianist he will present his "Concert Sound of Henry Mancini" show. It is early afternoon. In a little more than an hour Mancini will be rehearsing with an orchestra assembled especially for this performance by his friend and longtime colleague Al Cobine, a Bloomington-based bandleader and tenor saxophonist who frequently works with him as musical director and performer. Already the familiar sounds of the pre-rehearsal activities of the stage, lighting,

and sound crews fill the auditorium. As we get settled in the inner foyer, I marvel at the calmness with which Mancini has weathered the delays and problems of the morning's activities. He is a reserved, soft-spoken man who chooses his words carefully and thoughtfully. Yet beneath his quiet demeanor lurks a finely honed wit and subtle sense of humor, both of which he frequently directs at himself.

He begins our conversation with questions about the cassette machine on which the interview is being recorded. This, I learn later, is entirely characteristic and very much a part of his interest in keeping up with the latest developments in the music world: equipment, technology, performers, composers, compositional techniques and style, and every other aspect of the business.

In its earliest form this interest dates back to his childhood in the steel town of Aliquippa, Pennsylvania where, at the age of eight, he was introduced to the flute by his father, who played the instrument himself. When he was 12 he began studying piano and within a few years became interested in composing and arranging. "There was a teacher in Pittsburgh in the '30s whose name was Max Adkins. He was an arranger and conducted a pit band at the Stanley Theater in Pittsburgh, and he had a system for teaching arranging. I had been scuffling around, writing things on my own for little bands around town and I needed some kind of guidance, so I went to Max and studied with him for about three years. He was very influential; he took a kid out of a little town and put me in the right direction."

Other important early influences were the classic film composers, among them Victor Young, Miklos Rozsa, and Alfred Newman. "I was always curious about what they were doing, and I saw most all of the movies of those days." Mancini was also influenced by the music he studied and performed as a young instrumentalist. "I had two great influences: the classical influences that came through the flute, and the classical and jazz influences that came through the piano. I was a big-band fan; I knew all of the bands — who was on fourth trumpet and in what band and all of that. So I had a good feeling for both sides of the fence, which worked out fine when I finally got into movies."

At what point did he actually decide on a career in music? With the hint of a smile comes the deadpan reply: "I kind of always knew it, because I wasn't qualified for anything else." (He chuckles.) "I think I decided when I was in the service; that's where I met a lot of the friends who were to help me later to get into the various things that I did." An entry in his high school yearbook shows the beginnings of an even earlier commitment: "Henry Mancini, a true music lover, collects records, plays in the band and has even composed several beautiful selections. He wishes to continue his study of music and to have an orchestra of his own some day."

Following his graduation from Aliquippa High School, Mancini attended the Juilliard School of Music; but his studies were interrupted by the draft, leading to service overseas in the Air Force and later in the Infantry. After he was released from the service he joined the Glenn Miller-Tex Beneke Orchestra as pianist-arranger. It was there that he met the soon-to-be Mrs. Henry Mancini, Ginny O'Conner, who was singing with the band.

"Ginny was from California, so I came to California in 1947 to get married. In 1952 Universal Studios called me; they needed an arrangement for something they were doing. Then, about a month later, they called me back for two weeks and I stayed six years. They needed someone who had command of the popular idiom; then, in addition to popular things I was doing dramatic scores and all kinds of stuff. It was a great apprenticeship; you did everything — *everything!*

While at Universal Mancini contributed to more than 100 films, including *The Glenn Miller Story* (for which he received his first Academy Award nomination), *The Benny Goodman Story,* and Orson Welles's *Touch of Evil.* It was also on the Universal lot in 1958 that a chance encounter with producer-director Blake Edwards outside the studio barbershop resulted in the assignment that would bring Mancini to prominence: Edward's new detective series, *Peter Gunn.* Mancini's use of the jazz idiom in the *Peter Gunn* score represented a major stylistic departure from established Hollywood norms and won him an Emmy nomination; the album *Music from Peter Gunn* went gold, winning two Grammys in the process. In 1960 Mancini and Edwards continued their winning ways with their collaboration on *Mr. Lucky.* Another best-selling album resulted, and *Music from Mr. Lucky* also won two Grammys.

Now well-established, Mancini turned his attention back to film music; since that time he has scored more than 70 films, among them such favorites as *Breakfast At Tiffany's, Days of Wine and Roses, Charade, The Pink Panther* (and its numerous sequels), *Dear Heart, A Shot in the Dark, Bachelor in Paradise, Hatari!, The Great Race, Silver Streak, 10, Victor/Victoria, Wait Until Dark* and, most recently, *The Great Mouse Detective* and *A Fine Mess.* Currently he has two film projects in progress: *The Glass Menagerie,* directed by Paul Newman, and *Blind Date,* his 25th or 26th collaboration with Blake Edwards.

Mancini has continued his television work as well, and no fewer than five current shows — *Newhart, Remington Steele, Hotel, Ripley's Believe It Or Not,* and *What's Happening* — open and close each week with Mancini theme music. In addition, he's written a number of television film scores, including *The Thorn Birds, The Shadow Box, The Best Place To Be, The Money Changers,* and *A Family Upside Down.*

He admits to some favorites among his various efforts over the years, "things that I think have turned out well. *Wait Until Dark,* for example. I thought *The Great Race* turned out very well. *Two For The Road* was another one. Of the more recent ones I thought everything came together very well in *Victor/Victoria.*"

What about *The Pink Panther?* How did that theme, a perennial favorite among Mancini's many well-known compositions, come about? "It wasn't actually *The Pink Panther* theme at all in the beginning. It was the theme for the David Niven character when he was playing the part of the Phantom. Then Blake Edwards told me he was going to make an animated main title. Although I didn't know that when I first wrote the theme, everything pointed to that piece as the one that should be there, so it became *The Pink Panther* theme."

For Mancini, writing a film score begins with the big screen. "I always like to see the picture first in a big theater to get a feeling for the size of it and to see how it looks on a big screen, because when I'm working, I work from a VHS cassette; I talk to the people who are in charge first to see if they have any ideas, then we talk about where the music should be and where it shouldn't be. In the meantime, if I decide to take the picture, I will have been working on the thematic material; there's no reason to start writing until everybody knows what the thematic material is going to be. I put something on paper and then make a cassette of it to see if they like it; there's nothing worse than finishing a score and then having someone say that they don't like the theme. Then there's nothing left to do but do it again or get someone else."

Mancini's composing is done entirely on assignment. He writes each piece as needed and keeps no musical stockpile. "I wasn't trained to sit someplace and write my symphonies. I'm not geared that way, and I don't write like that. I have to have a phone call before I can work." Defining the Mancini style presents an interesting challenge. A composer of extraordinary versatility, he tailors his writing to the special demands of each of the individual projects he undertakes, although there seem to be stylistic features that characterize his work, regardless of genre. Not a man who wastes words, he describes his work as "melodic overall, rhythmic where needed."

Also reflected in his music is his commitment to keeping abreast of the latest developments in the field. In his book, *Sounds and Scores: A Practical Guide to Professional Orchestration*, he stresses the necessity for keeping an open mind and staying current:

> There was a time when the lines separating Pop, Jazz, Rock, Folk, Country, Latin, and Rhythm and Blues were clearly defined. These lines are crossed with increasing frequency as new and influential performers and writers emerge on the scene. A change in basic concept often follows innovation. We are involved in such a change of concept that, in time, will influence the entire orchestra — live amplified sound....To ignore this movement in the electronic field would be a serious mistake. Our job deals with musical sound, regardless of its source.
>
> The milk of sacred cows has a way of turning sour. The entire music scene is constantly changing, leaving the narrow-minded and the lazy behind. The truly professional writer must keep up with the ever-shifting scene. The man who writes for hire has an obligation, if only to himself, to keep an open mind and to absorb new ideas.

Electronic film scores fall into the category of new concepts; what does he think of them? "Just like orchestra scores, some are great and some are less than great," says Mancini, explaining that although the computer and the synthesizer have come into their own, use of them in films "is just starting to take hold." He cites examples: "The Giorgio Moroder score to *Midnight Express* was the first; then Kenneth Vangelis did *Chariots of Fire*. Those are examples of synthesizers being used extensively. Last year Maurice Jarre did a synthesized score for *Witness*; I though that turned out very well. I tend to use synthesizers in conjunction with the orchestra. That's my way, to find places where they can enhance; it's like having another section in the band. I used them on the album I did with Jimmy Galway (*In the Pink*) and also on an album of songs from Hollywood musicals I did recently with Johnny Mathis. I'm not adverse to them, and I certainly don't object to them. I do think, though, that economically there's a problem with having people do electronic scores. Without

the orchestra, someone, something has to suffer; technology always does that to people. And it's a myth about the synthesized score costing less than a regular score; that's not true."

The music of Henry Mancini appeals to a broad base of listeners, regardless of generation; and even very young instrumentalists are familiar with many of his compositions, especially those which have been published in simplified arrangements. While he recognizes that writing for beginning- and intermediate-level players must take their technical limitations into account, Mancini nevertheless expresses dismay over some of the changes he has seen made in adaptations of his music. "I question some of the arrangements that come across my desk from publishers. Sometimes they simplify rhythms or even change the melody in certain ways. I looked at one arrangement of *Peter Gunn* for beginning band and they had even changed the bass line."

One can readily understand his concern, particularly in light of the fact that Mancini is considered a master orchestrator and arranger himself. His book on the subject, *Sounds and Scores*, is now in its third printing and is recognized as an indispensible reference work for the serious writer.

As a performer with 20-some years of experience in various Mancini-led ensembles, Al Cobine has seen how well Mancini's writing is received by performers as well as listeners. He states: "The comment I always get from people in the orchestra is how well he writes for every instrument. In the popular field there are a lot of acts in the picture who perform with symphony orchestras, but he's probably the favorite because his music is so well written. The musicians really respect him for that. With a short rehearsal the orchestra sounds well rehearsed, really good, and most of that is in the writing. The concert sound of Henry Mancini is very practical, and as a writer myself I've learned a lot from that. I don't think anybody does it better than he does."

Strongly committed to encouraging and supporting talented young musicians, Mancini has established music scholarships and fellowships totalling $250,000 at the Juilliard School of Music, U.C.L.A., and U.S.C. From the perspective of an artist involved for more than 30 years in numerous areas of the music business, he passes on this advice for aspiring young performers and composers: "I think that it's very important to seek out the right teacher." Although he never went to college himself, he sees it as a necessity for anyone starting out now, "because most of the good teachers are in the universities and colleges. If you find a teacher who you really like who doesn't happen to be at a big name school, I think it's more important to get that teacher rather than go to a school and not be happy with what you're doing.

"When you're in college you're able to rehearse. Especially if you're an instrumentalist, you're able to have your choice of a lot of outlets: stage band, orchestras, concert bands, all kinds of groups. But what do you do after that? That's a move that everyone makes differently. I think at that point, depending on what you play or what you want to do, you have to go where the action is. If you want to do commercial work, you look to New York and L.A., and maybe Chicago. If you want to do symphonic work, it's different. Rarely do you step right into a major orchestra; you might have to do a little time in the tules. If you're in the rock area and you get a chance to go on the road with a group that's doing well playing *any* instrument, I'd say go and do it. Don't be choosy; keep working and don't wait for someone to hand you what you want, because it's probably not going to happen that way.

"For composers it's also important to go through a school course. Most music schools now have electronic set-ups I would definitely go into that, along with the acoustic side of it; if you can bring them both along at the same time, you've got a much better chance. But again, when you get out, you have to go where the action is and get into that fire.

"If you're interested in film writing, U.S.C. and U.C.L.A. have very good film music courses. Ray Wright has a good program at Eastman, and then there's the Dick Grove School of Music in the San Fernando Valley. There are others around, but those are the ones that stand out in my mind. Now you have to go to school; the studio system is gone, and you can't go there to learn it. Each studio used to have an extensive music department, but it's all done by piecework now. They don't have anyone under contract; everything is done on a personal basis."

Because he feels strongly about the need for music education, it concerns Mancini that California has eliminated grade school music programs. He sees that move as typical of a growing lack of support for the arts. "I think the present administration has done a great deal to break down the arts programs that we have built up over the years. Music, art, theater, dance, opera — these are all things people talk a great deal about, but not too many of them do much about it. It's something we need badly, but it's always the last thing on the agenda. Unfortunately, I don't see the trend going in the direction of aid for the arts, especially in the government sector."

He also sees some positive elements in the current picture. "To counter that, there's a great appreciation for music in all forms in this country, an appreciation that is steadily building and hopefully somehow will push the level of support up. I don't know how that's going to happen; it might be a pie-in-the-sky thing to think about, but there are thousands and thousands of people going through our schools and into professions who are much better than I ever was at that point, and that brings along a whole different audience with it. Who could have said in the 1940s that someone in the avant garde would fill an auditorium, and yet now Steve Reich does it and so does Philip Glass. So there's much more of an appreciation now, and a much more discerning audience.

When it comes to listening to music for his own enjoyment, Mancini rarely listens for fun; he's almost always listening for a specific purpose. "I read a lot of periodicals about records, and if I hear that there's a new recording of the Bartók *Concerto for Orchestra* that's outstanding, I'll go get it. When I heard about the new Paul Simon album, *Graceland*, I went out and got it. If I'm working on a picture, I'll do research on records." He does, however, have a large collection of solo piano jazz records, which he enjoys. "I love it because it's something I can't do. I'm in awe of anybody that can play jazz piano by himself."

Mancini's heavy schedule of compositional commitments and concert dates doesn't leave much time for other activities, but he nevertheless manages to pursue some fascinating outside interests. Along with skiing, photography, and painting, he has a great interest in art, and he has assembled a remarkable personal collection that includes four Rodin sculptures and oils by Dauchot, Caffe, Barnabe, Dubuffet, and others; his favorites are a small still life by James Cagney and a water color by Johnny Mercer. He is also an oenophile and his wine cellar is one of the best in Southern California. When I asked him if there was anything he'd like to do that he hadn't tried yet, I fully expected to hear about some new compositional technique or piece of equipment he found intriguing. Instead, the reply, delivered with a smile and a twinkle in his eye, was, "There's a new '85 Bordeaux I haven't tasted yet." ∎

Lida Belt Baker is a music researcher and lecturer at Indiana University and a free-lance musician and writer whose areas of specialization include jazz history and performance, ethnomusicology, oral history, and the creative process in music. She is the co-author of The Black Composer Speaks *and has written a number of articles on contemporary composers and musicians.*

TYRANTS OF

Shortly after he became the music director of the Minneapolis Symphony, Eugene Ormandy overheard several of his musicians make disparaging remarks about him.

Distraught, Ormandy met with his manager, Arthur Judson, and announced, "A.J., I must resign and resign at once. I overheard some of the men in the orchestra call me a little s.o.b."

Judson gave a hearty laugh, slapped Ormandy on the shoulder and said, "Congratulations, old man, now you're a real conductor!"

Ormandy represents the last of the podium tyrants, those maestros who transformed their batons into whips and terrorized musicians with their barbed rebukes. Their heyday came in the 1930s and '40s when Artur Rodzinski carried a loaded revolver to rehearsals, when Arturo Toscanini broke batons, when Victor de Sabata cursed players and spat in their faces, when Fritz Reiner pierced musicians with his laser-like eyes and George Szell slashed them with his razor-sharp tongue.

"Playing under them was like being in an open field during an electrical storm," recalls John de Lancie, director of the Curtis Institute of Music. De Lancie, who had been an oboist in the Philadelphia Orchestra, survived Stokowski, Reiner, Szell and Ormandy. He says times have changed. Today, a conductor's relationship with his musicians is characterized by affability, not antagonism.

"Back in the old days," comments Ted Dreher, director of the symphony department of the Ameri-

can Federation of Musicians, "conductors were autocratic, monarchical and totally controlled everything. That has gone like button shoes."

James Conlon, a young American maestro, agrees; "Conducting requires a great deal of sympathy. Musicians need a conductor's sympathy and his understanding. The old concept of a conductor standing god-like on an Olympian height dictating his will to musicians is outmoded. Conducting is a much more human and humanizing process."

"The conductor is king," says Ricardo Muti, Ormandy's successor with the Philadelphia Orchestra. "Not a dictator, but king."

None ever matched Toscanini for despotism. After he screamed obscenities at an offending musician during a rehearsal, the player stormed out — but not before he turned to shout, "Nuts to you!" Toscanini bellowed back, "It's too late to apologize!" The maestro once lined up the entire bass section of the NBC Symphony, screamed curses at them and then spat in their faces.

Robert Merrill thinks Toscanini planned his tantrums almost as thoroughly as he prepared his concerts.

"I once saw him jumping on and off the podium," recalls the baritone, "rehearsing the exact degree of rage he wanted to convey. His son, Walter, confirmed that he rehearsed that tirelessly, too. He was a perfectionist in everything."

After Toscanini, any conductor who wanted to be taken seriously had to behave like the fire-

THE PODIUM
by Robert Baxter

Legendary Maestros of Fury

breathing Italian. To his reed players in the Philadelphia Orchestra, Leopold Stokowski would cry out, "This is no sty. You are squealing like pigs!" In the men's room at the Academy of Music, Stokowski once discovered his name scrawled with an obscenity attached to it. Infuriated, he obtained samples of every player's handwriting and summoned an expert to pinpoint the culprit.

Fritz Reiner, like Stokowski, was notorious for firing musicians. One wag even contended that at his funeral Reiner fired two pallbearers. When he was the music director of the Pittsburgh Symphony, Reiner carried on feuds with several of his players. After subjecting a violinist to nonstop abuse for years, Reiner fired him. The violinist then joined the Chicago Symphony. Two years later Reiner, too, came to Chicago. At his first rehearsal, the conductor spied the violinist and yelled, "You're fired!"

Sometimes musicians tried to fight back. George Szell was prevented from conducting for one season in New York after musicians in the New York Philharmonic complained to the musicians' union and had his union card removed. When someone mentioned to the manager of the Metropolitan Opera, Rudolf Bing, that Szell was his own worst enemy, Bing replied, "Not while I'm alive."

When Eugene Ormandy left his post as the Philadelphia Orchestra's music director in 1980, an era came to an end.

Ormandy has always claimed that Toscanini

was his musical idol. Like Toscanini, Ormandy alternately terrorized and cajoled his musicians, and representatives of the musicians' union were sometimes called in to observe his rehearsals.

Ormandy's manner opened some unbridgeable rifts with guest soloists. Jascha Heifetz never returned to Philadelphia after Ormandy told him during a rehearsal, "You're just lucky I became a conductor. If I still played the violin, you would never even be heard of."

And Ormandy offended Eileen Farrell by asking the heavyset soprano how much she weighed. Farrell walked to the podium and said, "Gene, I'll tell you how much I weigh if you tell me how tall you are." The 5-foot-4 Ormandy remained silent.

Reprinted by permission from Horizon *Magazine and the Scripps-Howard News Service.*

Editor's note: Many of us know stories of tyrannical school band and orchestra directors, apparent admirers of Toscanini and others who berated their musicians. When discussing the subject with Sir Georg Solti after a concert he conducted with the Chicago Symphony Orchestra (*The Instrumentalist*, January 1975, pages 27-31), I said, "There are still some school people we know who emulate the tyrant type of conductor." Here is Solti's reply: "That is not necessary. It's stupid! Emulate the Toscanini spirit in its true essence — that he lived and breathed the score — all day — that's what young people should emulate, not the shouting. The shouting is wrong. . . ."

PERCY GRAINGER IN PERSPECTIVE

Stuart Uggen

George Percy Grainger was born on July 8, 1882, in Brighton, Australia, a small seashore community five miles from Melbourne. After five years of piano study with his mother, the 10 year-old Grainger became the pupil of Louis Pabst, a professor at the Melbourne Conservatory. At 12 he began a series of public performances which provided him with the means to travel to Europe for advanced study. During these early years he adopted the name by which he is now commonly known — Percy Aldridge Grainger.

Grainger began studying piano with James Kwast at Frankfurt am Main, Germany, in 1894. He began to study composition at the Frankfurt *Hochschule für Musik*, although he soon quit because of his inability to get along with the professor, Iwan Knorr.

"Grainger, then, did not trouble to learn the rules (as most of us do), in order to know how to break them — he merely broke them from the beginning."[1] He strayed from his early following of Handel to rather modern ideas for his time. Scott characterizes Grainger's writing as "at times excruciating to our pre-Debussyan ears."[2]

After the four years of European piano study, including some time with Feruccio Busoni, Grainger began his career as a concert pianist.

His first European concerts were in London, in 1900, "and from that time forward he was in great demand by all the important English orchestras and festivals. He met Grieg at the Leeds Festival in 1906; Grainger was Grieg's choice to play that famous Norwegian's *Piano Concerto in A Minor*, a work which Grainger played with a special eloquence, later becoming its chief exponent."

Grainger, as a composer, made his biggest public appearance at the Balfour Gardiner Concerts in London, in 1912. Two years later, after 15 years of maintaining residence in London, he moved to the United States, becoming a naturalized citizen in 1919.

Indicative of Grainger's repute as a composer was his selection as a judge, along with Victor Herbert, in the competition for the Edwin Franko Goldman prize in composition (for the best original band work of 1919).

In 1932 he was appointed head of the music depart-

Percy Grainger in later years.

Stuart Uggen received his B.S. degree in music education and his M.M. degree in French horn from Moorhead State College in Minnesota. He is presently on the faculty at Appalachian State University in Boone, North Carolina, where he conducts the concert band and teaches French horn. Uggen has taught public school music for three years in Minnesota.

ment of New York University, a post which he held only a short while. His natural gravitation towards his homeland led him to build, in 1935, the Grainger Museum at Melbourne. The museum was built for the preservation "of all things bearing on the musical life of Australia."

As further indication of Grainger's acceptance by contemporaries, his *The Power of Rome and the Christian Heart* was included in a program by the League of Composers at a Carnegie Hall concert on January 3, 1948, in honor of Edwin Franko Goldman's 70th birthday.

Grainger died at White Plains, New York, on February 20, 1961.

Grainger's personal music philosophy provides a point of departure into the character of Percy Grainger.

> I find no "modern" or "futuristic" music modern enough. All the new music I hear (in which I am vitally interested) sounds to me amazingly old-fashioned. Ever since I was about 10 or 11 years old (in Australia) I have heard in my imagination what I call "free music" — music that is not tied down to the slavery of scales, intervals, rhythm, harmony, but in which the tones dart, glide, curve like a bird in the air, a fish in the sea, and in which changes of pitch and changes of tone-strength can occur with the smooth gradualness we see in nature . . . At present (1937) I am writing such "free music" for six Theremins [5] — the Theremin being perfectly able to carry out my intentions. In the last few years I have become keenly interested in the older music of Europe . . . and in Asiatic music . . . I feel that all music (primitive music, folk-music, art-music in Asia and Europe) probably had a common origin, certainly should have a common appeal. I feel at home in music of all races, all periods, all styles. And I feel that every serious musician should know as wide a range of musics as we all know in the other arts (literature, sculpture, painting, architecture, etc.)
>
> But in spite of this universalist feeling for music, outlook upon music, I also feel that music should have local roots — should express the feelings of its country, race, nationality just as it also expresses the individual, personal feelings of its composer . . . I think I can express my view on universality and nationalism in music as follows: "Local sowing, universal harvest." [6]

The strength of Grainger's character and his persistent driving qualities are evidenced by his statement:

> I do not think my music, or my musical outlook has changed (essentially) since I was 10, in Australia. My life (as a composer and musician) has been an attempt to carry out the ideals and intentions I had formed at that age — ideals formed mainly upon Bach in music, the Icelandic Sagas, and Anglo-Saxon poetry in literature. [7]
>
> Grainger's personal sincerity and generosity are as remarkable as his talents. Paradoxically, his very sincerity has at times brought on him the completely undeserved charge of charlatanism. Thus, when he decided to marry, and wanted the whole world to know of the beauty of his bride and of his love for her . . . he wrote the piece *To a Nordic Princess*, dedicated to Ella Viola Strom Grainger, which was played at the wedding ceremonies, held in the Hollywood Bowl before an audience of some 20 thousand people. [8]

Scott saw a good deal of Kipling influence on Grainger. Grainger's relationship to Kipling is such that ". . . up to the present whenever Grainger elects to produce one of his Kipling's settings, be it song or chorus, he *becomes* Kipling in a manner which nobody else in the musical arena can approach." [9] According to Scott, Grainger found "a great part of himself" in finding Kipling.

One of Grainger's more interesting personal characteristics is labeled by Scott as a "spirit of athleticism."

> . . . he will run or jump, when other persons would be walking, and make the ordinary things of life, such as opening a door, into athletic feats by trying to turn the handle with his foot. [10]

The athleticism is carried into his music:

> Grainger insists on filling his catalogues and musical works, not only with golfing expressions but also with culinary phrases, so that his prospectus is a very masterpiece of slang and vulgarity, causing not a few people to dismiss him and his works as something not worthy of being taken seriously. [11]

In spite of these "defects" in his character (as Scott states) Grainger is said to have had hardly an enemy, "unless one could be found among those who never came in contact with him . . ." [12] Scott, in fact, credits him with "large-heartedness" and with a power to draw distinguished people in his direction.

In a subjective summary Scott states:

> In conclusion: contemplating Grainger's *entire* musical personality (for I would repeat this is essential) I see in him all those elements which make the "immortal artist." For he exists as something quite new in musical expressibility; he has invented new forms or considerably enlarged and transformed old ones; he is a great harmonic inventor, yet unlike Schoenberg he does not lead us into the excruciating. Furthermore, although at times he is a little too unafraid of the obvious, he is entirely consistent therein and one sees at once how little such a thing is the outcome of weakness. In addition to all these characteristics, he can equally show forth a poetry and pathos which speak in sublime dulcitude to the soul, and a rollicking liveliness which awakens energy almost in the limbs of the decrepit. Can one demand a more all-encompassing plane of emotions in one individuality than this? Truly it were difficult to find. [13]

Grainger's deep personal involvement in the folk music of many lands has a very practical basis: "incoming generations will not enjoy a first-hand experience of primitive music such as those amongst us can still obtain who are gifted with means, leisure, or fighting enthusiasm. Let us therefore not neglect to provide composers and students to come with the best second-hand material we can." [14]

That Grainger has taken action towards providing such material is certain. He notes that " . . . I have myself had to get under a bed in order to note down the singing of an old woman . . (wary) . . of passing on her accomplishments to any 'Tom, Dick or Harry.' [15] Grainger states that this reluctance to share original folk material is not at all uncommon among folksingers. The notator's problems are further complicated because " . . . a skilled notator will often have to repeat a phonographic record of . . . a performance some hundreds of times before he will have succeeded in extracting from it a representative picture on paper of its baffling, profuse characteristics." [16]

Through his studies of folk tunes in their native settings, Grainger has come to some interesting conclusions. For example:

> The music of all free peoples has a wide melodic sweep. By free I mean those people with string pioneer elements — people who live alone in isolated stations. This accounts for the great melodic fecundity of the Nordic race. Folk who live in congested districts cannot be expected to write melodies with wide melodic range. Their melodies are restricted by the group. The group can sing just so high or so low. It has a narrow range. The compass is short. On the other hand, the Scandinavian, the Englishman, the Scotchman, the Irishman, whether he be in his native land, an American cowboy or an Australian boundary rider, is often wholly solitary in his music-making; and his melodies have, therefore, wider range of melodic line . . . [17]

Grainger noticed in his folk singers that:

> . . . rhythmical irregularities of every kind are everywhere in evidence, and the folk-scales in which their so-called "modal" melodies move are not finally fixed as are our art-scales, but

abound with quickly alternating major and minor thirds, sharp and flat sevenths, and (more rarely) major and minor sixths, and whereas the sixth of the scale occurs usually merely as a passing note all the other intervals are attacked freely, either jumpingly from one to the other, or as initial notes in phrases. [18]

He also noted that some of the folk singers objected to singing more notes than syllables. To avoid this, nonsense syllables were used. [19]

That Grainger was observant of the physical aspects of the folk singers art is illustrated by his statement: "They . . . use their breath . . . as do some birds and animals, in short stabs and gushes of quickly contracted, twittering, pattering, and coughing sounds which (to my ears, at least) are as beautiful as they are amusing." [20]

In addition to his fondness for folk music of the singing type, Grainger had at least a practical respect for the medium of jazz.

If jazz had done nothing more than to break down certain old orchestral jail walls, it would be justified. It is in the instrumentation of the modern jazz orchestra that the musician is principally interested. This is momentous in every way. To me it represents an advance in instrumentation only to be compared in extent with that which occurred in another line between the instrumentation of Beethoven and the instrumentation of Wagner. It has opened up glorious instrumental possibilities.

It is amazing to me that the saxophone, the supreme achievement of the great instrument maker Adolphe Sax (the inventor of the bass clarinet and the perfector of the brass instruments which made many of the most beautiful passages of Wagner possible), should have to wait until this day and time to come into its own through the popular music of America. The same genius which Sax displayed with regard to wind instruments, America has displayed with regard to percussion instruments, such as the Deagan Xylophones and Marimbas, which I have prescribed for the score of my symphonic poem The Warriors. This American genius, taking the instruments from Africa, Asia and South America, has given them reliable pitch so that they may be legitimately employed, both in vaudeville and with great orchestras, in extremely beautiful effects. Most of the ancestors of these new American instruments may be traced in great collections, such as the Ethnographical Museum of Leyden, Holland, or the Crosby Brown collection at the Metropolitan Museum of Art in New York.

The Jazz orchestra has shown us how the percussion instruments add clarity to the orchestral mass. The instruments of the conventional symphony orchestra have something of a spongy character and lack the sharp, decisive qualities of the bells, xylophones and marimbas which have a clarity and sharpness, yet when well played seem to float on the mass of orchestral music. Bells and the percussion instruments I have mentioned cut through the tone mass but do not interfere with it. They seem to be in a different dimension of sound.

Another great achievement of Jazz is the introduction of vibrato in the wind instruments. All wind instruments should be played with vibrato; at least as much as the strings. [21]

The freedom Grainger found in his "folk" is readily seen in his own composition and performance practice:

. . . a tiny example of the sort of combinations that resulted from the individualistic use on the part of the various performers of the somewhat elastic material I had provided them with, remarking, however, that the effect of the actual performance was far warmer and less harsh than it appears on paper, largely owing to the transparent quality of the plucked sounds of the guitars, mandolins and mandolas, and the elusive and "non-adhesive" tone of the brighter percussion instruments. [22]

The same freedom is fully manifested in Grainger's widely diversified scoring. (Hughs [23] notes that Grainger is not often performed due to his lack of compliance with standard orchestration.) For example, in his Hill Song No. 1 [24] Grainger has included two flutes (piccolo), six oboes, six English horns, six bassoons, and one contrabassoon.

"In 1904 and 1905 Grainger borrowed a different reed instrument each week from the famous instrument company, Boosey of London. Hill Song No. 2, completed in 1907 and scored for 24 wind instruments, is a result of this study." [25]

Of particular interest to this writer is Grainger's music for the wind band. Although his offerings to this medium are relatively few in number, they represent some of the most vital elements of the repertoire. They are vital in the respect that they explore the colors and characteristics unique to the wind band in a manner far too seldom found in other composers for the medium. This writer attributes Grainger's vitality to his thorough knowledge of the instruments included in each score and to the fact that Grainger rarely doubles parts in his writing. Evidence of this may be found in Grainger's score for Lincolnshire Posy. [26]

Briefly, in conclusion, this writer has found the character of Percy Grainger to be unique. What else — more or less — could one expect from such a man?

[1] Scott, Cyril, "Percy Grainger, the Music and the Man," Musical Quarterly, July, 1916, p. 426.
[2] Ibid.
[3] Program notes from Percy Grainger Plays Grainger, Everest X-913.
[4] Encyclopedia Britannica, "Percy Grainger," Vol. X, 1965, p. 660d..
[5] A Theremin is a simple electronic device capable of producing variable tones (pitches) in variable intensities.
[6] Our Contemporary Composers, John Tasker Howard, T. Y. Crowell Co., New York, 1942.
[7] Ibid.
[8] Ibid.
[9] Op. cit., Scott, p. 427.
[10] Ibid., p. 429.
[11] Ibid. — Author's Note: Such vulgar terms as "bumpingly," "louden lots," "hold till blown," "dished up for piano" would doubtless be given a different reception in 1968.
[12] Ibid., p. 432.
[13] Ibid., p. 433.
[14] Grainger, Percy, "The Impress of Personality in Unwritten Music," Musical Quarterly, July, 1915, p. 434.
[15] Ibid., p. 420-21.
[16] Ibid., p. 422.
[17] Grainger, Percy, "What Effect is Jazz Likely to Have Upon the Music of the Future?, The Etude, 42:593, September, 1924.
[18] Op. cit., "The Impress of Personality . . . " p. 423.
[19] Ibid., p. 423.
[20] Ibid., p. 422.
[21] Op. cit. "What Effect is Jazz . . . "
[22] Op. cit. "The Impress of Personality . . . " p.433
[23] Hughs, Charles W., "Percy Grainger, Cosmopolitan Composer," Musical Quarterly, 23:127-36, April, 1937.
[24] Slattery, Thomas, "The Life and Work of Percy Grainger - Part I," The Instrumentalist, Vol. XXII, No. 4, November, 1967. pp. 42-3.
[25] Ibid.
[26] Grainger, Percy A., Lincolnshire Posy, Schott & Co., Ltd., London, 1940.

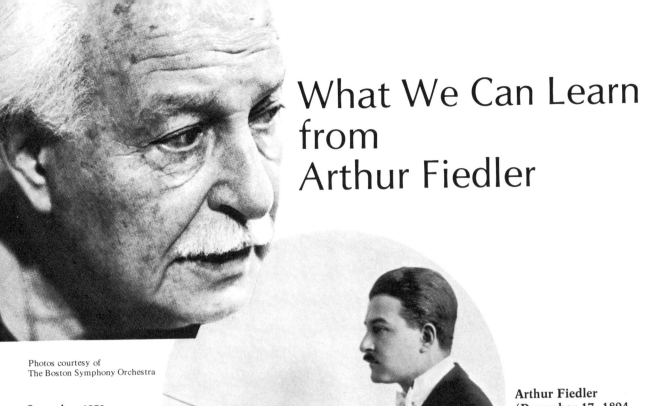

What We Can Learn from Arthur Fiedler

Photos courtesy of
The Boston Symphony Orchestra

September, 1979

**Arthur Fiedler
(December 17, 1894
— July 10, 1979)**

Traugott Rohner

Probably no one person has done more to sell good music than Arthur Fiedler during his 50 years as conductor of the Boston Pops Orchestra. Fiedler reached millions through his showmanship and unerring instincts as programmer for the people. He attracted a crowd of 400,000 to the banks of the Charles River in Boston for his Pops concert on the Bicentennial Fourth of July, and was a virtual institution in that city. But he also gained international recognition with his many recordings and television appearances. Even at the age of 82 he still made 164 appearances outside of Boston in his role as the chief proponent of light symphonic music in this country.

Some sophisticated classical music lovers may deplore his extensive programming of show tunes, popular classical music, and novelties. But Fiedler loved them and his programs built a bridge toward the appre-

Traugott Rohner is founder and publisher of The Instrumentalist.

ciation and understanding of serious music. We can do the same thing, attracting people to our school auditoriums with some popular programming so we can also expose them to the more serious works.

Arthur Fiedler was a superb salesman. While some school band and orchestra directors may object to being called salesmen, nevertheless one of our major purposes as music educators is to sell good music: to convince students, parents, administrators, board members, and others that good music deserves a place in the curriculum as well as financial support from the taxpayers.

Fiedler was not perfect. His baton technique was lacking and certainly should not be emulated by school music directors. Some of his players criticized him for other things. Still, he was a giant in the music world.

Yes, we aim to play the best in symphonic literature because that's the core of the best in music. But just as Fiedler's Boston Pops programs digressed from those of the Boston Symphony Orchestra, so too can we include some lighter music on our concerts. This does not mean a lowering of standards. To those band and orchestra conductors who play only serious classical music and still fill their houses, we wish only the best; but for most school concerts it seems to take some lighter programming to sell music to the community and students in order to maintain a successful music program. To this end we can learn a great lesson from Arthur Fiedler.

AMERICAN SALUTE

Kenneth L. Neidig

Morton Gould was born in 1913 in Richmond Hill, N.Y. Much of his early career was centered on composing, arranging, and conducting light orchestral works on radio and records; but it also included performances of more serious compositions by major symphonies. His *Chorale and Fugue in Jazz* (1931) was played by Stokowski and the Philadelphia Orchestra in 1936. His Second Symphonette (1936) contains the popular *Pavanne*. Other compositions familiar to school band and orchestra conductors include *American Salute* (1942), *Cowboy Rhapsody* (1940), *Jerico* (1941), *Prisms* (1968), and *Symphony for Band* (West Point - 1952).

Most of our readers know you from the band compositions they've played or conducted. But you had major composing credits long before that; in fact, I think you were probably one of the first prominent composers to get into the school music field.

That's right. Absolutely. In the middle and late '30s my works were being performed by Stokowski in Philadelphia, by the New York Philharmonic, and so on. I also was conducting and arranging relatively light music and writing lighter works for radio programs. At that time the school music field seemed to be a thing apart. There was a wide separation between the so-called music educator and the music professional.

Never the twain shall meet?

Exactly. Today, of course, the music educator and the professional musician is very often the same person, just as it's now accepted that one can write a symphonic work or write a lighter piece without one negating the other. But back in 1937-38, I knew

• An Interview With Morton Gould

nothing about symphonic bands, and I knew very little about school systems. I'm not a college graduate, so I was never in that atmosphere. I was born on Long Island in a little town called Richmond Hill right outside of New York City; my only knowledge of the band was what I'd heard as a kid growing up. I remember the American Legion Band practicing across the lot from where I lived, and the policemen's and firemen's bands in the Memorial Day parade. So the little band music I heard was basically from these sources. These bands often played out of tune and their sound was certainly not the most prepossessing thing I ever heard.

When Mills Music took me on as a composer in the '30s and suggested that I write some band music, I must confess I turned up my nose at the idea. I said, "Why do I want to write for band? I'm having enough problems with the professional orchestras." I was very young and was a little more volatile than I am now. I'd gotten into hassles as a young conductor, conducting men older than I was, arguing with them about intonation and tuning and so on — violent confrontations. And so I thought: I'm having enough problems right here, why should I have to deal with music for kids? But the general manager of Mills Music, Max Stark, convinced me to write a work and try it out with the University of Michigan Band. Dr. Revelli said they would love to have me as a guest conductor to do part of a concert and introduce my *Cowboy Rhapsody*. I remember saying to Max Stark: "Max, why am I doing this?" And he said, "You're going to be surprised, very surprised."

I remember all this so clearly. I walked into Hill Auditorium and met Bill Revelli and he said, "Why don't you go and sit in the auditorium. Let me warm the band up for you." I sat down very skeptically and saw this huge band tuning up, which impressed me because they were obviously tuning. There was no horsing around about that. I had never heard a professional orchestra tune that way. Then Bill gave a down beat and this beautiful sound came out — a Wagner transcription. I fell right out of my chair because I had heard something that was equivalent in quality to the finest professional orchestras of that time. Within one minute I was a convert. I realized what an important medium this was. And I felt that I, the so-called serious or symphonic composer, wanted to be part of this. It stimulated me. And from then on, as you know, I wrote a considerable amount of music in both large and small forms and many of my orchestral works were transcribed by other people for band. Yes, I wrote for band, and to this day I find it a fascinating medium.

Then Cowboy Rhapsody *was your first band composition?*

The very first that I wrote for band directly.

And you wrote it before you were converted in that miraculous minute?

Right.

In retrospect, did that affect the way you wrote it? I mean, you had the sound of that American Legion band in your ear, didn't you?

No, not too much, because you see I did not compromise. I proceeded to write in my major band works the same kind of music that I would write for regular orchestra performers. In those years there was a category called "educational music." Now I'm not putting it down because I think that category is important and there are areas in which students need certain kinds of material. But I found out very

---

When I write for three trumpets or three cornets, I mean three, I don't mean seven.

---

quickly that young players were often ahead of their directors in some instances. They were ready to do things, you see. But the directors had a tendency to stay with the tried and the relatively simple.

How important is it to you that the music be played with the exact instrumentation you indicate?

That's a very good question. There were a number of years where it was very difficult to avoid doubling because even if you didn't do it, the publisher put out double parts of everything and I understand the psychology of that. You don't want to tell half the trumpet section to stay home, because they want to play in the band the way everybody else does. But from the point of view of an actual concert performance, everybody has to realize that the band is an autonomous apparatus for making music that has its own qualities and its own guidelines the way an orchestra has. When you write a fast, articulated tonguing section for brass as an example, you cannot have seven trumpets or cornets playing on the same line; that's impossible. However, you could rehearse it that way in order for them to get the playing experience. But at the actual performance, the final target

has to be a balanced sound. I feel very strongly about this. When I write for three trumpets or three cornets, I mean three, I don't mean seven, and I don't mean somebody doubling on the first part or the third part. Please don't misunderstand what I'm saying. If you can make the piece sound, you can probably have eighty cornets on one part, even though that's obviously a much thicker sound than most composers anticipate. But if you are offering what's supposed to be a definitive performance of a work, and if that work is written by somebody who is very specific in his balancings — and I am — then I think you should stay as close to what somebody like me has put down on paper in terms of the number of players.

Is this true with all of your compositions for band?

All the ones that I write, yes. Now there have been transcriptions of my orchestral works done by others that are not balanced that crucially. They sound good, so I'm not taking anything away from them. That's a different thing, because what you're then doing is basically to transcribe a piece for band that has been popular, that has had a life of its own somewhere else; and this is a way of performing it so that everybody can get in on the act and have fun doing it. Of course in the band field we're mostly talking about things like the parts they put out for E♭ horns as well as F horns, and the D♭ piccolo parts they used to publish in the early days. I used to see these parts, and there wasn't one part that didn't have about six or seven doubles on it. For years there was a big campaign by people like Revelli to get the same quality control in the band that an orchestra had, to thin out the sound and not have this heavy way of scoring or playing.

You mentioned trumpets and cornets. Do you use them interchangeably?

No, there should be a difference. I write with that difference in mind. But in all fairness I must admit that I have heard brass in certain acoustical surroundings where it's very difficult to tell whether the sound is that of trumpets or cornets. But generally, I differentiate, I use them as two different sets of instruments.

I first became familiar with your music when I was in college as a bassoonist. I was always very grateful for American Salute, *because it gave me something to do in the band rather than play carbon copies of the trombone parts.*

That is an example of what I'm talking about. Many players have had the experience of playing pieces in which it really didn't make any difference what you played or whether you played at all.

Was American Salute *a transcription by someone else?*

Yes. Phil Lang did that from my score. Many transcriptions of my pieces were done under my supervision or from my orchestral score, and I would say, "Don't just transfer this directly. Use the winds just the way I've used them here, but for the strings do this." So it was done in consultation with me.

Are you generally pleased with that transcription?

Yes. There are things about it that I would have done perhaps a little differently, although it's had a lot of play the way it is. Sometimes I do what I as a writer think is a purer version and nobody touches it. *American Salute* is a work in both the orchestra and the band field that everybody seems to love — audiences, conductors, players. It keeps on going.

Which do you feel are your best compositions? Is there any qualitative difference in your mind between your band or your orchestra works?

I'm not the one to judge that. I think my band works qualify for the same aesthetic integrity that I hope my orchestra works have. To be specific, I think that my symphony for band, the *West Point Symphony,* is one of my major works. I wrote a thing called *Prisms* for a band a few years ago that is sort of a way-out piece along the lines of my *Jekyll and Hyde Variations* for orchestra in which I've gone into a serial type of writing. I hesitate to call it avant-garde because the word "avant-garde" becomes dated as soon as you say it. *Jekyll and Hyde Variations* rarely gets played, and yet I think that's one of my best pieces. On the other hand there are works of mine that have become sort of repertory pieces. I think we composers tend to be prejudiced in favor of those works that are not widely accepted. It's as if one of your children had a certain defect or was not liked by others, then maybe you tend to love that child more.

We composers tend to be prejudiced in favor of those of our works that are not widely accepted.

Do you plan to do more writing for bands?

Yes, I would love to do a lot more original band material. By the way, I'll also be doing some band versions of the score that I did for the television drama "Holocaust." The movie itself was a 9 1/2 hour film in four parts and oddly enough, very little of my music was in the final version. A lot of it is not there because they took out the filmed sequences that it accompanied. This often happens when you write for film or TV.

But the RCA Red Seal recording has all the movements complete. I've redone them for listening, because the film has many short scenes and half the time you don't even know the music is there, or there's a lot of talk over the music. I arranged the music into movements and I'm going to score some of that for band.

A lot of other top-level composers are now writing music for school groups, aren't they?

Yes, the band repertory is a very distinguished one today. When I came back from that Michigan experience years ago and I started to get into composing for band, I began to talk to some of my colleagues, some of the biggest names. I said, "You ought to write for band." And they all turned up their noses the way I had at first. "Why do you want

to write for band?" they asked me, and I explained that the country is full of these great bands on all different levels. Some of my colleagues became curious, and they put their toes in the water and started to write. So we have had, over the years, some wonderful contributions. And the repertory has developed very fast, thanks to some highly gifted directors and young players. Today's band literature and band programs are first-rate. It's become a field in which its normal to play much contemporary music. There's still a lot of flack in the symphony orchestra field about whether to perform new works; basically the orchestras are doing old works. But the band repertory and the band audiences have become conditioned to hearing new or relatively unfamiliar pieces. I think there is hardly a distinguished contemporary composer who has not written at least one or two band works, and in some cases they've written a great many.

Do you think writing for band is a good way for a young composer to get his works performed?

Certainly, in the sense that the band is the most accessible musical apparatus.

Do you play any of the instruments that you write for?

No, piano is my instrument. I'm sure that if I did know how to play other instruments, it would be of some benefit. I know some educators who probably play and teach every instrument, and they write music, too. But often they don't write particularly well, even for the instruments that they play. From the pure aesthetic viewpoint, it will not help either one's composing ability or the quality of the music one writes. It might be of help in a technical way. You might write a musical effect that you know is practical because you know what finger to put down or what hole to close up, but I think being able to compose is an instinctive talent. You must have a flair for it.

I never studied orchestration, but I do know the apparatus of the orchestra and the band. This instinct is something that I had when I did my first score, a score that could be played and that would sound. When I face the score paper, I light up, I know immediately what to do. However, before I get to the composing act itself, I spend a tremendous amount of time planning the smallest details of the composition in my mind. I sweat, I woodshed things, I agonize. I can get hung up on one bar, on one note, whether it should be D♭ or D♮. Then suddenly something will pour out almost complete just the way it is.

Are you writing any electronic music?

No. I'm not interested in it because the human element to me is basic. I know a very distinguished composer who writes electronic music, and he goes into a sound lab and puts things together. If it doesn't work, in one second he can change it. Once he decides on the final sound, then there's the performance, it's locked in, and it doesn't change. There's an input and there's an output, and that's it. He doesn't have to worry that somebody's going to play it slower or faster than he intended. When you compose that way, you're writing for a locked-in expression. I don't think it's necessarily negative. We're surrounded with that kind of thing in our daily life, technological sounds that come at us. Maybe it's because I'm also a conductor, but one of the intriguing things about music to me is the fantasy and the variablility of it, that you never know exactly how one performance will differ from another. That to me is the exciting part of music performance.

Can you remember how you discovered music?

My parents had a player piano and my earliest memories are of the piano rolls I heard. I was 4 1/2 years old when I started to play — suddenly. This thing had been stored up, I suppose, like data in a computer. And I started to play anything that was on piano rolls, transcriptions of *William Tell Overture, Light Cavalry Overture,* the *Prelude in C♯ Minor* of Rachmaninoff, Paderewski's *Minuet in G* — everything I'd heard on the piano rolls.

Were you doing it strictly by ear or were you following the depression of the player piano keys.

I don't remember. It must have been by ear, but obviously I saw the keys going down so I had an idea of where the notes were.

How do some selected few get this kind of talent?

I don't know. It's one of life's mysteries. Why do I hear sounds? Why does someone else see colors, or deal with words? Someone else is a great electronic technician. If it were left to me, we wouldn't even be up to the candle in our technological development. All of us, if we are blessed with a certain amount of intelligence and health, can function in our society. Aptitudes vary, and occasionally you run across a genius. There is no way of knowing how this happens. If we could know it and analyze it, we could plan it, and then everyone could do it. Everybody could be a composer, a painter, a poet, a bricklayer, or an electrician. With me composing is an instinct and defies close analysis of the exact process. There's no assurance that I'll wake up tomorrow and be able to compose. Sometimes I think, "What if nothing comes out?"

I know that you were a child prodigy, even composing a waltz at age 6. There may be other Morton Goulds sitting in classrooms around the country in bands and orchestras. How can a teacher recognize one? What can he do to help such a student_ How should he be treated? How were you treated?

Many prodigies have had rough childhoods, but I was very fortunate because my parents were sympathetic, and they recognized my gifts, as did many of the people around me. But when I was about eight or nine years old, I had an experience with one of my teachers that almost destroyed me. It did something to me that I have never forgotten.

I was not going to talk about that, but you opened up something which I think is very important, because it has to do with the educator. To me now, as a supposedly mature person, there's nobody that I respect more than the educator. I think a first-rate educator is on the same level as a composer or a performer. I say this because going back now to the question you asked me, I had really a relatively happy childhood. But one of the things that happened to

me — I won't go into details because I don't want to hurt anybody who might still be alive — but I did have a bad experience with one of my teachers . . . a much older person and I was very young. At a time when I should have had a teacher who understood what a young human being is and what he needs, this teacher was so tyrannical in approach that it really caused problems. One day I was on the way to my lesson, taking the subway from my home to the teacher's studio. I was so afraid, so worried about the ordeal I knew was coming. As I stood on the subway platform waiting for my train, I very seriously considered throwing myself onto the tracks, destroying myself. Luckily my parents got me away from the teacher and got help from a psychiatrist, so I was OK. But to this day I am reluctant to play the piano; and I was a very gifted pianist, and a large part of my career has been as a pianist.

I'm afraid there are still some of those tyrant teachers out there today.

The educator really has the life of a young human being in his or her hands. He can shape it, stimulate it, depress or discourage it. You know, young human beings have the same tribulations as older ones, except worse, because they haven't lived long enough to know that just because you're sad tonight it doesn't mean you'll be sad for the rest of your life. Students must be given sympathy, empathy, regard, and respect. If you give that, you'll get it back; it's a two-way return circuit. In the case of the young person who shows obvious gifts, the art of education is the art of getting a person to develop learning muscles and to use them, to get that student to learn on his own.

The educational process is more than just giving out a set of facts or putting something up on the board; there is a personal, living responsibility. It has to be a love affair in a way. It's part of the human relationship, and I think all teachers need to realize this. You can teach all about musical technique and all about theory and where the instruments go and what they do, and it means nothing. Meaningless. What is meaningful is to put stars in this young person's eyes and in this person's soul and to get students excited about the act of life, the act of living, and the act of communicating with other human beings.

Of course, you have to learn facts, too. If you want to compose or perform, you must develop certain muscles. There are certain things that you have to do, you cannot just sit down at an instrument, take off, and be satisfied with whatever comes out. No, there are certain procedures that must be mastered. But even then, before the instruction, there has to be the premise of "why." "Why is this important?" "Why should it be done in this way?" Students must have reasons, not just hard facts thrown at them.

Sometimes I regret that I didn't teach. I have some friends who teach, and I see them with their former students who come back for visits. It's very touching to watch. "We were with you in college, remember, we were in your class," and they love that teacher. I realize that all their lives these students will remember this teacher, because this teacher turned them on. I think that's great, that's what living is about. ■

MORTON GOULD

Musical Citizen

BY HARVEY PHILLIPS

Few American composers have succeeded as well in combining traditional and modern idioms as has Morton Gould. Since the 1930s, when he began composing and conducting for the "Music for Today" series on the Mutual Radio Network, Gould has been at the forefront of composers for the broadcast media, including radio, television, and film. His busy schedule and spiraling success have not, however, deterred him from writing in classical forms; he has produced concertos for piano, violin, and viola, along with numerous symphonic works.

Born in Richmond, New York in 1913 of immigrant Austrian and Russian parents, Gould began composing at six and presented a concert of his works in New York City at age 16. At 18 he became staff pianist at Radio City Music Hall and three years later joined the Mutual network. In 1942 Arturo Toscanini conducted the N.B.C. Symphony in Gould's Lincoln Legend, and three years later Gould conducted the Boston Symphony in a program of his own compositions.

Working for Mutual Radio for eight years had prepared Gould for the big break, which came in 1943, when C.B.S. Radio engaged him as music director of the "Chrysler Hour." Over the next few years Gould composed two Broadway musicals, three ballets, and several Hollywood film scores. With the advent of television, he began writing scores for historical productions such as World War I *and* Holocaust, *all the while maintaining his conducting career.*

In 1986 Morton Gould became president of the American Society of Composers, Authors, and Publishers.

When Morton Gould accepted the presidency of the American Society of Composers, Authors, and Publishers (A.S.C.A.P.), it seemed to many of his friends and admirers a drastic career change. What influenced him to take on such a responsibility?

"That's a loaded question," Gould begins with a smile. "Let me try to take it apart and answer it bit by bit. On the face of it, it may seem odd that a composer/conductor should become an executive; and yet, if you look closely at the background and varied involvements that have made up my career, it's not so far removed from what I've done before. I've always done things off the cuff – I have not had an orthodox or traditional career."

Even as an adolescent, having had formal training as a classical musician, Gould was already involved with commercial music. Growing up as a prodigy in a little town just outside New York City during the 1920s and finding himself a "serious composer" at an early age, he had to figure out what to do to survive economically.

"Many of my composer colleagues chose teaching to earn a living," he explains, "because in the '20s and '30s, even if your works were performed by symphony orchestras, it was unlikely that you would receive any kind of fee. (That was before A.S.C.A.P. began collecting fees for composers.) For that reason I chose to shape part of my career around income-producing possibilities, and at that time radio was an important one. I became active in live radio, conducting programs of light music that I arranged and sometimes composed. At the same time I was writing more extended pieces and getting them performed by

some great conductors and orchestras. I wrote, conducted, and recorded various kinds of music; so I was doing some unorthodox things early in my career."

Along with those activities, Gould has always been involved with what he calls musical citizenship: "I served on committees that had to do with the development and improvement of our musical culture. I have been a composer member of A.S.C.A.P. for over 50 years, and I have served on its Board of Directors for almost 30. I've also served on the board of the American Symphony Orchestra League and the National Endowment for the Arts. In short, I have been involved in the economics of music, which I believe is a very important subject. For a number of years there was talk of my becoming president of A.S.C.A.P. I was not sympathetic to the idea at first, but last year when my fellow board members asked me again to accept the presidency, it seemed like a natural thing for me to do. I look upon it as an extension of what I was already doing, yet it involves me in another area of the musical scene, in this case, as chief executive of the largest performing rights society in the world."

In the 35 years that I have known Morton Gould, he has always had free-spirited across-the-board concern for music. His open-mindedness is especially notable considering that when Morton Gould was getting his musical education, much of the music we now view as part of

the standard repertoire – important works of Bartók, and Copland, for example – had not been written. What music did he listen to as a student?

"The music I first heard as a child came from a player piano my parents had. Up until about the age of six or seven, the only music I heard was on player-piano rolls. This music consisted for the most part of pieces like Rachmaninoff's *Prelude in C♯ Minor*, Strauss waltzes, and transcriptions of overtures from works like *William Tell, Poet and Peasant*, and *Zampa*. There were no school music programs to speak of. The only bands I remember were the local policemen's and firemen's bands, which would march on the Fourth of July or Memorial Day. There was no concert series, and I don't remember any programs at school. At best we might sing words to the theme of Schubert's 'Unfinished' Symphony."

When he was eight years old, Morton received a scholarship to the Institute of Musical Art, which later became the Juilliard School. Before that he had only studied privately with a local piano teacher.

"One day when I was about four-and-a-half my parents heard me play what I had heard on the piano rolls and they took me to a local teacher. At the Institute of Musical Art I studied with a Hungarian pianist named Joseph Kardos, a wonderful teacher. We would play the Beethoven and Mozart Symphonies in piano four-hands.

943

Musical Citizen

From the age of 13 or 14 I studied piano with Abby Whiteside, a sort of maverick who was nevertheless well known and respected in pianistic circles. She had a fanatic dedication to her own way of doing things. Then I studied theory and composition with Dr. Vincent Jones at New York University. That was the extent of my formal musical training."

Morton Gould did not learn what he knows about popular music at the Institute of Musical Art. "Oh no," he explains, "we're talking about a period of our musical life when the basic musical influence was the Viennese Classic or German tradition. The idea of teaching, or hearing, or even being exposed to popular music was unheard of. There was a rigid belief that popular music was trash. It was tolerated, but it was considered to have nothing to do with 'serious' music.

"It was tremendously different from today's tolerance and concern for all music. Still, the truly great artists of that time didn't have such a narrow attitude. They appreciated genius whether it was found in a popular song or in a great symphonic work."

Gould's first composition, written when he was six years old, was appropriately titled *Just Six*. "It's not an epic contribution," he assures me, "but I have always been composing." A.S.C.A.P. was also six years old that year; the president is the same age as his organization. "I was not a member of A.S.C.A.P. when my first piece was published," Gould quips, "I became a member in 1936."

After having served on the policy-making Board of Directors for so long, Gould had some definite objectives in mind when he assumed the presidency. The battle against illegal copying, for instance, has escalated in recent years with the introduction of inexpensive desktop copiers.

"A.S.C.A.P. supports any action that restricts the possibilities of piracy; and piracy is exactly what we are talking about, whether inadvertent or intentional. With the growth in technology, there are increasing ways to misappropriate intellectual property — not only music, but all forms of art. At one time the whole idea of duplicating anything on tape was a highly technological feat that only the most skilled engineers could handle, but now people with simple tape machines can duplicate commercial recordings and record live."

With students bringing an increasing number of photocopies into their lessons, is this a problem our educational institutions need to address? Gould says it is. "It has been devastating for both composers and publishers, but it is most discouraging for the publishers. If, instead of buying additional copies of a work, students go out and photocopy them, they cut out any profit

to the publisher and thus any income to the composer. So why publish? Why make any material available at all?"

Gould's approach to composition has been inexorably bound up with the business of music. Over the years almost all his work has been done on commission. Does his new career allow time to compose?

"I have a lot of sketches lying around, and I hope I can shape my schedule here at A.S.C.A.P. to permit time to compose. This year I have had to cut back on the commissions I accepted, and on personal appearances, because this position is a full-time involvement; but I have always had full-time involvements along with other responsibilities."

As a film composer Gould is accustomed to meeting deadlines. The composer is usually called in after the film is shot, given a release date, and expected to meet it.

"The ideal would be for the composer to be involved right from the beginning," Gould explains, "but it doesn't usually work that way. What happened with *Holocaust* was that they called me in and showed me the rough cut of the film. To dramatize a very moving event like this you have to look at it objectively to determine where music should go and what the music can do to enhance the drama.

"The composer is restricted by a certain amount of time and film. There may be seven seconds here, eighteen there, and every now and then a scene may stretch out to two or three minutes. Within that framework there are certain gestures and events you have to pick up. You organize that in your mind and record it on a log sheet, using a stopwatch. Once you adjust to the time restraints, it's like writing anything else — ideas start to come to you and you hear music.

"Whether I am writing film music or a symphony or a band work, there is no guarantee that I will hear any original music in my head. I might just sit and stare at the wall. Oddly enough, though, it's usually the pressure of a deadline that produces something."

Whatever Gould composes, he does it with complete dedication to craftsmanship. "I treat it seriously, no matter what it is. I can sweat over a very simple short piece; I can get hung up over four bars, yet I often see myself labeled as facile. I think I do have a good technical command of my craft. I know instrumentation: I write for orchestra; I write for band; I write chamber music. I hear music already orchestrated: when I write an orchestral score, I don't write it and then orchestrate it. Then it is just a matter of calligraphy — getting the notes on the page. That doesn't mean that I don't sometimes have problems before I get to that stage, though."

Though modern computer technology has affected Gould less than some of his contemporaries — Pierre Boulez, for instance — Gould is open-minded about electronic music. "I've written very little of that," he explains, "because I found it difficult to find time to write all I wanted to write for traditional instruments and live musicians. Still, I am intrigued by all the possibilities that exist with synthesizers and computers. There is no doubt in my mind that they are valid new ways of producing musical sounds and textures.

"If I were younger, I would be very much a part of this new wave. Starting out in radio in the '30s, I was already experimenting with echo chambers and doing things with instruments that were slightly altered electronically; and throughout my years as a recording artist, I have stayed abreast of the developments in technology. Who knows, after I leave the presidency of A.S.C.A.P. I may become the next electronic composer. Anything is possible. Seriously, all these ways of putting sounds together are valid; it depends on how they are used and who uses them. It's a matter of what a person does with the talent and facilities he has at his disposal."

Morton Gould believes that young composers and instrumentalists should seek as broad a knowledge of music as possible if they want to succeed in the music business. "On every level there are exciting, wonderful, creative things going on. From the rock and pop field to the more esoteric music, new terrains are being opened up along with all the inherited ways of making music, from the traditional classical medium through twelve-tone and electronic composition. I think the composer and performer should be aware of all the possibilities and listen to all the great classical, jazz, rock, and other performers, because all those people have their own musicality. They enrich both the performer and the composer.

Students should be exposed to as many musical disciplines as possible, and it should be the choice of the individual which one to emphasize. It is significant how important popular music has been to young people over the years, even during periods when the establishment looked on it with a jaundiced eye."

Morton Gould has always been concerned about music education, and he is acutely aware of the problems that schools, from elementary through college, face today. It bothers him when people suggest that music is an extracurricular subject that is not so important as, say, the sciences. To Gould, the arts are what make us civilized.

"Music is an expression of the human spirit and of the spiritual quality unique to the human condition. Music is an intrinsic part of what we are, from the way we speak to the kinds of songs we sing. Babies are lulled to sleep with it; we grow up with it; we live with it as adults. For that reason, I believe that music in the schools — vocal ensembles, bands, orchestras, chamber ensembles, stage bands — should be an opportunity for young people to flex their talents in whatever form they choose to express themselves. Not all students will choose to be involved, but they must have the option; music must be part of the educational experience. Obviously, money must be available to sustain the programs.

Morton Gould and Jane Powell on the set of Delightfully Dangerous, 1945.

Photo courtesy A.S.C.A.P.

"Along with funding for the necessities of life — and I am certainly aware of the problems facing our society with the homeless, the sick, and the elderly — society must recognize the importance of museums, of libraries, of the arts, and of all those things that may not appear to have much to do with everyday survival. Money is needed to sustain and develop these institutions of human culture, and certainly I think that music education should be a part of that. One way to do this is to keep leaning on our legislators. Support for the musical arts should be one of their priorities."

Besides lobbying for legislation, A.S.C.A.P. is involved in music education in a number of ways. It provides funds for a number of musical organizations affiliated with educational institutions. A considerable amount of the money collected from users of the music it licenses is reinvested in music education.

It would seem that even a composer as prolific as Morton Gould would have some favorites among his compositions, but he claims to be neutral. "I really don't think much about my works once I have finished them," he says. "I continue to be aware of them, and I would like to think that they are being performed, that people hear and react to them, and that they get good critical reception; but you know, when it's done, it's finished.

"In the field of band repertoire I consider my *West Point Symphony* for band to be a good realization of the objective of that kind of piece. It was written to celebrate the 150th anniversary of the founding of the West Point Military Academy. Among orchestral compositions, I'm not sure...composers often have a particular awareness of works that do not get a lot of performances. For example, my *Jekyll and Hyde Variations*, which I wrote for Dmitri Mitropoulos and the New York Philharmonic in 1957, is a twelve-tone piece in my own style.

"I remember the *Tuba Suite* I wrote for you,

Harvey, and how you and your three colleagues played it for me after I hadn't heard it for a long time. As I listened, I thought, 'that's not a bad piece,' and I was happy to have written it."

After having conducted the world's great orchestras, often in performances of his own compositions, and after having been president of A.S.C.A.P., what is left for a man like Morton Gould to accomplish?

"I think the aspiration of any composer — of any creator — is to reach out over the horizon to try to achieve what you have not achieved before," says Gould. "As for me, I am still running after something, and I hope I can keep running, but not because I have any illusion of ever finding it. The horizon always moves; whenever you think you are getting close, you find it is still far away. That is what creative people are all about. I am very fortunate that I do what I like best, which is music; and I would hope that I have contributed something to an art that I love, one that affects me intellectually, emotionally, personally, and professionally. I feel lucky to have had a career in music." □

Harvey Phillips is Executive Editor of The Instrumentalist *and Distinguished Professor of Music at Indiana University. His career as tuba soloist, orchestral player, and chamber musician has spanned over 40 years.*

January, 1952

MORTON GOULD

"AN AMERICAN SUCCESS STORY" might be the title heading a sketch of the career of Morton Gould. All of his environment and study have been American, and most of his symphonic works have been based on some aspect of our national idiom.

At the age of six he had his first composition published, a waltz titled "Just Six." Two years before that he had started to play the piano and to improvise tunes of his own. At eight he won a scholarship to the Juilliard School of Music and at fifteen had finished his courses at the New York University School of Music, studying piano with Miss Abby Whiteside and composition with Dr. Vincent Jones.

When he was only seventeen, he entered the commercial music field, where he gained experience in playing routines for vaudeville, radio, dance band, and symphonic orchestra. In 1935, at the age of twenty-one, he was engaged by WOR to conduct and ar-

range his own programs with a large orchestra over the WOR-Mutual network.

In this activity Mr. Gould has had the opportunity to try out many of his creative ideas and to perfect techniques that have influenced both professional and school bands. Recently he has become more interested in the educational field and has conducted school orchestras in his own compositions, which have been increasingly popular with college and high school groups.

Among the symphony orchestras that have played Gould compositions are those conducted by Leopold Stokowski, John Barbirolli, Fritz Reiner, and Artur Rodzinski. Four "American Symphonettes," "Concerto for Piano and Orchestra," "A Lincoln Legend," "A Homespun Overture," "Cowboy Rhapsody," and "Spirituals for String Choir and Orchestra" are among his larger works.

When Mr. Gould was conducting the Cresta Blanca Hour, he composed a theme song for it, "Cresta Blanca Waltz." Orders resulted in its publication for string choir. Recently Simpson College in Iowa ordered one hundred copies of it for use in a spring festival in which two hundred string players were to participate.

Mr. Gould's "Pavanne" was the first serious work recorded by Glenn Miller in dance tempo. Published in 1938, this work is usually given credit for interesting serious writers in composing for jazz bands.

In 1944 Miss Shirley Bank became his wife, and the couple has three children. The family home is in Forest Hills, New York, where Mr. Gould composes music and enjoys model railroading during his spare time. as a textbook entitled "Arranging for School Bands." He is a member of the American Bandmasters Association, Beta Theta Pi, and Phi Beta Kappa.

946

Alfred Reed

Composer of Our Time

by Nicholas DeCarbo

Alfred Reed has published more than 200 works for concert band, wind ensemble, orchestra, and chamber music groups, and has guest-conducted throughout the United States, Europe, Canada, Mexico, South America, and Japan where he was the first American guest conductor of the Tokyo Kosei Wind Orchestra. Reed was also a staff composer/arranger at N.B.C. and A.B.C. studios in New York, and for 13 years was executive director for Hansen Publications, Inc.

Today he keeps a busy schedule with not only composing and guest conducting, but with teaching at the University of Miami, where he is conductor of the symphonic wind ensemble, director of the music merchandising program, and music publications executive editor.

What was your principal instrument?

As a student I played the trumpet, which I haven't touched for many years now. I also played piano, although I wouldn't dare let anyone hear me attempt to play either of these instruments today after so many years with the pencil. My trumpet teacher at Juilliard was very pleased that my major was composition and not trumpet.

What made you go into composition?

From a very early age I felt the desire, overwhelming at times, to communicate my ideas to other people. Although no one in my family was a musician, we loved good music and made it a part of everyday life. As a result I was always coming up with musical ideas, singing, whistling, and even imitating instruments. After seeing an instrument demonstration at school, I suppose it was only natural to tell my parents that I wanted to play the cornet. I was just 10 years old, and did not as yet have any bent towards writing. That came later, when I discovered I could write music easily and was better at it than I was at playing an instrument. From then on it was the pencil, rather than the horn, and the ideas began to come faster and faster. I always wanted people to listen to them, I wanted to share these ideas. To this day I feel composing is the strongest way I have of communicating with other people — communicating feelings and ideas that lie beyond the power of mere words to express fully and completely.

Who were your composition teachers?

Of all the teachers I had, between private study and at Juilliard and Baylor University, two stand out most strongly in my memory as influencing my outlook and my thinking — Paul Yartin and Vittorio Giannini. Yartin was a brilliant intellect, a pre-World War II Hungarian refugee. He impressed upon me the need for rigorous discipline and solid musical training. In effect, the greatest gift he gave me was the ability to teach myself as I went along. Giannini, whom I knew in New York when we worked at the National Youth Administration Radio Workshop before the war, and with whom I studied at Juilliard after the war, was for me a continuation of Yartin on an even more impressive scale. He said many times that the future of music lay in a fusion of Italian lyricism with solid German symphonic workmanship. Certainly his *Third Symphony* for band and the opera, *Taming of the Shrew*, would stand as examples of this approach. Somewhat of the same thing has been said about my own music, and, you know, you could do worse!

I understand that the writings of George Bernard Shaw and Richard Wagner have made important impressions upon you. Would you talk about them?

Because of the utter clarity of Shaw's thinking, both in musical and other matters, he exercised a strong influence on the development of my own outlook on life in general and on music and the arts in particular — perhaps even more than the teachers I've had. Although I didn't agree with everything he wrote, he consistently turned on lights in the confused and murky regions of my mind when I was groping for answers to questions that troubled me. Shaw helped me see matters clearly, and thereby gave me the opportunity of thinking things through for myself and coming to my own conclusions with something more than just wishful or hopeful thoughts to lean on.

Wagner, on the other hand, simply overwhelmed me with the sheer torrential drive and color of his music. My experience with his work came after having studied the classical composers. Since that time I have come to realize how many millions of people have had the same experience, whether they were musicians or just plain folks. It took me a long time, a very long time indeed, to work myself free of Wagner's overpowering musical personality to the point where I was able to say what I wanted and not imitate his style in any way. Also, his literary writings about art did a great deal to

open my eyes to the dramatic possibilities of music; that is, music in combination with extra-musical elements. Of course, his technical achievements in harmony, orchestration, and the development of musical textures, still based on traditional techniques that reached so far into the future, profoundly influenced my own studies in these areas then and later on.

What were your duties as staff composer/arranger for N.B.C. and A.B.C.?

My basic duties included writing both original music and arrangements of existing music for radio and television shows, and for the artists appearing on them. Original music was almost always required for major dramatic shows and sometimes for dance routines on musical comedy script shows or revues. Arrangements were required for such shows as well, but for the most part were confined to guest appearances by singers and instrumental performers.

Do you have a favorite anecdote about those days?

Yes, there is one pertaining to the advice given me at N.B.C. by an older colleague in the arranging department. I was speaking of the inordinate amount of time that it takes just to write down all of the notes on a score or part, the sheer physical labor required after the purely creative work of the composition or arrangement is completed. This colleague said, with a weary smile born of many years of writing, writing, writing, "There's only one thing I can tell you, Alfred, and that is, keep the pencil moving!" Some years later when I went to Hansen and entered the wonderful and, at times, crazy world of music publishing, I had our art department emblazon this saying as a motto for the arrangers' room, and it hung there for many years: "Keep the pencils moving!" It was even set to music as a four-part simple hymn:

"Keep the pencils moving
All the live long day.
Keep the pencils moving
Don't while the time away."

I wish I could remember the rest of it. We used to sing it whenever we had four voices handy to break the routine of writing.

As you guest conduct all over the country, what do you see as the most prominent weakness in high school instrumentalists?

Without question, the two most prominent weaknesses I encounter, and not just in high school instrumentalists, I might add, are rhythmic unsteadiness, and the inability to maintain a consistent *sostenuto* where the music demands it, such as in held tones or a long line. The two words that Toscanini used most often in his 60-plus years of conducting were "sostenuto" and "cantare," sustain and sing. To the end of his life he complained that there was not one orchestra he had ever conty of musical styles. No school or college orchestra I know of plays a steady diet of late Wagner, Strauss, Mahler, and Stravinsky, for the simple reasons that their string players can't perform that level of music. Therefore, the woodwind, brass, and percussion players, as a matter of course, consistently play far more music in actual notes and passages, and play far more demanding music in the band than they possibly could in the traditional orchestra. For this reason alone I would say that, as an educational experience, performance in a good band or wind ensemble under a conductor who knows the score, both literally and figuratively, is the most important training experience student performers can possibly have.

What developments are taking place with the band movement in Japan?

On the basis of two visits there during 1981 and '82, a great deal; perhaps even more, on a comparative basis, than in the United States. In Japan the wind band is solidly entrenched, not merely in the educational picture, but also in the concert-going and record-buying aspects of daily musical life. Of course, the fact that there are no less than nine fully professional wind orchestras in Japan already, two of them in Tokyo alone, argues louder than any mere statement can as to the support for and interest in wind music that the Japanese have.

ducted that could maintain a rock-steady rhythm without constantly being hammered at to do so. Therefore, it should not come as a surprise that younger, less mature players should experience the same problems.

Because there are no professional bands or wind ensembles, what alternative does the professional wind or percussion player have besides playing in an orchestra?

That's a difficult question. I assume, of course, that by the word "professional" you mean a person earning the entire or major portion of his income from playing an instrument. Leaving aside the possibility of playing in dance or jazz bands, there are always opportunities for studio work, although limited to be sure. If a player does want to perform in a concert band it has to be on a nonprofessional level such as in one of the slowly, but steadily growing number of community groups. He can also organize his own group as part of a teaching position in a school or college for example.

For students, the learning and practical playing experience obtained through performing in a wind group at school or in college will be of inestimable help to those who intend to become professionals. Only in the band or wind ensemble can such a player perfect and polish his technique and expand his physical and mental endurance while acquiring an intimate knowledge of the widest varie-

If you were to be remembered by one composition, which one would you want it to be?

Again, a difficult question — for a composer perhaps the most difficult of all because I believe he is best off speaking *through* his music and not *about* it. However, I should best like to be remembered by either the *Armenian Dances* or the *Second Symphony.* I honestly feel that in both of these works I have poured everything I know or feel about the wind orchestra — its capabilities and its future, at least the future I envision for it. Notice that I say the "wind orchestra" here and not the band. I am not, I hope, prejudiced against the band — far from it. After all, I owe my success as a serious writer for winds to the hundreds and hundreds of bands throughout the country that play my music. However, I am compelled to say that in my mind the true wind orchestra is the next step along the road to serious, large-scale composition for the large-scale wind group. It is to this end that I have been working during the past 30 years.

Of course, the above choices may change later on. I hope to remain active as a composer as long as I have anything to say. ■

Nicholas DeCarbo is an assistant professor of music education at the University of Miami in Coral Gables, Florida. He received his bachelors and masters degrees from Youngstown State University in Ohio and his doctorate from Kent State University.

Composer–Performer–Publisher–Audience: A Quadraphonic Relationship

BY ALFRED REED

One of the most prolific contemporary American composers, Alfred Reed has had over 200 works for concert band, wind ensemble, chorus, and chamber groups published. He is also one of the most frequently performed composers and has seen many of his pieces become standard repertoire for wind ensemble and band. Reed is active as a guest composer-conductor-clinician and has appeared in one or more of these capacities in 46 states, Europe, Canada, Mexico, and South America. Since 1966, he has been Professor of Music in Theory-Composition and Music Education at the University of Miami School of Music in Miami, Florida, where he also introduced a Music Merchandising degree program. In 1980 Reed succeeded Frederick Fennell as director of the University of Miami Wind Ensemble.

In addition to his concert works, Reed has written and directed music for radio and television shows, musical theatre, and motion picture sound tracks. He has also been active in music publishing; currently he is Executive Editor of the University of Miami Music Publications, and he previously held the same title at Hansen Publications for 11 years.

It is a saddening fact that most musicians (and nearly all of the public) remain in a state of ignorance of how the music industry really works. Yet without it, the whole continuum of musical life — composing and arranging of new music, dissemination of scores throughout the country (and, it is hoped, the world), performances, both live and recorded on disc or tape to bring music to audiences beyond the range of the immediate performing area — would almost instantly fade into silence.

We need to face certain truths at the outset, recognizing that they are not merely musical or artistic in nature, but arise from the very bedrock of the society in which we live today. These social, legal, and economic parameters establish the framework for all endeavors, and not just those in the arts. We must be willing to admit that the conditions under which a Bach, a Beethoven, a Wagner, even a Stravinsky, lived and worked are different today: that indeed, times have changed. It is the inability or unwillingness to face this single fact of life that accounts for more headaches, heartaches, and pocketbook aches, and more frustration and bitterness among composers and performers than any other.

The one essential truth from which everything else follows is this: that the single most important word as far as composer, publisher, and audience are concerned is performance. From the economic point of view there is a word even more vital than performance, and that is property.

Although the use of this word may offend some sensitive ears, property need not be a term of opprobrium when properly understood and used in a discussion such as this. All artists create properties when they write, draw, paint, sculpt, build, film, or compose; that is the nature of their endeavor. The artist's conception, however noble, significant, or beautiful it may be, cannot be responded to, judged, or enjoyed as long as it remains locked up inside his head. It may afford the artist great release or inner satisfaction to have fashioned a work completely in his mind, and he may even be content to leave it there forever; but as far as the rest of us are concerned, we cannot partake of it until it comes forth, or in the words of the copyright law, is "fixed" in some concrete medium, so that it becomes a work of permanent, and not just transient, nature. This act of literally bringing a work out of the artist's mind and "fixing" it in more or less permanent form, automatically creates a property.

Music, like drama and dance, must be performed to be grasped and responded to.

The twin ideas of property and performance have always been the essence of music. It is amazing to learn that every primitive society, including the oldest one still remaining on earth, has had very advanced notions of property and copyright. The creation and performance of songs and dances, even dreams and visions, have always been taken seriously indeed, with elaborate codes governing their legal use, exchange, sale, and inheritance. Implicit, and on occasion explicit, in these concepts is the idea of the artist not only creating a work, but also forging a bond between it and himself. There will always be something of the artist in the work, and this bond will remain a part of the work forever, regardless of who may own it in the future — a very advance concept indeed to find among the aborigines of Western Australia.

Today not only are the works the artist creates properties, the artist himself, or his name, can become a property. Since 1972, phonorecords (a relatively new legal word denoting all forms of records and tapes) have been recognized as copyrightable properties, along with printed music, books, films, and plays. Certain kinds of performances are even on their way to becoming properties in the eyes of the law.

The business of music is concerned primarily with handling these properties, and with those who make them, own them, and use them. In formal terms, it is concerned with the authors, copyright proprietors, and licensed users. The primary objective, however, has always been, and always will be performance. If a work is performed frequently enough, all else will follow as a matter of course, and the returns for all concerned will be limited only by the laws of the country, the agreements between the owners and users of the work (including the performers), and the continuing demand by audiences for more and more performances of it. Because of the continual interplay of all of these factors, it is the audience — much as some of us may not like to have to admit, or be willing to face this one fact — that in our society has the final say on everything: the work, the performers, and the performance. It is the public that decides the fate of the composer, the performer, the work, and the publisher together, in one fell swoop.

The publisher, then, is not just a printer, not just a seller of paper, but one who makes music available to anyone and everyone who wishes to own a copy of the musical work. It may come as a surprise that the two largest sources of income for most music publishers today are only peripheral to the printing and selling of paper. The fact is, performing rights and mechanical rights (the right to make phonorecords of a musical work) together yield the largest financial rewards and keep most publishing firms afloat. Both these areas have little direct connection with editing, engraving, proofreading, typesetting, artwork, photography, mechanical paste-up, layout, and printing, which together with sales and distribution, traditionally constitute the business of printing and selling paper. Unless the publisher specializes in the reprinting of works already in the public domain (where performing and mechanical rights do not apply because anyone and everyone "owns" such works, and therefore no royalties or license fees need be paid for their use), or publishes only so-called "educational music" (where even many performances of copyrighted works yield little or no return because they are overwhelmingly confined to non-profit use) he has no hope of realizing any significant return on his investments in new music without many performances. Naturally he will profit most if the performances are based on purchased copies, and if a few recordings that sell in sufficient quantity are made. If all this happens, he will not lose money, will break even at worst, and occasionally (hosanna!) manage to show a tiny profit.

It comes down to this: the publisher is the composer's agent, whose task it is to make the composer's music available to the world at large in the hope that the world will be so "turned on" (if I may so put it) that they will say again and again, "I like that; play it again, Sam." In this homespun, simple statement lies the essence of what makes any musical work a classic, whatever the length of its hair or depth of its philosophy.

Too often, especially in modern times, the diametrically opposed interests of the composer and publisher (as opposed to those of the performer) are misunderstood. The idea that a first performance, a premiere, is the be-all and end-all of the matter is simply not true — at least not for the composer, and most certainly not for the publisher. A first performance, a world-premiere performance, is ultimately of supreme importance, only to the conductor and the performers. If the work should become a classic, or at least gain wide popularity, it is the performers' names that will be forever associated with the piece and will appear, together with the composer's, in the program, the program notes, press criticisms, general articles, and future reference books, as well as on record jackets and in liner notes. Subsequent performances or recordings of the work may not be of great interest to the original performers, but for the composer and his publisher those subsequent performances are crucial. Both composer and publisher are far more concerned with the fifth performance than the first, the tenth than the fifth, the twentieth than the tenth, and so on. The fame of the composer (and the fortune of both composer and publisher together) rests right here: in the number of performances, and in their continuing on as steady a basis as possible.

This concept of a continuum of performances

brings us to yet another aspect of the matter. We have all seen and heard of at least some so-called smash hits: those works that not only were an instant success, but generated a tremendous number of performances, sold a great number of records, and went through three, four, or even more editions of sheet music, all within a period of a few months or less.

Like the supernovas they are, smash hits share a tendency to burn out after their initial impact. They either disappear from the scene altogether, or else they settle down and become what the music business refers to as standards or, in England, evergreens: works that will continue to sell more or less steadily, albeit never again in the tremendous numbers that they did during their "smash" period. Obviously the publisher lucky enough to have such a success on his hands must hope for the second of these alternatives. If the cooling supernova takes its place among the other steady income producers in his catalog, it will glorify its creator's name (and enrich his coffers) not just for a few hectic weeks or months, but steadily on into the future as well.

Another point that many composers seem not to realize whether they write pop songs or symphonies, is that when they bring a new piece to a publisher's office, they bring an investment largely of time, effort and talent; but when the publisher utters those magic words, "Yes, I'll take it!" he is committed to literally thousands of dollars in hard cash that must be spent before anyone can tell whether the investment will be worth anything at all. As a composer myself, I am not unaware of the fact that in addition to the time, effort, and talent, the blood, sweat and occasional tears that a composer invests in bringing forth a major work, there is also a certain amount of money involved as well ("living money" as one of my friends has called it); but the hard fact of the matter is that there can be no real comparison between the composer's purely financial investment and that of the publisher, who, incidentally, also must contribute his time, effort, and talent (in addition to his money) as well.

By accepting a work, a publisher commits himself up front to an investment of thousands of dollars. Certain expenses that he must incur in the publication of a new work, such as all of the preparation costs incurred before the presses can begin to print the first copy, remain the same whether he ultimately sells just that one copy, or a thousand, or none at all. In the case of a major work such as a symphony, a concerto, or an opera, these fixed preparation costs, all of which require extremely high-priced, highly skilled labor, can quickly mount, dictating a very high

price to the ultimate purchaser of the final printed copies. The only way in which the publisher can recoup all of his costs and still be able to sell copies at a reasonable price (so as to maximize the potential sales and thereby the resulting exposure of the composer's work to the public), is by spreading his total costs among as many buyers and users as possible. Assuming that there is sufficient public interest in the new work, and that a sufficient number of persons are willing to purchase copies when they become available in print, another factor enters the picture: the printing of subsequent editions of the music.

As with any other form of production, the more copies that are printed at any one time, the less each individual copy costs to print. This, of course, translates into greater profits for the publisher (if he manages to sell enough copies to cover his costs, and then continues selling more); it also means that he can recover his costs that much sooner, with relatively fewer copies having to be sold to reach that point. Even though each single copy may cost less to print in larger press runs the total printing bill still increases with the increasing size of the print order. This requires an even greater monetary commitment to the new work being published than a smaller press run would, whether it be the first edition or a subsequent one. The question then becomes: can the publisher afford it? The answer involves three interdependent considerations.

The publisher must first determine how many copies he can reasonably expect to sell, and in how short a period of time he can expect to recover his costs.

The second consideration is related to the first and varies with different firms, depending on the size of the company's catalog, its overall success, its financial structure, and its operating model. All of this translates into the simple question: How long can the firm afford to wait to recover any publishing investment it may make before running into trouble? The complexity of the question is the main reason why different decisions may be made by different firms considering the same work. One firm may be able to wait ten years and more before selling out the first edition of a new work without feeling a financial pinch; another firm may have to sell out the first edition within ten months to justify its investment in the work. Obviously, as in so many other areas of life, one man's meat may be another man's poison, and this is why certain firms simply cannot publish certain kinds of music at all: their financial structure and operating model will not permit it. There is a great

952

difference between selling 1,000 copies of a piece in ten months and in ten years.

The third consideration involves other possible income from the work, not just by selling printed paper (copies). This depends on how many public performances for profit the work may receive regardless of the total number of copies sold and how many recordings are likely to be made of it. We have already seen that it is in these two areas, performance and recording, that the largest financial returns are to be had, both for the publisher and the composer. It is entirely possible that a work that does not sell too many printed copies may yet generate a significant, even munificent, income for both parties *if* it receives a large number of public performances for profit or a number of commercially successful recordings. Naturally, an experienced publisher will carefully judge these aspects of a work he may be considering, along with its purely musical and artistic value.

There is a final consideration that may be involved, but which I did not include with the other three because it is so subjective. This is the publisher's intuition about a work. Publishers are only human after all, and their impressions of artistic works or experiences are sometimes very difficult to pin down to factual, assertive, direct statements. We all know that it is possible to be deeply impressed by something without being able to make provable comments about it. History is full of instances in which publishers (or patrons in earlier times) conceived a liking for, or an attachment to an artist or a work and continued to stick with him or it despite disappointments, losses, ridicule, or the contrary opinion of experts. This did not always result in a happy ending. Many times, in fact, it turned out just the opposite; but the attachment to, the belief in, the feeling for the artist or his work were certainly there.

It is, I suspect, this gut feeling about a work that impels a publisher to acquire it in the first place, invest a considerable amount of money in producing it, and invest still more money in promoting it. It is here, in the promotion or exploitation of a new work, that a publisher's commitment to the piece is really tested. There is an old saying among publishers (and not just music publishers, either) that you simply cannot spend more than a certain amount of money to produce a work, but there is absolutely no limit on what you can spend to promote it. You can easily spend over $100,000 to promote something that, if you succeed in selling each and every copy, will return only $10,000 in all. Surely it is obvious that no publisher, regardless of the purity or high-mindedness of his intentions, can stay in business very long at that rate.

Ultimately the composer, the performer, and the publisher are all in the audience's hands. Their hope is to be in its heart as well for a long time to come, and for the fortunate few, for all time. When that happens (and who can predict for certain just where, when, and to whom it will happen next?), regardless of the length of the composer's or the work's hair we will say of him or it, as of those of the previous generations, "Play that again, Sam, I like it!" Meanwhile, all four of us — composer, performer, publisher, and audience — must keep up the struggle; we must continue to make the investments each of us has to make in this continuing development leading only heaven knows where. There is no guarantee anytime, anywhere, for anyone. The most we can hope for is continuing opportunity; and if we can succeed in putting the common enrichment above our own personal hopes and ambitions (a difficult matter indeed), we may yet come to realize that the success, on so lofty a plane as this, of any single one of us during our own lifetime or thereafter is really a victory for all. It is this that makes the game, as it were, so exciting, and compels us all to continue playing, whether any single one of us wins, loses, or draws. □

November - December, 1948
November, 1985

Aaron Copland

—on—

Aaron Copland

When Aaron Copland's Symphony for Organ and Orchestra was premiered with the New York Philharmonic in 1924, the conductor, Walter Damrosch, turned to the audience and said, "If a young man at the age of 23 can write a symphony like that, at the end of five years he will be ready to commit murder!" That radical young composer became the leader of the American school of composers in the 1930s and today is considered the grand old man of American music. As a composer, teacher, lecturer, and writer Copland has influenced virtually every American composer living today either directly or indirectly. In honor of Copland's 85th birthday on November 14 we are reprinting the following excerpt from a television program called "A Copland Celebration" (produced by WQED/Pittsburgh). Following are some of the composer's remarks and thoughts about his life's work.

In the 1920s it seemed essential to me to have our composers in the serious field writing recognizable American music, just as the whole world recognized our popular music as being specifically American. It seemed a bit odd that if they could do that in the short forms of music, why we in the more serious music couldn't achieve the same thing.

For a period of perhaps 10 years I was preoccupied with that notion. Once I had written several scores of American quality, it satisfied me, and it didn't seem so important to stress that element in our so-called classical music. When I wanted to make some use of American atmosphere in music, I looked at a book. I had several books of American tunes. As a composer you look at a page of different folk tunes and you appreciate that this tune is very good, but you'll never be able to do anything with it. Then all of a sudden, some other tune sort of hits you and you say, "I'd like to work with this."

With the kind of life we have, it's a great help

to be able to borrow materials that the whole country recognizes as American in quality. Once I'd done several pieces it didn't seem so important to be doing the same thing. My *Music for the Theater* in 1925 and my Piano Concerto in 1927 definitely stressed the kind of jazz elements that I probably wouldn't have been thinking about if I weren't thinking about writing music that would be specifically recognizable as American.

My good friend Serge Koussevitzky, conductor of the Boston Symphony at the time, told me to write a piano concerto and play it myself. I'd never given a concert as a pianist and I was

rather hesitant, but he showed me that I could do it and was capable of playing it. So, I did it.

It caused a bit of excitement in Boston because I made use of jazz. In the 20s jazz was thought to be okay in its place, but the attitude was, "For heaven's sake — what is it doing in Symphony Hall in Boston?," as if you were playing jazz in a church. It was a shocker at the time, and I was highly amused and pleased.

El Salon Mexico

I don't think I could ever have been able to write *El Salon Mexico* (1936) unless I had actually been in Mexico. I spent several summers there

composing. I had a great friend in Mexico's greatest contemporary composer, Carlos Chavez. It was he who first invited me to come to Mexico, dangling before my eyes the possibility of an entire program of my own works played by the Mexican Symphony, which he conducted. I went to Mexico, and he did exactly that. I fell in love with the country.

The title of my composition was taken from a dance hall in Mexico City where I had found the best of the Mexican atmosphere, most characteristic and most lively. I remember it had a sign on the wall which said in Spanish, "Please don't drop your lighted cigarette on the floor so that the women don't burn their feet." It was a place to be remembered.

A Lincoln Portrait

A few years later I wanted to do a musical portrait of some outstanding American. I seem to remember having read a biography of Abraham Lincoln by an English lord. I was very taken by it — that an English lord would want to write about Lincoln and think him a great man. In that book I found various quotations from Lincoln's speeches and other things he had said. I gradually got the thought of doing a musical portrait of Lincoln and using some of his actual words to make it more particular. I'm very glad I had that idea. The work seems to have stood up quite well. I have spoken the words myself in performances conducted by others, and that's a great joy, too. I don't specifically remember where I got the idea of blending music and narrative, but it isn't that extraordinary.

A Fanfare for the Common Man

During the World War II years I think it was an idea of Eugene Goossens, conductor of the Cincinnati Symphony, to start a concert each week with a fanfare connected with the war effort. I remember a fanfare written for that series called *A Fanfare for the Fighting French*, which I thought was an inspired title. I remember how I got the idea of writing *A Fanfare for the Common Man* (1943) — it was the common man, after all, who was doing all the dirty work in the war and in the army. He deserved a fanfare. That, too, was a lucky day because I think the title sticks in the mind. Later on, I used it as an integral part of my Third Symphony.

Appalachian Spring

I've written several ballets. I lived through a period in the 1920s and 30s when we were very ballet conscious, maybe because of the fact that Igor Stravinsky was on the scene and present in our minds, and he was writing ballets. Writing for the ballet was very much in the front of our minds, more so than writing for the opera house which seemed almost too ambitious. Ballet companies are more friendly and more interested. I was pleased when I was invited to do a ballet, but I had actually written ballets before anyone asked me.

When choreographer Martha Graham asked me to write *Appalachian Spring* (1944), it had no title. She gave me an outline of what was going to happen and the nature of the dances. Many times people have said to me when they hear the music and see the ballet that they can just see the Appalachians and the springs. The fact of the matter is, when I wrote the music I didn't know a thing about the Appalachians — I was thinking about Martha Graham and her style of dancing. I was really putting Martha Graham to music. I remember that when I finished the score, I hadn't actually spoken to her about it, but the first time I saw her after that I asked her where she got the title "Appalachian Spring." She told me it was the title of a poem by a poet who had been forgotten at certain times. I said, "Well, does the ballet have anything to do specifically with the Appalachians?" and she said, "No, I just liked the title and decided to use it."

Composing for Films

I've written music for five Hollywood movies in all. It's rather fun to write music for a film if it's a really serious film with a serious point and well done. I wish more audiences could have the experience of watching the movie without any music and then seeing it the second time with music added. I think that would give them a full sense of what the music does for making the cold movie screen seem more humane, more touching, and more civilized, in the best sense of the word.

Once I had written the score for *The City*, it gave me a chance of being invited to do music for a regular Hollywood movie. The Hollywood score that I'm particularly proud of is the one I wrote for *The Heiress* (1949). The score won an Academy Award, and the whole picture was awarded.

I remember one particular scene in the film when the heiress is awaiting her boyfriend for the elopement, and she is in a state of high excitement. When carriages go by and don't stop, she naturally is disappointed. In a preview, to the amazement of the director, William Wyler, the audience laughed when the carriages passed by and none of them stopped.

Wyler said to me, "Copland, you've got to do something about that scene. We cannot have the audience laugh at that part — it means they are not taking it seriously and we have no picture. They're not having the feeling they should be having about her great disappointment. You've got to do something." I said, "I don't know what

to do with it." He said, "I don't care what you do, but do something to prevent everybody from laughing."

So, I threw out the music I had written for that scene and wrote a much more dissonant and tense kind of music. The whole orchestra recorded it, and it was pasted, so to speak, on that scene. They tried it out at another preview, and there wasn't a single sound after that same scene played. It worked. I gave Wyler a very vivid impression of what music can do in a film, even when the audience isn't really thinking about music.

Conducting and Leonard Bernstein

I move around America quite a bit in order to conduct symphony orchestras. I spent many years listening to other people conduct my own music. It was a great thrill to finally get up on stage and conduct it myself. I may not even think that I do better than some highly practiced conductor such as Leonard Bernstein, but nevertheless it's a personal joy to be able to do it in your own fashion and the tempo you think is exactly right for the place.

I remember the first time I ever heard of Leonard Bernstein was through some mutual friend who said to me, "There's a young Harvard student in Boston who plays your Piano Variations in a way you ought to hear." So I said casually, "Well, if he ever comes to New York, tell him to look me up. I'd like to hear him play it." Sure enough, he came. Looked me up and played them. I was honestly impressed.

I don't see any difference between that Leonard Bernstein at 18 and the gentleman, whatever he is, now. He seemed to know everything. He could do everything. Where he got it all from, I don't know. I met everybody in his family, his mother and father and sisters and brothers. I must say it's hard to imagine why that particular family could produce that particular Bernstein. They made some kind of miracle, and there he was. He's really a unique figure.

Music Education in America

America has a good number of well-known schools of music now in various parts of the country. We're turning out a large number of well-qualified musicians in a way that was not true 50 years ago when I began. So the scene seems very lively, and much more active than it did in the 1920s. Of course, the quality has to be good.

It's hard to keep track any longer of exactly what goes on in our country. It's so big and there are so many places where music is created. The important thing is that composers get a chance to hear their music in actual performance, well played, with an interesting audience.

A Copland Portrait

An Interview by Dana Davis

Aaron Copland is regarded as the American composer of his time. A brilliant and versatile writer, he has won many awards, including the Pulitzer Prize and an Academy Award. For the past 23 years, however, this gifted musician has been devoting most of his talents to conducting. In fact, at 78, Copland attributes his vibrant physical health to the "musical exercise" of wielding the baton.

This interview with Copland took place at California Institute of the Arts, Valencia, California, where he discussed the art of conducting.

Mr. Copland, you wear so many hats — composer, conductor, lecturer, author — which do you enjoy the most?

Well, they're a little hard to compare because they provide different satisfactions. When you compose you have the illusion, or anyhow the possibility, of composing forever. Your music is supposed to last far beyond you, and that's one of the excitements about composing. You feel you're putting something down that will go on.

Of course, if you're going to talk about sheer enjoyment, it is very exciting to conduct. In the first place, you're a performer, and that's always fun. Then again, with the audience behind you, you're up for approval, or disapproval; so if you're not a performer by nature I wouldn't advise you to pick up a stick — it's a risky place to be.

You're not composing right now, concentrating on conducting?

Yes, that's true. I've been composing for more than 50 years. That's a very long time to have to express yourself. It would be delightful to go on as if nothing had happened, but 50 years have happened.

If I had to write for a living, if I wanted to force myself, I could write; but I don't see any point in forcing myself. It probably wouldn't come out very well anyhow. So I just relax and let fate take its course.

How did you get started conducting?

I would have started conducting much earlier than I did but my great friend Sergei Koussevitzky was dead set against it. He used to point his finger at me and say, "You must not waste your time conducting. You must stay home and compose."

Of course it was very good advice, but as soon as he

Dana Davis is on leave from her position as band director at South Jr. High School in Anaheim, California. She is a graduate of California State University at Long Beach.

died I began conducting. It was a supressed passion. When you sit in an audience as many times as I do and watch other people conduct your music, finally you say, "Oh just once I'd like to get up there and do it the way I dreamt it."

Then you find that's not so easy to do because you have to develop a certain technique and feel comfortable up there in front of an orchestra. That's rather a nervous place to be, not even thinking about the audience. Having those 90 or more men and women staring at you when you're about to conduct something of your own puts you in an exposed position.

Still, it's a great joy to finally do a concert conducting a piece of one's own. It's as close as you can come to doing it the way you want it. I don't mean to say Leonard Bernstein can't do a work of mine better than I can; however he still adds his little bit. This addition might be very good, but as I say, it's just a profound satisfaction to do it in your own fashion.

Did you study conducting with anyone?

Well, I didn't formally study it but certainly I watched enough conductors and had been at enough rehearsals to get the idea of how to go about it. I knew best the conducting of Koussevitzky because I spent 25 summers at Tanglewood where he had the Boston Symphony each summer. I suppose I watched him conduct more than anybody else.

Do you think a conductor should be aware of the composer's intent when conducting?

Oh yes. That's the main idea.

What do you think of conductors who ignore the composer's intent?

I think conductors would all agree that they try to do what the composer would want, or they think they can do it better — faster, slower, or with the balance somewhat different. There are some conductors who don't admire the composer's idea of his own music, and think they can do it better than the composer's objective.

Are there any secrets to conducting the music of Aaron Copland?

No, I can't say I have any secret ways of doing my own things that I'd like other conductors to follow. I think it's interesting for a composer to hear different versions of his music, to see how it seems to somebody who's looking at it from his own standpoint. Sometimes the ideas might strike you as better than your own, sometimes not as good as your own way; but anyhow, it's always interesting to see how your own music is "read" by someone else.

Has that ever changed your own view?

Sometimes. I'll hear a conductor take a movement slower or faster than I take it and I think, "Gee, why didn't I think of that? It seems to fit the music better."

In your conducting engagements, do you conduct music other than your own?

It depends. Sometimes they ask me to do a one-man show, and sometimes they say do anything you like. In recent years more and more they've been asking me to do works of my own. When I do other works, I like to conduct the music of my fellow American composers, partly because I think we don't get played enough, and partly because I think being Americans together we ought to have a sense of how American music should sound. This is somewhat different than what a European would know about, not having lived here.

Do you memorize scores when you conduct?

No, I don't even memorize my own scores.

That's interesting. Why?

Why? Because it's tough to memorize if you don't have that kind of brain. You have to have a Bernstein brain to memorize everything. Of course you can't just open the score and start conducting, you have to study the score carefully. But to memorize a score and to be able to rehearse it from memory, that is quite a feat.

Would that tend to limit what you can do?

Definitely. That's one of the great disadvantages of always conducting without a score. It limits your repertoire. You can't learn everything by heart so you're reduced to playing those pieces you've memorized. Speaking generally, I'm against memorizing scores. I think it limits the repertoire the conductor makes use of. It's better to broaden your interests rather than to narrow them.

As a conductor, what makes a performance exciting?

I suppose one thing that makes it exciting is if everybody seems to be in the mood. That helps. And I think an orchestra has to want to play for you. They can either do a job because they're being paid and that's what they should do (they more or less do it willingly) or they do their best because they want to play for you, as if to say, "We'll show you what we can do." That kind of feeling makes a big difference in a performance.

Do you enjoy conducting a band as opposed to an orchestra?

It's very different. I haven't conducted bands often enough to know what working regularly with a band might be like. Except for the clarinets, there's nothing like 16 violins on one side of you and 14 on the other. That's quite a lot of performers. Just in size, a symphony orchestra normally would be larger than a band, with more people to think about and more balances to make. An orchestra is a more subtle instrument, I suppose.

Are there any conductors you admire particularly?

The conductor I was closest to was Sergei Koussevitzky. I knew in advance that anything I wrote he would conduct with the Boston Symphony. This was a terrific stimulus, of course, for a young composer. And he had lots of enthusiasm. He didn't just play it, but as soon as he finished performing something he'd say, "Now what are you going to write for us?" That was an enormous help.

Did you have any idols when you were a young man?

I don't know if I'd call him an idol, but a man greatly admired and who was "hot stuff" then was Stravinsky. When I was a student in Paris for three years, I'd see him walking on the street, and each new piece he wrote and had performed was a musical event. It was fascinating.

Is there anything you would like to say to a young conductor about conducting?

Aside from "work hard?" No, I don't think I have any magic formulas. I would like conductors to broaden their musical taste so they don't perform only the conventional repertoire. They should add to what is given the public with discoveries of their own.

The main problem with conductors is that they are more or less forced by the situation in the concert hall to a kind of over-dependence on the regular repertoire. There is terrific conventionality in the making of concert programs based mostly on the limited tastes of the audiences. The result is that our programs are not as fresh as they should be. Anything a young conductor could do — and it takes a certain amount of cleverness — to inject contemporary idioms into their programs would be a definite help.

Not all music is for everybody, but the gift of listening can be developed and conductors can be a strong influence in this development. ∎

Copland's Music Published for Concert Band*	
Date Published	Title
1944	Waltz from "Billy the Kid"
1948	Outdoor Overture
1951	A Lincoln Portrait
1960	Variations on a Shaker Melody
1965	Emblems
1969	Red Pony Suity
1974	El Salon Mexico
1975	Preamble for a Solemn Occasion
1975	Waltz & Celebration from "Billy the Kid"
*published by Boosey & Hawkes	

Meet the Composer: Vaclav Nelhybel

Meet the Composer: Vaclav Nelhybel

Vaclav Nelhybel is a favorite composer among student musicians and is also a colorful guest conductor. He has written some of the most widely played instrumental works, such as *Trittico, Sine Nomine* and *Symphonic Movement* for band. Players delight in his inventive rhythms and use of antiphonal choirs.

Nelhybel (whose full name is prounced VAHTS-clahv NELLY-bell) was born in Czechoslovakia and studied music in Prague, even though his parents tried to discourage him. His main instrument was organ, but he also studied many others (everything, he admits, except double reeds, saxophone, percussion, and string bass).

He gained valuable orchestration experience when he was house composer for Radio Prague, and he later got to experiment with electronic music while writing film scores as musical director for Radio Free Europe. He came to the U.S. in the late 1950s and it wasn't long before he "discovered" music education and began writing for school groups.

A dynamic man with a great sense of humor and dozens of fascinating anecdotes, he continues to be "interested in anything and everything."

What kind of musical opportunities did you have in school?

Absolutely none. Some students took private lessons, but there were no orchestras or any organized ensembles. I recruited my own group at the boarding school where I stayed so I could learn how to compose for an orchestra. At the same time I was devouring books about music, harmony, and counterpoint.

All on your own?

Yes, because I had no teacher, and my parents did not want me to go to the conservatory. I went to the university first in about 1938 and studied musicology. My parents thought I was actually a philosophy student.

But this was at the time of the Second World War, and Hitler soon closed the university. Then I was accepted as a student at the conservatory. It was an oppressive period musically, because Hitler wasn't allowing performances of works by Jewish composers, American composers, Stravinsky, or even Debussy and Ravel.

When did you write your first professional composition?

I was about 19 when I first heard the Czech Nonette, a woodwind quintet plus violin, viola, cello, and bass. I like the combination of instruments and so I wrote something for them; it was my first composition to be played by professionals.

From then on things seemed to go very fast. I had many compositions performed, including a combination ballet-opera when I was 27 years old. Once you get public recognition, commissions start coming in and everything rolls along.

Why did you start writing for school groups?

Well, in about 1962 when I'd been in the U.S. for five years, someone dragged me to my first music education convention. I was fascinated

959

with what I heard, especially the bands, which were a new medium for me. In Europe bands are just functional marching units.

The first band I heard played a piece by Persichetti, and it was so good I just caught fire. I was fascinated with the possibilities of what you can do with half an acre of clarinets, half an acre of flutes, and half an acre of percussion. So I said, why not try it? I did, and it seemed to open new creative channels in my mind.

What really inspired me was the great enthusiasm of the students, and after I visited a

---

"I am always collecting ideas, and I keep them in about 300 folders according to instruments, structure, rhythm, and so on."

---

few schools I tried writing one or two pieces for them.

The first piece was *Chorale,* the second was *Prelude and Fugue,* the third was *Trittico.* By then I was hooked forever on writing for students. I was also hooked because of the enthusiastic reaction from band directors; I especially love the way they all refer to "my kids," never to themselves.

You never studied percussion yourself, and yet your writing shows such great insight into what it's like to play the instruments. How did you learn that?

When I was first starting to write for bands I experimented with a very bad band at a school in New York City. I realized that when the percussion stops, the whole band stops. The percussion preserves the pulsation of the music. Very often composers use percussion as a kind of counterpoint against the rest of the band. What I did differently was to treat the percussion as a partner on the same level with the melody instruments. I never use percussion just to make noise or to cover something up — it is carefully chosen for structural reasons.

Percussionists tell me they like my music because they feel they are doing something important in it. Many of them have said, "You know, when I start playing, I feel as though the whole band is turning around to listen to me." That's happened often, with many different instruments. Music with interesting parts can make the players feel important.

Do you mean that everyone is a soloist at one time or another?

Not necessarily an actual soloist, but one who feels like a soloist. Once a young boy came up to me at a rehearsal and said, "Thank you for writing that solo for me." I thought he was a horn player or something, but it turned out that

he was an alto clarinet player. Just because his part was slightly different from the third clarinets, he thought he had a solo part.

How do you begin writing a composition?

I am a composer 24 hours a day. I don't have certain hours when I sit down and say, "Now I will compose." I am always collecting ideas, and I keep them in about 300 folders according to instruments, structure, rhythm, and so on.

How do I start a composition? There are two ways. First, if someone comes to me requesting a piece for string quartet and orchestra, certain channels in my brain are activated. Practically speaking, I will go home and take out my string quartet and orchestra idea folders, and see what happens. When I look over the ideas I immediately tune into something. That's why I'm a composer and not a bricklayer.

It is different every time. Sometimes the melody comes first, other times the harmonic structure, orchestration, or rhythmic pattern. I just start putting it all down on paper. Finally I sketch it out somehow, and then I put it away for awhile.

At first I have created a chunk of music. Then I begin to think about the musicians. I go back to make sure I didn't neglect the tenor saxophone or something. I think to myself, this player is sitting here and he hasn't played for 25 measures. Should his entrance be here or there? Loud or soft?

Do you compose at the piano?

No, I compose completely without piano, so when I write down something, it's always specifically for xylophone, trombone, clarinet, or tuba. Whenever I conceive a musical idea, I think of it in terms of the tonal color of a specific instrument.

As for musical material, I have always liked to incorporate modal scales, going back to Gregorian chant. My music also has always had enormous fluency with rhythm and meter; even in a simple piece the time signatures may constantly be changing between 5, 4, 6, 3, 2, or 4 beats per measure.

Have you had any "magic" moments of discovering something about music?

I remember one, when I was rehearsing a band in a lousy little bandroom where the students didn't know me, they weren't playing my music, and I could hardly speak English. But I suddenly realized that I could actually move them with the music. It was a shake-up for me, a major revelation. I felt that I was really accomplishing something.

Students have sent me thousands of letters, and I never will be blasé about them. Those letters mean so much to me. I'm close to 60 years old, but I don't think of the students as 12 or 16. They are people who want something bigger than life. I love to turn them on, to excite them. I want to addict them to music.

Gunther Schuller and His Many Worlds of Music

An Interview by Frank Battisti

Frank L. Battisti is a graduate of Ithaca College. He is conductor of wind ensembles and chairman of the music education department at the New England Conservatory.

In many ways, Gunther Schuller is a modern incarnation of the renaissance man, with his interests and abilities flowing from him like ripples in a pond. Born in New York in 1925, his prodigious musical talent surfaced rapidly. While still in his teens, he played solo French horn in the Cincinnati Symphony Orchestra. Soon after, he joined the Metropolitan Opera Orchestra as first horn, holding this position for 15 years.

As a composer, he has written in a wide variety of styles, often incorporating jazz techniques in symphonic compositions. His works include such widely diversified pieces as Seven Studies on Themes of Paul Klee (1959), Spectra (1958), Meditation for Wind Ensemble (1961), Conversations for Jazz Quartet and String Quartet, Symphony for Brass and Percussion (1949), and an opera The Visitation (1966).

He is a writer of distinction. His literary output includes Horn Technique (1962) and Early Jazz: Its Roots and Musical Development (1968). The latter work is the first part of a three volume story of jazz now in preparation.

In 1967 he was appointed president of the New England Conservatory of Music and in 1963 head of the composition department at the Berkshire Music Center, and has since become artistic director of Tanglewood.

In the short time since this interview took place Gunther Schuller has conducted the orchestras in Palermo, Italy, St. Louis, Fargo, North Dakota, and numerous concerts with the New York Philharmonic; he has composed a thirty-minute piece for three orchestras and spent two weeks in Japan in connection with its world premiere, served in residencies in New Mexico, Michigan State, Michigan University, SMU (Dallas), and he has given innumerable concerts with the New England Conservatory Ragtime Ensemble.

Tell us about your early musical experiences and influences.

I was fortunate to be born into a musical home. For 42 years my father was a violinist with the New York Philharmonic, and I was taken to concerts practically from the day that my mother brought me back from the hospital, from the cradle really. My father never was my formal teacher. It's just that I absorbed the musical influences around me in a sort of process of osmosis. I recall sitting in the bathtub at age 6 or so, playing with little plastic boats, singing the entire Tannhäuser Overture, imitating all the instruments. Later, when I began to study music in a more conscious and systematic way, I realized that I already knew a lot of things without ever having had to really learn them in a formal sense. I was very fortunate to be living in New York City in the late 1930s and 1940s. New York must have been one of the few cities at that time with three major classical music stations. That enabled me to hear and learn a tremendous amount of music at a very early age. When I was 13 I could identify almost any piece that came on the radio by hearing just half a measure or so of it, or sometimes just the opening chord. That wasn't because I was trying to break some kind of a learning record; it was just that I had such a voracious appetite for music. I began to spend all my allowance or earned money on records and began to accumulate what is now a substantial record collection. In those days — this was the days of 78's of course — I was buying every record I could get my hands on or afford. When I was eleven I attended St. Thomas Church Choir School in New York as a choir boy, and the organist and head of the school, Dr. T. Tertius Noble, was also my first theory and counterpoint teacher. It was at that time that I began to make my first attempts at composition. A piece I had written for string quartet was performed at a school concert. My father got three other members of the New York Philharmonic together and they played it. At 14 I left the school because my voice "broke" and I couldn't sing soprano any longer.

Did you study piano also?

Well, I did but not very successfully. My father thought I should learn to play the piano, not to become a pianist necessarily but just to "get around" on the keyboard. But I wouldn't put in the practice time that it required. I also didn't have the physical coordination to become a good pianist. Also at this time, I was literally surrounded by orchestra musicians of the New York Philharmonic, and was taken to concerts and rehearsals at Carnegie Hall and the Lewisohn Stadium. When I saw Joe Amans, the Philharmonic's Dutch-born first flutist, with his brand new shiny gold flute, I knew I wanted to play that instrument. Later, of course, in my last year at the Choir School, I fell in love with the French horn and began studying with Robert Schulze, fourth horn of the New York Philharmonic.

What were you composing at this time?

Of course, one begins by imitating. I remember one of the first things I tried to write was an imitation of a Mozartian-style etude, written by some anonymous German piano pedagogue. I must have been eleven or so. But I soon got more ambitious. Since my whole life was involved with the orchestra, what I wanted to write was orchestra pieces. And I did with a vengeance. I must have written a dozen or so very pompous, portentous orchestral openings of pieces, which I never finished. At that time I rarely wrote for smaller groups. I even wrote an opera based on a popular kid's novel of that time, one of those adventure stories, you know.

I had heard my father practice the violin all my life: I used to sit and watch him and follow the music. In this way I picked up a lot about string writing intuitively. Dr. Noble said that I had talent and he encouraged me to go on composing. So I became even more involved with music and really began to study scores. When people ask me, "How did you learn? How did you do all this by yourself?", I always answer that I had two teachers. The first was the musical scores themselves. I saved all my money and what I couldn't buy, I borrowed from the public library. I'd take out dozens of scores every week. My second teacher was playing in the orchestra. If you play and listen analytically as you play, that of course is the greatest kind of learning experience. I find it sad that there are so many musicians in orchestras who are playing but who have stopped listening. Listening was really how I learned.

How did you budget your time? You were composing, practicing, playing, and going to school. How did you work that out?

I learned to organize my time when I was a teenager. I was going to high school and of course I didn't want to fail any subjects. So I worked enough to maintain a B average and I guess I did shave some time off of my school studies in order to have time to compose and in order to study scores. And then I was also practicing the horn. At first I didn't practice enough; I was too occupied with composing. It was difficult for me to say, "Today I'm going to practice five hours on the horn" after coming home from high school when there was always that urge to compose. I gave it maybe an hour and a half or an hour, and sometimes I really short-changed my horn practicing. You have to steal from somewhere. I really didn't practice as much as my horn teacher wanted me to and he often had to reprimand me for what he regarded as throwing away my talent. But one period I remember very vividly when I put in three or four months of hard practicing during a summer vacation. Young players today may not realize that at some point they're going to have to put in that kind of real woodshedding work. It's what we call "paying your dues." Even if your lips feel like falling off, you've got to put in that kind of consecutive,

Gunther Schuller, 17, talking to two members of the Cincinnati Symphony, just after Schuller joined the orchestra.

hard, tough, absolutely critical, uncompromising practicing before you can go out and play all those auditions that you want to play, and before you can really survive in a professional context. Before that summer I had been a talent, I was developing, but I was also a little dilettantish and casual about it all. Suddenly there was that realization that, boy, if I want to play the French horn and make a living with that and face a lot of competition, I'd better do something really drastic about it. And I did. For half a year I almost gave up composing because I realized I couldn't do both at that time. Then at the end of that "paying-your-dues" period I took three auditions, one with the Philadelphia Orchestra, one with the Pittsburgh Symphony, and one with the Cincinnati Symphony. The best offer I had was for first horn in Cincinnati, so naturally I took that. Eugene Goossens was the conductor. I was very fortunate in that choice because Goossens planned and performed wonderful programs. He found a marvelous balance between the staples of the literature and exploring some of the less travelled byways. Being English, he also introduced a lot of contemporary English music — like Walton, Vaughan Williams, Bax, etc. — which we didn't know at that time. He also was a very fine composer himself. So I had in my two years in Cincinnati a richness and variety of repertory which most symphony orchestras couldn't match. Well, I took all of that music and studied it, and also studied anything else I could get my hands on.

How old were you when you went to Cincinnati?
I was seventeen.

You were so involved in music, but were there other things that you were interested in?
Well, first of all I should mention that I left high school when I was 16, because I got the chance to join the Ballet Theater Orchestra with Antal Dorati conducting. So you might say I was a high school dropout. That was a year before going to Cincinnati. But to answer your question, I was a voracious reader of literature at that time. I also went to museums a lot and even went so far as to frequent art galleries. Later, when I was making more money at the Met, I even bought some paintings by fairly famous European and American painters. I was an avid reader of all the artistic, cultural, literary and poetry magazines. I was living a very full life, not just dedicated singularly to performing or even to music but surrounding it with all these other things. I also became very interested in films as an art form, not merely as entertainment, and I used to study them avidly. I began to recognize the parallels between structure in film and structure in many forms of music. And then, of course, naturally I fell in love with a succession of girls and eventually married one of them. Although I loved bike riding, and some sports like soccer, handball, and hiking, I suppose I was not the typical American kid.

What were some of the musical influences that affected your work as a young composer?
Scriabin, Debussy, Ravel and early Stravinsky were very strong influences on me because one thing that characterizes my composing, conducting, and playing

is a strong predilection for thinking and hearing harmonically. I've come to realize over the years that in different people there are varying degrees of sensitivity to harmony. I can listen to pieces which have virtually nothing but harmonic interest and be quite satisfied, while I know that for other people such pieces (let's say by composers like Delius or Rachmaninoff) are anathema and boring. Maybe it's something in my genes. In any case, harmonic composers like Scriabin, Delius and Debussy really got to me. I was able in succeeding years to transfer that interest over to the non-twelve-tone works of Schoenberg and Berg and Webern, and to pieces like Schoenberg's *Five Pieces for Orchestra* or *Erwartung* or Berg's *Violin Concerto* and then later to twelve-tone music itself.

My generation of composers was confronted with a choice which now in retrospect seems slightly ridiculous; you had to choose between two camps in music, the Schoenbergians and the Stravinsky-Copland camp. You were not supposed to belong to both camps. Anyway, I thought that was nonsense because I felt that both were great masters. So I would have to say that my developing musical language was an amalgam of the influences of Stravinsky and Schoenberg, but with Ravel and Scriabin also in there.

Being self-taught it was only after I had developed to some degree a harmonic and melodic language of a particular quality, that I began to seriously study matters of musical form and structure, which I had been weak in up to that time. I must have been 19 or 20 before I really began to discipline myself as to those aspects of the craft of composition. And as I've already said, I learned these things not with a teacher, but by playing in orchestras and studying the scores of the great masters.

When did you start becoming interested in jazz?
In those days, the early 40s, the radio networks were all doing remote broadcasts of the famous big bands: Duke Ellington, Count Basie, Jimmy Lunceford, Harry James, Glenn Miller, etc. I began to listen to these air-checks, and to my amazement I saw absolutely no musical qualitative differences between the best of jazz and let's say a Dvorak symphony or a Strauss tone poem. Somehow I escaped the stigmatization that implied that jazz was to be listened to differently. Many people claimed that jazz wasn't as good as classical music and was somehow suspect or degenerate. My parents didn't approve of jazz. They thought it was kind of cheap music, but I don't think they really distinguished between real jazz and the various commercial derivatives. My mother berated me for liking Louis Armstrong's singing, for example. In her mind she contrasted his raspy, non-trained voice with operatic *bel canto* singing. But while my parents tried to dampen my enthusiasm for jazz, they never actually forbade me to listen to it. And that's how I heard things like Duke Ellington coming from the Hurricane Club in New York at 11:15 at night and I became as fascinated a listener to that music as I had been to Ravel's *Daphnis and Chloe* or Stravinsky's *Rite of Spring*.

Later I took Duke Ellington and Count Basie pieces and even some pop tunes of the day and made arrangements of them for the Cincinnati Symphony. Of course I had to put anything that resembled genuine jazz into my own French horn parts because the Cincinnati Symphony in 1943-44 was full of older musicians who were pretty far removed from jazz. I began to notate dozens of pieces from recordings because they did not exist in score form. For example, I made a serious study of Ellington performances for years, and I guess I haven't finished studying his music yet. The tragedy is that you can go into a music store in any large city and buy the Beethoven Fifth but you cannot buy *Cottontail* by Duke Ellington. I found that his compositions had wonderful form, tremendous melodic and harmonic sophistication; they had variety and terrific instrumentation — in short they had all the things that good music should have. Then I also began to play jazz on the French horn — this was still in Cincinnati — and I used to go down to a joint in one of the downtown alleys and sit in with a trio made up of piano, guitar, and bass. The first things I tried to play were blues because they contained elementary chord changes that I could handle.

Your interest in music has been extremely broad, from jazz to ragtime to country fiddle music to marches to classical music. How did you develop such wide-ranging interests?

I always knew the ragtime music and fooled around with it a little at the piano but not really being a pianist I never could get involved with it as a professional performer. Then later, around 1971, I realized that the orchestrated versions of Joplin's pieces would give me an opportunity to perform this marvelous ragtime music, at least as a conductor. And that was how the New England Conservatory Ragtime Ensemble actually got started; that is to say when I got a hold of the arrangements in the famous Red Back Book.

As to the other musics, those interests are all a combinations of having been first of all a listener for a long time and then through some accident of fate finding some reason to become actively involved with them. It was always the same reaction, always the same experience: I would hear this country fiddle music, for example, and say to myself: that's great music, it's clean, it's strong, it's beautiful, it does exactly what it says it's going to do. It may lack the development section of a Beethoven symphony but in its three or five minutes duration it sets its goals and perfectly accomplishes them. It's pure and honest music and deals with the same musical elements that all other music deals with. Whey should I have to put it into the country-fiddle bin, so to speak, and segregate it from the rest? With marches it's the same thing: a great march is as great an artistic achievement as the creation of any other kind of great music. Not everybody can just sit down and write a march; I wish that I could write a march as good as Sousa's. Naturally, if marches are merely played loudly without the dynamics and the contrasts that the composers wrote into them, then they appear to be a much lesser product. But that's not the composer's fault but rather the performer's. For me, the whole world of music consists of an immensely large spectrum of musical possibilities, philosophies, schools, concepts and techniques, in which there are great, good, not-so-good, and bad practitioners. I have never been able to see the qualitative differences between musical categories which many

people ascribe to them inherently. My view of music is pluralistic and it is a horizontal one, not a vertical one in which we pigeonhole or segregate different types of music. When I hear bad rock music or when I hear bad wind ensemble music or bad classical music, I don't then say that therefore all rock or all wind ensemble music is bad. One of the things that tells me that something is really getting through to me musically is when I get goosebumps, or when I am moved to tears or choke up. Well, I cried at Pete Turner singing the blues in Kansas City and I realized that it made me cry in the same way that Daphnis and Chloe did or Debussy's *Pelléas and Mélisande* or Wagner's music. At that level of physical response there's no way to argue that Pete Turner's music is a lesser creation.

Why do you write pieces for 16 French horns, 4 string basses, or 4 tubas?

I love to write for groups of similar instruments because of the particular sonority combinations that you can get that way. It's like the old renaissance consort tradition. To write for four tubas or five French horns or three oboes or three trombones or five saxophones is a special kind of sonoric problem of writing, and an interesting one. It's not necessarily better than writing for a mixed ensemble, but it's different. Also, I keep being asked by musicians to write for their instrument, most of them feeling that their instrument doesn't have a substantial enough literature. In other words it not only is very fulfilling for me, but there is a functional use for the music as well. I think it's very well for composers to dream of gigantic visions, of writing great timeless masterpieces, but it's nice to also take care of the immediate needs of tuba players and such.

Why haven't you gotten into electronic music in your compositions?

When I start writing electronic or synthesizer music I want to precede that by perhaps half a year of serious study of the medium so that I don't become just another dabbler and dial-twister. We have too many electronic music dabblers.

But electronic music does interest you?

Absolutely. In fact I've been one of the staunchest defenders of electronic music against those people who talk negatively about it. I constantly point to certain works which are masterpieces of the medium, such as some pieces by Milton Babbitt and Mario Davidovsky and Charles Wuorinen's *"Encomiums,"* for example. Before I would call myself a composer in the electronic medium, I would want to really do it right and that means a great deal of study of the medium which so far my life has not permitted me to do. On the other hand I must differ with some composers who feel the electronic medium is the only answer to their musical problems. They are often people who feel that the instrumental medium is exhausted. Now I don't feel that at all. On the contrary, I feel the orchestral medium is virtually inexhaustible. For me it would be a question of eventually balancing my composing between the two, with probably always a predilection for instrumental and vocal writing.

I know that you sometimes have aleatoric sections in the music you write, that there's a chance for the players to improvise. Do you feel that a totally aleatory piece is something that you would ever compose?

I see aleatory writing as one of the additional technical conceptual possibilities for the composer, but a minor one. I don't think that an entire piece consisting of only aleatoric procedures would be for me a totally valid musical experience. I hold to the belief that if the composer's name is on a composition he must retain the maximum responsibility for that piece. Now the average orchestral player hasn't the remotest idea of what it means to improvise or invent something. And therefore if you allow them too much freedom and give them too much responsibility, they will simply fall back on various remembered clichés of one kind or another. To my way of thinking, this in no way helps the creative process or the creative product. As a composer I don't wish to be held accountable for things over which I have no control, and knowing the paucity of invention of most classical musicians, I just will not abdicate that responsibility to them. Now when I say paucity I don't mean that critically; it's not their fault that they can't improvise or create spontaneously; they simply haven't been trained to be improvisers. Where in the average conservatory do you learn to improvise? Now when you're talking about jazz musicians that's different; that's a highly disci-

plined kind of improvisation with its own rules and techniques. That I like to work with.

There is a wide gap between present-day composers and their potential audiences. Can we blame this gap on the lack of student exposure to new music in our school programs? Or do you feel that composers themselves need to reconsider important issues in musical expression and communication?

Both. I think we have all defaulted on our responsibilities. The composers are guilty by not demanding enough of themselves and by not asking tough enough questions about what they are producing: like if what they are composing is not commmunicating, why isn't it? They just keep blaming the audience, the environment and the educational system and leave it at that. I think there's more to it than that and composers had better start worrying about what they're creating lest this gap will widen even more. Unless you can bring music to new audiences and can convince previously unconvinced people that what you're doing is worthwhile, you aren't making much progress.

Now, on the other side, the educational system indeed does not do enough to develop audiences and to teach us to be intelligent listeners. Our educational system simply does not produce musical literacy, a musical culture in the broadest, deepest sense. There's

965

little attention paid to music in most places in this country and even less to new music and the problems of how to hear and interpret it. In other words we have a classic situation of two opposing sides at a stand-off, frowning at each other and blaming each other: the composers and their audiences. The alienation of the composer from the audience is very serious now. The composers say the audiences are all dummies anyway and don't know anything about their kind of music, so the composers write for each other. And the audiences are saying composers don't care to communicate to them through their music and so they won't listen to it. Our educational system must attempt much harder to grapple with these issues and also to understand that there are some magnificent 20th-century works. Whether they equate ultimately with the level of the Beethoven *Eroica* or Bach's *St. Matthew Passion* doesn't even matter as long as they are of a certain quality relating them to our standard literature. Many composers are quite insensitive to the desperate plight of the audience. They don't seem to want to contribute anything to educating their potential audiences. They don't seem to want to meet them halfway, offering to help them to understand. Another thing, how do today's composers answer the same questions that Monteverdi, Bach, Beethoven, Schubert and Wagner or any other of the great masters not only had to constantly ask themselves but had to have an answer for? Questions like, how do I write this piece so it communicates or relates to an audience? Their answers were, the piece must have a melody or a theme; it must have harmony, form, clarity, and logic. Beethoven, for example, not only asked himself those questions but he also came up with some terrific answers, including some very innovative and radical ones. In other words, he wasn't just working with tried-and-true formulas.

Today, we seem to have rationalized all those tough questions out of existence. We simply say, "It's not necessary to have a melody, it's not necessary to have harmony, and the heck with audiences if they can't follow it." Well, I think we can no longer keep on just blithely saying that. We composers do not have to write down to the public, nor abdicate our originality or our individuality. The greatness of Beethoven partially resides in the fact that he was highly original. But he also answered all those tough questions brilliantly.

Your background is one of a symphonic musician and a jazz performer. What got you interested in the band and wind ensemble?

For the same reasons that I was interested in writing for 16 horns or 4 tubas, because it seemed to me that there was a sonority inherent in the wind ensemble which you do not have in the symphony orchestra, that there were unique expressive and technical possibilities which I'd never had an opportunity to exploit before. I believe that the acoustical hardware of the wind ensemble is one of the most fascinating innovations of our time. The possibility of that kind of a rich palette of instrumental colors fascinated me for years. Then in the early 1960s the College Band Directors National Association became involved in a commissioning program and I received some of those commis-

sions. In those days there was some opposition to the idea of twelve-tone composers writing for the wind ensemble. But others argued that it was absolutely necessary to keep the medium alive by giving it injections of new ideas, new techniques, new idioms. Since then, I think there have been some very fine additions to the wind ensemble literature. When you think back just 15 or 20 years, most everything was block chord writing. And then there were always these kinds of "chase" pieces as final movements, with the dum-dada-dum rhythms going on endlessly. If you compare them with the textural pieces that are being written now, you can see that there is a whole new sound which was previously unknown in the wind ensemble medium.

What qualities must a good conductor have and can these skills be taught?

That's a difficult question. I think that a lot of what ultimately makes a great conductor cannot be taught. Of course, the rudiments of baton technique and the elementary craft of how to study a score can be taught. But once you get past those stages it becomes a personalized art in which your own individual musical insights are a vital part of the end product. And there's a limit to how much of that can be taught.

How do you feel about music education in the schools? What do you think about the kind of music teachers we should be seeking to teach our young people?

That's also a complex question and problem. I guess we've done fairly well in this country in producing teachers, particularly those going into higher education. I'm much less happy about what I see in the primary and secondary educational levels because I do think there is a lot of inadequate teaching going on there. Most of this is caused by a lack of political or economic support, and by a great amount of public apathy concerning the teaching of music in our schools. There are some superb school systems, of course, but there are others that seem to be describable best as disaster areas. We must try to produce more teachers who are the finest musicians, performers, composers, or conductors that we can possibly train, and at the same time are people who are emotionally and psychologically totally committed to teaching, who love the act of teaching and working with young people, who feel fulfilled by it. It is important that the teacher continue his personal participation as a performer of music, otherwise fossilization takes place and you lose contact with what is happening in the front lines, so to speak. What you then end up teaching is only what you remember from the past, not what is happening in the present.

As a youth, perhaps Gunther Schuller was not the typical American kid. But elements of the many-faceted Schuller personality can be found in many music students: insatiable curiosity, talented musicianship, emotional sensitivity, wide-ranging interests. In a way Schuller represents a combination of qualities and talents found in varying degrees in many of the students we teach, though it is rare when they appear in one person. As teachers, we must be aware of and recognize these precious qualities when we find them, in whatever quantity. It might surprise us to learn that the typical American kids we see in our classrooms, rehearsal halls and private studios every day are very special indeed. ∎

Musical Dynamo

February, 1978

An Interview with W. Francis McBeth

Dana Davis

W. Francis McBeth is professor of music, chairman of the theory-composition department, and resident composer at Ouachita University in Arkadelphia, Arkansas as well as a well-known guest conductor. His compositions for concert band are highly respected, frequently appearing on festival programs.

To attend a clinic by W. Francis McBeth is to guarantee yourself two things: you will learn something new or refresh yourself on a technique you had forgotten, and you will be entertained. Dr. McBeth, who talks fast for a Texan, says "Nobody has ever learned anything he wasn't enjoying." He sprinkles his clinics with a stockpile of humorous anecdotes that help him make his points, but "funny" he is not. Behind the animated facade is a dedicated musician with a serious purpose: to improve the performance of band music in this country. I had a chance to talk to Dr.

McBeth when he was a clinician at the California Music Academy, California State University at Fullerton.

As you attend clinics and conduct bands across the country, what do you feel is the single biggest problem with bands today?

Interpretation. Much music is boring because of wrong interpretation. Wrong interpretation can make a good piece dull, and the greatest crime in teaching is to be dull. The problem is that technology took over. Now we've got to have technology; we've got to have good subdivision, balance, and pitch. But technology without musicality is just boring. It's not a musical experience, it's a competitive experience.

Dana Davis is a band director at South Jr. High School in Anaheim, California. She is a graduate of California State University-Long Beach.

967

When you say interpretation, what specifically are you referring to?

Interpretation is the recreation of the composer's intent, and 99 percent of this intent is written on the page. It is not a situation where the conductor has the prerogative to use his own interpretation.

The secret to interpretation is *volumes* [dynamics]. Interpretation is 20 percent tempos and 80 percent volumes.

In rehearsal I work on interpretation even before the notes. I don't care how good you are, if you don't have interpretation you might as well have not played.

What can band directors do to improve interpretation?

Number one, you must understand what the music says or does, and then you must change your attitude toward musicality. It's a step beyond technique.

Bad conductors conduct the score and not the band. They should try rehearsing from memory and get their head out of the score.

And you must use body effects when you conduct. Your body must do what the music does. Exaggerate everything in your conducting, and don't mirror your hands. Mirrored hands destroy the importance of your left hand. The left hand should say, "Band, look up, I have something to tell you."

Also, in off-contest time, play some simpler music that has fewer technical problems so you can have more opportunities to interpret.

After interpretation, what are some of the other big problems you are finding with bands today?

After interpretation would come balance and pitch, subdivision, and programming. Programming is part of our entertainment problem. We must not only be artists, we must entertain.

There is absolutely nothing in this world more boring than a poorly programmed concert. I hate to say this, but there aren't many band concerts I'd drive across town to listen to because they are so boring. And I love band music.

People tend to program what bands can play with little regard to the order or overall effect. You've got to program dramatically. You've got to get the audience's attention at the start, and then you have to use a slow work in there somewhere.

Slow music is where your band learns tone quality, breath support, interpretation, and balance. If you don't have a slow piece on your concert you're missing a large area of teaching.

With my clinic bands our programs are a little shorter than regular concerts. I usually do five pieces: an opener, a slow piece, a large work in the middle, a light number, and a large work at the end.

I never do an encore. I think an encore is the worst thing you can do. The audience likes to know when they can go, and you should leave the audience wanting more.

What do you look for in a rehearsal?

Discipline is the first order of business. A rehearsal should have an air of tension, and you can get it two ways: through fear or through excitement. Both are effective, but you can lose both ways.

With an atmosphere of pure fear the students get so tense that they never do well on a concert. With excitement they can get so high you'll never pull them down.

I prefer the excitement approach, but with the ability to tack a kid's hide to the wall when needed and then get back immediately to what you were doing. I think of it as the Dr. Jekyll - Mr. Hyde approach.

How do you develop a dynamic range in a band so that they can play what is written using a full range of volumes?

Lash them into it. I don't know of any other way. I work on interpretation constantly. It is almost an imprinting. The first time they do it should be right. Once we get the interpretation imprinted, we can work on other things.

Then you don't read through music completely the first time the band sees it?

I've never read through a whole piece because you are imprinting. I continue playing as far as possible so as not to make the rehearsal boring. After a stop or some isolated work with one group, I choose a starting place generally farther back than necessary. This method keeps a higher percentage of kids playing during these work periods.

The first time through we work on the high spots. We never try to perfect the piece the first time. The second time we work a little bit more specifically, and the third time still more.

How do you warm up a band?

I prefer that the kids warm up themselves. If you save ten minutes a day for nine months you've saved just about three to four weeks. Of course, with some school schedules you have to warm them up yourself.

There are a million different warm-up exercises. Whatever you like you can use. I would just suggest starting in the lower register.

I like to start the band warm-up on the F major scale, right down to the lowest F on the instrument. After we've done the F major, we do the C major. It's a little better register than the B♭.

Once I feel they are warmed up enough, we tune. I wouldn't work with balance, interpretation, and dynamics during warm-up. I work with them in the music.

How do you tune a band?

I tune to the first chair tuba. I know it's a little strange to use the tuba. I guess I started that, and others are doing it now. The reason is that if the tubas are out of pitch, everybody's wrong. That because the tubas can't be out of pitch.

Is that clear? Turn it upside down. If the tuba players are in pitch with each other, they are right. I don't care what else is determined, the tubas are right. They can't be wrong because they are at the bottom. You know that there is no such thing as the foundation being too short for the house. It is because it is.

But why not tune the tubas to the first clarinet or oboe? Why sound the tuning note from the bottom?

I've found that kids and professionals, too, can hear lower pitches better than higher ones. Tuba players have a hard time tuning to a clarinet, they really do. I think it is rather obvious when you think about it.

I like to bring the B♭ up through the band where nobody masks anybody else. In other words, I start with the first chair tuba, have all the tubas match that, then come up from the bottom, adding instruments till we reach the top.

The one thing you don't want is to have everyone play the tuning note at one time. When you do that the trumpets and the flutes usually play too loudly and the lower instruments can't hear.

The one thing I refuse to do is to go down the rows and tune individual kids. If you do that, you just deny then the ability to learn.

I noticed that as you worked with the clinic band you had them sing the B♭.

Singing is probably the best method of tuning that can be used. When you sing the tuning note, you relate it to the instrument a little better.

To use the tuning note singing idea, you should first have the tuba sound B♭ and then have the band sing "la" to match it in a comfortable register. In about three seconds you will hear this note come in tune. There is hardly a kid in a million who can't sing that B♭ in tune, and it is a very pure sound.

You can tune sections this way, and they can hear when they're off. Have the entire band sing the B♭, and when you cut them off, have the section play the same pitch alone. It really works. They heard a pure pitch from the singing and they'll hear when they're off.

What about pitch as you are playing?

Once the band starts playing, you really don't have any control over pitch. You have control over tempo, expression, and so forth, but you can't control the pitch. The band has to control the pitch.

The trick is that you don't work on pitch. You work on balance first. Pitch is a direct result of balance. I wouldn't say it is impossible to have good pitch without balance, but it is nearly impossible. To balance a band you must have a concept of what balance is.

In your book, Effective Performance of Band Music *(Southern) you explain your pyramid system of balance. Is this a new idea?*

It's not a new sound. It's as old as good bands. It's a new way of thinking it and teaching it, that's all.

Do you have any special secrets to a good performance on stage?

Number one, don't ever pull a curtain on your band. Their mouths will get dry, the adrenaline pumps, and they won't do well on the first number. Let them go on stage with the curtain open, find their chairs, and locate their mothers in the audience. Then they will be much more relaxed.

I believe in talking to the audience at concerts. If you talk to the audience about important works, they will enjoy them more. I've also talked a bad band through a good concert. The audience can't hear what you're saying if you talk to the band, so sometimes I'll look at a soloist and say, "Come on John, you can do it." It helps.

I also have a habit of stopping during a concert for dumb mistakes, like a keyboard percussion player with the wrong mallets. I'll just stop the music and turn around and tell the audience why. If the kids know you'll do that, they won't make dumb mistakes. I really should stop doing that though. It's getting so my wife won't come to my concerts.

As far as concert seating goes, I've been looking for 20 years for the best place for everybody. I know I don't want any brass on the outside. I want the brass blowing through warm bodies.

Some people come up with a new seating, but a new seating isn't going to change the sound that much. It isn't going to cure a lot, although you can use it to move the weak players out of the front row.

Do you have any suggestions for improving percussion sections?

First of all, don't let the same kid play the same instrument all year. You have to rotate them so everybody plays everything. Keep them on the same instrument on the same piece, but otherwise make them rotate.

Do not buy sticks for the kid. The only things you should buy are mallets and beaters for the gong, chimes, bass drum, and possibly the triangle. Everything else the kid owns.

You're talking about $75 per student when you include all the mallets they need to buy, but you have other kids sitting there who have paid $400 for an instrument, so $75 isn't much to ask.

If a kid doesn't own his sticks, he doesn't feel like part of the band. Once he owns those mallets he's suddenly going to start playing glockenspiel, xylophone, and timpani. You've got to make sure students buy a case for the mallets. It is vital psychologically.

If you do these things you'll start getting a percussion section instead of some drummers. I'll guarantee it works.

I also came up with something that helps mallet players learn to play without looking at the keys, and it works great. Buy a dark bed sheet or dye one black and throw it over the xylophone. The kids work right over the sheet as they practice. Sure, it ruins the tone quality, but who cares? They're practicing for kinesthetic accuracy.

Your son Matthew has played trumpet for nine months. If you had to move to another state or area, what qualities would you want to find in his new band director?

Number one is musicianship. He would have to be a good musician. Number two, and possibly on the same level, is sensitivity to a kid's needs and feelings. Those kids are tender. You can't treat them harshly without leaving a mark on them.

If you had one last word of advice to give band directors, what would it be?

The greatest sin a teacher can commit in the classroom is boredom, but the worst thing you can do to compensate is to relate to kids. Don't relate. Elevate! If you relate to someone musically you leave him where he is, and he goes down from there. And secondly, just because we are teachers doesn't mean we have to stop being professional musicians. Teachers are the real professionals. ■

Meet the Composer An Interview with CLARE GRUNDMAN

Did you have any special training in composition when you were in high school?

No, actually just living in the band and orchestra at school, listening to all the sounds going around, got me interested in arranging and scoring.

What instrument were you playing then?

I started playing clarinet when I was 13. I'd gotten free lessons from the music store when I bought the instrument, but I hated them because the teacher was dreadful. I put the clarinet in the attic immediately and didn't touch it for a year or two.

Then our high school music director in East Cleveland, Ohio, gave us a piece to try to get kids interested in the music program. I got the clarinet out of the attic and learned about 10 notes. The director let me join the orchestra where I had to play A parts on an Albert system clarinet, which is probably one of the hardest things you can ever try to do. That's how I got started. Pretty soon I got into the band and played saxophone in some good dance bands.

Did you do any composing while you were in high school?

Well, I did a lot of arranging for our dance band and some for the band. I didn't have any formal training. I bought a couple of books, one of them on dance band arranging, and then wrote as well as I could for the high school bands.

Did you ever get a chance to study composing with a teacher?

Sure, when I went to college at Ohio State University. I really got interested there in doing some decent scoring and original writing. When I finished school I taught high school music in Columbus for a year and then spent two hectic years in Lexington, Kentucky, where it seemed

Clare Grundman's quietly spectacular career has made him one of the most widely respected and most familiar composers in America. Almost everyone who has ever played in a band recognizes Grundman titles such as "Two Moods," "American Folk Rhapsody," "A Classical Overture," "English Suite," "The Black Knight," "Little Suite for Band," "March Processional," and "Trumpets Triumphant." Grundman learned his art through his experiences as a teacher in Ohio and a writer for Broadway and radio shows in New York City. But this modest master preferred to leave the big-city glamor so he could compose works for band, orchestra, chorus, and wind ensemble in a peaceful rural area of New York State.

like I was teaching music to the entire town. I taught five grade school bands, two in junior high, and the high school band. Some days I think I spent more time riding in my car than teaching.

Did you have any time to compose then?

Yes, in fact it was precisely *because* I was teaching that I started writing for school bands. I just couldn't find anything that the kids could play, especially in the lower grades. I started writing some original things and rescored written pieces so they would be easier to play and would sound better.

What was wrong with the works you needed to rescore?

It seemed that a lot of arrangers didn't know how to simplify running passages, especially for the woodwinds. They'd have every instrument playing all the notes instead of breaking up the lines among the various parts. The kids would throw up their hands and complain that they couldn't figure out how to play all the notes. The music would sound horrible too.

So was that the time you began developing your famous ability of writing music that sounds as if it were much more difficult to play than it actually is?

Well, I remember that when we used to go to band competitions some of the bands would sound dreadful, trying to struggle through. My band would sound really good because the music was scored simply and was pretty well divided between parts. The judges didn't even notice I'd split up the parts. You see, there are lots of good tricks that can be done with orchestrations to pull the music apart, most of which I learned through teaching. I found that little kids can learn almost anything if you just give them a chance by making it playable.

Did you get any experience teaching at a more advanced level?

Yes, after teaching in public schools I directed band and orchestra at Ohio State for four years. I took a brief leave-of-absence to study composition and counterpoint with the great master Paul Hindemith at Tanglewood in Massachusetts. By then I knew I really wanted to arrange and write music for radio and television. I went to New York and finally landed an arranging job with the Lucky Strike Hit Parade Program. I also got to write background music and bridges for the Helen Hayes Theatre, which is what I wanted to do most. I was just beginning to get really involved in New York when the war broke out.

Did you have to serve in World War II?

Yes, I joined the Coast Guard for four years. I played clarinet in the band and then got to teach and organize several army transport bands. I didn't compose much during that time, except for some background music for government propaganda movies. But I did meet a music publisher from Boosey & Hawkes in the service who suggested to me that I try writing an easy overture or something for a junior high school band. That's when I wrote "Two Moods."

That piece is still played by practically everyone who's ever been in a band! Is that really the first work you published?

Well, I'd actually written "American Folk Rhapsody" before "Two Moods," but the "Rhapsody" wasn't published until after the other.

Where did you go after the war?

I went back to New York and wrote some more for television, musicals, and ballets. The best experience for me, I think, was a musical called *Lend an Ear* starring Carol Channing — before she'd become a big name. I did all the orchestration and conducting in the pit for six months. I liked it for a while but then got tired of it.

What other shows did you work on?

Not too many. After *Lend an Ear* I didn't want to take on another whole show. Writing music for an entire show is too big of a job. Besides, I didn't like all that messing around taking a show on the road. So I just started helping out other composers to write parts when they get swamped. I did some work, for example, on Leonard Bernstein's *Mass* for its opening in New York City. Most of my time has been spent writing pieces for band and some for orchestra, chorus, and wind ensemble.

I've been trying to get completely out of the New York scene ever since I moved out in the country here in South Salem, N.Y., about 90 minutes outside New York City.

You weren't too impressed with the glamor of commercial music then?

No, it was a real rat race to me, especially TV. I got out as fast as I could. I'd had enough. Now I just write music at my own leisure — sometimes out here I even get *too* leisurely! I'm still writing under contract with Boosey & Hawkes. That is, they get first choice of whatever I write. To date, knock on wood, they haven't turned anything of mine down.

What advice would you give to a high school student who wants to become a composer?

To be good in any field, whether it may be art, literature, sports, or anything else, you've got to start with the basics. For a composer, the basics are an understanding of harmony, theory, and counterpoint. Later if you want to get away from the traditional framework, you can. But at least you have something to start writing from.

Then if you're going to write for a certain medium, such as the band, you should really get into that medium. It's hard for people to write or arrange for band when they haven't played in it and don't really know how it sounds. If they've only heard the band from the audience, sitting up front, they never learn what can and can't be done, and exactly what combination of instruments sounds good or bad. Probably the best composition lesson is to listen to the colors and sounds of music while you're sitting right in the middle of it all.

Claude T. Smith

On Composing, Conducting, and the Art of Teaching

BY JOHN THOMSON AND JAMES WARRICK

I n a musical world increasingly intent on ratings, technical skills, and bottom lines, Claude T. Smith is a refreshing voice from a saner past. Equally comfortable as a conductor and composer, he directed high school bands in the Kansas City area for 17 years, then taught orchestra for two years at Southwest Missouri State College before assuming his present position as staff composer for Jenson Publications, Inc., Editorial Consultant and Composer to Wingert-Jones Music, and Director of Music for the Blue Ridge Presbyterian Church in Kansas City, Missouri. On a brief layover in Chicago between flights, Smith shared his thoughts on enduring musical and personal values.

"My good friend Francis McBeth once told me that the two most influential people in a student's life are the coach and the music teacher," says Smith. "I think that's right, because at those two levels you're with the kids on a very personal basis. The other teachers see them for an hour and they're gone; some students might just be considered a name or a number in a grade book. Band directors get to know kids on a very personal level. When you run into kids so often and work with them year after year, you begin to know their personalities by the way they play, the way they react to you, and vice versa. After one hour with me," he adds, "they know exactly what kind of person I am."

In his long career leading high school bands, Smith says he tried to maintain a perspective that took into account the student's life as a whole, not simply his part in the school's music program. "I don't think it's fair for high school students to devote three hours a day to band, because they have other obligations. They need to study. I admire the band director who can do his job in the alloted time or

perhaps a little extra, but not to the point that the student dreads going to another after-school rehearsal. By the time that kid's a senior in high school, he will have had it. He won't have the enthusiasm, because of burnout.

"I admire the instrumental or choral director who has a large senior class, because that shows the director has done something right. I think the biggest compliment I ever had as a public school music teacher was when my seniors told me they were going to continue playing their instruments in college." Motivating students at all grade levels is important to Smith, both in his work as a composer and as a conductor. He points out that it can be difficult to write for junior high school students because of the limitations in their ranges, techniques, and rhythmic capabilities; but he says, "I work very hard on those pieces because I want that level of player to be as excited with the music as the skilled college or professional player."

Smith says that finding ways to maintain this kind of excitement about music in players can be difficult. Students can suffer from burnout; so can directors. Teachers who have become soured especially bother Smith. "I hear band directors say, 'Well, next year I'm going to get out of this high school business and go teach in the junior high.' I feel sorry for their junior high students, because they are probably going to get a burned-out teacher. Potential teachers need to be told about burnout and that it can be avoided if they are careful of the situations they create for themselves."

Smith is quick to offer further advice to ward off burnout. "Band directors," he cautions, "should schedule carefully what they do with their students, especially in relation to trips, competitions, and festivals. They should spend more time in rehearsals teaching music. It's the

things outside your program that wear you down. I'm convinced nobody gets out of band directing because of the music; it's the fund-raising, the trips, and the contests. These things are important, but too many of them divert you from what you love the most. We've got people still teaching who are 55 years old who have as much energy and love for their career, students, and music as they did when they started. Burnout is going to be a problem until people honestly confront what's happening to them."

Smith singles out competitions as potential hazards to the spirit of enjoying music. "Some directors are too competitive in their approaches to music," he says," and I'm not sure that competition is what the art is all about. Certainly the world is competitive, and that aspect is built into our human nature; but competition as the sole purpose of music education is not the way it should be.

"Naturally everyone wants to get the best rating he can, but the director and students shouldn't walk away from a competition where they received less than a '1' and feel like failures. A rating is just the judgment of two or three people as to how a group did that particular day. When I judge festivals myself, I always think, 'Here I am making a judgment on what these people are doing, while not knowing how much time they rehearse every day, the quality of their facilities, whether they have 10th, 11th, or 12th graders, or if the students study privately.' My judgments are just personal opinion. It's unfortunate that some directors live and die by ratings."

If excessive attention to ratings is the bane of the field, though, Smith still sees competitions as a potentially good experience. "I enjoy a good, healthy, festival where students can go to hear other ensembles play. If the director is serious about competition, then his group will be in

there listening to other bands or choirs perform. It's important to know what other people are doing and what the standards really are, instead of going in, playing, and never showing up at the hall again. That's the often-overlooked part of the learning experience that makes competitions and festivals valid."

Parents can be another challenge to the high school band director. "I remember a great quote by a good friend in Texas. He ran a majorette camp, and he asked the girls to give the 'majorette oath' every day before they started their routines. Here's how it goes:
"I will practice my horn daily,
I will practice my horn daily.
I will stay out of the way of the band,
I will stay out of the way of the band.
I will keep my mother at home,
I will keep my mother at home…"
Still, "Parents are an important part of the job," says Smith, "because they're looking out for the best interests of their children. I think we all sometimes need to stop, step back, and see what we are doing in relation to the child's overall growth. I'm tremendously concerned that many public school instrumental teachers are exploiting young people in the interest of winning trophies and prizes. Many parents' complaints about their children's band director are valid."

Community bands present a different set of considerations for the conductor. As a frequent guest conductor, Smith stresses that working with adults who pick up their horns only once a week calls for a sense of perspective as well as conducting expertise. As he explains, "The director can't always expect a professional level of performance from people who are there performing purely for their own enjoyment. Some of the players may not play very well, but there should be a place for those people to play, because something in music is speaking to them. It's like a church choir; the members vol-

unteer and really want to be there. The loyalty among the top-notch community bands is solid."

Claude Smith's composing clearly has benefitted from his long conducting experience. His *Emperata Overture*, frequently programmed by high school bands across the country, provides examples of modernist techniques that can challenge the high school student without overwhelming him. "I had written *Emperata* to be performed at a contest," he remembers. "Two weeks before the piece was to be performed I had an emergency appendectomy. While I was in the hospital, the choral director called and said, 'I'll be happy to take your band to the contest for you, what are you playing?' The next day he called back to say, 'I can't find the score and I keep running across measures that just don't feel right.' I had forgotten to tell him there was no score and that I had been rehearsing from sketches, so I ended up

copying the score for him and the judges just one day before the competition."

Unless a commission calls for a specific ensemble sound or instrumentation, Smith writes for a symphonic band of 65-70 players, the sonority with which he is most at home. "Certain things fit wind ensembles very well, especially if you want to write for piano, harp, intricate percussion sounds, or exotic instruments such as contrabassoon or English horn. Those instruments tend to get swallowed up in large ensembles.

"Some band directors don't realize that the instrumentation needs to be thinned down at certain times. It bothers me to hear school bands play two alto sax parts with seven alto saxes. With only one alto and tenor on a part, the sonority remains much clearer and cleaner. If you've played in an orchestra, then you realize that the winds don't play all the time. If you watch the fine high school, college, and service bands, you will see players resting and trading off. A brass player can't be expected to play every note of a two-hour concert, because it's physically impossible. It is important for the director to develop the teamwork that it takes for people in sections to work together."

Smith's music is filled with rhythmic challenges, such as ⅞ meter, that some high school musicians may not have seen before, but which provide good experience for their future encounters with 20th-century music. "Rhythmic variety and a contemporary flavor are important to 20th-century music," says Smith. "Much recent music, such as that of Stravinsky and Copland, uses asymmetrical rhythms. Students can get the feel of the odd-metered bars once it is carefully explained to them. It's important for the conductor to explain the beat pattern and how the measures are put together, so the players can feel the right rhythmic pulse. I once conducted *L'Histoire du Soldat*, and that cured me. Its complex rhythmic structure confused me for a

while, but it's fun and easy to do once you get into it.

"My conducting is much better since I left high school teaching, because I get to interpret more now. Many public school teachers are great teachers but they haven't had the opportunity to develop any interpretive conducting skill, because that's the last thing they get to in rehearsal. A 'class' organization is one where interpretation begins the first day the piece is rehearsed. You can do this even in the smallest of school bands; the secret is not to make the music too difficult. Many directors pick music that is one level too difficult for their groups. If the notes and rhythms are a problem, then the music itself is going to be a problem. It is wrong for the conductor to worry about a clarinet line that has never going right because it is technically too hard and then one day before the concert to announce, 'Oh, we've got it.' It is wrong because when it comes to the concert, the clarinet players probably won't have it.

"The best groups are the ones that can handle the pieces from a musical standpoint where everything is there early enough in the rehearsal process to work on molding lines and phrases. A lot of high school bands try my *Festival Variations*, but most teenagers don't have the physical stamina it takes even if they have the technique and range. They don't have the physical maturity that a 30, 35, or 40-year-old person has to make that much music happen in 10 minutes." Smith clarifies that he doesn't mean that a grade five band should always play grade four music, but rather that directors should judge whether their players can meet both the physical and the technical challenges of a piece."

Building and challenging students is the director's job, believes Smith. "We have a great amount of fine literature being written for symphonic band at every level, and it is important for the conductor to choose very carefully what he has his group perform. Directors have to be selective and give students the best opportunity to play the best possible music rather than just pulling a piece out of a drawer and playing it. Since the days of Clifton Williams, we have had a wealth of music written for band, and I think that is what has made band music become so popular. Band commissions are exploding in this country. Composers are booked up for a year or two in advance with commissions."

Smith would like to see benefits of this healthy state of affairs spill over into orchestral music. "If we were really serious about music education in this country," he says, "every school would have an orchestra. So much of the wealth of the great literature lies in the orchestra." Beyond that, Smith says, "We should look toward the students' futures as selective listeners, encouraging them not to just accept what the media gives them. Instrumental music students have a better appreciation for the best music because they have heard and worked on great music. They can have a higher degree of intelligence if they are aided by fine music teachers."

As a young man Smith says he was lucky to have helpful, encouraging music teachers. He supports activities such as the Oswald Competition that provide incentive to young composers. "I admire the high school or college band director who gets excited when a student says, 'I have written a piece; can the band play it for me so I can hear it?' " says Smith. "It is important for future writers to have directors who will take time and let their pieces be heard and recorded in a good fashion and not just a run-through."

Whether students are interested in composition or any other career in music, Smith advises them to "go where their hearts take them, not necessarily where the money is." He explains, "I see too many people who do not enjoy their adult years because they are doing something they do not enjoy. I think it is important that young people, with the help of parents and counselors, find out where their real interests and talents are and move in that direction.

"If students want to be professional performers I try to be frank with them. You have to be extremely good, competitive, and able to withstand many auditions. You have to be patient and want badly to perform. If you are good enough and have the right personality, I think you can succeed in professional music. Personality is a large part of it; people enjoy working with nice people who are not egotistical. The finest players I know are nice people. Many professionals are good people to be around. Because many students want to pursue performance as a career but are afraid to ask questions, I think it is important for high school music teachers to instill in students a sense of what the professional music world is all about. Students need to know what the standards are and what practical matters they will have to manage in music as a business."

If a student feels teaching is what he wants to do and he has both the desire and talent to do it well, Smith believes he should pursue his interest. This educator feels that "teaching really is no more difficult today than it has ever been. Directors often create their own situations. The school district may put obstacles in your way because of the lack of funds or facilities, but those problems have always been there, and the best teachers work around them. Successful teachers are able to take the good with the bad and be very happy."

Certainly Claude T. Smith qualifies as one of those well-adjusted people who have made the most of their talents. He's happy with the paths taken; as he recently told one band he guest-conducted, "I'm fortunate because I'm doing exactly what I want to do. . . . I don't envy anyone." He would like to be thought of, he says, as a good father, husband, and citizen — and as someone who enjoys working with people. "Everybody has some kind of problem in his life, and I think to be unkind to people only causes negative results. We have to work for as many positive results as we can, because in music we are dealing with human emotions. Musicians first get wrapped up in music because it is so emotional, but some directors become so demanding that they forget they are dealing with human beings. They consider the music first and the human beings second. If you are in education it is important to set a good example, like a parent. Students copy what their teachers do, and I think to show them how to be a good citizen we should be understanding of other people." ∎

John Thomson and James Warrick are the Wind Ensemble and Jazz Ensemble directors, respectively, of New Trier High School in Winnetka, Illinois. Both are also New Music Reviewers for The Instrumentalist.

Paul Yoder —
The Right Man at the Right Time

Andrew Balent

I grew up playing Paul Yoder's music. When I was in high school just about every band around was playing his arrangements of Joshua *and* Dry Bones.

It has been my privilege in recent years to get to know Paul and in December 1980 we finally got together with a tape recorder. He was at the Mid-West Clinic preparing folios for the Director's Band, a job he has carried out for many years. My months of anticipation were richly rewarded.

How has the school band business changed in the 50 years that you have been active in it?

There have been a lot of changes, most of them to the good, I would say. I started out with my first publication in 1933, for Rubank. I was teaching at the time in Aurora, Illinois, primarily in junior high and I found that there was not enough music that the kids could play. Most of the music was a holdover from the era of the professional bands and was too hard for the kids. So I became interested in writing for my own groups.

School bands had started some ten years before, around 1920-25. In fact, the first national contest was held in Chicago in 1925, promoted by the instrument companies. There were some good bands at that time, though not nearly as many as we have now, and they didn't have the repertoire that we now enjoy.

Henry Fillmore had written, under the name of Harold Bennett, in a very easy grade. It was understandable music, with a lot of canonic imitation, which the kids picked up readily. The professional arrangements before that time had a great deal of rhythm. For instance, the horns played nothing but rhythm. The 2nd and 3rd clarinets, the 2nd and 3rd cornets, and the 1st trombone often played rhythm. There was not much except an octave or so of lead in the 1st cornet, 1st clarinet, flute, and oboe, with perhaps a countermelody in the baritone or trombone, and a bass line. Otherwise it was pretty dull from the players point of view. Perhaps it was what the composer or arranger wanted to say, but the youngsters had to have a part that was interesting.

Andrew Balent is a band director in the Fitzgerald Public Schools of Warren, Michigan. He is active as a composer/arranger with over 200 published works.

I also found out that anything more than eight measures rest was a personal insult. They were ready to quit the band and their fathers ready to take the horn back to the store because they had paid all this money and their kid was just sitting there counting rests. All kinds of little things like that don't exist any more.

There were not too many musicians arranging for band who had experience with the school band; they were strictly from the professional ranks. If they wanted to write in the key of A, they wrote in the key of A. I found out that there were only four keys in which you could write: F, B♭, E♭, and A♭ as far as majors. None of our bands at that time played well in the minor keys, and a good many of them now don't have enough experience to understand the minor scales properly from the standpoint of intonation.

Later on, about the time of World War II, a good many more men and some women came into the field of arranging and composition; and they brought new ideas and in many cases changed the image of the band.

Now another thing that had a great influence on the band were the contests. In the 1920s there were the national contests in which bands that had won in their own states competed. That was the era when the Joliet High School band from Illinois became so famous by winning the national contest many times. Bill Revelli and the Hobart, Indiana high school band made their reputation so strong in Class B in the national contest. That was when Revelli made his first impact on the band field. Up to that time the band had been pretty much a military affair. *Mezzo forte* was about as low as they got in dynamic level and if they got lower the intensity of tone disappeared and it became a weak sound. Revelli had been a violinist, had been well trained, and had a good ear. He knew you could have tonal intensity on a wind instrument without sacrificing the sound, and that you could play softly and still have intensity. So that was the way he taught his players. His band came to the national contest and played Kenneth Alford's *Vanished Army* as a warm-up march and simply took the audience apart. They had never heard anything to equal the sound of that band: the intonation, the dynamic contrast, the excellent precision, everything.

Now from there a lot of fellows got the idea you had to have a soft band if you were going to win a contest. So everybody shooshed down all the players, but the results, many times, were far from what they were trying to imitate with the Hobart band. It was just a thin sound that didn't have any life, dynamic contrast, or intensity.

A whole evolution began to develop around bandmasters from across the country who had made a success and influenced other directors from their area. Clinics began to spring up. The first use of the word clinic, in reference to a band gathering of lectures, exhibitions, etc. was, as far as I know, at the University of Illinois. A.A. Harding used that as the title for his gathering, where bandmasters throughout the country would come to hear lectures and demonstrations. Harding was a master at transcribing material for the band. He had a wonderful band with full instrumentation and had a great influence on improving the caliber of literature that bands were able to obtain.

Students still had to start from whole notes for beginners in the fourth or fifth grade or wherever they were; and somebody had to have the method material where you could take a class of all instruments, piccolo to bass drum, start them one day and keep working with them. That's not an easy thing to do and it probably is not the best way to do it, but with one teacher in a school system it was impossible to have private lessons. Teachers were forced to have class lessons and that was the key to having numbers in the band and also the key to the band spreading.

How did you get started in music?

I began by playing in the junior high school band in Grand Forks, North Dakota. I was in the sixth grade, I think, and saw a toy drum in a store window. I asked my father, who was a teacher, if he would buy it for me for Christmas. Well, he did better than that. He wasn't necessarily enamored with the drum, but he thought that if I was going to be a drummer I should try to be a good one. He went to the music store, bought me a regular snare drum, and found that the clerk there was a drummer in the local theater. He arranged for me to have private lessons; I started out in the sixth grade practicing on the drum pad, and learned to read music. Before long I was invited to play in the junior high school band. This was about 1919.

We had an excellent bandmaster, Leo Hasley, a good solid German musician who had played on the road with the circus. He was one of H.A. VanderCook's early students and had the German attitude and practice of never telling you that you were any good. I knew him for years. After I had finished college and had music published, I would come back and sit in with the municipal band. He would refer to me as "Bells," or "Timpani," or "Drums," never calling me by name. He used to tell my Dad that I was doing pretty well, but he never told me that I knew anything. It was probably good psychology.

I got started that way and then went to the University of North Dakota where my father was on the faculty. I had a chance to be the student direc-

tor of the band for three years. There was a band director by the name of John Howard who was a very wonderful man, and became a very good friend of mine. He was very perceptive about a student who was thoroughly interested. I was excited because he let me conduct when he would go out on business or judging dates; I would have the University band for two or three rehearsals. I could go to the library and pick out anything I wanted and try to conduct it. I had a good bunch in the band, and they would stick with me and laugh if I made a mistake, but they'd give me a chance to get some experience.

I was also taking journalism, a field in which I had a great interest and some ambition, but I started playing in a local theater. In those days we had vaudeville and silent pictures, and every theater had an orchestra. We had four pieces for the matinee and five in the evening. I was playing drums, and of course in vaudeville, that is very important because you have all the cues and all the tempos to make. I remember my first year in college when Ginger Rogers came through. She had just won a Charleston contest in Texas and was on the vaudeville circuit with a dancing act of her own. I asked her mother, who was with her, if Ginger would dance at our fraternity party at the University on a Friday night. She was allowed to come out and dance for about five minutes with piano accompaniment. I paid her fifteen dollars. I don't suppose she would ever remember it.

I had a wonderful experience and was fascinated by show business. I loved it because the drummer had so much to do, taking all those cues and handling all that responsibility. I was ready to stay there; making $36 a week as a high school student in 1926 went a long way. I thought that it was the end of the world; I was never going to do anything else. Well in 1928 they came out with sound pictures and it wasn't more than six weeks until we were out completely. No more theater.

That was one factor which gave a boost to the school band business. In cities like Minneapolis, the biggest place in the world to me, they had a 60 piece orchestra in the State Theater playing for the stage show as well as background music for silent pictures. Then all of a sudden it was no more. Here were 60 men and women out of a job; instrument companies lost 60 professional people as a market. These people had to do something but none of them had a degree. Some would get permits to teach in the public schools and some taught privately. It gave an impetus to the school band because there were so many professional musicians that had to find some kind of work. Most of them wound up teaching groups or privately.

Then bands made this very fortunate tie up with football, when they would do the half-time performance. It started with college bands and became a real big thing. Men began training especially for the marching band. At the University of Illinois, which I mentioned before, Dr. Harding did the concert band, coming to the games perhaps to conduct a number, but Ray Dvorak was the marching band director. He would spend hours with the band every week in preparation for the show and hours on the field in drill. Glenn Cliffe Bainum also started at Illinois and then went to Northwestern. Both of them became very important leaders in the field of marching band as well as concert band.

The marching band caught on with people. Television is now giving it a rough time, but I feel the marching band is still a very important part of an athletic and music program, especially in the high school, because it brings so many people together. When you count up all the flag carriers, all the twirlers, rifles, etc., you'll find there are some high school bands with up to 300 pieces. That brings in many students from the school who are interested in the band, even if they are not doing the musical part. It has been a big factor in keeping the movement alive.

What was the first piece you had published?

It was called *The Family Band* — a novelty, and it had words. Let's see if I can remember it:

"Oh, it's always nice to hear a band play.
How I love the trumpet and trombone.
Bands are quite a treat,
Marching on the street,
But did you ever have one in your home?
My brother plays the trumpet, ta ta ta ta ta.
My sister likes to tease the saxophone.
My auntie and my uncle
Play clarinet duets,
My father likes to play the melophone.
But when grandpa bought a trombone
That's when I left home."

Pretty bad! I had one called *Stepping Out* with hand clapping and all that. The thing was, music was deadly serious. The Bennett books were great; they had some things with humor in them, but most everything else was very serious. The kids wanted to have some fun, relax at times, and do something that attracted the audience more. Humorous music was my holdover from being in vaudeville and the theater. I had a lot of novelty tunes; one went something like:

"See how he beats on the big bass drum
The great big drum
He hits it some —"

McAllister played that with the Joliet band at the contest out in Denver, not in the contest, but at a concert at the same time. That was published by Rubank; they gave me a chance to do a book of 16 pages, for which I was paid $400. On the strength of that I quit my teaching job and moved to Chicago. Conn got me a job starting a band at Loyola Academy. I was paid 15¢ a rehearsal, collected from the kids. Then Harold Bachman, my godfather really, introduced me to some other publishers and I went into the field of arranging popular music. There were plenty of arrangers in New York but they knew nothing about the school band. The pay was very low, about $35 for a number which would take me probably three days, and I had to copy all the parts. If I had used a union copyist, he would have charged me twice as much as what was paid for doing the arranging. So it was ridiculous. I had to do the work myself in

order to have any income. But I was very grateful and I did get in with some good firms. I had a book published by Sam Fox and some great tunes done with Harms: *Dancing in the Dark, Night and Day, Tea for Two,* and others.

I was proud of my work because I was trying to make a band sound better than it was. To do that, as you know very well, you need easy keys, you've got to know the registers, the range of the horns, the problems of crossing the break on the clarinet, the auxiliary positions on the trombone. You have to understand what the youngsters are going to do, so you can prevent as many errors as possible.

I have been criticized many times by other musicians. I had a joke at the American Bandmasters Association. They included me in a round table discussion with several pretty high-class composers and arrangers. I told them that I always like to come to the A.B.A. because I am insulted by such a high type of musician. Their problem was they felt that there was no balance in my arrangements. I had everybody blowing all the time. I replied, "Did you ever sit in a junior high school band as a player in fifth grade on 3rd cornet, and try to play low C♯ all by yourself with nobody else on that note? It's impossible." I would double things like that low C♯. I'd have the trombone on a B♭, or an alto sax on a G♯, or something that was not too difficult to do. When they were blowing in this kid's ear, he could get some idea of what was going on.

Of course you want to have rests, that's the way to get variety; you don't want to have everybody playing all the time. But the youngsters had to blow, they had to get their training, they had to be involved. As I said before, you couldn't give them more than eight measures rest without losing their interest.

That is why it's important to understand the instruments and particularly the problems of a young player. All that had to do with the arrangements. Where you might be criticized for writing too fully, the band would actually sound much better because it wasn't going to fall apart. You couldn't include the little interludes we used to have in professional show medleys when you had four bars of oboe and French horn. Probably neither one of the instruments were in the school band and you would be cuing in for somebody else. If they were there, they wouldn't be advanced enough to take a solo passage and be responsible for it being musical and in tune.

Did you make a living then as a full-time arranger and composer?

Yes. I expect that I was the only one who really made a living as a free-lancer. I taught from 1930 until 1936 in Aurora, Illinois and Evansville, Indiana, and then moved to Chicago and strictly went on my own. Except for that little job at Loyola I was making it on arranging.

I find that incredible when I see the prices of those old pieces, with full band sets at around $3.50 and marches at 75¢. You must have sold a tremendous amount of music to be able to make a living at it.

I didn't get many royalties. Neil Kjos was good to me and he gave me royalties from the begin-

A discussion with Edwin Franko Goldman at the 24th annual Band Clinic at the University of Illinois, 1953

ning. A little later on I did the *College Songs for School Bands* for a half royalty and was very fortunate to get that contract. That is, without question, the largest selling band book in the business, even more so than the Bennett books. It had all those good college songs that Walter Melrose had signed up: Illinois, Iowa, Michigan, Indiana, Wisconsin, Notre Dame, Southern Cal, Penn State. All the big schools were in there and they were tied up, nobody else could use those songs. Half a dozen of them are now public domain or out of copyright, but nobody can complete that same book for a long time. I had good luck with that one.

There's no opportunity now for anybody to make a living like I did as a free-lancer, I guarantee it. There isn't enough market to take one person's music for full time. Consequently we have many more people writing and many more ideas. Probably too much music is published, but it's better to have too much than too little. If there is plenty of music, the director has some chance to make choices and steer his band the way he wants it to go.

I remember playing some of your longer concert pieces around 1950 when I was in high school. Mountain Majesty *was one.*

That was my best effort at an overture. I started doing overtures for Belwin and Max Winkler. The number one Belwin edition was my original overture *Southern Cross.* Number two was my arrangement, *Rimsky-Korsakov.* That was an in-

teresting story. Max Winkler had been a music publisher for theater orchestras and he had devised the first cue sheets for silent pictures, suggesting music that should be played with the pictures. That all went out in 1928. He backed up about 12 big trucks and took all the music and sold it for scrap. He then started out, brand new, in the school business and I became associated with him then. He made a tremendous success along with his son later on. Anyway, those were the first two numbers he did in this area, and my first effort at writing an overture.

I didn't know what an overture was, except that it is a fairly free form, not like a symphony or a fugue or something which is definitely laid out in a pattern. In general, it's sort of a medley of tunes from the opera that is to follow, but these overtures were just from imaginary shows.

Anyhow, I did half a dozen overtures for Belwin, and Harold Bachman, my good friend who was working at Educational Music Bureau, would recommend them for sight-reading in the contests each spring, if the publisher would hold them back so they were new pieces. E.M.B. did that almost every year for one or two of these pieces, giving them a good start because they were exposed in a lot of contests. People who had played them usually went home and bought them to see how many mistakes they had made.

We are talking now in 1980 and have seen a lot of changes in original band music. There have been many new writers who have made an impression. It's dangerous to start listing names because there are so many, but I think Clifton Williams gave the first real shot in the arm to concert band music when he won the Ostwald Award for the first two years, some 25 years ago, with *Fanfare and Allegro* and *Symphonic Suite.* They were entirely original and had a strong masculine sound, strong form, striking dynamic effects, and a certain amount of dissonance. Not too much, but a certain amount. It wasn't the old medley type of overture anymore; it was a brand new picture.

Then a few years later Vaclav Nelhybel came along with an approach of his own. He had his own sound, too; it wasn't the Williams sound. It was a different way of combining instruments that he was championing. I think he had quite an influence — both of these men did. We have had so many others who have done creditable jobs in the more advanced field.

One fellow who I think has it all is Alfred Reed. He is able to write for the young students as well as the professional symphony orchestra. He is a very fine all-around musician with a tremendous creative imagination which he applies to arranging as well as composing. His compositions are not arrangements, they are real compositions; but his arrangements are very musical and he uses his talent to make the most of any tune.

I know you have been very interested in foreign bands with your travels around the world, especially Europe and Japan. How did you get involved in that?

My interest in Japan began when I started getting letters, about five years after World War II, from Japanese band directors saying they wanted their bands to play like the American service bands they had heard. They wanted to start band programs in their schools, and they were short of music. When I went over there in 1965 I found many pencilled copies of my music. I wasn't upset about the copyright angle; it was the fact that they could not get printed copies. Maybe one person in Japan would have a copy of *Mountain Majesty,* so all his friends would make a copy, including the score, so they would have something to play. There was no effort to beat us out of the price of the composition, they would have been delighted to pay.

In Europe I had an interesting experience because a couple of times I went to an international group called C.I.S.P.M. It stands for Confederation of International Societies of Popular Music, meaning music of the people. They had choruses, bands, and a few orchestras. I became acquainted with some of the publishers over there and got to see the kind of things they were doing.

England is very much enamored with the brass band. In the United States we hear people say, "Here comes a brass band." Well it is very seldom in America that we hear a brass band. That may be a term used for a band with clarinets, saxophones, and flutes, but a brass band has only brass instruments.

Do you find that English and European bands are trying to adopt American systems and techniques or are they working to develop their own?

They are going to stay with the brass band in England as far as the amateurs go. The guard bands that play for the Queen and the changing of the guard are called military bands, which are synonymous with our concert band. They march and also play concerts. That tradition is pretty solid in England.

There are countries like Norway, Holland, and Switzerland that have big school band programs. They are much like we are, and they use class methods in the schools.

What has been your greatest satisfaction over your long career in music?

I have received quite a few letters from people who have said that I've helped them and if it wasn't for me they wouldn't have had much to play. My biggest enjoyment has been in realizing that I have made that contribution, in spite of a lot of criticism that my music was too thick and not always the most inspiring musically. I took it seriously; I was writing the best I could and wasn't sluffing off the kids. I was trying to give them the very best kind of material I could. I know from hearing programs when other music (primarily professionally oriented) was used, that kids could play my music sooner, make it sound better, have it come off without any hitches, and the audience would think it was great.

Now you can't go on like that forever, but it's important that somebody was around to keep the thing moving with enough material so they all would have something to play. Forrest Buchtel did a lot of the same thing, and so did Joe Olivadoti.

I remember Oscar Anderson, who was the supervisor of instrumental music for the city of Chicago, probably around 1940, when they had contests for bands in the city. One morning he said, "I went to your recital last night." I replied, "What do you mean?" He explained, "I went to the band contest last night and 70% of the music was yours." Of course it made me happy. That's not true any more. I haven't had any numbers on the program at the Mid-West for several years. I used to be on at least a half dozen times and probably conducted a half dozen times. That was all a tremendous satisfaction then, but I don't think I'm a jealous old man now. There are two good examples of what can happen to a person. Sigmund Romberg and Rudolf Friml were two excellent operetta composers. Romberg went on a farewell tour with a symphony orchestra, was congratulated by everybody, and died happy. Rudolf Friml went to hear *My Fair Lady* and walked out because the tunes were "no good." Now that's just stupid. I've never met Friml, and I have great respect for his music; but you don't turn around and condemn the new people and the new sound just because you're not making it anymore. There's a time that comes when somebody else takes over. ∎

An Interview with
James D. Ployhar

Andrew Balent

Discussing projects with George Zepp
(right) of Byron-Douglas Publications.

James D. Ployhar is one of the most respected writers of school music in the business today. His hundreds of published pieces for band and orchestra as well as his many instruction books are used throughout the world. I have admired and been influenced by his works since the beginning of my teaching career.

We met for this interview one Sunday in January at the Detroit airport when Jim had a few hours between planes. He was returning to his home in Fargo, North Dakota from a guest conducting engagement in Montreal.

Jim is truly a gentleman in every sense of the word. His warm sense of humor and obvious love of people have won him friends throughout the country.

How has the school band field changed in the 30 or more years that you have been involved in it?

I think we have given more opportunities to youngsters over the years. The argument always exists as to whether bands are better or worse than before. You hear many people, senior members of our band fraternity, who will say, "Well, it's nothing like it used to be." But I contend that, by-and-large, there are many excellent programs where bands are actually better, playing better on better instruments, with better intonation.

One of the more definite changes is the use of more and more pop literature. I'm not against pop music because I've written a lot of it, but it is a matter of keeping the right balance of all types of music. Perhaps we, as writers and publishers, are a little guilty of promoting this because we have put so much pop music out for band.

Now, of course, we are into a period of budget restraint and in some cases there are fewer students in band programs. We are in an evolutionary

Andrew Balent is a band director in the Fitzgerald Public Schools of Warren, Michigan. He has been teaching for 28 years and is active as a composer and arranger for young bands.

period. I hope we will weather this financial strain and emerge with many really strong programs.

How did you get started in music?

I entered college after coming home from the Army in 1946. Even as a high school student, I had formed a little dance band, as many people do, and wrote for it. We had moderate success in a small town. Upon entering college I decided to study some music, and after studying it and enjoying it, I became a music major.

Where was this?

Valley City State College in Valley City, North Dakota. That was my home town, with the local college right in the community. I had played in the civic bands as a high school student before the war and in the early years of the war before I was drafted, so I knew the faculty and the school. I finally emerged with a degree in music education.

Where did you first teach?

My first two years were in Lakota, North Dakota, where I developed the band program and taught other subjects as well. I had saved some of my GI Bill and so decided to go to the University of Northern Colorado, in Greeley, to get my masters degree. I knew some people from there and my wife's parents lived in the area. Her father was on the faculty at the time (not in the music department), so it was sort of a second home. I stayed there for a year and received my Masters, but wasn't sure if I was going to go back into music. However I was really not qualified for anything else. A job opened up in Fargo, North Dakota. I accepted it and stayed there for 17 years, with the exception of one year that I took a sabbatical leave in California. I had a total of 19 years of teaching.

How did you get involved in writing for school bands?

It was really an accident, a fluke. When I was doing my Master's work I decided to write a piece for band. I was studying composition and just wanted to write something. Obviously I had done some writing before this time, but I wrote this piece and carried it around in my brief case. Finally, I took it up to Wayman Walker, our band director at Greeley. He agreed to play it at a rehearsal and of course I was very nervous. You know, being a writer yourself, that the minute you hear it played your whole soul is bared before the world. If it's good, that's fine, but if it isn't so good, you've got a lot of explaining to do — to yourself and to other people. They played the piece and the band, out of deference to me probably more than anything else, really liked it, or said they liked it. Wayman said that he was intending to use it on tour, so naturally my spirits were elevated very, very high, because I just didn't think that this would happen. I hired a young lady from the band to copy the piece for me. She was an excellent copyist; it looked like printed music. One of the band members suggested that I send it to a publisher but I sort of scoffed at the idea because I just didn't think there was any possibility that anyone would publish the piece. He kept urging, and I finally sent it to a publisher. The first one rejected it; but the second time it was published. Well, this whetted my appetite.

I was teaching, but I still found a little time to do some writing, so I proceeded to write a second piece and, lo and behold, that was accepted. Then I wrote a third piece and it was accepted. I guess I was off and running at that point.

What was the name of that first piece?

It was called *Rhumba Syncopada*. It got a lot of clinic play by Glenn Bainum and Paul Yoder. They were very kind and performed it for me often. Frankly, I haven't seen it for years and years. It was copyrighted somewhere around 1953 and went out of print a few years ago.

How did you get started writing originally, before you wrote for school bands?

It was mostly an avocation, a hobby, just something I did. I remember when I was in graduate school, a choral piece was needed the next day for a funeral. Nobody on the staff either wanted to do it or could do it, so I did. I wrote for a little dance band in college and I wrote for the high school band.

Did you take lessons or were you self-taught?

I guess that a lot of it was self-taught. I did study arranging in college just like everybody else. I maintain, and I don't mean this in a demeaning or critical way, that people who write and arrange basically do it by trial and error. You learn the ranges of the instruments and a little bit about how they go together, but beyond that, it's a stylistic trial-and-error thing by seeing what other people do as you develop your own style. Naturally the classes do help, but it's not the end-all of learning how to arrange, or compose for that matter.

To go back farther, how did you discover music in the first place?

My parents insisted that I study piano. We didn't even own a piano so I had to go next door to get my lessons. The piano teacher, a gentleman by the name of Art Lydell, would come to this house and teach me as well as other students. I went through the routine of playing, having lessons, and being in recitals up to about my sophomore year in high school. I was not a piano major but I took some lessons in college.

In junior high I played the cornet. I think I was the loudest cornet player in the junior high band, because I had an old instrument and in order to get any tone out of it at all, I had to blow with everything I had. When I got into high school it seemed that the band director had more cornets than he knew what to do with, so he asked if I would play baritone. Well, I really didn't care what I played, so I learned to play the baritone. When I went to college and throught I'd play in the band, they had all kinds of baritones — at least enough of them, but not enough French horns, so the director asked me to play French horn.

Let's pick up your writing career after you had your first few pieces published.

Many people have asked me if they should submit a piece for publication and I keep telling them that if it happened for me, it will probably happen for them. I encourage them to be persistent even though there are rejections. You never know because the next time it might be accepted.

My first published pieces did whet my appetite. As you well know, royalties build slowly, and I was nowhere near being a full-time writer. I was teaching with a gentleman by the name of George Zepp. After about my third piece was published I told George that maybe we should investigate the idea of starting our own publishing company. I suppose that everybody thinks that it's always greener in the other yard. So we did, and our first publication was called *A Marching Song*, which had moderate acceptance. The second one was an arrangement of *Nobody Knows The Trouble I've Seen* in which I used some different harmonies, more modern than the traditional ones. I don't know what I did, but the style of the piece and the nature of it seemed to get a lot of acceptance. Again, Glenn Bainum picked it up and performed it in many, many clinics. The sales started building and we were really encouraged. We then started a series of arrangements of folk songs. After about the first year of trying to be a part of this publishing venture, George and I both decided that it would be better if I were merely doing the writing and not so much involved in the publishing. So George bought out my interest in the company, Byron-Douglas, and he moved to Phoenix

Rafting down the Snake River in Grand Teton National Park with wife, Ruth, and three of five children

and set up shop there. I continued to write for him for a number of years until the firm was eventually sold. I guess that over the years I have written for ten or twelve different publishers, but now I'm concentrating on just one or two.

I first became aware of your work when I was starting out teaching young groups in a small town. My bands weren't very advanced and your pieces for young bands worked wonderfully well. Did you specialize in the easier material?

I don't think that it was necessarily planned that way, it sort of evolved and that's where my reputation lies. I became involved with the *First Division* band method through Frank Erickson and Fred Weber, and would get assignments for music for bands with young students, for beginning bands, and for second and third year bands. I tried to develop a style that would fit them, along with the guidelines that were set up for me by Fred Weber. Then my reputation really did emerge as one who could write for young bands as well as for junior high bands. Of course, there were some pieces that were more advanced. I felt that some of my earlier arrangements were not necessarily that difficult, but perhaps because of the harmonic content, or the style in which I did them, they were played by any number of bands on all levels, which was gratifying. It was nice to have that acceptance.

I played A Marching Song *in 1957 with my first band when I began teaching. I had a small group but did have a couple of strong trumpet players and one snare drummer who could hold the piece together.*

That piece was actually written for a grand march at a physical education demonstration. That was how it was conceived. We liked it, so decided to put it out when we started our publishing company. After all, we needed the manuscripts.

What types of schools and teaching situations have you had?

I've actually taught at only two schools in my career. One was a high school-junior high combination with some instrumental work in the grade school; it was all really one and the same. I did two

years of high school and then went away to get my Masters. The next 17 years were in a junior high, 7-8-9, which was later changed to a 6-7-8 middle school. During all those years I would start the beginning classes, usually a total of around 60 students.

I lived in an area where we had a very aggressive music dealer by the name of Nels Vogel. He would bring some of the top bands and top names in the band field into our area. For instance, I remember Edwin Franko Goldman visiting our school, as well as Frank Simon. I met Paul Yoder, who has been so kind to me over the years, and Glenn Bainum. I felt that I was very fortunate, even though we are not at any real crossroads of the nation in Fargo, North Dakota, that they managed to come up there and that I got to meet a lot of those people and get support from them.

What have your experiences been since you've left teaching?

Writing on a full time basis, which has given me opportunities for traveling and meeting so many band directors and people in the business that I could not have met otherwise. It has been most gratifying, especially since getting involved with the *Contemporary Band Course.* I visited Norway twice where it has been published in Norwegian, and is being used over there. I also visited Denmark and England to do a workshop. I guess the most flattering aspect of it is that all of these countries are using my music. I can walk into the publishing representatives and find my music on the shelves. I just didn't realize that this was going on, at least to that extent.

Have there been any special people who influenced you?

I think it all goes back to my teachers, both in high school and college. I hope that some of my students will say the same thing about me. I think a teacher has an element of immortality that is denied a lot of people. Now, many people believe in immortality in the theological sense, but I think there are other forms. I find myself emulating things that my own teachers did and saying things that they said; those things that I approve of and I think were good. I really enjoyed all of my teachers. I felt that they gave me a lot. I think that any teacher, if he's worth his salt, has a built-in immortality through the students that he leaves behind. It's a nice concept.

Teachers are in the people business, in the final analysis this is what it's all about. We're working with people, especially in the band field, and we do influence them. We hope the influence will be a good one. I think that is why this is such a fun profession, because we have that privilege, and therefore, we live on through these students, in one form or another.

Are there any writers who particularly influenced you?

I think that all of us who write look at other writers to see what they're doing. I know I was very closely associated with Frank Erickson during some of those early years and I sought advice from him. I don't believe I write like Frank, but I certainly was influenced, to a degree, by him and his successes. I developed my own style, but didn't do that intentionally. It just sort of happened. I've been told that I do have a particular style, although I would be hard pressed to tell you what it is. Apparently my writing can be identified. I think this is true of people who do make a success of this business. There is a certain (intangible perhaps) style that is there, that band directors will identify with and therefore program.

What do you think makes your music so popular and useful for schools?

I wish I could answer that properly, I really don't know. One of the answers I come up with is the fact that I did teach for 17 years in an elementary, junior high situation and perhaps this is the influence that is in my music, assuming it is accepted as you say. Maybe that experience in the actual classroom bodes well for me and carries through into my writing.

I know that you have done a lot of hymn settings. One of the facets of your work that I enjoy and admire are those different hymn tunes that you arrange for band. What led you in that direction?

I don't know why or when I did my first hymn. I guess that it was just a desire to embellish an otherwise good piece of music. Many times I would sit in church and thumb through the hymn book, or I might hear something played by the organist, and think it would make a good addition to band literature. So I did one. Then I found another. As they become successful you try to follow with another and so it goes.

What are your feelings on the benefits of band membership for children?

I am a real champion of music education, whether it be for winds, strings, or vocal. I really feel that we have a beautiful thing going in this country, and we are emulated by many other nations. I almost cringe when I hear people talking about music as a "frill" because I believe that if we are going to educate the complete person, music is a vital ingredient of the process. I really feel that it's a positive force. We all know that there are a lot of negative forces working in our society today, perhaps even more than we can fathom sometimes. Probably the one positive force that is going for us is the church. There are other positive forces that sort of keep us from becoming an uncivilized nation. I believe that both our public and our private school educational programs are certainly very positive forces in a society that needs something like that, and within those programs I think one of the best things going is the music program. Naturally because I'm associated with it I am probably quite prejudiced, but I believe the public school music program is by far and away a real star in the crown for the United States and its citizens. I think we are really doing a great thing. Now, I don't think that everyone can benefit from a wind instrument program any more than they can from a string program or even necessarily a choir program. I think, however, that everybody should have some exposure to music and the arts. We know that music is the most disciplined of all the arts and it has just been a phenomenon as to what has happened in our public schools with our band, string, and choir programs. I can't imagine these schools without them, I just can't. I don't think this country would be the same without them. So, I'm very proud to be associated with music education. I think that it's a strong, positive force in our whole social structure. I hope that it never goes away. It's suffering right now, but I hope that it will recover very, very fast.

What are your thoughts on the future for bands and instrumental music.

I have discussed this with many people and some are a little afraid. They feel that because of economics, school boards are just going to do away with what they consider to be the frills of bands and instrumental music. Of course there are programs that are suffering, but I know that in many places where we have innovative teachers with the strong desire to preserve their program, that the programs are becoming even stronger. We also are in a period of declining enrollments. There are just fewer bodies in some schools at the moment. Yet I have heard of many schools where the instrumental programs are actually growing. That is a credit to the teachers and supervisors who are heading those programs. I do feel that instrumental programs are going to be with us, and that the economy is going to definitely do a turnaround. We've had these ups and downs before. We know that there is now another slight baby boom in the offing and I think some of these youngsters going into kindergarten and first grade are beginning to swell the ranks of the school population. It's not going to be too many more years before they are going to be playing instruments, buying instruments and music, and going into music education programs. So I really feel upbeat about the whole thing, I think that it's going to move forward again very soon. ■

Frank Erickson
The Composer's Point of View

BY ANDREW BALENT

Band directors have been playing and conducting the music of Frank Erickson for a long time, possibly for the entire length of their musical careers. The man responsible for creating the music performed by so many young bands across the nation began his own musical career by taking piano lessons as a third grader, then two years later changed to trumpet. After attending high school in Spokane, Washington, and playing in dance bands, Erickson began college at the University of Washington in the fall of 1941.

Erickson traces his interest in writing music back to the time when he studied piano; his teacher would dictate words and the students would make up tunes to go with them. By playing popular songs on the piano, Erickson discovered he could combine the tunes with chords. As a teenager the budding composer began arranging for a couple of the bands he played with and in his senior year of high school composed Fall of Evening, *his first serious piece for concert band.*

After four years in the Army Air Corps, Erickson became seriously interested in composition and began studying with Mario Castelnuovo-Tedesco. In 1948 he entered the University of Southern California where he met the band director, Clarence Sawhill, who got him involved with band music. While at a meeting of the Music Educators National Conference in 1950, Ken Walker from Bourne heard Erickson's Little Suite for Band *and offered to publish it. A list of other publications followed --* Irish Folk Song Suite, Norwegian Folk Song Suite, *and* Deep River Suite. *His first big success was* Fantasy for Band, *followed by* Balladir, Air for Band, *and* Toccato for Band. *In the early 1960s Erickson moved to New York to work for Belwin where he joined Fred Weber to create the First Division Band Course. Erickson began his own publishing firm, Summit Publications, which he later sold to Belwin.*

During a recent interview with Frank Erickson, I asked him how he became interested in writing for younger bands.

Clarence Sawhill got me started composing for young bands. Working with Fred Weber on the First Division Band Course put me in touch with writing some elementary pieces, but I think that I have always been interested in young bands. *Little Suite for Band*, for example, was written for a young junior high or elementary group. However, there is another reason for my interest — I feel most comfortable with ideas that are rather simple and harmonically uncomplicated.

I have always looked at writing for younger bands as a challenge. The work has to interest young band members, be playable by them, and still express musically worthwhile ideas. Some people think that composers write for younger bands because there are more of them and, thus, the market is larger. Well, I have not found this to be necessarily true. The greatest commercial successes I have had are probably pieces that have been written for grade three or grade four groups.

What makes a young band piece successful? Do you work to produce something that is a musical achievement as well as an educational and commercial success?

Undoubtedly all three elements work together for almost any piece at any level. In a work that is a musical success, the melodies should be easy to play and well within the instruments' ranges. If a piece of music is appealing, it is commercial. I do not look at the commercial aspect of music publishing as being something unethical or undesirable; it is an important part of music. When I begin writing a piece, I try to come up with an idea that is exciting or interesting. Then I work to pass the idea on to the bands who are going to play it, and to their audiences.

I don't think in terms of writing music that is educational; rather I work to compose music that is appealing on a certain technical level. Of course, in the First Division Band Course we had some stringent writing limits in terms of the ranges and rhythms we taught. Directors can teach the fundamentals of music with almost any piece. I have had directors say, "One thing I like about some of your numbers is that I can teach with them. I can teach phrasing; I can teach rhythms." Again, I think this goes for almost any piece of music.

Composers should please themselves first, regardless of the level they are writing for. If the composer tries to write what he thinks someone else will like, suppressing his own feelings and intuition, he is second-guessing. If a composer does not sincerely like what he is creating and feels he is writing down to a younger group, his feelings will eventually become evident to everyone.

How has the school band movement changed in the 35 years that you have been involved in it?

At U.S.C. Clarence Sawhill played all of the standard works for band available at the time —

the Holst suite, the Vaughan Williams suite, the Schoenberg variations. We played the *French Quarter* of John Morrissey and Clare Grundman's *Folk Rhapsody*. Original band music was not readily available, and a good part of the literature at that time was transcriptions. One of the biggest changes I have seen is the change from playing transcriptions of orchestra and piano music to performing original works for band.

I have also seen quite a change in instrumentation. In 1948 most French horn sections were small, and I seldom saw a contrabass clarinet in any ensemble other than an advanced high school band. At that time there was a definite distinction between cornets and trumpets, with separate parts written for each instrument. Now, trumpets have taken over and you seldom find a cornet in a school band today.

In the last few years I have seen an increased growth in the wind ensemble, particularly at the college level, which is filtering down to the high schools. Today students generally are more proficient technically than they used to be. However, I remember hearing the Joliet High School Band at the Mid-West Band and Orchestra Clinic around 1953 or '54; more than 30 years later very few groups can surpass the music I heard on that program.

If I had to pick one instrument that has improved in quality, it would certainly be the saxophone. When I started composing, some of the saxophone sections were terribly weak and the instrument's quality left a lot to be desired; you would seldom see more than one saxophone on a part. I'm being somewhat facetious when I tell you that I once had a rule: score the music so you can't hear the saxophones. Needless to say, I have changed this philosophy. As a matter of fact, one of the works that I am the most proud of is the Saxophone Concerto that I wrote for Sigurd Rascher. Today saxophones are almost too numerous in our concert bands.

Another marked change in the concert band in the last 10 to 15 years is the use of percussion. Now, thanks to Vaclav Nelhybel and Frances McBeth, the percussion section is regarded as equal in importance to the brass or woodwind sections. Even in beginning band classes teaching percussion is handled differently. For instance, James Ployhar's method book, Band Today, has three separate percussion books — the drums, which is a traditional handling of snare and bass drum; auxiliary percussion, which presents work on such instruments as cymbals, triangle, tambourine; and mallet percussion.

Have there been any particularly strong influences — musical or non-musical — in your development as a composer?

A moment of relaxation for Erickson at home in Carlsbad, California.

The ideas that a composer expresses are the result of a great many influences, some of them he is probably not aware of. I began my musical career quite young in the jazz field and was certainly influenced by the popular music that I knew and grew up with. I would certainly have to say that my experiences in high school band were important to me, as was the time I spent at U.S.C.

Many of the people I met were tremendous influences. I remember some of the band directors whom I came to know, such as Bill Revelli, Mark Hindsley, Ed Kruth at San Francisco State, and Walter Wellkey from the University of Washington. I don't mean to leave anyone out because I could go on for a long time. A real favorite of mine was Glenn Cliffe Bainum. I also remember an experience from the first Mid-West Clinic I attended. Paul Yoder, whom I didn't know at the time, was sitting in front of me at the first performance of a piece of mine. Paul turned around, shook my hand, and said, "I think you should do very well." Experiences such as that one have been very important to me.

As far as the influence of music itself, I've been interested in many different kinds and styles. Through Halsey Stevens, whom I studied composition with at U.S.C., I became familiar with the well-known serious composers of the time. such as Stravinsky, Hindemith, Milhaud, and particularly Bartók. I don't think this influence shows in too many of my works, but I'm sure it's all there somewhere. Although Gustav Holst and Vaughan Williams are not my favorite composers by any means, I would have to say that these two men are probably the ones who have done the most to influence my own style of composing.

What do you think makes your music popular and useful for school bands?

Thank you for the compliment. Some numbers I've written have been popular and some of them not so popular. I am always conscious of several points when writing a piece of music. The first is keeping the scoring for each instrument in a good, practical range. I always start writing with a sketch, which is basically a three-line conductor's score. I usually put the upper woodwinds on the top line, the upper brass on the middle line, and a combination of low woodwinds and brass on the lower line. As I develop this sketch, I constantly make little notations as to which instruments are playing, so that I am aware of range. From there I go to a full score.

I try to make each part as interesting as possible for the players. There have been times when I've copied parts, only to see that the scoring was pretty dull, maybe with many whole notes or repetitious rhythms. Many times I rewrote a score just to correct some of these problems. I also try to keep all the parts as melodic as possible, while avoiding awkward intervals. I use interesting harmonies and rhythms, not just the conventional or expected ideas to surprise the players and director, adding to their interest.

I am also conscious of making sure that the piece has a good overall design, that the length is not too long or too short and that it reaches the climaxes at the right time. Also important, even in a short piece, is a variety of movement and style. I play almost every selection that I write before I send it to the publisher. I think

Mary and Frank Erickson enjoying the Pacific Ocean

that I have made more changes because of form than anything else.

What are your thoughts on the future for bands and band music?

Although there are many service and university bands of a very high professional caliber in this country, I feel that the future of bands is with the schools and the directions they take. At the present time band music is at a crossroads, things could go in almost any direction.

I am concerned because the school band movement seems to have become fragmented. In the 1930s the school band made its biggest thrust and became the main medium for teaching instrumental music in the public schools. Since that time, marching bands have been an integral part of the program, which is as it should be. Today, however, I am afraid that in many programs marching bands compete for the entire 12 months of the year and, in many cases, perform the same show. In these situations, the marching band seems to have replaced the concert band. The stage band became a part of the band program, in most cases, as an extracurricular activity. Currently, the jazz band is often considered the main focus of attention.

I am concerned about the shift from the concert band to the wind ensemble. There is no doubt that directors can achieve a cleaner, more transparent sound from a smaller group of players, but the big sonority of the full-fledged concert band is sacrificed. There are wind ensembles with as many as 50 or 60 players, but the memberships of many concert bands, both past and present, contain similar numbers. I am reminded of a remark made by Karl King about his Fort Dodge municipal band: "Here I've had a wind ensemble all these years and didn't even know it."

The main danger in this trend away from the concert band is in the motivation of students. If educators serve only a select group of students, those who are less qualified might become discouraged. Eventually we might not have even enough players for the wind ensemble.

Don't misunderstand me, I'm not against any of these organizations. Rather, I am concerned about the emphasis directors place on them. The main purpose of a school band program is to teach music. When the reason for the school band becomes basically one of public relations, entertainment, or marching, the entire program is in danger of collapsing. There is a place for all of these parts of a school music program, but they have to be kept in balance. ■

Andrew Balent is a band director in the Fitzgerald Public Schools of Warren, Michigan. He has been teaching for 29 years and is active as a composer and arranger for young bands.

Straight Ahead
with Sammy Nestico

BY JAMES WARRICK

I s it possible there is an arranger whose music has been heard by almost every person in America, or whose arrangements hve been performed by every jazz musician who has played in a jazz ensemble? Considering that Sammy Nestico has arranged or orchestrated music for more than 60 programs, including "M*A*S*H*," "The Mary Tyler Moore Show," "Love Boat," and "Mission Impossible," and has published more than 700 compositions or arrangements for school music groups, such a statement comes close to the truth.

Now 64 years old and living near Los Angeles, Sammy Nestico has never known life without music. As a 13-year-old trombonist at Oliver High School in Pittsburgh, he knew that he wanted a career in music. Encouraged by his mother who wanted him to become a teacher, Sammy graduated from Duquesne University as a music education major. After one year as the high school band director in Wilmerding, Pennsylvania, Sammy joined the Air Force in 1951. He recalls, "I remember how much I loved the kids while I was teaching, but I also remember how much I hated the administrative details and the paperwork."

Sammy then spent 15 years as a staff arranger for the Air Force Band in Washington, D.C. He was also the first arranger for the Airmen of Note, the official Air Force jazz ensemble. It was during this time that he perfected his unmistakable arranging style. For the next five years Sammy was the chief arranger for the United States

Last year James Warrick commissioned Sammy Nestico to compose Two Sides of the Coin *for his New Trier Jazz Ensemble. Jenson Music recently published the work, which was Nestico's first jazz commission. Warrick is Editor of the* Electronic Music Educator *and a Consulting Editor of* The Instrumentalist.

Marine Band and leader of the White House dance orchestra during the Kennedy and Johnson administrations. While in the Marines Sammy had his first encounter with Hollywood. "I directed the concert band on camera in the Gomer Pyle show when Gomer went to Washington to sing with the Marine Band."

On leaves from the service during the early 1950s Sammy took brief road trips as a trombonist in the Woody Herman and Tommy Dorsey bands. He says, "Tommy Dorsey was my idol. When I was in his band I just put my horn down and listened to him play. Don't forget, before Dorsey all you heard was gut bucket trombone, and then here came that golden Dorsey sound. He was an innovator."

Count Basie was introduced to Sammy's arrangements during this time. "My cousin Sal was playing tenor saxophone with Basie and said I ought to write something for the band, so I wrote 'Queen Bee' and sent it in," explains Nestico. "At 2 A.M. one morning I got a call from a band member telling me that Basie liked what I had written and wanted me to do some more charts for him." What followed was 10 albums of original Nestico music recorded by the Basie Band between 1968 and 1984, four of which

won Grammy Awards. Nestico says he had about 120 charts in the band's book by the time Basie died in 1984.

Sammy recalls his relationship with Basie as the musical highlight of his life. "I think Bill was the nicest person I've ever met; just a good, humble person — almost shy. Basie's band could take beautiful melodies and make them swing. That's what made his band different from the Herman or Kenton bands. While I admired Woody and Stan for having grown musically with each decade, Basie stuck with what he did best. One trouble a lot of writers had was that they wanted to write like Basie. Basie always told me, 'They should write like themselves and we'll play it like Basie.' "

At the age of 44 Sammy moved his family to Los Angeles in 1968. "My wife always said that if I was going to strike out, I should do it swinging with the bat in my hand. She said that I was going to get my shot in Los Angeles even if she had to scrub floors. I believe a break is what happens when preparation meets opportunity. A break will come so it's best to work hard and be prepared. If you should falter, then another break will come, but next time be ready."

Sammy doesn't have fond memories of his family's first few months in Los Angeles, but says he owes much to the Hollywood arranger Billy May, who gave him his first break. Nestico recalls, "Margie had back problems and was in a wheelchair, my three teenage kids didn't like California, our savings were gone, and there I sat trying to write cues for the Gomer Pyle show. Just as the water was up to my chin, Billy turned to me during a recording session and asked if I could copy a big band arrangement off an album. There was my break. He said Capitol Records was recording old swing-era tunes in stereo, so he gave me an album of Benny Goodman's 'Stealin' Apples' and I went to work. Billy had to arrange eight tunes a week, so he gave me three or four to do. I was with Capitol for four years and 63 albums."

Another break came when composer Pat Williams asked Sammy to orchestrate for him. Nestico says, "Pat would sketch out the melody and chords and then give me an almost blank sheet of manuscript paper to fill in the orchestral voicings and individual parts." The life of an orchestrator can be unpredictable and rather grueling, as Sammy recounts: "I once got a call from Universal Studios at 5 P.M. on Thanksgiving Day to come to the studio to orchestrate the television special 'It Happened One Christmas,' which featured Orson Wells and Marlo Thomas. I wrote all night long and was still writing when the orchestra walked in at 8 A.M. the next morning. I was still writing while they were recording at 2 P.M. that afternoon. I almost fell asleep going home on the freeway that night."

Another musical highlight was when he started to publish his own music. "My first publications were watered-down arrangements of my Basie charts. In those days Art Dedrick was the father of stage bands, and he was just starting Kendor Music. I've always regretted that we simplified the first Basie charts I published. We just figured they were too hard for kids. In fact, we didn't even publish 'Magic Flea' for quite a while and I think it sold more than any of the others when we finally published the recorded version."

Speaking of his current success as a published composer, Sammy says, "I'm very proud to be writing for the schools of America. I think that's terrific. There is something exciting about being able to write simple and melodic, but not bland pieces. It's a challenge and a thrill to write something that you know has some musicality to it and yet is playable by young people. I'll come out of my little studio and tell Margie that I really enjoyed that a lot more than writing a professional arrangement. A lot of love goes into the music I write for kids."

When Sammy writes for publishing companies he feels added pressure to get it right the first time. "My schedule in Los Angeles never gives me time to hear school groups play my music. It's almost always the publisher's promotional record that gives me my first hearing of my music, and then it's usually only 32 bars before it fades out. As I write I can hear the band in my head, but there are a few things that surprise me when I finally hear my music played by a band.

Sammy tries to write music that musicians will want to play. "Their enthusiasm for my music will spill over into the audience and the audience will like it. I like to write a piece that has everybody smiling after they hear it. I'm a happy person, and I like to write happy music. I guess that's why I don't write many minor key things." When asked to name his favorite big band compositions or arrangements, he names "Warm Breeze," "Basie Straight Ahead," "88 Basie Street," "Satin Doll," and "Sweet Georgia Brown."

Composers who influenced his style include Billy May, Bill Finegan, Bob Florence, Neal Hefti, Frank Foster, Nelson Riddle, and Thad Jones, most of whom wrote for the Basie band. Sammy now particularly enjoys the music of Bob Mintzer. "I think Mintzer's writing and band are terrific. His music doesn't sound like anything done before, even though he uses the same eight brass, five saxes, and rhythm section that everyone else uses. It's fresh."

The process of composing is not always easy for Sammy. "Two days a month I can't get the notes down fast enough on paper, the other 28

days it's really hard work. It's always a process of accepting and rejecting and it's not so much talent as it is persistence and desire. A young composer has to accept that there will be writer's blocks. I write better music in the car than I do at the piano because when I'm in the car I can sing melodies, but when I sit at the piano I get hung up playing chords."

Sammy regularly uses electronic instruments when he writes. "I use a synthesizer because it's easier, and I can use headphones; that way I can work late and not bother anybody. My son installed an 8-track tape recorder and a complete MIDI lab in my home studio. It makes writing more fun, but it takes me twice as long to put the music in the sequencer as to just write it out. It's just fun to hear the parts played back on a synthesizer. Still, it's not like a piano. The piano is the greatest instrument in the world."

Sammy believes that a young musician or composer shouldn't compare himself unfavorably with someone else. "Unfortunately, I always did this," he says. "I'll never forget the first time I worked with Hollywood composer Billy Byers. He called at 8 A.M. one morning and wanted me to help him write a complete show for Mama Cass, who needed the music the next day. A few minutes after we got started writing, I could hear Billy in the other room tearing off one score page after another. At 10 A.M. he was on the phone telling the copyist to come pick up some tunes. By 2 A.M. the next morning he had written three times the number of cues and arrangements I had. I went home and told Margie that after seeing Billy Byers work, I should be a plumber. That afternoon though, he called from the rehearsal to say that everybody loved my music. I felt like a million dollars. If you compare yourself to everyone else, you'll always come out second best."

One of Nestico's great thrills came in 1983 when he received the honorary Doctor of Music degree from Duquesne University, only the fourth person to receive such recognition from that school. "The others were Andre Previn, Henry Mancini, and Benny Goodman — pretty good company, wouldn't you say?" Sammy smiles.

What's in the future for Sammy Nestico? "At my age I can be more selective about who I write for. I won't write for night club acts, it's just too limiting. That's why I enjoy the writing I am doing now for Sarah Vaughan, Pia Zadora, and Toni Tennille: they use a full orchestra, which allows me to write exciting colors. I want to write music until the day I die. I've never really reached where I wanted to go, but I've had some good successes. You know it's all hittin' and missin'; I've done both, but hittin' is sure a lot more fun." □

Pablo Casals

(December 29, 1876 - October 22, 1973)

Henri Temianka

The Author records his own thoughts and memories,
and those of Gregor Piatigorsky, Sidney Harth and
Milton Thomas.

Pablo Casals was not only a giant among musicians, but among all of humanity. The moral courage and integrity which he demonstrated time and again are all the more impressive when contrasted with the corrupt standards of others in our ailing society. When Hitler came to power, Casals abruptly cancelled all his engagements in Germany, unlike so many musicians who gleefully exploited the opportunities created by the persecution of their Jewish colleagues. He refused to play in Mussolini's Italy. Finally, he became a voluntary exile from his own beloved Spain, refusing to bow to Franco's fascist dictatorship. Completely true to his principles, he even turned down urgent offers of engagements in those countries which actively, or through their silence, allied themselves with Spain's new regime. Withdrawing to a sleepy little town in the south of France (Prades) and living in the most modest style, Casals, then not quite sixty, had made the supreme sacrifice that any performing musician can make — he had put an end to his career at the height of his powers.

Pablo Casals
(1876-1973)

I am a man first, an artist second.
As a man, my first obligation is to the welfare of my fellow men.
My contribution to world peace may be small.
But at least I will have given all I can to an idea I hold sacred.

Had Casals died within the next decade, he would indeed have paid the price he was so willing and determined to pay. It is only thanks to his blessed longevity and to Alexander Schneider's efforts in seeking him out and organizing the Prades Festival that the last two decades of Casals' life became his greatest fulfillment. Thousands of people made the annual pilgrimage to Prades, and later to Puerto Rico, to pay homage to Pablo Casals, the musician and the man.

During the days immediately following the death of Casals, I spent many hours with my distinguished colleagues and friends, Gregor Piatigorsky, Sidney Harth, and Milton Thomas, reminiscing about Casals. All three were closely associated with him over the years. Here are some of the memories and thoughts we shared.

Gregor Piatigorsky: What can one say? When I was a child, I already knew the name. Maybe half a century ago, when I was 20, I went with Horowitz to a concert of Casals and Alfred Cortot, the great French pianist. We sat in the first row. It was too much for me to see the man at such close range — I was so overwhelmed by that alone. In the years that followed, we became friends. We would sit down to dinner, stay up until the early hours, we would play for each other, and we also played many duos. His preoccupation with technical details was extraordinary. He would ask: "How do you produce this spiccato?" There was a certain humility that everybody felt who met Casals.

I have often played solos with him when he was conducting. The last time was in Puerto Rico, just a few years ago. I played several works — Schumann Haydn and Don Quixote. And I also played the Schubert Quintet with him; it was a joy for me because for the first time (with Casals) I played the second cello.

Henri Temianka, leader of the famous Paganini Quartet for many years, is the founder/conductor of the California Chamber Symphony. In addition to his activities as violin soloist and conductor, he is The Instrumentalist's *string clinic editor.*

Gregor Piatigorsky, world renowned cello virtuoso, teaches at the University of Southern California in addition to his concert appearances.

Sidney Harth is Concertmaster of the Los Angeles Symphony Orchestra. He was formerly head of the Department of Music at Carnegie-Mellon University.

Milton Thomas, a member of the Los Angeles Symphony Orchestra, teaches viola at the University of Southern California.

Photographs by Paul Moor (Magnum), courtesy of Columbia Records.

I definitely feel more alone. I feel a personal loss. I mean, most people will say, he had such a marvelous, long life; but to me somehow, it is almost more tragic. Because his life was so beautiful, it should never have ended.

Henri Temianka: I first heard Casals under the most extraordinary circumstances. I was a student at the Curtis Institute in Philadelphia (where Piatigorsky taught for many years) and I went to a Casals recital. We waited, but no performer appeared. Finally, the manager came out on the stage and said, "we phoned Mr. Casals in his hotel room at the Bellevue-Stratford Hotel, and he was asleep!" We sat there in the auditorium for an hour and finally Casals came rushing out on the stage, terribly upset. One would be tempted to say that he looked "disheveled," but since he was completely bald, that wasn't possible. He told us that he had left a call for the operator to wake him up in time, but they had not called him. So he dressed in a wild hurry and rushed over. This must have been the only time in his life that he started out playing badly. He was so upset that he didn't even take time to tune his cello. The first piece was incredibly bad and then gradually he became Casals.

G.P.: I have a great many memories about one episode. It was when I met him for the first time. I wrote about it in my book.* Casals was staying in the Mendelssohn mansion in Berlin. Rudolph Serkin was also there. I played something with Serkin. It was not a good performance, but Casals was always interested in hearing talented young artists and he was enthusiastic. He asked me to play something alone and it was even worse, but he praised me and complimented me and asked me to play still more. And the more I played, the worse it got — but his enthusiasm increased! I was very unhappy knowing that I had played badly and disturbed because I took his compliments for a lack of sincerity. Shortly afterward, we met again in Paris and I couldn't help telling him my feelings. How could he have complimented me after such a poor performance? He got very angry. He took the cello and said, "You remember, you played this phrase with the third finger — it came right from the heart. It was so musical — and the bowing, you did it upbow. Most cellists play it downbow, but the way you did it fit the phrase so perfectly. I wasn't false, I was being sincere. Only bad people live for and remember bad things. I was very much impressed."

*Gregor Piatigorsky. Cellist (Garden City, NY: Doubleday and Co., Inc., 1965).

And then we met again in Barcelona. I played the Schumann Concerto with him and his orchestra. I arrived in Barcelona with the most dreadful cold. I was absolutely sick; I was perspiring and wet. What a mess! On the stage, Casals, who was so much shorter than I am, made a tremendous effort to raise himself up to my face and kiss me on the mouth, as Spaniards are accustomed to doing. I tried gently to push him away and to warn him that I carried the plague — but this only incited him to do it again, and in the Green room he embraced me still another time. And then two days later I gave a recital in Barcelona and he wanted to come. Suddenly there was a telephone call. I heard a dreadful cough. It was Casals. He was sick.

Sidney Harth: Actually I was one of the first players in Prades way back in 1950. It was very primitive that first festival, as I think back now. They put up egg cartons for the sound baffles. The rehearsals took place in an odd little room in a convent, as I remember, but the musical atmosphere was fantastic — great enthusiasm, great love of music. We did all the Bach Brandenburgs. All concerts were held in the church and there was *no* applause; but in the last concert (and it was a very long festival) the Abbot or Monseigneur stood up and applauded in the church, and so everybody else stood up and applauded.

I was there for two months. It wasn't a two-month festival, but there were recordings after it was over — I think 20 sides or more. Casals worked hard. He worried and worried over every little phrase, but we learned a lot.

I didn't go back to that festival again, since I was engrossed in other summer projects; but in 1957, when the Casals festival started in Puerto Rico, both my wife and I played. At the first rehearsal Casals was so excited and involved — but the next thing we knew he was in the back room and there was consternation, and the doctor came. To make a long story short, it was a heart attack, and he did no more conducting during that festival.

I played all the festivals as concertmaster and got to know the Casals techniques and his philosophy of playing music "naturally." One of his pet idiosyncrasies was that notes do not last a long time — they always come down. As though you're talking. Energy releases itself. I think he was inclined to exaggerate that. Frankly, it became, you know, like a religion. Therefore, every note that was long, had to drop, and drop almost completely. He never allowed a note to stick out, and I suppose in a way it is natural. Also, he paid very little attention to the basic dynamics. I mean you would never hear him "shushing" us, like so many conductors do. The main thing was that the music must sing. He put life into the music. For instance, the long notes in Bach — the very, very long sustained notes, pedal-point over or underneath the melody — he would make them come alive! They would have to come up and then go down again. Also, he liked the freedom in short notes. Always the short notes would go toward the long note.

A lot of people say that Casals was not a good conductor — probably thinking of the popular concept of conducting. But he made music and you could understand him. There were moments of fear naturally.

We had one this last summer when we did the Beethoven First. I don't know how we came in at one point, but we made it. It was the most beautiful kind of thing because everybody was so terribly alert. And I remember other instances, but they were far overshadowed by his ideas, which I would guess looking back now, were more or less explained to us verbally. You know, the baton is very limited in a sense, for any conductor, and he did a lot of explaining.

In 1965, as Head of the Music Department at Carnegie Institute of Technology (now Carnegie-Mellon) I invited Casals to Pittsburgh and he came for a month. It was a very big affair, a great event for the city. We did all the Bach Brandenburgs and as many suites as we could, in two concerts, which he conducted. Casals did those two concerts with great trepidation, because every moment before he was to go on, he was afraid of having a heart attack. He was always a hypochondriac, very careful, and always, always worried about his health. He worked hard and would forget himself in the music, but he was always complaining about his heart. My wife would go backstage and say to him, "Thank God, it's *beating*, it's fine."

By the way, Casals loved Pittsburgh. He found a good doctor there and thought it was a great town, although at first he was reluctant to come because he was afraid of the weather. He hated cold weather.

During his stay, he also gave master classes for cellists from all over the country, and there were some very good people. He was absolutely fantastic. Casals was then 89 and his left hand was so sure that it gravitated to the correct position, no matter what. I never saw such a natural instinct to get to a position. The right arm was a little shaky, but that left hand was there all the time. He knew every work that those cellists were playing — never referred to the music — and would join in and play along with them. From out of the blue everything would come back to him. Those were very inspiring sessions.

At the end of the festival, of course, he played his "Song of the Birds," which was his trademark, a very touching experience. The piece is really a Catalan folk song that he played at every festival, except the last

one, unaccompanied. It's a very quiet, introspective little piece, a kind of symbol for his fellow Spaniards, with political significance.

H.T.: Tell me about Casals' wife.

S.H.: Well, there was exactly 60 years difference in age. She is 36, and he was 96. He would have been 97 in December. I got to know Martita, and my wife especially got to know her quite well in Pittsburgh during that month. She is a very lovely woman. She took marvelous care of him, she really doted on him. They said he lived as long as he did, because of her.

H.T.: Is she a cellist?

S.H.: Yes, and a very good one, I understand. I've never heard her play, but a very fine, very elegant kind of cellist, they tell me. And she did play once or twice when he worked with her as conductor.

There's a cute little incident that happened while he was in Pittsburgh. It was on his first visit to the doctor he had met there, when both he and Martita went in for a medical examination. When they came out, my wife was waiting for them, and he said, with a twinkle in his eye, "She's the sick one, not I." It had been diagnosed that Martita had a nervous stomach and the doctor gave her medicine; but he gave Casals very little. That man had amazing resiliency. He was very strong.

Also during the time he was in Pittsburgh, he viewed color TV for the very first time — in my home. He loved it, especially the westerns, and said to his wife (but for all of us to hear), "I shall be the first one to own a color television in Puerto Rico."

Casals was a very stubborn man, stubborn about his politics, stubborn about his music, and you couldn't shake him. The story goes that he was once scheduled to play the Dvorak Concerto (which he loved) with Lamoureux conducting. Before they went on stage, Lamoureux made light of the piece and said, "Let's get it over with." Casals got angry and refused to play. There was a big to-do in the audience, but Casals wouldn't budge, and Lamoureux went out and made a speech to that effect. Debussy was in the audience and came back and asked what had happened. And so Casals told him the story and Debussy said, "Of course, Lamoureux is right, that's not really music." Well, of course, when he heard this — no more Debussy. And then on top of that, because Ravel was in a sense a disciple of Debussy, he never liked Ravel either.

H.T.: What about Casals' last festival?

S.H.: Casals did no conducting last year at all, except for the Beethoven First Symphony, and it was touch-and-go, but he did conduct at the first concert. He would stand up when the climax came, he got so excited. He had started rehearsals for the Mendelssohn Midsummer Night's Dream even though he had a cold and an ear problem that the doctors said affected his hearing. In the middle of the rehearsal he suddenly stopped and said, "I'm sorry, I cannot do any more."

Milton Thomas: I first went to Prades, in southern France, in the summer of 1949. I had made up my mind and was absolutely determined that I wanted to study with Casals, but I didn't even know whether he would accept any pupils. I remember those first lessons very vividly. I had a rather bloated and youthful opinion of myself and felt that he and I would have much in common. In the first lesson I played the Prelude from the C Minor Cello Suite for him. He let me finish without interruption, and then he stood up, his pipe in his mouth as usual. He picked up his cello, sat down and played the Prelude for me. I was literally stunned, having never heard him before in person. I then realized how little we had in common and how much I had to learn. It was an overwhelming, dynamic experience. The difference between what I had been trying to do, and what he did, was the sheer imagery and fantasy of his performance. It was a revelation! Then he described in words that this suite should sound like a Greek tragedy. Casals mentioned that he had played it for Edvard Grieg, who had made that comment half a century earlier. I took about ten lessons with him that summer, each lesson lasting about an hour and a half — the first five were devoted entirely to that one Bach Suite. He charged me $50 for each lesson. I would have paid anything, even if I had to borrow it. I remember thinking at that time that Casals was very old. He was 71, and I felt guilt-ridden to think that I was wearing him out. Well, I can tell you, he wore me out!

He lived very modestly then, in a tiny little house, actually the caretaker's house on a big property, and there was no telephone.

At one point I thought I was going to give up studying with him, because I simply could not do the things he asked. But then one evening we played chamber music. I think that was the first time we really hit it off. Casals commented that he had perceived something in my chamber music playing that had not been apparent to him until that evening. I felt very flattered and encouraged.

One day when he was again playing Bach for me in my lesson, just the two of us in the room, I said, "Maitre" (we all used to call him "Maitre" in those days; later in Puerto Rico we called him "Don Pablo"), "this was absolutely perfect." Casals' eyes sparkled, as he retorted, "No, Bach has yet to be interpreted." And that is an exact quote! It sounds so simple, but I realized that he really meant it sincerely.

I used to write down everything he said, and put down every single bowing he advised me to take. Imagine my astonishment when I heard him play the next year and he had changed all of his own bowings! One day I met Lajos Suk in Hollywood, and Lajos said, "Why doesn't Casals publish an edition of the Bach Sonatas? He of all people should establish a definitive edition." I answered, "I don't think he'll be interested in it, but if you like, write to him." He did, and got in reply a letter in Casals' typically miniscule handwriting.

> I would not dare,
> less be tempted, to do such a thing.
> The best edition is the original!

I would be inclined to define his attitude toward teaching as the old-fashioned, European approach, as opposed to more modern, progressive attitudes. I once asked him, point-blank, whether he didn't think that a student might have some good ideas of his own, which should be encouraged so that he could develop his individuality. He jumped up excitedly and went to the wall. "No!" he said, "the student must be like an apprentice. The Master draws the line, and the student re-traces it." He made a gesture with his arm, drawing an imaginary line along the wall. One of the memorable phrases he liked to use was: "A good imitation is better than a bad original."

When we played chamber music, instead of following the first violin, as is customary, everybody watched Casals. Even in the opening of the Brahms Sextet, where the viola has the lead phrase, I knew that nobody would change harmony until Casals changed his bow. When he was in a mood for playing slowly, that could be quite frustrating.

He had an almost naive sense of wonder about the music right until the end. Bach was his favorite. Of all the composers, he used to say, "Bach has the greatest variety and color." But some of my most exciting memories of his conducting are of his Brahms and Beethoven symphonies. His Mozart conducting sometimes became a little heavy-handed because he

got so carried away by the details of every lovely phrase. He was always admonishing us to play Mozart "beautifully" and with "love." Casals had such love and integrity in his music that one can say truthfully, he never in his life played a note that he did not believe in.

And that first festival in Prades, in 1950, is never-to-be-forgotten. When Casals played an unaccompanied Bach Sonata at every concert in the Cathedral, we all wept. ■

The Paradox of
PIERRE BOULEZ

Ralf-Finn Hestoft/Northwestern University

Boulez. The radical and outspoken *enfant terrible* who once advocated that concert halls and opera houses should be burned to the ground as dead monuments to an irrelevant past, but who ended up being known as one of the world's greatest conductors and interpreters of that past.

Boulez. The name of the leading serialist of his generation, the man who once advocated that serialism would become "the only musical direction of the future," and yet who later completely abandoned it as a compositional method.

Boulez. The frustrated artist who once vowed he'd never come back to an artistic position in his native France, and yet who for the past decade has headed the world's leading experimental music research center located in Paris at the Centre Pompidou.

Boulez. The defiant and arrogant lion in Nietzsche's *Also Sprach Zarathustra*, who once attacked all established systems, but who now is as diplomatic and subdued as a pussycat, and who has become the very system itself in contemporary music.

On the surface, it would seem we are dealing with a man of considerable contradiction. Rather, we are dealing with a man of genuine paradox. Boulez is a living parable: a walking 20th-century monument. Our greatest living figure in music, he is, in addition to being universally regarded as one of the century's greatest composers, a conductor and lecturer of international renown.

BY DENNIS POLKOW

Ralf-Finn Hestoft/Northwestern University

Now 62 years old, Boulez stands at the fore-front of the contemporary music movement. Born in Montbrison, France, his first important compositions date from the mid-1940s, as he emerged from compositional studies with Olivier Messiaen, and later, the serialist and former pupil of Schoenberg and Webern, René Leibo-witz. Boulez' now classic Second Piano Sonata (1947-8) marked his own radical and mature adaption of serial procedures.

Later, Boulez was to apply serial principles to all aspects of music (rhythm, register, dynamics, etc.) in *Structures I* for two pianos (1951-2), and he began work on large-scale pieces with literary influences such as the well-known *Le marteau sans maître* (1953-5) and *Pli selon pli* (1957-62).

From that time on Boulez turned more and more to conducting so that he could aggressively champion new music rarely heard on the podium, but by the end of the 1960s he had conducted works by composers of all periods, from Machaut to Beethoven to Wagner.

In 1971 Boulez simultaneously accepted music directorships of London's B.B.C. Symphony and the New York Philharmonic. The New York years were particularly stormy ones, with Boulez consistently taxing the ears, minds, and en-durance of post-Bernstein audiences with ex-perimental and unfamiliar scores.

By the mid-1970s Boulez began severely cur-tailing his conducting engagements so that he could return to experimental composition and the development of the new I.R.C.A.M. institu-tion that he returned to France to found. His new piece *Répons* is the culmination of a decade's worth of experimentation of combining music and technology at that institution, and was the centerpiece of last year's five-city U.S. tour of I.R.C.A.M.'s L'Ensemble InterContemporain that appropriately became a triumphant return of both Boulez the composer and Boulez the conductor. It was during that tour that I had the rare opportunity to have a conversation with a true 20th-century enigma.

997

Many of us were quite surprised when you left your post as Music Director of the New York Philharmonic to create IRCAM in Paris, because prior to that you hadn't been very involved in electronic music.

I had always been very interested in electronic music, but I had always been frustrated by the primitive technology. I tried writing an electronic piece in 1948, then again in 1951, 1958, and 1972. There seemed to be a lack of concentration within the major electronic centers on how technology could be developed further to serve musical purposes.

It was fortunate that, just as I was looking to find a way to create a new electronic institute, President Pompidou opened a large center in Paris for all of the arts. He was eager to do something unique in music at the new center, and we discussed what might be done.

I told him that if I came back to France, it would not be just to conduct, compose, or do things I had already been doing outside France. I would only come back if we could somehow set up the conditions for researching the most advanced technology for music. The idea appealed to him, and we integrated this as-yet-unnamed institute into the overall framework of the Centre Pompidou.

How did the name IRCAM come about, and what were its original goals?

IRCAM stands for *Institut de Recherche et Coor-* *dination Acoustique/Musique* [Institute for Research of Coordination between Acoustics and Music]. From its inception it was devoted to dialogue between musicians and scientists, as the name indicates.

I knew that there were some problems that the contemporary composer was fraught with daily that were not solved by a professional musical life. I saw this very clearly during my years as a conductor. I knew that what was needed was a cloistered environment where musicians would be protected and could think about their own problems and how to solve them without any pressure from the external world. An environment of protection with no deadlines, no obligations — just freedom.

If one just says "freedom" in an unqualified way, however, he runs the risk of being lost in a kind of freedom that is not very useful. Living in a fortress cuts one off from the world, which is dangerous. The scars that one develops in battles with the outside world are terribly important because they ultimately give one more strength. Too much protection and security are bad.

Research for its own sake doesn't exist for me, and the results of the research and the pieces now possible because of it must all be transmitted to the outside world. So research and protection go hand in hand, as does communication with an audience.

People who are really creative want to communicate with others. Truly creative people never want to discover for its own sake or only for themselves. Creativity is a form of generosity, albeit often mixed with egocentrism. Without this generosity, one is not creative.

The major specific goals of IRCAM were to expand the domain of musical instruments, and to expand the field of musical sounds. The contemporary composer has demands that are not really fulfilled by the construction of conventional instruments (the creation of multiphonic sounds, for example) because we have to fight against the instruments to produce sounds that might be produced by chance or by unstable conditions. We wanted to be able to provide these sounds within the instruments themselves, provided that we did not change the actual technique by which they were played. Rather, we were interested in adapting traditional techniques to electronic tools so that the composer could get what he wanted without fighting against the instrument.

Music based on intervals such as semitones and halftones is familiar to all of us, but suppose one wants music based not on halftones, but on some other intervalic relationship. From this point of view, our conventional instruments are difficult to change. If we take the violin, for example, one cannot manage smaller intervals in its high register because the fingers are simply too large to play them with precision. In the low register it is difficult because the physical space across the bridge is too large. If one wants to retune a harp with other intervals in mind it can be done, but it will quickly go out of tune, as will a piano, and so on. These instruments were all built for certain intervalic relationships, and you fight against them when you try to change this.

With the electronic media, one cannot only create new sounds and new timbres, one is free to fulfill all wishes, limited only by the imagination itself. If I want quarter tones or sixth tones, I can instantly have them, precisely and remaining perfectly in tune. This is something not possible on conventional instruments, and this is why technology appeals to me: not for its own sake, but because it makes music possible that would otherwise not be possible.

Enlarging the domain of musical instruments is something made necessary by the imagination. If imagination goes beyond the tools that we already have, then our path to create new tools and new materials becomes obvious.

Beyond this, new materials will dictate new uses as well. In the history of architecture, when the new materials of concrete, glass and steel came in, everything changed. One wouldn't build a Greek temple with steel and glass; one would not only rethink what to build, but how to build it. New building materials have affected everything from the lines of a building to its very construction or engineering.

Of course, the option to use stone and wood still exists today, but the really large buildings could not exist without the newer materials of concrete, glass, and steel.

It is the same with music. We cannot go on forever using the same materials as in the 17th and 18th centuries. We must invent new materials. These new materials also demand a new way of thinking that will be in phase with them. It's the chicken and the egg situation.

How did the computer come to have such a prominent role at IRCAM?

At first I had separate departments for voice, for instruments, for electronic sounds, and for the computer. Gradually I began to see the computer invading everything and even dominating the other departments. The computer is such a general tool and can help in so many ways: in creating new uses for music theory, in adapting acoustics, in synthesizing sounds, in creating programs for hanging sound in space, in expanding the sonorities of instruments, and even in expanding rhythmic figures and patterns. This demanded that we not only have one large in-house computer, but also banks of smaller, individual microcomputers as well. This solved the problem, which I had experienced myself, of having to wait three hours to hear one second of sound.

Another problem was the difference between the musical and the scientific imagination. When using a computer, even for musical purposes, one has to read a lot of figures, which are very abstract, and which do not correspond at all to one's musical imaginaton. There is musical culture, and then there is scientific culture, and it has always been a major goal of IRCAM to try and put the two cultures in phase so as to create a common language between them.

The more we worked with computers, the more the need arose for working in real time, that is, where a computer could figure out immediately — even if only in a rough way that could be perfected later — what the result of a particular sound transformation would be. This developed an interactive language between the

Ralf-Finn Hestoft/Northwestern University

Ralf-Finn Hestoft/Northwestern University

composer and the machine, which helped the composer's imagination to react.

You know, I conducted many works for instruments and tape, and I found myself in a schizophrenic situation. On the one hand, I could understand the need for tape — it could preserve complex sounds that, at least in the past, were difficult if not impossible to produce live. On the other hand, one becomes a prisoner to tape: if you conduct a score that is in complete synchronization with a tape, then your creative power as a performer is greatly reduced. Emphasizing a particular accent or adapting to the acoustics of a particular hall becomes impossible because the score on the tape is so stiff that it allows no freedom of interpretation. The performance becomes stiff because spontaneity, strength, and expression give way to anxiety over lining up every note precisely with the tape.

We wanted to solve such problems by introducing the notion of making the music on the stage itself, at the actual time of the performance. This creates a situation where the musician himself is the master, rather than the slave, of the technology. This is what the present 4X computer is all about, as well as its several predecessors over the years.

Tell us about your new work Répons *and what function the 4X fulfills in it.*

It is a work conceived completely along the direction that I have just outlined. It is set up with a small 24-piece orchestra of strings, woodwinds, and brass in the center of the hall, and their sound is not altered in any way, except to be slightly amplified in very large halls. Surrounding the orchestra is the audience itself. Surrounding the audience from behind, at various points around the hall, are the six soloists whose sounds are transformed by the 4X: piano I, cimbalom, piano II, vibraphone, harp, and glockenspiel. These six instruments were chosen because they are so resonant and therefore, at least for the moment, they are the easiest to transform through the 4X. They are transformed by being miked and processed through the 4X, the results of which are spatially distributed through a matrix and then transmitted 25 microseconds later through various loudspeakers placed at key points around the hall. The sound, often programmed to create the illusion of moving through space, literally surrounds the audience on all sides.

The work's title, *Répons* [Response], suggests a responsory, as in church between the priest and the congregation. It is structured basically as question/answer, and so forth. This idea is not strictly followed, but it was the springboard for the piece. It became a dialogue between direct sound and transformed sound — between the

Ralf-Finn Hestoft/Northwestern University

Jim Ziv/Northwestern University

Ralf-Finn Hestoft/Northwestern University

center group or collective playing, contrasted with the distant group of soloists, or individual playing.

The set-up for the piece is not simply a theatrical one; it is needed for the music itself. We bring everything that is needed to perform the piece, not only the instruments, the computer,

faces of the other puppeteers are covered. I am the main puppeteer because I am visible, and I manipulate the sound through computer assistants who transform each of the soloist's musical gestures.

The computer programs are an actual part of the structure of the music itself, and not something just tacked on at the end of the compositional process. Andrew Gerzso, our head technician, actually sits at the console of the 4X, pressing the various buttons for the programs at the appropriate time as marked by the score. There is another technician who handles all of the marked spatialization throughout the hall. Since both the technicians and the computers are physically there, and the sound is being transformed in real time, I am completely free as a conductor to emphasize anything I want, and I know that the computer programs will follow. This has given me, at last, a connection between music and technology that I have longed for for many years — to hear what I want to hear when I want to hear it. No longer am I a prisoner of tape; I am completely free. This is for me, a considerable achievement, but *Répons* is merely a first step in this direction.

Could you envision a time (many feel we are there already) where digital sampling technology, and other electronic innovations would eliminate the need or desire for performers as intermediaries in the compositional process?

Not for me, no. We need the performer, and I for one would not want to compose without taking into account the performer. I like the irrationality of the performer. Imprecision, after all, is the gift of the gods. Every instrumentalist and every soloist has his own characteristic and peculiar brand of irrationality. I have heard *Répons* done with six other soloists, and they each had a completely different approach to the music. That you could not reconstitute with any kind of technology or machinery. I could not overemphasize this point.

As a conductor I know that I have the reputation of being very strict, but I know also that being strict is really being just a little more precise, and that's all.

The performer can go beyond certain limits because of the elements of high complexity in his playing, elements that one would have great difficulty reconstituting through technology. And besides, why bother? Why be complicated when life can be simple? One could never constitute the exact sound of some individual who is performing according to the acoustical properties of an instrument and environment. There are many instant reactions that cannot be forseen and programmed.

What I expect from a machine is that which is

the matrix, etc., but even the various platforms, scaffolding, lights, and loudspeakers.

What is your relationship to the computer technicians who play such a vital role in Répons?

I tend to think of it all as Japanese puppetry. The main puppeter's face is uncovered, but the unique and specific to a machine, and what I expect from a performer is that which is unique and specific to a performer. In my own music I am interested in clashing the irrationality of the performer with the strict logic and possibilities of technology. It is this clash which I think makes the music interesting.

The original version of Répons *ran about 18 minutes, and your most recent version runs about 40 minutes. You have conjectured that the work could end up even longer. Why is it so difficult for you to consider this, as well as many other of your works, complete and finished?*

I suppose that I have the same problem that one of my favorite writers, Franz Kafka, had with his writing: Kafka could never finish a work. He was always revising, always reentering.

Any work I begin is its own world unto itself, and I always find it difficult to get out of these worlds. I often would like to, and of course, I have done it in that I have finished works and never returned to them; but when I think something can be improved or made more striking, stronger, and larger, I have to involve myself again. To me, each of my compositions is like a labyrinth, and a labyrinth can go on forever.

It would seem that being a 20th-century composer would be very discouraging in many ways. Not only does a composer of our time have to strive to create a new style or method of musical expression, but often an entirely new musical language as well. Such was not the case in the centuries immediately preceding our own, where composers of one age could simply work within an accepted and widely practiced musical language of a former age.

Yes, and that does make it more difficult to write music today. Nothing is taken for granted, and there are no standard conventions today as there once were — conventions that were once accepted and taken for granted for a long time. In fact, the history of European music can be seen as a gradual, progressive rejection or reduction of conventions. In Mahler the tonal conventions are much less visible than in Wagner, and in Wagner less than in Beethoven, in Beethoven less than in Mozart, and so on.

With modern or contemporary music from the beginning of the century, conventions are absent. The composer today must create the conventions of his own world. Of course, this is more difficult than just to accept something and work within an established frame.

Composers of the past took variations on the same scheme as their frame of musical reference with regard to form. A contemporary composer, however, invents a new scheme with each and every composition. They can be somewhat parallel or similar schemes, but they are to be fresh

each time. One has to find or create the form which fits the thought of a piece, or the particular way that one can express himself in that piece. Once found, the form cannot be repeated; but I enjoy this challenge. I'm not complaining at all to be a composer in this century. Quite the contrary, it is exciting. Our present ability to be able to expand the tools of music, in addition to the expanding musical language, is unique.

Speaking of musical languages, your name was synonymous for many years with serialism. What do you now see as the future of serialism?

Serialism actually has more of a past than a future. The pure serialists of my generation used it as a way of finding a new basis for musical language. We could not stay in this area because it was much too narrow. The more one wants to expand his expression, the more one has to be free with his materials. One must create ways of using the materials, which are not tied down to as tight a discipline as serialism.

Music has always had two ways of being written: freely, and strictly. With Bach for example, his free form was the prelude; his strict form was the fugue. There are parts in my own music where the relationships are very closed and tight — a more logical approach — and there are also parts that have a very open or free character. This is normal for all composers.

Would you then see serialism as simply one of a variety of strict forms available to the contemporary composer?

Yes, I would, but we must see serialism beyond Schoenberg's serialism of one note of a row at a time. We should see it expanded to chords, registers, and all of its implicit dimensions. That expands its usage considerably.

To borrow electronic music terminology, musical texture consists of a signal and an envelope. This is important to understand in composing, or in following new compositions.

The signal marks the turning point of the development of a piece. There might be a very loud, strong chord, which could continue to develop for a long time, then there might be another similar kind of chord, also played very loud and then developed. The form of a piece can be followed by tracing its signals.

The envelope is the register. One might compose a piece in a very high register, but later the envelope of the texture could become a very low register. Understanding a work's use of signal and envelope helps one to grasp the moments of a work.

You seem to be rejecting serialism, which I take to mean that you no longer want to hold to your polemical statements concerning serialism, particularly that serialism is "the only logical musical system of the future."

Such statements were made when I was in one process of my development, and I am now at another. If you take a picture of yourself from 30 years ago, that picture cannot be used as a picture of yourself today.

I'm sure you are aware of the fact that many of today's serialists use your polemical quotes to defend their use of that form, as if you had made the statement yesterday.

I know, and I don't want my statements to be frozen. The statements should always be tied to a date. They served a useful purpose in their day, but their day is past. Life must be in constant movement and flux, never static.

Would you also retract other famous radical quotes, notably the infamous "We must destroy the Mona Lisa?"

I never meant "destroy" in the literal sense of going inside the Louvre and actually physically destroying the painting. I meant "destroy" in the metaphorical sense of destroying within one's self: to keep us from being so obsessed with the past that we can't see the importance of the now.

What I said was that to add a moustache to the Mona Lisa [as Marcel Duchamp did] does not really get rid of history, it only makes fun of it. One would have to completely remove or destroy the image of the Mona Lisa from the consciousness altogether to remove it from history. That, in fact, is far more difficult than simply painting a moustache on the Mona Lisa!

The past is the past, and the more one simply absorbs it, the more free one is. For myself, conducting became my confrontation with the past, and it cured me about the past. One shouldn't ignore the past or be unaware of it from sloth or lack of study.

A composer's work will not be properly situated unless he has absorbed the past. Once that is done, he doesn't have to bother with it anymore. It becomes a part of him and will come out unconsciously or consciously in his compositions. It's important not to be preoccupied with what happened before. Confront the past, and then consciously forget it.

This must make specific influences difficult to trace for you.

For me, everything is an influence. Earlier works of mine such as *Le marteau sans maître* and *Pli selon pli* had obvious literary influences. I can look at an interesting painting today and unconsciously take something from it that I will use in a couple of months and then observe,

"Yes, I noticed that the day I saw that painting." A composer is a predator: he steals. Everything I find that is interesting I will steal, but I will use and transform it in such a way that it will not be recognized. At that point, it becomes part of myself and I myself can be surprised at the result and wonder how such a result was derived from that painting, or whatever may have inspired me.

With your interesting interpretation of the past and its significance, I would be curious to know your response to the current popularity of period-instrument performances of older music.

When performing older music, it is necessary to go back to the real value of the time. When music was conceived for a certain balance of instruments, that balance is important and it should be maintained.

One can go back too far, however, and can make music the property of historical fans. The more one consciously tries to be "historical," the further the music is removed from himself. One may think that he is getting back to the historical truth, but on the contrary he will end up with a frame of historical truth that makes the music more distant than if it had been played less faithfully.

Still, the 19th century standardized certain instruments, balances, and performance practices that we now know are no longer necessary for performing music of the Baroque era. As a composer, I find it very interesting to hear Bach, for example, on period instruments, to get a sense of the same timbres that he knew.

The Baroque era was very individualistic, and this individualism gradually disappeared during the 19th century, only to reappear again in the 20th century, as early as [Schoenberg's] *Pierrot lunaire*. This individualism has remained with us and has been further developed.

Is there any way that the negative response to your championing contemporary music during your years with the New York Philharmonic could have been avoided?

Given the present system of American education, I really don't think so. I'm not just talking about the audiences; it also lies very much on the shoulders of the performers. So many performers are simply not imaginative, even, I must say, for music of the past.

Is it your contention that if regular, qualitative performances of contemporary music were a regular staple of the American musical diet that audiences would learn to like it?

Yes. When people become accustomed to committed performances, they will enjoy contemporary music as long as the environment is correct and inviting and occurs within a presentation of diverse musical styles. Initial overdoses of contemporary music will serve to alienate many people, having an effect exactly opposite that one would like to have.

George Szell, for example, was a man who wasn't terribly interested in new music, and I can understand that a man in his seventies cannot completely change his musical landscape. His mind was open enough, though, that he realized that he was incapable of exposing his audiences to something new and foreign to him; he asked me to come and fulfill that role for his orchestra, which I did.

Are there things that we could be doing with children at even the elementary levels that would help them become open to new music?

Yes, certainly. They need an active education that will emphasize that both classical and contemporary music have the same roots. We should not be afraid to jump across centuries backwards and forwards with them, showing them very sharp contrasts, which actually makes music more accessible.

In New York we used to do a series of concerts for young people called the "Rug Concerts," so called because we would remove chairs and have the children sit on rugs on the floor. I tried to achieve a maximum of contrast in these concerts. I might, for example, begin with a Haydn Symphony, follow it perhaps by a Ligeti piece, and then conclude with something by Ravel: a real zig-zag approach. Everyone responded well because it held their interest to realize that there could be such variety in symphonic music.

Of course, this is true for older audiences as well. There is nothing more boring than an entire concert in E♭ major, despite what some of my [conductor] colleagues may think!

Do you think it is the complexity of much new music that often alienates audiences?

If so, it's often illusory. After all, a fugue from a Beethoven string quartet is highly complex. No contemporary composer has written music any more complex than that, and I for one wouldn't try to.

Simply because we at I.R.C.A.M., for example, are expanding the tools of music does not mean we are necessarily expanding its complexity. The technology itself and the thinking associated with it may be complex, but music written with the help of a computer may, in fact, be very simple; and why not?

I think that audiences would be much more comfortable with new music if it were programmed intelligently and played convincingly. If the performer himself is not convinced or even interested in the music and is just playing it to get rid of it as quickly as possible and move on, it will sound that way. You must be convincing!

It is sometimes difficult to perform new music in an intelligent way because of the inflexible rehearsal conditions of American symphony orchestras. Typically, there are four rehearsals for a program that will be repeated four times. If one is performing a new piece, which, by virtue of being new makes it difficult to rehearse because the musicians are being exposed to it for the first time, one has to compensate by programming it with a work that is very easy and that the orchestra will know very well: so-called symphonic war horses. The problem is that people interested in the new piece will not be attracted to the horses, and people brought in by the horses will not be interested in the new piece.

This is a constant dilemma: Do I mix antagonistic tastes, or do I give up and isolate new music in a ghetto for a small, though devoted, audience, and keep the rest of the larger audience quiet and content by not disturbing them?

As a matter of fact, we must disturb. We are here to disturb. All composers, however accepted they are now, were there to disturb within their own time. From the famous sentence of the Kaiser to Mozart ("Too many notes, my dear Mozart!"), to Wagner, to Schoenberg, there is always something disturbing in something new.

If we don't disturb, we do not grow. If we have nothing absolutely new, we are only recreating the past, which is not very intersting and, in fact, is very dangerous. As difficult as it may be to grasp, all old music was once new music.

What about the argument sometimes made that we can program the best of the past because it is time-tested, but we really don't know what scores being composed today are the best of what's out there today, and are therefore worth hearing?

You know, the other day I went back to the Art Institute [of Chicago], which I hadn't seen in nearly 15 years. I found it very interesting that in this, as most museums, extremely good paintings are shown next to only very good or just good paintings.

In music, however, we only perform and hear the top pieces, the peaks, if you will, and the rest of music is ignored. This repetition of the same pieces over and over, without even the curiosity of wanting the historical perspective that hearing other pieces would give us, creates a kind of Swiss cheese culture — that is, full of holes! Can you imagine an art museum with only a dozen or so paintings in it? I like Swiss cheese, but not when it comes to musical culture.

Therefore, when it comes to both new and older music, we need to hear the widest variety on every level. Otherwise, an overall perspective is lost, and we lose the criteria for what makes a great work of art.

Could you briefly comment on some of the present trends in new music? I know, for example, that minimalism is a movement that you have attacked.

Minimalism represents a view of things that is too simplistic and that really won't take us very far. I also now see, though, that the minimalists are beginning to maximalize a bit here and there, with bigger forces, bigger pieces, and so on. Of course, as this happens, whether they like it or not, the music becomes more interesting because it becomes more complex. You cannot skate on thin ice very long before falling into water.

Perhaps the minimalists are attempting to use minimalism in the same way that you and others of your generation used serialism: to help extend musical language. Perhaps they, like you, will outgrow the need for such a rigid formula, and will begin to employ it as one of several strict techniques available.

Yes, I could well imagine that being the case. I would also like to say that people who go back to something are, for me, not very interesting. The so-called Neoromantics for example, are exactly the same as the so-called Neoclassicists of the '20s in France. This is what I call "music for the antique market," and I find such scores unbearable.

How do you account for your involvement with some music of rock star Frank Zappa?

Because I have a wide variety of tastes and I don't want to be squeezed into the position of a serious musician who ignores the rest of the world. I don't want to be what the English call snooty.

I frankly didn't know too much about Frank Zappa — I had heard a little about him and a few of his recordings — but when I was told by a recording company that he wrote orchestral

scores and was asked if I would look at them, I said, "Yes, I'd like to see them." When we met I told him that if he wanted a piece for large orchestra to be performed by myself, he would have to wait at least a couple of years because I now conduct only two programs for large orchestra a year and next year's program is already full. I told him that if he wanted a performance in a shorter time that he should write something for our group, L'Ensemble InterContemporain, and he agreed.

As it turned out, I was very pleased with the result. Zappa is highly professional; he knows what he wants, and he hears very well. It was also a wonderful exercise of our musicians to go into another world of musical writing and to solve the unique problems of balance and ensemble that this music presented. We worked very hard to perform it as well as we could.

I did not, however, want to create a Zappa event where everyone would say, "Clever, clever, you are doing Zappa so you will attract and excite a lot of listeners you wouldn't ordinarily have." I put it in a very demanding context: an American music program that turned out to be Ives, Ruggles, Zappa, and Carter. Within that context, it was an enormous success, and that is what I had hoped.

How do your own tastes and views as a composer influence what is done at I.R.C.A.M. and how do other composers at the institution respond to your presence?

You would have to ask them! My own existence at I.R.C.A.M. is somewhat schizophrenic. On the one hand I am a composer with my own ideas on how to write music. On the other hand I am the head of an institution that I have created in such a way so that no one should feel an obligation to me, or to my ideas. Everyone can use all of the tools we have, and I will never object to anything done in the house, provided that it consists of quality and professionalism. That is

all I ask. Even then, if a young, inexperienced musician makes a mistake, all I ask is that learning should be the result.

I also have no interest in being idolized or put on a pedestal. I do not want disciples. I am much more interested in people who can legitimately criticize and show me things I had not seen, even in my own works.

As for how they respond to me as a composer, they don't need to at all. Perhaps my music says little to them; that's all right. That is not my problem. I try to do my best to express myself and I hope that it will effectively communicate with people, but if it doesn't, I've done my best.

Taste and personal attractions in music have little to do with actual music. I must again plead here for irrationality; this is simply not a logical matter. I find people are so surprised when they find out that I like Ravel. They look puzzled and say, "You really do?" and I respond, "Yes, I do." I like his approach. As a composition teacher I may prefer Debussy because his works are more refined and more interesting in terms of invention, but Ravel has, for me, such a unique and satisfying sound. I also find that I like Berg much more than Schoenberg, but that is me; it does not say Berg is a better composer than Schoenberg.

As far as my own music goes, I remember a quote that goes: "A writer should be happy when a reader has found himself in his writings." It is the same for me; I am happy when a listener finds part of himself in my music. The wonderful interactive side of this is that it is not for myself but for the listener to determine which part of himself that he may discover. ∎

Dennis Polkow holds degrees in music theory, composition, philosophy, and religious studies from DePaul University in Chicago. He is on the faculty of the College of DuPage in Glen Ellyn, Illinois. An author, journalist, and lecturer, he is also a columnist for The Chicago Musicale *and a critic for* The Chicago Reader.

Shinichi Suzuki
The Best of East and West

Katherine Johnson

The gait is slow, the teeth show signs of ever-present cigarettes, wrinkles are deeply etched in the narrow face. The kindness, humor, and energy that radiate from the slightly stooped frame belie his 86 years.

Shinichi Suzuki's schedule would cripple most people half his age. When in Japan, his day begins at 3:00 A.M. so he can listen to, and make comments about that day's portion of the 10,000 graduation tapes he receives yearly from all over. He expresses regret that this great number prevents him from continuing to paint, personally, the picture he sends to each child to acknowledge their accomplishment. "The scene of Matsumoto is of the beautiful mountains called the Japanese Alps." When complimented on the delicate warmth the painting conveys, he demurs modestly, saying "It is only decoration, not art." By 9:00 in the morning he is at work teaching his students, not just children but also *kenkyusei* (both seasoned and aspiring teachers from around the world), who have come to study with the *Sensei* (master teacher). Administrative chores, children's concert preparations, writing, and learning ("I am always studying to find new and better ways to explain what I am after") round out his arduous working day. When he travels, sleep is deferred, jet lag ignored; speeches, teaching, and consulting are the order of the day.

A Celebrity Abroad

While abroad Suzuki is a celebrity, hardly able to squeeze past those who seek to look at, touch, or speak to the legendary figure. When asked how it feels to be famous, his wry reply, "if I became famous, it is the fault of the American teachers," evades the answer even while being accurate. For in fact, this man who has become an American household word over the past 25 years has had, as many visionaries do, a serious recognition problem in his own land. Shinichi Suzuki, the 20th century's most influential pedagogue, is still confused in Japan with the former prime minister of the same name. Still more paradoxically, this Western popularity has come about despite musical results that pale in comparison to those in Japan.

From its inception the Suzuki method had difficulty gaining widespread endorsement in Japan. "It is not accepted by lots of musicians. Many Japanese who come to the United States on business hear about the Suzuki method for the first time in their life." Only when the city of Matsumoto hosted the International Suzuki Conference in 1983 did Japan's music establishment finally sit up and take notice. The fact that so many for-

eigners came to see Suzuki and that Japanese newspapers could preface articles with "In America...," "In Europe..." conferred upon the entire movement a new-found recognition and legitimacy. That fame at home should have been so delayed is astonishing. After all, even if the method is less widely used in Japan than in other parts of the world, the numbers still do add up. Suzuki estimates, "if we put together the last 37 or 38 years, there are many thousands of people who have studied in this way." Furthermore, the quality of the playing in Japan is higher than in the rest of the world. Western visitors report that the achievements they observe in Japan stagger their minds and ears. Why then have Suzuki and his method not had the same impact on his own country as they have had upon those in the West? Why are the results so different? Are there variations in the application of the method? These and several other puzzling questions revolving around East/West Comparisons were the focal point of my discussion with Suzuki when he attended the First American Suzuki Conference last May.

The "Mother Tongue Approach"

Suzuki has spent his entire life straddling the differences between East and West. He was brought up in Japan but at the age of 17 took up the study of the violin and its Western literature in Europe. He married a German woman with whom he has lived in Japan for over 50 years. When I asked whether traversing countries and cultures presented any problems, Suzuki maintained, "No, there is no difficulty with the adjustment except for the language." It is part of the Suzuki genius that he settled on this very liability and transformed it into an asset.

The core of the Suzuki method grew out of Suzuki's comparison of his own difficulties in learning German as an adult with the obvious ease with which all children mimic perfectly the most complex languages and dialects. One of the alternate terms for the method is "mother tongue approach," which aptly sums up the analogy of studying music and learning one's own language. Suzuki is unyielding in his conviction that the relationship between these two forms of learning is absolutely equal; yet my own experience as a Suzuki mother and teacher have been that children undergo far more frustration in learning music than in learning to speak. For the child who wants to be immediately perfect without working for a particular skill, Suzuki explains that learning anything isn't easy. "You cannot learn it in one practice session. If you are frustrated with yourself, then you have too much pride and too little modesty. First try it 10,000 times. Then if you can't do it, talk to me; but until you've done it that many times, I'm not going to accept any of the complaining." Actually Suzuki finds that it is most often the parent who is frustrated. If there is a difference in the results achieved by Japanese and American children, it is because Japanese mothers have more discipline. "Being a good mother means making the practice enjoyable. It comes down to the mother's creativity."

An Imaginative Mother

One of Suzuki's examples was about an imaginative mother who was having a hard time getting her daughter to repeat a passage of music. Because the child liked big noises, the mother allowed the youngster to throw a noisemaker into a large tub every time the child repeated the passage five times. The girl was getting such a kick out of the noise that she played the passage over and over. In a few days she could play it easily. The youngster never realized that she had actually been practicing; in her mind, she had just been making the noise.

Japanese mothers adopt a role that is significantly more extensive than their American counterparts. American mothers correctly form a triangle with the teacher and child. The mother who listens carefully, takes notes, uses the same terminology at home as that used by the teacher, and practices regularly with the child is considered an excellent Suzuki mother; but according to Suzuki, this is not enough. In Japan the mother is the teacher and the teacher is only an assistant. "Mother is to teach the piece at home. Only if there is something technical or musical that mother might not know, do we explain. American children are so much slower because the teacher tries to teach the music. That is the mother's job. If a mother does not know how to do this, then she must learn. She doesn't have to be able to play, but she does have to learn to read music. This can be difficult if the mother hasn't been learning all along. If the mother starts from the very beginning, the process is gradual and logical. She takes the music everywhere; if she has any time while waiting in a doctor's office, she is studying and putting in all the fingerings so she can teach her child. The lesson won't start until the child has learned the piece. Then the teacher points out what needs to be worked on: 'The tone is not so good here, change this fingering there, this passage you need to practice slower.' "

Our exchange of thoughts about practicing pointed to further differences between Eastern and Western habits. The teacher of an American three-year-old wouldn't dream of asking that child to practice more than an hour; yet Suzuki says, "If you are starting lessons, you are supposed to practice two hours per day from the beginning. At one hour you can maintain your same level of ability; two hours will allow you to make a little progress." This astounding figure does not include time spent listening to a recording of the music!

Music Reading

The Western controversy that rages among non-Su-zuki as well as Suzuki proponents on when and how to teach music reading perplexes Suzuki himself. The issue seems irrelevant in Japan for several reasons. "In Japan there is a lot of singing. All the parents and the grandmothers sing songs for the children from the time they are babies." Therefore, there seems to be no need for pre-reading pedagogies like Orff, Kodàly, and Dalcroze that have been so useful here in the United States. Japanese children are simply able to feel pulses, rhythms, and pitches through their early aural experiences as well as their own singing. Note reading comes later (most Japanese Suzuki students begin very young) and it is taught in Japanese schools. Whether the mother or the child has done the note deciphering is immaterial because the learned piece is expected to be memorized for the lesson. More significantly, there may be a conflict in the term "reading." When I pointed out the discrepancy in reading ability between pieces that are aurally familiar and those that are truly being read at sight, Suzuki was unconcerned. "There is a recording available" if one wants to play a piece not in the Suzuki repertoire. "When I look at an English word that I can't pronounce, I ask an American to pronounce it. Then I know, and the next time I see that word there is no problem in reading it."

Suzuki carried the language analogy further when I asked him about reading violin versus piano music. Because multiple-voice music is more complex and therefore more difficult to read, is it important for the piano student to start reading sooner than the violin student? "I think it is the same. It's because adults think it might be difficult because they themselves are not doing it. When the children do it, however, it's very easy. Just as any child can learn his own native language without any difficulty."

Guidelines to Ensure Quality

Our conversation turned to teaching quality. Because there is such a wide range of teaching skill in this country, I asked whether this is true also in Japan. Suzuki pointed out that all Japanese Suzuki teachers have to be accepted by him. "First you have to be an assistant to an established instructor and then work under me personally for a while. Then you are called an assistant instructor and can take your own students." After you are teaching a few years and Suzuki decides you are qualified, you finally can become an instructor. Even though the Suzuki Association of the Americas is attempting to establish some guidelines to ensure quality control in this country, uniform standards are difficult to achieve because there is no central figure comparable to Suzuki. He is saddened by teachers who claim to be using the method but lack real understanding "because the children are the victims." If the teacher is not good, then the students cannot learn correctly. In fact, his only regret is "all over the world people are using the Suzuki method but are not developing well. In language, when a child becomes five years old, he can speak very well; but in music it is just like the top of a mountain: there are very few good musicians who make it to the top of the mountain but many mediocre ones at the bottom — so not everybody is growing properly. Just as in mathematics or language, everybody has to be able to do it 100 percent right and get to the top of the mountain. The problem lies in the teaching; there is something mistaken in the movement."

When I asked whether he could be specific, he said "American teachers talk too much. They try to explain too much and the chidren become confused. We want the students to listen to the sound. We should demonstrate what we want the children to hear and imitate."

I pressed him about the technique of previewing tricky spots before the child gets to a particular piece. His reply once again placed the burden on the parent: "No, that's the mother's work." Returning once more to the aural aspect of the method, Suzuki indicated that the Japanese don't teach in as great detail as their American counterparts. After Book 1, for instance, the methods never present other information about bow divisions unless it is a necessity. The children are expected to listen to the recording and reproduce the sound, using whatever means are necessary to achieve the sound.

Suzuki's goal is to generate students who can hear and recreate a beautiful tone. Sometimes he is able to invent specific devices that help achieve this goal. "If the child is playing the violin too far from the bridge, I use a rubberband and pencil to help the student play closer to the bridge where the sound is bigger." Other times, he is not specific. "If you ask me how low a bow arm should be, you just have to come with ears." In any case, all roads lead to Rome and all efforts should seek to emulate the Kreisler tone.

Although some famous pedagogues feel that one should teach technique first and allow tone and musical feeling to develop, Suzuki's priorities are vehemently the reverse. He is not even particularly interested in supplemental technical exercises and generally recommends etudes only as a remedy for a particular problem with a specific individual. For example, Suzuki uses etudes to introduce shifting, usually around Book 3, so that the student will have already mastered second and third positions by the time he gets to the Vivaldi Concerto in A Minor. "Etudes were written to help play the concertos; but somehow people make the mistake of suffering through them for their own sake. When I was in Germany I spent hours and hours practicing them. If I practiced eight hours, I spent six hours practicing etudes. So I only had two hours to practice pieces. There are so many pieces in the world to learn and if you spend only two hours a day practicing them you can't learn them. The Brahms Concerto is a wonderful etude. If you can already play it without difficulty, why should you play etudes?"

Etudes or no, it is mind-boggling how many Japanese children graduate from the Suzuki system with dazzling techniques that would normally presage a career as a professional musician. Suzuki children, however, aren't encouraged along these lines. They are expected to practice seriously as long as they are studying. They are, therefore, highly advanced by the time they graduate from the Japanese educational system. If students give up music in order to prepare for another field, they can still return later in life as extremely well-versed amateur musicians. This, according to Suzuki, is the whole point of his method. His intent was never to produce legions of musicians, but rather to promote happiness among people through a love and understanding of music.

Most colleges and towns in Japan have orchestras filled with former Suzuki students, but there is not a widespread emphasis on orchestra and chamber music for young students. It is for this reason that Suzuki has not felt the need for a viola method in Japan. "When they are young, they can learn the violin and later change to the viola. The G string doesn't sound good on a small violin, so to replace it with an even lower C string for a viola is hopeless. I gave my permission for a viola book because American teachers wanted it for their chamber music and orchestral programs."

Performing Differences

As our comparisons drifted from the concrete to the more abstract, Suzuki and I agreed that the differences in playing levels between Oriental children both in the East and in this country could not be attributed only to more practice hours or to parents who participate in the process more actively. Certainly the formidable educational pride and discipline that are standard fare for Orientals play an important role. There is an acceptance of duty that transcends geographical boundaries and translates into tangible results. "The expectations of Oriental parents are very high for their children. American parents are so worried about pushing the children. They worry that their child might dislike them. I don't think parents should be afraid to tell the children what they're expected to do. As one person said, 'Is there any question about brushing teeth or not? Or going to school every day?' Those are things that have to be done. If the violin practice is supposed to be done, children will accept that. Then it's not difficult."

Even deeper than this, however, could it be that the Western mind, which depends upon logical, verbal explanations is simply not well-suited to an essentially Eastern idea? After all, Eastern philosophy defies verbalization and teases logical thought by thriving on riddles such as "What is the sound of one hand clapping?" Can Western teachers educate parents? Can Western instructors help instill in children a new-found respect for teacher and parent? Can they impart the importance of the undertaking while teaching an appreciation of the unimportance of the result? There are some in this country who have succeeded in doing just that, but what about the vast majority of us? Have we been fooled by the popularity of the Suzuki method into thinking we have been doing it right, just as the Emperor was deceived by the adulation of the crowds who dared not reveal his nakedness? The Japanese have been masters at taking Western ideas and adapting, even improving upon them. Can we not do the same? Shinichi Suzuki stands as a meeting point between East and West. The method, when used properly, blends the best of both. It is now up to the American Suzuki teachers to bring together these two divergent cultures in an ongoing cross-fertilization that will continue to benefit our children. ■

Katherine Johnson is a Suzuki piano teacher at the Music Center of the North Shore in Winnetka, Illinois. In addition to being an active recitalist and accompanist, she is a free-lance writer and author of the book, Accompanying the Violin (Kjos).

A special note of thanks to Yuko Honda for her help and translation that took place during the interview with Dr. Suzuki.

Philip Jones
The Prince of Brass

BY VINCENT CICHOWICZ

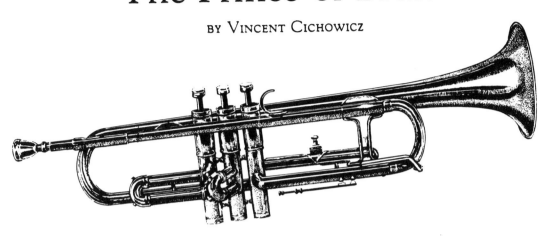

B rass players have a reputation, not altogether undeserved, for being an unruly and insensitive bunch. Those, however, who have played for Philip Jones for these past 35 years have never been allowed to give anything other than performances of the utmost discipline and refinement, even when the music has been essentially spectacular or humorous." Such were the reviews of the final concert given by the Philip Jones Brass Ensemble at the Queen Elizabeth Hall in London this June. After leading his internationally acclaimed brass ensemble for 35 years, Jones has decided to retire.

I met Philip in London during the Chicago Symphony's first European tour in 1971. Following our concert and a friendly gathering at a restaurant in Covent Garden, I was invited to his home where we talked until the early morning hours before I returned to Chicago. Since then we have met on several occasions, most of them during the Brass Ensemble's American tours. The group made its final tour to the States this spring, once again playing to a soldout crowd at Northwestern University. Just before the concert, Philip reminisced about the evolution of his ensemble, and went on to discuss brass playing, teaching, and his post-retirement activities. Vital and articulate, he seemed far from the realm of retiring.

Most of your early work was done with quintet wasn't it?

It was all quintet; I started mine in 1951, around the same time Bob Nagel started the New York Brass quintet. Of course there weren't any brass quintets in Europe at that time, so it was a new sound.

In the early stages I had two groups. One was a quartet — two trumpets, horn, and trombone — that played straight modern music, which was written for us, because there wasn't any modern music for brass quartet then. We played for the radio because no one would entertain the idea of attending brass concerts of any sort. The second group, which ran at the same time, was made up of two trumpets and three trombones, and we played the works of Petzel, Gabrieli, and so on, which was also brand new to us in those days.

After a while I became interested in using the tuba, but I never believed it could work in a small brass group; I thought the blends would be a problem. When Nagel and the New York Brass Quintet came to London in the early 60s with Harvey Phillips playing tuba, it was the first time I had heard that the instrument as part of the organization, instead of something outside the group playing the oompahs. Though I had an excellent tuba player, he was strictly an orchestral player and approached everything that way. Harvey Phillips had a sound and a flexibility that I had not heard before in tuba playing. I was absolutely knocked out by two things: the quintet's tremendous technical fluency and the fact that they could keep going for so long. We didn't know how to do that in those days; they showed me it was possible. Shortly after that I had the good luck of having John Fletcher appear on the horizon, out of nowhere from Cambridge. Someone said to me, "You should hear this crackpot Fletcher, who plays the tuba as you have not heard before," so I asked him to come and have a blow with us. We played a quintet through with the tuba, and I knew I was in business.

Phillips playing tuba, it was the first time I had heard that instrument as part of the organization, instead of something outside the group playing the oompahs. Though I had an excellent tuba player, he was strictly an orchestral player and approached everything that way. Harvey Phillips had a sound and a flexibility that I had not heard before in tuba playing. I was absolutely knocked out by two things: the quintet's tremendous technical fluency and the fact that they could keep going for so long. We didn't know how to do that in those days; they showed me it was possible. Shortly after that I had the good luck of having John Fletcher appear on the horizon, out of nowhere from Cambridge. Someone said to me, "You should hear this crackpot Fletcher, who plays the tuba as you have not heard before," so I asked him to come and have a blow with us. We played a quintet through with the tuba, and I knew I was in business.

Of course this is all told in *A Cheerful Noise*, a book about the history of the group, which has recently been published. It documents how the group evolved over 35 years, but in my opinion, the most interesting part will be the appendices at the end that include all the music we've played — the first performances, what each piece is scored for so other people can play it, and who publishes it.

My wife, Ursula, did all the research for the book, and we hired Donna McDonald to do the writing and the appendices. The history is quite amusing. I didn't tell any lies, and I did get into a few things that I thought were contentious. However, I think the only way to write about your colleagues in books is affirmatively. If their weaknesses are amusing, you can talk about them; if they are not amusing, you don't talk about them. I wouldn't call *A Cheerful Noise* a bland book, but it isn't an exposé; I am not going to have any libel suits.

I was threatened with one a long time ago. Amusingly, I heard that one of my horn players was irritated when, in an article I had written about the history of the group, I mentioned we had changed horn players because this chap did not want to practice. I wanted to get on with more adventurous music that required practice, and that annoyed him very much.

This is a problem, though, because the London scene is built principally on not practicing. Some brass players think it's not manly to practice, which is comically wrong. Anybody who is serious about playing doesn't make music that way.

I don't think that attitude should be relegated only to the London scene. I remember when I first joined the Chicago Symphony some of the older members of the orchestra would say, "Oh you're practicing; you must be insecure."

This is because a great deal of music making today is made instantly, whether it is commer-

cial or classical. In London a symphony concert often has a three-hour rehearsal and that's it. For instance, the first time I played the first cornet part in the *1812 Overture* in the London Philharmonic Orchestra, the conductor said, "Well, we all know this, gentlemen, don't we?" He closed the score, and I read it on the show. That is exactly the scene. You become a very fast sight-reader in London.

The danger about this is you can flip over a lot of music and never really get down to the nitty gritty. Some people, like my famous horn player, are terribly good players, but they don't want to practice. They think practicing is a waste of time and that they can bluff their way

through the music. You cannot bluff your way when playing chamber music; you have to sort it out.

During the time you were playing all this chamber music, I think you had every first trumpet position in London.

Well, I didn't actually hold the first trumpet chair of the L.S.O. I was offered it, but I declined because it wasn't my style, so I didn't go there. I did hold all the others.

When did you actually make the severance from orchestral playing to do the Brass Ensemble full time?

I made the break in 1972, which was very late when you consider I started the group in 1951. Until 1972 I was the first trumpet in an orchestra, although I would go out and be a freelancer occasionally and then go back into orchestras.

The Brass Ensemble was a hobby for me until

1972, but it got serious when it became my main occupation. At that point my wife began to take an interest in the group. She had stopped working as the general manager for the English Chamber Orchestra to become an archeologist, so for three years she was busy getting her degree. Then she thought "Why not use some of my contacts to get the Brass Ensemble a few jobs," because it is very hard to get jobs, especially abroad. All our work had been in England up until that time.

It was a difficult task, but things began to happen. Also, because the group had been going on a long time, the fellows knew how to handle the scene. When we were suddenly able to play in posh places for big audiences, nobody got frightened. From 1972 until now, I have been doing only the Brass Ensemble.

Were there things about the orchestral world that you felt had changed during your career, that you were disenchanted with?

I felt that the first trumpet orchestral world wasn't my scene anymore because in all ways it was definitely growing louder, faster, and noisier. The qualities of color and sensitivity were going out of the window for this sort of playing. Most of the younger conductors were interested in volume and not too much in sound.

I had been brought up with people who really cared about sound. Bruno Walter cared extraordinarily about sound. Sir Thomas Beecham was also extremely critical about sound, and I was hired by him because I had a nice sound. Otto Klemperer was very fussy about sound and control; he did not want you to blow your head off all the time. Sometimes you do have to blow quite loudly, but not all of the time. I got tired of the idea of being what I call just a "musical navvy"; I am not built that way. A German colleague said to my wife when he met me for the first time, "He's too thin. You have to feed him up with beer and sausages." I don't like beer or sausages so I stayed thin. Yet I could blow perfectly well over the top of the Philharmonia Orchestra which was a loud orchestra. It was a quality sound, but that was definitely out, so I became a bit disenchanted. It has come back again I am pleased to say. I hear more and more people asking for nice sounds again in the orchestras. There was a long period when trumpet sounds were nasty.

I was also fascinated with the development of the group at this time; I had good players around me, which excited me, and I still had a reasonable degree of energy left about playing lead trumpet parts. I really got going about 1972 with what was a very serious occupation.

When did Ray Premru and Gary Howarth join the group? They have been with you for quite a long time.

Ray joined in 1963; Gary joined a little later.

Ray used to play for me with the trumpet-trombone group when we did a lot of Gabrieli, Monteverdi, Schütz, and all that world. John Fletcher and Gary came around 1963, Ifor James joined then as our horn player, and shortly after that, John Iveson joined as tenor trombonist. Then we had a team that had the same language. We could play quintets quite differently; it was more the way I had imagined it, as though you were having a conversation instead of just getting through music. It got very exciting then.

Then Gary, of course, became interested in conducting.

He had always been interested in conducting, but he became more interested in modern music and in directing modern music because he was in the London Symphonietta when it was first formed. They always had one trumpet as a fixture in the group, and he got into conducting a bit there. He also conducted the Brass Ensemble when we had something like the Stravinsky Octet, so his career began to divide rather disastrously. At one of our concerts he said he couldn't face having to play the trumpet and being a conductor. I said, "You be a conductor because that will be much better than playing the trumpet," and so we agreed that he should stop.

Then Jimmy Watson joined the group; he was a protégé of Gary's from the Royal Philharmonic. Most of my players have come through the Opera House and the Royal Philharmonic, which have a gentler style of playing. The hardest and most brilliant style of playing in the town has always been in the L.S.O. Those people do not fit into my group at all. I've had them occasionally, as extras, and once a regular member of that orchestra joined us. It didn't work; the attacks were wrong for us. That's a different world all together.

I have always had a fascination with the orchestras of the world and have spent a great deal of time listening to them and admiring their qualities. The last time you were here we discussed the international style that is evolving where many orchestras are losing their individual characteristics.

I deplore that because it is fascinating to be able to go to a local area and hear something special that is representative of that particular place.

The French orchestras, for example, have had a unique quality, especially in the music of Debussy and Ravel, but that is disappearing.

The trouble is they've changed their instruments (woodwinds and brass), to get bigger, fatter sounds, and that is a mistake. You don't have to have everybody in the whole world playing with big, fat sounds.

Don't you suppose part of that is a result of the in-

ternational exchange of conductors who want to play the Bruckner symphonies and Wagnerian operas?

According to Barenboim, they hadn't played Bruckner symphonies in Paris until he went there; they didn't even know about them. They didn't own any Wagner tubas in Paris either; they had to buy them. They didn't know what Wagner tubas were, which puzzles me a bit because how did they manage to play *The Ring?* They must have played it at the opera; perhaps they made do with horns. The fact is that though Barenboim has done a lot of good things there, I think that if he has changed the basic sound of the French orchestra, it is a great shame. It has lost its distinctive color.

What will be your future plans now?

Everyone imagines I am going to conduct brass ensembles or something, when in fact I've never had any desire to conduct. I have met so many third-rate conductors in my life that I'm not joining that long queue. Because I have spent 40 years as a professional trumpeter, my interest in playing has waned. That is a long time, and unless you've got a fantastic ability (like a certain gentleman in your town), you are going to lose your real zip about the whole thing.

I have always been a first trumpet player. I detest being other than that, although I think I am quite clever at playing fourth trumpet, which is what I play in my own group. I do have the compensation of playing the flugelhorn in the group, so I still have some tunes to play. Basically, though, I don't want to continue playing the trumpet, because I don't think I play it well enough, and I want to stop before everybody else says so.

Everyone wants to know what I'll replace it with. For two years now I have had the very interesting job of running the wind department of the Guildhall School of Music. I have 120 students of the wind, brass, and percussion instruments and about 40 professors; and I run that whole scene. I don't even have a secretary, but I make up the syllabus and the exams, and I do all the auditions. I set the standards. I am interested in that because I set our standard in the Brass Ensemble.

At the Guildhall I hire people who can direct music much better than I can, although I have very definite ideas about how it should be done. I can sit in a group and say, "Play that longer, play it shorter, or let's try this"; that's one way. Fellows who have to use their hands and do it without talking (because the best ones do it without talking), are a special breed. I am always looking for people who can do that. My job, as I see it, is to get the best people to do the right job. That is what I have tried to do with the Brass Ensemble. I have always looked for people who get on with one another and play in a style I find acceptable.

I find this job quite interesting and it could run until I am 65 if I wanted it to. I have had a track record of leaving everything after four years, except the Brass Ensemble, which I am now leaving after 35 years. So, I am just wondering how long I can hold onto the Guildhall before my eyes wander somewhere else.

You have also been on a number of distinguished panels in international competitions and of course you have been involved in a number of workshops. What do you think about the current generation of musicians?

Certainly there has been a very distinct advance in technical dexterity on all the wind instruments since the War. However, there has not been and there never could be an equal advance in musicality. Some of the younger players' preoccupation with technical expertise at the expense of musicality is not good. I am pleased to say, though, that I always hear young players from around the world who have both dexterity and musicality. I am not referring to just the trumpet, but to all the wind instruments. The standard is fantastically good. Certainly there are more good players around than there were in my day, but there is not a greater percentage of musicians around than in my day.

I meet fewer people who have the courage of their own convictions to do their thing and not say, "I modeled my playing on Joe Blocks, and he taught me this." For example, the other day I had a gentleman ring me up to ask if I would give him a lesson. I said, "I don't give lessons, but I'll listen to you play while I'm on this tour." I listened to him and then asked who had taught him. He reeled off the names of umpteen people he'd had lessons from, which is all very well if finally you make those experiences into a synthesis of yourself. You should say, "OK, that was an interesting thing that man said, I wonder what that means to me," then take it inside yourself, and come out with your personality. Too many players are imitating somebody else's personality and, of course, the results mean nothing.

Jimmy Galway is a unique sort of flute player. It would be a silly chap or lady to play like Jimmy Galway. You can admire what he does and say, "That aspect of Jimmy Galway's playing I would like to take and I will do it my way." I feel there are too many people copying today.

Because of our extremely competitive situation here in the U.S., auditioning for orchestra positions often means playing in an absolutely definable way. The idea is not to slip up and introduce anything in your approach to the excerpts that will somehow offend this anonymous committee. As a result, there is a stereotyped way you have to play that becomes a mechanical approach to the literature. The problem is that the audition committees aren't necessarily go-

ing to be looking for unique personalities to fit into a section.

I think for a youngster it is a big problem. In the long run, however, if you want to be a real one-off, a unique player who projects something of his personality through the instrument, you have to do it for yourself; you can't just copy someone else. Every player I know who matters is a one-off, right up to the greatest, most famous people. Being a one-off myself I can only think about things this way.

I think this is true of the singers as well. All of the best singers are unique. There is not a second Joan Sutherland, or Kiri Te Kanawa, or Luciano Pavarotti. There is a Joe Blocks, who is the new Pavarotti. He's not Pavarotti; he's someone else, and we have to always think about that. I talk to students about being themselves. If they can't be individuals, they are never going to

versus musicality, but what are some of your other thoughts about this subject?

If you want to be a good musician on any instrument, you must go and listen to singers and to fiddle players. From them you can learn about line, about joining up notes in interesting ways, which we are not taught on our instruments.

Trumpet players are taught in a martial way, basically for brilliance and to produce different effects; in general we are not taught in a lyrical way. There is no singer who sings in the fashion that you hear many trumpet players playing, and that can't be right. That doesn't mean we have to play in a sloppy fashion, but the line has to be there. To get that, you listen to the great classics played on instruments other than your own. Then you can say to yourself, "Isn't

be anything more than fill-ins. Because they all maintain they want to be number ones, they had better think about being an individual. How else are they going to do it?

Of course you do have a situation in your country that we haven't really had to face in England yet, which is vastly too many people for too few jobs. So many play at a technical standard that is alarmingly good. Think about the tuba and all the people who could go in for a job, even in England now. If you owned a tuba when I began and could play oompah, oompah, you were a tuba player.

Now, it's very different. In the States you also have the I.T.G., the tuba farms, and all those other organizations, so there are even more interested players. It's wonderful so long as every person doesn't think he will become the tuba player of somebody's symphony orchestra. If they do it for fun and then become an insurance broker or something, that's fine. The terrible thing is that so many expect they will get into an orchestra and find out they can't.

Philip, what advice would you give to younger students now? You have mentioned technical proficiency

that marvelous? Now how can I do the equivalent, not the same, but the equivalent on my instrument?" I think that is important.

It's interesting that the French teach strong lyricism, but we still have a concept (and the French do as well) of the trumpet as principally being an over-brilliant instrument. It's not; that is just one of the instrument's characteristics.

Another thing I find with students is that few of them listen to themselves. If people don't listen to what they are doing when they practice, how are they going to get better? They think if they do six hours of the same exercise repetitively it is going to get better. It doesn't.

Youngsters should listen to quality of sound when playing their own instrument and when listening to everybody else. They should also listen to intonation because they seldom do. Only then can you start thinking of all the rest of it because if you can't play in tune and can't make a good sound, you'll never get a job worth having. Not in our world, not in the classical world.

Another facet of this awareness, which may be more true here than in England, is that our students don't appreciate the value of playing chamber music. Al-

though we have a lot of brass quintet activity, it is often very superficial.

In England it is just the same. So often chamber music just sounds like a mechanical exercise. Whenever I train a brass group, I immediately have to ask the players how they start. It hasn't occurred to them that five blokes actually have to start something in an organized fashion, like breathing in together and starting. They haven't even worked that bit out.

That puzzles me, but then you can talk about it. I also talk about eye contact. You can watch a fellow and see when he is going to do something; you don't have to be glued to the music all of the time. These are basic things, but they are not generally followed by students who hope somehow that magic will come down from heaven and suddenly they will all play together and it will sound great. Of course it doesn't. It's hard work just like anything else.

I had an interesting experience this week during a faculty search for a new violin teacher. There were three good candidates; two struck me as being good, but the third one was absolutely fantastic. She was trained in Russia and studied with David Oistrakh.

During a coaching session she listened to a student play some of the Mendelssohn Concerto, which I thought the student had played well. The teacher stopped and said, "How do you really want to play the opening bars of this piece?" to which the student replied, "I hadn't really thought about it." The teacher said, "I suspected as much. You know my dear," she continued "you must have a concept and you must make decisions about music before you can become an artist." That was the first statement she made.

As you said, students are misguided when they think repetition will somehow guarantee improvement. The thought process, the decision making, and the evaluation that comes through the ears has to be turned on. It is unfortunate when it's not.

Unless you can hear the sound you are trying to get in your head beforehand, how are you going to get it? If you haven't made that decision (which every artist makes), then you just take what comes. That is no way of playing music.

So you will not really be active in either a teaching capacity or a playing one?

I hope not; I'm basically an organizer. I've always said that I am the least good player in my group, but the best organizer by far. Certainly I'm the nastiest character, so I can afford to say "I think that's dreadful." I hope I say it in a nice way, though, because I really do mean it. I see myself as a chap who organizes other people with better talents than I have, but perhaps who are not using their talents very well.

For about two years now I have also been serving on the Arts Council, an honorary job that you can only hold for four years. I am one of 20 people who decide how all the money that the government gives the arts (music, theatre, dance, literature, and opera) will be spent throughout the country. It's a fascinating thing to do because we make many decisions. The most useful thing from the members' point of view is that they have a practicing and practical musician on the board saying, "But you can't do that because it doesn't work that way." They have never had someone like me before, so I am enjoying that enormously.

For a year I was awed by the group of people around me and didn't know how to make my points, but I have learned how to make them. I think this sort of activity is important for a professional to do, even though it's honorary. It's a good thing there is no money involved because of course you cannot possibly be bribed. As a professional you can draw from your experiences and actually pass on information that might do some good. It certainly can't do any harm. I have two more years to run with the Arts Council, and then I hope some other thing will knock on the door and I shall do something else.

Will the Brass Ensemble disband now?

I made a decision to stop 18 months in advance to make sure the group could continue once the fellows had gotten over the shock of the announcement. They thought I was going on forever, merely because I have been around forever. When they got over that shock I took on the job of organizer once again and said, "Now you will form a co-op. You will call yourselves London Brass, and you will continue this scene or however your scene develops, according to what you want to do."

There is one thing I couldn't do, however; I could not leave my name behind. The Philip Jones Brass Ensemble was a personal matter. I have good friends and colleagues in the group, but the standard of Philip Jones is Philip Jones', for good or for bad. For a little while the group will probably put in small letters, "Formerly P.J.B.E.," so people will realize it is the same outfit.

They will start straight away in June when I retire. I've already gotten the London Brass some jobs as a quintet. They played at the end of a couple of my recent tours in Europe — one in Norway and one in Germany. So the group is going to continue; they have my repertoire, my library, and all of our contacts. I hope the next 35 years will be quite an experience. ∎

Vincent Cichowicz is professor of trumpet at Northwestern University in Evanston, Illinois. A former member of the Chicago Symphony Orchestra, Cichowicz made the position of second trumpet as legendary as that of the first during his 22-year commitment to that orchestra. He also has performed with the Chicago Symphony Brass Quintet and the Grant Park Orchestra.

Woody Herman
Fifty Years and Still Swinging

by James Warrick

Long after a recent concert, when the stage had been cleared and the band bus was loaded, Woody Herman was still backstage signing autographs for young musicians in the audience. As his slow hand produced each signature, the kids waited patiently while the legendary jazz celebrity made his way to each of them. From the looks on their faces, the Woody Herman concert was one they would not soon forget.

Earlier that day, while some 300 high school musicians from 12 participating schools attended workshops presented by members of his band, The Young Thundering Herd, Woody relaxed with the jazz ensemble directors and several other invited guests in a rap session. Currently enjoying his 50th year as a band leader and performer, Woody offered entertaining and enlightening answers to our many questions.

What are your thoughts about jazz education in America's public schools?

Big band music is still played everywhere; and I believe college, high school, and junior high school music educators have kept it alive. Because of America's educational structure we are producing more great young players than ever before, and believe me, we are the envy of the world.

What country, do you think, plays a close second?

England would probably be the closest because of its structured educational system, although they are loosening it up a bit now. Louis Armstrong made a big impression there back in the early days. It's unfortunate, but as jazz players we are respected more in other parts of the world than we are here in America. I think the reasoning behind it is simple, though. In America we have too much of everything.

Do you think colleges produce too many jazz majors?

No, I don't think it's the fault of the colleges that there are so many great players; I think it's the fault of our society and our music world because they can't absorb all the good talent that's out there. For instance, we have a huge record industry whose bottom line is dollars and cents. It is run and controlled by lawyers and accountants instead of creative people who know music. They make what they think are masterful decisions about which group will be at the top of

the heap next month, while we have this overabundance of wonderful players who can't find work.

When high school kids ask me if they can make a career in music I strongly advise them to continue if they love it because in music, they have something real. The more deeply they get involved in it, the more music will do for them in their life. When you are involved in either playing or listening to music, you are completely on your own; you have complete solace from anything that might try to creep into your mind. I call it "the great escape."

At the same time, however, I advise young people to study something else like electronics or computers which will give them a way to make a living if they can't find a job performing music.

Where did you grow up? Did you ever play in a school band?

I was raised in Milwaukee, although I didn't spend much time there. By the time I was nine, I was on the road as a song and dance kid. My father was a frustrated ham, so he got me into the business.

I attended a parochial school in Milwaukee, but in my day they didn't have school bands. One of the nuns had a harmonica band which was as close as I came to playing in one. I remember the nun would say, "Woodrow, you must bring your saxophone to help us out."

In those days jazz was considered a dirty word. There was a young priest who played piano and would ghost around town playing jazz gigs in Milwaukee. His older brother was also a very good musician who had done a lot of legit study, so he attempted to help me with the more serious aspects of music such as theory. How much I learned I'll never know. Fortunately, though, I've always had big ears. I watched and listened to people who studied and worked over the years. I derived a lot from them by just being in their company.

Who were some of your favorite big bands?

When I was a teenager my biggest inspiration was a group known as The Washingtonians, an eight-piece band led by Duke Ellington. To this day the music he left us I enjoy playing more than anything else.

Does that mean much of your inspiration came from the group out of Harlem and the Cotton Club?

Not really, but as a teenager, I was excited when I first heard this kind of jungle sound. It didn't just turn me on, though; it turned music around.

I played opposite Duke on numerous occasions, and I got to know him well socially. I felt I derived many important things from Duke, but my band never tried to imitate him. To me, that wasn't the idea of it. I wanted to try to come up with something that had the same gay abandonment, but wasn't a copy.

If you hand out an arrangement that you haven't played in 35 years and give it to your present band to try, how much rehearsal time do you think you would need before the piece would be ready to perform?

We did something like that not long ago when we went out on a short tour to play the "Ebony Concerto" which Stravinsky wrote for us. That is one hard piece. I remember the first time we read it, Stravinsky was there to teach us. We

weren't great readers of that kind of music, but Stravinsky had the patience of Job. He hummed, whistled, sang, stomped his foot, and counted all at the same time.

I had great players, but they weren't used to playing that particular kind of music. The first time I played it I went to everyone I could possibly find for help, including Benny Goodman. One day we met on the street in New York City and Benny said, "How's the clarinet part in that Stravinsky piece?" I said, "Man, I have never seen anything like it. It's grotesque. I've called people to try and help me and no one has said 'yes'; it's wild." Soon after our meeting I got a mini-score and sent it to Benny. When I saw him about three months later all he could say was, "That's one hard part."

What about your present band's performance of the piece?

When they did it, it was like mincemeat. Oh, they ran through it quite a few times, but now it sounds like a different piece. One of the wisest things I ever did was to make an agreement with Richard Stoltzman to play the solo so I could hear how it should have been played. Richard is a young, great, legit clarinetist who has a fascination for jazz. It was something we could give to each other.

When I buy one of your charts published by Hal Leonard I get three trombone parts and four sax parts. How did you get into that instrumentation and why do you continue to use it now?

Until 1950 we had five saxophones, although we had already found a three-tenor and a baritone sound. The first tune we did was naturally "Four Brothers" and out of that came "Early Autumn." I felt this was a sound that belonged to us to a certain degree and I wanted to utilize it as much as possible.

When we started in 1950 with what I call the "Third Herd," Ralph Burns rewrote the book and voiced everything differently. I never did use four trombones except on a recording I did for a specific tune which was written like "Four Brothers."

As a music educator I know how valuable making such great music available to my students has been. Was promoting music education done out of the goodness of your heart, or was it done primarily for the economic benefit of the publishing company?

Originally, we worked with record companies

James Warrick is director of jazz studies at New Trier High School in Winnetka, Illinois. He also reviews new jazz publications for the New Music Review section of The Instrumentalist. Warrick holds music degrees from Ohio University.

that made our albums a part of the package that went along with the arrangement. That way the kids could hear what we were seeking from the arrangement. I think the premise was a great one. Everyone benefited, including the kids. I thought it was a great way to get kids doing something very simply with a good end result.

Unfortunately for the kids, there hasn't been much published lately, but that is not my choice. Tell band directors to let the publishing companies know our music is still wanted.

Do you believe that the technique of younger musicians has expanded, causing both the writing and the demands on the writer to expand?

Yes, but there is one basic rule that will never change and should not be forgotten. No matter who wrote it, if it doesn't swing, there is no sense in playing it. For 50 years I have tried to stay somewhere near where music is supposed to be and what we hope it is supposed to be.

Today when we play some of our earliest charts, they're not the same. Half of them were hits to begin with, but we always try to make them sound better than they did originally. Musically, my band has progressed over a long period of years.

What is the average age of your present band?

Most of the guys are in their mid to late 20s; some are in their early 30s.

You also have a few older folks.

Two guys in the band are closer to my age than the other guys. That's so I have somebody to talk to. I get along fine with the young kids and we never have any communication trouble as long as we only discuss music. I don't want to know what they did a week ago Thursday or whether they are thinking of getting married. They should keep that to themselves.

What do you expect of new players when they come onto your band and how does a new player get hired?

I expect to hear musicianship. We have a unique system in the band because we don't audition. Sometimes people send us their tapes and we listen to them, but that doesn't really make the decision for us. When we need to change a player or when a player is leaving, we go to the members of that section and ask them to make some suggestions. They are all aware that if you bring in one of your buddies and he doesn't cut it, it is no good for the soul because you are going to get the heat. When we decide

on a guy, we hire him. If something goes wrong after two weeks, he's out. That happens so seldom, though, it's remarkable. The system works very well for us.

How many weeks a year does your band work together?

We used to play 11 out of 12 months, but for the last 2 years we have worked less. This year we will be doing about 9 months out of 12. We break it up by playing in different locations.

For instance, we might go out on a cruise ship and stay two weeks. We've done this twice over the last two years on the S.S. Norway. They put together a jazz cruise with Dizzy Gillespie and almost anyone you can think of who is still available. It was very exciting for the guys in the band and for the people who could afford that kind of cruise.

Assuming that much of the cruise audience was made up of people who are retired, how much did this affect your choice of music to play?

It didn't affect it at all. When I was a kid in vaudeville I would share the same dressing room with people twice and three times my age. They spoke of every audience the same way; all vaudevillians called the audience "the great unwashed." Their reasoning was that a group should never play down to an audience. Instead, you let an audience try to catch on to your bootstraps and pull them up to where you want them to be. If you don't do that, you'll never be a very happy performer.

In Dizzy Gillespie's book, To Be or Not to Bop, *he mentions that he was proud to have written arrangements for your band. When did he write them?*

He wrote several things for us back in his younger days. Dizzy often tells the story that I was the first person to pay him $100 for one of his arrangements which he thought was a big amount. He wrote very well and after we played some of his music, he subbed with the band on a couple of occasions. When he had played with us for a number of days I suggested to him that he give up the trumpet and stick to writing; I didn't know what he was doing on the trumpet up there in the stratosphere. That was one of my many great judgments.

When a new arrangement comes into your book it is often from someone in the band. Does the composer rehearse the band?

Exactly.

So it's not always your job to actually rehearse them?

No, because I don't have that much time on the road. The band gets together for a few minutes and reads it down and then gives it a run on the gig that night. I'll pay attention to it and maybe have a suggestion or two after we've finished for the night.

What is the breakdown of concert and dance dates in your current schedule? What percentage of your gigs is dances?

One week's schedule might be completely different from the next week's. Over a nine-month period probably about 25% of our gigs are dances. That's reality, but fortunately there are more places to do concerts. We've opened a number of restored theatres in this country where they can afford the band for one night. We also play many concert halls where the symphony or the symphony society buys the band and sponsors a jazz concert.

Are you going to be releasing any records in the near future?

We just recorded a live album at the American Music Hall in San Francisco with perfect acoustics and a lively audience. In July we will be recording our 50th Anniversary Concert at the Hollywood Bowl with a live audience. We're going to do it in the Bowl because I live up on the hill and between tunes I can go up and take a nap. Besides, there's no reason to record in a studio today; recording techniques have improved so much you can record in the men's room and it will sound fine.

What can we as band directors tell our students about the future of playing in professional big bands?

I think there will always be professional big bands because there are so many young people who know how to play well, and want to play. As long as the desire is there and it is strong enough, these kids will move mountains to get it done. In addition, if someone is a big enough ham with a flair for catching audience attention, he will have a better shot at having his own band.

Can we expect to see a Woody Herman biography?

I know a few guys who have been attempting to write one for years now, but I haven't seen any end results. If they want to write one, fine, but I'm not particularly interested in writing one about myself.

How do you feel about bands that continue to play after the leader retires?

I once told my grandson, Tommy Littlefield, who is a 25-year-old guitarist, that if any of the family ever wanted to do this, it would be fine with me. I would want certain people in the band who would follow what we have tried to do, so the band would stay on track. I told Tommy I would like for him to stand and front the band because he would be the bloodline. He has been listening to me since he was a kid.

Do you have any memories that stand out over these 50 years?

That's a hard question. It's like asking, "What was your greatest band?" For that question I have a stock answer: the band I'm going to have next year. Otherwise I would have quit a long time ago. At 72, I'm living on borrowed time and loving every minute of it. ∎

Leonard Smith: One Man's Band

Doris Scharfenberg

"There's something about going to a band concert in the park that gives people a good 'American' feeling."

To one who plays only a typewriter in A♭, listening to Leonard Smith and the Detroit Concert Band rehearse is like visiting a candy factory: exciting, tempting, but you can't get your teeth into the product. Not here, anyway.

Again and again they play just enough of a selection for the eavesdropper to think, "Ah! One of my favorites!" Too bad. In seconds Smith raps his baton muttering, "That's fine, gentlemen. Now let's try number . . ." etc.

Left dangling, the lay listener blames it all on a shortage of time. This is the first rehearsal of the season; concerts begin in a week.

The Detroit Concert Band, however, is no assembly line operation, but one of the country's most professional concert bands and producer of some of the nation's finest band music. These top-caliber instrumentalists were chosen by the British Broadcasting Company to do the music portions of a documentary film on John Philip Sousa, and have received glowing reviews from countless music critics.

What the rehearsal visitor hears are snatches of an enormous repertoire which Detroit-area residents consume without charge, five nights a week from June to mid-August.

Summer, 1970, is year number 25 for the group. Like all 25 year olds, it has a story to tell and someone to thank; in this case founder and conductor Smith.

The Detroit Concert Band is Leonard Smith's own band. Virtuoso performer, composer, conductor, organizer, and teacher, the energetic, perfectionist Smith is an easy man to meet and a hard man to describe. Physically robust and genial as a professional host, he can put the visitor at ease even though he is apt to bound spring-like around the room fetching items he'd like you to see. His office is filled with mementos of his music triumphs. Cities have given him citations, colleges have given him honorary degrees, leading orchestras have thanked him with tokens of their esteem, and critics have praised him wholeheartedly.

One might ask Smith: "Why did you want to organize your own band?" (a question roughly akin to asking Peggy Fleming why she'd like her own skates).

The idea was part of his boyhood dream in Poughkeepsie, N.Y. It grew as Leonard Smith grew.

"I cherished three ambitions: to play with John Philip Sousa, to be first trumpet with a leading symphony, and to have my own band." He had the talent, good health, and passion for hard work that such grand planning required.

Sousa was along in years and Smith a little young for the first goal to work out. However, at 19 Leonard became cornet soloist and first chair with the popular Edwin Franko Goldman band, a post he held for six years. Goldman called him "the greatest cornet talent I have ever known."

With Goldman he established his reputation by playing 500 solos in 175 days, beginning at the Golden Gate International Exposition in San Francisco and closing the season in Central Park, New York.

The Smith talent was in demand. During the years between playing with the Goldman Band and coming to Detroit he played first chair or soloist with the Navy Band and the Philadelphia Symphony. He made appearances with the Metropolitan Opera, Bolshoi Ballet, and Radio City Music Hall. He recorded with RCA Victor and Fox Movietone News. Such random samples barely reflect his list of credits.

Remember when those familiar bars from the *William Tell Overture* told you that "The Lone Ranger" was about to ride again? That was Leonard Smith on the solo.

After three and one-half years in the Navy during World War II and several seasons as first trumpet with the Detroit Symphony (goal number two by now more than fulfilled), Smith was restless to get on with his third ambition. He wanted his own group. When the City of Detroit indicated a desire to inject new life into its summer concert programs, he speedily started organizing. As the city was ready with a new contract, Smith was ready with a new band.

Naturally, anyone whose life's project is the forming of a superior band keeps mental notes for recruiting purposes on the instrumentalists around him. Gathering his musicians required salesmanship, diplomacy, finesse, and auditions, but he had a band of which he was proud from the beginning.

Here is where an ingredient of the Leonard Smith success story shows up graphically. The man regards mediocrity as a major vice; his bandsmen have to be of the same ilk or forget it. Among the countless scores of players who have auditioned in hopes of finding a summer job with Smith, only a relative few have made the grade.

Along with assembling a band that met his stiff standards, there were other missions to perform. A certain rowdyism was taking over the park concert scene, and to add to the problem, the city of Detroit was reluctant to spend funds replacing a fast-disintegrating band shell.

The first concerts of the new group held a few bad moments. Lighting was poor, broken platform steps had to be carefully avoided, and a large proportion of the audience was restless with the selections offered.

"Hey! Give us some jazz!" "What kind of noise is that?" Smith met the situation head-on.

"This is a concert band," he announced. "I'm sorry but we are unable to play the numbers you request." With steely politeness he suggested places they might go to hear such music. Leonard Smith is a man who can glare while smiling and make you feel it at 100 yards. Concert by concert the disturbances decreased while the number of serious listeners coming to the park increased. His insistence on decorum has earned him much respect among the solid citizenry who appreciate seeing a firm hand at work.

Bureaucracy being what it is, sometimes civic improvements have to wait upon catastrophe before a community will act. The bandstand, tucked off on Belle Isle, Detroit's river park, kept getting older and more decrepit. Then one evening the drummer tapped his foot too hard and went through the floor. Even then it took some campaigning, but a beautiful new band shell was built.

As the longest-running summer group of its kind in the country, the Detroit Concert Band has stored up many collective and individual memories. There have been cold evenings when the wind swooped down from Canada and the hardy bandsmen outnumbered the audience, and rainy evenings when proceedings had to be hastily canceled. (This is in spite of the inevitable diehard in the audience who sits under a hood of newspapers believing that band concerts, like football games, should go on regardless of conditions.)

These weather-wrought upsets have been the rare exceptions. On endless starry nights the concert area has been overflowing with the pleased public. It is estimated that well over six million people have heard the band play more than 12 thousand selections in its 25 years of performing.

Like his boyhood hero, Sousa, Smith knows a thing or two about audiences. When a number is well received, he will beam at them and say, "If what we play is music to your ears, then be assured that your applause is music to *our* ears!" This seldom fails to trigger a lustier wave of clapping, the evening having been turned into a meeting of mutual admirers.

"It is impossible to satisfy everyone, but we try to present at least *one* item for every musical taste." For this the maestro calls on his extensive personal library plus the contents of unique "encore books" which contain more than 150 selections, enabling the band to grant a wide variety of requests. Every member has such a book at his side during the concert and it is used three or four times each evening.

A typical Smith-planned program begins with *The Star Spangled Banner* followed by a popular march and ends (before the encore) with a Strauss waltz. In between will be an overture, excerpts from a famous opera or Broadway musical, more marches (frequently Smith's own compositions), and a balance of fugues, tone poems, etc. Each concert is a study in variety.

The most requested encore is Sousa's *Stars and Stripes Forever*, which brings audiences to their feet cheering. Smith has the piccolos come to the front of the stage to play their famed obligato, then the cornets, trumpets, and trombones join in a line that sends the sound to the far corners of the park.

Clarinetist Edgar L. Barrow and flutist Anthony Ferrara were with Leonard Smith from the start. Kenneth Baldwin, percussionist and expert on the Sousa-Helmecke style of bass drumming, has been with the band for more than 21 years, and there are many 15 year members. Past rosters included such artists as Frank Elsass, Ned Mahoney, Gerhard Warms and others who give Smith part of the credit for their discovery and subsequent success.

When the man whose band this is starts musing about the positive effects of good music on the community, he comes across like Meredith Willson's Professor Harold Hill — but without the larceny.

"There's something about going to a band concert in the park, sitting around in your shirtsleeves under the stars, that gives people a good 'American' feeling. I want to do my bit to inculcate this feeling of community. Band concerts carry with them a certain pride."

It is a point well made. Detroit, in the throes of social upheaval as are all of today's cities, wonders anxiously about the future of its evening park programs: yet these concerts have been free from the incidents that have soured the reputation of other outdoor music gatherings.

J. Moore, former mayor of Philadelphia, put it this way: "Wherever there is good music, there is harmony. Wherever there is harmony there are good citizens and therefore we must provide all the good music that is possible."

Leonard Smith and the Detroit Concert Band offer good music, well played. Their effect is definitely settling, inspiring and, as the jargonists would have it, therapeutic.

May they play on and on and on. ∎

Doris Scharfenberg is a graduate of Hillsdale (Michigan) College. A free lance writer, her articles have appeared in several national publications. She received a national award for her radio play broadcast over CBS several years ago. As a life-long resident of the Detroit area, she has been a Detroit Band enthusiast for years.

From Toscanini to the Band of America

An Interview with Paul Lavalle

by Joseph Estock

Paul Lavalle, Don Butterfield, and Harvey Phillips.

Band lovers recognize Paul Lavalle as the director and organizer of the Band of America and McDonald's All-American High School Band. He also was clarinetist and saxophonist with the N.B.C. Symphony and played with George Gershwin, the Dorseys, Benny Goodman, and Glenn Miller. Lavalle created and conducted the 1940s radio programs Chamber Music Society of Lower Basin Street, Highways to Melody, and the All-Stradivari Orchestra. He was principal conductor of the Radio City Music Hall Orchestra, and guest conductor of many studio and symphony orchestras. As a composer of numerous marches and other instrumental music, Lavalle won several A.S.C.A.P. awards.

How did you become interested in music?

I was born into music; my two brothers studied at the Santa Cecilia Conservatory in Rome and were fine musicians when they came to this country. I was born in Beacon, New York on the Hudson River 60 miles north of New York City; when I was about seven years old, I was told I was going to take piano lessons. One brother conducted and played trumpet for the Beacon Municipal Band; the other brother played trombone, baritone horn, and drums. When I was 11 it was time to play in the band, and my first engagement was playing in my brother's band, but he didn't think I knew enough clarinet yet so I played bass drum. I was too short to carry the bass drum for parades, so they tied it around my back. The parade started, and I was way in the back, and walked into a hole for a gutter they were building alongside the road. I fell into it, and the band kept on going, minus the drum beat. When my brother noticed the absence of the beat, he came back and found me in the hole with my white uniform full of mud. He said, "Get up here and play," and ignored pleas that I was hurt and wet. I ran with the bass drum to catch up, and finished the parade.

How did you happen to attend Juilliard?

My father thought I should become a lawyer; that was that, there was no arguing with him. So I went to Columbia University, where I dated a girl who studied cello at Juilliard. She raved about the Juilliard orchestra and encouraged me to audition as first clarinet. After auditioning, I was accepted although I had only played in bands and dance orchestras before.

While at Juilliard I went to the musician's union every Wednesday afternoon to hear the guys talk about their engagements and became acquainted with them and played at society gigs.

How did your association with the union and commercial music lead to playing for Toscanini?

I played jobs to earn a living but always had wanted to be at N.B.C. When I graduated I got a job with a gypsy violinist named Dave Rubinoff and played with him for about a year at the Paramount Theater which had the first rising pit built in a theater. I told Rubinoff that I didn't want to continue playing four shows a

Joseph J. Estock is head of the department of music and professor of music at James Madison University. He holds a doctorate from the University of Iowa and has taught at the University of Wisconsin-Platteville, where he was department head from 1973-76.

day at the Paramount, but wanted to go to N.B.C.

When I gave my two weeks notice and went home to Beacon to practice, Dave said, "Listen, keed, you can't do this; if you do I'm finished with you." However, he called me after two weeks to say Rudy Vallee had just got him a commercial at N.B.C., and wanted me to play. "You know, keed, I always liked you," he added. That was my entrance into N.B.C., playing with Rubinoff for a Maxwell House coffee commercial. Rubinoff thought he had the best orchestra in radio: Tommy Dorsey, Jimmy Dorsey, Gene Krupa, Glenn Miller, and I was in there, too.

I read that Maestro Toscanini was coming back to New York to conduct the N.B.C. Symphony for General Sarnoff. I went to Frank Black, who was the musical director of all the N.B.C. stations and told him that I would love to audition for Maestro Toscanini. He warned me that they were getting the best musicians from all over the world who had been in the top symphonies but I persisted. Black set up an audition for three weeks before the symphony went on the air. I went down with my clarinet and saxophone, and was scared to death. I told Toscanini I was a student at Juilliard and would always be a student as long as I played music. He liked that and invited me to play clarinet and bass clarinet at the next rehearsal. He asked if I also played saxophone because the rehearsal included *Pictures at an Exhibition*. I sat next to Bill Polisi, the first bassoonist, and when the time came for the saxophone solo in "The Old Castle" I wondered whether to play it like a corny dance band and told Bill I was going to play with a vibrato. After about six bars Toscanini stopped, and this usually caused musicians to feel as though they were plummeting in an elevator from the eighth to the ground floor. Toscanini turned to Mischa Mischakoff, the concertmaster, looked down at him, and said, "Con vibrato. Saxophonist, vibrato! Molto bene, cosi me piace." That's the way he had always wanted it, he couldn't get enough vibrato at the right time.

I stayed with Toscanini for almost five years, but was also a house musician for N.B.C. playing in other things like the dance orchestra with Glenn Miller, Tommy and Jimmy Dorsey, and Benny Goodman.

What about the jam sessions with George Gershwin and Hoagy Carmichael?

George Gershwin sometimes came up to the station for a half hour or an hour when we were free between broadcasts and played piano for jam sessions; Gershwin played his tunes and we joined in. We thought he was great; we all did our little bit and there were times when some of us would hit on a nice lick. I could tell in some of his music, even *Rhapsody in Blue*, that he used a few notes from some of those licks.

Sometimes when we played a tune or piece that he had written he suddenly would start going in a different harmonic direction and we wondered what he was doing. He said that his numbers were played so much, he got a little tired of hearing them; he was reharmonizing his tunes. Instead of regular harmonies on the 7th chord, he might add a 9th, 11th, or 13th. It's a great memory.

When I met Gershwin I was still a student and asked about his reharmonization. He commented that he was studying with Joseph Schillinger, a Russian brought over by the Algebraic Society. I wondered what the Algebraic Society had to do with music, to which he replied that if you go to him, you'll understand. At that time he was writing *Porgy and Bess*. I called Schillinger and told him that what I had been writing was so academic. I wanted to progress in harmonizations and melody. After I started studying with Schillinger I knew what Gershwin was doing when he fooled around at the studio.

Schillinger wrote several books about his system based on mathematical principles. I studied with him about five years, using graph paper for rhythms; different results came from using the graph paper algebraically. One day at the Chamber Music Society of Lower Basin Street, Glenn Miller came to listen while we played jazz with Duke Ellington. After the broadcast Miller said he had never heard arrangements using just the woodwind section and asked who I studied with. When I responded with Schillinger's name and that Gershwin had recommended this teacher Glenn said, "Boy, I'd like to study with a guy like this." He was already an arranger, and looking for something to make his band sound different, as

Paul Lavalle and General Goodpaster at West Point, 1979.

1022

Tommy Dorsey did with his trombone solos. Glenn went to Schillinger for about three years and came into the studio while I was conducting to show me something. It was a five-part harmony that looked great. I offered to play it for him with the housemen if he would copy the parts. A week later, he brought in "White Serenade." It was a terrific sound with the clarinet on top and that five-part harmony that moved all the time. He wrote a letter thanking me for sending him to Schillinger.

This must have been a good time to have been in New York.

Yes, but it wasn't easy; I pounded a lot of pavement. No matter how much you know about music, others have to know how good you are. About the time that Toscanini came to New York for the N.B.C. Symphony in 1937, my friends Benny, Tommy, and Glenn left the N.B.C. station to start bands of their own. I did not want to be pegged as a musician who played just one kind of music by staying at N.B.C. After five years with Toscanini I considered conducting and playing for commercials and other work in New York City. I improved as a conductor and wanted to go further with it.

In 1944 I found out that Frank Black, who had been the conductor of the Cities Service Orchestra, had resigned. I made a pitch to Merlin H. Aylesworth, then president of N.B.C. and one of those people who loved music. We went together to the Cities Service office on Wall Street, where he talked with the president, who hesitated. "Paul, do you really think it is wise to follow Black and his big reputation?" I replied, "Well, I don't need a reputation; Cities Service has a reputation." He liked that. The Cities Service Orchestra was essentially Toscanini's symphony; the Maestro only used the orchestra on Saturdays for rehearsal and evening broadcasts, and naturally N.B.C. wanted to use the musicians during the week. The sponsor paid for about 60 musicians to play in the Cities Service Orchestra, which helped pay for the Toscanini broadcasts.

In our profession it is essential to think not only of the music but also of programming ideas so people will enjoy listening to your music. My idea for the Cities Service programs was "Highways to Melody" with a script to tell listeners where we were and what composers we encountered along the way, as in going up the east coast until we got to Boston, stopping in Westport to play Richard Rogers' music. Different soloists starred on "Highways to Melody," including Muriel Angelus, who later married Lavalle, Robert Merrill, Gordon MacRea, and Mario Lanza.

Both Aylesworth and W. Alton Jones, the president of Cities Service, were fans of John Philip Sousa, and wanted to start a band for the summer. This was in 1946 or 1947, and at first I did not want to conduct a band; but when Jones asked me about the first band I played in, I recalled my brother's band. He reminded me that as a youngster in the band, I probably thought it was the greatest band in the land.

I went home and told my wife Muriel about it, and she said there was nothing wrong with a band; the king and queen and the English love bands. "Your band will be the band of America." Just like that she gave me the idea. I went downtown and gave them the name, Cities Service Band of America. It took three or four weeks to organize the best players from the N.B.C. orchestra and a quartet of male singers. I wrote a march as a theme, and when we went on the air, we received mail from people in school bands across the country who liked the idea of a great band on coast-to-coast radio. After the summer N.B.C. wanted the band to continue; we were becoming famous and receiving invitations to travel. I got hundreds of invitations to conduct massed bands at football games. The band broadcasts continued for about ten years.

How was the Band of America chosen to play at the 1964 World's Fair?

Although we were off the air by then, Cities Service decided instead of having an exhibit to send the band to the fair on a mobile stage. We had about 50 players in two sections with me in the middle. Cities Service thought that was better than spending ten million dollars on an exhibit.

Band of America also made quite a few recordings that sold up to eight million copies and we went on a transcontinental tour after the World's Fair. I received invitations to conduct at schools and colleges and in 1965 got a call from the president of McDonalds, Ray Kroc, who loved bands and suggested forming a band with high school students. I asked him for some time to think about it and after a couple of weeks went to Chicago to talk with him. I got into education only then because I didn't have time for it during the Band of America years.

The McDonald's band was made up of two high school players from every state, recommended by their directors. I needed eight tubas, twenty clarinets, sixteen flutes; to get that balance I had an advisory board of three people to help select students. Sometimes we had a thousand tubas recommended when we needed only eight. I worked with the advisory board until we chose 100 players.

What differences do you perceive in music training over the years?

In my 15 years with the McDonalds band I noticed differences in discipline and training. Students in the later years weren't as disciplined as the earlier participants.

Why do you suppose that was?

In the first years there wasn't much interest in school jazz bands, partly because many conductors were not well-versed in jazz and could not get the same results as in concert bands. Students became confused when conductors just played a record of Harry James or someone, because listening is not enough. Such things as articulation are difficult to teach in jazz because they are not the same as in concert band music.

Some high schools and colleges don't have a separate jazz band leader. Youngsters often are stymied and don't know which style to pursue. They wonder if they are good enough in jazz to someday play in the equivalent of Tommy Dorsey's band, or whether they should try to be great concert band players and eventually play in a major symphony. Meager school budgets make it impossible for schools to afford two conductors for their ensembles.

Discipline is not as strict as it was when I started the All-American High School Band. Discipline and spending time on music are important because youngsters have too many things on their minds.

As a guest conductor in the early forties I saw and heard youngsters in high schools, and I was pleasantly surprised by their behavior, discipline, and training. In rehearsals I could suggest playing at the Presto and they understood, but in later years students did not know what such notations as staccato or legato meant. The earlier students recognized the nuances and dynamics and knew all the terms. When we rehearsed, they saw *mf*, and played *mezzo forte*.

Do you think training was better then, or were students just more serious about it?

They were taught better. Printed music still had these nuances, but more recently the students were not told what they meant. They knew the word, "trio", but not *fortissimo*.

How did you start a community orchestra in the 1960s?

When I moved to Wilton, a small Connecticut town about an hour from New York City, it had no music although there were many amateur musicians in the community. I advertised auditions to start an orchestra and even put an ad in the newspapers in Bridgeport, New Canaan, Danbury, and Norwalk. The string players, who were mainly doctors, lawyers, scientists, or professors played beautifully. These amateurs had discipline, and I asked how they could play so well as amateurs and keep up their professions. They practiced early in the morning or before going to bed.

There was a difference, however, between the high school members and middle-aged people. Very few students play string instruments now, and that is a shame, but I wanted at least to get some brass players from the high school. I asked a trumpeter to come in to play an audition and explained to him how playing dynamics, for example, was different in an orchestra from playing in a band. He said he had to ask his mother first. Here was a 17 year old who had to ask permission to play in an orchestra because he was so overloaded with basketball, hockey, and school work. Music was just one more thing to him.

You allude to discipline and commitment as important ingredients of music study and performance. Are they lacking today?

Discipline varies because there is so much distraction today, even aside from school. Rock and roll is the worst distraction musically; it is not educational. Thousands of guitarists play rock and roll or country music with just two or three chords. Student groups have electrical keyboards and other electrical instruments with big speakers but no brass or reeds. It takes trucks to bring in these big speakers that are placed all over the stage. How many people are up there with the speakers and electrical instruments? Five! There is too much emphasis on this kind of music; there is nothing wrong with it, but it is not educational.

Do you think it could be educational?

For what? Not for discipline. Good jazz is educational. I wish we had better teachers for these youngsters to show them how to play and approach it, and to make sure they don't play it literally the way it is written.

Perhaps we teach too many styles of music and lose focus with the diversity with marching band, jazz ensemble, woodwind quintet, a woodwind ensemble, and concert band.

I agree. There are too many drop-outs from music. These youngsters don't have enough motivation. Music is curricular icing; the arts are not even mentioned in education. President Bush charged the governors with the responsibility of creating national educational goals, but I read nothing about the arts. Why is it this way? Even though the President has invited well-known musicians to the White House to entertain guests, he does not mention music. Music to entertain the President's guests is just like curricular icing. We have had a wonderful dinner, and now we need something to entertain our guests; here comes the icing. They applaud, but it is not appreciated. It is only added, like putting a log on the fire.

Does the lack of discipline result from students having so much else to do in education?

Naturally I think back to my childhood, which was not so different, but the difference is discipline. Why hasn't that continued in music? Music is important; it creates a balance in life and provides more emphasis on discipline.

The key word is balance; how would you create a balance in the music curriculum?

We have marching bands, some of them great. There is a reason why these marching band youngsters play well. When I ask how directors find the time to do all this and do it well, the answer is, we're competing. Is that a form of discipline?

They rehearse to compete for awards. I question whether the players get a chance to play in concert band or jazz band or if they just concentrate on one thing. Band directors feel they have to show their bosses what a great job they are doing by winning the prize. The principal of the school doesn't see how much rehearsal it takes, only the marching and the prize. Too much value is placed on competition. Is what happens the rest of the semester music education?

Something else about this curricular icing, when football games are televised, the students think they will be on television and let family and friends know about it. They watch the game on television but don't see the bands. This hurts music motivation when announcers toss aside the bands with only a mention.

It's disgusting; music is extracurricular in the schools and that emphasis is terrible. The emphasis in education is only on English, mathematics, history, and science. Why is music not there? Years ago, no one was considered a gentleman unless he knew music; I cannot imagine how we have come this far away from music. □

February, 1989

Victor Herbert:
America's Forgotten Bandmaster

BY RONALD J. DIEKER

Can you name a turn-of-the-century American bandmaster who was also a virtuoso cellist, major symphony orchestra conductor and a prolific composer of both popular and serious music? Few modern musicians would name Victor Herbert, yet he filled all these categories.

Victor Herbert (1859-1924) was a consummate musician of uncommon versatility. Known primarily as a composer of popular operettas such as "Babes in Toyland" and "Naughty Marietta," Herbert's compositions also include cello concertos, orchestral works, operas, and band music. In addition to composing he worked as a cellist with the Metropolitan Opera and the New York Philharmonic; conducted the Pittsburgh Symphony Orchestra; and was bandmaster of the famous Gilmore band.

The choice of Herbert as the leader of the Gilmore Band was somewhat unusual; as there is no evidence he had ever conducted a band prior to his appointment. He was a serious musician who received the bulk of his musical training in the conservatory at Stuttgart, Germany.

The circumstances of Herbert's takeover of the Gilmore Band were unusual ones that required decisive action. Throughout the latter half of the 19th century Patrick Gilmore was widely acknowledged as America's finest bandmaster. From 1873 until his death in 1892 he led the Twenty-second Regiment Band of the New York National Guard, which became Gilmore's Band. His sudden death in 1892 during an engagement in St. Louis shocked music lovers across the country.

Two days after his death a new professional touring band under the direction of John Philip Sousa gave its first performance. Worried that this new band would be in direct competition with them, members of the Gilmore organization asked D. W. Reeves of the American Band of Providence, Rhode Island to be their new director.

His leadership proved to be both unsuccessful and controversial. Some of Gilmore's musicians abandoned the Twenty-second Regiment and joined with Sousa. Reeves reacted to the departure of these members in an angry letter published March 15, 1893 in the *Musical Courier*, New York's leading musical magazine.

In his letter Reeves claimed the former Gilmore players were "a few fossiled and worn out members...." He then went on to claim that the Sousa Band was under the control of a group of unscrupulous speculators whose only goals for the organization

---

Ronald J. Dieker is an associate professor of music and director of bands at Warner Pacific College in Portland, Oregon. He holds the Master of Music Degree from the University of Oregon and the Doctor of Musical Arts degree from Arizona State University. Dieker's doctoral research was concerned with Victor Herbert's contributions to American band history. His modern arrangement of The President's March *by Victor Herbert was published by the Theodore Presser Company in 1988.*

were to make money. Sensing the public interest in the controversy, the *Musical Courier* printed a rebuttal of the Reeves claims signed by 11 former Gilmore members who now worked for Sousa. Among the 11 signers was the famous cornet soloist, Herbert L. Clarke. His reputation tarnished, Reeves resigned. Victor Herbert was chosen as the band's new director.

Some would view conducting Gilmore's Band as a step down for a serious musician, but Herbert seized the opportunity to enhance his own popularity and fame by leading one of America's most well-loved attractions. He also saw the chance to develop his conducting career with a group of fine musicians.

It must be remembered this was a time before the advent of movies, radio and television. Bands were the leading form of entertainment in America. The large professional touring bands such as those of Gilmore and Sousa had budgets much larger than those of symphony orchestras. The bandmasters of these groups became national celebrities.

Herbert restored Gilmore's band to its previous stature. He managed to woo back several of the members who had defected to the Sousa Band, including Herbert L. Clarke. Victor Herbert appointed Clarke assistant director and Clarke also served as an arranger for the Gilmore organization.

The band's first performance under Victor Herbert was held in New York's Broadway Theater on November 26, 1893. The concert was well attended and received good reviews from the New York critics. Over the next five years, Gilmore's Band under the direction of Victor Herbert enjoyed great success. Each year the band toured America and Canada performing at resorts, parks, concert halls, and summer expositions.

The band's repertoire included transcriptions of famous orchestral works, dazzling instrumental solos (including Herbert performing on the cello), famous vocalists singing accompanied operatic arias and, of course, band marches.

During these years the Gilmore Band played to large and enthusiastic audiences and was universally praised by the critics. Many considered it to be the finest band in America. In its April 1, 1896 issue, the *Musical Courier* printed a review stating:

"Gilmore's is one of the first and greatest of the large band organizations, but — with the single exception of a short period immediately following the death of Mr. Gilmore — it has always contained the very best musicians that could be obtained. Its roster of famous artists has always been unapproachable. Victor Herbert has added to its quality vastly since he became director, and moreover has made of Gilmore's a far more artistic organization than it was ever before.... The band is today, without question, better that it ever was, and without equal."

Herbert was a gregarious and friendly leader, well-loved by the men in his band. He loved to eat, drink (especially imported German beer), and socialize with band members. Although he could act like one of the boys, in rehearsals he was a demanding conductor concerned with the fine details of performance. Herbert had the most extensive classical training of any bandmaster of the day, and this was reflected in his band's performance. He was also a conductor with an explosive temper who swore profusely in several languages so that the numerous European band members could understand him when things were not going well.

In 1897 Herbert's band received the honor of being chosen the official band of William McKinley's presidential inauguration. By this time the ensemble was being billed as Victor Herbert's Twenty-Second Regiment Band, although many still referred to it as Gilmore's Band.

Herbert and his men performed at the inauguration, and inaugural ball and gave five special "Inaugural Grand Concerts." Herbert composed the march "McKinley Inauguration," which was premiered during the festivities.

Another march written for President McKinley is one of Herbert's best band marches. "The President's March" first appeared in the July 1898 issue of the *Ladies' Home Journal* and was proposed as a new national march of America.

The introduction of the march uses the opening melody of the "Star Spangled Banner" in a rhythmically altered manner in an obvious attempt to unify the national anthem with this new national march. Whether or not Herbert's march was ever used during a McKinley administration in any official capacity is not known, but "Hail to the Chief" has remained as the march associated with the American presidency.

In 1898 Herbert's fame as a conductor had attracted the attention of trustees of the Pittsburgh Symphony Orchestra. Seeking a new conductor, the orchestra asked him to assume the leadership of its ensemble. Herbert accepted the offer and was the orchestra's conductor until March of 1904. Throughout his tenure at Pittsburgh there was criticism and controversy over his leadership, primarily by those who thought a band conductor not worthy of leading a serious artistic ensemble. However, Herbert succeeded in raising the musical quality of the orchestra as well as regaining its public following.

Herbert did not abandon his other musical activities while conducting in Pittsburgh. He was one of the leading operetta composers in America and busied himself conducting these popular works. Although he retained leadership of his band until 1900, after 1898 he had less time and energy to devote to it.

Herbert's band had difficulty competing with Sousa's for engagements at large summer expositions. A major blow to the organization was the resignation of cornetist Herbert L. Clarke, one of the band's leading attractions.

Sensing that the band's days of glory were coming to an end, Herbert resigned in June of 1900. Paul Henneberg, a flutist and band member, became the new conductor. The group never regained its national stature.

After 1900 Herbert's career included little contact with wind bands. He continued to write marches, many based on music from his early operettas. Throughout his career, Herbert composed at least 38 band marches, of which 35 have been preserved on microfilm in the Library of Congress.

Largely forgotten in modern times, Victor Herbert was one of America's premier bandmasters and contributed a great deal to band history. The compositional skill and craftsmanship that he displayed in his operatic and orchestral writing can also be seen in his band marches. These fine pieces unkown to many contemporary band directors, deserve to be performed at concerts today. □

Preparing for a Life in Music

An Interview With Harvey Phillips

by Bernard Dobroski

Many people have excelled on their instrument; others have become accomplished teachers, and a smaller number have done both. Few, though, have elevated their instrument from relative obscurity through their conduct and force of will. Because of Harvey Phillips the tuba has achieved a high level of excellence and respectability and a repertoire he singe-handedly commissioned and indirectly created by urging others to seek out commissions. Despite his abiding devotion to the tuba, Harvey is a modern renaissance man with interests and friendships that reach the far corners of the musical community. His address book lists an impressive diversity of musicians, all of whom are willing to take his calls.

If a high school senior asked you if he should pursue a career in music, what would you tell him?

I don't tell students whether to go into music, but I point out that some of us would not be happy if we did not follow our dreams and musical desires. Many people pursue careers in music but have no business doing so, except that they love music and want to continue serving that love. If students want a life in music, I can guarantee them one, but not necessarily as a player or teacher or even a combination of these. I tell students that there are three parts to our discipline: the art of music, the profession of music, and the business of music. We learn the art of music for credibility, the profession of music for participation, and the business of music for security.

If a person goes into music for financial remuneration, then he should leave music immediately because he will not become rich as an artist, even if he achieves international fame on a popular instrument. The business of music covers all of the aspects that serve performance: publicity, program selection, and management. One of the reasons our music profession has deteriorated is that musicians have given over decision-making to nonmusicians who make vital decisions affecting the future of music. Major symphonies have as many managers and administrators as they do musicians, and this is ridiculous. I remember when Julius Bloom was executive director of Carnegie Hall and had only a small staff. Today it takes a large staff to run that hall even with computers. There are no more days in the year; they can't produce any more concerts than they used to; it's an example of excessive management.

A musician with a good mind, dedication, and desire to learn the art and profession of music should consider a career. Instead of someone who has no musical training becoming the manager of a symphony orchestra, I would rather see a manager with a musical mind, someone sympathetic to performers' problems and who understands programming, public relations, and the needs of the public from a musician's perspective rather than from merely a business viewpoint.

Bernard Dobroski is dean of Northwestern University's School of Music and former dean at the University of Oregon, where he began the Oregon Bach Festival.

The president of a major instrument company spends his life in music; he isn't making his living playing an instrument, but he influences the quality of products musicians play. If he has musical training and an appreciation of musicians' problems, he is a better president of that corporation. This applies to every little pocket of people in our profession: music publishing, concert management, orchestra management, performance, instrument manufacturing, and sales of music or instruments. There's no end to it.

Is it because musicians don't have the talent or education that they surrender management responsibilities?

The public relations aspect of the music business has short-changed us. It's tragic when a great American symphony orchestra has a foreign contract because no American labels are willing to record it, but it's better for an orchestra to have a foreign contract than none. It is also ridiculous that we have three wealthy, powerful broadcasting corporations, but none maintain a symphony orchestra or staff of musicians. European television corporations have full symphony orchestras, chamber orchestras, jazz ensembles, and chamber ensembles on staff. Perhaps someday an aspiring young American musician will channel his interest into management, become head of a broadcasting corporation, and change this.

Are you suggesting a change in college requirements for a music major from 65-75% of courses in music to more courses in understanding himself?

Today many music students want to be soloists or concert artists, but few will reach their aspirations and pursue a career in chamber music or orchestral performance. Some realize how tough they must be to survive a performance career, but even in spite of their technical achievements, they will not be able to sustain the pressures of performance and need to investigate alternatives. The pressures of conductors and colleagues in the orchestra bearing down on them is difficult for many musicians to handle. I know players who had a lifelong career in music and were miserable because they came out on stage half an hour before the concert, got their reeds wet, and lived in fear of playing a wrong note. I can spot that in a player instantly. There are some mean people who see someone like that in the orchestra and just ride them. I saw an oboe player get up in the middle of a rehearsal and push over the clarinet player's chair; they got into a fist fight. The oboist was a nervous type and the clarinet player was one of those bravura players.

From the time a student enters as a freshman, he should be aware of a diversity of career possibilities. Students attend theory classes and see

how theory people think, and they experience conductors and players of other instruments the same way. Perhaps they should also take a course in self-awareness because this factor is missing in many students. Learning about your strengths spotlights your weaknesses; if students observe the strengths of others, they will also spotlight their own weaknesses. Every school of music should require a humanities course that teaches how serving the needs of others serves our own needs as well.

Member of the Voice of Firestone Orchestra, 1951

How do you guide a student who wants a career in music?

I encourage students to become experts in self-analysis. Every day they should analyze their present level of achievement and their potential in music, and not just as performers. Students learn about themselves by comparing their achievements to those of colleagues. A student may discover that others have achieved a superior technique that he can never achieve, no matter how hard he tries. However, he may have a great personality and be someone in whom others have confidence. This student should think about other areas of music in which he could become successful. I try to assess my students regularly to determine their strengths and weaknesses as well as their potential. I want students to talk with me about observations of themselves. By the time they are juniors and are more mature as people and musicians, we can plan for their musical futures and discuss the focus of each student's strengths. People don't win auditions or land jobs because of their weaknesses; they are hired for their strengths. Everyone has a closet full of weaknesses, to be opened when no one else is around, and each should take the time to turn them into strengths. I don't want students to become artistic robots, but human beings who are aware of their own strengths, weaknesses, and the needs of others.

I don't know of anyone in music who is involved in only one aspect of it. Most successful careers combine several aspects of music that draw on particular merits and abilities. Talent alone will never make a great musician. A great talent can be wasted without the investment of time, but a lesser talent who diligently puts in time can rise above more talented colleagues.

What do you teach in private lessons?

An applied teacher only does half his job if he ignores a student's personality and values. I always greet my students with "Hello, how are you? You look nice today," "Didn't you get your laundry done?" or "Have you heard from your parents and how are they?" I say these things in a friendly manner, and then ask to hear what they have prepared. I don't always hear the assigned lesson; instead I might hear about a major test or a challenging performance with the band, orchestra, or brass quintet that took up practice time. Those are acceptable reasons for not practicing for a lesson, but then I want to hear about that brass quintet concert and what was accomplished in the preparation for it.

The first thing I ask a student to play is a given scale, two octaves ascending and descending. I may ask for a whole tone scale, one of the modes, a major or minor scale in one of the three forms, or a chromatic scale. I'm concerned with his reflex knowledge of the scale patterns because this shows his innate musicality. A thinking player is aware of the position of half-and whole-steps in each scale and mode.

Almost every lesson includes music that is lyrical, technical, and I always include a study that explores range. The amount of time we spend on any of these areas depends on the student's needs. Generally we rehearse one or more excerpts, but we don't learn excerpts in isolation; we learn about composers. There are fewer composers than excerpts, so we learn about Berlioz, Wagner, Mahler, Strauss, Brahms, Stravinsky, and Bartók and listen to more than just the tuba parts. Teachers should pique students' interest, and students should know when composers lived, the important events that shaped their lives, and what else may have influenced them.

To prepare for your lessons, do students have to develop answers to questions in these areas?

They have to answer them or at least be interested in finding the answers. In all great music schools there is an enormous amount of knowledge students can gain by probing and asking questions. At Indiana University we have many great artists on violin, flute, cello, trumpet, and other instruments. If a student has contact only with me and other tuba students, he misses the benefits of experiencing and knowing these other artists. I encourage my students to develop relationships with other people on the faculty and their students. Each student has only one hour a week in applied lessons to shape purpose, drive, and talent. That's not a lot of time.

Musical maturity is the important thing for students to achieve, and precious few do — to be able to walk out on stage and play a Handel sonata, a Strauss tone poem, or a Brahms symphony and feel no remorse after the performance. With musical maturity they may play it differently every time but remain confident in themselves. That's when someone may walk up to them and say, "I've never heard that interpretation before; it's fantastic. I feel I've heard this music for the first time." When my students play for me, I want to know why they choose their interpretation; it doesn't matter whether I think it's great or rotten.

Bud Herseth broke the bounds of tradition and gave his interpretations of trumpet parts. He is such a genius as a musician that he is a hero. Another trumpet player who had that quality was Harry Glanz; there are others who are so secure with their own musicality that they never worry about their interpretations of any composer. That's something every young player should aspire to. The most important thing I aspire to is giving students self-reliance.

How do you give students a concept of sound?

I know of players who developed a wonderful sound without the benefit of tuba recordings or role models but who had the emotional experience of going to church and listening to great singing. Experiencing the sadness of a funeral or the joy of a basketball game influences our emotional makeup. Players are products of their environment and experience. The beautiful sound of a great flutist, violinist, cellist, or clarinetist influences a developing tuba sound. The most simple definition of music is organized sound. To develop a beautiful sound we have to be aware of all the possible shadings and draw on them in our playing. I've had students with incredible technique, range, and all the auxiliary skills of flutter-tonguing, circular breathing, staccato tonguing, and facility playing wide intervals, but whose basic tone left something to be desired. Avant garde music requires many techniques but not a great sound so those players can have careers as new music specialists.

Music is one language, but it has an infinite number of dialects. Just as actors learn to speak with certain dialects and inflections, musicians should master the dialects of the various historical periods in music: baroque, classical, romantic, contemporary, ragtime, Dixieland, swing, and be-bop.

Students should learn from listening to others and experimenting with what they hear. If they sit in a be-bop group but have only played Dixieland, they won't fit; but if they are sensitive they will soon adapt like chameleons. Without this experience be-bop will be a dialect missing from their repertoire.

Why did you choose the tuba as your instrument?

The tuba was selected for me. I grew up in a small community with a very small high school; between grades one and twelve we had just over 400 students, so you can imagine what our high school band was like. I took my father's violin to school and tried to play along with the band. In 1942, shortly after we entered World War II, our band's only Sousaphone player joined the Navy, and my high school band director asked me to play Sousaphone. I really inherited the tuba. That was one of the most wonderful things that ever happened to me. The tuba became my constant companion; I took it everywhere with me. I worked at a funeral home before school every day and even took it there. I rode my bicycle with the tuba; if I was riding into the wind I'd pull the bell in so the wind went straight over it. While riding away from the wind I used the bell to tack like a sailboat.

My high school band director talked me through the fingerings because I didn't have a fingering chart; my method book was a hymnal. In every free moment I sat at the piano and played hymns on the Sousaphone. My mother was often in the kitchen when I practiced and sang along. If I hit a clinker, she came in to make sure I knew it was a clinker. Because of her singing I paid attention to the words in the hymnal and became aware of how words influence phrasing. I ask my students to play lyrical melodies, popular songs, and hymns to develop phrasing. Students who do not develop a personal style to their phrasing are mimics of what they hear and what their teachers tell them. When people ask me why anyone plays the tuba, I usually think, why not? Those who say the tuba takes a lot of air, I ask if they had to spend the rest of their lives breathing through a straw, would they choose a small or big straw? Of course, they would choose a big straw; the tuba is a comfortable instrument and a natural extension of the human anatomy. All an instru-

ment can do, whether it is a violin or a tuba, is amplify and broadcast the musical intellect, talent and artistry of the person playing it. A Stradivarius violin has no talent; it is a beautiful work of art, but its musical personality is given to it by the musical intellect, dedication, talent, and resolve of the performer.

If Heifetz, Casals, or Horowitz played the tuba, would he have had less talent, musical intellect, or artistic potential? Any of them could have been incredible tuba players. Throughout the world there are young tuba players with the talent of a Heifetz, Horowitz, or Casals, but some in the musical community and the general public do not recognize them for their artistic achievements. Someday this situation will change.

Did you study with a private teacher?

I didn't study with anyone until I studied with George C. Wilson at the University of Missouri, where I attended classes only one semester. Before I entered Juilliard, I worked professionally for three years traveling with the Ringling Bros. Barnum and Bailey Circus Band and played with Johnny Evans, a great artist of the tuba and a former member of the Sousa Band. Sitting next to him was like taking six hours of private lessons every day. That was my apprenticeship, and my major study was with William Bell. He was my primary influence.

Do you influence your students' emotions, heart, and spirit?

Music is a dramatic art, and a good musical performance imparts the emotion of the performer to the audience. My students and I sometimes make up lyrics to a Bordogni Vocalise or a melody from a symphony because words help give emotional meaning to music. All music breathes. There are tensions; there are releases. You take in a breath, you create tension in your body. You let out a breath, it is relaxing. The tension and relaxation devices that composers use are simple and obvious: ascending scale for tension, descending for relaxation. They create tension with a crescendo and relaxation with a diminuendo, tension with accellerando, relaxation with rallentando. Once you make a student aware of this, he hears it in all music.

Although I can teach technique, interpretation, and sound, if I could ask the Lord for one special gift, it would be the ability to give talent to those students who are lacking. When I see a dreamy-eyed young musician, attractive, pleasant, intelligent, but with limited talent, I could just cry. I see other students with incredible potential who progress to a plateau and then stay there; nothing seems to raise them. Those are the difficult reconciliations of teaching.

What teaching problem is the most difficult?

Overcoming a student's bad habits, often developed because of the inattention of a teacher or director, is a challenge. A brass player's worst habit is puffing the cheeks; the next is pulling back the corners of the mouth when playing in the high register. These habits go hand-in-hand and are almost impossible to break. Sometimes making a student aware of what holds him back in developing range or uniform sound is the best I can do. While puffing his cheeks, he sounds like one player; when pulling his cheeks in, he sounds like another. Once a student is aware of the results from a change, he usually will pull through. If a student has a good sound in all registers I will accept that he alters his physical approach to the instrument to achieve a consistent sound in different registers. I don't expect any two players to play exactly the same way.

One dramatic success story is the European tuba student who came to study with me. He already had wonderful musical experience but had never learned any other way to articulate than the Arban approach, which is demonstrated by putting a pencil on the lips and touching it with the tip of the tongue for every articulation. This student spat out every note and wasn't aware of the many choices in articulation. He didn't use vowel sounds in lyrical playing, so I advised him to sing the horn solo from Tchaikovsky's 5th and pointed out the importance of using different vowel sounds; playing will never sound emotional if you use only one syllable. After putting vowel sounds into his lyrical playing, there weren't enough hours in the day for him to play. From ten in the morning until six at night we played duets and excerpts together, rediscovering music we already knew. Those four months were the happiest four months I've spent with any student.

I had another tuba player study with me, who was a member of the West Point Band. I've never had a student ask so many questions. When he visited for a weekend, I found myself trying to escape from him because every moment I was inundated with questions about playing, music, and composers. To this day he's one of the most intelligent musicians I know because he dreams up questions and seeks answers. I tell all my students how much their educations would improve if they sought the answers to just three questions every day.

Although symphony orchestras are the backbone of a tuba player's career, where should chamber music fit in?

The symphony orchestra has one tuba player who often stays there for 40 years; the Metropolitan Opera had Giovanni Manuti for 45 years. If every tuba player has that much longevity, then twice every hundred years there will be openings. We should stress chamber music more; most colleges leave brass and wind players on their own to organize quintets and while there is much to learn from organizing a brass quintet, students would benefit from a structured program.

In spite of our recording technology and the decline of the American classical music audience, do you think concert performances will continue?

I don't think concert performances will ever completely disappear because the experience of sitting in a hall listening to a performance cannot be duplicated by taking the orchestra off stage and putting a synthesizer in its place. I would rather hear an orchestra in a broadcast of a concert performance than from a recording because recording engineers generally separate the sections into different tracks and reassemble the parts with audio changes. It is the person at the dials, not the conductor and the orchestra, who determines the balance.

Where will all the students in our conservatories and schools of music find careers?

For every one of them there can be a life in music. If they want a life in medicine, law, or engineering but still want to be involved in music, it can be a great sideline that enhances their lives. Musicians who make their careers in music benefit from the support and interest of the audience, many of whom have avocations in music. There are no losers. It is immoral to tell every student he has the potential to be a major orchestral player; there should be honesty. I don't see how anyone can teach applied students without feeling involved with their lives. I hear from students who studied with me 25 or 30 years ago who want advice or want to tell me about a recent accomplishment. There is no greater enjoyment than the pleasure and fulfillment music brings to our lives.

From Battlefield to Concert Hall
The Career of Patrick S. Gilmore

by Rusty Hammer

When Patrick Sarsfield Gilmore (1829-1892) came to America from Ireland in 1849, he was an accomplished cornetist and eager to become a music leader. In time he became the father of the American band and one of the early directors to conduct with a baton. He began his career in the Boston area as director of the Aeolian Minstrals and bands in Charlestown, Suffolk, Boston, and Salem. He soon showed a passion for monster concerts, assembling several area bands into massed ensembles on the Boston Commons for July 4th celebrations. Gilmore also began a lifelong practice of touring when he took the Salem Band to Washington, D.C. for President Buchanan's inauguration. In 1857 he launched the first series of promenade concerts in America, which had the low ticket prices and light classical repertoire that were tremendously popular with Boston audiences. In 1858 he formed the first Gilmore Band with two woodwinds to each brass instrument, an unfamiliar sound to those used to brass bands. He drilled the musicians tirelessly, urging them to play the sweetest pianissimo and the most forceful fortissimo.

Gilmore took his band to the 1860 democratic national convention in Charleston, and the republican convention in Chicago that nominated Abraham Lincoln for President. At the start of the Civil War Gilmore's Band, attached to the Massachusetts

24th Regiment, joined General Burnside's expedition in North Carolina, where they played for the troops and helped care for wounded soldiers. They played "Dixie" and "Carry Me Back to Old Virginny" for Southern prisoners and the "Battle Hymn of the Republic" and "Hail, Columbia" for Northern troops. In Boston Gilmore introduced "When Johnny Comes Marching Home," ascribing it first to Louis Lambert, but later he claimed credit for writing the song, which was based on a traditional Irish melody.

During the war Gilmore served in New Orleans as director of all bands in the region. When called upon to produce the festivities for Governor Michael Hahn's inauguration, he assembled a chorus of 5,000 school children and a 500 piece band, the beginning of Gilmore's legendary large musical ensembles.

As a grand gesture to commemorate the Civil War's end, Gilmore organized the National Peace Jubilee in June 1869. He had a coliseum constructed in Boston's Back Bay with 35,000 seats, and he staged an overwhelming event with a thousand member orchestra and a chorus of ten thousand. An overwhelming success, it attracted enormous crowds for a week of concerts.

Gilmore outdid this three years later with a World's Peace Jubilee and International Music Festival at the end of the Franco-Prussian War in Europe. Another coliseum was built with seating for over 50,000. In addi-

tion to the orchestra of 2,000 instruments and the 20,000 voice chorus, the world's largest bass drum and organ were constructed for the month-long festivities. It was for this effort that Boston Mayor William A. Gaston presented a special baton to Gilmore, recognizing his tireless efforts to produce the stunning festival that hundreds of thousands of visitors attended. President U.S. Grant, Horace Greeley, Admiral Farragut, Oliver Wendell Holmes, and Ralph Waldo Emerson were there, but a highlight of the Jubilee was the guest conductor, waltz king Johann Strauss Jr., who made his only appearances in America at Gilmore's invitation for a fee of $100,000.

Gilmore was the star, however, and used his new baton to lead performances of the "Anvil Chorus" from Verdi's *Il Trovatore* with 100 Boston firemen playing the anvils. Batteries of cannons helped renditions of the "Star Spangled Banner," and the awesome chorus shone in "Hail, Columbia" and "Stabat Mater". To commemorate the event a gold band inscribed with the year 1872 was placed around Gilmore's baton. Although there are isolated references to a stick used for conducting as early as the 16th century, the baton only became

Rusty Hammer is executive director of the P.S. Gilmore Society and on the board of directors of the Richmond Concert Band. He received a degree in arts management from the University of Massachusetts.

popular in the 19th century as the size of performing ensembles increased. Berlioz used one to conduct his Requiem, and Verdi to direct his operas. Gilmore's group was the largest orchestra ever created, occasioning the special baton. His new baton accompanied him the following year when he, his wife Nellie, and daughter Minnie moved to New York where Gilmore directed the 22nd Regiment Band that became known as Gilmore's Band. Although they performed at the regiment's new armory on 14th Street, in 1875 Gilmore leased the Hippodrome building from P.T. Barnum, adding plants, fountains, walkways, and a bandstand in the middle to convert it into Gilmore's Concert Garden. His concerts were popular, and for the 150th one a crowd of 10,000 packed the Garden. When the lease ended in 1879, the building name was changed to Madison Square Garden, the first of five buildings to bear that name.

In 1876 Gilmore's Band had its first cross-country tour that included the Centennial Exposition in Philadelphia to celebrate the 100th anniversary of the Declaration of Independence. The Exposition commissioned Richard Wagner to compose the *Centennial March* and hired Jacques Offenbach to lead the Centennial Orchestra. They relied on Gilmore's Band to attract the audience, and placed them in the center of the main exhibition hall under a reflecting disk 34 feet in diameter so they could be heard throughout the hall. The large crowds that gathered to hear them obstructed views of the exhibits so they erected a special music pavillion. Gilmore also directed Philadelphia's Independence Square celebration on July 4, 1876, creating a musical spectacular complete with a 250 piece band and 1,200 singers. Once again he used the special baton, adding another gold band, inscribed with the year 1876.

Gilmore performed for every United States President of his day, starting with Buchanan and including Lincoln, Grant, Garfield, and Cleveland. His unusual relationship with Cleveland began shortly after the 1884 election, when the bachelor President Cleveland announced his engagement to the much younger Frances Folson. About that time he

reviewed a parade in New York, where the passing bands played national airs such as "See the Conquering Hero" and "Hail to the Chief." When Gilmore's Band stopped for its Presidential salute, throwing tradition to the wind they played "For He's Going to Marry Yum Yum," from Gilbert and Sullivan's *The Mikado*.

Another time, Cleveland returned to New York for a July 4th parade, without his new wife beside him on the reviewing stand. As Gilmore approached the platform, he bowed deeply, and struck up the band with "The Girl I Left Behind Me." The smile on Cleveland's usually stern face showed his approval of the musical joke. When the President and his wife, along with 40,000 people were guests at the 1886 dedication of the new music hall at the St. Louis Exposition, the lights went out as the President was about to be escorted through the crowd to his box. Gilmore started the band with "Oh Dear, What Can the Matter Be?" The audience and Cleveland believed the blackout was part of the program, although the cause was a circuit overload. Lights soon were restored, and Gilmore's quick program change averted a potentially disastrous panic.

In a San Francisco newspaper he said, "Figuratively speaking, the string orchestra is feminine, the military band is masculine. The string orchestra may be as coarse as a very coarse woman, or as refined as the most accomplished lady. So too, the military band may remain like a rough street tramp or he may undergo a polishing that will make him a perfect gentleman, equally fit, from a critical standpoint to occupy the concert room with his more sensitive sister. This is what I have tried to make of my band. Somebody may bring the string orchestra to such a degree of perfection as to make it a very queen among its kind, but my military band shall be king."

Gilmore's career continued to soar, and in 1878 he toured Europe. His band travelled in the United States regularly, also performing annually at the Manhattan Beach Hotel on Coney Island and at the St. Louis Exposition. In 1886 he was music director for the dedication of the Statue of Liberty.

Gilmore presented his baton to his solo flutist Fred Lax in 1888, but his

band continued performing for presidents and millions of Americans.

Gilmore made some of the first commercial recordings in 1891 at Thomas Edison's laboratory in New Jersey. He was named music director for the Columbian Exposition in Chicago, but on September 24, 1892, following a performance in St. Louis, P.S. Gilmore died of heart failure.

The story of the baton continues. Charles C. Donnelly, head of the musician's union in Lancaster, Pennsylvania, organized Gilmore Day on June 12, 1905. All of Lancaster's businesses closed for the day, and everybody came to the parade. Thirteen bands massed on the courthouse steps playing the *Star Spangled Banner* Gilmore-style, and Fred Lax sent Gilmore's baton to Donnelly along with a photograph of Gilmore's Band and a letter: "Since Gilmore died he has been imitated by charlatans, idiots, and acrobats. To you I beg to offer my thanks, as the only soloist left, for remembering poor old Pat Gilmore."

A committee headed by President Theodore Roosevelt, former President Grover Cleveland, and the mayor, governor, and senators of New York presented a benefit concert for Gilmore's wife and daughter in Madison Square Garden, New York on May 15, 1906. John Philip Sousa, Victor Herbert, and Walter and Frank Damrosh used Gilmore's baton, directing massed bands and chorus for an audience of 12,000. Gilmore Day celebrations continued in Lancaster in 1906-1908, ceasing because some manufacturers there complained about business disruptions.

Hartman's Hat Store displayed the baton in downtown Lancaster, and Arthur Pryor used it with his band in 1911, as did the Iroquois Band's leader. The National Federation of Music Clubs now has the baton at its national headquarters in Indianapolis.

There is a story of a stooped, old gentleman who approached Gilmore at the St. Louis Exposition just prior to the great band leader's death. "Why Gilmore," he exclaimed, "You and I are the same age, how is it we look so different?" "Easily explained my dear fellow," Gilmore countered, "I possess the secret of perpetual youth. You know as a matter of fact that time beats us all, but I (using suitable gestures with his baton) beat time." □

Stars and Stripes Forever

Memories of Sousa & His Men

FOREWORD

THIS series of articles is by no means an attempt to present to its readers the usual authentic biography of one of the world's foremost musicians. Rather it is the story of successive events, intended primarily as sheer enjoyment to the thousands of music lovers still living who recall the nostalgic era of bygone days when America's famous bandmasters thrilled millions up and down the length and width of the nation.

The author, formerly a semi-professional trumpeter, was so fortunate as to be personally acquainted with John Philip Sousa and other renowned directors of concert band fame. Many tales related herein have not been known to the public at large up to the time of this writing. The

1034

reader may be assured, however, of the authenticity of the events, set down not always in exact sequence, but with accurate knowledge of the facts.

The author was acquainted with quite a number of bandsmen, and was associated with Sousa, Pryor, Creatore, and other noted conductors of national renown. He also was a close friend for many years of Edwin J. Freudenvoll whose father, Mr. Charles W. Freudenvoll, was Patrick S. Gilmore's assistant director (1874-1892). With such a wealth of information available, our story should prove to be a source of genuine entertainment.

Memories of the March King and His Men

CHAPTER I

Ever since the early years of the 19th century the people of the United States have enjoyed listening to the music rendered by great bands and orchestras. Since 1915, during the years of the First World War, a new form of music has swept across the nations throughout the earth. We call it "jazz" or "jive." Legitimate concert bands are becoming scarcer as the years roll on. But an appreciable number of music lovers still live who recall the rich strains of such celebrated bands as those of "Pat" Gilmore, "Pat" Conway, Arthur Pryor, Giuseppe Creatore, Alessandro Liberati, and that of the foremost band of all time, John Philip Sousa's.

NOLBERT HUNT QUAYLE

Before going on directly with reminiscences concerning the Sousa Band, a few paragraphs relative to the organizations that preceded the Sousa era may well serve to enlarge the scope for the reader's understanding of America's band history.

The oldest known concert band in the United States, so far as the records show, was the Allentown (Pa.) Band, organized in 1828. The Repasz Band of Williamsport, Pa., named for Daniel Repasz, one of its first directors, was founded in 1831. Doubtless there existed quite a number of bands in this country that are unknown to us who "have been around a long time." Reading, Pa., boasts the Ringgold Band which began in 1852. This was the band which invited Mr. Sousa to act as its guest conductor on the occasion of its 80th anniversary concert on March 6, 1932.

Famous bandmasters during the second half of the 19th century included: David Wallace Reeves, leader of the band located at Providence, R. I.; Matthew Arbuckle, the most famous of all the cornet soloists with Gilmore's Band, directed the 9th Reg't N. Y. Nat'l Guard Band at the time of his death in 1883; John Hazel, a cornet virtuoso *par excellence* who was regarded as the legitimate rival of the great Jules Levy, conducted the "Repasz Band" from 1910 until his retirement in the early 1940s.

With such a background of fine concert bands which greatly served to acquaint the American public with the repertoire then available for truly inspiring band music, it is easy to observe the somewhat rapid rise to eminence of such outstanding leaders as Gilmore and Sousa. Although such musicians as Frederick N. Innes, Arthur Pryor, Bohumir Kryl, etc., added sterling impetus, so to speak, to the cause of high-class band music, the fact is generally acknowledged that Gilmore and Sousa, even to this day and generation, represent the epitome of band achievements, not only here in the United States, but throughout the world.

PART II

To MILLIONS OF MIDDLE-AGED and elderly music-lovers it seems incredible that a century has elapsed since John Philip Sousa was born in Washington, D.C., November 6, 1854, or that it is even more than twenty-two years since his death.

His biography is well-known, so let us consider actual events concerning his band. Sousa's original cornet soloist in 1892 at Plainfield was an English artist named Arthur Smith. One of the original saxophonists was Rudolph Becker. As late as 1952 he was the last survivor of the original Sousa Band. Frank Holton, the noted manufacturer of band instruments, was the first trombonist.

Sousa and His Band Before 1890

Shortly after Gilmore's death, about a dozen or more members of his band joined the new Sousa ensemble. Among them were such artists as Albert Bode, Herbert L. Clarke, Holly Wilder (cornet); E. A. Lefebre, Maxwell Davidson, Louis Knittle (saxophone); Michael Raffayolo (euphonium); Herman Conrad (tuba); etc.

Meanwhile a young trombonist named Arthur Pryor was making a name for himself at St. Joseph, Missouri, as a phenomenal "slide artist." Sons of a local bandmaster, Arthur and his two brothers (Samuel, a drummer, and Walter, a cornetist), inherited their dad's musical talents to the full. Arthur was born September 22, 1870. The first instruments he learned to play were the alto horn and the valve trombone. He did not see a slide trombone until he was sixteen years old. Charmed with the tone of this new instrument, at first he thought there were only two *positions* of the slide. One day he met a pool player who told him that there were as many as seven positions. Arthur quickly discovered them for himself.

It was not long before he abandoned all other instruments in favor of his new love, the "slip horn." At that time a small town showman named Bert Martin operated a vaudeville house in Arthur's home town. Mr. Martin presented *Amateur Night* each week on Friday evening. A prize of ten dollars was given to the contestant who elicited the loudest applause from the audience. Young Arthur was urged by his friends to enter the contest. He kept on winning prizes week after week, and the other "actors" were frantic with dismay. Although he was but seventeen years old, he was such a consummate artist on the slide trombone that he was eventually barred from further contests.

By 1892 Arthur Pryor had gained an enviable reputation as *The Trombone Wizard of the Corn Belt*. Sousa's Band had been in existence only a few weeks when Mr. Sousa sent for Arthur Pryor whose fame had, by then, spread to the Eastern seaboard. Young Pryor arrived in New York City with only 35¢ left in his purse and slept that first night on a park bench. At rehearsal the next day, Sousa knew that here was the peer of all trombonists.

Rich are the tales concerning Pryor as a trombone soloist *par excellence*.

In 1900 Sousa's Band was chosen as the official band to represent the United States at the Paris Exposition. The band also toured in several European countries that summer. A concert was given at Leipzig, Germany, in an open air grandstand before an audience of 25,000 persons. Pryor played one of his most *tricky* original solo compositions. At the close, the vast audience rose *en masse* and gave him the greatest ovation ever accorded an artist in that city. Musicians from the Leipzig Symphony Orchestra went up to the grandstand during the intermission and examined Pryor's instrument and mouthpiece thoroughly. They simply were unable to comprehend that any man could play a trombone with such incredible dexterity and thought it was some sort of *a Yankee trick.*

There were not more than four or five trombone soloists with Sousa's Band throughout the nearly forty years of its existence. Among the prominent first chair artists who played beneath Sousa's baton were: Leo Zimmerman (1903-1908), Ralph H. Corey (1908-1920), George Lucas (1910-1912), Jaroslav Cimera (1913), Richard Whitby (1914-1915), John Schuler (1920-1931). Although Arthur Pryor was rivalled only by Frederick Neil Innes, the celebrated soloist with Gilmore's Band, as a phenomenal virtuoso player, Leo Zimmerman was a more rounded performer playing band, opera and symphony orchestra.

When we recall the addition of so many outstanding stars to the new Sousa Band at the beginning of its career, by reason of Gilmore's sudden, tragic passing, it is no marvel that Mr. Sousa should have climbed immediately to the heights of success with his incomparable array of musicians.

In the fall of 1893, just one year after Mr. Gilmore's death, there was great excitement among the members of his dissolved band when the news came that Victor Herbert was about to reorganize the Gilmore Band under his own leadership. Herbert L. Clarke who was with Mr. Sousa at that time was offered the position of principal cornet soloist, and he accepted the offer immediately.

Mr. Herbert conducted the revived organization under its old, famous name—Gilmore's Band. However, the experiment lasted only four years.

Herbert was like a fish out of water while endeavoring to direct a brass band. A great cellist, also a composer of rarely delightful light operattas, he was far more "at home" while conducting his own music at the head of a symphony orchestra.

CHAPTER III

In 1898 the noted cornet virtuoso, Ernst A. Couturier, sought likewise to "resurrect" the old Gilmore Band by organizing a stock company for the purpose of selling shares in order to finance this new venture. Although the band was composed of the very greatest performers available, the project was doomed from the start. The new organization lasted only three weeks. Not one of the players ever received so much as one cent for his services. The magnetic Gilmore was no more, and his band simply perished with him. John Philip Sousa was now America's foremost bandmaster.

Many of Sousa's widely known marches were composed during the days when he directed the Marine Band. His reputation as the peer of all military march writers was unknown in those days. Some of his greatest marches sold for as little as $35, while his *Stars and Stripes Forever*, composed on Christmas Day in 1896, enriched him to the tune of $300,000 or more in royalties.

Many music lovers doubtless will agree with our statement that the Sousa Band which made such a triumphant tour of Europe in 1900 was perhaps the finest group of artists ever assembled by the *March King*. The 59-piece band included such renowned instrumentalists as Marshall Lufsky, Eugene Rose, Darius Lyons (flute), Louis Christie (clarinet), Jean Moeremans (saxophone), Anton Horner (French Horn), Franz Hell (fluegelhorn), Herbert L. Clarke, Walter B. Rogers, Holly Wilder, Henry Higginson (cornet), Pete Neilsen (trumpet), Arthur Pryor, Ross Chapman (trombone), Simone Mantia (euphonium), Herman Conrad, Lucius Del Negro, August Helleberg, Sr. (tuba), and Thomas Mills (tympani). It was indeed a magnificent ensemble.

There are so many stories concerning several of Sousa's cornet virtuosos that we shall skip over them and reserve them for a later chapter. Among the musicians whom Pryor took with him for his own band in 1903 was Simone Mantia who had

succeeded Michael Raffayolo in 1903 as Sousa's euphonium soloist. Mantia was Pryor's assistant conductor for many years. Professional musicians universally agree that Mantia never had an equal as a soloist on his instrument. Mr. Mantia was also an exceptional trombonist. His technique was such that even the majority of cornetists could not duplicate his *stunts.*

"Luke" Del Negro, one of the early Sousa veterans, also was a member of the LaBarre group in 1940, but he died in August during the Fair; and Stanley Green, an Englishman formerly with *Coldstream Guards Band* of London, England, replaced him. "Tom" Mills, who was with Sousa on the first foreign tour, must have been wonderful, for Mr. Sousa wrote, "Mills was the greatest drummer I ever heard."

In 1905 Sousa's Band made another tour on the Continent. As Walter B. Rogers had already left the band, Herman Bellstedt, the veteran cornetist from Cincinnati, Ohio, who at one time had been with "Pat" Gilmore, was engaged to sit beside Herbert L. Clarke on first chair. Years before he had played with the Cincinnati Orchestra as trumpet soloist. Bellstedt was also a fine composer and arranger of band music. His *Humoresques on Blue Bells of Scotland, Auld Lang Syne, Has Anybody Here Seen Kelly?* and other well known songs were a series of intricate variations for the various choirs of the band. He was one of the finest cornetists of his time. A few years ago Dr. Clarke told how Bellstedt would stand before the mantelpiece in his cold hotel room in London, wrapped in his overcoat, and would write his band arrangements by candlelight.

Leo Zimmerman, Arthur Pryor's immediate successor as Sousa's trombone soloist, was another one of the *greats* in his day. He doubtless could have remained with the band much longer than he did, but as "Zimmy" did not care a great deal for the constant travel required for the annual spring and autumn tours, to say naught concerning trips abroad, he quit after five years.

Ralph H. Corey, who followed Zimmerman, hailed from Boston. He was quite young at the time he signed on with Sousa. Ralph was a very handsome chap with curly black hair. Always natty in his Sousa uniform, he was the "Beau Brummel" of the band. It is not too much to state that he was probably more or less an idol of the members of the fairer sex. He came from a family of wealthy, society people in Boston, so Ralph evidently was a musician by choice rather than from the necessity of earning his living in this manner.

Although the writer heard John Schuler, Sousa's solo trombonist during the final years of the band's existence, he never met him. Other trombone players whom he saw and heard were Marc Lyons and Edward A. Williams. Both of these men played at least twenty-five years for Mr. Sousa. For many years professional musicians felt highly honored to become members of Sousa's band. Mr. Sousa was always considerate of his artists and paid them top salaries. If a man were a first-rate performer, he could remain with the band indefinitely. Sousa was loyal to the core and his players loved him. On the other hand, if a man were indifferent or played in a careless fashion, he was immediately dropped from the roster.

"Ed" Williams was a real veteran who had been a member of the U. S. Marine Band in his younger days. In 1892 he was released so that he could join the new Sousa Band. In 1918, the year following his retirement, Fred Blodgett, who for years was bass trombonist with the old New York Symphony Orchestra under Dr. Walter Damrosch, played one season with the band. The author knew Marc Lyons very well. He was second chair trombonist and baggagemaster of Sousa's Band for many years. In 1913 Jaroslav ("Jerry") Cimera, the great Bohemian artist, was with the band. He was one of the country's outstanding trombonists. For many years "Jerry" has made his own phonograph recordings in his laboratory, playing Arthur Pryor's own solos including the original *cadenzas.*

Joseph Norrito. the celebrated Italian clarinet virtuoso, was Sousa's soloist for many years. One of his last appearances with the band was at the Metropolitan Opera House on North Broad Street, Philadelphia, on March 6, 1922. On that occasion Mr. Sousa led a band of a hundred pieces. To be frank, however, the author, who was present that evening, much preferred to listen to the regular sized band of between fifty and sixty performers. The enlarged group sounded "top-heavy" with so many extra brasses.

Meredith Willson, a familiar figure in radio and TV circles now, was a flutist with the band at one time. After Jean Moereman's retirement, Ben Vereecken became the saxophone soloist. He also played with Pryor's Band.

Prior to 1919, the late H. Benne Henton, widely acclaimed as *The Saxophone Prince*, was a soloist for many seasons with Patrick Conway's Band. Although probably the greatest "sax" player in more modern times, he was given this title for the reason that Mr. Lefebre had long since been known as *The Saxophone King*. Back in 1906 he and Cimera were among the original members of Kryl's Band. Before his death, Henton headed a "sax" quartette which played with the Philadelphia Orchestra. The writer knew Benne very well.

Famous tuba players were John Kuhn, Emil Mix, Jack Richardson, Arthur von Storch and Emil Weber. Kuhn's real name was Red Cloud. A full-blooded American Indian, Kuhn was a superb artist. At one time he visited a band instruments factory in Indiana where he picked up a brand new Sousaphone and played one of Herbert L. Clarke's own cornet solos. Later he was with the Isham Jones Jazz Band.

The familiar huge bass tuba known as the *Sousaphone* was first manufactured in 1898 expressly for Sousa's Band. It was played by Herman Conrad during the European tour in 1900 and was a sensation wherever it was heard. The original Sousaphones were constructed with upright bells. The more modern bell front type was first built in 1908 though Sousa invariably preferred the older model. Whether he did so for musical reasons or from sentiment is not known.

Jack Richardson was with the band as far back as 1904 at the St. Louis Exposition and was still with Sousa twenty years later at Willow Grove Park near Philadelphia. As Richardson stood six feet and four inches in his socks, it seems fitting that he should have played the largest instrument in the band. For some reason, Jack did not accompany Mr. Sousa on the tour of the world in 1911. A player named Arthur Griswold substituted for him.

Sousa engaged female vocalists regularly during his annual tours. One of his early soloists was Bertha Bucklin who was at the Columbian Exposition in 1893. Perhaps the most famous of all the various sopranos with

Sousa's Band was Estelle Liebling who was with Mr. Sousa for a full decade and sang more than 10,000 solos with the band. In later years Mary Baker, Nora Fauchild and Marjorie Moody were among the singers. For a number of years prior to World War I, Sousa's soprano was Virginia Root. Miss Root, who later married a gentleman by the name of Adams, was a granddaughter of the American song-writer, George Frederick Root, who composed such songs as *The Battle-Cry of Freedom; Tramp, Tramp, Tramp, the Boys Are Marching; Just Before the Battle, Mother;* etc. Miss Root was with the band on the trip around the globe, as was Nicoline Zedeler, a violinist. After returning home to the United States, Miss Zedeler married the tubaist, Emil Mix. It may be of interest to note that the journey totalled 48,000 miles, mostly on water. This stupendous undertaking cost Mr. Sousa some $600,-000, yet he came home with a net profit of about $60,000.

Sousa was indeed a bandmaster of rare understanding. For example, if the band were rehearsing a new number for the first time, Mr. Sousa would first lead his men through the selection in routine manner. Next he would order it to be played in the way he thought the composer had planned. After the band had gone over the piece several times, Sousa would tell his players to rest for five minutes. On his way out of the room, he might overhear a certain artist run through his part a number of times until he was able to perform the melody to his own satisfaction. When the band returned to its task, the conductor would remark: "I overheard Jones going over his part just as I was leaving the room. His interpretation of the new number is much better than mine. Now then, fellows, I want you to listen carefully, please, as Mr. Jones plays it the way it should sound." Jones, beaming with pleasure, would play his part accordingly, then the others would follow his example. At one time Mr. Sousa asserted: "If I refused to avail myself of the individual genius of any one of my artists, I would be a very poor conductor. I am a better conductor now than I was last year and I hope to be an even better one next year." Is it any marvel that he is remembered as the *peer* of all bandmasters?

From 1903 until 1919, Sousa's euphonium soloist after Mantia's depart-

ure was John J. Perfetto. He was one of the foremost artists of his day. He was a fine trombonist also. The author knew him very well. During the seasons while he was with Sousa, he, like Ralph Corey, was a familiar figure to audiences who heard the band repeatedly. Mr. Perfetto sported a long waxed mustache and was impressive in his Sousa uniform. When he left the band in 1919, another friend of ours, Joseph DeLuca, was employed as the new euphonium soloist.

CHAPTER IV

IN 1893 WHEN VICTOR HERBERT reorganized the Gilmore Band, Herbert Clarke left Sousa to rejoin his former associates. In 1894 Bohumir Kryl, a nineteen-year-old cornetist and sculptor, emigrated to the United States from his native Bohemia. He went as far west as Indianapolis, Indiana, where his artistic talent was quickly recognized. Kryl had been there only a short time when the local authorities commissioned him to make a statue of the Civil War hero, General "Lew" Wallace, author of the famous novel, *Ben Hur*.

While the newcomer was busily engaged at his new task, Sousa's Band arrived in Indianapolis to play a concert. Young Bohumir had an idea that he could better himself as a cornetist by getting a bit of advice, and perhaps a lesson from Sousa's cornet soloist, who now was Albert Bode. He hurried over to the hotel where the visitors were stopping and went upstairs to Bode's room.

Some of the Sousa bandsmen had already been informed concerning the wonderful young cornetist who had come to town only a few short weeks earlier. When they learned that the *foreigner* had arrived at the hotel, a number of Sousa's men went upstairs and gathered outside Bode's room to poke fun at the youngster.

Suddenly the golden tones of a magnificently played cornet were heard in a rippling flood of trills and dazzling variations. The bandsmen stared at one another in sheer amazement. A moment later one of them exclaimed: "That can't be Bode! Albert never played that good in all his life."

Presently the music ceased and the door was opened. Bode came out into the hall with Kryl at his heels. The older man threw both of his arms above his head as he cried: "I can't teach this boy anything! He can play rings around me any day."

After the concert that evening, Bohumir abandoned his tools at the base of the statue and ran off to board the train in company with Sousa's Band. A month or so afterwards, the disgruntled Bode went on a spree and disappeared. He was never seen with the band after that. Young Kryl finished the season alone on the solo chair.

It is difficult to attempt to enumerate the sum total of all the many cornetists who played beneath Mr. Sousa's baton. We can only mention part of them herein. The list includes: Arthur Smith, Albert Bode, Herbert

L. Clarke, Bohumir Kryl, Emil Keneke, Herman Bellstedt, Walter B. Rogers, Ross Millhouse, Ira Holland, Ernest F. Pechin, Richard McCann, Frank Simon, Clarence A. Staigers, Eugene LaBarre, John Dolan, Richard Stross, William Tong, William Fees, etc., all of whom were solo chair occupants.

Walter B. Rogers, a native of Indiana, was born in 1865. He was only sixteen years old when he commenced to play solos with a band at Indianapolis. In 1893 Rogers was appointed bandmaster of the 7th Regiment N.Y. Nat'l Guard Band of New York City. Prior to that time the band was led by an Italian conductor named Cappa whose name has been perpetuated musically by Eddie Quinn who wrote the brilliant *Cappa's 7th Regiment March.*

Rogers joined Sousa's Band at the turn of the century in time to make the first foreign tour as Mr. Clarke's side partner. He remained with the band until 1905. During the remainder of his life he was active in phonograph work, both as a conductor and as a performer. His death occurred in 1939 at Brooklyn, N.Y.

From 1906 until 1912 Ross Millhouse was seated beside Herbert L. Clarke. Millhouse was a very able cornetist. After leaving Sousa, he settled in California where he lived for many years.

Not much is known concerning Ira Holland. He was with the band for a single season (1912). In 1913 Ernest F. Pechin teamed up with Clarke. Pechin was a star of the first magnitude. He also played quite a long time with Conway's Band where he had a greater opportunity to display his technical abilities as a soloist.

In 1914 Mr. Sousa engaged two newcomers as his solo cornetists. They were Richard McCann and Frank Simon. At that time Mr. Clarke was employed as an expert cornet and trumpet tester of instruments in one of the band instrument factories at Elkhart, Indiana, and at first it was believed that he would be unable to go on tour with Sousa's Band as usual. At the last moment, however, the manufacturer permitted Clarke to resign his position; but since McCann and Simon had already been signed, there were three men on hand for solo chair positions. Mr. Sousa solved the problem by assigning Frank Simon to play the fleugelhorn part on his *cornet*.

The author first heard "Dick" Mc-Cann with Edouarde's Band at Asbury Park in 1912. McCann hailed from Pittsburgh, Pa., where he had made an enviable reputation for himself as a brilliant cornet soloist. Later he went to New York City where he resided during the remainder of his life. He played two seasons with the band, and was present at the Panama-Pacific Exposition in 1915 at San Francisco. For that engagement Mr. Sousa employed four solo cornets. The other two cornetists, Clarence J. Russell and Guy Gaugler, were with the band for many years.

Frank Simon is better known today than many other former Sousa artists by reason of his radio activities. He was a pupil of the great Herman Bellstedt in Cincinnati. When Clarke retired from Sousa's Band in 1917, Mr. Simon became Sousa's new cornet soloist. Frank was a top-notch virtuoso and possessed a very beautiful tone. In 1919 he left Sousa and re-

Bohumir Kryl

turned to Cincinnati where, a number of years afterwards, he organized his famous "Armco Band," made up for the most part of players from the Cincinnati Symphony Orchestra. The name "Armco" comprises the first letters of the words, *American Rolling Mills Company*, located at Middletown, Ohio.

John Dolan, another great cornetist, joined Sousa in 1920. He had been a star performer for many years with "Pat" Conway. We first heard Dolan with Conway's Band on the Steel Pier in Atlantic City way back in the summer of 1907. "Jack" remained with Sousa for about nine or

ten years. He had a superb technique and possessed great powers of endurance. A few years ago, shortly before his death, Hale Ascher VanderCook, a nationally known Chicago bandmaster and founder of the VanderCook School of Music in that city, wrote to us as follows: "I once listened to John Dolan who played the most difficult cornet solo I ever heard in all my life." We should have asked "Uncle Van" to name that unknown selection, but it is too late now.

Dolan's first side partner was Richard Stross, a famous cornet virtuoso from Chicago, who played but one season with the Sousa Band. Stross was noted for his powerful "lip." Not so long ago we received a letter from the director of the Municipal Band at Kulm, North Dakota. In part it read: "I heard Stross many years ago while he was with a theatre orchestra in Chicago. During one of the intermissions the orchestra played the *Sextette from Lucia*. On the final E-flat above high C, Dick hit it with a thud. It sounded like a steam whistle."

There were four solo cornetists in 1919: Frank Simon, "Del" Staigers, Eugene LaBarre and Eugene Bishop. LaBarre was Pryor's soloist in 1916 at Asbury Park. It was his first *big time* job. Whenever Sousa's Band was "on the road," Frank Simon was *the* cornet soloist, but on long engagements at Willow Grove Park, etc., Mr. Sousa employed all four men in rotation, and players on other instruments as well.

"Gene" LaBarre's last tour with Sousa was in the fall of 1931. In 1934, two years after Mr. Sousa's death, LaBarre endeavored to revive the former Sousa Band in New York City. A brief series of concerts were played at Rockefeller Plaza before "crowded houses" out of doors. The newspapers stated that "it was a reincarnation of the world famous Sousa Band." LaBarre had high hopes that he could keep the revived organization together, but, unfortunately, as so often happens, jealousy reared and ruined the venture.

John Philip Sousa was not only a bandmaster of world renown: he was versatile in other fields of achievement. His compositions, in addition to about 150 marches, include operettas, intermezzos, suites for band, humoresques, scenic numbers and songs. He wrote at least three or four novels. He rode horseback frequently

Frank Simon

and was an expert rifleman. One might say that he was *a country gentleman*.

His earlier marches, written prior to World War One, remain the most popular in public estimation. The 1914-1918 conflict aroused Mr. Sousa to such a pitch of fervor that he composed a whole flock of marches with such warlike titles as *Bullets and Bayonets, Solid Men to the Front, U. S. Field Artillery, Who's Who in Navy Blue?* etc. Yet the good old standbys, *El Capitan, Fairest of the Fair, Hands Across the Sea, King Cotton, Liberty Bell, Manhattan Beach, Semper Fidelis*, and, of course, *The Stars and Stripes Forever*, and many more of his old time airs retain their gripping fascination as much as ever.

Sousa once asserted: "How my marches come, I cannot tell. At times I can shut my eyes and see, as in a vision, scenes of battle, troops marching, banners waving; and then I seem to hear brass bands playing on the march. At such times a new melody springs up in my mind and I usually make it a point to write it down at once before I may forget it. It is nothing less than sheer inspiration."

As Washington and Lincoln were our two greatest Presidents, we are sure that Gilmore and Sousa were our two foremost bandmasters. Herbert L. Clarke said: "When God creates a genius, He breaks the mold so that there can be no other. After Sousa, there can be no other."

Chapter V

Herbert Lincoln Clarke is probably the best-known cornet player who ever lived by reason of his many tours as a soloist with Sousa's Band for nearly a score of years.

Mr. Clarke came from a musical family. His father, William H. Clarke, was one of America's foremost church organists. Two of his brothers were nationally known as musicians. Ernest H. Clarke was Gilmore's trombone soloist for five years, 1887-1892. In 1900 he was the first trombonist of the Innes Band throughout the the summer season on the Steel Pier at Atlantic City. For twelve years he played first chair with the New York Symphony Orchestra under Walter Damrosch. Ernest was also a successful teacher of aspiring young trombone players.

Edwin G. Clarke played the fluegelhorn beside Franz Hell for several years in Sousa's Band. Later he was appointed as business manager of the band. Edwin had charge of the arrangements during the 1911 world tour which proved to be a great success.

Herbert was born in 1867, on September 12, in Massachusetts. Even as a young boy, he showed promise of his future greatness. When he was about twelve or thirteen years old, his father took the family to Indianapolis where he had obtained a new position in one of the churches. It was in that city where Herbert heard Walter B. Rogers for the first time. Walter, only two years older than Herbert, was already a brilliant cornet soloist with the local band. His great skill inspired the younger boy to practice harder than before.

The elder Clarke seems to have been widely known; for, it was not long before the family moved again, this time all the way to Toronto, Canada. Here Herbert joined the Queen's Rifle Regiment Band. There were twelve cornetists—and the newcomer was twelfth.

Clarke was twenty-four years old before he summoned up enough nerve to go to New York City on his own initiative. It had long been his secret ambition to become a member of "Pat" Gilmore's own band. His brother Ernest, born in 1865, had joined Gilmore's Band when he was only twenty-one years old.

It was during the month of February, 1892, when Herbert came to Manhattan unannounced. By then he was an experienced cornetist and serenely conscious of his exceptional talent. Even Ernest showed signs of amazement at the demonstration of Herbert's improvement on the cornet.

He took Herbert to Gilmore's home and introduced him to the bandmaster as a candidate for membership in the band.

Herbert could not have chosen a more favorable time for his application. Mr. Gilmore was even then planning to retire at the head of a gigantic 100-piece ensemble. He was trying to obtain a new cornet soloist to sit beside Albert Bode, and here was a young man who was anxious to secure that very position.

For nearly an hour, Herbert played continuously at Gilmore's behest. He knew all the selections called for. There was one cornet solo, a polka with variations, which he played with ease. At the finish, instead of winding up on the note as written, he played top F an octave above the staff. Gilmore was so enthused that he shouted "Bravo, bravo!"

Mr. Clarke wrote: "After an hour of continuous playing, I was exhausted. Then, without warning, Mr. Gilmore asked me to play the aria from *Robert the Devil*. Anybody who is familiar with this opera by Meyerbeer knows that the aria is exceedingly difficult. Bracing myself, after letting the water run out of the valve slides, I managed to play the aria straight through without a break."

A cornetist himself, Gilmore was well aware of the fact that the newcomer was on the verge of being *played out*, but he wanted final proof of the young man's stamina. When Herbert had played the aria, Mr. Gilmore patted him on the back and told him: "At last I have found a great cornetist who has both skill and endurance."

Rehearsals of the newly enlarged band were commenced in April at Madison Square Garden. In those days, long before the advent of radio and TV, a huge sounding board extended the full width of the stage at the rear. For a period of five weeks, beginning May 30, 1892, the great band played before crowded houses. Gilmore shared honors with Ida Klein, Signor Sartori and the noted tenor — Italo Campanini. It was, as we have stated previously, his final appearance in New York City. Throughout the summer, before going to St. Louis, the band played what proved to be its farewell engagement at Manhattan Beach. Owing to the increased size of the band, the concerts were given with greater acclaim than ever before.

As we have already noted, after Gilmore's death Clarke joined the new rising star, Sousa, but he played only about a year with the Sousa Band before he joined Victor Herbert with whom he was a soloist until 1898. Both Clarke and Pryor were featured soloists with Sousa's Band in 1893 at the World's Fair in Chicago.

After the Herbert sojourn, Clarke rejoined Sousa but left once again in 1902. He enlisted as a musician in the U. S. Navy and served with the band of the U. S. S. *Prairie* for two years. We are thus reminded of the fact that Mr. Sousa himself served in three branches of Government service: the Marine Corps, the Army, the Navy. He was with the Marine Band for nearly twenty-five years. In 1898, at the outbreak of the War with Spain, Sousa enlisted as an army bandmaster, but an attack of typhoid fever prevented him from taking part in his new duties. In 1917 he became leader of the Great Lakes U. S. Naval Band of 1,500 pieces with the rank of Lieutenant-Commander during World War I.

There is a tale in connection with Mr. Sousa's final military service. When he offered his services to the Government in 1917, the naval officer in charge of the recruiting told him: "Mr. Sousa, we know that you are a great musician, and we need you badly enough but we can pay you only $2,500 per year."

The famous director laughed as he replied: "Why, I sometimes earn as much as that in one day with my band." The officer was abashed. "How much would you want, if you should enlist as a bandmaster of a Navy band?" he inquired. "One dollar a month for the duration of the war," answered the visitor.

In 1904 Clarke rejoined Sousa's Band in time to play during the long engagement at the St. Louis Exposition. During his absence, Walter B. Rogers had been the featured soloist. From that time on, Clarke was assistant conductor and principal soloist of Sousa's Band until 1917 when he retired permanently as a bandman.

Many persons, including the author, looked forward to seeing and hearing Mr. Clarke play his own brilliant cornet solos fully as much as they wanted to hear Mr. Sousa lead his band. Years afterwards, when Clarke left Sousa for good, the band never seemed quite the same to us. "Sousa without Clarke" was

Herbert L. Clarke

just like "ham without mustard." True, Sousa's Band was always "meaty," so to speak, but Clarke gave it a "spicy flavor" which no other soloist, with the probable exception of Arthur Pryor, was ever able to duplicate.

Back in the year 1908, after years of public renown as one of the world's finest cornet soloists, Clarke began to practice a new method of "lip drills" devised by himself. His primary objective was to extend his range and render his embouchure far more flexible by a scientific regulation of the tension on his lips from the mouthpiece of his instrument.

There may have been soloists on a par with Herbert L. Clarke. Jules Arban, Paris Chambers, John Hazel, Bohumir Kryl, Jules Levy, "Del" Staigers—all of them were phenomenal. In 1911 we were very much privileged to hear Ernst Albert Couturier in a series of rare demonstrations on the cornet. This great artist possessed a range of more than six octaves; the normal range of either cornet or trumpet is only two

and one-half octaves. A few years before he died, Mr. Clarke wrote to us as follows: "Very few cornetists have been able to extend their compass to a full six octaves. I myself have done so to prove that it is possible." In *all-round* ability as virtuoso soloist and band performer, in opera and in symphony, Clarke was supreme. As such he never had an equal.

We heard Sousa's Band a number of times in 1912, 1913 and in 1914, mostly in New Jersey. In August, 1913, when the band played at the Ocean Grove Auditorium, Mr. Clarke handed us a printed copy of the fall tour itinerary. Amateur music lovers who enjoyed Mr. Clarke's original cornet solos would have appreciated his artistry even more, had they realized what physical difficulties beset him. Day after day, week after week, month after month, whenever he was on tour, Clarke stood up twice daily, matinee and evening, to play his own solo compositions with ease, often finishing on top Eb, F and even the second G above the staff. All this,

mind you, amidst continual train journeys with their concomitant strain. Sleeping-cars are by no means conducive to perfect rest. We recall that on that same tour the band traveled overnight via rail from Portland (Maine) to Albany (N. Y.). It was not an unusual experience.

In 1914 we heard four concerts by Sousa's Band at Ocean Grove in the Auditorium. We chatted a number of times with our beloved friend Clarke in his dressing-room. Once I told him: "I wish I could play trumpet as well as you play cornet; then I would never make any mistakes." The great soloist looked up with a quizzical smile and said: "If I had a dollar for every mistake I made this afternoon, I would be worth at least another thousand dollars." What Clarke regarded as mistakes are generally *passed up* by the overwhelming majority of cornetists. It is easy to understand why he was universally recognized as *The Old Master.*

One of the most amusing incidents which befell Mr. Clarke in those memorable days occurred in a small Midwestern city. While Sousa's Band was in town, a young boy called to see Mr. Clarke at the hotel. It seems that the lad had just purchased a new cornet of the same brand as that used by Clarke and the other Sousa cornetists. The other boys in the local high school band who had bought instruments of another "make" were teasing the poor fellow and making fun of his new cornet.

Mr. Clarke never hesitated. He inquired: "Are you coming to the concert this afternoon?" "Yes, of course," answered the boy. "Very well then," said Clarke; "lend me your cornet and I will try it out today for myself. If there is anything wrong with it, you won't have to worry. You will get another cornet free of charge."

The youngster was surprised, but he hurried home to get his cornet. During the matinee he sat on a seat in the first row. Sure enough, when Sousa's men took their places on the platform, there was Mr. Clarke with the boy's new cornet.

After the opening overture and encore, Clarke stood up for a solo as usual. He played with all his accustomed brilliancy and finished his solo on top F above high C as was his wont. At the close of the concert,

Arthur Pryor, one of Sousa's most famous soloists. He also directed his own band. His last appearance in public was in 1942. He died on June 18th of that year. The above photograph was taken when he was 70 (1941) at his New Jersey farm home.

Clarke invited the lad to accompany him to his dressing-room for a few moments.

Said Mr. Clarke: "How did your cornet sound when I played it?" The young chap was enthusiastic. "Gee, Mr. Clarke, I thought you were wonderful. It sounded great. I didn't know anybody could play on it that way."

"There is absolutely nothing wrong with your cornet," Clarke told him. "Now then, will you swap cornets with me?" "Not on your life," was the quick answer. Without further delay, the boy took his instrument and went on his way. The only difference between Clarke's cornet and that of the boy was that Clarke's was plated with gold and the boy's with silver.

The last time I heard Mr. Clarke play with Sousa's Band was at the Ocean Grove Auditorium on Saturday evening, August 22, 1914. I sat half way back on the main floor downstairs where I had a perfect view of the platform. Mr. Clarke's solo on that occasion was his *Sounds From the Hudson*. After he had played D above high C twice in succession, he finished his performance on the second G above the staff with a tone of thrilling beauty and power.

The next time I saw my dear friend was in Chicago during middle February in 1918. He had resigned from Sousa's Band the previous

autumn on Sunday, September 9th, at the conclusion of the annual engagement at Willow Grove Park, three days before his 50th birthday. Many years later he wrote: "In my younger days I observed that nearly all of the great cornetists whom I heard commenced to decline by the time they reached the age of fifty years. I determined that I would quit while I was still in my prime. When I informed Mr. Sousa of my determination, he could not understand it and seemed very much upset. However, my last solo with Sousa's Band was up to the mark."

In 1918 Mr. Clarke was employed as a tester of brass instruments for his old friend, Frank Holton. In company with a friend who was an amateur trombonist, I went to the factory where Mr. Clarke introduced us to Mr. Holton. Afterwards Mr. Clarke guided us on a tour through the factory where we watched the men making new instruments. It was an unusual experience for both of us.

Next we were escorted to Mr. Clarke's private testing room on the second floor where we enjoyed a lengthy conversation. While we were talking, I remembered that last solo I had heard my great friend play. I remarked: "I'll never forget that high note you played that night. To this day I don't know whether the thrill went up or down my spine, but I know that it *went*." Without a word, Mr. Clarke picked up his cornet from the table and commenced to play. After a few seconds he finished on the same top G which I had heard him play in 1914.

After leaving the factory, the trombonist and I returned to the boarding school where we were fellow students. There were several fellows in the front hall of the main building. Said McKinley: "I heard the greatest cornetist in the world today." Pointing a finger at me, he added: "This *gink* here just about made the old fellow do anything he wanted. I never saw anything like it." We had to laugh at that, of course, but we knew that

Clifton Webb in the role of John Philip Sousa in the motion picture "Stars and Stripes Forever." The film covers nine years in the life of Sousa. Done in Technicolor by Twentieth Century-Fox, it contains much of the spectacular, including such scenes as a White House reception and a Cotton States Exposition.

we had not been singled out for special favors, since Mr. Clarke was equally courteous to everybody.

Later that same year Clarke went to Huntsville, Ontario, Canada, where he conducted an industrial manufacturer's plant band for five years until he was called to Long Beach, California. Relieved of strenuous work as a Sousa bandman, Clarke continued to play cornet solos for several years with continued phenomenal dexterity. In 1922, while acting as one of the judges during a band clinic, Clarke joined one of the visiting bands at a given period and played one of Sousa's marches an octave higher than written. It was a stupendous feat for any player, particularly a man past his fiftieth year.

The last time the writer saw his old friend was on Broadway, New York City, on a Monday afternoon early in November of 1922. Clarke had come down for the week-end from Canada to renew his acquaintance with his old friends who were still playing for Sousa, and to enjoy the Sunday concerts at the famous New York Hippodrome.

During the entire season of 1915-1916, Sousa's Band was one of the main features of a gigantic Hippodrome spectacle, *The Big Show*. There were 1,200 people in the cast. The show was so successful that, at the close of the season, it was taken on tour through the Eastern States at a substantial profit. Mr. Clarke, of course, was a very busy cornetist that winter, playing solos at every matinee and evening performance six days a week, in addition to the regular band concerts which were given on Sundays at the Hippodrome.

From 1939 until his death in 1945, Mr. Clarke and the writer corresponded extensively. Much of the material which forms this present story can be credited to our old friend. Nowadays the majority of players in concert bands use trumpets instead of cornets. Way back in 1916, Mr. Clarke wrote: "Years ago, while I was playing at the Metropolitan Opera House, I used a trumpet because the parts called for a trumpet. But to play cornet parts on a trumpet —ye gods, that's all!" How the times have changed since then!

Herbert Lincoln Clarke passed away on January 30, 1945, in Los Angeles. His body was taken to Washington, D.C., for interment in the Congressional Cemetery. He lies buried close by the grave of his beloved Maestro, the immortal John Philip Sousa. The qualities of these two artists will ever be remembered by all who knew them.

Chapter VI

DOUBTLESS MANY READERS OF these memoirs are well-acquainted with the various instruments heard in concert or symphonic bands. Although there have been many changes amidst brass and woodwind choirs during the past seventy-five or eighty years, the over-all instrumentation has remained much the same as it was in the days of Gilmore, Reeves and their contemporaries.

However, several of the instruments which figured prominently in scores composed and arranged especially for brass bands have become obsolete. The Ab clarinet was used up to the beginning of the 20th century, about which time it was abandoned by the leading directors — whose influence was paramount with the instrument manufacturers.

The Eb clarinet still owns its place in the symphony orchestra, but it is seldom heard in bands today. The last time we saw this instrument in use in a concert band was at Asbury Park in 1944 and 1945 when the late Giuseppe Creatore played a series of week-end concerts on the boardwalk.

Old-time musicians recall Ur Matus, the Hungarian artist with Gilmore's Band. Matus was a supreme master of the little clarinet. Mr. Clarke wrote as follows: "Matus was a wizard on the Eb clarinet, and no one has ever taken his place in the world."

The Eb clarinet has a shrill, high, penetrating tone and is suitable only in special numbers. Richard Strauss, the noted composer of operettas and tone poems, features the instrument in his *Till Eulenspiegel*. The rascally *Till* meets his death at the close of the score by being hanged; and Strauss employs the shrieks of the Eb clarinet to depict *Till's* death agonies.

Gilmore included two Bb soprano saxophones in his band, and so did Sousa in the beginning; but by 1900, when Sousa's Band played abroad, only five saxes were used—first and second alto, a tenor, a baritone and a bass. Sousa had the same combination in 1919 at Willow Grove Park. LaBarre did likewise at the World's Fair in 1940.

Until about 1909 or 1910 such brasses as the Eb cornet, the Eb alto horn and the Bb tenor horn were commonly heard in bands throughout the country. Not one of these brasses was used by Sousa at any time. Gilmore, however, had one Eb cornet, two Eb alto horns and two Bb tenor horns in his great band at St. Louis in 1892.

The Bb fluegelhorn, which we have already discussed, is still manufactured in the United States; but school bandmasters apparently do not favor its inclusion in their ensembles. However, the popularity of this beautifully mellow brass instrument has not declined on the Continent. About nine or ten years ago, the late George M. Bundy. who was a well-known figure in musical circles for many years while he was associated with a leading instrument manufacturing firm, wrote to us as follows: "Each year when I visit Paris on business at the firm's headquarters, I never fail to hear the *Garde Républicaine Band* as often as possible. This great band uses fluegelhorns as solo brasses, and the effects are marvelous."

Not so many years ago a large band from Brussels was heard in the United States. Mr. Sousa and Mr. Goldman were present in the audience at Central Park in Manhattan. The Belgian band was instrumentated, of course, in the usual Continental manner. There were quite a few instruments which are practically unknown in this country, although they can be seen and heard in Canada.

During the intermission the two bandmasters were approached by a stranger who had recognized them. Evidently the man was possessed with a spirit of intense antagonism against the *foreigners*, who were so rash as to play such strange instruments here in the United States. We have no record of what he said, but, at any rate, he was so upset that he complained bitterly to the two American musicians concerning the *fantastic instrumentation*. When he was through speaking, Mr. Sousa replied quietly: "But did you notice how well they played?" Sousa and Goldman knew how to appreciate performances on *all* instruments.

Many years ago the author owned a recording of a fluegelhorn solo made abroad which always charmed him by its rich mellowness and depth of tone. Creatore used a fluegelhorn at Asbury Park, even though his band numbered only 34 pieces. The Italian maestro included an Eb contrabass sarrusophone as well. The latter-named instrument is really a contrabassoon made of brass. It provides additional bass foundation for the bassoons together with the contrabassoon. Neither Gilmore nor Sousa ever used this instrument which was invented by a Frenchman named Sarrus in 1856. Sarrus himself was a bandmaster.

Both Sousa and Prior used the E♭ tuba for many years, but toward the close of their careers they both seem to have dropped it entirely in favor of the larger BB♭ tuba which, of course, possesses a broader tone.

Many modern bandmasters use the string bass as a means of *smoothing the tuba section*. Among them are included such directors as Edwin Franko Goldman, Giuseppe Creatore and Frank Simon. However, such leaders as Gilmore, Sousa, Pryor, Conway, etc., never employed string basses at any time. The author believes that the harp is the sole string instrument essential to both bands and orchestras. There are many notable passages in overtures, tone poems, intermezzos, operatic excerpts, waltzes, etc., which require the use of the harp. There is no adequate substitute. The string bass is an orchestral instrument and, as such, it is—in my opinion—out of place in the band.

Gilmore never included a harp in his band. At first, Sousa, too, did not employ this instrument, but a short time prior to the world tour (1910-1911), Mr. Sousa added a harp to his ensemble. Thereafter he always made use of this noble instrument. Joseph Marthage, a musician of rare ability, was Sousa's harp soloist for many years. Later, the gifted young Canadian artist, Miss Genevieve Bambrick, was Sousa's harpist until the close of the bandmaster's life.

Both Gilmore and Sousa employed the contrabassoon in their bands. However, as many bandmasters do, they used the second oboist to double on the *cor Anglais*, English horn. This beautiful reed instrument, which, ironically enough, is neither English nor a horn, is in reality an alto oboe. We believe, emphatically, that the alto oboe should be played opposite the contrabassoon *in addition* to the two regular oboe performers. The oboe section is now, as it always has been, the most neglected choir within the band.

The bass trumpet seems to have

Winnie Brambrick, Sousa and Marjorie Moody. Both Miss Brambrick and Miss Moody appeared with Sousa's Band, the former as harpist and the latter as soprano.
Photo submitted by D. C. Gardner.

been built originally for use in Richard Wagner's operas. Such trumpets are now manufactured in this country. LaBarre used one regularly in his World's Fair Band with great effectiveness. In 1942 Pryor's baritone player was featured occasionally as a bass trumpet soloist.

It goes without saying that John Philip Sousa and Arthur Pryor, if they were living today and were still actively engaged in conducting, would avail themselves of every modern resource at their command, so as to improve their instrumentation whenever possible. Our good friend, LaBarre, did so in 1940. He used the contrabassoon, although he chose not to reinforce the oboes. Two modern woodwinds, the E♭ and the B♭ contrabass clarinets, unknown in Gilmore's time, are now available. LaBarre had a contrabass clarinet which was played by Ross Gorman, an unusually versatile artist who plays many woodwind instruments. Gorman is a valued member of the *Band of America*.

The B♭ contrabass clarinet proved a veritable sensation on display at the New York World's Fair. Its low register sounds for all the world like a pipe organ.

Of interest to the reader might be a list of the instruments which comprised Gilmore's Band in 1892.

4 Flutes (Piccolos)
4 E♭ Soprano Clarinets
1 A♭ Soprano Clarinet
29 B♭ Soprano Clarinets
(15 1st, 8 2nd, 6 3rd)
2 E♭ Alto Clarinets
2 B♭ Bass Clarinets

4 Oboes
4 Bassoons
1 Contrabassoon

2 B♭ Soprano Saxophones
2 E♭ Alto Saxophones
2 B♭ Tenor Saxophones
1 E♭ Baritone Saxophone
1 B♭ Bass Saxophone

4 French Horns
2 E♭ Alto Horns
2 Fluegelhorns
1 E♭ Solo Cornet
4 B♭ Solo Cornets
2 1st B♭ Cornets
2 2nd B♭ Trumpets
2 3rd B♭ Trumpets
2 B♭ Tenor Horns
3 Tenor Trombones
1 F Bass Trombone
1 B♭ Baritone
2 B♭ Euphoniums
4 E♭ Tubas
4 BB♭ Tubas

5 Percussion

———
100

The reader is already cognizant of the fact that the Sousaphone generally ousted the older basses. Nowadays, the Sousaphone itself has been displaced in many bands by the *recording model* tuba which has a superior intonation. LaBarre employed a quartette of these ultra-modern basses in 1940.

For the sake of the readers who may be fascinated by a comparison of the varying forms of band ensemble, we also include a chart showing the Sousa Band (1900) and the Goldman Band (1930).

SOUSA		GOLDMAN
4	Flutes (Piccolos)	4
1	E♭ Sop. Clarinet	1
7	1st B♭ Clarinets	8
4	2nd B♭ Clarinets	6
4	3rd B♭ Clarinets	6
2	E♭ Alto Clarinets	1
2	B♭ Bass Clarinets	1
2	Oboes	2
2	Bassoons	2
1	Contrabassoon	
2	E♭ Alto Saxes	
1	B♭ Tenor Sax	
1	E♭ Baritone Sax	
1	B♭ Bass Sax	
4	French Horns	5
2	Fluegelhorns	

2	Solo Bb Cornets	3	
2	1st Bb Cornets	2	
2	2nd-3rd Bb Trpts.	2	
3	Tenor Trombones	4	
1	F Bass Trombone	2	
2	Bb Euphoniums	2	
2	Eb Tubas	2	
2	BBb Tubas	2	
	String Basses	2	
	Harp	1	
3	Percussion	3	
59		61	

As Mr. Sousa added the harp to his instrumentation in later years, so

Mr. Goldman subsequently included the saxophones in his band. The saxophones have won their spurs in some symphony orchestras recently, and some modern composers write directly for these instruments within these *classical* organizations.

It is interesting to note that, although many people regard saxes as jazz instruments entirely, they were not used in jazz bands *at first*. Back in 1917 the famous *Dixieland Jazz Band* included a trumpet, a trombone, a clarinet, drums and piano, but no saxophones. Even as late as 1924 when the great trumpet player, the late Bix Beiderbecke, organized

his band, he did not use a saxophone.

But who can deny the ravishing beauty of tone heard on saxophones in such numbers as *Pictures from an Exhibition* by Moussorgsky, the sax solo in Ravel's *Bolero*, also the solo in Debussy's *Rhapsodie*, etc., as performed by such artists as Lucien Cailliet, Rolland Tapley, Leonard Schaller, Carroll Gillette, Maurice DeCruck, Cecil Leeson, Sigurd Rascher and other equally eminent symphony orchestra stars of national renown?

As we have seen, saxophones have been in constant use by the finest concert bands throughout the United States from Gilmore's time up to the present. Ironically enough, however, the credit for the widespread popularity of these brass-bodied instruments, which are played with reed mouthpieces, belongs neither to the old-fashioned *brass band* nor the ultra-modern *jive* or *swing* ensemble.

Veteran theater-goers who attended vaudeville shows as far back as 1911 should remember a musical skit known as *Tom Brown & His Saxophone Sextet*. Tom Brown organized his act that same year and continued with it until 1926, attaining a peak of popularity in 1924. It was he who taught Americans that the sax can moan, laugh, cackle, titter, squeal and grunt. The vaudeville stages from 1915 to 1925 were crowded with his imitators. To the uninitiated, such perversion of the instrument is synonymous with jazz but this is altogether untrue.

Much of the attraction of the saxophone for early audiences before which Tom Brown performed was the comparative novelty of the instrument. Apart from a few concert bands, it was practically unknown. But Brown was a great showman, and within a short time his combination of antics and music made the sax the most talked about instrument in America.

The saxophone has long since earned a solid place for itself in the concert or symphonic band. Sousa always used from four to eight of these instruments, depending upon the number of musicians in his famous organization. One time Mr. Sousa asserted: "There is much to be done in standardizing the saxophone with its strange sweetness of tone and its variety of effects."

Saint-Saens and John Philip Sousa. This photograph was taken in California in 1915 at an Exposition for which Saint-Saens had written a special oratorio for 500 voices and Sousa's Band and the Bendix Symphony Orchestra. This photograph was submitted by James Cimera (brother of Jaroslav Cimera).

Chapter VII

IT IS DIFFICULT TO STATE WHICH of the two bandmasters, Mr. Gilmore or Mr. Sousa, was the better showman. Gilmore was by no means Sousa's equal as a composer, but he was probably more successful as a presenter of spectacular effects in his music. Gilmore's personal magnetism was a powerful factor in his appeal to the public. Sousa, of course, was a magnetic figure, too, but he had the ears of his audiences itching to hear his incomparable marches.

Both Gilmore and Sousa knew the secret of programming their music so as to cater to the musical preferences of all sorts of people. They did not hesitate to play the classics and the more popular forms of music in constant juxtaposition. Both conductors possessed a highly developed sense of humor together with a sensitive flair for appropriate timing.

The passing of Gilmore, which coincided with the advent of Sousa, meant a decided change of program content, to say the least. The audiences in Gilmore's day were accustomed to hearing concert bands which performed much more classical music than do the modern groups.

It is quite likely that John Philip Sousa was responsible in a large measure for the more popular style of programming. Although Gilmore delighted in offering such eye-catching novelties as playing Verdi's *Anvil Chorus* with red-shirted firemen in the background, his music for the most part was planned to please the *highbrows*.

Mr. Sousa, as a matter of course, liberally flavored his programs with his own stirring marches as encores. He frequently included the Bellstedt *Humoresques* and such popular numbers as *Tres Moutarde* (*Too Much Mustard*) as a welcome relief from the heavier type of selections. More than this, Mr. Sousa himself composed not a few witty melodies. In 1919 we heard his band open the second part of an evening concert with his original satire entitled *Showing Off Before Company*. This commenced with a fanfare by the trumpets behind the scenes. Then the various sections of the band came out in front and played variations on a given theme, each section resuming its seats in turn. Frank Simon appeared with a long post horn (without valves) on which he blew a series of bugle calls. He finished his act on an extremely high note which he held a full minute. The writer vividly recalls hearing gasps of amazement here and there throughout the huge audience. The Indian artist, Red Cloud (John Kuhn) played a brilliant cadenza on the big sousaphone. At the close, Kuhn "went down into the basement" as though he would never stop. Just before he played the final amazingly

John Philip Sousa at his home in Sands Point, Long Island. This is one of the few photographs showing him without a uniform. This photograph is inscribed to Mr. A. A. Harding, former band director of the University of Illinois.

low note, he threw back his head and shouted "Ha, ha!"

Mr. Sousa possessed an acute consciousness of the dramatic in music. His scenic piece, *Sheridan's Ride*, is a classic example of inspiring melody. It is not to be wondered at that Mr. Sousa wrote so many marches with patriotic titles when we bear in mind the fact of his long apprenticeship with government bands.

Through the courtesy of our dear friend, Ed Freudenvoll, who died on August 8, 1953, at seventy-seven years of age, the author is in possession of a copy of the last program ever directed by Colonel Gilmore. The date of the concert was Friday evening, September 23, 1892, at the St. Louis Exposition. We present it to our readers so that they may know the type of programs given by Gilmore's Band.

1. Overture, "Tannhauser", Wagner.

2. Air, "Largo" from *Xerxes*, Handel.

3. Concerto, "Allegro Appassionato" (Concertstuck—Opus 47), Weber.

4. Old German Air, "Ein Vogel" (A musical wit's conception of how this air should have been composed by Bach, Haydn, Mozart, Strauss, Verdi, Gounod, Wagner), Ochs.

John Philip Sousa inspecting the national and state trophies that were awarded to the winners of the national contest in Denver, 1929. He is shown here with members of the contest committee: from left to right—Joseph E. Maddy, A. A. Harding, John Philip Sousa and the late C. M. Tremaine who was director of the National Bureau for the Advancement of Music.—Wide World Photo

5. Symphonic Poem, "Hungaria" (First rendition by a band), Liszt.

6. March, "Bay State Commandery" (Introducing *Adeste Fideles*), Burrell.

Another trait which endeared Mr. Sousa to all who knew him was his readiness at all times to be of service wherever possible. In the fall of 1922, the author was in Scranton, Pa. for a short time. During our visit, Sousa's Band came to town. On the morning of the band's appearance, we called at the office to renew acquaintance with a local violin instructor whom we had known for many years.

Said Theodore: "Say, have you heard the news? One of the local clarinetists who is only sixteen years old went up to Mr. Sousa today and asked for a job with the band, and Sousa has taken him on."

We were skeptical but said nothing. A short while afterwards, we met Jay Sims on the street. Sims, whom we knew fairly well, was Sousa's second trombonist and official examiner of applicants for membership in Sousa's Band.

When we told Jay what we had learned earlier, he replied: "That's right, your friend told you the truth." It seems that Mr. Sousa was so impressed by the lad's evident sincerity that he sent him at once to Sims for a tryout. After a thorough examination, Jay reported to the Maestro that the Scranton youngster was an A-1 clarinetist. Mr. Sousa engaged the boy on the spot. It was a typical Sousa gesture.

During that same autumn tour, Sousa's Band played a matinee and an evening concert on Sunday at Binghamton, N. Y. The members of the local *Ministerium* endeavored to prevent the concerts from being played as scheduled, but all in vain. When he was told of the efforts which had been put forth by the various pastors, Mr. Sousa cried: "There is more real inspiration in one of my marches than in all of their sermons put together."

All truly great musicians are invariably able to perform many "tricks of the trade" on their respective instruments. Couturier, during his cornet demonstrations in 1911 at Scranton, played three-part harmony throughout an entire melody that sounded as if a trio of cornetists were sounding off.

During our conversation with Mr. Clarke seven years afterwards in Chicago, we reminded him of Mr. Couturier's stunt. Our beloved friend immediately picked up his cornet and began to play a song in exactly the same fashion.

Chapter VIII, Conclusion

A funny incident occurred one season at Willow Grove Park. A cornet soloist with Sousa's Band was scheduled for a solo one night. We shall not mention his name, but he had a national reputation as an artist of top rank. On that occasion, however, a most peculiar thing happened. The soloist was in good form as usual, and he was playing as brilliantly as ever. But for some reason which neither he nor anyone else was ever able to explain, his final high note at the finish was a fluke. Instead of the beautifully clear and full tone which everybody naturally expected to hear, a hollow, ghostlike screech came out from the bell of the instrument. The poor fellow was so overcome with embarrassment that he actually slunk back to his seat like a whipped mongrel.

Many are the legends which have been told concerning the famous Jules Levy. Although Levy never played with Sousa's Band, he was a featured soloist with Gilmore. At one time he and Arbuckle were so envious of each other that they actually came to blows and had to be separated by their friends. Gilmore, with his flair for making the most of every opportunity, advertised a series of concerts featuring *two cornet soloists* simultaneously. He even went so far as to play up the rivalry between Levy and Arbuckle in the newspapers to assure himself of a packed house at every concert. The ruse was successful, and "Pat" was able to congratulate himself *as usual*.

A little later on, Levy played solos with a band conducted by Nahan Franko at Central Park in Manhattan. In those days bandsmen were paid by check on Saturday afternoons after the concerts. One week, however, Levy informed Mr. Franko: "I don't want any more checks. Pay me with *hard cash*."

Franko knew how to deal with Levy. "All right, Jules, you can have *hard cash*." Another Saturday rolled around and another matinee was given. The bandsmen waited on the platform as usual after the concert to receive their checks.

Levy stood there waiting for his money. As soon as all of the other musicians had been paid off, a large wagon drawn by a team of horses came up close and backed toward the platform. The driver climbed down and came over to the rear of the wagon and opened the tail-gate. A clinking sound was heard. "There is your *hard cash*, Levy," said the bandmaster. The little cornetist was dumfounded as he saw his money, which even in those days was one thousand dollars weekly, roll out on the platform in a shower of bright, new, golden *pennies*.

One time a friend asked Jules: "How would you like to be the President of the United States?" "Who, me?" cried Levy. "Not on your life! What, go to the White House for four years, and then get kicked out! Huh, look at me! I'm the greatest cornetist in the world ALL THE TIME."

Mr. Sousa's final moments were of significant interest, since his stirring marches attest his patriotism in such vigorous style. Early in 1932, the celebrated *March King* received an invitation to guest conduct the Ringgold Band of Reading, Pa., on the occasion of that band's 80th anniversary. On Saturday evening, March 5th, he led the band in a rehearsal of the scheduled Sunday concert. The final number played was *The Stars and Stripes Forever*, Sousa's own favorite march. Afterward Mr. Sousa returned to—of all places—the *Abraham Lincoln Hotel*. At 12:30 A.M., Sunday, March 6, 1932, a severe heart attack ended the career of the peerless bandmaster.

Sousa's fame and genius are enshrined forever in heart and in mind of whoever heard his incomparable band. The U.S. Marine Band participated in the solemnly impressive funeral services. During the ceremonies a veteran member of the Marine Band sobbed: "He was the best bandmaster I ever saw." Though his body and soul are at rest, John Philip Sousa's music *goes marching on*.

Sousa sitting with his dogs reveals some of the inner warmth that made him so much the complete man — composer, conductor, and father. Taken on a porch at the Sands Point home.

This picture, autographed, "To Jane, From Philip, 99" is one of the first portraits of Sousa in his Sousa Band uniform. The old English letter "S" is embroidered on the collar. His own band had only been organized some four or five years at this time but had rapidly established his reputation with the public. Mrs. Abert notes that *"this was Mother's favorite picture of Father."* The autograph "To Jane" is to his wife, Jennie.

"I believe this portrait was taken of Father in connection with his proposed service with the Army at the time of the Spanish American-War. He volunteered for the Army during the Spanish-American War, but caught 'walking typhoid' before he could report for acceptance for duty. He did not participate in the War and actually never left the country. 'Walking typhoid' was a term used in those days to mean those who had typhoid fever enough to make them ill, but not enough to hospitalize them. On the other hand, they were not well enough to serve on active duty."

An official tour picture taken in 1900 showing the Sousa Band uniform which remained unchanged for 30 years. It had a quiet dignity that set the pattern for other professional bands and for high school and college bands.

Index by Author